Table of Contents

Acknowledgements

This is a long and detailed publication containing thousands of facts and figures. It is only to be expected, despite continuous and repeated editing and checking, that errors may occur. In such cases, once we are aware of any, we publish a correction on our website.

Readers are encouraged to check regularly at www.dellam.com/books for any corrections and updates.

Although we take extreme care to ensure accuracy and being up-to-date, we cannot accept responsibility for any errors or omissions.

We appreciate your interest in our publications, and your comments and suggestions are always welcome. Please contact us at enquiries@dellam.com.

The Top 6000 Companies in Outer London

Companies with assets exceeding £5,000,000

John D Blackburn
Editor

dp

First Edition

Spring 2019

ISBN-13: 978-1-912736-25-6

ISBN-10: 1-912736-25-X

Printed in 8pt Nimbus Sans L

Designed by URW++ Design and Development GmbH

Dellam Publishing Limited

2 Heath Drive, Sutton, Surrey, SM2 5RP

Fax: 020 8770 7478 email: enquiries@dellam.com

SAN: 0177881 EAN/GLN: 5030670177882

Scotland
Northern Ireland
North East (England)
North West (England)
Yorkshire and The Humber
East Midlands (England)
West Midlands (England)
Wales
East of England
See London Inset
South East (England)
South West (England)

Scotland
North East (England)
North West (England)
Yorkshire and The Humber
East Midlands (England)
West Midlands (England)
Wales
East of England
South East (England)
South West (England)
London

Introduction

This study looks at all companies registered in Outer London and where their total assets are more than £5,000,000.

The statutory Outer London boroughs are: Barking and Dagenham, Barnet, Bexley, Brent, Bromley, Croydon, Ealing, Enfield, Haringey, Harrow, Havering, Hillingdon, Hounslow, Kingston upon Thames, Merton, Newham, Redbridge, Richmond upon Thames, Sutton and Waltham Forest. The population in 2011 was 4,942,040.

The aim of this study is to provide an overview of the key movers and shakers in the Outer London corporate sector. Only key data has been isolated, particularly the company's net worth and total assets, but also its full name, date incorporated, registered office, activities, shareholders, directors (with date of birth, occupation and nationality) and number of employees.

Two indicators of size are used: net worth and total assets. These are preferable to turnover which is influenced by profit margins and whether the companies are capital or labour intensive.

For Outer London, total output (GVA) is twice that of Wales and three times that of Northern Ireland. Thus, the total output (GVA) per boroughs was £12.3 billion in Hillingdon; £10.5 billion in Hounslow and £9.4 billion in Barnet.

For both Inner and Outer London, the population is 9 million (UK 66 million).

The total output (GVA), in 2016, was £408 billion (UK £1,748 billion). The total output (GVA) per head, in 2016, was £46,482 (UK £26,621). Economic Growth (GVA), 2010-2016, was 3.2% (UK 1.9%).

The number employed, May-July 2018, was 4,735,000 (UK 32,397,000) with an employment rate of 74.7% (UK 75.5%). The number unemployed was 235,000 (UK 1,361,000) with an unemployment rate of 4.7% (UK 4%). In 2017, there were 140,000 jobs in manufacturing (UK 2,685,000). Manufacturing employment, January-March 2018, was 2.4% of total jobs (UK 7.7%) Public sector employment was 13.6% (UK 16.6%).

The number of VAT/PAYE businesses were in 2016: 477,000 (18.7%); in 2017: 506,000 (18.9%) and in 2018: 506,000 (19%).

London at 1.1 million and South East England at 874,000 had the most private sector businesses, accounting for 35% of the UK.

In 2017, there were 92,300 new businesses (up 15%) and 86,270 businesses ceased trading (up 14%). In 2018, there were 1,096,000 businesses (UK 5,668,000) and 239,000 employers (UK 1,360,000). In the UK, in 2018, there were 1,059 businesses per 10,000 resident adults. In London there were 1,563 businesses per 10,000 residents, the highest number of business density in the UK.

London has a stronger service export than the rest of the UK. While London accounts for nearly half of UK service exports, it only accounts for 11% of goods exports, and for 27% of all UK exports. London's service exports are 29% of London's output, compared with 15% for the UK.

Standard cataloguing guidelines for company names in the profile section have been used, but there will be occurrences when the name may not be strictly alphabetical. A certain licence was adopted where it was felt that strictly alphabetical could lead to improper cataloguing. Some company names have been shortened in the league tables for aesthetic reasons.

John D Blackburn
Editor

This page is intentionally left blank

Total Assets League Table

Company	Value
DS (Holdings) 3 Limited	£700,200,189,952
BP International Limited	£160,948,404,224
GlaxoSmithKline Finance PLC	£135,010,271,232
GlaxoSmithKline Holdings Limited	£60,131,000,320
GlaxoSmithKline PLC	£56,381,001,728
BP Holdings North America Limited	£51,804,418,048
BP America Limited	£51,778,732,032
BP Exploration Operating Company Limited	£49,403,691,008
BP Capital Markets P.L.C.	£44,762,333,184
Setfirst Limited	£35,656,830,976
Canada Life Limited	£31,149,299,712
GlaxoSmithKline Consumer Healthcare Holdings	£20,771,000,320
ExxonMobil Holding Company Limited	£18,504,316,928
Heathrow Airport Holdings Limited	£18,395,000,832
Sky UK Limited	£18,364,999,680
FGP Topco Limited	£18,304,000,000
Sky Limited	£18,001,999,872
Heathrow Airport Limited	£17,422,000,128
Bottling Holdings Europe Limited	£16,759,967,744
British Airways PLC	£16,677,999,616
Coca-Cola European Partners PLC	£15,913,583,616
Heathrow Finance PLC	£15,616,000,000
Heathrow (SP) Limited	£15,258,000,384
Sony Global Treasury Services PLC	£14,148,797,440
Chromium Acquisitions Limited	£13,984,549,888
BP Global Investments Limited	£13,726,040,064
Cadbury Seven LLP	£13,519,614,976
Compass Group PLC	£12,266,000,384
BP Russian Investments Limited	£11,975,698,432
Heathrow Holdco Limited	£11,914,999,808
Compass Overseas Holdings No.2 Limited	£11,884,215,296
Glaxo Group Limited	£11,776,435,200
LHR Airports Limited	£11,187,999,744
Chubb Group Limited	£10,658,702,336
GlaxoSmithKline Capital PLC	£10,646,939,648
Hospitality Holdings Limited	£10,528,145,408
Kraft Foods Investment Holdings UK Limited	£10,462,016,512
Chubb Limited	£10,439,570,432
Six Continents Limited	£10,364,999,680
Cadbury Limited	£10,277,645,312
Direct Line Insurance Group PLC	£9,948,199,936
Sky Operational Finance Limited	£9,861,266,432
Vantas International Limited	£9,697,094,656
Mallinckrodt UK Ltd	£9,481,590,784
Compass Group Holdings PLC	£8,942,300,160
CCEP Holdings UK Limited	£8,796,600,320
Sky International Operations Limited	£8,306,297,344
Heathrow (AH) Limited	£8,156,000,256
BL Bottling Holdings UK Limited	£7,980,585,984
BP Exploration (Angola) Limited	£7,970,078,720
Cadbury Schweppes Overseas Limited	£7,902,595,072
Kenard Group Limited	£7,799,197,184
Xerox Overseas Holdings Limited	£7,706,999,808
Atlantica Yield PLC	£7,616,390,144
GlaxoSmithKline Intellectual Property Mngmnt	£7,432,076,800
ITW Holdings I Limited	£7,397,315,072
ITW Holdings VI Limited	£7,397,127,680
ITW Holdings III Limited	£7,103,780,352
ViiV Healthcare Limited	£7,080,999,936
BP Exploration (Caspian Sea) Limited	£7,042,281,472
ViiV Healthcare UK Limited	£7,015,779,840
Chromium Assets Limited	£6,845,971,968
GlaxoSmithKline Intellectual Property Limited	£6,631,912,960
GlaxoSmithKline Investment Holdings Limited	£6,483,027,968
BP Asia Pacific Holdings Limited	£6,405,887,488
Mondi PLC	£6,383,600,640
BP Australia Swaps Management Limited	£6,225,776,640
CNOOC UK Limited	£6,177,024,512
Toyota Financial Services (UK) PLC	£6,119,365,120
Six Continents Hotels International Limited	£5,887,932,928
BP Exploration (Azerbaijan) Limited	£5,863,719,424
Subsea 7 Treasury (UK) Limited	£5,851,809,280
BP Exploration (Delta) Limited	£5,733,650,944
ADI Finance 2 Limited	£5,717,000,192
RCI Financial Services Limited	£5,533,118,976
BP Corporate Holdings Limited	£5,420,483,584
Heathrow (DSH) Limited	£5,270,000,128
ADI Finance 1 Limited	£5,231,000,064
Hitachi Capital (UK) PLC	£5,090,800,128
TBC Bank Group PLC	£5,045,101,056
Pladis Foods Limited	£5,041,800,192
ITW Holdings II Limited	£4,805,328,896
Mondelez UK Holdings & Services Limited	£4,785,999,872
The Berkeley Group Holdings PLC	£4,776,500,224
BP Gas Marketing Limited	£4,760,592,896
Mallinckrodt Pharmaceuticals Limited	£4,702,202,368
GlaxoSmithKline Mercury Limited	£4,645,296,128
Berkeley Group PLC (The)	£4,548,788,224
BP Holdings Canada Limited	£4,533,431,808
Chromium Suchex LLP	£4,466,366,976
GlaxoSmithKline Intellectual Property Holdings Ltd	£4,385,067,008
ViiV Healthcare UK (No.3) Limited	£4,336,324,096
Xerox UK Holdings Limited	£4,295,000,064
Forester Life Limited	£4,291,504,128
Esso Exploration and Production UK Limited	£4,283,000,064
Bottling Great Britain Limited	£4,272,129,280
Cargill Global Funding PLC	£4,270,958,336
Subsea 7 Senior Holdings (UK) Limited	£4,240,687,360
GlaxoSmithKline IHC Limited	£4,119,490,048
United Biscuits (UK) Limited	£3,558,799,872
BP (Abu Dhabi) Limited	£3,456,190,976
ExxonMobil Finance Company Limited	£3,412,931,840
Xerox Limited	£3,376,000,000
BP Exploration (Alpha) Limited	£3,334,274,304
Mondi Investments Limited	£3,314,483,712
ViiV Healthcare Trading Services UK Limited	£3,306,328,064
Berkeley Homes Public Limited Company	£3,215,473,920
Hilton International IP Holding Limited	£3,080,324,096
The Canada Life Group (U.K.) Limited	£3,079,300,096
Esso UK Limited	£3,028,000,000
Asia Pacific Holdings Limited	£3,019,723,008
Igroup 8 Limited	£3,009,617,920
Hilton Worldwide Holding LLP	£2,958,253,056
Mondelez UK Limited	£2,928,550,912
Galliford Try PLC	£2,893,299,968
Compass Group North America Investments Ltd	£2,889,749,248
WIH UK Limited	£2,882,777,856
BP Exploration (Epsilon) Limited	£2,825,721,856
Mondelez UK Biscuit Financing Limited	£2,820,495,616
Nomad Foods Europe Midco Limited	£2,808,313,600
UMV Global Foods Holding Company Ltd.	£2,754,500,096
ITW Limited	£2,745,051,904
Esso Petroleum Company,Limited	£2,680,000,000
Brambles Holdings Unlimited	£2,660,660,480
GlaxoSmithKline Services Unlimited	£2,630,000,128
Nomad Foods Europe Limited	£2,627,912,960
Belron Finance Limited	£2,611,092,992
ITW Holdings IV Limited	£2,594,297,088
Subsea 7 Interim UK Holdings Limited	£2,577,399,296
Hilton Worldwide Manage Limited	£2,571,142,144
GR Bottling Holdings UK Limited	£2,541,998,592
Hilton International IP Holding 2 Limited	£2,523,724,800
SmithKline Beecham Limited	£2,496,000,000
Cadbury Eight LLP	£2,478,514,176
Subsea 7 Offshore Resources (UK) Limited	£2,468,395,520
Glaxochem (UK) Unlimited	£2,420,489,984
ITW Holdings VII Limited	£2,399,663,360
Hilton Worldwide Holding 2 Limited	£2,394,284,288
SNC-Lavalin (GB) Holdings Limited	£2,316,271,872
Suntory UK Holdings Limited	£2,312,583,424
ViiV Healthcare Finance Limited	£2,271,303,936
Brambles Finance PLC	£2,266,366,976
Intercontinental Hotels Group PLC	£2,262,524,160
SNC-Lavalin (GB) Limited	£2,262,006,272

Company	Value
ExxonMobil Financial Investment Company Ltd	£2,254,188,544
Brambles Investment Ltd.	£2,233,382,144
Mondi Finance PLC	£2,212,484,352
GlaxoSmithKline Holdings (Ireland) Limited	£2,196,562,944
Six Continents Overseas Holdings Limited	£2,185,080,064
UPS (UK) Limited	£2,179,633,664
UPS Global Treasury PLC	£2,141,116,800
CB Equity LLP	£2,114,128,512
United Biscuits Bidco Limited	£2,108,099,968
UMV Global Foods Company Ltd.	£2,077,799,936
Cross London Trains Limited	£1,989,815,040
Cross London Trains Holdco 2 Limited	£1,989,815,040
Intercontinental (PB) 1	£1,874,495,616
GlaxoSmithKline International Limited	£1,866,791,040
Spirit Norway Limited	£1,857,423,872
GlaxoSmithKline Consumer Healthcare (Overseas)	£1,856,691,968
Cadbury Nine LLP	£1,845,740,032
Wellcome Limited	£1,843,000,064
Parkview Treasury Services (UK) Limited	£1,834,680,960
Sky CP Limited	£1,830,000,000
Aryzta UK Holdings I Limited	£1,806,012,928
Spectris PLC	£1,798,899,968
GlaxoSmithKline Consumer Healthcare Finance	£1,798,552,960
Signet Group Limited	£1,798,029,184
Kellogg Brown & Root Limited	£1,787,815,936
BP Finance P.L.C	£1,781,024,000
Spectris Group Holdings Limited	£1,745,929,984
GlaxoSmithKline Research & Development Ltd	£1,721,917,952
De Lage Landen Leasing Limited	£1,721,616,000
Coca-Cola European Partners Hldgs Great Britain	£1,720,679,040
BP Shipping Limited	£1,682,076,032
GlaxoSmithKline Intellectual Property (No.2) Ltd	£1,679,232,000
Hilton Finance (UK) Limited	£1,676,255,104
Unilever UK Limited	£1,671,614,976
Compass Overseas Holdings Limited	£1,667,874,048
United Biscuits Holdco 2 Limited	£1,658,300,032
Fidelity China Special Situations PLC	£1,654,736,000
Kraft Foods UK IP & Production Holdings Limited	£1,648,612,992
Anno 2017 Joint Holding (UK) Limited	£1,611,495,936
Linden Limited	£1,588,732,032
Nomad Foods Europe Finco Limited	£1,585,529,856
Kellogg Brown & Root Holdings Limited	£1,585,053,056
GlaxoSmithKline Intellectual Property Development	£1,572,909,056
Hilton HHC Limited	£1,552,382,464
Mizzen Mezzco Limited	£1,551,892,992
Edwardian Group Limited	£1,551,187,968
GE Money Home Lending Holdings Limited	£1,547,659,136
SCIH Branston 3	£1,545,536,000
Spirit Energy Production UK Limited	£1,535,412,992
Premium Credit Limited	£1,533,364,992
CNOOC Petroleum Europe Limited	£1,519,397,376
BP Oil UK Limited	£1,510,000,000
Procter & Gamble Overseas Limited	£1,509,418,752
Firebolt RB Holdings Limited	£1,503,451,136
NBS Trade and Investment Limited	£1,501,340,416
Enterprise Rent-a-Car European Holdings Ltd	£1,499,531,008
Hilton International Hotels (UK) Limited	£1,487,772,288
Dairy Crest Limited	£1,479,000,064
Crest Nicholson Holdings PLC	£1,477,900,032
J D Wetherspoon PLC	£1,476,313,984
Capital Hospitals Ltd.	£1,476,226,944
Capital Hospitals (Holdings) Ltd.	£1,476,226,944
Procter & Gamble Finance (UK) Limited	£1,474,711,936
Enterprise Rent-a-Car UK Limited	£1,472,199,040
Connect Plus (M25) Limited	£1,469,575,040
Connect Plus (M25) Holdings Limited	£1,469,575,040
ExxonMobil Chemical Investment Company Limited	£1,466,121,984
Procter & Gamble Holdings (UK) Limited	£1,450,305,536
Capital Hospitals (Issuer) PLC	£1,446,487,040
Sky Telecommunications Services Limited	£1,444,999,936
Coats Group Finance Company Limited	£1,441,565,824
United Biscuits Holdco Limited	£1,439,299,968
Procter & Gamble Investment Company (UK) Ltd	£1,430,648,704
Cineworld Group PLC	£1,407,200,000
Belron Lending UK Limited	£1,406,666,624
Lucozade Ribena Suntory Limited	£1,394,434,944
Merck Holding Ltd.	£1,389,846,400
ITW Holdings V Limited	£1,387,344,768
Gallaher Limited	£1,385,600,000
TBG (3) 2009 Limited	£1,382,528,000
LGC Science Group Holdings Limited	£1,370,514,944
Elwy 2 Limited	£1,370,514,944
Elwy 3 Limited	£1,370,514,944
Intercontinental (PB) 3 Limited	£1,369,897,600
UB Overseas Limited	£1,367,154,048
Ceesail Limited	£1,354,002,944
Nomad Foods Europe Holdco Limited	£1,348,299,264
BFIM Limited	£1,344,396,032
Astellas Pharma Europe Ltd.	£1,343,135,104
Crest Nicholson PLC	£1,339,200,000
Hilton UK Hotels Limited	£1,338,172,928
Michael Page International Recruitment Limited	£1,333,287,936
Glaxo Operations UK Limited	£1,324,759,040
Chubb Group (International) Limited	£1,315,275,008
RAK Petroleum PLC	£1,310,131,840
Crest Nicholson Operations Limited	£1,309,500,032
Coca-Cola European Partners Great Britain Ltd	£1,293,049,984
PizzaExpress Financing 2 PLC	£1,280,556,032
JTI (UK) Management Ltd	£1,257,982,976
Alliance Healthcare (Distribution) Limited	£1,248,999,936
TJX UK	£1,234,300,032
PizzaExpress Group Holdings Limited	£1,233,755,008
PizzaExpress Financing 1 PLC	£1,233,755,008
AERL Holding Limited	£1,227,772,672
Galliford Try Construction & Investments Holdings	£1,224,300,032
PizzaExpress Operations Limited	£1,203,827,968
Signet Holdings Limited	£1,202,115,712
Sky Group Finance PLC	£1,193,028,992
Merck Sharp & Dohme Finance Europe Limited	£1,183,533,696
Safestore Holdings PLC	£1,156,600,064
Belron Finance Issuer Limited	£1,153,383,552
Subsea 7 Investments (UK) Limited	£1,149,899,776
Compass Group Finance No.2 Limited	£1,143,321,984
Mallinckrodt UK Finance LLP	£1,142,992,384
Subsea 7 Limited	£1,134,483,968
Cadbury Four LLP	£1,124,563,968
LGC (Holdings) Limited	£1,122,893,056
Samsung Electronics (UK) Limited	£1,121,426,048
PizzaExpress Group Limited	£1,113,291,008
St George PLC	£1,104,471,040
Sony Europe Limited	£1,102,010,112
BP Pipelines (SCP) Limited	£1,095,581,312
Equiniti Holdings Limited	£1,089,864,960
MC Treasury Limited	£1,086,730,624
Kidde International Limited	£1,084,392,960
Ultra Electronics Holdings PLC	£1,083,816,960
BP Chemicals East China Investments Limited	£1,083,757,312
Erac UK Finance Limited	£1,076,040,960
Mitsubishi Electric Finance Europe PLC	£1,049,174,016
Goodrich Inertial Limited	£1,042,073,024
Cargill Financial Markets Limited	£1,041,751,616
Fidelity European Values PLC	£1,038,979,968
ISS UK Limited	£1,033,267,008
Shilton Bidco Limited	£1,029,436,992
Six Continents Holdings Limited	£1,028,201,984
Atkins Limited	£1,027,699,968
London Airports 1992 Limited	£1,026,076,032
Senior Engineering Investments Limited	£1,019,582,976
Castle Bidco PLC	£1,019,200,000
Procter & Gamble UK Parent Company Limited	£1,013,041,408
Sky Television Limited	£1,006,201,024
Coats Group PLC	£1,002,335,232
Crown Agents Bank Limited	£993,044,992
Robert Bosch UK Holdings Limited	£988,782,016

Hilton Worldwide FS Treasury Limited	£986,574,848
PizzaExpress (Restaurants) Limited	£983,900,032
Societe Generale Equipment Finance Limited	£977,971,968
CALA Group (Holdings) Limited	£968,812,032
ExxonMobil Investment Company Limited	£964,005,312
Spirit Energy North Sea Limited	£956,955,008
Senior PLC	£950,800,000
Michael Page Holdings Limited	£948,027,008
Reed Business Information Limited	£946,572,992
RCL Cruises Ltd	£945,661,312
Brambles U.K. Limited	£920,161,024
ADT Finance Limited	£900,652,992
Coats Limited	£896,296,000
Costco Wholesale UK Limited	£895,956,992
Costco UK Holdings Limited	£893,710,016
Perform Group Limited	£892,328,000
Accord Healthcare Limited	£891,985,984
Skanska UK PLC	£891,872,000
Brambles Holdings (UK) Limited	£888,199,168
ExxonMobil UK Limited	£882,305,984
Hexagon Manufacturing Intelligence Management	£874,900,928
ViiV Healthcare Finance 2 Limited	£861,767,552
Sky Subscribers Services Limited	£858,601,024
Air Products Group Limited	£834,520,000
PizzaExpress Limited	£824,732,032
Harsco Infrastructure Group Limited	£824,603,200
Intercontinental Hotels Limited	£820,990,976
Premier Lotteries Capital UK Limited	£815,200,000
Premier Lotteries UK Limited	£814,899,968
Xerox Capital (Europe) Limited	£807,499,008
BP Biofuels Brazil Investments Limited	£800,981,376
Onix Investments UK Ltd	£795,908,160
Laing O'Rourke PLC.	£788,600,000
LGC Science Investments Limited	£787,196,032
Compass Hotels Chertsey	£783,217,024
GlaxoSmithKline Consumer Trading Services Ltd	£781,051,008
Air Products Public Limited Company	£778,465,984
Skanska Construction UK Limited	£774,459,008
Host Europe Group Limited	£771,225,024
Gallaher Group Limited	£769,382,976
United Technologies Holdings Limited	£768,590,016
Nissan Motor (GB) Limited	£767,649,024
ESPUG Finance Limited	£765,907,968
CP Holdings Limited	£762,854,976
ADT Fire and Security PLC	£761,942,016
Kidde UK	£761,939,968
Compass Group North America Investments No.2	£754,867,776
Superdrug Stores PLC	£753,222,016
WP Midco3 Limited	£752,249,984
nVent International (UK) Ltd	£749,903,168
Solai Holdings Limited	£745,441,984
St James Group Limited	£744,556,992
Britannic Trading Limited	£742,389,248
Hexagon Corporate Management Limited	£742,117,184
Galliard Group Limited	£741,121,024
Chubb International Holdings Limited	£740,940,032
Nuffield Health	£737,299,968
Air Products (BR) Limited	£736,190,016
Fidelity Special Values PLC	£733,105,024
Mott MacDonald Limited	£732,182,016
Sky Finance Europe Limited	£727,587,968
GlaxoSmithKline UK Limited	£723,723,008
Belron International Limited	£723,329,984
Toyota (G.B.) PLC	£721,769,024
Mott MacDonald Group Limited	£712,019,968
Port of Tilbury London Limited	£711,844,992
Safetykleen Group Services Limited	£710,739,008
Cineworld Cinemas Limited	£706,400,000
Laing O'Rourke Services Limited	£704,140,992
Wates Group Limited	£702,764,032
BP Senegal Investments Limited	£701,984,000
Automatic Data Processing Limited	£701,867,008
Colorcon European Holdings (No.5) Limited	£695,000,000
ISS Facility Services Limited	£694,902,016
Sky In-Home Service Limited	£689,548,032
GlaxoSmithKline Consumer Healthcare UK Trading	£685,875,968
DL Insurance Services Limited	£684,000,000
Tata Global Beverages Group Limited	£683,667,008
BP Exploration Beta Limited	£683,506,112
W.S. Atkins International Limited	£676,515,008
Cargill PLC	£676,387,008
Football Association Limited	£675,270,016
Augustus 2 Limited	£671,014,016
Xerox (UK) Limited	£667,699,968
UPS Limited	£664,441,984
Kellogg Brown & Root Overseas Projects Limited	£653,177,088
Camelot UK Lotteries Limited	£651,699,968
Sky Ventures Limited	£647,968,000
TJX Europe Limited	£643,612,992
DF Group Limited	£642,947,648
Arora Hotels Limited	£635,217,024
Dairy Crest Group PLC	£628,200,000
Cineworld Holdings Limited	£623,516,032
Nomad Foods BondCo PLC	£621,933,056
Renewable Energy Systems Holdings Limited	£620,592,000
The Hospital Company (Southmead) Limited	£620,545,984
Hospital Company (Southmead) Holdings Ltd	£620,545,984
Compass Group Finance No. 3 Limited	£619,163,008
Intralot Finance UK Limited	£618,260,544
WS Atkins Limited	£611,299,968
Trellis Acquisitions Limited	£610,833,984
Edwardian Hotel Finance Ltd	£610,369,024
Menzies Aviation PLC	£609,699,968
Merck Sharp & Dohme Limited	£607,619,008
Chubb Group Security Limited	£606,934,976
United Biscuits VInco Limited	£600,000,000
Coats Finance Co. Limited	£598,715,840
HCL EAS Ltd	£596,680,640
Perform Sports Media Limited	£595,744,000
Splendid Hospitality Group LLP	£593,888,832
Wates Construction Limited	£591,993,024
Laing O'Rourke Construction Limited	£591,195,008
Wembley National Stadium Limited	£589,750,976
Beecham Group P L C	£588,897,024
Amshold Group Limited	£587,838,016
Kellogg Brown & Root International Group Limited	£578,924,608
Galliford Try Building Limited	£576,496,000
Safestore Acquisition Limited	£576,177,024
Elysium Healthcare Holdings 2 Limited	£575,473,024
Beam Suntory UK Limited	£573,376,000
Runecorp Limited	£571,641,024
Senior Five Limited	£570,557,504
GlaxoSmithKline Investment Services Limited	£570,209,984
Dairy Crest UK Limited	£565,105,984
Cargill UK Holdings Limited	£556,501,952
Vinci PLC	£556,436,992
London May Fair Hotel Limited	£550,019,968
Innotech Advisers Limited	£549,925,120
Chubb Fire & Security Limited	£546,145,024
Vinci Construction UK Limited	£546,112,000
MGT Teesside Limited	£544,942,976
Safestore Group Limited	£543,182,976
Kerry Foods Limited	£538,807,168
BP Pipelines Tap Limited	£537,848,320
ADT Group Limited	£535,039,008
IHG Hotels Limited	£534,344,992
Tata Global Beverages Services Limited	£529,515,008
Wyevale Garden Centres Limited	£528,996,000
Rhombi Holdings Limited	£528,601,536
TBG (4) Limited	£525,227,008
BP Exploration (Shah Deniz) Limited	£522,955,648
International Transport Limited	£519,320,000
TWG Europe Limited	£519,175,008
St George Blackfriars Limited	£514,294,368

Company	Value
HIC Treasury Limited	£514,079,584
Kellogg Brown & Root Holdings (U.K.) Limited	£512,745,984
BP Pipelines (BTC) Limited	£509,718,560
Hotel Intercontinental London (Holdings) Limited	£508,111,008
TBG (1) 2009 Limited	£507,999,008
CTS Metropark Limited	£507,940,992
Network Treasury Services Limited	£506,721,056
Scentrics Information Security Technologies Limited	£505,965,952
ExxonMobil Chemical Limited	£502,000,000
Rhodia Holdings Limited	£501,308,992
Pagegroup PLC	£499,812,000
BP Exploration (Algeria) Limited	£499,201,024
HIC Racing (Chiswick) Limited	£499,137,952
Schering-Plough Holdings Limited	£498,076,992
London Square Developments (Holdings) Limited	£496,519,008
SmithKline Beecham (Investments) Limited	£495,331,008
PRA Group (UK) Limited	£492,511,008
Harsco (UK) Group Limited	£491,493,920
Belmont Green Ltd	£491,313,984
Spirit Energy Resources Limited	£488,572,992
Dairy Crest France Holdings 1 Limited	£487,660,000
First Rate Exchange Services Limited	£486,819,008
First Rate Exchange Services Holdings Limited	£484,660,992
ISS UK Holding Limited	£483,235,008
Audiotonix Group Limited	£479,676,288
Kia Motors (UK) Limited	£478,931,008
Smiths Interconnect Group Limited	£474,943,008
London Square Developments (Ventures) Limited	£473,415,008
London General Insurance Company Limited	£472,912,000
CEB Holdings UK 2 Limited	£472,727,008
Beam Suntory UK Holdings Limited	£470,887,008
Cine-UK Limited	£467,367,008
DS (Holdings) 2 Limited	£467,195,776
Harris Federation	£465,664,992
Perform Investment Limited	£464,953,984
Smith Kline & French Laboratories Limited	£464,873,984
Solvecorp Limited	£464,835,008
London Square Limited	£460,803,008
Wellcome Foundation Limited (The)	£457,700,992
Merck Sharp & Dohme (Holdings) Limited	£455,840,992
Wyevale Garden Centres Holdings Limited	£455,476,992
Spectris US Holdings Limited	£455,179,008
SSCP Spring Topco Limited	£450,452,992
Safestore Limited	£447,948,000
Ultra Electronics Limited	£447,919,008
GlaxoSmithKline Export Limited	£447,628,000
GDL Holdco Limited	£445,380,064
Tanjong Public Limited Company	£444,819,264
Gallaher Overseas (Holdings) Limited	£440,740,000
Regentrealm Limited	£439,400,000
Shilton Holdco Limited	£439,038,016
Kuehne + Nagel Limited	£436,123,008
Bio Products Laboratory Holdings Limited	£434,364,000
Procter & Gamble Product Supply (U.K.) Limited	£432,592,992
SAP (UK) Limited	£431,924,000
WDFG UK Holdings Limited	£429,328,000
Telford Homes PLC	£427,688,000
Caretech Holdings PLC	£426,992,000
WorleyParsons UK Finance Sub Limited	£426,903,008
Coventry and Rugby Hospital Company PLC	£423,859,008
Coventry and Rugby Hospital Company Holdings Ltd	£423,775,008
Wyevale Garden Centres Capital Limited	£422,868,000
Trellis Investments Limited	£422,860,992
Trellis Finance Limited	£422,680,000
Benson & Hedges Limited	£420,400,000
Kew Green Group Limited	£420,263,904
Lanber Properties LLP	£418,378,048
Future Electronics Limited	£418,320,000
EMC Computer Systems (U.K.) Limited	£417,184,992
Healthcare Support (North Staffs) Limited	£417,032,000
Healthcare Support (North Staffs) Holdings Limited	£417,032,000
Peterborough (Progress Health) Holdings Limited	£415,440,992
Peterborough (Progress Health) PLC	£415,440,992
Edwardian Finance Ltd	£411,384,992
Procter & Gamble (Health & Beauty Care) Limited	£411,360,000
Naga UK Topco Limited	£409,176,992
Kodak International Finance Limited	£408,733,472
HEL Bidco Ltd	£408,340,000
Lubricants UK Limited	£408,201,984
Tati Company Limited	£407,121,664
Derby Healthcare PLC	£405,967,008
Derby Healthcare (Holdings) Limited	£405,956,992
Healthcare Support (North Staffs) Finance PLC	£405,620,992
AGCO Finance Limited	£404,260,000
WorleyParsons Europe Limited	£401,252,992
O'Rourke Investments Holdings (UK) Limited	£400,808,000
Kellogg Brown & Root DH Limited	£399,282,432
Heathrow T5 Hotel Limited	£397,668,768
Consort Healthcare (Mid Yorkshire) Limited	£395,601,984
Consort Healthcare (Mid Yorkshire) Holdings Ltd	£395,601,984
A6 Audio Bidco Limited	£395,585,984
Forth Ports Finance PLC	£395,316,000
Nomad Foods Europe Holdings Limited	£394,835,936
IHC May Fair (Holdings) Limited	£392,679,008
ExxonMobil Gas Marketing Europe Limited	£392,000,000
Central Nottinghamshire Hospitals (Holdings) Ltd	£391,337,984
Central Nottinghamshire Hospitals PLC	£391,337,984
Galaxy Group Bidco Limited	£390,119,008
Schweppes Limited	£389,079,008
123-Reg Limited	£388,724,000
Consort Healthcare (Mid Yorkshire) Funding PLC	£386,988,992
Preziosa Cruise Limited	£386,967,136
Chubb Fire Limited	£385,910,016
Brighthouse Limited	£383,449,984
Kerry Holdings (U.K.) Limited	£382,593,792
Forth Health Holdings Limited	£382,000,992
Forth Health Limited	£381,987,008
GlaxoSmithKline Consumer Healthcare (UK) IP Ltd	£381,208,000
Healthcare Support (Newcastle) Limited	£381,011,008
Healthcare Support (Newcastle) Holdings Limited	£381,011,008
Healthcare Support (Newcastle) Finance PLC	£380,844,992
Elysium Healthcare Holdings 3 Limited	£377,808,992
Mentmore Limited	£376,945,984
Hill Holdings Limited	£376,777,984
Zoom Gas Pipelines Limited	£376,759,008
Endon Europe Power 3 Limited	£376,488,992
Zoom Infrastructure Limited	£375,833,984
Zoom Holding Limited	£375,684,992
BP Mauritania Investments Limited	£374,844,672
Tata Global Beverages Investments Limited	£371,004,000
London Square Developments Limited	£370,248,000
Synamedia Limited	£369,984,768
Perform Media Channels Ltd	£369,636,992
Signet Trading Limited	£369,443,008
Kellogg Brown & Root Group Limited	£366,753,312
Naga UK Bidco Limited	£364,713,984
F5 Networks Limited	£363,392,096
Edwardian Hotel Investments Ltd	£361,648,000
Galliford Try Partnerships Limited	£361,056,000
Perform Media Services Ltd	£360,615,008
GE Money Servicing Limited	£359,737,984
Fairview Holdings Limited	£356,788,992
Newhospitals (St Helens & Knowsley) Finance PLC	£355,201,984
Volkerwessels UK Limited	£351,801,984
Archer Daniels Midland (UK) Limited	£351,168,640
Teddington 2 Limited	£350,064,000
CEB Holdings UK 1 Limited	£349,908,000
Host Europe Investments Limited	£346,960,000
BA Cityflyer Limited	£346,233,984
LGC Science Holdings Limited	£345,708,992
Burnt Tree Group Limited	£345,360,000
Cardif Pinnacle Insurance Holdings PLC	£344,260,000
IHC Overseas (U.K.) Limited	£341,574,016
WDFG UK Limited	£340,180,000

Company	Value
Kellogg Brown & Root London Limited	£339,168,064
Renewable Energy Systems Limited	£336,766,016
LGC Limited	£336,591,008
Harsco Investment Limited	£333,897,984
Day Lewis PLC	£333,744,992
Accolade Wines Limited	£333,712,000
Caversham Finance Limited	£333,688,000
Verint Technology UK Limited	£333,026,240
Pinnacle Insurance PLC	£332,326,016
United Biscuits BondCo Limited	£331,800,000
WorleyParsons UK Finance Sub No. 2 Ltd	£330,134,528
Mondelez UK Finance Company Limited	£329,451,520
Newhospitals (St Helens and Knowsley) Limited	£327,828,992
Newhospitals (St Helens and Knowsley) Holdings Ltd	£327,828,992
Augustus 1 Limited	£325,528,992
Atkins Investments UK Limited	£325,300,000
BP Exploration Angola (Kwanza Benguela) Limited	£321,866,336
LG Electronics U.K. Ltd	£319,664,992
Toshiba of Europe Limited	£318,844,928
ACI Worldwide (EMEA) Limited	£316,646,016
Audley Group Limited	£315,832,992
Nexen Petroleum U.K. Holdings Limited	£315,630,880
Millipore UK Holdings LLP	£314,942,016
Skanska Construction Holdings UK Limited	£314,691,008
Tesla Motors Limited	£314,548,416
Laing O'Rourke Holdings Limited	£310,592,000
WP Safety-Kleen Limited	£310,040,000
CEB Global Holdings Limited	£309,841,984
Xerox Finance Limited	£309,790,016
Fairview New Homes Limited	£309,481,984
Amsprop Investments Limited	£308,055,968
Procter & Gamble Limited	£307,380,992
Signet UK Finance PLC	£306,881,696
BP Chemicals Investments Limited	£306,761,504
Hill Residential Limited	£305,825,984
DSTI Holdings Limited	£305,128,992
BTC Pipeline Holding Company Limited	£304,127,968
Optivo Finance PLC	£302,900,000
Bio Products Laboratory Limited	£302,643,008
Killinchy Aerospace Holdings Limited	£301,856,000
Host Europe Limited	£301,600,992
Endon Europe Power 1 Limited	£301,216,992
Renault U.K. Limited	£300,583,008
Cargill Investments	£300,479,424
Meritcape Limited	£300,435,936
Spirit Energy Southern North Sea Limited	£300,243,456
Galliard Holdings Limited	£299,718,112
Kew Green Hotels Limited	£297,879,168
Union Maritime Limited	£292,708,416
Audley Court Limited	£292,196,992
Bristol-Myers Squibb Holdings 2002 Limited	£291,864,992
Fidelity Asian Values PLC	£291,380,992
Best Holdings (UK) Limited	£291,121,248
BPH Finance Number 1 Limited	£289,932,000
The Vitec Group PLC.	£289,700,000
Phivco UK II Limited	£287,228,992
State Oil Limited	£286,220,000
DSTI Group LLP	£284,953,984
Hertz (U.K.) Limited	£282,980,992
Canada Life Finance (U.K.) Limited	£281,772,992
WP Midco1 Limited	£280,068,992
The Kemnal Academies Trust	£279,572,992
Hystead Limited	£278,608,736
Birds Eye Limited	£278,430,016
Bristol-Myers Squibb Pharmaceuticals Limited	£276,734,016
Mothercare PLC.	£276,700,000
Piramal Critical Care Limited	£276,387,680
Almus Pharmaceuticals Limited	£275,978,528
Riposte Limited	£275,720,992
Spirit Europe Limited	£271,979,104
ESP Utilities Group Limited	£271,476,000
Six Continents Investments Limited	£271,191,008
DHL Global Forwarding (UK) Limited	£270,824,000
BNK (UK) Limited	£269,637,024
St William Homes LLP	£269,284,000
South Central Property Limited	£268,950,304
Dairy Crest (Services) Limited	£268,000,992
WP Midco2 Limited	£267,900,000
Annes Gate Property PLC	£267,806,000
AGP Holdings (1) Limited	£267,806,000
Bluecastle Enterprises Limited	£267,046,032
Fizzy Enterprises LLP	£264,131,008
Dairy Crest France Holdings 2 Limited	£262,887,008
Abbey Developments Limited	£262,689,568
GE Money Home Finance Limited	£262,042,608
Vitec Investments Limited	£260,059,008
Select Plant Hire Company Limited	£259,896,992
HCL Technologies UK Limited	£259,556,000
Verint WS Holdings Limited	£257,842,000
Galliard Homes Limited	£257,703,344
Haymarket Media Group Ltd.	£256,752,000
ViiV Healthcare UK (No.4) Limited	£256,428,992
Flight Centre (UK) Limited	£255,576,992
Kodak Limited	£255,500,000
Brighthouse Holdings Limited	£254,842,000
British American Tobacco UK Limited	£254,247,008
Air BP Limited	£252,219,584
Majestic Wine PLC	£251,967,008
Procter & Gamble UK Group Holdings Limited	£251,772,000
William Grant & Sons Brands Limited	£251,652,000
Saipem Limited	£251,528,448
Shimtech Industries Holdco2 Limited	£248,446,000
PandoraExpress 2 Limited	£248,162,000
GPG (UK) Holdings Limited	£247,484,992
Subsea 7 International Contracting Limited	£247,003,392
PandoraExpress 4 Limited	£246,580,000
JCDecaux UK Limited	£246,292,000
CALA 1 Limited	£245,650,768
PandoraExpress 3 Limited	£244,707,008
JRL Group Holdings Limited	£244,142,128
BP Exploration Libya Limited	£244,057,344
Cipla (EU) Limited	£243,258,848
Cordant Group PLC	£242,836,992
Croudace Homes Group Limited	£242,700,992
PKA WLWF Holding (UK) Limited	£242,544,000
BP Aromatics Limited	£242,243,344
Tata Global Beverages GB Limited	£241,331,008
UPS (UK Holding) Limited	£239,067,920
Photo - Me International P L C	£238,908,992
Edwardian New Finance Limited	£238,123,008
Hamsard 3352 Limited	£237,866,800
United Technologies Finance (U.K.) Limited	£237,822,000
Rackspace Limited	£236,999,472
Reed Exhibitions Limited	£236,997,920
Procter & Gamble Technical Centres Limited	£234,520,000
Aura Finance Limited	£234,196,032
Brighthouse Group Limited	£233,292,000
Dhamecha Holdings Limited	£232,784,000
People Against Dirty Holdings Limited	£232,747,920
Mizzen Midco Limited	£232,080,992
Mothercare UK Limited	£231,000,000
Connect Plus (M25) Intermediate Limited	£230,339,008
Amoco (Fiddich) Limited	£229,542,288
JRL Group Limited	£229,338,288
Currie Motors Limited	£228,563,008
Shogun Finance Limited	£227,207,008
Adda Hotels	£226,913,728
Stiefel Consumer Healthcare (UK) Limited	£226,192,000
Tradex Insurance Holdings Limited	£224,988,992
Tradex Insurance Company Limited	£224,964,000
Hill Partnerships Limited	£224,531,008
Fidelity Japan Trust PLC	£224,475,008
WP SK Limited	£224,239,008
Noon Products Limited	£224,222,848

Company	Value
Paragon Treasury PLC	£224,140,000
Subsea 7 Finance (UK) PLC	£224,045,200
Chep UK Limited	£223,976,000
Safestore Properties Limited	£223,668,992
LGC Science Group Limited	£223,668,992
HH Global Group Limited	£223,102,000
E.S. Pipelines Limited	£223,075,008
Accolade Wines Holdings Europe Limited	£222,027,008
Manpower UK Limited	£220,271,008
Caretech Community Services Limited	£216,876,000
SK Hynix UK Limited	£216,451,216
BP Alternative Energy Investments Limited	£216,051,520
Atkins International Holdings Limited	£214,945,408
Atlantic 2/3 UK Holdings Limited	£214,789,936
British Airways Holidays Limited	£212,999,008
Medtronic Limited	£212,692,992
Hotel Inter-Continental London Limited	£212,570,000
Continental U.K. Group Holdings Limited	£212,311,008
Panther Securities P L C	£211,962,000
Rhodia Limited	£211,896,000
Volkerwessels Limited	£211,092,992
Hexagon Positioning Intelligence Limited	£210,702,000
Twentieth Century Fox Television Distribution (UK)	£209,570,784
Navigator Terminals Midco Limited	£209,240,000
Britair Holdings Limited	£209,104,992
Global Draw Limited	£208,888,000
Kone Public Limited Company	£208,575,008
Croudace Homes Limited	£207,668,000
Solvay Solutions UK Limited	£207,010,000
Finance Ireland Limited	£206,919,440
Treasury Wine Estates EMEA Limited	£205,760,000
Perform Group Financing PLC	£205,448,000
Petco Trading (UK) Limited	£205,126,992
Costco Limited	£205,079,008
Edwardian Pastoria Hotels Ltd	£204,695,008
Cargill UK Finance Limited	£204,367,008
TLC Group Limited	£203,683,040
Menzies Group Holdings Limited	£203,200,000
Cineworld Cinemas Holdings Limited	£202,770,000
Skanska Rashleigh Weatherfoil Limited	£202,738,000
Sharp Electronics (Europe) Limited	£202,510,208
GlaxoSmithKline Holdings (One) Limited	£202,339,008
Eskaylab Limited	£201,900,000
The Tower, One St George Wharf Limited	£201,730,000
Glasgow Learning Quarter Limited	£200,922,960
Wren Topco Limited	£200,296,992
Axon Group Limited	£199,728,000
Higgins Group PLC	£199,340,000
ISS Mediclean Limited	£198,944,992
KBR (U.K.) Investments Limited	£198,719,136
I.P. Clarke & Co. Limited	£198,687,008
Glasgow Learning Quarter (Holdings) Limited	£198,024,576
Delta Limited	£196,550,000
BH (City Forum) Limited	£196,340,000
RATP DEV UK Ltd	£195,572,992
Audio UK 2 Limited	£195,316,000
Audio UK 3 Limited	£195,316,000
Shurgard UK Limited	£194,987,392
Shimtech Industries Group Limited	£194,229,792
Celgene Limited	£190,243,632
GL Education Group Limited	£189,812,000
Tata Global Beverages Holdings Limited	£189,515,008
Trellis Holdco Limited	£189,350,000
UK Real Estate Limited	£189,299,520
Dhamecha Foods Limited	£188,968,992
Western United Investment Company Limited	£188,700,000
GLF Schools	£188,108,000
Prax Petroleum Limited	£188,040,848
Galliford Try Homes Limited	£186,766,000
Ardent Hire Solutions Limited	£186,712,000
Sogea Holdings (UK) Limited	£186,660,992
Transform Schools (Knowsley) Holdings Limited	£186,576,992

Company	Value
Transform Schools (Knowsley) Limited	£186,576,992
Haltermann Carless UK Limited	£186,391,008
Transform Schools (North Lanarkshire) Limited	£185,952,992
Transform Schools (North Lanarkshire) Holdings Ltd	£185,952,992
Tuskerdirect Limited	£185,849,040
P G S International Limited	£184,642,336
G4S Secure Solutions (UK) Limited	£184,500,992
Barnardo's	£184,364,000
Galvani Bioelectronics Limited	£183,852,000
The Gym Group PLC	£183,447,008
Senior Finance Four Limited	£183,024,992
Edwardian Investments Ltd	£182,242,000
Kellogg Brown & Root Overseas Operations Ltd	£181,719,616
Mallinckrodt Enterprises UK Limited	£181,503,984
Mushi UK Holdings Limited	£181,503,984
Eastbury Park Limited	£181,107,008
Eastbury Park (Holdings) Limited	£181,107,008
LSQ Holdco 3 Limited	£179,984,000
VolkerFitzpatrick Limited	£179,503,008
Elysium Healthcare No. 2 Limited	£179,348,992
Beko PLC	£179,327,008
Sun Valley Foods Limited	£177,972,000
Keltbray Group (Holdings) Limited	£177,407,840
Kingsway Asset Co Limited	£177,003,936
BP Exploration North Africa Limited	£176,713,184
Keltbray Group Limited	£176,649,984
WP SK Midco Limited	£176,288,992
Transform Schools (North Lanarkshire) Funding PLC	£175,468,992
Mizzen Bidco Limited	£175,308,992
A A Homes and Housing Ltd	£175,096,832
Berkeley (SQP) Limited	£174,989,664
Berkeley Homes (Southall) Limited	£174,928,992
Accolade Wines Europe No. 2 Limited	£172,960,000
Platinum Topco Limited	£171,971,168
Axiom Education (Edinburgh) Limited	£171,948,992
By Chelmer (Holdings) Limited	£171,388,992
By Chelmer PLC	£171,388,992
Sherrygreen Limited	£171,018,000
Blackstown Holdings Limited	£170,688,736
G4S Cash Solutions (UK) Limited	£169,738,000
Yang Ming (UK) Ltd	£169,668,224
Arora T5 Holdings Limited	£169,359,520
Gilead Sciences Europe Ltd.	£169,275,008
Watford Association Football Club Limited (The)	£168,852,896
Vestey Holdings Limited	£168,658,000
Manpower Public Limited Company	£168,376,000
SC Leisure Group Limited	£168,168,992
Del Monte Foods International Limited	£167,848,000
Advanced Elastomer Systems Limited	£165,834,000
Fulham Football Leisure Limited	£165,480,000
Cougar Holdco London Limited	£165,476,992
Mizzen Mezzco 2 Limited	£165,444,000
The Walsall Hospital Company (Holdings) Limited	£164,771,008
The Walsall Hospital Company PLC	£164,771,008
LGC Investments Limited	£164,500,992
Safety Kleen U.K. Limited	£164,420,000
Vitec Production Solutions Limited	£164,204,000
The Gym Group Midco1 Limited	£163,891,104
The Gym Group Midco2 Limited	£163,884,160
ADT (UK) Limited	£163,707,008
Graham Care (YB) Limited	£163,476,544
Endeavour SCH Holdings Limited	£163,332,000
Endeavour SCH PLC	£163,332,000
LGC Whirlwind Limited	£162,715,008
Tata Global Beverages Capital Limited	£162,334,000
Vitec Group Holdings Limited	£162,190,000
GDL (Millharbour) Limited	£162,070,064
Burroughs Wellcome International Limited	£162,024,000
Martin-Baker Aircraft Company Limited	£161,972,992
Del Monte Europe Limited	£161,174,000
Future Electronics Management Services Limited	£160,879,008
BP Middle East Limited	£160,749,520

Company	Turnover
DPSK Limited	£160,401,344
Retirement Villages Group Limited	£160,166,000
British Midland Airways Limited	£158,500,000
Kidde Finance Limited	£157,560,000
The Gym Limited	£156,844,000
Continental Tyre Group Ltd.	£155,530,000
Edwardian International Hotels Ltd	£154,612,000
All Metal Services Limited	£154,515,056
NEC Capital (UK) PLC	£154,100,000
The Spicers-Officeteam Group Limited	£153,911,008
Axiom Education (Perth & Kinross) Limited	£153,326,000
Moat Homes Finance PLC	£153,255,008
Galliard Developments Limited	£153,230,640
Care Management Group Limited	£152,823,120
ExxonMobil Marine Limited	£152,302,000
Menzies Aviation Holdings Limited	£151,800,000
BP Marine Limited	£151,731,200
NEC Europe Ltd	£151,679,792
Juniper Networks (UK) Limited	£151,603,760
Exploration Service Company Limited	£151,240,768
Adelie Foods Bidco Limited	£150,892,992
Console Bidco Limited	£150,419,008
John Guest Holdings Limited	£150,349,984
Safestore Investments Limited	£150,000,000
Platinum Acquisition Limited	£149,896,496
Senior UK Limited	£149,584,000
ExxonMobil International Limited	£149,532,000
ABJ Trading LLP	£148,512,000
SSCP Spring Midco 2 Limited	£148,200,992
RANC Holdings Limited	£148,106,368
Allocate Topco Limited	£147,862,000
Court Cavendish Limited	£147,824,000
Spectris UK Holdings Limited	£146,976,992
Forextra Developments Limited	£146,904,336
Burnfield Limited	£146,500,000
Equiniti Services Limited	£146,148,992
ABSL1 Limited	£146,092,176
Wolters Kluwer Holdings (UK) PLC	£146,081,552
Ruby Topco Limited	£145,100,000
ESSCI Limited	£145,068,992
Harvest Midco Limited	£145,030,000
Geodis FF United Kingdom Ltd.	£142,608,992
Durkan Holdings Limited	£142,434,064
Allocate Midco Limited	£142,212,992
BP Oil International Limited	£142,143,008
H & T Group PLC	£141,936,000
Kellogg Brown & Root (U.K.) Limited	£141,891,008
Alder Hey (Special Purpose Vehicle) Limited	£140,735,008
Alder Hey Holdco 3 Limited	£140,735,008
The Gym Group Operations Limited	£140,251,776
Onkar International Limited	£140,223,632
Teledyne Limited	£139,464,992
Majestic Wine Warehouses Limited	£138,679,008
RHP Finance PLC	£138,651,008
PMP Recruitment Limited	£138,570,784
GL Assessment Limited	£138,482,000
Consort Healthcare (Blackburn) Limited	£138,435,008
Consort Healthcare (Blackburn) Holdings Limited	£138,435,008
Harvey & Thompson Limited	£137,972,992
Allport Group Limited	£137,777,280
Sungard Availability Services (UK) Limited	£137,739,008
Elysium Healthcare LC Limited	£137,518,000
John Guest International Limited	£137,306,512
Macarthys Laboratories Limited	£137,148,992
Bourne Education Trust	£136,623,536
Fairview Hotels Limited	£136,622,640
Keltbray Limited	£135,913,392
KBC Process Technology Limited	£134,964,000
Porcelanosa U.K. Limited	£134,772,000
Wyevale Acquisitions Borrower Limited	£134,244,992
Kellogg Brown & Root International Group Holdings	£133,496,968
Astellas Pharma Ltd.	£133,302,000
Link Asset Services (Holdings) Limited	£133,232,328
GGI Holdings Limited	£133,229,000
Pentair UK Holdings Limited	£133,198,552
Papa Topco Limited	£133,039,000
Papa Midco Limited	£133,035,000
Kuehne + Nagel (UK) Limited	£132,956,480
United Living Group Limited	£132,833,000
Taylor Woodrow Construction	£132,612,000
Dnata World Travel Limited	£132,321,000
Avalon Cellars Two Limited	£132,179,000
Kingsway Mezz Hold Co Limited	£131,986,816
Link Market Services Limited	£131,760,304
Dealcyber Limited	£131,680,000
ViiV Healthcare Overseas Limited	£131,581,000
PB Topco Limited	£131,370,000
Aprite (GB) Limited	£131,193,000
CMG Holdco Limited	£131,002,000
Senior Finance Six Limited	£130,925,520
Imagination Technologies Group Limited	£130,912,000
St Mary's University, Twickenham	£130,741,000
Kaysail Limited	£130,549,824
Bynorth Limited	£130,389,000
Bynorth (Holdings) Limited	£130,389,000
Ali UK Limited	£130,357,000
Petroleum Geo-Services (UK) Limited	£130,185,000
Dormole Limited	£130,002,000
Hastoe Capital PLC	£129,685,000
Millipore (U.K.) Limited	£129,667,000
Reliance Vanco Group Limited	£129,491,488
DST Process Solutions Limited	£129,104,000
CNOOC Ettrick U.K. Limited	£129,054,616
NPL Management Limited	£128,708,000
Haymarket UK2 Limited	£128,682,680
Oki Europe Limited	£128,627,400
Housing Gateway Limited	£128,319,832
Medivet Group Limited	£128,100,616
Cramlington Renewable Energy Developments Hold	£127,721,000
Intercontinental Hotels Group Services Company	£127,499,000
Pandrol International Limited	£126,180,000
Procter & Gamble (L & CP) Limited	£125,951,000
Thorntons Limited	£125,707,000
Granitte Investments (UK) Limited	£125,554,400
Platinum Newco II Limited	£125,000,000
P.J. Carey (Contractors) Limited	£124,872,688
Allocate Bidco Limited	£124,390,000
Shure Europe Holdings Limited	£124,386,464
GD UK Holdings, Ltd	£124,193,000
The Howard Partnership Trust	£124,044,000
Newincco 1270 Limited	£123,700,328
Kellogg Brown & Root (Greenford) Limited	£123,680,904
Triplerose Limited	£123,471,992
Industrial Chemicals Group Limited	£121,617,424
Overseas Air Travel Limited	£121,246,000
Gartner U.K. Limited	£121,190,000
Higgins Construction PLC	£120,509,000
BP Technology Ventures Limited	£120,078,968
Cochlear Europe Limited	£120,014,048
CEB Global Limited	£119,790,000
BA and AA Holdings Limited	£119,417,072
Ferrero UK Limited	£119,285,000
ACS International Schools Limited	£119,153,392
Early Learning Centre Limited	£119,100,000
Caridon Holdings LLP	£118,772,880
Reliance Infra Projects (UK) Limited	£118,668,744
Travel Republic Ltd	£118,592,000
Chaptre Investments Limited	£118,546,072
Corona Energy Retail 4 Limited	£118,481,440
PizzaExpress Merchandising Limited	£118,259,000
Barcrest Group Limited	£118,188,000
Volex PLC	£117,791,552
ADT South Africa Holding Limited	£117,785,000
Eco Animal Health Group PLC	£117,185,000

Shiva Kingsway Limited	£117,024,896	BP Chemicals (Korea) Limited	£105,049,000
Hill Group Services Limited	£117,019,000	Officeteam Limited	£104,854,000
Meridian Hospital Company PLC	£116,998,000	Mitsubishi Heavy Industries Air-Conditioning Europe	£104,789,312
Meridian Hospital Company (Holdings) Limited	£116,998,000	Michael Page Recruitment Group Limited	£104,353,000
Quality Spirits International Limited	£116,992,000	Edwardian Hampshire Hotels Ltd	£104,171,000
Uniserve Holdings Limited	£116,781,000	Amsprop Bishopsgate Limited	£103,946,048
John Guest Limited	£116,658,504	Belton Associates (Group Holdings) Limited	£103,847,000
Sharp International Finance (U.K.) PLC	£116,652,608	VS Alliance Limited	£103,512,560
Skanska Project Developments Limited	£115,084,000	Alestra Limited	£103,388,792
PB Bidco Limited	£115,077,000	GCH Corporation Limited	£103,256,360
Legolas Debt Holdco Limited	£114,980,712	Grove HR Limited	£103,054,368
Western Wines Holdings Limited	£114,755,000	Alternative Bridging Corporation Limited	£103,020,976
Perform Media Sales Ltd	£114,639,000	BP Amoco Exploration (Faroes) Limited	£102,787,704
PB Holdco Limited	£114,291,000	Harsco Metals Group Limited	£102,759,000
PB Midco Limited	£114,290,000	GCP Cardale PFI Ltd	£102,363,056
United Living (South) Limited	£114,285,000	Mid Holding Co UK Limited	£102,321,984
P. Flannery Plant Hire (Oval) Limited	£114,142,808	Harsco Mole Valley Limited	£102,038,728
Fulham Stadium Limited	£113,179,000	Harsco Leatherhead Limited	£101,955,128
O'Halloran & O'Brien Limited	£113,127,728	BP Chemicals Limited	£101,846,000
Care Management Group (Acquisition) Limited	£113,076,000	Golden Leaves Limited	£101,814,112
Belton Associates Limited	£112,876,000	Cadbury Schweppes Finance Limited	£101,588,000
Cross London Trains Finance Company Limited	£112,677,000	Ferholding UK Ltd	£101,576,000
Hotel Management International (Holdings) Limited	£112,061,000	Expeditors International (UK) Limited	£101,461,000
The Gala Film Partners, LLP	£112,058,120	The Clancy Group PLC	£101,001,464
Bharat Forge International Limited	£112,049,960	Faithful+Gould Limited	£100,931,000
Education Management Corporation Limited	£111,891,240	Wren Midco Limited	£100,600,096
RO Trading Limited	£111,794,000	Samsung SDS Europe Limited	£100,519,000
Cargill Holdings	£111,631,192	Beck & Pollitzer Limited	£100,397,808
SME Group PLC	£111,588,000	Zotefoams PLC	£100,264,000
Ocobase Limited	£111,565,152	General Mills UK Limited	£100,212,000
Compass Group Finance No.4 Limited	£111,322,264	Belton Associates Holdings Limited	£99,935,000
Newship Limited	£111,119,000	Walker Greenbank PLC.	£99,653,000
Alliance Healthcare (IT Services) Limited	£111,040,000	Action for Children	£99,481,000
OTC Direct Limited	£111,000,000	The Invicta Film Partnership No.23, LLP	£99,070,112
Pandrol Finance Limited	£110,940,000	Moove Lubricants Limited	£99,059,000
BP Greece Limited	£110,869,536	Guangdong Investments Limited	£98,892,904
Harvest Energy Limited	£110,559,824	Kelvin Hughes Limited	£98,847,000
Pura Foods Limited	£110,393,752	Pearl River Delta Investments Limited	£98,754,248
BMT Group Limited	£110,380,000	Edwardian Grafton Hotel Ltd	£98,025,000
G4S Security Services (UK) Limited	£110,271,000	Berkeley Two Hundred and Three Limited	£97,515,000
PCL Bidco Limited	£109,900,000	The Invicta Film Partnership No.37, LLP	£97,431,904
Purelake Properties Limited	£109,685,592	Skanska J.V. Projects Ltd	£97,344,000
Laxmi BNS Holdings Limited	£109,609,696	Pizza Hut (U.K.) Limited	£97,308,000
Kew Green (LRG1) Limited	£109,454,512	Metaswitch Networks Ltd	£97,042,192
Allport Cargo Services Limited	£109,364,136	Wolters Kluwer (UK) Limited	£97,016,512
Newship Group Limited	£109,240,000	Synchro Clutch Company Limited	£96,960,448
Consort Healthcare (Blackburn) Funding PLC	£109,179,000	Space Truust UK Ltd	£96,950,280
Morrisroe Group Limited	£108,799,408	Grigny (UK) Limited	£96,418,048
Shimtech Industries Holdco Limited	£108,458,000	GCP Rooftop Solar Finance PLC	£96,093,096
GT NEPS (Holdings) Limited	£108,400,856	Vestey Group Limited	£95,996,000
GT NEPS Limited	£108,400,856	Transform Schools (Rotherham) Limited	£95,697,000
Sabre Global Technologies Limited	£108,301,144	Wates Developments Limited	£95,624,000
Panavision Europe Limited	£108,122,000	Parthenon Entertainment Limited	£95,502,000
Peak Securities Limited	£108,068,072	Spicers Limited	£95,105,000
Mulalley & Co. Limited	£107,964,000	PGS Exploration (UK) Limited	£94,821,744
RCL (UK) Ltd.	£107,839,368	EMC Europe Limited	£94,817,000
Edwardian Exclusive Hotels Ltd	£107,778,000	Mylan UK Healthcare Limited	£94,587,000
Sunny Topco Limited	£107,375,296	Edwardian Mercer Street Ltd	£94,290,000
Sunny Bidco Limited	£107,374,400	Edwardian Bloomsbury Street Limited	£94,130,000
Higgins Homes PLC	£106,665,000	Wren Buyerco Limited	£94,009,480
Kew Green (LRG2) Limited	£106,638,624	Step Academy Trust	£93,763,000
Emcor Group (UK) PLC	£106,556,000	S.S.S.Gears Limited	£93,697,616
Michael Page International Southern Europe Ltd	£106,235,000	IMCD UK Limited	£93,651,000
Mazda Motors UK Limited	£106,210,000	Kidde Limited	£93,275,000
Volkerrail Group Limited	£106,023,000	Cergold Limited	£93,224,952
UK Highways M40 (Holdings) Limited	£105,969,000	Hamsard 3353 Limited	£93,007,432
UK Highways M40 Limited	£105,964,000	TRAD Hire & Sales Limited	£92,950,464
Bryant Park Hospitality UK Limited	£105,830,000	Southall Travel Limited	£92,942,480
Corona Gas Management Limited	£105,769,296	Treasury Wine Estates UK Brands Limited	£92,878,672
Volga-Dnepr UK Ltd.	£105,627,016	Network Homes Investments Limited	£92,629,920
Audley Ellerslie Limited	£105,353,488	Shaneel Enterprises Limited	£92,480,160
Brentwick Limited	£105,310,128	Schindler Ltd.	£92,323,000

Company	Value
HH Global Limited	£92,304,000
UK Highways A55 Limited	£92,167,000
UK Highways A55 (Holdings) Limited	£92,167,000
Cadbury South Africa (Holdings)	£91,930,488
Alestra Group Holdings Limited	£91,926,704
Cosco Shipping (UK) Company Limited	£91,660,536
Skanska Infrastructure Investment UK Limited	£91,503,000
SLS Holding Company Limited	£91,498,000
Surrey Lighting Services Limited	£91,498,000
Verint Systems UK Limited	£91,495,000
Day Group Limited	£91,422,856
Balton CP Limited	£91,419,928
Greenshaw Learning Trust	£91,406,000
Ty Danjuma Family Office Limited	£91,351,000
Dunlop International Group Limited	£91,293,000
R O Ventures Limited	£91,076,080
ADM Pura Limited	£90,900,880
Galliford Try Services Limited	£90,749,000
IAG GBS Limited	£90,665,000
Countyroute Limited	£90,498,000
Countyroute (A130) PLC.	£90,498,000
Batt Cables Public Limited Company	£90,481,880
Kerneos Holding Northern Europe Limited	£90,405,000
Platinum Midco Limited	£90,332,704
Platinum Midco 2 Limited	£90,332,704
GCP Programme Funding 1 Limited	£90,294,408
The Regard Partnership Limited	£89,982,000
Counties Home Loan Management Limited	£89,916,704
Ability Hotels (III) Finance Limited	£89,742,664
CHG-Meridian UK Limited	£89,425,000
Yoplait UK Limited	£89,322,000
Amshold Securities Limited	£89,152,768
SITA Information Networking Computing UK Limited	£89,077,264
The Rosedale Hewens Academy Trust	£88,925,000
Loxford School Trust Limited	£88,856,584
A.G. Thames Holdings Limited	£88,771,000
Microlease Limited	£88,697,000
Coldunell Limited	£88,482,592
Tax Systems PLC	£88,376,000
Canon Europe Limited	£88,300,000
Orchard Hill College Academy Trust	£88,169,000
Rockley Dene Homes Limited	£88,143,448
Fulton Maritime Limited	£88,097,576
Lindt & Sprungli (U.K.) Limited	£87,928,000
Fulton Maritime Holdings Limited	£87,923,608
Skanska TAM Limited	£87,536,000
PHH 1 Limited	£87,468,000
Galliard Construction Limited	£87,221,768
Kew Green Intermediate One Limited	£87,110,312
Croydon and Lewisham Lighting Services (Holdings)	£87,063,000
Croydon and Lewisham Lighting Services Limited	£87,063,000
Akaal Group PLC	£86,872,256
Wandale Limited	£86,751,960
Signet Direct Diamond Sourcing Limited	£86,724,216
Bycentral Holdings Limited	£86,624,000
Bycentral Limited	£86,624,000
BP Exploration Indonesia Limited	£86,533,776
F.C. Stark Limited	£86,386,232
Garreg Lwyd Energy Limited	£86,383,000
Russell & Bromley Limited	£86,099,560
Pandrol Group Limited	£85,962,000
Linden Homes (Sherford) LLP	£85,858,000
Consolidated Timber Holdings Limited	£85,816,000
Offshore Containers Holdings Limited	£85,758,864
Adelie Foods Limited	£85,728,000
Pandrol Holdings Limited	£85,686,000
LGC Genomics Limited	£85,633,000
Pentagon Holdings Limited	£85,540,848
Caversham Trading Limited	£85,510,000
Purelake Investments Limited	£85,338,672
Generics (U.K.) Limited	£85,286,000
J. Reddington Ltd	£85,098,440

Company	Value
Volkerrail Limited	£84,958,000
Safety-Kleen UK (Europe) Limited	£84,911,000
IHC UK (Holdings) Limited	£84,874,000
Amshold International Limited	£84,816,392
Prospect Healthcare (Hairmyres) Limited	£84,789,000
Jato Dynamics Limited	£84,783,872
BP Car Fleet Limited	£84,655,000
Transform Schools (Bassetlaw) Limited	£84,582,000
Kreutzer Touristik GB Limited	£84,572,904
Tyco Fire Products Manufacturing Limited	£84,488,000
Forester Holdings (Europe) Limited	£84,484,000
Expanded Limited	£84,460,000
Imagination Technologies Limited	£84,409,000
Leeu London Limited	£84,405,816
Prospect Healthcare (Hairmyres) Group Limited	£84,352,000
Cosan Lubes Investments Limited	£84,226,000
Eco Animal Health Ltd.	£84,152,288
ESP Connections Limited	£84,047,000
J J Food Service Holdings Limited	£83,924,080
Tilda Limited	£83,850,000
DC Management Services Limited	£83,639,000
Services Support (Manchester) Holdings Limited	£83,626,000
Services Support (Manchester) Limited	£83,626,000
PandoraExpress 7 Limited	£83,505,000
Carlson Wagonlit UK Ltd	£83,417,200
A.J. Morrisroe & Sons Limited	£83,417,040
Newmarston Ltd	£83,385,696
Selecta UK Holding Limited	£83,043,000
LRH Care Homes Limited	£82,756,456
PizzaExpress (Wholesale) Limited	£82,605,000
Agility Logistics Limited	£82,599,000
Walgreens Boots Alliance Services Limited	£82,593,000
Voicevale Limited	£82,394,624
Ann Summers Ltd.	£82,357,000
Heathrow Enterprises Limited	£82,188,000
Hotel Management International Limited	£82,119,000
Console Midco Limited	£82,102,016
BP Africa Limited	£81,949,376
Travel Technology Investments Limited	£81,911,000
Gold Group International Limited	£81,888,840
Crown House Technologies Limited	£81,762,000
Colorcon Limited	£81,699,008
Durkan Limited	£81,418,736
Cross London Trains Holdco Limited	£81,268,000
Opal (Silvertown) LLP	£80,879,000
GCP Social Housing 1 Limited	£80,671,512
ADM Arkady Limited	£80,653,456
Jupiter Midco 1 Limited	£80,529,784
Wood Group Industrial Services Limited	£80,461,000
Ability Hotels (Cambridge) Limited	£80,440,672
Transform Schools (Birmingham) Limited	£80,415,000
Transform Schools (Birmingham) Holdings Limited	£80,415,000
Mott MacDonald International Limited	£80,366,896
ND1T Limited	£80,257,536
UK Assistance Accident Repair Centres Limited	£80,181,000
Haymarket Group Limited	£80,116,000
John Menzies Finance Limited	£80,100,000
S & B Herba Foods Limited	£79,704,000
Salaft Properties Limited	£79,544,768
Horlicks Limited	£79,499,000
Cordant People Limited	£79,454,632
Euro Alloys Limited	£79,417,480
QSC 1209 Limited	£79,262,000
LGC Group Holdings Limited	£79,252,000
De Lage Landen Limited	£79,230,000
Ralph Lauren UK Limited	£79,218,344
Masterson Holdings Limited	£78,976,696
Benecol Limited	£78,854,000
Inspiral Oldham Holding Company Limited	£78,819,000
Inspiral Oldham Limited	£78,819,000
Regenter Myatts Field North Holding Co Ltd	£78,731,000
Regenter Myatts Field North Limited	£78,731,000

Company	Value
Bowland Resources Limited	£78,598,000
RES UK & Ireland Limited	£78,506,000
IHC Hotel Limited	£78,290,000
Volkerstevin Group Limited	£78,214,000
CDK U.K. Limited	£78,097,000
London Residential Healthcare Limited	£78,004,168
Carpetright of London Limited	£77,989,000
ND2F Limited	£77,814,816
Cargill Financial Services Europe Limited	£77,807,256
ND3M Limited	£77,729,696
Toll Investments (NA) Ltd	£77,613,328
ViiV Healthcare UK (No.5) Limited	£77,537,000
Services Support (SEL) Limited	£77,453,000
Services Support (SEL) Holdings Limited	£77,453,000
John Menzies (108) Limited	£77,400,000
Jupiter Topco Limited	£77,377,568
City North (Telford Homes) Limited	£77,221,000
Britannia Refined Metals Limited	£77,058,000
Ethypharm Holdings UK Ltd	£76,845,232
HCL Great Britain Limited	£76,664,000
Consolidated Timber Holdings Group Limited	£76,628,080
Tax Systems Holdings Limited	£76,449,880
Heathrow Express Operating Company Limited	£76,440,000
Brentford FC Limited	£76,384,984
Nuffield Health Pension Trustees Limited	£76,287,696
Innisfree Schools (Secondary) Limited	£76,075,000
Harsco Metals Holdings Limited	£76,063,008
MBH Finco. Limited	£75,860,288
Cummins Cogeneration Limited	£75,777,608
Kelly Communications Group Limited	£75,496,664
London United Busways Limited	£75,454,000
Laxmico Limited	£75,175,608
Haig Housing Trust	£75,164,000
FBL Holdings Limited	£75,101,000
H. K. S. Holdings Limited	£74,859,520
Gravity Media Group Holdings Limited	£74,647,000
T G Products Limited	£74,453,000
Hertz Europe Limited	£74,385,000
Shimtech Industries Limited	£74,196,240
Edif Group Limited	£74,147,000
Photo-Me Limited	£73,950,312
B & P Buyco Limited	£73,912,480
SHL Group Limited	£73,779,000
Britannia Security Group Limited	£73,758,000
HCT Portland Limited	£73,717,096
Hudson Chemical Tankers Limited	£73,716,288
Girls' Learning Trust	£73,564,000
Sun Mark Limited	£73,485,520
TWG Services Limited	£73,476,000
Selecta U.K. Limited	£73,467,000
Del Monte (UK) Limited	£73,371,000
Ensign Holdco 1 Limited	£73,359,000
Innisfree Schools (F2C) Limited	£73,336,000
Ridgeland Properties Limited	£73,175,928
Clancy Docwra Limited	£73,155,760
Belmont Green Finance Ltd	£73,139,000
Five Star Inns Limited	£72,991,000
Subsea 7 Engineering Limited	£72,891,000
Armstrong World Industries Limited	£72,850,000
Bytes Software Services Limited	£72,827,568
Cresta Estates Limited	£72,809,952
Crosswater Limited	£72,733,000
KBC Advanced Technologies Limited	£72,729,000
Grove Developments Limited	£72,611,760
Complete Cover Group Limited	£72,565,000
Dhamecha Property Limited	£72,533,000
Medivet Partnership LLP	£72,368,000
KBR (Aspire Construction) Limited	£72,359,000
Chubb Group Properties Limited	£72,308,000
The Cloud Networks Limited	£72,240,000
Every Child, Every Day Academy Trust	£72,198,816
Mallinckrodt Chemical Limited	£72,142,376
Durkan Estates Limited	£72,139,800
SME Investments Limited	£71,963,288
Exagon Industries Limited	£71,939,616
Glaxo Wellcome UK Limited	£71,871,000
Royal Docks Property LLP	£71,380,480
Alphalarch Limited	£71,274,000
Hincroft Limited	£71,227,072
Nemo (UK) Holdco, Ltd.	£71,130,000
Midgard Ltd	£71,057,872
Rambler Metals and Mining PLC	£70,515,392
Lenta Properties Limited	£70,508,912
Flight Centre Robin Limited	£70,343,792
Ability Developments Limited	£70,342,472
Allocate Software Limited	£70,327,000
Cosco Maritime (UK) Limited	£70,223,720
Officeteam Group Limited	£70,184,000
Wyevale Garden Centres G & L Limited	£70,126,000
Mothercare Group Limited (The)	£70,013,000
NetApp UK Ltd	£69,980,512
Celgene Europe Limited	£69,875,936
Medequip Group Limited	£69,806,000
Linden/Downland Graylingwell LLP	£69,750,000
Heathrow Edwardian Hotel Ltd	£69,716,000
Waverley House Hotel Limited	£69,639,704
Travel Republic Holdings Ltd.	£69,617,000
National Football Centre Limited	£69,510,000
SmithKline Beecham (H) Limited	£69,504,000
Beam Global Finance UK Limited	£69,350,016
Agri-Chemicals Limited	£69,286,584
London Square (Crimscott Street) Limited	£69,164,000
PCL Holdco Limited	£68,861,000
Kidsprog Limited	£68,727,000
Schenker Limited	£68,653,000
Brown and Mason Holdings Limited	£68,638,608
Bathroom Brands Group Limited	£68,454,000
Ability Hotels (Liverpool) Limited	£68,349,192
Smiths Industries Industrial Group Limited	£68,211,000
Edwardian Free Trade Hall Ltd	£68,085,000
JLW Excellent Homes for Life Holding Co Ltd	£67,991,000
JLW Excellent Homes for Life Limited	£67,991,000
Carlson Wagonlit New Holdco Limited	£67,607,120
LSG/Sky Chefs Europe Holdings Limited	£67,589,000
Edwardian Ltd	£67,572,000
Quickdrop Limited	£67,552,240
Bristol-Myers Squibb Business Services Limited	£67,446,000
The Penspen Group Limited	£67,325,000
Diamond Corporation Limited	£67,295,496
The Park Federation Academy Trust	£67,274,000
Elysium Healthcare No. 3 Limited	£67,242,000
A24 Group Limited	£67,204,384
SGB Infrastructure Middle East Limited	£67,144,000
Sunny Midco Limited	£67,133,896
Kingston Technology Europe Co LLP	£66,927,244
Safety-Kleen Europe Limited	£66,915,000
B & P Acquisitionco Limited	£66,913,632
Technical Staffing Resources Limited	£66,808,688
Abaris Holdings Limited	£66,599,000
Racal Acoustics Limited	£66,500,000
Rackspace UK Leasing Limited	£66,431,580
Tour Partner Group Midco Limited	£66,387,204
Gate Gourmet London Limited	£66,306,000
Diomed Developments Limited	£66,227,728
Brown and Mason Limited	£66,133,708
Wyevale Garden Centres Acquisitions Limited	£66,081,000
Bandai Namco Holdings UK Limited	£65,900,000
Lorne Stewart PLC	£65,703,000
Curtis Holt Limited	£65,687,000
The Holmes Care (Group) Limited	£65,683,720
Edwardian Exclusive Ltd	£65,669,000
Arcus Investment Limited	£65,508,132
Lotus Flower Holdings Limited	£65,505,608
Street Family Group of Companies (Holdings) Ltd	£65,420,112

Company	Turnover
Nexus Education Schools Trust	£65,345,000
Abbey Total Care Group Limited	£65,309,764
The Invicta Film Partnership No.20, LLP	£65,264,124
PizzaExpress International Holdings Limited	£65,241,000
Retirement Villages Limited	£65,107,568
Betex LLP	£65,017,936
First Wave Housing Limited	£64,824,000
Tower Bridge Homes Care Limited	£64,816,460
Hy-Ten Group Limited	£64,761,272
Fieldrose Limited	£64,728,000
CHG-Meridian Computer Leasing UK Limited	£64,564,000
Ferring Laboratories Limited	£64,455,896
Tech 21 UK Limited	£64,286,460
Galldris Services Ltd	£64,286,348
Hill of Towie Limited	£64,152,000
Subsea 7 Crewing Limited	£63,792,680
The Principal London Limited	£63,768,000
Beck MBI Limited	£63,762,080
SME Holdings Limited	£63,635,392
Amsprop London Limited	£63,628,384
Erith Holdings Limited	£63,617,000
Aunt Bessie's Limited	£63,495,000
PFU (EMEA) Limited	£63,459,240
ENRA Group Limited	£63,454,864
Gillette U.K. Limited	£63,434,000
Education Support (Swindon) Limited	£63,428,000
Education Support (Swindon) Holdings Limited	£63,428,000
Topgolf Limited	£63,387,980
Penspen Limited	£63,387,000
Regentsmead Limited	£63,029,272
SES (Engineering Services) Limited	£62,982,000
JRL Plant and Logistics Limited	£62,889,348
Bathroom Brands Limited	£62,771,000
Ellenbrook Developments PLC	£62,760,000
Ellenbrook Holdings Limited	£62,760,000
Ability Housing Association	£62,583,428
GlaxoSmithKline Consumer Healthcare Finance No.2	£62,455,720
Axon Solutions Limited	£62,234,000
Trade Sale Ltd	£62,124,796
Laridge Investments Limited	£62,087,812
Thorn Security Limited	£61,857,000
New Ladderswood LLP	£61,847,616
Ability Hotels (III) Group Limited	£61,687,668
Acer U.K. Limited	£61,678,000
IAG Cargo Limited	£61,458,000
Omni Serv Limited	£61,331,000
Warborough Investments Limited	£61,271,024
Gardeners' Royal Benevolent Society	£61,241,000
Bridge Road Southall Limited	£61,180,600
Allocate Holdco Limited	£61,137,000
Samsung Semiconductor Europe Limited	£61,102,300
Six Continents Restaurants Limited	£61,100,000
GCP Biomass 1 Ltd	£61,095,576
Glenchamber Wind Energy Limited	£61,071,000
Marylebone Finco Limited	£61,022,936
Berkeley Homes (PCL) Limited	£61,021,000
Faber Prest Limited	£61,003,836
NFAG Limited	£60,975,000
Wates Living Space (Maintenance) Limited	£60,934,000
Minster Care Management Limited	£60,828,656
Modern Schools (Exeter) Limited	£60,781,000
Kedleston Group Limited	£60,707,804
Howitzer Acquisition Limited	£60,699,324
Amphora Acquisitions Limited	£60,684,000
TWE Finance (UK) Limited	£60,580,812
Camelot Global Lottery Solutions Limited	£60,554,000
ILB Investments Limited	£60,520,232
Harris Holdings (Grays) Limited	£60,435,548
Air Charter Service Group Limited	£60,419,000
Property Finance Capital Limited	£60,334,692
Sega Europe Limited	£60,303,000
Covidien UK Limited	£60,209,000
Kingston Bidco Limited	£60,137,024
Merck Serono Limited	£60,114,000
Explore Transport Limited	£60,020,000
Aluminium Services (UK) Limited	£60,000,024
Linden (York Road) LLP	£59,997,000
Fifty Shades Ltd	£59,905,328
Careys New Homes Limited	£59,838,172
Mountcharm Limited	£59,818,216
RO Property Management Limited	£59,752,972
Fairview Homes Limited	£59,639,000
Laing O'Rourke Infrastructure Limited	£59,629,000
Uniserve Limited	£59,599,056
Cineworld Estates Limited	£59,493,000
Ensign Holdco 4 Limited	£59,430,000
Ability Hotels (III) UK Limited	£59,399,856
Heidelberg Graphic Equipment Limited	£59,182,000
Richmond and Hillcroft Adult and Community College	£59,180,000
London Arena Investments Limited	£59,096,132
Alexander Fraser Holdings Limited	£58,880,576
Empower Learning Academy Trust	£58,780,768
Volkerstevin Limited	£58,728,000
Vendcrown Limited	£58,671,000
Raisio UK Limited	£58,564,000
BP Properties Limited	£58,560,000
Vinci UK Developments Limited	£58,511,000
GCP Rooftop Solar 6 PLC	£58,499,368
Beacon Multi-Academy Trust Limited	£58,470,000
Chrysalis Multi Academy Trust	£58,293,000
Anthony Nicholas (UK) Limited	£58,186,260
Harlequin FC Holdings Limited	£58,163,112
Sarena House LLP	£58,106,640
Hy-Ten Limited	£57,861,488
Wellmode Limited	£57,800,000
HEB Real Estate Limited	£57,800,000
The Whiteley Homes Trust	£57,607,644
Property Finance Nominees (No.3) Limited	£57,545,068
Neilcott Construction Limited	£57,488,768
Galldris Holdings Limited	£57,328,408
Regenter B3 Holdco Limited	£57,194,000
Regenter B3 Limited	£57,194,000
Digico UK Limited	£57,102,000
International Marine Transportation Limited	£57,075,828
Evolution (Shinfield) LLP	£56,992,000
QSC 1208 Limited	£56,909,872
BP Pension Trustees Limited	£56,905,000
BP Investment Management Limited	£56,856,624
Stephen James (Automotive) Limited	£56,729,000
Bywest (Holdings) Limited	£56,724,000
Bywest Limited	£56,723,000
Geo. Kingsbury Holdings Limited	£56,679,628
Nature Delivered Limited	£56,597,200
SmithKline Beecham Overseas Limited	£56,486,000
Wrist Holding UK Limited	£56,484,000
European Investments (Cornwall) Limited	£56,410,928
Avanti Schools Trust	£56,126,000
Rhodia International Holdings Limited	£55,991,000
Panther (VAT) Properties Limited	£55,986,056
Repair Funding Limited	£55,964,520
Wealmoor Limited	£55,834,576
Ability Hotels (IV) Finance Limited	£55,695,048
OH Logistics International (UK) Ltd	£55,658,144
Softwareone UK Limited	£55,639,360
Intelliflo Holdings 2013 Limited	£55,258,876
Intelliflo Midco Limited	£55,258,872
United Living (South) Group Limited	£55,203,000
United Healthcare (South Buckinghamshire) Group	£55,167,000
TJX Europe Buying Limited	£55,088,000
Dhamecha Group Limited	£54,941,000
D-Link (Europe) Limited	£54,911,244
A P P Wholesale PLC	£54,911,108
Cluff Oil Limited	£54,890,000
Pioneer DJ Europe Limited	£54,872,156

Company	Amount
APCOA Parking Holdings (UK) Limited	£54,863,068
McGrath Brothers (Holdings) Limited	£54,844,800
Borelli Tea Holdings Limited	£54,827,008
Victoria Docks Hotel Company (Number Two) Ltd	£54,760,104
Radnor House School (Holdings) Limited	£54,664,096
JBS Global (UK) Limited	£54,645,752
The National Fostering Agency Limited	£54,551,000
AG Retail Cards Limited	£54,537,000
Pandrol Limited	£54,439,000
Imagine Cruising Limited	£54,304,696
CNM Estates (Tolworth Tower MB) Limited	£54,246,356
Chaptre Finance PLC	£54,245,000
Boorley Green LLP	£54,241,000
Cerestar UK Ltd	£54,078,356
Kingsway Mezz Co Limited	£54,069,952
Sungard Availability Services (DR) Limited	£54,004,000
Anglo Suisse Investments Limited	£53,741,056
Millennium Cash & Carry Limited	£53,710,732
Dewhurst PLC	£53,657,000
Glendola Leisure (Holdings) Limited	£53,577,000
Safe Haven London	£53,576,304
Bytes Technology Group Limited	£53,560,000
Puma Heritage PLC	£53,540,000
Reyhold Limited	£53,438,000
Vestey Foods UK Limited	£53,420,000
Buyagift PLC	£53,391,976
Reynolds Catering Supplies Limited	£53,377,000
Thames Properties Ltd.	£53,337,912
Gruma Europe Limited	£53,273,000
Spaces Personal Storage Limited	£53,262,000
Heritage Square Limited	£53,244,000
Hinds Ltd	£53,229,980
Ravensale Limited	£53,164,788
Twickenham Experience Ltd	£53,160,000
Kingsway Senior Hold Co Limited	£53,024,576
Monster Energy Europe Limited	£53,013,208
Crest Nicholson Developments (Chertsey) Limited	£53,000,000
ADM Milling Limited	£52,998,376
London Inn Hotels (Stratford) Limited	£52,877,656
Gallaher Overseas Limited	£52,846,000
Bradenstoke Solar Park Limited	£52,818,064
Norwood Ravenswood	£52,817,000
S-P RIL Limited	£52,808,000
O.S.T.C. Limited	£52,668,920
KH Finance Limited	£52,648,000
B & P Holdings II Limited	£52,587,844
Alliance BMP Limited	£52,475,000
M New Holdings Limited	£52,452,424
Cementation Skanska Limited	£52,347,000
EWOS Limited	£52,320,000
Burhill Group Limited	£52,311,364
Enterprise Rent-a-Car UK Holdings Limited	£51,979,000
British Airways Associated Companies Limited	£51,810,000
Topgolf Group Limited	£51,660,136
Arora Management Services Limited	£51,631,480
Brasserie Bar Co Limited	£51,583,560
Kedleston Schools Limited	£51,455,176
Gravesend and District Real Estate Company Ltd	£51,402,836
Tricomm Housing (Portsmouth) Limited	£51,347,824
Elysium Healthcare (Lighthouse) Limited	£51,317,000
Nicholls & Clarke Limited	£51,268,684
Oyezstraker Group Limited	£51,260,000
Heart Internet Limited	£51,146,000
Daikin Airconditioning UK Limited	£51,144,000
Tata Global Beverages Overseas Holdings Limited	£51,138,000
Kingsway Hall Hotel Limited	£51,120,312
Sheikh Holdings Group (Investments) Limited	£51,078,424
Symmetry Logistics Holdings Limited	£51,057,244
Grosvenor Park 2002 Film LLP	£50,934,048
Spirit Resources (Armada) Limited	£50,855,000
Glenmark Pharmaceuticals Europe Limited	£50,697,828
The Willow Learning Trust	£50,639,000
Venson Automotive Solutions Limited	£50,620,388
Devine Holdings Limited	£50,540,040
Leisure Parks Real Estate (Holdings) Limited	£50,471,672
Cromwell Holdings Limited	£50,442,000
Impact Oil & Gas Limited	£50,431,184
Intelliflo Bidco Limited	£50,401,736
CSL Communications Group Limited	£50,398,536
JJ Food Service Limited	£50,369,880
KH Holdco Limited	£50,366,000
Needspace? Limited	£50,340,344
Shelfside Group LLP	£50,248,940
Metropolis Group Holdings Limited	£50,160,608
The Meller Educational Trust	£50,062,852
Hampton School	£50,031,768
Howard Hunt (City) Limited	£49,997,000
Good Harvest Group Limited	£49,967,744
St George's Weybridge	£49,638,200
Bathroom Brands Holdings UK Limited	£49,631,000
Ability Hotels (Syon Park) Limited	£49,532,904
D.J.Squire & Co.,Limited	£49,522,000
Clinisys Solutions Limited	£49,438,000
Kent EHFA Projectco Limited	£49,430,544
Al Jazeera International Limited	£49,428,116
Combined Counties Properties Limited	£49,416,748
Sword Soft Limited	£49,414,896
Albain Bidco UK Limited	£49,298,092
W.J.King (Garages) Limited	£49,264,216
Delice de France Limited	£49,231,404
Mouskos LLP	£49,201,652
Navigator Terminals Seal Sands Limited	£49,185,000
Jain International Foods Limited	£49,184,888
TY Properties (UK) Limited	£49,173,000
Generations Multi Academy Trust	£49,084,224
TCR New Limited	£48,970,824
Chemidex Pharma Limited	£48,929,356
Golf Entertainment International Limited	£48,893,816
Industrial Chemicals Limited	£48,816,096
Cooper Estates Limited	£48,811,544
Kingston Topco Limited	£48,750,108
Michael Page International Holdings Limited	£48,638,000
Wates Group Services Limited	£48,559,000
Kewsaw Limited	£48,544,000
Gladstone Court Developments Limited	£48,541,488
Strides Arcolab International Ltd	£48,504,460
Berkeley Ryewood Limited	£48,459,428
Robinson Webster (Holdings) Limited	£48,406,000
BP Kuwait Limited	£48,348,420
White Rock Land LLP	£48,318,000
European Investments (Cornwall) Holdings Limited	£48,295,900
Kent EHFA Holdco Limited	£48,288,048
Newman Street Hotel Limited	£48,265,764
McGee Group (Holdings) Limited	£48,231,040
CWT Holdco Limited	£48,218,652
Amsprop Portland Limited	£48,103,136
PDC Brands UK Limited	£48,029,652
Premier Fleet Management and Contract Hire Ltd	£47,869,992
Churchill Insurance Company Limited	£47,799,000
Longview Holding Parent UK Limited	£47,795,592
Beck & Pollitzer Engineering Limited	£47,730,452
Gateway Learning Community	£47,700,860
Cargill Cotton Limited	£47,646,000
Panalpina World Transport Limited	£47,638,000
Wadlow Energy Limited	£47,619,000
JCA Charitable Foundation	£47,593,000
Longview Holding UK Limited	£47,549,644
Wilsons Automobiles and Coachworks Limited	£47,490,304
Voluntary Service Overseas	£47,489,000
The Hoddesdon School Trust	£47,362,856
Octagon Group Limited	£47,297,000
Tour Partner Group Limited	£47,284,208
Brand Energy & Infrastructure Services UK, Ltd.	£47,269,000
CP Regents Park Two Limited	£47,227,640

Company	Amount
Tradewise Group of Companies Limited	£47,179,276
Sky SNI Limited	£47,161,000
Grouse Topco Limited	£47,114,000
Custodes Midco Limited	£47,083,628
Erith Contractors Limited	£47,079,216
Lea Redway Limited	£47,061,912
APCOA Parking (UK) Limited	£46,994,404
Grosvenor Park 2005 Film Partnership No.1 LLP	£46,802,520
Experis Group Limited	£46,643,000
RO Financing Company Limited	£46,587,744
Exela Technologies Limited	£46,578,000
Park Garage Group PLC	£46,549,408
Kingston Digital Europe Co LLP	£46,547,424
Mapeley Steps Contractor Limited	£46,538,000
Speyside Renewable Energy Finance PLC	£46,536,000
Europa Road Limited	£46,527,488
Alandale Holdings Limited	£46,485,568
Aim Academies Trust	£46,473,104
SintecMedia LON Ltd	£46,466,108
I4B Holdings Limited	£46,464,000
Collins 2017 Limited	£46,422,452
London Tower Crane Hire & Sales Limited	£46,363,016
Beck Interiors Limited	£46,355,192
B & P Midco 1 Limited	£46,345,424
The Invicta Film Partnership No.10, LLP	£46,335,496
Richstone Properties Limited	£46,332,496
TCR UK Limited	£46,323,968
Archer Daniels Midland Erith Limited	£46,321,200
The Harrodian School Limited	£46,261,300
Caligor Opco UK, Ltd	£46,252,908
Vink UK Limited	£46,216,000
Plexus Holdings PLC	£46,154,000
The Invicta Film Partnership No.14, LLP	£46,030,152
WP SK Holdings Limited	£46,000,000
United Healthcare (South Buckinghamshire) Ltd	£45,954,000
Bike Alert PLC	£45,941,720
Abbey Group Limited	£45,860,296
Digico Global Limited	£45,657,132
Firmenich UK Limited	£45,554,000
Howard Humphreys & Partners Limited	£45,467,092
Motor Parts Direct Limited	£45,425,640
Medlock Electrical Distributors Limited	£45,418,612
Tyrolese (751) Limited	£45,411,928
CeleritiFinTech Limited	£45,320,000
Woodcote Estates Limited	£45,316,128
BP Oil Vietnam Limited	£45,285,296
The Civil Service Benevolent Fund	£45,249,000
Transform Housing & Support	£45,192,000
Lighthouse Healthcare Group Limited	£45,142,000
J. Coffey Construction Limited	£45,137,436
Premier Fruit & Nut Limited	£45,135,876
Bellevue Education International Limited	£45,101,192
Europa Worldwide Group Limited	£45,062,596
Brookstream Properties Limited	£45,009,612
Green Hill Energy Limited	£45,007,000
Oakfield (Foods) Limited	£44,994,880
Swan Mill (Holdings) Limited	£44,979,000
Denland Limited	£44,881,004
Mingold Limited	£44,881,000
John F Hunt Group Ltd	£44,868,924
Dow Properties Limited	£44,860,032
New England Seafood International Limited	£44,779,000
Rocco Homes Limited	£44,745,772
Fasttrax Holdings Limited	£44,718,000
Fasttrax Limited	£44,712,000
Purelake New Homes Limited	£44,710,352
Octagon Developments Limited	£44,604,000
BP Investments Asia Limited	£44,532,652
Mylan Pharma UK Limited	£44,497,000
Nellsar Limited	£44,493,512
B & P Midco 2 Limited	£44,345,424
Brisko Scaffolding Limited	£44,339,620
Livingston Ltd	£44,311,000
Windmill Organics Limited	£44,271,744
Fourfront Holdings Limited	£44,251,040
F.Hinds Limited	£44,240,396
Stanmore Contractors Limited	£44,200,124
Coats Industrial Thread Limited	£44,122,168
Super Toughened Glass Limited	£44,073,320
Teddington School	£44,062,220
Street Property (Holdings) Limited	£44,051,604
KSEYE Group Limited	£44,022,188
MSV Group Limited	£43,991,000
Prefect Software LLP	£43,967,152
Medequip Assistive Technology Limited	£43,960,000
Templecare Limited	£43,912,432
Secom PLC	£43,885,000
Elysium Healthcare (Ultimate Care) Limited	£43,884,684
ESP Electricity Limited	£43,873,000
TGS Geophysical Company (UK) Limited	£43,833,228
Timeboard Investments LLP	£43,800,520
Hertswood Academy	£43,777,864
Flight Centre Travel Group (European Holdings) Ltd	£43,769,828
John Street & Company (Surrey) Limited	£43,769,624
CSL (Dualcom) Limited	£43,686,032
Henry Construction Projects Limited	£43,675,720
Coombe Academy Trust	£43,633,000
Tanita International Ltd.	£43,626,796
IMCD UK Acquisitions Limited	£43,591,000
Michael Page Partnership Limited	£43,563,000
Toshiba Tec U.K. Imaging Systems Limited	£43,535,000
City Link (Cardiff) Limited	£43,447,000
JCDecaux United Limited	£43,353,000
YMCA St Pauls Group	£43,328,256
South West Essex Community Education Trust Ltd	£43,314,000
Imperial Pharmaceuticals Limited	£43,295,732
Sumitomo Electric Europe Limited	£43,287,000
Laing Limited	£43,283,000
A.A.Fisher (Properties) Limited	£43,273,648
Edwardian Canary Wharf Hotel Limited	£43,167,000
Churchgate Estates Limited	£43,095,528
Evolution (Woking) Limited	£43,064,000
BRE Trust	£43,026,000
British Airways Maintenance Cardiff Limited	£42,889,000
The Invicta Film Partnership No.22, LLP	£42,851,436
Kenneth Green Associates Limited	£42,828,352
Doncaster School Solutions Limited	£42,817,000
Doncaster School Solutions (Holdings) Limited	£42,817,000
Gog Magog Partnership LLP	£42,817,000
Chemidex Generics Limited	£42,801,256
Abriand Limited	£42,796,000
Adelie Foods Group Limited	£42,783,000
KSEYE Capital Holdings Limited	£42,678,068
United Living (North) Holdings Limited	£42,618,000
Chingford Fruit Limited	£42,549,000
IHC May Fair Hotel Limited	£42,486,000
Security Monitoring Centres Limited	£42,449,000
Warrant Investments PLC	£42,415,112
Zionstone Limited	£42,309,000
London Pharma & Chemicals Holdings Ltd	£42,261,880
Langley Park Learning Trust	£42,240,000
Wryde Croft Wind Farm Limited	£42,107,000
CHEP Pallecon Solutions Limited	£42,080,944
Blessville Limited	£42,040,620
Edif Group Finance Limited	£42,035,000
Dashtag	£42,025,000
Aliunde Limited	£42,024,648
Bio-Rad Laboratories Limited	£41,961,000
Mizen Properties Limited	£41,955,016
Birmingham Schools Partnership Limited	£41,926,000
Volkerhighways Limited	£41,902,000
JTL	£41,899,648
Joseph Gallagher Group Limited	£41,862,936
Harepath Estates LLP	£41,831,352

Company	Value
Lincoln Plaza LLP	£41,818,000
Elite Mobile (Holdings) Limited	£41,816,000
City Lifting Limited	£41,766,104
International Society for Krishna Consciousness Ltd	£41,681,696
Essex Services Group Limited	£41,670,440
Econocom Limited	£41,658,000
Global Metcorp Limited	£41,590,520
Queens' School (Bushey)	£41,587,780
Epsom College	£41,569,000
RANC Care Homes Limited	£41,548,828
Hoole Hall Country Club Limited	£41,544,000
Harlequin Estates (Twickenham) Limited	£41,536,592
Explore Manufacturing Limited	£41,435,000
Erindale Limited	£41,399,480
Sloggett Group Limited	£41,359,968
K2M UK Limited	£41,350,028
Cargill Investments Holdings Limited	£41,304,000
ABC Drug Stores Limited	£41,183,192
Avicenna Holdings Ltd	£41,143,000
Bollore Logistics UK Ltd	£41,135,144
Linden Wates (Royston) LLP	£41,105,000
Linden (Northstowe) LLP	£41,094,000
Morley Finco Limited	£40,970,660
Dermal Laboratories Limited	£40,770,980
Medreich PLC	£40,756,208
Octagon Group Holdings Limited	£40,730,000
Howarth Homes PLC	£40,702,896
The Harrogate International Hotel Limited	£40,575,000
Metropolis International Group Ltd	£40,544,320
NEC (UK) Ltd.	£40,467,000
Drapers' Multi-Academy Trust	£40,456,000
MFG Parentco Limited	£40,391,000
ATP Media Operations Limited	£40,368,924
The Alec Reed Academy	£40,347,000
Burhill Golf and Leisure Limited	£40,325,740
Kingston Midco Limited	£40,253,276
BECAP Spicers (UK) Limited	£40,249,000
The Vernon Educational Trust Limited	£40,220,160
Trafalgar Leisure Ltd	£40,114,984
Tapi Carpets & Floors Limited	£40,078,868
AVMI Group Limited	£40,075,000
The Jewish Community Secondary School Trust	£40,056,592
Newschools (Merton) Limited	£39,979,000
Linden (Enfield) LLP	£39,953,000
Heathrow Airport Fuel Company Limited	£39,882,000
Services Support (Gravesend) Limited	£39,864,000
Services Support (Gravesend) Holdings Limited	£39,864,000
Pentagon Freight Services PLC	£39,823,044
CAE Technology Services Limited	£39,802,160
Menzies Aviation (ASIG) Limited	£39,800,000
Test Equipment Asset Management Limited	£39,761,000
The North London Collegiate School	£39,737,320
Domantis Limited	£39,719,000
Merchant Taylors' School	£39,653,028
The Lady Eleanor Holles School	£39,625,652
Menzies Aviation (UK) Limited	£39,600,000
Wind Farm Holdings Limited	£39,600,000
William Willett Learning Trust	£39,579,000
Westgate House Developments Limited	£39,558,556
Fleetwood Developments Limited	£39,505,720
Merton Acquisitions Limited	£39,461,368
D4T4 Solutions PLC	£39,416,000
Sega Publishing Europe Limited	£39,371,000
ABM Technical Solutions Limited	£39,368,328
Swiss Post Solutions Ltd	£39,237,000
G.R.Wright & Sons Limited	£39,198,168
Sirhowy Enterprise Way Limited	£39,123,000
Sirhowy Enterprise Way (Holdings) Limited	£39,123,000
St George Ealing Limited	£39,087,736
Synaptic Trust	£38,895,000
TBE (Southern) Limited	£38,875,668
Impact Multi Academy Trust	£38,875,000
Key Bidco Limited	£38,796,000
Elbrook (Cash & Carry) Limited	£38,748,460
Surrey Blue Limited	£38,712,928
Drift Bridge Garage Limited	£38,710,368
ATP Media Holdings Limited	£38,699,312
Prime Care Solutions (Kingston) Limited	£38,657,000
Prime Care Solutions (Kingston) Holdings Limited	£38,657,000
Russell Finex Limited	£38,615,720
Sevita (UK) Limited	£38,614,000
Picturehouse Cinemas Limited	£38,594,624
Hyperformance Limited	£38,561,000
Vanderbilt Hotels Limited	£38,533,000
Intelliflo Intermediate Holdings Limited	£38,501,876
Caretech Estates (No 7) Limited	£38,475,000
Toureen Group Limited	£38,441,624
ASIG Holdings Limited	£38,400,000
Truly Holdings Limited	£38,307,680
Cathedral Holdings Limited	£38,227,716
KLM Cityhopper UK Limited	£38,219,000
Parkdale Investments Limited	£38,207,036
RO Properties Limited	£38,183,000
Norwood Schools Ltd.	£38,106,000
S A Designer Parfums Limited	£38,092,696
Aitch Care Homes (London) Limited	£38,078,000
Kelly Communications Limited	£38,074,008
Pricketts Limited	£38,022,408
Brand Reputation Compliance Limited	£37,995,408
BP Subsea Well Response Limited	£37,991,692
Baik Agency Limited	£37,987,656
Hillary Bidco Limited	£37,972,000
GCP Rooftop Solar 4 Limited	£37,965,640
Focus Tankers Limited	£37,956,832
Prospects Group 2011 Limited	£37,933,000
Classic Cinemas Limited	£37,931,796
Gantrade Europe Limited	£37,915,792
Jaysam Contractors Limited	£37,892,284
Riverdale Developments Limited	£37,863,328
London Square (Streatham) Limited	£37,852,000
OPD Group Limited	£37,850,904
Jollyes Retail Group Limited	£37,843,816
Swan Mill Paper Company Limited	£37,843,000
DST Global Solutions (Realty) Limited	£37,835,000
Axiom Education (Edinburgh) Holdings Limited	£37,823,000
Tearfund	£37,725,000
Tandridge Learning Trust	£37,693,000
GlaxoSmithKline Caribbean Limited	£37,655,000
New Demipower Limited	£37,636,804
Alperton Community School	£37,629,564
Dame Alice Owen's School	£37,629,000
Netherhall Gardens Ltd	£37,621,308
Reliance Communications (U.K.) Limited	£37,609,052
Shelfside (Holdings) Limited	£37,585,772
Worldwide Flight Services Limited	£37,583,808
Scimitar Care Hotels PLC	£37,530,288
Fulham Football Club Limited	£37,528,000
Eagle 456 Limited	£37,521,620
Trans Global Limited	£37,490,000
Powergas Africa Limited	£37,415,864
Marsh Wall Limited	£37,376,164
W K Webster & Co Ltd	£37,320,556
Renatus Property Management Limited	£37,320,448
Trans Global Freight Management Limited	£37,289,880
Ability Hotels (Luton) Limited	£37,286,244
Toshiba Information Systems (UK) Limited	£37,230,544
Skillcrown Holdings Limited	£37,200,196
Prospects Services	£37,111,000
WLHC Projectco Limited	£37,067,272
EMC Consulting (UK) Limited	£37,052,000
Cadbury Ten LLP	£37,031,568
Gapsun Properties Limited	£36,992,648
Foundation Developments Limited	£36,966,392
Keltbray Plant Limited	£36,962,956

Company	Value
Premier Euro Hotels Limited	£36,904,408
B & P Midco Limited	£36,868,316
Victorygame Limited	£36,794,544
Synbra UK Limited	£36,775,304
Northwood Paper Sales Limited	£36,769,968
Apatech Limited	£36,755,124
Education for The 21st Century	£36,751,264
Nikon UK Limited	£36,741,208
Aurient Investments Limited	£36,616,536
Handsale Limited	£36,610,476
Beck & Pollitzer Holdings Limited	£36,608,288
Kellogg Brown & Root (Services) Limited	£36,539,200
TJX Germany Ltd.	£36,500,000
Cordant Security Limited	£36,478,744
Santray Limited	£36,447,964
Perform Sporting News Limited	£36,441,864
SEM Limited	£36,391,328
The Grand Central Hotel Glasgow Limited	£36,370,000
Deanplan Limited	£36,345,976
Key Midco Limited	£36,345,000
Olivegate Properties Limited	£36,333,076
Falcon Panel Products Limited	£36,302,428
Hilton UK Manage Limited	£36,292,152
Waters Limited	£36,251,000
Independent Inspections Limited	£36,191,000
Radnor House School (Property) Limited	£36,183,008
North Atlantic (Holdings) Limited	£36,138,724
Navigator Terminals UK Limited	£36,138,000
The European Film Partners III LLP	£36,126,636
The Richmond West Schools Trust	£36,118,740
Ash Properties Limited	£36,090,872
GCP Green Energy 1 Limited	£36,076,976
Chobham School Academy (Stratford)	£36,049,000
Evolution (Saffron Walden) LLP	£36,010,000
Transform Schools (Stoke) Holdings Limited	£36,008,000
Transform Schools (Stoke) Limited	£36,008,000
Crystal Windows & Doors Limited	£35,993,184
Thomas Bates & Son Limited	£35,982,312
Associated Lead Mills Ltd.	£35,974,448
Kedleston Wings Holdco Ltd	£35,954,744
The Principal Manchester Limited	£35,954,000
The Pegasus Academy Trust	£35,930,000
The Spring Partnership Trust	£35,905,352
TFC Holdings London Limited	£35,875,512
Chester International Hotel Limited	£35,808,000
Wembley Multi Academy Trust	£35,774,840
3VS UK Limited	£35,726,692
MSHA International Ltd.	£35,705,724
Continua Limited	£35,705,000
T.S.L. Finance Limited	£35,641,412
Imerys Aluminates Limited	£35,623,000
Palacath Limited	£35,614,168
Clearview Homes Limited	£35,594,368
NCMT Limited	£35,459,000
Kelly Services (UK) Limited	£35,458,000
Danu II Holdings Limited	£35,410,976
IHS Lothian Investments Limited	£35,402,000
IHS Lothian Holdings Limited	£35,402,000
Gowrie Laxmico Limited	£35,392,188
Vanguard Holdings Limited	£35,381,472
Science, Engineering and Mfg Technologies Alliance	£35,358,000
Unity Schools Trust	£35,321,000
Aquila MB3 Limited	£35,317,248
Aquila MB2 Limited	£35,316,752
Camelot Business Solutions Limited	£35,300,000
Bic U.K. Limited	£35,294,000
Shorterm Limited	£35,267,000
Sky Comedy Limited	£35,250,000
Telford Homes City North Limited	£35,179,000
Tyco Building Services Products (UK) Limited	£35,127,000
Net Pay (EUR) Limited	£35,109,772
United Living (North) Limited	£35,102,000
Brymore Investments Limited	£35,100,756
Endeavour MAT	£35,097,000
PPP Capital Limited	£35,069,812
Loudwater Management Limited	£35,059,456
Building Research Establishment Limited	£35,017,000
Hertz Holdings III UK Limited	£34,875,000
Leena Plaza Limited	£34,866,832
Meridian Residential Developments Limited	£34,862,720
Lionel Road Developments Ltd	£34,820,496
British Airways 777 Leasing Limited	£34,769,000
Flight Centre (UK) Wholesale Limited	£34,764,000
Runnymede Investments Limited	£34,758,336
Sky Home Communications Limited	£34,752,000
Alexion Pharma UK Limited	£34,744,548
Hoo Hing Holdings Limited	£34,708,916
Claremont Fan Court Foundation Limited (The)	£34,701,552
CAE Technology Holdings Limited	£34,676,052
Elite Mobile Limited	£34,514,000
North Atlantic Fishing Company Limited	£34,485,000
Metier Healthcare Limited	£34,452,380
Metier Holdings Limited	£34,452,380
Clancy Plant Limited	£34,449,128
The Bentley Wood Trust	£34,422,152
Sourcecode UK Limited	£34,420,536
Amsprop Central Limited	£34,407,408
Swakeleys School for Girls	£34,289,056
Marchase Limited	£34,260,184
Corona Energy Retail 1 Limited	£34,249,204
Citygate Holdings Limited	£34,243,736
Badger Holdings Limited	£34,243,216
Console Lowco Limited	£34,227,728
Collins Construction Ltd	£34,222,440
Achieving for Children Community Interest Company	£34,152,000
New River Holdings Limited	£34,151,528
Adilsons Properties Limited	£34,103,272
Atkins ATK Investments Limited	£34,102,000
British Limbless Ex-Service Men's Association	£34,064,508
Do & Co. Event & Airline Catering Limited	£34,036,388
Nicholas James Care Homes Ltd	£33,972,356
BBC Studioworks Limited	£33,958,312
NCMT Holdings Limited	£33,940,000
Brambles Enterprises Limited	£33,937,000
Sazerac UK Limited	£33,908,028
East Barnet School	£33,897,964
Aquila Estates Limited	£33,881,256
MSK Holdings Limited	£33,842,548
Linden (Brampton) LLP	£33,835,000
South Orpington Learning Alliance Multi-Academy	£33,824,152
The Invicta Film Partnership No.25, LLP	£33,805,844
Cooperscroft Care Home Limited	£33,605,224
Ensono Limited	£33,558,000
Coyle Personnel PLC	£33,545,504
Kedleston (Wings Education) Limited	£33,542,588
London South East Academies Trust	£33,542,000
Bowland Resources (No.2) Limited	£33,491,000
Comparex UK Limited	£33,477,328
Uniserve (Air Freight) Limited	£33,466,564
Hurstlane Limited	£33,431,456
Bonne Bouche Catering Limited	£33,374,368
Pyramid Schools (Sheffield) Limited	£33,368,000
Pharmaceuticals Direct Limited	£33,313,492
Roos Energy Limited	£33,296,000
Clarence Estates (London) Limited	£33,288,554
A-Roads Investments Limited	£33,247,534
BP Exploration China Limited	£33,227,468
TIGI International Limited	£33,217,912
Skanska Cementation International Limited	£33,210,000
Attewell Limited	£33,207,000
BP Shafag-Asiman Limited	£33,176,834
Seabrook Holdings Limited	£33,100,808
Citygate Automotive Limited	£33,090,256
Victoria Docks Hotel Company Limited	£33,074,908

Company	Amount
CLFIS (U.K.) Limited	£32,976,000
Campmoss Property Company Limited	£32,951,648
Wesco Distribution-International Limited	£32,930,000
ARRI (GB) Limited	£32,916,000
Haydon School	£32,915,100
Greenstone Oxford Limited	£32,909,552
Phoenix Software Limited	£32,899,000
Pinnacle Schools (Fife) Limited	£32,899,000
London Square (Putney) Limited	£32,865,840
Chesterhill Investments Limited	£32,855,708
Alder Hey Holdco 2 Limited	£32,808,000
Alder Hey Holdco 1 Limited	£32,808,000
Ferring Asset Management Limited	£32,750,000
Linden (Avery Hill) LLP	£32,658,000
Navigator Terminals North Tees Limited	£32,549,000
Yorkshire Transformations Limited	£32,537,000
Hawk-Eye Innovations Limited	£32,507,000
Jas Forwarding (UK) Limited	£32,490,200
Dwellcourt Limited	£32,484,010
Leven Wharf Limited	£32,341,948
Alfreds Way Investments (No. 2) Limited	£32,326,216
H.K.S. Motors Limited	£32,315,680
Splash Damage Limited	£32,278,618
Affinity (Reading) Limited	£32,271,964
Caterham School Limited	£32,258,000
Brymore Holdings Limited	£32,207,900
Merck Consumer Healthcare Limited	£32,178,000
The National Fostering Agency (Scotland) Limited	£32,132,000
Amshold Trading Limited	£32,109,412
Ranbaxy Holdings (UK) Limited	£32,096,450
Verifone (U.K.) Limited	£32,080,000
DB Investments Limited	£32,046,208
Hayes Point (Sully) Limited	£32,034,484
Dynama Solutions Ltd	£31,952,000
Defence Support (St Athan) Limited	£31,851,000
Defence Support (St Athan) Holdings Limited	£31,851,000
O'Neill Investments Limited	£31,838,832
Metro Global Holdings Limited	£31,833,718
The Collegiate Trust	£31,812,864
St Mary's CE Academy, Cheshunt	£31,793,000
Area Sq. Limited	£31,770,456
G4S Cash Centres (UK) Limited	£31,722,000
T.Choithram & Sons (London) Limited	£31,710,404
Orleans Park School	£31,701,936
Fairview Ventures Limited	£31,698,000
Preston Manor Academy Trust	£31,668,798
HRT UK Limited	£31,611,000
Brambles Nominees Limited	£31,579,820
ICS Incorporation Limited	£31,552,244
Collaborative Services Support (NE) Holdings Ltd	£31,484,000
Collaborative Services Support NE Limited	£31,484,000
The Children's Trust	£31,475,000
Simmons & Hawker Limited	£31,467,332
Yavneh College Academy Trust	£31,446,916
Folio Education Trust	£31,400,000
Bugler Group Limited	£31,377,884
Xtera Topco Limited	£31,366,754
Flair Leisure Products PLC	£31,356,000
The Jankel Group Limited	£31,346,048
Jankel Armouring Limited	£31,338,052
Pourshins Limited	£31,332,000
M & D Silk Properties Ltd	£31,327,848
Ensco 1212 Limited	£31,291,344
Best Commercial Properties Limited	£31,279,510
LSQ (Crimscott Street) Holdings Limited	£31,261,704
V.B. Investments Limited	£31,251,000
Aquila EHS Limited	£31,217,220
Mission Foods UK Limited	£31,083,000
Leisure Parks Real Estate Limited	£31,056,944
Donamount Limited	£31,020,032
Dentex Healthcare Group Limited	£31,000,684
Ensco 1214 Limited	£31,000,000
Sinek Global Finance & Trading LLP	£30,981,460
Motorsport Vision Limited	£30,917,884
Foundation and Friends of The Royal Botanic Gardens	£30,912,000
Fairview Estates (Housing) Limited	£30,832,000
Lyndon Scaffolding PLC	£30,829,792
Union Investcorp Limited	£30,790,780
Kendon Packaging Group Public Limited Company	£30,774,174
Saxonchart Limited	£30,768,108
CDB (U.K.) Limited	£30,763,000
Etcetera Construction Services Limited	£30,702,602
Domino Investments Limited	£30,686,856
BL Wind Limited	£30,665,000
AMG Healthcare Limited	£30,528,000
Nippon Express (U.K.) Limited	£30,495,964
Essential Pharma Limited	£30,423,222
Westfield Academy	£30,417,196
Padwicks Travel (Wembley) Limited	£30,341,244
Bostall Estates Limited	£30,305,232
ACR Investments Limited	£30,292,428
Capital Investment and Finance Ltd	£30,284,442
Bugler Developments Limited	£30,251,396
QED (Clacton) Limited	£30,126,000
Brobot Petroleum Limited	£30,122,572
IZH Holdings Ltd	£30,100,012
PCL Transport Limited	£30,098,416
SPD Moorgate Limited	£30,092,000
Chartco Limited	£30,067,000
AHL Holdings (Manchester) Limited	£30,064,000
Amey Highways Lighting (Manchester) Limited	£30,064,000
Elysium Healthcare Property 2 Limited	£30,056,000
Lampton School Academy Trust	£30,033,000
Dnata Travel (U.K.) Ltd.	£30,017,216
L P M (Professional Recruitment) Limited	£30,016,000
Lenham Storage Company Limited	£30,010,920
Crystal Home Improvements Holdings Limited	£29,984,880
GPS Food Group (UK) Limited	£29,946,258
Clece Care Services Limited	£29,932,040
Hanwha Techwin Europe Limited	£29,918,000
Prospect Healthcare (Reading) Limited	£29,903,000
SNC-Lavalin Rail & Transit Limited	£29,885,000
GCP Asset Finance 1 Limited	£29,873,892
Breyer Holdings Limited	£29,830,864
Liberata UK Limited	£29,794,000
KPIT Technologies (UK) Limited	£29,745,258
Cellarmaster Wines Holdings (UK) Limited	£29,715,000
Saxton Limited	£29,712,904
Academy Services (Waltham Forest) Limited	£29,670,000
Instalcom Limited	£29,624,182
Bellevue Education Group Limited	£29,585,864
TH UK & Ireland Limited	£29,562,736
Life Education Trust	£29,559,000
KGM Underwriting Services Limited	£29,555,680
Camberley Care Limited	£29,549,776
Erith School	£29,549,000
Silverson Machines Holdings Limited	£29,534,494
Seneca Environmental Solutions Ltd	£29,532,112
Gearhouse Broadcast Limited	£29,481,000
Sunlight PV Ltd	£29,480,514
Ennogen Healthcare Ltd	£29,465,110
Evolution Morpeth LLP	£29,457,000
Angel Care PLC	£29,445,680
Woodgavil Properties Limited	£29,440,504
Everest Limited	£29,419,000
Ganco Limited	£29,391,922
Towers & Co.,Limited	£29,375,000
R Stanton-Gleaves UK Limited	£29,330,048
Commercial Freeholds & Investments Ltd	£29,262,552
Modern Schools (Barnsley) Limited	£29,249,000
Royal British Legion Poppy Factory Limited (The)	£29,247,398
The Langley Park School for Boys Academy Trust	£29,243,000
Agility Project Logistics Limited	£29,237,988
Visual Impact (UK) Limited	£29,229,290

Company	Turnover
JRL Property Holdings Limited	£29,217,624
Goodwill SIP Limited	£29,198,068
Remy's Limited	£29,172,980
IBRC Asset Finance Limited	£29,145,804
The Invicta Film Partnership No.27, LLP	£29,141,476
F.J. Church & Sons Limited	£29,058,780
London Square (Fulham) Limited	£29,057,560
Manchester Jetline Limited	£29,029,000
Karium Ltd	£29,025,880
Breyer Group Public Limited Company	£29,019,344
Alandale Logistics Limited	£28,983,552
Jaysam Developments Borehamwood Limited	£28,973,820
Rex Partners LLP	£28,973,348
Teoco UK Limited	£28,921,400
Tchibo Coffee International Limited	£28,856,822
Jupiter Midco 2 Limited	£28,821,590
LGC (Teddington) Limited	£28,820,978
TES Enterprise Solutions Ltd	£28,815,054
Newmarket Promotions Limited	£28,809,550
MTALX Limited	£28,795,316
Gita Properties Limited	£28,789,296
Nucleus Financial Group PLC	£28,785,000
St Edward Homes Limited	£28,772,000
Air Menzies International Limited	£28,753,000
Saba Infra Holdings UK Limited	£28,750,320
West London YMCA	£28,731,302
Akari Therapeutics, PLC	£28,707,494
Amber Solar Parks Limited	£28,640,000
Danu Holding Limited	£28,618,104
Direct Line Group Limited	£28,597,000
Rollover Limited	£28,591,152
Joseph Gallagher Limited	£28,537,716
Amber Solar Parks (Holdings) Limited	£28,532,000
Fairview New Homes (Properties) Limited	£28,527,000
Hasbro U.K. Limited	£28,522,000
Blitzfair Limited	£28,516,492
Ensign Holdco 3 Limited	£28,515,000
Pharmadent Holdings Limited	£28,510,594
Broadway Malyan Employee Ownership Trustees Ltd	£28,492,000
Tristmire Limited	£28,489,294
Fizzy Canning Town LLP	£28,485,000
Orthopaedic Research UK	£28,451,824
Chrysalis (Stanhope) Limited	£28,434,720
Flexibon Limited	£28,428,516
Tradewise Insurance Services Limited	£28,386,768
Wood Hall Land & Properties Limited	£28,376,944
ACI Global Limited	£28,367,000
Ranbaxy (U.K.) Limited	£28,360,372
Longford Securities & Equities (K & T) Limited	£28,351,580
The Archbishop Lanfranc Academy - Coloma Trust	£28,295,168
Audley St George's Limited	£28,262,548
Harefield Academy Trust	£28,260,000
The Petersham Hotel Limited	£28,215,508
CNM Estates Holdings Limited	£28,212,946
Granherne Limited	£28,200,068
QED (Leeds) Limited	£28,176,000
EMAP Publishing Limited	£28,163,124
Lea Bridge Hill LLP	£28,153,000
Spark Property Assets LLP	£28,140,584
Trafficinvest Limited	£28,090,748
World Wise Foods Limited	£28,088,864
Kingston Grammar School	£28,075,000
J & E Hall Limited	£28,074,000
Volkerrail Specialist Businesses Limited	£28,070,000
Deltec International Courier Limited	£28,045,200
Cardiff Property Public Limited Company (The)	£28,043,000
Arcus Solutions (Holdings) Limited	£28,027,000
Harsco Metals 385 Limited	£27,980,780
Bookcash Trading Limited	£27,975,000
Milpharm Limited	£27,974,948
Bosch Automotive Service Solutions Ltd	£27,956,000
Broadway Malyan Holdings Limited	£27,942,000
Fairview New Homes (Charlton) Limited	£27,937,000
Readie Construction Limited	£27,932,864
Woldingham School	£27,910,932
Pepkor UK Retail Limited	£27,856,412
Lesser & Pavey Ltd.	£27,842,092
SFAET Ltd	£27,800,000
The Creative Assembly Limited	£27,756,866
Fizzy Stepney Green LLP	£27,755,000
Peterborough (Progress Health) Nominee Limited	£27,749,000
Try Homes Limited	£27,716,000
Grouse Bidco Limited	£27,680,528
Sauvello Limited	£27,625,672
DDD Investments Limited	£27,611,426
Kelly Property Company Limited	£27,588,656
Galliford Try Investments Limited	£27,541,000
Panther Investment Properties Limited	£27,539,376
London Square (Holdings) Limited	£27,528,478
Home and Comforts Limited	£27,512,000
Minster Care Group Limited	£27,477,660
Ability Hotels (Manchester) Limited	£27,470,850
P.C. Harrington Holdings Limited	£27,437,000
The Hill Company Limited	£27,435,568
RL Retail Services Limited	£27,429,290
PSN Holdco Limited	£27,428,000
Integrated Design Limited	£27,319,964
Creative Video Productions Limited	£27,303,416
Mouskos Holdings Limited	£27,300,036
B & T Plant Hire Limited	£27,256,760
The Invicta Film Partnership No.8, LLP	£27,248,724
GCP Biomass 4 Limited	£27,220,052
Centre for Engineering and Manufacturing Excellence	£27,218,968
Fishpools Holdings Limited	£27,214,488
Spectrum Franchising Limited	£27,182,000
Russell School Trust	£27,174,608
D.D.D. Limited	£27,138,234
Original Additions (Beauty Products) Limited	£27,130,652
Soul Coffee House Limited	£27,126,388
Samsung C & T U.K. Limited	£27,098,000
Bandai Namco Amusement Europe Limited	£27,074,000
John E.Fells & Sons Limited	£27,073,200
The Taunton Linac Company Limited	£27,053,000
Hoo Hing Limited	£27,048,712
Grouse Midco Limited	£27,037,648
Toureen Contractors Limited	£27,035,496
Kelly Comms Limited	£27,006,284
Ensign Bus Company Limited	£26,987,252
Transeur Properties Limited	£26,975,800
Excellence in Education Trust	£26,965,340
Sherrygreen Homes Ltd	£26,906,754
CNM Estates (Tolworth Tower SBP) Limited	£26,901,492
CNM Estates (Tolworth Tower MBP) Limited	£26,888,992
Tempur UK Limited	£26,838,000
Velji Bhovan & Sons (Trading) Limited	£26,832,736
Chigwell School	£26,811,000
Pace Academy Trust	£26,805,070
E & J Properties Limited	£26,794,584
Boston Limited	£26,768,804
Kings Langley School	£26,733,576
BP Eastern Mediterranean Limited	£26,727,732
Lanber Nursing Homes LLP	£26,723,600
Toshiba Global Commerce Solutions (U.K.) Limited	£26,720,284
Compagnie Fruitiere UK Limited	£26,638,000
TVH Fizzy Holdings Limited	£26,628,000
Queen Elizabeth's School Barnet	£26,613,764
ProAV Limited	£26,596,152
Honey Monster Foods Limited	£26,594,000
VGC Group Limited	£26,583,700
Lymington Precision Engineering (LPE) Limited	£26,579,000
Caskade Caterers Limited	£26,553,772
Spring Finance Limited	£26,494,268
Ability Hotels (Luton Inn) Limited	£26,448,556
Herbalife Europe Limited	£26,427,512

Company	Value
Miriad Property Investments Limited	£26,427,208
Link Market Services Trustees Limited	£26,423,796
Jollyes Group Limited	£26,417,982
Careprogress Limited	£26,391,724
London Care Partnership Limited	£26,390,636
Overton Grange School	£26,386,000
Melton House Investments Limited	£26,362,588
JF Hillebrand UK Limited	£26,352,304
Katrin Properties Limited	£26,322,198
Rooff Holdings Limited	£26,304,592
Grosvenor Park 2004 Film Partnership No.1 LLP	£26,292,000
Poland Street Properties Limited	£26,280,136
Therakos (UK), Ltd	£26,275,732
Advanced Lighting Technologies Europe Limited	£26,249,848
Towers Thompson Holdings Limited	£26,248,000
VFS Legal Limited	£26,235,670
Middlesex Learning Partnership	£26,233,772
Gould Publication Papers UK Limited	£26,193,992
McGrath Bros. (Environmental) Ltd.	£26,192,572
Devine Homes PLC	£26,191,474
Schinvest Limited	£26,172,000
AKA London Limited	£26,163,468
Elmwey Learning Trust	£26,149,000
Stapleford Commercial Group Limited	£26,114,722
Volkerservices Limited	£26,081,000
Grange Renewable Energy Limited	£26,079,000
Trochair Limited	£26,068,000
United Reformed Church (Southern Synod) Trust	£26,063,498
Harsco Rail Limited	£26,048,890
TRAD Properties LLP	£26,020,592
Hatch End High School	£26,020,154
Red Circle Security Services Limited	£25,980,226
The Victoria Foundation	£25,976,000
Longview Holding UK 2 Limited	£25,975,620
Reliance Globalcom (UK) Limited	£25,962,996
Designer M & E Services UK Limited	£25,962,836
Lufthansa Technik Landing Gear Services UK Limited	£25,961,000
Navitas Petroleum Limited	£25,953,000
Aquila BTE 1 Limited	£25,938,068
Ian Allan Group Limited	£25,894,818
Athena Care Homes (UK) Limited	£25,884,150
Coca-Cola European Partners Services Europe Ltd	£25,873,000
Deards Services Limited	£25,868,690
SmithKline Beecham Research Limited	£25,847,000
BP Turkey Refining Limited	£25,843,286
EHGT Limited	£25,817,214
Rowlandson Investments Limited	£25,810,204
Barking Power Limited	£25,810,000
Connect Schools Academy Trust	£25,744,576
Do & Co. International Catering Limited	£25,740,168
CSPH Limited	£25,739,364
Carnarvon Hotels Limited	£25,728,970
Chicken Cabins Limited	£25,707,024
Axis Group Integrated Services Limited	£25,680,000
Ocean Holidays Limited	£25,649,200
Nower Hill High School	£25,637,360
Paula Hawkins Limited	£25,613,192
Air Charter Service Limited	£25,593,000
Axiom Education (Perth & Kinross) Holdings Limited	£25,549,000
Masters of Beckenham Limited	£25,524,862
Bath Road Properties Limited	£25,498,034
Latchmere Academy Trust	£25,468,734
Fishdance Limited	£25,374,212
AVM Impact Ltd	£25,368,000
MCPA Limited	£25,347,940
Fork Rent Limited	£25,332,156
Graham Land & Developments Limited	£25,275,300
Ansa UK Limited	£25,275,000
Rush Hair Group Limited	£25,265,000
Metis Homes Limited	£25,263,516
ProAV Holdings Limited	£25,243,768
Buy 2 Let Cars Ltd	£25,240,802
SintecMedia WEM Ltd	£25,215,930
The Ockendon Academy	£25,208,908
Townhold Limited	£25,175,964
Clinisys Group Limited	£25,175,000
Lodge Bros. (Funerals) Limited	£25,171,020
APPT Corporation Limited	£25,133,720
Green Flag Holdings Limited	£25,087,408
Kimal Holdings Limited	£25,082,000
KH Finance No.2 Limited	£25,071,000
Strand Court Properties Limited	£25,068,000
Chislehurst and Sidcup Grammar School	£25,066,720
Odyssey Trust for Education	£25,015,000
Grand Union Multi Academy Trust	£25,014,368
Woodgavil Limited	£24,964,550
Dermalogica (UK) Limited	£24,956,168
The Invicta Film Partnership No.26, LLP	£24,924,640
St.Helen's School Northwood	£24,897,000
Pineridge Investments Limited	£24,892,824
L.E. Pritchitt & Company Limited	£24,888,000
Alternative Bridging (UK 1) Limited	£24,886,840
Safegold Properties Limited	£24,876,724
Lantern Services (Holdings) Ltd	£24,863,076
The New Victoria Hospital Limited	£24,828,000
TC Facilities Management Limited	£24,822,880
Motherwell Holdings Limited	£24,807,754
Cuffe Holdings Limited	£24,774,800
Blenheim Property Management Limited	£24,772,198
Project Tristar Limited	£24,763,000
Sky IQ Limited	£24,724,000
Ability Hotels (Liverpool Plaza) Limited	£24,713,962
Estates and Lets 2 LLP	£24,684,110
Wolters Kluwer Health (Medical Research) Limited	£24,669,000
Aitch Care Homes Holdco Limited	£24,653,000
Action Potential Venture Capital Limited	£24,652,604
First City Care (London) Limited	£24,632,024
Arcofina LLP	£24,628,286
Mood Media Limited	£24,609,000
The Waldegrave Trust	£24,606,262
Spar (UK) Limited	£24,605,934
Spar Food Distributors Limited	£24,605,884
United Healthcare (South Buckinghamshire) Holdings	£24,603,000
Chemilines Group Holdings Limited	£24,584,000
The Invicta Film Partnership No.13, LLP	£24,578,374
Specialist Equipment Solutions Limited	£24,535,000
Mobil Trading and Supply Limited	£24,515,328
Premier Rugby Limited	£24,510,050
World Mission Agency - Winners Chapel International	£24,500,488
Northamber PLC	£24,484,000
Flag Atlantic UK Limited	£24,482,128
Ethypharm UK Limited	£24,475,888
The Offer Group Ltd	£24,458,782
Bushey St James Trust	£24,446,866
Uxbridge High School Academy Trust	£24,446,592
Fizzy Lewisham LLP	£24,376,000
Francotyp-Postalia Limited	£24,351,000
MIQ Logistics Limited	£24,334,236
Kluman and Balter Holdings Limited	£24,322,160
Lapid Developments Limited	£24,292,516
Berkeley Homes (Fleet) Limited	£24,172,322
South Darenth Farms and Cold Store Co Ltd	£24,169,964
Reichhold UK Limited	£24,140,000
Blanc Brasseries Limited	£24,101,238
Buxton Building Contractors Limited	£24,079,828
Education Support (Enfield 2) Holdings Limited	£24,059,000
Education Support (Enfield 2) Limited	£24,059,000
Nextonline Limited	£24,053,180
Ability Hotels (Dunblane) Limited	£24,052,766
Gibson Propco Limited	£24,043,000
Openview Security Solutions Limited	£24,037,484
Fairview Enfield Limited	£24,004,000
Mouskos Capital Limited	£23,990,352
Croudace Portland Limited	£23,983,844

Www.Nakedwines.Com Limited £23,975,000
Sardar Properties (U.K.) Limited £23,952,000
Chelmer Foods Limited £23,947,330
Paragon Internet Group Limited £23,931,000
Yourway Transport Limited £23,926,840
Day Webster Limited £23,895,506
Chasemore Farm LLP £23,888,516
Demipower Limited £23,874,314
Prinhold Limited £23,869,468
Cordant Cleaning Limited £23,836,580
TMD Technologies Limited £23,829,000
Danes Educational Trust £23,811,000
Commodore Kitchens Limited £23,798,642
SNC-Lavalin Co. Ltd. £23,647,700
Carshalton Boys Sports College £23,633,000
Kelly Fleet Services Limited £23,571,540
Park High School £23,561,744
Cyberscience PLC £23,559,432
Shoppertrak Limited £23,559,000
Killoughery Holdings Limited £23,543,790
Nucleus Financial Services Limited £23,524,000
SF11 Limited £23,523,460
Canada Life (U.K.) Limited £23,519,000
Godrej UK Limited £23,470,900
N & C Building Products Limited £23,468,466
Wadlow Energy Holdings Limited £23,460,000
Kanta Enterprises Limited £23,451,408
Chicken Villas Limited £23,448,416
Canons High School £23,441,502
German School Association Limited £23,434,296
HML Holdings PLC £23,432,000
Newport Group (Holdings) Limited £23,408,532
Prospect Healthcare (Hinchingbrooke) Limited £23,405,000
Interdist Alliances Limited £23,395,220
St. Margaret's School Bushey £23,384,684
Salmon Management and Finance Limited £23,369,664
Heathland Whitefriars Federation £23,349,020
Compass Group Procurement Limited £23,340,000
Empire Bespoke Foods Limited £23,339,932
Infotech Trade Services Ltd £23,333,800
Oliver Bonas Limited £23,297,596
Cargobull Finance Limited £23,251,000
Goodman Family Investments Limited £23,247,308
Autosport Media UK Ltd £23,229,918
Necessity Supplies Limited £23,210,598
Drew Smith Homes Limited £23,192,174
Grosvenor Park 2007 S48 Film LLP £23,177,000
Mercury Land Holdings Limited £23,169,784
Heritage Care Limited £23,166,000
Highway Stops Retail Limited £23,157,496
GCP Rooftop Solar 5 Ltd £23,152,332
Linden (Biddenham) LLP £23,149,000
Canadian & West End Limited £23,143,928
Myatt's Field Development LLP £23,142,160
Yehudi Menuhin School Limited (The) £23,135,464
MIQ Logistics EU Limited £23,101,756
Sahara Presentation Systems PLC £23,098,064
Parallel Learning Trust £23,066,000
Laing Construction Limited £23,064,000
NSL (Holdings) Limited £23,043,112
St James Homes (Grosvenor Dock) Limited £23,036,194
Cellxion Ltd £23,014,504
Crest A2D (Walton Court) LLP £22,975,000
The Woodland Academy Trust £22,939,000
Karelia Tobacco Company (UK) Limited £22,936,140
Wolters Kluwer Tax and Accounting Limited £22,932,704
Fishpools Limited £22,924,174
IMCD Holding UK Ltd £22,885,000
The Automated Technology Group Limited £22,882,000
SG Equipment Finance (December) Limited £22,868,920
TRAD Scaffolding Co.Limited £22,854,960
Salisbury Holdings Limited £22,835,000
Epsilon Telecommunications Limited £22,832,492
Sapiens (UK) Limited £22,822,872
Skanska Major Projects Limited £22,816,000
P.J. Carey Plant Hire (Oval) Limited £22,805,350
G & O Securities Limited £22,798,464
Satco Investments Limited £22,797,708
Heathrow Hydrant Operating Company Limited £22,793,000
TMD Holdings Limited £22,778,000
Fujichem Sonneborn Limited £22,759,570
Avamore Limited £22,756,118
BP Exploration Personnel Company Limited £22,748,948
Jato Aviation Limited £22,716,352
Media 10 Holdings Limited £22,715,204
Network New Build Limited £22,708,172
Islam Channel Limited £22,683,580
McGrath Bros. (Waste Control) Limited £22,663,392
Sega Amusements International Limited £22,663,000
Wood Group Kenny Limited £22,648,000
Gentec Energy PLC £22,644,030
Vestey Foods Limited £22,644,000
Cricklewood Developments Limited £22,632,000
Notonthehighstreet Enterprises Ltd £22,616,844
Opecprime Properties Limited £22,600,000
Demipower (1991) Limited £22,569,406
Houlihan & Co. (Excavations) Limited £22,568,244
ESSCI Technical Services Limited £22,552,000
Derrin Brothers Properties Limited £22,542,756
Gould Paper Sales UK Limited £22,526,198
Thompsons (UK) Holdings Limited £22,517,220
Alliance Healthcare Management Services Limited £22,500,000
Munnelly Group PLC £22,497,000
Hansen Holdings Europe Ltd £22,496,672
Peppercorn Property Investments Limited £22,478,208
Openview Group Limited £22,470,132
Staten Investments Limited £22,459,124
Gould International UK Limited £22,452,140
Rowlands 2014 Limited £22,445,204
Skillcrown Homes (UK) LLP £22,443,164
Bancroft's School £22,429,332
Fizzy Lewisham B1 LLP £22,425,000
Brigade Electronics Group PLC £22,422,682
Brigade Holdings Limited £22,422,682
The Nuance Group (UK) Limited £22,405,000
Linden St Albans LLP £22,389,000
Site Sales Marketing Limited £22,387,996
Wrest Park Limited £22,351,964
ADM Trading (UK) Limited £22,346,016
Skanska Infrastructure Development UK Limited £22,338,000
Edif Group Management Limited £22,334,000
Comfort Hotels Limited £22,275,182
New Landmark Investment Limited £22,262,130
Sahara Holdings Limited £22,246,394
Acclaim DMW Holdings Limited £22,241,580
The Primary First Trust £22,201,000
Canadian & Arcadia Limited £22,179,252
Union Carriers Limited £22,164,462
Grosvenor Park (Harris & Trotter) 2002 Film LLP £22,162,680
QH Estates Ltd £22,161,596
Sea Cloud 1 Limited £22,157,740
Greystead Properties Limited £22,134,078
Edmonton Academy Trust £22,072,404
Corona Energy Limited £22,062,484
The Regard ACH Holdco Limited £22,046,000
Imtech Engineering Services London and South Ltd £22,040,000
LB Enterprises Limited £22,029,252
Lasted Limited £22,026,456
Rapid Action Packaging Limited £22,018,086
A A Homes and Housing (Exchange Court) Limited £22,000,000
Kallar Investments Limited £21,993,636
Yparho Investments Limited £21,981,840
Newacc (2014) Limited £21,972,700
Elmbridge Village Limited £21,961,660

Company	Amount
Vinayak Properties Limited	£21,953,264
Skynet (London) Limited	£21,945,900
254 Kilburn HR LLP	£21,930,924
Lituanica UK Ltd	£21,924,308
Wurth UK Limited	£21,901,000
Stem Healthcare Limited	£21,893,588
Zotefoams International Limited	£21,849,356
Audley Chalfont Limited	£21,840,756
Geo. Kingsbury Machine Tools Limited	£21,813,844
Bow Village Limited	£21,803,624
The Southern Motor Group Limited	£21,786,532
Atkins Properties Limited	£21,766,000
KSEYE Capital No.1 Limited	£21,745,690
Citizen Machinery UK Ltd	£21,732,640
Storm Technologies Limited	£21,701,044
Linden Barnet LLP	£21,685,000
Sussex Gardens Hotels Limited	£21,618,956
Great Park Developments Limited	£21,613,288
Acre 1176 Limited	£21,609,390
Namco UK Limited	£21,594,000
Primeeng Group Limited	£21,590,238
Agfa Healthcare UK Limited	£21,589,000
WNDirect Limited	£21,585,420
Robert Deards Limited	£21,579,480
Anzco Foods UK Limited	£21,575,996
Salisbury Workplace Services Limited	£21,566,000
Crystal Home Improvements Group Limited	£21,546,712
Majestic Securities Limited	£21,535,766
Residential Land Holdings Limited	£21,526,836
Filemaker International	£21,506,580
RO Regional Properties Limited	£21,486,416
John Laing Construction Limited	£21,434,000
Spencers Property Investments Limited	£21,419,826
World Duty Free Limited	£21,408,000
OLM Systems Limited	£21,406,962
Endon Europe Power 6 Limited	£21,397,000
Croudace Strategic Limited	£21,386,800
The Invicta Film Partnership No.9, LLP	£21,354,288
The Aldenham Foundation	£21,350,544
WWW Sunoptic Com UK Limited	£21,345,202
Samaritans	£21,331,000
Avantia Insurance Limited	£21,327,480
Equion Health (Newcastle) Limited	£21,325,000
London Irish Holdings Limited	£21,320,320
Tithe Academy	£21,301,552
Resham PLC	£21,289,094
Linden Wates (Kempshott) Limited	£21,224,000
Brook Hotels Group Limited	£21,216,716
Click Entertainment Limited	£21,210,268
Bamrose Enterprises Limited	£21,195,012
Duncan Lewis Solicitors Ltd	£21,194,938
Impact Africa Limited	£21,193,022
The Principal Edinburgh George Street Limited	£21,181,000
Atkins Holdings Limited	£21,170,000
Jablite Limited	£21,165,808
AER Rents Limited	£21,152,090
Mayday Healthcare PLC	£21,135,084
Blackfen School for Girls	£21,128,000
Champ Cargosystems (UK) Limited	£21,093,604
R. J. and D. E. Billings Limited	£21,091,332
Richard Cook Limited	£21,089,582
Sun Hotel Limited	£21,087,584
Myddleton London Limited	£21,065,404
Villachase Limited	£20,990,900
KSEYE Capital No.2 Limited	£20,979,084
The Invicta Film Partnership No.15, LLP	£20,950,716
FL Property Management Limited	£20,934,000
Isleworth and Syon School for Boys	£20,925,000
Endace Europe Limited	£20,908,974
Blenheim House Construction Limited	£20,895,484
P.F. Ahern & Sons Limited	£20,893,946
ACC Aviation Limited	£20,892,720
Zest Living Limited	£20,862,288
Penta Consulting Limited	£20,861,136
TASIS The American School in England	£20,860,680
TASIS UK Limited	£20,860,670
FT Technologies (UK) Ltd	£20,847,424
Adil Catering Limited	£20,837,032
Scape Opportunities Dublin Limited	£20,804,240
Watford Grammar School for Boys	£20,789,344
Anglogold Ashanti International Exploration Holdings	£20,789,270
Gate Gourmet Holdings U.K. Limited	£20,761,000
Asiatic Carpets Holdings Limited	£20,743,478
Sabre UK Marketing Limited	£20,741,318
Deneep Limited	£20,740,986
Aquila Chelmsford Limited	£20,735,054
Harvest Investments Solutions Limited	£20,705,364
Newmarket Holidays Limited	£20,701,376
Continental Investment Limited	£20,695,000
Kinedexe UK Limited	£20,690,110
Sky History Limited	£20,690,000
John Guest Speedfit Limited	£20,689,954
Brompton Bicycle Limited	£20,682,220
Invigia Limited	£20,665,000
LQAL UK Limited	£20,657,178
J Clubb Limited	£20,621,548
Ultimate Holdings Limited	£20,565,496
The Manor Trust	£20,544,000
Tallentire Energy Limited	£20,532,000
Glorious Solutions Limited	£20,526,442
Avocado Developments Limited	£20,517,598
Katsouris Brothers Limited	£20,508,800
Syscap Leasing Limited	£20,508,788
H.& G.Car Parks Limited	£20,502,416
Berkeley Seventy-Six Limited	£20,493,448
AMS Care Limited	£20,491,914
H.C. Jones & Co (Surrey) Limited	£20,491,104
Brymore Estates Limited	£20,468,156
Kimal PLC	£20,453,000
Sines Parks Ltd	£20,432,996
H & D Support Services (Holdings) Limited	£20,426,000
H & D Support Services Limited	£20,426,000
J.A. Phillips Holdings Limited	£20,419,454
Shields Environmental Group (Holdings) Ltd.	£20,411,000
Branden Solar Parks Limited	£20,407,000
Brentford School for Girls	£20,395,524
Stag Group Limited	£20,386,756
Thomas Sinden Limited	£20,384,588
Arcus FM Limited	£20,379,000
Combat Stress	£20,353,000
Strides Pharma Global (UK) Ltd	£20,348,244
Vanguard Learning Trust	£20,323,000
T.E.Scudder Limited	£20,308,644
Aerospares 2000 Limited	£20,302,044
London Distribution Park LLP	£20,301,448
Goal Group Limited	£20,300,352
Wagermotion Limited	£20,276,084
Bullers Wood Multi Academy Trust	£20,273,000
Bamboo Distribution Limited	£20,263,164
The Eden Academy	£20,257,000
Thames Reinforcements Limited	£20,254,036
Moss Electrical Holdings Limited	£20,248,884
A1 Pharmaceuticals Holdings Limited	£20,243,268
Fairview New Homes (South East) Limited	£20,231,000
Bellman Property Group Limited	£20,216,372
Laing O'Rourke Manufacturing Limited	£20,212,000
Travelpack Marketing & Leisure Services Limited	£20,189,584
Apex Medical Respiratory Ltd	£20,186,060
GCP Onshore Wind 3 Limited	£20,183,832
Grant Family Holdings Limited	£20,179,292
Grant Family Investments Limited	£20,179,292
Bishopshalt School	£20,159,984
Premiere Employment Group Limited	£20,152,888
MyTime Active	£20,130,700

Education Support (Newham) Limited £20,119,000
Education Support (Newham) Holdings Limited £20,119,000
Marbank Construction Limited £20,111,000
Newship Products Group Limited £20,071,000
Shadowgrade Developments Limited £20,069,988
Dalton Resources Limited £20,066,192
Mallinckrodt Medical Holdings (UK) Limited £20,057,250
Stema Shipping (UK) Limited £20,056,992
Goal Global Recoveries Limited £20,051,754
OLM Group Limited £20,030,796
Fresh Wharf Estates Limited £20,026,982
H.Evans & Sons Limited £20,012,294
Elysium Healthcare No. 4 Limited £20,008,000
John F Hunt Power Limited £20,003,154
Chem-Dry U.K. Limited £19,997,000
M.H.J. Limited £19,986,162
Petrocell Holdings Limited £19,946,964
SIP Group Limited £19,897,728
Regenter LCEP Limited £19,889,000
Regenter LCEP Holdco Limited £19,889,000
Brownlow Enterprises Limited £19,872,860
WPA Support Services Limited £19,869,000
Riverstone Pictures (Show Dogs) Limited £19,864,386
FJJ Limited £19,858,484
BP Exploration Orinoco Limited £19,852,416
Fairview Hotels Investments (2) Limited £19,836,746
The Solihull Hotel Company Limited £19,835,000
Eclerx Investments (UK) Limited £19,830,650
Optima Chemical Ltd £19,829,948
Mondi German Investments Limited £19,792,326
Fulton St James Limited £19,762,148
Shetson Property Developments Limited £19,743,774
Ansa Utilities Limited £19,743,000
Safety-Kleen UK (France) Limited £19,722,000
Pole To Win International Limited £19,717,092
Surebay Developments Limited £19,714,984
Duplo International Limited £19,697,648
Valley Wholesale Carpets (2004) Limited £19,697,338
Valley Wholesale Carpets Limited £19,690,298
Branden Solar Parks (Holdings) Limited £19,682,000
Desilu Group Limited £19,674,460
Watch It Come Down Limited £19,672,172
Griffon Land & Estates Limited £19,661,544
The Galaxy Trust £19,659,552
London Pharma & Chemicals Group Ltd £19,651,536
Exel Freight Management (UK) Limited £19,644,000
Solstor UK Limited £19,627,498
Globaltex Limited £19,624,000
Shirley High School £19,622,708
Solstor Holdings Limited £19,573,160
Jopate Estates Limited £19,564,136
Rugby Football Foundation £19,556,538
Thompsons (UK) Limited £19,549,700
Fizzy Epsom LLP £19,540,000
Grant & Bowman International Limited £19,532,718
Sunsave 25 (Wix Lodge Farm) Limited £19,526,000
Safedale Limited £19,517,820
The Holmes Care Limited £19,503,908
Independent Commercial Broking Group Limited £19,502,060
Highway Care Limited £19,497,688
United Living (North) Group Limited £19,465,000
Highway Care Group Limited £19,464,176
Derby School Solutions (Holdings) Limited £19,464,000
Derby School Solutions Limited £19,464,000
Charters Village Limited £19,463,878
British Airways Leasing Limited £19,460,000
Marwin Securities Limited £19,456,530
Newport Industries Limited £19,454,540
Al-Khair Foundation £19,436,840
Opus 2 International Limited £19,423,704
Bronzeshield Lifting Limited £19,404,582
Q.N. Hotels Limited £19,404,120
JSA Services Limited £19,393,340
Ranola Properties Limited £19,371,308
Cantillon Limited £19,370,000
Hinchley Wood School £19,369,000
Sparquote Limited £19,368,620
Grove T5 Limited £19,355,978
Delbanco Meyer & Company Limited £19,346,000
Facilicom UK Limited £19,340,324
Charco 2010 Limited £19,325,212
Volex Group Holdings Limited £19,312,000
Catalyst Academies Trust £19,307,262
Swanlea Limited £19,301,774
Charter Court (New Malden) Limited £19,297,172
Denecroft Estates Limited £19,275,098
Dunlop International Europe Limited £19,261,000
Nine Heathrow Ventures Limited £19,260,404
Ouhla Properties Limited £19,251,248
The Avenues Trust Group £19,249,000
Media 10 Limited £19,237,392
Denton Homes Limited £19,233,000
Easyfairs UK Limited £19,217,066
Homeguard Properties Limited £19,216,532
Shields Environmental Investment (Holdings) Ltd £19,212,000
Warrant Properties Limited £19,209,212
Films & Equipments Limited £19,207,570
The Brit School Limited £19,193,000
Audley St Elphins Limited £19,190,188
NFAP Limited £19,188,000
Petrolvalves (G.B.) Limited £19,184,008
Porcelanosa (South East) Limited £19,179,000
Inclusive Multi Academy Trust £19,169,036
Cranford Community College £19,142,560
Quinn Investment Holdings (London) Limited £19,140,008
FTX Logistics Limited £19,126,356
Drew Smith Limited £19,102,560
European Investments (Earlseat) Limited £19,100,000
Axis Security Services Limited £19,099,000
GDL (Slough Developments) Limited £19,077,416
T G Commodities Limited £19,073,816
Brightsun Travel (UK) Limited £19,070,808
Forester Investments Limited £19,066,772
Wates Foundation Limited (The) £19,036,852
Linden Wates (The Frythe) Limited £19,036,000
N.R.C. Plant Limited £19,035,140
Reach Academy Trust £19,028,760
Omavale Limited £19,027,584
Wickland (Holdings) Limited £19,022,956
Samax Resources Limited £19,018,806
SintecMedia Global Ltd £19,009,208
AA Property and Construction Services Limited £19,000,544
Harsco (U.K.) Limited £18,981,270
Mothers Ltd £18,980,012
Macquarie Corona Energy Holdings Limited £18,975,828
Saba Park Services UK Limited £18,971,592
Beechwood Investments Limited £18,971,092
Warrens Warehousing Group Limited £18,960,614
Queen Elizabeth's Girls' School (Barnet) £18,958,656
Ilot Investments UK Ltd £18,942,062
H H Associates Limited £18,923,000
Sotherby LLP £18,917,582
Norfolk Capital Group Limited £18,913,000
MRB Holdings Ltd £18,909,664
Creative Distribution Limited £18,892,476
Ilot Capital UK Ltd £18,871,134
PHH 2 Limited £18,859,400
Randall Watts London Limited £18,847,888
Investors in Ideas Ltd £18,840,764
Thumbzup UK Limited £18,839,764
Link Corporate Trustees (UK) Limited £18,837,716
Smiths Business Information Services Limited £18,836,000
Chadwell Heath Academy £18,834,648
MJF UK Holdings Limited £18,834,488

Kew Green Hotels (Speke) Limited	£18,805,734
Elliot Leigh Property Investments 2 Ltd	£18,802,786
Linden Wates (Ringwood) LLP	£18,788,000
Syd Bishop & Sons (Demolition) Limited	£18,787,870
Rickmansworth School	£18,782,918
Garrets Bidco Limited	£18,780,188
Houlihan & Co (Holdings) Limited	£18,773,256
Beck & Pollitzer Engineering Holdings Ltd.	£18,771,010
Planetree Developments Limited	£18,765,816
Aspect Software UK Limited	£18,731,000
Warrens' Warehousing & Distribution (Midlands) Ltd	£18,717,320
OGE Drilling & Investment Ltd	£18,709,168
Betcrown Limited	£18,706,236
Stirling Civil Engineering Limited	£18,700,000
Pirin Ltd	£18,658,932
Corinthia Investments Limited	£18,650,258
Reading Scientific Services Limited	£18,645,000
King Street Manchester Property LLP	£18,640,838
Countrywide Electrical Distributors Limited	£18,634,840
Universal Tyre Company (Deptford) Limited (The)	£18,616,326
Treetops Capital Limited	£18,612,568
Skanska Cementation International Holdings Limited	£18,610,000
Daarasp LLP	£18,595,234
EPI Global Ltd	£18,583,060
Abercorn Education Ltd	£18,561,468
J.Browne Construction Company Limited	£18,558,708
Hale Hamilton (Valves) Limited	£18,554,428
Audley Coopers Hill Limited	£18,554,176
S.J.M. Alloys & Metals Limited	£18,553,084
Feabrex Limited	£18,551,442
Earlseat Wind Farm Ltd	£18,545,000
Academy Services (Tendring) Limited	£18,510,000
Van Ameyde UK Holding Limited	£18,504,096
Amsprop City Properties Limited	£18,491,500
Birchwood Commercial Ltd	£18,487,676
Vinepost Limited	£18,481,164
Double A Group Services Limited	£18,480,432
Turnhold Properties Limited	£18,473,580
S N B Holdings Limited	£18,470,068
Lint Group Limited	£18,456,874
JEDS Investments Ltd	£18,450,604
Romans International Limited	£18,446,572
Martin Bunzl International Limited	£18,445,278
FIC Grand Plaza Ltd	£18,441,596
Churton Property Developments Limited	£18,413,018
Godiva Bearings (Southern) Limited	£18,397,750
Sines Parks Holdings Limited	£18,351,088
Cobalt Limited	£18,342,844
Whelan & Grant (Holdings) Limited	£18,338,496
Sutton Grammar School Trust	£18,337,000
H.Stain Limited	£18,329,352
Lumen Learning Trust	£18,325,380
Right Choice Insurance Brokers Limited	£18,314,632
Selecta Holding Limited	£18,314,000
European Investments (SCEL) Limited	£18,296,544
Northfield Avenue (Holdings) Limited	£18,292,048
Express Freight Services (U.K.) Limited	£18,283,578
Abbey View Produce Limited	£18,282,696
Woodgavil Estates Limited	£18,272,468
Ferring Pharmaceuticals Limited	£18,245,226
Asino Limited	£18,243,436
Full House Restaurants Holdings Limited	£18,240,940
M.Price Limited	£18,238,488
Hansgrohe Limited	£18,227,000
Wood Farm (Stanmore) Limited	£18,215,322
MY Construction & Carpentry Limited	£18,180,600
Korda Developments Limited	£18,174,750
Currie Finance and Leasing Company Limited	£18,167,000
Naked Wines International Limited	£18,161,000
IGUK Support Services Limited	£18,159,000
Runnymede Homes Limited	£18,157,632
Distell International Holdings Limited	£18,152,844
Reichmann Properties PLC	£18,139,238
Fizzy Poplar LLP	£18,133,000
The Continuity Company Limited	£18,122,000
Jessica House Developments Limited	£18,121,020
Hapag-Lloyd (U.K.) Limited	£18,103,140
Wood Hall Investments Limited	£18,096,462
Dabasia Estates LLP	£18,089,284
C.P. Hart & Sons Limited	£18,067,288
Radnor House Sevenoaks (Holdings) Limited	£18,054,304
Gillette Industries Limited	£18,051,000
Bramley Health Holding Company Limited	£18,036,060
HSP Investments Limited	£18,010,734
A1 Pharmaceuticals Public Limited Company	£18,008,192
Hertz Accident Support Ltd	£18,001,948
A A Homes and Housing (Metro Point) Property Ltd	£18,000,000
Healthcare Drugstores Limited	£17,998,800
Healthcare Support (Erdington) Limited	£17,985,000
Healthcare Support (Erdington) Holdings Limited	£17,985,000
John F Hunt Limited	£17,978,696
Family Funerals Trust Limited	£17,959,134
Catco Kids LLP	£17,944,464
New Way International Ltd	£17,938,606
Davroc Limited	£17,936,524
Angel Property Investments Limited	£17,917,088
Cochlear Research and Development Limited	£17,894,680
Currie Motors UK Limited	£17,879,000
Castlestone Investments Limited	£17,873,204
Charterhouse Simon Limited	£17,854,982
Subsea 7 West Africa Contracting Limited	£17,845,574
Shrewsbury House School Trust Limited	£17,830,712
Euromax Resources (Macedonia) UK Limited	£17,829,424
Pelham Academy Trust	£17,813,396
Fairview New Homes (Chase Road) Limited	£17,800,000
Ceros (Bradford) Limited	£17,794,986
Excelredstone Converged Solutions Limited	£17,792,348
Aquinas Church of England Education Trust Limited	£17,773,000
Twilight Real Estate Limited	£17,772,256
Queenwood Golf Club Limited	£17,762,472
RCL Investments Ltd	£17,751,788
Bayside Investment Company Limited	£17,717,552
Intelliflo Limited	£17,698,254
Robert Lee Distribution Limited	£17,693,266
Restate Management Ltd	£17,690,850
Kew Green Hotels (Gatwick) Limited	£17,682,292
Seacon Group Limited	£17,670,420
Oakburn European Properties Limited	£17,665,056
Crispin & Borst Limited	£17,656,000
Azurie Blue Limited	£17,652,464
Ruislip High School	£17,633,988
Vestey Foods International Limited	£17,628,000
Russell Education Trust	£17,602,000
Fairview New Homes (Developments) Limited	£17,592,000
The Invicta Film Partnership No. 17, LLP	£17,576,724
London and Hertfordshire Limited	£17,566,748
City & Southern Limited	£17,527,196
Soul Foods Limited	£17,520,264
H. Smith Food Group PLC	£17,509,352
Signet Group Services Limited	£17,505,000
Lensbury Limited	£17,482,000
Cranfield Technology Park Investments Limited	£17,481,700
Crown Holdings Limited	£17,480,976
Pleythorne Limited	£17,479,726
Everguard Limited	£17,474,784
BP Exploration Company (Middle East) Limited	£17,468,472
William Boyer & Sons, Limited	£17,465,312
Fulton Central Limited	£17,405,402
Princess Alice Hospice	£17,396,758
Bhaggo Limited	£17,396,412
Woodcote High School	£17,383,000
Former Reichmann Properties PLC	£17,363,948
Countrywide Developments (UK) PLC	£17,355,384
Woodford Heating Holdings Limited	£17,343,320

Company	Amount
E.G.T. Finance Limited	£17,331,720
Ability Hotels (III) Holdings Limited	£17,303,980
Chancery Education Trust	£17,303,000
Jablite Holdings Limited	£17,299,000
E92 Plus Limited	£17,296,402
Pantheon Hotels and Leisure Limited	£17,291,444
London General Life Company Limited	£17,264,000
ISS Damage Control Limited	£17,253,000
Baby Network Limited	£17,236,060
DSJ Homes Limited	£17,235,500
Richard Wright Music Limited	£17,229,790
BIP Industries Limited	£17,225,748
Brook Hotels No. 1 Limited	£17,218,070
Sunstar Group Limited	£17,213,568
Ergonomic Solutions Limited	£17,210,870
Harro Foods Limited	£17,200,028
Primat Recruitment Limited	£17,174,000
Alternative Bridging (UK 2) Limited	£17,161,092
NVSM Limited	£17,151,288
Regis 2000 Limited	£17,150,980
Truman Securities Limited	£17,147,800
M & H Properties London Limited	£17,137,336
London City Bond Limited	£17,133,680
Moss Electrical Co. Limited	£17,127,676
Hamton Environmental Services Limited	£17,124,328
Plymouth (Notte Street) Limited	£17,104,904
UHP Investments Limited	£17,104,812
Tower Hill Suffolk Limited	£17,103,280
Tri-Continental Limited	£17,101,246
S.T.C.Plumbing & Heating Merchants Limited	£17,098;472
L & M (Heating) Supplies Limited	£17,089,968
Tican (Chilled) Limited	£17,086,000
Chevaning Mining Company Limited	£17,081,086
Radical Investments Limited	£17,080,976
Lodge Hotels (London) Limited	£17,079,576
Standley Holdings Limited	£17,044,232
Roman Investments Limited	£17,029,512
Analog Devices Limited	£17,026,910
GHL (Hackney Wick) Limited	£17,026,062
Aura Finance (Holdco) Limited	£17,024,372
Skylight Investments Limited	£17,019,638
AVM Vision Investments Ltd	£17,005,000
Hurstmere School	£16,998,796
Fulton Hyde Limited	£16,997,012
Burwater Holdings Limited	£16,977,468
HAGS-SMP Limited	£16,971,164
Cygnus Academies Trust	£16,967,360
The Tiffin Girls' School	£16,959,000
Finer Limited	£16,949,120
The Harrow Academies Trust	£16,948,598
Galderma (U.K.) Limited	£16,943,000
Mallinckrodt Chemical Holdings (U.K.) Limited	£16,942,422
Radnor House Sevenoaks (Property) Limited	£16,933,416
GDL (Luton) Developments Limited	£16,923,480
Oasis Lending LLP	£16,915,680
Wise Trading Limited	£16,904,696
Y.A. Property Investments Limited	£16,903,558
McGee Civil Engineering Limited	£16,900,368
Thompson Bros. (Esher) Limited	£16,894,208
Shepperton Hotels Holdings Limited	£16,885,998
Metro Partners LLP	£16,880,308
GCP Healthcare 1 Limited	£16,878,376
Arora Heathrow Holdings Limited	£16,874,590
The Bishop Wand Church of England School	£16,846,754
Martlane Limited	£16,817,976
Verifone Services UK & Ireland Limited	£16,786,518
Elgon (Enfield) Limited	£16,779,368
Verisk International Holdings Limited	£16,769,658
Rose Film Partnership LLP	£16,761,960
Ability Hotels (Aberdeen) Limited	£16,760,660
BMT Defence and Security UK Limited	£16,753,000
Guardian IT	£16,751,000
Twickenham Studios Limited	£16,749,533
BP Services International Limited	£16,726,114
Institute of Grocery Distribution (The)	£16,713,299
Lay & Wheeler Limited	£16,707,000
Excitech Limited	£16,704,616
A.E.Thorogood Limited	£16,702,256
IBA Group Holdings Limited	£16,696,570
Pepper (UK) Limited	£16,696,472
Harouni Group of Companies Limited	£16,696,130
Fairview New Homes (Willow Way) Limited	£16,690,000
Milsom Hotels Limited	£16,689,450
Grange Walk LLP	£16,689,000
Tennay Properties Limited	£16,681,209
Optimum Group Services PLC	£16,675,437
Hills Group Enterprises Limited	£16,674,323
Renault Group U.K. Limited	£16,671,500
Startling Music Limited	£16,666,777
Enfield Fancy Goods Limited	£16,664,887
MA Securities London Limited	£16,654,916
Seven Seas Limited	£16,648,000
JSM Construction Limited	£16,643,443
JSM Group Holdings Limited	£16,643,443
Sovereign Equity Holdings Limited	£16,624,164
Tower Hill Investment Partners Limited	£16,623,895
Askham Village Community Limited	£16,619,195
Armstrong (U.K.) Investments	£16,617,000
Sky Retail Stores Limited	£16,616,000
Ziegler UK Limited	£16,594,064
Park Rutland Investments (London) Limited	£16,587,068
SmithKline Beecham Marketing & Technical Services	£16,581,000
RET Becket Keys Church of England Free School	£16,578,000
Galliford Try Plant Limited	£16,576,000
Denville Hall 2012	£16,574,064
J P C Mulligan Properties Limited	£16,566,412
One YMCA	£16,558,202
DP Poland PLC	£16,556,290
Pact Educational Trust Limited	£16,542,914
Durbin PLC	£16,542,647
BDL Group Public Limited Company (The)	£16,541,557
T Brown Group Limited	£16,537,778
Galamast Limited	£16,537,468
Corero Network Security PLC	£16,536,347
Panther Trading Limited	£16,531,522
Altomart Limited	£16,528,765
Vectra Limited	£16,518,368
Rivers Finance Group PLC	£16,517,509
Silverson Machines Limited	£16,510,545
SG Technologies Limited	£16,504,000
Silnat Holdings Limited	£16,500,291
Rivers Leasing PLC	£16,499,837
Tony Gee and Partners LLP	£16,488,747
Oatlands Investments Limited	£16,471,685
Brent Housing Ltd	£16,469,177
Europe Incoming Holdings Limited	£16,468,968
London Square Development Management Limited	£16,466,000
Westlake Estates Limited	£16,449,147
Crosswater Holdings Limited	£16,440,000
Garrets International Limited	£16,437,936
Facilicom Cleaning Services Limited	£16,436,873
NDK Europe Limited	£16,436,566
Sifcon International PLC	£16,430,931
TBG Holding C Limited	£16,413,738
Curo Charlotte House LLP	£16,408,843
MSC Cruises Limited	£16,397,508
B.A.T.S. Ilford Limited	£16,373,346
Sandhill Homes Limited	£16,372,683
Caretech Estates Limited	£16,363,000
Starbones Limited	£16,362,519
The Capital Dairy Company (Holdings) Limited	£16,357,963
Garusa Solutions U.K. Limited	£16,345,721
Thomas Aston Homes Limited	£16,313,521
D.M.C. Business Machines Limited	£16,312,805

Company	Amount
Elysium Healthcare Property 3 Limited	£16,310,000
TJX UK Property Limited	£16,295,000
Periworld Limited	£16,285,444
Ashill Land Limited	£16,274,051
Monarock Limited	£16,269,961
Alcedo Shipping Limited	£16,269,907
Dartford Grammar School	£16,266,000
EPI Group Holdings Ltd	£16,263,917
GCP Hydro 1 Limited	£16,258,949
Kubach & Sambrook (Metals) Limited	£16,255,821
Littleberries LLP	£16,251,027
Peacock Homes Limited	£16,250,122
Phoenix Property Development Co. Ltd.	£16,242,471
Alsford Timber Limited	£16,224,498
T.S.G. Building Services PLC	£16,224,464
Deco Design and Build Co. Limited	£16,201,423
Rina Consulting Ltd	£16,201,000
European Property Development Limited	£16,199,510
Glastry Advisory Partners Limited	£16,196,895
Caretech Estates (No. 5) Limited	£16,166,000
Supreme Hotels LLP	£16,153,491
Grey Bridge Holdings Limited	£16,130,590
British Danubian Trade Development Co Ltd	£16,129,190
SME Properties Limited	£16,102,450
Elysium Healthcare (Farndon) Limited	£16,087,000
Local Boy'z Group Holding Limited	£16,085,824
Grant & Boyd Limited	£16,081,908
TJX Europe Buying (Deutschland) Limited	£16,075,000
Otto Bock Healthcare PLC	£16,068,942
Norgine Pharmaceuticals Limited	£16,059,000
Amey Highways Lighting (Wakefield) Limited	£16,054,000
AHL Holdings (Wakefield) Limited	£16,054,000
D3O Holdings Ltd	£16,044,774
Kromachem Holdings Limited	£16,031,411
ATK Energy EU Limited	£16,028,000
Frelene Limited	£16,000,356
WJ Management Limited	£15,991,835
Prestolite Electric Limited	£15,957,000
Sunray Estates Limited	£15,948,466
GCP Rooftop Solar 2 Limited	£15,921,849
Black Arrow Group Limited	£15,912,484
Unity Academy Trust	£15,904,869
Morelli Group Limited	£15,901,264
Residential Land Management 2 Ltd	£15,896,826
NDEMIC Creations Ltd	£15,878,876
Vanneck Residential LLP	£15,878,174
Beths Grammar School	£15,874,000
Tazaki Foods Limited	£15,858,909
Viners Capital Properties Limited	£15,850,952
Rican Securities Limited	£15,836,983
Oliver Connell and Son Limited	£15,830,438
Ability Hotels (IV) UK Limited	£15,814,189
GCP Education 1 Limited	£15,803,246
Stonemanor Limited	£15,797,151
Ceragon (UK) Limited	£15,776,645
Orley Farm School Trust	£15,772,153
Viadex Limited	£15,767,877
Smartcomms SC Limited	£15,767,000
Precision Printing Co. Limited	£15,753,570
W & L Investments LLP	£15,752,335
Mapeley Columbus II Limited	£15,750,000
Sugarman Group Limited	£15,749,438
Emerson Crane Hire Limited	£15,747,388
Gade Property Developments Limited	£15,730,458
Port of London Properties Limited	£15,710,000
Toll Global Forwarding (UK) Limited	£15,702,000
The Church of Pentecost - UK	£15,687,379
Cargill Chocolate UK Limited	£15,683,290
Rent 2 Own Cars Ltd	£15,669,892
Country House Weddings Limited	£15,669,194
Skyline Arcomet Limited	£15,667,716
Bagga Holdings Limited	£15,664,758
Menzies Aviation (ASIG Ground Handling) Limited	£15,657,000
Apex Car Rental (Norwich) Limited	£15,656,083
Hildo Limited	£15,655,811
Watford Grammar School for Girls	£15,644,219
Central Property Investments Limited	£15,641,023
Hollin Hill Properties Limited	£15,640,747
NNR Global Logistics UK Limited	£15,637,087
Orbis Protect Limited	£15,612,000
Boxtrent Limited	£15,589,000
Kuflink Bridging Ltd	£15,577,400
Leitrim Properties Limited	£15,569,435
O'Hara Property Investment Holding Company Ltd	£15,568,922
Citipost Mail Limited	£15,567,773
Multitrust Property Investments Limited	£15,567,156
Stanley Dock Properties Limited	£15,561,307
Audley Stanbridge Earls Limited	£15,561,105
London Executive Aviation Limited	£15,557,000
J H Lorimer Limited	£15,554,778
Watts Farms Fresh Produce Holdings Limited	£15,553,254
PSSG Group Limited	£15,548,770
Marylebone Square Holdings Ltd	£15,528,017
Cadbury Six LLP	£15,519,000
QBS Software Limited	£15,515,417
Park Score Ltd	£15,513,085
Uniquehelp Limited	£15,501,395
Jabac Finances Limited	£15,498,803
Halliford School Limited	£15,493,779
Cappagh Browne Utilities Limited	£15,484,426
Kitewood (Creekside) Limited	£15,473,662
P.I.G. Holdings Limited	£15,448,000
Elysium Healthcare (St Mary's) Limited	£15,445,244
P. Johnson & Son (1976) Limited	£15,434,363
Grantol Investments Limited	£15,415,446
MNS Care PLC	£15,414,494
Berwen Limited	£15,401,277
SEJ Assets Limited	£15,391,768
Talbot House Business Centre Limited	£15,386,373
PS Foundation	£15,382,721
Atlas Cleaning Limited	£15,368,149
Blenheim Estates Limited	£15,362,492
Belsize Garages Project Limited	£15,362,346
Rugby Football Development Limited	£15,349,000
Laxkan Holdings Ltd	£15,322,764
Furlong Flooring (Southern) Ltd.	£15,317,550
Vetex Limited	£15,314,148
WJ Groundwater Limited	£15,310,471
Oatfield Limited	£15,303,548
Alan Day Investments LLP	£15,300,143
International Passenger Protection Limited	£15,271,911
Canada Life Asset Management Limited	£15,254,000
West Hatch High School Academy Trust	£15,242,000
Hudson Lisse Limited	£15,234,200
Broadway Malyan Limited	£15,231,000
JB & Ace Limited	£15,230,684
Oakray Limited	£15,224,925
Biggin Hill Hangar Company Limited	£15,209,881
WMF United Kingdom Limited	£15,209,381
Summit Media Limited	£15,199,332
Caretech Community Services (No.2) Limited	£15,198,000
MC Power Limited	£15,195,000
Caravel Trading Ltd	£15,192,947
Marymount International School	£15,182,470
Treebond Limited	£15,179,623
Ocourage Limited	£15,176,342
Munnelly Support Services Limited	£15,170,000
Vahnea Marolda Investments LLP	£15,168,396
Neilcott Group Holdings Limited	£15,166,838
Harlequin Football Club Limited	£15,166,016
Fibron BX Limited	£15,165,722
HCP Holdings Limited	£15,157,000
National Instruments Corporation (UK) Limited	£15,154,573
First Rented Housing Group Limited	£15,150,114

Company	Amount
V.G.Clements (Contractors) Limited	£15,146,263
R. & I. Grant & Co. Limited	£15,115,267
The Construction Workers Guild Limited	£15,103,765
Dialgreen Estates Limited	£15,080,637
GLS Global Logistics Solutions LLP	£15,074,162
Cornwall	£15,073,055
Z Hotel Poland Street Property LLP	£15,058,413
Kearns Premier Homes Ltd	£15,057,904
BR Pharma International Limited	£15,056,712
Croydon Logistics Limited	£15,052,000
The White Brasserie Company Ltd	£15,049,314
Perfect Smile Group Holding Limited	£15,048,207
Garfwish Limited	£15,036,886
Burney Realty Limited	£15,034,011
Timeboard Industrial Properties LLP	£15,028,699
Equatorial Traders Limited	£15,023,933
Belgrave Land (Sheffield) Limited	£15,021,822
GCP Biomass 2 Limited	£15,021,270
Wilman Universal Group Limited	£15,017,031
RPSD2 Limited	£15,011,804
UML Marylebone Limited	£15,011,344
Donald Russell Holdings Limited	£15,000,000
Simpson Marketing Limited	£14,996,613
Bible and Gospel Trust	£14,995,667
Sutton Group Holdings Limited	£14,986,647
West Bridgford JV LLP	£14,975,000
Vinci Environment UK Limited	£14,973,000
Bluestar Enterprise Limited	£14,963,473
Fairview New Homes (Colindale) Limited	£14,953,000
452 Finchley Road LLP	£14,943,261
Metrosold Limited	£14,919,094
Pizza Gogo Ltd	£14,916,840
Fineraid Limited	£14,906,744
Deltec Citimail Limited	£14,892,762
HRS Investments Limited	£14,872,608
Selborne Care Limited	£14,845,953
ARRI Rental Services UK Limited	£14,843,888
Pinden Limited	£14,831,102
SG Technologies Group Limited	£14,823,000
Via-Vox Limited	£14,821,082
Hudson Almere Limited	£14,802,959
Hawkspare Limited	£14,790,096
NBC Europe Ltd.	£14,784,000
First Coins Pawn LLP	£14,780,147
Nissin (U.K.) Limited	£14,769,000
Fresh Cash Pawn LLP	£14,767,824
Atlanta Trust Limited	£14,754,914
Kavo Dental Limited	£14,751,000
Levolux Limited	£14,732,000
Verde Agritech PLC	£14,730,166
United Kingdom Accreditation Service	£14,726,102
Avonpark Village (Care Homes) Limited	£14,721,223
MBM Forest Products Limited	£14,699,267
Payless Group Limited	£14,698,229
Grapes Direct Limited	£14,693,000
GCP Rooftop Solar 3 Limited	£14,681,043
Select Enterprises (Holdings) Limited	£14,678,742
Lineside Logistics (Southern) Ltd	£14,666,375
Karuna Care (TLC) Limited	£14,660,674
Embee Holdings Limited	£14,654,824
Summerhill Birmingham Limited	£14,644,183
The Valentine Group Limited	£14,636,649
FJC Topco Limited	£14,633,877
Sky LLU Assets Limited	£14,633,000
Good Harvest Properties (Southwark) Limited	£14,631,545
Mohan Building Services Limited	£14,630,588
Sherrygold No.1 Limited	£14,630,546
S.A.T.V. Publishing Limited	£14,630,000
Congregation of The Daughters of The Cross	£14,629,991
Sterndale Systems Limited	£14,628,791
Haymarket Publishing Services Limited	£14,620,000
Venture Lighting Europe Limited	£14,589,358
B Emerald Limited	£14,568,722
Purcell School (The)	£14,567,751
Amsik Limited	£14,564,792
Imperial Ductwork Services Limited	£14,560,906
JGC New Energy UK Limited	£14,560,236
Cedars Village Limited	£14,558,763
Volkerlaser Ltd	£14,555,000
Almirall Limited	£14,548,521
Leading Edge Labels Limited	£14,540,058
Stokes Marsh Solar Limited	£14,536,924
Mono Holdings Limited	£14,510,316
Veritas Educational Trust	£14,484,234
Passportcard Limited	£14,473,239
Davis and Dann Limited	£14,469,876
Truly Travel Limited	£14,463,172
Valley Trucks Holdings Limited	£14,455,042
Thames Industrial Estate Limited	£14,454,908
Epoch-Making Toys Limited	£14,451,114
PGG Properties Limited	£14,451,077
Grant & Bowman Limited	£14,443,814
Clifford Property Company Limited (The)	£14,443,479
HLT Stakis Operator Limited	£14,441,632
Saints Transport Limited	£14,438,034
Saints Transport GRP Limited	£14,438,034
SDJ Enterprises Limited	£14,420,452
Seebeck 133 Limited	£14,420,000
Premier PLC	£14,417,769
Manpower Services Limited	£14,417,000
Transform Schools (Knowsley) Intermediate Ltd	£14,414,000
The Arete Trust	£14,410,490
Transmec Properties Limited	£14,407,471
Sitecrest Limited	£14,391,378
Caretech Estates (No 2) Limited	£14,383,000
Coats Global Services Limited	£14,377,000
Sagoo & Takhar Limited	£14,367,279
Latimer Hill LLP	£14,366,000
Southdown Holdings Limited	£14,352,874
The Clay Oven UK Limited	£14,339,974
Defender No.1 Production LLP	£14,335,035
Saints Transport (Holdings) Limited	£14,327,330
PRP Architects LLP	£14,317,796
Fujikura Europe Limited	£14,314,800
UPS Air Couriers of America Limited	£14,312,000
West One Technology Ltd	£14,308,900
Bayti Properties Limited	£14,301,108
Newport School Solutions Limited	£14,298,000
Newport School Solutions (Holdings) Limited	£14,298,000
Cobalt Ground Solutions Limited	£14,275,416
Halcyon Offices Limited	£14,273,781
D R 4 Developments LLP	£14,272,000
LDBS Frays Academy Trust	£14,270,000
Contracting Made Easy Ltd	£14,269,625
Geyfords Limited	£14,251,847
Silverton Property Investments Limited	£14,247,594
Audley Binswood Limited	£14,245,001
Colts Cabs Limited	£14,243,478
Enfield Innovations Ltd	£14,227,513
Berkeley Residential Limited	£14,200,830
Geieonline Dafconsulting (UK) Ltd.	£14,194,706
F.H. Hale & Sons (Builders) Limited	£14,184,136
Insignia Investments Limited	£14,180,130
Aurient Investments N16 Ltd	£14,177,548
William Croxson & Son,Limited	£14,163,318
Bushey Developments Ltd	£14,161,799
D.Green & Co.(Stoke Newington) Limited	£14,160,731
Lefa Enterprises Limited	£14,158,972
Orbital Fasteners Holdings Limited	£14,158,778
Citipost Limited	£14,136,871
M - Integrated Solutions PLC	£14,134,020
Shooting Star Chase	£14,121,439
The Quest Academy - Coloma Trust	£14,101,000
Kore Wireless UK PLC	£14,098,949

Company	Amount
M.M.C. Investments Limited	£14,097,893
ATD Travel Services Limited	£14,082,404
The Siemon Company Limited	£14,080,926
Marine Point Property LLP	£14,048,415
Custodes Acqco Limited	£14,044,738
Henley Group Holdings Limited	£14,042,932
Riverstone Solutions 2 Limited	£14,035,968
J P Dunn Construction Limited	£14,029,537
Laxkan Ltd	£14,028,788
Fulton Grand Limited	£14,022,891
BRE Global Limited	£14,007,000
Oak Tree Schools Holdings Limited	£14,004,221
George Killoughery Limited	£13,998,409
Consulco Finance Ltd	£13,993,572
IMCD UK Investments Ltd	£13,980,000
Track Technology Limited	£13,974,000
The Derbyshire Hotel Derby Limited	£13,964,061
Hugh Langmead Limited	£13,960,168
Triplehigh Limited	£13,952,020
The Jewellery Channel Limited	£13,951,410
Sterling Relocation Limited	£13,950,000
Chemox Pound Limited	£13,944,316
Lismire LLP	£13,944,123
PizzaExpress (Franchises) Limited	£13,942,000
ISG Technology Limited	£13,937,000
Saint Francis Hospice	£13,928,000
Exmoore Financial Credit Co. Ltd.	£13,924,349
Trade Sale (Slough) Limited	£13,916,787
Cosco Shipping Lines (UK) Limited	£13,908,348
Defender No.1 Sale & Leaseback LLP	£13,907,090
Seacon Terminals Limited	£13,904,799
Early Learning Holdings Limited	£13,900,000
Chelsea Stores Holdings Limited	£13,900,000
Fitzjohns Avenue Ltd	£13,891,572
Harrow High School	£13,889,414
Baruch Investments Limited	£13,884,581
Blakley Electrics Limited	£13,857,786
Carrain Limited	£13,853,009
Pledream Properties Limited	£13,850,547
Alina Care Limited	£13,836,348
Bourne Court Properties Limited	£13,832,547
Saba Infra Cambridgeshire Limited	£13,827,983
CRK Finance Limited	£13,820,178
4th Dimension Innovation Limited	£13,811,714
Higgins Investments PLC	£13,784,537
Neopost Technologies Limited	£13,761,000
Farrington Care Homes Limited	£13,752,100
R. Maskell Limited	£13,745,360
Donald Russell Limited	£13,741,000
The Unstuffy Hotel Co Limited	£13,732,529
Java Asset Management Limited	£13,719,841
Vantage Volante Limited	£13,718,099
BSW Heating Ltd	£13,716,516
Oncoland Limited	£13,710,360
W.D.King Limited	£13,699,625
Container Providers International (UK) Limited	£13,690,848
Threshold Land & Estates Limited	£13,671,013
L & M Holding Ltd	£13,660,850
Abbey Mills Properties Ltd	£13,656,690
E.F.G. Housewares Limited	£13,650,907
KM Estates Limited	£13,638,141
Reliance Entertainment Productions 7 Ltd	£13,636,532
Paul Strickland Scanner Centre	£13,635,338
Mollart Group Limited	£13,630,071
Linden Wates (Westbury) Limited	£13,630,000
RA Securities London Limited	£13,602,942
Sartorius Stedim UK Limited	£13,602,207
Mallinckrodt Equinox Limited	£13,596,565
Ability Hotels (Syon) Limited	£13,593,305
Isleworth & Hounslow Charity Limited	£13,583,082
Vinci Fleet Services Limited	£13,580,000
Select Enterprises Limited	£13,570,220
KMP Holdings Limited	£13,568,670
Clarges Pharmaceuticals Limited	£13,568,000
British Airways Avionic Engineering Limited	£13,566,000
Trentpeak Limited	£13,564,798
Longmill Realty Limited	£13,562,213
Kellogg Brown & Root Projects Limited	£13,557,961
The Keswick Enterprises Group Limited	£13,552,875
Tax Computer Systems Limited	£13,543,293
Aster Healthcare Ltd.	£13,542,438
MK Windfarm Limited	£13,539,583
Tropical Sky Limited	£13,528,517
Prospect Healthcare (Hairmyres) Resources	£13,522,000
E Y C Limited	£13,492,361
Waystone Limited	£13,491,168
Siem Shipping UK Limited	£13,486,472
Darrick Wood School	£13,486,000
Bromley Business Centre (Holdings) Ltd.	£13,477,756
Mary Roxburghe Trust	£13,446,895
H.W.M. Limited	£13,434,019
Howard Hunt Mail Limited	£13,418,588
HCL Insurance BPO Services Limited	£13,412,000
Kingsmead School	£13,411,465
MJA Investments Limited	£13,410,765
Wear Point Wind Limited	£13,410,000
Urbanicity (No. 16) LLP	£13,404,916
Hart Homes Limited	£13,390,413
Marz Limited	£13,388,672
J.C.S. Developments Ltd.	£13,388,337
Thomas Lipton Ltd	£13,378,481
Hedgemans Limited	£13,375,961
Neptune Hotels Limited	£13,372,689
Chalk Farm Marine LLP	£13,372,217
Woodford Heating & Energy Limited	£13,368,076
Raue LLP	£13,365,174
Naked Wines Prepayments Trustee Company Ltd	£13,361,000
London School of Theology	£13,359,058
Silvermere Golf & Leisure Limited	£13,344,884
The Elstree UTC	£13,336,000
LE Packaging Ltd	£13,327,738
Workout Limited	£13,325,661
London Irish Consortium (2013) Ltd	£13,322,968
SMC Investcorp Limited	£13,316,588
Oak Narwana LLP	£13,316,127
Hill's Garages (Woodford) Limited	£13,312,039
Huntington House Limited	£13,311,652
Punjab House Associated Ltd	£13,301,499
Big Bear Group Limited	£13,295,000
Robert Gibbs (Contracting) Company Limited	£13,294,702
Ocean Gateway LLP	£13,291,004
Rocket Medical Group PLC	£13,290,275
Wind Assets LLP	£13,288,000
Garrets Bidco 2 Limited	£13,286,820
Menzies Aviation (NL) Limited	£13,282,000
Marsdens Caterers of Sheffield Limited	£13,265,836
Kelly Rail Group Ltd	£13,264,636
Cibi Investments Limited	£13,259,055
St Catherine's School Twickenham	£13,257,218
The Guild of Construction Workers Limited	£13,253,820
M.& R.Bowman Limited	£13,250,904
Fuel Oils (Holdings) Limited	£13,235,405
Equiniti Data Limited	£13,218,000
Foray 414 Limited	£13,200,000
The Foster Care Agency Limited	£13,199,000
Guardian DR (Overseas Holdings) Limited	£13,195,000
Opecprime Development Limited	£13,186,159
Neilcott Holdings Limited	£13,172,340
Multi Trade Links (UK) Ltd	£13,167,877
Rocket Medical PLC	£13,167,504
Thorn Security Group Limited	£13,155,000
Alandale Plant & Scaffolding Limited	£13,153,490
Caterham Cars Ltd.	£13,153,203
J. Gardner Holdings Limited	£13,144,440

Company	Amount
Marden Oak Limited	£13,144,341
Benfleet Scrap Co Limited	£13,142,642
Lionel Road Coalyard Ltd	£13,130,217
Dicky Birds Pre School Nurseries Limited	£13,128,583
Dip Systems (UK) Limited	£13,124,851
Courtlands Estate (Richmond) Limited	£13,123,755
Marchanson Limited	£13,118,397
St.Martins' (Northwood) Preparatory School Trust	£13,108,400
Simon Holdings PLC	£13,095,738
Lowery Group Limited	£13,088,788
Kelly Rail U.K. Ltd	£13,083,854
R V Moat House Limited	£13,077,738
Westway Services Holdings (2010) Ltd.	£13,072,953
R. Maskell (Holdings) Limited	£13,072,307
Imperial Ductwork Services Holdings Limited	£13,070,906
A. & A. 2000 Limited	£13,066,475
A & A Woodford Limited	£13,066,474
Livid Dare Limited	£13,061,452
Shepperton Hotels Limited	£13,060,999
GX Technology EAME Limited	£13,058,898
Oakburn Properties Limited	£13,053,889
Alderforce North Limited	£13,052,243
Pebble Beach Systems Group PLC	£13,047,000
D.K. Tools Limited	£13,045,581
Birmingham Resi Property LLP	£13,043,578
Epoch RJK Limited	£13,028,976
Go Daddy Europe Limited	£13,025,519
A.W. Champion Timber Limited	£13,022,213
A.W.Champion Limited	£13,022,001
Webley Holdings (UK) Limited	£13,016,285
Frisco (U.K.) Sales Limited	£13,002,582
Finepoint Broadcast Limited	£12,999,449
Deekay Investments Limited	£12,999,221
Arabella Health Staffing Limited	£12,985,053
Beam Suntory Operations Limited	£12,980,000
Fishnet Properties Limited	£12,971,217
Balgowan Primary School	£12,970,414
The AD Construction Group Limited	£12,942,864
TRAD Safety Systems Limited	£12,939,934
Avon Freeholds Limited	£12,934,297
Roberto Bucci (U.K.) Limited	£12,934,021
Manor IT (UK) Ltd	£12,924,616
E.G.T. Bridging Finance Limited	£12,921,594
Longmill Rickbost Ltd	£12,921,310
Gada Limited	£12,918,597
Sunsave 12 (Derriton Fields) Ltd	£12,917,000
Audley Inglewood Limited	£12,914,817
Architectural Decorators Limited	£12,913,852
Interlink Direct Limited	£12,912,190
The Invicta Film Partnership No.34, LLP	£12,911,442
KMI Brands Limited	£12,905,000
Warchest Limited	£12,903,055
Ram Parkash Sunderdass & Sons Ltd	£12,899,200
Sarr Investments Limited	£12,895,621
Legacy Broadcast Group Holdings Limited	£12,893,000
Richardson Roofing Holdings Limited	£12,888,130
Trueform Engineering Limited	£12,883,560
Symmetry Logistics Limited	£12,882,725
Valiant Holdings Limited	£12,875,541
J. B. Developments & Construction Limited	£12,874,032
IGD Services Limited	£12,871,688
Keltbray Aspire Limited	£12,870,681
FC JB Co Limited	£12,867,866
Cardiff Ground Rents Limited	£12,852,183
Fulton Clover Limited	£12,850,465
MJF Group Limited	£12,850,067
Swanbrae Limited	£12,828,343
Rushmon Limited	£12,817,257
Heley Holdings Limited	£12,813,648
Castle Village Limited	£12,810,467
Ability Hotels (IV) Holdings Limited	£12,810,345
Bulphan Developments LLP	£12,809,233
Your Healthcare Community Interest Company	£12,803,966
The John Apthorp Charity	£12,803,858
Leonard F.Jollye (Brookmans Park) Limited	£12,799,988
Whiteoak Developments Limited	£12,796,009
Shorterm Group Limited	£12,796,000
Datamede Limited	£12,795,938
Eskan Electronics Limited	£12,787,272
Opus 2 Magnum Holdings Limited	£12,786,475
The Parkside Group (Holdings) Limited	£12,784,806
Lester Hotels Group Limited	£12,769,418
Central Surrey Health Limited	£12,765,501
Bourn Investments Limited	£12,764,810
Limesquare Finance Limited	£12,764,580
Charles Austen Pumps Limited	£12,761,155
Ikarim Business Services Ltd	£12,753,014
Planshore Limited	£12,753,003
Galliford Try Employment Limited	£12,753,000
Crest Nicholson (Henley-on-Thames) Limited	£12,751,000
Mount Grace School	£12,742,163
Higgs International Limited	£12,740,000
Longview Holding Hedge UK Limited	£12,734,800
Senior Finance Seven Limited	£12,720,575
UML Wembley Limited	£12,715,205
Pandrol (Vortok) Limited	£12,715,000
CBee (Europe) Limited	£12,713,475
Excelredstone Services Limited	£12,712,179
H.K.S. Retail Limited	£12,704,044
Purple Surgical Holdings Limited	£12,701,356
SP Macbeth 5 Limited	£12,689,862
Entel Communications Holdings Limited	£12,683,989
Pure International Limited	£12,681,089
Advanced Logistics for Aerospace (UK) Limited	£12,680,232
Kew Green Hotels (Colchester) Limited	£12,676,711
Elvetham Hall (Property) Limited	£12,659,775
Chester Greyhound Retail Park LLP	£12,659,511
Oleoland Hotel Company Limited	£12,656,068
Bartlett Mitchell Services Limited	£12,653,534
CNOOC Petroleum Farragon U.K. Limited	£12,651,601
Cromwell (Wandsworth) Limited	£12,648,415
Cheam Academies Network	£12,640,000
Apollo Property Investment Limited	£12,639,118
Sims Milling Services Limited	£12,635,793
Thenhurst Agricultural Limited	£12,624,000
St George Healthcare Limited	£12,615,239
GCP Rooftop Solar 1 Limited	£12,612,083
Channeladvisor UK Limited	£12,609,516
Greenlight Credit Ltd	£12,607,538
Stapleford Frog Island (Rainham) Limited	£12,603,535
Centro PLC	£12,593,508
Camden Development Company Limited	£12,590,037
Electrosonic Limited	£12,590,000
Gulmay Holdings Limited	£12,586,596
KM Products Europe Limited	£12,583,808
Stonplan Limited	£12,579,420
Wolters Kluwer Health (Professional & Education)	£12,578,000
Homepines Investments Limited	£12,574,484
Musco (St Albans Place) Ltd	£12,563,735
KLDiscovery Ontrack Limited	£12,563,000
Ariyan Hotels Limited	£12,561,352
Citipost Holdings Limited	£12,556,510
Lime Tree Village Limited	£12,547,464
Rooff Ltd	£12,547,066
Smith and Byford Limited	£12,542,890
Gago Invest Limited	£12,525,304
Fujitsu General (U.K.) Co. Limited	£12,525,000
Trinitas Academy Trust	£12,525,000
Uavend Exeter LLP	£12,522,000
Wellsborough Developments Limited	£12,513,400
Genesis Pharmaceuticals Limited	£12,483,941
A.Martin Bunzl Limited	£12,480,718
Simat Properties Limited	£12,479,319
Allois Properties (Leatherhead) Limited	£12,479,118

Parkside Group Limited (The)	£12,473,392	Khosla Investments Limited	£11,966,858
Wolters Kluwer Health (Europe) Limited	£12,451,000	Plaut International Limited	£11,955,962
Education Support (Enfield) Limited	£12,442,000	Harringtons Builders PLC	£11,947,578
Education Support (Enfield) Holdings Limited	£12,442,000	The Headmasters Partnership Limited	£11,939,964
K K Investment Ltd	£12,435,536	Astor Lodge Holdings Limited	£11,938,191
Acclaim Handling Limited	£12,431,751	Daly Holdings Limited	£11,936,437
Radio Developments Ltd	£12,430,948	Lantern Recovery LLP	£11,918,358
Gerrard International Limited	£12,418,943	Saba Infra Gloucestershire Limited	£11,914,174
Balcraft Properties Limited	£12,418,675	Harris & Bailey Limited	£11,910,941
Up Offshore (UK) Limited	£12,396,296	Mountcharm (S.E.) Limited	£11,910,514
Maylands Green Limited	£12,394,912	Barrie Knitwear Limited	£11,908,000
The Tabor Group Ltd	£12,393,842	Limje Holdings Limited	£11,907,970
Stat Marine Limited	£12,380,829	Independent Commercial Broking Limited	£11,904,810
Greenswan Consultants Limited	£12,355,968	O G Holdings Limited	£11,902,151
The Good Shepherd Catholic Trust	£12,335,773	Tudor Williams (Holdings) Limited	£11,896,893
Subex (UK) Limited	£12,333,000	Interfleet Holdings Limited	£11,890,000
F. Copson Limited	£12,321,717	Skanska Construction (Regions) Limited	£11,881,000
Rainham Industrial Services Limited	£12,320,000	Amalgamated Property Holdings Limited	£11,876,038
Sword Charteris Limited	£12,313,559	T.W. White & Sons Limited	£11,857,114
European Springs and Pressings Limited	£12,311,045	T.W. White & Sons (Holdings) Limited	£11,857,114
NW3 Capital Ltd	£12,304,672	Notre Dame School Cobham	£11,855,000
Brown & Burk UK Limited	£12,304,449	Rangemist Limited	£11,854,180
Galldris Construction Limited	£12,304,427	Network Homes Investments (Stockwell) Limited	£11,853,693
Clancy Developments Limited	£12,297,739	STS Flooring Distributors Limited	£11,852,623
Gunpowder Mill Developments Limited	£12,296,000	NSL Group Limited	£11,843,620
Klassik Property Ltd	£12,276,857	Lantern Recovery Specialists PLC	£11,841,107
Capsicum Motorsport Holdings Limited	£12,272,907	Designplan Lighting Limited	£11,838,767
Kailas Hotel Finance Company Limited	£12,270,350	Albion Bunker and Trading LLP	£11,832,822
KBR (Aspire Services) Limited	£12,261,000	Crumlin Capital Limited	£11,830,296
Neilcott Construction Services Limited	£12,258,663	Jean-Luc Developments Ltd	£11,829,471
A.G.E. Nursing Homes Limited	£12,253,589	Dr Michael Prager Holdings Limited	£11,820,336
Carlton House Developments Limited	£12,252,801	Sharan Properties Limited	£11,806,635
Loxleigh Investments Limited	£12,247,300	Bandai UK Limited	£11,804,425
Green Mountain Estates Ltd	£12,238,257	Sea, Air & Land Forwarding Limited	£11,804,356
St James Media LLP	£12,236,442	Aprirose Trading Limited	£11,799,484
R.O'Rourke & Son Limited.	£12,234,000	Florence Nightingale Aid in Sickness Trust	£11,793,590
Acre 1144 Limited	£12,230,000	Thomas H. Collison Limited	£11,790,743
Blenheim High School	£12,225,000	Bayut Ltd	£11,788,630
T. Visaman & Sons Limited	£12,199,468	NeilMed Holding Company Limited	£11,773,630
Rock & Alluvium Limited	£12,198,000	Automatic Sales Limited	£11,771,722
Hilands Property Partners LLP	£12,190,634	MPM Connect Limited	£11,764,475
Attwell Business Inc. Limited	£12,185,503	Defender No.2 Production LLP	£11,763,425
Longford Securities & Equities Limited	£12,183,284	Chilworth Manor Limited	£11,761,986
UIDUK Ltd	£12,182,200	Katana Property Limited	£11,757,868
Pancredit Systems Ltd.	£12,178,000	B Crystal Limited	£11,756,635
Complete Coffee Limited	£12,168,002	Beale's Limited	£11,751,299
SME (Coffee) Limited	£12,153,441	Balgores Motors (1982) Limited	£11,746,194
BP Petrochemicals India Investments Limited	£12,139,216	Buckinghamshire Park Resort (Holdings) Limited	£11,744,633
The Principal York Limited	£12,133,000	Charlie Properties Limited	£11,733,035
Elysium Healthcare (Healthlinc) Limited	£12,118,000	Pearl Properties Limited	£11,731,613
Southborough High School	£12,097,168	Campmoss Property (Tangley Place) Limited	£11,726,604
DPA Support Services Limited	£12,091,000	Montpelier Properties Limited	£11,720,902
Advanced Group Holdings Limited	£12,084,024	McGinley Aviation Holdings Limited	£11,717,253
Angel Care (Orchid Care Homes) Ltd	£12,071,952	Rooff Property LLP	£11,712,768
Medipharmacy Limited	£12,058,420	Noble Gift Packaging Limited	£11,711,019
Phoenix Property Investment Company Limited	£12,054,792	Associated Coffee Merchants (International) Ltd	£11,704,136
Communications & Power Industries Europe Limited	£12,053,019	Belgrave Land (Perth) Limited	£11,700,486
Sines LLP	£12,040,737	Gargonay Limited	£11,695,779
Windcrest (U.K.) Limited	£12,035,480	Helius Investments Limited	£11,686,201
Newland House School Trust Limited	£12,030,060	Runnymede (Holdings) Limited	£11,685,084
S.Hille & Co.(Holdings) Limited	£12,025,737	G4S Aviation Services (UK) Limited	£11,685,000
Turner Properties Limited	£12,023,430	Fusion Global Limited	£11,682,306
Soda Studios Limited	£12,020,679	Bandai Namco Entertainment UK Ltd.	£11,672,175
Menzies World Cargo Limited	£12,020,000	Cloverton Property Ltd	£11,653,989
Cembrit Limited	£12,006,806	Sigma Sports Limited	£11,647,652
Aequitas Estates (Poyle) Limited	£12,003,844	Knowledge & Merchandising Inc. Ltd	£11,645,000
Intermay Management Ltd	£12,002,911	Wood End Academy	£11,642,451
A A Homes and Housing (5 Sydenham Road) Ltd	£12,000,001	KS SPV 3 Limited	£11,627,000
Kane Group Limited	£11,999,000	J. Van Vliet London Cash & Carry Limited	£11,620,717
Newschools (Swanscombe) Limited	£11,997,000	Broadfields Academy Trust	£11,617,000
Flahive Developments Limited	£11,993,425	Erith Haulage Company Limited	£11,616,903
BP+Amoco International Limited	£11,979,391	GBST Limited	£11,609,151

Company	Value
Charles Kalms, Henry Ronson Immanuel College	£11,606,515
Fujitsu General Air Conditioning (UK) Limited	£11,606,000
Phalarope Limited	£11,599,656
Orthene Holdings Limited	£11,594,368
Lymington Precision Engineers Co. Limited	£11,594,000
Mapal Limited	£11,589,465
Badger BC Investments Limited	£11,586,682
The Hive Football Centre Holdings Limited	£11,580,237
Explore Capital Limited	£11,574,000
Axcel Hospitality (Manchester) Limited	£11,558,945
Wheatland Cheese Co. Limited	£11,550,367
TES-AMM Europe Holdings Ltd	£11,549,366
Bosch Service Solutions Limited	£11,545,000
Sara (London) Limited	£11,542,600
Edwardian London Management Services Limited	£11,542,000
Brick Projects (Marland) Limited	£11,541,019
Fusion Business Solutions (UK) Limited	£11,540,497
Kara Designs Ltd	£11,538,804
Boon Group Limited	£11,538,419
J & J Transport Limited	£11,535,205
Allen (Concrete) Limited	£11,524,139
Audley Group Developments 1 Limited	£11,518,742
Love Productions Limited	£11,515,173
Highfield Junior School	£11,515,000
Maybury Media LLP	£11,514,990
Energypro Asset Management Limited	£11,500,334
Crane Investments Ltd	£11,493,055
Mollart Engineering Limited	£11,490,883
West Herts Community Free School Trust	£11,487,138
Giggs Hill Green Homes Limited	£11,479,945
Arihant Limited	£11,477,931
Corncrake Limited	£11,473,832
Manor Farm Solar Limited	£11,456,423
Union Glory Limited	£11,452,143
W. Humphreys Transport (London) Ltd	£11,443,584
Caretech Estates (No.4) Limited	£11,441,000
Pronovias UK Limited	£11,436,852
Purslow Investments Limited	£11,433,935
Mane Contract Services Limited	£11,432,055
J Devine Civil Engineering Ltd	£11,429,371
BPE Polandco Limited	£11,424,560
Mongas Kids Wear Limited	£11,421,086
Unifruit Limited	£11,420,123
ESSCI Ireland Limited	£11,420,000
CED Limited	£11,415,241
Appetite Holdings Limited	£11,407,620
Unifruit Group Limited	£11,405,024
GHL (Kilmorie) Limited	£11,403,809
Radia Estates Limited	£11,398,139
Harlequin Direct Limited	£11,393,563
Tustin Properties Ltd	£11,390,600
Whelan & Grant (Contractors) Limited	£11,389,643
Smart Card Software Limited	£11,382,703
Mortgage Guarantee Limited	£11,380,622
Volante Limited	£11,360,618
Peppercorn Investments Limited	£11,360,579
King's House School Trust (Richmond) Limited	£11,358,082
The Invicta Film Partnership No.11, LLP	£11,357,982
Aspire Investments and Property Developments LLP	£11,357,025
KFG Quickserve Limited	£11,356,000
A T & T (GB) Holdings Limited	£11,348,868
Grays Thurrock Properties Limited	£11,345,888
Forest Freight Limited	£11,339,004
Knight Strip Metals Limited	£11,338,008
Essex Motor Company Limited	£11,332,361
Kelly Communications Trading Group Limited	£11,321,408
All World Foods Limited	£11,321,115
Fedrigoni U.K. Limited	£11,317,673
Thamesmead School	£11,314,000
Concordia International Forwarding Limited	£11,298,617
Lowery Limited	£11,295,787
Van Ameyde UK Limited	£11,288,703
Esso Property Management Company, Limited	£11,278,000
The Leprosy Mission International	£11,277,626
Wilman Universal Industries Limited	£11,267,816
Filross Securities Limited	£11,264,200
Land Management Limited	£11,257,629
F. Copson (London) LLP	£11,253,393
Coniston Dartford Limited	£11,242,713
GAIAE Limited	£11,240,534
John Deere Forestry Limited	£11,238,019
Wenta	£11,234,375
Metro Properties Limited	£11,234,227
Opal (Earlsfield) LLP	£11,231,000
Ziji Productions Limited	£11,230,180
Buckinghamshire Golf Company Limited	£11,223,264
Arcese Real Estate UK Limited	£11,212,517
East Mediterranean Trading Limited	£11,212,367
Cosmos Tours Limited	£11,211,000
Vega Industries Limited	£11,210,557
Danjuma Collection Ltd	£11,205,738
E.F.R. Travel Limited	£11,199,832
Knight Noise Limited	£11,193,108
Clearview Homes (Western Avenue) Ltd	£11,188,561
Pass J. Holdings Limited	£11,181,216
Foodspeed Limited	£11,177,601
Jain (Europe) Limited	£11,175,979
Kew Green Hotels (Haydock) Limited	£11,166,727
Cressdene Limited	£11,166,000
TK Maxx	£11,160,000
Ernest Jackson & Co. Limited	£11,159,000
RBC Investments (Surrey) Limited	£11,156,863
Kestates Limited	£11,154,944
Ian Allan Travel Limited	£11,150,656
A T & T (GB) Limited	£11,146,514
Angelica Estates Limited	£11,145,977
Riverway Investments Limited	£11,138,222
Academia Limited	£11,136,415
Far East & Co Limited	£11,127,936
St. Dominic's Ltd.	£11,126,769
Luna Estates Limited	£11,116,017
Saffie Investments Limited	£11,110,722
66 Queen Square Limited	£11,106,000
Cousins Holdings Limited	£11,104,184
Glenageary Estates LLP	£11,102,064
R.T.Rate Limited	£11,092,069
Knight Precision Metals Limited	£11,088,492
Friars Developments Limited	£11,082,400
Field Marketing (UK) Holdings Limited	£11,078,000
Eurocity Properties (Central) Limited	£11,077,806
Carlton Group Developments Ltd	£11,074,216
Transmec UK Limited	£11,061,722
Nine Reading Hotel Limited	£11,058,695
Kirby Group Engineering (UK) Limited	£11,054,613
Kedleston (OS Education) Limited	£11,049,653
Grohe Limited	£11,046,584
Tulip Properties & Real Estate Ltd	£11,042,356
Aircom International Limited	£11,042,000
Plotplan Limited	£11,041,436
Direct Chauffeur Line Limited	£11,039,928
Parklight Properties Limited	£11,039,246
Bartlett Mitchell Limited	£11,027,017
Hoddesdon Developments Ltd	£11,024,788
A.S. Ashcroft Limited	£11,020,292
The Gateway Hotel Dunstable Limited	£11,005,747
Churchtown Farm Solar Limited	£11,001,576
A A Homes and Housing (Cygnet House) Limited	£11,000,001
Korea Foods Company Limited	£10,999,625
East Langford Solar Limited	£10,998,135
Watling Tyre Service Limited (The)	£10,993,567
Chubb (NI) Limited	£10,992,000
P. Colohan & Co. Limited	£10,987,848
Minton Holdings Limited	£10,979,686
T. Bro Investment Limited	£10,973,910

Company	Amount
E P I Limited	£10,965,568
M & J Charters LLP	£10,951,856
Mayfair Carpet Gallery Limited	£10,941,125
Loughton Care Centre Limited	£10,939,000
Togher Construction Limited	£10,937,303
GL Education (No.3) Limited	£10,929,000
Buildvantage Limited	£10,928,216
St. Luke's Hospice (Harrow & Brent) Ltd.	£10,918,000
Cremer (UK) Manufacturing Co. Ltd	£10,913,476
Crockford Park Properties Limited	£10,908,969
Culham Limited	£10,894,474
Edinburgh Sainsbury Holdings LLP	£10,892,010
Interport Limited	£10,890,231
WHTC Ltd	£10,884,137
Grove & Dean (Holdings) Limited	£10,878,883
Elegant Electronics Limited	£10,876,214
Shotfield Development Business Partnership Limited	£10,867,554
W.A. Truelove & Son Limited	£10,867,317
Grove & Dean Limited	£10,859,063
Orbital Fasteners Limited	£10,853,972
Magnet Harlequin Limited	£10,853,188
Feltonfleet School Trust Limited	£10,849,663
Goldex Investments Limited	£10,838,878
Syscap Limited	£10,834,499
Richmond & Hampshire Limited	£10,829,678
Ares Properties Ltd	£10,815,564
Cisilion Limited	£10,814,448
Green Hercules Trading Limited	£10,811,142
Heathrow Cargo Handling Limited	£10,806,000
Astonpalm Limited	£10,804,680
Britannia Row Productions Limited	£10,803,096
Hindu Education Authority Ltd	£10,800,594
Hel Group Limited	£10,800,524
Stora Enso Timber UK Limited	£10,799,000
Curo (West Campbell) LLP	£10,793,569
Premier Decorations Limited	£10,791,078
London Irish Rugby Football Ground Limited	£10,786,027
Farsound Aviation Limited	£10,781,000
Marcantonio Foods Limited	£10,779,802
Pitchset Limited	£10,778,681
DBCN Limited	£10,778,467
Stebiz Limited	£10,777,422
Defender No.2 Sale & Leaseback LLP	£10,773,785
Dock and Let Limited	£10,770,755
D & M Tools Limited	£10,761,907
Verex Insurance Services Limited	£10,754,122
Vidafresh Limited	£10,753,041
Crystal Group Limited	£10,749,148
O'Malley Haulage Limited	£10,745,246
Rose Bruford College of Theatre and Performance	£10,742,000
Verex Group Limited	£10,738,675
Nella Holdings Limited	£10,737,274
Charter UK Limited	£10,719,000
Good for Food Limited	£10,715,997
Optivo Development Services Limited	£10,715,000
Land & Water Services Ltd	£10,714,187
Offerco Limited	£10,707,692
Urban Enhance Limited	£10,705,299
Ace Investments Limited	£10,704,509
York Apartments Limited	£10,688,985
GPF Lewis PLC	£10,679,721
Hebridean Island Cruises Limited	£10,677,799
Compass Forest Products Limited	£10,677,546
Total Support Services Limited	£10,676,703
Atlas Contractors Limited	£10,675,306
A.L.Tozer Limited	£10,671,845
Lingerham Properties Limited	£10,670,186
Aitch Care Homes Topco Limited	£10,670,000
Twinglobe Limited	£10,668,499
DTW (Holdings) Limited	£10,659,219
TX Group Europe Ltd.	£10,658,000
City Link (Cardiff) Holdings Limited	£10,653,000
Goldfield Homes Limited	£10,650,994
UML Blandford Limited	£10,650,281
Norfolk Capital Hotels Limited	£10,649,000
Best Foods Limited	£10,647,870
Cadline Limited	£10,645,615
Chislehurst Care Limited	£10,642,002
12 Property FE Limited	£10,638,627
Property Finance Capital (No 2) Limited	£10,636,145
Watts Farms (Sales) Limited	£10,635,286
Hudson Camden Limited	£10,631,425
Brianco Services Limited	£10,631,070
Chep Intercontinental Containers Limited	£10,628,068
Ticketgrange Limited	£10,623,406
Letchworth Hall Hotel (Trading) Limited	£10,612,703
C.C. (Engineering) Limited	£10,604,654
Parry Murray & Company Limited	£10,604,473
Limesquare Vehicle Rental Limited	£10,598,619
S.L.E. Limited	£10,597,272
K.C.Y. Limited	£10,596,495
Saba Infra Hertfordshire Limited	£10,594,414
P & R Installation Company Limited	£10,594,075
Warren Road Primary School	£10,589,741
Caterham Enterprises Limited	£10,583,559
Bold-Rock Management and Investments Ltd	£10,582,725
Pet and Aquatics Properties Limited	£10,580,000
J.& J.Franks Limited	£10,579,189
Lanend Limited	£10,576,612
WVC Land & Developments Limited	£10,575,458
Stora Enso Holdings UK Limited	£10,573,000
B & H Worldwide (Holdings) Limited	£10,569,838
Westbrook Primary School	£10,569,545
Care Providers Recruitment Limited	£10,569,541
GDL (Aylesbury) Limited	£10,556,005
Spedition Services Limited	£10,552,391
Mayfield Grammar School, Gravesend	£10,527,136
Bucci Freight Services Limited	£10,526,289
Worldwide Energy Logistics Group Limited	£10,519,601
Harte Hanks UK Limited	£10,519,061
Mills Family Limited	£10,508,873
Evolution Newhall LLP	£10,502,000
Orthene Chemicals Limited	£10,497,679
Alba Broadcasting Corporation Limited	£10,496,773
Bexley Grammar School	£10,494,000
Antal International Limited	£10,492,515
KFM Holdings Limited	£10,487,314
Storefast Limited	£10,481,264
Ability Hotels (Glasgow) Limited	£10,477,622
Smart Transactions Group Limited	£10,473,000
Insurance Claims Accommodation Bureau Limited	£10,467,516
Robert Heath Group Limited	£10,464,710
DW Windsor Group Limited	£10,463,567
Hudson Richmond Limited	£10,457,273
Heathrow Aviation Engineering UTC	£10,451,370
Devitt Insurance Services Limited	£10,450,637
Mill Hill Properties Limited	£10,449,145
Kristal Enterprises Limited	£10,447,345
Newschools (Leyton) Limited	£10,445,000
Design Blue Limited	£10,440,480
Wenta Business Centres Limited	£10,438,055
Lint (Redington Road) Limited	£10,437,188
Shure UK Limited	£10,435,757
Grosvenor Park 2005 S42 Film LLP	£10,430,548
Megnum Limited	£10,416,754
Hudson Arnhem Limited	£10,414,724
Mega Fabrications Group Ltd	£10,413,398
Information Security Forum Limited	£10,403,608
Bromley Healthcare Community Interest Company	£10,401,709
Kew Green (Square) Limited	£10,393,802
Lipman Properties Limited	£10,387,718
Cleves Academy Trust	£10,384,000
Aerospace Tooling Limited	£10,382,058
Walsall Public Lighting Holding Company Limited	£10,374,000

Company	Amount
Walsall Public Lighting Limited	£10,374,000
The Global Logistics Group Ltd	£10,368,169
Kew Green (Norwich Property) Limited	£10,366,609
Raedex Consortium Limited	£10,360,206
Harrington (Properties) Limited	£10,359,064
Nestates Limited	£10,346,541
Castle Green Kendal Limited	£10,346,048
Shelfside Holding (Northern) Ltd	£10,345,071
GHL (Summerstown) Limited	£10,332,428
Saba Infra Cardiff Limited	£10,321,327
Purchase Group Limited	£10,320,000
OLR (UK) Limited	£10,314,193
RFU Injured Players Foundation	£10,297,275
Gosselin Mobility UK Limited	£10,295,396
Fieldside Associates Limited	£10,292,559
Hudson Brent Limited	£10,286,558
Kromachem Limited	£10,286,504
Ness Global Services Limited	£10,285,147
Pod-Trak Limited	£10,283,354
Thorney Leys Developments Limited	£10,282,169
Pinnacle Foods Limited	£10,280,604
P.I.E. Pharma Limited	£10,276,358
S. Franses Limited	£10,273,747
Amsprop Estates Limited	£10,272,408
Queensgate Finco Ltd	£10,264,102
Shopfittings Direct Limited	£10,263,358
JRL Property Limited	£10,257,168
Coex Properties LLP	£10,249,546
Shenley Park Trust	£10,235,764
F.W. Hipkin Limited	£10,233,493
Kent Capital Ltd	£10,232,784
Plutus Estates Limited	£10,229,884
Demiland Limited	£10,227,790
Terminus House Harlow LLP	£10,221,978
Neville UK Trading Holdings Limited	£10,216,238
Brausch & Co (UK) Limited	£10,213,438
Apexpost Limited	£10,210,034
Parrsouth Limited	£10,205,603
TCL Manufacturing Limited	£10,205,224
Manor Lodge School	£10,201,621
H & S Contractors Limited	£10,200,691
Seabrook Warehousing Limited	£10,200,498
Sunvil International Sales Limited	£10,197,099
M G 111 Ltd	£10,195,050
Gibson Bidco Limited	£10,194,000
Rimex Metals (U.K.) Limited	£10,193,596
Wood Group Kenny UK Limited	£10,190,000
Fulton Lincoln Limited	£10,182,852
Dalin Limited	£10,182,163
Paradine Holdings Limited	£10,175,627
Ikon Science Limited	£10,171,421
Tropical Marine Centre Limited	£10,168,000
The Original London Sightseeing Tour Limited	£10,163,000
Rashmian Limited	£10,162,573
Oakwood Finance London Limited	£10,161,086
Corbus Europe Limited	£10,153,909
Kentec Electronics Limited	£10,151,449
BW Foundation	£10,148,786
Anchor Bay Construction Products Limited	£10,137,870
Baruch Holdings Limited	£10,136,729
Fulton Regent Limited	£10,135,039
Highfield Infants' School	£10,134,000
AMS Care Wiltshire Limited	£10,127,908
SME Trading Limited	£10,123,182
Frontline Security Solutions Limited	£10,122,749
W.R.Newland & Sons Limited	£10,122,471
Fundamental Engineering Limited	£10,120,124
Multi Services Kent Limited	£10,117,161
Antoniou Investments Limited	£10,114,621
Chemilines Limited	£10,114,000
Positive Entertainment Ltd	£10,110,334
UML Moxon Limited	£10,108,995
Homes Caring for Autism Limited	£10,105,703
Albrin Capital Limited	£10,096,998
Letting International Limited	£10,095,509
Wurth Holding UK Ltd	£10,084,000
Trend Machinery & Cutting Tools Limited	£10,083,295
Kearns Property Management & Development Ltd	£10,068,127
Kolajola UK Ltd	£10,065,268
Equicap Estates Limited	£10,064,613
Pheechool Holdings Limited	£10,060,241
Rosetree Finance Limited	£10,056,309
D.W. Windsor Limited	£10,049,681
Hudson Kensington Limited	£10,048,801
Andgrove Property Investments Limited	£10,048,160
Cummins ESB Nigeria Limited	£10,045,365
Water Incorporated	£10,041,309
UML Eagle Limited	£10,039,261
Donatantonio Limited	£10,037,156
Regenter Bentilee District Centre (Holding) Limited	£10,035,000
Regenter Bentilee District Centre Limited	£10,035,000
Telecoms World (Group) Limited	£10,033,451
Chart Forte Holdings Ltd	£10,022,515
The Property Warehouse Limited	£10,018,453
St. Vincent's Charitable Trust	£10,010,634
Pebble Beach Systems Ltd	£10,006,000
Axcorp Limited	£10,005,154
The Watford UTC	£10,003,247
Worldwide Product Sourcing Limited	£10,001,640
PJG Developments Limited	£10,000,778
R A Insurance Brokers Limited	£10,000,237
Kelly Communications Enterprises Limited	£10,000,001
JTC Ventures Limited	£9,992,098
Ewell Castle School	£9,991,450
BPC Interiors Limited	£9,986,314
Burhill Estates Company Limited	£9,985,919
Atwood Primary Academy	£9,984,889
The Book Trade Charity (BTBS)	£9,978,932
Grupotec Renewables Limited	£9,976,242
St Catherine's Catholic School	£9,974,000
Elmex Sales Corporation Limited	£9,969,981
KFG Restaurants Limited	£9,961,000
Richardson Roofing Company Limited	£9,955,317
Ceros No.1 Limited	£9,950,112
Caskade Properties Limited	£9,944,650
Tudor Court Primary Academy Trust	£9,942,944
GlaxoSmithKline Consumer Healthcare (UK) (No.1)	£9,941,000
Frankham Holdings Limited	£9,939,966
Centaur Property Estates Limited	£9,934,622
Hillingdon House (UK) Limited	£9,931,481
Chessington Nurseries Holdings Company Limited	£9,925,878
Xavier Catholic Education Trust	£9,923,462
Denbourne Investments Limited	£9,918,081
Sportsworld Group Limited	£9,915,000
Martello (Holdings) Limited	£9,914,682
Palace Street Developments Limited	£9,913,686
LDD Construction Limited	£9,912,106
William Robinson Gravetye Charity	£9,904,080
The Grange Centre for People with Disabilities	£9,902,590
Cellecta Limited	£9,897,978
Cromwell Investments (Richmond) Limited	£9,894,491
Corley + Woolley Limited	£9,893,842
Central Developments (UK) Limited	£9,892,160
Conance Limited	£9,891,901
Emerson Park Academy	£9,891,558
Alderforce Limited	£9,890,436
Uniserve (Europe) Limited	£9,889,359
Scotline Limited	£9,884,397
DMC Contracts Limited	£9,877,729
Black Katz Eddy (Holdings) Limited	£9,877,369
Spence Refit Ltd	£9,874,049
Amana Trust	£9,873,503
Tram Operations Limited	£9,873,000
Xerox Products UK Limited	£9,866,195

Company	Amount
Aquifer Limited	£9,862,000
7e Communications Limited	£9,853,390
Killoughery Properties Limited	£9,851,207
Sines Parks (S.E.) Limited	£9,846,920
Miller & Miller (Chemicals) Limited	£9,843,544
British Marine Federation	£9,842,902
Masters Pharmaceuticals Limited	£9,841,748
Papa Entertainment Limited	£9,841,621
Mall School Trust (The)	£9,840,333
Zameen Ltd	£9,837,838
Howarth Homes (Farnham Close) Limited	£9,834,896
Arugula Spruce Limited	£9,832,582
Onslow Inc. Ltd	£9,831,311
Cobird Limited	£9,830,196
Kidiliz Group UK Ltd	£9,829,816
Sutton Winson Limited	£9,823,000
Goodmayes Properties Ltd	£9,820,061
Residential Management Group Limited	£9,818,000
Greensea Real Estate Management Limited	£9,814,826
Sports Interactive Limited	£9,807,884
Riverstone Europe LLP	£9,803,717
S and J Investments (Delivery Office Southall) Limited	£9,803,563
Wallacespace Limited	£9,803,414
T Gilmartin Holdings Limited	£9,800,848
Keswick European Holdings Limited	£9,794,534
Discover The World Limited	£9,794,014
Garves Wind Limited	£9,791,949
Broadham Care Limited	£9,789,000
Vandemoortele (U.K.) Limited	£9,783,000
Mouskos & Sons Co. Limited	£9,782,518
Wintertime Properties Limited	£9,776,739
South Mimms Services Limited	£9,763,739
Cardif Pinnacle Insurance Management Services	£9,760,000
XTO UK, Ltd	£9,759,258
Erinastar Limited	£9,754,188
Vitec Imaging Solutions UK Limited	£9,751,000
Chem-Dry Franchising Limited	£9,731,000
Hart Homes (Watford) Limited	£9,726,000
Purebond Limited	£9,725,268
Caunton Management Limited	£9,717,741
Anita Impex Limited	£9,717,001
Rokeby Educational Trust Limited	£9,714,597
NFAH Limited	£9,714,000
MWL International Limited	£9,711,590
One World Express Inc. Limited	£9,706,528
Fazal Fast Foods Limited	£9,695,077
Plastico Limited	£9,692,827
London Fluid System Technologies Limited	£9,684,841
Selwyns Travel Limited	£9,679,364
Gravity Media Group Limited	£9,672,000
Elgon Hotels Limited	£9,668,915
Morrisroe UK Ltd	£9,663,343
Baker Ross Limited	£9,660,612
Kew Green Hotels (York) Limited	£9,660,529
First Network Properties Ltd	£9,660,187
Unicorn Ingredients Ltd	£9,658,763
Anitass Limited	£9,653,028
Esin Cash & Carry Limited	£9,649,767
Mayfair Housing & Commercial Investments Ltd.	£9,642,696
Marron Civil Engineering Limited	£9,641,226
Aston Heating Limited	£9,641,046
Kelerbay Limited	£9,640,872
Noahs Ark Chemicals Limited	£9,640,393
Caretech Estates (No 3) Limited	£9,634,000
Ellis of Richmond (Holdings) Limited	£9,633,510
Playags UK Limited	£9,624,531
John Laing International Limited	£9,611,000
Cherubond Limited	£9,609,766
Kara Management Ltd	£9,607,503
Maple Hotels Management Company Limited	£9,606,547
Avon Estates (London) Limited	£9,606,368
Durkin and Sons Limited	£9,601,057
Transform Schools (Rotherham) Holdings Limited	£9,600,000
Unique Seafood Limited	£9,598,757
Aylesbury Vale Parkway Limited	£9,596,000
Rex Venture Resources Limited	£9,591,554
Hi-Spirits Ltd	£9,584,388
Erith Plant Services Limited	£9,584,385
Mechanical Services Limited	£9,582,701
Sovereign Recovery (UK) Limited	£9,582,107
Manichem Limited	£9,575,481
Bereta Investments Limited	£9,575,308
Norwood Green Junior School	£9,567,811
Landmark Civil Engineering Limited	£9,567,590
O.B.C. (Europe) Limited	£9,564,465
FBSE Finance Limited	£9,559,271
Norpap Property (Telford) Ltd	£9,556,848
The Mill Hotel Limited	£9,555,213
Consolidated Equities Limited	£9,551,268
Hilton Worldwide Manage Branchco Limited	£9,550,028
Millharbour Developments Limited	£9,549,624
Smithers Information Limited	£9,543,000
Remus White Limited	£9,537,541
Guru Nanak Sikh Academy Limited	£9,536,860
The London Outpost Limited	£9,531,085
Ping Pong Limited	£9,527,504
Langford Clinic Limited	£9,527,330
Brymec Ltd	£9,526,939
Carbon Solutions Global Ltd	£9,526,156
Yorkshire Dales Country Park Limited	£9,524,737
RDL1 Limited	£9,522,393
Popsoda Limited	£9,522,041
GCP Biomass 3 Limited	£9,521,851
Coniston Limited	£9,516,298
Bishopsgate School Limited	£9,515,538
Chessington Nurseries Limited	£9,513,799
Mono Properties Limited	£9,513,597
Skylord Travel PLC	£9,513,370
Kew Green Hotels (Lancaster) Limited	£9,513,116
Proper Music Distribution Limited	£9,507,494
The Invicta Film Partnership No.12, LLP	£9,506,957
Action for Children Services Limited	£9,506,013
Solight Limited	£9,505,534
Field Marketing (UK) Limited	£9,500,000
Automated Technology Group Holdings Limited	£9,500,000
Clinisupplies Limited	£9,498,135
Quebec Court Freehold Limited	£9,496,658
Celtic Contractors Limited	£9,487,491
Pridenature Limited	£9,487,002
Chesside Homes Limited	£9,484,207
Luce Limited	£9,483,999
Jenga (UK) Limited	£9,483,444
HJ Dhillon Ltd.	£9,474,914
Millennium Seacon Properties Limited	£9,474,587
Blenheim Consultancy Services Limited	£9,469,599
Meridian Wood Products Ltd.	£9,467,976
Landmark Groundworks Limited	£9,467,882
E. Feldman Limited	£9,467,060
Shakoor Capital Limited	£9,465,524
Prospect Healthcare (Hairmyres) Holdings Limited	£9,462,000
Ingenie Services Limited	£9,454,000
Kimberley Capital Limited	£9,447,750
SRCH Limited	£9,445,218
Hunn Holdings Limited	£9,444,976
The Langdon Foundation	£9,438,345
Abbeyfield Southern Oaks	£9,430,752
Liftec Lifts Limited	£9,417,350
Dallas Burston Ashbourne Holdings Limited	£9,415,455
Strongholding Limited	£9,400,342
Kingston Lodge Hotel Limited	£9,400,311
Assured Services Limited	£9,394,063
Audley Clevedon Limited	£9,389,327
Chellbrook Properties Limited	£9,386,257
Platinum Investments Surrey Limited	£9,385,228

Company	Value
Fascroft Limited	£9,383,104
O'Hara Bros. Surfacing Limited	£9,380,980
Queenscourt Limited	£9,379,244
Mizen Design/Build Ltd.	£9,377,231
BMG (Ashford) General Partner Limited	£9,374,191
Beauty Wholesale Limited	£9,373,346
E. Ivor Hughes Educational Foundation	£9,373,345
Elysium Healthcare (Acorn Care) Limited	£9,367,000
Turnlet Films (JN) Limited	£9,366,773
Namu Limited	£9,363,888
Medi-Shop Limited	£9,360,398
J. Isaacs Management Limited	£9,352,166
GCP RHI Boiler 1 Limited	£9,350,736
Enterprise Finance Limited	£9,350,643
Galleon Investments (Dartford) Limited	£9,345,729
Sinai (Antiques) Limited	£9,345,633
Amsair Aircraft Limited	£9,332,958
Gupta Brothers & Co Limited	£9,329,124
Upminster Academies Trust	£9,326,000
Sunrose Property Limited	£9,322,711
Honeycroft Hill Ltd	£9,321,304
Rijac Properties Limited	£9,321,262
Neville UK PLC	£9,318,385
Kew Green (LRG Property) Limited	£9,317,905
Bryen & Langley (Holdings) Ltd	£9,314,836
RSA Island Village Limited	£9,314,666
Bryen & Langley Limited	£9,314,236
Residential Loans Ltd.	£9,312,835
The Reedham Children's Trust	£9,309,253
Care Expertise Limited	£9,308,470
Aviation Business Continuity Limited	£9,301,021
Warren House Conference Centre Limited	£9,299,501
The Ursuline Academy Ilford	£9,295,986
Land Finance & Mortgage Corporation Limited (The)	£9,289,210
Algonquin Management Partners (UK) Ltd	£9,283,246
Symbio Energy Limited	£9,278,916
Walnut Estates Limited	£9,276,954
IDG International Marketing Services Europe Ltd	£9,276,675
Shazam Productions Limited	£9,265,620
FSI Global PLC	£9,259,638
SmithKline Beecham (Export) Limited	£9,255,000
Capsicum Leasing Limited	£9,254,731
Hills Prospect PLC	£9,251,692
Postgrad Limited	£9,250,281
Metro Mechanical Services Limited	£9,246,596
ITC Concepts Limited	£9,245,400
Camgate Holdings Limited	£9,244,177
Abhaya Limited	£9,243,277
Cisilion (Group) Limited	£9,242,792
Mason Pearson Bros. Limited	£9,241,883
Oneclickhr Limited	£9,241,000
Noodle Properties Limited	£9,237,281
Southern Counties Care Limited	£9,234,864
Himalaya Carpets Limited	£9,233,149
HFIS PLC	£9,232,645
Blackwater Securities Limited	£9,230,749
Forgefix Limited	£9,227,300
SOL Electronics Limited	£9,210,482
Limesquare Business Parks Limited	£9,205,388
Lynn Lewis Limited	£9,203,644
Aeropak (Chemical Products) Limited	£9,202,702
British Board of Agrement	£9,198,000
Sabre EMEA Marketing Limited	£9,196,465
Chai-Lifeline Cancer Care	£9,185,151
PE (Mount Carmel) Limited	£9,179,248
ATC Holdings Limited	£9,178,015
K.E.M. Property Services Limited	£9,165,317
ISG Technology Holdings Limited	£9,163,000
GH London Ground Handling Services Limited	£9,162,851
Perfect Practices Group Limited	£9,160,334
FBM Metals (UK) Limited	£9,155,639
Cranmore School	£9,151,864
Sensormatic Limited	£9,149,000
Abbey Investments Limited	£9,148,889
Merz Pharma UK Limited	£9,142,150
First Investments (UK) Limited	£9,140,244
Topfib Limited	£9,139,298
Steiner UK Limited	£9,136,322
Millennium Care Homes Limited	£9,133,727
Grunenthal Limited	£9,133,000
Chislehurst School for Girls	£9,130,000
Ripmax Limited	£9,129,936
Cranstoun	£9,123,000
ULS Living Limited	£9,118,000
Ashdown Care Limited	£9,117,736
UML Wigmore Limited	£9,117,172
Guarding UK Ltd	£9,113,401
Kidde Safety Europe Limited	£9,110,000
AMD Environmental Limited	£9,106,644
Clavering Care Limited	£9,105,500
Raven Promotions Limited	£9,104,190
Soloberry Limited	£9,104,000
Boyden & Co.Limited	£9,102,446
Ecover (UK) Limited	£9,099,000
Texcel Developments Ltd	£9,087,953
Al-Mubarakia Limited	£9,082,996
Uniserve (U.K.) Limited	£9,081,439
Active Travel Group Limited	£9,080,610
UML Westminster Limited	£9,067,016
Newham Family Dental Care Limited	£9,064,949
Fulca Limited	£9,060,190
Michael Spiers (Jewellers) Limited	£9,059,541
WD1A Limited	£9,054,424
Thomas Gibson Fine Art Limited	£9,049,142
Roseland Parc Limited	£9,044,142
Emcor (UK) Limited	£9,043,000
Maison Moti Limited	£9,041,150
Arora Manchester Limited	£9,036,850
Gold Group Properties Limited	£9,033,916
Green Space London Limited	£9,031,649
UML Chiltern Limited	£9,020,699
TRSL Limited	£9,014,810
Advanced Business Equipment Limited	£9,006,235
Sarr Noke Hospitality Limited	£9,005,375
Nicholls & Clarke Glass Limited	£9,004,226
GHL (Crescent Lane) Limited	£9,001,030
BNS Company (Property Holdings) Limited	£9,000,330
St. Aubyn's (Woodford Green) School Trust	£9,000,073
Belmont Green Funding 2 Limited	£9,000,000
Roomes Stores,Limited	£8,997,605
Ability Hotels (Newcastle) Limited	£8,995,615
Ezra Attia Limited	£8,991,860
Tarian Investment Co. Limited	£8,991,018
Excess Baggage Holdings Limited	£8,990,076
Cygnet Street Developments Limited	£8,983,481
Allandale Investments Limited	£8,978,322
Reach Active Group Limited	£8,969,035
Bow Wharf Development LLP	£8,964,035
Jalaram Limited	£8,962,572
Health & Case Management Limited	£8,962,478
Denton Homes Surrey Limited	£8,955,261
G.Purchase Construction Limited	£8,955,000
R K Property Investments Ltd.	£8,951,534
Pyramid Builders Limited	£8,950,507
HFS Investment Properties Limited	£8,945,114
Axis Cleaning and Support Services Limited	£8,939,000
Rex Trade Associates Limited	£8,937,277
Aylmer Road Limited	£8,935,402
Ergonomic Solutions International Limited	£8,931,379
Mitchells Holding Limited	£8,930,617
Redbridge Sports Centre Trust Limited	£8,929,152
Worthing Retail Limited Liability Partnership	£8,927,249
The Decus Educational Trust	£8,927,000
Worldwide Energy Logistics Limited	£8,926,375

Company	Value
Yomans (London) Limited	£8,925,338
Kew College	£8,922,496
MND Construction Services Limited	£8,916,024
Biz Karts Limited	£8,913,244
Crown House (Tadworth) Limited	£8,909,977
Mecon Holdings Limited	£8,900,836
Leonard F Jollye (Holdings) Limited	£8,900,390
ME Construction Limited	£8,899,760
Mr. Plant Hire PLC	£8,898,142
Rosebery House Developments Limited	£8,897,434
Flahive Brickwork Limited	£8,888,560
1st Step Solutions Limited	£8,885,864
Lee-Warren Fabrication and Design Limited	£8,885,668
Creative Car Park Ltd	£8,881,248
Metsa Tissue Limited	£8,878,979
Bytes Security Partnerships Limited	£8,866,845
Tican (UK) Holdings Limited	£8,861,939
Genuine Solutions International Limited	£8,860,812
D and D Property Company Limited	£8,842,019
Latif International Limited	£8,841,004
Direct Boot and Shoe Supplies Limited	£8,836,903
Beale's Hotels Limited	£8,832,589
Archway Apartments Limited	£8,830,916
JTI (RMS) Ltd	£8,815,000
Tavern Quay Developments LLP	£8,811,165
J P & S Servicess Ltd	£8,810,590
Florin Industrial Services Holdings Limited	£8,802,584
Kudos Catering (UK) Limited	£8,801,063
HJP Media LLP	£8,792,276
Austin (GB) Limited	£8,778,846
Yendall Hunter Limited	£8,776,678
Combe International Limited	£8,769,294
QOTD Film Investment Limited	£8,769,251
Robert Heath Heating Limited	£8,754,652
Business Systems (U.K.) Limited	£8,751,127
Olivewood Limited	£8,748,244
Fardaar LLP	£8,746,325
Motivair Compressors Limited	£8,746,272
Kimberley Property Investments Limited	£8,743,523
Metra Non-Ferrous Metals Limited	£8,738,862
Vassall Ventures Limited	£8,730,016
Advanced Industrial Technology Corporation Limited	£8,729,087
Grosvenor Park 2006 S48 Film LLP	£8,726,160
Cimbali UK Limited	£8,721,503
Greenfield Property Developments Limited	£8,718,012
JPO Communications Limited	£8,707,227
Investland Limited	£8,706,044
IGT U.K. Limited	£8,695,749
Only Care Limited	£8,694,155
World Transport Agency Limited	£8,690,108
Richmond Green Developments Limited	£8,688,500
Dilawar Property Ltd.	£8,687,118
Kingscote Construction Services Ltd	£8,677,842
Wedge Investments Limited	£8,677,694
Premier Quilting Company Limited	£8,675,334
Williams and Hill Group Ltd	£8,673,165
MSI Property Investments Limited	£8,671,877
Deal Partners Limited	£8,671,424
City Circle UK Limited	£8,669,000
St Edwards Court (Romford) Limited	£8,667,196
Trident Garages Limited	£8,666,887
Scimitar House (Holdings) Limited	£8,663,172
Uneek Forwarding Limited	£8,658,383
Arcus Solutions Limited	£8,657,000
Carmel (UK) Limited	£8,654,297
Gracilis Ltd.	£8,651,814
Kew Green Hotels (Portsmouth LRG1) Limited	£8,650,379
Kilmorie Investments LLP	£8,648,531
V.I.P. Limited	£8,646,623
Soho Loop Limited	£8,645,959
Kout Food Group Restaurants UK Limited	£8,641,000
Garden Centre Property Development Trading Ltd	£8,638,000
Acorn Truck Sales Limited	£8,636,166
P Energy Limited	£8,619,584
Kaybridge Construction (Barnet) Limited	£8,618,127
St. James The Great R.C. Primary and Nursery School	£8,618,000
Conneely Drylining Limited	£8,613,649
Gima (UK) Limited	£8,611,524
Excess Baggage Group Limited	£8,599,039
Seymour House Residential Care Homes Limited	£8,594,592
St.Michael's Manor Limited	£8,589,856
Silixa Ltd	£8,589,637
Quality Line Transport Limited	£8,589,000
Harris Commercial Repairs Limited	£8,581,317
Woodside Road Limited	£8,578,726
Sheargold Limited	£8,574,457
Manak Lawyers Limited	£8,573,651
Canterbury Homes Ltd	£8,571,169
Metro Investments (Stevenage) LLP	£8,568,294
Taylors Legal Limited	£8,566,699
A.W. Champion Properties Limited	£8,563,204
BMAK FX Limited	£8,562,174
Cromwell (Egham) Limited	£8,561,802
Mulcroft Limited	£8,559,722
Micro Plus Software Limited	£8,556,457
Huxley Global Limited	£8,538,746
Larkspur Investments Limited	£8,533,528
Satair UK Limited	£8,531,809
Econometric Limited	£8,531,089
Haymarket PR Publications LLP	£8,526,000
Air Products Renewable Energy Limited	£8,517,000
GDL (Romford) Limited	£8,516,545
DGC Limited	£8,511,552
Tone Group Limited	£8,504,401
Broadrich Limited	£8,500,139
UCL Frognal Limited	£8,496,399
London & District Limited	£8,493,728
Cook's Delights Limited	£8,493,234
Carigluz Investment Co Limited	£8,485,179
Gouhari Enterprises Limited	£8,481,895
Interiors with Art Limited	£8,479,317
Rhiannon Properties Limited	£8,473,616
Fraserfort Limited	£8,472,000
Aldwych Leisure Limited	£8,470,311
Gristwood and Toms Limited	£8,466,469
Donatantonio Group Limited	£8,466,016
IIAA Limited	£8,462,370
Applepeach Limited	£8,451,681
Nasco (UK) Ltd	£8,447,178
Lamrose Properties Limited	£8,439,290
Cossam Investment Co Ltd	£8,438,694
Kavanagh Retailing (UK) Limited	£8,437,741
Bricklehampton Classic Care Limited	£8,436,201
Pet Mate Limited	£8,430,761
E2X Limited	£8,423,975
Airclaims Group (Overseas) Limited	£8,422,823
Artic Building Services Limited	£8,420,528
Norsette Investment Co. Limited	£8,420,374
HEL Limited	£8,416,562
Edge Grove School Trust Limited	£8,415,870
Oblue Limited	£8,407,542
Sabichi Homewares Limited	£8,405,660
MH Foods Limited	£8,404,000
Kenwyn Solar Limited	£8,403,000
St Mark Homes PLC	£8,401,370
WVC Vehicle Solutions Limited	£8,399,972
PQW Brenley Corner Limited	£8,399,154
Ashcoe Holdings Limited	£8,396,189
A Russell (Farmers) Limited	£8,393,092
Starglade Parks Limited	£8,391,390
Marcus & Marcus Limited	£8,390,412
Simm Tronic Limited	£8,387,818
Heartlands Hotel Limited	£8,376,006
Community Stores Limited	£8,375,156

Cablesheer Group Limited	£8,374,506
Stanmore Implants Worldwide Limited	£8,373,000
3 Torland Drive Ltd	£8,370,794
Montreaux Maidenhead Limited	£8,370,225
Highrak Limited	£8,368,730
Sandkot Limited	£8,366,568
Apex Lifts (Group) Limited	£8,362,708
Mapcargo International Limited	£8,359,301
RDT Limited	£8,359,214
Hooper Homes West Well Limited	£8,355,430
Sahara Care Limited	£8,354,130
Road Tech Computer Systems Limited	£8,350,735
Road Tech Holdings Limited	£8,350,735
Premiere Coffee Limited	£8,348,895
Orbital Equipment Limited	£8,346,485
Moss Europe Limited	£8,344,625
Brandon House Limited	£8,344,554
Unicourt Properties Limited	£8,332,172
Orchard Plumbing Limited	£8,328,928
Trollope & Colls Limited	£8,326,000
London Irish Scottish Richmond Limited	£8,323,801
Bromcom Computers PLC	£8,323,456
Boon Building Services Ltd	£8,316,419
Q.F.S. Scaffolding Limited	£8,313,443
Audbern Limited	£8,311,586
Arem Investments Limited	£8,311,363
Snowflake 145 Limited	£8,306,165
Kingswood Corporation Limited	£8,305,064
W3 Insights Ltd	£8,303,000
Elia International Limited	£8,281,906
Metropolitan Electrical Services Limited	£8,281,332
Chard Properties (UK) Limited	£8,280,931
O.C. Tanner Limited	£8,276,004
Woodledge Limited	£8,275,650
Orbit Investment Securities Services PLC	£8,273,677
Eurostaff Group Limited	£8,271,575
Homefield Preparatory School Trust Limited	£8,266,591
UML Mayfair Limited	£8,264,092
BP Containment Response Limited	£8,263,789
John A.Taylor & Sons Limited	£8,263,199
Biz Group Holdings Limited	£8,256,077
Crown House Investments Limited	£8,255,170
Quivira Bridging No.1 LLP	£8,255,121
Parkside Leisure Limited	£8,252,080
Treno Investments Ltd	£8,250,949
Centaur Property Group Limited	£8,245,862
Highassets Limited	£8,245,822
Fairmile Homes Three Limited	£8,244,184
OCO Limited	£8,243,899
1 Big Data Management Limited	£8,240,972
Wood Green Investments Limited	£8,237,548
Barrowfen Properties Limited	£8,237,484
Blenheim Group Limited	£8,237,407
Cloud Possibilities Limited	£8,233,487
Specialist Learning Trust	£8,229,906
Berkeley Healthcare Limited	£8,228,880
Dunwoody Airline Services Limited	£8,223,528
Blackfriars Securities (Brighton) Limited	£8,214,600
Searchfield (Oatlands Court) Limited	£8,207,585
Everglade Windows Limited	£8,203,559
Directfield Limited	£8,202,084
Paramount 26 Limited	£8,201,855
Speed 9395 Limited	£8,195,488
Polar Audio Limited	£8,193,030
Pamina Estates Limited	£8,188,296
Gefco Forwarding UK Ltd.	£8,187,257
Aitch Demolition Co. Ltd	£8,186,222
Salient Investments Ltd.	£8,179,708
Brookpass Limited	£8,173,710
Audley Willicombe Limited	£8,173,247
Tomo Motor Parts Limited	£8,171,865
SME Corporation Limited	£8,170,117

Anderson Travel Limited	£8,168,312
G E Bowra Group Limited	£8,165,580
Whitestone Property Services Limited	£8,164,258
Sea Cloud 2 Limited	£8,158,525
Adil Property Investment Limited	£8,156,480
Centronic Limited	£8,155,625
Starna Limited	£8,149,187
Applied Laser Engineering Limited	£8,147,709
Burgess Furniture Ltd	£8,146,756
LHR Business Support Centre Limited	£8,146,000
Daylighting Power Limited	£8,141,984
Abbey Ravenscroft Park Limited	£8,138,937
Sugarman Family Limited	£8,130,931
Hi-Tec Europe Limited	£8,129,508
H.Stern (Jewellery) Limited	£8,128,656
Crystal Clear Group Limited	£8,128,493
Cargill Weybridge Limited	£8,128,384
Mosaic Estates Ltd	£8,128,177
Remus Construction & Development Limited	£8,117,962
Watts Farms Packers Limited	£8,116,563
Fleetmill Limited	£8,110,341
Linkhaven Estates Ltd	£8,105,050
Viewrose Limited	£8,103,932
Agrofertrans Ltd.	£8,098,485
Shurgard UK West London Limited	£8,097,269
Excellent Properties Ltd.	£8,097,003
Inspire Community Trust	£8,095,808
CP Kelco UK Limited	£8,092,000
Thomas,Arthur & Gordon,Limited	£8,091,394
Zian Hi-Tech (U.K.) Limited	£8,086,581
City & Westminster Developments Limited	£8,084,778
94 Camlet Way LLP	£8,084,432
Siya Properties Limited	£8,075,574
Beacon (Mimms) Limited	£8,075,082
Ability Hotels (Peterborough) Limited	£8,067,621
Mala Engineering Limited	£8,066,138
GCP Onshore Wind 1 Limited	£8,060,822
Tempur Sealy International Limited	£8,056,000
Rise Park Academy Trust	£8,047,842
Rooff Group Limited (The)	£8,047,577
Ellis of Richmond Limited	£8,047,245
Telida Limited	£8,044,808
Nacropolis (Langley) Ltd	£8,042,739
Sandhill Park Limited	£8,041,243
Riverside Bio Limited	£8,039,764
Benacre Investments Limited	£8,034,587
Marlborough Isleworth Properties Limited	£8,033,768
UML Hinde Limited	£8,028,726
Henley Group Finance Limited	£8,026,161
Via Global Limited	£8,025,002
RBR Property Investments Limited	£8,021,086
Golden Tours Sightseeing Ltd	£8,020,735
Saniflo Limited	£8,017,655
Artillery Properties Limited	£8,017,093
Himelight Limited	£8,014,373
Gracechurch Sports Management Limited	£8,001,742
TN (UK) Consultancy Ltd	£8,001,449
Coopers Investments Limited	£8,000,254
Lenta 2 Limited	£7,993,433
Cie PLC	£7,992,555
Agency Press Limited	£7,992,397
Adelmill Limited	£7,991,387
Herbalife (U.K.) Limited	£7,990,226
Maia Leisure Limited	£7,986,317
Dunkeld Trading Limited	£7,986,018
NUR Limited	£7,985,634
Prestige Nursing Limited	£7,982,079
Lambda Therapeutic Limited	£7,980,214
Sudbury Plastering Services Limited	£7,979,707
Stratford High Street Ventures Limited	£7,979,251
Promede Limited	£7,977,948
Parcelhero Group Limited	£7,977,296

Company	Amount
Thamesfield Limited	£7,970,297
Acre Invest (Sydenham) Limited	£7,968,526
E. Christian & Company (Holdings) Limited	£7,966,259
RO Enterprises Limited	£7,966,160
Starna Scientific Limited	£7,965,248
OMEC Holdings Limited	£7,962,508
Earndrive Limited	£7,961,032
Plutus Estates (Braintree) Limited	£7,960,062
Cyan Logistics Limited	£7,958,892
Templefields House LLP	£7,956,809
Sunbury Manor School	£7,955,217
RR Securities Limited	£7,951,924
Hive 1 Ltd	£7,951,500
True World Foods (UK) Ltd	£7,951,042
Regal Trading Ltd	£7,949,834
Wellstone Management Ltd	£7,941,923
Crestron (UK) Limited	£7,940,651
Hersham Green LLP	£7,940,642
Ebonyhill Limited	£7,940,283
Terra Trade and Engineering LLP	£7,939,795
Pexhurst Services Limited	£7,939,112
Toureen Plant Limited	£7,938,777
Palladio Estates Limited	£7,937,870
Calda Limited	£7,934,709
Apollo RPL Limited	£7,933,409
GBST Wealth Management Limited	£7,926,761
Bath Resorts Limited	£7,926,129
Supercraft Limited	£7,925,783
Sapna Caterers Limited	£7,924,180
Jetclub Limited	£7,921,420
Heritage Care Homes Limited	£7,920,047
Kew Green Hotels (Portsmouth) Limited	£7,918,901
Kap Homes Ltd.	£7,916,325
Cardinal International Limited	£7,915,285
Falcon Hotels Limited	£7,914,813
Alandale Scaffolding Group Limited	£7,914,164
NTS Retail Limited	£7,913,368
Bluecroft Riverdale LLP	£7,910,062
NPT Finance Limited	£7,908,908
HFMC Group Holdings Ltd	£7,908,027
Genuine Solutions Group Limited	£7,896,551
Olivanna Ltd	£7,895,756
Hadgate Limited	£7,894,461
Pan United Ltd	£7,889,665
Gibbs & Ball Limited	£7,884,859
T.H.G. & C.C. Limited	£7,875,000
Maxen Homes Limited	£7,874,786
St John's School, Northwood	£7,869,374
Landmark Global (UK) Limited	£7,862,401
Squire Energy Limited	£7,862,338
Sarr Hotels (Luton) Ltd	£7,857,898
Hunters Contracts Limited	£7,853,812
Concept Developments (Cobham) Limited	£7,849,804
V.S. Properties Limited	£7,849,039
Standard Wharf Limited	£7,847,730
Bizy Investments Limited	£7,840,886
Input Video Ltd	£7,837,000
Miko Coffee Limited	£7,834,074
Randall Watts Construction Ltd	£7,827,101
Stair Tread Holdings Limited	£7,822,533
Hayre Investments (Ealing) Ltd.	£7,819,855
Shun Cheong Lung Holding Company Limited	£7,816,680
Kellogg Brown & Root Overseas Limited	£7,816,431
Mitcham Garden Village	£7,816,407
UCAR Properties Limited	£7,816,139
STM Group (UK) Limited	£7,816,021
Dexter House Limited	£7,805,952
Meadvine Limited	£7,805,421
Fitton & Co Ltd	£7,802,679
Dunlop International Holdings Limited	£7,801,000
RSD Travel Limited	£7,793,221
Fourway Communication Limited	£7,788,776
Intuitive Holding Limited	£7,784,765
Delamere (Chelmsford) Limited	£7,783,706
Dennis Reed Limited	£7,782,264
Desilu Estates Limited	£7,781,546
Craneshaw House Limited	£7,780,498
Eight Investment Limited	£7,778,601
SR Developers Limited	£7,778,150
Gable Homes Lettings Limited	£7,773,595
W W Giles (Smithfield) Limited	£7,769,456
D.B. Rees (Builders) Limited	£7,768,971
James Blunt Limited	£7,762,015
Gatehall Services Limited	£7,761,302
Super Industries DMCC Metals Limited	£7,756,200
Tobacco Pipe Makers and Tobacco Trade Benevolent	£7,755,936
Sonata Europe Limited	£7,755,917
Neptune Subsea IP Limited	£7,753,757
Coxwell Care Limited	£7,753,283
Millcroft Services P.L.C.	£7,746,336
ATP Media Licensing Limited	£7,741,925
Travel Blue Limited	£7,732,154
Tancia (Holdings) Limited	£7,723,485
Saya Enterprises Limited	£7,719,311
Valeo Limited	£7,717,000
Marande Limited	£7,713,589
Sunshine Properties Limited	£7,711,588
Acorn Limited	£7,710,941
Orange Music Electronic Company Limited	£7,707,820
Roseview (London) Ltd.	£7,704,758
Portico UK Holdco Limited	£7,704,637
Kidspace Adventures Holdings Limited	£7,702,626
Sports Gambling Committee Ltd	£7,695,740
Aldis of Barking Limited	£7,694,073
Eda Quality Foods Limited	£7,693,200
The Royal Medical Foundation	£7,692,744
Vanco UK Limited	£7,690,985
MH Star UK Ltd	£7,686,471
TT Skate Properties Limited	£7,683,083
David Allen Holdings Limited	£7,682,259
Essex County Laundry,Limited	£7,679,252
Bazooka Candy Brands International Limited	£7,672,384
Land & Water Plant Limited	£7,671,025
Capital City Service Limited	£7,669,345
Calbrook Cars Limited	£7,669,213
Share and Debenture Trust Limited (The)	£7,668,025
Hollyhedge Limited	£7,667,922
Avantis Hotels Limited	£7,667,786
Standard Plant Hire Limited	£7,662,427
Flintridge Resources Limited	£7,657,675
Arlen Properties Limited	£7,657,585
Premier Moves Limited	£7,657,564
Outlook Fostering Services Limited	£7,653,000
Supercraft Holdings Limited	£7,647,385
Mentfield UK Limited	£7,646,787
Rambert School of Ballet and Contemporary Dance	£7,638,594
Hedge End Place (Durkan) LLP	£7,638,392
EID Limited	£7,635,910
Lascelles Leisure Limited	£7,634,435
The Campion School	£7,633,000
Watchingwell Farms Limited	£7,632,809
Renewable Energy Centre Limited	£7,632,000
Metrolink RATP Dev Limited	£7,630,000
Robore Cuts Limited	£7,629,258
Clearwater Property Company Limited	£7,625,644
TES-AMM UK Ltd	£7,622,408
Waterlow Business Supplies Limited	£7,620,913
Perpetuum Construction Limited	£7,619,679
Athona Limited	£7,618,419
Emson Haig Limited	£7,616,573
Spacemaker Group Limited	£7,613,709
Kesgrave Hall Limited	£7,611,809
Chawla's Limited	£7,611,808
UML Wimpole Limited	£7,610,585

Company	Amount
Lixmere Properties Limited	£7,607,366
Optimal Limited	£7,605,870
Unbar Rothon Limited	£7,604,267
DKH Investments Limited	£7,602,290
G3 Worldwide Mail (UK) Limited	£7,602,000
UCL Albion Limited	£7,597,164
Toly Products (U.K.) Limited	£7,595,494
Mizen (Nether Street) Limited	£7,594,383
Zing Leisure Limited	£7,592,303
Leez Priory Limited	£7,586,336
A & J Ryan Holdings Limited	£7,585,636
Amadeus Primary Academies Trust	£7,584,000
Playpower UK Limited	£7,575,839
Hazeldell Ltd	£7,575,497
Alto Property Investments Limited	£7,574,502
Aldro School Educational Trust Limited	£7,572,898
A.E. Thorogood Investments Limited	£7,570,718
Ilapak Limited	£7,566,220
Vinci Property Limited	£7,563,000
Property Finance Capital (No 3) Limited	£7,562,722
Ugo Foods Group Limited	£7,561,803
Penenden Heath Investments LLP	£7,559,659
RBH Hotel Management Limited	£7,558,867
Inner Town Homes Limited	£7,555,054
Vulcan Wharf Limited	£7,554,665
Abercorn School Limited	£7,553,742
Sunnyfield Veg Limited	£7,552,427
Mostell Limited	£7,548,000
Lesaffre UK and Ireland Limited	£7,547,099
Maybour Logistics Global Limited	£7,544,238
LPM Acquisitions Limited	£7,544,000
Wasteland Group Limited	£7,541,768
Grovepoint Properties Limited	£7,540,195
Niemans Holdings Limited	£7,538,275
Volkerinfra Limited	£7,537,000
Malibu Health Products Limited	£7,536,565
Milcars Limited	£7,533,655
Eco Regeneration LLP	£7,531,326
Rhenus Lupprians Limited	£7,520,852
Maysor LLP	£7,520,503
Gypcraft Drylining Contractors Limited	£7,520,161
Aitco Management Limited	£7,513,435
Kirkman and Jourdain Construction Limited	£7,513,392
Gulmay Limited	£7,512,643
Asia UK Property Fund LLP	£7,512,188
Yellow Brick Developments Limited	£7,506,531
Tara Mobile Ltd	£7,504,500
Eran Diamonds (UK) Limited	£7,502,391
Buxton Crescent Hotel and Thermal Spa Co Ltd	£7,500,021
Amal Investments Limited	£7,500,000
Khakharia Properties Limited	£7,498,665
Estates and Lets 3 LLP	£7,498,515
Cherryfield (Croydon) Limited	£7,497,352
Thames Ditton Sports and Squash Club Limited	£7,496,442
Frattro Limited	£7,495,305
PAAM Investments Limited	£7,494,018
High Park Investments Limited	£7,493,866
Polaris Ventures Ltd	£7,489,138
Mister Dee International Limited	£7,488,006
Scimitar House Limited	£7,487,943
Orlando Limited	£7,487,465
Capsicum Motorsport Limited	£7,486,443
Manors Sales and Lettings Limited	£7,481,970
The Royal Masonic School for Girls	£7,480,872
Mabel Properties LLP	£7,480,819
Beacon Hill Academy	£7,478,540
HH Global Corporate Services Limited	£7,477,000
First Network Ltd.	£7,476,027
Vision Homes Limited	£7,469,897
TCA Investments Limited	£7,467,735
Mullan Partnership Limited	£7,463,764
Lycee International de Londres	£7,462,000
L.M.H. Properties Limited	£7,457,705
Duke Street Church (Richmond-upon-Thames)	£7,457,286
Northstar Property Investment Limited	£7,456,388
Safestand Limited	£7,456,059
Wembley Tyres Limited	£7,453,510
F & J Arpino Limited	£7,452,500
Cobham Hall	£7,448,962
Marchent Limited	£7,448,284
R & R Asset Management Limited	£7,443,654
Speakerbus Limited	£7,443,590
G S A R Holdings Limited	£7,441,961
Nordic Properties Limited	£7,440,993
Saul D Harrison & Sons PLC	£7,438,411
Mapeley Estates Limited	£7,438,000
Maidensgrove Limited	£7,434,924
Burton Wold Wind Farm (Trading) Limited	£7,434,648
Rooted Architecture Limited	£7,430,538
Titan Containers Limited	£7,427,944
Birmingham Schools Partnership (Group) Limited	£7,424,000
Kennford Group Limited	£7,421,653
Meraj Limited	£7,421,019
McGinley Cep Ltd	£7,420,922
Innovate Services Limited	£7,416,251
Shrewsbury Hotel Limited	£7,414,865
U K Insurance Business Solutions Limited	£7,408,279
Suzo International (UK) Limited	£7,406,789
Star Reefers Trading Limited	£7,405,564
Fairchildes Academy Community Trust	£7,403,508
Ardour World Limited	£7,403,198
John S. Miller Limited	£7,402,610
Thames Recycling Limited	£7,398,556
Westbourne Academy Trust	£7,398,280
Austin Company of (U.K.) Limited (The)	£7,391,204
Bishopswood Estates Limited	£7,389,283
Roamquest Limited	£7,386,239
TRG Logistics Ltd	£7,383,882
West & Coe Limited	£7,376,552
S.S.A.T. Property Investments Limited	£7,373,126
Newserge Limited	£7,373,000
PES Group Limited	£7,369,898
Leonardo Holdings Limited	£7,369,471
Minesoft Ltd	£7,362,435
Swift Roofing Contracts Limited	£7,355,988
Xstro Investments Limited	£7,352,916
Kingswood Golf & Country Club Limited	£7,339,397
Football First Limited	£7,338,012
Kingston University Service Company Limited	£7,337,000
Everglade Holdings Limited	£7,332,032
Riches Ilford Ltd	£7,327,717
Islandbridge Chigwell Limited	£7,323,012
E Wood Holdings Limited	£7,321,000
Bal Holdings Limited	£7,320,954
MEI Properties Limited	£7,319,123
Advanced Access Platforms Ltd	£7,313,581
Hertz UK Receivables Ltd	£7,310,309
Tozer Seeds Limited	£7,308,062
Leisure and Outdoor Furniture Association Limited	£7,307,988
Vanneck Bros Limited	£7,307,832
Starcare Homes Limited	£7,298,812
Mangrove Global Limited	£7,298,294
Castledene Investments Limited	£7,296,653
Direct Supplies (2014) Limited	£7,294,925
Kenville Limited	£7,285,492
Crest Plus Operations Limited	£7,284,852
Rhenus High Tech UK Limited	£7,283,392
Hydro Cleansing Limited	£7,281,665
Renault Institute of Quality Management Limited	£7,275,986
KS SPV 4 Limited	£7,274,000
D.B.T. (Holdings) Limited	£7,273,498
Watts Farms Catering Limited	£7,267,568
Casewise Limited	£7,264,735
Pattinson Green Limited	£7,255,889

Company	Amount
Rubylake Investments Limited	£7,247,955
Kew Green Hotels (Derby/Nottingham) Limited	£7,246,036
Swift 100 Limited	£7,243,120
Arcplan UK Limited	£7,242,089
Days Lane Primary School	£7,237,905
Hawthorne Trust Limited	£7,232,833
JSA Properties (UK) Limited	£7,232,750
Operations Holdings Ltd	£7,225,985
I-Catering Management Services Limited	£7,223,758
Fairmont Property Developers UK Ltd	£7,220,559
Giesecke+Devrient Mobile Security GB Ltd	£7,218,592
Ruxley Holdings Limited	£7,218,070
Lavender Property Investments Limited	£7,214,798
Babington House School Limited	£7,209,231
Gerry Murphy Ltd	£7,201,928
Transputec Limited	£7,198,086
Mastermind Trading Limited	£7,197,928
Indiacast UK Ltd	£7,196,720
Rowhurst Limited	£7,196,458
Avantia Limited	£7,194,730
Air Products (Chemicals) Teesside Limited	£7,194,000
Derek Pobjoy Investments Limited	£7,188,864
SZ & W Limited	£7,186,782
Swakeleys Properties Limited	£7,185,590
Condor Group Limited	£7,185,582
C.L.T. Timber and Transport Limited	£7,180,056
Shire Properties (South East) Limited	£7,179,683
Catalina Investments Limited	£7,175,547
Tancia Limited	£7,172,905
Babcock Wanson UK Limited	£7,170,000
Alderforce SC Limited	£7,169,763
MacFarlane Media Limited	£7,169,753
Sale Service and Maintenance Ltd.	£7,168,501
John Steward Transport Limited	£7,162,291
G.A.F. Heley (Properties) Limited	£7,161,605
G & O Properties (London) Limited	£7,161,020
Residual and Brand Management Limited	£7,155,733
Griffon Land Holdings Limited	£7,155,578
St. George's Hill Lawn Tennis Club Limited	£7,155,003
James Development Company Limited	£7,151,389
Citigate Homes (UK) Ltd	£7,151,353
Clearway Environmental Services (U.K) Limited	£7,151,126
St. John's Preparatory & Senior School Limited	£7,148,655
Lowen Homes Limited	£7,148,000
Choice Wealth Management Limited	£7,145,170
Arcese UK Limited	£7,144,365
CFS-Zipp Limited	£7,142,722
Major Properties London Limited	£7,139,904
M D Properties Limited	£7,138,157
Polybags Limited	£7,130,483
J.J. Sweeney Limited	£7,130,090
Greenbond Properties Limited	£7,124,188
Euro Services Limited	£7,118,329
Watmough Brothers Investments Limited	£7,115,685
The Invicta Film Partnership No.32, LLP	£7,114,580
Jay Fostering Limited	£7,114,000
Hamilcourt Industrial Holdings Limited	£7,110,037
Currie Motors Kingston Limited	£7,106,000
Essential Harvest Limited	£7,093,909
Gittisham Care Limited	£7,082,092
Euron Developments (France) Limited	£7,080,350
Jobladder Limited	£7,080,172
Guru Nanak Limited	£7,079,858
Oakdene Holdings Limited	£7,074,628
Apex Lift & Escalator Engineers Limited	£7,072,768
SmithKline Beecham (SWG) Limited	£7,072,000
Owen Coyle Managements Limited	£7,068,644
Decadent Properties Limited	£7,065,042
Anglia Secure Homes (South East) Limited	£7,065,000
Leslie Rogers Investments Limited	£7,049,526
Visual Response Limited	£7,047,536
A L Properties Limited	£7,046,047
UML Portman Limited	£7,045,995
Inspireall Leisure and Family Support Services	£7,045,082
Giga Communications Limited	£7,044,715
Belgrave Land (Kilmarnock) Limited	£7,041,733
West Ten Properties (UK) Limited	£7,036,975
Trafalgar Square Investments Limited	£7,033,219
Gade Investments Limited	£7,032,070
J J Coughlan (Holdings) Limited	£7,028,243
Input Video Holdings Ltd	£7,027,000
A.E. Tyler Limited	£7,026,779
Active Travel Group Bidco Limited	£7,026,198
O'Hara Transport Limited	£7,025,443
Goodwin Associates Limited	£7,020,952
Marylebone Square Property Group Ltd	£7,018,478
Nelly Films (Christmas) Limited	£7,018,021
Acqua Plus Developments Limited	£7,017,257
Sliabh Construction Limited	£7,016,944
Mountbrook Properties Limited	£7,016,105
Ultimate Model Corporation Limited	£7,016,030
Amery Construction Limited	£7,015,458
Greencourt Property Group Limited	£7,014,087
Active Travel Group Midco Limited	£7,011,286
Sartra International Limited	£7,003,218
Purism Properties Limited	£7,002,459
George Potter House Ltd	£6,998,965
Keash Properties Limited	£6,998,037
Cort Business Services UK Limited	£6,993,836
Unitruc Limited	£6,992,959
Merligen Investments Limited	£6,992,358
Marblefloor Limited	£6,991,290
Aandatta Limited	£6,989,893
Kilofrequency Limited	£6,988,339
Neilmed Limited	£6,988,272
St Cross Developments Limited	£6,987,972
ET Enterprises Limited	£6,987,165
The Zentropa Film Partnership LLP	£6,984,795
H & H Care Home Investments Limited	£6,983,160
Rosemead Limited	£6,974,386
North Star (2000) Limited	£6,972,074
JRL Group (Ireland) Limited	£6,971,226
Parkwood Hall Co-operative Academy Trust	£6,968,000
Cousins Material House Limited	£6,966,693
SEJ Distribution Ltd	£6,960,997
Centro Group Limited	£6,959,212
Hazel Renewables Limited	£6,959,000
NK Image Limited	£6,958,479
Intuitive Limited	£6,957,338
Ashby & Croft Limited	£6,955,902
Seismic Exploration (Canada) Ltd	£6,950,169
Raglan Primary School	£6,948,000
RWW Holdings Limited	£6,947,460
S & D Pharma Limited	£6,941,872
KBR Property Investments Limited	£6,940,690
Bute Capital Limited	£6,936,925
UT (UK) Limited	£6,927,770
Pole To Win UK Limited	£6,925,578
Excelsior Textiles Limited	£6,923,131
The Sons of Divine Providence	£6,922,356
WLMG Limited	£6,920,921
Blossom House School Limited	£6,920,191
Dudley Properties Limited	£6,918,667
Caredeal Limited	£6,916,768
Alexandra Infant School	£6,915,000
Alhambra Hotel Limited	£6,913,835
Millers Bespoke Bakery Limited	£6,912,377
Nucleus Limited	£6,912,219
GDC (Holdings) Ltd	£6,912,177
G. D. Cooper & Co Ltd	£6,912,176
Cromwell Investments Limited	£6,912,050
Redab PLC	£6,910,246
Neelkanth Safe Deposit Ltd	£6,906,889
J P Investments London Ltd	£6,905,739

Company	Amount
Avon Lake Holdings Limited	£6,902,850
Surrey Rest Homes Limited	£6,897,092
Mashco Limited	£6,896,520
78A SW48BH Limited	£6,896,242
Paneurosys Limited	£6,894,992
Fortuna Frutos (UK) Limited	£6,894,370
Sutton Business Centre Limited	£6,893,231
Chromalox (UK) Limited	£6,886,675
Integrated Electronic Technologies Limited	£6,884,751
Eventist Group Limited	£6,882,200
E.D.S. Holdings Limited	£6,878,218
Anthony Property Co. Limited	£6,877,119
B K S Energy Limited	£6,875,000
Dilawar & Sons Limited	£6,873,485
Cherryfield Holdings Limited	£6,869,619
Railsite Holdings Limited	£6,869,107
Veriton Pharma Limited	£6,863,314
Odessa Print Group Ltd	£6,861,207
Blue Prop Ltd	£6,860,558
Jenga House Limited	£6,860,503
Fishpools (Finance) Limited	£6,860,445
Danly UK Limited	£6,855,790
The Natural Woodfloor Company Limited	£6,851,067
The Acclaim Handling Group Ltd	£6,849,648
Skanska Residential Development UK Limited	£6,849,000
Sancroft Properties Limited	£6,848,588
Thirsk Winton LLP	£6,846,768
Dial Investments Limited	£6,844,784
EA Consulting Group Ltd	£6,840,511
Ballward Limited	£6,838,773
Tropical Marine Centre (2012) Ltd	£6,838,000
J.A. Stott (Carpentry) Limited	£6,835,187
Brembury Properties Limited	£6,834,748
Summit Asset Management Limited	£6,833,000
Kew Green Hotels (Chester) Limited	£6,830,873
Chalford Property Company Limited	£6,829,758
Popat Stores Limited	£6,825,539
Purley Baptist Church	£6,823,335
Donovan Bros. Limited	£6,816,357
O'Rourke Civil & Structural Engineering Limited	£6,815,000
Plexus Europe Limited	£6,812,000
Highplus Limited	£6,811,895
ACM Eco Holdings Limited	£6,806,777
Stulz U.K. Limited	£6,804,769
RKPE Limited	£6,804,483
SI Electrical Limited	£6,800,209
Rian Properties Limited	£6,800,188
Cosco Shipping Crystal Logistics (UK) Co Ltd	£6,800,045
Henry Mansfield Limited	£6,798,638
H & V Serviceplan Limited	£6,797,108
Muniment Limited	£6,793,889
MCM Central Limited	£6,793,812
Fire Design Solutions Limited	£6,788,130
Berrite Limited	£6,782,426
Grovehawk Ltd	£6,782,277
Poliform UK Limited	£6,780,912
Raven Roofing and Building Supplies Limited	£6,776,495
Dimehome Limited	£6,769,935
HML PM Ltd	£6,769,609
Newstone International Limited	£6,768,214
Bamrose Properties Limited	£6,768,166
Kinsat Enterprises Ltd	£6,760,776
The Kendon Rope & Twine Co Limited	£6,759,090
Swanvale Management Limited	£6,758,181
Chalfont Coaches of Harrow Limited	£6,757,950
Belmont Castle Academy	£6,755,290
Anoopam Mission	£6,751,760
Secomak Limited	£6,751,012
Krinvest Limited	£6,749,775
Shepherd Harris & Co Limited	£6,749,598
Roadhouse Building & Civil Engineering Ltd.	£6,748,109
Elec-Mec (Wholesale) Limited	£6,747,611
National Animal Welfare Trust	£6,747,599
3pillar Global UK Limited	£6,744,751
Saville Services Limited	£6,738,240
DBT Property LLP	£6,737,096
Rosetta Investments Limited	£6,734,044
Leander Build Limited	£6,728,877
Butterworth Laboratories Limited	£6,725,596
Jennor Holdings Limited	£6,722,842
Vanwise Group Limited	£6,722,487
Moreland House Care Home Limited	£6,722,343
Gratia (Abbey Care Home) Limited	£6,717,526
Asgill House Trust Limited (The)	£6,716,509
Falcon Investment Ltd	£6,716,277
Gathercrest Properties Limited	£6,715,464
Saba Park Solutions UK Limited	£6,705,591
Harvard International Limited	£6,705,000
Stubbins Marketing Limited	£6,696,084
Learning Tree International Limited	£6,694,000
Vinstrata Builders (London) Limited	£6,687,975
Lee Park Estates Ltd	£6,684,847
Brinor Investments Limited	£6,684,423
West One Bathrooms Limited	£6,684,310
Blackstone City Ltd	£6,683,997
Lefroy Brooks Diffusion Limited	£6,682,677
Strandhaven Limited	£6,682,171
Friend's Property Portfolio Limited	£6,681,393
I.C.F. Finance Limited	£6,681,355
Chrome Dreams Media Ltd	£6,680,376
Pickhurst Infant Academy	£6,678,411
Bloomfield Terrace LLP	£6,678,285
Linden Wates (Horsham) LLP	£6,678,000
Uncle Buck Finance LLP	£6,677,132
E. T. Clay Products Limited	£6,675,633
Costco Online UK Limited	£6,675,000
The Zoroastrian Trust Funds of Europe (Incorporated)	£6,673,256
Ahmed Property Limited	£6,671,434
W.T. Partnership Limited	£6,668,090
Lodestar Properties Limited	£6,667,992
Universal Dispense Systems Limited	£6,667,852
Freshplant Limited	£6,667,716
Stealth Leisure Limited	£6,663,126
K2 Trading Limited	£6,662,291
Sheplord Limited	£6,658,804
Laurels Care Limited	£6,658,459
The Original Bedstead Co Limited	£6,654,791
Horn Cutting Tools Limited	£6,649,028
Mawpart Commercial Limited	£6,648,147
Aviation Servicing Company Ltd	£6,647,946
St James Contracts Limited	£6,646,083
Burnt Common Nurseries Limited	£6,646,000
Maison Maurice Limited	£6,645,845
Montreaux Redhill Limited	£6,642,553
Vivo Medical Care Limited	£6,641,173
Datamust Company Limited	£6,640,375
Garratt Services (Tooting) Limited	£6,638,789
Leander Construction Limited	£6,638,264
Croftwood Care (Cheshire) Limited	£6,637,540
Tudor Investments Limited	£6,636,222
Comwood Holdings Ltd.	£6,632,051
J.Browne Properties (UK) Limited	£6,631,355
Food Brands Group Limited	£6,628,000
South Coast Watch Fair Limited	£6,626,735
Belgrave Land (Armley) Limited	£6,617,794
Bulk Powder Terminals Limited	£6,617,656
Manpower Direct (UK) Ltd.	£6,612,683
Nicon Developments Limited	£6,612,531
Cobra Industries Limited	£6,610,292
Springhill Property Investments Limited	£6,607,496
TRAD Group Limited	£6,607,299
Services Support (Cleveland) Holdings Limited	£6,605,000
Services Support (Cleveland) Limited	£6,605,000
R S L (Slough) Limited	£6,600,238

Company	Amount
Corinthian Land (West Kent) Limited	£6,600,124
Glengall Limited	£6,598,885
Emerald Leather LLP	£6,596,751
Maxco London Limited	£6,596,168
Rhodehurst Limited	£6,591,610
A C Georgiades Ltd	£6,591,524
BML Utility Contractors Ltd	£6,590,824
West Dorset Leisure Holidays Limited	£6,588,743
Linkmart Limited	£6,584,276
Snowden Developments Limited	£6,583,988
Harry Motors Ltd	£6,582,425
ATK Energy EU Services Limited	£6,582,000
Key Mail (UK) Limited	£6,581,680
Trading Post Limited (The)	£6,580,669
London Wharf Limited	£6,577,012
Arboretum Partners LLP	£6,576,677
De Vere Care Limited	£6,569,492
Gordon Durham & Co.Limited	£6,566,000
Marke Creative Merchandise Ltd	£6,561,200
Brand Agency (London) Limited	£6,557,248
Peace Hospice Care	£6,556,619
Method Products Limited	£6,552,000
Braycote Ltd	£6,551,480
Fuller Leisure Limited	£6,550,197
Jaysam Developments Wembley Limited	£6,547,978
Artemis Interiors Limited	£6,543,849
M.E. Duffell Limited	£6,537,537
Porcelanosa Group Limited	£6,537,000
Boss & Co.Limited	£6,533,986
Watford FC's Community Sports & Education Trust	£6,531,742
Denton Wharf Properties Limited	£6,529,513
Etonbrook Properties PLC	£6,528,038
The Company of Animals Limited	£6,526,600
Giles Homes Limited	£6,523,706
Servotest Testing Systems Ltd	£6,523,431
Heley International Limited	£6,521,787
LGX Holdings Limited	£6,517,885
Ebury 106 Limited	£6,516,624
Portnall House Ltd	£6,515,047
Watches International Limited	£6,509,667
RBH Hotels UK Limited	£6,509,000
Body Works West at Lambton Place Limited	£6,507,787
Transcar Projects (Holdings) Ltd	£6,506,643
Harris Commercial Sales Limited	£6,504,159
T.C. Racing (Leisure) Limited	£6,503,667
Iceport Limited	£6,502,497
Melford Commercial Properties Ltd.	£6,488,000
Staines Preparatory School Trust	£6,487,510
Soul Coffee House (London) Limited	£6,485,169
Thew Arnott Group Limited	£6,483,862
Residential Care Services Limited	£6,482,979
Residential Properties Funds Limited	£6,478,264
E-Nova Healthcare Limited	£6,475,407
Strategic Shipping Company Limited	£6,474,720
A.E.Monk & Co.(London) Limited	£6,472,971
Oval Quarter Developments Limited	£6,462,950
UK 786 Limited	£6,459,313
Neogene Limited	£6,455,214
H.H.Keys Estates Limited	£6,454,158
Ospirit Limited	£6,453,463
Premier Work Support Limited	£6,452,410
Fairmile Homes One Limited	£6,450,498
Falco Construction Limited	£6,443,337
Badiani & Company Limited	£6,438,405
Actionmanor Limited	£6,436,137
Gordon Murray Design Limited	£6,425,639
South Manchester Energy Limited	£6,424,504
Daniel Johns Ltd	£6,424,088
Sharish Properties Limited	£6,420,497
Travellanda Ltd	£6,419,920
Saba Infra UK Limited	£6,418,772
Southcrown Limited	£6,413,976
H & S Contractors (Kent) Limited	£6,409,924
A E Properties Limited	£6,407,950
The Palace Theatre Watford Limited	£6,404,190
Community Support Project Limited	£6,403,000
KMS Holdings Limited	£6,401,892
HCL Investments (UK) Ltd	£6,400,598
HLT London Manage Limited	£6,394,006
Barilone Properties Limited	£6,393,807
JDM Investments Limited	£6,390,488
State Street HCL Holdings (UK) Limited	£6,386,137
Bell Theatre Services Limited	£6,386,008
Afinacorp Limited	£6,383,785
Coborn Engineering Company Limited	£6,378,450
Alium Medical Limited	£6,375,887
Hybrid Dining Limited	£6,374,000
Kew Green Hotels (Warrington) Limited	£6,371,180
Beecham Productions Limited	£6,370,898
Tumi (UK) Limited	£6,370,563
Roalco Limited	£6,370,382
JBG Enterprises Limited	£6,369,933
Maida Vale Leisure Limited	£6,362,068
Apollo Cleaning Services Limited	£6,361,361
Precision Engineering Plastics Ltd	£6,361,024
Dedalo1 Limited	£6,360,969
We Are Pentagon Limited	£6,359,886
Pinns Wharf Limited	£6,356,519
Abbey Care Complex Limited	£6,354,072
Bates Wharf Marine Sales Limited	£6,353,016
Clickatell Limited	£6,351,520
Kew Green Hotels (Norwich LRG1) Limited	£6,351,171
Worth More Limited	£6,350,088
Residential Land Limited	£6,344,970
Dentoptic Limited	£6,343,682
SAI Commodities Limited	£6,339,885
Crickmore Developments Limited	£6,337,396
Healy's ACR Limited	£6,332,491
WYM Legal Limited	£6,321,915
Transfleet Properties Limited	£6,319,710
Sunset Travel Limited	£6,319,660
Grovestream Limited	£6,319,545
Amaze Capital Limited	£6,316,534
Bet Invest Ltd	£6,316,111
Navigator Terminals Windmill Limited	£6,315,000
High Point Solutions Limited	£6,304,250
A. & G. P. Trading Limited	£6,303,141
VXR Imaging Limited	£6,302,189
Rusjon (UK) Limited	£6,299,958
L.M.H. (Management Services) Limited	£6,298,546
Hoopers Homes Limited	£6,297,663
Albert Darnell Limited	£6,293,896
Basis Technologies International Limited	£6,290,215
Pinder Developments Co. (Chislehurst) Limited	£6,287,922
Delivered on Time Limited	£6,287,252
TY Ventures (UK) Limited	£6,285,605
P.S.V. Transport Systems Limited	£6,284,917
Alim Caterers Limited	£6,278,011
Linkam Scientific Instruments Limited	£6,275,220
Ovationdata Limited	£6,273,280
SM Global Consultancy Limited	£6,273,002
Lanvin Trading Ltd	£6,272,822
Select Poultry & Meat Ltd	£6,272,146
R.G. Taylor Engineering Limited	£6,271,519
Laser Holdings Limited	£6,270,000
Boleyn Phoenix Limited	£6,266,357
Chiltern Court Properties Limited	£6,264,521
Anglo Scottish Leisure Limited	£6,260,970
Michael Franklin (Chemists) Limited	£6,259,426
EACG Holdings Limited	£6,252,897
Hayre Builders Company Limited	£6,252,216
SNC-Lavalin UK Holding Limited	£6,251,000
IAH Charity Company Limited	£6,248,384
Riso (U.K.) Limited	£6,247,527

Company	Value
Computer Financial Consultants Limited	£6,246,000
Sky Insurance Services Group Limited	£6,245,438
Lexcross Limited	£6,243,146
Innotrade Europe Limited	£6,242,189
Park Grove Residential Limited	£6,241,196
Siddharth Jewellery (U.K.) Limited	£6,240,844
Professor Puzzle Limited	£6,237,858
Riverstore Limited	£6,237,838
Vvoosh Limited	£6,234,973
Realmpark Health Care (Petworth) Limited	£6,231,796
Thames Honda Limited	£6,231,192
Envirotech Properties Limited	£6,225,186
FLW Holding Limited	£6,223,384
Erwin Technologies UK Limited	£6,221,276
I E Music Limited	£6,220,997
Brownings Electric Company Limited	£6,216,582
Abbeyman Investments Limited	£6,213,712
P.F. Ahern (London) Limited	£6,211,343
Philmont Properties UK Limited	£6,207,040
KECS Investments Limited	£6,201,688
Bellecity Limited	£6,201,420
A.A.Fisher Limited	£6,199,969
A.A. Fisher (Holdings) Limited	£6,199,969
Copley Limited	£6,198,962
Trading Scents Group Limited	£6,196,438
White Lodge Centre	£6,196,000
Second Shurgard UK Camberley Limited	£6,195,606
One for All (UK) Ltd.	£6,195,421
Thompsons Nursery Limited	£6,194,973
Parkside School Trust	£6,194,034
CK Property Developments Limited	£6,189,309
Universal Tyres and Spares Limited	£6,186,844
Remington Partners Ltd	£6,179,502
Harry A.Coff,Limited	£6,175,491
Heathrow Top Limited	£6,173,206
Taylor Wentworth Limited	£6,173,196
Blackford Media LLP	£6,172,750
Property Support Services UK Limited	£6,170,109
Oaks Academy Trust	£6,169,000
Penn Place Investments Limited	£6,167,780
Specialist Plant Associates Limited	£6,163,456
Walsingham Care	£6,160,904
S M E Enterprise Limited	£6,159,836
Safetell Limited	£6,158,809
Kimberley Peer Ventures One Ltd	£6,158,808
Ten Levels Ltd	£6,155,892
Good Harvest Properties (Hammersmith) Limited	£6,155,598
MJF Business Services Limited	£6,154,860
Citybond Holdings Limited	£6,151,729
Texcel (2011) Limited	£6,148,046
Texcel Technology PLC	£6,148,036
Proppertunity Limited	£6,147,803
Bishop & Sons' Depositories Limited	£6,145,373
Margiberg LLP	£6,142,265
Gilray Plant Limited	£6,139,814
Derby Pub Company Limited	£6,135,769
Stanmore Law Practice Limited	£6,134,805
Clivnars Limited	£6,130,867
Davton Holdings Ltd	£6,124,317
Cheyne Assets Ltd	£6,121,824
Diamed (G.B.) Ltd.	£6,120,000
Sunflower Healthcare (Greenford) LLP	£6,119,106
KMP Taste Limited	£6,118,466
Tone Scaffolding Services Limited	£6,115,418
Assetsky Limited	£6,114,948
Scan Corporation Limited	£6,111,041
Galliford Try HPS Limited	£6,111,000
Minverport Enterprises Limited	£6,110,945
Uponor Limited	£6,110,000
Ultrabrook Limited	£6,109,083
Asha (Camberley) Ltd	£6,105,803
Littlecroft Properties Limited	£6,104,684

Company	Value
Deacons Associates Limited	£6,104,214
Rilla Properties Limited	£6,101,841
Black River Asset Management (UK) Limited	£6,097,651
Crislex Limited	£6,094,047
Naked Fine Wine Bonds PLC	£6,093,000
Hungerburger Limited	£6,090,356
The Broxbourne School	£6,089,830
The Todd Group Limited	£6,089,086
JFD Developments Ltd	£6,087,602
Pharmacare (Europe) Limited	£6,085,796
Stat Holding International Limited	£6,083,324
Trans Global Group Limited	£6,082,895
Southfleet Investments Limited	£6,081,901
Burnt Ash Primary School	£6,081,409
Neston Court Limited	£6,078,685
Sukanya Holdings Limited	£6,078,417
Kentex Group Limited	£6,074,723
Goldace Investments LLP	£6,074,598
The Jersey Property Partnership LLP	£6,073,252
Metam Properties Limited	£6,071,924
Ostrider Limited	£6,071,151
Chesterton Education Limited	£6,070,187
Safe Properties Limited	£6,063,988
Ability Hotels (Southport) Limited	£6,061,836
GCH (St Katharine's) Limited	£6,060,562
Uavend Norris Castle Ltd	£6,060,357
Eiser Infrastructure Partners LLP	£6,060,000
Rapiergroup Limited	£6,058,819
Mesa Investment Limited	£6,056,051
Whisper Films Limited	£6,052,070
The Dewan Foundation Limited	£6,051,485
GH Land Developments Limited	£6,049,448
Trans-Britannia Properties Limited	£6,047,043
Ellenor	£6,045,613
East Central Limited	£6,043,423
Goldings Estates Limited	£6,041,148
Country House Weddings Holdings Ltd	£6,040,185
Servipharm Limited	£6,037,450
Axiom Wealth Management Limited	£6,036,983
Vine Investment Company Limited (The)	£6,036,134
Waterfront Cafe Benson Limited	£6,034,674
Blenheim Barnes Limited	£6,033,029
Barnardo Services Limited	£6,030,260
Ashley Homes Limited	£6,029,756
Rye Plant Hire Limited	£6,028,577
Frithsden Finance (Birmingham) Limited	£6,026,574
European Process Plant Limited	£6,024,882
360shareholders Limited	£6,023,618
BP Absheron Limited	£6,021,830
Panther Shop Investments Limited	£6,016,560
Frontline Technology Limited	£6,014,894
J M W Vicary Limited	£6,013,005
Quad Building Services (Southern) Limited	£6,011,935
King Street Manchester Holdings LLP	£6,009,403
Intercontinental Adjusters (Europe) Limited	£6,003,662
Caterham Cars Group Limited	£6,000,100
United Distributing Company (Coin Machine Sales)	£5,996,973
UCL Harrow Limited	£5,996,053
Boost Homes Ltd	£5,991,778
Freshasia Foods Ltd	£5,990,145
District One Estates Ltd	£5,985,587
Able Skills Limited	£5,984,085
Catalyst Corporate Development Limited	£5,975,343
Maxwelton House Property Company Limited	£5,973,850
Berea Limited	£5,970,043
Explore Living Limited	£5,970,000
Mark Luck Limited	£5,969,883
Todd Doors Limited	£5,968,875
Monks Way Development Limited	£5,965,534
Travel Nation Limited	£5,961,508
Excelsior Property Investments Limited	£5,961,307
T.C & D Construction Ltd.	£5,960,834

Company	Value
Wildview Limited	£5,957,525
Esteem Care Ltd	£5,957,139
D & M Audiovisual Ltd	£5,956,688
Armstrong Metal Ceilings Limited	£5,955,000
Dennys Uniforms Limited	£5,953,671
Verico Europe Holding Limited	£5,948,000
Raban Holdings Limited	£5,946,833
Clover Environmental Solutions Ltd	£5,944,463
Brookcast UK LLP	£5,943,286
Heatpoint Limited	£5,939,332
Hillier Hopkins LLP	£5,939,205
Soul Coffee House (West) Limited	£5,933,998
Kinetic IT Limited	£5,933,898
Sian Formwork Limited	£5,927,820
Trimite Limited	£5,919,281
Cuffe PLC	£5,918,315
Jasper Morrison Limited	£5,912,846
Capedeal Limited	£5,911,130
Anya House Limited	£5,907,660
Cromsource Ltd	£5,907,526
Butchoff Antiques Limited	£5,903,374
THMG Limited	£5,903,035
BMT Hi-Q Sigma Limited	£5,899,000
Residential Land Management Limited	£5,896,533
Hiretest Limited	£5,896,414
M3J Solutions Ltd	£5,893,925
Oforce Limited	£5,890,976
Al-Noor Foundation Limited	£5,881,852
Kays Limited	£5,881,485
Linden (Hartfield Road) LLP	£5,880,000
Silvertime Amusements Limited	£5,879,011
Reliance Entertainment Productions 5 Ltd	£5,878,711
Vadsala Limited	£5,874,752
La Nu-Range Ltd	£5,873,038
J. Devine Plant Hire Limited	£5,870,891
Fredereck Sage Holdings Limited	£5,867,409
York House Centre Limited	£5,864,904
The Magdi Yacoub Institute	£5,861,943
Lubkowski Saunders and Associates Limited	£5,851,923
APFS Property Ltd	£5,851,838
John F. Hunt Plant Hire Ltd	£5,848,818
Hurst Primary School	£5,848,621
Butlers Walsall Ltd	£5,846,833
Dovestone Estates Limited	£5,846,746
M.W. Helicopters Limited	£5,846,121
MCPE LLP	£5,841,596
Alexen Avocats (UK) Limited	£5,830,322
Movesell Limited	£5,829,247
K 2 Properties Limited	£5,827,508
Regina 2015 Limited	£5,826,872
Odris Investments Limited	£5,825,632
Tees Limited	£5,817,848
Goodshoeman Limited	£5,816,566
Lakedale Developments Limited	£5,816,530
Vizual Business Tools Limited	£5,815,000
Victory Lighting (UK) Limited	£5,814,978
Tan Sales (London) Limited	£5,814,732
Corumbe Investments Limited	£5,813,897
Schwing Stetter (UK) Ltd	£5,813,000
Osborn Securities (Braintree) Limited	£5,812,744
Mywalit (UK) Limited	£5,811,363
Syner-Med (Pharmaceutical Products) Limited	£5,802,189
Crown Design and Development Limited	£5,800,596
JSM Associates (LON) LLP	£5,798,804
Lorclon Limited	£5,797,065
CS Property and Consultancy Ltd.	£5,793,883
Meekland Limited	£5,790,732
Newfield Information Technology Limited	£5,786,559
DNC UK Limited	£5,786,092
P.C. Tustin & Company Limited	£5,785,387
Campaign Master (UK) Limited	£5,785,096
Party Invitation Limited	£5,784,211
Elcot Service Flats Limited	£5,780,534
Queensway Associates Limited	£5,769,975
M.A.C.-RK Precision Engineering Limited	£5,769,877
FPI Limited	£5,769,184
Foster Denovo Limited	£5,768,726
Kimberley Real Estate Limited	£5,768,360
Buckmead Limited	£5,767,531
Pickering Dental Surgeries Limited	£5,763,539
BEC (London) Limited	£5,762,005
Scalable Software Ltd	£5,760,396
Cherry Advertising Limited	£5,756,712
Kallarview Homes Limited	£5,756,203
Melville Hotel Limited	£5,755,474
Warm Hearth Limited	£5,752,265
Aerzen Machines Limited	£5,750,968
Armondi UK Limited	£5,749,594
Zenoffice Limited	£5,746,638
Soul Coffee House (South) Limited	£5,742,139
Clearwater Property Estates Limited	£5,739,230
Triland Properties Limited	£5,737,134
Blendhall Limited	£5,736,204
Spruce Investments Limited	£5,733,506
Vista Al Mar Limited	£5,732,761
Ralph Lauren London Limited	£5,726,423
Penasul UK Limited	£5,723,000
Dernagree Properties Limited	£5,720,320
Handspan Limited	£5,715,332
Newmir Limited	£5,714,000
Somers Hills Limited	£5,712,764
Pudfield Investments Ltd	£5,711,650
Epsomedical (Acquisitions) Limited	£5,710,372
Independent Group (UK) Limited	£5,710,000
Bernlite Limited	£5,705,289
Nine Hotel Ventures Limited	£5,705,190
L.W. (Developments) Limited	£5,704,754
Piazza Property LLP	£5,701,206
The Imaging Centre Holdings Limited	£5,698,608
Casewise Systems Limited	£5,689,329
GHH Estate Limited	£5,689,232
Normandy Court Development Limited	£5,687,711
Cover Up Clothing Limited	£5,686,340
Upgrade Investments Limited	£5,685,491
Caesar Management Limited	£5,683,843
Ambreck LLP	£5,680,390
Flowercloud Limited	£5,679,165
Alimar Limited	£5,674,702
Ultimate Care Limited	£5,674,592
Amar Property Services Limited	£5,667,093
Intercede 2052 Limited	£5,658,647
Medicrest Limited	£5,657,388
Vashisht Surgical Limited	£5,652,167
SME Fast Foods Limited	£5,645,431
Impulse Leisure	£5,644,884
Prima Tapes & Labels Ltd	£5,644,624
Medico-Dental Holdings Limited	£5,643,314
Ventford Limited	£5,643,158
Times Square Estates Limited	£5,641,898
EC Logistics Limited	£5,641,338
Kewbridge Trading Limited	£5,639,458
Davenant Foundation School	£5,639,000
Direct Link Worldwide Limited	£5,637,731
Chigwell (London) Limited	£5,636,940
Clion Limited	£5,636,021
Engineering, Logistics and Trading International UK	£5,634,761
Munster Limited	£5,631,508
Kew Green Hotels (Birmingham LRG1) Limited	£5,626,028
Panther Hinckley (VAT) Ltd	£5,625,048
Flowstop Services Limited	£5,623,909
Nine Hospitality 3 Ltd	£5,618,570
Sail Croatia Adventures Limited	£5,616,618
Weekes Brothers (Welling) Limited	£5,616,207
Croydon House Ltd	£5,615,354

KFG Holdings Limited	£5,615,000
Backstage Centre Limited	£5,612,141
Equiniti Global Payments Limited	£5,606,000
Dhiman Enterprises Limited	£5,603,556
Kew Green Hotels (Ashford) Limited	£5,602,048
Direct Supplies (London) Limited	£5,601,701
Retallack Holidays Limited	£5,599,709
Kenard Engineering Company Limited	£5,598,359
Trading Scents (2014) Limited	£5,596,729
Elektron Tower 3 Limited	£5,594,497
Four Quarters (Ingestre Road) Ltd	£5,593,395
Barry Stewart & Sons Limited	£5,592,325
Waystone 32 Limited	£5,591,806
Denver Building Services Limited	£5,591,312
Plan B Healthcare PLC	£5,591,085
Newmarket Transport Limited	£5,590,001
The Red Lion Hotel (Henley) Limited	£5,589,669
Rycote Microphone Holdings Limited	£5,589,196
Taylor Mac Limited	£5,584,204
Finefrance Holdings Limited	£5,583,943
Brooks Laundry LLP	£5,582,916
Ecohomes Development Limited	£5,581,372
Direct Supplies (2014) Group Limited	£5,576,913
Property Plus Investments Limited	£5,576,700
Shelly Motors Limited	£5,573,710
Kingrose Limited	£5,572,549
Q.N. Hotels (Wrexham) Limited	£5,572,337
Park House Residential Developments Limited	£5,570,006
Shoreland Limited	£5,566,853
Whitstable Homes Ltd	£5,566,109
Maker Properties Ltd	£5,565,570
Bimax Chemicals Limited	£5,562,399
Ambika Investments Limited	£5,561,992
Golden Meadows Limited	£5,561,509
Elmswood Properties Limited	£5,554,189
Crane Apartments Limited	£5,553,186
Empire Investment Capital Limited	£5,552,215
Kailash Estates Limited	£5,550,704
Queenring Limited	£5,549,835
Saiwil Limited	£5,549,344
Mew Investments Ltd	£5,548,671
Wilman Marine Limited	£5,546,963
Livingston Group Limited	£5,546,000
Valley Primary School	£5,540,000
Barrett Industrial Limited	£5,539,466
TFC Properties Limited	£5,533,989
Royal School of Needlework (The)	£5,531,215
Banks Hotel Limited	£5,530,537
Bickerton's Aerodromes Limited	£5,530,508
Gaat International Ltd	£5,530,147
Grayshott Investments Limited	£5,526,980
Burlodge Group Limited	£5,525,063
The Placement Group Healthcare Limited	£5,524,426
KGN Developments Limited	£5,520,146
Clinical Pathology Accreditation (UK) Limited	£5,518,351
Experis Resource Support Services Limited	£5,512,000
Photon Properties Limited	£5,511,915
Michael James Autos PLC	£5,511,761
Digico Europe Limited	£5,500,000
City & Docklands (W3) Limited	£5,498,526
Questmoor Limited	£5,493,129
Prosidion Limited	£5,491,000
IM Estates Limited	£5,490,976
Powerbase Management Company Limited	£5,489,501
Brimheath Developments Limited	£5,484,624
Kingpin Communications Limited	£5,484,196
Dee Gee Properties Limited	£5,483,769
Grafton Flats Limited	£5,481,298
Benja Properties Limited	£5,480,046
Zandera Ltd	£5,480,000
Country Rhythm Limited	£5,478,374
FSI (FM Solutions) Limited	£5,476,681
Reliance Entertainment Productions 12 Ltd	£5,471,271
Foster & Allen Holdings Limited	£5,470,476
Wandle Valley School	£5,469,279
Shellen Construction Limited	£5,468,128
Reliance Investments Ltd	£5,467,239
Charterhouse Ilford Limited	£5,463,553
Solai House Limited	£5,462,655
Park Green Investments Limited	£5,461,071
Lightwood Strategic Limited	£5,460,279
Lee Industrial Limited	£5,455,892
Propertycoe Limited	£5,449,220
Sweetland Properties Limited	£5,448,002
Healy Refrigeration & Air Conditioning Services Ltd	£5,444,528
Telbridge Motor Company Limited	£5,443,740
ABP Packaging Limited	£5,442,483
SME (Pizza) Limited	£5,442,398
Chawla & Gulati Property Investments Limited	£5,441,921
Dependable Homes Limited	£5,441,892
Butler & Young Approved Inspectors Limited	£5,441,700
Johnson Group Limited	£5,432,802
Van Gastel Beheer Limited	£5,432,310
MDJ Investments Limited	£5,432,072
Bio-Rad Services UK Limited	£5,430,000
Corporate Solutions Consulting Limited	£5,429,751
John Artis Limited	£5,426,653
AP Asset Management Limited	£5,426,557
Frankham Consultancy Group Limited	£5,425,870
Ahern Land Reclamation Limited	£5,424,626
Avocado Developments Wealdstone Limited	£5,420,805
City & Commercial Holdings Limited	£5,420,622
Express Toughening Ltd	£5,416,198
SAB Properties (London) Limited	£5,414,420
City Tool Hire Limited	£5,413,630
Thothaal Group Limited	£5,409,309
London Sovereign Limited	£5,405,000
Frankel Portfolio Property LLP	£5,404,210
Lester Hotels (Finchley) Limited	£5,403,184
Toroce Investments Ltd	£5,399,144
Cloudview Holdings Limited	£5,397,384
155 Staines Road Ltd	£5,396,709
Jancett Childcare & Jace Training Limited	£5,396,039
Zeco Limited	£5,394,586
Marco Polo Properties Limited	£5,392,937
ACM Environmental PLC	£5,392,608
Cummins Associates Limited	£5,384,231
Anglo-Dal Limited	£5,382,237
Velani & Velani Ltd	£5,382,199
Kewstone Limited	£5,381,082
Headmasters Salons Limited	£5,376,684
Aquila Maldon Limited	£5,374,980
Galliard Estates Limited	£5,373,307
Grace Baptist Trust Corporation	£5,371,942
Coyle Equipment Services Limited	£5,370,670
Koenig & Bauer (UK) Limited	£5,366,492
Grovetowns Southern Limited	£5,365,491
Earth-I Ltd	£5,364,741
Mont Rose College of Management and Sciences Ltd	£5,364,673
Globegold Limited	£5,364,310
De Vere Homes Limited	£5,361,375
Vlasak Holdings Limited	£5,358,957
Steel Yard Trading LLP	£5,358,324
Kalbro Investments Limited	£5,357,147
Barnardo Developments Limited	£5,356,357
Palmera Holdings Limited	£5,356,071
Riverstone Pictures (CMP) Limited	£5,352,066
Stonebourne Properties Limited	£5,351,899
Leyton Clubs (London) Limited	£5,349,771
Pegrid Limited	£5,347,549
VASBP Limited	£5,347,255
181 HR Chigwell LLP	£5,344,325
A & J Ryan Mechanical Services Limited	£5,339,412
Blackfriars Land Company Limited	£5,339,144

Company	Value
AMB Property Ltd	£5,338,070
Paje Limited	£5,336,165
Fieldgrange Properties Limited	£5,336,038
Green Homes Investment Ltd	£5,323,731
Heathcrest Limited	£5,322,930
Sienna Real Estate Ltd	£5,322,799
Full House Restaurants Limited	£5,321,236
Greenyard Prepared UK Limited	£5,317,355
Moyvale Properties Limited	£5,316,824
Chi-Chi Collection Limited	£5,312,494
Exterior Plas Limited	£5,310,691
Right Choice Property Holdings Limited	£5,309,494
RVT Group Limited	£5,304,061
Brickline Properties Limited	£5,303,700
FTE & M Limited	£5,302,270
Mercurius Synergy LLP	£5,300,906
Genesius Film Partners LLP	£5,300,569
Headstart 4 Life Limited	£5,300,209
Pink Fortress Limited	£5,297,371
Eurochoice Limited	£5,293,382
THS Group Limited	£5,290,555
Easymix Concrete UK Ltd	£5,289,799
Zebrak London Limited	£5,287,860
DBA Advisors Limited	£5,286,716
Forss Wind Farm Limited.	£5,286,000
Silvermead Properties Ltd	£5,283,786
Alim Investments Limited	£5,279,675
Panther AL (VAT) Limited	£5,279,398
BP Indonesia Investment Limited	£5,276,353
Global Business Trade LLP	£5,272,739
Fairway of Course Limited	£5,272,670
Beddington Park Academy Trust	£5,271,000
Besimcho Limited	£5,270,298
Broadberry Data Systems Limited	£5,269,613
Reliance Entertainment Productions Scandi Ltd	£5,269,034
Dalemead Care Home Limited	£5,266,979
HFSI Limited	£5,262,274
Tackle Guru Limited	£5,262,109
Ski Solutions Limited	£5,261,821
Platinum Gold Homes Limited	£5,260,407
Chantry Securities Limited	£5,258,013
Central Office and Commercial Properties Limited	£5,255,481
By Malene Birger UK Ltd.	£5,253,000
Marble Lending Limited	£5,251,412
Crossways Care (UK) Limited	£5,251,093
Oaktree Property Company Limited	£5,248,149
Taj Securities Company Number Two Limited	£5,247,047
Navblue Limited	£5,246,000
Sinclair House Properties Limited	£5,245,409
Lord Street Properties (Southport) Limited	£5,244,797
Ranks Enterprises Limited	£5,243,576
Roseplot Properties Limited	£5,241,738
The Whiter Smile Limited	£5,241,175
Transcar Projects Limited	£5,240,367
Crownstar Limited	£5,239,834
Netmac Limited	£5,239,671
Daleham Finance Limited	£5,239,033
SHL Product Ltd	£5,236,234
Seasoned Events Limited	£5,236,040
Aerial Scaffolding Limited	£5,235,914
Cassra LLP	£5,233,304
Dalco Developments Limited	£5,231,460
ESP Networks Limited	£5,228,180
Willco Properties Ltd	£5,223,241
Office Overload Limited	£5,222,438
Hi - Line Wines Limited	£5,220,125
Winscales Moor Windfarm Limited	£5,217,476
Anella Limited	£5,215,846
John F. Hunt Hire Centres Ltd	£5,215,564
Geomac Limited	£5,214,940
UK Addiction Treatment Group Limited	£5,210,883
Singer & James Limited	£5,210,532
TER AG Ltd.	£5,205,477
Milcars (Radlett) Limited	£5,202,368
Claremont Care Services Limited	£5,201,762
RSI Retail Solutions Limited	£5,200,737
Pharmvit Limited	£5,199,113
Cegal Limited	£5,198,228
Moriarty Haulage Limited	£5,197,901
Chainkey Limited	£5,197,000
Ealing Community Transport	£5,196,280
Distinction Investments Limited	£5,195,894
Sidan Trading Holdings Limited	£5,195,867
Rosewell Properties Limited	£5,194,984
Black Twig Limited	£5,194,787
Glansevern Properties Limited	£5,194,199
Raffingers Advisory Limited	£5,193,460
Yparho Limited	£5,193,124
Edinburgh Retail LLP	£5,190,414
B F Design Solutions Limited	£5,186,796
Monument Assets Limited	£5,184,438
Abode Hallam Ltd	£5,180,923
Coughlans Bakeries Limited	£5,179,547
Radiation Limited	£5,178,419
NCQ Developments Limited	£5,177,353
Hayre Investments & Developments Limited	£5,175,782
Nature's Finest Food Products Limited	£5,175,766
Ten Motives Limited	£5,173,000
Mundays LLP	£5,171,278
Essex Road Development Limited	£5,171,117
Tudor Bank Limited	£5,169,856
Easyoffice Rental Limited	£5,166,683
Bellis Homes Limited	£5,156,079
Belgrave Land (Management) Limited	£5,155,444
WK Properties Limited	£5,149,714
Hawthorn Crow Limited	£5,148,897
SHL People Solutions Group Holdings Ltd.	£5,147,000
William Hartley Group Limited	£5,145,296
Willhay Management Limited	£5,145,235
Southbeck Investment Company Limited	£5,143,405
Strategic Imperatives Limited	£5,140,402
Gibbs Gillespie Sales Limited	£5,138,329
Ghai & Co. Limited	£5,137,507
Guideline Lift Services Limited	£5,135,159
Upper Street Investments LLP	£5,135,076
Roseberry Property Development Company Limited	£5,134,838
Humberside Land Limited	£5,132,378
Asap Growth Limited	£5,131,800
Dakota Developments Limited	£5,129,770
Sovereign Business Integration Group PLC	£5,129,243
TPS Abbeydale Archway Limited	£5,126,106
Drayton Kirk Ltd	£5,125,571
Frasers and Son Ltd	£5,122,512
Johalian Property Limited	£5,120,760
West Thurrock Academy	£5,119,315
Brenray Holdings Ltd	£5,118,250
Humphrey & Stretton (Properties) Limited	£5,115,202
CIKU Construction Services Limited	£5,114,921
Perfect Smile Newcastle Limited	£5,114,778
Old Vicarage School Trust	£5,113,541
Pharmasure Limited	£5,113,464
Tyco European Metal Framing Limited	£5,113,000
Pure Bricks Limited	£5,112,774
Becontree Estates Ltd	£5,108,100
Genie Energy UK Ltd	£5,107,667
EDC Systems Limited	£5,107,031
RIG Medical Recruit Limited	£5,103,000
Stanbreck Properties Ltd	£5,101,975
CWR Capital Ltd	£5,100,729
Stafford-Miller Limited	£5,100,000
Oakburn Investment Holdings Limited	£5,100,000
Westfields Homes Limited	£5,098,134
Green Lane Goose Limited	£5,096,755
UK Salads Investments Limited	£5,094,427

Company	Amount
Nine Hotel Investments Limited	£5,094,129
The Offie Limited	£5,089,589
First Atlantic Finance Limited	£5,084,578
Audiotonix Limited	£5,084,000
Honister Capital Holdings I Limited	£5,082,527
Kew Green Hotels (Taunton) Limited	£5,082,451
Ist Developments Limited	£5,080,859
GMK Pepper Holdings Limited	£5,073,414
Unique Atlantic Seafood Limited	£5,070,586
Charteroak Estates Limited	£5,068,947
Ebenezer Bethel UK Limited	£5,064,121
Tracker Network (UK) Limited	£5,062,000
Court Lodge Epsom Limited	£5,061,527
City of London Holdings & Investments Limited	£5,058,013
Davenant Centre (The)	£5,053,757
London Urban Investments Limited	£5,053,673
C.V.J. Properties Ltd	£5,052,150
Financial Management Limited	£5,048,068
Mission Recordings Limited	£5,047,515
GVE London Ltd	£5,047,175
F A Firman (Harold Wood) Limited	£5,046,911
Lee Savell Properties Limited	£5,046,693
Interchemprod and Invest Ltd	£5,043,818
B & A Group Liverpool Street Limited	£5,040,265
MDJ Group Ltd.	£5,040,000
Millennium Property (London) Limited	£5,039,644
Mokarabia Limited	£5,034,080
Inspired Learning Group (UK) Limited	£5,033,773
Unit 2 (Rickmansworth) Limited	£5,025,641
Purley Point Limited	£5,023,712
Welcome To England (Hotels) Limited	£5,023,045
Kynoch Vets Limited	£5,020,084
Harlington Chambers Limited	£5,017,325
Manelia Limited	£5,016,539
LNOC Limited	£5,016,467
Profresh Solutions Limited	£5,012,472
Armitage BC1 Limited	£5,009,356
CML Projects Technology Limited	£5,007,346
Mini Club UK Limited	£5,007,000
Delta Membrane Systems Limited	£5,005,302
Haemonetics Asia UK Ltd	£5,005,103
Purfleet Commercials Limited	£5,002,097
Gall Holdings Limited	£5,000,200
Odris Holdings Limited	£5,000,200

Age of Companies

1800s [21]

Barnardo's
Beale's Limited
Cadbury Schweppes Overseas Ltd
Cardiff Property PLC
Chubb International Holdings Ltd
Coca-Cola European Partners GB Ltd
Delta Limited
Esso Petroleum Co Ltd
Faber Prest Limited
Humberside Land Limited
JCA Charitable Foundation
Kodak Limited
Lord Street Properties (Southport)
Mondelez UK Holdings & Services Ltd
N & C Building Products Ltd
Rhodia International Holdings Ltd
Royal School of Needlework
Smith Kline & French Laboratories
Solvay Solutions UK Limited
Towers & Co.,Limited
Walker Greenbank PLC.

1900-1909 [20]

Air Products PLC
Clarges Pharmaceuticals Ltd
I.P. Clarke & Co. Limited
Coats Group PLC
William Croxson & Son,Limited
Dashtag
Early Learning Centre Limited
Eskaylab Limited
Football Association Limited
Hilton UK Hotels Limited
Institute of Grocery Distribution
Lubricants UK Limited
Nicholls & Clarke Limited
Procter & Gamble Limited
Reedham Children's Trust
Renault U.K. Limited
Stora Enso Holdings UK Limited
Trollope & Colls Limited
Vestey Holdings Limited
Watford Association Football Club

1910-1919 [25]

Accolade Wines Limited
Agility Logistics Limited
Archer Daniels Midland Erith Ltd
BP Exploration Company (Middle East)
BP Shipping Limited
Benson & Hedges Limited
Chubb Fire Limited
D.D.D. Limited
Dewhurst PLC
Essex County Laundry,Limited
Esso Property Management Company,
GPG (UK) Holdings Limited
J. Gardner Holdings Limited
Harris & Bailey Limited
F.Hinds Limited
Ernest Jackson & Co. Limited
Reed Business Information Ltd
S & B Herba Foods Limited
SEM Limited
Share and Debenture Trust Ltd
Tati Co Ltd
Volex PLC
Western United Investment Co Ltd
World Transport Agency Limited
G.R.Wright & Sons Limited

1920-1929 [50]

Armstrong World Industries Ltd
BP Chemicals Limited
BP Greece Limited
BP Pension Trustees Limited
Thomas Bates & Son Limited
Beecham Group P L C
Bishop & Sons' Depositories Ltd
Bollore Logistics UK Ltd
Boyden & Co.Limited
William Boyer & Sons, Limited
Burhill Estates Co Ltd
Chep UK Limited
Clifford Property Co Ltd
Complete Coffee Limited
Del Monte Europe Limited
Esso Exploration and Production UK
John E.Fells & Sons Limited
Filross Securities Limited
A.A.Fisher Limited
Fresh Wharf Estates Limited
GlaxoSmithKline Finance PLC
Harsco Infrastructure Group Ltd
Horlicks Limited
John Laing Construction Ltd
Land Management Limited
Link Corporate Trustees (UK) Ltd
London Irish Rugby Football Ground
Merck Sharp & Dohme (Holdings) Ltd
Mondelez UK Limited
Mothercare Group Limited
Norfolk Capital Hotels Limited
North Atlantic Fishing Co Ltd
Parry Murray & Co Ltd
Rhodia Limited
Richmond and Hillcroft Adult and Community College
Rooff Group Limited
Roomes Stores,Limited
Royal British Legion Poppy Factory
Selecta UK Holding Limited
Skanska Construction (Regions) Ltd
Skanska Construction UK Ltd
SmithKline Beecham (SWG) Ltd
SmithKline Beecham Research Ltd
Stora Enso Timber UK Limited
Tanjong PLC
Thorntons Limited
Unbar Rothon Limited
United Technologies Finance (U.K.)
Vitec Group PLC.
Wellcome Foundation Limited

1930-1939 [82]

Abbey Developments Limited
Anglia Secure Homes (South East) Ltd
Anglo-Dal Limited
Austin Company of (U.K.) Ltd
BP Chemicals Investments Ltd
BP Exploration Operating Co Ltd
BP Global Investments Limited
BP Investment Management Ltd
BP Kuwait Limited
BP Oil International Limited
Beacon (Mimms) Limited
Bickerton's Aerodromes Limited
Birds Eye Limited
Britannia Refined Metals Ltd
F.J. Church & Sons Limited
Coats Industrial Thread Ltd
Harry A.Coff,Limited
Combat Stress
Condor Group Limited
Continental Tyre Group Ltd.
Cooper Estates Limited
Coughlans Bakeries Limited
Covidien UK Limited
Robert Deards Limited
Deards Services Limited
Delbanco Meyer & Co Ltd
Gordon Durham & Co.Limited
H.Evans & Sons Limited
Films & Equipments Limited
Fishpools Limited
G4S Cash Solutions (UK) Ltd
Gillette U.K. Limited
Glaxo Group Limited
Gould International UK Limited
Grange Centre for People with Disabilities
Grant & Boyd Limited
Gravesend and District Real Estate Co
Grays Thurrock Properties Ltd
H.W.M. Limited
Hapag-Lloyd (U.K.) Limited
Harsco (U.K.) Limited
Hawthorne Trust Limited
Haymarket Media Group Ltd.
F.W. Hipkin Limited
H.C. Jones & Co (Surrey) Ltd
Kendon Packaging Group PLC
W.D.King Limited
Land Finance & Mortgage Corporation
Lindt & Sprungli (U.K.) Ltd
Marsdens Caterers of Sheffield Ltd
Mentmore Limited
Mitcham Garden Village
A.E.Monk & Co.(London) Ltd
Nicholls & Clarke Glass Ltd
Panalpina World Transport Ltd
Panther Securities P L C
Panther Shop Investments Ltd
Quality Line Transport Limited
Dennis Reed Limited
Russell Finex Limited
Secomak Limited
Security Monitoring Centres Ltd
Senior PLC
Seven Seas Limited
Simmons & Hawker Limited
SmithKline Beecham (Investments) Ltd
D.J.Squire & Co.,Limited
Stafford-Miller Limited
F.C. Stark Limited
Swan Mill (Holdings) Limited
Trading Post Limited
Trochair Limited
W.A. Truelove & Son Limited
Ugo Foods Group Limited
Unilever UK Limited
Universal Tyre Company (Deptford)
Volkerinfra Limited
Volkerstevin Limited
Wates Group Services Limited
Wilsons Automobiles and Coachworks
Xerox (UK) Limited
Xerox Finance Limited

1940-1949 [69]

Aldis of Barking Limited
Architectural Decorators Ltd
BP Exploration (Caspian Sea) Ltd
BP Oil UK Limited
Berwen Limited

Bic U.K. Limited
Brentwick Limited
Brianco Services Limited
British Danubian Trade Development Co
British Midland Airways Ltd
Brownings Electric Co Ltd
Cadbury Schweppes Finance Ltd
Cargill Chocolate UK Limited
Centronic Limited
Chubb (NI) Limited
Clancy Docwra Limited
J Clubb Limited
Coborn Engineering Co Ltd
F. Copson Limited
Dairy Crest (Services) Limited
Day Group Limited
Denecroft Estates Limited
Dennys Uniforms Limited
Dependable Homes Limited
Donovan Bros. Limited
Elcot Service Flats Limited
Ellis of Richmond Limited
J.& J.Franks Limited
Fujichem Sonneborn Limited
John Guest Holdings Limited
Haltermann Carless UK Limited
Saul D Harrison & Sons PLC
Hill's Garages (Woodford) Ltd
ISS UK Limited
Jopate Estates Limited
Knight Strip Metals Limited
Hugh Langmead Limited
Lea Redway Limited
Lenham Storage Co Ltd
London School of Theology
J H Lorimer Limited
Henry Mansfield Limited
Marcantonio Foods Limited
Mayfair Housing & Commercial Investments
Medlock Electrical Distributors Ltd
Navigator Terminals Windmill Ltd
Norfolk Capital Group Limited
Pandrol International Limited
Poland Street Properties Ltd
Pricketts Limited
Procter & Gamble (Health & Beauty Care)
Ripmax Limited
Salmon Management and Finance Ltd
Schenker Limited
Schwing Stetter (UK) Ltd
Sifcon International PLC
Silverson Machines Limited
Skanska Cementation International
Spicers Limited
St.Helen's School Northwood
H.Stain Limited
Strand Court Properties Ltd
John Street & Company (Surrey) Ltd
Thomas,Arthur & Gordon,Limited
A.L.Tozer Limited
Wates Developments Limited
Weekes Brothers (Welling) Ltd
Wolters Kluwer (UK) Limited
E Wood Holdings Limited

1950-1959 [119]

Abbey Group Limited
Abbey Investments Limited
Ian Allan Travel Limited
Anthony Property Co. Limited
Charles Austen Pumps Limited
BP Exploration (Angola) Ltd
BP Exploration Orinoco Limited
BP International Limited
BP Middle East Limited
BP Oil Vietnam Limited
BP Turkey Refining Limited
Babcock Wanson UK Limited
Babington House School Limited
Black Arrow Group Limited
Blakley Electrics Limited
British Airways Associated Companies
British Airways Holidays Ltd
Burroughs Wellcome International Ltd
CED Limited
CP Holdings Limited
Cardiff Ground Rents Limited
Carigluz Investment Co Limited
A.W.Champion Limited
Chubb Fire & Security Limited
Chubb Group Limited
Cie PLC
Coldunell Limited
Collins Construction Ltd
Consolidated Equities Limited
Continental U.K. Group Holdings Ltd
Cossam Investment Co Ltd
Cresta Estates Limited
Croydon Logistics Limited
Curtis Holt Limited
Derrin Brothers Properties Ltd
Dial Investments Limited
European Springs and Pressings Ltd
Exel Freight Management (UK) Ltd
S. Franses Limited
Alexander Fraser Holdings Ltd
Fraserfort Limited
G3 Worldwide Mail (UK) Limited
GE Money Home Finance Limited
Geodis FF United Kingdom Ltd.
Glaxo Wellcome UK Limited
GlaxoSmithKline Caribbean Ltd
Grace Baptist Trust Corporation
Grafton Flats Limited
D.Green & Co.(Stoke Newington) Ltd
F.H. Hale & Sons (Builders) Ltd
Halliford School Limited
Harlington Chambers Limited
Harsco Metals Holdings Limited
Hertz (U.K.) Limited
Higgs International Limited
Howard Humphreys & Partners Ltd
Hy-Ten Limited
ITW Limited
Intercontinental Hotels Group Services Company
International Marine Transportation
J. Isaacs Management Limited
James Development Co Ltd
Kellogg Brown & Root Limited
H.H.Keys Estates Limited
King's House School Trust (Richmond)
Geo. Kingsbury Holdings Ltd
John Laing International Ltd
Lavender Property Investments Ltd
Lowery Limited
Macarthys Laboratories Limited
Manpower PLC
Marwin Securities Limited
Masters of Beckenham Limited
Minton Holdings Limited
Mobil Trading and Supply Ltd
Mood Media Limited
Mothercare UK Limited
New River Holdings Limited
Norwood Schools Ltd.
Nuffield Health
Oakburn Properties Limited
Orley Farm School Trust
Pandrol Limited
Park Rutland Investments (London)
Penspen Limited
Pickering Dental Surgeries Ltd
Premier Quilting Co Ltd
M.Price Limited
R.T.Rate Limited
Rimex Metals (U.K.) Limited
Rose Bruford College of Theatre and Performance
Russell & Bromley Limited
A Russell (Farmers) Limited
S.S.S.Gears Limited
Salaft Properties Limited
Schweppes Limited
T.E.Scudder Limited
Signet Group Limited
SmithKline Beecham Marketing and Technical Services
South Mimms Services Limited
Spar (UK) Limited
Stonebourne Properties Limited
Stonplan Limited
Sunshine Properties Limited
Sutton Winson Limited
Swakeleys Properties Limited
Tarian Investment Co. Limited
John A.Taylor & Sons Limited
Thompson Bros. (Esher) Limited
A.E.Thorogood Limited
Track Technology Limited
United Living (North) Limited
Universal Tyres and Spares Ltd
Vine Investment Co Ltd
Vlasak Holdings Limited
Volkerhighways Limited
Watch It Come Down Limited
Woodgavil Properties Limited
Xerox Limited

1960-1969 [242]

ACS International Schools Ltd
ADM Arkady Limited
ADM Pura Limited
ADM Trading (UK) Limited
Abbeyfield Southern Oaks
Adda Hotels
Aldro School Educational Trust Ltd
Alimar Limited
Ian Allan Group Limited
David Allen Holdings Limited
Allport Cargo Services Limited
Analog Devices Limited
Astellas Pharma Ltd.
Aston Heating Limited
Astor Lodge Holdings Limited
Atkins Limited
Atkins Properties Limited
Attewell Limited
Automatic Data Processing Ltd
BP (Abu Dhabi) Limited
BP Amoco Exploration (Faroes) Ltd
BP Car Fleet Limited
BP Exploration Beta Limited
BP Gas Marketing Limited
BP Properties Limited
Barilone Properties Limited

Barnardo Developments Limited
Bonne Bouche Catering Limited
Bosch Automotive Service Solutions Ltd
Boss & Co.Limited
M.& R.Bowman Limited
G E Bowra Group Limited
Breyer Group PLC
Brinor Investments Limited
Britannic Trading Limited
British Board of Agrement
Bromley Business Centre (Holdings) Ltd.
Brown and Mason Limited
Martin Bunzl International Ltd
Burnt Common Nurseries Limited
Calbrook Cars Limited
Camden Development Co Ltd
Cantillon Limited
P.J. Carey Plant Hire (Oval) Ltd
Carnarvon Hotels Limited
Castle Green Kendal Limited
Castlestone Investments Ltd
Caversham Finance Limited
Cellarmaster Wines Holdings (UK) Ltd
Cementation Skanska Limited
Chicken Cabins Limited
T.Choithram & Sons (London) Ltd
City & Commercial Holdings Ltd
Clancy Developments Limited
Clancy Plant Limited
Clearwater Property Co Ltd
V.G.Clements (Contractors) Ltd
Clivnars Limited
Cobham Hall
Compagnie Fruitiere UK Limited
Richard Cook Limited
Coopers Investments Limited
Cousins Holdings Limited
Owen Coyle Managements Ltd
Cressdene Limited
Crispin & Borst Limited
Crockford Park Properties Ltd
Cromwell Investments (Richmond) Ltd
Cromwell Investments Limited
Croudace Homes Limited
D & M Audiovisual Ltd
Davis and Dann Limited
Deanplan Limited
Designplan Lighting Limited
Diomed Developments Limited
Dovestone Estates Limited
Drift Bridge Garage Limited
Dunlop International Europe Ltd
Edge Grove School Trust Ltd
Electrosonic Limited
Emcor Group (UK) PLC
Equiniti Services Limited
Ewell Castle School
ExxonMobil Chemical Limited
Fairview Estates (Housing) Ltd
Feabrex Limited
Feltonfleet School Trust Ltd
Ferrero UK Limited
F A Firman (Harold Wood) Ltd
A.A.Fisher (Properties) Ltd
Fishpools (Finance) Limited
Five Star Inns Limited
Fourway Communication Limited
Michael Franklin (Chemists) Ltd
GBST Limited
Galderma (U.K.) Limited
Galliford Try PLC
Galliford Try Partnerships Ltd

Gibbs & Ball Limited
Gita Properties Limited
Glansevern Properties Limited
Glaxo Operations UK Limited
GlaxoSmithKline Consumer Healthcare (UK) (No.1)
GlaxoSmithKline Research & Development
Gold Group International Ltd
Grant & Bowman Limited
Greystead Properties Limited
Griffon Land Holdings Limited
Grohe Limited
John Guest Speedfit Limited
HAGS-SMP Limited
Hadgate Limited
Harsco Metals Group Limited
C.P. Hart & Sons Limited
Harvard International Limited
Haymarket Publishing Services Ltd
Helius Investments Limited
Higgins Construction PLC
Higgins Homes PLC
S.Hille & Co.(Holdings) Ltd
Hilton International Hotels (UK) Ltd
Homefield Preparatory School Trust
Hy-Ten Group Limited
ISS Facility Services Limited
Inner Town Homes Limited
International Society for Krishna Consciousness
JCDecaux United Limited
Jabac Finances Limited
Katsouris Brothers Limited
Kavo Dental Limited
Kellogg Brown & Root (Greenford) Ltd
Kenard Engineering Co Ltd
Killinchy Aerospace Holdings Ltd
George Killoughery Limited
Kimal PLC
W.J.King (Garages) Limited
Geo. Kingsbury Machine Tools Ltd
Koenig & Bauer (UK) Limited
Lingerham Properties Limited
Livingston Ltd
Lodestar Properties Limited
Lodge Bros. (Funerals) Limited
Lodge Hotels (London) Limited
Lyndon Scaffolding PLC
MBM Forest Products Limited
Manpower Services Limited
Martin-Baker Aircraft Co Ltd
McGee Civil Engineering Ltd
McGee Group (Holdings) Limited
Menzies Group Holdings Limited
Menzies World Cargo Limited
Merck Sharp & Dohme Limited
Motivair Compressors Limited
Mouskos & Sons Co. Limited
NCMT Limited
Navigator Terminals Seal Sands Ltd
Neopost Technologies Limited
W.R.Newland & Sons Limited
Nicon Developments Limited
Norsette Investment Co. Ltd
Office Overload Limited
Oncoland Limited
Parkdale Investments Limited
Parkside Group Limited
Parkside Leisure Limited
Parkside School Trust
Peacock Homes Limited
Peak Securities Limited

Photo - Me International P L C
Pleythorne Limited
Derek Pobjoy Investments Ltd
Polar Audio Limited
Polybags Limited
Purcell School
R O Ventures Limited
RO Property Management Limited
Reading Scientific Services Ltd
Reed Exhibitions Limited
D.B. Rees (Builders) Limited
Rian Properties Limited
Leslie Rogers Investments Ltd
Rokeby Educational Trust Ltd
Rowlandson Investments Limited
S-P RIL Limited
SC Leisure Group Limited
SES (Engineering Services) Ltd
Saints Transport Limited
Samaritans
Schindler Ltd.
Senior Engineering Investments Ltd
Shepperton Hotels Limited
Simat Properties Limited
Simon Holdings PLC
Six Continents Hotels International
Six Continents Investments Ltd
Six Continents Limited
Six Continents Restaurants Ltd
Skanska Cementation International Holdings
Skanska Rashleigh Weatherfoil Ltd
Skanska UK PLC
Smiths Industries Industrial Group
South Darenth Farms and Cold Store Co
Southbeck Investment Co Ltd
Southern Motor Group Limited
Southfleet Investments Limited
Michael Spiers (Jewellers) Ltd
St.Martins' (Northwood) Preparatory School Trust
St.Michael's Manor Limited
Starna Scientific Limited
Startling Music Limited
H.Stern (Jewellery) Limited
Stirling Civil Engineering Ltd
Sun Valley Foods Limited
Superdrug Stores PLC
Sweetland Properties Limited
TMD Technologies Limited
R.G. Taylor Engineering Ltd
Tchibo Coffee International Ltd
Tennay Properties Limited
Thorn Security Limited
A.E. Thorogood Investments Ltd
Threshold Land & Estates Ltd
Toshiba Information Systems (UK) Ltd
Toyota (G.B.) PLC
Trans Global Limited
Trident Garages Limited
UPS Air Couriers of America Ltd
United Living (South) Limited
United Technologies Holdings Ltd
V.S. Properties Limited
Vanguard Holdings Limited
Vinci PLC
Vinci Property Limited
Vinci UK Developments Limited
Voluntary Service Overseas
Warborough Investments Limited
Watchingwell Farms Limited
Watling Tyre Service Limited
Whelan & Grant (Contractors) Ltd

Wyevale Garden Centres Limited
Yehudi Menuhin School Limited
Yomans (London) Limited

1970-1979 [345]

A.G. Thames Holdings Limited
ADT Fire and Security PLC
Aandatta Limited
Abaris Holdings Limited
Abbey View Produce Limited
Ability Housing Association
Adelmill Limited
Aerial Scaffolding Limited
Aerzen Machines Limited
P.F. Ahern & Sons Limited
Air BP Limited
Albert Darnell Limited
Alfreds Way Investments (No. 2) Ltd
All Metal Services Limited
Amoco (Fiddich) Limited
Andgrove Property Investments Ltd
Anoopam Mission
Apex Lift & Escalator Engineers Ltd
Apollo Cleaning Services Ltd
Archer Daniels Midland (UK) Ltd
F & J Arpino Limited
John Artis Limited
Thomas Aston Homes Limited
W.S. Atkins International Ltd
Atlanta Trust Limited
BDL Group PLC
BP Africa Limited
BP Asia Pacific Holdings Ltd
BP Capital Markets P.L.C.
BP Exploration (Algeria) Ltd
BP Exploration (Alpha) Limited
BP Exploration (Delta) Limited
BP Exploration (Epsilon) Ltd
BP Exploration Indonesia Ltd
BP Marine Limited
BSW Heating Ltd
Badiani & Co Ltd
Balton CP Limited
Barnardo Services Limited
Batt Cables PLC
Berkeley Group PLC
Syd Bishop & Sons (Demolition) Ltd
Otto Bock Healthcare PLC
Body Works West at Lambton Place Ltd
Borelli Tea Holdings Limited
Brembury Properties Limited
Britannia Security Group Ltd
Brobot Petroleum Limited
Brompton Bicycle Limited
Brookpass Limited
T Brown Group Limited
J.Browne Construction Co Ltd
Brymore Investments Limited
A.Martin Bunzl Limited
Butterworth Laboratories Ltd
By Malene Birger UK Ltd.
CHG-Meridian Computer Leasing UK Ltd
CHG-Meridian UK Limited
CNOOC Petroleum Europe Limited
Canada Life (U.K.) Limited
Canada Life Limited
P.J. Carey (Contractors) Ltd
Careys New Homes Limited
Cargill Holdings
Cargill PLC
Caterham Cars Ltd.
Central Office and Commercial Properties
Chalfont Coaches of Harrow Ltd
Charterhouse Simon Limited
Cherryfield (Croydon) Limited
Chessington Nurseries Limited
Chesterhill Investments Ltd
Cimbali UK Limited
Citizen Machinery UK Ltd
City of London Holdings & Investments
Claremont Care Services Ltd
Claremont Fan Court Foundation Ltd
Cluff Oil Limited
Thomas H. Collison Limited
P. Colohan & Co. Limited
Colorcon Limited
Combe International Limited
Combined Counties Properties Ltd
Comfort Hotels Limited
Commodore Kitchens Limited
Concordia International Forwarding
Oliver Connell and Son Ltd
G. D. Cooper & Co Ltd
Cosmos Tours Limited
Crest Nicholson Operations Ltd
Crest Nicholson PLC
Currie Finance and Leasing Co Ltd
Currie Motors Kingston Limited
Currie Motors Limited
Cyberscience PLC
D.B.T. (Holdings) Limited
Day Lewis PLC
Deekay Investments Limited
Demiland Limited
Desilu Group Limited
J Devine Civil Engineering Ltd
Dhamecha Foods Limited
Diamed (G.B.) Ltd.
Dormole Limited
M.E. Duffell Limited
Dunwoody Airline Services Ltd
Durkan Holdings Limited
Durkan Limited
EMC Europe Limited
Edwardian Group Limited
Elysium Healthcare (Healthlinc) Ltd
Enfield Fancy Goods Limited
Erinastar Limited
Erith Contractors Limited
Erith Haulage Co Ltd
Essex Services Group Limited
Euro Services Limited
Europa Road Limited
European Process Plant Limited
Excelsior Textiles Limited
Exela Technologies Limited
Express Freight Services (U.K.) Ltd
FBM Metals (UK) Limited
E. Feldman Limited
Ferring Pharmaceuticals Ltd
P. Flannery Plant Hire (Oval) Ltd
Forest Freight Limited
Fujitsu General (U.K.) Co. Ltd
G4S Secure Solutions (UK) Ltd
Gade Property Developments Ltd
Galliford Try Services Limited
Garratt Services (Tooting) Ltd
German School Association Ltd
Geyfords Limited
Thomas Gibson Fine Art Ltd
Gillette Industries Limited
Gilray Plant Limited
GlaxoSmithKline Services Unlimited
Godiva Bearings (Southern) Ltd
Gould Paper Sales UK Limited
R. & I. Grant & Co. Limited
Griffon Land & Estates Limited
Grigny (UK) Limited
Grove & Dean Limited
John Guest Limited
Gulmay Limited
H.& G.Car Parks Limited
Hamton Environmental Services Ltd
Harlequin Estates (Twickenham) Ltd
Harris Commercial Repairs Ltd
Harris Commercial Sales Ltd
Harris Holdings (Grays) Ltd
Harsco Rail Limited
Heidelberg Graphic Equipment Ltd
Heley International Limited
Hertz Europe Limited
High Park Investments Limited
Himalaya Carpets Limited
Honeycroft Hill Ltd
Hoo Hing Holdings Limited
Hotel Inter-Continental London Ltd
Hotel Management International Ltd
Houlihan & Co. (Excavations) Ltd
Humphrey & Stretton (Properties) Ltd
W. Humphreys Transport (London) Ltd
Huntington House Limited
Ilapak Limited
Imagination Technologies Ltd
Industrial Chemicals Group Ltd
Jablite Limited
Jalaram Limited
Michael James Autos PLC
John S. Miller Limited
P. Johnson & Son (1976) Ltd
Leonard F.Jollye (Brookmans Park)
KBC Advanced Technologies Ltd
Kaybridge Construction (Barnet) Ltd
Kellogg Brown & Root (Services) Ltd
Keltbray Limited
Kelvin Hughes Limited
Kone PLC
Kubach & Sambrook (Metals) Ltd
Kuehne + Nagel (UK) Limited
L & M (Heating) Supplies Ltd
L.M.H. (Management Services) Ltd
L.W. (Developments) Limited
Lapid Developments Limited
Learning Tree International Ltd
Lee Industrial Limited
Lesser & Pavey Ltd.
Letchworth Hall Hotel (Trading) Ltd
Lynn Lewis Limited
Liberata UK Limited
Linden Limited
Littlecroft Properties Limited
Lorne Stewart PLC
Lubkowski Saunders and Associates
Mark Luck Limited
M.H.J. Limited
M.M.C. Investments Limited
MH Foods Limited
Maison Maurice Limited
Mala Engineering Limited
Manelia Limited
Marchanson Limited
Marke Creative Merchandise Ltd
R. Maskell Limited
Mason Pearson Bros. Limited
Maxwelton House Property Co Ltd
Medtronic Limited
Merck Consumer Healthcare Ltd

Merck Serono Limited
Metra Non-Ferrous Metals Ltd
Microlease Limited
Milcars (Radlett) Limited
Millcroft Services P.L.C.
Miller & Miller (Chemicals) Ltd
Mister Dee International Ltd
A.J. Morrisroe & Sons Limited
Mott MacDonald Group Limited
Mott MacDonald Limited
Moyvale Properties Limited
NEC (UK) Ltd.
Navigator Terminals UK Limited
Neilcott Construction Limited
Newland House School Trust Ltd
Newship Group Limited
Newship Products Group Limited
Nikon UK Limited
Nuance Group (UK) Limited
O'Halloran & O'Brien Limited
O'Hara Bros. Surfacing Limited
O'Rourke Civil & Structural Engineering
OCO Limited
Oakray Limited
Ocobase Limited
Octagon Developments Limited
Old Vicarage School Trust
Omavale Limited
Orange Music Electronic Co Ltd
Orbital Fasteners Limited
Orthene Chemicals Limited
Palacath Limited
Pan United Ltd
Pandrol (Vortok) Limited
Panther Investment Properties Ltd
Panther Trading Limited
Penspen Group Limited
Pentagon Freight Services PLC
Petrocell Holdings Limited
Pharmvit Limited
Pinder Developments Co. (Chislehurst)
Pinnacle Insurance PLC
Pirin Ltd
Pizza Hut (U.K.) Limited
PizzaExpress Limited
Pledream Properties Limited
Precision Printing Co. Limited
Prestige Nursing Limited
Prestolite Electric Limited
Prima Tapes & Labels Ltd
Purple Surgical Holdings Ltd
R K Property Investments Ltd.
Rashmian Limited
Raven Roofing and Building Supplies
Redbridge Sports Centre Trust Ltd
Rijac Properties Limited
Roalco Limited
Robinson Webster (Holdings) Ltd
Rooff Ltd
Royal Masonic School for Girls
Rushmon Limited
Russell School Trust
S.A.T.V. Publishing Limited
S.T.C.Plumbing & Heating Merchants
SHL Group Limited
Safety-Kleen U.K. Limited
Sagoo & Takhar Limited
Sahara Presentation Systems PLC
Saint Francis Hospice
Samsung C & T U.K. Limited
Saniflo Limited
Scimitar Care Hotels PLC
Selwyns Travel Limited
Shorterm Limited
Shrewsbury House School Trust Ltd
Sinai (Antiques) Limited
Singer & James Limited
Skanska Major Projects Limited
Smith and Byford Limited
Spar Food Distributors Limited
Specialist Equipment Solutions Ltd
Spectris Group Holdings Ltd
St. Aubyn's (Woodford Green) School Trust
St. George's Hill Lawn Tennis Club
Starna Limited
Strandhaven Limited
Subsea 7 Crewing Limited
Subsea 7 Treasury (UK) Limited
Ann Summers Ltd.
Sunvil International Sales Ltd
Sussex Gardens Hotels Limited
Swanbrae Limited
Synchro Clutch Co Ltd
TRAD Scaffolding Co.Limited
Tazaki Foods Limited
Tearfund
Thames Ditton Sports and Squash Club
Thenhurst Agricultural Limited
Thompsons (UK) Limited
Tilda Limited
Toly Products (U.K.) Limited
Trans Global Freight Management Ltd
Trans Global Group Limited
Trans-Britannia Properties Ltd
Transcar Projects Limited
Transform Housing & Support
Trend Machinery & Cutting Tools Ltd
Trentpeak Limited
Trueform Engineering Limited
A.E. Tyler Limited
Van Ameyde UK Limited
Vandemoortele (U.K.) Limited
Vantas International Limited
Vernon Educational Trust Ltd
Vink UK Limited
Volkerwessels UK Limited
W.T. Partnership Limited
Wates Living Space (Maintenance) Ltd
Watmough Brothers Investments Ltd
Wealmoor Limited
W K Webster & Co Ltd
Welcome To England (Hotels) Ltd
West Dorset Leisure Holidays Ltd
West One Bathrooms Limited
Whelan & Grant (Holdings) Ltd
T.W. White & Sons (Holdings) Ltd
T.W. White & Sons Limited
D.W. Windsor Limited
Wolters Kluwer Holdings (UK) PLC
Wood Group Kenny Limited
Richard Wright Music Limited
Wurth UK Limited
Zenoffice Limited
Zoroastrian Trust Funds of Europe (Incorporated)

1980-1989 [638]

7e Communications Limited
A E Properties Limited
ACI Worldwide (EMEA) Limited
ADM Milling Limited
ADT (UK) Limited
ADT Finance Limited
ADT South Africa Holding Ltd
AMD Environmental Limited
ARRI (GB) Limited
ARRI Rental Services UK Ltd
Ability Hotels (Syon Park) Ltd
Acclaim Handling Limited
Acer U.K. Limited
Acorn Truck Sales Limited
Action for Children Services Ltd
Adil Catering Limited
Advanced Logistics for Aerospace (UK)
Aeropak (Chemical Products) Ltd
Afinacorp Limited
Agri-Chemicals Limited
P.F. Ahern (London) Limited
Ahern Land Reclamation Limited
Airclaims Group (Overseas) Ltd
Aldenham Foundation
Alim Caterers Limited
Alim Investments Limited
Allen (Concrete) Limited
Amsik Limited
Amsprop London Limited
Anderson Travel Limited
Anglo Scottish Leisure Limited
Apex Car Rental (Norwich) Ltd
Apexpost Limited
Applied Laser Engineering Ltd
Asgill House Trust Limited
A.S. Ashcroft Limited
Askham Village Community Ltd
Aspect Software UK Limited
Assetsky Limited
Associated Coffee Merchants (International)
Atkins Holdings Limited
WS Atkins Limited
Atlas Cleaning Limited
Automatic Sales Limited
Axis Cleaning and Support Services
B & H Worldwide (Holdings) Ltd
BMT Defence and Security UK Ltd
BMT Group Limited
BMT Hi-Q Sigma Limited
BP Chemicals (Korea) Limited
BP Eastern Mediterranean Ltd
BP Exploration (Azerbaijan) Ltd
BP Technology Ventures Limited
Baker Ross Limited
Balgores Motors (1982) Limited
Ballward Limited
Bamrose Enterprises Limited
Bandai Namco Entertainment UK Ltd.
Bandai UK Limited
Barking Power Limited
Barrowfen Properties Limited
Beechwood Investments Limited
Beko PLC
Bell Theatre Services Limited
Belron International Limited
Bernlite Limited
Bike Alert PLC
R. J. and D. E. Billings Ltd
Bishopswood Estates Limited
Biz Karts Limited
Bizy Investments Limited
Blitzfair Limited
Bold-Rock Management and Investments Ltd
Brambles Enterprises Limited
Brambles U.K. Limited
Brausch & Co (UK) Limited
Brightsun Travel (UK) Limited
Bristol-Myers Squibb Business Services
Brit School Limited

Britannia Row Productions Ltd
British Airways Maintenance Cardiff
British Airways PLC
British American Tobacco UK Ltd
Bromcom Computers PLC
Bronzeshield Lifting Limited
Brown and Mason Holdings Ltd
Bryant Park Hospitality UK Ltd
Roberto Bucci (U.K.) Limited
Buckinghamshire Golf Co Ltd
Bugler Developments Limited
Burgess Furniture Ltd
Burhill Golf and Leisure Ltd
Burnfield Limited
Burnt Tree Group Limited
Burwater Holdings Limited
Business Systems (U.K.) Ltd
Buxton Building Contractors Ltd
Bytes Software Services Ltd
C.C. (Engineering) Limited
C.L.T. Timber and Transport Ltd
CDB (U.K.) Limited
CDK U.K. Limited
Campmoss Property Co Ltd
Canada Life Group (U.K.) Ltd
Cardinal International Limited
Carrain Limited
Casewise Systems Limited
Caskade Caterers Limited
Catalyst Corporate Development Ltd
Cembrit Limited
Centaur Property Estates Ltd
Central Property Investments Ltd
Centro PLC
Cerestar UK Ltd
Charlie Properties Limited
Charter UK Limited
Chellbrook Properties Limited
Chem-Dry Franchising Limited
Chemidex Pharma Limited
Chemilines Limited
Chep Intercontinental Containers Ltd
Cherubond Limited
Chester International Hotel Ltd
Chevaning Mining Co Ltd
Chicken Villas Limited
Children's Trust
Chilworth Manor Limited
Chubb Group (International) Ltd
Chubb Group Properties Limited
Churchill Insurance Co Ltd
Cineworld Cinemas Holdings Ltd
Cineworld Cinemas Limited
Citybond Holdings Limited
Clarence Estates (London) Ltd
Cobalt Limited
Company of Animals Limited
Compass Forest Products Ltd
Compass Group Holdings PLC
Conance Limited
Coniston Limited
Consolidated Timber Holdings Ltd
Continental Investment Limited
Cordant Cleaning Limited
Corinthia Investments Limited
Cosco Shipping (UK) Co Ltd
Counties Home Loan Management Ltd
Courtlands Estate (Richmond) Ltd
Coyle Personnel PLC
Creative Video Productions Ltd
Cromwell Holdings Limited
Croudace Portland Limited
Crown Agents Bank Limited
Crown House (Tadworth) Limited
Culham Limited
Currie Motors UK Limited
D.K. Tools Limited
D4T4 Solutions PLC
DC Management Services Limited
Dairy Crest Limited
Danly UK Limited
Davenant Centre
Davroc Limited
De Lage Landen Leasing Limited
De Vere Homes Limited
Dee Gee Properties Limited
John Deere Forestry Limited
Del Monte (UK) Limited
Del Monte Foods International Ltd
Delice de France Limited
Deltec Citimail Limited
Deltec International Courier Ltd
Demipower Limited
Denbourne Investments Limited
Denton Homes Limited
Dermal Laboratories Limited
Dermalogica (UK) Limited
Desilu Estates Limited
Devine Homes PLC
J. Devine Plant Hire Limited
Devitt Insurance Services Ltd
Dexter House Limited
Dimehome Limited
Direct Line Insurance Group PLC
Discover The World Limited
Dow Properties Limited
Durkan Estates Limited
Durkin and Sons Limited
Dwellcourt Limited
E92 Plus Limited
EMC Computer Systems (U.K.) Ltd
EWOS Limited
Eco Animal Health Group PLC
Elbrook (Cash & Carry) Limited
Elegant Electronics Limited
Elgon (Enfield) Limited
Elia International Limited
Elmbridge Village Limited
Emcor (UK) Limited
Eskan Electronics Limited
Esso UK Limited
Etcetera Construction Services Ltd
Etonbrook Properties PLC
Everglade Windows Limited
Excelredstone Converged Solutions
Excitech Limited
Expeditors International (UK) Ltd
Exterior Plas Limited
Facilicom Cleaning Services Ltd
Fairview Enfield Limited
Faithful+Gould Limited
Falcon Panel Products Limited
Family Funerals Trust Limited
Farsound Aviation Limited
Fazal Fast Foods Limited
Ferring Laboratories Limited
Fibron BX Limited
Finepoint Broadcast Limited
First Rented Housing Group Ltd
Flahive Brickwork Limited
Flahive Developments Limited
Fleetwood Developments Limited
Food Brands Group Limited
Forextra Developments Limited
Francotyp-Postalia Limited
Frelene Limited
Frisco (U.K.) Sales Limited
Frontline Technology Limited
Fuel Oils (Holdings) Limited
Fujikura Europe Limited
Fulham Football Club Limited
Future Electronics Limited
G & O Properties (London) Ltd
G4S Cash Centres (UK) Limited
G4S Security Services (UK) Ltd
GL Assessment Limited
Joseph Gallagher Limited
Gallaher Limited
Gallaher Overseas Limited
Galliard Homes Limited
Galliford Try Employment Ltd
Gantrade Europe Limited
Gartner U.K. Limited
Gate Gourmet Holdings U.K. Ltd
Generics (U.K.) Limited
Robert Gibbs (Contracting) Co Ltd
GlaxoSmithKline Capital PLC
GlaxoSmithKline Export Limited
GlaxoSmithKline International Ltd
Goal Group Limited
Golden Tours Sightseeing Ltd
Goodwin Associates Limited
Gouhari Enterprises Limited
Granherne Limited
Greencourt Property Group Ltd
Guideline Lift Services Ltd
H & S Contractors (Kent) Ltd
HEL Limited
HIC Racing (Chiswick) Limited
HIC Treasury Limited
Hale Hamilton (Valves) Limited
Hamilcourt Industrial Holdings Ltd
Handsale Limited
Harrington (Properties) Ltd
Harrogate International Hotel Ltd
Harsco Metals 385 Limited
Harte Hanks UK Limited
William Hartley Group Limited
Hasbro U.K. Limited
Hawkspare Limited
Healy Refrigeration & Air Conditioning Services
Robert Heath Heating Limited
Heathcrest Limited
Heathrow Airport Limited
Hedgemans Limited
Herbalife (U.K.) Limited
Higgins Group PLC
Higgins Investments PLC
Highrak Limited
Highway Care Group Limited
JF Hillebrand UK Limited
Hitachi Capital (UK) PLC
Homepines Investments Limited
Howarth Homes PLC
E. Ivor Hughes Educational Foundation
Hungerburger Limited
John F Hunt Limited
John F. Hunt Plant Hire Ltd
I E Music Limited
IDG International Marketing Services Europe
IHC Hotel Limited
IHC May Fair (Holdings) Ltd
IHC May Fair Hotel Limited
IHC Overseas (U.K.) Limited
IHC UK (Holdings) Limited

IMCD UK Limited
ISS Mediclean Limited
Imerys Aluminates Limited
Innotech Advisers Limited
Input Video Ltd
Inspired Learning Group (UK) Ltd
Integrated Design Limited
Interport Limited
JCDecaux UK Limited
JJ Food Service Limited
JSA Services Limited
JTC Ventures Limited
Jankel Armouring Limited
Jas Forwarding (UK) Limited
Jato Dynamics Limited
Jaysam Contractors Limited
Jetclub Limited
KBC Process Technology Limited
Kanta Enterprises Limited
Kedleston (OS Education) Ltd
Kellogg Brown & Root (U.K.) Ltd
Kellogg Brown & Root DH Ltd
Kellogg Brown & Root Holdings (U.K.)
Kellogg Brown & Root Overseas Operations
Kellogg Brown & Root Overseas Projects
Kellogg Brown & Root Projects Ltd
Kelly Communications Limited
Keltbray Plant Limited
Kentec Electronics Limited
Kenville Limited
Kerry Holdings (U.K.) Limited
Kew College
Kingswood Golf & Country Club Ltd
Kodak International Finance Ltd
Kromachem Holdings Limited
Kromachem Limited
Kuehne + Nagel Limited
L P M (Professional Recruitment) Ltd
L.M.H. Properties Limited
LG Electronics U.K. Ltd
LHR Airports Limited
Lantern Recovery Specialists PLC
Ralph Lauren London Limited
Robert Lee Distribution Ltd
Lee Savell Properties Limited
Lefroy Brooks Diffusion Ltd
Leisure and Outdoor Furniture Association
Lenta Properties Limited
Levolux Limited
Limesquare Business Parks Ltd
Linkam Scientific Instruments Ltd
London City Bond Limited
London General Insurance Co Ltd
London General Life Co Ltd
London Outpost Limited
London United Busways Limited
Longmill Realty Limited
Lymington Precision Engineers Co.
M.A.C.-RK Precision Engineering Ltd
Magnet Harlequin Limited
Majestic Wine PLC
Majestic Wine Warehouses Ltd
Mall School Trust
Mallinckrodt Chemical Limited
Mallinckrodt UK Ltd
Manchester Jetline Limited
Maple Hotels Management Co Ltd
Marande Limited
Marron Civil Engineering Ltd
Masters Pharmaceuticals Ltd
Mawpart Commercial Limited
Mayfair Carpet Gallery Limited
McGrath Bros. (Waste Control) Ltd
McGrath Brothers (Holdings) Ltd
Mechanical Services Limited
Medi-Shop Limited
Meekland Limited
Melford Commercial Properties Ltd.
Menzies Aviation (ASIG) Ltd
Meritcape Limited
Metaswitch Networks Ltd
Metro Mechanical Services Ltd
Metropolitan Electrical Services Ltd
Miko Coffee Limited
Milsom Hotels Limited
Mini Club UK Limited
Minverport Enterprises Limited
Mizen Design/Build Ltd.
Mizen Properties Limited
Mohan Building Services Ltd
Mollart Engineering Limited
Moove Lubricants Limited
Mortgage Guarantee Limited
Mothercare PLC.
Mott MacDonald International Ltd
Mr. Plant Hire PLC
Mulalley & Co. Limited
Mulcroft Limited
Munnelly Support Services Ltd
NDK Europe Limited
NEC Capital (UK) PLC
Necessity Supplies Limited
Neilcott Construction Services Ltd
Neilcott Holdings Limited
Neston Court Limited
Netmac Limited
Newmarket Holidays Limited
Newmarket Promotions Limited
Newmir Limited
Nippon Express (U.K.) Limited
Nissin (U.K.) Limited
Noon Products Limited
Northamber PLC
O'Hara Property Investment Holding Co
Oakburn Investment Holdings Ltd
Oakfield (Foods) Limited
Oatlands Investments Limited
Odessa Print Group Ltd
Offer Group Ltd
Oki Europe Limited
Onkar International Limited
Opecprime Development Limited
Opecprime Properties Limited
Optimum Group Services PLC
Original London Sightseeing Tour Ltd
Orlando Limited
Ovationdata Limited
PFU (EMEA) Limited
Padwicks Travel (Wembley) Ltd
Michael Page Holdings Limited
Michael Page International Holdings
Michael Page Partnership Ltd
Michael Page Recruitment Group Ltd
Palladio Estates Limited
Pancredit Systems Ltd.
Pantheon Hotels and Leisure Ltd
Paramount 26 Limited
Pass J. Holdings Limited
Peppercorn Property Investments Ltd
Periworld Limited
Pet Mate Limited
Petersham Hotel Limited
Petrolvalves (G.B.) Limited
Picturehouse Cinemas Limited
Planshore Limited
Plastico Limited
Plaut International Limited
Plexus Europe Limited
Porcelanosa Group Limited
Port of London Properties Ltd
Pourshins Limited
Precision Engineering Plastics Ltd
Premier Decorations Limited
Premier Fruit & Nut Limited
Premier PLC
Premium Credit Limited
Primat Recruitment Limited
Princess Alice Hospice
L.E. Pritchitt & Co Ltd
Pudfield Investments Ltd
Pura Foods Limited
Purfleet Commercials Limited
QBS Software Limited
Quality Spirits International Ltd
Queenring Limited
Questmoor Limited
RANC Care Homes Limited
Ravensale Limited
Red Circle Security Services Ltd
Redab PLC
Reichhold UK Limited
Remy's Limited
Renewable Energy Systems Ltd
Resham PLC
Residential Land Limited
Residential Management Group Ltd
Rhiannon Properties Limited
Richardson Roofing Co Ltd
Road Tech Computer Systems Ltd
Rock & Alluvium Limited
Rockley Dene Homes Limited
Roman Investments Limited
Roseberry Property Development Co Ltd
Rowhurst Limited
Donald Russell Limited
Ruxley Holdings Limited
A & J Ryan Mechanical Services Ltd
S M E Enterprise Limited
S.L.E. Limited
SAP (UK) Limited
SG Equipment Finance (December) Ltd
SG Technologies Limited
SME Fast Foods Limited
SME Group PLC
SME Trading Limited
Saba Park Services UK Limited
Safegold Properties Limited
Safetell Limited
Samax Resources Limited
Sandkot Limited
Sapiens (UK) Limited
Sara (London) Limited
Sartra International Limited
Satco Investments Limited
Schering-Plough Holdings Ltd
Schinvest Limited
Science, Engineering and Manufacturing Technologies Alliance
Scotline Limited
Sea, Air & Land Forwarding Ltd
Seabrook Holdings Limited
Seacon Terminals Limited
Sega Amusements International Ltd
Sega Europe Limited
Select Plant Hire Co Ltd
Senior UK Limited

Servipharm Limited
Setfirst Limited
Shadowgrade Developments Ltd
Shaneel Enterprises Limited
Sharan Properties Limited
Sheplord Limited
Sherrygreen Limited
Shogun Finance Limited
Shoppertrak Limited
Silvermere Golf & Leisure Ltd
Site Sales Marketing Limited
Sitecrest Limited
Ski Solutions Limited
Sky In-Home Service Limited
Sky Limited
Sky Subscribers Services Ltd
Sky Television Limited
Skylord Travel PLC
Sloggett Group Limited
Drew Smith Limited
SmithKline Beecham Limited
Solai Holdings Limited
Solihull Hotel Co Ltd
Sony Europe Limited
Southall Travel Limited
Southcrown Limited
Southern Counties Care Limited
Sparquote Limited
Speakerbus Limited
Specialist Plant Associates Ltd
Spectris PLC
Spectrum Franchising Limited
Sportsworld Group Limited
St. Dominic's Ltd.
St. Luke's Hospice (Harrow & Brent) Ltd.
Staines Preparatory School Trust
John Steward Transport Ltd
Barry Stewart & Sons Limited
Storefast Limited
Strategic Shipping Co Ltd
Paul Strickland Scanner Centre
Stubbins Marketing Limited
Stulz U.K. Limited
Sudbury Plastering Services Ltd
Sungard Availability Services (UK)
Sunset Travel Limited
Supercraft Limited
Sutton Group Holdings Limited
Swan Mill Paper Co Ltd
T.C. Racing (Leisure) Limited
T.H.G. & C.C. Limited
TASIS The American School in England
TASIS UK Limited
TBE (Southern) Limited
TRAD Safety Systems Limited
TWG Services Limited
Tan Sales (London) Limited
Tees Limited
Texcel Developments Ltd
Thames Properties Ltd.
Thompsons Nursery Limited
Ticketgrange Limited
Todd Doors Limited
Toll Global Forwarding (UK) Ltd
Toyota Financial Services (UK) PLC
Travel Blue Limited
Travelpack Marketing & Leisure Services
Treasury Wine Estates EMEA Ltd
Tri-Continental Limited
Trimite Limited
Turner Properties Limited
P.C. Tustin & Co Ltd
Twinglobe Limited
Tyco Fire Products Manufacturing Ltd
UB Overseas Limited
UK Real Estate Limited
UPS (UK) Limited
UPS Global Treasury PLC
UPS Limited
Uneek Forwarding Limited
Unifruit Limited
Uniquehelp Limited
Uniserve (Air Freight) Limited
Uniserve (Europe) Limited
Uniserve (U.K.) Limited
Uniserve Holdings Limited
Uniserve Limited
United Distributing Company (Coin Machine Sales)
United Reformed Church (Southern Synod) Trust
Unitruc Limited
V.I.P. Limited
Valley Wholesale Carpets Ltd
Vanco UK Limited
Verico Europe Holding Limited
Verifone (U.K.) Limited
Victoria Foundation
Victorygame Limited
Villachase Limited
Vinci Construction UK Limited
Vinci Fleet Services Limited
Vinstrata Builders (London) Ltd
Visual Impact (UK) Limited
Vitec Imaging Solutions UK Ltd
Vitec Production Solutions Ltd
Voicevale Limited
Volante Limited
VolkerFitzpatrick Limited
Volkerwessels Limited
WJ Groundwater Limited
Waterlow Business Supplies Ltd
Wates Construction Limited
Wates Foundation Limited
Wates Group Limited
Waystone Limited
Wellcome Limited
Wenta
West & Coe Limited
J D Wetherspoon PLC
Wheatland Cheese Co. Limited
White Lodge Centre
Wickland (Holdings) Limited
Wilman Marine Limited
Wise Trading Limited
Wolters Kluwer Health (Medical Research)
Wood Group Kenny UK Limited
A & A Woodford Limited
Wyevale Garden Centres Holdings Ltd
Zest Living Limited
Zionstone Limited

1990-1994 [444]

1 Big Data Management Limited
A A Homes and Housing Ltd
A.G.E. Nursing Homes Limited
A1 Pharmaceuticals PLC
ABC Drug Stores Limited
ADT Group Limited
AGCO Finance Limited
APCOA Parking (UK) Limited
AVM Impact Ltd
Accolade Wines Europe No. 2 Ltd
Advanced Business Equipment Ltd
Advanced Elastomer Systems Ltd
Advanced Industrial Technology Corporation
Agency Press Limited
Air Charter Service Limited
Air Menzies International Ltd
Air Products (BR) Limited
Alandale Scaffolding Group Ltd
Alba Broadcasting Corporation Ltd
Alhambra Hotel Limited
All World Foods Limited
Allocate Software Limited
Alsford Timber Limited
Altomart Limited
Amalgamated Property Holdings Ltd
Amsprop Estates Limited
Amsprop Investments Limited
Anita Impex Limited
Arlen Properties Limited
Assured Services Limited
Astellas Pharma Europe Ltd.
Atlas Contractors Limited
Avicenna Holdings Ltd
Axis Security Services Limited
Axon Solutions Limited
B & T Plant Hire Limited
BA Cityflyer Limited
BP Russian Investments Limited
Bandai Namco Holdings UK Ltd
Barrie Knitwear Limited
Baruch Holdings Limited
Bates Wharf Marine Sales Ltd
Bayside Investment Co Ltd
Beck & Pollitzer Engineering Ltd
Benacre Investments Limited
Berkeley Healthcare Limited
Berrite Limited
Bimax Chemicals Limited
Blendhall Limited
Bookcash Trading Limited
Boon Building Services Ltd
Bosch Service Solutions Ltd
Boston Limited
Bristol-Myers Squibb Pharmaceuticals
British Airways Avionic Engineering
British Marine Federation
Broadberry Data Systems Ltd
CAE Technology Services Ltd
Cadline Limited
Camelot UK Lotteries Limited
Camgate Holdings Limited
Cardif Pinnacle Insurance Holdings PLC
Cardif Pinnacle Insurance Management Services
Care Management Group Limited
Caredeal Limited
Caretech Community Services Ltd
Cargill Financial Markets Ltd
Cargill Global Funding PLC
Carlson Wagonlit UK Ltd
Carpetright of London Limited
Caunton Management Limited
Cedars Village Limited
Centro Group Limited
Chalford Property Co Ltd
Charles Kalms, Henry Ronson Immanuel College
Chelmer Foods Limited
Chem-Dry U.K. Limited
Chemox Pound Limited
E. Christian & Company (Holdings)
Chubb Group Security Limited
Churton Property Developments Ltd

Cineworld Estates Limited
Clavering Care Limited
Clearview Homes Limited
Clinical Pathology Accreditation (UK)
Coats Finance Co. Limited
J. Coffey Construction Ltd
Colts Cabs Limited
Comparex UK Limited
Compass Overseas Holdings Ltd
Computer Financial Consultants Ltd
Conneely Drylining Limited
Continua Limited
Continuity Co Ltd
Cordant People Limited
Corero Network Security PLC
Cornwall
Corona Energy Retail 4 Limited
Corona Gas Management Limited
Cosco Shipping Crystal Logistics (UK) Co
Costco Limited
Costco Wholesale UK Limited
Countrywide Electrical Distributors
Cover Up Clothing Limited
Cuffe PLC
D.M.C. Business Machines Ltd
DGC Limited
DL Insurance Services Limited
Datamust Co Ltd
De Lage Landen Limited
Demipower (1991) Limited
Dip Systems (UK) Limited
Direct Boot and Shoe Supplies Ltd
Direct Line Group Limited
Direct Link Worldwide Limited
Domino Investments Limited
E.D.S. Holdings Limited
E.G.T. Finance Limited
EC Logistics Limited
EMC Consulting (UK) Limited
ESP Networks Limited
ESP Utilities Group Limited
Eco Animal Health Ltd.
Ecover (UK) Limited
Edwardian Exclusive Hotels Ltd
Edwardian International Hotels Ltd
Edwardian London Management Services
Edwardian Ltd
Elec-Mec (Wholesale) Limited
Elite Mobile Limited
Ellis of Richmond (Holdings) Ltd
Elmex Sales Corporation Ltd
Elysium Healthcare No. 3 Ltd
Emerson Crane Hire Limited
Emson Haig Limited
Ensign Bus Co Ltd
Enterprise Rent-a-Car UK Holdings
Enterprise Rent-a-Car UK Ltd
Equatorial Traders Limited
Erac UK Finance Limited
Erith Holdings Limited
Euro Alloys Limited
Excellent Properties Ltd.
Experis Resource Support Services
ExxonMobil Gas Marketing Europe Ltd
Ezra Attia Limited
Fedrigoni U.K. Limited
Fidelity European Values PLC
Fidelity Japan Trust PLC
Fidelity Special Values PLC
Fieldrose Limited
Fieldside Associates Limited
Firmenich UK Limited
First City Care (London) Ltd
First Network Ltd.
Fleetmill Limited
Flight Centre (UK) Limited
Foray 414 Limited
Forester Investments Limited
Forester Life Limited
Forss Wind Farm Limited.
Foundation Developments Ltd
Foundation and Friends of The Royal Botanic Gardens, Kew
Frattro Limited
Furlong Flooring (Southern) Ltd.
G & O Securities Limited
G4S Aviation Services (UK) Ltd
GL Education Group Limited
Gada Limited
Galamast Limited
Galliford Try Building Limited
Garrets International Limited
Gearhouse Broadcast Limited
Gefco Forwarding UK Ltd.
Geieonline Dafconsulting (UK) Ltd.
Geomac Limited
Gerrard International Limited
Golden Leaves Limited
Golden Meadows Limited
Kenneth Green Associates Ltd
Greenswan Consultants Limited
Greenyard Prepared UK Limited
Gristwood and Toms Limited
H & V Serviceplan Limited
H H Associates Limited
Hansgrohe Limited
P.C. Harrington Holdings Ltd
Harro Foods Limited
Harrodian School Limited
Harvest Energy Limited
Harvey & Thompson Limited
Hawthorn Crow Limited
Haymarket Group Limited
Heathrow Enterprises Limited
Heathrow Hydrant Operating Co Ltd
G.A.F. Heley (Properties) Ltd
Highway Care Limited
Hill Partnerships Limited
Hiretest Limited
Holmes Care Limited
Hoo Hing Limited
Howard Hunt (City) Limited
John F. Hunt Hire Centres Ltd
Hunters Contracts Limited
IGT U.K. Limited
IIAA Limited
ITC Concepts Limited
Imagination Technologies Group Ltd
Imtech Engineering Services London and South
Independent Inspections Ltd
International Passenger Protection
International Transport Ltd
J & J Transport Limited
Johnson Group Limited
KLDiscovery Ontrack Limited
KM Products Europe Limited
Kane Group Limited
Karium Ltd
Kelerbay Limited
Kelly Services (UK) Limited
Keltbray Group (Holdings) Ltd
Kendon Rope & Twine Co Limited
Kerry Foods Limited
Kewstone Limited
Kidsprog Limited
Kingrose Limited
Knowledge & Merchandising Inc. Ltd
LGC Limited
Land & Water Services Ltd
Lanvin Trading Ltd
Ralph Lauren UK Limited
Leander Build Limited
Leander Construction Limited
Lefa Enterprises Limited
Lesaffre UK and Ireland Ltd
Limesquare Finance Limited
Link Market Services Limited
Link Market Services Trustees Ltd
London Airports 1992 Limited
London Sovereign Limited
London Wharf Limited
Longford Securities & Equities Ltd
MIQ Logistics Limited
MJA Investments Limited
MJF Group Limited
MSC Cruises Limited
MSHA International Ltd.
Mallinckrodt Chemical Holdings (U.K.)
Mallinckrodt Medical Holdings (UK)
Mane Contract Services Limited
Manor Lodge School
Mapal Limited
Marbank Construction Limited
Maylands Green Limited
John Menzies (108) Limited
Menzies Aviation PLC
Merck Sharp & Dohme Finance Europe
Meridian Wood Products Ltd.
Metropolis International Group Ltd
Metsa Tissue Limited
Micro Plus Software Limited
Mission Foods UK Limited
Mitsubishi Electric Finance Europe PLC
Morelli Group Limited
Moss Electrical Co. Limited
Mountcharm Limited
Multitrust Property Investments Ltd
NEC Europe Ltd
NNR Global Logistics UK Ltd
NPL Management Limited
Namco UK Limited
National Football Centre Ltd
National Instruments Corporation (UK)
Natural Woodfloor Co Ltd
NetApp UK Ltd
New England Seafood International
Nissan Motor (GB) Limited
Noble Gift Packaging Limited
North Atlantic (Holdings) Ltd
North London Collegiate School
Nucleus Limited
R.O'Rourke & Son Limited.
OLM Systems Limited
Oleoland Hotel Co Ltd
One for All (UK) Ltd.
Optimal Limited
Orbis Protect Limited
P.S.V. Transport Systems Ltd
PES Group Limited
PGS Exploration (UK) Limited
PJG Developments Limited
Palace Street Developments Ltd
Panavision Europe Limited
Paneurosys Limited
Park Green Investments Limited

Peace Hospice Care
Pearl Properties Limited
Petroleum Geo-Services (UK) Ltd
Pexhurst Services Limited
J.A. Phillips Holdings Ltd
Phoenix Software Limited
Pineridge Investments Limited
Pinns Wharf Limited
PizzaExpress (Franchises) Ltd
PizzaExpress (Restaurants) Ltd
PizzaExpress (Wholesale) Ltd
Port of Tilbury London Limited
ProAV Limited
Procter & Gamble UK Group Holdings
Proper Music Distribution Ltd
Purebond Limited
Purelake New Homes Limited
Purelake Properties Limited
Pyramid Builders Limited
Q.N. Hotels Limited
Quad Building Services (Southern)
RDT Limited
Ranbaxy (U.K.) Limited
Regentsmead Limited
Reliance Vanco Group Limited
Remus White Limited
Renault Group U.K. Limited
Residential Care Services Ltd
Residual and Brand Management Ltd
Reynolds Catering Supplies Ltd
Rhenus Lupprians Limited
Rican Securities Limited
Riso (U.K.) Limited
Robore Cuts Limited
Rollover Limited
Romans International Limited
Rosewell Properties Limited
Runnymede Investments Limited
Rye Plant Hire Limited
S & D Pharma Limited
S.J.M. Alloys & Metals Limited
Saba Infra Holdings UK Limited
Saba Park Solutions UK Limited
Sabichi Homewares Limited
Safedale Limited
Salient Investments Ltd.
Sandhill Park Limited
Sardar Properties (U.K.) Ltd
Saya Enterprises Limited
Scan Corporation Limited
Secom PLC
Selecta U.K. Limited
Sensormatic Limited
Sharp International Finance (U.K.) PLC
Sheargold Limited
Shenley Park Trust
Shetson Property Developments Ltd
Shooting Star Chase
Siem Shipping UK Limited
Siemon Co Ltd
Simm Tronic Limited
Six Continents Overseas Holdings Ltd
Sky Operational Finance Ltd
Sky Telecommunications Services Ltd
Sky UK Limited
H. Smith Food Group PLC
Drew Smith Homes Limited
SmithKline Beecham (Export) Ltd
SmithKline Beecham Overseas Ltd
South Central Property Limited
South Coast Watch Fair Limited
Sovereign Business Integration Group PLC
Spedition Services Limited
Spirit Energy Resources Ltd
Sports Interactive Limited
St Catherine's School Twickenham
St George PLC
St George's Weybridge
St. Vincent's Charitable Trust
Stanmore Contractors Limited
Stapleford Commercial Group Ltd
Star Reefers Trading Limited
Stat Marine Limited
Sterling Relocation Limited
Sterndale Systems Limited
J.A. Stott (Carpentry) Ltd
Subsea 7 West Africa Contracting Ltd
Summit Asset Management Ltd
Summit Media Limited
Sungard Availability Services (DR)
Sunstar Group Limited
Sutton Business Centre Limited
Swanlea Limited
Syner-Med (Pharmaceutical Products)
Syscap Leasing Limited
Syscap Limited
T G Products Limited
TC Facilities Management Ltd
TCL Manufacturing Limited
TK Maxx
TRSL Limited
TX Group Europe Ltd.
Tancia Limited
Tempur UK Limited
Texcel Technology PLC
Thorn Security Group Limited
Titan Containers Limited
Topfib Limited
Total Support Services Limited
Toureen Contractors Limited
Tracker Network (UK) Limited
Tradex Insurance Co Ltd
Transmec UK Limited
Triplehigh Limited
True World Foods (UK) Ltd
Try Homes Limited
Turnhold Properties Limited
Tyco Building Services Products (UK)
UCAR Properties Limited
UK Assistance Accident Repair Centres
UK Highways M40 (Holdings) Ltd
Ultra Electronics Holdings PLC
Ultra Electronics Limited
United Biscuits (UK) Limited
Van Ameyde UK Holding Limited
Vanderbilt Hotels Limited
Venson Automotive Solutions Ltd
Verifone Services UK & Ireland Ltd
Verint Systems UK Limited
Vestey Foods Limited
Victory Lighting (UK) Limited
Visual Response Limited
J. Van Vliet London Cash & Carry
Volex Group Holdings Limited
WDFG UK Limited
WVC Land & Developments Ltd
Wallacespace Limited
Warrant Investments PLC
Warrens' Warehousing & Distribution (Midlands)
Waters Limited
Wenta Business Centres Limited
Whiteoak Developments Limited
Wolters Kluwer Health (Europe) Ltd
Woodford Heating & Energy Ltd
Wurth Holding UK Ltd
YMCA St Pauls Group
Yoplait UK Limited
Zotefoams International Ltd
Zotefoams PLC

1995 [116]

Abercorn School Limited
Advanced Lighting Technologies Europe
Air Products Group Limited
Aircom International Limited
Anglogold Ashanti International Exploration Holdings
Armstrong Metal Ceilings Ltd
Automated Technology Group Ltd
Avon Estates (London) Limited
Badger Holdings Limited
Beck Interiors Limited
Benfleet Scrap Co Limited
Bio-Rad Laboratories Limited
Brookstream Properties Limited
Bucci Freight Services Limited
Cargill Investments
Celtic Contractors Limited
Cine-UK Limited
City Lifting Limited
Classic Cinemas Limited
Cobalt Ground Solutions Ltd
Cobra Industries Limited
Communications & Power Industries Europe
Compass Overseas Holdings No.2 Ltd
Corporate Solutions Consulting Ltd
Cosco Shipping Lines (UK) Ltd
Crystal Windows & Doors Ltd
D-Link (Europe) Limited
DB Investments Limited
Direct Supplies (London) Ltd
Dnata Travel (U.K.) Ltd.
Dunlop International Group Ltd
Dunlop International Holdings Ltd
Fairview Hotels Limited
Forester Holdings (Europe) Ltd
Former Reichmann Properties PLC
Graham Care (YB) Limited
J & E Hall Limited
Headmasters Partnership Ltd
Heathrow Cargo Handling Ltd
Henley Group Holdings Limited
IBRC Asset Finance Limited
IHG Hotels Limited
Interfleet Holdings Limited
Kailash Estates Limited
Kingston University Service Co Ltd
LGC (Holdings) Limited
LHR Business Support Centre Ltd
Laing Construction Limited
London Executive Aviation Ltd
M.W. Helicopters Limited
Mapcargo International Limited
Marden Oak Limited
Medicrest Limited
Medreich PLC
Mill Hotel Limited
Millennium Care Homes Limited
National Fostering Agency Ltd
Newmarket Transport Limited
OTC Direct Limited
Oak Tree Schools Holdings Ltd
Olivewood Limited
Overseas Air Travel Limited
Phoenix Property Investment Co Ltd

Pizza Gogo Ltd
Porcelanosa (South East) Ltd
Porcelanosa U.K. Limited
Premier Rugby Limited
Pridenature Limited
Procter & Gamble Product Supply (U.K.)
Prospects Services
Queenscourt Limited
Ranbaxy Holdings (UK) Limited
Renault Institute of Quality Management
Renewable Energy Centre Ltd
Rhodia Holdings Limited
SK Hynix UK Limited
SNC-Lavalin Rail & Transit Ltd
Saba Infra UK Limited
Sabre Global Technologies Ltd
Sabre UK Marketing Limited
Samsung Electronics (UK) Ltd
Satair UK Limited
Seabrook Warehousing Limited
Seismic Exploration (Canada) Ltd
Silvertime Amusements Limited
Skanska Infrastructure Development UK
Sky Comedy Limited
Sky History Limited
Sky LLU Assets Limited
Sky Ventures Limited
Spirit Energy Production UK Ltd
Stema Shipping (UK) Limited
Subsea 7 International Contracting
Sun Mark Limited
Swift Roofing Contracts Ltd
Synamedia Limited
T. Bro Investment Limited
TES-AMM UK Ltd
TJX Europe Buying (Deutschland) Ltd
TJX Europe Limited
TJX UK
Tata Global Beverages GB Ltd
Tata Global Beverages Overseas Holdings
Tata Global Beverages Services Ltd
Templecare Limited
Tram Operations Limited
Tristmire Limited
UK Highways M40 Limited
United Kingdom Accreditation Service
Vadsala Limited
Waverley House Hotel Limited
Waystone 32 Limited
Windcrest (U.K.) Limited
Wolters Kluwer Tax and Accounting
Woodledge Limited
Xerox Capital (Europe) Limited

1996 [136]

A24 Group Limited
ACM Environmental PLC
Ability Developments Limited
Alandale Holdings Limited
Alandale Logistics Limited
Aldwych Leisure Limited
Angel Care PLC
Aprite (GB) Limited
Armstrong (U.K.) Investments
BP Exploration (Shah Deniz) Ltd
BRE Trust
Beam Global Finance UK Limited
Berkeley Homes (Fleet) Limited
Blenheim House Construction Ltd
Blessville Limited
Brisko Scaffolding Limited
Brownlow Enterprises Limited
Buckmead Limited
Butler & Young Approved Inspectors
CS Property and Consultancy Ltd.
CSL (Dualcom) Limited
Casewise Limited
Castledene Investments Limited
Chesside Homes Limited
Chigwell (London) Limited
Churchgate Estates Limited
Cibi Investments Limited
City & Westminster Developments Ltd
Coca-Cola European Partners Holdings Great Britain
Coca-Cola European Partners Services Europe
Compass Group Finance No.2 Ltd
Cook's Delights Limited
Cordant Security Limited
Corona Energy Limited
Corona Energy Retail 1 Limited
DPA Support Services Limited
Dairy Crest France Holdings 1 Ltd
Dairy Crest Group PLC
Do & Co. International Catering Ltd
ESP Connections Limited
Ebonyhill Limited
Elysium Healthcare (Acorn Care) Ltd
Elysium Healthcare No. 4 Ltd
Ensono Limited
Ergonomic Solutions Limited
Eventist Group Limited
Fidelity Asian Values PLC
GX Technology EAME Limited
Galliard Construction Limited
Galliford Try Homes Limited
Gentec Energy PLC
Good Harvest Group Limited
Goodman Family Investments Ltd
Gracilis Ltd.
HCP Holdings Limited
HFIS PLC
Harlequin Direct Limited
Harlequin Football Club Ltd
Harry Motors Ltd
Heathrow Airport Fuel Co Ltd
Heathrow Express Operating Co Ltd
Herbalife Europe Limited
I.C.F. Finance Limited
Imperial Pharmaceuticals Ltd
JSA Properties (UK) Limited
Jain (Europe) Limited
KPIT Technologies (UK) Limited
Kelly Communications Group Ltd
Kelly Fleet Services Limited
Kingswood Corporation Limited
Lanend Limited
Limje Holdings Limited
MJF UK Holdings Limited
Maison Moti Limited
Millers Bespoke Bakery Limited
Minesoft Ltd
Multi Services Kent Limited
Newstone International Limited
Northstar Property Investment Ltd
Norwood Ravenswood
OLM Group Limited
OPD Group Limited
Oneclickhr Limited
Oyezstraker Group Limited
P.I.E. Pharma Limited
Pact Educational Trust Limited
Palace Theatre Watford Limited
Panther (VAT) Properties Ltd
Payless Group Limited
PizzaExpress Merchandising Ltd
Premier Moves Limited
Procter & Gamble (L & CP) Ltd
Procter & Gamble Technical Centres
Property Finance Nominees (No.3) Ltd
R A Insurance Brokers Limited
Rapid Action Packaging Limited
Realmpark Health Care (Petworth) Ltd
J. Reddington Ltd
Regard Partnership Limited
Rocket Medical PLC
STS Flooring Distributors Ltd
Saba Infra Cardiff Limited
Safestore Properties Limited
Shellen Construction Limited
Six Continents Holdings Ltd
SmithKline Beecham (H) Limited
Smiths Business Information Services
Spencers Property Investments Ltd
St Cross Developments Limited
St James Group Limited
St. Margaret's School Bushey
Stanmore Implants Worldwide Ltd
Stealth Leisure Limited
Sumitomo Electric Europe Ltd
Sunnyfield Veg Limited
J.J. Sweeney Limited
Synbra UK Limited
TIGI International Limited
Tata Global Beverages Holdings Ltd
Taylor Woodrow Construction
Tower Bridge Homes Care Ltd
Transcar Projects (Holdings) Ltd
Triplerose Limited
Ultimate Model Corporation Ltd
Velani & Velani Ltd
Vendcrown Limited
Volkerrail Limited
WDFG UK Holdings Limited
WLMG Limited
WWW Sunoptic Com UK Limited
Wagermotion Limited
Wembley Tyres Limited
West London YMCA
Xerox Overseas Holdings Ltd
Yellow Brick Developments Ltd
Yparho Limited

1997 [136]

A. & G. P. Trading Limited
ATC Holdings Limited
Agility Project Logistics Ltd
Air Products (Chemicals) Teesside
Al-Noor Foundation Limited
Alliance Healthcare (Distribution)
Alphalarch Limited
Amshold Securities Limited
Arihant Limited
Associated Lead Mills Ltd.
Astonpalm Limited
Axon Group Limited
Berkeley Residential Limited
Bishopsgate School Limited
Black Katz Eddy (Holdings) Ltd
Blackfriars Land Co Ltd
Blenheim Estates Limited
Blenheim Property Management Ltd
Brimheath Developments Limited
Building Research Establishment Ltd
Burney Realty Limited

CWT Holdco Limited
Centaur Property Group Limited
Citipost Limited
Clancy Group PLC
E. T. Clay Products Limited
Clinisys Solutions Limited
Cobird Limited
Construction Workers Guild Ltd
Cordant Group PLC
Cranstoun
Creative Assembly Limited
Cromwell (Wandsworth) Limited
Cummins Associates Limited
Cyan Logistics Limited
Dairy Crest France Holdings 2 Ltd
EHGT Limited
Empire Bespoke Foods Limited
Eurocity Properties (Central) Ltd
Fairview Homes Limited
Fairview New Homes (Chase Road) Ltd
Fairview New Homes (South East) Ltd
Football First Limited
Fulham Football Leisure Ltd
Fulham Stadium Limited
Full House Restaurants Limited
Gallaher Group Limited
Galliard Holdings Limited
Gate Gourmet London Limited
Giesecke+Devrient Mobile Security GB Ltd
Goldings Estates Limited
Gowrie Laxmico Limited
Grayshott Investments Limited
Guardian DR (Overseas Holdings) Ltd
HCL Great Britain Limited
Highplus Limited
Hollin Hill Properties Limited
IGD Services Limited
Imperial Ductwork Services Ltd
Instalcom Limited
Invigia Limited
JBG Enterprises Limited
Jasper Morrison Limited
Killoughery Holdings Limited
Kingpin Communications Limited
Leitrim Properties Limited
Letting International Limited
Liftec Lifts Limited
Linkmart Limited
London Irish Holdings Limited
London Residential Healthcare Ltd
Lufthansa Technik Landing Gear Services UK
MNS Care PLC
Mashco Limited
Medivet Group Limited
Merchant Taylors' School
Meridian Hospital Company (Holdings)
Meridian Hospital Company PLC
Metier Healthcare Limited
Milpharm Limited
Motorsport Vision Limited
N.R.C. Plant Limited
NK Image Limited
NUR Limited
Newport Industries Limited
North Star (2000) Limited
O'Hara Transport Limited
Olivanna Ltd
Openview Security Solutions Ltd
P & R Installation Co Ltd
PMP Recruitment Limited
Pagegroup PLC
Party Invitation Limited
Perform Media Services Ltd
Plexus Holdings PLC
Postgrad Limited
RCI Financial Services Limited
RSA Island Village Limited
Ridgeland Properties Limited
Roamquest Limited
SAB Properties (London) Ltd
SHL People Solutions Group Holdings Ltd.
SI Electrical Limited
Samsung Semiconductor Europe Ltd
Sancroft Properties Limited
Shepperton Hotels Holdings Ltd
Shire Properties (South East) Ltd
Shoreland Limited
Silverton Property Investments Ltd
Simpson Marketing Limited
Thomas Sinden Limited
Sogea Holdings (UK) Limited
Spacemaker Group Limited
Spruce Investments Limited
St John's School, Northwood
TRAD Group Limited
Tanita International Ltd.
Toshiba of Europe Limited
Towers Thompson Holdings Ltd
Trade Sale Ltd
Transputec Limited
Unique Seafood Limited
United Healthcare (South Buckinghamshire) Holdings
United Healthcare (South Buckinghamshire)
Upgrade Investments Limited
Uponor Limited
Venture Lighting Europe Ltd
Veriton Pharma Limited
WJ Management Limited
Watches International Limited
Wembley National Stadium Ltd
Wilman Universal Industries Ltd
World Duty Free Limited
Wyevale Garden Centres G & L Ltd
Yang Ming (UK) Ltd
Zeco Limited

1998 [156]

AA Property and Construction Services
ACI Global Limited
ATP Media Operations Limited
Adilsons Properties Limited
Ali UK Limited
Amal Investments Limited
Ansa UK Limited
Arcus Investment Limited
Artic Building Services Ltd
Artillery Properties Limited
Aurient Investments Limited
BBC Studioworks Limited
BMG (Ashford) General Partner Ltd
BP+Amoco International Limited
BR Pharma International Ltd
Balcraft Properties Limited
Bancroft's School
Barcrest Group Limited
Beck & Pollitzer Engineering Holdings
Bostall Estates Limited
Brentford FC Limited
Britair Holdings Limited
Broadway Malyan Limited
Bryen & Langley Limited
Butchoff Antiques Limited
Bytes Technology Group Limited
Cargill Investments Holdings Ltd
Chai-Lifeline Cancer Care
Chartco Limited
City Circle UK Limited
City Link (Cardiff) Limited
Complete Cover Group Limited
Contracting Made Easy Ltd
Country House Weddings Limited
Countyroute Limited
Crestron (UK) Limited
Crickmore Developments Limited
Crosswater Limited
DBA Advisors Limited
DF Group Limited
Dealcyber Limited
Delta Membrane Systems Limited
Dicky Birds Pre School Nurseries Ltd
Durbin PLC
E.F.G. Housewares Limited
E.G.T. Bridging Finance Ltd
EA Consulting Group Ltd
EID Limited
East Mediterranean Trading Ltd
Econocom Limited
Education Support (Enfield) Ltd
Elmswood Properties Limited
Endeavour SCH Holdings Limited
Endeavour SCH PLC
Endon Europe Power 1 Limited
Endon Europe Power 3 Limited
Endon Europe Power 6 Limited
Envirotech Properties Limited
Eran Diamonds (UK) Limited
Esteem Care Ltd
Everguard Limited
Exmoore Financial Credit Co Ltd
Experis Group Limited
FL Property Management Limited
Farrington Care Homes Limited
Fasttrax Limited
Filemaker International
Frontline Security Solutions Ltd
Fusion Business Solutions (UK) Ltd
Galldris Construction Limited
A C Georgiades Ltd
Gima (UK) Limited
Global Draw Limited
Green Flag Holdings Limited
Greenfield Property Developments Ltd
Grunenthal Limited
Guardian IT
H & S Contractors Limited
Homeguard Properties Limited
JSM Construction Limited
Kelly Comms Limited
Kentex Group Limited
Kidiliz Group UK Ltd
Kolajola UK Ltd
LB Enterprises Limited
LSG/Sky Chefs Europe Holdings Ltd
La Nu-Range Ltd
Laing Limited
Landmark Civil Engineering Ltd
Landmark Groundworks Limited
Latif International Limited
Leez Priory Limited
Lensbury Limited
Leprosy Mission International
MJF Business Services Limited
Maybour Logistics Global Ltd
Metier Holdings Limited

Mill Hill Properties Limited
Mills Family Limited
Minster Care Management Ltd
Mokarabia Limited
Monument Assets Limited
Motor Parts Direct Limited
Munster Limited
Ness Global Services Limited
Norgine Pharmaceuticals Ltd
Northwood Paper Sales Limited
O.B.C. (Europe) Limited
Oakburn European Properties Ltd
One World Express Inc. Limited
Original Bedstead Co Limited
Park Garage Group PLC
Parrsouth Limited
Penta Consulting Limited
Phoenix Property Development Co Ltd
Prospect Healthcare (Hairmyres) Holdings
Prospect Healthcare (Hairmyres) Ltd
Purelake Investments Limited
Queensway Associates Limited
Radiation Limited
Reichmann Properties PLC
Reliance Globalcom (UK) Ltd
Residential Loans Ltd.
Richardson Roofing Holdings Ltd
Rooff Holdings Limited
Safety-Kleen Europe Limited
Safety-Kleen UK (Europe) Ltd
Safety-Kleen UK (France) Ltd
Sapna Caterers Limited
Services Support (SEL) Limited
Shakoor Capital Limited
Shopfittings Direct Limited
Shorterm Group Limited
Sinclair House Properties Ltd
Skanska J.V. Projects Ltd
Societe Generale Equipment Finance
Spaces Personal Storage Ltd
Sugarman Group Limited
Super Toughened Glass Limited
T G Commodities Limited
TRAD Hire & Sales Limited
Tower Hill Suffolk Limited
Tozer Seeds Limited
UK Highways A55 (Holdings) Ltd
UK Highways A55 Limited
Unicourt Properties Limited
Vitec Investments Limited
WMF United Kingdom Limited
Walnut Estates Limited
Wellsborough Developments Ltd
Wesco Distribution-International Ltd
West One Technology Ltd
Westlake Estates Limited
Windmill Organics Limited
Xerox UK Holdings Limited
Zian Hi-Tech (U.K.) Limited

1999 [161]

A T & T (GB) Limited
A. & A. 2000 Limited
Amshold International Limited
Anchor Bay Construction Products Ltd
Ansa Utilities Limited
Area Sq. Limited
Arem Investments Limited
Avantia Limited
Avenues Trust Group
Axiom Wealth Management Ltd
BA and AA Holdings Limited
Bartlett Mitchell Limited
Beauty Wholesale Limited
Belron Finance Limited
Birmingham Schools Partnership Ltd
Oliver Bonas Limited
Bourn Investments Limited
Buyagift PLC
CK Property Developments Ltd
Canada Life Asset Management Ltd
Careprogress Limited
Caretech Community Services (No.2)
Castle Village Limited
Chantry Securities Limited
Chemidex Generics Limited
Chingford Fruit Limited
Citipost Mail Limited
Clay Oven UK Limited
Cochlear Europe Limited
Container Providers International (UK)
Country Rhythm Limited
Countyroute (A130) PLC.
Crest Nicholson (Henley-on-Thames)
Cromwell (Egham) Limited
DNC UK Limited
Decadent Properties Limited
Deco Design and Build Co. Ltd
Denton Homes Surrey Limited
Design Blue Limited
Dialgreen Estates Limited
Direct Chauffeur Line Limited
Dock and Let Limited
Donamount Limited
Duncan Lewis Solicitors Ltd
J P Dunn Construction Limited
E.S. Pipelines Limited
East Central Limited
ExxonMobil International Ltd
ExxonMobil Marine Limited
ExxonMobil UK Limited
F5 Networks Limited
Fairview New Homes (Colindale) Ltd
Fairview New Homes (Developments)
First Network Properties Ltd
Flag Atlantic UK Limited
Flair Leisure Products PLC
Forgefix Limited
Fortuna Frutos (UK) Limited
GE Money Servicing Limited
Joseph Gallagher Group Ltd
Genesis Pharmaceuticals Ltd
Gittisham Care Limited
GlaxoSmithKline PLC
Globaltex Limited
Good Harvest Properties (Hammersmith)
Grapes Direct Limited
Gravity Media Group Limited
Gruma Europe Limited
John Guest International Ltd
HRS Investments Limited
Heathrow T5 Hotel Limited
Hilton Finance (UK) Limited
Himelight Limited
Hyperformance Limited
ICS Incorporation Limited
Igroup 8 Limited
Industrial Chemicals Limited
Juniper Networks (UK) Limited
K.C.Y. Limited
Kara Designs Ltd
Kellogg Brown & Root Holdings Ltd
Key Mail (UK) Limited
Kingston Grammar School
Korea Foods Co Ltd
Land & Water Plant Limited
Landmark Global (UK) Limited
Laser Holdings Limited
Lee-Warren Fabrication and Design
Leonardo Holdings Limited
Lester Hotels Group Limited
London Irish Scottish Richmond Ltd
MWL International Limited
Major Properties London Ltd
Malibu Health Products Limited
Manpower UK Limited
Mapeley Estates Limited
Meadvine Limited
Menzies Aviation (NL) Limited
Metro Properties Limited
Metrosold Limited
Millennium Cash & Carry Ltd
Mono Holdings Limited
Mono Properties Limited
Mosaic Estates Ltd
Nellsar Limited
Neptune Hotels Limited
Newschools (Leyton) Limited
Notre Dame School Cobham
Orbital Equipment Limited
Orchard Plumbing Limited
Pandrol Finance Limited
Pandrol Group Limited
Pandrol Holdings Limited
Pharmaceuticals Direct Limited
Prospect Healthcare (Reading) Ltd
Queenwood Golf Club Limited
RL Retail Services Limited
Rackspace Limited
Ranks Enterprises Limited
Regentrealm Limited
Retirement Villages Limited
Runecorp Limited
Rusjon (UK) Limited
Sandhill Homes Limited
Signet Group Services Limited
Signet Holdings Limited
Signet Trading Limited
SintecMedia WEM Ltd
Siya Properties Limited
Smithers Information Limited
Solstor UK Limited
Solvecorp Limited
Spring Finance Limited
St George Healthcare Limited
St Mark Homes PLC
TLC Group Limited
Talbot House Business Centre Ltd
Tata Global Beverages Group Ltd
Taylor Wentworth Limited
Teledyne Limited
Tone Scaffolding Services Ltd
Topgolf Limited
Tower Hill Investment Partners Ltd
Townhold Limited
Trafalgar Leisure Ltd
Tudor Investments Limited
Tuskerdirect Limited
Tyco European Metal Framing Ltd
Vantage Volante Limited
Vashisht Surgical Limited
Vega Industries Limited
Vision Homes Limited
Vitec Group Holdings Limited
Vizual Business Tools Limited
Volga-Dnepr UK Ltd.

Volkerlaser Ltd
WVC Vehicle Solutions Limited
Wildview Limited
Wolters Kluwer Health (Professional & Education)
Wood Hall Investments Limited
Worldwide Flight Services Ltd

2000 [162]

A L Properties Limited
ABM Technical Solutions Ltd
Abercorn Education Ltd
Aerospares 2000 Limited
Air Charter Service Group Ltd
Alliance Healthcare (IT Services)
Amery Construction Limited
Anzco Foods UK Limited
Ardent Hire Solutions Limited
Asia Pacific Holdings Limited
Atlantic 2/3 UK Holdings Ltd
Aunt Bessie's Limited
BNS Company (Property Holdings) Ltd
BP Corporate Holdings Limited
Belgrave Land (Kilmarnock) Ltd
Berkeley Homes PLC
Blackfriars Securities (Brighton)
Blenheim Group Limited
Bluecastle Enterprises Limited
British Limbless Ex-Service Men's Association
Brown & Burk UK Limited
Burlodge Group Limited
Bywest (Holdings) Limited
Bywest Limited
CFS-Zipp Limited
CNOOC Ettrick U.K. Limited
CP Kelco UK Limited
Canon Europe Limited
Cargobull Finance Limited
Cathedral Holdings Limited
Chubb Limited
Cisilion Limited
Clearway Environmental Services (U.K)
Clinisupplies Limited
Compass Group PLC
Cosco Maritime (UK) Limited
Costco UK Holdings Limited
Coventry and Rugby Hospital Company (Holdings)
Crown Holdings Limited
D and D Property Co Ltd
DHL Global Forwarding (UK) Ltd
Devine Holdings Limited
Directfield Limited
Domantis Limited
Eagle 456 Limited
Epsom College
Exploration Service Co Ltd
Explore Manufacturing Limited
Express Toughening Ltd
FPI Limited
Fairview Holdings Limited
Fairview New Homes (Willow Way) Ltd
Fairview New Homes Limited
Flowstop Services Limited
Foodspeed Limited
Gallaher Overseas (Holdings) Ltd
Garden Centre Property Development Trading
Goodmayes Properties Ltd
Grovehawk Ltd
Harsco Investment Limited
Healthcare Support (Erdington) Holdings
Healthcare Support (Erdington) Ltd
Hospitality Holdings Limited
Hurstlane Limited
Hydro Cleansing Limited
Independent Commercial Broking Ltd
Intercontinental Adjusters (Europe)
Interlink Direct Limited
J J Food Service Holdings Ltd
JTL
Jato Aviation Limited
K 2 Properties Limited
Kays Limited
Kellogg Brown & Root Overseas Ltd
Kew Green Hotels Limited
Kidde Finance Limited
Kidde International Limited
Kidde Limited
Kidde Safety Europe Limited
Krinvest Limited
Kristal Enterprises Limited
Kudos Catering (UK) Limited
LGC (Teddington) Limited
Lakedale Developments Limited
Langford Clinic Limited
London Fluid System Technologies Ltd
Luce Limited
Magdi Yacoub Institute
Mapeley Columbus II Limited
Mapeley Steps Contractor Ltd
Marblefloor Limited
Menzies Aviation (UK) Limited
Menzies Aviation Holdings Ltd
Meraj Limited
Millipore (U.K.) Limited
Moss Europe Limited
Mostell Limited
Mountcharm (S.E.) Limited
Network New Build Limited
Neville UK PLC
Newfield Information Technology Ltd
Nextonline Limited
O G Holdings Limited
Orbit Investment Securities Services PLC
Ouhla Properties Limited
Michael Page International Recruitment
Michael Page International Southern Europe
Pebble Beach Systems Group PLC
Pebble Beach Systems Ltd
Pentagon Holdings Limited
Pharmasure Limited
Pinnacle Schools (Fife) Ltd
Pyramid Schools (Sheffield) Ltd
Randall Watts Construction Ltd
Regis 2000 Limited
Roseplot Properties Limited
Royal Medical Foundation
SITA Information Networking Computing UK
SME (Pizza) Limited
Sahara Care Limited
Sahara Holdings Limited
Sale Service and Maintenance Ltd.
Samsung SDS Europe Limited
Seasoned Events Limited
Services Support (Cleveland) Holdings
Services Support (Cleveland) Ltd
Services Support (Gravesend) Holdings
Services Support (Gravesend) Ltd
Services Support (SEL) Holdings Ltd
Shelfside (Holdings) Limited
SintecMedia Global Ltd
Skanska Construction Holdings UK Ltd
Sky Retail Stores Limited
Smart Transactions Group Ltd
Solight Limited
Sony Global Treasury Services PLC
Southdown Holdings Limited
St James Homes (Grosvenor Dock) Ltd
Starcare Homes Limited
State Oil Limited
Stebiz Limited
Storm Technologies Limited
T.S.G. Building Services PLC
T.S.L. Finance Limited
TRG Logistics Ltd
Tabor Group Ltd
Telford Homes PLC
Tican (Chilled) Limited
Toshiba Tec U.K. Imaging Systems Ltd
Transform Schools (Stoke) Holdings
Transform Schools (Stoke) Ltd
Twickenham Experience Ltd
Urban Enhance Limited
Valeo Limited
Vectra Limited
Verisk International Holdings Ltd
Vestey Foods UK Limited
Viadex Limited
Volkerservices Limited
Wasteland Group Limited
Woodside Road Limited
Ziji Productions Limited

2001 [164]

AGP Holdings (1) Limited
Academy Services (Tendring) Ltd
Adelie Foods Limited
Aitch Demolition Co. Ltd
Alexen Avocats (UK) Limited
Alium Medical Limited
Amsprop Central Limited
Amsprop City Properties Ltd
Annes Gate Property PLC
Apatech Limited
Aprirose Trading Limited
Aquila Chelmsford Limited
Ashdown Care Limited
Audley Willicombe Limited
Avantis Hotels Limited
BH (City Forum) Limited
BIP Industries Limited
BP Chemicals East China Investments
BP Finance P.L.C
BP Pipelines (BTC) Limited
Baruch Investments Limited
Bellecity Limited
Birchwood Commercial Ltd
Blackwater Securities Limited
James Blunt Limited
Brambles Holdings (UK) Limited
Brent Housing Ltd
British Airways Leasing Ltd
Bugler Group Limited
Bytes Security Partnerships Ltd
Capedeal Limited
Capital Investment and Finance Ltd
Cellecta Limited
Central Developments (UK) Ltd
Centre for Engineering and Manufacturing Excellence
Ceros (Bradford) Limited
Chemilines Group Holdings Ltd
Chislehurst Care Limited
Chromalox (UK) Limited

Chrome Dreams Media Ltd
Clickatell Limited
Clinisys Group Limited
Compass Hotels Chertsey
Court Cavendish Limited
Datamede Limited
Deacons Associates Limited
Denton Wharf Properties Ltd
Dewan Foundation Limited
Digico UK Limited
Dilawar Property Ltd.
Double A Group Services Ltd
E2X Limited
Early Learning Holdings Ltd
Econometric Limited
Ellenbrook Developments PLC
Ellenbrook Holdings Limited
Elvetham Hall (Property) Ltd
Enterprise Rent-a-Car European Holdings
Epoch RJK Limited
Essential Harvest Limited
European Film Partners III LLP
European Property Development Ltd
FTX Logistics Limited
Fairview Ventures Limited
Fairway of Course Limited
Fasttrax Holdings Limited
Financial Management Limited
Finer Limited
First Rate Exchange Services Holdings
First Rate Exchange Services Ltd
Foster Care Agency Limited
Galliard Estates Limited
GlaxoSmithKline Holdings (One) Ltd
GlaxoSmithKline UK Limited
Glaxochem (UK) Unlimited
Glendola Leisure (Holdings) Ltd
Global Metcorp Limited
Grosvenor Park (Harris & Trotter) 2002 Film LLP
Grosvenor Park 2002 Film LLP
Guild of Construction Workers Ltd
Gypcraft Drylining Contractors Ltd
HML PM Ltd
Hanwha Techwin Europe Limited
Harringtons Builders PLC
Hawk-Eye Innovations Limited
Heley Holdings Limited
Hill Holdings Limited
Hill Residential Limited
Hills Prospect PLC
Hotel Management International (Holdings)
IGUK Support Services Limited
IMCD UK Investments Ltd
ISS Damage Control Limited
Ikon Science Limited
Inspireall Leisure and Family Support Services
JBS Global (UK) Limited
Nicholas James Care Homes Ltd
Jankel Group Limited
KMI Brands Limited
Kidde UK
Kimberley Property Investments Ltd
Kingsway Hall Hotel Limited
Korda Developments Limited
Laing O'Rourke Construction Ltd
Laing O'Rourke Holdings Ltd
Laing O'Rourke Infrastructure Ltd
Laing O'Rourke PLC.
Lester Hotels (Finchley) Ltd
London Inn Hotels (Stratford) Ltd

M D Properties Limited
Maker Properties Ltd
Martlane Limited
Mastermind Trading Limited
Masterson Holdings Limited
Mazda Motors UK Limited
Medequip Assistive Technology Ltd
Melville Hotel Limited
Monarock Limited
NVSM Limited
National Animal Welfare Trust
Newmarston Ltd
Newschools (Swanscombe) Ltd
Newship Limited
Noahs Ark Chemicals Limited
Oatfield Limited
Octagon Group Limited
PRA Group (UK) Limited
Polaris Ventures Ltd
Poliform UK Limited
Powerbase Management Co Ltd
R S L (Slough) Limited
Radia Estates Limited
Raven Promotions Limited
Richmond & Hampshire Limited
S A Designer Parfums Limited
SME Holdings Limited
SOL Electronics Limited
Sabre EMEA Marketing Limited
Seacon Group Limited
Services Support (Manchester) Holdings
Services Support (Manchester) Ltd
Skynet (London) Limited
Smartcomms SC Limited
Sons of Divine Providence
Spirit Resources (Armada) Ltd
Splash Damage Limited
Stanbreck Properties Ltd
Subex (UK) Limited
Subsea 7 Limited
TCR UK Limited
O.C. Tanner Limited
Thames Industrial Estate Ltd
Times Square Estates Limited
Travel Nation Limited
ULS Living Limited
United Healthcare (South Buckinghamshire) Group
Victoria Docks Hotel Co Ltd
Volkerrail Specialist Businesses Ltd
Walsall Public Lighting Holding Co Ltd
Walsall Public Lighting Ltd
Wellmode Limited
Whiter Smile Limited
WorleyParsons Europe Limited
York Apartments Limited

2002 [177]

AD Construction Group Limited
AHL Holdings (Wakefield) Ltd
ATD Travel Services Limited
Abbeyman Investments Limited
Accord Healthcare Limited
Acorn Limited
Agrofertrans Ltd.
Aim Academies Trust
Alandale Plant & Scaffolding Ltd
Alestra Limited
Amana Trust
Amey Highways Lighting (Wakefield)
Angel Property Investments Ltd
Aquila EHS Limited

Aquila Estates Limited
Atkins ATK Investments Limited
Avantia Insurance Limited
BP Pipelines (SCP) Limited
Belgrave Land (Management) Ltd
Best Foods Limited
Velji Bhovan & Sons (Trading) Ltd
Bio Products Laboratory Holdings Ltd
Bottling Great Britain Limited
Brambles Finance PLC
Bristol-Myers Squibb Holdings 2002
Brymore Estates Limited
CLFIS (U.K.) Limited
Canada Life Finance (U.K.) Ltd
Caretech Holdings PLC
Cargill Weybridge Limited
Celgene Europe Limited
Chawla's Limited
Cipla (EU) Limited
Coats Limited
Consort Healthcare (Blackburn) Funding
Consort Healthcare (Blackburn) Holdings
Consort Healthcare (Blackburn) Ltd
Countrywide Developments (UK) PLC
Coventry and Rugby Hospital Company PLC
Crest Plus Operations Limited
Croudace Homes Group Limited
Crystal Home Improvements Group Ltd
Cuffe Holdings Limited
Daikin Airconditioning UK Ltd
Dallas Burston Ashbourne Holdings
Defence Support (St Athan) Holdings
Defence Support (St Athan) Ltd
Dentoptic Limited
Dhamecha Group Limited
Diamond Corporation Limited
District One Estates Ltd
E P I Limited
E.F.R. Travel Limited
Eda Quality Foods Limited
Education Support (Enfield 2) Holdings
Education Support (Enfield 2) Ltd
Education Support (Enfield) Holdings
Education Support (Newham) Holdings
Education Support (Newham) Ltd
Enterprise Finance Limited
Epsilon Telecommunications Ltd
Everest Limited
FSI (FM Solutions) Limited
Facilicom UK Limited
Fairview New Homes (Properties) Ltd
Fire Design Solutions Limited
First Wave Housing Limited
Frankham Consultancy Group Ltd
Fusion Global Limited
Galliford Try Construction & Investments Holdings
Garves Wind Limited
Ghai & Co. Limited
Glengall Limited
Gould Publication Papers UK Ltd
Gracechurch Sports Management Ltd
Grovestream Limited
Guangdong Investments Limited
Gunpowder Mill Developments Ltd
H.K.S. Motors Limited
Halcyon Offices Limited
Healthcare Support (Newcastle) Holdings
Healthcare Support (Newcastle) Ltd
Heritage Care Homes Limited
Hi-Spirits Ltd
Hills Group Enterprises Ltd

Hinds Ltd
Insurance Claims Accommodation Bureau
Interchemprod and Invest Ltd
Intercontinental Hotels Ltd
Interiors with Art Limited
Intermay Management Ltd
Invicta Film Partnership No.10, LLP
Invicta Film Partnership No.11, LLP
Invicta Film Partnership No.12, LLP
Invicta Film Partnership No.13, LLP
Invicta Film Partnership No.14, LLP
Invicta Film Partnership No.15, LLP
Invicta Film Partnership No.8, LLP
Invicta Film Partnership No.9, LLP
J.C.S. Developments Ltd.
JDM Investments Limited
Johalian Property Limited
KLM Cityhopper UK Limited
Karelia Tobacco Company (UK) Ltd
Kelly Rail U.K. Ltd
Kew Green Hotels (Portsmouth) Ltd
Kia Motors (UK) Limited
Laing O'Rourke Services Ltd
Lamrose Properties Limited
Laridge Investments Limited
Leading Edge Labels Limited
Lime Tree Village Limited
Marcus & Marcus Limited
Media 10 Limited
Metam Properties Limited
Mountbrook Properties Limited
Navblue Limited
New Demipower Limited
Newport School Solutions Ltd
Newschools (Merton) Limited
Niemans Holdings Limited
O'Neill Investments Limited
Olivegate Properties Limited
One YMCA
Outlook Fostering Services Ltd
PCL Transport Limited
Parthenon Entertainment Ltd
Pearl River Delta Investments Ltd
Prax Petroleum Limited
Professor Puzzle Limited
Prosidion Limited
G.Purchase Construction Ltd
RCL (UK) Ltd.
RIG Medical Recruit Limited
RO Regional Properties Limited
Rainham Industrial Services Ltd
The Alec Reed Academy
Regenter B3 Holdco Limited
Regenter B3 Limited
Reliance Communications (U.K.) Ltd
Remington Partners Ltd
Rivers Finance Group PLC
Rosetree Finance Limited
Rugby Football Foundation
S N B Holdings Limited
SCIH Branston 3
Sherrygold No.1 Limited
Shun Cheong Lung Holding Co Ltd
Silvermead Properties Ltd
Skanska Infrastructure Investment UK
Soul Foods Limited
Spectris UK Holdings Limited
Spectris US Holdings Limited
Speed 9395 Limited
Spirit Energy North Sea Ltd
St James Contracts Limited
St James Media LLP
Stat Holding International Ltd
Stonemanor Limited
Swanvale Management Limited
Swiss Post Solutions Ltd
Tesla Motors Limited
Thames Honda Limited
Tone Group Limited
Topgolf Group Limited
Tower, One St George Wharf Ltd
Trade Sale (Slough) Limited
Tradewise Insurance Services Ltd
Transeur Properties Limited
Triland Properties Limited
Valentine Group Limited
Vestey Group Limited
J M W Vicary Limited
W3 Insights Ltd
Western Wines Holdings Limited
Wilman Universal Group Limited
Yparho Investments Limited

2003 [214]

4th Dimension Innovation Ltd
AHL Holdings (Manchester) Ltd
Abbey Care Complex Limited
Abbey Total Care Group Limited
Academia Limited
Academy Services (Waltham Forest)
Acqua Plus Developments Ltd
Action for Children
Affinity (Reading) Limited
Al-Khair Foundation
Alderforce Limited
Amey Highways Lighting (Manchester)
The John Apthorp Charity
Ardour World Limited
Asiatic Carpets Holdings Ltd
Athona Limited
BTC Pipeline Holding Co Ltd
Bagga Holdings Limited
Baik Agency Limited
Basis Technologies International Ltd
Bellevue Education Group Ltd
Berkeley Ryewood Limited
Birmingham Schools Partnership (Group)
Black River Asset Management (UK)
Blanc Brasseries Limited
Bow Village Limited
Brambles Nominees Limited
Braycote Ltd
British Airways 777 Leasing Ltd
Bycentral Holdings Limited
Bycentral Limited
CEB Global Limited
Capital City Service Limited
Ceesail Limited
Cellxion Ltd
A.W. Champion Properties Ltd
A.W. Champion Timber Limited
City Link (Cardiff) Holdings Ltd
Cloverton Property Ltd
Coats Global Services Limited
Cochlear Research and Development
Corbus Europe Limited
Cousins Material House Limited
Creative Distribution Limited
Crest Nicholson Developments (Chertsey)
Crystal Home Improvements Holdings
DSJ Homes Limited
Dakota Developments Limited
Defender No.1 Production Limited Liability Partnership
Defender No.1 Sale & Leaseback Limited Liability Partnership
Defender No.2 Production Limited Liability Partnership
Defender No.2 Sale & Leaseback Limited Liability Partnership
Derby Healthcare (Holdings) Ltd
Derby Healthcare PLC
Do & Co. Event & Airline Catering
Donatantonio Limited
E Y C Limited
ESP Electricity Limited
Earndrive Limited
Elliot Leigh Property Investments 2 Ltd
Endace Europe Limited
Eurostaff Group Limited
Excess Baggage Group Limited
Fieldgrange Properties Limited
Fineraid Limited
Fuller Leisure Limited
Gaat International Ltd
Gala Film Partners, LLP
Ganco Limited
General Mills UK Limited
Golf Entertainment International Ltd
Grosvenor Park 2004 Film Partnership No.1 LLP
Guarding UK Ltd
HH Global Limited
HRT UK Limited
Hayes Point (Sully) Limited
Health & Case Management Ltd
Heart Internet Limited
Heatpoint Limited
Hi - Line Wines Limited
Highassets Limited
Hill Co Ltd
Hillier Hopkins LLP
Hollyhedge Limited
Hoopers Homes Limited
ISG Technology Limited
Information Security Forum Ltd
Intuitive Limited
Invicta Film Partnership No. 17, LLP
Islam Channel Limited
JRL Plant and Logistics Ltd
JRL Property Limited
Jay Fostering Limited
Jobladder Limited
K.E.M. Property Services Ltd
K2 Trading Limited
KBR Property Investments Ltd
Kalbro Investments Limited
Kallar Investments Limited
Kara Management Ltd
Katrin Properties Limited
Kedleston (Wings Education) Ltd
Kelly Property Co Ltd
Khakharia Properties Limited
Klassik Property Ltd
Kore Wireless UK PLC
LGC Group Holdings Limited
LGC Investments Limited
Limesquare Vehicle Rental Ltd
Lipman Properties Limited
Lituanica UK Ltd
Livingston Group Limited
London May Fair Hotel Limited
London Pharma & Chemicals Group Ltd
London Tower Crane Hire & Sales Ltd
Longford Securities & Equities (K & T)
MSV Group Limited

Macquarie Corona Energy Holdings Ltd
Manpower Direct (UK) Ltd.
Marchent Limited
Marlborough Isleworth Properties Ltd
Maybury Media LLP
Mayday Healthcare PLC
Megnum Limited
Merz Pharma UK Limited
Milcars Limited
Millennium Seacon Properties Ltd
Moreland House Care Home Ltd
Moss Electrical Holdings Ltd
Motherwell Holdings Limited
MyTime Active
Nasco (UK) Ltd
New Way International Ltd
Newport Group (Holdings) Ltd
Newport School Solutions (Holdings)
OGE Drilling & Investment Ltd
Offie Limited
Omni Serv Limited
PandoraExpress 2 Limited
PandoraExpress 3 Limited
PandoraExpress 4 Limited
PandoraExpress 7 Limited
Penasul UK Limited
PizzaExpress Operations Ltd
Popsoda Limited
Premiere Employment Group Ltd
Prime Care Solutions (Kingston) Holdings
Prime Care Solutions (Kingston) Ltd
Principal London Limited
Principal Manchester Limited
Principal York Limited
Property Warehouse Limited
Prospect Healthcare (Hairmyres) Group
Prospect Healthcare (Hinchingbrooke)
Q.F.S. Scaffolding Limited
QED (Clacton) Limited
QED (Leeds) Limited
Quickdrop Limited
RES UK & Ireland Limited
RO Enterprises Limited
Regenter Bentilee District Centre (Holding)
Remus Construction & Development Ltd
Renewable Energy Systems Holdings
Riposte Limited
Roseland Parc Limited
Rosemead Limited
Safe Properties Limited
Safestore Acquisition Limited
Safestore Group Limited
Safestore Holdings PLC
Sazerac UK Limited
Select Poultry & Meat Ltd
Seymour House Residential Care Homes
Shazam Productions Limited
Shure UK Limited
Shurgard UK Limited
Sian Formwork Limited
Sigma Sports Limited
Sines Parks Ltd
Sirhowy Enterprise Way (Holdings)
Sirhowy Enterprise Way Limited
Snowflake 145 Limited
Sourcecode UK Limited
Squire Energy Limited
Surrey Rest Homes Limited
Tax Systems PLC
Telbridge Motor Co Ltd
Tempur Sealy International Ltd
Trafalgar Square Investments Ltd
Transform Schools (Rotherham) Holdings
Transform Schools (Rotherham) Ltd
Travel Republic Ltd
Treebond Limited
Tudor Bank Limited
UHP Investments Limited
UPS (UK Holding) Limited
Ultrabrook Limited
Universal Dispense Systems Ltd
Unstuffy Hotel Co Limited
V.B. Investments Limited
Vanwise Group Limited
Verint WS Holdings Limited
Via-Vox Limited
Volkerrail Group Limited
WPA Support Services Limited
Warrant Properties Limited
Watford FC's Community Sports & Education Trust
Watts Farms (Sales) Limited
Whiteley Homes Trust
Wind Farm Holdings Limited
Woodcote Estates Limited
Workout Limited
Yorkshire Transformations Ltd
Zentropa Film Partnership LLP

2004 [193]

123-Reg Limited
1st Step Solutions Limited
3VS UK Limited
AMG Healthcare Limited
APCOA Parking Holdings (UK) Ltd
Accolade Wines Holdings Europe Ltd
Adil Property Investment Ltd
Aitch Care Homes (London) Ltd
Akari Therapeutics, PLC
Al Jazeera International Ltd
Allport Group Limited
Almus Pharmaceuticals Limited
Applepeach Limited
Aquifer Limited
Arora Manchester Limited
Atkins Investments UK Limited
Audley Court Limited
Augustus 1 Limited
Augustus 2 Limited
BP Exploration Personnel Co Ltd
BP Services International Ltd
Banks Hotel Limited
Beck & Pollitzer Holdings Ltd
Belgrave Land (Armley) Limited
Berkeley Group Holdings PLC
Berkeley Homes (PCL) Limited
Berkeley Seventy-Six Limited
Bhaggo Limited
Blackford Media LLP
Blossom House School Limited
Buxton Crescent Hotel and Thermal Spa Co
CP Regents Park Two Limited
Caesar Management Limited
Campaign Master (UK) Limited
Carmel (UK) Limited
Caterham Cars Group Limited
Ceros No.1 Limited
Chainkey Limited
Champ Cargosystems (UK) Ltd
Channeladvisor UK Limited
Chelsea Stores Holdings Ltd
Cineworld Group PLC
Cineworld Holdings Limited
Cloud Networks Limited
Compass Group Finance No.4 Ltd
Crown House Technologies Ltd
DDD Investments Limited
DMC Contracts Limited
DSTI Group LLP
DSTI Holdings Limited
Daarasp LLP
Delivered on Time Limited
Derby School Solutions (Holdings)
Derby School Solutions Limited
Dudley Properties Limited
Easyfairs UK Limited
Education Support (Swindon) Holdings
Education Support (Swindon) Ltd
Elysium Healthcare (Farndon) Ltd
Elysium Healthcare (St Mary's) Ltd
Equion Health (Newcastle) Ltd
Ergonomic Solutions International
Expanded Limited
Explore Capital Limited
ExxonMobil Finance Co Ltd
ExxonMobil Investment Co Ltd
Falco Construction Limited
Fardaar LLP
Finance Ireland Limited
First Investments (UK) Limited
Freshasia Foods Ltd
Future Electronics Management Services
GE Money Home Lending Holdings Ltd
Galliford Try Investments Ltd
Giga Communications Limited
Glenmark Pharmaceuticals Europe Ltd
Good Harvest Properties (Southwark)
Goodwill SIP Limited
Gratia (Abbey Care Home) Ltd
Greenbond Properties Limited
Grosvenor Park 2005 Film Partnership No.1 LLP
Grosvenor Park 2005 S42 Film LLP
H & D Support Services (Holdings)
H & D Support Services Limited
H & T Group PLC
HCL Insurance BPO Services Ltd
Harefield Academy Trust
Hart Homes Limited
Hayre Investments & Developments Ltd
Healthcare Support (Newcastle) Finance
Healthcare Support (North Staffs) Finance
Healthcare Support (North Staffs) Holdings
Healthcare Support (North Staffs)
Hindu Education Authority Ltd
Impulse Leisure
Inspire Community Trust
Intelliflo Limited
Intercontinental Hotels Group PLC
Invicta Film Partnership No.20, LLP
Invicta Film Partnership No.22, LLP
Invicta Film Partnership No.23, LLP
Invicta Film Partnership No.25, LLP
Invicta Film Partnership No.26, LLP
Invicta Film Partnership No.27, LLP
J P & S Servicess Ltd
J P Investments London Ltd
Jewish Community Secondary School Trust
K K Investment Ltd
Kaysail Limited
Keswick Enterprises Group Ltd
Kew Green (Square) Limited
Killoughery Properties Limited
Lambda Therapeutic Limited
Linkhaven Estates Ltd
Lixmere Properties Limited

Love Productions Limited
MIQ Logistics EU Limited
MK Windfarm Limited
MRB Holdings Ltd
Manors Sales and Lettings Ltd
Medipharmacy Limited
Mentfield UK Limited
Menzies Aviation (ASIG Ground Handling)
Modern Schools (Barnsley) Ltd
Modern Schools (Exeter) Ltd
Mondi German Investments Ltd
Mondi Investments Limited
Net Pay (EUR) Limited
Nexen Petroleum U.K. Holdings Ltd
Northfield Avenue (Holdings) Ltd
O'Rourke Investments Holdings (UK)
O.S.T.C. Limited
Officeteam Group Limited
Officeteam Limited
Openview Group Limited
Optivo Development Services Ltd
Original Additions (Beauty Products)
Peppercorn Investments Limited
Perform Media Sales Ltd
Pinden Limited
Ping Pong Limited
Piramal Critical Care Limited
Prefect Software LLP
Premier Work Support Limited
Premiere Coffee Limited
Procter & Gamble Finance (UK) Ltd
Procter & Gamble Holdings (UK) Ltd
Procter & Gamble Investment Company (UK)
Procter & Gamble Overseas Ltd
Profresh Solutions Limited
Prospect Healthcare (Hairmyres) Resources
Purchase Group Limited
Q.N. Hotels (Wrexham) Limited
RO Properties Limited
RO Trading Limited
Racal Acoustics Limited
Rambler Metals and Mining PLC
Regenter Bentilee District Centre
Residential Properties Funds Ltd
Rhenus High Tech UK Limited
Rhodehurst Limited
Riverdale Developments Limited
SIP Group Limited
Safestand Limited
Second Shurgard UK Camberley Ltd
Shurgard UK West London Ltd
Siddharth Jewellery (U.K.) Ltd
Sky Home Communications Ltd
Skyline Arcomet Limited
Smart Card Software Limited
Soloberry Limited
Spirit Europe Limited
St. John's Preparatory & Senior School
Strides Arcolab International Ltd
Sun Hotel Limited
Sunray Estates Limited
Supercraft Holdings Limited
Suzo International (UK) Ltd
Todd Group Limited
Togher Construction Limited
Tudor Williams (Holdings) Ltd
U K Insurance Business Solutions Ltd
Valley Wholesale Carpets (2004) Ltd
Vista Al Mar Limited
WP SK Holdings Limited
WP SK Limited
Winscales Moor Windfarm Ltd
Wintertime Properties Limited
Wood Group Industrial Services Ltd
Worldwide Energy Logistics Ltd
Wryde Croft Wind Farm Limited
Yourway Transport Limited
Zing Leisure Limited

2005 [194]

ATK Energy EU Limited
ATK Energy EU Services Limited
Abbey Ravenscroft Park Limited
Ability Hotels (Luton Inn) Ltd
Able Skills Limited
Aliunde Limited
Anglo Suisse Investments Ltd
Arabella Health Staffing Ltd
Arcese UK Limited
Arcofina LLP
Arora Hotels Limited
Arora Management Services Ltd
Ashley Homes Limited
Attwell Business Inc. Limited
Audley Clevedon Limited
Audley Inglewood Limited
Audley St Elphins Limited
Austin (GB) Limited
Axiom Education (Perth & Kinross) Holdings
Axiom Education (Perth & Kinross)
BEC (London) Limited
BP Exploration Libya Limited
BP Exploration North Africa Ltd
BP Investments Asia Limited
BPH Finance Number 1 Limited
Baby Network Limited
Bal Holdings Limited
Beam Suntory UK Holdings Ltd
Beam Suntory UK Limited
Belgrave Land (Perth) Limited
Belsize Garages Project Ltd
Berkeley (SQP) Limited
Betex LLP
Bible and Gospel Trust
Biz Group Holdings Limited
Broadham Care Limited
Broadway Malyan Holdings Ltd
J.Browne Properties (UK) Ltd
Burton Wold Wind Farm (Trading) Ltd
By Chelmer (Holdings) Limited
By Chelmer PLC
CNOOC Petroleum Farragon U.K. Ltd
Capital Hospitals (Holdings) Ltd.
Capital Hospitals (Issuer) PLC
Capital Hospitals Ltd.
Cargill Cotton Limited
Caterham School Limited
Caversham Trading Limited
Celgene Limited
Central Nottinghamshire Hospitals (Holdings)
Central Nottinghamshire Hospitals PLC
Chard Properties (UK) Limited
Charteroak Estates Limited
M & J Charters LLP
Cherry Advertising Limited
City & Docklands (W3) Limited
Citygate Automotive Limited
Citygate Holdings Limited
Compass Group North America Investments
Compass Group North America Investments No.2
Coxwell Care Limited
Creative Car Park Ltd
Croudace Strategic Limited
Crystal Group Limited
Dhiman Enterprises Limited
E-Nova Healthcare Limited
Easymix Concrete UK Ltd
Edinburgh Retail LLP
Elektron Tower 3 Limited
Elysium Healthcare Property 2 Ltd
Elysium Healthcare Property 3 Ltd
Equiniti Data Limited
Essex Motor Co Ltd
Explore Living Limited
FJJ Limited
A.A. Fisher (Holdings) Ltd
Fishnet Properties Limited
Fishpools Holdings Limited
Gable Homes Lettings Limited
Tony Gee and Partners LLP
Gilead Sciences Europe Ltd.
GlaxoSmithKline Holdings Ltd
Godrej UK Limited
Goldex Investments Limited
Grosvenor Park 2006 S48 Film LLP
Grosvenor Park 2007 S48 Film LLP
Gym Limited
H. K. S. Holdings Limited
H.K.S. Retail Limited
HFMC Group Holdings Ltd
Handspan Limited
Hertz Holdings III UK Limited
Homes Caring for Autism Ltd
John F Hunt Power Limited
IMCD Holding UK Ltd
ISG Technology Holdings Ltd
ISS UK Holding Limited
Intercede 2052 Limited
Invicta Film Partnership No.32, LLP
Invicta Film Partnership No.34, LLP
Invicta Film Partnership No.37, LLP
Isleworth & Hounslow Charity Ltd
Jewellery Channel Limited
Leonard F Jollye (Holdings) Ltd
KFG Quickserve Limited
KMP Holdings Limited
Kavanagh Retailing (UK) Ltd
Keash Properties Limited
Laurels Care Limited
Link Asset Services (Holdings) Ltd
Lint (Redington Road) Limited
Lint Group Limited
MY Construction & Carpentry Ltd
Maidensgrove Limited
Marchase Limited
Marymount International School
Marz Limited
McGrath Bros. (Environmental) Ltd.
Metrolink RATP Dev Limited
Millharbour Developments Ltd
Mothers Ltd
Mundays LLP
Munnelly Group PLC
National Fostering Agency (Scotland)
Needspace? Limited
Newhospitals (St Helens and Knowsley) Finance
Newhospitals (St Helens and Knowsley) Holdings
Newhospitals (St Helens and Knowsley)
Notonthehighstreet Enterprises Ltd
Nucleus Financial Group PLC
Nucleus Financial Services Ltd
O'Malley Haulage Limited
Oakwood Finance London Limited

Orthopaedic Research UK
PAAM Investments Limited
Park Score Ltd
Perform Media Channels Ltd
Playpower UK Limited
Principal Edinburgh George Street
Property Plus Investments Ltd
Property Support Services UK Ltd
RCL Investments Ltd
Rambert School of Ballet and Contemporary Dance Trust
Reach Active Group Limited
Regenter LCEP Holdco Limited
Regenter LCEP Limited
Retirement Villages Group Ltd
Riverstore Limited
Rubylake Investments Limited
Rugby Football Development Ltd
SME Investments Limited
SME Properties Limited
SRCH Limited
STM Group (UK) Limited
Safe Haven London
Safestore Limited
Sail Croatia Adventures Ltd
Sega Publishing Europe Limited
Selborne Care Limited
Select Enterprises Limited
SintecMedia LON Ltd
Sky Group Finance PLC
Spence Refit Ltd
St George Blackfriars Limited
Starglade Parks Limited
Strategic Imperatives Limited
Sunrose Property Limited
TMD Holdings Limited
Taunton Linac Co Ltd
Tax Computer Systems Limited
Tech 21 UK Limited
Thamesfield Limited
Thothaal Group Limited
Tomo Motor Parts Limited
Transform Schools (Bassetlaw) Ltd
Transform Schools (Birmingham) Holdings
Transform Schools (Birmingham) Ltd
Transform Schools (North Lanarkshire) Funding
Transform Schools (North Lanarkshire) Holdings
Transform Schools (North Lanarkshire)
Tricomm Housing (Portsmouth) Ltd
Tropical Sky Limited
UT (UK) Limited
United Living (North) Holdings Ltd
Up Offshore (UK) Limited
WP SK Midco Limited
Warren House Conference Centre Ltd
Wedge Investments Limited
Westfields Homes Limited
Wood Green Investments Limited
Worth More Limited
Worthing Retail Limited Liability Partnership
XTO UK, Ltd
Ziegler UK Limited

2006 [192]

A-Roads Investments Limited
ADI Finance 1 Limited
ADI Finance 2 Limited
AMS Care Limited
APPT Corporation Limited
Ace Investments Limited
Akaal Group PLC
Alexion Pharma UK Limited
Amsair Aircraft Limited
Amsprop Bishopsgate Limited
Amsprop Portland Limited
Antal International Limited
Arcese Real Estate UK Limited
Armondi UK Limited
Ashby & Croft Limited
Aster Healthcare Ltd.
Audley Group Developments 1 Ltd
Avamore Limited
Axiom Education (Edinburgh) Holdings
Axiom Education (Edinburgh) Ltd
Aylesbury Vale Parkway Limited
B.A.T.S. Ilford Limited
BFIM Limited
BP Alternative Energy Investments
BP Holdings North America Ltd
BPC Interiors Limited
Bandai Namco Amusement Europe Ltd
Barrett Industrial Limited
Berkeley Homes (Southall) Ltd
Big Bear Group Limited
Blenheim Consultancy Services Ltd
Boxtrent Limited
Brambles Holdings Unlimited
Brambles Investment Ltd.
Brasserie Bar Co Limited
CIKU Construction Services Ltd
Care Management Group (Acquisition)
Caretech Estates Limited
Carlson Wagonlit New Holdco Ltd
Castle Bidco PLC
Catco Kids LLP
Central Surrey Health Limited
Charco 2010 Limited
Chigwell School
Chrysalis (Stanhope) Limited
Community Support Project Ltd
Consort Healthcare (Mid Yorkshire) Funding
Consort Healthcare (Mid Yorkshire) Holdings
Consort Healthcare (Mid Yorkshire)
Crosswater Holdings Limited
Crystal Clear Group Limited
DS (Holdings) 2 Limited
Davton Holdings Ltd
Denver Building Services Ltd
Designer M & E Services UK Ltd
Doncaster School Solutions (Holdings)
Doncaster School Solutions Ltd
Duplo International Limited
Eastbury Park (Holdings) Ltd
Eastbury Park Limited
Education Management Corporation Ltd
Edwardian Hampshire Hotels Ltd
Edwardian Pastoria Hotels Ltd
Elysium Healthcare (Lighthouse) Ltd
Elysium Healthcare (Ultimate Care)
Excess Baggage Holdings Ltd
FGP Topco Limited
FSI Global PLC
Forth Health Holdings Limited
Forth Health Limited
Foster Denovo Limited
Freshplant Limited
Friend's Property Portfolio Ltd
GDC (Holdings) Ltd
GH Land Developments Limited
GPF Lewis PLC
Galliford Try Plant Limited
Gateway Learning Community
Genuine Solutions International Ltd
W W Giles (Smithfield) Ltd
Goldfield Homes Limited
Grantol Investments Limited
HML Holdings PLC
Harepath Estates LLP
Haymarket PR Publications LLP
Heathrow Airport Holdings Ltd
Hilton HHC Limited
Hoddesdon Developments Ltd
Holmes Care (Group) Limited
Honey Monster Foods Limited
Hoole Hall Country Club Ltd
Howitzer Acquisition Limited
John F Hunt Group Ltd
Integrated Electronic Technologies
JTI (UK) Management Ltd
Jersey Property Partnership LLP
KBR (Aspire Construction) Ltd
KBR (Aspire Services) Limited
Kallarview Homes Limited
Kedleston Schools Limited
Keltbray Aspire Limited
Kew Green Hotels (Gatwick) Ltd
Kilmorie Investments LLP
Kingscote Construction Services Ltd
Knight Noise Limited
LPM Acquisitions Limited
Lay & Wheeler Limited
Leena Plaza Limited
Lineside Logistics (Southern) Ltd
Lionel Road Developments Ltd
Lorclon Limited
MSK Holdings Limited
Method Products Limited
Midgard Ltd
Mondi Finance PLC
Mont Rose College of Management and Sciences
Morrisroe Group Limited
NFAG Limited
NFAH Limited
Neilmed Limited
New Victoria Hospital Limited
Newham Family Dental Care Ltd
Nomad Foods Europe Finco Ltd
Nomad Foods Europe Holdco Ltd
Nomad Foods Europe Holdings Ltd
Nomad Foods Europe Limited
Nomad Foods Europe Midco Ltd
Opus 2 International Limited
P G S International Limited
Philmont Properties UK Limited
Placement Group Healthcare Ltd
Premier Fleet Management and Contract Hire
Promede Limited
Pronovias UK Limited
QSC 1208 Limited
QSC 1209 Limited
RBR Property Investments Ltd
Raban Holdings Limited
Residential Land Holdings Ltd
Residential Land Management Ltd
Rex Partners LLP
Rooff Property LLP
SME (Coffee) Limited
Safestore Investments Limited
Saiwil Limited
Sartorius Stedim UK Limited
Seebeck 133 Limited
Shelly Motors Limited

Sherrygreen Homes Ltd
Skanska Project Developments Ltd
Sky Insurance Services Group Ltd
Sliabh Construction Limited
Sonata Europe Limited
Sovereign Recovery (UK) Ltd
Spirit Energy Southern North Sea Ltd
Spirit Norway Limited
St Edward Homes Limited
St Mary's University, Twickenham
Staten Investments Limited
Subsea 7 Engineering Limited
Sunflower Healthcare (Greenford) LLP
T.C & D Construction Ltd.
TGS Geophysical Company (UK) Ltd
Tata Global Beverages Capital Ltd
Tata Global Beverages Investments
Test Equipment Asset Management Ltd
Thames Reinforcements Limited
Toureen Group Limited
Toureen Plant Limited
Tumi (UK) Limited
Ultimate Care Limited
Union Maritime Limited
United Biscuits Bidco Limited
United Biscuits BondCo Limited
United Biscuits Holdco 2 Ltd
United Biscuits Holdco Limited
United Biscuits Vlnco Limited
VGC Group Limited
Van Gastel Beheer Limited
Vassall Ventures Limited
Verde Agritech PLC
Verex Insurance Services Ltd
Via Global Limited
Victoria Docks Hotel Company (Number Two)
T. Visaman & Sons Limited
Walsingham Care
Water Incorporated
West Ten Properties (UK) Ltd
Xstro Investments Limited
Zoom Gas Pipelines Limited
Zoom Holding Limited
Zoom Infrastructure Limited

2007 [187]

Ability Hotels (Cambridge) Ltd
Ability Hotels (Dunblane) Ltd
Ability Hotels (Glasgow) Ltd
Ability Hotels (Liverpool) Ltd
Acclaim Handling Group Ltd
Actionmanor Limited
Advanced Access Platforms Ltd
Aerospace Tooling Limited
Agfa Healthcare UK Limited
Ahmed Property Limited
Alliance BMP Limited
Almirall Limited
Aluminium Services (UK) Ltd
Anya House Limited
Aquila BTE 1 Limited
Aquila Maldon Limited
Atkins International Holdings Ltd
Audley Binswood Limited
Audley St George's Limited
Avalon Cellars Two Limited
Aviation Business Continuity Ltd
Avocado Developments Limited
B & P Acquisitionco Limited
B & P Holdings II Limited
B & P Midco Limited
BP Aromatics Limited
BW Foundation
Beck MBI Limited
Best Commercial Properties Ltd
Bloomfield Terrace LLP
Brighthouse Group Limited
Brighthouse Holdings Limited
Brighthouse Limited
Bynorth (Holdings) Limited
Bynorth Limited
CBee (Europe) Limited
Care Expertise Limited
Cargill Financial Services Europe
Cegal Limited
Clover Environmental Solutions Ltd
Compass Group Procurement Ltd
Concept Developments (Cobham) Ltd
Cort Business Services UK Ltd
Crownstar Limited
DS (Holdings) 3 Limited
Danu Holding Limited
Derbyshire Hotel Derby Limited
Digico Europe Limited
Donatantonio Group Limited
EDC Systems Limited
ET Enterprises Limited
Easyoffice Rental Limited
Ebury 106 Limited
Ellenor
Elysium Healthcare No. 2 Ltd
Embee Holdings Limited
Equiniti Global Payments Ltd
Equiniti Holdings Limited
Europa Worldwide Group Limited
FT Technologies (UK) Ltd
Fascroft Limited
Frithsden Finance (Birmingham) Ltd
Fujitsu General Air Conditioning (UK)
GGI Holdings Limited
Gatehall Services Limited
Go Daddy Europe Limited
Goal Global Recoveries Limited
Gold Group Properties Limited
Goldace Investments LLP
Green Hercules Trading Limited
Green Homes Investment Ltd
Green Space London Limited
Gulmay Holdings Limited
H & H Care Home Investments Ltd
HLT London Manage Limited
HLT Stakis Operator Limited
Hampton School
Harris Federation
Harsco (UK) Group Limited
Harsco Leatherhead Limited
Harsco Mole Valley Limited
Heartlands Hotel Limited
Heathrow (AH) Limited
Heathrow (DSH) Limited
Heathrow (SP) Limited
Heathrow Finance PLC
Heathrow Holdco Limited
Hilands Property Partners LLP
Hilton UK Manage Limited
Horn Cutting Tools Limited
Hotel Intercontinental London (Holdings)
Innovate Services Limited
Insignia Investments Limited
Intralot Finance UK Limited
Jancett Childcare & Jace Training
Java Asset Management Limited
Jollyes Group Limited
KFG Restaurants Limited
KH Finance Limited
KH Holdco Limited
KMS Holdings Limited
Kerneos Holding Northern Europe Ltd
Kesgrave Hall Limited
Kirby Group Engineering (UK) Ltd
Lantern Recovery LLP
Lascelles Leisure Limited
Leisure Parks Real Estate Ltd
Linden/Downland Graylingwell LLP
London Care Partnership Ltd
M - Integrated Solutions PLC
MC Treasury Limited
ME Construction Limited
MND Construction Services Ltd
Manichem Limited
Manor IT (UK) Ltd
Marsh Wall Limited
John Menzies Finance Limited
Metis Homes Limited
Mondi PLC
Monster Energy Europe Limited
Moriarty Haulage Limited
Gordon Murray Design Limited
Mywalit (UK) Limited
NCMT Holdings Limited
Nature Delivered Limited
Network Homes Investments (Stockwell)
Network Homes Investments Ltd
Network Treasury Services Ltd
Anthony Nicholas (UK) Limited
Oakdene Holdings Limited
Octagon Group Holdings Limited
PQW Brenley Corner Limited
Parkview Treasury Services (UK) Ltd
Perform Group Limited
Peterborough (Progress Health) Holdings
Peterborough (Progress Health) Nominee
Peterborough (Progress Health) PLC
Pharmacare (Europe) Limited
Pink Fortress Limited
Pinnacle Foods Limited
Plotplan Limited
Pod-Trak Limited
Project Tristar Limited
Proppertunity Limited
R V Moat House Limited
RFU Injured Players Foundation
Readie Construction Limited
Red Lion Hotel (Henley) Ltd
Reliance Investments Ltd
Rex Trade Associates Limited
Rex Venture Resources Limited
Right Choice Insurance Brokers Ltd
Riverstone Europe LLP
Rocco Homes Limited
Rose Film Partnership LLP
SAI Commodities Limited
SGB Infrastructure Middle East Ltd
SME Corporation Limited
Saints Transport GRP Limited
Santray Limited
Saxonchart Limited
Selecta Holding Limited
Servotest Testing Systems Ltd
Shrewsbury Hotel Limited
Silixa Ltd
Sines Parks (S.E.) Limited
Soda Studios Limited
Splendid Hospitality Group LLP
Starbones Limited
Stem Healthcare Limited

Sunlight PV Ltd
Sword Soft Limited
TFC Properties Limited
Terra Trade and Engineering LLP
Tican (UK) Holdings Limited
Transform Schools (Knowsley) Holdings
Transform Schools (Knowsley) Intermediate
Transform Schools (Knowsley) Ltd
Transmec Properties Limited
Travel Republic Holdings Ltd.
Vinci Environment UK Limited
Vinepost Limited
Walsall Hospital Company (Holdings)
Walsall Hospital Company PLC
Watts Farms Packers Limited
Willhay Management Limited
Wyevale Acquisitions Borrower Ltd

2008 [122]

A P P Wholesale PLC
ABP Packaging Limited
ASIG Holdings Limited
Ability Hotels (Luton) Limited
Ability Hotels (Syon) Limited
Arcus FM Limited
Aviation Servicing Co Ltd
BML Utility Contractors Ltd
BNK (UK) Limited
Backstage Centre Limited
Bamrose Properties Limited
Belgrave Land (Sheffield) Ltd
Biggin Hill Hangar Co Ltd
Book Trade Charity (BTBS)
Bowland Resources (No.2) Ltd
Breyer Holdings Limited
Brickline Properties Limited
Brook Hotels No. 1 Limited
Butlers Walsall Ltd
CSPH Limited
Cadbury Limited
Caretech Estates (No 2) Ltd
Caretech Estates (No 3) Ltd
Caretech Estates (No.4) Ltd
Church of Pentecost - UK
Connect Plus (M25) Holdings Ltd
Connect Plus (M25) Intermediate Ltd
Connect Plus (M25) Limited
Copley Limited
Crane Investments Ltd
Cromsource Ltd
DBT Property LLP
Dairy Crest UK Limited
Danu II Holdings Limited
De Vere Care Limited
Dhamecha Holdings Limited
Dhamecha Property Limited
Edwardian Bloomsbury Street Ltd
Edwardian New Finance Limited
Erindale Limited
Eurochoice Limited
Excelredstone Services Limited
FBL Holdings Limited
First Coins Pawn LLP
Fresh Cash Pawn LLP
GBST Wealth Management Limited
GPS Food Group (UK) Limited
Giggs Hill Green Homes Limited
Giles Homes Limited
Glenageary Estates LLP
Graham Land & Developments Ltd
Guru Nanak Limited
HCL EAS Ltd
Haig Housing Trust
Haymarket UK2 Limited
Robert Heath Group Limited
Host Europe Limited
I-Catering Management Services Ltd
ILB Investments Limited
Independent Group (UK) Limited
Intercontinental (PB) 1
Interdist Alliances Limited
Investland Limited
JRL Group Limited
JTI (RMS) Ltd
KFM Holdings Limited
Katana Property Limited
Kedleston Wings Holdco Ltd
Kew Green Hotels (Speke) Ltd
Khosla Investments Limited
Laing O'Rourke Manufacturing Ltd
Lanber Nursing Homes LLP
Lanber Properties LLP
Linden St Albans LLP
MGT Teesside Limited
Metro Partners LLP
Morrisroe UK Ltd
Multi Trade Links (UK) Ltd
NSL Group Limited
Naked Wines Prepayments Trustee Co Ltd
OH Logistics International (UK) Ltd
OLR (UK) Limited
Offshore Containers Holdings Ltd
PS Foundation
Pepper (UK) Limited
Petco Trading (UK) Limited
Purley Point Limited
Railsite Holdings Limited
Ram Parkash Sunderdass & Sons Ltd
Rangemist Limited
Reliance Infra Projects (UK) Ltd
SEJ Distribution Ltd
SHL Product Ltd
Safetykleen Group Services Ltd
Scalable Software Ltd
Scentrics Information Security Technologies
Seneca Environmental Solutions Ltd
Sevita (UK) Limited
Sinek Global Finance & Trading LLP
Smiths Interconnect Group Ltd
Softwareone UK Limited
Stag Group Limited
Stair Tread Holdings Limited
Stapleford Frog Island (Rainham) Ltd
Tackle Guru Limited
Ten Motives Limited
Ultimate Holdings Limited
Unicorn Ingredients Ltd
Union Glory Limited
Union Investcorp Limited
Valiant Holdings Limited
Verex Group Limited
WP Midco1 Limited
WP Midco2 Limited
WP Midco3 Limited
WP Safety-Kleen Limited
Westway Services Holdings (2010) Ltd.
Woldingham School
WorleyParsons UK Finance Sub Ltd
Wrest Park Limited
Www.Nakedwines.Com Limited
Your Healthcare CIC

2009 [162]

ACC Aviation Limited
Al-Mubarakia Limited
Alliance Healthcare Management Services
Alto Property Investments Ltd
Amar Property Services Limited
Anitass Limited
Apex Medical Respiratory Ltd
Arcus Solutions Limited
Arora Heathrow Holdings Ltd
Ash Properties Limited
Audbern Limited
Aurient Investments N16 Ltd
BPE Polandco Limited
Bamboo Distribution Limited
Bathroom Brands Holdings UK Ltd
Blue Prop Ltd
Bowland Resources Limited
Brand Agency (London) Limited
Brigade Electronics Group PLC
Bromley Healthcare CIC
Brook Hotels Group Limited
Brymore Holdings Limited
Bute Capital Limited
Cadbury South Africa (Holdings)
Capsicum Leasing Limited
Capsicum Motorsport Limited
Caretech Estates (No. 5) Ltd
Chobham School Academy (Stratford)
Chromium Acquisitions Limited
Chromium Assets Limited
Chromium Suchex LLP
Click Entertainment Limited
Coex Properties LLP
Collaborative Services Support (NE) Holdings
Collaborative Services Support NE
Community Stores Limited
Crest Nicholson Holdings PLC
Crossways Care (UK) Limited
Cummins Cogeneration Limited
Cummins ESB Nigeria Limited
Dalemead Care Home Limited
Day Webster Limited
Delamere (Chelmsford) Limited
Drapers' Multi-Academy Trust
Earlseat Wind Farm Ltd
Eiser Infrastructure Partners LLP
Elite Mobile (Holdings) Ltd
Estates and Lets 2 LLP
Estates and Lets 3 LLP
Europe Incoming Holdings Ltd
FBSE Finance Limited
Falcon Hotels Limited
Falcon Investment Ltd
Fitton & Co Ltd
Flexibon Limited
Flight Centre (UK) Wholesale Ltd
GCH (St Katharine's) Limited
GVE London Ltd
Galliford Try HPS Limited
GlaxoSmithKline Investment Holdings
GlaxoSmithKline Investment Services
GlaxoSmithKline Mercury Ltd
Glorious Solutions Limited
Goodrich Inertial Limited
Grand Central Hotel Glasgow Ltd
Green Hill Energy Limited
Harvest Investments Solutions Ltd
Headstart 4 Life Limited
Hertz Accident Support Ltd
Hill Group Services Limited
Hill of Towie Limited
Hospital Company (Southmead) Holdings

Hospital Company (Southmead) Ltd
Howard Hunt Mail Limited
Hybrid Dining Limited
Imagine Cruising Limited
Intercontinental (PB) 3 Ltd
J. B. Developments & Construction
JRL Group Holdings Limited
Jain International Foods Ltd
Jean-Luc Developments Ltd
K2M UK Limited
Kellogg Brown & Root Group Ltd
Kellogg Brown & Root International Group Holdings LLP
Kellogg Brown & Root International Group
Kelly Communications Trading Group
Kewsaw Limited
Kingston Lodge Hotel Limited
LDD Construction Limited
LGC Science Group Limited
LGC Science Investments Ltd
Lady Eleanor Holles School
Laxmico Limited
Local Boy'z Group Holding Ltd
London Pharma & Chemicals Holdings Ltd
MacFarlane Media Limited
Media 10 Holdings Limited
Medivet Partnership LLP
Meller Educational Trust
Millipore UK Holdings LLP
Mission Recordings Limited
Mongas Kids Wear Limited
NFAP Limited
Oaktree Property Co Ltd
Ocean Gateway LLP
Offerco Limited
Only Care Limited
Osborn Securities (Braintree) Ltd
Paje Limited
Panther AL (VAT) Limited
Pattinson Green Limited
Penenden Heath Investments LLP
Pet and Aquatics Properties Ltd
Phivco UK II Limited
Plan B Healthcare PLC
George Potter House Ltd
Purley Baptist Church
RR Securities Limited
William Robinson Gravetye Charity
SDJ Enterprises Limited
SLS Holding Co Ltd
Saba Infra Gloucestershire Ltd
Saville Services Limited
Saxton Limited
Senior Finance Four Limited
Shotfield Development Business Partnership
Sims Milling Services Limited
Sines LLP
Skillcrown Homes (UK) LLP
Standard Plant Hire Limited
Stanley Dock Properties Ltd
Steiner UK Limited
Surrey Lighting Services Ltd
TBG (1) 2009 Limited
TBG (3) 2009 Limited
TES-AMM Europe Holdings Ltd
TWG Europe Limited
TY Ventures (UK) Limited
Teddington 2 Limited
Thew Arnott Group Limited
Thirsk Winton LLP
Tropical Marine Centre Limited
Truly Travel Limited
Ty Danjuma Family Office Ltd
Valley Trucks Holdings Limited
ViiV Healthcare Limited
ViiV Healthcare Overseas Ltd
ViiV Healthcare Trading Services UK
ViiV Healthcare UK Limited
Vinayak Properties Limited
WLHC Projectco Limited
Walgreens Boots Alliance Services
Warrens Warehousing Group Ltd
Wind Assets LLP
Woodgavil Estates Limited
Woodgavil Limited
World Mission Agency - Winners Chapel International
Worldwide Energy Logistics Group Ltd
Worldwide Product Sourcing Ltd
Y.A. Property Investments Ltd
Yorkshire Dales Country Park Ltd
Zandera Ltd

January-June 2010 [90]

3pillar Global UK Limited
Alderforce North Limited
Alternative Bridging Corporation Ltd
Asia UK Property Fund LLP
Aspire Investments and Property Developments LLP
Avonpark Village (Care Homes) Ltd
Beale's Hotels Limited
Bereta Investments Limited
C.V.J. Properties Ltd
CAE Technology Holdings Ltd
CB Equity LLP
Campmoss Property (Tangley Place)
Capsicum Motorsport Holdings Ltd
Cargill UK Holdings Limited
Chi-Chi Collection Limited
Civil Service Benevolent Fund
F. Copson (London) LLP
Crane Apartments Limited
Crown Design and Development Ltd
DP Poland PLC
DST Global Solutions (Realty) Ltd
DST Process Solutions Limited
Alan Day Investments LLP
Duke Street Church (Richmond-upon-Thames)
EACG Holdings Limited
Ealing Community Transport
FC JB Co Limited
Fidelity China Special Situations PLC
Florin Industrial Services Holdings
GCH Corporation Limited
Gade Investments Limited
Galldris Services Ltd
Gateway Hotel Dunstable Ltd
GlaxoSmithKline IHC Limited
HFSI Limited
Healthcare Drugstores Limited
Henry Construction Projects Ltd
Heritage Care Limited
Impact Africa Limited
Inspiral Oldham Holding Co Ltd
Inspiral Oldham Limited
KS SPV 3 Limited
KS SPV 4 Limited
Kenard Group Limited
Kinetic IT Limited
LGC Science Holdings Limited
Laxmi BNS Holdings Limited
Leyton Clubs (London) Limited
London Square (Holdings) Ltd
London Square Developments Ltd
Loudwater Management Limited
MPM Connect Limited
MTALX Limited
McGinley Cep Ltd
Mercurius Synergy LLP
Montpelier Properties Limited
Mullan Partnership Limited
Pharmadent Holdings Limited
Pitchset Limited
Premier Lotteries Capital UK Ltd
Premier Lotteries UK Limited
Quebec Court Freehold Limited
Quest Academy - Coloma Trust
RATP DEV UK Ltd
Raisio UK Limited
Raue LLP
Residential Land Management 2 Ltd
Rooted Architecture Limited
Roseview (London) Ltd.
Saba Infra Hertfordshire Ltd
Saipem Limited
Skanska Residential Development UK
Sky IQ Limited
Spark Property Assets LLP
Surrey Blue Limited
TT Skate Properties Limited
TY Properties (UK) Limited
Tancia (Holdings) Limited
Tobacco Pipe Makers and Tobacco Trade Benevolent Fund
Toll Investments (NA) Ltd
Travel Technology Investments Ltd
Travellanda Ltd
Tustin Properties Ltd
United Living (South) Group Ltd
VXR Imaging Limited
Vidafresh Limited
Vvoosh Limited
WK Properties Limited
White Brasserie Co Ltd
World Wise Foods Limited

July-December 2010 [75]

AMB Property Ltd
AMS Care Wiltshire Limited
Abbey Mills Properties Ltd
Arcus Solutions (Holdings) Ltd
Asino Limited
Avon Freeholds Limited
B K S Energy Limited
Bazooka Candy Brands International
Beths Grammar School
Bexley Grammar School
Bharat Forge International Ltd
Bio Products Laboratory Ltd
Blenheim Barnes Limited
Bluestar Enterprise Limited
Robert Bosch UK Holdings Ltd
Bramley Health Holding Co Ltd
Broxbourne School
Burhill Group Limited
Cadbury Four LLP
Carlton Group Developments Ltd
Ceragon (UK) Limited
Chadwell Heath Academy
Cleves Academy Trust
Cranmore School
Darrick Wood School
Dartford Grammar School
Entel Communications Holdings Ltd

Erith School
Grove Developments Limited
Guru Nanak Sikh Academy Ltd
HEL Bidco Ltd
Hayre Builders Co Ltd
Headmasters Salons Limited
Hersham Green LLP
Hilton Worldwide Manage Ltd
Hunn Holdings Limited
IMCD UK Acquisitions Limited
Ingenie Services Limited
Investors in Ideas Ltd
JLW Excellent Homes for Life Holding Co
JLW Excellent Homes for Life Ltd
KFG Holdings Limited
KMP Taste Limited
Kellogg Brown & Root London Ltd
Kemnal Academies Trust
Kingsmead School
LNOC Limited
Lampton School Academy Trust
MH Star UK Ltd
Metro Global Holdings Limited
Ockendon Academy
Orthene Holdings Limited
Property Finance Capital Ltd
Purism Properties Limited
Queen Elizabeth's School Barnet
RBH Hotel Management Limited
RBH Hotels UK Limited
RCL Cruises Ltd
Radnor House School (Holdings) Ltd
Radnor House School (Property) Ltd
Right Choice Property Holdings Ltd
Rilla Properties Limited
Rina Consulting Ltd
Rivers Leasing PLC
Russell Education Trust
Sharish Properties Limited
Shure Europe Holdings Limited
M & D Silk Properties Ltd
TBG (4) Limited
Uncle Buck Finance LLP
Vestey Foods International Ltd
Wadlow Energy Limited
Watford Grammar School for Boys
Watford Grammar School for Girls
Whisper Films Limited

January-June 2011 [151]

66 Queen Square Limited
Acre 1144 Limited
Albion Bunker and Trading LLP
Amphora Acquisitions Limited
Aquinas Church of England Education Trust
Avanti Schools Trust
BECAP Spicers (UK) Limited
BP Biofuels Brazil Investments Ltd
BP Exploration Angola (Kwanza Benguela)
BP Shafag-Asiman Limited
Balgowan Primary School
Bayti Properties Limited
Bellman Property Group Limited
Black Twig Limited
Boost Homes Ltd
Bullers Wood Multi Academy Trust
Buy 2 Let Cars Ltd
Camelot Business Solutions Ltd
Camelot Global Lottery Solutions Ltd
Caravel Trading Ltd
Carshalton Boys Sports College
Caterham Enterprises Limited
Chancery Education Trust
Chart Forte Holdings Ltd
Charters Village Limited
Cheam Academies Network
Chislehurst School for Girls
Chislehurst and Sidcup Grammar School
Chrysalis Multi Academy Trust
Churchtown Farm Solar Limited
Congregation of The Daughters of The Cross International Generalate
Coyle Equipment Services Ltd
Cranford Community College
Croydon and Lewisham Lighting Services (Holdings)
Croydon and Lewisham Lighting Services
Dalco Developments Limited
Dame Alice Owen's School
Danes Educational Trust
Danjuma Collection Ltd
Davenant Foundation School
Deal Partners Limited
Decus Educational Trust
Dernagree Properties Limited
Dunkeld Trading Limited
East Barnet School
East Langford Solar Limited
Edif Group Finance Limited
Edif Group Limited
Edif Group Management Limited
Education for The 21st Century
Endeavour MAT
Essential Pharma Limited
Far East & Co Limited
Folio Education Trust
GCP Healthcare 1 Limited
GLF Schools
Genesius Film Partners LLP
Girls' Learning Trust
Global Business Trade LLP
Grange Renewable Energy Ltd
Greenlight Credit Ltd
Greenshaw Learning Trust
Grupotec Renewables Limited
Haydon School
Heathrow Aviation Engineering UTC
High Point Solutions Limited
Hoddesdon School Trust
Hooper Homes West Well Limited
Howard Partnership Trust
Hurstmere School
IAH Charity Co Ltd
Iceport Limited
Ikarim Business Services Ltd
Impact Multi Academy Trust
Impact Oil & Gas Limited
JFD Developments Ltd
Jollyes Retail Group Limited
KBR (U.K.) Investments Limited
Kelly Rail Group Ltd
Kent Capital Ltd
Kraft Foods Investment Holdings UK
Kraft Foods UK IP & Production Holdings
LGC Genomics Limited
LGC Whirlwind Limited
Langdon Foundation
Langley Park School for Boys Academy Trust
Lexcross Limited
London Square (Putney) Limited
Lymington Precision Engineering (LPE)
Manor Farm Solar Limited
Melton House Investments Ltd
J P C Mulligan Properties Ltd
New Ladderswood LLP
Overton Grange School
PRP Architects LLP
Papa Entertainment Limited
Paragon Internet Group Limited
Pegasus Academy Trust
Platinum Gold Homes Limited
Popat Stores Limited
Procter & Gamble UK Parent Co Ltd
QH Estates Ltd
Queens' School (Bushey)
RO Financing Co Ltd
RSD Travel Limited
Reach Academy Trust
Regenter Myatts Field North Holding Co
Regenter Myatts Field North Ltd
Rent 2 Own Cars Ltd
Rhombi Holdings Limited
Rickmansworth School
Roos Energy Limited
Rosedale Hewens Academy Trust
Select Enterprises (Holdings) Ltd
Sheikh Holdings Group (Investments)
Shelfside Holding (Northern) Ltd
Shimtech Industries Limited
Signet Direct Diamond Sourcing Ltd
Skylight Investments Limited
Space Truust UK Ltd
Spring Partnership Trust
Step Academy Trust
Sunbury Manor School
Sutton Grammar School Trust
Swakeleys School for Girls
Synaptic Trust
TJX Europe Buying Limited
TN (UK) Consultancy Ltd
TWE Finance (UK) Limited
Taylor Mac Limited
Technical Staffing Resources Ltd
Texcel (2011) Limited
Thamesmead School
Tiffin Girls' School
Tithe Academy
Treasury Wine Estates UK Brands Ltd
Trinitas Academy Trust
Unifruit Group Limited
Uxbridge High School Academy Trust
Viewrose Limited
Vivo Medical Care Limited
Wadlow Energy Holdings Limited
Warren Road Primary School
West Hatch High School Academy Trust
Westbourne Academy Trust
William Willett Learning Trust
Willow Learning Trust
Wood End Academy
Wood Farm (Stanmore) Limited
Wrist Holding UK Limited
Yavneh College Academy Trust

July-December 2011 [143]

Abriand Limited
Allandale Investments Limited
Automated Technology Group Holdings
Azurie Blue Limited
B F Design Solutions Limited
Beacon Multi-Academy Trust Ltd
Belton Associates (Group Holdings)
Belton Associates Holdings Ltd
Belton Associates Limited
Bentley Wood Trust
Bishopshalt School

Bourne Education Trust
CRK Finance Limited
CSL Communications Group Ltd
Cadbury Eight LLP
Cadbury Nine LLP
Cadbury Seven LLP
Cadbury Six LLP
Cadbury Ten LLP
Campion School
Canons High School
Care Providers Recruitment Ltd
City North (Telford Homes) Ltd
City Tool Hire Limited
Connect Schools Academy Trust
Cross London Trains Holdco 2 Ltd
Cross London Trains Limited
Curo Charlotte House LLP
Dalton Resources Limited
Digico Global Limited
Dnata World Travel Limited
EMAP Publishing Limited
Edwardian Canary Wharf Hotel Ltd
Edwardian Free Trade Hall Ltd
Edwardian Mercer Street Ltd
Elgon Hotels Limited
Emerson Park Academy
Empower Learning Academy Trust
Ennogen Healthcare Ltd
Field Marketing (UK) Holdings Ltd
Field Marketing (UK) Limited
Friars Developments Limited
GCP Rooftop Solar 1 Limited
GCP Rooftop Solar 2 Limited
Generations Multi Academy Trust
GlaxoSmithKline Intellectual Property Management
Good Shepherd Catholic Trust
Grand Union Multi Academy Trust
HCL Investments (UK) Ltd
Harouni Group of Companies Ltd
Harrow High School
Hatch End High School
Highway Stops Retail Limited
Hinchley Wood School
Home and Comforts Limited
Honister Capital Holdings I Ltd
Key Bidco Limited
Key Midco Limited
Kidspace Adventures Holdings Ltd
Kinsat Enterprises Ltd
Knight Precision Metals Ltd
Kuflink Bridging Ltd
Langley Park Learning Trust
Lasted Limited
London Square (Fulham) Limited
London Square Development Management
London Square Developments (Ventures)
London Square Limited
Loughton Care Centre Limited
Loxleigh Investments Limited
MC Power Limited
Manor Trust
R. Maskell (Holdings) Limited
Medico-Dental Holdings Limited
Merligen Investments Limited
Middlesex Learning Partnership
Moat Homes Finance PLC
Mount Grace School
Myddleton London Limited
Mylan Pharma UK Limited
NBC Europe Ltd.
Naked Wines International Ltd
Nature's Finest Food Products Ltd
Nower Hill High School
Odyssey Trust for Education
Opus 2 Magnum Holdings Limited
Oval Quarter Developments Ltd
Park High School
Pickhurst Infant Academy
Platinum Investments Surrey Ltd
Dr Michael Prager Holdings Ltd
Prinhold Limited
Prospects Group 2011 Limited
Punjab House Associated Ltd
Queen Elizabeth's Girls' School (Barnet)
RSI Retail Solutions Limited
Ranola Properties Limited
Reliance Entertainment Productions 5 Ltd
Reliance Entertainment Productions 7 Ltd
Renatus Property Management Ltd
Repair Funding Limited
Roadhouse Building & Civil Engineering
Runnymede Homes Limited
Donald Russell Holdings Ltd
S and J Investments (Delivery Office Southall)
SF11 Limited
SFAET Ltd
SG Technologies Group Limited
SNC-Lavalin UK Holding Limited
Senior Finance Six Limited
Senior Five Limited
Shirley High School
South West Essex Community Education Trust
Southborough High School
St Catherine's Catholic School
State Street HCL Holdings (UK) Ltd
Subsea 7 Interim UK Holdings Ltd
Subsea 7 Offshore Resources (UK) Ltd
Subsea 7 Senior Holdings (UK) Ltd
Supreme Hotels LLP
TCA Investments Limited
TER AG Ltd.
TFC Holdings London Limited
TRAD Properties LLP
Tara Mobile Ltd
Trellis Acquisitions Limited
UIDUK Ltd
United Living (North) Group Ltd
Unity Schools Trust
Ursuline Academy Ilford
VFS Legal Limited
Valley Primary School
Vanguard Learning Trust
Verint Technology UK Limited
Veritas Educational Trust
Volkerstevin Group Limited
WNDirect Limited
Wandle Valley School
Warchest Limited
Watts Farms Catering Limited
Watts Farms Fresh Produce Holdings
Woodland Academy Trust
Zebrak London Limited

January-March 2012 [67]

ACR Investments Limited
AVM Vision Investments Ltd
AVMI Group Limited
Adelie Foods Group Limited
Apollo Property Investment Ltd
BP Exploration China Limited
BP Subsea Well Response Ltd
Blackfen School for Girls
Blenheim High School
Bricklehampton Classic Care Ltd
Bushey St James Trust
Calda Limited
Coombe Academy Trust
Corumbe Investments Limited
Daylighting Power Limited
Elstree UTC
FTE & M Limited
Fifty Shades Ltd
Fizzy Enterprises LLP
Fizzy Epsom LLP
Galliard Group Limited
Garrets Bidco 2 Limited
Garrets Bidco Limited
Gog Magog Partnership LLP
Hastoe Capital PLC
Hazel Renewables Limited
Hertswood Academy
Hildo Limited
Hillary Bidco Limited
Isleworth and Syon School for Boys
JEDS Investments Ltd
Kimal Holdings Limited
Kluman and Balter Holdings Ltd
Lightwood Strategic Limited
Longmill Rickbost Ltd
Mayfield Grammar School, Gravesend
Maysor LLP
Mega Fabrications Group Ltd
Myatt's Field Development LLP
NDEMIC Creations Ltd
NTS Retail Limited
Oblue Limited
Oforce Limited
Optivo Finance PLC
Ospirit Limited
Parklight Properties Limited
RVT Group Limited
Raedex Consortium Limited
Retallack Holidays Limited
Richmond Green Developments Ltd
Rosetta Investments Limited
Salisbury Workplace Services Ltd
South Orpington Learning Alliance Multi-Academy Trust
St Mary's CE Academy, Cheshunt
St. James The Great R.C. Primary and Nursery School
Steel Yard Trading LLP
Symbio Energy Limited
TVH Fizzy Holdings Limited
Tallentire Energy Limited
Timeboard Investments LLP
Tradex Insurance Holdings Ltd
Trellis Finance Limited
Trellis Holdco Limited
Trellis Investments Limited
Wandale Limited
Wear Point Wind Limited
Wyevale Garden Centres Capital Ltd

April-June 2012 [47]

AG Retail Cards Limited
Amber Solar Parks (Holdings) Ltd
Amber Solar Parks Limited
Aryzta UK Holdings I Limited
Bellevue Education International Ltd
Broadrich Limited
Buildvantage Limited
Canterbury Homes Ltd

Carbon Solutions Global Ltd
Chasemore Farm LLP
Chawla & Gulati Property Investments
Collegiate Trust
Cosan Lubes Investments Ltd
Costco Online UK Limited
Crislex Limited
Cross London Trains Finance Co Ltd
Cross London Trains Holdco Ltd
Dalin Limited
Eden Academy
European Investments (Cornwall) Ltd
European Investments (SCEL) Ltd
Fizzy Canning Town LLP
Fulca Limited
GCP Rooftop Solar 3 Limited
GH London Ground Handling Services
Gladstone Court Developments Ltd
GlaxoSmithKline Consumer Trading Services
Grove HR Limited
Haemonetics Asia UK Ltd
Hincroft Limited
Hive Football Centre Holdings Ltd
IAG Cargo Limited
Kout Food Group Restaurants UK Ltd
Life Education Trust
Lismire LLP
Purslow Investments Limited
Quivira Bridging No.1 LLP
RET Becket Keys Church of England Free School Trust
Riverside Bio Limited
SP Macbeth 5 Limited
Sharp Electronics (Europe) Ltd
Sky International Operations Ltd
Thames Recycling Limited
Twickenham Studios Limited
Urbanicity (No. 16) LLP
Whitstable Homes Ltd
Woodcote High School

July-September 2012 [44]

ABJ Trading LLP
Alperton Community School
Ambreck LLP
Angel Care (Orchid Care Homes) Ltd
Audley Chalfont Limited
Audley Ellerslie Limited
Beacon Hill Academy
Berea Limited
Bishop Wand Church of England School
CEB Holdings UK 1 Limited
CEB Holdings UK 2 Limited
Cablesheer Group Limited
Cassra LLP
Cheyne Assets Ltd
Coniston Dartford Limited
Curo (West Campbell) LLP
Denville Hall 2012
Esin Cash & Carry Limited
Every Child, Every Day Academy Trust
Granitte Investments (UK) Ltd
Great Park Developments Ltd
HSP Investments Limited
Kedleston Group Limited
Larkspur Investments Limited
Latchmere Academy Trust
Mizzen Bidco Limited
Mizzen Mezzco 2 Limited
Mizzen Mezzco Limited
Neelkanth Safe Deposit Ltd
Neville UK Trading Holdings Ltd
Optima Chemical Ltd
Orleans Park School
Park Federation Academy Trust
Stokes Marsh Solar Limited
Sunsave 12 (Derriton Fields) Ltd
Teddington School
Toshiba Global Commerce Solutions (U.K.)
Upminster Academies Trust
VS Alliance Limited
WHTC Ltd
Waldegrave Trust
Wembley Multi Academy Trust
Wood Hall Land & Properties Ltd
Zameen Ltd

October-December 2012 [77]

Abhaya Limited
Algonquin Management Partners (UK) Ltd
Aura Finance Limited
BP Australia Swaps Management Ltd
BP Containment Response Ltd
BP Holdings Canada Limited
Belmont Castle Academy
Boon Group Limited
Branden Solar Parks (Holdings) Ltd
Branden Solar Parks Limited
Brentford School for Girls
CHEP Pallecon Solutions Ltd
Capital Dairy Company (Holdings) Ltd
Colorcon European Holdings (No.5)
Cooperscroft Care Home Limited
Corley + Woolley Limited
Derby Pub Co Ltd
Ecohomes Development Limited
Euromax Resources (Macedonia) UK Ltd
Flight Centre Robin Limited
GCP Rooftop Solar 4 Limited
GMK Pepper Holdings Limited
Garreg Lwyd Energy Limited
Glastry Advisory Partners Ltd
GlaxoSmithKline Intellectual Property (No.2)
GlaxoSmithKline Intellectual Property Development
GlaxoSmithKline Intellectual Property Holdings
GlaxoSmithKline Intellectual Property
Globegold Limited
Goodshoeman Limited
Independent Commercial Broking Group
Intuitive Holding Limited
Kailas Hotel Finance Co Ltd
Kelly Communications Enterprises Ltd
Kings Langley School
LDBS Frays Academy Trust
London Arena Investments Ltd
London Distribution Park LLP
MEI Properties Limited
Majestic Securities Limited
Mecon Holdings Limited
Meridian Residential Developments
Mew Investments Ltd
Mouskos LLP
ND1T Limited
ND2F Limited
ND3M Limited
NW3 Capital Ltd
Namu Limited
Neilcott Group Holdings Ltd
Ocourage Limited
Orbital Fasteners Holdings Ltd
Ostrider Limited
PCL Bidco Limited
PCL Holdco Limited
PHH 1 Limited
PHH 2 Limited
Pole To Win UK Limited
Puma Heritage PLC
Saba Infra Cambridgeshire Ltd
Sienna Real Estate Ltd
Sines Parks Holdings Limited
Sovereign Equity Holdings Ltd
Street Family Group of Companies (Holdings)
Street Property (Holdings) Ltd
TES Enterprise Solutions Ltd
Tandridge Learning Trust
Therakos (UK), Ltd
Treetops Capital Limited
Tropical Marine Centre (2012) Ltd
Tyrolese (751) Limited
UK Addiction Treatment Group Ltd
Ventford Limited
ViiV Healthcare UK (No.3) Ltd
We Are Pentagon Limited
West Herts Community Free School Trust
West Thurrock Academy

January-March 2013 [47]

Air Products Renewable Energy Ltd
Alder Hey (Special Purpose Vehicle)
Alder Hey Holdco 1 Limited
Alder Hey Holdco 2 Limited
Alder Hey Holdco 3 Limited
Arboretum Partners LLP
B Crystal Limited
B Emerald Limited
Best Holdings (UK) Limited
Bet Invest Ltd
CALA 1 Limited
CALA Group (Holdings) Limited
CNOOC UK Limited
Catalyst Academies Trust
Consulco Finance Ltd
Dilawar & Sons Limited
Equicap Estates Limited
First Atlantic Finance Limited
Foster & Allen Holdings Ltd
GCP Biomass 1 Ltd
GCP Onshore Wind 1 Limited
GCP RHI Boiler 1 Limited
GLS Global Logistics Solutions LLP
Glasgow Learning Quarter (Holdings)
Glasgow Learning Quarter Ltd
Heritage Square Limited
Howarth Homes (Farnham Close) Ltd
Indiacast UK Ltd
Innisfree Schools (F2C) Ltd
Innisfree Schools (Secondary) Ltd
Lantern Services (Holdings) Ltd
Leisure Parks Real Estate (Holdings)
Lincoln Plaza LLP
MCPA Limited
Mitsubishi Heavy Industries Air-Conditioning Europe,
Musco (St Albans Place) Ltd
Navitas Petroleum Limited
Newserge Limited
Pelham Academy Trust
Penn Place Investments Limited
Perform Sporting News Limited
Preston Manor Academy Trust
Rycote Microphone Holdings Ltd
SZ & W Limited
Skanska TAM Limited

Sky SNI Limited
Unique Atlantic Seafood Ltd

April-June 2013 [58]

A T & T (GB) Holdings Limited
A1 Pharmaceuticals Holdings Ltd
AP Asset Management Limited
Amshold Group Limited
Amshold Trading Limited
BL Wind Limited
BMAK FX Limited
BP Petrochemicals India Investments
Brookcast UK LLP
Cargill UK Finance Limited
Cergold Limited
Cisilion (Group) Limited
Earth-I Ltd
Epsomedical (Acquisitions) Ltd
Ethypharm UK Limited
ExxonMobil Holding Co Ltd
Fizzy Poplar LLP
Focus Tankers Limited
GCP Asset Finance 1 Limited
GCP Biomass 2 Limited
GCP Onshore Wind 3 Limited
Greensea Real Estate Management Ltd
Grove T5 Limited
Gym Group Midco1 Limited
Gym Group Midco2 Limited
Gym Group Operations Limited
Gym Group PLC
Host Europe Group Limited
Imperial Ductwork Services Holdings
Innotrade Europe Limited
Daniel Johns Ltd
Kingston Digital Europe Co LLP
Kingston Technology Europe Co LLP
Linden Homes (Sherford) LLP
Linden Wates (The Frythe) Ltd
London Square (Streatham) Ltd
MSI Property Investments Ltd
Merck Holding Ltd.
Metropolis Group Holdings Ltd
NBS Trade and Investment Ltd
Naga UK Bidco Limited
Naga UK Topco Limited
New Landmark Investment Ltd
Norwood Green Junior School
Ocean Holidays Limited
Orchard Hill College Academy Trust
P Energy Limited
Parcelhero Group Limited
RAK Petroleum PLC
S.S.A.T. Property Investments Ltd
St George Ealing Limited
Sunsave 25 (Wix Lodge Farm) Ltd
Symmetry Logistics Holdings Ltd
Symmetry Logistics Limited
Telida Limited
Westbrook Primary School
Westfield Academy
Wyevale Garden Centres Acquisitions

July-September 2013 [70]

Action Potential Venture Capital Ltd
Albain Bidco UK Limited
Ashill Land Limited
Bluecroft Riverdale LLP
Broadfields Academy Trust
CMG Holdco Limited
Caretech Estates (No 7) Ltd
Citigate Homes (UK) Ltd
Cougar Holdco London Limited
Edwardian Grafton Hotel Ltd
Edwardian Hotel Finance Ltd
Edwardian Hotel Investments Ltd
Emerald Leather LLP
Epoch-Making Toys Limited
Euron Developments (France) Ltd
European Investments (Earlseat) Ltd
Evolution (Woking) Limited
FIC Grand Plaza Ltd
FJC Topco Limited
Fizzy Stepney Green LLP
Flintridge Resources Limited
Garfwish Limited
Gathercrest Properties Limited
Good for Food Limited
Gupta Brothers & Co Limited
HCL Technologies UK Limited
HFS Investment Properties Ltd
Paula Hawkins Limited
Hayre Investments (Ealing) Ltd.
Heathrow Edwardian Hotel Ltd
Henley Group Finance Limited
Hexagon Corporate Management Ltd
Highfield Infants' School
Highfield Junior School
Host Europe Investments Ltd
Hurst Primary School
IM Estates Limited
Infotech Trade Services Ltd
Intelliflo Bidco Limited
Intelliflo Holdings 2013 Ltd
Intelliflo Intermediate Holdings Ltd
Intelliflo Midco Limited
KH Finance No.2 Limited
Kenwyn Solar Limited
London Square (Crimscott Street) Ltd
Lucozade Ribena Suntory Ltd
Lumen Learning Trust
Mangrove Global Limited
Margiberg LLP
Muniment Limited
Naked Fine Wine Bonds PLC
PB Bidco Limited
PB Holdco Limited
PB Midco Limited
PB Topco Limited
Parallel Learning Trust
Radio Developments Ltd
Raglan Primary School
Restate Management Ltd
Runnymede (Holdings) Limited
A & J Ryan Holdings Limited
SM Global Consultancy Limited
TBG Holding C Limited
TJX Germany Ltd.
Tavern Quay Developments LLP
Timeboard Industrial Properties LLP
Unit 2 (Rickmansworth) Limited
Watford UTC
White Rock Land LLP
Woodford Heating Holdings Ltd

October-December 2013 [55]

Aitch Care Homes Holdco Ltd
Aitch Care Homes Topco Limited
Alestra Group Holdings Limited
Alexandra Infant School
Ambika Investments Limited
Atlantica Yield PLC
Atwood Primary Academy
BP Indonesia Investment Ltd
Badger BC Investments Limited
Brand Energy & Infrastructure Services UK,
Brymec Ltd
CML Projects Technology Ltd
Clece Care Services Limited
Custodes Acqco Limited
ENRA Group Limited
Edwardian Exclusive Ltd
Edwardian Finance Ltd
Edwardian Investments Ltd
Essex Road Development Limited
Fishdance Limited
Forth Ports Finance PLC
Gardeners' Royal Benevolent Society
Genuine Solutions Group Ltd
Gibbs Gillespie Sales Limited
Grove & Dean (Holdings) Ltd
Harlequin FC Holdings Limited
Heathrow Top Limited
Hertz UK Receivables Ltd
Hexagon Positioning Intelligence Ltd
Kent EHFA Holdco Limited
Kent EHFA Projectco Limited
Keswick European Holdings Ltd
Kilofrequency Limited
Kingston Bidco Limited
Kingston Midco Limited
Kingston Topco Limited
Kynoch Vets Limited
London Irish Consortium (2013) Ltd
Lotus Flower Holdings Limited
Loxford School Trust Limited
MBH Finco. Limited
MCPE LLP
Mondelez UK Biscuit Financing Ltd
Newincco 1270 Limited
Nexus Education Schools Trust
Opal (Earlsfield) LLP
Positive Entertainment Ltd
Primary First Trust
QOTD Film Investment Limited
Quinn Investment Holdings (London)
SNC-Lavalin Co Ltd
Skillcrown Holdings Limited
Standard Wharf Limited
Teoco UK Limited
Tradewise Group of Companies Ltd

January-March 2014 [59]

Achieving for Children CIC
Alderforce SC Limited
Aura Finance (Holdco) Limited
BP America Limited
BRE Global Limited
Besimcho Limited
Boleyn Phoenix Limited
City & Southern Limited
Clion Limited
DKH Investments Limited
DPSK Limited
DW Windsor Group Limited
Days Lane Primary School
Direct Supplies (2014) Limited
EPI Global Ltd
EPI Group Holdings Ltd
Fairchildes Academy Community Trust
Fairmile Homes One Limited
Fizzy Lewisham LLP
Full House Restaurants Holdings Ltd
GAIAE Limited
GCP Biomass 3 Limited

GHL (Hackney Wick) Limited
Gapsun Properties Limited
William Grant & Sons Brands Ltd
Green Mountain Estates Ltd
Healy's ACR Limited
Hilton Worldwide FS Treasury Ltd
Hilton Worldwide Holding 2 Ltd
Hilton Worldwide Manage Branchco Ltd
Housing Gateway Limited
JPO Communications Limited
Jenga (UK) Limited
Kew Green (Norwich Property) Ltd
LE Packaging Ltd
Lighthouse Healthcare Group Ltd
London & District Limited
Longview Holding UK Limited
NSL (Holdings) Limited
Nine Hospitality 3 Ltd
Oaks Academy Trust
Pace Academy Trust
Pentair UK Holdings Limited
Perfect Smile Newcastle Ltd
Perpetuum Construction Limited
Photon Properties Limited
Primeeng Group Limited
ProAV Holdings Limited
Raffingers Advisory Limited
Randall Watts London Limited
Ruislip High School
Salisbury Holdings Limited
Senior Finance Seven Limited
Stratford High Street Ventures Ltd
Sword Charteris Limited
Telford Homes City North Ltd
VASBP Limited
Vahnea Marolda Investments LLP
WD1A Limited

April-June 2014 [94]

3 Torland Drive Ltd
Ability Hotels (Aberdeen) Ltd
Ability Hotels (Southport) Ltd
Alina Care Limited
Allocate Bidco Limited
Allocate Holdco Limited
Allocate Midco Limited
Allocate Topco Limited
Audiotonix Limited
Bartlett Mitchell Services Ltd
Bellis Homes Limited
Benecol Limited
Brigade Holdings Limited
Camberley Care Limited
Charterhouse Ilford Limited
Choice Wealth Management Ltd
Console Bidco Limited
Console Midco Limited
J J Coughlan (Holdings) Ltd
Croydon House Ltd
Direct Supplies (2014) Group Ltd
Eco Regeneration LLP
Ferring Asset Management Ltd
Frankham Holdings Limited
GCP Biomass 4 Limited
GCP Education 1 Limited
GCP Hydro 1 Limited
GCP Rooftop Solar 5 Ltd
GHL (Crescent Lane) Limited
Galleon Investments (Dartford) Ltd
GlaxoSmithKline Consumer Healthcare Holdings
Glenchamber Wind Energy Ltd
Harrow Academies Trust
Heathland Whitefriars Federation
Hilton Worldwide Holding LLP
Houlihan & Co (Holdings) Ltd
Karuna Care (TLC) Limited
Kew Green (LRG1) Limited
Kew Green Group Limited
Kew Green Hotels (Ashford) Ltd
Kew Green Hotels (Birmingham LRG1)
Kew Green Hotels (Chester) Ltd
Kew Green Hotels (Colchester) Ltd
Kew Green Hotels (Derby/Nottingham)
Kew Green Hotels (Haydock) Ltd
Kew Green Hotels (Lancaster) Ltd
Kew Green Hotels (Norwich LRG1) Ltd
Kew Green Hotels (Portsmouth LRG1)
Kew Green Hotels (Taunton) Ltd
Kew Green Hotels (Warrington) Ltd
Kew Green Hotels (York) Ltd
Kew Green Intermediate One Ltd
Kewbridge Trading Limited
LSQ Holdco 3 Limited
Linden (York Road) LLP
Livid Dare Limited
London South East Academies Trust
London Square Developments (Holdings)
Longview Holding UK 2 Limited
Lycee International de Londres
Mallinckrodt Enterprises UK Ltd
Mid Holding Co UK Limited
Mizzen Midco Limited
Morley Finco Limited
Mushi UK Holdings Limited
Florence Nightingale Aid in Sickness Trust
Nomad Foods BondCo PLC
PGG Properties Limited
Palmera Holdings Limited
Pegrid Limited
Perfect Smile Group Holding Ltd
Plutus Estates Limited
R & R Asset Management Limited
RANC Holdings Limited
Regal Trading Ltd
Richstone Properties Limited
Rise Park Academy Trust
Riverway Investments Limited
Ruby Topco Limited
SEJ Assets Limited
SNC-Lavalin (GB) Limited
Scimitar House Limited
Signet UK Finance PLC
Silnat Holdings Limited
Silverson Machines Holdings Ltd
Speyside Renewable Energy Finance PLC
Spicers-Officeteam Group Ltd
Trading Scents (2014) Limited
Trading Scents Group Limited
Tudor Court Primary Academy Trust
UK Salads Investments Limited
UML Eagle Limited
Viners Capital Properties Ltd
Webley Holdings (UK) Limited

July-September 2014 [67]

A A Homes and Housing (Exchange Court)
ABSL1 Limited
Ability Hotels (Newcastle) Ltd
Acre 1176 Limited
Apex Lifts (Group) Limited
Aquila MB2 Limited
Aquila MB3 Limited
Archbishop Lanfranc Academy - Coloma Trust
Archway Apartments Limited
Athena Care Homes (UK) Limited
Beam Suntory Operations Ltd
Brenray Holdings Ltd
Brick Projects (Marland) Ltd
Console Lowco Limited
Cricklewood Developments Ltd
Cygnet Street Developments Ltd
Dentex Healthcare Group Ltd
Empire Investment Capital Ltd
Erith Plant Services Limited
Ethypharm Holdings UK Ltd
Fairmont Property Developers UK Ltd
Fizzy Lewisham B1 LLP
Frasers and Son Ltd
Galliard Developments Limited
GlaxoSmithKline Consumer Healthcare (Overseas)
GlaxoSmithKline Consumer Healthcare (UK) IP
GlaxoSmithKline Consumer Healthcare (UK) Trading
GlaxoSmithKline Holdings (Ireland)
Grovepoint Properties Limited
HEB Real Estate Limited
Hazeldell Ltd
IAG GBS Limited
Jaysam Developments Borehamwood Ltd
Jaysam Developments Wembley Ltd
Kew Green (LRG Property) Ltd
Kew Green (LRG2) Limited
Kinedexe UK Limited
Kingsway Asset Co Limited
Kingsway Mezz Co Limited
Kingsway Mezz Hold Co Limited
Kingsway Senior Hold Co Ltd
Linden Wates (Kempshott) Ltd
Movesell Limited
Mylan UK Healthcare Limited
Netherhall Gardens Ltd
Newacc (2014) Limited
Pheechool Holdings Limited
Pioneer DJ Europe Limited
PizzaExpress Financing 1 PLC
PizzaExpress Financing 2 PLC
PizzaExpress Group Holdings Ltd
PizzaExpress Group Limited
Powergas Africa Limited
Riches Ilford Ltd
Rowlands 2014 Limited
SR Developers Limited
Shepherd Harris & Co Limited
Shiva Kingsway Limited
Subsea 7 Finance (UK) PLC
Subsea 7 Investments (UK) Ltd
Sugarman Family Limited
United Living Group Limited
Upper Street Investments LLP
Vanneck Bros Limited
Vanneck Residential LLP
Wellstone Management Ltd
Willco Properties Ltd

October-December 2014 [82]

12 Property FE Limited
155 Staines Road Ltd
360shareholders Limited
78A SW48BH Limited
94 Camlet Way LLP
AER Rents Limited

Ability Hotels (III) Finance Ltd
Ability Hotels (III) Group Ltd
Ability Hotels (III) Holdings Ltd
Ability Hotels (III) UK Ltd
Ability Hotels (IV) Finance Ltd
Ability Hotels (IV) Holdings Ltd
Ability Hotels (IV) UK Limited
Ability Hotels (Liverpool Plaza) Ltd
Ability Hotels (Manchester) Ltd
Ability Hotels (Peterborough) Ltd
Abode Hallam Ltd
Albrin Capital Limited
Alternative Bridging (UK 1) Ltd
Angelica Estates Limited
Antoniou Investments Limited
Ares Properties Ltd
Asha (Camberley) Ltd
Berkeley Two Hundred and Three Ltd
Blackstone City Ltd
Bow Wharf Development LLP
Bradenstoke Solar Park Limited
Cappagh Browne Utilities Ltd
Clearwater Property Estates Ltd
Corncrake Limited
Court Lodge Epsom Limited
DTW (Holdings) Limited
Daly Holdings Limited
Dedalo1 Limited
Enfield Innovations Ltd
GCP Green Energy 1 Limited
GCP Social Housing 1 Limited
GDL (Millharbour) Limited
GT NEPS (Holdings) Limited
GT NEPS Limited
Gago Invest Limited
Gargonay Limited
GlaxoSmithKline Consumer Healthcare Finance
Grange Walk LLP
Hamsard 3352 Limited
Hamsard 3353 Limited
IHS Lothian Holdings Limited
IHS Lothian Investments Ltd
Jablite Holdings Limited
Jenga House Limited
L & M Holding Ltd
Lea Bridge Hill LLP
Lionel Road Coalyard Ltd
London Urban Investments Ltd
Longview Holding Parent UK Ltd
Nine Heathrow Ventures Limited
Nine Hotel Ventures Limited
Opal (Silvertown) LLP
Papa Midco Limited
Papa Topco Limited
Paragon Treasury PLC
Passportcard Limited
Pepkor UK Retail Limited
Phalarope Limited
Pladis Foods Limited
Property Finance Capital (No 2) Ltd
RHP Finance PLC
RKPE Limited
SPD Moorgate Limited
SSCP Spring Topco Limited
Sarena House LLP
Shimtech Industries Group Ltd
Shimtech Industries Holdco Ltd
Shimtech Industries Holdco2 Ltd
St William Homes LLP
THMG Limited
Tapi Carpets & Floors Limited
Telecoms World (Group) Limited
Ten Levels Ltd
UMV Global Foods Co Ltd.
UMV Global Foods Holding Co Ltd.
York House Centre Limited

January 2015 [13]

Arcplan UK Limited
Blackstown Holdings Limited
Charter Court (New Malden) Ltd
Commercial Freeholds & Investments Ltd
Explore Transport Limited
RBC Investments (Surrey) Ltd
Radnor House Sevenoaks (Holdings)
Radnor House Sevenoaks (Property)
Soul Coffee House (South) Ltd
Soul Coffee House (West) Ltd
Soul Coffee House Limited
Treno Investments Ltd
Yendall Hunter Limited

February 2015 [13]

Adelie Foods Bidco Limited
Crumlin Capital Limited
Custodes Midco Limited
Fairmile Homes Three Limited
GCP Rooftop Solar 6 PLC
Harvest Midco Limited
Luna Estates Limited
Marco Polo Properties Limited
Pamina Estates Limited
Piazza Property LLP
Sky Finance Europe Limited
Stiefel Consumer Healthcare (UK) Ltd
Transfleet Properties Limited

March 2015 [25]

AERL Holding Limited
Bayut Ltd
Beddington Park Academy Trust
Benja Properties Limited
D3O Holdings Ltd
Eclerx Investments (UK) Ltd
Four Quarters (Ingestre Road) Ltd
Fundamental Engineering Ltd
HJP Media LLP
IZH Holdings Ltd
Imaging Centre Holdings Ltd
Linden Barnet LLP
Longview Holding Hedge UK Ltd
Lowery Group Limited
Maxco London Limited
Neogene Limited
Noodle Properties Limited
PSN Holdco Limited
Parkwood Hall Co-operative Academy Trust
PizzaExpress International Holdings
SSCP Spring Midco 2 Limited
Sky CP Limited
Super Industries DMCC Metals Ltd
Thumbzup UK Limited
UML Wigmore Limited

April 2015 [13]

Ariyan Hotels Limited
Bulk Powder Terminals Limited
Caridon Holdings LLP
Edinburgh Sainsbury Holdings LLP
Evolution (Shinfield) LLP
Medequip Group Limited
Premier Euro Hotels Limited
UML Blandford Limited
UML Chiltern Limited
UML Hinde Limited
UML Moxon Limited
Uavend Exeter LLP
Williams and Hill Group Ltd

May 2015 [19]

Bath Resorts Limited
Cherryfield Holdings Limited
Fork Rent Limited
GCP Cardale PFI Ltd
Hansen Holdings Europe Ltd
Ilot Capital UK Ltd
Ilot Investments UK Ltd
Leven Wharf Limited
Linden (Hartfield Road) LLP
PSSG Group Limited
Parkside Group (Holdings) Ltd
RWW Holdings Limited
SMC Investcorp Limited
Shields Environmental Group (Holdings)
Shields Environmental Investment (Holdings)
UML Marylebone Limited
Wren Buyerco Limited
Wren Midco Limited
Wren Topco Limited

June 2015 [23]

Aitco Management Limited
Amadeus Primary Academies Trust
Amaze Capital Limited
Asap Growth Limited
Cloud Possibilities Limited
Cloudview Holdings Limited
Cramlington Renewable Energy Developments Hold Co
Distinction Investments Ltd
Elmwey Learning Trust
Evolution Morpeth LLP
Evolution Newhall LLP
Ferholding UK Ltd
Grant Family Holdings Limited
Grant Family Investments Ltd
IBA Group Holdings Limited
Legacy Broadcast Group Holdings Ltd
Linden (Biddenham) LLP
Linden Wates (Horsham) LLP
Playags UK Limited
Regina 2015 Limited
Truman Securities Limited
UK 786 Limited
WYM Legal Limited

July 2015 [22]

A A Homes and Housing (Metro Point) Property
Avon Lake Holdings Limited
Aylmer Road Limited
Boorley Green LLP
CTS Metropark Limited
CeleritiFinTech Limited
Global Logistics Group Ltd
Hillingdon House (UK) Limited
M & H Properties London Ltd
Millennium Property (London) Ltd
NPT Finance Limited
Nine Hotel Investments Limited
Norpap Property (Telford) Ltd
Perform Group Financing PLC

Perform Investment Limited
Perform Sports Media Limited
Reliance Entertainment Productions 12
Reliance Entertainment Productions Scandi
Sarr Investments Limited
Strides Pharma Global (UK) Ltd
Tulip Properties & Real Estate Ltd
UML Portman Limited

August 2015 [20]

181 HR Chigwell LLP
Ashcoe Holdings Limited
Axcel Hospitality (Manchester) Ltd
Bulphan Developments LLP
CWR Capital Ltd
Coca-Cola European Partners PLC
Daleham Finance Limited
ESSCI Limited
ESSCI Technical Services Ltd
Input Video Holdings Ltd
JB & Ace Limited
Stephen James (Automotive) Ltd
KGN Developments Limited
Lenta 2 Limited
Mitchells Holding Limited
Nordic Properties Limited
Paradine Holdings Limited
R Stanton-Gleaves UK Limited
Thompsons (UK) Holdings Ltd
nVent International (UK) Ltd

September 2015 [18]

Axis Group Integrated Services Ltd
CEB Global Holdings Limited
CNM Estates (Tolworth Tower MB) Ltd
CNM Estates (Tolworth Tower MBP) Ltd
CNM Estates (Tolworth Tower SBP) Ltd
CNM Estates Holdings Limited
ESSCI Ireland Limited
Hive 1 Ltd
JSM Group Holdings Limited
MCM Central Limited
Mallinckrodt Pharmaceuticals Ltd
Mallinckrodt UK Finance LLP
Monks Way Development Limited
OMEC Holdings Limited
P.I.G. Holdings Limited
Rackspace UK Leasing Limited
Mary Roxburghe Trust
UML Wimpole Limited

October 2015 [21]

AKA London Limited
Belmont Green Finance Ltd
Belmont Green Ltd
Corinthian Land (West Kent) Ltd
Finefrance Holdings Limited
Flight Centre Travel Group (European Holdings)
G S A R Holdings Limited
KM Estates Limited
Kap Homes Ltd.
Keltbray Group Limited
King Street Manchester Holdings LLP
King Street Manchester Property LLP
M3J Solutions Ltd
Mesa Investment Limited
Radical Investments Limited
Scape Opportunities Dublin Ltd
Sotherby LLP
Tour Partner Group Limited
Tour Partner Group Midco Ltd
ViiV Healthcare Finance 2 Ltd
Warm Hearth Limited

November 2015 [16]

Allois Properties (Leatherhead) Ltd
Betcrown Limited
Denland Limited
Ebenezer Bethel UK Limited
ITW Holdings I Limited
Kestates Limited
Manak Lawyers Limited
Mercury Land Holdings Limited
Navigator Terminals Midco Ltd
Navigator Terminals North Tees Ltd
Nemo (UK) Holdco, Ltd.
Nestates Limited
People Against Dirty Holdings Ltd
Portico UK Holdco Limited
Reyhold Limited
TJX UK Property Limited

December 2015 [28]

Appetite Holdings Limited
Audley Group Limited
Axcorp Limited
Burnt Ash Primary School
Chaptre Finance PLC
Chaptre Investments Limited
Craneshaw House Limited
D & M Tools Limited
Elwy 2 Limited
Elwy 3 Limited
GDL (Slough Developments) Ltd
Hexagon Manufacturing Intelligence Management
Hystead Limited
ITW Holdings II Limited
ITW Holdings III Limited
ITW Holdings IV Limited
ITW Holdings V Limited
Jessica House Developments Ltd
LGC Science Group Holdings Ltd
LGX Holdings Limited
Mingold Limited
Odris Investments Limited
Park House Residential Developments
Propertycoe Limited
Queensgate Finco Ltd
Templefields House LLP
UML Wembley Limited
ViiV Healthcare UK (No.4) Ltd

January 2016 [22]

Audley Stanbridge Earls Ltd
B & A Group Liverpool Street Ltd
BP Absheron Limited
BP Senegal Investments Limited
Caligor Opco UK, Ltd
Canadian & Arcadia Limited
Canadian & West End Limited
Crest A2D (Walton Court) LLP
Cygnus Academies Trust
GDL (Luton) Developments Ltd
Jennor Holdings Limited
KECS Investments Limited
Kreutzer Touristik GB Limited
Mollart Group Limited
Pole To Win International Ltd
Saffie Investments Limited
THS Group Limited
Taylors Legal Limited
UML Mayfair Limited
UML Westminster Limited
ViiV Healthcare Finance Ltd
ViiV Healthcare UK (No.5) Ltd

February 2016 [28]

452 Finchley Road LLP
A A Homes and Housing (5 Sydenham Road)
A A Homes and Housing (Cygnet House)
Acre Invest (Sydenham) Limited
BP Pipelines Tap Limited
Clearview Homes (Western Avenue) Ltd
E & J Properties Limited
GHH Estate Limited
Galvani Bioelectronics Limited
Grey Bridge Holdings Limited
JSM Associates (LON) LLP
Kearns Premier Homes Ltd
Martello (Holdings) Limited
Marylebone Finco Limited
Mouskos Capital Limited
Mouskos Holdings Limited
Gerry Murphy Ltd
Newman Street Hotel Limited
Nuffield Health Pension Trustees Ltd
PE (Mount Carmel) Limited
PPP Capital Limited
Road Tech Holdings Limited
Rocket Medical Group PLC
Solstor Holdings Limited
TBC Bank Group PLC
TPS Abbeydale Archway Limited
Truly Holdings Limited
Vetex Limited

March 2016 [18]

Comwood Holdings Ltd.
Crown House Investments Ltd
Dabasia Estates LLP
Drayton Kirk Ltd
Exagon Industries Limited
Excellence in Education Trust
Flowercloud Limited
Fourfront Holdings Limited
Grant & Bowman International Ltd
Mallinckrodt Equinox Limited
PDC Brands UK Limited
Plutus Estates (Braintree) Ltd
Plymouth (Notte Street) Ltd
Richmond West Schools Trust
Soul Coffee House (London) Ltd
Strongholding Limited
Surebay Developments Limited
Westgate House Developments Ltd

April 2016 [31]

Aequitas Estates (Poyle) Ltd
Alternative Bridging (UK 2) Ltd
BL Bottling Holdings UK Ltd
Bushey Developments Ltd
Compass Group Finance No. 3 Ltd
Distell International Holdings Ltd
Fitzjohns Avenue Ltd
GDL Holdco Limited
GR Bottling Holdings UK Ltd
Gall Holdings Limited
Galldris Holdings Limited
Gibson Bidco Limited
Gibson Propco Limited
Islandbridge Chigwell Limited

KSEYE Capital Holdings Limited
KSEYE Capital No.1 Limited
KSEYE Capital No.2 Limited
KSEYE Group Limited
London and Hertfordshire Ltd
Mabel Properties LLP
Marble Lending Limited
Maxen Homes Limited
Mondelez UK Finance Co Ltd
Odris Holdings Limited
Property Finance Capital (No 3) Ltd
Sarr Hotels (Luton) Ltd
Sea Cloud 1 Limited
Sea Cloud 2 Limited
Terminus House Harlow LLP
W & L Investments LLP
WIH UK Limited

May 2016 [17]

Artemis Interiors Limited
Audley Coopers Hill Limited
Bottling Holdings Europe Ltd
CCEP Holdings UK Limited
Carlton House Developments Ltd
Ensign Holdco 1 Limited
Ensign Holdco 3 Limited
Ensign Holdco 4 Limited
Gravity Media Group Holdings Ltd
Ist Developments Limited
Littleberries LLP
Riverstone Pictures (Show Dogs) Ltd
Riverstone Solutions 2 Limited
Rosebery House Developments Ltd
Fredereck Sage Holdings Ltd
Springhill Property Investments Ltd
Trafficinvest Limited

June 2016 [23]

Apollo RPL Limited
Bath Road Properties Limited
Bathroom Brands Group Limited
Becontree Estates Ltd
Birmingham Resi Property LLP
Chester Greyhound Retail Park LLP
DBCN Limited
Engineering, Logistics and Trading International UK
GDL (Romford) Limited
Galaxy Trust
Hart Homes (Watford) Limited
Jupiter Midco 2 Limited
Jupiter Topco Limited
Marine Point Property LLP
NeilMed Holding Co Ltd
Normandy Court Development Ltd
Oak Narwana LLP
Scimitar House (Holdings) Ltd
Twentieth Century Fox Television Distribution (U.K.),
UCL Albion Limited
Uavend Norris Castle Ltd
Union Carriers Limited
Xavier Catholic Education Trust

July 2016 [20]

Advanced Group Holdings Ltd
Arora T5 Holdings Limited
Belmont Green Funding 2 Ltd
Croftwood Care (Cheshire) Ltd
Evolution (Saffron Walden) LLP
GCP Programme Funding 1 Ltd
Hedge End Place (Durkan) LLP
Hilton International IP Holding Ltd
Jupiter Midco 1 Limited
Linden (Brampton) LLP
Linden (Enfield) LLP
Linden (Northstowe) LLP
Metro Investments (Stevenage) LLP
Sarr Noke Hospitality Limited
St Edwards Court (Romford) Ltd
Swift 100 Limited
TH UK & Ireland Limited
Toroce Investments Ltd
Waterfront Cafe Benson Limited
Z Hotel Poland Street Property LLP

August 2016 [27]

Alcedo Shipping Limited
Arugula Spruce Limited
Autosport Media UK Ltd
B & P Buyco Limited
Bio-Rad Services UK Limited
HJ Dhillon Ltd.
Edmonton Academy Trust
Erwin Technologies UK Limited
GlaxoSmithKline Consumer Healthcare Finance No. 2
Hi-Tec Europe Limited
Kearns Property Management & Development
Linden (Avery Hill) LLP
MFG Parentco Limited
Miriad Property Investments Ltd
Photo-Me Limited
Platinum Acquisition Limited
Platinum Midco Limited
Platinum Newco II Limited
Platinum Topco Limited
RPSD2 Limited
Regard ACH Holdco Limited
Searchfield (Oatlands Court) Ltd
Shelfside Group LLP
Sunny Bidco Limited
Sunny Midco Limited
Sunny Topco Limited
Suntory UK Holdings Limited

September 2016 [15]

Acclaim DMW Holdings Limited
B & P Midco 1 Limited
B & P Midco 2 Limited
Beck & Pollitzer Limited
Broadway Malyan Employee Ownership Trustees
Firebolt RB Holdings Limited
Frankel Portfolio Property LLP
T Gilmartin Holdings Limited
Maida Vale Leisure Limited
McGinley Aviation Holdings Ltd
Platinum Midco 2 Limited
Pure Bricks Limited
Pure International Limited
Stanmore Law Practice Limited
Unity Academy Trust

October 2016 [23]

Buckinghamshire Park Resort (Holdings)
Catalina Investments Limited
Elysium Healthcare Holdings 2 Ltd
Elysium Healthcare Holdings 3 Ltd
ExxonMobil Chemical Investment Co Ltd
Fulton Maritime Holdings Ltd
Fulton Maritime Limited
Grouse Bidco Limited
Grouse Midco Limited
Grouse Topco Limited
Hebridean Island Cruises Ltd
Inclusive Multi Academy Trust
Kennford Group Limited
Kimberley Real Estate Limited
Linden Wates (Ringwood) LLP
Linden Wates (Westbury) Ltd
Montreaux Maidenhead Limited
Nacropolis (Langley) Ltd
Royal Docks Property LLP
Rush Hair Group Limited
Snowden Developments Limited
UCL Harrow Limited
West Bridgford JV LLP

November 2016 [26]

254 Kilburn HR LLP
Anella Limited
Brand Reputation Compliance Ltd
Coats Group Finance Co Ltd
Dynama Solutions Ltd
Elysium Healthcare LC Limited
Everglade Holdings Limited
Fairview New Homes (Charlton) Ltd
ITW Holdings VI Limited
ITW Holdings VII Limited
JRL Group (Ireland) Limited
LRH Care Homes Limited
Laxkan Holdings Ltd
Laxkan Ltd
M G 111 Ltd
MA Securities London Limited
Maia Leisure Limited
Mizen (Nether Street) Limited
NCQ Developments Limited
Nelly Films (Christmas) Ltd
Nine Reading Hotel Limited
Oasis Lending LLP
RA Securities London Limited
RDL1 Limited
Saints Transport (Holdings) Ltd
Sauvello Limited

December 2016 [21]

Active Travel Group Bidco Ltd
Active Travel Group Limited
Active Travel Group Midco Ltd
BP Mauritania Investments Ltd
Citipost Holdings Limited
Eight Investment Limited
Ensco 1212 Limited
ExxonMobil Financial Investment Co Ltd
GL Education (No.3) Limited
Greenstone Oxford Limited
Hilton International IP Holding 2
I4B Holdings Limited
Kitewood (Creekside) Limited
Lee Park Estates Ltd
Merton Acquisitions Limited
Portnall House Ltd
Preziosa Cruise Limited
South Manchester Energy Ltd
Standley Holdings Limited
WorleyParsons UK Finance Sub No. 2 Ltd
Xerox Products UK Limited

January 2017 [28]
A6 Audio Bidco Limited
APFS Property Ltd
Chesterton Education Limited
Collins 2017 Limited
Energypro Asset Management Ltd
Ensco 1214 Limited
Fairview Hotels Investments (2) Ltd
GDL (Aylesbury) Limited
Green Lane Goose Limited
Grovetowns Southern Limited
HCT Portland Limited
Hudson Almere Limited
Hudson Arnhem Limited
Hudson Brent Limited
Hudson Camden Limited
Hudson Chemical Tankers Ltd
Hudson Kensington Limited
Hudson Lisse Limited
Hudson Richmond Limited
KGM Underwriting Services Ltd
Marylebone Square Holdings Ltd
Marylebone Square Property Group Ltd
Neptune Subsea IP Limited
Onslow Inc. Ltd
Operations Holdings Ltd
Park Grove Residential Limited
Sports Gambling Committee Ltd
Xtera Topco Limited

February 2017 [21]
Audio UK 2 Limited
Audio UK 3 Limited
Audiotonix Group Limited
Brandon House Limited
Bridge Road Southall Limited
Chalk Farm Marine LLP
Consolidated Timber Holdings Group
Cremer (UK) Manufacturing Co. Ltd
Deneep Limited
Fulton Lincoln Limited
Fulton Regent Limited
GD UK Holdings, Ltd
Garusa Solutions U.K. Limited
JGC New Energy UK Limited
JRL Property Holdings Limited
Kimberley Peer Ventures One Ltd
Latimer Hill LLP
M New Holdings Limited
Nella Holdings Limited
Planetree Developments Limited
TCR New Limited

March 2017 [7]
Chessington Nurseries Holdings Co Ltd
Fulton Clover Limited
Fulton Hyde Limited
LSQ (Crimscott Street) Holdings Ltd
Leeu London Limited
Legolas Debt Holdco Limited
Twilight Real Estate Limited

April 2017 [13]
D R 4 Developments LLP
European Investments (Cornwall) Holdings
FLW Holding Limited
HH Global Corporate Services Ltd
Minster Care Group Limited
Perfect Practices Group Ltd
Riverstone Pictures (CMP) Ltd
SNC-Lavalin (GB) Holdings Ltd
Shilton Bidco Limited
Shilton Holdco Limited
Sukanya Holdings Limited
UCL Frognal Limited
Whitestone Property Services Ltd

May 2017 [19]
ACM Eco Holdings Limited
Arete Trust
Armitage BC1 Limited
Avocado Developments Wealdstone Ltd
Bourne Court Properties Ltd
Chiltern Court Properties Ltd
Cranfield Technology Park Investments
Excelsior Property Investments Ltd
Fulton Central Limited
Gosselin Mobility UK Limited
Linden Wates (Royston) LLP
MDJ Investments Limited
Montreaux Redhill Limited
Rapiergroup Limited
Soho Loop Limited
Solai House Limited
Taj Securities Company Number Two
Thorney Leys Developments Ltd
Turnlet Films (JN) Limited

June 2017 [10]
Anno 2017 Joint Holding (UK) Ltd
GCP Rooftop Solar Finance PLC
Kimberley Capital Limited
LQAL UK Limited
Thomas Lipton Ltd
Lowen Homes Limited
PKA WLWF Holding (UK) Limited
Somers Hills Limited
Tax Systems Holdings Limited
Vulcan Wharf Limited

July 2017 [13]
ATP Media Holdings Limited
ATP Media Licensing Limited
Brooks Laundry LLP
Bryen & Langley (Holdings) Ltd
Caskade Properties Limited
Fulton Grand Limited
Fulton St James Limited
GHL (Kilmorie) Limited
Genie Energy UK Ltd
HH Global Group Limited
MDJ Group Ltd.
Sidan Trading Holdings Limited
Specialist Learning Trust

August 2017
ESPUG Finance Limited
Onix Investments UK Ltd

September 2017
Huxley Global Limited
Panther Hinckley (VAT) Ltd
Summerhill Birmingham Limited

October 2017 [5]
Bathroom Brands Limited
Belron Finance Issuer Limited
Belron Lending UK Limited
Country House Weddings Holdings Ltd
Hel Group Limited

November 2017
GHL (Summerstown) Limited

December 2017
Galaxy Group Bidco Limited
Kirkman and Jourdain Construction

May 2018
Beecham Productions Limited

Company Profiles

1 Big Data Management Limited
Incorporated: 16 May 1994 *Employees:* 18
Net Worth: £4,407,770 *Total Assets:* £8,240,972
Registered Office: 1st Floor, Sheraton House, Lower Road, Chorleywood, Rickmansworth, Herts, WD3 5LH
Activities: Other letting and operating of own or leased real estate
Parent: Melsom Holdings Limited
Officers: David John Ridler, Secretary/Director; Clare Elizabeth Ridler [1969] Director; David John Ridler [1963] Director

12 Property FE Limited
Incorporated: 11 December 2014 *Employees:* 6
Net Worth: £2,062,063 *Total Assets:* £10,638,627
Registered Office: c/o Barnes Roffe LLP, 3 Brook Business Centre, Cowley Mill Road, Uxbridge, Middlesex, UB8 2FX
Activities: Hotels and similar accommodation
Officers: James Lewis Woolf [1964] Director

123-Reg Limited
Incorporated: 7 December 2004 *Employees:* 200
Previous: Webfusion Limited
Net Worth: £340,713,984 *Total Assets:* £388,724,000
Registered Office: 5th Floor, The Shipping Building, Old Vinyl Factory, 252-254 Blyth Road, Hayes, Middlesex, UB3 1HA
Activities: Data processing, hosting and related activities
Parent: Host Europe Limited
Officers: Richard Anthony Winslow [1979] Director; Jonathan Ying Kit Wong [1976] Director

155 Staines Road Ltd
Incorporated: 17 November 2014
Net Worth: £7,136 *Total Assets:* £5,396,709
Registered Office: Top Floor, Bridgewater House, 866-868 Uxbridge Road, Hayes, Middlesex, UB4 0RR
Activities: Buying and selling of own real estate
Parent: Reliance Investments Ltd
Officers: Rajinder Singh Makkar, Secretary; Manjot Singh Makkar [1992] Director; Paramjit Singh Makkar [1989] Director/Manager

181 HR Chigwell LLP
Incorporated: 15 August 2015
Net Worth: £2,638,868 *Total Assets:* £5,344,325
Registered Office: c/o Forward Financial Accounting, Catalyst House, 720 Centennial Court, Centennial Park, Elstree, Herts, WD6 3SY
Officers: Amir Adar [1957] Member; Igal Cafrey [1940] Member; Shlomit Lahad [1948] LLP Member; Daphna Slonim [1948] LLP Member

1st Step Solutions Limited
Incorporated: 22 June 2004 *Employees:* 112
Net Worth: £1,874,735 *Total Assets:* £8,885,864
Registered Office: West Hill House, West Hill, Dartford, Kent, DA1 2EU
Activities: Temporary employment agency activities
Officers: Leslie Fillery, Secretary; Andrew Brooks [1969] Operations Director; Simon Nicholas Cowdrey [1962] Director/Chairman; Leslie William Fillery [1963] Finance Director

254 Kilburn HR LLP
Incorporated: 22 November 2016
Net Worth: £8,299,500 *Total Assets:* £21,930,924
Registered Office: Suite 2, Fountain House, 1a Elm Park, Stanmore, Middlesex, HA7 4AU

3 Torland Drive Ltd
Incorporated: 15 April 2014 *Employees:* 3
Net Worth Deficit: £178,807 *Total Assets:* £8,370,794
Registered Office: Munro House, Portsmouth Road, Cobham, Surrey, KT11 1PP
Activities: Construction of domestic buildings
Shareholders: Parisa Ettehadi; Nader Farahati
Officers: Parisa Ettehadi [1964] Director/Immunologist; Dr Nader Farahati [1963] Director/Strategy Consultant

360shareholders Limited
Incorporated: 24 December 2014
Net Worth Deficit: £2,791,071 *Total Assets:* £6,023,618
Registered Office: Bourne House, Godstone Road, Whyteleafe, Surrey, CR3 0BL
Activities: Activities of head offices
Major Shareholder: Paul Adrian Stanley
Officers: Jane Barbara Tyler, Secretary; Paul Adrian Stanley [1956] Director

3pillar Global UK Limited
Incorporated: 24 May 2010 *Employees:* 2
Previous: Brickred Technologies UK Limited
Net Worth: £2,463,638 *Total Assets:* £6,744,751
Registered Office: Trident Court, 1 Oakcroft Road, Chessington, Surrey, KT9 1BD
Activities: Business and domestic software development
Officers: David Howard Dewolf [1978] Director [American]; Kevin Golden [1963] Director/Legal Counsel [American]

3VS UK Limited
Incorporated: 31 March 2004 *Employees:* 101
Net Worth: £6,089,738 *Total Assets:* £35,726,692
Registered Office: 39a Joel Street, Northwood Hills, Northwood, Middlesex, HA6 1NZ
Activities: Activities of head offices
Major Shareholder: Anuj Somchand Shah
Officers: Anuj Somchand Shah [1966] Director/Actuary

452 Finchley Road LLP
Incorporated: 1 February 2016
Net Worth: £4,041,383 *Total Assets:* £14,943,261
Registered Office: Grenville House, 4 Grenville Avenue, Broxbourne, Herts, EN10 7DH

4th Dimension Innovation Limited
Incorporated: 20 February 2003 *Employees:* 199
Net Worth: £5,399,207 *Total Assets:* £13,811,714
Registered Office: 5 Alpha Way, Thorpe Industrial Estate, Egham, Surrey, TW20 8RZ
Activities: Other activities auxiliary to insurance and pension funding
Major Shareholder: Neil Colin Foster
Officers: Neil Colin Foster, Secretary; Neil Colin Foster [1967] Director; Victoria Foster [1972] Director; Matt Oldfield [1976] Director

66 Queen Square Limited
Incorporated: 7 March 2011
Net Worth: £11,024,000 *Total Assets:* £11,106,000
Registered Office: Maple Cross House, Denham Way, Maple Cross, Rickmansworth, Herts, WD3 9SW
Activities: Development of building projects
Parent: Skanska Project Developments Limited
Officers: Steven Leven, Secretary; Culdip Kelly Kaur Gangotra [1970] Director/Accountant; Helen Katherine Martin [1975] Director/Civil Engineer; Martin George Neeson [1968] Director/Manager

78A SW48BH Limited
Incorporated: 4 December 2014
Net Worth Deficit: £51,926 *Total Assets:* £6,896,242
Registered Office: Unit 28 Sarum Complex, Salisbury Road, Uxbridge, Middlesex, UB8 2RZ
Activities: Construction of domestic buildings
Officers: Ishil Bharat Mehta [1987] Director

7e Communications Limited
Incorporated: 12 June 1987 *Employees:* 7
Net Worth: £4,501,521 *Total Assets:* £9,853,390
Registered Office: Signal House, 127 Molesey Avenue, West Molesey, Surrey, KT8 2FF
Activities: Satellite telecommunications activities
Shareholder: Peter Victor Francis Beardow
Officers: Peter Victor Francis Beardow [1955] Director

94 Camlet Way LLP
Incorporated: 16 December 2014
Net Worth: £1,679,477 *Total Assets:* £8,084,432
Registered Office: Grenville House, 4 Grenville Avenue, Broxbourne, Herts, EN10 7DH

A A Homes and Housing (5 Sydenham Road) Limited
Incorporated: 9 February 2016
Net Worth: £1,000,938 *Total Assets:* £12,000,001
Registered Office: The Lodge, Coombe Road, Croydon, Surrey, CR0 5RD
Activities: Other letting and operating of own or leased real estate
Officers: Dr Anwar Rauf Ansari [1957] Director/Doctor

A A Homes and Housing (Cygnet House) Limited
Incorporated: 10 February 2016
Net Worth: £1,000,001 *Total Assets:* £11,000,001
Registered Office: The Lodge, Coombe Road, Croydon, Surrey, CR0 5RD
Activities: Other letting and operating of own or leased real estate
Officers: Dr Anwar Rauf Ansari [1957] Director/Doctor

A A Homes and Housing (Exchange Court) Limited
Incorporated: 15 August 2014
Net Worth: £12,000,000 *Total Assets:* £22,000,000
Registered Office: The Lodge, Coombe Road, Croydon, Surrey, CR0 5RD
Activities: Development of building projects
Officers: Dr Anwar Rauf Ansari [1957] Director

A A Homes and Housing (Metro Point) Property Limited
Incorporated: 10 July 2015
Net Worth: £3,100,001 *Total Assets:* £18,000,000
Registered Office: The Lodge, Coombe Road, Croydon, Surrey, CR0 5RD
Activities: Other letting and operating of own or leased real estate
Officers: Dr Anwar Rauf Ansari [1957] Director

A A Homes and Housing Ltd
Incorporated: 13 May 1994 *Employees:* 1
Net Worth: £112,040,520 *Total Assets:* £175,096,832
Registered Office: The Lodge, Coombe Road, Croydon, Surrey, CR0 5RD
Activities: Other letting and operating of own or leased real estate
Officers: Sabeen Ansari, Secretary; Dr Anwar Rauf Ansari [1957] Director/Doctor

A E Properties Limited
Incorporated: 14 February 1989 *Employees:* 3
Net Worth: £1,798,634 *Total Assets:* £6,407,950
Registered Office: Unit 21 Kingspark Business Centre, 152-178 Kingston Road, New Malden, Surrey, KT3 3ST
Activities: Buying and selling of own real estate
Parent: Continental Assets Limited
Officers: Teck Siong Wong, Secretary; Tien Seng Law [1953] Director [Malaysian]; Wai Cheong Law [1986] Director/Lawyer [Malaysian]; Madam Geok Ngor Saw [1962] Director [Malaysian]

A L Properties Limited
Incorporated: 28 September 2000 *Employees:* 1
Net Worth: £2,311,431 *Total Assets:* £7,046,047
Registered Office: Harmile House, 54 St Marys Lane, Upminster, Essex, RM14 2QT
Activities: Other letting and operating of own or leased real estate
Parent: TDC Global Investors Limited
Officers: Andrew Charalambous, Secretary; Andrew Charalambous [1964] Director/Stockbroker; Jane Mary Charalambous [1963] Director

A P P Wholesale PLC
Incorporated: 2 April 2008 *Employees:* 159
Net Worth: £24,937,112 *Total Assets:* £54,911,108
Registered Office: Units 12-14 Sterling Industrial Estate, Rainham Road South, Dagenham, Essex, RM10 8TX
Activities: Wholesale of hardware, plumbing and heating equipment and supplies
Major Shareholder: Allan Paul Pierce
Officers: Michael John Brockman, Secretary; Michael John Brockman [1978] Director; David Fulton [1953] Director; Allan Paul Pierce [1947] Director; Matthew Pierce [1974] Director; Stuart Brian Snell [1961] Director

A T & T (GB) Holdings Limited
Incorporated: 5 April 2013 *Employees:* 3
Net Worth: £1,481,217 *Total Assets:* £11,348,868
Registered Office: Units 9 & 10, Phoenix Park, Brentford, Middlesex, TW8 9PL
Activities: Activities of other holding companies n.e.c.
Shareholders: Adrian Storr; Terence Anthony Brown
Officers: Adrian Storr, Secretary; Adrian Storr [1971] Director/Electrical Wholesaler

A T & T (GB) Limited
Incorporated: 8 April 1999 *Employees:* 3
Net Worth: £1,298,396 *Total Assets:* £11,146,514
Registered Office: Units 9 & 10 Phoenix Park, Ealing Road, Brentford, Middlesex, TW8 9PL
Activities: Wholesale of other machinery and equipment
Parent: A T & T (GB) Holdings Limited
Officers: Adrian Storr, Secretary; Terence Anthony Brown [1953] Director/Electrical Wholesaler; Steven David Habgood [1965] Director; Simon Pates [1965] Director; Adrian Storr [1971] Director/Electrical Wholesaler; John Williams [1971] Director

A-Roads Investments Limited
Incorporated: 19 December 2006
Net Worth: £26,386,576 *Total Assets:* £33,247,534
Registered Office: 36 James Bedford Close, Pinner, Middlesex, HA5 3TD
Activities: Activities of head offices
Parent: BIIF Bidco Limited
Officers: John Ivor Cavill [1972] Director; Matthew James Edwards [1985] Associate Director

A. & A. 2000 Limited
Incorporated: 29 October 1999 *Employees:* 57
Net Worth: £10,472,359 *Total Assets:* £13,066,475
Registered Office: 3rd Floor, Crown House, 151 High Road, Loughton, Essex, IG10 4LG
Activities: Activities of head offices
Shareholders: Ann Kathleen Warren; Alan Michael Warren
Officers: Alan Michael Warren, Secretary; Alan Michael Warren [1957] Director/Electrical Engineer; Ann Kathleen Warren [1956] Director/Sales Consultant

A. & G. P. Trading Limited
Incorporated: 1 April 1997 *Employees:* 51
Net Worth: £576,998 *Total Assets:* £6,303,141
Registered Office: 2 AC Court, High Street, Thames Ditton, Surrey, KT7 0SR
Activities: Manufacture of computers and peripheral equipment
Parent: A & GP Holdings Limited
Officers: Christopher Campbell [1981] Director; Philip Ernest Davis [1954] Director; Philip Raymond Emmerson [1971] Director; Andrew Phillip Pearson [1958] Director; Peter Pearson [1956] Director

A.G. Thames Holdings Limited
Incorporated: 19 August 1970 *Employees:* 462
Net Worth: £37,722,000 *Total Assets:* £88,771,000
Registered Office: Thames House, Thames Road, Crayford, Kent, DA1 4QP
Activities: Wholesale of fruit and vegetables
Major Shareholder: Leon Aichen
Officers: Christopher Oakley, Secretary; David Alex Aichen [1969] Director; Gwendolyn Ethel Aichen [1927] Director; Leon Aichen [1941] Director; Gary Raymond Linsell [1970] Managing Director; Christopher Richard Oakley [1963] Finance Director; John Walter Sutcliffe [1950] Director

A.G.E. Nursing Homes Limited
Incorporated: 5 December 1990 *Employees:* 254
Net Worth: £5,231,714 *Total Assets:* £12,253,589
Registered Office: 249 Cranbrook Road, Ilford, Essex, IG1 4TG
Activities: Residential nursing care facilities
Shareholders: Julia Rosalyn Hainsworth-Adams; Stewart Andrew Hainswoth
Officers: Julia Rosalyn Hainsworth-Adams, Secretary; Stewart Andrew Hainsworth [1969] Finance Director; Julia Rosalyn Hainsworth-Adams [1965] Managing Director

A1 Pharmaceuticals Holdings Limited
Incorporated: 30 April 2013 *Employees:* 37
Net Worth: £14,493,644 *Total Assets:* £20,243,268
Registered Office: Unit 20 & 21 Easter Industrial Park, Ferry Lane South, Rainham, Essex, RM13 9BP
Activities: Manufacture of basic pharmaceutical products
Officers: Carmen Lewis [1965] Director/Secretary Administrator; Gary Stephen Lewis [1960] Director/Pharmacist

A1 Pharmaceuticals Public Limited Company
Incorporated: 24 February 1992 *Employees:* 37
Net Worth: £14,392,724 *Total Assets:* £18,008,192
Registered Office: Unit 20 & 21 Easter Industrial Park, Ferry Lane South, Rainham, Essex, RM13 9BP
Activities: Wholesale of pharmaceutical goods
Shareholders: Gary Stephen Lewis; Carmen Lewis
Officers: Carmen Lewis, Secretary/Administrator; Carmen Lewis [1965] Director/Secretary Administrator; Gary Stephen Lewis [1960] Director/Pharmacist

A24 Group Limited
Incorporated: 11 October 1996 *Employees:* 355
Net Worth: £50,737,968 *Total Assets:* £67,204,384
Registered Office: 92-96 Lind Road, Sutton, Surrey, SM1 4PL
Activities: Temporary employment agency activities
Major Shareholder: Penelope Marion Streeter
Officers: Nishma Patel, Secretary; Charles Louis Rees [1960] Director/Chartered Accountant; Penelope Marion Streeter [1967] Director

A6 Audio Bidco Limited
Incorporated: 19 January 2017 *Employees:* 6
Net Worth: £166,402,000 *Total Assets:* £395,585,984
Registered Office: Unit 10 Silverglade Business Park, Leatherhead Road, Chessington, Surrey, KT9 2QL
Activities: Activities of other holding companies n.e.c.
Parent: Audio UK 3 Limited
Officers: Francois de Mitry, Secretary; James Barton [1970] Director; Michael Beetz [1982] Investor, Associate Director [German]; Helen Mary Culleton [1964] Director; Francois de Mitry [1966] Director/Investor, Partner [Luxembourger]; Stephane Epin [1978] Director/Investor, Partner [French]; James David Gordon [1972] Director

AA Property and Construction Services Limited
Incorporated: 27 February 1998
Net Worth: £4,948,101 *Total Assets:* £19,000,544
Registered Office: 115 London Road, Morden, Surrey, SM4 5HP
Activities: Other letting and operating of own or leased real estate
Major Shareholder: Ashfaq Ahmed Spaul
Officers: Ashfaq Ahmed Spaul [1955] Director/Property Developer

Aandatta Limited
Incorporated: 21 May 1979
Net Worth: £1,108,033 *Total Assets:* £6,989,893
Registered Office: Floor 2, Middlesex House, 130 College Road, Harrow, Middlesex, HA1 1BQ
Activities: Wholesale of household goods (other than musical instruments) n.e.c
Officers: Kiran Manilal Kotecha, Secretary; Mohamed Ismail Chogley [1951] Director; Parimal Ranchoddas Devani [1952] Director; Kiran Manilal Kotecha [1952] Director/Certified Accountant

Abaris Holdings Limited
Incorporated: 19 April 1974 *Employees:* 565
Net Worth: £30,998,000 *Total Assets:* £66,599,000
Registered Office: Chalfont House, Oxford Road, Denham, Bucks, UB9 4DX
Activities: Activities of head offices
Parent: Walker Greenbank PLC
Officers: Caroline Geary, Secretary; Michael David Gant [1969] Director; Christopher Charles Bevan Rogers [1960] Director; Terry George Stannard [1950] Director/Consultant

Abbey Care Complex Limited
Incorporated: 15 July 2003 *Employees:* 57
Net Worth: £1,563,925 *Total Assets:* £6,354,072
Registered Office: 9 Spareleaze Hill, Loughton, Essex, IG10 1BS
Activities: Residential nursing care facilities
Officers: Devyani Jayanti Patel, Secretary/Director; Devyani Jayanti Patel [1953] Director; Jayanti Mohanlal Patel [1949] Director

Abbey Developments Limited
Incorporated: 25 January 1939 *Employees:* 70
Net Worth: £181,635,776 *Total Assets:* £262,689,568
Registered Office: Abbey House, 2 Southgate Road, Potters Bar, Herts, EN6 5DU
Activities: Construction of domestic buildings
Parent: Abbey Group Limited
Officers: Jordan Lee Collison, Secretary; David John Dawson, Secretary; William Patrick Joseph Callinan [1958] Director; Edward John Costello [1959] Director [Irish]; Stuart David Critchell [1966] Director; David John Dawson [1964] Director; Lorenzo Guiseppe Fraquelli [1958] Director; Charles Hubert Gallagher [1959] Director [Irish]

Abbey Group Limited
Incorporated: 10 November 1954 *Employees:* 4
Net Worth: £27,561,040 *Total Assets:* £45,860,296
Registered Office: Abbey House, 2 Southgate Road, Potters Bar, Herts, EN6 5DU
Activities: Activities of head offices
Parent: Abbey Public Limited Company
Officers: David John Dawson, Secretary; David John Dawson [1964] Director/Accountant; Lorenzo Guiseppe Fraquelli [1958] Director; Charles Hubert Gallagher [1959] Director [Irish]

Abbey Investments Limited
Incorporated: 21 January 1955
Net Worth: £8,983,964 *Total Assets:* £9,148,889
Registered Office: Abbey House, 2 Southgate Road, Potters Bar, Herts, EN6 5DU
Activities: Other letting and operating of own or leased real estate
Parent: Abbe Group Limited
Officers: David John Dawson, Secretary; David John Dawson [1964] Director/Accountant; Lorenzo Guiseppe Fraquelli [1958] Director; Charles Hubert Gallagher [1959] Director [Irish]

Abbey Mills Properties Ltd
Incorporated: 10 August 2010
Net Worth: £9,517,519 *Total Assets:* £13,656,690
Registered Office: Unicorn House, Station Close, Potters Bar, Herts, EN6 1TL
Activities: Buying and selling of own real estate
Parent: Panther Securities PLC
Officers: Simon Jeffrey Peters, Secretary; Andrew Stewart Perloff [1944] Director; John Henry Perloff [1968] Director; Simon Jeffrey Peters [1977] Director

Abbey Ravenscroft Park Limited
Incorporated: 7 July 2005 *Employees:* 88
Net Worth: £1,816,617 *Total Assets:* £8,138,937
Registered Office: 9 Spareleaze Hill, Loughton, Essex, IG10 1BS
Activities: Residential nursing care facilities
Officers: Devyani Jayanti Patel, Company Secretary; Devyani Jayanti Patel [1953] Director/Secretary; Jayanti Mohanlal Patel [1949] Director/Businessman

Abbey Total Care Group Limited
Incorporated: 28 April 2003 *Employees:* 542
Net Worth: £34,179,184 *Total Assets:* £65,309,764
Registered Office: 9 Spareleaze Hill, Loughton, Essex, IG10 1BS
Activities: Activities of head offices
Officers: Devyani Jayanti Patel, Secretary/Director; Devyani Jayanti Patel [1953] Director/Secretary; Jayanti Mohanlal Patel [1949] Director

Abbey View Produce Limited
Incorporated: 14 September 1972 *Employees:* 132
Net Worth: £13,202,802 *Total Assets:* £18,282,696
Registered Office: Abbey View Nursery, Galley Hill Road, Waltham Abbey, Essex, EN9 2AG
Activities: Growing of other non-perennial crops
Major Shareholder: Brian John Hibberd
Officers: William James Worwood, Secretary/Accountant; Brian John Hibberd [1950] Director; Luke Hibberd [1984] Director; Scott Wilkinson [1974] Director

Abbeyfield Southern Oaks
Incorporated: 6 September 1962
Previous: Abbeyfield Purley Society Limited (The)
Net Worth: £8,078,880 *Total Assets:* £9,430,752
Registered Office: The Old House, Epsom Road, Ewell, Epsom, Surrey, KT17 1JZ
Activities: Other residential care activities n.e.c.
Officers: Margaret Christina Angus [1947] Director/Retired; Mary Boorman [1945] Director/Retired; Janet Fisher [1954] Director/Retired; Dr John Francis Flower [1942] Director/General Medical Practitioner (Locum); Dr Andrew Martin Hoy [1949] Director/Part-Time Medical Consultant; Nigel Colin Lock MacDonald [1945] Director; Lynette Maggs [1948] Director/Retired; Maurice Vondy Pagella [1946] Director/Retired; Jim Ratliff [1951] Director/Retired; William George Scott [1942] Director/Retired; John Anthony Shelton [1936] Director/Retired; Charles Nicholas Shore [1952] Director/Self Employed; Dr Malcolm William Wakerley OBE [1946] Director/Retired; Graham Arthur James Walker [1949] Director/Retired

Abbeyman Investments Limited
Incorporated: 28 March 2002 *Employees:* 3
Net Worth: £2,794,427 *Total Assets:* £6,213,712
Registered Office: 14 Queens Road, Hersham, Walton on Thames, Surrey, KT12 5LS
Activities: Other letting and operating of own or leased real estate
Major Shareholder: Paul Adrian Campfield
Officers: Paul Adrian Campfield, Secretary/Director; Caterina Maria Campfield [1957] Director; Marc Graham Campfield [1988] Director/Builder; Paul Adrian Campfield [1958] Director

ABC Drug Stores Limited
Incorporated: 10 June 1993 *Employees:* 185
Net Worth Deficit: £1,440,215 *Total Assets:* £41,183,192
Registered Office: 2 Peterwood Way, Croydon, Surrey, CR0 4UQ
Activities: Dispensing chemist in specialised stores
Parent: Healthcare Drugstores Limited
Officers: Ameetkumar Patel, Secretary; Dr Caroline Parkhurst [1965] Director/Pharmacist; Heena Patel [1963] Finance Director; Jayanti Chimanbhai Patel Junior [1984] Director

Abercorn Education Ltd
Incorporated: 16 February 2000
Net Worth: £10,041,089 *Total Assets:* £18,561,468
Registered Office: Elder House, St Georges Business Park, Brooklands Road, Weybridge, Surrey, KT13 0TS
Activities: Primary education
Parent: Sea Cloud 1 Limited
Officers: John David Clarke [1953] Director/Solicitor; Andrea Susan Greystoke [1946] Director/Headmistress [American/British]; David William Morse [1960] Director/Education Consultant; Sheila Patricia Redrupp [1959] Director/Chartered Accountant; Abigail Melinda Fawn Snell [1978] Director

Abercorn School Limited
Incorporated: 24 January 1995 *Employees:* 112
Net Worth: £1,928,563 *Total Assets:* £7,553,742
Registered Office: Elder House, St Georges Business Park, Brooklands Road, Weybridge, Surrey, KT13 0TS
Activities: Primary education
Parent: Sea Cloud 1 Limited
Officers: John David Clarke [1953] Director/Solicitor; Andrea Susan Greystoke [1946] Director/Headmistress [American/British]; David William Morse [1960] Director/Education Consultant; Sheila Patricia Redrupp [1959] Director/Chartered Accountant; Abigail Melinda Fawn Snell [1978] Director

Abhaya Limited
Incorporated: 1 November 2012
Net Worth: £9,004,658 *Total Assets:* £9,243,277
Registered Office: 65 Delamere Road, Hayes, Middlesex, UB4 0NN
Activities: Other professional, scientific and technical activities n.e.c.
Major Shareholder: Anil Kumar Sharma
Officers: Anil Kumar Sharma [1952] Director/Pharmacist; Sneh Sharma [1956] Director

Ability Developments Limited
Incorporated: 19 November 1996 *Employees:* 9
Net Worth: £62,655,208 *Total Assets:* £70,342,472
Registered Office: Hilton London, Syon Park, London Road, Brentford, Middlesex, TW8 8JF
Activities: Development of building projects
Officers: Juin Yong Chin, Secretary; Andreas Costas Panayiotou [1966] Director

Ability Hotels (Aberdeen) Limited
Incorporated: 9 May 2014 *Employees:* 90
Net Worth Deficit: £8,394,270 *Total Assets:* £16,760,660
Registered Office: Hilton London, Syon Park, London Road, Brentford, Middlesex, TW8 8JF
Activities: Hotels and similar accommodation
Parent: Ability Hotels (Aberdeen) Holdings Limited
Officers: Juin Yong Chin, Secretary; Andreas Costas Panayiotou [1966] Director/Property Developer

Ability Hotels (Cambridge) Limited
Incorporated: 5 November 2007 *Employees:* 83
Net Worth: £31,175,140 *Total Assets:* £80,440,672
Registered Office: Hilton London, Syon Park, London Road, Brentford, Middlesex, TW8 8JF
Activities: Hotels and similar accommodation
Parent: Ability Hotels (Luton) Limited
Officers: Juin Yong Chin, Secretary; Andreas Costas Panayiotou [1966] Director

Ability Hotels (Dunblane) Limited
Incorporated: 5 November 2007 *Employees:* 201
Net Worth Deficit: £12,345,912 *Total Assets:* £24,052,766
Registered Office: Hilton London, Syon Park, London Road, Brentford, Middlesex, TW8 8JF
Activities: Hotels and similar accommodation
Parent: Ability Hotels (III) Finance Limited
Officers: Juin Yong Chin, Secretary; Andreas Costas Panayiotou [1966] Director

Ability Hotels (Glasgow) Limited
Incorporated: 8 May 2007
Net Worth: £872,385 *Total Assets:* £10,477,622
Registered Office: Hilton London, Syon Park, London Road, Brentford, Middlesex, TW8 8JF
Activities: Activities of other holding companies n.e.c.
Parent: Ability Hotels (IV) Finance Limited
Officers: Juin Yong Chin, Secretary; Andreas Costas Panayiotou [1966] Director

Ability Hotels (III) Finance Limited
Incorporated: 24 November 2014
Net Worth Deficit: £422,095 *Total Assets:* £89,742,664
Registered Office: Hilton London, Syon Park, London Road, Brentford, Middlesex, TW8 8JF
Activities: Activities of other holding companies n.e.c.
Parent: Ability Hotels (III) UK Limited
Officers: Juin Yong Chin, Secretary; Andreas Costas Panayiotou [1966] Director

Ability Hotels (III) Group Limited
Incorporated: 24 November 2014
Net Worth: £3,043,469 *Total Assets:* £61,687,668
Registered Office: Hilton London, Syon Park, London Road, Brentford, Middlesex, TW8 8JF
Activities: Activities of other holding companies n.e.c.
Officers: Juin Yong Chin, Secretary; Andreas Costas Panayiotou [1966] Director

Ability Hotels (III) Holdings Limited
Incorporated: 24 November 2014
Net Worth: £706,273 *Total Assets:* £17,303,980
Registered Office: Hilton London, Syon Park, London Road, Brentford, Middlesex, TW8 8JF
Activities: Activities of other holding companies n.e.c.
Parent: Ability Hotels (III) Group Limited
Officers: Juin Yong Chin, Secretary; Andreas Costas Panayiotou [1966] Director

Ability Hotels (III) UK Limited
Incorporated: 24 November 2014
Net Worth: £2,905,710 *Total Assets:* £59,399,856
Registered Office: Hilton London, Syon Park, London Road, Brentford, Middlesex, TW8 8JF
Activities: Activities of other holding companies n.e.c.
Parent: Ability Hotels (III) Holdings Limited
Officers: Juin Yong Chin, Secretary; Andreas Costas Panayiotou [1966] Director

Ability Hotels (IV) Finance Limited
Incorporated: 1 December 2014
Net Worth Deficit: £748,245 *Total Assets:* £55,695,048
Registered Office: Hilton London, Syon Park, London Road, Brentford, Middlesex, TW8 8JF
Activities: Activities of other holding companies n.e.c.
Parent: Ability Hotels (IV) UK Limited
Officers: Juin Yong Chin, Secretary; Andreas Costas Panayiotou [1966] Director

Ability Hotels (IV) Holdings Limited
Incorporated: 1 December 2014
Net Worth: £272,319 *Total Assets:* £12,810,345
Registered Office: Hilton London, Syon Park, London Road, Brentford, Middlesex, TW8 8JF
Activities: Activities of other holding companies n.e.c.
Parent: Ability Hotels (IV) Group Limited
Officers: Juin Yong Chin, Secretary; Andreas Costas Panayiotou [1966] Director

Ability Hotels (IV) UK Limited
Incorporated: 1 December 2014
Net Worth Deficit: £101,121 *Total Assets:* £15,814,189
Registered Office: Hilton London, Syon Park, London Road, Brentford, Middlesex, TW8 8JF
Activities: Activities of other holding companies n.e.c.
Parent: Ability Hotels (IV) Holdings Limited
Officers: Juin Yong Chin, Secretary; Andreas Costas Panayiotou [1966] Director

Ability Hotels (Liverpool Plaza) Limited
Incorporated: 18 December 2014
Net Worth: £7,841,540 *Total Assets:* £24,713,962
Registered Office: Hilton London, Syon Park, London Road, Brentford, Middlesex, TW8 8JF
Activities: Other letting and operating of own or leased real estate
Parent: Ability Hotels (IV) Finance Limited
Officers: Juin Yong Chin, Secretary; Andreas Costas Panayiotou [1966] Director/Property Developer

Ability Hotels (Liverpool) Limited
Incorporated: 25 June 2007 *Employees:* 192
Net Worth: £9,165,320 *Total Assets:* £68,349,192
Registered Office: Hilton London, Syon Park, London Road, Brentford, Middlesex, TW8 8JF
Activities: Hotels and similar accommodation
Parent: Ability Hotels (III) Finance Limited
Officers: Juin Yong Chin, Secretary; Andreas Costas Panayiotou [1966] Director

Ability Hotels (Luton Inn) Limited
Incorporated: 26 January 2005 *Employees:* 32
Net Worth: £9,631,122 *Total Assets:* £26,448,556
Registered Office: Hilton London, Syon Park, London Road, Brentford, Middlesex, TW8 8JF
Activities: Development of building projects
Parent: Ability Hotels (Luton) Limited
Officers: Juin Yong Chin, Secretary; Andreas Costas Panayiotou [1966] Director

Ability Hotels (Luton) Limited
Incorporated: 9 May 2008
Net Worth Deficit: £6,667,929 *Total Assets:* £37,286,244
Registered Office: Hilton London, Syon Park, London Road, Brentford, Middlesex, TW8 8JF
Activities: Activities of other holding companies n.e.c.
Parent: Ability Hotels (Luton) Holdings Limited
Officers: Juin Yong Chin, Secretary; Andreas Costas Panayiotou [1966] Director

Ability Hotels (Manchester) Limited
Incorporated: 4 November 2014
Net Worth: £5,176,168 *Total Assets:* £27,470,850
Registered Office: Hilton London, Syon Park, London Road, Brentford, Middlesex, TW8 8JF
Activities: Other letting and operating of own or leased real estate
Parent: Ability Hotels (Manchester) Holdings Limited
Officers: Juin Yong Chin, Secretary; Andreas Costas Panayiotou [1966] Director/Property Developer

Ability Hotels (Newcastle) Limited
Incorporated: 20 August 2014
Net Worth: £1,058,919 *Total Assets:* £8,995,615
Registered Office: Hilton London, Syon Park, London Road, Brentford, Middlesex, TW8 8JF
Activities: Other letting and operating of own or leased real estate
Parent: Ability Hotels (Newcastle) Holdings Lmited
Officers: Juin Yong Chin, Secretary; Andreas Costas Panayiotou [1966] Director/Property Developer

Ability Hotels (Peterborough) Limited
Incorporated: 29 October 2014 *Employees:* 34
Net Worth: £1,653,416 *Total Assets:* £8,067,621
Registered Office: Hilton London, Syon Park, London Road, Brentford, Middlesex, TW8 8JF
Activities: Hotels and similar accommodation
Parent: Ability Hotels (Peterborough) Holdings Limited
Officers: Juin Yong Chin, Secretary; Andreas Costas Panayiotou [1966] Director/Property Developer

Ability Hotels (Southport) Limited
Incorporated: 4 June 2014
Net Worth: £738,650 *Total Assets:* £6,061,836
Registered Office: Hilton London, Syon Park, London Road, Brentford, Middlesex, TW8 8JF
Activities: Other letting and operating of own or leased real estate
Parent: Ability Hotels (Southport) Holdings Limited
Officers: Juin Yong Chin, Secretary; Andreas Costas Panayiotou [1966] Director/Property Developer

Ability Hotels (Syon Park) Limited
Incorporated: 5 December 1985 *Employees:* 124
Net Worth: £1,728,268 *Total Assets:* £49,532,904
Registered Office: Hilton London, Syon Park, London Road, Brentford, Middlesex, TW8 8JF
Activities: Hotels and similar accommodation
Parent: Ability Hotels (Syon) Limited
Officers: Juin Yong Chin, Secretary; Andreas Costas Panayiotou [1966] Director

Ability Hotels (Syon) Limited
Incorporated: 30 April 2008
Net Worth Deficit: £6,722,661 *Total Assets:* £13,593,305
Registered Office: Hilton London, Syon Park, London Road, Brentford, Middlesex, TW8 8JF
Activities: Hotels and similar accommodation
Parent: Ability Hotels (III) Finance Limited
Officers: Juin Yong Chin, Secretary; Andreas Costas Panayiotou [1966] Director

Ability Housing Association
Incorporated: 3 June 1976 *Employees:* 158
Net Worth: £16,961,960 *Total Assets:* £62,583,428
Registered Office: The Coach House, Gresham Road, Staines upon Thames, Middlesex, TW18 2AE
Activities: Renting and operating of Housing Association real estate
Officers: Peter Stuart Gardiner, Secretary; Jane Mary Harrison [1962] Director; Karen Hillhouse [1963] Director/Development Manager; Ian Lines [1965] Director/Asset Investment Manager; James MacIntyre [1970] Director; Vince John Mewett [1962] Director; Maureen Osborne [1967] Director; Nicola Philp [1968] Director/HR Specialist; Sally Jane Reay [1958] Finance Director; Gina Small [1963] Social Housing Director; Dominic Wallace [1964] Director/Chief Risk Officer

ABJ Trading LLP
Incorporated: 15 August 2012
Net Worth: £18,599,000 *Total Assets:* £148,512,000
Registered Office: 1st Floor, Midas House, 2 Knoll Rise, Orpington, Kent, BR6 0EL

Able Skills Limited
Incorporated: 27 June 2005
Net Worth: £4,153,256 *Total Assets:* £5,984,085
Registered Office: Unit K5, Riverside Industrial Estate, Riverside Way, Dartford, Kent, DA1 5BS
Activities: Other education n.e.c.
Major Shareholder: Gary Measures
Officers: Gary Measures [1960] Director; Angela Wright [1967] Director

ABM Technical Solutions Limited
Incorporated: 25 July 2000 *Employees:* 652
Previous: Westway Services Limited
Net Worth: £28,928,600 *Total Assets:* £39,368,328
Registered Office: Artemis Building, Odyssey Business Park, West End Road, South Ruislip, Middlesex, HA4 6QE
Activities: Other service activities n.e.c.
Parent: Westway Services Holdings (2010) Ltd
Officers: Mike Bindeman [1958] Director [American]; Jason Robert Pease [1970] Director; Colin Andrew Stevenson [1963] Finance Director

Abode Hallam Ltd
Incorporated: 17 December 2014 *Employees:* 3
Net Worth Deficit: £9,649 *Total Assets:* £5,180,923
Registered Office: 166 College Road, Harrow, Middlesex, HA1 1RA
Activities: Development of building projects
Parent: Hallam Student Investments Limited
Officers: Sean Peter O'Driscoll [1971] Director [Irish]; Bhavna Patel [1961] Director; Charlotte Anne Wyche [1960] Director

ABP Packaging Limited
Incorporated: 2 May 2008 *Employees:* 1
Net Worth: £4,663 *Total Assets:* £5,442,483
Registered Office: 21 Coopers Drive, Bexley Park, Dartford, Kent, DA2 7WS
Activities: Other business support service activities n.e.c.
Officers: Prasoon Patel, Secretary; Asmita Patel [1957] Director; Bhupendra Patel [1951] Director

Abriand Limited
Incorporated: 1 July 2011 *Employees:* 1,099
Net Worth Deficit: £32,419,000 *Total Assets:* £42,796,000
Registered Office: Wizard House, 2a Cambridge Road, Teddington, Middlesex, TW11 8DR
Activities: Activities of head offices
Parent: Core GP II LLP
Officers: Christopher Patrick Edward Guy, Secretary; Raymond Rene Alfred Blanc [1949] Director/Chef Patron [French]; Mark Derry [1960] Director/Chief Executive Officer; Stephen Peter Edwards [1964] Director; Christopher Patrick Edward Guy [1981] Finance Director; Helen Louise Melvin [1968] Director

ABSL1 Limited
Incorporated: 30 September 2014
Net Worth: £48,274,500 *Total Assets:* £146,092,176
Registered Office: 22 Barn Rise, Wembley, Middlesex, HA9 9NQ
Activities: Other letting and operating of own or leased real estate
Parent: ABSL Holdings Limited
Officers: Paul Gary Hirst, Secretary; Anthony David Chambers [1955] Director/Property Consultant; Daniel Freedman [1971] Director/Lawyer; Paul Gary Hirst [1961] Director/Property Consultant

Academia Limited
Incorporated: 20 May 2003 *Employees:* 103
Net Worth: £1,460,967 *Total Assets:* £11,136,415
Registered Office: 8 Kinetic Crescent, Innova Park, Enfield, Middlesex, EN3 7XH
Activities: Other information technology service activities
Major Shareholder: Michael Charles Bacon
Officers: Michael Charles Bacon, Secretary; Michael Charles Bacon [1967] Director; Ashley Bevan [1982] HR & Operations Director [South African]; James Matthew Dancer [1985] Technical Director; Christopher Anthony William Eaton [1977] Director/Sales; Timothy Alan Gillott [1974] Finance Director; Mark Anthony McCormack [1977] Director

Academy Services (Tendring) Limited
Incorporated: 16 May 2001
Net Worth Deficit: £5,050,000 *Total Assets:* £18,510,000
Registered Office: 8 White Oak Square, London Road, Swanley, Kent, BR8 7AG
Activities: Combined facilities support activities
Parent: Academy Services (Holdings) Limited
Officers: David John Brooking [1967] Investment Director; Benjamin Christopher Jacob Dean [1979] Director/Investment Manager

Academy Services (Waltham Forest) Limited
Incorporated: 5 November 2003
Net Worth Deficit: £5,514,000 *Total Assets:* £29,670,000
Registered Office: 8 White Oak Square, London Road, Swanley, Kent, BR8 7AG
Activities: Combined facilities support activities
Parent: Academy Services (Waltham Forest) (Holdings) Limited
Officers: Christopher James [1968] Investment Director; Alastair James Watson [1974] Investment Director

ACC Aviation Limited
Incorporated: 20 February 2009 *Employees:* 38
Net Worth: £5,082,243 *Total Assets:* £20,892,720
Registered Office: Belgrave House, 39-43 Monument Hill, Weybridge, Surrey, KT13 8RN
Activities: Other business support service activities n.e.c.
Parent: FLYACC Group Limited
Officers: Phillip John Aird-Mash [1975] Director

Acclaim DMW Holdings Limited
Incorporated: 22 September 2016 *Employees:* 103
Net Worth: £18,669,704 *Total Assets:* £22,241,580
Registered Office: Ellisam House, Purfleet Industrial Park, Purfleet, Essex, RM15 4YD
Activities: Other service activities n.e.c.
Major Shareholder: Carmel Frances Swift
Officers: Carmel Frances Swift [1959] Director; Samuel David Woods [1982] Director

The Acclaim Handling Group Ltd
Incorporated: 17 April 2007 *Employees:* 2
Net Worth: £199 *Total Assets:* £6,849,648
Registered Office: Ellisam House, Perfleet Industrial Park, Purfleet, Essex, RM15 4YD
Activities: Other letting and operating of own or leased real estate
Officers: Ian Raymond Foxall, Secretary; Carmel Frances Swift [1959] Director/Secretary; Samuel David Woods [1982] Director/Marketing Manager

Acclaim Handling Limited
Incorporated: 26 October 1988 *Employees:* 108
Net Worth: £3,490,044 *Total Assets:* £12,431,751
Registered Office: Ellisam House, Purfleet Industrial Park, A13, Purfleet, Essex, RM15 4YD
Activities: Renting and leasing of other machinery, equipment and tangible goods n.e.c.
Officers: Ian Raymond Foxall, Secretary; Richard David Bonser [1961] Operations Director; Stephen Kenneth Frost [1962] Regional Director; Philip Neil Hyslop [1955] Director/Sales & Marketing; Carmel Frances Swift [1959] Director/Secretary; Samuel David Woods [1982] Director

Accolade Wines Europe No. 2 Limited
Incorporated: 15 May 1992
Net Worth: £27,039,000 *Total Assets:* £172,960,000
Registered Office: Thomas Hardy House, 2 Heath Road, Weybridge, Surrey, KT13 8TB
Activities: Non-trading company
Parent: Accolade Wines Holdings Europe Limited
Officers: Anthony Graham Wood, Secretary; Adrian Francis McKeon [1963] Regional Managing Director, UKIR; Andrew Peter Smith [1974] Director/Accountant; Anthony Graham Wood [1975] Director/Financial Controller [Australian]

Accolade Wines Holdings Europe Limited
Incorporated: 21 July 2004 *Employees:* 676
Net Worth: £107,025,000 *Total Assets:* £222,027,008
Registered Office: Thomas Hardy House, 2 Heath Road, Weybridge, Surrey, KT13 8TB
Activities: Activities of head offices
Parent: Amphora Finance Limited
Officers: Adrian Francis McKeon [1963] Regional Managing Director, UKIR; Andrew Peter Smith [1974] Director/Accountant; Anthony Graham Wood [1975] Director/Financial Controller [Australian]

Accolade Wines Limited
Incorporated: 13 August 1914 *Employees:* 587
Net Worth: £158,856,000 *Total Assets:* £333,712,000
Registered Office: Thomas Hardy House, 2 Heath Road, Weybridge, Surrey, KT13 8TB
Activities: Manufacture of wine from grape
Parent: Accolade Brands Europe Limited
Officers: Anthony Graham Wood, Secretary; Adrian Francis McKeon [1963] Regional Managing Director, UKIR; Andrew Peter Smith [1974] Director/Accountant; Anthony Graham Wood [1975] Director/Financial Controller [Australian]

Accord Healthcare Limited
Incorporated: 21 November 2002 *Employees:* 1,197
Net Worth: £7,378,000 *Total Assets:* £891,985,984
Registered Office: Sage House, 319 Pinner Road, North Harrow, Middlesex, HA1 4HF
Activities: Manufacture of pharmaceutical preparations
Officers: Pradeep Bhagia, Secretary; Dr James Burt [1974] Director/Chemical Engineer; Binish Hasmukhbhai Chudgar [1963] Director/Businessman [Indian]; Anthony Leonard Cordrey [1961] Senior Director - EU Strategic Operations; Lord Jitesh Kishorekumar Gadhia [1970] Director; John Geoffrey Goddard [1951] Director; Roger Marquilles Escola [1975] Director/Head of Legal Affairs - Europe [Spanish]; Nilesh Parmar [1968] Director; Phillip Semmens [1971] Director/Vice President Hospitals - Europe

Ace Investments Limited
Incorporated: 14 August 2006 *Employees:* 15
Net Worth: £22,689 *Total Assets:* £10,704,509
Registered Office: Jubilee House, 7-9 The Oaks, Ruislip, Middlesex, HA4 7LF
Activities: Hotels and similar accommodation
Officers: Alim Amirali Janmohamed, Company Secretary; Alim Amirali Janmohamed [1981] Director; Amirali Hassanali Moledina Janmohamed [1952] Director/Hotelier

Acer U.K. Limited
Incorporated: 9 May 1988 *Employees:* 51
Net Worth: £28,186,000 *Total Assets:* £61,678,000
Registered Office: Acer House, Heathrow Boulevard 3, 282 Bath Road, West Drayton, Middlesex, UB7 0DQ
Activities: Wholesale of computers, computer peripheral equipment and software
Parent: Acer Europe B.V
Officers: Adam Gallop, Secretary; Emmanuel Pierre Marie Fromont [1967] Director [French]; Tai-Chi Shih [1965] Director [Taiwanese]

Achieving for Children Community Interest Company
Incorporated: 5 February 2014 *Employees:* 961
Net Worth Deficit: £39,189,000 *Total Assets:* £34,152,000
Registered Office: Gifford House, 67c St Helier Avenue, Morden, Surrey, SM4 6HY
Activities: General public administration activities
Shareholders: The London Borough of Richmond upon Thames; The Royal Borough of Kingston upon Thames
Officers: Ian Matthew Dodds, Secretary; David Cameron Archibald [1952] Director/Consultant; Elizabeth Ann Bruce [1957] Director of Adult Social Services; Nicola Charlotte Craig [1973] Director/Head of Human Resources; Ian Matthew Dodds [1970] Director/Deputy Chief Executive; Nina Hingorani-Crain [1973] Director/Chief Operating Officer; Sarah Jane Ireland [1966] Director/Local Government Officer; Catherine Ann Jervis [1965] Director/Chartered Accountant; Kevin Paul McDaniel [1967] Director of Children's Services; Jane Spencer [1958] Director/Magistrate; Christopher Charles Symons [1969] Director; Sian Elizabeth Wicks [1966] Director/Executive Nurse

ACI Global Limited
Incorporated: 11 September 1998 *Employees:* 193
Net Worth: £27,120,000 *Total Assets:* £28,367,000
Registered Office: 55-57 Clarendon Road, Watford, Herts, WD17 1FQ
Activities: Business and domestic software development
Parent: ACI Worldwide (EMEA) Limited
Officers: Dennis P. Byrnes, Secretary; Scott William Behrens [1971] Director/Accountant [American]; Dennis P. Byrnes [1963] Director/Attorney [American]; David Graham King [1966] Director/Businessman; Simon Paul Stokes [1965] Director/Corporate Executive

ACI Worldwide (EMEA) Limited
Incorporated: 28 October 1988 *Employees:* 340
Net Worth: £267,070,000 *Total Assets:* £316,646,016
Registered Office: 55-57 Clarendon Road, Watford, Herts, WD17 1FQ
Activities: Information technology consultancy activities
Parent: Applied Communications Inc. U.K. Holding Limited
Officers: Bryan Peterson, Secretary; Scott William Behrens [1971] Director/Accountant [American]; David Graham King [1966] Director/Businessman; Bryan Anthony Peterson [1962] Director/Certified Public Accountant [American]; Simon Paul Stokes [1965] Director/Corporate Executive

ACM Eco Holdings Limited
Incorporated: 22 May 2017 *Employees:* 64
Net Worth: £1,480,641 *Total Assets:* £6,806,777
Registered Office: Eco House, Lea Road, Waltham Abbey, Essex, EN9 1AS
Activities: Other business support service activities n.e.c.
Shareholders: Barry John Thomas Bolton; Andrew Jonathan Peter Jacobs
Officers: Barry John Thomas Bolton [1967] Director; Andrew Jonathan Peter Jacobs [1967] Director; Travis Damien Way [1975] Director

ACM Environmental PLC
Incorporated: 6 December 1996 *Employees:* 18
Net Worth: £739,871 *Total Assets:* £5,392,608
Registered Office: Eco House, Lea Road, Waltham Abbey, Essex, EN9 1AS
Activities: Remediation activities and other waste management services
Parent: ACM Eco Holdings Limited
Officers: Travis Damien Way, Secretary; Barry John Thomas Bolton [1967] Director; Andrew Jonathan Peter Jacobs [1967] Director; Travis Damien Way [1975] Director

Acorn Limited
Incorporated: 19 March 2002 *Employees:* 308
Net Worth: £1,821,731 *Total Assets:* £7,710,941
Registered Office: 1 Sherman Road, Bromley, Kent, BR1 3JH
Activities: Real estate agencies
Parent: Acorn (Holdings) Ltd
Officers: Hector Stavrinidis, Secretary; Alan Stephen Cornish [1955] Financial Director; Paul Stephen Deveney [1971] Director; Neil Charles Louth [1974] Group Managing Director; Robert Sargent [1964] Director/Chief Executive Officer; Hector Stavrinidis [1962] Director/Chartered Accountant

Acorn Truck Sales Limited
Incorporated: 25 April 1988 *Employees:* 106
Net Worth: £2,093,020 *Total Assets:* £8,636,166
Registered Office: 601 London Road, West Thurrock, Grays, Essex, RM20 4AU
Activities: Maintenance and repair of motor vehicles
Parent: Harris Holdings (Grays) Limited
Officers: Peter James Harlow, Secretary; Peter Joseph Greenyer [1956] Director/Certified Accountant; Francesca Emma Harlow [1986] Director; Peter James Harlow [1985] Director; Frank Douglas Harris [1964] Director; James Daniel Selway [1989] Director; Danielle Elizabeth Van Der Wiel [1962] Director

Acqua Plus Developments Limited
Incorporated: 20 January 2003 *Employees:* 5
Net Worth: £3,469,244 *Total Assets:* £7,017,257
Registered Office: Ground Floor, 100 College Road, Harrow, Middlesex, HA1 1BQ
Activities: Development of building projects
Major Shareholder: Raj Tankaria
Officers: Sapna Tankaria, Secretary; Rajesh Tankaria [1971] Director

ACR Investments Limited
Incorporated: 29 February 2012
Net Worth: £11,645,533 *Total Assets:* £30,292,428
Registered Office: Ground Floor, 4 Churchill Court, 58 Station Road, North Harrow, Middlesex, HA2 7SA
Activities: Other letting and operating of own or leased real estate
Shareholder: Bharat Mohanial Popat
Officers: Kishorkumar Mohanlal Ramji Popat, Secretary; Mohammad Akhtar [1962] Director/Property Investor; Bharat Mohanlal Popat [1962] Director/Consultant; Kishorkumar Mohanlal Ramji Popat [1959] Director/Estate Agent; Paul Stuart Weldon [1960] Director/Estate Agent

Acre 1144 Limited
Incorporated: 17 March 2011 *Employees:* 68
Net Worth: £10,126,000 *Total Assets:* £12,230,000
Registered Office: John Loftus House, Summer Road, Thames Ditton, Surrey, KT7 0QQ
Activities: Other business support service activities n.e.c.
Shareholders: Duncan McNeil; Nucleus Limited
Officers: Thomas MacKenzie Newton, Secretary; John Michael Morgan Holland [1963] Director; Peter Nicholas Matthews [1957] Director; Duncan McNeil [1952] Director; Adam Charles Smith [1964] Director [Australian]

Acre 1176 Limited
Incorporated: 9 September 2014 *Employees:* 7
Net Worth: £1,007,563 *Total Assets:* £21,609,390
Registered Office: Vista Centre, 50 Salisbury Road, Hounslow, Middlesex, TW4 6JQ
Activities: Other letting and operating of own or leased real estate
Shareholder: Sanjeet Singh Babbar
Officers: Waryam Singh Kakol [1970] Director [Dutch]; Gurmeet Singh Sethi [1983] Director

Acre Invest (Sydenham) Limited
Incorporated: 2 February 2016
Net Worth Deficit: £760,849 *Total Assets:* £7,968,526
Registered Office: 23 Harrow Fields Gardens, Harrow, Middlesex, HA1 3SN
Activities: Buying and selling of own real estate
Major Shareholder: Shahzad Khan
Officers: Shahzad Ahmad Khan [1966] Director/Businessman

ACS International Schools Limited
Incorporated: 5 July 1967 *Employees:* 1,019
Net Worth: £73,784,008 *Total Assets:* £119,153,392
Registered Office: Heywood, Portsmouth Road, Cobham, Surrey, KT11 1BL
Activities: General secondary education
Major Shareholder: David Terence Thomas
Officers: Gavin Charles, Secretary; Stefan Beurier [1973] Director/Divisional Chief Financial Officer [French]; Nicholas Edward Bobay [1963] Director/Consultant [American]; Jason Stuart Elsom [1974] Director/Consultant; Clare Joanna Elizabeth Ferguson [1970] Director/Consultant; Nicole Louis [1967] Director/Chief Marketing Officer; Robert Magnus MacNaughton [1963] Director/Chairman; Pamela Mundy [1959] Director; Russell Charles Prior [1964] Director/Head of Philanthropy and Social Investment; Jake Brangwyn Sheridan Swallow [1949] Director/Consultant; Corry Justina Wille [1960] Director/Consultant [Belgian]

Action for Children
Incorporated: 14 May 2003 *Employees:* 3,283
Net Worth: £78,775,000 *Total Assets:* £99,481,000
Registered Office: 3 The Boulevard, Ascot Road, Watford, Herts, WD18 8AG
Activities: Child day-care activities
Officers: Richard Hood, Secretary; Sheryl Milanda Anderson [1953] Director/Methodist Minister; Richard Anthony Cryer [1947] Director/Retired; Gillian Ellis [1958] Director/Retired; Evelyn Patricia Gordon [1956] Charity Director and Non-Executive Director; Tracy Ann Griffin [1962] Director; Kate Guthrie [1963] HR Director; Josephine Audrey Larbie [1956] Director/Management Consultant & Executive Coach; Deborah Jayne Morgan [1961] Director/Retired; Daleep Satyanand Mukarji [1946] Retired Director of Christian Aid; Sarika Bijendra Patel [1965] Director; Markus Hardy Ruetimann [1958] Director [British/Swiss]; Fiona Talitha Flora Thorne [1969] Director/Communications Advisor

Action for Children Services Limited
Incorporated: 3 January 1989 *Employees:* 5
Net Worth: £2,788,113 *Total Assets:* £9,506,013
Registered Office: 3 The Boulevard, Ascot Road, Watford, Herts, WD18 8AG
Activities: Other residential care activities n.e.c.
Parent: Action for Children
Officers: Richard Hood, Secretary; Julie Sandra Bentley [1969] Director/Chief Executive; Catherine Anne Guthrie [1963] HR Professional/Director; Carol Ann Iddon [1957] Managing Director of a Charity; Deborah Jayne Morgan [1961] Director/Retired

Action Potential Venture Capital Limited
Incorporated: 10 July 2013
Net Worth: £641,345 *Total Assets:* £24,652,604
Registered Office: 980 Great West Road, Brentford, Middlesex, TW8 9GS
Activities: Research and experimental development on biotechnology
Parent: Glaxo Group Limited
Officers: Dr Jens Eckstein [1963] Director [German/American]; Adam Walker [1967] Director

Actionmanor Limited
Incorporated: 29 March 2007
Net Worth: £1,325,748 *Total Assets:* £6,436,137
Registered Office: Nicholas House, River Front, Enfield, Middlesex, EN1 3FG
Activities: Buying and selling of own real estate
Shareholders: Aminmohamed Fazal Alidina Pabani; Akbarali Fazal Alidina Pabani
Officers: Amin Fazal Alidina Pabani [1948] Director/Property Investor; Omar Aminmohamed Pabani [1992] Director/Property Manager

Active Travel Group Bidco Limited
Incorporated: 13 December 2016 *Employees:* 6
Net Worth: £6,470,262 *Total Assets:* £7,026,198
Registered Office: 2nd Floor, Nucleus House, 2 Lower Mortlake Road, Richmond, Surrey, TW9 2JA
Activities: Financial management
Parent: Active Travel Group Midco Limited
Officers: Craig Murray Burton [1979] Director; Justin Haschel Maltz [1969] Director

Active Travel Group Limited
Incorporated: 13 December 2016
Net Worth: £320,076 *Total Assets:* £9,080,610
Registered Office: 2nd Floor, Nucleus House, 2 Lower Mortlake Road, Richmond, Surrey, TW9 2JA
Activities: Dormant company
Parent: Mobeus IV GP LLP
Officers: Craig Murray Burton [1979] Director; Paul Easto [1973] Director; Justin Haschel Maltz [1969] Director; John Wimbleton [1958] Director

Active Travel Group Midco Limited
Incorporated: 13 December 2016 *Employees:* 2
Net Worth: £412,435 *Total Assets:* £7,011,286
Registered Office: 2nd Floor, Nucleus House, 2 Lower Mortlake Road, Richmond, Surrey, TW9 2JA
Activities: Dormant company
Parent: Hamsard 3435 Limited
Officers: Craig Murray Burton [1979] Director; Justin Haschel Maltz [1969] Director

The AD Construction Group Limited
Incorporated: 27 March 2002 *Employees:* 109
Net Worth: £8,222,274 *Total Assets:* £12,942,864
Registered Office: Samuel House, 7 Powerscroft Road, Sidcup, Kent, DA14 5DT
Activities: Activities of head offices
Shareholders: Steven William Doyle; Nicholas Geoffrey Doyle
Officers: Peter Michael Conlan, Secretary; Richard Gordon, Secretary; Nicholas Geoffrey Doyle [1947] Director/Chairman; Steven William Doyle [1974] Managing Director

Adda Hotels
Incorporated: 17 May 1966
Net Worth Deficit: £73,370,872 *Total Assets:* £226,913,728
Registered Office: Maple Court, Central Park, Reeds Crescent, Watford, Herts, WD24 4QQ
Activities: Hotels and similar accommodation
Parent: Hilton Worldwide Limited
Officers: Stuart Beasley [1971] Director/Financial Controller; Richard Geoffrey Beeston [1982] Director/Chartered Accountant; Stephen Patrick Cassidy [1968] Director/SVP Operations UK & Ireland; Michelle Momdjian [1976] Director/Attorney; George Christopher Ogle [1974] Director/Attorney; James Owen Percival [1968] Director/Accountant; Brian McKay Wilson [1962] Director/Company Secretary

Adelie Foods Bidco Limited
Incorporated: 23 February 2015 *Employees:* 11
Net Worth: £49,878,000 *Total Assets:* £150,892,992
Registered Office: 2 The Square, Southall Lane, Heathrow, Southall, Middlesex, UB2 5NH
Activities: Activities of head offices
Parent: Harvest Midco Limited
Officers: Martin Johnson [1973] Director; Mark David Stott [1966] Director

Adelie Foods Group Limited
Incorporated: 24 February 2012 *Employees:* 2
Net Worth: £10,097,000 *Total Assets:* £42,783,000
Registered Office: 2 The Square, Southall Lane, Heathrow, Southall, Middlesex, UB2 5NH
Activities: Activities of other holding companies n.e.c.
Parent: Adelie Investco UK Limited
Officers: Martin Johnson [1973] Director; Mark David Stott [1966] Director

Adelie Foods Limited
Incorporated: 17 August 2001 *Employees:* 2,413
Previous: Buckingham Foods Limited
Net Worth: £4,008,000 *Total Assets:* £85,728,000
Registered Office: 2 The Square, Southall Lane, Heathrow, Southall, Middlesex, UB2 5NH
Activities: Manufacture of other food products n.e.c.
Parent: Adelie Foods Group Limited
Officers: Martin Johnson [1973] Director; Mark David Stott [1966] Director

Adelmill Limited
Incorporated: 18 May 1976
Net Worth: £1,522,184 *Total Assets:* £7,991,387
Registered Office: 1 Warner House, Harrovian Business Village, Bessborough Road, Harrow, Middlesex, HA1 3EX
Activities: Development of building projects
Officers: Maureen Franklin, Secretary; Maureen Peggy Franklin [1933] Director

ADI Finance 1 Limited
Incorporated: 28 February 2006
Net Worth: £2,486,000,128 *Total Assets:* £5,231,000,064
Registered Office: The Compass Centre, Nelson Road, Hounslow, Middlesex, TW6 2GW
Activities: Activities of head offices
Parent: FGP Topco Limited
Officers: Ahmed Ali Al-Hammadi [1981] Director [Qatari]; Stuart Harvey Baldwin [1969] Director/Investment Manager; Christopher William Beale [1947] Director [American]; Jinhong Chen [1990] Director [Chinese]; Samuel Coxe [1975] Alternate Director [American]; Olivier Georges Xavier Fortin [1974] Director [French]; Jorge Gil Villen [1972] Director/Lawyer/Economist [Spanish]; Mr Deven Arvind Karnik [1967] Alternate Director; Tom Kelly [1989] Director [Irish]; Alexander Leonard [1985] Director; Inigo Meiras [1963] Alternate Director [Spanish]; Michael James Powell [1972] Director; David Jinlin Xie [1978] Alternate Director [American]

ADI Finance 2 Limited
Incorporated: 28 February 2006
Net Worth: £5,624,000,000 *Total Assets:* £5,717,000,192
Registered Office: The Compass Centre, Nelson Road, Hounslow, Middlesex, TW6 2GW
Activities: Activities of head offices
Parent: ADI Finance 1 Limited
Officers: Ahmed Ali Al-Hammadi [1981] Director [Qatari]; Stuart Harvey Baldwin [1969] Director/Investment Manager; Christopher William Beale [1947] Director [American]; Jinhong Chen [1990] Director [Chinese]; Samuel Coxe [1975] Alternate Director [American]; Olivier Georges Xavier Fortin [1974] Director [French]; Jorge Gil Villen [1972] Director/Lawyer/Economist [Spanish]; Mr Deven Arvind Karnik [1967] Alternate Director; Tom Kelly [1989] Director [Irish]; Alexander Leonard [1985] Director; Inigo Meiras [1963] Alternate Director [Spanish]; Michael James Powell [1972] Director; David Jinlin Xie [1978] Alternate Director [American]

Adil Catering Limited
Incorporated: 17 May 1983 *Employees:* 210
Net Worth: £12,802,922 *Total Assets:* £20,837,032
Registered Office: 34-36 London Road, Wembley, Middlesex, HA9 7EX
Activities: Unlicenced restaurants and cafes
Parent: Adil Restaurants Limited
Officers: Irshad Adil, Secretary; Irshad Adil [1950] Director/Housewife; Mohammed Adil [1945] Director/Caterer

Adil Property Investment Limited
Incorporated: 19 February 2004
Net Worth: £3,208,502 *Total Assets:* £8,156,480
Registered Office: 91 Wellesley Road, Ilford, Essex, IG1 4LJ
Activities: Other letting and operating of own or leased real estate
Major Shareholder: Syed Adil Hussain Shah
Officers: Shazia Batool Shah, Secretary; Mumtaz Begum Shah [1954] Director; Shahzia Batool Shah [1982] Director/Secretary; Syed Adil Hussain Shah [1955] Director

Adilsons Properties Limited
Incorporated: 3 February 1998 *Employees:* 5
Net Worth: £17,684,168 *Total Assets:* £34,103,272
Registered Office: 34-36 London Road, Wembley, Middlesex, HA9 7EX
Activities: Other letting and operating of own or leased real estate
Parent: Adilson Limited
Officers: Zahair Adil [1976] Director

ADM Arkady Limited
Incorporated: 1 May 1967 *Employees:* 24
Net Worth: £48,857,644 *Total Assets:* £80,653,456
Registered Office: 5 Hercules Way, Leavesden Park, Watford, Herts, WD25 7GS
Activities: Wholesale of grain, unmanufactured tobacco, seeds and animal feeds
Parent: Archer Daniels Midland Company
Officers: Paul William Briggs, Secretary; Graham Lawrence Atkinson [1960] Director/Commodity Trader; Paul William Briggs [1958] Director

ADM Milling Limited
Incorporated: 21 November 1989 *Employees:* 440
Net Worth: £30,101,084 *Total Assets:* £52,998,376
Registered Office: ADM International Limited, Church Manorway, Erith, Kent, DA8 1DL
Activities: Grain milling
Parent: Archer Daniels Midland (UK) Limited
Officers: Timothy James Cook [1957] Managing Director; Mark Lee Kolkhorst [1964] Director/President [American]; Orla Margaret Muldoon [1969] Managing Director [Irish]; Fabian James Dunbar Somerville-Cotton [1964] Managing Director

ADM Pura Limited
Incorporated: 19 May 1965
Net Worth: £88,303,544 *Total Assets:* £90,900,880
Registered Office: ADM International Offices, Church Manorway, Erith, Kent, DA8 1DL
Activities: Activities of production holding companies
Parent: Archer Daniels Midland (UK) Limited
Officers: Helen Louise McLelland [1975] Director/Financial Controller; Lance Thomas Rogers [1973] Director/Financial Controller

ADM Trading (UK) Limited
Incorporated: 9 September 1964 *Employees:* 28
Net Worth: £13,876,150 *Total Assets:* £22,346,016
Registered Office: Church Manorway, Erith, Kent, DA8 1DL
Activities: Wholesale of dairy products, eggs and edible oils and fats
Parent: Archer Daniels Midland (UK) Limited
Officers: Marcus Degen [1966] Director/General Manager [Dutch]; Martin Paul Farrow [1956] Director/General Manager; Phillipa Girard [1980] Director/UK Oilseeds Country Controller; Dr Martin Kropp [1965] Director/Vice President [German]; Orla Margaret Muldoon [1969] Managing Director [Irish]; Lance Thomas Rogers [1973] Director/Financial Controller

ADT (UK) Limited
Incorporated: 6 August 1984
Net Worth Deficit: £709,883,008 *Total Assets:* £163,707,008
Registered Office: Security House, The Summit, Hanworth Road, Sunbury on Thames, Middlesex, TW16 5DB
Activities: Activities of head offices
Parent: ADT Group Limited
Officers: Mark Ayre [1963] Finance Director; Peter Schieser [1967] Director [German]

ADT Finance Limited
Incorporated: 8 August 1985
Previous: ADT Finance Public Limited Company
Net Worth: £159,860,000 *Total Assets:* £900,652,992
Registered Office: Security House, The Summit, Hanworth Road, Sunbury on Thames, Middlesex, TW16 5DB
Activities: Financial intermediation not elsewhere classified
Parent: ADT (UK) Limited
Officers: Mark Ayre [1963] Finance Director; Peter Schieser [1967] Director [German]

ADT Fire and Security PLC
Incorporated: 22 February 1974 *Employees:* 3,270
Net Worth: £578,139,008 *Total Assets:* £761,942,016
Registered Office: Security House, The Summit, Hanworth Road, Sunbury on Thames, Middlesex, TW16 5DB
Activities: Other service activities n.e.c.
Parent: Tyco Holdings (UK) Limited
Officers: Mark Ayre, Secretary; James Paul Earnshaw [1976] Finance Director; Andrew John Ellis [1961] Director; Richard Hilton Jones [1964] Director; Moosa Farook Meah [1965] Director

ADT Group Limited
Incorporated: 1 March 1990
Previous: ADT Group Public Limited Company
Net Worth: £511,744,000 *Total Assets:* £535,039,008
Registered Office: Security House, The Summit, Hanworth Road, Sunbury on Thames, Middlesex, TW16 5DB
Activities: Activities of head offices
Parent: ADT (UK) Holdings Limited
Officers: Mark Ayre [1963] Finance Director; Peter Schieser [1967] Director [German]

ADT South Africa Holding Limited
Incorporated: 16 October 1984
Net Worth: £117,390,000 *Total Assets:* £117,785,000
Registered Office: Security House, The Summit, Hanworth Road, Sunbury on Thames, Middlesex, TW16 5DB
Activities: Non-trading company
Parent: Tyco Holdings (UK) Limited
Officers: Mark Ayre [1963] Finance Director; Peter Schieser [1967] Director [German]

Advanced Access Platforms Ltd
Incorporated: 4 September 2007 *Employees:* 18
Net Worth: £595,002 *Total Assets:* £7,313,581
Registered Office: c/o CWM, 1a High Street, Epsom, Surrey, KT19 8DA
Activities: Other specialised construction activities n.e.c.
Shareholders: John Anthony Corcoran; Joanne Louise Corcoran
Officers: John Anthony Corcoran, Secretary; Joanne Louise Corcoran [1968] Director/Housewife; John Anthony Corcoran [1967] Director/General Manager

Advanced Business Equipment Limited
Incorporated: 5 July 1991 *Employees:* 41
Net Worth: £4,697,371 *Total Assets:* £9,006,235
Registered Office: Tavistock House, 5 Rockingham Road, Uxbridge, Middlesex, UB8 2UB
Activities: Photocopying, document preparation and other specialised office support activities
Shareholders: Philip Michael Tucker; John George Emery
Officers: Joseph Sean Gallagher [1963] Sales Director; Philip Michael Tucker [1961] Sales Director

Advanced Elastomer Systems Limited
Incorporated: 15 June 1990 *Employees:* 85
Net Worth: £149,600,000 *Total Assets:* £165,834,000
Registered Office: Ermyn House, Ermyn Way, Leatherhead, Surrey, KT22 8UX
Activities: Manufacture of plastics in primary forms
Parent: ExxonMobil Chemical Investment Company Limited
Officers: Fiona Harness, Secretary; Richard Robert Henderson [1966] Director/Oil Company Executive; Andrew Mark Johnson [1976] Director/Oil Company Executive; Tom Van Nuland [1974] Director/Oil Company Executive [Belgian]

Advanced Group Holdings Limited
Incorporated: 13 July 2016 *Employees:* 41
Net Worth: £3,350,635 *Total Assets:* £12,084,024
Registered Office: Tavistock House, 5 Rockingham Road, Uxbridge, Middlesex, UB8 2UB
Activities: Activities of head offices
Major Shareholder: Philip Michael Tucker
Officers: Joseph Sean Gallagher [1963] Director; Philip Michael Tucker [1961] Sales Director

Advanced Industrial Technology Corporation Limited
Incorporated: 26 January 1993 *Employees:* 2
Net Worth: £1,641,786 *Total Assets:* £8,729,087
Registered Office: 249 Cranbrook Road, Ilford, Essex, IG1 4TG
Activities: Other service activities n.e.c.
Officers: James McKenzie Morrison Denney, Secretary; Diane Elizabeth Slack [1946] Director; Karl Dudley Slack [1945] Director/Finance

Advanced Lighting Technologies Europe Limited
Incorporated: 20 June 1995 *Employees:* 61
Net Worth: £7,515,482 *Total Assets:* £26,249,848
Registered Office: c/o Venture Lighting Europe Ltd, Trinity Court, Batchworth Island, Church Street, Rickmansworth, Herts, WD3 1RT
Activities: Activities of head offices
Officers: Philip Colin Croker [1978] Managing Director; Sabu Krishnan [1958] Director/Engineer [American]; Richard John Morris [1963] Managing Director

Advanced Logistics for Aerospace (UK) Limited
Incorporated: 6 June 1988 *Employees:* 42
Previous: Specialist Technologies Ltd
Net Worth: £5,263,498 *Total Assets:* £12,680,232
Registered Office: 1 Lyon Road, Walton on Thames, Surrey, KT12 3PU
Activities: Wholesale of other intermediate products
Parent: ALA (Advanced Logistics Aerospace) S.P.A
Officers: Gennaro di Capua [1954] Director/Chief Executive [Italian]; Vittorio Genna [1961] Director [Italian]; Fulvio Scannapieco [1952] Director [Italian]; Adolfo Varini [1964] Director [Italian]

Aequitas Estates (Poyle) Limited
Incorporated: 12 April 2016
Net Worth Deficit: £29,571 *Total Assets:* £12,003,844
Registered Office: 3rd Floor, Sterling House, Langston Road, Loughton, Essex, IG10 3TS
Activities: Other business support service activities n.e.c.
Parent: GDL (Aylesbury) Limited
Officers: Allan William Porter, Secretary; John Cole [1971] Director; Stephen Stuart Solomon Conway [1948] Director; Jonathan Simon Goldstein [1966] Director; Donagh O'Sullivan [1968] Director [Irish]

AER Rents Limited
Incorporated: 26 November 2014 *Employees:* 66
Net Worth: £2,141,526 *Total Assets:* £21,152,090
Registered Office: Lynwood House, 373-375 Station Road, Harrow, Middlesex, HA1 2AW
Activities: Activities of other holding companies n.e.c.
Parent: Hailstone Holdings Limited
Officers: Siobhan Shaw, Secretary; Ciaran Mahon [1967] Director [Irish]; Stephen O'Flaherty [1961] Director [Irish]

Aerial Scaffolding Limited
Incorporated: 12 January 1972 *Employees:* 33
Net Worth: £3,299,497 *Total Assets:* £5,235,914
Registered Office: 12 Hatherley Road, Sidcup, Kent, DA14 4DT
Activities: Scaffold erection
Major Shareholder: Scott Robert Clark
Officers: James Donald Clark [1987] Director/Engineer; Scott Robert Clark [1982] Director/Scaffolder

AERL Holding Limited
Incorporated: 10 March 2015
Net Worth: £801,287,744 *Total Assets:* £1,227,772,672
Registered Office: Waterside, Harmondsworth, West Drayton, Middlesex, UB7 0GB
Activities: Activities of head offices
Parent: International Consolidated Airlines Group S.A.
Officers: Enrique Dupuy de Lome Chavarr [1957] Director/Chief Financial Officer [Spanish]; Christopher Mark Haynes [1970] Director/General Counsel; Marcia Yor Ing Lin [1971] Director

Aeropak (Chemical Products) Limited
Incorporated: 28 August 1980 *Employees:* 92
Net Worth: £5,716,137 *Total Assets:* £9,202,702
Registered Office: Haslers, Old Station Road, Loughton, Essex, IG10 4PL
Activities: Manufacture of other chemical products n.e.c.
Parent: Diomed Developments Limited
Officers: Andrew James Head, Secretary; Elizabeth Kennedy [1947] Director/Head of Purchasing and Supply; Michael Jonathan Yarrow [1947] Director

Aerospace Tooling Limited
Incorporated: 9 January 2007 *Employees:* 75
Net Worth: £8,977,637 *Total Assets:* £10,382,058
Registered Office: Charles Lake House, Claire Causeway, Crossways Business Park, Dartford, Kent, DA2 6QA
Activities: Manufacture of other special-purpose machinery n.e.c.
Parent: Aerospace Tooling Corporation Limited
Officers: Andrew Adams [1971] Sales Director; Dale Warren Harris [1972] Director/Chief Executive Officer; Robert Michael Jones [1984] Director/Investment Manager; Donald Miller MacLeod [1959] Finance Director; William Kerr Picken [1963] Director/Chairman; Maurice Rutten [1972] Sales Director [Dutch]; John Gavin Seaton [1942] Director/Engineer

Aerospares 2000 Limited
Incorporated: 26 June 2000 *Employees:* 16
Net Worth: £15,022,468 *Total Assets:* £20,302,044
Registered Office: 3 Caxton Way, Watford Business Park, Watford, Herts, WD18 8UA
Activities: Service activities incidental to air transportation
Parent: Nextgen Limited
Officers: Adam Meir Nemenyi, Secretary; Adam Meir Nemenyi [1981] Director/Aviator

Aerzen Machines Limited
Incorporated: 13 September 1973 *Employees:* 48
Net Worth: £2,895,525 *Total Assets:* £5,750,968
Registered Office: Aerzen House, Langston Road, Loughton, Essex, IG10 3SL
Activities: Repair of machinery
Shareholders: Klaus Hasso Heller; Katrin Normann
Officers: Clive Stephen Barnes, Secretary; Klaus Hasso Heller [1967] Managing Director [German]; Matthew George Morey [1968] Director

Affinity (Reading) Limited
Incorporated: 30 July 2003
Net Worth: £4,911,562 *Total Assets:* £32,271,964
Registered Office: 8 White Oak Square, London Road, Swanley, Kent, BR8 7AG
Activities: Combined facilities support activities
Shareholders: Affinity (Reading) Holdings Limited; Affinity (Reading) Holdings Limited
Officers: Susanne Coleman [1965] Director/Regional Operations Manager; Malcolm Robert Lambert [1977] Director/Accountant; Christopher James Neil [1985] Director/Financial Controller; Josephine Ruth Roberts [1971] Director/Head of Specialist Housing

Afinacorp Limited
Incorporated: 7 July 1986
Net Worth Deficit: £8,330,619 *Total Assets:* £6,383,785
Registered Office: Kingswood House, 15 Linksway, Northwood, Middlesex, HA6 2XA
Activities: Security dealing on own account
Shareholder: Anish Anil Doshi
Officers: Nisha Anish Doshi, Secretary; Anil Jayantilal Doshi [1944] Director; Anish Anil Doshi [1972] Director

AG Retail Cards Limited
Incorporated: 29 May 2012 *Employees:* 3,405
Net Worth Deficit: £51,977,000 *Total Assets:* £54,537,000
Registered Office: The Crystal Building, Langston Road, Loughton, Essex, IG10 3TH
Activities: Other retail sale of new goods in specialised stores (not commercial art galleries and opticians)
Parent: Lakeshore Lending Limited
Officers: Edward Michael Shepherd [1971] Director/Chief Executive Officer; Jeff Weiss [1963] Director [American]; Morry Weiss [1940] Director [American]; Zev Weiss [1966] Director/CEO of American Greetings Corporation [American]

AGCO Finance Limited
Incorporated: 11 July 1990 *Employees:* 35
Net Worth: £30,421,000 *Total Assets:* £404,260,000
Registered Office: Building 7, Croxley Park, Hatters Lane, Watford, Herts, WD18 8YN
Activities: Financial intermediation not elsewhere classified
Shareholders: De Lage Landen Leasing Limited; AGCO International Limited
Officers: Julia Laura Kortz, Secretary; Mark Albert Casement [1965] Director; Duncan John Hullis [1963] Director; Saul Brendan Jones [1974] Director

Agency Press Limited
Incorporated: 9 August 1991 *Employees:* 36
Net Worth: £3,461,570 *Total Assets:* £7,992,397
Registered Office: Gladstone House, 77-79 High Street, Egham, Surrey, TW20 9HY
Activities: Advertising agencies
Shareholders: Adrian MacKenserey Francis; Sharon Ann Francis
Officers: Elaine Cosette Quinn, Secretary; Helen Collins [1968] Director/Advertising Agent; James Robert Faint [1973] Director/Media Planning Executive; Adrian MacKensery Francis [1957] Managing Director; Elaine Cosette Quinn [1949] Finance Director

Agfa Healthcare UK Limited
Incorporated: 18 July 2007 *Employees:* 96
Net Worth: £13,545,000 *Total Assets:* £21,589,000
Registered Office: 6-9 The Square, Stockley Park, Uxbridge, Middlesex, UB11 1FW
Activities: Other information technology service activities
Parent: Agfa Healthcare NV
Officers: Iskandar Emile Accaoui [1961] Director/General Manager - Imaging [French]; Peter Maria Victor Gielen [1960] Sales Director and Support Manager [Belgian]

Agility Logistics Limited
Incorporated: 29 October 1910 *Employees:* 352
Net Worth: £23,693,000 *Total Assets:* £82,599,000
Registered Office: Unit 6 North Radius Park, Faggs Road, Feltham, Middlesex, TW14 0NG
Activities: Other transportation support activities
Parent: Agility Logistics Holdings Limited
Officers: Colm Patrick McAlinden [1968] Director/Forwarder; Sait Mohammed Esa Oomer [1972] Director [Indian]; Hitesh Nathwani [1970] Director/Accountant; Paul Terence O'Keefe [1960] Director; Steven John Ryan [1972] Director/Accountant

Agility Project Logistics Limited
Incorporated: 18 August 1997 *Employees:* 26
Net Worth: £11,489,193 *Total Assets:* £29,237,988
Registered Office: Unit 6 North Radius Park, Faggs Road, Feltham, Middlesex, TW14 0NG
Activities: Agents involved in the sale of a variety of goods
Parent: Transoceanic Holdings BV
Officers: Colm Patrick McAlinden [1968] Director; Hitesh Nathwani [1970] Director/Accountant

AGP Holdings (1) Limited
Incorporated: 1 February 2001
Net Worth: £18,345,000 *Total Assets:* £267,806,000
Registered Office: 8 White Oak Square, London Road, Swanley, Kent, BR8 7AG
Activities: Buying and selling of own real estate
Parent: Infrastructure Investments Holdings Limited
Officers: David John Carr [1969] Finance Director; Glynn Newby [1966] Director/Business Management; Natalia Poupard [1977] Director/Asset Manager; Mark Christopher Wayment [1958] Director

Agri-Chemicals Limited
Incorporated: 23 July 1982
Net Worth: £20,984,856 *Total Assets:* £69,286,584
Registered Office: Portland House, 69-71 Wembley Hill Road, Wembley, Middlesex, HA9 8BU
Activities: Wholesale of agricultural machinery, equipment and supplies
Parent: Solai Holdings Limited
Officers: Bhupendra Shantilal Kansagra, Secretary; Bhupendra Shantilal Kansagra [1956] Director; Ramesh Shantilal Kansagra [1950] Director

Agrofertrans Ltd.
Incorporated: 6 August 2002 *Employees:* 37
Net Worth: £1,011,169 *Total Assets:* £8,098,485
Registered Office: Leonard House, 5-7 Newman Road, Bromley, Kent, BR1 1RJ
Activities: Agents selling agricultural raw materials, livestock, textile raw materials and semi-finished goods
Officers: Peter Clive Cawthorne, Secretary; Maria Mondel-Watrak [1966] Director/Economist [Polish]

P.F. Ahern & Sons Limited
Incorporated: 7 October 1975 *Employees:* 65
Net Worth: £16,409,204 *Total Assets:* £20,893,946
Registered Office: 106 Charter Avenue, Ilford, Essex, IG2 7AD
Activities: Activities of head offices
Shareholders: Patrick Brian Ahern; Lilian Beatrice Scott
Officers: Lilian Beatrice Scott, Secretary; Patrick Brian Ahern [1947] Director; Lilian Beatrice Scott [1948] Director; Peter Ryan Scott [1978] Director/Chief Executive

P.F. Ahern (London) Limited
Incorporated: 6 December 1985 *Employees:* 42
Net Worth: £799,289 *Total Assets:* £6,211,343
Registered Office: 106 Charter Avenue, Ilford, Essex, IG2 7AD
Activities: Freight transport by road
Parent: P F Ahern & Sons Limited
Officers: Lilian Beatrice Scott, Secretary; Patrick Brian Ahern [1947] Director; Lilian Beatrice Scott [1948] Director; Peter Ryan Scott [1978] Director/Chief Executive

Ahern Land Reclamation Limited
Incorporated: 24 June 1982
Net Worth: £4,841,606 *Total Assets:* £5,424,626
Registered Office: 106 Charter Avenue, Ilford, Essex, IG2 7AD
Activities: Other mining and quarrying n.e.c.
Parent: P F Ahern & Sons Limited
Officers: Lilian Beatrice Scott, Secretary; Patrick Brian Ahern [1947] Director; Lilian Beatrice Scott [1948] Director; Peter Ryan Scott [1978] Director/Chief Executive

AHL Holdings (Manchester) Limited
Incorporated: 17 April 2003
Net Worth Deficit: £2,425,000 *Total Assets:* £30,064,000
Registered Office: 8 White Oak Square, London Road, Swanley, Kent, BR8 7AG
Activities: Construction of commercial buildings
Shareholders: Amey Ventures Investments Limited; JLIF (GP) Limited
Officers: Neeti Mukundrai Anand [1984] Director; Carl Harvey Dix [1966] Operations Director; Asif Ghafoor [1970] Director; Katherine Pearman [1961] Director/Chartered Accountant; Carlos Vela Lazaga [1989] Director/Junior Valuation Analyst [Spanish]

AHL Holdings (Wakefield) Limited
Incorporated: 15 April 2002
Net Worth Deficit: £1,248,000 *Total Assets:* £16,054,000
Registered Office: 8 Whiteoak Square, London Road, Swanley, Kent, BR8 7AG
Activities: Other business support service activities n.e.c.
Shareholders: Amey Ventures Investments Limited; JLIF (GP) Limited
Officers: Neeti Mukundrai Anand [1984] Director; Carl Harvey Dix [1966] Operations Director; Asif Ghafoor [1970] Director; Katherine Pearman [1961] Director/Chartered Accountant; Carlos Vela Lazaga [1989] Director/Junior Valuation Analyst [Spanish]

Ahmed Property Limited
Incorporated: 22 June 2007 *Employees:* 3
Net Worth: £6,544,813 *Total Assets:* £6,671,434
Registered Office: 35 Amp House, Dingwall Road, East Croydon, Surrey, CR0 2LX
Activities: Renting and operating of Housing Association real estate
Shareholders: Waqar Ahmed; Waqar Ahmed
Officers: Salma Ahmed, Secretary/Director; Iftikhar Ahmed [1939] Director; Salma Ahmed [1944] Director; Waqar Ahmed [1969] Director

Aim Academies Trust
Incorporated: 7 March 2002 *Employees:* 241
Previous: Barnet City Academy
Net Worth: £42,662,272 *Total Assets:* £46,473,104
Registered Office: London Academy, Spur Road, Edgware, Middlesex, HA8 8DE
Activities: General secondary education
Officers: Jeremy Menell, Secretary; Lord Howard Darryl Leigh [1959] Director/Investment Banker; Paddy McGrath [1977] Director/Teacher; Jeremy Menell [1970] Director/Chartered Accountant; Philip O'Hear [1949] Director/Education Consultant; Dr Michael Harris Platt [1935] Director/Dental Surgeon; Simon Joseph Pollins [1964] Finance Director; Neville John Portelli [1959] Creative Director; Michael Brian Shalson [1943] Director; Peter Shalson [1957] Director; Michael Henry Van Praagh [1961] Director/Chartered Accountant

Air BP Limited
Incorporated: 11 December 1973
Net Worth: £64,494,364 *Total Assets:* £252,219,584
Registered Office: Chertsey Road, Sunbury on Thames, Middlesex, TW16 7BP
Activities: Wholesale of other fuels and related products
Parent: BP Global Investments Limited
Officers: Matthew Howard Elliott [1972] Director/Oil Company Executive [New Zealander]; Jonathan Peter Platt [1967] Director/Oil Company Executive; Jonathan William Winston Wood [1962] Director/Oil Company Executive

Air Charter Service Group Limited
Incorporated: 6 July 2000 *Employees:* 386
Previous: Air Charter Service Group PLC
Net Worth: £11,982,000 *Total Assets:* £60,419,000
Registered Office: Millbank House, 171-185 Ewell Road, Surbiton, Surrey, KT6 6AP
Activities: Non-scheduled passenger air transport
Parent: Mountfitchet Group Limited
Officers: Omar Saeed, Secretary; Justin Christopher Bowman [1972] Director/Executive; William Andrew Christie [1976] Director; Ruan Patrick Courtney [1972] Director/Executive; Justin James Lancaster [1977] Director/Sales Executive; Christopher Denis Stephen Leach [1949] Director/Executive; Stewart Pitt [1972] Finance Director

Air Charter Service Limited
Incorporated: 27 July 1990 *Employees:* 155
Previous: Air Charter Service PLC
Net Worth: £7,927,000 *Total Assets:* £25,593,000
Registered Office: Millbank House, 171-185 Ewell Road, Surbiton, Surrey, KT6 6AP
Activities: Non-scheduled passenger air transport
Parent: Air Charter Service Group Limited
Officers: Omar Saeed, Secretary; James Cristofoli [1982] Director; Georgina June Heron [1984] Director; Taylor Holloman [1988] Director/Financial Controller; Justin James Lancaster [1977] Director; James Jonathan Leach [1984] Marketing Director; Katie Mansfield [1982] Commercial Jets Director; Matthew Edward Purton [1980] Director/Sales Executive

Air Menzies International Limited
Incorporated: 23 February 1994 *Employees:* 155
Net Worth: £2,566,000 *Total Assets:* £28,753,000
Registered Office: 2 World Business Centre Heathrow, Newall Road, London Heathrow Airport, Hounslow, Middlesex, TW6 2SF
Activities: Other service activities n.e.c.
Parent: Menzies Aviation PLC
Officers: Mark Edward Lawrence [1959] Director/Accountant; Mark Rhynes [1981] Director/Accountant; Sharon Wright [1957] Director

Air Products (BR) Limited
Incorporated: 17 August 1990
Net Worth: £70,965,000 *Total Assets:* £736,190,016
Registered Office: Hersham Place Technology Park, Molesey Road, Walton on Thames, Surrey, KT12 4RZ
Activities: Manufacture of industrial gases
Officers: Mark Jamie Sambrook, Secretary; Richard John Boocock [1961] Director/President, Industrial Gases-Middle East, India; Charles George Stinner [1963] Director/Vice President, Taxes [American]; Gregory Earl Weigard [1954] Director/Vice President and Corporate Treasurer [American]

Air Products (Chemicals) Teesside Limited
Incorporated: 12 November 1997
Net Worth: £7,146,000 *Total Assets:* £7,194,000
Registered Office: Hersham Place Technology Park, Molesey Road, Walton on Thames, Surrey, KT12 4RZ
Activities: Other manufacturing n.e.c.
Officers: Mark Jamie Sambrook, Secretary; Richard John Boocock [1961] Director/President, Industrial Gases-Middle East, India; Charles George Stinner [1963] Director/Vice President, Taxes [American]; Gregory Earl Weigard [1954] Director/Vice President and Corporate Treasurer [American]

Air Products Group Limited
Incorporated: 13 September 1995
Net Worth: £566,960,000 *Total Assets:* £834,520,000
Registered Office: Hersham Place Technology Park, Molesey Road, Hersham, Walton on Thames, Surrey, KT12 4RZ
Activities: Activities of head offices
Officers: Mark Jamie Sambrook, Secretary; Richard John Boocock [1961] Director/President, Industrial Gases-Middle East, India; Charles George Stinner [1963] Director/Vice President, Taxes [American]; Gregory Earl Weigard [1954] Director/Vice President and Corporate Treasurer [American]

Air Products Public Limited Company
Incorporated: 5 July 1909 *Employees:* 1,378
Net Worth: £421,652,000 *Total Assets:* £778,465,984
Registered Office: Hersham Place Technology Park, Molesey Road, Walton on Thames, Surrey, KT12 4RZ
Activities: Manufacture of industrial gases
Parent: Air Products Group Limited
Officers: Mark Jamie Sambrook, Secretary; Richard John Boocock [1961] Director/President, Industrial Gases-Middle East, India; David Leney [1967] Director/Financial Controller; Charles George Stinner [1963] Director/Vice President, Taxes [American]; Gregory Earl Weigard [1954] Director/Vice President and Corporate Treasurer [American]

Air Products Renewable Energy Limited
Incorporated: 13 March 2013
Net Worth Deficit: £9,451,000 *Total Assets:* £8,517,000
Registered Office: Hersham Place Technology Park, Molesey Road, Walton on Thames, Surrey, KT12 4RZ
Activities: Production of electricity
Parent: Air Products PLC
Officers: David Leney [1967] Director/Financial Controller; Damian John Meadows [1975] Director/Asset Manager; Mark Jamie Sambrook [1971] Director/Solicitor

Airclaims Group (Overseas) Limited
Incorporated: 30 August 1983
Net Worth: £2,786,808 *Total Assets:* £8,422,823
Registered Office: 1 World Business Centre, Newall Road, London Heathrow Airport, Hounslow, Middlesex, TW6 2AS
Activities: Activities of other holding companies n.e.c.
Parent: MYI Acquiror Limited
Officers: Elizabeth Janet Mary Tubb, Secretary; Gary Brown [1966] Director [American]; Ross Glenn Landsbaum [1962] Director [American]; Nigel Paul Minett [1957] Managing Director

Aircom International Limited
Incorporated: 1 May 1995 *Employees:* 63
Net Worth: £2,343,000 *Total Assets:* £11,042,000
Registered Office: Pascal Place, Randalls Research Park, Randalls Way, Leatherhead, Surrey, KT22 7TW
Activities: Other telecommunications activities
Major Shareholder: Atul Jain
Officers: Philip Merritt Giuntini [1946] Director/Vice Chairman [American]; Avraham Goldstein [1965] Director [American]

Aitch Care Homes (London) Limited
Incorporated: 15 January 2004 *Employees:* 629
Net Worth: £17,983,000 *Total Assets:* £38,078,000
Registered Office: Unit 6 & 7 Princeton Mews, 167-169 London Road, Kingston upon Thames, Surrey, KT2 6PT
Activities: Other business support service activities n.e.c.
Parent: Aitch Care Homes Holdco Limited
Officers: Garry John Fitton, Secretary; Garry John Fitton [1972] Finance Director; Nicola Rosemary Lucy Hopkins [1968] Director/Chartered Accountant; Peter Kinsey [1964] Director

Aitch Care Homes Holdco Limited
Incorporated: 26 November 2013
Previous: Montreux Almayer Limited
Net Worth Deficit: £8,602,000 *Total Assets:* £24,653,000
Registered Office: Unit 6 & 7 Princeton Mews, 167-169 London Road, Kingston upon Thames, Surrey, KT2 6PT
Activities: Residential care activities for the elderly and disabled
Parent: Aitch Care Homes Topco Limited
Officers: Garry John Fitton, Secretary; Garry John Fitton [1972] Finance Director; Nicola Rosemary Lucy Hopkins [1968] Director/Chartered Accountant; Peter Kinsey [1964] Director

Aitch Care Homes Topco Limited
Incorporated: 9 December 2013
Previous: Montreux Nostromo Limited
Net Worth: £10,670,000 *Total Assets:* £10,670,000
Registered Office: Unit 6 & 7 Princeton Mews, 167-169 London Road, Kingston upon Thames, Surrey, KT2 6PT
Activities: Residential care activities for the elderly and disabled
Parent: The Regard (Group) Bidco Limited
Officers: Garry John Fitton, Secretary; Garry John Fitton [1972] Finance Director; Nicola Rosemary Lucy Hopkins [1968] Director/Chartered Accountant; Peter Kinsey [1964] Director

Aitch Demolition Co. Ltd
Incorporated: 20 September 2001 *Employees:* 8
Net Worth: £5,238,288 *Total Assets:* £8,186,222
Registered Office: First Floor, Radius House, 51 Clarendon Road, Watford, Herts, WD17 1HP
Activities: Site preparation
Parent: Aitch Plant and Equipment Limited
Officers: Rennee Allen, Secretary; Harold Talbot John Allen [1962] Director/Demolition Contractor

Aitco Management Limited
Incorporated: 18 June 2015
Net Worth: £4,641,870 *Total Assets:* £7,513,435
Registered Office: 249 Cranbrook Road, Ilford, Essex, IG1 4TG
Activities: Other business support service activities n.e.c.
Major Shareholder: Diane Elizabeth Slack
Officers: Diane Elizabeth Slack [1946] Director; Karl Dudley Slack [1945] Director

AKA London Limited
Incorporated: 29 October 2015
Net Worth Deficit: £442,005 *Total Assets:* £26,163,468
Registered Office: Morton House, Coombe Park, Kingston upon Thames, Surrey, KT2 7JB
Activities: Buying and selling of own real estate
Major Shareholder: Aibibula Nuermaimaiti
Officers: Aibibula Nuermaimaiti [1989] Director [Chinese]; Aibibula Paliwanmuhaimaiti [1991] Director [Chinese]

Akaal Group PLC
Incorporated: 5 October 2006 *Employees:* 288
Net Worth: £66,641,928 *Total Assets:* £86,872,256
Registered Office: 3 Roberts Mews, Orpington, Kent, BR6 0JP
Activities: Activities of head offices
Major Shareholder: Rajbir Singh Manak
Officers: Tanya Maria Barrett, Secretary; Harbhajan Kaur Manak [1940] Director [Indian]; Rajbir Singh Manak [1966] Managing Director [Indian]

Akari Therapeutics, PLC
Incorporated: 7 October 2004 *Employees:* 21
Previous: Celsus Therapeutics PLC
Net Worth: £23,538,988 *Total Assets:* £28,707,494
Registered Office: Elder House, St Georges Business Park, 207 Brooklands Road, Weybridge, Surrey, KT13 0TS
Activities: Other business support service activities n.e.c.
Officers: Dov Elefant, Secretary; David Anthony Byrne [1959] Director; Peter Feldschreiber [1943] Director; Michael Grissinger [1953] Director [American]; Dr James Ferguson Hill [1945] Director/Retired; Raymond Richard Prudo-Chlebosz [1944] Director/Doctor [Canadian]; Clive Stuart Richardson [1965] Director; Stuart Charles Ungar [1943] Director; Donald Allen Williams [1958] Director [American]

Al Jazeera International Limited
Incorporated: 16 September 2004 *Employees:* 136
Net Worth: £33,798,856 *Total Assets:* £49,428,116
Registered Office: Premier Suite, 4 Churchill Court, 58 Station Road, North Harrow, Middlesex, HA2 7ST
Activities: Television programming and broadcasting activities
Officers: Jankhana Jaydeep Desai, Secretary; Mandan Safdari, Secretary; Muftah Al Suwaidan [1959] Director [Qatari]; Khalid Abdulla M Al-Mulla [1967] Director [Qatari]

Al-Khair Foundation
Incorporated: 3 July 2003 *Employees:* 154
Net Worth: £18,865,636 *Total Assets:* £19,436,840
Registered Office: 109-117 Cherry Orchard Road, Croydon, Surrey, CR0 6BE
Activities: General secondary education
Officers: Mohmed Ayyub Shaikh, Secretary; Qasim Rashid Ahmad [1970] Director/Minister of Religion; Basil Saad Abdulwahab Nader [1965] Director; Dr Mohammed Jafer Hussain Qureshi [1945] Director/Consultant Psychiatrist; Mohmed Ayyub Shaikh [1954] Director/Teacher

Al-Mubarakia Limited
Incorporated: 22 April 2009 *Employees:* 10
Net Worth Deficit: £9,566,025 *Total Assets:* £9,082,996
Registered Office: 3rd Floor, Chancery House, St Nicholas Way, Sutton, Surrey, SM1 1JB
Activities: Management of real estate on a fee or contract basis
Officers: Mohammed Al Besharah [1986] Director [Kuwaiti]; Abdulaziz Albesharah [1984] Director [Kuwaiti]; Fawzia Mubarak Al Hassawi [1953] Director [Kuwaiti]

Al-Noor Foundation Limited
Incorporated: 13 January 1997 *Employees:* 38
Net Worth: £861,203 *Total Assets:* £5,881,852
Registered Office: Newton Industrial Estate, Eastern Avenue, Romford, Essex, RM6 5SD
Activities: Primary education
Officers: Imran Hafiz, Secretary; Zulfiqar Ahmed [1954] Director; Juneja Daud [1954] Director/Buyer; Imran Hafiz [1974] Director; Reza Jugon [1974] Director; Imran Khan [1977] Director; Sadiq Yakub Kothia [1966] Director; Muhammed Ilyas Mirza [1968] Director/IT Consultancy; Khalil Rahman [1966] Director/Restaurateur

Alandale Holdings Limited
Incorporated: 15 November 1996 *Employees:* 187
Net Worth: £16,652,806 *Total Assets:* £46,485,568
Registered Office: 1 Brook Court, Blakeney Road, Beckenham, Kent, BR3 1HG
Activities: Other specialised construction activities n.e.c.
Major Shareholder: Perry Edward Morgan
Officers: David Trevor Bulman [1969] Director; Barbara Ann Morgan [1964] Director; Michael John Stocker-Harris [1965] Financial Director

Alandale Logistics Limited
Incorporated: 18 November 1996 *Employees:* 158
Net Worth: £5,698,987 *Total Assets:* £28,983,552
Registered Office: 1 Brook Court, Blakeney Road, Beckenham, Kent, BR3 1HG
Activities: Other specialised construction activities n.e.c.
Officers: David Trevor Bulman [1969] Director/Health & Safety; Michael John Stocker-Harris [1965] Financial Director

Alandale Plant & Scaffolding Limited
Incorporated: 23 May 2002 *Employees:* 26
Net Worth: £2,939,198 *Total Assets:* £13,153,490
Registered Office: 1 Brook Court, Blakeney Road, Beckenham, Kent, BR3 1HG
Activities: Scaffold erection
Officers: David Trevor Bulman [1969] Director; Michael John Stocker-Harris [1965] Financial Director; Lee Scott Jason Wright [1967] Operations Director

Alandale Scaffolding Group Limited
Incorporated: 1 May 1992
Previous: Alandale Recycling Limited
Net Worth: £34,873 *Total Assets:* £7,914,164
Registered Office: 1 Brook Court, Blakeney Road, Beckenham, Kent, BR3 1HG
Activities: Renting and leasing of other machinery, equipment and tangible goods n.e.c.
Officers: David Trevor Bulman [1969] Director; Michael John Stocker-Harris [1965] Financial Director

Alba Broadcasting Corporation Limited
Incorporated: 13 July 1990 *Employees:* 11
Net Worth Deficit: £35,162,268 *Total Assets:* £10,496,773
Registered Office: Suite 105a, Citibase Watford, 42-44 Clarendon Road, Watford, Herts, WD17 1JJ
Activities: Wholesale of radio, television goods & electrical household appliances (other than records, tapes, CDs)
Parent: Harvard International Limited
Officers: Lei Li [1978] Director [Chinese]; Zhuoyan Xu [1985] Director [Chinese]; Xuhui Zhou [1968] Director/Chairman [Chinese]

Albain Bidco UK Limited
Incorporated: 25 September 2013
Net Worth: £48,576,400 *Total Assets:* £49,298,092
Registered Office: Velocity V1, Brooklands Drive, Weybridge, Surrey, KT13 0SL
Activities: Activities of other holding companies n.e.c.
Officers: Dena Michelle L O'Bue, Secretary; Stephen James Hamilton [1969] Director/Country Tax Manager, UK & Ireland; Holly Caroline Webster [1974] Director/Lawyer

Albert Darnell Limited
Incorporated: 1 March 1971 *Employees:* 115
Net Worth Deficit: £560,954 *Total Assets:* £6,293,896
Registered Office: 48 Cox Lane, Chessington, Surrey, KT9 1TW
Activities: Retail sale of fish, crustaceans and molluscs in specialised stores
Parent: Albert Darnell Holdings Limited
Officers: Iain Murray Imray, Secretary; Daniel Thomas Aherne [1977] Director; Iain Murray Imray [1957] Director; James Robinson [1971] Director

Albion Bunker and Trading LLP
Incorporated: 19 April 2011
Net Worth: £11,734,288 *Total Assets:* £11,832,822
Registered Office: Suite 1, The Studio, St Nicholas Close, Elstree, Herts, WD6 3EW

Albrin Capital Limited
Incorporated: 8 December 2014
Net Worth: £687,573 *Total Assets:* £10,096,998
Registered Office: 2 Villiers Court, 40 Upper Mulgrave Road, Cheam, Sutton, Surrey, SM2 7AJ
Activities: Activities of other holding companies n.e.c.
Shareholders: Steven Paul Fenn; Sarah Louise Fenn
Officers: Sarah Louise Fenn [1965] Director; Steven Paul Fenn [1965] Director

Alcedo Shipping Limited
Incorporated: 18 August 2016 *Employees:* 13
Net Worth: £10,910,627 *Total Assets:* £16,269,907
Registered Office: Long Reach House, London Road, Purfleet, Essex, RM19 1PD
Activities: Sea and coastal freight water transport
Parent: Priveq Limited
Officers: Michael Gray Esq [1948] Director; Karel Van Bellingen [1984] Director [Belgian]

The Aldenham Foundation
Incorporated: 10 September 1984 *Employees:* 255
Net Worth: £13,741,699 *Total Assets:* £21,350,544
Registered Office: Aldenham School, Aldenham Road, Elstree, Borehamwood, Herts, WD6 3AJ
Activities: Pre-primary education
Officers: Karl Mahon, Secretary; Sarah Elizabeth Altman [1967] Finance & Operations Director; Joseph Trevor Barton [1957] Director; Anthony John Bingham [1950] Director/Chartered Accountant; Andrew Js Cox [1960] Director/Chartered Surveyor; Fiona Cuttell [1970] Director/Assistant Company Secretary; Alan Charles Day [1956] Director/Chartered Surveyor; Ian Andrew Dewar [1957] Director/Chartered Accountant; Anthony Graham Hellman [1958] Director/Investment Manager; David Stephen Lambert [1945] Director/Herts County Councillor; Retired University Lecturer; Ronak Mashru [1978] Sales Director; Michael O'Dwyer [1967] Director; Dr Deborah Anne Price-Williams [1957] Director/Doctor; Vandana Mayank Shah [1960] Director/Solicitor; Harriet Simmons [1961] Director/Food Law Consultant; Torquil Charles Fflorance Barrow Sligo-Young [1959] Director; The Venerable Jonathan Peter Smith [1955] Director/Archdeacon; David Thomas Tidmarsh [1962] Director/Headmaster; Thomas Franey Wells [1951] Director

Alder Hey (Special Purpose Vehicle) Limited
Incorporated: 6 February 2013
Net Worth: £611,000 *Total Assets:* £140,735,008
Registered Office: 8 White Oak Square, London Road, Swanley, Kent, BR8 7AG
Activities: Construction of commercial buildings
Parent: Alder Hey Holdco 1 Limited
Officers: Robert James Marsden [1955] Director; Tristan James Meredith [1980] Bid Director; Andrew Stephen Pearson [1964] Managing Director; Alan Travis [1971] Director

Alder Hey Holdco 1 Limited
Incorporated: 5 February 2013
Net Worth: £30,000 *Total Assets:* £32,808,000
Registered Office: 8 White Oak Square, London Road, Swanley, Kent, BR8 7AG
Activities: Activities of head offices
Parent: Alder Hey Holdco 2 Limited
Officers: Robert James Marsden [1955] Director; Tristan James Meredith [1980] Bid Director; Andrew Stephen Pearson [1964] Managing Director; Alan Travis [1971] Director

Alder Hey Holdco 2 Limited
Incorporated: 4 February 2013
Net Worth: £30,000 *Total Assets:* £32,808,000
Registered Office: 8 White Oak Square, London Road, Swanley, Kent, BR8 7AG
Activities: Activities of head offices
Parent: Alder Hey Holdco 3 Limited
Officers: Robert James Marsden [1955] Director; Tristan James Meredith [1980] Bid Director; Andrew Stephen Pearson [1964] Managing Director; Alan Travis [1971] Director

Alder Hey Holdco 3 Limited
Incorporated: 20 February 2013
Net Worth: £611,000 *Total Assets:* £140,735,008
Registered Office: 8 White Oak Square, London Road, Swanley, Kent, BR8 7AG
Activities: Activities of head offices
Shareholders: John Laing Investments Limited; Laing O'Rourke PLC
Officers: Robert James Marsden [1955] Director; Tristan James Meredith [1980] Bid Director; Andrew Stephen Pearson [1964] Managing Director; Alan Travis [1971] Director

Alderforce Limited
Incorporated: 20 November 2003 *Employees:* 388
Net Worth: £5,876,899 *Total Assets:* £9,890,436
Registered Office: 34-36 London Road, Wembley, Middlesex, HA9 7EX
Activities: Unlicenced restaurants and cafes
Major Shareholder: Raja Jameel Adil
Officers: Mohammed Adil, Secretary; Raja Jameel Adil [1971] Director/Solicitor

Alderforce North Limited
Incorporated: 17 February 2010 *Employees:* 695
Net Worth: £779,735 *Total Assets:* £13,052,243
Registered Office: 34-36 London Road, Wembley, Middlesex, HA9 7EX
Activities: Unlicenced restaurants and cafes
Major Shareholder: Raja Jameel Adil
Officers: Mohammed Adil, Secretary; Raja Jameel Adil [1971] Director/Solicitor

Alderforce SC Limited
Incorporated: 11 March 2014 *Employees:* 390
Net Worth: £1,211,743 *Total Assets:* £7,169,763
Registered Office: 34-36 London Road, Wembley, Middlesex, HA9 7EX
Activities: Unlicenced restaurants and cafes
Major Shareholder: Raja Jameel Adil
Officers: Mohammed Adil, Secretary; Raja Jameel Adil [1971] Director

Aldis of Barking Limited
Incorporated: 27 March 1946
Net Worth: £3,013,004 *Total Assets:* £7,694,073
Registered Office: Orbital House, 20 Eastern Road, Romford, Essex, RM1 3DP
Activities: Development of building projects
Major Shareholder: Linda Irene Aldis
Officers: Jane Sylvia Alltimes, Secretary; Jane Sylvia Alltimes [1965] Director; Nigel Robert Alltimes [1960] Director

Aldro School Educational Trust Limited
Incorporated: 27 August 1968 *Employees:* 76
Net Worth: £6,625,718 *Total Assets:* £7,572,898
Registered Office: 5 Robin Hood Lane, Sutton, Surrey, SM1 2SW
Activities: Other education n.e.c.
Officers: Magdalena Jackson, Secretary; James Benjamin Henry Geffen [1962] Director/Retired; Sarah Louise Hunt [1983] Director/Barrister; Timothy Rowland Johns [1957] Director/Retired; Brian Robert Kirkpatrick [1948] Director/Chartered Accountant; Reverend Philip Vernon Parker [1960] Director/Vicar; Jonathan Freeman Perry [1969] Director/Headmaster; Edward Reid [1976] Director/Housemaster; Reverend Margot Spencer [1948] Director/Assistant Minister; Garth Taylor Williams [1968] Director/Teacher; Timothy George Nicolas Woodhouse [1973] Director/Underwriter

Aldwych Leisure Limited
Incorporated: 26 July 1996
Net Worth: £6,334,407 *Total Assets:* £8,470,311
Registered Office: Runway House, The Runway, Ruislip, Middlesex, HA4 6SE
Activities: Other accommodation
Shareholder: SME Group PLC
Officers: Aly Mohamed Esmail, Secretary; Salim Jivraj, Secretary/Director; Aly Mohamed Esmail [1982] Director; Sayed Mohamed Esmail [1986] Director; Salim Jivraj [1948] Director

Alestra Group Holdings Limited
Incorporated: 9 December 2013 *Employees:* 445
Net Worth: £36,892,584 *Total Assets:* £91,926,704
Registered Office: 1 Princeton Mews, 167-169 London Road, Kingston upon Thames, Surrey, KT2 6PT
Activities: Other business support service activities n.e.c.
Officers: Monika Anna Marie Carlsson [1974] Director [American]; Manuela Dina Maria Eleuteri [1952] Director; Erik Staffan Encrantz [1951] Director [Swedish]; Donata Van Der Veen [1954] Director/Administrator [Italian]

Alestra Limited
Incorporated: 19 November 2002 *Employees:* 3
Net Worth: £101,180,712 *Total Assets:* £103,388,792
Registered Office: 1 Princeton Mews, 167-169 London Road, Kingston upon Thames, Surrey, KT2 6PT
Activities: Non-trading company
Parent: Alestra Group Holdings Limited
Officers: Monika Anna Marie Carlsson [1974] Director [American]; Manuela Dina Maria Eleuteri [1952] Director/Corporate Consultant; Staffan Encrantz [1951] Director [Swedish]; Donata Van Der Veen [1954] Director/Administrator [Italian]

Alexandra Infant School
Incorporated: 4 November 2013 *Employees:* 34
Net Worth: £6,242,000 *Total Assets:* £6,915,000
Registered Office: Alexandra Infant School, Kent House Road, Beckenham, Kent, BR3 1JG
Activities: Primary education
Officers: Irene Patricia Morley, Secretary; Ian Anderson [1979] Director/Accountant; Andrew Philip Bostridge [1961] Director/Royal Mail Processing Engineer; Maria Elizabeth Cenayko [1978] Director/Assistant Headteacher; Jenna Fishwick [1976] Director/Teacher; Alison Louise Hills [1981] Director/Headteacher; Duncan Shrubsole [1978] Director/Senior Manager

Alexen Avocats (UK) Limited
Incorporated: 30 August 2001 *Employees:* 1
Previous: Alister Avocats (UK) Limited
Net Worth: £5,463,471 *Total Assets:* £5,830,322
Registered Office: 59 Victoria Road, Surbiton, Surrey, KT6 4NQ
Activities: Other business support service activities n.e.c.
Major Shareholder: Remi Turcon
Officers: Eric Turcon, Secretary; Remi Turcon [1963] Director [French]

Alexion Pharma UK Limited
Incorporated: 17 October 2006 *Employees:* 74
Net Worth: £3,460,531 *Total Assets:* £34,744,548
Registered Office: 3 Furzeground Way, Stockley Park, Uxbridge, Middlesex, UB11 1EZ
Activities: Other business support service activities n.e.c.
Parent: Alexion Pharmaceuticals, Inc.
Officers: Philippe Dufaux, Secretary; Michael Ira Kenneth Elloian [1972] Director/VP, Chief of Tax, Finance [American]; Vivien Ruth Greer [1976] Director Finance [Irish]; Sean Richardson [1970] Director/General Manager - Pharmaceuticals

Alfreds Way Investments (No. 2) Limited
Incorporated: 1 November 1972
Net Worth: £24,610,448 *Total Assets:* £32,326,216
Registered Office: Atlas House, 28 Great Cambridge Road, Enfield, Middlesex, EN1 1UU
Activities: Development of building projects
Officers: Judith Erlich, Secretary; Baruch Erlich [1962] Director/Solicitor; Judith Erlich [1960] Director/Secretary

Algonquin Management Partners (UK) Ltd
Incorporated: 25 October 2012 *Employees:* 10
Previous: Algonquin (UK) Limited
Net Worth: £7,431,381 *Total Assets:* £9,283,246
Registered Office: 5 Elstree Gate, Elstree Way, Borehamwood, Herts, WD6 1JD
Activities: Hotels and similar accommodation
Officers: Frederic de Brem [1975] Director [French]; Melinda Lu San Knatchbull [1975] Director/Chartered Accountant [Malaysian]

Alhambra Hotel Limited
Incorporated: 13 April 1992 *Employees:* 16
Net Worth: £6,668,040 *Total Assets:* £6,913,835
Registered Office: CKR House, 70 East Hill, Dartford, Kent, DA1 1RZ
Activities: Hotels and similar accommodation
Shareholders: Martine Yolande Valoti; Francesco Valoti
Officers: Martine Yolande Josette Valoti, Secretary; Bruno Miguel Pereira Cabral [1974] Director/Hotelier [Portuguese]; Francesco Valoti [1951] Director/Hotelier; Martine Yolande Josette Valoti [1952] Director/Hotelier [French]

Ali UK Limited
Incorporated: 20 February 1998 *Employees:* 3
Net Worth: £81,506,000 *Total Assets:* £130,357,000
Registered Office: 60 Barwell Business Park, Leatherhead Road, Chessington, Surrey, KT9 2NY
Activities: Other food services
Major Shareholder: Filippo Berti
Officers: Michael Hans May, Secretary; Maurizio Anastasia [1970] Director [Italian]; Michael Hans May [1951] Director; Angelo Speranza [1962] Director

Alim Caterers Limited
Incorporated: 7 April 1986 *Employees:* 89
Net Worth: £1,656,301 *Total Assets:* £6,278,011
Registered Office: Runway House, The Runway, Ruislip, Middlesex, HA4 6SE
Activities: Unlicenced restaurants and cafes
Parent: SME Investments Ltd
Officers: Aly Mohamed Esmail, Secretary; Sayed Mohamed Esmail, Secretary; Aly Mohamed Esmail [1982] Director; Sayed Mohamed Esmail [1986] Director

Alim Investments Limited
Incorporated: 14 January 1985 *Employees:* 25
Net Worth: £3,240,401 *Total Assets:* £5,279,675
Registered Office: Runway House, The Runway, Ruislip, Middlesex, HA4 6SE
Activities: Unlicenced restaurants and cafes
Parent: SME Investments Ltd
Officers: Aly Mohamed Esmail, Secretary; Sayed Mohamed Esmail, Secretary; Ali Mohamed Esmail [1982] Director; Sayed Mohamed Esmail [1986] Director

Alimar Limited
Incorporated: 13 August 1962 *Employees:* 2
Net Worth: £5,287,897 *Total Assets:* £5,674,702
Registered Office: York House, Empire Way, Wembley, Middlesex, HA9 0FQ
Activities: Other letting and operating of own or leased real estate
Parent: Astor Lodge Holdings Limited
Officers: David Lessman, Secretary/Director; Julia Ruth Bekhor [1960] Director; David Lessman [1925] Director

Alina Care Limited
Incorporated: 28 April 2014 *Employees:* 16
Net Worth Deficit: £2,351,487 *Total Assets:* £13,836,348
Registered Office: Manor House, Church Street, Leatherhead, Surrey, KT22 8DN
Activities: Other human health activities
Parent: Alina Care Holdings Limited
Officers: Paul James Steadman, Secretary; James Richard Deeley [1963] Director; Katherine Francis Ford [1973] Director; Fergus Alexander Kee [1960] Director [Irish]; Justine Carolyn Pickford [1968] Director; Paul James Steadman [1966] Director/Chartered Accountant

Alium Medical Limited
Incorporated: 12 June 2001 *Employees:* 33
Net Worth: £5,263,362 *Total Assets:* £6,375,887
Registered Office: Haslers, Old Station Road, Loughton, Essex, IG10 4PL
Activities: Wholesale of pharmaceutical goods
Shareholder: Bennie Rabin
Officers: Kyriacos Costas Kyriacou, Secretary; Kyriacos Costas Kyriacou [1958] Director/Accountant; Bennie Rabin [1942] Director/Pharmacist; Ruth Moira Rabin [1950] Director/Company Secretary

Aliunde Limited
Incorporated: 29 July 2005 *Employees:* 1
Net Worth: £1,453,004 *Total Assets:* £42,024,648
Registered Office: 12 Hatherley Road, Sidcup, Kent, DA14 4DT
Activities: Security and commodity contracts dealing activities
Major Shareholder: Bertrand Velge
Officers: Bertrand Roger Velge [1959] Director

All Metal Services Limited
Incorporated: 8 February 1974 *Employees:* 305
Net Worth: £90,441,312 *Total Assets:* £154,515,056
Registered Office: Unit 6 Horton Industrial Park, Horton Road, West Drayton, Middlesex, UB7 8JD
Activities: Agents involved in the sale of machinery, industrial equipment, ships and aircraft
Officers: James Donald Hoffman [1958] Director/Chief Executive Officer [American]; Karla Renee Lewis [1965] Director/Chief Financial Officer [American]; William Sales [1957] Director [American]; Sara Williams [1967] Financial Director

All World Foods Limited
Incorporated: 27 June 1994 *Employees:* 3
Net Worth: £8,613,026 *Total Assets:* £11,321,115
Registered Office: 3rd Floor Left, Elizabeth House, 54-58 High Street, Edgware, Middlesex, HA8 7EJ
Activities: Agents involved in the sale of food, beverages and tobacco
Shareholders: Lucila Tania Lara Acosta; Isabel Cristina O'Reilly Cana
Officers: Jose Antonio Goncalves Da Silva, Secretary; Alejandro Cardet Chaveco [1973] Director [Cuban]

Ian Allan Group Limited
Incorporated: 1 November 1962 *Employees:* 144
Net Worth: £19,245,572 *Total Assets:* £25,894,818
Registered Office: Terminal House, Station Approach, Shepperton, Surrey, TW17 8AS
Activities: Activities of head offices
Officers: Derek Arthur Hart, Secretary; David Ian Allan [1954] Executive Director; Edwin Paul Allan [1957] Executive Director; Gillian Susan Allan [1957] Director; Michael Andrew Smith [1960] Director/Chartered Accountant; Anthony Douglas Watkins [1944] Director/Chartered Accountant

Ian Allan Travel Limited
Incorporated: 19 April 1951 *Employees:* 89
Net Worth: £6,496,020 *Total Assets:* £11,150,656
Registered Office: Terminal House, Station Approach, Shepperton, Surrey, TW17 8AS
Activities: Travel agency activities
Parent: Ian Allan Group Limited
Officers: Derek Arthur Hart, Secretary; David Ian Allan [1954] Executive Director; Edwin Paul Allan [1957] Executive Director; Patrick Joseph O'Neill [1960] Director; Michael Andrew Smith [1960] Director/Chartered Accountant; Anthony Douglas Watkins [1944] Director/Chartered Accountant

Allandale Investments Limited
Incorporated: 8 August 2011
Net Worth Deficit: £587,394 *Total Assets:* £8,978,322
Registered Office: 54 The Enterprise Centre, Cranborne Road, Potters Bar, Herts, EN6 3DQ
Activities: Financial intermediation not elsewhere classified
Major Shareholder: Aleksei Bazhenov
Officers: Nigel David Rowlinson, Secretary; Patrick Joseph Albert Hansen [1972] Director [Luxembourger]

Allen (Concrete) Limited
Incorporated: 8 April 1987
Net Worth: £9,917,458 *Total Assets:* £11,524,139
Registered Office: 38 Willow Lane, Mitcham, Surrey, CR4 4NA
Activities: Other manufacturing n.e.c.
Parent: Topcrete Limited
Officers: Michael Ignatius Roddy [1979] Director [Irish]; Charles Edmund Trigg [1980] Director/Operations Manager; Clinton John White [1965] Director

David Allen Holdings Limited
Incorporated: 30 August 1966 *Employees:* 8
Net Worth: £6,433,044 *Total Assets:* £7,682,259
Registered Office: 991 Great West Road, Brentford, Middlesex, TW8 9DN
Activities: Advertising agencies
Officers: Joanne Elred Grant, Secretary; Patrick Joseph Mannion [1969] Commercial Director [Irish]; Julie Patricia Mulleady [1972] Property & Logistics Director [Irish]; Tony O'Flanagan [1970] Marketing Director [Irish]; Nicholas Joseph Roberts [1969] APC Director [Irish]; Andy Joseph Sherry [1973] Director/Chartered Accountant [Irish]

Alliance BMP Limited
Incorporated: 17 January 2007 *Employees:* 1
Net Worth: £36,571,000 *Total Assets:* £52,475,000
Registered Office: 2 The Heights, Brooklands, Weybridge, Surrey, KT13 0NY
Activities: Other business support service activities n.e.c.
Parent: WBA Group Limited
Officers: Frank Standish, Secretary [Irish]; Mattia D'Alessandro [1975] Director [Italian]; Alexandro Depau [1970] Director [American]; John Kallend [1959] Director

Alliance Healthcare (Distribution) Limited
Incorporated: 7 October 1997
Net Worth: £258,000,000 *Total Assets:* £1,248,999,936
Registered Office: 43 Cox Lane, Chessington, Surrey, KT9 1SN
Activities: Wholesale of pharmaceutical goods
Parent: Alliance Boots Holdings Limited
Officers: Lucie Charlotte Massart, Secretary; Alexandro Depau [1970] Director [American]; Julian David Mount [1965] Director; Pablo Cortes Rivas [1972] Director [Spanish]

Alliance Healthcare (IT Services) Limited
Incorporated: 13 March 2000
Net Worth: £9,290,000 *Total Assets:* £111,040,000
Registered Office: 2 The Heights, Brooklands, Weybridge, Surrey, KT13 0NY
Activities: Other information technology service activities
Parent: Alliance Boots Holdings Limited
Officers: Frank Standish, Secretary [Irish]; Mark Francis Muller [1964] Director; Steven Rempel [1961] Director [American]; Anthony Charles Roberts [1962] Director

Alliance Healthcare Management Services Limited
Incorporated: 11 November 2009 *Employees:* 4,563
Net Worth: £6,700,000 *Total Assets:* £22,500,000
Registered Office: 43 Cox Lane, Chessington, Surrey, KT9 1SN
Activities: Other business support service activities n.e.c.
Parent: Alliance Boots Holdings Limited
Officers: Frank Standish, Secretary; Claude Louis Joseph Bahoshy [1973] Director; Pablo Cortes Rivas [1972] Director [Spanish]; Frank Standish [1963] Company Secretary/Director [Irish]

Allocate Bidco Limited
Incorporated: 1 May 2014 *Employees:* 5
Net Worth Deficit: £24,430,000 *Total Assets:* £124,390,000
Registered Office: 2nd Floor, 1 Church Road, Richmond, Surrey, TW9 2QE
Activities: Information technology consultancy activities
Parent: Allocate Midco Limited
Officers: Ryan Friedman Atlas [1984] Director [American]; Nicholas Stephen Wilson [1971] Director/Chief Executive Officer

Allocate Holdco Limited
Incorporated: 1 May 2014
Net Worth Deficit: £821,000 *Total Assets:* £61,137,000
Registered Office: 2nd Floor, 1 Church Road, Richmond, Surrey, TW9 2QE
Activities: Information technology consultancy activities
Parent: Allocate Topco Limited
Officers: Ryan Friedman Atlas [1984] Director [American]; Nicholas Stephen Wilson [1971] Director/Chief Executive Officer

Allocate Midco Limited
Incorporated: 1 May 2014 *Employees:* 408
Net Worth Deficit: £27,971,000 *Total Assets:* £142,212,992
Registered Office: 2nd Floor, 1 Church Road, Richmond, Surrey, TW9 2QE
Activities: Information technology consultancy activities
Parent: Allocate Holdco Limited
Officers: Ryan Friedman Atlas [1984] Director [American]; Nicholas Stephen Wilson [1971] Director/Chief Executive Officer

Allocate Software Limited
Incorporated: 5 May 1993 *Employees:* 378
Previous: Allocate Software PLC
Net Worth: £20,600,000 *Total Assets:* £70,327,000
Registered Office: 2nd Floor, 1 Church Road, Richmond, Surrey, TW9 2QE
Activities: Information technology consultancy activities
Parent: Allocate Bidco Limited
Officers: Ryan Friedman Atlas [1984] Director [American]; Jonathan James Harston [1976] Director/Chief Financial Officer; Nicholas Stephen Wilson [1971] Director/Chief Executive Officer

Allocate Topco Limited
Incorporated: 1 May 2014 *Employees:* 413
Net Worth Deficit: £29,458,000 *Total Assets:* £147,862,000
Registered Office: 2nd Floor, 1 Church Road, Richmond, Surrey, TW9 2QE
Activities: Information technology consultancy activities
Parent: Antidote Bidco Limited
Officers: Ryan Friedman Atlas [1984] Director [American]; Nicholas Stephen Wilson [1971] Director/Chief Executive Officer

Allois Properties (Leatherhead) Limited
Incorporated: 18 November 2015
Net Worth Deficit: £468,013 *Total Assets:* £12,479,118
Registered Office: Belgrave House, 39-43 Monument Hill, Weybridge, Surrey, KT13 8RN
Activities: Development of building projects
Parent: KH111 Properties 618 Limited
Officers: Russel Neale Warburton, Secretary; Andrew John Pettit [1968] Director/Banker; Caroline Jane Porter [1963] Director/Surveyor; Neil Lettington Porter [1962] Director; Nicholas Ashley West [1972] Director/Chartered Surveyor

Allport Cargo Services Limited
Incorporated: 3 September 1963 *Employees:* 649
Net Worth: £21,362,684 *Total Assets:* £109,364,136
Registered Office: Allport House, 1 Cowley Business Park, High Street, Cowley, Middlesex, UB8 2AD
Activities: Other transportation support activities
Parent: Allport Group Limited
Officers: Shek Yau John Lau [1947] Director [Chinese]; Charles Frater McGurin [1965] Director; David James Thomas [1962] Director; William Alfred John Toye [1942] Freight Forwarder Director; Heath Brian Zarin [1975] Director/Finance [Kittitian]

Allport Group Limited
Incorporated: 15 January 2004 *Employees:* 915
Net Worth: £35,517,076 *Total Assets:* £137,777,280
Registered Office: Allport House, 1 Cowley Business Park, High Street, Cowley, Middlesex, UB8 2AD
Activities: Activities of head offices
Major Shareholder: Heath Brian Zarin
Officers: Mark Davis, Secretary; Clyde Buntrock [1972] Director; Shek Yau John Lau [1947] Director [Chinese]; Charles Frater McGurin [1965] Director; Simon Richard Pearson [1967] Director; David James Thomas [1962] Director; William Alfred John Toye [1942] Freight Forwarder-Director; Steve John Williams [1972] Director; Heath Brian Zarin [1975] Director/Finance [American]

Almirall Limited
Incorporated: 23 July 2007 *Employees:* 35
Net Worth: £8,029,066 *Total Assets:* £14,548,521
Registered Office: 1 George Street, Uxbridge, Middlesex, UB8 1QQ
Activities: Wholesale of perfume and cosmetics
Parent: Almirall S.A.
Officers: Alfredo Baron de Juan [1967] Senior Director [Spanish]

Almus Pharmaceuticals Limited
Incorporated: 6 February 2004 *Employees:* 13
Net Worth: £274,858,464 *Total Assets:* £275,978,528
Registered Office: 2 The Heights, Brooklands, Weybridge, Surrey, KT13 0NY
Activities: Other business support service activities n.e.c.
Parent: Alliance Boots Holdings Limited
Officers: Frank Standish, Company Secretary [Irish]; Alexandro Depau [1970] Director [American]; Richard Joseph Anthony Gorsuch [1970] Director/Chartered Accountant; Careen Elizabeth Snadden [1967] Director

Alperton Community School
Incorporated: 31 July 2012 *Employees:* 187
Net Worth: £32,979,520 *Total Assets:* £37,629,564
Registered Office: Alperton Community School, Stanley Avenue, Wembley, Middlesex, HA0 4JE
Activities: General secondary education
Officers: Suresh Chandra Jatla, Secretary; Safoora Ahmed [1980] Director/Homemaker; Frances Jeanne Edwards [1981] Director/Teacher; Maureen Griffith [1945] Director/Retired; Michael Jonathan Heiser [1957] Director/Senior Adviser (Finance); Nevia Johnson [1981] Director/Councillor; Sujatha Jothi [1971] Director/Software Engineer [Indian]; Gerard Patrick McKenna [1961] Director/Headteacher; Vijesh Patel [1972] Director/Senior Manager - Business Intelligence; Mona Shah [1963] Director/Legal Department Co-ordinator; Ian Spencer Slade [1967] Director/Teacher; Vimalkumar Tailor [1970] Director/Bank Manager; Daksha Mahendrarai Thanki [1965] Director

Alphalarch Limited
Incorporated: 22 July 1997
Net Worth: £20,005,000 *Total Assets:* £71,274,000
Registered Office: 161 Chertsey Road, Twickenham, Middlesex, TW1 1ER
Activities: Other letting and operating of own or leased real estate
Parent: Curfin (Netherlands Antilles) B.V.
Officers: Joseph Michael Jaffe [1955] Director/Business Executive; Derek Jonathan Murray [1960] Director/Company Executive; Glenn Robert Bruce Pitzer [1968] Director/Company Executive

Alsford Timber Limited
Incorporated: 16 June 1993 *Employees:* 237
Net Worth: £10,984,176 *Total Assets:* £16,224,498
Registered Office: 45 Portsmouth Road, Cobham, Surrey, KT11 1JQ
Activities: Wholesale of wood, construction materials and sanitary equipment
Parent: Geo. Kingsbury Timber Ltd
Officers: Mark William Kingsbury, Secretary; Neil Anthony Fuller [1965] Managing Director; Christopher Kingsbury [1937] Director; Mark William Kingsbury [1964] Director; Michael George Kingsbury [1934] Director

Alternative Bridging (UK 1) Limited
Incorporated: 15 October 2014
Net Worth: £109,388 *Total Assets:* £24,886,840
Registered Office: 1st Floor, Healthaid House, Marlborough Hill, Harrow, Middlesex, HA1 1UD
Activities: Financial intermediation not elsewhere classified
Parent: Alternative Bridging Corporation Limited
Officers: Robert Jeffrey Piper, Secretary; Stephen Daniel Meller [1967] Director; Brian Leslie Rubins [1939] Director; Jonathan Rubins [1967] Director

Alternative Bridging (UK 2) Limited
Incorporated: 8 April 2016
Net Worth: £15,945 *Total Assets:* £17,161,092
Registered Office: 1st Floor, Healthaid House, Marlborough Hill, Harrow, Middlesex, HA1 1UD
Activities: Financial intermediation not elsewhere classified
Parent: Alternative Bridging Corporation Limited
Officers: Robert Jeffrey Piper, Secretary; Stephen Daniel Meller [1967] Director; Brian Leslie Rubins [1939] Director; Jonathan Rubins [1967] Director

Alternative Bridging Corporation Limited
Incorporated: 18 March 2010 *Employees:* 2
Net Worth: £488,333 *Total Assets:* £103,020,976
Registered Office: 1st Floor, Healthaid House, Marlborough Hill, Harrow, Middlesex, HA1 1UD
Activities: Financial intermediation not elsewhere classified
Parent: Southern Group Limited
Officers: Robert Jeffrey Piper, Secretary; Allan Howard Kay [1963] Director/Chief Operating Officer; Stephen Daniel Meller [1967] Director; Brian Leslie Rubins [1939] Director; Jonathan Rubins [1967] Director; Steven Sharpe [1967] Director

Alto Property Investments Limited
Incorporated: 25 June 2009
Net Worth: £31,310 *Total Assets:* £7,574,502
Registered Office: 19-20 Bourne Court, Southend Road, Woodford Green, Essex, IG8 8HD
Activities: Other business support service activities n.e.c.
Shareholders: Abraham Aharon Dodi; Abraham Rosenberg
Officers: Abraham Aharon Dodi [1963] Director/Chairman; Abraham Rosenberg [1948] Director

Altomart Limited
Incorporated: 31 December 1991 *Employees:* 3
Net Worth: £12,654,108 *Total Assets:* £16,528,765
Registered Office: Suite 2, Rama Apartments, 17 St Anns Road, Harrow, Middlesex, HA1 1JU
Activities: Sale of new cars and light motor vehicles
Officers: Rekha Soni, Secretary; Raajnish Mahendra Soni [1971] Director

Aluminium Services (UK) Limited
Incorporated: 2 March 2007
Net Worth: £26,703,060 *Total Assets:* £60,000,024
Registered Office: Unit 6 Horton Industrial Park, Horton Road, West Drayton, Middlesex, UB7 8JD
Activities: Activities of head offices
Parent: Reliance Steel and Aluminum
Officers: Karla Renee Lewis [1965] Director/Chief Financial Officer [American]; Gregg James Mollins [1954] Director [American]; David Leslie Potts [1946] Director; William Sales [1957] Director [American]; Sara Williams [1967] Financial Director

Amadeus Primary Academies Trust
Incorporated: 29 June 2015 *Employees:* 223
Net Worth: £5,040,000 *Total Assets:* £7,584,000
Registered Office: Old Bexley Church of England Primary School, Hurst Road, Bexley, Kent, DA5 3JR
Activities: Primary education
Officers: Paul Albert Allen [1947] Director/Chartered Engineer; Julie Elizabeth Bowen [1964] Director/Anglican Priest; Janice Collins [1958] Director/Retired; Ida Marcia Philbin [1964] Assistant Director; John Francis Simms [1971] Bank Director; Father Philip Anthony Wells [1983] Director/Clerk in Holy Orders; Peter Martin Wilson [1957] Director/Executive Headteacher

Amal Investments Limited
Incorporated: 29 July 1998
Net Worth: £7,499,397 *Total Assets:* £7,500,000
Registered Office: Stoneham House, 17 Scarbrook Road, Croydon, Surrey, CR0 1SQ
Activities: Activities of extraterritorial organisations and bodies
Officers: Riaz Datoo [1950] Director; Mohsen Mousavi [1955] Director

Amalgamated Property Holdings Limited
Incorporated: 16 June 1993
Net Worth: £6,909,809 *Total Assets:* £11,876,038
Registered Office: 6 Park Road, Hampton Hill, Middlesex, TW12 1HB
Activities: Other letting and operating of own or leased real estate
Parent: Amalgamated Holdco Ltd
Officers: Derek George Cormack, Secretary; Derek George Cormack [1959] Director [Irish]; Clifford Andrew William Hamilton [1962] Director

Amana Trust
Incorporated: 5 February 2002 *Employees:* 113
Net Worth: £8,816,988 *Total Assets:* £9,873,503
Registered Office: Bower House, Orange Tree Hill, Romford, Essex, RM4 1PB
Activities: Activities of religious organisations
Officers: Samuel Petrus Alexander, Secretary; Paul Cooke [1949] Director/Christian Worker; Joseph Harold Davis [1943] Director; Curtis James Kennard [1958] Director/Bible School Administrator

Amar Property Services Limited
Incorporated: 20 April 2009 *Employees:* 2
Net Worth: £3,826,903 *Total Assets:* £5,667,093
Registered Office: c/o Haslers, Old Station Road, Loughton, Essex, IG10 4PL
Activities: Management of real estate on a fee or contract basis
Officers: Amrik Singh Kahlon, Secretary; Amrik Singh Kahlon [1962] Director; Kanbir Kaur Kahlon [1968] Director/Housewife

Amaze Capital Limited
Incorporated: 9 June 2015 *Employees:* 2
Net Worth: £181,343 *Total Assets:* £6,316,534
Registered Office: 22 Birds Hill Drive, Oxshott, Surrey, KT22 0SP
Activities: Other service activities n.e.c.
Major Shareholder: Douglas Steven Lawrence
Officers: Douglas Steven Lawrence [1971] Director/Financial Trader; Dr John Brian Lawrence [1945] Director/Retired

AMB Property Ltd
Incorporated: 21 October 2010
Net Worth Deficit: £69,689 *Total Assets:* £5,338,070
Registered Office: 195a Kenton Road, Harrow, Middlesex, HA3 0HD
Activities: Other letting and operating of own or leased real estate
Major Shareholder: Minaxi Bathia
Officers: Minaxi Bathia [1958] Director

Amber Solar Parks (Holdings) Limited
Incorporated: 25 May 2012
Net Worth: £9,689,000 *Total Assets:* £28,532,000
Registered Office: 8 White Oak Square, London Road, Swanley, Kent, BR8 7AG
Activities: Production of electricity
Parent: John Laing Environmental Assets Group (UK) Limited
Officers: Giuseppe La Loggia [1975] Director/Entrepreneur [Italian]; Joseph Mark Linney [1958] Director/Chartered Quantity Surveyor; Christopher James Tanner [1972] Investment Director

Amber Solar Parks Limited
Incorporated: 25 May 2012
Net Worth: £9,783,000 *Total Assets:* £28,640,000
Registered Office: 8 White Oak Square, London Road, Swanley, Kent, BR8 7AG
Activities: Production of electricity
Parent: Amber Solar Parks (Holdings) Limited
Officers: Giuseppe La Loggia [1975] Director/Entrepreneur [Italian]; Joseph Mark Linney [1958] Director/Chartered Quantity Surveyor; Christopher James Tanner [1972] Investment Director

Ambika Investments Limited
Incorporated: 7 November 2013 *Employees:* 1
Net Worth: £1,492,630 *Total Assets:* £5,561,992
Registered Office: Devonshire House, 582 Honeypot Lane, Stanmore, Middlesex, HA7 1JS
Activities: Development of building projects
Shareholders: Mitul Popat; Sneha Patel; Beejal Popat; Mitul Popat
Officers: Shivani Popat, Secretary; Mitul Popat [1980] Director

Ambreck LLP
Incorporated: 14 September 2012
Net Worth: £3,203,266 *Total Assets:* £5,680,390
Registered Office: 6-10 Outram Road, Croydon, Surrey, CR0 6XE
Officers: Gordon Henry Phillips [1947] Member; Hilary Jewel Phillips [1948] Member

AMD Environmental Limited
Incorporated: 4 December 1989 *Employees:* 46
Net Worth: £3,256,119 *Total Assets:* £9,106,644
Registered Office: Jupiter House, Orbital One, Green Street, Green Road, Dartford, Kent, DA1 1QG
Activities: Electrical installation
Shareholders: Jon Andrew King; Marcus Gordon Sullivan
Officers: Jonathan Andrew King [1961] Director; Darren Barry Peachey [1980] Director/Chartered Accountant; Daniel John Pearce [1969] Director

Amery Construction Limited
Incorporated: 10 January 2000 *Employees:* 6
Net Worth: £4,930,707 *Total Assets:* £7,015,458
Registered Office: 27a Maxwell Road, Northwood, Middlesex, HA6 2XY
Activities: Other business support service activities n.e.c.
Major Shareholder: Martin Christopher Flannery
Officers: Caroline Carmel Brown, Secretary; Martin Christopher Flannery [1978] Director; Patrick Francis Sheehan [1974] Director [Irish]

Amey Highways Lighting (Manchester) Limited
Incorporated: 17 April 2003
Net Worth Deficit: £2,425,000 *Total Assets:* £30,064,000
Registered Office: 8 White Oak Square, London Road, Swanley, Kent, BR8 7AG
Activities: Construction of commercial buildings
Parent: AHL Holdings (Manchester) Limited
Officers: Neeti Mukundrai Anand [1984] Director; Carl Harvey Dix [1966] Operations Director; Asif Ghafoor [1970] Director; Katherine Pearman [1961] Director/Chartered Accountant; Carlos Vela Lazaga [1989] Director/Junior Valuation Analyst [Spanish]

Amey Highways Lighting (Wakefield) Limited
Incorporated: 15 April 2002
Net Worth Deficit: £1,248,000 *Total Assets:* £16,054,000
Registered Office: 8 White Oak Square, London Road, Swanley, Kent, BR8 7AG
Activities: Other business support service activities n.e.c.
Parent: AHL Holdings (Wakefield) Limited
Officers: Neeti Mukundrai Anand [1984] Director; Carl Harvey Dix [1966] Operations Director; Asif Ghafoor [1970] Director; Katherine Pearman [1961] Director/Chartered Accountant; Carlos Vela Lazaga [1989] Director/Junior Valuation Analyst [Spanish]

AMG Healthcare Limited
Incorporated: 5 March 2004 *Employees:* 165
Net Worth: £16,082,000 *Total Assets:* £30,528,000
Registered Office: 1st Floor, Selsdon House, 212-220 Addington Road, South Croydon, Surrey, CR2 8LD
Activities: Dispensing chemist in specialised stores
Parent: Avicenna Holdings Ltd
Officers: Shiraz Kassam Hirji [1947] Director; Salim Kassamali Esmail Jetha [1953] Director/Pharmacist; Jayanti Chimanbhai Patel Junior [1984] Director

Amoco (Fiddich) Limited
Incorporated: 19 March 1971
Net Worth: £82,234,152 *Total Assets:* £229,542,288
Registered Office: Chertsey Road, Sunbury on Thames, Middlesex, TW16 7BP
Activities: Extraction of crude petroleum
Parent: Britoil Limited
Officers: Karen MacLennan [1971] Director/Oil Company Executive; Sandra Jean MacRae [1963] Director/Oil Company Executive

Amphora Acquisitions Limited
Incorporated: 21 June 2011 *Employees:* 3
Net Worth: £25,553,000 *Total Assets:* £60,684,000
Registered Office: One London Road, Staines upon Thames, Middlesex, TW18 4EX
Activities: Information technology consultancy activities
Parent: Ensono Opco Holdings Limited
Officers: Peter John Bazil [1972] Director/General Counsel [American]; Norman Smagley [1958] Director/Chief Financial Officer [American]

AMS Care Limited
Incorporated: 8 March 2006 *Employees:* 123
Net Worth: £10,735,931 *Total Assets:* £20,491,914
Registered Office: 2 Ambassador House, Wolseley Road, Harrow, Middlesex, HA3 5RT
Activities: Residential nursing care facilities
Major Shareholder: Saloni Chotai
Officers: Saloni Chotai, Secretary/Lawyer; Manish Chotai [1961] Director/Chartered Accountant; Saloni Chotai [1963] Director/Lawyer

AMS Care Wiltshire Limited
Incorporated: 6 September 2010 *Employees:* 62
Net Worth: £4,897,600 *Total Assets:* £10,127,908
Registered Office: 2 Ambassador House, Wolseley Road, Harrow, Middlesex, HA3 5RT
Activities: Residential care activities for the elderly and disabled
Major Shareholder: Saloni Chotai
Officers: Saloni Chotai, Secretary; Manish Chotai [1961] Director/Chartered Accountant; Saloni Chotai [1963] Director/Lawyer

Amsair Aircraft Limited
Incorporated: 13 June 2006
Net Worth Deficit: £4,513,165 *Total Assets:* £9,332,958
Registered Office: Amshold House, Goldings Hill, Loughton, Essex, IG10 2RW
Activities: Non-scheduled passenger air transport
Parent: Amshold Trading Limited
Officers: Michael Edward Ray, Secretary; Roger George Adams [1950] Director/Certified Accountant; Claude Manuel Littner [1949] Director [British/American]; Michael Edward Ray [1963] Director/Chartered Accountant; Daniel Paul Sugar [1971] Director; Simon Sugar [1969] Director

Amshold Group Limited
Incorporated: 5 June 2013 *Employees:* 23
Net Worth: £535,119,008 *Total Assets:* £587,838,016
Registered Office: Amshold House, Goldings Hill, Loughton, Essex, IG10 2RW
Activities: Buying and selling of own real estate
Major Shareholder: Alan Michael Sugar
Officers: Michael Edward Ray, Secretary; Roger George Adams [1950] Director/Certified Accountant; Michael Edward Ray [1963] Director/Certified Accountant; Lord Alan Michael Sugar [1947] Director/Chairman; Daniel Paul Sugar [1971] Director; Simon Sugar [1969] Director

Amshold International Limited
Incorporated: 10 February 1999
Net Worth: £4,156,491 *Total Assets:* £84,816,392
Registered Office: Amshold House, Goldings Hill, Loughton, Essex, IG10 2RW
Activities: Buying and selling of own real estate
Parent: Amsprop London Limited
Officers: Michael Edward Ray, Secretary; Roger George Adams [1950] Director/Certified Accountant; Andrew Norman Cohen [1961] Director/Chartered Surveyor; Claude Manuel Littner [1949] Director [British/American]; Michael Edward Ray [1963] Director/Chartered Accountant; Lord Alan Michael Sugar [1947] Chairman and Managing Director; Daniel Paul Sugar [1971] Director; Louise Jane Sugar [1974] Director; Simon Sugar [1969] Director

Amshold Securities Limited
Incorporated: 21 March 1997
Net Worth: £188,758 *Total Assets:* £89,152,768
Registered Office: Amshold House, Goldings Hill, Loughton, Essex, IG10 2RW
Activities: Activities of other holding companies n.e.c.
Parent: Amshold Group Limited
Officers: Michael Edward Ray, Secretary; Claude Manuel Littner [1949] Director [British/American]; Michael Edward Ray [1963] Director/Chartered Accountant

Amshold Trading Limited
Incorporated: 5 June 2013 *Employees:* 58
Net Worth: £4,769,068 *Total Assets:* £32,109,412
Registered Office: Amshold House, Goldings Hill, Loughton, Essex, IG10 2RW
Activities: Activities of head offices
Major Shareholder: Alan Michael Sugar
Officers: Michael Edward Ray, Secretary; Roger George Adams [1950] Director/Certified Accountant; Michael Edward Ray [1963] Director/Certified Accountant; Lord Alan Michael Sugar [1947] Director/Chairman; Daniel Paul Sugar [1971] Director; Simon Sugar [1969] Director

Amsik Limited
Incorporated: 15 May 1989
Net Worth: £6,546,743 *Total Assets:* £14,564,792
Registered Office: 79 College Road, Harrow, Middlesex, HA1 1BD
Activities: Buying and selling of own real estate
Major Shareholder: Sandeep Singh Sahni
Officers: Priyaneet Sahni, Secretary; Sandeep Singh Sahni [1972] Director/Property Dealer

Amsprop Bishopsgate Limited
Incorporated: 1 August 2006
Net Worth: £53,309,284 *Total Assets:* £103,946,048
Registered Office: Amshold House, Goldings Hill, Loughton, Essex, IG10 2RW
Activities: Buying and selling of own real estate
Parent: Amsprop Limited
Officers: Michael Edward Ray, Secretary; Roger George Adams [1950] Director/Certified Accountant; Andrew Norman Cohen [1961] Director/Chartered Surveyor; James Hughes [1963] Estates Director; Claude Manuel Littner [1949] Director [British/American]; Michael Edward Ray [1963] Director/Chartered Accountant; Daniel Paul Sugar [1971] Director; Simon Sugar [1969] Director

Amsprop Central Limited
Incorporated: 26 September 2001
Net Worth: £18,543,966 *Total Assets:* £34,407,408
Registered Office: Amshold House, Goldings Hill, Loughton, Essex, IG10 2RW
Activities: Buying and selling of own real estate
Parent: Amsprop Limited
Officers: Michael Edward Ray, Secretary; Roger George Adams [1950] Director/Certified Accountant; Andrew Norman Cohen [1961] Director/Chartered Surveyor; James Hughes [1963] Estates Director; Claude Manuel Littner [1949] Director [British/American]; Michael Edward Ray [1963] Director/Chartered Accountant; Daniel Paul Sugar [1971] Director; Louise Jane Sugar [1974] Director; Simon Sugar [1969] Director

Amsprop City Properties Limited
Incorporated: 23 April 2001
Net Worth: £13,232,221 *Total Assets:* £18,491,500
Registered Office: Amshold House, Goldings Hill, Loughton, Essex, IG10 2RW
Activities: Buying and selling of own real estate
Parent: Amsprop Limited
Officers: Michael Edward Ray, Secretary; Roger George Adams [1950] Director/Certified Accountant; Andrew Norman Cohen [1961] Director/Chartered Surveyor; James Hughes [1963] Estates Director; Claude Manuel Littner [1949] Director [British/American]; Michael Edward Ray [1963] Director/Chartered Accountant; Daniel Paul Sugar [1971] Director; Louise Jane Sugar [1974] Director; Simon Sugar [1969] Director

Amsprop Estates Limited
Incorporated: 19 March 1993
Net Worth: £9,796,504 *Total Assets:* £10,272,408
Registered Office: Amshold House, Goldings Hill, Loughton, Essex, IG10 2RW
Activities: Buying and selling of own real estate
Parent: Amsprop Limited
Officers: Michael Edward Ray, Secretary; Roger George Adams [1950] Director/Certified Accountant; Andrew Norman Cohen [1961] Director/Chartered Surveyor; James Hughes [1963] Estates Director; Claude Manuel Littner [1949] Director [British/American]; Michael Edward Ray [1963] Director/Chartered Accountant; Daniel Paul Sugar [1971] Director; Louise Jane Sugar [1974] Director; Simon Sugar [1969] Director

Amsprop Investments Limited
Incorporated: 5 March 1990
Net Worth: £199,924,304 *Total Assets:* £308,055,968
Registered Office: Amshold House, Goldings Hill, Loughton, Essex, IG10 2RW
Activities: Buying and selling of own real estate
Parent: Amsprop Limited
Officers: Michael Edward Ray, Secretary; Roger George Adams [1950] Director/Certified Accountant; Andrew Norman Cohen [1961] Director/Chartered Surveyor; James Hughes [1963] Estates Director; Claude Manuel Littner [1949] Director [British/American]; Michael Edward Ray [1963] Director/Chartered Accountant; Daniel Paul Sugar [1971] Director; Louise Jane Sugar [1974] Director; Simon Sugar [1969] Director

Amsprop London Limited
Incorporated: 8 February 1989
Net Worth: £59,940,132 *Total Assets:* £63,628,384
Registered Office: Amshold House, Goldings Hill, Loughton, Essex, IG10 2RW
Activities: Buying and selling of own real estate
Parent: Amshold Group Limited
Officers: Michael Edward Ray, Secretary; Roger George Adams [1950] Director/Certified Accountant; Andrew Norman Cohen [1961] Director/Chartered Surveyor; James Hughes [1963] Estates Director; Claude Manuel Littner [1949] Director [British/American]; Michael Edward Ray [1963] Director/Chartered Accountant; Lord Alan Michael Sugar [1947] Chairman and Managing Director; Daniel Paul Sugar [1971] Director; Louise Jane Sugar [1974] Director; Simon Sugar [1969] Director

Amsprop Portland Limited
Incorporated: 1 August 2006
Net Worth: £20,478,624 *Total Assets:* £48,103,136
Registered Office: Amshold House, Goldings Hill, Loughton, Essex, IG10 2RW
Activities: Buying and selling of own real estate
Parent: Amsprop Limited
Officers: Michael Edward Ray, Secretary; Roger George Adams [1950] Director/Certified Accountant; Andrew Norman Cohen [1961] Director/Chartered Surveyor; James Hughes [1963] Estates Director; Claude Manuel Littner [1949] Director [British/American]; Michael Edward Ray [1963] Director/Chartered Accountant; Daniel Paul Sugar [1971] Director; Simon Sugar [1969] Director

Analog Devices Limited
Incorporated: 6 January 1967 *Employees:* 111
Net Worth: £6,634,203 *Total Assets:* £17,026,910
Registered Office: Unit 3 Horizon Business Village, 1 Brooklands Road, Weybridge, Surrey, KT13 0TJ
Activities: Manufacture of electronic components
Parent: Analog Devices Holdings BV
Officers: Elizabeth Marion Mathieson, Secretary; Thomas Edward Cribben [1965] Global Tax Director [American]; Kevin Paul Lanouette [1970] Director [American]; Eileen Marie Wynne [1966] Director/VP, Corporate Controller [American]

Anchor Bay Construction Products Limited
Incorporated: 14 June 1999 *Employees:* 75
Net Worth: £6,380,458 *Total Assets:* £10,137,870
Registered Office: Building B and C, Centurion Way, Erith, Kent, DA18 4AF
Activities: Agents involved in the sale of timber and building materials
Parent: Threesixty Holdco 1 Limited
Officers: Paul William Jeal, Secretary; Paul William Jeal [1969] Finance Director; Chay Kinslow [1979] Operations Director; Marcus Parnham [1968] Managing Director; Peter James Raybould [1965] Director; John Neville Whitfield [1966] Director

Anderson Travel Limited
Incorporated: 4 April 1988 *Employees:* 63
Net Worth: £2,399,750 *Total Assets:* £8,168,312
Registered Office: 9 Carlton Road, New Malden, Surrey, KT3 3AJ
Activities: Other passenger land transport
Parent: M. S. Anderson Holdings Limited
Officers: Hannah Jo Anne Gray, Secretary; Mark Stephen Anderson [1962] Director

Andgrove Property Investments Limited
Incorporated: 20 July 1977 *Employees:* 1
Net Worth: £8,625,170 *Total Assets:* £10,048,160
Registered Office: 2nd Floor, Hygeia House, 66 College Road, Harrow, Middlesex, HA1 1BE
Activities: Development of building projects
Shareholders: Anthony David Gross; Helena Gross
Officers: Anthony David Gross [1938] Director; Helena Gross [1939] Director; Robert Lawrence Gross [1963] Director

Anella Limited
Incorporated: 3 November 2016 *Employees:* 2
Net Worth: £221,381 *Total Assets:* £5,215,846
Registered Office: 2 Royston Road, Richmond, Surrey, TW10 6LT
Activities: Activities of other holding companies n.e.c.
Shareholders: Andrew Kirkland Bassadone; Anne Charlotte Bassadone
Officers: Andrew Kirkland Bassadone [1957] Director; Anne Charlotte Bassadone [1962] Director

Angel Care (Orchid Care Homes) Ltd
Incorporated: 12 September 2012 *Employees:* 93
Net Worth: £5,992,633 *Total Assets:* £12,071,952
Registered Office: 116 Headstone Drive, Harrow, Middlesex, HA1 4UH
Activities: Residential nursing care facilities
Major Shareholder: Sandip Ruparelia
Officers: Sandip Ruparelia [1963] Director

Angel Care PLC
Incorporated: 16 January 1996 *Employees:* 245
Net Worth: £16,481,334 *Total Assets:* £29,445,680
Registered Office: 116 Headstone Drive, Harrow, Middlesex, HA1 4UH
Activities: Residential nursing care facilities
Shareholders: Sandip Ruparelia; Priti Ruparelia
Officers: Priti Ruparelia, Secretary/Care Home Operator; Priti Ruparelia [1963] Director/Care Home Operator; Sandip Ruparelia [1963] Director/Care Home Operator

Angel Property Investments Limited
Incorporated: 19 September 2002 *Employees:* 3
Net Worth: £9,680,686 *Total Assets:* £17,917,088
Registered Office: Churchill House, Stirling Way, Borehamwood, Herts, WD6 2HP
Activities: Other letting and operating of own or leased real estate
Officers: Richard Ian Basch, Secretary; Richard Ian Basch [1978] Director/Accountant; Adam James Margolis [1979] Director/Self Employed; Laura Margolis [1978] Director/Administrator

Angelica Estates Limited
Incorporated: 30 December 2014
Net Worth: £5,202,693 *Total Assets:* £11,145,977
Registered Office: 50 Lancaster Road, Enfield, Middlesex, EN2 0BY
Activities: Other letting and operating of own or leased real estate
Shareholders: Gerald Anthony Malton; Annabel Susan Malton
Officers: Annabel Susan Malton [1960] Director; Generald Anthony Malton [1960] Director

Anglia Secure Homes (South East) Limited
Incorporated: 13 January 1936 *Employees:* 8
Net Worth: £4,843,000 *Total Assets:* £7,065,000
Registered Office: 50 Lancaster Road, Enfield, Middlesex, EN2 0BY
Activities: Development of building projects
Parent: Fairview New Homes Limited
Officers: Jonathan Mark Baxter, Secretary; Michael Blakey [1963] Director; Nicholas Martin Dulcken [1967] Director; Generald Anthony Malton [1960] Director; Darren Lee McCormack [1982] Sales Director; Richard James Paterson [1957] Director; Martin Richard Smith [1955] Director; Jonathan Andrew Spring [1972] Land Buying Director; Michael Raymond Walker [1958] Director; Robert Kenneth Williams [1964] Finance Director

Anglo Scottish Leisure Limited
Incorporated: 24 May 1988 *Employees:* 55
Net Worth: £2,499,421 *Total Assets:* £6,260,970
Registered Office: Regency House, 33 Wood Street, Barnet, Herts, EN5 4BE
Activities: Other amusement and recreation activities n.e.c.
Shareholders: Country House Weddings Ltd; Country House Weddings Limited
Officers: Harry Bramer, Secretary; Harry Bramer [1949] Director; Nicholas Bramer [1983] Director

Anglo Suisse Investments Limited
Incorporated: 28 February 2005 *Employees:* 5
Net Worth: £20,918,286 *Total Assets:* £53,741,056
Registered Office: B E Roberts & Co, 3 Kirkleas Road, Surbiton, Surrey, KT6 6QJ
Activities: Activities of venture and development capital companies
Shareholder: Geoffrey John de Jager
Officers: Benjamin Thomas Geoffrey de Jager, Secretary; Jonathan Geoffrey de Jager, Secretary; Benjamin Thomas Geoffrey de Jager [1996] Director; Caroline Mary de Jager [1961] Director; Geoffrey John de Jager [1950] Director; Jonathan Geoffrey de Jager [1977] Director

Anglo-Dal Limited
Incorporated: 26 April 1939
Net Worth: £4,686,747 *Total Assets:* £5,382,237
Registered Office: Anglo Dal House, 5 Spring Villa Road, Edgware, Middlesex, HA8 7EB
Activities: Non-specialised wholesale trade
Officers: Marek Cichecki, Secretary [Polish]; Stanislaw Mirgos [1931] Director [Polish]

Anglogold Ashanti International Exploration Holdings Limited
Incorporated: 7 December 1995
Net Worth: £897,950 *Total Assets:* £20,789,270
Registered Office: 4th Floor, Communications House, South Street, Staines upon Thames, Surrey, TW18 4PR
Activities: Activities of head offices
Officers: Kevin Patrick Ernest Davies, Secretary; Kevin Patrick Ernest Davies [1957] Director/Transitional Manager

Anita Impex Limited
Incorporated: 5 October 1993
Net Worth: £4,171,377 *Total Assets:* £9,717,001
Registered Office: 60 Burns Way, Hounslow, Middlesex, TW5 9BA
Activities: Development of building projects
Officers: Suresh Chandra Pandya, Secretary; Anita Niraj Chandra [1982] Director/Student - Self Employed; Anjali Samarth Chandra [1989] Director/Student; Amar Suresh Pandya [1982] Director/Student; Suresh Pandya [1957] Director

Anitass Limited
Incorporated: 3 December 2009
Net Worth: £3,019,260 *Total Assets:* £9,653,028
Registered Office: Progress House, 404 Brighton Road, South Croydon, Surrey, CR2 6AN
Activities: Other letting and operating of own or leased real estate
Officers: Richard Henry Ballard [1949] Director; John Phelim Henry [1962] Director; David Michael Phillips [1945] Director

Annes Gate Property PLC
Incorporated: 31 January 2001
Net Worth: £18,345,000 *Total Assets:* £267,806,000
Registered Office: 8 White Oak Square, London Road, Swanley, Kent, BR8 7AG
Activities: Other business support service activities n.e.c.
Parent: AGP Holdings (1) Limited
Officers: David John Carr [1969] Director/Chartered Accountant; Glynn Newby [1966] Director/Business Management; Natalia Poupard [1977] Director/Asset Manager; Mark Christopher Wayment [1958] Director

Anno 2017 Joint Holding (UK) Limited
Incorporated: 20 June 2017
Net Worth: £244,512,000 *Total Assets:* £1,611,495,936
Registered Office: 8 White Oak Square, London Road, Swanley, Kent, BR8 7AG
Activities: Activities of other holding companies n.e.c.
Shareholders: PFA Neptune Holding (UK) Limited; PKA WLWF Holding (UK) Limited
Officers: James Edward Burbidge [1975] Director/Chartered Accountant; Mark Alan Cade [1972] Director/Chartered Engineer; Christian Krogsgaard [1974] Director [Danish]; Domenico Tripodi [1984] Director [Italian]

Anoopam Mission
Incorporated: 22 November 1977
Net Worth: £2,117,240 *Total Assets:* £6,751,760
Registered Office: Brahmajyoti, The Lea, Western Avenue, Denham, Bucks, UB9 4NA
Activities: Activities of religious organisations
Officers: Himatlal V Sakaria, Secretary; Satish Jamnadas Chatwani [1953] Director; Kiran Nakarja [1953] Director/Accounts Clerk; Vinodkant Nakarja [1946] Director/Sub-Postmaster; Ashwin Popat [1948] Director/Optometrist; Jayendra Sakaria [1967] Director/IT Consultant

Ansa UK Limited
Incorporated: 14 April 1998 *Employees:* 12
Net Worth: £3,996,000 *Total Assets:* £25,275,000
Registered Office: 2 AC Court, High Street, Thames Ditton, Surrey, KT7 0SR
Activities: Other specialised construction activities n.e.c.
Parent: IGUK Support Services Limited
Officers: Alan Albert Horton [1963] Director; Stuart Pace [1962] Director

Ansa Utilities Limited
Incorporated: 21 June 1999 *Employees:* 32
Net Worth: £2,901,000 *Total Assets:* £19,743,000
Registered Office: 2 AC Court, High Street, Thames Ditton, Surrey, KT7 0SR
Activities: Other specialised construction activities n.e.c.
Parent: IGUK Support Services Limited
Officers: Alan Albert Horton [1963] Director; Stuart Pace [1962] Director

Antal International Limited
Incorporated: 6 December 2006 *Employees:* 365
Net Worth: £3,309,035 *Total Assets:* £10,492,515
Registered Office: First Floor, Radius House, 51 Clarendon Road, Watford, Herts, WD17 1HP
Activities: Temporary employment agency activities
Major Shareholder: Anthony Michael Goodwin
Officers: Sagar Ramnik Ruparelia, Secretary; Anthony Michael Goodwin [1962] Director; Sagar Ramnik Ruparelia [1983] Group Financial Director

Anthony Property Co. Limited
Incorporated: 24 November 1954
Net Worth: £6,106,960 *Total Assets:* £6,877,119
Registered Office: Northside House, Mount Pleasant, Barnet, Herts, EN4 9EE
Activities: Buying and selling of own real estate
Parent: ATS Group Limited
Officers: Rayner Norma Caplan, Secretary; Andrew Simon Davis [1960] Director/Accountant; Diana Smith [1947] Director

Antoniou Investments Limited
Incorporated: 9 December 2014
Net Worth: £497,695 *Total Assets:* £10,114,621
Registered Office: Toronto Suite, Maple House, High Street, Potters Bar, Herts, EN6 5BS
Activities: Other letting and operating of own or leased real estate
Shareholders: Demetrios Antoniou; Harry Zenonos Antoniou; Maria Zenonos Polycarpou
Officers: Demetrios Antoniou [1976] Director; Harry Zenonos Antoniou [1983] Director; Maria Zenonos Polycarpou [1978] Director

Anya House Limited
Incorporated: 2 May 2007
Net Worth: £2,143,261 *Total Assets:* £5,907,660
Registered Office: 9a The Broadway, Stanmore, Middlesex, HA7 4DA
Activities: Other letting and operating of own or leased real estate
Parent: Brentpark Limited
Officers: Mahesh Raojibhai Patel, Secretary; Mahesh Raojibhai Patel [1968] Director/Property Developer; Hitenkumar Mansukhlal Shah [1968] Director/Consultant

Anzco Foods UK Limited
Incorporated: 10 August 2000 *Employees:* 16
Net Worth: £7,475,652 *Total Assets:* £21,575,996
Registered Office: Unit 7 Bates Industrial Estate, Church Road, Harold Wood, Romford, Essex, RM3 0HU
Activities: Wholesale of meat and meat products
Officers: Peter William Conley [1967] Director/COO Sales and Marketing [New Zealander]; Poh Ying Loke [1955] Director/General Manager Finance [New Zealander]; Richard William Walker [1972] Director/General Manager of Marketing [New Zealander]

AP Asset Management Limited
Incorporated: 18 April 2013 *Employees:* 1
Net Worth: £518,827 *Total Assets:* £5,426,557
Registered Office: 400 Dashwood Lang Road, Weybridge, Surrey, KT15 2HJ
Activities: Development of building projects
Major Shareholder: Adrian Michael Pitts
Officers: Adrian Michael Pitts [1966] Director

Apatech Limited
Incorporated: 1 March 2001 *Employees:* 65
Net Worth: £34,201,144 *Total Assets:* £36,755,124
Registered Office: 370 Centennial Avenue, Centennial Park, Elstree, Herts, WD6 3TJ
Activities: Manufacture of other chemical products n.e.c.
Parent: Baxter Holding BV
Officers: Andrew Neil Goldney [1968] Director/General Manager; Brian Keith Morgan [1969] Director/Business Executive [American]

APCOA Parking (UK) Limited
Incorporated: 11 January 1991 *Employees:* 1,821
Net Worth: £333,820 *Total Assets:* £46,994,404
Registered Office: Wellington House, 4-10 Cowley Road, Uxbridge, Middlesex, UB8 2XW
Activities: Other business support service activities n.e.c.
Parent: APCOA Parking Holdings (UK) Limited
Officers: David Ian Carruthers, Secretary; David Ian Carruthers [1959] Director/Solicitor; Kamini Challis [1970] Director; John Peter Goodwin [1976] Director

APCOA Parking Holdings (UK) Limited
Incorporated: 25 June 2004
Net Worth: £18,171,076 *Total Assets:* £54,863,068
Registered Office: Wellington House, 4-10 Cowley Road, Uxbridge, Middlesex, UB8 2XW
Activities: Other business support service activities n.e.c.
Parent: APCOA Parking Holdings GmbH
Officers: David Ian Carruthers, Secretary; David Ian Carruthers [1959] Director/Solicitor; Kamini Challis [1970] Director; John Peter Goodwin [1976] Director

Apex Car Rental (Norwich) Limited
Incorporated: 7 February 1989 *Employees:* 25
Net Worth: £10,043,921 *Total Assets:* £15,656,083
Registered Office: 8 Overcliffe, Gravesend, Kent, DA11 0HJ
Activities: Renting and leasing of cars and light motor vehicles
Shareholders: Richard Paul Nash; Lynn Julie Nash
Officers: Richard Paul Nash, Secretary; Lynn Julie Nash [1961] Director/Company Secretary; Richard Paul Nash [1956] Director

Apex Lift & Escalator Engineers Limited
Incorporated: 17 August 1973 *Employees:* 113
Net Worth: £4,215,817 *Total Assets:* £7,072,768
Registered Office: Art's House, Banks Lane, Bexleyheath, Kent, DA6 7BH
Activities: Other specialised construction activities n.e.c.
Parent: Apex Lifts (Group) Limited
Officers: Elsie Lilian Jenchner, Secretary; Lesley Anne Hughes [1962] Director; Elsie Lilian Jenchner [1941] Financial Director; Warren Jenchner [1966] Director/Lift Sales Manager; Gary Lee Poynter [1960] Director/Construction Manager; Kevin Thomas Warnock [1960] Director

Apex Lifts (Group) Limited
Incorporated: 1 July 2014 *Employees:* 113
Net Worth: £5,049,687 *Total Assets:* £8,362,708
Registered Office: Art's House, Banks Lane, Bexleyheath, Kent, DA6 7BH
Activities: Activities of other holding companies n.e.c.
Officers: Warren Jenchner [1966] Director

Apex Medical Respiratory Ltd
Incorporated: 10 October 2009
Previous: Apex Medical Limited
Net Worth: £20,184,000 *Total Assets:* £20,186,060
Registered Office: Unit 21 Optima Park, Thames Road, Crayford, Kent, DA1 4QX
Activities: Agents involved in the sale of a variety of goods
Parent: Apex Medical Global Cooperatie UA
Officers: Ying-Chieh Hsu [1963] Director [Taiwanese]; Daniel Lee [1958] Director [Taiwanese]

Apexpost Limited
Incorporated: 10 March 1989 *Employees:* 8
Net Worth: £1,735,266 *Total Assets:* £10,210,034
Registered Office: 166 College Road, Harrow, Middlesex, HA1 1RA
Activities: Other business support service activities n.e.c.
Shareholders: Simon Hiro Punjabi; Michael Punjabi
Officers: Michael Punjabi, Secretary; Michael Punjabi [1963] Director; Simon Hiro Punjabi [1971] Director

APFS Property Ltd
Incorporated: 17 January 2017
Net Worth: £40,638 *Total Assets:* £5,851,838
Registered Office: 215 Lower Addiscombe Road, Croydon, Surrey, CR0 6RB
Activities: Other letting and operating of own or leased real estate
Officers: Akeem Fabunmi, Secretary; Ade Fabunmi-Stone [1964] Director/Accounts Manager; Bryce Fabunmi-Stone [1994] Director/Administrator; Pauline Jennifer Fabunmi-Stone [1957] Director

Apollo Cleaning Services Limited
Incorporated: 21 January 1975 *Employees:* 1
Net Worth: £5,847,501 *Total Assets:* £6,361,361
Registered Office: Unit 7 Bourne Court, Southend Road, Woodford Green, Essex, IG8 8HD
Activities: Other cleaning services
Parent: Apollo RPL Limited
Officers: Richard Paul Lundy, Secretary/Quality Control Manager; Richard Paul Lundy [1963] Director/Quality Control Manager

Apollo Property Investment Limited
Incorporated: 14 February 2012 *Employees:* 1
Net Worth: £106,599 *Total Assets:* £12,639,118
Registered Office: 188 High Road, Loughton, Essex, IG10 1DN
Activities: Development of building projects
Major Shareholder: Gary Patrick Couch
Officers: Gary Patrick Couch [1962] Director

Apollo RPL Limited
Incorporated: 27 June 2016 *Employees:* 678
Net Worth: £7,036,729 *Total Assets:* £7,933,409
Registered Office: Unit 7 Bourne Court, Southend Road, Woodford Green, Essex, IG8 8HD
Activities: Activities of other holding companies n.e.c.
Major Shareholder: Richard Paul Lundy
Officers: Richard Paul Lundy [1963] Director

Appetite Holdings Limited
Incorporated: 7 December 2015 *Employees:* 131
Net Worth: £3,601,851 *Total Assets:* £11,407,620
Registered Office: 1 Hertsmere Industrial Park, Warwick Road, Borehamwood, Herts, WD6 1GT
Activities: Manufacture of other food products n.e.c.
Major Shareholder: Paul Luigi Ugo
Officers: Paul Luigi Ugo [1966] Director

Applepeach Limited
Incorporated: 19 March 2004 *Employees:* 9
Net Worth: £4,407,042 *Total Assets:* £8,451,681
Registered Office: CP House, Otterspool Way, Watford Bypass, Watford, Herts, WD25 8JJ
Activities: Management of real estate on a fee or contract basis
Shareholders: Lenta Properties Limited; Searchgrade Limited
Officers: Eric Lewis, Secretary; Paul Andrew Filer [1957] Director; Mark Gibbor [1988] Director; Michael Robert Goldberger [1956] Director; David Alan Pearlman [1945] Director

Applied Laser Engineering Limited
Incorporated: 16 November 1989 *Employees:* 32
Net Worth: £4,878,156 *Total Assets:* £8,147,709
Registered Office: Aissela, 46 High Street, Esher, Surrey, KT10 9QY
Activities: Manufacture of electronic measuring, testing etc. equipment, not for industrial process control
Shareholders: Brendan Thomas Pollard; Philip Walter Limberger
Officers: Sara Penelope Pollard, Secretary; Alison Birch [1963] Director; Philip Walter Limberger [1964] Director; Brendan Thomas Pollard [1956] Director; Sara Penelope Pollard [1957] Director/Company Secretary

APPT Corporation Limited
Incorporated: 10 May 2006 *Employees:* 2,947
Net Worth: £2,873,413 *Total Assets:* £25,133,720
Registered Office: McDonald's, Uxbridge Road Iron Bridge, Southall, Middlesex, UB1 3EG
Activities: Unlicenced restaurants and cafes
Shareholders: Atul Pathak; McDonald's Restaurants Limited
Officers: Tarspal Pathak, Secretary; Christopher John English [1971] Director; Alistair Macrow [1970] Director; Atul Pathak [1961] Managing Director; Tarspal Pathak [1960] Director

Aprirose Trading Limited
Incorporated: 3 September 2001 *Employees:* 7
Net Worth: £7,771,837 *Total Assets:* £11,799,484
Registered Office: Aprirose House, 48a High Street, Edgware, Middlesex, HA8 7EQ
Activities: Agents specialised in the sale of other particular products
Parent: Aprirose Trading Holding Limited
Officers: Mansukhlal Gosar Gudka, Secretary; Manish Mansukhlal Gudka [1970] Director; Mansukhlal Gosar Gudka [1941] Director; Parag Mansukhlal Gudka [1971] Director/Export Manager

Aprite (GB) Limited
Incorporated: 10 October 1996 *Employees:* 586
Net Worth: £13,363,000 *Total Assets:* £131,193,000
Registered Office: The Rivers Office Park, Denham Way, Rickmansworth, Herts, WD3 9YS
Activities: Sale of new cars and light motor vehicles
Parent: Nissan Motor (GB) Limited
Officers: Steven Neil Tiffin, Secretary; Laurent Frank Christian David [1971] Director [French]; Gareth John Main [1967] Director/General Manager; Jordi Vila Onses [1963] Director/Vice President Sales [Spanish]

The John Apthorp Charity
Incorporated: 30 December 2003
Net Worth: £12,800,648 *Total Assets:* £12,803,858
Registered Office: Egale 1, 80 St Albans Road, Watford, Herts, WD17 1DL
Activities: Other education n.e.c.
Officers: Kate Arnold, Secretary; Duncan Mark Apthorp [1960] Director/Engineer; John Dorrington Apthorp [1935] Director; Justin James Apthorp [1962] Director; Kate Arnold [1967] Director/Service Resource Administrator

Aquifer Limited
Incorporated: 10 February 2004 *Employees:* 2,303
Net Worth: £3,496,000 *Total Assets:* £9,862,000
Registered Office: Q3 The Square, Randalls Way, Leatherhead, Surrey, KT22 7TW
Activities: Other business support service activities n.e.c.
Officers: David Roy Wood, Secretary; Peter Hesketh [1962] Director; Stanley Hwami Musesengwa [1952] Director; David Roy Wood [1961] Director/Chartered Accountant

Aquila BTE 1 Limited
Incorporated: 2 May 2007
Net Worth: £7,755,020 *Total Assets:* £25,938,068
Registered Office: 22 Barn Rise, Wembley, Middlesex, HA9 9NQ
Activities: Other letting and operating of own or leased real estate
Parent: Aquila House Property Limited
Officers: Paul Gary Hirst, Secretary/Surveyor; Anthony David Chambers [1955] Director/Surveyor; Daniel Freedman [1971] Director/Lawyer; Paul Gary Hirst [1961] Director/Surveyor

Aquila Chelmsford Limited
Incorporated: 21 February 2001
Net Worth: £12,027,747 *Total Assets:* £20,735,054
Registered Office: 22 Barn Rise, Wembley, Middlesex, HA9 9NQ
Activities: Other letting and operating of own or leased real estate
Parent: Aquila House Property Limited
Officers: Anne Shirley Chambers, Secretary; Anthony David Chambers [1955] Director/Chartered Surveyor; Daniel Freedman [1971] Director/Lawyer; Paul Gary Hirst [1961] Director

Aquila EHS Limited
Incorporated: 23 January 2002 *Employees:* 3
Net Worth: £5,168,227 *Total Assets:* £31,217,220
Registered Office: 22 Barn Rise, Wembley, Middlesex, HA9 9NQ
Activities: Other letting and operating of own or leased real estate
Parent: Aquila House Property Limited
Officers: Anne Shirley Chambers, Secretary; Anthony David Chambers [1955] Director/Surveyor; Daniel Freedman [1971] Director/Lawyer; Paul Gary Hirst [1961] Director

Aquila Estates Limited
Incorporated: 3 December 2002 *Employees:* 3
Net Worth Deficit: £3,367,769 *Total Assets:* £33,881,256
Registered Office: 22 Barn Rise, Wembley, Middlesex, HA9 9NQ
Activities: Other letting and operating of own or leased real estate
Parent: Aquila House Property Limited
Officers: Paul Gary Hirst, Secretary/Director; Anthony David Chambers [1955] Director/Chartered Surveyor; Daniel Freedman [1971] Director/Lawyer; Paul Gary Hirst [1961] Director

Aquila Maldon Limited
Incorporated: 29 November 2007
Net Worth: £3,588,143 *Total Assets:* £5,374,980
Registered Office: 22 Barn Rise, Wembley, Middlesex, HA9 9NQ
Activities: Development of building projects
Parent: Aquila House Holdings Limited
Officers: Paul Gary Hirst, Secretary; Anthony David Chambers [1955] Director; Daniel Freedman [1971] Director/Lawyer; Paul Gary Hirst [1961] Director

Aquila MB2 Limited
Incorporated: 30 September 2014 *Employees:* 3
Previous: ABSL2 Limited
Net Worth Deficit: £118 *Total Assets:* £35,316,752
Registered Office: 22 Barn Rise, Wembley, Middlesex, HA9 9NQ
Activities: Activities of other holding companies n.e.c.
Parent: Aquila MB3 Limited
Officers: Paul Gary Hirst, Secretary; Anthony David Chambers [1955] Director/Property Consultant; Daniel Freedman [1971] Director/Lawyer; Paul Gary Hirst [1961] Director/Property Consultant

Aquila MB3 Limited
Incorporated: 30 September 2014
Previous: ABSL3 Limited
Net Worth Deficit: £1,184,910 *Total Assets:* £35,317,248
Registered Office: 22 Barn Rise, Wembley, Middlesex, HA9 9NQ
Activities: Activities of other holding companies n.e.c.
Parent: Aquila House Holdings Limited
Officers: Paul Gary Hirst, Secretary; Anthony David Chambers [1955] Director/Property Consultant; Daniel Freedman [1971] Director/Lawyer; Paul Gary Hirst [1961] Director/Property Consultant

Aquinas Church of England Education Trust Limited
Incorporated: 10 February 2011 *Employees:* 636
Net Worth: £12,433,000 *Total Assets:* £17,773,000
Registered Office: Bishop Justus Church of England School, Magpie Hall Lane, Bromley, Kent, BR2 8HZ
Activities: Pre-primary education
Officers: Mary Capon, Secretary; David Wilson Bridger [1944] Director/Retired; Victoria Cliff [1950] Director/Consultant; Kathy Donna Griffiths [1965] Director/Headteacher; Anna Lind [1979] Marketing and Business Development Director [Australian]; Sue Mordecai [1948] Director/Consultant; Richard Jonathan Norman [1988] Director/Vicar; Simon Derek Parker [1963] Director/Consultant; Alexander Paul [1980] Director/Banker; Sui-Te Wu [1955] Director/Architect

Arabella Health Staffing Limited
Incorporated: 2 June 2005
Net Worth: £11,266,009 *Total Assets:* £12,985,053
Registered Office: Ambition House, 92-96 Lind Road, Sutton, Surrey, SM1 4PL
Activities: Temporary employment agency activities
Officers: Nishma Patel, Secretary; Charles Louis Rees [1960] Director/Chartered Accountant; Penelope Marion Streeter [1967] Director/Businesswomen

Arboretum Partners LLP
Incorporated: 28 January 2013
Net Worth: £6,536,250 *Total Assets:* £6,576,677
Registered Office: Sans Souci, Southview Road, Pinner, Middlesex, HA5 3YD
Officers: Esther Sharon Sutcliffe [1949] Member; James Harry Sutcliffe [1956] Member

Arcese Real Estate UK Limited
Incorporated: 6 June 2006
Net Worth: £6,729,259 *Total Assets:* £11,212,517
Registered Office: Thurrock Parkway, Thurrock Park Industrial Estate, Tilbury, Essex, RM18 7HY
Activities: Other letting and operating of own or leased real estate
Parent: Arcese Immobiliare SpA
Officers: Alberto Dejana [1959] Director/Chief Executive [Italian]; Michele Nascetti [1969] Managing Director [Italian]

Arcese UK Limited
Incorporated: 15 July 2005 *Employees:* 125
Net Worth: £1,719,203 *Total Assets:* £7,144,365
Registered Office: Thurock Parkway, Thurock Park Industrial Estate, Tilbury, Essex, RM18 7HY
Activities: Freight transport by road
Parent: Arcese SpA
Officers: Matteo Arcese [1974] Managing Director [Italian]; Alberto Dejana [1959] Director/Chief Executive [Italian]; Michele Nascetti [1969] Director [Italian]

The Archbishop Lanfranc Academy - Coloma Trust
Incorporated: 22 August 2014 *Employees:* 61
Net Worth: £25,766,664 *Total Assets:* £28,295,168
Registered Office: The Archbishop Lanfranc School, Mitcham Road, Croydon, Surrey, CR9 3AS
Activities: General secondary education
Officers: Thomas James Bateman [1987] Director/Teacher; Alan Nigel Buckland [1961] Director/Actuary; Michael Paul Juan Del Rio [1973] Director/Headteacher; Ronald James Huggett [1950] Director/Chief Executive Officer; Jacqueline Rose Johnson [1964] Director/Headteacher; Christopher Anthony Kinch [1953] Director/Judge; Matthew Jordan Morley [1990] Director/Civil Servant; Ahmed Osman [1964] Director; Generaldine Dominica Ozah [1949] Director/Retired [Irish]; Fiona Ann Smith [1962] Director; Clare Nicola Tillson [1958] Director/Retired; Sister Felice Anne Bowker Wright [1943] Director/Religious Sister

Archer Daniels Midland (UK) Limited
Incorporated: 15 January 1973 *Employees:* 69
Net Worth: £304,771,360 *Total Assets:* £351,168,640
Registered Office: Church Manorway, Erith, Kent, DA8 1DL
Activities: Wholesale of grain, unmanufactured tobacco, seeds and animal feeds
Parent: Archer Daniels Midland Company
Officers: Gary Thomas McGuigan [1971] Director [Irish]; Orla Margaret Muldoon [1969] Managing Director [Irish]; John Patrick Stott [1967] Director/Accountant

Archer Daniels Midland Erith Limited
Incorporated: 10 October 1919 *Employees:* 110
Net Worth: £34,342,700 *Total Assets:* £46,321,200
Registered Office: Erith Oil Works, Church Manorway, Erith, Kent, DA8 1DL
Activities: Other processing and preserving of fruit and vegetables
Parent: Archer Daniels Midland (UK) Limited
Officers: Martin Paul Farrow [1956] Director/General Manager; Dr Martin Kropp [1965] Director/Vice President [German]

Architectural Decorators Limited
Incorporated: 6 April 1944 *Employees:* 109
Net Worth: £8,195,986 *Total Assets:* £12,913,852
Registered Office: Samuel House, 7 Powerscroft Road, Sidcup, Kent, DA14 5DT
Activities: Other construction installation
Officers: Richard Gordon, Secretary; Steven William Doyle [1974] Director; Richard Gordon [1965] Director for Health & Safety; Aaron Lee Mitchell [1975] Director

Archway Apartments Limited
Incorporated: 19 August 2014
Net Worth Deficit: £1,630,570 *Total Assets:* £8,830,916
Registered Office: 42 Lytton Road, Barnet, Herts, EN5 5BY
Activities: Buying and selling of own real estate
Officers: Joseph Peter Gerrard [1954] Director; Michael Gerrard [1957] Director

Arcofina LLP
Incorporated: 8 February 2005
Net Worth Deficit: £14,976 *Total Assets:* £24,628,286
Registered Office: Suite 105, Viglen House, Alperton Lane, Wembley, Middlesex, HA0 1HD
Officers: Jerome Joliat [1935] Member; Mohamed Abdelouahab Rahim [1952] Member

Arcplan UK Limited
Incorporated: 14 January 2015
Net Worth: £7,190,845 *Total Assets:* £7,242,089
Registered Office: Nexus House, Station Road, Egham, Surrey, TW20 9LB
Activities: Business and domestic software development
Parent: Longview Holding Hedge UK Limited
Officers: Jerome Jon Dolinsky [1965] Director [American]; Grant Bennett Schachter [1984] Director/Private Equity [American]; Michael Edward Wilkinson [1986] Director/Private Equity

Arcus FM Limited
Incorporated: 17 January 2008 *Employees:* 693
Net Worth: £5,185,000 *Total Assets:* £20,379,000
Registered Office: Enterprise House, 168-170 Upminster Road, Upminster, Essex, RM14 2RB
Activities: Management of real estate on a fee or contract basis
Officers: Paul Duckels [1977] Director; Ian David Ellis [1955] Director; David Furness [1966] Director; Christopher Mark Green [1965] Managing Director; Joanne Hall [1981] Director/Regional Manager; Samantha Holmes [1971] HSQE Director; Samantha Lambton [1966] HR Director; Danny Malyon [1969] Director/Head of FM Sainsbury's Supermarkets Ltd; Anthony Benedict Mars [1968] Director/Head of Design Construction and Delivery, Property; Neil Pearce [1967] Director; Stephen Terence Patrick Willis [1965] Director

Arcus Investment Limited
Incorporated: 11 June 1998 *Employees:* 16
Net Worth: £53,075,240 *Total Assets:* £65,508,132
Registered Office: Elder House, St Georges Business Park, 207 Brooklands Road, Weybridge, Surrey, KT13 0TS
Activities: Security and commodity contracts dealing activities
Shareholder: Peter Tasker
Officers: Mark Anthony Pearson [1960] Director; Steven Wheeler [1960] Director/Chief Operating Officer

Arcus Solutions (Holdings) Limited
Incorporated: 25 October 2010 *Employees:* 1,664
Net Worth: £8,873,000 *Total Assets:* £28,027,000
Registered Office: Enterprise House, 168-170 Upminster Road, Upminster, Essex, RM14 2RB
Activities: Activities of head offices
Officers: Terry Douglas [1966] Director; Ian David Ellis [1955] Director; Richard John Fabian [1956] Director; Christopher Mark Green [1965] Director; Neil Pearce [1967] Director; Stephen Terence Patrick Willis [1965] Director

Arcus Solutions Limited
Incorporated: 22 September 2009 *Employees:* 320
Net Worth: £1,971,000 *Total Assets:* £8,657,000
Registered Office: Enterprise House, 168-170 Upminster Road, Upminster, Essex, RM14 2RB
Activities: Repair of machinery
Officers: Paul Duckels [1977] Director; Ian David Ellis [1955] Director; David Furness [1966] Director; Christopher Mark Green [1965] Director; Joanne Hall [1981] Director/Regional Manager; Samantha Holmes [1971] HSQE Director; Samantha Lambton [1966] HR Director; Danny Malyon [1969] Director/Head of FM Sainsbury's Supermarkets Ltd; Anthony Benedict Mars [1968] Director/Head of Design Construction and Delivery, Property; Neil Pearce [1967] Director; Stephen Terence Patrick Willis [1965] Director

Ardent Hire Solutions Limited
Incorporated: 8 May 2000 *Employees:* 278
Previous: One Call Hire Limited
Net Worth: £66,224,000 *Total Assets:* £186,712,000
Registered Office: Ardent House, 32 Crown Road, Enfield, Middlesex, EN1 1TH
Activities: Renting and leasing of construction and civil engineering machinery and equipment
Officers: Jeremy Peter Fish [1965] Director/Chief Executive Officer; Greg Paul FitzGenerald [1964] Director/Chairman; Julian Alexander O'Neill [1971] Director/Chief Financial Officer

Ardour World Limited
Incorporated: 22 April 2003 *Employees:* 13
Net Worth: £3,738,099 *Total Assets:* £7,403,198
Registered Office: Grove House, 55 Lowlands Road, Harrow on the Hill, Middlesex, HA1 3AW
Activities: Wholesale of metals and metal ores
Shareholder: Ashish Chaudhari
Officers: Ashish Chaudhari, Secretary/Trader [Indian]; Ashish Chaudhari [1979] Director [Indian]; Sundip Goyal [1971] Director [Indian]

Area Sq. Limited
Incorporated: 5 November 1999 *Employees:* 263
Net Worth: £4,352,085 *Total Assets:* £31,770,456
Registered Office: The Old Post Office, 33 Station Road, Egham, Surrey, TW20 9LA
Activities: Other specialised construction activities n.e.c.
Parent: Fourfront Group Ltd
Officers: Paul Ames [1964] Contracts Director; Steven Vincent Baldock [1956] Managing Director; Justin Marc Bass [1968] Managing Director; Gary James Chandler [1969] Managing Director; James Elwin Cornwell [1964] Director; Sion Davies [1976] Managing Director; Lee Richard Marple [1968] Operations Director; Simon Pearson [1969] Contracts Director; Colin Christopher Pye [1964] Director; Mark Joseph Scott [1968] Director/Chief Financial Officer; Aki Stamatis [1960] Director; Christopher Stewart [1973] Divisional Director

Arem Investments Limited
Incorporated: 27 April 1999 *Employees:* 2
Net Worth: £3,767,131 *Total Assets:* £8,311,363
Registered Office: Ibex House, Baker Street, Weybridge, Surrey, KT13 8AH
Activities: Other letting and operating of own or leased real estate
Major Shareholder: Rajat Mehta
Officers: Rajeev Mehta, Secretary; Anita Mehta [1954] Director/Property Consultant [Indian]; Rajat Mehta [1980] Director/Executive [Indian]

Ares Properties Ltd
Incorporated: 13 November 2014
Net Worth: £3,884,290 *Total Assets:* £10,815,564
Registered Office: Floor 2, 555-557 Cranbrook Road, Ilford, Essex, IG2 6HE
Activities: Buying and selling of own real estate
Parent: Albrox Limited
Officers: Ghulam Asghar Alahi [1970] Director

The Arete Trust
Incorporated: 9 May 2017 *Employees:* 124
Net Worth: £13,105,268 *Total Assets:* £14,410,490
Registered Office: The Arete Trust, Dartford Grammar School for Girls, Shepherds Lane, Dartford, Kent, DA1 2NT
Activities: General secondary education
Officers: Janice Brooke [1955] Finance Director; Robert Charles Chapman [1948] Director/Retired Senior Manager; Generald King [1966] Director/Manager with Her Majesty's Prison Service; Sharon Jane Pritchard [1971] Director/Headteacher; David William Smith [1947] Director/Retired Headteacher and Education Consultant

Arihant Limited
Incorporated: 15 December 1997 *Employees:* 9
Net Worth: £5,839,376 *Total Assets:* £11,477,931
Registered Office: 18 Parkfield Gardens, North Harrow, Middlesex, HA2 6JR
Activities: Other letting and operating of own or leased real estate
Officers: Himanshu Anantrai Shah, Secretary; Himanshu Anantrai Shah [1966] Director/Self Employed & Lettings; Sejal Himanshu Shah [1971] Director/Employed and Lettings

Ariyan Hotels Limited
Incorporated: 23 April 2015 *Employees:* 20
Net Worth: £95,206 *Total Assets:* £12,561,352
Registered Office: Jubilee House, 7-9 The Oaks, Ruislip, Middlesex, HA4 7LF
Activities: Hotels and similar accommodation
Officers: Alim Amirali Janmohamed, Secretary; Alim Amirali Janmohamed [1981] Director; Amirali Hassanali Moledina Janmohamed [1952] Director/Hotelier

Arlen Properties Limited
Incorporated: 6 September 1991 *Employees:* 5
Previous: Arlen Properties PLC
Net Worth: £5,204,405 *Total Assets:* £7,657,585
Registered Office: Suite A, 10th Floor, Maple House, High Street, Potters Bar, Herts, EN6 5BS
Activities: Management of real estate on a fee or contract basis
Major Shareholder: Samuel Hayek
Officers: Marilyn Waisman, Secretary; Samuel Hayek [1953] Director; Simon Hayek [1949] Director

Armitage BC1 Limited
Incorporated: 9 May 2017 *Employees:* 3
Net Worth: £4,868,752 *Total Assets:* £5,009,356
Registered Office: 1 Armitage Business Centre, Delamare Road, Cheshunt, Waltham Cross, Herts, EN8 9FN
Activities: Other letting and operating of own or leased real estate
Parent: ABC1 Holdco Limited
Officers: Darren Mustafa [1979] Director; Deniz Mustafa [1983] Director; Ozay Mustafa [1956] Director

Armondi UK Limited
Incorporated: 3 August 2006 *Employees:* 28
Net Worth: £123,735 *Total Assets:* £5,749,594
Registered Office: Francis House, 2 Park Road, Barnet, Herts, EN5 5RN
Activities: Manufacture of other women's outerwear
Shareholder: Robert Ian Telson
Officers: Robert Ian Telson [1953] Sales Director

Armstrong (U.K.) Investments
Incorporated: 21 August 1996 *Employees:* 3
Net Worth: £16,559,000 *Total Assets:* £16,617,000
Registered Office: 2nd Floor, Harman House, 1 George Street, Uxbridge, Middlesex, UB8 1QQ
Activities: Non-trading company
Officers: Michael James Bignell, Secretary; Mark Alan Laikin [1968] Finance Director; Willem Antonius Middel [1967] VP and Managing Director EMEA [Dutch]; William Mark Willis Jones [1957] Director/Barrister

Armstrong Metal Ceilings Limited
Incorporated: 19 July 1995 *Employees:* 61
Net Worth: £4,658,000 *Total Assets:* £5,955,000
Registered Office: 2nd Floor, Harman House, 1 George Street, Uxbridge, Middlesex, UB8 1QQ
Activities: Manufacture of other fabricated metal products n.e.c.
Parent: Armstrong World Industries Limited
Officers: Michael James Bignell, Secretary; Mark Alan Laikin [1968] Finance Director; Willem Antonius Middel [1967] VP and Managing Director EMEA [Dutch]

Armstrong World Industries Limited
Incorporated: 7 August 1925 *Employees:* 179
Net Worth: £57,900,000 *Total Assets:* £72,850,000
Registered Office: 2nd Floor, Harman House, 1 George Street, Uxbridge, Middlesex, UB8 1QQ
Activities: Manufacture of other non-metallic mineral products n.e.c.
Parent: Armstrong (U.K.) Investments
Officers: Michael James Bignell, Secretary; Sara Joanne Carter [1976] HR Director; Lee Alan Davidson [1973] Director/Chartered Accountant; Mark Alan Laikin [1968] Finance Director; Stephen Francis McNamara [1966] Director/Controller [American]; Willem Antonius Middel [1967] VP and Managing Director EMEA [Dutch]; Yang Ming Tham [1982] Director [American]; William Mark Willis Jones [1957] Director/Barrister

Arora Heathrow Holdings Limited
Incorporated: 24 February 2009
Previous: Heathrow T5 Hotel Limited
Net Worth Deficit: £7,034,209 *Total Assets:* £16,874,590
Registered Office: World Business Centre, 3 Newall Road, London Heathrow Airport, Hounslow, Middlesex, TW6 2TA
Activities: Other letting and operating of own or leased real estate
Parent: Arora Investments Limited
Officers: Athos George Yiannis, Secretary; Surinder Arora [1958] Director; Carlton Jeffrey Brown [1972] Director/Chartered Accountant; Athos George Yiannis [1963] Director/Chartered Accountant

Arora Hotels Limited
Incorporated: 29 July 2005 *Employees:* 1,467
Previous: Arora Staff Houses Limited
Net Worth: £293,436,992 *Total Assets:* £635,217,024
Registered Office: World Business Centre, 3 Newall Road, London Heathrow Airport, Hounslow, Middlesex, TW6 2TA
Activities: Activities of other holding companies n.e.c.
Parent: Grove Acquisitions Limited
Officers: Athos George Yiannis, Secretary; Sunita Arora [1964] Director; Surinder Arora [1958] Director; Carlton Jeffrey Brown [1972] Director/Chartered Accountant; Athos George Yiannis [1963] Director/Chartered Accountant

Arora Management Services Limited
Incorporated: 27 November 2005 *Employees:* 62
Net Worth: £20,519,416 *Total Assets:* £51,631,480
Registered Office: World Business Centre, 3 Newall Road, London Heathrow Airport, Hounslow, Middlesex, TW6 2TA
Activities: Activities of head offices
Parent: Grove Acquisitions Limited
Officers: Athos George Yiannis, Secretary; Sanjay Arora [1989] Director; Sunita Arora [1964] Director; Surinder Arora [1958] Director; Carlton Jeffrey Brown [1972] Director/Chartered Accountant; Athos George Yiannis [1963] Director/Chartered Accountant

Arora Manchester Limited
Incorporated: 26 February 2004
Net Worth: £9,036,850 *Total Assets:* £9,036,850
Registered Office: World Business Centre, 3 Newall Road, London Heathrow Airport, Hounslow, Middlesex, TW6 2TA
Activities: Dormant company
Officers: Athos George Yiannis, Secretary; Sanjay Arora [1989] Director; Athos George Yiannis [1963] Director/Chartered Accountant

Arora T5 Holdings Limited
Incorporated: 13 July 2016
Net Worth: £128,193,832 *Total Assets:* £169,359,520
Registered Office: World Business Centre, 3 Newall Road, London Heathrow Airport, Hounslow, Middlesex, TW6 2TA
Activities: Activities of head offices
Parent: Arora Hotels Limited
Officers: Athos George Yiannis, Secretary; Carlton Jeffrey Brown [1972] Director/Chartered Accountant; Athos George Yiannis [1963] Director/Chartered Accountant

F & J Arpino Limited
Incorporated: 5 September 1973 *Employees:* 51
Previous: F. & J. Arpino Limited
Net Worth: £4,099,130 *Total Assets:* £7,452,500
Registered Office: 5 Theobald Court, Theobald Street, Elstree, Herts, WD6 4RN
Activities: Wholesale of household goods (other than musical instruments) n.e.c
Officers: Aamer Johar, Secretary; Aamer Johar [1959] Director; Rafia Aamer Johar [1966] Director

ARRI (GB) Limited
Incorporated: 23 December 1982 *Employees:* 82
Net Worth: £18,619,000 *Total Assets:* £32,916,000
Registered Office: 2 Highbridge, Oxford Road, Uxbridge, Middlesex, UB8 1LX
Activities: Wholesale of household goods (other than musical instruments) n.e.c
Shareholders: Christoph Stahl; Carolin Stahl; Florian Stahl
Officers: Dawn Melanie Oatley [1963] Finance Director; Dr. Jorg Pohlman [1963] Managing Director [German]

ARRI Rental Services UK Limited
Incorporated: 6 August 1986 *Employees:* 62
Previous: Media Film Service Limited
Net Worth: £10,018,999 *Total Assets:* £14,843,888
Registered Office: 2 Highbridge, Oxford Road, Uxbridge, Middlesex, UB8 1LX
Activities: Renting and leasing of other machinery, equipment and tangible goods n.e.c.
Parent: ARRI (GB) Limited
Officers: Russell David Allen [1966] Director of Operations; Dawn Melanie Oatley [1963] Finance Director

Artemis Interiors Limited
Incorporated: 10 May 2016 *Employees:* 18
Net Worth: £306,319 *Total Assets:* £6,543,849
Registered Office: Unit A, Oyo Business Units, Dagenham, Essex, RM9 6LP
Activities: Activities of other holding companies n.e.c.
Shareholders: Anthony David Martin; Alan Martin
Officers: Norman Campbell, Secretary; Alan Martin [1968] Director; Anthony David Martin [1959] Director

Artic Building Services Limited
Incorporated: 18 March 1998 *Employees:* 109
Net Worth: £2,301,385 *Total Assets:* £8,420,528
Registered Office: 16-17 Schooner Court, Crossways Business Park, Dartford, Kent, DA2 6NW
Activities: Electrical installation
Officers: Zehra McAnallen, Secretary; Vincent McAnallen [1968] Director/Contracts Manager

Artillery Properties Limited
Incorporated: 15 May 1998
Net Worth: £2,512,356 *Total Assets:* £8,017,093
Registered Office: 1 Beauchamp Court, 10 Victors Way, Barnet, Herts, EN5 5TZ
Activities: Development of building projects
Major Shareholder: Selwyn Howard David Tarn
Officers: Selwyn Howard David Tarn [1961] Director

John Artis Limited
Incorporated: 26 February 1975 *Employees:* 44
Net Worth: £3,219,915 *Total Assets:* £5,426,653
Registered Office: Artis Glassworks, Cox Lane, Chessington, Surrey, KT9 1SF
Activities: Manufacture and processing of other glass, including technical glassware
Parent: BHS Tabletop AG
Officers: Gernot Harald Egretzberger [1977] Financial Director [German]; Noel Ralph Grundy [1960] Managing Director; Stefan Janicke [1964] Director [German]; Christian Strootmann [1963] Director [German]

Arugula Spruce Limited
Incorporated: 17 August 2016 *Employees:* 1
Net Worth Deficit: £158,938 *Total Assets:* £9,832,582
Registered Office: Suite 2, Viscount House, 6a Love Lane, Pinner, Middlesex, HA5 3EF
Activities: Buying and selling of own real estate
Major Shareholder: Zareen Syed Habib
Officers: Zareen Syed Habib, Secretary; Zareen Syed Habib [1971] Director [Canadian]

Aryzta UK Holdings I Limited
Incorporated: 12 April 2012
Net Worth: £1,805,984,768 *Total Assets:* £1,806,012,928
Registered Office: Delice House, 149 Brent Road, Southall, Middlesex, UB2 5LJ
Activities: Activities of head offices
Officers: Sean Timothy Murphy, Secretary; Thierry Cacaly [1971] Director/Head of Aryzta Food Solutions UK [French]; John McNiff [1976] Director [Irish]; Sean Timothy Murphy [1969] Director/Accountant [Irish]

Asap Growth Limited
Incorporated: 1 June 2015
Net Worth Deficit: £3,850 *Total Assets:* £5,131,800
Registered Office: 65 Delamere Road, Hayes, Middlesex, UB4 0NN
Activities: Activities of other holding companies n.e.c.
Shareholders: Anil Kumar Sharma; Jolanta Barbara Patel
Officers: Jagjeet Kaur Ahluwalia [1962] Director/Manager; Amit Hasmukh Raojibhai Patel [1975] Director/Manager; Anil Kumar Sharma [1952] Director

Asgill House Trust Limited (The)
Incorporated: 22 February 1983
Net Worth: £3,578,803 *Total Assets:* £6,716,509
Registered Office: Asgill House, Old Palace Lane, Richmond upon Thames, Surrey, TW9 1PQ
Activities: Operation of historical sites and buildings and similar visitor attractions
Officers: Faqrul Islam, Secretary; Albert F Hauptfuhrer [1937] Director/Retired [American/British]; Petina Leigh Sumner [1959] Director; Alan David Taylor [1941] Director/Solicitor; Dr Farouk Rajabali Walji [1950] Director/Educationalist

Ash Properties Limited
Incorporated: 20 March 2009 *Employees:* 2
Net Worth: £14,399,855 *Total Assets:* £36,090,872
Registered Office: 38 The Drive, Ickenham, Middlesex, UB10 8AG
Activities: Residents property management
Shareholders: Sital Kaur; Kuldeep Singh
Officers: Sital Kaur, Secretary; Kuldeep Singh [1967] Director/Businessman

Asha (Camberley) Ltd
Incorporated: 13 November 2014
Net Worth Deficit: £5,115 *Total Assets:* £6,105,803
Registered Office: Top Floor, Bridgewater House, 866-868 Uxbridge Road, Hayes, Middlesex, UB4 0RR
Activities: Development of building projects
Parent: Reliance Investments Ltd
Officers: Rajinder Singh Makkar [1963] Director

Ashby & Croft Limited
Incorporated: 17 May 2006 *Employees:* 40
Net Worth: £1,268,832 *Total Assets:* £6,955,902
Registered Office: Yard 5, Oliver Road, Riverside Industrial Estate, West Thurrock, Grays, Essex, RM20 3ED
Activities: Construction of utility projects for fluids
Shareholder: David Langford
Officers: David Langford, Secretary/Director; David Langford [1965] Director; Victoria Jane Leadbetter [1971] Director

Ashcoe Holdings Limited
Incorporated: 19 August 2015 *Employees:* 14
Net Worth: £217,866 *Total Assets:* £8,396,189
Registered Office: 53-63 Redbridge Lane East, Ilford, Essex, IG4 5EY
Activities: Activities of other holding companies n.e.c.
Major Shareholder: John Maitland Coe
Officers: Ashley Katherine Coe [1986] Director/Wine and Spirit Merchant; Jacqueline Coe [1957] Director; John Maitland Coe [1955] Director/Wine and Spirit Merchant

A.S. Ashcroft Limited
Incorporated: 8 June 1989 *Employees:* 18
Net Worth: £10,504,315 *Total Assets:* £11,020,292
Registered Office: 64 Cottimore Lane, Walton on Thames, Surrey, KT12 2BP
Activities: Construction of domestic buildings
Shareholder: Nicholas Antony Perrin
Officers: Rebecca Adele Perrin, Secretary; Michael Adrian Perrin [1942] Director; Nicholas Perrin [1964] Director

Ashdown Care Limited
Incorporated: 16 February 2001 *Employees:* 141
Net Worth: £2,856,305 *Total Assets:* £9,117,736
Registered Office: c/o MCAK & Co, 1st Floor, 15 Princeton Mews, 167-169 London Road, Kingston upon Thames, Surrey, KT2 6PT
Activities: Residential care activities for the elderly and disabled
Officers: Naseem Pradhan, Secretary; Arif Sultanali Pradhan [1957] Director/Businessman

Ashill Land Limited
Incorporated: 6 September 2013 *Employees:* 9
Net Worth: £9,314,018 *Total Assets:* £16,274,051
Registered Office: Aissela, 46 High Street, Esher, Surrey, KT10 9QY
Activities: Buying and selling of own real estate
Shareholder: Stephen Ryan Lavers
Officers: Benjamin Oliver Boyce [1980] Director; Philip James Davies [1950] Director; Steven James Foreman [1979] Director; Stephen Ryan Lavers [1973] Director

Ashley Homes Limited
Incorporated: 5 January 2005 *Employees:* 3
Net Worth: £1,987,285 *Total Assets:* £6,029,756
Registered Office: Corner Oak, Weybridge Park, Weybridge, Surrey, KT13 8SH
Activities: Construction of domestic buildings
Shareholders: Michael Gordon Scott; Graham Richard Scott

Asia Pacific Holdings Limited
Incorporated: 7 March 2000
Net Worth: £2,143,913,984 *Total Assets:* £3,019,723,008
Registered Office: Broadwater Park, Denham, Bucks, UB9 5HR
Activities: Other business support service activities n.e.c.
Parent: Six Continents Limited
Officers: Fiona Cuttell, Secretary; Michael Jon Cockcroft [1974] Director/Accountant; Michael Todd Glover [1971] Director/Financial Controller [American]; Nicolette Henfrey [1969] Director

Asia UK Property Fund LLP
Incorporated: 2 February 2010
Net Worth: £7,448,451 *Total Assets:* £7,512,188
Registered Office: Upminster Court, 133 Hall Lane, Upminster, Essex, RM14 1AL
Officers: Iain Robert Liddell [1963] Member

Asiatic Carpets Holdings Limited
Incorporated: 25 March 2003 *Employees:* 36
Net Worth: £15,014,914 *Total Assets:* £20,743,478
Registered Office: 42 Lytton Road, Barnet, Herts, EN5 5BY
Activities: Retail sale of textiles in specialised stores
Shareholders: Sharon Mozell Kelaty; Frederick Sion Kelaty
Officers: Frederick Sion Kelaty, Secretary; Frederick Sion Kelaty [1968] Director; Sharon Mozell Kelaty [1964] Director

ASIG Holdings Limited
Incorporated: 20 March 2008
Net Worth: £37,600,000 *Total Assets:* £38,400,000
Registered Office: 2 World Business Centre Heathrow, Newall Road, London Heathrow Airport, Hounslow, Middlesex, TW6 2SF
Activities: Scheduled passenger air transport
Parent: BBA Holdings Limited
Officers: John Francis Alexander Geddes, Secretary; Deon Van Niekerk [1972] Director/Accountant [South African]; Laura Relf [1982] Director/Accountant

Asino Limited
Incorporated: 14 December 2010
Net Worth Deficit: £4,856,154 *Total Assets:* £18,243,436
Registered Office: Hill House, Lowlands Road, Harrow, Middlesex, HA1 3EQ
Activities: Development of building projects
Major Shareholder: Donovan Gijsbertus Wijsmuller
Officers: Brian Martin Comer [1960] Director [Irish]; Luke Andrew Comer [1957] Director [Irish]

Askham Village Community Limited
Incorporated: 23 August 1988 *Employees:* 156
Net Worth: £6,522,597 *Total Assets:* £16,619,195
Registered Office: Suite 2B, 4th Floor, Congress House, 14 Lyon Road, Harrow, Middlesex, HA1 2EN
Activities: Residential nursing care facilities
Shareholders: Salim Kamrudin Punjani Giga; Salma Salim Giga
Officers: Salma Salim Giga, Secretary; Salim Kamrudin Punjani Giga [1949] Director; Salma Salim Giga [1954] Director; Aliyyah-Begum Nasser [1983] Director/Consultant; Rabiyyah-Begum Raval [1981] Director/Optometrist

Aspect Software UK Limited
Incorporated: 21 October 1987 *Employees:* 141
Net Worth: £7,406,000 *Total Assets:* £18,731,000
Registered Office: Record Store Building, 15 Pressing Lane, Hayes, Middlesex, UB3 1EP
Activities: Other telecommunications activities
Officers: Stephen Mathew Ball [1969] Director/Business Executive; Sherri Lynn Moyen [1976] Director [American]

Aspire Investments and Property Developments LLP
Incorporated: 4 March 2010 *Employees:* 14
Net Worth: £32,005 *Total Assets:* £11,357,025
Registered Office: Bank Chambers, 2 Bridge Street, Leatherhead, Surrey, KT22 8BZ
Officers: Gary Edward Brine [1964] Member; Alyson Lumb [1976] Member; Lisa Jane Brine [1969] LLP Member

Assetsky Limited
Incorporated: 25 May 1988 *Employees:* 4
Net Worth: £3,758,852 *Total Assets:* £6,114,948
Registered Office: Gladstone House, 77-79 High Street, Egham, Surrey, TW20 9HY
Activities: Development of building projects
Officers: Michael John Birch, Secretary; Amanda Jones [1964] Director; Leonard Jones [1946] Director/Manager

Associated Coffee Merchants (International) Limited
Incorporated: 28 April 1980 *Employees:* 13
Net Worth: £1,871,584 *Total Assets:* £11,704,136
Registered Office: Corinthian House, 17 Lansdowne Road, Croydon, Surrey, CR0 2BX
Activities: Activities of head offices
Shareholder: Ian Ernest Anthony Breminer
Officers: David John Eagle, Secretary; Ian Ernest Anthony Breminer [1952] Director/Coffee Merchant; Kristine Elise Antonia Breminer Isgren [1980] Director/Marketing Executive

Associated Lead Mills Ltd.
Incorporated: 6 June 1997 *Employees:* 51
Net Worth: £10,360,480 *Total Assets:* £35,974,448
Registered Office: Unit B, Bingley Road, Hoddesdon, Herts, EN11 0NX
Activities: Wholesale of metals and metal ores
Parent: Envirolead Distribution Limited
Officers: Maurice Elliot Sherling [1949] Director [Irish]; Barry Howard Smith [1956] Director/General Manager

Assured Services Limited
Incorporated: 10 November 1994 *Employees:* 77
Net Worth: £6,083,573 *Total Assets:* £9,394,063
Registered Office: Tudor House, 4 Birdhurst Road, South Croydon, Surrey, CR2 7EA
Activities: Other accommodation
Shareholders: Piyoosh Amin; Vipul Patel
Officers: Piyoosh Amin, Secretary/Certified Accountant; Hemangini Amin [1961] Director/Administrator; Piyoosh Amin [1957] Director/Accountant; Priti Patel [1965] Director/Administrator; Vipul Patel [1963] Director

Astellas Pharma Europe Ltd.
Incorporated: 29 March 1990 *Employees:* 399
Net Worth: £870,882,368 *Total Assets:* £1,343,135,104
Registered Office: 2000 Hillswood Drive, Chertsey, Surrey, KT16 0RS
Activities: Wholesale of pharmaceutical goods
Parent: Astellas Pharma Inc.
Officers: Sally Anne Hinchliffe, Secretary; Jochen Norbert Bohner [1971] Director/SVP Finance, Procurement & IS EMEA [German]; Masaaki Hirano [1967] Director/Businessman [Japanese]; Dr Dirk Armin Kosche [1963] Director/President EMEA Operations [German]; Daniel Benjamin Matthias Schulze [1975] Director/Vice President and General Counsel [German]; Toru Yoshimitsu [1963] Director [Japanese]

Astellas Pharma Ltd.
Incorporated: 10 January 1964 *Employees:* 195
Net Worth: £49,799,000 *Total Assets:* £133,302,000
Registered Office: 2000 Hillswood Drive, Chertsey, Surrey, KT16 0RS
Activities: Wholesale of pharmaceutical goods
Parent: Astellas Pharma Inc.
Officers: Ian Michael Hall [1966] Director/Chartered Accountant; Dr Jose Maria Sanz [1972] Director/General Manager

Aster Healthcare Ltd.
Incorporated: 30 March 2006 *Employees:* 6
Net Worth: £2,914,107 *Total Assets:* £13,542,438
Registered Office: Image Court, 328-334 Moseley Road, Walton-on-Thames, Surrey, KT12 3LT
Activities: Residential nursing care facilities
Shareholder: Sheth Jeebun
Officers: Zainah Jeebun, Secretary; Sheth Jeebun [1961] Director/Entrepreneur; Zainah Jeebun [1961] Director/Entrepreneur

Aston Heating Limited
Incorporated: 18 March 1964
Net Worth: £3,860,757 *Total Assets:* £9,641,046
Registered Office: Moss Lodge, Moss Lane, Romford, Essex, RM1 2PT
Activities: Plumbing, heat and air-conditioning installation
Shareholders: Evan Charles Ivey; Lyn Dalton
Officers: Michael William John Thomas, Secretary; Evan Charles Ivey [1959] Director; Alan Thomas [1960] Director/Heating Engineer; Michael William John Thomas [1951] Director/Plumbing Engineer

Thomas Aston Homes Limited
Incorporated: 8 February 1973 *Employees:* 2
Net Worth: £16,051,865 *Total Assets:* £16,313,521
Registered Office: P O Box 10, Denbigh Close, Chislehurst, Kent, BR7 5ZE
Activities: Development of building projects
Major Shareholder: William John Thomas
Officers: Fiona Wendy Thomas, Secretary; Fiona Wendy Thomas [1948] Director; William John Thomas [1942] Director/Property Negotiator

Astonpalm Limited
Incorporated: 20 October 1997
Net Worth: £6,482,390 *Total Assets:* £10,804,680
Registered Office: Alton House, 66-68 High Street, Northwood, Middlesex, HA6 1BL
Activities: Development of building projects
Major Shareholder: Barry Attarzadeh
Officers: Peter William Johnson, Secretary; Barry Attarzadeh [1956] Director [Canadian]

Astor Lodge Holdings Limited
Incorporated: 19 December 1962 *Employees:* 2
Net Worth: £9,986,970 *Total Assets:* £11,938,191
Registered Office: York House, Empire Way, Wembley, Middlesex, HA9 0FQ
Activities: Other letting and operating of own or leased real estate
Parent: Hydecourt Developments Limited
Officers: David Lessman, Secretary/Director; Julia Ruth Bekhor [1960] Director; David Lessman [1925] Director

ATC Holdings Limited
Incorporated: 29 May 1997
Net Worth: £5,725,075 *Total Assets:* £9,178,015
Registered Office: Aero Engine Centre, 109 Green Lane, Hounslow, Middlesex, TW4 6DF
Activities: Other service activities n.e.c.
Shareholders: James Francis Cook; Nicolas Victor Cook
Officers: Nicolas Victor Cook, Secretary/Director; James Francis Cook [1979] Director/Engineer; Nicolas Victor Cook [1951] Director/Engineer

ATD Travel Services Limited
Incorporated: 8 March 2002 *Employees:* 132
Net Worth: £5,288,399 *Total Assets:* £14,082,404
Registered Office: 2nd Floor, Nucleus House, 2 Lower Mortlake Road, Richmond, Surrey, TW9 2JA
Activities: Other reservation service activities n.e.c.
Major Shareholder: Oliver Henry Brendon
Officers: Matthew James Reynolds, Secretary; Christopher Bradshaw [1975] Director/Travel Executive; Oliver Henry Brendon [1974] Director/Account Manager; David Charles Wiseman [1957] Director

Athena Care Homes (UK) Limited
Incorporated: 3 September 2014 *Employees:* 443
Net Worth: £8,222,314 *Total Assets:* £25,884,150
Registered Office: Unit 2 Rima House, A13 Approach, Ripple Road, Barking, Essex, IG11 0RH
Activities: Activities of head offices
Shareholders: Udayan Agarwal; Mala Agarwal
Officers: Mala Agarwal, Secretary; Mala Agarwal [1969] Director; Udayan Agarwal [1969] Director

Athona Limited
Incorporated: 1 August 2003 *Employees:* 113
Net Worth: £909,767 *Total Assets:* £7,618,419
Registered Office: Orbital House, 20 Eastern Road, Romford, Essex, RM1 3PJ
Activities: Temporary employment agency activities
Shareholders: Tina London; Stewart David London
Officers: Stewart David London [1976] Director; Tina London [1973] Director

ATK Energy EU Limited
Incorporated: 4 November 2005
Previous: Atkins Energy EU Limited
Net Worth: £5,994,000 *Total Assets:* £16,028,000
Registered Office: Woodcote Grove, Ashley Road, Epsom, Surrey, KT18 5BW
Activities: Activities of head offices
Parent: Atkins Limited
Officers: Louise Mary McAllister, Secretary; Elliot Michael Nobelen, Secretary; Mark Stephen Anderson [1965] Director/Accountant; Christopher Ball [1973] Director; Simon Glenister Cole [1965] Director/Accountant; Alan James Cullens [1963] Group HR Director

ATK Energy EU Services Limited
Incorporated: 25 May 2005
Previous: Atkins Energy EU Services Limited
Net Worth: £2,330,000 *Total Assets:* £6,582,000
Registered Office: Woodcote Grove, Ashley Road, Epsom, Surrey, KT18 5BW
Activities: Treatment and disposal of hazardous waste
Parent: ATK Energy EU Limited
Officers: Louise Mary McAllister, Secretary; Elliot Michael Nobelen, Secretary; Mark Stephen Anderson [1965] Director/Accountant; Simon Glenister Cole [1965] Director/Accountant; Alan James Cullens [1963] Group HR Director

Atkins ATK Investments Limited
Incorporated: 26 March 2002
Previous: Atkins Investments UK Limited
Net Worth: £33,122,000 *Total Assets:* £34,102,000
Registered Office: Woodcote Grove, Ashley Road, Epsom, Surrey, KT18 5BW
Activities: Other business support service activities n.e.c.
Parent: WS Atkins Limited
Officers: Louise Mary McAllister, Secretary; Elliot Michael Nobelen, Secretary; Mark Stephen Anderson [1965] Director/Accountant; Simon Glenister Cole [1965] Director/Accountant; Alan James Cullens [1963] Group HR Director

Atkins Holdings Limited
Incorporated: 6 March 1985 *Employees:* 9
Net Worth: £18,409,000 *Total Assets:* £21,170,000
Registered Office: Cedars Cottage, 16 Church Street, Epsom, Surrey, KT17 4QB
Activities: Activities of head offices
Shareholders: William Stewart Gregg; Bruce Meredith Caporn
Officers: Charles Elliott Marr, Secretary; Catherine Clare Butler [1962] Director; Bruce Meredith Caporn [1934] Director/Solicitor; William Stewart Gregg [1949] Director/Chartered Accountant; Charles Elliott Marr [1958] Director/Chartered Accountant; Christopher Charles Micklethwaite [1958] Director; Reverend Peter William Micklethwaite [1962] Director/Minister of Religion; Nicholas Robert Worthington [1960] Director

Atkins International Holdings Limited
Incorporated: 22 November 2007
Previous: Atkins Gamma Limited
Net Worth: £72,040,000 *Total Assets:* £214,945,408
Registered Office: Woodcote Grove, Ashley Road, Epsom, Surrey, KT18 5BW
Activities: Other business support service activities n.e.c.
Parent: WS Atkins Limited
Officers: Louise Mary McAllister, Secretary; Elliot Michael Nobelen, Secretary; Mark Stephen Anderson [1965] Director/Accountant; Simon Glenister Cole [1965] Director/Accountant; Alan James Cullens [1963] Group HR Director

W.S. Atkins International Limited
Incorporated: 23 January 1973 *Employees:* 13
Net Worth: £240,802,000 *Total Assets:* £676,515,008
Registered Office: Woodcote Grove, Ashley Road, Epsom, Surrey, KT18 5BW
Activities: Other business support service activities n.e.c.
Parent: Atkins International Holdings Limited
Officers: Louise Mary McAllister, Secretary; Elliot Michael Nobelen, Secretary; Mark Stephen Anderson [1965] Director/Accountant; Christopher Ball [1973] Director; Christopher Laine Birdsong [1952] Director/Project Manager [American]; Martin Alexander Chalmers [1964] Director/Manager; Simon Glenister Cole [1965] Director/Accountant; Alan James Cullens [1963] Group HR Director; Martin MacDonald Grant [1958] Director/Mechanical Engineer; Philip David Hoare [1970] Director/Chartered Civil Engineer; Michael McNicholas [1961] Director/Civil Engineer; Nicholas John Roberts [1968] Director/Chartered Geologist; Neil James Corfield Thomas [1962] Director/Chartered Engineer

Atkins Investments UK Limited
Incorporated: 14 December 2004
Previous: Atkins Beta Limited
Net Worth: £120,300,000 *Total Assets:* £325,300,000
Registered Office: Woodcote Grove, Ashley Road, Epsom, Surrey, KT18 5BW
Activities: Other business support service activities n.e.c.
Parent: WS Atkins Limited
Officers: Louise Mary McAllister, Secretary; Elliot Michael Nobelen, Secretary; Mark Stephen Anderson [1965] Director/Accountant; Simon Glenister Cole [1965] Director/Accountant; Alan James Cullens [1963] Group HR Director

Atkins Limited
Incorporated: 30 March 1961 *Employees:* 7,144
Net Worth: £298,900,000 *Total Assets:* £1,027,699,968
Registered Office: Woodcote Grove, Ashley Road, Epsom, Surrey, KT18 5BW
Activities: Management consultancy activities other than financial management
Parent: Atkins Investments UK Limited
Officers: Louise Mary McAllister, Secretary; Elliot Michael Nobelen, Secretary; Mark Stephen Anderson [1965] Director/Accountant; Christopher Ball [1973] Director; Martin Alexander Chalmers [1964] Director/Manager; Simon Glenister Cole [1965] Director/Accountant; Alan James Cullens [1963] Group HR Director; Martin MacDonald Grant [1958] Director/Mechanical Engineer; Philip David Hoare [1970] Director/Chartered Civil Engineer; Michael McNicholas [1961] Director/Civil Engineer; Nicholas John Roberts [1968] Director/Chartered Geologist; Neil James Corfield Thomas [1962] Director/Chartered Engineer

WS Atkins Limited
Incorporated: 13 February 1985
Previous: WS Atkins PLC
Net Worth: £235,300,000 *Total Assets:* £611,299,968
Registered Office: Woodcote Grove, Ashley Road, Epsom, Surrey, KT18 5BW
Activities: Activities of head offices
Parent: SNC-Lavalin (GB) Holdings Limited
Officers: Louise Mary McAllister, Secretary; Elliot Michael Nobelen, Secretary; Mark Stephen Anderson [1965] Director/Accountant; Christopher Ball [1973] Director; Simon Glenister Cole [1965] Director/Accountant; James Richard Compston [1965] Director/Executive; Alan James Cullens [1963] Group HR Director; Martin MacDonald Grant [1958] Director/Mechanical Engineer

Atkins Properties Limited
Incorporated: 7 March 1961 *Employees:* 9
Net Worth: £20,011,000 *Total Assets:* £21,766,000
Registered Office: Cedars Cottage, 16 Church Street, Epsom, Surrey, KT17 4QB
Activities: Other letting and operating of own or leased real estate
Parent: Atkins Holdings Limited
Officers: Charles Elliott Marr, Secretary; Charles Elliott Marr [1958] Director/Chartered Accountant; Christopher Charles Micklethwaite [1958] Director; Roderick Stephen Milne [1959] Director/Chartered Surveyor

Atlanta Trust Limited
Incorporated: 16 December 1976 *Employees:* 13
Net Worth: £14,214,693 *Total Assets:* £14,754,914
Registered Office: 615-623 Princes Road, Dartford, Kent, DA2 6HH
Activities: Manufacture of other machine tools
Major Shareholder: Jean Isabelle Cameron Suckling
Officers: Mary Irene Wright, Secretary; Carole King [1963] Director; Amy Elizabeth Nicholas [1979] Director; Christopher Paul Nicholas [1964] Director/Engineer; Robert Wilson Nicholas [1981] Director/Electrical Engineer; Jean Isabelle Cameron Suckling [1932] Director; Mary Irene Wright [1954] Director/Accountant

Atlantic 2/3 UK Holdings Limited
Incorporated: 20 September 2000
Net Worth: £214,780,416 *Total Assets:* £214,789,936
Registered Office: Chertsey Road, Sunbury on Thames, Middlesex, TW16 7BP
Activities: Non-trading company
Parent: BP Exploration Operating Company Limited
Officers: David Alan Rider [1964] Director/Oil Company Executive; Katherine Anne Thomson [1968] Director/Oil Company Executive

Atlantica Yield PLC
Incorporated: 17 December 2013 *Employees:* 181
Previous: Abengoa Yield PLC
Net Worth: £1,276,755,200 *Total Assets:* £7,616,390,144
Registered Office: Great West House, (GW1), Great West Road, Brentford, Middlesex, TW8 9DF
Activities: Production of electricity
Shareholder: ACIL Luxco 1 S.A.
Officers: Irene Maria Hernandez Martin de Arriva, Secretary; Andrea Brentan [1949] Director [Italian]; Christopher Kenneth Jarratt [1958] Director [Canadian]; Francisco Jose Martinez [1958] Director [Spanish]; Ian Edward Robertson [1959] Director [Canadian]; Jackson Robinson [1942] Director [American]; Santiago Seage [1969] Director/Chief Executive Officer [Spanish]; Daniel Villalba [1947] Director [Spanish]

Atlas Cleaning Limited
Incorporated: 5 March 1986 *Employees:* 2,487
Net Worth: £3,466,465 *Total Assets:* £15,368,149
Registered Office: 82 Hampton Road West, Hanworth, Middlesex, TW13 6DZ
Activities: Other building and industrial cleaning activities
Officers: Theresa Helen Earley, Secretary; Nicholas James Earley [1956] Director/Cleaning Contractor; Raymond William Empson [1959] Director/Cleaning Contractor

Atlas Contractors Limited
Incorporated: 29 July 1991 *Employees:* 2
Net Worth: £6,252,477 *Total Assets:* £10,675,306
Registered Office: 82 Hampton Road West, Hanworth, Feltham, Middlesex, TW13 6DZ
Activities: General cleaning of buildings
Parent: Atlas FM Limited
Officers: Theresa Helen Earley, Secretary; Nicholas James Earley [1956] Director/Accountant; Raymond William Empson [1959] Director/Marketing Manager

ATP Media Holdings Limited
Incorporated: 18 July 2017 *Employees:* 32
Net Worth: £4,933,332 *Total Assets:* £38,699,312
Registered Office: Thames House, Portsmouth Road, Esher, Surrey, KT10 9AD
Activities: Activities of other holding companies n.e.c.
Officers: Tom Bullock, Secretary; Andrea Gaudenzi [1973] Director/Entrepreneur [Italian]; Stuart James Watts [1965] Director/Chief Operating Officer; Mark Andrew Webster [1962] Director/Chief Executive Officer; Mark Vernon Young [1958] Director/Sports Executive [American]; Gavin Ziv [1975] Director/Vice President, Tennis Canada [Canadian]

ATP Media Licensing Limited
Incorporated: 18 July 2017
Net Worth: £729 *Total Assets:* £7,741,925
Registered Office: Thames House, Portsmouth Road, Esher, Surrey, KT10 9AD
Activities: Media representation services
Parent: ATP Media Tennis Limited
Officers: Tom Bullock, Secretary; Andrea Gaudenzi [1973] Director/Entrepreneur [Italian]; Stuart James Watts [1965] Director/Chief Operating Officer; Mark Andrew Webster [1962] Director/Chief Executive Officer; Mark Vernon Young [1958] Director/Sports Executive [American]; Gavin Ziv [1975] Director/Vice President, Tennis Canada [Canadian]

ATP Media Operations Limited
Incorporated: 15 October 1998 *Employees:* 32
Previous: Tennis Properties Limited
Net Worth: £4,963,838 *Total Assets:* £40,368,924
Registered Office: Thames House, Portsmouth Road, Esher, Surrey, KT10 9AD
Activities: Television programme production activities
Officers: Thomas Bullock, Secretary; Andrea Gaudenzi [1973] Director/Entrepreneur [Italian]; Stuart James Watts [1965] Director/Chief Operating Officer; Mark Andrew Webster [1962] Director/Chief Executive Officer; Mark Vernon Young [1958] Director/Attorney/Business Executive [American]; Gavin Ziv [1975] Director/Vice President Tennis Canada [Canadian]

Attewell Limited
Incorporated: 11 December 1962 *Employees:* 102
Net Worth: £23,432,000 *Total Assets:* £33,207,000
Registered Office: 7 A/B, Millington Road, Hayes, Middlesex, UB3 4AZ
Activities: Other manufacturing n.e.c.
Parent: Shimtech Industries Limited
Officers: Heath Denis Batwell [1983] Director/Accountant [Irish]; Alastair Scott Fanning [1967] Director/Chartered Accountant; Matthew Giggle [1967] Director; Christopher Eric Smith [1971] Director

Attwell Business Inc. Limited
Incorporated: 5 August 2005
Net Worth: £7,007,468 *Total Assets:* £12,185,503
Registered Office: Unit 90 Kingspark Business Centre, 152-178 Kingston Road, New Malden, Surrey, KT3 3ST
Activities: Wholesale of chemical products
Major Shareholder: Andrii Vietokha
Officers: Richard Laurence Cooper [1968] Director/Consultant

Atwood Primary Academy
Incorporated: 28 November 2013 *Employees:* 46
Net Worth: £9,126,624 *Total Assets:* £9,984,889
Registered Office: Atwood Primary School, Limpsfield Road, South Croydon, Surrey, CR2 9EE
Activities: Primary education
Officers: Abi Lynn, Secretary; Samit Bhat [1976] Director; Anna Carroll [1977] Director/Underwriter; Vincent Chan [1974] Director/Financial Controller; Andrew Henderson [1977] Operations Director; Carl Joseph Knightly [1979] Managing Director; Amanda Lawrence [1956] Director/School Assistant; Philip Luff [1972] Director/Solicitor; Neil McKenzie [1963] Director/Retired; Kerry McSweeney [1973] Marketing Director; Alison Morgan [1944] Director/Retired; Sophie Skelley [1993] Director/Teacher; Robert Veale [1974] Director/Headmaster

Audbern Limited
Incorporated: 15 December 2009 *Employees:* 2
Net Worth: £2,139,716 *Total Assets:* £8,311,586
Registered Office: Old Bishops' College, Churchgate, Cheshunt, Herts, EN8 9XP
Activities: Activities of other holding companies n.e.c.
Shareholder: Wayne Christopher Rolfe
Officers: Audrey Helen Rolfe [1933] Director; Wayne Christopher Rolfe [1966] Director

Audio UK 2 Limited
Incorporated: 23 February 2017
Net Worth: £167,315,008 *Total Assets:* £195,316,000
Registered Office: Unit 10 Silverglade Business Park, Leatherhead Road, Chessington, Surrey, KT9 2QL
Activities: Activities of other holding companies n.e.c.
Parent: Audiotonix Group Limited
Officers: Francois de Mitry, Secretary; James Barton [1970] Director; Michael Beetz [1982] Investor, Associate Director [German]; Helen Mary Culleton [1964] Director; Francois de Mitry [1966] Director/Investor, Partner [Luxembourger]; Stephane Epin [1978] Director/Investor, Partner [French]; James David Gordon [1972] Director

Audio UK 3 Limited
Incorporated: 23 February 2017
Net Worth: £167,315,008 *Total Assets:* £195,316,000
Registered Office: Unit 10 Silverglade Business Park, Leatherhead Road, Chessington, Surrey, KT9 2QL
Activities: Activities of other holding companies n.e.c.
Parent: Audio UK 2 Limited
Officers: Francois de Mitry, Secretary; James Barton [1970] Director; Michael Beetz [1982] Investor, Associate Director [German]; Helen Mary Culleton [1964] Director; Francois de Mitry [1966] Director/Investor, Partner [Luxembourger]; Stephane Epin [1978] Director/Investor, Partner [French]; James David Gordon [1972] Director

Audiotonix Group Limited
Incorporated: 23 February 2017
Net Worth: £7,373,979 *Total Assets:* £479,676,288
Registered Office: Unit 10 Silverglade Business Park, Leatherhead Road, Chessington, Surrey, KT9 2QL
Activities: Activities of other holding companies n.e.c.
Officers: Francois de Mitry, Secretary; James Barton [1970] Director; Michael Beetz [1982] Investor, Associate Director [German]; Helen Mary Culleton [1964] Director; Francois de Mitry [1966] Director/Investor, Partner [Luxembourger]; Stephane Epin [1978] Director/Investor, Partner [French]; James David Gordon [1972] Director

Audiotonix Limited
Incorporated: 13 June 2014
Total Assets: £5,084,000
Registered Office: Unit 10 Silverglade Business Park, Leatherhead Road, Chessington, Surrey, KT9 2QL
Activities: Activities of other holding companies n.e.c.
Parent: A6 Audio Bidco Limited
Officers: James Barton [1970] Director; Helen Mary Culleton [1964] Director; James David Gordon [1972] Managing Director; Neil Alexander Hooper [1962] Director; Anthony Williams [1965] Director

Audley Binswood Limited
Incorporated: 23 November 2007 *Employees:* 3
Net Worth: £5,122,466 *Total Assets:* £14,245,001
Registered Office: 65 High Street, Egham, Surrey, TW20 9EY
Activities: Buying and selling of own real estate
Parent: Audley Court Limited
Officers: Jonathan Martin Austen [1956] Director/Chief Financial Officer; Paul David Morgan [1969] Operations Director; John William Nettleton [1970] Director/Chartered Surveyor; Katherine Elizabeth Rose [1964] Marketing Director; Malcolm Nicholas Sanderson [1959] Director/Property Developer; Kevin Anthony Shaw [1977] Sales Director

Audley Chalfont Limited
Incorporated: 4 July 2012 *Employees:* 3
Net Worth: £19,244,864 *Total Assets:* £21,840,756
Registered Office: 65 High Street, Egham, Surrey, TW20 9EY
Activities: Buying and selling of own real estate
Parent: Audley Court Limited
Officers: Jonathan Martin Austen [1956] Director/Chief Financial Officer; Paul David Morgan [1969] Operations Director; John William Nettleton [1970] Director/Chartered Surveyor; Katherine Elizabeth Rose [1964] Marketing Director; Malcolm Nicholas Sanderson [1959] Director/Property Developer; Kevin Anthony Shaw [1977] Sales Director

Audley Clevedon Limited
Incorporated: 27 October 2005 *Employees:* 1
Net Worth: £2,611,954 *Total Assets:* £9,389,327
Registered Office: 65 High Street, Egham, Surrey, TW20 9EY
Activities: Buying and selling of own real estate
Parent: Audley Court Limited
Officers: Jonathan Martin Austen [1956] Director/Chief Financial Officer; Paul David Morgan [1969] Director/Operations Manager; John William Nettleton [1970] Director/Chartered Surveyor; Katherine Elizabeth Rose [1964] Marketing Director; Malcolm Nicholas Sanderson [1959] Director/Property Developer; Kevin Anthony Shaw [1977] Sales Director

Audley Coopers Hill Limited
Incorporated: 3 May 2016
Net Worth Deficit: £936,335 *Total Assets:* £18,554,176
Registered Office: 65 High Street, Egham, Surrey, TW20 9EY
Activities: Buying and selling of own real estate
Parent: Audley Court Limited
Officers: Jonathan Martin Austen [1956] Director/Chief Financial Officer; Paul David Morgan [1969] Operations Director; John William Nettleton [1970] Director/Chartered Surveyor; Katherine Elizabeth Rose [1964] Marketing Director; Malcolm Nicholas Sanderson [1959] Director/Chief Executive; Kevin Anthony Shaw [1977] Sales Director

Audley Court Limited
Incorporated: 22 June 2004 *Employees:* 373
Net Worth: £145,519,008 *Total Assets:* £292,196,992
Registered Office: 65 High Street, Egham, Surrey, TW20 9EY
Activities: Buying and selling of own real estate
Parent: Audley Group Limited
Officers: Jonathan Martin Austen [1956] Director/Chief Financial Officer; Nicholas William John Edwards [1973] Finance Director; Marc Edward Charles Gilbard [1962] Director/CEO of Private Equity Real Estate Fund Manager; Paul David Morgan [1969] Operations Director; John William Nettleton [1970] Director/Chartered Surveyor; Katherine Elizabeth Rose [1964] Director; Malcolm Nicholas Sanderson [1959] Director/Property Developer; Kevin Anthony Shaw [1977] Sales and Development Director

Audley Ellerslie Limited
Incorporated: 4 July 2012
Previous: Audley Malvern Limited
Net Worth Deficit: £3,587,511 *Total Assets:* £105,353,488
Registered Office: 65 High Street, Egham, Surrey, TW20 9EY
Activities: Buying and selling of own real estate
Parent: Audley Court Limited
Officers: Jonathan Martin Austen [1956] Director/Chief Financial Officer; Paul David Morgan [1969] Operations Director; John William Nettleton [1970] Director/Chartered Surveyor; Katherine Elizabeth Rose [1964] Marketing Director; Malcolm Nicholas Sanderson [1959] Director/Property Developer; Kevin Anthony Shaw [1977] Sales Director

Audley Group Developments 1 Limited
Incorporated: 16 October 2006 *Employees:* 1
Previous: Audley Mote Limited
Net Worth Deficit: £8,785,666 *Total Assets:* £11,518,742
Registered Office: 65 High Street, Egham, Surrey, TW20 9EY
Activities: Buying and selling of own real estate
Parent: Audley Court Limited
Officers: Jonathan Martin Austen [1956] Director/Chief Financial Officer; Paul David Morgan [1969] Operations Director; John William Nettleton [1970] Director/Chartered Surveyor; Katherine Elizabeth Rose [1964] Marketing Director; Malcolm Nicholas Sanderson [1959] Director/Property Developer; Kevin Anthony Shaw [1977] Sales Director

Audley Group Limited
Incorporated: 8 December 2015 *Employees:* 375
Net Worth: £239,752,000 *Total Assets:* £315,832,992
Registered Office: 65 High Street, Egham, Surrey, TW20 9EY
Activities: Activities of other holding companies n.e.c.
Parent: Maref Topco Limited
Officers: Jonathan Martin Austen [1956] Director/Chief Financial Officer; Michael Bruhn [1959] Director [Danish]; Nicholas William John Edwards [1973] Director; Marc Edward Charles Gilbard [1962] Director; Paul David Morgan [1969] Director; Malcolm Nicholas Sanderson [1959] Director; Kevin Anthony Shaw [1977] Director

Audley Inglewood Limited
Incorporated: 15 September 2005 *Employees:* 2
Net Worth: £3,804,567 *Total Assets:* £12,914,817
Registered Office: 65 High Street, Egham, Surrey, TW20 9EY
Activities: Buying and selling of own real estate
Parent: Audley Court Limited
Officers: Jonathan Martin Austen [1956] Director/Chief Financial Officer; Paul David Morgan [1969] Operations Director; John William Nettleton [1970] Director/Chartered Surveyor; Katherine Elizabeth Rose [1964] Marketing Director; Malcolm Nicholas Sanderson [1959] Director/Property Developer; Kevin Anthony Shaw [1977] Sales Director

Audley St Elphins Limited
Incorporated: 31 May 2005 *Employees:* 2
Net Worth Deficit: £3,132,867 *Total Assets:* £19,190,188
Registered Office: 65 High Street, Egham, Surrey, TW20 9EY
Activities: Buying and selling of own real estate
Parent: Audley Court Limited
Officers: Jonathan Martin Austen [1956] Director/Chief Financial Officer; Paul David Morgan [1969] Operations Director; John William Nettleton [1970] Director/Chartered Surveyor; Katherine Elizabeth Rose [1964] Marketing Director; Malcolm Nicholas Sanderson [1959] Director/Property Developer; Kevin Anthony Shaw [1977] Sales Director

Audley St George's Limited
Incorporated: 19 September 2007
Previous: Audley Edgbaston Limited
Net Worth Deficit: £1,314,224 *Total Assets:* £28,262,548
Registered Office: 65 High Street, Egham, Surrey, TW20 9EY
Activities: Buying and selling of own real estate
Parent: Audley Court Limited
Officers: Jonathan Martin Austen [1956] Director/Chief Financial Officer; Paul David Morgan [1969] Operations Director; John William Nettleton [1970] Director/Chartered Surveyor; Katherine Elizabeth Rose [1964] Marketing Director; Malcolm Nicholas Sanderson [1959] Director/Property Developer; Kevin Anthony Shaw [1977] Sales Director

Audley Stanbridge Earls Limited
Incorporated: 11 January 2016 *Employees:* 3
Net Worth Deficit: £1,123,614 *Total Assets:* £15,561,105
Registered Office: 65 High Street, Egham, Surrey, TW20 9EY
Activities: Buying and selling of own real estate
Parent: Audley Court Limited
Officers: Jonathan Martin Austen [1956] Director/Chief Financial Officer; Paul David Morgan [1969] Operations Director; John William Nettleton [1970] Director/Chartered Surveyor; Katherine Elizabeth Rose [1964] Marketing Director; Malcolm Nicholas Sanderson [1959] Director/Chief Executive; Kevin Anthony Shaw [1977] Sales Director

Audley Willicombe Limited
Incorporated: 22 February 2001
Net Worth: £4,712,957 *Total Assets:* £8,173,247
Registered Office: 65 High Street, Egham, Surrey, TW20 9EY
Activities: Management of real estate on a fee or contract basis
Parent: Audley Court Limited
Officers: Jonathan Martin Austen [1956] Director/Chief Financial Officer; Paul David Morgan [1969] Operations Director; John William Nettleton [1970] Director/Chartered Surveyor; Katherine Elizabeth Rose [1964] Marketing Director; Malcolm Nicholas Sanderson [1959] Director/Property Developer; Kevin Anthony Shaw [1977] Sales Director

Augustus 1 Limited
Incorporated: 23 August 2004
Net Worth: £30,824,000 *Total Assets:* £325,528,992
Registered Office: 8th Floor, Vantage London, Great West Road, Brentford, Middlesex, TW8 9AG
Activities: Activities of other holding companies n.e.c.
Parent: Crown UK Holdco Limited
Officers: Fiona Elizabeth Smith, Secretary; Nisan Cohen [1972] Director [Israeli]; Israel Greidinger [1961] Director/Cinema Proprietor [Israeli]; Shaun Alan Jones [1970] Director; Nir Lion [1981] Director [Israeli]

Augustus 2 Limited
Incorporated: 26 August 2004
Net Worth: £108,211,000 *Total Assets:* £671,014,016
Registered Office: 8th Floor, Vantage London, Great West Road, Brentford, Middlesex, TW8 9AG
Activities: Activities of other holding companies n.e.c.
Parent: Augustus 1 Limited
Officers: Fiona Elizabeth Smith, Secretary; Nisan Cohen [1972] Director [Israeli]; Israel Greidinger [1961] Director/Cinema Proprietor [Israeli]; Shaun Alan Jones [1970] Director; Nir Lion [1981] Director [Israeli]

Aunt Bessie's Limited
Incorporated: 12 April 2000 *Employees:* 393
Net Worth: £36,243,000 *Total Assets:* £63,495,000
Registered Office: 1 New Square, Feltham, Middlesex, TW14 8HA
Activities: Manufacture of other food products n.e.c.
Parent: Nomad Foods Europe Limited
Officers: Edward John Heaton Marriott, Secretary; Wayne Brian Hudson [1964] Director; Sarah Pollard [1974] Finance Director

Aura Finance (Holdco) Limited
Incorporated: 11 February 2014 *Employees:* 3
Net Worth: £3,274,523 *Total Assets:* £17,024,372
Registered Office: 3rd Floor, Premiere House, Elstree Way, Borehamwood, Herts, WD6 1JH
Activities: Credit granting by non-deposit taking finance houses and other specialist consumer credit grantors
Parent: January Loan Services Limited
Officers: Emily Henrietta Gestetner [1967] Director; Harry Leon Landy [1978] Director; Danny Stephen Waters [1984] Director

Aura Finance Limited
Incorporated: 11 December 2012 *Employees:* 4
Net Worth: £29,113,396 *Total Assets:* £234,196,032
Registered Office: 3rd Floor, Premiere House, Elstree Way, Borehamwood, Herts, WD6 1JH
Activities: Other business support service activities n.e.c.
Parent: Aura Finance (Holdco) Limited
Officers: Emily Henrietta Gestetner [1967] Director; David Stewart [1965] Director; Stephen Bryan Wasserman [1984] Director; Danny Stephen Waters [1984] Director

Aurient Investments Limited
Incorporated: 16 June 1998
Net Worth: £19,288,732 *Total Assets:* £36,616,536
Registered Office: 1st Floor, Argyle House, South Entrance, Joel Street, Northwood Hills, Northwood, Middlesex, HA6 1NW
Activities: Buying and selling of own real estate
Parent: Milestone Properties UK Limited
Officers: Menal Mahendra Mehta, Secretary; Menal Mahendra Mehta [1972] Director/Businessman; Richard Lewis Whitehorn [1950] Director/Property Consultant

Aurient Investments N16 Ltd
Incorporated: 4 February 2009
Net Worth: £3,740,346 *Total Assets:* £14,177,548
Registered Office: 1st Floor, Argyle House, South Entrance, Joel Street, Northwood Hills, Northwood, Middlesex, HA6 1NW
Activities: Other letting and operating of own or leased real estate
Parent: Aurient Investments Ltd
Officers: Menal Mahendra Mehta [1972] Director; Richard Lewis Whitehorn [1950] Director/Surveyor

Charles Austen Pumps Limited
Incorporated: 21 January 1957 *Employees:* 75
Net Worth: £8,323,824 *Total Assets:* £12,761,155
Registered Office: 100 Royston Road, Byfleet, Weybridge, Surrey, KT14 7NY
Activities: Manufacture of pumps
Shareholder: William Eric Shepherd
Officers: William Eric Shepherd, Secretary; Paula Jane Shepherd [1966] Director/Engineer; William Eric Shepherd [1956] Director/Engineer

Austin (GB) Limited
Incorporated: 15 December 2005 *Employees:* 37
Net Worth: £2,413,422 *Total Assets:* £8,778,846
Registered Office: Cardinal Point, Park Road, Rickmansworth, Herts, WD3 1RE
Activities: Construction of commercial buildings
Major Shareholder: Sunita Davda
Officers: Prakash Chandra Jayantilal Davda [1960] Director; Adrian Thomas Ward [1963] Director/Senior Project Construction Manager

Austin Company of (U.K.) Limited (The)
Incorporated: 17 August 1938 *Employees:* 36
Net Worth: £1,015,786 *Total Assets:* £7,391,204
Registered Office: Cardinal Point, Park Road, Rickmansworth, Herts, WD3 1RE
Activities: Construction of commercial buildings
Officers: Prakash Chandra Jayantilal Davda [1960] Managing Director

Automated Technology Group Holdings Limited
Incorporated: 5 December 2011 *Employees:* 5
Net Worth: £8,866,000 *Total Assets:* £9,500,000
Registered Office: Compass Point, Kingston Road, Staines upon Thames, Middlesex, TW18 1DT
Activities: Activities of head offices
Parent: Wood Group Engineering & Operations Support Limited
Officers: Iain Angus Jones, Secretary; William Saxon Greenhalgh [1956] Director/Accountant; Leslie John Hinder [1956] Director; Andrew Robinson [1968] Director; William George Setter [1975] Director

The Automated Technology Group Limited
Incorporated: 3 October 1995 *Employees:* 261
Net Worth: £10,866,000 *Total Assets:* £22,882,000
Registered Office: Compass Point, Kingston Road, Staines upon Thames, Middlesex, TW18 1DT
Activities: Manufacture of electricity distribution and control apparatus
Parent: Automated Technology Group Holdings Limited
Officers: Iain Angus Jones, Secretary; Darren Ashford [1966] Installations Director; Nigel Brookes [1962] Sales Director; Ian Paul Farmer [1969] Technical Director; Leslie John Hinder [1956] Director; Simon Litchfield [1967] Operations Director; Andrew Robinson [1968] Director

Automatic Data Processing Limited
Incorporated: 11 March 1969 *Employees:* 651
Net Worth: £13,556,000 *Total Assets:* £701,867,008
Registered Office: Syward Place, Pyrcroft Road, Chertsey, Surrey, KT16 9JT
Activities: Other information technology service activities
Parent: ADP Network Services Limited
Officers: Peter Hadley [1972] Director; Jeffrey Lewis Phipps [1968] Managing Director; Lorna Wake [1976] Director/Accountant

Automatic Sales Limited
Incorporated: 27 October 1980
Net Worth: £2,787,154 *Total Assets:* £11,771,722
Registered Office: Heath House, West Drayton Road, Hillingdon, Middlesex, UB8 3LA
Activities: Other service activities n.e.c.
Officers: Balbinder Kaur Takhar, Secretary; Balbinder Kaur Takhar [1961] Director; Gurmeet Kaur Takhar [1934] Director; Ravinder Singh Takhar [1956] Director/Businessman

Autosport Media UK Ltd
Incorporated: 9 August 2016 *Employees:* 103
Net Worth Deficit: £3,019,014 *Total Assets:* £23,229,918
Registered Office: 1 Eton Street, Richmond, Surrey, TW9 1EF
Activities: Publishing of consumer and business journals and periodicals
Parent: Autosport.Com, LLC
Officers: Timothy Keith Chadwick, Secretary; Yura V Barabash [1974] Director [American]

Avalon Cellars Two Limited
Incorporated: 10 January 2007
Net Worth: £38,473,000 *Total Assets:* £132,179,000
Registered Office: Thomas Hardy House, 2 Heath Road, Weybridge, Surrey, KT13 8TB
Activities: Activities of head offices
Parent: Accolade Wines Europe No. 2 Limited
Officers: Anthony Graham Wood, Secretary; Adrian Francis McKeon [1963] Regional Managing Director, UKIR; Andrew Peter Smith [1974] Director/Accountant; Anthony Graham Wood [1975] Director/Financial Controller [Australian]

Avamore Limited
Incorporated: 13 September 2006 *Employees:* 10
Net Worth: £4,734,240 *Total Assets:* £22,756,118
Registered Office: 1st Floor, 44-50 The Broadway, Southall, Middlesex, UB1 1QB
Activities: Buying and selling of own real estate
Major Shareholder: Sant Ram Ghai
Officers: Sant Ram Ghai [1966] Director/Businessman

Avanti Schools Trust
Incorporated: 26 January 2011 *Employees:* 323
Net Worth: £51,890,000 *Total Assets:* £56,126,000
Registered Office: Avanti House Secondary School, Wemborough Road, Stanmore, Middlesex, HA7 2EQ
Activities: Pre-primary education
Officers: Shamita Kumar, Secretary; Dr James William Biddulph [1976] Director/Headteacher; Gerard Vincent Irwin Davis [1948] Director/Retired (Local Government Officer); Vijay Doshi [1967] Director of Finance; Nitesh Bipinchandra Gor [1975] Director/Consultant; Mayurkumar Parsuram Manibhai Patel [1959] Director/Solicitor; Dr Krutika Pau [1961] Director/Children's Services Consultant; Kumar Sureshchandra Raval [1971] Director and Founder, Faith in Leadership; Bavaani Vadivale-Nanthabalan [1957] Director/Executive Headteacher [Singaporean]; Dr Molly Jane Warrington [1949] Director/Retired University Lecturer; Michael Robert Younger [1948] Director/Retired University Professor

Avantia Insurance Limited
Incorporated: 21 October 2002 *Employees:* 122
Net Worth: £14,579,135 *Total Assets:* £21,327,480
Registered Office: Avantia House, 29 Thames Street, Kingston upon Thames, Surrey, KT1 1PH
Activities: Activities of insurance agents and brokers
Parent: Avantia Limited
Officers: Mark Robert Eastham [1972] Director; Daniel Philip Huddart [1982] Director; Shahid Mahmood [1969] Director; Jason Paschalides [1972] Director/Chief Underwriting Officer; Richard Wilson [1975] Director/Chief Commercial Officer

Avantia Limited
Incorporated: 6 August 1999
Net Worth: £6,902,784 *Total Assets:* £7,194,730
Registered Office: Avantia House, 29 Thames Street, Kingston upon Thames, Surrey, KT1 1PH
Activities: Non-trading company
Parent: Kingston Bidco Limited
Officers: Mark Eastham [1972] Director; Shahid Mahmood [1969] Director

Avantis Hotels Limited
Incorporated: 1 March 2001 *Employees:* 23
Net Worth: £4,383,004 *Total Assets:* £7,667,786
Registered Office: Sunmil House, Northgate, Northwood, Middlesex, HA6 2TH
Activities: Hotels and similar accommodation
Officers: Annette Majithia, Secretary; Kishor Majithia [1950] Director; Mukesh Chatrabhuj Majithia [1954] Director; Rajnikant Chatrabhuj Majithia [1952] Director

The Avenues Trust Group
Incorporated: 9 July 1999 *Employees:* 1,812
Net Worth: £7,228,000 *Total Assets:* £19,249,000
Registered Office: River House, 1 Maidstone Road, Sidcup, Kent, DA14 5TA
Activities: Other human health activities
Officers: Lauren Osman, Secretary; Andrew Bruce Calderwood [1954] Director/Retired Civil Servant; Janet Elaine Coltman [1956] Director/Homemaker; Nicola Ford [1980] Finance Director; Evlynne Gilvarry [1957] Director/Senior Executive Manager [Irish]; Jeffrey Robin Gritzman [1951] Director/Retired; Lynne Margaret Holmes [1957] Human Resources Director; Stephen Paul James [1955] Director/Group Chief Executive; Helen Sarah Louise John [1965] Director/Chartered Accountant; Joanne Land [1961] Group Director of Organisational Development; Alistair Oag [1952] Director/Certified Chartered Accountant; Terence Andrew Rich [1953] Director/Consultant; Peter Snelling [1958] Group Director of Operations

Aviation Business Continuity Limited
Incorporated: 18 October 2007 *Employees:* 42
Net Worth: £2,390,485 *Total Assets:* £9,301,021
Registered Office: The Mill Heathrow, Horton Road, Stanmoor, Staines upon Thames, Middlesex, TW19 6BJ
Activities: Service activities incidental to air transportation
Major Shareholder: Grant Thompson
Officers: Peter Jones, Secretary; Grant David Thompson [1967] Director/Management Consultant

Aviation Servicing Company Ltd
Incorporated: 15 May 2008 *Employees:* 70
Previous: Azerbaijan Airlines UK Limited
Net Worth Deficit: £3,552,258 *Total Assets:* £6,647,946
Registered Office: Building 582, Sandringham Road, London Heathrow Airport, Hounslow, Middlesex, TW6 3SN
Activities: Cargo handling for air transport activities
Major Shareholder: Ignazio Coraci
Officers: Ignazio Coraci, Secretary; Ignazio Coraci [1980] Director [Italian]

Avicenna Holdings Ltd
Incorporated: 24 August 1994 *Employees:* 198
Previous: Avicenna Holdings PLC
Net Worth: £25,888,000 *Total Assets:* £41,143,000
Registered Office: Selsdon House, 212-220 Addington Road, South Croydon, Surrey, CR2 8LD
Activities: Dispensing chemist in specialised stores
Officers: Anita Larsen, Secretary; Ian Archie Gray [1953] Director; Shiraz Kassam Hirji [1947] Director; Salim Kassamali Esmail Jetha [1953] Director/Pharmacist

AVM Impact Ltd
Incorporated: 8 February 1990 *Employees:* 382
Net Worth: £5,075,000 *Total Assets:* £25,368,000
Registered Office: Europe House, 170 Windmill Road, Sunbury on Thames, Middlesex, TW16 7HB
Activities: Other professional, scientific and technical activities n.e.c.
Parent: AVM Limited
Officers: John Allen, Secretary; John Allen [1961] Director; Edward Charles Peregrine Phelps Cook [1967] Director

AVM Vision Investments Ltd
Incorporated: 20 March 2012 *Employees:* 4
Net Worth Deficit: £7,640,000 *Total Assets:* £17,005,000
Registered Office: Europe House, Windmill Road, Sunbury on Thames, Middlesex, TW16 7HB
Activities: Activities of head offices
Parent: AVMI Group Ltd
Officers: John Allen [1961] Director; Edward Charles Peregrine Phelps Cook [1967] Director; Adrian Paul Lurie [1973] Director/Investment Management; Nick Richard Motum Seaman [1981] Director/Investment Professional

AVMI Group Limited
Incorporated: 20 March 2012 *Employees:* 414
Net Worth Deficit: £11,375,000 *Total Assets:* £40,075,000
Registered Office: Europe House, Windmill Road, Sunbury on Thames, Middlesex, TW16 7HB
Activities: Activities of head offices
Officers: John Allen [1961] Director; Edward Charles Peregrine Phelps Cook [1967] Director; Adrian Paul Lurie [1973] Director/Investment Management; Nick Richard Motum Seaman [1981] Director/Investment Professional

Avocado Developments Limited
Incorporated: 6 February 2007
Net Worth: £6,088,453 *Total Assets:* £20,517,598
Registered Office: Kimberley House, 31 Burnt Oak Broadway, Edgware, Middlesex, HA8 5LD
Activities: Development of building projects
Officers: Harish Keshra Halai [1971] Director; Shital Mansukhlal Haria [1971] Director; Bipin Mohanlal Shah [1958] Director/Certified Chartered Accountant; Hiren Hasmukh Shah [1979] Director/Certified Chartered Accountant

Avocado Developments Wealdstone Limited
Incorporated: 15 May 2017
Net Worth Deficit: £16,825 *Total Assets:* £5,420,805
Registered Office: Kimberley House, 31 Burnt Oak Broadway, Edgware, Middlesex, HA8 5LD
Activities: Development of building projects
Parent: Avocado Developments Limited
Officers: Harish Keshra Halai [1971] Director; Shital Mansukhlal Haria [1971] Director; Bipin Mohanlal Shah [1958] Director; Hiren Hasmukh Shah [1979] Director

Avon Estates (London) Limited
Incorporated: 19 May 1995
Net Worth: £6,745,353 *Total Assets:* £9,606,368
Registered Office: 88 Edgware Way, Edgware, Middlesex, HA8 8JS
Activities: Buying and selling of own real estate
Shareholder: Israel Moskovitz
Officers: Israel Moskovitz, Secretary [Canadian]; Chavi Moskovitz [1964] Director/Housewife

Avon Freeholds Limited
Incorporated: 7 October 2010
Net Worth: £6,977,019 *Total Assets:* £12,934,297
Registered Office: 88 Edgware Way, Edgware, Middlesex, HA8 8JS
Activities: Other letting and operating of own or leased real estate
Officers: Chavi Moskovitz, Secretary; Israel Moskovitz [1964] Director [Canadian]

Avon Lake Holdings Limited
Incorporated: 28 July 2015
Net Worth Deficit: £152,774 *Total Assets:* £6,902,850
Registered Office: 1 Beauchamp Court, 10 Victors Way, Barnet, Herts, EN5 5TZ
Activities: Management of real estate on a fee or contract basis
Major Shareholder: Munundev Gunputh
Officers: Devika Gunputh, Secretary; Devika Gunputh [1957] Director [Mauritian]; Munundev Gunputh [1958] Director [Mauritian]

Avonpark Village (Care Homes) Limited
Incorporated: 11 January 2010 *Employees:* 53
Net Worth: £1,061,582 *Total Assets:* £14,721,223
Registered Office: 1st Floor, Brunswick House, Regent Park, 297-299 Kingston Road, Leatherhead, Surrey, KT22 7LU
Activities: Other business support service activities n.e.c.
Parent: Retirement Villages Group Limited
Officers: Sally Irene Rees, Secretary; Sarah Denise Burgess [1971] Director; Neil Donaldson [1966] Director/Accountant; Andrew George Esmond Ovey [1971] Director/Investment Manager

Axcel Hospitality (Manchester) Limited
Incorporated: 5 August 2015 *Employees:* 1
Net Worth Deficit: £582,329 *Total Assets:* £11,558,945
Registered Office: 2nd Floor, 29 Dingwall Road, Croydon, Surrey, CR0 2NB
Activities: Hotels and similar accommodation
Parent: Axcel Group Limited
Officers: Shamir Patel [1970] Director; Sunil Patel [1968] Director

Axcorp Limited
Incorporated: 30 December 2015
Net Worth Deficit: £3,989 *Total Assets:* £10,005,154
Registered Office: 36 South Approach, Northwood, Middlesex, HA6 2ET
Activities: Management consultancy activities other than financial management
Major Shareholder: Derrick Williams
Officers: Derrick Alexander Williams [1963] Director

Axiom Education (Edinburgh) Holdings Limited
Incorporated: 15 September 2006
Net Worth: £27,617,000 *Total Assets:* £37,823,000
Registered Office: c/o Galliford Try PLC, Cowley Business Park, Cowley, Uxbridge, Middlesex, UB8 2AL
Activities: Activities of other holding companies n.e.c.
Parent: Zealburg Holdings Limited
Officers: Mark Geoffrey David Holden [1957] Director; Natalia Poupard [1977] Investment Director

Axiom Education (Edinburgh) Limited
Incorporated: 28 November 2006
Net Worth Deficit: £53,286,000 *Total Assets:* £171,948,992
Registered Office: Cowley Business Park, Cowley, Uxbridge, Middlesex, UB8 2AL
Activities: Management of real estate on a fee or contract basis
Parent: Axiom Education (Edinburgh) Holdings Limited
Officers: Mark Geoffrey David Holden [1957] Director; Natalia Poupard [1977] Investment Director

Axiom Education (Perth & Kinross) Holdings Limited
Incorporated: 28 July 2005
Net Worth: £16,860,000 *Total Assets:* £25,549,000
Registered Office: Cowley Business Park, Cowley, Uxbridge, Middlesex, UB8 2AL
Activities: Activities of other holding companies n.e.c.
Parent: Yorker Holdings PKR Limited
Officers: Mark Geoffrey David Holden [1957] Director; Natalia Poupard [1977] Investment Director

Axiom Education (Perth & Kinross) Limited
Incorporated: 4 August 2005
Net Worth Deficit: £84,243,000 *Total Assets:* £153,326,000
Registered Office: c/o Galliford Try PLC, Cowley Business Park, Cowley, Uxbridge, Middlesex, UB8 2AL
Activities: Management of real estate on a fee or contract basis
Parent: Axiom Education (Perth & Kinross) Holdings Limited
Officers: Mark Geoffrey David Holden [1957] Director; Natalia Poupard [1977] Investment Director

Axiom Wealth Management Limited
Incorporated: 13 May 1999
Net Worth: £4,456,494 *Total Assets:* £6,036,983
Registered Office: 3rd Floor Northside, Argyle House, Joel Street, Northwood Hills, Northwood, Middlesex, HA6 1NW
Activities: Security and commodity contracts dealing activities
Major Shareholder: Paulspencer Courtney
Officers: Paul Spencer Courtney [1967] Director/Financial

Axis Cleaning and Support Services Limited
Incorporated: 21 February 1985 *Employees:* 603
Net Worth Deficit: £1,293,000 *Total Assets:* £8,939,000
Registered Office: Ground Floor Suite, River House, Maidstone Road, Sidcup, Kent, DA14 5RH
Activities: General cleaning of buildings
Officers: Simon Kenneth Giles, Secretary; Simon Kenneth Giles [1974] Finance Director; Jonathan Stephen Levine [1952] Director/Chief Executive Officer

Axis Group Integrated Services Limited
Incorporated: 24 September 2015 *Employees:* 2,683
Net Worth: £5,431,000 *Total Assets:* £25,680,000
Registered Office: Ground Floor Suite, River House, Maidstone Road, Sidcup, Kent, DA14 5RH
Activities: Other business support service activities n.e.c.
Shareholder: Jonathan Stephen Levine
Officers: Roger Leonard Burdett [1950] Director; Simon Kenneth Giles [1974] Finance Director; Jonathan Stephen Levine [1952] Director/Chief Executive Officer; David John Mundell [1957] Director

Axis Security Services Limited
Incorporated: 27 May 1994 *Employees:* 2,028
Net Worth: £3,067,000 *Total Assets:* £19,099,000
Registered Office: Ground Floor Suite, River House, Maidstone Road, Sidcup, Kent, DA14 5RH
Activities: Security systems service activities
Officers: Simon Kenneth Giles, Secretary; Simon Kenneth Giles [1974] Finance Director; Jonathan Stephen Levine [1952] Director; David John Mundell [1957] Director

Axon Group Limited
Incorporated: 14 August 1997 *Employees:* 5
Net Worth: £199,672,000 *Total Assets:* £199,728,000
Registered Office: Axoncentre, Church Road, Egham, Surrey, TW20 9QB
Activities: Activities of head offices
Parent: HCL EAS Ltd
Officers: Manish Anand [1968] Director [Indian]; Prahlad Rai Bansal [1957] Director/Service [Indian]; Ajit Krishnan Kutty Kumar [1964] Director [Indian]; Rahul Singh [1963] Director [Indian]; Shiv Kumar Walia [1969] Director [Australian]

Axon Solutions Limited
Incorporated: 7 October 1994 *Employees:* 497
Net Worth: £36,359,000 *Total Assets:* £62,234,000
Registered Office: Axon Centre, Church Road, Egham, Surrey, TW20 9QB
Activities: Information technology consultancy activities
Parent: Axon Group Limited
Officers: Manish Anand [1968] Director [Indian]; Subramanian Gopalakrishnan [1967] Director [Indian]; Ajit Krishnan Kutty Kumar [1964] Director [Indian]; Rahul Singh [1963] Director [Indian]; Shiv Kumar Walia [1969] Director [Australian]

Aylesbury Vale Parkway Limited
Incorporated: 8 June 2006
Net Worth: £1,782,000 *Total Assets:* £9,596,000
Registered Office: 8 White Oak Square, London Road, Swanley, Kent, BR8 7AG
Activities: Construction of commercial buildings
Parent: JLIF Holdings (Avp & C) Limited
Officers: Julian Denzil Sutcliffe [1968] Life Cycle Asset Director; Neil Woodburn [1979] Director/Chartered Building Surveyor

Aylmer Road Limited
Incorporated: 3 July 2015
Net Worth Deficit: £52,943 *Total Assets:* £8,935,402
Registered Office: C K R House, 70 East Hill, Dartford, Kent, DA1 1RZ
Activities: Buying and selling of own real estate
Shareholders: Grahame Donald Crisp Seaman; Permjit Singh Sulh; Giles William Underhill
Officers: Grahame Donald Crisp Seaman [1946] Director/Property Developer; Permjit Singh Sulh [1968] Director/Property Developer; Giles William Underhill [1964] Director/Property Developer

Azurie Blue Limited
Incorporated: 26 October 2011 *Employees:* 4
Net Worth: £4,714,171 *Total Assets:* £17,652,464
Registered Office: Enterprise House, Beesons Yard, Bury Lane, Rickmansworth, Herts, WD3 1DS
Activities: Other business support service activities n.e.c.
Officers: Dominique Elisabeth Jacqueline Sharpe [1953] Director [French]; Edward Adrian Sharpe [1975] Director/Solicitor; Georgina Alexandra Sharpe [1978] Director; William John Ashdown Sharpe [1947] Director

B & A Group Liverpool Street Limited
Incorporated: 22 January 2016 *Employees:* 1
Net Worth: £3,723,386 *Total Assets:* £5,040,265
Registered Office: The Retreat, 406 Roding Lane South, Woodford Green, Essex, IG8 8EY
Activities: Other business support service activities n.e.c.
Officers: Sati Simon Riahi [1967] Clinical Director [British/Iranian]

B & H Worldwide (Holdings) Limited
Incorporated: 18 March 1988 *Employees:* 141
Net Worth: £5,843,063 *Total Assets:* £10,569,838
Registered Office: 1 Saxon Way Trading Estate, Harmondsworth, West Drayton, Middlesex, UB7 0LW
Activities: Scheduled passenger air transport
Major Shareholder: Stuart David Allen
Officers: Stuart David Allen [1969] Director; Seth Zachary Profit [1978] Director [American]; Paul David Wakefield [1972] Director; Gary James Wilson [1962] Director/Accountant

B & P Acquisitionco Limited
Incorporated: 19 September 2007 *Employees:* 3
Net Worth Deficit: £19,906,980 *Total Assets:* £66,913,632
Registered Office: Burnham Road, Dartford, Kent, DA1 5BD
Activities: Activities of other holding companies n.e.c.
Parent: B & P Midco Limited
Officers: Ivo Vesselinov, Secretary; Andrew Hodgson [1965] Director; Romain Jean Patrick Prouvost [1979] Director [French]; Ivo Vesselinov [1976] Financial Director

B & P Buyco Limited
Incorporated: 16 August 2016 *Employees:* 3
Net Worth: £475,817 *Total Assets:* £73,912,480
Registered Office: Burnham Road, Sandpit Road, Dartford, Kent, DA1 5BD
Activities: Activities of venture and development capital companies
Parent: Graphite Capital Management LLP
Officers: Andrew Hodgson [1965] Director; Romain Jean Patrick Prouvost [1979] Director [French]; Ivo Vesselinov [1976] Finance Director

B & P Holdings II Limited
Incorporated: 15 August 2007 *Employees:* 4
Previous: Beck & Pollitzer Limited
Net Worth: £481,003 *Total Assets:* £52,587,844
Registered Office: Burnham Road, Dartford, Kent, DA1 5BD
Activities: Activities of other holding companies n.e.c.
Parent: Burgundy Buyco Limited
Officers: Ivo Vesselinov, Secretary; Andrew Hodgson [1965] Director; Janusz Lach [1963] Director [Polish]; Romain Jean Patrick Prouvost [1979] Director [French]; Ivo Vesselinov [1976] Finance Director

B & P Midco 1 Limited
Incorporated: 2 September 2016 *Employees:* 3
Net Worth Deficit: £1,491,461 *Total Assets:* £46,345,424
Registered Office: Burnham Road, Sandpit Road, Dartford, Kent, DA1 5BD
Activities: Activities of venture and development capital companies
Parent: Graphite Capital Management LLP
Officers: Andrew Hodgson [1965] Director; Romain Jean Patrick Prouvost [1979] Director [French]; Ivo Vesselinov [1976] Finance Director

B & P Midco 2 Limited
Incorporated: 2 September 2016
Net Worth: £1,869,913 *Total Assets:* £44,345,424
Registered Office: Burnham Road, Sandpit Road, Dartford, Kent, DA1 5BD
Activities: Activities of venture and development capital companies
Parent: Graphite Capital Management LLP
Officers: Andrew Hodgson [1965] Director; Romain Jean Patrick Prouvost [1979] Director [French]; Ivo Vesselinov [1976] Finance Director

B & P Midco Limited
Incorporated: 15 August 2007 *Employees:* 3
Net Worth: £657,280 *Total Assets:* £36,868,316
Registered Office: Burnham Road, Dartford, Kent, DA1 5BD
Activities: Activities of other holding companies n.e.c.
Officers: Ivo Vesselinov, Secretary; Andrew Hodgson [1965] Director; Romain Jean Patrick Prouvost [1979] Director [French]; Ivo Vesselinov [1976] Finance Director

B & T Plant Hire Limited
Incorporated: 8 January 1992 *Employees:* 39
Net Worth: £16,370,529 *Total Assets:* £27,256,760
Registered Office: O'Brien House, 197-199 Garth Road, Morden, Surrey, SM4 4NE
Activities: Other specialised construction activities n.e.c.
Parent: OHOB Group Ltd
Officers: Colin David Southey, Secretary; Thomas Jason O'Brien [1976] Director/Company Manager; Thomas Francis O'Brien [1947] Director/Builder [Irish]; Colin David Southey [1959] Director

B Crystal Limited
Incorporated: 13 March 2013
Net Worth: £4,528,279 *Total Assets:* £11,756,635
Registered Office: Portland House, 69-71 Wembley Hill Road, Wembley, Middlesex, HA9 8BU
Activities: Sea and coastal freight water transport
Parent: Union Maritime Limited
Officers: Bhupendra Shantilal Kansagra, Secretary; Laurent Elie Cadji [1977] Director/Businessman; Lewis Levy Cadji [1938] Director/Businessman; Bhupendra Shantilal Kansagra [1956] Director/Businessman; Ramesh Shantilal Kansagra [1950] Director/Businessman

B Emerald Limited
Incorporated: 13 March 2013
Net Worth: £5,434,628 *Total Assets:* £14,568,722
Registered Office: Portland House, 69-71 Wembley Hill Road, Wembley, Middlesex, HA9 8BU
Activities: Sea and coastal freight water transport
Parent: Union Maritime Limited
Officers: Bhupendra Shantilal Kansagra, Secretary; Laurent Elie Cadji [1977] Director/Businessman; Lewis Levy Cadji [1938] Director/Businessman; Bhupendra Shantilal Kansagra [1956] Director/Businessman; Ramesh Shantilal Kansagra [1950] Director/Businessman

B F Design Solutions Limited
Incorporated: 8 August 2011
Net Worth: £1,105,575 *Total Assets:* £5,186,796
Registered Office: 1 Beauchamp Court, 10 Victors Way, Barnet, Herts, EN5 5TZ
Activities: Other business support service activities n.e.c.
Shareholders: Gordon William Bell; Tristan Dominic Frampton
Officers: Tristan Frampton, Secretary; Gordon William Bell [1956] Director; Tristan Dominic Frampton [1966] Director

B K S Energy Limited
Incorporated: 5 November 2010
Net Worth: £662,000 *Total Assets:* £6,875,000
Registered Office: Beaufort Court, Egg Farm Lane, Kings Langley, Herts, WD4 8LR
Activities: Production of electricity
Parent: European Investments Solar Holdings 2 Limited
Officers: Dominic James Hearth, Secretary; Steven William Hughes [1972] Global Support Services Director, UK&I - Commercial; Mitesh Raj Patel [1982] Director/Group Financial Controller; Tracy Jane Scott [1976] Director/Delivery Project Manager - New Technologies UK&I; Mark Christopher Wayment [1958] Director

B.A.T.S. Ilford Limited
Incorporated: 1 September 2006 *Employees:* 2
Net Worth: £10,762,027 *Total Assets:* £16,373,346
Registered Office: 48 Westmoreland Avenue, Hornchurch, Essex, RM11 2EE
Activities: Other letting and operating of own or leased real estate
Parent: BATS Holdings Limited
Officers: Maria Bernadette Seaton, Secretary; Spencer Brian Seaton [1962] Director

BA and AA Holdings Limited
Incorporated: 13 September 1999
Net Worth: £119,286,808 *Total Assets:* £119,417,072
Registered Office: British Airways PLC, P O Box 365, Waterside, Harmondsworth, West Drayton, Middlesex, UB7 0GB
Activities: Activities of head offices
Parent: British Airways PLC
Officers: Luke Alexander Michael Straver, Secretary; Andrew Ian Fleming [1979] Director/Company Secretary; Simon Philcox [1979] Director/Accountant

BA Cityflyer Limited
Incorporated: 2 January 1991 *Employees:* 538
Net Worth: £61,009,000 *Total Assets:* £346,233,984
Registered Office: P O Box 365, Waterside, Harmondsworth, West Drayton, Middlesex, UB7 0GB
Activities: Scheduled passenger air transport
Parent: British Airways PLC
Officers: Katie Louise Bishop, Secretary; Neil Alan Chernoff [1973] Director [American]; Colm Leo Lacy [1970] Director/Airline Executive [Irish]; Rebecca Louise Napier [1980] Director/Accountant; Thomas David Stoddart [1979] Director/Airline Manager

Babcock Wanson UK Limited
Incorporated: 6 November 1956 *Employees:* 59
Net Worth: £2,238,000 *Total Assets:* £7,170,000
Registered Office: 7 Elstree Way, Borehamwood, Herts, WD6 1SA
Activities: Other manufacturing n.e.c.
Officers: Carole Anne Humphreys, Secretary; Patrick Richard Brunet [1969] Director [French]; Cyrille Marie-Francois Fournier-Montgieux [1965] Managing Director [French]; Christopher Horsley [1959] Director/Engineer

Babington House School Limited
Incorporated: 1 September 1958 *Employees:* 91
Net Worth: £4,157,757 *Total Assets:* £7,209,231
Registered Office: Babington House School, Grange Drive, Chislehurst, Kent, BR7 5ES
Activities: Primary education
Officers: Nicola Georgina Howard [1975] Director/Investment Banker; William James Magill [1950] Director/Retired; Hayley Jane Porter-Aslet [1980] Finance Director; Steven Thompson [1956] Director/Quantity Surveyor; Christopher Lloyd Turner [1953] Director/Management Consultant; Justin Turner [1981] Director/Head of IT

Baby Network Limited
Incorporated: 28 February 2005 *Employees:* 15
Net Worth: £11,470,030 *Total Assets:* £17,236,060
Registered Office: 5 Elstree Gate, Elstree Way, Borehamwood, Herts, WD6 1JD
Activities: Video production activities
Parent: Twenty-First Century Fox, Inc.
Officers: Kathryn Frances Fink [1966] Director [Australian]; Jan Koeppen [1970] Executive Director [Dutch]; Diego Fernando Londono [1970] Executive Director [Colombian]

Backstage Centre Limited
Incorporated: 24 June 2008 *Employees:* 5
Previous: Creative and Cultural Industries Trading Limited
Net Worth Deficit: £139,750 *Total Assets:* £5,612,141
Registered Office: The Backstage Centre, High House Production Park, Vellacott Close, Purfleet, Essex, RM19 1RJ
Activities: Cultural education
Parent: The National College for The Creative and Cultural Industries
Officers: Melissa Jane Drayson, Secretary; Althea Joy Efunshile [1956] Director/Arts Administrator; Edward Robin Moore [1963] Director/Stage Engineering; Bryan Alan Raven [1964] Director; Gary Raymond Sparkes [1967] Director/Theatre Consultant

Badger BC Investments Limited
Incorporated: 8 November 2013
Net Worth: £1,632,146 *Total Assets:* £11,586,682
Registered Office: Borough Offices, Churchgate, Cheshunt, Herts, EN8 9XJ
Activities: Other letting and operating of own or leased real estate
Parent: Broxbourne Borough Council
Officers: Nathalie Loretta Boateng, Secretary; Sandra Lesley Beck [1966] Director/Head of Financial Services; Nathalie Loretta Boateng [1969] Director/Solicitor; Jeffrey Thomas Stack [1961] Director/Local Government Officer

Badger Holdings Limited
Incorporated: 11 August 1995 *Employees:* 30
Net Worth: £5,979,297 *Total Assets:* £34,243,216
Registered Office: Unit 2 Wintersells Road, Byfleet, West Byfleet, Surrey, KT14 7LF
Activities: Real estate agencies
Shareholders: Alchemy Special Opportunities LLP; Badger Group (Holdings) Limited
Officers: Nicholas Anthony Robert Dunning [1962] Director; Graham Martin Harrison [1957] Director; Julian Matthew Irby [1966] Director/Chief Financial Officer

Badiani & Company Limited
Incorporated: 11 September 1978 *Employees:* 21
Net Worth: £5,627,444 *Total Assets:* £6,438,405
Registered Office: 54 Istead Rise, Northfleet, Kent, DA13 9JF
Activities: Dispensing chemist in specialised stores
Major Shareholder: Rajendra Vithaldas Badiani
Officers: Rajendra Vithaldas Badiani, Secretary; Bindu Rajendra Badiani [1955] Director; Rajendra Vithaldas Badiani [1953] Director/Pharmacist; Sachin Badiani [1981] Director

Bagga Holdings Limited
Incorporated: 22 September 2003 *Employees:* 42
Net Worth: £10,570,406 *Total Assets:* £15,664,758
Registered Office: Sabichi House, 5 Wadsworth Road, Perivale, Middlesex, UB6 7JD
Activities: Other letting and operating of own or leased real estate
Shareholder: Tarsem Bagga
Officers: Mukesh Lata Bagga, Secretary; Mukesh Lata Bagga [1956] Director/Secretary; Sachin Bagga [1982] Director; Tarsem Bagga [1953] Director; Sabrina Phull [1981] Director/Manager

Baik Agency Limited
Incorporated: 28 July 2003 *Employees:* 97
Net Worth: £4,776,542 *Total Assets:* £37,987,656
Registered Office: 19-20 Bourne Court, Southend Road, Woodford Green, Essex, IG8 8HD
Activities: Activities of head offices
Major Shareholder: Thierry Andre Victor Cohen
Officers: Nathalie Izumi Cohen [1970] Director [Italian]

Baker Ross Limited
Incorporated: 15 December 1981 *Employees:* 73
Net Worth: £3,860,810 *Total Assets:* £9,660,612
Registered Office: Treviot House, 186-192 High Road, Ilford, Essex, IG1 1JQ
Activities: Retail sale via mail order houses or via Internet
Officers: Patricia Ann Baker, Secretary; Patricia Ann Baker [1947] Managing Director; Paul Emerson Baker [1968] Sales Director

Bal Holdings Limited
Incorporated: 4 April 2005
Net Worth: £6,805 *Total Assets:* £7,320,954
Registered Office: 170 Tudor Drive, Kingston upon Thames, Surrey, KT2 5QG
Activities: Activities of other holding companies n.e.c.
Shareholders: Ashok Kumar Tanna; Bhagyachandra Jivandas Tanna; Lalit Kumar Tanna
Officers: Ashok Kumar Tanna, Secretary; Ashok Kumar Tanna [1956] Director/Pharmacist; Bhagyachandra Jivandas Tanna [1951] Director/Pharmacy; Lalit Kumar Tanna [1956] Director/Pharmacy

Balcraft Properties Limited
Incorporated: 18 June 1998
Net Worth: £8,526,763 *Total Assets:* £12,418,675
Registered Office: Hill House, Lowlands Road, Harrow, Middlesex, HA1 3EQ
Activities: Development of building projects
Major Shareholder: Donovan Gijsbertus Wijsmuller
Officers: Brian Martin Comer [1960] Director [Irish]; Luke Andrew Comer [1957] Director [Irish]; Thomas Donnellan [1960] Director [Irish]

Balgores Motors (1982) Limited
Incorporated: 14 July 1982 *Employees:* 242
Net Worth: £7,580,233 *Total Assets:* £11,746,194
Registered Office: 1 Bryant Avenue, Gallows Corner, Romford, Essex, RM3 0AP
Activities: Other service activities incidental to land transportation, n.e.c.
Major Shareholder: Paul Alfred Austin
Officers: Paul Alfred Austin, Secretary; Paul Alfred Austin [1952] Director/Engineer; Steven Arthur Austin [1957] Director/Engineer

Balgowan Primary School
Incorporated: 16 June 2011 *Employees:* 88
Net Worth: £11,923,299 *Total Assets:* £12,970,414
Registered Office: Balgowan Primary School, Balgowan Road, Beckenham, Kent, BR3 4HJ
Activities: Primary education
Officers: Jeremy Richard Adams [1972] Director/PR Consultant; Simon Armstrong [1967] Director/Lawyer; Stacey Alexandra Bell [1979] Director/Business Owner; Samantha Coles [1985] Director/Senior Education Policy Adviser; Julie Margaret Freeth [1957] Director; Jessica Owen [1991] Director/Teacher; Daniel Benjamin Radov [1974] Director/Consulting Economist [American]; Emma Rigby [1973] Director/Head of a National Health Charity; Patricia Spedding [1956] Director/Teacher; Linda Stenning [1963] Director/Teaching Assistant; Maria Veysey [1974] Director/Headteacher [Russian]

Ballward Limited
Incorporated: 8 September 1986 *Employees:* 3
Net Worth: £5,942,793 *Total Assets:* £6,838,773
Registered Office: Ballward House, 3 Liberty Centre, Mount Pleasant, Wembley, Middlesex, HA0 1TX
Activities: Non-specialised wholesale trade
Shareholders: Executors of Suresh Ramlal Kotecha; Prafulla Kotecha
Officers: Prafulla Kotecha, Secretary; Vipul Suresh Kotecha [1968] Director

Balton CP Limited
Incorporated: 22 December 1976 *Employees:* 1,209
Net Worth: £21,451,602 *Total Assets:* £91,419,928
Registered Office: CP House, Otterspool Way, Watford, Herts, WD25 8HU
Activities: Non-specialised wholesale trade
Parent: Premier Telecommunication International Limited
Officers: Eric Lewis, Secretary; Andrew Joseph Baker [1965] Director/Chief Executive Officer; Paul Andrew Filer [1957] Director/Chartered Accountant; Alexei James Schreier [1976] Director; Kevin Edgar Torlage [1964] Director/Chief Finance Officer

Bamboo Distribution Limited
Incorporated: 12 June 2009 *Employees:* 97
Net Worth: £7,689,995 *Total Assets:* £20,263,164
Registered Office: Unit 5 IO Centre, Lea Road, Waltham Abbey, Essex, EN9 1AS
Activities: Non-specialised wholesale trade
Major Shareholder: Cuney Ahmet Mistiki
Officers: Paula Hansson, Secretary; Adrian Bryant [1960] Director/Chartered Accountant; Dervish Dervish [1968] Director; Cuney Ahmet Mistiki [1971] Director

Bamrose Enterprises Limited
Incorporated: 22 May 1985 *Employees:* 2
Net Worth: £19,232,510 *Total Assets:* £21,195,012
Registered Office: 34 West Drive, Harrow Weald, Middlesex, HA3 6TS
Activities: Administration of financial markets
Officers: Chandrabala Dalia, Secretary; Chandrabala Dalia [1946] Director; Sheetal Dalia-Patel [1972] Director; Heena Rajiv Sodha [1969] Director

Bamrose Properties Limited
Incorporated: 31 January 2008 *Employees:* 1
Net Worth: £2,479,767 *Total Assets:* £6,768,166
Registered Office: 34 West Drive, Harrow Weald, Middlesex, HA3 6TS
Activities: Buying and selling of own real estate
Shareholder: Chandrabala Dalia
Officers: Chandrabala Dalia, Secretary/Director; Chandrabala Dalia [1946] Director; Sheetal Dalia-Patel [1972] Director; Heena Rajiv Sodha [1969] Director

Bancroft's School
Incorporated: 19 February 1998 *Employees:* 228
Net Worth: £16,635,126 *Total Assets:* £22,429,332
Registered Office: High Road, Woodford Green, Essex, IG8 0RF
Activities: Primary education
Officers: Lionel Green, Secretary; Rejpaul Singh Bhumbra [1973] Director/Surgeon; Bernadette Sarah Conroy [1966] Director; Raymond John Gooding [1950] Director/Councillor; Professor Peter Graham Kopelman [1951] Director/University Principal; James Michael Rose [1971] Director/Stockbroker; Ed Sautter [1958] Director/Solicitor; Saheeda Begum Siddiqui [1956] Director/Solicitor; Councillor Michael John Stark [1942] Director/Councillor; Richard Van Maanen [1960] Director/Chartered Surveyor; Richard Williamson [1972] Strategy Director; Lizzie Wingham [1978] Director/TV Production

Bandai Namco Amusement Europe Limited
Incorporated: 27 October 2006 *Employees:* 117
Net Worth: £14,950,000 *Total Assets:* £27,074,000
Registered Office: 37-39 Kew Foot Road, Richmond, Surrey, TW9 2SS
Activities: Other business support service activities n.e.c.
Parent: Bandai Namco Holdings UK Ltd.
Officers: Raymond Bradley, Secretary; Raymond Bradley [1965] Finance Director; Iwanaga Kato [1967] Director [Japanese]; John McKenzie [1965] Director

Bandai Namco Entertainment UK Ltd.
Incorporated: 21 May 1987 *Employees:* 18
Previous: Bandai Namco Games UK Ltd
Net Worth: £4,789,067 *Total Assets:* £11,672,175
Registered Office: 37-39 Kew Foot Road, Richmond, Surrey, TW9 2SS
Activities: Business and domestic software development
Parent: Bandai Namco Holdings Inc.
Officers: Mark Jonathan Passam, Secretary; John Galloway [1963] Director; Naoki Katashima [1961] Director [Japanese]; Mark Passam [1964] Director/Accountant

Bandai Namco Holdings UK Limited
Incorporated: 5 November 1991 *Employees:* 7
Net Worth: £64,654,000 *Total Assets:* £65,900,000
Registered Office: 37-39 Kew Foot Road, Richmond, Surrey, TW9 2SS
Activities: Non-specialised wholesale trade
Parent: Bandai Namco Holdings Inc.
Officers: Raymond Bradley, Secretary; Raymond Bradley [1965] Finance Director; Masaaki Tsuji [1953] Director [Japanese]

Bandai UK Limited
Incorporated: 29 April 1982 *Employees:* 17
Net Worth: £9,216,556 *Total Assets:* £11,804,425
Registered Office: 37-39 Kew Foot Road, Richmond, Surrey, TW9 2SS
Activities: Wholesale of household goods (other than musical instruments) n.e.c
Parent: Bandai Namco Holdings UK Limited
Officers: Simon Fettes, Secretary; Nicolas Ernest Lloyd Aldridge [1978] Managing Director; Nobuhiko Momoi [1968] Director [Japanese]

Banks Hotel Limited
Incorporated: 13 April 2004 *Employees:* 11
Net Worth: £1,317,473 *Total Assets:* £5,530,537
Registered Office: 114-116 Goodmayes Road, Ilford, Essex, IG3 9UZ
Activities: Hotels and similar accommodation
Shareholders: Sukhbinder Singh Takhar; Sukhbinder Singh Takhar
Officers: Iqbal Kaur Takhar, Secretary; Iqbal Kaur Takhar [1960] Director; Pirthipal Singh Takhar [1982] Director; Sukhbinder Singh Takhar [1954] Director

Barcrest Group Limited
Incorporated: 22 January 1998 *Employees:* 176
Net Worth: £56,411,000 *Total Assets:* £118,188,000
Registered Office: SG House, 1 Dukes Green Avenue, Feltham, Middlesex, TW14 0LR
Activities: Gambling and betting activities
Parent: Scientific Games International Holdings Limited
Officers: Phillip Douglas Horne [1961] Managing Director; Paul Phillips [1978] Finance Director

Barilone Properties Limited
Incorporated: 22 September 1960 *Employees:* 2
Net Worth: £5,659,954 *Total Assets:* £6,393,807
Registered Office: Leonard House, 5-7 Newman Road, Bromley, Kent, BR1 1RJ
Activities: Other letting and operating of own or leased real estate
Shareholders: Antonio Stephen Barilone; Margaret Barilone
Officers: Margaret Barilone, Secretary; Antonio Stephen Barilone [1952] Director; Margaret Barilone [1950] Director/Antiques Retailer

Barking Power Limited
Incorporated: 2 March 1989
Net Worth: £14,213,000 *Total Assets:* £25,810,000
Registered Office: Barking Power Station, Chequers Lane, Dagenham, Essex, RM9 6PF
Activities: Production of electricity
Parent: The Mayor and Commonalty and Citizens of The City of London
Officers: Philip Gregory [1980] Director; Paul Graham Wilkinson [1962] Director/Surveyor; Peter Derek Young [1966] Director/Chartered Surveyor

Barnardo Developments Limited
Incorporated: 28 October 1969
Net Worth: £100 *Total Assets:* £5,356,357
Registered Office: Barnardo House, Tanners Lane, Barkingside, Ilford, Essex, IG6 1QG
Activities: Development of building projects
Parent: Barnardo Holdings Limited
Officers: David Mark Cunningham, Secretary; Anthony Malcolm Cripps [1957] Director/Property Manager; Richard Michael Moore [1967] Director/Chartered Accountant

Barnardo Services Limited
Incorporated: 26 September 1975
Net Worth: £100 *Total Assets:* £6,030,260
Registered Office: Barnardo House, Tanners Lane, Barkingside, Ilford, Essex, IG6 1QG
Activities: Other social work activities without accommodation n.e.c.
Parent: Barnardo Holdings Limited
Officers: David Mark Cunningham, Secretary; Martin Alistair Crewe [1960] Corporate Director Children's Services; Liam Patrick Duffy [1955] Director of Business Development; Javed Akhtar Khan [1963] Director

Barnardo's
Incorporated: 20 April 1899 *Employees:* 8,128
Net Worth: £2,038,000 *Total Assets:* £184,364,000
Registered Office: Barnardo House, Tanners Lane, Barkingside, Ilford, Essex, IG6 1QG
Activities: Other social work activities without accommodation n.e.c.
Officers: David Mark Cunningham, Secretary; John Harold Bartlett [1953] Director/Head of Tax; Neil Braithwaite [1959] Managing Director; Alexis Jane Cleveland [1954] Director/Retired Cabinet Officer; Amanda Ellingworth [1957] Director; Zoe Elizabeth Harris [1975] Marketing Director; Dennis Vincent Hone [1958] Finance Director; Sheikh Mansurah Tal-At Mannings [1963] Director/Lawyer; Darra Singh [1959] Director/Partner; Colin James Walsh [1955] Director/Chief Executive

Barrett Industrial Limited
Incorporated: 22 February 2006
Net Worth: £7,300 *Total Assets:* £5,539,466
Registered Office: Office 216, Regico Offices, The Old Bank, 153 The Parade, High Street, Watford, Herts, WD17 1NA
Activities: Other service activities n.e.c.
Officers: Carlos Alberto Weand Ortiz [1963] Director [Panamanian]

Barrie Knitwear Limited
Incorporated: 2 December 1994 *Employees:* 249
Net Worth: £7,565,000 *Total Assets:* £11,908,000
Registered Office: 5 Queensway, Croydon, Surrey, CR9 4DL
Activities: Manufacture of other knitted and crocheted apparel
Officers: Paul Stuart Gaff, Secretary; Eric Dupont [1968] Director [French]; Bruno Andre Jean Pavlovsky [1962] Director/President [French]; Jan Young [1965] Managing Director

Barrowfen Properties Limited
Incorporated: 6 July 1984 *Employees:* 2
Net Worth: £4,183,936 *Total Assets:* £8,237,484
Registered Office: First Floor, Kirkland House, 11-15 Peterborough Road, Harrow, Middlesex, HA1 2AX
Activities: Construction of commercial buildings
Shareholder: Prashant Rajnikant Patel
Officers: Prashant Rajnikant Patel [1976] Director [Australian]; Prashant Rajnikant Patel [1976] Director [Australian]; Suresh Patel [1953] Director/Merchant [Singaporean]

Bartlett Mitchell Limited
Incorporated: 19 August 1999 *Employees:* 764
Net Worth: £2,066,527 *Total Assets:* £11,027,017
Registered Office: 80 High Street, Egham, Surrey, TW20 9HE
Activities: Other food services
Major Shareholder: Wendy Pamela Bartlett
Officers: Irene Crawford Douglas, Secretary; Wendy Pamela Bartlett [1960] Director/Caterer; Ian Maxwell Robert Mitchell [1949] Director/Caterer; Ian Lincoln Thomas [1972] Director

Bartlett Mitchell Services Limited
Incorporated: 20 June 2014 *Employees:* 774
Net Worth: £2,725,393 *Total Assets:* £12,653,534
Registered Office: 80 High Street, Egham, Surrey, TW20 9HE
Activities: Activities of head offices
Major Shareholder: Wendy Pamela Bartlett
Officers: Wendy Bartlett [1960] Director; Ian Maxwell Robert Mitchell [1949] Director/Caterer; Ian Lincoln Thomas [1972] Director

Baruch Holdings Limited
Incorporated: 5 October 1993
Net Worth: £3,257,529 *Total Assets:* £10,136,729
Registered Office: York House, Empire Way, Wembley, Middlesex, HA9 0FQ
Activities: Other letting and operating of own or leased real estate
Parent: Baruch Investments Limited
Officers: Emil Baruch, Secretary/Director; Emil Baruch [1960] Director; Robert Baruch [1963] Director

Baruch Investments Limited
Incorporated: 28 March 2001 *Employees:* 36
Net Worth: £10,163,017 *Total Assets:* £13,884,581
Registered Office: York House, Empire Way, Wembley, Middlesex, HA9 0FQ
Activities: Activities of head offices
Shareholders: Emil Baruch; Robert Baruch
Officers: Emil Baruch, Secretary/Director; Emil Baruch [1960] Director; Robert Baruch [1963] Director

Basis Technologies International Limited
Incorporated: 24 June 2003 *Employees:* 32
Net Worth: £1,496,671 *Total Assets:* £6,290,215
Registered Office: Spencer House, 23 Sheen Road, Richmond, Surrey, TW9 1BN
Activities: Business and domestic software development
Parent: Basis Technologies Holdings Limited
Officers: Richard Anthony Bayliss, Secretary; Richard Anthony Bayliss [1969] Director; Martin Edward Metcalf [1959] Director; Craig Douglas Oliver [1975] Director

Thomas Bates & Son Limited
Incorporated: 3 January 1927 *Employees:* 15
Net Worth: £28,555,750 *Total Assets:* £35,982,312
Registered Office: The Old Brickworks, Church Road, Harold Wood, Romford, Essex, RM3 0JA
Activities: Buying and selling of own real estate
Shareholders: Michael Bates; Joshua James Bates
Officers: James David Clark, Secretary; Joshua James Bates [1969] Director/Farmer; Michael Bates [1936] Director/Farmer; James David Clark [1983] Finance Director; Joseph Jackson [1982] Director

Bates Wharf Marine Sales Limited
Incorporated: 28 February 1992 *Employees:* 14
Net Worth: £1,379,600 *Total Assets:* £6,353,016
Registered Office: Bridge Wharf, Chertsey, Surrey, KT16 8LG
Activities: Other retail sale not in stores, stalls or markets
Major Shareholder: Richard Anthony Barrett Bates
Officers: David Campbell de Vere, Secretary; Richard Anthony Barret Bates [1966] Director; David Campbell de Vere [1942] Director

Bath Resorts Limited
Incorporated: 6 May 2015 *Employees:* 4
Net Worth: £622,690 *Total Assets:* £7,926,129
Registered Office: Kirkland House, 11-15 Peterborough Road, Harrow, Middlesex, HA1 2AX
Activities: Hotels and similar accommodation
Officers: Dinesh Gordhandas Bhattessa [1946] Director/Businessman; Haider Ladhu Jaffer [1940] Director; Dr Manoj Raman [1960] Director/Businessman; Hassanali Amirali Dawood Suleman [1954] Director

Bath Road Properties Limited
Incorporated: 7 June 2016
Net Worth Deficit: £1,159,321 *Total Assets:* £25,498,034
Registered Office: 3rd Floor, Sterling House, Langston Road, Loughton, Essex, IG10 3TS
Activities: Development of building projects
Parent: Galliard Developments Limited
Officers: Allan William Porter, Secretary; John Cole [1971] Director; Stephen Stuart Solomon Conway [1948] Director; Rory Anthony O'Connor [1959] Director [Irish]; Donagh O'Sullivan [1968] Director [Irish]

Bathroom Brands Group Limited
Incorporated: 20 June 2016
Net Worth: £34,000,000 *Total Assets:* £68,454,000
Registered Office: Lake View House, Rennie Drive, Dartford, Kent, DA1 5FU
Activities: Activities of other holding companies n.e.c.
Officers: Vikram Kant, Secretary; David John Anning [1966] Director; Clive Aubrey Charles Chaplin [1951] Director/Lawyer; Vikram Kant [1984] Director [Indian]

Bathroom Brands Holdings UK Limited
Incorporated: 11 May 2009 *Employees:* 12
Previous: Crosswater Holdings UK Limited
Net Worth: £10,485,000 *Total Assets:* £49,631,000
Registered Office: Lake View House, Rennie Drive, Dartford, Kent, DA1 5FU
Activities: Wholesale of hardware, plumbing and heating equipment and supplies
Parent: Bathroom Brands Group Limited
Officers: Vikram Kant, Secretary; David Richard Hance [1965] Director/Group Chairman; Vikram Kant [1984] Director [Indian]

Bathroom Brands Limited
Incorporated: 11 October 2017 *Employees:* 285
Net Worth: £26,859,000 *Total Assets:* £62,771,000
Registered Office: Lake View House, Rennie Drive, Dartford, Kent, DA1 5FU
Activities: Activities of other holding companies n.e.c.
Officers: Vikram Kant, Secretary; David John Anning [1966] Director; Jeremy Guy Nicholas Bird [1961] Director; Clive Aubrey Charles Chaplin [1951] Director/Lawyer; Philip Roger Cooper [1948] Director/Consultant; Tanis Lee Crosby [1983] Group Director [South African]; Nico Albert de Beer [1960] Group Director; David Richard Hance [1965] Group Director; Vikram Kant [1984] Director [Indian]; Timothy Martin Powell [1972] Director [Australian]; Derek Patrick Riley [1961] Executive Director [Irish]

Batt Cables Public Limited Company
Incorporated: 17 February 1978 *Employees:* 299
Net Worth: £54,032,940 *Total Assets:* £90,481,880
Registered Office: The Belfry, Fraser Road, Erith, Kent, DA8 1QH
Activities: Wholesale of other intermediate products
Major Shareholder: Peter John Holm
Officers: Stephen Martin Brown, Secretary; Stephen Martin Brown [1968] Financial Director; Peter John Holm [1958] Director; Robert Waddington [1955] Sales Director

Bayside Investment Company Limited
Incorporated: 23 August 1993
Net Worth: £16,165,393 *Total Assets:* £17,717,552
Registered Office: 198 Lower Addiscombe Road, Croydon, Surrey, CR0 7AB
Activities: Other letting and operating of own or leased real estate
Major Shareholder: Clare Louise Upward
Officers: Paul David Upward, Secretary/Director; Clare Louise Upward [1963] Director; Paul David Upward [1962] Director

Bayti Properties Limited
Incorporated: 12 January 2011
Net Worth: £3,223,989 *Total Assets:* £14,301,108
Registered Office: 77 Nork Way, Banstead, Surrey, SM7 1HN
Activities: Other letting and operating of own or leased real estate
Officers: Tarik Al-Abdeen [1979] Director

Bayut Ltd
Incorporated: 17 March 2015
Net Worth: £7,083,290 *Total Assets:* £11,788,630
Registered Office: Spirit House, 8 High Street, West Molesey, Surrey, KT8 2NA
Activities: Management consultancy activities other than financial management
Officers: Derek Williamson, Secretary; Imran Ali Khan [1978] Director/Businessman

Bazooka Candy Brands International Limited
Incorporated: 3 December 2010 *Employees:* 18
Net Worth: £436,383 *Total Assets:* £7,672,384
Registered Office: 15 Petersham Road, Richmond, Surrey, TW10 6TP
Activities: Wholesale of sugar and chocolate and sugar confectionery
Parent: Topps MK Holdings Ltd
Officers: Andrew Barnes, Secretary; Michael Neil Brandstaedter [1970] Director/VP COO [American]; David Alexander Collier [1960] Commercial Director

BBC Studioworks Limited
Incorporated: 1 July 1998 *Employees:* 94
Previous: BBC Studios and Post Production Limited
Net Worth: £24,250,308 *Total Assets:* £33,958,312
Registered Office: Room N101, Neptune House, BBC Elstree Centre, Eldon Avenue, Borehamwood, Herts, WD6 1NL
Activities: Television programme production activities
Parent: BBC Commercial Holdings Limited
Officers: Peter John Ranyard, Secretary; David Conway [1976] Managing Director; Robert Glyn Isherwood [1968] Group Finance and Operations Director

BDL Group Public Limited Company (The)
Incorporated: 8 November 1977 *Employees:* 128
Net Worth: £7,892,398 *Total Assets:* £16,541,557
Registered Office: Carey House, Great Central Way, Wembley, Middlesex, HA9 0HR
Activities: Construction of commercial buildings
Parent: Carey Group PLC
Officers: Fiona Mary O'Donnell, Secretary; Timothy Joseph Barnes [1954] Director; John Carey [1941] Director [Irish]; Denis Patrick Deacy [1965] Group Managing Director

Beacon (Mimms) Limited
Incorporated: 7 January 1938 *Employees:* 1
Net Worth: £7,031,778 *Total Assets:* £8,075,082
Registered Office: Plantagenet House, 4 Plantagenet Road, New Barnet, Herts, EN5 5JQ
Activities: Other letting and operating of own or leased real estate
Major Shareholder: Christopher Edward Scarfe
Officers: Nicholas James Scarfe, Secretary; Nicholas James Scarfe [1992] Director

Beacon Hill Academy
Incorporated: 17 August 2012 *Employees:* 80
Net Worth: £4,998,194 *Total Assets:* £7,478,540
Registered Office: Beacon Hill School, Erriff Drive, South Ockendon, Essex, RM15 5AY
Activities: Other education n.e.c.
Officers: Linda Jennifer Bostock [1951] Director; Fiona Louise Margaret Carter [1989] Director/Teacher; Wallace Generald Cope [1933] Director/Retired Chartered Surveyor; Susan Elliott [1976] Director; Anthony William Fish [1957] Director/Borough Councillor; Sue Hewitt [1964] Director/Principal; Deanne Lodge [1972] Director/Product Developer; Vyramuthu Rattinam Loganathan [1957] Director of Operations [Colombian]; John Hugh Paddick [1958] Director; Emma Saunders [1970] Director

Beacon Multi-Academy Trust Limited
Incorporated: 4 November 2011 *Employees:* 502
Previous: Beal Multi-Academy Trust Limited
Net Worth: £53,741,000 *Total Assets:* £58,470,000
Registered Office: Beal High School, Woodford Bridge Road, Ilford, Essex, IG4 5LP
Activities: General secondary education
Officers: Suda Ratnam, Secretary; Nadjie Carol Butler [1960] Director; Michelle Fuller [1970] Director; Dr Simon James Gibbons [1970] Director; Balbinder Ranbir Singh Panesar [1952] Director/Retired; Shona Ramsay [1958] Director; Suda Ratnam [1968] Director; Jatinder Saini [1954] Director; Dr Elizabeth Sidwell [1949] Director; Elizabeth Slattery [1958] Director/Lawyer; Michael Roderick Stokes [1969] Director/Manager; Alan Edward Weinberg [1946] Director/Councillor

Beale's Hotels Limited
Incorporated: 11 February 2010 *Employees:* 158
Net Worth: £3,563,816 *Total Assets:* £8,832,589
Registered Office: West Lodge Park, Cockfosters Road, Barnet, Herts, EN4 0PY
Activities: Hotels and similar accommodation
Shareholder: Beale Trust
Officers: Michael George Pettit, Secretary; Andrew Edward Beale [1963] Director; Nicholas Henderson Beale [1969] Director/Surveyor; Antony Peter King [1953] Director

Beale's Limited
Incorporated: 15 February 1895 *Employees:* 158
Net Worth: £6,482,426 *Total Assets:* £11,751,299
Registered Office: Beales Ltd, West Lodge Park, Cockfosters Road, Barnet, Herts, EN4 0PY
Activities: Hotels and similar accommodation
Parent: Beales Hotels Limited
Officers: Michael George Pettit, Secretary; Andrew Edward Beale [1963] Director/Hotelier; Nicholas Henderson Beale [1969] Director/Surveyor

Beam Global Finance UK Limited
Incorporated: 13 August 1996
Net Worth: £9,475,752 *Total Assets:* £69,350,016
Registered Office: 2 Longwalk Road, Stockley Park, Uxbridge, Middlesex, UB11 1BA
Activities: Other service activities n.e.c.
Officers: Aoife Clarke [1980] Public Affairs Director - International [Irish]; Richard Dalton [1962] Director/General Manager - Cooley Distillery [Irish]; William Lindquist [1977] Director [Irish]; Leonard John Mathews [1975] Director/Financial Controller [Irish]

Beam Suntory Operations Limited
Incorporated: 10 September 2014 *Employees:* 1
Net Worth Deficit: £1,727,000 *Total Assets:* £12,980,000
Registered Office: 2 Longwalk Road, Stockley Park, Uxbridge, Middlesex, UB11 1BA
Activities: Other business support service activities n.e.c.
Parent: Beam Suntory UK Limited
Officers: Jose Padilla Munoz [1959] Senior Director, International Supply Chain Finance [Spanish]; Michael John Ord [1965] Director of Scotch & Irish Whiskies

Beam Suntory UK Holdings Limited
Incorporated: 1 November 2005
Previous: Beam Inc UK Holdings Limited
Net Worth: £464,076,992 *Total Assets:* £470,887,008
Registered Office: 2 Longwalk Road, Stockley Park, Uxbridge, Middlesex, UB11 1BA
Activities: Activities of other holding companies n.e.c.
Officers: Nadim Assi [1967] Director/CFO International [Canadian]; Madame Del Pino Bermudez de La Puente Sanchez-Aguilera [1974] Director/Associate General Counsel [Spanish]

Beam Suntory UK Limited
Incorporated: 13 October 2005 *Employees:* 186
Previous: Beam Inc UK Limited
Net Worth: £474,952,000 *Total Assets:* £573,376,000
Registered Office: 2 Longwalk Road, Stockley Park, Uxbridge, Middlesex, UB11 1BA
Activities: Distilling, rectifying and blending of spirits
Parent: Beam Suntory UK Holdings Limited
Officers: Nadim Assi [1967] Director/CFO International [Canadian]; Madame Del Pino Bermudez de La Puente Sanchez-Aguilera [1974] Director/Associate General Counsel [Spanish]; Pryce William David Greenow [1970] Director/President International; Jose Padilla Munoz [1959] Senior Director International Supply Chain Finance [Spanish]; David William James Wilson [1964] Director/MD Global Travel Retail

Beauty Wholesale Limited
Incorporated: 8 June 1999 *Employees:* 29
Net Worth: £1,738,514 *Total Assets:* £9,373,346
Registered Office: 3 George Street, Watford, Herts, WD18 0BX
Activities: Wholesale of perfume and cosmetics
Parent: KMS Holdings Limited
Officers: Gulam Nasser [1965] Director

BEC (London) Limited
Incorporated: 7 February 2005 *Employees:* 72
Net Worth: £626,370 *Total Assets:* £5,762,005
Registered Office: 11 Thames Road, Barking, Essex, IG11 0HG
Activities: Repair of machinery
Shareholders: Lawrence Toni Galea; Brian Edward Kemp; Sudash Lal Damney
Officers: Sudash Lal Damney, Secretary/Engineer; Sudash Lal Damney [1961] Director/Engineer; Lawrence Toni Galea [1955] Director/Engineer; Brian Edward Kemp [1958] Director/Engineer; Jeffrey George Lake [1946] Director

BECAP Spicers (UK) Limited
Incorporated: 7 April 2011
Net Worth Deficit: £1,659,000 *Total Assets:* £40,249,000
Registered Office: c/o OfficeTeam, Unit 4, 500 Purley Way, Croydon, Surrey, CR0 4NZ
Activities: Activities of head offices
Major Shareholder: Jonathan Paul Moulton
Officers: Philippa Anne Maynard, Secretary; Andrew Graham Mobbs [1978] Director

Beck & Pollitzer Engineering Holdings Ltd.
Incorporated: 20 February 1998 *Employees:* 3
Net Worth: £8,444,008 *Total Assets:* £18,771,010
Registered Office: Burnham Road, Dartford, Kent, DA1 5BD
Activities: Activities of other holding companies n.e.c.
Parent: Beck & Pollitzer Holdings Ltd
Officers: Ivo Vesselinov, Secretary; Andrew Hodgson [1965] Director; Romain Jean Patrick Prouvost [1979] Director [French]; Ivo Vesselinov [1976] Finance Director

Beck & Pollitzer Engineering Limited
Incorporated: 22 November 1993 *Employees:* 144
Net Worth: £32,209,252 *Total Assets:* £47,730,452
Registered Office: Burnham Road, Dartford, Kent, DA1 5BD
Activities: Installation of industrial machinery and equipment
Parent: Beck & Pollitzer Engineering Holdings Ltd
Officers: Ivo Vesselinov, Secretary; Andrew Hodgson [1965] Director; Romain Jean Patrick Prouvost [1979] Director [French]; Ivo Vesselinov [1976] Finance Director

Beck & Pollitzer Holdings Limited
Incorporated: 25 October 2004 *Employees:* 3
Net Worth: £26,480,580 *Total Assets:* £36,608,288
Registered Office: Burnham Road, Dartford, Kent, DA1 5BD
Activities: Activities of other holding companies n.e.c.
Parent: B & P Acquisitionco Limited
Officers: Ivo Vesselinov, Secretary; Andrew Hodgson [1965] Director; Romain Jean Patrick Prouvost [1979] Director [French]; Ivo Vesselinov [1976] Finance Director

Beck & Pollitzer Limited
Incorporated: 1 September 2016 *Employees:* 860
Net Worth Deficit: £1,611,941 *Total Assets:* £100,397,808
Registered Office: Burnham Road, Sandpit Road, Dartford, Kent, DA1 5BD
Activities: Activities of venture and development capital companies
Parent: Graphite Capital Management LLP
Officers: Andrew Hodgson [1965] Director; Charles Lewis Matthews [1953] Director; Romain Jean Patrick Prouvost [1979] Director [French]; Ivo Vesselinov [1976] Finance Director

Beck Interiors Limited
Incorporated: 21 February 1995 *Employees:* 194
Net Worth: £21,243,542 *Total Assets:* £46,355,192
Registered Office: Victory House, Cox Lane, Chessington, Surrey, KT9 1SG
Activities: Joinery installation
Parent: Beck MBI Ltd
Officers: Edward Corrigan, Secretary; Mark Andrew Banham [1971] Director; Robert Andrew Bishop [1954] Commercial Director; Shaun Carvalho [1964] Director; Dalbir Chana [1979] Board Director; Jonathan Embling Dart [1959] Director; Christopher Sinclair Galloway [1972] Operations Director; Brian Paul Hutchison [1964] Director; Edward Kent [1976] Board Director

Beck MBI Limited
Incorporated: 23 October 2007 *Employees:* 258
Net Worth: £34,185,200 *Total Assets:* £63,762,080
Registered Office: Victory House, Cox Lane, Chessington, Surrey, KT9 1SG
Activities: Other specialised construction activities n.e.c.
Parent: Beck MBI2 Ltd
Officers: Jonathan Dart, Secretary; Mark Andrew Banham [1971] Director; Jonathan Embling Dart [1959] Financial Director; Christopher Sinclair Galloway [1972] Director; Robert Horvath [1956] Director/Chairman

Becontree Estates Ltd
Incorporated: 21 June 2016
Net Worth Deficit: £620 *Total Assets:* £5,108,100
Registered Office: 148 Cranbrook Road, Ilford, Essex, IG1 4LZ
Activities: Buying and selling of own real estate
Major Shareholder: Herjit Singh Kataria
Officers: Herjit Singh Kataria [1967] Director

Beddington Park Academy Trust
Incorporated: 19 March 2015 *Employees:* 55
Net Worth: £3,991,000 *Total Assets:* £5,271,000
Registered Office: Mallinson Road, Beddington, Surrey, CR0 4UL
Activities: Primary education
Officers: Rosalind Redman, Secretary; Emma Jane Browne [1974] Director/Teaching Assistant; Toby Cooke [1971] Director/Headteacher; Lucy Elizabeth Davey [1977] Director/Class Teacher; Jeremy Dearmer [1950] Director/Retired Rail Manager; Michael Fort [1963] Director/Financial Services; Andrew Halm-Owoo [1973] Director/Mechanical Design Engineer; Julie Anne Hendry [1965] Director/Senior Lecturer; Rachel Muir-Nelson [1976] Director/Children with Disabilities Practitioner; Elizabeth Margaret Swinton [1943] Director/Retired Solicitor

Beecham Group P L C
Incorporated: 23 January 1928
Net Worth: £587,270,016 *Total Assets:* £588,897,024
Registered Office: 980 Great West Road, Brentford, Middlesex, TW8 9GS
Activities: Other business support service activities n.e.c.
Parent: SmithKline & French Laboratories Limited
Officers: Victoria Anne Whyte, Secretary; Adam Walker [1967] Director

Beecham Productions Limited
Incorporated: 8 May 2018
Net Worth: £1,035,001 *Total Assets:* £6,370,898
Registered Office: c/o Malde & Co, 99 Kenton Road, Harrow, Middlesex, HA3 0AN
Activities: Television programme production activities
Parent: Carrot Cake Television Limited
Officers: Bharti Satish Padharia [1963] Director; Sandra Shuttleworth [1970] Director/Production Executive

Beechwood Investments Limited
Incorporated: 14 July 1983 *Employees:* 1
Net Worth: £15,544,738 *Total Assets:* £18,971,092
Registered Office: Beechwood, 57 Church Street, Epsom, Surrey, KT17 4PX
Activities: Financial intermediation not elsewhere classified
Shareholders: Penelope Jane Sheen; Mervyn Llewellyn Sheen
Officers: Penelope Jane Sheen, Secretary; Mervyn Llewellyn Sheen [1944] Director; Penelope Jane Sheen [1947] Director

Beko PLC
Incorporated: 22 August 1989 *Employees:* 238
Net Worth: £30,350,000 *Total Assets:* £179,327,008
Registered Office: Beko House, 1 Greenhill Crescent, Watford, Herts, WD18 8QU
Activities: Manufacture of electric domestic appliances
Parent: Arcelik A.S.
Officers: Gul Arslanoglu, Secretary; Mehmet Ragip Balcioglu [1967] Director; Hakan Hamdi Bulgurlu [1972] Director/Mechanical Engineer [Turkish]; Levent Cakiroglu [1967] Director [Turkish]; Fatih Kemal Ebiclioglu [1967] Director [Turkish]; Mustafa Rahmi Koc [1930] Director [Turkish]; Sir David Norman Reddaway [1953] Director; Polat SEN [1976] Director [Turkish]

Belgrave Land (Armley) Limited
Incorporated: 22 July 2004 *Employees:* 3
Net Worth: £2,110,523 *Total Assets:* £6,617,794
Registered Office: First Floor, Radius House, 51 Clarendon Road, Watford, Herts, WD17 1HP
Activities: Development of building projects
Shareholders: John Fearnley Hoyle; Richard David Swaine; Jonathan James Willoughby
Officers: Richard David Swaine, Secretary; John Fearnley Hoyle [1947] Director; Richard David Swaine [1962] Director; Jonathan James Willoughby [1966] Director

Belgrave Land (Kilmarnock) Limited
Incorporated: 3 August 2000 *Employees:* 2
Net Worth: £2,231,449 *Total Assets:* £7,041,733
Registered Office: First Floor, Radius House, 51 Clarendon Road, Watford, Herts, WD17 1HP
Activities: Development of building projects
Shareholders: Richard David Swaine; Jonathan James Willoughby
Officers: Richard David Swaine, Secretary; Richard David Swaine [1962] Director; Jonathan James Willoughby [1966] Director

Belgrave Land (Management) Limited
Incorporated: 30 September 2002 *Employees:* 3
Net Worth: £1,187,343 *Total Assets:* £5,155,444
Registered Office: First Floor, Radius House, 51 Clarendon Road, Watford, Herts, WD17 1HP
Activities: Development of building projects
Parent: BL (Grimsby) Limited
Officers: Richard David Swaine, Secretary; John Fearnley Hoyle [1947] Director; Richard David Swaine [1962] Director; Jonathan James Willoughby [1947] Director

Belgrave Land (Perth) Limited
Incorporated: 13 June 2005 *Employees:* 3
Net Worth: £3,928,176 *Total Assets:* £11,700,486
Registered Office: First Floor, Radius House, 51 Clarendon Road, Watford, Herts, WD17 1HP
Activities: Development of building projects
Shareholders: John Hoyle; Richard Swaine; Jonathan Willoughby
Officers: Richard David Swaine, Secretary; John Fearnley Hoyle [1947] Director; Richard David Swaine [1962] Director; Jonathan James Willoughby [1966] Director

Belgrave Land (Sheffield) Limited
Incorporated: 28 March 2008 *Employees:* 3
Net Worth: £4,771,292 *Total Assets:* £15,021,822
Registered Office: First Floor, Radius House, 51 Clarendon Road, Watford, Herts, WD17 1HP
Activities: Other letting and operating of own or leased real estate
Shareholders: John Fearnley Hoyle; Richard David Swaine; Jonathan James Willoughby
Officers: Richard David Swaine, Secretary; John Fearnley Hoyle [1947] Director; Richard David Swaine [1962] Director; Jonathan James Willoughby [1966] Director

Bell Theatre Services Limited
Incorporated: 8 May 1987 *Employees:* 14
Net Worth: £5,620,184 *Total Assets:* £6,386,008
Registered Office: 9b Chester Road, Borehamwood, Herts, WD6 1LT
Activities: Motion picture projection activities
Major Shareholder: Charles Maximilian Bell
Officers: Charles Maximilian Bell [1940] Director/Sound Engineer; Thomas James Bell [1943] Director; Sean Downey [1965] Director; Stephen Murray Mitchell [1939] Director/Solicitor; Robert Neil Surman [1949] Director/Chartered Accountant

Bellecity Limited
Incorporated: 9 August 2001 *Employees:* 1
Net Worth: £815,423 *Total Assets:* £6,201,420
Registered Office: Unit 1 Loughton Business Centre, 5 Langston Road, Loughton, Essex, IG10 3FL
Activities: Development of building projects
Major Shareholder: Stephen Mucklow
Officers: Stephen Mucklow [1962] Director

Bellevue Education Group Limited
Incorporated: 7 October 2003
Net Worth: £17,023,974 *Total Assets:* £29,585,864
Registered Office: 1 Wolsey Road, East Molesey, Surrey, KT8 9EL
Activities: Educational support services
Parent: Bellevue Education International Limited
Officers: Nicholas Edward Holt [1980] Director; Mark William Malley [1974] Director; Jay Sunny Varkey [1984] Director [Indian]

Bellevue Education International Limited
Incorporated: 12 April 2012 *Employees:* 607
Net Worth: £11,269,233 *Total Assets:* £45,101,192
Registered Office: Ground Floor, 1 Wolsey Road, East Molesey, Surrey, KT8 9EL
Activities: Pre-primary education
Parent: Project Beta Limited
Officers: Nicholas Edward Holt [1980] Director; Mark William Malley [1974] Director; Jay Sunny Varkey [1984] Director [Indian]

Bellis Homes Limited
Incorporated: 13 May 2014 *Employees:* 11
Net Worth: £684,087 *Total Assets:* £5,156,079
Registered Office: Grenville House, 4 Grenville Avenue, Broxbourne, Herts, EN10 7DH
Activities: Development of building projects
Shareholders: Alan James Fordham; Henry William Alan Fordham
Officers: Mark Hedley, Secretary; Alan James Fordham [1953] Director/Developer; Henry William Alan Fordham [1990] Director

Bellman Property Group Limited
Incorporated: 10 February 2011 *Employees:* 2
Net Worth: £8,559,297 *Total Assets:* £20,216,372
Registered Office: Ground Floor, Unit 501 Centennial Park, Centennial Avenue, Elstree, Borehamwood, Herts, WD6 3FG
Activities: Other service activities n.e.c.
Shareholder: Laurence Alan Bellman
Officers: Sarah Jane Bellman, Secretary; Laurence Alan Bellman [1956] Director, Surveyor and Property Manager; Neil Andrew Evans [1954] Director/Solicitor

Belmont Castle Academy
Incorporated: 3 October 2012 *Employees:* 119
Net Worth: £4,598,949 *Total Assets:* £6,755,290
Registered Office: Belmont Castle Academy, Parker Road, Grays, Essex, RM17 5YN
Activities: Primary education
Officers: Clare Anne Clarke, Secretary; Sagayarani Arokiasamy [1984] Director/Self Employed [Sri Lankan]; Pamela Charlesworth [1964] Director/Nurse; Mark Jones [1963] Director/Headteacher; Sarah Jane Joynes [1973] Director/Assistant Headteacher; Jacqueline Mays [1949] Director/Retired; James Edward Sinclair [1961] Director/Self Employed; Steve Smith [1968] Director/Civil Servant; Daren Timson-Hunt [1965] Director/Civil Servant

Belmont Green Finance Ltd
Incorporated: 22 October 2015 *Employees:* 137
Net Worth: £57,771,000 *Total Assets:* £73,139,000
Registered Office: 1 Bridge Street, Staines upon Thames, Surrey, TW18 4TW
Activities: Activities of mortgage finance companies
Parent: Belmont Green Midco Ltd
Officers: Helen Trott, Secretary; David Basra [1969] Finance Director; Stephen William Haggerty [1954] Director; Nicholaos Constantinos Krenteras [1970] Director [American]; Alan Martin Newton [1957] Director/Solicitor; David William Paterson Tweedy [1958] Director; Ethan Wang [1985] Director [American]; Dr Peter Richard Williams [1946] Director

Belmont Green Funding 2 Limited
Incorporated: 11 July 2016
Net Worth: £9,000,000 *Total Assets:* £9,000,000
Registered Office: 1 Bridge Street, Staines upon Thames, Surrey, TW18 4TW
Activities: Activities of mortgage finance companies
Parent: Belmont Green Finance Ltd
Officers: Helen Trott, Secretary; Adrian Scragg [1976] Director; Mel Taylor [1964] Director; David William Paterson Tweedy [1958] Director

Belmont Green Ltd
Incorporated: 16 October 2015 *Employees:* 137
Net Worth: £50,908,000 *Total Assets:* £491,313,984
Registered Office: 1 Bridge Street, Staines upon Thames, Surrey, TW18 4TW
Activities: Activities of financial services holding companies
Officers: David Basra [1969] Finance Director; Nicholaos Constantinos Krenteras [1985] Director [American]; David William Paterson Tweedy [1958] Director; Ethan Jay Wang [1985] Director [American]

Belron Finance Issuer Limited
Incorporated: 20 October 2017
Net Worth: £105,792 *Total Assets:* £1,153,383,552
Registered Office: Milton Park, Stroude Road, Egham, Surrey, TW20 9EL
Activities: Management consultancy activities other than financial management
Parent: Belron Finance Limited
Officers: Claire Dakin, Secretary; Rebecca Scudamore, Secretary; Gary Lubner [1959] Director/Business Executive; David Brian Meller [1966] Finance Director

Belron Finance Limited
Incorporated: 21 September 1999
Net Worth: £1,234,381,440 *Total Assets:* £2,611,092,992
Registered Office: Milton Park, Stroude Road, Egham, Surrey, TW20 9EL
Activities: Management consultancy activities other than financial management
Parent: Belron Lending UK Limited
Officers: Robert Bass, Secretary; Gary Lubner [1959] Director; David Brian Meller [1966] Finance Director

Belron International Limited
Incorporated: 13 November 1989 *Employees:* 184
Net Worth: £680,422,976 *Total Assets:* £723,329,984
Registered Office: Milton Park, Stroude Road, Egham, Surrey, TW20 9EL
Activities: Activities of head offices
Parent: Belron Finance Limited
Officers: Robert Bass, Secretary; Gary Lubner [1959] Director/Business Executive; David Brian Meller [1966] Finance Director; Richard Robert Tyler [1971] Group Operations & Supply Chain Director

Belron Lending UK Limited
Incorporated: 20 October 2017
Net Worth: £1,406,666,624 *Total Assets:* £1,406,666,624
Registered Office: Milton Park, Stroude Road, Egham, Surrey, TW20 9EL
Activities: Management consultancy activities other than financial management
Parent: S.A. D'Ieteren N.V.
Officers: Claire Elizabeth Dakin, Secretary; Rebecca Scudamore, Secretary; Gary Lubner [1959] Director/Business Executive; David Brian Meller [1966] Finance Director

Belsize Garages Project Limited
Incorporated: 11 July 2005
Net Worth Deficit: £275,618 *Total Assets:* £15,362,346
Registered Office: Suite 2, Fountain House, 1a Elm Park, Stanmore, Middlesex, HA7 4AU
Activities: Construction of domestic buildings
Parent: Belsize Ltd
Officers: Paul Simon Godfrey [1980] Director; Tal Orly [1963] Director [Israeli]

Belton Associates (Group Holdings) Limited
Incorporated: 8 December 2011 *Employees:* 3
Net Worth Deficit: £1,131,000 *Total Assets:* £103,847,000
Registered Office: Frays Court, 71 Cowley Road, Uxbridge, Middlesex, UB8 2AE
Activities: Other social work activities without accommodation n.e.c.
Parent: SSCP Spring Bidco Limited
Officers: Helen Elizabeth Lecky, Secretary; Antony Vincent Holt [1959] Director/Chartered Accountant; Jean-Luc Emmanuel Janet [1970] Director [French]; David Jon Leatherbarrow [1969] Director/Group Chief Executive Officer

Belton Associates Holdings Limited
Incorporated: 9 December 2011 *Employees:* 3
Net Worth Deficit: £3,912,000 *Total Assets:* £99,935,000
Registered Office: Frays Court, 71 Cowley Road, Uxbridge, Middlesex, UB8 2AE
Activities: Other social work activities without accommodation n.e.c.
Parent: Belton Associates Group Limited
Officers: Helen Elizabeth Lecky, Secretary; Antony Vincent Holt [1959] Director/Chartered Accountant; Jean-Luc Emmanuel Janet [1970] Director [French]; David Jon Leatherbarrow [1969] Director/Group Chief Executive Officer

Belton Associates Limited
Incorporated: 12 December 2011 *Employees:* 8
Net Worth: £26,806,000 *Total Assets:* £112,876,000
Registered Office: Frays Court, 71 Cowley Road, Uxbridge, Middlesex, UB8 2AE
Activities: Other social work activities without accommodation n.e.c.
Parent: Belton Associates Holdings Limited
Officers: Helen Elizabeth Lecky, Secretary; Antony Vincent Holt [1959] Director/Chartered Accountant; Jean-Luc Emmanuel Janet [1970] Director/Chief Financial Officer [French]; David Jon Leatherbarrow [1969] Director/Group Chief Executive Officer

Benacre Investments Limited
Incorporated: 6 March 1992
Net Worth: £5,704,188 *Total Assets:* £8,034,587
Registered Office: 1 Tower House, Tower Centre, Hoddesdon, Herts, EN11 8UR
Activities: Other letting and operating of own or leased real estate
Major Shareholder: Steven John Dale
Officers: Steven John Dale [1957] Director/Travel Consultant

Benecol Limited
Incorporated: 29 May 2014 *Employees:* 15
Net Worth: £56,775,000 *Total Assets:* £78,854,000
Registered Office: The Mille, 1000 Great West Road, Brentford, Middlesex, TW8 9DW
Activities: Manufacture of other food products n.e.c.
Parent: Raisio UK Limited
Officers: Merja Sisko Lumme [1961] Director/VP Human Resources [Finnish]; Iiro Tapio Wester [1963] Director/Chief Commercial Officer [Finnish]

Benfleet Scrap Co Limited
Incorporated: 10 March 1995 *Employees:* 79
Net Worth: £9,416,076 *Total Assets:* £13,142,642
Registered Office: St James's House, 8 Overcliffe, Gravesend, Kent, DA11 0HJ
Activities: Wholesale of waste and scrap
Major Shareholder: Richard Brian Leeman
Officers: Leo Brian Leeman, Secretary; Richard Brian Leeman [1964] Director

Benja Properties Limited
Incorporated: 9 March 2015 *Employees:* 2
Net Worth: £292,515 *Total Assets:* £5,480,046
Registered Office: 28 Watersfield Way, Edgware, Middlesex, HA8 6RZ
Activities: Other letting and operating of own or leased real estate
Major Shareholder: Benjamin Sam Caplan
Officers: Benjamin Sam Caplan [1995] Director; Adam Kaye [1968] Director

Benson & Hedges Limited
Incorporated: 24 December 1910 *Employees:* 7
Net Worth: £420,400,000 *Total Assets:* £420,400,000
Registered Office: Members Hill, Brooklands Road, Weybridge, Surrey, KT13 0QU
Activities: Activities of head offices
Parent: Gallaher Overseas (Holdings) Limited
Officers: Nicholas Charles David Craig, Secretary; Andrew Chamberlain [1965] Director/Accountant; Charles Ashley Cunningham-Reid [1968] Director; Alison Maria Hawkett [1968] Director/Accountant; Paul Bernard Hennessy [1980] Director [Irish]; Jeroen Rusbach [1977] Director/Accountant [Dutch]; Daniel Sciamma [1970] Director [French]

The Bentley Wood Trust
Incorporated: 5 July 2011 *Employees:* 256
Net Worth: £30,126,728 *Total Assets:* £34,422,152
Registered Office: Bentley Wood High School, Bridges Road, Stanmore, Middlesex, HA7 3NA
Activities: Pre-primary education
Officers: Marcello Borgese [1966] Director/House Husband; Calvin Niklaus Hardy [1969] Director; Dr Janice Karen Howkins [1955] Director; Andrew McLeod Lewis [1959] Director/Government Service; Raakhi Patel [1978] Director/Accountant; Iram Qazi [1967] Director/Homemaker; Clive Westall [1965] Director/Headteacher

Berea Limited
Incorporated: 20 July 2012 *Employees:* 2
Net Worth: £387,148 *Total Assets:* £5,970,043
Registered Office: 7 Jardine House, Harrovian Business Village, Bessborough Road, Harrow, Middlesex, HA1 3EX
Activities: Other letting and operating of own or leased real estate
Officers: Hilton Lewis [1952] Director; Leslie Jonathan Sieff [1947] Director

Bereta Investments Limited
Incorporated: 18 January 2010
Net Worth: £820,368 *Total Assets:* £9,575,308
Registered Office: Unit H1, Imperial Business Park, Gravesend, Kent, DA11 0DQ
Activities: Management of real estate on a fee or contract basis
Major Shareholder: Michael Duncan Brown
Officers: Michael Duncan Brown, Secretary; Ian Anthony Barwick [1968] Director; Michael Duncan Brown [1971] Director

Berkeley (SQP) Limited
Incorporated: 4 March 2005
Previous: Berkeley Eighty-Eight Limited
Net Worth: £79,180,176 *Total Assets:* £174,989,664
Registered Office: Berkeley House, 19 Portsmouth Road, Cobham, Surrey, KT11 1JG
Activities: Non-trading company
Parent: Berkeley Homes (Capital) PLC
Officers: Jared Stephen Philip Cranney, Secretary; Antony Ball [1975] Director; Peter John Davidson [1982] Director; James Matthew Davies [1975] Finance Director; David Anthony Fox [1967] Finance Director; Sean James Gavin [1971] Director [Irish]; David Hall [1970] Director; Harry James Hulton Lewis [1975] Director; Edward Patrick McKenna [1970] Director [Irish]; David Michael Mullin [1981] Director; Robert Charles Grenville Perrins [1965] Director; Anthony William Pidgley [1947] Director; Richard James Stearn [1968] Director; Justin Tibaldi [1970] Director

The Berkeley Group Holdings PLC
Incorporated: 7 July 2004 *Employees:* 2,617
Net Worth: £2,620,000,000 *Total Assets:* £4,776,500,224
Registered Office: Berkeley House, 19 Portsmouth Road, Cobham, Surrey, KT11 1JG
Activities: Activities of head offices
Officers: Jared Stephen Philip Cranney, Secretary; Sir John Alexander Armitt [1946] Director; Glyn Barker [1953] Director; Diana Sarah Brightmore-Armour [1954] Director; Rachel Sara Downey [1969] Director; Sean Ellis [1968] Director; Adrian Man-Kiu Li [1973] Director; Andrew William Myers [1964] Director; Alison Nimmo [1964] Director; Robert Charles Grenville Perrins [1965] Director; Anthony William Pidgley [1947] Director; Richard James Stearn [1968] Director; Justin Tibaldi [1970] Director; Paul Mark Vallone [1964] Director; Peter Sean Vernon [1959] Director; Veronica Judith Colleton Wadley [1952] Director; Karl Whiteman [1965] Director

Berkeley Group PLC (The)
Incorporated: 15 October 1979
Net Worth: £2,001,586,048 *Total Assets:* £4,548,788,224
Registered Office: Berkeley House, 19 Portsmouth Road, Cobham, Surrey, KT11 1JG
Activities: Activities of head offices
Parent: The Berkeley Group Holdings PLC
Officers: Jared Stephen Philip Cranney, Secretary; Sean Ellis [1968] Director; Robert Charles Grenville Perrins [1965] Director; Anthony William Pidgley [1947] Director; Richard James Stearn [1968] Director; Justin Tibaldi [1970] Director; Paul Mark Vallone [1964] Director; Karl Whiteman [1965] Director

Berkeley Healthcare Limited
Incorporated: 9 November 1994 *Employees:* 33
Net Worth: £5,255,182 *Total Assets:* £8,228,880
Registered Office: Castle House, Victoria Street, Englefield Green, Surrey, TW20 0QX
Activities: Residential nursing care facilities
Shareholders: Amar Sheikh; Momin Sheikh
Officers: Amar Sheikh, Secretary; Amar Sheikh [1961] Director; Momin Sheikh [1963] Director

Berkeley Homes (Fleet) Limited
Incorporated: 18 March 1996
Net Worth: £19,405,992 *Total Assets:* £24,172,322
Registered Office: Berkeley House, 19 Portsmouth Road, Cobham, Surrey, KT11 1JG
Activities: Development of building projects
Parent: The Berkeley Group PLC
Officers: Jared Stephen Philip Cranney, Secretary; Stuart Bainbridge [1975] Director; Jeremy Paul Chapman [1974] Director; Graham John Chivers [1980] Director; Daniel Cooper [1971] Director; Christopher Lee Gilbert [1971] Director; Andrew Blair McPhillips [1967] Director; Robert Charles Grenville Perrins [1965] Director; Anthony William Pidgley [1947] Director; Richard James Stearn [1968] Director

Berkeley Homes (PCL) Limited
Incorporated: 15 September 2004
Net Worth: £56,945,000 *Total Assets:* £61,021,000
Registered Office: Berkeley House, 19 Portsmouth Road, Cobham, Surrey, KT11 1JG
Activities: Non-trading company
Parent: Berkeley Homes (Central London) Limited
Officers: Jared Stephen Philip Cranney, Secretary; Simon Piers Howard [1974] Director; Allen Edmond Michaels [1981] Director; Angus James Michie [1966] Director; Robert Charles Grenville Perrins [1965] Director; Anthony William Pidgley [1947] Director; Richard James Stearn [1968] Director; Paul Mark Vallone [1964] Director; Karl Whiteman [1965] Director; Dexter Whiting [1978] Director

Berkeley Homes (Southall) Limited
Incorporated: 29 November 2006 *Employees:* 62
Previous: St James West London Limited
Net Worth Deficit: £9,345,000 *Total Assets:* £174,928,992
Registered Office: Berkeley House, 19 Portsmouth Road, Cobham, Surrey, KT11 1JG
Activities: Development of building projects
Parent: Berkeley Homes Public Limited Company
Officers: Jared Stephen Philip Cranney, Secretary; Nigel Graham Davis [1968] Finance Director; Alison Jane Dowsett [1966] Director; Sean Ellis [1968] Director; Peter Kemkers [1971] Director; Damian Joseph Leydon [1967] Director; Robert Charles Grenville Perrins [1965] Director; Anthony William Pidgley [1947] Director; Richard James Stearn [1968] Director; Karl Whiteman [1965] Director

Berkeley Homes Public Limited Company
Incorporated: 6 October 2000 *Employees:* 1,529
Net Worth: £1,831,058,944 *Total Assets:* £3,215,473,920
Registered Office: 19 Portsmouth Road, Cobham, Surrey, KT11 1JG
Activities: Activities of head offices
Parent: TBG (3) 2009 Limited
Officers: Jared Stephen Philip Cranney, Secretary; Christopher Lee Gilbert [1971] Director; Angus James Michie [1966] Development Director; Robert Charles Grenville Perrins [1965] Director; Anthony William Pidgley [1947] Director; Andrew Michael Saunders-Davies [1958] Director; Peter James Smith [1971] Director; Richard James Stearn [1968] Director; Justin Tibaldi [1970] Director; Paul Mark Vallone [1964] Director; Karl Whiteman [1965] Director

Berkeley Residential Limited
Incorporated: 8 May 1997
Net Worth: £8,263,161 *Total Assets:* £14,200,830
Registered Office: Berkeley House, 19 Portsmouth Road, Cobham, Surrey, KT11 1JG
Activities: Activities of head offices
Parent: The Berkeley Group PLC
Officers: Jared Stephen Philip Cranney, Secretary; Robert Charles Grenville Perrins [1965] Director; Anthony William Pidgley [1947] Director; Richard James Stearn [1968] Director

Berkeley Ryewood Limited
Incorporated: 13 April 2003
Net Worth: £34,126,796 *Total Assets:* £48,459,428
Registered Office: Berkeley House, 19 Portsmouth Road, Cobham, Surrey, KT11 1JG
Activities: Development of building projects
Parent: The Berkeley Group PLC
Officers: Jared Stephen Philip Cranney, Secretary; Neil Leslie Eady [1977] Director; Karrina Stella Oki [1981] Director; Robert Charles Grenville Perrins [1965] Director; Anthony William Pidgley [1947] Director; Peter James Smith [1971] Director; Richard James Stearn [1968] Director

Berkeley Seventy-Six Limited
Incorporated: 16 September 2004
Net Worth: £20,252,492 *Total Assets:* £20,493,448
Registered Office: Berkeley House, 19 Portsmouth Road, Cobham, Surrey, KT11 1JG
Activities: Non-trading company
Shareholders: Berkeley Homes Public Limited Company; St James Group Limited
Officers: Jared Stephen Philip Cranney, Secretary; David Martin Lowry [1981] Director; Robert Charles Grenville Perrins [1965] Director; Anthony William Pidgley [1947] Director; Richard James Stearn [1968] Director

Berkeley Two Hundred and Three Limited
Incorporated: 23 October 2014
Net Worth: £1,851,499 *Total Assets:* £97,515,000
Registered Office: Berkeley House, 19 Portsmouth Road, Cobham, Surrey, KT11 1JG
Activities: Other business support service activities n.e.c.
Parent: The Berkeley Group PLC
Officers: Jared Stephen Philip Cranney, Secretary; Alison Jane Dowsett [1966] Director; Sean Ellis [1968] Director; Peter Kemkers [1971] Director; Robert Charles Grenville Perrins [1965] Director; Anthony William Pidgley [1947] Director; Richard James Stearn [1968] Director

Bernlite Limited
Incorporated: 2 July 1984 *Employees:* 20
Net Worth: £4,587,977 *Total Assets:* £5,705,289
Registered Office: Unit 2 The Eclipse Industrial Estate, 20 Sandown Road, Watford, Herts, WD24 7AE
Activities: Non-specialised wholesale trade
Major Shareholder: Barry Sydney Glazer
Officers: Donna Fuell, Secretary; Donna Fuell [1964] Financial Director; Barry Sydney Glazer [1945] Director/Chairman; Jason Scott Glazer [1970] Sales Director

Berrite Limited
Incorporated: 6 March 1990 *Employees:* 4
Net Worth: £6,438,224 *Total Assets:* £6,782,426
Registered Office: 79 High Street, Teddington, Middlesex, TW11 8HG
Activities: Other letting and operating of own or leased real estate
Officers: Christina Ann Fothergill, Secretary/Administrator; Christina Ann Fothergill [1951] Director/Administrator; Charles Julian Halford [1950] Director/Computer Engineer; Sir Michael James Harwood Harrison [1936] Director/Chairman

Berwen Limited
Incorporated: 11 February 1946 *Employees:* 4
Net Worth: £13,141,085 *Total Assets:* £15,401,277
Registered Office: Estate House, Marsh Way, Fairview Industrial Park, Rainham, Essex, RM13 8UH
Activities: Buying and selling of own real estate
Officers: Elizabeth Mary Berry, Secretary; John Berry [1943] Director; Simon John Berry [1969] Director

Besimcho Limited
Incorporated: 6 February 2014 *Employees:* 1
Net Worth Deficit: £18,271 *Total Assets:* £5,270,298
Registered Office: 19-20 Bourne Court, Southend Road, Woodford Green, Essex, IG8 8HD
Activities: Dormant company
Major Shareholder: Pesha Halberstam
Officers: Mozes Halberstam [1983] Director [Belgian]

Best Commercial Properties Limited
Incorporated: 6 December 2007 *Employees:* 1
Net Worth: £17,756,132 *Total Assets:* £31,279,510
Registered Office: 166 College Road, Harrow, Middlesex, HA1 1RA
Activities: Buying and selling of own real estate
Parent: Best Holdings (UK) Limited
Officers: Ian Michael Farr, Secretary; Alfred William Best [1970] Director; Waseem Hanif [1967] Director

Best Foods Limited
Incorporated: 5 September 2002 *Employees:* 17
Net Worth: £5,348,965 *Total Assets:* £10,647,870
Registered Office: GW Business Centre, Great West Road, London, TW8 9DF
Activities: Wholesale of fruit and vegetables
Shareholders: Radomir Szwed; Radomir Szwed
Officers: Stuart Hinchliffe [1974] Commercial Director; Radomir Szwed [1977] Director [Polish]

Best Holdings (UK) Limited
Incorporated: 31 January 2013 *Employees:* 123
Net Worth: £143,520,192 *Total Assets:* £291,121,248
Registered Office: 166 College Road, Harrow, Middlesex, HA1 1RA
Activities: Activities of other holding companies n.e.c.
Major Shareholder: Alfred William Best
Officers: Ian Michael Farr, Secretary; Alfred William Best [1970] Director; Waseem Hanif [1967] Director

Bet Invest Ltd
Incorporated: 7 January 2013
Net Worth: £45,559 *Total Assets:* £6,316,111
Registered Office: 15 Foxfield Close, Northwood, Middlesex, HA6 3NU
Activities: Other business support service activities n.e.c.
Major Shareholder: Andrii Matiukha
Officers: Andrii Matiukha [1972] Director [Ukrainian]

Betcrown Limited
Incorporated: 25 November 2015
Net Worth Deficit: £1,082,391 *Total Assets:* £18,706,236
Registered Office: Hill House, Lowlands Road, Harrow, Middlesex, HA1 3EQ
Activities: Development of building projects
Major Shareholder: Donovan Gijsbertus Wijsmuller
Officers: Brian Martin Comer [1960] Director [Irish]; Luke Andrew Comer [1957] Director [Irish]

Betex LLP
Incorporated: 19 February 2005
Net Worth: £26,000,100 *Total Assets:* £65,017,936
Registered Office: 166 College Road, Harrow, Middlesex, HA1 1RA
Officers: Tom Bennet [1966] LLP Member; Warrick Richard Booth [1964] LLP Member; Samuel Brodovcky [1978] LLP Member; Nicholas Exarchos [1964] LLP Member; Vittorio Fazio [1969] LLP Member; Alastair Keith MacKeith [1958] LLP Member; Edward Maravanyika [1975] LLP Member; Janardan Nedyam Menon [1967] LLP Member; Nilesh Ambalal Patel [1961] LLP Member; Matthieu Prevot [1978] LLP Member; Suresh Sadasivan [1968] LLP Member; Alexander Michael Trojanow [1976] LLP Member; Julian Max Rupert Trott [1964] LLP Member; Daniel Paul Wray [1976] LLP Member; Oleksandr Zakharchenko [1968] LLP Member

Beths Grammar School
Incorporated: 17 September 2010 *Employees:* 132
Net Worth: £14,274,000 *Total Assets:* £15,874,000
Registered Office: Beths Grammar School, Hartford Road, Bexley, Kent, DA5 1NE
Activities: General secondary education
Officers: Lisa Kay Gibson, Secretary; Malcolm Peter Appleby [1956] Director/Civil Engineer; Richard James Blyghton [1966] Director/Headmaster; Julie Elizabeth Bowen [1964] Director/Reverend; Jonathan Brock [1991] Director/Programme Manager; Maria Teresa Espindola [1974] Director/Barrister; Catherine Guest [1964] Director/Head of Business Development for National Literacy; Christopher Hares [1989] Director/Parliamentary and Stakeholder Engagement Officer; Stephen Mulvaney [1957] Assistant Director in The NHS; Oluwasanmi Anthony Obafaiye [1966] Director/Businessman; Dr Maria Pack [1972] Director/Education; Michael Charles Pack [1947] Director/Retired; Cathy Palmer [1974] Director/Intervention Manager; Raymond Ramsay [1987] Finance Director; Kim Patrice Sangster [1957] Director; Theresa Anne Tolhurst [1987] Director/Teacher [Irish]

Bexley Grammar School
Incorporated: 30 November 2010 *Employees:* 174
Net Worth: £8,624,000 *Total Assets:* £10,494,000
Registered Office: Bexley Grammar School, Danson Lane, Welling, Kent, DA16 2BL
Activities: General secondary education
Officers: Ann Julie Gibbs, Secretary; Ian James Beattie [1960] Director/Finance Manager; Savithri Khandige Bhat [1975] Director/Senior Clinical Healthcare Professional; Donna Briant [1964] Director/Admissions Officer at University of Greenwich; Olubunmi Diya [1970] Director/Academic Solutions Officer; Stephen Charles Elphick [1965] Director/Headteacher; Alice Fisher [1967] Director/Teacher; Cllr Richard Michael Gillespie [1953] Director/Schedules Manager; Thomas Callum Gorrard-Smith [1986] Director/Solicitor; Matthew Lines [1978] Director/Secondary School Teacher; Thomas Andrew Martin [1987] Director/Teacher; Moyra McDonald Pickering [1953] Deputy Director of Finance; Baljit Kaur Sangha [1976] Director/Marketing Professional; Alison Mary Saridogan [1961] Director/Education; Eileen Mary Elizabeth Stagg [1949] Director/Retired; Ian John Tonks [1971] Director/IT Project Manager; Anthony John Woodcock [1954] Director/Solicitor; Michael James Woodhall [1971] Director/Psychologist

BFIM Limited
Incorporated: 11 October 2006
Net Worth: £902,698,944 *Total Assets:* £1,344,396,032
Registered Office: 2nd Floor, 400 Dashwood Lang Road, Bourne Business Park, Addlestone, Surrey, KT15 2HJ
Activities: Activities of other holding companies n.e.c.
Parent: Brambles Investment Ltd.
Officers: Peter Jonathon Caisley Bruford [1964] Director/Accountant; Pascal Huart [1963] Director/Regional Treasurer [Belgian]; Rafe Anthony Warren [1959] Director/Accountant

BH (City Forum) Limited
Incorporated: 22 February 2001
Net Worth Deficit: £2,642,000 *Total Assets:* £196,340,000
Registered Office: Berkeley House, 19 Portsmouth Road, Cobham, Surrey, KT11 1JG
Activities: Construction of domestic buildings
Parent: Berkeley Homes (Capital) PLC
Officers: Jared Stephen Philip Cranney, Secretary; Christopher Abel [1974] Director; Louis Charles Aldred [1984] Director; Brian Benfield [1958] Director; James Matthew Davies [1975] Finance Director; David Anthony Fox [1967] Finance Director; Harry James Hulton Lewis [1975] Director; Brian Keith McKenzie [1976] Director; Robert Charles Grenville Perrins [1965] Director; Anthony William Pidgley [1947] Director; Blake Sanders [1984] Director; John Paul Sanders [1971] Director; Richard James Stearn [1968] Director; Justin Tibaldi [1970] Director; Mark David Tomlinson [1962] Director

Bhaggo Limited
Incorporated: 17 May 2004 *Employees:* 7
Net Worth: £6,655,917 *Total Assets:* £17,396,412
Registered Office: 114-116 Goodmayes Road, Ilford, Essex, IG3 9UZ
Activities: Growing of cereals (except rice), leguminous crops and oil seeds
Shareholders: Pirthipal Singh Takhar; Pirthipal Singh Takhar
Officers: Iqbal Kaur Takhar, Secretary; Pirthipal Singh Takhar [1982] Director

Bharat Forge International Limited
Incorporated: 3 December 2010 *Employees:* 13
Net Worth: £9,000,902 *Total Assets:* £112,049,960
Registered Office: Boston House, Business Center, 69-75 Boston Manor Road, Brentford, Middlesex, TW8 9JJ
Activities: Wholesale trade of motor vehicle parts and accessories
Officers: Kedar Prakash Dixit [1976] Director [Indian]; Sanjeev Gajanan Joglekar [1957] Director [Indian]; Amit Babasaheb Kalyani [1975] Director [Indian]; Babasaheb Neelkanth Kalyani [1949] Director [Indian]

Velji Bhovan & Sons (Trading) Limited
Incorporated: 22 November 2002 *Employees:* 187
Net Worth: £19,431,612 *Total Assets:* £26,832,736
Registered Office: VB House, Woodside End, Alperton, Wembley, Middlesex, HA0 1UR
Activities: Non-specialised wholesale of food, beverages and tobacco
Officers: Chunilal Velji Nathwani, Secretary; Chandulal Velji Nathwani [1938] Director/Sales Executive; Chunilal Velji Nathwani [1936] Director/Sales Executive; Mahendra Velji Nathwani [1946] Director/Sales Executive; Manharlal Velji Nathwani [1949] Director/Sales Executive; Natwarlal Velji Nathwani [1940] Director/Sales Executive

Bible and Gospel Trust
Incorporated: 9 June 2005 *Employees:* 31
Net Worth: £13,162,947 *Total Assets:* £14,995,667
Registered Office: Chelwood House, Cox Lane, Chessington, Surrey, KT9 1DN
Activities: Printing n.e.c.
Officers: Clive Vernon Anderson [1958] Director/Printer; Donald Franklin Druckenmiller [1958] Director/Commercial Interior Contractor [American]; Kevin Noel Dunlop [1948] Director/Accountant [Australian]; William Hugh George Hathorn [1946] Director/Furniture Manufacturer; Graham Ronald Olsson [1957] Director/Business Manager [Australian]; Bernard Graham Reiner [1956] Director/Merchant; Glen Jonathan Stacey [1976] Director/Business Development Manager; Murray James Walker [1946] Director; Simon Whiley [1976] Director

Bic U.K. Limited
Incorporated: 4 August 1944 *Employees:* 37
Net Worth: £13,859,000 *Total Assets:* £35,294,000
Registered Office: Bic UK Limited, Chaplin House, Widewater Place, Moorhall Road, Harefield, Middlesex, UB9 6NS
Activities: Wholesale of household goods (other than musical instruments) n.e.c
Parent: Societe Bic SA
Officers: Andrea Serafini, Secretary; Gonzalve Marie Leon Bich [1979] Director/General Manager [American]; Benoit Arnaud Marotte [1966] Director/General Manager [French]; Henri Claude Nicolau-Guillaumet [1969] Director/General Manager [French]

Bickerton's Aerodromes Limited
Incorporated: 14 November 1938 *Employees:* 10
Net Worth: £5,015,843 *Total Assets:* £5,530,508
Registered Office: Denham Aerodrome, Tilehouse Lane, Denham, Uxbridge, Middlesex, UB9 5DF
Activities: Service activities incidental to air transportation
Shareholders: Thomas Paul; Beatrice Amy Paul
Officers: Amy Elizabeth Paul, Secretary; Eva Alexandra Ceh [1975] Director/Pilot; Amy Elizabeth Paul [1974] Director/Solicitor; Beatrice Amy Paul [1940] Director; Thomas Ian Myles Paul [1970] Director/Pilot

Big Bear Group Limited
Incorporated: 17 October 2006 *Employees:* 2
Net Worth: £13,211,000 *Total Assets:* £13,295,000
Registered Office: Benecol Limited, The Mille, 1000 Great West Road, Brentford, Middlesex, TW8 9DW
Activities: Activities of head offices
Parent: Glisten Limited
Officers: Merja Sisko Lumme [1961] Director/VP Human Resources [Finnish]; Iiro Tapio Wester [1963] Director/Chief Commercial Officer [Finnish]

Biggin Hill Hangar Company Limited
Incorporated: 28 October 2008
Net Worth Deficit: £3,702,457 *Total Assets:* £15,209,881
Registered Office: Endeavour House, 78 Stafford Road, Wallington, Surrey, SM6 9AY
Activities: Other letting and operating of own or leased real estate
Officers: Ghanim Bin Saad Alsaad M Al-Kuwari [1964] Director [Qatari]; Carla Hanna [1977] Director [Lebanese]

Bike Alert PLC
Incorporated: 21 December 1989 *Employees:* 36
Net Worth: £40,452,492 *Total Assets:* £45,941,720
Registered Office: 30 Optima Park, Thames Road, Crayford, Dartford, Kent, DA1 4QX
Activities: Sale, maintenance and repair of motorcycles and related parts and accessories
Major Shareholder: Chris Boyiantzeas
Officers: Susan Olive Marsh, Secretary; Chris Boyiantzeas [1955] Director/Import/Export Manager [Greek]; Christophoros Constantinou [1975] Director/Accountant [Cypriot]; Susan Olive Marsh [1957] Director/Import/Export Manager

R. J. and D. E. Billings Limited
Incorporated: 13 May 1986 *Employees:* 7
Net Worth: £4,824,991 *Total Assets:* £21,091,332
Registered Office: Gay Dawn Offices, Pennis Lane, Fawkham, Longfield, Kent, DA3 8LY
Activities: Hotels and similar accommodation
Officers: Stephen John Billings, Secretary; Andrew John Billings [1964] Director; Clive John Billings [1955] Director; Ronald John Billings [1960] Director/Manager; Stephen John Billings [1961] Director

Bimax Chemicals Limited
Incorporated: 8 April 1993 *Employees:* 3
Net Worth: £3,706,217 *Total Assets:* £5,562,399
Registered Office: Suite 43-45, Airport House, Croydon, Surrey, CR0 0XZ
Activities: Manufacture of other organic basic chemicals
Shareholders: Cristian Marius Sghibartz; Evelyn Sghibartz
Officers: Evelyn Sghibartz, Secretary/Director; Caroline Annabelle Sghibartz [1992] Director; Christina Amanda Sghibartz [1986] Director; Dr Cristian Marius Sghibartz [1950] Managing Director; Evelyn Sghibartz [1949] Director

Bio Products Laboratory Holdings Limited
Incorporated: 16 October 2002 *Employees:* 2,893
Net Worth: £149,928,000 *Total Assets:* £434,364,000
Registered Office: Bio Products Laboratory, Dagger Lane, Elstree, Herts, WD6 3BX
Activities: Other human health activities
Shareholders: Naga UK Bidco Limited; Naga UK Bidco Limited
Officers: Kieu Hoang [1944] Director [American]; Kevin Lane [1961] Director/President [American]; Xu Wu [1967] Director [Chinese]

Bio Products Laboratory Limited
Incorporated: 11 August 2010
Net Worth: £74,935,000 *Total Assets:* £302,643,008
Registered Office: c/o Bio Products Laboratory, Dagger Lane, Elstree, Herts, WD6 3BX
Activities: Other business support service activities n.e.c.
Parent: Bio Products Laboratory Holdings Limited
Officers: Kieu Hoang [1944] Director [American]; Kevin Lane [1961] Director/President [American]; Xu Wu [1967] Director [Chinese]

Bio-Rad Laboratories Limited
Incorporated: 11 April 1995 *Employees:* 146
Net Worth: £21,641,000 *Total Assets:* £41,961,000
Registered Office: 3rd and 4th Floor, The Junction, Station Road, Watford, Herts, WD17 1ET
Activities: Non-specialised wholesale trade
Parent: Bio-Metrics (U.K.) Limited
Officers: Philip Howard [1957] Director/Regional Sales Manager; Norman David Schwartz [1950] Director/C.E.O. & President [American]

Bio-Rad Services UK Limited
Incorporated: 26 August 2016 *Employees:* 101
Net Worth: £769,000 *Total Assets:* £5,430,000
Registered Office: 3rd and 4th Floor, The Junction, Station Road, Watford, Herts, WD17 1ET
Activities: Other business support service activities n.e.c.
Parent: Bio-Rad Laboratories, Inc.
Officers: Rajinder Kumar Chopra [1966] Director/Marketing Professional; Norman David Schwartz [1950] Director/C.E.O. & President [American]

BIP Industries Limited
Incorporated: 3 January 2001
Net Worth: £17,192,940 *Total Assets:* £17,225,748
Registered Office: 2nd Floor, 400 Dashwood Lang Road, Bourne Business Park, Addlestone, Surrey, KT15 2HJ
Activities: Activities of other holding companies n.e.c.
Parent: Brambles Investment Ltd.
Officers: Peter Jonathon Caisley Bruford [1964] Director/Accountant; Pascal Huart [1963] Director/Regional Treasurer [Belgian]; Rafe Anthony Warren [1959] Director/Accountant

Birchwood Commercial Ltd
Incorporated: 18 October 2001 *Employees:* 2
Net Worth: £4,672,288 *Total Assets:* £18,487,676
Registered Office: Ibex House, Baker Street, Weybridge, Surrey, KT13 8AH
Activities: Management of real estate on a fee or contract basis
Shareholders: David Paul Steen; Rosario Angelo Minerva
Officers: David Paul Steen, Secretary/Developer; Rosario Angelo Minerva [1964] Director/Developer; David Paul Steen [1963] Director/Developer

Birds Eye Limited
Incorporated: 18 August 1938 *Employees:* 578
Net Worth: £194,418,000 *Total Assets:* £278,430,016
Registered Office: 1 New Square, Bedfont Lakes Business Park, Feltham, Middlesex, TW14 8HA
Activities: Manufacture of other food products n.e.c.
Parent: Nomad Foods Europe Limited
Officers: Edward John Heaton Marriott, Secretary; Craig Hamilton [1971] Director/Factory General Manager; Wayne Brian Hudson [1964] Managing Director; Sarah Ann Pollard [1974] Finance Director

Birmingham Resi Property LLP
Incorporated: 22 June 2016
Net Worth: £13,043,578 *Total Assets:* £13,043,578
Registered Office: Aprirose House, 48a High Street, Edgware, Middlesex, HA8 7EQ
Officers: Manish Mansukhlal Gudka [1970] Member; Gareth Jones [1973] Member; Suraj Rashmikant Shah [1982] LLP Member

Birmingham Schools Partnership (Group) Limited
Incorporated: 23 January 2003
Net Worth Deficit: £93,000 *Total Assets:* £7,424,000
Registered Office: 8 White Oak Square, London Road, Swanley, Kent, BR8 7AG
Activities: Activities of financial services holding companies
Parent: Innisfree M & G PPP LLP
Officers: Gaynor Birley Smith [1966] Investment Director; Richard Keith Sheehan [1975] Investment Director

Birmingham Schools Partnership Limited
Incorporated: 14 October 1999
Net Worth Deficit: £1,576,000 *Total Assets:* £41,926,000
Registered Office: 8 White Oak Square, London Road, Swanley, Kent, BR8 7AG
Activities: Development of building projects
Parent: Birmingham Schools Partnership (Holdings) Limited
Officers: Gaynor Birley Smith [1966] Investment Director; Richard Keith Sheehan [1975] Investment Director

Syd Bishop & Sons (Demolition) Limited
Incorporated: 24 January 1973 *Employees:* 140
Net Worth: £5,041,393 *Total Assets:* £18,787,870
Registered Office: Waldens Depot, Waldens Road, Orpington, Kent, BR5 4EU
Activities: Demolition
Shareholder: Terence Malcolm Bishop
Officers: Stephen Edward Bishop [1959] Director/Estimating Manager; Sydney Michael Bishop [1956] Director/Contracts Manager; Terrence Malcolm Bishop [1941] Director/Demolition Contractor; Thomas James Bishop [1965] Director/Manager

Bishop & Sons' Depositories Limited
Incorporated: 3 December 1927 *Employees:* 169
Net Worth Deficit: £1,083,400 *Total Assets:* £6,145,373
Registered Office: Unit 2 HQ3, 223 Hook Rise South, Surbiton, Surrey, KT6 7LD
Activities: Removal services
Shareholder: Peter William Bishop
Officers: Kevin Francis Osullivan, Secretary; Alistair Paul Robert Bingle [1965] Managing Director; Grant Hamilton Bishop [1972] International Director; Neil Paul Bishop [1974] Business Development Director; Peter William Bishop [1966] ICT Director; David William Guiel [1967] Operations Director; Christopher James Marshall [1970] Marketing Director; Kevin Francis Osullivan [1962] Finance Director [Irish]; Stuart Martin Philp [1974] Business Relocation Director

The Bishop Wand Church of England School
Incorporated: 16 July 2012 *Employees:* 125
Net Worth: £14,712,972 *Total Assets:* £16,846,754
Registered Office: Bishop Wand Cofe School, Laytons Lane, Sunbury on Thames, Surrey, TW16 6LT
Activities: General secondary education
Officers: Lynne Denny, Secretary; Daniel Nigel Aldridge [1977] Director/Headteacher; Professor Margaret Jayne Barlow [1960] Director/University Professor; Catherine Esther Batt [1978] Director/Learning Mentor; Maria Bramhall [1965] Director/Teacher; Matthew Charles Church [1970] Director/Accountant; Tracey-Anne Joy Cutbush [1968] Director/Teacher; Russell John Dickens [1973] Director; The Reverend Andrew Victor John Downes [1965] Director/Vicar; Christopher John Fowler [1971] Director/Head of Complaints (Bank); Peter David Frith [1971] Director/Teacher; Caroline Gill [1947] Director/Retired; Brian Peter Grew [1966] Director/Commercial Manager; Darinka Howley [1956] Director; Ian James Kirk [1971] Director/IT Operations Manager; Andrew Saville [1966] Director/Vicar and Area Dean of Spelthorne; Charlotte Anne Watmore [1975] Director/Learning and Development Partner; Toby James Graham Wood [1986] Director/Teacher

Bishopsgate School Limited
Incorporated: 17 January 1997 *Employees:* 73
Net Worth: £8,899,941 *Total Assets:* £9,515,538
Registered Office: Bishopsgate Road, Englefield Green, Egham, Surrey, TW20 0YJ
Activities: Primary education
Officers: Charles Michael Barnard Carver, Secretary; Barbara Breedon [1967] Director/Teacher; Linda Susan Buchanan [1962] Director/Counsellor; Jonathan Aspull Carroll [1961] Director/Headmaster; Vanessa Cresswell [1966] Director/Chartered Accountant; Timothy Eddis [1969] Director/Teacher; Marc David Fisher [1958] Director/Quantity Surveyor; David Andrew Henderson Williams [1958] Director/Chartered Surveyor; Nicholas Derrick Jamison [1959] Director/Solicitor; Christiian Paul Marriott [1970] Director/Financier; Dudley John Mills [1965] Director; Claire Robertson [1974] Director; Simon Sydenham [1967] Director; Shirley Madeleine Winson [1934] Director

Bishopshalt School
Incorporated: 6 October 2011 *Employees:* 165
Net Worth: £17,860,696 *Total Assets:* £20,159,984
Registered Office: Royal Lane, Hillingdon, Uxbridge, Middlesex, UB8 3RF
Activities: General secondary education
Officers: Irene Denise Warnock, Secretary; Abdi Abby [1964] Director; Tahira Naheed Ansari [1970] Director; Gail Bond [1957] Director; Lyndon Bray [1969] Director/Police Officer; Andrew Brown [1950] Director/Teacher; Michelle Brown [1969] Director/School Administrator; Peter Charles Coombs [1955] Director/Teacher; Michael John Deighton [1962] Director/Teacher; Lydia Mary Holland [1952] Director/Retired; Professor William Leahy [1959] Director/Academic; Nancy Kirsten Rawlings [1967] Director; Kim David Rowe [1961] Director/Headteacher; Julie Ann Spikings [1967] Director/Deputy Headteacher; Nicola St Paul [1980] Director/International Marketing Manager; Peter Charles William Underwood [1937] Director/Retired; Stephen White [1989] Director/Student Welfare Officer

Bishopswood Estates Limited
Incorporated: 23 July 1981
Net Worth: £351,149 *Total Assets:* £7,389,283
Registered Office: Portland House, 69-71 Wembley Hill Road, Wembley, Middlesex, HA9 8BU
Activities: Construction of commercial buildings
Parent: Solai Holdings Limited
Officers: Rajni Shantilal Kansagra, Secretary; Bhupendra Shantilal Kansagra [1956] Director; Rajni Shantilal Kansagra [1942] Director/Engineer; Ramesh Shantilal Kansagra [1950] Director; Sunil Rajni Kansagra [1976] Director/Developer

Biz Group Holdings Limited
Incorporated: 17 August 2005 *Employees:* 2
Net Worth Deficit: £487,105 *Total Assets:* £8,256,077
Registered Office: Millmarsh Lane, Brimsdown, Enfield, Middlesex, EN3 7QA
Activities: Combined office administrative service activities
Officers: Michael Stuart Smith, Secretary/Manager; Graham Paul Smith [1959] Director/Manager; Michael Stuart Smith [1962] Director/Manager

Biz Karts Limited
Incorporated: 6 November 1987 *Employees:* 33
Net Worth: £4,696,388 *Total Assets:* £8,913,244
Registered Office: Millmarsh Lane, Brimsdown, Enfield, Middlesex, EN3 7QA
Activities: Other manufacturing n.e.c.
Officers: Michael Stuart Smith, Secretary/Director; Christopher Smith [1988] Director/Manager; Graham Paul Smith [1959] Director/Manager; Michael Stuart Smith [1962] Director/Manager

Bizy Investments Limited
Incorporated: 19 March 1987 *Employees:* 7
Net Worth: £7,743,776 *Total Assets:* £7,840,886
Registered Office: Centrum House, 36 Station Road, Egham, Surrey, TW20 9LF
Activities: Financial intermediation not elsewhere classified
Shareholders: Denize Fiona Cameron Hawkes; Michael John Cameron Hawkes; Suzanna Louise Cameron Watt; Edward Jonathan Cameron Hawkes
Officers: Michael John Cameron Hawkes, Secretary; Suzanna Louise Cameron Watt [1974] Director/Executive; Denize Fiona Cameron Hawkes [1948] Director; Edward Jonathan Cameron Hawkes [1977] Director; Michael John Cameron Hawkes [1946] Director; Tania Maxine Cameron McLuckie [1985] Director/Student; Laura Katherine Cameron Temple-Mills [1981] Director/Make Up Artist

BL Bottling Holdings UK Limited
Incorporated: 21 April 2016
Net Worth: £6,767,248,384 *Total Assets:* £7,980,585,984
Registered Office: Pemberton House, Bakers Road, Uxbridge, Middlesex, UB8 1EZ
Activities: Activities of other holding companies n.e.c.
Parent: Bottling Holdings Europe Limited
Officers: Paul Van Reesch, Secretary; Frank Govaerts [1961] Director [Belgian]; Joyce Marie King-Lavinder [1959] Director [American]; Paul Van Reesch [1976] Director; Edward Owen Walker [1967] Director

BL Wind Limited
Incorporated: 9 May 2013
Net Worth Deficit: £5,939,000 *Total Assets:* £30,665,000
Registered Office: 8 White Oak Square, London Road, Swanley, Kent, BR8 7AG
Activities: Production of electricity
Parent: JLEAG Wind Limited
Officers: Christopher Holmes [1976] Investment Adviser/Director; Joseph Mark Linney [1958] Director/Chartered Quantity Surveyor

Black Arrow Group Limited
Incorporated: 1 May 1959 *Employees:* 8
Net Worth: £12,412,528 *Total Assets:* £15,912,484
Registered Office: 3rd Floor, Profile West, 950 Great West Road, Brentford, Middlesex, TW8 9ES
Activities: Financial leasing
Shareholders: Maurice Edward; Arnold Edward
Officers: Arnold Edward [1926] Director/Chairman; Ian Edward [1959] Director/Financial Advisor; Maurice Edward [1929] Director/Deputy Chairman; Paul Edward [1959] Director/Sales Executive; David Oliver Horne [1932] Director; Simon Geoffrey Lake [1959] Director/Chartered Accountant

Black Katz Eddy (Holdings) Limited
Incorporated: 14 July 1997 *Employees:* 3
Net Worth: £6,831,062 *Total Assets:* £9,877,369
Registered Office: 94 Orchard Gate, Greenford, Middlesex, UB6 0QP
Activities: Other letting and operating of own or leased real estate
Shareholders: Andrew Noel Black; Christian Stephen Eddy; Juliette Rachel Katz
Officers: Juliette Rachel Katz, Secretary; Andrew Noel Black [1964] Director/Property Agent; Christian Stephen Eddy [1963] Sales Director; Juliette Rachel Katz [1968] Director/Property Agent

Black River Asset Management (UK) Limited
Incorporated: 14 August 2003
Net Worth: £6,097,651 *Total Assets:* £6,097,651
Registered Office: Velocity V1, Brooklands Drive, Weybridge, Surrey, KT13 0SL
Activities: Fund management activities
Officers: Dena Michelle L O'Bue, Secretary; Peter Robert Goodwin [1979] Director/Controller and Finance Lead [American]; David Alexander Robertson [1960] Director/Assistant General Counsel [American]

Black Twig Limited
Incorporated: 17 February 2011 *Employees:* 2
Previous: Leighcroft Limited
Net Worth: £5,144,583 *Total Assets:* £5,194,787
Registered Office: Nicholas House, River Front, Enfield, Middlesex, EN1 3FG
Activities: Other business support service activities n.e.c.
Officers: John Alan Silvester [1948] Director/General Manager

Blackfen School for Girls
Incorporated: 2 March 2012 *Employees:* 157
Net Worth: £19,230,000 *Total Assets:* £21,128,000
Registered Office: Blackfen School for Girls, Blackfen Road, Sidcup, Kent, DA15 9NU
Activities: General secondary education
Officers: Jane Andrews [1954] Director; Launa Joy Ashdown [1960] Director/Delivery Driver; Kim Brewer [1973] Director/Teacher; Matthew Francis William Brown [1964] Director/Teacher; Anita Dhorajiwala [1972] Director/Regulatory Manager; Stuart James Fitz Generald [1950] Director/Lecturer; Danielle Moore [1972] Director/Local Government Employee - School Improvement; Trevor Victor Perrin [1947] Director/Semi Retired; Janet Mary Phelps [1950] Director/Casual Clerk - Bexley Clerkship Practice; Robert Joseph Shaw [1980] Director/Teacher; William Anthony Stone [1959] Director; Lee Christopher Thomas [1971] Director; Carol Susan Townsend [1954] Director/Housewife; Louise Clare Twiner [1973] Director/Relationship Support Manager

Blackford Media LLP
Incorporated: 23 April 2004
Net Worth: £6,172,750 *Total Assets:* £6,172,750
Registered Office: 99 Kenton Road, Harrow, Middlesex, HA3 0AN
Officers: John Boyle [1952] LLP Member; Gillian Kay Christie [1958] LLP Member; Steven Christie [1965] LLP Member; Peter David Cook [1964] LLP Member; Andrew John Forryan [1960] LLP Member; Peter Glenn [1963] LLP Member; Bruce Malcolm Gordon [1959] LLP Member; George Heydon [1961] LLP Member; Michael Makepeace Eugene Jeffries [1944] LLP Member; Andrew Christopher Lapping [1963] LLP Member; Graham Richard David Lay [1956] LLP Member; Johan Mjallby [1971] LLP Member; Nicholas Charles Munday [1959] LLP Member; Mark Robert Newall [1966] LLP Member; Nicholas John Preston [1955] LLP Member; Jacqueline Stephens [1960] LLP Member; Stephen William Vaughan [1960] LLP Member; Peter Maurice Watson [1956] LLP Member; Mark Benjamin Wells [1955] LLP Member; James Ian Wilkes [1945] LLP Member; Iestyn Milton Williams [1951] LLP Member

Blackfriars Land Company Limited
Incorporated: 3 April 1997 *Employees:* 5
Net Worth: £2,433,159 *Total Assets:* £5,339,144
Registered Office: c/o Messrs Elliot Woolfe & Rose, 1st Floor, Equity House, 128-136 High Street, Edgware, Middlesex, HA8 7TT
Activities: Other business support service activities n.e.c.
Officers: Michelle Mary Sands, Secretary; John Donald Garrett [1964] Director; Justin Garrett [1971] Director/Retailer; Mark Charles Richard Garrett [1963] Director/Draughtsman; Michelle Mary Sands [1966] Director/Housewife

Blackfriars Securities (Brighton) Limited
Incorporated: 28 April 2000 *Employees:* 2
Net Worth: £3,734,330 *Total Assets:* £8,214,600
Registered Office: Park Place House, 24 Church Street, Epsom, Surrey, KT17 4QB
Activities: Other letting and operating of own or leased real estate
Parent: Albemarle Securities Ltd
Officers: Darren Colin Bradley [1969] Director/Chartered Surveyor; James Perry Hallam [1978] Director; Michael Stuart Hastings [1942] Director

Blackstone City Ltd
Incorporated: 4 December 2014 *Employees:* 1
Net Worth Deficit: £240,371 *Total Assets:* £6,683,997
Registered Office: Vista Centre, 50 Salisbury Road, Hounslow, Middlesex, TW4 6JQ
Activities: Other letting and operating of own or leased real estate
Shareholders: Waryam Singh Kakol; Waryam Singh Kakol
Officers: Wender Kour Kakar [1977] Director/Manager

Blackstown Holdings Limited
Incorporated: 8 January 2015 *Employees:* 701
Previous: Graham Care Group Limited
Net Worth: £101,012,120 *Total Assets:* £170,688,736
Registered Office: 20 Cranley Road, Hersham, Walton on Thames, Surrey, KT12 5BP
Activities: Activities of other holding companies n.e.c.
Shareholders: William Ernest Graham; Karen Elizabeth Graham
Officers: Dr Karen Elizabeth Graham [1962] Director/Medical Doctor; William Ernest Graham [1961] Director

Blackwater Securities Limited
Incorporated: 16 October 2001 *Employees:* 3
Net Worth: £2,137,417 *Total Assets:* £9,230,749
Registered Office: York House, Empire Way, Wembley, Middlesex, HA9 0FQ
Activities: Development of building projects
Parent: Newcroft Investments Limited
Officers: Vivian Emmy Taylor, Secretary; Simon Mark Collins [1974] Director; Allan Raymond Taylor [1948] Director; Vivian Emmy Taylor [1949] Director/Company Secretary

Blakley Electrics Limited
Incorporated: 21 October 1957 *Employees:* 101
Net Worth: £8,546,964 *Total Assets:* £13,857,786
Registered Office: 1 Thomas Road, Optima Park, Crayford, Kent, DA1 4QX
Activities: Manufacture of electricity distribution and control apparatus
Major Shareholder: Peter John Blakley
Officers: Daniel Alexander Slater, Secretary/Director; Andrew Robert Baker [1964] Projects Director; Marion Nellie Blakley [1928] Director; Peter John Blakley [1958] Director; Alan Mark Milton [1966] Director; Daniel Alexander Slater [1965] Director

Blanc Brasseries Limited
Incorporated: 30 May 2003 *Employees:* 604
Net Worth Deficit: £22,155,240 *Total Assets:* £24,101,238
Registered Office: Wizard House, 2a Cambridge Road, Teddington, Middlesex, TW11 8DR
Activities: Licenced restaurants
Parent: Brasserie Bar Co Limited
Officers: Raymond Rene Alfred Blanc [1949] Director/Chef Patron [French]; Jeremy Brown [1966] Director; Kathryn Coury [1964] Director; Mark Derry [1960] Restaurant Group Managing Director; Clive Andrew Fretwell [1961] Director/Executive Chef; Christopher Patrick Edward Guy [1981] Finance Director; Helen Louise Melvin [1968] Director/Accountant

Blendhall Limited
Incorporated: 13 March 1990 *Employees:* 2
Net Worth: £1,835,269 *Total Assets:* £5,736,204
Registered Office: Hadley Hurst, Hadley Common, Barnet, Herts, EN5 5QG
Activities: Activities of head offices
Parent: Wellmode Limited
Officers: Farrokh Mahboubian, Secretary; Anthony George Bunker [1944] Director/Tax Consultant; Alexander Mahboubian [1972] Director; Farrokh Mahboubian [1932] Director [Iranian]

Blenheim Barnes Limited
Incorporated: 29 November 2010
Net Worth: £908,826 *Total Assets:* £6,033,029
Registered Office: 22 Barn Rise, Wembley, Middlesex, HA9 9NQ
Activities: Development of building projects
Officers: Anthony David Chambers [1955] Director/Property Developer/Investor; Daniel Freedman [1971] Director/Lawyer; Paul Gary Hirst [1961] Director/Property Development/Investor

Blenheim Consultancy Services Limited
Incorporated: 28 March 2006 *Employees:* 4
Net Worth: £6,559,293 *Total Assets:* £9,469,599
Registered Office: 22 Barn Rise, Wembley, Middlesex, HA9 9NQ
Activities: Management of real estate on a fee or contract basis
Major Shareholder: Anthony David Chambers
Officers: Paul Gary Hirst, Secretary; Anthony David Chambers [1955] Director; Daniel Freedman [1971] Director/Lawyer; Paul Gary Hirst [1961] Director

Blenheim Estates Limited
Incorporated: 1 October 1997
Net Worth: £8,066,735 *Total Assets:* £15,362,492
Registered Office: 28 Church Road, Stanmore, Middlesex, HA7 4XR
Activities: Other letting and operating of own or leased real estate
Parent: Blenheim Property Management Ltd
Officers: Jacqueline Smith, Secretary; Dennis Isaac Warwick [1952] Director

Blenheim Group Limited
Incorporated: 13 September 2000
Net Worth: £3,377,541 *Total Assets:* £8,237,407
Registered Office: Bytes House, Randalls Way, Leatherhead, Surrey, KT22 7TW
Activities: Activities of other holding companies n.e.c.
Parent: Bytes Technology Group Limited
Officers: Paul David Emms [1967] Director; Samantha Jayne Mudd [1969] Director; Neil Robert Murphy [1964] Director; Keith Alan Richardson [1959] Director; Robert Eben Venter [1960] Director [South African]

Blenheim High School
Incorporated: 9 February 2012 *Employees:* 188
Net Worth: £8,965,000 *Total Assets:* £12,225,000
Registered Office: Blenheim High School, Longmead Road, Epsom, Surrey, KT19 9BH
Activities: General secondary education
Officers: Karam Bhogal, Secretary; Sandra Balkwill [1958] Director/QCF Assessor; Anthony Bodell [1971] Director/Headteacher; Laura Maria Caldwell [1964] Director/Parent Governor [Dutch]; Sandra Christine Darey [1969] Director/Charity Worker; Robin Keith Dear [1957] Finance Director; Louise Margaret Footner [1962] Director/Civil Servant; Claire Elizabeth Hadcocks [1960] Director/Management Consultant; Jeff Richard Lloyd [1952] Director/Retired Primary Headteacher; Dr Polycarp Samuel Luke [1962] Civil Engineering Director; David Murden [1975] Director/Deputy Headteacher; Alastair Whitby [1990] Director/Customer Experience Manager

Blenheim House Construction Limited
Incorporated: 4 October 1996 *Employees:* 76
Net Worth: £3,620,501 *Total Assets:* £20,895,484
Registered Office: The Old Bank House, 11-13 London Street, Chertsey, Surrey, KT16 8AP
Activities: Construction of commercial buildings
Shareholders: David Huw Pearce; Anne Pearce; Michael Curtis
Officers: Michael Curtis, Secretary; Ian Roland Bosley [1970] Director/Quantity Surveyor; Anthony Peter Francis Brewester [1971] Director/Quantity Surveyor; Michael Curtis [1965] Commercial Director; Richard David Jones [1962] Director/Civil Engineer; Marc Matthews [1969] Director/Quantity Surveyor; David Huw Pearce [1955] Managing Director; Richard Henderson Taylor [1966] Director/Civil Engineer

Blenheim Property Management Limited
Incorporated: 1 October 1997
Net Worth: £16,120,106 *Total Assets:* £24,772,198
Registered Office: 28 Church Road, Stanmore, Middlesex, HA7 4XR
Activities: Other letting and operating of own or leased real estate
Shareholders: Alan Harold Warwick; Sheldon Andrew Cordell
Officers: Jacqueline Smith, Secretary; Dennis Isaac Warwick [1952] Director

Blessville Limited
Incorporated: 22 October 1996
Net Worth Deficit: £3,622,067 *Total Assets:* £42,040,620
Registered Office: Hill House, Lowlands Road, Harrow, Middlesex, HA1 3EQ
Activities: Development of building projects
Major Shareholder: Donovan Gijsbertus Wijsmuller
Officers: Brian Martin Comer [1960] Director [Irish]; Luke Andrew Comer [1957] Director [Irish]

Blitzfair Limited
Incorporated: 28 January 1985 *Employees:* 3
Net Worth: £13,044,592 *Total Assets:* £28,516,492
Registered Office: c/o Messrs Elliot Woolfe & Rose, 1st Floor, Equity House, 128-136 High Street, Edgware, Middlesex, HA8 7TT
Activities: Development of building projects
Major Shareholder: Geoffrey Harvey Toms
Officers: Benjamin George Harvey Toms, Secretary; Geoffrey Harvey Toms [1946] Director/Property Executive; Stephen Nathaniel Toms [1966] Director/Chartered Surveyor

Bloomfield Terrace LLP
Incorporated: 26 January 2007
Net Worth: £1,263,259 *Total Assets:* £6,678,285
Registered Office: 168 Ember Lane, Esher, Surrey, KT10 8EJ
Officers: Henry Norman Lewis [1939] Member; Steven Robert Sharp [1957] Member

Blossom House School Limited
Incorporated: 5 August 2004 *Employees:* 183
Previous: Blossom Lower School Limited
Net Worth: £157,209 *Total Assets:* £6,920,191
Registered Office: Station Road, Motspur Park, New Malden, Surrey, KT3 6JJ
Activities: Other business support service activities n.e.c.
Parent: Lanend Limited
Officers: Joanna Briant Burgess, Secretary; Joanna Briant Burgess [1950] Director/Teacher; Dr Timothy Evans [1955] Director, General Practitioner

Blue Prop Ltd
Incorporated: 26 October 2009 *Employees:* 2
Net Worth: £11,393 *Total Assets:* £6,860,558
Registered Office: Suite 2, Fountain House, 1a Elm Park, Stanmore, Middlesex, HA7 4AU
Activities: Development of building projects
Major Shareholder: Claudia Michelle Magid
Officers: Michael Magid, Secretary; Claudia Michelle Magid [1970] Director [Irish]; Michael Magid [1967] Director [Irish]

Bluecastle Enterprises Limited
Incorporated: 20 December 2000
Net Worth Deficit: £29,417,268 *Total Assets:* £267,046,032
Registered Office: Suite No 2, First Floor, Kenwood House, 77a Shenley Road, Borehamwood, Herts, WD6 1AG
Activities: Tax consultancy
Major Shareholder: Vadim Giner
Officers: Jennifer Elizabeth Westmoreland [1967] Director/Financial Controller

Bluecroft Riverdale LLP
Incorporated: 23 July 2013
Net Worth: £277,938 *Total Assets:* £7,910,062
Registered Office: 3rd Floor, Sterling House, Langston Road, Loughton, Essex, IG10 1JA
Officers: Mario Micheal Ttakoushis [1966] Member

Bluestar Enterprise Limited
Incorporated: 27 September 2010
Net Worth: £1,260,832 *Total Assets:* £14,963,473
Registered Office: Unit 4 Imperial Park, Stonefield Way, South Ruislip, Middlesex, HA4 0JW
Activities: Wholesale of perfume and cosmetics
Major Shareholder: Manisha Thakrar
Officers: Nayan Thakrar [1960] Director

James Blunt Limited
Incorporated: 15 January 2001 *Employees:* 3
Net Worth: £4,102,274 *Total Assets:* £7,762,015
Registered Office: Munro House, Portsmouth Road, Cobham, Surrey, KT11 1PP
Activities: Other business support service activities n.e.c.
Major Shareholder: James Hillier Blount
Officers: Jane Ann Farran Blount, Secretary/Director; Charles Blount [1946] Director; James Hillier Blount [1974] Director/Musician; Jane Ann Farran Blount [1950] Director

BMAK FX Limited
Incorporated: 7 May 2013
Net Worth: £571,477 *Total Assets:* £8,562,174
Registered Office: 4 The Headway, Ewell, Epsom, Surrey, KT17 1UJ
Activities: Activities of financial services holding companies
Officers: Alexandra Lawrence [1991] Director/Accountant; Bernadette Lawrence [1958] Director; Kenneth William Lawrence [1958] Director; Matthew William Lawrence [1989] Director

BMG (Ashford) General Partner Limited
Incorporated: 24 July 1998
Net Worth: £1,939,393 *Total Assets:* £9,374,191
Registered Office: The Compass Centre, Nelson Road, Hounslow, Middlesex, TW6 2GW
Activities: Buying and selling of own real estate
Parent: Heathrow Enterprises Limited
Officers: Ross Findlay Scott Baker [1974] Director

BML Utility Contractors Ltd
Incorporated: 29 April 2008 *Employees:* 15
Net Worth: £5,622,061 *Total Assets:* £6,590,824
Registered Office: Devonshire House, 582 Honeypot Lane, Stanmore, Middlesex, HA7 1JS
Activities: Other specialised construction activities n.e.c.
Major Shareholder: Brendan McNicholas
Officers: Karen McNicholas, Secretary; Brendan McNicholas [1967] Director/Utility and Groundworks Contractor

BMT Defence and Security UK Limited
Incorporated: 8 December 1988 *Employees:* 313
Previous: BMT Defence Services Limited
Net Worth: £7,807,000 *Total Assets:* £16,753,000
Registered Office: Third Floor, 1 Park Road, Teddington, Middlesex, TW11 0AP
Activities: Other engineering activities
Parent: BMT Group Limited
Officers: Trudy Michelle Grey, Secretary; Jeremy Mark Alan Berwick [1967] Director; Sarah Louise Kenny [1973] Director; David Keith McSweeney [1958] Director

BMT Group Limited
Incorporated: 18 February 1985 *Employees:* 1,450
Net Worth: £31,667,000 *Total Assets:* £110,380,000
Registered Office: Third Floor, 1 Park Road, Teddington, Middlesex, TW11 0AP
Activities: Management consultancy activities other than financial management
Officers: Trudy Michelle Grey, Secretary; Wendy Jacqueline Barnes [1957] Director; Sir John Antony Hood [1952] Chairman & Director [New Zealander]; Sarah Louise Kenny [1973] Director; David Keith McSweeney [1958] Director; Charles Max Packshaw [1952] Director; Minoo Homi Patel [1949] Director/Professor of Mechanical Engineering; Douglas Russell Webb [1961] Director

BMT Hi-Q Sigma Limited
Incorporated: 28 August 1987 *Employees:* 115
Net Worth: £3,429,000 *Total Assets:* £5,899,000
Registered Office: Third Floor, 1 Park Road, Teddington, Middlesex, TW11 0AP
Activities: Management consultancy activities other than financial management
Parent: BMT Group Limited
Officers: Trudy Michelle Grey, Secretary; Jeremy Mark Alan Berwick [1967] Director; Sarah Louise Kenny [1973] Director; David Keith McSweeney [1958] Director

BNK (UK) Limited
Incorporated: 7 March 2008 *Employees:* 15
Net Worth: £6,603,691 *Total Assets:* £269,637,024
Registered Office: Salatin House, 19 Cedar Road, Sutton, Surrey, SM2 5DA
Activities: Wholesale of other fuels and related products
Officers: Andrei Dashutin [1957] Director [Belarusian]

BNS Company (Property Holdings) Limited
Incorporated: 21 December 2000
Net Worth: £6,943,524 *Total Assets:* £9,000,330
Registered Office: World Business Centre, 3 Newall Road, London Heathrow Airport, Hounslow, Middlesex, TW6 2TA
Activities: Treatment and disposal of non-hazardous waste
Parent: Bath Road Holdings Limited
Officers: Surinder Arora, Secretary; Sunita Arora [1964] Director; Surinder Arora [1958] Director

Otto Bock Healthcare PLC
Incorporated: 5 August 1976 *Employees:* 133
Net Worth: £2,934,393 *Total Assets:* £16,068,942
Registered Office: 32 Parsonage Road, Englefield Green, Egham, Surrey, TW20 0LD
Activities: Manufacture of medical and dental instruments and supplies
Major Shareholder: Hans Georg Nader
Officers: Gregor John Bates, Secretary; Gregor John Bates [1969] Director; Graeme Goody [1962] Director/Clinical Management; Andrew Philip McLean [1966] Director; Hans Georg Nader [1961] Director/Bachelor of Commerce [German]; Philip Anthony Yates [1963] Director/Manager of Orthopaedic Company

Body Works West at Lambton Place Limited
Incorporated: 19 July 1972 *Employees:* 21
Net Worth: £3,348,001 *Total Assets:* £6,507,787
Registered Office: 5 Elstree Gate, Elstree Way, Borehamwood, Herts, WD6 1JD
Activities: Other amusement and recreation activities n.e.c.
Parent: Lambton Squash Holdings Limited
Officers: Elizabeth Margaret Greenwood, Secretary/Director; Elizabeth Margaret Greenwood [1952] Director; Alan James Rivers [1945] Director; Alexander Henry James Rivers [1987] Director

Bold-Rock Management and Investments Ltd
Incorporated: 26 October 1987 *Employees:* 2
Net Worth: £2,510,200 *Total Assets:* £10,582,725
Registered Office: Ground Floor, Elizabeth House, 54-58 High Street, Edgware, Middlesex, HA8 7EJ
Activities: Other business support service activities n.e.c.
Major Shareholder: Corinne Lena Davin Evens
Officers: Alon Bar [1980] Director [Israeli]; Corinne Evens [1955] Director [Belgian]

Boleyn Phoenix Limited
Incorporated: 30 January 2014
Net Worth Deficit: £45,663 *Total Assets:* £6,266,357
Registered Office: 3rd Floor, Sterling House, Langston Road, Loughton, Essex, IG10 3TS
Activities: Development of building projects
Shareholders: Galliard Holdings Limited; Mount Pleasant Development Limited
Officers: Allan William Porter, Secretary; David Edward Conway [1976] Director; Stephen Stuart Solomon Conway [1948] Director; Donagh O'Sullivan [1968] Construction Director [Irish]; Allan William Porter [1957] Director/Accountant

Bollore Logistics UK Ltd
Incorporated: 17 August 1928 *Employees:* 438
Previous: SDV Ltd
Net Worth: £9,248,027 *Total Assets:* £41,135,144
Registered Office: Unit 1 Skyline, Great South West Road, Heathrow, Feltham, Middlesex, TW14 8NT
Activities: Other transportation support activities
Parent: Bollore
Officers: John David Gavin Love, Secretary; Thierry Joseph Ehrenbogen [1960] Director/CEO Europe [French]; Henri Antoine Le Gouis [1967] Director/CEO Western Europe [French]; David Smith [1965] Director

Oliver Bonas Limited
Incorporated: 1 July 1999 *Employees:* 599
Net Worth: £6,198,048 *Total Assets:* £23,297,596
Registered Office: Unit F, Davis Road Industrial Park, Davis Road, Chessington, Surrey, KT9 1TQ
Activities: Other retail sale in non-specialised stores
Shareholders: Oliver James Mark Tress; Timothy Richard Naunton Hollidge
Officers: Timothy Richard Naunton Hollidge, Secretary; Timothy Richard Naunton Hollidge [1967] Director/Chief Operating Officer; Oliver James Mark Tress [1967] Managing Director

Bonne Bouche Catering Limited
Incorporated: 29 July 1965 *Employees:* 49
Net Worth: £22,410,320 *Total Assets:* £33,374,368
Registered Office: Unit 23 Fleetway Business Park, 14-16 Wadsworth Road, Perivale, Middlesex, UB6 7JD
Activities: Manufacture of bread; manufacture of fresh pastry goods and cakes
Major Shareholder: Rolf Ferdinand Biller
Officers: Marcia Biller, Secretary; Marcia Biller [1946] Director; Rolf Ferdinand Biller [1942] Director [German]

The Book Trade Charity (BTBS)
Incorporated: 15 October 2008 *Employees:* 6
Net Worth: £9,896,463 *Total Assets:* £9,978,932
Registered Office: The Foyle Centre, The Retreat, Kings Langley, Herts, WD4 8LT
Activities: Other service activities n.e.c.
Officers: David Hicks, Secretary; Elise Burns [1974] Sales Director; Isobel Margaret Dixon [1969] Director/Literary Agent [British/South African]; David Warwick Graham [1960] Managing Director; Kate Patricia McFarlan [1957] Director/Business Operations; David Edward Henry Neale [1943] Director/Retired; Jonathan Charles Peter Nowell [1958] Director; Peter Fraser Tanner [1952] Director; Emily-Jane Taylor [1980] Finance Director; Ann Veronica Woodhall [1951] HR/Facilities Director; Gemma Leigh Woodward [1972] Director/Investment Manager

Bookcash Trading Limited
Incorporated: 4 January 1994 *Employees:* 71
Net Worth: £12,771,000 *Total Assets:* £27,975,000
Registered Office: Hunton House, Highbridge Estate, Oxford Road, Uxbridge, Middlesex, UB8 1LX
Activities: Licenced restaurants
Parent: PizzaExpress (Restaurants) Limited
Officers: Andrew David Pellington, Secretary; Andrew David Pellington [1964] Director; Jinlong Wang [1957] Director [American]

Boon Building Services Ltd
Incorporated: 3 December 1990 *Employees:* 86
Net Worth: £1,300,674 *Total Assets:* £8,316,419
Registered Office: Floor 2, Swan Court, Kingsbury Crescent, Watermans Business Park, Staines upon Thames, Middlesex, TW18 3BA
Activities: Electrical installation
Parent: Boon Group Limited
Officers: Amanda Jane Boon, Secretary; Matthew Edward Boon [1970] Director/Engineer; Corinne Cordery [1978] Financial Director; Mark Fisher [1970] Director; Stuart Neale [1964] Director; Gary Dene Slade [1961] Director; Peter Darren Walker [1977] Director

Boon Group Limited
Incorporated: 5 December 2012 *Employees:* 91
Previous: Boon Building Holdings Limited
Net Worth: £2,958,642 *Total Assets:* £11,538,419
Registered Office: 2nd Floor, Swan Court, Watermans Business Park, The Causeway, Staines upon Thames, Middlesex, TW18 3BA
Activities: Activities of other holding companies n.e.c.
Shareholders: Matthew Edward Boon; Amanda Jane Boon
Officers: Matthew Edward Boon [1970] Director/Engineer

Boorley Green LLP
Incorporated: 20 July 2015
Net Worth Deficit: £126,000 *Total Assets:* £54,241,000
Registered Office: Cowley Business Park, Cowley, Uxbridge, Middlesex, UB8 2AL

Boost Homes Ltd
Incorporated: 28 January 2011 *Employees:* 7
Net Worth: £158,244 *Total Assets:* £5,991,778
Registered Office: Ibex House, Baker Street, Weybridge, Surrey, KT13 8AH
Activities: Other specialised construction activities n.e.c.
Shareholders: Samuel Edward Steen; Jayson James Ware
Officers: Barbara Steen [1961] Director; David Paul Steen [1963] Director/Property Developer; Samuel Edward Steen [1989] Director/Property Developer; Jayson James Ware [1983] Director/Property Developer

Borelli Tea Holdings Limited
Incorporated: 19 March 1976
Net Worth: £39,460,080 *Total Assets:* £54,827,008
Registered Office: Woodlands, 79 High Street, Greenhithe, Kent, DA9 9RD
Activities: Activities of agricultural holding companies
Parent: McLeod Russel India Limited
Officers: Dilsher SEN, Secretary/Solicitor; Kamal Kishore Baheti [1963] Director/Company Executive [Indian]; Aditya Khaitan [1968] Director/Industrialist [Indian]; Stephen Knight [1960] Director; Barry John Ruck [1959] Director; Dilsher SEN [1968] Director/Solicitor

Bosch Automotive Service Solutions Ltd
Incorporated: 25 May 1966 *Employees:* 201
Net Worth: £17,895,000 *Total Assets:* £27,956,000
Registered Office: Robert Bosch Ltd, Broadwater Park, North Orbital Road, Denham, Uxbridge, Middlesex, UB9 5HJ
Activities: Non-specialised wholesale trade
Parent: Robert Bosch UK Holdings Limited
Officers: Jonathan David Burton, Secretary; David Roy Butterworth [1969] Managing Director; Robert Josef Hilbert [1965] Director/Manager [German]; Dr Steffen Tobias Hoffmann [1965] Director [German]; Fedra Ribeiro [1972] Director/Vice President Global [Portuguese]

Bosch Service Solutions Limited
Incorporated: 25 October 1993 *Employees:* 200
Previous: Bosch Security Systems Limited
Net Worth: £5,786,000 *Total Assets:* £11,545,000
Registered Office: P O Box 750, Uxbridge, Middlesex, UB9 5ZJ
Activities: Wholesale of electronic and telecommunications equipment and parts
Parent: Robert Bosch UK Holdings Limited
Officers: Jonathan Burton, Secretary; Dr Steffen Tobias Hoffmann [1965] Director [German]; John Milburn [1973] Director/Manager; Georg Bernhard Wessels [1959] Director/Vice President Europe, Middle East, Africa (EMEA) [German]

Robert Bosch UK Holdings Limited
Incorporated: 1 October 2010 *Employees:* 53
Net Worth: £613,361,024 *Total Assets:* £988,782,016
Registered Office: Broadwater Park, North Orbital Road, Denham, Uxbridge, Middlesex, UB9 5HJ
Activities: Activities of head offices
Parent: Robert Bosch Investment Nederland BV
Officers: Jonathan Burton, Secretary; Andrew Ralph Castle [1957] Director; Dr Steffen Tobias Hoffmann [1965] Director [German]

Boss & Co.Limited
Incorporated: 29 September 1967
Net Worth: £2,312,864 *Total Assets:* £6,533,986
Registered Office: The Caxton House, 110 Kew Green, Richmond, Surrey, TW9 3AP
Activities: Manufacture of weapons and ammunition
Officers: Arthur Stephen Demoulas [1958] Director/Self Employed [American]

Bostall Estates Limited
Incorporated: 15 June 1998 *Employees:* 3
Net Worth: £16,322,744 *Total Assets:* £30,305,232
Registered Office: 3 Montpelier Avenue, Bexley, Kent, DA5 3AP
Activities: Development of building projects
Major Shareholder: Manjit Singh Heer
Officers: Manjit Singh Heer [1968] Director/Businessman

Boston Limited
Incorporated: 8 December 1992 *Employees:* 154
Net Worth: £4,792,572 *Total Assets:* £26,768,804
Registered Office: 5 Theobald Court, Theobald Street, Elstree, Herts, WD6 4RN
Activities: Other information technology service activities
Officers: Ashok Uttamlal Chauhan, Secretary; Manojkumar Nayee [1963] Director/Computer Sales

Bottling Great Britain Limited
Incorporated: 11 September 2002
Net Worth: £2,462,513,408 *Total Assets:* £4,272,129,280
Registered Office: Pemberton House, Bakers Road, Uxbridge, Middlesex, UB8 1EZ
Activities: Activities of head offices
Officers: Huma Allana, Secretary; Huma Allana [1975] Company Secretary/Director; Michael Clark [1970] Director; Leendert Pieter Den Hollander [1969] Director/Vice President & General Manager CCE Ltd [Dutch]; Frank Govaerts [1961] Director [Belgian]; Angela Corina Sabadus [1979] Director [French]; Florian Tornow [1974] Director [German]; Kathleen Veirman [1965] Director [Belgian]; Ed Owen Walker [1967] Director

Bottling Holdings Europe Limited
Incorporated: 25 May 2016
Net Worth: £15,390,483,456 *Total Assets:* £16,759,967,744
Registered Office: Pemberton House, Bakers Road, Uxbridge, Middlesex, UB8 1EZ
Activities: Activities of other holding companies n.e.c.
Shareholders: CCEP Holdings UK Limited; Coca-Cola European Partners PLC
Officers: Paul Van Reesch, Secretary; Frank Govaerts [1961] Director [Belgian]; Paul Van Reesch [1976] Director; Edward Owen Walker [1967] Director

Bourn Investments Limited
Incorporated: 25 February 1999 *Employees:* 4
Net Worth: £5,853,827 *Total Assets:* £12,764,810
Registered Office: Bourn Reach, 9 Montrose Gardens, Oxshott, Leatherhead, Surrey, KT22 0UU
Activities: Other letting and operating of own or leased real estate
Major Shareholder: Rita Elizabeth Karoline Clarke
Officers: Rita Elisabeth Karoline Clarke, Secretary; Douglas Staward Clarke [1968] Director; Graham Staward Clarke [1937] Director/Chairman; Rita Elisabeth Karoline Clarke [1939] Director [German]; Tessa Ellen Staward Mayes Clarke [1965] Director

Bourne Court Properties Limited
Incorporated: 3 May 2017
Net Worth: £140,715 *Total Assets:* £13,832,547
Registered Office: 3rd Floor, Sterling House, Langston Road, Loughton, Essex, IG10 3TS
Activities: Development of building projects
Parent: Galliard Holdings
Officers: Allan William Porter, Secretary; David Edward Conway [1976] Director; Stephen Stuart Solomon Conway [1948] Director; Jonathan Michael Morgan [1978] Director; Donagh O'Sullivan [1968] Construction Director [Irish]

Bourne Education Trust
Incorporated: 9 September 2011 *Employees:* 841
Net Worth: £123,260,240 *Total Assets:* £136,623,536
Registered Office: Epsom and Ewell High School, Ruxley Lane, Epsom, Surrey, KT19 9JW
Activities: Primary education
Officers: Kathrine Sanders, Secretary; Peter Charles Deane [1956] Director; Stephen Dennison [1953] Director/Retired; Susan Mary Gibbin [1963] Director/Management Consultant; Sara Elizabeth Anne Lipscombe-Nott [1966] Communications Director; Chris Marston [1964] Director/Commercial Manager; Christopher Ross Munro [1960] Director/Business Development Manager; Sarah Louise Pittam [1968] Director/Education Consultant; Alex Russell [1962] Director/Headteacher; Audrey Wade [1971] Director/Chartered Accountant

Bow Village Limited
Incorporated: 17 April 2003
Net Worth: £14,992,647 *Total Assets:* £21,803,624
Registered Office: 1 Beauchamp Court, 10 Victors Way, Barnet, Herts, EN5 5TZ
Activities: Management of real estate on a fee or contract basis
Major Shareholder: Santokh Singh Chima
Officers: Mohinder Kaur Chima, Secretary; Santokh Singh Chima [1959] Director/Solicitor

Bow Wharf Development LLP
Incorporated: 23 December 2014
Net Worth: £5,878,361 *Total Assets:* £8,964,035
Registered Office: 3rd Floor, The Granary, 80 Abbey Road, Barking, Essex, IG11 7BT

Bowland Resources (No.2) Limited
Incorporated: 25 April 2008
Net Worth Deficit: £3,565,000 *Total Assets:* £33,491,000
Registered Office: 1st Floor, 20 Kingston Road, Staines upon Thames, Middlesex, TW18 4LG
Activities: Support activities for petroleum and natural gas mining
Officers: Nicola MacLeod, Secretary; Generald Martin Harrison [1954] Director; Andrew Daryl Le Poidevin [1958] Director; Nicola Jane MacLeod [1974] Director/General Counsel

Bowland Resources Limited
Incorporated: 5 February 2009
Net Worth: £4,636,000 *Total Assets:* £78,598,000
Registered Office: 1st Floor, 20 Kingston Road, Staines upon Thames, Middlesex, TW18 4LG
Activities: Support activities for petroleum and natural gas mining
Parent: Spirit North Sea Gas Limited
Officers: Nicola MacLeod, Secretary; Generald Martin Harrison [1954] Director; Andrew Daryl Le Poidevin [1958] Director; Nicola Jane MacLeod [1974] Director/General Counsel

M.& R.Bowman Limited
Incorporated: 4 March 1963 *Employees:* 7
Net Worth: £8,027,363 *Total Assets:* £13,250,904
Registered Office: 1st Floor, Sheraton House, Lower Road, Chorleywood, Rickmansworth, Herts, WD3 5LH
Activities: Construction of commercial buildings
Major Shareholder: Raymond Valentine Mawhood
Officers: Lisa Jane Ashton-Jones, Secretary; Lisa Jane Ashton-Jones [1966] Director/Landlord & Property Developer; Philip Ashton-Jones [1964] Director/Barrister; Barbara Ann Mawhood [1943] Director; Raymond Valentine Mawhood [1942] Director

G E Bowra Group Limited
Incorporated: 24 June 1960
Net Worth: £4,535,355 *Total Assets:* £8,165,580
Registered Office: Cranfields, First Floor, 43 Friends Road, Croydon, Surrey, CR0 1ED
Activities: Buying and selling of own real estate
Shareholders: Christopher Edward Bowra; George Edward Alan Bowra
Officers: George Edward Alan Bowra [1977] Director; Joanne Manning [1967] Director/Company Secretary

Boxtrent Limited
Incorporated: 20 March 2006 *Employees:* 30
Net Worth: £2,268,000 *Total Assets:* £15,589,000
Registered Office: 2 Wintersells Road, Byfleet, West Byfleet, Surrey, KT14 7LF
Activities: Construction of commercial buildings
Major Shareholder: Mark James Edward Woods
Officers: Stephen Andrew Brown, Secretary; Stephen Andrew Brown [1954] Director/Chartered Accountant; Mark James Edward Woods [1964] Director

Boyden & Co.Limited
Incorporated: 20 July 1925 *Employees:* 52
Net Worth: £7,890,247 *Total Assets:* £9,102,446
Registered Office: 108 Beddington Lane, Croydon, Surrey, CR0 4YY
Activities: Non-specialised wholesale trade
Parent: Boyden Investments Limited
Officers: Margaret Eunice Frei [1930] Director; Peter Lancaster [1964] Director/Accountant; Andrew Paul Williamson [1957] Director; Joanne Elizabeth Williamson [1959] Director/Office Manager

William Boyer & Sons, Limited
Incorporated: 12 February 1926 *Employees:* 5
Net Worth: £15,303,154 *Total Assets:* £17,465,312
Registered Office: Trout Road, West Drayton, Middlesex, UB7 7SN
Activities: Operation of gravel and sand pits; mining of clays and kaolin
Shareholders: Miranda Jane Taylor; Kenneth Frank Morgan; Gillian Ann Dutfield
Officers: Mary Theresa Woods, Secretary; Penelope Jane Boyer [1959] Director; Gillian Ann Dutfield [1927] Director; Miranda Jane Taylor [1959] Director/Company Secretary

BP (Abu Dhabi) Limited
Incorporated: 18 September 1962
Net Worth: £662,224,192 *Total Assets:* £3,456,190,976
Registered Office: Chertsey Road, Sunbury on Thames, Middlesex, TW16 7BP
Activities: Support activities for petroleum and natural gas mining
Parent: BP Exploration Company Limited
Officers: Andrew James Alexander McAuslan [1961] Director/Oil Company Executive; John Myers [1967] Director/Oil Company Executive

BP Absheron Limited
Incorporated: 26 January 2016
Net Worth: £1,168,061 *Total Assets:* £6,021,830
Registered Office: Chertsey Road, Sunbury on Thames, Middlesex, TW16 7BP
Activities: Activities of head offices
Parent: BP Exploration Operating Company Limited
Officers: Jaqui Freeman [1968] Director/Oil Company Executive; Robert Gary Jones [1960] Director/Oil Company Executive

BP Africa Limited
Incorporated: 10 November 1971
Net Worth: £40,856,280 *Total Assets:* £81,949,376
Registered Office: Chertsey Road, Sunbury on Thames, Middlesex, TW16 7BP
Activities: Activities of head offices
Parent: BP PLC.
Officers: Guy Jan Julia Moeyens [1965] Director/Oil Company Executive [Belgian]; Thierry Jose Henri Rondeau [1959] Director/Oil Company Executive [French]

BP Alternative Energy Investments Limited
Incorporated: 14 November 2006
Previous: BP Biofuels UK Limited
Net Worth: £161,085,632 *Total Assets:* £216,051,520
Registered Office: Chertsey Road, Sunbury on Thames, Middlesex, TW16 7BP
Activities: Activities of head offices
Parent: BP International Limited
Officers: David Thomas Anderson [1964] Director/Oil Company Executive; Mario Lindenhayn [1964] Director/Oil Company Executive [Brazilian/German]; Nicholas James Wayth [1973] Director/Oil Company Executive

BP America Limited
Incorporated: 13 January 2014
Net Worth: £51,778,691,072 *Total Assets:* £51,778,732,032
Registered Office: Chertsey Road, Sunbury on Thames, Middlesex, TW16 7BP
Activities: Activities of head offices
Parent: BP Holdings North America Limited
Officers: Jens Bertelsen [1959] Director/Deputy Secretary; Jan Clayton Lyons [1965] Director/Oil Company Executive [American]; Peter James Mather [1960] Director/Oil Company Executive

BP Amoco Exploration (Faroes) Limited
Incorporated: 10 August 1965
Net Worth: £69,042,400 *Total Assets:* £102,787,704
Registered Office: Chertsey Road, Sunbury on Thames, Middlesex, TW16 7BP
Activities: Extraction of crude petroleum
Parent: BP Exploration Operating Company Limited
Officers: Ariel David Flores [1977] Director/Oil Company Executive [American]

BP Aromatics Limited
Incorporated: 25 April 2007 *Employees:* 20
Net Worth: £143,959,152 *Total Assets:* £242,243,344
Registered Office: Chertsey Road, Sunbury on Thames, Middlesex, TW16 7BP
Activities: Manufacture of other inorganic basic chemicals
Parent: BP Aromatics Holdings Limited
Officers: Alessia Alberoni [1977] Director/Oil Company Executive [Italian]; Graham Michael Knights [1969] Director/Oil Company Executive; David Jozef Vermylen [1972] Director/Oil Company Executive [Belgian]

BP Asia Pacific Holdings Limited
Incorporated: 5 February 1973
Net Worth: £3,637,187,840 *Total Assets:* £6,405,887,488
Registered Office: Chertsey Road, Sunbury on Thames, Middlesex, TW16 7BP
Activities: Activities of head offices
Parent: BP Global Investments Limited
Officers: David Alan Rider [1964] Director/Oil Company Executive; Katherine Anne Thomson [1968] Director/Oil Company Executive

BP Australia Swaps Management Limited
Incorporated: 19 November 2012
Net Worth: £4,722,393,088 *Total Assets:* £6,225,776,640
Registered Office: Chertsey Road, Sunbury on Thames, Middlesex, TW16 7BP
Activities: Financial intermediation not elsewhere classified
Parent: BP International Limited
Officers: Kathryn Mary Berry [1967] Director/Oil Company Executive; Jan Clayton Lyons [1965] Director/Oil Company Executive [American]

BP Biofuels Brazil Investments Limited
Incorporated: 23 February 2011
Net Worth: £800,981,376 *Total Assets:* £800,981,376
Registered Office: Chertsey Road, Sunbury on Thames, Middlesex, TW16 7BP
Activities: Activities of head offices
Parent: BP Asia Pacific Holdings Limited
Officers: David Thomas Anderson [1964] Director/Oil Company Executive; Mario Lindenhayn [1964] Director/Oil Company Executive [Brazilian/German]; Nicholas James Wayth [1973] Director/Oil Company Executive

BP Capital Markets P.L.C.
Incorporated: 14 December 1976
Net Worth: £562,711,872 *Total Assets:* £44,762,333,184
Registered Office: Chertsey Road, Sunbury on Thames, Middlesex, TW16 7BP
Activities: Financial intermediation not elsewhere classified
Parent: BP International Limited
Officers: Dr Brian Gilvary [1962] Director; Jayne Angela Hodgson [1969] Director/Oil Company Executive; Katherine Anne Thomson [1968] Director/Oil Company Executive

BP Car Fleet Limited
Incorporated: 8 March 1960
Previous: BP Car Finance Limited
Net Worth: £84,639,000 *Total Assets:* £84,655,000
Registered Office: Chertsey Road, Sunbury on Thames, Middlesex, TW16 7BP
Activities: Financial leasing
Parent: BP PLC.
Officers: Dr Brian Gilvary [1962] Director; Katherine Anne Thomson [1968] Director/Oil Company Executive

BP Chemicals (Korea) Limited
Incorporated: 11 November 1988
Net Worth: £104,169,000 *Total Assets:* £105,049,000
Registered Office: Chertsey Road, Sunbury on Thames, Middlesex, TW16 7BP
Activities: Activities of head offices
Shareholder: BP Chemicals Limited
Officers: Nigel Clifford Dunn [1967] Director/Oil Company Executive; Catherine Ann McCann [1966] Director/Oil Company Executive; Terence Michael Thornton [1963] Director/Oil Company Executive

BP Chemicals East China Investments Limited
Incorporated: 2 February 2001
Net Worth: £1,083,322,880 *Total Assets:* £1,083,757,312
Registered Office: Chertsey Road, Sunbury on Thames, Middlesex, TW16 7BP
Activities: Activities of head offices
Parent: BP Global Investments Limited
Officers: Nicholas John Charles Evans [1969] Director/Oil Company Executive; Rita Elizabeth Griffin [1963] Director/Oil Company Executive [American]; Terence Michael Thornton [1963] Director/Oil Company Executive

BP Chemicals Investments Limited
Incorporated: 2 September 1935
Net Worth: £245,367,824 *Total Assets:* £306,761,504
Registered Office: Chertsey Road, Sunbury on Thames, Middlesex, TW16 7BP
Activities: Activities of head offices
Parent: BP International Limited
Officers: Rita Elizabeth Griffin [1963] Director/Oil Company Executive [American]; Catherine Ann McCann [1966] Director/Oil Company Executive; Terence Michael Thornton [1963] Director/Oil Company Executive

BP Chemicals Limited
Incorporated: 9 January 1924 *Employees:* 439
Net Worth: £95,729,000 *Total Assets:* £101,846,000
Registered Office: Chertsey Road, Sunbury on Thames, Middlesex, TW16 7BP
Activities: Manufacture of other inorganic basic chemicals
Parent: BP Chemicals Investments Limited
Officers: Nigel Clifford Dunn [1967] Director/Oil Company Executive; Catherine Ann McCann [1966] Director/Oil Company Executive; Terence Michael Thornton [1963] Director/Oil Company Executive

BP Containment Response Limited
Incorporated: 14 December 2012
Net Worth: £46,711 *Total Assets:* £8,263,789
Registered Office: Chertsey Road, Sunbury on Thames, Middlesex, TW16 7BP
Activities: Support activities for petroleum and natural gas mining
Parent: BP Exploration Operating Company Limited
Officers: Gordon Young Birrell [1963] Director/Oil Company Executive; Jaqui Freeman [1968] Director/Oil Company Executive; Timothy Robert Schofield [1963] Director/Oil Company Executive

BP Corporate Holdings Limited
Incorporated: 23 November 2000
Net Worth: £5,403,174,400 *Total Assets:* £5,420,483,584
Registered Office: Chertsey Road, Sunbury on Thames, Middlesex, TW16 7BP
Activities: Activities of head offices
Parent: BP International Limited
Officers: Dr Brian Gilvary [1962] Director; Jayne Angela Hodgson [1969] Director/Oil Company Executive; Katherine Anne Thomson [1968] Director/Oil Company Executive

BP Eastern Mediterranean Limited
Incorporated: 4 April 1988 *Employees:* 33
Net Worth: £16,192,415 *Total Assets:* £26,727,732
Registered Office: Chertsey Road, Sunbury on Thames, Middlesex, TW16 7BP
Activities: Wholesale of other fuels and related products
Parent: BP Global Investments Limited
Officers: Amir Saadeddin Ibrahim [1975] Director/Oil Company Executive; Stavros Photiou [1972] Director/Oil Company Executive [Cypriot]; Jonathan Peter Platt [1967] Director/Oil Company Executive

BP Exploration (Algeria) Limited
Incorporated: 19 February 1970 *Employees:* 6
Net Worth: £499,087,200 *Total Assets:* £499,201,024
Registered Office: Chertsey Road, Sunbury on Thames, Middlesex, TW16 7BP
Activities: Extraction of crude petroleum
Parent: BP Exploration Operating Company Limited
Officers: Amna Bon [1980] Director [Australian]; Timothy King [1978] Director/Oil Company Executive [Irish]; Wissam Al Monthiry [1980] Director/Oil Company Executive [Canadian]

BP Exploration (Alpha) Limited
Incorporated: 16 August 1971 *Employees:* 43
Net Worth: £2,852,660,480 *Total Assets:* £3,334,274,304
Registered Office: Chertsey Road, Sunbury on Thames, Middlesex, TW16 7BP
Activities: Extraction of crude petroleum
Parent: BP Exploration Operating Company Limited
Officers: Ariel David Flores [1977] Director/Oil Company Executive [American]; Sandra Jean MacRae [1963] Director/Oil Company Executive; Sashi Kumar Mukundan [1957] Director/Oil Company Executive [American]; David Alan Rider [1964] Director/Oil Company Executive; Dr Bryan David Ritchie [1975] Director/Oil Company Executive

BP Exploration (Angola) Limited
Incorporated: 24 November 1958
Net Worth: £6,367,930,880 *Total Assets:* £7,970,078,720
Registered Office: Chertsey Road, Sunbury on Thames, Middlesex, TW16 7BP
Activities: Extraction of crude petroleum
Parent: BP Exploration Operating Company Limited
Officers: Sandra Jean MacRae [1963] Director/Oil Company Executive; David Alan Rider [1964] Director/Oil Company Executive; Stephen Willis [1962] Director/Oil Company Executive

BP Exploration (Azerbaijan) Limited
Incorporated: 2 September 1987
Net Worth: £5,288,811,008 *Total Assets:* £5,863,719,424
Registered Office: Chertsey Road, Sunbury on Thames, Middlesex, TW16 7BP
Activities: Extraction of crude petroleum
Parent: BP Exploration Operating Company Limited
Officers: Jaqui Freeman [1968] Director/Oil Company Executive; Robert Gary Jones [1960] Director/Oil Company Executive

BP Exploration (Caspian Sea) Limited
Incorporated: 11 February 1946 *Employees:* 3,226
Net Worth: £4,594,371,584 *Total Assets:* £7,042,281,472
Registered Office: Chertsey Road, Sunbury on Thames, Middlesex, TW16 7BP
Activities: Extraction of crude petroleum
Parent: BP Exploration Operating Company Limited
Officers: Jaqui Freeman [1968] Director/Oil Company Executive; Robert Gary Jones [1960] Director/Oil Company Executive

BP Exploration (Delta) Limited
Incorporated: 6 July 1970
Net Worth: £4,603,390,464 *Total Assets:* £5,733,650,944
Registered Office: Chertsey Road, Sunbury on Thames, Middlesex, TW16 7BP
Activities: Extraction of crude petroleum
Parent: BP Exploration Operating Company Limited
Officers: Hesham Saad Mekawi [1960] Director/Oil Company Executive [Egyptian]; John Myers [1967] Director/Oil Company Executive; Karim Mohamed Alaaeldin Abdelhakim Youssef [1981] Director/Oil Company Executive [Egyptian]

BP Exploration (Epsilon) Limited
Incorporated: 17 March 1971 *Employees:* 388
Net Worth: £2,364,617,728 *Total Assets:* £2,825,721,856
Registered Office: Chertsey Road, Sunbury on Thames, Middlesex, TW16 7BP
Activities: Extraction of crude petroleum
Parent: BP Exploration Operating Company Limited
Officers: Andrew James Alexander McAuslan [1961] Director/Oil Company Executive; Yousuf Mohamed Salim Al Ojaili [1963] Director/Oil Company Executive [Omani]; Michael Andrew Wenham [1959] Director/Oil Company Executive

BP Exploration (Shah Deniz) Limited
Incorporated: 3 July 1996
Net Worth: £2 *Total Assets:* £522,955,648
Registered Office: Chertsey Road, Sunbury on Thames, Middlesex, TW16 7BP
Activities: Extraction of crude petroleum
Parent: BP Exploration Operating Company Limited
Officers: Jaqui Freeman [1968] Director/Oil Company Executive; Robert Gary Jones [1960] Director/Oil Company Executive

BP Exploration Angola (Kwanza Benguela) Limited
Incorporated: 8 February 2011
Net Worth: £300,309,120 *Total Assets:* £321,866,336
Registered Office: Chertsey Road, Sunbury on Thames, Middlesex, TW16 7BP
Activities: Test drilling and boring
Parent: BP Exploration Operating Company Limited
Officers: Howard Leach [1962] Director/Oil Company Executive; David Alan Rider [1964] Director/Oil Company Executive; Stephen Willis [1962] Director/Oil Company Executive

BP Exploration Beta Limited
Incorporated: 12 January 1967
Net Worth: £521,550,272 *Total Assets:* £683,506,112
Registered Office: Chertsey Road, Sunbury on Thames, Middlesex, TW16 7BP
Activities: Extraction of crude petroleum
Parent: BP Exploration Operating Company Limited
Officers: Ariel David Flores [1977] Director/Oil Company Executive [American]; Howard Leach [1962] Director/Oil Company Executive; Sandra Jean MacRae [1963] Director/Oil Company Executive; David Alan Rider [1964] Director/Oil Company Executive; Stephen Willis [1962] Director/Oil Company Executive

BP Exploration China Limited
Incorporated: 2 March 2012
Net Worth Deficit: £2,959,859 *Total Assets:* £33,227,468
Registered Office: Chertsey Road, Sunbury on Thames, Middlesex, TW16 7BP
Activities: Support activities for petroleum and natural gas mining
Parent: BP Exploration Operating Company Limited
Officers: Edward Gallatin Bryant [1960] Director/Oil Company Executive [American]; Sandra Jean MacRae [1963] Director/Oil Company Executive; Dr Lorna Taryn Malcolm [1972] Director/Oil Company Executive

BP Exploration Company (Middle East) Limited
Incorporated: 12 June 1914
Net Worth: £17,450,016 *Total Assets:* £17,468,472
Registered Office: Chertsey Road, Sunbury on Thames, Middlesex, TW16 7BP
Activities: Support activities for petroleum and natural gas mining
Parent: BP Exploration Company Limited
Officers: Andrew James Alexander McAuslan [1961] Director/Oil Company Executive; John Myers [1967] Director/Oil Company Executive

BP Exploration Indonesia Limited
Incorporated: 3 May 1971
Net Worth: £19,343,708 *Total Assets:* £86,533,776
Registered Office: Chertsey Road, Sunbury on Thames, Middlesex, TW16 7BP
Activities: Extraction of crude petroleum
Parent: BP Exploration Operating Company Limited
Officers: Sandra Jean MacRae [1963] Director/Oil Company Executive; Alan Philip Martin [1971] Director/Oil Company Executive; Svetlana Pereverzeva [1972] Director/Oil Company Executive; Alison Sheila Young [1965] Director/Oil Company Executive; Nader Zaki [1973] Director/Oil Company Executive [Egyptian]

BP Exploration Libya Limited
Incorporated: 18 January 2005 *Employees:* 1
Net Worth: £175,523,264 *Total Assets:* £244,057,344
Registered Office: Chertsey Road, Sunbury on Thames, Middlesex, TW16 7BP
Activities: Extraction of crude petroleum
Parent: BP Exploration Operating Company Limited
Officers: Andrew James Alexander McAuslan [1961] Director/Oil Company Executive; Jasper Adrianus Marinus Matthaeus Peijs [1969] Director/Oil Company Executive [Dutch]; Karim Mohamed Alaaeldin Abdelhakim Youssef [1981] Director/Oil Company Executive [Egyptian]

BP Exploration North Africa Limited
Incorporated: 18 January 2005
Net Worth: £174,196,880 *Total Assets:* £176,713,184
Registered Office: Chertsey Road, Sunbury on Thames, Middlesex, TW16 7BP
Activities: Extraction of crude petroleum
Parent: BP Exploration Operating Company Limited
Officers: Hesham Saad Mekawi [1960] Director/Oil Company Executive [Egyptian]; John Myers [1967] Director/Oil Company Executive; Karim Mohamed Alaaeldin Abdelhakim Youssef [1981] Director/Oil Company Executive [Egyptian]

BP Exploration Operating Company Limited
Incorporated: 12 October 1935 *Employees:* 3,625
Net Worth: £43,361,202,176 *Total Assets:* £49,403,691,008
Registered Office: Chertsey Road, Sunbury on Thames, Middlesex, TW16 7BP
Activities: Extraction of crude petroleum
Parent: BP Exploration Company Limited
Officers: Emma Louise Delaney-Mc Knight [1973] Director/Oil Company Executive [Irish]; Ariel David Flores [1977] Director/Oil Company Executive [American]; Dr Andrew Beaton Johnston [1959] Director/Oil Company Executive; Karen MacLennan [1971] Director/Oil Company Executive; Sandra Jean MacRae [1963] Director/Oil Company Executive; Peter James Mather [1960] Director/Oil Company Executive; Peter William Anderson Miller [1968] Director/Oil Company Executive; Doris Friederike Reiter [1970] Director/Oil Company Executive [Austrian/American]

BP Exploration Orinoco Limited
Incorporated: 31 January 1958
Net Worth: £19,763,408 *Total Assets:* £19,852,416
Registered Office: Chertsey Road, Sunbury on Thames, Middlesex, TW16 7BP
Activities: Extraction of crude petroleum
Parent: BP Exploration Company Limited
Officers: Felipe Arbelaez [1969] Director/Oil Company Executive; Andres Manuel Guevara de La Vega [1977] Director/Oil Company Executive [Venezuelan]; Sandra Jean MacRae [1963] Director/Oil Company Executive

BP Exploration Personnel Company Limited
Incorporated: 22 December 2004
Net Worth: £5,837,197 *Total Assets:* £22,748,948
Registered Office: Chertsey Road, Sunbury on Thames, Middlesex, TW16 7BP
Activities: Non-trading company
Parent: BP Global Investments Limited
Officers: Peter Anthony Charow [1954] Director/Oil Company Executive [American]; David Alan Rider [1964] Director/Oil Company Executive

BP Finance P.L.C
Incorporated: 22 January 2001
Net Worth: £1,780,986,624 *Total Assets:* £1,781,024,000
Registered Office: Chertsey Road, Sunbury on Thames, Middlesex, TW16 7BP
Activities: Financial intermediation not elsewhere classified
Parent: BP International Limited
Officers: Martin Francis Giles [1961] Director/Oil Company Executive; Dr Brian Gilvary [1962] Director; Richard Alastair Hubbard [1963] Director/Oil Company Executive; Katherine Anne Thomson [1968] Director/Oil Company Executive

BP Gas Marketing Limited
Incorporated: 22 June 1967
Net Worth: £1,105,419,008 *Total Assets:* £4,760,592,896
Registered Office: Chertsey Road, Sunbury on Thames, Middlesex, TW16 7BP
Activities: Support activities for petroleum and natural gas mining
Parent: BP Exploration Operating Company Limited
Officers: Robert John Harrison [1964] Director/Oil Company Executive; David William Knipe [1974] Director/Oil Company Executive; Robert Stephen Lawson [1970] Director/Oil Company Executive

BP Global Investments Limited
Incorporated: 24 March 1932
Net Worth: £9,464,045,568 *Total Assets:* £13,726,040,064
Registered Office: Chertsey Road, Sunbury on Thames, Middlesex, TW16 7BP
Activities: Activities of head offices
Parent: BP PLC.
Officers: David James Bucknall [1968] Director/Oil Company Executive; Dr Brian Gilvary [1962] Director; Jayne Angela Hodgson [1969] Director/Oil Company Executive; Jan Clayton Lyons [1965] Director/Oil Company Executive [American]; Michael John O'Sullivan [1964] Director/Oil Company Executive; Katherine Anne Thomson [1968] Director/Oil Company Executive

BP Greece Limited
Incorporated: 7 September 1921
Net Worth: £108,807,912 *Total Assets:* £110,869,536
Registered Office: Chertsey Road, Sunbury on Thames, Middlesex, TW16 7BP
Activities: Activities of head offices
Parent: BP Global Investments Limited
Officers: Nicholas John Charles Evans [1969] Director/Oil Company Executive; David Alan Rider [1964] Director/Oil Company Executive; Terence Michael Thornton [1963] Director/Oil Company Executive

BP Holdings Canada Limited
Incorporated: 30 October 2012
Net Worth: £4,533,431,808 *Total Assets:* £4,533,431,808
Registered Office: Chertsey Road, Sunbury on Thames, Middlesex, TW16 7BP
Activities: Activities of head offices
Parent: BP PLC.
Officers: Martin Francis Giles [1961] Director/Oil Company Executive; Jan Clayton Lyons [1965] Director/Oil Company Executive [American]; Katherine Anne Thomson [1968] Director/Oil Company Executive

BP Holdings North America Limited
Incorporated: 20 December 2006
Net Worth: £51,804,327,936 *Total Assets:* £51,804,418,048
Registered Office: Chertsey Road, Sunbury on Thames, Middlesex, TW16 7BP
Activities: Activities of head offices
Parent: BP P L C
Officers: Dr Brian Gilvary [1962] Director; Jayne Angela Hodgson [1969] Director/Oil Company Executive; Katherine Anne Thomson [1968] Director/Oil Company Executive

BP Indonesia Investment Limited
Incorporated: 3 October 2013
Net Worth: £5,276,353 *Total Assets:* £5,276,353
Registered Office: Chertsey Road, Sunbury on Thames, Middlesex, TW16 7BP
Activities: Activities of head offices
Parent: Britannic Strategies Limited
Officers: Carol-Lee Howle [1972] Director/Oil Company Executive; Brian Michael Puffer [1969] Director/Oil Company Executive [British/American]; Sharon Hyman Weintraub [1965] Director/Oil Company Executive [American]

BP International Limited
Incorporated: 29 December 1954
Net Worth: £43,699,302,400 *Total Assets:* £160,948,404,224
Registered Office: Chertsey Road, Sunbury on Thames, Middlesex, TW16 7BP
Activities: Wholesale of other fuels and related products
Parent: BP PLC.
Officers: David James Bucknall [1968] Director/Group Treasurer; Dr Brian Gilvary [1962] Director; Jayne Angela Hodgson [1969] Director/Oil Company Executive; Jan Clayton Lyons [1965] Director/Oil Company Executive [American]; Michael John O'Sullivan [1964] Director/Oil Company Executive; Katherine Anne Thomson [1968] Director/Oil Company Executive

BP Investment Management Limited
Incorporated: 7 December 1936
Net Worth: £52,308,912 *Total Assets:* £56,856,624
Registered Office: Chertsey Road, Sunbury on Thames, Middlesex, TW16 7BP
Activities: Other business support service activities n.e.c.
Parent: BP Pension Trustees Limited
Officers: Diana Patricia Legge, Secretary; Douglas Roderick MacLeod [1953] Director/Oil Company Executive; Paul Jonathan Reed [1956] Director; Shane Michael Roche [1976] Director/Oil Company Executive [Irish]; Mark Edward Stageman [1953] Managing Director - GIR Limited

BP Investments Asia Limited
Incorporated: 29 November 2005
Net Worth: £44,532,648 *Total Assets:* £44,532,652
Registered Office: Chertsey Road, Sunbury on Thames, Middlesex, TW16 7BP
Activities: Activities of head offices
Parent: BP Global Investments Limited
Officers: Jonathan Peter Platt [1967] Director/Oil Company Executive; Clive Colin Gerard Sinnott [1963] Director/Oil Company Executive

BP Kuwait Limited
Incorporated: 2 February 1934 *Employees:* 31
Net Worth: £40,179,536 *Total Assets:* £48,348,420
Registered Office: Chertsey Road, Sunbury on Thames, Middlesex, TW16 7BP
Activities: Support activities for petroleum and natural gas mining
Parent: BP Exploration Operating Company Limited
Officers: Andrew James Alexander McAuslan [1961] Director/Oil Company Executive; John Myers [1967] Director/Oil Company Executive; David Alan Rider [1964] Director/Oil Company Executive

BP Marine Limited
Incorporated: 29 May 1975
Net Worth: £116,557,536 *Total Assets:* £151,731,200
Registered Office: Chertsey Road, Sunbury on Thames, Middlesex, TW16 7BP
Activities: Wholesale of other fuels and related products
Parent: BP International Limited
Officers: Jens Jacob Andersen [1970] Director/Oil Company Executive [Danish]; Robert David Mutchell [1974] Director/Oil Company Executive; Kamuran Yazganoglu [1976] Director/Oil Company Executive [Turkish]

BP Mauritania Investments Limited
Incorporated: 9 December 2016
Net Worth: £321,781,760 *Total Assets:* £374,844,672
Registered Office: c/o BP Exploration (West Africa) Limited, Chertsey Road, Sunbury on Thames, Middlesex, TW16 7BP
Activities: Activities of other holding companies n.e.c.
Parent: BP Exploration Operating Company Limited
Officers: Emma Louise Delaney-McKnight [1973] Director/Oil Company Executive [Irish]; Andrew Charles Lane [1963] Director/Oil Company Executive; Russell Irving Smith [1960] Director/Oil Company Executive

BP Middle East Limited
Incorporated: 30 September 1957
Net Worth: £25,116,584 *Total Assets:* £160,749,520
Registered Office: Chertsey Road, Sunbury on Thames, Middlesex, TW16 7BP
Activities: Wholesale of other fuels and related products
Parent: BP PLC.
Officers: Jens Bertelsen [1959] Director/Deputy Secretary; Nicholas John Charles Evans [1969] Director/Oil Company Executive; Terence Michael Thornton [1963] Director/Oil Company Executive

BP Oil International Limited
Incorporated: 28 December 1936
Net Worth: £142,143,008 *Total Assets:* £142,143,008
Registered Office: Chertsey Road, Sunbury on Thames, Middlesex, TW16 7BP
Activities: Wholesale of other fuels and related products
Parent: BP International Limited
Officers: Alan Henry Haywood [1966] Director; Carol-Lee Howle [1972] Director/Oil Company Executive; Robert Stephen Lawson [1970] Director/Oil Company Executive; Brian Michael Puffer [1969] Director/Oil Company Executive [British/American]; Geir Patrick Robinson [1968] Director/Oil Company Executive

BP Oil UK Limited
Incorporated: 20 December 1947 *Employees:* 341
Net Worth: £816,000,000 *Total Assets:* £1,510,000,000
Registered Office: Chertsey Road, Sunbury on Thames, Middlesex, TW16 7BP
Activities: Mineral oil refining
Parent: BP International Limited
Officers: Neil Emmett [1970] Director/Oil Company Executive; Nicola Louise Grady-Smith [1973] Director/Oil Company Executive; William George Warren Harland [1975] Director/Oil Company Executive; Peter James Mather [1960] Director/Oil Company Executive

BP Oil Vietnam Limited
Incorporated: 8 June 1956
Net Worth: £45,285,296 *Total Assets:* £45,285,296
Registered Office: Chertsey Road, Sunbury on Thames, Middlesex, TW16 7BP
Activities: Wholesale of other fuels and related products
Parent: BP Asia Pacific Holdings Limited
Officers: Sandra Jean MacRae [1963] Director/Oil Company Executive

BP Pension Trustees Limited
Incorporated: 25 May 1928
Net Worth: £52,000,000 *Total Assets:* £56,905,000
Registered Office: Chertsey Road, Sunbury on Thames, Middlesex, TW16 7BP
Activities: Pension funding
Parent: BP PLC.
Officers: Diana Legge, Secretary; Grahame Paul Cook [1963] Director; Emma Louise Delaney-McKnight [1973] Director/Oil Company Executive [Irish]; Catherine Sarah Gillam [1979] Director/Oil Company Executive; David John Jackson [1953] Director/Solicitor; Jan Clayton Lyons [1965] Director/Oil Company Executive [American]; Peter James Mather [1960] Director/Oil Company Executive; Sir Ian Maurice Gray Prosser [1943] Director; Mark Edward Stageman [1953] Director; Angus James Walker [1963] Director

BP Petrochemicals India Investments Limited
Incorporated: 25 June 2013
Net Worth: £12,043,362 *Total Assets:* £12,139,216
Registered Office: Chertsey Road, Sunbury on Thames, Middlesex, TW16 7BP
Activities: Other business support service activities n.e.c.
Parent: BP Global Investments Limited
Officers: Nigel Clifford Dunn [1967] Director/Oil Company Executive; Catherine Ann McCann [1966] Director/Oil Company Executive; Terence Michael Thornton [1963] Director/Oil Company Executive

BP Pipelines (BTC) Limited
Incorporated: 5 November 2001
Net Worth: £475,656,736 *Total Assets:* £509,718,560
Registered Office: Chertsey Road, Sunbury on Thames, Middlesex, TW16 7BP
Activities: Activities of head offices
Parent: BTC Pipeline Holding Company Limited
Officers: Jaqui Freeman [1968] Director/Oil Company Executive; Robert Gary Jones [1960] Director/Oil Company Executive

BP Pipelines (SCP) Limited
Incorporated: 23 May 2002
Net Worth: £1,095,581,312 *Total Assets:* £1,095,581,312
Registered Office: Chertsey Road, Sunbury on Thames, Middlesex, TW16 7BP
Activities: Activities of head offices
Parent: BP Global Investments Limited
Officers: Jaqui Freeman [1968] Director/Oil Company Executive; Robert Gary Jones [1960] Director/Oil Company Executive

BP Pipelines Tap Limited
Incorporated: 25 February 2016
Net Worth: £338,963,616 *Total Assets:* £537,848,320
Registered Office: Chertsey Road, Sunbury on Thames, Middlesex, TW16 7BP
Activities: Activities of head offices
Parent: BP Exploration Operating Company Limited
Officers: Jaqui Freeman [1968] Director/Oil Company Executive; Robert Gary Jones [1960] Director/Oil Company Executive

BP Properties Limited
Incorporated: 27 July 1961
Net Worth: £56,512,000 *Total Assets:* £58,560,000
Registered Office: Chertsey Road, Sunbury on Thames, Middlesex, TW16 7BP
Activities: Buying and selling of own real estate
Parent: BP PLC
Officers: Juliet Nadine Filose [1960] Director/Oil Company Executive; David Alan Rider [1964] Director/Oil Company Executive; Katherine Anne Thomson [1968] Director/Oil Company Executive

BP Russian Investments Limited
Incorporated: 5 December 1990
Net Worth: £11,790,125,056 *Total Assets:* £11,975,698,432
Registered Office: Chertsey Road, Sunbury on Thames, Middlesex, TW16 7BP
Activities: Activities of head offices
Parent: BP International Limited
Officers: Joanne Elizabeth Cross [1965] Director/Oil Company Lawyer; Sandra Jean MacRae [1963] Director/Oil Company Executive; David Alan Rider [1964] Director/Oil Company Executive; Lord George Islay MacNeill Robertson [1946] Director

BP Senegal Investments Limited
Incorporated: 29 January 2016 *Employees:* 1
Net Worth: £640,183,808 *Total Assets:* £701,984,000
Registered Office: Chertsey Road, Sunbury on Thames, Middlesex, TW16 7BP
Activities: Support activities for petroleum and natural gas mining
Parent: BP Exploration Operating Company Limited
Officers: Emma Louise Delaney-Mc Knight [1973] Director/Oil Company Executive [Irish]; Andrew Charles Lane [1963] Director/Oil Company Executive; Russell Irving Smith [1960] Director/Oil Company Executive

BP Services International Limited
Incorporated: 22 December 2004 *Employees:* 85
Net Worth: £16,285,472 *Total Assets:* £16,726,114
Registered Office: Chertsey Road, Sunbury on Thames, Middlesex, TW16 7BP
Activities: Non-trading company
Parent: BP Exploration Company Limited
Officers: Jaqui Freeman [1968] Director/Oil Company Executive

BP Shafag-Asiman Limited
Incorporated: 11 April 2011
Net Worth: £32,254,938 *Total Assets:* £33,176,834
Registered Office: Chertsey Road, Sunbury on Thames, Middlesex, TW16 7BP
Activities: Support activities for petroleum and natural gas mining
Parent: BP Exploration Operating Company Limited
Officers: Jaqui Freeman [1968] Director/Oil Company Executive; Robert Gary Jones [1960] Director/Oil Company Executive

BP Shipping Limited
Incorporated: 30 April 1915
Net Worth: £1,602,840,704 *Total Assets:* £1,682,076,032
Registered Office: Chertsey Road, Sunbury on Thames, Middlesex, TW16 7BP
Activities: Sea and coastal freight water transport
Parent: BP International Limited
Officers: Carol-Lee Howle [1972] Director/Oil Company Executive; Roderick Guy Mason [1964] Director/Oil Company Executive; Aleida Garza Rios [1968] Director/Oil Company Executive [American]; Katherine Anne Thomson [1968] Director/Oil Company Executive; Chunming Zhao [1966] Director/Oil Company Executive [Chinese]

BP Subsea Well Response Limited
Incorporated: 2 March 2012
Net Worth: £35,110,936 *Total Assets:* £37,991,692
Registered Office: Chertsey Road, Sunbury on Thames, Middlesex, TW16 7BP
Activities: Other business support service activities n.e.c.
Parent: BP Exploration Operating Company Limited
Officers: Gordon Young Birrell [1963] Director/Oil Company Executive; Jaqui Freeman [1968] Director/Oil Company Executive; Timothy Robert Schofield [1963] Director/Oil Company Executive

BP Technology Ventures Limited
Incorporated: 27 March 1981
Previous: BP Alternative Energy International Limited
Net Worth: £68,475,040 *Total Assets:* £120,078,968
Registered Office: Chertsey Road, Sunbury on Thames, Middlesex, TW16 7BP
Activities: Activities of head offices
Parent: BP International Limited
Officers: David Geoffrey Philip Eyton [1961] Director/Oil Company Executive; Anna Marie Floyer-LEA [1976] Director/Oil Company Executive; David Ian Gilmour [1960] Sales & Marketing Director

BP Turkey Refining Limited
Incorporated: 15 August 1958
Net Worth: £16,496,006 *Total Assets:* £25,843,286
Registered Office: Chertsey Road, Sunbury on Thames, Middlesex, TW16 7BP
Activities: Mineral oil refining
Parent: BP PLC.
Officers: Nicholas John Charles Evans [1969] Director/Oil Company Executive; Richard James Lord [1980] Director/Oil Company Executive; Terence Michael Thornton [1963] Director/Oil Company Executive

BP+Amoco International Limited
Incorporated: 27 July 1998
Net Worth: £6,994,002 *Total Assets:* £11,979,391
Registered Office: Chertsey Road, Sunbury on Thames, Middlesex, TW16 7BP
Activities: Wholesale of other fuels and related products
Parent: BP PLC.
Officers: Christopher Jon Humes [1962] Director/Oil Company Executive [American]; Jonathan William Winston Wood [1962] Director/Oil Company Executive

BPC Interiors Limited
Incorporated: 24 July 2006 *Employees:* 14
Net Worth: £1,348,551 *Total Assets:* £9,986,314
Registered Office: 19-20 Bourne Court, Southend Road, Woodford Green, Essex, IG8 8HD
Activities: Other business support service activities n.e.c.
Parent: BPC Interiors Holdings Limited
Officers: Anne Knight, Secretary; Nicola Parmenter, Secretary; Paul John Johnson [1965] Director; Barry Knight [1960] Director/Chartered Surveyor

BPE Polandco Limited
Incorporated: 29 August 2009 *Employees:* 3
Net Worth: £10,327,442 *Total Assets:* £11,424,560
Registered Office: c/o Beck & Pollitzer Engineering Limited, Burnham Road, Dartford, Kent, DA1 5BD
Activities: Non-trading company
Parent: Beck and Pollitzer Polska SP.Z.O.O
Officers: Ivo Vesselinov, Secretary; Andrew Hodgson [1965] Director; Romain Jean Patrick Prouvost [1979] Director [French]; Ivo Vesselinov [1976] Finance Director

BPH Finance Number 1 Limited
Incorporated: 18 January 2005 *Employees:* 939
Net Worth: £192,563,008 *Total Assets:* £289,932,000
Registered Office: Queens Court, 9-17 Eastern Road, Romford, Essex, RM1 3NG
Activities: Activities of head offices
Parent: BPH Subholdco Limited
Officers: Jonathan Patrick Braidley [1965] Director/Investment Professional; Christopher Andre Kula [1983] Director/Chartered Accountant [German/Canadian]

BR Pharma International Limited
Incorporated: 1 July 1998 *Employees:* 36
Net Worth: £12,410,152 *Total Assets:* £15,056,712
Registered Office: Haslers, Old Station Road, Loughton, Essex, IG10 4PL
Activities: Wholesale of pharmaceutical goods
Shareholders: Joel Rabin; Rebecca Eleanor Blinston-Jones; Fabienne Rabin
Officers: Fabienne Rabin, Secretary; Sheryl Anne Glanvill [1970] Operations Director [New Zealander]; Joel Rabin [1974] Director; Christina White [1967] Finance Director

Bradenstoke Solar Park Limited
Incorporated: 5 November 2014
Net Worth Deficit: £15,324,218 *Total Assets:* £52,818,064
Registered Office: 40 Brighton Road, Sutton, Surrey, SM2 5BN
Activities: Production of electricity
Officers: Charles Bondi [1972] Director/Accountant; Kenneth Reid Ross [1968] Director

Brambles Enterprises Limited
Incorporated: 21 December 1988 *Employees:* 80
Net Worth: £8,135,000 *Total Assets:* £33,937,000
Registered Office: 2nd Floor, 400 Dashwood Lang Road, Bourne Business Park, Addlestone, Surrey, KT15 2HJ
Activities: Activities of head offices
Parent: Cyan Logistics Limited
Officers: Daniel Robert Berry [1973] Director/Lawyer; Michael Bruce Pooley [1967] Director/President, CHEP Europe

Brambles Finance PLC
Incorporated: 31 October 2002
Net Worth: £120,559,008 *Total Assets:* £2,266,366,976
Registered Office: 2nd Floor, 400 Dashwood Lang Road, Bourne Business Park, Addlestone, Surrey, KT15 2HJ
Activities: Financial intermediation not elsewhere classified
Parent: Brambles Holdings Unlimited
Officers: Peter Jonathon Caisley Bruford [1964] Director/Accountant; Pascal Huart [1963] Director/Treasurer [Belgian]; Rafe Anthony Warren [1959] Director/Accountant

Brambles Holdings (UK) Limited
Incorporated: 23 February 2001 *Employees:* 130
Net Worth: £845,748,032 *Total Assets:* £888,199,168
Registered Office: 2nd Floor, 400 Dashwood Lang Road, Bourne Business Park, Addlestone, Surrey, KT15 2HJ
Activities: Activities of head offices
Parent: Brambles U.K. Limited
Officers: Peter Jonathon Caisley Bruford [1964] Director/Accountant; Pascal Huart [1963] Director/Treasurer [Belgian]; Rafe Anthony Warren [1959] Director/Accountant

Brambles Holdings Unlimited
Incorporated: 10 October 2006
Net Worth: £2,419,762,688 *Total Assets:* £2,660,660,480
Registered Office: 2nd Floor, 400 Dashwood Lang Road, Bourne Business Park, Addlestone, Surrey, KT15 2HJ
Activities: Activities of other holding companies n.e.c.
Officers: Peter Jonathon Caisley Bruford [1964] Director/Accountant; Pascal Huart [1963] Director/Regional Treasurer [Belgian]; Rafe Anthony Warren [1959] Director/Accountant

Brambles Investment Ltd.
Incorporated: 11 October 2006
Net Worth: £1,455,966,848 *Total Assets:* £2,233,382,144
Registered Office: 2nd Floor, 400 Dashwood Lang Road, Bourne Business Park, Addlestone, Surrey, KT15 2HJ
Activities: Activities of other holding companies n.e.c.
Parent: Brambles Holdings Unlimited
Officers: Peter Jonathon Caisley Bruford [1964] Director/Accountant; Pascal Huart [1963] Director/Regional Treasurer [Belgian]; Rafe Anthony Warren [1959] Director/Accountant

Brambles Nominees Limited
Incorporated: 6 June 2003
Net Worth Deficit: £5,942,102 *Total Assets:* £31,579,820
Registered Office: 2nd Floor, 400 Dashwood Lang Road, Bourne Business Park, Addlestone, Surrey, KT15 2HJ
Activities: Activities of other holding companies n.e.c.
Parent: Brambles Holdings (UK) Limited
Officers: Peter Jonathon Caisley Bruford [1964] Director/Accountant; Pascal Huart [1963] Director/Regional Treasurer [Belgian]; Rafe Anthony Warren [1959] Director/Accountant

Brambles U.K. Limited
Incorporated: 3 December 1980
Net Worth: £786,406,016 *Total Assets:* £920,161,024
Registered Office: 2nd Floor, 400 Dashwood Lang Road, Bourne Business Park, Addlestone, Surrey, KT15 2HJ
Activities: Activities of other holding companies n.e.c.
Parent: BFIM Limited
Officers: Peter Jonathon Caisley Bruford [1964] Director/Accountant; Pascal Huart [1963] Director/Treasurer [Belgian]; Rafe Anthony Warren [1959] Director/Accountant

Bramley Health Holding Company Limited
Incorporated: 28 September 2010 *Employees:* 117
Previous: Glen Care Supported Living Services Limited
Net Worth: £8,392,072 *Total Assets:* £18,036,060
Registered Office: 6-10 Outram Road, Croydon, Surrey, CR0 6XE
Activities: Other human health activities
Major Shareholder: Gordon Henry Phillips
Officers: Gordon Henry Phillips [1947] Director

Brand Agency (London) Limited
Incorporated: 10 September 2009 *Employees:* 26
Net Worth Deficit: £609,605 *Total Assets:* £6,557,248
Registered Office: Batchworth House, Batchworth Place, Church Street, Rickmansworth, Herts, WD3 1JE
Activities: Wholesale of perfume and cosmetics
Parent: PBS Brand Agency Limited
Officers: Charlotte Knight [1979] Director

Brand Energy & Infrastructure Services UK, Ltd.
Incorporated: 11 October 2013 *Employees:* 1,043
Net Worth: £11,948,000 *Total Assets:* £47,269,000
Registered Office: Regent Park, 299 Kingston Road, Leatherhead, Surrey, KT22 7SG
Activities: Other service activities n.e.c.
Major Shareholder: Donald J. Gogel
Officers: Michael Edward Herke [1964] Director [Irish]; James David Maskell [1972] Director; Christopher McGalpine [1962] Director/VP Engineering, Asset and Project Management; Benjamin Stevenson Read [1974] Director/Chartered Accountant

Brand Reputation Compliance Limited
Incorporated: 21 November 2016 *Employees:* 35
Net Worth Deficit: £5,397,430 *Total Assets:* £37,995,408
Registered Office: LGC, Queens Road, Teddington, Middlesex, TW11 0LY
Activities: Other professional, scientific and technical activities n.e.c.
Shareholders: LGC (Holdings) Limited; LGC (Holdings) Limited
Officers: Navneet Kaur Ogle, Secretary; Steven Esom [1960] Director; Tessa Leueen Anne Kelly [1953] Director; Euan Ralph Herbert O'Sullivan [1979] Managing Director; Manish Patel [1971] Director; Mark Christopher Proctor [1960] Director; Edward Smyth [1973] Director/Accountant

Branden Solar Parks (Holdings) Limited
Incorporated: 24 October 2012
Net Worth Deficit: £2,777,000 *Total Assets:* £19,682,000
Registered Office: 8 White Oak Square, London Road, Swanley, Kent, BR8 7AG
Activities: Production of electricity
Parent: John Laing Environmental Assets Group (UK) Limited
Officers: Giuseppe La Loggia [1975] Director/Entrepreneur [Italian]; Joseph Mark Linney [1958] Director/Chartered Quantity Surveyor; Yit Ho Tang [1974] Director/Investment Manager [Singaporean]; Christopher James Tanner [1972] Investment Director

Branden Solar Parks Limited
Incorporated: 25 October 2012
Net Worth: £576,000 *Total Assets:* £20,407,000
Registered Office: 8 White Oak Square, London Road, Swanley, Kent, BR8 7AG
Activities: Production of electricity
Parent: Branden Solar Parks (Holdings) Limited
Officers: Giuseppe La Loggia [1975] Director/Entrepreneur [Italian]; Joseph Mark Linney [1958] Director/Chartered Quantity Surveyor; Yit Ho Tang [1974] Director/Investment Manager [Singaporean]; Christopher James Tanner [1972] Investment Director

Brandon House Limited
Incorporated: 9 February 2017
Net Worth Deficit: £27,305 *Total Assets:* £8,344,554
Registered Office: 104 College Road, Harrow, Middlesex, HA1 1BQ
Activities: Letting and operating of conference and exhibition centres
Officers: Kishorkant Bhattessa [1941] Director/Hotelier; Jitendrakumar Maganbhai Patel [1952] Director; Vinodrai Harmanbhai Patel [1938] Director/Retired; Yogesh Patel [1956] Director; Dr Mayank Ramanlal Shah [1958] Director/Doctor

Brasserie Bar Co Limited
Incorporated: 6 February 2006 *Employees:* 35
Net Worth Deficit: £3,022,373 *Total Assets:* £51,583,560
Registered Office: Wizard House, 2a Cambridge Road, Teddington, Middlesex, TW11 8DR
Activities: Licenced restaurants
Parent: Abriand Ltd
Officers: Jeremy Brown [1966] Director; Kathryn Coury [1964] Director; Mark Derry [1960] Director; Stephen Peter Edwards [1964] Director/Venture Capitalist; Clive Andrew Fretwell [1961] Director; Christopher Patrick Edward Guy [1981] Finance Director; Helen Louise Melvin [1968] Director/Accountant

Brausch & Co (UK) Limited
Incorporated: 11 November 1985 *Employees:* 62
Net Worth: £5,821,013 *Total Assets:* £10,213,438
Registered Office: Unit 4 Great West Trading Estate, Great West Road, Brentford, Middlesex, TW8 9DN
Activities: Wholesale of wood, construction materials and sanitary equipment
Major Shareholder: Ghassan Hussein Taher Fadlallah
Officers: Richard Mark Jones [1975] Director; Talal Naji Kanafani [1952] Director; Azzam Masri [1975] Director; Zouheir Ghassan Taher-Fadlallah [1978] Marketing Director [Lebanese]

Braycote Ltd
Incorporated: 20 March 2003
Net Worth: £4,190,725 *Total Assets:* £6,551,480
Registered Office: 9a Sandy Lodge Road, Rickmansworth, Herts, WD3 1LP
Activities: Buying and selling of own real estate
Officers: Chandra Vadan Ganatra, Secretary/Chartered Accountant; Chandra Vadan Ganatra [1949] Director/Chartered Accountant; Mahendra Vithaldas Ganatra [1951] Director/Accountant

BRE Global Limited
Incorporated: 26 March 2014 *Employees:* 292
Net Worth: £8,788,000 *Total Assets:* £14,007,000
Registered Office: Bucknalls Lane, Garston, Watford, Herts, WD25 9XX
Activities: Technical testing and analysis
Parent: BRE Group Ltd
Officers: Anthony Richard Tanner, Secretary; Nicholas Brian Farrimond [1965] Director/Chief Finance Officer; Dr Deborah Anita Smith [1960] Director/Scientist

BRE Trust
Incorporated: 22 November 1996 *Employees:* 638
Net Worth Deficit: £17,176,000 *Total Assets:* £43,026,000
Registered Office: Bucknalls Lane, Garston, Watford, Herts, WD25 9XX
Activities: Other research and experimental development on natural sciences and engineering
Officers: Anthony Richard Tanner, Secretary; June Mary Barnes [1954] Non-Executive Director of Urban and Civic PLC; Julia Bernadette Barrett [1966] Director of Sustainability; Francesca Anne Howard Berriman [1964] Director/Chief Executive; Professor Nicholas Robert Jennings [1966] Director/Academic; Peter William MacDonald Lobban [1947] Director/Chief Executive; James Garwood Michael Wates [1960] Director; Philip George Wilbraham [1960] Expansion Programme Director; Gary Wingrove [1960] Projects and Construction Director

Brembury Properties Limited
Incorporated: 21 August 1973
Net Worth: £4,140,989 *Total Assets:* £6,834,748
Registered Office: 1 Beauchamp Court, Victors Way, Barnet, Herts, EN5 5TZ
Activities: Buying and selling of own real estate
Parent: Maxwelton House Property Company Limited
Officers: Gillian Diana Jamieson, Secretary/Executive; Gillian Diana Jamieson [1936] Director/Executive; Simon Charles Jamieson [1961] Director/Executive; Victor Charles Jamieson [1928] Director/Surveyor

Brenray Holdings Ltd
Incorporated: 21 August 2014
Net Worth: £3,000,000 *Total Assets:* £5,118,250
Registered Office: Aissela, 46 High Street, Esher, Surrey, KT10 9QY
Activities: Activities of other holding companies n.e.c.
Shareholders: Nicola Julia Moore; Leon Joseph Moore
Officers: Leon Joseph Moore [1970] Director/Business Manager; Nicola Julia Moore [1974] Director

Brent Housing Ltd
Incorporated: 20 November 2001
Net Worth: £10,209,922 *Total Assets:* £16,469,177
Registered Office: c/o Dattani Chartered Accountants, Scottish Provident House, 76-80 College Road, Harrow, Middlesex, HA1 1BQ
Activities: Other letting and operating of own or leased real estate
Officers: Brendan Michael Monaghan [1951] Director/Builder [Irish]

Brentford FC Limited
Incorporated: 1 October 1998 *Employees:* 132
Net Worth: £2,600,290 *Total Assets:* £76,384,984
Registered Office: Griffin Park, Braemar Road, Brentford, Middlesex, TW8 0NT
Activities: Activities of sport clubs
Major Shareholder: Matthew Alexander Benham
Officers: Lisa Jane Skelhorn, Secretary; Rasmus Ankersen [1983] Sporting Director, Club Director [Danish]; Monique Choudhuri [1961] Director/Personal Development Consultant; Clifford Crown [1956] Finance Director; Philip Robert Giles [1979] Sporting Director, Club Director; Donald Gilbert Kerr [1952] Director/Marketing Consultant; Michael John Power [1947] Director/Retired Business Executive; Stewart Peter Purvis [1947] Director; Nityajit Saidev Raj [1973] Director/Lawyer

Brentford School for Girls
Incorporated: 8 November 2012 *Employees:* 103
Net Worth: £16,604,538 *Total Assets:* £20,395,524
Registered Office: Brentford School for Girls, 5 Boston Manor Road, Brentford, Middlesex, TW8 0PG
Activities: General secondary education
Officers: Caren Benn, Secretary; Shamiala Amin [1989] Director/Teacher; Marie Elizabeth Anderson [1977] Director/Marketing Consultant; Dr Katia Babbar [1978] Director/Banker; Renu Badiani [1978] Director/Solicitor; Paul Chambers [1974] Director/Procurement Manager; Simon French [1981] Director/Economist; Terri George [1965] Director/Teacher; Nicola Faye Gouldstone [1962] Director/Branding Consultant; Rosemary Ann Griffiths [1976] Director/Housewife; Nancy Horsnell [1954] Director/School Administrator; Sameem Malek [1970] Director/Teacher; Anna Moore [1979] Director/Solicitor; Sari-Maries Nesbeth [1970] Director/Headteacher; Julie Woodward [1976] Director/Programme Manager; Alison Wren [1980] Director/Housewife

Brentwick Limited
Incorporated: 28 February 1940
Net Worth: £105,310,128 *Total Assets:* £105,310,128
Registered Office: Cadbury House, Sanderson Road, Uxbridge, Middlesex, UB8 1DH
Activities: Other business support service activities n.e.c.
Parent: Kraft Foods Investment Holdings UK Limited
Officers: Adrian John Paul Arrighi [1978] Tax Director; Michael Brendan Foye [1965] Treasury Director; John Michael Hladusz [1972] Director/Chartered Accountant; Carole Noelle Keene [1966] Director

Breyer Group Public Limited Company
Incorporated: 2 December 1963 *Employees:* 300
Net Worth: £6,235,903 *Total Assets:* £29,019,344
Registered Office: Faringdon Avenue, Harold Hill, Romford, Essex, RM3 8ST
Activities: Construction of domestic buildings
Parent: Breyer Holdings Limited
Officers: Hilda May Breyer, Secretary; Timothy Breyer [1961] Director; Anne Sarah Dyer [1962] HR Director; Neil Ian Fisher [1963] Finance Director; Warren Michael Sean Hand [1966] Director/Quantity Surveyor; John Andrew Patrick Walsh [1962] Construction Director

Breyer Holdings Limited
Incorporated: 29 July 2008 *Employees:* 300
Net Worth: £7,044,296 *Total Assets:* £29,830,864
Registered Office: Faringdon Avenue, Harold Hill, Romford, Essex, RM3 8ST
Activities: Activities of construction holding companies
Major Shareholder: Timothy Breyer
Officers: Timothy Breyer [1961] Director; Neil Ian Fisher [1963] Finance Director; Warren Michael Sean Hand [1966] Director

Brianco Services Limited
Incorporated: 23 November 1943 *Employees:* 4
Net Worth: £8,706,179 *Total Assets:* £10,631,070
Registered Office: Newmans House, Queens Road, Barnet, Herts, EN5 4DL
Activities: Other letting and operating of own or leased real estate
Parent: Nufrend Limited
Officers: Derek Robert Newman [1984] Director; Janice Newman [1986] Director; Martha Newman [1952] Director

Brick Projects (Marland) Limited
Incorporated: 21 July 2014
Net Worth: £1,638,174 *Total Assets:* £11,541,019
Registered Office: Kimberley House, 31 Burnt Oak Broadway, Edgware, Middlesex, HA8 5LD
Activities: Other letting and operating of own or leased real estate
Parent: St Katherine Investment Group Limited
Officers: Sunil Premchand Hemraj Shah [1960] Director/Chartered Accountant; Terence John Williams [1947] Director

Bricklehampton Classic Care Limited
Incorporated: 7 March 2012 *Employees:* 76
Net Worth: £2,019,263 *Total Assets:* £8,436,201
Registered Office: 6 Highbanks Road, Pinner, Middlesex, HA5 4AR
Activities: Other letting and operating of own or leased real estate
Officers: Jabriel Ejaz Raja, Secretary; Ejaz Nabi Raja [1940] Director; Jabriel Ejaz Raja [1977] Director

Brickline Properties Limited
Incorporated: 9 September 2008 *Employees:* 2
Net Worth: £1,304,248 *Total Assets:* £5,303,700
Registered Office: c/o William & Co, 8-10 South Street, Epsom, Surrey, KT18 7PF
Activities: Other letting and operating of own or leased real estate
Major Shareholder: Claudio Pulze
Officers: Lori Pulze, Secretary; Lori Catherine Kelly-Pulze [1965] Director/Accountant [American]; Claudio Pulze [1949] Director/Restaurateur [Italian]

Bridge Road Southall Limited
Incorporated: 7 February 2017
Net Worth Deficit: £542,148 *Total Assets:* £61,180,600
Registered Office: 3rd Floor, Sterling House, Langston Road, Loughton, Essex, IG10 3TS
Activities: Development of building projects
Parent: Galliard Developments Limited
Officers: Allan William Porter, Secretary; John Cole [1971] Director; Stephen Stuart Solomon Conway [1948] Director; Jonathan Simon Goldstein [1966] Director; Rory Anthony O'Connor [1959] Director [Irish]; Donagh O'Sullivan [1968] Construction Director [Irish]

Brigade Electronics Group PLC
Incorporated: 17 December 2009 *Employees:* 176
Net Worth: £13,659,569 *Total Assets:* £22,422,682
Registered Office: Brigade House, The Mills, Station Road, South Darenth, Kent, DA4 9BD
Activities: Wholesale trade of motor vehicle parts and accessories
Parent: Brigade Holdings Ltd
Officers: John Harris, Secretary; Thomas Craig Brett [1975] Marketing Director; Christopher Philip Hanson-Abbott [1934] Director; Philip Julian Hanson-Abbott [1959] Director; John Lewis David Harris [1960] Director; Rachel Emma Hutson [1974] Director; Stuart Andrew Matthews [1975] Engineering Director; Noel Philip Moody [1949] Sales Director

Brigade Holdings Limited
Incorporated: 16 May 2014 *Employees:* 176
Net Worth: £13,829,582 *Total Assets:* £22,422,682
Registered Office: The Mills, Station Road, South Darenth, Kent, DA4 9BD
Activities: Activities of head offices
Shareholders: Christopher Philip Hanson-Abbott; Philip Julian Hanson-Abbott
Officers: Ian Wilson Sillars, Secretary; Christopher Philip Hanson-Abbott [1934] Director; Philip Julian Hanson-Abbott [1959] Director; Ian Wilson Sillars [1948] Director

Brighthouse Group Limited
Incorporated: 16 May 2007 *Employees:* 2,526
Previous: Brighthouse Group PLC
Net Worth: £71,324,000 *Total Assets:* £233,292,000
Registered Office: 5 Hercules Way, Leavesden, Watford, Herts, WD25 7GS
Activities: Retail sale of audio and video equipment in specialised stores
Officers: David John Harwood, Secretary; Graeme James Campbell [1972] Finance Director; Hamish Stewart Paton [1976] Director

Brighthouse Holdings Limited
Incorporated: 17 May 2007
Net Worth: £196,879,008 *Total Assets:* £254,842,000
Registered Office: 5 Hercules Way, Leavesden, Watford, Herts, WD25 7GS
Activities: Retail sale of audio and video equipment in specialised stores
Parent: Brighthouse Group PLC
Officers: David John Harwood, Secretary; Graeme James Campbell [1972] Finance Director; Hamish Stewart Paton [1976] Director

Brighthouse Limited
Incorporated: 30 January 2007 *Employees:* 2,526
Net Worth: £222,264,000 *Total Assets:* £383,449,984
Registered Office: 5 Hercules Way, Leavesden, Watford, Herts, WD25 7GS
Activities: Retail sale of electrical household appliances in specialised stores
Parent: Brighthouse Holdings Ltd
Officers: David John Harwood, Secretary; Graeme James Campbell [1972] Finance Director; Hamish Stewart Paton [1976] Director

Brightsun Travel (UK) Limited
Incorporated: 30 May 1986 *Employees:* 42
Net Worth: £3,739,543 *Total Assets:* £19,070,808
Registered Office: 14 Hanworth Road, Hounslow, Middlesex, TW3 1UA
Activities: Travel agency activities
Major Shareholder: Deepak Nangla
Officers: Veena Nangla, Secretary; Deepak Nangla [1970] Director/Travel Agent

Brimheath Developments Limited
Incorporated: 4 November 1997
Net Worth: £4,269,301 *Total Assets:* £5,484,624
Registered Office: 11-17 Fowler Road, Ilford, Essex, IG6 3UJ
Activities: Public houses and bars
Major Shareholder: Michael Victor Burgess
Officers: Maria Bather, Secretary; Michael Victor Burgess [1957] Director/Caterer

Brinor Investments Limited
Incorporated: 18 October 1960 *Employees:* 6
Net Worth: £5,764,212 *Total Assets:* £6,684,423
Registered Office: 255 Cranbrook Road, Ilford, Essex, IG1 4TG
Activities: Development of building projects
Shareholder: John Peter William Maidman
Officers: David Macaree [1945] Director; Philip James Macaree [1978] Director/Surveyor; Jessica Louise Maidman [1987] Director/Chartered Surveyor; John Peter William Maidman [1956] Director/Chartered Surveyor; Ronald William Maidman [1928] Director; Annika Clare Woodcock [1985] Director/Dietician

Brisko Scaffolding Limited
Incorporated: 24 October 1996 *Employees:* 43
Net Worth: £2,472,482 *Total Assets:* £44,339,620
Registered Office: Unit 16 Kingsmill Business Park, Chapel Mill Lane, Kingston upon Thames, Surrey, KT1 3GZ
Activities: Other specialised construction activities n.e.c.
Officers: Shanmuganathan Subramaniam, Secretary; Lalit Premchandani [1974] Director; Anil Munish Kumar Arjan Taurani [1968] Director/Business Person [Indian]; Arjan Taurani [1936] Director/Business Person [Indian]; Lalit Arjan Taurani [1974] Director/Business Person [Indian]

Bristol-Myers Squibb Business Services Limited
Incorporated: 29 September 1986 *Employees:* 324
Net Worth Deficit: £5,028,000 *Total Assets:* £67,446,000
Registered Office: Uxbridge Business Park, Sanderson Road, Uxbridge, Middlesex, UB8 1DH
Activities: Other business support service activities n.e.c.
Parent: Bristol-Myers Squibb Holdings 2002 Limited
Officers: Bruno Marie Pierre Lauras [1961] Director/Head of Business and Finance Services, Europe [French]; Joanne Elizabeth Rishworth [1977] Director

Bristol-Myers Squibb Holdings 2002 Limited
Incorporated: 31 October 2002 *Employees:* 3
Net Worth: £291,720,992 *Total Assets:* £291,864,992
Registered Office: Uxbridge Business Park, Sanderson Road, Uxbridge, Middlesex, UB8 1DH
Activities: Activities of head offices
Officers: Bertrand Pierre Marie Grosjean [1969] Finance Director [French]; Katherine Reynolds Kelly [1976] Director/Vice President & Assistant General Counsel [American]; Veronique Maguin EP Walsh [1961] Director/General Manager (UK & Ireland) [French]

Bristol-Myers Squibb Pharmaceuticals Limited
Incorporated: 2 April 1990 *Employees:* 414
Net Worth: £165,060,992 *Total Assets:* £276,734,016
Registered Office: Uxbridge Business Park, Sanderson Road, Uxbridge, Middlesex, UB8 1DH
Activities: Manufacture of basic pharmaceutical products
Parent: Bristol-Myers Squibb Holdings 2002 Limited
Officers: Bertrand Pierre Marie Grosjean [1969] Finance Director [French]; Veronique Maguin EP Walsh [1961] Director/General Manager (UK & Ireland) [French]

The Brit School Limited
Incorporated: 6 April 1989 *Employees:* 162
Net Worth: £16,723,000 *Total Assets:* £19,193,000
Registered Office: The Brit School, 60 The Cresent, Croydon, Surrey, CR0 2HN
Activities: Technical and vocational secondary education
Officers: Richard Giles Elliott, Secretary; Christopher John Ancliff [1965] Director/Solicitor; Paul Jeffery Burger [1955] Director; David Robert Carter [1952] Director; Joanna Fitzmaurice Charrington [1970] Director/Executive Vice President A&R; Olivia Natalie Chew [1982] Director/Teacher; Madelaine Louise Cooper [1957] Director/Talent Broker; John Andrew Craig [1944] Director; Maggie Crowe [1966] Director/Event Manager; Marianne Saleisha Cwynarski [1967] Director/Senior Manager, Public Sector; Angela Ferreira [1961] Director/Television Producer; Felicity Hamblyn [1961] Director; Adina Marilena Havard [1966] Director/Learning Support Assistant [Romanian]; Matthew James Hilton [1967] Director/Consultant; Martin Frank Locket [1970] Director; Professor Sally Patricia Mackey [1956] Director/Lecturer; Ayodeji Christopher Renner Mahoney [1963] Director; Jonathan Charles Lutwyche Morrish [1950] Director/PR Executive; Simon Paul Thomas Presswell [1970] Managing Director; Louise Marcelle Victoria Soden [1952] Director/Education Consultant; Geoffrey Michael Windsor Taylor [1968] Director/Chief Executive Officer; Horace Trubridge [1957] Director/Trades Union Officer; Antony Ronald Wadsworth [1956] Director

Britair Holdings Limited
Incorporated: 25 March 1998
Net Worth: £112,907,000 *Total Assets:* £209,104,992
Registered Office: P O Box 365, Waterside, Harmondsworth, Middlesex, UB7 0GB
Activities: Activities of head offices
Parent: British Airways PLC
Officers: Luke Alexander Michael Straver, Secretary; Andrew Ian Fleming [1979] Director/Company Secretary; Simon Philcox [1979] Director/Accountant

Britannia Refined Metals Limited
Incorporated: 4 December 1930 *Employees:* 161
Net Worth: £48,243,000 *Total Assets:* £77,058,000
Registered Office: Botany Road, Northfleet, Kent, DA11 9BG
Activities: Precious metals production
Parent: Xstrata Limited
Officers: Howard Stephen Gilroy, Secretary; Anna Carson [1970] Director/Fluorspar Manager; Carole Anne Constant [1961] Director/IT Superintendent; Howard Stephen Gilroy [1955] Director/Accountant; Jeffrey William Henderson [1961] Director/Compliance Manager; Carlos Navalpotro [1985] Director/Asset Manager [Spanish]; Florian Jurgen Bogislaw Von Steinkeller [1979] Director/Economist [German]

Britannia Row Productions Limited
Incorporated: 12 September 1984 *Employees:* 57
Net Worth: £5,710,845 *Total Assets:* £10,803,096
Registered Office: 104 The Green, Twickenham, Middlesex, TW2 5AG
Activities: Renting and leasing of media entertainment equipment
Officers: Nicola Amoruso [1980] Director/General Manager [Italian]; Christina Sarah Bosch [1986] Director/Financial Controller; Matthew Ronald Clair [1985] Director/CIO Live Sound Reinforcement [American]; Shaun Eugene Clair [1983] Director/VP Sales Live Sound Reinforcement [American]; Troy Anthony Clair [1960] Director/President Live Sound Reinforcement [American]; Stuart Andrew Robert Dickson [1949] Financial Director; Leslie John Dwight [1969] Sales Director; Bryan David Grant [1950] Director; Michael John Lowe [1949] Director

Britannia Security Group Limited
Incorporated: 11 September 1978
Net Worth: £42,066,000 *Total Assets:* £73,758,000
Registered Office: Security House, The Summit, Hanworth Road, Sunbury on Thames, Middlesex, TW16 5DB
Activities: Activities of head offices
Parent: ADT Group Limited
Officers: Mark Ayre [1963] Finance Director; Peter Schieser [1967] Director [German]

Britannic Trading Limited
Incorporated: 21 February 1966
Net Worth: £421,945,568 *Total Assets:* £742,389,248
Registered Office: Chertsey Road, Sunbury on Thames, Middlesex, TW16 7BP
Activities: Other business support service activities n.e.c.
Parent: BP International Limited
Officers: Alan Henry Haywood [1966] Director; Carol-Lee Howle [1972] Director/Oil Company Executive; Robert Stephen Lawson [1970] Director/Oil Company Executive; Brian Michael Puffer [1969] Director/Oil Company Executive [British/American]; Geir Patrick Robinson [1968] Director/Oil Company Executive

British Airways 777 Leasing Limited
Incorporated: 5 November 2003
Net Worth Deficit: £12,705,000 *Total Assets:* £34,769,000
Registered Office: P O Box 365, Waterside, Harmondsworth, Middlesex, UB7 0GB
Activities: Financial leasing
Parent: British Airways PLC
Officers: Luke Alexander Michael Straver, Secretary; Andrew Ian Fleming [1979] Director/Company Secretary; Simon Philcox [1979] Director/Accountant

British Airways Associated Companies Limited
Incorporated: 6 September 1957
Net Worth: £51,727,000 *Total Assets:* £51,810,000
Registered Office: P O Box 365, Waterside, Harmondsworth, Middlesex, UB7 0GB
Activities: Activities of head offices
Parent: British Airways PLC
Officers: Luke Alexander Michael Straver, Secretary; Andrew Ian Fleming [1979] Director/Company Secretary; Simon Philcox [1979] Director/Accountant

British Airways Avionic Engineering Limited
Incorporated: 4 January 1993 *Employees:* 193
Net Worth: £12,707,000 *Total Assets:* £13,566,000
Registered Office: P O Box 365, Waterside, Harmondsworth, Middlesex, UB7 0GB
Activities: Repair and maintenance of aircraft and spacecraft
Parent: British Airways PLC
Officers: Carole Hibbs, Secretary; William Armstrong [1971] Director/Manager; Robert Llewellyn Crew [1964] Director/Engineer; Sian Louise Davies [1973] Director/Accountant; Melanie Jane Grant-Stevens [1962] Director/Human Resources Advisor; Jason Patrick Mahoney [1971] Director/Engineer [Irish]; Louise Anne Street [1974] Director/Manager

British Airways Holidays Limited
Incorporated: 6 September 1955 *Employees:* 260
Net Worth: £43,694,000 *Total Assets:* £212,999,008
Registered Office: P O Box 365, Waterside HBB3, Harmondsworth, West Drayton, Middlesex, UB7 0GB
Activities: Scheduled passenger air transport
Parent: British Airways PLC
Officers: Katie Louise Bishop, Secretary; Claire Marie Elizabeth Bentley [1968] Director/Airline Executive; Andrew Peter David Brem [1968] Director [Swiss]; Colm Leo Lacy [1970] Director/Airline Executive [Irish]; Sarah Elizabeth Mussenden [1965] Director; Duncan Alexander John Roberts [1973] Commercial Director; Jack Robert Smith [1977] Director

British Airways Leasing Limited
Incorporated: 30 January 2001
Net Worth: £11,608,000 *Total Assets:* £19,460,000
Registered Office: P O Box 365, Waterside, Harmondsworth, Middlesex, UB7 0GB
Activities: Renting and leasing of air passenger transport equipment
Parent: British Airways PLC
Officers: Luke Alexander Michael Straver, Secretary; Andrew Ian Fleming [1979] Director/Company Secretary; Simon Philcox [1979] Director/Accountant

British Airways Maintenance Cardiff Limited
Incorporated: 10 December 1987 *Employees:* 625
Net Worth: £36,436,000 *Total Assets:* £42,889,000
Registered Office: P O Box 365, Waterside, Harmondsworth, Middlesex, UB7 0GB
Activities: Repair and maintenance of aircraft and spacecraft
Parent: British Airways PLC
Officers: Carole Hibbs, Secretary; William Armstrong [1971] Director/Manager; Robert Llewellyn Crew [1964] Director/Engineer; Sian Louise Davies [1973] Director/Accountant; Melanie Jane Grant-Stevens [1962] Director/Human Resources Advisor; Jason Patrick Mahoney [1971] Director/Engineer [Irish]; Louise Anne Street [1974] Director/Manager

British Airways PLC
Incorporated: 13 December 1983 *Employees:* 43,125
Net Worth: £5,774,000,128 *Total Assets:* £16,677,999,616
Registered Office: P O Box 365, Waterside, Harmondsworth, Middlesex, UB7 0GB
Activities: Scheduled passenger air transport
Shareholders: LDC (NCS) Limited; International Consolidated Airlines Group S.A
Officers: Andrew Ian Fleming, Secretary; Alejandro Cruz de Llano [1966] Director/Chairman and CEO [Spanish]; Lynne Louise Embleton [1969] Director/Airline Executive; Stephen William Lawrence Gunning [1967] Director/Chief Financial Officer; Gavin Echlin Patterson [1967] Director; Alison Clare Reed [1956] Director/Accountant; Julia Elizabeth Simpson [1958] Director

British American Tobacco UK Limited
Incorporated: 13 February 1989 *Employees:* 198
Net Worth: £36,803,000 *Total Assets:* £254,247,008
Registered Office: One Eton Street, Richmond upon Thames, London, TW9 1EF
Activities: Wholesale of tobacco products
Parent: Weston Investment Company Limited
Officers: Jessica Munday, Secretary; Christopher Mathew John Barraclough [1982] Director/Head of HR; Nigel Graeme Hardy [1968] Director/General Manager; William Richard Darvell Hill [1977] Director/Head of Legal & External Affairs, UK&I; Dimitri Alexandros Tounis [1980] Director/Head of Finance; Gemma Bridget Webb [1963] Director/Business Manager [Irish]

British Board of Agrement
Incorporated: 2 May 1966 *Employees:* 153
Net Worth Deficit: £944,000 *Total Assets:* £9,198,000
Registered Office: Bucknalls Lane, Garston, Watford, Herts, WD25 9BA
Activities: Other professional, scientific and technical activities n.e.c.
Officers: Claire Curtis-Thomas [1958] Director/Chief Executive; Richard Vincent Gunning [1953] Director; Neil Roberts Hannah [1955] Director; Valerie Ellen Le Vaillant [1957] Director; Professor Robert John Lowe [1955] Director/Professor of Energy & Building Science; Brian Desmond Patrick Moore [1959] Operations Director; Helen Rachael Wylde [1968] Director

British Danubian Trade Development Company Limited
Incorporated: 18 July 1946 *Employees:* 3
Net Worth: £16,112,434 *Total Assets:* £16,129,190
Registered Office: Lygon House, 50 London Road, Bromley, Kent, BR1 3RA
Activities: Financial intermediation not elsewhere classified
Major Shareholder: Stephen Anthony John Carew Deverell
Officers: Marina Lys Carew Deverell, Secretary; Stephen Anthony John Carew Deverell [1957] Director

British Limbless Ex-Service Men's Association
Incorporated: 6 November 2000 *Employees:* 34
Net Worth: £33,258,056 *Total Assets:* £34,064,508
Registered Office: Frankland Moore House, 185-187 High Road, Chadwell Heath, Romford, Essex, RM6 6NA
Activities: Activities of other membership organisations n.e.c.
Officers: Barry John Le Grys, Secretary; Miles Courtenay Ambler [1960] Director/Financial Consultant; Adrian John Bradshaw [1958] Director/Army Officer; William Lloyd Dixon [1984] Director/Banker; Alison Laura Grant [1968] Director/Retired; Anthony John Harris [1981] Director/Leadership and Development Consultant; Rebecca Charlotte Maciejewska [1967] Director/Trust Secretary; Philip David Monkhouse [1968] Director/Factory Operative; Andrew Kenneth Mudd [1956] Director/Retired; Mark Nicholas Pillans [1971] Director/Communications Consultant; Colin Rouse [1957] Director/Retired; Robert John Watts [1952] Director/Retired

British Marine Federation
Incorporated: 18 March 1991 *Employees:* 53
Net Worth: £2,134,272 *Total Assets:* £9,842,902
Registered Office: Marine House, Thorpe Lea Road, Egham, Surrey, TW20 8BF
Activities: Activities of business and employers membership organisations
Officers: Alice Elisabeth Allen [1965] Director/PR Consultant; Will Hugh Alex Blagdon [1970] Director/Boat Builder; Ian David Cooke [1972] Director; Paul Douglas Maxfield Gullett [1955] Director; Edward John Helps [1953] Director; Bryan William Jones [1967] Director/Marketing Manager; Christopher Paul Manners [1968] Managing Director; Paul Gavin Martin [1968] Managing Director; Alan Morgan [1950] Director/Consultant; Greg Munford [1966] Director/Chief Executive; David Anthony Pougher [1955] Director/Div Manager; Johann Lesley Robinson [1961] Director/Chief Executive Officer; Dean Trevor Smith [1968] Commercial Director; Philippa Woods [1972] Managing Director

British Midland Airways Limited
Incorporated: 16 February 1949
Net Worth: £47,900,000 *Total Assets:* £158,500,000
Registered Office: P O Box 365, Waterside, Speedbird Way, Harmondsworth, Middlesex, UB7 0GB
Activities: Renting and leasing of air passenger transport equipment
Parent: British Midland Limited
Officers: Andrew Ian Fleming, Secretary; Sian Louise Davies [1973] Director/Accountant; Simon Philcox [1979] Director/Accountant

Broadberry Data Systems Limited
Incorporated: 20 December 1993
Net Worth: £3,952,133 *Total Assets:* £5,269,613
Registered Office: 3 Sheen Road, Richmond, Surrey, TW9 1AD
Activities: Wholesale of computers, computer peripheral equipment and software
Major Shareholder: Colin Peter Broadberry
Officers: Peter John Broadberry, Secretary; Colin Peter Broadberry [1971] Director

Broadfields Academy Trust
Incorporated: 6 August 2013 *Employees:* 148
Net Worth: £9,898,000 *Total Assets:* £11,617,000
Registered Office: Broadfields Primary School, Roseberry Drive, Edgware, Middlesex, HA8 8JP
Activities: Primary education
Officers: Robin Archibald [1964] Director/Headteacher; Manoj Parmar [1970] Director/Regional Finance Manager; Kajal Shah [1973] Director

Broadham Care Limited
Incorporated: 3 May 2005 *Employees:* 112
Net Worth: £5,170,000 *Total Assets:* £9,789,000
Registered Office: c/o Elysium Healthcare, 2 Imperial Place, Maxwell Road, Borehamwood, Herts, WD6 1JN
Activities: Residential care activities for the elderly and disabled
Parent: Elysium Healthcare Holdings 3 Limited
Officers: Sarah Juliette Livingston, Secretary; Lesley Joy Chamberlain [1963] Director/Group Chief Executive; Dr Quazi Shams Mahfooz Haque [1968] Executive Medical Director; Steven John Woolgar [1955] Director of Policy and Regulation

Broadrich Limited
Incorporated: 13 April 2012 *Employees:* 3
Net Worth: £4,147,333 *Total Assets:* £8,500,139
Registered Office: Northside House, Mount Pleasant, Barnet, Herts, EN4 9EE
Activities: Other letting and operating of own or leased real estate
Parent: Mountcharm Group Limited
Officers: Jason Robert Cooper, Secretary; Adam Cooper [1971] Director; Jason Robert Cooper [1947] Director; Melvyn Frank Cooper [1941] Director

Broadway Malyan Employee Ownership Trustees Limited
Incorporated: 2 September 2016 *Employees:* 495
Net Worth: £3,459,000 *Total Assets:* £28,492,000
Registered Office: Unit 3 Weybridge Business Park, Addlestone Road, Weybridge, Surrey, KT15 2BW
Activities: Other business support service activities n.e.c.
Officers: Francesca Yeomans, Secretary; Antonio Miguel Condeco de Sousa [1978] Director/Architect [Portuguese]; Peter Anthony Crossley [1957] Director/Architect; David Campbell McDonald [1976] Director; James Edward Tanswell Rayner [1963] Director/Architect; Kate Stone [1968] Director/UK Bid Leader; Philip Peter Stone [1972] Director/Technician; Daniela Viloria [1984] Director/Architect [Spanish]

Broadway Malyan Holdings Limited
Incorporated: 8 April 2005 *Employees:* 495
Net Worth: £11,354,000 *Total Assets:* £27,942,000
Registered Office: 3 Weybridge Business Park, Addlestone Road, Weybridge, Surrey, KT15 2BW
Activities: Activities of head offices
Parent: Broadway Malyan Employee Ownership Trustees Limited
Officers: Francesca Yeomans, Secretary; David Hugh Anderson [1962] Director/Architect; Ian Apsley [1973] Director/Architect; Edward Luke Baker [1973] Director/Urban Designer; Martin Bates [1974] Director/Architect; Margarida de Ordaz Caldeira [1962] Director/Architect [Portuguese]; Peter Anthony Crossley [1957] Director/Architect; Anne Kathryn Howard [1969] Finance Director; John Charles Oliver [1955] Director/Accountant; Jorge Eduardo Ponce Dawson Petrocelli [1963] Director/Architect [Spanish]; James Edward Tanswell Rayner [1963] Director/Masterplanner; Stuart Rough [1960] Director; Jeremy John Salmon [1968] Director/Architect; Ian Andrew Simpson [1966] Director/Architect; Peter Anthony Vaughan [1960] Director/Architect; Gary Whittle [1959] Director/Architect

Broadway Malyan Limited
Incorporated: 6 April 1998 *Employees:* 232
Net Worth: £3,782,000 *Total Assets:* £15,231,000
Registered Office: 3 Weybridge Business Park, Addlestone Road, Weybridge, Surrey, KT15 2BW
Activities: Other engineering activities
Parent: Broadway Malyan Holdings Limited
Officers: Francesca Yeomans, Secretary; David Hugh Anderson [1962] Director/Architect; Ian Apsley [1973] Director/Architect; Martin Bates [1974] Director/Architect; Stuart Bertie [1975] Director/Architect; Monika Bik [1976] Director/Masterplanner; Laura Cassullo [1975] Director/Architect [Italian]; Nicholas James Davies [1970] Director/Architect; Hugo Charles Maurice FitzGenerald [1971] Director/Masterplanner; Anne Kathryn Howard [1969] Finance Director; Stephen Ignatius McGrath [1968] Director/Part 2 Architect; Jeff Alan Nottage [1976] Director/Masterplanner; James Edward Tanswell Rayner [1963] Director/Urban Planner; Philip Peter Stone [1972] Director/Technician; Peter Anthony Vaughan [1960] Director/Architect; Charlotte Ann Wilson [1971] Director/Architect; Joseph Witchell [1972] Director/Architect

Brobot Petroleum Limited
Incorporated: 23 January 1978 *Employees:* 275
Net Worth: £20,887,252 *Total Assets:* £30,122,572
Registered Office: Prax House, Horizon Business Village, 1 Brooklands Road, Weybridge, Surrey, KT13 0TJ
Activities: Retail sale of automotive fuel in specialised stores
Parent: Brobot Group Limited
Officers: Arani Soosaipillai, Secretary; Don Camillo Emilio Borneo [1957] Director; Winston Sanjeevkumar Soosaipillai [1973] Director

Bromcom Computers PLC
Incorporated: 24 July 1986 *Employees:* 40
Net Worth: £4,912,096 *Total Assets:* £8,323,456
Registered Office: Rutland House, 44 Masons Hill, Bromley, Kent, BR2 9JG
Activities: Wholesale of computers, computer peripheral equipment and software
Major Shareholder: Ali Guryel
Officers: Serap Bayramoglu, Secretary; Ali Guryel [1948] Director/Computer Consultant

Bromley Business Centre (Holdings) Ltd.
Incorporated: 14 November 1960 *Employees:* 4
Net Worth: £9,033,352 *Total Assets:* £13,477,756
Registered Office: Enterprise House, 27 Hastings Road, Bromley, Kent, BR2 8NA
Activities: Other business support service activities n.e.c.
Parent: Beechwood Properties Limited
Officers: David Robert Garmson, Secretary/Property Developer; David Mark Garmson [1972] Director; David Robert Garmson [1945] Director/Property Developer; Liam Dominic Williams [1974] Director

Bromley Healthcare Community Interest Company
Incorporated: 11 February 2009 *Employees:* 813
Net Worth: £4,882,182 *Total Assets:* £10,401,709
Registered Office: Global House, 10 Station Approach, Hayes, Bromley, Kent, BR2 7EH
Activities: Other human health activities
Officers: Janet Christine Ettridge [1964] Operations Director; Andrew Mark Hardman [1965] Director of Strategy & Business Development; Dr Catherine Michaela Jenson [1969] Director/Doctor; Elizabeth Anne Jones [1970] Director of Finance; Andrew Michael Naish [1965] Director/Management Consultant; Charanjit Kaur Yogeshbhai Patel [1954] Director; Raoul Michael Pinnell [1951] Director; Jacqueline Ann Scott [1968] Director/Chief Executive Officer

Brompton Bicycle Limited
Incorporated: 3 June 1976 *Employees:* 266
Net Worth: £16,327,471 *Total Assets:* £20,682,220
Registered Office: Brompton Bicycle Ltd, Ockham Drive, Greenford, Middlesex, UB6 0FD
Activities: Manufacture of bicycles and invalid carriages
Officers: Richard Francis Townsend Coles, Secretary; William Butler Adams [1974] Director/Engineer; William Geoffrey Carleysmith [1981] Director/Engineer; Timothy Whitmore Newton Guinness [1947] Director/Investment Management; Luke Oliver Johnson [1962] Director; Robert Bradley Kendall [1973] Director; Stephen Desmond Loftus [1973] Director/Sales and Marketing; John Alan Stenton-Putt [1951] Director/Consultant; Lorne Alan Vary [1972] Finance Director

Bronzeshield Lifting Limited
Incorporated: 16 January 1986 *Employees:* 61
Net Worth: £10,719,636 *Total Assets:* £19,404,582
Registered Office: Crayford Mill, Thames Road, Crayford, Kent, DA1 4QH
Activities: Other specialised construction activities n.e.c.
Major Shareholder: William Charles Albert Frost
Officers: William Charles Albert Frost [1944] Director/Engineer; Martin Jones [1960] Director/Accountant; Malcolm James Stevens [1958] Director/Salesman

Brook Hotels Group Limited
Incorporated: 3 February 2009 *Employees:* 144
Net Worth: £3,836,977 *Total Assets:* £21,216,716
Registered Office: 94 Kingston Hill, Kingston upon Thames, Surrey, KT2 7NP
Activities: Hotels and similar accommodation
Major Shareholder: Umesh Ummat
Officers: Ashok Kumar Ummat [1953] Director/Hotelier; Umesh Ummat [1957] Director

Brook Hotels No. 1 Limited
Incorporated: 10 April 2008 *Employees:* 101
Net Worth: £3,656,311 *Total Assets:* £17,218,070
Registered Office: 94 Kingston Hill, Kingston upon Thames, Surrey, KT2 7NP
Activities: Hotels and similar accommodation
Parent: Brook Hotels Group Limited
Officers: Ashok Kumar Ummat, Secretary; Mervyn Humphries [1953] Director/Accountant; Ashok Kumar Ummat [1953] Director; Umesh Ummat [1957] Director; Denise Anne Unmat [1960] Director

Brookcast UK LLP
Incorporated: 24 May 2013
Net Worth: £2,683,930 *Total Assets:* £5,943,286
Registered Office: 38 Ducketts Road, Crayford, Dartford, Kent, DA1 4BA
Officers: Ramil Mavlyutov [1973] Member

Brookpass Limited
Incorporated: 13 December 1978 *Employees:* 3
Net Worth: £6,156,985 *Total Assets:* £8,173,710
Registered Office: 20b Cross Road, Tadworth, Surrey, KT20 5SR
Activities: Development of building projects
Officers: Kenneth Charles Newman, Secretary/Joint Managing Director/Chairman; Gordon Edward Newman [1975] Director/Accounts Manager; Kenneth Charles Newman [1936] Chairman and Managing Director

Brooks Laundry LLP
Incorporated: 7 July 2017
Net Worth: £952,590 *Total Assets:* £5,582,916
Registered Office: 3rd Floor, Sterling House, Langston Road, Loughton, Essex, IG10 3TS

Brookstream Properties Limited
Incorporated: 14 July 1995
Net Worth: £15,940,611 *Total Assets:* £45,009,612
Registered Office: Hill House, Lowlands Road, Harrow, Middlesex, HA1 3EQ
Activities: Development of building projects
Shareholders: Luke Andrew Comer; Brian Martin Comer
Officers: Brian Martin Comer [1960] Director [Irish]; Luke Andrew Comer [1957] Director [Irish]

Brown & Burk UK Limited
Incorporated: 2 October 2000 *Employees:* 7
Net Worth: £2,455,673 *Total Assets:* £12,304,449
Registered Office: Micro House, 5 Marryat Close, Hounslow, Middlesex, TW4 5DQ
Activities: Manufacture of pharmaceutical preparations
Officers: Preetham Sharma Hiremat [1973] Director [Indian]; Badarinath Ibrampur [1966] Director [Indian]; Ashok Kumar Jain [1956] Director [Indian]

Brown and Mason Holdings Limited
Incorporated: 17 January 1984 *Employees:* 425
Net Worth: £11,462,295 *Total Assets:* £68,638,608
Registered Office: Anson House, Schooner Court, Crossways Business Park, Dartford, Kent, DA2 6QQ
Activities: Other business support service activities n.e.c.
Officers: Laura Ann Hadden, Secretary; Nicholas Terry Brown [1974] Director; Terry Alfred Brown [1944] Director/Demolition Contractor

Brown and Mason Limited
Incorporated: 14 March 1961 *Employees:* 425
Net Worth: £10,865,878 *Total Assets:* £66,133,708
Registered Office: Anson House, Schooner Court, Crossways Business Park, Dartford, Kent, DA2 6QQ
Activities: Demolition
Parent: Brown and Mason Holdings Limited
Officers: Laura Ann Hadden, Secretary; Lee Fredrick Alfred Brown [1978] Director; Nicholas Terry Brown [1974] Director; Richard William Brown [1976] Director; Terry Alfred Brown [1944] Director/Demolition Contractor; Charles Ernest Buckingham [1954] Director; Alex Hadden [1967] Safety Director; Laura Ann Hadden [1980] Director; Miles Hamilton Jacob [1961] Director; John Anthony Payton [1954] Director/Contracts Manager

T Brown Group Limited
Incorporated: 1 April 1971 *Employees:* 371
Net Worth: £6,272,307 *Total Assets:* £16,537,778
Registered Office: 24 High Street, Ewell, Surrey, KT17 1SJ
Activities: Plumbing, heat and air-conditioning installation
Parent: TBG Holding C Limited
Officers: Jonathan Daniel Brown, Secretary/Director; Christian Brown [1962] Director; Jonathan Daniel Brown [1967] Director/Heating Engineer; Simon Terence Brown [1960] Director/Heating Engineer; David John Williams [1962] Director

J.Browne Construction Company Limited
Incorporated: 21 January 1971 *Employees:* 176
Net Worth: £10,557,858 *Total Assets:* £18,558,708
Registered Office: Meelin House, Unit 2 Pavilion Business Centre, 6 Kinetic Crescent, Enfield, Middlesex, EN3 7FJ
Activities: Construction of water projects
Parent: J. Browne Group Holdings Limited
Officers: Norah Carmel Browne, Secretary; Jeremy Browne [1971] Director [Irish]; Jonathan Mark Dodd [1973] Director; Paul Denis McMahon [1966] Managing Director

J.Browne Properties (UK) Limited
Incorporated: 6 July 2005 *Employees:* 1
Net Worth: £4,682,571 *Total Assets:* £6,631,355
Registered Office: Kings Parade, Lower Coombe Street, Croydon, Surrey, CR0 1AA
Activities: Other letting and operating of own or leased real estate
Parent: J. Browne Holdings Limited
Officers: Jeremy Browne [1971] Director [Irish]

Brownings Electric Company Limited
Incorporated: 5 August 1940 *Employees:* 5
Net Worth: £1,380,932 *Total Assets:* £6,216,582
Registered Office: 11 Thames Road, Barking, Essex, IG11 0HG
Activities: Repair of electrical equipment
Parent: BEC (London) Limited
Officers: Sudashlal Damney, Secretary; Sudash Lal Damney [1961] Director; Lawrence Toni Galea [1955] Director; Sharon Elizabeth Heaton [1961] Finance Director; Brian Edward Kemp [1958] Director; Jeffrey George Lake [1946] Director

Brownlow Enterprises Limited
Incorporated: 27 November 1996 *Employees:* 129
Net Worth: £14,629,377 *Total Assets:* £19,872,860
Registered Office: Salisbury House, 81 High Street, Potters Bar, Herts, EN6 5AS
Activities: Residential care activities for the elderly and disabled
Shareholders: William Heneghan; Margaret Heneghan
Officers: Damien Heneghan [1975] Director [Irish]; David Heneghan [1979] Director [Irish]; Liam James Heneghan [1975] Director; Margaret Heneghan [1945] Director/Nurse [Irish]; William Heneghan [1945] Director [Irish]

The Broxbourne School
Incorporated: 22 November 2010 *Employees:* 138
Net Worth: £4,315,248 *Total Assets:* £6,089,830
Registered Office: The Broxbourne School, High Road, Broxbourne, Herts, EN10 7DD
Activities: General secondary education
Officers: Christine Beverley Jarman, Secretary; Charles John Bradbrook [1951] Director; Catherine Mary Campany [1965] Director/Banker; Richard William Davies [1971] Director/Chartered Accountant; David William Holliday [1957] Director/Senior Technical Manager; David Horner [1949] Director/Retired Solicitor; Paula Humphreys [1965] Director/Headteacher; Enid June Ingrey [1950] Director/Business Manager; Malcolm James [1955] Director; Jonathan Marcus Lawn [1971] Director/Software Engineer; Angela Martino [1976] Director/Teacher; Debra McNicholas [1960] Director/Retired; Christine Pepper [1952] Director; Allison Jayne Pilbeam [1965] Director/Teacher; Peter Michael Shawyer [1950] Director/Retired; Robert Neil Smith [1972] Director/Chartered Surveyor; Karen Trew [1962] Director/Magistrate; Graeme Simon Troll [1965] Director; Patricia Ann Waddington [1956] Director/Part-Time Nurse

Bryant Park Hospitality UK Limited
Incorporated: 13 November 1985
Net Worth: £17,027,000 *Total Assets:* £105,830,000
Registered Office: Queens Court, 9-17 Eastern Road, Romford, Essex, RM1 3NG
Activities: Hotels and similar accommodation
Parent: BPH Finance Number 1 Limited
Officers: Jonathan Patrick Braidley [1965] Director/Investment Professional; Christopher Andre Kula [1983] Director/Chartered Accountant [German/Canadian]

Bryen & Langley (Holdings) Ltd
Incorporated: 6 July 2017 *Employees:* 116
Net Worth: £2,840,308 *Total Assets:* £9,314,836
Registered Office: 6 Lagoon Road, Orpington, Kent, BR5 3QX
Activities: Activities of construction holding companies
Shareholders: Alan Escudier; Paul McMahon; David George Wrighton
Officers: Alan Escudier [1954] Director/Manager; Paul McMahon [1964] Director/Surveyor; David George Wrighton [1955] Director/Surveyor

Bryen & Langley Limited
Incorporated: 13 March 1998 *Employees:* 116
Net Worth: £2,844,543 *Total Assets:* £9,314,236
Registered Office: 6 Lagoon Road, Orpington, Kent, BR5 3QX
Activities: Other building completion and finishing
Shareholders: Alan Escudier; Paul McMahon; David George Wrighton
Officers: David Chalk, Secretary; Alan Escudier [1954] Director/Manager; Paul McMahon [1964] Director/Surveyor; David George Wrighton [1955] Director/Surveyor

Brymec Ltd
Incorporated: 20 December 2013 *Employees:* 78
Net Worth: £2,633,861 *Total Assets:* £9,526,939
Registered Office: Unit C, Redlands, Coulsdon, Surrey, CR5 2HT
Activities: Wholesale of other machinery and equipment
Officers: Glen Reiner [1979] Director/Business Manager; Graham Reiner [1956] Director; Luke Reiner [1987] Director

Brymore Estates Limited
Incorporated: 30 January 2002 *Employees:* 13
Net Worth: £17,676,952 *Total Assets:* £20,468,156
Registered Office: 8 Tavistock Court, Tavistock Road, Croydon, Surrey, CR9 2ED
Activities: Renting and operating of Housing Association real estate
Parent: Brymore Investments Limited
Officers: Lucinda Jane Lewis, Secretary; Leonard Sidney Lewis [1956] Director; Miles Jason Webber [1969] Director

Brymore Holdings Limited
Incorporated: 24 September 2009
Net Worth: £23,788,044 *Total Assets:* £32,207,900
Registered Office: 8 Tavistock Court, Tavistock Road, Croydon, Surrey, CR9 2ED
Activities: Activities of head offices
Parent: Brymore Organisation Ltd
Officers: Lucinda Jane Lewis, Secretary; Leonard Sidney Lewis [1956] Director; Miles Jason Webber [1969] Director

Brymore Investments Limited
Incorporated: 28 February 1973
Net Worth: £28,959,942 *Total Assets:* £35,100,756
Registered Office: 8 Tavistock Court, Tavistock Road, Croydon, Surrey, CR9 2ED
Activities: Renting and operating of Housing Association real estate
Parent: Brymore Holdings Limited
Officers: Lucinda Jane Lewis, Secretary; Leonard Sidney Lewis [1956] Director; Miles Jason Webber [1969] Non-Executive Director

BSW Heating Ltd
Incorporated: 28 March 1972 *Employees:* 322
Net Worth: £7,032,516 *Total Assets:* £13,716,516
Registered Office: 3 Old Barn Lane, Kenley, Surrey, CR8 5AT
Activities: Plumbing, heat and air-conditioning installation
Officers: Michael Paul Belliere, Secretary/Managing Director; Robert Serioj Bazil [1960] Director; Guy James Belliere [1973] Managing Director; Matthew Charles Belliere [1975] Operations Director; Michael Paul Belliere [1943] Director/Executive Chairman; Leslie Joseph Finucane [1952] Business Development Director

BTC Pipeline Holding Company Limited
Incorporated: 3 November 2003
Net Worth: £304,127,968 *Total Assets:* £304,127,968
Registered Office: Chertsey Road, Sunbury on Thames, Middlesex, TW16 7BP
Activities: Activities of head offices
Parent: BP Global Investments Limited
Officers: Jaqui Freeman [1968] Director/Oil Company Executive; Robert Gary Jones [1960] Director/Oil Company Executive; Katherine Anne Thomson [1968] Director/Oil Company Executive

Roberto Bucci (U.K.) Limited
Incorporated: 22 March 1982 *Employees:* 13
Net Worth: £9,721,387 *Total Assets:* £12,934,021
Registered Office: 1 Town Quay Wharf, Abbey Road, Barking, Essex, IG11 7BZ
Activities: Other transportation support activities
Officers: Gebhard Boito [1944] Director [Italian]; Roberto Bucci [1936] Director [Italian]; Davide Gnerre [1994] Director [Italian]

Bucci Freight Services Limited
Incorporated: 27 November 1995 *Employees:* 10
Net Worth: £8,069,141 *Total Assets:* £10,526,289
Registered Office: 1 Town Quay Wharf, Abbey Road, Barking, Essex, IG11 7BZ
Activities: Other service activities incidental to land transportation, n.e.c.
Officers: Gebhard Boito [1944] Director [Italian]; Roberto Bucci [1936] Director [Italian]; Davide Gnerre [1994] Director [Italian]

Buckinghamshire Golf Company Limited
Incorporated: 15 June 1989 *Employees:* 71
Net Worth: £9,568,286 *Total Assets:* £11,223,264
Registered Office: World Business Centre, 3 Newall Road, London Heathrow Airport, Hounslow, Middlesex, TW6 2TA
Activities: Operation of sports facilities
Parent: Buckinghamshire Park Resort (Holdings) Ltd
Officers: Athos George Yiannis, Secretary; Sanjay Arora [1989] Director; Athos George Yiannis [1963] Director/Chartered Accountant

Buckinghamshire Park Resort (Holdings) Limited
Incorporated: 27 October 2016 *Employees:* 71
Net Worth Deficit: £441,076 *Total Assets:* £11,744,633
Registered Office: World Business Centre, 3 Newall Road, London Heathrow Airport, Hounslow, Middlesex, TW6 2TA
Activities: Hotels and similar accommodation
Parent: Arora Hotels Limited
Officers: Athos George Yiannis, Secretary; Sanjay Arora [1989] Director

Buckmead Limited
Incorporated: 19 September 1996
Net Worth: £3,301,258 *Total Assets:* £5,767,531
Registered Office: Alton House, 66-68 High Street, Northwood, Middlesex, HA6 1BL
Activities: Development of building projects
Major Shareholder: Barry Attarzadeh
Officers: Peter William Johnson, Secretary; Barry Attarzadeh [1956] Director [Canadian]

Bugler Developments Limited
Incorporated: 30 July 1981 *Employees:* 66
Net Worth: £10,335,437 *Total Assets:* £30,251,396
Registered Office: Bugler House, 25 High Street, Rickmansworth, Herts, WD3 1ET
Activities: Development of building projects
Parent: Bugler Group Limited
Officers: Andrew Philip Hawkins, Secretary; Andrew Thomas Bugler [1968] Director/Solicitor; Denis Patrick Bugler [1961] Director/Builder; Kieran Thomas Bugler [1963] Director; Jeremy Graham [1969] Construction Director; Steven James Tough [1973] Surveying Director

Bugler Group Limited
Incorporated: 22 March 2001 *Employees:* 66
Previous: Bugler Holdings Limited
Net Worth: £11,384,305 *Total Assets:* £31,377,884
Registered Office: Bugler House, 25 High Street, Rickmansworth, Herts, WD3 1ET
Activities: Development of building projects
Shareholders: Andrew Thomas Bugler; Denis Patrick Bugler; Kieran Thomas Bugler
Officers: Andrew Philip Hawkins, Secretary; Andrew Thomas Bugler [1968] Director/Solicitor; Denis Patrick Bugler [1961] Director/Builder; Kieran Thomas Bugler [1963] Director/Builder; Steven James Tough [1973] Commercial Director

Building Research Establishment Limited
Incorporated: 17 February 1997 *Employees:* 339
Net Worth Deficit: £29,692,000 *Total Assets:* £35,017,000
Registered Office: Bucknalls Lane, Garston, Watford, Herts, WD25 9XX
Activities: Other research and experimental development on natural sciences and engineering
Parent: BRE Group Ltd
Officers: Anthony Richard Tanner, Secretary; Nicholas Brian Farrimond [1965] Director/Chief Finance Officer; Niall Gerard Trafford [1962] Director/Chief Operating Officer

Buildvantage Limited
Incorporated: 1 May 2012
Net Worth: £1,103,756 *Total Assets:* £10,928,216
Registered Office: Orion House, 104-106 Cranbrook Road, Ilford, Essex, IG1 4LZ
Activities: Development of building projects
Officers: Ravi Kumar [1966] Director

Bulk Powder Terminals Limited
Incorporated: 14 April 2015 *Employees:* 4
Net Worth Deficit: £683,149 *Total Assets:* £6,617,656
Registered Office: Spencer House, 23 Sheen Road, Richmond upon Thames, Surrey, TW9 1BN
Activities: Operation of warehousing and storage facilities for water transport activities
Parent: Newport Group (Holdings) Limited
Officers: Rajesh Kumar Patel [1970] Managing Director

Bullers Wood Multi Academy Trust
Incorporated: 1 April 2011
Previous: Bullers Wood School
Net Worth: £18,206,000 *Total Assets:* £20,273,000
Registered Office: Bullers Wood School, St Nicholas Lane, Logs Hill, Chislehurst, Kent, BR7 5LJ
Activities: General secondary education
Officers: Isobel Sophia Cattermole [1949] Director/Consultant Education and Social Care; Ben Greene [1970] Director/Headteacher; Katharine Howell [1988] Director/Special Adviser (Currently on Maternity Leave); Susan Simons [1952] Director; Jeffrey Simon Ward [1960] Director/Chartered Accountant; Leonard John Webb [1953] Director/Retired (Part-Time Consultant)

Bulphan Developments LLP
Incorporated: 13 August 2015
Net Worth: £2,189,517 *Total Assets:* £12,809,233
Registered Office: No 1 Railshead Road, St Margarets, Old Isleworth, Middlesex, TW7 7EP
Officers: Michael John Norcross [1963] Member

Martin Bunzl International Limited
Incorporated: 16 February 1965 *Employees:* 177
Net Worth: £13,059,005 *Total Assets:* £18,445,278
Registered Office: St George's House, 2 Bromley Road, Beckenham, Kent, BR3 5JE
Activities: Activities of head offices
Shareholder: Ward Nominees (Abingdon) Limited
Officers: Vanita Jayne Buxton, Secretary; John Martin Bunzl [1957] Director/Marketing Office Consumables; Vanita Jayne Buxton [1963] Director/Secretary; Michael Peter Simms [1969] Director/Executive

A.Martin Bunzl Limited
Incorporated: 1 April 1970 *Employees:* 11
Net Worth: £9,842,807 *Total Assets:* £12,480,718
Registered Office: St George's House, 2 Bromley Road, Beckenham, Kent, BR3 5JE
Activities: Non-specialised wholesale trade
Parent: Martin Bunzl International Limited
Officers: Vanita Jayne Buxton, Secretary; John Martin Bunzl [1957] Director/Marketing Office Consumables; Vanita Jayne Buxton [1963] Director/Secretary; Kam Cheong Fok [1982] Director/Trader; Michael Peter Simms [1969] Director

Burgess Furniture Ltd
Incorporated: 16 February 1988 *Employees:* 124
Net Worth: £5,769,853 *Total Assets:* £8,146,756
Registered Office: Hanworth Trading Estate, Feltham, Middlesex, TW13 6EH
Activities: Manufacture of other furniture
Major Shareholder: Jeremy Nutland Burgess
Officers: Ashley Paul Taylor, Secretary; Jeremy Nutland Burgess [1955] Managing Director; Craig Andrew Kent [1976] Director/Engineer; Ashley Paul Taylor [1983] Finance Director

Burhill Estates Company Limited
Incorporated: 15 December 1926 *Employees:* 2
Net Worth: £9,180,975 *Total Assets:* £9,985,919
Registered Office: Burhill, Walton on Thames, Surrey, KT12 4BX
Activities: Buying and selling of own real estate
Parent: Burhill Group Limited
Officers: James Conlan, Secretary/Chartered Accountant/Director; James Conlan [1956] Chartered Accountant & Director; Colin Michael Mayes [1955] Director/Chief Executive

Burhill Golf and Leisure Limited
Incorporated: 19 May 1980 *Employees:* 530
Net Worth: £24,871,794 *Total Assets:* £40,325,740
Registered Office: Burhill, Walton on Thames, Surrey, KT12 4BX
Activities: Operation of sports facilities
Parent: Burhill Group Limited
Officers: James Conlan, Secretary/Chartered Accountant/Director; James Conlan [1956] Chartered Accountant & Director; Colin Michael Mayes [1955] Director/Chief Executive

Burhill Group Limited
Incorporated: 22 November 2010 *Employees:* 679
Net Worth: £38,474,208 *Total Assets:* £52,311,364
Registered Office: Burhill, Burwood Road, Walton on Thames, Surrey, KT12 4BX
Activities: Activities of head offices
Officers: James Conlan, Secretary; Edward George Clive [1968] Director; James Conlan [1956] Chartered Accountant & Director; Georgia Honor Fanshawe [1966] Director; Arthur Edward Rory Guinness [1969] Director [Irish]; Robin Ivan Howard [1955] Director; Colin Michael Mayes [1955] Director/Chief Executive; Lady Honor Victoria Montagu [1979] Director; Simon O'Donnell [1952] Director

Burlodge Group Limited
Incorporated: 15 November 2000
Net Worth: £5,525,060 *Total Assets:* £5,525,063
Registered Office: 60 Barwell Business Park, Leatherhead Road, Chessington, Surrey, KT9 2NY
Activities: Activities of head offices
Parent: ALI UK Limited
Officers: Angelo Speranza, Secretary; Maurizio Anastasia [1970] Director [Italian]; Michael Hans May [1951] Director; Angelo Speranza [1962] Director

Burney Realty Limited
Incorporated: 12 May 1997 *Employees:* 4
Net Worth: £7,305,370 *Total Assets:* £15,034,011
Registered Office: 249 Cranbrook Road, Ilford, Essex, IG1 4TG
Activities: Other business support service activities n.e.c.
Shareholders: Daren Mark Burney; Paula Tracey Burney
Officers: Paula Tracey Burney, Secretary; Daren Mark Burney [1964] Director; Paula Tracey Burney [1963] Director/Company Secretary; Sarah Mellissa Burney [1993] Director/Business Executive

Burnfield Limited
Incorporated: 16 October 1980
Net Worth: £145,872,000 *Total Assets:* £146,500,000
Registered Office: Heritage House, Church Road, Egham, Surrey, TW20 9QD
Activities: Other business support service activities n.e.c.
Parent: Spectris US Holdings Limited
Officers: Rebecca Louise Dunn, Secretary; Anthony William Dumpleton [1969] Director/Accountant; Clive Graeme Watson [1958] Director

Burnt Ash Primary School
Incorporated: 1 December 2015 *Employees:* 66
Net Worth: £5,241,620 *Total Assets:* £6,081,409
Registered Office: Burnt Ash Primary School, Rangefield Road, Bromley, Kent, BR1 4QX
Activities: Primary education
Officers: Leah Zoe Crawley [1962] Director/Headteacher; Byron Danahay [1966] Director/Sales Manager; Dinesh Gnanapragasam [1973] Sales Director; Christine Ann Hollis [1948] Director/Headteacher (Retired); Andrew Junaid [1967] Director/Minister of Religion; Richard Ian Lockyer [1967] Director; Susan Mary Matthews [1960] Director/Retired

Burnt Common Nurseries Limited
Incorporated: 25 March 1966 *Employees:* 4
Net Worth: £5,068,000 *Total Assets:* £6,646,000
Registered Office: Fernside Place, 179 Queens Road, Weybridge, Surrey, KT13 0AH
Activities: Buying and selling of own real estate
Parent: Newship Products Limited
Officers: Andrew St Clair Harrison, Secretary/Accountant; Jeremy David Clarkson [1961] Director; John Watson Newman [1945] Director/Accountant; Richard John Newman [1979] Director; David Anthony Thornton [1971] Finance Director

Burnt Tree Group Limited
Incorporated: 15 May 1989
Net Worth: £37,238,000 *Total Assets:* £345,360,000
Registered Office: Enterprise House, Vicarage Road, Egham, Surrey, TW20 9FB
Activities: Renting and leasing of cars and light motor vehicles
Parent: Enterprise Rent-a-Car UK Limited
Officers: Teresa Anne Holderer, Secretary; Ricky Allan Short [1958] Director [American]

Burroughs Wellcome International Limited
Incorporated: 26 January 1955
Net Worth: £161,970,000 *Total Assets:* £162,024,000
Registered Office: 980 Great West Road, Brentford, Middlesex, TW8 9GS
Activities: Activities of head offices
Parent: Wellcome Consumer Healthcare Limited
Officers: James Borger [1963] Director/VP, Group Financial Planning and Analysis [American]; Alan George Burns [1975] Director

Burton Wold Wind Farm (Trading) Limited
Incorporated: 16 March 2005 *Employees:* 5
Net Worth: £6,713,487 *Total Assets:* £7,434,648
Registered Office: Munro House, Portsmouth Road, Cobham, Surrey, KT11 1PP
Activities: Production of electricity
Parent: Burton Wold Wind Farm Limited
Officers: Stephen Campbell Joseph Ellis [1959] Director; Rollo Andrew Johnstone Wright [1976] Director; Philip William Kent [1984] Director; Ronan Niall Kierans [1978] Director [Irish]; Nicholas Simon Parker [1969] Director

Burwater Holdings Limited
Incorporated: 8 May 1980 *Employees:* 50
Net Worth: £3,657,528 *Total Assets:* £16,977,468
Registered Office: Bridge Motor Works, New Zealand Avenue, Walton on Thames, Surrey, KT12 1AT
Activities: Sale of new cars and light motor vehicles
Major Shareholder: Michael Peter Harting
Officers: Neil Andrew Harting, Secretary; Michael Peter Harting [1930] Director/Garage Proprietor; Neil Andrew Harting [1961] Director

Bushey Developments Ltd
Incorporated: 1 April 2016
Net Worth Deficit: £2,960 *Total Assets:* £14,161,799
Registered Office: Montreaux House, The Hythe, Staines upon Thames, Middlesex, TW18 3JQ
Activities: Buying and selling of own real estate
Major Shareholder: David Burke
Officers: David Burke [1965] Director

Bushey St James Trust
Incorporated: 3 January 2012 *Employees:* 227
Net Worth: £21,397,720 *Total Assets:* £24,446,866
Registered Office: c/o Bushey Meads School, Coldharbour Lane, Bushey, Herts, WD23 4PA
Activities: Primary education
Officers: Imelda Dempsey, Secretary; Richard Daryl Abrahams [1965] Director/Regional Manager; Dinah Foster Hoeksma [1945] Director; Janet Elspeth Buchanan McNulty [1948] Director/Retired; Samuel Charles Russell [1984] Director; Nicholas Adam Smith [1978] Director/Chief Financial Officer; Sir Alan William Steer [1948] Director/Education; Jeremy William Turner [1965] Director/Executive Principal

Business Systems (U.K.) Limited
Incorporated: 27 November 1987 *Employees:* 81
Net Worth: £3,193,924 *Total Assets:* £8,751,127
Registered Office: 462 London Road, Isleworth, Middlesex, TW7 4ED
Activities: Repair of other equipment
Officers: Stephen Thurston, Secretary; Richard Peter Mill [1951] Director; Stephen Thurston [1954] Director

Butchoff Antiques Limited
Incorporated: 10 September 1998 *Employees:* 3
Net Worth: £4,767,782 *Total Assets:* £5,903,374
Registered Office: Lynwood House, 373-375 Station Road, Harrow, Middlesex, HA1 2AW
Activities: Retail sale of antiques including antique books in stores
Shareholders: Ian Michael Butchoff; Adam Philip Kaye
Officers: James Kaye, Secretary; Ian Michael Butchoff [1952] Director/Antique Dealer; Adam Philip Kaye [1975] Director/Antique Dealer; James Kaye [1979] Director

Bute Capital Limited
Incorporated: 28 January 2009 *Employees:* 5
Net Worth: £930,330 *Total Assets:* £6,936,925
Registered Office: P O Box 687, Weybridge, Surrey, KT13 3GG
Activities: Other business support service activities n.e.c.
Officers: Julian Anthony Harrison [1970] Director/Financier

Butler & Young Approved Inspectors Limited
Incorporated: 4 April 1996 *Employees:* 85
Previous: Butler & Young Limited
Net Worth: £2,997,650 *Total Assets:* £5,441,700
Registered Office: Airport House, Unit 10 Purley Way, Croydon, Surrey, CR0 0XZ
Activities: Other engineering activities
Parent: Butler & Young Group Ltd
Officers: Dilshard Mansoor, Secretary; Charles Craven [1972] Director/Chartered Surveyor; Owen Edwards [1964] Technical and Training Director; Geoffrey Elliman [1960] Regional Director

Butlers Walsall Ltd
Incorporated: 19 May 2008
Net Worth: £734,722 *Total Assets:* £5,846,833
Registered Office: 204 Field End Road, Pinner, Middlesex, HA5 1RD
Activities: Buying and selling of own real estate
Shareholder: Amar Singh Mehli
Officers: Amarveer Singh Dhatt [1982] Director; Amar Singh Mehli [1959] Director

Butterworth Laboratories Limited
Incorporated: 25 September 1974 *Employees:* 68
Net Worth: £5,494,545 *Total Assets:* £6,725,596
Registered Office: 54-56 Waldegrave Road, Teddington, Middlesex, TW11 8NY
Activities: Other professional, scientific and technical activities n.e.c.
Major Shareholder: Doris Emily Butterworth
Officers: John Marchant Gearey, Secretary; Doris Emily Butterworth [1924] Director/Micro Analyst; John Marchant Gearey [1938] Director/Chartered Accountant; David John Hawkins [1967] Managing Director; David Andrew Riches [1963] Technical Director; Patrick David Stewart [1958] Director/Solicitor

Buxton Building Contractors Limited
Incorporated: 23 May 1988 *Employees:* 109
Net Worth: £5,745,826 *Total Assets:* £24,079,828
Registered Office: Cedar House, 91 High Street, Caterham, Surrey, CR3 5UH
Activities: Development of building projects
Shareholders: Marie Therese Pagan; Keith Malcolm Pagan
Officers: Mark Alan Freeland, Secretary; Mark Alan Freeland [1978] Director; Stephen Michael Holland [1959] Director; Gregory William Lynn [1964] Director; David John Norman [1967] Director; Keith Malcolm Pagan [1958] Director; Bhadresh Kumar Shukla [1962] Director; Pauline Warnes [1958] Director

Buxton Crescent Hotel and Thermal Spa Company Limited
Incorporated: 18 June 2004 *Employees:* 6
Net Worth Deficit: £5,314,201 *Total Assets:* £7,500,021
Registered Office: CP House, Otterspool Way, Watford, Herts, WD25 8JJ
Activities: Hotels and similar accommodation
Shareholders: CP Holdings Limited; Osborne (Buxton) Limited
Officers: Eric Lewis, Secretary/Solicitor; Paul Andrew Filer [1957] Director/Chartered Accountant; Philip Hoffbrand [1967] Director; Trevor Osborne [1943] Director/Surveyor; Andrew James Gerard Ryan [1965] Director

Buy 2 Let Cars Ltd
Incorporated: 12 May 2011
Net Worth: £1,607,406 *Total Assets:* £25,240,802
Registered Office: 1 Bell Parade, Glebe Way, West Wickham, Kent, BR4 0RH
Activities: Renting and leasing of cars and light motor vehicles
Parent: Raedex Consortium Limited
Officers: Reginald Larry-Cole [1970] Director/Car Salesman; Scott Andrew Martin [1978] Director/Car Salesman

Buyagift PLC
Incorporated: 25 November 1999 *Employees:* 125
Net Worth: £7,119,070 *Total Assets:* £53,391,976
Registered Office: 4 Imperial Place, Maxwell Road, Borehamwood, Herts, WD6 1JN
Activities: Retail sale via mail order houses or via Internet
Major Shareholder: Pierre-Edouard Robert Raymond Marie-Joseph Sterin
Officers: Daniel Jeremy Mountain, Secretary; Syed Kashif Abbas [1979] Director [Pakistani]; Pierre Charles Boccon-Liaudet [1969] Director [French]; Daniel Jeremy Mountain [1974] Managing Director; John Richard Perkins [1964] Director

BW Foundation
Incorporated: 25 July 2007
Net Worth: £8,897,445 *Total Assets:* £10,148,786
Registered Office: 336 Pinner Road, Harrow, Middlesex, HA1 4LB
Activities: Activities of religious organisations
Officers: Mohamed Iqbal Asaria [1950] Director/Economist; Riazali Esmail [1957] Director/Pharmacist; Sabira Mohamed Kanji [1957] Director/Accountant; Mukhtar Manji [1965] Director/Pharmacist; Murtaza Versi [1952] Director/Engineer

By Chelmer (Holdings) Limited
Incorporated: 29 June 2005
Net Worth Deficit: £14,769,000 *Total Assets:* £171,388,992
Registered Office: 8 White Oak Square, London Road, Swanley, Kent, BR8 7AG
Activities: Activities of head offices
Parent: Infrared Infrastructure Yield Holdings Limited
Officers: James Christopher Heath [1975] Director; Mark Geoffrey David Holden [1957] Director; Mark Christopher Wayment [1958] Director; Elena Giorgiana Wegener [1975] Director/Investment Executive

By Chelmer PLC
Incorporated: 21 July 2005
Net Worth Deficit: £14,769,000 *Total Assets:* £171,388,992
Registered Office: 8 White Oak Square, London Road, Swanley, Kent, BR8 7AG
Activities: Non-trading company
Parent: By Chelmer (Holdings) Limited
Officers: Anthony Robert Faulkner [1973] Director/Chartered Accountant; James Christopher Heath [1975] Director; Mark Geoffrey David Holden [1957] Director; Mark Christopher Wayment [1958] Director; Elena Giorgiana Wegener [1975] Director/Investment Executive

By Malene Birger UK Ltd.
Incorporated: 4 October 1978 *Employees:* 12
Previous: ICGroup UK Ltd
Net Worth: £4,440,000 *Total Assets:* £5,253,000
Registered Office: c/o Godley & Co, 5th Floor, Congress House, 14 Lyon Road, Harrow, Middlesex, HA1 2EN
Activities: Wholesale of clothing and footwear
Parent: IC Group A/S
Officers: Anders Boelskift [1972] Director [Danish]; Martin Sahner Gundestrup Christiansen [1974] Director [Danish]; Morten Linnet [1970] Director [Danish]; Alexander Martensen-Larsen [1975] Director/Senior Vice President [Danish]

Bycentral Holdings Limited
Incorporated: 10 March 2003
Net Worth Deficit: £43,957,000 *Total Assets:* £86,624,000
Registered Office: 8 White Oak Square, London Road, Swanley, Kent, BR8 7AG
Activities: Activities of head offices
Parent: Infrastructure Investments Holdings Limited
Officers: David John Carr [1969] Finance Director; Sarah Louise Gledhill [1975] Director; Mark Geoffrey David Holden [1957] Director; Stephen Howard McDonald [1968] Director

Bycentral Limited
Incorporated: 10 March 2003
Net Worth Deficit: £43,957,000 *Total Assets:* £86,624,000
Registered Office: 8 White Oak Square, London Road, Swanley, Kent, BR8 7AG
Activities: Other service activities n.e.c.
Parent: Bycentral Holdings Limited
Officers: David John Carr [1969] Finance Director; Sarah Louise Gledhill [1975] Director; Mark Geoffrey David Holden [1957] Director; Stephen Howard McDonald [1968] Director

Bynorth (Holdings) Limited
Incorporated: 3 May 2007
Net Worth Deficit: £65,396,000 *Total Assets:* £130,389,000
Registered Office: 8 White Oak Square, London Road, Swanley, Kent, BR8 7AG
Activities: Activities of head offices
Parent: Infrared Infrastructure Yield Holdings Limited
Officers: Anthony Robert Faulkner [1973] Director; Mark Christopher Wayment [1958] Director; Elena Giorgiana Wegener [1975] Director/Investment Executive

Bynorth Limited
Incorporated: 3 May 2007
Net Worth Deficit: £65,396,000 *Total Assets:* £130,389,000
Registered Office: 8 White Oak Square, London Road, Swanley, Kent, BR8 7AG
Activities: Construction of commercial buildings
Parent: Bynorth (Holdings) Limited
Officers: Anthony Robert Faulkner [1973] Director; Mark Christopher Wayment [1958] Director; Elena Giorgiana Wegener [1975] Director/Investment Executive

Bytes Security Partnerships Limited
Incorporated: 14 August 2001 *Employees:* 47
Net Worth: £3,400,750 *Total Assets:* £8,866,845
Registered Office: Bytes House, Randalls Way, Leatherhead, Surrey, KT22 7TW
Activities: Information technology consultancy activities
Officers: Tina Elizabeth Sexton, Secretary; John Gilbertson [1975] Sales Director; Neil Robert Murphy [1964] Managing Director; David Rawle [1976] Technical Director; Keith Alan Richardson [1959] Director; Robert Eben Venter [1960] Director [South African]

Bytes Software Services Limited
Incorporated: 25 February 1982 *Employees:* 266
Net Worth: £17,470,788 *Total Assets:* £72,827,568
Registered Office: Bytes House, Randalls Way, Leatherhead, Surrey, KT22 7TW
Activities: Other information technology service activities
Officers: Tina Elizabeth Sexton, Secretary; Neil Robert Murphy [1964] Sales Director; Amanda Jane Nicholson [1967] Director; Keith Alan Richardson [1959] Finance Director; Robert Eben Venter [1960] Director [South African]

Bytes Technology Group Limited
Incorporated: 28 September 1998 *Employees:* 6
Net Worth: £14,625,000 *Total Assets:* £53,560,000
Registered Office: Bytes House, Randalls Way, Leatherhead, Surrey, KT22 7TW
Activities: Information technology consultancy activities
Officers: Tina Elizabeth Sexton, Secretary; Andrew Holden [1967] Director [South African]; David Nicholas Maw [1950] Director/Accountant; Neil Robert Murphy [1964] Managing Director; Mteto Nyati [1964] Director [South African]; Keith Alan Richardson [1959] Director; Robert Eben Venter [1960] Director/Chief Executive [South African]

Bywest (Holdings) Limited
Incorporated: 22 September 2000
Net Worth Deficit: £9,712,000 *Total Assets:* £56,724,000
Registered Office: 8 White Oak Square, London Road, Swanley, Kent, BR8 7AG
Activities: Activities of head offices
Parent: Infrastructure Investments Holdings Limited
Officers: Sarah Louise Gledhill [1975] Director; Mark John Griffiths [1967] Operations Director; Mark Geoffrey David Holden [1957] Director; Glynn Newby [1966] Director; Rachel Louise Turnbull [1978] Director

Bywest Limited
Incorporated: 25 September 2000
Net Worth Deficit: £7,083,000 *Total Assets:* £56,723,000
Registered Office: 8 White Oak Square, London Road, Swanley, Kent, BR8 7AG
Activities: Other service activities n.e.c.
Parent: Bywest (Holdings) Limited
Officers: Sarah Louise Gledhill [1975] Director; Mark John Griffiths [1967] Operations Director; Mark Geoffrey David Holden [1957] Director; Glynn Newby [1966] Director; Rachel Louise Turnbull [1978] Director

C.C. (Engineering) Limited
Incorporated: 28 March 1985 *Employees:* 158
Net Worth: £2,517,156 *Total Assets:* £10,604,654
Registered Office: Technology House, 215 High Street, Yiewsley, West Drayton, Middlesex, UB7 7QP
Activities: Repair of computers and peripheral equipment
Major Shareholder: Giles Damian Thorpe
Officers: Andrew John Grosse, Secretary; Peter Fincham [1967] Sales Director; Andrew John Grosse [1968] Finance Director; Giles Damian Thorpe [1967] Managing Director; Roger Henry Thorpe [1938] Director/Chairman

C.L.T. Timber and Transport Limited
Incorporated: 26 November 1980 *Employees:* 71
Net Worth: £5,181,886 *Total Assets:* £7,180,056
Registered Office: 4 Olds Approach, Tolpits Lane, Watford, Herts, WD18 9RE
Activities: Other letting and operating of own or leased real estate
Major Shareholder: Richard Neil Thomas Coles
Officers: Richard Neil Thomas Coles, Secretary; Richard Neil Thomas Coles [1948] Director; Montague John Meyer [1944] Director

C.V.J. Properties Ltd
Incorporated: 22 March 2010
Net Worth: £5,052,150 *Total Assets:* £5,052,150
Registered Office: Suite 2, Fountain House, 1a Elm Park, Stanmore, Middlesex, HA7 4AU
Activities: Activities of other holding companies n.e.c.
Officers: Jane Elizabeth Putt [1953] Director; Charles William Vaughan-Jones [1953] Director

Cablesheer Group Limited
Incorporated: 3 August 2012 *Employees:* 113
Net Worth: £4,016,032 *Total Assets:* £8,374,506
Registered Office: Cablesheer House, Murray Road, Orpington, Kent, BR5 3QY
Activities: Dormant company
Major Shareholder: Donald Robert Brown
Officers: Donald Robert Brown [1953] Director

Cadbury Eight LLP
Incorporated: 18 August 2011
Net Worth: £2,478,514,176 *Total Assets:* £2,478,514,176
Registered Office: Cadbury House, Sanderson Road, Uxbridge, Middlesex, UB8 1DH

Cadbury Four LLP
Incorporated: 5 November 2010
Net Worth: £1,124,563,968 *Total Assets:* £1,124,563,968
Registered Office: Cadbury House, Sanderson Road, Uxbridge, Middlesex, UB8 1DH

Cadbury Limited
Incorporated: 7 February 2008
Net Worth: £10,277,645,312 *Total Assets:* £10,277,645,312
Registered Office: Cadbury House, Sanderson Road, Uxbridge, Middlesex, UB8 1DH
Activities: Activities of head offices
Parent: Chromium Acquisitions Limited
Officers: Adrian John Paul Arrighi [1978] Tax Director; Michael Brendan Foye [1965] Treasury Director; John Michael Hladusz [1972] Director/Chartered Accountant; Carole Noelle Keene [1966] Director

Cadbury Nine LLP
Incorporated: 9 August 2011
Net Worth: £1,845,699,968 *Total Assets:* £1,845,740,032
Registered Office: Cadbury House, Sanderson Road, Uxbridge, Middlesex, UB8 1DH

Cadbury Schweppes Finance Limited
Incorporated: 24 February 1949
Net Worth: £83,496,000 *Total Assets:* £101,588,000
Registered Office: Cadbury House, Sanderson Road, Uxbridge, Middlesex, UB8 1DH
Activities: Activities of head offices
Parent: Mondelez UK Holdings & Services Limited
Officers: Adrian John Paul Arrighi [1978] Tax Director; Michael Brendan Foye [1965] Treasury Director; John Michael Hladusz [1972] Director/Chartered Accountant; Carole Noelle Keene [1966] Director

Cadbury Schweppes Overseas Limited
Incorporated: 13 June 1899
Net Worth: £7,902,566,912 *Total Assets:* £7,902,595,072
Registered Office: Cadbury House, Sanderson Road, Uxbridge, Middlesex, UB8 1DH
Activities: Activities of head offices
Parent: Chromium Assets Limited
Officers: Adrian John Paul Arrighi [1978] Tax Director; Michael Brendan Foye [1965] Treasury Director; John Michael Hladusz [1972] Director/Chartered Accountant; Carole Noelle Keene [1966] Director

Cadbury Seven LLP
Incorporated: 19 December 2011
Net Worth: £13,519,614,976 *Total Assets:* £13,519,614,976
Registered Office: Cadbury House, Sanderson Road, Uxbridge, Middlesex, UB8 1DH

Cadbury Six LLP
Incorporated: 5 December 2011
Net Worth: £15,420,000 *Total Assets:* £15,519,000
Registered Office: Cadbury House, Sanderson Road, Uxbridge, Middlesex, UB8 1DH

Cadbury South Africa (Holdings)
Incorporated: 16 December 2009
Net Worth: £91,929,080 *Total Assets:* £91,930,488
Registered Office: Cadbury House, Sanderson Road, Uxbridge, Middlesex, UB8 1DH
Activities: Activities of head offices
Parent: Cadbury Schweppes Overseas Limited
Officers: David John Groves [1963] Director/Finance Controller [South African]; Karol Leszek Jozwicki [1980] Director/Financial Controller [Polish]

Cadbury Ten LLP
Incorporated: 19 December 2011
Net Worth: £36,659,304 *Total Assets:* £37,031,568
Registered Office: Cadbury House, Sanderson Road, Uxbridge, Middlesex, UB8 1DH

Cadline Limited
Incorporated: 29 March 1990 *Employees:* 88
Net Worth: £3,893,743 *Total Assets:* £10,645,615
Registered Office: Cadline House, Drake Avenue, Staines upon Thames, Middlesex, TW18 2AP
Activities: Business and domestic software development
Major Shareholder: Deborah Peppin
Officers: Deborah Peppin, Secretary; Nicholas Harris [1974] Director; Nick Harris [1974] Director; Barry Colin Lewis [1959] Managing Director; Deborah Peppin [1962] Director; Claire Robertson [1974] Director; Richard John Robertson [1972] Director; Scott Woolven [1972] Commercial Director

CAE Technology Holdings Limited
Incorporated: 18 May 2010 *Employees:* 242
Net Worth: £4,650,611 *Total Assets:* £34,676,052
Registered Office: CAE House, Colonial Way, Watford, Herts, WD24 4PT
Activities: Activities of other holding companies n.e.c.
Parent: Caerus Assets Limited
Officers: Richard Behan [1978] Director; Justin Matthew Harling [1973] Director

CAE Technology Services Limited
Incorporated: 7 February 1992 *Employees:* 242
Net Worth: £9,711,106 *Total Assets:* £39,802,160
Registered Office: CAE House, Colonial Way, Watford, Herts, WD24 4PT
Activities: Other information technology service activities
Parent: Seckloe 194 Limited
Officers: Richard Behan [1978] Director; Umesh Chauhan [1965] Finance Director; Justin Matthew Harling [1973] Managing Director

Caesar Management Limited
Incorporated: 8 April 2004 *Employees:* 44
Net Worth: £2,728,299 *Total Assets:* £5,683,843
Registered Office: c/o Turbervilles, Hill House, 118 High Street, Uxbridge, Middlesex, UB8 1JT
Activities: Hotels and similar accommodation
Shareholders: Jorge Clos Llombart; Montserrat Casellas Castellvi
Officers: Jorge Clos Llombart [1950] Director [Spanish]

CALA 1 Limited
Incorporated: 4 March 2013 *Employees:* 7
Net Worth: £17,284,766 *Total Assets:* £245,650,768
Registered Office: Cala House, 54 The Causeway, Staines upon Thames, Surrey, TW18 3AX
Activities: Construction of domestic buildings
Parent: CALA Group (Holdings) Limited
Officers: Jasan Fitzpatrick, Secretary; Matteo Charles Colombo [1980] Director/Investment Professional; Neil John Stoddart [1969] Finance Director; Geoffrey Julian Timms [1960] Director/Solicitor; Kevin Whitaker [1969] Director

CALA Group (Holdings) Limited
Incorporated: 4 March 2013 *Employees:* 873
Net Worth: £338,294,016 *Total Assets:* £968,812,032
Registered Office: Cala House, 54 The Causeway, Staines upon Thames, Surrey, TW18 3AX
Activities: Construction of domestic buildings
Parent: Haut Investments 2 Limited
Officers: Jasan Fitzpatrick, Secretary; Matteo Charles Colombo [1980] Director/Investment Professional; Emma Hardaker-Jones [1973] Director; Kerrigan William Procter [1969] Director; Neil John Stoddart [1969] Finance Director; Geoffrey Julian Timms [1960] Director/Solicitor; Kevin Whitaker [1969] Director

Calbrook Cars Limited
Incorporated: 1 May 1967 *Employees:* 22
Net Worth: £6,984,834 *Total Assets:* £7,669,213
Registered Office: 42 Lytton Road, Barnet, Herts, EN5 5BY
Activities: Wholesale trade of motor vehicle parts and accessories
Major Shareholder: Dennis John Fernie
Officers: Dennis John Fernie, Secretary; Dennis John Fernie [1943] Director; Judith Mary Fernie [1946] Director

Calda Limited
Incorporated: 31 January 2012
Net Worth Deficit: £2,320,169 *Total Assets:* £7,934,709
Registered Office: Hill House, Lowlands Road, Harrow, Middlesex, HA1 3EQ
Activities: Development of building projects
Major Shareholder: Donovan Gijsbertus Wijsmuller
Officers: Brian Martin Comer [1960] Director [Irish]; Luke Andrew Comer [1957] Director [Irish]

Caligor Opco UK, Ltd
Incorporated: 7 January 2016
Net Worth: £13,782,084 *Total Assets:* £46,252,908
Registered Office: Caligor Opco UK Ltd, Unit 8 Masthead, Capstan Court, Crossways Business Park, Dartford, Kent, DA2 6QG
Activities: Other service activities n.e.c.
Officers: Kevin Daekyung Ma [1985] Director/Investor [American]; Ron Nayot [1978] Director/Finance [Canadian]

Camberley Care Limited
Incorporated: 14 May 2014 *Employees:* 93
Net Worth: £14,661,314 *Total Assets:* £29,549,776
Registered Office: 36 Railway Approach, Harrow, Middlesex, HA3 5AA
Activities: Residential nursing care facilities
Parent: TLC Group Limited
Officers: Gagan Puri, Secretary; William Charles Neal [1986] Director; Paavan Popat [1985] Managing Director; Honourable Shivaan Shillin Popat [1988] Director; Gagan Puri [1978] Finance Director

Camden Development Company Limited
Incorporated: 7 May 1963 *Employees:* 5
Net Worth: £10,419,700 *Total Assets:* £12,590,037
Registered Office: 1 Beauchamp Court, Victors Way, Barnet, Herts, EN5 5TZ
Activities: Development of building projects
Parent: Embleton Trust Corporation Limited
Officers: Olive May Herman, Secretary; Julia Deborah Burton [1962] Director; Rosalind Carol Gelbart [1958] Director; Charles Robert Herman [1956] Director/Investment Manager; Olive May Herman [1931] Director; Paul Philip Herman [1968] Director

Camelot Business Solutions Limited
Incorporated: 7 March 2011 *Employees:* 87
Net Worth: £2,900,000 *Total Assets:* £35,300,000
Registered Office: Magdalen House, Tolpits Lane, Watford, Herts, WD18 9RN
Activities: Gambling and betting activities
Parent: Premier Lotteries UK Limited
Officers: John Edward Michael Dillon, Secretary; John Edward Michael Dillon [1963] Legal Director and Company Secretary; Ilya Kachko [1979] Director/Portfolio Manager [Canadian]; Andrew Jonathan Mark Taylor [1961] Director/Private Equity Investor

Camelot Global Lottery Solutions Limited
Incorporated: 7 March 2011 *Employees:* 209
Previous: Camelot Strategic Solutions Limited
Net Worth Deficit: £11,544,000 *Total Assets:* £60,554,000
Registered Office: Magdalen House, Tolpits Lane, Watford, Herts, WD18 9RN
Activities: Gambling and betting activities
Parent: Premier Lotteries UK Limited
Officers: John Edward Michael Dillon, Secretary; Bogdan Cenanovic [1976] Director/Vice President, Technology, Media & Telecom [Canadian]; Ilya Kachko [1979] Director/Portfolio Manager [Canadian]; Dr David Thomas Kelly [1963] Non-Executive Director; Michael Charles Lightman [1963] Director [American]; John Henderson McNeil [1968] Director [American]; Wayne Lawrence Pickup [1976] Director/Chief Executive [New Zealander]; Jane Sarah Rowe [1959] Director/Senior Vice President [Canadian]; Robert Oscar Rowley [1949] Director

Camelot UK Lotteries Limited
Incorporated: 27 May 1993 *Employees:* 667
Net Worth: £33,600,000 *Total Assets:* £651,699,968
Registered Office: Tolpits Lane, Watford, Herts, WD18 9RN
Activities: Gambling and betting activities
Parent: Premier Lotteries UK Limited
Officers: John Edward Michael Dillon, Secretary; Ilya Kachko [1979] Director/Portfolio Manager [Canadian]; David Thomas Kelly [1963] Non-Executive Director; Nigel Railton [1967] Director/Chief Executive; Sir Hugh Michael Robertson [1962] Director/Chairman; Sarah Jane Rowe [1959] Director/Senior Vice President [Canadian]; Robert Oscar Rowley [1949] Director; Andrew Jonathan Mark Taylor [1961] Regional Managing Director; Jennelle Lisa Tilling [1969] Director [Australian/British]; Robert Malcolm Walker [1945] Director/Deputy Chairman

Camgate Holdings Limited
Incorporated: 21 January 1993 *Employees:* 5
Net Worth: £7,418,538 *Total Assets:* £9,244,177
Registered Office: 2 Raeburn Avenue, Dartford, Kent, DA1 3BG
Activities: Other letting and operating of own or leased real estate
Major Shareholder: Thomas Albert Howse
Officers: Peter Charles Relf, Secretary; Claire Louise Howse [1977] Director; Stephen George Howse [1973] Director; Suzanna Christie Howse [1969] Director; Thomas Albert Howse [1937] Director

Campaign Master (UK) Limited
Incorporated: 5 October 2004 *Employees:* 19
Net Worth: £5,563,839 *Total Assets:* £5,785,096
Registered Office: 4th Floor, Hygeia, 66-68 College Road, Harrow, Middlesex, HA1 1BE
Activities: Business and domestic software development
Shareholders: Gurjeet Dhillon; Hardeep Dhillon
Officers: Hardeep Dhillon, Secretary; Gurjeet Dhillon [1965] Director

The Campion School
Incorporated: 5 July 2011 *Employees:* 167
Net Worth: £4,981,000 *Total Assets:* £7,633,000
Registered Office: Wingletye Lane, Hornchurch, Essex, RM11 3BX
Activities: General secondary education
Officers: Christine Noddings, Secretary; Duncan George Bartlett [1970] Owner/Director, Taylor James Resourcing; Patrick Wolfe Davis [1968] Director/Solicitor; Alexandra Claire Giesen [1975] Director/Teacher; Maureen Margaret Leech [1947] Director/Retired Assistant Bursar; Colin Charles Miles [1954] Director/Chartered Civil Engineer; Robert Lester Pearn [1966] Director/Teacher; Deirdre Elizabeth Pembroke [1966] Director; Reverend Jean-Claude Gaston Selvini [1946] Director/Priest [French]; Niall Tiernan [1969] Director/Solicitor; Robert George Townsend [1950] Retired Bank Area Director; Richard Tucker [1965] Director/Detective Chief Superintendent; Brenda Underwood [1966] Director/Solicitor; Keith Williams [1961] Director/Headteacher; Nicholas Pym Williamson [1951] Director/Retired

Campmoss Property (Tangley Place) Limited
Incorporated: 22 January 2010
Net Worth: £11,723,904 *Total Assets:* £11,726,604
Registered Office: 56 Station Road, Egham, Surrey, TW20 9LF
Activities: Buying and selling of own real estate
Parent: Campmoss Property Company Limited
Officers: Karen Louise Chandler, Secretary; Edward Richard Goodwin [1939] Director; John Richard Wollenberg [1948] Director

Campmoss Property Company Limited
Incorporated: 16 January 1987 *Employees:* 1
Net Worth: £16,956,708 *Total Assets:* £32,951,648
Registered Office: 56 Station Road, Egham, Surrey, TW20 9LF
Activities: Buying and selling of own real estate
Shareholder: Christabel Scott-Balls
Officers: Karen Louise Chandler, Secretary; Edward Richard Goodwin [1939] Director; John Richard Wollenberg [1948] Director

Canada Life (U.K.) Limited
Incorporated: 4 April 1974
Net Worth: £23,515,000 *Total Assets:* £23,519,000
Registered Office: Canada Life Place, Potters Bar, Herts, EN6 5BA
Activities: Activities of head offices
Parent: Canada Life Limited
Officers: Kathryn Louise Bateman [1964] Director/Chief Financial Officer; Douglas Allan Brown [1971] Director; Ashleigh Martin Kewney [1966] Director/Head of Tax

Canada Life Asset Management Limited
Incorporated: 23 September 1999
Net Worth: £12,384,000 *Total Assets:* £15,254,000
Registered Office: Canada Life Place, High Street, Potters Bar, Herts, EN6 5BA
Activities: Security and commodity contracts dealing activities
Parent: The Canada Life Group (U.K.) Limited
Officers: Narmadha Dharshini Riley, Secretary; Douglas Allan Brown [1971] Director/Chief Executive; Alan Henry Clifton [1946] Director; Ian Gilmour [1952] Director; David John Marchant [1964] Director

Canada Life Finance (U.K.) Limited
Incorporated: 24 July 2002
Net Worth: £39,058,000 *Total Assets:* £281,772,992
Registered Office: Canada Life Place, Potters Bar, Herts, EN6 5BA
Activities: Financial intermediation not elsewhere classified
Shareholders: Sophie Desmarais; Paul Desmarais, Jr; Andre Desmarais; Michael Plessis-Belair; Guy Fortin
Officers: Kathryn Louise Bateman [1964] Director; Douglas Allan Brown [1971] Director; Ashleigh Martin Kewney [1966] Director/Head of Taxation

The Canada Life Group (U.K.) Limited
Incorporated: 9 March 1988
Net Worth: £2,751,300,096 *Total Assets:* £3,079,300,096
Registered Office: Canada Life Place, Potters Bar, Herts, EN6 5BA
Activities: Other business support service activities n.e.c.
Shareholders: Sophie Desmarais; Paul Desmarais, Jr; Andre Desmarais; Michel Plessis-Belair; Guy Fortin
Officers: Lisa Annette Rodriguez, Secretary; Marcia Dominic Campbell [1959] Director; Cecil Hayes [1956] Director [Irish]; Arshil Jamal [1967] Director [Canadian]; Paul Anthony Mahon [1963] Director [Canadian]; Susan Jane McArthur [1963] Director [Canadian]; Nathan Moss [1955] Director; Derek Nigel Donald Netherton [1945] Director; Robert Jeffrey Orr [1958] Director [Canadian]; Siim Alden Vanaselja [1956] Director [Canadian]

Canada Life Limited
Incorporated: 25 February 1970
Net Worth: £2,854,799,872 *Total Assets:* £31,149,299,712
Registered Office: Canada Life Place, Potters Bar, Herts, EN6 5BA
Activities: Life insurance
Parent: The Canada Life Group (U.K.) Limited
Officers: Lisa Annette Rodriguez, Secretary; Keith William Abercromby [1964] Director; Douglas Allan Brown [1971] Director/Chief Executive; Marcia Dominic Campbell [1959] Director; Arshil Jamal [1967] Director [Canadian]; Paul Anthony Mahon [1963] Director [Canadian]; Susan Jane McArthur [1963] Director [Canadian]; Mary-Anne Bridget McIntyre [1961] Director; Derek Nigel Donald Netherton [1945] Director; Siim Alden Vanaselja [1956] Director [Canadian]

Canadian & Arcadia Limited
Incorporated: 8 January 2016 *Employees:* 2
Net Worth Deficit: £3,622,659 *Total Assets:* £22,179,252
Registered Office: 8-10 South Street, Epsom, Surrey, KT18 7PF
Activities: Buying and selling of own real estate
Parent: Canadian & Portland Estates (Holdings) Limited
Officers: Samantha Clark, Secretary; Emma Tiptaft, Secretary; Samantha Clark [1968] Director/Surveyor; John Paul Miles [1953] Director/Surveyor

Canadian & West End Limited
Incorporated: 8 January 2016 *Employees:* 2
Net Worth: £7,795,778 *Total Assets:* £23,143,928
Registered Office: 8-10 South Street, Epsom, Surrey, KT18 7PF
Activities: Buying and selling of own real estate
Parent: Canadian & Portland Estates (Holdings) Limited
Officers: Samantha Clark, Secretary; Emma Tiptaft, Secretary; Samantha Clark [1968] Director; John Paul Miles [1953] Director

Canon Europe Limited
Incorporated: 20 October 2000 *Employees:* 797
Net Worth: £60,299,000 *Total Assets:* £88,300,000
Registered Office: 3 The Square, Stockley Park, Uxbridge, Middlesex, UB11 1ET
Activities: Manufacture of other electrical equipment
Parent: Canon Inc
Officers: David John Bateson, Secretary/Director; Jeppe Frandsen [1960] Director [Danish]; Yuichi Ishizuka [1955] Director [Japanese]; Takanobu Nakamasu [1958] Director [Japanese]; Alessandro Stanzani [1962] Director [Italian]; Aitake Wakiya [1955] Director [Japanese]; Stefano Zenti [1961] Director [Italian]

Canons High School
Incorporated: 5 July 2011 *Employees:* 143
Net Worth: £21,116,816 *Total Assets:* £23,441,502
Registered Office: Shaldon Road, Edgware, Middlesex, HA8 6AN
Activities: General secondary education
Officers: Kevin Andrew Bartle [1972] Director/Teacher; Jacqueline Brennan [1969] Director/PA; Audrey Anne Brightwell [1937] Director; Natalie Cain [1979] Director/Assistant Facilities Manager; Jennifer Hart [1982] Director/Teacher; Anthony Bernard Richard Hickin [1957] Director; David Esseh Inyang [1953] Director/Engineering/Management Consultant; Dimple Khagram [1972] Managing Director; George Kynaston [1988] Director/Education Professional; Alexandra Joanne Mawson [1983] Director/Teacher [Australian]; Heni Patel [1978] Director/Neurophysiology Medical Secretary; Athena Pitsillis [1988] Director/Teacher; Keith Edward Rutter [1948] Director/Retired; Ronald Derrick Warshaw [1926] Director; Stephen John Leete Wright [1946] Director/Councillor

Canterbury Homes Ltd
Incorporated: 4 May 2012
Net Worth Deficit: £714,567 *Total Assets:* £8,571,169
Registered Office: 30 Station Road, Orpington, Kent, BR6 0SA
Activities: Development of building projects
Major Shareholder: Kanagaratnam Rajakanthan
Officers: Kanagaratnam Rajakanthan [1955] Managing Director

Cantillon Limited
Incorporated: 28 September 1967 *Employees:* 73
Net Worth: £8,340,000 *Total Assets:* £19,370,000
Registered Office: 10 Elton Way, Watford, Herts, WD25 8HH
Activities: Demolition
Parent: Cantillon Holdings Limited
Officers: Michael William Cantillon [1963] Director; Paul Andrew Cluskey [1973] Managing Director

Capedeal Limited
Incorporated: 28 March 2001
Net Worth: £4,294,461 *Total Assets:* £5,911,130
Registered Office: 103 High Street, Waltham Cross, Herts, EN8 7AN
Activities: Buying and selling of own real estate
Shareholders: Karen Elaine Jacobs; Michelle Lucas
Officers: Gary Stephen Lucas, Secretary; Stuart Martin Jacobs [1952] Director/Solicitor

Capital City Service Limited
Incorporated: 4 March 2003 *Employees:* 43
Net Worth: £3,249,879 *Total Assets:* £7,669,345
Registered Office: 54 Clarendon Road, Watford, Herts, WD17 1DU
Activities: Wired telecommunications activities
Shareholder: Alexandru Taracanov
Officers: Alexandru Taracanov [1953] Director/Businessman [Russian]

The Capital Dairy Company (Holdings) Limited
Incorporated: 12 October 2012 *Employees:* 44
Net Worth: £13,208,263 *Total Assets:* £16,357,963
Registered Office: 38 The Drive, Ickenham, Middlesex, UB10 8AG
Activities: Activities of other holding companies n.e.c.
Shareholders: Kuldeep Singh; Sital Kaur
Officers: Kuldeep Singh [1967] Director

Capital Hospitals (Holdings) Ltd.
Incorporated: 25 May 2005
Net Worth: £14,919,000 *Total Assets:* £1,476,226,944
Registered Office: 8 White Oak Square, London Road, Swanley, Kent, BR8 7AG
Activities: Combined facilities support activities
Parent: Innisfree Nominees Ltd
Officers: Paul Alan Bannister [1959] Director; Gaynor Birley Smith [1966] Investment Director; Louis Javier Falero [1977] Director; Jennifer Kathryn Fegan [1973] Director/Lawyer; Martine Caroline Gagnon [1963] Portfolio Director [French]; Nils Ulf Henrik Norehn [1955] Director [Swedish]; Timothy Richard Pearson [1962] Director; Sabrina Sidhu [1979] Investment Director

Capital Hospitals (Issuer) PLC
Incorporated: 25 May 2005
Net Worth: £50,000 *Total Assets:* £1,446,487,040
Registered Office: 8 White Oak Square, London Road, Swanley, Kent, BR8 7AG
Activities: Other credit granting n.e.c.
Parent: Capital Hospitals (Holdings) Ltd
Officers: Paul Alan Bannister [1959] Director; Gaynor Birley Smith [1966] Investment Director; Louis Javier Falero [1977] Director; Jennifer Kathryn Fegan [1973] Director/Lawyer; Nils Ulf Henrik Norehn [1955] Director [Swedish]; Timothy Richard Pearson [1962] Director; Sabrina Sidhu [1979] Investment Director

Capital Hospitals Ltd.
Incorporated: 25 May 2005
Net Worth: £14,869,000 *Total Assets:* £1,476,226,944
Registered Office: 8 White Oak Square, London Road, Swanley, Kent, BR8 7AG
Activities: Combined facilities support activities
Parent: Capital Hospitals (Holdings) Ltd
Officers: Paul Alan Bannister [1959] Director; Gaynor Birley Smith [1966] Investment Director; Louis Javier Falero [1977] Director; Jennifer Kathryn Fegan [1973] Director/Lawyer; Nils Ulf Henrik Norehn [1955] Director [Swedish]; Timothy Richard Pearson [1962] Director; Sabrina Sidhu [1979] Investment Director

Capital Investment and Finance Ltd
Incorporated: 6 July 2001
Net Worth: £169,972 *Total Assets:* £30,284,442
Registered Office: 52a Spring Grove Road, Hounslow, Middlesex, TW3 4BN
Activities: Buying and selling of own real estate
Major Shareholder: Sivarajah Manivannan
Officers: Manivannan Meenadharshani, Secretary; Sivarajah Manivannan [1960] Director

Cappagh Browne Utilities Limited
Incorporated: 3 November 2014 *Employees:* 201
Net Worth Deficit: £1,831,947 *Total Assets:* £15,484,426
Registered Office: Meelin House, Unit 2 Pavilion Business Centre, 6 Kinetic Crescent, Enfield, Middlesex, EN3 7FJ
Activities: Other business support service activities n.e.c.
Shareholders: Cappagh Contractors Construction (London) Limited; J.Brown Construction Company Limited
Officers: Jeffrey Paul Birtwhistle [1963] Director/Civil Engineer; Jeremy Browne [1971] Director [Irish]; Jonathan Mark Dodd [1973] Director; Michael John Ferncombe [1967] Director; Thomas Augustine Ferncombe [1942] Director [Irish]; Matthew Simon Guest [1972] Director; Paul Denis McMahon [1966] Director

Capsicum Leasing Limited
Incorporated: 24 December 2009 *Employees:* 2
Net Worth: £645,619 *Total Assets:* £9,254,731
Registered Office: Suffolk House, George Street, Croydon, Surrey, CR0 0YN
Activities: Financial leasing
Parent: Capsicum Motorsport Holdings Limited
Officers: Grahame David Chilton [1959] Director; Rupert William Swallow [1967] Director

Capsicum Motorsport Holdings Limited
Incorporated: 4 January 2010 *Employees:* 92
Net Worth Deficit: £5,726,276 *Total Assets:* £12,272,907
Registered Office: Suffolk House, George Street, Croydon, Surrey, CR0 0YN
Activities: Activities of other holding companies n.e.c.
Major Shareholder: Grahame David Chilton
Officers: Grahame David Chilton [1959] Director; Rupert William Swallow [1967] Director

Capsicum Motorsport Limited
Incorporated: 16 October 2009 *Employees:* 61
Net Worth Deficit: £5,409,949 *Total Assets:* £7,486,443
Registered Office: Capsicum Motorsport Limited, c/o Simpson Wreford & Partners, Suffolk House, George Street, Croydon, Surrey, CR0 0YN
Activities: Other business support service activities n.e.c.
Parent: Capsicum Motorsport Holdings Limited
Officers: Grahame David Chilton [1959] Director; Rupert William Swallow [1967] Director

Caravel Trading Ltd
Incorporated: 1 June 2011 *Employees:* 1
Net Worth: £5,007,736 *Total Assets:* £15,192,947
Registered Office: Unit 1 St Margarets Business Centre, Moor Mead Road, Twickenham, Middlesex, TW1 1JS
Activities: Other business support service activities n.e.c.
Major Shareholder: Marco Zanetti
Officers: Marco Zanetti [1968] Director/Consultant [Italian]

Carbon Solutions Global Ltd
Incorporated: 12 June 2012
Net Worth: £7,040,450 *Total Assets:* £9,526,156
Registered Office: CKR House, 70 East Hill, Dartford, Kent, DA1 1RZ
Activities: Environmental consulting activities
Shareholder: Peter Gaspar
Officers: Ria Kamras [1966] Director [Hungarian]

Cardif Pinnacle Insurance Holdings PLC
Incorporated: 5 May 1992 *Employees:* 245
Net Worth: £142,234,000 *Total Assets:* £344,260,000
Registered Office: Pinnacle House, A1 Barnet Way, Borehamwood, Herts, WD6 2XX
Activities: Life insurance
Parent: BNP Paribas Cardif
Officers: Matthew Justin Lorimer, Secretary; Gerard Binet [1953] Development and Strategy Director [French]; Peter John Box [1952] Director; Stanislas Louis Paul Francois Chevalet [1961] Director [French]; Marie Haderer [1979] Director/Actuary [French]; Matthew Justin Lorimer [1967] Director/Solicitor; Nicholas Dutfield Rochez [1954] Director; Andrew Miles Wigg [1972] Director

Cardif Pinnacle Insurance Management Services PLC
Incorporated: 2 July 1992 *Employees:* 188
Net Worth: £2,184,000 *Total Assets:* £9,760,000
Registered Office: Pinnacle House, A1 Barnet Way, Borehamwood, Herts, WD6 2XX
Activities: Other business support service activities n.e.c.
Parent: Cardif Pinnacle Insurance Holdings PLC
Officers: Matthew Justin Lorimer, Secretary; Gerard Binet [1953] Development and Strategy Director [French]; Peter John Box [1952] Director; Stanislas Louis Paul Francois Chevalet [1961] Director/Exco Member COO BNPPC [French]; Marie Haderer [1979] Director/Actuary [French]; Matthew Justin Lorimer [1967] Director/Solicitor; Nicholas Dutfield Rochez [1954] Director; Andrew Miles Wigg [1972] Director

Cardiff Ground Rents Limited
Incorporated: 4 February 1958 *Employees:* 5
Net Worth: £8,518,198 *Total Assets:* £12,852,183
Registered Office: 141 Stanmore Hill, Stanmore, Middlesex, HA7 3ED
Activities: Other letting and operating of own or leased real estate
Officers: Stephen Samuel, Secretary; Babara Ruth Cohen [1960] Director/Secretary; Gideon Elisha Cohen [1985] Director/Student; Simon Charles Cohen [1962] Director/Solicitor; Judith Samuel [1950] Director; Stephen Samuel [1948] Director/Chartered Accountant

Cardiff Property Public Limited Company (The)
Incorporated: 31 May 1886 *Employees:* 6
Net Worth: £27,290,000 *Total Assets:* £28,043,000
Registered Office: 56 Station Road, Egham, Surrey, TW20 9LF
Activities: Buying and selling of own real estate
Shareholder: John Richard Wollenberg
Officers: Karen Louise Chandler, Secretary; Karen Louise Chandler [1972] Finance Director; Nigel Dare Jamieson [1950] Director/Chartered Surveyor; John Richard Wollenberg [1948] Director

Cardinal International Limited
Incorporated: 26 January 1981 *Employees:* 8
Net Worth Deficit: £1,171,174 *Total Assets:* £7,915,285
Registered Office: Ridgecourt, The Ridge, Epsom, Surrey, KT18 7EP
Activities: Activities of head offices
Officers: Christopher Paul Baker, Secretary; Jeremy Graham Paul Campling [1969] Director/Chartered Surveyor; Sandra Jane Pope [1963] Director/Accountant

Care Expertise Limited
Incorporated: 21 May 2007 *Employees:* 8
Net Worth: £4,469,228 *Total Assets:* £9,308,470
Registered Office: 1070-1072 London Road, Thornton Heath, Surrey, CR7 7ND
Activities: Activities of head offices
Shareholders: Ian Jones; Mussarat Awan
Officers: Mussarat Awan [1956] Director; Dr Ian Jones [1956] Director

Care Management Group (Acquisition) Limited
Incorporated: 5 July 2006 *Employees:* 3
Net Worth: £14,076,000 *Total Assets:* £113,076,000
Registered Office: Ground Floor, Q1 The Square, Randalls Way, Leatherhead, Surrey, KT22 7TW
Activities: Activities of head offices
Parent: CMG Holdco Limited
Officers: Garry John Fitton, Secretary; Garry John Fitton [1972] Director/Chartered Accountant; Peter Kinsey [1964] Director; David Andrew Spruzen [1967] Director

Care Management Group Limited
Incorporated: 22 November 1994 *Employees:* 2,241
Net Worth: £67,697,648 *Total Assets:* £152,823,120
Registered Office: Ground Floor, Q1 The Square, Randalls Way, Leatherhead, Surrey, KT22 7TW
Activities: Residential care activities for learning difficulties, mental health and substance abuse
Parent: CMG Holdco Limited
Officers: Garry John Fitton, Secretary; Garry John Fitton [1972] Director/Chartered Accountant; Peter Kinsey [1964] Director; David Andrew Spruzen [1967] Director

Care Providers Recruitment Limited
Incorporated: 5 July 2011 *Employees:* 3
Net Worth: £2,302,823 *Total Assets:* £10,569,541
Registered Office: Treviot House, 186-192 High Road, Ilford, Essex, IG1 1LR
Activities: Other residential care activities n.e.c.
Parent: Day Webster Limited
Officers: Hugh Woods Ballard, Secretary; Wayne Arthur St John [1974] Director; Daniel Jonathan Wise [1982] Director; Hugh William Woods Ballard [1968] Director

Caredeal Limited
Incorporated: 21 July 1993
Net Worth: £2,967,045 *Total Assets:* £6,916,768
Registered Office: The Hive, Camrose Avenue, London, HA8 6AG
Activities: Other letting and operating of own or leased real estate
Parent: WD1A Limited
Officers: Mahendra Patel, Secretary; Anthony Andrew Kleanthous [1966] Director

Careprogress Limited
Incorporated: 26 October 1999 *Employees:* 207
Net Worth: £13,218,546 *Total Assets:* £26,391,724
Registered Office: c/o Elysium Healthcare, 2 Imperial Place, Maxwell Road, Borehamwood, Herts, WD6 1JN
Activities: Residential care activities for the elderly and disabled
Parent: Elysium Healthcare Holdings 3 Limited
Officers: Sarah Juliette Livingston, Secretary; Lesley Joy Chamberlain [1963] Director/Group Chief Executive; Dr Quazi Shams Mahfooz Haque [1968] Executive Medical Director; Steven John Woolgar [1955] Director of Policy and Regulation

Caretech Community Services (No.2) Limited
Incorporated: 15 December 1999 *Employees:* 436
Net Worth: £229,000 *Total Assets:* £15,198,000
Registered Office: 5th Floor, Metropolitan House, 3 Darkes Lane, Potters Bar, Herts, EN6 1AG
Activities: Other human health activities
Officers: Gareth Dufton, Secretary; Gareth Dufton [1976] Director/Chartered Accountant; Farouq Rashid Sheikh [1958] Director; Haroon Rashid Sheikh [1956] Director

Caretech Community Services Limited
Incorporated: 29 March 1993 *Employees:* 969
Net Worth: £6,922,000 *Total Assets:* £216,876,000
Registered Office: 5th Floor, Metropolitan House, 3 Darkes Lane, Potters Bar, Herts, EN6 1AG
Activities: Other human health activities
Parent: Caretech Holdings PLC
Officers: Gareth Dufton, Secretary; Gareth Dufton [1976] Director/Chartered Accountant; Farouq Rashid Sheikh [1958] Director; Haroon Rashid Sheikh [1956] Director

Caretech Estates (No 2) Limited
Incorporated: 29 February 2008
Net Worth: £656,000 *Total Assets:* £14,383,000
Registered Office: 5th Floor, Metropolitan Houe, 3 Darkes Lane, Potters Bar, Herts, EN6 1AG
Activities: Other letting and operating of own or leased real estate
Parent: Caretech Holdings PLC
Officers: Gareth Dufton, Secretary; Gareth Dufton [1976] Director/Chartered Accountant; Farouq Rashid Sheikh [1958] Director

Caretech Estates (No 3) Limited
Incorporated: 29 February 2008
Net Worth: £400,000 *Total Assets:* £9,634,000
Registered Office: 5th Floor, Metropolitan House, 3 Darkes Lane, Potters Bar, Herts, EN6 1AG
Activities: Other letting and operating of own or leased real estate
Parent: Caretech Holdings PLC
Officers: Gareth Dufton, Secretary; Gareth Dufton [1976] Director/Chartered Accountant; Farouq Rashid Sheikh [1958] Director

Caretech Estates (No 7) Limited
Incorporated: 29 July 2013
Net Worth: £3,480,000 *Total Assets:* £38,475,000
Registered Office: 5th Floor, Metropolitan House, 3 Darkes Lane, Potters Bar, Herts, EN6 1AG
Activities: Other letting and operating of own or leased real estate
Parent: Caretech Holdings PLC
Officers: Gareth Dufton, Secretary; Gareth Dufton [1976] Director/Chartered Accountant; Farouq Rashid Sheikh [1958] Director; Haroon Rashid Sheikh [1956] Director

Caretech Estates (No. 5) Limited
Incorporated: 23 September 2009
Net Worth: £786,000 *Total Assets:* £16,166,000
Registered Office: 5th Floor, Metropolitan House, Darkes Lane, Potters Bar, Herts, EN6 1AG
Activities: Other letting and operating of own or leased real estate
Parent: Caretech Holdings PLC
Officers: Gareth Dufton, Secretary; Gareth Dufton [1976] Director/Chartered Accountant; Farouq Rashid Sheikh [1958] Director; Haroon Rashid Sheikh [1956] Director

Caretech Estates (No.4) Limited
Incorporated: 26 March 2008
Net Worth: £420,000 *Total Assets:* £11,441,000
Registered Office: 5th Floor, Metropolitan House, 3 Darkes Lane, Potters Bar, Herts, EN6 1AG
Activities: Other letting and operating of own or leased real estate
Parent: Caretech Holdings PLC
Officers: Gareth Dufton, Secretary; Gareth Dufton [1976] Director/Chartered Accountant; Farouq Rashid Sheikh [1958] Director

Caretech Estates Limited
Incorporated: 12 October 2006
Net Worth: £1,337,000 *Total Assets:* £16,363,000
Registered Office: 5th Floor, Metropolitan House, 3 Darkes Lane, Potters Bar, Herts, EN6 1AG
Activities: Other letting and operating of own or leased real estate
Parent: Caretech Holdings PLC
Officers: Gareth Dufton, Secretary; Gareth Dufton [1976] Director/Chartered Accountant; Farouq Rashid Sheikh [1958] Director; Haroon Rashid Sheikh [1956] Director

Caretech Holdings PLC
Incorporated: 10 June 2002 *Employees:* 5,439
Net Worth: £207,594,000 *Total Assets:* £426,992,000
Registered Office: 5th Floor, Metropolitan House, 3 Darkes Lane, Potters Bar, Herts, EN6 1AG
Activities: Activities of head offices
Officers: Gareth Dufton, Secretary; Michael John Adams [1971] Director; James Stuart Cumming [1950] Director; Gareth Dufton [1976] Director/Chartered Accountant; Karl Upton Monaghan [1962] Director [Irish]; Farouq Rashid Sheikh [1958] Director; Haroon Rashid Sheikh [1956] Director

P.J. Carey (Contractors) Limited
Incorporated: 9 November 1979 *Employees:* 982
Net Worth: £56,466,940 *Total Assets:* £124,872,688
Registered Office: Carey House, Great Central Way, Wembley, Middlesex, HA9 0HR
Activities: Construction of commercial buildings
Parent: Carey Group PLC
Officers: Fiona Mary O'Donnell, Secretary; Bjourn Bigley [1979] Director [Irish]; Jason Anthony Carey [1975] Director [Irish]; John Anthony Carey [1964] Director [Irish]; John Carey [1941] Director [Irish]; Patrick Joseph Carey [1945] Director [Irish]; Thomas Noel Carey [1973] Director; Thomas Carey [1943] Director [Irish]; Denis Patrick Deacy [1965] Director; Paul Albert Johnson [1970] Director/Health & Safety Officer; Martin James McGuire [1972] Director; Joe O'Hagan [1967] Director; Paul Quigley [1958] Estimating Director [Irish]; Steven John Regan [1974] Director; Stephen Peter Smith [1957] Director

P.J. Carey Plant Hire (Oval) Limited
Incorporated: 29 October 1968 *Employees:* 61
Net Worth: £3,621,148 *Total Assets:* £22,805,350
Registered Office: Carey House, Great Central Way, Wembley, Middlesex, HA9 0HR
Activities: Renting and leasing of cars and light motor vehicles
Parent: Carey Group PLC
Officers: Fiona Mary O'Donnell, Secretary; John Carey [1941] Director [Irish]; Patrick Joseph Carey [1945] Director [Irish]; Thomas Noel Carey [1973] Director; Thomas Carey [1943] Director [Irish]; Gary Condon [1961] Managing Director

Careys New Homes Limited
Incorporated: 5 December 1975 *Employees:* 4
Previous: Maxplan Properties Limited
Net Worth: £9,953,778 *Total Assets:* £59,838,172
Registered Office: Carey House, Great Central Way, Wembley, Middlesex, HA9 0HR
Activities: Development of building projects
Parent: Carey Group PLC
Officers: Fiona Mary O'Donnell, Secretary; John Carey [1941] Director [Irish]; Thomas Carey [1943] Director [Irish]; Denis Patrick Deacy [1965] Group Managing Director; Gregory Charles Ketteridge [1958] Director

Cargill Chocolate UK Limited
Incorporated: 10 June 1941 *Employees:* 60
Previous: ADM Cocoa UK Limited
Net Worth: £14,169,753 *Total Assets:* £15,683,290
Registered Office: Velocity V1, Brooklands Drive, Weybridge, Surrey, KT13 0SL
Activities: Manufacture of cocoa and chocolate confectionery
Parent: Cargill PLC
Officers: Dena Michelle L O'Bue, Secretary; Stephen James Hamilton [1969] Director/Country Tax Manager UK and Ireland; Michael James Timewell [1974] Director/Solicitor

Cargill Cotton Limited
Incorporated: 15 September 2005 *Employees:* 13
Net Worth: £6,322,000 *Total Assets:* £47,646,000
Registered Office: Velocity V1, Brooklands Drive, Weybridge, Surrey, KT13 0SL
Activities: Growing of fibre crops
Parent: Cargill PLC
Officers: Dena Michelle L O'Bue, Secretary; Stephen James Hamilton [1969] Director/Country Tax Manager UK & Ireland; Carl Patrick Peltzer [1966] Director/UK Cotton Commercial Manager

Cargill Financial Markets Limited
Incorporated: 26 April 1990
Net Worth: £447,032,256 *Total Assets:* £1,041,751,616
Registered Office: Velocity V1, Brooklands Drive, Weybridge, Surrey, KT13 0SL
Activities: Financial intermediation not elsewhere classified
Parent: Cargill Holdings
Officers: Dena Michelle L O'Bue, Secretary; Paul Justin Robert Bothamley [1965] Director, EMEA Tax; Clifford Andrew Bottomley [1970] Director, Treasury Europe

Cargill Financial Services Europe Limited
Incorporated: 30 May 2007
Net Worth: £16,537,606 *Total Assets:* £77,807,256
Registered Office: Velocity V1, Brooklands Drive, Weybridge, Surrey, KT13 0SL
Activities: Activities auxiliary to financial intermediation n.e.c.
Officers: Dena Michelle L O'Bue, Secretary; Keith Livingston Milne [1964] Director/Marketing Manager, EMEA Cargill Risk Management; Federico Urquidi Negron [1965] Director/UK & Ireland Country Controller [Spanish]; Raymond Geoffrey Ward [1964] Director/Derivatives Compliance Senior Adviser

Cargill Global Funding PLC
Incorporated: 24 September 1993 *Employees:* 51
Net Worth: £196,052,288 *Total Assets:* £4,270,958,336
Registered Office: Velocity V1, Brooklands Drive, Weybridge, Surrey, KT13 0SL
Activities: Financial intermediation not elsewhere classified
Parent: Cargill Holdings
Officers: Dena Michelle L O'Bue, Secretary; Judith Helen Mawhood [1959] Director/Accountant; Alison Mulholland [1970] Director/EMEA Regional Lead, Treasury Services Group; Jayme Donald Olson [1956] Director/Financial Manager [American]

Cargill Holdings
Incorporated: 10 August 1970
Net Worth: £55,574,784 *Total Assets:* £111,631,192
Registered Office: Velocity V1, Brooklands Drive, Weybridge, Surrey, KT13 0SL
Activities: Non-trading company
Officers: Dena Michelle L O'Bue, Secretary; Stephen James Hamilton [1969] Director/Country Tax Manager UK & Ireland; Michael James Timewell [1974] Director/Solicitor

Cargill Investments
Incorporated: 7 February 1995 *Employees:* 2
Net Worth: £237,169,728 *Total Assets:* £300,479,424
Registered Office: Velocity V1, Brooklands Drive, Weybridge, Surrey, KT13 0SL
Activities: Financial intermediation not elsewhere classified
Parent: Cargill Investments Holdings Limited
Officers: Dena Michelle L O'Bue, Secretary; Paul Justin Robert Bothamley [1965] Director; Clifford Andrew Bottomley [1970] Director, Treasury Europe

Cargill Investments Holdings Limited
Incorporated: 2 June 1998
Net Worth: £41,296,000 *Total Assets:* £41,304,000
Registered Office: Velocity V1, Brooklands Drive, Weybridge, Surrey, KT13 0SL
Activities: Non-trading company
Parent: Cargill Holdings
Officers: Dena Michelle L O'Bue, Secretary; Paul Justin Robert Bothamley [1965] Director; Clifford Andrew Bottomley [1970] Director, Treasury Europe

Cargill PLC
Incorporated: 6 September 1978 *Employees:* 599
Net Worth: £356,444,000 *Total Assets:* £676,387,008
Registered Office: Velocity V1, Brooklands Drive, Weybridge, Surrey, KT13 0SL
Activities: Wholesale of other intermediate products
Parent: Cargill UK Holdings Limited
Officers: Dena Michelle L O'Bue, Secretary; Peter de Braal [1959] Director/Accountant [Dutch]; Paul Jonathan Kingston [1970] Director/Chemical Engineer; Samina Kosar [1970] Director/Global Head, Cargill Risk Operations and Execution; Melanie Ann Pollard [1970] Director/General Manager, Cargill Grain and Oilseeds UK; Michael James Timewell [1974] Director/Solicitor

Cargill UK Finance Limited
Incorporated: 23 May 2013
Net Worth: £203,440,992 *Total Assets:* £204,367,008
Registered Office: Velocity V1, Brooklands Drive, Weybridge, Surrey, KT13 0SL
Activities: Financial intermediation not elsewhere classified
Officers: Dena Michelle L O'Bue, Secretary; Paul Justin Robert Bothamley [1965] Director, EMEA Tax; Clifford Andrew Bottomley [1970] Director, Treasury Europe

Cargill UK Holdings Limited
Incorporated: 25 March 2010
Net Worth: £314,753,664 *Total Assets:* £556,501,952
Registered Office: Velocity V1, Brooklands Drive, Weybridge, Surrey, KT13 0SL
Activities: Non-trading company
Officers: Dena Michelle L O'Bue, Secretary; Stephen James Hamilton [1969] Director/Country Tax Manager UK & Ireland; Michael James Timewell [1974] Director/Solicitor

Cargill Weybridge Limited
Incorporated: 25 July 2002
Previous: Cargill Schokinag UK Limited
Net Worth: £8,055,862 *Total Assets:* £8,128,384
Registered Office: Velocity V1, Brooklands Drive, Weybridge, Surrey, KT13 0SL
Activities: Wholesale of sugar and chocolate and sugar confectionery
Parent: Cargill PLC
Officers: Dena Michelle L O'Bue, Secretary; Stephen James Hamilton [1969] Director/Country Tax Manager UK and Ireland; Michael James Timewell [1974] Director/Solicitor

Cargobull Finance Limited
Incorporated: 11 December 2000 *Employees:* 1
Net Worth: £9,228,000 *Total Assets:* £23,251,000
Registered Office: Building 7, Croxley Park, Hatters Lane, Watford, Herts, WD18 8YN
Activities: Renting and leasing of cars and light motor vehicles
Officers: Thies Johannes Philipp Engering [1974] Director [German]; Duncan John Hullis [1963] Director/General Manager; Simon John Trudgeon [1968] Director/Credit Risk Officer

Caridon Holdings LLP
Incorporated: 1 April 2015
Net Worth: £25,965,504 *Total Assets:* £118,772,880
Registered Office: Wrencote House, 123 High Street, Croydon, Surrey, CR0 0XJ
Officers: Abbas Alidina [1979] Member; Mario Joseph Carrozzo [1972] Member; Roy Andrew Ledgister [1973] LLP Member

Carigluz Investment Co Limited
Incorporated: 16 April 1953 *Employees:* 3
Net Worth: £7,518,058 *Total Assets:* £8,485,179
Registered Office: Unit 5 Manor Farm, Manor Road North, Thames Ditton, Surrey, KT7 0BH
Activities: Other letting and operating of own or leased real estate
Officers: Denis Rossiter Carpenter, Secretary/Hotel Proprietor; Rodney Duncan Jones [1940] Director/Builder; Simon Harvey Jones [1967] Director/Property Manager

Carlson Wagonlit New Holdco Limited
Incorporated: 23 May 2006
Net Worth: £31,605,128 *Total Assets:* £67,607,120
Registered Office: Maple House, High Street, Potters Bar, Herts, EN6 5RF
Activities: Travel agency activities
Shareholders: Marilyn Arleen Nelson; Barbara Ann Carlson Gage
Officers: Narinder Sanotra, Secretary; Christopher Bowen [1960] Director; Denise Harman [1970] Director [Irish]; Sanjay Kapoor [1967] Director [British/Australian]; Rhodri Llewelyn Hollister Turner [1977] Director/Chief Financial Officer

Carlson Wagonlit UK Ltd
Incorporated: 12 May 1994 *Employees:* 944
Net Worth: £20,163,888 *Total Assets:* £83,417,200
Registered Office: Maple House, High Street, Potters Bar, Herts, EN6 5RF
Activities: Travel agency activities
Parent: CWT Holdco Limited
Officers: Narinder Sanotra, Secretary; Christopher Bowen [1960] Director; Denise Harman [1970] Commercial Director [Irish]; Sanjay Kapoor [1967] Director [British/Australian]; Rhodri Llewelyn Hollister Turner [1977] Director/Chief Financial Officer

Carlton Group Developments Ltd
Incorporated: 8 July 2010
Net Worth Deficit: £56,393 *Total Assets:* £11,074,216
Registered Office: 501 High Road, Ilford, Essex, IG1 1TZ
Activities: Management of real estate on a fee or contract basis
Major Shareholder: Paul Waraich
Officers: Amar Waraich, Secretary; Swinder Paul Waraich [1952] Director

Carlton House Developments Limited
Incorporated: 23 May 2016
Net Worth Deficit: £1,349,644 *Total Assets:* £12,252,801
Registered Office: 3rd Floor, Sterling House, Langston Road, Loughton, Essex, IG10 3TS
Activities: Development of building projects
Parent: Galliard Holdings Limited
Officers: Allan William Porter, Secretary; Stephen Stuart Solomon Conway [1948] Director; Jonathan Michael Morgan [1978] Director; Donagh O'Sullivan [1968] Director [Irish]; Michael William Watson [1952] Director

Carmel (UK) Limited
Incorporated: 14 July 2004 *Employees:* 111
Net Worth: £2,110,908 *Total Assets:* £8,654,297
Registered Office: Unit A, Blenheim House, 1 Blenheim Road, Epsom, Surrey, KT19 9BE
Activities: Electrical installation
Officers: Melvyn Spelling, Secretary; Christopher Clarke [1972] Director; Anthony Hurst [1971] Director; David Charles Tippetts [1955] Director/Engineer

Carnarvon Hotels Limited
Incorporated: 24 November 1967 *Employees:* 171
Net Worth: £10,346,123 *Total Assets:* £25,728,970
Registered Office: 17 Bourne Court, Southend Road, Woodford Green, Essex, IG8 8HD
Activities: Hotels and similar accommodation
Shareholders: Michael Anthony Harris; Albert Harris
Officers: Robert Phaidonos Aristotelous, Secretary; Albert Harris [1922] Director/Hotelier; Daniel Harris [1984] Director/Hotelier; Gregory Lewis Ralph Harris [1947] Director/Hotelier; Michael Anthony Harris [1954] Director/Hotelier

Carpetright of London Limited
Incorporated: 17 December 1992
Net Worth: £35,068,000 *Total Assets:* £77,989,000
Registered Office: Purfleet By Pass, Purfleet, Essex, RM19 1TT
Activities: Activities of other holding companies n.e.c.
Parent: Carpetright PLC
Officers: Neil Lloyd Page [1963] Director/Accountant; Jeremy Andrew Sampson [1968] Director/Solicitor

Carrain Limited
Incorporated: 19 August 1982 *Employees:* 5
Net Worth: £9,210,941 *Total Assets:* £13,853,009
Registered Office: 1 Beauchamp Court, Victors Way, Barnet, Herts, EN5 5TZ
Activities: Development of building projects
Officers: Olive May Herman, Secretary; Julia Deborah Burton [1962] Director; Rosalind Carol Gelbart [1958] Director; Charles Robert Herman [1956] Director; Olive May Herman [1931] Director; Paul Philip Herman [1968] Director

Carshalton Boys Sports College
Incorporated: 16 May 2011 *Employees:* 141
Net Worth: £21,205,000 *Total Assets:* £23,633,000
Registered Office: Carshalton Boys Sport College, Winchcombe Road, Carshalton, Surrey, SM5 1RW
Activities: General secondary education
Officers: Jenny Gaylor, Secretary; Daniel Olumide Ayeni [1976] Director/Team Manager (Education), Cognus Limited; Simon Barber [1957] Director/Principal; David Baron [1959] Director/Retail Management; Stephen Bosdet [1979] Director/Teacher; Joanne Damianou [1971] Director/SHC & Procurement Co-ordinator; Catherine Suzanne Fontinelle [1969] Director/Biomedical Scientist; Alan Forder [1955] Director/Education; Jenny Gaylor [1971] Director/Vice Principal; Jean Carole Knight [1939] Director; Andrew Lee [1970] Project Director Construction; Deborah Anne Martin [1964] Director/School Business Manager; Nicholas Maybanks [1985] Director/Teacher; Rebecca McGowan [1978] Director/Pension Consultant; Susan Eleanor O'Neill [1948] Director; Chris O'Sullivan [1968] Director/Senior Network Support Engineer; Valerie Verona Roberts [1966] Director/Senior Curriculum Support Officer; Edwina Rozek [1964] Director/Administrative Manager; Graham Skipp [1962] Director/Operations Manager; Mark William Twigg [1975] Executive Director of Cicero Group; Oliver Wilson-Hughes [1984] Director/English Teacher; Hayley Margaret Anne Wood [1964] Director/Lab Technician Manager

Casewise Limited
Incorporated: 19 November 1996 *Employees:* 12
Net Worth: £35,677 *Total Assets:* £7,264,735
Registered Office: 1 The Green, Richmond, Surrey, TW9 1PL
Activities: Information technology consultancy activities
Shareholders: Casewise Systems Limited; Casewise Systems Limited
Officers: Richard Norman Campbell [1961] Director/Accountant [Canadian]; James McGarry [1969] Director/Manager [American]

Casewise Systems Limited
Incorporated: 17 October 1989 *Employees:* 6
Net Worth Deficit: £412,055 *Total Assets:* £5,689,329
Registered Office: 1 The Green, Richmond, Surrey, TW9 1PL
Activities: Business and domestic software development
Officers: Richard Norman Campbell [1961] Director/Accountant [Canadian]; James McGarry [1969] Director/Manager [American]

Caskade Caterers Limited
Incorporated: 16 October 1984 *Employees:* 788
Net Worth: £6,578,674 *Total Assets:* £26,553,772
Registered Office: The Pavilion, 56 Rosslyn Crescent, Harrow, Middlesex, HA1 2SZ
Activities: Licenced restaurants
Parent: MSHA International Limited
Officers: Hamid Ali [1956] Director

Caskade Properties Limited
Incorporated: 24 July 2017
Net Worth: £4,389,597 *Total Assets:* £9,944,650
Registered Office: The Pavilion, Rosslyn Crescent, Harrow, Middlesex, HA1 2SZ
Activities: Buying and selling of own real estate
Major Shareholder: Hamid Ali
Officers: Hamid Ali [1956] Director

Cassra LLP
Incorporated: 14 September 2012
Net Worth: £3,847,391 *Total Assets:* £5,233,304
Registered Office: 6-10 Outram Road, Croydon, Surrey, CR0 6XE
Officers: Gordon Henry Phillips [1947] Member; Hilary Jewel Phillips [1948] Member

Castle Bidco PLC
Incorporated: 3 November 2006
Previous: Castle Bidco Limited
Net Worth: £512,000,000 *Total Assets:* £1,019,200,000
Registered Office: Crest House, Pyrcroft Road, Chertsey, Surrey, KT16 9GN
Activities: Activities of head offices
Parent: Crest Nicholson Holdings PLC
Officers: Kevin Maguire, Secretary; Patrick Joseph Bergin [1966] Director/Group Financial Controller; Robin Patrick Hoyles [1954] Group Land & Planning Director; Stephen Stone [1954] Managing Director; Nigel Christopher Tinker [1960] Urban Land Director

Castle Green Kendal Limited
Incorporated: 22 December 1964 *Employees:* 112
Net Worth: £2,526,520 *Total Assets:* £10,346,048
Registered Office: Kirkland House, 11-15 Peterborough Road, Harrow, Middlesex, HA1 2AX
Activities: Hotels and similar accommodation
Officers: Haider Ladhu Jaffer [1940] Director; Dr Manoj Raman [1960] Director; Hassanali Amirali Dawood Suleman [1954] Director

Castle Village Limited
Incorporated: 3 November 1999 *Employees:* 3
Net Worth: £10,414,464 *Total Assets:* £12,810,467
Registered Office: 1st Floor, Brunswick House, Regent Park, 297-299 Kingston Road, Leatherhead, Surrey, KT22 7LU
Activities: Other business support service activities n.e.c.
Parent: Retirement Villages Management Limited
Officers: Sally Irene Rees, Secretary; Sarah Denise Burgess [1971] Director; Neil Donaldson [1966] Director/Accountant; Andrew George Esmond Ovey [1971] Director/Investment Manager

Castledene Investments Limited
Incorporated: 17 December 1996 *Employees:* 2
Net Worth: £2,145,144 *Total Assets:* £7,296,653
Registered Office: 19 Coombehurst Close, Hadley Wood, Herts, EN4 0JU
Activities: Development of building projects
Major Shareholder: Paul Lawrence Balcombe
Officers: Paul Lawrence Balcombe [1941] Director; Nigel Kingsley [1957] Director

Castlestone Investments Limited
Incorporated: 3 December 1965 *Employees:* 4
Net Worth: £15,964,458 *Total Assets:* £17,873,204
Registered Office: Enterprise House, Beesons Yard, Bury Lane, Rickmansworth, Herts, WD3 1DS
Activities: Development of building projects
Parent: Miaglen Limited
Officers: Sandra Estella Lask, Secretary; Ronald John Joseph Lask [1939] Director/Surveyor; Sandra Estella Lask [1943] Director

Catalina Investments Limited
Incorporated: 17 October 2016
Net Worth: £119,311 *Total Assets:* £7,175,547
Registered Office: 1 Tower House, Tower Centre, Hoddesdon, Herts, EN11 8UR
Activities: Activities of open-ended investment companies
Shareholders: Anne Marie Revell; Richard Revell
Officers: Anne Marie Revell [1966] Director

Catalyst Academies Trust
Incorporated: 18 February 2013 *Employees:* 254
Net Worth: £15,202,873 *Total Assets:* £19,307,262
Registered Office: Dilkes Academy, Garron Lane, South Ockendon, Essex, RM15 5JQ
Activities: Primary education
Officers: Sarah Jane Coote [1967] Operations Director; Timothy Richard Drakes [1979] Director/Financial Consultant; Tony Reg Parfett [1977] Director/Headteacher; LEA Tyler [1965] Director/Deputy Headteacher; Darren Antony Walters [1972] Director/Engineer; Keith Charles Williams [1957] Director/NGA Planning Manager

Catalyst Corporate Development Limited
Incorporated: 20 January 1989
Net Worth: £34,578 *Total Assets:* £5,975,343
Registered Office: 139 Richmond Park Road, Kingston upon Thames, Surrey, KT2 6AG
Activities: Other retail sale not in stores, stalls or markets
Major Shareholder: Kenneth Adrian Raymond Wilson
Officers: Georgina Rachel Hall, Secretary; Kenneth Adrian Raymond Wilson [1957] Director/Corporate Financier/Management Consultant

Catco Kids LLP
Incorporated: 4 January 2006
Net Worth: £7,173,211 *Total Assets:* £17,944,464
Registered Office: 166 College Road, Harrow, Middlesex, HA1 1RA
Officers: Simon Marcus Bottle [1973] LLP Member; Johnny Byrne [1935] LLP Member; Sandy Rivera [1971] LLP Member; Doctor Vishwas Murlidhar Sapatnekar [1947] LLP Member

Caterham Cars Group Limited
Incorporated: 11 November 2004 *Employees:* 3
Net Worth: £5,945,997 *Total Assets:* £6,000,100
Registered Office: 2 Kennet Road, Dartford, Kent, DA1 4QN
Activities: Manufacture of motor vehicles
Parent: Caterham Enterprises Limited
Officers: Trevor David Steel, Secretary; Karena Fernandes [1975] Director/General Manager [Malaysian]; Graham Alastair MacDonald [1964] Director; Kamarudin Bin Meranun [1961] Director [Malaysian]

Caterham Cars Ltd.
Incorporated: 23 May 1974 *Employees:* 122
Net Worth: £2,632,200 *Total Assets:* £13,153,203
Registered Office: 2 Kennet Road, Dartford, Kent, DA1 4QN
Activities: Manufacture of motor vehicles
Officers: Trevor David Steel, Secretary; Karena Fernandes [1975] Director/General Manager [Malaysian]; Graham Alastair MacDonald [1964] Director/Group CEO; Kamarudin Bin Meranun [1961] Director [Malaysian]; Dixon Wong Kit Seng [1989] Director/Corporate Finance Manager [Malaysian]

Caterham Enterprises Limited
Incorporated: 9 February 2011 *Employees:* 122
Net Worth Deficit: £219,538,800 *Total Assets:* £10,583,559
Registered Office: 2-3 Kennet Road, Crayford, Dartford, Kent, DA1 4QN
Activities: Activities of other holding companies n.e.c.
Shareholders: Tan Sri Anthony Francis Fernandes; Datuk Kamarudin Bin Meranun
Officers: Karena Fernandes [1975] Director/General Manager [Malaysian]; Kamarudin Bin Meranun [1961] Director [Malaysian]

Caterham School Limited
Incorporated: 1 April 2005 *Employees:* 335
Net Worth: £18,623,000 *Total Assets:* £32,258,000
Registered Office: Caterham School, Harestone Valley Road, Caterham, Surrey, CR3 6YA
Activities: Pre-primary education
Officers: Angela Denise Higgs, Secretary; Dr Stephen Richard Critchley [1951] Director; Ian Robert Michael Edwards [1954] Director; Tracey Frances Eldridge-Hinmers [1962] Director/Solicitor; Anne Margaret Fletcher [1955] Director; Revd Nicola Jayne Furley-Smith [1961] Director/Minister of Religion; Monisha Amrit Shah [1969] Director; John Edward Kitson Smith [1954] Director/Chartered Accountant; Mark Haskett Peplow Smith [1981] Director; Ewan Paul Russell Turney [1980] Director; Mary Lavinia Whenman [1969] Director; Suzi Mary Whittle [1954] Director/Accountant; Anthony Peter Wilson [1966] Director/Clerk to The Skinners Company

Cathedral Holdings Limited
Incorporated: 14 April 2000 *Employees:* 2
Net Worth: £35,525,804 *Total Assets:* £38,227,716
Registered Office: 22 Barn Rise, Wembley, Middlesex, HA9 9NQ
Activities: Development of building projects
Parent: Monument Assets Limited
Officers: Anthony David Chambers, Secretary/Director; Anthony David Chambers [1955] Director; Sarah Davies [1976] Director/Chartered Accountant

Caunton Management Limited
Incorporated: 3 December 1992 *Employees:* 21
Net Worth: £8,905,526 *Total Assets:* £9,717,741
Registered Office: c/o Haslers, Old Station Road, Loughton, Essex, IG10 4PL
Activities: Buying and selling of own real estate
Shareholders: Nicholas Charles Pearce; Sarah Jane Hill
Officers: Nicholas Charles Pearce [1962] Managing Director

Caversham Finance Limited
Incorporated: 24 December 1963 *Employees:* 1,868
Net Worth: £134,201,000 *Total Assets:* £333,688,000
Registered Office: 5 Hercules Way, Leavesden, Watford, Herts, WD25 7GS
Activities: Retail sale of electrical household appliances in specialised stores
Parent: Brighthouse Limited
Officers: David John Harwood, Secretary; Brian Edward Brodie [1965] Director; Graeme James Campbell [1972] Director; Stuart John Deane [1965] Director; Lysa Maria Hardy [1970] Director; Hugh John Harvey [1959] Director; Ian David Larkin [1968] Director [Irish]; Lars Magnus Mattsson [1973] Director [Swedish]; Hamish Stewart Paton [1976] Commercial Director; David Anthony Poole [1969] Director

Caversham Trading Limited
Incorporated: 17 March 2005 *Employees:* 658
Net Worth: £73,485,000 *Total Assets:* £85,510,000
Registered Office: 5 Hercules Way, Leavesden, Watford, Herts, WD25 7GS
Activities: Retail sale of electrical household appliances in specialised stores
Parent: Caversham Finance Ltd
Officers: David John Harwood, Secretary; Graeme James Campbell [1972] Finance Director; Hamish Stewart Paton [1976] Director

CB Equity LLP
Incorporated: 5 January 2010
Net Worth: £2,114,017,408 *Total Assets:* £2,114,128,512
Registered Office: 1 Princeton Mews, 167-169 London Road, Kingston upon Thames, Surrey, KT2 6PT

CBee (Europe) Limited
Incorporated: 23 January 2007 *Employees:* 44
Net Worth: £2,539,023 *Total Assets:* £12,713,475
Registered Office: Eton House, 18-24 Paradise Road, Richmond, Surrey, TW9 1SE
Activities: Wholesale of china and glassware and cleaning materials
Parent: Burt's Bees International Holdings, Inc
Officers: Charlotte Marie Bailey, Secretary; Todd Lawrence Brock [1966] Director/VP/General Manager [American]; Ajaz Ahmad Khan [1962] Director/General Manager; Giles Addis Malone [1966] Director/Accountant [Irish]

CCEP Holdings UK Limited
Incorporated: 13 May 2016
Net Worth: £8,683,429,888 *Total Assets:* £8,796,600,320
Registered Office: Pemberton House, Bakers Road, Uxbridge, Middlesex, UB8 1EZ
Activities: Activities of other holding companies n.e.c.
Parent: Coca-Cola European Partners PLC
Officers: Paul Van Reesch, Secretary; Frank Govaerts [1961] Director [Belgian]; Paul Van Reesch [1976] Director; Edward Owen Walker [1967] Director

CDB (U.K.) Limited
Incorporated: 8 December 1983
Net Worth: £29,797,000 *Total Assets:* £30,763,000
Registered Office: c/o Hold Store Limited, Unit 33a Enterprise House, 44-46 Terrace Road, Walton on Thames, Surrey, KT12 2SD
Activities: Activities of financial services holding companies
Parent: Irish Government (Minister for Finance)
Officers: James Ednie Brydie [1959] Director/Banker; Robert Dix [1953] Director [Irish]

CDK U.K. Limited
Incorporated: 5 August 1988
Net Worth: £77,989,000 *Total Assets:* £78,097,000
Registered Office: Building 9, Croxley Park, Hatters Lane, Watford, Herts, WD18 8WW
Activities: Activities of head offices
Officers: Joanne Pascucci, Secretary; Oliver Ellis [1972] Sales & Marketing Director; Mark Justin Elsey [1967] Finance Director; Jacqueline Fielding [1964] Vice President (Director)

CEB Global Holdings Limited
Incorporated: 8 September 2015
Net Worth: £309,825,984 *Total Assets:* £309,841,984
Registered Office: Tamesis, The Glanty, Egham, Surrey, TW20 9AH
Activities: Activities of other holding companies n.e.c.
Parent: CEB Holdings UK 1 Limited
Officers: William Joseph Dorgan [1967] Director/GVP Legal Operations [American]; Craig Safian [1969] Director [American]

CEB Global Limited
Incorporated: 1 October 2003 *Employees:* 371
Previous: The Corporate Executive Board Company (UK) Ltd.
Net Worth: £6,544,000 *Total Assets:* £119,790,000
Registered Office: Tamesis, The Glanty, Egham, Surrey, TW20 9AH
Activities: Other information service activities n.e.c.
Parent: Gartner U.K. Limited
Officers: William Joseph Dorgan [1967] Director/Group Vice President of Legal Operations [American]; Craig Warren Safian [1969] Director/CFO, Chief Operations [American]

CEB Holdings UK 1 Limited
Incorporated: 26 July 2012
Net Worth: £61,109,000 *Total Assets:* £349,908,000
Registered Office: Tamesis, The Glanty, Egham, Surrey, TW20 9AH
Activities: Management consultancy activities other than financial management
Parent: CEB Inc.
Officers: William Joseph Dorgan [1967] Director/Group Vice President of Legal Operations [American]; Craig Warren Safian [1969] Director/CFO, Financial Operations [American]

CEB Holdings UK 2 Limited
Incorporated: 27 July 2012
Net Worth: £472,687,008 *Total Assets:* £472,727,008
Registered Office: Tamesis, The Glanty, Egham, Surrey, TW20 9AH
Activities: Management consultancy activities other than financial management
Parent: CEB Global Holdings Limited
Officers: William Joseph Dorgan [1967] Director/Global Vice President of Legal Operations [American]; Craig Warren Safian [1969] Director/CFO Financial Operations [American]

CED Limited
Incorporated: 3 April 1959 *Employees:* 111
Net Worth: £2,532,364 *Total Assets:* £11,415,241
Registered Office: 728 London Road, West Thurrock, Grays, Essex, RM20 3LU
Activities: Agents involved in the sale of timber and building materials
Major Shareholder: Michael Elliott Walley Heap
Officers: Richard Robert Davies, Secretary; Ian John Burridge [1970] Director; Richard Robert Davies [1950] Director; Gary Ewing [1965] Director/Manager; Calum Stuart Fraser [1961] Director/Manager; Giles Elliott James Walley Heap [1972] Director; Michael Elliott Walley Heap [1946] Director; Patrick Robert Courtney Parker [1942] Director; Antony Richard Spink [1970] Director/Company Accountant; Howard White [1964] Director/Operations Manager

Cedars Village Limited
Incorporated: 20 June 1994 *Employees:* 3
Net Worth: £11,502,389 *Total Assets:* £14,558,763
Registered Office: 1st Floor, Brunswick House, Regent Park, 297-299 Kingston Road, Leatherhead, Surrey, KT22 7LU
Activities: Other service activities n.e.c.
Parent: Retirement Villages Management Limited
Officers: Sally Irene Rees, Secretary; Sarah Denise Burgess [1971] Director; Neil Donaldson [1966] Director/Accountant; Andrew George Esmond Ovey [1971] Director/Investment Manager

Ceesail Limited
Incorporated: 22 January 2003
Net Worth: £1,345,713,024 *Total Assets:* £1,354,002,944
Registered Office: 1st Floor, Ash House, Littleton Road, Ashford, Middlesex, TW15 1TZ
Activities: Activities of head offices
Parent: Beesail Limited
Officers: Lynne Banis, Secretary; Christian Bruno Jean Idczak [1963] Director/Business Executive [French]; James Terence George Laurence [1964] Financial Director; Patricia Catherine Moran [1964] Finance Director [American]; Louise Kay Thompson [1983] Director/Chartered Management Accountant

Cegal Limited
Incorporated: 14 November 2007 *Employees:* 40
Previous: Blueback Reservoir Limited
Net Worth: £3,618,962 *Total Assets:* £5,198,228
Registered Office: Two Furlongs, Portsmouth Road, Esher, Surrey, KT10 9AA
Activities: Other business support service activities n.e.c.
Parent: Cegal Geoscience AS
Officers: Anny Erfjord, Secretary; Jan Egil Fivelstad [1970] Managing Director [Norwegian]; Mitchell William Sutherland [1968] Director/Manager

CeleritiFinTech Limited
Incorporated: 8 July 2015
Net Worth: £36,475,000 *Total Assets:* £45,320,000
Registered Office: Axon Centre, Church Road, Egham, Surrey, TW20 9QB
Activities: Information technology consultancy activities
Shareholders: Computer Sciences Corporation; HCL Technologies UK Limited
Officers: Prateek Aggarwal [1967] Director [Indian]; Joanne Mason [1967] Director/Service; Sunil Sharma [1966] Director; Rahul Singh [1963] Director [Indian]; Shiv Kumar Walia [1969] Director/Service [Australian]

Celgene Europe Limited
Incorporated: 13 February 2002 *Employees:* 102
Net Worth: £57,526,308 *Total Assets:* £69,875,936
Registered Office: 1 Longwalk Road, Stockley Park, Uxbridge, Middlesex, UB11 1DB
Activities: Other research and experimental development on natural sciences and engineering
Parent: Celgene Corporation
Officers: Jonathan Prim Biller [1963] Director [American]; Jurg Oehen [1966] Director [Swiss]; Tuomo Tapani Patsi [1964] Director [Finnish]; Anne Patricia Janine Pellier [1956] Director [French]; Nakisa Serry [1965] Director [American]

Celgene Limited
Incorporated: 2 June 2005 *Employees:* 152
Net Worth: £83,576,944 *Total Assets:* £190,243,632
Registered Office: 1 Longwalk Road, Stockley Park, Uxbridge, Middlesex, UB11 1DB
Activities: Wholesale of pharmaceutical goods
Parent: Celgene UK Manufacturing (II) Limited
Officers: Jonathan Prim Biller [1963] Director [American]; Remo Gujer [1973] Director [Swiss]; Jurg Oehen [1966] Director [Swiss]; Tuomo Tapani Patsi [1964] Director [Finnish]; Nakisa Serry [1965] Director [American]

Cellarmaster Wines Holdings (UK) Limited
Incorporated: 29 January 1968
Net Worth: £29,715,000 *Total Assets:* £29,715,000
Registered Office: 9th Floor, Regal House, 70 London Road, Twickenham, Middlesex, TW1 3QS
Activities: Manufacture of wine from grape
Officers: Michelle Elizabeth Brampton [1972] Finance Director; Richard John Renwick [1969] Director/Chief Financial Officer Europe

Cellecta Limited
Incorporated: 14 May 2001 *Employees:* 46
Net Worth: £8,735,299 *Total Assets:* £9,897,978
Registered Office: c/o Myrus Smith, Norman House, 8 Burnell Road, Sutton, Surrey, SM1 4BW
Activities: Other construction installation
Major Shareholder: Andrew William Fry
Officers: Andrew William Fry [1967] Director/Construction Sales

Cellxion Ltd
Incorporated: 29 May 2003 *Employees:* 15
Net Worth: £14,655,038 *Total Assets:* £23,014,504
Registered Office: Hallmark House, 2 Timber Hill Road, Caterham, Surrey, CR3 6LD
Activities: Wireless telecommunications activities
Shareholders: Anthony Richard Timson; Mark William Brumpton
Officers: Tobias Mark Brumpton, Secretary; Mark Brumpton [1957] Director/Telecommunications; Paul Moore [1969] Director; Anthony Richard Timson [1968] Director

Celtic Contractors Limited
Incorporated: 18 October 1995 *Employees:* 27
Net Worth: £4,032,765 *Total Assets:* £9,487,491
Registered Office: Celtic House, 167 Garth Road, Morden, Surrey, SM4 4LF
Activities: Other construction installation
Major Shareholder: John Whyte
Officers: Sinead Kelly Theresa Malik, Secretary; Mark Avis [1979] Contracts Director; Martin John Brennan [1962] Director [Irish]; Martin John Stripe [1970] Contracts Director; John Whyte [1955] Director/Building Contractor [Irish]; Jon Christopher Whyte [1982] Director/Manager

Cembrit Limited
Incorporated: 4 December 1985 *Employees:* 54
Net Worth: £3,275,621 *Total Assets:* £12,006,806
Registered Office: Studio 39, Thames Innovation Centre, 2 Veridion Way, Erith, Kent, DA18 4AL
Activities: Wholesale of wood, construction materials and sanitary equipment
Parent: Cembrit Holding AS
Officers: Oleg Stukalov-Stone, Secretary; Karsten Riis Anderson [1970] Director/CFO of Cembrit Group A/S [Danish]; Philip Geoffrey Archer [1953] Sales Director; Thomas Heldgaard [1969] Managing Director [Danish]; Jorn Morkeberg Nielsen [1961] Director/CEO of Cembrit Group A/S [Danish]

Cementation Skanska Limited
Incorporated: 21 August 1968 *Employees:* 378
Net Worth: £25,968,000 *Total Assets:* £52,347,000
Registered Office: Maple Cross House, Denham Way, Maple Cross, Rickmansworth, Herts, WD3 9SW
Activities: Construction of commercial buildings
Parent: Skanska Construction UK Limited
Officers: Steven Leven, Secretary; James Maxwell Dunbar [1964] Director; Dr Jonathan David Morris [1973] Director

Centaur Property Estates Limited
Incorporated: 22 April 1981
Net Worth: £5,245,118 *Total Assets:* £9,934,622
Registered Office: 20 Park Avenue, Farnborough, Orpington, Kent, BR6 8LL
Activities: Other letting and operating of own or leased real estate
Officers: Alan Geoffrey Fernback [1947] Director

Centaur Property Group Limited
Incorporated: 21 January 1997
Net Worth: £1,090,171 *Total Assets:* £8,245,862
Registered Office: 20 Park Avenue, Farnborough, Orpington, Kent, BR6 8LL
Activities: Other letting and operating of own or leased real estate
Officers: Alan Geoffrey Fernback [1947] Director

Central Developments (UK) Limited
Incorporated: 19 March 2001 *Employees:* 3
Net Worth: £2,715,733 *Total Assets:* £9,892,160
Registered Office: 20 Greenhill Park, New Barnet, Barnet, Herts, EN5 1HP
Activities: Development of building projects
Shareholders: John Andreou Papadouris; Servas Developments Ltd
Officers: Joseph Servas, Secretary; John Andrea Papadouris [1945] Director/Civil Engineer; Joseph Servas [1941] Director/Civil Engineer; Stavros Servas [1981] Director/Office Administrator

Central Nottinghamshire Hospitals (Holdings) Limited
Incorporated: 19 May 2005
Net Worth Deficit: £129,000 *Total Assets:* £391,337,984
Registered Office: 8 White Oak Square, London Road, Swanley, Kent, BR8 7AG
Activities: Activities of other holding companies n.e.c.
Shareholders: Innisfree Secondary Partners 1 LLP; Innisfree Secondary Partners 2 LLP
Officers: Gaynor Birley Smith [1966] Investment Director; Sabrina Sidhu [1979] Investment Director; Benjamin Michael Watson [1985] Director/Portfolio Manager

Central Nottinghamshire Hospitals PLC
Incorporated: 25 May 2005
Net Worth Deficit: £129,000 *Total Assets:* £391,337,984
Registered Office: 8 White Oak Square, London Road, Swanley, Kent, BR8 7AG
Activities: Hospital activities
Parent: Central Nottinghamshire Hospitals (Holdings) Limited
Officers: Gaynor Birley Smith [1966] Investment Director; Michael Davis [1946] Director; Sabrina Sidhu [1979] Investment Director; Benjamin Michael Watson [1985] Director/Portfolio Manager

Central Office and Commercial Properties Limited
Incorporated: 26 September 1973
Net Worth: £4,277,888 *Total Assets:* £5,255,481
Registered Office: c/o Parker Cavendish, 28 Church Road, Stanmore, Middlesex, HA7 4XR
Activities: Development of building projects
Parent: Sandringham Investments Limited
Officers: Zalina Dewan, Secretary; Ramesh Dewan [1947] Director/Publisher; Sheena Selina Dewan [1973] Director

Central Property Investments Limited
Incorporated: 29 September 1987 *Employees:* 7
Net Worth: £9,386,067 *Total Assets:* £15,641,023
Registered Office: Northside House, Mount Pleasant, Barnet, Herts, EN4 9EE
Activities: Other letting and operating of own or leased real estate
Shareholders: Michael Christopher Moniatis; Nicos Christopher Moniatis
Officers: Louise Anne Moniatis [1981] Director; Michael Christopher Moniatis [1950] Director; Nicos Christopher Moniatis [1952] Director

Central Surrey Health Limited
Incorporated: 7 February 2006 *Employees:* 1,681
Net Worth: £2,229,762 *Total Assets:* £12,765,501
Registered Office: Ewell Court Clinic, Ewell Court Avenue, Ewell, Epsom, Surrey, KT19 0DZ
Activities: Hospital activities
Officers: William Frederick Caplan [1958] Director; Clinton Edwin Everard [1961] Director; Stephen David Flanagan [1960] Director; Peter James Lock [1980] Director; Dr Caroline Mary Shuldham [1953] Director/Nurse

Centre for Engineering and Manufacturing Excellence Ltd
Incorporated: 21 June 2001 *Employees:* 23
Net Worth: £24,749,272 *Total Assets:* £27,218,968
Registered Office: CEME Campus, Marsh Way, Rainham, Essex, RM13 8EU
Activities: Other letting and operating of own or leased real estate
Officers: Harjeet Singh Sadheura, Secretary; Judith Jane Armitt [1953] Director/Civil Servant; Martin Tilston Broadhurst [1953] Director; Dr Keyvan Mehdi Djamarani [1961] Director/General Manager; Rachel Hadley [1975] Director/HR Manager; Yvonne Kelly [1964] Director/Principal & CEO; Findlay Cameron MacAlpine [1964] Director/Chartered Surveyor; Barak Maoz [1957] Director/Management Consultant; Geoffrey Simon Richman [1966] Director/Finance Manager Ford Motor Co; Harjeet Singh Sadheura [1959] Director/Chief Financial Officer; Mark Peter Williams [1964] Director/Chief Executive

Centro Group Limited
Incorporated: 29 October 1991 *Employees:* 3
Net Worth: £5,472,986 *Total Assets:* £6,959,212
Registered Office: Mid-Day Court, 30 Brighton Road, Sutton, Surrey, SM2 5BN
Activities: Development of building projects
Officers: M/S Doreen Evelyn Walker, Secretary; Paul Raymond Harwood [1965] Director/Commercial Surveyor; Raymond Philip Harwood [1939] Director/Chartered Surveyor; Paul MacAinsh [1980] Director of Property Management; M/S Doreen Evelyn Walker [1937] Director

Centro PLC
Incorporated: 17 June 1988 *Employees:* 54
Net Worth: £7,362,158 *Total Assets:* £12,593,508
Registered Office: Mid-Day Court, 30 Brighton Road, Sutton, Surrey, SM2 5BN
Activities: Other business support service activities n.e.c.
Officers: M/S Doreen Evelyn Walker, Secretary; Paul Raymond Harwood [1965] Director; Raymond Philip Harwood [1939] Director/Chartered Surveyor; Paul MacAinsh [1980] Director of Property Management; M/S Doreen Evelyn Walker [1937] Director/Company Secretary

Centronic Limited
Incorporated: 22 June 1949 *Employees:* 117
Net Worth: £7,045,968 *Total Assets:* £8,155,625
Registered Office: Centronic House, King Henry's Drive, New Addington, Croydon, Surrey, CR9 0BG
Activities: Manufacture of electronic components
Parent: Centronic Holdings Limited
Officers: Neil Charles Foreman [1961] Director; Dr Robert David McKeag [1971] Director/Engineer; Stephen Sawle [1963] Operations Director

Ceragon (UK) Limited
Incorporated: 31 December 2010
Net Worth: £15,776,645 *Total Assets:* £15,776,645
Registered Office: Egale 1, 80 St Albans Road, Watford, Herts, WD17 1DL
Activities: Non-trading company
Parent: Ceragon Networks (UK) Limited
Officers: Doron Ovadia Arazi [1963] Director/Deputy CEO & CFO [Israeli]; Ira Palti [1957] Director/CEO & President [Israeli]

Cerestar UK Ltd
Incorporated: 22 June 1987
Net Worth: £53,920,024 *Total Assets:* £54,078,356
Registered Office: Velocity V1, Brooklands Drive, Weybridge, Surrey, KT13 0SL
Activities: Non-trading company
Officers: Dena Michelle L O'Bue, Secretary; Stephen James Hamilton [1969] Director/Country Tax Manager UK & Ireland; Michael James Timewell [1974] Director/Solicitor

Cergold Limited
Incorporated: 2 April 2013
Net Worth: £8,888,329 *Total Assets:* £93,224,952
Registered Office: Hill House, Lowlands Road, Harrow, Middlesex, HA1 3EQ
Activities: Buying and selling of own real estate
Major Shareholder: Donovan Gijsbertus Wijsmuller
Officers: Brian Martin Comer [1960] Director [Irish]; Luke Andrew Comer [1957] Director [Irish]

Ceros (Bradford) Limited
Incorporated: 18 October 2001 *Employees:* 1
Net Worth: £10,464,082 *Total Assets:* £17,794,986
Registered Office: Munro House, Portsmouth Road, Cobham, Surrey, KT11 1PP
Activities: Development of building projects
Parent: Ceros No 1 Ltd
Officers: Christopher Roupell [1957] Director/Estate Agent

Ceros No.1 Limited
Incorporated: 10 June 2004 *Employees:* 1
Net Worth Deficit: £19,277,620 *Total Assets:* £9,950,112
Registered Office: Munro House, Portsmouth Road, Cobham, Surrey, KT11 1PP
Activities: Other business support service activities n.e.c.
Major Shareholder: Christopher Roupell
Officers: Christopher Roupell [1957] Director/Estate Agent

CFS-Zipp Limited
Incorporated: 14 February 2000
Net Worth: £4,778,315 *Total Assets:* £7,142,722
Registered Office: 790 Uxbridge Road, Hayes, Middlesex, UB4 0RS
Activities: Financial intermediation not elsewhere classified
Parent: St.Georges BK Ltd
Officers: Uma Venkatesh, Secretary; Robert Edmund Courtneidge [1964] Director; Srinivasan Venkatesh [1953] Director; Uma Venkatesh [1957] Director

Chadwell Heath Academy
Incorporated: 16 August 2010 *Employees:* 135
Net Worth: £18,014,352 *Total Assets:* £18,834,648
Registered Office: Christie Gardens, Chadwell Heath, Romford, Essex, RM6 4RS
Activities: General secondary education
Officers: Norman Ernest Abbott [1936] Director; Teresa Ann Banks [1958] Director/School Manager; Peter Michael Brewster [1951] Director/Civil Engineer; Stephen Nicholas Bull [1957] Director/Headmaster; Farzana Chowdhury [1976] Director/Solicitor; Abdus Samad Hamid [1973] Director/Network Security Analyst; Nicola Dionne Merry [1972] Director/Production Manager; Yasmeen Sattar [1980] Director/Secretary; Dhirajlal Velji Shah [1951] Director/Business Owner (Retail); Paul Southcott [1958] Director/Design Technology Technician; Philip Terry [1954] Director/Clerical Officer; Keith Edward Wilkinson [1947] Director/Retired

Chai-Lifeline Cancer Care
Incorporated: 24 September 1998 *Employees:* 25
Net Worth: £8,954,543 *Total Assets:* £9,185,151
Registered Office: York House, Empire Way, Wembley, Middlesex, HA9 0FQ
Activities: Other human health activities
Officers: Louise Hager [1955] Director; Jonathan Andrew Hodes [1968] Director/Chartered Accountant and Chartered Tax Adviser; Lady Pamela Audrey Kalms [1931] Director; Richard Lawrence Segal [1963] Director/Company Chairman; Susan Lesley Shipman [1948] Director; Dr Adrian Tookman [1953] Director/Doctor of Medicine; Philip David Weinstein [1953] Director; Lord Lord of Graffham David Young [1932] Director

Chainkey Limited
Incorporated: 6 January 2004
Net Worth: £1,684,264 *Total Assets:* £5,197,000
Registered Office: 4th Floor, Amba House, 15 College Road, Harrow, Middlesex, HA1 1BA
Activities: Other letting and operating of own or leased real estate
Shareholders: Ajay Kumar Gokani; Ketan Chandulal Gokani
Officers: Ajay Kumar Gokani, Secretary; Ajay Kumar Gokani [1965] Director; Ketan Chandulal Gokani [1974] Sales Director

Chalfont Coaches of Harrow Limited
Incorporated: 31 December 1971 *Employees:* 85
Net Worth: £2,769,838 *Total Assets:* £6,757,950
Registered Office: 200 Featherstone Road, Southall, Middlesex, UB2 5AQ
Activities: Other passenger land transport
Major Shareholder: Christopher James Shears
Officers: Gill Shears, Secretary; Christopher James Shears [1946] Director/Executive; Ivan Christopher Shears [1974] Director; Mark James Shears [1975] Director/MOT Tester; Vera June Stevens [1977] Director/Manager

Chalford Property Company Limited
Incorporated: 26 January 1994 *Employees:* 2
Net Worth: £5,932,115 *Total Assets:* £6,829,758
Registered Office: 2 Castle Business Village, Station Road, Hampton, Surrey, TW12 2BX
Activities: Buying and selling of own real estate
Parent: Ember Estates Limited
Officers: Martyn Hickman, Secretary/Property Director; James Martyn Hickman [1970] Director/Accountant; Martyn Hickman [1944] Property Director; Vivienne Marie Hickman [1945] Director/Housewife

Chalk Farm Marine LLP
Incorporated: 10 February 2017
Net Worth: £4,745,914 *Total Assets:* £13,372,217
Registered Office: Grenville House, 4 Grenville Avenue, Broxbourne, Herts, EN10 7DH

Champ Cargosystems (UK) Limited
Incorporated: 18 October 2004 *Employees:* 110
Net Worth: £6,991,237 *Total Assets:* £21,093,604
Registered Office: The Old Vinyl Factory, 252-254 Blyth Road, Hayes, Middlesex, UB3 1HA
Activities: Other information technology service activities
Parent: Champ Cargosystems SA
Officers: Alain Brodeur, Secretary; Lee Booth [1962] Director/Vice President Global Products; Gabriel Florea [1975] Director/Chief Financial Officer [Belgian]; Arnaud Lambert [1968] Managing Director [Belgian]

A.W.Champion Limited
Incorporated: 26 February 1953 *Employees:* 218
Net Worth: £9,477,899 *Total Assets:* £13,022,001
Registered Office: Champion House, Burlington Road, New Malden, Surrey, KT3 4NB
Activities: Wholesale of wood, construction materials and sanitary equipment
Parent: A W Champion Timber Limited
Officers: Stephen Patrick Bowden, Secretary; Phillip William Aron Champion [1952] Director/Timber Merchant; Steven Bernard Lewis Lister [1954] Director/Business Consultant; Martin Edward Saunders [1951] Director/Yard Manager

A.W. Champion Properties Limited
Incorporated: 30 July 2003 *Employees:* 4
Net Worth: £8,251,403 *Total Assets:* £8,563,204
Registered Office: Champion House, Burlington Road, New Malden, Surrey, KT3 4NB
Activities: Other letting and operating of own or leased real estate
Shareholders: Philip William Aron Champion; John Spencer McCuin; William Frank Clifton Simmonds
Officers: Stephen Patrick Bowden, Secretary; Phillip William Aron Champion [1952] Director/Timber Merchant; Steven Bernard Lewis Lister [1954] Director/Business Consultant

A.W. Champion Timber Limited
Incorporated: 24 July 2003 *Employees:* 218
Net Worth: £9,478,225 *Total Assets:* £13,022,213
Registered Office: Champion House, Burlington Road, New Malden, Surrey, KT3 4NB
Activities: Wholesale of wood, construction materials and sanitary equipment
Major Shareholder: Philip William Aron Champion
Officers: Stephen Patrick Bowden, Secretary; Phillip William Aron Champion [1952] Director/Timber Merchant; Steven Bernard Lewis Lister [1954] Director/Business Consultant; Martin Edward Saunders [1951] Director/Yard Manager

Chancery Education Trust
Incorporated: 15 June 2011 *Employees:* 126
Previous: Pickhurst Junior School
Net Worth: £15,014,000 *Total Assets:* £17,303,000
Registered Office: Pickhurst Junior School, Pickhurst Lane, West Wickham, Kent, BR4 0HL
Activities: Primary education
Officers: Stephen Generald Hills [1959] Director/Financial Services; Philip Jefferies [1978] Director/University Lecturer; Shelley Muscatt [1962] Director/Office Manager; Marie Powell [1959] Director/Executive Leader Chief Technology Officer; Matthew Peter Rampton [1967] Director/Headteacher

Channeladvisor UK Limited
Incorporated: 25 November 2004 *Employees:* 96
Net Worth Deficit: £12,478,205 *Total Assets:* £12,609,516
Registered Office: 400 Dashwood Lang Road, Weybridge, Surrey, KT15 2HJ
Activities: Other information technology service activities
Parent: ChannelAdvisor Europe Limited
Officers: Jon Christian Maury [1969] Director/Executive [British/American]; David John Spitz [1972] Director/Executive [American]

Chantry Securities Limited
Incorporated: 15 July 1999
Net Worth: £1,745,294 *Total Assets:* £5,258,013
Registered Office: 10 Teddington Business Park, Station Road, Teddington, Middlesex, TW11 9BQ
Activities: Development of building projects
Parent: Chantry Securities Holding Company Limited
Officers: Carol Dawn Doble, Secretary; Jeffrey Ian Doble [1959] Director/Estate Agent

Chaptre Finance PLC
Incorporated: 23 December 2015
Net Worth: £50,000 *Total Assets:* £54,245,000
Registered Office: 8 White Oak Square, London Road, Swanley, Kent, BR8 7AG
Activities: Financial intermediation not elsewhere classified
Parent: Chaptre Holdings Limited
Officers: Matthew James Spencer Booth [1971] Director/Investment Banker; Jens Christian Clausen [1948] Director/Consultant [Danish]; Kasper Hansen [1978] Director [Danish]; Andrew Horsley Clifford Hartley [1958] Director; David Jensen [1974] Director/Senior Asset Manager [Danish]

Chaptre Investments Limited
Incorporated: 9 December 2015
Net Worth: £26,230,500 *Total Assets:* £118,546,072
Registered Office: 8 White Oak Square, London Road, Swanley, Kent, BR8 7AG
Activities: Financial intermediation not elsewhere classified
Parent: Chaptre Greenco Limited
Officers: Matthew John Edgar [1985] Director/Senior Vice President [Australian]; Andrew Horsley Clifford Hartley [1958] Managing Director; Adam Cade Nancarrow [1975] Director [Australian]

Charco 2010 Limited
Incorporated: 8 November 2006 *Employees:* 254
Net Worth: £9,669,328 *Total Assets:* £19,325,212
Registered Office: Unit 40 Charles Park, Claire Causeway, Crossways, Dartford, Kent, DA2 6QA
Activities: Non-trading company
Shareholders: Kevin Michael Ohle; Richard Hugh Reynolds
Officers: Richard Hugh Reynolds, Secretary; Fredrik Ulf Cappelen [1957] Director [Swedish]; Kevin Ohle [1957] Director [Irish]; George William Hugo Reynolds [1986] Director/Commercial Manager; Richard Hugh Reynolds [1955] Director

Chard Properties (UK) Limited
Incorporated: 20 May 2005 *Employees:* 10
Net Worth: £5,584,038 *Total Assets:* £8,280,931
Registered Office: 35a High Street, Ruislip, Middlesex, HA4 7AU
Activities: Retail of furniture, lighting, and similar (not musical instruments or scores) in specialised store
Shareholders: Amarjit Singh Chard; Narinder Kaur Chard
Officers: Balraj Chard, Secretary; Amarjit Singh Chard [1949] Director [Indian]; Narinder Kaur Chard [1948] Director

The Charles Kalms, Henry Ronson Immanuel College
Incorporated: 12 April 1990 *Employees:* 157
Net Worth: £6,817,146 *Total Assets:* £11,606,515
Registered Office: 87-91 Elstree Road, Bushey, Herts, WD23 4EB
Activities: Primary education
Officers: Antony Berkin, Secretary; Dr Daphna Regina Atar [1972] Director/Scientist [British/Swiss]; Keith Philip Barnett [1961] Director/Solicitor; Hannah Ruth Boyden [1977] Director; Lynda Gail Dullop [1962] Director; Valerie Helen Eppel [1968] Director/Chartered Accountant; Annette Hilary Deborah Koslover [1964] Director/Solicitor; Erica Marks [1964] Operations Director; Lucy Gabrielle Marks [1971] Director/Solicitor; Neal Menashe [1972] Director [Italian]; Edward Misrahi [1969] Director/Fund Management; Michelle Laura Sint [1965] Director/Teacher; Professor Anthony Nigel Warrens [1959] Director/University Professor; Eliezer Zobin [1975] Director/Rabbi

Charlie Properties Limited
Incorporated: 1 October 1982 *Employees:* 4
Net Worth: £9,901,579 *Total Assets:* £11,733,035
Registered Office: Old Station Road, Loughton, Essex, IG10 4PL
Activities: Development of building projects
Officers: Christina Hilliard, Secretary; Philipos Andrea [1967] Director/Solicitor; Christina Hilliard [1962] Director/Company Secretary; Laura McManus Andrea [1969] Director

Chart Forte Holdings Ltd
Incorporated: 14 June 2011
Net Worth: £5,937,296 *Total Assets:* £10,022,515
Registered Office: Cervantes House, 5-9 Headstone Road, Harrow, Middlesex, HA1 1PD
Activities: Other service activities n.e.c.
Shareholders: Jalaluddin Kajani; Mawash Kajani
Officers: Mawash Kajani, Secretary; Jalaluddin Kajani [1957] Director [Irish]; Mawash Kajani [1966] Director [Irish]

Chartco Limited
Incorporated: 14 October 1998 *Employees:* 130
Net Worth: £18,133,000 *Total Assets:* £30,067,000
Registered Office: Unit 4 Voltage, Mollison Avenue, Enfield, Middlesex, EN3 7XQ
Activities: Non-specialised wholesale trade
Parent: Ensign Holdco 4 Limited
Officers: Sukhjeevan Singh Samra [1976] Finance Director; Martin Stuart Taylor [1967] Director, KH Charts

Charter Court (New Malden) Limited
Incorporated: 30 January 2015
Net Worth: £95,028 *Total Assets:* £19,297,172
Registered Office: Crown House Mews, Chequers Lane, Walton on the Hill, Tadworth, Surrey, KT20 7ST
Activities: Other letting and operating of own or leased real estate
Parent: Woodgavil Ltd
Officers: David Mark Pay, Secretary; Martin James Morris [1963] Director

Charter UK Limited
Incorporated: 19 December 1989 *Employees:* 26
Net Worth: £6,312,000 *Total Assets:* £10,719,000
Registered Office: Elder House, St Georges Business Park, Brooklands Road, Weybridge, Surrey, KT13 0TS
Activities: Information technology consultancy activities
Parent: Invigia Limited
Officers: Katherine Cong, Secretary; Seema Sangar [1976] Finance Director; John Stier [1966] Director/Chief Financial Officer

Charterhouse Ilford Limited
Incorporated: 13 June 2014 *Employees:* 1
Net Worth: £3,830,897 *Total Assets:* £5,463,553
Registered Office: 166 College Road, Harrow, Middlesex, HA1 1RA
Activities: Development of building projects
Parent: Estates and Lets 2 LLP
Officers: Mr. Michael Spencer Docker [1963] Director

Charterhouse Simon Limited
Incorporated: 12 September 1973 *Employees:* 2
Net Worth: £14,463,325 *Total Assets:* £17,854,982
Registered Office: 52 Alston Road, Barnet, Herts, EN5 4EY
Activities: Other letting and operating of own or leased real estate
Major Shareholder: Richard Stephen Leslie
Officers: Kim Mulvey, Secretary; Claudia Ruth Leslie [1955] Director/Consultant; Richard Stephen Leslie [1943] Director/Chartered Accountant

Charteroak Estates Limited
Incorporated: 7 January 2005 *Employees:* 10
Net Worth Deficit: £2,310,449 *Total Assets:* £5,068,947
Registered Office: Graham House, 7 Wyllyotts Place, Potters Bar, Herts, EN6 2JD
Activities: Construction of other civil engineering projects n.e.c.
Parent: RO Group Property Ventures Limited
Officers: Edward Thomas Morton Rowlandson [1974] Director; Richard Woodman-Bailey [1950] Director

M & J Charters LLP
Incorporated: 23 March 2005 *Employees:* 2
Net Worth: £7,600,000 *Total Assets:* £10,951,856
Registered Office: Watergate, Broxhill Road, Havering-Atte-Bower, Romford, Essex, RM4 1QH
Officers: Lawrence Jefferson Gilbert [1948] Member; Richard Henry Maskell [1943] Member

Charters Village Limited
Incorporated: 29 June 2011 *Employees:* 93
Net Worth: £4,116,169 *Total Assets:* £19,463,878
Registered Office: 1st Floor, Brunswick House, Regent Park, 297-299 Kingston Road, Leatherhead, Surrey, KT22 7LU
Activities: Other service activities n.e.c.
Parent: Retirement Villages Group Limited
Officers: Sally Irene Rees, Secretary; Sarah Denise Burgess [1971] Director; William Edwin John Crawford [1970] Director/Development; Neil Donaldson [1966] Director/Accountant; Andrew George Esmond Ovey [1971] Director/Investment Manager

Chasemore Farm LLP
Incorporated: 18 April 2012 *Employees:* 27
Net Worth: £23,487,880 *Total Assets:* £23,888,516
Registered Office: Chasemore Farm, Bookham Road, Downside, Surrey, KT11 3JT
Officers: Andrew Wilson Black [1963] Member; Jane Elizabeth Black [1966] Member

Chawla & Gulati Property Investments Limited
Incorporated: 2 April 2012
Net Worth: £470,766 *Total Assets:* £5,441,921
Registered Office: First Floor, 10 College Road, Harrow, Middlesex, HA1 1BE
Activities: Other service activities n.e.c.
Officers: Ajit Singh Chawla [1975] Director; Kulwant Singh Gulati [1966] Director

Chawla's Limited
Incorporated: 2 July 2002
Net Worth: £2,495,388 *Total Assets:* £7,611,808
Registered Office: 249 Bath Road, Hounslow, Middlesex, TW3 3DA
Activities: Real estate agencies
Officers: Raminder Singh Chawla, Secretary/Manager; Parmesh Kaur Chawla [1937] Director/Self Employed; Raminder Singh Chawla [1976] Director/Manager; Surinder Singh Chawla [1961] Director/Self Employed

Cheam Academies Network
Incorporated: 1 April 2011 *Employees:* 246
Previous: Cheam High School
Net Worth: £8,503,000 *Total Assets:* £12,640,000
Registered Office: Cheam High School, Chatsworth Road, Cheam, Surrey, SM3 8PW
Activities: General secondary education
Officers: Susan Elizabeth Norton, Secretary; Rebecca Joyce Allott [1962] Director/Headteacher; Richard Alan Beer [1967] Finance Director; Jane Susan Etheridge [1961] Director; Brian Peter Forsyth Goldie [1947] Director/Consultant; Susan Mary Lyden [1959] Director/HR Consultant; Peter Charles Naudi [1970] Director/Headteacher; Barbara Kathleen Rayment [1953] Director/Charity CEO; Dr Rosemary Sally Satchell [1935] Director

Chellbrook Properties Limited
Incorporated: 1 February 1988 *Employees:* 6
Previous: Chellbrook Properties PLC
Net Worth: £4,818,088 *Total Assets:* £9,386,257
Registered Office: 16 St Philips Road, Surbiton, Surrey, KT6 4DX
Activities: Other letting and operating of own or leased real estate
Shareholder: Timothy Rupert Ward
Officers: Timothy Rupert Ward, Secretary; David Gibson [1947] Director; Haydn Ward [1934] Director/Property Manager & Owner; Janet Gwendoline Ward [1937] Director/Property Manager & Owner; Timothy Rupert Ward [1963] Director/Property Owner & Manager

Chelmer Foods Limited
Incorporated: 6 April 1992 *Employees:* 21
Net Worth: £18,153,100 *Total Assets:* £23,947,330
Registered Office: 1st Floor, Upminster Library, 26 Corbets Tey Road, Upminster, Essex, RM14 2BB
Activities: Other processing and preserving of fruit and vegetables
Major Shareholder: Roger Arthur Weaire
Officers: Paul William Pleasant, Secretary; Simon John Heather [1986] Sales Director; Paul William Pleasant [1979] Financial Director; Anthony Julian Smith [1965] Director; James Weaire [1978] Director/Manager; Roger Arthur Weaire [1945] Director; Christopher Edward Wilding [1986] Sales Director

Chelsea Stores Holdings Limited
Incorporated: 11 March 2004
Net Worth Deficit: £24,500,000 *Total Assets:* £13,900,000
Registered Office: Cherry Tree Road, Watford, Herts, WD24 6SH
Activities: Activities of head offices
Parent: Mothercare PLC
Officers: Lynne Samatha Medini, Secretary; Kirsty Rowena Homer [1974] HR Director; Daniel Juckes [1982] Director/Chartered Accountant

Chem-Dry Franchising Limited
Incorporated: 27 November 1987 *Employees:* 4
Net Worth: £8,770,000 *Total Assets:* £9,731,000
Registered Office: 2 AC Court, High Street, Thames Ditton, Surrey, KT7 0SR
Activities: Other service activities n.e.c.
Parent: Aghoco 1022 Limited
Officers: Alan Albert Horton [1963] Director; Stuart Pace [1962] Director

Chem-Dry U.K. Limited
Incorporated: 9 February 1993 *Employees:* 29
Net Worth: £8,258,000 *Total Assets:* £19,997,000
Registered Office: 2 AC Court, High Street, Thames Ditton, Surrey, KT7 0SR
Activities: General cleaning of buildings
Parent: Aghoco 1022 Limited
Officers: Alan Albert Horton [1963] Director; Stuart Pace [1962] Director

Chemidex Generics Limited
Incorporated: 23 July 1999 *Employees:* 1
Net Worth: £41,655,200 *Total Assets:* £42,801,256
Registered Office: Chemidex House, Unit 7 Egham Business Village, Crabtree Road, Egham, Surrey, TW20 8RB
Activities: Wholesale of pharmaceutical goods
Shareholders: Navinchandra Jamnadas; Varsha Navinchandas Engineer
Officers: Nikesh Engineer [1985] Director/Doctor

Chemidex Pharma Limited
Incorporated: 8 November 1982 *Employees:* 20
Net Worth: £29,905,596 *Total Assets:* £48,929,356
Registered Office: Chemidex House, Unit 7 Egham Business Village, Crabtree Road, Egham, Surrey, TW20 8RB
Activities: Manufacture of basic pharmaceutical products
Shareholders: Navinchandra Jamnadas; Varsha Navinchandra
Officers: Nikesh Engineer [1985] Director/Doctor

Chemilines Group Holdings Limited
Incorporated: 30 November 2001 *Employees:* 113
Net Worth: £18,482,000 *Total Assets:* £24,584,000
Registered Office: Chemilines House, Alperton Lane, Wembley, Middlesex, HA0 1DX
Activities: Wholesale of pharmaceutical goods
Shareholders: Ravindra Prabhudas Karia; Jagdish Prabhudas Karia
Officers: Ravindra Prabhudas Karia, Secretary; Jagdish Prabhudas Karia [1958] Director; Ravindra Prabhudas Karia [1953] Director

Chemilines Limited
Incorporated: 28 July 1987 *Employees:* 84
Net Worth: £6,462,000 *Total Assets:* £10,114,000
Registered Office: Chemilines House, Alperton Lane, Wembley, Middlesex, HA0 1DX
Activities: Wholesale of pharmaceutical goods
Parent: Chemilines Group Holdings Limited
Officers: Ravindra Prabhudas Karia, Secretary; Sadhana Ravindra Karia, Secretary; Jagdish Prabhudas Karia [1958] Director; Ravindra Prabhudas Karia [1953] Director

Chemox Pound Limited
Incorporated: 22 January 1993 *Employees:* 26
Net Worth: £6,148,317 *Total Assets:* £13,944,316
Registered Office: Gladstone House, 77-79 High Street, Egham, Surrey, TW20 9HY
Activities: Non-specialised wholesale trade
Shareholder: Chemox Pound Investment Limited
Officers: David George Barnby, Secretary; David George Barnby [1963] Director/Accountant; Michelle Abina Bourke [1977] Director/Accountant [Irish]; Philip Charles Hinton [1967] Director; Gordon Dominic Victor Pound [1968] Director; Generald William Schell [1968] Director/International Business Manager [South African]; Gavin David Westley [1970] Director

Chep Intercontinental Containers Limited
Incorporated: 16 April 1981 *Employees:* 5
Net Worth: £1,168,526 *Total Assets:* £10,628,068
Registered Office: 2nd Floor, 400 Dashwood Lang Road, Bourne Business Park, Addlestone, Surrey, KT15 2HJ
Activities: Renting and leasing of other machinery, equipment and tangible goods n.e.c.
Parent: Brambles Investment Ltd.
Officers: Daniel Robert Berry [1973] Director/Lawyer; Carla Mae Brocklehurst [1975] Finance Director; Murray Gilder [1978] Director/Vice President Automotive EMEA

CHEP Pallecon Solutions Limited
Incorporated: 4 December 2012 *Employees:* 119
Net Worth: £2,991,387 *Total Assets:* £42,080,944
Registered Office: 2nd Floor, 400 Dashwood Lang Road, Bourne Business Park, Addlestone, Surrey, KT15 2HJ
Activities: Other transportation support activities
Parent: Brambls Holdings (UK) Ltd
Officers: Daniel Robert Berry [1973] Director/Lawyer; Steven John McGhee [1971] Senior Director, Sales and Marketing; Craig Patrick Willmott [1973] Director/Finance Professional [Australian]

Chep UK Limited
Incorporated: 8 May 1924 *Employees:* 906
Net Worth: £87,173,000 *Total Assets:* £223,976,000
Registered Office: 2nd Floor, 400 Dashwood Lang Road, Bourne Business Park, Addlestone, Surrey, KT15 2HJ
Activities: Renting and leasing of other machinery, equipment and tangible goods n.e.c.
Parent: Cyan Logistics Limited
Officers: Maureen Barwell [1968] Human Resources Director; Daniel Robert Berry [1973] Director/Lawyer; Carla Mae Brocklehurst [1975] Finance Director; Helen Victoria Lane [1981] Director/VP Northern Europe

Cherry Advertising Limited
Incorporated: 13 October 2005 *Employees:* 55
Net Worth: £2,780,641 *Total Assets:* £5,756,712
Registered Office: 18 Camden Park Road, Chislehurst, Kent, BR7 5HG
Activities: Advertising agencies
Parent: Madano Partnership Limited
Officers: Valerie Beauregard [1964] Director [Canadian]; John Ralph Goundry [1963] Director/Advertising Consultant; Royal Poulin [1972] Director [Canadian]; Ralph Sutton [1965] Director [Irish]; Jean-Pierre Vasseur [1959] Director [Canadian]

Cherryfield (Croydon) Limited
Incorporated: 19 September 1972 *Employees:* 66
Net Worth: £4,260,502 *Total Assets:* £7,497,352
Registered Office: 44-60 Cherry Orchard Road, East Croydon, Surrey, CR0 6BA
Activities: Wholesale of meat and meat products
Parent: Cherryfield Holdings Limited
Officers: Miles John Rudham [1966] Director/Meat Trader

Cherryfield Holdings Limited
Incorporated: 11 May 2015 *Employees:* 66
Net Worth: £3,195,110 *Total Assets:* £6,869,619
Registered Office: 44-60 Cherry Orchard Road, East Croydon, Surrey, CR0 6BA
Activities: Wholesale of meat and meat products
Major Shareholder: Miles John Rudham
Officers: Miles John Rudham [1966] Director/Meat Trader

Cherubond Limited
Incorporated: 22 January 1981 *Employees:* 5
Net Worth: £6,963,068 *Total Assets:* £9,609,766
Registered Office: 1 Park Road, Hampton Wick, Kingston upon Thames, Surrey, KT1 4AS
Activities: Development of building projects
Shareholder: Andrew Michael
Officers: Rex Valins, Secretary; Andrew Michael [1946] Director/Accountant; Ruth Michael [1949] Director/Secretary

Chesside Homes Limited
Incorporated: 4 June 1996 *Employees:* 2
Net Worth: £4,206,233 *Total Assets:* £9,484,207
Registered Office: Enterprise House, Beesons Yard, Bury Lane, Rickmansworth, Herts, WD3 1DS
Activities: Development of building projects
Shareholders: Edward John Costello; Ann Patricia Costello
Officers: Ann Patricia Costello, Secretary/Director; Ann Patricia Costello [1941] Director; Edward John Costello [1937] Director [Irish]

Chessington Nurseries Holdings Company Limited
Incorporated: 31 March 2017 *Employees:* 178
Net Worth: £6,463,545 *Total Assets:* £9,925,878
Registered Office: Chessington Nurseries Ltd, Leatherhead Road, Chessington, Surrey, KT9 2NG
Activities: Other retail sale in non-specialised stores
Major Shareholder: Jolyon Paul Martin
Officers: Stephen Mark Fleming [1964] Director; Alexander Keith Martin [1941] Director; Jolyon Paul Martin [1971] Director

Chessington Nurseries Limited
Incorporated: 9 August 1973 *Employees:* 178
Net Worth: £6,084,766 *Total Assets:* £9,513,799
Registered Office: Leatherhead Road, Chessington, Surrey, KT9 2NG
Activities: Other retail sale of new goods in specialised stores (not commercial art galleries and opticians)
Parent: Chessington Nurseries Holdings Company Limited
Officers: Stephen Mark Fleming [1964] Financial Director; Timothy John Hickman [1959] Operations Director; Jolyon Paul Martin [1971] Director; Paul Antony Smith [1972] Buying Director; Elaine Joyce Sorensen [1959] Director/Accountant

Chester Greyhound Retail Park LLP
Incorporated: 22 June 2016
Net Worth: £12,659,511 *Total Assets:* £12,659,511
Registered Office: Aprirose House, 48a High Street, Edgware, Middlesex, HA8 7EQ
Officers: Manish Mansukhlal Gudka [1970] Member; Gareth Jones [1973] Member; Suraj Rashmikant Shah [1982] LLP Member

Chester International Hotel Limited
Incorporated: 13 March 1986 *Employees:* 71
Net Worth: £30,993,000 *Total Assets:* £35,808,000
Registered Office: Queens Court, 9-17 Eastern Road, Romford, Essex, RM1 3NG
Activities: Hotels and similar accommodation
Parent: BPH Finance Number 1 Limited
Officers: Jonathan Patrick Braidley [1965] Director/Investment Professional; Christopher Andre Kula [1983] Director/Chartered Accountant [German/Canadian]

Chesterhill Investments Limited
Incorporated: 26 January 1972 *Employees:* 7
Net Worth: £19,187,268 *Total Assets:* £32,855,708
Registered Office: Albany House, 10 Wood Street, Barnet, Herts, EN5 4BW
Activities: Buying and selling of own real estate
Major Shareholder: Brian Alan Binstock
Officers: Stephen David Cole, Secretary; Brian Alan Binstock [1947] Director/Accountant; Pauline Elizabeth Binstock [1947] Director/Secretary; Stephen David Cole [1959] Director/Property Consultant

Chesterton Education Limited
Incorporated: 24 January 2017 *Employees:* 27
Net Worth: £236,761 *Total Assets:* £6,070,187
Registered Office: 1 Wolsey Road, East Molesey, Surrey, KT8 9EL
Activities: Primary education
Parent: Bellevue Schools Group Limited
Officers: Mark William Malley [1974] Director; Jerry Sterling Stover Jr [1950] Director/Lawyer; Steven John York Wade [1970] Director/Teacher

Chevaning Mining Company Limited
Incorporated: 7 December 1981
Net Worth: £17,081,084 *Total Assets:* £17,081,086
Registered Office: 4th Floor, Communications House, South Street, Staines upon Thames, Surrey, TW18 4PR
Activities: Activities of head offices
Officers: Kevin Patrick Ernest Davies, Secretary; Kevin Patrick Ernest Davies [1957] Director/Transitional Manager

Cheyne Assets Ltd
Incorporated: 3 August 2012
Net Worth: £961,051 *Total Assets:* £6,121,824
Registered Office: The Cedars, 82 Camden Park Road, Chislehurst, Kent, BR7 5HF
Activities: Buying and selling of own real estate
Major Shareholder: Adewale Adeyemi Ogunyemi
Officers: Adewale Adeyemi Ogunyemi, Secretary; Adewale Adeyemi Ogunyemi [1967] Director

CHG-Meridian Computer Leasing UK Limited
Incorporated: 6 September 1976
Net Worth: £973,000 *Total Assets:* £64,564,000
Registered Office: Barons Court, 22 The Avenue, Egham, Surrey, TW20 9AB
Activities: Financial leasing
Officers: Declan Martin McGlone [1965] Director [Irish]; Dr Mathias Wagner [1971] Director/Chief Sales Officer International [German]; Simon Young [1976] Sales Director

CHG-Meridian UK Limited
Incorporated: 3 September 1971 *Employees:* 47
Net Worth: £37,885,000 *Total Assets:* £89,425,000
Registered Office: Barons Court, 22 The Avenue, Egham, Surrey, TW20 9AB
Activities: Financial leasing
Officers: Declan Martin McGlone [1965] Director [Irish]; Dr Mathias Wagner [1971] Director/Chief Sales Officer International [German]; Simon Young [1976] Sales Director

Chi-Chi Collection Limited
Incorporated: 11 February 2010
Net Worth: £1,362,844 *Total Assets:* £5,312,494
Registered Office: Unit 5 Redburn Industrial Estate, Woodall Road, Enfield, Middlesex, EN3 4LE
Activities: Wholesale of clothing and footwear
Shareholders: Jamal Najar; Daniel Najar
Officers: Jamal Najar, Secretary; Daniel Najar [1984] Director; Jehad William Najar [1987] Director

Chicken Cabins Limited
Incorporated: 8 December 1965 *Employees:* 690
Net Worth: £12,908,308 *Total Assets:* £25,707,024
Registered Office: 64 Wolsey Road, Northwood, Middlesex, HA6 2EH
Activities: Unlicenced restaurants and cafes
Major Shareholder: Aly Hassanali Moleaina Janmohamed
Officers: Samirah Janmohamed, Secretary; Aly Hassanali Moleaina Janmohamed [1957] Director; Shehzad Janmohamed [1984] Director

Chicken Villas Limited
Incorporated: 16 December 1982 *Employees:* 2
Net Worth: £1,996,626 *Total Assets:* £23,448,416
Registered Office: First Floor, Kirkland House, 11-15 Peterborough Road, Harrow, Middlesex, HA1 2AX
Activities: Other letting and operating of own or leased real estate
Parent: Mulcroft Limited
Officers: Maya Bharat Patel, Secretary; Bharat Chandubhai Patel [1964] Director/Businessman; Maya Bharat Patel [1965] Director/Secretary

Chigwell (London) Limited
Incorporated: 9 July 1996
Net Worth: £2,085,264 *Total Assets:* £5,636,940
Registered Office: Aaron House, Unit 8 Hainault Business Park, Forest Road, Hainault, Essex, IG6 3JP
Activities: Activities of head offices
Major Shareholder: Dean Anthony Floyd
Officers: Dean Anthony Floyd [1966] Director/Builder

Chigwell School
Incorporated: 14 June 2006 *Employees:* 190
Net Worth: £24,517,000 *Total Assets:* £26,811,000
Registered Office: Chigwell School, High Road, Chigwell, Essex, IG7 6QF
Activities: Primary education
Officers: Claire Jones, Secretary; Susannah Louise Aliker [1966] Director/Accountant; Emma Brett [1970] Director/Chartered Accountant; John Frederick Cullis [1941] Director/University Tutor; Rev Christopher Mark Davies [1976] Director/Clerk in Holy Orders; Dr Graham Peter Dixon [1956] Director/Head of Radio EBU; Nicholas Antony Garnish [1965] Director; Jennifer Mary Gwinn [1950] Director/Retired; Martin James Higgins [1960] Director; Robin William John Howard [1959] Director/Barrister; Andrew Neil Howat [1959] Director/Group Treasurer; Melody Jones [1975] Director/Teacher; Reverend Benjamin William King [1976] Director/Minister of Religion; David Morriss [1942] Director/Consultant; Isobel Peck [1968] Marketing Director; Meera Ragha [1990] Director/Solicitor; Purmima SEN [1971] Director; Roseanne Serrelli [1968] Director/Solicitor

The Children's Trust
Incorporated: 30 September 1983 *Employees:* 505
Net Worth: £28,932,000 *Total Assets:* £31,475,000
Registered Office: Tadworth Court, Tadworth, Surrey, KT20 5RU
Activities: Primary education
Officers: Colin Kerr, Secretary; Elizabeth Sarah Baker [1959] Director/Healthcare Consultant; Tim John Davies [1955] Director/Retired; Michael David Gercke [1952] Director/Chartered Accountant; Duncan George Ingram [1955] Former FTSE100 Director; Denise Elizabeth Matthams [1958] Director/Independent Governing Body Board Nurse; Toby Jonathan Mullins [1961] Director/Executive Headteacher; Nigel Keith Lethbridge Scott [1952] Director/Charity Consultant; Katherine Anne Walker [1959] Director/Consultant

Chiltern Court Properties Limited
Incorporated: 3 May 2017
Net Worth Deficit: £5,769 *Total Assets:* £6,264,521
Registered Office: 3rd Floor, Sterling House, Langston Road, Loughton, Essex, IG10 3TS
Activities: Development of building projects
Parent: Galliard Developments Limited
Officers: Allan William Porter, Secretary; David Edward Conway [1976] Director; Stephen Stuart Solomon Conway [1948] Director; Jonathan Michael Morgan [1978] Director; Donagh O'Sullivan [1968] Construction Director [Irish]

Chilworth Manor Limited
Incorporated: 15 December 1988 *Employees:* 106
Net Worth: £5,311,920 *Total Assets:* £11,761,986
Registered Office: Kirkland House, 11-15 Peterborough Road, Harrow, Middlesex, HA1 2AX
Activities: Hotels and similar accommodation
Officers: Dinesh Gordhandas Bhattessa [1946] Director/Businessman; Haider Ladhu Jaffer [1940] Director/Businessman; Dr Manoj Raman [1960] Director/Businessman; Hassanali Amirali Dawood Suleman [1954] Director/Businessman

Chingford Fruit Limited
Incorporated: 20 September 1999 *Employees:* 263
Net Worth: £27,328,000 *Total Assets:* £42,549,000
Registered Office: Thames House, Thames Road, Crayford, Kent, DA1 4QP
Activities: Wholesale of fruit and vegetables
Parent: AG Thames Holdings Limited
Officers: Christopher Oakley, Secretary; David Alex Aichen [1969] Director; Leon Aichen [1941] Director; Gary Raymond Linsell [1970] Managing Director; Christopher Richard Oakley [1963] Finance Director

Chislehurst and Sidcup Grammar School
Incorporated: 1 June 2011 *Employees:* 123
Net Worth: £23,947,378 *Total Assets:* £25,066,720
Registered Office: Hurst Road, Sidcup, Kent, DA15 9AG
Activities: General secondary education
Officers: June Rose Ben Rabah [1958] Director; Dawn Burton [1966] Director/Primary School Teacher; Helen Everett [1964] Director/Teacher; Jason Gardiner [1963] Director/Compliance Consultant; Jane Elizabeth Gritt [1963] Director/Human Resources Manager; Joe Henry [1970] Director/Management Consultant; Janice Power [1958] Director/Administrator; Michael Sradling [1974] Director/Barrister; Lindsey Stewart [1969] Director/Doctoral Researcher; Amanda Lisa Sutton [1965] Director; Nigel Austin Walker [1966] Director/Headteacher; Richard Anthony Wallbridge [1969] Director; Susan Margaret Watson [1955] Director

Chislehurst Care Limited
Incorporated: 2 April 2001 *Employees:* 115
Net Worth: £3,924,029 *Total Assets:* £10,642,002
Registered Office: The Old Exchange, 3 London Road, Farningham, Kent, DA4 0JP
Activities: Residential care activities for the elderly and disabled
Officers: Sarah Jacqueline Mills, Secretary; Martin Gregory Mills [1963] Director; Sarah Jacqueline Mills [1968] Director

Chislehurst School for Girls
Incorporated: 11 February 2011 *Employees:* 138
Net Worth: £7,599,000 *Total Assets:* £9,130,000
Registered Office: Chislehurst School for Girls, Beaverwood Road, Chislehurst, Kent, BR7 6HE
Activities: General secondary education
Shareholder: Sheryl Orchard
Officers: Linda Day, Secretary; Emma Linda Downes [1987] Director/Businesswoman; Peter Luis Frampton [1977] Director/Manager; Jatin Ranjitlal Mehta [1975] Director/Accountant; Elizabeth Mensah [1983] Director; Sheryl Orchard [1970] Director/Self Employed/Run Plumbing Business; Hamesh Patel [1976] Director/Chartered Accountant; Luke Paul Picknett [1987] Director/Management Consultant; Karen Jayne Raven [1958] Director; John Richard Wafer [1963] Director/Land Manager; Dawn Lindsay Wakefield [1974] Director/Manager

Chobham School Academy (Stratford)
Incorporated: 13 March 2009 *Employees:* 185
Net Worth: £31,975,000 *Total Assets:* £36,049,000
Registered Office: 4th Floor, Norfolk House, Wellesley Road, Croydon, Surrey, CR0 1LH
Activities: General secondary education
Officers: Alan John Bates [1970] Project Director; Angela Marie Forbes [1979] Commercial Director; Jeremy Stuart Fraser [1958] Director/Vicar; Duncan Cowan Gray [1983] Director/Strategy Consultant; William Nigel Hugill [1958] Director/Consultant

Choice Wealth Management Limited
Incorporated: 10 April 2014
Net Worth Deficit: £19,466 *Total Assets:* £7,145,170
Registered Office: Haresfoot, 177 Barnet Road, Arkely, Herts, EN5 3JZ
Activities: Fund management activities
Major Shareholder: Anjim Iqbal
Officers: Anjim Iqbal [1972] Director

T.Choithram & Sons (London) Limited
Incorporated: 31 October 1960 *Employees:* 265
Net Worth: £10,076,252 *Total Assets:* £31,710,404
Registered Office: Unit 5 Silverdale Road, Pump Lane, Hayes, Middlesex, UB3 3BL
Activities: Non-specialised wholesale of food, beverages and tobacco
Officers: Ramesh Pohumal Thanwani, Secretary; Kanhaya Azad [1953] Director [Indian]; Lekhraj Thakurdas Pagarani [1954] Director/Merchant; Luke Pagarani [1983] Director/Merchant; Ramchand Dharamdas Rajwani [1930] Director/Merchant [Indian]; Ramesh Pohumal Thanwani [1946] Director/Merchant [Indian]

E. Christian & Company (Holdings) Limited
Incorporated: 9 April 1991 *Employees:* 56
Net Worth: £6,384,473 *Total Assets:* £7,966,259
Registered Office: EC Group, Europa Park, Magnet Road, Grays, Essex, RM20 4DN
Activities: Activities of distribution holding companies
Major Shareholder: Christopher John Long
Officers: Christopher John Long, Secretary/Accountant; Jacqueline Eve Curtis Casadella [1951] Director; Christopher John Long [1958] Director/Accountant; Karen Joy Long [1960] Director

Chromalox (UK) Limited
Incorporated: 20 November 2001 *Employees:* 41
Net Worth: £3,094,571 *Total Assets:* £6,886,675
Registered Office: 2nd Floor, Amp House, Dingwall Road, Croydon, Surrey, CR0 2LX
Activities: Manufacture of electronic industrial process control equipment
Parent: Heat Holding (UK) Limited
Officers: Thierry Desseignes, Secretary; Kevin James Boyd [1964] Finance Director; Neil Harvey Daws [1962] Director - EMEA; Thierry Desseignes [1962] Managing Director Chromolox EMEIA [French]; Michael Charles Sutter [1961] Director [American]

Chrome Dreams Media Ltd
Incorporated: 14 November 2001 *Employees:* 15
Net Worth: £6,338,575 *Total Assets:* £6,680,376
Registered Office: 12 Seaforth Avenue, New Malden, Surrey, KT3 6JP
Activities: Video production activities
Major Shareholder: Robert Alexander Johnstone
Officers: Robert Alexander Johnstone [1961] Director/Company Chairman

Chromium Acquisitions Limited
Incorporated: 5 October 2009
Net Worth: £9,493,148,672 *Total Assets:* £13,984,549,888
Registered Office: Cadbury House, Sanderson Road, Uxbridge, Middlesex, UB8 1DH
Activities: Activities of other holding companies n.e.c.
Parent: Mondelez International, Inc
Officers: Adrian John Paul Arrighi [1978] Tax Director; Michael Brendan Foye [1965] Treasury Director; John Michael Hladusz [1972] Director/Chartered Accountant; Carole Noelle Keene [1966] Director

Chromium Assets Limited
Incorporated: 5 October 2009
Net Worth: £6,845,971,968 *Total Assets:* £6,845,971,968
Registered Office: Cadbury House, Sanderson Road, Uxbridge, Middlesex, UB8 1DH
Activities: Activities of head offices
Parent: Kraft Foods Investment Holdings UK Limited
Officers: Adrian John Paul Arrighi [1978] Tax Director; Michael Brendan Foye [1965] Treasury Director; John Michael Hladusz [1972] Director/Chartered Accountant; Carole Noelle Keene [1966] Director

Chromium Suchex LLP
Incorporated: 27 October 2009
Net Worth: £4,466,366,976 *Total Assets:* £4,466,366,976
Registered Office: Cadbury House, Sanderson Road, Uxbridge, Middlesex, UB8 1DH

Chrysalis (Stanhope) Limited
Incorporated: 16 October 2006
Net Worth: £67,176 *Total Assets:* £28,434,720
Registered Office: 8 White Oak Square, London Road, Swanley, Kent, BR8 7AG
Activities: Other business support service activities n.e.c.
Parent: Chrysalis (Stanhope) Holdings Limited
Officers: Neeti Mukundrai Anand [1984] Director; Stewart Chalmers Grant [1951] Director; Angela Louise Roshier [1975] Director/Asset Management

Chrysalis Multi Academy Trust
Incorporated: 9 March 2011 *Employees:* 267
Previous: Claremont High School Academy Trust
Net Worth: £54,264,000 *Total Assets:* £58,293,000
Registered Office: Claremont High School, Claremont Avenue, Kenton, Harrow, Middlesex, HA3 0UH
Activities: General secondary education
Officers: Steven Raphael Brunswick [1954] Director/Structural Engineer; Raxita Kapashi [1964] Director/Chartered Accountant; Shyamal Kishan Kataria [1984] Director/Chartered Accountant; Olivia Louisy [1988] Director/Recruitment Consultant; Reverend Grenville Thomas [1966] Director/Vicar

Chubb (NI) Limited
Incorporated: 14 May 1942 *Employees:* 52
Net Worth: £54,000 *Total Assets:* £10,992,000
Registered Office: Littleton Road, Ashford, Middlesex, TW15 1TZ
Activities: Security systems service activities
Parent: Chubb Group Security Limited
Officers: Robert John Sloss, Secretary/Director; Anthony Brennan [1966] Finance Director [Irish]; David Byrne [1965] Managing Director [Irish]; Craig Alexander Forbes [1963] Finance Director

Chubb Fire & Security Limited
Incorporated: 9 October 1953 *Employees:* 1,853
Net Worth: £166,360,000 *Total Assets:* £546,145,024
Registered Office: Littleton Road, Ashford, Middlesex, TW15 1TZ
Activities: Activities of head offices
Parent: Chubb Group Security Limited
Officers: Robert John Sloss, Secretary; Laura Jayne Wilcock, Secretary; Anthony Brennan [1966] Finance Director [Irish]; Craig Alexander Forbes [1963] Director

Chubb Fire Limited
Incorporated: 25 February 1914 *Employees:* 109
Net Worth: £356,032,992 *Total Assets:* £385,910,016
Registered Office: Littleton Road, Ashford, Middlesex, TW15 1TZ
Activities: Fire service activities
Shareholders: United Technologies Holdings Limited; Chubb Group Security Limited
Officers: Robert John Sloss, Secretary/Solicitor; Anthony Brennan [1966] Finance Director [Irish]; Craig Alexander Forbes [1963] Finance Director

Chubb Group (International) Limited
Incorporated: 25 August 1988
Net Worth: £170,246,000 *Total Assets:* £1,315,275,008
Registered Office: 1st Floor, Ash House, Littleton Road, Ashford, Middlesex, TW15 1TZ
Activities: Activities of head offices
Parent: Chubb Group Limited
Officers: Robert Sloss, Secretary; Laura Wilcock, Secretary; Neil Andrew Vincent Gregor MacGregor [1955] Director/Accounting and Controls Manager; Robert John Sloss [1967] Director/Solicitor

Chubb Group Limited
Incorporated: 18 June 1957 *Employees:* 4
Net Worth: £2,884,808,960 *Total Assets:* £10,658,702,336
Registered Office: 1st Floor, Ash House, Littleton Road, Ashford, Middlesex, TW15 1TZ
Activities: Activities of head offices
Parent: Chubb Limited
Officers: Robert Sloss, Secretary; Laura Wilcock, Secretary; Neil Andrew Vincent Gregor MacGregor [1955] Director/Accounting and Controls Manager; Robert John Sloss [1967] Director/Solicitor

Chubb Group Properties Limited
Incorporated: 21 April 1987
Net Worth: £30,906,000 *Total Assets:* £72,308,000
Registered Office: 1st Floor, Ash House, Littleton Road, Ashford, Middlesex, TW15 1TZ
Activities: Activities of head offices
Parent: Chubb Group Limited
Officers: Robert Sloss, Secretary; Laura Wilcock, Secretary; Neil Andrew Vincent Gregor MacGregor [1955] Director/Accounting and Controls Manager; Robert John Sloss [1967] Director/Solicitor

Chubb Group Security Limited
Incorporated: 1 November 1994 *Employees:* 54
Net Worth: £593,108,992 *Total Assets:* £606,934,976
Registered Office: Littleton Road, Ashford, Middlesex, TW15 1TZ
Activities: Activities of head offices
Parent: Goodrich Aftermarket Services Limited
Officers: Laura Wilcock, Secretary; Anthony Brennan [1966] Finance Director [Irish]; Robert John Sloss [1967] Director/Senior Counsel

Chubb International Holdings Limited
Incorporated: 14 December 1882
Net Worth: £687,595,008 *Total Assets:* £740,940,032
Registered Office: 1st Floor, Ash House, Littleton Road, Ashford, Middlesex, TW15 1TZ
Activities: Activities of head offices
Parent: Chubb Limited
Officers: Robert Sloss, Secretary; Laura Wilcock, Secretary; Neil Andrew Vincent Gregor MacGregor [1955] Director/Accounting and Controls Manager; Robert John Sloss [1967] Director/Solicitor

Chubb Limited
Incorporated: 17 July 2000
Net Worth: £388,857,984 *Total Assets:* £10,439,570,432
Registered Office: 1st Floor, Ash House, Littleton Road, Ashford, Middlesex, TW15 1TZ
Activities: Activities of head offices
Parent: Goodrich Inertial Limited
Officers: Robert Sloss, Secretary; Laura Wilcock, Secretary; Neil Andrew Vincent Gregor MacGregor [1955] Director/Accounting and Controls Manager; Robert John Sloss [1967] Director/Solicitor

F.J. Church & Sons Limited
Incorporated: 4 January 1937 *Employees:* 55
Net Worth: £20,493,550 *Total Assets:* £29,058,780
Registered Office: Centenary Works, Manor Way, Rainham, Essex, RM13 8RH
Activities: Recovery of sorted materials
Parent: FJC Topco Ltd
Officers: Patrick John Church [1957] Director; Ian Simon Magson [1967] Managing Director

The Church of Pentecost - UK
Incorporated: 31 March 2008 *Employees:* 54
Net Worth: £11,204,913 *Total Assets:* £15,687,379
Registered Office: 746 Green Lane, Dagenham, Essex, RM8 1YX
Activities: Activities of religious organisations
Officers: Reverend James Kofi Sam, Secretary; Kwaku Joe Adomako [1962] Director/Lecturer; Revd Osei Owusu Afriyie [1955] Director/Minister of Religion; Reverend Kwame Twumasi Appiah [1955] Director/Minister of Religion [Ghanaian]; Alex Appenteng Boateng [1978] Director/Pharmacist [Ghanaian]; Reverend Emmanuel Danso [1963] Director/Minister of Religion; Reverend George Kwaku Korankye [1968] Director/Minister of Religion; Reverend James Kofi Sam [1957] Director/Minister of Religion

Churchgate Estates Limited
Incorporated: 6 November 1996
Net Worth: £43,075,132 *Total Assets:* £43,095,528
Registered Office: 227 London Road, Romford, Essex, RM7 9BQ
Activities: Activities of head offices
Officers: Ameet Kotecha, Secretary; Ameet Kotecha [1973] Director; Ranjan Madhusudan Kotecha [1947] Director/Business Consultant

Churchill Insurance Company Limited
Incorporated: 17 May 1988
Net Worth: £12,780,000 *Total Assets:* £47,799,000
Registered Office: Churchill Court, Westmoreland Road, Bromley, Kent, BR1 1DP
Activities: Non-life insurance
Parent: U K Insurance Limited
Officers: Roger Cheston Clifton, Secretary; Michael Nicholas Biggs [1952] Director/Chartered Accountant; Paul Robert Geddes [1969] Director/Bank Official; Danuta Gray [1958] Director; Mark Julian Gregory [1963] Director; Jane Carolyn Hanson [1967] Director; Michael Anthony Holliday-Williams [1970] Director; Penelope Jane James [1969] Director; Sebastian Richard Edward Cuthbert James [1966] Director/Group CEO; Fiona Catherine McBain [1961] Director; Gregor Ninian Stewart [1964] Director; Clare Eleanor Thompson [1954] Director; Doctor Richard Churchill Ward [1957] Director

Churchtown Farm Solar Limited
Incorporated: 20 April 2011
Net Worth Deficit: £2,278,562 *Total Assets:* £11,001,576
Registered Office: Beaufort Court, Egg Farm Lane, off Station Road, Kings Langley, Herts, WD4 8LR
Activities: Production of electricity
Parent: European Investments (Cornwall) Limited
Officers: Dominic Hearth, Secretary; Steven William Hughes [1972] Global Support Services Director, UK&I - Commercial; Mitesh Raj Patel [1982] Director/Chartered Accountant; Tracy Jane Scott [1976] Director/Delivery Project Manager; Mark Christopher Wayment [1958] Director

Churton Property Developments Limited
Incorporated: 16 August 1994
Net Worth: £11,037,154 *Total Assets:* £18,413,018
Registered Office: 47 Canons Drive, Edgware, Harrow, Middlesex, HA8 7RG
Activities: Other letting and operating of own or leased real estate
Shareholders: John O'Connor; Patrick Thomas Osullivan
Officers: Patrick Thomas O'Sullivan, Secretary/Management Consultant; John O'Connor [1951] Director; Patrick Thomas O'Sullivan [1950] Director

Cibi Investments Limited
Incorporated: 5 August 1996 *Employees:* 2
Net Worth: £3,938,460 *Total Assets:* £13,259,055
Registered Office: Centrum House, 36 Station Road, Egham, Surrey, TW20 9LF
Activities: Development of building projects
Parent: Delamere Estates Limited
Officers: William Archibald Harkness, Secretary; Tessa Jane Harkness [1948] Director; William Archibald Harkness [1951] Director/Chartered Surveyor

Cie PLC
Incorporated: 3 February 1959 *Employees:* 22
Net Worth: £4,028,226 *Total Assets:* £7,992,555
Registered Office: Acorn House, Gumley Road, Grays, Essex, RM20 4XP
Activities: Joinery installation
Parent: CIE UK (Holdings) Limited
Officers: Nicola Jane Hardcastle, Secretary; Antony Lawrence Amodio [1965] Director; Daniel Arthur Edward Carr [1975] Finance Director; Peter Kane [1965] Managing Director; Kristoffer Ljungfelt [1977] Director [Swedish]; David Roberts [1949] Director

CIKU Construction Services Limited
Incorporated: 20 November 2006 *Employees:* 4
Net Worth: £2,049,834 *Total Assets:* £5,114,921
Registered Office: 63a Hawks Road, Kingston upon Thames, Surrey, KT1 3EF
Activities: Demolition
Shareholders: Bujar Ciku; Arif Ciku
Officers: Bujar Ciku, Secretary; Arif Ciku [1979] Director [Albanian]; Bujar Ciku [1973] Director

Cimbali UK Limited
Incorporated: 1 February 1973 *Employees:* 102
Net Worth: £2,117,485 *Total Assets:* £8,721,503
Registered Office: Unit 280 Centennial Park, Centennial Avenue, Elstree, Herts, WD6 3ST
Activities: Non-specialised wholesale trade
Officers: Maurizio Cimbali [1945] Director/President [Italian]; Daniel Joseph Clarke [1981] Director; Franco Panno [1958] Director [Italian]

Cine-UK Limited
Incorporated: 4 January 1995 *Employees:* 2,877
Net Worth: £66,303,000 *Total Assets:* £467,367,008
Registered Office: 8th Floor, Vantage London, Great West Road, Brentford, Middlesex, TW8 9AG
Activities: Motion picture distribution activities
Parent: Cineworld Holdings Limited
Officers: Fiona Smith, Secretary; Israel Greidinger [1961] Director/Cinema Proprietor [Israeli]; Mr Moshe Joseph Greidinger [1952] Director/Cinema Proprietor [Israeli]; Shaun Alan Jones [1970] Director; Nir Lion [1981] Director [Israeli]

Cineworld Cinemas Holdings Limited
Incorporated: 16 April 1986
Net Worth: £56,227,000 *Total Assets:* £202,770,000
Registered Office: 8th Floor, Vantage London, Great West Road, Brentford, Middlesex, TW8 9AG
Activities: Activities of head offices
Parent: Cineworld Holdings Limited
Officers: Fiona Elizabeth Smith, Secretary; Nisan Cohen [1972] Director [Israeli]; Israel Greidinger [1961] Director/Cinema Proprietor [Israeli]; Mr Moshe Joseph Greidinger [1952] Director/Cinema Proprietor [Israeli]; Shaun Alan Jones [1970] Director; Nir Lion [1981] Finance Director [Israeli]

Cineworld Cinemas Limited
Incorporated: 22 May 1985 *Employees:* 2,418
Net Worth: £66,213,000 *Total Assets:* £706,400,000
Registered Office: 8th Floor, Vantage London, Great West Road, Brentford, Middlesex, TW8 9AG
Activities: Motion picture distribution activities
Parent: Cineworld Cinemas Holdings Limited
Officers: Fiona Smith, Secretary; Israel Greidinger [1961] Director/Cinema Proprietor [Israeli]; Mr Moshe Joseph Greidinger [1952] Director/Cinema Proprietor [Israeli]; Shaun Alan Jones [1970] Director; Nir Lion [1981] Director [Israeli]

Cineworld Estates Limited
Incorporated: 23 March 1990
Net Worth: £59,475,000 *Total Assets:* £59,493,000
Registered Office: 8th Floor, Vantage London, Great West Road, Brentford, Middlesex, TW8 9AG
Activities: Other business support service activities n.e.c.
Parent: Cineworld Cinemas Limited
Officers: Fiona Elizabeth Smith, Secretary; Shaun Alan Jones [1970] Director; Nir Lion [1981] Director [Israeli]

Cineworld Group PLC
Incorporated: 23 August 2004 *Employees:* 10,232
Net Worth: £778,600,000 *Total Assets:* £1,407,200,000
Registered Office: 8th Floor, Vantage London, Great West Road, Brentford, Middlesex, TW8 9AG
Activities: Activities of other holding companies n.e.c.
Officers: Fiona Smith, Secretary; Anthony Herbert Bloom [1939] Director; Nisan Cohen [1972] Director [Israeli]; Camela Galano [1957] Director [American]; Israel Greidinger [1961] Director/Cinema Proprietor [Israeli]; Mr Moshe Joseph Greidinger [1952] Director/Cinema Proprietor [Israeli]; Alicja Kornasiewicz [1951] Director [Polish]; Dean Roderick Moore [1957] Director; Scott S. Rosenblum [1949] Director/Attorney at Law [American]; Arni Samuelsson [1942] Director/Cinema Proprietor [Icelander]; Eric Hartley Senat [1949] Director; Julie Helen Southern [1959] Director; Renana Teperberg [1977] Director [Israeli]

Cineworld Holdings Limited
Incorporated: 23 August 2004
Net Worth: £290,352,000 *Total Assets:* £623,516,032
Registered Office: 8th Floor, Vantage London, Great West Road, Brentford, Middlesex, TW8 9AG
Activities: Activities of head offices
Parent: Augustus 2 Limited
Officers: Fiona Elizabeth Smith, Secretary; Nisan Cohen [1972] Director [Israeli]; Israel Greidinger [1961] Director/Cinema Proprietor [Israeli]; Shaun Alan Jones [1970] Director; Nir Lion [1981] Director [Israeli]

Cipla (EU) Limited
Incorporated: 16 August 2002 *Employees:* 10
Net Worth: £48,950,488 *Total Assets:* £243,258,848
Registered Office: Dixcart House, Addlestone Road, Bourne Business Park, Addlestone, Surrey, KT15 2LE
Activities: Other business support service activities n.e.c.
Officers: Peter Anthony Robertson, Secretary; Christos Kartalis [1962] Director/Service [Greek]; Gillian Mary Latham [1958] Director of Regulatory Affairs; Anchal Sultania [1983] Director [Indian]; Samina Vaziralli [1975] Director/Service [Indian]

Cisilion (Group) Limited
Incorporated: 30 May 2013 *Employees:* 97
Net Worth: £3,522,712 *Total Assets:* £9,242,792
Registered Office: Cisilion House, Guildford Road, Leatherhead, Surrey, KT22 9UT
Activities: Other information technology service activities
Major Shareholder: Roger David Paul
Officers: Roger David Paul [1958] Director

Cisilion Limited
Incorporated: 4 January 2000 *Employees:* 97
Net Worth: £5,130,766 *Total Assets:* £10,814,448
Registered Office: Cisilion House, Guildford Road, Leatherhead, Surrey, KT22 9UT
Activities: Other information technology service activities
Parent: Cisilion (Group) Limited
Officers: Roger David Paul [1958] Director

Citigate Homes (UK) Ltd
Incorporated: 30 August 2013
Net Worth Deficit: £4,293 *Total Assets:* £7,151,353
Registered Office: 112 Kirkland Avenue, Clayhall, Ilford, Essex, IG5 0TN
Activities: Development of building projects
Major Shareholder: Mian Abdul Sattar
Officers: Lakhwinder Singh Roopra [1978] Director [Indian]; Mohammad Sohail Sattar [1965] Director

Citipost Holdings Limited
Incorporated: 5 December 2016 *Employees:* 131
Net Worth Deficit: £474,572 *Total Assets:* £12,556,510
Registered Office: 51 Hailey Road, Erith, Kent, DA18 4AA
Activities: Activities of other holding companies n.e.c.
Shareholders: Daniel Charlesworth; Gregory Charlesworth
Officers: Daniel Charlesworth [1979] Director; Gregory Charlesworth [1984] Director

Citipost Limited
Incorporated: 16 October 1997 *Employees:* 131
Net Worth: £1,105,790 *Total Assets:* £14,136,871
Registered Office: 51 Hailey Road, Erith, Kent, DA18 4AA
Activities: Other service activities n.e.c.
Parent: Citipost Holdings Limited
Officers: Lisa Jannine Blatch, Secretary; Daniel Albert Charlesworth [1951] Director; Gregory Charlesworth [1984] Director; Daniel Charlesworth Jnr [1979] Director

Citipost Mail Limited
Incorporated: 21 April 1999 *Employees:* 39
Net Worth: £71,619 *Total Assets:* £15,567,773
Registered Office: 51 Hailey Road, Erith, Kent, DA18 4AA
Activities: Licensed carriers
Officers: Lisa Jannine Blatch, Secretary; Robert Bradford [1969] Director; Daniel Albert Charlesworth [1951] Director; Gregory Charlesworth [1984] Director; Linda Joan Charlesworth [1947] Director; Daniel Charlesworth Jnr [1979] Director

Citizen Machinery UK Ltd
Incorporated: 24 June 1974 *Employees:* 48
Net Worth: £10,542,794 *Total Assets:* £21,732,640
Registered Office: 1 Park Avenue, Bushey, Herts, WD23 2DA
Activities: Agents involved in the sale of machinery, industrial equipment, ships and aircraft
Parent: Citizen Machinery Co., Ltd.
Officers: Jonathan Matthew Hart [1979] Director; Edward Harry James [1969] Managing Director; Hiromitsu Kamata [1963] Director/Financial Manager [Japanese]; Toshiyuki Nagasawa [1957] Director/General Manager [Japanese]; Darren Michael John Wilkins [1965] Deputy Managing Director

City & Commercial Holdings Limited
Incorporated: 14 January 1960
Net Worth: £4,647,307 *Total Assets:* £5,420,622
Registered Office: Fourways, Mount Park Road, Harrow on the Hill, Middlesex, HA1 3JY
Activities: Financial intermediation not elsewhere classified
Officers: Ruth Soloway, Secretary; Jane Diane Rome [1963] Director; Julian Nigel Soloway [1959] Director; Ruth Soloway [1936] Director; Seymour Soloway [1930] Director

City & Docklands (W3) Limited
Incorporated: 5 April 2005 *Employees:* 1
Net Worth: £5,457,526 *Total Assets:* £5,498,526
Registered Office: Aldenham Wood Lodge, Watling Street, Elstree, Borehamwood, Herts, WD6 3AA
Activities: Development of building projects
Parent: City & Docklands Property Holdings Limited
Officers: Gary Hilton Sacks, Secretary; Gary Hilton Sacks [1965] Director

City & Southern Limited
Incorporated: 13 February 2014 *Employees:* 3
Net Worth: £13,056,545 *Total Assets:* £17,527,196
Registered Office: Duffy House, 1 Mount Road, Feltham, Middlesex, TW13 6AR
Activities: Development of building projects
Parent: Duffy Group Holdings Limited
Officers: Donal Corbett [1959] Director/Quantity Surveyor [Irish]; Jonathan Bernard Duffy [1978] Director; Stephen Peter Vincett [1980] Director/Accountant

City & Westminster Developments Limited
Incorporated: 1 August 1996 *Employees:* 4
Net Worth: £5,005,607 *Total Assets:* £8,084,778
Registered Office: Handel House, 95 High Street, Edgware, Middlesex, HA8 7DB
Activities: Development of building projects
Shareholders: Francis Henry Jones; Shaida Nagsh-Jones
Officers: Shaida Nagsh-Jones, Secretary; Francis Henry Jones [1948] Director

City Circle UK Limited
Incorporated: 2 December 1998 *Employees:* 80
Net Worth: £3,901,000 *Total Assets:* £8,669,000
Registered Office: 4 Millington Road, Hyde Park, Hayes, Middlesex, UB3 4AZ
Activities: Other passenger land transport
Parent: JTB Europe Limited
Officers: Niranjan Aleti [1981] Director/Business Executive [Indian]; Noboru Nakasone [1957] Director/Business Executive; Neil Jonathan Pegg [1965] Director/Business Executive

City Lifting Limited
Incorporated: 15 May 1995 *Employees:* 175
Net Worth: £10,816,432 *Total Assets:* £41,766,104
Registered Office: 9 Juliette Way, Purfleet Industrial Park, South Ockendon, Essex, RM15 4YD
Activities: Other specialised construction activities n.e.c.
Shareholders: Trevor Mark Jepson; Clare Gillian Jepson
Officers: Clare Gillian Jepson [1959] Director; Trevor Mark Jepson [1958] Director; Robert John Jones [1963] Director/Crane Hire Manager

City Link (Cardiff) Holdings Limited
Incorporated: 29 January 2003
Net Worth: £3,313,000 *Total Assets:* £10,653,000
Registered Office: Astral House, Imperial Way, Watford, Herts, WD24 4WW
Activities: Activities of head offices
Parent: Vinci Pensions Limited
Officers: Ian David Hudson [1964] Director/Chartered Accountant; Rory John Murphy [1969] Director/Chartered Surveyor

City Link (Cardiff) Limited
Incorporated: 22 April 1998
Net Worth Deficit: £104,000 *Total Assets:* £43,447,000
Registered Office: Astral House, Imperial Way, Watford, Herts, WD24 4WW
Activities: Activities of head offices
Parent: City Link (Cardiff) Holdings Limited
Officers: Ian David Hudson [1964] Director/Chartered Accountant; Rory John Murphy [1969] Director/Chartered Surveyor

City North (Telford Homes) Limited
Incorporated: 23 November 2011
Previous: United House City North Limited
Net Worth: £36,055,000 *Total Assets:* £77,221,000
Registered Office: Telford House, Britannia Road, Queensgate, Waltham Cross, Herts, EN8 7TF
Activities: Activities of construction holding companies
Shareholders: City North Islington Holdings Limited; Telford Homes City North Limited
Officers: Joseph Mullee, Secretary; David Myles Campbell [1965] Group Sales and Marketing Director; Jonathan Graham Di-Stefano [1974] Director/Chief Executive; John Anthony FitzGenerald [1971] Group Managing Director; Dominic Richard Albert Ismael Jones [1967] Director; Jack Anthony Morris [1956] Director; Joseph Mullee [1978] Director/Accountant; Katie Rogers [1981] Finance Director

City of London Holdings & Investments Limited
Incorporated: 15 November 1973 *Employees:* 1
Net Worth: £1,346,500 *Total Assets:* £5,058,013
Registered Office: Suite 3, Amba House, 15 College Road, Harrow, Middlesex, HA1 1BA
Activities: Other letting and operating of own or leased real estate
Parent: Beaulieu Ltd
Officers: Daniel Max Bloom, Secretary; Daniel Max Bloom [1970] Director/Surveyor; Dr Natalia Bogatcheva [1977] Director

City Tool Hire Limited
Incorporated: 15 September 2011 *Employees:* 62
Net Worth: £3,180,415 *Total Assets:* £5,413,630
Registered Office: 5-6 Boeing Way International Business Park, Southall, Middlesex, UB2 5LB
Activities: Renting and leasing of construction and civil engineering machinery and equipment
Shareholders: Warren Burgess; Lionel Burgess; Richard Burgess; Rosemary Burgess
Officers: Rosemary Burgess, Secretary; Lionel Burgess [1978] Director; Richard Burgess [1952] Director; Warren Burgess [1986] Director

Citybond Holdings Limited
Incorporated: 11 February 1980 *Employees:* 70
Previous: Citybond Holdings PLC
Net Worth: £3,934,479 *Total Assets:* £6,151,729
Registered Office: 109 Elmers End Road, Beckenham, Kent, BR3 4SY
Activities: Financial intermediation not elsewhere classified
Major Shareholder: Mansukh Gordhandas Ganatra
Officers: Jeremy James Jonathan Jones, Secretary; Mansukh Gordhandas Ganatra [1949] Director/Certified Accountant; Satishchandra Gordhandas Ganatra [1947] Director/Insurance Broker; Jeremy James Jonathan Jones [1977] Director/Accountant; Anil Kumar [1947] Director/Chartered Accountant; Hugh John Watchorn [1963] Director/Accountant

Citygate Automotive Limited
Incorporated: 8 November 2005 *Employees:* 456
Net Worth: £4,156,558 *Total Assets:* £33,090,256
Registered Office: 664 Victoria Road, Ruislip, Middlesex, HA4 0LN
Activities: Sale of new cars and light motor vehicles
Parent: Citygate Holdings Limited
Officers: Peter Dickey, Secretary; Peter Dickey [1956] Company Secretary/Director; Jonathan Kevin Smith [1965] Director

Citygate Holdings Limited
Incorporated: 8 November 2005 *Employees:* 496
Net Worth: £4,581,340 *Total Assets:* £34,243,736
Registered Office: 664 Victoria Road, Ruislip, Middlesex, HA4 0LN
Activities: Activities of head offices
Major Shareholder: Jonathan Kevin Smith
Officers: Peter Dickey, Secretary; Peter Dickey [1956] Director; Stephen Paul Shepherd [1954] Director/Management Consultant; Jonathan Kevin Smith [1965] Director; Timothy John Worrall [1946] Director

The Civil Service Benevolent Fund
Incorporated: 16 June 2010
Net Worth: £42,772,000 *Total Assets:* £45,249,000
Registered Office: 5 Anne Boleyns Walk, Cheam, Sutton, Surrey, SM3 8DY
Activities: Other business support service activities n.e.c.
Officers: Elizabeth Lucy Dymond, Secretary; Mark Eric Addison [1951] Director/Retired; Janet Mary Aiston [1965] Director of Personal Tax; Selvin Brown [1971] Director/Civil Servant; Barry Thomas Burton [1958] Director/Civil Servant; Ross Stuart Campbell [1968] Director; Vivienne Margaret Dews [1952] Director/Civil Servant; Deborah Jane Loudon [1955] Director/Recruitment Consultant; Susan Jane Owen [1955] Director/Permanent Secretary; Wendy Sara Coltman Proctor [1954] Director/Civil Servant; Jonathan Michael Russell [1963] Director/Civil Servant; Kevin Ian Sadler [1962] Director/Civil Servant; Mal Singh [1961] Director/Civil Servant

CK Property Developments Limited
Incorporated: 3 March 1999 *Employees:* 21
Net Worth: £4,134,830 *Total Assets:* £6,189,309
Registered Office: Haslers, Old Station Road, Loughton, Essex, IG10 4PL
Activities: Development of building projects
Parent: CK Property Holdings Limited
Officers: Keith William Renew, Secretary/Director; Keith William Renew [1952] Director; Colin Anthony Sullivan [1963] Director/Property Developer

Clancy Developments Limited
Incorporated: 5 June 1963 *Employees:* 20
Net Worth: £49,266 *Total Assets:* £12,297,739
Registered Office: Coppermill Lane, Harefield, Middlesex, UB9 6HZ
Activities: Construction of domestic buildings
Parent: The Clancy Group PLC
Officers: David Pegg, Secretary; Matthew Stephen Canon [1979] Director/Chief Executive Officer; Dermot Michael Clancy [1951] Joint Managing Director; Kevin Thomas Clancy [1950] Contracts Director [Irish]

Clancy Docwra Limited
Incorporated: 31 March 1947 *Employees:* 2,195
Net Worth: £14,777,747 *Total Assets:* £73,155,760
Registered Office: Coppermill Lane, Harefield, Middlesex, UB9 6HZ
Activities: Construction of water projects
Parent: The Clancy Group PLC
Officers: David Pegg, Secretary; Matthew Bailey [1970] Director; Nicholas John Blaber [1968] Director/Chief Financial Officer; Matthew Stephen Canon [1979] Director/Chief Executive Officer; Dermot Michael Clancy [1951] Joint Managing Director; Kevin Thomas Clancy [1950] Contracts Director [Irish]; James Bernard Davey [1964] Director; James Seamus Augustine Keogh [1961] Director [Irish]; Jonathan Loveday [1969] Director/Chief Commercial Officer

The Clancy Group PLC
Incorporated: 25 March 1997 *Employees:* 2,314
Net Worth: £29,175,624 *Total Assets:* £101,001,464
Registered Office: Clare House, Coppermill Lane, Harefield, Middlesex, UB9 6HZ
Activities: Activities of construction holding companies
Shareholders: Kevin Thomas Clancy; Dermot Michael Clancy
Officers: David Pegg, Secretary; Nicholas John Blaber [1968] Director/Chief Financial Officer; Matthew Stephen Canon [1979] Director/Chief Executive; Dermot Michael Clancy [1951] Director/Civil Engineer; Kathleen Philomena Clancy [1925] Director/Housewife [Irish]; Kevin Thomas Clancy [1950] Director/Civil Engineer [Irish]; Mary Philomena Clancy [1948] Director/Administrator; Ian Archie Gray [1953] Director; James Seamus Augustine Keogh [1961] Director [Irish]; Jonathan Loveday [1969] Director; David Pegg [1961] Director

Clancy Plant Limited
Incorporated: 21 February 1962 *Employees:* 230
Previous: Clancy Plant Hire Limited
Net Worth: £8,433,524 *Total Assets:* £34,449,128
Registered Office: Coppermill Lane, Harefield, Middlesex, UB9 6HZ
Activities: Renting and leasing of construction and civil engineering machinery and equipment
Shareholders: Kevin Thomas Clancy; Dermot Michael Clancy; Mary Philomena Clancy
Officers: David Pegg, Secretary; Matthew Stephen Canon [1979] Director/Chief Executive Officer; Dermot Michael Clancy [1951] Joint Managing Director; Kevin Thomas Clancy [1950] Contracts Director [Irish]; Mary Philomena Clancy [1948] Director/Secretary; Bernard John Stack [1958] Director

Claremont Care Services Limited
Incorporated: 4 August 1971 *Employees:* 102
Net Worth: £2,324,545 *Total Assets:* £5,201,762
Registered Office: 63 De Vere House, Woodland Way, Kingswood, Surrey, KT20 6NN
Activities: Medical nursing home activities
Officers: Yasheen Rajan, Secretary; Mehboob Mohomedali Rajan [1948] Director; Yasheen Rajan [1979] Director/Self Employed; Zeenat Mehboob Rajan [1947] Director

Claremont Fan Court Foundation Limited (The)
Incorporated: 10 June 1976 *Employees:* 201
Net Worth: £31,804,604 *Total Assets:* £34,701,552
Registered Office: Claremont Fan Court School, Claremont Drive, Esher, Surrey, KT10 9LY
Activities: Pre-primary education
Officers: Jane Mary Jenkins, Secretary; Jeremy David Alton Bachelor [1948] Director/Retired; Nigel Beavor [1950] Director/Voluntary Worker; Stephen Charles Eggins [1950] Director/Business Executive; David Alan Ford [1949] Director/Retired Teacher [American]; Julian John Gall [1955] Director/Project Manager; Gordon Frederick Hunt [1945] Director/Retired; Catherine Lindsay Jackson [1964] Director/Management Consultant; Jennifer Frances Long [1977] Director/Senior Bank Executive; Patricia Ann Rickard [1959] Director/Retired; Dr Generald Smart [1943] Director/Retired; John Andrew Sutherland [1947] Director/Educationalist and Teacher

Clarence Estates (London) Limited
Incorporated: 1 March 1984 *Employees:* 5
Net Worth: £20,902,912 *Total Assets:* £33,288,554
Registered Office: Lynwood House, 373-375 Station Road, Harrow, Middlesex, HA1 2AW
Activities: Development of building projects
Major Shareholder: Ali Tekin Atalar
Officers: Kerem Benjamin Atalar, Secretary; Dr Ali Tekin Atalar [1947] Director; Kerem Benjamin Atalar [1981] Director; Sara Elisabeth Atalar [1986] Director

Clarges Pharmaceuticals Limited
Incorporated: 9 December 1908
Net Worth: £11,303,000 *Total Assets:* £13,568,000
Registered Office: 980 Great West Road, Brentford, Middlesex, TW8 9GS
Activities: Non-trading company
Parent: Glaxo Group Limited
Officers: James Borger [1963] Director/VP, Group Financial Planning and Analysis [American]; Alan George Burns [1975] Director

I.P. Clarke & Co. Limited
Incorporated: 17 May 1907
Total Assets: £198,687,008
Registered Office: 1 The Square, Stockley Park, Uxbridge, Middlesex, UB11 1TD
Activities: Activities of head offices
Parent: Coats Holdings Ltd
Officers: Richard Charles Reade [1973] Director; Claire Thompson [1984] Director/Solicitor

Classic Cinemas Limited
Incorporated: 21 September 1995
Net Worth: £33,365,648 *Total Assets:* £37,931,796
Registered Office: 8th Floor, Vantage London, Great West Road, Brentford, Middlesex, TW8 9AG
Activities: Data processing, hosting and related activities
Parent: Cineworld Cinemas Limited
Officers: Fiona Elizabeth Smith, Secretary; Shaun Alan Jones [1970] Director; Nir Lion [1981] Director [Israeli]

Clavering Care Limited
Incorporated: 27 January 1993
Net Worth: £6,390,325 *Total Assets:* £9,105,500
Registered Office: 36 Railway Approach, Harrow, Middlesex, HA3 5AA
Activities: Residential nursing care facilities
Parent: TLC Group Ltd
Officers: Gagan Puri, Secretary; William Charles Neal [1986] Director; Paavan Popat [1985] Managing Director; Honourable Shivaan Shillin Popat [1988] Director; Gagan Puri [1978] Finance Director

The Clay Oven UK Limited
Incorporated: 24 June 1999 *Employees:* 35
Net Worth: £4,235,801 *Total Assets:* £14,339,974
Registered Office: Garlands, Sandy Lane, Northwood, Middlesex, HA6 3ES
Activities: Event catering activities
Officers: Veena Khanna, Secretary; Neal Khanna [1979] Director/Restaurateur; Veena Khanna [1949] Director/Restaurateur; Vinod Kumar Khanna [1948] Director/Restaurateur

E. T. Clay Products Limited
Incorporated: 19 May 1997 *Employees:* 44
Net Worth: £1,352,556 *Total Assets:* £6,675,633
Registered Office: Hangman's Wood Industrial Park, Stifford Road, South Ockendon, Essex, RM15 6RL
Activities: Agents involved in the sale of timber and building materials
Major Shareholder: Edmund Turze
Officers: David Edward Blitz [1980] Commercial Director; James Ernest Hawkins [1957] Sales Director; Melvyn Jeremy John Hillstead [1963] Director/Sales Representative; Imran Khalid [1975] Director/Accountant; Edmund Turze [1958] Director; Sharon Francine Turze [1956] Director

Clearview Homes (Western Avenue) Ltd
Incorporated: 10 February 2016
Net Worth: £2 *Total Assets:* £11,188,561
Registered Office: 201 Clearview House, Pinner Road, Northwood, Middlesex, HA6 1BX
Activities: Buying and selling of own real estate
Officers: Ramon Juan Dias [1962] Director; Stephen John Murphy [1960] Director

Clearview Homes Limited
Incorporated: 2 April 1991 *Employees:* 36
Net Worth: £15,867,783 *Total Assets:* £35,594,368
Registered Office: Clearview House, 201 Pinner Road, Northwood, Middlesex, HA6 1BX
Activities: Development of building projects
Officers: Donna Murphy, Secretary; Ramon Juan Dias [1962] Director; Stephen John Murphy [1960] Director

Clearwater Property Company Limited
Incorporated: 12 July 1960 *Employees:* 3
Net Worth: £5,739,229 *Total Assets:* £7,625,644
Registered Office: Kenbury, Hamm Court, Weybridge, Surrey, KT13 8YA
Activities: Other letting and operating of own or leased real estate
Parent: Clearwater Property Estates Limited
Officers: Gary Robert Hall [1967] Director/Surveyor

Clearwater Property Estates Limited
Incorporated: 20 October 2014
Net Worth: £5,739,230 *Total Assets:* £5,739,230
Registered Office: Kenbury, Hamm Court, Weybridge, Surrey, KT13 8YA
Activities: Activities of other holding companies n.e.c.
Shareholders: Georgina Emma Clapton-Hall; Gary Robert Hall
Officers: Gary Robert Hall [1967] Director; Georgina Emma Hall [1969] Director

Clearway Environmental Services (U.K) Limited
Incorporated: 17 August 2000 *Employees:* 73
Net Worth: £4,438,002 *Total Assets:* £7,151,126
Registered Office: Fountain House, Anchor Boulevard, Crossways Business Park, Dartford, Kent, DA2 6QH
Activities: Renting and leasing of other machinery, equipment and tangible goods n.e.c.
Parent: GI Investments UK Ltd
Officers: Catrin Jones, Secretary; Matthew Robert Crook [1969] Director; David Martin Gratton [1960] Director; Gideon Ian Israel [1948] Director; Ian Quinlan [1950] Director; Phillip Owen Sexton [1957] Director

Clece Care Services Limited
Incorporated: 4 October 2013 *Employees:* 458
Net Worth: £6,859,207 *Total Assets:* £29,932,040
Registered Office: 3rd Floor, Quest House, 125-135 Staines Road, Hounslow, Middlesex, TW3 3JB
Activities: Other service activities incidental to land transportation, n.e.c.
Parent: ACS Actividades de Construccion y Servicios, S.A.
Officers: Lamberto Fresnillo Lobo, Secretary; Mario Abajo Menguez [1972] Managing Director [Spanish]; Lamberto Fresnillo Lobo [1966] Director/Lawyer [Spanish]

V.G.Clements (Contractors) Limited
Incorporated: 1 March 1960 *Employees:* 1,153
Net Worth: £7,737,540 *Total Assets:* £15,146,263
Registered Office: Cardinal House, Bury Street, Ruislip, Middlesex, HA4 7GD
Activities: Construction of commercial buildings
Parent: VGC Group Limited
Officers: Olivia Fitzpatrick, Secretary; Matthew John Fitzpatrick [1945] Director [Irish]; Laurence Richard McKidd [1955] Director; Ciara Melanie Pryce [1979] Director; Christopher Edward Ryan [1979] Director

Cleves Academy Trust
Incorporated: 11 October 2010 *Employees:* 91
Net Worth: £9,077,000 *Total Assets:* £10,384,000
Registered Office: Cleves School, Oatlands Avenue, Weybridge, Surrey, KT13 9TS
Activities: Primary education
Officers: Moya Susan Tytherleigh, Secretary; Hilary Bennett [1953] Director/Retired; Emma Jane Calow [1974] Director/Management Accountant; Rebecca Jane Flaherty [1967] Director/Teacher; Susan Warner Foster [1959] Director/Property Manager; Wayne Terry Giddens [1970] Finance Director; James Graham [1978] Director/Manager; Christopher Owen Hodges [1968] Director/Headteacher; Elaine Jones [1962] Director/School Governor; Simon Andrew Matthews [1967] Director/Computer Consultant; Alistair Nelson [1978] Director/Teacher; Doris Bell Neville-Davies [1943] Director/School Governor

CLFIS (U.K.) Limited
Incorporated: 18 January 2002 *Employees:* 1,024
Net Worth Deficit: £95,076,000 *Total Assets:* £32,976,000
Registered Office: Canada Life Place, High Street, Potters Bar, Herts, EN6 5BA
Activities: Other business support service activities n.e.c.
Parent: The Canada Life Group (U.K.) Limited
Officers: Lisa Annette Rodriguez, Secretary; Kathryn Louise Bateman [1964] Director; Douglas Allan Brown [1971] Director/Chief Operating Officer; Robert Craig Fazzini-Jones [1974] Director; David John Marchant [1964] Director; Karen Helen Pengelly [1973] Director; Richard Paul Priestley [1971] Director; Timothy James Stoves [1980] Director

Click Entertainment Limited
Incorporated: 9 March 2009 *Employees:* 32
Net Worth: £5,100,896 *Total Assets:* £21,210,268
Registered Office: Unit 5 ZK Park, 23 Commerce Way, Croydon, Surrey, CR0 4ZS
Activities: Wholesale of electronic and telecommunications equipment and parts
Shareholder: Jake Wright
Officers: Anders Aagaard Andresen [1961] Director [Danish]; Karsten Vagn Olsen [1971] Director/Chief Operational Officer [Danish]; Jake Wright [1986] Director

Clickatell Limited
Incorporated: 7 November 2001
Net Worth: £3,688,963 *Total Assets:* £6,351,520
Registered Office: Bank House, 81 St Judes Road, Englefield Green, Surrey, TW20 0DF
Activities: Other telecommunications activities
Shareholders: Pieter Wouter de Villiers; Deon Van Heerden; Philip Rogers; Nick Pianim
Officers: Pieter Wouter de Villiers [1972] Managing Director [South African]; Deon Van Heerden [1972] Director/Management Consultant

Clifford Property Company Limited (The)
Incorporated: 28 March 1924 *Employees:* 6
Net Worth: £12,422,986 *Total Assets:* £14,443,479
Registered Office: Leonard House, 5-7 Newman Road, Bromley, Kent, BR1 1RJ
Activities: Buying and selling of own real estate
Officers: Sandra Ellen Greenfield Astley, Secretary; Sandra Ellen Greenfield Astley [1957] Director; Catherine Antoinette Bishop [1961] Director; Philip Raymond Hawkins [1962] Director/Stockbroker; Ellen Mary Hurst [1936] Director; Graham Arthur Hurst [1966] Director/Banker; Nicholas Ian Maynard [1954] Director/Surveyor

Clinical Pathology Accreditation (UK) Limited
Incorporated: 6 January 1992 *Employees:* 22
Net Worth: £5,146,782 *Total Assets:* £5,518,351
Registered Office: 2 Pine Trees, Chertsey Lane, Staines upon Thames, Middlesex, TW18 3HR
Activities: Other business support service activities n.e.c.
Officers: Georgia Alsop [1970] Director/Accountant; James Randolph Lindsay [1955] Director

Clinisupplies Limited
Incorporated: 13 June 2000 *Employees:* 74
Net Worth: £6,676,006 *Total Assets:* £9,498,135
Registered Office: Qualitas House, 100 Elmgrove Road, Harrow, Middlesex, HA1 2RW
Activities: Other human health activities
Officers: Samik Basu [1985] Director [Indian]; Paul Joseph Cook [1979] Director

Clinisys Group Limited
Incorporated: 18 December 2001 *Employees:* 3
Net Worth: £652,000 *Total Assets:* £25,175,000
Registered Office: Two Bridges, Guildford Street, Chertsey, Surrey, KT16 9AU
Activities: Business and domestic software development
Parent: QSC 1209 Limited
Officers: Jason Phillip Conley [1975] Finance Director [American]; Robert Christopher Crisci [1975] Finance Director [American]; Robin Tarquinn Morris-Weston [1970] Director; John Kenneth Stipancich [1968] Director/Vice President, General Counsel and Secretary [American]

Clinisys Solutions Limited
Incorporated: 8 December 1997 *Employees:* 120
Net Worth: £19,643,000 *Total Assets:* £49,438,000
Registered Office: Two Bridges, Guildford Street, Chertsey, Surrey, KT16 9AU
Activities: Business and domestic software development
Officers: Jason Phillip Conley [1975] Finance Director [American]; Robert Christopher Crisci [1975] Finance Director [American]; Robin Tarquinn Morris-Weston [1970] Director; John Kenneth Stipancich [1968] Director/Vice President, General Counsel and Secretary [American]

Clion Limited
Incorporated: 21 March 2014
Net Worth: £5,154,616 *Total Assets:* £5,636,021
Registered Office: Portland House, 69-71 Wembley Hill Road, Wembley, Middlesex, HA9 8BU
Activities: Sea and coastal freight water transport
Parent: Focus Tankers Ltd
Officers: Bhupendra Shantilal Kansagra, Secretary; Laurent Elie Cadji [1977] Director/Businessman; Lewis Levy Cadji [1938] Director/Businessman; Bhupendra Shantilal Kansagra [1956] Director/Businessman; Ramesh Shantilal Kansagra [1950] Director/Businessman

Clivnars Limited
Incorporated: 15 March 1967 *Employees:* 33
Net Worth: £5,370,286 *Total Assets:* £6,130,867
Registered Office: Pindar Road, Hoddesdon, Herts, EN11 0EA
Activities: Other manufacturing n.e.c.
Shareholders: Kim Squires; Mark Squires
Officers: Kim Squires, Secretary; Kim Squires [1957] Director/Double Glazing Specialist; Mark Squires [1962] Director/Double Glazing Specialist

The Cloud Networks Limited
Incorporated: 28 May 2004 *Employees:* 61
Net Worth: £47,020,000 *Total Assets:* £72,240,000
Registered Office: Grant Way, Isleworth, Middlesex, TW7 5QD
Activities: Other telecommunications activities
Parent: Sky UK Limited
Officers: Christopher Jon Taylor, Secretary; David Nicholas Rey [1970] Managing Director; Colin Smith [1973] Finance Director

Cloud Possibilities Limited
Incorporated: 2 June 2015
Net Worth: £5,984,021 *Total Assets:* £8,233,487
Registered Office: 506 Centennial Park, Centennial Avenue, Elstree, Herts, WD6 3FG
Activities: Activities of other holding companies n.e.c.
Major Shareholder: Mehool Harshadray Sanghrajka
Officers: Professor Stephen John Heppell [1950] Director; David Leonard Prais [1964] Director; Mehool Harshadray Sanghrajka [1966] Director/IT Consultant; Vijay Narendra Shah [1981] Director; Vishaal Narendra Shah [1984] Director/Entrepreneur

Cloudview Holdings Limited
Incorporated: 8 June 2015 *Employees:* 13
Net Worth: £2,215,719 *Total Assets:* £5,397,384
Registered Office: Enterprise House, Beesons Yard, Bury Lane, Rickmansworth, Herts, WD3 1DS
Activities: Other business support service activities n.e.c.
Officers: Simon Peter Dudley Barker [1959] Accountant and Director; Christopher Stephen Burke [1960] Director; Richard Wilson Jewson [1944] Director; Husam Faisal Sorour [1979] Director/Finance Consultant; James Nicholas Becher Wickes [1960] Director

Clover Environmental Solutions Ltd
Incorporated: 13 February 2007 *Employees:* 61
Net Worth: £4,932,196 *Total Assets:* £5,944,463
Registered Office: Units 8 and 9 First Quarter, Blenheim Road, Epsom, Surrey, KT19 9QN
Activities: Collection of non-hazardous waste
Officers: Michael Welton, Secretary; Paul James Freshwater [1973] Director; Mark Perry [1960] Director; Brian Michael Regan [1972] Director/Vice President [American]; Michael Welton [1971] Director/Management [American]

Cloverton Property Ltd
Incorporated: 4 February 2003
Net Worth: £1,998,166 *Total Assets:* £11,653,989
Registered Office: 10 Broadfield Way, Buckhurst Hill, Essex, IG9 5AG
Activities: Other letting and operating of own or leased real estate
Officers: George Somogyi, Secretary/Director; George Somogyi [1953] Director; Thomas David Somogyi [1983] Director

J Clubb Limited
Incorporated: 30 September 1947 *Employees:* 62
Net Worth: £14,981,999 *Total Assets:* £20,621,548
Registered Office: Church Hill, Wilmington, Dartford, Kent, DA2 7DZ
Activities: Operation of gravel and sand pits; mining of clays and kaolin
Parent: Deneep Limited
Officers: Simon William Clubb [1960] Managing Director, F.C.C.A; Colin Dring [1957] Works Director; Jonathan James Lovett [1955] Commercial Director

Cluff Oil Limited
Incorporated: 18 December 1972
Net Worth: £54,890,000 *Total Assets:* £54,890,000
Registered Office: 4th Floor, Communications House, South Street, Staines upon Thames, Surrey, TW18 4PR
Activities: Activities of head offices
Officers: Kevin Patrick Ernest Davies, Secretary; Kevin Patrick Ernest Davies [1957] Director/Transitional Manager

CMG Holdco Limited
Incorporated: 19 September 2013 *Employees:* 2,242
Net Worth: £39,477,000 *Total Assets:* £131,002,000
Registered Office: Ground Floor, Q1 The Square, Randalls Way, Leatherhead, Surrey, KT22 7TW
Activities: Residential care activities for learning difficulties, mental health and substance abuse
Parent: Galaxy Group Bidco Limited
Officers: Garry Fitton, Secretary; Ruben Kumar Bhagobati [1971] Director/Partner; Malcolm Brown [1967] Director/Senior Principal; Garry John Fitton [1972] Director/Chartered Accountant; Peter Kinsey [1964] Director; Adam Ringer [1980] Investment Director; David Andrew Spruzen [1967] Director

CML Projects Technology Limited
Incorporated: 7 November 2013 *Employees:* 2
Net Worth: £2,143,844 *Total Assets:* £5,007,346
Registered Office: c/o Hillier Hopkins LLP, First Floor, Radius House, 51 Clarendon Road, Watford, Herts, WD17 1HP
Activities: Television programming and broadcasting activities
Major Shareholder: Paul Antony Brett
Officers: Paul Antony Brett [1969] Director/Businessman; Yngrid Darey Rico Florez [1976] Director/Administration [Venezuelan]

CNM Estates (Tolworth Tower MB) Limited
Incorporated: 8 September 2015
Net Worth: £13,510,236 *Total Assets:* £54,246,356
Registered Office: Aissela, 46 High Street, Esher, Surrey, KT10 9QY
Activities: Development of building projects
Parent: CNM Estates (Tolworth Tower MBP) Limited
Officers: Wahid Samady [1961] Director/Consultant

CNM Estates (Tolworth Tower MBP) Limited
Incorporated: 7 September 2015
Net Worth: £13,506,661 *Total Assets:* £26,888,992
Registered Office: Aissela, 46 High Street, Esher, Surrey, KT10 9QY
Activities: Development of building projects
Parent: CNM Estates Holdings Limited
Officers: Wahid Samady [1961] Director/Consultant

CNM Estates (Tolworth Tower SBP) Limited
Incorporated: 7 September 2015
Net Worth: £13,516,786 *Total Assets:* £26,901,492
Registered Office: Aissela, 46 High Street, Esher, Surrey, KT10 9QY
Activities: Development of building projects
Parent: CNM Estates (Tolworth Tower MB) Limited
Officers: Wahid Samady [1961] Director/Consultant

CNM Estates Holdings Limited
Incorporated: 7 September 2015
Net Worth: £13,408,390 *Total Assets:* £28,212,946
Registered Office: Aissela, 46 High Street, Esher, Surrey, KT10 9QY
Activities: Development of building projects
Major Shareholder: Wahid Samady
Officers: Wahid Samady [1961] Director/Consultant

CNOOC Ettrick U.K. Limited
Incorporated: 13 April 2000
Previous: CNOOC Ettrick U.K Limited
Net Worth: £108,092,656 *Total Assets:* £129,054,616
Registered Office: Prospect House, 97 Oxford Road, Uxbridge, Middlesex, UB8 1LU
Activities: Extraction of crude petroleum
Parent: Nexen Petroleum U.K. Limited
Officers: Jamie David Doyle, Secretary; Jamie David Doyle [1975] Director; Zhi Fang [1962] Director [Chinese]; Ray Christopher John Riddoch [1961] Managing Director; Ian Michael Smale [1960] Director; Brent Christian Tilford [1978] Finance Director

CNOOC Petroleum Europe Limited
Incorporated: 24 April 1972 *Employees:* 590
Previous: Nexen Petroleum U.K. Limited
Net Worth: £235,028,256 *Total Assets:* £1,519,397,376
Registered Office: Prospect House, 97 Oxford Road, Uxbridge, Middlesex, UB8 1LU
Activities: Extraction of crude petroleum
Parent: CNOOC UK Limited
Officers: Jamie David Doyle, Secretary; Jamie David Doyle [1975] Director; Zhi Fang [1962] Director [Chinese]; Ray Christopher John Riddoch [1961] Managing Director; Ian Michael Smale [1960] Director; Brent Christian Tilford [1978] Finance Director

CNOOC Petroleum Farragon U.K. Limited
Incorporated: 6 December 2005
Previous: Nexen Petroleum Dragon U.K. Limited
Net Worth: £6,217,702 *Total Assets:* £12,651,601
Registered Office: Prospect House, 97 Oxford Road, Uxbridge, Middlesex, UB8 1LU
Activities: Extraction of crude petroleum
Parent: Nexen Petroleum U.K. Limited
Officers: Jamie David Doyle, Secretary; Jamie David Doyle [1975] Director; Zhi Fang [1962] Director [Chinese]; Ray Christopher John Riddoch [1961] Managing Director; Ian Michael Smale [1960] Director; Brent Christian Tilford [1978] Finance Director

CNOOC UK Limited
Incorporated: 6 February 2013
Net Worth: £5,234,651,648 *Total Assets:* £6,177,024,512
Registered Office: Prospect House, 97 Oxford Road, Uxbridge, Middlesex, UB8 1LU
Activities: Other business support service activities n.e.c.
Parent: CNOOC Limited
Officers: Jamie David Doyle, Secretary; Jamie David Doyle [1975] Director; Zhi Fang [1962] Director [Chinese]; Ray Christopher John Riddoch [1961] Managing Director; Brent Christian Tilford [1978] Finance Director

Coats Finance Co. Limited
Incorporated: 13 March 1991
Net Worth: £162,464,816 *Total Assets:* £598,715,840
Registered Office: 1 The Square, Stockley Park, Uxbridge, Middlesex, UB11 1TD
Activities: Other business support service activities n.e.c.
Parent: Coats Holdings Ltd
Officers: Nicholas James Kidd [1977] Director; Andrew James Stockwell [1966] Director

Coats Global Services Limited
Incorporated: 4 November 2003
Net Worth: £13,175,000 *Total Assets:* £14,377,000
Registered Office: 1 The Square, Stockley Park, Uxbridge, Middlesex, UB11 1TD
Activities: Activities of head offices
Parent: Coats Group Finance Company Limited
Officers: Adrian John Elliott [1965] Director; Yael Gairola [1973] Director

Coats Group Finance Company Limited
Incorporated: 7 November 2016 *Employees:* 3
Net Worth: £1,156,718,208 *Total Assets:* £1,441,565,824
Registered Office: 1 The Square, Stockley Park, Uxbridge, Middlesex, UB11 1TD
Activities: Activities of financial services holding companies
Parent: Coats PLC
Officers: Stuart John Morgan, Secretary; Simon Boddie [1960] Director; Rajiv Sharma [1966] Director [Singaporean]; Andrew James Stockwell [1966] Director

Coats Group PLC
Incorporated: 17 June 1909 *Employees:* 19,085
Previous: Guinness Peat Group PLC
Net Worth: £215,216,576 *Total Assets:* £1,002,335,232
Registered Office: 1 The Square, Stockley Park, Uxbridge, Middlesex, UB11 1TD
Activities: Activities of head offices
Officers: Stuart John Morgan, Secretary; Michael Nicholas Allen [1959] Director [New Zealander]; Simon Boddie [1960] Director; Nicholas James Douglas Bull [1952] Director; Michael Clasper [1953] Director; Anne Kathleen Fahy [1960] Director [Irish]; David Peter Gosnell [1957] Director; Hongyan Echo Lu [1974] Director [Chinese]; Frances Paxson Philip [1958] Director [American]; Richard Alan Rosling [1962] Director; Rajiv Sharma [1966] Director [Singaporean]

Coats Industrial Thread Limited
Incorporated: 13 October 1937
Net Worth: £39,971,380 *Total Assets:* £44,122,168
Registered Office: 1 The Square, Stockley Park, Uxbridge, Middlesex, UB11 1TD
Activities: Activities of head offices
Parent: Coats Group Finance Company Limited
Officers: Wai Kuen Chiang [1968] Director [Singaporean]; Richard Charles Reade [1973] Director

Coats Limited
Incorporated: 18 December 2002 *Employees:* 2
Previous: Coats PLC
Net Worth: £815,443,968 *Total Assets:* £896,296,000
Registered Office: 1 The Square, Stockley Park, Uxbridge, Middlesex, UB11 1TD
Activities: Activities of head offices
Parent: Coats Group PLC
Officers: Stuart John Morgan, Secretary; Simon Boddie [1960] Director; Rajiv Sharma [1966] Director [Singaporean]

Cobalt Ground Solutions Limited
Incorporated: 29 March 1995 *Employees:* 862
Net Worth: £8,838,445 *Total Assets:* £14,275,416
Registered Office: 2 World Business Centre, Newall Road, London Heathrow Airport, Hounslow, Middlesex, TW6 2SF
Activities: Service activities incidental to air transportation
Officers: Robert Leslie David Baker, Secretary; Claude Guedj [1938] Director [French]; Karine Guedj [1962] Director [French]; Nathalie Jaoui [1963] Director [French]; Marc Lemaitre [1962] Director [French]; Darren Moloney [1976] Director [Irish]

Cobalt Limited
Incorporated: 22 August 1984 *Employees:* 2
Net Worth: £13,626,708 *Total Assets:* £18,342,844
Registered Office: 1 Sherman Road, Bromley, Kent, BR1 3JH
Activities: Other letting and operating of own or leased real estate
Shareholders: Alan Stephen Cornish; Robert Sargent
Officers: Alan Stephen Cornish, Secretary; Robert Sargent, Secretary/Director; Alan Stephen Cornish [1955] Director; Robert Sargent [1964] Director

Cobham Hall
Incorporated: 16 March 1961 *Employees:* 92
Net Worth: £4,687,244 *Total Assets:* £7,448,962
Registered Office: Cobham Hall, Cobham, Gravesend, Kent, DA12 3BL
Activities: Other accommodation
Officers: David Standen, Secretary; John Anderson Calder Dick [1954] Director; Sarah Charlotte Jane McRitchie [1966] Editorial Director; Dr Katrina O'Neill-Byrne [1961] Director/Medical Doctor [Irish]; Martin David Pennell [1963] Director/Solicitor; Graham Francis Smith [1963] Director/Consultant; Colin Sykes [1943] Director/Civil Servant; Susan Anne Margaret Grace Webb [1956] Director/Retired Headteacher

Cobird Limited
Incorporated: 28 August 1997
Net Worth: £8,360,542 *Total Assets:* £9,830,196
Registered Office: Salisbury House, 20 Queens Road, Weybridge, Surrey, KT13 9XE
Activities: Other research and experimental development on natural sciences and engineering
Shareholders: Corncrake Limited; Gargonay Limited; Phalarope Limited
Officers: Martin Richard Tracey Church, Secretary/Doctor; Dr Susannah Margaret Blundell [1965] Director; Jonathan Christian Martin Church [1960] Director/Engineer; Martin Richard Tracey Church [1962] Director/Doctor

Coborn Engineering Company Limited
Incorporated: 13 October 1942 *Employees:* 79
Net Worth: £2,961,557 *Total Assets:* £6,378,450
Registered Office: Chesham Close, Romford, Essex, RM7 7PJ
Activities: Manufacture of other machine tools
Parent: Trochilics Limited
Officers: Carolyn Phyllis Innocent, Secretary; Richard Cox [1959] Director; John Lewis Innocent [1941] Director/Engineer; Matthew Lewis Innocent [1977] Director; Vincent Leatt [1954] Director/Electronics Engineer; Daniel Lyons [1975] Director/Finance Manager; Stephen Westlake [1958] Managing Director

Cobra Industries Limited
Incorporated: 16 February 1995 *Employees:* 49
Net Worth: £5,531,263 *Total Assets:* £6,610,292
Registered Office: Pindar Road, Hoddesdon, Herts, EN11 0JX
Activities: Manufacture of sports goods
Officers: Damian Sebastian Ara [1980] Director/Sales Manager; Colin John Harris [1956] Director; Geoffrey Colin Paxman [1965] Director/Sales Manager; Robert James St Clair Pringle [1955] Director/Sales Manager

Coca-Cola European Partners Great Britain Limited
Incorporated: 24 July 1888 *Employees:* 3,440
Previous: Coca-Cola Enterprises Limited
Net Worth: £739,393,024 *Total Assets:* £1,293,049,984
Registered Office: Pemberton House, Bakers Road, Uxbridge, Middlesex, UB8 1EZ
Activities: Manufacture of soft drinks; production of mineral waters and other bottled waters
Parent: Coca-Cola European Partners Holdings Great Britain Limited
Officers: Huma Allana, Secretary; Huma Allana [1975] Company Secretary/Director; Michael Clark [1970] Director; Leendert Pieter Den Hollander [1969] Director/Vice President & General Manager CCE Ltd [Dutch]; Frank Govaerts [1961] Director/European General Counsel [Belgian]; Ed Owen Walker [1967] Director

Coca-Cola European Partners Holdings Great Britain Limited
Incorporated: 15 March 1996
Previous: Coca-Cola Enterprises Great Britain Limited
Net Worth: £1,429,897,984 *Total Assets:* £1,720,679,040
Registered Office: Pemberton House, Bakers Road, Uxbridge, Middlesex, UB8 1EZ
Activities: Activities of head offices
Parent: Bottling Great Britain Limited
Officers: Huma Allana, Secretary; Huma Allana [1975] Company Secretary/Director; Michael Clark [1970] Director; Leendert Pieter Den Hollander [1969] Director/Vice President & General Manager CCE Ltd [Dutch]; Frank Govaerts [1961] Director/European General Counsel [Belgian]; Ed Owen Walker [1967] Director

Coca-Cola European Partners PLC
Incorporated: 4 August 2015 *Employees:* 24
Net Worth: £5,847,109,120 *Total Assets:* £15,913,583,616
Registered Office: Pemberton House, Bakers Road, Uxbridge, Middlesex, UB8 1EZ
Activities: Manufacture of soft drinks; production of mineral waters and other bottled waters
Officers: Clare Wardle, Secretary; Jan Bennink [1956] Director [Dutch]; Francisco Javier Crespo Benitez [1965] Director [American]; Christine Cross [1951] Director; Sol Daurella [1966] Director/Chairperson; Javier Ferran [1956] Director; Irial Finan [1957] Director/Executive Vice President [Irish]; Damian Paul Gammell [1970] Director [Irish]; Nathalie Laurence Gaveau [1975] Director [French]; Alvaro Gomez-Trenor Aguilar [1952] Director [Spanish]; Philip Humann [1945] Director [American]; Orrin Henry Ingram II [1960] Director [American]; Thomas Johnson [1949] Director [American]; Alfonso Libano Daurella [1954] Director [Spanish]; Mario Rotllant Sola [1951] Director [Spanish]; Jose Ignacio Comenge Sanchez Real [1951] Director [Spanish]; Garry Watts [1956] Director/Chairman of BTG PLC; Curtis Welling [1949] Director [American]

Coca-Cola European Partners Services Europe Limited
Incorporated: 19 July 1996 *Employees:* 326
Previous: Coca-Cola Enterprises Europe Limited
Net Worth: £10,440,000 *Total Assets:* £25,873,000
Registered Office: Pemberton House, Bakers Road, Uxbridge, Middlesex, UB8 1EZ
Activities: Activities of head offices
Parent: Coca-Cola European Partners Holdings Great Britain Limited
Officers: Huma Allana, Secretary; Huma Allana [1975] Company Secretary/Director; Michael Clark [1970] Director; Frank Govaerts [1961] Director/European General Counsel [Belgian]; Stephen James Lusk [1970] Director; Ed Owen Walker [1967] Director

Cochlear Europe Limited
Incorporated: 10 November 1999 *Employees:* 127
Net Worth: £77,203,344 *Total Assets:* £120,014,048
Registered Office: 6 Dashwood Lang Road, Bourne Business Park, Addlestone, Surrey, KT15 2HJ
Activities: Other human health activities
Officers: David Thomas Mark Ashton, Secretary; David Thomas Mark Ashton [1959] Director/Vice President Business Operations; Richard John Brook [1963] Director/President Europe Middle East; Brent Andrew Cubis [1964] Director [Australian]; Christian Paul Zuscak [1975] Director/Finance Manager [Australian]

Cochlear Research and Development Limited
Incorporated: 29 May 2003 *Employees:* 84
Net Worth: £6,964,754 *Total Assets:* £17,894,680
Registered Office: 6 Dashwood Lang Road, Bourne Business Park, Addlestone, Surrey, KT15 2HJ
Activities: Other human health activities
Parent: Cochlear Europe Limited
Officers: David Thomas Mark Ashton, Secretary; David Thomas Mark Ashton [1959] Director/VP Business Operations; Richard John Brook [1963] Director; Brent Andrew Cubis [1964] Director [Australian]; Christian Paul Zuscak [1975] Director/Finance Manager [Australian]

Coex Properties LLP
Incorporated: 5 May 2009 *Employees:* 2
Net Worth: £6,002,571 *Total Assets:* £10,249,546
Registered Office: c/o Haslers, Old Station Road, Loughton, Essex, IG10 4PL
Officers: Lovisa Elina Elisabet Pelosi [1990] Member; Andrew John Sheen [1959] Member; Karola Elisabet Sheen [1957] Member; Lukas Wilhelm Sheen [1985] Member

Harry A.Coff,Limited
Incorporated: 12 April 1937 *Employees:* 3
Net Worth: £6,103,655 *Total Assets:* £6,175,491
Registered Office: Ludwell House, 2 Guildford Street, Chertsey, Surrey, KT16 9BQ
Activities: Other letting and operating of own or leased real estate
Parent: Coff Holdings Ltd
Officers: Richard Paul Coff, Secretary; Lynda Coff [1960] Director/Administrator; Richard Paul Coff [1960] Director

J. Coffey Construction Limited
Incorporated: 10 June 1994 *Employees:* 105
Net Worth: £16,315,123 *Total Assets:* £45,137,436
Registered Office: 93-95 Greenford Road, Harrow, Middlesex, HA1 3QF
Activities: Other specialised construction activities n.e.c.
Major Shareholder: James Anthony Coffey
Officers: Edward Generald Barrett [1965] Director/Surveyor [Irish]; James Anthony Coffey [1954] Director/Building Contractor [Irish]; Mary Teresa Coffey [1957] Director/Secretary [Irish]; Thomas Patrick Mitchell [1958] Director [Irish]

Coldunell Limited
Incorporated: 8 January 1959
Net Worth: £52,519,100 *Total Assets:* £88,482,592
Registered Office: Dawes Court House, Dawes Court, High Street, Esher, Surrey, KT10 9QD
Activities: Other letting and operating of own or leased real estate
Shareholder: David Henry Dunsdon
Officers: John Aoun, Secretary; Rita Vivienne O'Rourke, Secretary; David Henry Dunsdon [1982] Director; Rita Vivienne O'Rourke [1928] Director

Collaborative Services Support (NE) Holdings Limited
Incorporated: 16 February 2009
Net Worth Deficit: £6,785,000 *Total Assets:* £31,484,000
Registered Office: 8 White Oak Square, London Road, Swanley, Kent, BR8 7AG
Activities: Activities of head offices
Parent: Palio (No 14) Limited
Officers: Keerthana Sivanathan [1988] Director/Senior Management Accountant; Neil Woodburn [1979] Director/Chartered Building Surveyor

Collaborative Services Support NE Limited
Incorporated: 5 March 2009
Net Worth Deficit: £6,785,000 *Total Assets:* £31,484,000
Registered Office: 8 White Oak Square, London Road, Swanley, Kent, BR8 7AG
Activities: Construction of commercial buildings
Parent: Collaborative Services Support (NE) Holdings Limited
Officers: Keerthana Sivanathan [1988] Director/Senior Management Accountant; Neil Woodburn [1979] Director/Chartered Building Surveyor

The Collegiate Trust
Incorporated: 4 May 2012 *Employees:* 258
Previous: Riddlesdown Collegiate Academy Trust
Net Worth: £27,989,108 *Total Assets:* £31,812,864
Registered Office: Riddlesdown Collegiate, Honister Heights, Purley, Surrey, CR8 1EX
Activities: General secondary education
Officers: David Clarke, Secretary; Keith Charles Beattie [1974] Director/Management Consultant; Philip Richard Hogan [1959] Director/Retired; Fiona Margaret McSorley [1953] Director/Retired; Sylvia Doreen Moys [1959] Director/Chartered Secretary; Alastair Roseweir [1975] Director/IT; Gordon Hodge Smith [1966] Director/Headteacher

Collins 2017 Limited
Incorporated: 30 January 2017 *Employees:* 124
Net Worth: £9,313,874 *Total Assets:* £46,422,452
Registered Office: No 1 Croydon, 12-16 Addiscombe Road, Croydon, Surrey, CR0 0XT
Activities: Development of building projects
Shareholders: Christopher David Bartram; Hannah Frances Bartram
Officers: Michael Maximillian Barrett [1970] Director/Contracts Manager; Christopher David Bartram [1967] Director/Surveyor; Hannah Frances Bartram [1968] Director/Housewife; Mary Louise Brooks [1971] Director/Chartered Accountant; Stephen Davies [1971] Director; Mark Joseph Dockery [1967] Director; Stuart James Johnson [1972] Director; Colin Payne [1969] Director; Jason Mark Warren [1968] Director

Collins Construction Ltd
Incorporated: 25 January 1956 *Employees:* 124
Previous: Collins Construction PLC
Net Worth: £7,337,646 *Total Assets:* £34,222,440
Registered Office: No 1 Croydon, 12-16 Addiscombe Road, Croydon, Surrey, CR0 0XT
Activities: Other specialised construction activities n.e.c.
Parent: Collins 2017 Limited
Officers: Christopher David Bartram, Secretary; Michael Maximillian Barrett [1970] Director/Contracts Manager; Christopher David Bartram [1967] Director/Surveyor; Hannah Frances Bartram [1968] Director/Housewife; Mary Louise Brooks [1971] Director/Chartered Accountant; Stephen Davies [1971] Director; Mark Joseph Dockery [1967] Director; Stuart James Johnson [1972] Director; Colin Payne [1969] Director; Jason Mark Warren [1968] Director

Thomas H. Collison Limited
Incorporated: 30 July 1975 *Employees:* 47
Net Worth: £11,273,723 *Total Assets:* £11,790,743
Registered Office: Chateau Vingt, Firfields, Cobbetts Hill, Weybridge, Surrey, KT13 0UD
Activities: Other human health activities
Shareholder: Brian Thomas Collison
Officers: Brian Collison, Secretary; Brian Thomas Collison [1951] Director/Dispensing Optician

P. Colohan & Co. Limited
Incorporated: 7 December 1973 *Employees:* 18
Net Worth: £9,655,396 *Total Assets:* £10,987,848
Registered Office: 238 Station Road, Addlestone, Surrey, KT15 2PS
Activities: Construction of commercial buildings
Major Shareholder: Patrick Benedictus Colohan
Officers: Margaret Mary Colohan, Secretary [Irish]; Margaret Mary Colohan [1944] Director [Irish]; Patrick Benedictus Colohan [1942] Director/Carpenter/Contractor [Irish]

Colorcon European Holdings (No.5) Limited
Incorporated: 2 November 2012
Net Worth: £642,689,152 *Total Assets:* £695,000,000
Registered Office: Flagship House, Victory Way, Crossways, Dartford, Kent, DA2 6QD
Activities: Activities of other holding companies n.e.c.
Parent: Colorcon European Holdings (No.4) Limited
Officers: Stephen John Bachelor, Secretary; David Francis Bain [1971] Managing Director - EMEA; Stephen John Bachelor [1967] Director; Martti Tapani Hedman [1958] Director/Chief Executive Officer [Finnish]

Colorcon Limited
Incorporated: 7 January 1971 *Employees:* 252
Net Worth: £35,843,076 *Total Assets:* £81,699,008
Registered Office: Flagship House, Victory Way, Crossways, Dartford, Kent, DA2 6QD
Activities: Manufacture of basic pharmaceutical products
Parent: Colorcon European Holdings (No.5) Limited
Officers: Stephen John Bachelor, Secretary; David Francis Bain [1971] Managing Director - EMEA; Stephen John Bachelor [1967] Finance Director; Martti Tapani Hedman [1958] Director/Chief Executive Officer [Finnish]

Colts Cabs Limited
Incorporated: 26 July 1991
Net Worth: £5,593,067 *Total Assets:* £14,243,478
Registered Office: 5 Elstree Gate, Elstree Way, Borehamwood, Herts, WD6 1JD
Activities: Taxi operation
Major Shareholder: Michael Glassman
Officers: Michael Glassman [1963] Director/Taxi Fleet Operator

Combat Stress
Incorporated: 11 May 1931 *Employees:* 312
Previous: Ex-Services Mental Welfare Society
Net Worth: £19,510,000 *Total Assets:* £20,353,000
Registered Office: Tyrwhitt House, Oaklawn Road, Leatherhead, Surrey, KT22 0BX
Activities: Specialists medical practice activities
Officers: Jeffrey Malcolm Harrison, Secretary; Peter Allen [1946] Director; Sally Goldthorpe [1961] Director/HR Business Partner; Lieutenant General Andrew John Noble Graham [1956] Director; Mark Andrew Izatt [1969] Director/Communications; Calvin Cheuk Lun Manager [1973] Director/Consultant; Christian Kenneth Bowring Melville [1965] Director/Lawyer; Mary Molesworth-St.Aubyn [1942] Director/Chairman NHS Trust; Michael Peter Morrissey [1959] Director/Head of Distribution; Jan Janusz Sobieraj [1957] Director/Head of Leadership; Dr Suzy Nicola Walton [1963] Director; Professor Sir Simon Charles Wessely [1956] Director/Doctor

Combe International Limited
Incorporated: 13 March 1974 *Employees:* 10
Net Worth: £3,571,132 *Total Assets:* £8,769,294
Registered Office: Cedar Court, Guildford Road, Leatherhead, Surrey, KT22 9RX
Activities: Manufacture of perfumes and toilet preparations
Officers: Adrian McCulloch, Secretary; Keech Combe-Shetty [1977] Director/Co-Chief Executive Officer [American]; Akshay Anand Shetty [1977] Director/SVP Global Operations Co-Head Asia & Latin America [Indian]; Clare Want [1966] Managing Director

Combined Counties Properties Limited
Incorporated: 22 March 1978 *Employees:* 10
Net Worth: £45,769,784 *Total Assets:* £49,416,748
Registered Office: Coldunell House, Dawes Court, Esher, Surrey, KT10 9QD
Activities: Buying and selling of own real estate
Officers: John Aoun, Secretary; Rita Vivienne O'Rourke, Secretary; David Henry Dunsdon [1982] Director; Sarah Hildred Gay Dunsdon [1949] Director

Comfort Hotels Limited
Incorporated: 31 January 1978
Net Worth: £22,275,182 *Total Assets:* £22,275,182
Registered Office: Maple Court, Central Park, Reeds Crescent, Watford, Herts, WD24 4QQ
Activities: Hotels and similar accommodation
Parent: Hilton Worldwide Limited
Officers: Stuart Beasley [1971] Director/Financial Controller; Richard Geoffrey Beeston [1982] Director/Chartered Accountant; Michelle Momdjian [1976] Director/Attorney; George Christopher Ogle [1974] Director/Attorney; James Owen Percival [1968] Director/Accountant

Commercial Freeholds & Investments Ltd
Incorporated: 12 January 2015 *Employees:* 5
Net Worth: £1,743,297 *Total Assets:* £29,262,552
Registered Office: 5 Elstree Gate, Elstree Way, Borehamwood, Herts, WD6 1JD
Activities: Development of building projects
Major Shareholder: Christopher Richard Cradock
Officers: Samantha Bolton [1972] Director; Christopher Richard Cradock [1942] Director; Francis Christoper Richard Cradock [1962] Director; Susan Margret Drake Cradock [1942] Director; Tracy Margaret Joannie MacDonald [1964] Director

Commodore Kitchens Limited
Incorporated: 9 May 1979 *Employees:* 152
Net Worth: £9,970,740 *Total Assets:* £23,798,642
Registered Office: Acorn House, Gumley Road, Grays, Essex, RM20 4XP
Activities: Manufacture of kitchen furniture
Parent: Nobia Holdings UK Limited
Officers: Nicola Jane Hardcastle, Secretary; Antony Lawrence Amodio [1965] Director; Daniel Arthur Edward Carr [1975] Finance Director; Peter Kane [1965] Managing Director; Kristoffer Ljungfelt [1977] Director [Swedish]; Darren James Mahoney [1966] Design Director; Jasdip Nijjar [1986] Director

Communications & Power Industries Europe Limited
Incorporated: 16 June 1995 *Employees:* 20
Net Worth: £10,969,372 *Total Assets:* £12,053,019
Registered Office: Abbey House, Wellington Way, Brooklands Business Park, Weybridge, Surrey, KT13 0TT
Activities: Agents involved in the sale of machinery, industrial equipment, ships and aircraft
Officers: John Beighley, Secretary/Vice President of Sales [American]; Stephen Paul Mummert, Secretary; John Beighley [1952] Director/Vice President of Sales [American]; Robert Kemp [1954] Director/Chief Financial Officer [American]; Wolfgang Alfred Tschunke [1966] Director [German]

Community Stores Limited
Incorporated: 4 November 2009
Net Worth: £5,020,971 *Total Assets:* £8,375,156
Registered Office: 2 Peterwood Way, Croydon, Surrey, CR0 4UQ
Activities: Activities of head offices
Parent: ABC Drug Stores Limited
Officers: Ameetkumar Patel, Secretary; Heena Patel [1963] Finance Director; Jayantibhai Chimanbhai Patel [1945] Director; Jayanti Chimanbhai Patel Junior [1984] Director

Community Support Project Limited
Incorporated: 20 September 2006
Net Worth: £2,925,000 *Total Assets:* £6,403,000
Registered Office: 5th Floor, Metropolitan House, Darkes Lane, Potters Bar, Herts, EN6 1AG
Activities: Other residential care activities n.e.c.
Parent: Caretech Holdings PLC
Officers: Gareth Dufton, Secretary; Gareth Dufton [1976] Director/Chartered Accountant; Farouq Rashid Sheikh [1958] Director; Haroon Rashid Sheikh [1956] Director

Compagnie Fruitiere UK Limited
Incorporated: 30 December 1969 *Employees:* 113
Net Worth: £18,376,000 *Total Assets:* £26,638,000
Registered Office: 12 Newtons Court, Galleon Boulevard, Crossways Business Park, Dartford, Kent, DA2 6QL
Activities: Wholesale of fruit and vegetables
Major Shareholder: Robert Elie Gabriel Fabre
Officers: Jerome Ferdinand Laurent Pierre Fabre [1978] Director [French]; William Francis Feeney [1942] Director [French/American]; Gautier Christian Philippe Fischel [1982] Director/Vice President Distribution and Marketing [French]; Keith Ernest Sadler [1958] Director; Jan Baptist Van Opstal [1951] Director [French]

The Company of Animals Limited
Incorporated: 24 June 1986 *Employees:* 36
Net Worth: £2,036,006 *Total Assets:* £6,526,600
Registered Office: Ruxbury Farm, St Anns Hill Road, Chertsey, Surrey, KT16 9NL
Activities: Non-specialised wholesale trade
Major Shareholder: Roger Arthur Mugford
Officers: Paul Marshall, Secretary; Paul Marshall [1960] Director/Chartered Accountant; Roger Arthur Mugford [1946] Director/Animal Psychologist; Paul John Christopher Nolan [1986] Operations Director

Comparex UK Limited
Incorporated: 5 October 1994 *Employees:* 48
Net Worth: £1,480,642 *Total Assets:* £33,477,328
Registered Office: OneSixSix, 166 College Road, Harrow, Middlesex, HA1 1BH
Activities: Information technology consultancy activities
Officers: Richard Best [1973] Managing Director; Marcel Kloeppner [1977] Finance Director [German]

Compass Forest Products Limited
Incorporated: 8 March 1985 *Employees:* 13
Net Worth: £3,604,888 *Total Assets:* £10,677,546
Registered Office: Clock House, Station Approach, Shepperton, Surrey, TW17 8AN
Activities: Wholesale of wood, construction materials and sanitary equipment
Parent: Consolidated Timber Holdings Ltd
Officers: David John Colman [1962] Director/Chartered Accountant; Peter Corlett [1964] Director/Sales Executive; Simon David Holdsworth [1956] Director/Chartered Accountant; Stephen Peter Sabine [1963] Director; Andrew Peter Smith [1959] Director; David Alan Whitehill [1969] Sales Director

Compass Group Finance No. 3 Limited
Incorporated: 21 April 2016
Net Worth: £615,609,984 *Total Assets:* £619,163,008
Registered Office: Compass House, Guildford Street, Chertsey, Surrey, KT16 9BQ
Activities: Activities of head offices
Shareholders: Compass Overseas Holdings Limited; Compass Overseas Holdings No.2 Limited
Officers: Sarah Jane Sergeant [1973] Director/Accountant; Alison Rebecca Yapp [1965] Director/Solicitor

Compass Group Finance No.2 Limited
Incorporated: 28 February 1996
Net Worth: £392,780,992 *Total Assets:* £1,143,321,984
Registered Office: Compass House, Guildford Street, Chertsey, Surrey, KT16 9BQ
Activities: Activities of head offices
Parent: Compass Group PLC
Officers: Sarah Jane Sergeant [1973] Director/Accountant; Alison Rebecca Yapp [1965] Director/Solicitor

Compass Group Finance No.4 Limited
Incorporated: 25 February 2004
Net Worth: £104,034,168 *Total Assets:* £111,322,264
Registered Office: Compass House, Guildford Street, Chertsey, Surrey, KT16 9BQ
Activities: Non-trading company
Shareholders: Compass Group PLC; Compass Group Finance No.5 Limited; Walbrook Asset Management Limited
Officers: Sarah Jane Sergeant [1973] Director/Accountant; Alison Rebecca Yapp [1965] Director/Solicitor

Compass Group Holdings Public Limited Company
Incorporated: 16 January 1987
Net Worth: £3,901,499,904 *Total Assets:* £8,942,300,160
Registered Office: Compass House, Guildford Street, Chertsey, Surrey, KT16 9BQ
Activities: Event catering activities
Parent: Hospitality Holdings Limited
Officers: Alison Rebecca Yapp, Secretary; Dominic William Blakemore [1969] Director; Charles Palmer Brown [1971] Director/Accountant and Lawyer [American]; Alison Rebecca Yapp [1965] Director/Solicitor

Compass Group North America Investments Limited
Incorporated: 8 September 2005
Net Worth: £2,650,300,672 *Total Assets:* £2,889,749,248
Registered Office: Compass House, Guildford Street, Chertsey, Surrey, KT16 9BQ
Activities: Non-trading company
Parent: Compass Overseas Holdings No.2 Limited
Officers: Sarah Jane Sergeant [1973] Director/Accountant; Alison Rebecca Yapp [1965] Director/Solicitor

Compass Group North America Investments No.2
Incorporated: 16 February 2005
Net Worth: £1,572,128 *Total Assets:* £754,867,776
Registered Office: Compass House, Guildford Street, Chertsey, Surrey, KT16 9BA
Activities: Non-trading company
Parent: Compass Group Holdings PLC
Officers: Sarah Jane Sergeant [1973] Director/Accountant

Compass Group PLC
Incorporated: 29 September 2000 *Employees:* 595,841
Net Worth: £2,615,000,064 *Total Assets:* £12,266,000,384
Registered Office: Compass House, Guildford Street, Chertsey, Surrey, KT16 9BQ
Activities: Activities of head offices
Officers: Alison Rebecca Yapp, Secretary; Carol Ann Arrowsmith [1954] Director/Partner, Deloitte; John George Bason [1957] Director; Dominic William Blakemore [1969] Director; Stefan Bomhard [1967] Director [German]; John Anthony Bryant [1965] Director [American]; Gary Richard Green [1957] Director; Anne-Francoise Nesmes [1971] Director [French]; Nelson Luiz Costa Silva [1955] Director [Brazilian]; Ireena Vittal [1968] Director [Indian]; Paul Steven Walsh [1955] Director

Compass Group Procurement Limited
Incorporated: 21 February 2007
Net Worth: £9,469,000 *Total Assets:* £23,340,000
Registered Office: Compass House, Guildford Street, Chertsey, Surrey, KT16 9BQ
Activities: Event catering activities
Parent: Compass Group Holdings PLC
Officers: Paul Martin Baker [1969] Director; Sarah Jane Sergeant [1973] Director/Accountant; Venkatesh Shantaram [1972] Managing Director

Compass Hotels Chertsey
Incorporated: 4 July 2001
Net Worth: £773,878,016 *Total Assets:* £783,217,024
Registered Office: Compass House, Guildford Street, Chertsey, Surrey, KT16 9BQ
Activities: Non-trading company
Parent: Compass Overseas Holdings No.2 Limited
Officers: Sarah Jane Sergeant [1973] Director/Accountant

Compass Overseas Holdings Limited
Incorporated: 11 May 1992
Net Worth: £1,488,889,984 *Total Assets:* £1,667,874,048
Registered Office: Compass House, Guildford Street, Chertsey, Surrey, KT16 9BQ
Activities: Activities of head offices
Parent: Compass Overseas Holdings No.2 Limited
Officers: Sarah Jane Sergeant [1973] Director/Accountant; Alison Rebecca Yapp [1965] Director/Solicitor

Compass Overseas Holdings No.2 Limited
Incorporated: 11 July 1995
Net Worth: £7,930,598,912 *Total Assets:* £11,884,215,296
Registered Office: Compass House, Guildford Street, Chertsey, Surrey, KT16 9BQ
Activities: Activities of head offices
Parent: Compass Group Holdings PLC
Officers: Sarah Jane Sergeant [1973] Director/Accountant; Alison Rebecca Yapp [1965] Director/Solicitor

Complete Coffee Limited
Incorporated: 4 March 1929 *Employees:* 13
Net Worth: £2,359,831 *Total Assets:* £12,168,002
Registered Office: Corinthian House, 17 Lansdowne Road, Croydon, Surrey, CR0 2BX
Activities: Wholesale of coffee, tea, cocoa and spices
Parent: Associated Coffee Merchants International Ltd
Officers: David John Eagle, Secretary; Mark Phillip Ayling [1960] Director/Coffee Trader; Ian Ernest Anthony Breminer [1952] Director/Coffee Merchant; Kristine Elise Antonia Breminer Isgren [1980] Director

Complete Cover Group Limited
Incorporated: 9 June 1998 *Employees:* 267
Previous: The A & A Group Limited
Net Worth: £14,609,000 *Total Assets:* £72,565,000
Registered Office: Elmbrook House, 18-19 Station Road, Sunbury on Thames, Surrey, TW16 6SU
Activities: Non-life insurance
Parent: Key Bidco Limited
Officers: Angela Margaret Darling [1959] Compliance Director; Shaun Ian Hooper [1972] Director/Chief Executive; Tim Paul Wills [1972] Finance Director

Computer Financial Consultants Limited
Incorporated: 4 August 1993 *Employees:* 13
Net Worth: £5,191,000 *Total Assets:* £6,246,000
Registered Office: Tamesis, The Glanty, Egham, Surrey, TW20 9AH
Activities: Other information technology service activities
Parent: Gartner U.K. Limited
Officers: William Joseph Dorgan [1967] Director/Lawyer [American]; Craig Warren Safian [1969] Director/Senior VP and CFO, Gartner Inc [American]

Comwood Holdings Ltd.
Incorporated: 24 March 2016
Net Worth: £1,380,586 *Total Assets:* £6,632,051
Registered Office: JSW Associates Ltd, Harrow Business Centre, 429-433 Pinner Road, Harrow, Middlesex, HA1 4HN
Activities: Buying and selling of own real estate
Officers: Prudence Margret Burletson, Secretary; Lawrence Michael Alkin [1939] Director; Bryan Richard Burletson [1941] Director

Conance Limited
Incorporated: 28 November 1985 *Employees:* 8
Net Worth: £2,750,895 *Total Assets:* £9,891,901
Registered Office: Hatherley House, 15-17 Wood Street, Barnet, Herts, EN5 4AT
Activities: Credit granting by non-deposit taking finance houses and other specialist consumer credit grantors
Shareholders: Graeme David Sands; Christopher Seabrooke
Officers: Brian Gitlin [1944] Director; Nigel Stuart Hamilton Hughes [1954] Commercial Director [Australian]; Spencer Harry Saffer [1965] Director; Graeme David Sands [1962] Director; Christopher Stefan Seabrooke [1953] Director/Financier [South African]; Albert Johan Walraven [1945] Director [Dutch]

Concept Developments (Cobham) Limited
Incorporated: 31 August 2007 *Employees:* 18
Net Worth: £83,618 *Total Assets:* £7,849,804
Registered Office: 2 AC Court, High Street, Thames Ditton, Surrey, KT7 0SR
Activities: Other specialised construction activities n.e.c.
Shareholder: Nicholas James Daley
Officers: Helle Andersen, Secretary; Jan Bech Andersen, Secretary; Nicholas James Daley [1979] Director

Concordia International Forwarding Limited
Incorporated: 5 July 1978 *Employees:* 60
Net Worth: £319,109 *Total Assets:* £11,298,617
Registered Office: Shackleton House, Challenge Road, Ashford, Middlesex, TW15 1AX
Activities: Other transportation support activities
Officers: Brian Nixon, Secretary; Wayne Bolton [1963] Director; Paul Emposimato [1937] Director [American]; Brian Nixon [1943] Director; Keith Wright [1969] Director

Condor Group Limited
Incorporated: 20 January 1939 *Employees:* 37
Net Worth: £1,196,820 *Total Assets:* £7,185,582
Registered Office: Condor House, 700 Great Cambridge Road, Enfield, Middlesex, EN1 3EA
Activities: Wholesale of watches and jewellery
Parent: Condor Group Holdings Ltd
Officers: Hiru Halai, Secretary; Indira Bhoja [1960] Director/Manager; Narshi Bhoja [1957] Director/Wholesale Jeweller

Congregation of The Daughters of The Cross International Generalate
Incorporated: 15 March 2011
Net Worth: £12,917,588 *Total Assets:* £14,629,991
Registered Office: International Generalate, St Joseph's Convent, 801 London Road, North Cheam, Surrey, SM3 9AT
Activities: Other social work activities without accommodation n.e.c.
Officers: Sister Mary Alice McLaughlin [1943] Director/Trustee [Irish]; Sister Valerie Miranda [1950] Director/Trustee [Indian]; Sr Maureen O'Brien [1939] Director/Trustee; Sister Pushpa Elishwa Purathur [1948] Director/Trustee [Indian]; Sister Zeenat Shangara [1966] Director/Trustee [Pakistani]

Coniston Dartford Limited
Incorporated: 18 July 2012 *Employees:* 88
Net Worth: £2,321,059 *Total Assets:* £11,242,713
Registered Office: Collingwood House, Schooner Court, Crossways, Dartford, Kent, DA2 6QQ
Activities: Activities of head offices
Major Shareholder: John Peter Rathbone
Officers: Steven Leslie Clarke [1963] Director; John Peter Rathbone [1955] Director

Coniston Limited
Incorporated: 21 December 1982 *Employees:* 84
Net Worth: £3,059,281 *Total Assets:* £9,516,298
Registered Office: Collingwood House, Schooner Court, Crossways, Dartford, Kent, DA2 6QQ
Activities: Construction of other civil engineering projects n.e.c.
Officers: Steven Leslie Clark [1963] Contracts Director; Gary Frederick Evans [1962] Commercial Director; John Peter Rathbone [1955] Director/Builder; Mustafa Serdar Ulla [1965] Operations Director

Connect Plus (M25) Holdings Limited
Incorporated: 29 August 2008
Net Worth Deficit: £175,590,000 *Total Assets:* £1,469,575,040
Registered Office: Connect Plus House, St Albans Road, South Mimms, Herts, EN6 3NP
Activities: Activities of construction holding companies
Shareholders: BBDE Orbital Holdings LLP; Edge Orbital Holdings Ltd
Officers: Alastair John Campbell, Secretary; Sofia Athanassiou [1977] Director/Civil Engineer [British/Greek]; Abdellha Benhatta [1956] Director [French]; Philip Michael Bentley [1972] Assurance Director; Alastair John Campbell [1969] Director/Chartered Accountant; Andrew Maxwell Dean [1967] Director; Jane Elizabeth Guyett [1959] Director/Banker; Richard Daniel Knight [1974] Director; Barry Paul Millsom [1974] Director; Philip Arthur Skerman [1988] Director [Australian]; Brian Roland Walker [1955] Director; Stephen Douglas Worthy [1976] Director/Chartered Accountant

Connect Plus (M25) Intermediate Limited
Incorporated: 3 October 2008
Total Assets: £230,339,008
Registered Office: Connect Plus House, St Albans Road, South Mimms, Herts, EN6 3NP
Activities: Financial intermediation not elsewhere classified
Shareholders: BBDE Orbital Holdings LLP; Edge Orbital Holdings Ltd
Officers: Alastair John Campbell, Secretary; Sofia Athanassiou [1977] Director/Civil Engineer [British/Greek]; Abdellah Benhatta [1968] Director [French]; Philip Michael Bentley [1972] Assurance Director; Alastair John Campbell [1969] Director/Chartered Accountant; Andrew Maxwell Dean [1967] Director; Jane Elizabeth Guyett [1959] Director/Banker; Richard Daniel Knight [1974] Director; Barry Paul Millsom [1974] Director; Brian Roland Walker [1955] Director; Stephen Douglas Worthy [1976] Director/Chartered Accountant

Connect Plus (M25) Limited
Incorporated: 29 August 2008
Net Worth Deficit: £175,590,000 *Total Assets:* £1,469,575,040
Registered Office: Connect Plus House, St Albans Road, South Mimms, Herts, EN6 3NP
Activities: Construction of roads and motorways
Parent: Connect Plus (M25) Holdings Limited
Officers: Alastair John Campbell, Secretary; Sofia Athanassiou [1977] Director/Civil Engineer [British/Greek]; Abdellah Benhatta [1968] Director [French]; Philip Michael Bentley [1972] Assurance Director; Alastair John Campbell [1969] Director/Chartered Accountant; Andrew Maxwell Dean [1967] Director; Jane Elizabeth Guyett [1959] Director/Banker; Richard Daniel Knight [1974] Director; Barry Paul Millsom [1974] Director; Philip Arthur Skerman [1988] Director [Australian]; Brian Roland Walker [1955] Director; Stephen Douglas Worthy [1976] Director/Chartered Accountant

Connect Schools Academy Trust
Incorporated: 26 October 2011 *Employees:* 378
Previous: Crofton Schools Academy Trust
Net Worth: £23,927,272 *Total Assets:* £25,744,576
Registered Office: Crofton Junior School, Towncourt Lane, Orpington, Kent, BR5 1EL
Activities: Primary education
Officers: Marie Ghansah-Poku, Secretary; Andrea Jane Carter [1963] Director Headteacher; Sandra Rosemary Clements [1950] Director/Retired Deputy Headteacher; Scott Anthony George [1973] Director/IT Manager; Susan Jacqueline Hannay [1958] Research Services Director/Relate Counsellor; Naureen Khalid [1961] Director; William John Mitchell [1963] Director; Diane Patricia Moss [1966] Director/Administrator; Christopher Thomas Munday [1965] Director/Solicitor; Scott James Pinder [1980] Director/Actuary

Conneely Drylining Limited
Incorporated: 18 November 1993 *Employees:* 52
Net Worth: £2,534,356 *Total Assets:* £8,613,649
Registered Office: Gautam House, 1-3 Shenley Avenue, Ruislip Manor, Middlesex, HA4 6BP
Activities: Other service activities n.e.c.
Shareholders: Conneely Services Limited; John Melvyn Cockerton; Michael James Cockerton
Officers: John Melvyn Cockerton, Secretary/Director; John Melvyn Cockerton [1974] Director; Michael James Cockerton [1976] Director; Eamon Conneely [1960] Director [Irish]

Oliver Connell and Son Limited
Incorporated: 2 May 1974 *Employees:* 72
Net Worth: £4,963,584 *Total Assets:* £15,830,438
Registered Office: Zanrose House, Perivale Industrial Estate, Horsenden Lane South, Greenford, Middlesex, UB6 7RH
Activities: Construction of other civil engineering projects n.e.c.
Officers: Gregory Connell, Secretary; Gregory Connell [1971] Director/Accountant [Irish]; James Thomas Connell [1978] Operations Director; Oliver Connell [1945] Director [Irish]; Patrick Brendon Connell [1952] Director [Irish]; Thomas Joseph Connell [1980] Director [Irish]

Console Bidco Limited
Incorporated: 13 June 2014
Net Worth Deficit: £22,771,000 *Total Assets:* £150,419,008
Registered Office: Unit 10 Silverglade Business Park, Leatherhead Road, Chessington, Surrey, KT9 2QL
Activities: Management consultancy activities other than financial management
Parent: Console Lowco Limited
Officers: Helen Mary Culleton, Secretary; Helen Mary Culleton [1964] Director; James David Gordon [1972] Managing Director

Console Lowco Limited
Incorporated: 10 July 2014
Net Worth: £1 *Total Assets:* £34,227,728
Registered Office: Unit 10 Silverglade Business Park, Leatherhead Road, Chessington, Surrey, KT9 2QL
Activities: Dormant company
Parent: Console Midco Limited
Officers: Helen Mary Culleton [1964] Director; James David Gordon [1972] Managing Director

Console Midco Limited
Incorporated: 13 June 2014
Net Worth Deficit: £24,255,224 *Total Assets:* £82,102,016
Registered Office: Unit 10 Silverglade Business Park, Leatherhead Road, Chessington, Surrey, KT9 2QL
Activities: Activities of other holding companies n.e.c.
Parent: Audiotonix Limited
Officers: Helen Mary Culleton [1964] Director; James David Gordon [1972] Managing Director

Consolidated Equities Limited
Incorporated: 1 April 1954 *Employees:* 2
Net Worth: £9,139,145 *Total Assets:* £9,551,268
Registered Office: 173 Hempstead Road, Watford, Herts, WD17 3HG
Activities: Other letting and operating of own or leased real estate
Shareholder: Telford Thomas Rice
Officers: Margaret Jamieson Rice, Secretary; Margaret Jamieson Rice [1940] Director; Telford Thomas Rice [1960] Director/Building Manager

Consolidated Timber Holdings Group Limited
Incorporated: 8 February 2017 *Employees:* 210
Net Worth: £9,983,359 *Total Assets:* £76,628,080
Registered Office: Clock House, Station Approach, Shepperton, Surrey, TW17 8AN
Activities: Activities of head offices
Officers: David John Colman [1962] Director; Jonathan David Leigh Gregory [1961] Director/Chartered Accountant; Simon David Holdsworth [1956] Director/Chartered Accountant; Michael James Laughlin [1961] Director; Montague John Meyer [1944] Director; Stephen Peter Sabine [1963] Director; Andrew Peter Smith [1959] Director; Andrew James Tilbury [1959] Director

Consolidated Timber Holdings Limited
Incorporated: 12 September 1988 *Employees:* 210
Net Worth: £26,268,436 *Total Assets:* £85,816,000
Registered Office: Clock House, Station Approach, Shepperton, Surrey, TW17 8AN
Activities: Activities of head offices
Parent: Consolidated Timber Holdings Group Limited
Officers: David John Colman [1962] Director/Chartered Accountant; Jonathan David Leigh Gregory [1961] Director/Chartered Accountant; Simon David Holdsworth [1956] Director/Chartered Accountant; Michael James Laughlin [1961] Director; Stephen Peter Sabine [1963] Director/Sales Executive; Andrew Peter Smith [1959] Director; Andrew James Tilbury [1959] Director/Sales Executive

Consort Healthcare (Blackburn) Funding PLC
Incorporated: 26 September 2002
Net Worth: £57,000 *Total Assets:* £109,179,000
Registered Office: 8 White Oak Square, Swanley, Kent, BR8 7AG
Activities: Other business support service activities n.e.c.
Parent: Consort Healthcare (Blackburn) Holdings Limited
Officers: James Christopher Heath [1975] Director; Mark Geoffrey David Holden [1957] Director/Asset Manager; Elena Giorgiana Wegener [1975] Director [Romanian]

Consort Healthcare (Blackburn) Holdings Limited
Incorporated: 26 September 2002
Net Worth: £4,223,000 *Total Assets:* £138,435,008
Registered Office: 8 White Oak Square, Swanley, Kent, BR8 7AG
Activities: Activities of head offices
Parent: Infrastructure Investments Holdings Limited
Officers: James Christopher Heath [1975] Director; Mark Geoffrey David Holden [1957] Director/Asset Manager; Elena Giorgiana Wegener [1975] Director [Romanian]

Consort Healthcare (Blackburn) Limited
Incorporated: 26 September 2002
Net Worth: £4,173,000 *Total Assets:* £138,435,008
Registered Office: Unit 8 White Oak Square, Swanley, Kent, BR8 7AG
Activities: Other business support service activities n.e.c.
Parent: Consort Healthcare (Blackburn) Holdings Limited
Officers: James Christopher Heath [1975] Director; Mark Geoffrey David Holden [1957] Director/Asset Manager; Elena Giorgiana Wegener [1975] Director [Romanian]

Consort Healthcare (Mid Yorkshire) Funding PLC
Incorporated: 21 November 2006
Net Worth: £50,000 *Total Assets:* £386,988,992
Registered Office: 8 White Oak Square, London Road, Swanley, Kent, BR8 7AG
Activities: Hospital activities
Parent: Consort Healthcare (Mid Yorkshire) Holdings Limited
Officers: Richard Martin Goulder [1971] Director; Mark Geoffrey David Holden [1957] Investment Director, Infrastructure

Consort Healthcare (Mid Yorkshire) Holdings Limited
Incorporated: 12 December 2006
Net Worth: £1,638,000 *Total Assets:* £395,601,984
Registered Office: 8 White Oak Square, London Road, Swanley, Kent, BR8 7AG
Activities: Hospital activities
Parent: Infrastructure Investments Holdings Limited
Officers: Richard Martin Goulder [1971] Director; Mark Geoffrey David Holden [1957] Investment Director, Infrastructure

Consort Healthcare (Mid Yorkshire) Limited
Incorporated: 21 November 2006
Net Worth: £1,588,000 *Total Assets:* £395,601,984
Registered Office: 8 White Oak Square, London Road, Swanley, Kent, BR8 7AG
Activities: Hospital activities
Parent: Consort Healthcare (Mid Yorkshire) Holdings Limited
Officers: Richard Martin Goulder [1971] Director; Mark Geoffrey David Holden [1957] Investment Director, Infrastructure

The Construction Workers Guild Limited
Incorporated: 22 April 1997
Net Worth: £577,913 *Total Assets:* £15,103,765
Registered Office: 2 Mountside, Stanmore, Middlesex, HA7 2DT
Activities: Other business support service activities n.e.c.
Parent: Guild Corporate Services Group Limited
Officers: Derek Stephen Reynolds [1959] Managing Director

Consulco Finance Ltd
Incorporated: 21 March 2013 *Employees:* 6
Net Worth: £4,582,916 *Total Assets:* £13,993,572
Registered Office: The Business Centre, 758 Great Cambridge Road, Enfield, Middlesex, EN1 3GN
Activities: Other business support service activities n.e.c.
Shareholders: Marios Hadjiroussos; Hermioni Khenkin
Officers: Marios Hadjiroussos [1966] Director/Businessman [Cypriot]; Elena Karina Hajiroussou [1970] Director/Lawyer; Dmitry Khenkin [1965] Director/Businessman [Cypriot]

Container Providers International (UK) Limited
Incorporated: 11 August 1999
Net Worth: £328,203 *Total Assets:* £13,690,848
Registered Office: 308 High Street, Croydon, Surrey, CR0 1NG
Activities: Sea and coastal freight water transport
Shareholder: Henning Fahlmann Nielsen
Officers: Henning Nielsen [1945] Director [Danish]

Continental Investment Limited
Incorporated: 14 April 1989
Net Worth: £20,687,000 *Total Assets:* £20,695,000
Registered Office: Continental House, 191 High Street, Yiewsley, West Drayton, Middlesex, UB7 7XW
Activities: Non-trading company
Parent: Continental U.K. Group Holdings Limited
Officers: Matthew Owen, Secretary; David Thomas Smith [1965] Finance Director; Johannes Suttmeyer [1959] Director/Lawyer [German]

Continental Tyre Group Ltd.
Incorporated: 28 January 1935 *Employees:* 160
Net Worth: £50,891,000 *Total Assets:* £155,530,000
Registered Office: Continental House, 191 High Street, Yiewsley, West Drayton, Middlesex, UB7 7XW
Activities: Wholesale trade of motor vehicle parts and accessories
Parent: Continental Tyres Limited
Officers: Matthew Owen, Secretary; Arthur Jordan Gregg [1962] Sales & Marketing Director; David Thomas Smith [1965] Managing Director

Continental U.K. Group Holdings Limited
Incorporated: 15 May 1956
Net Worth: £51,527,000 *Total Assets:* £212,311,008
Registered Office: 191-195 High Street, Yiewsley, West Drayton, Middlesex, UB7 7XW
Activities: Activities of head offices
Parent: Continental Aktiengesellschaft
Officers: Matthew Owen, Secretary; Gerd Bartels [1967] Director/Business Executive [German]; David Thomas Smith [1965] Managing Director; Johannes Suttmeyer [1959] Director/Lawyer [German]

Continua Limited
Incorporated: 14 November 1994 *Employees:* 15
Net Worth: £33,536,000 *Total Assets:* £35,705,000
Registered Office: Riverview, Oxford Road, Uxbridge, Middlesex, UB8 1HS
Activities: Other business support service activities n.e.c.
Parent: Xerox Limited
Officers: Mark Christopher Canons [1963] Managing Director; Stephen Charles Dillon [1944] Director/Solicitor; David Brian Dyas [1963] Director/President, UK & Ireland, Eurasia, India, MEA; Rodney Noonoo [1962] Director/CFO, UK & Ireland, Eurasia, India, MEA [American]

The Continuity Company Limited
Incorporated: 3 January 1991 *Employees:* 101
Net Worth: £7,179,000 *Total Assets:* £18,122,000
Registered Office: Heathrow House, 785 Bath Road, Hounslow, Middlesex, TW5 9AT
Activities: Other retail sale not in stores, stalls or markets
Major Shareholder: Richard Beattie
Officers: Ton Schipperijn, Secretary; Ton Schipperijn [1961] Finance Director [Dutch]

Contracting Made Easy Ltd
Incorporated: 11 February 1998
Net Worth: £756,860 *Total Assets:* £14,269,625
Registered Office: Anglo Dal House, 5 Spring Villa Park, Edgware, Middlesex, HA8 7EB
Activities: Other business support service activities n.e.c.
Shareholders: Victor Korman; Denise Korman
Officers: Denise Korman, Secretary; Eli Korman [1982] Director; Victor Korman [1958] Director/Accountant

Richard Cook Limited
Incorporated: 27 May 1964 *Employees:* 5
Net Worth: £20,034,740 *Total Assets:* £21,089,582
Registered Office: 26 Windsor Street, Chertsey, Surrey, KT16 8AS
Activities: Buying and selling of own real estate
Shareholders: Richard Cook; Henry Richard Cook; Chania Victoria Cook
Officers: Henry Richard Cook, Secretary; Chania Victoria Cook [1982] Marketing Director; Henry Richard Cook [1973] Director/Property Dealer; Richard Cook [1943] Director; Susan Camilla Cook [1946] Director/Business Executive

Cook's Delights Limited
Incorporated: 5 June 1996 *Employees:* 90
Net Worth: £891,160 *Total Assets:* £8,493,234
Registered Office: Lynwood House, 373-375 Station Road, Harrow, Middlesex, HA1 2AW
Activities: Wholesale of meat and meat products
Parent: Catering 328 Limited
Officers: Sue Shuk Yin Liu, Secretary; Ronny Wai Kin Liu [1960] Director; Sue Shuk Yin Liu [1961] Director; Andrew Pao [1964] Director

Coombe Academy Trust
Incorporated: 11 January 2012 *Employees:* 311
Previous: The Coombe Secondary Schools Academy Trust
Net Worth: £39,844,000 *Total Assets:* £43,633,000
Registered Office: c/o Coombe Boys School, College Gardens, Blakes Lane, New Malden, Surrey, KT3 6NU
Activities: General secondary education
Officers: Diana Mary Brotherston [1955] Director/Retired; Alan David Burbridge [1944] Director/Consultant; Judith Catherine Davies [1945] Director/Retired; Janet Elizabeth Galloway [1966] Director/Solicitor; Margaret Hunnaball [1960] Director/Retired; Derek James Morgan [1953] Director/Businessman; Naomi Vijeyarani Sellayah [1960] Director/Accountant; Emma Katherine Thomas [1979] Deputy Director of Finance; Deborah Ann Walls [1964] Director/Headteacher; Marion Webb [1950] Director/Retired

G. D. Cooper & Co Ltd
Incorporated: 23 June 1978 *Employees:* 36
Net Worth: £5,025,521 *Total Assets:* £6,912,176
Registered Office: 20 Progress Way, Croydon, Surrey, CR0 4XD
Activities: Wholesale of pharmaceutical goods
Parent: GDC (Holdings) Ltd
Officers: Mahendra Meghji Shah, Secretary; Khilan Mahendra Shah [1973] Director; Mahendra Meghji Shah [1945] Director/Businessman; Rahul Mahendra Shah [1977] Director

Cooper Estates Limited
Incorporated: 14 December 1933 *Employees:* 13
Net Worth: £39,523,572 *Total Assets:* £48,811,544
Registered Office: Claremont House, 65c Main Road, Longfield, Kent, DA3 7QT
Activities: Development of building projects
Officers: Wendy Caroline Parker, Secretary; David Gough Cooper [1975] Director/Surveyor; George Ian Gough Cooper [1948] Director/Builder; Henry William Gough-Cooper [1950] Director/Farmer; James Henry Gough-Cooper [1968] Director/Accountant; Jennifer Gough-Cooper [1942] Director/Exhibition Organiser; Malcolm Keith Honey [1946] Director/Chartered Surveyor; David Howard Scotton [1955] Director/Architect

Coopers Investments Limited
Incorporated: 16 December 1968 *Employees:* 5
Net Worth: £6,555,192 *Total Assets:* £8,000,254
Registered Office: 10 Union Street, Barnet, Herts, EN5 4HZ
Activities: Other letting and operating of own or leased real estate
Shareholder: Simon Ashley Cooper
Officers: Vanessa Jane Wennell, Secretary; Simon Ashley Cooper [1960] Director/Surveyor; Stanley Cooper [1929] Director/Building Surveyor

Cooperscroft Care Home Limited
Incorporated: 13 November 2012 *Employees:* 153
Net Worth: £20,119,264 *Total Assets:* £33,605,224
Registered Office: 36 Railway Approach, Harrow, Middlesex, HA3 5AA
Activities: Residential nursing care facilities
Parent: TLC Group Ltd
Officers: Gagan Puri, Secretary; William Charles Neal [1986] Director; Paavan Popat [1985] Managing Director; Honourable Shivaan Shillin Popat [1988] Director; Gagan Puri [1978] Finance Director

Copley Limited
Incorporated: 4 November 2008
Net Worth: £5,511,249 *Total Assets:* £6,198,962
Registered Office: 104 High Street, West Wickham, Kent, BR4 0NF
Activities: Other building completion and finishing
Major Shareholder: Colin Richard Copley
Officers: Colin Richard Copley, Secretary; Colin Richard Copley [1968] Director; Raymond Alfred Crane [1963] Director/Project Manager

F. Copson (London) LLP
Incorporated: 25 May 2010
Net Worth Deficit: £39,442 *Total Assets:* £11,253,393
Registered Office: Kanta Hose, Victoria Road, South Ruislip, Middlesex, HA4 0JQ

F. Copson Limited
Incorporated: 26 April 1947
Net Worth: £11,597,960 *Total Assets:* £12,321,717
Registered Office: Kanta House, Victoria Road, South Ruislip, Middlesex, HA4 0JQ
Activities: Other letting and operating of own or leased real estate
Officers: Bhasker Tailor, Secretary; Jawahar Jamnadas Chatwani [1948] Director; Rashmi Jamnadas Chatwani [1954] Director; Satish Jamnadas Chatwani [1953] Director

Corbus Europe Limited
Incorporated: 15 July 2003
Net Worth Deficit: £258,093 *Total Assets:* £10,153,909
Registered Office: 66 Montpelier Rise, Wembley, Middlesex, HA9 8RQ
Activities: Information technology consultancy activities
Parent: Corbus LLC
Officers: Rajesh Kumar Soin [1947] Director [American]; Vishal Soin [1973] Director [American]

Cordant Cleaning Limited
Incorporated: 23 June 1981 *Employees:* 2,649
Previous: Dynamiq Cleaning Limited
Net Worth: £5,075,506 *Total Assets:* £23,836,580
Registered Office: Chevron House, 346 Long Lane, Hillingdon, Middlesex, UB10 9PF
Activities: General cleaning of buildings
Parent: Cordant Security Limited
Officers: Alan Connor, Secretary; Chris Martin Kenneally [1960] Director; Jack Rainer Ullmann [1928] Director; Phillip Lionel Ullmann [1964] Director

Cordant Group PLC
Incorporated: 12 June 1997 *Employees:* 39,513
Net Worth: £19,937,000 *Total Assets:* £242,836,992
Registered Office: Chevron House, 346 Long Lane, Hillingdon, Middlesex, UB10 9PF
Activities: Other service activities n.e.c.
Shareholders: Jack Ullmann; Marianne Flora Ullmann; Phillip Ullmann
Officers: Alan Connor, Secretary; Alan Connor [1976] Director; Richard Mark Gerver [1969] Director; Chris Martin Kenneally [1960] Director; Daniel Liebert [1964] Director; Ken Steers [1969] Director; Deborah Miriam Ullman [1968] Director; Harry Ullmann [1931] Director; Jack Rainer Ullmann [1928] Director; Phillip Lionel Ullmann [1964] Director; Uri Ullmann [1976] Director

Cordant People Limited
Incorporated: 9 August 1991 *Employees:* 4,921
Previous: Prime Time Recruitment Limited
Net Worth: £9,203,971 *Total Assets:* £79,454,632
Registered Office: Chevron House, 346 Long Lane, Hillingdon, Middlesex, UB10 9PF
Activities: Temporary employment agency activities
Parent: Cordant Group PLC
Officers: Alan Connor, Secretary; Chris Martin Kenneally [1960] Director; Jack Rainer Ullmann [1928] Director; Phillip Lionel Ullmann [1964] Director

Cordant Security Limited
Incorporated: 31 January 1996 *Employees:* 4,123
Previous: Advance Security UK Limited
Net Worth: £12,959,835 *Total Assets:* £36,478,744
Registered Office: Chevron House, Long Lane, Hillingdon, Uxbridge, Middlesex, UB10 9PF
Activities: Other service activities n.e.c.
Parent: Cordant Group PLC
Officers: Alan Connor, Secretary/Director; Chris Martin Kenneally [1960] Director; Jack Rainer Ullmann [1928] Director; Phillip Lionel Ullmann [1964] Director

Corero Network Security PLC
Incorporated: 14 November 1991 *Employees:* 61
Net Worth: £13,155,556 *Total Assets:* £16,536,347
Registered Office: Regus House, Highbridge, Oxford Road, Uxbridge, Middlesex, UB8 1HR
Activities: Management consultancy activities other than financial management
Shareholder: Jens Peter Montanana
Officers: Duncan Swallow, Secretary; Peter George [1959] Director [American]; Richard Last [1957] Director; Andrew Douglas Miller [1964] Director; Jens Peter Montanana [1960] Director; Robert Ashley Stephenson [1959] Director

Corinthia Investments Limited
Incorporated: 21 November 1985
Net Worth: £18,319,664 *Total Assets:* £18,650,258
Registered Office: Aissela, 46 High Street, Esher, Surrey, KT10 9QY
Activities: Other service activities n.e.c.
Officers: Reginald Cuschieri, Secretary; Reginald Alfred Cuschieri [1933] Director/Company Executive [Maltese]; Joseph Fenech [1956] Director/Company Executive [Maltese]; Alfred Pisani [1939] Director/Company Chairman [Maltese]; George Pisani [1940] Director [Maltese]; Joseph Pisani [1937] Director [Maltese]; Victor Pisani [1941] Director [Maltese]

Corinthian Land (West Kent) Limited
Incorporated: 28 October 2015 *Employees:* 4
Net Worth Deficit: £901,076 *Total Assets:* £6,600,124
Registered Office: Gay Dawn Farm, Pennis Lane, Fawkham, Longfield, Dartford, Kent, DA3 8LY
Activities: Other business support service activities n.e.c.
Officers: Andrew John Billings [1964] Director; Clive John Billings [1955] Director; Ronald John Billings [1960] Director; Stephen John Billings [1961] Director

Corley + Woolley Limited
Incorporated: 1 November 2012 *Employees:* 27
Net Worth: £1,983,606 *Total Assets:* £9,893,842
Registered Office: Suite D, The Business Centre, Faringdon Avenue, Romford, Essex, RM3 8EN
Activities: Other construction installation
Shareholders: John Christopher Corley; Mark Robert Woolley
Officers: John Christopher Corley [1967] Director; Andrew Thomas Greenway [1984] Director/Pre-Construction Manager; Mark Robert Woolley [1972] Director

Corncrake Limited
Incorporated: 16 December 2014
Net Worth: £11,304,453 *Total Assets:* £11,473,832
Registered Office: Salisbury House, 20 Queens Road, Weybridge, Surrey, KT13 9XE
Activities: Financial intermediation not elsewhere classified
Major Shareholder: Susannah Margaret Blundell
Officers: Dr Susannah Margaret Blundell [1965] Director

Cornwall
Incorporated: 27 August 1994
Net Worth: £15,035,106 *Total Assets:* £15,073,055
Registered Office: 5 Elstree Gate, Elstree Way, Borehamwood, Herts, WD6 1JD
Activities: Activities of other holding companies n.e.c.
Officers: Graham David Hill, Secretary; Bruce Victor Grakal [1940] Director [American]; John Gwilym Hemingway [1931] Director; Graham David Hill [1946] Director/Accountant

Corona Energy Limited
Incorporated: 22 August 1996
Net Worth: £15,665,727 *Total Assets:* £22,062,484
Registered Office: Building 2, Level 2, Croxley Park, Watford, Herts, WD18 8YA
Activities: Activities of head offices
Parent: Macquarie Corona Energy Holdings Limited
Officers: Shaheda Begum Thomas, Secretary; Neil Trevor Mitchell [1974] Commercial Director; Philip Morton [1968] Finance Director; Paul Christian Plewman [1972] Director/Banker [Irish]

Corona Energy Retail 1 Limited
Incorporated: 22 August 1996 *Employees:* 212
Net Worth: £11,361,115 *Total Assets:* £34,249,204
Registered Office: Building 2, Level 2, Croxley Park, Watford, Herts, WD18 8YA
Activities: Trade of gas through mains
Parent: Corona Energy Limited
Officers: Shaheda Begum Thomas, Secretary; Neil Trevor Mitchell [1974] Commercial Director; Philip Morton [1968] Finance Director; Paul Christian Plewman [1972] Director/Banker [Irish]

Corona Energy Retail 4 Limited
Incorporated: 11 March 1993
Net Worth: £7,582,111 *Total Assets:* £118,481,440
Registered Office: Building 2, Level 2, Croxley Park, Watford, Herts, WD18 8YA
Activities: Trade of electricity
Parent: Corona Energy Limited
Officers: Shaheda Begum Thomas, Secretary; Neil Trevor Mitchell [1974] Commercial Director; Philip Morton [1968] Finance Director; Paul Christian Plewman [1972] Director/Banker [Irish]

Corona Gas Management Limited
Incorporated: 10 December 1993
Net Worth: £1,048,717 *Total Assets:* £105,769,296
Registered Office: Building 2, Level 2, Croxley Park, Watford, Herts, WD18 8YA
Activities: Wholesale of other fuels and related products
Parent: Corona Energy Retail 1 Limited
Officers: Shaheda Begum Thomas, Secretary; Neil Trevor Mitchell [1974] Commercial Director; Philip Morton [1968] Finance Director; Paul Christian Plewman [1972] Director/Banker [Irish]

Corporate Solutions Consulting Limited
Incorporated: 18 January 1995 *Employees:* 13
Net Worth: £2,748,474 *Total Assets:* £5,429,751
Registered Office: Unit 2 Artisan Place, 23 Ladysmith Road, Harrow, Middlesex, HA3 5FE
Activities: Management consultancy activities other than financial management
Shareholders: Kayvon Adhami; Ebrahim Adhami
Officers: Kayvon Adhami, Secretary; Ebrahim Adhami [1957] Director/Management Consultant; Kayvon Adhami [1963] Director/Management Consultant

Cort Business Services UK Limited
Incorporated: 10 December 2007 *Employees:* 55
Net Worth: £5,562,703 *Total Assets:* £6,993,836
Registered Office: Unit 28 Barwell Business Park, Leatherhead Road, Chessington, Surrey, KT9 2NY
Activities: Agents involved in the sale of furniture, household goods, hardware and ironmongery
Parent: Berkshire Hathaway Inc
Officers: Deborah Lansford, Secretary; Deborah Lansford [1958] Director [American]; Jeffrey Pederson [1959] Director/Company President [American]; Graham Michael Smith [1956] Director; Brian Stahl [1956] Director [American]

Corumbe Investments Limited
Incorporated: 26 January 2012
Net Worth Deficit: £72,777 *Total Assets:* £5,813,897
Registered Office: Lynfield House, Lyne Lane, Lyne, Chertsey, Surrey, KT16 0AN
Activities: Development of building projects
Shareholders: Marco Brustio; Silvia Orsi Mazzucchelli
Officers: Marco Brustio [1954] Director [Italian]; Torsten Michael Hallerstrom [1952] Director/Manager [Swedish]; Silvia Orsi Mazzucchelli [1951] Director [Italian]

Cosan Lubes Investments Limited
Incorporated: 3 April 2012
Net Worth: £13,893,000 *Total Assets:* £84,226,000
Registered Office: Moove, Dering Way, Gravesend, Kent, DA12 2QX
Activities: Activities of head offices
Parent: Cosan Limited
Officers: Gary Michael Sands, Secretary; Michael Winston Bewsey [1965] Director; Marcelo de Souza Scarcela Portela [1961] Director [Brazilian]; Renato Aparecido Fontalva [1967] Director/Business Administration [Brazilian]; Nelson Roseira Gomes Neto [1971] Director [Brazilian]; Marcos Marinho Lutz [1969] Director [Brazilian]; Marcelo Eduardo Martins [1966] Director [Brazilian]; Rubens Ometto Silveira Mello [1950] Director [Brazilian]; Gary Michael Sands [1961] Director

Cosco Maritime (UK) Limited
Incorporated: 13 June 2000 *Employees:* 15
Net Worth: £16,433,450 *Total Assets:* £70,223,720
Registered Office: Cosco House, Vicarage Drive, Barking, Essex, IG11 7NA
Activities: Sea and coastal freight water transport
Parent: Cosco Shipholdings (UK) Limited
Officers: Romeo Abenes Mendoza, Secretary; Li Sun [1975] Director/Accounting Manager [Chinese]; Gang Wang [1971] Director [Chinese]

Cosco Shipping (UK) Company Limited
Incorporated: 2 February 1988 *Employees:* 54
Previous: Cosco (UK) Limited
Net Worth: £34,897,472 *Total Assets:* £91,660,536
Registered Office: Cosco House, Vicarage Drive, Barking, Essex, IG11 7NA
Activities: Other transportation support activities
Parent: State-Owned Assets Supervision and Administration Commission of The State Council (SASAC)
Officers: Romeo Abenes Mendoza, Secretary; Jing Guo [1961] Director/Shipping [Chinese]; Ji Lin [1970] Director [Chinese]; Li Sun [1975] Director/Accounting Manager [Chinese]; Gang Wang [1971] Director [Chinese]; Haihua Yu [1963] Director [Chinese]

Cosco Shipping Crystal Logistics (UK) Company Limited
Incorporated: 6 December 1991 *Employees:* 27
Previous: Cosco Crystal Logistics (UK) Limited
Net Worth: £3,615,308 *Total Assets:* £6,800,045
Registered Office: Vicarage Drive, Barking, Essex, IG11 7NA
Activities: Freight transport by road
Parent: Cosco Shipping (UK) Company Limited
Officers: Romeo Mendoza, Secretary; Romeo Abenes Mendoza [1951] Director/Accounts Manager; Roman Plewa [1957] Director/Deputy General Manager; Gang Wang [1971] Director [Chinese]

Cosco Shipping Lines (UK) Limited
Incorporated: 3 March 1995 *Employees:* 63
Previous: Coscon (UK) Ltd
Net Worth: £6,572,329 *Total Assets:* £13,908,348
Registered Office: Cosco House, Vicarage Drive, Barking, Essex, IG11 7NA
Activities: Sea and coastal freight water transport
Parent: Cosco Container Lines Europe GmbH
Officers: Thambyah Wignarajah, Secretary; Dongxiang Li [1977] Director [Chinese]; Ji Lin [1970] Director/Chairman [Chinese]; Jun Shi [1976] Director [Chinese]; Yong Wang [1973] Director [Chinese]; Zhendong Zhang [1968] Managing Director [Chinese]

Cosmos Tours Limited
Incorporated: 25 June 1974 *Employees:* 82
Net Worth: £2,477,000 *Total Assets:* £11,211,000
Registered Office: First Floor, Wells House, 15 Elmfield Road, Bromley, Kent, BR1 1LT
Activities: Tour operator activities
Shareholders: Sergio Antonio Mantegazza; Mario Albek
Officers: Samuel Kodjo Parker, Secretary; Giles James Martin Hawke [1969] Director; Claire Rose Hazle [1977] Director; Samuel Kodjo Parker [1969] Finance Director; Janet Linda Parton [1978] Sales Director; Lesley Anne Smith [1971] Director; Tristram Henry John Yarde-Leavett [1964] Director

Cossam Investment Co Ltd
Incorporated: 26 June 1958 *Employees:* 5
Previous: Cossam Investment Co.,Limited
Net Worth: £5,014,541 *Total Assets:* £8,438,694
Registered Office: 141 Stanmore Hill, Stanmore, Middlesex, HA7 3ED
Activities: Other letting and operating of own or leased real estate
Officers: Stephen Samuel, Secretary; Babara Ruth Cohen [1960] Director/Speech Therapist; Gideon Elisha Cohen [1985] Director/Student; Simon Charles Cohen [1962] Director/Solicitor; Judith Samuel [1950] Director; Stephen Samuel [1948] Director/Chartered Accountant; Stephen Samuel [1948] Director/Chartered Accountant

Costco Limited
Incorporated: 23 December 1992
Net Worth: £203,444,000 *Total Assets:* £205,079,008
Registered Office: Hartspring Lane, Watford, Herts, WD25 8JS
Activities: Other letting and operating of own or leased real estate
Parent: Costco Wholesale UK Limited
Officers: Magan Khushalbhai Chauhan, Secretary; Magan Khushalbhai Chauhan [1951] Director; James Patrick Murphy [1952] Managing Director [American]; Stephen Michael Pappas [1954] Director [American]

Costco Online UK Limited
Incorporated: 2 May 2012 *Employees:* 72
Net Worth Deficit: £8,938,000 *Total Assets:* £6,675,000
Registered Office: UK Home Office, Hartspring Lane, Watford, Herts, WD25 8JS
Activities: Non-specialised wholesale trade
Parent: Costco UK Holdings Limited
Officers: Magan Khushalbhai Chauhan, Secretary; Magan Khushalbhai Chauhan [1951] Director; Garth Andrew Morris [1965] Director/General Merchandising Manager; James Patrick Murphy [1952] Managing Director [American]; Stephen Michael Pappas [1954] Director [American]

Costco UK Holdings Limited
Incorporated: 28 February 2000 *Employees:* 6,628
Net Worth: £590,630,976 *Total Assets:* £893,710,016
Registered Office: UK Home Office, Hartspring Lane, Watford, Herts, WD25 8JS
Activities: Non-specialised wholesale trade
Parent: Costco Wholesale Corporation
Officers: Magan Khushalbhai Chauhan, Secretary; Richard Galanti [1956] Director/Chief Financial Officer [American]; James Patrick Murphy [1952] Director/Senior Vice President - Europe [American]

Costco Wholesale UK Limited
Incorporated: 6 August 1991 *Employees:* 6,556
Net Worth: £595,078,016 *Total Assets:* £895,956,992
Registered Office: UK Home Office, 213 Hartspring Lane, Watford, Herts, WD25 8JS
Activities: Non-specialised wholesale trade
Parent: Costco UK Holdings Limited
Officers: Magan Khushalbhai Chauhan, Secretary; Walter Craig Jelinek [1952] Director [American]; James Patrick Murphy [1952] Director [American]; Stephen Michael Pappas [1954] Director [American]

Cougar Holdco London Limited
Incorporated: 8 July 2013 *Employees:* 270
Net Worth Deficit: £9,800,000 *Total Assets:* £165,476,992
Registered Office: The Training Ground, Motspur Park, New Malden, Surrey, KT3 6PT
Activities: Other sports activities
Shareholders: The Shahid Rafiq Khan Family Trust A; The Shahid Rafiq Khan Family Trust B
Officers: Neville Darren Preston, Secretary; Shahid Rafiq Khan [1950] Director/Executive [American]; Mark Lamping [1958] Director/President Jacksonville Jaguars [American]

J J Coughlan (Holdings) Limited
Incorporated: 26 June 2014
Net Worth: £3,801,211 *Total Assets:* £7,028,243
Registered Office: 12 Walmgate Road, Perivale, Greenford, Middlesex, UB6 7LH
Activities: Activities of other holding companies n.e.c.
Shareholders: Francis Deely; John Joseph McGarry
Officers: Mr John Joseph McGarry, Secretary; Mr Francis Deely [1954] Director [Irish]; Mr John Joseph McGarry [1950] Director [Irish]

Coughlans Bakeries Limited
Incorporated: 4 October 1937 *Employees:* 177
Net Worth: £3,488,376 *Total Assets:* £5,179,547
Registered Office: 21-29 Sandringham Road, Thornton Heath, Surrey, CR7 7AX
Activities: Manufacture of bread; manufacture of fresh pastry goods and cakes
Officers: Virginia Tracy Coughlan, Secretary; Peter John Coughlan [1939] Director/Master Baker; Sean Patrick Coughlan [1971] Director/Master Baker; Virginia Tracy Coughlan [1964] Director/Company Secretary; Jacqueline Jane Taylor [1968] Director/Office Manager

Counties Home Loan Management Limited
Incorporated: 26 October 1989
Net Worth: £194,008 *Total Assets:* £89,916,704
Registered Office: 30 Church Street, Epsom, Surrey, KT17 4NL
Activities: Banks
Parent: National Counties Building Society
Officers: Andrew David Barnard [1971] Finance Director; Christopher Rendell Croft [1951] Solicitor and Director; Rodger Grant Hughes [1948] Director

Country House Weddings Holdings Ltd
Incorporated: 3 October 2017
Net Worth: £10,185 *Total Assets:* £6,040,185
Registered Office: Regency House, 33 Wood Street, Barnet, Herts, EN5 4BE
Activities: Activities of other holding companies n.e.c.
Major Shareholder: Harry Bramer
Officers: Harry Bramer [1949] Director

Country House Weddings Limited
Incorporated: 12 August 1998 *Employees:* 248
Net Worth: £9,225,184 *Total Assets:* £15,669,194
Registered Office: Regency House, 33 Wood Street, Barnet, Herts, EN5 4BE
Activities: Other business support service activities n.e.c.
Parent: Country House Weddings Holdings Ltd
Officers: Harry Bramer, Secretary/Director; Harry Bramer [1949] Director; Nicholas Bramer [1983] Director

Country Rhythm Limited
Incorporated: 1 September 1999 *Employees:* 4
Net Worth: £3,358,640 *Total Assets:* £5,478,374
Registered Office: Field End, Ridgeway Close, Oxshott, Leatherhead, Surrey, KT22 0LQ
Activities: Development of building projects
Shareholder: Rodney Frederick Frost
Officers: Janet Sandra Frost, Secretary; Janet Sandra Frost [1962] Director/Accountant; Rodney Frederick Frost [1962] Director

Countrywide Developments (UK) PLC
Incorporated: 28 January 2002 *Employees:* 4
Net Worth: £9,213,167 *Total Assets:* £17,355,384
Registered Office: 416 Green Lane, Ilford, Essex, IG3 9JX
Activities: Buying and selling of own real estate
Major Shareholder: Glenn Howard Cohen
Officers: Laurence Melvin Cohen, Secretary; Glenn Howard Cohen [1970] Director; Laurence Melvyn Cohen [1939] Director

Countrywide Electrical Distributors Limited
Incorporated: 5 January 1994 *Employees:* 47
Net Worth: £13,813,023 *Total Assets:* £18,634,840
Registered Office: 44-48 Freshwater Road, Dagenham, Essex, RM8 1RX
Activities: Wholesale of household goods (other than musical instruments) n.e.c
Major Shareholder: Ravinder Kumar Sood
Officers: Ravinder Kumar Sood, Secretary; Ravinder Kumar Sood [1947] Managing Director; Jayantilal Velani [1958] Director

Countyroute (A130) PLC.
Incorporated: 28 September 1999
Net Worth Deficit: £24,508,000 *Total Assets:* £90,498,000
Registered Office: 8 White Oak Square, London Road, Swanley, Kent, BR8 7AG
Activities: Construction of roads and motorways
Parent: Countyroute Limited
Officers: Alexander David Gates [1973] Director/Investment Manager; Andrew Stephen Pearson [1964] Managing Director

Countyroute Limited
Incorporated: 8 December 1998
Net Worth Deficit: £24,508,000 *Total Assets:* £90,498,000
Registered Office: 8 White Oak Square, London Road, Swanley, Kent, BR8 7AG
Activities: Construction of roads and motorways
Parent: John Laing Infrastructure Limited
Officers: Alexander David Gates [1973] Director/Investment Manager; Andrew Stephen Pearson [1964] Managing Director

Court Cavendish Limited
Incorporated: 20 September 2001 *Employees:* 2,269
Net Worth: £40,159,000 *Total Assets:* £147,824,000
Registered Office: River Bridge House, Guildford Road, Leatherhead, Surrey, KT22 9AD
Activities: Management consultancy activities other than financial management
Major Shareholder: Chaitanya Bhupendra Patel
Officers: Catherine Assunta Valenti, Secretary; Chaitanya Bhupendra Patel [1954] Director; Katharine Anne Patel [1963] Director; Catherine Assunta Valenti [1961] Director/Chartered Accountant

Court Lodge Epsom Limited
Incorporated: 1 December 2014
Net Worth Deficit: £7,416 *Total Assets:* £5,061,527
Registered Office: 14 First Quarter, Blenheim Road, Epsom, Surrey, KT19 9QN
Activities: Buying and selling of own real estate
Major Shareholder: Richard Ewart Dunstan
Officers: Richard Ewart Dunstan [1951] Director/Mortgage Broker; Andries Christoffel Stricker [1958] Director [South African]

Courtlands Estate (Richmond) Limited
Incorporated: 19 May 1982 *Employees:* 15
Net Worth: £11,333,683 *Total Assets:* £13,123,755
Registered Office: 27 Norfolk House, Courtlands, Sheen Road, Richmond, Surrey, TW10 5AT
Activities: Other letting and operating of own or leased real estate
Officers: Kenneth George Hassan, Secretary; Jenifer Megan Fellows [1946] Director/Administrator/Retired Teacher/JP; Oliver Knox [1970] Director/Retail Manager; Mark Lucas [1947] Director/Deal Leader; Esfandiar Mafy [1961] Director/Senior Financial Analyst; John Chuka Mbanefo [1948] Director/Retired Banking; Dr Christine Alice Margrit Pickard [1938] Director/Doctor; Anne Falconer Pringle [1958] Director/Manager; Simon Anthony Sanders [1962] Finance Director; Lynda May Waters [1949] Director/Marketing Research Consultant

Cousins Holdings Limited
Incorporated: 19 March 1964
Net Worth: £9,606,975 *Total Assets:* £11,104,184
Registered Office: Five Ways, 57-59 Hatfield Road, Potters Bar, Herts, EN6 1HS
Activities: Activities of head offices
Shareholder: Alexander Eric Gordon Cousins
Officers: Rory Alexander John Cousins [1981] Director

Cousins Material House Limited
Incorporated: 8 September 2003 *Employees:* 34
Net Worth: £6,051,887 *Total Assets:* £6,966,693
Registered Office: Unit J, Chesham Close, Romford, Essex, RM7 7PJ
Activities: Non-specialised wholesale trade
Major Shareholder: Anthony Edward Cousins
Officers: Anthony Edward Cousins [1963] Director/Horological Wholesaler; Christine Cousins [1964] Director; Samuel Cousins [1989] Director

The Coventry and Rugby Hospital Company (Holdings) Limited
Incorporated: 22 December 2000
Net Worth Deficit: £48,684,000 *Total Assets:* £423,775,008
Registered Office: 8 White Oak Square, London Road, Swanley, Kent, BR8 7AG
Activities: Activities of financial services holding companies
Parent: Innisfree Continuation Partners LLP
Officers: Sheila Jamieson Clark [1973] Director; Nicholas John Edward Crowther [1960] Investment Director; Benjamin Christopher Jacob Dean [1979] Director/Investment Manager

The Coventry and Rugby Hospital Company PLC
Incorporated: 12 August 2002
Net Worth Deficit: £48,601,000 *Total Assets:* £423,859,008
Registered Office: 8 White Oak Square, London Road, Swanley, Kent, BR8 7AG
Activities: Combined facilities support activities
Parent: The Coventry and Rugby Hospital Company (Holdings) Limited
Officers: Sheila Jamieson Clark [1973] Director; Nicholas John Edward Crowther [1960] Investment Director; Benjamin Christopher Jacob Dean [1979] Director/Investment Manager; Michael Edward Fry [1958] Director

Cover Up Clothing Limited
Incorporated: 28 November 1990 *Employees:* 47
Net Worth: £1,753,541 *Total Assets:* £5,686,340
Registered Office: East Wing, Goffs Oak House, Goffs Lane, Goffs Oak, Waltham Cross, Herts, EN7 5BW
Activities: Manufacture of other wearing apparel and accessories n.e.c.
Major Shareholder: Rachel Elizabeth Mary Heather
Officers: Norman Percival Heather, Secretary; Tracy Jane Green [1965] Director; Rachel Elizabeth Mary Heather [1964] Managing Director

Covidien UK Limited
Incorporated: 29 January 1937
Net Worth: £2,376,000 *Total Assets:* £60,209,000
Registered Office: Building 9, Croxley Park, Hatters Lane, Watford, Herts, WD18 8WW
Activities: Manufacture of knitted and crocheted hosiery
Parent: CDK U.K. Limited
Officers: Joanne Pascucci, Senior Corporate Secretary; Mark Justin Elsey [1967] Finance Director; Jacqueline Fielding [1964] Vice President (Director)

Coxwell Care Limited
Incorporated: 10 October 2005
Net Worth: £3,599,761 *Total Assets:* £7,753,283
Registered Office: Castle House, 69-70 Victoria, Street, Englefield Green, Surrey, TW20 0QX
Activities: Other residential care activities n.e.c.
Shareholders: Amar Sheikh; Momin Sheikh
Officers: Amar Sheikh, Secretary; Amar Sheikh [1961] Director; Momin Sheikh [1963] Director

Coyle Equipment Services Limited
Incorporated: 14 February 2011 *Employees:* 4
Net Worth: £3,271,877 *Total Assets:* £5,370,670
Registered Office: Unit 1 Canal Wharf, Horsenden Lane North, Greenford, Middlesex, UB6 7PH
Activities: Repair of machinery
Major Shareholder: William Coyle
Officers: William Bernard Coyle [1988] Director [Irish]

Owen Coyle Managements Limited
Incorporated: 22 May 1969 *Employees:* 5
Net Worth: £6,091,889 *Total Assets:* £7,068,644
Registered Office: Alpha Works, Blyth Road, Hayes, Middlesex, UB3 1DE
Activities: Development of building projects
Major Shareholder: Sharon Longman
Officers: Sharon Longman, Secretary; Eileen Esther Coyle [1936] Director; Graeme Clive Longman [1966] Director; Sharon Longman [1965] Director/Company Secretary

Coyle Personnel PLC
Incorporated: 27 July 1988 *Employees:* 156
Net Worth: £16,604,924 *Total Assets:* £33,545,504
Registered Office: Hygeia, 66-68 College Road, Harrow, Middlesex, HA1 1BE
Activities: Temporary employment agency activities
Major Shareholder: Kevin Michael Coyle
Officers: Howard Pepperdine, Secretary; Richard James Button [1973] Director/Operations Manager; Anna Louise Cooper [1978] Director; Ashling Michelle Coyle [1989] Director; Christopher John Coyle [1984] Director; Kevin Michael Coyle [1956] Chairman and Managing Director; Noreen Patricia Coyle [1959] Director [Irish]; Roger Andrew Stewart [1965] Director/Consultant

CP Holdings Limited
Incorporated: 22 March 1957 *Employees:* 7,059
Net Worth: £395,296,000 *Total Assets:* £762,854,976
Registered Office: CP House, Otterspool Way, Watford, Herts, WD25 8JJ
Activities: Activities of head offices
Shareholders: Lady Lilly Schreier; Iris Gibbor; Mark Gibbor; Robert Glatter; Michael Montague Wreschner; Alexei James Schreier
Officers: Eric Lewis, Secretary; Paul Andrew Filer [1957] Director/Chartered Accountant; Iris Gibbor [1951] Director; Mark Gibbor [1988] Director; Robert Glatter [1937] Director; Mark Hennebry [1966] Director [Irish]; Michael Barry Hirst OBE [1943] Director; Philip Hoffbrand [1967] Director/Solicitor; Eric Lewis [1927] Director/Solicitor; Alexei James Schreier [1976] Director/Executive; Lady Lilly Schreier [1924] Director; John Ernest Smith [1949] Director

CP Kelco UK Limited
Incorporated: 10 April 2000 *Employees:* 18
Net Worth: £6,816,000 *Total Assets:* £8,092,000
Registered Office: River Bridge House, Guildford Road, Fetcham, Leatherhead, Surrey, KT22 9AD
Activities: Agents specialised in the sale of other particular products
Officers: Jerome Bera [1968] Director [French]; Victor Dean [1964] Director [American]

CP Regents Park Two Limited
Incorporated: 8 December 2004 *Employees:* 124
Net Worth: £1,011,530 *Total Assets:* £47,227,640
Registered Office: CP House, Otterspool Way, Watford, Herts, WD25 8JJ
Activities: Hotels and similar accommodation
Parent: CP Holdings Limited
Officers: Eric Lewis, Secretary; Paul Andrew Filer [1957] Director/Chartered Accountant; Iris Gibbor [1951] Director; Mark Gibbor [1988] Director; Mark Hennebry [1966] Director [Irish]; Eric Lewis [1927] Director/Solicitor; Alexei James Schreier [1976] Director

Cramlington Renewable Energy Developments Hold Co Limited
Incorporated: 4 June 2015
Net Worth Deficit: £7,284,000 *Total Assets:* £127,721,000
Registered Office: 8 White Oak Square, London Road, Swanley, Kent, BR8 7AG
Activities: Activities of other holding companies n.e.c.
Shareholders: Equitix ESI CHP 2 Limited; John Laing Investments Limited
Officers: Maxwell Francis Aitken [1977] Director; David Richard Bradbury [1969] Director/Senior Investment Manager; Benjamin Matthew Cashin [1972] Director; Paul John Ireland [1979] Director; David Adam Whitehurst [1971] Director/Investment Professional

Crane Apartments Limited
Incorporated: 11 March 2010
Net Worth: £2,196,879 *Total Assets:* £5,553,186
Registered Office: 10 Durham Avenue, Gidea Park, Romford, Essex, RM2 6JS
Activities: Other letting and operating of own or leased real estate
Parent: Crane Investments Limited
Officers: Sharanjit Patel, Secretary; Aprajay Patel [1984] Director; Ashok Kumar Patel [1950] Director

Crane Investments Ltd
Incorporated: 24 October 2008 *Employees:* 1
Net Worth: £6,038,894 *Total Assets:* £11,493,055
Registered Office: 10 Durham Avenue, Gidea Park, Romford, Essex, RM2 6JS
Activities: Other letting and operating of own or leased real estate
Major Shareholder: Ashok Kumar Patel
Officers: Aprajay Patel [1984] Director; Ashok Kumar Patel [1950] Director/Solicitor

Craneshaw House Limited
Incorporated: 8 December 2015
Net Worth Deficit: £243,801 *Total Assets:* £7,780,498
Registered Office: 3rd Floor, Sterling House, Langston Road, Loughton, Essex, IG10 3TS
Activities: Development of building projects
Parent: Galliard Developments Limited
Officers: Allan William Porter, Secretary; John Cole [1971] Director; Stephen Stuart Solomon Conway [1948] Director; Adam Max Dreyfuss [1991] Director/Property Analyst; Robert Mark Dreyfuss [1966] Director; Jonathan Simon Goldstein [1966] Director; Donagh O'Sullivan [1968] Construction Director [Irish]

Cranfield Technology Park Investments Limited
Incorporated: 4 May 2017 *Employees:* 4
Net Worth: £2,231,357 *Total Assets:* £17,481,700
Registered Office: 7th Floor, Metropolitan House, 3 Darkes Lane, Potters Bar, Herts, EN6 1AG
Activities: Buying and selling of own real estate
Parent: Sheikh Holdings Group (Investments) Limited
Officers: Gareth Norman Dufton [1976] Director/Chartered Accountant; Akbar Sheikh [1989] Director; Farouq Rashid Sheikh [1958] Director; Yusuf Sheikh [1992] Director

Cranford Community College
Incorporated: 10 March 2011 *Employees:* 165
Net Worth: £13,168,971 *Total Assets:* £19,142,560
Registered Office: Cranford Community College, High Street, Cranford, Hounslow, Middlesex, TW5 9PD
Activities: General secondary education
Officers: Bernadette Catherine Moir, Secretary; Shafia Haroon [1977] Director/Manager; Aftab Hussain [1972] Director/Operations Manager; Jennifer Lewis [1978] Director/Teacher; Jennifer Lewis [1946] Director/Retired; Barbara Lodge [1971] Director/Teacher; John Rodger Lyden [1958] Director/Examinations Officer; Daanish Saeed [1965] Director

Cranmore School
Incorporated: 21 September 2010 *Employees:* 94
Net Worth: £7,874,994 *Total Assets:* £9,151,864
Registered Office: Cranmore School, Epsom Road, West Horsley, Surrey, KT24 6AT
Activities: Primary education
Officers: Claire Louise Minikin, Secretary; Michael Edward Agius [1944] Director/Retired; Nina Katrin Brenninkmeijer [1970] Director/Psychologist [German]; Brendan Alistair Cook [1962] Director/Banker; Anne Marie Fort [1957] Director/Freelance Translator; Michael John Glidden Henderson [1938] Director/Chartered Accountant; Dr Catherine-Anne McMullan [1950] Director/Retired; Edmund Anthony Middlehurst [1952] Director/Solicitor

Cranstoun
Incorporated: 23 January 1997 *Employees:* 391
Net Worth: £3,612,000 *Total Assets:* £9,123,000
Registered Office: Thames Mews, Portsmouth Road, Esher, Surrey, KT10 9AD
Activities: Other human health activities
Officers: Martin Holly, Secretary; Franklin Jay Apfel [1945] Director/Consultant; Cees Cornelius Goos [1941] Director/Consultant [Dutch]; Malcolm Wayne Haywood [1961] Director; Faith Stella Jenner [1947] Director; Katharine Patel [1974] Director/Chartered Accountant; Richard James Charles Pertwee [1955] Director/Solicitor

The Creative Assembly Limited
Incorporated: 28 August 1997 *Employees:* 372
Net Worth: £19,971,728 *Total Assets:* £27,756,866
Registered Office: 27 Great West Road, Brentford, Middlesex, TW8 9BW
Activities: Ready-made interactive leisure and entertainment software development
Parent: Sega Sammy Holdings Inc
Officers: Nicola Ormrod, Secretary; Gary Robert Dale [1961] Director/Chief Operating Officer; Tatsuyuki Miyazaki [1967] Director [Japanese]; David Jonathon Ward [1965] Director/Chief Financial Officer

Creative Car Park Ltd
Incorporated: 22 September 2005 *Employees:* 58
Net Worth: £3,604,534 *Total Assets:* £8,881,248
Registered Office: The Studio, St Nicholas Close, Elstree, Borehamwood, Herts, WD6 3EW
Activities: Other business support service activities n.e.c.
Parent: Creative Technologies and Systems Limited
Officers: Willem Marthinus de Beer [1967] Director/Consultant [South African]

Creative Distribution Limited
Incorporated: 13 June 2003 *Employees:* 62
Net Worth: £15,346,783 *Total Assets:* £18,892,476
Registered Office: Unit 2 Beddington Industrial Estate, 119 Beddington Lane, Croydon, Surrey, CR0 4TD
Activities: Wholesale of computers, computer peripheral equipment and software
Shareholders: Gareth Dain; Mark Nielsen
Officers: Anthony Hogarth, Secretary; Gareth Lloyd Dain [1978] Director; Anthony Hogarth [1978] Director/Accountant; Craig Francis Lewis [1982] Director; Samuel Richard John Wilson [1989] Director

Creative Video Productions Limited
Incorporated: 2 June 1989 *Employees:* 120
Net Worth: £13,791,374 *Total Assets:* £27,303,416
Registered Office: 23 Shield Drive, West Cross Industrial Estate, Brentford, Middlesex, TW8 9EX
Activities: Motion picture production activities
Parent: Infinity Media Group Limited
Officers: Mark Andrew Forth [1969] Director; Jon Fry [1973] Director; Mansukh Kerai [1971] Director; Darren Simpson [1974] Director; Yevgeny Subbotin [1974] Director

Cremer (UK) Manufacturing Co. Ltd
Incorporated: 24 February 2017 *Employees:* 26
Net Worth: £2,444,303 *Total Assets:* £10,913,476
Registered Office: c/o Procter & Gamble, London Plant West Office, Hedley Avenue, West Thurrock, Essex, RM20 4AL
Activities: Other manufacturing n.e.c.
Parent: Cremer Oleo Management GmbH
Officers: Mr Andrew Brian Aylwin [1969] Director/Chief Production Officer; Ullrich Wegner [1964] Director/Chief Executive Officer [German]

Cressdene Limited
Incorporated: 26 November 1969
Net Worth: £9,487,000 *Total Assets:* £11,166,000
Registered Office: Claygate House, Littleworth Road, Esher, Surrey, KT10 9PN
Activities: Non-trading company
Parent: Dairy Crest Limited
Officers: Isobel Jean Hinton, Secretary; Mark Allen [1959] Managing Director; Thomas Alexander Atherton [1970] Director/Deputy Chief Executive

Crest A2D (Walton Court) LLP
Incorporated: 22 January 2016
Net Worth: £1,461,000 *Total Assets:* £22,975,000
Registered Office: Crest House, Pyrcroft Road, Chertsey, Surrey, KT16 9GN

Crest Nicholson (Henley-on-Thames) Limited
Incorporated: 20 August 1999
Previous: Associated Properties UK Limited
Net Worth: £2,027,000 *Total Assets:* £12,751,000
Registered Office: Crest House, Pyrcroft Road, Chertsey, Surrey, KT16 9GN
Activities: Development of building projects
Parent: Crest Nicholson (Highlands Farm) Ltd
Officers: Kevin Maguire, Secretary; Patrick Joseph Bergin [1966] Director/Group Financial Controller; Robin Patrick Hoyles [1954] Group Land and Planning Director; Stephen Stone [1954] Managing Director; Chris Tinker [1960] Urban Land Director

Crest Nicholson Developments (Chertsey) Limited
Incorporated: 23 March 2003
Net Worth: £13,700,000 *Total Assets:* £53,000,000
Registered Office: Crest House, Pyrcroft Road, Chertsey, Surrey, KT16 9GN
Activities: Non-trading company
Parent: Crest Nicholson PLC
Officers: Kevin Maguire, Secretary; Patrick Joseph Bergin [1966] Director/Group Financial Controller; Anil Bungar [1972] Director; Stephen Stone [1954] Managing Director; Nigel Christopher Tinker [1960] Urban Land Director

Crest Nicholson Holdings PLC
Incorporated: 23 January 2009 *Employees:* 905
Net Worth: £817,800,000 *Total Assets:* £1,477,900,032
Registered Office: Crest House, Pyrcroft Road, Chertsey, Surrey, KT16 9GN
Activities: Activities of head offices
Officers: Kevin Maguire, Secretary; Lucinda Margaret Bell [1964] Director; Patrick Joseph Bergin [1966] Director/Group Financial Controller; Sharon Emma Flood [1965] Director; Louise Jane Hardy [1966] Director; Octavia Kate Morley [1968] Director; Stephen Stone [1954] Managing Director; Nigel Christopher Tinker [1960] Urban Land Director; Philippe Leslie Van de Walle [1956] Director/Deputy Chairman [French]

Crest Nicholson Operations Limited
Incorporated: 26 April 1974 *Employees:* 895
Net Worth: £503,200,000 *Total Assets:* £1,309,500,032
Registered Office: Crest House, Pyrcroft Road, Chertsey, Surrey, KT16 9GN
Activities: Development of building projects
Parent: Crest Nicholson PLC
Officers: Kevin Maguire, Secretary; Patrick Joseph Bergin [1966] Director/Group Financial Controller; Robin Patrick Hoyles [1954] Group Land & Planning Director; Stephen Stone [1954] Managing Director; Nigel Christopher Tinker [1960] Urban Land Director

Crest Nicholson PLC
Incorporated: 31 January 1972 *Employees:* 905
Net Worth: £742,800,000 *Total Assets:* £1,339,200,000
Registered Office: Crest House, Pyrcroft Road, Chertsey, Surrey, KT16 9GN
Activities: Activities of head offices
Parent: Castle Bidco Limited
Officers: Kevin Maguire, Secretary; Patrick Joseph Bergin [1966] Director/Group Financial Controller; Robin Patrick Hoyles [1954] Group Land & Planning Director; Stephen Stone [1954] Managing Director; Nigel Christopher Tinker [1960] Urban Land Director

Crest Plus Operations Limited
Incorporated: 18 December 2002 *Employees:* 2,338
Net Worth: £1,431,909 *Total Assets:* £7,284,852
Registered Office: 4th Floor, Radius House, Clarendon Road, Watford, Herts, WD17 1HP
Activities: Other professional, scientific and technical activities n.e.c.
Parent: JSA Services Limited
Officers: Derek John Harling [1956] Director; John Hugo Hoskin [1974] Director; Valerie Ann Lawton [1971] Finance Director; Paul Anthony McDonnell [1970] Director/Businessman; Kwasi Martin Missah [1969] Director

Cresta Estates Limited
Incorporated: 7 June 1952
Net Worth: £10,876,705 *Total Assets:* £72,809,952
Registered Office: Atlas House, 28 Great Cambridge Road, Enfield, Middlesex, EN1 1UU
Activities: Other letting and operating of own or leased real estate
Shareholder: Baruch Erlich
Officers: Judith Erlich, Secretary; Baruch Erlich [1962] Director/Solicitor

Crestron (UK) Limited
Incorporated: 18 March 1998 *Employees:* 52
Net Worth: £1,652,104 *Total Assets:* £7,940,651
Registered Office: Munro House, Portsmouth Road, Cobham, Surrey, KT11 1TF
Activities: Other information technology service activities
Major Shareholder: Robin Anthony Van Meeuwen
Officers: Robin Anthony Van Meeuwen, Secretary; Robin Anthony Van Meeuwen [1971] Director

Cricklewood Developments Limited
Incorporated: 25 July 2014 *Employees:* 7
Net Worth Deficit: £605,000 *Total Assets:* £22,632,000
Registered Office: 50 Lancaster Road, Enfield, Middlesex, EN2 0BY
Activities: Development of building projects
Parent: Fairview New Homes Limited
Officers: Jonathan Mark Baxter, Secretary; Michael Blakey [1963] Director; Nicholas Martin Dulcken [1967] Director; Generald Anthony Malton [1960] Director; Darren Lee McCormack [1982] Sales Director; Richard James Paterson [1957] Director; Jonathan Andrew Spring [1972] Land Buying Director; Michael Raymond Walker [1958] Director; Robert Kenneth Williams [1964] Director

Crickmore Developments Limited
Incorporated: 11 December 1998 *Employees:* 6
Net Worth: £354,335 *Total Assets:* £6,337,396
Registered Office: 166 College Road, Harrow, Middlesex, HA1 1RA
Activities: Development of building projects
Major Shareholder: Colin Crickmore
Officers: Colin Crickmore, Secretary/Car Salesman; Colin Crickmore [1958] Director/Businessman; Rebecca Crickmore [1958] Director/Secretary

Crislex Limited
Incorporated: 24 May 2012
Net Worth: £6,093,982 *Total Assets:* £6,094,047
Registered Office: 8 Langley Grove, New Malden, Surrey, KT3 3AL
Activities: Activities of other holding companies n.e.c.
Shareholders: Christopher Hogg; Alexander Hogg
Officers: Christopher John Hogg [1978] Director

Crispin & Borst Limited
Incorporated: 23 January 1964
Net Worth: £15,801,000 *Total Assets:* £17,656,000
Registered Office: Astral House, Imperial Way, Watford, Herts, WD24 4WW
Activities: Construction of commercial buildings
Parent: C & B Holdings Limited
Officers: Barry John Boxall [1957] Director/Construction Manager; Christopher Carl Brennan [1969] Director/Accountant; Generald James Smith [1956] Director/Chartered Builder

CRK Finance Limited
Incorporated: 4 November 2011
Net Worth: £13,746,638 *Total Assets:* £13,820,178
Registered Office: 116 Goodmayes Road, Ilford, Essex, IG3 9UZ
Activities: Other credit granting n.e.c.
Officers: Sundesh Kudhail, Secretary; Sundesh Kumar Kudhail [1959] Director; Surinder Kudhail [1960] Director

Crockford Park Properties Limited
Incorporated: 6 June 1969
Net Worth: £9,276,062 *Total Assets:* £10,908,969
Registered Office: The Pantiles, Ottershaw Park, Chobham Road, Ottershaw, Chertsey, Surrey, KT16 0QG
Activities: Other business support service activities n.e.c.
Major Shareholder: Raymond James Vincent
Officers: Marguerite Susan Vincent, Secretary/Director; Marguerite Susan Vincent [1944] Director; Raymond James Vincent [1943] Director/Contractor

Croftwood Care (Cheshire) Limited
Incorporated: 6 July 2016 *Employees:* 359
Net Worth: £5,896,748 *Total Assets:* £6,637,540
Registered Office: 238 Station Road, Addlestone, Surrey, KT15 2PS
Activities: Other residential care activities n.e.c.
Parent: Minster Care Group Limited
Officers: John Neal Alflatt, Secretary; Colin William Farebrother [1965] Operations Director; Mahesh Shivabhai Patel [1953] Managing Director; Surendra Shivabhai Patel [1945] Operations Director

Cromsource Ltd
Incorporated: 5 February 2008 *Employees:* 35
Net Worth: £337,087 *Total Assets:* £5,907,526
Registered Office: 6-9 The Square, Stockley Park, Hayes, Uxbridge, Middlesex, UB11 1FW
Activities: Other professional, scientific and technical activities n.e.c.
Parent: Cromsource S.R.L
Officers: Kerry Dyson [1969] Director/Head UK Operations; Oriana Maria Zerbini [1953] Director/Doctor [Italian]

Cromwell (Egham) Limited
Incorporated: 18 January 1999 *Employees:* 2
Net Worth: £2,109,397 *Total Assets:* £8,561,802
Registered Office: Park Place House, 24 Church Street, Epsom, Surrey, KT17 4QB
Activities: Other letting and operating of own or leased real estate
Parent: Precious Metal Coin Co. Ltd
Officers: Darren Colin Bradley [1969] Director/Chartered Surveyor; James Perry Hallam [1978] Director; Michael Stuart Hastings [1942] Director

Cromwell (Wandsworth) Limited
Incorporated: 11 August 1997 *Employees:* 3
Net Worth: £12,158,371 *Total Assets:* £12,648,415
Registered Office: Park Place House, 24 Church Street, Epsom, Surrey, KT17 4QB
Activities: Other letting and operating of own or leased real estate
Parent: Precious Metal Coin Co. Ltd
Officers: Darren Colin Bradley [1969] Director/Chartered Surveyor; James Perry Hallam [1978] Director; Michael Stuart Hastings [1942] Director; Albert Richard Perry [1924] Director

Cromwell Holdings Limited
Incorporated: 21 March 1983 *Employees:* 14
Net Worth: £36,299,000 *Total Assets:* £50,442,000
Registered Office: Park Place House, 24 Church Street, Epsom, Surrey, KT17 4QB
Activities: Activities of head offices
Major Shareholder: James Perry Hallam
Officers: Alison Hedges, Secretary; Darren Colin Bradley [1969] Director/Chartered Surveyor; James Perry Hallam [1978] Director; Michael Stuart Hastings [1942] Director/Certified Accountant; Albert Richard Perry [1924] Director

Cromwell Investments (Richmond) Limited
Incorporated: 29 October 1963 *Employees:* 3
Net Worth: £6,059,458 *Total Assets:* £9,894,491
Registered Office: Park Place House, 24 Church Street, Epsom, Surrey, KT17 4QB
Activities: Other letting and operating of own or leased real estate
Parent: Cromwell (2003) Ltd
Officers: Darren Colin Bradley [1969] Director/Chartered Surveyor; James Perry Hallam [1978] Director; Michael Stuart Hastings [1942] Director/Certified Accountant; Albert Richard Perry [1924] Director

Cromwell Investments Limited
Incorporated: 30 March 1965 *Employees:* 2
Net Worth: £6,909,767 *Total Assets:* £6,912,050
Registered Office: Park Place House, 24 Church Street, Epsom, Surrey, KT17 4QB
Activities: Activities of head offices
Parent: Kempletyne Limited
Officers: James Perry Hallam [1978] Director; Michael Stuart Hastings [1942] Director/Certified Accountant; Albert Richard Perry [1924] Director

Cross London Trains Finance Company Limited
Incorporated: 19 June 2012
Net Worth Deficit: £63,000 *Total Assets:* £112,677,000
Registered Office: 8 White Oak Square, London Road, Swanley, Kent, BR8 7AG
Activities: Financial leasing
Parent: Cross London Trains Holdco Limited
Officers: Graham Maurice Beazley-Long [1960] Director/Investment Manager; John Ivor Cavill [1972] Director; Timothy John Kashem [1970] Director/Fund Manager; Scott Bruce Michael Moseley [1978] Director/Partner; Andrew Christopher Pitt [1959] Director; Petra Regge [1973] Director/Investment Manager [German]; Basil Justin Bromley Wetters [1967] Director

Cross London Trains Holdco 2 Limited
Incorporated: 17 October 2011 *Employees:* 2
Net Worth Deficit: £236,660,000 *Total Assets:* £1,989,815,040
Registered Office: 8 White Oak Square, London Road, Swanley, Kent, BR8 7AG
Activities: Financial leasing
Shareholders: 3i Infrastructure PLC; Project Ventures Rail Investments I Limited; Innisfree Secondary Partners 2 LLP
Officers: Graham Maurice Beazley-Long [1960] Director/Investment Manager; John Ivor Cavill [1972] Director; Timothy John Kashem [1970] Director/Fund Manager; Scott Bruce Michael Moseley [1978] Director/Partner; Andrew Christopher Pitt [1959] Director; Petra Regge [1973] Director/Investment Manager [German]; Basil Justin Bromley Wetters [1967] Director

Cross London Trains Holdco Limited
Incorporated: 19 June 2012
Net Worth: £30,392,000 *Total Assets:* £81,268,000
Registered Office: 8 White Oak Square, London Road, Swanley, Kent, BR8 7AG
Activities: Financial leasing
Parent: Cross London Trains Holdco 2 Limited
Officers: Graham Maurice Beazley-Long [1960] Director/Investment Manager; John Ivor Cavill [1972] Director; Timothy John Kashem [1970] Director/Fund Manager; Scott Bruce Michael Moseley [1978] Director/Partner; Andrew Christopher Pitt [1959] Director; Petra Regge [1973] Director/Investment Manager [German]; Basil Justin Bromley Wetters [1967] Director

Cross London Trains Limited
Incorporated: 17 October 2011 *Employees:* 2
Net Worth Deficit: £236,596,992 *Total Assets:* £1,989,815,040
Registered Office: 8 White Oak Square, London Road, Swanley, Kent, BR8 7AG
Activities: Financial leasing
Parent: Cross London Trains Holdco Limited
Officers: Graham Maurice Beazley-Long [1960] Director/Investment Manager; John Ivor Cavill [1972] Director; Timothy John Kashem [1970] Director/Fund Manager; Scott Bruce Michael Moseley [1978] Director/Partner; Andrew Christopher Pitt [1959] Director; Petra Regge [1973] Director/Investment Manager [German]; Basil Justin Bromley Wetters [1967] Director

Crosswater Holdings Limited
Incorporated: 24 March 2006
Net Worth: £432,000 *Total Assets:* £16,440,000
Registered Office: Lake View House, Rennie Drive, Dartford, Kent, DA1 5FU
Activities: Other business support service activities n.e.c.
Parent: Bathroom Brands Holdings UK Limited
Officers: Vikram Kant, Secretary; David John Anning [1966] Director; Vikram Kant [1984] Director [Indian]

Crosswater Limited
Incorporated: 20 August 1998 *Employees:* 203
Net Worth: £20,590,000 *Total Assets:* £72,733,000
Registered Office: Lake View House, Rennie Drive, Dartford, Kent, DA1 5FU
Activities: Wholesale of hardware, plumbing and heating equipment and supplies
Parent: Bathroom Brands Holdings UK Limited
Officers: Vikram Kant, Secretary; David John Anning [1966] Director; David Michael Button [1966] Director; David Richard Hance [1965] Director/Group Chairman; Vikram Kant [1984] Director [Indian]

Crossways Care (UK) Limited
Incorporated: 14 October 2009
Net Worth: £1,781,463 *Total Assets:* £5,251,093
Registered Office: 69 Squirrels Heath Road, Romford, Essex, RM3 0LS
Activities: Other residential care activities n.e.c.
Major Shareholder: Mahmood Dewji
Officers: Parviz Dewji, Secretary; Mahmood Dewji [1961] Director

Croudace Homes Group Limited
Incorporated: 13 February 2002 *Employees:* 274
Net Worth: £143,644,992 *Total Assets:* £242,700,992
Registered Office: Croudace House, Tupwood Lane, Caterham, Surrey, CR3 6XQ
Activities: Construction of domestic buildings
Officers: Caroline Jane Bailey Boakes, Secretary; Anthony Brotherton-Ratcliffe [1950] Director; Allan Robert Carey [1956] Director/Chartered Accountant; Russell Kane Denness [1959] Director; Richard John Holmans [1959] Director; Steven Michael Thomas [1975] Finance Director

Croudace Homes Limited
Incorporated: 22 July 1964 *Employees:* 274
Net Worth: £134,716,992 *Total Assets:* £207,668,000
Registered Office: Croudace House, Caterham, Surrey, CR3 6XQ
Activities: Construction of domestic buildings
Parent: Croudace Homes Group Limited
Officers: Caroline Jane Bailey Boakes, Secretary; Simon John Boakes [1966] Director; Ian John Burgess [1977] Director; Allan Robert Carey [1956] Director/Chartered Accountant; Jason Alexander Cross [1976] Director; Russell Kane Denness [1959] Director; Stuart Alan Elvidge [1968] Director; Richard John Holmans [1959] Director; Matthew Robert Houson [1970] Director; Matthew Adam Norris [1975] Director; Steven Michael Thomas [1975] Finance Director; Benjamin William Yallop [1976] Director

Croudace Portland Limited
Incorporated: 19 January 1983
Net Worth: £714,709 *Total Assets:* £23,983,844
Registered Office: Croudace House, Tupwood Lane, Caterham, Surrey, CR3 6XQ
Activities: Construction of domestic buildings
Parent: Croudace Homes Group Limited
Officers: Caroline Jane Bailey Boakes, Secretary; Allan Robert Carey [1956] Director/Chartered Accountant; Russell Kane Denness [1959] Director; Steven Michael Thomas [1975] Finance Director

Croudace Strategic Limited
Incorporated: 12 December 2005
Net Worth: £6,139,723 *Total Assets:* £21,386,800
Registered Office: Croudace House, Tupwood Lane, Caterham, Surrey, CR3 6XQ
Activities: Development of building projects
Parent: Croudace Homes Group Limited
Officers: Caroline Jane Bailey Boakes, Secretary; Simon John Boakes [1966] Director; Allan Robert Carey [1956] Director; Russell Kane Denness [1959] Director; Richard John Holmans [1959] Director; Steven Michael Thomas [1975] Finance Director; Benjamin William Yallop [1976] Director

Crown Agents Bank Limited
Incorporated: 12 January 1989 *Employees:* 118
Net Worth: £57,664,000 *Total Assets:* £993,044,992
Registered Office: Quadrant House, The Quadrant, Sutton, Surrey, SM2 5AS
Activities: Financial intermediation not elsewhere classified
Parent: Cabim Limited
Officers: Nicholas Charles Beecroft [1960] Director/Financial Consultant; Rajesh Bhatia [1963] Director/Banker; Susanne Chishti [1971] Director [Austrian]; Arnold Onyekwere Ekpe [1953] Director; Richard Charles Hallett [1966] Director/Accountant; Albert Cornelis Maasland [1960] Director [Dutch]; Carole Machell [1962] Director/Chartered Accountant; Douglas Davidson MacLennan [1964] Director; Derek Neil McMenamin [1955] Director; Jeremy Parrish [1955] Director; Simon Hilliard Poole [1966] Director

Crown Design and Development Limited
Incorporated: 6 April 2010
Net Worth: £1,089,857 *Total Assets:* £5,800,596
Registered Office: Coveham House, Downside Bridge Road, Cobham, Surrey, KT11 3EP
Activities: Other business support service activities n.e.c.
Major Shareholder: Kerry Amanda Stone
Officers: Kerry Stone [1963] Director

Crown Holdings Limited
Incorporated: 4 September 2000 *Employees:* 751
Net Worth: £7,490,740 *Total Assets:* £17,480,976
Registered Office: Crown House, 855 London Road, Grays, Essex, RM20 3LG
Activities: Activities of head offices
Major Shareholder: Russell Lee Christopher Morgan
Officers: Javed Taher, Secretary; Charles Nicholas Beer [1971] Managing Director; Deirdre Morgan [1952] Director; Russell Lee Christopher Morgan [1952] Director/Chairman; Christopher John Sullivan [1956] Director

Crown House (Tadworth) Limited
Incorporated: 28 January 1980
Net Worth: £3,075,320 *Total Assets:* £8,909,977
Registered Office: Crown House Mews, Chequers Lane, Walton on the Hill, Tadworth, Surrey, KT20 7ST
Activities: Other letting and operating of own or leased real estate
Major Shareholder: Martin James Morris
Officers: David Mark Pay, Secretary; Martin James Morris [1963] Director

Crown House Investments Limited
Incorporated: 12 March 2016
Net Worth: £347,042 *Total Assets:* £8,255,170
Registered Office: Crown House, 151 High Road, Loughton, Essex, IG10 4LF
Activities: Other letting and operating of own or leased real estate
Major Shareholder: Lee Steven Newton
Officers: Jane Louise Musgrove, Secretary; Lee Steven Newton [1965] Director; Eric John William Wenham [1950] Director/Accountant

Crown House Technologies Limited
Incorporated: 24 March 2004
Net Worth: £49,503,000 *Total Assets:* £81,762,000
Registered Office: Bridge Place, Anchor Boulevard, Admirals Park, Dartford, Kent, DA2 6SN
Activities: Construction of commercial buildings
Parent: Laing O'Rourke Holdings Limited
Officers: Robert Edward Turner, Secretary; Stephen John Harley [1951] Director; Alexander Stewart McIntyre [1956] Director; Hubert Desmond O'Rourke [1949] Director/Structural Engineer [Irish]

Crownstar Limited
Incorporated: 22 August 2007
Net Worth: £2,594,006 *Total Assets:* £5,239,834
Registered Office: Suite 2B, 4th Floor, Congress House, Lyon Road, Harrow, Middlesex, HA1 2EN
Activities: Security dealing on own account
Shareholders: Kamal Oswal; Jawahar Lal Oswal
Officers: Dinesh Gogna, Secretary; Dinesh Gogna [1953] Finance Director [Indian]; Dinesh Oswal [1965] Director [Indian]; Jawaharlal Oswal [1943] Director [Indian]; Kamal Oswal [1962] Director [Indian]; Sambhav Oswal [1993] Director [Indian]

William Croxson & Son,Limited
Incorporated: 21 November 1901 *Employees:* 28
Net Worth: £5,454,763 *Total Assets:* £14,163,318
Registered Office: Alpha Place, Garth Road, Morden, Surrey, SM4 4LX
Activities: Non-specialised wholesale trade
Major Shareholder: James Edward Croxson
Officers: Christopher John Dalley, Secretary; James Edward Croxson [1951] Managing Director; Timothy James Croxson [1982] Director; Andrew Martin Giles [1948] Director/Chartered Accountant; David Benjamin Giles [1981] Director/Chartered Accountant; Paul Francis McGrane [1980] Director; George O'Brien [1966] Director

Croydon and Lewisham Lighting Services (Holdings) Limited
Incorporated: 8 February 2011
Net Worth Deficit: £19,106,000 *Total Assets:* £87,063,000
Registered Office: 8 White Oak Square, London Road, Swanley, Kent, BR8 7AG
Activities: Activities of head offices
Shareholders: JLIF Holdings (Croydon and Lewisham Street Lighting) Limited; Skanska TAM Limited
Officers: Paul Alan Bannister [1959] Director/Accountant; David Richard Bradbury [1969] Director/Senior Investment Manager; Jennifer Kathryn Fegan [1973] Director/Lawyer; Katherine Mary Rae [1980] Director/Legal Advisor; Paul Sydney Shadbolt [1957] Asset Management Director; Keerthana Sivanathan [1988] Director/Senior Management Accountant

Croydon and Lewisham Lighting Services Limited
Incorporated: 9 February 2011
Net Worth Deficit: £19,106,000 *Total Assets:* £87,063,000
Registered Office: 8 White Oak Square, London Road, Swanley, Kent, BR8 7AG
Activities: Other business support service activities n.e.c.
Parent: Croydon and Lewisham Lighting Services (Holdings) Limited
Officers: Paul Alan Bannister [1959] Director/Accountant; David Richard Bradbury [1969] Director/Senior Investment Manager; Jennifer Kathryn Fegan [1973] Director/Lawyer; Katherine Mary Rae [1980] Director/Legal Advisor; Paul Sydney Shadbolt [1957] Asset Management Director; Keerthana Sivanathan [1988] Director/Senior Management Accountant

Croydon House Ltd
Incorporated: 4 June 2014
Net Worth: £1,734,646 *Total Assets:* £5,615,354
Registered Office: Wrencote House, 123 High Street, Croydon, Surrey, CR0 0XJ
Activities: Other letting and operating of own or leased real estate
Shareholders: Abbas Alidina; Mario Joseph Carrozzo
Officers: Abbas Alidina [1979] Director; Mario Joseph Carrozzo [1972] Director

Croydon Logistics Limited
Incorporated: 23 November 1956 *Employees:* 157
Net Worth: £13,395,000 *Total Assets:* £15,052,000
Registered Office: 5 Queensway, Croydon, Surrey, CR9 4DL
Activities: Freight transport by road
Parent: Chanel Limited
Officers: Paul Stuart Gaff, Secretary; Pia Marie Therese Dekkers [1962] H R Director; Alberto Fasanotti [1974] Finance Director [Italian]; Paul Stuart Gaff [1975] Director/General Counsel; Martin Hamilton [1953] Director/Solicitor; Andrew Brian Lilley [1964] Operations Director; Olivier Nicolay [1957] Director [French]; Gerard Paul Philippe Wertheimer [1951] Director [French]; Steven Antony Wright [1980] Director/Accountant

Crumlin Capital Limited
Incorporated: 16 February 2015
Net Worth: £5,240,732 *Total Assets:* £11,830,296
Registered Office: St Andrew's House, Portsmouth Road, Esher, Surrey, KT10 9TA
Activities: Activities of other holding companies n.e.c.
Officers: Peter James Burnside [1965] Director/Chartered Accountant; Brendan Martin Kerr [1965] Director [Irish]

Crystal Clear Group Limited
Incorporated: 20 December 2006 *Employees:* 90
Net Worth: £1,059,330 *Total Assets:* £8,128,493
Registered Office: 42 Lytton Road, Barnet, Herts, EN5 5BY
Activities: Manufacture of other plastic products
Major Shareholder: Martin John Randall
Officers: Sandra Ann Randall, Secretary/Director; Timothy Peter Allen [1955] Director; Tim Goldspink [1968] Director; Steve John Halford [1964] Director; Kevin Paul Morgan [1972] Director; Martin John Randall [1963] Director; Sandra Ann Randall [1967] Director

Crystal Group Limited
Incorporated: 2 September 2005 *Employees:* 251
Net Worth: £3,975,662 *Total Assets:* £10,749,148
Registered Office: Crystal House, Unit 1 King George Close, Romford, Essex, RM7 7PN
Activities: Other manufacturing n.e.c.
Shareholder: John Ettore Antonio Oddi
Officers: Michael Brian Ballard [1965] Director/Accountant; Agostina Boland [1965] Director

Crystal Home Improvements Group Limited
Incorporated: 6 February 2002
Net Worth Deficit: £227,441 *Total Assets:* £21,546,712
Registered Office: Crystal House, Unit 1 King George Close, Romford, Essex, RM7 7PN
Activities: Other manufacturing n.e.c.
Parent: Crystal Home Improvements Holdings Ltd
Officers: Michael Brian Ballard [1965] Director/Accountant; Agostina Boland [1965] Director

Crystal Home Improvements Holdings Limited
Incorporated: 2 December 2003
Net Worth: £4,561,855 *Total Assets:* £29,984,880
Registered Office: Crystal House, Unit 1 King George Close, Romford, Essex, RM7 7PN
Activities: Other manufacturing n.e.c.
Parent: Crystal Group Ltd
Officers: Michael Brian Ballard [1965] Director/Accountant; Agostina Boland [1965] Director

Crystal Windows & Doors Limited
Incorporated: 2 August 1995 *Employees:* 251
Net Worth: £16,671,328 *Total Assets:* £35,993,184
Registered Office: Crystal House, Unit 1 King George Close, Eastern Avenue, Romford, Essex, RM7 7PN
Activities: Other manufacturing n.e.c.
Parent: Crystal Home Improvement Group Ltd
Officers: Michael Brian Ballard [1965] Finance Director; Agostina Boland [1965] Director; Michael Charles Farley [1976] Director; Mark Raynor [1962] Director

CS Property and Consultancy Ltd.
Incorporated: 26 February 1996 *Employees:* 2
Net Worth: £59,814 *Total Assets:* £5,793,883
Registered Office: 2 Parham Drive, Gants Hill, Ilford, Essex, IG2 6LZ
Activities: Development of building projects
Officers: Chaya Kiritkumar Shah, Secretary; Kirit Nandlal Shah [1961] Director/Accountancy

CSL (Dualcom) Limited
Incorporated: 6 February 1996 *Employees:* 96
Net Worth: £23,684,504 *Total Assets:* £43,686,032
Registered Office: Salamander Quay West, Park Lane, Harefield, Middlesex, UB9 6NZ
Activities: Other manufacturing n.e.c.
Parent: Dualcom Holdings Limited
Officers: Simon James Banks [1967] Director; Santosh Satish Chandorkar [1974] Director; Robert John Evans [1968] Director; Edward Heale [1973] Director; Philip Hollett [1961] Director; Thomas William Elliott Leigh [1971] Director; Anthony Edward Mann [1970] Director; Jon Shipp [1967] Director

CSL Communications Group Limited
Incorporated: 2 December 2011
Net Worth Deficit: £19,988,428 *Total Assets:* £50,398,536
Registered Office: Salamander Quay West, Park Lane, Harefield, Middlesex, UB9 6NZ
Activities: Activities of head offices
Parent: Sunny Bidco Limited
Officers: Simon James Banks [1967] Director; Paraag Dave [1975] Director; Edward Heale [1973] Director; Philip Hollett [1961] Director; Thomas William Elliott Leigh [1971] Director

CSPH Limited
Incorporated: 7 March 2008 *Employees:* 82
Net Worth: £1,772,423 *Total Assets:* £25,739,364
Registered Office: Duffy House, 1 Mount Road, Feltham, Middlesex, TW13 6AR
Activities: Activities of head offices
Major Shareholder: Jonathan Bernard Duffy
Officers: Joanna Margaret Duffy, Secretary; Donal Corbett [1959] Director/Quantity Surveyor [Irish]; Jonathan Bernard Duffy [1978] Director; Stephen Peter Vincett [1980] Director/Accountant

CTS Metropark Limited
Incorporated: 29 July 2015 *Employees:* 2,285
Net Worth: £2,438,000 *Total Assets:* £507,940,992
Registered Office: 1 Towers Place, Eton Street, Richmond, Surrey, TW9 1EG
Activities: Hotels and similar accommodation
Parent: China National Travel Service Group Corporation
Officers: Rong Chen [1966] Director [Chinese]; Weihong Feng [1970] Director [Chinese]; Peng Huang [1967] Director/General Manager [Chinese]; Yan Huang [1967] Director [Chinese]; Jamie Andrew Lamb [1972] Director/Chartered Accountant; Alex Edward Pritchard [1976] Director/Chief Operating Officer; Yiyin Sun [1962] Director [Chinese]

Cuffe Holdings Limited
Incorporated: 22 March 2002 *Employees:* 37
Net Worth: £16,714,759 *Total Assets:* £24,774,800
Registered Office: 19 Penrhyn Road, Kingston upon Thames, Surrey, KT1 2BZ
Activities: Other letting and operating of own or leased real estate
Major Shareholder: Arthur Charles Cowdery
Officers: Ian Maxwell Dodd, Secretary; Arthur Charles Cowdery [1953] Director

Cuffe PLC
Incorporated: 22 October 1991 *Employees:* 38
Net Worth: £1,120,099 *Total Assets:* £5,918,315
Registered Office: 19 Penrhyn Road, Kingston upon Thames, Surrey, KT1 2BZ
Activities: Development of building projects
Parent: Cuffe Holdings Ltd
Officers: Ian Maxwell Dodd, Secretary; Simon David Cook [1967] Construction Director; Ian Maxwell Dodd [1963] Director/Certified Accountant

Culham Limited
Incorporated: 21 January 1983
Net Worth: £5,482,296 *Total Assets:* £10,894,474
Registered Office: 7 Coombehurst Close, Hadley Wood, Herts, EN4 0JU
Activities: Other letting and operating of own or leased real estate
Shareholders: Twinglobe 2008 Ltd; Twinglobe Holdings Limited
Officers: Mihir Kantilal Thakerar, Secretary; Dipak Thakerar [1965] Director/Accountant; Mihir Kantilal Thakerar [1963] Director

Cummins Associates Limited
Incorporated: 26 August 1997 *Employees:* 2
Net Worth: £2,621,741 *Total Assets:* £5,384,231
Registered Office: 18 The Fairway, Northwood, Middlesex, HA6 3DY
Activities: Financial management
Officers: Nizar Kanji, Secretary; Andrew Douglas Cummins [1949] Director/Business Executive [Australian]; Jennifer Muriel Cummins [1951] Director/Business Executive [Australian]

Cummins Cogeneration Limited
Incorporated: 13 July 2009 *Employees:* 29
Net Worth Deficit: £42,491,624 *Total Assets:* £75,777,608
Registered Office: Unit 7 Chancery Gate Close, Stonefield Way, South Ruislip, Middlesex, HA4 0JS
Activities: Production of electricity
Officers: Navaratnarajah Navendrha, Secretary; Gino Butera [1963] Director [Australian]; Aditya Khilnani [1990] Director; Asha Khilnani [1959] Director; Deepak Khilnani [1959] Director/Company Secretary; Alexandre Savelli [1968] Executive Director [American]

Cummins ESB Nigeria Limited
Incorporated: 13 July 2009 *Employees:* 4
Net Worth: £7,454,613 *Total Assets:* £10,045,365
Registered Office: Unit 7 Chancery Gate Business Park, Stonefield Way, South Ruislip, Middlesex, HA4 0JS
Activities: Trade of electricity
Officers: Navaratnarajah Navendrha, Secretary; Alok Joshi [1970] Director [Indian]; Aditya Khilnani [1990] Director; Deepak Khilnani [1959] Director/Company Secretary; Chris Oberholster [1962] Director/Company Executive [South African]

Curo (West Campbell) LLP
Incorporated: 17 July 2012
Net Worth: £2,321,741 *Total Assets:* £10,793,569
Registered Office: Kopshop, 6 Old London Road, Kingston upon Thames, Surrey, KT2 6QF
Officers: Kevin William Crighton [1961] Member; Neil Stuart Gullan [1958] Member; Philip John Addington [1960] LLP Member; Jonathon Edward Allum [1976] LLP Member; Dr Duncan Alexander Baines [1974] LLP Member; John Paul Bennett [1980] LLP Member; Andrew Guy Blackwood [1970] LLP Member; Jonathan Kingsley Borrill [1967] LLP Member; George Pattullo Brewster [1960] LLP Member; Edward Martin Brown [1980] LLP Member; Ian Winton Cameron [1960] LLP Member; Christopher John Chatterton [1963] LLP Member; Rakesh Charles Chhabra [1966] LLP Member; Neil Christie [1962] LLP Member; Janet Marilyn Cooke [1950] LLP Member; Michel John Crane [1950] LLP Member; Derrick Ralph Dale [1966] LLP Member; Anthony Francis Davidson [1964] LLP Member; David Matthew Davies [1979] LLP Member; Dr. Georges Duponcheele [1970] LLP Member; Richard John Eschwege [1983] LLP Member; David Fairs [1962] LLP Member; Ian James Fergusson [1965] LLP Member; Christopher Newton Fox [1970] LLP Member; John Gerard Goonan [1953] LLP Member; Christopher John Grinyer [1967] LLP Member; Ian Francis Hannon [1967] LLP Member; Sunil Harji [1971] LLP Member; Jonathan George Henry [1966] LLP Member; David Nigel Hicks [1971] LLP Member; Riaz Hussain [1978] LLP Member; Christopher Steele Jamieson [1971] LLP Member; Laura Elizabeth John [1981] LLP Member; Paul Allan Kirkbright [1967] LLP Member; Matthew Charles Lawrence [1977] LLP Member; Geoffrey Charles Maddock [1964] LLP Member; Lloyds Derek Massey [1966] LLP Member; Scott Douglas McDonald [1983] LLP Member; Paul Anthony McGrath [1970] LLP Member; David Monksfield [1952] LLP Member; Jennifer Bridget Morrison [1971] LLP Member; Edward Jonathan Palmer [1974] LLP Member; Kim Darryl Papworth [1959] LLP Member; Nathan Charles Pillow [1974] LLP Member; Richard Anthony Rawlinson [1957] LLP Member; Mark Anthony Read [1971] LLP Member; Mark Douglas Reeves [1968] LLP Member; Michael Stuart Robinson [1962] LLP Member; Benjamin Olivier Rostein [1974] LLP Member; James Edmund Rutherford [1959] LLP Member; David Anthony Sayer [1956] LLP Member; David William John Scorey [1973] LLP Member; Akhil Shah [1965] LLP Member; Richard John Slade [1961] LLP Member; Michael Jonathan Smedley [1969] LLP Member; Graeme Francis Stewart [1972] LLP Member; Anant Kuman Shantilal Suchak [1959] LLP Member; Bankim Thanki [1964] LLP Member; Jason David Thiel [1967] LLP Member; Alexis Edward Tobin [1973] LLP Member; Jonathan Richard Turner [1963] LLP Member; Rene Hendrik Vanhaesendonck [1970] LLP Member; Mark James Vanhegan [1966] LLP Member; Steven John Walker [1971] LLP Member; Matthew Stuart Andrew Wilson [1967] LLP Member; Crispin David Richard Winser [1978] LLP Member; Anthony Christopher Bowes Young [1953] LLP Member

Curo Charlotte House LLP
Incorporated: 4 October 2011
Net Worth: £8,512,453 *Total Assets:* £16,408,843
Registered Office: Kopshop, 6 Old London Road, Kingston upon Thames, Surrey, KT2 6QF
Officers: Kevin William Crighton [1961] Member; Neil Stuart Gullan [1958] Member; Amadeo Alentorn Farre [1978] LLP Member; Christopher Francis Henry Baker [1955] LLP Member; Richard Bennison [1958] LLP Member; Philip Benjamin Bergman [1966] LLP Member; Stanley Boland [1960] LLP Member; Thomas Burley [1965] LLP Member; Michael John Burton [1971] LLP Member; Logan James Campbell [1975] LLP Member; Scott Wilson Cardno [1976] LLP Member; Andrew James Carmichael [1957] LLP Member; Jint Hung Chan [1973] LLP Member; David Anthony Collins [1965] LLP Member; Kenneth Cooke [1949] LLP Member; Nicholas John Cox [1966] LLP Member; Timothy Eric Cox [1960] LLP Member; Gautamkumar Kamur Dave [1949] LLP Member; Dominic Joseph Jonathan de Lord [1962] LLP Member; Christopher Ronald Derby [1954] LLP Member; Andrew Richard Docker [1967] LLP Member; Generald Vincent Doherty [1958] LLP Member; John Martin Downie [1963] LLP Member; John Buchan Duthie [1968] LLP Member; Stephen Philip Dyer [1962] LLP Member; Richard Paul Emerton [1960] LLP Member; Kevin Peter Esplin [1952] LLP Member; David John Farrer [1943] LLP Member; Duncan James MacKenzie Fergusson [1980] LLP Member; Lawrence Bruce Fletcher [1968] LLP Member; George William Frier [1962] LLP Member; Patricia Carolina Garces Monterrubio [1975] LLP Member; Nicholas David Gatfield [1960] LLP Member; Robert John Gilraine [1978] LLP Member; Dr Wail Rizk Girgis [1967] LLP Member; Ralph Godley [1949] LLP Member; Richard Alan James Gustard [1974] LLP Member; John Michael Hall [1961] LLP Member; Paul Brendan Hanratty [1961] LLP Member; Iain David Henry [1969] LLP Member; Jonathan Hitchin [1963] LLP Member; Joseph Robert Holderness [1967] LLP Member; Robert Andrew Holms [1941] LLP Member; Dominc Edward Wakelin Hubble [1963] LLP Member; John William Hunter [1950] LLP Member; Deepti Jerath [1980] LLP Member; James Gerard Kenny [1967] LLP Member; Derek Arthur Arrowsmith Kersey [1943] LLP Member; Peter Murray Kirk [1959] LLP Member; James Terence Kyle [1946] LLP Member; Robert Hugh Jeremy Lascelles [1955] LLP Member; Graham Richard David Lay [1956] LLP Member; Sally Victoria Lock [1944] LLP Member; Dr Julian Cannell Martin [1961] LLP Member; Bruce Matthews [1956] LLP Member; John Tasker McKee [1946] LLP Member; Jonathan Jackson Moore [1979] LLP Member; David Mulroy [1973] LLP Member; Paul Stephen Musgrove [1967] LLP Member; Trevor Summers Mutch [1971] LLP Member; Dr Janaki Kutty Nayar [1945] LLP Member; Nicholas Nicholson [1968] LLP Member; Cyrus Nikkhah [1972] LLP Member; Shane Patrick O'Cuinn [1971] LLP Member; Jonathan Hugh O'Neill [1957] LLP Member; Siobhan Anne Oudahar [1964] LLP Member; Dr Ronald Stanley Parr [1964] LLP Member; Dr Ian Robert Pearson [1960] LLP Member; Paul Michael Phillips [1961] LLP Member; Amanda Felicity Poorta [1963] LLP Member; Richard Probert [1970] LLP Member; Brian Michael Puffer [1969] LLP Member; Shonah Margaret Raffan [1961] LLP Member; Alessandro Ricci [1974] LLP Member; Peter James Rimer [1969] LLP Member; Jamie Richard Sambruck [1980] LLP Member; Amrik Singh Sandhu [1966] LLP Member; Shaun William Sargent [1967] LLP Member; Timothy Edward Scanlan [1966] LLP Member; Professor John Howard Scholefield [1959] LLP Member; Palvi Shah [1961] LLP Member; Martin Haddow Sim [1968] LLP Member; Colin Maurice Sloman [1961] LLP Member; Joanna Angela Smith [1968] LLP Member; Philip Patrick Smith [1957] LLP Member; Robin Simon Southwell [1960] LLP Member; John Watt Stevenson [1940] LLP Member; Archie James Struthers [1973] LLP Member; Anant Kuman Shantilal Suchak [1959] LLP Member; Michael Andrew Sullivan [1963] LLP Member; Eric Summers [1947] LLP Member; Geoffrey Peter Taylor [1956] LLP Member; Oliver Talbot Taylor-Higginson [1976] LLP Member; David Thomson [1964] LLP Member; Kerry John Tomlinson [1949] LLP Member; Paul Frederick Tutin [1962] LLP Member; Bobby Uberoi [1972] LLP Member; Pepijn Jochem Van Kasteren [1975] LLP Member; Mar James Vanegan [1966] LLP Member; Richard John Ward [1959] LLP Member

Currie Finance and Leasing Company Limited
Incorporated: 13 July 1972
Net Worth: £16,269,000 *Total Assets:* £18,167,000
Registered Office: 161 Chertsey Road, Twickenham, Middlesex, TW1 1ER
Activities: Activities of head offices
Parent: Curfin (Netherlands Antilles) B.V.
Officers: Joseph Michael Jaffe [1955] Director; Derek Jonathan Murray [1960] Director/Company Executive; Glenn Robert Bruce Pitzer [1968] Director/Company Executive

Currie Motors Kingston Limited
Incorporated: 12 November 1974
Net Worth: £6,746,000 *Total Assets:* £7,106,000
Registered Office: 161 Chertsey Road, Twickenham, Middlesex, TW1 1ER
Activities: Other letting and operating of own or leased real estate
Parent: Curfin (Netherlands Antilles) B.V.
Officers: Joseph Michael Jaffe [1955] Director; Derek Jonathan Murray [1960] Director/Company Executive; Glenn Robert Bruce Pitzer [1968] Director/Company Executive

Currie Motors Limited
Incorporated: 13 July 1979 *Employees:* 614
Net Worth: £123,356,000 *Total Assets:* £228,563,008
Registered Office: 161 Chertsey Road, Twickenham, Middlesex, TW1 1ER
Activities: Other letting and operating of own or leased real estate
Parent: Curfin (Netherlands Antilles) B.V.
Officers: Joseph Michael Jaffe [1955] Director/Business Executive; Derek Jonathan Murray [1960] Director/Company Executive; Glenn Robert Bruce Pitzer [1968] Director/Company Executive

Currie Motors UK Limited
Incorporated: 2 October 1989 *Employees:* 201
Net Worth: £10,409,000 *Total Assets:* £17,879,000
Registered Office: 161 Chertsey Road, Twickenham, Middlesex, TW1 1ER
Activities: Sale of new cars and light motor vehicles
Parent: Currie Motors Limited
Officers: Hannah Louise Bicknell [1970] Director/Business Executive; Kiranjit Chance [1961] Director/Company Executive; Neil Alistair Elkins [1958] Director/Company Executive; Joseph Michael Jaffe [1955] Director; Derek Jonathan Murray [1960] Director/Company Executive; Glenn Robert Bruce Pitzer [1968] Director/Company Executive

Curtis Holt Limited
Incorporated: 5 March 1954 *Employees:* 532
Net Worth: £50,736,000 *Total Assets:* £65,687,000
Registered Office: Long Reach, Galleon Boulevard, Crossways Business Park, Dartford, Kent, DA2 6QE
Activities: Non-specialised wholesale trade
Parent: Dormole Ltd
Officers: Robert David Rowe, Secretary; Andrew James Thomas Strong [1955] Director; Timothy John Strong [1958] Director; John Randall Charles Twallin [1933] Director

Custodes Acqco Limited
Incorporated: 17 December 2013
Net Worth Deficit: £12,828,432 *Total Assets:* £14,044,738
Registered Office: River House, Maidstone Road, Sidcup, Kent, DA14 5RH
Activities: Residential nursing care facilities
Parent: Custodes Midco Limited
Officers: Colin Leslie Stokes [1975] Director; Nicholas John Yarrow [1967] Director

Custodes Midco Limited
Incorporated: 16 February 2015 *Employees:* 1,300
Net Worth: £21,658,990 *Total Assets:* £47,083,628
Registered Office: River House, Maidstone Road, Sidcup, Kent, DA14 5RH
Activities: Residential nursing care facilities
Parent: Custodes Pikco Limited
Officers: Nils Ian Stoesser [1974] Managing Director [German]; Colin Leslie Stokes [1975] Director; Nicholas John Yarrow [1967] Director

CWR Capital Ltd
Incorporated: 14 August 2015 *Employees:* 1
Net Worth: £160,868 *Total Assets:* £5,100,729
Registered Office: 92 Station Lane, Hornchurch, Essex, RM12 6LX
Activities: Other business support service activities n.e.c.
Major Shareholder: Christopher William Roase
Officers: Christopher William Roase [1974] Director/Commodity Trader

CWT Holdco Limited
Incorporated: 7 May 1997
Net Worth: £44,286,420 *Total Assets:* £48,218,652
Registered Office: Maple House, High Street, Potters Bar, Herts, EN6 5RF
Activities: Travel agency activities
Parent: Carlson Wagonlit New Holdco Limited
Officers: Narinder Sanotra, Secretary; Christopher Bowen [1960] Director; Denise Harman [1970] Director [Irish]; Sanjay Kapoor [1967] Director [British/Australian]; Rhodri Llewelyn Hollister Turner [1977] Director/Chief Financial Officer

Cyan Logistics Limited
Incorporated: 19 December 1997
Net Worth: £7,944,760 *Total Assets:* £7,958,892
Registered Office: 2nd Floor, 400 Dashwood Lang Road, Bourne Business Park, Addlestone, Surrey, KT15 2HJ
Activities: Activities of other holding companies n.e.c.
Parent: Brambles Holdings (UK) Limited
Officers: Daniel Robert Berry [1973] Director/Lawyer; Peter Jonathon Caisley Bruford [1964] Director/Accountant; Michael Bruce Pooley [1967] Director/President, CHEP Europe

Cyberscience PLC
Incorporated: 28 December 1977 *Employees:* 45
Net Worth: £16,976,632 *Total Assets:* £23,559,432
Registered Office: Rawdon House, High Street, Hoddesdon, Herts, EN11 8BD
Activities: Business and domestic software development
Major Shareholder: Paul John Rogers
Officers: Simon Mathew Foden, Secretary; Simon Mathew Foden [1972] Operations Director; Julia Sarah Pyper [1958] Director/Consultant

Cygnet Street Developments Limited
Incorporated: 2 September 2014
Net Worth: £5,075,405 *Total Assets:* £8,983,481
Registered Office: 3rd Floor, Sterling House, Langston Road, Loughton, Essex, IG10 3TS
Activities: Development of building projects
Parent: Galliard Holdings Limited
Officers: Allan William Porter, Secretary; David Edward Conway [1976] Director; Stephen Stuart Solomon Conway [1948] Director

Cygnus Academies Trust
Incorporated: 13 January 2016 *Employees:* 184
Net Worth: £15,288,042 *Total Assets:* £16,967,360
Registered Office: c/o Manor Community Primary School, Keary Road, Swanscombe, Kent, DA10 0BU
Activities: Primary education
Officers: Trixie Dianne Ball [1944] Director; Susan Elizabeth Constant [1966] Director/Quality and Compliance Manager; Larissa Cesar [1978] Director/Civil Servant; Sandra Irene Herbert [1943] Director/Retired; David Edwin Lloyd [1963] Director/Executive Headteacher; Amanda Dianne McMullen [1976] Director/Teacher; Paul Stephen Wilkins [1976] Director/Accountant

D & M Audiovisual Ltd
Incorporated: 21 April 1964 *Employees:* 36
Net Worth: £1,102,795 *Total Assets:* £5,956,688
Registered Office: Cell 6 & 7 Kopshop, 6 Old London Road, Kingston upon Thames, Surrey, KT2 6QF
Activities: Wholesale of radio, television goods & electrical household appliances (other than records, tapes, CDs)
Parent: D & M Europe B.V.
Officers: Jason Edward Hartley Dear [1971] Director/Brand Manager; Peter Harper [1961] Director [American]; Mairead Terrie O'Connell [1959] Director [Irish]; Joseph Tristani [1966] Director [American]

D & M Tools Limited
Incorporated: 15 December 2015 *Employees:* 25
Net Worth: £9,863,895 *Total Assets:* £10,761,907
Registered Office: 73-81 Heath Road, Twickenham, Middlesex, TW1 4AW
Activities: Other retail sale of new goods in specialised stores (not commercial art galleries and opticians)
Major Shareholder: Paul David Dowding
Officers: David Dowding [1940] Director; Jennifer Louise Dowding [1969] Director/Head of Finance; Mary Elizabeth Dowding [1941] Director; Paul David Dowding [1965] Director; Elizabeth June Richards [1962] Director

D and D Property Company Limited
Incorporated: 19 September 2000 *Employees:* 2
Net Worth Deficit: £188,224 *Total Assets:* £8,842,019
Registered Office: 12 Hatherley Road, Sidcup, Kent, DA14 4DT
Activities: Buying and selling of own real estate
Shareholders: David Paul Mark Andrew Hadden; Denise Roberts
Officers: David Paul Mark Andrew Hadden [1963] Director/Landlord; Denise Roberts [1958] Director

D R 4 Developments LLP
Incorporated: 28 April 2017
Net Worth Deficit: £376,000 *Total Assets:* £14,272,000
Registered Office: Cowley Business Park, Cowley, Uxbridge, Middlesex, UB8 2AL

D-Link (Europe) Limited
Incorporated: 30 May 1995 *Employees:* 258
Net Worth: £29,288,148 *Total Assets:* £54,911,244
Registered Office: First Floor, Artemis Building, Odyssey Business Park, West End Road, South Ruislip, Middlesex, HA4 6QE
Activities: Other information technology service activities
Parent: D-Link Corporation
Officers: Rick Ching Yei Chen, Secretary; Gen-Kwo Lee [1958] Director [Taiwanese]; Kevin Wen Huang Wen [1961] Director/Businessman [Australian]; Shu-Chen Yu [1971] Director [Taiwanese]

D.B.T. (Holdings) Limited
Incorporated: 3 August 1972 *Employees:* 3
Net Worth: £6,547,621 *Total Assets:* £7,273,498
Registered Office: Charles Lake House, Claire Causeway, Crossways Business Park, Dartford, Kent, DA2 6QA
Activities: Other letting and operating of own or leased real estate
Shareholders: Christopher Anthony Dougal; Douglas Andrew Dougal; Martin James Dougal
Officers: Martin James Dougal, Secretary/General Administrator; Christopher Anthony Dougal [1953] Director/Haulage Contractor; Douglas Andrew Dougal [1951] Director/Haulage Contractor; Martin James Dougal [1957] Director/General Administrator

D.D.D. Limited
Incorporated: 16 May 1912 *Employees:* 304
Net Worth: £4,715,009 *Total Assets:* £27,138,234
Registered Office: 94 Rickmansworth Road, Watford, Herts, WD18 7JJ
Activities: Manufacture of basic pharmaceutical products
Parent: DDD Investments Limited
Officers: Carl Atkinson [1974] Director; Hanna Joy Coonagh [1972] Director; Digby Lawrence Spence Halsby [1976] Non Executive Director; Roger Harrison [1969] Managing Director; Simon Morris [1973] HR Director; Charles Philip Wadsworth [1962] Finance Director

D.K. Tools Limited
Incorporated: 19 January 1989 *Employees:* 29
Net Worth: £8,588,531 *Total Assets:* £13,045,581
Registered Office: Unit 1 & 2 North Point Business Centre, Horton Road, West Drayton, Middlesex, UB7 8EQ
Activities: Non-specialised wholesale trade
Shareholder: Deepak Kalra
Officers: Chander Kanta Kalra, Secretary; Deepak Kalra [1954] Director; Ishan Devraj Kalra [1988] Operations Director

D.M.C. Business Machines Limited
Incorporated: 16 November 1990 *Employees:* 151
Previous: D.M.C. Business Machines PLC
Net Worth: £9,749,106 *Total Assets:* £16,312,805
Registered Office: Kings Parade, Lower Coombe Street, Croydon, Surrey, CR0 1AA
Activities: Other service activities n.e.c.
Parent: Tokyo Bidco Limited
Officers: Jonathan Edmond David Hill, Secretary; Simon Alan Davey [1974] Director; Jonathan Edmond David Hill [1960] Managing Director; Philip Andrew Kavanagh [1959] Director; Justin James Nicholson [1968] Sales Director

D3O Holdings Ltd
Incorporated: 11 March 2015 *Employees:* 44
Net Worth: £12,107,046 *Total Assets:* £16,044,774
Registered Office: The Lab, 7-8 Commerce Way, Croydon, Surrey, CR0 4XA
Activities: Other manufacturing n.e.c.
Shareholder: Entrepreneurs Fund LP
Officers: Colin David Smith, Secretary; Alexander Hardtmuth [1972] Director/Investment Manager [Austrian]; Karen Ann McCormick [1976] Director/Chief Investment Officer [American]; Stuart Sawyer [1962] Director/Consultant; Colin David Smith [1971] Director; Jeremy Werner [1990] Investor Director [American]

D4T4 Solutions PLC
Incorporated: 6 March 1985 *Employees:* 122
Previous: I S Solutions PLC
Net Worth: £20,985,000 *Total Assets:* £39,416,000
Registered Office: Windmill House, 91-93 Windmill Road, Sunbury upon Thames, Middlesex, TW16 7EF
Activities: Other information technology service activities
Officers: James Henry Thorne, Secretary; Mark Geoffrey Boxall [1963] Operations Director; James Lloyd Dodkins [1956] Director; Peter John Kear [1955] Sales Director; John Lythall [1948] Director; Roger Steven McDowell [1955] Director; Peter Anthony Simmonds [1958] Director/Accountant; Mathew Tod [1964] Director; Carmel Elizabeth Warren [1964] Finance Director; Peter Frederick Whiting [1966] Director

Daarasp LLP
Incorporated: 17 February 2004
Net Worth: £18,337,988 *Total Assets:* £18,595,234
Registered Office: 166 College Road, Harrow, Middlesex, HA1 1RA
Officers: John Alan Hall [1949] LLP Member; Niresh Patel [1956] LLP Member

Dabasia Estates LLP
Incorporated: 10 March 2016
Net Worth: £13,283,921 *Total Assets:* £18,089,284
Registered Office: c/o Albury Associates Limited, 79 College Road, Harrow, Middlesex, HA1 1BD
Officers: Davendra Laxmidas Dabasia [1979] Member; Laxmidas Premji Dabasia [1954] Member; Rama Laxmidas Dabasia [1957] Member; Sima Dabasia [1979] Member

Daikin Airconditioning UK Limited
Incorporated: 13 December 2002 *Employees:* 261
Net Worth: £18,119,000 *Total Assets:* £51,144,000
Registered Office: The Heights, Brooklands, Weybridge, Surrey, KT13 0NY
Activities: Steam and air conditioning supply
Parent: Daikin Europe N.V.
Officers: Hendrik Jan Van Den Berg, Secretary; Wim de Schacht [1968] Director/Manager [Belgian]; Mark Dyer [1972] Director/Sales Management; Hiroyasu Ishikawa [1977] Director [Japanese]; Angela McGinlay [1963] Managing Director; Toshitaka Tsubouchi [1958] Director/Manager [Japanese]; Junji Umamoto [1961] Director [Japanese]

Dairy Crest (Services) Limited
Incorporated: 31 March 1943
Net Worth: £257,376,992 *Total Assets:* £268,000,992
Registered Office: Claygate House, Littleworth Road, Esher, Surrey, KT10 9PN
Activities: Non-trading company
Parent: Dairy Crest France Holdings 1
Officers: Isobel Jean Hinton, Secretary; Mark Allen [1959] Managing Director; Thomas Alexander Atherton [1970] Director/Chartered Accountant

Dairy Crest France Holdings 1 Limited
Incorporated: 21 June 1996
Net Worth: £337,920,000 *Total Assets:* £487,660,000
Registered Office: Claygate House, Littleworth Road, Esher, Surrey, KT10 9PN
Activities: Other business support service activities n.e.c.
Parent: Dairy Crest Limited
Officers: Isobel Jean Hinton, Secretary; Mark Allen [1959] Managing Director; Thomas Alexander Atherton [1970] Director/Chartered Accountant; Robert Thomas Arthur Willock [1966] Director

Dairy Crest France Holdings 2 Limited
Incorporated: 24 November 1997
Net Worth: £115,949,000 *Total Assets:* £262,887,008
Registered Office: Claygate House, Littleworth Road, Esher, Surrey, KT10 9PN
Activities: Liquid milk and cream production
Parent: Dairy Crest France Holdings 1 Limited
Officers: Isobel Jean Hinton, Secretary; Mark Allen [1959] Managing Director; Thomas Alexander Atherton [1970] Director/Chartered Accountant

Dairy Crest Group PLC
Incorporated: 22 February 1996 *Employees:* 1,097
Net Worth: £243,700,000 *Total Assets:* £628,200,000
Registered Office: Claygate House, Littleworth Road, Esher, Surrey, KT10 9PN
Activities: Manufacture of margarine and similar edible fats
Officers: Roger James Robotham, Secretary; Stephen Harold Alexander [1955] Director; Mark Allen [1959] Director; Thomas Alexander Atherton [1970] Director/Chartered Accountant; Adam Braithwaite [1975] Director; Susan Jane Farr [1956] Director; John Michael Gibney [1960] Director; Richard Auld MacDonald [1954] Director/Consultant; Sheikh Mansurah Tal-At Mannings [1963] Director

Dairy Crest Limited
Incorporated: 23 December 1986 *Employees:* 1,047
Net Worth: £176,100,000 *Total Assets:* £1,479,000,064
Registered Office: Claygate House, Littleworth Road, Esher, Surrey, KT10 9PN
Activities: Manufacture of margarine and similar edible fats
Parent: Dairy Crest UK Limited
Officers: Roger James Robotham, Secretary; Mark Allen [1959] Director/MD Cheese; Thomas Alexander Atherton [1970] Director/Chartered Accountant; Richard Steven Jones [1969] Procurement Director; Robert Thomas Arthur Willock [1966] Director

Dairy Crest UK Limited
Incorporated: 22 August 2008
Net Worth: £235,256,000 *Total Assets:* £565,105,984
Registered Office: Claygate House, Littleworth Road, Esher, Surrey, KT10 9PN
Activities: Other business support service activities n.e.c.
Parent: Dairy Crest Group
Officers: Isobel Jean Hinton, Secretary; Thomas Alexander Atherton [1970] Director/Chartered Accountant; Richard Steven Jones [1969] Procurement Director

Dakota Developments Limited
Incorporated: 4 September 2003
Net Worth: £4,294,607 *Total Assets:* £5,129,770
Registered Office: Aissela, 46 High Street, Esher, Surrey, KT10 9QY
Activities: Development of building projects
Major Shareholder: Graham David Wick
Officers: Graham David Wick, Secretary; Graham David Wick [1948] Director

Dalco Developments Limited
Incorporated: 5 May 2011
Net Worth Deficit: £86,995 *Total Assets:* £5,231,460
Registered Office: 101 Wanstead Park Road, Ilford, Essex, IG1 3TH
Activities: Development of building projects
Officers: Dalbir Singh Sanger [1965] Director/Businessman; Kuldip Singh Sanger [1961] Director/Businessman

Daleham Finance Limited
Incorporated: 18 August 2015
Net Worth: £5,234,968 *Total Assets:* £5,239,033
Registered Office: York House, Empire Way, Wembley, Middlesex, HA9 0FQ
Activities: Security dealing on own account
Shareholder: Andrew Joseph Kisiel
Officers: Andrew Joseph Kisiel [1939] Director; Brigitte Margarete Kisiel [1938] Director; Timothy Bronek Kisiel [1969] Director/Company Secretary

Dalemead Care Home Limited
Incorporated: 3 April 2009
Net Worth: £4,019,586 *Total Assets:* £5,266,979
Registered Office: 42 Kew Court, Richmond Road, Kingston upon Thames, Surrey, KT2 5BF
Activities: Medical nursing home activities
Shareholders: Anwar Phul; Bibi Raseeda Roucksana Phul
Officers: Amreen Phul [1984] Director/Administrator; Anwar Phul [1953] Director/Care Home Manager; Bibi Raseeda Roucksana Phul [1952] Director/Housewife

Dalin Limited
Incorporated: 8 June 2012
Net Worth Deficit: £10,614,570 *Total Assets:* £10,182,163
Registered Office: Hill House, Lowlands Road, Harrow, Middlesex, HA1 3EQ
Activities: Development of building projects
Major Shareholder: Donovan Gijsbertus Wijsmuller
Officers: Brian Martin Comer [1960] Director [Irish]; Luke Andrew Comer [1957] Director [Irish]

Dallas Burston Ashbourne Holdings Limited
Incorporated: 13 May 2002
Net Worth: £8,691,742 *Total Assets:* £9,415,455
Registered Office: Bampton Road, Harold Hill, Romford, Essex, RM3 8UG
Activities: Wholesale of pharmaceutical goods
Parent: Ethypharm Holdings UK Ltd
Officers: Roseline Georgette Joannesse [1959] Director/Vice President Legal Affairs [French]; Jean-Hugues Louis Marie Lecat [1956] Director [French]

Dalton Resources Limited
Incorporated: 26 October 2011
Net Worth Deficit: £647,768 *Total Assets:* £20,066,192
Registered Office: Suite 1, The Studio, St Nicholas Close, Elstree, Herts, WD6 3EW
Activities: Construction of commercial buildings
Major Shareholder: Iryna Simonchuk
Officers: Christiana Savva [1974] Director/Private Employee [Cypriot]; Iryna Simonchuk [1968] Deputy Director [Ukrainian]

Daly Holdings Limited
Incorporated: 23 December 2014 *Employees:* 86
Previous: Sky Holdings (UK) Limited
Net Worth: £5,350,709 *Total Assets:* £11,936,437
Registered Office: 167 Turners Hill, Cheshunt, Herts, EN8 9BH
Activities: Activities of insurance agents and brokers
Major Shareholder: Michael James Daly
Officers: Michael James Daly [1955] Director; Scott Forrester [1980] Director/Insurance Broker; Jae LEA Pearse [1975] Director/Insurance Broker

Dame Alice Owen's School
Incorporated: 10 March 2011 *Employees:* 194
Net Worth: £35,776,000 *Total Assets:* £37,629,000
Registered Office: Dame Alice Owen's School, Dugdale Hill Lane, Potters Bar, Herts, EN6 2DU
Activities: General secondary education
Officers: Lona Hennigan, Secretary; Lucy Amelia Bailie [1972] Director/School Administrator; Nicholas Matthew Barnes [1974] Director; Timothy Eric Bonham [1952] Director; David John Barrington Burrowes [1969] Director/Lawyer; Monique Choudhuri [1961] Director/Management Consultant; Richard Hamilton Fleetwood Fuller [1960] Sales and Personnel Director, Fuller's; Seamus Joseph Gillen [1959] Director; Stephen Frederick Goodyear [1955] Director/CEO Youngs Brewery; Gary Kenneth Haigh [1964] Director/Retired; Sandra Dawn Huckle [1964] Director/Chartered Accountant; Peter Frederick John Knell [1945] Director/Hertsmere Borough Councillor; Daniel Latham [1993] Director/Teacher; Peter James Martin [1952] Director; Hannah Nemko [1975] Director/Headteacher; Andrew James Porter [1972] Director/Partner at Communications Agency; Jonathan Robinson [1975] Director/Teacher; Sally Louise Tanner [1964] Director/IBM Employee; Glenn Taylor [1967] Director; Charles Mortimer Tracy [1962] Director/Education Manager; Jacqueline Tyler [1971] Director/Administrator; Paul Richard Wells [1958] Director

Danes Educational Trust
Incorporated: 16 June 2011 *Employees:* 135
Previous: St. Clement Danes School
Net Worth: £22,237,000 *Total Assets:* £23,811,000
Registered Office: St Clement Danes School, Chenies Road, Chorleywood, Herts, WD3 6EW
Activities: General secondary education
Officers: Nils Michael Blythe [1956] Director/Communications Consultant; Rosemary Faunch [1954] Director/Management Consultant; Darren Franklin [1971] Contract Director; Rachel Gauke [1972] Director/Lawyer; Doctor Malcolm Frederick Green [1951] Director/Retired; Rosemary Elizabeth Hadfield [1946] Director; Rachel Althea Rodney Hatfield [1963] Director/Lawyer; Louise Marcelle Victoria Soden [1952] Director/Educational Consultant; Kathleen Maeve Unger [1956] Director/HR Manager; Dr Josephine Anne Valentine [1958] Director/Headteacher

Danjuma Collection Ltd
Incorporated: 19 May 2011 *Employees:* 2
Net Worth: £5,134,501 *Total Assets:* £11,205,738
Registered Office: 1st Floor, Two Furlongs, Esher, Surrey, KT10 9AA
Activities: Other retail sale not in stores, stalls or markets
Shareholders: Theophilus Yakubu Danjuma; Theophilus Danjuma; TY Ventures (UK) Limited
Officers: Theophilus Danjuma [1985] Director [Nigerian]; Simon Miles Foster [1968] Director/Accountant

Danly UK Limited
Incorporated: 10 July 1989
Net Worth: £2,792,518 *Total Assets:* £6,855,790
Registered Office: 2 Aintree Road, Perivale, Greenford, Middlesex, UB6 7LA
Activities: Other manufacturing n.e.c.
Officers: James C Danly [1943] Director/Manager [American]; Arumugadas Kumaradas [1957] Group Director Controller

Danu Holding Limited
Incorporated: 7 December 2007
Net Worth Deficit: £8,204,993 *Total Assets:* £28,618,104
Registered Office: Munro House, Portsmouth Road, Cobham, Surrey, KT11 1PP
Activities: Other business support service activities n.e.c.
Parent: Gravis Onshore Wind 1 Limited
Officers: Stephen Campbell Joseph Ellis [1959] Director; Rollo Andrew Johnstone Wright [1976] Director; Philip William Kent [1984] Director; Ronan Niall Kierans [1978] Director [Irish]; Nicholas Simon Parker [1969] Director

Danu II Holdings Limited
Incorporated: 17 December 2008 *Employees:* 5
Net Worth Deficit: £11,944,455 *Total Assets:* £35,410,976
Registered Office: Munro House, Portsmouth Road, Cobham, Surrey, KT11 1PP
Activities: Other business support service activities n.e.c.
Parent: Gravis Onshore Wind 2 Limited
Officers: Stephen Campbell Joseph Ellis [1959] Director; Rollo Andrew Johnstone Wright [1976] Director; Philip William Kent [1984] Director; Ronan Niall Kierans [1978] Director [Irish]; Nicholas Simon Parker [1969] Director

Darrick Wood School
Incorporated: 30 September 2010 *Employees:* 233
Net Worth: £11,310,000 *Total Assets:* £13,486,000
Registered Office: Darrick Wood School, Lovibonds Avenue, Orpington, Kent, BR6 8ER
Activities: General secondary education
Officers: Anne Carey, Secretary; Dr Martin Airey [1970] Director/Headteacher; Lesley-Anne Avis [1959] Director/Lawyer; Paul Cook [1974] Director/Teacher; Professor Peter Dale Earley [1949] Director/University Professor; James Goatcher [1954] Director/Chartered Accountant; Michael John Green [1946] Director; Warren Harris [1959] Director/School Inclusion Unit Manager; Jane Razina Hewitt [1960] Director/Greeting Card Publisher; Michael Brian Hewitt [1942] Director/Educational Consultant; Kathleen Morris [1950] Director/Consultant Clinical Psychologist; Mandy Piper-Killick [1965] Director/HR Business Partner; Elizabeth Thornton [1964] Director/Local Government Officer; John Tuck [1963] Director/Teacher; Allan Joseph Tweddle [1975] Director/Chartered Accountant; Robert Arthur Voyce [1947] Director; David Charles Wilcox [1949] Director

Dartford Grammar School
Incorporated: 13 October 2010 *Employees:* 200
Net Worth: £13,870,000 *Total Assets:* £16,266,000
Registered Office: Dartford Grammar School, West Hill, Dartford, Kent, DA1 2HW
Activities: General secondary education
Officers: Jacqueline Ann Roblett, Secretary; Nicola Jane Booker [1973] Director/Business Manager; Wendy Margaret Carey [1946] Director; Derek James Eastley [1935] Director; Warren Fernandez [1986] Director/Solicitor; Sarah Louise Golding [1967] Osteopath/Director; Reverend Martin John Henwood [1958] Director; Ailsa Marie Hughes [1947] Director/Retired; Mary Cynthia Jacobs [1946] Director; Martin Johnson [1987] Director/Chartered Accountant; Dr David John Lawrence [1955] Director/Doctor; Anna Metcalf [1966] Director/Teacher; William John Oakes [1956] Director/Headmaster; Robert Tibbott [1951] Director/Teacher; Councillor David Harold Winston Turner [1942] Director

Dashtag
Incorporated: 31 October 1906
Net Worth: £15,005,000 *Total Assets:* £42,025,000
Registered Office: West Hill, Hertford Road, Hoddesdon, Herts, EN11 9BU
Activities: Activities of head offices
Parent: Schering-Plough Holdings Limited
Officers: Richard Robinski, Secretary; Louise Jane Houson [1976] Director; Simon Nicholson [1975] Director; Ebru Can Temucin [1972] Director [Turkish]

Datamede Limited
Incorporated: 7 February 2001 *Employees:* 1
Net Worth: £2,452,965 *Total Assets:* £12,795,938
Registered Office: Unit 8 West London Industrial Park, Iver Lane, Uxbridge, Middlesex, UB8 2JG
Activities: Other letting and operating of own or leased real estate
Major Shareholder: Fil Levi Gray
Officers: Fil Levi Gray [1958] Director

Datamust Company Limited
Incorporated: 12 November 1993
Net Worth: £5,892,809 *Total Assets:* £6,640,375
Registered Office: 37 Cottingham Chase, Ruislip, Middlesex, HA4 0BZ
Activities: Other letting and operating of own or leased real estate
Parent: Datamere Holdings UC
Officers: Koren Sinead Hickey, Secretary; Michael John Hickey [1944] Director [Irish]; Patrick Joseph Rowan [1954] Director/Consultant [Irish]

Davenant Centre (The)
Incorporated: 13 March 1984
Net Worth: £4,295,757 *Total Assets:* £5,053,757
Registered Office: 114-116 Goodmayes Road, Ilford, Essex, IG3 9UZ
Activities: Other social work activities without accommodation n.e.c.
Officers: Martin Ebbs, Secretary; Graham Keith Collins [1968] Director; Anita Louise Hurrell [1983] Director; Jacqueline Ruth Odunoye [1957] Director/Local Government Officer; John Alfred Pulford [1943] Director; Andrew Charles Scott [1964] Director

Davenant Foundation School
Incorporated: 23 February 2011 *Employees:* 173
Net Worth: £2,442,000 *Total Assets:* £5,639,000
Registered Office: Davenant Foundation School, Chester Road, Loughton, Essex, IG10 2LD
Activities: General secondary education
Officers: Jacqueline Ruth Beaumont, Secretary; Ade Aderemi [1967] Director/Local Government Officer; Juliet Claire Anderson [1970] Director/Physiotherapist; Glynne Kenneth Anthony [1971] Director/Chartered Surveyor; Rev Christopher Mark Davies [1976] Director/Clerk in Holy Orders; John Patrick Doherty [1971] Director; Christine Rosemary Folkes [1960] Director/Chartered Accountant; Michael Hicks [1959] Director/Chartered Accountant; David Prosser [1972] Director/Self Employed; Howard James Smith [1961] Director/Barrister; Sally-Ann Temple [1971] Director/Home Maker; Adam Reese Thorne [1971] Director/Headteacher; Mary Teresa Vine-Morris [1959] Director; Debra Williams [1967] Director/Teacher

Davis and Dann Limited
Incorporated: 26 March 1965 *Employees:* 9
Net Worth: £5,725,378 *Total Assets:* £14,469,876
Registered Office: Kanta House, Victoria Road, South Ruislip, Middlesex, HA4 0JQ
Activities: Wholesale of pharmaceutical goods
Officers: Satish Jamnadas Chatwani, Secretary; Jawahar Jamnadas Chatwani [1948] Director; Rashmi Jamnadas Chatwani [1954] Director; Satish Jamnadas Chatwani [1953] Director

Davroc Limited
Incorporated: 7 February 1980 *Employees:* 186
Net Worth: £14,847,193 *Total Assets:* £17,936,524
Registered Office: Ibroc House, Essex Road, Hoddesdon, Herts, EN11 0QS
Activities: Agents involved in the sale of timber and building materials
Shareholders: Pietro Corbisiero; Giuseppe Corbisiero
Officers: Pietro Corbisiero, Secretary [Italian]; Giuseppe Corbisiero [1955] Director [Italian]; Pietro Corbisiero [1953] Director [Italian]

Davton Holdings Ltd
Incorporated: 13 June 2006 *Employees:* 583
Net Worth: £3,602,412 *Total Assets:* £6,124,317
Registered Office: 184 Broadway, Bexleyheath, Kent, DA6 7BT
Activities: Unlicenced restaurants and cafes
Shareholders: David Michael Catterall; Ratnarajah Anton Jebaharan
Officers: David Michael Catterall, Secretary/Shop Manager; David Michael Catterall [1964] Director/Area Manager; Ratnarajah Anton Jebaharan [1964] Director/Shop Manager

Day Group Limited
Incorporated: 2 April 1947 *Employees:* 466
Net Worth: £33,562,568 *Total Assets:* £91,422,856
Registered Office: Day Group House, Transport Avenue, Brentford, Middlesex, TW8 9HF
Activities: Manufacture of other non-metallic mineral products n.e.c.
Officers: David Spencer Churchill, Secretary; Adam Michael Day [1968] Contracting Director; Alan John Day [1941] Director/Chairman; Dominic Peter Day [1973] Director; James Alan Day [1965] Managing Director; Jonathan Matthew Day [1967] Director

Alan Day Investments LLP
Incorporated: 5 March 2010
Net Worth: £15,134,329 *Total Assets:* £15,300,143
Registered Office: Green Close Cottage, The Green, Sarratt, Rickmansworth, Herts, WD3 6AY
Officers: Alan Christian Day [1973] Member; Alan Edwin Day [1933] Member; Michael John Day [1963] Member; Stephen Robert Day [1958] Member

Day Lewis PLC
Incorporated: 7 March 1975 *Employees:* 2,501
Net Worth: £91,534,000 *Total Assets:* £333,744,992
Registered Office: 2 Peterwood Way, Croydon, Surrey, CR0 4UQ
Activities: Dispensing chemist in specialised stores
Shareholders: Naliniben Kiritkumar Patel; Rupa Patel; Jayanti Chimanbhai Patel Jnr; Kirit Chimanbhai Tulsibhai Patel Jnr
Officers: Ameetkumar Ramananbhai Patel, Secretary; Jayantibhai Chimanbhai Patel, Secretary; Carey Charles Edwards [1955] Director; Peter James Glover [1947] Director; Heena Patel [1963] Finance Director; Jayanti Chimanbhai Patel Junior [1984] Director; Kirit Chimanbhai Patel Junior [1980] Director

Day Webster Limited
Incorporated: 29 October 2009 *Employees:* 205
Net Worth: £3,710,449 *Total Assets:* £23,895,506
Registered Office: Treviot House, 186-192 High Road, Ilford, Essex, IG1 1LR
Activities: Other activities of employment placement agencies
Officers: Rebecca Louisa Woods Ballard, Secretary; Wayne Arthur St John [1974] Director; Daniel Jonathan Wise [1982] Director; Hugh William Woods Ballard [1968] Director

Daylighting Power Limited
Incorporated: 20 January 2012
Net Worth Deficit: £2,208,875 *Total Assets:* £8,141,984
Registered Office: 57 Belmont Lane, Stanmore, Middlesex, HA7 2PU
Activities: Other manufacturing n.e.c.
Officers: Alka Jasooja, Secretary; Alka Jasooja [1977] Director/Employee [Indian]

Days Lane Primary School
Incorporated: 28 February 2014 *Employees:* 80
Net Worth: £6,367,879 *Total Assets:* £7,237,905
Registered Office: Days Lane Primary School, Days Lane, Sidcup, Kent, DA15 8JU
Activities: Primary education
Officers: Chimeine Ali [1981] Director/Educational Adviser; Simon Allen [1979] Director/Teacher; Susan Govier [1966] Director/Nurse; Luke Jobson [1987] Director/Teacher; Shirley Ann Moore [1954] Director/Retired; Susan Georgina Self [1952] Director/Retired; Joanna Trusty [1968] Director/Acting Headteacher; Stephan John Williams [1981] Director; Jamie Michael Wood [1978] Director/IT Team Leader; Janine Wooster [1959] Director/Acting SENCO Teacher

DB Investments Limited
Incorporated: 23 November 1995 *Employees:* 3
Net Worth: £24,287,684 *Total Assets:* £32,046,208
Registered Office: Haslers, Old Station Road, Loughton, Essex, IG10 4PL
Activities: Other business support service activities n.e.c.
Shareholders: David Howard Sanders; Barry Roy Peterson
Officers: David Howard Sanders, Secretary; Barry Roy Peterson [1953] Director; David Howard Sanders [1958] Director

DBA Advisors Limited
Incorporated: 27 July 1998
Net Worth: £3,244,053 *Total Assets:* £5,286,716
Registered Office: 9 Bridle Close, Surbiton Road, Kingston upon Thames, Surrey, KT1 2JW
Activities: Buying and selling of own real estate
Major Shareholder: David Solomon Baroukh
Officers: David Solomon Baroukh [1971] Director/Surveyor; Melissa Baroukh [1976] Director

DBCN Limited
Incorporated: 16 June 2016
Net Worth: £808,541 *Total Assets:* £10,778,467
Registered Office: Ground Floor, Unit 501 Centennial Park, Centennial Avenue, Elstree, Borehamwood, Herts, WD6 3FG
Activities: Fund management activities
Major Shareholder: Nicola Scott Knight
Officers: Nathaniel Julian Scott Knight [1973] Director/Media Consultant; Adrian Jeremy Scott Knight [1940] Director/Retired; Benedict John Scott Knight [1969] Director; Nicola Scott Knight [1945] Director/Retired

DBT Property LLP
Incorporated: 13 August 2008
Net Worth: £6,663,609 *Total Assets:* £6,737,096
Registered Office: Charles Lake House, Claire Causeway, Crossways Business Park, Dartford, Kent, DA2 6QA
Officers: Christopher Anthony Dougal [1953] Member; Douglas Andrew Dougal [1951] Member; Martin James Dougal [1957] Member

DC Management Services Limited
Incorporated: 3 September 1986 *Employees:* 413
Net Worth: £23,249,000 *Total Assets:* £83,639,000
Registered Office: Unit 1 Martinbridge Estate, Lincoln Road, Enfield, Middlesex, EN1 1SP
Activities: Other letting and operating of own or leased real estate
Parent: DCMS Holdings Limited
Officers: Benjamin James Collins [1977] Managing Director; Jodie Collins [1980] Director; Megan Sarah Collins [1986] Director; Nicholas John Davis [1978] Director; Richard Ennis [1975] Director; Patrick James O'Donnell [1949] Director; Peter David Williams [1971] Director/Accountant [Australian]

DDD Investments Limited
Incorporated: 1 June 2004 *Employees:* 304
Net Worth: £5,322,656 *Total Assets:* £27,611,426
Registered Office: 94 Rickmansworth Road, Watford, Herts, WD18 7JJ
Activities: Activities of head offices
Officers: Carl Atkinson [1974] Director; Hanna Joy Coonagh [1972] Director; Digby Lawrence Spence Halsby [1976] Director; Roger Harrison [1969] Managing Director; Simon Morris [1973] HR Director; Charles Philip Wadsworth [1962] Finance Director

De Lage Landen Leasing Limited
Incorporated: 4 May 1989 *Employees:* 176
Net Worth: £153,748,992 *Total Assets:* £1,721,616,000
Registered Office: Building 7, Croxley Park, Hatters Lane, Watford, Herts, WD18 8YN
Activities: Financial leasing
Parent: De Lage Landen Limited
Officers: Duncan John Hullis [1963] Director/General Manager; Vijay Chandulal Shah [1969] Director/Country Finance Manager; Simon John Trudgeon [1968] Director/Credit Risk Officer

De Lage Landen Limited
Incorporated: 17 December 1992
Net Worth: £78,956,000 *Total Assets:* £79,230,000
Registered Office: Building 7, Croxley Park, Hatters Lane, Watford, Herts, WD18 8YN
Activities: Activities of head offices
Parent: De Lage Landen International B.V.
Officers: Duncan John Hullis [1963] Director/General Manager; Simon John Trudgeon [1968] Director/Credit Risk Officer; Bas Van Asseldonk [1977] Director/Executive Vice President [Dutch]

De Vere Care Limited
Incorporated: 22 April 2008
Net Worth: £3,008,681 *Total Assets:* £6,569,492
Registered Office: Capital Gate, 320 New North Road, Hainault, Essex, IG6 3ES
Activities: Residential nursing care facilities
Shareholders: Ajvinder Singh Sandhu; Rajwinder Kaur Sandhu
Officers: Ajvinder Singh Sandhu [1971] Director/Businessman; Rajwinder Kaur Sandhu [1974] Director/Care Manager

De Vere Homes Limited
Incorporated: 28 January 1986 *Employees:* 1
Net Worth: £1,337,277 *Total Assets:* £5,361,375
Registered Office: 19 Amwell Street, Hoddesdon, Herts, EN11 8TS
Activities: Development of building projects
Major Shareholder: John Walter Couling
Officers: John Walter Couling [1948] Director/Builder

Deacons Associates Limited
Incorporated: 19 April 2001 *Employees:* 3
Net Worth: £237,038 *Total Assets:* £6,104,214
Registered Office: Charles Lake House, Claire Causeway, Crossways Business Park, Dartford, Kent, DA2 6QA
Activities: Other business support service activities n.e.c.
Shareholders: Farah Zuberi; Shahina Zuberi
Officers: Shahina Zuberi, Secretary; Muhamed Umar Qureshi [1984] Director; Farah Zuberi [1987] Director; Shahina Zuberi [1984] Director

Deal Partners Limited
Incorporated: 3 June 2011 *Employees:* 4
Net Worth: £8,280,042 *Total Assets:* £8,671,424
Registered Office: The Powerhouse, 21 Woodthorpe Road, Ashford, Middlesex, TW15 2RP
Activities: Non-specialised wholesale trade
Officers: Richard Robert Cochrane [1964] Director; Clive Richard Morris [1958] Director; Charles Rodney Reynolds [1958] Managing Director

Dealcyber Limited
Incorporated: 7 April 1998
Net Worth: £77,538,000 *Total Assets:* £131,680,000
Registered Office: 980 Great West Road, Brentford, Middlesex, TW8 9GS
Activities: Other business support service activities n.e.c.
Parent: SmithKline Beecham Limited
Officers: Adam Walker [1967] Director

Deanplan Limited
Incorporated: 3 April 1969
Net Worth: £2,945,082 *Total Assets:* £36,345,976
Registered Office: Atlas House, 28 Great Cambridge Road, Enfield, Middlesex, EN1 1UU
Activities: Other letting and operating of own or leased real estate
Officers: Judith Erlich, Secretary; Baruch Erlich [1962] Director/Solicitor; Judith Erlich [1960] Director/Secretary

Robert Deards Limited
Incorporated: 4 June 1931 *Employees:* 3
Net Worth: £20,599,876 *Total Assets:* £21,579,480
Registered Office: Plantagenet House, 4 Plantagenet Road, New Barnet, Herts, EN5 5JQ
Activities: Other letting and operating of own or leased real estate
Major Shareholder: Christopher Edward Scarfe
Officers: Nicholas James Scarfe, Secretary; Nicholas James Scarfe [1992] Director

Deards Services Limited
Incorporated: 6 March 1937 *Employees:* 1
Net Worth: £22,508,088 *Total Assets:* £25,868,690
Registered Office: Plantagenet House, 4 Plantagenet Road, New Barnet, Herts, EN5 5JQ
Activities: Other letting and operating of own or leased real estate
Major Shareholder: Christopher Edward Scarfe
Officers: Nicholas James Scarfe, Secretary; Nicholas James Scarfe [1992] Director

Decadent Properties Limited
Incorporated: 8 September 1999
Net Worth: £2,450,390 *Total Assets:* £7,065,042
Registered Office: Lynwood House, 373-375 Station Road, Harrow, Middlesex, HA1 2AW
Activities: Development of building projects
Major Shareholder: Karen Ruth Emanuel
Officers: Karen Ruth Emanuel, Secretary; Colin James Currie [1976] Director/IT Consultant; Karen Ruth Emanuel [1965] Director

Deco Design and Build Co. Limited
Incorporated: 28 January 1999
Net Worth: £12,371,420 *Total Assets:* £16,201,423
Registered Office: North Star House, 11 London Road, Bromley, Kent, BR1 1BY
Activities: Construction of other civil engineering projects n.e.c.
Shareholders: Robert Francis Copper; Marco Williams
Officers: Sara Copper, Secretary; Robert Francis Copper [1956] Director/Developer; Marco Williams [1963] Director/Developer

The Decus Educational Trust
Incorporated: 28 June 2011 *Employees:* 252
Previous: Gravesend Grammar School Academies Trust
Net Worth: £6,191,000 *Total Assets:* £8,927,000
Registered Office: Gravesend Grammar School, Church Walk, Gravesend, Kent, DA12 2PR
Activities: General secondary education
Officers: Janet Helen Carmody, Secretary; Sally Anne Banks [1951] Director/Self Employed; Mark Philip Law [1961] Director/Chartered Accountant; Anne Lesley McLean [1961] Director/HR Consultant; Graham Peter Ralph [1967] Director/Civil Servant; Anne Mary Robinson [1962] Director/Governance Services Manager; Dr Sukhwinder Singh Shergill [1966] Director/Psychiatrist; Brian Simpson [1955] Director/Retired; John Christopher Stone [1953] Director/Clergy; Dr Katharine Mary Scott Winstone [1956] Director/Dental Surgeon; Geoffrey Stewart Wybar [1958] Director/Headteacher

Dedalo1 Limited
Incorporated: 11 December 2014
Net Worth: £1,452 *Total Assets:* £6,360,969
Registered Office: 107 Hindes Road, Harrow, Middlesex, HA1 1RU
Activities: Other letting and operating of own or leased real estate
Officers: Manuel Alsoni [1982] Director [Italian]

Dee Gee Properties Limited
Incorporated: 24 April 1984 *Employees:* 3
Net Worth: £4,475,976 *Total Assets:* £5,483,769
Registered Office: Nicholas House, River Front, Enfield, Middlesex, EN1 3FG
Activities: Development of building projects
Major Shareholder: Robin Edward Worby
Officers: Sara Gina Bensusan, Secretary; Davina Bensusan [1933] Director/Property Manager; Sara Gina Bensusan [1958] Director; Lisa Aviva Sefton [1961] Director

Deekay Investments Limited
Incorporated: 27 June 1972 *Employees:* 4
Net Worth: £7,491,810 *Total Assets:* £12,999,221
Registered Office: Kimberley House, 31 Burnt Oak Broadway, Edgware, Middlesex, HA8 5LD
Activities: Other letting and operating of own or leased real estate
Parent: Paru Limited
Officers: Neel Mahendra Shah, Secretary; Khimchand Hansraj Chandaria [1935] Director; Nirmala Khimcand Chandaria [1937] Director; Bindi Holding [1956] Director; Neel Mahendra Shah [1974] Director

John Deere Forestry Limited
Incorporated: 9 February 1988 *Employees:* 29
Net Worth: £6,822,263 *Total Assets:* £11,238,019
Registered Office: 400 Dashwood Lang Road, Weybridge, Surrey, KT15 2HJ
Activities: Support services to forestry
Parent: John Deere Forestry Limited
Officers: Janne Tapani Markala [1969] Director/General Manager EU/Retail Sales [Finnish]; John McKie [1975] Managing Director; Pertti Juhani Rauva [1959] Director/General Manager EU/Retail Aftersales [Finnish]; Maria Heleena Virtanen [1979] Director/Group Controller Europe Forestry Retail; Timo Vaino Ylanen [1963] Director WWCTL Products and Forestry Europe [Finnish]

Defence Support (St Athan) Holdings Limited
Incorporated: 19 April 2002
Net Worth Deficit: £920,000 *Total Assets:* £31,851,000
Registered Office: 8 White Oak Square, London Road, Swanley, Kent, BR8 7AG
Activities: Activities of head offices
Parent: John Laing Social Infrastructure Limited
Officers: Guy Frederick Walker [1984] Director/Accountant

Defence Support (St Athan) Limited
Incorporated: 19 April 2002
Net Worth Deficit: £920,000 *Total Assets:* £31,851,000
Registered Office: 8 White Oak Square, London Road, Swanley, Kent, BR8 7AG
Activities: Construction of commercial buildings
Parent: Defence Support (St Athan) Holdings Limited
Officers: Guy Frederick Walker [1984] Director/Accountant

Defender No.1 Production Limited Liability Partnership
Incorporated: 25 September 2003
Net Worth: £11,651,940 *Total Assets:* £14,335,035
Registered Office: 99 Kenton Road, Harrow, London, HA3 0AN
Officers: Joerg Birkholz [1964] LLP Member; Nicholas Mark Brown [1962] LLP Member; Neil John Campbell [1970] LLP Member; Stephen Brian Dainton [1967] LLP Member; David Michael Gorton [1963] LLP Member; Tahir Roland Khan Gandapur [1961] LLP Member; John Robert King [1960] LLP Member; Luigi La Vecchia [1967] LLP Member; Vittorio Martino [1965] LLP Member; Ian James McBride [1961] LLP Member; Adrian Mutu [1979] LLP Member; Michael Alexander Northeast Roffey [1966] LLP Member; Angus John Drennan Wink [1967] LLP Member

Defender No.1 Sale & Leaseback Limited Liability Partnership
Incorporated: 25 September 2003
Net Worth: £13,889,142 *Total Assets:* £13,907,090
Registered Office: 99 Kenton Road, Harrow, London, HA3 0AN
Officers: Joerg Birkholz [1964] LLP Member; Nicholas Mark Brown [1962] LLP Member; Neil John Campbell [1970] LLP Member; Stephen Brian Dainton [1967] LLP Member; David Michael Gorton [1963] LLP Member; Tahir Roland Khan-Gandapur [1961] LLP Member; John Robert King [1960] LLP Member; Luigi La Vecchia [1967] LLP Member; Vittorio Martino [1965] LLP Member; Ian James McBride [1961] LLP Member; Adrian Mutu [1979] LLP Member; Michael Alexander Northeast Roffey [1966] LLP Member; Angus John Drennan Wink [1967] LLP Member

Defender No.2 Production Limited Liability Partnership
Incorporated: 25 September 2003
Net Worth: £9,593,878 *Total Assets:* £11,763,425
Registered Office: 99 Kenton Road, Harrow, London, HA3 0AN
Officers: Martin Jeffrey Stewart Bates [1970] LLP Member; Stuart Andrew Clark [1971] LLP Member; Bobby Console-Verma [1966] LLP Member; Jevin John Davis [1970] LLP Member; Thomas Stefan Duetoft [1964] LLP Member; Justin Garth Excell [1965] LLP Member; Kevin Lindsay Fordham [1954] LLP Member; Matthew Haigh [1972] LLP Member; John Hitchcox [1961] LLP Member; Trevor Neil Hubner [1968] LLP Member; Jeremy Griffith Hughes [1962] LLP Member; Stephanie Judith Jerron-Quarshie [1965] LLP Member; Tom Martin Johannessen [1970] LLP Member; David Michael Kingham [1967] LLP Member; Timothy John Peat [1961] LLP Member; Margaret Robertson [1962] LLP Member; Darren John Sharp [1967] LLP Member

Defender No.2 Sale & Leaseback Limited Liability Partnership
Incorporated: 25 September 2003
Net Worth: £10,766,310 *Total Assets:* £10,773,785
Registered Office: 99 Kenton Road, Harrow, London, HA3 0AN
Officers: Martin Jeffrey Stewart Bates [1970] LLP Member; Bobby Console-Verma [1966] LLP Member; Jevin John Davis [1970] LLP Member; Thomas Stefan Duetoft [1964] LLP Member; Justin Garth Excell [1965] LLP Member; Kevin Lindsay Fordham [1954] LLP Member; Matthew Haigh [1972] LLP Member; John Hitchcox [1961] LLP Member; Trevor Neil Hubner [1968] LLP Member; Jeremy Griffith Hughes [1962] LLP Member; Tom Martin Johannessen [1970] LLP Member; Timothy John Peat [1961] LLP Member; Margaret Robertson [1962] LLP Member; Darren John Sharp [1967] LLP Member

Del Monte (UK) Limited
Incorporated: 23 August 1989 *Employees:* 172
Net Worth: £59,015,000 *Total Assets:* £73,371,000
Registered Office: 240 London Road, Staines upon Thames, Middlesex, TW18 4JD
Activities: Wholesale of fruit and vegetables
Parent: Del Monte Fresh Produce SARL
Officers: Cecelia Dempsey, Secretary; Richard Contreras [1950] Director/Businessman [American]; Martin John Selley [1961] Director; Youssef Zakharia [1961] Director/VP [Lebanese]

Del Monte Europe Limited
Incorporated: 28 December 1926 *Employees:* 5
Net Worth: £51,574,000 *Total Assets:* £161,174,000
Registered Office: 240 London Road, Staines upon Thames, Middlesex, TW18 4JD
Activities: Other processing and preserving of fruit and vegetables
Parent: Del Monte Foods International Ltd
Officers: Cecelia Dempsey, Secretary; Richard Contreras [1950] Director/Businessman [American]; Gianpaolo Renino [1968] Director/VP Europe and Africa [Italian]; Youssef Zakharia [1961] Director/VP [Lebanese]

Del Monte Foods International Limited
Incorporated: 27 December 1989
Net Worth: £223,000 *Total Assets:* £167,848,000
Registered Office: 240 London Road, Staines upon Thames, Middlesex, TW18 4JD
Activities: Wholesale of fruit and vegetables
Parent: Del Monte Fresh Produce SARL
Officers: Cecelia Dempsey, Secretary; Gianpaolo Renino [1968] Director/VP Europe and Africa [Italian]; Youssef Zakharia [1961] Director/VP [Lebanese]

Delamere (Chelmsford) Limited
Incorporated: 18 March 2009 *Employees:* 1
Net Worth: £3,016,925 *Total Assets:* £7,783,706
Registered Office: Centrum House, 36 Station Road, Egham, Surrey, TW20 9LF
Activities: Development of building projects
Major Shareholder: William Archibald Harkness
Officers: Tessa Jane Harkness, Secretary; William Archibald Harkness [1951] Director/Chartered Surveyor

Delbanco Meyer & Company Limited
Incorporated: 27 August 1936 *Employees:* 2
Net Worth: £18,656,000 *Total Assets:* £19,346,000
Registered Office: P O Box 772, 8 Beechwood Avenue, Chorleywood, Rickmansworth, Herts, WD3 5RL
Activities: Development of building projects
Shareholder: Jonathan Hugh Rose
Officers: Edmund Anthony William Kramers, Secretary; Edmund Anthony William Kramers [1953] Director; Jonathan Hugh Rose [1958] Director/Chairman

Delice de France Limited
Incorporated: 20 July 1987 *Employees:* 382
Net Worth: £19,953,060 *Total Assets:* £49,231,404
Registered Office: 149 Brent Road, Southall, Middlesex, UB2 5LJ
Activities: Non-specialised wholesale of food, beverages and tobacco
Officers: Thierry Cacaly, Secretary; Thierry Cacaly [1971] Director/Head of Aryzta Food Solutions UK [French]; Sean Timothy Murphy [1969] Director/Accountant [Irish]; James Anthony Proctor [1972] Director [Irish]

Delivered on Time Limited
Incorporated: 24 February 2004
Net Worth: £2,956,478 *Total Assets:* £6,287,252
Registered Office: Eastworth House, Eastworth Road, Chertsey, Surrey, KT16 8SH
Activities: Cargo handling for air transport activities
Parent: Deutsche Post AG
Officers: Vari Isabel Cameron [1961] Director; Paul Anthony Fowler [1969] Director; Michael Paul Young [1972] Director

Delta Limited
Incorporated: 12 March 1888
Net Worth: £55,339,000 *Total Assets:* £196,550,000
Registered Office: Elder House, St Georges Business Park, Brooklands Road, Weybridge, Surrey, KT13 0TS
Activities: Activities of head offices
Parent: Valmont Industries, Inc.
Officers: Timothy Perry Francis [1976] Director/VP Corporate Controller [American]; Mark Charles Jaksich [1957] Director/Corporate Controller [American]; Gary Steven Lebens [1963] Director/Corporate Finance [American]; Roger Andrew Massey [1969] Director/Corporate Attorney [American]; Karen Colleen Potts [1980] Director/Corporate Attorney [American]; Jamie Austin Taylor [1971] Financial Director

Delta Membrane Systems Limited
Incorporated: 27 March 1998 *Employees:* 23
Net Worth: £2,071,729 *Total Assets:* £5,005,302
Registered Office: 10 Western Road, Romford, Essex, RM1 3JT
Activities: Agents specialised in the sale of other particular products
Shareholder: Delta Membrane Holdings Limited
Officers: Brian George Davison, Secretary/Sales Consultant; Christopher Sidney Burbridge [1963] Director; Brian George Davison [1951] Director; Kevin Nigel Dodds [1964] Director; David Symes [1970] Director

Deltec Citimail Limited
Incorporated: 25 May 1988
Net Worth: £2,426,488 *Total Assets:* £14,892,762
Registered Office: Skynet House, 18-21 Pulborough Way, Hounslow, Middlesex, TW4 6DE
Activities: Buying and selling of own real estate
Shareholders: John Barry Ellis; Dianne Joy Ellis
Officers: Dianne Joy Ellis, Secretary; Dianne Joy Ellis [1956] Courier Director; John Barry Ellis [1939] Director/General Manager

Deltec International Courier Limited
Incorporated: 24 June 1985 *Employees:* 231
Net Worth: £18,172,252 *Total Assets:* £28,045,200
Registered Office: Skynet House, 18-21 Pulborough Way, Hounslow, Middlesex, TW4 6DE
Activities: Unlicensed carriers
Shareholders: John Barry Ellis; Dianne Joy Ellis
Officers: Dianne Joy Ellis, Secretary; John Barry Ellis [1939] Director/General Manager

Demiland Limited
Incorporated: 13 November 1979 *Employees:* 2
Net Worth: £8,613,990 *Total Assets:* £10,227,790
Registered Office: Estate House, Marsh Way, Fairview Industrial Park, Rainham, Essex, RM13 8UH
Activities: Buying and selling of own real estate
Parent: Berwen Limited
Officers: Elizabeth Mary Berry, Secretary; John Berry [1943] Director; Simon John Berry [1969] Director

Demipower (1991) Limited
Incorporated: 7 November 1991 *Employees:* 609
Net Worth: £1,107,776 *Total Assets:* £22,569,406
Registered Office: Jubilee House, 7-9 The Oaks, Ruislip, Middlesex, HA4 7LF
Activities: Unlicenced restaurants and cafes
Shareholders: Amirali Hassanali Moledina Janmohamed; Alim Amirali Janmohamed
Officers: Alim Amirali Janmohamed, Company Secretary; Alim Amirali Janmohamed [1981] Director; Amirali Hassanali Moledina Janmohamed [1952] Director

Demipower Limited
Incorporated: 31 January 1989 *Employees:* 776
Net Worth: £3,531,754 *Total Assets:* £23,874,314
Registered Office: Jubilee House, 7-9 The Oaks, Ruislip, Middlesex, HA4 7LF
Activities: Unlicenced restaurants and cafes
Shareholders: Amirali Hassanali Moledina Janmohamed; Alim Amirali Janmohamed
Officers: Alim Amirali Janmohamed, Company Secretary; Alim Amirali Janmohamed [1981] Director; Amirali Hassanali Moledina Janmohamed [1952] Director/Fast Food Catering

Denbourne Investments Limited
Incorporated: 20 November 1980 *Employees:* 4
Net Worth: £7,013,955 *Total Assets:* £9,918,081
Registered Office: Salisbury House, 81 High Street, Potters Bar, Herts, EN6 5AS
Activities: Buying and selling of own real estate
Shareholders: Kyriacos Neocleous; Keti Neocleous
Officers: Keti Neocleous, Company Secretary; Kyriacos Neocleous [1955] Director

Denecroft Estates Limited
Incorporated: 31 July 1947 *Employees:* 4
Net Worth: £14,240,615 *Total Assets:* £19,275,098
Registered Office: York House, Empire Way, Wembley, Middlesex, HA9 0FQ
Activities: Development of building projects
Parent: UK Real Estate Limited
Officers: Jeremy Louis Landau, Secretary; Nicholas John Capstick-Dale [1962] Director

Deneep Limited
Incorporated: 24 February 2017 *Employees:* 62
Net Worth: £14,803,929 *Total Assets:* £20,740,986
Registered Office: Church Hill, Wilmington, Dartford, Kent, DA2 7DZ
Activities: Activities of construction holding companies
Shareholder: Simon William Clubb
Officers: James Spencer Clubb [1954] Director; Simon William Clubb [1960] Director; Colin Dring [1957] Director; Alexandra Mary Fernyhough [1959] Director; Sarah Jane Gillan [1961] Director; Jonathan James Lovett [1955] Director; Iris Nash [1935] Director; Caroline Ann Reynolds [1963] Director

Denland Limited
Incorporated: 25 November 2015
Net Worth: £3 *Total Assets:* £44,881,004
Registered Office: Hill House, Lowlands Road, Harrow, Middlesex, HA1 3EQ
Activities: Development of building projects
Major Shareholder: Donovan Gijsbertus Wijsmuller
Officers: Brian Martin Comer [1960] Director [Irish]; Luke Andrew Comer [1957] Director [Irish]

Dennys Uniforms Limited
Incorporated: 5 November 1946 *Employees:* 70
Previous: Denny's Uniforms Limited
Net Worth: £2,774,642 *Total Assets:* £5,953,671
Registered Office: 128 Kingston Road, Leatherhead, Surrey, KT22 7PU
Activities: Wholesale of clothing and footwear
Major Shareholder: Peter Nicholas Jubert
Officers: Dominic Noel Green [1965] Sales Director; Mark Gregory [1961] Director [New Zealander]; Peter Nicholas Jubert [1951] Director

Dentex Healthcare Group Limited
Incorporated: 3 July 2014 *Employees:* 16
Net Worth: £25,708,708 *Total Assets:* £31,000,684
Registered Office: Nicholas House, River Front, Enfield, Middlesex, EN1 3FG
Activities: Dental practice activities
Officers: Mark Frederick Bonar Cockburn [1956] Director; Barry Koors Lanesman [1959] Director [South African]; Justin Colin Rodrigues [1987] Director; Eben Andries Van Heerden [1970] Director [South African]; David Allan Vinokur [1979] Director/Private Equity [South African]; Michael Brent Zurowski [1965] Director/Chief Financial Officer

Denton Homes Limited
Incorporated: 6 August 1986 *Employees:* 28
Net Worth: £4,053,911 *Total Assets:* £19,233,000
Registered Office: Upper Deck Admiral's Quarters, Portsmouth Road, Thames Ditton, Surrey, KT7 0XA
Activities: Construction of domestic buildings
Major Shareholder: David Philip Erskine Padden
Officers: Alison Rachel Armstrong, Secretary; David Philip Erskine Padden [1961] Director/Property Developer

Denton Homes Surrey Limited
Incorporated: 20 April 1999
Net Worth: £468,499 *Total Assets:* £8,955,261
Registered Office: Upper Deck Admirals Quarters, Portsmouth Road, Thames Ditton, Surrey, KT7 0XA
Activities: Buying and selling of own real estate
Officers: Alison Rachel Armstrong, Secretary; David Philip Erskine Padden [1961] Director

Denton Wharf Properties Limited
Incorporated: 20 August 2001
Net Worth: £5,150,835 *Total Assets:* £6,529,513
Registered Office: Coopers House, 65a Wingletye Lane, Hornchurch, Essex, RM11 3AT
Activities: Renting and leasing of trucks and other heavy vehicles
Shareholders: Michael John Verrechia; Ian Jeffrey McKellar; Michael John Verrechia
Officers: Ian Jeffrey McKellar [1945] Director; Michael John Verrechia [1951] Director; Michael John Verrechia [1969] Director

Dentoptic Limited
Incorporated: 17 October 2002 *Employees:* 2
Net Worth: £1,953,642 *Total Assets:* £6,343,682
Registered Office: 132 Coombe Lane West, Kingston upon Thames, Surrey, KT2 7DD
Activities: Other letting and operating of own or leased real estate
Officers: Meghna Chirag Patel, Secretary/Optometrist; Chirag Subhashchandra Patel [1977] Director/Dentist; Meghna Chirag Patel [1979] Director/Optician

Denver Building Services Limited
Incorporated: 20 April 2006 *Employees:* 3
Net Worth Deficit: £970,834 *Total Assets:* £5,591,312
Registered Office: Bank House, 81 St Judes Road, Englefield Green, Surrey, TW20 0DF
Activities: Other specialised construction activities n.e.c.
Major Shareholder: Caroline Uloego Haladu
Officers: Caroline Uloego Haladu [1973] Director [Nigerian]

Denville Hall 2012
Incorporated: 9 August 2012 *Employees:* 63
Net Worth: £16,390,921 *Total Assets:* £16,574,064
Registered Office: Denville Hall, 62 Ducks Hill Road, Northwood, Middlesex, HA6 2SB
Activities: Residential care activities for the elderly and disabled
Officers: Richard Langley Berry [1950] Director/Retired; Hemlata Bountra [1960] Director/Accountant; Joanna David [1940] Director/Actress; Generaldine James Blatchley OBE [1950] Director/Actress; Derek Lamden [1949] Director/Front of House Manager; Louisa MacGregor Rix [1955] Director/Interior Designer; The Honourable Sarah Jill Ward [1951] Director/Actor and Artist

Dependable Homes Limited
Incorporated: 27 July 1949 *Employees:* 7
Net Worth: £4,793,401 *Total Assets:* £5,441,892
Registered Office: 172 Greenford Road, Harrow, Middlesex, HA1 3QZ
Activities: Development of building projects
Shareholders: Leigh of Hurley; Trevor Quentin Leigh
Officers: Lord Leigh of Hurley, Secretary; Jacqueline Maureen Harris [1935] Director; Trevor Quentin Leigh [1960] Director; Lord Leigh of Hurley [1959] Director/Chartered Accountant

Derby Healthcare (Holdings) Limited
Incorporated: 11 February 2003
Net Worth Deficit: £35,439,000 *Total Assets:* £405,956,992
Registered Office: 8 White Oak Square, London Road, Swanley, Kent, BR8 7AG
Activities: Combined facilities support activities
Parent: Innisfree Nominees Limited (as Nominee for Innisfree PFI Continuation Fund)
Officers: Gaynor Birley Smith [1966] Investment Director; Richard Keith Sheehan [1975] Investment Director

Derby Healthcare PLC
Incorporated: 17 February 2003
Net Worth Deficit: £35,429,000 *Total Assets:* £405,967,008
Registered Office: 8 White Oak Square, London Road, Swanley, Kent, BR8 7AG
Activities: Development of building projects
Parent: Derby Healthcare (Holdings) Limited
Officers: Gaynor Birley Smith [1966] Investment Director; Michael Davis [1946] Director; Richard Keith Sheehan [1975] Investment Director

Derby Pub Company Limited
Incorporated: 9 November 2012 *Employees:* 85
Net Worth: £5,624,687 *Total Assets:* £6,135,769
Registered Office: Elder House, St Georges Business Park, 207 Brooklands Road, Weybridge, Surrey, KT13 0TS
Activities: Public houses and bars
Officers: Robert Keith Finlay Thomson [1962] Director/Accountant; Alexander Rupert West [1981] Director/Financier

Derby School Solutions (Holdings) Limited
Incorporated: 10 March 2004
Net Worth Deficit: £2,788,000 *Total Assets:* £19,464,000
Registered Office: Astral House, Imperial Way, Watford, Herts, WD24 4WW
Activities: Activities of head offices
Parent: Infrastructure Investments Holdings Limited
Officers: Ian Hudson, Secretary; David Wyn Davies [1968] Director/Accountant; Hannah Holman [1980] Director

Derby School Solutions Limited
Incorporated: 12 March 2004
Net Worth Deficit: £2,788,000 *Total Assets:* £19,464,000
Registered Office: Astral House, Imperial Way, Watford, Herts, WD24 4WW
Activities: Combined facilities support activities
Parent: Derby School Solutions (Holdings) Limited
Officers: Ian Hudson, Secretary; David Wyn Davies [1968] Director/Accountant; Hannah Holman [1980] Director

The Derbyshire Hotel Derby Limited
Incorporated: 25 June 2007
Previous: Venice Regal Derby Limited
Net Worth: £456,969 *Total Assets:* £13,964,061
Registered Office: 1st Floor, Monument House, 215 Marsh Road, Pinner, Middlesex, HA5 5NE
Activities: Hotels and similar accommodation
Parent: Serani Hotels Ltd
Officers: Rajiv Dhirendra Nathwani [1988] Director/Financier

Dermal Laboratories Limited
Incorporated: 2 November 1981 *Employees:* 146
Net Worth: £30,581,380 *Total Assets:* £40,770,980
Registered Office: Haslers, Old Station Road, Loughton, Essex, IG10 4PL
Activities: Manufacture of pharmaceutical preparations
Parent: Diomed Developments Limited
Officers: Andrew James Head, Secretary; Michael Jonathan Yarrow [1947] Director

Dermalogica (UK) Limited
Incorporated: 1 June 1988 *Employees:* 342
Net Worth: £19,056,980 *Total Assets:* £24,956,168
Registered Office: The Manser Building, Thorncroft Manor, Thorncroft Drive, Dorking Road, Leatherhead, Surrey, KT22 8JB
Activities: Wholesale of perfume and cosmetics
Parent: Unilever Overseas Holdings Limited
Officers: James Oliver Earley, Secretary; Richard Clive Hazell, Secretary; Pamela Dickson [1968] Finance Director; Stuart Colin Parkinson Hill [1979] Director/CFO Dermalogica; Glenn Derrick Poy [1957] Director/General Manager [Canadian]; Anthony Colin Rudd [1975] Finance Director

Dernagree Properties Limited
Incorporated: 19 May 2011
Net Worth: £470,803 *Total Assets:* £5,720,320
Registered Office: 19 Abbotsford Gardens, Woodford Green, Essex, IG8 9HW
Activities: Buying and selling of own real estate
Major Shareholder: John Vincent Burton
Officers: John Vincent Burton [1955] Director

Derrin Brothers Properties Limited
Incorporated: 19 May 1959 *Employees:* 3
Net Worth Deficit: £6,142,571 *Total Assets:* £22,542,756
Registered Office: 1 Princeton Mews, 167-169 London Road, Kingston upon Thames, Surrey, KT2 6PT
Activities: Non-trading company
Major Shareholder: Willy Schaperkotter
Officers: Winny Borgas [1938] Director [Belgian]; John Donnelly [1973] Director/Chartered Accountant [Irish]; Carine Martinez [1961] Director/Accountant [Swiss]

Design Blue Limited
Incorporated: 21 June 1999 *Employees:* 44
Net Worth Deficit: £5,292,686 *Total Assets:* £10,440,480
Registered Office: The Lab, 7-8 Commerce Way, Croydon, Surrey, CR0 4XA
Activities: Other professional, scientific and technical activities n.e.c.
Parent: D3O Holdings Ltd
Officers: Colin David Smith, Secretary; Stuart Sawyer [1962] Director/Consultant; Colin David Smith [1971] Director

Designer M & E Services UK Limited
Incorporated: 22 March 2006 *Employees:* 115
Net Worth: £3,546,531 *Total Assets:* £25,962,836
Registered Office: 1st Floor, Egale 1, 80 St Albans Road, Watford, Herts, WD17 1RP
Activities: Construction of commercial buildings
Parent: Designer Group Engineering Contractors Holdings DAC
Officers: Jonathan Panton, Secretary; Nicholas James Baish [1972] Director/M & E Contractors; Benedict Edward Gandee [1967] Commercial Director; Michael Charles Stone [1968] Managing Director [Irish]; Niall Christopher Stone [1975] Director [Irish]

Designplan Lighting Limited
Incorporated: 11 December 1963 *Employees:* 152
Net Worth: £7,829,969 *Total Assets:* £11,838,767
Registered Office: 16 Kimpton Park Way, Sutton, Surrey, SM3 9QS
Activities: Manufacture of electric lighting equipment
Parent: Fagerhults Belysning AB
Officers: David Kevin Barnes [1968] Director; Antony Osborne Browne [1964] Managing Director; Braden Lee Harris [1981] Finance Director [Australian]; Alex Hawkins [1974] Customer Service Director; Philip George Muir [1969] Design & Technology Director; Bodil Sonesson [1968] Director/President & CEO [Swedish]; Dr Geert Jan Van Der Meer [1965] Director/Manager [Dutch]; Michael Wood [1964] Director/Chief Financial Officer

Desilu Estates Limited
Incorporated: 6 April 1988 *Employees:* 2
Net Worth: £4,130,257 *Total Assets:* £7,781,546
Registered Office: First Floor, Woodgate Studios, 2-8 Games Road, Cockfosters, Barnet, Herts, EN4 9HN
Activities: Buying and selling of own real estate
Parent: Desilu Group Limited
Officers: Elenor Joseph, Secretary/Sales Executive; George Josife [1962] Director

Desilu Group Limited
Incorporated: 19 April 1971
Net Worth: £16,563,979 *Total Assets:* £19,674,460
Registered Office: First Floor, Woodgate Studios, 2-8 Games Road, Cockfosters, Barnet, Herts, EN4 9HN
Activities: Buying and selling of own real estate
Shareholder: Christopher Joseph
Officers: Eleanor Joseph, Secretary; George Josife [1962] Director

J Devine Civil Engineering Ltd
Incorporated: 3 July 1974 *Employees:* 28
Net Worth: £2,635,276 *Total Assets:* £11,429,371
Registered Office: 133 Church Hill Road, Cheam, Sutton, Surrey, SM3 8NE
Activities: Construction of other civil engineering projects n.e.c.
Parent: Devine Holdings Limited
Officers: Brian Philip Beckett, Secretary; James Timothy Devine [1949] Director [Irish]; Nigel Frank Jordan [1956] Director

Devine Holdings Limited
Incorporated: 22 March 2000 *Employees:* 51
Net Worth: £29,658,414 *Total Assets:* £50,540,040
Registered Office: 133 Church Hill Road, Sutton, Surrey, SM3 8NE
Activities: Activities of head offices
Major Shareholder: James Timothy Devine
Officers: Brian Philip Beckett, Secretary; James Timothy Devine [1949] Managing Director [Irish]

Devine Homes PLC
Incorporated: 31 January 1985 *Employees:* 17
Net Worth: £14,802,987 *Total Assets:* £26,191,474
Registered Office: 133 Church Hill Road, Sutton, Surrey, SM3 8NE
Activities: Construction of domestic buildings
Parent: Devine Holdings Limited
Officers: Brian Philip Beckett, Secretary; James Timothy Devine [1949] Director [Irish]; Christopher Allen Posgate [1957] Director

J. Devine Plant Hire Limited
Incorporated: 19 February 1982 *Employees:* 6
Net Worth: £5,104,685 *Total Assets:* £5,870,891
Registered Office: 133 Church Hill Road, Cheam, Sutton, Surrey, SM3 8NE
Activities: Renting and leasing of construction and civil engineering machinery and equipment
Parent: Devine Holdings Limited
Officers: Brian Philip Beckett, Secretary; James Timothy Devine [1949] Managing Director [Irish]

Devitt Insurance Services Limited
Incorporated: 2 November 1989 *Employees:* 138
Net Worth: £3,010,486 *Total Assets:* £10,450,637
Registered Office: North House, St Edwards Way, Romford, Essex, RM1 3PP
Activities: Activities of insurance agents and brokers
Parent: CKH Limited
Officers: Anthony Edward Chapman [1962] Director/Accountant; William James Hughes [1971] Managing Director

The Dewan Foundation Limited
Incorporated: 14 August 2001
Net Worth: £6,041,698 *Total Assets:* £6,051,485
Registered Office: 28 Church Road, Stanmore, Harrow, Middlesex, HA7 4XR
Activities: Other social work activities without accommodation n.e.c.
Officers: Zalina Dewan, Secretary; Naresh Dewan [1950] Director/Retired [American]; Ramesh Dewan [1947] Director/Publisher; Sheena Selina Dewan [1973] Director/Publisher; Zalina Dewan [1942] Director/Teacher

Dewhurst PLC
Incorporated: 5 November 1919 *Employees:* 395
Net Worth: £35,951,000 *Total Assets:* £53,657,000
Registered Office: Unit 9 Hampton Business Park, Hampton Road West, Feltham, Middlesex, TW13 6DB
Activities: Manufacture of other electrical equipment
Officers: Jared Conan Sinclair, Secretary; John Robert Bailey [1970] Director; David Dewhurst [1961] Director/Export Sales Manager; Richard Melbourne Dewhurst [1956] Director/Accountant; Jared Conan Sinclair [1970] Director/Accountant; Peter Alfred Tett [1939] Director; Alan Michael Warren [1957] Director; Richard John Young [1956] Director/Engineer

Dexter House Limited
Incorporated: 31 May 1985 *Employees:* 32
Net Worth: £4,628,706 *Total Assets:* £7,805,952
Registered Office: Southbridge House, Southbridge Place, Croydon, Surrey, CR0 4HA
Activities: Other business support service activities n.e.c.
Officers: Dominique Sasha Metcalfe, Secretary/Director; Samuel Thomas James Knights [1982] Director/Press Officer; Gemma Rose Leader [1980] Director/Recruitment Consultant; April Linda McErlain [1950] Director/Administrator; Dominique Sasha Metcalfe [1973] Director; Ian Derek Peadon [1964] Director/Manager

DF Group Limited
Incorporated: 3 June 1998
Net Worth: £610,102,464 *Total Assets:* £642,947,648
Registered Office: 417 Bridport Road, Greenford, Middlesex, UB6 8UA
Activities: Other business support service activities n.e.c.
Parent: Ultra Electronics Holdings PLC
Officers: Anant Prakash, Secretary; Mark Richard Nelson [1966] Director Group Finance; Simon Charles Conrad Pryce [1961] Director; Amitabh Sharma [1967] Finance Director

DGC Limited
Incorporated: 4 December 1990 *Employees:* 9
Net Worth: £1,926,222 *Total Assets:* £8,511,552
Registered Office: 93 Beddington Lane, Croydon, Surrey, CR0 4TD
Activities: Renting and leasing of trucks and other heavy vehicles
Parent: Ballyvesey Holdings Limited
Officers: Harold Hugh Montgomery, Secretary; David Nigel Birkmyre [1942] Director; Paul Anthony Irving [1961] Director; Harold Hugh Montgomery [1948] Director/Haulier

Dhamecha Foods Limited
Incorporated: 20 March 1974 *Employees:* 628
Net Worth: £76,463,000 *Total Assets:* £188,968,992
Registered Office: 2 Hathaway Close, Stanmore, Middlesex, HA7 3NR
Activities: Wholesale of wine, beer, spirits and other alcoholic beverages
Parent: Dhamecha Group Limited
Officers: Mukesh Manilal Vithlani, Secretary; Khodidas Ratanshi Dhamecha [1930] Director; Shantilal Ratanshi Dhamecha [1931] Director; Jitendra Patel [1959] Director

Dhamecha Group Limited
Incorporated: 4 March 2002
Net Worth: £41,816,000 *Total Assets:* £54,941,000
Registered Office: 2 Hathaway Close, Stanmore, Middlesex, HA7 3NR
Activities: Activities of head offices
Parent: Dhamecha Holdings Limited
Officers: Mukesh Manilal Vithlani, Secretary; Khodidas Ratanshi Dhamecha [1930] Director; Shantilal Ratanshi Dhamecha [1931] Director

Dhamecha Holdings Limited
Incorporated: 1 March 2008 *Employees:* 628
Net Worth: £100,586,000 *Total Assets:* £232,784,000
Registered Office: 2 Hathaway Close, Stanmore, Middlesex, HA7 3NR
Activities: Activities of head offices
Shareholders: Khodidas Ratanshi Dhamecha; Shantilal Ratanshi Dhamecha
Officers: Mukesh Manilal Vithlani, Secretary; Khodidas Ratanshi Dhamecha [1930] Director; Shantilal Ratanshi Dhamecha [1931] Director; Jitendra Patel [1959] Director/Accountant

Dhamecha Property Limited
Incorporated: 3 March 2008
Net Worth: £14,927,000 *Total Assets:* £72,533,000
Registered Office: 2 Hathaway Close, Stanmore, Middlesex, HA7 3NR
Activities: Renting and operating of Housing Association real estate
Parent: Dhamecha Group Limited
Officers: Mukesh Manilal Vithlani, Secretary; Khodidas Ratanshi Dhamecha [1930] Director; Shantilal Ratanshi Dhamecha [1931] Director; Jitendra Patel [1959] Director/Accountant

HJ Dhillon Ltd.
Incorporated: 22 August 2016
Net Worth: £9,138,170 *Total Assets:* £9,474,914
Registered Office: 46 The Drive, Ickenham, Uxbridge, Middlesex, UB10 8AG
Activities: Management of real estate on a fee or contract basis
Shareholders: Harbhajan Singh Dhillon; Jasber Kaur Dhillon
Officers: Anita Kaur Dhillon [1986] Director; Benjeev Singh Dhillon [1982] Director; Harbhajan Singh Dhillon [1947] Director; Jasber Kaur Dhillon [1953] Director

Dhiman Enterprises Limited
Incorporated: 24 February 2005
Net Worth: £4,463,942 *Total Assets:* £5,603,556
Registered Office: Unit 5 Triangle Centre, 399 Uxbridge Road, Southall, Middlesex, UB1 3EJ
Activities: Non-specialised wholesale trade
Shareholder: Gurinder Dhiman
Officers: Manjit Dhiman, Secretary; Gurinder Dhiman [1959] Director/Salesman; Harjinder Dhiman [1981] Director; Narinder Dhiman [1985] Director

DHL Global Forwarding (UK) Limited
Incorporated: 15 August 2000 *Employees:* 944
Net Worth: £104,168,000 *Total Assets:* £270,824,000
Registered Office: Eastworth House, Eastworth Road, Chertsey, Surrey, KT16 8SH
Activities: Other transportation support activities
Officers: Vari Isabel Cameron [1961] Finance Director; Remco Pieter Van Oerle [1966] Director [Dutch]; Michael Paul Young [1972] Director

Dial Investments Limited
Incorporated: 4 August 1959 *Employees:* 2
Net Worth: £5,223,705 *Total Assets:* £6,844,784
Registered Office: Deal House, 3 Willow Grove, Chislehurst, Kent, BR7 5BN
Activities: Other letting and operating of own or leased real estate
Officers: Brenda Ann Osborn, Secretary; Sarah Anne Aucamp [1969] Director; Brenda Ann Osborn [1945] Director/Secretary; Guy Stuart Osborn [1970] Director; Michael John Osborn [1942] Director

Dialgreen Estates Limited
Incorporated: 14 July 1999 *Employees:* 2
Net Worth: £9,724,599 *Total Assets:* £15,080,637
Registered Office: 5 Beauchamp Court, Victors Way, Barnet, Herts, EN5 5TZ
Activities: Other letting and operating of own or leased real estate
Major Shareholder: Francis Jarlath Burke
Officers: Francis Jarlath Burke [1946] Director [Irish]

Diamed (G.B.) Ltd.
Incorporated: 30 June 1975 *Employees:* 24
Net Worth: £4,545,000 *Total Assets:* £6,120,000
Registered Office: 3rd and 4th Floor, The Junction, Station Road, Watford, Herts, WD17 1ET
Activities: Other business support service activities n.e.c.
Parent: Bio-Rad Laboratories Limited
Officers: Philip Howard [1957] Director/Regional Sales Manager; Norman David Schwartz [1950] Director/President and CEO [American]

Diamond Corporation Limited
Incorporated: 19 March 2002 *Employees:* 2
Net Worth: £29,463,552 *Total Assets:* £67,295,496
Registered Office: Toronto Suite, Maple House, High Street, Potters Bar, Herts, EN6 5BS
Activities: Other letting and operating of own or leased real estate
Shareholders: Demetrios Zenonos Antoniou; Harry Zenonos Antoniou
Officers: Demetrios Antoniou [1976] Director/Administrator; Harry Antoniou [1983] Director/Administrator

Dicky Birds Pre School Nurseries Limited
Incorporated: 16 April 1998 *Employees:* 286
Net Worth: £6,848,034 *Total Assets:* £13,128,583
Registered Office: Anchor House, Burgoine Quay, 8 Lower Teddington Road, Kingston upon Thames, Surrey, KT1 4EU
Activities: Pre-primary education
Parent: Berry Holdings (London) Ltd
Officers: Rachel Berry, Secretary; Christopher Berry [1951] Director; Rachel Berry [1962] Director

Digico Europe Limited
Incorporated: 1 June 2007
Net Worth: £3,738,131 *Total Assets:* £5,500,000
Registered Office: Unit 10 Silverglade Business Park, Leatherhead Road, Chessington, Surrey, KT9 2QL
Activities: Manufacture of communication equipment other than telegraph, and telephone apparatus and equipment
Parent: Digico Global Limited
Officers: Helen Mary Culleton, Secretary/Director; Helen Mary Culleton [1964] Director; James David Gordon [1972] Managing Director; John Robert Stadius [1956] Technical Director

Digico Global Limited
Incorporated: 23 September 2011
Net Worth: £14,845,678 *Total Assets:* £45,657,132
Registered Office: Unit 10 Silverglade Business Park, Leatherhead Road, Chessington, Surrey, KT9 2QL
Activities: Dormant company
Parent: Console Bidco Limited
Officers: Helen Mary Culleton [1964] Director; James David Gordon [1972] Managing Director; John Robert Stadius [1956] Technical Director

Digico UK Limited
Incorporated: 7 December 2001 *Employees:* 103
Net Worth: £47,599,000 *Total Assets:* £57,102,000
Registered Office: Unit 10 Silverglade Business Park, Chessington, Surrey, KT9 2QL
Activities: Manufacture of other electrical equipment
Parent: Digico Europe Limited
Officers: Helen Mary Culleton, Secretary/Director; Helen Mary Culleton [1964] Director; James David Gordon [1972] Managing Director; John Robert Stadius [1956] Director

Dilawar & Sons Limited
Incorporated: 15 January 2013
Net Worth: £142,919 *Total Assets:* £6,873,485
Registered Office: 416 Green Lane, Ilford, Essex, IG3 9JX
Activities: Other letting and operating of own or leased real estate
Officers: Dilawar Singh [1945] Director

Dilawar Property Ltd.
Incorporated: 13 June 2001
Net Worth: £3,370,270 *Total Assets:* £8,687,118
Registered Office: 416 Green Lane, Ilford, Essex, IG3 9JX
Activities: Other letting and operating of own or leased real estate
Officers: Krishan Kaur, Secretary; Dilawar Singh [1945] Director/Property Consultant

Dimehome Limited
Incorporated: 26 April 1989
Net Worth: £5,580,689 *Total Assets:* £6,769,935
Registered Office: c/o Parker Cavendish, 28 Church Road, Stanmore, Middlesex, HA7 4XR
Activities: Development of building projects
Shareholders: Sheena Dewan; Zalina Dewan
Officers: Shaileshkumar Naik, Secretary; Zalina Dewan [1942] Director/Teacher

Diomed Developments Limited
Incorporated: 2 January 1963 *Employees:* 238
Net Worth: £54,324,936 *Total Assets:* £66,227,728
Registered Office: Haslers, Old Station Road, Loughton, Essex, IG10 4PL
Activities: Manufacture of basic pharmaceutical products
Major Shareholder: Michael Jonathan Yarrow
Officers: Heather Jennifer Yarrow, Secretary; Heather Jennifer Yarrow [1949] Director; Michael Jonathan Yarrow [1947] Director; Nicola Irene Yarrow [1987] Director

Dip Systems (UK) Limited
Incorporated: 18 July 1994 *Employees:* 3
Net Worth: £8,116,658 *Total Assets:* £13,124,851
Registered Office: 3 Montpelier Avenue, Bexley, Kent, DA5 3AP
Activities: Development of building projects
Shareholders: Kamaldip Heer; Lakhbir Singh Heer
Officers: Kamaldip Heer, Secretary; Lakhbir Singh Heer [1966] Managing Director

Direct Boot and Shoe Supplies Limited
Incorporated: 2 December 1994 *Employees:* 29
Net Worth: £4,806,379 *Total Assets:* £8,836,903
Registered Office: 1-3 Woodford Avenue, Gants Hill, Ilford, Essex, IG2 6UF
Activities: Wholesale of clothing and footwear
Major Shareholder: Mark Redvers Cooper
Officers: Ann Cooper, Secretary; Mark Redvers Cooper [1953] Director/Shoe Retailer and Embroiderer

Direct Chauffeur Line Limited
Incorporated: 18 January 1999 *Employees:* 44
Net Worth: £1,484,504 *Total Assets:* £11,039,928
Registered Office: 308 High Street, Croydon, Surrey, CR0 1NG
Activities: Activities of insurance agents and brokers
Major Shareholder: Andrew Anthony Hussey
Officers: Jacqueline Hussey, Secretary/Director; Andrew Anthony Hussey [1960] Director; Jacqueline Hussey [1960] Director

Direct Line Group Limited
Incorporated: 21 April 1993
Net Worth: £28,588,000 *Total Assets:* £28,597,000
Registered Office: Churchill Court, Westmoreland Road, Bromley, Kent, BR1 1DP
Activities: Activities of head offices
Parent: Direct Line Insurance Group PLC
Officers: Roger Cheston Clifton, Secretary; Roger Cheston Clifton [1964] Director/Secretary; Helen Clare O'Murchu [1967] Director; Humphrey Michael Tomlinson [1962] Director/General Counsel & Company Secretary

Direct Line Insurance Group PLC
Incorporated: 26 July 1988 *Employees:* 10,949
Net Worth: £3,061,600,000 *Total Assets:* £9,948,199,936
Registered Office: Churchill Court, Westmoreland Road, Bromley, Kent, BR1 1DP
Activities: Activities of head offices
Officers: Roger Cheston Clifton, Secretary; Michael Nicholas Biggs [1952] Director/Chartered Accountant; Paul Robert Geddes [1969] Director/Bank Official; Danuta Gray [1958] Director; Mark Julian Gregory [1963] Director; Jane Carolyn Hanson [1967] Director; Michael Anthony Holliday-Williams [1970] Director; Penelope Jane James [1969] Director; Sebastian Richard Edward Cuthbert James [1966] Director/Group CEO; Fiona Catherine McBain [1961] Director; Gregor Ninian Stewart [1964] Director; Clare Eleanor Thompson [1954] Director; Doctor Richard Churchill Ward [1957] Director

Direct Link Worldwide Limited
Incorporated: 22 March 1994 *Employees:* 49
Net Worth: £2,273,057 *Total Assets:* £5,637,731
Registered Office: Fairview Business Centre, 25 Clayton Road, Hayes, Middlesex, UB3 1AN
Activities: Licensed carriers
Officers: Karin Lisa Falkentoft, Secretary/Managing Director [Danish]; Karin Lisa Falkentoft [1964] Managing Director [Danish]; Mats Ingmar Johansson [1960] Director [Swedish]; Tim Jornsen [1966] Director [Norwegian]

Direct Supplies (2014) Group Limited
Incorporated: 14 April 2014
Net Worth: £4,312,999 *Total Assets:* £5,576,913
Registered Office: 166 College Road, Harrow, Middlesex, HA1 1RA
Activities: Other business support service activities n.e.c.
Major Shareholder: Samuel Bazini
Officers: Samuel Bazini [1963] Director; Sara Lisa Bazini [1964] Director

Direct Supplies (2014) Limited
Incorporated: 31 March 2014 *Employees:* 2
Net Worth: £2,263,064 *Total Assets:* £7,294,925
Registered Office: 166 College Road, Harrow, Middlesex, HA1 1RA
Activities: Wholesale of perfume and cosmetics
Parent: Direct Supplies (2014) Group Limited
Officers: Samuel Bazini [1963] Director; Sara Lisa Bazini [1964] Director

Direct Supplies (London) Limited
Incorporated: 10 July 1995
Net Worth: £5,538,377 *Total Assets:* £5,601,701
Registered Office: 166 College Road, Harrow, Middlesex, HA1 1RA
Activities: Other business support service activities n.e.c.
Parent: Direct Supplies (2014) Limited
Officers: Sara Lisa Bazini, Secretary/Director; Samuel Bazini [1963] Director; Sara Lisa Bazini [1964] Director

Directfield Limited
Incorporated: 14 March 2000
Net Worth: £2,188,476 *Total Assets:* £8,202,084
Registered Office: Moorcroft House, Wilderness Road, Chislehurst, Kent, BR7 5EY
Activities: Buying and selling of own real estate
Shareholders: Anthony David Allan; Peter Cooper Smith
Officers: Peter Cooper Smith, Secretary/Chartered Surveyor; Peter Cooper Smith [1957] Director/Chartered Surveyor; Lance James Gainsford [1973] Director/Office Manager; Lionel Hayes [1963] Director

Discover The World Limited
Incorporated: 13 September 1988 *Employees:* 100
Net Worth: £604,089 *Total Assets:* £9,794,014
Registered Office: Arctic House, 8 Bolters Lane, Banstead, Surrey, SM7 2AR
Activities: Tour operator activities
Officers: Mark Leaney, Secretary/Accountant; Paul Andrzej Furlepa [1964] Finance Director; Georgina Hancock [1973] Director/Tour Operator; Mark Leaney [1951] Director/Accountant; Clive Lindsay Stacey [1953] Director/Tour Operator; Daniel Clive James Stacey [1983] Director/Tour Operator

Distell International Holdings Limited
Incorporated: 8 April 2016
Net Worth: £16,970,308 *Total Assets:* £18,152,844
Registered Office: Avalon House, 72 Lower Mortlake Road, Richmond, Surrey, TW9 2JY
Activities: Distilling, rectifying and blending of spirits
Parent: Distell Group Limited
Officers: Nwavudu Constance Ekebuisi, Secretary; Christopher John Blandford-Newson [1964] Director/Asset Management [British/South African]; Steven Jeffrey Nathan [1962] Director [South African]; Werner Nolte [1976] Finance Director [South African]; Fraser John Thornton [1969] Managing Director; Leonard Jacobus Volschenk [1971] Managing Director [South African]

Distinction Investments Limited
Incorporated: 22 June 2015
Net Worth: £134,272 *Total Assets:* £5,195,894
Registered Office: Springfield House, 99-101 Crossbrook Street, Waltham Cross, Herts, EN8 8JR
Activities: Financial intermediation not elsewhere classified
Shareholders: Mark Andrew Elliott; Clare Adrienne Elliott
Officers: Clare Adrienne Elliott [1957] Director; Mark Andrew Elliott [1957] Director

District One Estates Ltd
Incorporated: 19 July 2002
Net Worth: £3,437,102 *Total Assets:* £5,985,587
Registered Office: 40 Greenleafe Drive, Ilford, Essex, IG6 1LL
Activities: Other letting and operating of own or leased real estate
Shareholder: Askir Ali
Officers: Kamru Ali, Secretary/Director; Askir Ali [1970] Director; Kamru Ali [1973] Director

DKH Investments Limited
Incorporated: 25 March 2014
Net Worth: £4,683,575 *Total Assets:* £7,602,290
Registered Office: 5-7 Bath Road, Heathrow, Hounslow, Middlesex, TW6 2AA
Activities: Development of building projects
Officers: Dalpreet Kaur Grewal, Secretary; Kavanjit Singh Hayre [1989] Director

DL Insurance Services Limited
Incorporated: 15 December 1994 *Employees:* 10,949
Net Worth: £449,400,000 *Total Assets:* £684,000,000
Registered Office: Churchill Court, Westmoreland Road, Bromley, Kent, BR1 1DP
Activities: Non-life insurance
Parent: Direct Line Insurance Group PLC
Officers: Roger Cheston Clifton, Secretary; Paul Robert Geddes [1969] Director/Bank Official; Jonathan Paul Greenwood [1968] Director/Bank Official; Penelope Jane James [1969] Director; Steven Maddock [1968] Director/Bank Official; Neil Manser [1974] Director/Accountant; Humphrey Michael Tomlinson [1962] Director/General Counsel & Company Secretary

DMC Contracts Limited
Incorporated: 8 July 2004 *Employees:* 23
Net Worth: £4,712,255 *Total Assets:* £9,877,729
Registered Office: Unit 17 The Capstan Centre, Tilbury, Essex, RM18 7HH
Activities: Floor and wall covering
Shareholders: David Andrew McCartney; Michelle McCartney
Officers: Michelle McCartney, Secretary; Lee Bird [1973] Director; Edward Conor McCann [1970] Director [Irish]; David Andrew McCartney [1971] Director; Alexander Eugene Morrissey [1975] Director

Dnata Travel (U.K.) Ltd.
Incorporated: 6 March 1995 *Employees:* 49
Net Worth: £2,951,790 *Total Assets:* £30,017,216
Registered Office: Clarendon House, 147 London Road, Kingston upon Thames, Surrey, KT2 6NH
Activities: Tour operator activities
Officers: Niel Alobaidi [1974] Director/Manager; Iain Charles Richard Andrew [1965] Director/Divisional Senior Vice President - Travel; Ailsa Elizabeth Pollard [1976] Director

Dnata World Travel Limited
Incorporated: 1 December 2011
Net Worth Deficit: £3,890,000 *Total Assets:* £132,321,000
Registered Office: Clarendon House, 147 London Road, Kingston upon Thames, Surrey, KT2 6NH
Activities: Activities of head offices
Officers: Iain Andrew [1965] Director; Asif Hamza Parkar [1974] Director/Finance Manager

DNC UK Limited
Incorporated: 28 January 1999 *Employees:* 23
Net Worth: £2,014,711 *Total Assets:* £5,786,092
Registered Office: 51 Princes Road, Weybridge, Surrey, KT13 9BN
Activities: Other business support service activities n.e.c.
Shareholders: Giovanni Matteini; Andrew O'Neill
Officers: Filippo Cattani [1964] Director [Italian]; Simone Cattani [1958] Director [Italian]; Alan William Johnson [1960] Finance & Operations Director; David Lisi [1957] Director [Italian]; Andrew O'Neill [1962] Director/Sales and Marketing Manager

Do & Co. Event & Airline Catering Limited
Incorporated: 8 September 2003 *Employees:* 423
Net Worth: £6,734,809 *Total Assets:* £34,036,388
Registered Office: Unit 2 Girling Way, Feltham, Middlesex, TW14 0PH
Activities: Other food services
Parent: Do & Co. International Investments Limited
Officers: Harald Hrastnig [1959] Director/Manager [Austrian]

Do & Co. International Catering Limited
Incorporated: 13 September 1996 *Employees:* 5
Net Worth: £3,579,965 *Total Assets:* £25,740,168
Registered Office: Unit 2 Girling Way, Feltham, Middlesex, TW14 0PH
Activities: Event catering activities
Parent: Do & Co. International Investments Limited
Officers: Gert Kretschmeier, Secretary [Austrian]; Attila Dogudan [1959] Director/Business Manager [Austrian]

Dock and Let Limited
Incorporated: 2 March 1999 *Employees:* 3
Net Worth: £848,528 *Total Assets:* £10,770,755
Registered Office: 166 College Road, Harrow, Middlesex, HA1 1RA
Activities: Development of building projects
Major Shareholder: Michael Spencer Docker
Officers: Michele Docker, Secretary; Michael Spencer Docker [1963] Director/Property Developer

Domantis Limited
Incorporated: 17 January 2000
Net Worth: £39,675,000 *Total Assets:* £39,719,000
Registered Office: 980 Great West Road, Brentford, Middlesex, TW8 9GS
Activities: Other research and experimental development on natural sciences and engineering
Parent: Glaxo Group Limited
Officers: Victoria Anne Whyte, Secretary; James Borger [1963] Director/VP, Group Financial Planning and Analysis [American]; Alan George Burns [1975] Director

Domino Investments Limited
Incorporated: 12 February 1993 *Employees:* 138
Net Worth: £18,046,308 *Total Assets:* £30,686,856
Registered Office: 17 Aden Road, Enfield, Middlesex, EN3 7SU
Activities: Activities of production holding companies
Major Shareholder: Keith Childs
Officers: Timothy John Childs, Secretary; Brenda Ann Childs [1941] Director; Keith Childs [1941] Director; Timothy John Childs [1966] Director; Georgina Elizabeth Hofer [1969] Director; Jacquiline Louise Squire [1969] Director

Donamount Limited
Incorporated: 30 September 1999
Net Worth Deficit: £20,872,466 *Total Assets:* £31,020,032
Registered Office: NJHco, Suite 1, The Sanctuary, 23 Oak Hill Grove, Surbiton, Surrey, KT6 6DU
Activities: Activities of other holding companies n.e.c.
Major Shareholder: Klaas Johannes Zwart
Officers: Paul Emmanuel O'Neill [1978] Director [Irish]; Adrian Relph [1967] Director; Stuart William Wilson [1967] Director

Donatantonio Group Limited
Incorporated: 6 November 2007 *Employees:* 33
Net Worth: £521,596 *Total Assets:* £8,466,016
Registered Office: Lupa House, York Way, Borehamwood, Herts, WD6 1PX
Activities: Activities of other holding companies n.e.c.
Shareholders: Proven VCT PLC; Proven Growth and Income VCT PLC
Officers: Manish Mandavia, Secretary; Simon Bell [1964] Director; Peter Maurice Crystal [1948] Director/Lawyer; Manish Jayant Mandavia [1972] Director; Malcolm Kennedy Hunt Moss [1959] Director/Venture Fund Manager; Elizabeth Catherine Scarborough [1968] Director; Timothy Ross Scarborough [1968] Commercial Director

Donatantonio Limited
Incorporated: 16 October 2003 *Employees:* 33
Net Worth: £4,294,745 *Total Assets:* £10,037,156
Registered Office: Lupa House, York Way, Borehamwood, Herts, WD6 1PX
Activities: Non-specialised wholesale of food, beverages and tobacco
Parent: Donatantonio Group Ltd
Officers: Manish Mandavia, Secretary; Simon Bell [1964] Director; Peter Maurice Crystal [1948] Director/Solicitor; Manish Jayant Mandavia [1972] Director; Malcolm Kennedy Hunt Moss [1959] Director/Founding Partner; Elizabeth Catherine Scarborough [1968] Director; Timothy Ross Scarborough [1968] Commercial Director

Doncaster School Solutions (Holdings) Limited
Incorporated: 28 November 2006
Net Worth Deficit: £11,247,000 *Total Assets:* £42,817,000
Registered Office: Astral House, Imperial Way, Watford, Herts, WD24 4WW
Activities: Activities of head offices
Parent: Vinci Pensions Limited
Officers: Ian David Hudson [1964] Director/Chartered Accountant; Rory John Murphy [1969] Director/Chartered Surveyor

Doncaster School Solutions Limited
Incorporated: 28 November 2006
Net Worth Deficit: £11,247,000 *Total Assets:* £42,817,000
Registered Office: Astral House, Imperial Way, Watford, Herts, WD24 4WW
Activities: Development of building projects
Parent: Doncaster School Solutions (Holdings) Limited
Officers: Ian David Hudson [1964] Director/Chartered Accountant; Rory John Murphy [1969] Director/Chartered Surveyor

Donovan Bros. Limited
Incorporated: 5 December 1947 *Employees:* 36
Net Worth: £4,923,218 *Total Assets:* £6,816,357
Registered Office: 5 Lagoon Road, Orpington, Kent, BR5 3QX
Activities: Wholesale of china and glassware and cleaning materials
Shareholders: McHael Donovan; John Edward Anthony Olney
Officers: Anne Elizabeth Donovan, Secretary; Anne Elizabeth Donovan [1950] Director/Manager; Maureen Kathleen Donovan [1936] Director/Manager; Michael John Donovan [1950] Director/Manager; John Edward Anthony Olney [1947] Director/Manager

Dormole Limited
Incorporated: 10 January 1974 *Employees:* 934
Net Worth: £94,078,000 *Total Assets:* £130,002,000
Registered Office: Long Reach, Galleon Boulevard, Crossways Business Park, Dartford, Kent, DA2 6QE
Activities: Activities of head offices
Officers: Robert David Rowe, Secretary; Barry Gordon Karl Brice [1948] Director/Solicitor; John Nicholas Christie [1942] Director/Chartered Accountant; Stephen John Clemson [1951] Director; Andrew James Thomas Strong [1955] Director; Timothy John Strong [1958] Director; John Randall Charles Twallin [1933] Director

Double A Group Services Limited
Incorporated: 26 March 2001
Previous: U2013 Limited
Net Worth: £11,339,020 *Total Assets:* £18,480,432
Registered Office: The Hive, Camrose Avenue, London, HA8 6AG
Activities: Operation of sports facilities
Parent: Double A Group Ltd
Officers: Mahendra Patel, Secretary; Anthony Andrew Kleanthous [1966] Director

Dovestone Estates Limited
Incorporated: 17 October 1963 *Employees:* 67
Net Worth: £3,749,951 *Total Assets:* £5,846,746
Registered Office: Kenton House, 666 Kenton Road, Harrow, Middlesex, HA3 9QN
Activities: Medical nursing home activities
Shareholders: Renee Rose Segal; Stanley Irving Segal
Officers: Debra Michelle Messulam, Secretary; Howard Benson Segal [1966] Director/Nursing Home Operator; Rene Rose Segal [1944] Director; Stanley Irving Segal [1940] Director/Nursing Home Proprietor

Dow Properties Limited
Incorporated: 13 November 1987 *Employees:* 6
Net Worth: £20,748,246 *Total Assets:* £44,860,032
Registered Office: 195 Hale Lane, Edgware, Middlesex, HA8 9QN
Activities: Buying and selling of own real estate
Shareholders: Kazi Mohammed Morad Arefin; Dimitra Arefin
Officers: Dr Kazi Mohammed Morad Arefin, Secretary; Dimitra Arefin [1942] Director

DP Poland PLC
Incorporated: 9 June 2010 *Employees:* 96
Net Worth: £14,497,231 *Total Assets:* £16,556,290
Registered Office: Elder House, St Georges Business Park, 207 Brooklands Road, Weybridge, Surrey, KT13 0TS
Activities: Licenced restaurants
Officers: Patrick Bodenham, Secretary; Nicholas John Donaldson [1953] Director; Dr Generald William Ford [1957] Director [American]; Maciej Adam Jania [1972] Director [Polish]; Christopher Humphrey Robertson Moore [1959] Director; Robert Nicholas Lutwyche Morrish [1949] Director/Accountant; Peter John Edward Shaw [1960] Director

DPA Support Services Limited
Incorporated: 17 September 1996
Net Worth Deficit: £1,544,000 *Total Assets:* £12,091,000
Registered Office: Astral House, Imperial Way, Watford, Herts, WD24 4WW
Activities: Activities of head offices
Parent: DPASS Holdings Limited
Officers: Ian David Hudson [1964] Director/Chartered Accountant; Rory John Murphy [1969] Director/Chartered Surveyor

DPSK Limited
Incorporated: 28 March 2014 *Employees:* 97
Net Worth: £106,917,944 *Total Assets:* £160,401,344
Registered Office: Fortune House, Crabtree Office Village, Eversley Way, Egham, Surrey, TW20 8RY
Activities: Other food services
Officers: Gurprit Dhaliwal [1982] Director; Surinderjit Singh Kandola [1965] Director

Drapers' Multi-Academy Trust
Incorporated: 30 September 2009 *Employees:* 311
Net Worth: £35,643,000 *Total Assets:* £40,456,000
Registered Office: Drapers' Academy, Settle Road, Harold Hill, Romford, Essex, RM3 9XR
Activities: Primary education
Officers: Philip Norman, Secretary; Patrick Beddows [1961] Director/Partner, Land Management; Professor Alison Mary Blunt [1969] Director/Professor of Geography; Professor Virginia Grace Davis [1958] Director/Professor of Medieval History [Irish]; Stephen Peter Foakes [1950] Director/Retired; Gillian Kemp [1972] Director of Education; Jonathan David Morgan [1972] Director/Academic Registrar and Council Secretary; Timothy Gerard Orchard [1963] Director; Professor Kim Mary Piper [1967] Director/Professor of Pathology; Professor Morag Elizabeth Shiach [1958] Director/Professor; David Michael Sumner [1971] Finance Director

Drayton Kirk Ltd
Incorporated: 11 March 2016
Net Worth: £27,291 *Total Assets:* £5,125,571
Registered Office: 92-98 Lower Mortlake Road, Richmond, Surrey, TW9 2JG
Activities: Other letting and operating of own or leased real estate
Major Shareholder: Liasos Antonakis Lianos
Officers: Liasos Antonakis Lianos [1956] Director/Architect

Drift Bridge Garage Limited
Incorporated: 15 August 1961 *Employees:* 308
Net Worth: £6,134,811 *Total Assets:* £38,710,368
Registered Office: Drift Bridge Garage, Reigate Road, Epsom, Surrey, KT17 3LA
Activities: Sale of new cars and light motor vehicles
Parent: Drift Bridge Group Holdings Limited
Officers: Edwin John Frost [1939] Director/Garage Proprietor; Michael Vernon Frost [1939] Director/Garage Proprietor

DS (Holdings) 2 Limited
Incorporated: 28 September 2006
Previous: Office Depot (Holdings) 2 Limited
Net Worth Deficit: £236,439,968 *Total Assets:* £467,195,776
Registered Office: Allen House, 1 Westmead Road, Sutton, Surrey, SM1 4LA
Activities: Activities of head offices
Major Shareholder: Chi Wai Tammy Lam
Officers: Stewart Roland Hussey [1958] Director

DS (Holdings) 3 Limited
Incorporated: 20 December 2007
Previous: Office Depot (Holdings) 3 Limited
Net Worth: £700,200,189,952 *Total Assets:* £700,200,189,952
Registered Office: Allem House, 1 Westmead Road, Sutton, Surrey, SM1 4LA
Activities: Activities of head offices
Parent: Office Depot (Holdings) 2 Limited
Officers: Stewart Roland Hussey [1958] Director

DSJ Homes Limited
Incorporated: 6 November 2003
Net Worth: £3,035,303 *Total Assets:* £17,235,500
Registered Office: 555-557 Cranbrook Road, Gants Hill, Ilford, Essex, IG2 6HE
Activities: Buying and selling of own real estate
Shareholders: Jasbir Singh Jhumat; Pardeep Singh Jhumat
Officers: Pardeep Singh Jhumat, Secretary; Jasbir Singh Jhumat [1968] Director; Pardeep Singh Jhumat [1971] Director

DST Global Solutions (Realty) Limited
Incorporated: 24 May 2010 *Employees:* 1
Net Worth: £36,528,000 *Total Assets:* £37,835,000
Registered Office: DST House, St Marks Hill, Surbiton, Surrey, KT6 4QD
Activities: Buying and selling of own real estate
Parent: DST Process Solutions Limited
Officers: Patrick John Louis Pedonti [1951] Director [American]

DST Process Solutions Limited
Incorporated: 1 June 2010 *Employees:* 35
Net Worth: £109,323,000 *Total Assets:* £129,104,000
Registered Office: DST House, St Mark's Hill, Surbiton, Surrey, KT6 4QD
Activities: Information technology consultancy activities
Parent: DSTI Holdings Limited
Officers: Patrick John Louis Pedonti [1951] Director [American]

DSTI Group LLP
Incorporated: 11 August 2004
Net Worth: £277,791,008 *Total Assets:* £284,953,984
Registered Office: DST House, St Marks Hill, Surbiton, Surrey, KT6 4QD

DSTI Holdings Limited
Incorporated: 23 August 2004 *Employees:* 116
Net Worth: £174,487,008 *Total Assets:* £305,128,992
Registered Office: DST House, St Marks Hill, Surbiton, Surrey, KT6 4QD
Activities: Activities of head offices
Officers: Patrick John Louis Pedonti [1961] Director [American]; William Slattery [1955] Director [Irish]

DTW (Holdings) Limited
Incorporated: 18 November 2014 *Employees:* 100
Net Worth: £2,485,221 *Total Assets:* £10,659,219
Registered Office: Arctic House, 8 Bolters Lane, Banstead, Surrey, SM7 2AR
Activities: Tour operator activities
Shareholder: Mark Leaney
Officers: Mark Leaney, Secretary; Mark Leaney [1951] Director; Clive Lindsay Stacey [1953] Director

Dudley Properties Limited
Incorporated: 23 April 2004
Net Worth: £3,363,750 *Total Assets:* £6,918,667
Registered Office: 167 Turners Hill, Cheshunt, Herts, EN8 9BH
Activities: Other letting and operating of own or leased real estate
Shareholders: Christopher Sean Wickman Dudley; Katie Jane Dudley
Officers: Katie Jane Dudley, Secretary/Designer; Christopher Sean Wickman Dudley [1968] Director/Consultant Engineer; Katie Jane Dudley [1970] Director/Designer

M.E. Duffell Limited
Incorporated: 15 December 1972 *Employees:* 97
Net Worth: £1,636,334 *Total Assets:* £6,537,537
Registered Office: Unit 3 Commerce Park, 19 Commerce Way, Croydon, Surrey, CR0 4YL
Activities: Wholesale of hardware, plumbing and heating equipment and supplies
Shareholders: Natasha Bartholomew; Alex Kuness; James Craig Kuness
Officers: Karen Kuness, Secretary; Natasha Bartholomew [1973] Managing Director; Alexander Kuness [1980] Director; James Craig Kuness [1982] Director; Karen Kuness [1954] Director/Secretary; Patrick Kuness [1955] Director/Manager

Duke Street Church (Richmond-upon-Thames)
Incorporated: 7 January 2010 *Employees:* 13
Net Worth: £6,464,784 *Total Assets:* £7,457,286
Registered Office: Duke Street Church, Duke Street, Richmond, Surrey, TW9 1DH
Activities: Activities of religious organisations
Officers: Ali Azzopardi [1943] Director/Retired; Ivan Baird [1968] Director/Teacher; Gareth Batten [1982] Director/Project Manager; Simon Buss [1979] Director/Architect; Paul Chambers [1975] Project Director; Lisa Coleridge [1947] Director; Alex Forbes [1980] Director/Civil Servant; Philip Chay Suang Long [1965] Director/Head of Risk; Jonathan Peter Niblett [1967] Director/Chartered Accountant; John Leith Samuel [1955] Director/Minister of Religion; David Joseph Shafik [1942] Director/Quantity Surveyor; John Taylor [1953] Director/Bursar; Johan Van Wijgerden [1974] Director/Health Professional [Dutch]; Angie Vincent [1970] Nursing Director

Duncan Lewis Solicitors Ltd
Incorporated: 23 February 1999 *Employees:* 462
Previous: Duncan Lewis (Solicitors) Limited
Net Worth: £6,761,083 *Total Assets:* £21,194,938
Registered Office: Spencer House, 29 Grove Hill Road, Harrow on the Hill, Harrow, Middlesex, HA1 3BN
Activities: Solicitors
Major Shareholder: Amarpal Singh Gupta
Officers: Vinia Majaba, Secretary; Bernadette Adusei [1980] Director/Solicitor; Vanketaramana Appalakondiah [1950] Director/Solicitor; Bahar Ata [1980] Director/Chartered Legal Executive; Manjinder Kaur Atwal [1982] Director/Solicitor; Ahmed Hassan Aydeed [1987] Director/Solicitor; Tamana Aziz [1976] Director/Solicitor; Lail Bhunndoo [1969] Director/Solicitor; Jason Charles Bruce [1978] Director/Solicitor; Rachel Caswell [1981] Director/Solicitor; Bernadette Chikwe [1971] Director/Solicitor; Dianne Cowie [1976] Director/Solicitor; Nicholas de Freitas [1981] Director/Solicitor; Sobashni de Silva [1973] Director/Solicitor; James de Vere Moss [1974] Director/Solicitor; Hardeep Singh Dhaliwal [1970] Director/Solicitor; Sheena Donlon [1984] Director/Solicitor; Sara Dowie [1979] Director/Solicitor; Zofia Eugenia Duszynska [1964] Director/Solicitor; Sophie Vivienne Fretten [1983] Director/Solicitor; Richard Gray [1968] Director/Solicitor; Amarpal Singh Gupta [1973] Director/Solicitor; Forida Hakim [1978] Director/Solicitor; Trevor James Hatton [1974] Director/Solicitor; David Mark Head [1963] Director/Solicitor; Toufique Hossain [1979] Director/Solicitor; Heather Iqbal Rayner [1972] Director/Solicitor; Rubin Italia [1971] Director/Solicitor; Nina Joshi [1971] Director/Solicitor; Meeta Kumari [1977] Director/Solicitor; Julie Margaret Leslie [1961] Director/Solicitor; Alia Lewis [1980] Director/Solicitor; Ravi Mahey [1978] Director/Solicitor; Abbid Majeed [1983] Director/Solicitor; Jenna McKinney [1978] Director/Solicitor; Emine Mehmet [1976] Director/Solicitor; Gabor Nagy [1979] Director/Solicitor; Adeeba Naseem [1978] Director/Solicitor; Anthony Okumah [1977] Director/Solicitor; Chinedu Orogbu [1974] Director/Solicitor; James Richard Packer [1969] Director/Solicitor; Krina Parmar [1983] Director; Alexander Peebles [1980] Director/Solicitor; Satya Sridhar Ponnada [1969] Director/IT Manager; Syed Talha Hamad Rafique [1940] Director/Solicitor; Vicash Ramkissoon [1974] Director/Solicitor; Caroline Roche [1984] Director/Solicitor; Sangita Shah [1971] Director/Solicitor; Subbiah Kandasamy Sivapunniyam [1960] Director/Solicitor [Indian]; Vinita Templeton [1975] Director/Solicitor; Rebecca Thomas [1965] Director/Solicitor; Randolph Anthony Thompson [1963] Director/Solicitor; Kathy Katholiki Walker [1977] Director/Solicitor; Rohena Wallace [1983] Director/Solicitor; Lorick Winarskie [1965] Director/Solicitor; Ayan Yalchin [1974] Director/Solicitor

Dunkeld Trading Limited
Incorporated: 24 February 2011
Net Worth: £7,945,618 *Total Assets:* £7,986,018
Registered Office: Elder House, St Georges Business Park, 207 Brooklands Road, Weybridge, Surrey, KT13 0TS
Activities: Other service activities n.e.c.
Officers: Eliot Charles Kaye, Secretary; Eliot Charles Kaye [1974] Director; Michael Alfred Litman [1945] Director; Terence Roberts [1955] Director/Project Coordinator

Dunlop International Europe Limited
Incorporated: 7 October 1963 *Employees:* 75
Previous: Dunlop Slazenger International Limited
Net Worth Deficit: £91,195,000 *Total Assets:* £19,261,000
Registered Office: Thorncroft Manor, Thorncroft Drive, Leatherhead, Surrey, KT22 8JB
Activities: Manufacture of sports goods
Parent: Dunlop International Group Limited
Officers: Seiichi Izawa, Secretary; Masahiro Asahino [1963] Director/Chief Executive [Japanese]; Yasutaka Doko [1970] Director [Japanese]; Yasuo Watanabe [1962] Director/General Manager [Japanese]

Dunlop International Group Limited
Incorporated: 4 September 1995 *Employees:* 4
Previous: Dunlop Slazenger Group Limited
Net Worth: £24,784,000 *Total Assets:* £91,293,000
Registered Office: Thorncroft Manor, Thorncroft Drive, Dorking Road, Leatherhead, Surrey, KT22 8JB
Activities: Non-trading company
Parent: Dunlop International Group Holdings Limited
Officers: Tetsuo Shimizu, Secretary; Masahiro Asahino [1963] Director/Chief Executive Officer [Japanese]; Takuya Inabetsu [1967] Director/General Manager [Japanese]; Hidekazu Nishiguchi [1960] Director [Japanese]; Yasuo Watanabe [1962] Director/General Manager [Japanese]

Dunlop International Holdings Limited
Incorporated: 20 December 1995
Previous: Dunlop Slazenger Holdings Limited
Net Worth: £7,801,000 *Total Assets:* £7,801,000
Registered Office: Thorncroft Manor, Thorncroft Drive, Dorking Road, Leatherhead, Surrey, KT22 8JB
Activities: Activities of head offices
Parent: Dunlop International Group Limited
Officers: Tetsuo Shimizu, Secretary; Takuya Inabetsu [1967] Director/General Manager [Japanese]; Yasuo Watanabe [1962] Director/General Manager [Japanese]

J P Dunn Construction Limited
Incorporated: 23 February 1999 *Employees:* 31
Net Worth: £7,764,588 *Total Assets:* £14,029,537
Registered Office: 5 AC Court, High Street, Thames Ditton, Surrey, KT7 0SR
Activities: Construction of commercial buildings
Officers: Orla Mary Dunn, Secretary; Jonathan Paul Dunn [1961] Director; Nicholas Jacks [1975] Pre Contracts Director; Kevin Patrick McSweeney [1967] Contracts Director; Yllka Uruci [1976] Surveying Director

Dunwoody Airline Services Limited
Incorporated: 19 June 1979 *Employees:* 264
Net Worth: £3,113,117 *Total Assets:* £8,223,528
Registered Office: Building 552, Shoreham Road East, London Heathrow Airport, Hounslow, Middlesex, TW6 3UA
Activities: Freight air transport
Officers: Steven Greenhalgh, Secretary/Director; John Andrew Batten [1960] Director/CEO for WFS Cargo EMEAA; Lewis Ian Girdwood [1967] Director/CFO for IAG Cargo; Steven Greenhalgh [1974] Director/Secretary; Lynn Fiona McClelland [1968] Director of Operations IAG; Patrick Ian Roberts [1950] Director

Duplo International Limited
Incorporated: 31 January 2006 *Employees:* 122
Previous: Duplo International Group Limited
Net Worth: £10,486,764 *Total Assets:* £19,697,648
Registered Office: Automated Precision House, Hamm Moor Lane, Addlestone, Surrey, KT15 2SD
Activities: Repair of machinery
Officers: Glyn Adrian Nutting, Secretary/Director; Alan David John Greenhalgh [1954] Director; Philip William Greenhalgh [1956] Director; Robin David Vincent Greenhalgh [1962] Director; Glyn Adrian Nutting [1959] Director; Judith Sally Thomson [1969] HR Director

Durbin PLC
Incorporated: 4 September 1998 *Employees:* 121
Net Worth: £10,044,928 *Total Assets:* £16,542,647
Registered Office: Durbin House, Unit 5 Swallowfield Way, Hayes, Middlesex, UB3 1DQ
Activities: Wholesale of pharmaceutical goods
Parent: Durbin Group PLC
Officers: Carmen Gleen, Secretary/Director; Carmen Gleen [1947] Director; Leslie Morgan [1954] Director/Pharmacist

Gordon Durham & Co.Limited
Incorporated: 23 May 1936
Net Worth: £5,852,000 *Total Assets:* £6,566,000
Registered Office: Astral House, Imperial Way, Watford, Herts, WD24 4WW
Activities: Construction of commercial buildings
Parent: Gordon Durham Holdings Limited
Officers: Charistopher Carl Brennan [1969] Director/Accountant; Ruth Elizabeth Tilbrook [1968] Director/Accountant

Durkan Estates Limited
Incorporated: 19 May 1987 *Employees:* 9
Net Worth: £12,984,717 *Total Assets:* £72,139,800
Registered Office: 4 Elstree Gate, Elstree Way, Borehamwood, Herts, WD6 1JD
Activities: Development of building projects
Officers: Ronan Patrick Murphy, Secretary; Daniel Gerard Durkan [1964] Director - Sales [Irish]; Ronan Patrick Murphy [1969] Director/Chartered Accountant [Irish]

Durkan Holdings Limited
Incorporated: 9 June 1977 *Employees:* 175
Net Worth: £58,871,960 *Total Assets:* £142,434,064
Registered Office: 4 Elstree Gate, Elstree Way, Borehamwood, Herts, WD6 1JD
Activities: Development of building projects
Officers: Ronan Patrick Murphy, Secretary; Daniel Gerard Durkan [1964] Director/Chief Executive [Irish]; Ronan Patrick Murphy [1969] Director/Chartered Accountant [Irish]

Durkan Limited
Incorporated: 15 December 1970 *Employees:* 171
Net Worth: £37,842,612 *Total Assets:* £81,418,736
Registered Office: 4 Elstree Gate, Elstree Way, Borehamwood, Herts, WD6 1JD
Activities: Development of building projects
Officers: Ronan Patrick Murphy, Secretary; James Philip Briggs [1960] Managing Director; Ian Philip Cresswell [1965] Health & Safety Director; Daniel Gerard Durkan [1964] Director/Chief Executive [Irish]; Dean Martin [1968] Construction Director; Ronan Patrick Murphy [1969] Director/Chartered Accountant [Irish]; Shane Rooney [1965] Commercial Director [Irish]; Jason Russell Mark Smith [1978] Technical Director

Durkin and Sons Limited
Incorporated: 6 June 1983 *Employees:* 71
Net Worth: £7,758,808 *Total Assets:* £9,601,057
Registered Office: Suite 10, Second Floor, Alperton House, Bridgewater Road, Wembley, Middlesex, HA0 1EH
Activities: Construction of other civil engineering projects n.e.c.
Major Shareholder: Michael Edward Durkin
Officers: Edward Durkin, Secretary; Edward Durkin [1956] Director/Company Secretary; Michael Durkin [1954] Director; Monica Durkin [1935] Director [Irish]

DW Windsor Group Limited
Incorporated: 16 January 2014 *Employees:* 126
Net Worth: £6,368,523 *Total Assets:* £10,463,567
Registered Office: DW Windsor, Pindar Road, Hoddesdon, Herts, EN11 0DX
Activities: Other business support service activities n.e.c.
Shareholders: Nikola Susan Thompson; Thomas Walter David Webster
Officers: Terence Albert Dean [1959] Director; Nikola Susan Thompson [1962] Director; Thomas Walter David Webster [1961] Director

Dwellcourt Limited
Incorporated: 17 August 1984 *Employees:* 188
Net Worth: £21,016,544 *Total Assets:* £32,484,010
Registered Office: Downs Farm, Reigate Road, Ewell, Surrey, KT17 3BY
Activities: Activities of head offices
Major Shareholder: Thomas Albert Hilliard
Officers: Jeffrey Thomas Hilliard, Secretary; James Michael Bowry [1987] Finance Director; Jeffrey Thomas Hilliard [1964] Development Director; Douglas William McClelland [1949] Director; Terry Kirk Sims [1971] Director; Steven John Turnbull [1976] Director

Dynama Solutions Ltd
Incorporated: 1 November 2016 *Employees:* 31
Net Worth: £830,000 *Total Assets:* £31,952,000
Registered Office: 2nd Floor, 1 Church Road, Richmond, Surrey, TW9 2QE
Activities: Other business support service activities n.e.c.
Parent: Allocate Bidco Limited
Officers: Jonathan James Harston [1976] Director/Chief Financial Officer; Charles George Munro [1975] Director/Accountant; Nicholas Stephen Wilson [1971] Director/Chief Executive Officer

E & J Properties Limited
Incorporated: 25 February 2016 *Employees:* 2
Net Worth: £23,081,994 *Total Assets:* £26,794,584
Registered Office: Treviot House, 186-192 High Road, Ilford, Essex, IG1 1LR
Activities: Renting and operating of Housing Association real estate
Shareholders: Intertrust Trustee 2 (Guernsey) Ltd as Trustee for The Heaven Scent QNUPS; Intertrust Trustee 2 (Guernsey) Ltd as Trustee for The Kleg QNUPS
Officers: Barry Albert Elvidge [1949] Director; Howard Victor Jones [1950] Director

E P I Limited
Incorporated: 11 June 2002 *Employees:* 21
Net Worth: £9,783,353 *Total Assets:* £10,965,568
Registered Office: 25 High Street, Cobham, Surrey, KT11 3DH
Activities: Other professional, scientific and technical activities n.e.c.
Parent: EPI Group Holdings Ltd
Officers: Richard Bradley, Secretary; Richard Bradley [1981] Director; Rupert James Brown [1983] Director; Anthony Dickin [1970] Director; Dr Mark Andrew Enfield [1960] Director; Ian Michael Langley [1962] Director; Andrew Stuart James Smart [1962] Land Director; Richard Thompson [1976] Director

E Y C Limited
Incorporated: 17 October 2003 *Employees:* 64
Net Worth Deficit: £665,631 *Total Assets:* £13,492,361
Registered Office: Ambassador House, Paradise Road, Richmond, Surrey, TW9 1SQ
Activities: Data processing, hosting and related activities
Officers: Andrew Young, Secretary; Pallab Kumar Chatterjee [1950] Managing Director [American]; Mathilde Millies-Lacroix [1976] Director/Lawyer [French]

E-Nova Healthcare Limited
Incorporated: 16 November 2005 *Employees:* 40
Net Worth: £1,006,329 *Total Assets:* £6,475,407
Registered Office: Congress House, 14 Lyon Road, Harrow, Middlesex, HA1 2EN
Activities: Other business support service activities n.e.c.
Shareholders: Milan Ashwin Kumar Patel; Prashant Ashwin Kumar Patel
Officers: Milan Ashwin Kumar Patel, Secretary/Pharmacy HCare; Milan Ashwin Kumar Patel [1975] Director/Pharmacy HCare; Prashant Ashwin Kumar Patel [1976] Director/Pharmacy HCare

E.D.S. Holdings Limited
Incorporated: 14 December 1993 *Employees:* 3
Net Worth: £6,074,955 *Total Assets:* £6,878,218
Registered Office: Centrum House, 36 Station Road, Egham, Surrey, TW20 9LF
Activities: Other letting and operating of own or leased real estate
Major Shareholder: Eric Christopher Edwards
Officers: Ryan Edwards, Secretary; Michaela Christian [1965] Director; Eric Christopher Edwards [1949] Director; Greg Edwards [1978] Director; Ryan Edwards [1976] Director

E.F.G. Housewares Limited
Incorporated: 13 March 1998 *Employees:* 78
Net Worth: £8,588,254 *Total Assets:* £13,650,907
Registered Office: 55 High Street, Hoddesdon, Herts, EN11 8TQ
Activities: Wholesale of china and glassware and cleaning materials
Parent: Enfield Fancy Goods Limited
Officers: Alan Brian Shipton, Secretary/Wholesaler; Alan Brian Shipton [1938] Director/Wholesaler; Daren Shipton [1968] Director/Manager; Mark William Shipton [1973] Director/Manager; Trevor Roderick Shipton [1943] Director/Wholesaler

E.F.R. Travel Limited
Incorporated: 16 May 2002 *Employees:* 47
Net Worth: £4,134,190 *Total Assets:* £11,199,832
Registered Office: 2nd Floor, Nucleus House, 2 Lower Mortlake Road, Richmond, Surrey, TW9 2JA
Activities: Travel agency activities
Shareholders: Edward Richard Rom; Melanie Ruth Rom
Officers: Melanie Ruth Rom, Secretary; John Albert McEwan [1946] Director; Marlene Anne Newman [1941] Director; Sydney Newman [1938] Director; Edward Richard Rom [1963] Director

E.G.T. Bridging Finance Limited
Incorporated: 1 September 1998 *Employees:* 3
Net Worth: £12,019 *Total Assets:* £12,921,594
Registered Office: 35 Glanleam Road, Stanmore, Middlesex, HA7 4NW
Activities: Credit granting by non-deposit taking finance houses and other specialist consumer credit grantors
Parent: E.G.T. Finance Limited
Officers: Dana Houri [1997] Director; Leanne Houri [1996] Director/Trainee; Shaoul Houri [1957] Director; Talia Houri [1990] Director/Teacher

E.G.T. Finance Limited
Incorporated: 27 January 1993 *Employees:* 5
Net Worth: £5,171,496 *Total Assets:* £17,331,720
Registered Office: 35 Glanleam Road, Stanmore, Middlesex, HA7 4NW
Activities: Other credit granting n.e.c.
Shareholder: Shaoul Houri
Officers: Shaoul Houri [1957] Director

E.S. Pipelines Limited
Incorporated: 10 August 1999 *Employees:* 55
Net Worth: £71,257,000 *Total Assets:* £223,075,008
Registered Office: 1st Floor, Bluebird House, Mole Business Park, Leatherhead, Surrey, KT22 7BA
Activities: Transport via pipeline
Parent: ESPUG Finance Limited
Officers: Thomas William Butler [1959] Finance Director [Irish]; Nicholas John Clark [1960] Director; Anna Louise Dellis [1973] Director/Investment Executive; Paul Miles [1971] Director/Chief Financial Officer; Kevin O'Connor [1976] Director/Chief Executive Officer; Sebastian Schwengber [1979] Director/Investment Professional [German]; Victoria Caroline Spiers [1969] Director/Manager; Stuart Peter Williams [1965] Operations Director

E2X Limited
Incorporated: 26 July 2001 *Employees:* 46
Net Worth: £7,090,918 *Total Assets:* £8,423,975
Registered Office: 137 Ireton Avenue, Walton on Thames, Surrey, KT12 1EN
Activities: Business and domestic software development
Shareholders: Christine Anne Spalding; James Hugh Ferguson Spalding
Officers: Christine Anne Spalding, Secretary; James Hugh Ferguson Spalding, Secretary/Director; James Hugh Ferguson Spalding [1966] Director

E92 Plus Limited
Incorporated: 12 September 1989 *Employees:* 52
Net Worth: £4,090,337 *Total Assets:* £17,296,402
Registered Office: Unit C & Unit D, Argent Court, Hook Rise South, Surbiton, Surrey, KT6 7NL
Activities: Wholesale of computers, computer peripheral equipment and software
Officers: Mukesh Kumar Gupta, Secretary; Jeremy Stuart Gascoine [1967] Director/Accountant; Mukesh Kumar Gupta [1965] Director

EA Consulting Group Ltd
Incorporated: 26 January 1998 *Employees:* 34
Net Worth: £2,204,388 *Total Assets:* £6,840,511
Registered Office: 2 Oriel Court, 106 The Green, Twickenham, Middlesex, TW2 5AG
Activities: Management consultancy activities other than financial management
Major Shareholder: Stephen Gregory Robson
Officers: Jon Murphy [1959] Director; Cheryl Denise Robson [1957] Director/Publisher; Stephen Gregory Robson [1956] Director/Management Consultant

EACG Holdings Limited
Incorporated: 17 March 2010 *Employees:* 34
Net Worth: £1,616,774 *Total Assets:* £6,252,897
Registered Office: 2 Oriel Court, 106 The Green, Twickenham, Middlesex, TW2 5AG
Activities: Activities of other holding companies n.e.c.
Major Shareholder: Stephen Gregory Robson
Officers: Jon Murphy [1959] Director; Cheryl Denise Robson [1957] Director/Publisher [Australian]; Stephen Gregory Robson [1956] Director/Management Consultant

Eagle 456 Limited
Incorporated: 18 April 2000 *Employees:* 3
Net Worth: £14,599,464 *Total Assets:* £37,521,620
Registered Office: 22 Barn Rise, Wembley, Middlesex, HA9 9NQ
Activities: Other letting and operating of own or leased real estate
Parent: Aquila House Property Limited
Officers: Paul Gary Hirst, Secretary/Director; Anthony David Chambers [1955] Director; Daniel Freedman [1971] Director/Lawyer; Paul Gary Hirst [1961] Director

Ealing Community Transport
Incorporated: 1 April 2010 *Employees:* 198
Net Worth: £3,655,818 *Total Assets:* £5,196,280
Registered Office: Greenford Depot, Greenford Road, Greenford, Middlesex, UB6 9AP
Activities: Other passenger land transport
Officers: Paul Andrew Creasey [1965] Director/Chartered Accountant; Sonia Krishna [1974] Director/Chemical Engineer; Patrick O'Keeffe [1951] Director/Retired [Irish]; Christian Tilleray [1971] Director/Freelance Consultant; David Tinnion [1980] Director/Operations Manager; Timothy John Harold West [1969] Director/Editor

Earlseat Wind Farm Ltd
Incorporated: 9 April 2009
Net Worth: £1,089,000 *Total Assets:* £18,545,000
Registered Office: Beaufort Court, Egg Farm Lane, Kings Langley, Herts, WD4 8LR
Activities: Production of electricity
Parent: European Investments (Earlseat) Limited
Officers: Dominic James Hearth, Secretary; Steven William Hughes [1972] Generation and Asset Management Director; Fraser Stephen Merry [1968] Director/Chartered Surveyor; Mitesh Raj Patel [1982] Director/Group Financial Controller

Early Learning Centre Limited
Incorporated: 25 March 1909 *Employees:* 24
Net Worth Deficit: £114,600,000 *Total Assets:* £119,100,000
Registered Office: Cherry Tree Road, Watford, Herts, WD24 6SH
Activities: Other retail sale of new goods in specialised stores (not commercial art galleries and opticians)
Parent: Early Learning Holdings Limited
Officers: Lynne Samatha Medini, Secretary; Kirsty Rowena Homer [1974] HR Director; William Glyn Lawrence Hughes [1976] Director/Chief Financial Officer; Mark Newton-Jones [1967] Director; Kevin Jonathan Rusling [1977] Managing Director, International

Early Learning Holdings Limited
Incorporated: 29 March 2001
Net Worth Deficit: £4,800,000 *Total Assets:* £13,900,000
Registered Office: Cherry Tree Road, Watford, Herts, WD24 6SH
Activities: Non-trading company
Parent: Chelsea Stores Holdings Limited
Officers: Lynne Samatha Medini, Secretary; Kirsty Rowena Homer [1974] HR Director; Daniel Juckes [1982] Director/Chartered Accountant

Earndrive Limited
Incorporated: 1 October 2003 *Employees:* 2
Net Worth: £1,902,948 *Total Assets:* £7,961,032
Registered Office: 102 Weston Drive, Stanmore, Middlesex, HA7 2EN
Activities: Other letting and operating of own or leased real estate
Officers: Ansuya Shah, Secretary; Navinchandra Keshavlal Shah [1949] Director/Businessman

Earth-I Ltd
Incorporated: 29 April 2013 *Employees:* 18
Previous: Satellite Resources Limited
Net Worth: £4,792,689 *Total Assets:* £5,364,741
Registered Office: Northside House, 69 Tweedy Road, Bromley, Kent, BR1 3WA
Activities: Other information service activities n.e.c.
Shareholders: Richard Timothy Blain; Hassan Abdulhadi Taher
Officers: Richard Timothy Blain [1969] Director; Joseph Charles French [1949] Consultant and Director; Archibald Frederick Smith [1949] Director/Company Executive; Alexander James Herbert Stott [1962] Director; Hassan Abdulhadi Taher [1987] Director/Entrepreneur [Saudi Arabian]

East Barnet School
Incorporated: 4 March 2011 *Employees:* 173
Net Worth: £31,794,992 *Total Assets:* £33,897,964
Registered Office: East Barnet School, 5 Chestnut Grove, Barnet, Herts, EN4 8PU
Activities: General secondary education
Officers: Susan Waters, Secretary; Deborah Ann Brazier [1967] Director/Accountant; Debbie Jane Cuthbert [1951] Director/Educational Consultant; Theodoulos Lakis Diamandis [1971] Director/Learning & Development Manager; Stuart Morrison Gates [1959] Director/Self Employed, Sole Trader; Scott Michael Harrison [1949] Director/Education Consultant; Major John Bernard Ireton [1957] Director/Head of Department Veolia Water Central; Susan Patricia McDonald [1968] Charity Director; Nicholas John Mottershead [1958] Director/Dubbing Mixer; Caroline Roncarati [1971] Director/Teacher; Joanna Ray Tambourides [1948] Director/Councillor and P.A; Claire Elizabeth Thomas [1963] Deputy Director of Charity; Timothy John Beech Williamson [1960] Director/Civil Servant; Mariam Zaman [1989] Director/Teacher; Ingrid Zanchetta [1972] Director/Programme Development Manager [Italian]

East Central Limited
Incorporated: 8 September 1999 *Employees:* 2
Net Worth: £3,268,289 *Total Assets:* £6,043,423
Registered Office: York House, Empire Way, Wembley, Middlesex, HA9 0FQ
Activities: Other letting and operating of own or leased real estate
Parent: Multi Commerce International Limited
Officers: Stephen Ian Greenman, Secretary/Director; Stephen Ian Greenman [1946] Director; Jerry Shatzkes [1945] Director [American/British]

East Langford Solar Limited
Incorporated: 20 April 2011
Net Worth Deficit: £1,851,968 *Total Assets:* £10,998,135
Registered Office: Beaufort Court, Egg Farm Lane, off Station Road, Kings Langley, Herts, WD4 8LR
Activities: Production of electricity
Parent: European Investments (Cornwall) Limited
Officers: Dominic Hearth, Secretary; Steven William Hughes [1972] Global Support Services Director, UK&I - Commercial; Mitesh Raj Patel [1982] Director/Chartered Accountant; Tracy Jane Scott [1976] Director/Delivery Project Manager; Mark Christopher Wayment [1958] Director

East Mediterranean Trading Limited
Incorporated: 21 October 1998
Net Worth: £11,175,077 *Total Assets:* £11,212,367
Registered Office: Velocity V1, Brooklands Drive, Weybridge, Surrey, KT13 0SL
Activities: Financial intermediation not elsewhere classified
Officers: Dena Michelle L O'Bue, Secretary; Sanem Bilgin [1965] Director, Risk Investors Group-EMEA, TSF [Turkish]; Rajesh Kumar Daruka [1980] Director - Global Trade Credit Insurance [Indian]; Marina Haidar Chede Carton [1985] Director/Senior Trader, Risk Investors Group [Brazilian]; Michael Joseph Wilkins [1967] Director/Head of European Bank Relation

Eastbury Park (Holdings) Limited
Incorporated: 7 June 2006
Net Worth Deficit: £36,378,000 *Total Assets:* £181,107,008
Registered Office: 8 White Oak Square, London Road, Swanley, Kent, BR8 7AG
Activities: Activities of head offices
Shareholders: Infrared Infrastructure Yield Holdings Limited; Infrastructure Investments Holdings Limited
Officers: Ross William Driver [1981] Director; Mark Christopher Wayment [1958] Director/Investment Banker

Eastbury Park Limited
Incorporated: 7 June 2006
Net Worth Deficit: £36,378,000 *Total Assets:* £181,107,008
Registered Office: 8 White Oak Square, London Road, Swanley, Kent, BR8 7AG
Activities: Defence activities
Parent: Eastbury Park (Holdings) Limited
Officers: Ross William Driver [1981] Director; Mark Christopher Wayment [1958] Director/Investment Banker

Easyfairs UK Limited
Incorporated: 9 March 2004 *Employees:* 82
Net Worth Deficit: £4,376,004 *Total Assets:* £19,217,066
Registered Office: Second Floor, Regal House, 70 London Road, Twickenham, Middlesex, TW1 3QS
Activities: Other business support service activities n.e.c.
Parent: Easyfairs NV
Officers: Matthew Edward Benyon [1973] Director; Eric Patrick Christian Ettenne Everard [1964] Director [Belgian]

Easymix Concrete UK Ltd
Incorporated: 1 August 2005 *Employees:* 25
Net Worth: £1,704,071 *Total Assets:* £5,289,799
Registered Office: Unit 12 Enterprise Close, Croydon, Surrey, CR0 3RZ
Activities: Other specialised construction activities n.e.c.
Major Shareholder: Steven George Brown
Officers: Nicola Ann Brown, Secretary; Steven George Brown [1964] Director

Easyoffice Rental Limited
Incorporated: 22 January 2007
Net Worth: £2,538,650 *Total Assets:* £5,166,683
Registered Office: 249 Cranbrook Road, Ilford, Essex, IG1 4TG
Activities: Residents property management
Major Shareholder: Diane Elizabeth Slack
Officers: Dilys Marion Denney, Secretary; James McKenzie Morrison Denney [1956] Director/Consultant

Ebenezer Bethel UK Limited
Incorporated: 4 November 2015
Net Worth: £80,703 *Total Assets:* £5,064,121
Registered Office: Kajaine House, 57-67 High Street, Edgware, Middlesex, HA8 7DD
Activities: Other letting and operating of own or leased real estate
Major Shareholder: Anando Mukerjee
Officers: Anando Mukerjee [1977] Director [Indian]

Ebonyhill Limited
Incorporated: 31 October 1996
Net Worth: £3,803,732 *Total Assets:* £7,940,283
Registered Office: 19-20 Bourne Court, Unity Trading Estate, Southend Road, Woodford Green, Essex, IG8 8HD
Activities: Buying and selling of own real estate
Major Shareholder: Edward James Andrews
Officers: Anthony Edward Andrews, Secretary; Edward James Andrews [1936] Director

Ebury 106 Limited
Incorporated: 3 January 2007 *Employees:* 11
Net Worth: £2,163,817 *Total Assets:* £6,516,624
Registered Office: 116 Goodmayes Road, Ilford, Essex, IG3 9UZ
Activities: Hotels and similar accommodation
Shareholder: Raksha Ramaiah Mathikere Seetharam
Officers: Seetharam Mathikere Ramaiah, Secretary; Seetharam Mathikere Ramaiah [1956] Director/Business Promoter [Indian]; Raksha Ramaiah Mathikere Seetharam [1985] Director/Business Promoter [Indian]; Sunder Ram Mathikere Seetharam [1989] Director/Business Promoter [Indian]; Shruthy Seetharam [1960] Director/Business Promoter [Indian]

EC Logistics Limited
Incorporated: 8 April 1991 *Employees:* 5
Net Worth: £4,006,998 *Total Assets:* £5,641,338
Registered Office: EC Group, Europa Park, Magnet Road, Grays, Essex, RM20 4DN
Activities: Freight transport by road
Parent: E.Christian & Company (Holdings) Limited
Officers: Christopher John Long, Secretary/Accountant; Jacqueline Eve Curtis Casadella [1951] Director; Alexander Edmund Long [1986] Director/Investment Banker; Christopher John Long [1958] Director/Accountant; Edward Anthony Long [1989] Director/Chartered Surveyor; Karen Joy Long [1960] Director

Eclerx Investments (UK) Limited
Incorporated: 14 March 2015 *Employees:* 1
Net Worth: £19,801,992 *Total Assets:* £19,830,650
Registered Office: 4 Red Lion Court, Alexandra Road, Hounslow, Middlesex, TW3 1JS
Activities: Activities of open-ended investment companies
Parent: Eclerx Services Limited
Officers: Anjan Malik [1970] Director; Baljit Phull [1971] Director/Administrator

Eco Animal Health Group PLC
Incorporated: 22 May 1984 *Employees:* 207
Net Worth: £99,690,000 *Total Assets:* £117,185,000
Registered Office: 78 Coombe Road, New Malden, Surrey, KT3 4QS
Activities: Wholesale of pharmaceutical goods
Officers: Julia Trouse, Secretary; Brett Timothy Clemo [1962] Global Operations Director; Dr Andrew Alfred Jones [1960] Director/Management Consultant; Peter Anthony Lawrence [1948] Director; Marc Denham Loomes [1961] Director; Anthony Paul Rawlinson [1957] Director/Chartered Accountant; Kevin Anthony Stockdale [1965] Finance Director; Julia Trouse [1966] Director

Eco Animal Health Ltd.
Incorporated: 22 November 1991 *Employees:* 51
Net Worth: £26,555,696 *Total Assets:* £84,152,288
Registered Office: 78 Coombe Road, New Malden, Surrey, KT3 4QS
Activities: Manufacture of basic pharmaceutical products
Officers: Julia Trouse, Secretary; Andrew Buglass [1972] Global Sales Director; Brett Timothy Clemo [1962] Director; Peter Anthony Lawrence [1948] Director; Marc Denham Loomes [1961] Managing Director; Kevin Anthony Stockdale [1965] Finance Director

Eco Regeneration LLP
Incorporated: 1 May 2014
Net Worth: £2,769,478 *Total Assets:* £7,531,326
Registered Office: 21-23 Croydon Road, Caterham, Surrey, CR3 6PA
Officers: Mark Edward Smith [1982] Member

Ecohomes Development Limited
Incorporated: 10 December 2012
Net Worth Deficit: £11,382 *Total Assets:* £5,581,372
Registered Office: 14 Ham Common, Forbes Cottage, Richmond, Surrey, TW10 7JB
Activities: Other business support service activities n.e.c.
Major Shareholder: Erika Chernavskaya
Officers: Jurijus Slepciukas [1977] Director [Lithuanian]

Econocom Limited
Incorporated: 25 February 1998 *Employees:* 34
Net Worth: £7,533,000 *Total Assets:* £41,658,000
Registered Office: Eton House, 18-24 Paradise Road, Richmond upon Thames, Surrey, TW9 1SE
Activities: Renting and leasing of office machinery and equipment (including computers)
Parent: Econocom Group SE
Officers: Laurent Olivier Caparros [1966] Managing Director [French]; Chris Labrey [1969] Director; Nicolas Noquet [1980] Financial Director [French]; Galliane Edmee Anne Colette Touze [1972] Director [French]

Econometric Limited
Incorporated: 23 August 2001 *Employees:* 3
Net Worth: £6,464,668 *Total Assets:* £8,531,089
Registered Office: 27 Beechcroft Road, Bushey, Herts, WD23 2JU
Activities: Remediation activities and other waste management services
Major Shareholder: Kelly Holland
Officers: Mark Freeman Freeman, Secretary; Kelly Holland [1974] Director/Contractor

Ecover (UK) Limited
Incorporated: 9 October 1992 *Employees:* 16
Net Worth Deficit: £120,000 *Total Assets:* £9,099,000
Registered Office: 1 Eton Street, Richmond, Surrey, TW9 1AG
Activities: Wholesale of household goods (other than musical instruments) n.e.c
Parent: People Against Dirty Holdings Limited
Officers: Timothy Earl Bailey [1962] Director/Executive VP [American]; Audrey Sue Ditter [1962] Director/Senior Vice President [American]; Christoph Wolfgang Schulze-Melander [1974] Managing Director

Eda Quality Foods Limited
Incorporated: 3 September 2002 *Employees:* 85
Net Worth: £1,926,170 *Total Assets:* £7,693,200
Registered Office: Unit 1-8 Centenary Industrial Estate, Jeffreys Road, Enfield, Middlesex, EN3 7UD
Activities: Other processing and preserving of fruit and vegetables
Parent: TFC Holdings London Limited
Officers: Eran Ucur, Secretary; Ercan Ucur [1970] Director; Huseyin Ucur [1945] Director

EDC Systems Limited
Incorporated: 21 August 2007 *Employees:* 38
Net Worth: £792,676 *Total Assets:* £5,107,031
Registered Office: First Floor, Healthaid House, Marlborough Hill, Harrow, Middlesex, HA1 1UD
Activities: Retail sale of telecommunications equipment other than mobile telephones
Shareholder: Traffilog Limited
Officers: Liat Copitch, Secretary; Benjamin Simon Copitch [1979] Director/General Manager; Yaniv Giron [1974] Director [Israeli]; Paul Gefferson Louis-Fernand [1969] Managing Director; Yaron Tal [1969] Director [Israeli]

The Eden Academy
Incorporated: 18 April 2012 *Employees:* 330
Net Worth: £14,639,000 *Total Assets:* £20,257,000
Registered Office: Grangewood School, Fore Street, Eastcote, Pinner, Middlesex, HA5 2JQ
Activities: Primary education
Officers: Keith James Holroyd, Secretary; Hardip Singh Begol [1971] Director/Senior Civil Servant; James Kempe Clarke [1963] Director/Retired; Victoria Collis [1970] Director/Consultant; Karen Deacon [1960] Director of Education and Social Care; Susan Frances Douglas [1970] Director/Educational Consultant; Brian David Eaton [1957] Director/University Lecturer; Helen Marion Susan Milner [1957] Director/Project Manager; Barry Joseph Nolan [1968] Director/Banker; Angela St John [1959] Director; Collette Gwendoline Stone [1956] Director/Civil Servant

Edge Grove School Trust Limited
Incorporated: 31 January 1969 *Employees:* 106
Net Worth: £5,517,645 *Total Assets:* £8,415,870
Registered Office: Edge Grove School, Aldenham, Herts, WD25 8NL
Activities: Primary education
Officers: Martin Gregory Montague Sims, Secretary; Christopher Howard John Clayden [1961] Finance Director; Dr Lucy Ann Dexter [1980] Director/Teacher; Ian Stewart Elliott [1944] Director/Retired Headmaster; Amanda Jane Godfrey [1962] Director/Executive Headteacher; Paul Ashley Kendall [1962] Managing Director; Charles Edward Lilley [1963] Director/Solicitor; Trefor Wilmot Llewellyn [1947] Director/Chartered Accountant; Samantha O'Sullivan [1974] Director/Teacher; Andrew James Robson [1963] Director/Chartered Surveyor; Ian Alastair Sheldon [1977] Director/School Teacher; Jeremy Laurence Stevens [1959] Director/Chartered Surveyor; John Wilson Tweddle [1958] Director/Retired Investment Manager; Dr Susan Barbara Whiting [1951] Director/Memory Consultant; David Anthony Ellis Williams [1953] Director/Accountant

Edif Group Finance Limited
Incorporated: 19 January 2011
Net Worth: £7,492,000 *Total Assets:* £42,035,000
Registered Office: Era Building, Cleeve Road, Leatherhead, Surrey, KT22 7SA
Activities: Activities of head offices
Parent: Edif Group Limited
Officers: Roberto Cavanna [1961] Director [Italian]; Annelie Du Plessis [1972] Director/Financial Controller

Edif Group Limited
Incorporated: 19 January 2011
Net Worth: £74,147,000 *Total Assets:* £74,147,000
Registered Office: Era Building, Cleeve Road, Leatherhead, Surrey, KT22 7SA
Activities: Engineering related scientific and technical consulting activities
Officers: Roberto Cavanna [1961] Director [Italian]; Annelie Du Plessis [1972] Director/Financial Controller

Edif Group Management Limited
Incorporated: 19 January 2011 *Employees:* 2
Net Worth Deficit: £51,472,000 *Total Assets:* £22,334,000
Registered Office: Era Building, Cleeve Road, Leatherhead, Surrey, KT22 7SA
Activities: Activities of head offices
Parent: Edif Group Finance Limited
Officers: Roberto Cavanna [1961] Director [Italian]; Annelie Du Plessis [1972] Director/Financial Controller

Edinburgh Retail LLP
Incorporated: 28 April 2005
Net Worth Deficit: £5,547,292 *Total Assets:* £5,190,414
Registered Office: Philip Harris House, 1a Spur Road, Orpington, Kent, BR6 0PH

Edinburgh Sainsbury Holdings LLP
Incorporated: 27 April 2015 *Employees:* 5
Net Worth: £10,892,010 *Total Assets:* £10,892,010
Registered Office: Aprirose House, 48a High Street, Edgware, Middlesex, HA8 7EQ
Officers: Manish Mansukhlal Gudka [1970] Member; Gareth Jones [1973] Member; Suraj Rashmikant Shah [1982] LLP Member

Edmonton Academy Trust
Incorporated: 4 August 2016 *Employees:* 240
Net Worth: £19,442,016 *Total Assets:* £22,072,404
Registered Office: Edmonton County School, Great Cambridge Road, Enfield, Middlesex, EN1 1HQ
Activities: Primary education
Officers: Peter Quentin Blane [1969] Finance Sales Director; Konrad Hogarth Halls [1961] Director/Facilities Management; Rob Leak [1951] Director/Retired; Dr Christine Maria Martin [1965] Director/Software Engineer [British/American]; Salih Suavi [1960] Director/IT Manager; Dr Susan Mary Tranter [1963] Director/Executive Headteacher; Elizabeth Nicola Whale [1980] Director/Merchandiser

Education for The 21st Century
Incorporated: 10 March 2011 *Employees:* 349
Net Worth: £33,393,884 *Total Assets:* £36,751,264
Registered Office: The Ravensbourne School, Hayes Lane, Bromley, Kent, BR2 9EH
Activities: General secondary education
Officers: Mark Benjamin Anderson [1960] Director/Retired Solicitor; Michael Atkinson [1972] Director/Accountant; Richard Defriend [1949] Director/Retired; Ann Patricia Dempsey [1955] Director/Retired; Paul Featherstone [1967] Director of IT and Digital Transformation; David John McKivett [1957] Director/Consultant; Mark Whitby [1964] Director/Education Consultant

Education Management Corporation Limited
Incorporated: 21 December 2006 *Employees:* 1,725
Net Worth Deficit: £13,604,114 *Total Assets:* £111,891,240
Registered Office: 2nd Floor, Hygeia Building, 66 College Road, Harrow, Middlesex, HA1 1BE
Activities: Activities of other holding companies n.e.c.
Officers: Derek Russell Smith [1962] Director

Education Support (Enfield 2) Holdings Limited
Incorporated: 22 March 2002
Net Worth Deficit: £2,086,000 *Total Assets:* £24,059,000
Registered Office: 8 White Oak Square, London Road, Swanley, Kent, BR8 7AG
Activities: Construction of commercial buildings
Parent: Palio (No 17) Limited
Officers: Gresa Daullxhi [1986] Director/Chartered Accountant (ACA); Neil Woodburn [1979] Director/Chartered Building Surveyor

Education Support (Enfield 2) Limited
Incorporated: 19 April 2002
Net Worth Deficit: £2,086,000 *Total Assets:* £24,059,000
Registered Office: 8 White Oak Square, London Road, Swanley, Kent, BR8 7AG
Activities: Construction of commercial buildings
Parent: Education Support (Enfield 2) Holdings Limited
Officers: Gresa Daullxhi [1986] Director/Chartered Accountant (ACA); Neil Woodburn [1979] Director/Chartered Building Surveyor

Education Support (Enfield) Holdings Limited
Incorporated: 4 February 2002
Net Worth Deficit: £248,000 *Total Assets:* £12,442,000
Registered Office: 8 White Oak Square, London Road, Swanley, Kent, BR8 7AG
Activities: Activities of head offices
Parent: JLIF (GP) Limited
Officers: Gresa Daullxhi [1986] Director/Chartered Accountant (ACA); Neil Woodburn [1979] Director/Chartered Building Surveyor

Education Support (Enfield) Limited
Incorporated: 20 July 1998
Net Worth Deficit: £248,000 *Total Assets:* £12,442,000
Registered Office: 8 White Oak Square, London Road, Swanley, Kent, BR8 7AG
Activities: Other business support service activities n.e.c.
Parent: Education Support (Enfield) Holdings Limited
Officers: Gresa Daullxhi [1986] Director/Chartered Accountant (ACA); Neil Woodburn [1979] Director/Chartered Building Surveyor

Education Support (Newham) Holdings Limited
Incorporated: 19 April 2002
Net Worth Deficit: £2,001,000 *Total Assets:* £20,119,000
Registered Office: 8 White Oak Square, London Road, Swanley, Kent, BR8 7AG
Activities: Construction of commercial buildings
Parent: Palio (No 18) Limited
Officers: Gresa Daullxhi [1986] Director/Chartered Accountant; Neil Woodburn [1979] Director/Chartered Building Surveyor

Education Support (Newham) Limited
Incorporated: 19 April 2002
Net Worth Deficit: £2,001,000 *Total Assets:* £20,119,000
Registered Office: 8 White Oak Square, London Road, Swanley, Kent, BR8 7AG
Activities: Construction of commercial buildings
Parent: Education Support (Newham) Holdings Limited
Officers: Gresa Daullxhi [1986] Director/Chartered Accountant (ACA); Neil Woodburn [1979] Director/Chartered Building Surveyor

Education Support (Swindon) Holdings Limited
Incorporated: 6 July 2004
Net Worth Deficit: £8,330,000 *Total Assets:* £63,428,000
Registered Office: 8 White Oak Square, London Road, Swanley, Kent, BR8 7AG
Activities: Activities of head offices
Parent: Palio (No 16) Limited
Officers: Carl Harvey Dix [1966] Operations Director; Vikki Louise Everett [1971] Director/Project Manager

Education Support (Swindon) Limited
Incorporated: 6 July 2004
Net Worth Deficit: £8,330,000 *Total Assets:* £63,428,000
Registered Office: 8 White Oak Square, London Road, Swanley, Kent, BR8 7AG
Activities: Construction of commercial buildings
Parent: Education Support (Swindon) Holdings Limited
Officers: Carl Harvey Dix [1966] Operations Director; Vikki Louise Everett [1971] Director/Project Manager

Edwardian Bloomsbury Street Limited
Incorporated: 18 February 2008 *Employees:* 129
Net Worth: £52,511,000 *Total Assets:* £94,130,000
Registered Office: 140 Bath Road, Hayes, Middlesex, UB3 5AW
Activities: Hotels and similar accommodation
Parent: Edwardian Hotel Investments Ltd
Officers: Vijay Wason, Secretary; John Robert Morley [1945] Director/Financial Consultant; Jasminder Singh [1951] Director/Hotelier

Edwardian Canary Wharf Hotel Limited
Incorporated: 28 September 2011 *Employees:* 132
Net Worth: £27,377,000 *Total Assets:* £43,167,000
Registered Office: Radisson Edwardian Heathrow, 140 Bath Road, Hayes, Middlesex, UB3 5AW
Activities: Hotels and similar accommodation
Parent: Edwardian Hotel Investments Ltd
Officers: Vijay Wason, Secretary; John Robert Morley [1945] Director/Financial Consultant; Jasminder Singh [1951] Director/Hotelier

Edwardian Exclusive Hotels Ltd
Incorporated: 8 April 1993 *Employees:* 91
Net Worth: £65,220,000 *Total Assets:* £107,778,000
Registered Office: 140 Bath Road, Hayes, Middlesex, UB3 5AW
Activities: Hotels and similar accommodation
Parent: Edwardian Exclusive Ltd
Officers: Vijay Wason, Secretary; John Robert Morley [1945] Director/Financial Consultant; Shashi Merag Shah [1945] Director; Jasminder Singh [1951] Director/Hotelier; Vijay Wason [1948] Director/Company Secretary

Edwardian Exclusive Ltd
Incorporated: 16 October 2013
Net Worth: £28,123,000 *Total Assets:* £65,669,000
Registered Office: 140 Bath Road, Hayes, Middlesex, UB3 5AW
Activities: Activities of other holding companies n.e.c.
Parent: Edwardian Group Limited
Officers: Vijay Wason, Secretary; John Robert Morley [1945] Director/Financial Consultant; Jasminder Singh [1951] Director/Hotelier

Edwardian Finance Ltd
Incorporated: 16 October 2013
Net Worth: £262,532,992 *Total Assets:* £411,384,992
Registered Office: 140 Bath Road, Hayes, Middlesex, UB3 5AW
Activities: Activities of other holding companies n.e.c.
Parent: Edwardian Group Limited
Officers: Vijay Wason, Secretary; John Robert Morley [1945] Director/Financial Consultant; Jasminder Singh [1951] Director/Hotelier

Edwardian Free Trade Hall Ltd
Incorporated: 27 September 2011 *Employees:* 229
Net Worth: £51,466,000 *Total Assets:* £68,085,000
Registered Office: Radisson Edwardian Heathrow, 140 Bath Road, Hayes, Middlesex, UB3 5AW
Activities: Hotels and similar accommodation
Parent: Edwardian Hotel Finance Ltd
Officers: Vijay Wason, Secretary; John Robert Morley [1945] Director/Financial Consultant; Jasminder Singh [1951] Director/Hotelier

Edwardian Grafton Hotel Ltd
Incorporated: 27 August 2013 *Employees:* 174
Net Worth: £46,032,000 *Total Assets:* £98,025,000
Registered Office: 140 Bath Road, Hayes, Middlesex, UB3 5AW
Activities: Hotels and similar accommodation
Parent: Edwardian Hotel Investments Ltd
Officers: Vijay Wason, Secretary; John Robert Morley [1945] Director/Financial Consultant; Jasminder Singh [1951] Director/Hotelier

Edwardian Group Limited
Incorporated: 2 June 1977 *Employees:* 2,349
Net Worth: £945,161,984 *Total Assets:* £1,551,187,968
Registered Office: 140 Bath Road, Hayes, Middlesex, UB3 5AW
Activities: Activities of other holding companies n.e.c.
Major Shareholder: George Robinson Machan
Officers: Vijay Wason, Secretary; Andrew Hart [1947] Director/Solicitor Consultant; John Robert Morley [1945] Director/Financial Consultant; Shashi Merag Shah [1945] Director; Amrit Singh [1959] Director; Inderneel Singh [1984] Managing Director; Jasminder Singh [1951] Director/Hotelier

Edwardian Hampshire Hotels Ltd
Incorporated: 2 November 2006 *Employees:* 156
Net Worth: £52,712,000 *Total Assets:* £104,171,000
Registered Office: 140 Bath Road, Hayes, Middlesex, UB3 5AW
Activities: Hotels and similar accommodation
Parent: Edwardian New Finance Limited
Officers: Vijay Wason, Secretary; John Robert Morley [1945] Director/Financial Consultant; Jasminder Singh [1951] Director/Hotelier

Edwardian Hotel Finance Ltd
Incorporated: 27 August 2013
Net Worth: £262,551,008 *Total Assets:* £610,369,024
Registered Office: 140 Bath Road, Hayes, Middlesex, UB3 5AW
Activities: Activities of other holding companies n.e.c.
Parent: Edwardian Finance Ltd
Officers: Vijay Wason, Secretary; John Robert Morley [1945] Director/Financial Consultant; Shashi Merag Shah [1945] Director; Jasminder Singh [1951] Director/Hotelier; Vijay Wason [1948] Director/Company Secretary

Edwardian Hotel Investments Ltd
Incorporated: 27 August 2013
Net Worth: £126,940,000 *Total Assets:* £361,648,000
Registered Office: 140 Bath Road, Hayes, Middlesex, UB3 5AW
Activities: Activities of other holding companies n.e.c.
Parent: Edwardian Investments Ltd
Officers: Vijay Wason, Secretary; John Robert Morley [1945] Director/Financial Consultant; Shashi Merag Shah [1945] Director; Jasminder Singh [1951] Director/Hotelier; Vijay Wason [1948] Director/Company Secretary

Edwardian International Hotels Ltd
Incorporated: 8 April 1993 *Employees:* 73
Net Worth: £152,712,992 *Total Assets:* £154,612,000
Registered Office: 140 Bath Road, Hayes, Middlesex, UB3 5AW
Activities: Hotels and similar accommodation
Parent: Edwardian Group Limited
Officers: Vijay Wason, Secretary; John Robert Morley [1945] Director/Financial Consultant; Jasminder Singh [1951] Director/Hotelier

Edwardian Investments Ltd
Incorporated: 16 October 2013
Net Worth: £126,919,000 *Total Assets:* £182,242,000
Registered Office: 140 Bath Road, Hayes, Middlesex, UB3 5AW
Activities: Activities of other holding companies n.e.c.
Parent: Edwardian Group Limited
Officers: Vijay Wason, Secretary; John Robert Morley [1945] Director/Financial Consultant; Jasminder Singh [1951] Director/Hotelier

Edwardian London Management Services Limited
Incorporated: 18 March 1993 *Employees:* 125
Net Worth: £5,351,000 *Total Assets:* £11,542,000
Registered Office: 140 Bath Road, Hayes, Middlesex, UB3 5AW
Activities: Other business support service activities n.e.c.
Parent: Edwardian Group Limited
Officers: Vijay Wason, Secretary; Andrew Hart [1947] Director; John Robert Morley [1945] Director/Financial Consultant; Shashi Merag Shah [1945] Director; Jasminder Singh [1951] Director/Hotelier

Edwardian Ltd
Incorporated: 8 April 1993 *Employees:* 111
Net Worth: £40,780,000 *Total Assets:* £67,572,000
Registered Office: 140 Bath Road, Hayes, Middlesex, UB3 5AW
Activities: Hotels and similar accommodation
Parent: Edwardian Hotel Investments Ltd
Officers: Vijay Wason, Secretary; John Robert Morley [1945] Director/Financial Consultant; Jasminder Singh [1951] Director/Hotelier

Edwardian Mercer Street Ltd
Incorporated: 27 September 2011 *Employees:* 128
Net Worth: £45,835,000 *Total Assets:* £94,290,000
Registered Office: Radisson Edwardian Heathrow, 140 Bath Road, Hayes, Middlesex, UB3 5AW
Activities: Hotels and similar accommodation
Parent: Edwardian Hotel Investments Ltd
Officers: Vijay Wason, Secretary; John Robert Morley [1945] Director/Financial Consultant; Jasminder Singh [1951] Director/Hotelier

Edwardian New Finance Limited
Incorporated: 26 March 2008
Net Worth: £87,109,000 *Total Assets:* £238,123,008
Registered Office: 140 Bath Road, Hayes, Middlesex, UB3 5AW
Activities: Activities of other holding companies n.e.c.
Parent: Edwardian Group Limited
Officers: Vijay Wason, Secretary; John Robert Morley [1945] Director/Financial Consultant; Shashi Merag Shah [1945] Director; Jasminder Singh [1951] Director/Hotelier; Vijay Wason [1948] Director/Company Secretary

Edwardian Pastoria Hotels Ltd
Incorporated: 2 November 2006
Net Worth: £3,384,000 *Total Assets:* £204,695,008
Registered Office: 140 Bath Road, Hayes, Middlesex, UB3 5AW
Activities: Hotels and similar accommodation
Parent: Edwardian New Finance Limited
Officers: Vijay Wason, Secretary; John Robert Morley [1945] Director/Financial Consultant; Jasminder Singh [1951] Director/Hotelier

EHGT Limited
Incorporated: 10 November 1997
Net Worth: £25,813,604 *Total Assets:* £25,817,214
Registered Office: Wyevale Garden Centres, Syon Park, London Road, Brentford, Middlesex, TW8 8JF
Activities: Activities of head offices
Parent: Wyevale Garden Centres Limited
Officers: Laura Harradine-Greene, Secretary; Anthony Generald Jones [1973] Director; Richard MacLachlan [1976] Director

EID Limited
Incorporated: 13 January 1998
Net Worth: £1,367,722 *Total Assets:* £7,635,910
Registered Office: Elm Park House, Elm Park Court, Pinner, Middlesex, HA5 3NN
Activities: Wholesale of metals and metal ores
Shareholders: Arieh Isaac Edel; Uri Dov Edel; Rafael Natan Edel
Officers: Sandra Alberta Hinds, Secretary; Martin Barry Lee [1960] Director

Eight Investment Limited
Incorporated: 2 December 2016 *Employees:* 3
Net Worth: £229,383 *Total Assets:* £7,778,601
Registered Office: 400 Dashwood Lang Road, Weybridge, Surrey, KT15 2HJ
Activities: Other business support service activities n.e.c.
Major Shareholder: Bill Lee
Officers: Bill Lee [1992] Director [Chinese]

Eiser Infrastructure Partners LLP
Incorporated: 12 November 2009 *Employees:* 15
Net Worth: £2,377,000 *Total Assets:* £6,060,000
Registered Office: Kajaine House, 57-67 High Street, Edgware, Middlesex, HA8 7DD
Officers: Hans Rupprecht Wilhelm Meissner [1954] Member; Vivian Kin Fon Nicoli [1966] Member

Elbrook (Cash & Carry) Limited
Incorporated: 9 August 1984 *Employees:* 63
Net Worth: £22,717,016 *Total Assets:* £38,748,460
Registered Office: 105 Bond Road, Mitcham, Surrey, CR4 3HG
Activities: Retail sale in non-specialised stores with food, beverages or tobacco predominating
Shareholder: Fukhera Khalid
Officers: Amjad Khalid [1983] Director; Fukhera Khalid [1968] Managing Director

Elcot Service Flats Limited
Incorporated: 6 February 1945 *Employees:* 2
Net Worth: £4,368,464 *Total Assets:* £5,780,534
Registered Office: York House, Empire Way, Wembley, Middlesex, HA9 0FQ
Activities: Other letting and operating of own or leased real estate
Parent: Alimar Limited
Officers: David Lessman, Secretary/Director; Julia Ruth Bekhor [1960] Director; David Lessman [1925] Director

Elec-Mec (Wholesale) Limited
Incorporated: 10 July 1991
Net Worth: £5,381,624 *Total Assets:* £6,747,611
Registered Office: Floor 2, Middlesex House, 130 College Road, Harrow, Middlesex, HA1 1BQ
Activities: Other retail sale of new goods in specialised stores (not commercial art galleries and opticians)
Shareholders: Purshotam Gami; Devila Gami
Officers: Devila Gami, Secretary; Pursotham Gami [1953] Director

Electrosonic Limited
Incorporated: 3 March 1964 *Employees:* 279
Net Worth: £3,225,000 *Total Assets:* £12,590,000
Registered Office: Hawley Mill, Hawley Road, Dartford, Kent, DA2 7SY
Activities: Manufacture of other electrical equipment
Parent: Electrosonic Group Limited
Officers: Marc Adrian Russell Cooke [1976] Director; Jonathan Peter Hancock [1971] Director/Chief Executive; Donald Clive Stuart [1968] Managing Director; Christopher Graham Ward [1971] Director/Chief Finance Officer

Elegant Electronics Limited
Incorporated: 7 February 1984 *Employees:* 4
Net Worth: £4,652,565 *Total Assets:* £10,876,214
Registered Office: 16 Astons Road, Northwood, Middlesex, HA6 2LD
Activities: Retail sale of computers, peripheral units and software in specialised stores
Shareholders: Deepak Kumar; Niranjana Kumar
Officers: Deepak Kumar, Secretary; Deepak Kumar [1961] Director; Niranjana Kumar [1956] Director; Sham Kumar [1990] Director/Editorial Assistant

Elektron Tower 3 Limited
Incorporated: 20 December 2005 *Employees:* 1
Net Worth: £3,708,985 *Total Assets:* £5,594,497
Registered Office: 166 College Road, Harrow, Middlesex, HA1 1RA
Activities: Development of building projects
Major Shareholder: Michael Spencer Docker
Officers: Michele Docker, Secretary; Michael Spencer Docker [1963] Director/Property Developer

Elgon (Enfield) Limited
Incorporated: 1 November 1984
Net Worth: £9,634,732 *Total Assets:* £16,779,368
Registered Office: Eagle House Surgery, 291 High Street, Enfield, Middlesex, EN3 4DN
Activities: Dispensing chemist in specialised stores
Major Shareholder: Jayesh Jayantilal Lakhani
Officers: Anil Jayantilal Lakhani, Secretary; Anil Jayantilal Lakhani [1957] Director/Pharmacist; Jayesh Jayantilal Lakhani [1959] Director/Pharmacist

Elgon Hotels Limited
Incorporated: 25 October 2011
Net Worth: £5,852,380 *Total Assets:* £9,668,915
Registered Office: 29-31 Mayfield Road, Sutton, Surrey, SM2 5DU
Activities: Hotels and similar accommodation
Shareholder: Nazim Manji
Officers: Ajay Kumar Gokani [1965] Director; Nazim Manji [1958] Director

Elia International Limited
Incorporated: 3 January 1986
Net Worth: £6,690,849 *Total Assets:* £8,281,906
Registered Office: 10 Aintree Road, Perivale, Middlesex, London, UB6 7LA
Activities: Wholesale of household goods (other than musical instruments) n.e.c
Officers: Myung Ju Kim, Secretary; Myung Yel Kim [1951] Director [South Korean]; Myung Ju Kim [1957] Director/Secretary [South Korean]

Elite Mobile (Holdings) Limited
Incorporated: 9 March 2009 *Employees:* 203
Net Worth: £29,723,000 *Total Assets:* £41,816,000
Registered Office: Kings Suite, 4th Floor, Amba House, 15 College Road, Harrow, Middlesex, HA1 1BA
Activities: Activities of other holding companies n.e.c.
Shareholder: Ketan Chandulal Gokani
Officers: Ketan Chandulal Gokani [1974] Director

Elite Mobile Limited
Incorporated: 7 November 1994 *Employees:* 93
Net Worth: £23,572,000 *Total Assets:* £34,514,000
Registered Office: Wembley Stadium Industrial Estate, First Way, Wembley, Middlesex, HA9 0TU
Activities: Non-specialised wholesale trade
Parent: Elite Mobile (Holdings) Limited
Officers: Ketan Gokani, Secretary; Amit Kumar Shantilal Dhamecha [1969] Director; Ketan Chandulal Gokani [1974] Director

Ellenbrook Developments PLC
Incorporated: 7 November 2001
Net Worth: £1,918,000 *Total Assets:* £62,760,000
Registered Office: 8 White Oak Square, Swanley, Kent, BR8 7AG
Activities: Other business support service activities n.e.c.
Parent: Ellenbrook Holdings Limited
Officers: Neeti Mukundrai Anand [1984] Director; Angela Louise Roshier [1975] Director/Finance

Ellenbrook Holdings Limited
Incorporated: 7 November 2001
Net Worth: £1,918,000 *Total Assets:* £62,760,000
Registered Office: 8 White Oak Square, Swanley, Kent, BR8 7AG
Activities: Activities of other holding companies n.e.c.
Parent: DIF Infra Yield 1 UK Limited
Officers: Neeti Mukundrai Anand [1984] Director; Angela Louise Roshier [1975] Director/Finance

Ellenor
Incorporated: 4 July 2007 *Employees:* 177
Previous: Ellenor Lions Hospices
Net Worth: £5,477,064 *Total Assets:* £6,045,613
Registered Office: Coldharbour Road, Northfleet, Gravesend, Kent, DA11 7HQ
Activities: General medical practice activities
Officers: Timothy Michael Hammond, Secretary; Ann Christine Barnes [1945] Director/Retired; Nancy Jean MacKenzie Cogswell [1954] Director/Architect & Management Consultant [Canadian]; Serena Gaye St Clair Cooper [1952] Director/Specialist Palliative Care Nurse; Bryan Arthur Edward Harris [1941] Director/Journalist; Mary Victoria Kirk [1963] Director/Registered Nurse Lecturer; Kerry-Jane Packman [1976] Fundraising Director; Glynis Mary Rogers [1955] Director/Retired; Catherine Jane Rossiter [1976] Director/Financial Controller; Janet Elizabeth Stanton [1952] Director/Solicitor; Dr. Bhargawa Vasudaven [1954] Director/Retired Cop/Trustee; Andrew Roger Wedderburn-Day [1962] Director/Retired

Elliot Leigh Property Investments 2 Ltd
Incorporated: 21 July 2003 *Employees:* 16
Previous: Elliot Leigh Property Management Limited
Net Worth: £8,901,201 *Total Assets:* £18,802,786
Registered Office: 19-20 Bourne Court, Southend Road, Woodford Green, Essex, IG8 8HD
Activities: Management of real estate on a fee or contract basis
Parent: EL Property Holdings Limited
Officers: Elliot James Altman, Secretary; Elliot James Altman [1976] Director/Property Consultant; Leigh Ryce Young [1972] Director/Self Employed

Ellis of Richmond (Holdings) Limited
Incorporated: 21 July 1994 *Employees:* 75
Net Worth: £6,249,680 *Total Assets:* £9,633,510
Registered Office: Richmond House, Unit 1 The Links, Popham Close, Hanworth, Middlesex, TW13 6JE
Activities: Wholesale of wine, beer, spirits and other alcoholic beverages
Shareholder: Guy Maxwell Cunningham
Officers: William Derek Ellis, Secretary; Guy Maxwell Cunningham [1969] Director/Wine Merchant; Henry James Ellis [1960] Director/Wine Merchant; John Robert Henry Ellis [1963] Director/Wine Merchant; William Derek Ellis [1965] Director/Chartered Accountant; Graham Peter Triefus [1952] Director/Chartered Accountant

Ellis of Richmond Limited
Incorporated: 8 January 1944 *Employees:* 69
Net Worth: £3,879,142 *Total Assets:* £8,047,245
Registered Office: Richmond House, Unit 1 The Links, Popham Close, Hanworth, Middlesex, TW13 6JE
Activities: Wholesale of wine, beer, spirits and other alcoholic beverages
Parent: Ellis of Richmond (Holdings) Ltd
Officers: Henry James Ellis, Secretary; Guy Maxwell Cunningham [1969] Director/Wine Merchant; Henry James Ellis [1960] Director/Wine Merchant; John Robert Henry Ellis [1963] Director/Wine Merchant; William Derek Ellis [1965] Director/Chartered Accountant; Peter John Harwood [1953] Director/Wine Merchant; Martin Paul Longley [1947] Director/Wine Merchant; Graham Peter Triefus [1952] Director/Chartered Accountant

Elmbridge Village Limited
Incorporated: 6 March 1980 *Employees:* 4
Net Worth: £12,419,001 *Total Assets:* £21,961,660
Registered Office: 1st Floor, Brunswick House, Regent Park, 297-299 Kingston Road, Leatherhead, Surrey, KT22 7LU
Activities: Development of building projects
Parent: Retirement Villages Management Limited
Officers: Sally Irene Rees, Secretary; Sarah Denise Burgess [1971] Director; William Edwin John Crawford [1970] Director/Development; Neil Donaldson [1966] Director/Accountant; Andrew George Esmond Ovey [1971] Director/Investment Manager

Elmex Sales Corporation Limited
Incorporated: 4 February 1994 *Employees:* 17
Net Worth: £1,577,208 *Total Assets:* £9,969,981
Registered Office: 3 Brook Business Centre, Cowley Mill Road, Uxbridge, Middlesex, UB8 2FX
Activities: Activities of other holding companies n.e.c.
Shareholders: Deborah Lynn Hill; Daryl Andrew Hill; Howard Michael Charles Jupp
Officers: Daryl Andrew Hill [1964] Director; Howard Michael Charles Jupp [1965] Director/Freight Forwarder

Elmswood Properties Limited
Incorporated: 7 July 1998 *Employees:* 3
Net Worth: £2,777,916 *Total Assets:* £5,554,189
Registered Office: Lynwood House, 373-375 Station Road, Harrow, Middlesex, HA1 2AW
Activities: Buying and selling of own real estate
Parent: Gerko Limited
Officers: Mark Jason Crader [1962] Director/Property Developer; Aron Grisha Gelbard [1982] Director/Management Consultant; Elimelech Kopilov [1953] Director/Engineer [Israeli]; Ron Gershon Kopilov [1984] Director [Israeli]

Elmwey Learning Trust
Incorporated: 5 June 2015 *Employees:* 132
Net Worth: £23,871,000 *Total Assets:* £26,149,000
Registered Office: Heathside School, Brooklands Lane, Weybridge, Surrey, KT13 8UZ
Activities: General secondary education
Officers: Rebecca Harris, Secretary; Maria Cicero-Scott [1963] Director/Head of HR & Recruitment; Helen France Cooper [1983] Director/Actuary; Anne Louise Cullum [1962] Director/Principal; Francis Michael Nicholas [1972] Commercial Director; Nathan George Roberts [1972] Director/IT Consultant [American]; Guy Jonathan Solway [1964] Director/Chartered Quantity Surveyor; Dr Robert Alan Wright [1949] Director

The Elstree UTC
Incorporated: 11 January 2012 *Employees:* 8
Net Worth: £12,199,000 *Total Assets:* £13,336,000
Registered Office: Elstree UTC, Studio Way, Borehamwood, Herts, WD6 5NN
Activities: General secondary education
Officers: Alexander Hall, Secretary; Geoffrey Keith Butler [1951] Director/Retired/Part Time Educational Consultant; Geoffrey Dominic Bygate [1961] Director/University Lecturer; Claire Charles [1973] Director/Professional Coach; Judy Glasman [1957] Director/University Academic Manager; Brian Gunner Larholm [1974] Director/Entrepreneur [Danish]; Anne Elisabeth Lean [1960] Director/Projects and Partnerships Manager; Christopher William Mitchell [1979] Director/Headteacher; Roger William Morris [1949] Managing Director; Dalia Smith [1970] Director/Landlord and Author; David Zerafa [1987] Director/Company Member of Staff

Elvetham Hall (Property) Limited
Incorporated: 12 March 2001
Net Worth: £3,236,987 *Total Assets:* £12,659,775
Registered Office: The Petersham, Nightingale Lane, Richmond, Surrey, TW10 6UZ
Activities: Hotels and similar accommodation
Officers: Greville Richard Hugh Dare, Secretary/Hotel Owner; Sir Euan Hamilton Anstruther-Gough-Calthorpe BT [1966] Director/Principal; Greville Richard Hugh Dare [1963] Director/Hotelier; Philip David Warden [1963] Director/Hotelier

Elwy 2 Limited
Incorporated: 7 December 2015 *Employees:* 2,626
Net Worth Deficit: £181,108,992 *Total Assets:* £1,370,514,944
Registered Office: Queens Road, Teddington, Middlesex, TW11 0LY
Activities: Other business support service activities n.e.c.
Parent: Elwy 1 Limited
Officers: Navneet Kaur Ogle, Secretary; Mark Simon Danzey [1979] Director, KKR Capital Markets; Edouard Jean Charles Pillot [1977] Director [French]

Elwy 3 Limited
Incorporated: 7 December 2015 *Employees:* 2,626
Net Worth: £494,812,992 *Total Assets:* £1,370,514,944
Registered Office: LGC, Queens Road, Teddington, Middlesex, TW11 0LY
Activities: Other business support service activities n.e.c.
Parent: Elwy 2 Limited
Officers: Navneet Kaur Ogle, Secretary; Edouard Jean Charles Pillot [1977] Director [French]

Elysium Healthcare (Acorn Care) Limited
Incorporated: 17 January 1996 *Employees:* 240
Previous: Acorn Care Limited
Net Worth: £6,373,000 *Total Assets:* £9,367,000
Registered Office: 2 Imperial Place, Maxwell Road, Borehamwood, Herts, WD6 1JN
Activities: Specialists medical practice activities
Parent: Elysium Healthcare (Lighthouse) Limited
Officers: Sarah Juliette Livingston, Secretary; Lesley Joy Chamberlain [1963] Director/Group Chief Executive; Dr Quazi Shams Mahfooz Haque [1968] Executive Medical Director; Steven John Woolgar [1955] Director of Policy and Regulation

Elysium Healthcare (Farndon) Limited
Incorporated: 11 October 2004 *Employees:* 126
Previous: Raphael Health Care Ltd
Net Worth: £7,518,000 *Total Assets:* £16,087,000
Registered Office: c/o Elysium Healthcare, 2 Imperial Place, Maxwell Road, Borehamwood, Herts, WD6 1JN
Activities: Other human health activities
Parent: Elysium Healthcare Holdings 3 Limited
Officers: Sarah Juliette Livingston, Secretary; Lesley Joy Chamberlain [1963] Director/Group Chief Executive; Dr Quazi Shams Mahfooz Haque [1968] Group Medical Director; Steven John Woolgar [1955] Director of Policy and Regulation

Elysium Healthcare (Healthlinc) Limited
Incorporated: 30 July 1979 *Employees:* 324
Previous: Healthlinc Individual Care Limited
Net Worth: £9,581,000 *Total Assets:* £12,118,000
Registered Office: 2 Imperial Place, Maxwell Road, Borehamwood, Herts, WD6 1JN
Activities: Specialists medical practice activities
Parent: Elysium Healthcare (Lighthouse) Limited
Officers: Sarah Juliette Livingston, Secretary; Lesley Joy Chamberlain [1963] Director/Group Chief Executive; Dr Quazi Shams Mahfooz Haque [1968] Executive Medical Director; Steven John Woolgar [1955] Director of Policy and Regulation

Elysium Healthcare (Lighthouse) Limited
Incorporated: 18 May 2006 *Employees:* 15
Previous: Lighthouse Healthcare Limited
Net Worth: £48,078,000 *Total Assets:* £51,317,000
Registered Office: 2 Imperial Place, Maxwell Road, Borehamwood, Herts, WD6 1JN
Activities: Activities of head offices
Parent: Lighthouse Healthcare Group Limited
Officers: Sarah Juliette Livingston, Secretary; Lesley Joy Chamberlain [1963] Director/Group Chief Executive; Dr Quazi Shams Mahfooz Haque [1968] Executive Medical Director; Steven John Woolgar [1955] Director of Policy and Regulation

Elysium Healthcare (St Mary's) Limited
Incorporated: 18 May 2004 *Employees:* 377
Previous: St Mary's Hospitals Limited
Net Worth: £2,297,465 *Total Assets:* £15,445,244
Registered Office: c/o Elysium Healthcare, 2 Imperial Place, Maxwell Road, Borehamwood, Herts, WD6 1JN
Activities: Hospital activities
Parent: Elysium Healthcare (Ultimate Care) Limited
Officers: Sarah Juliette Livingston, Secretary; Lesley Joy Chamberlain [1963] Director/Group Chief Executive; Dr Quazi Shams Mahfooz Haque [1968] Executive Medical Director; Steven John Woolgar [1955] Director of Policy and Regulation

Elysium Healthcare (Ultimate Care) Limited
Incorporated: 20 February 2006 *Employees:* 654
Previous: St George Ultimate Care Limited
Net Worth: £4,425,032 *Total Assets:* £43,884,684
Registered Office: c/o Elysium Healthcare, 2 Imperial Place, Maxwell Road, Borehamwood, Herts, WD6 1JN
Activities: Other human health activities
Parent: Elysium Healthcare Holdings 3 Limited
Officers: Sarah Juliette Livingston, Secretary; Lesley Joy Chamberlain [1963] Director/Group Chief Executive; Dr Quazi Shams Mahfooz Haque [1968] Executive Medical Director; Steven John Woolgar [1955] Director of Policy and Regulation

Elysium Healthcare Holdings 2 Limited
Incorporated: 10 October 2016 *Employees:* 3,290
Net Worth: £63,930,000 *Total Assets:* £575,473,024
Registered Office: 2 Imperial Place, Maxwell Road, Borehamwood, Herts, WD6 1JN
Activities: Non-trading company
Parent: Elysium Healthcare Holdings 1 Limited
Officers: Sarah Juliette Livingston, Secretary; Lesley Joy Chamberlain [1963] Director/Chief Executive Officer; Dr Quazi Shams Mahfooz Haque [1968] Executive Medical Director; Steven John Woolgar [1955] Director of Policy and Regulation

Elysium Healthcare Holdings 3 Limited
Incorporated: 10 October 2016 *Employees:* 11
Net Worth: £54,745,000 *Total Assets:* £377,808,992
Registered Office: 2 Imperial Place, Maxwell Road, Borehamwood, Herts, WD6 1JN
Activities: Non-trading company
Parent: Elysium Healthcare Holdings 2 Limited
Officers: Sarah Juliette Livingston, Secretary; Lesley Joy Chamberlain [1963] Director/Chief Executive Officer; Dr Quazi Shams Mahfooz Haque [1968] Executive Medical Director; Steven John Woolgar [1955] Director of Policy and Regulation

Elysium Healthcare LC Limited
Incorporated: 22 November 2016
Net Worth: £134,075,000 *Total Assets:* £137,518,000
Registered Office: 2 Imperial Place, Maxwell Road, Borehamwood, Herts, WD6 1JN
Activities: Non-trading company
Parent: Elysium Healthcare Holdings 3 Limited
Officers: Sarah Juliette Livingston, Secretary; Lesley Joy Chamberlain [1963] Director/Chief Executive Officer; Dr Quazi Shams Mahfooz Haque [1968] Executive Medical Director

Elysium Healthcare No. 2 Limited
Incorporated: 11 May 2007 *Employees:* 1,356
Previous: Priory Secure Services Limited
Net Worth: £23,858,000 *Total Assets:* £179,348,992
Registered Office: 2 Imperial Place, Maxwell Road, Borehamwood, Herts, WD6 1JN
Activities: Hospital activities
Parent: Elysium Healthcare Holdings 3 Limited
Officers: Sarah Juliette Livingston, Secretary; Lesley Joy Chamberlain [1963] Director/Chief Executive Officer; Dr Quazi Shams Mahfooz Haque [1968] Executive Medical Director; Steven John Woolgar [1955] Director of Policy and Regulation

Elysium Healthcare No. 3 Limited
Incorporated: 14 November 1994 *Employees:* 176
Previous: Craegmoor Hospitals Limited
Net Worth: £24,619,000 *Total Assets:* £67,242,000
Registered Office: 2 Imperial Place, Maxwell Road, Borehamwood, Herts, WD6 1JN
Activities: Other human health activities
Parent: Elysium Healthcare Holdings 3 Limited
Officers: Sarah Juliette Livingston, Secretary; Lesley Joy Chamberlain [1963] Director/Chief Executive Officer; Dr Quazi Shams Mahfooz Haque [1968] Executive Medical Director; Steven John Woolgar [1955] Director of Policy and Regulation

Elysium Healthcare No. 4 Limited
Incorporated: 26 September 1996 *Employees:* 107
Previous: Speciality Care (Care Homes) Limited
Net Worth: £7,037,000 *Total Assets:* £20,008,000
Registered Office: 2 Imperial Place, Maxwell Road, Borehamwood, Herts, WD6 1JN
Activities: Other human health activities
Parent: Elysium Healthcare No. 3 Limited
Officers: Sarah Juliette Livingston, Secretary; Lesley Joy Chamberlain [1963] Director/Chief Executive Officer; Dr Quazi Shams Mahfooz Haque [1968] Executive Medical Director; Steven John Woolgar [1955] Director of Policy and Regulation

Elysium Healthcare Property 2 Limited
Incorporated: 29 March 2005
Previous: Partnerships in Care Property 13 Limited
Net Worth: £9,098,000 *Total Assets:* £30,056,000
Registered Office: 2 Imperial Place, Maxwell Road, Borehamwood, Herts, WD6 1JN
Activities: Hospital activities
Parent: Elysium Healthcare Limited
Officers: Sarah Juliette Livingston, Secretary; Lesley Joy Chamberlain [1963] Director/Chartered Accountant; Dr Quazi Shams Mahfooz Haque [1968] Group Medical Director

Elysium Healthcare Property 3 Limited
Incorporated: 4 November 2005
Previous: Partnerships in Care Property 18 Limited
Net Worth: £6,687,000 *Total Assets:* £16,310,000
Registered Office: 2 Imperial Place, Maxwell Road, Borehamwood, Herts, WD6 1JN
Activities: Hospital activities
Parent: Elysium Healthcare Limited
Officers: Sarah Juliette Livingston, Secretary; Lesley Joy Chamberlain [1963] Director/Chartered Accountant; Dr Quazi Shams Mahfooz Haque [1968] Group Medical Director

EMAP Publishing Limited
Incorporated: 14 December 2011 *Employees:* 217
Net Worth: £20,133,616 *Total Assets:* £28,163,124
Registered Office: 7th Floor, Vantage London, Great West Road, Brentford, Middlesex, TW8 9AG
Activities: Other publishing activities
Parent: Metropolis Group Holdings Limited
Officers: Richard Hutchinson, Secretary; Richard Hutchinson [1966] Director; Robert Andrew Marr [1965] Director/Chief Executive Officer

Embee Holdings Limited
Incorporated: 11 October 2007 *Employees:* 322
Net Worth: £8,135,431 *Total Assets:* £14,654,824
Registered Office: 3 Old Barn Lane, Kenley, Surrey, CR8 5AT
Activities: Activities of head offices
Officers: Michael Paul Belliere, Secretary; Robert Serioj Bazil [1960] Director; Guy James Belliere [1973] Director; Matthew Charles Belliere [1975] Director; Michael Paul Belliere [1943] Director; Leslie Joseph Finucane [1952] Director

EMC Computer Systems (U.K.) Limited
Incorporated: 1 September 1986 *Employees:* 729
Net Worth: £76,230,000 *Total Assets:* £417,184,992
Registered Office: Dell EMC Tower, Great West Road, Brentford, Middlesex, TW8 9AN
Activities: Other information technology service activities
Parent: Dell Technologies Inc
Officers: Fiona Margaret Dibley, Secretary; Janet Merritt Bawcom [1964] Director/Vice President & Assistant Secretary [American]; Richard William Rawcliffe [1964] Director/VP - Sales

EMC Consulting (UK) Limited
Incorporated: 8 April 1991 *Employees:* 29
Net Worth: £8,053,000 *Total Assets:* £37,052,000
Registered Office: Dell EMC Tower, Great West Road, Brentford, Middlesex, TW8 9AN
Activities: Information technology consultancy activities
Parent: Dell Technologies Inc.
Officers: Fiona Margaret Dibley, Secretary; Janet Merritt Bawcom [1964] Director/Vice President and Assistant Secretary [American]; Richard William Rawcliffe [1964] Director/VP - Sales

EMC Europe Limited
Incorporated: 2 October 1970 *Employees:* 520
Net Worth: £74,017,000 *Total Assets:* £94,817,000
Registered Office: Dell EMC Tower, Great West Road, Brentford, Middlesex, TW8 9AN
Activities: Information technology consultancy activities
Parent: Dell Technologies Inc
Officers: Fiona Margaret Dibley, Secretary; Janet Merritt Bawcom [1964] Director/Vice President & Assistant Secretary [American]; Richard William Rawcliffe [1964] Director/VP - Sales

Emcor (UK) Limited
Incorporated: 28 February 1989
Net Worth: £9,043,000 *Total Assets:* £9,043,000
Registered Office: 1 The Crescent, Surbiton, Surrey, KT6 4BN
Activities: Activities of head offices
Officers: Michael Lawrence Walker, Secretary; Keith Chanter [1958] Director; Anthony J Guzzi [1964] Director/Executive [American]; Christopher John Howse [1961] Director/Business Executive; Maxine Lum Mauricio [1971] Director/Business Executive [American]; Mark Pompa [1958] Director/Businessman [American]

Emcor Group (UK) PLC
Incorporated: 27 May 1964 *Employees:* 3,870
Net Worth: £3,513,000 *Total Assets:* £106,556,000
Registered Office: 1 The Crescent, Surbiton, Surrey, KT6 4BN
Activities: Electrical installation
Officers: Michael Lawrence Walker, Secretary; Keith Chanter [1958] Director; Christopher John Howse [1961] Director/Business Executive; Christopher Kehoe [1972] Director/Executive; David John Parker [1967] Director/Executive

Emerald Leather LLP
Incorporated: 10 September 2013
Net Worth: £3,874,759 *Total Assets:* £6,596,751
Registered Office: 1st Floor, Midas House, 2 Knoll Rise, Orpington, Kent, BR6 0EL

Emerson Crane Hire Limited
Incorporated: 18 April 1991 *Employees:* 108
Net Worth: £4,651,103 *Total Assets:* £15,747,388
Registered Office: Emerson House, Freshwater Road, Dagenham, Essex, RM8 1RX
Activities: Renting and leasing of construction and civil engineering machinery and equipment
Major Shareholder: Edward Clancy
Officers: Liam Clancy [1981] Director/Manager; Paul Clancy [1962] Director/Crane Hire; Robert Thomas Jackson [1971] Director/Crane Hire Technical Representative

Emerson Park Academy
Incorporated: 2 August 2011 *Employees:* 98
Net Worth: £8,294,083 *Total Assets:* £9,891,558
Registered Office: Wych Elm Road, Hornchurch, Essex, RM11 3AD
Activities: General secondary education
Officers: Ian Richard Buckmaster, Secretary; Veedoula Kumarl Bharaj [1973] Director/Civil Servant; Terrence Lee Huff [1968] Director/Health Service Official; John Peter Luff [1962] Director/Management Consultant; Scott McGuinness [1972] Director/Headteacher; Sarah Jane Meacher [1971] Director/Headteacher; Carol Jane Newton [1961] Director/Teacher; Victoria Anne O'Connor [1967] Director; Neil Robert Rebeugeot-Smith [1969] Director/Architect; Martin Tilbury [1955] Director/Retired

Empire Bespoke Foods Limited
Incorporated: 11 August 1997 *Employees:* 63
Net Worth: £12,313,349 *Total Assets:* £23,339,932
Registered Office: 45 Rowdell Road, Europa House, Northolt, Middlesex, UB5 6AG
Activities: Wholesale of sugar and chocolate and sugar confectionery
Shareholder: Jitendra Maganbhai Patel
Officers: Anil Gunvantbhai Patel, Secretary/Director; Anil Gunvantbhai Patel [1954] Director; Chandresh Patel [1958] Director; Jitendrakumar Maganbhai Patel [1952] Director

Empire Investment Capital Limited
Incorporated: 11 September 2014 *Employees:* 1
Previous: Empire Investments 2014 Limited
Net Worth: £4,931,119 *Total Assets:* £5,552,215
Registered Office: Richmond Bridge House, 419 Richmond Road, Twickenham, Middlesex, TW1 2EX
Activities: Other letting and operating of own or leased real estate
Major Shareholder: Raymond William Empson
Officers: Raymond William Empson [1959] Director

Empower Learning Academy Trust
Incorporated: 12 July 2011 *Employees:* 442
Previous: Hall Mead School
Net Worth: £51,636,392 *Total Assets:* £58,780,768
Registered Office: Hall Mead School, Marlborough Gardens, Upminster, Essex, RM14 1SF
Activities: General secondary education
Officers: Paula Garner, Secretary; James Brooks [1952] Director/Retired; Keith Butcher [1972] Director/Chartered Surveyor; Anthony Farrow [1975] Director/Business Manager; David Nicholas Harries [1960] Director; Simon London [1970] Director/Headteacher; Keith James Stewart [1961] Director/Shipping Manager; Stuart Mark Walton [1970] Director/Operations Manager

Emson Haig Limited
Incorporated: 21 November 1990 *Employees:* 110
Net Worth: £4,113,242 *Total Assets:* £7,616,573
Registered Office: 19-20 Bourne Court, Southend Road, Woodford Green, Essex, IG8 8HD
Activities: Other retail sale of new goods in specialised stores (not commercial art galleries and opticians)
Major Shareholder: David Philip Shone
Officers: David Philip Shone [1962] Director/Jeweller

Endace Europe Limited
Incorporated: 16 July 2003 *Employees:* 11
Net Worth: £2,940,797 *Total Assets:* £20,908,974
Registered Office: Squires House, 205a High Street, West Wickham, Kent, BR4 0PH
Activities: Other information technology service activities
Officers: Andrew Dean Harsant [1973] Director/Accountant [New Zealander]; Stuart Timothy Wilson [1959] Director/Engineer [Australian]

Endeavour MAT
Incorporated: 24 June 2011 *Employees:* 204
Previous: Wilmington Grammar School for Girls
Net Worth: £32,248,000 *Total Assets:* £35,097,000
Registered Office: Wilmington Grange, Parsons Lane, Wilmington, Dartford, Kent, DA2 7BB
Activities: General secondary education
Officers: Paul Clark [1967] Director/Bank Professional; Diane Elizabeth Connell [1948] Director; Shereen Daniels [1981] Director/HR Professional; John Bernard Gerard Horgan [1950] Director/Consultant; Sara Nadine Kemsley [1955] Director/Retired; Donna Lodge [1962] Director/Headmistress; Professor Graeme Gregery Maidment [1967] Director/Mechanical Engineer; Susan Yvonne Mavin [1957] Director/Head of Compliance & Systems; David Alistair Strachan [1965] Director/Chartered Accountant

Endeavour SCH Holdings Limited
Incorporated: 23 November 1998
Net Worth: £11,021,000 *Total Assets:* £163,332,000
Registered Office: 8 White Oak Square, London Road, Swanley, Kent, BR8 7AG
Activities: Activities of other holding companies n.e.c.
Shareholders: Innisfree M & G PPP LLP; Semperian PPP Investment Partners No.2 Limited
Officers: David John Brooking [1967] Investment Director; Neil Rae [1971] Director; Mr Terrence Ryan [1957] Director; Alastair James Watson [1974] Investment Director

Endeavour SCH PLC
Incorporated: 23 November 1998
Net Worth: £11,021,000 *Total Assets:* £163,332,000
Registered Office: 8 White Oak Square, London Road, Swanley, Kent, BR8 7AG
Activities: Hospital activities
Parent: Endeavour SCH Holdings Limited
Officers: David John Brooking [1967] Investment Director; Neil Rae [1971] Director; Mr Terrence Ryan [1957] Director; Alastair James Watson [1974] Investment Director

Endon Europe Power 1 Limited
Incorporated: 5 June 1998 *Employees:* 2
Net Worth Deficit: £93,074,000 *Total Assets:* £301,216,992
Registered Office: Velocity V1, Brooklands Drive, Weybridge, Surrey, KT13 0SL
Activities: Non-trading company
Parent: Endon Europe Power 3 Limited
Officers: Dena Michelle L O'Bue, Secretary; Asim Iftikhar Chohan [1973] Director of Operations; Michael James Timewell [1974] Director/Solicitor

Endon Europe Power 3 Limited
Incorporated: 19 August 1998 *Employees:* 2
Net Worth Deficit: £150,242,000 *Total Assets:* £376,488,992
Registered Office: Velocity V1, Brooklands Drive, Weybridge, Surrey, KT13 0SL
Activities: Non-trading company
Shareholders: Endon Europe Power 4 Limited; Endon Europe Power 6 Limited
Officers: Dena Michelle L O'Bue, Secretary; Asim Iftikhar Chohan [1973] Director of Operations; Michael James Timewell [1974] Director/Solicitor

Endon Europe Power 6 Limited
Incorporated: 24 December 1998 *Employees:* 2
Net Worth Deficit: £20,997,000 *Total Assets:* £21,397,000
Registered Office: Velocity V1, Brooklands Drive, Weybridge, Surrey, KT13 0SL
Activities: Non-trading company
Parent: Endon Europe Power 5 Limited
Officers: Dena Michelle L O'Bue, Secretary; Asim Iftikhar Chohan [1973] Director of Operations; Michael James Timewell [1974] Director/Solicitor

Energypro Asset Management Limited
Incorporated: 17 January 2017 *Employees:* 4
Net Worth: £5,947,750 *Total Assets:* £11,500,334
Registered Office: Nicholas House, River Front, Enfield, Middlesex, EN1 3FG
Activities: Other business support service activities n.e.c.
Shareholder: Steven Derrick Fawkes
Officers: David Anderson [1953] Director; Dr Steven Derrick Fawkes [1959] Director; Delvin Martin Lane [1974] Director; Stephen Michael Packer [1968] Director; Matthew William Pumfrey [1971] Director; Michael Anthony Tivey [1970] Director

Enfield Fancy Goods Limited
Incorporated: 2 March 1978 *Employees:* 82
Net Worth: £9,762,571 *Total Assets:* £16,664,887
Registered Office: 55 High Street, Hoddesdon, Herts, EN11 8TQ
Activities: Activities of head offices
Parent: EFG SIP
Officers: Alan Brian Shipton, Secretary; Alan Brian Shipton [1938] Director; Daren Shipton [1968] Director; Mark William Shipton [1973] Director; Trevor Roderick Shipton [1943] Director

Enfield Innovations Ltd
Incorporated: 3 October 2014 *Employees:* 2
Net Worth: £686,418 *Total Assets:* £14,227,513
Registered Office: 50 Civic Centre, Silver Street, Enfield, Middlesex, EN1 3XA
Activities: Buying and selling of own real estate
Parent: London Borough of Enfield
Officers: Matthew Bowmer [1965] Director/Accountant; Mark Timothy Bradbury [1961] Director/Chartered Surveyor; Joanna Michelle Embling [1949] Director; Sally Ann McTernan [1963] Director; Jayne Middleton-Albooye [1963] Director/Solicitor; Peter Chukuaduom Madako Nwosu [1965] Director/Chartered Accountant; Sabri Ozaydin [1968] Director/Manufacturer

Engineering, Logistics and Trading International UK Limited
Incorporated: 6 June 2016
Net Worth: £3,197,626 *Total Assets:* £5,634,761
Registered Office: c/o Brayne Williams & Barnard Limited, Rosemount House, Rosemount Avenue, West Byfleet, Surrey, KT14 6LB
Activities: Agents involved in the sale of a variety of goods
Major Shareholder: Pascal Raymond Joseph Bosquillon de Jenlis
Officers: Edouard de Jenlis [1975] Director [French]; Guillaume de Jenlis [1977] Director [French]; Nicolas Debavelaere [1966] Director [French]

Ennogen Healthcare Ltd
Incorporated: 14 October 2011 *Employees:* 10
Net Worth: £21,729,260 *Total Assets:* £29,465,110
Registered Office: Unit G4, Riverside Way, Dartford, Kent, DA1 5BS
Activities: Manufacture of basic pharmaceutical products
Major Shareholder: Gurdev Singh Rurai
Officers: Gurdev Singh Ruprai [1960] Director/Pharmacist

ENRA Group Limited
Incorporated: 13 November 2013 *Employees:* 2
Previous: ENRA Group Ltd
Net Worth Deficit: £358,797 *Total Assets:* £63,454,864
Registered Office: 3rd Floor, Premiere House, Elstree Way, Borehamwood, Herts, WD6 1JH
Activities: Other business support service activities n.e.c.
Parent: Newincco 1270 Limited
Officers: Emily Henrietta Gestetner [1967] Director; Harry Leon Landy [1978] Director; Danny Stephen Waters [1984] Director

Ensco 1212 Limited
Incorporated: 28 December 2016 *Employees:* 2
Net Worth Deficit: £450,709 *Total Assets:* £31,291,344
Registered Office: c/o Otto Bock Healthcare PLC, 32 Parsonage Road, Englefield Green, Egham, Surrey, TW20 0LD
Activities: Non-trading company
Parent: Ensco 1214 Limited
Officers: Gregor John Bates [1969] Director; Philip Anthony Yates [1963] Director

Ensco 1214 Limited
Incorporated: 12 January 2017 *Employees:* 2
Net Worth: £31,000,000 *Total Assets:* £31,000,000
Registered Office: c/o Otto Bock Healthcare PLC, 32 Parsonage Road, Englefield Green, Egham, Surrey, TW20 0LD
Activities: Non-trading company
Major Shareholder: Hans Georg Nader
Officers: Gregor John Bates [1969] Director; Philip Anthony Yates [1963] Director

Ensign Bus Company Limited
Incorporated: 23 October 1991 *Employees:* 213
Net Worth: £21,773,740 *Total Assets:* £26,987,252
Registered Office: The Rifle Range, Juliette Close, Purfleet Industrial Park, Aveley, South Ockendon, Essex, RM15 4YF
Activities: Other passenger land transport
Major Shareholder: Peter Ivor Newman
Officers: Louise Amy Pirie, Secretary; Roger Frederick Jackson [1958] Engineering Director; Peter Ivor Newman [1940] Director; Ross Christopher Newman [1970] Operations Director; Stephen Philip Newman [1972] Director/Operations Manager

Ensign Holdco 1 Limited
Incorporated: 10 May 2016 *Employees:* 202
Net Worth Deficit: £7,514,000 *Total Assets:* £73,359,000
Registered Office: Unit 4 Voltage, Mollison Avenue, Enfield, Middlesex, EN3 7XQ
Activities: Activities of head offices
Shareholders: Equistone General Partner V LLP; Equistone Partners Europe Limited
Officers: Christopher Nicholas Sebastian Jehan Candfield [1985] Investment Director [British/German]; Sukhjeevan Singh Samra [1976] Director; Tim Allan Swales [1978] Director; Martin Stuart Taylor [1967] Director

Ensign Holdco 3 Limited
Incorporated: 10 May 2016
Net Worth: £88,000 *Total Assets:* £28,515,000
Registered Office: Unit 4 Voltage, Mollison Avenue, Enfield, Middlesex, EN3 7XQ
Activities: Activities of head offices
Parent: Ensign Holdco 2 Limited
Officers: Sukhjeevan Singh Samra [1976] Commercial Director; Martin Stuart Taylor [1967] Director

Ensign Holdco 4 Limited
Incorporated: 10 May 2016
Net Worth: £22,320,000 *Total Assets:* £59,430,000
Registered Office: Unit 4 Voltage, Mollison Avenue, Enfield, Middlesex, EN3 7XQ
Activities: Activities of head offices
Parent: Ensign Holdco 3 Limited
Officers: Sukhjeevan Singh Samra [1976] Director; Martin Stuart Taylor [1967] Commercial Director

Ensono Limited
Incorporated: 12 November 1996 *Employees:* 304
Previous: Attenda Limited
Net Worth: £12,769,000 *Total Assets:* £33,558,000
Registered Office: One London Road, Staines upon Thames, Middlesex, TW18 4EX
Activities: Information technology consultancy activities
Parent: Amphora Acquisitions Ltd
Officers: Peter John Bazil [1972] Director/General Counsel [American]; Norman Smagley [1958] Director/Chief Financial Officer [American]

Entel Communications Holdings Limited
Incorporated: 3 December 2010 *Employees:* 201
Net Worth: £9,403,630 *Total Assets:* £12,683,989
Registered Office: 320 Centennial Avenue, Centennial Park, Elstree, Borehamwood, Herts, WD6 3TJ
Activities: Activities of head offices
Major Shareholder: Metin Pallenberg
Officers: Metin Luke Pallenberg [1970] Director

Enterprise Finance Limited
Incorporated: 16 May 2002 *Employees:* 60
Net Worth: £8,228,437 *Total Assets:* £9,350,643
Registered Office: 3rd Floor, Premiere House, Elstree Way, Borehamwood, Herts, WD6 1JH
Activities: Banks
Parent: ENRA Group Limited
Officers: Emily Henrietta Gestetner [1967] Director; Harry Leon Landy [1978] Director; David Stewart [1965] Director; Danny Stephen Waters [1984] Director

Enterprise Rent-a-Car European Holdings Limited
Incorporated: 2 July 2001 *Employees:* 4,955
Net Worth: £198,180,000 *Total Assets:* £1,499,531,008
Registered Office: Enterprise House, Vicarage Road, Egham, Surrey, TW20 9FB
Activities: Activities of head offices
Officers: Teresa Anne Holderer, Secretary; Ricky Allan Short [1958] Director [American]

Enterprise Rent-a-Car UK Holdings Limited
Incorporated: 21 June 1994
Net Worth: £48,041,000 *Total Assets:* £51,979,000
Registered Office: Enterprise House, Vicarage Road, Egham, Surrey, TW20 9FB
Activities: Activities of head offices
Parent: Enterprise Rent-a-Car European Holdings Limited
Officers: Teresa Anne Holderer, Secretary; Ricky Allan Short [1958] Director [American]

Enterprise Rent-a-Car UK Limited
Incorporated: 4 July 1994 *Employees:* 4,951
Net Worth: £202,119,008 *Total Assets:* £1,472,199,040
Registered Office: Enterprise House, Vicarage Road, Egham, Surrey, TW20 9FB
Activities: Renting and leasing of cars and light motor vehicles
Parent: Enterprise Rent-a-Car UK Holdings Limited
Officers: Teresa Anne Holderer, Secretary; Ricky Allan Short [1958] Director [American]

Envirotech Properties Limited
Incorporated: 1 July 1998
Net Worth: £6,218,866 *Total Assets:* £6,225,186
Registered Office: 187 Ashley Park Avenue, Walton on Thames, Surrey, KT12 1ET
Activities: Other letting and operating of own or leased real estate
Officers: Linda Fay McGivern, Secretary; David Ashley McBean [1959] Director

EPI Global Ltd
Incorporated: 13 March 2014 *Employees:* 1
Net Worth Deficit: £38,911 *Total Assets:* £18,583,060
Registered Office: 25 High Street, Cobham, Surrey, KT11 3DH
Activities: Other business support service activities n.e.c.
Parent: EPI Group Holdings Ltd
Officers: Richard Bradley, Secretary; Richard Bradley [1981] Director; Rupert James Brown [1983] Director; Anthony Dickin [1970] Director; Ian Michael Langley [1962] Director; Andrew Stuart James Smart [1962] Director

EPI Group Holdings Ltd
Incorporated: 26 March 2014 *Employees:* 32
Net Worth Deficit: £10,010,143 *Total Assets:* £16,263,917
Registered Office: 25 High Street, Cobham, Surrey, KT11 3DH
Activities: Activities of head offices
Parent: Palatine Private Equity LLP
Officers: Richard Bradley, Secretary; Richard Bradley [1981] Director; Rupert James Brown [1983] Director; Anthony Dickin [1970] Director; Ian Michael Langley [1962] Director; Andrew Stuart James Smart [1962] Director

Epoch RJK Limited
Incorporated: 15 November 2001
Net Worth: £11,033,645 *Total Assets:* £13,028,976
Registered Office: Chemilines House, Alperton Lane, Wembley, Middlesex, HA0 1DX
Activities: Other letting and operating of own or leased real estate
Parent: Chemilines Group Holdings Limited
Officers: Ravindra Prabhudas Karia, Secretary; Jagdish Prabhudas Karia [1958] Director; Ravindra Prabhudas Karia [1953] Director

Epoch-Making Toys Limited
Incorporated: 29 July 2013 *Employees:* 18
Net Worth Deficit: £973,185 *Total Assets:* £14,451,114
Registered Office: Capital Court, 30 Windsor Street, Uxbridge, Middlesex, UB8 1AB
Activities: Wholesale of household goods (other than musical instruments) n.e.c
Shareholder: Michihiro Maeda
Officers: Daniel Martyn Tavender, Secretary; Neil John Grant Bandtock [1961] Managing Director; Michihiro Maeda [1958] Director/Manufacturer of Toys [Japanese]; Daniel Martyn Tavender [1975] Finance Director

Epsilon Telecommunications Limited
Incorporated: 7 August 2002 *Employees:* 60
Net Worth: £6,257,648 *Total Assets:* £22,832,492
Registered Office: 400 Dashwood Lang Road, Weybridge, Surrey, KT15 2HJ
Activities: Other telecommunications activities
Officers: Thomas William Slack [1965] Director; Jerzy Szlosarek [1976] Director/Manager; Long Peng Wu [1953] Director [Singaporean]

Epsom College
Incorporated: 6 June 2000 *Employees:* 422
Net Worth: £22,995,000 *Total Assets:* £41,569,000
Registered Office: Epsom College, College Road, Epsom, Surrey, KT17 4JQ
Activities: General secondary education
Officers: Sarah Elizabeth Teasdale, Secretary; Dr Jeremy Shaw Bolton [1943] Director/Medical Practitioner; Tania Alison Louise Botting [1965] Director/Headmistress; Fiona Jane Boulton [1964] Director/Headmistress; Doctor Hywel Henry Bowen Perkins [1952] Director/GP; Edward James Chandler [1954] Director/Financial Consultant; Belinda Jane Dolbear [1965] Director/Solicitor; The Very Reverend Dianna Lynn Gwilliams [1957] Director/Dean of Guildford; John Hay [1948] PR Director; Dr Suzannah Rebecca Gabriella Lipscomb [1978] Director/Historian and Senior Lecturer; Ayodeji Christopher Renner Mahoney [1963] Director/Legal Consultant; Andrew John Pianca [1951] Director/Accountant; George Pincus [1942] Director/Recruitment Consultant; Alexander Murray Russell [1962] Director; Paul Andrew Stanford [1967] Managing Director; Karen Elizabeth Thomas [1958] Director/Consultant Surgeon; Clive Royston Watson [1961] Director; Dr Alastair James Wells [1960] Director/General Medical Practitioner

Epsomedical (Acquisitions) Limited
Incorporated: 8 May 2013 *Employees:* 2
Net Worth: £3,762,769 *Total Assets:* £5,710,372
Registered Office: Cobham Hospital, 168 Portsmouth Road, Cobham, Surrey, KT11 1HS
Activities: Activities of head offices
Shareholder: Timothy James Lang Taylor
Officers: Angela Ruth Pearce, Secretary; Doctor Richard John Cowlard [1959] Director/Medical Practitioner; Timothy James Lang Taylor [1956] Director

Equatorial Traders Limited
Incorporated: 14 June 1991 *Employees:* 14
Net Worth: £7,272,039 *Total Assets:* £15,023,933
Registered Office: 2nd Floor, Grove House, 55 Lowlands Road, Harrow, Middlesex, HA1 3AW
Activities: Wholesale of coffee, tea, cocoa and spices
Major Shareholder: Rupen Manherlal Soochak
Officers: Sona Mehta, Secretary; Chandrika Manherlal Soochak [1949] Director; Manherlal Pradhan Soochak [1944] Director; Rupen Manherlal Soochak [1971] Director/Commodity Trader

Equicap Estates Limited
Incorporated: 14 February 2013
Net Worth: £3,549,770 *Total Assets:* £10,064,613
Registered Office: Fairfield, London Road, Rickmansworth, Herts, WD3 1JS
Activities: Security dealing on own account
Parent: Equicap Limited
Officers: Sarika Luthra, Secretary; Arun Luthra [1964] Director

Equiniti Data Limited
Incorporated: 2 February 2005 *Employees:* 47
Previous: Marketing Source Ltd
Net Worth: £10,252,000 *Total Assets:* £13,218,000
Registered Office: Elder House, St Georges Business Park, Brooklands Road, Weybridge, Surrey, KT13 0TS
Activities: Information technology consultancy activities
Parent: Equiniti Holdings Limited
Officers: Katherine Cong, Secretary; Adam Charles Green [1978] Director/Chief Risk Officer; Guy Edward Looker [1978] Director; Stuart Robb [1972] Director; Seema Sangar [1976] Finance Director; Guy Wakeley [1970] Director

Equiniti Global Payments Limited
Incorporated: 2 March 2007 *Employees:* 1
Previous: Transglobal Payment Solutions Limited
Net Worth: £3,917,000 *Total Assets:* £5,606,000
Registered Office: Elder House, St Georges Business Park, Brooklands Road, Weybridge, Surrey, KT13 0TS
Activities: Financial intermediation not elsewhere classified
Parent: Equiniti Holdings Limited
Officers: Katherine Cong, Secretary; Harshna Cayley [1979] Managing Director; Neil Kinnon [1973] Operations Director; Liam Scott Forrest McGrath [1970] Director; Seema Sangar [1976] Finance Director; Guy Richard Wakeley [1970] Director

Equiniti Holdings Limited
Incorporated: 23 April 2007 *Employees:* 16
Net Worth: £104,386,000 *Total Assets:* £1,089,864,960
Registered Office: Elder House, St Georges Business Park, Brooklands Road, Weybridge, Surrey, KT13 0TS
Activities: Activities of head offices
Parent: Equiniti Group PLC
Officers: Katherine Cong, Secretary; John Stier [1966] Director/Chief Financial Officer; Guy Richard Wakeley [1970] Director

Equiniti Services Limited
Incorporated: 5 April 1963 *Employees:* 528
Net Worth: £42,038,000 *Total Assets:* £146,148,992
Registered Office: Elder House, St Georges Business Park, Brooklands Road, Weybridge, Surrey, KT13 0TS
Activities: Activities of other holding companies n.e.c.
Parent: Equiniti Limited
Officers: Katherine Cong, Secretary; Robert David Bloor [1968] Director/Accountant; John Stier [1966] Director/Chief Financial Officer; Guy Richard Wakeley [1970] Director

Equion Health (Newcastle) Limited
Incorporated: 15 December 2004
Net Worth: £41,000 *Total Assets:* £21,325,000
Registered Office: 8 White Oak Square, London Road, Swanley, Kent, BR8 7AG
Activities: Activities of head offices
Parent: Innisfree Nominees Limited
Officers: Gaynor Birley-Smith [1966] Investment Director; David Richard Bradbury [1969] Asset Director; Alastair James Watson [1974] Investment Director

Erac UK Finance Limited
Incorporated: 18 July 1994
Net Worth: £16,000 *Total Assets:* £1,076,040,960
Registered Office: Enterprise House, Vicarage Road, Egham, Surrey, TW20 9FB
Activities: Financial management
Parent: Enterprise Rent-a-Car UK Holdings Limited
Officers: Teresa Anne Holderer, Secretary; Ricky Allan Short [1958] Director [American]

Eran Diamonds (UK) Limited
Incorporated: 11 November 1998 *Employees:* 4
Net Worth: £2,280,523 *Total Assets:* £7,502,391
Registered Office: 88 North Street, Hornchurch, Essex, RM11 1SR
Activities: Wholesale of watches and jewellery
Officers: Indrani Nahar, Secretary; Sailendra Nahar [1971] Director

Ergonomic Solutions International Limited
Incorporated: 28 July 2004 *Employees:* 18
Net Worth: £6,354,290 *Total Assets:* £8,931,379
Registered Office: B1 Longmead Business Centre, Blenheim Road, Epsom, Surrey, KT19 9QQ
Activities: Information technology consultancy activities
Parent: Ergonomic Solutions Limited
Officers: Robert Buchler, Secretary; Christopher William Arthur Davis [1948] Financial Director; Ian Campbell Dewar [1961] Director/Sales Agent Consultant; Morten Jensen [1961] Director/Lawyer [Danish]; Heather Ann McSharry [1961] Director [Irish]; Patrick Brendan Prior [1943] Financial Director [Irish]; Kieron Alfred Tonge [1949] Director [Irish]

Ergonomic Solutions Limited
Incorporated: 4 July 1996 *Employees:* 134
Net Worth: £8,844,762 *Total Assets:* £17,210,870
Registered Office: B1 Longmead Business Centre, Blenheim Road, Epsom, Surrey, KT19 9QQ
Activities: Manufacture of other fabricated metal products n.e.c.
Major Shareholder: Keiron Alfred Tonge
Officers: Ian Campbell Dewar [1961] Director/Manager; Patrick Brendan Prior [1943] Director [Irish]; Kieron Alfred Tonge [1949] Director [Irish]

Erinastar Limited
Incorporated: 2 January 1976 *Employees:* 4
Net Worth: £9,692,969 *Total Assets:* £9,754,188
Registered Office: Cavendish House, 369 Burnt Oak Broadway, Edgware, Middlesex, HA8 5AW
Activities: Activities of religious organisations
Officers: Dov Cohen [1981] Director/Property Manager; Richard Simon Lewis [1949] Director; David Reichmann [1962] Director; Dov Reichmann [1930] Director

Erindale Limited
Incorporated: 30 April 2008 *Employees:* 1
Net Worth: £13,443,007 *Total Assets:* £41,399,480
Registered Office: 34-36 London Road, Wembley, Middlesex, HA9 7EX
Activities: Other letting and operating of own or leased real estate
Major Shareholder: Raja Jameel Adil
Officers: Mohammed Adil, Secretary; Raja Jameel Adil [1971] Director/Solicitor

Erith Contractors Limited
Incorporated: 15 March 1973 *Employees:* 421
Net Worth: £12,801,829 *Total Assets:* £47,079,216
Registered Office: Erith House, 7 Queen Street, Erith, Kent, DA8 1RP
Activities: Treatment and disposal of hazardous waste
Parent: Erith Holdings Limited
Officers: Steven Thomas Darsey, Secretary; David John Darsey [1969] Director; Tony Darsey [1961] Director; Steven May [1985] Director; Barry Menzies [1957] Director/Chartered Quantity Surveyor; Victoria Stokes [1974] Finance Director

Erith Haulage Company Limited
Incorporated: 24 September 1971 *Employees:* 69
Net Worth: £1,696,785 *Total Assets:* £11,616,903
Registered Office: Erith House, 7 Queen Street, Erith, Kent, DA8 1RP
Activities: Collection of non-hazardous waste
Parent: Erith Holdings Ltd
Officers: Steven Thomas Darsey, Secretary; Steven Thomas Darsey [1958] Director; Steven Richard Head [1956] Director/Transport Manager; Steve Martin [1971] Director; Victoria Stokes [1974] Finance Director

Erith Holdings Limited
Incorporated: 27 February 1991 *Employees:* 626
Net Worth: £16,877,000 *Total Assets:* £63,617,000
Registered Office: Erith House, 7 Queen Street, Erith, Kent, DA8 1RP
Activities: Activities of head offices
Parent: Erith Holdings Trustee Limited
Officers: Steven Thomas Darsey, Secretary; David John Darsey [1969] Director; Steven Thomas Darsey [1958] Director; Tony Darsey [1961] Contract Director; Victoria Stokes [1974] Finance Director

Erith Plant Services Limited
Incorporated: 10 July 2014 *Employees:* 76
Net Worth: £409,794 *Total Assets:* £9,584,385
Registered Office: Erith House, Queen Street, Erith, Kent, DA8 1RP
Activities: Other specialised construction activities n.e.c.
Parent: Erith Haulage Company Ltd
Officers: Victoria Stokes, Secretary; Steven Richard Head [1956] Director; Steve Martin [1971] Director; Victoria Stokes [1974] Finance Director

Erith School
Incorporated: 10 September 2010 *Employees:* 220
Net Worth: £25,767,000 *Total Assets:* £29,549,000
Registered Office: Erith School, Avenue Road, Erith, Kent, DA8 3BN
Activities: General secondary education
Officers: Stephanie Allen [1964] Director/Headteacher; Monica Cane [1953] Director/Retired; Peter Francis Thomas Carter [1955] Director/Retired; Yvonne Enoe [1959] Director/Lecturer; Wendy Lynne Maietta-Turner [1967] Director/Community Nursery Nurse; Maria Fatima Frazao Freitas Melder [1965] Director/HR Administrator; Ann Janet Nuckley [1947] Director/Retired; Adeola Olatokunbo Apeke Olojo [1957] Director/Senior Business Manager CPS

Erwin Technologies UK Limited
Incorporated: 4 August 2016 *Employees:* 20
Net Worth: £29,509 *Total Assets:* £6,221,276
Registered Office: 1 The Green, Richmond, Surrey, TW9 1PL
Activities: Other information service activities n.e.c.
Parent: Erwin Inc
Officers: Richard Norman Campbell [1961] Director/Chief Financial Officer [Canadian]; James P McGarry [1969] Director/Manager [American]

Esin Cash & Carry Limited
Incorporated: 12 September 2012 *Employees:* 2
Net Worth: £2,256,122 *Total Assets:* £9,649,767
Registered Office: Unit 1-8 Centenary Industrial Estate, Jeffreys Road, Enfield, Middlesex, EN3 7UF
Activities: Retail sale in non-specialised stores with food, beverages or tobacco predominating
Parent: TFC Holdings London Limited
Officers: Ercan Ucur [1970] Director; Huseyin Ucur [1945] Director

Eskan Electronics Limited
Incorporated: 26 February 1988 *Employees:* 10
Net Worth: £10,225,143 *Total Assets:* £12,787,272
Registered Office: Unit 3b Kelvin Industrial Estate, Long Drive, Greenford, Middlesex, UB6 8WA
Activities: Manufacture of communication equipment other than telegraph, and telephone apparatus and equipment
Major Shareholder: Shaun Anderson
Officers: Shaun Anderson [1956] Director/Engineer

Eskaylab Limited
Incorporated: 29 July 1908
Net Worth: £201,868,992 *Total Assets:* £201,900,000
Registered Office: 980 Great West Road, Brentford, Middlesex, TW8 9GS
Activities: Other business support service activities n.e.c.
Parent: SmithKline Beecham Limited
Officers: James Borger [1963] Director/VP, Group Financial Planning and Analysis [American]; Alan George Burns [1975] Director

ESP Connections Limited
Incorporated: 1 August 1996
Net Worth: £18,321,000 *Total Assets:* £84,047,000
Registered Office: 1st Floor, Bluebird House, Mole Business Park, Leatherhead, Surrey, KT22 7BA
Activities: Other business support service activities n.e.c.
Parent: E.S. Pipelines Limited
Officers: Thomas William Butler [1959] Finance Director [Irish]; Nicholas John Clark [1960] Director; Paul Miles [1971] Director/Chief Financial Officer; Kevin O'Connor [1976] Director/Chief Executive Officer; Victoria Caroline Spiers [1969] Director/Manager; Stuart Peter Williams [1965] Operations Director

ESP Electricity Limited
Incorporated: 1 April 2003 *Employees:* 19
Net Worth: £9,511,000 *Total Assets:* £43,873,000
Registered Office: 1st Floor, Bluebird House, Mole Business Park, Leatherhead, Surrey, KT22 7BA
Activities: Distribution of electricity
Parent: ESPUG Finance Limited
Officers: Thomas William Butler [1959] Finance Director [Irish]; Nicholas John Clark [1960] Director; Paul Miles [1971] Director/Chief Financial Officer; Kevin O'Connor [1976] Director/Chief Executive Officer; Victoria Caroline Spiers [1969] Director/Manager; Stuart Peter Williams [1965] Operations Director

ESP Networks Limited
Incorporated: 22 October 1993
Net Worth: £3,538,926 *Total Assets:* £5,228,180
Registered Office: 1st Floor, Bluebird House, Mole Business Park, Leatherhead, Surrey, KT22 7BA
Activities: Transport via pipeline
Parent: E.S. Pipelines Limited
Officers: Thomas William Butler [1959] Finance Director [Irish]; Nicholas John Clark [1960] Director; Paul Miles [1971] Director/Chief Financial Officer; Kevin O'Connor [1976] Director/Chief Executive Officer; Victoria Caroline Spiers [1969] Director/Manager; Stuart Peter Williams [1965] Operations Director

ESP Utilities Group Limited
Incorporated: 17 May 1991 *Employees:* 74
Net Worth Deficit: £14,482,000 *Total Assets:* £271,476,000
Registered Office: 1st Floor, Bluebird House, Mole Business Park, Leatherhead, Surrey, KT22 7BA
Activities: Activities of head offices
Parent: Zoom Gas Pipelines Limited
Officers: Thomas William Butler [1959] Finance Director [Irish]; Nicholas John Clark [1960] Director; Anna Louise Dellis [1973] Director; Nicholas Wenham Horler [1959] Director/Chairman; Paul Miles [1971] Director/Chief Financial Officer; Kevin O'Connor [1976] Director/Chief Executive Officer; Sebastian Schwengber [1979] Director/Investment Professional [German]; Bernardo de SA Braamcamp Sobral Sottomayor [1973] Director [Portuguese]; Victoria Caroline Spiers [1969] Director/Manager; Stuart Peter Williams [1965] Operations Director

ESPUG Finance Limited
Incorporated: 25 August 2017
Net Worth: £512,523,008 *Total Assets:* £765,907,968
Registered Office: 1st Floor, Bluebird House, Mole Business Park, Leatherhead, Surrey, KT22 7BA
Activities: Activities of other holding companies n.e.c.
Parent: ESP Utilities Group Limited
Officers: Thomas William Butler [1959] Finance Director [Irish]; Nicholas John Clark [1960] Development Director; Anna Louise Dellis [1973] Director/Accountant; Paul Miles [1971] Director/Chief Financial Officer; Kevin O'Connor [1976] Director/Chief Executive Officer; Sebastian Schwengber [1979] Director/Investment Professional [German]; Bernardo de SA Braamcamp Sobral Sottomayor [1973] Director [Portuguese]; Victoria Caroline Spiers [1969] Director/Manager; Stuart Peter Williams [1965] Operations Director

ESSCI Ireland Limited
Incorporated: 3 September 2015
Net Worth Deficit: £965,000 *Total Assets:* £11,420,000
Registered Office: Twenty, Kingston Road, Staines upon Thames, Middlesex, TW18 4LG
Activities: Electrical installation
Parent: ESSCI Limited
Officers: Michael Andrew Booth [1974] Director/Chief Financial Officer; Paul John Patrick Paul Kavanagh [1957] Director/Chief Executive [Irish]

ESSCI Limited
Incorporated: 27 August 2015 *Employees:* 2,170
Net Worth Deficit: £1,796,000 *Total Assets:* £145,068,992
Registered Office: Twenty, Kingston Road, Staines upon Thames, Middlesex, TW18 4LG
Activities: Electrical installation
Parent: EDF Energy Services Limited
Officers: Michael Andrew Booth [1974] Director/Chief Financial Officer; Michael Edward Harris [1962] Director; Gautier Jacob [1974] Director [French]; Paul John Patrick Paul Kavanagh [1957] Director/Chief Executive [Irish]; John Joseph Kelly [1969] Commercial Director; Michael Kennedy [1956] Director/Chief Operations Officer [Irish]; William Alexander Sloan [1957] HR Director

ESSCI Technical Services Limited
Incorporated: 27 August 2015 *Employees:* 24
Net Worth Deficit: £2,349,000 *Total Assets:* £22,552,000
Registered Office: Twenty, Kingston Road, Staines upon Thames, Middlesex, TW18 4LG
Activities: Electrical installation
Parent: ESSCI Limited
Officers: Michael Andrew Booth [1974] Finance Director; Paul John Patrick Paul Kavanagh [1957] Director/Chief Executive [Irish]

Essential Harvest Limited
Incorporated: 28 August 2001
Net Worth: £377,985 *Total Assets:* £7,093,909
Registered Office: Old Barn House, High Road, Eastcote, Pinner, Middlesex, HA5 2EW
Activities: Other letting and operating of own or leased real estate
Parent: Good Harvest Group Limited
Officers: Michael Richard Cowen, Secretary; Paul Allan Beer [1948] Director/Chartered Accountant; Michael Richard Cowen [1961] Director/Chief Financial Officer; Anthony Ronald William Parfitt [1952] Director/Chartered Accountant

Essential Pharma Limited
Incorporated: 2 February 2011 *Employees:* 1
Net Worth: £10,300,627 *Total Assets:* £30,423,222
Registered Office: 7 Egham Business Village, Crabtree Road, Egham, Surrey, TW20 8RB
Activities: Manufacture of basic pharmaceutical products
Shareholders: Navinchandra Jamnadas; Varsha Navinchandra
Officers: Nikesh Engineer [1985] Director/Doctor

Essex County Laundry,Limited
Incorporated: 21 April 1915 *Employees:* 101
Net Worth: £740,801 *Total Assets:* £7,679,252
Registered Office: Westcott House, Selinas Lane, Dagenham, Essex, RM8 1QH
Activities: Washing and (dry-)cleaning of textile and fur products
Officers: Christopher Mark Westcott, Secretary; James Andrew Lincoln [1982] Director/MD; Christopher Mark Westcott [1956] Director/Manager

Essex Motor Company Limited
Incorporated: 26 April 2005 *Employees:* 67
Net Worth: £3,264,296 *Total Assets:* £11,332,361
Registered Office: 54 Sun Street, Waltham Abbey, Essex, EN9 1EJ
Activities: Sale of new cars and light motor vehicles
Shareholders: William Gary Cook; Darren Lowe; Karen Cook
Officers: William Gary Cook, Secretary; William Gary Cook [1957] Director; Darren Lowe [1969] Director; Simon Nicholas Ross [1966] Director/Accountant

Essex Road Development Limited
Incorporated: 3 October 2013 *Employees:* 2
Net Worth: £2,287,033 *Total Assets:* £5,171,117
Registered Office: 119 High Street, Loughton, Essex, IG10 4LT
Activities: Buying and selling of own real estate
Shareholders: Beech Two Limited; RGK Properties Limited; Tommo Properties Ltd
Officers: Vincent Daniel Goldstein [1960] Director; Russell George Kilikita [1960] Director

Essex Services Group Limited
Incorporated: 1 September 1975 *Employees:* 194
Previous: Essex Services Group PLC
Net Worth: £9,849,633 *Total Assets:* £41,670,440
Registered Office: Viking Business Centre, Danes Road, Romford, Essex, RM7 0HL
Activities: Electrical installation
Parent: Essex Group Holdings Limited
Officers: James Hansford, Secretary; James Hansford [1978] Director/Accountant; John Sylvester Sampson [1944] Director/Electrical Contractor; Mark Peter Sampson [1978] Director; Michael John Ventham [1951] Director/Chartered Accountant

Esso Exploration and Production UK Limited
Incorporated: 22 July 1925
Net Worth: £880,000,000 *Total Assets:* £4,283,000,064
Registered Office: Ermyn House, Ermyn Way, Leatherhead, Surrey, KT22 8UX
Activities: Extraction of crude petroleum
Parent: Esso UK Limited
Officers: Fiona Harness, Secretary; Robert Michael Cooper [1961] Director/Oil Company Executive; Jay Loren Jackson [1962] Director/Oil Company Executive [American]; Andrew Mark Johnson [1976] Director/Oil Company Executive

Esso Petroleum Company,Limited
Incorporated: 27 April 1888 *Employees:* 1,291
Net Worth: £1,264,000,000 *Total Assets:* £2,680,000,000
Registered Office: Ermyn House, Ermyn Way, Leatherhead, Surrey, KT22 8UX
Activities: Extraction of crude petroleum
Parent: ExxonMobil UK Limited
Officers: Fiona Harness, Secretary; Robert Michael Cooper [1961] Director/Oil Company Executive; Simon Peter Downing [1964] Director/Oil Company Executive; Andrew Mark Johnson [1976] Director/Oil Company Executive

Esso Property Management Company, Limited
Incorporated: 15 July 1919
Net Worth: £8,718,000 *Total Assets:* £11,278,000
Registered Office: Ermyn House, Ermyn Way, Leatherhead, Surrey, KT22 8UX
Activities: Management of real estate on a fee or contract basis
Parent: Exxon Mobil Corporation
Officers: Fiona Henderson Harness, Secretary; Robert Michael Cooper [1961] Director/Oil Company Executive; Andrew Mark Johnson [1976] Director/Oil Company Executive; Steven Adam Oldfield [1972] Director/Oil Company Executive

Esso UK Limited
Incorporated: 6 October 1981
Net Worth: £1,744,000,000 *Total Assets:* £3,028,000,000
Registered Office: Ermyn House, Ermyn Way, Leatherhead, Surrey, KT22 8UX
Activities: Extraction of crude petroleum
Parent: Exxon Mobil Corporation
Officers: Fiona Harness, Secretary; Robert Michael Cooper [1961] Director/Oil Company Executive; Simon Peter Downing [1964] Director/Oil Company Executive; Jay Loren Jackson [1962] Director/Oil Company Executive [American]; Andrew Mark Johnson [1976] Director/Oil Company Executive

Estates and Lets 2 LLP
Incorporated: 10 March 2009
Net Worth: £13,385,354 *Total Assets:* £24,684,110
Registered Office: 166 College Road, Harrow, Middlesex, HA1 1RA
Officers: Michael Docker [1963] Member; Michele Docker [1965] Member; Charles Sedgwick Pear [1983] LLP Member

Estates and Lets 3 LLP
Incorporated: 13 July 2009
Net Worth: £1,614,641 *Total Assets:* £7,498,515
Registered Office: 166 College Road, Harrow, Middlesex, HA1 1RA
Officers: Michael Spencer Docker [1963] Member; Michele Docker [1965] Member

Esteem Care Ltd
Incorporated: 29 October 1998 *Employees:* 86
Net Worth: £5,542,049 *Total Assets:* £5,957,139
Registered Office: 1st Floor, 44-50 The Broadway, Southall, Middlesex, UB1 1QB
Activities: Residential nursing care facilities
Officers: Palani Ketheeswaran [1968] Director; Sharmili Seevarajah [1977] Director; Nadarajah Bernard Suresparan [1959] Director/Company Secretary; Vathsala Suresparan [1961] Director

ET Enterprises Limited
Incorporated: 5 February 2007 *Employees:* 89
Net Worth: £3,640,351 *Total Assets:* £6,987,165
Registered Office: 45 Riverside Way, Cowley, Uxbridge, Middlesex, UB8 2YF
Activities: Other manufacturing n.e.c.
Parent: Ludlum Measurements Inc
Officers: Gary Chambers, Secretary; Dr Andrew James Cormack [1971] Managing Director; Laurence Merl Ludlum [1957] Director/Engineer [American]

Etcetera Construction Services Limited
Incorporated: 17 April 1986 *Employees:* 6
Net Worth: £28,465,444 *Total Assets:* £30,702,602
Registered Office: Riverside House, 1-5 Como Street, Romford, Essex, RM7 7DN
Activities: Construction of other civil engineering projects n.e.c.
Shareholder: Michael Harkins
Officers: Janet Margaret Harkins, Secretary; Darren Michael Harkins [1972] Director; Janet Margaret Harkins [1954] Director

Ethypharm Holdings UK Ltd
Incorporated: 4 July 2014 *Employees:* 1
Net Worth: £24,243,340 *Total Assets:* £76,845,232
Registered Office: Bampton Road, Harold Hill, Romford, Essex, RM3 8UG
Activities: Dormant company
Parent: Ethypharm S.A.
Officers: Roseline Georgette Joannesse [1959] Director/Vice President Legal Affairs [French]; Jean-Hugues Louis Marie Lecat [1956] Director [French]

Ethypharm UK Limited
Incorporated: 11 June 2013 *Employees:* 17
Previous: DB Ashbourne Limited
Net Worth: £5,230,574 *Total Assets:* £24,475,888
Registered Office: Bampton Road, Harold Hill, Romford, Essex, RM3 8UG
Activities: Wholesale of pharmaceutical goods
Parent: Dallas Burston Ashbourne Holdings Limited
Officers: Roseline Georgette Joannesse [1959] Director/Vice President Legal Affairs [French]; Jean-Hugues Louis Marie Lecat [1956] Director [French]; Lisa Elaine Tomkins [1978] Finance Director

Etonbrook Properties PLC
Incorporated: 14 February 1985
Net Worth: £5,465,714 *Total Assets:* £6,528,038
Registered Office: Unicorn House, Station Close, Potters Bar, Herts, EN6 1TL
Activities: Dormant company
Parent: Panther Securities PLC
Officers: Simon Jeffrey Peters, Secretary/Director; Peter Michael Kellner [1942] Director; Andrew Stewart Perloff [1944] Director; Simon Jeffrey Peters [1977] Director

Euro Alloys Limited
Incorporated: 26 February 1990 *Employees:* 14
Net Worth: £12,266,735 *Total Assets:* £79,417,480
Registered Office: 9th Floor, One Croydon, 12-16 Addiscombe Road, Croydon, Surrey, CR0 0XT
Activities: Wholesale of metals and metal ores
Major Shareholder: Alfredo Riviere
Officers: Stuart Reginald Brothers, Secretary; David Charles Hogan [1948] Director/Accountant; Kevin John Rhodes [1965] Director; Alfredo Luis Riviere Rodriguez [1969] Director [Italian]

Euro Services Limited
Incorporated: 3 August 1979 *Employees:* 64
Net Worth: £3,188,540 *Total Assets:* £7,118,329
Registered Office: Unit 2c, Twickenham Trading Estate, Rugby Road, Twickenham, Middlesex, TW1 1DG
Activities: Retail sale of carpets, rugs, wall and floor coverings in specialised stores
Shareholder: Rolfi Kandioti
Officers: Rolfi Kandioti [1954] Director/Importer and Exporter; Nicholas James Laudrum [1967] Sales and Marketing Director; David Andrew Payne [1952] Finance Director

Eurochoice Limited
Incorporated: 1 December 2008
Net Worth: £41,271 *Total Assets:* £5,293,382
Registered Office: Continental House, 497 Sunleigh Road, Wembley, Middlesex, HA0 4LY
Activities: Wholesale of wine, beer, spirits and other alcoholic beverages
Officers: Salmon Ahmed [1970] Director

Eurocity Properties (Central) Limited
Incorporated: 3 September 1997
Net Worth: £131,547 *Total Assets:* £11,077,806
Registered Office: Unicorn House, Station Close, Potters Bar, Herts, EN6 1TL
Activities: Buying and selling of own real estate
Parent: Panther Securities PLC
Officers: Simon Jeffrey Peters, Company Secretary; Andrew Stewart Perloff [1944] Director; John Henry Perloff [1968] Director; Simon Jeffrey Peters [1977] Director

Euromax Resources (Macedonia) UK Limited
Incorporated: 20 November 2012
Net Worth: £9,429,545 *Total Assets:* £17,829,424
Registered Office: 5-9 Eden Street, Kingston upon Thames, Surrey, KT1 1BQ
Activities: Mining of other non-ferrous metal ores
Parent: Euromax Resources Limited
Officers: Varshan Baboolal Gokool, Secretary; Patrick William Forward [1967] Director; Varshan Baboolal Gokool [1976] Director

Euron Developments (France) Limited
Incorporated: 9 July 2013
Net Worth Deficit: £3,009,309 *Total Assets:* £7,080,350
Registered Office: 480 Great West Road, Hounslow, Middlesex, TW5 0TA
Activities: Other letting and operating of own or leased real estate
Parent: Radha Soami Satsang Beas British Isles
Officers: William Kahn [1946] Director [American]; Sunita Naidoo [1965] Director/Dentist; Surender Shyam Uttamsingh [1981] Director [French]; Santosh Singh Vaswani [1935] Director

Europa Road Limited
Incorporated: 17 November 1975 *Employees:* 598
Previous: Europa Worldwide Logistics Ltd
Net Worth: £7,760,865 *Total Assets:* £46,527,488
Registered Office: Littlebrook DC1, Shield Road, Dartford, Kent, DA1 5UR
Activities: Freight transport by road
Parent: Europa Worldwide Group Limited
Officers: Robert William Gilbert Ross, Secretary; Andrew Neville Baxter [1975] Managing Director; Daniel Paul Cook [1974] Director; Dionne Redpath [1973] Director; Robert William Gilbert Ross [1982] Finance Director

Europa Worldwide Group Limited
Incorporated: 18 January 2007 *Employees:* 600
Previous: EWG Limited
Net Worth: £6,814,644 *Total Assets:* £45,062,596
Registered Office: Littlebrook DC1, Shield Road, Dartford, Kent, DA1 5UR
Activities: Activities of head offices
Major Shareholder: Andrew Neville Baxter
Officers: Robert William Gilbert Ross, Secretary; Andrew Neville Baxter [1975] Managing Director; Richard Stephen Litchfield [1976] IT Director; Carl John Potter [1959] HR and Facilities Director; Robert William Gilbert Ross [1982] Finance Director

Europe Incoming Holdings Limited
Incorporated: 22 October 2009 *Employees:* 29
Previous: Europe Incoming Limited
Net Worth: £5,184,489 *Total Assets:* £16,468,968
Registered Office: 166 College Road, Harrow, Middlesex, HA1 1RA
Activities: Activities of other holding companies n.e.c.
Major Shareholder: Uma Patel
Officers: Uma Somia, Secretary; Dylan Lall [1980] Director; Staffan Nilsson [1968] Director [Swedish]; Uma Somia [1964] Director

The European Film Partners III LLP
Incorporated: 14 December 2001
Net Worth: £32,776,124 *Total Assets:* £36,126,636
Registered Office: 99 Kenton Road, Harrow, Middlesex, HA3 0AN
Officers: Andrew Iain Bennett [1966] LLP Member; Paul St John Brine [1950] LLP Member; Daniel William Deschamps Chamier [1964] LLP Member; Stephen Trevor Din [1964] LLP Member; Jeremy Ryton Drax [1960] LLP Member; Gavin Colunba Dredge [1973] LLP Member; Michael John Thornton Dudley [1957] LLP Member; Gavin Rhys Eddy [1967] LLP Member; Richard Oliver Fagan [1945] LLP Member; Benjamin James Ernest Guest [1973] LLP Member; Gerrard Leslie Henry [1953] LLP Member; John Edward Inglis [1961] LLP Member; John Anthony Maloney [1964] LLP Member; Christopher Ator Potts [1967] LLP Member; Martin Vincent Quinn [1964] LLP Member; Manfred Johan Schepers [1960] LLP Member; Tariq Shaikh [1969] LLP Member; Peter Skinner [1930] LLP Member; Rupert Peregrine Austin Tyer [1963] LLP Member; Thomas Henry Wiggin [1969] LLP Member

European Investments (Cornwall) Holdings Limited
Incorporated: 7 April 2017
Net Worth Deficit: £6,142,855 *Total Assets:* £48,295,900
Registered Office: Beaufort Court, Egg Farm Lane, off Station Road, Kings Langley, Herts, WD4 8LR
Activities: Financial intermediation not elsewhere classified
Parent: The Renewables Infrastructure Group (UK) Investments Limited
Officers: Dominic James Hearth, Secretary; Steven William Hughes [1972] Global Support Services Director, UK&I - Commercial; Mitesh Raj Patel [1982] Director/Chartered Accountant; Tracy Jane Scott [1976] Director/Delivery Project Manager; Mark Christopher Wayment [1958] Director

European Investments (Cornwall) Limited
Incorporated: 13 April 2012
Net Worth: £2,565,519 *Total Assets:* £56,410,928
Registered Office: Beaufort Court, Egg Farm Lane, off Station Road, Kings Langley, Herts, WD4 8LR
Activities: Other business support service activities n.e.c.
Parent: European Investments (SCEL) Limited
Officers: Dominic Hearth, Secretary; Steven William Hughes [1972] Global Support Services Director, UK&I - Commercial; Mitesh Raj Patel [1982] Director/Chartered Accountant; Tracy Jane Scott [1976] Director/Delivery Project Manager; Mark Christopher Wayment [1958] Director

European Investments (Earlseat) Limited
Incorporated: 9 September 2013
Net Worth: £1,595,000 *Total Assets:* £19,100,000
Registered Office: Beaufort Court, Egg Farm Lane, Kings Langley, Herts, WD4 8LR
Activities: Other business support service activities n.e.c.
Parent: European Investments Solar Holdings Limited
Officers: Dominic James Hearth, Secretary; Steven William Hughes [1972] Generation & Asset Management Director; Fraser Stephen Merry [1968] Director/Chartered Surveyor; Mitesh Raj Patel [1982] Director/Group Financial Controller

European Investments (SCEL) Limited
Incorporated: 5 April 2012
Net Worth: £7,893,309 *Total Assets:* £18,296,544
Registered Office: Beaufort Court, Egg Farm Lane, off Station Road, Kings Langley, Herts, WD4 8LR
Activities: Other business support service activities n.e.c.
Parent: The Renewables Infrastructure Group (UK) Investments Limited
Officers: Dominic Hearth, Secretary; Steven William Hughes [1972] Global Support Services Director, UK&I; Mitesh Raj Patel [1982] Director/Chartered Accountant; Tracy Jane Scott [1976] Director/Delivery Project Manager

European Process Plant Limited
Incorporated: 17 February 1972 *Employees:* 23
Net Worth: £2,769,839 *Total Assets:* £6,024,882
Registered Office: EPP House, 8-9 Epsom Business Park, Kiln Lane, Epsom, Surrey, KT17 1JF
Activities: Installation of industrial machinery and equipment
Major Shareholder: Keith James Stalker
Officers: Josephine Dorothy Mitchell, Secretary; Melissa James [1966] Business Support Director; Stephen Charles Merritt [1965] Managing Director; Josephine Dorothy Mitchell [1949] Director; Stewart William Morris [1966] Director; Roger William Mott [1954] Director; Keith James Stalker [1951] Director

European Property Development Limited
Incorporated: 20 August 2001
Net Worth Deficit: £2,323,856 *Total Assets:* £16,199,510
Registered Office: 54 Oaks Road, Croydon, Surrey, CR0 5HL
Activities: Activities of venture and development capital companies
Officers: Pankaj Patel [1953] Director/Certified Chartered Accountant

European Springs and Pressings Limited
Incorporated: 9 May 1955 *Employees:* 175
Net Worth: £8,729,177 *Total Assets:* £12,311,045
Registered Office: Chaffinch Business Park, Croydon Road, Beckenham, Kent, BR3 4DW
Activities: Manufacture of wire products, chain and springs
Parent: ESP Holdings (UK) Limited
Officers: Michael Ralph Gibbs, Secretary; Howard Malcolm Downs [1959] Director; Michael Ralph Gibbs [1975] Director; Kjell-Arne Gunnar Lindback [1952] Director [Swedish]; Stuart Patrick McSheehy [1969] Director

Eurostaff Group Limited
Incorporated: 10 January 2003 *Employees:* 62
Net Worth Deficit: £348,132 *Total Assets:* £8,271,575
Registered Office: Chevron House, Long Lane, Hillingdon, Uxbridge, Middlesex, UB10 9PF
Activities: Other activities of employment placement agencies
Parent: Staffgroup Limited
Officers: Chris Martin Kenneally [1960] Director; Jack Rainer Ullmann [1928] Director; Phillip Lionel Ullmann [1964] Director

H.Evans & Sons Limited
Incorporated: 6 July 1936 *Employees:* 280
Net Worth: £14,251,905 *Total Assets:* £20,012,294
Registered Office: Ruxley Manor Nursery, Maidstone Road, Sidcup, Kent, DA14 5BQ
Activities: Activities of head offices
Shareholders: James Sebastian Evans; Andrew Richard Brodie Evans; Richard Thornton Evans
Officers: Richard Thornton Evans, Secretary; Kevin Baker [1957] Director/Accountant; Andrew Richard Brodie Evans [1974] Director; James Sebastian Evans [1975] Director; Richard Thornton Evans [1940] Director/Nursery Manager

Eventist Group Limited
Incorporated: 7 June 1996 *Employees:* 290
Previous: Best Parties Ever Limited
Net Worth: £763,413 *Total Assets:* £6,882,200
Registered Office: Units 1-4 Trade City, Brooklands Industrial Estate, Weybridge, Surrey, KT13 0YF
Activities: Event catering activities
Major Shareholder: Timothy Peter Stevens
Officers: Timothy Peter Stevens [1967] Director; Steven John Turnbull [1976] Finance Director

Everest Limited
Incorporated: 18 October 2002 *Employees:* 661
Net Worth Deficit: £5,593,000 *Total Assets:* £29,419,000
Registered Office: Everest House, Sopers Road, Cuffley, Potters Bar, Herts, EN6 4SG
Activities: Glazing
Parent: Hillary Bidco Ltd
Officers: Robert Alexander Asplin [1979] Director; Joanne Maria Holland [1960] Director [Australian]; Karl Sean Munns [1970] Director

Everglade Holdings Limited
Incorporated: 17 November 2016 *Employees:* 86
Net Worth: £637,482 *Total Assets:* £7,332,032
Registered Office: 22 Wadsworth Road, Perivale, Greenford, Middlesex, UB6 7JD
Activities: Glazing
Officers: Bhavik Dabasia [1979] Technical Director; Reena Gjoci [1980] Operations Director; Yogesh Gopal [1985] Managing Director; Jayesh Hirji Hirani [1978] Commercial Director; Jayesh Ravji Patel [1983] Sales Director

Everglade Windows Limited
Incorporated: 14 November 1989 *Employees:* 86
Net Worth: £3,632,930 *Total Assets:* £8,203,559
Registered Office: 22 Wadsworth Road, Perivale, Greenford, Middlesex, UB6 7JD
Activities: Glazing
Parent: Everglade Holdings Limited
Officers: Bhavik Dabasia [1979] Technical Director; Reena Gjoci [1980] Operations Director; Yogesh Gopal [1985] Managing Director; Jayesh Hirji Hirani [1978] Commercial Director; Jayesh Ravji Patel [1983] Sales Director

Everguard Limited
Incorporated: 25 June 1998 *Employees:* 4
Net Worth: £14,457,477 *Total Assets:* £17,474,784
Registered Office: 2nd Floor, Katherine House, 11 Wyllyotts Place, Potters Bar, Herts, EN6 2JD
Activities: Other letting and operating of own or leased real estate
Shareholders: Chrysanthos Zacharia; Andreas Zacharia; Paraskevou Pamela Gumuskaya
Officers: Paraskevou Pamela Gumuskaya [1980] Director/Senior Manager; Andreas Zacharia [1976] Director/Property Manager; Chrysanthos Zacharia [1974] Director/Property Manager

Every Child, Every Day Academy Trust
Incorporated: 20 August 2012 *Employees:* 385
Previous: Grey Court School
Net Worth: £67,949,216 *Total Assets:* £72,198,816
Registered Office: Grey Court School, Ham Street, Ham, Richmond upon Thames, Surrey, TW10 7HN
Activities: General secondary education
Officers: Neil Knox-Hall, Secretary; Robert Alexander [1959] Director/Accountant; Margaret Mary Michel Bernadette Bailey [1960] Director/Headteacher; David Bealing [1964] Commercial Director; Elaine England [1954] Director/Education Advisor; Donald Henry Farquharson [1954] Director; Dr Lorna Jillian Goodwin [1961] Academic Director; Anthony Francis Cloudsley Kitson [1958] Director/Civil Servant; Penny St Martin [1972] Director/HR Manager; Bill Watkin [1958] Director

Evolution (Saffron Walden) LLP
Incorporated: 4 July 2016
Net Worth: £1,071,000 *Total Assets:* £36,010,000
Registered Office: Cowley Business Park, Cowley, Uxbridge, Middlesex, UB8 2AL

Evolution (Shinfield) LLP
Incorporated: 20 April 2015
Net Worth: £1,637,000 *Total Assets:* £56,992,000
Registered Office: Cowley Business Park, Cowley, Uxbridge, Middlesex, UB8 2AL

Evolution (Woking) Limited
Incorporated: 25 September 2013
Net Worth Deficit: £8,894,000 *Total Assets:* £43,064,000
Registered Office: Premier House, 52 London Road, Twickenham, Middlesex, TW1 3RP
Activities: Construction of domestic buildings
Parent: Evolution (Woking) Holdings Limited
Officers: Peter Nicholas Bowden [1968] Director; Howard Peter Dawson [1970] Housing Director; Stephen Noel King [1964] Finance Director; Karen Sheedy [1961] Director/Head of Treasury

Evolution Morpeth LLP
Incorporated: 11 June 2015
Net Worth: £699,000 *Total Assets:* £29,457,000
Registered Office: Cowley Business Park, Cowley, Uxbridge, Middlesex, UB8 2AL

Evolution Newhall LLP
Incorporated: 11 June 2015
Net Worth: £9,362,000 *Total Assets:* £10,502,000
Registered Office: Cowley Business Park, Cowley, Uxbridge, Middlesex, UB8 2AL

Ewell Castle School
Incorporated: 22 January 1964 *Employees:* 95
Net Worth: £7,397,380 *Total Assets:* £9,991,450
Registered Office: Ewell Castle School, Church Street, Ewell, Surrey, KT17 2AW
Activities: Pre-primary education
Officers: Janet Mercia Barnett, Secretary; Nigel Geoffrey David Bird [1961] Director; Anthony John Evans [1951] Director/Retired; Colin Alfred Griffith [1947] Director/Retired; Jennifer Gray Moran [1954] Director/Assistant Headmistress [Irish]; Doreen Parker [1953] Director/Freelance Trainer; Antony Peter Shawyer [1967] Director/Teacher; Sean Barry Sullivan [1981] Director/Barrister; David Michael Tucker [1942] Director/Retired

EWOS Limited
Incorporated: 17 May 1982 *Employees:* 76
Net Worth: £36,955,000 *Total Assets:* £52,320,000
Registered Office: Velocity V1, Brooklands Drive, Weybridge, Surrey, KT13 0SL
Activities: Support activities for animal production (other than farm animal boarding)
Parent: Albain Bidco UK Limited
Officers: Dena Michelle L O'Bue, Secretary; David Morrice [1970] Country Director; Federico Urquidi Negron [1965] Director/UK & Ireland Country Controller [Spanish]

Exagon Industries Limited
Incorporated: 3 March 2016 *Employees:* 1
Net Worth: £1,299,392 *Total Assets:* £71,939,616
Registered Office: Charles Lake House, Claire Causeway, Crossways Business Park, Dartford, Kent, DA2 6QA
Activities: Research and experimental development on biotechnology
Major Shareholder: Fabrizio Tonna
Officers: Fabrizio Tonna [1964] Director [Italian]

Excellence in Education Trust
Incorporated: 1 March 2016 *Employees:* 180
Net Worth: £24,017,226 *Total Assets:* £26,965,340
Registered Office: c/o Oakington Manor Primary School, Oakington Manor Drive, Wembley, Middlesex, HA9 6NF
Activities: Primary education
Officers: Sheila Ann Campbell, Secretary; Cyril Copitch [1947] Director/Facilities Manager; Ivan Deshumkh [1942] Director/Retired; Jo Jhally [1949] Director/Retired; Sylvia Libson OBE [1948] Director/Executive Headteacher; Narinder Nathan [1948] Director/Retired [Malaysian]; Waleed Shamki [1962] Director/Office Manager; Everton Sharpe [1957] Director/Headteacher; Darren David Singer [1969] Director/Accountant; Uwem Utip [1960] Director/Lawyer

Excellent Properties Ltd.
Incorporated: 8 April 1991
Net Worth: £7,717,729 *Total Assets:* £8,097,003
Registered Office: 2 AC Court, High Street, Thames Ditton, Surrey, KT7 0SR
Activities: Renting and operating of Housing Association real estate
Shareholder: Thomas Anthony Ignatius Fitzpatrick
Officers: Thomas Anthony Ignatius Fitzpatrick [1939] Director; David Johns [1938] Director

Excelredstone Converged Solutions Limited
Incorporated: 11 June 1986 *Employees:* 273
Previous: Redstone Converged Solutions Limited
Net Worth: £8,383,835 *Total Assets:* £17,792,348
Registered Office: Trafalgar House, 712 London Road, Grays, Essex, RM20 3JT
Activities: Information technology consultancy activities
Parent: Excelredstone Comunica Limited
Officers: Barry John Horgan [1971] Director [Irish]; Brendan Loughrey [1961] Managing Director; Jakob Moeller-Jensen [1973] Director [Danish]; Matthew Salter [1971] Operations Director [New Zealander]; Steven Williams [1979] Finance Director

Excelredstone Services Limited
Incorporated: 9 January 2008 *Employees:* 140
Previous: Excel I.T Services Limited
Net Worth: £7,283,940 *Total Assets:* £12,712,179
Registered Office: Trafalgar House, 712 London Road, Grays, Essex, RM20 3JT
Activities: Other information technology service activities
Officers: Barry John Horgan, Secretary; Barry John Horgan [1971] Director [Irish]; Jakob Moeller-Jensen [1973] Director [Danish]; Simon Hobart Charles Morrish [1974] Director; Matthew Porter [1960] Director [Irish]

Excelsior Property Investments Limited
Incorporated: 31 May 2017 *Employees:* 2
Net Worth: £91,060 *Total Assets:* £5,961,307
Registered Office: Torwood, 8 Beech Hill Avenue, Barnet, Herts, EN4 0LW
Activities: Other letting and operating of own or leased real estate
Officers: Mukesh Zaverchand Shah [1960] Director; Ninna Shah [1964] Director

Excelsior Textiles Limited
Incorporated: 28 May 1971 *Employees:* 7
Net Worth: £6,297,629 *Total Assets:* £6,923,131
Registered Office: 666 Kenton Road, Harrow, Middlesex, HA3 9QN
Activities: Wholesale of textiles
Major Shareholder: Tobi Mahalla
Officers: Karen Mahalla, Secretary; Karen Mahalla [1957] Director/Secretary; Tobi Mahalla [1947] Director/Retail Textile Dealer

Excess Baggage Group Limited
Incorporated: 20 June 2003 *Employees:* 301
Net Worth: £2,898,315 *Total Assets:* £8,599,039
Registered Office: 2 Provident Industrial Estate, Pump Lane, Hayes, Middlesex, UB3 3NE
Activities: Activities of head offices
Major Shareholder: David Christopher George Elliott
Officers: Maire Brid Ann Elliott, Secretary/Director [Irish]; David Christopher George Elliott [1955] Director; Maire Brid Ann Elliott [1962] Director [Irish]

Excess Baggage Holdings Limited
Incorporated: 26 October 2006 *Employees:* 301
Net Worth: £4,889,244 *Total Assets:* £8,990,076
Registered Office: 2 Provident Industrial Estate, Pump Lane, Hayes, Middlesex, UB3 3NE
Activities: Activities of head offices
Major Shareholder: David Christopher George Elliott
Officers: David Christopher George Elliott, Secretary/Director; David Christopher George Elliott [1955] Director; Maire Brid Ann Elliott [1962] Director [Irish]

Excitech Limited
Incorporated: 11 March 1985 *Employees:* 118
Net Worth: £8,271,259 *Total Assets:* £16,704,616
Registered Office: Design Technology Centre, 8 Kinetic Crescent, Innova Business Park, Enfield, Middlesex, EN3 7XH
Activities: Business and domestic software development
Major Shareholder: Adrian Robert Atkinson
Officers: Peter Blake, Secretary; Adrian Robert Atkinson [1956] Director/Chairman; Leigh Atkinson [1958] Strategic Director; Peter Blake [1976] Director/Accountant; David Aled Hughes [1965] Managing Director

Exel Freight Management (UK) Limited
Incorporated: 17 January 1957 *Employees:* 3
Net Worth: £19,643,000 *Total Assets:* £19,644,000
Registered Office: Eastworth House, Eastworth Road, Chertsey, Surrey, KT16 8SH
Activities: Other transportation support activities
Parent: DHL Global Forwarding (UK) Limited
Officers: Vari Isabel Cameron [1961] Director; Michael Paul Young [1972] Director

Exela Technologies Limited
Incorporated: 27 October 1976 *Employees:* 536
Previous: BancTec Limited
Net Worth: £6,136,000 *Total Assets:* £46,578,000
Registered Office: Baronsmede, The Avenue, Egham, Surrey, TW20 9AB
Activities: Business and domestic software development
Parent: BTC International Holdings Inc
Officers: Jaymin Chhaya, Secretary; Jaymin Chhaya [1966] Director/Chartered Accountant; Stephen John Downey [1963] Managing Director

Exmoore Financial Credit Co. Ltd.
Incorporated: 13 February 1998
Net Worth Deficit: £154,111 *Total Assets:* £13,924,349
Registered Office: 1st Floor, Midas House, 2 Knoll Rise, Orpington, Kent, BR6 0EL
Activities: Other credit granting n.e.c.
Parent: Geieonline Dafconsulting (UK) Ltd
Officers: Helen Louise Roue, Secretary; Sarah Louise Oldershaw [1990] Director; Helen Louise Roue [1967] Director

Expanded Limited
Incorporated: 4 May 2004
Net Worth: £35,632,000 *Total Assets:* £84,460,000
Registered Office: Bridge Place, Anchor Boulevard, Admirals Park, Crossways, Dartford, Kent, DA2 6SN
Activities: Activities of head offices
Parent: Laing O'Rourke Holdings Limited
Officers: Robert Edward Turner, Secretary; Matthew Clement Hugh Gill [1971] Director/Group Financial Controller; Declan James McGeeney [1978] Director/General Manager [Irish]; Alexander Stewart McIntyre [1956] Director; Hubert Desmond O'Rourke [1949] Director/Structural Engineer [Irish]

Expeditors International (UK) Limited
Incorporated: 18 December 1984 *Employees:* 550
Net Worth: £12,036,000 *Total Assets:* £101,461,000
Registered Office: 1 Ascot Road, Bedfont, Middlesex, TW14 8QH
Activities: Other transportation support activities
Parent: Expeditors International of Washington Inc
Officers: John Joseph Hayes, Secretary; Tim Barber [1959] Director/Business Executive [American]; Philip Michael Coughlin [1960] Director [American]; Jeffrey Scott Musser [1966] Managing Director [American]

Experis Group Limited
Incorporated: 28 September 1998 *Employees:* 5
Net Worth: £33,855,000 *Total Assets:* £46,643,000
Registered Office: Capital Court, Windsor Street, Uxbridge, Middlesex, UB8 1AB
Activities: Other information technology service activities
Parent: Manpower Public Limited Company
Officers: Mark Anthony Cahill [1958] Commercial Director; Mark Joseph Donnelly [1968] Finance Director; Stefano Scabbio [1964] Director [Italian]; Damian Paul Whitham [1967] Commercial Director

Experis Resource Support Services Limited
Incorporated: 11 November 1992 *Employees:* 1
Net Worth: £5,104,000 *Total Assets:* £5,512,000
Registered Office: Capital Court, Windsor Street, Uxbridge, Middlesex, UB8 1AB
Activities: Temporary employment agency activities
Officers: Mark Anthony Cahill [1958] Director; Mark Joseph Donnelly [1968] Finance Director; Damian Paul Whitham [1967] Commercial Director

Exploration Service Company Limited
Incorporated: 9 March 2000
Net Worth: £151,140,352 *Total Assets:* £151,240,768
Registered Office: Chertsey Road, Sunbury on Thames, Middlesex, TW16 7BP
Activities: Activities of head offices
Parent: BP Global Investments Limited
Officers: Terence Michael Thornton [1963] Director/Oil Company Executive; David Jozef Vermylen [1972] Director/Oil Company Executive [Belgian]

Explore Capital Limited
Incorporated: 13 October 2004
Net Worth Deficit: £43,360,000 *Total Assets:* £11,574,000
Registered Office: Bridge Place, Anchor Boulevard, Admirals Park, Crossways, Dartford, Kent, DA2 6SN
Activities: Activities of head offices
Parent: Laing O'Rourke PLC
Officers: Robert Turner, Secretary; Alexander Stewart McIntyre [1956] Director

Explore Living Limited
Incorporated: 18 March 2005
Net Worth Deficit: £554,000 *Total Assets:* £5,970,000
Registered Office: Bridge Place, Anchor Boulevard, Admirals Park, Crossways, Dartford, Kent, DA2 6SN
Activities: Development of building projects
Parent: Explore Capital Limited
Officers: Robert Edward Turner, Secretary; Alexander Stewart McIntyre [1956] Director

Explore Manufacturing Limited
Incorporated: 26 July 2000
Net Worth Deficit: £22,223,000 *Total Assets:* £41,435,000
Registered Office: Bridge Place, Anchor Boulevard, Admirals Park, Crossways, Dartford, Kent, DA2 6SN
Activities: Construction of commercial buildings
Parent: R O'Rourke & Son Limited
Officers: Robert Edward Turner, Secretary; Stephen John Harley [1951] Director; Alexander Stewart McIntyre [1956] Director; Paul William McNerney [1977] Director/Business Unit Leader

Explore Transport Limited
Incorporated: 23 January 2015 *Employees:* 223
Net Worth: £7,243,000 *Total Assets:* £60,020,000
Registered Office: Bridge Place, Anchor Boulevard, Admirals Park, Crossways, Dartford, Kent, DA2 6SN
Activities: Freight transport by road
Shareholders: Select Plant Hire Company Limited; WS Transport Limited
Officers: Emma Rigler, Secretary; Bradley George Cooper [1976] Finance Director; David Norman Cox [1979] Director; Douglas Jurrien Heynen [1967] Director

Express Freight Services (U.K.) Limited
Incorporated: 29 August 1979 *Employees:* 68
Net Worth: £14,225,159 *Total Assets:* £18,283,578
Registered Office: Armada House, Tilbury Freeport, Tilbury, Essex, RM18 7ET
Activities: Freight transport by road
Parent: R Swain & Sons Limited
Officers: Andrew John Baxter [1966] Director; Matthew Deer [1975] Director; Stuart James Rigby [1963] Director

Express Toughening Ltd
Incorporated: 27 October 2000 *Employees:* 89
Net Worth: £3,083,131 *Total Assets:* £5,416,198
Registered Office: 51-55 Fowler Road, Hainault, Ilford, Essex, IG6 3XE
Activities: Other manufacturing n.e.c.
Major Shareholder: Geoffrey Stephen Curtis
Officers: Philip Simon Curtis, Secretary; Adam Wayne Curtis [1983] Director; Daniel Robert Curtis [1978] Director; Geoffrey Stephen Curtis [1948] Director; Philip Simon Curtis [1951] Director; George Anthony Howard [1960] Director/Chief Executive [Irish]

Exterior Plas Limited
Incorporated: 15 August 1988 *Employees:* 21
Net Worth: £2,932,442 *Total Assets:* £5,310,691
Registered Office: Haslers, Old Station Road, Loughton, Essex, IG10 4PL
Activities: Construction of commercial buildings
Parent: EP Construction Services Limited
Officers: Andrew John Sheen, Secretary; Andrew John Sheen [1959] Director; Karola Elisabet Sheen [1957] Director [Swedish]

ExxonMobil Chemical Investment Company Limited
Incorporated: 7 October 2016
Net Worth: £860,182,976 *Total Assets:* £1,466,121,984
Registered Office: Ermyn House, Ermyn Way, Leatherhead, Surrey, KT22 8UX
Activities: Other business support service activities n.e.c.
Parent: Esso Exploration and Production UK Limited
Officers: Fiona Henderson Harness, Secretary; Robert Michael Cooper [1961] Director/Oil Company Executive; Andrew Mark Johnson [1976] Director/Oil Company Executive; Steven Adam Oldfield [1972] Director/Oil Company Executive

ExxonMobil Chemical Limited
Incorporated: 21 December 1965 *Employees:* 512
Net Worth: £366,000,000 *Total Assets:* £502,000,000
Registered Office: Ermyn House, Ermyn Way, Leatherhead, Surrey, KT22 8UX
Activities: Manufacture of other organic basic chemicals
Parent: ExxonMobil Chemical Investment Company Limited
Officers: Fiona Harness, Secretary; Richard Robert Henderson [1966] Director/Oil Company Executive; Andrew Mark Johnson [1976] Director/Oil Company Executive; Larry Jacob McAlister [1978] Director/Oil Company Executive [American]

ExxonMobil Finance Company Limited
Incorporated: 26 November 2004
Net Worth: £182,122,480 *Total Assets:* £3,412,931,840
Registered Office: Ermyn House, Ermyn Way, Leatherhead, Surrey, KT22 8UX
Activities: Other business support service activities n.e.c.
Parent: ExxonMobil Investment Company Limited
Officers: Fiona Harness, Secretary; Robert Michael Cooper [1961] Director/Oil Company Executive; Andrew Mark Johnson [1976] Director/Oil Company Executive; Steven Adam Oldfield [1972] Director/Oil Company Executive

ExxonMobil Financial Investment Company Limited
Incorporated: 7 December 2016
Net Worth: £226,104,976 *Total Assets:* £2,254,188,544
Registered Office: Ermyn House, Ermyn Way, Leatherhead, Surrey, KT22 8UX
Activities: Other business support service activities n.e.c.
Parent: ExxonMobil Finance Company Limited
Officers: Fiona Henderson Harness, Secretary; Robert Michael Cooper [1961] Director/Oil Company Executive; Andrew Mark Johnson [1976] Director/Oil Company Executive; Steven Adam Oldfield [1972] Director/Oil Company Executive

ExxonMobil Gas Marketing Europe Limited
Incorporated: 1 July 1990
Net Worth: £182,000,000 *Total Assets:* £392,000,000
Registered Office: Ermyn House, Ermyn Way, Leatherhead, Surrey, KT22 8UX
Activities: Wholesale of other fuels and related products
Parent: ExxonMobil UK Limited
Officers: Fiona Henderson Harness, Secretary; Stefan Ihnen [1966] Director/Oil Company Executive [German]; Andrew Mark Johnson [1976] Director/Oil Company Executive; Alex Volkov [1972] Director/Oil Company Executive [American]

ExxonMobil Holding Company Limited
Incorporated: 6 June 2013
Net Worth: £16,606,653,440 *Total Assets:* £18,504,316,928
Registered Office: Ermyn House, Ermyn Way, Leatherhead, Surrey, KT22 8UX
Activities: Other business support service activities n.e.c.
Shareholder: Exxon Mobil Corporation
Officers: Fiona Henderson Harness, Secretary; Robert Michael Cooper [1961] Director/Oil Company Executive; Andrew Mark Johnson [1976] Director/Oil Company Executive; Steven Adam Oldfield [1972] Director/Oil Company Executive

ExxonMobil International Limited
Incorporated: 1 September 1999 *Employees:* 252
Net Worth: £138,574,000 *Total Assets:* £149,532,000
Registered Office: Ermyn House, Ermyn Way, Leatherhead, Surrey, KT22 8UX
Activities: Extraction of crude petroleum
Parent: Esso UK Limited
Officers: Fiona Harness, Secretary; Robert Michael Cooper [1961] Director/Oil Company Executive; Jay Loren Jackson [1962] Director/Oil Company Executive [American]; Andrew Mark Johnson [1976] Director/Oil Company Executive

ExxonMobil Investment Company Limited
Incorporated: 26 November 2004
Net Worth: £493,449,216 *Total Assets:* £964,005,312
Registered Office: Ermyn House, Ermyn Way, Leatherhead, Surrey, KT22 8UX
Activities: Other business support service activities n.e.c.
Parent: Exxon Mobil Corporation
Officers: Fiona Harness, Secretary; Robert Michael Cooper [1961] Director/Oil Company Executive; Andrew Mark Johnson [1976] Director/Oil Company Executive; Steven Adam Oldfield [1972] Director/Oil Company Executive

ExxonMobil Marine Limited
Incorporated: 20 December 1999 *Employees:* 4
Net Worth: £2,204,000 *Total Assets:* £152,302,000
Registered Office: Ermyn House, Ermyn Way, Leatherhead, Surrey, KT22 8UX
Activities: Mineral oil refining
Parent: ExxonMobil UK Limited
Officers: Fiona Harness, Secretary; Frans Bert Horjus [1967] Director/Oil Company Executive [Dutch]; Andrew Mark Johnson [1976] Director/Oil Company Executive; Luca Volta [1969] Director/Oil Company Executive [Italian]; Iain White [1962] Director/Oil Company Executive

ExxonMobil UK Limited
Incorporated: 15 December 1999
Net Worth: £881,830,976 *Total Assets:* £882,305,984
Registered Office: Ermyn House, Ermyn Way, Leatherhead, Surrey, KT22 8UX
Activities: Other business support service activities n.e.c.
Parent: Esso UK Limited
Officers: Fiona Harness, Secretary; Robert Michael Cooper [1961] Director/Oil Company Executive; Andrew Mark Johnson [1976] Director/Oil Company Executive; Steven Adam Oldfield [1972] Director/Oil Company Executive

Ezra Attia Limited
Incorporated: 21 January 1993
Net Worth: £5,338,538 *Total Assets:* £8,991,860
Registered Office: Ground Floor, Elizabeth House, 54-58 High Street, Edgware, Middlesex, HA8 7EJ
Activities: Other business support service activities n.e.c.
Officers: Lee Maurice Gold [1987] Director

F5 Networks Limited
Incorporated: 26 July 1999 *Employees:* 383
Net Worth: £112,087,384 *Total Assets:* £363,392,096
Registered Office: Chertsey Gate West, 43-47 London Street, Chertsey, Surrey, KT16 8AP
Activities: Other information technology service activities
Parent: F5 Networks, Inc.
Officers: Steven Irving Grieger [1963] Director [American]; Scot Frazier Rogers [1967] Director/Executive Vice President, General Counsel [American]; Kunwarjit Suri [1966] Director/EMEA Corporate Controller; Chad Michael Whalen [1971] Director [American]

Faber Prest Limited
Incorporated: 29 July 1892
Net Worth: £43,625,916 *Total Assets:* £61,003,836
Registered Office: Harsco House, Regent Park, 299 Kingston Road, Leatherhead, Surrey, KT22 7SG
Activities: Activities of head offices
Parent: Harsco Metals Group Limited
Officers: Christopher Claude Lashmer Whistler, Secretary; Stephen Richard Cooper [1966] Director/Accountant; Christopher Claude Lashmer Whistler [1958] Director/Accountant

Facilicom Cleaning Services Limited
Incorporated: 20 February 1987 *Employees:* 2,169
Net Worth: £6,725,913 *Total Assets:* £16,436,873
Registered Office: Sargasso Level 2, Five Arches Business Centre, Maidstone Road, Sidcup, Kent, DA14 5AE
Activities: General cleaning of buildings
Shareholders: Martine Jolande Sophia Geurts; Walter Paul Geurts
Officers: Philip Joseph Lockwood-Taylor, Secretary; Lesley Joan Coates [1954] Administration Director; Johannes Adrianus Gennissen [1960] Director [Dutch]

Facilicom UK Limited
Incorporated: 3 December 2002
Net Worth: £11,162,509 *Total Assets:* £19,340,324
Registered Office: Sargasso Level 2, Five Arches Business Centre, Maidstone Road, Sidcup, Kent, DA14 5AE
Activities: Activities of head offices
Shareholders: Martine Jolande Sophia Geurts; Walter Paul Geurts
Officers: Lesley Joan Coates, Secretary; Johannes Adrianus Gennissen [1960] Director [Dutch]

Fairchildes Academy Community Trust
Incorporated: 12 March 2014 *Employees:* 211
Net Worth: £4,388,638 *Total Assets:* £7,403,508
Registered Office: Fairchildes Primary School, Fairchildes Avenue, New Addington, Croydon, Surrey, CR0 0AH
Activities: Primary education
Officers: Roxana Huque-Dowlet, Secretary; Kathleen Conroy [1981] Director/Solicitor; Roseanne Ellis [1947] Director/Education Consultant; Robert Hitchcock [1986] Director/Financial Controller; Natalie Patel [1981] Director/Civil Servant; Ros Sandell [1960] Director/Headteacher

Fairmile Homes One Limited
Incorporated: 20 January 2014
Net Worth: £1,739,157 *Total Assets:* £6,450,498
Registered Office: Fairmile House, Claremont Lane, Esher, Surrey, KT10 9DA
Activities: Development of building projects
Shareholders: Rodney Aldridge; Fairmile Homes Ltd
Officers: Lady Carol Frances Aldridge [1963] Director; Sir Rod Aldridge [1947] Director; Matthew Estwick [1978] Director; Paul Gillam [1978] Director

Fairmile Homes Three Limited
Incorporated: 6 February 2015
Net Worth: £1,000 *Total Assets:* £8,244,184
Registered Office: Fairmile House, Claremont Lane, Esher, Surrey, KT10 9DA
Activities: Development of building projects
Shareholders: Fairmile Homes Ltd; Aldridge Capital Ltd
Officers: Lady Carol Frances Aldridge [1963] Director; Sir Rod Aldridge [1947] Director; Matthew Estwick [1978] Director; Paul Gillam [1978] Director

Fairmont Property Developers UK Ltd
Incorporated: 16 July 2014
Net Worth Deficit: £15,377 *Total Assets:* £7,220,559
Registered Office: 4th Floor, Amba House, 15 College Road, Harrow, Middlesex, HA1 1BA
Activities: Other letting and operating of own or leased real estate
Major Shareholder: Nicholas John Gerard
Officers: Sandeep Gohil, Secretary; Nicholas John Gerard [1959] Director; Sundeep Gohil [1967] Director

Fairview Enfield Limited
Incorporated: 17 February 1984
Net Worth: £23,333,000 *Total Assets:* £24,004,000
Registered Office: 50 Lancaster Road, Enfield, Middlesex, EN2 0BY
Activities: Development of building projects
Parent: Fairview New Homes Limited
Officers: Jonathan Mark Baxter, Secretary; Michael Blakey [1963] Director; Nicholas Martin Dulcken [1967] Director; Generald Anthony Malton [1960] Director; Darren Lee McCormack [1982] Sales Director; Richard James Paterson [1957] Director; Jonathan Andrew Spring [1972] Land Buying Director; Michael Raymond Walker [1958] Director; Robert Kenneth Williams [1964] Finance Director

Fairview Estates (Housing) Limited
Incorporated: 6 August 1963 *Employees:* 219
Net Worth: £9,068,000 *Total Assets:* £30,832,000
Registered Office: 50 Lancaster Road, Enfield, Middlesex, EN2 0BY
Activities: Construction of domestic buildings
Parent: Fairview New Homes Limited
Officers: Jonathan Mark Baxter, Secretary; Daniel John Carroll [1980] Director; Rhys Bernard Davies [1982] Director/Land Buyer; Steven Eastwood [1967] Commercial Director; Mark John Jackson [1971] Planning Director; Generald Anthony Malton [1960] Director; Vasos Ptohopoulos [1975] Director [Greek]; John Andrew Barker Reid [1966] Design Director; Timothy Simon Sellens [1959] Director/Head of Affordable Housing; Martin Richard Smith [1955] Director; Robert Kenneth Williams [1964] Finance Director; John Wood [1958] Director

Fairview Holdings Limited
Incorporated: 2 October 2000 *Employees:* 226
Net Worth: £252,863,008 *Total Assets:* £356,788,992
Registered Office: 50 Lancaster Road, Enfield, Middlesex, EN2 0BY
Activities: Activities of construction holding companies
Shareholders: Michael Raymond Walker; Robert Kenneth Williams; Michael Blakey; Nicholas Martin Dulcken; Gerald Anthony Malton; Richard James Paterson
Officers: Jonathan Mark Baxter, Secretary; Michael Blakey [1963] Director; Dennis John Cope [1933] Director; Nicholas Martin Dulcken [1967] Director; Generald Anthony Malton [1960] Director; Darren Lee McCormack [1982] Sales Director; Richard James Paterson [1957] Director; Jonathan Andrew Spring [1972] Land Buying Director; Michael Raymond Walker [1958] Director; Robert Kenneth Williams [1964] Finance Director

Fairview Homes Limited
Incorporated: 22 April 1997 *Employees:* 9
Net Worth Deficit: £266,000 *Total Assets:* £59,639,000
Registered Office: 50 Lancaster Road, Enfield, Middlesex, EN2 0BY
Activities: Development of building projects
Parent: Fairview New Homes Limited
Officers: Jonathan Mark Baxter, Secretary; Michael Blakey [1963] Director; Nicholas Martin Dulcken [1967] Director; Generald Anthony Malton [1960] Director; Darren Lee McCormack [1982] Sales Director; Richard James Paterson [1957] Director; Martin Richard Smith [1955] Director; Jonathan Andrew Spring [1972] Land Buying Director; Michael Raymond Walker [1958] Director; Robert Kenneth Williams [1964] Finance Director

Fairview Hotels Investments (2) Limited
Incorporated: 26 January 2017
Net Worth: £1,518,115 *Total Assets:* £19,836,746
Registered Office: Kanta House, Victoria Road, South Ruislip, Middlesex, HA4 0JQ
Activities: Activities of real estate investment trusts
Parent: Fairview Hotels Limited
Officers: Bhasker Tailor, Secretary; Jawahar Jamnadas Chatwani [1948] Director; Rashmi Jamnadas Chatwani [1954] Director; Satish Jamnadas Chatwani [1953] Director

Fairview Hotels Limited
Incorporated: 4 July 1995 *Employees:* 534
Previous: Fairview Hotels & Healthcare Limited
Net Worth: £53,232,356 *Total Assets:* £136,622,640
Registered Office: Kanta House, Victoria Road, South Ruislip, Middlesex, HA4 0JQ
Activities: Hotels and similar accommodation
Officers: Bhasker Tailor, Secretary; Jawahar Jamnadas Chatwani [1948] Director; Rashmi Jamnadas Chatwani [1954] Director; Satish Jamnadas Chatwani [1953] Director

Fairview New Homes (Charlton) Limited
Incorporated: 18 November 2016
Net Worth: £405,000 *Total Assets:* £27,937,000
Registered Office: 50 Lancaster Road, Enfield, Middlesex, EN2 0BY
Activities: Development of building projects
Parent: Fairview New Homes Limited
Officers: Jonathan Mark Baxter, Secretary; Michael Blakey [1963] Director; Nicholas Martin Dulcken [1967] Director; Generald Anthony Malton [1960] Director; Darren Lee McCormack [1982] Sales Director; Richard James Paterson [1957] Director; Jonathan Andrew Spring [1972] Land Buying Director; Michael Raymond Walker [1958] Director; Robert Kenneth Williams [1964] Director

Fairview New Homes (Chase Road) Limited
Incorporated: 5 December 1997 *Employees:* 9
Net Worth: £573,000 *Total Assets:* £17,800,000
Registered Office: 50 Lancaster Road, Enfield, Middlesex, EN2 0BY
Activities: Development of building projects
Parent: Fairview New Homes Limited
Officers: Jonathan Mark Baxter, Secretary; Michael Blakey [1963] Director; Nicholas Martin Dulcken [1967] Director; Generald Anthony Malton [1960] Director; Darren Lee McCormack [1982] Sales Director; Richard James Paterson [1957] Director; Martin Richard Smith [1955] Director; Jonathan Andrew Spring [1972] Land Buying Director; Michael Raymond Walker [1958] Director; Robert Kenneth Williams [1964] Finance Director

Fairview New Homes (Colindale) Limited
Incorporated: 10 May 1999 *Employees:* 9
Net Worth: £4,478,000 *Total Assets:* £14,953,000
Registered Office: 50 Lancaster Road, Enfield, Middlesex, EN2 0BY
Activities: Development of building projects
Parent: Fairview New Homes Limited
Officers: Jonathan Mark Baxter, Secretary; Michael Blakey [1963] Director; Nicholas Martin Dulcken [1967] Director; Generald Anthony Malton [1960] Director; Darren Lee McCormack [1982] Sales Director; Richard James Paterson [1957] Director; Martin Richard Smith [1955] Director; Jonathan Andrew Spring [1972] Land Buying Director; Michael Raymond Walker [1958] Director; Robert Kenneth Williams [1964] Finance Director

Fairview New Homes (Developments) Limited
Incorporated: 2 November 1999
Net Worth: £2,358,000 *Total Assets:* £17,592,000
Registered Office: 50 Lancaster Road, Enfield, Middlesex, EN2 0BY
Activities: Development of building projects
Parent: Fairview New Homes Limited
Officers: Jonathan Mark Baxter, Secretary; Michael Blakey [1963] Director; Nicholas Martin Dulcken [1967] Director; Generald Anthony Malton [1960] Director; Darren Lee McCormack [1982] Sales Director; Richard James Paterson [1957] Director; Jonathan Andrew Spring [1972] Land Buying Director; Michael Raymond Walker [1958] Director; Robert Kenneth Williams [1964] Finance Director

Fairview New Homes (Properties) Limited
Incorporated: 19 December 2002 *Employees:* 9
Net Worth: £1,264,000 *Total Assets:* £28,527,000
Registered Office: 50 Lancaster Road, Enfield, Middlesex, EN2 0BY
Activities: Development of building projects
Parent: Fairview New Homes Limited
Officers: Jonathan Mark Baxter, Secretary; Michael Blakey [1963] Director; Nicholas Martin Dulcken [1967] Director; Generald Anthony Malton [1960] Director; Darren Lee McCormack [1982] Sales Director; Richard James Paterson [1957] Director; Martin Richard Smith [1955] Director; Jonathan Andrew Spring [1972] Land Buying Director; Michael Raymond Walker [1958] Director; Robert Kenneth Williams [1964] Finance Director

Fairview New Homes (South East) Limited
Incorporated: 2 September 1997
Net Worth: £19,954,000 *Total Assets:* £20,231,000
Registered Office: 50 Lancaster Road, Enfield, Middlesex, EN2 0BY
Activities: Development of building projects
Parent: Fairview Enfield Limited
Officers: Jonathan Mark Baxter, Secretary; Michael Blakey [1963] Director; Nicholas Martin Dulcken [1967] Director; Generald Anthony Malton [1960] Director; Darren Lee McCormack [1982] Sales Director; Richard James Paterson [1957] Director; Jonathan Andrew Spring [1972] Land Buying Director; Michael Raymond Walker [1958] Director; Robert Kenneth Williams [1964] Finance Director

Fairview New Homes (Willow Way) Limited
Incorporated: 8 March 2000
Net Worth: £1,058,000 *Total Assets:* £16,690,000
Registered Office: 50 Lancaster Road, Enfield, Middlesex, EN2 0BY
Activities: Development of building projects
Parent: Fairview New Homes Limited
Officers: Jonathan Mark Baxter, Secretary; Michael Blakey [1963] Director; Nicholas Martin Dulcken [1967] Director; Generald Anthony Malton [1960] Director; Darren Lee McCormack [1982] Sales Director; Richard James Paterson [1957] Director; Martin Richard Smith [1955] Director; Jonathan Andrew Spring [1972] Land Buying Director; Michael Raymond Walker [1958] Director; Robert Kenneth Williams [1964] Finance Director

Fairview New Homes Limited
Incorporated: 2 October 2000 *Employees:* 9
Net Worth: £238,704,992 *Total Assets:* £309,481,984
Registered Office: 50 Lancaster Road, Enfield, Middlesex, EN2 0BY
Activities: Activities of construction holding companies
Parent: Fairview Holdings Limited
Officers: Jonathan Mark Baxter, Secretary; Michael Blakey [1963] Director; Dennis John Cope [1933] Director; Nicholas Martin Dulcken [1967] Director; Generald Anthony Malton [1960] Director; Darren Lee McCormack [1982] Sales Director; Richard James Paterson [1957] Director; Jonathan Andrew Spring [1972] Land Buying Director; Michael Raymond Walker [1958] Development Director; Robert Kenneth Williams [1964] Finance Director

Fairview Ventures Limited
Incorporated: 11 September 2001 *Employees:* 8
Net Worth: £1,247,000 *Total Assets:* £31,698,000
Registered Office: 50 Lancaster Road, Enfield, Middlesex, EN2 0BY
Activities: Development of building projects
Parent: Fairview New Homes Limited
Officers: Jonathan Mark Baxter, Secretary; Michael Blakey [1963] Director; Nicholas Martin Dulcken [1967] Director; Generald Anthony Malton [1960] Director/Accountant; Darren Lee McCormack [1982] Sales Director; Richard James Paterson [1957] Director; Jonathan Andrew Spring [1972] Land Buying Director; Michael Raymond Walker [1958] Director; Robert Kenneth Williams [1964] Finance Director

Fairway of Course Limited
Incorporated: 5 June 2001 *Employees:* 24
Net Worth: £4,268,054 *Total Assets:* £5,272,670
Registered Office: Woodfield House, 506-508 Honeypot Lane, Stanmore, Middlesex, HA7 1JS
Activities: Other retail sale not in stores, stalls or markets
Officers: Deep Bhaichand Patani, Secretary/Director; Deep Bhaichand Patani [1965] Director; Nihar Indravadan Devchand Patani [1975] Director/Management Consultant; Rajnikant Devchand Patani [1947] Director/Businessman; Rumit Rajnikant Patani [1978] Director/Computer Systems Engineer; Samit Rajnikant Patani [1977] Director/IT Consultant

Faithful+Gould Limited
Incorporated: 28 March 1988 *Employees:* 1,286
Net Worth: £62,140,000 *Total Assets:* £100,931,000
Registered Office: Woodcote Grove, Ashley Road, Epsom, Surrey, KT18 5BW
Activities: Management consultancy activities other than financial management
Parent: Faithful+Gould (Holdings) Limited
Officers: Louise Mary McAllister, Secretary; Elliot Michael Nobelen, Secretary; Mark Stephen Anderson [1965] Director/Accountant; Adam Brooks [1965] Director/Chartered Surveyor; Neil William Clemson [1962] Director/Project Manager; Simon Glenister Cole [1965] Director/Accountant; Andrew Stephen Constable [1957] Director/Chartered Quantity Surveyor; Alan James Cullens [1963] Group HR Director; Nicholas Kenneth Gray [1966] Director/Chartered Quantity Surveyor; Andrew Clifford Green [1959] Director/Surveyor; Jonathan Mark Sealy [1966] Director/Chartered Surveyor; John Wood [1957] Director/Quantity Surveyor

Falco Construction Limited
Incorporated: 12 November 2004 *Employees:* 21
Net Worth: £4,192,940 *Total Assets:* £6,443,337
Registered Office: 2 Mountside, Stanmore, Middlesex, HA7 2DT
Activities: Other construction installation
Major Shareholder: Brendan Anthony Griffin
Officers: Jana Griffin, Secretary; Brendan Anthony Griffin [1967] Director; Alan Seyfi [1965] Director

Falcon Hotels Limited
Incorporated: 6 July 2009
Net Worth: £372,141 *Total Assets:* £7,914,813
Registered Office: Kirkland House, 11-15 Peterborough Road, Harrow, Middlesex, HA1 2AX
Activities: Hotels and similar accommodation
Officers: Dinesh Gordhandas Bhattessa [1946] Director/Businessman; Haider Ladhu Jaffer [1940] Director/Businessman; Mohmed Jetha [1958] Director/Businessman; Dr Manoj Raman [1960] Director/Businessman; Hassanali Amirali Dawood Suleman [1954] Director/Businessman

Falcon Investment Ltd
Incorporated: 20 August 2009
Net Worth Deficit: £1,000,879 *Total Assets:* £6,716,277
Registered Office: 404 Staines Road, Bedfont, Middlesex, TW14 8BT
Activities: Development of building projects
Major Shareholder: Gurdial Singh Mann
Officers: Gurdial Singh Mann [1955] Director

Falcon Panel Products Limited
Incorporated: 24 April 1986 *Employees:* 69
Net Worth: £8,658,491 *Total Assets:* £36,302,428
Registered Office: Clock House, Station Approach, Shepperton, Surrey, TW17 8AN
Activities: Wholesale of wood, construction materials and sanitary equipment
Parent: Consolidated Timber Holdings Ltd
Officers: Ann Bowler [1954] Director/Sales Executive; David John Colman [1962] Director/Chartered Accountant; Simon David Holdsworth [1956] Director/Chartered Accountant; Aidan George Hudson [1969] Operations Director; Gary Miller [1969] Sales Director; Mark Lee Percival [1958] Director/Sales Executive; Martin James Perry [1982] Strategy Director; Andrew Peter Smith [1959] Director/Salesman; Andrew James Tilbury [1959] Director/Salesman

Family Funerals Trust Limited
Incorporated: 15 March 1988 *Employees:* 6
Net Worth: £1,866,406 *Total Assets:* £17,959,134
Registered Office: Ludlow House, Ludlow Road, Feltham, Middlesex, TW13 7JF
Activities: Funeral and related activities
Parent: Lodge Bros (Funerals) Ltd
Officers: Michael Lodge, Secretary; Beverley Ann Harris [1960] Director; Andrew John Lodge [1969] Director; Christopher David Lodge [1970] Director; Janet Rachel Lodge [1969] Director; Michael James Lodge [1966] Financial Director; Robert John Lodge [1965] Director

Far East & Co Limited
Incorporated: 16 May 2011 *Employees:* 1
Net Worth: £7,788,353 *Total Assets:* £11,127,936
Registered Office: Ibex House, Baker Street, Weybridge, Surrey, KT13 8AH
Activities: Other business support service activities n.e.c.
Major Shareholder: Jean-Paul Riviere
Officers: Jonathan Farrow [1965] Director

Fardaar LLP
Incorporated: 27 March 2004 *Employees:* 6
Net Worth: £8,739,090 *Total Assets:* £8,746,325
Registered Office: 166 College Road, Harrow, Middlesex, HA1 1RA
Officers: Naishad Patel [1963] LLP Member; Meera Nalin Shah [1973] LLP Member; Priya Nalin Kantilal Shah [1972] LLP Member; Edward Watson [1971] LLP Member

Farrington Care Homes Limited
Incorporated: 18 February 1998 *Employees:* 368
Net Worth: £8,953,928 *Total Assets:* £13,752,100
Registered Office: Sai Villa, 1 Farrington Place, Northwood, Middlesex, HA6 3SW
Activities: Residential nursing care facilities
Officers: Paren Chuni Nathwani, Secretary; Kiran Chuni Nathwani [1962] Director; Paren Chuni Nathwani [1965] Director

Farsound Aviation Limited
Incorporated: 17 February 1986 *Employees:* 35
Net Worth: £8,269,000 *Total Assets:* £10,781,000
Registered Office: 15 Ashton Gate, Ashton Road, Romford, Essex, RM3 8UF
Activities: Agents involved in the sale of a variety of goods
Parent: Farsound Investments Limited
Officers: Jonathan Charles Richardson, Secretary; Joseph Boucher [1983] Director/Chartered Accountant; Andrew Olaf Fischer [1964] Director [German]; Ian Fisher [1950] Director; Lee Kelsey [1976] Sales Director; Christopher Terence Knott [1979] Director/Accountant; Jonathan Mark Medhurst [1973] Procurement Director; Philip Charles Northfield [1952] Technical Director; Daniel O'Neill [1983] Director [Irish]; Jonathan Charles Richardson [1960] Director; Kevin Stephen Sargent [1961] Director; David Skinner [1962] Director

Fascroft Limited
Incorporated: 30 May 2007
Net Worth: £1,848,103 *Total Assets:* £9,383,104
Registered Office: 9 Bridle Close, Kingston upon Thames, Surrey, KT1 2JW
Activities: Development of building projects
Shareholders: The Jersey Property Partnership LLP; Flodrive Holdings Ltd
Officers: Ashok Kumar Tanna, Secretary; David Solomon Baroukh [1971] Director/Property Consultant; Anthony Menashi Khalastchi [1961] Director; Ephraim Menashi Frank Khalastchi [1933] Director; Peter Salim David Khalastchi [1963] Director

Fasttrax Holdings Limited
Incorporated: 30 November 2001 *Employees:* 4
Net Worth: £8,827,000 *Total Assets:* £44,718,000
Registered Office: Hill Park Court, Springfield Drive, Leatherhead, Surrey, KT22 7NL
Activities: Activities of other holding companies n.e.c.
Parent: Kellogg Brown & Root Limited
Officers: Larry Jay Henry, Secretary/Director [American]; Richard Sean Card [1961] Project Director; John Ivor Cavill [1972] Director; Larry Jay Henry [1953] Director [American]; Peter John Sheldrake [1959] Director

Fasttrax Limited
Incorporated: 12 May 1998 *Employees:* 4
Net Worth: £8,821,000 *Total Assets:* £44,712,000
Registered Office: Hill Park Court, Springfield Drive, Leatherhead, Surrey, KT22 7NL
Activities: Manufacture of bodies (coachwork) for motor vehicles (except caravans)
Parent: Fasttrax Holdings Limited
Officers: Larry Jay Henry, Secretary/Director [American]; Richard Sean Card [1961] Project Director; John Ivor Cavill [1972] Director; Larry Jay Henry [1953] Director [American]; Peter John Sheldrake [1959] Director

Fazal Fast Foods Limited
Incorporated: 20 November 1984 *Employees:* 128
Net Worth: £6,923,403 *Total Assets:* £9,695,077
Registered Office: Runway House, The Runway, Ruislip, Middlesex, HA4 6SE
Activities: Unlicenced restaurants and cafes
Parent: SME Holdings Limited
Officers: Aly Mohamed Esmail, Secretary; Sayed Mohamed Esmail, Secretary; Aly Mohamed Esmail [1982] Director; Sayed Mohamed Esmail [1986] Director

FBL Holdings Limited
Incorporated: 20 June 2008
Net Worth Deficit: £30,647,000 *Total Assets:* £75,101,000
Registered Office: 9th Floor, Regal House, 70 London Road, Twickenham, Middlesex, TW1 3QS
Activities: Manufacture of wine from grape
Parent: Treasury Wine Estates EMEA Limited
Officers: Michelle Elizabeth Brampton [1972] Finance Director; Richard John Renwick [1969] Director/Chief Financial Officer Europe

FBM Metals (UK) Limited
Incorporated: 12 August 1975 *Employees:* 1
Net Worth: £6,572,047 *Total Assets:* £9,155,639
Registered Office: 5 Beauchamp Court, 10 Victors Way, Barnet, Herts, EN5 5TZ
Activities: Recovery of sorted materials
Parent: FBM Holdings Limited
Officers: Henry Edward Wilkinson, Secretary; Michael Stephen Gawne [1983] Director/Metal Broker; Henry Edward Wilkinson [1976] Director

FBSE Finance Limited
Incorporated: 20 March 2009 *Employees:* 7
Net Worth: £1,823,379 *Total Assets:* £9,559,271
Registered Office: Ground Floor, Regent House, Theobald Street, Borehamwood, Herts, WD6 4RS
Activities: Activities of mortgage finance companies
Major Shareholder: Dorian Grant Nineberg
Officers: Rosalind Caroline Nineberg, Secretary; Dorian Grant Nineberg [1958] Director/Financier; Hayley Nineberg [1985] Director; Rosalind Caroline Nineberg [1958] Director/Administrator

FC JB Co Limited
Incorporated: 23 March 2010
Net Worth: £12,525,247 *Total Assets:* £12,867,866
Registered Office: 2 AC Court, High Street, Thames Ditton, Surrey, KT7 0SR
Activities: Other business support service activities n.e.c.
Parent: Tribal Energy Limited
Officers: John Charles Bodenham [1957] Director/Conference Organiser

Feabrex Limited
Incorporated: 29 December 1964 *Employees:* 3
Net Worth: £17,438,036 *Total Assets:* £18,551,442
Registered Office: Albion Engineering Works (South), Albion Parade, Gravesend, Kent, DA12 2RN
Activities: Development of building projects
Major Shareholder: Ronald William Nash
Officers: Paul Nash, Secretary; Ronald William Nash [1941] Director/Plater

Fedrigoni U.K. Limited
Incorporated: 19 November 1992 *Employees:* 38
Net Worth: £4,871,321 *Total Assets:* £11,317,673
Registered Office: 1 Princeton Mews, 167-169 London Road, Kingston upon Thames, Surrey, KT2 6PT
Activities: Non-specialised wholesale trade
Parent: Fabric (BC) Holdco Limited
Officers: Gabriele Alfonsi [1962] Director [Italian]; Chiara Medioli [1971] Director/Entrepreneur [Italian]

E. Feldman Limited
Incorporated: 25 September 1978 *Employees:* 12
Net Worth: £9,207,161 *Total Assets:* £9,467,060
Registered Office: Unit 6 Barking Industrial Estate, Alfreds Way, Barking, Essex, IG11 0TJ
Activities: Wholesale of clothing and footwear
Shareholders: Emanuel Feldman; Thelma Feldman
Officers: Thelma Feldman, Secretary; Emanuel Feldman [1936] Director/Merchant; Thelma Feldman [1939] Director

John E.Fells & Sons Limited
Incorporated: 1 May 1920 *Employees:* 50
Net Worth: £10,591,224 *Total Assets:* £27,073,200
Registered Office: Fells House, Station Road, Kings Langley, Herts, WD4 8LH
Activities: Wholesale of wine, beer, spirits and other alcoholic beverages
Parent: Atlantis Wine Holdings Ltd
Officers: Louise Catherine Rimes, Secretary; Alan Robert Campbell [1962] Sales Director; Nicholas John Gurney [1970] Director/Certified Chartered Accountant; Robert Wyndham Hill-Smith [1951] Managing Director [Australian]; Stephen Antony Moody [1960] Managing Director; John Andrew Douglas Symington [1960] Director/Port Producer; Paul Douglas Symington [1953] Director/Port Producer; Edward Jared MacLeod Thornton [1965] Development Director; Simon William Michael Thorpe [1966] Commercial Director; Miguel Torres Maczassek [1974] Director [Spanish]

Feltonfleet School Trust Limited
Incorporated: 28 July 1967 *Employees:* 88
Net Worth: £7,982,414 *Total Assets:* £10,849,663
Registered Office: Feltonfleet School, Byfleet Road, Cobham, Surrey, KT11 1DR
Activities: Pre-primary education
Officers: Jason Player McKinlay, Secretary; Elizabeth Anderson Forsyth Anderson [1960] Director; Giles Douglas Ashbee [1959] Director; David Joseph Barry [1963] Director/Chief Executive [Irish]; Rosaleen Mary Bishop [1965] Director/Chief Executive [Irish]; Richard Murray Bray [1944] Director/Solicitor; Tina Louise Harvey [1961] Director/Headteacher; Paul Arthur Howard [1969] Director; Sarah Humphrey [1970] Director/Deputy Head of a School; Hilary Frances Shapland Humphry Baker [1958] Director/Deputy Headteacher; Mary Jenner [1947] Director/Self Employed; Graeme Robert Owton [1970] Director/Headmaster; Michael George Sadler [1947] Director/Retired; Caroline St Gallay [1971] Director/Teacher

Ferholding UK Ltd
Incorporated: 12 June 2015
Net Worth Deficit: £10,635,000 *Total Assets:* £101,576,000
Registered Office: 889 Greenford Road, Greenford, Middlesex, UB6 0HE
Activities: Activities of other holding companies n.e.c.
Officers: Tim John Shirley, Secretary; Salvatore Castelli [1971] Finance Director [Italian]; Pieraldo Oldano [1965] Managing Director [Italian]; Marco Pescarolo [1957] Director/Global Treasurer [Italian]

Ferrero UK Limited
Incorporated: 4 April 1966 *Employees:* 203
Net Worth Deficit: £26,873,000 *Total Assets:* £119,285,000
Registered Office: 889 Greenford Road, Greenford, Middlesex, UB6 0HE
Activities: Manufacture of cocoa and chocolate confectionery
Officers: Tim John Shirley, Secretary; Salvatore Castelli [1971] Director [Italian]; Pieraldo Oldano [1965] Director/Business Manager [Italian]; Marco Pescarolo [1957] Director [Italian]

Ferring Asset Management Limited
Incorporated: 10 June 2014 *Employees:* 1
Net Worth: £32,533,996 *Total Assets:* £32,750,000
Registered Office: Drayton Hall, Church Road, West Drayton, Middlesex, UB7 7PS
Activities: Non-trading company
Parent: Ferring Laboratories Limited
Officers: Raphael Cretegny, Secretary; Frank Christoph Lindenmann [1959] Director/Tax Lawyer [Swiss]

Ferring Laboratories Limited
Incorporated: 18 July 1980 *Employees:* 192
Net Worth Deficit: £17,292,892 *Total Assets:* £64,455,896
Registered Office: Drayton Hall, Church Road, West Drayton, Middlesex, UB7 7PS
Activities: Activities of head offices
Officers: Raphael Cretegny, Secretary; Jean Marie Duvall [1961] Director [American]; Dr Peter Wilden [1957] Director [German]

Ferring Pharmaceuticals Limited
Incorporated: 28 January 1975 *Employees:* 107
Net Worth: £3,635,637 *Total Assets:* £18,245,226
Registered Office: Drayton Hall, Church Road, West Drayton, Middlesex, UB7 7PS
Activities: Wholesale of pharmaceutical goods
Parent: Ferring Asset Management Limited
Officers: Raphael Cretegny, Secretary; Michel Lucien Pettigrew [1953] Director/Business Executive [Canadian]; Gilles Pluntz [1957] Director/Senior Vice President [French]

FGP Topco Limited
Incorporated: 28 February 2006 *Employees:* 6,740
Net Worth: £922,000,000 *Total Assets:* £18,304,000,000
Registered Office: The Compass Centre, Nelson Road, Hounslow, Middlesex, TW6 2GW
Activities: Activities of head offices
Officers: Ahmed Ali Al-Hammadi [1981] Director [Qatari]; Stuart Harvey Baldwin [1969] Director/Investment Manager; Christopher William Beale [1947] Director [American]; Jinhong Chen [1990] Director [Chinese]; Samuel Coxe [1975] Alternate Director [American]; Olivier Georges Xavier Fortin [1974] Director [French]; Jorge Gil Villen [1972] Director/Lawyer/Economist [Spanish]; Mr Deven Arvind Karnik [1967] Alternate Director; Tom Kelly [1989] Director [Irish]; Alexander Leonard [1985] Director; Inigo Meiras [1963] Alternate Director [Spanish]; Michael James Powell [1972] Director; David Jinlin Xie [1978] Alternate Director [American]

Fibron BX Limited
Incorporated: 28 January 1987 *Employees:* 90
Previous: Cortland Fibron BX Limited
Net Worth: £8,668,543 *Total Assets:* £15,165,722
Registered Office: Unit 2 R D Park, Stephenson Close, Hoddesdon, Herts, EN11 0BW
Activities: Other manufacturing n.e.c.
Parent: Cortland U.K. Holdings Limited
Officers: Andrew James Finch, Secretary; Bruno Cianfini [1970] Commercial Director; Andrew Olaf Fischer [1964] Director [German]; Balraj Singh Virdi [1986] Director

FIC Grand Plaza Ltd
Incorporated: 31 July 2013 *Employees:* 47
Net Worth: £2,959,539 *Total Assets:* £18,441,596
Registered Office: Delson Suite, 2nd Floor, Amba House, 15 College Road, Harrow, Middlesex, HA1 1BA
Activities: Hotels and similar accommodation
Parent: BHD
Officers: Mohammed Jeffri [1962] Director/Manager [Malaysian]; AB Ghani Mohd Ali [1957] Director/Admin Officer [Malaysian]; Mohd Shahrin Mohd Ali [1969] Director [Malaysian]; Bin Mohd Nor Muzzammil [1971] Director [Malaysian]

Fidelity Asian Values PLC
Incorporated: 2 April 1996
Net Worth: £287,974,016 *Total Assets:* £291,380,992
Registered Office: Beech Gate, Millfield Lane, Lower Kingswood, Tadworth, Surrey, KT20 6RB
Activities: Activities of investment trusts
Officers: Katherine Blanche Mary Bolsover [1958] Director/Retired; Timothy Scholefield [1963] Director; Philip David Smiley [1951] Director; Grahame Stott [1954] Director/Actuary; Michael Sturrock Warren [1961] Director/Investment Professional

Fidelity China Special Situations PLC
Incorporated: 22 January 2010
Net Worth: £1,502,866,048 *Total Assets:* £1,654,736,000
Registered Office: Beech Gate, Millfield Lane, Lower Kingswood, Tadworth, Surrey, KT20 6RP
Activities: Activities of investment trusts
Officers: Michael Warren Balfour [1960] Director; Nicholas James Douglas Bull [1952] Director; David John Causer [1950] Director; The Hon Peter John Pleydell-Bouverie [1958] Director; Elisabeth Charlotte Scott [1962] Director

Fidelity European Values PLC
Incorporated: 16 August 1991
Net Worth: £1,030,048,000 *Total Assets:* £1,038,979,968
Registered Office: Beech Gate, Millfield Lane, Lower Kingswood, Tadworth, Surrey, KT20 6RB
Activities: Activities of investment trusts
Officers: Vivian Paul Bazalgette [1951] Director; Fleur Meijs [1971] Director [Dutch]; Robin Christian Howard Niblett [1961] Director; Marion Jane Sears [1962] Director; Paul Tennant Yates [1957] Director

Fidelity Japan Trust PLC
Incorporated: 7 January 1994
Previous: Fidelity Japanese Values PLC
Net Worth: £222,527,008 *Total Assets:* £224,475,008
Registered Office: Beech Gate, Millfield Lane, Lower Kingswood, Tadworth, Surrey, KT20 6RB
Activities: Activities of investment trusts
Officers: David Rowley Graham [1955] Director; Philip Bruce Kay [1955] Director; Sarah Juliet MacAulay [1962] Director; Sir Laurence Henry Philip Magnus [1955] Director and Charity Trustee; David Anthony Robins [1949] Director; Dominic Martin Matthew Ziegler [1961] Director

Fidelity Special Values PLC
Incorporated: 27 September 1994
Net Worth: £724,969,984 *Total Assets:* £733,105,024
Registered Office: Beech Gate, Millfield Lane, Lower Kingswood, Tadworth, Surrey, KT20 6RP
Activities: Activities of investment trusts
Officers: Sharon Mary Brown [1968] Director; Dean Robert Buckley [1960] Director; Nigel Foster [1952] Director; Andrew Robertson Irvine [1951] Director; Nicola Joanne McCabe [1969] Executive Director

Field Marketing (UK) Holdings Limited
Incorporated: 17 November 2011 *Employees:* 76
Net Worth: £8,242,000 *Total Assets:* £11,078,000
Registered Office: 1 Parkshot, Richmond, Surrey, TW9 2RD
Activities: Other professional, scientific and technical activities n.e.c.
Officers: Sean Marc Roberts, Secretary; Paul Boyle [1978] Director/Chief Executive; Mian Hua Chen [1976] Investment Director [Malaysian]; Philip Peter Latham [1960] Director of Private Equity Advisor [British/Australian]; Kelvin Mak [1985] Director/Investment Manager [Australian]; David Norbury [1958] Director

Field Marketing (UK) Limited
Incorporated: 28 October 2011 *Employees:* 5
Net Worth: £7,188,000 *Total Assets:* £9,500,000
Registered Office: 1 Parkshot, Richmond, Surrey, TW9 2RD
Activities: Other professional, scientific and technical activities n.e.c.
Officers: Sean Marc Roberts, Secretary; Paul Boyle [1978] Director/Chief Executive; Mian Hua Chen [1976] Investment Director [Malaysian]; Philip Peter Latham [1960] Director of Private Equity Advisor [British/Australian]; Kelvin Mak [1985] Director/Investment Manager [Australian]; David Norbury [1958] Director

Fieldgrange Properties Limited
Incorporated: 20 November 2003
Net Worth Deficit: £7,169,018 *Total Assets:* £5,336,038
Registered Office: Hill House, Lowlands Road, Harrow, Middlesex, HA1 3EQ
Activities: Development of building projects
Major Shareholder: Donovan Gijsbertus Wijsmuller
Officers: Brian Martin Comer [1960] Director [Irish]; Luke Andrew Comer [1957] Director [Irish]

Fieldrose Limited
Incorporated: 7 July 1992 *Employees:* 1,510
Net Worth: £11,166,164 *Total Assets:* £64,728,000
Registered Office: First Floor, Kirkland House, 11-15 Peterborough Road, Harrow, Middlesex, HA1 2AX
Activities: Unlicenced restaurants and cafes
Shareholders: Bharat Chandubhai Patel; Maya Bharat Patel
Officers: Maya Bharat Patel, Secretary; Bharat Chandubhai Patel [1964] Director/Businessman; Maya Bharat Patel [1965] Director/Secretary

Fieldside Associates Limited
Incorporated: 26 April 1991 *Employees:* 2
Net Worth: £5,856,304 *Total Assets:* £10,292,559
Registered Office: Aissela, 46 High Street, Esher, Surrey, KT10 9QY
Activities: Development of building projects
Major Shareholder: Gillian Elaine Spiero Burns
Officers: James Stewart Burns, Secretary/Property Developer; Gillian Elaine Spiero Burns [1959] Director

Fifty Shades Ltd
Incorporated: 3 February 2012 *Employees:* 2
Net Worth: £58,444,604 *Total Assets:* £59,905,328
Registered Office: Russell House, 140 High Street, Edgware, Middlesex, HA8 7LW
Activities: Artistic creation
Major Shareholder: Erika Lena Mitchell
Officers: Niall Patrick Leonard, Secretary; Erika Mitchell [1963] Director

Filemaker International
Incorporated: 24 April 1998 *Employees:* 17
Net Worth: £7,884,902 *Total Assets:* £21,506,580
Registered Office: 2 Furzeground Way, Stockley Park, Uxbridge, Middlesex, UB11 1BB
Activities: Other software publishing
Officers: Sophia Crystal Yungen, Secretary; William Young Epling [1959] Director/Business Executive [American]; Roger Andrew Hale [1966] Director/Businessman; Sophia Crystal Yungen [1987] Director/Businesswoman [American]

Films & Equipments Limited
Incorporated: 1 May 1934 *Employees:* 3
Net Worth: £18,961,764 *Total Assets:* £19,207,570
Registered Office: STC House, 7 Elmfield Road, Bromley, Kent, BR1 1LT
Activities: Fund management activities
Officers: Adrian Hollands, Secretary; Wendy Jacqueline Forrester [1933] Director; Adrian Hollands [1952] Director/Chartered Accountant; Melissa Wendy Jones [1950] Director/Retired

Filross Securities Limited
Incorporated: 20 September 1927
Net Worth: £7,843,940 *Total Assets:* £11,264,200
Registered Office: 28 Church Road, Stanmore, Middlesex, HA7 4XR
Activities: Development of building projects
Major Shareholder: Lawrence Michael Alkin
Officers: Kim Min Chong, Secretary; Lawrence Michael Alkin [1939] Director

Finance Ireland Limited
Incorporated: 3 June 2004 *Employees:* 99
Net Worth: £70,072,600 *Total Assets:* £206,919,440
Registered Office: The Registry, Beckenham Road, Beckenham, Kent, BR3 4TU
Activities: Activities of head offices
Shareholders: National Treasury Management Agency; Allianz SE
Officers: Lily MacKenna, Secretary; Joshua Michael Anderson [1972] Managing Director [American]; Daniel Ballen [1982] Director/Private Equity Investor [American]; Ian Alexander Black [1963] Director [Irish]; Frank Donnellan [1958] Director [Irish]; John Humphrey Gunn [1942] Director; James Hickey [1968] Director [Irish]; William Kane [1955] Director [Irish]; Kristofer Kraus [1970] Director/Investment Manager [American]; Fergal McAleavey [1970] Director [Irish]

Financial Management Limited
Incorporated: 3 July 2001
Net Worth: £2,239,156 *Total Assets:* £5,048,068
Registered Office: 42 Lytton Road, Barnet, Herts, EN5 5BY
Activities: Financial management
Officers: Jeffrey Ian Lermer [1964] Director/Accountant

Finefrance Holdings Limited
Incorporated: 8 October 2015
Net Worth: £212,881 *Total Assets:* £5,583,943
Registered Office: 29 Ullswater Crescent, Coulsdon, Surrey, CR5 2HR
Activities: Activities of head offices
Parent: Vestey Holdings Limited
Officers: Neil Thornton, Secretary; Colin George Copland [1954] Director/Chartered Accountant; George Moubray William Vestey [1964] Director

Finepoint Broadcast Limited
Incorporated: 26 January 1984 *Employees:* 16
Previous: Fine Point Broadcast Limited
Net Worth: £8,451,768 *Total Assets:* £12,999,449
Registered Office: Nightingale House, 46-48 East Street, Epsom, Surrey, KT17 1HQ
Activities: Other service activities n.e.c.
Shareholders: Allen Bendig; Wendy Patricia Bendig
Officers: Wendy Patricia Bendig, Secretary; Allen Bendig [1930] Director/Chairman; Giles Christopher Allen Bendig [1982] Director; Dr Justin William Allen Bendig [1957] Director/Medical Practitioner; Wendy Patricia Bendig [1930] Director

Finer Limited
Incorporated: 17 December 2001
Net Worth: £11,016,095 *Total Assets:* £16,949,120
Registered Office: 35a High Street, Ruislip, Middlesex, HA4 7AU
Activities: Other letting and operating of own or leased real estate
Shareholders: Jaswir Singh Malhi; Inderjit Kaur Malhi
Officers: Amandeep Malhi, Secretary; Amandeep Malhi [1980] Director; Baljinder Kaur Malhi [1982] Director; Inderjit Kaur Malhi [1957] Director; Jaswir Singh Malhi [1953] Marketing Director [Indian]

Fineraid Limited
Incorporated: 5 December 2003 *Employees:* 3
Net Worth: £9,543,034 *Total Assets:* £14,906,744
Registered Office: Northside House, Mount Pleasant, Barnet, Herts, EN4 9EE
Activities: Other service activities n.e.c.
Shareholder: Melvyn Frank Cooper
Officers: Jason Robert Cooper, Secretary; Adam Cooper [1971] Director; Jason Robert Cooper [1967] Director; Melvyn Frank Cooper [1941] Director

Fire Design Solutions Limited
Incorporated: 13 June 2002 *Employees:* 43
Net Worth: £3,365,733 *Total Assets:* £6,788,130
Registered Office: 152-154 London Road, Greenhithe, Dartford, Kent, DA9 9JW
Activities: Other construction installation
Parent: G S A R Holdings Limited
Officers: Andrew Graham Riley [1975] Director; Samantha Christine Riley [1975] Marketing Director; Gerard Joseph Sheridan [1966] Director; Nicholas Matthew Waterfield [1963] Managing Director

Firebolt RB Holdings Limited
Incorporated: 19 September 2016
Net Worth: £232,766,976 *Total Assets:* £1,503,451,136
Registered Office: 8 White Oak Square, London Road, Swanley, Kent, BR8 7AG
Activities: Activities of other holding companies n.e.c.
Officers: Erin Kate Eisenberg [1978] Director [American]; Charles John Gore Hazelwood [1963] Director; Philip William Kent [1984] Director; Christoph Friedrich Mertens [1969] Director [German]; David Paul Tilstone [1969] Director; Koji Wakabayashi [1973] Director [Japanese]

F A Firman (Harold Wood) Limited
Incorporated: 8 September 1960
Net Worth: £3,408,135 *Total Assets:* £5,046,911
Registered Office: 19 Bates Road, Harold Wood, Romford, Essex, RM3 0JH
Activities: Shaping and processing of flat glass
Major Shareholder: Jody Hodgson
Officers: Keith Robin Tanner, Secretary; Jody Hodgson [1975] Director/Glass Manufacturer

Firmenich UK Limited
Incorporated: 18 May 1990 *Employees:* 166
Net Worth: £25,586,000 *Total Assets:* £45,554,000
Registered Office: Hayes Road, Southall, Middlesex, UB2 5NN
Activities: Manufacture of perfumes and toilet preparations
Officers: Elodie Josiane Bouchard [1972] Senior Director Finance Europe [French]; Gary Charles Nelson [1961] Director; Paulo Sergio Menoita Nogueira [1966] Director [Brazilian/Portuguese]; Laetitia Christabel Pictet [1970] Director/Legal Counsel [Swiss]; Dominique Florence Zundel [1963] Director/VP Europe, Perfumery BHC [French]

First Atlantic Finance Limited
Incorporated: 18 March 2013
Net Worth: £109,628 *Total Assets:* £5,084,578
Registered Office: 9 Handel Parade, Whitchurch Lane, Edgware, Middlesex, HA8 6LD
Activities: Other credit granting n.e.c.
Major Shareholder: Nimesh Khiroya
Officers: Neesha Khiroya [1954] Director/Accountant

First City Care (London) Limited
Incorporated: 21 September 1993 *Employees:* 35
Previous: First City Care (London) PLC
Net Worth: £6,929,578 *Total Assets:* £24,632,024
Registered Office: Security House, The Summit, Hanworth Road, Sunbury on Thames, Middlesex, TW16 5DB
Activities: Other business support service activities n.e.c.
Parent: Amberwell Holdings Limited
Officers: Moosa Farook Meah [1965] Director

First Coins Pawn LLP
Incorporated: 17 September 2008
Net Worth: £14,744,799 *Total Assets:* £14,780,147
Registered Office: Unit 90 Kingspark Business Centre, 152-178 Kingston Road, New Malden, Surrey, KT3 3ST

First Investments (UK) Limited
Incorporated: 4 June 2004
Net Worth: £3,118,104 *Total Assets:* £9,140,244
Registered Office: Unit 1 Rowdell Road, Northolt, Middlesex, UB5 5QR
Activities: Buying and selling of own real estate
Parent: FIUKL (Holdings) Limited
Officers: Daljit Singh Sohal, Secretary; Dennis Georgiou [1957] Director; George Georgiou [1954] Director/Reinsurance Broker; Daljit Singh Sohal [1956] Finance Director

First Network Ltd.
Incorporated: 6 February 1992 *Employees:* 19
Net Worth: £6,384,397 *Total Assets:* £7,476,027
Registered Office: Unit 1 Rowdell Road, Northolt, Middlesex, UB5 5QR
Activities: Artistic creation
Parent: FNL (Holdings) Limited
Officers: Daljit Singh Sohal, Secretary; Dennis Georgiou [1957] Managing Director; George Georgiou [1954] Director/Reinsurance Broker; Claire Joanne Maisey [1979] Director; Daljit Singh Sohal [1956] Finance Director

First Network Properties Ltd
Incorporated: 14 October 1999
Net Worth: £4,177,816 *Total Assets:* £9,660,187
Registered Office: Unit 1 Rowdell Road, Northolt, Middlesex, UB5 5QR
Activities: Other letting and operating of own or leased real estate
Parent: FNPL (Holdings) Limited
Officers: Daljit Singh Sohal, Secretary; Dennis Georgiou [1957] Director; George Georgiou [1954] Director/Reinsurance Broker; Daljit Singh Sohal [1956] Finance Director

First Rate Exchange Services Holdings Limited
Incorporated: 14 September 2001 *Employees:* 282
Net Worth: £132,922,000 *Total Assets:* £484,660,992
Registered Office: Great West House, Great West Road, Brentford, Middlesex, TW8 9DF
Activities: Banks
Shareholders: Bank of Ireland (UK) PLC; Post Office Limited
Officers: Jane Elizabeth MacLeod, Secretary; Amy Burke [1975] HR Director [Irish]; Desmond Edward Crowley [1959] Director/Banker [Irish]; Gary Fitton [1968] Director/Chief Executive Officer; Neil Anthony Fuller [1966] Director; Roger William Gale [1957] Director; Andrew James MacGregor Hardie [1967] Director; Deborah Kay Smith [1965] Director/Chief Executive; John Tudor [1969] Director; Henk Van Hulle [1971] Director, Post Office Money [Belgian]; The Reverend Paula Anne Vennells [1959] Director; Owen Pearson Woodley [1967] Managing Director, Post Office Money

First Rate Exchange Services Limited
Incorporated: 14 September 2001 *Employees:* 282
Net Worth: £135,082,000 *Total Assets:* £486,819,008
Registered Office: Great West House, Great West Road, Brentford, Middlesex, TW8 9DF
Activities: Banks
Parent: First Rate Exchange Services Holdings Limited
Officers: Jane Elizabeth MacLeod, Secretary; Amy Burke [1975] HR Director [Irish]; Desmond Edward Crowley [1959] Director/Banker [Irish]; Gary Fitton [1968] Director/Chief Executive Officer; Neil Anthony Fuller [1966] Director; Roger William Gale [1957] Director; Andrew James MacGregor Hardie [1967] Director; Deborah Kay Smith [1965] Director/Chief Executive; John Tudor [1969] Director; Henk Van Hulle [1971] Director, Post Office Money [Belgian]; The Reverend Paula Anne Vennells [1959] Director; Owen Pearson Woodley [1967] Managing Director, Post Office Money

First Rented Housing Group Limited
Incorporated: 20 October 1988
Net Worth: £5,992,080 *Total Assets:* £15,150,114
Registered Office: Global House, 1 Ashley Avenue, Epsom, Surrey, KT18 5FL
Activities: Buying and selling of own real estate
Parent: The Valentine Group Limited
Officers: Joanna Katie Hunt, Secretary; Richard John Burgess [1946] Director/Chartered Accountant; John Charles Bentlif South [1937] Director/Solicitor (Retired)

First Wave Housing Limited
Incorporated: 12 September 2002 *Employees:* 118
Previous: Brent Housing Partnership Limited
Net Worth: £24,790,000 *Total Assets:* £64,824,000
Registered Office: Brent Civic Centre, Engineers Way, Wembley, Middlesex, HA9 0FJ
Activities: Management of real estate on a fee or contract basis
Parent: London Borough of Brent
Officers: Peter Gadsdon, Secretary; George Crane [1949] Director/Councillor; Akintoye Mobolaji Durowoju [1969] Director/Chartered Surveyor; Peter Gadsdon [1962] Director; Martin Frank Smith [1960] Director; Gail Elizabeth Tolley [1957] Director

Fishdance Limited
Incorporated: 9 October 2013
Net Worth: £4,843,392 *Total Assets:* £25,374,212
Registered Office: 2 Castle Business Village, Station Road, Hampton, Surrey, TW12 2BX
Activities: Raising of horses and other equines
Shareholders: David Fish; Linda Fish
Officers: Dr David John Fish [1948] Director; Linda Pamela Fish [1953] Director/Housewife

A.A. Fisher (Holdings) Limited
Incorporated: 3 February 2005
Net Worth: £6,199,969 *Total Assets:* £6,199,969
Registered Office: Unit 3 Fishers Industrial Estate, Wiggenhall Road, Watford, Herts, WD18 0FE
Activities: Activities of head offices
Shareholder: William Moorton Fisher
Officers: Pamela Jill Ryman, Secretary/Director; William Moorton Fisher [1951] Director; Pamela Jill Ryman [1954] Director

A.A.Fisher (Properties) Limited
Incorporated: 20 March 1962 *Employees:* 2
Net Worth: £31,120,048 *Total Assets:* £43,273,648
Registered Office: Unit 3 Fisher's Industrial Estate, Wiggenhall Road, Watford, Herts, WD18 0FE
Activities: Renting and operating of Housing Association real estate
Parent: A A Fisher Limited
Officers: Pamela Ann Saunders, Secretary; William Moorton Fisher [1951] Director; Pamela Jill Ryman [1954] Director

A.A.Fisher Limited
Incorporated: 26 January 1927
Net Worth: £6,199,969 *Total Assets:* £6,199,969
Registered Office: Unit 3 Fisher's Industrial Estate, Wiggenhall Road, Watford, Herts, WD18 0FE
Activities: Activities of head offices
Parent: A A Fisher (Holdings) Limited
Officers: William Moorton Fisher, Secretary; William Moorton Fisher [1951] Director; Pamela Jill Ryman [1954] Director

Fishnet Properties Limited
Incorporated: 25 April 2005 *Employees:* 1
Net Worth: £4,284,997 *Total Assets:* £12,971,217
Registered Office: 3a Chestnut House, Farm Close, Shenley, Herts, WD7 9AD
Activities: Buying and selling of own real estate
Shareholders: Lawrence Marcel Albonico; Heather Elizabeth Scanlan
Officers: Lawrence Marcel Albonico, Secretary; Lawrence Marcel Albonico [1964] Director/Property; Heather Elizabeth Scanlan [1968] Director/Media Consultant

Fishpools (Finance) Limited
Incorporated: 18 November 1965
Net Worth: £6,726,463 *Total Assets:* £6,860,445
Registered Office: 107-115 High Street, Waltham Cross, Herts, EN8 7AL
Activities: Other letting and operating of own or leased real estate
Parent: Fishpools Holdings Limited
Officers: Edward Duggan, Secretary; John Ernest Fishpool [1938] Director/Home Furnisher

Fishpools Holdings Limited
Incorporated: 28 April 2005 *Employees:* 199
Net Worth: £19,692,528 *Total Assets:* £27,214,488
Registered Office: 107-115 High Street, Waltham Cross, Herts, EN8 7AL
Activities: Activities of head offices
Shareholders: Ian Carson; John Ernest Fishpool
Officers: Edward Duggan, Secretary; Ian Carson [1938] Director; John Ernest Fishpool [1938] Director; Simon John Fishpool [1963] Director

Fishpools Limited
Incorporated: 10 July 1935 *Employees:* 197
Net Worth: £12,352,475 *Total Assets:* £22,924,174
Registered Office: 107-115 High Street, Waltham Cross, Herts, EN8 7AL
Activities: Retail of furniture, lighting, and similar (not musical instruments or scores) in specialised store
Parent: Fishpools Holdings Limited
Officers: Edward Duggan, Secretary; Ian Carson [1938] Director/Solicitor; John Ernest Fishpool [1938] Director/Home Furnisher; Simon John Fishpool [1963] Director/Home Furnisher

Fitton & Co Ltd
Incorporated: 23 October 2009
Net Worth: £7,413,736 *Total Assets:* £7,802,679
Registered Office: 6 Pembroke Villas, The Green, Richmond, Surrey, TW9 1QF
Activities: Activities of other holding companies n.e.c.
Major Shareholder: Andrew Charles Fitton
Officers: Andrew Charles Fitton [1956] Director; Rosalind Clare Fitton [1959] Director

Fitzjohns Avenue Ltd
Incorporated: 25 April 2016
Net Worth: £3 *Total Assets:* £13,891,572
Registered Office: Suite 2, Fountain House, 1a Elm Park, Stanmore, Middlesex, HA7 4AU
Activities: Development of building projects
Officers: Paul Simon Godfrey [1980] Director/Property Developer

Five Star Inns Limited
Incorporated: 2 April 1964 *Employees:* 300
Net Worth: £35,015,000 *Total Assets:* £72,991,000
Registered Office: Queens Court, 9-17 Eastern Road, Romford, Essex, RM1 3NG
Activities: Hotels and similar accommodation
Parent: BPH Finance Number 1 Limited
Officers: Jonathan Patrick Braidley [1965] Director/Investment Professional; Christopher Andre Kula [1983] Director/Chartered Accountant [German/Canadian]

Fizzy Canning Town LLP
Incorporated: 26 June 2012
Net Worth: £19,617,000 *Total Assets:* £28,485,000
Registered Office: Premier House, 52 London Road, Twickenham, Middlesex, TW1 3RP

Fizzy Enterprises LLP
Incorporated: 22 March 2012
Net Worth: £215,772,000 *Total Assets:* £264,131,008
Registered Office: Premier House, 52 London Road, Twickenham, Middlesex, TW1 3RP
Officers: Henry Charles Rupert Downes [1955] LLP Member

Fizzy Epsom LLP
Incorporated: 23 March 2012
Net Worth: £11,515,000 *Total Assets:* £19,540,000
Registered Office: Premier House, 52 London Road, Twickenham, Middlesex, TW1 3RP

Fizzy Lewisham B1 LLP
Incorporated: 4 September 2014
Net Worth: £21,176,000 *Total Assets:* £22,425,000
Registered Office: Premier House, 52 London Road, Twickenham, Middlesex, TW1 3RP

Fizzy Lewisham LLP
Incorporated: 6 February 2014
Net Worth: £14,157,000 *Total Assets:* £24,376,000
Registered Office: Premier House, 52 London Road, Twickenham, Middlesex, TW1 3RP

Fizzy Poplar LLP
Incorporated: 20 May 2013
Net Worth: £11,498,000 *Total Assets:* £18,133,000
Registered Office: Premier House, 52 London Road, Twickenham, Middlesex, TW1 3RP

Fizzy Stepney Green LLP
Incorporated: 20 September 2013
Net Worth: £18,201,000 *Total Assets:* £27,755,000
Registered Office: Premier House, 52 London Road, Twickenham, Middlesex, TW1 3RP

FJC Topco Limited
Incorporated: 31 July 2013 *Employees:* 55
Net Worth: £1,164,568 *Total Assets:* £14,633,877
Registered Office: Centenary Works, Manor Way, New Road, Rainham, Essex, RM13 8RH
Activities: Remediation activities and other waste management services
Shareholder: Patrick John Church
Officers: Patrick John Church [1957] Director; Ian Magson [1967] Director

FJJ Limited
Incorporated: 18 March 2005 *Employees:* 114
Net Worth: £14,077,576 *Total Assets:* £19,858,484
Registered Office: 36 Kingsleigh Place, Mitcham, Surrey, CR4 4NU
Activities: Activities of head offices
Major Shareholder: Brigid Gertrude McHugh
Officers: Alison Elizabeth Chaffey, Secretary; Michael Cronin [1941] Director - Non-Executive; Brigid Gertrude McHugh [1945] Director/Chairman - Non-Executive [Irish]; James Bernard John McHugh [1978] Senior Managing Director

FL Property Management Limited
Incorporated: 28 April 1998
Net Worth: £14,418,000 *Total Assets:* £20,934,000
Registered Office: Fulham Football Club Training Ground, Motspur Park, New Malden, Surrey, KT3 6PT
Activities: Operation of sports facilities
Shareholders: Shahid Rafiq Khan Family Trust A; Shahid Rafiq Khan Family Trust B
Officers: Neville Darren Preston, Secretary; Shahid Rafiq Khan [1950] Director/Executive [American]; Mark Lamping [1958] Director/President, Jacksonville Jaguars [American]; Alistair Julian Mackintosh [1970] Director/Chief Executive Officer

Flag Atlantic UK Limited
Incorporated: 30 April 1999
Net Worth Deficit: £34,085,640 *Total Assets:* £24,482,128
Registered Office: Sovereign Court, 635 Sipson Road, Sipson, West Drayton, Middlesex, UB7 0JE
Activities: Wired telecommunications activities
Shareholder: Anil Dhirubhai Ambani
Officers: Rodney Hardwicke Riley, Secretary; Andrew Peter Goldie [1960] Director/Service in Private Sector; Bipendra Kumar Sinha [1971] Director/Service [Indian]

Flahive Brickwork Limited
Incorporated: 5 December 1985 *Employees:* 51
Net Worth: £6,915,325 *Total Assets:* £8,888,560
Registered Office: Unit 28 Orbital 25 Business Park, Dwight Road, Watford, Herts, WD18 9DA
Activities: Construction of commercial buildings
Major Shareholder: Kevin Flahive
Officers: Kevin Flahive [1975] Director; Patricia Flahive [1948] Director; Karen Heffer [1977] Director/Teacher; Joanna Wallace [1974] Director; Catherine Ann Wright [1971] Director

Flahive Developments Limited
Incorporated: 23 February 1981 *Employees:* 4
Net Worth: £10,746,826 *Total Assets:* £11,993,425
Registered Office: Unit 28 Orbital 25 Business Park, Dwight Road, Watford, Herts, WD18 9DA
Activities: Other letting and operating of own or leased real estate
Officers: Kevin Flahive [1975] Director/Surveyor; Patricia Flahive [1948] Director; Karen Heffer [1977] Director/Advertising Account Co-ordinator; Joanna Wallace [1974] Director/Accounts Clerk; Catherine Ann Wright [1971] Director/Accounts Clerk

Flair Leisure Products PLC
Incorporated: 22 January 1999 *Employees:* 52
Net Worth: £14,445,000 *Total Assets:* £31,356,000
Registered Office: Anne Boleyn House, 9-13 Ewell Road, Cheam, Surrey, SM3 8BZ
Activities: Manufacture of other games and toys, n.e.c.
Major Shareholder: Enrico Preziosi
Officers: Carl Patrick Moran, Secretary/Director; Dario Berte [1955] Director [Italian]; Peter Brown [1944] Director; Simon John Hedge [1966] Director; Marco Lischetti [1966] Group Financial Director [Italian]; Antonella Robaldo [1959] Director [Italian]

P. Flannery Plant Hire (Oval) Limited
Incorporated: 16 June 1972 *Employees:* 107
Net Worth: £60,040,660 *Total Assets:* £114,142,808
Registered Office: 27a Maxwell Road, Northwood, Middlesex, HA6 2XY
Activities: Other specialised construction activities n.e.c.
Major Shareholder: Patrick Flannery
Officers: Gareth Austin Corbett [1979] Director [Irish]; Martin Christopher Flannery [1978] Director; Patrick Flannery [1980] Director; Patrick Flannery [1950] Director/Plant Hire Contractor [Irish]; John Anthony Moran [1961] Director

Fleetmill Limited
Incorporated: 16 July 1992 *Employees:* 52
Net Worth: £6,957,814 *Total Assets:* £8,110,341
Registered Office: 10 B Lyon Way, Greenford, Middlesex, UB6 0BN
Activities: Retail sale of leather goods in specialised stores
Officers: Hossein Rezvani [1960] Director

Fleetwood Developments Limited
Incorporated: 18 May 1983 *Employees:* 3
Net Worth: £16,317,953 *Total Assets:* £39,505,720
Registered Office: 2 AC Court, High Street, Thames Ditton, Surrey, KT7 0SR
Activities: Other letting and operating of own or leased real estate
Major Shareholder: Roger Kilby
Officers: Maureen Elizabeth Stopher, Secretary; Roger Frederick Kilby [1946] Director/Property Development/Investment

Flexibon Limited
Incorporated: 30 January 2009
Net Worth: £832,558 *Total Assets:* £28,428,516
Registered Office: 8-10 South Street, Epsom, Surrey, KT18 7PF
Activities: Activities of venture and development capital companies
Major Shareholder: Jonathan Philip Feuer
Officers: Jonathan Philip Feuer [1962] Director

Flight Centre (UK) Limited
Incorporated: 9 June 1994 *Employees:* 1,813
Net Worth: £105,521,000 *Total Assets:* £255,576,992
Registered Office: Level 6, CI Tower, St Georges Square, High Street, New Malden, Surrey, KT3 4TE
Activities: Travel agency activities
Officers: Adam Murray, Secretary; Chris Adrian Galanty [1974] Director/Executive GM; Graham Francis Turner [1949] Director/Travel Agent [Australian]

Flight Centre (UK) Wholesale Limited
Incorporated: 2 April 2009
Net Worth: £2,000 *Total Assets:* £34,764,000
Registered Office: Level 6, CI Tower, St Georges Square, High Street, New Malden, Surrey, KT3 4TE
Activities: Travel agency activities
Parent: Flight Centre (UK) Limited
Officers: Adam Murray, Secretary; Chris Adrian Galanty [1974] Director/Executive GM; Graham Francis Turner [1949] Director/Travel Agent [Australian]

Flight Centre Robin Limited
Incorporated: 7 December 2012
Net Worth: £70,013,456 *Total Assets:* £70,343,792
Registered Office: Level 6, CI Tower, St Georges Square, High Street, New Malden, Surrey, KT3 4TE
Activities: Other credit granting n.e.c.
Officers: Adam Murray, Secretary; Chris Adrian Galanty [1974] Director/Executive General Manager; Adam Murray [1973] Director/Chief Financial Officer; Graham Francis Turner [1949] Director/Travel Agent [Australian]

Flight Centre Travel Group (European Holdings) Ltd
Incorporated: 28 October 2015
Net Worth: £41,705,128 *Total Assets:* £43,769,828
Registered Office: Level 6, CI Tower, St Georges Square, High Street, New Malden, Surrey, KT3 4TE
Activities: Activities of other holding companies n.e.c.
Officers: Adam Murray, Secretary; Chris Adrian Galanty [1974] Managing Director; Adam Murray [1973] Director

Flintridge Resources Limited
Incorporated: 26 September 2013 *Employees:* 17
Net Worth Deficit: £6,902,335 *Total Assets:* £7,657,675
Registered Office: 3a St Kildas Road, Harrow, Middlesex, HA1 1QD
Activities: Mining of other non-ferrous metal ores
Parent: Galantas Gold Corporation
Officers: Leo O'Shaughnessy [1950] Director/Chartered Accountant [Irish]; Roland Frank Phelps [1953] Director/Chartered Engineer

Florin Industrial Services Holdings Limited
Incorporated: 25 February 2010 *Employees:* 740
Net Worth: £506,187 *Total Assets:* £8,802,584
Registered Office: 245 Main Road, Sidcup, Kent, DA14 6QS
Activities: Other business support service activities n.e.c.
Parent: Meredith Corporation Limited
Officers: Ian Perfect [1961] Director

Flowercloud Limited
Incorporated: 22 March 2016
Net Worth: £14,202 *Total Assets:* £5,679,165
Registered Office: 1 Park Road, Hampton Wick, Kingston upon Thames, Surrey, KT1 4AS
Activities: Activities of other holding companies n.e.c.
Shareholders: Jan Van Den Berghe; Evelyne Callens
Officers: Jan Van Den Berghe, Secretary; Evelyne Callens [1974] Director [Belgian]; Jan Van Den Berghe [1971] Director [Belgian]

Flowstop Services Limited
Incorporated: 15 December 2000 *Employees:* 9
Net Worth: £1,792,915 *Total Assets:* £5,623,909
Registered Office: 8 Kennet Road, Dartford, Kent, DA1 4QN
Activities: Construction of utility projects for fluids
Shareholders: John Eastwood Junior; Patricia Joy
Officers: John Eastwood, Secretary; John Eastwood [1952] Director/Pipeline Contractor; John Eastwood Jr [1978] Director/Pipeline Contractor

FLW Holding Limited
Incorporated: 26 April 2017
Net Worth: £1,080,238 *Total Assets:* £6,223,384
Registered Office: The Lodge, Portsmouth Road, Cobham, Surrey, KT11 1TA
Activities: Service activities incidental to water transportation
Officers: Christopher Michael Bates Fraser [1971] Director; Rodney Basil Loyd [1966] Director; James Robert Woolfson [1984] Director

Focus Tankers Limited
Incorporated: 28 June 2013
Net Worth: £37,948,716 *Total Assets:* £37,956,832
Registered Office: Portland House, 69-71 Wembley Hill Road, Wembley, Middlesex, HA9 8BU
Activities: Other service activities n.e.c.
Parent: Union Maritime Limited
Officers: Bhupendra Shantilal Kansagra, Secretary; Laurent Elie Cadji [1977] Director/Businessman; Lewis Levy Cadji [1938] Director/Businessman; Bhupendra Shantilal Kansagra [1956] Director/Businessman; Ramesh Shantilal Kansagra [1950] Director/Businessman

Folio Education Trust
Incorporated: 9 May 2011 *Employees:* 247
Previous: WCGS Academy Trust
Net Worth: £26,883,000 *Total Assets:* £31,400,000
Registered Office: Coombe Wood School, 30 Melville Avenue, South Croydon, Surrey, CR2 7HY
Activities: General secondary education
Officers: Richard Calverley Baker, Secretary; Dr Tim Crayford [1964] Director/Doctor; Paul Huitson [1958] Director/Police Officer; Vinoo John [1972] Director/Analyst; Jane Elizabeth Speller [1966] Director/Development Manager; Jonathan James Wilden [1976] Director/Headmaster

Food Brands Group Limited
Incorporated: 11 July 1983 *Employees:* 11
Net Worth: £4,406,000 *Total Assets:* £6,628,000
Registered Office: Unit 4 Fika House, Horton Road, West Drayton, Middlesex, UB7 8JD
Activities: Wholesale of coffee, tea, cocoa and spices
Parent: AB Anders Lofberg
Officers: Tony Wilson, Secretary; Lars Christer Appelqvist [1974] Director [Swedish]; Fredrik Nilsson [1974] Director/Chief Financial Officer [Swedish]

Foodspeed Limited
Incorporated: 3 April 2000 *Employees:* 67
Net Worth: £9,929,497 *Total Assets:* £11,177,601
Registered Office: Unit 7-8 Hexagon Business Centre, Springfield Road, Hayes, Middlesex, UB4 0TH
Activities: Wholesale of dairy products, eggs and edible oils and fats
Shareholders: Manpreet Singh Bawa; Gurmit Kaur Bawa
Officers: Manpreet Singh Bawa, Secretary/Director; Gurmit Kaur Bawa [1974] Director; Mandeep Kaur Bawa [1968] Director; Manpreet Singh Bawa [1967] Director

Football Association Limited
Incorporated: 23 June 1903 *Employees:* 1,062
Net Worth: £146,243,008 *Total Assets:* £675,270,016
Registered Office: Wembley Stadium, Wembley, Middlesex, HA9 0WS
Activities: Other sports activities
Officers: Richard James McDermott, Secretary; Rupinder Bains [1974] Director/Solicitor; Stacey Cartwright [1963] Director; Gregory Clarke [1957] Director/Chairman Football Association Limited; Robert Malcolm Cotter [1949] Director/Retired; Martin Richard Glenn [1960] Director/Chief Executive Officer; Mervyn Reginald Leggett [1949] Director/Company Secretary; Peter David Godfrey McCormick [1952] Director/Solicitor; John David Pearce [1949] Director/Football Manager; James Richard Rodwell [1970] Director/Chief Executive Officer; Kate Helena Tinsley [1976] Director/Chief Executive Officer

Football First Limited
Incorporated: 27 November 1997
Net Worth: £309,112 *Total Assets:* £7,338,012
Registered Office: The Hive, Camrose Avenue, London, HA8 6AG
Activities: Operation of sports facilities
Parent: The Hive Football Centre Holdings Limited
Officers: Mahendra Patel, Secretary; Anthony Andrew Kleanthous [1966] Director

Foray 414 Limited
Incorporated: 8 April 1992
Net Worth Deficit: £3,900,000 *Total Assets:* £13,200,000
Registered Office: United Technologies House, Guildford Road, Fetcham, Leatherhead, Surrey, KT22 9UT
Activities: Non-trading company
Parent: United Technologies Holdings Limited
Officers: Simon Boniface, Secretary; Nordine Benzakour [1974] Finance Director [French]; Didier Genois [1969] Director of Marketing [French]; Archibald Ziwanemoyo Hungwe [1973] Director/General Manager

Forest Freight Limited
Incorporated: 30 December 1971 *Employees:* 104
Net Worth: £4,977,059 *Total Assets:* £11,339,004
Registered Office: Barlow Way South, Manor Way, Rainham, Essex, RM13 8RH
Activities: Freight transport by road
Major Shareholder: George Malcolm Stuart Fullerton
Officers: Andrew Richard Saltwell, Secretary; George Malcolm Stuart Fullerton [1943] Director; Andrew Richard Saltwell [1958] Director/Accountant; Nicholas Richard Saltwell [1986] Operational Director

Forester Holdings (Europe) Limited
Incorporated: 23 January 1995
Net Worth: £70,213,000 *Total Assets:* £84,484,000
Registered Office: 2 Cromwell Avenue, Bromley, Kent, BR2 9BF
Activities: Activities of head offices
Parent: The Independent Order of Foresters
Officers: Jason Christopher Rose, Secretary; Euan Thomas Allison [1958] Director/Chief Executive Officer; Michael Christophers [1942] Director/Consultant; Robert Edward Lamoureux [1947] Director [Canadian]; John Todd Young [1957] Director/Retired Solicitor

Forester Investments Limited
Incorporated: 2 December 1994
Net Worth: £19,064,036 *Total Assets:* £19,066,772
Registered Office: Foresters House, Cromwell Avenue, Bromley, Kent, BR2 9BF
Activities: Non-trading company
Parent: Forester Life Limited
Officers: Jason Christopher Rose, Secretary; Euan Thomas Allison [1958] Director/Financial Services Executive; Latinka Pilipovic [1969] Director/Chief Finance Officer

Forester Life Limited
Incorporated: 2 December 1994 *Employees:* 162
Net Worth: £121,211,000 *Total Assets:* £4,291,504,128
Registered Office: 2 Cromwell Avenue, Bromley, Kent, BR2 9BF
Activities: Life insurance
Parent: Forester Holdings (Europe) Limited
Officers: Jason Christopher Rose, Secretary; Euan Thomas Allison [1958] Director/Chief Executive Officer; Michael Christophers [1942] Director/Consultant; Robert Edward Lamoureux [1947] Director [Canadian]; John Todd Young [1957] Director/Retired Solicitor

Forextra Developments Limited
Incorporated: 22 July 1986 *Employees:* 6
Net Worth: £80,567,624 *Total Assets:* £146,904,336
Registered Office: 8 Highbridge Close, Radlett, Herts, WD7 7GW
Activities: Other letting and operating of own or leased real estate
Parent: Frelene Limited
Officers: Freddy Salem [1941] Director/Buying Agent; Philip Joseph Salem [1981] Director

Forgefix Limited
Incorporated: 19 February 1999 *Employees:* 47
Net Worth: £3,374,497 *Total Assets:* £9,227,300
Registered Office: Long Reach, Galleon Boulevard, Crossways Business Park, Dartford, Kent, DA2 6QE
Activities: Manufacture of fasteners and screw machine products
Parent: Galleon Investments (Dartford) Ltd
Officers: Robert David Rowe, Secretary; Anthony John Armitt [1965] Director; Michael John William Brown [1959] Managing Director

Fork Rent Limited
Incorporated: 14 May 2015 *Employees:* 4
Previous: Wren Rollco Limited
Net Worth: £25,332,156 *Total Assets:* £25,332,156
Registered Office: 32 Crown Road, Enfield, Middlesex, EN1 1TH
Activities: Renting and leasing of construction and civil engineering machinery and equipment
Officers: Francois Dekker [1975] Director [Dutch]; Jeremy Peter Fish [1965] Director/Chief Executive Officer; Stuart Russell McMinnies [1968] Investment Director; Julian Alexander O'Neill [1971] Director

Former Reichmann Properties PLC
Incorporated: 21 November 1995
Previous: Reichmann Properties PLC
Net Worth: £3,903,969 *Total Assets:* £17,363,948
Registered Office: 5 Elstree Gate, Elstree Way, Borehamwood, Herts, WD6 1JD
Activities: Other business support service activities n.e.c.
Officers: Dov Reichmann, Secretary; Daniel Reichmann [1988] Director; Dov Reichmann [1930] Director

Forss Wind Farm Limited.
Incorporated: 29 April 1994
Net Worth: £3,186,000 *Total Assets:* £5,286,000
Registered Office: Beaufort Court, Egg Farm Lane, off Station Road, Kings Langley, Herts, WD4 8LR
Activities: Other business support service activities n.e.c.
Parent: Wind Farm Holdings Limited
Officers: Dominic James Hearth, Secretary; Steven William Hughes [1972] Generation & Asset Management Director; Fraser Stephen Merry [1968] Director/Chartered Surveyor; Mitesh Raj Patel [1982] Director/Group Financial Controller

Forth Health Holdings Limited
Incorporated: 2 November 2006
Net Worth Deficit: £114,618,000 *Total Assets:* £382,000,992
Registered Office: 8 White Oak Square, London Road, Swanley, Kent, BR8 7AG
Activities: Construction of commercial buildings
Parent: Palio (No 11) Limited
Officers: Carl Harvey Dix [1966] Operations Director; Jamie Pritchard [1971] Director/Investment Manager

Forth Health Limited
Incorporated: 2 November 2006
Net Worth Deficit: £114,619,000 *Total Assets:* £381,987,008
Registered Office: 8 White Oak Square, London Road, Swanley, Kent, BR8 7AG
Activities: Construction of commercial buildings
Parent: Forth Health Holdings Limited
Officers: Carl Harvey Dix [1966] Operations Director; Jamie Pritchard [1971] Director/Investment Manager

Forth Ports Finance PLC
Incorporated: 16 October 2013
Net Worth: £57,000 *Total Assets:* £395,316,000
Registered Office: Leslie Ford House, Tilbury Freeport, Tilbury, Essex, RM18 7EH
Activities: Activities of other holding companies n.e.c.
Parent: Forth Ports Limited
Officers: Pamela June Smyth, Secretary; Simon Daniel Beer [1980] Director/Asset Manager; Diana Callebaut [1980] Director/Investments [Australian]; Richard Wing-Eng Chang [1971] Director/Investment Professional [British/Australian]; Patrick Charbonneau [1978] Managing Director [Canadian]; Carole Jean Cran [1970] Director/Chief Financial Officer; Simon George Davy [1970] Director/Investment Manager; Charles Graham Hammond [1961] Director; Stephen Kynaston [1978] Director/Investment Manager; Patrick Samson [1971] Director [Canadian]; Lord Robert Smith [1944] Managing Director; Stuart James Wallace [1970] Director/Chief Operating Officer

Fortuna Frutos (UK) Limited
Incorporated: 30 June 1999 *Employees:* 13
Net Worth: £2,250,142 *Total Assets:* £6,894,370
Registered Office: Suite 14 & 15, Airport House, Purley Way, Croydon, Surrey, CR0 0XZ
Activities: Wholesale of fruit and vegetables
Officers: Juan Guerra, Secretary [Spanish]; Jose Hernandez Morales [1968] Director [Spanish]

Foster & Allen Holdings Limited
Incorporated: 20 February 2013
Net Worth: £864,280 *Total Assets:* £5,470,476
Registered Office: Suite 43-45, Airport House, Purley Way, Croydon, Surrey, CR0 0XZ
Activities: Other business support service activities n.e.c.
Major Shareholder: Mark Mitchell
Officers: Kevin Allen [1969] Director/Electrical Contractor; Marc Barrett [1982] Director/Project Manager; Paul Foster [1969] Director/Electrical Contractor; Mark Mitchell [1981] Director/Project Manager

The Foster Care Agency Limited
Incorporated: 13 June 2001 *Employees:* 8
Net Worth: £5,633,000 *Total Assets:* £13,199,000
Registered Office: Frays Court, 71 Cowley Road, Uxbridge, Middlesex, UB8 2AE
Activities: Other social work activities without accommodation n.e.c.
Parent: NFAG Limited
Officers: Helen Elizabeth Lecky, Secretary; Antony Vincent Holt [1959] Director/Chartered Accountant; Isabella Mary Hutchison [1956] Managing Director; Jean-Luc Emmanuel Janet [1970] Director [French]; David Jon Leatherbarrow [1969] Director/Group Chief Executive Officer

Foster Denovo Limited
Incorporated: 18 October 2006 *Employees:* 152
Net Worth: £1,555,340 *Total Assets:* £5,768,726
Registered Office: Ruxley House, 2 Hamm Moor Lane, Addlestone, Surrey, KT15 2SA
Activities: Financial intermediation not elsewhere classified
Parent: Foster Denovo Group Limited
Officers: Richard Paul Horton, Secretary; Roger Nicholas Brosch [1962] Director/Chief Executive Officer; David Scott Currie [1969] Non-Executive Director Chairman; Richard Paul Horton [1952] Director/Chartered Accountant; Andre Robert Jordache [1965] Director; Helen Marie Lovett [1967] Director/Chief Operating Officer; Alan Taylor [1948] Non-Executive Director

The Foundation and Friends of The Royal Botanic Gardens, Kew
Incorporated: 3 May 1990 *Employees:* 47
Net Worth: £27,490,000 *Total Assets:* £30,912,000
Registered Office: 47 Kew Green, Kew, Richmond, Surrey, TW9 3AB
Activities: Activities of other membership organisations n.e.c.
Officers: Marcus Ambrose Paul Agius [1946] Director; Ian Karet [1963] Director/Solicitor; Kristina Louise Kenworthy [1958] Director/Solicitor; Jan Stephen Pethick [1947] Director/Chair, Troy Asset Management; Charles Nigel Cross Sherwood [1959] Director/Private Equity

Foundation Developments Limited
Incorporated: 2 October 1990 *Employees:* 37
Net Worth: £7,588,021 *Total Assets:* £36,966,392
Registered Office: Foundation House, Clarendon Road, Wallington, Surrey, SM6 8QX
Activities: Other specialised construction activities n.e.c.
Parent: Hickey Group Limited
Officers: Anne Hickey, Secretary/Director [Irish]; Stewart Paul Adcock [1965] Pre Construction Director; Anne Hickey [1951] Director [Irish]; Patrick Hickey [1954] Director/Building Contractor [Irish]; Trina Anne Hickey [1981] Finance & HR Director [Irish]; Martin Joseph McDonagh [1967] Director/Quantity Surveyor [Irish]; Shane Nicholson [1975] Construction Director [Irish]

Four Quarters (Ingestre Road) Ltd
Incorporated: 13 March 2015
Net Worth Deficit: £24,042 *Total Assets:* £5,593,395
Registered Office: Varsani Joseph, 18 The Broadway, Wembley, Middlesex, HA9 8JU
Activities: Buying and selling of own real estate
Major Shareholder: Pravin Shah
Officers: Pravin Shah [1954] Director

Fourfront Holdings Limited
Incorporated: 22 March 2016 *Employees:* 301
Net Worth: £5,255,836 *Total Assets:* £44,251,040
Registered Office: The Old Post Office, 33 Station Road, Egham, Surrey, TW20 9LA
Activities: Activities of other holding companies n.e.c.
Officers: Gary James Chandler [1969] Director/Chief Executive; James Elwin Cornwell [1967] Director; Mark Joseph Scott [1968] Director; Aki Stamatis [1960] Director

Fourway Communication Limited
Incorporated: 5 February 1962 *Employees:* 60
Net Worth: £2,839,701 *Total Assets:* £7,788,776
Registered Office: Delamare Road, Cheshunt, Herts, EN8 9SH
Activities: Construction of utility projects for electricity and telecommunications
Parent: The Fourway Group Limited
Officers: Ingrid Anne Snell, Secretary; Charles Edward Codrington [1967] Director/Sales Management; Guy Neville Snell [1965] Director/Project Manager; Ingrid Anne Snell [1941] Director/Housewife; Lance Gordon Christopher Snell [1967] Director/Engineer; Leon Neville Snell [1931] Director/Master Toolmaker

FPI Limited
Incorporated: 24 August 2000 *Employees:* 176
Net Worth: £2,204,973 *Total Assets:* £5,769,184
Registered Office: 18a Falcon Business Centre, Ashton Road, Romford, Essex, RM3 8UR
Activities: Other retail sale of new goods in specialised stores (not commercial art galleries and opticians)
Officers: Rebecca Jarman, Secretary; Richard James Boxall [1968] Director; Colin Campbell [1942] Director; James Russell Hamilton [1958] Director; Andrew David Oddie [1972] Director; Kenneth Penman [1957] Director

Francotyp-Postalia Limited
Incorporated: 22 November 1989 *Employees:* 101
Net Worth: £7,356,000 *Total Assets:* £24,351,000
Registered Office: 74 Questor, Powder Mill Lane, Dartford, Kent, DA1 1EF
Activities: Other business support service activities n.e.c.
Parent: Francotyp-Postalia International GmbH
Officers: Adam Joseph Branch [1968] Sales Director; Leonard James Fletcher [1949] Managing Director; Leanne Tyrrell [1971] Marketing Director; Nicola Jane Walford [1971] Operations Director

Frankel Portfolio Property LLP
Incorporated: 30 September 2016
Net Worth: £5,404,210 *Total Assets:* £5,404,210
Registered Office: Aprirose House, 48a High Street, Edgware, Middlesex, HA8 7EQ
Officers: Manish Mansukhlal Gudka [1970] Member; Gareth Jones [1973] Member; Suraj Rashmikant Shah [1982] LLP Member

Frankham Consultancy Group Limited
Incorporated: 4 April 2002 *Employees:* 106
Net Worth: £918,060 *Total Assets:* £5,425,870
Registered Office: Irene House, Five Arches Business Park, Sidcup, Kent, DA14 5AE
Activities: Other engineering activities
Parent: Frankham Holdings Limited
Officers: John Clifton Gardner, Secretary/Director; Richard John Chitty [1968] Director; Steven John Frankham [1951] Director; John Clifton Gardner [1951] Director

Frankham Holdings Limited
Incorporated: 30 May 2014 *Employees:* 132
Net Worth: £1,787,470 *Total Assets:* £9,939,966
Registered Office: 1st Floor, Leonard House, 5-7 Newman Road, Bromley, Kent, BR1 1RJ
Activities: Activities of construction holding companies
Major Shareholder: Stephen John Frankham
Officers: John Gardner, Secretary; Richard John Chitty [1968] Director; Steven John Frankham [1951] Director; John Clifton Gardner [1951] Director

Michael Franklin (Chemists) Limited
Incorporated: 17 December 1962 *Employees:* 95
Net Worth: £1,830,155 *Total Assets:* £6,259,426
Registered Office: Elthorne Gate, 64 High Street, Pinner, Middlesex, HA5 5QA
Activities: Dispensing chemist in specialised stores
Officers: Kalpesh Kanubhai Patel, Secretary; Amar Shilan Kalpesh Patel [1991] Director; Chhaya Patel [1962] Director/Pharmacist; Kalpesh Kanubhai Patel [1959] Director; Minesh Kanubhai Patel [1956] Director; Priti Patel [1961] Director/Businesswoman; Sharda Kanubhai Patel [1933] Director/Housewife

J.& J.Franks Limited
Incorporated: 25 June 1941
Net Worth: £8,445,295 *Total Assets:* £10,579,189
Registered Office: 69-71 East Street, Epsom, Surrey, KT17 1BP
Activities: Operation of gravel and sand pits; mining of clays and kaolin
Major Shareholder: Peter David Crate
Officers: Helen Crate, Secretary; Peter David Crate [1961] Director; Paul Laurence Lewis [1958] Director

S. Franses Limited
Incorporated: 17 August 1959 *Employees:* 11
Net Worth: £5,793,923 *Total Assets:* £10,273,747
Registered Office: York House, Empire Way, Wembley, Middlesex, HA9 0FQ
Activities: Wholesale of household goods (other than musical instruments) n.e.c
Major Shareholder: David Sidney Franses
Officers: Sara Rebecca Franses, Secretary; David Sidney Franses [1926] Director; Sara Rebecca Franses [1962] Director; Simon Franses [1960] Director

Alexander Fraser Holdings Limited
Incorporated: 11 December 1959 *Employees:* 314
Net Worth: £47,080,652 *Total Assets:* £58,880,576
Registered Office: Foxhills, Stonehills Road, Ottershaw, Surrey, KT16 0EL
Activities: Activities of head offices
Major Shareholder: Pamela Lillian Hayton
Officers: Pamela Lillian Hayton, Secretary [Australian]; Marc Alexander Hayton [1964] Director/Marketing; Pamela Lillian Hayton [1939] Director [Australian]

Fraserfort Limited
Incorporated: 15 March 1956
Net Worth: £8,363,000 *Total Assets:* £8,472,000
Registered Office: Queens Court, 9-17 Eastern Road, Romford, Essex, RM1 3NG
Activities: Non-trading company
Parent: BPH Finance Number 1 Limited
Officers: Jonathan Patrick Braidley [1965] Director/Investment Professional; Christopher Andre Kula [1983] Director/Chartered Accountant [German/Canadian]

Frasers and Son Ltd
Incorporated: 23 July 2014
Net Worth: £5,100,000 *Total Assets:* £5,122,512
Registered Office: Fraser House, 184 South Park Road, Ilford, Essex, IG1 2XR
Activities: Other human health activities
Major Shareholder: Arh Warishaully
Officers: Arh Warishaully [1969] Director

Frattro Limited
Incorporated: 29 March 1993
Net Worth: £2,963,349 *Total Assets:* £7,495,305
Registered Office: Pennyweights, Welcomes Road, Kenley, Surrey, CR8 5HB
Activities: Other letting and operating of own or leased real estate
Shareholders: Paul Tropea; Frank Tropea
Officers: Paul Tropea, Secretary/Property Owner [Italian]; Frank Tropea [1961] Director/Property Owner; Paul Tropea [1958] Director/Property Owner [Italian]

Frelene Limited
Incorporated: 7 May 1985
Net Worth: £10,790,866 *Total Assets:* £16,000,356
Registered Office: 8 Highbridge Close, Radlett, Herts, WD7 7GW
Activities: Other letting and operating of own or leased real estate
Parent: Rothschild & Co
Officers: Freddy Salem, Secretary; Freddy Salem [1941] Director/Buying Agent; Philip Joseph Salem [1981] Director

Fresh Cash Pawn LLP
Incorporated: 17 September 2008
Net Worth: £14,758,987 *Total Assets:* £14,767,824
Registered Office: Unit 90 Kingspark Business Centre, 152-178 Kingston Road, New Malden, Surrey, KT3 3ST

Fresh Wharf Estates Limited
Incorporated: 5 October 1928 *Employees:* 9
Net Worth: £15,354,778 *Total Assets:* £20,026,982
Registered Office: Studio F5, The Granary, Abbey Road, Barking, Essex, IG11 7BT
Activities: Other letting and operating of own or leased real estate
Officers: Doctor Christopher Douglas Hewett [1938] Director/Veterinary Surgeon; Julian John Hewett [1954] Director/Analyst; Rodney Muirhead Goodwin Hewett [1941] Director/Civil Engineer; Flavia Penelope Sophia Jokic [1963] Director; Andrew Michael Leahy [1963] Director; Timothy John Muirhead Sanders Hewett [1950] Director

Freshasia Foods Ltd
Incorporated: 16 November 2004 *Employees:* 127
Net Worth: £2,901,517 *Total Assets:* £5,990,145
Registered Office: 21 Hailey Road, Erith, Kent, DA18 4AA
Activities: Processing and preserving of meat
Major Shareholder: Jian Lan
Officers: Jian Lan [1975] Director

Freshplant Limited
Incorporated: 5 April 2006
Net Worth Deficit: £1,846,614 *Total Assets:* £6,667,716
Registered Office: 3rd Floor, Sterling House, Langston Road, Loughton, Essex, IG10 3TS
Activities: Development of building projects
Parent: Galliard Holdings Limited
Officers: Allan William Porter, Secretary; David Edward Conway [1976] Director; Donagh O'Sullivan [1968] Construction Director [Irish]; Stephen Stuart Conway [1948] Director; Michael William Watson [1952] Architectural Director

Friars Developments Limited
Incorporated: 19 September 2011
Net Worth Deficit: £2,180,795 *Total Assets:* £11,082,400
Registered Office: 3rd Floor, Sterling House, Langston Road, Loughton, Essex, IG10 3TS
Activities: Other business support service activities n.e.c.
Parent: Galliard Holdings Limited
Officers: Allan William Porter, Secretary; Stephen Stuart Solomon Conway [1948] Director; Donagh O'Sullivan [1968] Construction Director [Irish]

Friend's Property Portfolio Limited
Incorporated: 6 June 2006
Net Worth: £435,407 *Total Assets:* £6,681,393
Registered Office: 20 Queens Road, Morden, Surrey, SM4 5DF
Activities: Buying and selling of own real estate
Officers: Dr Sameer Zar, Secretary/Doctor; Dr Mian Zubair Ahmed [1962] Director/Doctor; Dr. Kashif Hamid Aziz [1972] Director/Doctor; Dr Amer Hafeez [1962] Director/GP [Irish]

Frisco (U.K.) Sales Limited
Incorporated: 20 March 1981 *Employees:* 49
Net Worth: £6,888,001 *Total Assets:* £13,002,582
Registered Office: 14 Pindar Road, Hoddesdon, Herts, EN11 0DE
Activities: Other service activities n.e.c.
Parent: Insignia Investments Limited
Officers: Marc Flynn, Secretary/Chairman; Marc Flynn [1964] Director; Simon Gary Foord [1978] Operations Director; Gary Zubiena [1958] Sales Director

Frithsden Finance (Birmingham) Limited
Incorporated: 29 May 2007
Net Worth: £2,850,791 *Total Assets:* £6,026,574
Registered Office: First Floor, Radius House, 51 Clarendon Road, Watford, Herts, WD17 1HP
Activities: Financial intermediation not elsewhere classified
Major Shareholder: Raymond Charles Russell Dalton
Officers: Georgina Jane Dalton, Secretary; Raymond Charles Russell Dalton [1934] Director; William Raymond Dalton [1985] Director/Chartered Surveyor; Christopher Michael Sheedy [1964] Director/Chartered Surveyor

Frontline Security Solutions Limited
Incorporated: 25 March 1998 *Employees:* 114
Net Worth: £3,982,079 *Total Assets:* £10,122,749
Registered Office: Oak House, Littleton Road, Ashford, Middlesex, TW15 1TZ
Activities: Security systems service activities
Parent: Chubb Fire & Security Limited
Officers: Robert Sloss, Secretary; Tracy Cordes [1963] Director [American]; Craig Alexander Forbes [1963] Director; Graeme Heanan [1968] Director

Frontline Technology Limited
Incorporated: 23 July 1986
Net Worth: £2,808,298 *Total Assets:* £6,014,894
Registered Office: Rutland House, 44 Masons Hill, Bromley, Kent, BR2 9JG
Activities: Wholesale of computers, computer peripheral equipment and software
Major Shareholder: Ali Guryel
Officers: Ali Guryel [1948] Director/Computer Consultant

FSI (FM Solutions) Limited
Incorporated: 25 June 2002 *Employees:* 130
Net Worth: £1,687,013 *Total Assets:* £5,476,681
Registered Office: 5 White Oak Square, London Road, Swanley, Kent, BR8 7AG
Activities: Business and domestic software development
Parent: FSI Global PLC
Officers: Christopher Robert Harvey, Secretary; Paul Richard Bullard [1978] Director/IT Consultant; Compton Elwyn Darlington [1959] Sales and Marketing Director [British/Guyanese]; Kevin John Shipp [1970] Professional Services Director; Peter Tyler [1972] Director; Gesina Dorethea Van Den Ende [1977] Client Services Director [British/South African]

FSI Global PLC
Incorporated: 21 September 2006 *Employees:* 157
Net Worth: £4,194,572 *Total Assets:* £9,259,638
Registered Office: 5 White Oak Square, London Road, Swanley, Kent, BR8 7AG
Activities: Business and domestic software development
Major Shareholder: Patrick Brian Curran
Officers: Christopher Robert Harvey, Secretary; Patrick Brian Curran [1947] Director; John Moriaty [1960] Director

FT Technologies (UK) Ltd
Incorporated: 9 November 2007 *Employees:* 85
Net Worth: £19,325,516 *Total Assets:* £20,847,424
Registered Office: Sunbury House, Brooklands Close, Sunbury on Thames, Surrey, TW16 7DX
Activities: Manufacture of other electrical equipment
Shareholders: Savvas Kapartis; Stephen John Norton; Peter Frederick Elgar
Officers: Peter Frederick Elgar [1949] Director; Dr Savvas Kapartis [1955] Director; Dr Stephen John Norton [1955] Director

FTE & M Limited
Incorporated: 17 February 2012
Net Worth: £3,201,425 *Total Assets:* £5,302,270
Registered Office: Frederick Thomas House, 39 Belmont Road, Erith, Kent, DA8 1JY
Activities: Other business support service activities n.e.c.
Major Shareholder: Derrick Charlesworth
Officers: Chloe Charlesworth [1988] Director; Derrick John Charlesworth [1960] Director; Grant Charlesworth [1990] Director; Sandra Charlesworth [1961] Director

FTX Logistics Limited
Incorporated: 23 January 2001 *Employees:* 95
Net Worth: £16,193,281 *Total Assets:* £19,126,356
Registered Office: Hill Park Court, Springfield Drive, Leatherhead, Surrey, KT22 7NL
Activities: Freight transport by road
Parent: Kellogg Brown & Root Limited
Officers: Sharon Mason, Secretary; Peter Derek Aston [1966] Director; James Arthur Barret [1965] Director/Accountant; Ian William Bryant [1952] Director/Accountant; Richard Sean Card [1961] Project Director; Sharon Mason [1970] Director

Fuel Oils (Holdings) Limited
Incorporated: 23 March 1983 *Employees:* 61
Net Worth: £6,906,366 *Total Assets:* £13,235,405
Registered Office: Unit 3-4 Darent Industrial Park, Burnet Road, Erith, Kent, DA8 2JZ
Activities: Wholesale of other fuels and related products
Officers: Corinne Geering, Secretary; Royston Thomas Durell [1940] Director/Oil Distributor; Stuart John Durell [1973] Director/IT Administration

Fujichem Sonneborn Limited
Incorporated: 25 June 1947 *Employees:* 142
Net Worth: £13,261,350 *Total Assets:* £22,759,570
Registered Office: Jaxa Works, 91-95 Peregrine Road, Hainault, Essex, IG6 3XH
Activities: Manufacture of paints, varnishes and similar coatings, mastics and sealants
Parent: Fujikura Kasei Co. Ltd
Officers: Edward Vincent Cox, Secretary; Edward Vincent Cox [1951] Director and Company Secretary; Hiroya Dejima [1961] Director/Chief Executive Officer [Japanese]; Hisashi Kajiwara [1959] Director [Japanese]; Hiroshi Kawai [1958] Director/Chief Finance Officer [Japanese]; Keith Mannas [1967] Director; Robert Frank Sheppard [1957] Director/Chief Operations Officer

Fujikura Europe Limited
Incorporated: 30 March 1988 *Employees:* 47
Net Worth: £3,217,856 *Total Assets:* £14,314,800
Registered Office: C51 Barwell Business Park, Leatherhead Road, Chessington, Surrey, KT9 2NY
Activities: Manufacture of electronic components
Parent: Fujikura Limited
Officers: Hideyuki Hosoya [1959] Director [Japanese]; Masaaki Kimpara [1959] Director [Japanese]; Takeaki Kitajima [1957] Director [Japanese]; Akira Saita [1959] Director/Businessman [Japanese]

Fujitsu General (U.K.) Co. Limited
Incorporated: 20 July 1977 *Employees:* 4
Net Worth: £11,620,000 *Total Assets:* £12,525,000
Registered Office: Unit 330 Centennial Park, Centennial Avenue, Elstree, Herts, WD6 3TJ
Activities: Manufacture of other electrical equipment
Officers: Andrew Gaffar, Secretary; Hirofumi Fuji [1954] Director/Chief Executive Officer [Japanese]; Takashi Harada [1970] Director [Japanese]

Fujitsu General Air Conditioning (UK) Limited
Incorporated: 12 June 2007 *Employees:* 30
Previous: FG Eurofred Limited
Net Worth: £3,111,000 *Total Assets:* £11,606,000
Registered Office: Unit 150 Centennial Park, Centennial Avenue, Elstree, Herts, WD6 3SG
Activities: Other professional, scientific and technical activities n.e.c.
Officers: Ignacio Franquesa Castrillo [1966] Director [Spanish]; Hirofumi Fuji [1954] Director [Japanese]; Takashi Harada [1970] Director [Japanese]; Marc Sabe Richer [1969] Director/Board Advisor [Spanish]

Fulca Limited
Incorporated: 8 June 2012
Net Worth Deficit: £3,318,941 *Total Assets:* £9,060,190
Registered Office: Hill House, Lowlands Road, Harrow, Middlesex, HA1 3EQ
Activities: Development of building projects
Major Shareholder: Donovan Gijsbertus Wijsmuller
Officers: Brian Martin Comer [1960] Director [Irish]; Luke Andrew Comer [1957] Director [Irish]

Fulham Football Club Limited
Incorporated: 24 March 1987 *Employees:* 270
Net Worth Deficit: £49,657,000 *Total Assets:* £37,528,000
Registered Office: Fulham Football Club, Training Ground, Motspur Park, New Malden, Surrey, KT3 6PT
Activities: Activities of sport clubs
Shareholders: Shahid Rafiq Khan Family Trust A; Shahid Rafiq Khan Family Trust B
Officers: Neville Darren Preston, Secretary; David John Daly [1959] Director; Antony Rafiq Khan [1982] Director [American]; Shahid Rafiq Khan [1950] Director/Executive [American]; Mark Lamping [1958] Director/President, Jacksonville Jaguars [American]; Alistair Julian Mackintosh [1970] Director/Chief Executive Officer

Fulham Football Leisure Limited
Incorporated: 21 May 1997 *Employees:* 270
Net Worth: £76,984,000 *Total Assets:* £165,480,000
Registered Office: Fulham Football Club, Training Ground, Motspur Park, New Malden, Surrey, KT3 6PT
Activities: Activities of sport clubs
Shareholders: Shahid Rafiq Khan Family Trust A; Shahid Rafiq Khan Family Trust B
Officers: Neville Darren Preston, Secretary; Shahid Rafiq Khan [1950] Director/Executive [American]; Mark Lamping [1958] Director/President, Jacksonville Jaguars [American]; Alistair Julian Mackintosh [1970] Director/Chief Executive Officer

Fulham Stadium Limited
Incorporated: 23 May 1997
Net Worth: £104,166,000 *Total Assets:* £113,179,000
Registered Office: Fulham Football Club, Training Ground, Motspur Park, New Malden, Surrey, KT3 6PT
Activities: Operation of sports facilities
Shareholders: Shahid Rafiq Khan Family Trust A; Shahid Rafiq Khan Family Trust B
Officers: Neville Darren Preston, Secretary; Shahid Rafiq Khan [1950] Director/Executive [American]; Mark Lamping [1958] Director/President, Jacksonville Jaguars [American]; Alistair Julian Mackintosh [1970] Director/Chief Executive Officer

Full House Restaurants Holdings Limited
Incorporated: 14 February 2014 *Employees:* 1,000
Net Worth: £6,080,865 *Total Assets:* £18,240,940
Registered Office: 34 Anyards Road, Cobham, Surrey, KT11 2LA
Activities: Take-away food shops and mobile food stands
Shareholders: John Edward Shedden; Dominos Pizza UK & Ireland Limited
Officers: Christine Jane Shedden, Secretary; Stephen Glen Hemsley [1957] Director/Chartered Accountant; Bradley Shedden [1975] Director/Operations Manager; John Edward Shedden [1947] Director

Full House Restaurants Limited
Incorporated: 25 April 1997 *Employees:* 540
Net Worth: £3,460,777 *Total Assets:* £5,321,236
Registered Office: 34 Anyards Road, Cobham, Surrey, KT11 2LA
Activities: Take-away food shops and mobile food stands
Parent: Full House Restaurants Holdings Limited
Officers: Christine Jane Shedden, Secretary; Stephen Glen Hemsley [1957] Director/Chartered Accountant; John Edward Shedden [1947] Director/Delivered Pizza

Fuller Leisure Limited
Incorporated: 7 March 2003 *Employees:* 21
Net Worth: £3,041,016 *Total Assets:* £6,550,197
Registered Office: Haslers, Old Station Road, Loughton, Essex, IG10 4PL
Activities: Sale of other motor vehicles
Parent: Caunton Management Limited
Officers: Nicholas Charles Pearce, Secretary; Nicholas Charles Pearce [1962] Managing Director

Fulton Central Limited
Incorporated: 20 May 2017
Net Worth: £9,757,355 *Total Assets:* £17,405,402
Registered Office: Portland House, 69-71 Wembley Hill Road, Wembley, Middlesex, HA9 8BU
Activities: Other business support service activities n.e.c.
Parent: Fulton Maritime Holdings Limited
Officers: Bhupendra Shantilal Kansagra, Secretary; Laurent Elie Cadji [1977] Director/Businessman; Lewis Levy Cadji [1938] Director/Businessman; Bhupendra Shantilal Kansagra [1956] Director/Businessman; Ramesh Shantilal Kansagra [1950] Director/Businessman

Fulton Clover Limited
Incorporated: 29 March 2017
Net Worth: £7,511,983 *Total Assets:* £12,850,465
Registered Office: Portland House, 69-71 Wembley Hill Road, Wembley, Middlesex, HA9 8BU
Activities: Other business support service activities n.e.c.
Officers: Bhupendra Shantilal Kansagra, Secretary; Laurent Elie Cadji [1977] Director/Businessman; Lewis Levy Cadji [1938] Director/Businessman; Bhupendra Shantilal Kansagra [1956] Director/Businessman; Ramesh Shantilal Kansagra [1950] Director/Businessman

Fulton Grand Limited
Incorporated: 21 July 2017
Net Worth: £7,696,419 *Total Assets:* £14,022,891
Registered Office: Portland House, 69-71 Wembley Hill Road, Wembley, Middlesex, HA9 8BU
Activities: Other business support service activities n.e.c.
Officers: Bhupendra Shantilal Kansagra, Secretary; Laurent Elie Cadji [1977] Director/Businessman; Lewis Levy Cadji [1938] Director/Businessman; Bhupendra Shantilal Kansagra [1956] Director/Businessman; Ramesh Shantilal Kansagra [1950] Director/Businessman

Fulton Hyde Limited
Incorporated: 29 March 2017
Net Worth: £9,619,591 *Total Assets:* £16,997,012
Registered Office: Portland House, 69-71 Wembley Hill Road, Wembley, Middlesex, HA9 8BU
Activities: Other business support service activities n.e.c.
Officers: Bhupendra Shantilal Kansagra, Secretary; Laurent Elie Cadji [1977] Director/Businessman; Lewis Levy Cadji [1938] Director/Businessman; Bhupendra Shantilal Kansagra [1956] Director/Businessman; Ramesh Shantilal Kansagra [1950] Director/Businessman

Fulton Lincoln Limited
Incorporated: 1 February 2017
Net Worth: £6,434,414 *Total Assets:* £10,182,852
Registered Office: Portland House, 69-71 Wembley Hill Road, Wembley, Middlesex, HA9 8BU
Activities: Other business support service activities n.e.c.
Officers: Bhupendra Shantilal Kansagra, Secretary; Laurent Elie Cadji [1977] Director/Businessman; Lewis Levy Cadji [1938] Director/Businessman; Bhupendra Shantilal Kansagra [1956] Director/Businessman; Ramesh Shantilal Kansagra [1950] Director/Businessman

Fulton Maritime Holdings Limited
Incorporated: 25 October 2016 *Employees:* 3
Net Worth: £50,441,992 *Total Assets:* £87,923,608
Registered Office: Portland House, 69-71 Wembley Hill Road, Wembley, Middlesex, HA9 8BU
Activities: Sea and coastal freight water transport
Parent: Fulton Maritime Limited
Officers: Tristan Frisell, Secretary; Laurent Elie Cadji [1977] Director/Businessman; Lewis Levy Cadji [1938] Director/Businessman; Ramesh Shantilal Kansagra [1950] Director/Businessman

Fulton Maritime Limited
Incorporated: 19 October 2016
Net Worth: £13,392,910 *Total Assets:* £88,097,576
Registered Office: Portland House, 69-71 Wembley Hill Road, Wembley, Middlesex, HA9 8BU
Activities: Sea and coastal freight water transport
Officers: Tristan Frisell, Secretary; Laurent Elie Cadji [1977] Director/Businessman; Lewis Levy Cadji [1938] Director/Businessman; Ramesh Shantilal Kansagra [1950] Director/Businessman

Fulton Regent Limited
Incorporated: 1 February 2017
Net Worth: £6,302,328 *Total Assets:* £10,135,039
Registered Office: Portland House, 69-71 Wembley Hill Road, Wembley, Middlesex, HA9 8BU
Activities: Other business support service activities n.e.c.
Officers: Bhupendra Shantilal Kansagra, Secretary; Laurent Elie Cadji [1977] Director/Businessman; Lewis Levy Cadji [1938] Director/Businessman; Bhupendra Shantilal Kansagra [1956] Director/Businessman; Ramesh Shantilal Kansagra [1950] Director/Businessman

Fulton St James Limited
Incorporated: 13 July 2017
Net Worth: £10,580,521 *Total Assets:* £19,762,148
Registered Office: Portland House, 69-71 Wembley Hill Road, Wembley, Middlesex, HA9 8BU
Activities: Other business support service activities n.e.c.
Officers: Bhupendra Shantilal Kansagra, Secretary; Laurent Elie Cadji [1977] Director/Businessman; Lewis Levy Cadji [1938] Director/Businessman; Bhupendra Shantilal Kansagra [1956] Director/Businessman; Ramesh Shantilal Kansagra [1950] Director/Businessman

Fundamental Engineering Limited
Incorporated: 20 March 2015 *Employees:* 120
Net Worth: £4,632,379 *Total Assets:* £10,120,124
Registered Office: 38 Furham Field, Hatch End, London, HA5 4DZ
Activities: Machining
Officers: Alexander Dunn [1953] Director; Surojit Ghosh [1951] Director; Daniel Julian Kalms [1974] Director/Chartered Accountant; David Mark Taylor [1963] Director

Furlong Flooring (Southern) Ltd.
Incorporated: 7 April 1992 *Employees:* 95
Net Worth: £8,725,860 *Total Assets:* £15,317,550
Registered Office: Unit 6 Bridge Close, Edisons Park, Crossways Industrial Park, Dartford, Kent, DA2 6QN
Activities: Wholesale of furniture, carpets and lighting equipment
Parent: Furlong Holdings (UK) Ltd
Officers: Victoria Rose Wells, Secretary; Ian Michael Collacott [1977] Sales Director; Noel Furlong [1937] Director; Muir Martin O'Loghlen [1950] Director [Irish]; Michael Geoffrey Symonds [1971] Managing Director

Fusion Business Solutions (UK) Limited
Incorporated: 11 February 1998 *Employees:* 56
Net Worth: £7,464,028 *Total Assets:* £11,540,497
Registered Office: 55 Staines Road West, Sunbury on Thames, Surrey, TW16 7AH
Activities: Information technology consultancy activities
Major Shareholder: Mark Kelvin Lyttle
Officers: John Christopher Mohan, Secretary/Director [Irish]; Mark Kelvin Lyttle [1963] Director [Irish]; John Christopher Mohan [1968] Director [Irish]

Fusion Global Limited
Incorporated: 5 July 2002 *Employees:* 64
Net Worth: £6,814,540 *Total Assets:* £11,682,306
Registered Office: 55 Staines Road West, Sunbury on Thames, Surrey, TW16 7AH
Activities: Activities of head offices
Major Shareholder: Mark Kelvin Lyttle
Officers: John Christopher Mohan, Secretary [Irish]; Mark Kelvin Lyttle [1963] Director [Irish]; John Christopher Mohan [1968] Director [Irish]

Future Electronics Limited
Incorporated: 9 January 1987 *Employees:* 341
Net Worth: £190,015,008 *Total Assets:* £418,320,000
Registered Office: Future House, The Glanty, Egham, Surrey, TW20 9AH
Activities: Wholesale of electronic and telecommunications equipment and parts
Officers: Keith Carton, Secretary; Gary Bruce Oliver [1965] Director; Ann Shepherd [1970] Director/HR & Business Operations

Future Electronics Management Services Limited
Incorporated: 22 December 2004 *Employees:* 3
Net Worth: £148,179,008 *Total Assets:* £160,879,008
Registered Office: Future House, The Glanty, Egham, Surrey, TW20 9AH
Activities: Activities of head offices
Officers: Keith Carton, Secretary; Gary Bruce Oliver [1965] Director; Ann Shepherd [1970] HR Business Director

G & O Properties (London) Limited
Incorporated: 1 March 1989 *Employees:* 2
Net Worth: £4,856,430 *Total Assets:* £7,161,020
Registered Office: 60 Kingston Road, New Malden, Surrey, KT3 3JG
Activities: Buying and selling of own real estate
Parent: G & O Securities Limited
Officers: Christopher John O'Dell, Secretary; Ferdous Sultana Gossain [1962] Director; Christopher John O'Dell [1952] Director

G & O Securities Limited
Incorporated: 18 August 1994 *Employees:* 2
Net Worth: £10,497,599 *Total Assets:* £22,798,464
Registered Office: 60 Kingston Road, New Malden, Surrey, KT3 3JG
Activities: Buying and selling of own real estate
Parent: G & O Group Limited
Officers: Christopher John O'Dell, Secretary/Consultant; Ferdous Sultana Gossain [1962] Director; Christopher John O'Dell [1952] Director/Consultant

G S A R Holdings Limited
Incorporated: 19 October 2015 *Employees:* 56
Net Worth: £5,067,256 *Total Assets:* £7,441,961
Registered Office: 152-154 London Road, Greenhithe, Kent, DA9 9JW
Activities: Activities of other holding companies n.e.c.
Shareholders: Andrew Graham Riley; Gerard Joseph Sheridan
Officers: Andrew Graham Riley [1975] Director; Gerard Joseph Sheridan [1966] Director

G3 Worldwide Mail (UK) Limited
Incorporated: 4 March 1955 *Employees:* 78
Net Worth: £1,334,000 *Total Assets:* £7,602,000
Registered Office: Unit 9 Trident Way, International Trading Estate, Southall, Middlesex, UB2 5LF
Activities: Licensed carriers
Parent: G3 Worldiwde Mail NV
Officers: Alan Thomas O'Halloran, Secretary; Stephen Mark Ferguson [1966] Director; Alan Thomas O'Halloran [1966] Finance Director

G4S Aviation Services (UK) Limited
Incorporated: 19 July 1993 *Employees:* 1,523
Net Worth Deficit: £4,324,000 *Total Assets:* £11,685,000
Registered Office: Sutton Park House, Carshalton Road, Sutton, Surrey, SM1 4LD
Activities: Private security activities
Parent: G4S Regional Management (UK & I) Limited
Officers: Vaishali Jagdish Patel, Secretary; Douglas Charles Hewitson [1963] Director; Graham Austen Levinsohn [1962] Director; David Paul Lobley [1965] Finance Director

G4S Cash Centres (UK) Limited
Incorporated: 13 March 1980 *Employees:* 1,297
Net Worth: £20,705,000 *Total Assets:* £31,722,000
Registered Office: Sutton Park House, 15 Carshalton Road, Sutton, Surrey, SM1 4LD
Activities: Private security activities
Parent: G4S UK Holdings Limited
Officers: Vaishali Jagdish Patel, Secretary; John Michael Joseph Campbell [1967] Managing Director [Irish]; Jodie Louise France [1977] Finance Director; John William Lennox [1960] Operations Director

G4S Cash Solutions (UK) Limited
Incorporated: 10 July 1939 *Employees:* 3,305
Net Worth: £108,017,000 *Total Assets:* £169,738,000
Registered Office: Sutton Park House, 15 Carshalton Road, Sutton, Surrey, SM1 4LD
Activities: Private security activities
Shareholders: G4S UK Holdings Limited; G4S UK Holdings Limited
Officers: Vaishali Jagdish Patel, Secretary; John Michael Joseph Campbell [1967] Managing Director [Irish]; Jodie Louise France [1977] Finance Director; John William Lennox [1960] Director

G4S Secure Solutions (UK) Limited
Incorporated: 14 March 1972 *Employees:* 13,555
Net Worth: £37,315,000 *Total Assets:* £184,500,992
Registered Office: Sutton Park House, 15 Carshalton Road, Sutton, Surrey, SM1 4LD
Activities: Private security activities
Parent: G4S Regional Management (UK & I) Limited
Officers: Vaishali Jagdish Patel, Secretary; Douglas Charles Hewitson [1963] Director; Graham Austen Levinsohn [1962] Director; David Paul Lobley [1965] Finance Director

G4S Security Services (UK) Limited
Incorporated: 8 May 1989 *Employees:* 4,209
Net Worth: £69,080,000 *Total Assets:* £110,271,000
Registered Office: Sutton Park House, 15 Carshalton Road, Sutton, Surrey, SM1 4LD
Activities: Private security activities
Parent: G4S Secure Solutions (UK) Limited
Officers: Vaishali Jagdish Patel, Secretary; Douglas Charles Hewitson [1963] Managing Director; Graham Austen Levinsohn [1962] Director; David Paul Lobley [1965] Finance Director

Gaat International Ltd
Incorporated: 26 September 2003 *Employees:* 7
Net Worth: £1,499,358 *Total Assets:* £5,530,147
Registered Office: Northside House, 69 Tweedy Road, Bromley, Kent, BR1 3WA
Activities: Wholesale of clothing and footwear
Major Shareholder: Atila Turkmen
Officers: Aysen Deniz Soyaslan, Secretary; Cem Ciprut [1983] Director [Turkish]; Atila Turkmen [1950] Director [Turkish]; Dogu Turkmen [1979] Director [Turkish]; Onder Turkmen [1977] Director [Turkish]; Yaman Turkmen [1995] Director [Turkish]

Gable Homes Lettings Limited
Incorporated: 12 October 2005
Net Worth: £3,387,017 *Total Assets:* £7,773,595
Registered Office: 4 Queens Road, Hersham, Walton on Thames, Surrey, KT12 5LS
Activities: Other letting and operating of own or leased real estate
Major Shareholder: Keith Whybrow
Officers: Keith Whybrow [1959] Director/Builder

Gada Limited
Incorporated: 4 October 1993 *Employees:* 5
Net Worth: £12,765,527 *Total Assets:* £12,918,597
Registered Office: 11 Chestnut Avenue, Northwood, Middlesex, HA6 1HR
Activities: Other letting and operating of own or leased real estate
Shareholders: Dipen Hasmukhlal Shah; Sheilina Shah
Officers: Dipen Hasmukhlal Shah, Secretary/Chartered Accountant; Dipen Hasmukhlal Shah [1967] Director/Chartered Accountant; Radhika Shah [1969] Director/Chartered Accountant; Sheilina Shah [1972] Director/Management Accountant

Gade Investments Limited
Incorporated: 14 June 2010
Net Worth: £2,701,538 *Total Assets:* £7,032,070
Registered Office: First Floor, Radius House, 51 Clarendon Road, Watford, Herts, WD17 1HP
Activities: Activities of head offices
Shareholders: Raymond Charles Russell Dalton; Anita Jane Dalton
Officers: Sonia Whitehead, Secretary; Anita Jane Dalton [1945] Director; Raymond Charles Russell Dalton [1934] Director; William Raymond Dalton [1985] Director/Property Development

Gade Property Developments Limited
Incorporated: 15 April 1971 *Employees:* 9
Net Worth: £8,457,943 *Total Assets:* £15,730,458
Registered Office: First Floor, Radius House, 51 Clarendon Road, Watford, Herts, WD17 1HP
Activities: Development of building projects
Officers: Sonia Whitehead, Secretary; Anita Jane Dalton [1945] Director; Raymond Charles Russell Dalton [1934] Director; William Raymond Dalton [1985] Director/Property Development

Gago Invest Limited
Incorporated: 5 November 2014 *Employees:* 5
Net Worth: £12,506,046 *Total Assets:* £12,525,304
Registered Office: 5 Elstree Gate, Elstree Way, Borehamwood, Herts, WD6 1JD
Activities: Other service activities n.e.c.
Shareholders: Frederic Gastaldo-Nigra; Francoise Gastaldo-Nigra
Officers: Nathalie Gastaldo-Godeau [1972] Director [French]; Francoise Gastaldo-Nigra [1946] Director [French]; Frederic Gastaldo-Nigra [1977] Director [French]; Philippe Godeau [1961] Director [French]; Sylvain Lagneaux [1957] Director/Lawyer Associate [French]

GAIAE Limited
Incorporated: 25 March 2014
Net Worth: £246,673 *Total Assets:* £11,240,534
Registered Office: 107 Hindes Road, Harrow, Middlesex, HA1 1RU
Activities: Activities of other holding companies n.e.c.
Officers: Manuel Alsoni [1982] Director [Italian]

The Gala Film Partners, LLP
Incorporated: 7 May 2003
Net Worth: £112,058,120 *Total Assets:* £112,058,120
Registered Office: 99 Kenton Road, Harrow, Middlesex, HA3 0AN
Officers: Junghwa Aitken [1960] LLP Member; Thomas David Guy Arculus [1946] LLP Member; Lisa Arnold [1962] LLP Member; Niall Richard Bamford [1966] LLP Member; John Edward Gilder Bateson [1948] LLP Member; Abraham Bejerano [1947] LLP Member; Alan Richard Bekhor [1960] LLP Member; Charles Louis Berman [1958] LLP Member; George Boateng [1975] LLP Member; James Everett Burgess [1964] LLP Member; William Patrick Cadogan [1947] LLP Member; Roger William Carey [1944] LLP Member; Steven John Bentley Carr [1961] LLP Member; Stephen Leonard Conn [1946] LLP Member; Nick Criticos [1958] LLP Member; Gael de Boissard [1967] LLP Member; Thomas Dicker [1953] LLP Member; Marcus Benjamin Donn [1973] LLP Member; Derek James Duffy [1954] LLP Member; Ian Keith Fisher [1959] LLP Member; Dr Stephen Garnett [1957] LLP Member; Michael David Goldman [1949] LLP Member; Colin Stewart Grassie [1961] LLP Member; Richard William John Hardie [1948] LLP Member; Robin Leonard Henshall [1959] LLP Member; Francis Paul Henri Pie Herve [1953] LLP Member; Nicola Karina Christina Horlick [1960] LLP Member; Marc Ronald Hotimsky [1956] LLP Member; Yann Le Garrec [1962] LLP Member; Barry Lewis [1954] LLP Member; Susan Jane Livesey [1959] LLP Member; Jonathan Angus MacDonald [1960] LLP Member; Christopher John Mallet [1957] LLP Member; Christopher Mary Masterson [1956] LLP Member; John Anthony McLevy [1949] LLP Member; Andrew McMillan [1965] LLP Member; Pierre Jean Henri Mirat [1965] LLP Member; Patrick Jacques Elkin Mocatta [1949] LLP Member; Kenneth Morton [1942] LLP Member; Michael Murphy [1965] LLP Member; Michael Darren Murphy [1965] LLP Member; Alan Daniel Neilson [1957] LLP Member; David Leslie Newland [1968] LLP Member; Craig Wyndham Orr [1962] LLP Member; Peter Edward Owen [1946] LLP Member; Gillian Mary Payne [1937] LLP Member; Humphrey Richard Percy [1956] LLP Member; Thomas Martin Harwood Reid [1960] LLP Member; Terence Ian Sadler [1948] LLP Member; Rajiv Sharma [1970] LLP Member; Trevor Hugh Silver [1953] LLP Member; Roderick John Sinclair [1944] LLP Member; Colin Spencer Smith [1946] LLP Member; Alison Mary Straszewski [1963] LLP Member; Jonathan William Summers [1971] LLP Member; Rhoderick Martin Swire [1951] LLP Member; Oliver Robert Takacs [1969] LLP Member; Hugh Ian Taylor [1945] LLP Member; Ian John Thacker [1957] LLP Member; Guy Henry Toller [1958] LLP Member; Stanislav Varga [1972] LLP Member; Alan Edward Westall [1947] LLP Member; Manjit Wolstenholme [1964] LLP Member; Alan James Wood [1958] LLP Member; Mark John Lyon Wyllie [1963] LLP Member

Galamast Limited
Incorporated: 12 September 1991 *Employees:* 244
Net Worth: £9,847,231 *Total Assets:* £16,537,468
Registered Office: Park House, Cowper Road, Bromley, Kent, BR2 9RT
Activities: Construction of roads and motorways
Shareholder: Michael Frederick Gallagher
Officers: Michael Frederick Gallagher, Secretary; Michael Frederick Gallagher [1954] Director/Civil Engineer; Kieran Thomas Masterson [1963] Director/Civil Engineer

Galaxy Group Bidco Limited
Incorporated: 14 December 2017 *Employees:* 2,538
Net Worth: £89,760,000 *Total Assets:* £390,119,008
Registered Office: Units 6 & 7 Princeton Mews, 167-169 London Road, Kingston upon Thames, Surrey, KT2 6PT
Activities: Activities of other holding companies n.e.c.
Parent: Galaxy Group Midco Limited
Officers: Garry John Fitton, Secretary; Ruben Kumar Bhagobati [1971] Director/Principal; Malcolm Brown [1967] Director/Head of Asset Management Europe; Garry John Fitton [1972] Finance Director; Nicola Rosemary Lucy Hopkins [1968] Director/Chartered Accountant; Peter Kinsey [1964] Director; Julie-Anne Marie Mizzi [1969] Director [Australian]; Adam Ringer [1980] Investment Director; David Andrew Spruzen [1967] Director

The Galaxy Trust
Incorporated: 24 June 2016 *Employees:* 248
Net Worth: £16,716,747 *Total Assets:* £19,659,552
Registered Office: Oakfield Community Primary School, Oakfield Lane, Dartford, Kent, DA1 2SW
Activities: Primary education
Officers: Akua Agyepong [1977] Director/Local Authority Employee; Hannah Susan Delany [1980] Director/HR; Victoria Dennis [1978] Director/Social Worker; Adrian Marcus Denny [1972] Director/Solicitor; Dawn Funge [1955] Director/Retired; Victoria Faith Stretton [1979] Director/Education; David John Taffs [1948] Director/Retired Accountant; Noflsat Ayotola Tiamiyu [1978] Director/Auditor; Tom Whelan [1979] Director/Accountant

Galderma (U.K.) Limited
Incorporated: 14 February 1962 *Employees:* 81
Net Worth: £2,385,000 *Total Assets:* £16,943,000
Registered Office: Meridien House, 69-71 Clarendon Road, Watford, Herts, WD17 1DS
Activities: Wholesale of pharmaceutical goods
Officers: Jacques Bodevin [1961] Director/Chief Financial Officer Nestle Skin Health [Swiss]; Can Davut Ongen [1965] Director/Regional VP EMEA [Swiss]; Alexandra Tretyakova [1972] Director/General Manager [Russian]

Gall Holdings Limited
Incorporated: 15 April 2016
Net Worth: £5,000,200 *Total Assets:* £5,000,200
Registered Office: 166 College Road, Harrow, Middlesex, HA1 1RA
Activities: Activities of other holding companies n.e.c.
Major Shareholder: Donal Gallagher
Officers: Donal Gallagher [1972] Director [Irish]

Joseph Gallagher Group Limited
Incorporated: 21 June 1999 *Employees:* 231
Net Worth: £15,421,579 *Total Assets:* £41,862,936
Registered Office: Neagron House, Stanford Road, Orsett, Essex, RM16 3BX
Activities: Non-trading company
Shareholders: Joseph Jude Gallagher; Mrs Agnes Teresa Gallagher
Officers: Agnes Theresa Gallagher, Secretary; Agnes Teresa Gallagher [1954] Director; Joseph Jude Gallagher [1945] Director [Irish]; Paul Joseph Gallagher [1981] Director; Steven Keith Harvey [1963] Managing Director

Joseph Gallagher Limited
Incorporated: 2 March 1982 *Employees:* 192
Net Worth: £11,078,520 *Total Assets:* £28,537,716
Registered Office: Neagron House, Stanford Road, Orsett, Essex, RM16 3BX
Activities: Construction of bridges and tunnels
Parent: Joseph Gallagher Group Limited
Officers: Agnes Theresa Gallagher, Secretary; Claire Elaine Dale [1983] Director/Quantity Surveyor; Agnes Theresa Gallagher [1946] Director; Joseph Jude Gallagher [1945] Director [Irish]; Paul Joseph Gallagher [1981] Director; Steven Harvey [1963] Director/Civil Engineer; Anthony Andrew Matheson [1968] Group Commercial Director; John Timothy O'Dwyer [1970] Contracts Director; Clive Wigley [1946] Director/Civil Engineer

Gallaher Group Limited
Incorporated: 2 January 1997 *Employees:* 5
Net Worth: £724,998,976 *Total Assets:* £769,382,976
Registered Office: Members Hill, Brooklands Road, Weybridge, Surrey, KT13 0QU
Activities: Activities of head offices
Parent: JTI (UK) Management Ltd
Officers: Nicholas Charles David Craig, Secretary; Charles Ashley Cunningham-Reid [1968] Director; Paul Bernard Hennessy [1980] Director [Irish]; Jeroen Rusbach [1977] Director/Accountant [Dutch]; Daniel Sciamma [1970] Director [French]

Gallaher Limited
Incorporated: 12 June 1980 *Employees:* 651
Net Worth: £303,400,000 *Total Assets:* £1,385,600,000
Registered Office: Members Hill, Brooklands Road, Weybridge, Surrey, KT13 0QU
Activities: Manufacture of tobacco products
Parent: Benson & Hedges Limited
Officers: Nicholas Charles David Craig, Secretary; Stephane Berset [1975] Director [Swiss]; Charles Ashley Cunningham-Reid [1968] Director; Paul Bernard Hennessy [1980] Director [Irish]; Ross Michael Hennessy [1981] Director [Irish]; Jason Robert Melling [1971] HR Director; Daniel Sciamma [1970] Director [French]

Gallaher Overseas (Holdings) Limited
Incorporated: 10 May 2000
Net Worth: £440,740,000 *Total Assets:* £440,740,000
Registered Office: Members Hill, Brooklands Road, Weybridge, Surrey, KT13 0QU
Activities: Activities of head offices
Parent: Gallaher Group Limited
Officers: Nicholas Charles David Craig, Secretary; Charles Ashley Cunningham-Reid [1968] Director; Paul Bernard Hennessy [1980] Director [Irish]; Jeroen Rusbach [1977] Director/Accountant [Dutch]; Daniel Sciamma [1970] Director [French]

Gallaher Overseas Limited
Incorporated: 17 August 1988 *Employees:* 6
Net Worth: £37,150,000 *Total Assets:* £52,846,000
Registered Office: Members Hill, Brooklands Road, Weybridge, Surrey, KT13 0QU
Activities: Activities of head offices
Parent: Gallaher Overseas (Holdings) Limited
Officers: Nicholas Charles David Craig, Secretary; Mohammed Junab Ali [1981] Director/Accountant; Andrew Chamberlain [1965] Director/Accountant; Alison Maria Hawkett [1968] Director/Accountant; Paul Bernard Hennessy [1980] Director [Irish]; Jeroen Rusbach [1977] Director/Accountant [Dutch]; Daniel Sciamma [1970] Director [French]

Galldris Construction Limited
Incorporated: 23 March 1998 *Employees:* 4
Previous: Sedo Holdings 2016 Limited
Net Worth: £338,507 *Total Assets:* £12,304,427
Registered Office: 166 College Road, Harrow, Middlesex, HA1 1RA
Activities: Other specialised construction activities n.e.c.
Shareholders: Donal Gallagher; Sean Peter O'Driscoll
Officers: Sean Peter O'Driscoll, Secretary/Civil Engineer [Irish]; Donal Gallagher [1972] Director/Construction Manager [Irish]; Martin McDonough [1958] Health & Safety Director; Sean Peter O'Driscoll [1971] Director/Civil Engineer [Irish]; Jeremy Charles Pasley [1961] Construction Director [Irish]

Galldris Holdings Limited
Incorporated: 15 April 2016 *Employees:* 48
Net Worth: £4,579,660 *Total Assets:* £57,328,408
Registered Office: 166 College Road, Harrow, Middlesex, HA1 1RA
Activities: Activities of other holding companies n.e.c.
Major Shareholder: Donal Gallagher
Officers: Donal Gallagher [1972] Director [Irish]; Sean Peter O'Driscoll [1971] Director [Irish]

Galldris Services Ltd
Incorporated: 24 March 2010 *Employees:* 42
Previous: Galldris Construction Limited
Net Worth: £11,303,958 *Total Assets:* £64,286,348
Registered Office: 166 College Road, Harrow, Middlesex, HA1 1RA
Activities: Activities of head offices
Parent: Galldris Holdings Limited
Officers: Sean O'Driscoll, Secretary; Donal Gallagher [1972] Director [Irish]; Sean Peter O'Driscoll [1971] Director/Civil Engineer [Irish]

Galleon Investments (Dartford) Limited
Incorporated: 19 June 2014
Net Worth: £2,618,923 *Total Assets:* £9,345,729
Registered Office: Long Reach, Galleon Boulevard, Crossways Business Park, Dartford, Kent, DA2 6QE
Activities: Non-trading company
Parent: Dormole Ltd
Officers: Andrew James Thomas Strong [1955] Director; Timothy John Strong [1958] Director

Galliard Construction Limited
Incorporated: 7 February 1996
Net Worth: £31,742,446 *Total Assets:* £87,221,768
Registered Office: 3rd Floor, Sterling House, Langston Road, Loughton, Essex, IG10 3TS
Activities: Development of building projects
Parent: Galliard Holdings Limited
Officers: Allan William Porter, Secretary; Victoria Elizabeth Anthony [1977] Group HR Director; John Leslie August [1939] Director/Project Manager; David Edward Conway [1976] Director; Stephen Stuart Solomon Conway [1948] Director; Robin Hawkins [1957] Director/Contracts Manager; Darren Paul Maguire [1970] Construction Director; Donagh O'Sullivan [1968] Construction Director [Irish]; Allan William Porter [1957] Director/Accountant; Michael William Watson [1952] Director/Architectural Technologist

Galliard Developments Limited
Incorporated: 1 August 2014
Net Worth: £66,038,056 *Total Assets:* £153,230,640
Registered Office: 3rd Floor, Sterling House, Langston Road, Loughton, Essex, IG10 3TS
Activities: Other business support service activities n.e.c.
Parent: GDL Holdco Limited
Officers: Allan William Porter, Secretary; John Cole [1971] Director; Stephen Stuart Solomon Conway [1948] Director; Jonathan Simon Goldstein [1966] Director; Donagh O'Sullivan [1968] Director [Irish]

Galliard Estates Limited
Incorporated: 27 April 2001
Net Worth Deficit: £723,842 *Total Assets:* £5,373,307
Registered Office: 3rd Floor, Sterling House, Langston Road, Loughton, Essex, IG10 3TS
Activities: Development of building projects
Shareholder: Galliard Homes Limited
Officers: Allan William Porter, Secretary; Gary Alexander Conway [1973] Director/Property Investor; Richard Matthew Conway [1978] Director; Stephen Stuart Solomon Conway [1948] Director; Trevor Jonathan Racke [1969] Director

Galliard Group Limited
Incorporated: 13 February 2012 *Employees:* 567
Previous: Galliard (Group) Limited
Net Worth: £239,578,000 *Total Assets:* £741,121,024
Registered Office: 3rd Floor, Sterling House, Langston Road, Loughton, Essex, IG10 3TS
Activities: Activities of other holding companies n.e.c.
Shareholder: Stephen Stuart Solomon Conway
Officers: Allan William Porter, Secretary; Low See Ching [1975] Director/Deputy CEO [Singaporean]; David Edward Conway [1976] Director; Gary Alexander Conway [1973] Director; Richard Matthew Conway [1978] Director; Stephen Stuart Solomon Conway [1948] Director; Paul Laurence Huberman [1961] Director/Chartered Accountant; Luke Oliver Johnson [1962] Director/Restaurateur; Ching Chiat Kwong [1965] Director/Chairman & CEO [Singaporean]; Jonathan Michael Morgan [1978] Director; Donagh O'Sullivan [1968] Construction Director [Irish]; Michael William Watson [1952] Director/Architectural Technologist; Jonathan Paul White [1951] Director

Galliard Holdings Limited
Incorporated: 9 May 1997
Net Worth: £44,670,496 *Total Assets:* £299,718,112
Registered Office: 3rd Floor, Sterling House, Langston Road, Loughton, Essex, IG10 3TS
Activities: Activities of head offices
Parent: Galliard Group Limited
Officers: Allan William Porter, Secretary; David Edward Conway [1976] Director; Stephen Stuart Solomon Conway [1948] Director; Paul Laurence Huberman [1961] Director/Chartered Accountant; Jonathan Michael Morgan [1978] Director; Donagh O'Sullivan [1968] Construction Director [Irish]; Michael William Watson [1952] Director/Architectural Technologist; Jonathan Paul White [1951] Director

Galliard Homes Limited
Incorporated: 28 August 1987 *Employees:* 427
Net Worth: £11,531,404 *Total Assets:* £257,703,344
Registered Office: 3rd Floor, Sterling House, Langston Road, Loughton, Essex, IG10 3TS
Activities: Development of building projects
Parent: Galliard Holdings Limited
Officers: Allan William Porter, Secretary; Victoria Elizabeth Anthony [1977] Group HR Director; David Edward Conway [1976] Director/Property Developer; Stephen Stuart Solomon Conway [1948] Director; Amanda Louise Dijk [1976] Director/Group Financial Controller; David Galman [1963] Sales Director; David Joseph Hirschfield [1985] Director/Solicitor; Paul Laurence Huberman [1961] Director/Chartered Accountant; Jonathan Michael Morgan [1978] Director; Donagh O'Sullivan [1968] Construction Director [Irish]; Allan William Porter [1957] Director/Accountant; Michael John Watson [1974] Architectural & Technical Director; Michael William Watson [1952] Director/Architectural Technologist

Galliford Try Building Limited
Incorporated: 20 February 1990 *Employees:* 1,682
Net Worth: £57,387,000 *Total Assets:* £576,496,000
Registered Office: Cowley Business Park, Cowley, Uxbridge, Middlesex, UB8 2AL
Activities: Construction of commercial buildings
Parent: Galliford Try Construction & Investments Holdings Limited
Officers: Mark Baxter [1972] Director/Finance Manager; Michael Charles Bruce [1969] Director; Simon Burton [1963] Regional Managing Director; Neil David Cocker [1966] Director; Martin Cooper [1971] Director/Chartered Accountant; Bill Hocking [1963] Director; Ian Thomas Jubb [1964] Director/Senior Management; Michael Laws [1970] Director; Jonathan Frank Marston [1970] Director/Quantity Surveyor; Donald James McLachlan [1961] Director; James Robert Parker [1959] Director/Quantity Surveyor; Matthew Malcolm Pool [1965] Director/Chartered Surveyor; Edward James Robertson [1961] Director; Stephen Paul Scard [1966] Construction Director; Christopher Mark Slidel [1962] Director/Quantity Surveyor; Graham William West [1970] Director/Commercial Manager; Clifford James Wheatley [1977] Director/Quantity Surveyor

Galliford Try Construction & Investments Holdings Limited
Incorporated: 10 September 2002 *Employees:* 3,079
Net Worth: £113,200,000 *Total Assets:* £1,224,300,032
Registered Office: Cowley Business Park, High Street, Cowley, Uxbridge, Middlesex, UB8 2AL
Activities: Activities of head offices
Parent: Galliford Try PLC
Officers: Mark Baxter [1972] Director/Finance Manager; Martin Cooper [1971] Director/Chartered Accountant; Kevin Allan Corbett [1960] Director/Solicitor; Bill Hocking [1963] Director; Ian Thomas Jubb [1964] Director/Senior Management; Michael Laws [1970] Director; Nicholas James Salt [1970] Director

Galliford Try Employment Limited
Incorporated: 9 May 1988 *Employees:* 5,506
Net Worth Deficit: £15,000 *Total Assets:* £12,753,000
Registered Office: Cowley Business Park, Cowley, Uxbridge, Middlesex, UB8 2AL
Activities: Construction of commercial buildings
Parent: Galliford Try Services Limited
Officers: Kevin Allan Corbett [1960] Director/Solicitor; Stuart Alexander Waldman [1968] Finance Director

Galliford Try Homes Limited
Incorporated: 14 February 1996
Net Worth: £4,078,000 *Total Assets:* £186,766,000
Registered Office: Cowley Business Park, Cowley, Uxbridge, Middlesex, UB8 2AL
Activities: Construction of commercial buildings
Parent: Galliford Try PLC
Officers: Andrew James Duxbury [1975] Director/Accountant; Mark Robert Farnham [1965] Director/Accountant; Andrew Richard Hammond [1970] Director; Tom Marshall Nicholson [1965] Director; Stephen John Teagle [1959] Director; Peter Martin Truscott [1962] Director

Galliford Try HPS Limited
Incorporated: 13 August 2009
Net Worth Deficit: £685,000 *Total Assets:* £6,111,000
Registered Office: Cowley Business Park, Cowley, Uxbridge, Middlesex, UB8 2AL
Activities: Construction of commercial buildings
Parent: Galliford Try Building Limited
Officers: Martin Cooper [1971] Director/Chartered Accountant; Kevin Allan Corbett [1960] Director/Solicitor; Bill Hocking [1963] Director; Ian Thomas Jubb [1964] Director/Senior Management; Michael Laws [1970] Director; Graham William West [1970] Director/Commercial Manager

Galliford Try Investments Limited
Incorporated: 17 February 2004 *Employees:* 45
Net Worth: £11,141,000 *Total Assets:* £27,541,000
Registered Office: Cowley Business Park, Cowley, Uxbridge, Middlesex, UB8 2AL
Activities: Activities of head offices
Parent: Galliford Try Construction & Investments Holdings Limited
Officers: Mark Baxter [1972] Director; Philip Jonathan Harris [1971] Director; Brian Love [1979] Director; Paul James McGirk [1959] Director; Philip McVey [1960] Director; Lee Richard Simmons [1970] Director

Galliford Try Partnerships Limited
Incorporated: 10 April 1964 *Employees:* 746
Net Worth: £39,368,000 *Total Assets:* £361,056,000
Registered Office: Cowley Business Park, Cowley, Uxbridge, Middlesex, UB8 2AL
Activities: Construction of commercial buildings
Parent: Galliford Try Homes Limited
Officers: Clare Helen Crawford [1977] Director; Mark Robert Farnham [1965] Director/Accountant; Stephen John Teagle [1959] Director; Peter Martin Truscott [1962] Director

Galliford Try Plant Limited
Incorporated: 28 June 2006 *Employees:* 14
Net Worth: £8,644,000 *Total Assets:* £16,576,000
Registered Office: Cowley Business Park, Cowley, Uxbridge, Middlesex, UB8 2AL
Activities: Renting and leasing of trucks and other heavy vehicles
Parent: Galliford Try Construction & Investments Holdings Limited
Officers: Martin Cooper [1971] Director/Chartered Accountant; Bill Hocking [1963] Director

Galliford Try PLC
Incorporated: 3 February 1965 *Employees:* 5,485
Net Worth: £776,499,968 *Total Assets:* £2,893,299,968
Registered Office: Cowley Business Park, Cowley, Uxbridge, Middlesex, UB8 2AL
Activities: Construction of commercial buildings
Officers: Kevin Allan Corbett, Secretary; Maria Luisa Cassoni [1951] Director/Accountant; Therese Lynn Miller [1951] Director; Graham Prothero [1961] Director/Chartered Accountant; Gavin Slark [1965] Director; Jeremy Charles Douglas Townsend [1964] Director; Peter Martin Truscott [1962] Director; Peter John Ventress [1960] Director

Galliford Try Services Limited
Incorporated: 5 April 1977 *Employees:* 312
Net Worth: £30,742,000 *Total Assets:* £90,749,000
Registered Office: Cowley Business Park, Cowley, Uxbridge, Middlesex, UB8 2AL
Activities: Development of building projects
Parent: Galliford Try PLC
Officers: Kevin Allan Corbett [1960] Director/Solicitor; Graham Prothero [1961] Director; Stuart Alexander Waldman [1968] Finance Director

Galvani Bioelectronics Limited
Incorporated: 3 February 2016 *Employees:* 26
Net Worth: £162,342,000 *Total Assets:* £183,852,000
Registered Office: 980 Great West Road, Brentford, Middlesex, TW8 9GS
Activities: Other research and experimental development on natural sciences and engineering
Shareholders: Alphabet Inc.; Setfirst Limited
Officers: Dr Andrew Jason Conrad [1963] Director/President & CEO, Verily Life Sciences LLC [American]; Dr Christopher Corsico [1962] Director [American]; Dr Kaigham Jacob Gabriel [1955] Director/President & CEO, Draper [American]; Dr Brian Partick Otis [1977] Director/Chief Technology Officer, Verily Life Sciences [American]; Dr Jordi Parramon [1971] Director of Medical Devices [Spanish/American]; Dr Mohamed Moncef Slaoui [1959] Director/Chairman Global Vaccines [Belgian]; Subesh Ronald Williams [1962] Director/SVP, Global Corporate Development

Ganco Limited
Incorporated: 6 February 2003 *Employees:* 4
Net Worth: £13,016,661 *Total Assets:* £29,391,922
Registered Office: 1 Commonside West, Mitcham, Surrey, CR4 4HA
Activities: Development of building projects
Parent: Ganco (Holdings) Limited
Officers: Rukshana Nowsad Gani, Secretary; Muhammed Sufiyan Gani [1992] Director; Nowsad Abdul Gani [1963] Director/Property Consultant; Rukshana Nowsad Gani [1961] Director/Property Consultant

Gantrade Europe Limited
Incorporated: 5 April 1983 *Employees:* 15
Net Worth: £11,656,942 *Total Assets:* £37,915,792
Registered Office: 3rd Floor, Birch House, Fairfield Avenue, Staines upon Thames, Middlesex, TW18 4AB
Activities: Wholesale of chemical products
Major Shareholder: Mahendra Parekh
Officers: Jaikumar Moorthy [1962] Director [American]; Hemal Aaron Parekh [1969] Director [American]; Nayan Gregory Parekh [1968] Director/Executive [American]

Gapsun Properties Limited
Incorporated: 12 February 2014
Net Worth: £31,743,996 *Total Assets:* £36,992,648
Registered Office: Hawke House, Old Station Road, Loughton, Essex, IG10 4PL
Activities: Dormant company
Parent: TRAD Properties LLP
Officers: Doretta Smith, Secretary; Doretta Smith [1943] Director; Hayden Francis Smith [1939] Director

Garden Centre Property Development Trading Limited
Incorporated: 4 December 2000
Previous: Garden Centre Property Development Trading PLC
Net Worth: £7,889,000 *Total Assets:* £8,638,000
Registered Office: Wyevale Garden Centres, Syon Park, London Road, Brentford, Middlesex, TW8 8JF
Activities: Buying and selling of own real estate
Parent: Garden Centre Holdings Limited
Officers: Laura Harradine-Greene, Secretary; Anthony Generald Jones [1973] Director; Richard MacLachlan [1976] Director

Gardeners' Royal Benevolent Society
Incorporated: 31 December 2013 *Employees:* 41
Net Worth: £60,854,000 *Total Assets:* £61,241,000
Registered Office: 115-117 Kingston Road, Leatherhead, Surrey, KT22 7SU
Activities: Other letting and operating of own or leased real estate
Officers: Peter John Newman, Secretary; Heather Anne Barrett-Mold [1948] Director/Consultant; Carole Mary Baxter [1957] Director/Horticulturist; Thomas Alan Cole [1966] Director/Horticultural Lecturer; Maureen Hart [1953] Director/Retired; Mark Lane [1959] Director/Gardens Manager; Cynthia Isabel Margaret Leslie [1951] Director/Solicitor; Steven Mark Palmer [1960] Finance Director; Carol Paris [1966] Director/Chief Executive; Dougal Ramsay George Philip [1953] Director/Retailer; James Portland Robinson [1947] Director/Retired; Neville John Stein [1960] Director/Business Consultant; Emma Natalie Tinker [1975] Director/Investment Management

J. Gardner Holdings Limited
Incorporated: 22 January 1913 *Employees:* 3
Net Worth: £12,061,004 *Total Assets:* £13,144,440
Registered Office: Gladstone House, 77-79 High Street, Egham, Surrey, TW20 9HY
Activities: Development of building projects
Officers: William George Henry Fuller, Secretary; William George Henry Fuller [1944] Director/Chartered Accountant; Stephen John Christie Gardner [1962] Director; David Arthur Preston [1939] Director/Chartered Accountant; Geoffrey Nigel Mitford Taunton [1939] Director/Chartered Surveyor

Garfwish Limited
Incorporated: 29 July 2013 *Employees:* 2
Net Worth Deficit: £4,565,360 *Total Assets:* £15,036,886
Registered Office: York House, Empire Way, Wembley, Middlesex, HA9 0FQ
Activities: Development of building projects
Parent: Wishgarf Limited
Officers: John Stuart Godwin Garfield [1949] Director; Charles George MacKenzie Wishart [1948] Director

Gargonay Limited
Incorporated: 16 December 2014 *Employees:* 1
Net Worth: £11,673,142 *Total Assets:* £11,695,779
Registered Office: c/o McBrides Accountants LLP, Nexus House, 2 Cray Road, Sidcup, Kent, DA14 5DA
Activities: Activities of investment trusts
Shareholders: Jonathan Christian Martin Church; Eleanor Church
Officers: Eleanor Church [1962] Director; Jonathan Christian Martin Church [1960] Director/Engineer

Garratt Services (Tooting) Limited
Incorporated: 29 March 1978 *Employees:* 4
Net Worth: £5,696,046 *Total Assets:* £6,638,789
Registered Office: Allen House, 1 Westmead Road, Sutton, Surrey, SM1 4LA
Activities: Development of building projects
Shareholders: Michael John Holden; William Alexander Reid
Officers: William Alexander Reid, Secretary; Michael John Holden [1945] Director; William Alexander Reid [1941] Director

Garreg Lwyd Energy Limited
Incorporated: 23 October 2012
Net Worth Deficit: £3,186,000 *Total Assets:* £86,383,000
Registered Office: Beaufort Court, Egg Farm Lane, Kings Langley, Herts, WD4 8LR
Activities: Other business support service activities n.e.c.
Parent: European Wind Investments Group Limited
Officers: Dominic James Hearth, Secretary; Steven William Hughes [1972] Global Support Services Director, UK&I - Commercial; Fraser Stephen Merry [1968] Director/Chartered Surveyor; Mitesh Raj Patel [1982] Director/Group Financial Controller

Garrets Bidco 2 Limited
Incorporated: 17 February 2012
Previous: Garrets (Holdings) Limited
Net Worth: £9,365,943 *Total Assets:* £13,286,820
Registered Office: 3rd Floor, South Wing, St James House, 27-43 Eastern Road, Romford, Essex, RM1 3NH
Activities: Activities of other holding companies n.e.c.
Parent: Garrets Holding Limited
Officers: Robert Steen Kledal [1969] Director/Chief Executive Officer [Danish]; Anders Skipper [1967] Director/Chief Financial Officer [Danish]

Garrets Bidco Limited
Incorporated: 17 February 2012
Net Worth: £18,473,512 *Total Assets:* £18,780,188
Registered Office: 3rd Floor, South Wing, St James House, 27-43 Eastern Road, Romford, Essex, RM1 3NH
Activities: Other service activities n.e.c.
Parent: Garrets Bidco 2 Limited
Officers: Geoffrey Brian Battersby [1960] Director; Robert Steen Kledal [1969] Director/Chief Executive Officer [Danish]; Anders Skipper [1967] Director/Chief Executive Officer [Danish]

Garrets International Limited
Incorporated: 19 May 1993 *Employees:* 52
Net Worth: £4,152,419 *Total Assets:* £16,437,936
Registered Office: 3rd Floor, South Wing, St James House, 27-43 Eastern Road, Romford, Essex, RM1 3NH
Activities: Operation of warehousing and storage facilities for land transport activities
Parent: Garrets Bidco Limited
Officers: Geoffrey Brian Battersby [1960] Director; Soeren Joergensen [1974] Director/Chief Commercial Officer [Danish]; Robert Steen Kledal [1969] Director/Chief Executive Officer [Danish]; Stanley Watt Morrice [1963] Director; Richard Owen Page [1965] Operations Director; Anders Skipper [1967] Director/Chief Financial Officer [Danish]; Niels Mors Snog [1971] Director/Chief Executive Officer [Danish]

Gartner U.K. Limited
Incorporated: 9 June 1988 *Employees:* 1,198
Net Worth: £11,656,000 *Total Assets:* £121,190,000
Registered Office: Tamesis, The Glanty, Egham, Surrey, TW20 9AH
Activities: Data processing, hosting and related activities
Parent: Gartner Inc
Officers: Patrick Busby [1966] Director; William Joseph Dorgan [1967] Director/Lawyer [American]; Michael Lithgow [1958] Director; Craig Warren Safian [1969] Director/Senior VP and CFO, Gartner Inc [American]

Garusa Solutions U.K. Limited
Incorporated: 28 February 2017
Net Worth: £16,343,964 *Total Assets:* £16,345,721
Registered Office: 3 Montpelier Avenue, Bexley, Kent, DA5 3AP
Activities: Wholesale of pharmaceutical goods
Major Shareholder: Kalvinder Singh Ruprai
Officers: Kalvinder Singh Ruprai [1969] Director

Garves Wind Limited
Incorporated: 24 May 2002 *Employees:* 5
Net Worth: £9,015,815 *Total Assets:* £9,791,949
Registered Office: Munro House, Portsmouth Road, Cobham, Surrey, KT11 1PP
Activities: Production of electricity
Parent: Danu Holding Limited
Officers: Stephen Campbell Joseph Ellis [1959] Director; Rollo Andrew Johnstone Wright [1976] Director; Philip William Kent [1984] Director; Ronan Niall Kierans [1978] Director [Irish]; Nicholas Simon Parker [1969] Director

Gate Gourmet Holdings U.K. Limited
Incorporated: 22 August 1986
Net Worth: £5,914,000 *Total Assets:* £20,761,000
Registered Office: Building 1071, Heathrow West, Southampton Road, Heathrow Airport, Hounslow, Middlesex, TW6 3AQ
Activities: Activities of other holding companies n.e.c.
Officers: Sreekumar Nair, Secretary; Stephen Philip Corr [1960] Managing Director; Thomas William Fountain [1969] Director/Chartered Accountant; Willem Hendrik Human [1982] Finance Director [British/South African]

Gate Gourmet London Limited
Incorporated: 20 October 1997 *Employees:* 1,882
Net Worth: £30,185,000 *Total Assets:* £66,306,000
Registered Office: Heathrow West, Building 1071, Southampton Road, Heathrow Airport, Hounslow, Middlesex, TW6 3AQ
Activities: Event catering activities
Officers: Sreekumar Nair, Secretary; Stephen Philip Corr [1960] Managing Director; Thomas William Fountain [1969] Director/Chartered Accountant; Willem Hendrik Human [1982] Finance Director [British/South African]

Gatehall Services Limited
Incorporated: 19 October 2007
Net Worth: £1,948,932 *Total Assets:* £7,761,302
Registered Office: 74 Shenley Hill, Radlett, Herts, WD7 7BD
Activities: Other letting and operating of own or leased real estate
Shareholders: Pritpal Singh Millan; Jagjeet Singh Midha
Officers: Pritpal Singh Millan, Secretary/Solicitor; Jagjeet Singh Midha [1983] Director/Caseworker; Pritpal Singh Millan [1971] Director/Solicitor

The Gateway Hotel Dunstable Limited
Incorporated: 22 June 2010 *Employees:* 26
Net Worth: £902,621 *Total Assets:* £11,005,747
Registered Office: 10th Floor, The Mille, 1000 Great West Road, Brentford, Middlesex, TW8 9DW
Activities: Development of building projects
Shareholder: RBH Hotel Group Limited (BVI)
Officers: David Robert Hart [1978] Director/Accountant; Helder Ricardo Silva Pereira [1955] Director [Portuguese]

Gateway Learning Community
Incorporated: 21 June 2006 *Employees:* 512
Net Worth: £36,530,428 *Total Assets:* £47,700,860
Registered Office: The Gateway Academy, Marshfoot Road, Grays, Essex, RM16 4LU
Activities: Primary education
Officers: Joanna Susan Jones, Secretary; Paul Victor Connew [1957] Director/Consultant; Graham Foster [1952] Director/Education Adviser; Lucy Emma Harris [1968] Director/Administrator; Hilary Ruth Hodgson [1960] Charity Director; Victoria Jane Reid [1971] Director/Headteacher; Kevin John Sadler [1961] Director/Headteacher; Margaret Christine Smith [1945] Director/Analytical Chemist (Retired); Peter John Ward [1964] Commercial Director

Gathercrest Properties Limited
Incorporated: 2 September 2013
Net Worth: £6,993 *Total Assets:* £6,715,464
Registered Office: Lynton House, 304 Bensham Lane, Thornton Heath, Surrey, CR7 7EQ
Activities: Other letting and operating of own or leased real estate
Officers: Meena Mahesha Patel, Secretary; Amish Dinkar Patel [1970] Director; Priya Mahesha Patel [1976] Director

GBST Limited
Incorporated: 18 August 1964 *Employees:* 38
Net Worth: £4,033,024 *Total Assets:* £11,609,151
Registered Office: Building 3, Hatters Lane, Croxley Green Business Park, Watford, Herts, WD18 8YG
Activities: Business and domestic software development
Parent: GBST Holdings Limited
Officers: Jillian Glenda Bannan, Secretary; Robert Dedominicis [1965] Director [Australian]; David Simpson [1969] Director/Business Executive

GBST Wealth Management Limited
Incorporated: 4 August 2008 *Employees:* 55
Net Worth: £6,556,589 *Total Assets:* £7,926,761
Registered Office: Building 3, Hatters Lane, Croxley Green Business Park, Watford, Herts, WD18 8YG
Activities: Business and domestic software development
Parent: GBST UK Holdings Ltd
Officers: Jillian Glenda Bannan, Secretary; Robert Dedominicis [1965] Director [Australian]; David Simpson [1969] Director/Business Executive

GCH (St Katharine's) Limited
Incorporated: 12 March 2009 *Employees:* 66
Net Worth: £1,930,061 *Total Assets:* £6,060,562
Registered Office: Gidar House, 13 The Crossway, Uxbridge, Middlesex, UB10 0JH
Activities: Residential nursing care facilities
Officers: Sukhvinder Singh Gidar, Secretary; Jaskiran Kaur Gidar [1964] Director; Ravinder Singh Gidar [1959] Director/Pharmacist; Sheetal Kaur Gidar [1973] Director; Sukhvinder Singh Gidar [1968] Director/Pharmacist

GCH Corporation Limited
Incorporated: 23 March 2010 *Employees:* 837
Previous: GCH Capital Limited
Net Worth: £64,205,408 *Total Assets:* £103,256,360
Registered Office: 2 Castle Business Village, Station Road, Hampton, Surrey, TW12 2BX
Activities: Activities of other holding companies n.e.c.
Major Shareholder: Gregory Frederick Hutchings
Officers: Cassie Hutchings, Secretary; Cassie Olivia Hutchings [1983] Director; Gregory Frederick Hutchings [1947] Director/Businessman

GCP Asset Finance 1 Limited
Incorporated: 17 June 2013 *Employees:* 3
Net Worth Deficit: £2,002,282 *Total Assets:* £29,873,892
Registered Office: Munro House, Portsmouth Road, Cobham, Surrey, KT11 1PP
Activities: Other business support service activities n.e.c.
Parent: GCP Intermediary Holdings Limited
Officers: Stephen Campbell Joseph Ellis [1959] Director; Nicholas Simon Parker [1969] Director; Rollo Andrew Johnstone Wright [1976] Director

GCP Biomass 1 Ltd
Incorporated: 23 January 2013 *Employees:* 3
Net Worth Deficit: £9,091,509 *Total Assets:* £61,095,576
Registered Office: Munro House, Portsmouth Road, Cobham, Surrey, KT11 1PP
Activities: Other business support service activities n.e.c.
Parent: GCP Intermediary Holdings Limited
Officers: Stephen Campbell Joseph Ellis [1959] Director; Ronan Niall Kierans [1978] Director [Irish]; Rollo Andrew Johnstone Wright [1976] Director

GCP Biomass 2 Limited
Incorporated: 25 June 2013 *Employees:* 3
Net Worth Deficit: £229,011 *Total Assets:* £15,021,270
Registered Office: Munro House, Portsmouth Road, Cobham, Surrey, KT11 1PP
Activities: Other business support service activities n.e.c.
Parent: GCP Intermediary Holdings Limited
Officers: Stephen Campbell Joseph Ellis [1959] Director; Ronan Niall Kierans [1978] Director/Chartered Accountant [Irish]; Rollo Andrew Johnstone Wright [1976] Director

GCP Biomass 3 Limited
Incorporated: 20 February 2014 *Employees:* 3
Net Worth Deficit: £9,783,184 *Total Assets:* £9,521,851
Registered Office: Munro House, Portsmouth Road, Cobham, Surrey, KT11 1PP
Activities: Other business support service activities n.e.c.
Parent: GCP Intermediary Holdings Limited
Officers: Stephen Campbell Joseph Ellis [1959] Director; Ronan Niall Kierans [1978] Director/Chartered Accountant [Irish]; Rollo Andrew Johnstone Wright [1976] Director

GCP Biomass 4 Limited
Incorporated: 13 May 2014 *Employees:* 3
Net Worth: £162,600 *Total Assets:* £27,220,052
Registered Office: Munro House, Portsmouth Road, Cobham, Surrey, KT11 1PP
Activities: Other business support service activities n.e.c.
Parent: GCP Intermediary Holdings Limited
Officers: Stephen Campbell Joseph Ellis [1959] Director; Ronan Niall Kierans [1978] Director/Chartered Accountant [Irish]; Rollo Andrew Johnstone Wright [1976] Director

GCP Cardale PFI Ltd
Incorporated: 27 May 2015 *Employees:* 4
Net Worth Deficit: £1,058,115 *Total Assets:* £102,363,056
Registered Office: Munro House, Portsmouth Road, Cobham, Surrey, KT11 1PP
Activities: Other business support service activities n.e.c.
Parent: GCP Intermediary Holdings Limited
Officers: Stephen Campbell Joseph Ellis [1959] Director; Ronan Niall Kierans [1978] Director [Irish]; Nicholas Simon Parker [1969] Director; Rollo Andrew Johnstone Wright [1976] Director

GCP Education 1 Limited
Incorporated: 28 May 2014 *Employees:* 3
Net Worth Deficit: £49,538 *Total Assets:* £15,803,246
Registered Office: Munro House, Portsmouth Road, Cobham, Surrey, KT11 1PP
Activities: Other business support service activities n.e.c.
Parent: GCP Intermediary Holdings Limited
Officers: Stephen Campbell Joseph Ellis [1959] Director; Ronan Niall Kierans [1978] Director/Chartered Accountant [Irish]; Rollo Andrew Johnstone Wright [1976] Director

GCP Green Energy 1 Limited
Incorporated: 7 October 2014 *Employees:* 4
Net Worth: £59,751 *Total Assets:* £36,076,976
Registered Office: Munro House, Portsmouth Road, Cobham, Surrey, KT11 1PP
Activities: Other business support service activities n.e.c.
Parent: GCP Intermediary Holdings Limited
Officers: Stephen Campbell Joseph Ellis [1959] Director; Ronan Niall Kierans [1978] Director/Chartered Accountant [Irish]; Nicholas Simon Parker [1969] Director; Rollo Andrew Johnstone Wright [1976] Director

GCP Healthcare 1 Limited
Incorporated: 24 March 2011 *Employees:* 3
Net Worth Deficit: £971,383 *Total Assets:* £16,878,376
Registered Office: Munro House, Portsmouth Road, Cobham, Surrey, KT11 1PP
Activities: Other business support service activities n.e.c.
Parent: GCP Intermediary Holdings Limited
Officers: Stephen Campbell Joseph Ellis [1959] Director; Ronan Niall Kierans [1978] Director [Irish]; Rollo Andrew Johnstone Wright [1976] Director

GCP Hydro 1 Limited
Incorporated: 3 April 2014 *Employees:* 3
Net Worth Deficit: £31,080 *Total Assets:* £16,258,949
Registered Office: Munro House, Portsmouth Road, Cobham, Surrey, KT11 1PP
Activities: Other business support service activities n.e.c.
Parent: GCP Intermediary Holdings Limited
Officers: Stephen Campbell Joseph Ellis [1959] Director; Nicholas Simon Parker [1969] Director; Rollo Andrew Johnstone Wright [1976] Director

GCP Onshore Wind 1 Limited
Incorporated: 13 February 2013 *Employees:* 3
Net Worth: £46,284 *Total Assets:* £8,060,822
Registered Office: Munro House, Portsmouth Road, Cobham, Surrey, KT11 1PP
Activities: Other business support service activities n.e.c.
Parent: GCP Intermediary Holdings Limited
Officers: Stephen Campbell Joseph Ellis [1959] Director; Nicholas Simon Parker [1969] Director; Rollo Andrew Johnstone Wright [1976] Director

GCP Onshore Wind 3 Limited
Incorporated: 10 June 2013 *Employees:* 3
Net Worth: £16,538 *Total Assets:* £20,183,832
Registered Office: Munro House, Portsmouth Road, Cobham, Surrey, KT11 1PP
Activities: Other business support service activities n.e.c.
Parent: GCP Intermediary Holdings Limited
Officers: Stephen Campbell Joseph Ellis [1959] Director; Nicholas Simon Parker [1969] Director; Rollo Andrew Johnstone Wright [1976] Director

GCP Programme Funding 1 Limited
Incorporated: 19 July 2016 *Employees:* 4
Net Worth: £45,500 *Total Assets:* £90,294,408
Registered Office: Munro House, Portsmouth Road, Cobham, Surrey, KT11 1PP
Activities: Other business support service activities n.e.c.
Parent: GCP Intermediary Holdings Limited
Officers: Stephen Campbell Joseph Ellis [1959] Director; Ronan Niall Kierans [1978] Director [Irish]; Nicholas Simon Parker [1969] Director; Rollo Andrew Johnstone Wright [1976] Director

GCP RHI Boiler 1 Limited
Incorporated: 15 February 2013 *Employees:* 3
Net Worth Deficit: £103,815 *Total Assets:* £9,350,736
Registered Office: Munro House, Portsmouth Road, Cobham, Surrey, KT11 1PP
Activities: Other business support service activities n.e.c.
Parent: GCP Intermediary Holdings Limited
Officers: Stephen Campbell Joseph Ellis [1959] Director; Nicholas Simon Parker [1969] Director; Rollo Andrew Johnstone Wright [1976] Director

GCP Rooftop Solar 1 Limited
Incorporated: 26 August 2011 *Employees:* 3
Net Worth Deficit: £3,249 *Total Assets:* £12,612,083
Registered Office: Munro House, Portsmouth Road, Cobham, Surrey, KT11 1PP
Activities: Other business support service activities n.e.c.
Parent: GCP Intermediary Holdings Limited
Officers: Stephen Campbell Joseph Ellis [1959] Director; Nicholas Simon Parker [1969] Director; Rollo Andrew Johnstone Wright [1976] Director

GCP Rooftop Solar 2 Limited
Incorporated: 18 November 2011 *Employees:* 3
Net Worth Deficit: £35,340 *Total Assets:* £15,921,849
Registered Office: Munro House, Portsmouth Road, Cobham, Surrey, KT11 1PP
Activities: Other business support service activities n.e.c.
Parent: GCP Intermediary Holdings Limited
Officers: Stephen Campbell Joseph Ellis [1959] Director; Nicholas Simon Parker [1969] Director/Accountant; Rollo Andrew Johnstone Wright [1976] Director

GCP Rooftop Solar 3 Limited
Incorporated: 1 June 2012 *Employees:* 3
Net Worth: £5,643 *Total Assets:* £14,681,043
Registered Office: Munro House, Portsmouth Road, Cobham, Surrey, KT11 1PP
Activities: Other business support service activities n.e.c.
Parent: GCP Intermediary Holdings Limited
Officers: Stephen Campbell Joseph Ellis [1959] Director; Nicholas Simon Parker [1969] Director; Rollo Andrew Johnstone Wright [1976] Director

GCP Rooftop Solar 4 Limited
Incorporated: 2 October 2012 *Employees:* 3
Net Worth Deficit: £5,430 *Total Assets:* £37,965,640
Registered Office: Munro House, Portsmouth Road, Cobham, Surrey, KT11 1PP
Activities: Other business support service activities n.e.c.
Parent: GCP Intermediary Holdings Limited
Officers: Stephen Campbell Joseph Ellis [1959] Director; Nicholas Simon Parker [1969] Director; Rollo Andrew Johnstone Wright [1976] Director

GCP Rooftop Solar 5 Ltd
Incorporated: 8 April 2014 *Employees:* 3
Net Worth: £4,272 *Total Assets:* £23,152,332
Registered Office: Munro House, Portsmouth Road, Cobham, Surrey, KT11 1PP
Activities: Other business support service activities n.e.c.
Parent: GCP Intermediary Holdings Limited
Officers: Stephen Campbell Joseph Ellis [1959] Director; Nicholas Simon Parker [1969] Director; Rollo Andrew Johnstone Wright [1976] Director

GCP Rooftop Solar 6 PLC
Incorporated: 27 February 2015 *Employees:* 4
Net Worth Deficit: £2,742,624 *Total Assets:* £58,499,368
Registered Office: Munro House, Portsmouth Road, Cobham, Surrey, KT11 1PP
Activities: Other business support service activities n.e.c.
Parent: GCP Intermediary Holdings Limited
Officers: David George Conlon, Secretary; Stephen Campbell Joseph Ellis [1959] Director; Ronan Niall Kierans [1978] Director/Chartered Accountant [Irish]; Nicholas Simon Parker [1969] Director; Rollo Andrew Johnstone Wright [1976] Director

GCP Rooftop Solar Finance PLC
Incorporated: 8 June 2017 *Employees:* 4
Net Worth Deficit: £1,332,193 *Total Assets:* £96,093,096
Registered Office: Munro House, Portsmouth Road, Cobham, Surrey, KT11 1PP
Activities: Other business support service activities n.e.c.
Parent: GCP Solar Finance Holdings Limited
Officers: David George Conlon, Secretary; Stephen Campbell Joseph Ellis [1959] Director; Ronan Niall Kierans [1978] Director/Chartered Accountant [Irish]; Nicholas Simon Parker [1969] Director; Rollo Andrew Johnstone Wright [1976] Director

GCP Social Housing 1 Limited
Incorporated: 2 December 2014 *Employees:* 4
Net Worth Deficit: £314,322 *Total Assets:* £80,671,512
Registered Office: Munro House, Portsmouth Road, Cobham, Surrey, KT11 1PP
Activities: Other business support service activities n.e.c.
Parent: GCP Intermediary Holdings Limited
Officers: Stephen Campbell Joseph Ellis [1959] Director; Ronan Niall Kierans [1978] Director/Chartered Accountant [Irish]; Nicholas Simon Parker [1969] Director; Rollo Andrew Johnstone Wright [1976] Director

GD UK Holdings, Ltd
Incorporated: 17 February 2017
Net Worth: £124,193,000 *Total Assets:* £124,193,000
Registered Office: 5th Floor, The Shipping Building, Old Vinyl Factory, 252-254 Blyth Road, Hayes, Middlesex, UB3 1HA
Activities: Other information technology service activities
Parent: Go Daddy Operating Company, LLC
Officers: Richard Anthony Winslow [1979] Director; Jonathan Ying Kit Wong [1976] Group Director Finance

GDC (Holdings) Ltd
Incorporated: 22 December 2006 *Employees:* 36
Net Worth: £5,025,522 *Total Assets:* £6,912,177
Registered Office: 20 Progress Way, Croydon, Surrey, CR0 4XD
Activities: Activities of head offices
Shareholders: Khilan Mahendra Shah; Rahul Mahendra Shah; Mahendra Meghji Shah
Officers: Khilan Mahendra Shah [1973] Director; Mahendra Meghji Shah [1945] Director/Businessman; Rahul Mahendra Shah [1977] Director

GDL (Aylesbury) Limited
Incorporated: 27 January 2017
Net Worth Deficit: £2,000 *Total Assets:* £10,556,005
Registered Office: 3rd Floor, Sterling House, Langston Road, Loughton, Essex, IG10 3TS
Activities: Development of building projects
Parent: Galliard Developments Limited
Officers: Allan William Porter, Secretary; Edward Azouz [1949] Director; John Cole [1971] Director; Stephen Stuart Solomon Conway [1948] Director; Scott Matthew Franklin [1966] Director; Jonathan Simon Goldstein [1966] Director; Rory Anthony O'Connor [1959] Director [Irish]; Donagh O'Sullivan [1968] Construction Director [Irish]

GDL (Luton) Developments Limited
Incorporated: 20 January 2016
Net Worth Deficit: £261,245 *Total Assets:* £16,923,480
Registered Office: 3rd Floor, Sterling House, Langston Road, Loughton, Essex, IG10 3TS
Activities: Development of building projects
Parent: Galliard Developments Limited
Officers: Allan William Porter, Secretary; John Cole [1971] Director; Stephen Stuart Solomon Conway [1948] Director; Jonathan Simon Goldstein [1966] Director; Donagh O'Sullivan [1968] Director [Irish]; Sabeeta Thukral [1973] Director

GDL (Millharbour) Limited
Incorporated: 8 October 2014
Net Worth: £41,253,264 *Total Assets:* £162,070,064
Registered Office: 3rd Floor, Sterling House, Langston Road, Loughton, Essex, IG10 3TS
Activities: Development of building projects
Parent: Galliard Developments Limited
Officers: Allan William Porter, Secretary; John Cole [1971] Director; Stephen Stuart Solomon Conway [1948] Director; Jonathan Simon Goldstein [1966] Director; Donagh O'Sullivan [1968] Director [Irish]

GDL (Romford) Limited
Incorporated: 11 June 2016
Net Worth: £349,837 *Total Assets:* £8,516,545
Registered Office: 3rd Floor, Sterling House, Langston Road, Loughton, Essex, IG10 3TS
Activities: Development of building projects
Parent: Galliard Developments Limited
Officers: Allan William Porter, Secretary; John Cole [1971] Director; Stephen Stuart Solomon Conway [1948] Director; Jonathan Simon Goldstein [1966] Director; Donagh O'Sullivan [1968] Director [Irish]

GDL (Slough Developments) Limited
Incorporated: 17 December 2015
Net Worth Deficit: £1,014,053 *Total Assets:* £19,077,416
Registered Office: 3rd Floor, Sterling House, Langston Road, Loughton, Essex, IG10 3TS
Activities: Development of building projects
Parent: Galliard Developments Limited
Officers: Allan William Porter, Secretary; John Cole [1971] Director; Stephen Stuart Solomon Conway [1948] Director; Jonathan Simon Goldstein [1966] Director; Donagh O'Sullivan [1968] Director [Irish]

GDL Holdco Limited
Incorporated: 26 April 2016
Net Worth: £46,763,844 *Total Assets:* £445,380,064
Registered Office: 3rd Floor, Sterling House, Langston Road, Loughton, Essex, IG10 3TS
Activities: Activities of construction holding companies
Shareholders: Galliard (Group) Limited; Todd Boehly
Officers: Alan William Porter, Secretary; John Cole [1971] Director; Stephen Stuart Solomon Conway [1971] Director; Jonathan Simon Goldstein [1966] Director; Donagh O'Sullivan [1968] Director [Irish]

GE Money Home Finance Limited
Incorporated: 4 November 1957
Net Worth: £242,772,912 *Total Assets:* £262,042,608
Registered Office: P O Box 2497, Building 4, Hatters Lane, Watford, Herts, WD18 1YY
Activities: Financial intermediation not elsewhere classified
Parent: GE Money Home Lending Finance Limited
Officers: Samantha Jones [1981] Director; Jonathan Edward Taylor [1980] Director/Risk and Compliance Leader

GE Money Home Lending Holdings Limited
Incorporated: 14 May 2004
Net Worth: £1,547,659,136 *Total Assets:* £1,547,659,136
Registered Office: P O Box 2497, Building 4, Hatters Lane, Watford, Herts, WD18 1YY
Activities: Activities of head offices
Shareholders: GE Capital International 2 Limited; GE Capital International 6 Limited; GE Capital International Holdings Limited
Officers: Paul Kilrain Goudie [1964] Director [American]; Samantha Jones [1981] Director; Jonathan Edward Taylor [1980] Director/Risk and Compliance Leader

GE Money Servicing Limited
Incorporated: 11 October 1999 *Employees:* 95
Net Worth: £265,084,000 *Total Assets:* £359,737,984
Registered Office: P O Box 2497, Building 4, Hatters Lane, Watford, Herts, WD18 1YY
Activities: Other business support service activities n.e.c.
Parent: Igroup8 Limited
Officers: Samantha Jones [1981] Director; Jonathan Edward Taylor [1980] Director/Risk and Compliance Leader

Gearhouse Broadcast Limited
Incorporated: 29 September 1993 *Employees:* 99
Net Worth: £18,893,000 *Total Assets:* £29,481,000
Registered Office: 32-34 Greenhill Crescent, Watford, Herts, WD18 8JU
Activities: Television programming and broadcasting activities
Parent: Gravity Media Group UK Holdings Limited
Officers: Nikki Petken, Secretary; Eamonn MacArten Dowdall [1963] Director; Elliot Saul Kaye [1971] Director; Kevin Moorhouse [1958] Director; John Richard Newton [1963] Director/Chief Executive; Nicholas Peter Newton [1962] Commercial Director

Tony Gee and Partners LLP
Incorporated: 8 December 2005 *Employees:* 281
Net Worth: £12,416,508 *Total Assets:* £16,488,747
Registered Office: Hardy House, 140 High Street, Esher, Surrey, KT10 9QJ
Officers: Nicholas Johan Southward [1966] Member; Lee Paul Barraclough [1983] LLP Member; Timothy Richard Burgess [1980] LLP Member; Christopher James Thomas Burton [1968] LLP Member; Iain Ward Fletcher [1959] LLP Member; Alasdair MacLeod Fowler [1970] LLP Member; Colin Mark Fowler [1981] LLP Member; Dr Ian Richard Hackman [1981] LLP Member; Edward James Helsby [1963] LLP Member; Eng Siang Ho [1973] LLP Member; Michael Ian Lacy [1969] LLP Member; Andrew Paul Marshall [1976] LLP Member; Chun Wai Mo-Yung [1979] LLP Member; Jonathan Timothy Powell [1978] LLP Member; Richard James Prosser [1972] LLP Member; Peter Bill Reeves-Toy [1981] LLP Member; Justin Ryan [1969] LLP Member; Philip Thomas Simmonds [1984] LLP Member; Cyrus Jeremy Toms [1967] LLP Member

Gefco Forwarding UK Ltd.
Incorporated: 3 February 1993 *Employees:* 124
Previous: IJS Global UK Ltd.
Net Worth: £2,166,062 *Total Assets:* £8,187,257
Registered Office: Unit 1 Mereside Park, Shield Road, Ashford, Middlesex, TW15 1BL
Activities: Cargo handling for water transport activities
Parent: IJS Global EMEA Holding BV
Officers: Gary Ford Roche [1963] Director/Logistics

Geieonline Dafconsulting (UK) Ltd.
Incorporated: 8 October 1992
Net Worth Deficit: £29,968 *Total Assets:* £14,194,706
Registered Office: 1st Floor, Midas House, 2 Knoll Rise, Orpington, Kent, BR6 0EL
Activities: Activities of other holding companies n.e.c.
Officers: Claudia Von Fellenberg [1957] Director [Swiss]

General Mills UK Limited
Incorporated: 10 January 2003 *Employees:* 262
Net Worth: £21,640,000 *Total Assets:* £100,212,000
Registered Office: Harman House, 1 George Street, Uxbridge, Middlesex, UB8 1QQ
Activities: Agents involved in the sale of food, beverages and tobacco
Parent: General Mills, Inc
Officers: Jana Gaffaney, Secretary; Jana Marie-Rose Gaffaney [1980] Legal Director [American]; Natasha Laul [1978] Finance Director [American]; Benjamin John Pearman [1972] Vice President, Managing Director

Generations Multi Academy Trust
Incorporated: 1 September 2011 *Employees:* 196
Previous: Goffs School
Net Worth: £46,114,864 *Total Assets:* £49,084,224
Registered Office: Goffs School, Goffs Lane, Cheshunt, Waltham Cross, Herts, EN7 5QW
Activities: General secondary education
Officers: Ian David Denchfield, Secretary; Andrew Bertram Clarke [1956] Director/Queen's Counsel; Lisa Claire Joanna Clowes [1978] Director/Project Manager; Donna Marie Cooper [1974] Director; Kathy Dunnett [1957] Director/Governance Officer; Ian Peter Fish [1971] Director; Giovanna Formoso [1966] Director; Alison Garner [1965] Director/Headteacher; Francoise Grote [1966] Director/Attendance and Parent Support Officer [French]; Jean Margaret Holt [1955] Director; Martin Peter Jackson [1970] Director/HR Manager; John Joseph O'Sullivan [1943] Director/Human Resources Manager; Toyin Oyelade [1978] Director/Teacher [Nigerian]; Patrick James Philpott [1989] Managing Director; Sandra Skinner [1964] Director/Student Support Officer; Vanessa Wright [1972] Director/Vice President

Generics (U.K.) Limited
Incorporated: 29 April 1981 *Employees:* 262
Net Worth: £45,680,000 *Total Assets:* £85,286,000
Registered Office: Station Close, Potters Bar, Herts, EN6 1TL
Activities: Manufacture of basic pharmaceutical products
Parent: Mylan Group BV
Officers: Caroline Rebecca Louise Dixon, Finance Director; Jean-Yves Brault [1967] Director/Area Head Northern Europe [Canadian]; Jose Javier Cotarelo [1972] Director/Commercial Head of Northern & Western Europe [American]; Caroline Rebecca Louise Dixon [1968] Finance Director; Balwant Singh Heer [1959] Director/Global Head - Product Safety & Risk Management

Genesis Pharmaceuticals Limited
Incorporated: 29 September 1999 *Employees:* 10
Net Worth: £3,607,776 *Total Assets:* £12,483,941
Registered Office: 3rd Floor, Scottish Provident House, 76-80 College Road, Harrow, Middlesex, HA1 1BQ
Activities: Wholesale of pharmaceutical goods
Parent: Genethics Europe Limited
Officers: Nilesh Prataprai Mehta, Secretary/Director; Patrick Anthony Kingsford Chubb [1956] Commercial Director; Bharat Prataprai Mehta [1952] Director; Nilesh Prataprai Mehta [1962] Director; Dr David Louis Charles Solomon [1970] Director

Genesius Film Partners LLP
Incorporated: 5 April 2011
Net Worth: £5,281,934 *Total Assets:* £5,300,569
Registered Office: 99 Kenton Road, Harrow, Middlesex, HA3 0AN

Genie Energy UK Ltd
Incorporated: 11 July 2017 *Employees:* 3
Net Worth Deficit: £537,467 *Total Assets:* £5,107,667
Registered Office: c/o Sable International, 13th Floor, One Croydon, 12-16 Addiscombe Road, Croydon, Surrey, CR0 0XT
Activities: Other business support service activities n.e.c.
Parent: Genie Energy Ltd
Officers: Michael Menachem Stein [1984] Director [American]

Gentec Energy PLC
Incorporated: 12 August 1996 *Employees:* 80
Net Worth: £10,036,925 *Total Assets:* £22,644,030
Registered Office: Unit 7 Chancery Gate Close, Stonefield Way, South Ruislip, Middlesex, HA4 0JS
Activities: Agents involved in the sale of machinery, industrial equipment, ships and aircraft
Officers: Navaratnarajah Navendrha, Secretary; Asha Khilnani [1959] Director; Colin Richard Walker [1951] Managing Director

Genuine Solutions Group Limited
Incorporated: 19 December 2013 *Employees:* 100
Net Worth: £2,654,168 *Total Assets:* £7,896,551
Registered Office: Unit 1, Solutions House, 223 Hook Rise South, Surbiton, Surrey, KT6 7LD
Activities: Activities of head offices
Shareholders: Christian McBride; Bhavnesh Majithia
Officers: Bhavnesh Majithia [1973] Director; Christian James McBride [1980] Director

Genuine Solutions International Limited
Incorporated: 7 February 2006
Net Worth: £5,794,002 *Total Assets:* £8,860,812
Registered Office: Solutions House, Unit 1 HQ3, 223 Hook Rise South, Surbiton, Surrey, KT6 7LD
Activities: Activities of head offices
Parent: Genuine Solutions Group Limited
Officers: Bhavnesh Majithia [1973] Director; Christian James McBride [1980] Director

Geodis FF United Kingdom Ltd.
Incorporated: 23 February 1959 *Employees:* 368
Previous: Geodis Wilson UK Limited
Net Worth Deficit: £20,755,000 *Total Assets:* £142,608,992
Registered Office: LHRL, 145 Faggs Road, Feltham, Middlesex, TW14 0LZ
Activities: Freight transport by road
Parent: Geodis International SA
Officers: Gareth Adrian Harries, Secretary; Gareth Adrian Harries [1976] Finance Director; Thomas Walter Kraus [1966] Director [German]; Yann Robert Noyon [1972] Director [French]; Christopher John Packwood [1975] Managing Director

Geomac Limited
Incorporated: 2 April 1991 *Employees:* 5
Net Worth: £2,158,948 *Total Assets:* £5,214,940
Registered Office: 98 Station Road, Sidcup, Kent, DA15 7BY
Activities: Other professional, scientific and technical activities n.e.c.
Shareholders: Richard Edward Fitzharding Melhuish; James Alexander MacLean
Officers: Roger Browning, Secretary; James Alexander MacLean [1969] Director/Plant Contractor; Richard Edward Fitzharding Melhuish [1946] Director

A C Georgiades Ltd
Incorporated: 24 December 1998 *Employees:* 28
Net Worth: £1,133,918 *Total Assets:* £6,591,524
Registered Office: Unit 2, 32-34 Station Close, Potters Bar, Herts, EN6 1TL
Activities: Agents involved in the sale of food, beverages and tobacco
Officers: Bronya Georgiades, Secretary; Anastassis Christos Georgiades [1955] Director/Manager; Bronya Georgiades [1958] Director/Secretary

German School Association Limited
Incorporated: 13 July 1970 *Employees:* 133
Net Worth: £10,301,606 *Total Assets:* £23,434,296
Registered Office: Douglas House, Petersham Road, Petersham, Richmond, Surrey, TW10 7AH
Activities: Pre-primary education
Officers: Matthias Krauss, Secretary; Baethke Beate [1962] Director/Self Employed [German]; Michael Frieser [1970] Director/Banker [Austrian]; Lynda Funke [1964] Director/Senior Administrative Officer [American]; Markus Nitsche [1967] Director/Banker [German]; Colin Thomann [1974] Director/Barrister; Charlotte Von Der Goltz [1969] Director/Housewife [German]; Peter Weiland [1974] Director/Solicitor [German]

Gerrard International Limited
Incorporated: 26 February 1992 *Employees:* 117
Net Worth: £10,928,076 *Total Assets:* £12,418,943
Registered Office: 47 Theobald Street, Borehamwood, Herts, WD6 4RT
Activities: Other business support service activities n.e.c.
Shareholders: Ian Gerrard; Susan Angela Gerrard
Officers: Susan Angela Gerrard, Secretary/Director; Amanda Eileen Cook [1958] Director/National Sales Manager; Ian Gerrard [1944] Director; Lisa Gerrard [1967] Director; Susan Angela Gerrard [1945] Director

Geyfords Limited
Incorporated: 29 January 1971 *Employees:* 9
Net Worth: £13,406,093 *Total Assets:* £14,251,847
Registered Office: 1 Stafford Road, Wallington, Surrey, SM6 9AQ
Activities: Sale of new cars and light motor vehicles
Officers: David James Wisden, Secretary; David Charles Wisden [1980] Director; David James Wisden [1942] Director; Jane Wisden [1966] Director

GGI Holdings Limited
Incorporated: 28 September 2007 *Employees:* 1,388
Net Worth: £81,992,000 *Total Assets:* £133,229,000
Registered Office: Gold Group House, Godstone Road, Whyteleafe, Surrey, CR3 0GG
Activities: Activities of head offices
Major Shareholder: David Gold
Officers: David Gold [1936] Director; Jacqueline Gold [1960] Director; Vanessa Gold [1967] Director

GH Land Developments Limited
Incorporated: 14 March 2006
Net Worth Deficit: £67,649 *Total Assets:* £6,049,448
Registered Office: 11 Whitchurch Parade, Whitchurch Lane, Edgware, Middlesex, HA8 6LR
Activities: Construction of domestic buildings
Major Shareholder: Stuart Jerrold Ifield
Officers: Hilarie Ruth Ifield [1955] Director/Housewife; Stuart Jerrold Ifield [1947] Director/Chartered Accountant; Joe Shack [1940] Director/Property Developer

GH London Ground Handling Services Limited
Incorporated: 23 May 2012 *Employees:* 520
Previous: Azzurra Ground Handling Services Limited
Net Worth: £1,800,057 *Total Assets:* £9,162,851
Registered Office: 249 Cranbrook Road, Ilford, Essex, IG1 4TG
Activities: Service activities incidental to air transportation
Officers: Paolo de Ruggiero [1968] Director of Operations [Italian]; Vittorio Mazza [1968] Director [Italian]; Marco Tierno [1971] Director [Italian]; Paolo Zincone [1961] Director [Italian]

Ghai & Co. Limited
Incorporated: 14 November 2002 *Employees:* 1
Net Worth: £1,543,485 *Total Assets:* £5,137,507
Registered Office: 1 Agincourt Villas, Uxbridge Road, Hillingdon, Middlesex, UB10 0NX
Activities: Development of building projects
Shareholder: Kamal Kumar Ghai
Officers: Kamal Kumar Ghai [1989] Director [Indian]

GHH Estate Limited
Incorporated: 24 February 2016 *Employees:* 2
Net Worth: £5,515,359 *Total Assets:* £5,689,232
Registered Office: Lynwood House, 373-375 Station Road, Harrow, Middlesex, HA1 2AW
Activities: Buying and selling of own real estate
Shareholders: Florence Beatrice Mary Mather; Frederick James George Mather
Officers: Frederick James George Mather [1987] Director

GHL (Crescent Lane) Limited
Incorporated: 9 May 2014
Net Worth Deficit: £887,303 *Total Assets:* £9,001,030
Registered Office: 3rd Floor, Sterling House, Langston Road, Loughton, Essex, IG10 3TS
Activities: Development of building projects
Shareholders: Aria Investments Limited; Galliard Holdings Limited
Officers: Allan William Porter, Secretary; David Edward Conway [1976] Director; Stephen Stuart Solomon Conway [1948] Director; Jonathan Michael Morgan [1978] Director

GHL (Hackney Wick) Limited
Incorporated: 7 February 2014
Net Worth Deficit: £6,952 *Total Assets:* £17,026,062
Registered Office: 3rd Floor, Sterling House, Langston Road, Loughton, Essex, IG10 3TS
Activities: Other business support service activities n.e.c.
Parent: Galliard Holdings Limited
Officers: Allan William Porter, Secretary; David Edward Conway [1976] Director; Stephen Stuart Solomon Conway [1948] Director; Rory Anthony O'Connor [1959] Director [Irish]

GHL (Kilmorie) Limited
Incorporated: 12 July 2017
Net Worth Deficit: £116,026 *Total Assets:* £11,403,809
Registered Office: 3rd Floor, Sterling House, Langston Road, Loughton, Essex, IG10 3TS
Activities: Development of building projects
Parent: Galliard Holdings Limited
Officers: Allan William Porter, Secretary; David Edward Conway [1976] Director; Stephen Stuart Solomon Conway [1948] Director; Donagh O'Sullivan [1968] Construction Director [Irish]

GHL (Summerstown) Limited
Incorporated: 8 November 2017
Net Worth Deficit: £29,119 *Total Assets:* £10,332,428
Registered Office: 3rd Floor, Sterling House, Langston Road, Loughton, Essex, IG10 3TS
Activities: Development of building projects
Parent: Galliard Holdings Limited
Officers: Allan William Porter, Secretary; Stephen Stuart Solomon Conway [1948] Director; Donagh O'Sullivan [1968] Construction Director [Irish]

Gibbs & Ball Limited
Incorporated: 1 November 1961 *Employees:* 12
Net Worth: £5,817,574 *Total Assets:* £7,884,859
Registered Office: St Margarets Farm, St Margarets Road, Dartford, Kent, DA4 9LB
Activities: Operation of warehousing and storage facilities for land transport activities
Parent: Favourquick Ltd
Officers: Yvonne Suzette Maria Hawkins Houiller, Company Secretary; Alison Eleanor Hawkins [1958] Director; Derek George Hawkins [1955] Director; Lisa Jane Alexandra Hawkins [1969] Director; Yvonne Suzette Maria Hawkins Houiller [1962] Director; Sharon Claretta Angela Kirby [1957] Director; Fiona Kathryn Louise Taylor [1964] Director

Robert Gibbs (Contracting) Company Limited
Incorporated: 9 December 1986 *Employees:* 61
Net Worth: £10,370,444 *Total Assets:* £13,294,702
Registered Office: Bridge Works, Normandy Way, off Pindar Road, Hoddesdon, Herts, EN11 0EW
Activities: Wholesale of waste and scrap
Shareholders: Barry Albert Elvidge; Howard Victor Jones
Officers: Barry Albert Elvidge, Secretary; Howard Victor Jones, Secretary/Scrap Metal Merchant; David Maskell [1966] Director

Gibbs Gillespie Sales Limited
Incorporated: 22 November 2013 *Employees:* 133
Net Worth: £1,084,217 *Total Assets:* £5,138,329
Registered Office: Batchworth House, Batchworth Place, Church Street, Rickmansworth, Herts, WD3 1JE
Activities: Real estate agencies
Shareholders: James Graham Gibbs; Paul James Gillespie
Officers: James Graham Gibbs [1955] Director/Estate Agent; Ronald William Gibbs [1957] Director; Paul James Gillespie [1969] Director/Estate Agent

Gibson Bidco Limited
Incorporated: 8 April 2016 *Employees:* 2
Net Worth: £9,807,000 *Total Assets:* £10,194,000
Registered Office: Regal House, Royal Crescent, Ilford, Essex, IG2 7JY
Activities: Activities of other holding companies n.e.c.
Parent: Gibson Topco Limited
Officers: Harnoop Singh Atkar [1986] Director; Daren Dalmedo [1978] Director

Thomas Gibson Fine Art Limited
Incorporated: 26 August 1970 *Employees:* 5
Net Worth: £5,626,908 *Total Assets:* £9,049,142
Registered Office: 19 Coombehurst Close, Hadley Wood, Herts, EN4 0JU
Activities: Retail sale in commercial art galleries
Major Shareholder: Benjamin Hugh George Gibson
Officers: Benjamin Hugh George Gibson [1973] Director

Gibson Propco Limited
Incorporated: 15 April 2016 *Employees:* 2
Net Worth: £8,928,000 *Total Assets:* £24,043,000
Registered Office: Regal House, Royal Crescent, Ilford, Essex, IG2 7JY
Activities: Activities of other holding companies n.e.c.
Parent: Gibson Bidco Limited
Officers: Harnoop Singh Atkar [1986] Director; Daren Dalmedo [1978] Director

Giesecke+Devrient Mobile Security GB Ltd
Incorporated: 8 July 1997 *Employees:* 146
Previous: Giesecke & Devrient GB Ltd
Net Worth: £3,029,337 *Total Assets:* £7,218,592
Registered Office: Globe House, Unit 1 Westlinks, Alperton Lane, Wembley, Middlesex, HA0 1ER
Activities: Other manufacturing n.e.c.
Officers: Claus Wagner, Secretary; Carsten Ahrens [1963] Director [German]; Christian Bellsolell Rosich [1972] Director [Spanish]; Axel Lange [1963] Managing Director [German]

Giga Communications Limited
Incorporated: 9 March 2004 *Employees:* 32
Net Worth: £3,229,169 *Total Assets:* £7,044,715
Registered Office: 417 Bridport Road, Greenford, Middlesex, UB6 8UA
Activities: Satellite telecommunications activities
Parent: Ultra Electronics Holdings PLC
Officers: Anant Prakash, Secretary; Simon Charles Conrad Pryce [1961] Director; Carlos Santiago [1955] Director [American]; Amitabh Sharma [1967] Finance Director

Giggs Hill Green Homes Limited
Incorporated: 5 December 2008
Net Worth Deficit: £340,802 *Total Assets:* £11,479,945
Registered Office: Coveham House, Downside Bridge Road, Cobham, Surrey, KT11 3EP
Activities: Construction of domestic buildings
Shareholders: Barbara Taylor; Robert Patrick Taylor
Officers: Barbara Taylor [1951] Director/Solicitor [Polish]; Robert Patrick Taylor [1956] Director/Surveyor

Gilead Sciences Europe Ltd.
Incorporated: 15 July 2005 *Employees:* 287
Net Worth: £79,709,000 *Total Assets:* £169,275,008
Registered Office: 2 Roundwood Avenue, Stockley Park, Uxbridge, Middlesex, UB11 1AF
Activities: Other business support service activities n.e.c.
Parent: Gilead Sciences, Inc.
Officers: Johanna Henry, Secretary; Rudolf Ertl [1960] Director [German]; Brett Pletcher [1968] Director [American]; Robin Washington [1962] Director [American]

W W Giles (Smithfield) Limited
Incorporated: 8 August 2006 *Employees:* 17
Net Worth: £1,183,779 *Total Assets:* £7,769,456
Registered Office: 1 Warner House, Harrovian Business Village, Bessborough Road, Harrow, Middlesex, HA1 3EX
Activities: Wholesale of meat and meat products
Shareholder: Victor William Harmer
Officers: Victor William Harmer, Secretary; Gillian Rosemary Harmer [1942] Director; Guy Aston William Harmer [1976] Director; Victor William Harmer [1947] Director; Laura Margaret Turral [1963] Director/Sales Manager

Giles Homes Limited
Incorporated: 19 November 2008 *Employees:* 9
Net Worth: £114,964 *Total Assets:* £6,523,706
Registered Office: 148 Queens Road, Watford, Herts, WD17 2NX
Activities: Other business support service activities n.e.c.
Shareholders: Andrew Richard Taylor; Giles William Murphy; Julie Angela Kelley
Officers: Julie Angela Kelley, Secretary; Ian John Berney [1968] Director; Julie Angela Kelley [1974] Director; Giles William Murphy [1965] Director/Contracts Manager; Andrew Richard Taylor [1972] Director

Gillette Industries Limited
Incorporated: 21 December 1977 *Employees:* 3
Net Worth: £10,436,000 *Total Assets:* £18,051,000
Registered Office: The Heights, Brooklands, Weybridge, Surrey, KT13 0XP
Activities: Activities of head offices
Parent: Procter & Gamble Limited
Officers: Anthony Joseph Appleton, Secretary; Anthony Joseph Appleton [1962] Director/Solicitor; Alexander George Buckthorp [1973] Finance Director; Vijay Indroo Sitlani [1975] Finance Director [Singaporean]

Gillette U.K. Limited
Incorporated: 17 March 1931 *Employees:* 168
Net Worth: £29,559,000 *Total Assets:* £63,434,000
Registered Office: The Heights, Brooklands, Weybridge, Surrey, KT13 0XP
Activities: Manufacture of perfumes and toilet preparations
Parent: Gilette Industries Limited
Officers: Anthony Joseph Appleton, Secretary; Anthony Joseph Appleton [1962] Director/Solicitor; Alexander George Buckthorp [1973] Finance Director; Vijay Indroo Sitlani [1975] Finance Director [Singaporean]; Husnu Yilmaz [1971] Director/Plant Manager [Turkish]; Christopher John Young [1974] HR Director

T Gilmartin Holdings Limited
Incorporated: 15 September 2016 *Employees:* 144
Net Worth: £4,956,561 *Total Assets:* £9,800,848
Registered Office: c/o Hillier Hopkins LLP, First Floor, Radius House, 51 Clarendon Road, Watford, Herts, WD17 1HP
Activities: Activities of other holding companies n.e.c.
Major Shareholder: Terence Martin Gilmartin
Officers: Terence Martin Gilmartin [1965] Director

Gilray Plant Limited
Incorporated: 12 April 1973 *Employees:* 17
Net Worth: £3,118,232 *Total Assets:* £6,139,814
Registered Office: Cedar Depot, Church Manorway, Erith, Kent, DA8 1DE
Activities: Wholesale of wood, construction materials and sanitary equipment
Major Shareholder: Ralph Wilson
Officers: Sarah Generaldine Wilson, Secretary; Ralph Wilson [1959] Director; Sarah Generaldine Wilson [1966] Director/Office Manager

Gima (UK) Limited
Incorporated: 25 September 1998 *Employees:* 166
Net Worth: £2,375,690 *Total Assets:* £8,611,524
Registered Office: Unit 4 Gima House, Rippleside Commercial Estate, A13 Ripple Road, off Renwick Road, Barking, Essex, IG11 0RH
Activities: Non-specialised wholesale of food, beverages and tobacco
Shareholders: Erol Ozkan; Vebhi Keles
Officers: Erol Ozkan, Secretary; Vehbi Keles [1971] Director/Manager

Girls' Learning Trust
Incorporated: 10 May 2011 *Employees:* 400
Previous: Nonsuch and Wallington Education Trust
Net Worth: £65,023,000 *Total Assets:* £73,564,000
Registered Office: Nonsuch High School for Girls, Ewell Road, Cheam, Sutton, Surrey, SM3 8AB
Activities: General secondary education
Officers: Caroline Helen Latham, Secretary; Jane Victoria Burton [1965] Director/Executive Headteacher; Alexander Philip Clark [1966] Director/Executive Headteacher; Sandra Anne Gillett [1951] Director/Independent HR Consultant; Marie Josephine Grant [1951] Director/Self Employed [Irish]; Antony Robert Hyams-Parish [1965] Director/Solicitor; Malcolm Bruce Munro [1965] Director/Senior Project Manager; Nigel Sandon Pepper [1970] Director/Financial Consultant; Philip Julian Taylor [1965] Director/Sales Manager

Gita Properties Limited
Incorporated: 5 January 1968 *Employees:* 7
Net Worth: £24,510,924 *Total Assets:* £28,789,296
Registered Office: Treviot House, 186-192 High Road, Ilford, Essex, IG1 1LR
Activities: Buying and selling of own real estate
Shareholders: Joseph Henri Szlezinger; Kathrin Jane Szlezinger
Officers: Kathrine Jane Szlezinger, Secretary; Jason Szlezinger [1970] Director; Joseph Henri Szlezinger [1935] Managing Director; Kathrine Jane Szlezinger [1944] Director/Secretary

Gittisham Care Limited
Incorporated: 24 September 1999 *Employees:* 41
Net Worth: £5,900,784 *Total Assets:* £7,082,092
Registered Office: 1st Floor, Brunswick House, Regent Park, 297-299 Kingston Road, Leatherhead, Surrey, KT22 7LU
Activities: Other human health activities
Parent: RV Wessex Limited
Officers: Sally Irene Rees, Secretary; Sarah Denise Burgess [1971] Director; Neil Donaldson [1966] Director/Accountant; Andrew George Esmond Ovey [1971] Director/Investment Manager

GL Assessment Limited
Incorporated: 31 October 1980 *Employees:* 100
Net Worth: £72,068,000 *Total Assets:* £138,482,000
Registered Office: 1st Floor, Vantage London, Great West Road, Brentford, Middlesex, TW8 9AG
Activities: Other publishing activities
Parent: GL Education Group Limited
Officers: Robert Dargue [1975] Director/Chartered Accountant; Gregor Stanley Watson [1965] Director

GL Education (No.3) Limited
Incorporated: 19 December 2016 *Employees:* 2
Net Worth Deficit: £196,000 *Total Assets:* £10,929,000
Registered Office: 1st Floor, Vantage London, Great West Road, Brentford, Middlesex, TW8 9AG
Activities: Activities of head offices
Parent: GL Education Group Limited
Officers: Robert Dargue [1975] Director/Chartered Accountant; Gregor Stanley Watson [1965] Director

GL Education Group Limited
Incorporated: 19 April 1991 *Employees:* 77
Net Worth Deficit: £932,000 *Total Assets:* £189,812,000
Registered Office: 1st Floor, Vantage London, Great West Road, Brentford, Middlesex, TW8 9AG
Activities: Other publishing activities
Parent: Assessments Bidco Limited
Officers: Robert Dargue [1975] Director/Chartered Accountant; Gregor Stanley Watson [1965] Director

Gladstone Court Developments Limited
Incorporated: 24 April 2012
Net Worth Deficit: £28,421,760 *Total Assets:* £48,541,488
Registered Office: 3rd Floor, Sterling House, Langston Road, Loughton, Essex, IG10 3TS
Activities: Other business support service activities n.e.c.
Parent: Gladstone Holdings Limited
Officers: Allan William Porter, Secretary; David Edward Conway [1976] Director; Stephen Stuart Solomon Conway [1948] Director; Donagh O'Sullivan [1968] Construction Director [Irish]

Glansevern Properties Limited
Incorporated: 8 April 1964 *Employees:* 7
Net Worth: £3,893,627 *Total Assets:* £5,194,199
Registered Office: London & Thames House, 70-72 Croydon Road, Caterham, Surrey, CR3 6QD
Activities: Development of building projects
Parent: London & Thames Counties Securities Ltd
Officers: Dasa Sumberova, Secretary; David Peter Goodwin [1958] Director/Solicitor; Raymond Martin Pothecary [1948] Director/Property Manager & Consultant; Dasa Sumberova [1974] Finance Director [Czech]

Glasgow Learning Quarter (Holdings) Limited
Incorporated: 21 February 2013
Net Worth Deficit: £20,316,298 *Total Assets:* £198,024,576
Registered Office: 8 White Oak Square, London Road, Swanley, Kent, BR8 7AG
Activities: Activities of head offices
Shareholders: FES Resources Limited; Robert McAlpine Capital Ventures Limited
Officers: Dylan Fletcher [1971] Director; David Honeyman [1967] Director/Accountant; David Niall Smith [1971] Director; Robert John William Wotherspoon [1967] Director/Accountant

Glasgow Learning Quarter Limited
Incorporated: 21 February 2013
Net Worth Deficit: £20,316,296 *Total Assets:* £200,922,960
Registered Office: 8 White Oak Square, London Road, Swanley, Kent, BR8 7AG
Activities: Other business support service activities n.e.c.
Parent: Glasgow Learning Quarter (Holdings) Limited
Officers: Dylan Fletcher [1971] Director; David Honeyman [1967] Director/Accountant; David MacDonald [1961] National Programme Director; David Niall Smith [1971] Director; Robert John William Wotherspoon [1967] Director/Accountant

Glastry Advisory Partners Limited
Incorporated: 20 November 2012 *Employees:* 1
Net Worth: £16,128,881 *Total Assets:* £16,196,895
Registered Office: 5 Elstree Gate, Elstree Way, Borehamwood, Herts, WD6 1JD
Activities: Management consultancy activities other than financial management
Major Shareholder: Joyce Anne Smyth
Officers: Joyce Anne Smyth [1957] Director/Solicitor

Glaxo Group Limited
Incorporated: 14 October 1935
Net Worth: £11,255,962,624 *Total Assets:* £11,776,435,200
Registered Office: 980 Great West Road, Brentford, Middlesex, TW8 9GS
Activities: Activities of head offices
Parent: GlaxoSmithKline Finance PLC
Officers: Victoria Anne Whyte, Secretary; Simon Paul Dingemans [1963] Director; Adam Walker [1967] Director

Glaxo Operations UK Limited
Incorporated: 1 January 1962 *Employees:* 4,160
Net Worth: £858,684,032 *Total Assets:* £1,324,759,040
Registered Office: 980 Great West Road, Brentford, Middlesex, TW8 9GS
Activities: Manufacture of pharmaceutical preparations
Parent: Glaxo Group Limited
Officers: Victoria Anne Whyte, Secretary; Alan George Burns [1975] Director; Freek Jongen [1980] Director [Dutch]; Regis Jean-Pierre Simard [1965] Director/Head of Supply Chain [French]

Glaxo Wellcome UK Limited
Incorporated: 25 March 1950
Net Worth: £69,164,000 *Total Assets:* £71,871,000
Registered Office: 980 Great West Road, Brentford, Middlesex, TW8 9GS
Activities: Wholesale of pharmaceutical goods
Parent: Glaxo Group Limited
Officers: Victoria Anne Whyte, Secretary; James Borger [1963] Director/VP, Group Financial Planning and Analysis [American]; Alan George Burns [1975] Director

Glaxochem (UK) Unlimited
Incorporated: 4 October 2001
Net Worth: £2,418,490,880 *Total Assets:* £2,420,489,984
Registered Office: 980 Great West Road, Brentford, Middlesex, TW8 9GS
Activities: Financial intermediation not elsewhere classified
Shareholders: GlaxoSmithKline SL LP; Setfirst Limited
Officers: Simon Paul Dingemans [1963] Director

GlaxoSmithKline Capital PLC
Incorporated: 16 May 1988
Net Worth: £37,635,000 *Total Assets:* £10,646,939,648
Registered Office: 980 Great West Road, Brentford, Middlesex, TW8 9GS
Activities: Financial intermediation not elsewhere classified
Officers: Victoria Anne Whyte, Secretary; Simon Paul Dingemans [1963] Director

GlaxoSmithKline Caribbean Limited
Incorporated: 28 July 1953 *Employees:* 49
Net Worth: £34,652,000 *Total Assets:* £37,655,000
Registered Office: 980 Great West Road, Brentford, Middlesex, TW8 9GS
Activities: Wholesale of pharmaceutical goods
Parent: SmithKline Beecham Limited
Officers: Adam Walker [1967] Director

GlaxoSmithKline Consumer Healthcare (Overseas) Limited
Incorporated: 26 September 2014 *Employees:* 53
Net Worth: £1,200,146,048 *Total Assets:* £1,856,691,968
Registered Office: 980 Great West Road, Brentford, Middlesex, TW8 9GS
Activities: Activities of other holding companies n.e.c.
Parent: GlaxoSmithKline Consumer Healthcare Holdings Limited
Officers: Richard Green [1974] Director/Head of Reporting; Tobias Hestler [1972] Director [German/Swiss]

GlaxoSmithKline Consumer Healthcare (UK) (No.1) Limited
Incorporated: 13 March 1963
Previous: Novartis Consumer Health UK Limited
Net Worth: £9,921,000 *Total Assets:* £9,941,000
Registered Office: 980 Great West Road, Brentford, Middlesex, TW8 9GS
Activities: Non-trading company
Parent: GlaxoSmithKline Consumer Healthcare Holdings Limited
Officers: Richard Green [1974] Director; Terence O'Neill [1965] Finance Director

GlaxoSmithKline Consumer Healthcare (UK) IP Limited
Incorporated: 26 September 2014
Net Worth: £260,424,000 *Total Assets:* £381,208,000
Registered Office: 980 Great West Road, Brentford, Middlesex, TW8 9GS
Activities: Activities of other holding companies n.e.c.
Parent: GlaxoSmithKline Consumer Healthcare Holdings Limited
Officers: Richard Green [1974] Director; Tobias Hestler [1972] Director [German/Swiss]

GlaxoSmithKline Consumer Healthcare (UK) Trading Limited
Incorporated: 26 September 2014 *Employees:* 1,379
Net Worth: £201,250,000 *Total Assets:* £685,875,968
Registered Office: 980 Great West Road, Brentford, Middlesex, TW8 9GS
Activities: Manufacture of pharmaceutical preparations
Parent: GlaxoSmithKline Consumer Healthcare Holdings Limited
Officers: Richard Green [1974] Director; Aidan Lynch [1964] Managing Director - Trading Partners [Irish]; Terence O'Neill [1965] Finance Director; Eugene Prokopchuk [1981] Finance Director [Ukrainian]

GlaxoSmithKline Consumer Healthcare Finance Limited
Incorporated: 6 November 2014
Net Worth: £231,710,000 *Total Assets:* £1,798,552,960
Registered Office: 980 Great West Road, Brentford, Middlesex, TW8 9GS
Activities: Financial intermediation not elsewhere classified
Parent: GlaxoSmithKline Consumer Healthcare Holdings Limited
Officers: Richard Green [1974] Director; Tobias Hestler [1972] Director [German/Swiss]

GlaxoSmithKline Consumer Healthcare Finance No. 2 Limited
Incorporated: 4 August 2016
Net Worth: £47,269,888 *Total Assets:* £62,455,720
Registered Office: 980 Great West Road, Brentford, Middlesex, TW8 9GS
Activities: Financial intermediation not elsewhere classified
Parent: GlaxoSmithKline Consumer Healthcare (Overseas) Limited
Officers: Richard Green [1974] Director; Tobias Hestler [1972] Director [German/Swiss]

GlaxoSmithKline Consumer Healthcare Holdings Limited
Incorporated: 15 April 2014
Net Worth: £20,770,000,896 *Total Assets:* £20,771,000,320
Registered Office: 980 Great West Road, Brentford, Middlesex, TW8 9GS
Activities: Activities of head offices
Parent: Setfirst Limited
Officers: Simon Paul Dingemans [1963] Director; Tobias Hestler [1972] Director/Chief Financial Officer [German/Swiss]; Brian McNamara [1966] Director/Head of Americas and Europe [American]; David Simon Redfern [1966] Director

GlaxoSmithKline Consumer Trading Services Limited
Incorporated: 21 June 2012
Net Worth: £19,491,000 *Total Assets:* £781,051,008
Registered Office: 980 Great West Road, Brentford, Middlesex, TW8 9GS
Activities: Wholesale of pharmaceutical goods
Parent: GlaxoSmithKline Consumer Healthcare Holdings Limited
Officers: Victoria Anne Whyte, Secretary; Richard Green [1974] Director; Tobias Hestler [1972] Director [German/Swiss]; Neil O'Hara [1973] Director

GlaxoSmithKline Export Limited
Incorporated: 18 October 1989 *Employees:* 1,214
Net Worth: £94,567,000 *Total Assets:* £447,628,000
Registered Office: 980 Great West Road, Brentford, Middlesex, TW8 9GS
Activities: Wholesale of pharmaceutical goods
Parent: Glaxo Group Limited
Officers: Victoria Anne Whyte, Secretary; Dylan Jackson [1972] Director/General Manager; Adam Walker [1967] Director; Jane Mary Whitmore [1968] Finance Director

GlaxoSmithKline Finance PLC
Incorporated: 2 October 1929
Net Worth: £61,286,526,976 *Total Assets:* £135,010,271,232
Registered Office: 980 Great West Road, Brentford, Middlesex, TW8 9GS
Activities: Financial intermediation not elsewhere classified
Parent: GlaxoSmithKline Holdings Limited
Officers: Victoria Anne Whyte, Secretary; Simon Paul Dingemans [1963] Director; Adam Walker [1967] Director

GlaxoSmithKline Holdings (Ireland) Limited
Incorporated: 5 August 2014
Net Worth: £2,183,034,880 *Total Assets:* £2,196,562,944
Registered Office: 980 Great West Road, Brentford, Middlesex, TW8 9GS
Activities: Financial management
Parent: Setfirst Limited
Officers: Alan George Burns [1975] Director; Adam Walker [1967] Director

GlaxoSmithKline Holdings (One) Limited
Incorporated: 7 June 2001
Net Worth: £55,996,000 *Total Assets:* £202,339,008
Registered Office: 980 Great West Road, Brentford, Middlesex, TW8 9GS
Activities: Activities of head offices
Parent: GlaxoSmithKline PLC
Officers: Victoria Anne Whyte, Secretary; Adam Walker [1967] Director

GlaxoSmithKline Holdings Limited
Incorporated: 7 December 2005
Net Worth: £15,292,999,680 *Total Assets:* £60,131,000,320
Registered Office: 980 Great West Road, Brentford, Middlesex, TW8 9GS
Activities: Activities of head offices
Parent: GlaxoSmithKline PLC
Officers: Simon Paul Dingemans [1963] Director

GlaxoSmithKline IHC Limited
Incorporated: 18 May 2010
Net Worth: £174,892,000 *Total Assets:* £4,119,490,048
Registered Office: 980 Great West Road, Brentford, Middlesex, TW8 9GS
Activities: Financial intermediation not elsewhere classified
Parent: GlaxoSmithKline Finance PLC
Officers: Victoria Anne Whyte, Secretary; James Borger [1963] Director/VP, Group Financial Planning and Analysis [American]; Alan George Burns [1975] Director; Adam Walker [1967] Director

GlaxoSmithKline Intellectual Property (No.2) Limited
Incorporated: 6 November 2012
Net Worth: £1,487,657,984 *Total Assets:* £1,679,232,000
Registered Office: 980 Great West Road, Brentford, Middlesex, TW8 9GS
Activities: Activities of other holding companies n.e.c.
Parent: GlaxoSmithKline Intellectual Property Holdings Limited
Officers: Jerome Charles Maurice Andries [1969] Director [French]; Simon Paul Dingemans [1963] Director; Kate Sophie Priestman [1973] Director/Strategy Professional; Adam Walker [1967] Director/Accountant

GlaxoSmithKline Intellectual Property Development Limited
Incorporated: 6 November 2012
Net Worth Deficit: £8,606,166,016 *Total Assets:* £1,572,909,056
Registered Office: 980 Great West Road, Brentford, Middlesex, TW8 9GS
Activities: Activities of other holding companies n.e.c.
Parent: GlaxoSmithKline Intellectual Property Mangement Limited
Officers: Jerome Charles Maurice Andries [1969] Director [French]; Simon Paul Dingemans [1963] Director; Kate Sophie Priestman [1973] Director/Strategy Professional; Adam Walker [1967] Director/Accountant

GlaxoSmithKline Intellectual Property Holdings Limited
Incorporated: 6 November 2012
Net Worth: £4,383,954,944 *Total Assets:* £4,385,067,008
Registered Office: 980 Great West Road, Brentford, Middlesex, TW8 9GS
Activities: Activities of other holding companies n.e.c.
Shareholders: Glaxo Group Limited; GlaxoSmithKline Finance PLC
Officers: Jerome Charles Maurice Andries [1969] Director [French]; Simon Paul Dingemans [1963] Director; Kate Sophie Priestman [1973] Director/Strategy Professional; Adam Walker [1967] Director/Accountant

GlaxoSmithKline Intellectual Property Limited
Incorporated: 6 November 2012
Net Worth: £6,002,445,824 *Total Assets:* £6,631,912,960
Registered Office: 980 Great West Road, Brentford, Middlesex, TW8 9GS
Activities: Activities of other holding companies n.e.c.
Parent: Glaxo Group Limited
Officers: Jerome Charles Maurice Andries [1969] Director [French]; Simon Paul Dingemans [1963] Director; Kate Sophie Priestman [1973] Director/Strategy Professional; Adam Walker [1967] Director/Accountant

GlaxoSmithKline Intellectual Property Management Limited
Incorporated: 12 August 2011
Net Worth: £7,026,833,920 *Total Assets:* £7,432,076,800
Registered Office: 980 Great West Road, Brentford, Middlesex, TW8 9GS
Activities: Other business support service activities n.e.c.
Parent: GlaxoSmithKline Intellectual Property Holdings Limited
Officers: Jerome Charles Maurice Andries [1969] Director [French]; Simon Paul Dingemans [1963] Director/Chief Financial Officer; Kate Sophie Priestman [1973] Director/Strategy Professional; Adam Walker [1967] Director/Accountant (Senior Vice President - Finance)

GlaxoSmithKline International Limited
Incorporated: 21 September 1988
Net Worth: £1,419,955,968 *Total Assets:* £1,866,791,040
Registered Office: 980 Great West Road, Brentford, Middlesex, TW8 9GS
Activities: Other business support service activities n.e.c.
Parent: Setfirst Limited
Officers: James Borger [1963] Director/VP, Group Financial Planning and Analysis [American]; Alan George Burns [1975] Director

GlaxoSmithKline Investment Holdings Limited
Incorporated: 27 November 2009
Net Worth: £6,467,611,136 *Total Assets:* £6,483,027,968
Registered Office: 980 Great West Road, Brentford, Middlesex, TW8 9GS
Activities: Activities of head offices
Parent: Setfirst
Officers: Adam Walker [1967] Director

GlaxoSmithKline Investment Services Limited
Incorporated: 21 July 2009
Net Worth: £552,454,016 *Total Assets:* £570,209,984
Registered Office: 980 Great West Road, Brentford, Middlesex, TW8 9GS
Activities: Other business support service activities n.e.c.
Parent: Setfirst Limited
Officers: Adam Walker [1967] Director

GlaxoSmithKline Mercury Limited
Incorporated: 28 August 2009
Net Worth: £4,642,886,144 *Total Assets:* £4,645,296,128
Registered Office: 980 Great West Road, Brentford, Middlesex, TW8 9GS
Activities: Activities of head offices
Parent: GlaxoSmithKline PLC
Officers: Victoria Anne Whyte, Secretary; James Borger [1963] Director/VP, Group Financial Planning and Analysis [American]; Alan George Burns [1975] Director

GlaxoSmithKline PLC
Incorporated: 6 December 1999 *Employees:* 99,349
Net Worth Deficit: £68,000,000 *Total Assets:* £56,381,001,728
Registered Office: 980 Great West Road, Brentford, Middlesex, TW8 9GS
Activities: Activities of head offices
Officers: Victoria Anne Whyte, Secretary; Manvinder Singh Banga [1954] Director [Indian]; Dr Hal Barron [1962] Director [American]; Dr Vivienne Cox [1959] Director/Businesswoman; Simon Paul Dingemans [1963] Director/Chief Financial Officer; Lynn Laverty Elsenhans [1956] Director [American]; Dr Laurie Glimcher [1951] Director [American]; Dr Jesse Goodman [1951] Director/Physician/Scientist [American]; Sir Philip Roy Hampton [1953] Director; Judith Carol Lewent [1949] Director [American]; Iain James MacKay [1961] Director; Urs Rohner [1959] Director [Swiss]; Emma Natasha Walmsley [1969] Director

GlaxoSmithKline Research & Development Limited
Incorporated: 22 January 1965 *Employees:* 3,831
Net Worth: £1,145,257,984 *Total Assets:* £1,721,917,952
Registered Office: 980 Great West Road, Brentford, Middlesex, TW8 9GS
Activities: Other research and experimental development on natural sciences and engineering
Parent: Glaxo Group Limited
Officers: Victoria Whyte, Secretary; David George Allen [1959] Director/SVP Respiratory Therapy Area; Jerome Andries [1969] Director [French]

GlaxoSmithKline Services Unlimited
Incorporated: 23 March 1972 *Employees:* 14,424
Net Worth: £1,592,000,000 *Total Assets:* £2,630,000,128
Registered Office: 980 Great West Road, Brentford, Middlesex, TW8 9GS
Activities: Activities of head offices
Parent: GlaxoSmithKline PLC
Officers: Victoria Anne Whyte, Secretary; Simon Paul Dingemans [1963] Director

GlaxoSmithKline UK Limited
Incorporated: 24 October 2001 *Employees:* 499
Net Worth: £617,320,000 *Total Assets:* £723,723,008
Registered Office: 980 Great West Road, Brentford, Middlesex, TW8 9GS
Activities: Wholesale of pharmaceutical goods
Parent: Glaxo Group Limited
Officers: Simon Paul Dingemans [1963] Director; Ville Kullervo Maukonen [1978] Finance Director [Finnish]

Glenageary Estates LLP
Incorporated: 26 February 2008
Net Worth: £11,097,579 *Total Assets:* £11,102,064
Registered Office: 4 Elstree Gate, Elstree Way, Borehamwood, Herts, WD6 1JD

Glenchamber Wind Energy Limited
Incorporated: 8 April 2014
Net Worth Deficit: £10,402,000 *Total Assets:* £61,071,000
Registered Office: Beaufort Court, Egg Farm Lane, Kings Langley, Herts, WD4 8LR
Activities: Production of electricity
Parent: Boreas Energy Limited
Officers: Dominic James Heath, Secretary; Peter Edward Dias [1981] Director; Christopher Peter Gaydon [1978] Director [Hungarian]; Paul Stephen Latham [1956] Director; Thomas James Rosser [1985] Director

Glendola Leisure (Holdings) Limited
Incorporated: 16 November 2001 *Employees:* 601
Net Worth: £24,574,000 *Total Assets:* £53,577,000
Registered Office: 364 High Street, Harlington, Heathrow, Hayes, Middlesex, UB3 5LF
Activities: Activities of head offices
Major Shareholder: Peter Nicholas Salussolia
Officers: Graeme John Ramsay, Secretary; Graeme John Ramsay [1967] Director/Chartered Accountant; Alexander Salussolia [1968] Director; Christina Salussolia [1950] Director/Executive Secretary; Peter Nicholas Salussolia [1968] Director

Glengall Limited
Incorporated: 1 November 2002
Net Worth: £2,828,118 *Total Assets:* £6,598,885
Registered Office: 61 Twickenham Road, Isleworth, Middlesex, TW7 6AR
Activities: Freight transport by road
Shareholder: Amrik Singh Padda
Officers: Amrik Singh Padda, Secretary/Self Employed; Amrik Padda [1943] Director/Self Employed; Harbans Padda [1943] Director [Indian]

Glenmark Pharmaceuticals Europe Limited
Incorporated: 10 February 2004 *Employees:* 83
Net Worth: £12,932,667 *Total Assets:* £50,697,828
Registered Office: Laxmi House, 2B Draycott Avenue, Kenton, Harrow, Middlesex, HA3 0BU
Activities: Wholesale of pharmaceutical goods
Shareholders: Blanche Saldanha; Cherylann Pinto; Glenn Saldanha
Officers: Fiona Hill, Secretary; Oliver Henry Bourne [1980] Director; Achin Gupta [1976] Director [Indian]

GLF Schools
Incorporated: 4 March 2011 *Employees:* 217
Previous: The Glyn Learning Foundation
Net Worth: £166,894,000 *Total Assets:* £188,108,000
Registered Office: Claygate House, Littleworth Road, Esher, Surrey, KT10 9PN
Activities: Primary education
Officers: Sarah Lynagh, Secretary; Jacqueline Elizabeth Adams [1963] Director/Human Resources Manager; Adam Braithwaite [1975] Executive Director; Martin Joseph Burke [1952] Director/Retired; Paul Duncan Carpenter [1958] Director/Solicitor; Jonathan Michael Chaloner [1969] Director/Headteacher; Colin David Charles [1959] Director/Accountant; Bruce Alan Ray Ely-Johnston [1975] Financial Director; Helen Elizabeth Mannion [1980] Director/Head of Business Intelligence; Lynne Hazel O'Reilly [1962] Director/Retired

Global Business Trade LLP
Incorporated: 14 June 2011
Net Worth: £3,725,168 *Total Assets:* £5,272,739
Registered Office: Suite 1, The Studio, St Nicholas Close, Elstree, Herts, WD6 3EW

Global Draw Limited
Incorporated: 12 May 1998 *Employees:* 343
Net Worth: £52,396,000 *Total Assets:* £208,888,000
Registered Office: SG House, 1 Dukes Green Avenue, Feltham, Middlesex, TW14 0LR
Activities: Ready-made interactive leisure and entertainment software development
Parent: Scientific Games International Holdings Limited
Officers: Phillip Douglas Horne [1961] Managing Director; Paul Phillips [1978] Finance Director

The Global Logistics Group Ltd
Incorporated: 15 July 2015 *Employees:* 141
Net Worth: £5,641,394 *Total Assets:* £10,368,169
Registered Office: 1 Saxon Way, Harmondsworth, West Drayton, Middlesex, UB7 0LW
Activities: Activities of distribution holding companies
Major Shareholder: Stuart David Allen
Officers: Gary James Wilson, Secretary; Stuart David Allen [1969] Director; Seth Zachary Profit [1978] Director [American]; Paul David Wakefield [1972] Director; Gary James Wilson [1962] Director/Accountant

Global Metcorp Limited
Incorporated: 30 August 2001 *Employees:* 17
Net Worth: £10,149,544 *Total Assets:* £41,590,520
Registered Office: Grove House, 55 Lowlands Road, Harrow on the Hill, Middlesex, HA1 3AW
Activities: Wholesale of waste and scrap
Parent: Greta Investments Limited
Officers: Ritesh Shah, Secretary; Ashish Chaudhari [1979] Director [Indian]; Gaurav Chaudhary [1984] Director [Indian]; Rajan Choudhary [1985] Director [Indian]

Globaltex Limited
Incorporated: 7 December 1999 *Employees:* 72
Net Worth: £16,348,000 *Total Assets:* £19,624,000
Registered Office: Chalfont House, Oxford Road, Denham, Uxbridge, Middlesex, UB9 4DX
Activities: Wholesale of textiles
Parent: Globaltex 2015 Limited
Officers: Caroline Geary, Secretary; Michael David Gant [1969] Director; Christopher Charles Bevan Rogers [1960] Director

Globegold Limited
Incorporated: 31 October 2012
Net Worth: £1,129,330 *Total Assets:* £5,364,310
Registered Office: Westgate Chambers, 8a Elm Park Road, Pinner, Middlesex, HA5 3LA
Activities: Other letting and operating of own or leased real estate
Shareholder: Malcolm John Harrison
Officers: Jack Harrison [1985] Director; Laura Harrison [1956] Director; Malcolm John Harrison [1951] Director; William Harrison [1987] Director

Glorious Solutions Limited
Incorporated: 7 May 2009 *Employees:* 43
Net Worth: £3,111,186 *Total Assets:* £20,526,442
Registered Office: Media Park, 40b River Road, Barking, Essex, IG11 0DW
Activities: Activities of other holding companies n.e.c.
Officers: Ofir Mor, Secretary; Ofir Mor [1969] Director/Sales Manager

GLS Global Logistics Solutions LLP
Incorporated: 15 March 2013
Net Worth Deficit: £137,305 *Total Assets:* £15,074,162
Registered Office: Suite 1, The Studio, St Nicholas Close, Elstree, Herts, WD6 3EW

GMK Pepper Holdings Limited
Incorporated: 9 November 2012
Net Worth: £3,572,564 *Total Assets:* £5,073,414
Registered Office: Unit 12 Epsom Business Park, Kiln Lane, Epsom, Surrey, KT17 1JF
Activities: Activities of head offices
Parent: Intralan Investments Limited
Officers: Joe Bennett [1987] Director; Dave Hersom [1962] Director [American]; Phillip Frank Mitchell [1961] Director

Go Daddy Europe Limited
Incorporated: 13 March 2007
Net Worth: £4,210 *Total Assets:* £13,025,519
Registered Office: 5th Floor, The Shipping Building, The Old Vinyl Factory, 252-254 Blyth Road, Hayes, Middlesex, UB3 1HA
Activities: Information technology consultancy activities
Parent: Go Daddy Operating Company, LLC
Officers: Jessica Leinhardt Hately [1972] Director [American]; Nima Jacobs Kelly [1962] Director/General Counsel [American]; Paul William John McDowell [1973] Director; Rebecca Morrow [1973] Director/Vice President, Accounting Policy Planning [American]

Goal Global Recoveries Limited
Incorporated: 12 January 2007 *Employees:* 12
Net Worth Deficit: £2,200,101 *Total Assets:* £20,051,754
Registered Office: Ground Floor, 69 Park Lane, Croydon, Surrey, CR9 1BG
Activities: Other business support service activities n.e.c.
Parent: Goal Group Limited
Officers: Stephen Mark Everard, Secretary; John Michael Croft [1953] Director; Stephen Mark Everard [1959] Managing Director; Elliot Spencer Blades Howard [1969] Director/Sales; David Lindon Wilkinson [1956] Director

Goal Group Limited
Incorporated: 1 November 1989 *Employees:* 44
Net Worth Deficit: £6,160,713 *Total Assets:* £20,300,352
Registered Office: 69 Ground Floor, Park Lane, Croydon, Surrey, CR9 1BG
Activities: Management consultancy activities other than financial management
Officers: Stephen Mark Everard, Secretary; John Michael Croft [1953] Director; Stephen Mark Everard [1959] Managing Director; Elliot Spencer Blades Howard [1969] Director; David Lindon Wilkinson [1956] Director

Godiva Bearings (Southern) Limited
Incorporated: 7 January 1977 *Employees:* 51
Net Worth: £13,756,406 *Total Assets:* £18,397,750
Registered Office: Unit 3 Shepperton Business Park, Govett Avenue, Shepperton, Surrey, TW17 8BA
Activities: Non-specialised wholesale trade
Parent: Godiva Bearings Limited
Officers: Trevor John Brain, Secretary; Trevor John Brain [1954] Director/Accountant; Paul Cuthill [1962] Director; Thomas William Hamlett [1972] Director

Godrej UK Limited
Incorporated: 24 October 2005
Net Worth: £23,470,900 *Total Assets:* £23,470,900
Registered Office: Falcon House, 115-123 Staines Road, Hounslow, Middlesex, TW3 3LL
Activities: Non-trading company
Parent: Godrej Netherlands BV
Officers: Thomas Dawes [1982] Director; Dorab Erach Mistry [1953] Director/Business Executive; Anand Rangaswamy [1971] Director [Indian]

Gog Magog Partnership LLP
Incorporated: 21 February 2012
Net Worth: £12,528,000 *Total Assets:* £42,817,000
Registered Office: The Power House, Gunpowder Mill, Powdermill Lane, Waltham Abbey, Essex, EN9 1BN

Gold Group International Limited
Incorporated: 5 August 1965 *Employees:* 10
Net Worth: £26,546,364 *Total Assets:* £81,888,840
Registered Office: Gold Group House, Godstone Road, Whyteleafe, Surrey, CR3 0GG
Activities: Activities of head offices
Major Shareholder: David Gold
Officers: David Gold [1936] Director; Jacqueline Gold [1960] Director; Vanessa Gold [1967] Acting Managing Director

Gold Group Properties Limited
Incorporated: 11 October 2007 *Employees:* 2
Net Worth: £8,344,267 *Total Assets:* £9,033,916
Registered Office: Gold Group House, Godstone Road, Whyteleafe, Surrey, CR3 0GG
Activities: Activities of head offices
Major Shareholder: David Gold
Officers: Bradley Gold [1964] Director; Ralph Gold [1938] Director

Goldace Investments LLP
Incorporated: 6 August 2007
Net Worth: £3,040,383 *Total Assets:* £6,074,598
Registered Office: 352b Green Lane, Seven Kings, Ilford, Essex, IG3 9JS
Officers: Zahoor Hussain [1953] Member; Abbas Zahoor [1975] Member; Idris Zahoor [1979] Member; Parveen Hussain [1954] LLP Member; Saima Zahoor [1982] LLP Member; Syqa Zahoor [1977] LLP Member

Golden Leaves Limited
Incorporated: 3 June 1994 *Employees:* 27
Net Worth: £19,686,596 *Total Assets:* £101,814,112
Registered Office: 5 Robin Hood Lane, Sutton, Surrey, SM1 2SW
Activities: Funeral and related activities
Major Shareholder: Stephen Neil Anthony Rowland
Officers: Stephen Neil Anthony Rowland, Secretary/Director; Barry William Floyd [1967] Director/Head of Operations and Marketing; Anthony Brian Arthur Rowland [1938] Funeral Director; Stephen Neil Anthony Rowland [1965] Director/Funeral Director

Golden Meadows Limited
Incorporated: 4 September 1990
Net Worth: £3,745,534 *Total Assets:* £5,561,509
Registered Office: 68 St Margarets Road, Edgware, Middlesex, HA8 9UU
Activities: Non-specialised wholesale of food, beverages and tobacco
Shareholders: Dilip Sheth; Nila D Sheth
Officers: Nila D Sheth, Secretary; Dilip Shantilal Sheth [1954] Director; Nila D Sheth [1956] Director

Golden Tours Sightseeing Ltd
Incorporated: 16 February 1984 *Employees:* 40
Previous: Golden Tours (Transport) Limited
Net Worth: £6,442,943 *Total Assets:* £8,020,735
Registered Office: Unit 2 The Axis, 40 Athlon Industrial Estate, 338 Athlon Road, Wembley, Middlesex, HA0 1YJ
Activities: Other passenger land transport
Officers: Kamu Palan, Secretary; Kamu Palan [1955] Director/Secretary; Nitin Ratilalbhai Palan [1954] Director/Businessman

Goldex Investments Limited
Incorporated: 14 October 2005 *Employees:* 278
Net Worth: £6,320,811 *Total Assets:* £10,838,878
Registered Office: Warwick House, Park Corner Road, Southfleet, Gravesend, Kent, DA13 9LN
Activities: Unlicenced restaurants and cafes
Major Shareholder: Diljit Singh Brar
Officers: Diljit Singh Brar [1963] Director/Property & Retail; Satnam Brar [1965] Director

Goldfield Homes Limited
Incorporated: 27 July 2006
Net Worth: £2,574,682 *Total Assets:* £10,650,994
Registered Office: 1st Floor, 44-50 The Broadway, Southall, Middlesex, UB1 1QB
Activities: Buying and selling of own real estate
Major Shareholder: Sant Ram Ghai
Officers: Sant Ram Ghai [1966] Director/Businessman

Goldings Estates Limited
Incorporated: 4 March 1997 *Employees:* 2
Net Worth: £3,097,920 *Total Assets:* £6,041,148
Registered Office: Suite D, The Business Centre, Faringdon Avenue, Romford, Essex, RM3 8EN
Activities: Development of building projects
Major Shareholder: Patrick Eugene Flannery
Officers: Krysia Lake, Secretary; Patrick Eugene Flannery [1955] Director/Property Developer [Irish]

Golf Entertainment International Limited
Incorporated: 22 December 2003
Net Worth: £48,893,816 *Total Assets:* £48,893,816
Registered Office: Kinetic House, Theobold Street, Elstree, Herts, WD6 4PJ
Activities: Operation of sports facilities
Parent: Topgolf UK Holdings Limited Partnership
Officers: Kieren Charles Mildwaters, Secretary; Eldridge Allen Burns [1969] Director/General Counsel [American]; William Barry Davenport [1971] Finance Director [American]

Good for Food Limited
Incorporated: 22 August 2013 *Employees:* 1
Net Worth: £3,884,871 *Total Assets:* £10,715,997
Registered Office: 42 Lytton Road, Barnet, Herts, EN5 5BY
Activities: Other letting and operating of own or leased real estate
Shareholders: Wayne Michael Selt; Lewis Selt
Officers: Lewis Selt [1963] Director; Wayne Michael Selt [1958] Director

Good Harvest Group Limited
Incorporated: 8 July 1996 *Employees:* 4
Net Worth: £32,322,438 *Total Assets:* £49,967,744
Registered Office: Old Barn House, High Road, Eastcote, Pinner, Middlesex, HA5 2EW
Activities: Other letting and operating of own or leased real estate
Officers: Michael Richard Cowen, Secretary; Paul Allan Beer [1948] Director/Chartered Accountant; Michael Richard Cowen [1961] Director/Chief Financial Officer; Anthony Ronald William Parfitt [1952] Director/Chartered Accountant

Good Harvest Properties (Hammersmith) Limited
Incorporated: 1 September 1999
Net Worth: £6,138,401 *Total Assets:* £6,155,598
Registered Office: Old Barn House, High Road, Eastcote, Pinner, Middlesex, HA5 2EW
Activities: Other letting and operating of own or leased real estate
Parent: Good Harvest Group Limited
Officers: Michael Richard Cowen, Secretary; Paul Allan Beer [1948] Director/Chartered Accountant; Michael Richard Cowen [1961] Director/Chief Financial Officer; Anthony Ronald William Parfitt [1952] Director/Chartered Accountant

Good Harvest Properties (Southwark) Limited
Incorporated: 11 August 2004
Net Worth: £9,841,946 *Total Assets:* £14,631,545
Registered Office: Old Barn House, High Road, Eastcote, Pinner, Middlesex, HA5 2EW
Activities: Other letting and operating of own or leased real estate
Parent: Good Harvest Group Limited
Officers: Michael Richard Cowen, Secretary; Paul Allan Beer [1948] Director/Chartered Accountant; Michael Richard Cowen [1961] Director/Chief Financial Officer; Anthony Ronald William Parfitt [1952] Director/Chartered Accountant

The Good Shepherd Catholic Trust
Incorporated: 7 July 2011 *Employees:* 140
Previous: The Palmer Catholic Academy
Net Worth: £11,455,245 *Total Assets:* £12,335,773
Registered Office: The Palmer Catholic Academy, Aldborough Road South, Seven Kings, Ilford, Essex, IG3 8EU
Activities: General secondary education
Officers: Nazmul Islam, Secretary; Thomas Alexander [1967] Director/HR Officer; John Anthony [1949] Director; Joseph Daniel Bau-Mann [1966] Director; Father Sean Connolly [1964] Director/Priest; Michael Corcoran [1974] Director; Gerard Adrian Durcan [1960] Director; Reverend Andrew Michael John Headon [1966] Director/Priest; John Jacobson [1965] Director/Administrator; Marian Leslie-Povoas [1961] Director/Bank Manager [Irish]; Eoin McHugh [1979] Director/Teacher; Roger Melder [1965] Director/Technical Administrator; George Reynolds [1963] Director/Accountant; Natasha Scott [1977] Director/Headteacher

Goodman Family Investments Limited
Incorporated: 2 August 1996 *Employees:* 5,251
Previous: J S A Group Limited
Net Worth: £5,662,656 *Total Assets:* £23,247,308
Registered Office: 4th Floor, Radius House, 51 Clarendon Road, Watford, Herts, WD17 1HP
Activities: Non-trading company
Parent: JSA Newco Limited
Officers: Andrew Graham Goodman [1962] Director/Chairman/Investor; John Hugo Hoskin [1974] Director; Kwasi Martin Missah [1969] Director

Goodmayes Properties Ltd
Incorporated: 15 February 2000
Net Worth: £6,040,538 *Total Assets:* £9,820,061
Registered Office: 148 Cranbrook Road, Ilford, Essex, IG1 4LZ
Activities: Other letting and operating of own or leased real estate
Major Shareholder: Pavneet Kaur Kataria
Officers: Gurvinder Kataria, Secretary; Pavneet Kaur Kataria [1970] Director

Goodrich Inertial Limited
Incorporated: 9 December 2009
Net Worth: £151,528,000 *Total Assets:* £1,042,073,024
Registered Office: 1st Floor, Ash House, Littleton Road, Ashford, Middlesex, TW15 1TZ
Activities: Non-trading company
Parent: United Technologies Corporation
Officers: Christian Bruno Jean Idczak [1963] Director/Business Executive [French]; Patricia Catherine Moran [1964] Finance Director [American]; Peter Ross [1964] Finance Director; Louise Kay Thompson [1983] Director/Chartered Management Accountant

Goodshoeman Limited
Incorporated: 24 December 2012
Net Worth: £2,256,110 *Total Assets:* £5,816,566
Registered Office: 3 Theobald Court, Theobald Street, Borehamwood, Herts, WD6 4RN
Activities: Other letting and operating of own or leased real estate
Shareholders: Andrew Graham Goodman; Jonathan Floyd Schuman
Officers: Andrew Graham Goodman [1962] Director; Jonathan Floyd Schuman [1969] Director

Goodwill SIP Limited
Incorporated: 14 April 2004 *Employees:* 5
Net Worth: £4,625,101 *Total Assets:* £29,198,068
Registered Office: 114-116 Goodmayes Road, Ilford, Essex, IG3 9UZ
Activities: Hotels and similar accommodation
Shareholder: Sukhbinder Singh Takhar
Officers: Iqbal Kaur Takhar, Secretary; Iqbal Kaur Takhar [1960] Director; Pirthipal Singh Takhar [1982] Director; Sukhbinder Singh Takhar [1954] Director

Goodwin Associates Limited
Incorporated: 10 November 1983 *Employees:* 1
Net Worth: £6,263,479 *Total Assets:* £7,020,952
Registered Office: Trinity Court, 34 West Street, Sutton, Surrey, SM1 1SH
Activities: Development of building projects
Major Shareholder: Steven Raylar Adkins
Officers: Susan Ellen Peck, Secretary; Steven Raylar Adkins [1956] Director/Property Developer

Gosselin Mobility UK Limited
Incorporated: 4 May 2017
Net Worth: £5,214,307 *Total Assets:* £10,295,396
Registered Office: 49 Wates Way, Mitcham, Surrey, CR4 4HR
Activities: Activities of other holding companies n.e.c.
Major Shareholder: Marc Smet
Officers: Marcel Jorg [1974] Director [Swiss]; Nicholas Kerr [1956] Director/Household Mover; Marc Smet [1958] Director [Belgian]

Gouhari Enterprises Limited
Incorporated: 28 March 1989
Net Worth: £4,322,810 *Total Assets:* £8,481,895
Registered Office: 135 Jersey Road, Isleworth, Middlesex, TW7 4QP
Activities: Other letting and operating of own or leased real estate
Shareholders: Nand Kumar Gouhari; Rajni Gouhari
Officers: Nand Kumar Gouhari, Secretary; Nand Kumar Gouhari [1946] Director/Accountant; Rajni Gouhari [1951] Director/Housewife; Sumit Gouhari [1977] Director/Accountant; Sarika Rallan [1982] Director/Housewife

Gould International UK Limited
Incorporated: 29 August 1934 *Employees:* 43
Net Worth: £12,832,384 *Total Assets:* £22,452,140
Registered Office: Brunswick House, Regent Park, 299 Kingston Road, Leatherhead, Surrey, KT22 7LU
Activities: Wholesale of other intermediate products
Officers: Josephine Morley, Secretary; David Hillel Berkowitz [1946] Director/Chief Executive [American]; Nicholas Christopher Henry [1969] Managing Director; Edward Lawrence Silver [1969] Director/Chief Financial Officer [American]; Michael David Trachtenberg [1965] Director [American]; Darren James Wheeler [1971] Director

Gould Paper Sales UK Limited
Incorporated: 3 August 1979 *Employees:* 14
Net Worth: £5,218,247 *Total Assets:* £22,526,198
Registered Office: Brunswick House, Regent Park, 299 Kingston Road, Leatherhead, Surrey, KT22 7LU
Activities: Wholesale of other intermediate products
Parent: Gould International UK Limited
Officers: Josephine Morley, Secretary; David Hillel Berkowitz [1946] Director/Chief Executive [American]; Nicholas Christopher Henry [1969] Director; Edward Lawrence Silver [1969] Director/Chief Financial Officer [American]; Michael David Trachtenberg [1965] Director [American]; Michael David Trachtenberg [1962] Director [American]

Gould Publication Papers UK Limited
Incorporated: 2 October 2002 *Employees:* 26
Net Worth: £8,813,394 *Total Assets:* £26,193,992
Registered Office: Brunswick House, Regent Park, 299 Kingston Road, Leatherhead, Surrey, KT22 7LU
Activities: Wholesale of other intermediate products
Parent: Gould International UK Limited
Officers: Josephine Morley, Secretary; David Hillel Berkowitz [1946] Director/Chief Executive [American]; Dominic Karl Kristian Blakey [1968] Sales Director; Edward Lawrence Silver [1969] Director/Chief Financial Officer [American]; Michael David Trachtenberg [1965] Director [American]; Darren James Wheeler [1971] Director

Gowrie Laxmico Limited
Incorporated: 8 October 1997 *Employees:* 297
Previous: Gowrie Limited
Net Worth: £17,930,260 *Total Assets:* £35,392,188
Registered Office: Unit 4 Bradfield Road, Ruislip, Middlesex, HA4 0NU
Activities: Wholesale of pharmaceutical goods
Officers: Govindji Thakershi Hathi, Secretary; Alpa Hathi [1968] Director/HR; Govindji Thakershi Hathi [1941] Director; Samit Hathi [1967] Director/Chief Executive

GPF Lewis PLC
Incorporated: 7 November 2006 *Employees:* 48
Previous: G P F Lewis Contracts PLC
Net Worth: £1,075,941 *Total Assets:* £10,679,721
Registered Office: GPF Lewis House, Olds Approach, Tolpits Lane, Watford, Herts, WD18 9AB
Activities: Other construction installation
Shareholders: Joe Lewis Ringart; Rory Gerard Fitzgerald
Officers: Belinda George, Secretary; Jacob Alexander Colliss [1981] Commercial Director; Rory FitzGenerald [1977] Director/Entrepreneur; David Andrew Morford [1974] Pre-Construction Director; Joe Lewis Ringart [1977] Director/Construction

GPG (UK) Holdings Limited
Incorporated: 25 October 1919
Previous: GPG (UK) Holdings PLC
Net Worth: £5,077,000 *Total Assets:* £247,484,992
Registered Office: 1 The Square, Stockley Park, Uxbridge, Middlesex, UB11 1TD
Activities: Activities of head offices
Parent: Coats Group PLC
Officers: John Sinclair Lovell [1967] Group Pensions Director

GPS Food Group (UK) Limited
Incorporated: 4 June 2008 *Employees:* 43
Net Worth: £6,180,140 *Total Assets:* £29,946,258
Registered Office: Windsor House, Queensgate, Britannia Road, Waltham Cross, Herts, EN8 7NX
Activities: Wholesale of meat and meat products
Parent: GPS Food Group Holdings Limited
Officers: Padraig Anthony McCarthy, Secretary; Padraig McCarthy [1967] Director [Irish]; Brian Perkins [1962] Director; Fergus Quinn-Smith [1965] Director

GR Bottling Holdings UK Limited
Incorporated: 21 April 2016
Net Worth: £2,541,987,328 *Total Assets:* £2,541,998,592
Registered Office: Pemberton House, Bakers Road, Uxbridge, Middlesex, UB8 1EZ
Activities: Activities of other holding companies n.e.c.
Parent: Coca-Cola European Partners PLC
Officers: Paul Van Reesch, Secretary; Frank Govaerts [1961] Director [Belgian]; Paul Van Reesch [1976] Director; Edward Owen Walker [1967] Director

Grace Baptist Trust Corporation
Incorporated: 24 October 1957 *Employees:* 2
Net Worth: £5,363,128 *Total Assets:* £5,371,942
Registered Office: 19 Croydon Road, Caterham, Surrey, CR3 6PA
Activities: Activities of religious organisations
Officers: Eric John Cousins, Secretary; Jonathan Neil Broome [1968] Director/Chartered Surveyor; Peter Canty [1950] Director/Consultant Engineer; Alan Richard Copeman [1945] Director/Chartered Building Surveyor; Andrew Brian Keen [1964] Director/Solicitor; Simon Anthony Partington [1969] Director/Architect; Robert Edward Powell [1969] Director/Chartered Insurer; Paul Relf [1962] Director/Baptist Minister; John Arthur Henry Risbridger [1931] Director/Solicitor; David William James Skull [1934] Director/Chartered Quantity Surveyor; David John Steere [1943] Director/Minister of Religion; Kevin Charles William Wiltshire [1960] Director

Gracechurch Sports Management Limited
Incorporated: 17 September 2002
Net Worth: £1,350,267 *Total Assets:* £8,001,742
Registered Office: 2 Linksway, Northwood, Middlesex, HA6 2XB
Activities: Development of building projects
Officers: Donald Owen Scott, Secretary/Chartered Accountant; Michael Charles Grahame Davey [1946] Director/Retired Chartered Surveyor; Manoj Kumar Saluja [1959] Director/Accountant; Reva Saluja [1963] Director/Manager

Gracilis Ltd.
Incorporated: 27 June 1996
Net Worth: £7,622,676 *Total Assets:* £8,651,814
Registered Office: Southerns House, 133 Church Hill Road, Cheam, Sutton, Surrey, SM3 8NE
Activities: Other letting and operating of own or leased real estate
Shareholders: Barry James Devine; James Timothy Devine
Officers: Brian Philip Beckett, Secretary; Barry James Devine [1971] Director; James Timothy Devine [1949] Director [Irish]

Grafton Flats Limited
Incorporated: 25 March 1957
Net Worth: £2,221,796 *Total Assets:* £5,481,298
Registered Office: Canada House, 29 Hampton Road, Twickenham, Middlesex, TW2 5QE
Activities: Development of building projects
Officers: John Simon Moore, Secretary; Jamie Cooper [1970] Director/Property Developer; Joanna Elizabeth Grant [1970] Director

Graham Care (YB) Limited
Incorporated: 4 October 1995 *Employees:* 565
Previous: Graham Care Limited
Net Worth: £84,549,256 *Total Assets:* £163,476,544
Registered Office: 20 Cranley Road, Hersham, Walton on Thames, Surrey, KT12 5BP
Activities: Residential nursing care facilities
Parent: Graham Care Group Limited
Officers: William Ernest Graham, Secretary/Business Manager; Dr Karen Elizabeth Graham [1962] Director/Medical Doctor; William Ernest Graham [1961] Director/Business Manager

Graham Land & Developments Limited
Incorporated: 6 March 2008
Net Worth: £306,263 *Total Assets:* £25,275,300
Registered Office: 20 Cranley Road, Hersham, Walton on Thames, Surrey, KT12 5BP
Activities: Development of building projects
Parent: Graham Care Group Limited
Officers: William Ernest Graham, Secretary/Director; Dr Karen Elizabeth Graham [1962] Director/Doctor; William Ernest Graham [1961] Director

The Grand Central Hotel Glasgow Limited
Incorporated: 9 April 2009 *Employees:* 280
Previous: Troy Management Services (Glasgow) Limited
Net Worth: £15,074,000 *Total Assets:* £36,370,000
Registered Office: Broadwater Park, Denham, Bucks, UB9 5HR
Activities: Hotels and similar accommodation
Parent: IHC May Fair Hotel Limited
Officers: Catherine Elizabeth Lindsay, Secretary; Michael Todd Glover [1971] Director [American]; Nicolette Henfrey [1969] Director; Geoffrey Howard Lee [1955] Director [Australian]; Daisy Eleanor Loveday Caroline Llewellyn [1971] Director; David James Taylor [1976] Director; Matthew Woollard [1985] Director

Grand Union Multi Academy Trust
Incorporated: 6 October 2011 *Employees:* 232
Previous: Featherstone High School
Net Worth: £18,337,616 *Total Assets:* £25,014,368
Registered Office: Featherstone High School, 11 Montague Waye, Southall, Middlesex, UB2 5HF
Activities: General secondary education
Officers: Shahbaz Haider, Secretary; Christine Rose Dickson [1954] Managing Director and Chartered Accountant; Shahbaz Haider [1983] Finance Director; Manish Madhas [1976] Director/Head of Regulatory Performance; Denise Joy Maloney [1958] Director/Governance Consultant; David Millican [1952] Director/Elected Councillor; Jan Moorhouse [1963] Director/Lecturer; Gerry Wadwa [1957] Director/Headteacher

The Grange Centre for People with Disabilities
Incorporated: 11 January 1939 *Employees:* 109
Net Worth: £7,799,968 *Total Assets:* £9,902,590
Registered Office: The Grange Centre, Rectory Lane, Bookham, Leatherhead, Surrey, KT23 4DZ
Activities: Other accommodation
Officers: Eloise Appleby, Secretary; Pamela Jane Barrett [1949] Director/Retired; Anna Louise Coss [1943] Director/Retired; Denis Michel Coulon [1949] Director/Retired [British/French]; Paul Joseph Cullen [1963] Director/Owner of Telecommunications Business; Linda Ann Ferguson [1964] Director; Deborah Ann Gowns [1958] Director/Retired; Peter Alan Grose [1953] Director/Lawyer; John Clovis Pagella [1943] Director/Retired Chartered Surveyor; Dr Carol Riddington [1954] Director/Health and Social Care; Christopher Tailby [1949] Director/Retired; David John Turner [1950] Director/Retired

Grange Renewable Energy Limited
Incorporated: 18 May 2011
Net Worth Deficit: £4,550,000 *Total Assets:* £26,079,000
Registered Office: Beaufort Court, Egg Farm Lane, Kings Langley, Herts, WD4 8LR
Activities: Production of electricity
Parent: Trafalgar Wind Holdings Limited
Officers: Dominic James Hearth, Secretary; Steven William Hughes [1972] Generation & Asset Management Director; Fraser Stephen Merry [1968] Director/Chartered Surveyor; Mitesh Raj Patel [1982] Director/Group Financial Controller

Grange Walk LLP
Incorporated: 16 October 2014
Net Worth: £6,509,000 *Total Assets:* £16,689,000
Registered Office: Cowley Business Park, Cowley, Uxbridge, Middlesex, UB8 2AL

Granherne Limited
Incorporated: 22 May 1980
Net Worth Deficit: £5,491,393 *Total Assets:* £28,200,068
Registered Office: Hill Park Court, Springfield Drive, Leatherhead, Surrey, KT22 7NL
Activities: Construction of other civil engineering projects n.e.c.
Parent: Granherne International (Holdings) Limited
Officers: Martin Nelhams, Secretary; Stephen Peet [1966] Director; Alan Gwilliam Williams [1958] Director/Engineer

Granitte Investments (UK) Limited
Incorporated: 30 July 2012
Net Worth: £125,548,904 *Total Assets:* £125,554,400
Registered Office: Ground Floor, Unit 501 Centennial Park, Centennial Avenue, Elstree, Borehamwood, Herts, WD6 3FG
Activities: Activities of other holding companies n.e.c.
Officers: Ying-Chou Yang [1955] Director [Taiwanese]

Grant & Bowman International Limited
Incorporated: 10 March 2016 *Employees:* 10
Net Worth: £1,533,840 *Total Assets:* £19,532,718
Registered Office: 1st Floor, Sheraton House, Lower Road, Chorleywood, Rickmansworth, Herts, WD3 5LH
Activities: Activities of distribution holding companies
Shareholders: Malcolm Bowman; Myles David Jaakko Bowman
Officers: David Alistair Bowman [1957] Director; Malcolm Bowman [1935] Director; Myles David Jaakko Bowman [1973] Director

Grant & Bowman Limited
Incorporated: 18 October 1967 *Employees:* 19
Net Worth: £9,923,470 *Total Assets:* £14,443,814
Registered Office: 1st Floor, Sheraton House, Lower Road, Chorleywood, Herts, WD3 5LH
Activities: Non-specialised wholesale trade
Shareholder: David Alistair Bowman
Officers: Maria Hajineocli, Secretary; David Alistair Bowman [1957] Director; Malcolm Bowman [1935] Director; Myles David Jaakko Bowman [1973] Director; Daniel Barrie Estrin [1971] Director; Raymond Mark Estrin [1946] Director

Grant & Boyd Limited
Incorporated: 9 November 1938 *Employees:* 8
Net Worth: £11,215,276 *Total Assets:* £16,081,908
Registered Office: York House, Empire Way, Wembley, Middlesex, HA9 0FQ
Activities: Other letting and operating of own or leased real estate
Shareholders: Grant Family Holdings Limited; Grant Family Investments Limited
Officers: Roger Lloyd Jamie Grant, Company Secretary; Benjamin Paul Grant [1980] Director; Daniel Scot Grant [1978] Director; Ian Douglas Grant [1953] Director; Roger Lloyd Jamie Grant [1947] Director

R. & I. Grant & Co. Limited
Incorporated: 27 July 1973 *Employees:* 7
Net Worth: £9,161,270 *Total Assets:* £15,115,267
Registered Office: York House, Empire Way, Wembley, Middlesex, HA9 0FQ
Activities: Other letting and operating of own or leased real estate
Shareholders: Grant Family Holdings Limited; Grant Family Investments Limited
Officers: Roger Lloyd Jamie Grant, Secretary/Director; Ian Douglas Grant [1953] Director; Roger Lloyd Jamie Grant [1947] Director; Susan Melanie Grant [1958] Director; Victoria Sharon Grant [1947] Director

William Grant & Sons Brands Limited
Incorporated: 31 January 2014 *Employees:* 115
Net Worth: £100,693,000 *Total Assets:* £251,652,000
Registered Office: Independence House, 84 Lower Mortlake Road, Richmond, Surrey, TW9 2HS
Activities: Wholesale of wine, beer, spirits and other alcoholic beverages
Parent: William Grant & Sons Limited
Officers: Gregory Justin Bargeton, Secretary; Douglas John Bagley [1967] Director [Australian]; Gregory Justin Bargeton [1973] Director/Global Head of Legal; Gary William Brewer [1961] Director; Philip Andrew Gladman [1970] Marketing Director; Rita Marie Greenwood [1968] Director; Ewan John Henderson [1968] Director; Simon John Hunt [1971] Director [Australian/British]; Michael Lamont [1960] Director/Accountant; Christopher Wesley Mason [1953] Director; Paul Henry Rochford [1963] Director/Accountant; Jonathan Mark Yusen [1970] Director [American]

Grant Family Holdings Limited
Incorporated: 25 June 2015
Net Worth: £20,087,692 *Total Assets:* £20,179,292
Registered Office: York House, Empire Way, Wembley, Middlesex, HA9 0FQ
Activities: Activities of head offices
Shareholder: Roger Lloyd Jamie Grant
Officers: Benjamin Paul Grant [1980] Director; Roger Lloyd Jamie Grant [1947] Director; Victoria Sharon Grant [1947] Director

Grant Family Investments Limited
Incorporated: 25 June 2015
Net Worth: £20,087,692 *Total Assets:* £20,179,292
Registered Office: York House, Empire Way, Wembley, Middlesex, HA9 0FQ
Activities: Activities of head offices
Shareholder: Ian Douglas Grant
Officers: Daniel Scot Grant [1978] Director; Ian Douglas Grant [1953] Director; Susan Melanie Grant [1958] Director

Grantol Investments Limited
Incorporated: 9 February 2006
Net Worth Deficit: £7,120,166 *Total Assets:* £15,415,446
Registered Office: First Floor, Woodgate Studios, 2-8 Games Road, Cockfosters, Barnet, Herts, EN4 9HN
Activities: Other business support service activities n.e.c.
Major Shareholder: Friese Wolfgang Rudiker
Officers: Maria Papaioannou [1979] Director/Employee [Cypriot]

Grapes Direct Limited
Incorporated: 5 October 1999 *Employees:* 12
Net Worth: £4,622,000 *Total Assets:* £14,693,000
Registered Office: Thames House, Thames Road, Crayford, Dartford, Kent, DA1 4QP
Activities: Wholesale of fruit and vegetables
Parent: AG Thames Holdings Limited
Officers: Christopher Oakley, Secretary; Leon Aichen [1941] Director

Gratia (Abbey Care Home) Limited
Incorporated: 8 September 2004
Net Worth: £17,790 *Total Assets:* £6,717,526
Registered Office: Suite 4-5, Second Floor, Congress House, 14 Lyon Road, Harrow, Middlesex, HA1 2EN
Activities: Other letting and operating of own or leased real estate
Major Shareholder: Brijesh Patel
Officers: Brijesh Patel [1988] Director

Gravesend and District Real Estate Company Limited (The)
Incorporated: 19 September 1930
Net Worth: £33,172,356 *Total Assets:* £51,402,836
Registered Office: 49 & 50 Windmill Street, Gravesend, Kent, DA12 1BG
Activities: Development of building projects
Officers: Neil Wilson Chatterton, Secretary; Alexander Guy Chambers [1968] Director; Peter Guy Chambers [1943] Director; Neil Wilson Chatterton [1963] Director/Chartered Surveyor; Brian Frederick Cradick [1949] Director/Chartered Surveyor; William John Bullen Meakin [1945] Director; Philip Stephen Rothwell [1953] Director/Solicitor

Gravity Media Group Holdings Limited
Incorporated: 19 May 2016 *Employees:* 308
Net Worth Deficit: £8,771,000 *Total Assets:* £74,647,000
Registered Office: 32-34 Greenhill Crescent, Watford, Herts, WD18 8JU
Activities: Activities of head offices
Major Shareholder: John Richard Newton
Officers: Nikki Petken, Secretary; David Wayne Checketts [1955] Director/Executive Investor [American]; Paul John Greensmith [1967] Director/Chief Financial Officer; Gordon Andrew Holmes [1969] Managing Director [Irish]; Peter Joseph Lewis [1964] Director [Australian]; Kevin Moorhouse [1958] Director; John Richard Newton [1963] Director

Gravity Media Group Limited
Incorporated: 18 November 1999 *Employees:* 6
Net Worth: £2,022,000 *Total Assets:* £9,672,000
Registered Office: 32-34 Greenhill Crescent, Watford, Herts, WD18 8JU
Activities: Activities of head offices
Parent: Gravity Media Group Holdings Limited
Officers: Nikki Petken, Secretary; Eamonn MacArten Dowdall [1963] Director; Paul John Greensmith [1967] Director/Chief Financial Officer; Elliot Saul Kaye [1971] Finance Director; Kevin Moorhouse [1958] Director; John Richard Newton [1963] Director; Nicholas Peter Newton [1962] Commercial Director

Grays Thurrock Properties Limited
Incorporated: 14 January 1935 *Employees:* 22
Net Worth: £5,387,826 *Total Assets:* £11,345,888
Registered Office: Gay Dawn Offices, Pennis Lane, Fawkham, Longfield, Kent, DA3 8LZ
Activities: Development of building projects
Parent: F.C. Stark Limited
Officers: Stephen John Billings, Secretary; Andrew John Billings [1964] Director/Manager; Ronald John Billings [1960] Director

Grayshott Investments Limited
Incorporated: 17 June 1997 *Employees:* 1
Net Worth: £1,673,321 *Total Assets:* £5,526,980
Registered Office: 298 Ewell Road, Surbiton, Surrey, KT6 7AQ
Activities: Other letting and operating of own or leased real estate
Shareholders: Harold John Bebbington; Paul Ian Chevalier
Officers: Paul Ian Chevalier, Secretary; Harold John Bebbington [1944] Director/Property Manager; Paul Ian Chevalier [1950] Director/Solicitor

Great Park Developments Limited
Incorporated: 3 July 2012
Net Worth: £1,629,211 *Total Assets:* £21,613,288
Registered Office: Probyns, Wick Lane, Englefield Green, Surrey, TW20 0HU
Activities: Construction of domestic buildings
Shareholders: Oakgate Developments Ltd; Applegate Homes Limited; Imperative Management Company Limited
Officers: Darrin George Goff [1966] Director/Developer; Sergey Kuznetsov [1977] Director/Developer; Alexander Myachin [1968] Director/Developer; Catarina Inga Maria Simon [1962] Director/Developer [Swedish]; Lee Robert Simon [1959] Director/Developer

D.Green & Co.(Stoke Newington) Limited
Incorporated: 30 October 1952 *Employees:* 128
Net Worth: £4,751,620 *Total Assets:* £14,160,731
Registered Office: First Floor, 110-112 Morden Road, Mitcham, Surrey, CR4 4DA
Activities: Activities of head offices
Major Shareholder: Eileen June Wiggins
Officers: Eileen June Wiggins, Secretary/Business Owner; Caroline Alicia Wiggins [1960] Director/Chief Executive; Eileen June Wiggins [1930] Director/Chairperson

Kenneth Green Associates Limited
Incorporated: 30 September 1992 *Employees:* 310
Net Worth: £26,602,820 *Total Assets:* £42,828,352
Registered Office: Hill House, Monument Hill, Weybridge, Surrey, KT13 8RX
Activities: Wholesale of perfume and cosmetics
Shareholders: Susan Esther Green; Kenneth Charles Green
Officers: Philip John Stokes, Secretary; Kenneth Charles Green [1945] Director/Business Consultant; Brian John Stanton [1978] Managing Director [New Zealander]; Philip John Stokes [1956] Finance Director

Green Flag Holdings Limited
Incorporated: 8 June 1998
Net Worth: £25,084,020 *Total Assets:* £25,087,408
Registered Office: Churchill Court, Westmoreland Road, Bromley, Kent, BR1 1DP
Activities: Activities of other holding companies n.e.c.
Parent: Direct Line Group Limited
Officers: Roger Cheston Clifton, Secretary; Roger Cheston Clifton [1964] Director/Secretary; Helen Clare O'Murchu [1967] Director/Bank Official; Humphrey Michael Tomlinson [1962] Director/General Counsel & Company Secretary

Green Hercules Trading Limited
Incorporated: 3 May 2007
Net Worth: £457,253 *Total Assets:* £10,811,142
Registered Office: Velocity V1, Brooklands Drive, Weybridge, Surrey, KT13 0SL
Activities: Financial intermediation not elsewhere classified
Parent: Cargill Holdings
Officers: Dena Michelle L O'Bue, Secretary; Stephen James Hamilton [1969] Director/Country Tax Manager UK and Ireland; Michael James Timewell [1974] Director/Solicitor

Green Hill Energy Limited
Incorporated: 6 July 2009
Net Worth Deficit: £1,998,000 *Total Assets:* £45,007,000
Registered Office: Beaufort Court, Egg Farm Lane, Kings Langley, Herts, WD4 8LR
Activities: Other business support service activities n.e.c.
Parent: Trafalgar Wind Holdings Limited
Officers: Dominic James Hearth, Secretary; Steven William Hughes [1972] Generation & Asset Management Director; Fraser Stephen Merry [1968] Director/Chartered Surveyor; Mitesh Raj Patel [1982] Director/Group Financial Controller

Green Homes Investment Ltd
Incorporated: 22 March 2007
Net Worth: £72,706 *Total Assets:* £5,323,731
Registered Office: 3 Woodstock Avenue, Sutton, Surrey, SM3 9EG
Activities: Other letting and operating of own or leased real estate
Officers: Akeel Ahmed Rehman, Secretary; Shahin Sarwar Ali [1969] Director/Businesswoman

Green Lane Goose Limited
Incorporated: 25 January 2017 *Employees:* 2
Net Worth Deficit: £62,746 *Total Assets:* £5,096,755
Registered Office: Nexus House, 2 Cray Road, Sidcup, Kent, DA14 5DA
Activities: Non-trading company
Major Shareholder: Andrew Stewart Needham
Officers: Madhu Ahluwalia [1966] Director; Andrew Stewart Needham [1970] Director

Green Mountain Estates Ltd
Incorporated: 25 February 2014
Net Worth: £2,863,998 *Total Assets:* £12,238,257
Registered Office: 5 Elstree Gate, Elstree Way, Borehamwood, Herts, WD6 1JD
Activities: Other business support service activities n.e.c.
Major Shareholder: Marc Shalam
Officers: Marc Shalam [1977] Director/Property Investment [American]

Green Space London Limited
Incorporated: 27 February 2007 *Employees:* 5
Net Worth: £3,920,572 *Total Assets:* £9,031,649
Registered Office: Price Mann and Co, 447 Kenton Road, London, HA3 0XY
Activities: Other business support service activities n.e.c.
Officers: Abbas Mosawi [1985] Director/Hotelier; Ali Reza Mosawi [1992] Director/Hotelier

Greenbond Properties Limited
Incorporated: 23 March 2004
Net Worth: £7,044,668 *Total Assets:* £7,124,188
Registered Office: 1 Beauchamp Court, 10 Victors Way, Barnet, Herts, EN5 5TZ
Activities: Buying and selling of own real estate
Major Shareholder: Norman Henry Slater
Officers: Nicholas Maurice Slater [1965] Director; Norman Henry Slater [1938] Director/Solicitor

Greencourt Property Group Limited
Incorporated: 6 March 1987
Net Worth: £4,708,535 *Total Assets:* £7,014,087
Registered Office: 42 Lytton Road, Barnet, Herts, EN5 5BY
Activities: Development of building projects
Shareholders: Michael Greenfield; Jacqueline Touba Greenfield
Officers: Jacqueline Greenfield, Secretary; Michael Greenfield [1937] Director

Greenfield Property Developments Limited
Incorporated: 26 February 1998 *Employees:* 3
Net Worth: £1,492,261 *Total Assets:* £8,718,012
Registered Office: Park Place House, 24 Church Street, Epsom, Surrey, KT17 4QB
Activities: Other letting and operating of own or leased real estate
Parent: Richmond Securities Ltd
Officers: Darren Colin Bradley [1969] Director/Chartered Surveyor; James Perry Hallam [1978] Director; Michael Stuart Hastings [1942] Director; Albert Richard Perry [1924] Director

Greenlight Credit Ltd
Incorporated: 4 March 2011 *Employees:* 17
Net Worth: £2,572,551 *Total Assets:* £12,607,538
Registered Office: Suite 43-45, Airport House, Purley Way, Croydon, Surrey, CR0 0XZ
Activities: Other credit granting n.e.c.
Shareholders: Katherine Jane Margaret Clark; Rebecca Lee; Surrey Dragons Limited
Officers: Joseph Robert Clark [1980] Director; Peter Justin Rickenberg [1963] Director

Greensea Real Estate Management Limited
Incorporated: 30 April 2013 *Employees:* 3
Net Worth: £908,412 *Total Assets:* £9,814,826
Registered Office: First Floor, Kirkland House, 11-15 Peterborough Road, Harrow, Middlesex, HA1 2AX
Activities: Management of real estate on a fee or contract basis
Parent: Greenrock, SGPS, S.A.
Officers: Gibran Sikander Sattar [1990] Director [Portuguese]; Nadia Sikander Sattar [1992] Director [Portuguese]; Shaira Sikander Sattar [1970] Director

Greenshaw Learning Trust
Incorporated: 13 May 2011 *Employees:* 148
Net Worth: £69,028,000 *Total Assets:* £91,406,000
Registered Office: Greenshaw Learning Trust, Grennell Road, Sutton, Surrey, SM1 3DY
Activities: General secondary education
Officers: Julie Adams, Secretary; Diana Coman [1958] Director/Consultant; Michael Cooper [1960] Director/Management Consultant; Gary Martin Miles [1955] Former Director of Management Institute; Roger Charles Mills [1956] Director/Publisher/Consultant; Ingrid Percy [1965] Director/Strategic Workforce Planner; Professor Darren Reynolds [1968] Director/University Professor; Karen Lesley Roche [1956] Director/Ofsted Inspector; William George Stewart Smith [1969] Director/Headteacher

Greenstone Oxford Limited
Incorporated: 6 December 2016 *Employees:* 2
Net Worth: £68,572 *Total Assets:* £32,909,552
Registered Office: c/o Hillier Hopkins LLP, First Floor, Radius House, 51 Clarendon Road, Watford, Herts, WD17 1HP
Activities: Other letting and operating of own or leased real estate
Parent: Greenstone Property Holdings Limited
Officers: Stephen Barrow [1956] Director; Simon Richard Hope [1964] Director

Greenswan Consultants Limited
Incorporated: 23 March 1994 *Employees:* 168
Net Worth: £4,399,857 *Total Assets:* £12,355,968
Registered Office: Trinity House, Foxes Parade, Sewardstone Road, Waltham Abbey, Essex, EN9 1PH
Activities: Residential nursing care facilities
Shareholders: Nasreen Begum Raja; Mohammed Moazam Raja
Officers: Nasreen Begum Raja, Secretary/Administration; Mohammed Moazam Raja [1953] Director/Businessman; Nasreen Begum Raja [1953] Director/Administration

Greenyard Prepared UK Limited
Incorporated: 29 October 1991 *Employees:* 2
Previous: Noliko Limited
Net Worth: £4,915,233 *Total Assets:* £5,317,355
Registered Office: 306 High Street, Croydon, Surrey, CR0 1NG
Activities: Non-specialised wholesale trade
Officers: John Richard Burton, Secretary; John Richard Burton [1955] Director; Karl Peeters [1957] Director [Belgian]

Grey Bridge Holdings Limited
Incorporated: 18 February 2016
Net Worth: £15,930,590 *Total Assets:* £16,130,590
Registered Office: Lygon House, 50 London Road, Bromley, Kent, BR1 3RA
Activities: Activities of other holding companies n.e.c.
Major Shareholder: Richard Francis Berridge
Officers: Richard Francis Berridge [1970] Director

Greystead Properties Limited
Incorporated: 17 August 1962 *Employees:* 5
Net Worth: £18,178,450 *Total Assets:* £22,134,078
Registered Office: The Old Brickworks, Church Road, Harold Wood, Romford, Essex, RM3 0JA
Activities: Other letting and operating of own or leased real estate
Officers: Irene Yolande Krantz, Secretary; Joshua James Bates [1969] Director; Michael Bates [1936] Director/Building Contractor; Irene Yolande Krantz [1940] Director/Archivist; Jeremy Robert Maurice Krantz [1968] Director/Property Consultant; Dr Allan Robert Salem [1944] Director; Zoe Warren [1963] Director

Griffon Land & Estates Limited
Incorporated: 19 April 1973 *Employees:* 3
Net Worth: £13,423,395 *Total Assets:* £19,661,544
Registered Office: 1 Towers Place, Eton Street, Richmond upon Thames, Surrey, TW9 1EG
Activities: Other letting and operating of own or leased real estate
Officers: Pauline Miles, Secretary; Michael Jeremy Denholm [1942] Director/Chartered Surveyor; David Graham Kilby [1962] Director

Griffon Land Holdings Limited
Incorporated: 12 February 1965 *Employees:* 3
Net Worth: £6,813,418 *Total Assets:* £7,155,578
Registered Office: 1 Towers Place, Eton Street, Richmond upon Thames, Surrey, TW9 1EG
Activities: Other letting and operating of own or leased real estate
Officers: Pauline Miles, Secretary; Michael Jeremy Denholm [1942] Director/Chartered Surveyor; David Graham Kilby [1962] Director

Grigny (UK) Limited
Incorporated: 1 December 1977 *Employees:* 2
Net Worth: £840,275 *Total Assets:* £96,418,048
Registered Office: The Rivers Office Park, Denham Way, Maple Cross, Herts, WD3 9YS
Activities: Other professional, scientific and technical activities n.e.c.
Shareholders: Renault SA; Renault SA
Officers: James Alexander Blendis, Secretary; Cyril Francois Roger Abiteboul [1977] Managing Director [French]; El-Hassan Aitsaid [1964] Finance Director [Belgian]

Gristwood and Toms Limited
Incorporated: 22 November 1991 *Employees:* 155
Net Worth: £6,142,024 *Total Assets:* £8,466,469
Registered Office: c/o Hillier Hopkins LLP, First Floor, Radius House, 51 Clarendon Road, Watford, Herts, WD17 1HP
Activities: Support services to forestry
Shareholders: Andrew Philip Toms; David Charles Gristwood
Officers: Andrew Philip Toms, Secretary/Tree Surgeon; David Charles Gristwood [1953] Director/Tree Surgeon; Andrew Philip Toms [1953] Director/Tree Surgeon

Grohe Limited
Incorporated: 14 August 1963 *Employees:* 63
Net Worth: £1,671,985 *Total Assets:* £11,046,584
Registered Office: World Business Centre, 2 Newall Road, London Heathrow Airport, Hounslow, Middlesex, TW6 2SF
Activities: Wholesale of hardware, plumbing and heating equipment and supplies
Parent: Grohe AG
Officers: Matthew Brown, Secretary; Matthew Brown [1975] Finance Director; Ina Susanne Sielemann [1971] Managing Director [German]; Garry Smith [1965] Sales Director

Grosvenor Park (Harris & Trotter) 2002 Film LLP
Incorporated: 24 October 2001
Net Worth: £22,162,680 *Total Assets:* £22,162,680
Registered Office: 99 Kenton Road, Harrow, Middlesex, HA3 0AN
Officers: David Thomas Bassett [1944] LLP Member; John David Burns [1944] LLP Member; Mark Stephen Butterworth [1958] LLP Member; Guy Antony Chambers [1963] LLP Member; Craig Laurence Feldman [1963] LLP Member; Stephen Michael Garbutta [1949] LLP Member; Andrew Graham Goodman [1961] LLP Member; Andrew Hale [1962] LLP Member; Julio Salomon Harari [1962] LLP Member; Nicholas Piers Killeen [1959] LLP Member; Alexander Justin Krzeczunowicz [1967] LLP Member; Bruce Charles Nicholas Lane [1953] LLP Member; Hugh Michael Lask [1957] LLP Member; Jack David Linton [1955] LLP Member; Ian Alexander MacDonald [1939] LLP Member; Jason Maratos [1959] LLP Member; Ian David Myers [1954] LLP Member; Richard Francis Jackson Park [1948] LLP Member; Patrick Ranger [1959] LLP Member; Ahmet Vedat Ratib [1963] LLP Member; Harold James Redknapp [1947] LLP Member; Jamie Frank Redknapp [1973] LLP Member; David Henry Rosen [1955] LLP Member; Jayant Sanghrajka [1955] LLP Member; Donald Arthur Starr [1948] LLP Member; Giles Storey [1954] LLP Member; Daniel James Breden Taylor [1958] LLP Member; Alan Keith Thomas [1946] LLP Member; John Patrick Thomson [1969] LLP Member; Paul Anthony Tipton [1954] LLP Member; Richard John Waller [1961] LLP Member; Malcolm Webber [1949] LLP Member

Grosvenor Park 2002 Film LLP
Incorporated: 18 October 2001
Net Worth: £50,934,048 *Total Assets:* £50,934,048
Registered Office: 99 Kenton Road, Harrow, Middlesex, HA3 0AN

Grosvenor Park 2004 Film Partnership No.1 LLP
Incorporated: 21 May 2003
Net Worth: £26,292,000 *Total Assets:* £26,292,000
Registered Office: 99 Kenton Road, Harrow, Middlesex, HA3 0AN
Officers: Peter Minshull Armstrong [1949] LLP Member; Brian Atkinson [1951] LLP Member; Richard Andrew Baker [1962] LLP Member; Eric Edmund Barnett [1961] LLP Member; Susanne Barron [1966] LLP Member; Andrew Gratrix Bennison [1959] LLP Member; Jonathan David Berger [1962] LLP Member; David John Bermingham [1962] LLP Member; Anthony John Best [1960] LLP Member; Carolyn Anne Blore Mitchell [1961] LLP Member; Winston Bogarde [1970] LLP Member; Mark Boothright [1964] LLP Member; Patrick Thomas Joseph Brooke [1947] LLP Member; Olivier Brousse [1965] LLP Member; Richard Brown [1953] LLP Member; David Nigel Caplan [1954] LLP Member; Nigel Alexander Carter [1968] LLP Member; Dominic Kern Chambers [1963] LLP Member; Jeremy John Champion [1962] LLP Member; Mark Gerard Clough [1953] LLP Member; Ian Stuart Cohen [1967] LLP Member; Angus Christopher Calvert Collett [1964] LLP Member; Daniel John Cunliffe [1971] LLP Member; Giles Roderick Dealtry [1963] LLP Member; Dr Yogeshkumar Shantilal Desai [1949] LLP Member; Nicolas Dossiter [1966] LLP Member; Anthony Charles Stephen Druttman [1951] LLP Member; Anthony Due [1970] LLP Member; Andrew John Dunlop [1966] LLP Member; Gillian Anne Dunlop [1965] LLP Member; Andrew David Eady [1964] LLP Member; Robert Elliot [1952] LLP Member; Patrick Noel Farrelly [1955] LLP Member; Nigel Andrew Foster [1958] LLP Member; Paul David Friedman [1966] LLP Member; Richard Peter Garnett [1960] LLP Member; Brian Gaunt [1958] LLP Member; Richard Henry George [1954] LLP Member; Raymond Neil Goodman [1955] LLP Member; Charles Richard Gray [1955] LLP Member; Barry Ludlow Green [1943] LLP Member; Robert Alan Hall [1949] LLP Member; Christopher Hancock [1965] LLP Member; Neil Hugh Thomas Hart [1972] LLP Member; Andrew Peter Joseph Edward Hogan [1973] LLP Member; John Charles Hollis [1953] LLP Member; Richard Halliday Jackson [1965] LLP Member; Thomas Stuart Jackson [1937] LLP Member; Philippe Pierre Jacquemard [1971] LLP Member; Robert Terence Johnson [1962] LLP Member; Robert Hylton Jolliffe [1960] LLP Member; Stephen Ransford Jones [1962] LLP Member; Stephen Frederick Joynes [1935] LLP Member; James Christopher Kaberry [1970] LLP Member; Paul George Kirtley [1959] LLP Member; Arno Kitts [1963] LLP Member; Markos Komondouros [1963] LLP Member; Laura Lawrence [1965] LLP Member; Kenneth Charles Leeper [1965] LLP Member; Jack David Linton [1955] LLP Member; Charles Marcus Sykes Longbottom [1969] LLP Member; John Dyer Lumley [1960] LLP Member; Donald James MacKay [1949] LLP Member; Gaurang Majmudar [1960] LLP Member; David Thomas Joseph Mansfield [1976] LLP Member; Ashley Terence Marston [1960] LLP Member; Philip Joseph McLaughlin [1948] LLP Member; John James McPhillips [1957] LLP Member; Tej Bahadur Singh Metha [1953] LLP Member; Emmanuelle Michels [1967] LLP Member; Timothy John Miller [1957] LLP Member; Andrew Robert Mitchell [1954] LLP Member; John Robert Morgan [1943] LLP Member; Tom Mark Harmer Nichols [1974] LLP Member; David Hase Osborne [1957] LLP Member; Christopher Adrian Palmer [1956] LLP Member; Biagino Palmeri [1967] LLP Member; Naishad Patel [1963] LLP Member; Dr Rashmika Patel [1959] LLP Member; Leslie Joseph Phillips [1958] LLP Member; David Riley [1950] LLP Member; Jocelyn Riley [1950] LLP Member; Jeffery Roberts [1961] LLP Member; Mark James Sadie [1969] LLP Member; Timothy Sice [1959] LLP Member; Paul Anthony Smith [1956] LLP Member; Nigel John Stacey [1970] LLP Member; Donald Arthur Starr [1948] LLP Member; Graham Stedman [1956] LLP Member; Mark Paul Stradling [1965] LLP Member; Andrew David Taylor [1956] LLP Member; Daniel James Breden Taylor [1958] LLP Member; Paul Anthony Tipton [1954] LLP Member; Joanna Trollope [1943] LLP Member; Christopher Richard Underwood [1954] LLP Member; Paul Jeffrey Vann [1947] LLP Member; Helen Walker [1966] LLP Member

Grosvenor Park 2005 Film Partnership No.1 LLP
Incorporated: 6 April 2004
Net Worth: £46,802,168 *Total Assets:* £46,802,520
Registered Office: 99 Kenton Road, Harrow, Middlesex, HA3 0AN
Officers: Hani Al Salih [1946] LLP Member; Shiblee Alam [1971] LLP Member; Steven Kenneth Allport [1971] LLP Member; Peter Minshull Armstrong [1949] LLP Member; Nicholas Anthony Athanasou [1953] LLP Member; Vincent Francis Baczor [1956] LLP Member; John Adam Ball [1969] LLP Member; Wendy Ball [1970] LLP Member; Deborah Bangay [1957] LLP Member; Fiona Margaret Anne Barlow [1959] LLP Member; Eric Edmund Barnett [1961] LLP Member; Jonathan David Berger [1962] LLP Member; David John Bermingham [1962] LLP Member; Thomas Bjorn [1971] LLP Member; Roderick James Blackwell [1958] LLP Member; Nicholas Blezard [1944] LLP Member; Andrew John Booth [1964] LLP Member; Mark Boothright [1964] LLP Member; Paul Martin Boston [1967] LLP Member; Simon Laurence Bowen [1966] LLP Member; Richard Brown [1953] LLP Member; John Scott Cameron [1965] LLP Member; David Nigel Caplan [1954] LLP Member; Giovanni Lorenzo Centi Colella [1976] LLP Member; Dominic Kern Chambers [1963] LLP Member; Gillian Kay Christie [1958] LLP Member; Steven Christie [1965] LLP Member; Lee Robert Clark [1972] LLP Member; Kevin Coogan [1951] LLP Member; Peter Thomas Cook [1956] LLP Member; Rodney Wayne Correia [1956] LLP Member; Stephen Hugh Stapleton Cotton [1949] LLP Member; Daniel John Cunliffe [1971] LLP Member; Julien Francois Olivier Dauchez [1972] LLP Member; Antony Charles William Davis [1964] LLP Member; Simon Henry Davis [1966] LLP Member; Giles Roderick Dealtry [1963] LLP Member; Gary John Dillon [1966] LLP Member; William Douglass Dodd [1946] LLP Member; Jonathan Downes [1961] LLP Member; Anthony Due [1970] LLP Member; John Stanley Durham [1939] LLP Member; Tonianne Dwyer [1962] LLP Member; Paul Anthony Stuart Dyke [1951] LLP Member; David Baron Eccleston [1964] LLP Member; Colin Benjamin Ettinger [1952] LLP Member; Roderick Clifford Evans [1964] LLP Member; Craig Laurence Feldman [1963] LLP Member; Daniel John Finestein [1965] LLP Member; Andrew Flounders [1958] LLP Member; Richard Henry George [1954] LLP Member; Thomas George [1960] LLP Member; Robert Malcolm Gilbert [1965] LLP Member; Sean David Gilbert [1964] LLP Member; Bruce Malcolm Gordon [1959] LLP Member; Ian Gray [1960] LLP Member; Barry Ludlow Green [1943] LLP Member; Patrick Green [1947] LLP Member; Massimo Guiati [1972] LLP Member; Pankaj Gupta [1972] LLP Member; David Gerard Heffron [1965] LLP Member; George Heydon [1961] LLP Member; Stuart William Hindle [1955] LLP Member; Alistair James Hollingdale [1970] LLP Member; Stephen Martyn Hopkins [1960] LLP Member; Jennifer Pamela Houghton [1946] LLP Member; Harvinderpal Singh Hungin [1960] LLP Member; Iain Catleugh Hutchinson [1965] LLP Member; Trevor John Immelman [1979] LLP Member; Kevin David Jackson [1956] LLP Member; Richard Halliday Jackson [1965] LLP Member; Prof Howard Saul Jacobs [1938] LLP Member; Philippe Pierre Jacquemard [1971] LLP Member; Rajat Jain [1965] LLP Member; Sean St John James [1965] LLP Member; Nils Eric Johansson [1980] LLP Member; Robert Terence Johnson [1962] LLP Member; Gareth Jones [1951] LLP Member; Ian Martin Jones [1955] LLP Member; Stephen Ransford Jones [1962] LLP Member; Timothy Francis Comyn Jordan [1960] LLP Member; Stephen Frederick Joynes [1935] LLP Member; Sean Gary Kenwrick [1965] LLP Member; David William Kerr [1963] LLP Member; Jodie Elizabeth Kidd [1978] LLP Member; Arno Kitts [1963] LLP Member; Barry Douglas Lane [1960] LLP Member; Andrew John Leake [1957] LLP Member; Bruce Lightbody [1962] LLP Member; David Patrick Lumley [1958] LLP Member; Bruce John MacDonald [1967] LLP Member; Magdalena Maczan [1975] LLP Member; Mark Joseph Massetti [1959] LLP Member; Karita Mattila [1960] LLP Member; Kevin Connal McGeeney [1970] LLP Member; Alister Hugh Mellor [1962] LLP Member

Grosvenor Park 2005 S42 Film LLP
Incorporated: 6 April 2004
Net Worth: £10,430,000 *Total Assets:* £10,430,548
Registered Office: 99 Kenton Road, Harrow, Middlesex, HA3 0AN
Officers: Colin Steven Braid [1966] LLP Member; Ian Anthony Brown [1974] LLP Member; Peter Harry Dunsby [1969] LLP Member; James Leslie Hayman Joyce [1945] LLP Member; Robert Warwick Hetherington [1964] LLP Member; Brian Eric Charles Lynch [1970] LLP Member; Bruce John MacDonald [1967] LLP Member; Mark Jeremy Melville Naylor [1959] LLP Member; Rudolph Jack Paul Alfred Reginiano [1949] LLP Member; Christopher Andrew Stainton [1970] LLP Member

Grosvenor Park 2006 S48 Film LLP
Incorporated: 18 April 2005
Net Worth: £8,726,160 *Total Assets:* £8,726,160
Registered Office: 99 Kenton Road, Harrow, Middlesex, HA3 0AN
Officers: Cecil Ashe [1944] LLP Member; James Neil Bargeron [1964] LLP Member; Matthew George Butcher [1976] LLP Member; Dominic Kern Chambers [1963] LLP Member; John Bernard Clare [1955] LLP Member; Andrew John Clark [1961] LLP Member; Stuart Douglas Cooper [1966] LLP Member; Nicholas Cusworth [1964] LLP Member; David Richard William Good [1948] LLP Member; Colin Walsh Graham [1970] LLP Member; Tessa Christine Hopkins [1952] LLP Member; Stuart Lindsay Isaacs [1952] LLP Member; Prof Howard Saul Jacobs [1938] LLP Member; Harald Torbjorn Gabriel Jakob Kinde [1958] LLP Member; Howard Martin King [1969] LLP Member; Arno Kitts [1963] LLP Member; Michael Angelo Le Houx [1959] LLP Member; Philip George Llewellyn [1961] LLP Member; Stewart Cameron McAndie [1973] LLP Member; Andrew Gwyn Menary [1959] LLP Member; Andrew Robert Mitchell [1954] LLP Member; Martin James Gerard Moore [1953] LLP Member; Andrew Raymond Moorfield [1966] LLP Member; Peter Anthony Parker [1959] LLP Member; Marcus Ewart Ronksley Potts [1960] LLP Member; Philip James Sweetland [1964] LLP Member; Alan Malcolm Thompson [1951] LLP Member; Raymond Clive Tooth [1940] LLP Member; John Alexander Yule [1964] LLP Member

Grosvenor Park 2007 S48 Film LLP
Incorporated: 1 December 2005
Net Worth: £23,177,000 *Total Assets:* £23,177,000
Registered Office: 99 Kenton Road, Harrow, Middlesex, HA3 0AN
Officers: Omar Mohammed Bachir Abdellaoui [1972] LLP Member; Riccardo Branchetti [1966] LLP Member; Vincent David Robin [1963] LLP Member; Filippo de Nicolais [1966] LLP Member; Leif Oveson Hoegh [1963] LLP Member; Morten Westye Hoegh [1973] LLP Member; Thomas Christian Hoegh [1966] LLP Member; Roberto Hoornweg [1968] LLP Member; Dr Christoph Michael Ladanyi [1956] LLP Member; Guy Delemere Lafferty [1954] LLP Member; Anders Larsen [1967] LLP Member; Anthony Henry Alfred Laubi [1965] LLP Member; Philip Lynch [1965] LLP Member; Alexandre Cyrille Araze Mouradian [1970] LLP Member; Emanuele Ravano [1964] LLP Member; Jerome Roussel [1965] LLP Member

Grouse Bidco Limited
Incorporated: 18 October 2016 *Employees:* 2
Net Worth: £2,073,010 *Total Assets:* £27,680,528
Registered Office: The Barn, Philpots Close, West Drayton, Middlesex, UB7 7RY
Activities: Activities of other holding companies n.e.c.
Parent: Grouse Midco Limited
Officers: Stephen Gallucci [1969] Director; Patrick Finbarr Keenan [1967] Director/Accountant [Irish]

Grouse Midco Limited
Incorporated: 18 October 2016 *Employees:* 2
Net Worth Deficit: £2,475,063 *Total Assets:* £27,037,648
Registered Office: The Barn, Philpots Close, West Drayton, Middlesex, UB7 7RY
Activities: Activities of other holding companies n.e.c.
Parent: Grouse Topco Limited
Officers: Stephen Gallucci [1969] Director; Patrick Finbarr Keenan [1967] Director/Accountant [Irish]

Grouse Topco Limited
Incorporated: 18 October 2016 *Employees:* 140
Net Worth Deficit: £545,000 *Total Assets:* £47,114,000
Registered Office: The Barn, Philpots Close, West Drayton, Middlesex, UB7 7RY
Activities: Activities of other holding companies n.e.c.
Parent: Growth Capital Partners Nominees Limited
Officers: Stephen Gallucci [1969] Director; Nicholas Horler [1959] Director; Patrick Finbarr Keenan [1967] Director/Accountant [Irish]; John Edward Marsh [1979] Director

Grove & Dean (Holdings) Limited
Incorporated: 4 December 2013 *Employees:* 139
Net Worth: £3,560,278 *Total Assets:* £10,878,883
Registered Office: Tollgate House, 96 Market Place, Romford, Essex, RM1 3ER
Activities: Non-life insurance
Shareholder: Damian Paul Collett
Officers: Richard Ernest Brewster [1946] Director; Damian Paul Collett [1970] Managing Director; Matthew Paul Collett [1974] Director; Hannah Louise Thomson [1972] Director

Grove & Dean Limited
Incorporated: 17 April 1974 *Employees:* 138
Net Worth: £3,542,759 *Total Assets:* £10,859,063
Registered Office: Tollgate House, 96 Market Place, Romford, Essex, RM1 3ER
Activities: Non-life insurance
Parent: Grove & Dean (Holdings) Ltd
Officers: Richard Ernest Brewster [1946] Director; Damian Paul Collett [1970] Director/Insurance Consultant; Matthew Paul Collett [1974] Director; Gordon Robert Pratt [1959] Director; Hannah Louise Thomson [1972] Director

Grove Developments Limited
Incorporated: 3 December 2010 *Employees:* 38
Net Worth: £34,245,664 *Total Assets:* £72,611,760
Registered Office: World Business Centre, 3 Newall Road, London Heathrow Airport, Hounslow, Middlesex, TW6 2TA
Activities: Development of building projects
Parent: Grove Acquisitions Limited
Officers: Athos George Yiannis, Secretary; Surinder Arora [1958] Director; Carlton Jeffrey Brown [1972] Director/Chartered Accountant; Sinead Hughes [1965] Director [Irish]; Athos George Yiannis [1963] Director/Chartered Accountant

Grove HR Limited
Incorporated: 28 June 2012 *Employees:* 742
Net Worth: £49,777,560 *Total Assets:* £103,054,368
Registered Office: World Business Centre, 3 Newall Road, London Heathrow Airport, Hounslow, Middlesex, TW6 2TA
Activities: Hotels and similar accommodation
Parent: Arora Hotels Limited
Officers: Athos George Yiannis, Secretary; Sanjay Arora [1989] Director; Surinder Arora [1958] Director; Carlton Jeffrey Brown [1972] Director/Chartered Accountant; Athos George Yiannis [1963] Director/Chartered Accountant

Grove T5 Limited
Incorporated: 8 April 2013 *Employees:* 372
Net Worth: £12,785,261 *Total Assets:* £19,355,978
Registered Office: World Business Centre, 3 Newall Road, London Heathrow Airport, Hounslow, Middlesex, TW6 2TA
Activities: Hotels and similar accommodation
Parent: Arora T5 Holdings Limited
Officers: Athos George Yiannis, Secretary; Surinder Arora [1958] Director; Carlton Jeffrey Brown [1972] Director/Chartered Accountant; Sanjeev Kumar Roda [1969] Director/IT and Procurement Consultant; Athos George Yiannis [1963] Director/Chartered Accountant

Grovehawk Ltd
Incorporated: 9 March 2000
Net Worth Deficit: £32,785 *Total Assets:* £6,782,277
Registered Office: 1st Floor, Healthaid House, Marlborough Hill, Harrow, Middlesex, HA1 1UD
Activities: Other accommodation
Major Shareholder: Neethi Shantesh Gureddi
Officers: Neethi Shantesh Gureddi [1982] Director/Scientist

Grovepoint Properties Limited
Incorporated: 1 July 2014 *Employees:* 1
Net Worth Deficit: £16,599 *Total Assets:* £7,540,195
Registered Office: 1 Warner House, Harrovian Business Village, Bessborough Road, Harrow, Middlesex, HA1 3EX
Activities: Development of building projects
Officers: Haaron Soud Al-Mishwit [1984] Director/Investment Strategist [American]

Grovestream Limited
Incorporated: 27 August 2002 *Employees:* 1
Net Worth: £619,243 *Total Assets:* £6,319,545
Registered Office: Unit 14, 142 Johnson Street, Southall, Middlesex, UB2 5FD
Activities: Other business support service activities n.e.c.
Major Shareholder: Marhab Mohammad Ali Abu Nayla
Officers: Silvia Helena Oliveira, Secretary/Director [Brazilian]; Marhab Mohammad Ali Abu Nayla [1955] Director

Grovetowns Southern Limited
Incorporated: 31 January 2017
Net Worth: £5,365,491 *Total Assets:* £5,365,491
Registered Office: 381 Ewell Road, Tolworth, Surbiton, Surrey, KT6 7DF
Activities: Activities of other holding companies n.e.c.
Major Shareholder: Calvin Gilmore Crane
Officers: Calvin Gilmore Crane, Secretary; Calvin Gilmore Crane [1950] Director/Property Investor

Gruma Europe Limited
Incorporated: 9 August 1999 *Employees:* 367
Net Worth: £45,401,000 *Total Assets:* £53,273,000
Registered Office: Second Floor, Heathrow Boulevard 4, 282 Bath Road, Sipson, West Drayton, Middlesex, UB7 0DQ
Activities: Manufacture of bread; manufacture of fresh pastry goods and cakes
Shareholders: Graciela Silvia Gonzalez Moreno; Mayra Adela Gonzalez Moreno; Juan Antonio de Jesus Gonzalez Moreno
Officers: Amy Lucy Ashman, Secretary; Dannie Lee Burke [1969] Director/Treasurer [American]; Simon Mark Colaco [1975] Procurement Director; Peter Hall Ellis [1965] Managing Director; Rodolfo Maldonado [1953] Director/Chief Executive Officer [American]; Mohammed Saeed [1969] HR Director

Grunenthal Limited
Incorporated: 29 October 1998 *Employees:* 113
Net Worth: £3,298,000 *Total Assets:* £9,133,000
Registered Office: Regus, Lakeside House, 1 Furzeground Way, Stockley Park, Uxbridge, Middlesex, UB11 1BD
Activities: Wholesale of pharmaceutical goods
Parent: Grunenthal GmbH
Officers: Mark Fladrich [1959] Director/Pharmacist [Australian]; Amanda Flanagan [1971] Managing Director [Irish]; Thomas Spindler [1973] Finance Director [German]

Grupotec Renewables Limited
Incorporated: 25 February 2011 *Employees:* 18
Net Worth: £3,290,144 *Total Assets:* £9,976,242
Registered Office: Otterman House, 12 Petersham Road, Richmond, Surrey, TW10 6UW
Activities: Other specialised construction activities n.e.c.
Parent: Grupotec Servicios Avanzados, SA
Officers: Cesar Alejandro Moreyra Martinez [1970] Engineer Director [Spanish]

GT NEPS (Holdings) Limited
Incorporated: 10 November 2014
Net Worth: £1,176,652 *Total Assets:* £108,400,856
Registered Office: Cowley Business Park, Cowley, Uxbridge, Middlesex, UB8 2AL
Activities: Construction of commercial buildings
Parent: Infrastructure Investments Holdings Limited
Officers: Jayesh Gajendra Doshi [1968] Director/Head of Portfolio Management; Joanna Lisette Fox [1970] Director; Mark Geoffrey David Holden [1957] Director; Elena Giorgiana Wegener [1975] Director

GT NEPS Limited
Incorporated: 11 November 2014
Net Worth: £1,176,652 *Total Assets:* £108,400,856
Registered Office: Cowley Business Park, Cowley, Uxbridge, Middlesex, UB8 2AL
Activities: Construction of commercial buildings
Parent: GT NEPS (Holdings) Limited
Officers: Jayesh Gajendra Doshi [1968] Director/Head of Portfolio Management; Joanna Lisette Fox [1970] Director; Mark Geoffrey David Holden [1957] Director; Elena Giorgiana Wegener [1975] Director

Guangdong Investments Limited
Incorporated: 20 December 2002
Net Worth: £98,089,368 *Total Assets:* £98,892,904
Registered Office: Chertsey Road, Sunbury on Thames, Middlesex, TW16 7BP
Activities: Activities of head offices
Parent: BP Global Investments Limited
Officers: David William Knipe [1974] Director/Oil Company Executive

Guardian DR (Overseas Holdings) Limited
Incorporated: 3 February 1997
Net Worth Deficit: £40,922,000 *Total Assets:* £13,195,000
Registered Office: Unit B, Heathrow Corporate Park, Green Lane, Hounslow, Middlesex, TW4 6ER
Activities: Activities of head offices
Parent: Guardian IT
Officers: Susan Diane Lynch [1961] Director/Chief Financial Officer [American]; Michael John Threlfall [1961] Director/Senior Vice President - Global Consulting

Guardian IT
Incorporated: 1 January 1998
Net Worth: £16,286,000 *Total Assets:* £16,751,000
Registered Office: Unit B, Heathrow Corporate Park, Green Lane, Hounslow, Middlesex, TW4 6ER
Activities: Activities of head offices
Parent: Sungard Availability Services Limited
Officers: Susan Diane Lynch [1961] Director/Chief Financial Officer [American]; Michael John Threlfall [1961] Director/Senior Vice President - Global Consulting

Guarding UK Ltd
Incorporated: 19 February 2003 *Employees:* 737
Net Worth: £2,070,174 *Total Assets:* £9,113,401
Registered Office: 249 Cranbrook Road, Ilford, Essex, IG1 4TG
Activities: Public order and safety activities
Officers: Michael John Rust [1947] Director

John Guest Holdings Limited
Incorporated: 29 June 1943 *Employees:* 1,299
Net Worth: £109,191,368 *Total Assets:* £150,349,984
Registered Office: Head Office, Horton Road, West Drayton, Middlesex, UB7 8JL
Activities: Activities of production holding companies
Officers: Robert Gerard Bollman [1968] Director [American]; Jonathan Blayr Munz [1961] Director [Australian]; Heath Graham Sharp [1968] Director [Australian]

John Guest International Limited
Incorporated: 16 November 1999 *Employees:* 1,289
Net Worth: £96,891,888 *Total Assets:* £137,306,512
Registered Office: John Guest Ltd, Horton Road, West Drayton, Middlesex, UB7 8JL
Activities: Activities of production holding companies
Officers: Pernille Fabricius [1966] Director/Chief Financial Officer [Danish]; Jonathan Blayr Munz [1961] Director [Australian]; Heath Graham Sharp [1968] Director [Australian]

John Guest Limited
Incorporated: 9 August 1979 *Employees:* 908
Net Worth: £89,210,688 *Total Assets:* £116,658,504
Registered Office: Horton Road, West Drayton, Middlesex, UB7 8JL
Activities: Manufacture of other plastic products
Officers: Pernille Fabricius [1966] Director/Chief Financial Officer [Danish]; Jonathan Blayr Munz [1961] Director [Australian]; Heath Graham Sharp [1968] Director [Australian]

John Guest Speedfit Limited
Incorporated: 8 October 1962 *Employees:* 59
Net Worth: £5,705,472 *Total Assets:* £20,689,954
Registered Office: Horton Road, West Drayton, Middlesex, UB7 8JL
Activities: Agents specialised in the sale of other particular products
Officers: Pernille Fabricius [1966] Director/Chief Financial Officer [Danish]; Jonathan Blayr Munz [1961] Director [Australian]; Heath Graham Sharp [1968] Director [Australian]

Guideline Lift Services Limited
Incorporated: 31 October 1989 *Employees:* 97
Net Worth: £2,767,504 *Total Assets:* £5,135,159
Registered Office: Unit C, White Oak Technology Park, London Road, Swanley, Kent, BR8 7AG
Activities: Other specialised construction activities n.e.c.
Shareholders: Timothy Peter Jepheart; Simon Derek Jepheart
Officers: Lawrence Anthony Willsey, Secretary/Accounts Manager; Simon Derek Jepheart [1968] Service Accounts Director; Timothy Peter Jepheart [1966] Technical Repair Director; John Martin Oliver [1963] Service Sales Director; Lawrence Anthony Willsey [1962] Finance Director

The Guild of Construction Workers Limited
Incorporated: 3 April 2001
Net Worth: £77,975 *Total Assets:* £13,253,820
Registered Office: Fifth Floor, 79 College Road, Harrow, Middlesex, HA1 1BD
Activities: Other business support service activities n.e.c.
Parent: Guild Corporate Services Group Limited
Officers: Derek Stephen Reynolds [1959] Managing Director

Gulmay Holdings Limited
Incorporated: 14 March 2007 *Employees:* 105
Net Worth: £8,303,806 *Total Assets:* £12,586,596
Registered Office: Cyan House, Canada Road, Byfleet, West Byfleet, Surrey, KT14 7JL
Activities: Manufacture of other electrical equipment
Parent: Stuart William Duncan
Officers: Janice Kay Duncan, Secretary; Janice Kay Duncan [1948] Director Secretary; Stuart William Duncan [1948] Director

Gulmay Limited
Incorporated: 22 June 1976 *Employees:* 60
Net Worth: £5,767,145 *Total Assets:* £7,512,643
Registered Office: Cyan House, 1 Canada Road, Byfleet, Surrey, KT14 7JL
Activities: Manufacture of telegraph and telephone apparatus and equipment
Parent: Gulmay Holdings Limited
Officers: Janice Kay Duncan, Secretary; Stuart William Duncan [1948] Managing Director; Mark Jewell [1961] Director [American]; Ian Wilson [1963] Operations Director

Gunpowder Mill Developments Limited
Incorporated: 19 November 2002 *Employees:* 1
Net Worth: £6,239,000 *Total Assets:* £12,296,000
Registered Office: The Power House, Gunpowder Mill, Powdermill Lane, Waltham Abbey, Essex, EN9 1BN
Activities: Other letting and operating of own or leased real estate
Major Shareholder: Andrew Richard Hill
Officers: Neil Stuart Williams, Secretary; Andrew Richard Hill [1958] Director

Gupta Brothers & Co Limited
Incorporated: 20 August 2013 *Employees:* 4
Net Worth: £8,089,669 *Total Assets:* £9,329,124
Registered Office: Flat 112, Altitude 25, 9 Altyre Road, Croydon, Surrey, CR0 5BP
Activities: Security and commodity contracts dealing activities
Shareholders: Amit Gupta; Rahul Gupta
Officers: Amit Gupta [1981] Director; Rahul Gupta [1981] Director; Reema Mahajan [1983] Director [Indian]

Guru Nanak Limited
Incorporated: 15 September 2008
Net Worth Deficit: £1,989,719 *Total Assets:* £7,079,858
Registered Office: 545 Uxbridge Road, Hayes, Middlesex, UB4 8HP
Activities: Activities of head offices
Shareholder: Satpal Singh
Officers: Saptal Singh Singh, Secretary; Harmeet Singh Arora [1985] Director/Market Owner; Satpal Singh Sethi [1984] Director; Satpal Singh [1977] Director

Guru Nanak Sikh Academy Limited
Incorporated: 22 October 2010 *Employees:* 204
Net Worth: £6,372,144 *Total Assets:* £9,536,860
Registered Office: Guru Nanak Sikh Academy, Springfield Road, Hayes, Middlesex, UB4 0LT
Activities: General secondary education
Officers: Gurpreet Sidhu, Secretary; Dr Parvez Abraham Afzal [1981] Director/Doctor [Indian]; Gurvinder Singh Ahluwalia [1961] Director/Real Estate Developer; Dr Punamdip Kaur Bhullar [1980] Director; Amarpal Singh Gakhal [1977] Director/Senior Subject Matter Expert; Kulwant Singh Mann [1947] Director/Hotelier; Manjeet Mendhir [1953] Director/Barrister; Peter Michael Ryerson [1937] Director; Rajinder Singh Sandhu [1952] Director; Ranjit Singh Sandhu [1972] Director/Ground Operations Officer [Malaysian]; Gurpreet Sidhu [1981] Director; Jaskamal Sidhu [1981] Director/Teacher [Indian]; Arun Thakur [1961] Director/Customer Services Department

GVE London Ltd
Incorporated: 11 November 2009 *Employees:* 9
Net Worth: £1,110,047 *Total Assets:* £5,047,175
Registered Office: Unit 15 Tradecity, Cowley Mill Road, Uxbridge, Middlesex, UB8 2DB
Activities: Sale of new cars and light motor vehicles
Major Shareholder: Dilraj Singh Rai
Officers: Sarina Kaur Lally, Secretary; Dilraj Singh Rai [1984] Director/Accountant

GX Technology EAME Limited
Incorporated: 10 October 1996 *Employees:* 51
Net Worth: £11,769,845 *Total Assets:* £13,058,898
Registered Office: 31 Windsor Street, Chertsey, Surrey, KT16 8AT
Activities: Data processing, hosting and related activities
Parent: GX Technology Corporation
Officers: Alistair David Guthrie Arnot [1966] Director/Accountant; Matthew Roger Powers [1975] Director/General Counsel [American]

The Gym Group Midco1 Limited
Incorporated: 15 May 2013
Net Worth: £156,360,320 *Total Assets:* £163,891,104
Registered Office: Fifth Floor, No 1 Croydon, 12-16 Addiscombe Road, Croydon, Surrey, CR0 0XT
Activities: Activities of other holding companies n.e.c.
Parent: The Gym Group PLC
Officers: Richard James Darwin [1967] Director; Mark Alexander George [1974] Director/Chief Financial Officer

The Gym Group Midco2 Limited
Incorporated: 15 May 2013
Net Worth: £156,244,608 *Total Assets:* £163,884,160
Registered Office: Fifth Floor, No 1 Croydon, 12-16 Addiscombe Road, Croydon, Surrey, CR0 0XT
Activities: Activities of other holding companies n.e.c.
Parent: The Gym Group Midco 1 Limited
Officers: Richard James Darwin [1967] Director; Mark Alexander George [1974] Director/Chief Financial Officer

The Gym Group Operations Limited
Incorporated: 15 May 2013 *Employees:* 10
Previous: The Gym Group Limited
Net Worth: £132,308,544 *Total Assets:* £140,251,776
Registered Office: Fifth Floor, No 1 Croydon, 12-16 Addiscombe Road, Croydon, Surrey, CR0 0XT
Activities: Activities of head offices
Parent: The Gym Group Midco2 Limited
Officers: Richard James Darwin [1967] Director; Mark Alexander George [1974] Director/Chief Financial Officer

The Gym Group PLC
Incorporated: 14 May 2013
Previous: The Gym Group Limited
Net Worth: £141,846,000 *Total Assets:* £183,447,008
Registered Office: Fifth Floor, No 1 Croydon, 12-16 Addiscombe Road, Croydon, Surrey, CR0 0XT
Activities: Activities of other holding companies n.e.c.
Officers: Richard Darwin, Secretary; Richard James Darwin [1967] Director; Mark Alexander George [1974] Director/Chief Financial Officer; Paul John Thomas Gilbert [1962] Director; Penelope Lesley Hughes [1959] Director; Dr David Thomas Kelly [1963] Director; John Robert Treharne [1954] Director; Emma Margaret Woods [1968] Group Marketing and Digital Director

The Gym Limited
Incorporated: 21 December 2005 *Employees:* 272
Net Worth: £97,775,000 *Total Assets:* £156,844,000
Registered Office: Fifth Floor, No 1 Croydon, 12-16 Addiscombe Road, Croydon, Surrey, CR0 0XT
Activities: Fitness facilities
Parent: The Gym Group Operations Limited
Officers: Richard James Darwin [1967] Director; Mark Alexander George [1974] Director/Chief Financial Officer; Nicholas Charles Henwood [1968] Operations Director; Jasper Angus McIntosh [1973] Director/Chief Information Officer; Jonathan Guy Spaven [1958] Director/Chartered Surveyor

Gypcraft Drylining Contractors Limited
Incorporated: 20 April 2001 *Employees:* 33
Net Worth: £3,286,373 *Total Assets:* £7,520,161
Registered Office: Lynwood House, Crofton Road, Orpington, Kent, BR6 8QE
Activities: Other building completion and finishing
Parent: Gypcraft Holdings Limited
Officers: Mark Derek Adams [1972] Director

H & D Support Services (Holdings) Limited
Incorporated: 8 January 2004
Net Worth Deficit: £5,424,000 *Total Assets:* £20,426,000
Registered Office: Astral House, Imperial Way, Watford, Herts, WD24 4WW
Activities: Activities of head offices
Parent: Infrastructure Investments Holdings Limited
Officers: Ian Hudson, Secretary; David Wyn Davies [1968] Director/Accountant; Hannah Holman [1980] Director

H & D Support Services Limited
Incorporated: 8 January 2004
Net Worth Deficit: £5,424,000 *Total Assets:* £20,426,000
Registered Office: Astral House, Imperial Way, Watford, Herts, WD24 4WW
Activities: Combined facilities support activities
Parent: H & D Support Services (Holdings) Limited
Officers: Ian Hudson, Secretary; David Wyn Davies [1968] Director/Accountant; Hannah Holman [1980] Director

H & H Care Home Investments Limited
Incorporated: 13 April 2007
Net Worth: £2,044,895 *Total Assets:* £6,983,160
Registered Office: Zone G, Salamander Quay West, Park Lane, Harefield, Uxbridge, Middlesex, UB9 6NZ
Activities: Buying and selling of own real estate
Parent: Handsale Limited
Officers: Bharat Chunilal Sodha [1959] Director

H & S Contractors (Kent) Limited
Incorporated: 24 March 1981 *Employees:* 57
Net Worth: £2,724,111 *Total Assets:* £6,409,924
Registered Office: First Floor, Cranfields, 43 Friends Road, Croydon, Surrey, CR0 1ED
Activities: Other specialised construction activities n.e.c.
Parent: H & S Contractors Ltd
Officers: Valerie Anne Pallet, Secretary; Valerie Anne Pallet [1944] Director/Secretary; Neil Stephen Pallett [1962] Director/Contracts Supervisor

H & S Contractors Limited
Incorporated: 2 June 1998 *Employees:* 59
Net Worth: £6,276,791 *Total Assets:* £10,200,691
Registered Office: 1st Floor, 43 Friends Road, Croydon, Surrey, CR0 1ED
Activities: Other specialised construction activities n.e.c.
Major Shareholder: Neil Stephen Pallet
Officers: Valerie Anne Pallet, Secretary/Director; Valerie Anne Pallet [1944] Director; Neil Stephen Pallett [1962] Director

H & T Group PLC
Incorporated: 23 July 2004 *Employees:* 1,102
Net Worth: £107,622,000 *Total Assets:* £141,936,000
Registered Office: Harvey & Thompson Ltd, Times House, Throwley Way, Sutton, Surrey, SM1 4AF
Activities: Activities of financial services holding companies
Officers: Stephen Anthony Fenerty, Secretary; Elaine Frances Draper [1963] Director; Stephen Anthony Fenerty [1973] Commercial Director; Peter Denis McNamara [1951] Director/Finance; John Graham Nichols [1950] Director; Mark Smith [1958] Director; James FitzGenerald Thornton [1957] Director/Chartered Accountant

H & V Serviceplan Limited
Incorporated: 25 March 1992 *Employees:* 8
Net Worth: £4,116,135 *Total Assets:* £6,797,108
Registered Office: Endeavour House, 78 Stafford Road, Wallington, Surrey, SM6 9AY
Activities: Plumbing, heat and air-conditioning installation
Shareholders: Alan John Coldwell Jnr; David James Coldwell; James Pennington
Officers: David James Coldwell, Company Secretary; Alan James Coldwell [1937] Managing Director; David James Coldwell [1972] Director/Company Secretary; Alan John Coldwell Jnr [1964] Director; James Pennington [1969] Director/Contracts Manager

H H Associates Limited
Incorporated: 16 December 1991 *Employees:* 298
Net Worth Deficit: £614,000 *Total Assets:* £18,923,000
Registered Office: Grove House, Guildford Road, Fetcham, Leatherhead, Surrey, KT22 9DF
Activities: Public relations and communications activities
Parent: HH Global Limited
Officers: Reinhard Schu, Secretary; Kevin Dunckley [1966] Director/Chief Information Officer; Lee Graham Humphreys [1976] Director; Robert John Fergus Macmillan [1972] Managing Director; Stephen Christopher Charles Nunn [1963] Director CEO - EMEA; Edward James Parsons [1967] Financial Director; Michael Edward Perez [1973] Director [American]

H. K. S. Holdings Limited
Incorporated: 26 May 2005 *Employees:* 573
Net Worth: £21,978,640 *Total Assets:* £74,859,520
Registered Office: Prax House, Horizon Business Village, 1 Brooklands Road, Weybridge, Surrey, KT13 0TJ
Activities: Other service activities n.e.c.
Parent: Harvest Energy Retail Limited
Officers: Arani Soosaipillai, Secretary; Don Camillo Emilio Borneo [1957] Director; Winston Sanjeevkumar Soosaipillai [1973] Director

H.& G.Car Parks Limited
Incorporated: 30 April 1971 *Employees:* 4
Net Worth: £15,499,260 *Total Assets:* £20,502,416
Registered Office: Coopers House, 65a Wingletye Lane, Hornchurch, Essex, RM11 3AT
Activities: Other service activities incidental to land transportation, n.e.c.
Parent: Step Property Group Limited
Officers: Mark William Perkins, Secretary; Gary Perkins [1959] Director

H.K.S. Motors Limited
Incorporated: 27 May 2002 *Employees:* 3
Net Worth: £16,252,962 *Total Assets:* £32,315,680
Registered Office: Prax House, Horizon Business Village, 1 Brooklands Road, Weybridge, Surrey, KT13 0TJ
Activities: Other service activities n.e.c.
Parent: H.K.S. Holdings Limited
Officers: Arani Soosaipillai, Secretary; Don Camillo Emilio Borneo [1957] Director; Winston Sanjeevkumar Soosaipillai [1973] Director

H.K.S. Retail Limited
Incorporated: 10 May 2005 *Employees:* 291
Net Worth: £2,749,144 *Total Assets:* £12,704,044
Registered Office: Prax House, Horizon Business Village, 1 Brooklands Road, Weybridge, Surrey, KT13 0TJ
Activities: Other retail sale in non-specialised stores
Parent: H.K.S. Holdings Limited
Officers: Arani Soosaipillai, Secretary; Don Camillo Emilio Borneo [1957] Director; Winston Sanjeevkumar Soosaipillai [1973] Director

H.W.M. Limited
Incorporated: 10 February 1938 *Employees:* 37
Net Worth: £1,562,851 *Total Assets:* £13,434,019
Registered Office: Bridge Motor Works, New Zealand Avenue, Walton on Thames, Surrey, KT12 1AT
Activities: Sale of new cars and light motor vehicles
Parent: Burwater Holdings Limited
Officers: Neil Andrew Harting, Secretary; Michael Peter Harting [1930] Director/Garage Proprietor; Neil Andrew Harting [1961] Director; Neil Anthony Hayfield [1975] Finance Director; Guy Jenner [1979] Managing Director

Hadgate Limited
Incorporated: 23 December 1963
Net Worth: £2,859,818 *Total Assets:* £7,894,461
Registered Office: 792 Wickham Road, Croydon, Surrey, CR0 8EA
Activities: Other letting and operating of own or leased real estate
Shareholders: Abolghasm Tehranchian; Kurosh Tehranchian
Officers: Kurosh Tehranchian, Secretary; Abolghasm Tehranchian [1923] Director [Iranian]; Kurosh Tehranchian [1962] Director

Haemonetics Asia UK Ltd
Incorporated: 26 April 2012
Net Worth: £4,969,947 *Total Assets:* £5,005,103
Registered Office: Lynwood House, 373-375 Station Road, Harrow, Middlesex, HA1 2AW
Activities: Other business support service activities n.e.c.
Parent: Haemonetics Corporation
Officers: William Patrick Burke [1968] Director [American]; Dan Goldstein [1976] Director/Finance/Corporate Controller [American]

HAGS-SMP Limited
Incorporated: 8 June 1967 *Employees:* 132
Net Worth: £7,493,750 *Total Assets:* £16,971,164
Registered Office: Clockhouse Nurseries, Clockhouse Lane East, Egham, Surrey, TW20 8PG
Activities: Manufacture of other special-purpose machinery n.e.c.
Officers: Anne Coleman, Secretary; Mark John Andrew Grace [1973] Managing Director; Mark Leslie Hoskins [1964] Director; Stephen Geoffrey Lyon [1966] Financial Director; Andrew Bryan Yates [1964] Director/Engineer

Haig Housing Trust
Incorporated: 14 May 2008 *Employees:* 41
Net Worth: £70,334,000 *Total Assets:* £75,164,000
Registered Office: Alban Dobson House, Green Lane, Morden, Surrey, SM4 5NS
Activities: Other letting and operating of own or leased real estate
Officers: Rakesh Gulati, Secretary; Stephen Michael Elliott [1973] Director; Fiona Marie Gordon [1968] Director/Civil Servant and Army Reservist; Cathy Lester-Walker [1953] Director; Luise Margaret Stirling Locke [1955] Director/Advocate; John Douglas Stokoe [1947] Director/Retired; Ian Alexander Vere Nicoll [1952] Director; Andrew Bruce Weir [1961] Communications Strategy Director; Dr Mark James Stewart Weir [1965] Director/Medical Practitioner; Neil Graham White [1952] Director; David Gareth Williams [1960] Director

Halcyon Offices Limited
Incorporated: 11 July 2002
Net Worth: £5,785,147 *Total Assets:* £14,273,781
Registered Office: Thorncroft Manor, Thorncroft Drive, Leatherhead, Surrey, KT22 8JB
Activities: Other letting and operating of own or leased real estate
Shareholders: Miles Dobson; James Fairclough Sheppard
Officers: Karen Temple, Secretary; Miles Dobson [1966] Director; James Fairclough Sheppard [1967] Director

F.H. Hale & Sons (Builders) Limited
Incorporated: 7 April 1959 *Employees:* 5
Net Worth: £12,704,299 *Total Assets:* £14,184,136
Registered Office: First Floor, Radius House, 51 Clarendon Road, Watford, Herts, WD17 1HP
Activities: Buying and selling of own real estate
Shareholders: Alison Featherstone Hale; Sheila Eleanor Gillett
Officers: Alison Featherstone Hale, Secretary; Amanda Dodd [1965] Director/Teacher; Barry Gillett [1950] Director/Retired; Sheila Eleanor Gillett [1930] Director; Alison Featherstone Hale [1939] Director

Hale Hamilton (Valves) Limited
Incorporated: 26 May 1981 *Employees:* 134
Net Worth: £14,848,982 *Total Assets:* £18,554,428
Registered Office: Frays Mill Works, Cowley Road, Uxbridge, Middlesex, UB8 2AF
Activities: Manufacture of taps and valves
Parent: Howitzer Acquisition Limited
Officers: Peter Graham Crawford Harvey, Secretary; Andrew Craig Delves [1965] Sales Director; Jason Alexander Fenn [1966] Managing Director; Peter Graham Crawford Harvey [1957] Finance Director; David Mullen [1968] Director/SVP, Finance & Corporate Controller [American]; Christopher Michael Skarbek-Wazynski [1955] Director/Chartered Engineer

J & E Hall Limited
Incorporated: 1 November 1995 *Employees:* 266
Net Worth Deficit: £18,020,000 *Total Assets:* £28,074,000
Registered Office: Questor House, 191 Hawley Road, Dartford, Kent, DA1 1PU
Activities: Manufacture of non-domestic cooling and ventilation equipment
Parent: AAF McQuay UK Ltd
Officers: Ian Phillip Creasey, Secretary; Andrew Bowden [1971] Managing Director; Voon Ping Chen [1965] Director/Corporate Controller [Malaysian]; Ian Phillip Creasey [1961] Director/Accountant; Benny Woon Khin Liow [1957] Director [Malaysian]; Alan Dale Proffitt [1972] Director/Corporate Controller [American]

Halliford School Limited
Incorporated: 7 December 1956 *Employees:* 94
Net Worth: £11,206,174 *Total Assets:* £15,493,779
Registered Office: Halliford House, Russell Road, Shepperton, Surrey, TW17 9HX
Activities: General secondary education
Officers: Elspeth Wilson Mackie Sanders, Secretary; Norma Frances Cook [1946] Director/Retired; Michael Anthony Crosby [1948] Director/Architect; Richard Cowper Davison [1946] PR Director; Katherine Gulliver [1972] Director/Partner Consulting; Brian Thomas Harris [1951] Director/Local Government Officer; Andrew Philip Hirst [1956] Director; Pamela Ann Horner [1952] Director/Solicitor; Alex Lenoel [1974] Director; Nigel Jonathan Maud [1966] Director/Solicitor; Richard James Parsons [1948] Director/Newspaper Editor; Professor Jonathan Pitt Phillips [1965] Director/University Professor; Peter Roberts [1958] Director/Headmaster; Doctor Millan Sachania [1972] Director/Headmaster; Colin Stuart Squire [1936] Director; Kenneth Harry Woodward [1944] Director/Retired

Haltermann Carless UK Limited
Incorporated: 8 February 1947 *Employees:* 192
Previous: Petrochem Carless Limited
Net Worth: £108,173,000 *Total Assets:* £186,391,008
Registered Office: Grove House, Guildford Road, Leatherhead, Surrey, KT22 9DF
Activities: Manufacture of other chemical products n.e.c.
Parent: PCL Bidco Limited
Officers: Christopher Michael Higgs, Secretary; Christopher Michael Higgs [1956] Finance Director; Duncan Paul Stonehouse [1970] Operations Director

Hamilcourt Industrial Holdings Limited
Incorporated: 22 September 1980 *Employees:* 2
Net Worth: £6,913,411 *Total Assets:* £7,110,037
Registered Office: 297 Richmond Road, Kingston on Thames, Surrey, KT2 5QU
Activities: Development of building projects
Shareholders: Brian Lewis Thomas Harcourt-Jones; Peter David Harcourt-Jones
Officers: Peter David Harcourt-Jones, Secretary; Brian Lewis Thomas Harcourt-Jones [1936] Director/Garage Proprietor; Peter David Harcourt-Jones [1945] Director/Garage Proprietor

Hampton School
Incorporated: 31 May 2007 *Employees:* 376
Net Worth: £35,174,604 *Total Assets:* £50,031,768
Registered Office: Hampton School, Hanworth Road, Hampton, Surrey, TW12 3HD
Activities: Pre-primary education
Officers: Michael Alan King, Secretary; Stuart Alan Bull [1953] Director/Retired; Mona Choueiri [1962] Marketing Director; Marie-Louise Ellis [1953] Director/Self Employed; Laurence Richard Llewellyn [1948] Director/Strategic Consultant; Revd Ben Robert Lovell [1982] Director/Vicar; Helen Anne Lowe [1960] Director/Headmistress; Christine Ruth Mercer [1962] Director/Headmistress; Andrew Hugh Munday [1950] Director/Barrister; John Sinclair Perry [1953] Director/Solicitor; Anthony John Roberts [1944] Director; Nigel John Spooner [1950] Director/Retired; Robert Malcolm Walker [1945] Director; Richard James Keith Washington [1974] Director/Banking; Leslie Hunter Welch [1950] Director/Retired; Alice Victoria Yandle [1989] Director/Solicitor

Hamsard 3352 Limited
Incorporated: 9 October 2014 *Employees:* 177
Net Worth Deficit: £21,065,030 *Total Assets:* £237,866,800
Registered Office: Building 4, Hatters Lane, Croxley Green Business Park, Watford, Herts, WD18 8YF
Activities: Renting and leasing of cars and light motor vehicles
Officers: Laura Catherine Elizabeth Alexander [1979] Director/Chief Financial Officer; Clive Andrew Whistler Baker [1974] Director [British/South African]; Paul Gilshan [1975] Director; David Hosking [1963] Managing Director; Paul Dominic Ian McCreadie [1979] Director; Richard John Prosser [1957] Director/Chairman

Hamsard 3353 Limited
Incorporated: 9 October 2014 *Employees:* 5
Net Worth Deficit: £27,635,996 *Total Assets:* £93,007,432
Registered Office: Building 4, Hatters Lane, Croxley Green Business Park, Watford, Herts, WD18 8YF
Activities: Renting and leasing of cars and light motor vehicles
Parent: Hamsard 3352 Limited
Officers: Laura Catherine Elizabeth Alexander [1979] Director/Chief Financial Officer; Paul Gilshan [1975] Director; Paul Dominic Ian McCreadie [1979] Director

Hamton Environmental Services Limited
Incorporated: 12 July 1973 *Employees:* 599
Net Worth: £11,128,644 *Total Assets:* £17,124,328
Registered Office: 249 Cranbrook Road, Ilford, Essex, IG1 4TG
Activities: Combined facilities support activities
Major Shareholder: Antoinette Carter
Officers: Louise Jane Beenham, Secretary; Jessica Elizabeth Beenham [1981] Director; Antoinette Carter [1955] Director; Michelle Denise Carter [1959] Director; Philip Michael Joslin [1964] Director; Terence Arthur Vincent [1952] Director

Handsale Limited
Incorporated: 7 July 1987 *Employees:* 583
Net Worth: £12,977,782 *Total Assets:* £36,610,476
Registered Office: Zone G, Salamander Quay West, Park Lane, Harefield, Middlesex, UB9 6NZ
Activities: Buying and selling of own real estate
Shareholders: Bharat Chunilal Sodha; Bindu Sodha
Officers: Bindu Sodha, Secretary; Bharat Chunilal Sodha [1959] Director; Bindu Sodha [1961] Director/Secretary; Rishi Sodha [1989] Director

Handspan Limited
Incorporated: 7 March 2005
Net Worth Deficit: £7,819,712 *Total Assets:* £5,715,332
Registered Office: 3rd Floor, Sterling House, Langston Road, Loughton, Essex, IG10 3TS
Activities: Buying and selling of own real estate
Parent: Zestplan Limited
Officers: Allan William Porter, Secretary; David Edward Conway [1976] Director; Christopher John Duffy [1968] Director/Property Developer; Donagh O'Sullivan [1968] Director [Irish]

Hansen Holdings Europe Ltd
Incorporated: 7 May 2015
Net Worth: £18,688,568 *Total Assets:* £22,496,672
Registered Office: 3rd Floor, Harlequin House, 7 High Street, Teddington, Middlesex, TW11 8EE
Activities: Other information technology service activities
Officers: Julia Chand, Secretary; Andrew Alexander Hansen [1959] Director [Australian]; John William May [1961] Director [Australian]; Scott James Andrew Weir [1970] Director

Hansgrohe Limited
Incorporated: 26 March 1990 *Employees:* 77
Net Worth: £11,022,000 *Total Assets:* £18,227,000
Registered Office: Units D1 and D2, Sandown Park Trading Estate, Royal Mills, Esher, Surrey, KT10 8BL
Activities: Wholesale of hardware, plumbing and heating equipment and supplies
Officers: Martin James Mongan, Secretary; Martin James Mongan [1966] Managing Director

Hanwha Techwin Europe Limited
Incorporated: 20 December 2001 *Employees:* 102
Previous: Samsung Techwin Europe Limited
Net Worth: £16,677,000 *Total Assets:* £29,918,000
Registered Office: Heriot House, Heriot Road, Chertsey, Surrey, KT16 9DT
Activities: Wholesale of electronic and telecommunications equipment and parts
Parent: Hanwha Techwin Company Limited
Officers: Chang Baek Lee, Secretary; Ho Yon Hwang [1961] Managing Director [South Korean]; Chang Baek Lee [1976] Director/Chief Financial Officer [South Korean]

Hapag-Lloyd (U.K.) Limited
Incorporated: 15 January 1936 *Employees:* 203
Net Worth: £3,890,553 *Total Assets:* £18,103,140
Registered Office: Hapag Lloyd House, Cambridge Road, Barking, Essex, IG11 8HH
Activities: Other transportation support activities
Parent: Hapag-Lloyd Aktiengesellschaft
Officers: Roberto Falleni, Secretary; Jason Paul Clarke [1969] Managing Director; Michael Pradel [1967] Managing Director [German]

Harefield Academy Trust
Incorporated: 20 February 2004 *Employees:* 93
Net Worth: £25,604,000 *Total Assets:* £28,260,000
Registered Office: The Harefield Academy, Northwood Way, Harefield, Uxbridge, Middlesex, UB9 6ET
Activities: General secondary education
Officers: Peter James Wastall, Secretary; Jonathan Michael Green [1960] Director/Fund Manager; Haig Bertrand Oundjian [1949] Director; Michael Sidney Sherwood [1965] Director/Investment Banker

Harepath Estates LLP
Incorporated: 19 January 2006 *Employees:* 3
Net Worth: £14,490,184 *Total Assets:* £41,831,352
Registered Office: 8-10 South Street, Epsom, Surrey, KT18 7PF
Officers: Christopher Paul Ackley [1962] Member; Charlotte Iskjaer-Ackley [1961] Member; Patricia Hazel Whiteway [1961] Member; Peter James Whiteway [1958] Member

Harlequin Direct Limited
Incorporated: 25 September 1996 *Employees:* 1
Net Worth: £8,283,941 *Total Assets:* £11,393,563
Registered Office: 1 Beauchamp Court, Victors Way, Barnet, Herts, EN5 5TZ
Activities: Other business support service activities n.e.c.
Major Shareholder: Garry Michael Brandt
Officers: Suzanne Brandt, Secretary; Garry Michael Brandt [1964] Director/Importer; Suzanne Brandt [1961] Director

Harlequin Estates (Twickenham) Limited
Incorporated: 22 February 1971
Net Worth: £19,624,588 *Total Assets:* £41,536,592
Registered Office: Twickenham Stoop Stadium, Langhorn Drive, Twickenham, Middlesex, TW2 7SX
Activities: Other letting and operating of own or leased real estate
Shareholders: Duncan Paul Saville; Charles David Owen Jillings; Alasdair Relph Younie
Officers: Nicholas Mark Butterworth, Secretary; Jeremy Graham Paul Campling [1969] Director/Chartered Surveyor; David Armstrong Ellis [1975] Director/Chief Executive; David John Morgan [1957] Director; Sandra Jane Pope [1963] Director/Accountant

Harlequin FC Holdings Limited
Incorporated: 20 December 2013 *Employees:* 286
Previous: Harlequin RFC Holdings Limited
Net Worth: £8,210,094 *Total Assets:* £58,163,112
Registered Office: Twickenham Stoop Stadium, Langhorn Drive, Twickenham, Middlesex, TW2 7SX
Activities: Activities of other holding companies n.e.c.
Shareholders: Duncan Paul Saville; Charles David Owen Jillings; Alasdair Relph Younie
Officers: Nicholas Mark Butterworth, Secretary; Charles David Owen Jillings [1955] Director/Fund Manager; Sandra Jane Pope [1963] Director/Accountant; Duncan Paul Saville [1957] Director/Chartered Accountant

Harlequin Football Club Limited
Incorporated: 12 June 1996 *Employees:* 286
Previous: Blue Sky Leisure Limited
Net Worth: £1,195,827 *Total Assets:* £15,166,016
Registered Office: Twickenham Stoop Stadium, Langhorn Drive, Twickenham, Middlesex, TW2 7SX
Activities: Other sports activities
Shareholders: Duncan Paul Saville; Charles David Owen Jillings; Alasdair Relph Younie
Officers: Nicholas Mark Butterworth, Secretary; David Armstrong Ellis [1975] Director/Chief Executive; Charles David Owen Jillings [1955] Director/Consultant; David John Morgan [1957] Director/Retired Banker; Sandra Jane Pope [1963] Director/Accountant

Harlington Chambers Limited
Incorporated: 18 December 1958 *Employees:* 2
Net Worth: £4,404,974 *Total Assets:* £5,017,325
Registered Office: Ground Floor, Unit 501 Centennial Park, Centennial Avenue, Elstree, Borehamwood, Herts, WD6 3FG
Activities: Buying and selling of own real estate
Major Shareholder: Christopher Henry Douglas Jackson
Officers: Christopher Henry Douglas Jackson, Secretary/Surveyor; Christopher Henry Douglas Jackson [1966] Director/Surveyor; Joan Elizabeth Jackson [1928] Director/Secretary

Harouni Group of Companies Limited
Incorporated: 16 November 2011
Net Worth Deficit: £739,725 *Total Assets:* £16,696,130
Registered Office: 2nd Floor, Unicorn House, Station Close, Potters Bar, Herts, EN6 1TL
Activities: Management of real estate on a fee or contract basis
Major Shareholder: Ester Louise Nassiv
Officers: David Samuel Harouni [1977] Director; Ester Louise Nassiv [1952] Director

Harrington (Properties) Limited
Incorporated: 20 January 1982
Net Worth: £8,452,884 *Total Assets:* £10,359,064
Registered Office: Harrington House, Exhibition Grounds, Fourth Way, Wembley, Middlesex, HA9 0UQ
Activities: Construction of commercial buildings
Shareholders: Cornelius Francis Harrington; Anthony Francis Harrington
Officers: Anthony Francis Harrington, Secretary; Anthony Francis Harrington [1975] Company Secretary/Director; Cornelius Francis Harrington [1940] Director/Building Contractor [Irish]

P.C. Harrington Holdings Limited
Incorporated: 21 October 1991 *Employees:* 126
Net Worth: £9,495,000 *Total Assets:* £27,437,000
Registered Office: Harrington House, 7 Dean Way, Great Western Industrial Park, Southall, Middlesex, UB2 4SB
Activities: Activities of construction holding companies
Major Shareholder: Patrick Christopher Harrington
Officers: Eileen Harrington, Secretary; Patrick Christopher Harrington [1937] Director/Contractor [Irish]; Anne Marie McGann [1966] Director

Harringtons Builders PLC
Incorporated: 18 January 2001 *Employees:* 48
Net Worth: £8,771,173 *Total Assets:* £11,947,578
Registered Office: 27a Maxwell Road, Northwood, Middlesex, HA6 2XY
Activities: Other building completion and finishing
Shareholders: Cornelius Francis Harrington; Anthony Francis Harrington
Officers: Anthony Francis Harrington, Secretary/Director; Gary Fagg [1966] Director; Anthony Francis Harrington [1975] Director; Cornelius Francis Harrington [1940] Director/Building Contractor [Irish]; James Patrick Kavanagh [1969] Director

Harris & Bailey Limited
Incorporated: 1 July 1913 *Employees:* 73
Net Worth: £10,326,552 *Total Assets:* £11,910,941
Registered Office: 50 Hastings Road, Croydon, Surrey, CR9 6BR
Activities: Agents involved in the sale of timber and building materials
Shareholder: Joanna Jane Southgate
Officers: Sheila Anne Harris, Secretary/Director; Caroline Cartwright [1971] Director; Daryl John Gasson [1964] IT Director; Sheila Anne Harris [1942] Director; Thomas Generald Hayman [1959] Managing Director; Neville Horsfield [1967] Deputy Managing Director; Brian William Richardson [1935] Director/Chairman; Jonathan Southgate [1971] Finance Director; Nicholas Wadey [1956] Sales Director

Harris Commercial Repairs Limited
Incorporated: 2 January 1974 *Employees:* 123
Net Worth: £5,663,272 *Total Assets:* £8,581,317
Registered Office: 601 London Road, West Thurrock, Essex, RM20 4AU
Activities: Sale of other motor vehicles
Parent: Harris Holdings (Grays) Limited
Officers: Peter James Harlow, Secretary; Gary John Carpenter [1971] Director/Engineer; Peter Joseph Greenyer [1956] Director/Certified Accountant; Francesca Emma Harlow [1986] Director; Peter James Harlow [1985] Director; Frank Douglas Harris [1964] Director; James Daniel Selway [1989] Director; Danielle Elizabeth Van Der Wiel [1962] Director

Harris Commercial Sales Limited
Incorporated: 24 May 1976 *Employees:* 14
Net Worth: £398,276 *Total Assets:* £6,504,159
Registered Office: 601 London Road, West Thurrock, Essex, RM20 4AU
Activities: Sale of other motor vehicles
Parent: Harris Holdings (Grays) Ltd
Officers: Peter James Harlow, Secretary; Dean Luke Crane [1959] Director/Salesman; Peter Joseph Greenyer [1956] Director; Francesca Emma Harlow [1986] Director; Peter James Harlow [1985] Director; Frank Douglas Harris [1964] Director; James Daniel Selway [1989] Director; Danielle Elizabeth Van Der Wiel [1962] Director

Harris Federation
Incorporated: 26 April 2007 *Employees:* 3,228
Net Worth: £395,575,008 *Total Assets:* £465,664,992
Registered Office: 4th Floor, Norfolk House, Wellesley Road, Croydon, Surrey, CR0 1LH
Activities: Other education n.e.c.
Officers: Mike Antoniou, Secretary; Robin Keith Alcock [1946] Director/Management Consultant; Anthony Peter Bayon [1948] Director/Retired; Dorothy Elliott [1959] Project Director; Lord Philip Charles Harris of Peckham [1942] Director; Karl James Hoods [1973] Director/Civil Servant; Paul Jacobs [1968] Director; Angela Lewina Pamela Kail [1981] Director/Management Consultant; Timothy David Moore [1965] Director/Marketing Consultant; Daniel Moynihan [1960] Director/Teacher; Dr Nigel David Rata [1973] Director/IT Manager; Philip John Saunders [1955] Director; Rosalyn Susan Wilton [1952] Director

Harris Holdings (Grays) Limited
Incorporated: 23 October 1973 *Employees:* 541
Net Worth: £34,019,276 *Total Assets:* £60,435,548
Registered Office: 601 London Road, West Thurrock, Essex, RM20 4AU
Activities: Activities of head offices
Shareholder: Danielle Elizabeth van der Wiel
Officers: Peter James Harlow, Secretary; Peter Joseph Greenyer [1956] Director/Certified Accountant; Francesca Emma Harlow [1986] Director/Accounts Manager; Peter James Harlow [1985] Director/Chartered Accountant; Frank Douglas Harris [1964] Director; Norman Sydney Harris [1937] Director; James Daniel Selway [1989] Director/Engineer; Danielle Elizabeth Van Der Wiel [1962] Director

Saul D Harrison & Sons PLC
Incorporated: 21 July 1947 *Employees:* 51
Net Worth: £4,659,397 *Total Assets:* £7,438,411
Registered Office: 4 Langley Close, Harold Hill Industrial Estate, Romford, Essex, RM3 8XB
Activities: Manufacture of non-wovens and articles made from non-wovens, except apparel
Major Shareholder: Stephen David Harrison
Officers: Lisa Caron Harrison, Secretary; Lisa Caron Harrison [1962] Director; Stephen David Harrison [1961] Director

Harro Foods Limited
Incorporated: 14 August 1992 *Employees:* 87
Net Worth: £3,376,928 *Total Assets:* £17,200,028
Registered Office: Oak Point, Oakcroft Road, Chessington, Surrey, KT9 1RH
Activities: Other food services
Major Shareholder: Yoshiro Susaki
Officers: Matthew Martin Stone, Secretary; Mototsugu Ichikawa [1970] Managing Director [Japanese]; Maki Itazu [1973] Deputy Managing Director [Japanese]; Takayuki Kanai [1959] Director [Japanese]; Atsuhiko Kimura [1958] Financial Director [Japanese]; Akinori Kitanaka [1976] Director [Japanese]

The Harrodian School Limited
Incorporated: 25 January 1993 *Employees:* 219
Net Worth: £27,614,340 *Total Assets:* £46,261,300
Registered Office: c/o Hill Wooldridge & Co, 107 Hindes Road, Harrow, Middlesex, HA1 1RU
Activities: General secondary education
Major Shareholder: Thomas Alford Houstoun-Boswall
Officers: Sir Thomas Alford Houstoun-Boswall [1947] Director; Amber Georgina Moore [1946] Director/House Manager

The Harrogate International Hotel Limited
Incorporated: 8 April 1982 *Employees:* 194
Net Worth: £19,460,000 *Total Assets:* £40,575,000
Registered Office: Queens Court, 9-17 Eastern Road, Romford, Essex, RM1 3NG
Activities: Hotels and similar accommodation
Parent: BPH Finance Number 1 Limited
Officers: Jonathan Patrick Braidley [1965] Director/Investment Professional; Christopher Andre Kula [1983] Director/Chartered Accountant [German/Canadian]

The Harrow Academies Trust
Incorporated: 6 May 2014 *Employees:* 21
Net Worth: £16,600,512 *Total Assets:* £16,948,598
Registered Office: Pinner High School, Beaulieu Drive, Pinner, Middlesex, HA5 1NB
Activities: Primary education
Officers: Dr Andleeb Ahmed [1970] Director/Doctor; David Chappell [1963] Director/Academy Head, Holland Park School; Paul Stuart Gamble [1973] Director/Headteacher; Susan Hammond [1962] Director/Headteacher; Dr Janice Karen Howkins [1955] Director; Susan Mary Maguire [1966] Director/Headteacher; Dr John Reavley [1958] Director; James Andrew Varley [1962] Director/Chartered Accountant; Christopher David Woolf [1977] Director/Headteacher

Harrow High School
Incorporated: 6 July 2011 *Employees:* 110
Net Worth: £11,269,925 *Total Assets:* £13,889,414
Registered Office: Harrow High School, Gayton Road, Harrow, Middlesex, HA1 2JG
Activities: General secondary education
Officers: Pete Bains [1958] Director/Retired; Donna Campbell [1967] Director; Stefan Arthur Clayton [1958] Director/Managing Agent; Andrew Steven Desai [1985] Director/Teacher; Stephen Fisher [1953] Director/Site Supervisor; Paul Stuart Gamble [1973] Director; Josephine Lang [1950] Director/Retired; Kishan Bhimji Patel [1987] Director/Actuarial Trainee; Mavji Patel [1971] Director/Teacher; Nigel William Rowlands [1961] Director/Headteacher Consultant

Harry Motors Ltd
Incorporated: 8 November 1996 *Employees:* 19
Net Worth: £3,157,813 *Total Assets:* £6,582,425
Registered Office: Maple House, 382 Kenton Road, Kenton, Harrow, Middlesex, HA3 9DP
Activities: Maintenance and repair of motor vehicles
Shareholders: Sunil Pindoria; Vijay Pindoria
Officers: Sunil Pindoria, Secretary/Director; Sunil Pindoria [1969] Director; Vijay Pindoria [1971] Director

Harsco (U.K.) Limited
Incorporated: 28 November 1938
Net Worth: £16,555,635 *Total Assets:* £18,981,270
Registered Office: Harsco House, Regent Park, 299 Kingston Road, Leatherhead, Surrey, KT22 7SG
Activities: Activities of head offices
Parent: Harsco Europa B.V.
Officers: Matthew James Flint, Secretary; Stephen Richard Cooper [1966] Director/Accountant; Christopher Claude Lashmer Whistler [1958] Director

Harsco (UK) Group Limited
Incorporated: 12 September 2007 *Employees:* 3
Net Worth: £108,478,232 *Total Assets:* £491,493,920
Registered Office: Harsco House, Regent Park, 299 Kingston Road, Leatherhead, Surrey, KT22 7SG
Activities: Activities of head offices
Officers: Graham Richard Smith, Secretary; Stephen Richard Cooper [1966] Director/Accountant; John Joseph Sweeney [1952] International Tax Director; Christopher Claude Lashmer Whistler [1958] Director/Vice President and Controller

Harsco Infrastructure Group Limited
Incorporated: 18 February 1920 *Employees:* 3
Net Worth: £173,612,752 *Total Assets:* £824,603,200
Registered Office: Harsco House, Regent Park, 299 Kingston Road, Leatherhead, Surrey, KT22 7SG
Activities: Activities of head offices
Parent: Harsco Investment Limited
Officers: Graham Richard Smith, Secretary; Stephen Richard Cooper [1966] Director/Accountant; John Joseph Sweeney [1952] International Tax Director; Christopher Claude Lashmer Whistler [1958] Director/Accountant

Harsco Investment Limited
Incorporated: 4 May 2000 *Employees:* 6
Net Worth: £212,752,000 *Total Assets:* £333,897,984
Registered Office: Harsco House, Regent Park, 299 Kingston Road, Leatherhead, Surrey, KT22 7SG
Activities: Activities of head offices
Parent: Harsco Holdings, Inc.
Officers: Graham Richard Smith, Secretary; Stephen Richard Cooper [1966] Director/Accountant; William Ian Mullen [1966] Director; John Joseph Sweeney [1952] International Tax Director

Harsco Leatherhead Limited
Incorporated: 5 October 2007 *Employees:* 4
Net Worth: £4,118,092 *Total Assets:* £101,955,128
Registered Office: Harsco House, Regent Park, 299 Kingston Road, Leatherhead, Surrey, KT22 7SG
Activities: Activities of head offices
Officers: Graham Richard Smith, Secretary; Stephen Richard Cooper [1966] Director/Accountant; William Ian Mullen [1966] Director; John Joseph Sweeney [1952] International Tax Director; Christopher Claude Lashmer Whistler [1958] Director/Vice President and Controller

Harsco Metals 385 Limited
Incorporated: 2 June 1988 *Employees:* 2
Net Worth: £27,912,736 *Total Assets:* £27,980,780
Registered Office: Harsco House, Regent Park, 299 Kingston Road, Leatherhead, Surrey, KT22 7SG
Activities: Activities of head offices
Officers: Graham Richard Smith, Secretary; Stephen Richard Cooper [1966] Director/Accountant; Christopher Claude Lashmer Whistler [1958] Director/Accountant

Harsco Metals Group Limited
Incorporated: 8 September 1961 *Employees:* 928
Net Worth: £52,229,000 *Total Assets:* £102,759,000
Registered Office: Harsco House, Regent Park, 299 Kingston Road, Leatherhead, Surrey, KT22 7SG
Activities: Activities of head offices
Officers: Stephen Richard Cooper [1966] Director/Accountant; Mauro Curi [1970] Director [Italian]; Albert Russell Mitchell [1966] Director [American]; William Ian Mullen [1966] Director; Christophe Nicolas Reitemeier [1965] Director [French]; John Joseph Sweeney [1952] International Tax Director; Christopher Claude Lashmer Whistler [1958] Director/Accountant

Harsco Metals Holdings Limited
Incorporated: 2 August 1956 *Employees:* 5
Net Worth: £72,286,552 *Total Assets:* £76,063,008
Registered Office: Harsco House, Regent Park, 299 Kingston Road, Leatherhead, Surrey, KT22 7SG
Activities: Activities of head offices
Officers: Stephen Richard Cooper [1966] Director/Accountant; William Ian Mullen [1966] Director; John Joseph Sweeney [1952] International Tax Director; Christopher Claude Lashmer Whistler [1958] Director/Accountant

Harsco Mole Valley Limited
Incorporated: 10 October 2007 *Employees:* 2
Net Worth: £99,986,448 *Total Assets:* £102,038,728
Registered Office: Harsco House, Regent Park, 299 Kingston Road, Leatherhead, Surrey, KT22 7SG
Activities: Activities of head offices
Officers: Graham Richard Smith, Secretary; Stephen Richard Cooper [1966] Director/Accountant; Christopher Claude Lashmer Whistler [1958] Director/Vice President and Controller

Harsco Rail Limited
Incorporated: 14 April 1970 *Employees:* 200
Net Worth: £15,485,124 *Total Assets:* £26,048,890
Registered Office: Harsco House, Regent Park, 299 Kingston Road, Leatherhead, Surrey, KT22 7SG
Activities: Manufacture of other general-purpose machinery n.e.c.
Parent: Ballagio S.A.R.L.
Officers: Matthew James Flint, Secretary; Matthew James Flint [1973] Director/Chartered Accountant; David Raymond Geering [1955] Director; David Charles Marsh [1969] Director; Hugo Van Audenaerde [1963] Director [Belgian]

C.P. Hart & Sons Limited
Incorporated: 17 October 1966 *Employees:* 254
Net Worth: £8,482,275 *Total Assets:* £18,067,288
Registered Office: Unit 40 Charles Park, Claire Causeway, Crossways, Dartford, Kent, DA2 6QA
Activities: Wholesale of household goods (other than musical instruments) n.e.c
Parent: Charco 2010 Ltd.
Officers: Richard Hugh Reynolds, Secretary; Stephen Broomhead [1954] Director of Operations; Rachel Ann Martin [1971] Merchandising & Showroom Development Director; Kevin Ohle [1957] Director [Irish]; Richard Hugh Reynolds [1955] Director; Paul Francis Harrison Rowland [1960] Managing Director (Contracts)

Hart Homes (Watford) Limited
Incorporated: 24 June 2016
Net Worth: £4,764,000 *Total Assets:* £9,726,000
Registered Office: Gateway House, 59 Clarendon Road, Watford, Herts, WD17 1LA
Activities: Other accommodation
Officers: Tina Barnard, Secretary; Tina Jane Barnard [1963] Director/Chief Executive of Housing Association; Alan Victor Gough [1965] Director/Head of Community & Customer; Paul Richmond [1978] Finance Director; Joanne Wagstaffe [1967] Director/Accountant

Hart Homes Limited
Incorporated: 17 March 2004 *Employees:* 1
Net Worth: £1,338,169 *Total Assets:* £13,390,413
Registered Office: Corner Oak, Weybridge Park, Weybridge, Surrey, KT13 8SH
Activities: Construction of domestic buildings
Shareholders: Graham Scott; Michael Gordon Scott

Harte Hanks UK Limited
Incorporated: 25 October 1989 *Employees:* 68
Net Worth: £4,525,827 *Total Assets:* £10,519,061
Registered Office: Wyvern House, Wyvern Way, Rockingham Road, Uxbridge, Middlesex, UB8 2XN
Activities: Activities of call centres
Officers: Jon Biro [1966] Director/Vice President [American]; Sydney Hoffman [1958] Director/Chief Financial Officer [American]; Peter John Kitley [1956] Finance Director

William Hartley Group Limited
Incorporated: 16 April 1985
Net Worth: £2,139,429 *Total Assets:* £5,145,296
Registered Office: Nicholas House, River Front, Enfield, Middlesex, EN1 3FG
Activities: Other letting and operating of own or leased real estate
Major Shareholder: Mario Cilia
Officers: Stephen Cilia [1976] Director/Property [Maltese]

Harvard International Limited
Incorporated: 2 April 1963 *Employees:* 14
Net Worth: £4,198,000 *Total Assets:* £6,705,000
Registered Office: Suite 105a, Citibase Watford, 42-44 Clarendon Road, Watford, Herts, WD17 1JJ
Activities: Activities of head offices
Major Shareholder: Xuhui Zhou
Officers: Lei Li [1978] Director [Chinese]; Zhuoyan Xu [1985] Director [Chinese]; Xuhui Zhou [1968] Director/Chairman [Chinese]

Harvest Energy Limited
Incorporated: 7 December 1994
Net Worth: £12,105,732 *Total Assets:* £110,559,824
Registered Office: Prax House, Horizon Business Village, 1 Brooklands Road, Weybridge, Surrey, KT13 0TJ
Activities: Wholesale of petroleum and petroleum products
Officers: Arani Soosaipillai, Secretary; Don Camillo Emilio Borneo [1957] Director/Oil Trader; Winston Sanjeev Kumar Soosaipillai [1973] Director

Harvest Investments Solutions Limited
Incorporated: 28 April 2009
Net Worth: £10,801 *Total Assets:* £20,705,364
Registered Office: 13 Clarence Lodge, Taverners Way, Hoddesdon, Herts, EN11 8TH
Activities: Management consultancy activities other than financial management
Major Shareholder: Hartmut Jacob
Officers: Phoebus Papapetrou [1950] Director

Harvest Midco Limited
Incorporated: 23 February 2015 *Employees:* 2,422
Net Worth: £55,818,000 *Total Assets:* £145,030,000
Registered Office: 2 The Square, Southall Lane, Southall, Middlesex, UB2 5NH
Activities: Activities of head offices
Parent: New Midco Limited
Officers: Martin Johnson [1973] Director; Mark Stott [1966] Director

Harvey & Thompson Limited
Incorporated: 9 August 1991 *Employees:* 1,102
Net Worth: £103,989,000 *Total Assets:* £137,972,992
Registered Office: Times House, Throwley Way, Sutton, Surrey, SM1 4AF
Activities: Financial intermediation not elsewhere classified
Officers: Stephen Anthony Fenerty, Secretary; Elaine Frances Draper [1963] Director; Stephen Anthony Fenerty [1973] Commercial Director; Mark Peter Harrold [1976] Operations Director; Peter Denis McNamara [1951] Director; John Graham Nichols [1950] Managing Director; Mark Joseph Smith [1958] Director; James FitzGenerald Thornton [1957] Director/Chartered Accountant

Hasbro U.K. Limited
Incorporated: 23 January 1986 *Employees:* 218
Net Worth: £20,521,000 *Total Assets:* £28,522,000
Registered Office: 4 The Square, Stockley Park, Uxbridge, Middlesex, UB11 1ET
Activities: Operation of warehousing and storage facilities for land transport activities
Officers: Julia Rachel Runnacles, Secretary; Kay Jackie Green [1969] Director/Business Executive; Nigel George Hutton [1952] Director/Senior VP Legal Counsel

Hastoe Capital PLC
Incorporated: 6 March 2012
Net Worth: £50,000 *Total Assets:* £129,685,000
Registered Office: Marina House, 17 Marina Place, Hampton Wick, Kingston upon Thames, Surrey, KT1 4BH
Activities: Financial intermediation not elsewhere classified
Parent: Hastoe Housing Association
Officers: William Roberts, Secretary; Andrew Potter [1971] Director/Chief Executive; William Jeremy Roberts [1970] Finance Director; Robert Rutledge [1954] Director/Retired

Hatch End High School
Incorporated: 1 July 2011 *Employees:* 178
Net Worth: £21,715,824 *Total Assets:* £26,020,154
Registered Office: Headstone Lane, Harrow, Middlesex, HA3 6NR
Activities: General secondary education
Officers: Maria Abrams [1954] Director/Pastoral Manager; Rebecca Ann Cleary [1986] Director/Teacher; Anton Collyer [1951] Director/Retired; Timothy Matthew Dalton [1979] Director/Teacher; Catherine Mary Deed [1954] Director; Christopher Firth [1985] Director/Pastoral Support Manager; Sayed Hamid [1972] Director/Teacher [Afghan]; Oky Lee [1976] Director/Project Manager; Clement Alexander Lewis [1928] Director/Retired; Susan Mary Maguire [1966] Director; Edwin Solomon [1950] Director; Ketan Chandrakant Varia [1968] Director/Management Consultant; Dr Nandini Varma [1945] Director/Retired Community Paediatrician; Emma Wennington [1985] Director/Brand Marketing; Catherine Garnons Williams [1952] Director

Hawk-Eye Innovations Limited
Incorporated: 17 July 2001 *Employees:* 224
Net Worth: £21,256,000 *Total Assets:* £32,507,000
Registered Office: Legal Department, The Heights, Brooklands, Weybridge, Surrey, KT13 0XW
Activities: Ready-made interactive leisure and entertainment software development
Parent: Sony Europe Limited
Officers: Richard James Waite, Secretary; Stephen James Carter [1979] Managing Director; Adam Charles Fry [1964] Director/Businessman; Romona Liddiard [1971] Finance Director; David McIntosh [1962] Finance Director

Paula Hawkins Limited
Incorporated: 18 July 2013 *Employees:* 1
Net Worth: £21,973,516 *Total Assets:* £25,613,192
Registered Office: c/o Alderwick James & Co, 4 The Sanctuary, 23 Oakhill Grove, Surbiton, Surrey, KT6 6DU
Activities: Book publishing
Major Shareholder: Paula Bawden Hawkins
Officers: Paula Bawden Hawkins [1972] Director

Hawkspare Limited
Incorporated: 26 August 1986 *Employees:* 9
Net Worth: £8,191,135 *Total Assets:* £14,790,096
Registered Office: Green Street, Green Road, Dartford, Kent, DA2 8DP
Activities: Agents involved in the sale of machinery, industrial equipment, ships and aircraft
Parent: Forgekind Limited
Officers: Laura Eloise Hicken, Secretary; Derek George Hawkins [1955] Director; Elliot David Hawkins [1990] Director/Sales Manager; Laura Eloise Hicken [1985] Director/Property Manager

Hawthorn Crow Limited
Incorporated: 25 February 1992 *Employees:* 3
Net Worth: £4,839,597 *Total Assets:* £5,148,897
Registered Office: F W Berringer & Co, Lygon House, 50 London Road, Bromley, Kent, BR1 3RA
Activities: Development of building projects
Shareholders: Alan Baker; June Virginia Baker
Officers: Alan Baker, Secretary; Jonathan Baker [1969] Director/Artist; June Virginia Baker [1937] Director

Hawthorne Trust Limited
Incorporated: 3 November 1934 *Employees:* 28
Net Worth: £7,129,265 *Total Assets:* £7,232,833
Registered Office: Charton Manor, Gorse Hill, Farningham, Kent, DA4 0JT
Activities: Other residential care activities n.e.c.
Officers: Alan Michael Holland, Secretary; Dr Brian Blandford [1945] Director/Consultant; Margaret Chaplin [1942] Director/Retired; Peter Adrian Ramsbottom [1959] Director/Christian Science Practitioner; Jim Weaver [1951] Director/Graphic Designer

Haydon School
Incorporated: 9 March 2011 *Employees:* 208
Net Worth: £30,342,600 *Total Assets:* £32,915,100
Registered Office: Haydon School, Wiltshire Lane, Eastcote, Pinner, Middlesex, HA5 2LX
Activities: General secondary education
Officers: Beyhan Ercan-Razvi, Secretary; Claire Louise Barry [1972] Director/Strategy Manager; Stuart John Burnaby [1978] Director/Teacher; Jane Elizabeth Davies [1958] Director/School Pastoral Assistant Leader; Angela Amelda Dennie [1958] Director/Bookkeeper; Steven Edwards [1981] Director/Government; Dr Christopher Hayes [1973] Director/Barrister; Derek Honeygold [1936] Director/Senior University Lecturer (Retired); Dr Tanya Yvonne Huehns [1965] Director/Doctor; Robert William Jones [1967] Director/Headteacher; Carol Anne Katugampola [1968] Director/PCJ Fast Food Limited; Janet Ann Keal [1962] Director/Housewife; Sandeep Kumar [1967] Director/IT Analyst; Giuseppe Schettino [1970] Director/Scientist [Italian]

Hayes Point (Sully) Limited
Incorporated: 5 December 2003
Net Worth Deficit: £34,712,076 *Total Assets:* £32,034,484
Registered Office: 3rd Floor, Sterling House, Langston Road, Loughton, Essex, IG10 3TS
Activities: Other business support service activities n.e.c.
Shareholder: Zestplan Limited
Officers: Allan William Porter, Secretary; Stephen Stuart Solomon Conway [1948] Director; Donagh O'Sullivan [1968] Construction Director [Irish]

Haymarket Group Limited
Incorporated: 14 April 1993 *Employees:* 1,440
Net Worth: £19,210,000 *Total Assets:* £80,116,000
Registered Office: Bridge House, 69 London Road, Twickenham, Middlesex, TW1 3SP
Activities: Activities of head offices
Major Shareholder: Michael Ray Dibdin Heseltine
Officers: Kevin Costello [1964] Director; David Baird Fraser [1939] Director/Chartered Accountant; Brian John Freeman [1954] Director/Accountant; Mark Gibson [1953] Director/Chief Executive Charity; Lord Michael Ray Dibdin Heseltine [1933] Director/Publisher; Hon Rupert Heseltine [1967] Director/Publisher; Lord Peter Keith Levene [1941] Director

Haymarket Media Group Ltd.
Incorporated: 22 July 1932 *Employees:* 782
Net Worth: £95,681,000 *Total Assets:* £256,752,000
Registered Office: Bridge House, 69 London Road, Twickenham, Middlesex, TW1 3SP
Activities: Publishing of consumer and business journals and periodicals
Parent: Haymarket Group Limited
Officers: Kevin Costello [1964] Publishing Director; Brian John Freeman [1964] Director/Accountant; Lord Michael Ray Dibdin Heseltine [1933] Director/Publisher; Hon Rupert Heseltine [1967] Director/Publisher

Haymarket PR Publications LLP
Incorporated: 28 November 2006 *Employees:* 12
Net Worth: £8,502,000 *Total Assets:* £8,526,000
Registered Office: Bridge House, 69 London Road, Twickenham, Middlesex, TW1 3SP

Haymarket Publishing Services Limited
Incorporated: 23 July 1964 *Employees:* 2
Net Worth: £14,620,000 *Total Assets:* £14,620,000
Registered Office: Bridge House, 69 London Road, Twickenham, Middlesex, TW1 3SP
Activities: Activities of head offices
Parent: Haymarket Media Group Limited
Officers: Philip Stanley Goodman, Secretary; Brian John Freeman [1964] Director/Accountant; Philip Stanley Goodman [1959] Director/Chartered Accountant

Haymarket UK2 Limited
Incorporated: 2 July 2008
Net Worth: £128,164,784 *Total Assets:* £128,682,680
Registered Office: Bridge House, 69 London Road, Twickenham, Middlesex, TW1 3SP
Activities: Other business support service activities n.e.c.
Parent: Haymarket Media Group Limited
Officers: Philip Stanley Goodman, Secretary; Brian John Freeman [1964] Director/Accountant

Hayre Builders Company Limited
Incorporated: 17 August 2010 *Employees:* 6
Net Worth: £1,069,535 *Total Assets:* £6,252,216
Registered Office: Hayre House, 5-7 Bath Road, Heathrow, Hounslow, Middlesex, TW6 2AA
Activities: Other building completion and finishing
Officers: Talwinder Singh Hayre [1965] Director/Estate Manager

Hayre Investments & Developments Limited
Incorporated: 18 March 2004
Net Worth: £2,036,222 *Total Assets:* £5,175,782
Registered Office: Hayre House, 5-7 Bath Road, Heathrow, Hounslow, Middlesex, TW6 2AA
Activities: Management of real estate on a fee or contract basis
Officers: Talwinder Singh Hayre, Secretary/Manager; Amit Singh Chhokar [1993] Director; Talwinder Singh Hayre [1965] Director/Manager

Hayre Investments (Ealing) Ltd.
Incorporated: 23 August 2013
Net Worth: £4,649,024 *Total Assets:* £7,819,855
Registered Office: Hayre House, 5-7 Bath Road, Heathrow, Hounslow, Middlesex, TW6 2AA
Activities: Other letting and operating of own or leased real estate
Officers: Talwinder Singh Hayre [1965] Director/Property Investor

Hazel Renewables Limited
Incorporated: 6 February 2012
Net Worth: £236,000 *Total Assets:* £6,959,000
Registered Office: Beaufort Court, Egg Farm Lane, off Station Road, Kings Langley, Herts, WD4 8LR
Activities: Production of electricity
Parent: European Investments Solar Holdings 2 Limited
Officers: Dominic Hearth, Secretary; Steven William Hughes [1972] Global Support Services Director, UK&I - Commercial; Mitesh Raj Patel [1982] Director/Group Financial Controller; Tracy Jane Scott [1976] Director/Delivery Project Manager - New Technologies UK&I; Mark Christopher Wayment [1958] Director

Hazeldell Ltd
Incorporated: 7 August 2014 *Employees:* 49
Net Worth: £325,989 *Total Assets:* £7,575,497
Registered Office: 51 Parkstone Avenue, Emerson Park, Hornchurch, Essex, RM11 3LN
Activities: Medical nursing home activities
Shareholders: Krishan Parkash Sohal; Harjinder Kaur; Karn Inder Singh Sohal
Officers: Harjinder Kaur [1954] Director; Karn Inder Singh Sohal [1987] Director; Krishan Parkash Sohal [1949] Director

HCL EAS Ltd
Incorporated: 11 September 2008
Net Worth: £118,785,144 *Total Assets:* £596,680,640
Registered Office: Axoncentre, Church Road, Egham, Surrey, TW20 9QB
Activities: Activities of head offices
Major Shareholder: Sivaprasad Sivasubramaniam Nadar
Officers: Manish Anand [1968] Director [Indian]; Subramanian Gopalakrishnan [1967] Director [Indian]; Ajit Krishnan Kutty Kumar [1964] Director [Indian]; Rahul Singh [1963] Director [Indian]; Shiv Kumar Walia [1969] Director [Australian]

HCL Great Britain Limited
Incorporated: 7 January 1997 *Employees:* 607
Net Worth: £31,126,000 *Total Assets:* £76,664,000
Registered Office: Axon Centre, Church Road, Egham, Surrey, TW20 9QB
Activities: Information technology consultancy activities
Parent: HCL Technologies UK Limited
Officers: Prateek Aggarwal [1967] Director [Indian]; Prahlad Rai Bansal [1957] Director [Indian]; Ajit Krishnan Kutty Kumar [1964] Director [Indian]; Rahul Singh [1963] Director [Indian]; Shiv Kumar Walia [1969] Director [Australian]

HCL Insurance BPO Services Limited
Incorporated: 1 December 2004 *Employees:* 366
Net Worth: £5,763,000 *Total Assets:* £13,412,000
Registered Office: HCL House, 28-36 Eastern Road, Romford, Essex, RM1 3PJ
Activities: Other activities auxiliary to insurance and pension funding
Major Shareholder: Sivaprasad Sivasubramaniam Nadar
Officers: Nicholas Adrian Dumonde [1968] Director/Chief Operating Officer; Subramanian Gopalakrishnan [1967] Director [Indian]; Sugata Gupta [1965] Director [Irish]; Vijay Udupi Mallya [1964] Director [Indian]

HCL Investments (UK) Ltd
Incorporated: 9 November 2011
Net Worth: £6,373,422 *Total Assets:* £6,400,598
Registered Office: Axon Centre, Church Road, Egham, Surrey, TW20 9QB
Activities: Information technology consultancy activities
Parent: Axon Solutions Limited
Officers: Subramanian Gopalakrishnan [1967] Director [Indian]; Ajit Krishnan Kutty Kumar [1964] Director [Indian]; Rahul Singh [1963] Director [Indian]; Shiv Kumar Walia [1969] Director [Australian]

HCL Technologies UK Limited
Incorporated: 20 August 2013 *Employees:* 1,068
Net Worth: £48,883,000 *Total Assets:* £259,556,000
Registered Office: Axon Centre, Church Road, Egham, Surrey, TW20 9QB
Activities: Activities of head offices
Major Shareholder: Sivaprasad Sivasubramaniam Nadar
Officers: Manish Anand [1968] Director [Indian]; Ajit Krishnan Kutty Kumar [1964] Director [Indian]; Rahul Singh [1963] Director [Indian]; Shiv Kumar Walia [1969] Director [Australian]

HCP Holdings Limited
Incorporated: 7 June 1996 *Employees:* 300
Net Worth: £7,206,000 *Total Assets:* £15,157,000
Registered Office: 8 White Oak Square, London Road, Swanley, Kent, BR8 7AG
Activities: Activities of head offices
Parent: Innisfree M & G PPP LLP
Officers: Donna Lucia McCormack, Secretary; Donald a Bourgeois [1963] Director [Canadian]; Nicholas John Edward Crowther [1960] Investment Director; Martin James Lennon [1970] Director/Investment Prof; Donna Lucia McCormack [1961] Director; Timothy Richard Pearson [1962] Director/Investment Manager; Matthew James Webber [1963] Director/Fund Manager; Michael Paul Woodhead [1956] Director

HCT Portland Limited
Incorporated: 13 January 2017 *Employees:* 4
Net Worth: £3,979,384 *Total Assets:* £73,717,096
Registered Office: Portland House, 69-71 Wembley Hill Road, Wembley, Middlesex, HA9 8BU
Activities: Other business support service activities n.e.c.
Parent: South Central Property Limited
Officers: Bhupendra Shantilal Kansagra, Secretary; Laurent Elie Cadji [1977] Director/Businessman; Lewis Levy Cadji [1938] Director/Businessman; Bhupendra Shantilal Kansagra [1956] Director/Businessman; Ramesh Shantilal Kansagra [1950] Director/Businessman

The Headmasters Partnership Limited
Incorporated: 27 September 1995 *Employees:* 88
Net Worth: £5,702,335 *Total Assets:* £11,939,964
Registered Office: 1 Tolworth Broadway, Surbiton, Surrey, KT6 7DQ
Activities: Hairdressing and other beauty treatment
Officers: Trevor Sanders, Secretary; Timothy James Binnington [1969] Director; Mark Adrian Foster [1958] Director; John Sanders [1955] Director/Salon Owner; Trevor Sanders [1957] Director; Michael Stanley Taylor [1960] Director

Headmasters Salons Limited
Incorporated: 9 November 2010 *Employees:* 634
Net Worth: £2,282,877 *Total Assets:* £5,376,684
Registered Office: 1 Tolworth Broadway, Surbiton, Surrey, KT6 7DQ
Activities: Hairdressing and other beauty treatment
Officers: Timothy James Binnington [1969] Director; Mark Adrian Foster [1958] Director; John Sanders [1955] Director; Trevor Sanders [1957] Director; Michael Stanley Taylor [1960] Director

Headstart 4 Life Limited
Incorporated: 14 August 2009
Net Worth: £2,061,529 *Total Assets:* £5,300,209
Registered Office: 634 Green Lane, Ilford, Essex, IG3 9RZ
Activities: Real estate agencies
Major Shareholder: Harpal Lakhan
Officers: Harpal Lakhan [1960] Director

Health & Case Management Limited
Incorporated: 19 March 2003 *Employees:* 112
Net Worth: £3,889,103 *Total Assets:* £8,962,478
Registered Office: Melrose House, 42 Dingwall Road, Croydon, Surrey, CR0 2NE
Activities: General medical practice activities
Parent: Ballard Investment Company Limited
Officers: Rhoslyn Moore, Secretary; Keith Alan Bushnell [1955] Director; Maurice David Henchey [1945] Director

Healthcare Drugstores Limited
Incorporated: 25 May 2010 *Employees:* 3
Net Worth Deficit: £1,273,513 *Total Assets:* £17,998,800
Registered Office: 2 Peterwood Way, Croydon, Surrey, CR0 4UQ
Activities: Activities of head offices
Parent: Day Lewis PLC
Officers: Ameetkumar Patel, Secretary; Heena Patel [1963] Finance Director; Jayantibhai Chimanbhai Patel [1945] Director; Jayanti Chimanbhai Patel Junior [1984] Director

Healthcare Support (Erdington) Holdings Limited
Incorporated: 17 February 2000
Net Worth: £924,000 *Total Assets:* £17,985,000
Registered Office: 8 White Oak Square, London Road, Swanley, Kent, BR8 7AG
Activities: Activities of head offices
Parent: JLIF Investments Limited
Officers: Carlos Vela Lazaga [1989] Director/Junior Valuation Analyst [Spanish]; Neil Woodburn [1979] Director/Chartered Building Surveyor

Healthcare Support (Erdington) Limited
Incorporated: 25 January 2000
Net Worth: £924,000 *Total Assets:* £17,985,000
Registered Office: 8 White Oak Square, London Road, Swanley, Kent, BR8 7AG
Activities: Other service activities n.e.c.
Parent: Healthcare Support (Erdington) Holdings Limited
Officers: Carlos Vela Lazaga [1989] Director/Junior Valuation Analyst [Spanish]; Neil Woodburn [1979] Director/Chartered Building Surveyor

Healthcare Support (Newcastle) Finance PLC
Incorporated: 15 December 2004
Net Worth: £429,000 *Total Assets:* £380,844,992
Registered Office: 8 White Oak Square, London Road, Swanley, Kent, BR8 7AG
Activities: Financial intermediation not elsewhere classified
Parent: Healthcare Support (Newcastle) Holdings Limited
Officers: Gaynor Birley-Smith [1966] Investment Director; David Richard Bradbury [1969] Asset Director; Robert James Marsden [1955] Projects Director; Hannah O'Gorman [1971] Director; Alastair James Watson [1974] Investment Director

Healthcare Support (Newcastle) Holdings Limited
Incorporated: 19 April 2002
Net Worth: £4,060,000 *Total Assets:* £381,011,008
Registered Office: 8 White Oak Square, London Road, Swanley, Kent, BR8 7AG
Activities: Construction of commercial buildings
Parent: Equion Health (Newcastle) Limited
Officers: Gaynor Birley-Smith [1966] Investment Director; David Richard Bradbury [1969] Asset Director; Robert James Marsden [1955] Projects Director; Hannah O'Gorman [1971] Director; Alistair James Watson [1974] Investment Director

Healthcare Support (Newcastle) Limited
Incorporated: 22 March 2002
Net Worth: £3,631,000 *Total Assets:* £381,011,008
Registered Office: 8 White Oak Square, London Road, Swanley, Kent, BR8 7AG
Activities: Construction of commercial buildings
Parent: Healthcare Support (Newcastle) Holdings Limited
Officers: Gaynor Birley-Smith [1966] Investment Director; David Richard Bradbury [1969] Asset Director; Robert James Marsden [1955] Projects Director; Hannah O'Gorman [1971] Director; Alastair James Watson [1974] Investment Director

Healthcare Support (North Staffs) Finance PLC
Incorporated: 10 December 2004
Net Worth: £733,000 *Total Assets:* £405,620,992
Registered Office: 8 White Oak Square, London Road, Swanley, Kent, BR8 7AG
Activities: Banks
Parent: Healthcare Support (North Staffs) Holdings Limited
Officers: Stuart Anthony Carter [1965] Project Director; Jonathan Nigel Edward Cowdell [1966] Director/Chartered Accountant; Jamie Pritchard [1971] Director/Investment Manager; Neil Woodburn [1979] Director/Chartered Building Surveyor

Healthcare Support (North Staffs) Holdings Limited
Incorporated: 10 December 2004
Net Worth: £7,466,000 *Total Assets:* £417,032,000
Registered Office: 8 White Oak Square, London Road, Swanley, Kent, BR8 7AG
Activities: Activities of head offices
Parent: JLIF Investments Limited
Officers: Stuart Anthony Carter [1965] Project Director; Jonathan Nigel Edward Cowdell [1966] Director/Chartered Accountant; Jamie Pritchard [1971] Director/Investment Manager; Neil Woodburn [1979] Director/Chartered Building Surveyor

Healthcare Support (North Staffs) Limited
Incorporated: 9 December 2004
Net Worth: £6,733,000 *Total Assets:* £417,032,000
Registered Office: 8 White Oak Square, London Road, Swanley, Kent, BR8 7AG
Activities: Construction of commercial buildings
Parent: Healthcare Support (North Staffs) Holdings Limited
Officers: Stuart Anthony Carter [1965] Project Director; Jonathan Nigel Edward Cowdell [1966] Director/Chartered Accountant; Jamie Pritchard [1971] Director/Investment Manager; Neil Woodburn [1979] Director/Chartered Building Surveyor

Healy Refrigeration & Air Conditioning Services Limited
Incorporated: 18 February 1985 *Employees:* 6
Net Worth: £4,981,845 *Total Assets:* £5,444,528
Registered Office: Unit 5 Epsom Downs Metro Centre, Waterfield, Tadworth, Surrey, KT20 5LR
Activities: Electrical installation
Parent: Healy's ACR Limited
Officers: Richard Healy [1974] Director

Healy's ACR Limited
Incorporated: 27 March 2014 *Employees:* 1
Net Worth: £8,527 *Total Assets:* £6,332,491
Registered Office: Ashcombe House, 5 The Crescent, Leatherhead, Surrey, KT22 8DY
Activities: Steam and air conditioning supply
Major Shareholder: Richard Healy
Officers: Richard Healy [1974] Director

Heart Internet Limited
Incorporated: 14 August 2003 *Employees:* 78
Net Worth: £44,174,000 *Total Assets:* £51,146,000
Registered Office: 5th Floor, The Shipping Building, Old Vinyl Factory, 252-254 Blyth Road, Hayes, Middlesex, UB3 1HA
Activities: Data processing, hosting and related activities
Parent: HEL Bidco Ltd
Officers: Sara Silveira Da Costa Da Cunha Rego [1973] Director [Portuguese]; Jonathan Ying Kit Wong [1976] Director

Heartlands Hotel Limited
Incorporated: 6 November 2007
Net Worth: £647,135 *Total Assets:* £8,376,006
Registered Office: 1 Towers Place, Eton Street, Richmond, Surrey, TW9 1EG
Activities: Buying and selling of own real estate
Parent: China National Travel Service Group Corporation
Officers: Jameson Andrew Lamb [1972] Director; Alex Edward Pritchard [1976] Director

Robert Heath Group Limited
Incorporated: 2 October 2008 *Employees:* 340
Net Worth: £2,210,193 *Total Assets:* £10,464,710
Registered Office: Heath House, 264 Burlington Road, New Malden, Surrey, KT3 4NN
Activities: Other business support service activities n.e.c.
Major Shareholder: Robert Bernard Heath
Officers: Michael Lloyd Heath [1978] Managing Director; Robert Bernard Heath [1949] Director/Chairman

Robert Heath Heating Limited
Incorporated: 29 November 1983 *Employees:* 331
Net Worth: £2,562,693 *Total Assets:* £8,754,652
Registered Office: Heath House, 264 Burlington Road, New Malden, Surrey, KT3 4NN
Activities: Plumbing, heat and air-conditioning installation
Parent: Robert Heath Group Limited
Officers: Michael Lloyd Heath [1978] Managing Director; Robert Bernard Heath [1949] Director/Engineer; William Gary McIntosh [1960] Director

Heathcrest Limited
Incorporated: 30 April 1987
Net Worth: £4,676,422 *Total Assets:* £5,322,930
Registered Office: 47 Canons Drive, Edgware, Harrow, Middlesex, HA8 7RG
Activities: Renting and operating of Housing Association real estate
Shareholders: Patrick Thomas O'Sullivan; Knightingale Estates Limited
Officers: Patrick Thomas O'Sullivan, Secretary; James O'Sullivan [1981] Director; Patrick Thomas O'Sullivan [1950] Director/Computer Operator

Heathland Whitefriars Federation
Incorporated: 2 June 2014 *Employees:* 224
Net Worth: £19,973,672 *Total Assets:* £23,349,020
Registered Office: Healthland School, Eastcote Lane, Harrow, Middlesex, HA2 9AG
Activities: Pre-primary education
Officers: Angela Rosalind Bowd, Secretary; Lucy Emma Caswell [1971] Director/Executive Headteacher; Anup Chalisey [1979] Director/Mechanical Engineer; Roulla Chandarana [1974] Director/Pharmacist; Fiona Ruth Hopkins [1985] Director/Associate Headteacher; Thangavadivelu Jegatheesan [1974] Director; Lynne Malzard [1965] Director/Learning Support Assistant; David Harris Mattison [1948] Director/Retired; Marie-Louise Straub Nolan [1958] Director; Jonathan Robert Watson [1981] Director/Associate Headteacher

Heathrow (AH) Limited
Incorporated: 20 December 2007
Net Worth: £8,156,000,256 *Total Assets:* £8,156,000,256
Registered Office: The Compass Centre, Nelson Road, Hounslow, Middlesex, TW6 2GW
Activities: Activities of head offices
Parent: Heathrow (SP) Limited
Officers: Yuanyuan Ding [1979] Director; Javier Echave Espot [1980] Director [Spanish]; Nicholas Francis Golding [1963] Director

Heathrow (DSH) Limited
Incorporated: 20 December 2007
Net Worth: £4,674,999,808 *Total Assets:* £5,270,000,128
Registered Office: The Compass Centre, Nelson Road, Hounslow, Middlesex, TW6 2GW
Activities: Activities of head offices
Parent: LHR Airports Limited
Officers: Yuanyuan Ding [1979] Director; Javier Echave Espot [1980] Director [Spanish]; Nicholas Francis Golding [1963] Director

Heathrow (SP) Limited
Incorporated: 20 December 2007 *Employees:* 6,605
Net Worth Deficit: £2,635,000,064 *Total Assets:* £15,258,000,384
Registered Office: The Compass Centre, Nelson Road, Hounslow, Middlesex, TW6 2GW
Activities: Activities of head offices
Parent: Heathrow Finance PLC
Officers: Yuanyuan Ding [1979] Director; Javier Echave Espot [1980] Director [Spanish]; Charlotte Emma Tiffany Gilthorpe [1970] Director/Employed Barrister; Nicholas Francis Golding [1963] Director

Heathrow Airport Fuel Company Limited
Incorporated: 23 April 1996
Net Worth: £13,615,000 *Total Assets:* £39,882,000
Registered Office: Building 1204, Sandringham Road, Heathrow Airport, Hounslow, Middlesex, TW6 3SH
Activities: Non-trading company
Officers: Victoria Guy [1971] Director/General Manager; Mark Stephen Hayward [1979] Director/Manager; Mary Marshall Henderson [1959] Director/Oil Company Executive; Rupert Leland Agnar Hone [1966] Director/Oil Company Executive; Stephen Jonathan Newton [1961] Director; Calum James Stacey [1986] Director/Solicitor; Andrew Charles Francis Taylor [1965] Director/Oil Company Executive; Paul William Vowell [1971] Director/Manager [New Zealander]

Heathrow Airport Holdings Limited
Incorporated: 27 March 2006 *Employees:* 6,740
Net Worth: £703,000,000 *Total Assets:* £18,395,000,832
Registered Office: The Compass Centre, Nelson Road, Hounslow, Middlesex, TW6 2GW
Activities: Activities of head offices
Parent: ADI Finance 2 Limited
Officers: Carol Hui, Secretary; Akbar Abbas Al Baker [1960] Director/Chief Executive Officer [Qatari]; Ahmed Ali Al-Hammadi [1981] Director [Qatari]; Stuart Harvey Baldwin [1969] Director/Investment Manager; Christopher William Beale [1947] Director [American]; David Andrew Begg [1956] Director; Ali Bouzarif [1978] Director [Belgian]; Maria Cristina Casero Borges [1960] Director [Spanish]; Jinhong Chen [1990] Director [Chinese]; Samuel Coxe [1975] Alternate Director [American]; Lord Paul Clive Deighton [1956] Director/Company Chairman; Javier Echave Espot [1980] Director [Spanish]; Olivier Georges Xavier Fortin [1974] Director [French]; Ignacio Aitor Garcia Bilbao [1970] Alternate Director [Spanish]; Jorge Gil Villen [1972] Director/Lawyer/Economist [Spanish]; John William Holland-Kaye [1965] Director/Chief Executive Officer; Mr Deven Arvind Karnik [1967] Alternate Director; Tom Kelly [1989] Director [Irish]; Alexander Leonard [1985] Director; Rachel Janis Lomax [1945] Director; Ernesto Lopez [1964] Director/Chief Financial Officer; Inigo Meiras [1963] Alternate Director [Spanish]; Michael James Powell [1972] Director; David Jinlin Xie [1978] Alternate Director [American]; Gonzalo Velasco Zabalza [1979] Alternate Director [Spanish]

Heathrow Airport Limited
Incorporated: 19 February 1986
Net Worth: £2,430,000,128 *Total Assets:* £17,422,000,128
Registered Office: The Compass Centre, Nelson Road, Hounslow, Middlesex, TW6 2GW
Activities: Scheduled passenger air transport
Parent: Heathrow (AH) Limited
Officers: Ross Findlay Scott Baker [1974] Director; William Stuart Birrell [1964] Director/Chief Information Officer; Javier Echave Espot [1980] Director [Spanish]; Christopher Charles Garton [1961] Director; Charlotte Emma Tiffany Gilthorpe [1970] Director/Employed Barrister; John William Holland Kaye [1965] Director/Chief Executive Officer; Carol Hui [1956] Director/Lawyer; Andrew Hugh Macmillan [1975] Director; Paula Stannett [1965] HR Director

Heathrow Aviation Engineering UTC
Incorporated: 31 January 2011 *Employees:* 30
Net Worth: £8,821,438 *Total Assets:* £10,451,370
Registered Office: Heathrow Aviation Engineering UTC, Potter Street, Northwood, Middlesex, HA6 1QG
Activities: General secondary education
Officers: Robert John Bush, Secretary; Jennifer Body [1953] Director/Retired; Joanne Stephanie Harper [1970] Director/Teacher; Dr Sarmin Hossain [1971] Director/University Lecturer; Prof Geoffrey John Rodgers [1963] Director/Academic; Dr Rosa Scoble [1961] Director of Planning [Italian]; Paula Stannett [1965] Director/Chief People Officer

Heathrow Cargo Handling Limited
Incorporated: 5 July 1995 *Employees:* 124
Net Worth: £5,890,000 *Total Assets:* £10,806,000
Registered Office: Building 558, Shoreham Road West, Heathrow Airport, Hounslow, Middlesex, TW6 3RN
Activities: Cargo handling for air transport activities
Shareholders: Air France KLM; Swissport Group UK Limited
Officers: Ariane Appe [1962] Director/Affiliates and Subsidiaries, Investment Strategy [French]; Darren Beamer [1974] Commercial Director; Stephane Patrick Paul Bretaudeau [1971] Director/VP Finance [French]; Jean-Yves Chaumet [1966] Director/Air France Cargo Vice President Operations [French]; Jason Gaskell [1971] Director; Raphael Lebreton de Vannoise [1980] Director [French]; Luzius Wirth [1974] Director [Swiss]

Heathrow Edwardian Hotel Ltd
Incorporated: 27 August 2013 *Employees:* 329
Net Worth: £56,853,000 *Total Assets:* £69,716,000
Registered Office: 140 Bath Road, Hayes, Middlesex, UB3 5AW
Activities: Hotels and similar accommodation
Parent: Edwardian Hotel Finance Ltd
Officers: Vijay Wason, Secretary; John Robert Morley [1945] Director/Financial Consultant; Jasminder Singh [1951] Director/Hotelier

Heathrow Enterprises Limited
Incorporated: 24 November 1992 *Employees:* 22
Net Worth: £68,422,000 *Total Assets:* £82,188,000
Registered Office: The Compass Centre, Nelson Road, Hounslow, Middlesex, TW6 2GW
Activities: Activities of head offices
Parent: LHR Airports Limited
Officers: Ross Findlay Scott Baker [1974] Director; Yuanyuan Ding [1979] Director; Javier Echave Espot [1980] Director [Spanish]

Heathrow Express Operating Company Limited
Incorporated: 11 January 1996 *Employees:* 460
Net Worth: £69,501,000 *Total Assets:* £76,440,000
Registered Office: The Compass Centre, Nelson Road, Hounslow, Middlesex, TW6 2GW
Activities: Passenger rail transport, interurban
Parent: Heathrow Airport Limited
Officers: Ross Findlay Scott Baker [1974] Director; Phillip Alan Bearpark [1966] Director; Anthony Joseph Caccavone [1972] Director; Stephen Paul Chambers [1971] Director; Leslie Freer [1966] Director; Michael Peter Hodson [1951] Director; Andrew Hugh Macmillan [1975] Director

Heathrow Finance PLC
Incorporated: 20 December 2007
Net Worth Deficit: £1,070,000,000 *Total Assets:* £15,616,000,000
Registered Office: The Compass Centre, Nelson Road, Hounslow, Middlesex, TW6 2GW
Activities: Activities of head offices
Parent: Heathrow (DSH) Limited
Officers: Patrick Dawe-Lane, Secretary; Yuanyuan Ding [1979] Director; Javier Echave Espot [1980] Director [Spanish]; Nicholas Francis Golding [1963] Director

Heathrow Holdco Limited
Incorporated: 24 October 2007
Net Worth: £3,782,000,128 *Total Assets:* £11,914,999,808
Registered Office: The Compass Centre, Nelson Road, Hounslow, Middlesex, TW6 2GW
Activities: Activities of head offices
Parent: Heathrow Airport Holdings Limited
Officers: Yuanyuan Ding [1979] Director; Javier Echave Espot [1980] Director [Spanish]; John William Holland-Kaye [1965] Commercial Director

Heathrow Hydrant Operating Company Limited
Incorporated: 21 June 1993 *Employees:* 28
Net Worth: £18,177,000 *Total Assets:* £22,793,000
Registered Office: Building 1204, Sandringham Road, Heathrow Airport, Hounslow, Middlesex, TW6 3SH
Activities: Other service activities n.e.c.
Officers: Victoria Guy [1971] Director/General Manager; Mark Stephen Hayward [1979] Director/Manager; Mary Marshall Henderson [1959] Director/Oil Company Executive; Rupert Leland Agnar Hone [1966] Director/Oil Company Executive; Malachy Joseph Murphy [1963] Director/Company Executive; Stephen Jonathan Newton [1961] Director; Calum James Stacey [1986] Director/Solicitor; Andrew Charles Francis Taylor [1965] Director/Oil Company Executive; Paul William Vowell [1971] Director/Manager [New Zealander]

Heathrow T5 Hotel Limited
Incorporated: 20 December 1999 *Employees:* 5
Previous: Arora Heathrow Holdings Limited
Net Worth: £196,350,688 *Total Assets:* £397,668,768
Registered Office: World Business Centre, 3 Newall Road, London Heathrow Airport, Hounslow, Middlesex, TW6 2TA
Activities: Activities of head offices
Parent: Arora T5 Holdings Limited
Officers: Athos George Yiannis, Secretary; Sunita Arora [1964] Director; Surinder Arora [1958] Director; Carlton Jeffrey Brown [1972] Director/Chartered Accountant; Sanjeev Kumar Roda [1969] Director/IT and Procurement Consultant; Athos George Yiannis [1963] Director/Chartered Accountant

Heathrow Top Limited
Incorporated: 9 December 2013 *Employees:* 5
Net Worth Deficit: £68,059 *Total Assets:* £6,173,206
Registered Office: Long Drive, Station Approach, South Ruislip, Middlesex, HA4 0HN
Activities: Activities of head offices
Parent: Savera London Holdings Limited
Officers: Balkar Singh Johal [1946] Director; Balraj Singh Johal [1948] Director; Iqbal Singh Johal [1954] Director; Jasbir Singh Johal [1953] Director; Sarnpal Singh Johal [1957] Director

Heatpoint Limited
Incorporated: 20 August 2003
Net Worth: £1,689,975 *Total Assets:* £5,939,332
Registered Office: 3rd Floor, Sterling House, Langston Road, Loughton, Essex, IG10 3TS
Activities: Buying and selling of own real estate
Shareholders: Frogmore Property Company Joint Ventures Limited; Galliard Holdings Limited
Officers: Allan William Porter, Secretary; David Edward Conway [1976] Director/Property Developer; Stephen Stuart Solomon Conway [1948] Director

HEB Real Estate Limited
Incorporated: 17 September 2014
Net Worth: £18,187,812 *Total Assets:* £57,800,000
Registered Office: 21 Fulton Road, Wembley, Middlesex, HA9 0GA
Activities: Activities of other holding companies n.e.c.
Major Shareholder: Hasibullah Akbary
Officers: Hasibullah Akbary [1965] Director [Canadian]

Hebridean Island Cruises Limited
Incorporated: 19 October 2016 *Employees:* 14
Net Worth: £3,600,417 *Total Assets:* £10,677,799
Registered Office: 2nd Floor, Nucleus House, 2 Lower Mortlake Road, Richmond, Surrey, TW9 2JA
Activities: Tour operator activities
Officers: Christopher Photi, Secretary; Roger Jeffrey Allard [1954] Director; Kenneth Harvey Charleson [1966] Director; Nigel John Jenkins [1952] Director

Hedge End Place (Durkan) LLP
Incorporated: 20 July 2016
Net Worth Deficit: £7,403 *Total Assets:* £7,638,392
Registered Office: 4 Elstree Gate, Elstree Way, Borehamwood, Herts, WD6 1JD

Hedgemans Limited
Incorporated: 11 December 1984
Net Worth: £11,557,513 *Total Assets:* £13,375,961
Registered Office: 15 Woodlands Avenue, Hornchurch, Essex, RM11 2QT
Activities: Buying and selling of own real estate
Shareholder: Virendra Patel
Officers: Virendra Patel [1958] Director/Pharmacist

Heidelberg Graphic Equipment Limited
Incorporated: 12 July 1974 *Employees:* 246
Net Worth: £22,763,000 *Total Assets:* £59,182,000
Registered Office: 69-76 High Street, Brentford, Middlesex, TW8 0AA
Activities: Installation of industrial machinery and equipment
Officers: Simon Richard Gamble [1967] Finance Director; Axel Lammer [1963] Director/Chairman [German]; James Robert Todd [1956] Director; Ian Terence Wilcock [1963] Service Director

HEL Bidco Ltd
Incorporated: 13 July 2010
Net Worth: £393,815,008 *Total Assets:* £408,340,000
Registered Office: 5th Floor, The Shipping Building, Old Vinyl Factory, 252-254 Blyth Road, Hayes, Middlesex, UB3 1HA
Activities: Activities of head offices
Parent: Host Europe Group Limited
Officers: Richard Anthony Winslow [1979] Director; Jonathan Ying Kit Wong [1976] Director

Hel Group Limited
Incorporated: 26 October 2017 *Employees:* 6
Net Worth Deficit: £452,099 *Total Assets:* £10,800,524
Registered Office: 9-10 Capital Business Park, Manor Way, Borehamwood, Herts, WD6 1GW
Activities: Non-trading company
Parent: Ensco 1261 Limited
Officers: Andrew Roger Dixey [1950] Director; Louise Madden [1971] Director; Luke Edward Matthews [1982] Director; Dr Jasbir Singh [1953] Director; Paul Stuart Sturgeon [1966] Finance Director

HEL Limited
Incorporated: 14 July 1987 *Employees:* 7
Net Worth: £6,545,851 *Total Assets:* £8,416,562
Registered Office: 9-10 Capital Business Park, Manor Way, Borehamwood, Herts, WD6 1GW
Activities: Other research and experimental development on natural sciences and engineering
Parent: Ensco 1262 Limited
Officers: Paul Stuart Sturgeon, Secretary; Mark Stewart Appleton [1960] Director; Gurchetan Singh Dhallu [1966] Director; Roy Eggleston [1967] Director; Gerard Terence Bowker Gardner [1970] Director; Louise Madden [1971] Director; Dr Jasbir Singh [1953] Director; Paul Stuart Sturgeon [1966] Finance Director

G.A.F. Heley (Properties) Limited
Incorporated: 3 August 1992 *Employees:* 3
Net Worth: £2,702,599 *Total Assets:* £7,161,605
Registered Office: Trafalgar House, 712 London Road, Grays, Essex, RM20 3JT
Activities: Other letting and operating of own or leased real estate
Parent: Heley Holdings Limited
Officers: Michael Schultz, Secretary; George Alexander Frederick Heley [1938] Director; George Heley [1957] Managing Director

Heley Holdings Limited
Incorporated: 27 November 2001 *Employees:* 53
Net Worth: £6,215,829 *Total Assets:* £12,813,648
Registered Office: 712 London Road, West Thurrock, Grays, Essex, RM20 3JT
Activities: Non-trading company
Shareholders: George Heley; George Alexander Frederick Heley
Officers: Michael Schultz, Secretary; George Heley [1957] Director; George Alexander Frederick Heley [1938] Director

Heley International Limited
Incorporated: 2 September 1976 *Employees:* 50
Net Worth: £3,048,778 *Total Assets:* £6,521,787
Registered Office: 712 London Road, Grays, Essex, RM20 3JT
Activities: Non-specialised wholesale of food, beverages and tobacco
Parent: Heley Holdings Limited
Officers: Michael Schultz, Secretary; David George Heley [1978] Buying Director; George Heley [1957] Director; George Alexander Frederick Heley [1938] Director; Michael Thomas Heley [1982] Warehouse & Distribution Director; Paul John Manley [1968] Sales Director-Food Wholesaler

Helius Investments Limited
Incorporated: 16 April 1963
Net Worth: £10,668,037 *Total Assets:* £11,686,201
Registered Office: 1 Victoria Parade, Sandycombe Road, Richmond, Surrey, TW9 3NB
Activities: Buying and selling of own real estate
Major Shareholder: Maureen Rowlands
Officers: Maureen Rowlands [1933] Director; Rachel Charlotte Louise Rowlands [1970] Landlord/Director

Henley Group Finance Limited
Incorporated: 2 July 2013 *Employees:* 1
Net Worth: £78,859 *Total Assets:* £8,026,161
Registered Office: 28 Church Road, Stanmore, Middlesex, HA7 4XR
Activities: Financial intermediation not elsewhere classified
Parent: Henley Group Holdings Limited
Officers: Julian Mark Miller [1966] Director/Manager

Henley Group Holdings Limited
Incorporated: 13 March 1995 *Employees:* 1
Net Worth: £14,022,806 *Total Assets:* £14,042,932
Registered Office: 28 Church Road, Stanmore, Middlesex, HA7 4XR
Activities: Activities of head offices
Major Shareholder: Peter Gordon Watts
Officers: Julian Mark Miller [1966] Director/Manager

Henry Construction Projects Limited
Incorporated: 14 June 2010 *Employees:* 12
Net Worth: £9,247,834 *Total Assets:* £43,675,720
Registered Office: Parkway Farm, Church Road, Cranford, Hounslow, Middlesex, TW5 9RY
Activities: Construction of commercial buildings
Parent: Henry Group Holdings Limited
Officers: Elizabeth Mary Henry, Secretary; Mark James Henry [1978] Director [Irish]; William Anthony Henry [1945] Director [Irish]; John Noone [1971] Director [Irish]

Herbalife (U.K.) Limited
Incorporated: 28 March 1983 *Employees:* 24
Net Worth: £2,153,947 *Total Assets:* £7,990,226
Registered Office: The Atrium, 1 Harefield Road, Uxbridge, Middlesex, UB8 1HB
Activities: Other retail sale of food in specialised stores
Parent: Herbalife Ltd.
Officers: Martin James Bartlett [1959] Director/Vice President, Finance and Operations, EMEA; Richard Paul Goudis [1961] Director/Chief Executive Officer [American]; Paul Kambanaros [1969] Director/Vice President - Regional Controller EMEA; Neil Spiers [1970] Director/Vice President

Herbalife Europe Limited
Incorporated: 22 February 1996 *Employees:* 109
Net Worth: £1,500,011 *Total Assets:* £26,427,512
Registered Office: The Atrium, 1 Harefield Road, Uxbridge, Middlesex, UB8 1HB
Activities: Other service activities n.e.c.
Parent: Herbalife (U.K.) Limited
Officers: Martin James Bartlett [1959] Director/Vice President, Finance and Operations, EMEA; Richard Paul Goudis [1961] Director/Chief Executive Officer [American]; Paul Kambanaros [1969] Director/Vice President - Regional Controller EMEA

Heritage Care Homes Limited
Incorporated: 22 February 2002 *Employees:* 82
Net Worth: £4,124,352 *Total Assets:* £7,920,047
Registered Office: 1st Floor, 5 Century Court, Tolpits Lane, Watford, Herts, WD18 9PX
Activities: Residential nursing care facilities
Shareholders: Sheikh Mubashir Hussain; Razia Begum Hussain
Officers: Razia Begum Hussain, Secretary; Razia Begum Hussain [1952] Director/Businesswoman; Sheikh Mubashir Hussain [1950] Director/Businessman

Heritage Care Limited
Incorporated: 1 April 2010 *Employees:* 1,461
Net Worth: £10,241,000 *Total Assets:* £23,166,000
Registered Office: Connaught House, 112-120 High Road, Loughton, Essex, IG10 4HJ
Activities: Social work activities without accommodation for the elderly and disabled
Officers: Mark Timothy Milton, Secretary; Alan Twan Bates [1979] Director/Barrister; Nigel Owen Fletcher [1976] HR Director; Simon William Paul Griffiths [1961] Director/NHS Manager; Scott Thomas Haldane [1959] Finance Director; Richard James Edward Jones [1961] Director/Business Executive; Margaret Mary Lally [1953] Director/Retired; Jeanette Mitchell [1949] Director/Retired/Sessional Community Support Worker; Iain Francis O'Neil [1974] Director/Civil Servant; Lorraine Reynolds [1954] Director/Consultant [American]; John Peter Schuster [1950] Director/Retired; Richard John Smallwood [1955] Director/Retired

Heritage Square Limited
Incorporated: 17 January 2013 *Employees:* 1
Net Worth: £2,295,000 *Total Assets:* £53,244,000
Registered Office: Elder House, St Georges Business Park, Brooklands Road, Weybridge, Surrey, KT13 0TS
Activities: Financial intermediation not elsewhere classified
Parent: Puma Heritage PLC
Officers: James Ednie Brydie [1959] Director; Michael David Posen [1944] Director; Michael Laurent Van Messel [1964] Director

Hersham Green LLP
Incorporated: 20 August 2010
Net Worth: £2,574,712 *Total Assets:* £7,940,642
Registered Office: 2 AC Court, High Street, Thames Ditton, Surrey, KT7 0SR
Officers: Timothy David Edwards [1958] Member; Darren Matthew Johns [1971] Member

Hertswood Academy
Incorporated: 15 March 2012 *Employees:* 154
Net Worth: £39,391,384 *Total Assets:* £43,777,864
Registered Office: Cowley Hill, Borehamwood, Herts, WD6 5LG
Activities: General secondary education
Officers: Joy Linda Wells Cox [1957] Director; Martin Wolfgang Doe [1966] Director/Computer Programmer; Peter Gillett [1970] Director; Fiona Helen Gubb Blackwood [1974] Director/Children's Centre Manager; Ann Muriel Harrison [1946] Director; Richard Arthur Kirk [1942] Director; Elizabeth Longworth [1968] Director/Teacher; Julie Dawn Smith [1966] Director/Sales Programme Support Manager; Christine Wainright [1954] Director/KS3 Co-ordinator

Hertz (U.K.) Limited
Incorporated: 28 January 1958 *Employees:* 413
Net Worth: £16,640,000 *Total Assets:* £282,980,992
Registered Office: Hertz House, 11 Vine Street, Uxbridge, Middlesex, UB8 1QE
Activities: Renting and leasing of cars and light motor vehicles
Parent: Hertz Holdings III UK Limited
Officers: John Christopher Finch, Secretary; Bhaven Ashok Taylor [1980] Finance Director

Hertz Accident Support Ltd
Incorporated: 15 December 2009
Previous: CCL Vehicle Rentals Ltd
Net Worth: £6,706,991 *Total Assets:* £18,001,948
Registered Office: Hertz House, 11 Vine Street, Uxbridge, Middlesex, UB8 1QE
Activities: Renting and leasing of cars and light motor vehicles
Parent: Hertz (U.K.) Limited
Officers: John Christopher Finch, Secretary; David Andrew Hayward [1967] Director; Bhaven Ashok Taylor [1980] Finance Director

Hertz Europe Limited
Incorporated: 22 April 1971 *Employees:* 204
Net Worth: £33,627,000 *Total Assets:* £74,385,000
Registered Office: Hertz House, 11 Vine Street, Uxbridge, Middlesex, UB8 1QE
Activities: Other service activities n.e.c.
Parent: Hertz (U.K.) Limited
Officers: John Christopher Finch, Secretary; John Christopher Finch [1965] Director; Tracy Ann Gehlan [1968] Director; Michel Maurice Taride [1956] Director/Executive [French]

Hertz Holdings III UK Limited
Incorporated: 6 December 2005
Net Worth: £34,875,000 *Total Assets:* £34,875,000
Registered Office: Hertz House, 11 Vine Street, Uxbridge, Middlesex, UB8 1QE
Activities: Other business support service activities n.e.c.
Officers: John Christopher Finch, Secretary; Michel Maurice Taride [1956] Director/Executive [French]

Hertz UK Receivables Ltd
Incorporated: 25 November 2013
Net Worth: £159,600 *Total Assets:* £7,310,309
Registered Office: 11 Vine Street, Uxbridge, Middlesex, UB8 1QE
Activities: Factoring
Parent: Hertz Holdings III UK Limited
Officers: John Christopher Finch, Secretary; Bryn Davies [1973] Director/Treasurer; Bhaven Ashok Taylor [1980] Finance Director

Hexagon Corporate Management Limited
Incorporated: 12 September 2013
Net Worth: £738,456,704 *Total Assets:* £742,117,184
Registered Office: Cedar House, 78 Portsmouth Road, Cobham, Surrey, KT11 1AN
Activities: Financial management
Parent: Hexagon Metrology Services Ltd
Officers: Helen Elizabeth Peall, Secretary; David Anthony Mills [1972] Director/CFO, Hexagon Metrology

Hexagon Manufacturing Intelligence Management Limited
Incorporated: 22 December 2015
Net Worth: £871,914,560 *Total Assets:* £874,900,928
Registered Office: 78 Cedar House, Portsmouth Road, Cobham, Surrey, KT11 1AN
Activities: Financial management
Shareholders: Hexagon Metrology Services Ltd; Hexagon AB
Officers: Helen Elizabeth Peall, Secretary; David Anthony Mills [1972] Director/CFO Hexagon Metrology

Hexagon Positioning Intelligence Limited
Incorporated: 17 October 2013
Net Worth: £119,576,000 *Total Assets:* £210,702,000
Registered Office: Cedar House, 78 Portsmouth Road, Cobham, Surrey, KT11 1AN
Activities: Activities of head offices
Parent: Hexagon AB
Officers: Helen Elizabeth Peall, Secretary; David Anthony Mills [1972] Director

HFIS PLC
Incorporated: 20 September 1996 *Employees:* 215
Net Worth: £4,381,265 *Total Assets:* £9,232,645
Registered Office: First Floor, Lumiere, Elstree Way, Borehamwood, Herts, WD6 1JH
Activities: Non-life insurance
Major Shareholder: Simon Fox
Officers: David Anthony Jacobs, Secretary; Graham Marshall Coates [1956] Director/Management Consultant; Teresa Anne Dunne [1964] Human Resources Director; Edward William Hooker [1967] Director/Insurance Consultant; David Anthony Jacobs [1958] Director/Accountant; Ben John Terrett [1972] Finance Director

HFMC Group Holdings Ltd
Incorporated: 20 June 2005 *Employees:* 100
Previous: HFM Columbus Group Holdings Limited
Net Worth: £4,430,371 *Total Assets:* £7,908,027
Registered Office: Russell House, 140 High Street, Edgware, Middlesex, HA8 7LW
Activities: Financial intermediation not elsewhere classified
Shareholder: Jacqueline Elizabeth Suzanne Hoyland
Officers: Lee Anthony Robert Paris, Secretary; Marcus Reinhard Anthony Carlton [1959] Director; Gary John Festa [1952] Director; John Nicolas Jeremy Hoyland [1958] Director; Ross Hamilton Ibbotson [1976] Director; Lee Anthony Robert Paris [1959] Director; Philip Patient [1975] Director/Chief Operating Officer; Mark Ellis Waller [1973] Director

HFS Investment Properties Limited
Incorporated: 12 August 2013
Net Worth: £1,893,404 *Total Assets:* £8,945,114
Registered Office: Haslers, Old Station Road, Loughton, Essex, IG10 4PL
Activities: Other business support service activities n.e.c.
Shareholders: Jacqueline Walker; Christopher Hayden Smith
Officers: Doretta Smith [1943] Director; Hayden Francis Smith [1939] Managing Director

HFSI Limited
Incorporated: 27 April 2010
Net Worth: £358,497 *Total Assets:* £5,262,274
Registered Office: Haslers, Old Station Road, Loughton, Essex, IG10 4PL
Activities: Credit granting by non-deposit taking finance houses and other specialist consumer credit grantors
Shareholders: Doretta Smith; Hayden Francis Smith; Christopher Hayden Smith; Jacqueline Walker
Officers: Doretta Smith [1943] Director; Hayden Francis Smith [1939] Director

HH Global Corporate Services Limited
Incorporated: 4 April 2017
Net Worth: £490,000 *Total Assets:* £7,477,000
Registered Office: Grove House, Guildford Road, Fetcham, Leatherhead, Surrey, KT22 9DF
Activities: Other business support service activities n.e.c.
Parent: HH Global Limited
Officers: Reinhard Schu, Secretary; Kevin Dunckley [1966] Director/Chief Digital Officer; Robert John Fergus Macmillan [1972] Managing Director; Edward James Parsons [1967] Financial Director

HH Global Group Limited
Incorporated: 26 July 2017 *Employees:* 866
Net Worth: £96,801,000 *Total Assets:* £223,102,000
Registered Office: Grove House, Guildford Road, Fetcham, Leatherhead, Surrey, KT22 9DF
Activities: Activities of other holding companies n.e.c.
Major Shareholder: Robert John Fergus Macmillan
Officers: Reinhard Schu, Secretary; Justin Glenn Barton [1963] Director; Robert John Fergus Macmillan [1972] Director; Edward James Parsons [1967] Director

HH Global Limited
Incorporated: 27 February 2003 *Employees:* 877
Net Worth: £855,000 *Total Assets:* £92,304,000
Registered Office: Grove House, Guildford Road, Fetcham, Leatherhead, Surrey, KT22 9DF
Activities: Activities of other holding companies n.e.c.
Parent: HH Global Group Limited
Officers: Reinhard Schu, Secretary; Justin Glenn Barton [1963] Director; Nicholas William Dixon [1961] Director; Kevin Dunckley [1966] Technical Director; Lee Graham Humphreys [1976] Director; Robert John Fergus Macmillan [1972] Director; Stephen Christopher Charles Nunn [1963] Director CEO - EMEA; Edward James Parsons [1967] Financial Director; Michael Edward Perez [1973] Director [American]; Andrew John Price [1963] Director [Australian]

Hi - Line Wines Limited
Incorporated: 6 November 2003 *Employees:* 50
Net Worth: £528,808 *Total Assets:* £5,220,125
Registered Office: Unit 2, 40 Purley Way, Croydon, Surrey, CR0 3JP
Activities: Wholesale of wine, beer, spirits and other alcoholic beverages
Major Shareholder: Sharmmila Jeganmogan
Officers: Sharmmila Jeganmogan [1979] Director

Hi-Spirits Ltd
Incorporated: 13 August 2002 *Employees:* 25
Net Worth: £4,355,371 *Total Assets:* £9,584,388
Registered Office: 60 Marina Place, Hampton Wick, Kingston upon Thames, Surrey, KT1 4BH
Activities: Wholesale of wine, beer, spirits and other alcoholic beverages
Major Shareholder: William Alan Goldring
Officers: Christopher Douglas Ritchie [1972] Director [Canadian]; Christopher Robin Skinger [1974] Director [American]; Magdalena Ewa Tadych [1978] Director [Polish]

Hi-Tec Europe Limited
Incorporated: 31 August 2016 *Employees:* 58
Net Worth: £465,245 *Total Assets:* £8,129,508
Registered Office: Unit 1 Colonial Business Park, Colonial Way, Watford, Herts, WD24 4PR
Activities: Other retail sale in non-specialised stores
Major Shareholder: Rajiv Batra
Officers: Rajesh Batra [1955] Director [Indian]; Rajiv Batra [1961] Director; Ian McDonald McLean Cameron [1967] Director; Poopalasingham Rudran [1961] Finance Director

HIC Racing (Chiswick) Limited
Incorporated: 25 November 1981
Net Worth: £499,114,144 *Total Assets:* £499,137,952
Registered Office: Maple Court, Central Park, Reeds Crescent, Watford, Herts, WD24 4QQ
Activities: Non-trading company
Parent: Hilton Worldwide Holdings, Inc
Officers: Stuart Beasley [1971] Director/Financial Controller; Richard Geoffrey Beeston [1982] Director/Chartered Accountant; Michelle Momdjian [1976] Director/Attorney; George Christopher Ogle [1974] Director/Attorney; James Owen Percival [1968] Director/Accountant

HIC Treasury Limited
Incorporated: 29 June 1982
Net Worth: £512,404,288 *Total Assets:* £514,079,584
Registered Office: Maple Court, Central Park, Reeds Crescent, Watford, Herts, WD24 4QQ
Activities: Non-trading company
Parent: Hilton Finance (UK) Limited
Officers: Stuart Beasley [1971] Director/Financial Controller; Richard Geoffrey Beeston [1982] Director/Chartered Accountant; Michelle Momdjian [1976] Director/Attorney; George Christopher Ogle [1974] Director/Attorney; James Owen Percival [1968] Director/Accountant

Higgins Construction PLC
Incorporated: 27 February 1961 *Employees:* 306
Net Worth: £31,662,000 *Total Assets:* £120,509,000
Registered Office: One Langston Road, Loughton, Essex, IG10 3SD
Activities: Development of building projects
Parent: Higgins Group PLC
Officers: Mark Kevin Francis, Secretary; Stephen Bailess [1969] Director; Mark William Bradbury [1961] Construction Director; Philip David Burrows [1962] Director; Mark Kevin Francis [1980] Director; Declan Graham Higgins [1992] Director; Richard Graham Higgins [1956] Director; Stephen John Leakey [1969] Director/Construction; Antony Millidge [1961] Construction Director; Sean David Robinson [1975] Commercial Director

Higgins Group PLC
Incorporated: 16 February 1989 *Employees:* 379
Net Worth: £56,196,000 *Total Assets:* £199,340,000
Registered Office: One Langston Road, Loughton, Essex, IG10 3SD
Activities: Activities of head offices
Shareholders: Richard Graham Higgins; Martin James Higgins; Stephen Peter Higgins
Officers: Mark Kevin Francis, Secretary; Mark Kevin Francis [1980] Director; Martin James Higgins [1960] Director; Richard Graham Higgins [1956] Director; Stephen Peter Higgins [1958] Director

Higgins Homes PLC
Incorporated: 29 March 1965 *Employees:* 60
Net Worth: £21,425,000 *Total Assets:* £106,665,000
Registered Office: One Langston Road, Loughton, Essex, IG10 3SD
Activities: Development of building projects
Parent: Higgins Group PLC
Officers: Mark Kevin Francis, Secretary; Stephen James Boreham [1973] Construction Director; Mark Kevin Francis [1980] Director/Accountant; Steven Hancocks [1957] Director/Chartered Surveyor; Martin James Higgins [1960] Director; Richard Graham Higgins [1956] Director; William Michael Higgins [1986] Director; Jeremy Paul Marcus [1964] Sales Director; Christopher Miller [1966] Commercial Director; Malcolm Stuart Wallace [1958] Construction Director

Higgins Investments PLC
Incorporated: 5 December 1989 *Employees:* 3
Net Worth: £3,998,016 *Total Assets:* £13,784,537
Registered Office: One Langston Road, Loughton, Essex, IG10 3SD
Activities: Buying and selling of own real estate
Parent: Higgins Group PLC
Officers: Mark Kevin Francis, Secretary; Mark Kevin Francis [1980] Director/Accountant; Martin James Higgins [1960] Director; Richard Graham Higgins [1956] Director

Higgs International Limited
Incorporated: 17 February 1956 *Employees:* 42
Net Worth: £8,966,000 *Total Assets:* £12,740,000
Registered Office: Eastworth House, Eastworth Road, Chertsey, Surrey, KT16 8SH
Activities: Other service activities n.e.c.
Parent: DHL Global Forwarding (UK) Limited
Officers: Vari Isabel Cameron [1961] Director/Chief Executive Officer; Darren John Starkey [1966] Director; Michael Paul Young [1972] Director

High Park Investments Limited
Incorporated: 7 April 1972
Net Worth: £2,549,239 *Total Assets:* £7,493,866
Registered Office: 88 Edgware Way, Edgware, Middlesex, HA8 8JS
Activities: Other letting and operating of own or leased real estate
Shareholders: Robert Grussgott; Solomon Grussgott
Officers: Solomon Grussgott, Secretary; Robert Grussgott [1944] Director; Solomon Grussgott [1943] Director

High Point Solutions Limited
Incorporated: 27 January 2011 *Employees:* 28
Net Worth Deficit: £51,746 *Total Assets:* £6,304,250
Registered Office: 5 Ockham Drive, Greenford Park, Greenford, Middlesex, UB6 0FD
Activities: Repair of other equipment
Shareholders: Michael Mendiburu; Thomas Mendiburu
Officers: Michael Mendiburu [1968] Director/Company Owner [American]; Thomas Mendiburu [1971] Director [American]

Highassets Limited
Incorporated: 21 November 2003
Net Worth Deficit: £290,616 *Total Assets:* £8,245,822
Registered Office: c/o S2 Asset Management Ltd, 3rd Floor, Argyle House, Northside, Joel Street, Northwood Hills, Northwood, Middlesex, HA6 1NW
Activities: Buying and selling of own real estate
Parent: Milebank Ltd
Officers: Hardip Singh [1973] Director; Bharat Kumar Hirji Thakrar [1957] Director

Highfield Infants' School
Incorporated: 1 August 2013 *Employees:* 41
Net Worth: £9,717,000 *Total Assets:* £10,134,000
Registered Office: Highfield Infants' School, Highfield Drive, Bromley, Kent, BR2 0RX
Activities: Primary education
Officers: Annick Zella Smith, Secretary; Joanna Abigail Addison [1972] Director/School Governor; Nick Aziz [1962] HR Director; Nathan Giles Bavidge [1975] Director/Finance Controller; Anthony Martin Chase [1952] Director/Chartered Surveyor; Zoe Anne Frankis [1960] Director/Teacher; Kira Gabbert [1979] Director/Management Consultant; Ann Winifred Golding [1958] Director/Headteacher; Nicola Susan Williamson [1968] Director/Teacher

Highfield Junior School
Incorporated: 20 August 2013 *Employees:* 54
Net Worth: £11,255,000 *Total Assets:* £11,515,000
Registered Office: Highfield Junior School, South Hill Road, Shortlands, Bromley, Kent, BR2 0RL
Activities: Primary education
Officers: Mohit Aiyar [1977] Regional Sales Director [Indian]; Timothy Ayres [1988] Director/Teacher; Nick Aziz [1962] HR Director; Fiona Valerie Eleanor Bratt [1961] Director/Teacher; Fiona Mary Cape [1958] Director/Debt Counsellor; Ann Winifred Golding [1958] Director/Headteacher; Don Gihantha Jayasinghe [1971] Director/Marketing; Nicola Osinaike [1978] Director; Jonathan Alexander Matthew Patterson [1961] Director/Retired; Orla Penruddocke [1976] Director [Irish]; Alastair Taylor [1975] Director/Deputy Headteacher; Tim Edward Yendell [1969] Director/Consultant

Highplus Limited
Incorporated: 21 August 1997
Net Worth: £450,014 *Total Assets:* £6,811,895
Registered Office: Regency House, 33 Wood Street, Barnet, Herts, EN5 4BE
Activities: Management consultancy activities other than financial management
Shareholders: Ian Barry Abrams; Karen Abrams
Officers: Ian Barry Abrams, Secretary; Ian Barry Abrams [1950] Director/Actuary; Karen Abrams [1952] Director/Lawyer

Highrak Limited
Incorporated: 2 November 1988 *Employees:* 7
Net Worth: £4,876,098 *Total Assets:* £8,368,730
Registered Office: Runway House, The Runway, Ruislip, Middlesex, HA4 6SE
Activities: Hotels and similar accommodation
Parent: SME Holdings Ltd
Officers: Aly Mohamed Esmail, Secretary; Sayed Mohamed Esmail, Secretary; Aly Mohamed Esmail [1982] Director; Sayed Mohamed Esmail [1986] Director

Highway Care Group Limited
Incorporated: 27 November 1980 *Employees:* 87
Net Worth: £5,698,475 *Total Assets:* £19,464,176
Registered Office: Trinity House, 3 Bullace Lane, Dartford, Kent, DA1 1BB
Activities: Other service activities n.e.c.
Shareholders: John Edward Talbot; Esther Jeanette Talbot
Officers: John Edward Talbot, Secretary/Director; Peter Alan Ranson [1953] Contracts Manager/Director; Esther Jeanette Talbot [1958] Director/Payroll Administrator; John Edward Talbot [1942] Director/Chemical Engineer

Highway Care Limited
Incorporated: 29 May 1990 *Employees:* 87
Net Worth: £8,428,435 *Total Assets:* £19,497,688
Registered Office: Trinity House, 3 Bullace Lane, Dartford, Kent, DA1 1BB
Activities: Other service activities n.e.c.
Parent: Highway Care Group Limited
Officers: Antony William Frederick Butcher, Secretary; Adrian Bullock [1971] Engineering Director; Antony William Frederick Butcher [1975] Director/Chartered Accountant; Benjamin James Duncker [1983] Director - International Sales; Norman Arthur Farrell [1950] Director/Consultant [New Zealander]; Andrew MacCuish [1986] Operations Director; Peter Alan Ranson [1953] Contracts Manager/Director; Esther Jeanette Talbot [1958] Director/Payroll Administrator; John Edward Talbot [1942] Director/Chemical Engineer

Highway Stops Retail Limited
Incorporated: 8 August 2011 *Employees:* 3
Net Worth: £12,992,547 *Total Assets:* £23,157,496
Registered Office: Unit 11 Metro Trading Centre, Second Way, Wembley, Middlesex, HA9 0YJ
Activities: Other business support service activities n.e.c.
Major Shareholder: Sharad Mohanlal Raja
Officers: Anthony David Head [1968] Director; Sharad Mohanlal Raja [1949] Director; Shilan Raja [1986] Director; Shobhana Sharad Raja [1953] Director

Hilands Property Partners LLP
Incorporated: 30 March 2007 *Employees:* 2
Net Worth: £12,183,434 *Total Assets:* £12,190,634
Registered Office: Enterprise House, Eastern Road, Romford, Essex, RM1 3PJ
Officers: Dennis Edward Myers [1950] Member; Patricia Anne Myers [1948] Member

Hildo Limited
Incorporated: 31 January 2012
Net Worth: £13,342,024 *Total Assets:* £15,655,811
Registered Office: Hill House, Lowlands Road, Harrow, Middlesex, HA1 3EQ
Activities: Development of building projects
Major Shareholder: Donovan Gijsbertus Wijsmuller
Officers: Brian Martin Comer [1960] Director [Irish]; Luke Andrew Comer [1957] Director [Irish]

The Hill Company Limited
Incorporated: 11 November 2003 *Employees:* 63
Net Worth: £5,416,503 *Total Assets:* £27,435,568
Registered Office: Solus 31, Motherwell Way, West Thurrock, Essex, RM20 3LB
Activities: Archives activities
Parent: Motherwell Holdings Ltd
Officers: James Douglas Hill, Secretary/Director; Ryan James Brazier [1989] Director; Andrew Douglas Hill [1931] Director; James Douglas Hill [1968] Director; Sarah Jane Hill [1966] Director; David Victor Malempre [1949] Director/Corporate Lawyer; Roger Joseph McGlynn [1957] Director/Company Accountant

Hill Group Services Limited
Incorporated: 14 April 2009 *Employees:* 26
Net Worth: £4,022,000 *Total Assets:* £117,019,000
Registered Office: The Power House, Gunpowder Mill, Powdermill Lane, Waltham Abbey, Essex, EN9 1BN
Activities: Other business support service activities n.e.c.
Parent: Hill Holdings Limited
Officers: Andrew Richard Hill [1958] Director; Gregory James Hill [1986] Director; Kieran Thomas Larkin [1953] Director; Neil Stuart Williams [1961] Finance Director

Hill Holdings Limited
Incorporated: 20 April 2001 *Employees:* 432
Net Worth: £128,543,000 *Total Assets:* £376,777,984
Registered Office: The Power House, Gunpowder Mill, Powdermill Lane, Waltham Abbey, Essex, EN9 1BN
Activities: Activities of construction holding companies
Major Shareholder: Andrew Richard Hill
Officers: Neil Stuart Williams, Secretary; Ernest Stephen Battey [1959] Director; Andrew Richard Hill [1958] Director; Gregory James Hill [1986] Director; Kieran Thomas Larkin [1953] Director; Neil Stuart Williams [1961] Finance Director

Hill of Towie Limited
Incorporated: 6 July 2009
Net Worth Deficit: £16,366,000 *Total Assets:* £64,152,000
Registered Office: Beaufort Court, Egg Farm Lane, Kings Langley, Herts, WD4 8LR
Activities: Other business support service activities n.e.c.
Parent: Trafalgar Wind Holdings Limited
Officers: Dominic James Hearth, Secretary; Steven William Hughes [1972] Generation & Asset Management Director; Fraser Stephen Merry [1968] Director/Chartered Surveyor; Mitesh Raj Patel [1982] Director/Group Financial Controller

Hill Partnerships Limited
Incorporated: 8 April 1991 *Employees:* 319
Net Worth: £35,963,000 *Total Assets:* £224,531,008
Registered Office: The Power House, Gunpowder Mill, Powdermill Lane, Waltham Abbey, Essex, EN9 1BN
Activities: Construction of domestic buildings
Parent: Hill Holdings Limited
Officers: Neil Stuart Williams, Secretary; Andrew Richard Hill [1958] Managing Director; Gregory James Hill [1986] Director; Thomas Hill [1988] Director; Ian Jamie Hunter [1967] Director; Robert Allan Jack [1974] Director; Paul Robert Jordan [1964] Director; Stephen John Kane [1964] Commercial Director; Kieran Thomas Larkin [1953] Director; Simon William Trice [1978] Director; Neil Stuart Williams [1961] Finance Director

Hill Residential Limited
Incorporated: 13 July 2001 *Employees:* 78
Net Worth: £97,007,000 *Total Assets:* £305,825,984
Registered Office: The Power House, Gunpowder Mill, Powdermill Lane, Waltham Abbey, Essex, EN9 1BN
Activities: Buying and selling of own real estate
Parent: Hill Holdings Limited
Officers: Neil Stuart Williams, Secretary; David Stewart Eardley [1968] Director; Robert Hall [1967] Director; Ryan Paul Harris [1982] Director; Andrew Richard Hill [1958] Director; Gregory James Hill [1986] Director; Ian Jamie Hunter [1967] Director; Stephen John Kane [1964] Director; Kieran Thomas Larkin [1953] Director; Amanda Miller [1964] Director/Solicitor; Damian O'Hara [1964] Director; Anthony Charles Parker [1971] Director/Chartered Accountant; Nicholas Parkinson [1960] Design Director; Cain Peters [1972] Director; Jon Thistlethwaite [1969] Director; Neil Stuart Williams [1961] Finance Director; Anthony John Woodman [1960] Director

Hill's Garages (Woodford) Limited
Incorporated: 6 June 1945 *Employees:* 108
Net Worth: £4,302,805 *Total Assets:* £13,312,039
Registered Office: 536-564 High Road, Woodford Green, Essex, IG8 0PR
Activities: Sale of new cars and light motor vehicles
Parent: Hills Group Enterprises Limited
Officers: Rosanna Hill, Secretary; Ashley Boyd Humphries, Secretary; Rosanna Francesca Hill [1988] Director; Ashley Boyd Humphries [1959] Director

Hillary Bidco Limited
Incorporated: 23 March 2012 *Employees:* 661
Net Worth Deficit: £45,515,000 *Total Assets:* £37,972,000
Registered Office: Everest House, Sopers Road, Cuffley, Potters Bar, Herts, EN6 4SG
Activities: Activities of head offices
Major Shareholder: Jonathan Paul Moulton
Officers: Robert Alexander Asplin [1979] Director; Joanne Maria Holland [1960] Director [Australian]; Karl Sean Munns [1970] Director

S.Hille & Co.(Holdings) Limited
Incorporated: 20 October 1964 *Employees:* 5
Net Worth: £11,208,170 *Total Assets:* £12,025,737
Registered Office: 132 St Albans Road, Watford, Herts, WD24 4AE
Activities: Other letting and operating of own or leased real estate
Officers: Ian Scheer, Secretary; Brian Ivan Leaver [1936] Director/Chartered Surveyor; Cherrill Sheila Scheer [1939] Director; Ian Scheer [1933] Director/Printer; Terence Ivan Scheer [1968] Director/Printer

JF Hillebrand UK Limited
Incorporated: 13 January 1982 *Employees:* 133
Net Worth: £5,352,729 *Total Assets:* £26,352,304
Registered Office: Dissegna House, Weston Avenue, West Thurrock, Grays, Essex, RM20 3ZP
Activities: Other transportation support activities
Officers: Joanne Christina Kelly, Secretary; Thorsten Beer [1971] Director/Chief Financial Officer [German]; Gavin Herman [1967] Director/Chief Operating Officer; Joanne Christina Kelly [1979] Finance Director; Cornelis Sigmund Van Gent [1962] Director/Chief Executive [Dutch]

Hillier Hopkins LLP
Incorporated: 16 January 2003 *Employees:* 125
Net Worth: £3,195,946 *Total Assets:* £5,939,205
Registered Office: Radius House, 51 Clarendon Road, Watford, Herts, WD17 1HP

Hillingdon House (UK) Limited
Incorporated: 29 July 2015
Net Worth: £2,099,268 *Total Assets:* £9,931,481
Registered Office: Top Floor, Bridgewater House, 866-868 Uxbridge Road, Hayes, Middlesex, UB4 0RR
Activities: Other letting and operating of own or leased real estate
Shareholders: Rajinder Singh Makkar; Inderpal Kaur Makkar
Officers: Rajinder Singh Makkar, Secretary; Inderpal Kaur Makkar [1967] Director; Rajinder Singh Makkar [1963] Director

Hills Group Enterprises Limited
Incorporated: 19 November 2002 *Employees:* 108
Net Worth: £7,664,311 *Total Assets:* £16,674,323
Registered Office: 536-564 High Road, Woodford Green, Essex, IG8 0PR
Activities: Activities of head offices
Major Shareholder: Richard Martin Hill
Officers: Rosanna Hill, Secretary; Ashley Boyd Humphries, Secretary; Rosanna Francesca Hill [1988] Director; Ashley Boyd Humphries [1959] Director

Hills Prospect PLC
Incorporated: 23 July 2001 *Employees:* 144
Net Worth: £3,471,074 *Total Assets:* £9,251,692
Registered Office: Hills Prospect PLC, Consolidated House, Faringdon Avenue, Romford, Essex, RM3 8SP
Activities: Wholesale of wine, beer, spirits and other alcoholic beverages
Officers: Michael Lomotey, Secretary; Trevor Bowers [1958] Director; Nicholas Callaghan [1970] Director; Lisa Richards [1966] Director; Darren Smart [1969] Director; Collette Whittington-Bowers [1967] Director

Hilton Finance (UK) Limited
Incorporated: 18 November 1999
Net Worth: £1,663,046,016 *Total Assets:* £1,676,255,104
Registered Office: Maple Court, Central Park, Reeds Crescent, Watford, Herts, WD24 4QQ
Activities: Other business support service activities n.e.c.
Parent: Hilton UK Hotels Limited
Officers: Stuart Beasley [1971] Director/Financial Controller; Richard Geoffrey Beeston [1982] Director/Chartered Accountant; Michelle Momdjian [1976] Director/Attorney; George Christopher Ogle [1974] Director/Attorney; James Owen Percival [1968] Director/Accountant

Hilton HHC Limited
Incorporated: 19 January 2006
Net Worth: £1,552,382,464 *Total Assets:* £1,552,382,464
Registered Office: Maple Court, Central Park, Reeds Crescent, Watford, Herts, WD24 4QQ
Activities: Activities of head offices
Parent: Hilton HIH Limited
Officers: Stuart Beasley [1971] Director/Financial Controller; Richard Geoffrey Beeston [1982] Director/Chartered Accountant; Michelle Momdjian [1976] Director/Attorney; George Christopher Ogle [1974] Director/Attorney; Brian McKay Wilson [1962] Director/Company Secretary

Hilton International Hotels (UK) Limited
Incorporated: 12 June 1961
Net Worth: £666,311,040 *Total Assets:* £1,487,772,288
Registered Office: Maple Court, Central Park, Reeds Crescent, Watford, Herts, WD24 4QQ
Activities: Hotels and similar accommodation
Parent: Hilton International IP Holding Limited
Officers: Stuart Beasley [1971] Director/Financial Controller; Richard Geoffrey Beeston [1982] Director/Chartered Accountant; Stephen Patrick Cassidy [1968] Director/SVP Operations UK & Ireland; Michelle Momdjian [1976] Director/Attorney; George Christopher Ogle [1974] Director/Attorney; James Owen Percival [1968] Director/Accountant; Simon Robert Vincent [1963] Director; Brian McKay Wilson [1962] Director/Company Secretary

Hilton International IP Holding 2 Limited
Incorporated: 6 December 2016
Net Worth: £2,394,365,184 *Total Assets:* £2,523,724,800
Registered Office: Maple Court, Central Park, Reeds Crescent, Watford, Herts, WD24 4QQ
Activities: Hotels and similar accommodation
Parent: Hilton International Master Holding Limited
Officers: Stuart Beasley [1971] Director/Financial Controller; Richard Geoffrey Beeston [1982] Director/Chartered Accountant; Stephen Patrick Cassidy [1968] Director/Senior Vice President Operations; Michelle Momdjian [1976] Director/Attorney; George Christopher Ogle [1974] Director/Attorney; James Owen Percival [1968] Director/Accountant; Brian McKay Wilson [1962] Director/Company Secretary

Hilton International IP Holding Limited
Incorporated: 8 July 2016
Net Worth: £2,694,447,104 *Total Assets:* £3,080,324,096
Registered Office: Maple Court, Central Park, Reeds Crescent, Watford, Herts, WD24 4QQ
Activities: Hotels and similar accommodation
Parent: Hilton International IP Holding 2 Limited
Officers: Stuart Beasley [1971] Director/Financial Controller; Richard Geoffrey Beeston [1982] Director/Chartered Accountant; Stephen Patrick Cassidy [1968] Director/Senior Vice President Operations; Michelle Momdjian [1976] Director/Attorney; George Christopher Ogle [1974] Director/Attorney; James Owen Percival [1968] Director/Accountant; Brian McKay Wilson [1962] Director/Company Secretary

Hilton UK Hotels Limited
Incorporated: 18 May 1904
Net Worth: £1,272,785,152 *Total Assets:* £1,338,172,928
Registered Office: Maple Court, Central Park, Reeds Crescent, Watford, Herts, WD24 4QQ
Activities: Hotels and similar accommodation
Parent: Hilton Worldwide Holding 2 Limited
Officers: Stuart Beasley [1971] Director/Financial Controller; Richard Geoffrey Beeston [1982] Director/Chartered Accountant; Stephen Patrick Cassidy [1968] Senior Vice President and Managing Director; Michelle Momdjian [1976] Director/Attorney; George Christopher Ogle [1974] Director/Attorney; James Owen Percival [1968] Director/Accountant; Simon Robert Vincent [1963] Director; Brian McKay Wilson [1962] Director/Company Secretary

Hilton UK Manage Limited
Incorporated: 15 October 2007
Net Worth: £28,088,258 *Total Assets:* £36,292,152
Registered Office: Maple Court, Central Park, Reeds Crescent, Watford, Herts, WD24 4QQ
Activities: Hotels and similar accommodation
Parent: Hilton Worldwide Limited
Officers: Stuart Beasley [1971] Director/Financial Controller; Richard Geoffrey Beeston [1982] Director/Chartered Accountant; Michelle Momdjian [1976] Director/Attorney; George Christopher Ogle [1974] Director/Attorney; James Owen Percival [1968] Director/Accountant; Simon Robert Vincent [1963] Director; Brian McKay Wilson [1962] Director/Company Secretary

Hilton Worldwide FS Treasury Limited
Incorporated: 18 February 2014
Net Worth: £9,563,753 *Total Assets:* £986,574,848
Registered Office: Maple Court, Central Park, Reeds Crescent, Watford, Herts, WD24 4QQ
Activities: Other business support service activities n.e.c.
Parent: Hilton Worldwide Manage Limited
Officers: Stuart Beasley [1971] Director/Financial Controller; Richard Geoffrey Beeston [1982] Director/Chartered Accountant; Stephen Patrick Cassidy [1968] Director/Senior Vice President Operations; Michelle Momdjian [1976] Director/Attorney; George Christopher Ogle [1974] Director/Attorney; James Owen Percival [1968] Director/Accountant; Brian McKay Wilson [1962] Director/Attorney

Hilton Worldwide Holding 2 Limited
Incorporated: 12 February 2014
Net Worth: £397,220,800 *Total Assets:* £2,394,284,288
Registered Office: Maple Court, Central Park, Reeds Crescent, Watford, Herts, WD24 4QQ
Activities: Hotels and similar accommodation
Parent: Hilton HHC Limited
Officers: Stuart Beasley [1971] Director/Financial Controller; Richard Geoffrey Beeston [1982] Director/Chartered Accountant; Stephen Patrick Cassidy [1968] Director/Senior Vice President Operations UK & Ireland; Michelle Momdjian [1976] Director/Attorney; George Christopher Ogle [1974] Director/Attorney; James Owen Percival [1968] Director/Accountant; Brian McKay Wilson [1962] Director/Attorney

Hilton Worldwide Holding LLP
Incorporated: 4 April 2014
Net Worth: £2,958,252,800 *Total Assets:* £2,958,253,056
Registered Office: Maple Court, Central Park, Reeds Crescent, Watford, Herts, WD24 4QQ

Hilton Worldwide Manage Branchco Limited
Incorporated: 12 February 2014
Net Worth: £4,843,892 *Total Assets:* £9,550,028
Registered Office: Maple Court, Central Park, Reeds Crescent, Watford, Herts, WD24 4QQ
Activities: Hotels and similar accommodation
Parent: Hilton Worldwide Manage Limited
Officers: Stuart Beasley [1971] Director/Financial Controller; Richard Geoffrey Beeston [1982] Director/Chartered Accountant; Stephen Patrick Cassidy [1968] Director/Senior Vice President Operations; Michelle Momdjian [1976] Director/Attorney; George Christopher Ogle [1974] Director/Attorney; James Owen Percival [1968] Director/Accountant; Brian McKay Wilson [1962] Director/Attorney

Hilton Worldwide Manage Limited
Incorporated: 7 December 2010 *Employees:* 32
Net Worth: £1,429,282,432 *Total Assets:* £2,571,142,144
Registered Office: Maple Court, Central Park, Reeds Crescent, Watford, Herts, WD24 4QQ
Activities: Hotels and similar accommodation
Shareholders: Hilton International IP Holding Limited; Hilton International Hotels (UK) Limited
Officers: Stuart Beasley [1971] Director/Financial Controller; Richard Geoffrey Beeston [1982] Director/Chartered Accountant; Stephen Patrick Cassidy [1968] Director/Senior Vice President Operations UK & Ireland; Michelle Momdjian [1976] Director/Attorney; George Christopher Ogle [1974] Director/Attorney; James Owen Percival [1968] Director/Accountant; Brian McKay Wilson [1962] Director/Company Secretary

Himalaya Carpets Limited
Incorporated: 25 July 1979 *Employees:* 17
Net Worth: £7,849,149 *Total Assets:* £9,233,149
Registered Office: 7 The Triangle Centre, Uxbridge Road, Southall, Middlesex, UB1 3ET
Activities: Wholesale of household goods (other than musical instruments) n.e.c
Shareholders: Surjit Singh Pandher; Valveer Kaur Pandher
Officers: Valveer Kaur Pandher, Secretary; Jaswinder Singh Pandher [1977] Director; Surjit Singh Pandher [1954] Director/Company Secretary; Tersham Singh Pandher [1975] Director; Valveer Kaur Pandher [1956] Director/Company Secretary

Himelight Limited
Incorporated: 28 April 1999 *Employees:* 1
Net Worth: £5,583,437 *Total Assets:* £8,014,373
Registered Office: 1 Warner House, Harrovian Business Village, Bessborough Road, Harrow, Middlesex, HA1 3EX
Activities: Renting and operating of Housing Association real estate
Shareholder: Robert Milton Fu
Officers: Robert Milton Fu, Secretary; Robert Milton Fu [1964] Director [Brazilian]

Hinchley Wood School
Incorporated: 19 December 2011 *Employees:* 173
Net Worth: £16,328,000 *Total Assets:* £19,369,000
Registered Office: Hinchley Wood School, Claygate Lane, Esher, Surrey, KT10 0AQ
Activities: General secondary education
Officers: Claudette Alethea Atkinson [1967] Director/Business Development Manager; Benjamin Nicholas Bartlett [1968] Director/Headteacher; Paul John Camp [1967] Director/Accountant; Alison Patricia Cruthers [1966] Director/Veterinary Surgeon; Peter James Drysdale [1949] Director/Accountant; Professor Becky Jane Francis [1969] Director/Academic; June Hall [1957] Sales Director; Robert David Mutchell [1974] Director/Chief Financial Officer; Lucy Josephine Richardson [1968] Director/Marketing Consultant; Jonathan Stuart Ross [1979] Director/Teacher; Andrew John Robert Sellers [1958] Director/Security Consultant; Timothy Ben Smytheman [1989] Director/Teacher; Karen Lloyd Walker [1957] Director/Security Controller/(S.H.E.); Marcus Weedon [1966] Human Resources Director; Nick Weston-Jones [1957] Director/Project Manager; Doctor Caroline Alicia Whitehouse [1971] Director/Teacher; Alexander Campbell Wright [1978] Public Affairs Director

Hincroft Limited
Incorporated: 8 June 2012
Net Worth Deficit: £18,032,442 *Total Assets:* £71,227,072
Registered Office: Hill House, Lowlands Road, Harrow, Middlesex, HA1 3EQ
Activities: Development of building projects
Parent: Mingold Limited
Officers: Brian Martin Comer [1960] Director [Irish]; Luke Andrew Comer [1957] Director [Irish]

F.Hinds Limited
Incorporated: 5 January 1918 *Employees:* 722
Net Worth: £28,058,012 *Total Assets:* £44,240,396
Registered Office: 24 Park Road, Uxbridge, Middlesex, UB8 1NH
Activities: Other retail sale of new goods in specialised stores (not commercial art galleries and opticians)
Parent: Hinds Ltd
Officers: Benedetto Mario Colucci [1959] Director/Retail Management; Stephen Barrie Cornwall [1970] Director/Chartered Accountant; Andrew Frank Hinds [1967] Director/Jeweller; David Royden Harcourt Hinds [1959] Director/Jeweller; Jeremy David Hinds [1987] Marketing Director; Neil Alexander Hinds [1960] Director/Chartered Surveyor; Paul Harcourt Hinds [1986] IT Director; Martin Jeffrey Preston [1962] Director/Jeweller

Hinds Ltd
Incorporated: 11 April 2002 *Employees:* 726
Net Worth: £36,342,864 *Total Assets:* £53,229,980
Registered Office: 24 Park Road, Uxbridge, Middlesex, UB8 1NH
Activities: Activities of head offices
Shareholder: Andrew Frank Hinds
Officers: Stephen Barrie Cornwall, Secretary; Andrew Frank Hinds [1967] Director/Retail Jeweller; David Royden Harcourt Hinds [1959] Retail Jeweller (Managing Director); Neil Alexander Hinds [1960] Director/Chartered Surveyor

Hindu Education Authority Ltd
Incorporated: 25 May 2004 *Employees:* 7
Previous: IFoundation Ltd
Net Worth: £9,811,863 *Total Assets:* £10,800,594
Registered Office: Bhaktivedanta Manor, Dharam Marg, Hilfield Lane, Aldenham, Watford, Herts, WD25 8EZ
Activities: Primary education
Officers: Dhruva-Kusa Shah, Secretary; Dr Sanjiv Kumar Agarwal [1963] Director/Consultant Surgeon; Sulabh Agarwal [1977] Director/Consultant; Dr Kapil Chawla [1976] Director/Doctor; William John Martin Fleming [1954] Director/Businessman; Upendra Kalan [1953] Director/Chartered Accountant; Kartik Rajen Khandwala [1979] Director/Consultant; Shailesh Patel [1958] Director/Priest

F.W. Hipkin Limited
Incorporated: 1 January 1937 *Employees:* 48
Net Worth: £4,082,694 *Total Assets:* £10,233,493
Registered Office: Acorn House, Coppen Road, off Selinas Lane, Chadwell Heath, Dagenham, Essex, RM8 1NU
Activities: Non-specialised wholesale trade
Parent: Hipkin Holdings Limited
Officers: Frank Dulson Lafford [1928] Director; Simon Lafford-Walker [1972] Director; Peter Rolland [1964] Director

Hiretest Limited
Incorporated: 15 October 1991 *Employees:* 22
Net Worth: £2,599,421 *Total Assets:* £5,896,414
Registered Office: 10 Western Road, Romford, Essex, RM1 3JT
Activities: Construction of commercial buildings
Shareholders: Frank Martin Sugrue; Michael Joseph Sugrue
Officers: Jerom Patrick Sugrue, Secretary; Christopher Robert Allan [1967] Contracts Director; John Joseph McGinty [1959] Contracts Director; Ann Philomena Smith [1948] Director; Anthony Soave [1951] Surveying Director; Frank Martin Sugrue [1944] Director/Accountant; Michael Joseph Sugrue [1946] Director/Manager; James David Allan Woodley [1962] Commercial Director

Hitachi Capital (UK) PLC
Incorporated: 21 April 1982 *Employees:* 1,238
Net Worth: £590,600,000 *Total Assets:* £5,090,800,128
Registered Office: Hitachi Capital House, Thorpe Road, Staines upon Thames, Surrey, TW18 3HP
Activities: Financial leasing
Parent: Hitachi Capital Corporation
Officers: John Nathaniel McDowall Sims, Secretary; Hiroyuki Fukuro [1958] Director [Japanese]; Robert Douglas Gordon [1961] Director [Australian]; Alan Renatus Frederick Hughes [1951] Director; Gavin Russell Cameron Munnoch [1952] Director; Yoshikazu Ohashi [1962] Director [Japanese]; Anne Whitaker [1958] Director

Hive 1 Ltd
Incorporated: 10 September 2015
Net Worth: £3,584,696 *Total Assets:* £7,951,500
Registered Office: Ground Floor, Elizabeth House, 54-58 High Street, Edgware, Middlesex, HA8 7EJ
Activities: Construction of domestic buildings
Officers: Lee Maurice Gold [1987] Director; Robert Grantham McGregor [1969] Director

The Hive Football Centre Holdings Limited
Incorporated: 26 June 2012
Previous: The Hive London Holdings Limited
Net Worth: £1,013,305 *Total Assets:* £11,580,237
Registered Office: The Hive, Camrose Avenue, London, HA8 6AG
Activities: Operation of sports facilities
Parent: Double A Group Ltd
Officers: Mahendra Patel, Secretary; Anthony Andrew Kleanthous [1966] Director

HJP Media LLP
Incorporated: 17 March 2015 *Employees:* 2
Net Worth: £8,237,433 *Total Assets:* £8,792,276
Registered Office: 166 College Road, Harrow, Middlesex, HA1 1RA
Officers: Paul John Hollywood [1966] Member

HLT London Manage Limited
Incorporated: 15 October 2007
Net Worth: £6,001,749 *Total Assets:* £6,394,006
Registered Office: Maple Court, Central Park, Reeds Crescent, Watford, Herts, WD24 4QQ
Activities: Hotels and similar accommodation
Parent: Hilton Worldwide Limited
Officers: Stuart Beasley [1971] Director/Financial Controller; Richard Geoffrey Beeston [1982] Director/Chartered Accountant; Michelle Momdjian [1976] Director/Attorney; George Christopher Ogle [1974] Director/Attorney; James Owen Percival [1968] Director/Accountant; Simon Robert Vincent [1963] Director; Brian McKay Wilson [1962] Director/Company Secretary

HLT Stakis Operator Limited
Incorporated: 15 October 2007
Net Worth Deficit: £48,437,320 *Total Assets:* £14,441,632
Registered Office: Maple Court, Central Park, Reeds Crescent, Watford, Herts, WD24 4QQ
Activities: Hotels and similar accommodation
Parent: Hilton Worldwide Limited
Officers: Stuart Beasley [1971] Director/Financial Controller; Richard Geoffrey Beeston [1982] Director/Chartered Accountant; Stephen Patrick Cassidy [1968] Director/SVP Operations UK & Ireland; Michelle Momdjian [1976] Director/Attorney; George Christopher Ogle [1974] Director/Attorney; James Owen Percival [1968] Director/Accountant

HML Holdings PLC
Incorporated: 2 March 2006 *Employees:* 507
Net Worth: £14,111,000 *Total Assets:* £23,432,000
Registered Office: 9-11 The Quadrant, Richmond, Surrey, TW9 1BP
Activities: Activities of head offices
Officers: James Alfred Lloyd Howgego, Secretary; Geoffrey John Griggs [1954] Director/Chartered Accountant; Charles Alec Guthrie [1964] Director/Chief Operating Officer; Elizabeth Jane Dilwihs Holden [1967] Director/Lawyer; James Alfred Lloyd Howgego [1968] Director/Chartered Accountant; Robert Henry Charles Plumb [1954] Director/Chartered Accountant; Richard Gwynne Smith [1952] Director

HML PM Ltd
Incorporated: 11 June 2001 *Employees:* 184
Previous: HML Andertons Limited
Net Worth: £3,793,042 *Total Assets:* £6,769,609
Registered Office: 9-11 The Quadrant, Richmond, Surrey, TW9 1BP
Activities: Management of real estate on a fee or contract basis
Parent: HML Holdings PLC
Officers: James Alfred Lloyd Howgego, Secretary; Alan John Coates [1952] Director; Hamilton Robert Comely [1955] Director/Property Manager; Alec Guthrie [1964] Director/Property Manager; Michael Hehir [1984] Director/Head of Accounts; James Alfred Lloyd Howgego [1968] Director/Chartered Accountant; Robert Henry Charles Plumb [1954] Managing Director

Hoddesdon Developments Ltd
Incorporated: 27 October 2006 *Employees:* 2
Net Worth: £7,463,800 *Total Assets:* £11,024,788
Registered Office: 57-59 High Street, Hoddesdon, Herts, EN11 8TQ
Activities: Other letting and operating of own or leased real estate
Shareholders: Giuseppe Ricotta; Giuseppina Ricotta
Officers: Joe Ricotta, Secretary/Director; Giuseppina Ricotta [1969] Director; Joe Ricotta [1966] Director

The Hoddesdon School Trust
Incorporated: 8 March 2011 *Employees:* 256
Previous: The John Warner School
Net Worth: £45,248,412 *Total Assets:* £47,362,856
Registered Office: The Hoddesdon School Trust, Stanstead Road, Hoddesdon, Herts, EN11 0QF
Activities: Primary education
Officers: David Andrew Allman, Secretary; Jane Eileen Margaret Carson [1953] Director/Headteacher; Peter Cuffaro [1957] Director/Solicitor; Graeme Alan Dykes [1965] Director/Chartered Accountant; Alison Heal [1963] Director/Retired; Sarah Anne Hurwood [1965] Director/Headteacher; Fiona Louise Ives [1956] Director; David James Patrick Kennedy [1958] Director/Headteacher [Irish]; Anthony Clive Lebaigue [1958] Director; Robert McCarthy [1961] Director/Civil Engineer; Rachel Elizabeth Semark [1967] Director/Headteacher; Adrian Shah-Cundy [1973] Corporate Responsibility Director; Mary Catherine Sykes [1965] Marketing Director [Canadian/British]

Hollin Hill Properties Limited
Incorporated: 9 May 1997 *Employees:* 1
Net Worth: £8,696,075 *Total Assets:* £15,640,747
Registered Office: 2nd Floor, 29 Dingwall Road, Croydon, Surrey, CR0 2NB
Activities: Hotels and similar accommodation
Parent: Axcel Group Limited
Officers: Shamir Patel [1970] Director/Hotelier; Sunil Patel [1968] Director/Hotelier

Hollyhedge Limited
Incorporated: 13 April 2003
Net Worth: £3,493,083 *Total Assets:* £7,667,922
Registered Office: 7 Churchill Court, 58 Station Road, Harrow, Middlesex, HA2 7SA
Activities: Development of building projects
Shareholders: Joshna Pankhania; Vraj Pankhania
Officers: Joshna Pankhania, Secretary; Kamal Pankhania [1977] Director; Sunil Pankhania [1982] Director; Vraj Pankhania [1950] Director/Property Developer

The Holmes Care (Group) Limited
Incorporated: 25 April 2006 *Employees:* 1,192
Net Worth: £24,918,116 *Total Assets:* £65,683,720
Registered Office: 228 St Marys Lane, Upminster, Essex, RM14 3DH
Activities: Activities of head offices
Shareholders: Shiraz Lakhani; Indumati Lakhani
Officers: Indumati Lakhani [1942] Director; Sharifa Lakhani [1987] Managing Director; Shiraz Lakhani [1945] Director

The Holmes Care Limited
Incorporated: 3 November 1994 *Employees:* 72
Net Worth Deficit: £444,843 *Total Assets:* £19,503,908
Registered Office: 228 St Mary's Lane, Upminster, Essex, RM14 3DH
Activities: Other human health activities
Parent: Holmes Care (Group) Limited
Officers: Indumati Lakhani, Secretary; Shiraz Lakhani [1945] Director

Home and Comforts Limited
Incorporated: 22 September 2011
Net Worth: £9,442,000 *Total Assets:* £27,512,000
Registered Office: 2 AC Court, High Street, Thames Ditton, Surrey, KT7 0SR
Activities: Other service activities n.e.c.
Parent: Home and Comforts Holdings Limited
Officers: Alan Albert Horton [1963] Director; Stuart Pace [1962] Director

Homefield Preparatory School Trust Limited
Incorporated: 15 September 1966 *Employees:* 79
Net Worth: £7,769,179 *Total Assets:* £8,266,591
Registered Office: Homefield School, Western Road, Sutton, Surrey, SM1 2TE
Activities: Primary education
Officers: Robin Angus Harper, Secretary; Asif Ahmed [1970] Director/Multi Asset Class Product Specialist; Dr Gillian Bamford [1954] Director/Teacher; Inderpreet Singh Dhingra [1960] Director/Retired Banker; Margaret Gardiner [1987] Director/Business Manager; Marjorie Heather Harris [1948] Director/ISI School Inspector; David Hutchings [1985] Director/Accountant; Anthony Edgar Jeans [1946] Director/Chartered Accountant; Paul Anthony Kavanagh [1962] Director/Solicitor; Michael Andrew Lestrange [1971] Director/Architect; Jacqueline Whittingham [1970] Director Bursar; Dr Adrian Hervey Wilcox [1950] Director/Consultant Pathologist

Homeguard Properties Limited
Incorporated: 13 January 1998 *Employees:* 3
Net Worth: £10,198,001 *Total Assets:* £19,216,532
Registered Office: 5 Elstree Gate, Elstree Way, Borehamwood, Herts, WD6 1JD
Activities: Other letting and operating of own or leased real estate
Officers: Daniel Naftali Reichmann [1988] Director

Homepines Investments Limited
Incorporated: 12 November 1985 *Employees:* 3
Net Worth: £2,862,807 *Total Assets:* £12,574,484
Registered Office: Suite 105, Viglen House, Alperton Lane, Wembley, Middlesex, HA0 1HD
Activities: Other business support service activities n.e.c.
Major Shareholder: Augusto Montanari
Officers: William Robert Hawes [1945] Director

Homes Caring for Autism Limited
Incorporated: 19 May 2005 *Employees:* 312
Net Worth: £10,105,703 *Total Assets:* £10,105,703
Registered Office: Ground Floor, Q1 The Square, Randalls Way, Leatherhead, Surrey, KT22 7TW
Activities: Residential care activities for learning difficulties, mental health and substance abuse
Parent: Care Management Group Limited
Officers: Garry John Fitton, Secretary; Garry John Fitton [1972] Director; Peter Kinsey [1962] Director

Honey Monster Foods Limited
Incorporated: 13 September 2006 *Employees:* 2
Net Worth: £23,425,000 *Total Assets:* £26,594,000
Registered Office: Benecol Limited, The Mille, 1000 Great West Road, Brentford, Middlesex, TW8 9DW
Activities: Manufacture of breakfast cereals and cereals-based food
Parent: Big Bear Group Limited
Officers: Merja Sisko Lumme [1961] Director/VP Human Resources [Finnish]; Iiro Tapio Wester [1963] Director/Chief Commercial Officer [Finnish]

Honeycroft Hill Ltd
Incorporated: 20 January 1972
Net Worth: £9,258,080 *Total Assets:* £9,321,304
Registered Office: 24 Park Road, Uxbridge, Middlesex, UB8 1NH
Activities: Other letting and operating of own or leased real estate
Parent: Hinds Ltd
Officers: Stephen Barrie Cornwall, Secretary; Andrew Frank Hinds [1967] Director/Jeweller; David Royden Harcourt Hinds [1959] Director/Jeweller; Neil Alexander Hinds [1960] Director/Chartered Surveyor

Honister Capital Holdings I Limited
Incorporated: 24 October 2011
Net Worth: £5,078,527 *Total Assets:* £5,082,527
Registered Office: Ground Floor, Unit 2, 507 Centennial Business Park, Elstree, Herts, WD6 3FG
Activities: Activities of financial services holding companies
Major Shareholder: Peter Michael Simon
Officers: Jason Chapman [1968] Managing Director; Mark Grahame Holloway [1963] Director

Hoo Hing Holdings Limited
Incorporated: 6 June 1978 *Employees:* 293
Net Worth: £26,456,588 *Total Assets:* £34,708,916
Registered Office: Hoo Hing House, Freshwater Road, Dagenham, Essex, RM8 1RX
Activities: Non-specialised wholesale trade
Shareholder: Tim Fuk Poon
Officers: Caroline Poon, Secretary; Caroline Poon [1963] Director/Trader; Ken Poon [1964] Director; Tim Fuk Poon [1941] Director/Trader

Hoo Hing Limited
Incorporated: 1 July 1991 *Employees:* 293
Net Worth: £18,786,808 *Total Assets:* £27,048,712
Registered Office: Hoo Hing House, Freshwater Road, Dagenham, Essex, RM8 1RX
Activities: Non-specialised wholesale trade
Parent: Hoo Hing Holdings Ltd
Officers: Caroline Poon, Secretary; Caroline Poon [1963] Director/Trader; Ken Poon [1964] Director/Trader; Tim Fuk Poon [1941] Director/Trader

Hoole Hall Country Club Limited
Incorporated: 22 November 2006 *Employees:* 131
Net Worth: £814,000 *Total Assets:* £41,544,000
Registered Office: Queen Court, 9-17 Eastern Road, Romford, Essex, RM1 3NG
Activities: Hotels and similar accommodation
Officers: Jonathan Patrick Braidley [1965] Director/Real Estate Investment and Finance Professional; Christopher Andre Kula [1983] Director/Chartered Accountant [German/Canadian]

Hooper Homes West Well Limited
Incorporated: 16 March 2011 *Employees:* 1
Net Worth: £723,574 *Total Assets:* £8,355,430
Registered Office: 77 Church Road, Ashford, Surrey, TW15 2PE
Activities: Development of building projects
Major Shareholder: Darren Hooper
Officers: Darren Hooper [1978] Director

Hoopers Homes Limited
Incorporated: 13 May 2003 *Employees:* 3
Net Worth: £10,297 *Total Assets:* £6,297,663
Registered Office: 77 Church Road, Ashford, Surrey, TW15 2PE
Activities: Development of building projects
Major Shareholder: Darren Hooper
Officers: Darren Hooper [1978] Director

Horlicks Limited
Incorporated: 11 December 1925
Net Worth: £79,499,000 *Total Assets:* £79,499,000
Registered Office: 980 Great West Road, Brentford, Middlesex, TW8 9GS
Activities: Other business support service activities n.e.c.
Parent: SmithKline Beecham Limited
Officers: Adam Walker [1967] Director

Horn Cutting Tools Limited
Incorporated: 15 November 2007 *Employees:* 51
Net Worth: £3,871,666 *Total Assets:* £6,649,028
Registered Office: Palmerston House, 814 Brighton Road, Purley, Surrey, CR8 2BR
Activities: Manufacture of other machine tools
Major Shareholder: Lothar Horn
Officers: Andreas Vollmer [1968] Director/Export Manager [German]

The Hospital Company (Southmead) Holdings Limited
Incorporated: 19 November 2009
Net Worth Deficit: £106,240,000 *Total Assets:* £620,545,984
Registered Office: 8 White Oak Square, London Road, Swanley, Kent, BR8 7AG
Activities: Activities of head offices
Shareholders: Aberdeen Infrastructure Investments (Southmead) Limited; Infrastructure Investments (Health) Limited
Officers: Nicholas Tommy Cole [1978] Investment Director; Andrew Brian Deacon [1980] Portfolio Director, Infrastructure; Mark Christopher Wayment [1958] Director/Investment Banker; Edward Arthur Wilson [1964] Director/Investment Manager

The Hospital Company (Southmead) Limited
Incorporated: 18 November 2009
Net Worth Deficit: £106,240,000 *Total Assets:* £620,545,984
Registered Office: 8 White Oak Square, London Road, Swanley, Kent, BR8 7AG
Activities: Medical nursing home activities
Parent: The Hospital Company (Southmead) Holdings Limited
Officers: Nicholas Tommy Cole [1978] Investment Director; Andrew Brian Deacon [1980] Portfolio Director, Infrastructure; Mark Christopher Wayment [1958] Director/Investment Banker; Edward Arthur Wilson [1964] Director/Investment Manager

Hospitality Holdings Limited
Incorporated: 30 March 2000
Net Worth: £3,117,755,904 *Total Assets:* £10,528,145,408
Registered Office: Compass House, Guildford Street, Chertsey, Surrey, KT16 9BQ
Activities: Activities of head offices
Parent: Compass Group PLC
Officers: Dominic William Blakemore [1969] Director; Alison Rebecca Yapp [1965] Director/Solicitor

Host Europe Group Limited
Incorporated: 30 April 2013 *Employees:* 3
Net Worth: £282,908,000 *Total Assets:* £771,225,024
Registered Office: 5th Floor, The Shipping Building, Old Vinyl Factory, 252-254 Blyth Road, Hayes, Middlesex, UB3 1HA
Activities: Activities of head offices
Parent: Host Europe Investments Limited
Officers: Richard Anthony Winslow [1979] Director; Jonathan Ying Kit Wong [1976] Director

Host Europe Investments Limited
Incorporated: 18 July 2013
Net Worth: £346,612,000 *Total Assets:* £346,960,000
Registered Office: 5th Floor, The Shipping Building, Old Vinyl Factory, 252-254 Blyth Road, Hayes, Middlesex, UB3 1HA
Activities: Dormant company
Parent: Host Europe Finance Co. Limited
Officers: Richard Anthony Winslow [1979] Director; Jonathan Ying Kit Wong [1976] Director

Host Europe Limited
Incorporated: 7 March 2008
Net Worth: £295,087,008 *Total Assets:* £301,600,992
Registered Office: 5th Floor, The Shipping Building, Old Vinyl Factory, 252-254 Blyth Road, Hayes, Middlesex, UB3 1HA
Activities: Activities of head offices
Parent: HEL Bidco Ltd
Officers: Richard Anthony Winslow [1979] Director; Jonathan Ying Kit Wong [1976] Director

Hotel Inter-Continental London Limited
Incorporated: 4 January 1972
Net Worth: £211,520,992 *Total Assets:* £212,570,000
Registered Office: Broadwater Park, Denham, Bucks, UB9 5HR
Activities: Hotels and similar accommodation
Parent: Six Continents Limited
Officers: Fiona Cuttell, Secretary; Michael Jon Cockcroft [1974] Director/Accountant; Michael Todd Glover [1971] Director/Financial Controller [American]; Nicolette Henfrey [1969] Director; George Turner [1971] Director

Hotel Intercontinental London (Holdings) Limited
Incorporated: 11 December 2007
Net Worth: £506,536,000 *Total Assets:* £508,111,008
Registered Office: Broadwater Park, Denham, Bucks, UB9 5HR
Activities: Other business support service activities n.e.c.
Parent: Six Continents Holdings Limited
Officers: Fiona Cuttell, Secretary; Michael Jon Cockcroft [1974] Director/Accountant; Michael Todd Glover [1971] Director/Financial Controller [American]; Nicolette Henfrey [1969] Director

Hotel Management International (Holdings) Limited
Incorporated: 16 November 2001 *Employees:* 379
Net Worth: £75,446,000 *Total Assets:* £112,061,000
Registered Office: 364 High Street, Harlington, Heathrow, Hayes, Middlesex, UB3 5LF
Activities: Activities of head offices
Major Shareholder: Peter Nicholas Salussolia
Officers: Graeme John Ramsay, Secretary; Graeme John Ramsay [1967] Director/Chartered Accountant; Christina Salussolia [1950] Director/Executive Secretary; Peter Nicholas Salussolia [1968] Director

Hotel Management International Limited
Incorporated: 24 April 1972 *Employees:* 5
Net Worth: £74,755,000 *Total Assets:* £82,119,000
Registered Office: 364 High Street, Harlington, Heathrow, Hayes, Middlesex, UB3 5LF
Activities: Hotels and similar accommodation
Major Shareholder: Peter Nicholas Salussolia
Officers: Graeme John Ramsay, Secretary; Graeme John Ramsay [1967] Director/Chartered Accountant; Alexander Salussolia [1968] Director; Peter Nicholas Salussolia [1968] Director

Houlihan & Co (Holdings) Limited
Incorporated: 29 May 2014 *Employees:* 87
Net Worth: £3,941,013 *Total Assets:* £18,773,256
Registered Office: Unit J2, Brooklands Close, Sunbury on Thames, Surrey, TW16 7DX
Activities: Activities of other holding companies n.e.c.
Major Shareholder: Richard Mark Knight
Officers: Thomas Christopher Hunt [1985] Director; Richard Knight [1972] Director/Construction Surveyor; David Shine [1963] Director

Houlihan & Co. (Excavations) Limited
Incorporated: 11 August 1972 *Employees:* 87
Net Worth: £8,479,035 *Total Assets:* £22,568,244
Registered Office: Unit J2, Brooklands Close, Sunbury on Thames, Surrey, TW16 7DX
Activities: Construction of other civil engineering projects n.e.c.
Parent: Houlihan and Co (Holdings) Ltd
Officers: Richard Mark Knight, Secretary; Thomas Christopher Hunt [1985] Director; Richard Mark Knight [1972] Director/Construction Surveyor; David Shine [1963] Director

Housing Gateway Limited
Incorporated: 13 March 2014 *Employees:* 2
Net Worth: £8,501,047 *Total Assets:* £128,319,832
Registered Office: Civic Centre, Silver Street, Enfield, Middlesex, EN1 3XA
Activities: Buying and selling of own real estate
Parent: The Mayor and Burgesses of The London Borough of Enfield
Officers: Joanne Drew [1968] Director/Local Government Officer; Joanna Michelle Embling [1949] Director; Timothy Leaver [1966] Director/Chartered Accountant; Sally Ann McTernan [1963] Director/Local Government Officer; Jayne Middleton-Albooye [1963] Director/Solicitor; Peter Chukuaduom Madako Nwosu [1965] Director/Chartered Accountant

The Howard Partnership Trust
Incorporated: 8 April 2011 *Employees:* 930
Net Worth: £109,256,000 *Total Assets:* £124,044,000
Registered Office: c/o Howard of Effingham School, Lower Road, Effingham, Leatherhead, Surrey, KT24 5JR
Activities: Primary education
Officers: Rhona Julia Barnfield [1953] Director/Executive Head; Paul Conrad Belok [1960] Director/Actuary; Tina Barbara Crombie [1969] Director/Civil Servant; Jane Heather Cunliffe [1979] Director/Civil Servant; Joseph Jerry Liow Yune Loy [1969] Director/Chartered Accountant; Mark Joseph Clarence Swyny [1965] Director/Banker; Miles Howard Templeman [1947] Director; Christopher Williamson [1952] Director/Retired; Ian Stuart Wilson [1951] Director/Education Consultant

Howarth Homes (Farnham Close) Limited
Incorporated: 8 March 2013 *Employees:* 2
Net Worth: £797,252 *Total Assets:* £9,834,896
Registered Office: Waterside House, 20 Riverside Way, Cowley, Uxbridge, Middlesex, UB8 2YF
Activities: Development of building projects
Parent: Howarth Homes PLC
Officers: Adam Peter Howarth [1963] Director; Brig Eric Howarth [1968] Director

Howarth Homes PLC
Incorporated: 6 July 1988 *Employees:* 45
Net Worth: £6,817,747 *Total Assets:* £40,702,896
Registered Office: Waterside House, 20 Riverside Way, Uxbridge, Middlesex, UB8 2YF
Activities: Development of building projects
Major Shareholder: Adam Peter Howarth
Officers: Adam Peter Howarth, Secretary; Adam Peter Howarth [1963] Director/Property Developer; Brig Eric Howarth [1968] Director

Howitzer Acquisition Limited
Incorporated: 23 January 2006
Net Worth: £23,343,062 *Total Assets:* £60,699,324
Registered Office: Frays Mill Works, Cowley Road, Uxbridge, Middlesex, UB8 2AF
Activities: Activities of other holding companies n.e.c.
Parent: Circor Luxembourg Holdings S.A.R.L
Officers: Peter Graham Crawford Harvey, Secretary; Peter Graham Crawford Harvey [1957] Finance Director; David Mullen [1968] Director/SVP, Finance & Corporate Controller [American]

HRS Investments Limited
Incorporated: 19 March 1999 *Employees:* 179
Net Worth: £3,747,879 *Total Assets:* £14,872,608
Registered Office: HRS House, 10-12 Caxton Way, Watford Business Park, Watford, Herts, WD18 8JY
Activities: Activities of head offices
Major Shareholder: Steven Edward Pither
Officers: Robert Michael Twydle, Secretary; Francisco Javier Abad Ruiz [1969] Director/Accountant [Spanish]; Linda Amanda Galdes [1964] Director; Catherine Elizabeth Pither [1991] Director; Jack Edward Pither [1994] Director; Steven Edward Pither [1957] Director

HRT UK Limited
Incorporated: 6 October 2003 *Employees:* 2
Net Worth: £31,611,000 *Total Assets:* £31,611,000
Registered Office: Osprey House, 63 Station Road, Addlestone, Surrey, KT15 2AR
Activities: Activities of production holding companies
Parent: HRT SAS
Officers: Jonathan Baxter, Secretary; Olivier Vincent Antille [1971] Director [French]; Brian Forster [1953] Director

HSP Investments Limited
Incorporated: 14 September 2012 *Employees:* 4
Previous: 95&97 Harley Street Properties Limited
Net Worth: £17,386,618 *Total Assets:* £18,010,734
Registered Office: 3 Kirkleas Road, Surbiton, Surrey, KT6 6QJ
Activities: Activities of venture and development capital companies
Parent: Anglo Suisse Investments Ltd
Officers: Benjamin Thomas Geoffrey de Jager, Secretary; Benjamin Thomas Geoffrey de Jager [1996] Company Secretary/Director; Caroline Mary de Jager [1961] Director; Geoffrey John de Jager [1950] Director; Jonathan Geoffrey de Jager [1977] Director

Hudson Almere Limited
Incorporated: 17 January 2017
Net Worth: £699,948 *Total Assets:* £14,802,959
Registered Office: Portland House, 69-71 Wembley Hill Road, Wembley, Middlesex, HA9 8BU
Activities: Other business support service activities n.e.c.
Officers: Bhupendra Shantilal Kansagra, Secretary; Laurent Elie Cadji [1977] Director/Businessman; Lewis Levy Cadji [1938] Director/Businessman; Bhupendra Shantilal Kansagra [1956] Director/Businessman; Ramesh Shantilal Kansagra [1950] Director/Businessman

Hudson Arnhem Limited
Incorporated: 17 January 2017
Net Worth Deficit: £7,979 *Total Assets:* £10,414,724
Registered Office: Portland House, 69-71 Wembley Hill Road, Wembley, Middlesex, HA9 8BU
Activities: Other business support service activities n.e.c.
Officers: Bhupendra Shantilal Kansagra, Secretary; Laurent Elie Cadji [1977] Director/Businessman; Lewis Levy Cadji [1938] Director/Businessman; Bhupendra Shantilal Kansagra [1956] Director/Businessman; Ramesh Shantilal Kansagra [1950] Director/Businessman

Hudson Brent Limited
Incorporated: 17 January 2017
Net Worth: £1,289,010 *Total Assets:* £10,286,558
Registered Office: Portland House, 69-71 Wembley Hill Road, Wembley, Middlesex, HA9 8BU
Activities: Other business support service activities n.e.c.
Officers: Bhupendra Shantilal Kansagra, Secretary; Laurent Elie Cadji [1977] Director/Businessman; Lewis Levy Cadji [1938] Director/Businessman; Bhupendra Shantilal Kansagra [1956] Director/Businessman; Ramesh Shantilal Kansagra [1950] Director/Businessman

Hudson Camden Limited
Incorporated: 17 January 2017
Net Worth: £1,026,544 *Total Assets:* £10,631,425
Registered Office: Portland House, 69-71 Wembley Hill Road, Wembley, Middlesex, HA9 8BU
Activities: Other business support service activities n.e.c.
Officers: Bhupendra Shantilal Kansagra, Secretary; Laurent Elie Cadji [1977] Director/Businessman; Lewis Levy Cadji [1938] Director/Businessman; Bhupendra Shantilal Kansagra [1956] Director/Businessman; Ramesh Shantilal Kansagra [1950] Director/Businessman

Hudson Chemical Tankers Limited
Incorporated: 17 January 2017 *Employees:* 4
Net Worth: £5,307,836 *Total Assets:* £73,716,288
Registered Office: Portland House, 69-71 Wembley Hill Road, Wembley, Middlesex, HA9 8BU
Activities: Other business support service activities n.e.c.
Shareholder: Shipping and Intermodal Investment Fund II LLC
Officers: Bhupendra Shantilal Kansagra, Secretary; Laurent Elie Cadji [1977] Director/Businessman; Edwin Erik Gelbert Jager [1966] Managing Director [Dutch]; Bhupendra Shantilal Kansagra [1956] Director/Businessman; Ramesh Shantilal Kansagra [1950] Director/Businessman

Hudson Kensington Limited
Incorporated: 17 January 2017
Net Worth: £605,679 *Total Assets:* £10,048,801
Registered Office: Portland House, 69-71 Wembley Hill Road, Wembley, Middlesex, HA9 8BU
Activities: Sea and coastal freight water transport
Officers: Bhupendra Shantilal Kansagra, Secretary; Laurent Elie Cadji [1977] Director/Businessman; Lewis Levy Cadji [1938] Director/Businessman; Bhupendra Shantilal Kansagra [1956] Director/Businessman; Ramesh Shantilal Kansagra [1950] Director/Businessman

Hudson Lisse Limited
Incorporated: 17 January 2017
Net Worth: £584,616 *Total Assets:* £15,234,200
Registered Office: Portland House, 69-71 Wembley Hill Road, Wembley, Middlesex, HA9 8BU
Activities: Sea and coastal freight water transport
Officers: Bhupendra Shantilal Kansagra, Secretary; Laurent Elie Cadji [1977] Director/Businessman; Lewis Levy Cadji [1938] Director/Businessman; Bhupendra Shantilal Kansagra [1956] Director/Businessman; Ramesh Shantilal Kansagra [1950] Director/Businessman

Hudson Richmond Limited
Incorporated: 17 January 2017
Net Worth: £798,401 *Total Assets:* £10,457,273
Registered Office: Portland House, 69-71 Wembley Hill Road, Wembley, Middlesex, HA9 8BU
Activities: Sea and coastal freight water transport
Officers: Bhupendra Shantilal Kansagra, Secretary; Laurent Elie Cadji [1977] Director/Businessman; Lewis Levy Cadji [1938] Director/Businessman; Bhupendra Shantilal Kansagra [1956] Director/Businessman; Ramesh Shantilal Kansagra [1950] Director/Businessman

E. Ivor Hughes Educational Foundation
Incorporated: 9 January 1986 *Employees:* 32
Net Worth: £9,138,793 *Total Assets:* £9,373,345
Registered Office: Buckingham College Preparatory School, 458 Rayners Lane, Pinner, Middlesex, HA5 5DT
Activities: Pre-primary education
Officers: Quinton Mark Poulton, Secretary; Robert John Brock [1942] Director/Property Consultant; John Corcut [1946] Director/School Teacher; Lynn Denise Grimes [1950] Marketing Director; Andrew Robert Olins [1964] Director/Solicitor

Humberside Land Limited
Incorporated: 22 September 1864 *Employees:* 2
Net Worth: £5,071,125 *Total Assets:* £5,132,378
Registered Office: Hill House, 49 The Ridgeway, Fetcham, Leatherhead, Surrey, KT22 9BN
Activities: Other letting and operating of own or leased real estate
Shareholders: John Ridgill Trout; Humberside Investments Limited
Officers: Anitra Generaldine Margaret Trout, Secretary; Anitra Generaldine Margaret Trout [1947] Director; John Ridgill Trout [1945] Managing Director

Humphrey & Stretton (Properties) Limited
Incorporated: 15 November 1973 *Employees:* 5
Net Worth: £4,312,882 *Total Assets:* £5,115,202
Registered Office: Pindar Road Industrial Estate, Pindar Road, Hoddesdon, Herts, EN11 0EU
Activities: Other letting and operating of own or leased real estate
Parent: Humphrey & Stretton Holdings Limited
Officers: Scott David Carter Humphrey, Secretary; Brad Kenneth James Humphrey [1996] Director; David John Humphrey [1965] Director; Doreen Winifred Humphrey [1934] Director; Kenneth William Humphrey [1935] Director; Scott David Carter Humphrey [1998] Director

Howard Humphreys & Partners Limited
Incorporated: 1 June 1959
Net Worth: £45,433,888 *Total Assets:* £45,467,092
Registered Office: Hill Park Court, Springfield Drive, Leatherhead, Surrey, KT22 7NL
Activities: Activities of other holding companies n.e.c.
Parent: Kellogg Brown & Root Group Limited
Officers: Martin Nelhams, Secretary; James Arthur Barrett [1965] Director/Accountant; Martin Nelhams [1960] Director/Solicitor

W. Humphreys Transport (London) Ltd
Incorporated: 6 March 1975 *Employees:* 2
Net Worth: £11,033,080 *Total Assets:* £11,443,584
Registered Office: 64 Bromley Common, Bromley, Kent, BR2 9PF
Activities: Freight transport by road
Major Shareholder: Patricia Ellen Humphreys
Officers: William Humphreys, Secretary; Patricia Ellen Humphreys [1936] Director/Secretary; Williams Humphreys [1958] Director

Hungerburger Limited
Incorporated: 29 May 1985
Net Worth: £5,823,776 *Total Assets:* £6,090,356
Registered Office: Asghar House, 24a Station Parade, Barking, Essex, IG11 8DR
Activities: Hotels and similar accommodation
Major Shareholder: Ali Kholghi
Officers: Parisa Jahanpanah, Secretary; Parisa Jahanpanah [1970] Director/Hotelier; Ali Asghar Kadkhodayi-Kholghi [1952] Director/General Manager

Hunn Holdings Limited
Incorporated: 4 October 2010 *Employees:* 50
Net Worth: £4,194,070 *Total Assets:* £9,444,976
Registered Office: Suite D, The Business Centre, Faringdon Avenue, Romford, Essex, RM3 8EN
Activities: Activities of other holding companies n.e.c.
Shareholders: Ricky George Hunn; Karen Patricia Frost
Officers: Karen Patricia Frost [1965] Director; Ricky George Hunn [1953] Director

Howard Hunt (City) Limited
Incorporated: 28 August 1990 *Employees:* 268
Net Worth: £12,863,000 *Total Assets:* £49,997,000
Registered Office: 3rd Floor, Crown House, 151 High Road, Loughton, Essex, IG10 4LG
Activities: Printing n.e.c.
Shareholders: Martin Albert Pigott; Howard Hunt Mail Limited
Officers: Luke Martin Pigott, Secretary/Managing Director; Daniel Clarke [1981] Sales Director; Paul Kemp [1969] Operations Director; Luke Martin Pigott [1972] Managing Director; Martin Albert Pigott [1944] Director; Keith Edwin Whitehead [1958] Production Director

John F Hunt Group Ltd
Incorporated: 3 May 2006 *Employees:* 403
Previous: John F Hunt Ltd
Net Worth: £22,005,184 *Total Assets:* £44,868,924
Registered Office: Europa Park, London Road, Grays, Essex, RM20 4DB
Activities: Other specialised construction activities n.e.c.
Major Shareholder: John Alan Hall
Officers: Charles Richard Green, Secretary; Janet Hall, Secretary; Ian David Saville, Secretary; John Alan Hall [1949] Director; Ian David Saville [1968] Finance Director

John F. Hunt Hire Centres Ltd
Incorporated: 24 June 1994 *Employees:* 40
Net Worth: £3,022,329 *Total Assets:* £5,215,564
Registered Office: Europa Park, London Road, Grays, Essex, RM20 4DB
Activities: Renting and leasing of trucks and other heavy vehicles
Parent: John F Hunt Group Ltd
Officers: Charles Richard Green, Secretary; Ian David Saville, Secretary; Leon Carter [1978] Sales Director; John Alan Hall [1949] Director; Martin Lavery [1961] Director/Plant Hire Manager; Ian David Saville [1968] Finance Director; Keith Andrew Scott [1963] Director/Plant Manager

John F Hunt Limited
Incorporated: 9 December 1981 *Employees:* 167
Previous: John F. Hunt Demolition Ltd
Net Worth: £9,993,262 *Total Assets:* £17,978,696
Registered Office: Europa Park, London Road, Grays, Essex, RM20 4DB
Activities: Demolition
Parent: John F Hunt Ltd
Officers: Charles Richard Green, Secretary; Ian David Saville, Secretary; Paul Bland [1972] Managing Director; Michael John Blizzard [1964] Divisional Director; Glen Clark [1967] Managing Director; John Alan Hall [1949] Director; Jason Mark Hill [1970] Commercial Director; Ian David Saville [1968] Finance Director

Howard Hunt Mail Limited
Incorporated: 18 August 2009 *Employees:* 54
Net Worth: £4,312,632 *Total Assets:* £13,418,588
Registered Office: 3rd Floor, Crown House, 151 High Road, Loughton, Essex, IG10 4LG
Activities: Other business support service activities n.e.c.
Shareholders: Martin Albert Pigott; Luke Martin Pigott
Officers: Luke Martin Pigott [1972] Managing Director; Martin Albert Pigott [1944] Director; Catherine Jane Wozencroft [1962] Director

John F. Hunt Plant Hire Ltd
Incorporated: 9 October 1986 *Employees:* 14
Net Worth: £4,374,168 *Total Assets:* £5,848,818
Registered Office: Europa Park, London Road, Grays, Essex, RM20 4DB
Activities: Other specialised construction activities n.e.c.
Parent: John F Hunt Ltd
Officers: Charles Richard Green, Secretary; Ian David Saville, Secretary; John Alan Hall [1949] Director; Ian David Saville [1968] Finance Director; Keith Andrew Scott [1963] Director/Plant Manager

John F Hunt Power Limited
Incorporated: 10 June 2005 *Employees:* 53
Net Worth: £6,761,469 *Total Assets:* £20,003,154
Registered Office: Europa Park, London Road, Grays, Essex, RM20 4DB
Activities: Renting and leasing of construction and civil engineering machinery and equipment
Major Shareholder: John Alan Hall
Officers: Charles Richard Green, Secretary; Janet Hall, Secretary; Ian David Saville, Secretary; Kevin Davies [1957] Director; John Alan Hall [1949] Director; David Paul Hunt [1966] Sales Director; Ian David Saville [1968] Finance Director; Keith Andrew Scott [1963] Director

Hunters Contracts Limited
Incorporated: 13 August 1990 *Employees:* 44
Net Worth: £898,956 *Total Assets:* £7,853,812
Registered Office: Unit A, Oyo Business Units, Hindmans Way, Dagenham, Essex, RM9 6LP
Activities: Other business support service activities n.e.c.
Shareholders: Martin Playell; Gary Mark Thomas
Officers: Norman Campbell, Secretary; Stefan John Brennan [1979] Sales Director; Norman Campbell [1970] Finance Director; Lewis Mathew Harman [1982] A&D Director; Martin Playell [1961] Director; Gary Mark Thomas [1966] Director

Huntington House Limited
Incorporated: 24 August 1973 *Employees:* 121
Net Worth: £5,530,147 *Total Assets:* £13,311,652
Registered Office: The Old Rectory, Church Street, Weybridge, Surrey, KT13 8DE
Activities: Residential nursing care facilities
Parent: Huntington House (Hldgs) Limited
Officers: Geoffrey Peter Hoare, Secretary; Sarah Elizabeth Chapman [1985] Director; Charles Goodall Nicholas Hoare [1984] Director; Geoffrey Peter Hoare [1956] Director; Marilyn Florence Maud Hoare [1948] Director

Hurst Primary School
Incorporated: 20 August 2013 *Employees:* 93
Net Worth: £4,998,184 *Total Assets:* £5,848,621
Registered Office: Hurst Primary School, Dorchester Avenue, Bexley, Kent, DA5 3AJ
Activities: Primary education
Officers: Esther Marianne Box [1977] Director/Midwife; Tazmeen Dhillon [1973] Director/Project Manager; Julian Colin Freeman [1952] Director/Retired; Susan Ann Goudie [1952] Director/Retired; Claire Louise Mortimer [1982] Director/Assistant Headteacher; Sarah Jane Mortimer [1964] Director/Assistant Headteacher; Iain Scott [1980] Director/Reward Consultant; Charlotte Ann-Marie Sharp [1976] Director/Housewife; Jayne Imelda Smith [1967] Director/Assistant Headteacher; Warren Daniel Valentine [1991] Director/Teacher; Trevor John Wald [1952] Director/Retired; Maire Bernadette Williams [1954] Director/School Business Manager

Hurstlane Limited
Incorporated: 12 July 2000
Net Worth: £20,669,440 *Total Assets:* £33,431,456
Registered Office: Castle House, 69-70 Victoria Street, Englefield Green, Surrey, TW20 0QX
Activities: Renting and operating of Housing Association real estate
Shareholders: Amar Sheikh; Momin Sheikh
Officers: Momin Sheikh, Secretary/Director; Amar Sheikh [1961] Director; Momin Sheikh [1963] Director

Hurstmere School
Incorporated: 1 June 2011 *Employees:* 113
Net Worth: £15,463,555 *Total Assets:* £16,998,796
Registered Office: Hurst Road, Sidcup, Kent, DA15 9AW
Activities: General secondary education
Officers: Carmel Murphy, Secretary; Eleanor Allen [1955] Director; Thomas Edward Clarke Baston [1985] Director/Teacher; David Mark Chatt [1960] Director/Bank Concierge; Natalie Judith Coney [1965] Director/Teacher; Iain Phillip Coombes [1968] Director/Accountant; John Peter Cutts [1936] Director/Retired; Robert Pavey [1947] Director/Estate Manager; Lucie Rignier Notton [1975] Director/Teacher [French]; Ian Simpson [1961] Director/Retired; George Christopher Stollery [1963] Director/Principal

Huxley Global Limited
Incorporated: 7 September 2017
Net Worth: £27,004 *Total Assets:* £8,538,746
Registered Office: Potland House, 69-71 Wembley Hill Road, Wembley, Middlesex, HA9 8BU
Activities: Non-specialised wholesale trade
Parent: Solai Holdings Limited
Officers: Bhupendra Shantilal Kansagra, Secretary; Bhupendra Shantilal Kansagra [1956] Director; Ramesh Shantilal Kansagra [1950] Director; Rishi Ramesh Kansagra [1981] Director; Ronak Kansagra [1987] Director

Hy-Ten Group Limited
Incorporated: 25 October 1965 *Employees:* 320
Net Worth: £31,780,204 *Total Assets:* £64,761,272
Registered Office: 12 The Green, Richmond, Surrey, TW9 1PX
Activities: Manufacture of metal structures and parts of structures
Major Shareholder: Adrian Charles Larkins
Officers: Michael Dennis Shattock, Secretary; Adrian Charles Larkins [1967] Director; Michael Dennis Shattock [1951] Director

Hy-Ten Limited
Incorporated: 17 February 1958 *Employees:* 283
Net Worth: £26,252,548 *Total Assets:* £57,861,488
Registered Office: 12 The Green, Richmond, Surrey, TW9 1PX
Activities: Manufacture of metal structures and parts of structures
Parent: Hy-Ten Group Limited
Officers: Michael Dennis Shattock, Secretary; Ian Thomas Dennis Jeffries [1970] Director/Branch Manager Steel Manufacturing; Adrian Charles Larkins [1967] Director; William Macpherson Brooks Mackay [1958] Sales Director; Paul William Nicholls [1957] Director; Michael Dennis Shattock [1951] Director; Richard Keith Webster [1966] Director

Hybrid Dining Limited
Incorporated: 10 December 2009
Net Worth: £5,834,000 *Total Assets:* £6,374,000
Registered Office: 100-102 High Street, Ruislip, Middlesex, HA4 8LS
Activities: Activities of head offices
Officers: Madam Fadwa Al Homaizi [1957] Director [Kuwaiti]

Hydro Cleansing Limited
Incorporated: 31 January 2000 *Employees:* 119
Net Worth: £1,534,517 *Total Assets:* £7,281,665
Registered Office: HCL House, Beddington Farm Road, Beddington, Croydon, Surrey, CR0 4XB
Activities: Sewerage
Major Shareholder: Steven Hoad
Officers: Graham Peter Brady [1975] Director [Irish]; Steven Hoad [1967] Projects Director; Steven Alistair Roake [1976] Director

Hyperformance Limited
Incorporated: 26 April 1999 *Employees:* 155
Net Worth: £4,949,000 *Total Assets:* £38,561,000
Registered Office: Elmbrook House, 18-19 Station Road, Sunbury on Thames, Surrey, TW16 6SU
Activities: Non-life insurance
Parent: Key Bidco Limited
Officers: Angela Margaret Darling [1959] Compliance Director; Shaun Ian Hooper [1972] Director/Chief Executive; Tim Paul Wills [1972] Finance Director

Hystead Limited
Incorporated: 3 December 2015
Previous: Hystead PLC
Net Worth Deficit: £147,398,000 *Total Assets:* £278,608,736
Registered Office: Doran & Minehane, 3rd Floor, WM Promus, 132-144 High Street, Bromley, Kent, BR1 1EZ
Activities: Management consultancy activities other than financial management
Officers: Wessel Johannes Hamman [1972] Director; Louis Norval [1956] Director [Australian]; Rabia Shihab [1979] Director/Chief Financial Officer [Israeli]; Morne Cornelius Wilken [1971] Director [South African]

I E Music Limited
Incorporated: 18 August 1989 *Employees:* 19
Net Worth: £4,324,166 *Total Assets:* £6,220,997
Registered Office: 5 Jardine House, Harrovian Business Village, Bessborough Road, Harrow, Middlesex, HA1 3EX
Activities: Other service activities n.e.c.
Parent: De:Ream Global Limited
Officers: Timothy Howard Clark, Secretary; Timothy Howard Clark [1945] Director; Michael Dennis Loney [1978] Director/Artist Manager; Daniel Medland [1980] Director/Manager; Stephen O'Reilly [1977] Director; Nina Parnaby [1977] Director/Administrator

I-Catering Management Services Limited
Incorporated: 15 April 2008 *Employees:* 646
Net Worth: £2,208,715 *Total Assets:* £7,223,758
Registered Office: Phoenix House, Pyrford Road, West Byfleet, Surrey, KT14 6RA
Activities: Combined office administrative service activities
Parent: Manilva International Limited
Officers: Michele Sara Callcut [1959] Finance Director; Kenneth John Navin [1962] Director; Geoffrey Owen Peppiatt [1953] Director

I.C.F. Finance Limited
Incorporated: 28 June 1996
Net Worth: £4,294,090 *Total Assets:* £6,681,355
Registered Office: Northside House, Mount Pleasant, Barnet, Herts, EN4 9EE
Activities: Other business support service activities n.e.c.
Shareholders: Melvyn Stewart Becker; Ian Leonard Rhodes
Officers: Ian Leonard Rhodes, Secretary; Melvyn Stewart Becker [1951] Director; Gary Robert Platt [1956] Director; Ian Leonard Rhodes [1951] Director

I4B Holdings Limited
Incorporated: 16 December 2016
Net Worth: £11,301,000 *Total Assets:* £46,464,000
Registered Office: Civic Centre, 9 Engineers Way, Wembley, Middlesex, HA9 0FJ
Activities: Other business support service activities n.e.c.
Parent: London Borough of Brent
Officers: George Crane [1949] Director; Akintoye Mobolaji Durowoju [1969] Director/Chartered Surveyor; Peter Gadsdon [1962] Director; Martin Frank Smith [1960] Director; Gail Elizabeth Tolley [1957] Director

IAG Cargo Limited
Incorporated: 18 May 2012 *Employees:* 344
Net Worth: £1,805,000 *Total Assets:* £61,458,000
Registered Office: P O Box 99, Carrus Cargo Centre, Sealand Road, London Heathrow Airport, Hounslow, Middlesex, TW6 2JS
Activities: Freight air transport
Parent: International Consolidated Airlines Group S.A.
Officers: Luke Alexander Michael Straver, Secretary; Jose Antonio Barrionuevo Urgel [1972] Director [Spanish]; Robert Boyle [1964] Director; Lynne Louise Embleton [1969] Director/Airline Executive; Lewis Ian Girdwood [1967] Director/Chief Financial Officer; Stephen William Lawrence Gunning [1967] Managing Director; William David Shepherd [1971] Director/Head of Commercial

IAG GBS Limited
Incorporated: 15 August 2014 *Employees:* 157
Net Worth Deficit: £16,232,000 *Total Assets:* £90,665,000
Registered Office: Waterside, Harmondsworth, West Drayton, Middlesex, UB7 0GB
Activities: Other business support service activities n.e.c.
Parent: International Consolidated Airlines Group SA
Officers: Luke Alexander Michael Straver, Secretary; Sian Louise Davies [1973] Director/Accountant; William John Francis [1962] Director; Stephen William Lawrence Gunning [1967] Director/British Airways PLC - Chief Financial Officer; Marcia Yor Ing Lin [1971] Director

IAH Charity Company Limited
Incorporated: 3 May 2011 *Employees:* 5
Net Worth: £6,227,284 *Total Assets:* £6,248,384
Registered Office: Congress House, 14 Lyon Road, Harrow, Middlesex, HA1 2EN
Activities: Physical well-being activities
Officers: George David Astor [1958] Director/Chief Investment Officer; Timothy Nicolas Carter [1952] Director; Dr Rosalyn Anne Davies [1955] Director/Hospital Consultant; Susan Rosemary Douthwaite [1947] Director/University Lecturer; William Alexander Mavourn Francklin [1958] Director/Investment Manager; Professor Jennifer Rosemary Harrow [1947] Director/University Professor; Professor Linda Maitland Luxon [1948] Director/Medical Consultant Physician; Anthony Richard Wilson [1949] Director/Retired

IBA Group Holdings Limited
Incorporated: 12 June 2015 *Employees:* 2
Net Worth: £3,696,570 *Total Assets:* £16,696,570
Registered Office: IBA House, 7 The Crescent, Leatherhead, Surrey, KT22 8DY
Activities: Activities of head offices
Officers: Gregory Raymond Allen [1986] Director; Philip Leslie Seymour [1959] Director

IBRC Asset Finance Limited
Incorporated: 14 August 1995
Net Worth: £28,976,064 *Total Assets:* £29,145,804
Registered Office: Unit 33a Enterprise House, 44-46 Terrace Road, Walton on Thames, Surrey, KT12 2SD
Activities: Other credit granting n.e.c.
Parent: CDB (U.K.) Limited
Officers: James Ednie Brydie [1959] Director/Banker

Iceport Limited
Incorporated: 5 January 2011
Net Worth: £1,954,076 *Total Assets:* £6,502,497
Registered Office: Portland House, 69-71 Wembley Hill Road, Wembley, Middlesex, HA9 8BU
Activities: Other letting and operating of own or leased real estate
Parent: Solai Holdings Limited
Officers: Bhupendra Shantilal Kansagra, Secretary; Bhupendra Shantilal Kansagra [1956] Director/Businessman; Rajni Shantilal Kansagra [1942] Director/Businessman; Ramesh Shantilal Kansagra [1950] Director/Businessman; Sunil Rajni Kansagra [1976] Director/Developer

ICS Incorporation Limited
Incorporated: 11 June 1999
Net Worth Deficit: £23,939,552 *Total Assets:* £31,552,244
Registered Office: Unit 6 North Radius Park, Faggs Road, Feltham, Middlesex, TW14 0NG
Activities: Other business support service activities n.e.c.
Officers: Bassam Salim Khoury, Secretary/Financial Officer [Lebanese]; Ernie Vibas Cayubit [1983] Director/Accountant [Filipino]; Manu Chennattu Kuriakose [1976] Director/Accountant [Indian]; Charmaine Dela Cerna Encabo [1983] Director/Secretary [Filipino]; Samuel Kutty John [1974] Director/Accountant [Indian]; Bassam Salim Khoury [1963] Director/Financial Officer [Lebanese]

IDG International Marketing Services Europe Ltd
Incorporated: 20 March 1987 *Employees:* 72
Net Worth: £4,207,850 *Total Assets:* £9,276,675
Registered Office: Staines One, Station Approach, Staines upon Thames, Middlesex, TW18 4LY
Activities: Advertising agencies
Officers: Peter Augustine Bradley, Secretary; Keith James Arnot [1955] Director/Chartered Accountant; John Peter Omalley [1965] Director [Irish]

IGD Services Limited
Incorporated: 22 April 1997
Net Worth: £652,052 *Total Assets:* £12,871,688
Registered Office: Grange Lane, Letchmore Heath, Watford, Herts, WD25 8GD
Activities: Other information service activities n.e.c.
Parent: The Institute of Grocery Distribution
Officers: Julia Clare Bastiman, Secretary; Ann Michelle Bell [1971] People Director, International; Nicolas Paul Michael Angelo Mills-Hicks [1971] Food Commercial Director; Bradley Moore [1972] Grocery Sales Director; Ian Douglas Morley [1966] Group Sales Director; David O'Flynn [1970] Director/Chief Financial Officer [Irish]; Jill Margaret Ross [1973] Director/Vice President, Customer Development; Philip John Tenney [1970] Director/Vice President and CIO; Mark John Webster [1972] Director/Financial Controller

Igroup 8 Limited
Incorporated: 10 December 1999
Net Worth: £1,434,001,024 *Total Assets:* £3,009,617,920
Registered Office: P O Box 2497, Building 4, Hatters Lane, Watford, Herts, WD18 1YY
Activities: Other business support service activities n.e.c.
Parent: GE Money Home Lending Finance Limited
Officers: Samantha Jones [1981] Director; Jonathan Edward Taylor [1980] Director/Risk and Compliance Leader

IGT U.K. Limited
Incorporated: 5 March 1993 *Employees:* 61
Previous: GTECH U.K. Limited
Net Worth: £7,227,343 *Total Assets:* £8,695,749
Registered Office: 1st Floor, Building 3, Croxley Green Business Park, Hatters Lane, Watford, Herts, WD18 8YG
Activities: Business and domestic software development
Parent: International Game Technology PLC
Officers: Declan James Harkin [1961] Director [American]

IGUK Support Services Limited
Incorporated: 23 August 2001 *Employees:* 39
Net Worth Deficit: £29,257,000 *Total Assets:* £18,159,000
Registered Office: 2 AC Court, High Street, Thames Ditton, Surrey, KT7 0SR
Activities: Other business support service activities n.e.c.
Parent: IGUK Limited
Officers: Alan Albert Horton [1963] Director; Stuart Pace [1962] Director

IHC Hotel Limited
Incorporated: 29 November 1988
Net Worth: £78,266,000 *Total Assets:* £78,290,000
Registered Office: Broadwater Park, Denham, Bucks, UB9 5HR
Activities: Activities of head offices
Parent: Six Continents Limited
Officers: Fiona Cuttell, Secretary; Michael Jon Cockcroft [1974] Director/Accountant; Michael Todd Glover [1971] Director/Financial Controller [American]; Nicolette Henfrey [1969] Director

IHC May Fair (Holdings) Limited
Incorporated: 29 November 1988
Net Worth Deficit: £30,827,000 *Total Assets:* £392,679,008
Registered Office: Broadwater Park, Denham, Bucks, UB9 5HR
Activities: Activities of head offices
Parent: IHC UK (Holdings) Limited
Officers: Fiona Cuttell, Secretary; Michael Jon Cockcroft [1974] Director/Accountant; Michael Todd Glover [1971] Director/Financial Controller [American]; Nicolette Henfrey [1969] Director

IHC May Fair Hotel Limited
Incorporated: 29 November 1988
Net Worth: £42,473,000 *Total Assets:* £42,486,000
Registered Office: Broadwater Park, Denham, Bucks, UB9 5HR
Activities: Activities of head offices
Parent: Six Continents Limited
Officers: Fiona Littlebury-Cuttell, Secretary; Michael Jon Cockcroft [1974] Director/Accountant; Michael Todd Glover [1971] Director/Financial Controller [American]; Nicolette Henfrey [1969] Director

IHC Overseas (U.K.) Limited
Incorporated: 28 November 1988
Net Worth: £341,419,008 *Total Assets:* £341,574,016
Registered Office: Broadwater Park, Denham, Bucks, UB9 5HR
Activities: Activities of head offices
Parent: Six Continents Limited
Officers: Fiona Cuttell, Secretary; Michael Jon Cockcroft [1974] Director/Accountant; Michael Todd Glover [1971] Director/Financial Controller [American]; Nicolette Henfrey [1969] Director

IHC UK (Holdings) Limited
Incorporated: 28 November 1988
Net Worth: £84,858,000 *Total Assets:* £84,874,000
Registered Office: Broadwater Park, Denham, Bucks, UB9 5HR
Activities: Activities of head offices
Parent: Six Continents Limited
Officers: Fiona Cuttell, Secretary; Michael Jon Cockcroft [1974] Director/Accountant; Michael Todd Glover [1971] Director/Financial Controller [American]; Nicolette Henfrey [1969] Director

IHG Hotels Limited
Incorporated: 24 November 1995
Net Worth: £489,766,016 *Total Assets:* £534,344,992
Registered Office: Broadwater Park, Denham, Bucks, UB9 5HR
Activities: Other business support service activities n.e.c.
Parent: Six Continents Holdings Limited
Officers: Fiona Cuttell, Secretary; Michael Jon Cockcroft [1974] Director/Accountant; Michael Todd Glover [1971] Director/Financial Controller [American]; Nicolette Henfrey [1969] Director; Daisy Eleanor Loveday Caroline Llewellyn [1976] Director; George Turner [1971] Director

IHS Lothian Holdings Limited
Incorporated: 18 December 2014
Total Assets: £35,402,000
Registered Office: 8 White Oak Square, London Road, Swanley, Kent, BR8 7AG
Activities: Activities of construction holding companies
Officers: Mark Dening Bradshaw [1975] Director/Banker [Australian]; John Stephen Gordon [1962] Director; John McDonagh [1969] Director; Richard Osborne [1979] Alternate Director

IHS Lothian Investments Limited
Incorporated: 18 December 2014
Total Assets: £35,402,000
Registered Office: 8 White Oak Square, London Road, Swanley, Kent, BR8 7AG
Activities: Activities of other holding companies n.e.c.
Officers: Mark Dening Bradshaw [1975] Director/Banker [Australian]; John Stephen Gordon [1962] Director; John McDonagh [1969] Director; Richard Osborne [1979] Alternate Director

IIAA Limited
Incorporated: 20 April 1993 *Employees:* 182
Net Worth: £2,703,949 *Total Assets:* £8,462,370
Registered Office: 1st Floor, Stanmore House, 15-19 Church Road, Stanmore, Middlesex, HA7 4AR
Activities: Non-specialised wholesale trade
Major Shareholder: David Alpert
Officers: David Alpert, Secretary; David Alpert [1969] Director; Tracy Alpert [1968] Director; Nicola Louise Bell [1972] Sales Director; Martin Evans [1956] Director/Accountant

Ikarim Business Services Ltd
Incorporated: 12 January 2011 *Employees:* 4
Net Worth: £301 *Total Assets:* £12,753,014
Registered Office: The Coach House, Powell Road, Buckhurst Hill, Essex, IG9 5RD
Activities: Other information technology service activities
Major Shareholder: Mohammed Shakeel Mughal
Officers: Mohammed Shakeel Mughal [1965] Director

Ikon Science Limited
Incorporated: 26 February 2001 *Employees:* 111
Net Worth: £3,080,039 *Total Assets:* £10,171,421
Registered Office: 1st Floor, 1 The Crescent, Surbiton, Surrey, KT6 4BN
Activities: Other information technology service activities
Parent: Ikon Intermediate Limited
Officers: Charlotte Roche, Secretary; Mark Anthony Bashforth [1963] Director; Steven Alec Hunt [1957] Director/Chief Operating Officer; Martyn Frederick Millwood Hargrave [1958] Director/Geophysicist; Dr Denis Robert Michel Saussus [1974] Director/Chief Technology Officer [Belgian]

Ilapak Limited
Incorporated: 25 August 1970 *Employees:* 32
Net Worth: £1,418,475 *Total Assets:* £7,566,220
Registered Office: 29 Riverside Way, Uxbridge, Middlesex, UB8 2YF
Activities: Manufacture of other special-purpose machinery n.e.c.
Parent: Ilapak International SA
Officers: Michael Rowland Vail, Secretary; Sergio Marzo [1966] Director/IMA Group CFO [Italian]; Filippo Melandri [1961] Director [Italian]

ILB Investments Limited
Incorporated: 3 September 2008 *Employees:* 4
Net Worth: £3,520,188 *Total Assets:* £60,520,232
Registered Office: C P House, Otterspool Way, Watford By-Pass, Watford, Herts, WD25 8JJ
Activities: Other letting and operating of own or leased real estate
Shareholders: Iris Gibbor; Lady Lilly Schreier
Officers: Eric Lewis, Secretary; Iris Gibbor [1951] Director; Mark Gibbor [1988] Director/Accountant; Lady Lilly Schreier [1924] Director

Ilot Capital UK Ltd
Incorporated: 29 May 2015
Net Worth: £5,618,447 *Total Assets:* £18,871,134
Registered Office: First Floor, Sheraton House, Lower Road, Chorleywood, Herts, WD3 5LH
Activities: Financial intermediation not elsewhere classified
Parent: Intralot S.A Integrated Lottery Systems and Services
Officers: Evangelos Raptis [1969] Director [Greek]

Ilot Investments UK Ltd
Incorporated: 29 May 2015
Net Worth: £5,543,211 *Total Assets:* £18,942,062
Registered Office: First Floor, Sheraton House, Lower Road, Chorleywood, Herts, WD3 5LH
Activities: Financial intermediation not elsewhere classified
Parent: Intralot S.A Integrated
Officers: Evangelos Raptis [1969] Director [Greek]

IM Estates Limited
Incorporated: 24 July 2013 *Employees:* 1
Net Worth: £5,486,601 *Total Assets:* £5,490,976
Registered Office: 168 Thornbury Road, Isleworth, Middlesex, TW7 4QE
Activities: Activities of other holding companies n.e.c.
Major Shareholder: Isabelle Marie Mathew
Officers: Isabelle Marie Mathew [1954] Director

Imagination Technologies Group Limited
Incorporated: 18 April 1994 *Employees:* 1,068
Previous: Imagination Technologies Group PLC
Net Worth: £85,375,000 *Total Assets:* £130,912,000
Registered Office: Imagination House, Home Park Estate, Kings Langley, Herts, WD4 8LZ
Activities: Other information service activities n.e.c.
Parent: CBFI Investment Limited
Officers: Ray Bingham [1945] Director [American]; Ronald Douglas Black [1963] Director [American]; John Kao [1969] Director [Chinese]; Peter Kuo [1971] Director [Chinese]

Imagination Technologies Limited
Incorporated: 1 April 1977 *Employees:* 661
Net Worth: £7,923,000 *Total Assets:* £84,409,000
Registered Office: Imagination House, Home Park Estate, Kings Langley, Herts, WD4 8LZ
Activities: Other information technology service activities
Parent: Imagination Technologies Group PLC
Officers: Ronald Douglas Black [1963] Director [American]

Imagine Cruising Limited
Incorporated: 27 January 2009 *Employees:* 158
Net Worth: £3,040,158 *Total Assets:* £54,304,696
Registered Office: 2nd Floor, Nucleus House, 2 Lower Mortlake Road, Richmond, Surrey, TW9 2JA
Activities: Travel agency activities
Parent: Imagine Enterprises Limited
Officers: Iain Charles Richard Andrew [1965] Director; Robin John Deller [1967] Managing Director; Natalie Ann Maye [1981] Director; Sarah Elizabeth McAllister [1979] Director; Asif Hamza Parkar [1974] Director/Finance Manager; Geoffrey Peter Wood [1957] Director

The Imaging Centre Holdings Limited
Incorporated: 17 March 2015
Net Worth: £1,327,350 *Total Assets:* £5,698,608
Registered Office: The Hive, Camrose Avenue, London, HA8 6AG
Activities: Other human health activities
Parent: Double A Group Ltd
Officers: Mahendra Patel, Secretary; Anthony Andrew Kleanthous [1966] Director

IMCD Holding UK Ltd
Incorporated: 17 August 2005
Net Worth: £17,580,000 *Total Assets:* £22,885,000
Registered Office: 5th Floor, Times House, Throwley Way, Sutton, Surrey, SM1 4AF
Activities: Activities of head offices
Parent: IMCD UK Acquisitions Limited
Officers: Hendrikus Jacobus Jozef Kooijmans, Secretary/Director [Dutch]; Monsieur Olivier Philippe Champault [1967] Managing Director [French]; Paul Christopher Hanbury [1976] Managing Director; Hendrikus Jacobus Jozef Kooijmans [1961] Director [Dutch]

IMCD UK Acquisitions Limited
Incorporated: 10 December 2010
Net Worth: £23,881,000 *Total Assets:* £43,591,000
Registered Office: Times House, Throwley Way, Sutton, Surrey, SM1 4AF
Activities: Activities of head offices
Parent: IMCD N.V.
Officers: Monsieur Olivier Philippe Champault [1967] Managing Director [French]; Paul Christopher Hanbury [1976] Managing Director; Hendrikus Jacobus Jozef Kooijmans [1961] Director/Chief Financial Officer [Dutch]

IMCD UK Investments Ltd
Incorporated: 22 February 2001
Net Worth: £5,014,000 *Total Assets:* £13,980,000
Registered Office: Times House, Throwley Way, Sutton, Surrey, SM1 4AF
Activities: Activities of head offices
Parent: IMCD N.V.
Officers: Hendrikus Jacobus Jozef Kooijmans, Secretary; Monsieur Olivier Philippe Champault [1967] Managing Director [French]; Paul Christopher Hanbury [1976] Managing Director; Hendrikus Jacobus Jozef Kooijmans [1961] Director [Dutch]

IMCD UK Limited
Incorporated: 19 September 1988 *Employees:* 134
Net Worth: £55,915,000 *Total Assets:* £93,651,000
Registered Office: Times House, Throwley Way, Sutton, Surrey, SM1 4AF
Activities: Wholesale of chemical products
Parent: IMCD N.V.
Officers: Hans Kooijmans, Secretary; Paul Christopher Hanbury [1976] Managing Director; Hans Kooijmans [1961] Financial Director [Dutch]; Richard John Mell [1968] Finance Director

Imerys Aluminates Limited
Incorporated: 31 December 1985 *Employees:* 63
Previous: Kerneos Limited
Net Worth: £19,779,000 *Total Assets:* £35,623,000
Registered Office: Kerneos, Dolphin Way, Purfleet, Essex, RM19 1NZ
Activities: Manufacture of cement
Parent: Kerneos Holding Northern Europe Limited
Officers: Ian William Adamson, Secretary; Paul Bottomley [1958] Director/Commercial Manager; Patrick Michael Molitor [1967] Director [German]; Tony Vivian Newton [1959] Director/Commercial Manager; Peter Arthur Odendaal [1968] Works Director

Impact Africa Limited
Incorporated: 24 March 2010 *Employees:* 2
Net Worth Deficit: £6,194,732 *Total Assets:* £21,193,022
Registered Office: Elder House, St Georges Business Park, Brooklands Road, Weybridge, Surrey, KT13 0TS
Activities: Extraction of crude petroleum
Parent: Impact Oil & Gas Limited
Officers: Siraj Ahmed, Secretary; Philip Lloyd Birch [1958] Director; Robert Wilde [1964] Finance Director

Impact Multi Academy Trust
Incorporated: 7 March 2011 *Employees:* 389
Previous: Apollo Learning Trust
Net Worth: £35,493,000 *Total Assets:* £38,875,000
Registered Office: Ravens Wood School, Oakley Road, Bromley, Kent, BR2 8HP
Activities: General secondary education
Officers: Joanne Elizabeth Marriott, Secretary; Jeremy Richard Marlow Allen [1966] Director/Computer Programmer; Nicholas Alastair Cross [1968] Director of Education; Lucy Marjorie Jeffreys [1957] Director/Education Consultant; Harendra Madugalle [1980] Director/Accountant; Andrew Michael Naish [1965] Director; Kieran Jude Osborne [1953] Director/Education Consultant; Peter Lewis Ostacchini [1960] Director/Chief Executive Officer, Bank

Impact Oil & Gas Limited
Incorporated: 11 April 2011 *Employees:* 15
Net Worth: £39,841,028 *Total Assets:* £50,431,184
Registered Office: Elder House, St Georges Business Park, Brooklands Road, Weybridge, Surrey, KT13 0TS
Activities: Extraction of crude petroleum
Officers: Siraj Ahmed, Secretary; Siraj Ahmed [1982] Director; Andrew Donald Bartlett [1957] Director; Philip Lloyd Birch [1958] Director; John Anthony Copelyn [1950] Director/Chief Executive Officer HCI [South African]; Michael James Doherty [1949] Director [Irish]; Keith Charles Hill [1959] Director/Businessman [Canadian]; James Robert Nicolella [1968] Director [South African/British]; Charles Richard Theodore Ramsden [1953] Director/Geophysicist [South African]; Robert Wilde [1964] Finance Director

Imperial Ductwork Services Holdings Limited
Incorporated: 11 April 2013 *Employees:* 45
Net Worth: £1,532,948 *Total Assets:* £13,070,906
Registered Office: Numeric House, 98 Station Road, Sidcup, Kent, DA15 7BY
Activities: Activities of other holding companies n.e.c.
Shareholder: Tracy Jane Farmer
Officers: Dean John Barnes [1981] Commercial Director; Tracy Jane Farmer [1970] Director; Anthony O'Connell [1969] Director; Rodney Michael Silke [1972] Operations Director; John Smith [1968] Contracts Director

Imperial Ductwork Services Limited
Incorporated: 11 July 1997 *Employees:* 45
Net Worth: £3,022,948 *Total Assets:* £14,560,906
Registered Office: Numeric House, 98 Station Road, Sidcup, Kent, DA15 7BY
Activities: Other specialised construction activities n.e.c.
Parent: Imperial Ductwork Sevices Holdings Limited
Officers: Tracy Jane Farmer, Secretary; Keith Barclay [1967] Associate Director; Dean John Barnes [1981] Commercial Director; John Anthony Barnes [1955] Managing Director; Jamie Donnelly [1971] Associate Director; Terry Hussey [1986] Director; Dean Morris [1981] Associate Director; Anthony O'Connell [1969] Contracts Director; Rodney Michael Silke [1972] Operations Director; John Smith [1968] Contracts Director; Scott Strutton [1968] Director

Imperial Pharmaceuticals Limited
Incorporated: 14 August 1996 *Employees:* 14
Net Worth: £21,344,456 *Total Assets:* £43,295,732
Registered Office: Unit 4 Imperial Park, Stonefield Way, South Ruislip, Middlesex, HA4 0JW
Activities: Wholesale of perfume and cosmetics
Shareholder: Manisha Thakrar
Officers: Manisha Thakrar, Secretary; Nayan Thakrar [1960] Director; Shivani Thakrar [1987] Director/Dentist

Impulse Leisure
Incorporated: 2 September 2004 *Employees:* 379
Net Worth: £3,960,208 *Total Assets:* £5,644,884
Registered Office: Blackshots Leisure Centre, Blackshots Lane, Grays, Essex, RM16 2JU
Activities: Operation of sports facilities
Officers: Jonathan Nicholas Tatchell, Secretary; Generald Hodgson [1943] Director of Events; Christopher David Seamark [1980] Director/Local Government Officer; John Robert Huckson Seymour [1941] Director/Retired [Australian]; Dr Peter Wilson [1938] Director/Architect

Imtech Engineering Services London and South Ltd
Incorporated: 3 May 1994 *Employees:* 159
Net Worth Deficit: £5,697,000 *Total Assets:* £22,040,000
Registered Office: Twenty, 20 Kingston Road, Staines upon Thames, Middlesex, TW18 4LG
Activities: Electrical installation
Parent: ESSCI Engineering Services Ltd
Officers: Maritz Naude, Secretary; Michael Andrew Booth [1974] Director; Martin McEvoy [1965] Managing Director [Irish]; Maritz Naude [1973] Finance Director

Inclusive Multi Academy Trust
Incorporated: 5 October 2016 *Employees:* 141
Net Worth: £16,874,984 *Total Assets:* £19,169,036
Registered Office: Laurance Haines School, Vicarage Road, Watford, Herts, WD18 0DD
Activities: Primary education
Officers: Rebecca Blackstaffe [1977] Director/Teacher; Jessie Bruce [1962] Director/Headteacher; Andrew John Chappell [1963] Director/Chartered Accountant; Richard Andrew Jones [1980] Director; Elizabeth Mary Leeman [1957] Director/Business Executive; James Thomas Roach [1979] Director

Independent Commercial Broking Group Limited
Incorporated: 25 October 2012 *Employees:* 112
Net Worth: £7,698,286 *Total Assets:* £19,502,060
Registered Office: Virginia House, 35-51 Station Road, Egham, Surrey, TW20 9LB
Activities: Activities of financial services holding companies
Parent: SAS Verlingue
Officers: Hilary Burrow, Secretary; Anthony John Barnett [1951] Director/Accountant; Richard George Peter Bevins [1977] Director/Insurance Broker; Neil Allen Campling [1961] Director/Insurance Broker; Kevin Peter Chairman [1967] Director/Insurance Broker; Craig Paul Kitchen [1968] Director/Insurance Broker; Jason George Laslett [1969] Director/Independent Financial Advisor; Ian Livingstone [1960] Director/Insurance Broker; Eric Maurice Maumy [1966] Director [French]; Mark Julian Treasure [1958] Director/Insurance Broker; Jacques Henri Verlingue [1953] Director [French]

Independent Commercial Broking Limited
Incorporated: 30 June 2000 *Employees:* 95
Net Worth: £4,870,870 *Total Assets:* £11,904,810
Registered Office: Virginia House, 35-51 Station Road, Egham, Surrey, TW20 9LB
Activities: Non-life insurance
Parent: Independent Commercial Broking Group Limited
Officers: Hilary Burrow, Secretary; Anthony John Barnett [1951] Director/Accountant; Richard George Peter Bevins [1977] Director/Insurance Broker; Neil Allen Campling [1961] Director/Insurance Broker; Kevin Peter Chairman [1967] Director/Insurance Broker; Craig Paul Kitchen [1968] Director/Insurance Broker; Ian Livingstone [1960] Director/Insurance Broker; Mark Julian Treasure [1958] Director/Insurance Broker

Independent Group (UK) Limited
Incorporated: 24 October 2008 *Employees:* 248
Net Worth Deficit: £4,407,000 *Total Assets:* £5,710,000
Registered Office: 2 AC Court, High Street, Thames Ditton, Surrey, KT7 0SR
Activities: Activities of head offices
Shareholder: Jamie Christopher Constable
Officers: Jamie Constable, Secretary; Steve Curtis, Secretary; Christopher Campbell [1981] Director; Philip Raymond Emmerson [1971] Director; Alan Albert Horton [1963] Director; Stuart Pace [1962] Director

Independent Inspections Limited
Incorporated: 1 July 1993 *Employees:* 131
Net Worth: £6,125,000 *Total Assets:* £36,191,000
Registered Office: 2 AC Court, High Street, Thames Ditton, Surrey, KT7 0SR
Activities: Other service activities n.e.c.
Parent: Independent Inspections Holdings Limited
Officers: Alan Albert Horton [1963] Director; Stuart Pace [1962] Director

Indiacast UK Ltd
Incorporated: 22 January 2013 *Employees:* 8
Net Worth: £688,327 *Total Assets:* £7,196,720
Registered Office: Suite 02.13, Avanta Harrow, 79 College Road, Harrow, Middlesex, HA1 1BD
Activities: Television programme distribution activities
Parent: Indiacast Media Distribution Private Limited
Officers: Anuj Gandhi [1968] Director [Indian]; Govind Keshav Shahi [1972] Director

Industrial Chemicals Group Limited
Incorporated: 10 March 1976 *Employees:* 511
Net Worth: £48,226,352 *Total Assets:* £121,617,424
Registered Office: Titan Works, Hogg Lane, Grays, Essex, RM17 5DU
Activities: Manufacture of other chemical products n.e.c.
Shareholders: John William Carver; Allen Rodney Carver; Charles Daryl Carver
Officers: Benjamin James Lowthian, Secretary; Allen Rodney Carver [1947] Director; Charles Daryl Carver [1964] Director; John William Carver [1945] Director; Edwin John Strang [1958] Finance Director

Industrial Chemicals Limited
Incorporated: 30 November 1999 *Employees:* 495
Net Worth: £17,625,142 *Total Assets:* £48,816,096
Registered Office: Titan Works, Titan Industrial Estate, Hogg Lane, Grays, Essex, RM17 5DU
Activities: Manufacture of other inorganic basic chemicals
Shareholders: John William Carver; Allen Rodney Carver; Charles Daryl Carver
Officers: Benjamin James Lowthian, Secretary; Allen Rodney Carver [1947] Director; Charles Daryl Carver [1964] Director; John William Carver [1945] Director; Edwin John Strang [1958] Finance Director

Information Security Forum Limited
Incorporated: 6 July 2003 *Employees:* 28
Net Worth: £3,211,128 *Total Assets:* £10,403,608
Registered Office: Elder House, St Georges Business Park, 207 Brooklands Road, Weybridge, Surrey, KT13 0TS
Activities: Other business support service activities n.e.c.
Officers: Rory Magnus Alsop [1971] Director/Head of Information Security Risk Oversight [British/Australian]; Thorsten Delbrouck-Konetzko [1970] Director/Corporate Chief Information Security Officer [German]; Steven Robert Durbin [1961] Managing Director; Werner Gutau [1958] Director Business Continuity - Information Security [German]; Gareth James Lindahl-Wise [1973] Director/Group Information Security Manager; Jari Pirhonen [1962] Security Director [Finnish]; Josef Johannes Van Wyk [1970] Director Information Security and Privacy [American]

Infotech Trade Services Ltd
Incorporated: 19 September 2013
Net Worth: £3,778 *Total Assets:* £23,333,800
Registered Office: Suite 121, Wey House, 15 Church Street, Weybridge, Surrey, KT13 8NA
Activities: Other business support service activities n.e.c.
Shareholders: Christiana Chioma Ekeh; Leonard Nnamdi Ekeh
Officers: Christiana Chioma Ekeh [1964] Director/Accountant [Nigerian]; Leonard Nnamdi Ekeh [1957] Director/Economist [Nigerian]

Ingenie Services Limited
Incorporated: 9 December 2010
Net Worth: £5,201,000 *Total Assets:* £9,454,000
Registered Office: The Stables, Thorncroft Manor, Thorncroft Drive, Leatherhead, Surrey, KT22 8JB
Activities: Activities of insurance agents and brokers
Parent: Ingenie Limited
Officers: Christopher Francis Woodall, Secretary; Selim Damian Cavanagh [1971] Director; Mark Pritchard Williams [1965] Director; Christopher Francis Woodall [1965] Director/Accountant; David Thomas McAree Young [1961] Director

Inner Town Homes Limited
Incorporated: 17 July 1962 *Employees:* 3
Net Worth: £7,095,837 *Total Assets:* £7,555,054
Registered Office: Suite 2, West Hill House, West Hill, Epsom, Surrey, KT19 8JD
Activities: Other letting and operating of own or leased real estate
Parent: Street Family Group of Companies (Holdings) Limited
Officers: Andrew Mark Munday, Secretary; Patricia Jane French [1951] Managing Director; Rivkah Hazel McCullough [1980] Director/Commercial Portfolio Executive; Andrew Mark Munday [1969] Director/Property Manager; Jonathan Justin Selig Symons [1949] Director

Innisfree Schools (F2C) Limited
Incorporated: 22 March 2013
Net Worth: £35,460,000 *Total Assets:* £73,336,000
Registered Office: 8 White Oak Square, London Road, Swanley, Kent, BR8 7AG
Activities: Activities of other holding companies n.e.c.
Parent: Innisfree Continuation Partners LLP
Officers: Nicholas John Edward Crowther [1960] Investment Director; Burton David [1978] Director

Innisfree Schools (Secondary) Limited
Incorporated: 22 March 2013
Net Worth: £40,924,000 *Total Assets:* £76,075,000
Registered Office: 8 White Oak Square, London Road, Swanley, Kent, BR8 7AG
Activities: Activities of other holding companies n.e.c.
Shareholders: Innisfree Secondary Partners 1 LLP; Innisfree Secondary Partners 2 LLP
Officers: Nicholas John Edward Crowther [1960] Investment Director; Burton David [1978] Director

Innotech Advisers Limited
Incorporated: 23 November 1982 *Employees:* 13
Net Worth: £117,243,408 *Total Assets:* £549,925,120
Registered Office: Q3, The Square, Randalls Way, Leatherhead, Surrey, KT22 7TW
Activities: Financial intermediation not elsewhere classified
Major Shareholder: David John Sainsbury
Officers: Michael David Langford Smith, Secretary; Joseph Christopher Burns [1978] Director; Baron David John Sainsbury of Turville [1940] Director; James Frederick Shea [1964] Director; David Roy Wood [1961] Director

Innotrade Europe Limited
Incorporated: 18 June 2013
Net Worth: £6,214,179 *Total Assets:* £6,242,189
Registered Office: 167 Turners Hill, Cheshunt, Herts, EN8 9BH
Activities: Activities of mortgage finance companies
Parent: Investex Group Ltd
Officers: Daniel Mark Neumann [1967] Director; Paul Nicholas Neumann [1961] Director

Innovate Services Limited
Incorporated: 7 November 2007 *Employees:* 646
Net Worth: £3,712,895 *Total Assets:* £7,416,251
Registered Office: Phoenix House, Pyrford Road, West Byfleet, Surrey, KT14 6RA
Activities: Other food services
Parent: I Catering Management Services Ltd
Officers: Michele Sara Callcut [1959] Finance Director; John Hamill [1966] Director; Phillip James Morris [1978] Director; Kenneth John Navin [1962] Director; Geoffrey Owen Peppiatt [1953] Director

Input Video Holdings Ltd
Incorporated: 11 August 2015
Net Worth: £4,403,000 *Total Assets:* £7,027,000
Registered Office: 32-34 Greenhill Crescent, Watford, Herts, WD18 8JU
Activities: Television programming and broadcasting activities
Parent: Gravity Media Group UK Holdings Limited
Officers: Nikki Jane Petken, Secretary; Elliot Saul Kaye [1971] Director; Kevin Moorhouse [1958] Director; Nick Newton [1962] Director; Neil Jonathan Oughton [1958] Director/Television Producer

Input Video Ltd
Incorporated: 18 December 1987 *Employees:* 122
Net Worth: £5,461,000 *Total Assets:* £7,837,000
Registered Office: 32-34 Greenhill Crescent, Watford, Herts, WD18 8JU
Activities: Television programme production activities
Parent: Input Video Holdings Limited
Officers: Nikki Jane Petken, Secretary; Elliot Saul Kaye [1971] Director; Kevin Moorhouse [1958] Director; Nick Newton [1962] Director; Neil Jonathan Oughton [1958] Director/Television Producer

Insignia Investments Limited
Incorporated: 11 October 2007 *Employees:* 52
Net Worth: £6,552,756 *Total Assets:* £14,180,130
Registered Office: 14 Pindar Road, Hoddesdon, Herts, EN11 0DE
Activities: Activities of head offices
Shareholders: Tara Flynn; Marc Flynn
Officers: James Flynn [1941] Director/Retired [Irish]; Marc Flynn [1964] Director; Ian Andrew Wright [1955] Director

Inspiral Oldham Holding Company Limited
Incorporated: 29 January 2010
Net Worth Deficit: £8,282,000 *Total Assets:* £78,819,000
Registered Office: 8 White Oak Square, London Road, Swanley, Kent, BR8 7AG
Activities: Activities of head offices
Parent: JLIF Holdings (Regeneration and Social Housing) Limited
Officers: Guy James Cresswell [1966] Director of Housing; Philip Howard Elvy [1967] Finance Director; Vikki Louise Everett [1971] Director/Project Manager; Julian Denzil Sutcliffe [1968] Life Cycle Asset Director

Inspiral Oldham Limited
Incorporated: 4 February 2010
Net Worth Deficit: £8,282,000 *Total Assets:* £78,819,000
Registered Office: 8 White Oak Square, London Road, Swanley, Kent, BR8 7AG
Activities: Other business support service activities n.e.c.
Parent: Inspiral Oldham Holding Company Limited
Officers: Guy James Cresswell [1966] Director of Housing; Philip Howard Elvy [1967] Finance Director; Vikki Louise Everett [1971] Director/Project Manager; Julian Denzil Sutcliffe [1968] Life Cycle Asset Director

Inspire Community Trust
Incorporated: 24 November 2004 *Employees:* 72
Net Worth: £7,739,654 *Total Assets:* £8,095,808
Registered Office: 20 Whitehall Lane, Slade Green, Kent, DA8 2DH
Activities: Other human health activities
Officers: Vinod Kumar Khanna, Secretary [Indian]; Ranjit Singh Bhamra [1957] Director/Voluntary Worker; Anne Bramley [1931] Director/Retired; Dr. Peter Paul Catterall [1961] Director/Lecturer; Andrew Thomas Crawford [1955] Director/Local Government Officer (Retired); Pamila Crawford [1954] Director/Retired; Roland Horace French [1932] Director/Retired; Vinod Kumar Khanna [1953] Director/Chief Executive; Hugh Neville Miller [1953] Director/Accountant; Peter Onley [1946] Director/Retired

Inspireall Leisure and Family Support Services
Incorporated: 19 December 2001 *Employees:* 941
Previous: Hertsmere Leisure Temp
Net Worth: £1,467,893 *Total Assets:* £7,045,082
Registered Office: The Venue, Elstree Way, Borehamwood, Herts, WD6 1JY
Activities: Operation of arts facilities
Officers: Clifford Mark Hedley, Secretary; Christine Anne Ayrton [1952] Director; Miranda Fleur Barnett [1970] Director; Michael Gibson [1954] Director/Bursar [Irish]; Ruth Anelena Huda [1980] Director; Anthony John Keating [1959] Director; Gavin Key [1976] Director/Accountant; Kevin John O'Malley [1956] Director/Chartered Accountant; Alison Muriel Sinclair [1953] Director/Retired Solicitor; Colin Neil Warne [1956] Director/Retired

Inspired Learning Group (UK) Limited
Incorporated: 13 March 1981 *Employees:* 65
Previous: Timedance Limited
Net Worth: £1,016,346 *Total Assets:* £5,033,773
Registered Office: 75 Park Lane, Croydon, Surrey, CR9 1XS
Activities: Primary education
Parent: Oakseal Ltd.
Officers: Hemal Lukha [1979] Early Years Director; Amitkumar Mehta [1971] Director

Instalcom Limited
Incorporated: 19 August 1997 *Employees:* 81
Net Worth: £15,067,343 *Total Assets:* £29,624,182
Registered Office: 467 Rayners Lane, Pinner, Middlesex, HA5 5ET
Activities: Other specialised construction activities n.e.c.
Parent: OCU Group Limited
Officers: Timothy Gerard O'Connor, Secretary/Contractor [Irish]; John McVeigh [1964] Managing Director [Irish]; Thomas Joseph O'Connor [1961] Director [Irish]; Timothy Gerard O'Connor [1960] Director [Irish]

Institute of Grocery Distribution (The)
Incorporated: 1 November 1909 *Employees:* 149
Net Worth: £9,113,861 *Total Assets:* £16,713,299
Registered Office: Grange Lane, Letchmore Heath, Watford, Herts, WD25 8GD
Activities: Other professional, scientific and technical activities n.e.c.
Officers: Julia Clare Bastiman, Secretary; Ann Michelle Bell [1971] People Director, International; Andrew James Clappen [1965] Corporate Services Director; Bradley Moore [1972] Grocery Sales Director; Ian Douglas Morley [1966] Group Sales Director; David Oflynn [1970] Director/Chief Financial Officer [Irish]; Jill Margaret Ross [1973] Director/Vice President, Customer Development; Philip John Tenney [1970] Director/Vice President and CIO; Mark John Webster [1972] Director/Financial Controller; Christopher Paul Whitfield [1969] Director/Chief Operating Officer

Insurance Claims Accommodation Bureau Limited
Incorporated: 23 October 2002 *Employees:* 34
Net Worth: £1,113,009 *Total Assets:* £10,467,516
Registered Office: Second Floor, Galley House, Moon Lane, Barnet, Herts, EN5 5YL
Activities: Other reservation service activities n.e.c.
Shareholders: Gary Michael Goodman; Angela Marilyn Goodman
Officers: Angela Marilyn Goodman, Secretary; Gary Michael Goodman [1948] Managing Director; Joel Peter Goodman [1974] Director; Timothy Scott Goodman [1975] Director/Manager

Integrated Design Limited
Incorporated: 30 May 1985 *Employees:* 45
Net Worth: £26,147,046 *Total Assets:* £27,319,964
Registered Office: Feltham Point, Air Park Way, Browells Lane, Feltham, Middlesex, TW13 7EQ
Activities: Manufacture of other special-purpose machinery n.e.c.
Shareholders: Derek Graham Huff; Lorraine Margaret Huff
Officers: Lorraine Margaret Huff, Secretary; Philip Andrew Coombes [1965] Production Director; Derek Graham Huff [1957] Managing Director; Lorraine Margaret Huff [1961] Director; Shane Naish [1960] Operations Director

Integrated Electronic Technologies Limited
Incorporated: 27 September 2006
Previous: Able Applied Technologies Ltd
Net Worth: £4,799,691 *Total Assets:* £6,884,751
Registered Office: Unit 2 Beverley Court, 26 Elmtree Road, Teddington, Middlesex, TW11 8ST
Activities: Manufacture of electronic components
Shareholders: Michael McNamara; Roberto Santini
Officers: Roger Chowen [1960] Director

Intelliflo Bidco Limited
Incorporated: 15 July 2013
Net Worth Deficit: £13,294,405 *Total Assets:* £50,401,736
Registered Office: Third Floor, Drapers Court, Kingston Hall Road, Kingston upon Thames, Surrey, KT1 2BQ
Activities: Activities of other holding companies n.e.c.
Parent: Intelliflo Midco Limited
Officers: Robert Rigsby, Secretary; Bryan Patrick Perryman [1979] Director [American]; Hamish John Purdey [1975] Director [Australian/British]

Intelliflo Holdings 2013 Limited
Incorporated: 15 July 2013 *Employees:* 169
Net Worth Deficit: £13,613,391 *Total Assets:* £55,258,876
Registered Office: Third Floor, Drapers Court, Kingston Hall Road, Kingston upon Thames, Surrey, KT1 2BQ
Activities: Activities of other holding companies n.e.c.
Parent: Invesco Holding Company Limited
Officers: Robert Rigsby, Secretary; Akeel Ahmed [1976] Director/Software Consultant; Nick Eatock [1968] IT Director; Bryan Patrick Perryman [1979] Director [American]; Hamish John Purdey [1975] Director [Australian/British]

Intelliflo Intermediate Holdings Limited
Incorporated: 15 July 2013
Net Worth Deficit: £2,731,094 *Total Assets:* £38,501,876
Registered Office: Third Floor, Drapers Court, Kingston Hall Road, Kingston upon Thames, Surrey, KT1 2BQ
Activities: Activities of other holding companies n.e.c.
Parent: Intelliflo Holdings 2013 Ltd
Officers: Robert Rigsby, Secretary; Bryan Patrick Perryman [1979] Director [American]; Hamish John Purdey [1975] Director [Australian/British]

Intelliflo Limited
Incorporated: 16 August 2004 *Employees:* 169
Net Worth: £13,117,960 *Total Assets:* £17,698,254
Registered Office: Third Floor, Drapers Court, Kingston Hall Road, Kingston upon Thames, Surrey, KT1 2BQ
Activities: Other information technology service activities
Parent: Intelliflo Bidco Ltd
Officers: Robert Rigsby, Secretary; Akeel Ahmed [1976] Director/Software Consultant; Mike Anthony Clifford [1966] Director; Nick Eatock [1968] IT Director; Bryan Patrick Perryman [1979] Director [American]; Hamish John Purdey [1975] Director [Australian/British]

Intelliflo Midco Limited
Incorporated: 15 July 2013 *Employees:* 169
Net Worth Deficit: £8,947,798 *Total Assets:* £55,258,872
Registered Office: Third Floor, Drapers Court, Kingston Hall Road, Kingston upon Thames, Surrey, KT1 2BQ
Activities: Activities of other holding companies n.e.c.
Parent: Intelliflo Intermediate Holdings Limited
Officers: Robert Rigsby, Secretary; Bryan Patrick Perryman [1979] Director [American]; Hamish John Purdey [1975] Director [Australian/British]

Intercede 2052 Limited
Incorporated: 21 June 2005 *Employees:* 10
Net Worth: £3,441,388 *Total Assets:* £5,658,647
Registered Office: 313 Boston Manor Road, Brentford, Middlesex, TW8 9LX
Activities: Other passenger land transport
Shareholder: Joseph Justin Bitran
Officers: Louise Bitran, Secretary/Solicitor; Joseph Justin Bitran [1970] Director; Louise Hilary Bitran [1977] Director/Legal Adviser

Interchemprod and Invest Ltd
Incorporated: 27 March 2002
Net Worth Deficit: £11,753,833 *Total Assets:* £5,043,818
Registered Office: First Floor, Woodgate Studios, 2-8 Games Road, Cockfosters, Barnet, Herts, EN4 9HN
Activities: Other business support service activities n.e.c.
Shareholders: Andreas Sofocleous; Friese Wolfgang Rudiger
Officers: Antri Lamprou, Secretary; Andreas Sofocleous [1967] Director [Cypriot]

Intercontinental (PB) 1
Incorporated: 15 October 2008
Net Worth: £1,865,974,400 *Total Assets:* £1,874,495,616
Registered Office: Broadwater Park, Denham, Bucks, UB9 5HR
Activities: Activities of head offices
Parent: Six Continents Hotels International Limited
Officers: Fiona Cuttell, Secretary; Colin Philip Garwood [1961] Director; Michael Todd Glover [1971] Director/Financial Controller [American]; Nicolette Henfrey [1969] Director

Intercontinental (PB) 3 Limited
Incorporated: 29 June 2009
Net Worth: £1,364,837,632 *Total Assets:* £1,369,897,600
Registered Office: Broadwater Park, Denham, Bucks, UB9 5HR
Activities: Activities of head offices
Parent: Six Continents Hotels International Limited
Officers: Fiona Cuttell, Secretary; Colin Philip Garwood [1961] Director; Michael Todd Glover [1971] Director/Financial Controller [American]; Nicolette Henfrey [1969] Director

Intercontinental Adjusters (Europe) Limited
Incorporated: 11 February 2000 *Employees:* 13
Net Worth: £2,117,179 *Total Assets:* £6,003,662
Registered Office: 2nd Floor, Building A, Turnford Place, Great Cambridge Road, Broxbourne, Herts, EN10 6NH
Activities: Other business support service activities n.e.c.
Shareholders: Sally Anne Hart; Alistair James Hart
Officers: Sally Anne Hart, Secretary; Alistair James Hart [1967] Director/Insurance Loss Adjuster; Brian David Hart [1940] Director/Loss Adjuster; Sally Anne Hart [1954] Director

Intercontinental Hotels Group PLC
Incorporated: 21 May 2004 *Employees:* 6,658
Net Worth Deficit: £611,415,936 *Total Assets:* £2,262,524,160
Registered Office: Broadwater Park, Denham, Bucks, UB9 5HR
Activities: Hotels and similar accommodation
Officers: Nicolette Henfrey, Secretary; Keith Barr [1970] Director [American]; Anne Busquet [1950] Director [American]; Patrick Jean Pierre Cescau [1948] Director [French]; Ian Dyson [1962] Director; Paul Russell Edgecliffe-Johnson [1972] Director/Certified Chartered Accountant; Jo Nell Harlow [1962] Director [American]; Elie Wajih Maalouf [1964] Director [American]; Malina Ngai Man Lin [1969] Director [Chinese]; Christopher Luke Mayhew [1953] Director; Gillian Clare McDonald [1964] Director; Dale Frederick Morrison [1949] Director [American]

Intercontinental Hotels Group Services Company
Incorporated: 3 December 1956 *Employees:* 568
Net Worth: £99,131,000 *Total Assets:* £127,499,000
Registered Office: Broadwater Park, Denham, Bucks, UB9 5HR
Activities: Other service activities n.e.c.
Parent: IHG Hotels Limited
Officers: Fiona Cuttell, Secretary; Michael Jon Cockcroft [1974] Director; Michael Todd Glover [1971] Director/Financial Controller [American]; Nicolette Henfrey [1969] Director

Intercontinental Hotels Limited
Incorporated: 2 October 2002
Net Worth: £820,241,984 *Total Assets:* £820,990,976
Registered Office: Broadwater Park, Denham, Bucks, UB9 5HR
Activities: Other business support service activities n.e.c.
Parent: Intercontinental Hotels Group PLC
Officers: Fiona Cuttell, Secretary; Paul Russell Edgecliffe-Johnson [1972] Director/Certified Chartered Accountant; Michael Todd Glover [1971] Director/Financial Controller [American]; Nicolette Henfrey [1969] Director; George Turner [1971] Director

Interdist Alliances Limited
Incorporated: 14 February 2008 *Employees:* 46
Net Worth: £1,838,960 *Total Assets:* £23,395,220
Registered Office: 2nd Floor, Nucleus House, 2 Lower Mortlake Road, Richmond, Surrey, TW9 2JA
Activities: Other information technology service activities
Shareholder: Susan Tierney
Officers: Antoine Kareh [1952] Director/Manager [Lebanese]

Interfleet Holdings Limited
Incorporated: 24 April 1995
Net Worth Deficit: £4,455,000 *Total Assets:* £11,890,000
Registered Office: Woodcote Grove, Ashley Road, Epsom, Surrey, KT18 5BW
Activities: Activities of head offices
Parent: SNC-Lavalin UK Holding Ltd
Officers: Louise Mary McAllister, Secretary; Elliot Michael Nobelen, Secretary; Richard Thomas Glandon George [1955] Director/MD

Interiors with Art Limited
Incorporated: 15 August 2002 *Employees:* 32
Net Worth: £5,376,193 *Total Assets:* £8,479,317
Registered Office: 505 Pinner Road, Harrow, Middlesex, HA2 6EH
Activities: Other business support service activities n.e.c.
Shareholders: Sanjay Dev Sharma; Shailja Vohora
Officers: Pius Chirayathu Thomas, Secretary; Sanjay Dev Sharma [1968] Director/Consultant [Indian]; Shailja Vohora [1963] Director

Interlink Direct Limited
Incorporated: 2 March 2000 *Employees:* 37
Net Worth: £6,153,980 *Total Assets:* £12,912,190
Registered Office: 402-404 Roding Lane South, Woodford Green, Essex, IG8 8EY
Activities: Agents involved in the sale of food, beverages and tobacco
Major Shareholder: Yin Ha Kwok
Officers: Fu Kit Kwok, Secretary; Fu Kit Kwok [1966] Director/Office Manager; Fu Leung Kwok [1967] Director/Operation Manager; Yin Ha Kwok [1957] Director

Intermay Management Ltd
Incorporated: 23 May 2002
Net Worth: £11,646,867 *Total Assets:* £12,002,911
Registered Office: First Floor, Woodgate Studios, 2-8 Games Road, Cockfosters, Barnet, Herts, EN4 9HN
Activities: Other professional, scientific and technical activities n.e.c.
Major Shareholder: Oksana Marchenko
Officers: Anzelika Pasenidou, Secretary; Andreas Sofocleous [1967] Director [Cypriot]

International Marine Transportation Limited
Incorporated: 3 April 1952 *Employees:* 11
Net Worth: £40,897,032 *Total Assets:* £57,075,828
Registered Office: Ermyn House, Ermyn Way, Leatherhead, Surrey, KT22 8UX
Activities: Sea and coastal freight water transport
Parent: Esso UK Limited
Officers: Fiona Harness, Secretary; Jonathan Maxwell Evans [1957] Director/Oil Company Executive; Andrew Mark Johnson [1976] Director/Oil Company Executive; Cory Emil Quarles [1975] Director/Oil Company Executive [American]

International Passenger Protection Limited
Incorporated: 3 May 1990 *Employees:* 15
Net Worth: £1,995,462 *Total Assets:* £15,271,911
Registered Office: IPP House, 22-26 Station Road, West Wickham, Kent, BR4 0PR
Activities: Non-life insurance
Major Shareholder: Brian James McLean
Officers: Brian McLean, Secretary; Brian McLean [1949] Director; Paul Brian James McLean [1969] Director

International Society for Krishna Consciousness Limited
Incorporated: 15 September 1969 *Employees:* 230
Net Worth: £38,726,092 *Total Assets:* £41,681,696
Registered Office: Oak House, 1 Watford Road, Radlett, Herts, WD7 8LA
Activities: Activities of religious organisations
Officers: Grace Olapoju, Secretary; Terry Michael Anderson [1959] Director/Priest; Anthony William Howchin [1956] Director/Priest Branch Manager; George Thomas McMullan [1963] Director/Voluntary Worker; Paul Patrick Murphy [1961] Director/Restaurateur [Irish]; Kamlesh Kumar Maheshwar Patel [1962] Director/Corporate Financial Advisor

International Transport Limited
Incorporated: 14 November 1991
Net Worth: £99,061,000 *Total Assets:* £519,320,000
Registered Office: Leslie Ford House, Tilbury, Essex, RM18 7EH
Activities: Activities of other holding companies n.e.c.
Parent: Forth Ports Limited
Officers: Pamela June Smyth, Secretary; Carole Jean Cran [1970] Director/Chief Financial Officer; Charles Graham Hammond [1961] Director/Solicitor

Interport Limited
Incorporated: 26 March 1981 *Employees:* 31
Net Worth: £7,303,536 *Total Assets:* £10,890,231
Registered Office: Brandon House, Marlowe Way, Croydon, Surrey, CR0 4XS
Activities: Wholesale of pharmaceutical goods
Major Shareholder: Harshadrai Ishwarbhai Ashabhai Patel
Officers: Snehlata Satish Patel, Secretary; Harshadrai Ishwarbhai Ashabhai Patel [1944] Director/Chemist; Dr Natasha Harshad Patel [1974] Director/Doctor/Consultant

Intralot Finance UK Limited
Incorporated: 11 December 2007 *Employees:* 2
Previous: Intralot Finance UK PLC
Net Worth Deficit: £4,683,278 *Total Assets:* £618,260,544
Registered Office: 1st Floor, Sheraton House, Lower Road, Chorleywood, Rickmansworth, Herts, WD3 5LH
Activities: Other business support service activities n.e.c.
Parent: Intralot SA Integrated Lottery Systems and Services
Officers: Antonios Kerastaris [1969] Director/Chief Financial Officer [Greek]; Evangelos Raptis [1969] Director/Treasurer [Greek]; Vasileios Vasdaris [1957] Director/Economist [Greek]

Intuitive Holding Limited
Incorporated: 14 November 2012
Net Worth Deficit: £4,465,909 *Total Assets:* £7,784,765
Registered Office: Davis House, Robert Street, Croydon, Surrey, CR0 1QQ
Activities: Business and domestic software development
Officers: Andrew Keeley [1979] Director; Timothy Roland Levett [1949] Director; Paul Stuart Nixon [1970] Director

Intuitive Limited
Incorporated: 12 August 2003 *Employees:* 41
Net Worth: £6,217,096 *Total Assets:* £6,957,338
Registered Office: 7th Floor, Davis House, Robert Street, Croydon, Surrey, CR0 1QE
Activities: Business and domestic software development
Officers: Neil Alexander Gibson [1977] Director/Chartered Accountant; Andrew Keeley [1979] Director; Paul Stuart Nixon [1970] Director; Alan Frederick Stevens [1976] Director/Operations Manager

Investland Limited
Incorporated: 27 June 2008 *Employees:* 8
Net Worth: £100,260 *Total Assets:* £8,706,044
Registered Office: 42 Lytton Road, Barnet, Herts, EN5 5BY
Activities: Other business support service activities n.e.c.
Shareholders: Sassoon Raymond; Suraia Gorjian; Michael Gerrard; Joseph Peter Gerrard
Officers: Joseph Peter Gerrard [1954] Director/Accountant; Michael Gerrard [1957] Director/Textile Merchant

Investors in Ideas Ltd
Incorporated: 20 July 2010
Net Worth: £7,070,337 *Total Assets:* £18,840,764
Registered Office: 1000 The Mille, Great West Road, Brentford, Middlesex, TW8 9DW
Activities: Management consultancy activities other than financial management
Major Shareholder: Alan John Balmer
Officers: Alan John Balmer [1963] Director

The Invicta Film Partnership No. 17, LLP
Incorporated: 1 September 2003
Net Worth: £15,699,488 *Total Assets:* £17,576,724
Registered Office: 99 Kenton Road, Harrow, Middlesex, HA3 0AN
Officers: Paul Anderson [1956] LLP Member; Caroline Susan Bailey [1961] LLP Member; James Edward Baird [1952] LLP Member; John Beare [1953] LLP Member; Mary Catherine Best [1960] LLP Member; Nicholas Charles Birch [1959] LLP Member; Alan James Brydon [1954] LLP Member; James Robert Burgess [1956] LLP Member; Stephen James Burnhope [1956] LLP Member; David John Cameron [1942] LLP Member; Dr Joseph Chandy [1941] LLP Member; Lee Robert Clark [1972] LLP Member; Dr Mark Nathaniel Collins [1952] LLP Member; John Robert Davy [1955] LLP Member; Andrew David Dick [1965] LLP Member; Alexander Charles Duncan [1960] LLP Member; Ralph Godley [1949] LLP Member; Robert David Goffman [1960] LLP Member; Bryan Neil Grainger [1951] LLP Member; Doctor Philip Gerard Guest [1957] LLP Member; Philippa Ryan Hamilton James [1968] LLP Member; Charles Dominic Hazlehurst [1966] LLP Member; Iain Catleugh Hutchinson [1965] LLP Member; Renaud Hugues Edmond Isman [1963] LLP Member; Victoria Reynolds Jenkinson [1962] LLP Member; Seth Art Maurice Johnson [1979] LLP Member; Maria Zofia Kempinska-Davy [1953] LLP Member; Ian David Kennedy [1947] LLP Member; Nicholas John Kirk [1943] LLP Member; Leighton Richard Lloyd [1963] LLP Member; Dr Craig Howard Macmillan [1958] LLP Member; Gaetano William Mammana [1962] LLP Member; Roger Frank Millett [1952] LLP Member; Malcolm Bruce Oastler [1959] LLP Member; Ranjan Madhukar Patwardhan [1959] LLP Member; Dominic Paul Price [1967] LLP Member; Michael David Pryke Smith [1967] LLP Member; Mudalagiri Dasappa Ramakrishna Gupta [1945] LLP Member; David Ernest Henry Robson [1940] LLP Member; Shaun William Sargent [1967] LLP Member; Guduthur Raghavendra Setty [1942] LLP Member; Rajiv Sharma [1970] LLP Member; Adrian Vaughan Shipman Sharpe [1948] LLP Member; Ronald William Southern [1956] LLP Member; Alan Stubbs [1971] LLP Member; Geoffrey Peter Taylor [1956] LLP Member; Manoj Vadhera [1970] LLP Member; Maria Genevieve Vardy [1967] LLP Member; Richard John Ward [1959] LLP Member; Alexandra Patricia Wilson [1955] LLP Member; Stephen John Yarwood [1961] LLP Member

The Invicta Film Partnership No.10, LLP
Incorporated: 20 May 2002
Net Worth: £42,361,056 *Total Assets:* £46,335,496
Registered Office: 99 Kenton Road, Harrow, Middlesex, HA3 0AN
Officers: Adam Paul Apter [1962] LLP Member; Colin Ian McMillan Armstrong Bell [1969] LLP Member; Nicholas Anthony Athanasou [1953] LLP Member; James Edward Baird [1952] LLP Member; John Beare [1953] LLP Member; Primo Bertorelli [1953] LLP Member; Winston Bogarde [1970] LLP Member; Andrew Giles Finlinson Brash [1956] LLP Member; David Richard Brooke [1958] LLP Member; Alan Neil Brown [1957] LLP Member; Alan James Brydon [1954] LLP Member; James Robert Burgess [1956] LLP Member; Stuart Alan Charles Cakebread [1954] LLP Member; Nigel Alexander Carter [1968] LLP Member; Susanne Carter [1966] LLP Member; James Patrick Casiddy [1966] LLP Member; Celine Ann Cassidy [1966] LLP Member; Dr Joseph Chandy [1941] LLP Member; Dr Mark Nathaniel Collins [1952] LLP Member; David Ashley Cook [1944] LLP Member; David Craggs [1955] LLP Member; Jonathan Charles Creagh Coen [1964] LLP Member; Simon Csoka [1968] LLP Member; Adrienne Lesley de Vos [1962] LLP Member; Nicholas Thomas de Winton [1960] LLP Member; Laurent Delorge [1979] LLP Member; Damien Devine [1960] LLP Member; Thomas Dicker [1953] LLP Member; Anthony Charles Stephen Druttman [1951] LLP Member; Alexander Charles Duncan [1960] LLP Member; Peter David Ebdon [1970] LLP Member; Robert Willoughby Elias [1955] LLP Member; Christopher Evangeli [1967] LLP Member; Nicholas Evangeli [1939] LLP Member; Roderick Clifford Evans [1964] LLP Member; Frank Geoffrey Fielding [1947] LLP Member; Michael Lawrence Filer [1960] LLP Member; Malcolm Foulis [1953] LLP Member; Helen Mary Fryer [1963] LLP Member; Roy Anthony Gabbie [1953] LLP Member; David Gibbs [1969] LLP Member; Charles Richard Gray [1955] LLP Member; Matthew Robert Green [1967] LLP Member; Nicholas David Anthony Greenstone [1944] LLP Member; William Robert Griffiths [1948] LLP Member; Alain Leopold Grisay [1954] LLP Member; Doctor Philip Gerard Guest [1957] LLP Member; John Norman Harris [1957] LLP Member; Pamela Mary Harris [1958] LLP Member; Peter Hennell [1947] LLP Member; Gerrard Leslie Henry [1953] LLP Member; Robin Jeremy Charles Higham [1956] LLP Member; Michael Hilton [1970] LLP Member; Stephen Benjamin Howard [1970] LLP Member; Christopher Martin Huggett [1964] LLP Member; Michael Makepeace Eugene Jeffries [1944] LLP Member; Victoria Reynolds Jenkinson [1962] LLP Member; Mohammed Hassan Jiva [1974] LLP Member; Seth Art Maurice Johnson [1979] LLP Member; Geoffrey Arthur Jordan [1946] LLP Member; Georgina Susanne Keene [1971] LLP Member; Gabriel Choon Moi Kow [1948] LLP Member; Karl Nicholas Langhorne [1969] LLP Member; Nadir Sikander Latif [1962] LLP Member; Geoffrey Richard Long [1960] LLP Member; David Charles Longley [1945] LLP Member; Kieran Looney [1967] LLP Member; Timothy Geoffrey Fraser Lord [1953] LLP Member; John Dyer Lumley [1960] LLP Member; Andrew John Magson [1960] LLP Member; Elaine Ann Magson [1955] LLP Member; Sanjiv Mahal [1961] LLP Member; James Bruce McKendrick [1962] LLP Member; James Measures [1931] LLP Member; David Miles Middleton [1935] LLP Member; John Morrison Robert Millar [1962] LLP Member; David Christopher Morris [1925] LLP Member; Ramakrishna Mudadagiri [1945] LLP Member; Alan Stewart Nedas [1938] LLP Member; Patrick Gerard Newton [1957] LLP Member; Nicholas Nicholson [1968] LLP Member; Matthew John Northover [1971] LLP Member; Gerard Anthony O'Brien [1957] LLP Member; Malcolm Bruce Oastler [1959] LLP Member; Edward Martin Burgess Olley [1967] LLP Member; Petra Katherine Osborne Fardon [1969] LLP Member; Rajesh Parkash [1970] LLP Member; Martin George Parker [1952] LLP Member; Prashant Babubhai Patel [1956] LLP Member; Leslie James Patient [1958] LLP Member; Humphrey Richard Percy [1956] LLP Member; David Rhodes [1959] LLP Member; Jonathan Rhodes [1966] LLP Member; David Ernest Henry Robson [1940] LLP Member; Amanda Ross [1962] LLP Member; Simon John Ross [1958] LLP Member; Josephine June Rowley [1938] LLP Member; Kenneth John Rowley [1950] LLP Member

The Invicta Film Partnership No.11, LLP
Incorporated: 28 May 2002
Net Worth: £11,357,982 *Total Assets:* £11,357,982
Registered Office: 99 Kenton Road, Harrow, Middlesex, HA3 0AN
Officers: Trevor Steven Allan [1965] LLP Member; Francoise Ellen Atherton [1947] LLP Member; Dr Peter Granville Atherton [1944] LLP Member; Neville James Buckley [1958] LLP Member; Stephen Leonard Conn [1946] LLP Member; Thomas Dicker [1953] LLP Member; Roger Michael Gabb [1938] LLP Member; David Hall [1951] LLP Member; Julian Alexander Robert Jakobi [1951] LLP Member; Victoria Reynolds Jenkinson [1962] LLP Member; Andrew James McIntyre [1956] LLP Member; Jeremy Nicholas Roff [1959] LLP Member; Joanna Trollope [1943] LLP Member; Giammarco Vela [1968] LLP Member

The Invicta Film Partnership No.12, LLP
Incorporated: 1 August 2002
Net Worth: £8,706,501 *Total Assets:* £9,506,957
Registered Office: 99 Kenton Road, Harrow, Middlesex, HA3 0AN
Officers: Maria Theresa Barlow [1953] LLP Member; Peter George Barlow [1953] LLP Member; Primo Bertorelli [1953] LLP Member; Anthony Mark Biggs [1957] LLP Member; Mark Dominic Dempsey [1963] LLP Member; Marc Joel Duschenes [1975] LLP Member; Alfred Michael Dwan [1959] LLP Member; Christopher Evangeli [1967] LLP Member; Nicholas Evangeli [1939] LLP Member; Sheldon Barry Neil Fagelman [1961] LLP Member; Frank Geoffrey Fielding [1947] LLP Member; Richard Ian Griffiths [1966] LLP Member; Christopher Hancock [1965] LLP Member; David Jonathan Healy [1979] LLP Member; Robin Jeremy Charles Higham [1956] LLP Member; Michael Hilton [1970] LLP Member; Iain Catleugh Hutchinson [1965] LLP Member; Geoffrey Arthur Jordan [1946] LLP Member; Daniel Kerven [1975] LLP Member; Geoffrey Richard Long [1960] LLP Member; John Dyer Lumley [1960] LLP Member; James Bruce McKendrick [1962] LLP Member; Alister Hugh Mellor [1962] LLP Member; Ian George Nicoll [1947] LLP Member; Matthew John Northover [1963] LLP Member; Leslie James Patient [1958] LLP Member; Richard Sheridan [1956] LLP Member; Lee Martin Stenson [1954] LLP Member; Alan Stubbs [1971] LLP Member; Manoj Vadhera [1970] LLP Member; Mark Andrew Woods [1964] LLP Member; Andrew Hylton Young [1962] LLP Member; Dr Antonios Camille Zamar [1965] LLP Member

The Invicta Film Partnership No.13, LLP
Incorporated: 1 August 2002
Net Worth: £21,920,020 *Total Assets:* £24,578,374
Registered Office: 99 Kenton Road, Harrow, Middlesex, HA3 0AN
Officers: Rajesh Kumar Bhardwaj [1969] LLP Member; Ian George Bradley [1959] LLP Member; Valerie Josephine Bradley [1943] LLP Member; Michael Dudley Moran Davies [1957] LLP Member; Anthony Arthur Dove [1946] LLP Member; Rupert Alexander Lendon English [1966] LLP Member; Raymond Charles Eyre [1955] LLP Member; Andrew Jason Fearon [1969] LLP Member; Susan Garrard [1957] LLP Member; Stephen Gutteridge [1954] LLP Member; Andrew Charles Hodson [1966] LLP Member; Ashley John King [1967] LLP Member; John Henry King [1945] LLP Member; Philip Alexander Mastriforte [1965] LLP Member; Paris Moayedi [1938] LLP Member; Mark Stephen Edward Ryan [1965] LLP Member; Steven Paul Sharp [1962] LLP Member; Hugh Ian Taylor [1945] LLP Member; Anthony Oliver Thorold [1945] LLP Member; Paul Augustus Warren [1968] LLP Member; Hugh Mark Warrender [1968] LLP Member; Andrew James Willoughby [1965] LLP Member; Christopher David Winfield [1964] LLP Member; Shaun Michael Wyles [1965] LLP Member

The Invicta Film Partnership No.14, LLP
Incorporated: 1 August 2002
Net Worth: £46,022,276 *Total Assets:* £46,030,152
Registered Office: 99 Kenton Road, Harrow, Middlesex, HA3 0AN
Officers: Sami Al Sayed [1956] LLP Member; Adam Paul Apter [1962] LLP Member; David Banks [1969] LLP Member; Maria Theresa Barlow [1953] LLP Member; David Robert Beaton [1968] LLP Member; Primo Bertolli [1953] LLP Member; Mary Catherine Best [1960] LLP Member; Stephen Best [1957] LLP Member; Anthony Mark Biggs [1957] LLP Member; David Bonner [1959] LLP Member; Olivier Brousse [1965] LLP Member; Peter Alfred Brown [1952] LLP Member; Robert Mark Hartley Camping [1968] LLP Member; Anthony Edwin Carlisle [1947] LLP Member; Joseph Wayne Case [1944] LLP Member; Ailene Margaret Charlton [1962] LLP Member; James Edward Chilcott [1971] LLP Member; Lee Robert Clark [1972] LLP Member; James Coldwell [1964] LLP Member; Terence Shelby Cole [1932] LLP Member; David Paul Couch [1966] LLP Member; Robert James Curson [1951] LLP Member; Nikos Dabizas [1973] LLP Member; Oliver Dacourt [1974] LLP Member; Alok Dhanda [1962] LLP Member; Ivan Richard Dunn [1945] LLP Member; Marcelino Elena Sierra [1971] LLP Member; Nicholas Paul Farrell [1966] LLP Member; Lord Gary Blair Farrow [1955] LLP Member; Andrew Charles Fisher [1961] LLP Member; Christopher David Fishwick [1961] LLP Member; Gordon William Galloway French [1955] LLP Member; Bhupendra Gandhi [1964] LLP Member; Howard Leslie Gant [1961] LLP Member; Keith Howard Garber [1962] LLP Member; Susan Barbara Garrad [1957] LLP Member; Ian William Gibson [1957] LLP Member; Martin James Gilbert [1955] LLP Member; Peter Frank Gosling [1951] LLP Member; Alan Gray [1958] LLP Member; Alain Leopold Grisay [1954] LLP Member; Andrew Marshall Halmer [1958] LLP Member; Anders Hansen [1970] LLP Member; Christopher Richard Scott Hardie [1957] LLP Member; Keith Reginald Harris [1953] LLP Member; Geoffrey Demaine Hill [1947] LLP Member; John Robert Hutt [1967] LLP Member; Wendy Johnston [1962] LLP Member; Paul John Kavanagh [1969] LLP Member; Michael Kelly [1961] LLP Member; Paul Geoffrey Killik [1947] LLP Member; Timothy Anthony Kilroe [1964] LLP Member; George Brian Kirk [1940] LLP Member; Christopher Peter Lane [1948] LLP Member; Henry Norman Lewis [1939] LLP Member; Joan Alison Linney [1955] LLP Member; John Linney [1957] LLP Member; Robert Ross Linney [1971] LLP Member; Gary Lloyd [1961] LLP Member; Andrew Douglas Lloyd-Skinner [1954] LLP Member; Paul Mason [1960] LLP Member; Angus McLanders [1964] LLP Member; Glenn George McCrory [1964] LLP Member; Catherine Lynda McLanders [1963] LLP Member; Stanley Leslie Miller [1961] LLP Member; William Robert Moody [1956] LLP Member; Kenneth John Morris [1961] LLP Member; Michael David Moss [1950] LLP Member; David Charles Moulsdale [1968] LLP Member; Elizabeth Patricia Norton [1954] LLP Member; Grant Notman [1959] LLP Member; Gordon Edward Orr [1949] LLP Member; Martin Orr [1964] LLP Member; Matthew Nicholson Orr [1962] LLP Member; David Hase Osborne [1957] LLP Member; John Michael Osborne [1953] LLP Member; Jonathan William Frederic Peart [1965] LLP Member; Julian Henry Ponsonby [1963] LLP Member; Mark Price [1971] LLP Member; Steven Patrick Ronksley [1958] LLP Member; Mrs Jm Ruddle 1997 Discretionary Settlement [2003] LLP Member; Jonathan Andrew Sadler [1965] LLP Member; James Denis Saunders [1960] LLP Member; David Lee Scorah [1951] LLP Member; Peter Glenn Sellars [1952] LLP Member; Ann Elizabeth Shankland [1950] LLP Member; Adrian Vaughan Shipman Sharpe [1948] LLP Member; Anthony Slimmings [1963] LLP Member; Ronald William Southern [1956] LLP Member; Mark Neil Steinberg [1959] LLP Member; Robert Michael Storey [1960] LLP Member; James Sweeney [1960] LLP Member; Alan Malcolm Thompson [1951] LLP Member; David Hugh Thompson [1950] LLP Member; Martin John Edward Tidd [1960] LLP Member; Stephen William Vaughan [1960] LLP Member; Dr Graham John Walker [1962] LLP Member

The Invicta Film Partnership No.15, LLP
Incorporated: 1 August 2002
Net Worth: £20,950,716 *Total Assets:* £20,950,716
Registered Office: 99 Kenton Road, Harrow, Middlesex, HA3 0AN
Officers: Edward Oscar Belgeonne [1962] LLP Member; Philip Charles Easter [1953] LLP Member; Raymond Charles Eyre [1955] LLP Member; Robert Blackburn Gray [1950] LLP Member; William Robert Griffiths [1948] LLP Member; Dr Eric Yves Leon [1947] LLP Member; Philip Alexander Mastriforte [1965] LLP Member; Humphrey Richard Percy [1956] LLP Member; Roderick John Sinclair [1944] LLP Member; Andrew Nicholas Sutton [1954] LLP Member; Hugh Ian Taylor [1945] LLP Member; Constantine Thanassoulas [1952] LLP Member

The Invicta Film Partnership No.20, LLP
Incorporated: 15 March 2004
Net Worth: £61,241,400 *Total Assets:* £65,264,124
Registered Office: 99 Kenton Road, Harrow, Middlesex, HA3 0AN
Officers: Mark Stephen Adams [1962] LLP Member; Charmian Ali [1954] LLP Member; Stephen Charles Ashworth [1967] LLP Member; Nicholas Anthony Athanasou [1953] LLP Member; Christopher Francis Henry Baker [1955] LLP Member; Nigel Robert James Baker [1942] LLP Member; Richard John Beale [1959] LLP Member; Sanjeev Lalji Bhanderi [1971] LLP Member; Jonathan David Bowes [1966] LLP Member; Edward Leonard Bradley [1957] LLP Member; Peter Lincoln Breitenbach [1954] LLP Member; Duncan Broadbent [1963] LLP Member; Ian Blaine Brook [1949] LLP Member; Richard James Emmett Bryan [1970] LLP Member; Richard James Butland [1971] LLP Member; James Aldo Campanini [1968] LLP Member; Clive Stephen Carpenter [1953] LLP Member; Clive Anderson Carr [1954] LLP Member; Barry Gareth Cashman [1966] LLP Member; Michael Chesterton [1970] LLP Member; Richard Childs [1959] LLP Member; Mark Gerard Clough [1953] LLP Member; Christopher Cole [1968] LLP Member; Stephen Leonard Conn [1946] LLP Member; Peter David Cook [1964] LLP Member; David John Courtley [1957] LLP Member; Ian Curtis [1968] LLP Member; Martin Sinclair Davies [1956] LLP Member; Peter John Day [1966] LLP Member; Paul di Leo [1962] LLP Member; Gary Anthony Dugan [1961] LLP Member; Peter David Ebdon [1970] LLP Member; Neal Errington [1956] LLP Member; Christopher Evangeli [1967] LLP Member; Jonathan Howard Fine [1974] LLP Member; David Martin Fletcher [1963] LLP Member; John Foster [1970] LLP Member; Mark Haakon Gaunt [1961] LLP Member; Andrew Gavan [1960] LLP Member; Charles Philip Gaynor [1961] LLP Member; Brian Grant [1947] LLP Member; Dr Philip Raymond Greene [1948] LLP Member; Bruce John Hanton [1962] LLP Member; Andrew John Harrison [1970] LLP Member; Mark Charles Haswell [1965] LLP Member; Mark Hollister [1962] LLP Member; Ian Horsley [1974] LLP Member; Susan Deborah Howard [1964] LLP Member; Christopher Martin Huggett [1964] LLP Member; Gary Hulme [1975] LLP Member; John Denby Robert Jakeways [1962] LLP Member; Roisin Helen Anne Jordan [1962] LLP Member; Simon William Judd [1964] LLP Member; Harold Kahan [1945] LLP Member; Leo Kane [1950] LLP Member; Peter Kane [1961] LLP Member; Jonathan David Keating [1963] LLP Member; Anil Kumar Khiani [1972] LLP Member; Cyrus Mohan Korat [1972] LLP Member; Graham Richard David Lay [1956] LLP Member; Matthew Robert Layton [1961] LLP Member; Elizabeth Anne Linton [1949] LLP Member; Gary Lloyd [1961] LLP Member; Phillip Stephen Loach [1967] LLP Member; Martin John Lockyer [1967] LLP Member; Jamieson John Logie [1961] LLP Member; Mark Adrian Lubbock [1958] LLP Member; Angus John Elsom MacCormick [1965] LLP Member; Avril Catherine Burns Martindale [1961] LLP Member; Richard Andrew Matthews [1966] LLP Member; Donald Stuart McClumpha [1964] LLP Member; Adrian McDonald [1964] LLP Member; Thomas Wardrope McEwan [1958] LLP Member; Frank McHugh [1958] LLP Member; Brian Patrick Meehan [1967] LLP Member; Symon David Meikle [1972] LLP Member; David John Moore [1958] LLP Member; Dr Timothy Marcus Mulchay [1969] LLP Member; Paul Alexander Murdoch [1947] LLP Member; Guy Timothy Napier [1961] LLP Member; Mark Robert Newall [1966] LLP Member; Mark Brian Nichols [1963] LLP Member; Kathryn Trudy Norris-Grey [1960] LLP Member; Patricia Helen Nuttall [1944] LLP Member; Catherine Lena Peterson [1963] LLP Member; Richard William Philips [1966] LLP Member; Russell James Platts [1975] LLP Member; Adnrew David Raikes [1972] LLP Member; Gavin Robert Duthie Ralston [1960] LLP Member; Howard Reece-Smith [1951] LLP Member; Ron Victor Reeves [1952] LLP Member; Jonathan Richard Reynolds [1954] LLP Member; Ian David Richards [1945] LLP Member; Stephen Mark Rodney [1965] LLP Member; Kenneth James Gordon Harvey Ross [1971] LLP Member; Jeffrey Arron Rubinoff [1965] LLP Member; Simeon Spencer Perrott Rudin [1961] LLP Member

The Invicta Film Partnership No.22, LLP
Incorporated: 15 March 2004
Net Worth: £39,226,080 *Total Assets:* £42,851,436
Registered Office: 99 Kenton Road, Harrow, Middlesex, HA3 0AN
Officers: Steven Kenneth Allport [1971] LLP Member; Dirk Posthumus Anthony [1963] LLP Member; Christopher Francis Henry Baker [1955] LLP Member; Patrick George Barker [1947] LLP Member; Michael Andrew Bradley [1961] LLP Member; Jennifer Bryant [1957] LLP Member; Clive Stephen Carpenter [1953] LLP Member; Nicholas John Chaffey [1969] LLP Member; Simon Charles [1970] LLP Member; Robin Raj Chhabra Chhabra [1970] LLP Member; Richard Childs [1959] LLP Member; Steven Lindsay Cloran [1964] LLP Member; Estelle Conron [1970] LLP Member; David John Courtley [1957] LLP Member; Timothy Eric Cox [1960] LLP Member; James Henry Davey [1962] LLP Member; Giles Roderick Dealtry [1963] LLP Member; Nicholas Dennys [1951] LLP Member; Richard Andrew Fellows [1960] LLP Member; Paul Gregory Franklin [1956] LLP Member; John Gardner [1959] LLP Member; Andrew Gavan [1960] LLP Member; Ian Charles Gibson [1958] LLP Member; John Anthony Goodey [1972] LLP Member; Nicholas Edward Greenwood [1970] LLP Member; Neil Hugh Thomas Hart [1972] LLP Member; Peter Charles Hill [1952] LLP Member; Andrew James Hough [1972] LLP Member; Susan Deborah Howard [1964] LLP Member; Steven Hull [1963] LLP Member; James Anthony Hyde [1962] LLP Member; Nicholas St John Isitt [1964] LLP Member; John Denby Robert Jakeways [1962] LLP Member; Christopher Basil Johnson [1967] LLP Member; Robert Francis Raymond Jolliffe [1968] LLP Member; Gareth Neil Jones [1958] LLP Member; Mark Royce Jones [1969] LLP Member; Peter Francis Kenyon [1953] LLP Member; John Jeremy King [1962] LLP Member; Nicholas John Kirk [1943] LLP Member; John Jekabs Krumins [1964] LLP Member; Richard Guy Rafe Lister [1966] LLP Member; Richard Brian Lowe [1954] LLP Member; Stephen Paul Lundy [1956] LLP Member; Marcus Charles MacKenzie [1965] LLP Member; Christopher Peter Milligan [1970] LLP Member; David Allan Murray [1964] LLP Member; David Anthony Nickson [1971] LLP Member; Paul Robert Norris [1963] LLP Member; Dominic Kevin O'Carroll [1960] LLP Member; Timothy Simon Oldfield [1964] LLP Member; Kevin Bryan Orgill [1962] LLP Member; David Hase Osborne [1957] LLP Member; Sir Michael Parkinson [1935] LLP Member; Gary Senior [1962] LLP Member; Bernard Francis Seymour [1960] LLP Member; David Charles Simpson [1960] LLP Member; David Stanley Spillane [1950] LLP Member; Alasdair Bruce Stewart [1954] LLP Member; Kenneth Paul Tollet [1954] LLP Member; Paul Frederick Tutin [1962] LLP Member; Garry Tibbott Veale [1960] LLP Member; Simon Walker [1964] LLP Member; Richard John Ward [1959] LLP Member; Trevor Ward [1961] LLP Member; Guy Rodney Warrington [1957] LLP Member; Christopher Ian Watson [1957] LLP Member; Andrew Roger Wedderburn-Day [1962] LLP Member; Ross Kirkwood Williams [1974] LLP Member

The Invicta Film Partnership No.23, LLP
Incorporated: 15 March 2004
Net Worth: £89,952,400 *Total Assets:* £99,070,112
Registered Office: 99 Kenton Road, Harrow, Middlesex, HA3 0AN
Officers: Masood Ahmad [1942] LLP Member; Nuzhat Ahmad [1945] LLP Member; Jahangeer Ahmed [1956] LLP Member; Dr Peter Russell Allamby [1958] LLP Member; Claude Edward Ashmore [1974] LLP Member; Joseph Colin Aspinall [1960] LLP Member; Steven Mark Avery Gee [1953] LLP Member; Ruth Bailey [1961] LLP Member; Christopher Bailey-Woods [1971] LLP Member; Niall Richard Bamford [1966] LLP Member; Dr Khalid Barakat [1966] LLP Member; Gary James Barber [1960] LLP Member; Philip John Barnatt [1949] LLP Member; Michael Forsyth Barnett [1970] LLP Member; Peter John Beddis [1952] LLP Member; David Frank Bell [1962] LLP Member; Michael George Bell [1967] LLP Member; Marcus Peter Bemrose [1956] LLP Member; Duncan Howard Blatch [1963] LLP Member; John Alan Booth [1970] LLP Member; Richard James Bowskill [1964] LLP Member; Michael Andrew Bradley [1961] LLP Member; William Angus Bridger [1968] LLP Member; Simon Anthony Briggs [1962] LLP Member; Andrew Christopher Briscoe [1971] LLP Member; Paul Antony Broadhurst [1960] LLP Member; Garry Burden [1958] LLP Member; Alastair Butler [1973] LLP Member; Robert Paul Camping [1973] LLP Member; David Nigel Caplan [1954] LLP Member; Christopher John Chandler [1958] LLP Member; Satnam Singh Chase [1966] LLP Member; Pratim Kumar Chaudhury [1948] LLP Member; Sushma Chopra [1957] LLP Member; Peter Charlton Christie [1951] LLP Member; Patrick Alan Clarke [1965] LLP Member; Carlyle Cyril Clump [1953] LLP Member; Harvey Stewart Cohen [1965] LLP Member; James Winston Collings [1965] LLP Member; Kevin Cooke [1961] LLP Member; John Benedict Leodoghar Cooper [1955] LLP Member; Dr David Richard Cox [1957] LLP Member; Philip John Craven [1958] LLP Member; Cheryl Ann Cribbin [1966] LLP Member; Nicholas Cusworth [1964] LLP Member; Rodney Graeme Dacomb [1955] LLP Member; Miles John Davidson [1963] LLP Member; Ian Charles Davies [1952] LLP Member; Aidan Christopher Goddard Day [1962] LLP Member; Gareth Wyn Derbyshire [1962] LLP Member; Hugh Philip Egerton Dumas [1942] LLP Member; Stuart William Duncan [1948] LLP Member; Steven Peter Eccleston [1964] LLP Member; Richard Jeffrey Ellingworth [1968] LLP Member; Paul Jeremy Epstein [1963] LLP Member; James William Farrand [1947] LLP Member; Oliver Paul Farrer [1963] LLP Member; Gary Michael Finn [1957] LLP Member; Kaye Forsythe [1961] LLP Member; Fiona Claire Foster [1962] LLP Member; Andrew Foxley [1962] LLP Member; Justin Paul Martin Gale [1964] LLP Member; Grant Gardner [1960] LLP Member; Stephen Paul Gelder [1966] LLP Member; Christopher John Gerber [1959] LLP Member; Mark Govan [1972] LLP Member; Paul Richard Greaney [1970] LLP Member; Barry Ludlow Green [1943] LLP Member; Brian Rex Green [1934] LLP Member; Philip Stuart Hanna [1962] LLP Member; Elizabeth Kay Harriman [1956] LLP Member; Andrew John Harvey [1964] LLP Member; Mark Vernon Henderson [1969] LLP Member; Rebecca Jane Hewetson [1974] LLP Member; Paul Joseph Higgins [1955] LLP Member; James Andrew Paul Hines [1960] LLP Member; Kausar Hirani [1967] LLP Member; John Walter Holmes [1958] LLP Member; Nicholas St John Isitt [1964] LLP Member; Michael Makepeace Eugene Jeffries [1944] LLP Member; Thomas Arthur John Jenkins [1972] LLP Member; Eric William Jones [1952] LLP Member; Gareth Wyn Jones [1960] LLP Member; Bruce Douglas King [1955] LLP Member; Paul George Kirtley [1959] LLP Member; Doctor Ormala Krishnan [1969] LLP Member; Nicholas Ronald Lancaster [1948] LLP Member; Graeme Neil Langford [1961] LLP Member; Michael Angelo Le Houx [1959] LLP Member; Amanda Jane Lipman [1962] LLP Member; Matthew Louis Lorenzo [1958] LLP Member; Laurence Bruce Lovat [1962] LLP Member; Andrew Lumley [1953] LLP Member; Stephen Paul Lundy [1956] LLP Member; Denis James Anthony MacDaid [1944] LLP Member; Kirankumar Vardhaman Malde [1954] LLP Member; Rajesh Vardhaman Malde [1959] LLP Member; Sirishkumar Vardhaman Malde [1951] LLP Member

The Invicta Film Partnership No.25, LLP
Incorporated: 18 March 2004
Net Worth: £30,980,424 *Total Assets:* £33,805,844
Registered Office: 99 Kenton Road, Harrow, Middlesex, HA3 0AN
Officers: Georgina Jane Agnew [1949] LLP Member; Niall Richard Bamford [1966] LLP Member; Raymond James Batters [1950] LLP Member; Kirsty Bell [1966] LLP Member; Jonathan David Berger [1962] LLP Member; Mary Catherine Best [1960] LLP Member; Nicholas Charles Birch [1959] LLP Member; Stephen Boylan [1952] LLP Member; Anthony Omer Browne [1950] LLP Member; Robert James Buckland [1968] LLP Member; Dr Joseph Chandy [1941] LLP Member; Shahid Mahmood Choudry [1971] LLP Member; Salvatore Ciullo [1958] LLP Member; Lee Robert Clark [1972] LLP Member; David Paul Couch [1966] LLP Member; Simon Christopher Cowie [1969] LLP Member; Anthony Maurice Cross [1958] LLP Member; Tapan Kumar Datta [1958] LLP Member; Christopher Daw [1970] LLP Member; Alok Dhanda [1962] LLP Member; Dr Simon John Dolin [1952] LLP Member; Christopher William Duffy [1957] LLP Member; Peter David Ebdon [1970] LLP Member; John Brynmor Edwards [1957] LLP Member; Dr Antony Michael Esprey [1950] LLP Member; Christopher Evangel [1967] LLP Member; Nicholas Evangeli [1939] LLP Member; Ian Keith Fisher [1959] LLP Member; James Alistair Fok [1979] LLP Member; Doctor Anton Franckeiss [1956] LLP Member; Susan Garrard [1957] LLP Member; Ian Gray [1960] LLP Member; Nicholas John Hall [1960] LLP Member; Nicola Jane Harris [1969] LLP Member; Michael Heppell [1967] LLP Member; George Heydon [1961] LLP Member; Timothy Charles Hill [1963] LLP Member; Dr Wayne Kevin Hirschowitz [1965] LLP Member; David Edmund Hoggett [1962] LLP Member; Nicholas Hopkin [1955] LLP Member; Steven Hull [1963] LLP Member; Quentin John Hunt [1975] LLP Member; Dr Roy Richard Huson [1973] LLP Member; Keith Martin Jobson [1959] LLP Member; Robert Terence Johnson [1962] LLP Member; Simon Henry Kenner [1962] LLP Member; David Kerr [1963] LLP Member; Adrian Geoffrey Knight [1957] LLP Member; Lisa Gillian Claire Knight [1961] LLP Member; Gabriel Choon Moi Kow [1948] LLP Member; Nadir Sikander Latif [1962] LLP Member; Andrew John Leake [1957] LLP Member; Bruce Lightbody [1962] LLP Member; Robert John Llewellyn [1962] LLP Member; Simon Timothy Lofthouse [1966] LLP Member; Roy Maplesden [1960] LLP Member; Paul Robert Marshall [1954] LLP Member; Andrew Charles Arthur McBride [1960] LLP Member; Spiros Michael [1974] LLP Member; David Miles Middleton [1935] LLP Member; Peter Minshull Armstrong [1949] LLP Member; Andrew Robert Mitchell [1954] LLP Member; Edward David South Morse [1960] LLP Member; David Charles Moulsdale [1968] LLP Member; Philip O'Hagan [1961] LLP Member; Paul Theodore Orchart [1953] LLP Member; Dr Hemant Kumar Patel [1968] LLP Member; Jayantibhai Chimanbhai Patel [1945] LLP Member; Dr Katherine Mary Patel [1968] LLP Member; Kirit Chimanbhai Patel [1949] LLP Member; Jane Ann Peace [1961] LLP Member; Michael Robert Pedder [1949] LLP Member; Pieter Daniel Pienaar [1956] LLP Member; Michael David Prince [1947] LLP Member; Dorothy Rose Purdew [1932] LLP Member; Stephen James Purdew [1959] LLP Member; David Rhodes [1959] LLP Member; Jonathan Rhodes [1968] LLP Member; Eamonn Joseph Rice [1963] LLP Member; Nicholas John Robinson [1956] LLP Member; Christopher Gregory Rodgers [1957] LLP Member; Josephine June Rowley [1938] LLP Member; Kenneth John Rowley [1950] LLP Member; Dominic James Ryder [1968] LLP Member; John Ryder [1955] LLP Member; Martin Paul Sasada [1958] LLP Member; Guduthur Raghavendra Setty [1942] LLP Member; Richard Anthony Sharp [1966] LLP Member; Robert Douglas Shears [1953] LLP Member; Richard Graham Simons [1965] LLP Member; Ian Simpson [1970] LLP Member; Neil James Smith [1965] LLP Member; Jeremy Lewis Charles Spencer [1958] LLP Member; Paul David Robert Spraggs [1963] LLP Member; Graham Stedman [1956] LLP Member; Douglas Mark Stuart [1961] LLP Member; Stephen Lee Sweet [1951] LLP Member; Christine Ann Taylor [1960] LLP Member

The Invicta Film Partnership No.26, LLP
Incorporated: 18 March 2004
Net Worth: £22,715,108 *Total Assets:* £24,924,640
Registered Office: 99 Kenton Road, Harrow, Middlesex, HA3 0AN
Officers: Richard John Julian Addison [1961] LLP Member; Justin Martyn Anim [1968] LLP Member; Niall Richard Bamford [1966] LLP Member; Raymond James Batters [1950] LLP Member; Kirsty Bell [1966] LLP Member; Mark Andrew Binns [1961] LLP Member; Stephen Boylan [1952] LLP Member; William George Bush [1954] LLP Member; David Joseph Chadwick [1944] LLP Member; Gillian Jean Bird Cottam [1956] LLP Member; Gary Steven Cottle [1966] LLP Member; Shaun Christopher Craig Coulson [1963] LLP Member; Anthony Maurice Cross [1958] LLP Member; Alok Dhanda [1962] LLP Member; Paul William Henry Dixon [1943] LLP Member; Simon Timothy Dixon [1966] LLP Member; Dr Simon John Dolin [1952] LLP Member; Peter David Ebdon [1970] LLP Member; John Brynmor Edwards [1957] LLP Member; Dr Antony Michael Esprey [1950] LLP Member; Christopher Evangeli [1967] LLP Member; Nicholas Evangeli [1939] LLP Member; Rodley Evans [1953] LLP Member; Andrew Jason Fearon [1969] LLP Member; Anthony John Blakeley Fogg [1950] LLP Member; Doctor Anton Franckeiss [1956] LLP Member; Christopher Thomas Freeman [1961] LLP Member; Roy Anthony Gabbie [1953] LLP Member; Irena Greaves [1952] LLP Member; Nyasha Gwatidzo [1962] LLP Member; Nicholas John Hall [1960] LLP Member; Nicola Jane Harris [1969] LLP Member; Christopher Alan Harrison [1955] LLP Member; Michael Heppell [1967] LLP Member; Sally Ann Horrox [1967] LLP Member; Steven Hull [1963] LLP Member; Roy Richard Huson [1973] LLP Member; Prof Howard Saul Jacobs [1938] LLP Member; Keith Martin Jobson [1959] LLP Member; Roy Johnson [1952] LLP Member; Robert Frances Raymond Joliffe [1968] LLP Member; Matthew George Justice [1965] LLP Member; Sean Gary Kenwrick [1965] LLP Member; Adrian Geoffrey Knight [1957] LLP Member; Lisa Gillian Claire Knight [1961] LLP Member; William George Lane [1960] LLP Member; Robert John Llewellyn [1962] LLP Member; Leighton Richard Lloyd [1963] LLP Member; Rosalind Loveridge [1972] LLP Member; Spiros Michael [1974] LLP Member; Spiros Michael [1974] LLP Member; Ramakrishna Mudalagiri [1945] LLP Member; Ronald Edward Clayton Myland [1946] LLP Member; Paul NG [1967] LLP Member; Philip O'Hagan [1961] LLP Member; Jayantibhai Chimanbhai Patel [1945] LLP Member; Kirit Chimanbhai Patel [1949] LLP Member; John Richard Peace [1956] LLP Member; Michael Robert Pedder [1949] LLP Member; Michael David Prince [1947] LLP Member; Dorothy Rose Purdew [1932] LLP Member; Stephen James Purdew [1959] LLP Member; Peter Elisa Roos [1953] LLP Member; Magnus Scaddan [1972] LLP Member; Richard Graham Simons [1965] LLP Member; Dr Jacob Francois Smit [1962] LLP Member; Anthony Bernard Solomon [1956] LLP Member; Dr Paul John Rackham Soper [1943] LLP Member; Matteo Stefanel [1975] LLP Member; Dipak Maganlal Thakrar [1966] LLP Member; Rachana Thakrar [1965] LLP Member; Anthony Harold Todd [1947] LLP Member; Paul Harold MacKenzie Turner [1958] LLP Member; Gyles Turrell [1966] LLP Member; Paul Vallance [1946] LLP Member; Diane Walton [1952] LLP Member; Philip George Walton [1949] LLP Member; Peter Lawrence Warne [1968] LLP Member; Peter Gilhespy Willey [1951] LLP Member; Adrian Mark Williamson [1957] LLP Member; Nigel James Yates [1949] LLP Member

The Invicta Film Partnership No.27, LLP
Incorporated: 18 March 2004
Net Worth: £27,615,968 *Total Assets:* £29,141,476
Registered Office: 99 Kenton Road, Harrow, Middlesex, HA3 0AN
Officers: Yvonne Kathleen Agha [1968] LLP Member; David John Allonby [1978] LLP Member; Cecil Ashe [1944] LLP Member; John Adam Ball [1969] LLP Member; Anthony Paul Barnfather [1964] LLP Member; Robert Ashley Barrett [1962] LLP Member; Raymond James Batters [1950] LLP Member; Jonathan Paul Beacon [1946] LLP Member; Charles James Bennett [1962] LLP Member; Charles Jefferis Woodburn Benson [1962] LLP Member; Nicholas Blezard [1944] LLP Member; Stephen Boylan [1952] LLP Member; Ian Alan Bull [1961] LLP Member; Christopher Jordan Carlson [1978] LLP Member; Mr Robert Carlyle [1961] LLP Member; Dr Joseph Chandy [1941] LLP Member; Michael Chesterton [1970] LLP Member; Barry Alan Church [1947] LLP Member; William David Clouston [1946] LLP Member; Peter Cole [1967] LLP Member; Ian Curtis [1968] LLP Member; Nicholas Cusworth [1964] LLP Member; Colin Davies [1959] LLP Member; Simon Downing de Lacy Adams [1961] LLP Member; Alok Dhanda [1962] LLP Member; Dr Alan Joseph Dobkin [1943] LLP Member; Ellis George Downes [1965] LLP Member; Neal Errington [1956] LLP Member; Paul Francis Fraser [1960] LLP Member; Thomas George [1960] LLP Member; Arthur Edward Goddard [1948] LLP Member; David Joseph Goddard [1953] LLP Member; Gaias Gozem [1950] LLP Member; Nicholas Hopkin [1955] LLP Member; Ian Horsley [1974] LLP Member; Keith Jackson [1957] LLP Member; Christopher Basil Johnson [1967] LLP Member; Rachel Daisy Jones [1968] LLP Member; Roy Barry Jones [1962] LLP Member; Rosalind Elisabeth Kendall [1950] LLP Member; Michael Warwick Lawrence [1955] LLP Member; Michael Angelo Le Houx [1959] LLP Member; Michael Phillip David Lording [1958] LLP Member; Gregor Lachlan MacLean [1971] LLP Member; Andrew Charles Arthur McBride [1960] LLP Member; Kevin Connal McGeeney [1970] LLP Member; Jarlath James McHale [1958] LLP Member; Andrew Gwyn Menary [1959] LLP Member; Bryan Edward Mouat [1967] LLP Member; David Charles Moulsdale [1968] LLP Member; Susan Vanessa Noble [1970] LLP Member; Philip O'Hagan [1961] LLP Member; John Patrick O'Sullivan [1937] LLP Member; Giles Martin Oberheim [1970] LLP Member; Peter Anthony Parker [1959] LLP Member; Jayantibhai Chimanbhai Patel [1945] LLP Member; Kirit Chimanbhai Patel [1949] LLP Member; Angus Thien Siang Phang [1961] LLP Member; Dr Julian Mark Potter [1963] LLP Member; Michael David Prince [1947] LLP Member; Dorothy Rose Purdew [1932] LLP Member; Stephen James Purdew [1959] LLP Member; Dr Monica Reinach [1968] LLP Member; Diana Clare Robson [1954] LLP Member; Josephine June Rowley [1938] LLP Member; Kenneth John Rowley [1950] LLP Member; Ian Scarr-Hall [1938] LLP Member; Timothy James Scoble [1957] LLP Member; Mark Anthony Sensier [1966] LLP Member; Richard Anthony Sharp [1966] LLP Member; Robert Douglas Shears [1953] LLP Member; Richard Graham Simons [1965] LLP Member; Richard Charles Smith [1957] LLP Member; Robert Anthony Stiles [1976] LLP Member; Stuart Timmins [1958] LLP Member; Graham Stewart Alexander Walker [1971] LLP Member; Philip Alan Wander [1943] LLP Member; Dr Stuart Charles Webb [1950] LLP Member; Alistair Stevenson Webster [1953] LLP Member; Antony Paul Christopher Williams [1972] LLP Member; Robert Darren Withecombe [1965] LLP Member; Alastair David Wright [1967] LLP Member; Nigel James Yates [1949] LLP Member

The Invicta Film Partnership No.32, LLP
Incorporated: 17 January 2005
Net Worth: £6,544,322 *Total Assets:* £7,114,580
Registered Office: 99 Kenton Road, Harrow, Middlesex, HA3 0AN
Officers: Nigel Robert James Baker [1942] LLP Member; Robert Ashley Barrett [1962] LLP Member; Stephen Boylan [1952] LLP Member; Jonathan Maxfield Buchan [1969] LLP Member; Gillian Carrick [1943] LLP Member; Dr Noureen Chaudery [1960] LLP Member; Djibril Cisse [1981] LLP Member; Barry Cooper [1953] LLP Member; Simon Csoka [1968] LLP Member; Indriraben Arun Gohil [1950] LLP Member; Simon Vivian Goodman [1968] LLP Member; Dr Shiba Hameed [1956] LLP Member; Tariq Hameed [1953] LLP Member; Dr Sarjit Kumar Handa [1941] LLP Member; David John Moore [1958] LLP Member; Susan Vanessa Noble [1970] LLP Member; Philip O'Hagan [1961] LLP Member; Harshadrai Ishwarbhai Ashabhai Patel [1944] LLP Member; Jaimin Purushottam Patel [1961] LLP Member; Dr Dinesh Panachand Shah [1947] LLP Member; Dr Kalpesh Shah [1968] LLP Member; Kaushik Shah [1962] LLP Member; Smita Suresh Thanki [1961] LLP Member; Suresh Meghji Thanki [1957] LLP Member; Stuart Timmins [1958] LLP Member; Graham Stewart Alexander Walker [1947] LLP Member; Nigel James Yates [1949] LLP Member

The Invicta Film Partnership No.34, LLP
Incorporated: 4 April 2005
Net Worth: £11,915,357 *Total Assets:* £12,911,442
Registered Office: 99 Kenton Road, Harrow, Middlesex, HA3 0AN
Officers: Robert Fredrik Martin Adair [1956] LLP Member; Shiblee Alam [1971] LLP Member; Jean Felix Aniel Quiroga [1968] LLP Member; Charles Jefferis Woodburn Benson [1962] LLP Member; Jean Marc Blankert [1970] LLP Member; Philip Charles Barry Bruce [1949] LLP Member; Alastair Andrew Bertram Cade [1972] LLP Member; Gillian Carrick [1943] LLP Member; William David Clouston [1946] LLP Member; Carlyle Cyril Clump [1953] LLP Member; Roger William Cowell [1972] LLP Member; Steven John Cowling [1960] LLP Member; Alok Dhanda [1962] LLP Member; Robert Stephen Dodds [1952] LLP Member; Brendan Paul Farmer [1965] LLP Member; Robert Steven Fountain [1954] LLP Member; John Gordon [1952] LLP Member; Barry Ludlow Green [1943] LLP Member; Norma Frances Heyman [1937] LLP Member; David Edmund Hoggett [1962] LLP Member; Leonard Simon Horwich [1956] LLP Member; David William Jinks [1966] LLP Member; Andrew Ian Kennedy [1965] LLP Member; Michael Warwick Lawrence [1955] LLP Member; Leighton Richard Lloyd [1963] LLP Member; Esme Charles Harlowe Lowe [1962] LLP Member; David Rugbinder Singh Mattu [1958] LLP Member; Andrew Gwyn Menary [1959] LLP Member; Dr Ramakrishnagupta Dasappagupta Mudalagiri [1945] LLP Member; Susanne Vanessa Noble [1970] LLP Member; Sameer Satish Patel [1976] LLP Member; Dr Julian Mark Potter [1963] LLP Member; Mark Graham Pullen [1963] LLP Member; The Executors of The Estate of David Ernest Henry Robson [1940] LLP Member; Kenneth John Rowley [1950] LLP Member; Ravi Sher Singh [1969] LLP Member; Geoffrey Robert Spiller [1951] LLP Member; Paul David Robert Spraggs [1963] LLP Member; Nicholas John Symons [1969] LLP Member; Raymond Clive Tooth [1940] LLP Member; Karl Brian Vella [1959] LLP Member; Guy Michael Linsley Weaver [1961] LLP Member; James John Wheeler [1965] LLP Member; Kenneth Grant Williamson [1967] LLP Member

The Invicta Film Partnership No.37, LLP
Incorporated: 4 April 2005
Net Worth: £89,910,760 *Total Assets:* £97,431,904
Registered Office: 99 Kenton Road, Harrow, Middlesex, HA3 0AN
Officers: Michael Anthony Acratopulo [1968] LLP Member; Robert Fredrik Martin Adair [1956] LLP Member; Rawle Hamilton Adams [1966] LLP Member; Richard John Julian Addison [1961] LLP Member; Bhikam Chand Agarwal [1952] LLP Member; Dr Sarmid Abdul Karim Al Kamil [1965] LLP Member; Dr Peter Russell Allamby [1958] LLP Member; Charles John Maynard Andrews [1960] LLP Member; Jean Felix Aniel Quiroga [1968] LLP Member; Daniel Andre Arbili [1971] LLP Member; Carol Claire Ashton [1962] LLP Member; Robert John Charles Astley [1979] LLP Member; Edward Samuel Awty [1951] LLP Member; Andrew Baird [1964] LLP Member; David Michael Baker [1960] LLP Member; Philip John Barnatt [1949] LLP Member; Doctor Christopher John Batty [1963] LLP Member; Grant Martin Eugene Beglan [1964] LLP Member; John Charles Bentley [1964] LLP Member; Rajesh Kumar Bhardwaj [1969] LLP Member; Michael Francis Antony Borrelli [1954] LLP Member; Willem Albertus Botha [1964] LLP Member; Giovanni Brighi [1965] LLP Member; Kelvin John Bromley [1955] LLP Member; Paul Andrew Buckland [1965] LLP Member; John Campbell [1960] LLP Member; Lucy Campbell [1959] LLP Member; Dominic Francis John Cheetham [1966] LLP Member; Sven Martin Chipchase [1967] LLP Member; Andrew John Clark [1961] LLP Member; James Anthony Clegg [1966] LLP Member; Graham Richard Cockroft [1959] LLP Member; David Anthony Collins [1965] LLP Member; Dr Yogesh Contractor [1965] LLP Member; John Patrick Costello [1970] LLP Member; Philip John Craven [1958] LLP Member; Nicholas James Cross [1976] LLP Member; Miles John Davidson [1965] LLP Member; Andrew William Dawson [1963] LLP Member; Antony Peter di Lorenzo [1962] LLP Member; Peter Harry Dunsby [1969] LLP Member; Richard Colin Ellis [1969] LLP Member; Stephen Christopher Alesbury Ellis [1959] LLP Member; Pieter Esterhuysen [1967] LLP Member; Raymond Charles Eyre [1955] LLP Member; Brendan Paul Farmer [1965] LLP Member; Sean Thomas Farrell [1973] LLP Member; Kenneth Rodney Ferguson [1963] LLP Member; Gary Michael Finn [1957] LLP Member; Alan Roy Fitzpatrick [1939] LLP Member; Martin Alan Charles Fitzpatrick [1969] LLP Member; Andrew Fraser [1972] LLP Member; Andrew Gavan [1960] LLP Member; Peter James Gerrard [1962] LLP Member; Vijay Narendra Gohil [1976] LLP Member; Christopher Gunning [1944] LLP Member; Simon David Hague [1966] LLP Member; Dr Shiba Hameed [1956] LLP Member; Christopher Hancock [1965] LLP Member; Peter Edward Joseph Hansell [1966] LLP Member; Dr Grant Richard Harris [1968] LLP Member; Keith John Harvey [1966] LLP Member; John Simon Helfgott [1958] LLP Member; Alan James Highton [1957] LLP Member; James Andrew Paul Hines [1960] LLP Member; Wallace Simon Duthie Hinshelwood [1963] LLP Member; Dr Mohammad Altaf Hossain [1941] LLP Member; Laurence Gerrad Howard [1957] LLP Member; Jonathan Richard Jeff [1974] LLP Member; Richard Mark Jones [1968] LLP Member; Timothy Francis Comyn Jordan [1960] LLP Member; Abu Yousuf Fazlul Karim [1944] LLP Member; Geoffrey Arthur Kent [1954] LLP Member; Arno Kitts [1963] LLP Member; Karl Roderick Knipe [1966] LLP Member; Pietro Lamberti [1961] LLP Member; Richard Gwilym Langley [1953] LLP Member; Nadir Sikander Latif [1962] LLP Member; Michael Angelo Le Houx [1959] LLP Member; Mitchel Andrew Lenson [1954] LLP Member; Keith Malcolm Lewin [1957] LLP Member; Sean Richard Ormsby Lindsay [1967] LLP Member; Gordon Ionwy David Llewelyn [1956] LLP Member; Linda Jane Lord [1970] LLP Member; Peter John Lowless [1952] LLP Member; Richard Lucas James [1964] LLP Member; Geoffrey Charles Maddock [1964] LLP Member; Kirankumar Vardhaman Malde [1954] LLP Member; Rajesh Vardhaman Malde [1959] LLP Member; Sirishkumar Vardhaman Malde [1951] LLP Member; Simon Charles Caldwell Marsh [1959] LLP Member; John Russell Mathers [1956] LLP Member; David Scott Meads [1966] LLP Member; Nigel Headley Meredith [1953] LLP Member; Richard John Mitchell [1970] LLP Member; Andrew Raymond Moorfield [1966] LLP Member; Frank Murphy [1941] LLP Member; Dr Philip John Naish [1951] LLP Member

The Invicta Film Partnership No.8, LLP
Incorporated: 19 March 2002
Net Worth: £27,242,708 *Total Assets:* £27,248,724
Registered Office: 99 Kenton Road, Harrow, Middlesex, HA3 0AN
Officers: Fatima Albizua Ureta [1971] LLP Member; Suneel Bakhshi [1958] LLP Member; David Keith Bee [1961] LLP Member; Winston Bogarde [1970] LLP Member; Martin Major Bradford [1942] LLP Member; Graham Maxwell Brown [1958] LLP Member; Trevor Brown [1942] LLP Member; Stewart James Cameron [1969] LLP Member; Duncan Campbell [1952] LLP Member; Neil Robert Chamberlain [1958] LLP Member; Peter Robert Chapman [1943] LLP Member; William Clutterbuck [1959] LLP Member; Wayne Anthony Cook [1966] LLP Member; Martin John Crabtree [1960] LLP Member; Julian Charles Desmond Culhane [1966] LLP Member; Jeremy Jenkin Davies [1963] LLP Member; Mark Andrew Deane [1956] LLP Member; Graeme Ryland Frederick Dell [1964] LLP Member; Martin Jeremy Dyer [1956] LLP Member; Robert Simon Ford [1965] LLP Member; Brian John Forster [1950] LLP Member; Iain Fraser [1965] LLP Member; Brian Gaunt [1958] LLP Member; Helen Green [1961] LLP Member; John Harding [1973] LLP Member; Robert Mark Hartley [1968] LLP Member; Mark Colin Heaney [1967] LLP Member; Peter Hennell [1947] LLP Member; Stephen Benjamin Howard [1970] LLP Member; Harvinderpal Singh Hungin [1960] LLP Member; Richard George Hurdley [1968] LLP Member; John Jekabs Krumins [1964] LLP Member; Gillian Lancaster [1964] LLP Member; Frederick Mark Latham [1959] LLP Member; Philip Anthony Leaper [1965] LLP Member; Stavros Loizou [1964] LLP Member; Graham Jack Longhurst [1957] LLP Member; Angus John Elsom MacCormick [1965] LLP Member; Donald Hugh MacLiver [1956] LLP Member; Donald Robert Mark [1956] LLP Member; Granville Robert May [1947] LLP Member; Mario Dino Patrick Melchiot [1976] LLP Member; Kazuichi Mihara [1946] LLP Member; Timothy John Miller [1957] LLP Member; Deborah Jane Monks [1959] LLP Member; Malcolm Colin Monks [1956] LLP Member; Richard Morgan [1957] LLP Member; Ian Morris [1961] LLP Member; Steven Neat [1961] LLP Member; Colin Vincent Austin Nunn [1963] LLP Member; Malcolm Bruce Oastler [1959] LLP Member; Peter James Palmer [1953] LLP Member; Matthew Richard Peachey [1967] LLP Member; Timothy Hugh Pitcher [1965] LLP Member; John Roden Plimmer [1958] LLP Member; William Jean Marie Pratt [1953] LLP Member; Ahmet Vedat Ratib [1963] LLP Member; Andrew Lawrence Reay [1971] LLP Member; Bennett Riley [1972] LLP Member; Pamela Florence Roberts [1946] LLP Member; Malcolm Murray Robertson [1954] LLP Member; Brian Ralph Shubrook [1950] LLP Member; Calvin Francis Smith [1968] LLP Member; Robert Ian Dickson Strong [1970] LLP Member; Gordon McKenzie Stuart [1963] LLP Member; Hutton Daniel John Swinglehurst [1970] LLP Member; Robert Emile Morley Taussig [1950] LLP Member; Nicholas John Thurlow [1961] LLP Member; Craig Francis Tillotson [1964] LLP Member; Brian John Twigger [1954] LLP Member; Richard Francis Usmar [1946] LLP Member; Peter Edwin Villa [1944] LLP Member; Lewis FitzGenerald Watts [1964] LLP Member; Alistair Stevenson Webster [1953] LLP Member; Barry John Westwood [1951] LLP Member; Peter George Wilson [1953] LLP Member; Andrew Winfield [1958] LLP Member; Curtis Woodhouse [1980] LLP Member

The Invicta Film Partnership No.9, LLP
Incorporated: 20 May 2002
Net Worth: £21,350,728 *Total Assets:* £21,354,288
Registered Office: 99 Kenton Road, Harrow, Middlesex, HA3 0AN
Officers: Michael Adcock [1962] LLP Member; Nicholas Anthony Athanasou [1953] LLP Member; Suneel Bakhshi [1958] LLP Member; David Keith Bee [1961] LLP Member; Nicola Jane Blakemore [1966] LLP Member; Winston Bogarde [1970] LLP Member; David Bonner [1959] LLP Member; Steve John Brigden [1962] LLP Member; Steven Astley Brown [1959] LLP Member; Sally Ann Carre [1961] LLP Member; William Clutterbuck [1959] LLP Member; James Coldwell [1964] LLP Member; Malcolm Alan Cook [1948] LLP Member; Peter David Cook [1964] LLP Member; Trevor John Cook [1958] LLP Member; Martin John Crabtree [1960] LLP Member; Julian Charles Desmond Culhane [1966] LLP Member; Jeremy Jenkin Davies [1963] LLP Member; Michael John Trefor Davies [1960] LLP Member; Bradley James Edward Day [1962] LLP Member; Paul di Leo [1962] LLP Member; Brian Gaunt [1958] LLP Member; Peter John Bradford Gibson [1956] LLP Member; Jonathan Martin Grantham [1962] LLP Member; Richard Haining [1951] LLP Member; Richard John Stephen Hart [1948] LLP Member; Ian Allison Henderson [1957] LLP Member; Stephen Benjamin Howard [1970] LLP Member; Michael Makepeace Eugene Jeffries [1944] LLP Member; Graham Douglas Kendrick [1946] LLP Member; Janis Jekabs Krumins [1964] LLP Member; William George Lane [1960] LLP Member; Frederick Mark Latham [1959] LLP Member; Angus John Elsom MacCormick [1965] LLP Member; Donald Hugh MacLiver [1956] LLP Member; Gaetano William Mammana [1962] LLP Member; David Scott Meads [1966] LLP Member; Mario Dino Patrick Melchiot [1976] LLP Member; Timothy John Miller [1957] LLP Member; Linda Karen Morey Smith [1963] LLP Member; Margaret Morrison [1961] LLP Member; Timothy Paul Murray [1963] LLP Member; Steven Neat [1961] LLP Member; Mark Neil [1954] LLP Member; Guy Jeremy Norgrove [1951] LLP Member; Malcolm Bruce Oastler [1959] LLP Member; Donald Kennedy Pepper [1961] LLP Member; Karl Gregory Pick [1967] LLP Member; John Roden Plimmer [1958] LLP Member; Karen Linda Anne Richardson [1955] LLP Member; Bennett Riley [1972] LLP Member; Pamela Florence Roberts [1946] LLP Member; Malcolm Murray Robertson [1954] LLP Member; Trudi Ometha Ryan Dawes [1960] LLP Member; Daman Marcus Sanders [1964] LLP Member; Adrian Vaughan Shipman Sharpe [1948] LLP Member; Gavin Sinclair [1952] LLP Member; Calvin Francis Smith [1968] LLP Member; Robin Simon Southwell [1960] LLP Member; Mark Neil Steinberg [1959] LLP Member; Robert Emile Morley Taussig [1950] LLP Member; David Taylor [1962] LLP Member; Craig Francis Tillotson [1964] LLP Member; Richard Francis Usmar [1946] LLP Member; John Michael Vickerman [1961] LLP Member; Peter George Wilson [1953] LLP Member; Andrew Winfield [1958] LLP Member; Ian Leslie Zant-Boer [1953] LLP Member

Invigia Limited
Incorporated: 14 February 1997
Net Worth: £9,880,000 *Total Assets:* £20,665,000
Registered Office: Elder House, St Georges Business Park, Brooklands Road, Weybridge, Surrey, KT13 0TS
Activities: Business and domestic software development
Parent: Equiniti Holdings Limited
Officers: Katherine Cong, Secretary; Seema Sangar [1976] Finance Director; John Stier [1966] Director/Chief Financial Officer

J. Isaacs Management Limited
Incorporated: 2 October 1958 *Employees:* 6
Net Worth: £8,971,791 *Total Assets:* £9,352,166
Registered Office: Suite 117, Catalyst House, 720 Centennial Court, Centennial Park, Elstree, Herts, WD6 3SY
Activities: Other letting and operating of own or leased real estate
Shareholder: J Isaacs Israel Ltd
Officers: Laurence Joseph Gordon, Secretary; Leah Miriam Besser [1972] Director/Pharmacist; Adam Samuel Isaacs [1971] Director; Nathan David Isaacs [1936] Director/Retired [Israeli]; Michelle Anne Lawrence [1967] Director/Fundraising Property; Jonathan Maurice Paull [1962] Director/Chartered Marketer

ISG Technology Holdings Limited
Incorporated: 19 January 2005 *Employees:* 5
Net Worth Deficit: £3,412,000 *Total Assets:* £9,163,000
Registered Office: Ashmead House, Eversley Way, Crabtree Office Village, Egham, Surrey, TW20 8RY
Activities: Other information technology service activities
Parent: Coupra Limited
Officers: Jeremy Buckton [1970] Director; Michael John Morrison [1956] Director; Andrew James Webb [1962] Director

ISG Technology Limited
Incorporated: 18 September 2003 *Employees:* 90
Net Worth: £7,359,000 *Total Assets:* £13,937,000
Registered Office: Ashmead House, Eversley Way, Crabtree Office Village, Egham, Surrey, TW20 8RY
Activities: Other information technology service activities
Parent: ISG Technology Holdings Limited
Officers: Michael John Morrison [1956] Director; Andrew James Webb [1962] Director

Islam Channel Limited
Incorporated: 6 February 2003 *Employees:* 15
Net Worth: £19,919,676 *Total Assets:* £22,683,580
Registered Office: 428-432 Ley Street, Ilford, Essex, IG2 7BS
Activities: Television programming and broadcasting activities
Major Shareholder: Mohamed Ali Harrath
Officers: Mohamed Ali Harrath [1963] Director/Businessman

Islandbridge Chigwell Limited
Incorporated: 8 April 2016
Net Worth Deficit: £3,522 *Total Assets:* £7,323,012
Registered Office: 188 High Road, Loughton, Essex, IG10 1DN
Activities: Other business support service activities n.e.c.
Parent: Apollo Property Investment Limited
Officers: Stephen John Allen [1956] Director; Gary Patrick Couch [1962] Director

Isleworth & Hounslow Charity Limited
Incorporated: 29 September 2005 *Employees:* 3
Net Worth: £13,251,124 *Total Assets:* £13,583,082
Registered Office: Executive Clerk's Office, Tolson House, Parthenia Drive, Isleworth, Middlesex, TW7 6GT
Activities: Other accommodation
Officers: Barry John Newitt, Secretary; Ronald John Bartholomew [1945] Director/Retired; Angela Carroll [1964] Director/Solicitor; Emma Cartwright [1966] Director/Chief Executive of a Charity; Helena Davidson [1976] Director/Accountant; Peter George Dodkins [1952] Director/Administrator; Linda Anne Green [1958] Director/Councillor; Cllr Antonios Louki [1959] Director/Charity Administrator; Rev David MacLure [1980] Director/Clerk in Holy Orders; Anthony Charles McKendry [1937] Director/Retired; Shirley Sylvester [1959] Director/Housing Association; Dr John Tippins [1950] Director/Retired; Paul Turner [1932] Director/Retired; Rev Alison Claire Walton [1959] Director/Vicar; David George Woods [1960] Director of Development, Octavia Housing

Isleworth and Syon School for Boys
Incorporated: 23 February 2012 *Employees:* 115
Net Worth: £17,640,000 *Total Assets:* £20,925,000
Registered Office: Isleworth and Syon School for Boys, Ridgeway Road, Isleworth, Middlesex, TW7 5LJ
Activities: General secondary education
Officers: Premilla George, Secretary; Tamsin Leigh Billimoria [1970] Director/Assistant Headteacher - ICT; Amal Moawad Ahmed Bolbol [1976] Director/Learning Support Assistant; Fergus Euan Ferguson [1960] Director/Headteacher; Dr Roy Gardner [1932] Director/Educational Consultant; Catherine Patrice Gower [1968] Director/University Lecturer in Education; Sophie Hannon [1989] Director/Teacher; Dr Derek Michael Healy [1978] Director/H&S & Environmental Officer & GILO Brunel University; Martin David King [1969] Director/Senior Learning Technologist; Raymond Henry O'Neill [1956] Director/Teacher; Alan John Smith [1948] Director/Local Government Officer; Vanessa Katherine Smith [1947] Director; Dr Emily Jane Tomlinson [1974] Director/Charity Management; Dr Iris Turner [1941] Director/Academic Adviser External Examinations

ISS Damage Control Limited
Incorporated: 18 January 2001 *Employees:* 104
Net Worth: £14,547,000 *Total Assets:* £17,253,000
Registered Office: Velocity, 1 Brooklands Drive, Brooklands, Weybridge, Surrey, KT13 0SL
Activities: Specialised cleaning services
Parent: ISS UK Limited
Officers: Matthew Edward Stanley Brabin [1965] Director/Chief Executive Officer; Kenneth Ian Mackintosh [1962] Director; Stephen Graham Mitchell [1964] Operations Director; Barbara Plucnar Jensen [1971] Director/Chief Financial Officer [Danish]

ISS Facility Services Limited
Incorporated: 31 October 1966 *Employees:* 24,852
Net Worth: £108,124,000 *Total Assets:* £694,902,016
Registered Office: Velocity, 1 Brooklands Drive, Brooklands, Weybridge, Surrey, KT13 0SL
Activities: Unlicenced restaurants and cafes
Parent: ISS UK Limited
Officers: Matthew Edward Stanley Brabin [1965] Director/Chief Executive Officer; Andrew Owen Chappell [1975] Director/Chief Operating Officer; Philip John Leigh [1967] Director/Chief Operating Officer; Barbara Plucnar Jensen [1971] Director/Chief Financial Officer [Danish]; Robert David Stanley [1976] Director/Chief Operating Officer

ISS Mediclean Limited
Incorporated: 23 August 1982 *Employees:* 15,984
Net Worth: £86,044,000 *Total Assets:* £198,944,992
Registered Office: Velocity, 1 Brooklands Drive, Brooklands, Weybridge, Surrey, KT13 0SL
Activities: Other food services
Parent: ISS UK Ltd
Officers: Michael Barker, Secretary; Michael Barker [1963] Director; Matthew Edward Stanley Brabin [1965] Director/Chief Executive Officer; Philip John Leigh [1967] Director/Chief Operating Officer; Barbara Plucnar Jensen [1971] Director/Chief Financial Officer [Danish]; Wendy Stowell [1966] Commercial Director [New Zealander]

ISS UK Holding Limited
Incorporated: 24 August 2005 *Employees:* 4
Net Worth: £263,684,000 *Total Assets:* £483,235,008
Registered Office: Velocity, 1 Brooklands Drive, Brooklands, Weybridge, Surrey, KT13 0SL
Activities: Activities of head offices
Parent: ISS Global A/S
Officers: Matthew Edward Stanley Brabin [1965] Director/Chief Executive Officer; Barbara Plucnar Jensen [1971] Director/Chief Financial Officer [Danish]; Richard Ian Sykes [1970] Director; Jorn Vestergaard [1968] Director [Danish]

ISS UK Limited
Incorporated: 27 January 1949 *Employees:* 173
Net Worth: £149,790,000 *Total Assets:* £1,033,267,008
Registered Office: Velocity, 1 Brooklands Drive, Brooklands, Weybridge, Surrey, KT13 0SL
Activities: Activities of head offices
Parent: ISS UK Holding Limited
Officers: Matthew Edward Stanley Brabin [1965] Director/Chief Executive Officer; Andrew Owen Chappell [1975] Director/Chief Operating Officer; Stephanie Louise Hamilton [1971] Director/Head People & Culture; Philip John Leigh [1967] Director/Chief Operating Officer; Barbara Plucnar Jensen [1971] Director/Chief Financial Officer [Danish]; Robert David Stanley [1976] Director/Chief Operating Officer

Ist Developments Limited
Incorporated: 21 May 2016 *Employees:* 3
Net Worth: £1,980,256 *Total Assets:* £5,080,859
Registered Office: 32 Byron Hill Road, Harrow, Middlesex, HA2 0HY
Activities: Other letting and operating of own or leased real estate
Officers: Abul Kalam Shumsuddin Choudhury, Secretary; Shumon Salauddin Choudhury [1973] Director; Tamanna Choudhury [1956] Director; Tasneem Choudhury [1988] Director

ITC Concepts Limited
Incorporated: 15 April 1992 *Employees:* 64
Net Worth: £2,573,607 *Total Assets:* £9,245,400
Registered Office: Annecy Court, Ferry Works, Summer Road, Thames Ditton, Surrey, KT7 0QJ
Activities: Other engineering activities
Shareholder: Ian Thomas Conway
Officers: Christine Mary Evans, Secretary; Ian Thomas Conway [1958] Managing Director; Nicholas Conway [1984] Director; Martin John Paul [1964] Director/Accountant; Antony Edward Smith [1965] Director-Electrical/Mechanical

ITW Holdings I Limited
Incorporated: 4 November 2015
Net Worth: £2,136,424,192 *Total Assets:* £7,397,315,072
Registered Office: Nexus House, Station Road, Egham, Surrey, TW20 9LB
Activities: Activities of other holding companies n.e.c.
Parent: ITW Holdings Inc.
Officers: Ryan Ronald Dale, Secretary; Giles Matthew Hudson [1972] Director/Chartered Accountant; Stephen James Rowell [1967] Director of International Corporate Finance

ITW Holdings II Limited
Incorporated: 10 December 2015
Net Worth: £4,805,328,896 *Total Assets:* £4,805,328,896
Registered Office: Nexus House, Station Road, Egham, Surrey, TW20 9LB
Activities: Activities of other holding companies n.e.c.
Parent: ITW Holdings I Limited
Officers: Ryan Ronald Dale, Secretary; Giles Matthew Hudson [1972] Director/Chartered Accountant; Stephen James Rowell [1967] Director of International Corporate Finance

ITW Holdings III Limited
Incorporated: 10 December 2015
Net Worth: £7,103,780,352 *Total Assets:* £7,103,780,352
Registered Office: Nexus House, Station Road, Egham, Surrey, TW20 9LB
Activities: Activities of other holding companies n.e.c.
Parent: ITW Holdings VIII Limited
Officers: Ryan Ronald Dale, Secretary; Giles Matthew Hudson [1972] Director/Chartered Accountant; Stephen James Rowell [1967] Director of International Corporate Finance

ITW Holdings IV Limited
Incorporated: 10 December 2015
Net Worth: £2,562,002,432 *Total Assets:* £2,594,297,088
Registered Office: Nexus House, Station Road, Egham, Surrey, TW20 9LB
Activities: Activities of other holding companies n.e.c.
Parent: ITW Holdings I Limited
Officers: Ryan Ronald Dale, Secretary; Giles Matthew Hudson [1972] Director/Chartered Accountant; Stephen James Rowell [1967] Director of International Corporate Finance

ITW Holdings V Limited
Incorporated: 18 December 2015
Net Worth: £1,385,645,312 *Total Assets:* £1,387,344,768
Registered Office: Nexus House, Station Road, Egham, Surrey, TW20 9LB
Activities: Activities of other holding companies n.e.c.
Parent: ITW Holdings II Limited
Officers: Ryan Ronald Dale, Secretary; Giles Matthew Hudson [1972] Director/Chartered Accountant; Stephen James Rowell [1967] Director of International Corporate Finance

ITW Holdings VI Limited
Incorporated: 22 November 2016
Net Worth: £7,397,127,680 *Total Assets:* £7,397,127,680
Registered Office: Nexus House, Station Road, Egham, Surrey, TW20 9LB
Activities: Activities of other holding companies n.e.c.
Shareholders: ITW Holdings III Limited (in Trust for ITW Holdings LP); ITW Holdings III Limited
Officers: Ryan Ronald Dale, Secretary; Giles Matthew Hudson [1972] Director/Chartered Accountant; Stephen James Rowell [1967] Director of International Corporate Finance

ITW Holdings VII Limited
Incorporated: 22 November 2016
Net Worth: £2,399,663,360 *Total Assets:* £2,399,663,360
Registered Office: Nexus House, Station Road, Egham, Surrey, TW20 9LB
Activities: Activities of other holding companies n.e.c.
Parent: ITW (EU) Holdings SARL
Officers: Ryan Ronald Dale, Secretary; Giles Matthew Hudson [1972] Director/Chartered Accountant; Stephen James Rowell [1967] Director of International Corporate Finance

ITW Limited
Incorporated: 6 January 1956 *Employees:* 2,322
Net Worth: £1,521,196,032 *Total Assets:* £2,745,051,904
Registered Office: Nexus House, Station Road, Egham, Surrey, TW20 9LB
Activities: Manufacture of other chemical products n.e.c.
Parent: Berrington UK
Officers: Ryan Ronald Dale, Secretary; Giles Matthew Hudson, Secretary/Chartered Accountant; Giles Matthew Hudson [1972] Director/Chartered Accountant; Stephen James Rowell [1967] Director of International Corporate Finance

IZH Holdings Ltd
Incorporated: 17 March 2015
Net Worth: £28,835,992 *Total Assets:* £30,100,012
Registered Office: Spirit House, 8 High Street, West Molesey, Surrey, KT8 2NA
Activities: Management consultancy activities other than financial management
Officers: Derek Williamson, Secretary; Gilles Christophe Marc Blanchard [1964] Director/Businessman [French]; Afonso Manuel Leao Da Costa Campos [1986] Director [Portuguese]; Imran Ali Khan [1978] Director/Businessman; Zeeshan Ali Khan [1977] Director

J & J Transport Limited
Incorporated: 24 March 1993
Net Worth: £8,952,664 *Total Assets:* £11,535,205
Registered Office: Unit 1 Station Approach, Oldfield Lane North, Greenford, Middlesex, UB6 0AL
Activities: Site preparation
Shareholders: John Malachy McDaid; Kathleen McDaid
Officers: John Malachy McDaid, Secretary/Haulage Contractor [Irish]; John Malachy McDaid [1962] Director [Irish]; Kathleen McDaid [1962] Director [Irish]

J J Food Service Holdings Limited
Incorporated: 4 October 2000
Net Worth: £65,140,624 *Total Assets:* £83,924,080
Registered Office: 7 Solar Way, Innova Park, Enfield, Middlesex, EN3 7XY
Activities: Other letting and operating of own or leased real estate
Major Shareholder: Mustafa Hussein Kiamil
Officers: Mustafa Hussein Kiamil, Secretary; Mustafa Hussein Kiamil [1956] Director; Rifat Kiamil [1983] Director/IT Manager

J P & S Servicess Ltd
Incorporated: 24 March 2004 *Employees:* 55
Net Worth: £1,463,452 *Total Assets:* £8,810,590
Registered Office: Accountancy Solutions, 797 Harrow Road, Sudbury Town, Wembley, Middlesex, HA0 2LP
Activities: Retail sale in non-specialised stores with food, beverages or tobacco predominating
Shareholders: Jeyakumary Yoganathan; Visvanathan Yoganathan
Officers: Jeyakumary Yoganathan, Secretary; Visvanathan Yoganathan [1960] Director/Retail Consultant

J P Investments London Ltd
Incorporated: 26 November 2004 *Employees:* 1
Net Worth Deficit: £112,963 *Total Assets:* £6,905,739
Registered Office: Unit 7 Triangle Centre, Uxbridge Road, Southall, Middlesex, UB1 3ED
Activities: Buying and selling of own real estate
Major Shareholder: Jaswinder Singh Pandher
Officers: Tersham Singh Pandher, Secretary; Jaswinder Singh Pandher [1978] Director

J. B. Developments & Construction Limited
Incorporated: 27 November 2009 *Employees:* 13
Net Worth: £5,566,289 *Total Assets:* £12,874,032
Registered Office: Printing House, 66 Lower Road, Harrow, Middlesex, HA2 0DH
Activities: Development of building projects
Shareholders: John Patrick Barrett; Brendan Barrett
Officers: Brendan Barrett [1983] Director/Builder; John Patrick Barrett [1959] Director/Builder [Irish]; Mark Sweeney [1971] Director [Irish]

J.C.S. Developments Ltd.
Incorporated: 18 December 2002 *Employees:* 5
Net Worth: £5,226,185 *Total Assets:* £13,388,337
Registered Office: 1 Brook Court, Blakeney Road, Beckenham, Kent, BR3 1HG
Activities: Development of building projects
Major Shareholder: Jason Charles Spearing
Officers: Deborah Ann Garrett, Secretary; Jason Charles Spearing [1970] Director

Jabac Finances Limited
Incorporated: 31 August 1962 *Employees:* 5
Net Worth: £4,484,334 *Total Assets:* £15,498,803
Registered Office: Lynwood House, 373-375 Station Road, Harrow, Middlesex, HA1 2AW
Activities: Banks
Officers: Adam Craig Newman [1965] Director; Clive Barry Newman [1960] Director; Harold Maurice Newman [1934] Director/Chartered Accountant; Paul Newman [1963] Director/Accounts Administrator

Jablite Holdings Limited
Incorporated: 20 October 2014 *Employees:* 175
Net Worth: £2,898,000 *Total Assets:* £17,299,000
Registered Office: Infinity House, Anderson Way, Belvedere, Kent, DA17 6BG
Activities: Activities of head offices
Officers: Matthew David Groom, Secretary; Wayne Robert Brown [1961] Manufacturing Director; John Graham Colley [1954] Director; Richard Peter Simon Lee [1968] Managing Director; Edward Aston Wass [1971] Director/Fund Manager

Jablite Limited
Incorporated: 26 September 1972 *Employees:* 97
Net Worth: £9,331,333 *Total Assets:* £21,165,808
Registered Office: Infinity House, Anderson Way, Belvedere, Kent, DA17 6BG
Activities: Manufacture of other inorganic basic chemicals
Parent: Synbra UK Ltd
Officers: M Matthew David Groom, Secretary; Wayne Robert Brown [1961] Manufacturing Director; Matthew David Groom [1979] Finance Director; Richard Peter Simon Lee [1968] Director

Ernest Jackson & Co. Limited
Incorporated: 20 June 1916 *Employees:* 117
Net Worth: £6,829,000 *Total Assets:* £11,159,000
Registered Office: Cadbury House, Sanderson Road, Uxbridge, Middlesex, UB8 1DH
Activities: Manufacture of cocoa and chocolate confectionery
Parent: Kraft Foods UK IP & Production Holdings Limited
Officers: Louise Anne Stigant [1967] Category Development & Market Activation Director; David Mark Walter [1971] Director/General Manager

Jain (Europe) Limited
Incorporated: 21 June 1996 *Employees:* 3
Net Worth: £7,664,171 *Total Assets:* £11,175,979
Registered Office: 3rd Floor, Rear Right, Regal House, 70 London Road, Twickenham, Middlesex, TW1 3QS
Activities: Wholesale of other intermediate products
Parent: Jain Irrigation Systems Ltd
Officers: Jitendra Shah, Secretary; Anil Bhavarlal Jain [1965] Director [Indian]; Atul Jain [1969] Director [Indian]

Jain International Foods Limited
Incorporated: 15 October 2009 *Employees:* 11
Previous: SQF 2009 Limited
Net Worth: £8,092,352 *Total Assets:* £49,184,888
Registered Office: 3rd Floor, Rear Right, Regal House, 70 London Road, Twickenham, Middlesex, TW1 3QS
Activities: Manufacture of other food products n.e.c.
Parent: Jain Irrigation Systems Ltd
Officers: Paul David Lawlor, Secretary; James Patrick Arnold [1965] Director; Anil Bhavarlal Jain [1965] Managing Director [Indian]; Atul Bhavarial Jain [1969] Marketing Director [Indian]; Suvan Kumar Sharma [1972] Director/V.P. Food Products

Jalaram Limited
Incorporated: 15 August 1974
Net Worth: £6,145,302 *Total Assets:* £8,962,572
Registered Office: 39 South Parade, Mollison Way, Edgware, Middlesex, HA8 5QL
Activities: Dispensing chemist in specialised stores
Officers: Ramesh Manibhai Patel, Secretary; Hement Manibhai Patel [1942] Director; Jayendra Patel [1948] Director; Ramesh Manibhai Patel [1937] Director

Stephen James (Automotive) Limited
Incorporated: 18 August 2015 *Employees:* 413
Net Worth: £11,172,000 *Total Assets:* £56,729,000
Registered Office: Unit 1 Martinbridge Estate, Lincoln Road, Enfield, Middlesex, EN1 1SP
Activities: Sale of new cars and light motor vehicles
Parent: DC Management Services Limited
Officers: Benjamin James Collins [1977] Managing Director; Richard Ennis [1975] Director; Peter David Williams [1971] Director/Accountant [Australian]

Michael James Autos PLC
Incorporated: 11 June 1974 *Employees:* 39
Net Worth: £5,226,775 *Total Assets:* £5,511,761
Registered Office: 9 Cheam Road, Epsom, Surrey, KT17 1SP
Activities: Sale of used cars and light motor vehicles
Shareholders: Adam James Garrett; Jack Michael Garrett
Officers: Jack Michael Garrett, Secretary; Adam James Garrett [1984] Director/Business Executive; Jack Michael Garrett [1983] Director/Accountant; Michael Edward Garrett [1947] Director/Motor Dealer

Nicholas James Care Homes Ltd
Incorporated: 5 December 2001 *Employees:* 327
Net Worth: £15,635,696 *Total Assets:* £33,972,356
Registered Office: 30 Station Road, Orpington, Kent, BR6 0SA
Activities: Residential nursing care facilities
Major Shareholder: Kanagaratnam Rajakanthan
Officers: Kanagaratnam Rajakanthan [1955] Director

James Development Company Limited
Incorporated: 19 May 1959
Net Worth: £6,087,236 *Total Assets:* £7,151,389
Registered Office: 123 Victoria Road, Romford, Essex, RM1 2NL
Activities: Development of building projects
Major Shareholder: Eugene James Brian Cooper
Officers: Michele Jane Feneley, Secretary; Christian Sheridan Giles Cooper [1973] Director/Architect & Property Developer; Eugene James Brian Cooper [1935] Director/Architect & Property Developer [British/Swiss]; Julien James Barrington Cooper [1967] Director/Property Developer; Marcel Eugene Barrington Cooper [1962] Director/Civil Engineer; Margaretha Katherina Cooper [1936] Director; Michele Jane Feneley [1959] Director/Company Secretary

Jancett Childcare & Jace Training Limited
Incorporated: 1 August 2007 *Employees:* 231
Net Worth: £2,704,078 *Total Assets:* £5,396,039
Registered Office: Graylaw House, 42-54 Manor Road, Wallington, Surrey, SM6 0AB
Activities: Technical and vocational secondary education
Officers: Stephen Alexander Drummond [1964] Director; Nicola Christine Hopper [1967] Director; Christine Eileen Pritchard [1941] Director/Training Day Care; John Alfred Pritchard [1936] Director/Child Day Care; Kirsty Elaine Pritchard [1972] Director; Trevor John Pritchard [1964] Director/Chef; Tracy Ann Pritchard-Drummond [1965] Director/Child Day Care Manager

Jankel Armouring Limited
Incorporated: 3 February 1987 *Employees:* 120
Net Worth: £17,709,924 *Total Assets:* £31,338,052
Registered Office: Belgrave House, 39-43 Monument Hill, Weybridge, Surrey, KT13 8RN
Activities: Defence activities
Parent: The Jankel Group Limited
Officers: Anthony Louis Harry Jankel, Secretary; Daniel Crosby [1981] Business Development Director; Andrew Jankel [1968] Director; Anthony Louis Harry Jankel [1950] Director; Jennifer Anne Jankel [1940] Director; Michael Patrick Mullen [1961] Director/Engineer

The Jankel Group Limited
Incorporated: 22 January 2001 *Employees:* 120
Net Worth: £17,744,046 *Total Assets:* £31,346,048
Registered Office: Belgrave House, 39-43 Monument Hill, Weybridge, Surrey, KT13 8RN
Activities: Activities of head offices
Officers: Anthony Louis Harry Jankel, Secretary; Jonathan Mark Farrow [1965] Director; Andrew Jankel [1968] Sales and Marketing Director; Anthony Louis Harry Jankel [1950] Director; Jennifer Anne Jankel [1940] Director

Jas Forwarding (UK) Limited
Incorporated: 14 June 1984 *Employees:* 115
Net Worth: £22,150,768 *Total Assets:* £32,490,200
Registered Office: Cargo Point, Bedfont Road, Stanwell, Middlesex, TW19 7NZ
Activities: Other transportation support activities
Officers: Noel Rex Broadbent, Secretary; Noel Rex Broadbent [1957] Managing Director; Biagio Bruni [1945] Director [Italian]; Tahira Fumo [1966] Director/Chief Financial Officer [American]; Marco Rebuffi [1961] Director/President and CEO [Italian]

Jasper Morrison Limited
Incorporated: 23 October 1997 *Employees:* 4
Net Worth: £862,331 *Total Assets:* £5,912,846
Registered Office: Mill House, 58 Guildford Street, Chertsey, Surrey, KT16 9BE
Activities: Other business support service activities n.e.c.
Major Shareholder: Jasper Charles Morrison
Officers: Jasper Morrison [1959] Director/Designer

Jato Aviation Limited
Incorporated: 29 November 2000 *Employees:* 3
Net Worth Deficit: £3,458,817 *Total Assets:* £22,716,352
Registered Office: Hunton House, Highbridge Industrial Estate, Oxford Road, Uxbridge, Middlesex, UB8 1LX
Activities: Non-scheduled passenger air transport
Major Shareholder: Jacob Baruch Shafran
Officers: Matthew William Hall [1971] Director; Helene Marie Shafran [1966] Director [American]; Jacob Baruch Shafran [1952] Director

Jato Dynamics Limited
Incorporated: 26 May 1988 *Employees:* 684
Net Worth: £27,845,398 *Total Assets:* £84,783,872
Registered Office: Hunton House, Highbridge Industrial Estate, Oxford Road, Uxbridge, Middlesex, UB8 1LX
Activities: Market research and public opinion polling
Major Shareholder: Jacob Baruch Shafran
Officers: Fiona Lesley Sandford, Secretary; Matthew William Hall [1971] Director/Chartered Accountant; Helene Marie Shafran [1966] Director [American]; Jacob Baruch Shafran [1952] Director

Java Asset Management Limited
Incorporated: 23 March 2007
Net Worth: £2,055,871 *Total Assets:* £13,719,841
Registered Office: Montreaux House, The Hythe, Staines upon Thames, Middlesex, TW18 3JQ
Activities: Buying and selling of own real estate
Major Shareholder: David Burke
Officers: David Burke [1965] Director

Jay Fostering Limited
Incorporated: 6 July 2003 *Employees:* 22
Net Worth: £6,941,000 *Total Assets:* £7,114,000
Registered Office: Frays Court, 71 Cowley Road, Uxbridge, Middlesex, UB8 2AE
Activities: Other social work activities without accommodation n.e.c.
Parent: NFAP Limited
Officers: Helen Elizabeth Lecky, Secretary; Antony Vincent Holt [1959] Director/Chartered Accountant; Isabella Mary Hutchison [1956] Managing Director; Jean-Luc Emmanuel Janet [1970] Director [French]; David Jon Leatherbarrow [1969] Director/Group Chief Executive Officer

Jaysam Contractors Limited
Incorporated: 3 July 1986 *Employees:* 56
Net Worth: £18,337,174 *Total Assets:* £37,892,284
Registered Office: 14 Oxford Road, Wealdstone, Middlesex, HA3 7RG
Activities: Construction of domestic buildings
Major Shareholder: Samji Shivji Patel
Officers: Chhaya Gorsia, Secretary; Dhiraj Dabasia [1984] Director/Chartered Surveyor; Sundip Samji Dabasia [1983] Director/Office Manager; Samji Shivji Patel [1956] Director/Carpenter

Jaysam Developments Borehamwood Limited
Incorporated: 17 July 2014
Net Worth Deficit: £719,381 *Total Assets:* £28,973,820
Registered Office: 14 Oxford Road, Wealdstone, Middlesex, HA3 7RG
Activities: Construction of domestic buildings
Officers: Dhiraj Dabasia [1984] Director/Commercial Manager; Hitesh Samji Dabasia [1980] Director/Orthopaedic Surgeon; Sundip Samji Dabasia [1983] Director/Purchasing Manager; Samji Shivji Patel [1956] Director/Businessman; Gaurang Babulal Velani [1973] Director/Development Manager

Jaysam Developments Wembley Limited
Incorporated: 29 July 2014
Net Worth Deficit: £305,713 *Total Assets:* £6,547,978
Registered Office: 14 Oxford Road, Wealdstone, Harrow, Middlesex, HA3 7RG
Activities: Construction of domestic buildings
Officers: Dhiraj Dabasia [1984] Director/Commercial Manager; Hitesh Samji Dabasia [1980] Director/Orthopedic Surgeon; Sundip Samji Dabasia [1983] Director/Procurement Manager; Samji Shivji Patel [1956] Director/Businessman; Gaurang Babulal Velani [1973] Director/Development Manager

JB & Ace Limited
Incorporated: 3 August 2015 *Employees:* 2
Net Worth: £1,532,369 *Total Assets:* £15,230,684
Registered Office: Belgrave House, 39-43 Monument Hill, Weybridge, Surrey, KT13 8RN
Activities: Management consultancy activities other than financial management
Shareholders: John Charles Maynard; Bridget Maynard
Officers: Bridget Maynard [1959] Director [New Zealander]; John Charles Maynard [1948] Director

JBG Enterprises Limited
Incorporated: 9 June 1997
Net Worth: £664,698 *Total Assets:* £6,369,933
Registered Office: Riverside House, 1-5 Como Street, Romford, Essex, RM7 7DN
Activities: Financial management
Shareholder: John Bernard Giannotti
Officers: Susan Linda Giannotti, Secretary; John Bernard Giannotti [1951] Director; Susan Linda Giannotti [1952] Director

JBS Global (UK) Limited
Incorporated: 11 September 2001 *Employees:* 24
Net Worth: £28,589,878 *Total Assets:* £54,645,752
Registered Office: 2nd Floor, Building 1, Imperial Place, Maxwell Road, Borehamwood, Herts, WD6 1JN
Activities: Wholesale of meat and meat products
Officers: Ian Geoffrey Kemp, Secretary/Administration Manager; Wesley Mendonca Batista Filho [1991] Director [Brazilian]; Marcus Enda O'Sullivan [1970] Director [Irish]

JCA Charitable Foundation
Incorporated: 10 September 1891 *Employees:* 2
Net Worth: £47,497,000 *Total Assets:* £47,593,000
Registered Office: 39 Church Meadow, Long Ditton, Surbiton, Surrey, KT6 5EP
Activities: Other social work activities without accommodation n.e.c.
Officers: Timothy Robin Martin, Secretary; Yaffa Ben-Amt [1954] Director/Council Member [Israeli]; Jacques Capelluto [1949] Director/Private Investor [Belgian]; William Arthur Lionel Cohen [1961] Director/Lawyer; Geoffrey Sigmund Gestetner [1965] Director; Avner Hermoni [1947] Director [Israeli]; Beatrice Anne Jouan [1957] Director/Consultant [French]; Tal Kvatinsky [1985] Director [Israeli]; Peter Anthony Lawrence [1948] Director; Jacques Martin Paul Marie Tim Philippson [1972] Managing Director Blue Squares Holding [Belgian]; Marc Vellay [1954] Director/Sculptor [French]; Sir Stephen Harry Waley-Cohen [1946] Director; Doron Weiss [1955] Director [Israeli]; Prof Smuel Wolf [1954] Director/Professor [Israeli]

JCDecaux UK Limited
Incorporated: 19 November 1982 *Employees:* 704
Net Worth: £34,628,000 *Total Assets:* £246,292,000
Registered Office: 991 Great West Road, Brentford, Middlesex, TW8 9DN
Activities: Advertising agencies
Officers: Philip Idris James Thomas, Secretary/Financial Director; Spencer Berwin [1961] Managing Director of Sales; Jean-Francois Decaux [1959] Director/Chief Executive [French]; Philip Stewart Drye [1965] Director; Xavier Dupre [1963] Managing Director [French]; Neil Allan Eddleston [1961] Director; Thibaut Huon de Kermadec [1973] Finance Director [French]; Helena Mary Kavanagh [1959] Director [Irish]; David McEvoy [1961] Director; Alan Sullivan [1973] Director; Philip Idris James Thomas [1958] Financial Director

JCDecaux United Limited
Incorporated: 20 March 1964
Net Worth: £26,768,000 *Total Assets:* £43,353,000
Registered Office: 991 Great West Road, Brentford, Middlesex, TW8 9DN
Activities: Advertising agencies
Officers: Philip Idris James Thomas, Secretary/Financial Director; Thibaut Huon de Kermadec [1973] Finance Director [French]; Helena Mary Kavanagh [1959] Director [Irish]; Philip Idris James Thomas [1958] Financial Director

JDM Investments Limited
Incorporated: 5 December 2002 *Employees:* 1
Net Worth: £3,207,458 *Total Assets:* £6,390,488
Registered Office: First Floor, Radius House, 51 Clarendon Road, Watford, Herts, WD17 1HP
Activities: Public houses and bars
Major Shareholder: John Denis McGowan
Officers: Eithne Bridget McGowan, Secretary [Irish]; John Denis McGowan [1966] Director/Public House Entrepreneur [Irish]

Jean-Luc Developments Ltd
Incorporated: 3 February 2009 *Employees:* 77
Net Worth: £2,736,749 *Total Assets:* £11,829,471
Registered Office: First Floor, Radius House, 51 Clarendon Road, Watford, Herts, WD17 1HP
Activities: Construction of commercial buildings
Major Shareholder: Nicola Louise Spence
Officers: Russell Jonathan James Spence, Secretary; Andrew Hill [1966] Director; Luke Johnson Spence [1988] Director; Russell Jonathon James Spence [1985] Director

JEDS Investments Ltd
Incorporated: 15 March 2012 *Employees:* 3
Net Worth: £5,424,401 *Total Assets:* £18,450,604
Registered Office: 1 Albany Close, Blackhills Private Estate, Esher, Surrey, KT10 9JR
Activities: Development of building projects
Officers: Eamonn Donald Coleman [1980] Managing Director [Irish]; Siobhan Teresa Coleman [1981] Director

Jenga (UK) Limited
Incorporated: 27 February 2014
Net Worth Deficit: £111,521 *Total Assets:* £9,483,444
Registered Office: 9a The Broadway, Stanmore, Middlesex, HA7 4DA
Activities: Real estate agencies
Shareholders: Hitenkumar Mansukhlal Shah; Mahesh Raojibhai Patel; Navika Hitenkumar Shah; Alpa Mahesh Patel
Officers: Mahesh Raojibhai Patel, Secretary; Alpa Mahesh Patel [1972] Director/Pharmacist; Mahesh Raojibhai Patel [1968] Director/Businessman; Hitenkumar Mansukhlal Shah [1968] Director/Businessman; Navika Hitenkumar Shah [1972] Director/Pharmacist

Jenga House Limited
Incorporated: 6 October 2014
Net Worth: £1,188,704 *Total Assets:* £6,860,503
Registered Office: 9a The Broadway, Stanmore, Middlesex, HA7 4DA
Activities: Real estate agencies
Shareholders: Hitenkumar Mansukhlal Shah; Mahesh Raojibhai Patel
Officers: Mahesh Raojibhai Patel, Secretary; Mahesh Raojibhai Patel [1968] Director/Businessman; Hitenkumar Mansukhlal Shah [1968] Director/Businessman

Jennor Holdings Limited
Incorporated: 28 January 2016
Net Worth: £5,701,186 *Total Assets:* £6,722,842
Registered Office: Jennor House, Lockfield Avenue, Enfield, Middlesex, EN3 7QL
Activities: Activities of other holding companies n.e.c.
Officers: David Jenkins [1978] Director; James Jenkins [1981] Director; Karen Jenkins [1978] Director; Philip Evan Jenkins [1976] Director; Robert Jenkins [1984] Director

The Jersey Property Partnership LLP
Incorporated: 29 March 2006 *Employees:* 1
Net Worth: £1,286,832 *Total Assets:* £6,073,252
Registered Office: 9 Bridle Close, Surbiton Road, Kingston upon Thames, Surrey, KT1 2JW

Jessica House Developments Limited
Incorporated: 21 December 2015
Net Worth Deficit: £1,136,190 *Total Assets:* £18,121,020
Registered Office: 3rd Floor, Sterling House, Langston Road, Loughton, Essex, IG10 3TS
Activities: Development of building projects
Parent: Galliard Developments Limited
Officers: Allan William Porter, Secretary; John Cole [1971] Director; Stephen Stuart Solomon Conway [1948] Director; Jonathan Simon Goldstein [1966] Director; Donagh O'Sullivan [1968] Director [Irish]

Jetclub Limited
Incorporated: 31 March 1983 *Employees:* 80
Net Worth: £784,179 *Total Assets:* £7,921,420
Registered Office: 75 Corbets Tey Road, Upminster, Essex, RM14 2AJ
Activities: Travel agency activities
Parent: Inspearational Travels Ltd
Officers: Derek Adams, Secretary; Derek Adams [1962] Director/Travel Agent; Janet Maria Byng [1967] Director/Accountant; Elizabeth Ann Cookson [1956] Director/Travel Agent; Peter Richard Hatton Cookson [1953] Director/Travel Agent

The Jewellery Channel Limited
Incorporated: 15 December 2005 *Employees:* 105
Net Worth: £3,337,166 *Total Assets:* £13,951,410
Registered Office: Surrey House, Plane Tree Crescent, Feltham, Middlesex, TW13 7HF
Activities: Other retail sale of new goods in specialised stores (not commercial art galleries and opticians)
Parent: Genoa Jewellers Ltd
Officers: Nitin Panwad, Secretary; Amit Agarwal [1978] Managing Director; Sanjeev Agrawal [1965] Director [Indian]; Harsh Bahadur [1955] Director [Indian]; Rahim Ullah [1956] Director [Indian]

The Jewish Community Secondary School Trust
Incorporated: 15 December 2004
Net Worth: £39,723,764 *Total Assets:* £40,056,592
Registered Office: JCoSS School, Castlewood Road, Cockfosters, Barnet, Herts, EN4 9GE
Activities: General secondary education
Officers: Jamie Robert Cassell, Secretary; Nicole Julia Ronson Allalouf [1972] Director/CEO Nicron Productions Ltd; Jamie Robert Cassell [1973] Director/Chartered Accountant; Stephen Alan Clayman [1968] Director/Police Superintendent; Joel Anthony Courts [1982] Director/Chartered Accountant; Mark David Freedman [1970] Director/Solicitor; Graham Andrew Harris [1963] Managing Director; Tamara Margaret Isaacs [1967] Director/Civil Servant; Jeremy Paul Kosky [1968] Director/Solicitor; David Mark Kyte [1960] Director; Stephen David Moss [1952] Director

JFD Developments Ltd
Incorporated: 3 March 2011 *Employees:* 2
Net Worth: £275,390 *Total Assets:* £6,087,602
Registered Office: Parker House, 44 Stafford Road, Wallington, Surrey, SM6 9AA
Activities: Construction of domestic buildings
Shareholders: Dee Ann Davis; Jason Rodney Foy
Officers: Dee Ann Davis [1985] Director/Secretary; Jason Rodney Foy [1967] Director/Builder

JGC New Energy UK Limited
Incorporated: 14 February 2017 *Employees:* 6
Net Worth: £302,857 *Total Assets:* £14,560,236
Registered Office: 4th Floor, Hyde Park Hayes 3, 11 Millington Road, Hayes, Middlesex, UB3 4AZ
Activities: Other engineering activities
Parent: JGC Corporation
Officers: Tsutomu Akabane [1955] Director [Japanese]; Kazuyoshi Muto [1953] Director [Japanese]; Hiroki Suzuki [1974] Director [Japanese]; Akio Yoshida [1959] Director [Japanese]

JJ Food Service Limited
Incorporated: 23 December 1988 *Employees:* 823
Net Worth: £34,158,096 *Total Assets:* £50,369,880
Registered Office: 7 Solar Way, Innova Park, Enfield, Middlesex, EN3 7XY
Activities: Non-specialised wholesale of food, beverages and tobacco
Parent: JJ Food Service Holdings Limited
Officers: Mustafa Hussein Kiamil, Secretary; Mustafa Hussein Kiamil [1956] Director; Rifat Kiamil [1983] Director/IT Manager

JLW Excellent Homes for Life Holding Company Limited
Incorporated: 1 December 2010
Net Worth Deficit: £6,733,000 *Total Assets:* £67,991,000
Registered Office: 8 White Oak Square, London Road, Swanley, Kent, BR8 7AG
Activities: Activities of head offices
Parent: JLIF Holdings (Regeneration and Social Housing) Limited
Officers: Vikki Louise Everett [1971] Director/Project Manager; Julian Denzil Sutcliffe [1968] Life Cycle Asset Director

JLW Excellent Homes for Life Limited
Incorporated: 3 December 2010
Net Worth Deficit: £6,733,000 *Total Assets:* £67,991,000
Registered Office: 8 White Oak Square, London Road, Swanley, Kent, BR8 7AG
Activities: Other business support service activities n.e.c.
Parent: JLW Excellent Homes for Life Holding Company Limited
Officers: Vikki Louise Everett [1971] Director/Project Manager; Julian Denzil Sutcliffe [1968] Life Cycle Asset Director

Jobladder Limited
Incorporated: 20 February 2003 *Employees:* 31
Net Worth: £6,625,277 *Total Assets:* £7,080,172
Registered Office: Milton House, 33a Milton Road, Hampton, Surrey, TW12 2LL
Activities: Advertising agencies
Shareholders: Stephen Wexler; Raya Wexler
Officers: Stephen Wexler, Secretary; Raya Wexler [1961] Director/Public Relations Consultant; Stephen Wexler [1955] Director/Web Site Manager

Johalian Property Limited
Incorporated: 14 November 2002 *Employees:* 1
Net Worth: £1,338,587 *Total Assets:* £5,120,760
Registered Office: 1 Warner House, Harrovian Business Village, Bessborough Road, Harrow, Middlesex, HA1 3EX
Activities: Other building completion and finishing
Major Shareholder: Nauman Javid
Officers: Nauman Javid [1972] Director

John S. Miller Limited
Incorporated: 6 May 1974 *Employees:* 13
Net Worth: £5,971,236 *Total Assets:* £7,402,610
Registered Office: Haslers, Old Station Road, Loughton, Essex, IG10 4PL
Activities: Renting and operating of Housing Association real estate
Shareholder: John Simon Miller
Officers: Natalie Laura Livingston, Secretary; Natalie Laura Livingston [1972] Director; David Miller [1974] Sales Director; John Simon Miller [1943] Director/Dispensing Chemist

Daniel Johns Ltd
Incorporated: 6 June 2013
Net Worth: £660,901 *Total Assets:* £6,424,088
Registered Office: CEME, Marsh Way, Rainham, Essex, RM13 8EU
Activities: Buying and selling of own real estate
Major Shareholder: Khalid Iqbal Bhatti
Officers: Khalid Iqbal Bhatti [1982] Director [Pakistani]; Peter Summersgill [1948] Director

P. Johnson & Son (1976) Limited
Incorporated: 23 June 1976 *Employees:* 11
Net Worth: £11,192,556 *Total Assets:* £15,434,363
Registered Office: The Estate Office, Highams Hill Farm, Sheepbarn Lane, Warlingham, Surrey, CR6 9PQ
Activities: Remediation activities and other waste management services
Shareholder: Adam Leonard Johnson
Officers: Adam Leonard Johnson [1969] Director/Estate Manager; Michelle Bernice Johnson [1967] Director/Estate Manager; Teresa Johnson [1943] Director/Secretary

Johnson Group Limited
Incorporated: 4 April 1990
Net Worth: £334,691 *Total Assets:* £5,432,802
Registered Office: 15 Home Farm Road, Rickmansworth, Herts, WD3 1JU
Activities: Other letting and operating of own or leased real estate
Shareholders: Patrick James Johnson; Patrick James Johnson; Maria Theresa Johnson
Officers: Maria-Louisa Christina Manton, Secretary; Patrick James Johnson [1944] Director

Leonard F.Jollye (Brookmans Park) Limited
Incorporated: 24 June 1971 *Employees:* 604
Net Worth: £4,396,229 *Total Assets:* £12,799,988
Registered Office: 1 Lea Road, Waltham Abbey, Essex, EN9 1AS
Activities: Retail sale of flowers, plants, seeds, fertilizers, pet animals and pet food in specialised stores
Parent: Leonard F Jollye (Holdings) Limited
Officers: David Leslie Hutchinson [1969] Director; Warwick Richard Thresher [1974] Director; Christian Robert Philip Ward [1972] Director

Leonard F Jollye (Holdings) Limited
Incorporated: 9 September 2005
Net Worth: £8,899,890 *Total Assets:* £8,900,390
Registered Office: 1 Lea Road, Waltham Abbey, Essex, EN9 1AS
Activities: Activities of other holding companies n.e.c.
Parent: Jollyes Group Limited
Officers: David Leslie Hutchinson [1969] Director; Warwick Richard Thresher [1974] Director; Christian Robert Philip Ward [1972] Director

Jollyes Group Limited
Incorporated: 21 December 2007
Net Worth: £21,738,400 *Total Assets:* £26,417,982
Registered Office: 1 Lea Road, Waltham Abbey, Essex, EN9 1AS
Activities: Activities of other holding companies n.e.c.
Parent: Jollyes Retail Group Limited
Officers: David Leslie Hutchinson [1969] Director; Warwick Richard Thresher [1974] Director; Christian Robert Philip Ward [1972] Director

Jollyes Retail Group Limited
Incorporated: 21 June 2011 *Employees:* 604
Net Worth: £19,382,716 *Total Assets:* £37,843,816
Registered Office: 1 Lea Road, Waltham Abbey, Essex, EN9 1AS
Activities: Activities of other holding companies n.e.c.
Parent: Jaguar Bidco Limited
Officers: David Leslie Hutchinson [1969] Director; Warwick Richard Thresher [1974] Director; Christian Robert Philip Ward [1972] Director

H.C. Jones & Co (Surrey) Limited
Incorporated: 29 March 1930 *Employees:* 4
Net Worth: £18,644,404 *Total Assets:* £20,491,104
Registered Office: Unit 5 Manor Farm, Manor Road North, Thames Ditton, Surrey, KT7 0BH
Activities: Other letting and operating of own or leased real estate
Officers: Clare Ann Jones, Secretary; Denis Rossiter Carpenter [1938] Director/Property; Rodney Duncan Jones [1940] Director/Builder; Simon Harvey Jones [1967] Director

Jopate Estates Limited
Incorporated: 12 June 1947 *Employees:* 4
Net Worth: £17,998,132 *Total Assets:* £19,564,136
Registered Office: 69 Highlands Road, Leatherhead, Surrey, KT22 8NW
Activities: Other letting and operating of own or leased real estate
Officers: John William Hewlett, Secretary; Gareth Seamus Prickett [1962] Managing Director; William Leighton Whittaker [1957] Director/Retired

JPO Communications Limited
Incorporated: 28 March 2014 *Employees:* 79
Net Worth: £2,560,677 *Total Assets:* £8,707,227
Registered Office: 7 Pier Road, Feltham, Middlesex, TW14 0TW
Activities: Activities of other holding companies n.e.c.
Shareholder: Samuel James Neal
Officers: Charlotte Elizabeth Neal [1977] Director; Samuel James Neal [1977] Director

JRL Group (Ireland) Limited
Incorporated: 16 November 2016 *Employees:* 3
Net Worth: £220,859 *Total Assets:* £6,971,226
Registered Office: 4 Elstree Way, Borehamwood, Herts, WD6 1RN
Activities: Activities of other holding companies n.e.c.
Parent: JRL Group Holdings Limited
Officers: Ronan Gleeson, Secretary; Ronan Joseph Gleeson [1976] Director/Chartered Accountant [Irish]; Kevin William Keegan [1963] Director [Irish]; John James Reddington [1972] Director [Irish]

JRL Group Holdings Limited
Incorporated: 16 October 2009 *Employees:* 871
Net Worth: £41,824,040 *Total Assets:* £244,142,128
Registered Office: 4 Elstree Way, Borehamwood, Herts, WD6 1RN
Activities: Activities of construction holding companies
Shareholder: Kevin William Keegan
Officers: Ronan Joseph Gleeson, Secretary [Irish]; Ronan Joseph Gleeson [1976] Director [Irish]; Kevin William Keegan [1963] Director [Irish]; John James Reddington [1972] Director [Irish]

JRL Group Limited
Incorporated: 26 March 2008 *Employees:* 871
Net Worth: £39,052,300 *Total Assets:* £229,338,288
Registered Office: 4 Elstree Way, Borehamwood, Herts, WD6 1RN
Activities: Activities of construction holding companies
Parent: JRL Group Holdings Ltd
Officers: Ronan Joseph Gleeson, Secretary [Irish]; Ronan Joseph Gleeson [1976] Director/Chartered Accountant [Irish]; Kevin William Keegan [1963] Director [Irish]; John James Reddington [1972] Director [Irish]

JRL Plant and Logistics Limited
Incorporated: 17 April 2003 *Employees:* 148
Net Worth: £968,887 *Total Assets:* £62,889,348
Registered Office: 4 Elstree Way, Borehamwood, Herts, WD6 1RN
Activities: Renting and leasing of construction and civil engineering machinery and equipment
Parent: JRL Group Ltd
Officers: Ronan Joseph Gleeson, Secretary/Director [Irish]; Ronan Joseph Gleeson [1976] Director [Irish]; Kevin William Keegan [1963] Director/Estimator [Irish]; John James Reddington [1972] Director/Formwork [Irish]

JRL Property Holdings Limited
Incorporated: 24 February 2017 *Employees:* 3
Net Worth: £4,660,324 *Total Assets:* £29,217,624
Registered Office: 4 Elstree Way, Borehamwood, Herts, WD6 1RN
Activities: Activities of other holding companies n.e.c.
Parent: JRL Group Holdings Limited
Officers: Ronan Gleeson, Secretary; Ronan Joseph Gleeson [1976] Director/Chartered Accountant [Irish]; Kevin William Keegan [1963] Director [Irish]; John James Reddington [1972] Director [Irish]

JRL Property Limited
Incorporated: 21 November 2003 *Employees:* 3
Net Worth: £4,342,742 *Total Assets:* £10,257,168
Registered Office: 4 Elstree Way, Borehamwood, Herts, WD6 1RN
Activities: Other letting and operating of own or leased real estate
Parent: JRL Property Holdings Limited
Officers: Ronan Joseph Gleeson, Secretary/Director [Irish]; Ronan Joseph Gleeson [1976] Director [Irish]; Kevin William Keegan [1963] Director [Irish]; John James Reddington [1972] Director/Formwork [Irish]

JSA Properties (UK) Limited
Incorporated: 30 January 1996 *Employees:* 3
Net Worth: £3,552,385 *Total Assets:* £7,232,750
Registered Office: Treviot House, 186-192 High Road, Ilford, Essex, IG1 1LR
Activities: Development of building projects
Major Shareholder: Leslie Steven Gilbert
Officers: Leslie Steven Gilbert [1964] Director

JSA Services Limited
Incorporated: 24 July 1989 *Employees:* 5,251
Net Worth: £2,865,712 *Total Assets:* £19,393,340
Registered Office: 4th Floor, Radius House, 51 Clarendon Road, Watford, Herts, WD17 1HP
Activities: Accounting and auditing activities
Shareholders: Goodman Family Investments Limited; JSA Newco Limited
Officers: Katherine Mary Rogers, Secretary; Andrew Graham Goodman [1962] Director; John Hugo Hoskin [1974] Director; Kwasi Martin Missah [1969] Legal Director; Katherine Mary Rogers [1953] Director

JSM Associates (LON) LLP
Incorporated: 3 February 2016
Net Worth: £245,957 *Total Assets:* £5,798,804
Registered Office: 7 Clairvale, Hornchurch, Essex, RM11 3NA
Officers: Baldev Lullian Kaur Johal [1951] Member; Mavinda Kaur Johal [1991] Member; Parmjit Singh Johal [1955] Member

JSM Construction Limited
Incorporated: 1 July 1998 *Employees:* 191
Net Worth: £8,117,488 *Total Assets:* £16,643,443
Registered Office: Sterling House, Mutton Lane, Potters Bar, Herts, EN6 3AR
Activities: Construction of utility projects for electricity and telecommunications
Parent: JSM Group Holdings Limited
Officers: John Joseph Scanlon, Secretary; John Joseph Scanlon [1968] Director; Mark Vincent Scanlon [1969] Director; Stuart Wiltshire [1965] Director

JSM Group Holdings Limited
Incorporated: 4 September 2015 *Employees:* 191
Net Worth: £8,117,488 *Total Assets:* £16,643,443
Registered Office: c/o Hillier Hopkins LLP, First Floor, Radius House, 51 Clarendon Road, Watford, Herts, WD17 1HP
Activities: Activities of other holding companies n.e.c.
Shareholder: Mark Vincent Scanlon
Officers: John Joseph Scanlon [1968] Director; Mark Vincent Scanlon [1969] Director; Stuart Wiltshire [1965] Director

JTC Ventures Limited
Incorporated: 18 January 1988 *Employees:* 10
Previous: Junior Tennis Centres Ventures Limited
Net Worth: £6,111,061 *Total Assets:* £9,992,098
Registered Office: 1 Park Road, Hampton Wick, Kingston upon Thames, Surrey, KT1 4AS
Activities: Other letting and operating of own or leased real estate
Shareholder: James Alexander Sohl
Officers: Jennifer Susan Sohl, Secretary; James Alexander Sohl [1977] Development Director; Jennifer Susan Sohl [1947] Director; Keith James Sohl [1948] Managing Director; Natascha Emile Sohl Williams [1979] Director; Nathalia Ingrid Speake [1979] Director

JTI (RMS) Ltd
Incorporated: 5 March 2008 *Employees:* 14
Net Worth: £1,866,000 *Total Assets:* £8,815,000
Registered Office: Members Hill, Brooklands Road, Weybridge, Surrey, KT13 0QU
Activities: Other business support service activities n.e.c.
Parent: Japan Tobacco Inc.
Officers: Christopher Peter Hill [1978] Director/Lawyer; Mark Vincent Phillips [1970] Human Resources Director [Australian]; Bertrand Henri Tamisier [1966] Director [Swiss]

JTI (UK) Management Ltd
Incorporated: 3 November 2006 *Employees:* 4
Net Worth: £1,055,300,992 *Total Assets:* £1,257,982,976
Registered Office: Members Hill, Brooklands Road, Weybridge, Surrey, KT13 0QU
Activities: Activities of head offices
Parent: Japan Tobacco Inc.
Officers: Nicholas Charles David Craig, Secretary; Charles Ashley Cunningham-Reid [1968] Director; Paul Bernard Hennessy [1980] Director [Irish]; Jeroen Rusbach [1977] Director/Accountant [Dutch]; Daniel Sciamma [1970] Director [French]

JTL
Incorporated: 23 March 2000 *Employees:* 295
Net Worth: £36,310,576 *Total Assets:* £41,899,648
Registered Office: Stafford House, 120-122 High Street, Orpington, Kent, BR6 0JS
Activities: Technical and vocational secondary education
Officers: Caroline Anne Turner, Secretary; John Allott [1962] Director/Trades Union Official; Paul Graham Bird [1971] Finance Director; John Alexander Burrows [1954] HR Director; Richard Jeremy Clarke [1972] Director/Trade Union Official; Andrew Colin Eldred [1969] Director/Manager; Christopher Victor Fenton [1962] Director; Bernard McAulay [1951] Director/Trade Union Official; Paul Campbell McNaughton [1958] Managing Director; Geoffrey Russell [1958] Director; Tracey Elaine Shelley [1968] Director/Chief Executive and Company Secretary; William Cameron Spiers [1946] Director/Approved Electrician

Juniper Networks (UK) Limited
Incorporated: 16 September 1999
Net Worth: £64,392,344 *Total Assets:* £151,603,760
Registered Office: Building 1, Aviator Park, Station Road, Addlestone, Surrey, KT15 2PG
Activities: Other information technology service activities
Parent: Juniper Networks, Inc.
Officers: Julie Ann Appelbe [1967] Finance Director; Ketan Kumar Vithalbhai Rambhai Patel [1962] Director; Terrance Floyd Spidell [1968] Director/Chief Accounting Officer [American]

Jupiter Midco 1 Limited
Incorporated: 26 July 2016 *Employees:* 1,808
Net Worth Deficit: £4,505,099 *Total Assets:* £80,529,784
Registered Office: Charta House, 30-38 Church Street, Staines upon Thames, Middlesex, TW18 4EP
Activities: Activities of other holding companies n.e.c.
Parent: Jupiter Topco Limited
Officers: Christopher John Clasper [1981] Director/Investment Professional; Christopher John Wilmot [1973] Director/Investment Professional; Ayal Zylberman [1975] Director [Israeli/French]

Jupiter Midco 2 Limited
Incorporated: 17 June 2016
Net Worth: £624,090 *Total Assets:* £28,821,590
Registered Office: Charta House, 30-38 Church Street, Staines upon Thames, Middlesex, TW18 4EP
Activities: Activities of other holding companies n.e.c.
Parent: Jupiter Midco 1 Limited
Officers: Christopher John Clasper [1981] Director/Investment Professional; Christopher John Wilmot [1973] Director/Investment Professional; Ayal Zylberman [1975] Director [Israeli/French]

Jupiter Topco Limited
Incorporated: 17 June 2016 *Employees:* 1,808
Net Worth Deficit: £4,445,099 *Total Assets:* £77,377,568
Registered Office: Charta House, 30-38 Church Street, Staines upon Thames, Middlesex, TW18 4EP
Activities: Other business support service activities n.e.c.
Officers: Martin Harold Blackburn [1967] Director; Jan Olivier Fillols [1980] Director; Shawn Allister McMorran [1963] Director/Investment Professional [Canadian]; Edward Thomas Richards [1975] Director; Michael Edward Wilkinson [1986] Director; Ayal Zylberman [1975] Director/President, Qualitest Group [Israeli/French]

K 2 Properties Limited
Incorporated: 8 June 2000
Net Worth: £1,387,677 *Total Assets:* £5,827,508
Registered Office: Crown House, 24-25 Turners Hill, Cheshunt, Herts, EN8 8NJ
Activities: Other letting and operating of own or leased real estate
Shareholders: Thomas Paine; Karl Roderick Knipe
Officers: Thomas Paine, Secretary; Karl Roderick Knipe [1966] Director; Thomas Paine [1966] Director

K K Investment Ltd
Incorporated: 6 April 2004
Net Worth: £839,355 *Total Assets:* £12,435,536
Registered Office: 7 The Broadway, Preston Road, Wembley, Middlesex, HA9 8JT
Activities: Development of building projects
Major Shareholder: Khosrow Khosravani
Officers: Khosrow Khosravani Shiri [1962] Director/Building Developer

K.C.Y. Limited
Incorporated: 23 September 1999 *Employees:* 1
Net Worth: £5,649,118 *Total Assets:* £10,596,495
Registered Office: 10 Long Drive, South Ruislip, Middlesex, HA4 0HG
Activities: Other letting and operating of own or leased real estate
Shareholders: Christos Yiannakis; Christos Yiannakis
Officers: Julia Yiannakis, Secretary; Christina Louise Yiannakis [1989] Director; Christos Yiannakis [1951] Director/Restaurateur [Greek]; Katherine Elissa Yiannakis [1987] Director

K.E.M. Property Services Limited
Incorporated: 24 January 2003 *Employees:* 5
Net Worth: £5,706,766 *Total Assets:* £9,165,317
Registered Office: 36a Goodmayes Road, Goodmayes, Essex, IG3 9UR
Activities: Management of real estate on a fee or contract basis
Major Shareholder: Ashley Parker
Officers: Nitan Bafna, Secretary; Ashley Parker [1962] Director/Manager; Edward Charles Parker-Bancroft [1957] Director/Acquisitions Manager

K2 Trading Limited
Incorporated: 12 November 2003 *Employees:* 5
Net Worth: £1,061,348 *Total Assets:* £6,662,291
Registered Office: Wrotham Business Park, Barnet, Herts, EN5 4SB
Activities: Agents selling agricultural raw materials, livestock, textile raw materials and semi-finished goods
Shareholders: Houry Kazanjian; Nicole Laurence
Officers: Parul Shah, Secretary; Irfan Ellahi Shamsi [1950] Director

K2M UK Limited
Incorporated: 2 July 2009 *Employees:* 50
Net Worth: £33,707,376 *Total Assets:* £41,350,028
Registered Office: Ground Floor, 1 Roundwood Avenue, Stockley Park, Uxbridge, Middlesex, UB11 1FG
Activities: Retail sale of medical and orthopaedic goods in specialised stores (not incl. hearing aids) n.e.c.
Parent: K2M Inc
Officers: Luke Russell Miller, Secretary [American]; Eric David Major [1969] Director [American]; Luke Russell Miller [1979] Director [American]

Kailas Hotel Finance Company Limited
Incorporated: 19 November 2012
Net Worth: £1 *Total Assets:* £12,270,350
Registered Office: 505 Pinner Road, Harrow, Middlesex, HA2 6EH
Activities: Other letting and operating of own or leased real estate
Officers: Denise Olival, Secretary; Rishi Ramesh Sachdev [1976] Director; Uday Vyas [1978] Director

Kailash Estates Limited
Incorporated: 23 June 1995 *Employees:* 1
Net Worth: £5,172,860 *Total Assets:* £5,550,704
Registered Office: Regent House, Allum Gate, Theobald Street, Elstree, Borehamwood, Herts, WD6 4RS
Activities: Management of real estate on a fee or contract basis
Shareholder: Ramesh Govindji Sachdev
Officers: Uday Vyas, Secretary; David Arthur Osborne [1960] Director/Surveyor; Pratibha Ramesh Sachdev [1948] Director; Ramesh Chandra Govindji Sachdev [1945] Director/Certified Accountant

Kalbro Investments Limited
Incorporated: 1 September 2003
Net Worth: £1,149,578 *Total Assets:* £5,357,147
Registered Office: 46 Yeading Fork, Hayes, Middlesex, UB4 9DQ
Activities: Other letting and operating of own or leased real estate
Officers: Raaj Kalaria, Secretary/Accounts Assistant; Raaj Kalaria [1979] Managing Director; Shradha Kaneria [1982] Director; Dr Binita Shah [1980] Director/Medical Doctor

Kallar Investments Limited
Incorporated: 23 July 2003 *Employees:* 2
Net Worth: £7,718,104 *Total Assets:* £21,993,636
Registered Office: 148 The Office, Station Road, Sidcup, Kent, DA15 7AB
Activities: Buying and selling of own real estate
Shareholders: Lakhbinder Kallar; Sukhjeev Kallar
Officers: Sukhjeev Kallar, Secretary; Lakhbinder Kallar [1973] Director/Estate Agent; Sukhjeev Kallar [1981] Director

Kallarview Homes Limited
Incorporated: 27 April 2006 *Employees:* 1
Net Worth: £2,648,611 *Total Assets:* £5,756,203
Registered Office: 148 The Office, Station Road, Sidcup, Kent, DA15 7AB
Activities: Buying and selling of own real estate
Major Shareholder: Lakhbinder Kallar
Officers: Sarbjit Kallar, Secretary; Lakhbinder Kallar [1973] Director/Estate Agent

Kane Group Limited
Incorporated: 23 September 1991 *Employees:* 204
Net Worth: £2,889,000 *Total Assets:* £11,999,000
Registered Office: Hartfield Place, 40-44 High Street, Northwood, Middlesex, HA6 1BN
Activities: Activities of head offices
Shareholders: Jonathan Stephen Henry Arthur Kane; Grace Ventures LLC
Officers: Robert Christopher Clow [1948] Director/Chartered Accountant; Jonathan Stephen Henry Arthur Kane [1965] Director; Michael John Paul Charles Kane [1960] Director [American]

Kanta Enterprises Limited
Incorporated: 26 January 1982 *Employees:* 34
Net Worth: £9,001,002 *Total Assets:* £23,451,408
Registered Office: Kanta House, Victoria Road, South Ruislip, Middlesex, HA4 0JQ
Activities: Wholesale of pharmaceutical goods
Officers: Satish Jamnadas Chatwani, Secretary; Jawahar Jamnadas Chatwani [1948] Director; Rashmi Jamnadas Chatwani [1954] Director; Satish Jamnadas Chatwani [1953] Director

Kap Homes Ltd.
Incorporated: 16 October 2015
Net Worth Deficit: £1,503,654 *Total Assets:* £7,916,325
Registered Office: Floor 2, Middlesex House, 130 College Road, Harrow, Middlesex, HA1 1BQ
Activities: Other letting and operating of own or leased real estate
Shareholder: Deepak Khullar
Officers: Deepak Khullar [1973] Director

Kara Designs Ltd
Incorporated: 26 March 1999 *Employees:* 22
Net Worth: £10,195,480 *Total Assets:* £11,538,804
Registered Office: Unit 6 Haslemere Business Centre, Lincoln Way, Enfield, Middlesex, EN1 1TE
Activities: Manufacture of other women's outerwear
Shareholders: Ahmet Karaman; Yee Yoke Karaman; Huseyin Karaman
Officers: Yee Yoke Karaman, Secretary; Ahmet Karaman [1974] Director/Production Manager

Kara Management Ltd
Incorporated: 14 March 2003
Net Worth: £1,879,268 *Total Assets:* £9,607,503
Registered Office: Unit 6 Haslemere Business Centre, Lincoln Way, Enfield, Middlesex, EN1 1TE
Activities: Other letting and operating of own or leased real estate
Shareholders: Ahmet Karaman; Yee Yoke Karaman; Huseyin Karaman
Officers: Yee Yoke Karaman, Secretary; Ahmet Karaman [1974] Director/Dressmaker

Karelia Tobacco Company (UK) Limited
Incorporated: 13 August 2002 *Employees:* 6
Net Worth: £2,006,714 *Total Assets:* £22,936,140
Registered Office: Parkshot House, 5 Kew Road, Richmond, Surrey, TW9 2PR
Activities: Manufacture of tobacco products
Parent: Karelia Tobacco Company Inc
Officers: Andreas George Karelias [1966] Managing Director [Greek]; Efstathios George Karelias [1969] Director/General Manager [Greek]; Anthony Edward Peter Mulcrone [1959] Director

Karium Ltd
Incorporated: 14 August 1990 *Employees:* 61
Previous: Godrej Consumer Products (UK) Limited
Net Worth: £14,725,599 *Total Assets:* £29,025,880
Registered Office: Falcon House, 115-123 Staines Road, Hounslow, Middlesex, TW3 3LL
Activities: Wholesale of perfume and cosmetics
Parent: JZ Consumer Brands Limited
Officers: Benjamin David Hammersley, Secretary; Lee Graham Gelderd [1974] Managing Director; Jock Green-Armytage [1945] Director; Benjamin David Hammersley [1970] Finance Director; Alexander James MacGillivray Langmuir [1985] Director; Richard Reverdy Otley [1974] Director/Chairman [British Virgin Islander]; Miguel Rueda Hernando [1967] Director [Spanish]; Martin Stephen Northcote Wright [1968] Director

Karuna Care (TLC) Limited
Incorporated: 14 May 2014 *Employees:* 104
Net Worth: £5,039,160 *Total Assets:* £14,660,674
Registered Office: 36 Railway Approach, Harrow, Middlesex, HA3 5AA
Activities: Residential nursing care facilities
Parent: TLC Group Limited
Officers: Gagan Puri, Secretary; William Charles Neal [1986] Director; Paavan Popat [1985] Managing Director; Honourable Shivaan Shillin Popat [1988] Director; Gagan Puri [1978] Finance Director

Katana Property Limited
Incorporated: 12 March 2008 *Employees:* 2
Net Worth: £3,817,975 *Total Assets:* £11,757,868
Registered Office: Centrum House, 36 Station Road, Egham, Surrey, TW20 9LF
Activities: Buying and selling of own real estate
Major Shareholder: Adrian Stuart Brennan Dyball
Officers: Henry Lawrence Flint, Secretary; Adrian Stuart Brennan Dyball [1968] Property Director; Henry Lawrence Flint [1960] Director/Chartered Accountant

Katrin Properties Limited
Incorporated: 15 January 2003 *Employees:* 5
Net Worth: £13,645,954 *Total Assets:* £26,322,198
Registered Office: 834 Hertford Road, Enfield, Middlesex, EN3 6UE
Activities: Other letting and operating of own or leased real estate
Shareholder: Kerem Yavuzarslan
Officers: Kerem Yavuzarslan [1961] Managing Director

Katsouris Brothers Limited
Incorporated: 22 October 1964 *Employees:* 216
Net Worth: £10,970,954 *Total Assets:* £20,508,800
Registered Office: 98-100 Queensbury Road, Wembley, Middlesex, HA0 1QG
Activities: Non-specialised wholesale trade
Parent: Katsouris Brothers Limited
Officers: Katerina Charalambous, Secretary; Costas Constantinou [1957] Director/Consultant [Cypriot]; Loizos Constantinou [1958] Director; Demos Habeshis [1951] Director/Manager; Alexander Katsouris [1980] Director/Manager; Antonios Prodromou Yerolemou [1942] Director

Kavanagh Retailing (UK) Limited
Incorporated: 25 July 2005 *Employees:* 115
Net Worth: £4,339,544 *Total Assets:* £8,437,741
Registered Office: Budgens Hinchley Wood, 10-12 Manor Road North, Hinchley Wood, Esher, Surrey, KT10 0SH
Activities: Retail sale in non-specialised stores with food, beverages or tobacco predominating
Officers: Noel Jnr Kavanagh, Secretary; Marian Kavanagh [1954] Director [Irish]; Noel Kavanagh Jnr [1983] Director [Irish]

Kavo Dental Limited
Incorporated: 31 December 1969 *Employees:* 17
Net Worth: £12,237,000 *Total Assets:* £14,751,000
Registered Office: 3 Furzeground Way, Stockley Park, Uxbridge, Middlesex, UB11 1EZ
Activities: Dental practice activities
Parent: Kerr U.K. Limited
Officers: Amir Aghdaei [1958] Director [American]; Keith Graham Ward [1953] Director; Henner Witte [1961] Director [German]

Kaybridge Construction (Barnet) Limited
Incorporated: 19 July 1972 *Employees:* 7
Net Worth: £5,950,277 *Total Assets:* £8,618,127
Registered Office: Tudor House, 24 Cecil Road, Enfield, Middlesex, EN2 6TG
Activities: Construction of domestic buildings
Officers: Philomena Mary O'Connor, Secretary [Irish]; Joseph Paul Hurley [1947] Director; Siobhan Michelle Joyce [1973] Director; Ann Marie O'Connor [1966] Director; Michael O'Connor [1942] Director [Irish]; Philomena Mary O'Connor [1943] Director [Irish]; Sean Gerard O'Connor [1969] Director; Gary Peter Robinson [1971] Director

Kays Limited
Incorporated: 16 May 2000 *Employees:* 2
Net Worth: £4,851,569 *Total Assets:* £5,881,485
Registered Office: Suite 2, Fountain House, 1a Elm Park, Stanmore, Middlesex, HA7 4AU
Activities: Book publishing
Major Shareholder: Jayne Hatfield
Officers: Jayne Hatfield, Secretary/Publisher; Jayne Hatfield [1962] Director/Publisher; Bernard Lawrence Kay [1954] Director/Publisher

Kaysail Limited
Incorporated: 20 October 2004
Net Worth: £85,301,648 *Total Assets:* £130,549,824
Registered Office: 1st Floor, Ash House, Littleton Road, Ashford, Middlesex, TW15 1TZ
Activities: Activities of head offices
Parent: Goodrich Inertial Limited
Officers: Lynn Banis, Secretary; Christian Bruno Jean Idczak [1963] Director/Business Executive [French]; James Terence George Laurence [1964] Director/Accountant; Patricia Catherine Moran [1964] Finance Director [American]; Peter Ross [1964] Finance Director

KBC Advanced Technologies Limited
Incorporated: 15 March 1978 *Employees:* 253
Previous: KBC Advanced Technologies PLC
Net Worth: £33,149,000 *Total Assets:* £72,729,000
Registered Office: 42-50 Hersham Road, Hersham, Walton on Thames, Surrey, KT12 1RZ
Activities: Activities of head offices
Officers: James Richard Jordan, Secretary; Andrew John Howell [1968] Board Director; Satoru Kurosu [1960] Director/Company Executive [Japanese]; Matthew Curtis Ray [1966] Director/Financial Executive [American]; Simon Michael Rogers [1964] Director; Masataka Tomonaga [1973] Director/HR Manager [Japanese]

KBC Process Technology Limited
Incorporated: 10 April 1984 *Employees:* 95
Net Worth: £7,501,000 *Total Assets:* £134,964,000
Registered Office: 42-50 Hersham Road, Hersham, Walton on Thames, Surrey, KT12 1RZ
Activities: Other engineering activities
Parent: KBC Advanced Technologies PLC
Officers: James Richard Jordan, Secretary; Mark Patrick Henry Anderson [1959] Director/Chemical Engineer; James Richard Jordan [1965] Director/Accountant; Allan Rudman [1963] Director/Chemical Engineer

KBR (Aspire Construction) Limited
Incorporated: 9 February 2006
Net Worth Deficit: £2,561,000 *Total Assets:* £72,359,000
Registered Office: Hill Park Court, Springfield Drive, Leatherhead, Surrey, KT22 7NL
Activities: Other service activities n.e.c.
Parent: KBR (Aspire Construction) Holdings Limited
Officers: Susan Meirion Owen, Secretary; Stephen John Arthur [1956] Director; James Arthur Barrett [1965] Director/Accountant; Robert Paul Kerry [1956] Director/Senior Commercial Manager

KBR (Aspire Services) Limited
Incorporated: 9 February 2006
Net Worth: £1,255,000 *Total Assets:* £12,261,000
Registered Office: Hill Park Court, Springfield Drive, Leatherhead, Surrey, KT22 7NL
Activities: Other service activities n.e.c.
Parent: KBR (Aspire Services) Holdings Limited
Officers: Susan Meirion Owen, Secretary; James Arthur Barrett [1965] Director/Accountant; Colin Kenneth Kenton [1957] Director; Robert Paul Kerry [1956] Commercial Director

KBR (U.K.) Investments Limited
Incorporated: 10 March 2011
Net Worth: £187,851,424 *Total Assets:* £198,719,136
Registered Office: Hill Park Court, Springfield Drive, Leatherhead, Surrey, KT22 7NL
Activities: Activities of other holding companies n.e.c.
Parent: Kellogg Brown & Root Limited
Officers: Susan Meirion Owen, Secretary; James Arthur Barrett [1965] Director/Chartered Accountant; Farhan Mujib [1963] Director [Australian]

KBR Property Investments Limited
Incorporated: 14 October 2003
Net Worth: £299,224 *Total Assets:* £6,940,690
Registered Office: 20 Priory Gardens, Wembley, Middlesex, HA0 2QG
Activities: Buying and selling of own real estate
Shareholder: Kishor Ruparelia
Officers: Bhavna Ruparelia, Secretary; Kishor Ruparelia [1956] Director

Kearns Premier Homes Ltd
Incorporated: 17 February 2016
Net Worth Deficit: £308,393 *Total Assets:* £15,057,904
Registered Office: 33 Highfield Drive, Ickenham, Uxbridge, Middlesex, UB10 8AW
Activities: Construction of domestic buildings
Shareholders: Goldform Enterprises Limited; Kearns Property Management & Development Ltd
Officers: Majid Khalil Ibrahim [1956] Director; Peter Paul Kearns [1954] Director [Irish]

Kearns Property Management & Development Ltd
Incorporated: 10 August 2016 *Employees:* 5
Net Worth: £587,489 *Total Assets:* £10,068,127
Registered Office: 33 Highfield Drive, Ickenham, Uxbridge, Middlesex, UB10 8AW
Activities: Construction of domestic buildings
Major Shareholder: Peter Paul Kearns
Officers: Peter Paul Kearns [1954] Director [Irish]

Keash Properties Limited
Incorporated: 22 April 2005
Net Worth: £1,824,967 *Total Assets:* £6,998,037
Registered Office: First Floor, Radius House, 51 Clarendon Road, Watford, Herts, WD17 1HP
Activities: Other letting and operating of own or leased real estate
Major Shareholder: Therese Woulfe
Officers: Elizabeth Mary Henry [1951] Director/Bookkeeper; Therese Woulfe [1978] Director [Irish]

KECS Investments Limited
Incorporated: 25 January 2016
Net Worth Deficit: £89,047 *Total Assets:* £6,201,688
Registered Office: The Fold, 114 Station Road, Sidcup, Kent, DA15 7AE
Activities: Other letting and operating of own or leased real estate
Officers: Can Tekinalp [1987] Director [Turkish]

Kedleston (OS Education) Limited
Incorporated: 6 April 1987 *Employees:* 89
Previous: OS Education Limited
Net Worth: £8,775,546 *Total Assets:* £11,049,653
Registered Office: Unit 8 Brook Business Centre, Cowley Mill Road, Uxbridge, Middlesex, UB8 2FX
Activities: General secondary education
Parent: Kedleston Schools Limited
Officers: Anthony Robert Hurran, Secretary/Director; Denis Brosnan [1944] Director [Irish]; Paul Brosnan [1975] Director [Irish]; Anthony Robert Hurran [1976] Finance Director

Kedleston (Wings Education) Limited
Incorporated: 2 January 2003 *Employees:* 189
Previous: Wings Education Limited
Net Worth: £28,059,390 *Total Assets:* £33,542,588
Registered Office: Unit 8 Brook Business Centre, Cowley Mill Road, Uxbridge, Middlesex, UB8 2FX
Activities: General secondary education
Parent: Kedleston Wings Holdco Ltd
Officers: Anthony Robert Hurran, Secretary/Director; Denis Brosnan [1944] Director [Irish]; Paul Brosnan [1975] Director [Irish]; Anthony Robert Hurran [1976] Finance Director

Kedleston Group Limited
Incorporated: 13 August 2012 *Employees:* 472
Previous: Kedleston Education Limited
Net Worth Deficit: £8,163,156 *Total Assets:* £60,707,804
Registered Office: Unit 8 Brook Business Centre, Cowley Mill Road, Uxbridge, Middlesex, UB8 2FX
Activities: Activities of head offices
Officers: Denis Brosnan [1944] Director/Businessman [Irish]; Paul Brosnan [1975] Director [Irish]; Lesley Claire Cox [1959] Director; Anthony Robert Hurran [1976] Director/FD; Angela Marion Nightingale [1953] Director; Lee Nigel Reed [1963] Director/Chief Operating Officer; Richard Guy Murray Tassell [1947] Director

Kedleston Schools Limited
Incorporated: 12 April 2006 *Employees:* 472
Net Worth: £13,753,541 *Total Assets:* £51,455,176
Registered Office: Unit 8 Brook Business Centre, Cowley Mill Road, Uxbridge, Middlesex, UB8 2FX
Activities: Educational support services
Parent: Kedleston Group Limited
Officers: Anthony Robert Hurran, Finance Director; Denis Brosnan [1944] Director [Irish]; Paul Brosnan [1975] Director [Irish]; Anthony Robert Hurran [1976] Finance Director

Kedleston Wings Holdco Ltd
Incorporated: 4 March 2008
Net Worth: £4,659,965 *Total Assets:* £35,954,744
Registered Office: Unit 8 Brook Business Centre, Cowley Mill Road, Uxbridge, Middlesex, UB8 2FX
Activities: Activities of other holding companies n.e.c.
Parent: Kedlestson Schools Limited
Officers: Anthony Robert Hurran, Finance Director; Denis Brosnan [1944] Director [Irish]; Paul Brosnan [1975] Director [Irish]; Anthony Robert Hurran [1976] Finance Director

Kelerbay Limited
Incorporated: 1 November 1994 *Employees:* 191
Net Worth: £3,454,778 *Total Assets:* £9,640,872
Registered Office: International House, 19 Kennet Road, Dartford, Kent, DA1 4QN
Activities: Removal services
Parent: Doree Bonner Holdings Limited
Officers: Gordon Miller Lyall [1962] Director/Manager; William Robert John Rawkins [1974] Director; Geoffrey Peter Watson [1960] Director/Manager

Kellogg Brown & Root (Greenford) Limited
Incorporated: 5 July 1967
Net Worth: £82,622,720 *Total Assets:* £123,680,904
Registered Office: Hill Park Court, Springfield Drive, Leatherhead, Surrey, KT22 7NL
Activities: Other professional, scientific and technical activities n.e.c.
Parent: Kellogg Brown & Root DH Limited
Officers: Gregor Andrej Kosak, Secretary; David Lindsay Gibson [1962] Director/VP Operations; Farhan Mujib [1963] Director [Australian]; Martin Simmonite [1969] Director/Vice President Operations; Richard Francis Sullivan [1971] Director/Chartered Accountant

Kellogg Brown & Root (Services) Limited
Incorporated: 9 July 1975
Net Worth: £36,504,440 *Total Assets:* £36,539,200
Registered Office: Hill Park Court, Springfield Drive, Leatherhead, Surrey, KT22 7NL
Activities: Activities of construction holding companies
Parent: Laurel Financial Services B.V
Officers: Maya Diana Sutorius Feijen, Secretary/Manager Accounting [Dutch]; Maya Diana Sutorius Feijen [1971] Director/Manager Accounting [Dutch]

Kellogg Brown & Root (U.K.) Limited
Incorporated: 21 May 1986 *Employees:* 1,050
Net Worth Deficit: £598,273,024 *Total Assets:* £141,891,008
Registered Office: Hill Park Court, Springfield Drive, Leatherhead, Surrey, KT22 7NL
Activities: Other specialised construction activities n.e.c.
Parent: Kellogg Brown & Root Holdings (U.K.) Limited
Officers: Martin Nelhams, Secretary/Solicitor; James Arthur Barrett [1965] Director/Accountant; Jan Egil Braendeland [1967] Director [Norwegian]; Jalal Jay Ibrahim [1960] Director [American]; James Edward Lewis [1977] QHSE Director; Farhan Mujib [1963] Director [Australian]; Martin Nelhams [1960] Director/Solicitor; Martin Simmonite [1969] Director; Richard Francis Sullivan [1971] Director/Chartered Accountant

Kellogg Brown & Root DH Limited
Incorporated: 28 July 1987
Net Worth: £399,282,432 *Total Assets:* £399,282,432
Registered Office: Hill Park Court, Springfield Drive, Leatherhead, Surrey, KT22 7NL
Activities: Activities of other holding companies n.e.c.
Parent: Kellogg Brown & Root London Limited
Officers: Martin Nelhams, Secretary/Solicitor; James Arthur Barrett [1965] Director/Accountant; Martin Nelhams [1960] Director/Solicitor

Kellogg Brown & Root Group Limited
Incorporated: 27 October 2009
Net Worth Deficit: £253,736,176 *Total Assets:* £366,753,312
Registered Office: Hill Park Court, Springfield Drive, Leatherhead, Surrey, KT22 7NL
Activities: Activities of construction holding companies
Parent: Kellogg Brown & Root Overseas Projects Limited
Officers: Martin Nelhams, Secretary; James Arthur Barrett [1965] Director/Chartered Accountant; Martin Nelhams [1960] Director/Solicitor

Kellogg Brown & Root Holdings (U.K.) Limited
Incorporated: 11 December 1984
Net Worth: £25,794,000 *Total Assets:* £512,745,984
Registered Office: Hill Park Court, Springfield Drive, Leatherhead, Surrey, KT22 7NL
Activities: Activities of construction holding companies
Parent: Kellogg Brown & Root Holdings Limited
Officers: Martin Nelhams, Secretary/Solicitor; James Arthur Barrett [1965] Director/Accountant; Martin Nelhams [1960] Director/Solicitor

Kellogg Brown & Root Holdings Limited
Incorporated: 1 June 1999 *Employees:* 1,335
Net Worth: £966,976,000 *Total Assets:* £1,585,053,056
Registered Office: Hill Park Court, Springfield Drive, Leatherhead, Surrey, KT22 7NL
Activities: Activities of construction holding companies
Parent: Kellogg Brown & Root International Group Limited
Officers: Martin Nelhams, Secretary/Solicitor; James Arthur Barrett [1965] Director/Accountant; Martin Nelhams [1960] Director/Solicitor

Kellogg Brown & Root International Group Holdings LLP
Incorporated: 4 November 2009 *Employees:* 2
Net Worth: £133,496,432 *Total Assets:* £133,496,968
Registered Office: Hill Park Court, Springfield Drive, Leatherhead, Surrey, KT22 7NL

Kellogg Brown & Root International Group Limited
Incorporated: 26 October 2009
Net Worth: £77,243,056 *Total Assets:* £578,924,608
Registered Office: Hill Park Court, Springfield Drive, Leatherhead, Surrey, KT22 7NL
Activities: Activities of construction holding companies
Parent: Kellogg Brown & Root International Group Holdings LLP
Officers: Martin Nelhams, Secretary; James Arthur Barrett [1965] Director/Chartered Accountant; Martin Nelhams [1960] Director/Solicitor

Kellogg Brown & Root Limited
Incorporated: 22 December 1959 *Employees:* 110
Net Worth: £1,342,550,016 *Total Assets:* £1,787,815,936
Registered Office: Hill Park Court, Springfield Drive, Leatherhead, Surrey, KT22 7NL
Activities: Other engineering activities
Parent: Kellogg Brown Root Holdings (U.K.) Limited
Officers: Martin Nelhams, Secretary; James Arthur Barrett [1965] Director/Accountant; Jan Egil Braendeland [1967] Director [Norwegian]; David Lindsay Gibson [1962] Director/Vice President Operations EAME; Jalal Jay Ibrahim [1960] Director [American]; James Edward Lewis [1977] QHSE Director; Farhan Mujib [1963] Director [Australian]; Martin Simmonite [1969] Director; Richard Francis Sullivan [1971] Director/Chartered Accountant

Kellogg Brown & Root London Limited
Incorporated: 16 December 2010
Net Worth: £189,882,800 *Total Assets:* £339,168,064
Registered Office: Hill Park Court, Springfield Drive, Leatherhead, Surrey, KT22 7NL
Activities: Activities of other holding companies n.e.c.
Parent: Kellogg Brown & Root London Holdings Limited
Officers: Susan Meirion Owen, Secretary; James Arthur Barrett [1965] Director/Chartered Accountant; Farhan Mujib [1963] Director [Australian]

Kellogg Brown & Root Overseas Limited
Incorporated: 29 June 2000 *Employees:* 4
Net Worth Deficit: £17,936,552 *Total Assets:* £7,816,431
Registered Office: Hill Park Court, Springfield Drive, Leatherhead, Surrey, KT22 7NL
Activities: Other specialised construction activities n.e.c.
Parent: Kellogg Brown & Root Investment Holdings Limited
Officers: Susan Meirion Owen, Secretary; Jalal Jay Ibrahim [1960] Director [American]; Martin Nelhams [1960] Director/Solicitor; Martin Simmonite [1969] Director

Kellogg Brown & Root Overseas Operations Limited
Incorporated: 8 July 1986 *Employees:* 5
Net Worth: £116,061,104 *Total Assets:* £181,719,616
Registered Office: Hill Park Court, Springfield Drive, Leatherhead, Surrey, KT22 7NL
Activities: Other engineering activities
Parent: Kellogg Brown & Root Group Limited
Officers: Susan Meirion Owen, Secretary; Jan Egil Braendeland [1967] Director [Norwegian]; Jalal Jay Ibrahim [1960] Director [American]; Martin Simmonite [1969] Director; Richard Francis Sullivan [1971] Director/Chartered Accountant

Kellogg Brown & Root Overseas Projects Limited
Incorporated: 29 August 1986
Net Worth: £648,128,512 *Total Assets:* £653,177,088
Registered Office: Hill Park Court, Springfield Drive, Leatherhead, Surrey, KT22 7NL
Activities: Other engineering activities
Parent: Kellogg Brown & Root Limited
Officers: Martin Nelhams, Secretary; James Arthur Barrett [1965] Director/Chartered Accountant; Martin Nelhams [1960] Director/Solicitor

Kellogg Brown & Root Projects Limited
Incorporated: 18 September 1984
Net Worth: £249,777 *Total Assets:* £13,557,961
Registered Office: Hill Park Court, Springfield Drive, Leatherhead, Surrey, KT22 7NL
Activities: Other engineering activities
Parent: Kellogg Brown & Root Limited
Officers: Susan Meirion Owen, Secretary; Jalal Jay Ibrahim [1960] Director [American]; Martin Simmonite [1969] Director; Richard Francis Sullivan [1971] Director/Chartered Accountant

Kelly Comms Limited
Incorporated: 17 April 1998 *Employees:* 257
Net Worth: £2,518,773 *Total Assets:* £27,006,284
Registered Office: Kelly House, Fourth Way, Wembley, Middlesex, HA9 0LH
Activities: Other business support service activities n.e.c.
Parent: Kelly Communications Trading Group Limited
Officers: James Patrick Bradley, Secretary; Timothy Joseph Kelly [1954] Director [Irish]

Kelly Communications Enterprises Limited
Incorporated: 10 October 2012 *Employees:* 1
Net Worth: £1 *Total Assets:* £10,000,001
Registered Office: Kelly House, Fourth Way, Wembley, Middlesex, HA9 0LH
Activities: Non-trading company
Parent: Kelly Communications Group Limited
Officers: Timothy Joseph Kelly [1954] Director [Irish]

Kelly Communications Group Limited
Incorporated: 18 November 1996 *Employees:* 846
Net Worth: £32,972,540 *Total Assets:* £75,496,664
Registered Office: Kelly House, Fourth Way, Wembley, Middlesex, HA9 0LH
Activities: Other specialised construction activities n.e.c.
Major Shareholder: Timothy Kelly
Officers: James Patrick Bradley, Secretary; Timothy Patrick Kelly [2000] Director; Timothy Joseph Kelly [1954] Director [Irish]; Rosita Westropp-Bennett [1965] Finance Director [Irish]

Kelly Communications Limited
Incorporated: 9 June 1988 *Employees:* 364
Net Worth: £2,494,419 *Total Assets:* £38,074,008
Registered Office: Kelly House, Fourth Way, Wembley, Middlesex, HA9 0LH
Activities: Other construction installation
Parent: Kelly Communications Trading Group Limited
Officers: James Patrick Bradley, Secretary; Timothy Joseph Kelly [1954] Director [Irish]

Kelly Communications Trading Group Limited
Incorporated: 1 May 2009 *Employees:* 12
Net Worth: £1 *Total Assets:* £11,321,408
Registered Office: Kelly House, Fourth Way, Wembley, Middlesex, HA9 0LH
Activities: Non-trading company
Parent: Kelly Communications Enterprises Limited
Officers: James Bradley, Secretary; Timothy Joseph Kelly [1954] Director [Irish]; Larry McGrane [1968] Director

Kelly Fleet Services Limited
Incorporated: 24 June 1996 *Employees:* 62
Net Worth: £1,898,484 *Total Assets:* £23,571,540
Registered Office: Kelly House, Fourth Way, Wembley, Middlesex, HA9 0LH
Activities: Other specialised construction activities n.e.c.
Parent: Kelly Communications Trading Group Limited
Officers: James Patrick Bradley, Secretary; Timothy Joseph Kelly [1954] Director [Irish]; Larry McGrane [1968] Director

Kelly Property Company Limited
Incorporated: 11 July 2003
Net Worth: £5,506,194 *Total Assets:* £27,588,656
Registered Office: Kelly House, Fourth Way, Wembley, Middlesex, HA9 0LH
Activities: Other letting and operating of own or leased real estate
Parent: Kelly Communications Group Limited
Officers: James Patrick Bradley, Secretary; Timothy Joseph Kelly [1954] Director [Irish]

Kelly Rail Group Ltd
Incorporated: 24 January 2011 *Employees:* 65
Previous: Kelly Integrated Ltd
Net Worth: £5,026,420 *Total Assets:* £13,264,636
Registered Office: Kelly House, Fourth Way, Wembley, Middlesex, HA9 0LH
Activities: Other specialised construction activities n.e.c.
Major Shareholder: Timothy Joseph Kelly
Officers: James Patrick Bradley, Secretary; Timothy Patrick Kelly [2000] Director; Timothy Joseph Kelly [1954] Director [Irish]; Rosita Westropp-Bennett [1965] Finance Director [Irish]

Kelly Rail U.K. Ltd
Incorporated: 8 April 2002 *Employees:* 65
Previous: Kelly Integrated Transport Services Ltd
Net Worth: £2,908,631 *Total Assets:* £13,083,854
Registered Office: Kelly House, Fourth Way, Wembley, Middlesex, HA9 0LH
Activities: Construction of commercial buildings
Parent: Kelly Rail UK Services Ltd
Officers: James Patrick Bradley, Secretary; Timothy Joseph Kelly [1954] Director [Irish]

Kelly Services (UK) Limited
Incorporated: 23 September 1992 *Employees:* 176
Net Worth Deficit: £811,000 *Total Assets:* £35,458,000
Registered Office: Apple Market House, 17 Union Street, Kingston upon Thames, Surrey, KT1 1RR
Activities: Temporary employment agency activities
Parent: Kelly Services Inc
Officers: Richard Bradley, Secretary; Berendina Maria Bekhuis [1969] Director/VP and Operations Leader [Dutch]; Richard Bradley [1971] Managing Director; George Steven Corona [1958] Director/President and Chief Executive [American]; Olivier Thirot [1961] Director/Business Executive [Swiss]

Keltbray Aspire Limited
Incorporated: 16 November 2006 *Employees:* 155
Previous: Keltbray Aspire Rail Limited
Net Worth: £1,959,885 *Total Assets:* £12,870,681
Registered Office: St Andrew's House, Portsmouth Road, Esher, Surrey, KT10 9TA
Activities: Repair and maintenance of other transport equipment n.e.c.
Parent: Keltbray Ltd
Officers: Peter James Burnside, Secretary; Martin James Brown [1976] Director; Peter James Burnside [1965] Director/Chartered Accountant; Vincent Corrigan [1961] Director; Philip Reginald Price [1962] Director

Keltbray Group (Holdings) Limited
Incorporated: 20 April 1993 *Employees:* 1,393
Net Worth: £34,107,904 *Total Assets:* £177,407,840
Registered Office: St Andrew's House, Portsmouth Road, Esher, Surrey, KT10 9TA
Activities: Construction of other civil engineering projects n.e.c.
Parent: Keltbray Group Ltd
Officers: Peter James Burnside, Secretary; Vincent Corrigan [1961] Director; Paul Francis Deacy [1965] Director; Antony John Douglas [1963] Director; John Patrick Keehan [1955] Director/Accountant; Brendan Martin Kerr [1965] Director [Irish]; John Richard Price [1959] Director/Construction; Philip Reginald Price [1962] Director; Peter Konrad Suchy [1961] Director/Quantity Surveyor

Keltbray Group Limited
Incorporated: 28 October 2015 *Employees:* 1,393
Net Worth: £25,580,930 *Total Assets:* £176,649,984
Registered Office: St Andrews House, Portsmouth Road, Esher, Surrey, KT10 9TA
Activities: Activities of construction holding companies
Major Shareholder: Brendan Martin Kerr
Officers: Peter James Burnside, Secretary; Peter James Burnside [1965] Director/Chartered Accountant; John Patrick Keehan [1955] Director/Chartered Accountant; Brendan Martin Kerr [1965] Director [Irish]

Keltbray Limited
Incorporated: 23 August 1976 *Employees:* 882
Net Worth: £30,592,034 *Total Assets:* £135,913,392
Registered Office: St Andrew's House, Portsmouth Road, Esher, Surrey, KT10 9TA
Activities: Demolition
Parent: Keltbray Group (Holdings) Limited
Officers: Peter James Burnside, Secretary; Peter James Burnside [1965] Director/Chartered Accountant; Paul Francis Deacy [1965] Director; David Anthony Harrison [1982] Director; John Patrick Keehan [1955] Director/Accountant; Brendan Martin Kerr [1965] Director [Irish]; Andrew John McClafferty [1971] Director [Irish]; Holly Price [1979] Director; John Richard Price [1959] Director; Philip Reginald Price [1962] Director; Peter Konrad Suchy [1961] Director/Quantity Surveyor

Keltbray Plant Limited
Incorporated: 3 November 1982 *Employees:* 174
Net Worth: £5,312,376 *Total Assets:* £36,962,956
Registered Office: St Andrew's House, Portsmouth Road, Esher, Surrey, KT10 9TA
Activities: Renting and leasing of construction and civil engineering machinery and equipment
Parent: Keltbray Group (Holdings) Limited
Officers: Peter James Burnside, Secretary; Peter James Burnside [1965] Director/Chartered Accountant; Paul Francis Deacy [1965] Director; Brendan Martin Kerr [1965] Director [Irish]; John Richard Price [1959] Director

Kelvin Hughes Limited
Incorporated: 8 November 1971 *Employees:* 168
Net Worth: £83,414,000 *Total Assets:* £98,847,000
Registered Office: Voltage, Mollison Avenue, Enfield, Middlesex, EN3 7XQ
Activities: Manufacture of other electrical equipment
Shareholders: KKR & Co Inc; KH Finance Limited
Officers: David John Millard, Secretary; Russell Charles Gould [1963] Director/Chief Executive; David John Millard [1970] Finance Director

The Kemnal Academies Trust
Incorporated: 17 August 2010 *Employees:* 3,355
Net Worth: £232,782,000 *Total Assets:* £279,572,992
Registered Office: The Atkins Centre, Kemnal Technology College, Sevenoaks Way, Sidcup, Kent, DA14 5AA
Activities: Other education n.e.c.
Officers: Claire Louise Lee, Secretary; John Peter Atkins [1949] Director/Chief Executive; Gaenor Anne Bagley [1964] Director/Senior Partner; Peter Anthony Baines [1962] Director/Chief Executive; Aruna Anand Mehta [1962] Director/Retired Banker; Dr Karen Louise Roberts [1968] Director/Chief Executive Officer; Elaine Marie Thomas [1971] Global HR Director

Kenard Engineering Company Limited
Incorporated: 27 November 1964 *Employees:* 78
Net Worth: £3,310,123 *Total Assets:* £5,598,359
Registered Office: Green Street, Green Road, Dartford, Kent, DA1 1QE
Activities: Machining
Parent: Kenard Group Limited
Officers: Keith John Ellis, Secretary; Daniel Booth-Adams [1976] Director; Keith John Ellis [1957] Director/Company Secretary; Dr Raymond Reginald Ellis [1947] Technical Director; Neil Ransom [1966] Director

Kenard Group Limited
Incorporated: 9 February 2010 *Employees:* 155
Net Worth: £3,564,387,072 *Total Assets:* £7,799,197,184
Registered Office: Kenard Group Limited, Green Street, Green Road, Dartford, Kent, DA1 1QE
Activities: Activities of head offices
Shareholders: Keith John Ellis; Raymond Reginald Ellis
Officers: Keith John Ellis, Secretary; Matthew Donald Cornford [1952] Director; Keith John Ellis [1957] Director; Dr Raymond Reginald Ellis [1947] Director; John William Trueman [1961] Director/Business Consultant

Kendon Packaging Group Public Limited Company
Incorporated: 21 September 1933 *Employees:* 107
Net Worth: £23,068,222 *Total Assets:* £30,774,174
Registered Office: 7 Innova Way, Innova Park, Enfield, Middlesex, EN3 7FL
Activities: Packaging activities
Shareholders: Alistair John Kendon; Edwin Alexander Kendon
Officers: Alistair John Kendon, Secretary; Alistair John Kendon [1944] Executive Director; Edwin Alexander Kendon [1941] Executive Director; Frazer Alistair John Kendon [1977] Director; John Proctor [1966] Director

The Kendon Rope & Twine Co Limited
Incorporated: 27 March 1992 *Employees:* 17
Net Worth: £6,414,037 *Total Assets:* £6,759,090
Registered Office: 7 Innova Way, Innova Park, Enfield, Middlesex, EN3 7FL
Activities: Packaging activities
Shareholders: Alistair John Kendon; Edwin Alexander Kendon
Officers: Edwin Alexander Kendon, Secretary/Director; Alistair John Kendon [1944] Director; Edwin Alexander Kendon [1941] Director

Kennford Group Limited
Incorporated: 4 October 2016
Net Worth Deficit: £110,944 *Total Assets:* £7,421,653
Registered Office: 2nd Floor, Dunwoody House, 396 Kenton Road, Harrow, Middlesex, HA3 9DH
Activities: Activities of head offices
Officers: Roy Lawrence Hawkins [1951] Director; Kantesh Amarshi Popat [1960] Director; Rekha Popat [1967] Director

Kent Capital Ltd
Incorporated: 15 June 2011 *Employees:* 2
Net Worth: £101,723 *Total Assets:* £10,232,784
Registered Office: 36 Farnaby Road, Bromley, Kent, BR1 4BJ
Activities: Financial intermediation not elsewhere classified
Shareholder: David Kinane
Officers: David Kinane [1962] Director

Kent EHFA Holdco Limited
Incorporated: 10 December 2013 *Employees:* 4
Net Worth Deficit: £11,906,579 *Total Assets:* £48,288,048
Registered Office: Cowley Business Park, Cowley, Uxbridge, Middlesex, UB8 2AL
Activities: Activities of construction holding companies
Parent: PPDI Assetco 2 Limited
Officers: Rory Christie [1958] Director; John Stephen Gordon [1962] Director

Kent EHFA Projectco Limited
Incorporated: 10 December 2013 *Employees:* 2
Net Worth Deficit: £11,906,678 *Total Assets:* £49,430,544
Registered Office: Cowley Business Park, Cowley, Uxbridge, Middlesex, UB8 2AL
Activities: Development of building projects
Parent: Kent EHFA Holdco Limited
Officers: Rory Christie [1958] Director; John Stephen Gordon [1962] Director

Kentec Electronics Limited
Incorporated: 8 August 1985 *Employees:* 217
Net Worth: £6,356,782 *Total Assets:* £10,151,449
Registered Office: Unit 25-27 Fawkes Avenue, Questor, Dartford, Kent, DA1 1JQ
Activities: Manufacture of other electrical equipment
Parent: Hochiki Corporation
Officers: Rie Schembri Ishita, Secretary; Patrick Agbakpe [1964] Director [Japanese]; Tomoki Ikeda [1956] Director [Japanese]; Tomohiko Seki [1968] Director [Japanese]; Kevin Swann [1960] Managing Director; Junichi Uozumi [1969] Director [Japanese]

Kentex Group Limited
Incorporated: 7 September 1998 *Employees:* 34
Net Worth: £2,171,777 *Total Assets:* £6,074,723
Registered Office: Melbury House, 34 Southborough Road, Bickley, Bromley, Kent, BR1 2EB
Activities: Activities of head offices
Shareholders: Guiseppe Marinaro; Tina Marinaro
Officers: Tina Marinaro, Secretary; Giuseppe Marinaro [1957] Director/Electrician

Kenville Limited
Incorporated: 24 November 1983 *Employees:* 5
Net Worth: £7,252,786 *Total Assets:* £7,285,492
Registered Office: Kenville House, Spring Villa Road, Spring Villa Business Park, Edgware, Middlesex, HA8 7EB
Activities: Buying and selling of own real estate
Parent: Varosi Investments Ltd
Officers: Zela Photini Marina Gardiner, Secretary; Zela Photini Marina Gardiner [1989] Director/Property Manager

Kenwyn Solar Limited
Incorporated: 16 August 2013
Net Worth: £275,000 *Total Assets:* £8,403,000
Registered Office: Beaufort Court, Egg Farm Lane, Kings Langley, Herts, WD4 8LR
Activities: Production of electricity
Parent: European Investments Solar Holdings 2 Limited
Officers: Dominic James Hearth, Secretary; Steven William Hughes [1972] Global Support Services Director, UK&I - Commercial; Mitesh Raj Patel [1982] Director/Group Financial Controller; Tracy Jane Scott [1976] Director/Delivery Project Manager - New Technologies UK&I; Mark Christopher Wayment [1958] Director

Kerneos Holding Northern Europe Limited
Incorporated: 16 October 2007
Net Worth: £51,310,000 *Total Assets:* £90,405,000
Registered Office: Kerneos Ltd, Dolphin Way, Purfleet, Essex, RM19 1NZ
Activities: Non-trading company
Parent: Kerneos SA
Officers: Ian William Adamson, Secretary; Philippe Guy Pascal Bourg [1967] Director/Senior Vice President [French]

Kerry Foods Limited
Incorporated: 23 April 1991 *Employees:* 2,969
Net Worth: £62,272,828 *Total Assets:* £538,807,168
Registered Office: Thorpe Lea Manor, Thorpe Lea Road, Egham, Surrey, TW20 8HY
Activities: Production of meat and poultry meat products
Parent: Kerry Holdings (U.K.) Limited
Officers: Ronan Deasy, Secretary; Ronan Deasy [1964] Director/Accountant [Irish]; Trevor James Horan [1972] EMEA Country Compliance Director [Irish]; Marguerite Larkin [1971] Director/Chief Financial Officer [Irish]

Kerry Holdings (U.K.) Limited
Incorporated: 10 September 1982
Net Worth: £231,849,504 *Total Assets:* £382,593,792
Registered Office: Thorpe Lea Manor, Thorpe Lea Road, Egham, Surrey, TW20 8HY
Activities: Activities of head offices
Parent: Kerry Group PLC
Officers: Ronan Deasy, Secretary; Ronan Deasy [1964] Director/Accountant [Irish]; Duncan Everett [1971] Director; Cathal Henry Gunton [1977] Director/Accountant [Irish]; Trevor James Horan [1972] EMEA Country Compliance Director [Irish]; Marguerite Larkin [1971] Director/Chief Financial Officer [Irish]

Kesgrave Hall Limited
Incorporated: 28 August 2007 *Employees:* 84
Net Worth: £1,736,371 *Total Assets:* £7,611,809
Registered Office: 400 Dashwood Lang Road, Weybridge, Surrey, KT15 2HJ
Activities: Hotels and similar accommodation
Shareholders: Milsom Hotels Limited; Hills Residential Construction Limited
Officers: Jonathan Alan Hills, Secretary; Jonathan Alan Hills [1968] Director; Paul John Milsom [1964] Director

Kestates Limited
Incorporated: 5 November 2015
Net Worth Deficit: £1,129,770 *Total Assets:* £11,154,944
Registered Office: Portland House, 69-71 Wembley Hill Road, Wembley, Middlesex, HA9 8BU
Activities: Other letting and operating of own or leased real estate
Parent: Solai Holdings Limited
Officers: Bhupendra Shantilal Kansagra, Secretary; Bhupendra Shantilal Kansagra [1956] Director; Ramesh Shantilal Kansagra [1950] Director

The Keswick Enterprises Group Limited
Incorporated: 23 June 2004 *Employees:* 168
Net Worth: £6,239,616 *Total Assets:* £13,552,875
Registered Office: 19-20 Bourne Court, Southend Road, Woodford Green, Essex, IG8 8HD
Activities: Management consultancy activities other than financial management
Major Shareholder: John Harvey
Officers: Geoffrey Michael Gillo, Secretary/Executive; Geoffrey Michael Gillo [1952] Director/Executive; John Anthony Harvey [1935] Director/Consultant; Michael Wallis [1958] Director; Gavin David Withers [1965] Director/Consultant

Keswick European Holdings Limited
Incorporated: 10 October 2013
Net Worth: £9,794,534 *Total Assets:* £9,794,534
Registered Office: 19-20 Bourne Court, Southend Road, Woodford Green, Essex, IG8 8HD
Activities: Activities of other holding companies n.e.c.
Shareholders: Yusen Logistics Co., Ltd.; Nippon Yusen Kabushiki Kaisha
Officers: Kenichiro Miyamoto [1968] Director [Japanese]; Willem Emiel Pauwels [1955] Director [Belgian]

Kew College
Incorporated: 17 November 1982 *Employees:* 54
Net Worth: £6,047,621 *Total Assets:* £8,922,496
Registered Office: 24-26 Cumberland Road, Kew, Richmond, Surrey, TW9 3HQ
Activities: Primary education
Officers: Joanna Helen Brackenbury, Secretary; Serena Alexander [1954] Director/Reporting Inspector for ISI; Susan Mary Bourne [1958] Director/Retired; Aylsa Geeson [1958] Director/Retired; David John Imrie [1954] Director/Retired Bursar; Cllr Generald Alexander Richard McGregor [1948] Director/Organising Partner of Business Consultancy; Paula Helena Vanninen [1967] Director/Teacher [Finnish]

Kew Green (LRG Property) Limited
Incorporated: 6 August 2014 *Employees:* 2
Net Worth: £2,417,346 *Total Assets:* £9,317,905
Registered Office: 1 Towers Place, Eton Street, Richmond, Surrey, TW9 1EG
Activities: Hotels and similar accommodation
Parent: China National Travel Service Group Corporation
Officers: Jamie Andrew Lamb, Secretary; Jamie Andrew Lamb [1972] Director/Chartered Accountant; Alex Edward Pritchard [1976] Director

Kew Green (LRG1) Limited
Incorporated: 20 June 2014 *Employees:* 2
Net Worth: £108,336,608 *Total Assets:* £109,454,512
Registered Office: 1 Towers Place, Eton Street, Richmond, Surrey, TW9 1EG
Activities: Hotels and similar accommodation
Parent: China National Travel Service Group Corporation
Officers: Jamie Andrew Lamb, Secretary; Jamie Andrew Lamb [1972] Director/Chartered Accountant; Alex Edward Pritchard [1976] Director

Kew Green (LRG2) Limited
Incorporated: 3 July 2014
Net Worth: £106,638,624 *Total Assets:* £106,638,624
Registered Office: 1 Towers Place, Eton Street, Richmond, Surrey, TW9 1EG
Activities: Hotels and similar accommodation
Shareholders: China National Travel Service Group Corporation; China National Travel Service Group Corporation
Officers: Jamie Andrew Lamb, Secretary; Jamie Andrew Lamb [1972] Director/Chartered Accountant; Alex Edward Pritchard [1976] Director

Kew Green (Norwich Property) Limited
Incorporated: 10 March 2014 *Employees:* 2
Net Worth: £9,833,289 *Total Assets:* £10,366,609
Registered Office: 1 Towers Place, Eton Street, Richmond, Surrey, TW9 1EG
Activities: Hotels and similar accommodation
Parent: China National Travel Service Group Corporation
Officers: Jamie Andrew Lamb, Secretary; Jamie Andrew Lamb [1972] Director/Chartered Accountant; Alex Edward Pritchard [1976] Director

Kew Green (Square) Limited
Incorporated: 20 October 2004 *Employees:* 420
Net Worth Deficit: £19,904,456 *Total Assets:* £10,393,802
Registered Office: 1 Towers Place, Eton Street, Richmond, Surrey, TW9 1EG
Activities: Hotels and similar accommodation
Parent: China National Travel Service Group Corporation
Officers: Jameson Andrew Lamb, Secretary; Jameson Andrew Lamb [1972] Finance Director; Alex Edward Pritchard [1976] Director

Kew Green Group Limited
Incorporated: 7 May 2014 *Employees:* 110
Net Worth: £283,917,568 *Total Assets:* £420,263,904
Registered Office: 1 Towers Place, Eton Street, Richmond, Surrey, TW9 1EG
Activities: Hotels and similar accommodation
Parent: China National Travel Service Group Corporation
Officers: Jamie Andrew Lamb, Secretary; Jamie Andrew Lamb [1972] Director/Chartered Accountant; Alex Edward Pritchard [1976] Director

Kew Green Hotels (Ashford) Limited
Incorporated: 20 June 2014 *Employees:* 30
Net Worth: £1,312,383 *Total Assets:* £5,602,048
Registered Office: 1 Towers Place, Eton Street, Richmond, Surrey, TW9 1EG
Activities: Hotels and similar accommodation
Parent: China National Travel Service Group Corporation
Officers: Jamie Andrew Lamb, Secretary; Jamie Andrew Lamb [1972] Director/Chartered Accountant; Alex Edward Pritchard [1976] Director

Kew Green Hotels (Birmingham LRG1) Limited
Incorporated: 20 June 2014 *Employees:* 63
Net Worth: £2,455,389 *Total Assets:* £5,626,028
Registered Office: 1 Towers Place, Eton Street, Richmond, Surrey, TW9 1EG
Activities: Hotels and similar accommodation
Parent: China National Travel Service Group Corporation
Officers: Jamie Andrew Lamb, Secretary; Jamie Andrew Lamb [1972] Director/Chartered Accountant; Alex Edward Pritchard [1976] Director

Kew Green Hotels (Chester) Limited
Incorporated: 20 June 2014 *Employees:* 46
Net Worth: £2,176,538 *Total Assets:* £6,830,873
Registered Office: 1 Towers Place, Eton Street, Richmond, Surrey, TW9 1EG
Activities: Hotels and similar accommodation
Parent: China National Travel Service Group Corporation
Officers: Jamie Andrew Lamb, Secretary; Jamie Andrew Lamb [1972] Director/Chartered Accountant; Alex Edward Pritchard [1976] Director

Kew Green Hotels (Colchester) Limited
Incorporated: 20 June 2014 *Employees:* 43
Net Worth Deficit: £1,147,334 *Total Assets:* £12,676,711
Registered Office: 1 Towers Place, Eton Street, Richmond, Surrey, TW9 1EG
Activities: Hotels and similar accommodation
Parent: China National Travel Service Group Corporation
Officers: Jamie Andrew Lamb, Secretary; Jamie Andrew Lamb [1972] Director/Chartered Accountant; Alex Edward Pritchard [1976] Director

Kew Green Hotels (Derby/Nottingham) Limited
Incorporated: 20 June 2014 *Employees:* 41
Net Worth: £63,571 *Total Assets:* £7,246,036
Registered Office: 1 Towers Place, Eton Street, Richmond, Surrey, TW9 1EG
Activities: Hotels and similar accommodation
Parent: China National Travel Service Group Corporation
Officers: Jamie Andrew Lamb, Secretary; Jamie Andrew Lamb [1972] Director/Chartered Accountant; Alex Edward Pritchard [1976] Director

Kew Green Hotels (Gatwick) Limited
Incorporated: 22 June 2006 *Employees:* 46
Net Worth Deficit: £2,471,371 *Total Assets:* £17,682,292
Registered Office: 1 Towers Place, Eton Street, Richmond, Surrey, TW9 1EG
Activities: Hotels and similar accommodation
Parent: China National Travel Service Group Corporation
Officers: Jameson Andrew Lamb, Secretary; Jameson Andrew Lamb [1972] Director/Company Secretary; Alex Edward Pritchard [1976] Director

Kew Green Hotels (Haydock) Limited
Incorporated: 20 June 2014 *Employees:* 66
Net Worth: £1,679,599 *Total Assets:* £11,166,727
Registered Office: 1 Towers Place, Eton Street, Richmond, Surrey, TW9 1EG
Activities: Hotels and similar accommodation
Parent: China National Travel Service Group Corporation
Officers: Jamie Andrew Lamb, Secretary; Jamie Andrew Lamb [1972] Director/Chartered Accountant; Alex Edward Pritchard [1976] Director

Kew Green Hotels (Lancaster) Limited
Incorporated: 20 June 2014 *Employees:* 59
Net Worth: £1,679,696 *Total Assets:* £9,513,116
Registered Office: 1 Towers Place, Eton Street, Richmond, Surrey, TW9 1EG
Activities: Hotels and similar accommodation
Parent: China National Travel Service Group Corporation
Officers: Jamie Andrew Lamb, Secretary; Jamie Andrew Lamb [1972] Director/Chartered Accountant; Alex Edward Pritchard [1976] Director

Kew Green Hotels (Norwich LRG1) Limited
Incorporated: 20 June 2014 *Employees:* 42
Net Worth: £2,022,624 *Total Assets:* £6,351,171
Registered Office: 1 Towers Place, Eton Street, Richmond, Surrey, TW9 1EG
Activities: Hotels and similar accommodation
Parent: China National Travel Service Group Corporation
Officers: Jamie Andrew Lamb, Secretary; Jamie Andrew Lamb [1972] Director/Chartered Accountant; Alex Edward Pritchard [1976] Director

Kew Green Hotels (Portsmouth LRG1) Limited
Incorporated: 20 June 2014 *Employees:* 54
Net Worth: £1,260,104 *Total Assets:* £8,650,379
Registered Office: 1 Towers Place, Richmond, Surrey, TW9 1EG
Activities: Hotels and similar accommodation
Parent: China National Travel Service Group Corporation
Officers: Jamie Andrew Lamb, Secretary; Jamie Andrew Lamb [1972] Director/Chartered Accountant; Alex Edward Pritchard [1976] Director

Kew Green Hotels (Portsmouth) Limited
Incorporated: 22 May 2002 *Employees:* 18
Net Worth: £7,104,009 *Total Assets:* £7,918,901
Registered Office: 1 Towers Place, Eton Street, Richmond, Surrey, TW9 1EG
Activities: Hotels and similar accommodation
Parent: China National Travel Service Group Corporation
Officers: Jameson Andrew Lamb, Secretary; Jameson Andrew Lamb [1972] Finance Director; Alex Edward Pritchard [1976] Director

Kew Green Hotels (Speke) Limited
Incorporated: 26 March 2008
Net Worth Deficit: £10,275,547 *Total Assets:* £18,805,734
Registered Office: 1 Towers Place, Eton Street, Richmond, Surrey, TW9 1EG
Activities: Hotels and similar accommodation
Parent: China National Travel Service Group Corporation
Officers: Jameson Andrew Lamb, Secretary; Jameson Andrew Lamb [1972] Finance Director; Alex Edward Pritchard [1976] Director

Kew Green Hotels (Taunton) Limited
Incorporated: 20 June 2014 *Employees:* 62
Net Worth: £2,925,814 *Total Assets:* £5,082,451
Registered Office: 1 Towers Place, Eton Street, Richmond, Surrey, TW9 1EG
Activities: Hotels and similar accommodation
Parent: China National Travel Service Group Corporation
Officers: Jamie Andrew Lamb, Secretary; Jamie Andrew Lamb [1972] Director/Chartered Accountant; Alex Edward Pritchard [1976] Director

Kew Green Hotels (Warrington) Limited
Incorporated: 20 June 2014 *Employees:* 36
Net Worth: £1,056,315 *Total Assets:* £6,371,180
Registered Office: 1 Towers Place, Eton Street, Richmond, Surrey, TW9 1EG
Activities: Hotels and similar accommodation
Parent: China National Travel Service Group Corporation
Officers: Jamie Andrew Lamb, Secretary; Jamie Andrew Lamb [1972] Director/Chartered Accountant; Alex Edward Pritchard [1976] Director

Kew Green Hotels (York) Limited
Incorporated: 20 June 2014 *Employees:* 55
Net Worth: £380,520 *Total Assets:* £9,660,529
Registered Office: 1 Towers Place, Eton Street, Richmond, Surrey, TW9 1EG
Activities: Hotels and similar accommodation
Parent: China National Travel Service Group Corporation
Officers: Jamie Andrew Lamb, Secretary; Jamie Andrew Lamb [1972] Director/Chartered Accountant; Alex Edward Pritchard [1976] Director

Kew Green Hotels Limited
Incorporated: 15 May 2000 *Employees:* 2
Net Worth: £292,185,280 *Total Assets:* £297,879,168
Registered Office: 1 Towers Place, Eton Street, Richmond, Surrey, TW9 1EG
Activities: Hotels and similar accommodation
Parent: China National Travel Service Group Corporation
Officers: Jameson Andrew Lamb, Secretary; Jameson Andrew Lamb [1972] Finance Director; Alex Edward Pritchard [1976] Director

Kew Green Intermediate One Limited
Incorporated: 15 May 2014
Net Worth: £86,315,656 *Total Assets:* £87,110,312
Registered Office: 1 Towers Place, Eton Street, Richmond, Surrey, TW9 1EG
Activities: Hotels and similar accommodation
Parent: China National Travel Service Group Corporation
Officers: Jamie Andrew Lamb, Secretary; Jamie Andrew Lamb [1972] Director/Chartered Accountant; Alex Edward Pritchard [1976] Director

Kewbridge Trading Limited
Incorporated: 30 May 2014
Net Worth Deficit: £676,575 *Total Assets:* £5,639,458
Registered Office: 75 Park Lane, Croydon, Surrey, CR9 1XS
Activities: Development of building projects
Shareholders: Bejal Mehta; Arun Soni
Officers: Bejal Mehta [1969] Director; Arun Soni [1958] Director

Kewsaw Limited
Incorporated: 21 May 2009 *Employees:* 1,077
Net Worth: £9,694,000 *Total Assets:* £48,544,000
Registered Office: 159 Mortlake Road, Kew, Richmond, Surrey, TW9 4AW
Activities: Non-trading company
Major Shareholder: John Graham Robinson
Officers: Charles Spencer James Atterton, Secretary; Charles Spencer James Atterton [1956] Director; Belle Robinson [1964] Director; John Graham Robinson [1947] Director/Chairman

Kewstone Limited
Incorporated: 13 October 1994
Net Worth: £3,099,863 *Total Assets:* £5,381,082
Registered Office: Meridian House, 114 Oak Hill Crescent, Woodford Green, Essex, IG8 9PQ
Activities: Other letting and operating of own or leased real estate
Shareholders: Andrew Cushway; Denise Cushway; Mark Vernon Cushway; Caterina Tedeschi
Officers: Andrew Cushway, Secretary; Andrew Cushway [1958] Director; Denise Cushway [1960] Director; Mark Vernon Cushway [1955] Director/Business Manager; Caterina Tedeschi [1962] Director

Key Bidco Limited
Incorporated: 2 November 2011
Net Worth: £18,038,000 *Total Assets:* £38,796,000
Registered Office: Elmbrook House, 18-19 Station Road, Sunbury on Thames, Surrey, TW16 6SU
Activities: Non-life insurance
Parent: Key Midco Limited
Officers: James Richard Hastie Cumming [1980] Finance Director; Alan David Maynard [1965] Director

Key Mail (UK) Limited
Incorporated: 21 April 1999 *Employees:* 12
Net Worth: £2,476,589 *Total Assets:* £6,581,680
Registered Office: Unit 12 Saxon Way, Harmondsworth, West Drayton, Middlesex, UB7 0LW
Activities: Postal activities under universal service obligation
Shareholders: Harphjan Singh Rooprah; Jaswinder Kaur Rooprah
Officers: Kaliya Perumal Servoo Ravishanker, Secretary; Harphjan Singh Rooprah [1963] Director; Jaswinder Kaur Rooprah [1963] Director

Key Midco Limited
Incorporated: 14 December 2011
Net Worth Deficit: £40,731,000 *Total Assets:* £36,345,000
Registered Office: Elmbrook House, 18-19 Station Road, Sunbury on Thames, Surrey, TW16 6SU
Activities: Non-life insurance
Parent: Key Topco Lmited
Officers: James Richard Hastie Cumming [1980] Finance Director; Alan David Maynard [1965] Director

H.H.Keys Estates Limited
Incorporated: 27 November 1957 *Employees:* 2
Net Worth: £6,154,078 *Total Assets:* £6,454,158
Registered Office: 27 St Albans Crescent, Woodford Green, Essex, IG8 9EJ
Activities: Buying and selling of own real estate
Shareholder: John Richard Keys
Officers: John Richard Keys, Secretary; John Richard Keys [1932] Director/Estate Manager; Roger Hayman Keys [1960] Director/Surveyor

KFG Holdings Limited
Incorporated: 6 October 2010
Net Worth: £5,615,000 *Total Assets:* £5,615,000
Registered Office: 100-102 High Street, Ruislip, Middlesex, HA4 8LS
Activities: Activities of other holding companies n.e.c.
Officers: Abdul-Mohsen Mohsen Al Homaizi [1967] Director [Kuwaiti]; Madam Fadwa Al Homaizi [1957] Director [Kuwaiti]

KFG Quickserve Limited
Incorporated: 6 July 2005 *Employees:* 832
Net Worth: £1,635,000 *Total Assets:* £11,356,000
Registered Office: 100-102 High Street, Ruislip, Middlesex, HA4 8LS
Activities: Other retail sale of food in specialised stores
Officers: Abdul-Mohsen Mohsen Al Homaizi [1967] Director [Kuwaiti]; Madam Fadwa Al Homaizi [1957] Director [Kuwaiti]

KFG Restaurants Limited
Incorporated: 3 September 2007 *Employees:* 21
Net Worth Deficit: £3,303,000 *Total Assets:* £9,961,000
Registered Office: 100-102 High Street, Ruislip, Middlesex, HA4 8LS
Activities: Licenced restaurants
Officers: Madam Fadwa Al Homaizi [1957] Director [Kuwaiti]

KFM Holdings Limited
Incorporated: 8 January 2008
Previous: Timbmet Holdings Limited
Net Worth: £8,681,114 *Total Assets:* £10,487,314
Registered Office: Suite 1, Leavesden Park, Hercules Way, Leavesden, Watford, Herts, WD25 7GS
Activities: Wholesale of wood, construction materials and sanitary equipment
Shareholders: Simon Lewis Fineman; Evelyn Frances Kemp; Ashwani Malham
Officers: Simon Lewis Fineman [1959] Operations Director; Dr Evelyn Frances Kemp [1961] Director; Ashwani Malhan [1968] Director; Sunit Malhan [1962] Director

KGM Underwriting Services Limited
Incorporated: 24 January 2017
Net Worth Deficit: £914,559 *Total Assets:* £29,555,680
Registered Office: 2nd Floor, St James House, 27-43 Eastern Road, Romford, Essex, RM1 3NH
Activities: Activities of insurance agents and brokers
Parent: Trafalgar Bidco Limited
Officers: Andrew Galbraith, Secretary; James Maxwell Carruthers [1954] Director; Andrew James Galbraith [1970] Director; Clive Adam Nathan [1965] Director; Matthew James Puttick [1979] Director; Carl Anthony Shuker [1961] Director

KGN Developments Limited
Incorporated: 19 August 2015 *Employees:* 1
Net Worth: £192,087 *Total Assets:* £5,520,146
Registered Office: The Old Barn, off Wood Street, Swanley Village, Kent, BR8 7PA
Activities: Development of building projects
Major Shareholder: Thomas Joseph Doran
Officers: Thomas Joseph Doran [1960] Director/Property Developer [Irish]

KH Finance Limited
Incorporated: 5 October 2007
Net Worth Deficit: £45,944,000 *Total Assets:* £52,648,000
Registered Office: Voltage, Mollison Avenue, Enfield, Middlesex, EN3 7XQ
Activities: Activities of head offices
Shareholders: KKR & Co Inc; KH Finance No.2 Limited
Officers: David John Millard, Secretary; Russell Charles Gould [1963] Director/Chief Executive; David John Millard [1970] Finance Director

KH Finance No.2 Limited
Incorporated: 18 July 2013
Net Worth: £17,962,000 *Total Assets:* £25,071,000
Registered Office: Voltage, Mollison Avenue, Enfield, Middlesex, EN3 7XQ
Activities: Activities of head offices
Shareholders: KKR & Co Inc; KH Holdco Limited
Officers: David John Millard, Secretary; Russell Charles Gould [1963] Director/Chief Executive; David John Millard [1970] Finance Director

KH Holdco Limited
Incorporated: 5 October 2007
Net Worth: £43,257,000 *Total Assets:* £50,366,000
Registered Office: Voltage, Mollison Avenue, Enfield, Middlesex, EN3 7XQ
Activities: Activities of head offices
Officers: David John Millard, Secretary; Russell Charles Gould [1963] Director/Chief Executive; David John Millard [1970] Finance Director; Erwin Manfred Paulus [1961] Director/Head of Radar [German]; Joerg Sigurd Ristow [1957] Director [German]; Christoph Erich Ruffner [1977] Director [German]

Khakharia Properties Limited
Incorporated: 21 August 2003
Net Worth: £1,566,760 *Total Assets:* £7,498,665
Registered Office: 451 Alexandra Avenue, Rayners Lane, Harrow, Middlesex, HA2 9SE
Activities: Buying and selling of own real estate
Shareholders: Paresh Khakharia; Rashmi Khakharia
Officers: Rashmi Khakharia, Secretary; Paresh Khakharia [1960] Director/Estate Agent Property Investor; Rashmi Khakharia [1963] Director/Estate Agent

Khosla Investments Limited
Incorporated: 17 January 2008
Net Worth: £5,518,611 *Total Assets:* £11,966,858
Registered Office: The White House, Cranford Lane, Harlington, Middlesex, UB3 5HD
Activities: Buying and selling of own real estate
Major Shareholder: Rajesh Kumar Khosla
Officers: Rajesh Kumar Khosla, Secretary/Director; Rajesh Kumar Khosla [1949] Director/Property Investor

Kia Motors (UK) Limited
Incorporated: 12 April 2002 *Employees:* 223
Net Worth: £94,641,000 *Total Assets:* £478,931,008
Registered Office: Walton Green, Walton on Thames, Surrey, KT12 1FJ
Activities: Sale of new cars and light motor vehicles
Officers: Paul Jonathan Philpott, Secretary; Woojai Kim [1973] Director [South Korean]; Jin Young Park [1977] Director [South Korean]; Paul Jonathan Philpott [1966] Director

Kidde Finance Limited
Incorporated: 16 August 2000
Net Worth: £25,440,000 *Total Assets:* £157,560,000
Registered Office: 1st Floor, Ash House, Littleton Road, Ashford, Middlesex, TW15 1TZ
Activities: Other business support service activities n.e.c.
Parent: Kidde UK
Officers: Robert Sloss, Secretary; Laura Wilcock, Secretary; Neil Andrew Vincent Gregor MacGregor [1955] Director/Accounting and Controls Manager; Robert John Sloss [1967] Director/Solicitor

Kidde International Limited
Incorporated: 21 December 2000
Net Worth: £1,022,465,024 *Total Assets:* £1,084,392,960
Registered Office: 1st Floor, Ash House, Littleton Road, Ashford, Middlesex, TW15 1TZ
Activities: Activities of head offices
Parent: Goodrich Aftermarket Services Limited
Officers: Robert Sloss, Secretary; Laura Wilcock, Secretary; Neil Andrew Vincent Gregor MacGregor [1955] Director/Accounting and Controls Manager; Robert John Sloss [1967] Director/Solicitor

Kidde Limited
Incorporated: 24 July 2000
Net Worth: £92,981,000 *Total Assets:* £93,275,000
Registered Office: 1st Floor, Ash House, Littleton Road, Ashford, Middlesex, TW15 1TZ
Activities: Activities of head offices
Parent: Goodrich Inertial Limited
Officers: Robert Sloss, Secretary; Laura Wilcock, Secretary; Neil Andrew Vincent Gregor MacGregor [1955] Director/Accounting and Controls Manager; Robert John Sloss [1967] Director/Solicitor

Kidde Safety Europe Limited
Incorporated: 7 March 2000 *Employees:* 20
Net Worth: £236,000 *Total Assets:* £9,110,000
Registered Office: 1st Floor, Ash House, Littleton Road, Ashford, Middlesex, TW15 1TZ
Activities: Manufacture of other electrical equipment
Parent: United Technologies Holdings Limited
Officers: Frederick Patrick Collins [1961] Managing Director; Paul Anthony Fraipont [1964] Director/Vice President and General Manager [American]

Kidde UK
Incorporated: 22 June 2001
Net Worth: £619,134,016 *Total Assets:* £761,939,968
Registered Office: 1st Floor, Ash House, Littleton Road, Ashford, Middlesex, TW15 1TZ
Activities: Activities of head offices
Parent: Goodrich Aftermarket Services Limited
Officers: Robert Sloss, Secretary; Laura Wilcock, Secretary; Neil Andrew Vincent Gregor MacGregor [1955] Director/Accounting and Controls Manager

Kidiliz Group UK Ltd
Incorporated: 3 June 1998 *Employees:* 42
Previous: Groupe Zannier UK Limited
Net Worth: £5,574,379 *Total Assets:* £9,829,816
Registered Office: Warren Place, Birch Vale, Cobham, Surrey, KT11 2PX
Activities: Retail sale of clothing in specialised stores
Officers: Michael Alan Farndon, Secretary/Accountant; Pascal Claude Gardin [1970] Director [French]; Loic Rene Francis Josse [1965] Director [French]

Kidspace Adventures Holdings Limited
Incorporated: 30 September 2011 *Employees:* 236
Net Worth: £782,982 *Total Assets:* £7,702,626
Registered Office: Horton Park Childrens Farm, Horton Lane, Epsom, Surrey, KT19 8PT
Activities: Other amusement and recreation activities n.e.c.
Shareholders: Nicholas Simon Vully de Candole; Richard Farley
Officers: Richard Farley, Secretary; Paul Joseph Beaumont [1964] Director; Mark Andrew Vully de Candole [1953] Director; Nicholas Simon Vully de Candole [1969] Director; Richard Miles Farley [1969] Director

Kidsprog Limited
Incorporated: 24 November 1992
Net Worth: £63,200,000 *Total Assets:* £68,727,000
Registered Office: Grant Way, Isleworth, Middlesex, TW7 5QD
Activities: Activities of head offices
Parent: Sky Ventures Limited
Officers: Christopher Jon Taylor, Secretary; Karl Holmes [1973] Director/Finance Professional; Colin Robert Jones [1964] Director; Christopher Jon Taylor [1971] Director/Company Secretary

Killinchy Aerospace Holdings Limited
Incorporated: 5 November 1965 *Employees:* 977
Net Worth: £270,612,992 *Total Assets:* £301,856,000
Registered Office: Aircraft Works, Lower Road, Higher Denham, Uxbridge, Middlesex, UB9 5AJ
Activities: Manufacture of metal structures and parts of structures
Officers: William John Henderson Deeves, Secretary; Amanda Barrington [1975] Director; Charles Merrick Burrell [1981] Director; Daniel David Hess [1979] Director; Andrew James Martin [1973] Director; James William Martin [1942] Director; John Stephen Martin [1942] Director; Robert John Martin [1969] Director/Engineer; Robert Keith Morgan [1975] Director; Ian Steele [1956] Director/Chartered Accountant; Mark Thomas Wearden [1957] Director/Certified Accountant

Killoughery Holdings Limited
Incorporated: 23 January 1997 *Employees:* 32
Net Worth: £9,783,366 *Total Assets:* £23,543,790
Registered Office: 43a Willow Lane, Mitcham, Surrey, CR4 4NA
Activities: Construction of other civil engineering projects n.e.c.
Major Shareholder: George Joseph Killoughery
Officers: Joseph Killoughery, Secretary; Joseph George Killoughery [1965] Director/Manager; Mary Killoughery [1932] Director/Manager

George Killoughery Limited
Incorporated: 20 May 1965 *Employees:* 32
Net Worth: £7,506,368 *Total Assets:* £13,998,409
Registered Office: 43a Willow Lane, Mitcham, Surrey, CR4 4NA
Activities: Other specialised construction activities n.e.c.
Parent: Killoughery Holdings Limited
Officers: Joseph Killoughery, Secretary; George Joseph Killoughery [1965] Director/Manager; Mary Killoughery [1932] Director/Secretary

Killoughery Properties Limited
Incorporated: 4 November 2004
Net Worth: £2,353,219 *Total Assets:* £9,851,207
Registered Office: 43a Willow Lane, Mitcham, Surrey, CR4 4NA
Activities: Buying and selling of own real estate
Parent: Killoughery Holdings Limited
Officers: Joseph Killoughery, Secretary; Maura Doran [1960] Director/Public Servant; Joseph George Killoughery [1965] Director

Kilmorie Investments LLP
Incorporated: 4 December 2006
Net Worth: £1,319,501 *Total Assets:* £8,648,531
Registered Office: 3rd Floor, Sterling House, Langston Road, Loughton, Essex, IG10 3TS

Kilofrequency Limited
Incorporated: 22 November 2013 *Employees:* 71
Net Worth: £1,286,795 *Total Assets:* £6,988,339
Registered Office: Unit D, Chesham Close, Cedar Road, Romford, Essex, RM7 7PJ
Activities: Activities of other holding companies n.e.c.
Shareholders: John Lewis Innocent; Carolyn Phyllis Innocent
Officers: Stephen Paul Attridge [1954] Director/Engineer; John Lewis Innocent [1941] Director/Engineer; Vincent Leatt [1954] Director/Electronics Engineer; Mark John Treadgold [1972] Director; Stephen Westlake [1958] Director

Kimal Holdings Limited
Incorporated: 17 January 2012 *Employees:* 314
Net Worth: £18,783,000 *Total Assets:* £25,082,000
Registered Office: Kimal, Arundel Road, Uxbridge, Middlesex, UB8 2SA
Activities: Activities of head offices
Shareholder: James Anthony Martin
Officers: Anthony William Wilson, Secretary; Neil Duncan Eaton [1946] Director; Joseph Frederick Fleischhaker [1954] Director [American]; Geoffrey Charles Redmond Morris [1957] Director; Mark Ronald Pettitt [1961] Director; Alan Christopher Press [1953] Director; Andrew George Press [1966] Director; Matthew James Press [1978] Director; Anthony William Wilson [1956] Finance Director

Kimal PLC
Incorporated: 19 November 1964 *Employees:* 273
Net Worth: £15,027,000 *Total Assets:* £20,453,000
Registered Office: Kimal, Arundel Road, Uxbridge, Middlesex, UB8 2SA
Activities: Manufacture of medical and dental instruments and supplies
Parent: Kimal Group PLC
Officers: Anthony William Wilson, Secretary; Damian Paul Donnelly [1976] Business Unit Director; Stephen Cavan Eccles [1968] Operations Director; Claire Louise Nicholson [1983] Sales Director; Mark Ronald Pettitt [1961] Managing Director; Alan Christopher Press [1953] Director; Matthew James Press [1978] Director; Anthony William Wilson [1956] Director

Kimberley Capital Limited
Incorporated: 23 June 2017
Net Worth: £8,757 *Total Assets:* £9,447,750
Registered Office: Kimberley House, 31 Burnt Oak Broadway, Edgware, Middlesex, HA8 5LD
Activities: Other credit granting n.e.c.
Parent: Deekay Holdings (UK) Limited
Officers: Khimchand Hansraj Chandaria [1935] Director; Bhavik Patel [1984] Director; Neel Mahendra Shah [1974] Director

Kimberley Peer Ventures One Ltd
Incorporated: 1 February 2017
Net Worth Deficit: £1,942 *Total Assets:* £6,158,808
Registered Office: Kimberley House, 31 Burnt Oak Broadway, Edgware, Middlesex, HA8 5LD
Activities: Financial intermediation not elsewhere classified
Officers: Khimchand Hansraj Chandaria [1935] Director; Bhavik Patel [1984] Director; Neel Mahendra Shah [1974] Director

Kimberley Property Investments Limited
Incorporated: 4 December 2001 *Employees:* 2
Net Worth: £3,143,298 *Total Assets:* £8,743,523
Registered Office: Kimberley House, 31 Burnt Oak Broadway, Edgware, Middlesex, HA8 5LD
Activities: Other letting and operating of own or leased real estate
Officers: Bipin Shah, Secretary; Bipin Mohanlal Shah [1958] Director/Certified Chartered Accountant; Hiren Hasmukh Shah [1979] Director/Accountant

Kimberley Real Estate Limited
Incorporated: 11 October 2016
Net Worth: £1,173,513 *Total Assets:* £5,768,360
Registered Office: 19-20 Bourne Court, Southend Road, Woodford Green, Essex, IG8 8HD
Activities: Buying and selling of own real estate
Parent: Spring Properties (UK) Holdings Limited
Officers: Joel Wider [1980] Director/Business Person

Kinedexe UK Limited
Incorporated: 17 July 2014 *Employees:* 7
Net Worth: £19,799,890 *Total Assets:* £20,690,110
Registered Office: 65 Delamere Road, Hayes, Middlesex, UB4 0NN
Activities: Other professional, scientific and technical activities n.e.c.
Major Shareholder: Anil Kumar Sharma
Officers: Jagjeet Kaur Ahluwalia [1962] Director/Manager; Anil Kumar Sharma [1952] Director; Sneh Sharma [1956] Director/Manager

Kinetic IT Limited
Incorporated: 16 March 2010 *Employees:* 18
Net Worth: £5,164,633 *Total Assets:* £5,933,898
Registered Office: The Base, Dartford Business Park, Victoria Road, Dartford, Kent, DA1 5FS
Activities: Wired telecommunications activities
Major Shareholder: Tommy Micheal Cella
Officers: Tommy Micheal Cella [1979] Director; Stuart Packer [1973] Director

W.J.King (Garages) Limited
Incorporated: 14 January 1960 *Employees:* 365
Net Worth: £35,305,592 *Total Assets:* £49,264,216
Registered Office: 70-88 Park View Road, Welling, Kent, DA16 1SF
Activities: Sale of new cars and light motor vehicles
Shareholder: William John King
Officers: Jane Atkins, Secretary; Olivia King [1950] Director/Administrator; William John King [1992] Director/Administrator; William John King [1955] Director/Administrator

W.D.King Limited
Incorporated: 25 February 1935 *Employees:* 4
Net Worth: £6,598,792 *Total Assets:* £13,699,625
Registered Office: 120 High Street, Edgware, Middlesex, HA8 7EL
Activities: Development of building projects
Parent: Kingrose Limited
Officers: Jeffrey Lionel Rosenbaum [1940] Director; Joshua Da Silva Rosenbaum [1986] Director

King Street Manchester Holdings LLP
Incorporated: 19 October 2015
Net Worth: £6,009,403 *Total Assets:* £6,009,403
Registered Office: Aprirose House, 48a High Street, Edgware, Middlesex, HA8 7EQ
Officers: Manish Mansukhlal Gudka [1970] Member; Gareth Jones [1973] Member

King Street Manchester Property LLP
Incorporated: 21 October 2015
Net Worth: £8,343,913 *Total Assets:* £18,640,838
Registered Office: Aprirose House, 48a High Street, Edgware, Middlesex, HA8 7EQ

King's House School Trust (Richmond) Limited
Incorporated: 17 September 1957 *Employees:* 122
Net Worth: £8,998,560 *Total Assets:* £11,358,082
Registered Office: 68 King's Road, Richmond, Surrey, TW10 6ES
Activities: Primary education
Officers: Kim Golightly, Secretary; David James Barbour [1966] Director/Investment Manager; Nicholas John Collins [1962] Director; John Julian Davison [1960] Director/Private Equity Partner; Jennifer Ann George [1965] Director/Self-Employed HR Consultant; Brian Richard Girvan [1978] Director/Surmaster; Dr Stephen Harrison [1976] Director/Housemaster; Sarah Ann Hendry [1977] Director/Teacher; Christine Mary Laverty [1961] Director/Accountant [Australian]; James Wintringham Owen [1950] Director/Retired; Jane Shalders [1965] Director/Barrister; Catherine Urch [1965] Director/Medical Practitioner; Jeffrey Peter Van Der Eems [1962] Director; Doctor Richard Churchill Ward [1957] Director

Kingpin Communications Limited
Incorporated: 11 June 1997 *Employees:* 20
Net Worth: £678,777 *Total Assets:* £5,484,196
Registered Office: Ashcome House, 5 The Crescent, Leatherhead, Surrey, KT22 8DY
Activities: Advertising agencies
Parent: Kingpin Communications Holdings Limited
Officers: Mirza Fur, Company Secretary/Director; James Foulkes [1972] Director; Mirza Adnan Fur [1972] Company Secretary/Director

Kingrose Limited
Incorporated: 27 January 1992 *Employees:* 2
Net Worth Deficit: £5,287,017 *Total Assets:* £5,572,549
Registered Office: 120 High Street, Edgware, Middlesex, HA8 7EL
Activities: Financial intermediation not elsewhere classified
Shareholders: Jeffrey Lionel Rosenbaum; Barry Akin
Officers: Joshua Da Silva Rosenbaum [1986] Director; Jeffrey Lionel Rosenbaum [1940] Director

Kings Langley School
Incorporated: 29 October 2012 *Employees:* 163
Net Worth: £24,540,424 *Total Assets:* £26,733,576
Registered Office: Kings Langley School, Love Lane, Kings Langley, Herts, WD4 9HN
Activities: General secondary education
Officers: Diane Marie Bell, Secretary; David Bernard Ash Butler [1966] Bank Director; Graham James Craggs [1965] Director/Chartered Surveyor; Dawn Helfgott [1968] Director/Financial Advisor; Mark John Hutchings [1968] Director; Gary Michael Lewis [1957] Director/Headteacher; Mark Morant [1968] Director/Head of Supply Chain; Joanne Clare O'Sullivan [1974] Director/Customer Service Executive; Simon Matthew Setterfield [1964] Commercial Director; Frances Stickley [1956] Director/Facilities Management; Lisa Welling [1972] Franchise Director; Angela Westlake [1956] Director/Business Support Manager; Simon Christopher Wood [1963] Director/Chartered Surveyor; Helen Young [1985] Director/Solicitor

Geo. Kingsbury Holdings Limited
Incorporated: 28 September 1956 *Employees:* 302
Net Worth: £38,828,804 *Total Assets:* £56,679,628
Registered Office: 45 Portsmouth Road, Cobham, Surrey, KT11 1JQ
Activities: Activities of head offices
Shareholders: Christopher Kingsbury; Michael George Kingsbury
Officers: Mark William Kingsbury, Secretary; Christopher Kingsbury [1937] Director; Mark William Kingsbury [1964] Director; Michael George Kingsbury [1934] Director; Peter James Kingsbury [1967] Director; Richard George Kingsbury [1963] Director

Geo. Kingsbury Machine Tools Limited
Incorporated: 7 March 1963 *Employees:* 49
Net Worth: £10,559,175 *Total Assets:* £21,813,844
Registered Office: 45 Portsmouth Road, Cobham, Surrey, KT11 1JQ
Activities: Wholesale of machine tools
Parent: Geo Kingsbury Holdings Ltd
Officers: Mark William Kingsbury, Secretary; Christopher Kingsbury [1937] Director; Michael George Kingsbury [1934] Director; Peter James Kingsbury [1967] Director; Richard George Kingsbury [1963] Director/Engineer; David John McGrath [1957] Finance Director

Kingscote Construction Services Ltd
Incorporated: 15 November 2006 *Employees:* 11
Net Worth: £4,724,446 *Total Assets:* £8,677,842
Registered Office: Unit 4 Oaks Court, Warwick Road, Borehamwood, Herts, WD6 1GS
Activities: Renting and leasing of other machinery, equipment and tangible goods n.e.c.
Major Shareholder: Brian Quinlan Morrisroe
Officers: Gerard Marapao, Secretary; Brian Quinlan Morrisroe [1955] Director

Kingsmead School
Incorporated: 17 September 2010 *Employees:* 168
Net Worth: £12,429,796 *Total Assets:* £13,411,465
Registered Office: 196 Southbury Road, Enfield, Middlesex, EN1 1YQ
Activities: General secondary education
Officers: Andrea Gajadhar, Secretary; Alok Kumar Agrawal [1945] Director; David Philip Boothroyd [1947] Director/Teacher; Denise Chan [1969] Director/Governor [Malaysian]; Joanne Eaton [1974] Director/Governor; Rhodoulla Flindall [1978] Director/Teacher; Carmien Gharbaoui [1974] Director/Governor; Ken Gregory [1936] Director/Retired; Usman Haroon [1994] Director/Volunteer; Dr Rachel Andromache Harris [1969] Director/Governor; Randolph Hoyte [1972] Director/Teacher; David Medway [1980] Director/Headteacher; Andrew Calder Nicholas [1955] Director; Samantha Ojokor [1967] Director/Governor; Kim Pickering [1958] Director/Retired; Lesley Pitcher [1962] Director/Data Manager; George Rhoden [1961] Director/Retired; Angela Velasco [1988] Director/Teacher; Deborah Ann Watson [1960] Director/Governor

Kingston Bidco Limited
Incorporated: 19 November 2013
Net Worth Deficit: £8,108,360 *Total Assets:* £60,137,024
Registered Office: Avantia House, 29 Thames Street, Kingston upon Thames, Surrey, KT1 1PH
Activities: Non-trading company
Parent: Kingston Midco Limited
Officers: Mark Robert Eastham [1972] Director; Shahid Mahmood [1969] Director

Kingston Digital Europe Co LLP
Incorporated: 6 April 2013 *Employees:* 54
Net Worth: £40,691,228 *Total Assets:* £46,547,424
Registered Office: Kingston Court, Brooklands Close, Sunbury on Thames, Middlesex, TW16 7EP

Kingston Grammar School
Incorporated: 22 November 1999 *Employees:* 214
Net Worth: £14,759,000 *Total Assets:* £28,075,000
Registered Office: Kingston Grammar School, London Road, Kingston upon Thames, Surrey, KT2 6PY
Activities: General secondary education
Officers: Lorraine Tanya Adam [1968] Director/Marketing Consultant; Mark Annesley [1956] Director/Chartered Accountant; Catherine Julie Chevallier [1966] Director/HR Manager; Duncan Paul David Combe [1979] Director/Management Consultant; Michael Dohler [1975] Director/University Professor [German]; Andrew David Evans [1979] Director/Accountant; Jatinder Singh Harchowal [1969] Director/Pharmacist; Nima Khandan-Nia [1968] Director/Manager; Frances Claire Le Grys [1964] Director/Lawyer; Robert George O'Dowd [1961] Director/Chief Executive; Diana Rose [1955] Director/Teacher; Kerstin Sonnemann [1966] Director/Architect [German]

Kingston Lodge Hotel Limited
Incorporated: 27 October 2009 *Employees:* 43
Net Worth: £2,755,296 *Total Assets:* £9,400,311
Registered Office: 94 Kingston Hill, Kingston upon Thames, Surrey, KT2 7NP
Activities: Hotels and similar accommodation
Parent: Brook Hotels Group Limited
Officers: Mervyn Humphries, Secretary; Ashok Kumar Ummat [1953] Director; Umesh Ummat [1957] Director

Kingston Midco Limited
Incorporated: 19 November 2013
Net Worth: £2,753,331 *Total Assets:* £40,253,276
Registered Office: Avantia House, 29 Thames Street, Kingston upon Thames, Surrey, KT1 1PH
Activities: Non-trading company
Parent: Kingston Topco Limited
Officers: Mark Robert Eastham [1972] Director; Shahid Mahmood [1969] Director

Kingston Technology Europe Co LLP
Incorporated: 8 April 2013 *Employees:* 195
Net Worth: £50,012,828 *Total Assets:* £66,927,244
Registered Office: Kingston Court, Brooklands Close, Sunbury on Thames, Middlesex, TW16 7EP

Kingston Topco Limited
Incorporated: 18 November 2013 *Employees:* 124
Net Worth Deficit: £7,373,254 *Total Assets:* £48,750,108
Registered Office: Avantia House, 29 Thames Street, Kingston upon Thames, Surrey, KT1 1PH
Activities: Non-trading company
Officers: Stephen David Ashton [1963] Director; Mark Robert Eastham [1972] Director; Shahid Mahmood [1969] Director; Paul Dominic Ian McCreadie [1979] Director; David Jonathan Haddon Walker [1965] Director

Kingston University Service Company Limited
Incorporated: 5 December 1995 *Employees:* 212
Net Worth: £2,740,000 *Total Assets:* £7,337,000
Registered Office: Kings' Stone House, 12 High Street, Kingston upon Thames, Surrey, KT1 1HD
Activities: Management of real estate on a fee or contract basis
Parent: Kingston University Higher Education Corporation
Officers: Keith Gerard Brennan [1968] Director/Registrar and University Secretary; Heather Joanne Woods [1967] Finance Director

Kingsway Asset Co Limited
Incorporated: 10 September 2014
Net Worth Deficit: £3,769,037 *Total Assets:* £177,003,936
Registered Office: 505 Pinner Road, Harrow, Middlesex, HA2 6EH
Activities: Activities of other holding companies n.e.c.
Officers: Rishi Ramesh Sachdev [1976] Director; Uday Vyas [1978] Director

Kingsway Hall Hotel Limited
Incorporated: 10 September 2001
Net Worth: £51,107,112 *Total Assets:* £51,120,312
Registered Office: 505 Pinner Road, Harrow, Middlesex, HA2 6EH
Activities: Hotels and similar accommodation
Officers: Rishi Ramesh Sachdev [1976] Director; Uday Vyas [1978] Director

Kingsway Mezz Co Limited
Incorporated: 10 September 2014
Net Worth: £1,357,354 *Total Assets:* £54,069,952
Registered Office: 505 Pinner Road, Harrow, Middlesex, HA2 6EH
Activities: Activities of other holding companies n.e.c.
Officers: Rishi Ramesh Sachdev [1976] Director; Uday Vyas [1978] Director

Kingsway Mezz Hold Co Limited
Incorporated: 10 September 2014 *Employees:* 88
Net Worth Deficit: £2,098,473 *Total Assets:* £131,986,816
Registered Office: 505 Pinner Road, Harrow, Middlesex, HA2 6EH
Activities: Activities of other holding companies n.e.c.
Officers: Rishi Ramesh Sachdev [1976] Director; Uday Vyas [1978] Director

Kingsway Senior Hold Co Limited
Incorporated: 10 September 2014
Net Worth Deficit: £23,400 *Total Assets:* £53,024,576
Registered Office: 505 Pinner Road, Harrow, Middlesex, HA2 6EH
Activities: Activities of other holding companies n.e.c.
Officers: Rishi Ramesh Sachdev [1976] Director; Uday Vyas [1978] Director

Kingswood Corporation Limited
Incorporated: 20 December 1996 *Employees:* 116
Net Worth: £6,219,887 *Total Assets:* £8,305,064
Registered Office: Westgate Chambers, 8a Elmpark Road, Pinner, Middlesex, HA5 3LA
Activities: Activities of head offices
Shareholder: Malcolm John Harrison
Officers: Malcolm John Harrison [1951] Director

Kingswood Golf & Country Club Limited
Incorporated: 15 May 1985 *Employees:* 60
Net Worth: £2,965,142 *Total Assets:* £7,339,397
Registered Office: Downs Farm, Reigate Road, Ewell, Surrey, KT17 3BY
Activities: Operation of sports facilities
Parent: Dwellcourt Ltd
Officers: Jeffrey Thomas Hilliard, Secretary; James Michael Bowry [1987] Finance Director; Jeffrey Thomas Hilliard [1964] Development Director; Douglas William McClelland [1949] Director; Steven John Turnbull [1976] Director

Kinsat Enterprises Ltd
Incorporated: 15 September 2011
Net Worth: £3,805,229 *Total Assets:* £6,760,776
Registered Office: 42 Lytton Road, Barnet, Herts, EN5 5BY
Activities: Financial intermediation not elsewhere classified
Shareholders: Michael Gerrard; Taskin Ahmet Izzet; Joseph Peter Gerrard
Officers: Joseph Peter Gerrard [1954] Director; Michael Gerrard [1957] Director; Taskin Ahmet Izzet [1976] Director

Kirby Group Engineering (UK) Limited
Incorporated: 24 April 2007
Net Worth: £3,501,416 *Total Assets:* £11,054,613
Registered Office: Profile West, 950 Great West Road, London, TW8 9ES
Activities: Other engineering activities
Parent: Kirby Group Engineering Unlimited Company
Officers: Derry McMahon, Secretary; Mark Flanagan [1968] Director [Irish]; James Kirby [1966] Director [Irish]; Derry McMahon [1967] Director [Irish]; Conor O'Brien [1976] Director [Irish]; Raymond Ryan [1962] Director [Irish]

Kirkman and Jourdain Construction Limited
Incorporated: 20 December 2017
Net Worth: £3,168,537 *Total Assets:* £7,513,392
Registered Office: 150 Brooker Road, Waltham Abbey, Essex, EN9 1JH
Activities: Construction of commercial buildings
Shareholders: Philip Stanley Hayward; Kevin Michael Grehan; Mark James Downey
Officers: Mark James Downey [1971] Director; Kevin Michael Grehan [1965] Director; Philip Stanley Hayward [1965] Director

Kitewood (Creekside) Limited
Incorporated: 15 December 2016
Net Worth Deficit: £2,474,957 *Total Assets:* £15,473,662
Registered Office: 3rd Floor, Sterling House, Langston Road, Loughton, Essex, IG10 3TS
Activities: Buying and selling of own real estate
Parent: GDL (Creekside) Limited
Officers: Allan Porter, Secretary; John Cole [1971] Director; Stephen Stuart Solomon Conway [1948] Director; John Stephen Faith [1948] Director/Chartered Surveyor; Jonathan Goldstein [1971] Director; Philip Owen Van Reyk [1958] Director

Klassik Property Ltd
Incorporated: 3 September 2003 *Employees:* 4
Net Worth: £4,638,528 *Total Assets:* £12,276,857
Registered Office: 96-98 Braemar Avenue, South Croydon, Surrey, CR2 0QB
Activities: Other letting and operating of own or leased real estate
Major Shareholder: Michael Dennis Slack
Officers: Alison Jane Crane, Secretary; Michael Dennis Slack [1942] Director/Insurance Broker

KLDiscovery Ontrack Limited
Incorporated: 10 December 1991
Previous: Kroll Ontrack Limited
Net Worth: £7,951,197 *Total Assets:* £12,563,000
Registered Office: Global House, 1 Ashley Avenue, Epsom, Surrey, KT18 5AD
Activities: Other professional, scientific and technical activities n.e.c.
Parent: LD International Holdings Limited
Officers: Philip Neil Bridge [1972] Managing Director; Christopher Weiler [1962] Director/Chief Executive [American]; Dawn Wilson [1966] Director/Chief Financial Officer [American]

KLM Cityhopper UK Limited
Incorporated: 7 August 2002 *Employees:* 45
Net Worth Deficit: £57,509,000 *Total Assets:* £38,219,000
Registered Office: Plesman House, Cains Lane, Bedfont, Feltham, Middlesex, TW14 9RL
Activities: Scheduled passenger air transport
Officers: Kirsten Pronk, Secretary; Farah Khan [1979] Director/HR Manager; Warner Arnoud Rootliep [1961] Managing Director [Dutch]; Nigel Hilton Tyson [1962] Director of Finance North Europe

Kluman and Balter Holdings Limited
Incorporated: 15 March 2012 *Employees:* 62
Net Worth: £7,834,214 *Total Assets:* £24,322,160
Registered Office: Unit 8 The IO Centre, Lea Road, Waltham Abbey, Essex, EN9 1AS
Activities: Activities of head offices
Shareholder: DK Investments Limited
Officers: Simon Douglas, Secretary; Diana Kluman, Secretary; Omer Tahir, Secretary; Danny Kluman [1975] Director; Jamie Kluman [1978] Director

KM Estates Limited
Incorporated: 22 October 2015 *Employees:* 2
Net Worth: £10,601,569 *Total Assets:* £13,638,141
Registered Office: Nicholas House, River Front, Enfield, Middlesex, EN1 3FG
Activities: Other letting and operating of own or leased real estate
Shareholders: Aminmohamed Fazal Alidina Pabani; Shabnam Pabani
Officers: Omar Aminmohamed Pabani, Secretary; Amin Fazal Alidina Pabani [1948] Director; Omar Aminmohamed Pabani [1992] Director

KM Products Europe Limited
Incorporated: 27 November 1992 *Employees:* 60
Net Worth: £7,440,384 *Total Assets:* £12,583,808
Registered Office: Aissela, 46 High Street, Esher, Surrey, KT10 9QY
Activities: Wholesale of agricultural machinery, equipment and supplies
Parent: KMP Holdings Limited
Officers: Bhaskar Bhushan Basu, Secretary; Bhaskar Bhushan Basu [1965] Director - Accounts and Finance; Joseph Eisenberg [1939] Director; Michael Dawes LEA [1956] Director/Engineer; Virendra Mundra [1953] Director/Sales; Maurizio Paserman [1968] Director [Italian]; David Scrivener [1973] Director/Sales

KMI Brands Limited
Incorporated: 24 August 2001 *Employees:* 32
Net Worth: £4,664,000 *Total Assets:* £12,905,000
Registered Office: Floor 1, Harlequin House, 7 High Street, Teddington, Middlesex, TW11 8EE
Activities: Wholesale of perfume and cosmetics
Parent: Knowledge & Merchandising Inc Limited
Officers: Charlotte Amy Lee, Secretary; Hiten Jackis Dayal [1958] Director; Lorna Mitchell [1975] Product and Brand Director; Rachel Lisa Parsonage [1974] Managing Director

KMP Holdings Limited
Incorporated: 10 August 2005 *Employees:* 78
Net Worth: £7,555,321 *Total Assets:* £13,568,670
Registered Office: Aissela, 46 High Street, Esher, Surrey, KT10 9QY
Activities: Activities of head offices
Major Shareholder: Joseph Eisenberg
Officers: Ziva Eisenberg, Secretary; Joseph Eisenberg [1939] Director; Maurizio Paserman [1968] Director [Italian]

KMP Taste Limited
Incorporated: 2 December 2010 *Employees:* 505
Net Worth: £389,047 *Total Assets:* £6,118,466
Registered Office: Regus Cardinal Point, Park Road, Rickmansworth, Herts, WD3 1RE
Activities: Take-away food shops and mobile food stands
Parent: Zaf Holdings Limited
Officers: Arif Abdul Jivraj [1964] Director; Kishore Jukhoop [1984] Director [Mauritian]

KMS Holdings Limited
Incorporated: 12 June 2007
Net Worth: £2,905,683 *Total Assets:* £6,401,892
Registered Office: 3 George Street, Watford, Herts, WD18 0BX
Activities: Activities of head offices
Major Shareholder: Gulam Nasser
Officers: Gulam Nasser [1965] Director

Knight Noise Limited
Incorporated: 2 June 2006 *Employees:* 130
Net Worth Deficit: £822,280 *Total Assets:* £11,193,108
Registered Office: Allcures House, Arisdale Avenue, South Ockendon, Essex, RM15 5TT
Activities: Non-trading company
Officers: Jaipal Singh Cheema [1956] Director

Knight Precision Metals Limited
Incorporated: 1 September 2011 *Employees:* 59
Net Worth: £9,063,258 *Total Assets:* £11,088,492
Registered Office: Linkside Summit Road, Cranborne Road, Potters Bar, Herts, EN6 3JL
Activities: Manufacture of metal structures and parts of structures
Officers: Judith Maxine Townsend, Secretary; Sophie Harrieth Blyth [1966] Director; Carolyn Yvette Ferguson [1961] Director; Brien Walter Knight [1929] Director; Darrell Edward Alfred Knight [1963] Director; Christopher Smyth [1941] Director; Judith Maxine Townsend [1964] Director; Emma Louise Wright [1966] Director

Knight Strip Metals Limited
Incorporated: 29 September 1943 *Employees:* 54
Net Worth: £9,464,157 *Total Assets:* £11,338,008
Registered Office: Linkside Business Centre, Summit Road, Cranborne Road, Potters Bar, Herts, EN6 3JL
Activities: Manufacture of metal structures and parts of structures
Parent: Knight Precision Metals Limited
Officers: Judith Maxine Townsend, Secretary; Brien Walter Knight [1929] Director; Michael Stephen O'Neill [1961] Director; Christopher Smyth [1941] Director; Martin Ken Wiltshire [1962] Financial Director

Knowledge & Merchandising Inc. Ltd
Incorporated: 13 April 1993 *Employees:* 34
Net Worth: £3,353,000 *Total Assets:* £11,645,000
Registered Office: Floor 1, Harlequin House, 7 High Street, Teddington, Middlesex, TW11 8EE
Activities: Non-trading company
Shareholders: Douglas King; Patrick Maris
Officers: Charlotte Amy Lee, Secretary; Hiten Jackis Dayal [1958] Director; Douglas Richard John King [1967] Director/Fund Manager; Rachel Parsonage [1974] Managing Director

Kodak International Finance Limited
Incorporated: 30 March 1983
Net Worth: £56,501,848 *Total Assets:* £408,733,472
Registered Office: Building 8, Croxley Green Business Park, Hatters Lane, Watford, Herts, WD18 8PX
Activities: Financial intermediation not elsewhere classified
Officers: Helen Veronica Griffiths, Secretary; Evelina Latuta [1973] Director/Financial Controller; William George Love [1956] Director/Finance/Treasurer [American]; Manfred Hubert Stegmaier [1957] Director/EAMER Controller [German]

Kodak Limited
Incorporated: 15 November 1898 *Employees:* 205
Net Worth: £95,900,000 *Total Assets:* £255,500,000
Registered Office: Building 8, Croxley Green Business Park, Hatters Lane, Watford, Herts, WD18 8PX
Activities: Other publishing activities
Officers: Helen Veronica Griffiths, Secretary; Helen Veronica Griffiths [1962] Legal Director; John Gerard O'Grady [1964] Director/General Manager WW Sales, Senior Vice President [Irish]; Susan White [1972] HR Director

Koenig & Bauer (UK) Limited
Incorporated: 17 June 1960 *Employees:* 41
Previous: K B A (UK) Limited
Net Worth: £60,272 *Total Assets:* £5,366,492
Registered Office: 5 Century Court, Tolpits Lane, Watford, Herts, WD18 9PX
Activities: Installation of industrial machinery and equipment
Parent: Koenig and Bauer Aktiengesellschaft
Officers: Stephanie Louise Nicklin, Secretary; Thomas Longhino [1973] Director/Chief Financial Officer [Austrian]; Andrew James Pang [1967] Director; Ralf Sammeck [1962] Sales Director [German]; Christopher Scully [1965] Sales Director

Kolajola UK Ltd
Incorporated: 5 May 1998 *Employees:* 3
Net Worth: £4,090,748 *Total Assets:* £10,065,268
Registered Office: 97 Lower Addiscombe Road, Croydon, Surrey, CR0 6PT
Activities: Other letting and operating of own or leased real estate
Major Shareholder: Kolajo Adebayo Lawal
Officers: Omowunmi F Lawal, Secretary; Kolajo Adebayo Lawal [1966] Director

Kone Public Limited Company
Incorporated: 13 June 1978 *Employees:* 1,721
Net Worth: £93,244,000 *Total Assets:* £208,575,008
Registered Office: Global House, Station Place, Fox Lane North, Chertsey, Surrey, KT16 9HW
Activities: Other manufacturing n.e.c.
Parent: Kone Corporation
Officers: Tebogo Brenda Msi, Secretary; Thomas Hinnerskov [1971] Director [Danish]; Tim John Joyce [1965] Managing Director [American]; Gerard Keith Loty [1972] Director [Australian]; Andrew Brian Miles [1981] Finance Director; Andrew James Todd [1972] Director; Patrick Weil [1971] Director; Michael Anthony Williams [1965] Managing Director [Australian]

Korda Developments Limited
Incorporated: 7 December 2001 *Employees:* 67
Net Worth: £13,197,962 *Total Assets:* £18,174,750
Registered Office: Orbital House, 20 Eastern Road, Romford, Essex, RM1 3PJ
Activities: Other retail sale not in stores, stalls or markets
Major Shareholder: Daniel William Fairbrass
Officers: Damian Keith Clarke [1971] Director/Head of Operations; Daniel William Fairbrass [1970] Director/Angling Consultant

Kore Wireless UK PLC
Incorporated: 11 March 2003 *Employees:* 13
Previous: Wyless Europe PLC
Net Worth: £13,138,657 *Total Assets:* £14,098,949
Registered Office: Drayton Hall, Church Road, West Drayton, Middlesex, UB7 7PS
Activities: Other business support service activities n.e.c.
Officers: Romil Bahl [1968] Director [American]; Richard Jacob Burston [1960] Director; Terence James Jarman [1951] Director [Canadian]; Robert Joseph Nicewicz Jr [1985] Director [American]

Korea Foods Company Limited
Incorporated: 20 December 1999 *Employees:* 250
Net Worth: £688,327 *Total Assets:* £10,999,625
Registered Office: Unit 5 Wyvern Industrial Estate, Beverley Way, New Malden, Surrey, KT3 4PH
Activities: Non-specialised wholesale of food, beverages and tobacco
Shareholder: Bernard Suh
Officers: Anna Suh, Secretary; Bernard Suh [1946] Director/Manager; Daniel Suh [1975] Director

Kout Food Group Restaurants UK Limited
Incorporated: 22 May 2012
Net Worth Deficit: £16,985,000 *Total Assets:* £8,641,000
Registered Office: 100-102 High Street, Ruislip, Middlesex, HA4 8LS
Activities: Activities of other holding companies n.e.c.
Officers: Fadwa Alhomaiz [1957] Director/Chairwoman [Kuwaiti]

KPIT Technologies (UK) Limited
Incorporated: 17 October 1996 *Employees:* 160
Net Worth: £15,863,656 *Total Assets:* £29,745,258
Registered Office: Gautam House, 1-3 Shenley Avenue, Ruislip Manor, Middlesex, HA4 6BP
Activities: Other business support service activities n.e.c.
Parent: KPIT Technologies Limited
Officers: Amit Avinash Bhave, Secretary; Deepak Koshal [1951] Director/Chartered Accountant; Kishore Parshuram Patil [1962] Director/Chartered Accountant [Indian]; Pankaj Sathe [1967] Director/Management Professional [Indian]

Kraft Foods Investment Holdings UK Limited
Incorporated: 24 March 2011
Net Worth: £7,831,298,048 *Total Assets:* £10,462,016,512
Registered Office: Cadbury House, Sanderson Road, Uxbridge, Middlesex, UB8 1DH
Activities: Activities of head offices
Parent: Vantas International Limited
Officers: Adrian John Paul Arrighi [1978] Tax Director; Michael Brendan Foye [1965] Treasury Director; John Michael Hladusz [1972] Director/Chartered Accountant; Carole Noelle Keene [1966] Director

Kraft Foods UK IP & Production Holdings Limited
Incorporated: 25 March 2011
Net Worth: £1,648,612,992 *Total Assets:* £1,648,612,992
Registered Office: Cadbury House, Sanderson Road, Uxbridge, Middlesex, UB8 1DH
Activities: Activities of head offices
Parent: Kraft Foods Investment Holdings UK Limited
Officers: Adrian John Paul Arrighi [1978] Tax Director; Michael Brendan Foye [1965] Treasury Director; John Michael Hladusz [1972] Director/Chartered Accountant; Carole Noelle Keene [1966] Director

Kreutzer Touristik GB Limited
Incorporated: 13 January 2016 *Employees:* 2
Net Worth Deficit: £16,506 *Total Assets:* £84,572,904
Registered Office: Queens Court, 9-17 Eastern Road, Romford, Essex, RM1 3NH
Activities: Other reservation service activities n.e.c.
Major Shareholder: Menachem Shaked
Officers: Anna Dubro [1977] Director [Latvian]

Krinvest Limited
Incorporated: 7 April 2000 *Employees:* 91
Net Worth: £2,416,915 *Total Assets:* £6,749,775
Registered Office: 60 Central Road, Morden, Surrey, SM4 5RP
Activities: Primary education
Major Shareholder: Krishnan Julian Satkunam
Officers: Krishnan Julian Satkunam [1976] Director/General Business

Kristal Enterprises Limited
Incorporated: 7 September 2000 *Employees:* 25
Net Worth: £8,408,488 *Total Assets:* £10,447,345
Registered Office: Doshi Accountants Ltd, 6th Floor, Amp House, Dingwall Road, Croydon, Surrey, CR0 2LX
Activities: Other business support service activities n.e.c.
Major Shareholder: Muslim Jaffer
Officers: Muslim Jaffer [1959] Director/Pharmacist

Kromachem Holdings Limited
Incorporated: 30 November 1989 *Employees:* 42
Net Worth: £14,218,621 *Total Assets:* £16,031,411
Registered Office: Unit 10 Moor Park Industrial Centre, Tolpits Lane, Watford, Herts, WD18 9ER
Activities: Activities of head offices
Major Shareholder: Ewald Josef Kensbock
Officers: Ewald Josef Kensbock [1939] Director/Industrial Chemist [German]; Margrit Doris Kensbock [1941] Director [German]; Uwe Kensbock [1971] Managing Director [German]

Kromachem Limited
Incorporated: 6 September 1982 *Employees:* 30
Net Worth: £9,631,276 *Total Assets:* £10,286,504
Registered Office: Unit 10 Moor Park Industrial Centre, Tolpits Lane, Watford, Herts, WD18 9ER
Activities: Manufacture of paints, varnishes and similar coatings, mastics and sealants
Parent: Kromachem Holdings Ltd
Officers: Ewald Josef Kensbock [1939] Director/Industrial Chemist [German]; Uwe Kensbock [1971] Managing Director [German]

KS SPV 3 Limited
Incorporated: 25 June 2010
Net Worth Deficit: £1,973,000 *Total Assets:* £11,627,000
Registered Office: 8 White Oak Square, London Road, Swanley, Kent, BR8 7AG
Activities: Other manufacturing n.e.c.
Parent: Branden Solar Parks Limited
Officers: Giuseppe La Loggia [1975] Director/Entrepreneur [Italian]; Joseph Mark Linney [1958] Director/Chartered Quantity Surveyor; Yit Ho Tang [1974] Director/Investment Manager [Singaporean]; Christopher James Tanner [1972] Investment Director

KS SPV 4 Limited
Incorporated: 25 June 2010
Net Worth Deficit: £1,139,000 *Total Assets:* £7,274,000
Registered Office: 8 White Oak Square, London Road, Swanley, Kent, BR8 7AG
Activities: Other manufacturing n.e.c.
Parent: Branden Solar Parks Limited
Officers: Giuseppe La Loggia [1975] Director/Entrepreneur [Italian]; Joseph Mark Linney [1958] Director/Chartered Quantity Surveyor; Yit Ho Tang [1974] Director/Investment Manager [Singaporean]; Christopher James Tanner [1972] Investment Director

KSEYE Capital Holdings Limited
Incorporated: 26 April 2016 *Employees:* 2
Net Worth: £609,122 *Total Assets:* £42,678,068
Registered Office: 1 Kenyngton Place, Harrow, Middlesex, HA3 0DW
Activities: Activities of financial services holding companies
Parent: KSEYE Group Limited
Officers: Jitendra Khagram [1971] Director/Business Adviser; Nikes Khagram [1984] Director/Consultant

KSEYE Capital No.1 Limited
Incorporated: 27 April 2016 *Employees:* 2
Net Worth: £269,487 *Total Assets:* £21,745,690
Registered Office: 1 Kenyngton Place, Harrow, Middlesex, HA3 0DW
Activities: Other credit granting n.e.c.
Parent: KSEYE Capital Holdings Limited
Officers: Jitendra Khagram [1971] Director/Business Adviser; Nikes Khagram [1984] Director/Consultant

KSEYE Capital No.2 Limited
Incorporated: 27 April 2016 *Employees:* 2
Net Worth: £325,207 *Total Assets:* £20,979,084
Registered Office: 1 Kenyngton Place, Harrow, Middlesex, HA3 0DW
Activities: Other credit granting n.e.c.
Parent: KSEYE Capital Holdings Limited
Officers: Jitendra Khagram [1971] Director/Business Adviser; Nikes Khagram [1984] Director/Consultant

KSEYE Group Limited
Incorporated: 26 April 2016 *Employees:* 4
Net Worth: £6,187,885 *Total Assets:* £44,022,188
Registered Office: 1 Kenyngton Place, Harrow, Middlesex, HA3 0DW
Activities: Activities of other holding companies n.e.c.
Shareholders: Jitendra Khagram; Nikes Khagram
Officers: Jitendra Khagram [1971] Director/Business Adviser; Nikes Khagram [1984] Director/Consultant

Kubach & Sambrook (Metals) Limited
Incorporated: 28 February 1973 *Employees:* 11
Net Worth: £4,151,229 *Total Assets:* £16,255,821
Registered Office: 57 Manor Park Crescent, Edgware, Middlesex, HA8 7LY
Activities: Manufacture of basic iron and steel and of ferro-alloys
Officers: Pareshkumar Dahyabhai Patel, Secretary; Ajay Arunkant Doshi [1958] Director [Australian]

Kudos Catering (UK) Limited
Incorporated: 17 August 2000 *Employees:* 427
Net Worth: £4,248,051 *Total Assets:* £8,801,063
Registered Office: Crown House, 855 London Road, Grays, Essex, RM20 3LG
Activities: Event catering activities
Parent: Crown Holdings Limited
Officers: Javed Taher, Secretary; Charles Nicholas Beer [1971] Director/Catering Hospitality; Matthew Erich Herter [1972] Director [American]; Nigel Mark Hutson [1958] Managing Director; Deirdre Morgan [1952] Director; Russell Lee Christopher Morgan [1952] Director/Co Chairman; Christopher John Sullivan [1956] Director

Kuehne + Nagel (UK) Limited
Incorporated: 26 November 1979
Net Worth: £24,484,014 *Total Assets:* £132,956,480
Registered Office: 1 Roundwood Avenue, Stockley Park, Uxbridge, Middlesex, UB11 1FG
Activities: Other business support service activities n.e.c.
Parent: Kuehne + Nagel International AG
Officers: Tristan Richard Michael Stokes, Secretary; Martin Arzethauser [1965] Director/Head of Group Tax [Swiss]; Allison Michelle Best [1969] Finance Director; Brian Cox [1969] Director

Kuehne + Nagel Limited
Incorporated: 11 May 1983 *Employees:* 9,181
Net Worth: £68,401,000 *Total Assets:* £436,123,008
Registered Office: 1 Roundwood Avenue, Stockley Park, Uxbridge, Middlesex, UB11 1FG
Activities: Other transportation support activities
Parent: Kuehne + Nagel (UK) Limited
Officers: Tristan Richard Michael Stokes, Secretary; Allison Michelle Best [1969] Finance Director; Brian Cox [1969] Managing Director; Mark David James Jenkins [1962] Director

Kuflink Bridging Ltd
Incorporated: 21 December 2011 *Employees:* 39
Previous: Alpha Bridging Solutions Ltd
Net Worth: £4,909,350 *Total Assets:* £15,577,400
Registered Office: 21 West Street, Gravesend, Kent, DA11 0BF
Activities: Other business support service activities n.e.c.
Parent: Kuflink Group PLC
Officers: Tejwant Singh Chattha [1978] Director; Nattalie Jane Weeks [1970] Director

Kynoch Vets Limited
Incorporated: 11 October 2013 *Employees:* 7
Net Worth: £2,731,700 *Total Assets:* £5,020,084
Registered Office: 4 Mowat Industrial Estate, Sandown Road, Watford, Herts, WD24 7UY
Activities: Veterinary activities
Officers: Arnold Stephen Levy, Secretary; Arnold Stephen Levy [1959] Director/Veterinary Surgeon; Kevin Lance Morris [1973] Director/Veterinary Surgeon; John William Hampden Smithers [1963] Director/Veterinary Surgeon

L & M (Heating) Supplies Limited
Incorporated: 27 April 1970 *Employees:* 40
Net Worth: £11,093,762 *Total Assets:* £17,089,968
Registered Office: 103 Lockfield Avenue, Enfield, Middlesex, EN3 7PY
Activities: Non-specialised wholesale trade
Parent: L & M Holding Limited
Officers: Hasnain Ali [1978] Director; Michael Leonard Louis Jones [1949] Director; Muhammad Ali Makkani [1976] Director [Pakistani]

L & M Holding Ltd
Incorporated: 16 December 2014 *Employees:* 40
Net Worth: £4,894,165 *Total Assets:* £13,660,850
Registered Office: 795 St Albans Road, Watford, Herts, WD25 9LA
Activities: Activities of head offices
Officers: Hasnain Ali [1978] Director; Muhammad Ali Makkani [1976] Director [Pakistani]

L P M (Professional Recruitment) Limited
Incorporated: 21 November 1980 *Employees:* 2
Net Worth: £23,183,000 *Total Assets:* £30,016,000
Registered Office: Page House, 1 Dashwood Lang Road, Bourne Business Park, Addlestone, Surrey, KT15 2QW
Activities: Other activities of employment placement agencies
Parent: Michael Page International Southern Europe Limited
Officers: Kaye Maguire, Secretary; Kaye Elizabeth Maguire [1977] Director/General Counsel and Company Secretary; Kelvin John Stagg [1971] Director/Accountant; Jeremy Paul Tatham [1969] Director/Accountant

L.M.H. (Management Services) Limited
Incorporated: 19 August 1976
Net Worth: £248,125 *Total Assets:* £6,298,546
Registered Office: 110-112 Lancaster Road, New Barnet, Herts, EN4 8AL
Activities: Management consultancy activities other than financial management
Officers: Daniel Philip Harvey [1985] Director/Property Development Manager; Rebecca Louise Harvey [1987] Director/Accounts Manager

L.M.H. Properties Limited
Incorporated: 9 February 1984
Net Worth: £296,466 *Total Assets:* £7,457,705
Registered Office: 110-112 Lancaster Road, New Barnet, Herts, EN4 8AL
Activities: Other letting and operating of own or leased real estate
Officers: Carol Jane Piper, Secretary; Daniel Harvey [1985] Director; Rebecca Harvey [1987] Director

L.W. (Developments) Limited
Incorporated: 22 November 1979 *Employees:* 10
Net Worth: £506,435 *Total Assets:* £5,704,754
Registered Office: Springfield House, 99-101 Crossbrook Street, Waltham Cross, Herts, EN8 8JR
Activities: Construction of domestic buildings
Parent: Williamson Investment Group Limited
Officers: Dean Andrew Williamson [1979] Director; Deborah Jane Williamson [1958] Director; Glen Andrew Williamson [1982] Director; Lee Andrew Williamson [1958] Director/Builder

La Nu-Range Ltd
Incorporated: 15 June 1998 *Employees:* 5
Net Worth: £4,411,733 *Total Assets:* £5,873,038
Registered Office: 30 Sylvan Avenue, Hornchurch, Essex, RM11 2PN
Activities: Other letting and operating of own or leased real estate
Shareholders: Arun Kumar Sharma; Angela Sharma
Officers: Dr Arun Kumar Sharma, Secretary; Angela Sharma [1970] Director/Solicitor; Dr Arun Kumar Sharma [1964] Director/Doctor

The Lady Eleanor Holles School
Incorporated: 6 April 2009 *Employees:* 268
Net Worth: £19,280,730 *Total Assets:* £39,625,652
Registered Office: The Bursary, The Lady Eleanor Holles School, Hanworth Road, Hampton, Surrey, TW12 3HF
Activities: Primary education
Officers: Sarah Whitehouse, Secretary; Annabel Emma Blair [1977] Executive Director; David Harold King [1951] Director/Retired; Neil Dewar Lewis [1962] Director/Solicitor; Dr Sophia Jane Aubrey McCormick [1950] Director/Educational Consultant Retired Voluntary Worker; Alison Hamilton Meyric Hughes [1944] Director/University Lecturer; Robert John Milburn [1956] Director/Accountant; Catherine Ann Millis [1971] HR Director; Barbara Anne Parson [1953] Director/Retired; Christopher Stanley Stokes [1949] Director/IP Rights Specialist [Irish]; Catherine Susan Thomas [1965] Director/Management Consultant; Charlotte Victoria Thomas [1983] Director/Architect; Sister Paula Susan Thomas [1956] Director/Headmistress; Wendy Jennifer Wildman [1945] Director/Retired

Laing Construction Limited
Incorporated: 29 June 1995
Net Worth: £23,064,000 *Total Assets:* £23,064,000
Registered Office: Bridge Place, Anchor Boulevard, Admirals Park, Crossways, Dartford, Kent, DA2 6SN
Activities: Construction of commercial buildings
Parent: Laing O'Rourke Holdings Limited
Officers: Robert Edward Turner, Secretary; Alexander Stewart McIntyre [1956] Director

John Laing Construction Limited
Incorporated: 21 December 1920
Net Worth: £1,121,000 *Total Assets:* £21,434,000
Registered Office: Bridge Place, Anchor Boulevard, Admirals Park, Crossways, Dartford, Kent, DA2 6SN
Activities: Construction of commercial buildings
Parent: Laing Construction Limited
Officers: Robert Edward Turner, Secretary; Alexander Stewart McIntyre [1956] Director

John Laing International Limited
Incorporated: 16 March 1959 *Employees:* 19
Net Worth Deficit: £746,000 *Total Assets:* £9,611,000
Registered Office: Bridge Place, Anchor Boulevard, Admirals Park, Crossways, Dartford, Kent, DA2 6SN
Activities: Construction of commercial buildings
Parent: Laing Limited
Officers: Robert Edward Turner, Secretary; Alexander Stewart McIntyre [1956] Director; Raymond Gabriel O'Rourke [1947] Director/Structural Engineer [Irish]; John Christopher Oconnor [1965] Director

Laing Limited
Incorporated: 24 September 1998
Net Worth: £43,283,000 *Total Assets:* £43,283,000
Registered Office: Bridge Place, Anchor Boulevard, Admirals Park, Crossways, Dartford, Kent, DA2 6SN
Activities: Construction of commercial buildings
Shareholders: John Laing Construction Limited; R O'Rourke & Son Limited
Officers: Robert Edward Turner, Secretary; Alexander Stewart McIntyre [1956] Director

Laing O'Rourke Construction Limited
Incorporated: 23 October 2001
Net Worth: £53,559,000 *Total Assets:* £591,195,008
Registered Office: Bridge Place, Anchor Boulevard, Admirals Park, Crossways, Dartford, Kent, DA2 6SN
Activities: Construction of commercial buildings
Parent: Laing O'Rourke Holdings Limited
Officers: Robert Edward Turner, Secretary; Liam John Cummins [1970] Director; Alexander Stewart McIntyre [1956] Director; Hubert Desmond O'Rourke [1949] Director/Structural Engineer [Irish]

Laing O'Rourke Holdings Limited
Incorporated: 23 May 2001
Net Worth: £13,141,000 *Total Assets:* £310,592,000
Registered Office: Bridge Place, Anchor Boulevard, Admirals Park, Crossways, Dartford, Kent, DA2 6SN
Activities: Construction of commercial buildings
Parent: Laing O'Rourke PLC
Officers: Robert Edward Turner, Secretary; Alexander Stewart McIntyre [1956] Director

Laing O'Rourke Infrastructure Limited
Incorporated: 23 October 2001
Net Worth: £22,417,000 *Total Assets:* £59,629,000
Registered Office: Bridge Place, Anchor Boulevard, Admirals Park, Crossways, Dartford, Kent, DA2 6SN
Activities: Construction of other civil engineering projects n.e.c.
Parent: Laing O'Rourke Holdings Limited
Officers: Robert Edward Turner, Secretary; Alexander Stewart McIntyre [1956] Director

Laing O'Rourke Manufacturing Limited
Incorporated: 16 October 2008
Previous: Bison Manufacturing Limited
Net Worth: £15,640,000 *Total Assets:* £20,212,000
Registered Office: Bridge Place, Anchor Boulevard, Admirals Park, Crossways, Dartford, Kent, DA2 6SN
Activities: Manufacture of concrete products for construction purposes
Parent: Bison Holdings Limited
Officers: Robert Edward Turner, Secretary; Stephen John Harley [1951] Director; Alexander Stewart McIntyre [1956] Director; Paul William McNerney [1977] Director/Business Unit Leader

Laing O'Rourke PLC.
Incorporated: 23 May 2001 *Employees:* 7,669
Net Worth Deficit: £217,900,000 *Total Assets:* £788,600,000
Registered Office: Bridge Place, Anchor Boulevard, Admirals Park, Crossways, Dartford, Kent, DA2 6SN
Activities: Construction of commercial buildings
Parent: O'Rourke Investments Limited
Officers: Robert Edward Turner, Secretary; Declan James McGeeney [1978] Director/General Manager [Irish]; Alexander Stewart McIntyre [1956] Director; Paul William McNerney [1977] Director/Business Unit Leader; Hugh Desmond O'Rourke [1949] Director/Structural Engineer [Irish]; Raymond Gabriel O'Rourke [1947] Director/Structural Engineer [Irish]

Laing O'Rourke Services Limited
Incorporated: 1 February 2002 *Employees:* 7,640
Net Worth: £859,000 *Total Assets:* £704,140,992
Registered Office: Bridge Place, Anchor Boulevard, Admirals Park, Crossways, Dartford, Kent, DA2 6SN
Activities: Construction of commercial buildings
Parent: Laing O'Rourke Holdings Limited
Officers: Robert Edward Turner, Secretary; Alexander Stewart McIntyre [1956] Director; John Christopher O'Connor [1965] Commercial Director

Lakedale Developments Limited
Incorporated: 16 November 2000
Net Worth Deficit: £39,166 *Total Assets:* £5,816,530
Registered Office: 18 Crook Log, Bexleyheath, Kent, DA6 8BP
Activities: Development of building projects
Major Shareholder: Paul Desmond McCauley
Officers: Paul Desmond McCauley [1961] Director

Lambda Therapeutic Limited
Incorporated: 4 May 2004 *Employees:* 6
Net Worth: £761,356 *Total Assets:* £7,980,214
Registered Office: Sage House, 319 Pinner Road, North Harrow, Middlesex, HA1 4HF
Activities: Technical testing and analysis
Shareholders: Binish Hasmukhbhai Chudgar; Bindi Binish Chudgar
Officers: Nilesh Parmar, Secretary; Bindi Binish Chudgar [1964] Director [Indian]; Nilesh Parmar [1968] Director

Lampton School Academy Trust
Incorporated: 13 August 2010 *Employees:* 146
Net Worth: £24,262,000 *Total Assets:* £30,033,000
Registered Office: Lampton School, Lampton Avenue, Hounslow, Middlesex, TW3 4EP
Activities: General secondary education
Officers: Rina Sehgal, Secretary; Sharan Bangar [1976] Director/Senior Administrator; Harjinder Singh Chaudry [1969] Director/IT Consultant; Stephen Davis [1974] Director/Headteacher; Elizabeth Ellis [1965] Director/Librarian [American]; Dr Parvinder Singh Garcha [1958] Director/G.P; Glen Grace [1971] Director/Health and Safety Officer; Raghav Gupta-Chaudhary [1987] Director/Chartered Accountant; Birna Helgadottir [1964] Director/Teacher [Icelander]; Edward Jonathan Locke [1953] Director/Landscape Gardener; Ruby Mir [1987] Director; Thomas Peter Samuel [1989] Director/Financial Consultant; Dorina Scott [1955] Director/Headteacher; Gurjit Sisodia [1971] Director; Moira Stuart [1951] Director; Ruth Williams [1970] Director/Teacher; Natasha Woolman [1978] Director

Lamrose Properties Limited
Incorporated: 18 November 2002 *Employees:* 2
Net Worth: £3,781,535 *Total Assets:* £8,439,290
Registered Office: 45 Rowdell Road, Europa House, Northolt, Middlesex, UB5 6AG
Activities: Buying and selling of own real estate
Officers: Anil Gunvantbhai Patel, Company Secretary; Anil Gunvantbhai Patel [1954] Director; Jitendrakumar Maganbhai Patel [1952] Director; Maheshkumar Mohanbhai Patel [1949] Director

Lanber Nursing Homes LLP
Incorporated: 16 September 2008
Net Worth: £7,634,926 *Total Assets:* £26,723,600
Registered Office: 47 Canons Drive, Edgware, Middlesex, HA8 7RG

Lanber Properties LLP
Incorporated: 16 September 2008
Net Worth: £149,818,208 *Total Assets:* £418,378,048
Registered Office: 47 Canons Drive, Edgware, Middlesex, HA8 7RG

Land & Water Plant Limited
Incorporated: 15 October 1999 *Employees:* 16
Net Worth: £2,956,818 *Total Assets:* £7,671,025
Registered Office: Numeric House, 98 Station Road, Sidcup, Kent, DA15 7BY
Activities: Renting and leasing of other machinery, equipment and tangible goods n.e.c.
Parent: M H J Limited
Officers: Roger Browning, Secretary; James Alexander MacLean [1969] Director; Richard Charles MacLean [1971] Director/Plant Hire; Richard Edward Fitzharding Melhuish [1946] Director

Land & Water Services Ltd
Incorporated: 24 December 1992 *Employees:* 116
Net Worth: £2,527,700 *Total Assets:* £10,714,187
Registered Office: Numeric House, 98 Station Road, Sidcup, Kent, DA15 7BY
Activities: Other professional, scientific and technical activities n.e.c.
Parent: M.H.J Limited
Officers: Roger Browning, Secretary; David Jonathan Bligh [1953] Director; Adrian Barrie Gascoyne [1967] Director/Quantity Surveyor; William James Gush [1951] Director/Civil Engineer; Kevin James Kirkland [1974] Director; James Alexander MacLean [1969] Director; Richard Edward Fitzharding Melhuish [1946] Director

Land Finance & Mortgage Corporation Limited (The)
Incorporated: 29 June 1933 *Employees:* 5
Net Worth: £6,479,620 *Total Assets:* £9,289,210
Registered Office: 84 Market Place, Romford, Essex, RM1 3JE
Activities: Buying and selling of own real estate
Parent: Romford Construction Company Ltd
Officers: Nicholas Hilbery Chaplin, Secretary; Sir Malcolm Hilbery Chaplin [1934] Director/Chartered Surveyor; Nicholas Hilbery Chaplin [1965] Director/Chartered Surveyor; Ruth Mary Chaplin [1966] Director/Chartered Surveyor

Land Management Limited
Incorporated: 29 April 1922
Net Worth: £9,817,464 *Total Assets:* £11,257,629
Registered Office: 43 Market Place, Romford, Essex, RM1 3AB
Activities: Other letting and operating of own or leased real estate
Shareholder: William D'Urban Sunnucks
Officers: Conor O'Mahony, Secretary; Shaun David Barker [1971] Director; William D'Urban Sunnucks [1956] Director/Accountant

Landmark Civil Engineering Limited
Incorporated: 22 July 1998 *Employees:* 1
Net Worth: £2,309,303 *Total Assets:* £9,567,590
Registered Office: 2 AC Court, High Street, Thames Ditton, Surrey, KT7 0SR
Activities: Construction of commercial buildings
Major Shareholder: Michael George Johnson
Officers: Deina Johnson, Secretary; Michael George Johnson [1964] Director

Landmark Global (UK) Limited
Incorporated: 8 October 1999 *Employees:* 52
Previous: Bpost International (UK) Limited
Net Worth Deficit: £2,502,674 *Total Assets:* £7,862,401
Registered Office: Unit A1, Parkway, Cranford Lane, Heston, Middlesex, TW5 9QA
Activities: Other service activities incidental to land transportation, n.e.c.
Parent: Bpost SA/NV
Officers: Luc Camiel Cloet [1959] Director [Belgian]; Henri Baudry Charles Marie de Romree de Vichenet [1975] Director [Belgian]

Landmark Groundworks Limited
Incorporated: 30 July 1998 *Employees:* 47
Net Worth: £1,877,945 *Total Assets:* £9,467,882
Registered Office: 2 AC Court, High Street, Thames Ditton, Surrey, KT7 0SR
Activities: Construction of commercial buildings
Shareholders: Deina Johnson; Michael George Johnson
Officers: Deina Johnson, Secretary; Kyle Michael Johnson [1986] Director/Quantity Surveyor; Michael George Johnson [1964] Director; Kevin Lynch [1969] Director [Irish]; David Timothy McCarthy [1981] Director/Quantity Surveyor [Irish]

Lanend Limited
Incorporated: 1 May 1996
Previous: Blossom House School Limited
Net Worth: £9,241,013 *Total Assets:* £10,576,612
Registered Office: Station Road, Motspur Park, New Malden, Surrey, KT3 6JJ
Activities: Development of building projects
Major Shareholder: Joanna Briant Burgess
Officers: Joanna Briant Burgess, Secretary; Joanna Briant Burgess [1950] Director/Teacher

The Langdon Foundation
Incorporated: 4 May 2011 *Employees:* 229
Net Worth: £6,343,278 *Total Assets:* £9,438,345
Registered Office: Camrose House, 2a Camrose Avenue, Edgware, London, HA8 6EG
Activities: Other business support service activities n.e.c.
Officers: Barry Clive Shine, Secretary; Michael Lawrence Blane [1938] Director [American]; Jeremy William Bolchover [1963] Director; Richard Davis [1977] Director/Accountant; Nicholas Ian Doffman [1961] Director/Solicitor; Sophie Isabel Frais [1988] Director/Social Worker; Nigel John Henry [1964] Director/Property Developer; Jonathan Lionel Joseph [1950] Director/Property Developer; Benjamin Mark Miller [1970] Director/Software Executive; Antonia Leila Mitchell [1982] Director/Fundraiser; Samuel Boruch Salomon [1979] Director/Management Consultant; Samuel Shaerf [1982] Director/Retail Head Office; Shelley Hilary Chieff [1957] Director/Counsellor

Langford Clinic Limited
Incorporated: 3 February 2000 *Employees:* 116
Net Worth: £3,019,519 *Total Assets:* £9,527,330
Registered Office: 6-10 Outram Road, Croydon, Surrey, CR0 6XE
Activities: Other human health activities
Parent: Bramley Health Holding Company Limited
Officers: Simon James Frederic Judd, Secretary; Gordon Henry Phillips [1947] Director; Hilary Jewel Phillips [1948] Director; James Phillips [1979] Director

Langley Park Learning Trust
Incorporated: 7 July 2011 *Employees:* 320
Previous: Langley Park Academies
Net Worth: £39,185,000 *Total Assets:* £42,240,000
Registered Office: Langley Park School for Girls, Hawksbrook Lane, South Eden Park Road, Beckenham, Kent, BR3 3BE
Activities: Primary education
Officers: Micon Metcalfe, Secretary; David Laurence Appleton [1947] Director/Retired; John Budden [1971] Director/Headteacher; Andrea Felicity Carr [1964] Director; George Thomas Chalmers [1988] Director; Gareth Scott Fendick [1980] HR Director; Barbara Florence Hart [1949] Director/Retired; Enkanah Soobadoo [1953] Director/Retired; James Edward Weatherill [1983] Director

The Langley Park School for Boys Academy Trust
Incorporated: 7 March 2011 *Employees:* 173
Net Worth: £27,744,000 *Total Assets:* £29,243,000
Registered Office: Langley Park School for Boys, Hawksbrook Lane, Beckenham, Kent, BR3 3BP
Activities: General secondary education
Officers: Leonard Edmund Blomstrand [1947] Director/Education Consultant; Wendy Anne Coello [1970] Director/Civil Servant; Alana Dave [1964] Director/Education Officer; Caroline Sarah Davies [1968] Director/School Business Manager; Mario di Clemente [1963] Director/College Principal; Sandra Lauren Dodds [1946] Director/NHS Officer; Lee Terence Game [1990] Director/Teacher; Julia Garvey [1969] Director/Marketing Consultant; Lawrence Richard Gold [1965] Director; Sian Elizabeth Henderson [1964] Director/Civil Servant; Paul Michael Monaghan [1972] Director/Bank Manager; Stephen Ivor James Parsons [1974] Director/Headmaster; Claudette Thomas [1965] Director/People and Operations Manager

Hugh Langmead Limited
Incorporated: 20 September 1946 *Employees:* 1
Net Worth: £11,469,242 *Total Assets:* £13,960,168
Registered Office: Ashcombe House, 5 The Crescent, Leatherhead, Surrey, KT22 8DY
Activities: Other letting and operating of own or leased real estate
Major Shareholder: Langmead Hugh
Officers: Hugh Langmead, Secretary; Hugh Langmead [1946] Director

Lantern Recovery LLP
Incorporated: 27 September 2007
Net Worth: £11,606,733 *Total Assets:* £11,918,358
Registered Office: Lantern House, 39-41 High Street, Potters Bar, Herts, EN6 5AJ
Officers: Raymond Michael Coleman [1956] Member

Lantern Recovery Specialists PLC
Incorporated: 2 November 1987
Net Worth: £6,534,051 *Total Assets:* £11,841,107
Registered Office: Lantern House, 39-41 High Street, Potters Bar, Herts, EN6 5AJ
Activities: Maintenance and repair of motor vehicles
Parent: Lantern Services (Holdings) Ltd
Officers: Craig Coleman, Secretary; Craig Coleman [1976] Director; Lee Coleman [1977] Director; Raymond Michael Coleman [1956] Director; Ryan Coleman [1982] Director

Lantern Services (Holdings) Ltd
Incorporated: 8 February 2013 *Employees:* 145
Net Worth: £20,017,228 *Total Assets:* £24,863,076
Registered Office: 39-41 High Street, Potters Bar, Herts, EN6 5AJ
Activities: Activities of other holding companies n.e.c.
Shareholder: Raymond Michael Coleman
Officers: Craig Coleman, Secretary; Craig Coleman [1976] Director; Lee Coleman [1977] Director; Raymond Michael Coleman [1956] Director; Ryan Coleman [1982] Director

Lanvin Trading Ltd
Incorporated: 25 April 1990 *Employees:* 3
Net Worth: £5,221,719 *Total Assets:* £6,272,822
Registered Office: Suite A, 10th Floor, Maple House, High Street, Potters Bar, Herts, EN6 5BS
Activities: Activities of head offices
Shareholders: Stuart Vincent Cove; Nicola Maxine Cove
Officers: Stuart Vincent Cove, Secretary; Nicola Maxine Cove [1964] Director/Computer Consultant; Stuart Vincent Cove [1951] Director/Engineering Consultant; Michael John Stroud [1960] Director

Lapid Developments Limited
Incorporated: 29 January 1971
Net Worth: £21,827,756 *Total Assets:* £24,292,516
Registered Office: 5 Elstree Gate, Elstree Way, Borehamwood, Herts, WD6 1JD
Activities: Renting and operating of Housing Association real estate
Parent: Meekport Limited
Officers: Eldad Aizenberg, Secretary; Eldad Aizenberg [1957] Managing Director; Naomi Braybrooke [1967] Director/Museum Education; Daniel Cigman [1969] Director; Julie Cigman [1954] Director/Advisory Teacher; Dr Ruth Cigman [1951] Director/University Lecturer

Laridge Investments Limited
Incorporated: 21 November 2002
Net Worth: £62,080,636 *Total Assets:* £62,087,812
Registered Office: First Floor, Woodgate Studios, 2-8 Games Road, Cockfosters, Barnet, Herts, EN4 9HN
Activities: Other business support service activities n.e.c.
Major Shareholder: Oksana Marcheno
Officers: Anna Korelidou, Secretary; Menelaos Sazos [1974] Director/Advocate [Cypriot]

Larkspur Investments Limited
Incorporated: 24 July 2012
Net Worth: £7,678 *Total Assets:* £8,533,528
Registered Office: 68 St Margarest Road, Edgware, Middlesex, HA8 9UU
Activities: Buying and selling of own real estate
Major Shareholder: Bina Raju Kishinani
Officers: Bina Kishinani, Secretary; Bina Raju Kishinani [1960] Director

Lascelles Leisure Limited
Incorporated: 26 September 2007 *Employees:* 1
Net Worth: £1,630,214 *Total Assets:* £7,634,435
Registered Office: Endeavour House, 78 Stafford Road, Wallington, Surrey, SM6 9AY
Activities: Activities of head offices
Shareholders: Martyn Booth; Elaine Booth
Officers: Elaine Booth, Secretary; Elaine Booth [1965] Director; Martyn Booth [1950] Director

Laser Holdings Limited
Incorporated: 1 October 1999
Previous: Lastminute.Com Limited
Net Worth: £4,108,000 *Total Assets:* £6,270,000
Registered Office: 3rd Floor, 1 Church Road, Richmond, Surrey, TW9 2QE
Activities: Activities of other holding companies n.e.c.
Parent: TVL Europe
Officers: Steve Milton, Secretary; Brian Scott Evans [1974] Director/CFA, VP Treasury [American]

Lasted Limited
Incorporated: 7 September 2011 *Employees:* 3
Net Worth: £8,072,313 *Total Assets:* £22,026,456
Registered Office: Northside House, Mount Pleasant, Barnet, Herts, EN4 9EE
Activities: Other letting and operating of own or leased real estate
Shareholders: Melvyn Frank Cooper; Jason Robert Cooper
Officers: Adam Cooper, Secretary; Adam Cooper [1971] Director; Jason Robert Cooper [1971] Director; Melvyn Frank Cooper [1941] Director

Latchmere Academy Trust
Incorporated: 9 July 2012 *Employees:* 217
Previous: Latchmere School
Net Worth: £23,026,212 *Total Assets:* £25,468,734
Registered Office: Latchmere School, Latchmere Road, Kingston upon Thames, Surrey, KT2 5TT
Activities: Primary education
Officers: Clare Blake, Secretary; Justin Jacobs [1976] Director/Financial Services Regulation; Bethlyn Killey [1975] Director; Madeline Maguire [1953] Director/Retired; Sarah Elizabeth McCarthy [1974] Marketing Director; Stephen Edward Pritchard [1979] Director; Clare Reeve [1985] Director; Julie Denise Ritchie [1953] Director/Headteacher; Lisa Stone [1979] Director/Clerical Officer; Raghu Venkatesam [1973] Director/IT Consultant

Latif International Limited
Incorporated: 2 September 1998
Net Worth: £975,970 *Total Assets:* £8,841,004
Registered Office: Latif House, First Way, Wembley, Middlesex, HA9 0JD
Activities: Manufacture of woven or tufted carpets and rugs
Major Shareholder: Abdul Abraham Latif
Officers: Latifa Latif [1972] Director

Latimer Hill LLP
Incorporated: 15 February 2017
Net Worth: £8,756,000 *Total Assets:* £14,366,000
Registered Office: The Power House, Gunpowder Mill, Powdermill Lane, Waltham Abbey, Essex, EN9 1BN

Laurels Care Limited
Incorporated: 10 October 2005
Net Worth: £1,849,020 *Total Assets:* £6,658,459
Registered Office: Castle House, 69-79 Victoria Street, Englefield Green, Surrey, TW20 0QX
Activities: Other residential care activities n.e.c.
Shareholders: Amar Sheikh; Momin Sheikh
Officers: Amar Sheikh, Secretary; Amar Sheikh [1961] Director; Momin Sheikh [1963] Director

Ralph Lauren London Limited
Incorporated: 23 March 1983
Net Worth: £5,443,896 *Total Assets:* £5,726,423
Registered Office: 46 Clarendon Road, Watford, Herts, WD17 1HE
Activities: Retail sale of clothing in specialised stores
Parent: Ralph Lauren Corporation
Officers: Aldo Alex Fleri [1961] Director/Vice President Sales UK; Carmel Ann Pedatella [1974] Director/Business Executive [American]

Ralph Lauren UK Limited
Incorporated: 17 August 1994
Net Worth: £8,572,470 *Total Assets:* £79,218,344
Registered Office: 46 Clarendon Road, Watford, Herts, WD1 1DR
Activities: Wholesale of clothing and footwear
Parent: RL Retail Services Limited
Officers: Aldo Alex Fleri [1961] Director/Vice President Sales UK; Carmel Ann Pedatella [1974] Director/Business Executive [American]; Robert Patrick Ranftl [1971] Director/Business Executive [American]; Andrew Howard Smith [1971] Director/Business Executive

Lavender Property Investments Limited
Incorporated: 27 November 1953 *Employees:* 3
Net Worth: £1,113,849 *Total Assets:* £7,214,798
Registered Office: Ashcombe House, 5 The Crescent, Leatherhead, Surrey, KT22 8DY
Activities: Development of building projects
Major Shareholder: Mark Edward Woodruff
Officers: Lucy Mary Woodruff, Secretary; Lucy Mary Woodruff [1961] Property Designer Director; Mark Edward Woodruff [1959] Director

Laxkan Holdings Ltd
Incorporated: 30 November 2016
Net Worth: £126,006 *Total Assets:* £15,322,764
Registered Office: Kimberley House, 31 Burnt Oak Broadway, Edgware, Middlesex, HA8 5LD
Activities: Other service activities n.e.c.
Officers: Premchand Kantilal Shah [1937] Director; Vinay Shah [1974] Director

Laxkan Ltd
Incorporated: 30 November 2016
Net Worth: £8,328,111 *Total Assets:* £14,028,788
Registered Office: Kimberley House, 31 Burnt Oak Broadway, Edgware, Middlesex, HA8 5LD
Activities: Other service activities n.e.c.
Parent: Laxkan Holdings Limited
Officers: Premchand Kantilal Shah [1937] Director; Vinay Shah [1974] Director

Laxmi BNS Holdings Limited
Incorporated: 10 February 2010 *Employees:* 646
Net Worth: £22,051,180 *Total Assets:* £109,609,696
Registered Office: Unit 4 Bradfield Road, Ruislip, Middlesex, HA4 0NU
Activities: Manufacture of basic pharmaceutical products
Officers: Govindji Hathi, Secretary; Alpa Hathi [1968] Director/HR; Govindji Thakershi Hathi [1941] Director; Samit Govindji Hathi [1967] Director

Laxmico Limited
Incorporated: 21 April 2009 *Employees:* 234
Net Worth: £3,491,584 *Total Assets:* £75,175,608
Registered Office: Unit 4 Bradfield Road, Ruislip, Middlesex, HA4 0NU
Activities: Wholesale of pharmaceutical goods
Major Shareholder: Samit Govindji Hathi
Officers: Govindji Hathi, Secretary; Alpa Hathi [1968] Director/HR; Govindji Thakershi Hathi [1941] Director; Samit Hathi [1967] Director/Pharmacist

Lay & Wheeler Limited
Incorporated: 6 March 2006 *Employees:* 24
Net Worth: £3,603,000 *Total Assets:* £16,707,000
Registered Office: Majestic House, The Belfry, Colonial Way, Watford, Herts, WD24 4WH
Activities: Wholesale of wine, beer, spirits and other alcoholic beverages
Parent: Majestic Wine Warehouses Limited
Officers: Alex Iapichino, Secretary; James Crawford [1977] Finance Director; Rowan Gormley [1962] Director [Irish]; Kathryn Dibble Andersen Keating [1986] Director/Businesswoman [American]

LB Enterprises Limited
Incorporated: 30 March 1998 *Employees:* 117
Net Worth: £12,461,668 *Total Assets:* £22,029,252
Registered Office: 118-126 Ilford Lane, Ilford, Essex, IG1 2LE
Activities: Retail sale in non-specialised stores with food, beverages or tobacco predominating
Shareholders: Arvind Bachubhai Sedani; Vipul Bachubhai Sedani; Pius Bachubhai Sedani
Officers: Arvind Bachubhai Sedani, Secretary; Arvind Bachubhai Sedani [1952] Director/Businessman [Kenyan]; Vipul Bachubhai Sedani [1963] Director/Businessman

LDBS Frays Academy Trust
Incorporated: 18 December 2012 *Employees:* 226
Net Worth: £10,933,000 *Total Assets:* £14,270,000
Registered Office: Cowley St Laurence CofE Primary School, Worcester Road, Cowley, Uxbridge, Middlesex, UB8 3TH
Activities: Primary education
Officers: Catherine Jane Mosdell, Secretary; Angie Brett [1964] Director/Banker [Irish]; Father Ken Buckler [1950] Director/Clergymen; Christopher Brian Cole [1967] Director/Executive Headteacher; Daniella Dean [1973] Director/Office Manager; Janet Susan Marion Duncan [1942] Director/Retired; Rebecca Hughes [1972] Managing Director; Inigo Rodney Milman Woolf [1946] Finance Director

LDD Construction Limited
Incorporated: 17 February 2009 *Employees:* 133
Previous: London Diamond Drilling Services Ltd.
Net Worth: £1,685,059 *Total Assets:* £9,912,106
Registered Office: 19-20 Bourne Court, Southend Road, Woodford Green, Essex, IG8 8HD
Activities: Other specialised construction activities n.e.c.
Parent: London Diamond Drilling Holdings Ltd
Officers: Daniel Ian McIver [1977] Director; Caroline Seagroatt [1975] Director; Marc David Seagroatt [1976] Director; Kang Hung Yau [1972] Financial Director

LE Packaging Ltd
Incorporated: 17 February 2014 *Employees:* 144
Net Worth: £6,069,504 *Total Assets:* £13,327,738
Registered Office: Unit H1, Imperial Retail Park, Gravesend, Kent, DA11 0DQ
Activities: Printing n.e.c.
Officers: Carmel Mulvey, Secretary; Ian Anthony Barwick [1968] Director; Michael Duncan Brown [1971] Director

Lea Bridge Hill LLP
Incorporated: 1 December 2014
Total Assets: £28,153,000
Registered Office: The Power House, Gunpowder Mill, Powdermill Lane, Waltham Abbey, Essex, EN9 1BN

Lea Redway Limited
Incorporated: 25 March 1943 *Employees:* 502
Net Worth: £40,047,336 *Total Assets:* £47,061,912
Registered Office: 59a Mosslea Road, Whyteleafe, Surrey, CR3 0DS
Activities: Activities of head offices
Shareholder: Nigel Beddgood
Officers: Maria Adaway, Secretary; Maria Adaway [1965] Director/Board Member; Luke Edward Victor Beddgood [1974] Director/Board Member; Margaret Anne Beddgood [1945] Director/Administrator [Australian]; Nigel Edward Lawrence Beddgood [1941] Director/Engineer; Carol Ann Catt [1944] Director/Administrator

Leading Edge Labels Limited
Incorporated: 24 December 2002 *Employees:* 144
Net Worth: £8,178,177 *Total Assets:* £14,540,058
Registered Office: Imperial Retail Park, Gravesend, Kent, DA11 0DQ
Activities: Printing n.e.c.
Officers: Carmel Mulvey, Secretary; Ian Anthony Barwick [1968] Director; Michael Duncan Brown [1971] Director; Paul Barry Brown [1967] Technical Director; Carmel Mary Mulvey [1971] Finance Director [Irish]; Scott Terriss [1975] Operations Director

Leander Build Limited
Incorporated: 7 November 1994
Net Worth: £757,844 *Total Assets:* £6,728,877
Registered Office: Ashtead House, Business Park 8, Barnett Wood Lane, Leatherhead, Surrey, KT22 7DG
Activities: Construction of commercial buildings
Parent: Leander Group Limited
Officers: Iain Hugh Prain, Secretary/Quantity Surveyor; Scott John Hillman [1973] Director/Quantity Surveyor; Barry Johnson [1973] Director/Engineering Surveyor; Iain Hugh Prain [1964] Director/Quantity Surveyor; Edmund Quinton Shepherd [1959] Director/Freelance Engineer

Leander Construction Limited
Incorporated: 30 March 1992 *Employees:* 34
Net Worth: £809,732 *Total Assets:* £6,638,264
Registered Office: Ashtead House, Business Park 8, Barnett Wood Lane, Leatherhead, Surrey, KT22 7DG
Activities: Construction of commercial buildings
Parent: Leander Group Limited
Officers: Iain Hugh Prain, Secretary; Scott John Hillman [1973] Director/Quantity Surveyor; Barry Johnson [1973] Director/Engineering Surveyor; Iain Hugh Prain [1964] Director; Edmund Quinton Shepherd [1959] Director/Freelance Engineer

Learning Tree International Limited
Incorporated: 5 October 1978 *Employees:* 56
Net Worth: £1,763,000 *Total Assets:* £6,694,000
Registered Office: Leatherhead House, Station Road, Leatherhead, Surrey, KT22 7FG
Activities: Other education n.e.c.
Shareholders: Kevin Gruneich; Donna Gruneich
Officers: Jonas Tor Larsson, Secretary; Robert John Harvey [1966] Finance Director; Benjamin Kite [1976] Director; Jonas Tor Larsson [1967] Director [Swedish]; Magnus Nylund [1970] Director [Swedish]; Richard Andrew Spires [1961] Director [American]

Robert Lee Distribution Limited
Incorporated: 30 April 1984 *Employees:* 200
Net Worth: £9,495,839 *Total Assets:* £17,693,266
Registered Office: Riverside Place, Lea Road, Waltham Abbey, Essex, EN9 1AS
Activities: Wholesale of wood, construction materials and sanitary equipment
Parent: New River Holdings Limited
Officers: Robert Alfred Ellender, Secretary; Barrie Colston Brackstone [1961] Director/Operations Manager; Martin Stewart Earle [1946] Director/Manager; Matthew Richard Earle [1973] Commercial Director; David John Ground [1963] Director; Charles William Valens Smith [1949] Director/Manager; Timothy John Wayman [1960] Managing Director

Lee Industrial Limited
Incorporated: 27 August 1976 *Employees:* 24
Net Worth: £3,941,249 *Total Assets:* £5,455,892
Registered Office: 78 Suez Road, Brimsdown, Enfield, Middlesex, EN3 7PS
Activities: Non-specialised wholesale trade
Major Shareholder: John Henry Chance
Officers: Blanche Chance, Secretary; Blanche Chance [1944] Director; Jason Jonathan Chance [1966] Director; John Henry Chance [1943] Director

Lee Park Estates Ltd
Incorporated: 1 December 2016 *Employees:* 5
Net Worth: £15,773 *Total Assets:* £6,684,847
Registered Office: Wayside, London Road, Upper Ruxley, Sidcup, Kent, DA14 5AR
Activities: Recreational vehicle parks, trailer parks and camping grounds
Shareholders: Albert Lee; Corinna Lee
Officers: Albert Lee [1972] Director; Corinna Lee [1973] Director

Lee Savell Properties Limited
Incorporated: 16 January 1989 *Employees:* 4
Net Worth: £4,741,983 *Total Assets:* £5,046,693
Registered Office: 41 Stanley Road, Carshalton, Surrey, SM5 4LE
Activities: Development of building projects
Major Shareholder: Edmund Buglass Rogers
Officers: Edmund Buglass Rogers, Secretary/Director; Edmund Buglass Rogers [1945] Director; Margaret Rogers [1953] Director; Richard Stuart Williams [1988] Director/Chartered Accountant

Lee-Warren Fabrication and Design Limited
Incorporated: 22 November 1999 *Employees:* 101
Net Worth: £4,052,041 *Total Assets:* £8,885,668
Registered Office: Units 6 7 & 8 Silverdale Road Industrial Estate, Silverdale Road, Hayes, Middlesex, UB3 3BL
Activities: Manufacture of metal structures and parts of structures
Parent: Lee-Warren Fabrication and Design Holdings Limited
Officers: Caroline Few, Secretary; Hugo Mendelssohn Cox [1980] SHEQ Director; Caroline Few [1946] Director; John Few [1947] Director; Warren Few [1973] Director/Chief Executive Officer; Jonathan Henry Lambert [1984] Managing Director; Paul Oram [1973] Director; Alex Pollock [1957] Production Director; Leslie Purdy [1958] Business Development Director; Richard Smith [1976] Director

Leena Plaza Limited
Incorporated: 28 April 2006 *Employees:* 3
Net Worth: £2,590,369 *Total Assets:* £34,866,832
Registered Office: Kirkland House, 11-15 Peterborough Road, Harrow, Middlesex, HA1 2AX
Activities: Hotels and similar accommodation
Officers: Haider Ladhu Jaffer [1940] Director/Businessman; Hassanali Amirali Dawood Suleman [1954] Director/Businessman; Cameron Beresford Sunter [1956] Director/Solicitor

Leeu London Limited
Incorporated: 13 March 2017
Net Worth: £14,132,330 *Total Assets:* £84,405,816
Registered Office: Dixcart House, Addlestone Road, Bourne Business Park, Addlestone, Surrey, KT15 2LE
Activities: Hotels and similar accommodation
Shareholders: Analjit Singh; Neelu Singh
Officers: Analjit Singh [1954] Director [Indian]

Leez Priory Limited
Incorporated: 13 March 1998 *Employees:* 128
Net Worth: £3,803,724 *Total Assets:* £7,586,336
Registered Office: Regency House, 33 Wood Street, Barnet, Herts, EN5 4BE
Activities: Other business support service activities n.e.c.
Parent: Country House Weddings Limited
Officers: Harry Bramer, Secretary; Harry Bramer [1949] Director; Nicholas Bramer [1983] Director

Lefa Enterprises Limited
Incorporated: 10 October 1991 *Employees:* 10
Net Worth: £12,361,138 *Total Assets:* £14,158,972
Registered Office: Planwell House, Edgington Way, Sidcup, Kent, DA14 5EF
Activities: Financial management
Officers: William Martin Benedict O'Doherty, Secretary; Edward Henry Arthur [1981] Director/Chief Executive; Jessie Arthur [1919] Director; Jean Crichton O'Doherty [1947] Director; William Martin Benedict O'Doherty [1980] Director; Esther Maud Prosser [1946] Director/Teacher

Lefroy Brooks Diffusion Limited
Incorporated: 24 December 1982 *Employees:* 11
Net Worth: £5,588,964 *Total Assets:* £6,682,677
Registered Office: Ibroc House, Essex Road, Hoddesdon, Herts, EN11 0QS
Activities: Non-specialised wholesale trade
Parent: Davroc Limited
Officers: Pietro Corbisiero, Secretary [Italian]; Andrew Russell Christopher [1971] Managing Director; Giuseppe Corbisiero [1955] Director [Italian]; Pietro Corbisiero [1953] Director [Italian]

Legacy Broadcast Group Holdings Limited
Incorporated: 15 June 2015 *Employees:* 2
Previous: Vislink Group Holdings Limited
Net Worth: £8,057,000 *Total Assets:* £12,893,000
Registered Office: 12 Horizon Business Village, 1 Brooklands Road, Weybridge, Surrey, KT13 0TJ
Activities: Activities of head offices
Parent: Pebble Beach Systems Group PLC
Officers: Robin Beatham Howe [1947] Director; John Charles Varney [1956] Director

Legolas Debt Holdco Limited
Incorporated: 7 March 2017 *Employees:* 4
Net Worth: £3,772,068 *Total Assets:* £114,980,712
Registered Office: Munro House, Portsmouth Road, Cobham, Surrey, KT11 1PP
Activities: Financial intermediation not elsewhere classified
Parent: GCP Bridge Holdings Ltd
Officers: Stephen Campbell Joseph Ellis [1959] Director; Ronan Niall Kierans [1978] Director [Irish]; Nicholas Simon Parker [1969] Director; Rollo Andrew Johnstone Wright [1976] Director

Leisure and Outdoor Furniture Association Limited
Incorporated: 1 January 1986 *Employees:* 1
Net Worth: £6,950,174 *Total Assets:* £7,307,988
Registered Office: 54 Sun Street, Waltham Abbey, Essex, EN9 1EJ
Activities: Activities of professional membership organisations
Officers: Michael James Brand [1973] Director; Hannah Mary Brown [1981] Director; Martin Jonathon Carnaby [1969] Managing Director; Stephen Mark Davies [1960] Director; Paul William Facey [1962] Sales Director; Richard Paul Grimmer [1950] Managing Director; Mark David Osborne [1963] Director/BBQ and Accessory Manufacturer; Pravin Patel [1961] Director; Tim Pennell [1979] Director/Sales Manager

Leisure Parks Real Estate (Holdings) Limited
Incorporated: 7 February 2013 *Employees:* 3
Net Worth: £18,800,268 *Total Assets:* £50,471,672
Registered Office: 166 College Road, Harrow, Middlesex, HA1 1RA
Activities: Activities of other holding companies n.e.c.
Shareholder: Maurice Sines
Officers: Colin Crickmore [1958] Director; James Robert Crickmore [1980] Director; Maurice Sines [1962] Director

Leisure Parks Real Estate Limited
Incorporated: 13 August 2007 *Employees:* 3
Net Worth: £8,169,301 *Total Assets:* £31,056,944
Registered Office: 166 College Road, Harrow, Middlesex, HA1 1RA
Activities: Recreational vehicle parks, trailer parks and camping grounds
Parent: Leisure Parks Real Estate (Holdings) Limited
Officers: James Robert Crickmore, Secretary; Colin Crickmore [1958] Director; James Robert Crickmore [1980] Director; Maurice Sines [1962] Director

Leitrim Properties Limited
Incorporated: 31 October 1997 *Employees:* 2
Net Worth: £9,142,493 *Total Assets:* £15,569,435
Registered Office: 101 Rowlands Avenue, Hatch End, Pinner, Middlesex, HA5 4AW
Activities: Other letting and operating of own or leased real estate
Parent: Rowlands 2014 Limited
Officers: Noreen O'Hara, Secretary; Michael O'Hara [1947] Director/Public Works Contractor [Irish]

Lenham Storage Company Limited
Incorporated: 22 January 1949 *Employees:* 422
Net Worth: £17,332,368 *Total Assets:* £30,010,920
Registered Office: Ashcombe House, 5 The Crescent, Leatherhead, Surrey, KT22 8DY
Activities: Freight transport by road
Shareholders: Dorothy Janet Abrehart; Rodney Frederic Tolhurst
Officers: Anthony Michael Burgess, Secretary; Dorothy Janet Abrehart [1946] Director; Keith Nicholas Abrehart [1972] Managing Director; Anthony Michael Burgess [1963] Financial Director; Andrew Charles Fulcher [1968] Operational Director; Stephen Leslie Phibbs [1951] Director; Christopher Frederick Tolhurst [1973] IT Director; Rodney Frederic Tolhurst [1943] Director

Lensbury Limited
Incorporated: 30 September 1998 *Employees:* 193
Net Worth: £7,370,000 *Total Assets:* £17,482,000
Registered Office: Broom Road, Teddington, Middlesex, TW11 9NU
Activities: Activities of sport clubs
Parent: The Shell Petroleum Company Limited
Officers: Robert William Birchall [1958] Director/Oil Company Executive; Jane Lacy Curtis-Ward [1956] Director/Oil Company Executive [American]; Timothy Harte [1962] Director/Oil Company Executive; Roland Alexander Ilube [1971] Director/Oil Company Executive; Sandra Kay Perlaki [1959] Director/Oil Company Executive

Lenta 2 Limited
Incorporated: 20 August 2015 *Employees:* 4
Net Worth: £3,239,913 *Total Assets:* £7,993,433
Registered Office: CP House, Otterspool Way, Watford, Herts, WD25 8HR
Activities: Other information technology service activities
Parent: Lenta Properties Limited
Officers: Eric Lewis, Secretary; Paul Andrew Filer [1957] Finance Director; Mark Gibbor [1988] Director; Geoffrey Grodner [1961] Director

Lenta Properties Limited
Incorporated: 4 March 1981 *Employees:* 55
Net Worth: £54,831,952 *Total Assets:* £70,508,912
Registered Office: CP House, Otterspool Way, Watford, Herts, WD25 8HR
Activities: Other letting and operating of own or leased real estate
Parent: Lenta Business Space Limited
Officers: Eric Lewis, Secretary/Solicitor; Paul Andrew Filer [1957] Director/Chartered Accountant; Ian Leslie Gibbor [1950] Director; Iris Gibbor [1951] Director; Mark Gibbor [1988] Director; Geoffrey Grodner [1961] Director/Chartered Accountant; Eric Lewis [1927] Director/Solicitor; Alexei James Schreier [1976] Director; Sarra Gay Temple [1959] Commercial Director

Leonardo Holdings Limited
Incorporated: 1 November 1999 *Employees:* 32
Net Worth Deficit: £204,046 *Total Assets:* £7,369,471
Registered Office: Leonardo House, Fawkes Avenue, Dartford Trade Park, Dartford, Kent, DA1 1JQ
Activities: Activities of head offices
Major Shareholder: Julian Allemby Hunt
Officers: Derek Howard Fieldman [1949] Director; Julian Allemby Hunt [1958] Director/Importer; Ronald Frank Pavey [1948] Director/Importer

The Leprosy Mission International
Incorporated: 2 July 1998 *Employees:* 30
Net Worth: £9,882,485 *Total Assets:* £11,277,626
Registered Office: 80 Windmill Road, Brentford, Middlesex, TW8 0QH
Activities: Other human health activities
Officers: Brent John Morgan, Secretary; Dr Nalini Abraham [1947] Director/Medical Doctor [Indian]; Ashok Adhikari [1974] Director/Pastor [Nepalese]; Dr Warwick John Britton [1948] Director/Professor of Medicine [Australian]; Eric Chollet [1947] Director/Retired [Swiss]; Paul Emans [1949] Director/Management Consultant [Dutch]; Alan David Gray [1954] Director/Retired; Dr Colin Leonard Martin [1953] Director/Retired [Australian]; Dr Shem Zagbayi Nuhu [1956] Director/Pharmacist [Nigerian]; Colin Osborne [1949] Director; Philip Michael Putman [1950] Director/Retired; Anne Ratliff [1958] Director/HR Management Consultant [New Zealander]; Amar Timalsina [1977] Director/Headteacher [Nepalese]

Lesaffre UK and Ireland Limited
Incorporated: 27 April 1992 *Employees:* 18
Previous: DCL Yeast Limited
Net Worth: £5,015,552 *Total Assets:* £7,547,099
Registered Office: Trinity Court, 34 West Street, Sutton, Surrey, SM1 1SH
Activities: Non-specialised wholesale trade
Parent: Algist Bruggeman NV
Officers: Marie-Cecile Perchereau [1973] Director [French]; Vincent Pascal Sainger [1969] Director [French]

Lesser & Pavey Ltd.
Incorporated: 4 January 1971 *Employees:* 32
Net Worth: £23,670,144 *Total Assets:* £27,842,092
Registered Office: Leonardo House, Fawkes Avenue, Dartford Trade Park, Dartford, Kent, DA1 1JQ
Activities: Wholesale of china and glassware and cleaning materials
Parent: Leonardo Group Limited
Officers: Derek Howard Fieldman [1949] Director; Julian Allemby Hunt [1958] Director/Importer; Ronald Frank Pavey [1948] Director/Importer

Lester Hotels (Finchley) Limited
Incorporated: 17 August 2001 *Employees:* 22
Net Worth: £1,402,634 *Total Assets:* £5,403,184
Registered Office: St John House, The Walk, Potters Bar, Herts, EN6 1QQ
Activities: Hotels and similar accommodation
Officers: Martin Johnstone, Secretary; Martin Johnstone [1958] Finance Director; Simon Mark Lester [1964] Director

Lester Hotels Group Limited
Incorporated: 9 September 1999 *Employees:* 206
Net Worth: £6,255,133 *Total Assets:* £12,769,418
Registered Office: St John House, The Walk, Potters Bar, Herts, EN6 1QQ
Activities: Non-trading company
Major Shareholder: Simon Mark Lester
Officers: Martin Johnstone, Secretary; Linda Lester [1963] Director; Simon Mark Lester [1964] Director

Letchworth Hall Hotel (Trading) Limited
Incorporated: 27 July 1976 *Employees:* 45
Net Worth Deficit: £1,303,751 *Total Assets:* £10,612,703
Registered Office: Kanta House, Victoria Road, South Ruislip, Middlesex, HA4 0JQ
Activities: Hotels and similar accommodation
Officers: Satish Jamnadas Chatwani, Secretary/Director; Jawahar Jamnadas Chatwani [1948] Director; Rashmi Jamnadas Chatwani [1954] Director; Satish Jamnadas Chatwani [1953] Director

Letting International Limited
Incorporated: 27 August 1997 *Employees:* 53
Net Worth: £2,520,060 *Total Assets:* £10,095,509
Registered Office: Gabrielle House, 332-336 Perth Road, Ilford, Essex, IG2 6FF
Activities: Management of real estate on a fee or contract basis
Parent: Lint Group Limited
Officers: Tarsaim Chand, Secretary/Director; Tarsaim Chand [1967] Director; Rizwan Patel [1974] Director

Leven Wharf Limited
Incorporated: 1 May 2015
Net Worth Deficit: £77,764 *Total Assets:* £32,341,948
Registered Office: C K R House, 70 East Hill, Dartford, Kent, DA1 1RZ
Activities: Construction of domestic buildings
Shareholders: Giles William Underhill; Permjit Singh Sulh; Grahame Donald Crisp Seaman
Officers: Grahame Donald Crisp Seaman [1946] Director/Property Developer; Permjit Singh Sulh [1968] Director/Property Developer; Giles William Underhill [1964] Director/Property Developer

Levolux Limited
Incorporated: 19 July 1984 *Employees:* 103
Net Worth: £9,198,000 *Total Assets:* £14,732,000
Registered Office: 1 Forward Drive, Harrow, Middlesex, HA3 8NT
Activities: Other specialised construction activities n.e.c.
Parent: The Alumasc Group PLC
Officers: Andrew Magson, Secretary; David Patrick Gordon [1953] Sales & Marketing Director; Graham Paul Hooper [1956] Director; Andrew Magson [1966] Director; Stephen James Smith [1965] Finance Director; Katie Stewart [1987] Director/Accountant

Lynn Lewis Limited
Incorporated: 14 April 1976 *Employees:* 95
Net Worth: £3,290,602 *Total Assets:* £9,203,644
Registered Office: Ferry Works, Ferry Lane, Shepperton on Thames, Surrey, TW17 9LQ
Activities: Activities of head offices
Shareholder: Lynn Alexander Lewis
Officers: Lynn Alexander Lewis [1937] Director; Valerie Elaine Lewis [1939] Director; Carol Elaine Murdoch [1959] Director; Christopher John Murdoch [1961] Director

Lexcross Limited
Incorporated: 24 January 2011
Net Worth: £975,167 *Total Assets:* £6,243,146
Registered Office: 3rd Floor Northside, Argyle House, Joel Street, Northwood Hills, Northwood, Middlesex, HA6 1NW
Activities: Management consultancy activities other than financial management
Major Shareholder: Bharat Kumar Hirji Thakrar
Officers: Bharat Thakrar, Secretary; Bharat Kumar Hirji Thakrar [1957] Director

Leyton Clubs (London) Limited
Incorporated: 22 March 2010
Net Worth: £915,370 *Total Assets:* £5,349,771
Registered Office: 249 Cranbrook Road, Ilford, Essex, IG1 4TG
Activities: Other business support service activities n.e.c.
Officers: Michael Greenfield [1937] Director; Marc Jonathan Herman [1967] Director; Garry Jon Simpson [1967] Director/Property Developer; Elise Ruth Summers [1966] Director/Personal Assistant

LG Electronics U.K. Ltd
Incorporated: 1 July 1987 *Employees:* 229
Net Worth: £52,531,000 *Total Assets:* £319,664,992
Registered Office: Velocity 2, Brooklands Drive, Weybridge, Surrey, KT13 0SL
Activities: Wholesale of electronic and telecommunications equipment and parts
Parent: LG Electronics European Holding B.V.
Officers: Jae Ho Min, Secretary; Byeongseon Ban [1968] Director/CFO - Europe [South Korean]; Bum Seop Lee [1968] Director/President of UK Subsidiary [South Korean]; Jae Ho Min [1975] Director [South Korean]

LGC (Holdings) Limited
Incorporated: 27 December 1995 *Employees:* 10
Net Worth: £557,251,008 *Total Assets:* £1,122,893,056
Registered Office: Queens Road, Teddington, Middlesex, TW11 0LY
Activities: Other business support service activities n.e.c.
Parent: LGC Investments Limited
Officers: Navneet Kaur Ogle, Secretary; Simon Lawrence Parsons [1969] Finance Director; Timothy Michael Robinson [1963] Director

LGC (Teddington) Limited
Incorporated: 13 October 2000 *Employees:* 2
Net Worth Deficit: £8,171,949 *Total Assets:* £28,820,978
Registered Office: Queens Road, Teddington, Middlesex, TW11 0LY
Activities: Non-trading company
Parent: LGC (Holdings) Limited
Officers: Navneet Kaur Ogle, Secretary; Ian David Burrell [1975] Director/Chartered Accountant; Simon Lawrence Parsons [1969] Finance Director

LGC Genomics Limited
Incorporated: 28 June 2011 *Employees:* 116
Net Worth: £67,616,000 *Total Assets:* £85,633,000
Registered Office: LGC, Queens Road, Teddington, Middlesex, TW11 0LY
Activities: Research and experimental development on biotechnology
Parent: KBiosciences Limited
Officers: Navneet Kaur Ogle, Secretary; Ross Frazer Finlay [1971] Director/Chartered Accountant; Simon Lawrence Parsons [1969] Finance Director

LGC Group Holdings Limited
Incorporated: 26 June 2003 *Employees:* 2
Net Worth: £79,056,000 *Total Assets:* £79,252,000
Registered Office: LGC, Queens Road, Teddington, Middlesex, TW11 0LY
Activities: Activities of head offices
Parent: LGC Science Investments Limited
Officers: Navneet Kaur Ogle, Secretary; Simon Lawrence Parsons [1969] Finance Director; Timothy Michael Robinson [1963] Director

LGC Investments Limited
Incorporated: 23 July 2003 *Employees:* 2
Net Worth Deficit: £53,447,000 *Total Assets:* £164,500,992
Registered Office: LGC, Queens Road, Teddington, Middlesex, TW11 0LY
Activities: Other business support service activities n.e.c.
Parent: LGC Group Holdings Limited
Officers: Navneet Kaur Ogle, Secretary; Simon Lawrence Parsons [1969] Finance Director; Timothy Michael Robinson [1963] Director

LGC Limited
Incorporated: 18 November 1994 *Employees:* 1,265
Net Worth: £18,057,000 *Total Assets:* £336,591,008
Registered Office: Queens Road, Teddington, Middlesex, TW11 0LY
Activities: Other professional, scientific and technical activities n.e.c.
Parent: LGC Holdings Limited
Officers: Navneet Kaur Ogle, Secretary; Julian Hugh Braybrook [1963] Director/Scientific Management; Simon Lawrence Parsons [1969] Finance Director; Timothy Michael Robinson [1963] Director

LGC Science Group Holdings Limited
Incorporated: 4 December 2015 *Employees:* 2,626
Net Worth: £494,812,992 *Total Assets:* £1,370,514,944
Registered Office: LGC, Queens Road, Teddington, Middlesex, TW11 0LY
Activities: Activities of head offices
Parent: Elwy 3 Limited
Officers: Navneet Kaur Ogle, Secretary; Dr Derek Harry Craston [1961] Director/Chemist; Mark Simon Danzey [1979] Director, KKR Capital Markets; Brian Kim [1970] Director/Life Science Executive [American]; Euan Ralph Herbert O'Sullivan [1979] Director/Executive; Simon Lawrence Parsons [1969] Director/Chief Financial Officer; Edouard Jean Charles Pillot [1977] Director [French]; Timothy Michael Robinson [1963] Director; Nicolas Henry Roelofs [1958] Director [American]; Kugan Sathiyanandarajah [1986] Director/Principal, Private Equity

LGC Science Group Limited
Incorporated: 22 December 2009 *Employees:* 2
Net Worth: £118,281,000 *Total Assets:* £223,668,992
Registered Office: LGC, Queens Road, Teddington, Middlesex, TW11 0LY
Activities: Activities of head offices
Parent: LGC Science Group Holdings Limited
Officers: Navneet Kaur Ogle, Secretary; Simon Lawrence Parsons [1969] Finance Director; Timothy Michael Robinson [1963] Director

LGC Science Holdings Limited
Incorporated: 4 January 2010 *Employees:* 2
Net Worth: £221,244,992 *Total Assets:* £345,708,992
Registered Office: LGC, Queens Road, Teddington, Middlesex, TW11 0LY
Activities: Other business support service activities n.e.c.
Parent: Teddington 2 Limited
Officers: Navneet Kaur Ogle, Secretary; Simon Lawrence Parsons [1969] Finance Director; Timothy Michael Robinson [1963] Director

LGC Science Investments Limited
Incorporated: 6 November 2009
Net Worth: £154,780,000 *Total Assets:* £787,196,032
Registered Office: LGC, Queens Road, Teddington, Middlesex, TW11 0LY
Activities: Other business support service activities n.e.c.
Parent: LGC Science Holdings Limited
Officers: Navneet Kaur Ogle, Secretary; Simon Lawrence Parsons [1969] Finance Director; Timothy Michael Robinson [1963] Director

LGC Whirlwind Limited
Incorporated: 28 June 2011
Net Worth: £37,773,000 *Total Assets:* £162,715,008
Registered Office: LGC, Queens Road, Teddington, Middlesex, TW11 0LY
Activities: Other business support service activities n.e.c.
Parent: LGC (Holdings) Limited
Officers: Navneet Kaur Ogle, Secretary; Ian David Burrell [1975] Director/Chartered Accountant; Simon Lawrence Parsons [1969] Chief Financial Director

LGX Holdings Limited
Incorporated: 21 December 2015 *Employees:* 40
Net Worth: £1,031,589 *Total Assets:* £6,517,885
Registered Office: Unit 20 Bourne Industrial Park, Bourne Road, Crayford, Dartford, Kent, DA1 4BZ
Activities: Activities of production holding companies
Shareholders: Simon James Lyon; Robert Buxton
Officers: Robert Andrew Buxton [1978] Director; Richard Hargreaves [1955] Director; Stanley David Harris [1964] Director; Simon James Lyon [1978] Director

LHR Airports Limited
Incorporated: 13 December 1985 *Employees:* 7
Net Worth: £9,772,999,680 *Total Assets:* £11,187,999,744
Registered Office: The Compass Centre, Nelson Road, Hounslow, Middlesex, TW6 2GW
Activities: Scheduled passenger air transport
Parent: Heathrow Holdco Limited
Officers: Ross Findlay Scott Baker [1974] Director; William Stuart Birrell [1964] Director/Chief Information Officer; Javier Echave Espot [1980] Director [Spanish]; Christopher Charles Garton [1961] Director; Charlotte Emma Tiffany Gilthorpe [1970] Director/Employed Barrister; John William Holland Kaye [1965] Director/Chief Executive Officer; Carol Hui [1956] Director/Lawyer; Andrew Hugh Macmillan [1975] Director; Paula Stannett [1965] HR Director

LHR Business Support Centre Limited
Incorporated: 6 June 1995 *Employees:* 107
Net Worth: £6,380,000 *Total Assets:* £8,146,000
Registered Office: The Compass Centre, Nelson Road, Hounslow, Middlesex, TW6 2GW
Activities: Combined facilities support activities
Parent: LHR Airports Limited
Officers: Yuanyuan Ding [1979] Director; Javier Echave Espot [1980] Director [Spanish]; Nicholas Francis Golding [1963] Director; Paula Stannett [1965] HR Director; Richard John White [1973] Director

Liberata UK Limited
Incorporated: 22 December 1975 *Employees:* 1,403
Net Worth: £7,627,000 *Total Assets:* £29,794,000
Registered Office: 5th Floor, Knollys House, 17 Addiscombe Road, Croydon, Surrey, CR0 6SR
Activities: Management consultancy activities other than financial management
Parent: Outsourcing UK Limited
Officers: Timothy John Francis Collins, Secretary; Charles Edward Bruin [1971] Business Director; Masaki Motegi [1978] Director [Japanese]; Yuya Ono [1977] Director/General Manager [Japanese]; Robert David Price [1974] Finance Director; Kazuhiko Suzuki [1969] Director [Japanese]; Allan Leigh Wood [1964] Director

Life Education Trust
Incorporated: 12 June 2012 *Employees:* 211
Previous: The Frances Bardsley Academy for Girls
Net Worth: £27,527,000 *Total Assets:* £29,559,000
Registered Office: The Frances Bardsley Academy for Girls, Brentwood Road, Romford, Essex, RM1 2RR
Activities: General secondary education
Officers: Toni Juanita Burrowes-Cromwell [1965] Director/Management Consultant; Mary Cherry [1967] Director/Bursar; Michael Debens [1946] Director/Retired; Louise Douglas [1967] Director/Consultant; Julian Dutnall [1971] Director/Headteacher; Sophia Malik [1979] Director/Lawyer; David Mansfield [1959] Director/Executive Headteacher; Steve Odart [1968] Director/Founder & VP Sales

Liftec Lifts Limited
Incorporated: 4 June 1997 *Employees:* 154
Net Worth: £4,421,920 *Total Assets:* £9,417,350
Registered Office: Unit 7 Orbital One, Green Street, Green Road, Dartford, Kent, DA1 1QG
Activities: Other construction installation
Shareholder: Otis Limited
Officers: David McAllen, Secretary; John Emery [1950] Director; David McAllen [1973] Director; Jon David Morrissey [1962] Director; Jeffrey Ernest Nokes [1965] Director

Lighthouse Healthcare Group Limited
Incorporated: 21 March 2014
Net Worth: £11,832,000 *Total Assets:* £45,142,000
Registered Office: 2 Imperial Place, Maxwell Road, Borehamwood, Herts, WD6 1JN
Activities: Activities of head offices
Parent: Elysium Healthcare Holdings 3 Limited
Officers: Sarah Juliette Livingston, Secretary; Lesley Joy Chamberlain [1963] Director/Group Chief Executive; Dr Quazi Shams Mahfooz Haque [1968] Executive Medical Director; Steven John Woolgar [1955] Director of Policy and Regulation

Lightwood Strategic Limited
Incorporated: 17 January 2012
Net Worth: £3,921,253 *Total Assets:* £5,460,279
Registered Office: 9 Bridle Close, Surbiton Road, Kingston upon Thames, Surrey, KT1 2JW
Activities: Buying and selling of own real estate
Shareholder: Monopro Ltd
Officers: Philip James Chichester [1978] Director; Michael Arthur Jonathan Dangoor [1951] Director; Gian Paolo James Sorrentino [1971] Director/Property Development

Lime Tree Village Limited
Incorporated: 31 May 2002 *Employees:* 4
Net Worth: £7,736,926 *Total Assets:* £12,547,464
Registered Office: 1st Floor, Brunswick House, Regent Park, 297-299 Kingston Road, Leatherhead, Surrey, KT22 7LU
Activities: Other business support service activities n.e.c.
Parent: Retirement Villages Developments Limited
Officers: Sally Irene Rees, Secretary; Sarah Denise Burgess [1971] Director; William Edwin John Crawford [1970] Director/Development; Neil Donaldson [1966] Director/Accountant; Andrew George Esmond Ovey [1971] Director/Investment Manager

Limesquare Business Parks Limited
Incorporated: 29 March 1984 *Employees:* 2
Net Worth: £6,396,161 *Total Assets:* £9,205,388
Registered Office: P O Box 208, Old Avenue, Weybridge, Surrey, KT13 0TU
Activities: Development of building projects
Parent: Limesquare Holdings Limited
Officers: Walter Thomas Webb, Secretary/Property Manager; Johanna Louisa Cornelia Webb [1956] Director/Secretary [Dutch]; Walter Thomas Webb [1951] Director/Property Manager

Limesquare Finance Limited
Incorporated: 31 May 1990 *Employees:* 4
Net Worth: £4,133,279 *Total Assets:* £12,764,580
Registered Office: P O Box 208, Old Avenue, Weybridge, Surrey, KT13 0TU
Activities: Renting and leasing of cars and light motor vehicles
Parent: Limesquare Holdings Ltd
Officers: Walter Thomas Webb, Secretary/Rental Agent; Walter Thomas Webb [1951] Director

Limesquare Vehicle Rental Limited
Incorporated: 12 September 2003 *Employees:* 59
Net Worth: £2,301,566 *Total Assets:* £10,598,619
Registered Office: Limesquare House, Downside, off Guildford Street, Chertsey, Surrey, KT16 9DS
Activities: Renting and leasing of cars and light motor vehicles
Parent: Limesquare Holdings Limited
Officers: Walter Thomas Webb, Secretary; Walter Thomas Webb [1951] Director/Property Developer

Limje Holdings Limited
Incorporated: 30 September 1996 *Employees:* 104
Net Worth: £2,596,802 *Total Assets:* £11,907,970
Registered Office: Wh Matthews & Co, 19 Penrhyn Road, Kingston upon Thames, Surrey, KT1 2BZ
Activities: Activities of head offices
Major Shareholder: Emil Mahendra Kumar
Officers: Maria Gnanamathy Christopher, Secretary; Murugesu Arumugam [1948] Director/Business Executive [Sri Lankan]; Emil Mahendra Kumar [1950] Chartered Accountant/Director; Alan Kenneth Skinner [1948] Director/Accountant

Lincoln Plaza LLP
Incorporated: 7 February 2013 *Employees:* 2
Net Worth: £2,782,000 *Total Assets:* £41,818,000
Registered Office: Regent House, Allum Gate, Theobald Street, Borehamwood, Herts, WD6 4RS
Officers: Ramesh Chandra Govindji Sachdev [1945] Member; Rishi Ramesh Sachdev [1976] Member; Meenal Hasmukh Sachdev [1979] LLP Member; Pratibha Ramesh Chandra Sachdev [1948] LLP Member

Linden (Avery Hill) LLP
Incorporated: 1 August 2016
Net Worth: £579,000 *Total Assets:* £32,658,000
Registered Office: Cowley Business Park, Cowley, Uxbridge, Middlesex, UB8 2AL

Linden (Biddenham) LLP
Incorporated: 24 June 2015
Net Worth: £599,000 *Total Assets:* £23,149,000
Registered Office: Cowley Business Park, Cowley, Uxbridge, Middlesex, UB8 2AL

Linden (Brampton) LLP
Incorporated: 27 July 2016
Net Worth Deficit: £253,000 *Total Assets:* £33,835,000
Registered Office: Cowley Business Park, Cowley, Uxbridge, Middlesex, UB8 2AL

Linden (Enfield) LLP
Incorporated: 11 July 2016
Net Worth Deficit: £1,121,000 *Total Assets:* £39,953,000
Registered Office: Cowley Business Park, Cowley, Uxbridge, Middlesex, UB8 2AL

Linden (Hartfield Road) LLP
Incorporated: 20 May 2015
Net Worth: £5,011,000 *Total Assets:* £5,880,000
Registered Office: Cowley Business Park, Cowley, Uxbridge, Middlesex, UB8 2AL

Linden (Northstowe) LLP
Incorporated: 19 July 2016
Net Worth: £592,000 *Total Assets:* £41,094,000
Registered Office: Cowley Business Park, Cowley, Uxbridge, Middlesex, UB8 2AL

Linden (York Road) LLP
Incorporated: 17 April 2014
Net Worth Deficit: £1,404,000 *Total Assets:* £59,997,000
Registered Office: Cowley Business Park, Cowley, Uxbridge, Middlesex, UB8 2AL

Linden Barnet LLP
Incorporated: 13 March 2015
Net Worth: £3,346,000 *Total Assets:* £21,685,000
Registered Office: Cowley Business Park, Cowley, Uxbridge, Middlesex, UB8 2AL

Linden Homes (Sherford) LLP
Incorporated: 18 April 2013
Previous: Sherford Developments LLP
Net Worth Deficit: £3,171,000 *Total Assets:* £85,858,000
Registered Office: Cowley Business Park, Cowley, Uxbridge, Middlesex, UB8 2AL

Linden Limited
Incorporated: 16 April 1973 *Employees:* 989
Net Worth: £200,251,008 *Total Assets:* £1,588,732,032
Registered Office: Cowley Business Park, Cowley, Uxbridge, Middlesex, UB8 2AL
Activities: Construction of commercial buildings
Parent: Galliford Try Homes Limited
Officers: Andrew James Duxbury [1975] Director/Accountant; Andrew Richard Hammond [1970] Director; Tom Marshall Nicholson [1965] Director; Stephen John Teagle [1959] Director; Peter Martin Truscott [1962] Director

Linden St Albans LLP
Incorporated: 26 June 2008
Net Worth: £21,091,000 *Total Assets:* £22,389,000
Registered Office: Cowley Business Park, Cowley, Uxbridge, Middlesex, UB8 2AL

Linden Wates (Horsham) LLP
Incorporated: 5 June 2015
Net Worth: £4,258,000 *Total Assets:* £6,678,000
Registered Office: Cowley Business Park, Cowley, Uxbridge, Middlesex, UB8 2AL

Linden Wates (Kempshott) Limited
Incorporated: 22 September 2014
Net Worth: £6,200,000 *Total Assets:* £21,224,000
Registered Office: Cowley Business Centre, Cowley, Uxbridge, Middlesex, UB8 2AL
Activities: Construction of domestic buildings
Shareholders: Wates Group Limited; Linden Limited
Officers: David Alexander Bowen [1967] Director/Accountant; David Michael Brocklebank [1970] Managing Director; Natalie Jane Flint [1969] Sales Marketing Director; Andrew Richard Hammond [1970] Director; Suzanne Irons [1964] Director; Martin Geoffrey Leach [1965] Operations Director; Andrew Colin Modle [1967] Director; Stephen Charles Swinscoe [1976] Director/Residential Developer; Trevor Wicks [1974] Managing Director

Linden Wates (Ringwood) LLP
Incorporated: 4 October 2016
Net Worth Deficit: £84,000 *Total Assets:* £18,788,000
Registered Office: Cowley Business Park, Cowley, Uxbridge, Middlesex, UB8 2AL

Linden Wates (Royston) LLP
Incorporated: 10 May 2017
Net Worth Deficit: £79,000 *Total Assets:* £41,105,000
Registered Office: Cowley Business Park, Cowley, Uxbridge, Middlesex, UB8 2AL

Linden Wates (The Frythe) Limited
Incorporated: 23 May 2013
Net Worth: £11,291,000 *Total Assets:* £19,036,000
Registered Office: Cowley Business Park, Cowley, Uxbridge, Middlesex, UB8 2AL
Activities: Construction of domestic buildings
Shareholders: Wates Group Limited; Linden Limited
Officers: David Alexander Bowen [1967] Director/Accountant; David Michael Brocklebank [1967] Director; Nichola Chapman [1979] Sales and Marketing Director; Natalie Jane Flint [1969] Sales Marketing Director; Nicholas James Laugharne [1983] Director; Martin Geoffrey Leach [1965] Director; Sharon Christine Marwick [1971] Director; Andrew Colin Modle [1967] Director; Tom Marshall Nicholson [1965] Director; Adrian Justin Sims [1970] Director

Linden Wates (Westbury) Limited
Incorporated: 31 October 2016
Net Worth Deficit: £49,000 *Total Assets:* £13,630,000
Registered Office: Cowley Business Park, Cowley, Uxbridge, Middlesex, UB8 2AL
Activities: Construction of commercial buildings
Shareholders: Wates Group Limited; Galliford Try Homes Limited
Officers: David Alexander Bowen [1967] Director/Accountant; David Michael Brocklebank [1967] Director; Andrew James Duxbury [1975] Director/Accountant; Benjamin John Engley [1975] Director/Head of Commercial; Natalie Jane Flint [1969] Sales Marketing Director; Christopher James Harris [1976] Director; Martin Geoffrey Leach [1965] Director; Andrew Colin Modle [1967] Director; Susan Scholfield [1965] Sales and Marketing Director; Martin John White [1964] Director

Linden/Downland Graylingwell LLP
Incorporated: 19 December 2007
Net Worth Deficit: £62,867,000 *Total Assets:* £69,750,000
Registered Office: Cowley Business Park, Cowley, Uxbridge, Middlesex, UB8 2AL

Lindt & Sprungli (U.K.) Limited
Incorporated: 20 June 1932 *Employees:* 331
Net Worth: £23,421,000 *Total Assets:* £87,928,000
Registered Office: Top Floor, 4 New Square, Bedfont Lakes, Feltham, Middlesex, TW14 8HA
Activities: Wholesale of sugar and chocolate and sugar confectionery
Parent: Chocoladefabriken Lindt & Sprungli AG
Officers: Alain Germiquet [1971] Director/Group Management Member [Swiss]; Dieter Weisskopf [1955] Director

Lineside Logistics (Southern) Ltd
Incorporated: 16 June 2006 *Employees:* 305
Net Worth: £5,300,283 *Total Assets:* £14,666,375
Registered Office: 249 Cranbrook Road, Ilford, Essex, IG1 4TG
Activities: Other business support service activities n.e.c.
Shareholder: Antoinette Carter
Officers: Antoinette Carter [1955] Managing Director

Lingerham Properties Limited
Incorporated: 29 April 1969
Net Worth: £10,434,964 *Total Assets:* £10,670,186
Registered Office: STC House, 7 Elmfield Road, Bromley, Kent, BR1 1LT
Activities: Management of real estate on a fee or contract basis
Major Shareholder: Pamela June Foster
Officers: Pamela June Foster, Secretary; Pamela June Foster [1967] Director/Company Secretary

Link Asset Services (Holdings) Limited
Incorporated: 12 July 2005 *Employees:* 1
Previous: Capita International Financial Services Holdings Limited
Net Worth: £44,999,328 *Total Assets:* £133,232,328
Registered Office: The Registry, 34 Beckenham Road, Beckenham, Kent, BR3 4TU
Activities: Other business support service activities n.e.c.
Parent: Link Market Services (EMEA) Limited
Officers: Jacqueline Millan [1966] Finance Director [Canadian]; Howard Alan Montagu [1970] Director; Anthony Patrick O'Keeffe [1965] Director

Link Corporate Trustees (UK) Limited
Incorporated: 22 May 1929 *Employees:* 57
Previous: Capita Trust Company Limited
Net Worth: £13,350,003 *Total Assets:* £18,837,716
Registered Office: The Registry, 34 Beckenham Road, Beckenham, Kent, BR3 4TU
Activities: Other business support service activities n.e.c.
Parent: Link Asset Services (Holdings) Limited
Officers: Colin Arthur Benford [1962] Director; Sean Peter Martin [1965] Director; Howard Alan Montagu [1970] Finance Director

Link Market Services Limited
Incorporated: 26 April 1991 *Employees:* 906
Previous: Capita Registrars Limited
Net Worth: £47,041,840 *Total Assets:* £131,760,304
Registered Office: The Registry, 34 Beckenham Road, Beckenham, Kent, BR3 4TU
Activities: Other business support service activities n.e.c.
Parent: Link Market Services (EMEA) Limited
Officers: Justin Ashley Cooper [1969] Managing Director; Nigel Timothy Fish [1967] Finance Director; Michael John Kempe [1970] Director [German]; David John Kilmartin [1968] Director; Graham Philip Renn [1957] Director

Link Market Services Trustees Limited
Incorporated: 7 July 1992 *Employees:* 238
Previous: Capita IRG Trustees Limited
Net Worth: £23,336,708 *Total Assets:* £26,423,796
Registered Office: The Registry, 34 Beckenham Road, Beckenham, Kent, BR3 4TU
Activities: Other service activities n.e.c.
Parent: Link Market Services (EMEA) Limited
Officers: Justin Ashley Cooper [1969] Managing Director; Nigel Timothy Fish [1967] Finance Director; Maureen Hadaway [1957] Director; Michael John Kempe [1970] Director [German]; Nicholas Michael Sharrock [1963] Director; Antony John Stuart [1952] Director

Linkam Scientific Instruments Limited
Incorporated: 14 October 1982 *Employees:* 39
Net Worth: £4,978,114 *Total Assets:* £6,275,220
Registered Office: Unit 8 Epsom Downs Metro Centre, Waterfield, Tadworth, Surrey, KT20 5LR
Activities: Manufacture of electronic measuring, testing etc. equipment, not for industrial process control
Major Shareholder: Arnold Cornelius Francois Kamp
Officers: Helen Kenward, Secretary; Ross Browne [1967] Managing Director; Arnoldus Cornelius Francois Kamp [1940] Technical Director [Dutch]; Vincent Bernard Kamp [1975] Managing Director [Dutch]

Linkhaven Estates Ltd
Incorporated: 23 April 2004
Net Worth: £4,299,521 *Total Assets:* £8,105,050
Registered Office: 148 Cranbrook Road, Ilford, Essex, IG1 4LZ
Activities: Other letting and operating of own or leased real estate
Major Shareholder: Pavneet Kaur Kataria
Officers: Gurvinder Kataria, Secretary; Pavneet Kaur Kataria [1970] Director/Developer

Linkmart Limited
Incorporated: 20 May 1997 *Employees:* 1
Net Worth: £240,600 *Total Assets:* £6,584,276
Registered Office: Suite A, 10th Floor, Maple House, High Street, Potters Bar, Herts, EN6 5BS
Activities: Other business support service activities n.e.c.
Major Shareholder: Dragan Blagojevic
Officers: Milomir Ilic, Secretary/Finance Manager; Dragan Blagojevic [1959] Director [British/Serbian]

Lint (Redington Road) Limited
Incorporated: 13 April 2005
Net Worth Deficit: £65,922 *Total Assets:* £10,437,188
Registered Office: Gabrielle House, 332-336 Perth Road, Ilford, Essex, IG2 6FF
Activities: Construction of domestic buildings
Parent: Lint Group Limited
Officers: Tarsaim Chand, Secretary/Director; Tarsaim Chand [1967] Director; Rizwan Patel [1974] Managing Director

Lint Group Limited
Incorporated: 22 April 2005 *Employees:* 57
Net Worth: £2,413,998 *Total Assets:* £18,456,874
Registered Office: Gabrielle House, 332-336 Perth Road, Ilford, Essex, IG2 6FF
Activities: Activities of other holding companies n.e.c.
Shareholders: Tarsaim Chand; Rizwan Patel
Officers: Tarsaim Chand, Director and Secretary; Tarsaim Chand [1967] Director & Secretary; Rizwan Patel [1974] Director

Lionel Road Coalyard Ltd
Incorporated: 5 December 2014
Net Worth: £16,248 *Total Assets:* £13,130,217
Registered Office: Griffin Park, Braemar Road, Brentford, Middlesex, TW8 0NT
Activities: Buying and selling of own real estate
Parent: Lionel Road Developments Ltd
Officers: Clifford Crown [1956] Finance Director; Conor Hayes [1954] Director/Chairman and Corporate Adviser [Irish]

Lionel Road Developments Ltd
Incorporated: 24 March 2006
Net Worth: £1,729,939 *Total Assets:* £34,820,496
Registered Office: Griffin Park, Braemar Road, Brentford, Middlesex, TW8 0NT
Activities: Buying and selling of own real estate
Parent: Brentford FC Ltd
Officers: Clifford Crown [1956] Finance Director; Conor Hayes [1954] Director/Corporate Adviser [Irish]

Lipman Properties Limited
Incorporated: 20 November 2003 *Employees:* 3
Net Worth Deficit: £390,987 *Total Assets:* £10,387,718
Registered Office: c/o Forward Financial Accounting Limited, Catalyst House, 720 Centennial Court, Centennial Park, Elstree, Herts, WD6 3SY
Activities: Real estate agencies
Major Shareholder: Steven Roy Lipman
Officers: Miriam Lipman, Secretary; Adam Lipman [1989] Director; Miriam Lipman [1965] Director [Danish]; Steven Roy Lipman [1962] Director

Thomas Lipton Ltd
Incorporated: 22 June 2017
Net Worth Deficit: £551,884 *Total Assets:* £13,378,481
Registered Office: 1st Floor, Woodgate Studios, 2-8 Games Road, Cockfosters, Barnet, Herts, EN4 9HN
Activities: Development of building projects
Major Shareholder: George Philippou
Officers: George Philippou [1965] Director

Lismire LLP
Incorporated: 16 May 2012
Net Worth: £13,920,003 *Total Assets:* £13,944,123
Registered Office: Old Bishops' College, Churchgate, Cheshunt, Herts, EN8 9XP
Officers: Richard John Murphy [1956] Member; Colette Helen Murphy [1989] LLP Member; Daniel Richard Murphy [1987] LLP Member; Siobhan Murphy [1985] LLP Member

Littleberries LLP
Incorporated: 26 May 2016
Net Worth: £2,460,000 *Total Assets:* £16,251,027
Registered Office: Grenville House, 4 Grenville Avenue, Broxbourne, Herts, EN10 7DH

Littlecroft Properties Limited
Incorporated: 14 November 1978 *Employees:* 6
Net Worth: £1,254,253 *Total Assets:* £6,104,684
Registered Office: 9-11 High Beech Road, Loughton, Essex, IG10 4BN
Activities: Development of building projects
Major Shareholder: Howard Ralph Winston
Officers: Michael John Weston [1980] Director/Manager; Hannah Louise Winston [1987] Director; Howard Ralph Winston [1953] Director

Lituanica UK Ltd
Incorporated: 6 November 2003 *Employees:* 144
Net Worth: £13,654,582 *Total Assets:* £21,924,308
Registered Office: 3 Gallions Close, Barking, Essex, IG11 0JD
Activities: Non-specialised wholesale of food, beverages and tobacco
Shareholders: Ruta Sakauskiene; Aurimas Sidlauskas
Officers: Ruta Sakauskiene, Secretary; Rasa Apostol [1968] Director [Lithuanian]; Rolandas Sakauskas [1972] Director [Lithuanian]; Ruta Sakauskiene [1972] Director [Lithuanian]

Livid Dare Limited
Incorporated: 21 May 2014 *Employees:* 3
Net Worth: £12,599,850 *Total Assets:* £13,061,452
Registered Office: Burgoine House, 8 Lower Teddington Road, Hampton Wick, Surrey, KT1 4ER
Activities: Other letting and operating of own or leased real estate
Shareholders: Claire Offer; Harry John Miles Offer
Officers: Claire Offer, Secretary; Claire Offer [1969] Director; Daisy Offer [1933] Director; Harry John Miles Offer [1962] Director/Chartered Surveyor

Livingston Group Limited
Incorporated: 1 June 2003
Net Worth Deficit: £9,524,000 *Total Assets:* £5,546,000
Registered Office: Unit 1 Waverley Industrial Park, Hailsham Drive, Harrow, Middlesex, HA1 4TR
Activities: Activities of head offices
Parent: Microlease Limited
Officers: Nigel Brown [1957] Director; John Joseph Hafferty [1956] Director/Chief Financial Officer [American]

Livingston Ltd
Incorporated: 22 August 1967 *Employees:* 46
Net Worth: £21,995,000 *Total Assets:* £44,311,000
Registered Office: Unit 1 Waverley Industrial Park, Hailsham Drive, Harrow, Middlesex, HA1 4TR
Activities: Renting and leasing of other machinery, equipment and tangible goods n.e.c.
Officers: Nigel Brown [1957] Director; Masten Gregory Evans [1960] Director; John Joseph Hafferty [1956] Director/Chief Financial Officer [American]; David Whitfield [1959] Director

Lixmere Properties Limited
Incorporated: 21 January 2004 *Employees:* 3
Net Worth: £2,896,903 *Total Assets:* £7,607,366
Registered Office: Lixmere House, 211 Kenton Road, Harrow, Middlesex, HA3 0HD
Activities: Buying and selling of own real estate
Shareholder: Jayendra Kumar Shah
Officers: Anya Shah Spellward, Secretary/Property Consultant; Jayendra Kumar Shah [1938] Director/Exporter; Sybille Shah [1939] Director/Housewife [German]; Anya Shah Spellward [1968] Director/Property Consultant

LNOC Limited
Incorporated: 24 September 2010
Net Worth: £439,379 *Total Assets:* £5,016,467
Registered Office: Centrum House, 36 Station Road, Egham, Surrey, TW20 9LF
Activities: Other service activities n.e.c.
Shareholders: Nicholas Roose Francis; Lesley Francis
Officers: Lesley Francis [1958] Director; Nicholas Roose Francis [1959] Director

Local Boy'z Group Holding Limited
Incorporated: 11 September 2009 *Employees:* 28
Net Worth: £11,016,244 *Total Assets:* £16,085,824
Registered Office: 1 Beauchamp Court, Victors Way, Barnet, Herts, EN5 5TZ
Activities: Other business support service activities n.e.c.
Major Shareholder: Stephen Mucklow
Officers: Muhammad Naeem, Secretary; Stephen Mucklow [1962] Director

Lodestar Properties Limited
Incorporated: 5 November 1962 *Employees:* 3
Net Worth: £5,761,095 *Total Assets:* £6,667,992
Registered Office: Oaks Farm, Vicarage Lane, Chigwell, Essex, IG7 6LT
Activities: Development of building projects
Officers: Rosanna Clare Spero, Secretary; Daniel Spero [1968] Director; Patricia Spero [1942] Director; Rosanna Clare Spero [1970] Director/Journalist

Lodge Bros. (Funerals) Limited
Incorporated: 1 January 1965 *Employees:* 156
Net Worth: £7,316,040 *Total Assets:* £25,171,020
Registered Office: Ludlow House, Ludlow Road, Feltham, Middlesex, TW13 7JF
Activities: Funeral and related activities
Officers: Michael Lodge, Secretary; Beverley Ann Harris [1960] Director; Andrew John Lodge [1969] Director; Christopher David Lodge [1970] Director; Janet Rachel Lodge [1969] Director; Michael James Lodge [1966] Financial Director; Robert John Lodge [1965] Director

Lodge Hotels (London) Limited
Incorporated: 15 November 1960 *Employees:* 35
Net Worth: £12,606,028 *Total Assets:* £17,079,576
Registered Office: 2 Castle Business Village, Station Road, Hampton, Surrey, TW12 2BX
Activities: Hotels and similar accommodation
Shareholders: John Jack Krall; Ben Robert Charles Hirschfeld; Anthony Gustav Hirschfeld
Officers: Ben Robert Charles Hirschfeld, Secretary; Anthony Gustav Hirschfeld [1948] Director/Hotelier; Ben Robert Charles Hirschfeld [1978] Director/Company Manager

London & District Limited
Incorporated: 18 March 2014 *Employees:* 3
Net Worth: £3,604,027 *Total Assets:* £8,493,728
Registered Office: Nightingale House, 46-48 East Street, Epsom, Surrey, KT17 1HQ
Activities: Other letting and operating of own or leased real estate
Shareholders: Meyrick Edward Douglas Ferguson; Niall Ferguson; Katherine Jane Margaret Ferguson
Officers: Katherine Jane Margaret Ferguson [1980] Director; Meyrick Edward Douglas Ferguson [1975] Director; Niall Ferguson [1977] Director

London Airports 1992 Limited
Incorporated: 3 August 1992
Net Worth: £996,345,984 *Total Assets:* £1,026,076,032
Registered Office: The Compass Centre, Nelson Road, Hounslow, Middlesex, TW6 2GW
Activities: Activities of head offices
Parent: LHR Airports Limited
Officers: Yuanyuan Ding [1979] Director; Javier Echave Espot [1980] Director [Spanish]; Nicholas Francis Golding [1963] Director

London and Hertfordshire Limited
Incorporated: 19 April 2016
Net Worth Deficit: £43,011 *Total Assets:* £17,566,748
Registered Office: The Lodge, Heriots, The Common, Stanmore, Middlesex, HA7 3HG
Activities: Buying and selling of own real estate
Shareholders: TPS Abbeydale St Albans Limited; KIG St Albans Limited
Officers: Marc Simon Franks [1981] Director; Gary Hackner [1982] Director [South African]; Lee Richard Joseph Portnoi [1959] Director

London Arena Investments Limited
Incorporated: 16 November 2012
Net Worth: £59,036,132 *Total Assets:* £59,096,132
Registered Office: World Business Centre, 3 Newall Road, London Heathrow Airport, Hounslow, Middlesex, TW6 2TA
Activities: Activities of other holding companies n.e.c.
Parent: Grove Acquisitions Limited
Officers: Athos George Yiannis, Secretary; Surinder Arora [1958] Director; Carlton Jeffrey Brown [1972] Director/Chartered Accountant; Athos George Yiannis [1963] Director/Chartered Accountant

London Care Partnership Limited
Incorporated: 9 January 2007 *Employees:* 207
Net Worth: £14,114,941 *Total Assets:* £26,390,636
Registered Office: c/o Elysium Healthcare, 2 Imperial Place, Maxwell Road, Borehamwood, Herts, WD6 1JN
Activities: Other residential care activities n.e.c.
Parent: Careprogress Limited
Officers: Sarah Juliette Livingston, Secretary; Lesley Joy Chamberlain [1963] Director/Group Chief Executive; Dr Quazi Shams Mahfooz Haque [1968] Executive Medical Director; Steven John Woolgar [1955] Director of Policy and Regulation

London City Bond Limited
Incorporated: 20 April 1988 *Employees:* 367
Net Worth: £2,073,670 *Total Assets:* £17,133,680
Registered Office: Olympus, 91-101 River Road, Barking, Essex, IG11 0EG
Activities: Operation of warehousing and storage facilities for land transport activities
Shareholders: Benjamin Arthur Crawshay Jones; Alexandra Jones
Officers: Alfred John Allington [1960] Director/Warehouse Manager; Brian John Davis [1953] Director/Business Development Manager; David Hogg [1955] Sales Director; Nicholas Andrew Joyce [1958] Finance Director

London Distribution Park LLP
Incorporated: 19 November 2012
Net Worth: £20,208,632 *Total Assets:* £20,301,448
Registered Office: Leslie Ford House, Tilbury Freeport, Tilbury, Essex, RM18 7EH

London Executive Aviation Limited
Incorporated: 24 October 1995 *Employees:* 88
Net Worth Deficit: £2,676,000 *Total Assets:* £15,557,000
Registered Office: Lea Office Building, Stapleford Aerodrome, Stapleford Tawney, Romford, Essex, RM4 1SJ
Activities: Non-scheduled passenger air transport
Parent: Executive Aviation Group Limited
Officers: Anthony George Medlock, Secretary; Aleksei Bazhenov [1973] Director; George Christos Galanopoulos [1963] Director; Patrick Joseph Albert Hansen [1972] Director [Luxembourger]; Patrick Joseph George Margetson-Rushmore [1959] Director; Charlotte Pedersen [1970] Director [Danish]

London Fluid System Technologies Limited
Incorporated: 28 June 2000 *Employees:* 47
Net Worth: £7,413,554 *Total Assets:* £9,684,841
Registered Office: Kingley Park, Station Road, Kings Langley, Herts, WD4 8GW
Activities: Manufacture of other fabricated metal products n.e.c.
Major Shareholder: Adrian Wynne
Officers: Deborah Ann Cridford, Secretary; Adrian Wynne [1961] Managing Director

London General Insurance Company Limited
Incorporated: 22 November 1984 *Employees:* 1
Net Worth: £126,461,000 *Total Assets:* £472,912,000
Registered Office: Twenty Kingston Road, Staines upon Thames, Surrey, TW18 4LG
Activities: Non-life insurance
Parent: TWG Europe Limited
Officers: Natalie Ann Paddock, Secretary; George Derek Wilson Bartlett [1948] Director; Michael John Carter [1981] Director; Colin Martin Kersley [1956] Director; Ricardo Jesus Morales-Gomez [1970] Director [American]; Andrew James Morris [1971] Director/Chief Executive Officer; Claude Kwasi Sarfo-Agyare [1969] Director

London General Life Company Limited
Incorporated: 16 November 1989
Net Worth: £5,291,000 *Total Assets:* £17,264,000
Registered Office: Twenty Kingston Road, Staines upon Thames, Surrey, TW18 4LG
Activities: Life insurance
Parent: TWG Europe Limited
Officers: Natalie Ann Paddock, Secretary; George Derek Wilson Bartlett [1948] Director; Michael John Carter [1981] Director; Colin Martin Kersely [1956] Director; Ricardo Jesus Morales-Gomez [1970] Director [American]; Andrew James Morris [1971] Director/Chief Executive Officer; Claude Kwasi Sarfo-Agyare [1969] Director

London Inn Hotels (Stratford) Limited
Incorporated: 13 July 2001 *Employees:* 51
Net Worth: £28,282,488 *Total Assets:* £52,877,656
Registered Office: 36 Railway Approach, Harrow, Middlesex, HA3 5AA
Activities: Hotels and similar accommodation
Parent: TLC Group Limited
Officers: Gagan Puri, Secretary; William Charles Neal [1986] Director; Paavan Popat [1985] Managing Director; Honourable Shivaan Shillin Popat [1988] Director; Gagan Puri [1978] Finance Director

London Irish Consortium (2013) Ltd
Incorporated: 3 December 2013
Net Worth: £3,008,593 *Total Assets:* £13,322,968
Registered Office: Hazelwood, Hazelwood Drive, Sunbury on Thames, Middlesex, TW16 6QU
Activities: Other business support service activities n.e.c.
Parent: Powerday PLC
Officers: Mark Laurence Bensted [1958] Director; Michael Rowland Crossan [1956] Director; Brian William Ernest Facer [1970] Director/Chief Executive Officer

London Irish Holdings Limited
Incorporated: 1 April 1997 *Employees:* 89
Net Worth: £7,340,591 *Total Assets:* £21,320,320
Registered Office: Hazelwood, Hazelwood Drive, Sunbury on Thames, Middlesex, TW16 6QU
Activities: Activities of head offices
Parent: London Irish Consortium (2013) Limited
Officers: Paul Forsyth, Secretary; Mark Laurence Bensted [1958] Director; Michael Rowland Crossan [1956] Director; Brian William Ernest Facer [1970] Director/Chief Executive; Nigel Northridge [1956] Director; Michael O'Hagan [1964] Director [Irish]; Allan Robson [1954] Director; Jonathan Robert Turner [1975] Director [Irish]

London Irish Rugby Football Ground Limited
Incorporated: 14 November 1927
Net Worth: £10,777,897 *Total Assets:* £10,786,027
Registered Office: Hazelwood Centre, Croysdale Avenue, Sunbury on Thames, Middlesex, TW16 6QU
Activities: Activities of sport clubs
Parent: London Irish Holdings Limited
Officers: Paul Forsyth, Secretary; Mark Laurence Bensted [1958] Director; Michael Rowland Crossan [1956] Director; Brian William Ernest Facer [1970] Director/Chief Executive

London Irish Scottish Richmond Limited
Incorporated: 1 June 1999 *Employees:* 89
Net Worth Deficit: £17,804,016 *Total Assets:* £8,323,801
Registered Office: Hazelwood, Hazelwood Drive, Sunbury on Thames, Middlesex, TW16 6QU
Activities: Activities of sport clubs
Parent: London Irish Holdings Limited
Officers: Paul Forsyth, Secretary; Mark Laurence Bensted [1958] Director; Michael Rowland Crossan [1956] Director; Brian William Ernest Facer [1970] Director/Chief Executive; Allan Robson [1954] Director

London May Fair Hotel Limited
Incorporated: 17 July 2003 *Employees:* 483
Net Worth: £367,048,992 *Total Assets:* £550,019,968
Registered Office: 140 Bath Road, Hayes, Middlesex, UB3 5AW
Activities: Hotels and similar accommodation
Parent: Edwardian Hotel Finance Ltd
Officers: Vijay Wason, Secretary; John Robert Morley [1945] Director/Financial Consultant; Inderneel Singh [1984] Director; Jasminder Singh [1951] Director/Hotelier; Vijay Wason [1948] Director/Company Secretary

The London Outpost Limited
Incorporated: 14 March 1984
Net Worth Deficit: £8,926,094 *Total Assets:* £9,531,085
Registered Office: Unit 2 Capital Business Park, Manor Way, Borehamwood, Herts, WD6 1GW
Activities: Other business support service activities n.e.c.
Parent: Pipestone Properties Limited
Officers: Karen Millie-James, Secretary; Moustapha El Solh [1970] Director [Lebanese]; Marc Thevenoux [1956] Director [French]

London Pharma & Chemicals Group Ltd
Incorporated: 11 February 2003 *Employees:* 9
Net Worth: £11,520,712 *Total Assets:* £19,651,536
Registered Office: Unit 10 Delta Court, Manor Way, Borehamwood, Herts, WD6 1FJ
Activities: Bookkeeping activities
Parent: London Pharma & Chemicals Holdings Ltd
Officers: Alan Edward Eastwood [1955] Director; Christian Leemann [1958] Director/Chief Executive Officer [Swiss]; Jamie Andrew Sandler [1976] Finance Director; Daniel Reuben Straus [1972] Director/Business Manager

London Pharma & Chemicals Holdings Ltd
Incorporated: 18 November 2009 *Employees:* 131
Net Worth: £21,623,834 *Total Assets:* £42,261,880
Registered Office: Unit 10 Delta Court, Manor Way, Borehamwood, Herts, WD6 1FJ
Activities: Activities of head offices
Shareholders: Claire Joanne Sharon Straus; Daniel Reuben Straus
Officers: Claire Joanne Sharon Straus [1969] Director; Daniel Reuben Straus [1972] Director/Business Manager

London Residential Healthcare Limited
Incorporated: 18 February 1997 *Employees:* 796
Net Worth: £43,950,320 *Total Assets:* £78,004,168
Registered Office: 12-14 Langley Avenue, Surbiton, Surrey, KT6 6QL
Activities: Development of building projects
Parent: LRH Care Homes Limited
Officers: Eirik Peter Robson [1958] Director; Arnon Nir Rubinstein [1964] Director

London School of Theology
Incorporated: 25 June 1943 *Employees:* 64
Net Worth: £11,476,952 *Total Assets:* £13,359,058
Registered Office: Green Lane, Northwood, Middlesex, HA6 2UW
Activities: First-degree level higher education
Officers: Ruwani Christine Gunawardene, Secretary; Rev Bunmi Yemi Adedeji [1961] Director of The One People Commission, Minister; Graham Alan Cray [1947] Director/Minister; Rev Jonathan William Dixon Douglas [1975] Director/Minister; Margaret Marian Doyle [1953] Director/School Tutor; Steve Hughes [1949] Director/Retired; Revd Dr Alex Irving [1987] Director/Minister; Malcolm Douglas Peckham [1946] Director/Retired; Paul Maurice Smith [1945] Director/Consultant Electrical Engineer; Ian Thompson [1968] Director/Banker; Professor Hugh Godfrey Maturin Williamson [1947] Director/Regius Professor

London South East Academies Trust
Incorporated: 7 May 2014 *Employees:* 177
Previous: Bromley Educational Trust
Net Worth: £29,381,000 *Total Assets:* £33,542,000
Registered Office: Bromley College, Rookery Lane, Bromley, Kent, BR2 8HE
Activities: Other education n.e.c.
Officers: John Peter Hunt, Secretary; Maxwell Bero [1971] Director/Chief Internal Auditor; Corinne Botten [1952] Director/Chair of Governors, New Horizons Federation; Mark Burnett [1984] Director/Chief Operating Officer; David Lambert [1970] Director/Vice Principal, LSEC; Helen Samantha Parrett [1969] Director/Principal and Chief Executive; Joanna Power [1982] Director/Leveraged Finance Officer; Peter Charles Reeves [1954] Director/Retired

London Sovereign Limited
Incorporated: 5 February 1990 *Employees:* 505
Net Worth: £2,083,000 *Total Assets:* £5,405,000
Registered Office: Busways House, Wellington Road, Twickenham, Middlesex, TW2 5NX
Activities: Other urban, suburban or metropolitan passenger land transport (not underground, metro or similar)
Parent: RATP DEV UK Ltd
Officers: Catherine Marie-Jeanne Chardon [1970] Transformation Director [French]; Romain Ferriere [1975] Director/Chief Financial Officer [French]; Karen Rose Fuller [1968] HR Director; Howard Charles Goodbourn [1961] Director/Chief Financial Officer; David Andrew Kaye [1962] Director; Kuldeep Singh Nothey [1965] Service Delivery Director; Peter Richardson [1974] Finance Director; Florence Rodet [1969] Director/Secretary General - Public Relations [French]; Fiona Jacqueline Taylor [1962] Managing Director

London Square (Crimscott Street) Limited
Incorporated: 1 August 2013
Net Worth: £2,485,000 *Total Assets:* £69,164,000
Registered Office: One York Road, Uxbridge, Middlesex, UB8 1RN
Activities: Development of building projects
Parent: LSQ (Crimscott Street) Holdings Ltd
Officers: Adam Lawrence, Secretary; Scott Douglas Brown [1968] Director [Australian]; Mark Stewart Evans [1969] Director/Chief Operating Officer; Steven Simon Hudson [1970] Commercial Director; Adam Paul Lawrence [1970] Director; Rebecca Susan Littler [1982] Sales and Marketing Director; Andy Maciejewski [1965] Construction Director; Matthew Steven Phillips [1979] Technical Director; Mark Clive Smith [1973] Development and Technical Director

London Square (Fulham) Limited
Incorporated: 27 September 2011
Net Worth: £17,429,564 *Total Assets:* £29,057,560
Registered Office: One York Road, Uxbridge, Middlesex, UB8 1RN
Activities: Development of building projects
Parent: London Square Developments (Ventures) Ltd
Officers: Adam Paul Lawrence, Secretary; Scott Douglas Brown [1968] Director [Australian]; Mark Stewart Evans [1969] Director/Chief Operating Officer; Adam Paul Lawrence [1970] Director

London Square (Holdings) Limited
Incorporated: 16 February 2010
Net Worth: £27,498,476 *Total Assets:* £27,528,478
Registered Office: One York Road, Uxbridge, Middlesex, UB8 1RN
Activities: Development of building projects
Parent: London Square Developments (Ventures) Ltd
Officers: Adam Lawrence, Secretary; Scott Douglas Brown [1968] Director [Australian]; Mark Stewart Evans [1969] Director/Chief Operating Officer; Adam Paul Lawrence [1970] Director

London Square (Putney) Limited
Incorporated: 10 May 2011
Net Worth: £23,652,620 *Total Assets:* £32,865,840
Registered Office: One York Road, Uxbridge, Middlesex, UB8 1RN
Activities: Development of building projects
Parent: London Square Developments Ltd
Officers: Adam Lawrence, Secretary; Scott Douglas Brown [1968] Director [Australian]; Mark Stewart Evans [1969] Director/Chief Operating Officer; Steven Simon Hudson [1970] Commercial Director; Adam Paul Lawrence [1970] Director; Rebecca Susan Littler [1982] Sales and Marketing Director; Andy Maciejewski [1965] Construction Director; Matthew Steven Phillips [1979] Technical Director; Mark Clive Smith [1973] Development and Technical Director

London Square (Streatham) Limited
Incorporated: 18 June 2013
Net Worth: £17,003,000 *Total Assets:* £37,852,000
Registered Office: One York Road, Uxbridge, Middlesex, UB8 1RN
Activities: Development of building projects
Parent: London Square (Investments) Ltd
Officers: Adam Lawrence, Secretary; Scott Douglas Brown [1968] Director [Australian]; Mark Stewart Evans [1969] Director/Chief Operating Officer; Steven Simon Hudson [1970] Commercial Director; Adam Paul Lawrence [1970] Director; Rebecca Susan Littler [1982] Sales and Marketing Director; Andy Maciejewski [1965] Construction Director; Matthew Steven Phillips [1979] Technical Director; Mark Clive Smith [1973] Development and Technical Director

London Square Development Management Limited
Incorporated: 27 September 2011
Net Worth: £3,690,000 *Total Assets:* £16,466,000
Registered Office: One York Road, Uxbridge, Middlesex, UB8 1RN
Activities: Development of building projects
Parent: London Square Developments (Ventures) Ltd
Officers: Adam Lawrence, Secretary; Scott Douglas Brown [1968] Director [Australian]; Mark Stewart Evans [1969] Director/Chief Operating Officer; Steven Simon Hudson [1970] Commercial Director; Adam Paul Lawrence [1970] Director; Rebecca Susan Littler [1982] Sales and Marketing Director; Andy Maciejewski [1965] Construction Director; Matthew Steven Phillips [1979] Technical Director; Mark Clive Smith [1973] Development and Technical Director

London Square Developments (Holdings) Limited
Incorporated: 20 June 2014 *Employees:* 142
Net Worth Deficit: £59,871,000 *Total Assets:* £496,519,008
Registered Office: One York Road, Uxbridge, Middlesex, UB8 1RN
Activities: Construction of domestic buildings
Parent: LSQ Holdings (Luxembourg) SARL
Officers: William Stephen Benjamin [1964] Director [American]; Scott Douglas Brown [1968] Director [Australian]; Mark Buckland [1960] Director [American]; Stephen Charles Casey [1949] Director; Mark Stewart Evans [1969] Director/Chief Operating Officer; Adam Paul Lawrence [1970] Director; Mark Andrew Pain [1961] Director; Charles Richard Arklay Steel [1975] Director; William Gowanloch Westbrook [1976] Director

London Square Developments (Ventures) Limited
Incorporated: 15 September 2011 *Employees:* 142
Net Worth: £98,451,000 *Total Assets:* £473,415,008
Registered Office: One York Road, Uxbridge, Middlesex, UB8 1RN
Activities: Development of building projects
Parent: London Square Ltd
Officers: Adam Paul Lawrence, Secretary; Scott Douglas Brown [1968] Director [Australian]; Mark Stewart Evans [1969] Director/Chief Operating Officer; Adam Paul Lawrence [1970] Director

London Square Developments Limited
Incorporated: 17 February 2010 *Employees:* 142
Net Worth Deficit: £17,185,000 *Total Assets:* £370,248,000
Registered Office: One York Road, Uxbridge, Middlesex, UB8 1RN
Activities: Development of building projects
Parent: London Square (Holdings) Ltd
Officers: Adam Lawrence, Secretary; Scott Douglas Brown [1968] Director [Australian]; Mark Stewart Evans [1969] Director/Chief Operating Officer; Steven Simon Hudson [1970] Commercial Director; Adam Paul Lawrence [1970] Director; Rebecca Susan Littler [1982] Sales and Marketing Director; Andy Maciejewski [1965] Construction Director; Matthew Steven Phillips [1979] Technical Director; Mark Clive Smith [1973] Development and Technical Director

London Square Limited
Incorporated: 14 September 2011 *Employees:* 142
Net Worth: £157,144,992 *Total Assets:* £460,803,008
Registered Office: One York Road, Uxbridge, Middlesex, UB8 1RN
Activities: Development of building projects
Parent: LSQ Holdco 3 Ltd
Officers: Adam Paul Lawrence, Secretary; Scott Douglas Brown [1968] Director [Australian]; Stephen Charles Casey [1949] Director/Executive; Mark Stewart Evans [1969] Director/Chief Operating Officer; Steven Simon Hudson [1970] Commercial Director; Adam Paul Lawrence [1970] Director; Rebecca Susan Littler [1982] Sales & Marketing Director; Andy Maciejewski [1965] Construction Director; Mark Andrew Pain [1961] Director; Matthew Steven Phillips [1979] Technical Director; Mark Clive Smith [1973] Development Director

London Tower Crane Hire & Sales Limited
Incorporated: 25 April 2003 *Employees:* 58
Net Worth: £21,214,614 *Total Assets:* £46,363,016
Registered Office: 4 Elstree Way, Borehamwood, Herts, WD6 1RN
Activities: Renting and leasing of construction and civil engineering machinery and equipment
Parent: JRL Group Ltd
Officers: Ronan Joseph Gleeson, Secretary/Director [Irish]; Ronan Joseph Gleeson [1976] Director [Irish]; Martin Harvey [1972] Director/Operations Manager; Kevin William Keegan [1963] Director/Estimator [Irish]; John James Reddington [1972] Director/Formwork [Irish]

London United Busways Limited
Incorporated: 14 December 1988 *Employees:* 2,556
Net Worth: £47,625,000 *Total Assets:* £75,454,000
Registered Office: Busways House, Wellington Road, Twickenham, Middlesex, TW2 5NX
Activities: Other urban, suburban or metropolitan passenger land transport (not underground, metro or similar)
Parent: RATP DEV UK Ltd
Officers: Catherine Marie-Jeanne Chardon [1970] Transformation Director [French]; Romain Ferriere [1975] Director/Chief Financial Officer [French]; Karen Rose Fuller [1968] HR Director; Howard Charles Goodbourn [1961] Director/Chief Financial Officer; David Andrew Kaye [1962] Director; Kuldeep Singh Nothey [1965] Service Delivery Director; Peter Richardson [1974] Finance Director; Florence Rodet [1969] Director/Secretary General - Public Relations [French]; Fiona Jacqueline Taylor [1962] Managing Director

London Urban Investments Limited
Incorporated: 17 October 2014
Net Worth Deficit: £8,297 *Total Assets:* £5,053,673
Registered Office: Delson Suite, 2nd Floor, Amba House, 15 College Road, Harrow, Middlesex, HA1 1BA
Activities: Other letting and operating of own or leased real estate
Shareholders: Sara Castelao; Gloria Monroy
Officers: Sara Castelao [1969] Director/Senior Coordinator; Gloria Monroy [1960] Director/Senior Financial Accountant

London Wharf Limited
Incorporated: 5 January 1993 *Employees:* 5
Previous: London Wharf PLC
Net Worth: £6,456,536 *Total Assets:* £6,577,012
Registered Office: York House, Empire Way, Wembley, Middlesex, HA9 0FQ
Activities: Construction of commercial buildings
Officers: David Lewin [1962] Director/Property Dealer; Peter Malcolm Wharfe [1958] Director/Builder

Longford Securities & Equities (K & T) Limited
Incorporated: 3 March 2003
Net Worth: £6,045,536 *Total Assets:* £28,351,580
Registered Office: Alton House, 66-68 High Street, Northwood, Middlesex, HA6 1BL
Activities: Development of building projects
Major Shareholder: Barry Attarzadeh
Officers: Peter William Johnson, Secretary; Barry Attarzadeh [1956] Director/Property Developer [Canadian]

Longford Securities & Equities Limited
Incorporated: 17 June 1993
Net Worth Deficit: £712,672 *Total Assets:* £12,183,284
Registered Office: Alton House, 66 High Street, Northwood, Middlesex, HA6 1BL
Activities: Development of building projects
Major Shareholder: Barry Attarzadeh
Officers: Peter William Johnson, Secretary; Barry Attarzadeh [1956] Director/Property Developer [Canadian]; Peter William Johnson [1948] Director/Chartered Quantity Surveyor

Longmill Realty Limited
Incorporated: 31 October 1984 *Employees:* 11
Net Worth: £5,246,337 *Total Assets:* £13,562,213
Registered Office: 5 Elstree Gate, Elstree Way, Borehamwood, Herts, WD6 1JD
Activities: Non-specialised wholesale trade
Major Shareholder: David Yamin-Joseph
Officers: Veerasingham Ganeshan Jeyabavan, Secretary/Director; Veerasingham Ganeshan Jeyabavan [1960] Director; David Yamin-Joseph [1965] Director/Merchant [Italian]

Longmill Rickbost Ltd
Incorporated: 9 January 2012
Net Worth: £451,390 *Total Assets:* £12,921,310
Registered Office: 5 Elstree Gate, Elstree Way, Borehamwood, Herts, WD6 1JD
Activities: Buying and selling of own real estate
Parent: Longmill Realty Limited
Officers: Veerasingham Ganeshan Jeyabavan [1960] Director; David Yamin-Joseph [1965] Director [Italian]

Longview Holding Hedge UK Limited
Incorporated: 17 March 2015
Net Worth Deficit: £1,662,194 *Total Assets:* £12,734,800
Registered Office: Nexus House, Station Road, Egham, Surrey, TW20 9LB
Activities: Business and domestic software development
Parent: Longview Holding UK 2 Limited
Officers: Nick Kaiser [1976] Director/Private Equity [American]; Grant Bennett Schachter [1984] Director/Private Equity [American]; Michael Edward Wilkinson [1986] Director/Private Equity

Longview Holding Parent UK Limited
Incorporated: 18 December 2014 *Employees:* 187
Net Worth Deficit: £37,752,428 *Total Assets:* £47,795,592
Registered Office: Nexus House, Station Road, Egham, Surrey, TW20 9LB
Activities: Business and domestic software development
Officers: Nick Kaiser [1976] Director/Private Equity [American]; Grant Bennett Schachter [1964] Director/Private Equity [American]; Michael Edward Wilkinson [1986] Director/Private Equity

Longview Holding UK 2 Limited
Incorporated: 14 April 2014
Net Worth: £18,459,710 *Total Assets:* £25,975,620
Registered Office: Nexus House, Station Road, Egham, Surrey, TW20 9LB
Activities: Business and domestic software development
Parent: Longview Holding UK Limited
Officers: Jerome Jon Dolinsky [1965] Director [American]; Nick Kaiser [1976] Director/Private Equity [American]; Grant Bennett Schachter [1984] Director/Private Equity [American]; Michael Edward Wilkinson [1986] Director/Private Equity

Longview Holding UK Limited
Incorporated: 3 March 2014 *Employees:* 187
Net Worth Deficit: £35,288,660 *Total Assets:* £47,549,644
Registered Office: Nexus House, Station Road, Egham, Surrey, TW20 9LB
Activities: Business and domestic software development
Parent: Longview Holding Parent UK Limited
Officers: Nick Kaiser [1976] Director/Private Equity [American]; Grant Bennett Schachter [1984] Director/Private Equity [American]; Michael Edward Wilkinson [1986] Director/Private Equity

Lorclon Limited
Incorporated: 12 April 2006 *Employees:* 11
Net Worth: £2,729,380 *Total Assets:* £5,797,065
Registered Office: 2 Mountside, Stanmore, Middlesex, HA7 2DT
Activities: Other specialised construction activities n.e.c.
Shareholders: Kevin Leahy; Michael James O'Meara
Officers: Kevin Leahy, Secretary; Kevin Leahy [1965] Director/Manager; Keith Joseph Morgan [1958] Managing Director; Michael James O'Meara [1972] Director/Civil Engineer [Irish]

Lord Street Properties (Southport) Limited
Incorporated: 8 December 1896
Net Worth: £5,156,033 *Total Assets:* £5,244,797
Registered Office: Unicorn House, Station Close, Potters Bar, Herts, EN6 1TL
Activities: Other letting and operating of own or leased real estate
Parent: Panther Securities PLC
Officers: Simon Peters, Secretary; Andrew Stewart Perloff [1944] Director; John Perloff [1977] Director; Simon Jeffrey Peters [1977] Director

J H Lorimer Limited
Incorporated: 30 July 1949 *Employees:* 104
Net Worth: £12,045,377 *Total Assets:* £15,554,778
Registered Office: Unit B2, Ullswater Crescent, Ullswater Industrial Estate, Coulsdon, Surrey, CR5 2HR
Activities: Other retail sale in non-specialised stores
Parent: PAAM Investments Ltd
Officers: Rajan Virendrabhai Patel, Secretary; Bhavini Udhyam Amin [1963] Director/Pharmacist; Udhyam Babubhai Amin [1961] Director/Businessman; Dipesh Virendrabhai Patel [1966] Director; Kiren Virendrabhai Patel [1970] Director; Rajan Virendrabhai Patel [1972] IT Consultant Director; Virendra Chhotabhai Patel [1938] Director

Lorne Stewart PLC
Incorporated: 16 January 1978 *Employees:* 727
Net Worth: £13,031,000 *Total Assets:* £65,703,000
Registered Office: Stewart House, Kenton Road, Harrow, Middlesex, HA3 9TU
Activities: Electrical installation
Parent: LSRM Holdings Ltd
Officers: Inbaraj Rajakumar, Secretary; Tarek Fuad Abuzayyad [1969] Director/Finance; Gary Heitmann [1970] Group Business Development Director; Paul James Hughes [1956] Group Commercial Director; Jacob Kurian [1958] Director/Group Financial Controller [Australian]; Puliyelethu Mathai Mathew [1952] Director/Group Vice Chairman [Indian]; Ramesh Krishna Murthy [1962] Director/Group Chief Financial Officer [Indian]; Simon Roopchand [1973] Director/Group Chief Executive Officer; David Webb [1971] Managing Director - FM; Gary Robert Worrall [1959] Director/CEO - Contracting Division

Lotus Flower Holdings Limited
Incorporated: 4 December 2013 *Employees:* 2,472
Net Worth: £33,848,784 *Total Assets:* £65,505,608
Registered Office: Jetha House, Unit 5 Auriol Drive, Greenford Park, Greenford, Middlesex, UB6 0TP
Activities: Activities of head offices
Major Shareholder: Leena Avnish Malde
Officers: Leena Malde, Secretary; Avnish Amritlal Malde [1965] Director; Leena Avnish Malde [1966] Director

Loudwater Management Limited
Incorporated: 24 May 2010 *Employees:* 16
Net Worth: £4,047,119 *Total Assets:* £35,059,456
Registered Office: Lynwood House, 373-375 Station Road, Harrow, Middlesex, HA1 2AW
Activities: Activities of distribution holding companies
Shareholders: Rishy Investments Limited; Loudwater Trade and Finance Limited
Officers: Anthony Herman Stimler [1971] Director; Maurice Stimler [1978] Director; Stanley Stimler [1955] Director

Loughton Care Centre Limited
Incorporated: 25 November 2011 *Employees:* 63
Net Worth: £3,071,000 *Total Assets:* £10,939,000
Registered Office: Regal House, Royal Crescent, Ilford, Essex, IG2 7JY
Activities: Residential nursing care facilities
Parent: Gibson Propco Limited
Officers: Harnoop Singh Atkar [1986] Director; Daren Dalmedo [1978] Director

Love Productions Limited
Incorporated: 3 September 2004 *Employees:* 57
Net Worth: £4,619,302 *Total Assets:* £11,515,173
Registered Office: Grant Way, Isleworth, Middlesex, TW7 5QD
Activities: Television programme production activities
Parent: Sky Ventures Limited
Officers: Christopher Jon Taylor, Secretary; Caroline Lindsay Cooper [1980] Finance Director; Laetitia Ellen Kavanagh [1974] Managing Director [Irish]; Richard McKerrow [1964] Director/TV Producer; Jane Helen Millichip [1965] Managing Director; Dominic Richard Shorrocks [1972] Director

Lowen Homes Limited
Incorporated: 22 June 2017
Net Worth: £24,000 *Total Assets:* £7,148,000
Registered Office: Marina House, 17 Marina Place, Hampton Wick, Kingston upon Thames, Surrey, KT1 4BH
Activities: Development of building projects
Parent: Hastoe Housing Association Limited
Officers: William Jeremy Mostyn Roberts, Secretary; Andrew Potter [1971] Director/Chief Executive; William Jeremy Roberts [1970] Finance Director

Lowery Group Limited
Incorporated: 4 March 2015 *Employees:* 56
Net Worth: £3,364,146 *Total Assets:* £13,088,788
Registered Office: Ashley Place, Hanworth Lane, Chertsey, Surrey, KT16 9JX
Activities: Dormant company
Shareholders: Daniel Napier Burge; Kenneth George Henson; Mark Gubbins
Officers: Daniel Napier Burge [1974] Director; Mark Gubbins [1964] Director; Kenneth George Henson [1955] Director

Lowery Limited
Incorporated: 17 August 1950 *Employees:* 41
Net Worth: £7,051,494 *Total Assets:* £11,295,787
Registered Office: Ashley Place, Hanworth Lane, Chertsey, Surrey, KT16 9JX
Activities: Construction of other civil engineering projects n.e.c.
Parent: Lowery Holdings Limited
Officers: Daniel Napier Burge [1974] Director; Mark Gubbins [1964] Director; Kenneth George Henson [1955] Director

Loxford School Trust Limited
Incorporated: 22 October 2013 *Employees:* 776
Net Worth: £78,953,616 *Total Assets:* £88,856,584
Registered Office: Loxford School, Loxford Lane, Ilford, Essex, IG1 2UT
Activities: Other education n.e.c.
Officers: Peter William Ballard [1948] Director; David Francis Hubbard [1948] Director; Anita Johnson [1965] Director; David Anthony Low [1950] Director/Retired; Michael McIntyre [1957] Director/Project Management and Mentoring

Loxleigh Investments Limited
Incorporated: 20 October 2011
Net Worth: £1,316,696 *Total Assets:* £12,247,300
Registered Office: 3 Montpelier Avenue, Bexley, Kent, DA5 3AP
Activities: Development of building projects
Major Shareholder: Lakhbir Singh Heer
Officers: Lakhbir Singh Heer [1966] Managing Director

LPM Acquisitions Limited
Incorporated: 10 November 2006
Net Worth Deficit: £8,226,000 *Total Assets:* £7,544,000
Registered Office: Ground Floor Suite, River House, Maidstone Road, Sidcup, Kent, DA14 5RH
Activities: Activities of head offices
Officers: Simon Kenneth Giles, Secretary; Simon Kenneth Giles [1974] Finance Director; Jonathan Stephen Levine [1952] Director/Chief Executive

LQAL UK Limited
Incorporated: 14 June 2017
Net Worth: £18,954,204 *Total Assets:* £20,657,178
Registered Office: 2 Victoria Works, 6 Fairway, Orpington, Kent, BR5 1EG
Activities: Hotels and similar accommodation
Officers: Michael Bornitz [1982] Director [American]; Andrew Steven Lazzaro [1971] Director [American]

LRH Care Homes Limited
Incorporated: 24 November 2016 *Employees:* 796
Net Worth: £24,630,758 *Total Assets:* £82,756,456
Registered Office: 12-14 Langley Avenue, Surbiton, Surrey, KT6 6QL
Activities: Other business support service activities n.e.c.
Officers: Eirik Peter Robson [1958] Director/Surveyor; Arnon Nir Rubinstein [1964] Managing Director

LSG/Sky Chefs Europe Holdings Limited
Incorporated: 4 February 1998 *Employees:* 14
Net Worth: £16,558,000 *Total Assets:* £67,589,000
Registered Office: Heathrow Boulevard 2, 284 Bath Road, Sipson, West Drayton, Middlesex, UB7 0DQ
Activities: Event catering activities
Shareholders: LSG South America GmbH; LSG Lufthansa Service Europa/Africa GmbH
Officers: Muhammad Waqas, Secretary; Matteo Bagliani [1966] Managing Director [Italian]

LSQ (Crimscott Street) Holdings Limited
Incorporated: 9 March 2017
Net Worth: £2 *Total Assets:* £31,261,704
Registered Office: 1 York Road, Uxbridge, Middlesex, UB8 1RN
Activities: Development of building projects
Parent: London Square (Investments) Limited
Officers: Scott Douglas Brown [1968] Director/Chief Financial Officer [Australian]; Mark Stewart Evans [1969] Director/Chief Operating Officer; Adam Paul Lawrence [1970] Director/Chief Executive Officer

LSQ Holdco 3 Limited
Incorporated: 20 June 2014
Net Worth Deficit: £73,047,000 *Total Assets:* £179,984,000
Registered Office: One York Road, Uxbridge, Middlesex, UB8 1RN
Activities: Construction of domestic buildings
Parent: LSQ Holdco 2 Ltd
Officers: Scott Douglas Brown [1968] Director [Australian]; Mark Stewart Evans [1969] Director/Chief Operating Officer; Adam Paul Lawrence [1970] Director; Charles Richard Arklay Steel [1975] Director; William Gowanloch Westbrook [1976] Director

Lubkowski Saunders and Associates Limited
Incorporated: 10 December 1973 *Employees:* 68
Net Worth: £4,017,022 *Total Assets:* £5,851,923
Registered Office: Unit C2, Dolphin Estate, Windmill Road West, Sunbury on Thames, Middlesex, TW16 7HE
Activities: Manufacture and processing of other glass, including technical glassware
Major Shareholder: Monika Ewa Lubkowska-Jonas
Officers: Malcolm Julian Foreman, Secretary; Malcolm Julian Foreman [1964] Director/Accountant; Mark Jonas [1961] Director; Monika Ewa Lubkowska-Jonas [1960] Director; Richard Andrew Smedley [1967] Managing Director

Lubricants UK Limited
Incorporated: 13 March 1908 *Employees:* 721
Net Worth: £189,942,000 *Total Assets:* £408,201,984
Registered Office: Chertsey Road, Sunbury on Thames, Middlesex, TW16 7BP
Activities: Mineral oil refining
Parent: Burmah Castrol PLC
Officers: Peter James Mather [1960] Director/Oil Company Executive; Andrew Michael Moore [1964] Director/Oil Company Executive; Daniel Chukumah Odogwu [1966] Director/Oil Company Executive; Paul Ian Winton Turner [1963] Director/Oil Company Executive

Luce Limited
Incorporated: 27 June 2000
Net Worth: £2,701,142 *Total Assets:* £9,483,999
Registered Office: Donal Lucey Lawlor, 61 The Base, Victoria Road, Dartford, Kent, DA1 5FS
Activities: Other letting and operating of own or leased real estate
Major Shareholder: Donal Finbarr Lucey
Officers: Donal Finbarr Lucey [1958] Director/Chartered Accountant [Irish]

Mark Luck Limited
Incorporated: 28 February 1977 *Employees:* 55
Net Worth: £1,775,429 *Total Assets:* £5,969,883
Registered Office: Numeric House, 98 Station Road, Sidcup, Kent, DA15 7BY
Activities: Other building completion and finishing
Parent: Mark Luck (Holdings) Ltd
Officers: Mark Lennard James Luck, Secretary; Guy Alan James Archbutt [1978] Director; Elizabeth Louise Carter [1985] Director; Mark Lennard James Luck [1984] Director/Haulier

Lucozade Ribena Suntory Limited
Incorporated: 10 July 2013 *Employees:* 720
Net Worth: £864,452,992 *Total Assets:* £1,394,434,944
Registered Office: 2 Longwalk Road, Stockley Park, Uxbridge, Middlesex, UB11 1BA
Activities: Manufacture of soft drinks; production of mineral waters and other bottled waters
Parent: Suntory Beverage & Food Limited
Officers: Mary Guest, Secretary; Mary Elizabeth Guest [1980] Director and Company Secretary; Peter John Harding [1964] Director/Chief Operating Officer; Toby Peter McKeever [1969] Director; Jaime Antonio Mussons Freixas [1961] Director/Chief Marketing Officer [Spanish]; Carol Robert [1979] Director; Takayuki Sanno [1968] Director [Japanese]; Craig William Shelden [1964] Director/Chief Financial Officer [Australian]; Tetsu Tanaka [1967] Director [Japanese]; Peter James Thomlinson [1967] Director/Chief Financial Officer; Yuji Yamazaki [1957] Director [Japanese]

Lufthansa Technik Landing Gear Services UK Limited
Incorporated: 3 November 1997 *Employees:* 278
Net Worth Deficit: £5,843,000 *Total Assets:* £25,961,000
Registered Office: Unit 3 Dawley Park, Kestrel Way, Hayes, Middlesex, UB3 1HP
Activities: Repair and maintenance of aircraft and spacecraft
Shareholders: Lufthansa Technik A.G.; Deutsche Lufthansa AG
Officers: Olaf Behn, Secretary; Sandra Ecksten [1973] Director [German]; Robert Gaag [1960] Director [German]; Klaus Wachholz [1968] Director [German]

Lumen Learning Trust
Incorporated: 30 August 2013 *Employees:* 239
Net Worth: £15,604,725 *Total Assets:* £18,325,380
Registered Office: Saxon Primary School, Briar Road, Shepperton, Surrey, TW17 0JB
Activities: Primary education
Officers: Elizabeth Helen Wilkins, Secretary; Laura Ellis-Philip [1965] IT Director; Ian Thomas Ingham [1952] Director/Business Executive; Mary Ellen McCarthy [1964] Director/Executive Principal (Education); Alison Osmond [1961] Director/Human Resources; Peter Anthony Rodin [1956] Director/Retired; Wendy Sedgwick [1968] Director/Public Relations Consultant; Raymond Edward Vango [1953] Director/Retired; Wendy Sylvia Walford [1978] Director/Actuary

Luna Estates Limited
Incorporated: 6 February 2015
Net Worth: £5,145,296 *Total Assets:* £11,116,017
Registered Office: 50 Lancaster Road, Enfield, Middlesex, EN2 0BY
Activities: Other letting and operating of own or leased real estate
Shareholders: Richard James Paterson; Janet Margaret Paterson
Officers: Janet Margaret Paterson [1957] Director/Housewife; Richard James Paterson [1957] Director

Lycee International de Londres
Incorporated: 9 May 2014 *Employees:* 92
Net Worth: £2,357,000 *Total Assets:* £7,462,000
Registered Office: 54 Forty Lane, Wembley, Middlesex, HA9 9LY
Activities: Primary education
Officers: Jennifer Kathleen Hasnip, Secretary; Jennifer Ann Banks Oughourlian [1969] Director; Laurent Bigorgne [1974] Managing Director [French]; Lionel Gerard Marie Bouvard [1964] Director/International Mobility Manager [French]; Jane Anne Camblin [1952] Executive Director [British/American]; Emmanuel Yann Simon Caradec [1974] Director/Head of Legal [French]; Loic Pierre Marie Henriot [1978] Director [French]; Bertrand Marie Henri Benoit Michaud [1958] Managing Director [French]; Michael Penrose [1972] Executive Director; Arnaud Paul Alain Vaissie [1954] Director [French]; Emma Elizabeth Lawson Vaslet de Fontaubert [1969] Director/Member and Chief Operating Officer [New Zealander]

Lymington Precision Engineering (LPE) Limited
Incorporated: 1 February 2011
Net Worth: £26,576,000 *Total Assets:* £26,579,000
Registered Office: 59-61 High Street, Rickmansworth, Herts, WD3 1RH
Activities: Manufacture of other fabricated metal products n.e.c.
Parent: Senior UK Limited
Officers: Andrew John Bodenham, Secretary; Martin John Barnes [1966] Director; Andrew John Bodenham [1966] Director; Bindi Jayantilal Jivraj Foyle [1973] Director

Lymington Precision Engineers Co. Limited
Incorporated: 6 February 1981 *Employees:* 174
Net Worth: £6,019,000 *Total Assets:* £11,594,000
Registered Office: 59-61 High Street, Rickmansworth, Herts, WD3 1RH
Activities: Manufacture of other fabricated metal products n.e.c.
Parent: Lymington Precision Engineering (LPE) Limited
Officers: Andrew John Bodenham, Secretary; Martin John Barnes [1966] Director; Andrew John Bodenham [1966] Director; Bindi Jayantilal Jivraj Foyle [1973] Director

Lyndon Scaffolding PLC
Incorporated: 26 June 1968 *Employees:* 635
Net Worth: £21,534,798 *Total Assets:* £30,829,792
Registered Office: Regent Park, 299 Kingston Road, Leatherhead, Surrey, KT22 7SG
Activities: Scaffold erection
Major Shareholder: Donald Gogel
Officers: Andreas Akhtar, Secretary; Andreas Akhtar [1974] Director [German]; Michael Edward Herke [1964] Director [Irish]; Marcus Paul Leonardus Marie Niederer [1963] Director [Dutch]; Benjamin Stevenson Read [1974] Director

M & H Properties London Limited
Incorporated: 1 July 2015 *Employees:* 2
Net Worth: £3,579,592 *Total Assets:* £17,137,336
Registered Office: RAB House, 102-104 Park Lane, Croydon, Surrey, CR0 1JB
Activities: Other letting and operating of own or leased real estate
Shareholder: Sunil Tandon
Officers: Balraj Tandon [1959] Director/Businessman; Sunil Tandon [1962] Director/Businessman

M - Integrated Solutions PLC
Incorporated: 12 July 2007 *Employees:* 72
Net Worth: £4,529,455 *Total Assets:* £14,134,020
Registered Office: Home House, 10 Church Street, Old Isleworth, London, TW7 6DA
Activities: Other service activities n.e.c.
Major Shareholder: James Richard Harold Curley
Officers: Gillian Curley, Secretary; Sean Paul Buckley [1970] Director; James Richard Harold Curley [1967] Director; Nigel Engeham [1961] Director; John Walton Young [1966] Director

M D Properties Limited
Incorporated: 7 November 2001
Net Worth: £2,291,004 *Total Assets:* £7,138,157
Registered Office: 78 Nibthwaite Road, Harrow, Middlesex, HA1 1TG
Activities: Other letting and operating of own or leased real estate
Major Shareholder: Mukesh Chhatrabhuj Dalia
Officers: David John Thomas Ford, Secretary; Mukesh Chhatrabhuj Dalia [1960] Director/Property Developer

M G 111 Ltd
Incorporated: 22 November 2016
Net Worth Deficit: £43,462 *Total Assets:* £10,195,050
Registered Office: 364-368 Cranbrook Rd, Gants Hill, London, IG2 6HY
Activities: Other business support service activities n.e.c.
Parent: Millennium Cash & Carry Limited
Officers: Rishi Lakhani [1982] Director

M New Holdings Limited
Incorporated: 14 February 2017 *Employees:* 364
Net Worth: £20,691,348 *Total Assets:* £52,452,424
Registered Office: 7th Floor, Vantage London, Great West Road, Brentford, Middlesex, TW8 9AG
Activities: Activities of other holding companies n.e.c.
Major Shareholder: Jonathan George Mills
Officers: Richard Hutchinson, Secretary; Edmund Lazarus [1968] Director; Jonathan George Mills [1968] Director

M.A.C.-RK Precision Engineering Limited
Incorporated: 22 May 1989 *Employees:* 23
Net Worth: £3,434,218 *Total Assets:* £5,769,877
Registered Office: Unit A1, Bridge Road Industrial Estate, Bridge Road, Southall, Middlesex, UB2 4AB
Activities: Manufacture of other fabricated metal products n.e.c.
Major Shareholder: Ramesh Kumar Sharma
Officers: Rita Sharma, Secretary; Ramesh Kumar Sharma [1950] Director/Mechanical Engineer; Rita Sharma [1955] Director/Secretary

M.H.J. Limited
Incorporated: 31 October 1979 *Employees:* 154
Net Worth: £5,562,058 *Total Assets:* £19,986,162
Registered Office: Numeric House, 98 Station Road, Sidcup, Kent, DA15 7BY
Activities: Activities of head offices
Shareholders: Richard Edward Fitzharding Melhuish; James Alexander MacLean
Officers: Roger Browning, Secretary; James Alexander MacLean [1969] Contracts Director; Richard Edward Fitzharding Melhuish [1946] Managing Director

M.M.C. Investments Limited
Incorporated: 9 March 1973
Net Worth: £12,358,915 *Total Assets:* £14,097,893
Registered Office: 12 Castle Business Village, Station Road, Hampton, Surrey, TW12 2BX
Activities: Activities of head offices
Shareholder: John Hugh Londal
Officers: Edward Albert Mills, Secretary; Colin Mervyn Cox [1957] Director; Mervyn Marcus Cox [1937] Director; John Hugh Londal [1945] Director [Norwegian]

M.W. Helicopters Limited
Incorporated: 13 April 1995 *Employees:* 11
Net Worth: £2,060,124 *Total Assets:* £5,846,121
Registered Office: 110 Lancaster Road, Barnet, Herts, EN4 8AL
Activities: Other service activities n.e.c.
Officers: Martin Wood, Secretary/Haulage Contractor; Alison Jane Wood [1959] Director; Martin Wood [1958] Director

M3J Solutions Ltd
Incorporated: 20 October 2015 *Employees:* 15
Net Worth: £4,404,910 *Total Assets:* £5,893,925
Registered Office: Melbury House, 34 Southborough Road, Bromley, Kent, BR1 2EB
Activities: Freight transport by road
Major Shareholder: Sapna Panchal
Officers: Sapna Amit Panchal [1972] Director [Indian]

MA Securities London Limited
Incorporated: 17 November 2016
Net Worth: £100 *Total Assets:* £16,654,916
Registered Office: 166 College Road, Harrow, Middlesex, HA1 1RA
Activities: Other business support service activities n.e.c.
Major Shareholder: Mark Stuart Allan
Officers: Mark Stuart Allan [1962] Director

Mabel Properties LLP
Incorporated: 11 April 2016 *Employees:* 1
Net Worth: £28,629 *Total Assets:* £7,480,819
Registered Office: Northside House, 69 Tweedy Road, Bromley, Kent, BR1 3WA
Officers: Colin George Watson [1932] Member; Gillian Margaret Watson [1938] Member; Philip Charles Watson [1967] Member; Stephen Watson [1969] Member

Macarthys Laboratories Limited
Incorporated: 30 January 1959 *Employees:* 440
Net Worth: £112,461,000 *Total Assets:* £137,148,992
Registered Office: Bampton Road, Harold Hill, Romford, Essex, RM3 8UG
Activities: Manufacture of basic pharmaceutical products
Parent: Orphea Limited
Officers: Michael Christopher James Harris [1970] Director/Chief Executive; Roseline Georgette Joannesse [1959] Director/Vice President Legal Affairs [French]; Philip Edward Parry [1965] Director/Quality Assurance Professional

MacFarlane Media Limited
Incorporated: 16 October 2009 *Employees:* 20
Net Worth: £2,812,586 *Total Assets:* £7,169,753
Registered Office: Bank House, 81 St Judes Road, Englefield Green, Surrey, TW20 0DF
Activities: Media representation services
Major Shareholder: Grant MacFarlane
Officers: Grant MacFarlane [1973] Director; Marketa MacFarlane [1979] Director

Macquarie Corona Energy Holdings Limited
Incorporated: 2 May 2003
Net Worth: £12,107,631 *Total Assets:* £18,975,828
Registered Office: Building 2, Level 2, Croxley Park, Watford, Herts, WD18 8YA
Activities: Activities of head offices
Parent: Macquarie Investments 2 Limited
Officers: Shaheda Begum Thomas, Secretary; Neil Trevor Mitchell [1974] Commercial Director; Philip Morton [1968] Finance Director; Paul Christian Plewman [1972] Director/Banker [Irish]

The Magdi Yacoub Institute
Incorporated: 30 August 2000 *Employees:* 12
Net Worth: £5,636,318 *Total Assets:* £5,861,943
Registered Office: Heart Science Centre, Harefield, Middlesex, UB9 6JH
Activities: Research and experimental development on biotechnology
Officers: Alan Hargreaves, Secretary; Dr Assem Allam [1939] Director; Professor Kim Michael Fox [1948] Director/Doctor; Lord Grey Gowrie [1939] Director; Alan Hargreaves [1946] Director/Retired; Dr Magdy Adib Ishak-Hanna [1947] Director/President of The Egyptian Medical Society; Asghar Khaghani [1947] Director/Surgeon; Dr Rosemary Claire Radley-Smith [1939] Director/Physician; Professor Sir Magdi Habib Yacoub [1935] Director/Surgeon

Magnet Harlequin Limited
Incorporated: 22 March 1983 *Employees:* 130
Net Worth: £5,249,978 *Total Assets:* £10,853,188
Registered Office: Unit F, Tomo Estate, Packet Boat Lane, Cowley, Uxbridge, Middlesex, UB8 2JP
Activities: Printing n.e.c.
Parent: Writtle Holdings Limited
Officers: Matthew John Gilmore, Secretary; Jason Steven Allen [1969] Director; Robert Thomas Tickler Essex [1960] Director; Graeme Richard Harris [1966] Director; Anthony Edward Knight [1971] Production Director; Jamie Trevor Richards [1976] Director; Andrew William Williamson [1963] Finance Director; Alan John Wright [1959] Managing Director

Maia Leisure Limited
Incorporated: 9 November 2016
Net Worth: £1,013,680 *Total Assets:* £7,986,317
Registered Office: c/o Prohal Ltd, 54 Clarendon Road, Watford, Herts, WD17 1DU
Activities: Other sports activities
Officers: Allan Saud [1986] Director

Maida Vale Leisure Limited
Incorporated: 7 September 2016
Net Worth: £4,864,974 *Total Assets:* £6,362,068
Registered Office: 1st Floor, Healthaid House, Marlborough Hill, Harrow, Middlesex, HA1 1UD
Activities: Public houses and bars
Parent: Ducalian Capital Ltd
Officers: Robert Charles Cherry [1982] Director; James Oliver Hancock [1980] Director; James Anthony McCulloch [1981] Director; Rachel Jane Rossiter [1973] Finance Director

Maidensgrove Limited
Incorporated: 23 February 2005
Net Worth: £3,634,535 *Total Assets:* £7,434,924
Registered Office: The Old Rectory, Church Street, Weybridge, Surrey, KT13 8DE
Activities: Buying and selling of own real estate
Officers: Rupert Stuart Frank Coltart [1978] Director

Maison Maurice Limited
Incorporated: 21 January 1977 *Employees:* 35
Net Worth: £5,183,348 *Total Assets:* £6,645,845
Registered Office: K1-K5 Northfleet Industrial Estate, Lower Road, Northfleet, Gravesend, Kent, DA11 9BL
Activities: Wholesale of wine, beer, spirits and other alcoholic beverages
Shareholders: Adrian John Sundin; Jonathan Mark Sundin
Officers: Jonathan Mark Sundin, Secretary; Adrian John Sundin [1955] Director/Executive; Jonathan Mark Sundin [1956] Director/Executive

Maison Moti Limited
Incorporated: 31 October 1996 *Employees:* 74
Net Worth: £4,408,931 *Total Assets:* £9,041,150
Registered Office: 8a Southbury Road, Enfield, Middlesex, EN1 1YT
Activities: Other service activities n.e.c.
Major Shareholder: Maya Mahtani
Officers: Mostak Ahmed [1971] Managing Director; Maya Mahtani [1946] Director; Vinod Mahtani [1969] Director/Doctor

Majestic Securities Limited
Incorporated: 21 December 2012 *Employees:* 66
Net Worth: £19,716,844 *Total Assets:* £21,535,766
Registered Office: 7-9 Stafford Road, Wallington, Surrey, SM6 9AN
Activities: Activities of head offices
Major Shareholder: Parminder Singh Dosanjh
Officers: Arjan Singh Dosanjh [1987] Director; Parminder Singh Dosanjh [1955] Director; Sarvjeet Kaur Dosanjh [1960] Director/Accounts Manager

Majestic Wine PLC
Incorporated: 28 July 1988 *Employees:* 1,528
Net Worth: £121,761,000 *Total Assets:* £251,967,008
Registered Office: Majestic House, The Belfry, Colonial Way, Watford, Herts, WD24 4WH
Activities: Wholesale of wine, beer, spirits and other alcoholic beverages
Officers: Alex Iapichino, Secretary; Justin James Apthorp [1962] Director/Buyer; James Crawford [1977] Finance Director; Rowan Gormley [1962] Director/Chief Executive Officer [Irish]; Ian Andrew Harding [1964] Director/Company Executive; Brian Gregory Hodder [1952] Director; David Anthony Stead [1958] Director/Auditor

Majestic Wine Warehouses Limited
Incorporated: 30 October 1981 *Employees:* 1,168
Net Worth: £86,652,000 *Total Assets:* £138,679,008
Registered Office: Majestic House, The Belfry, Colonial Way, Watford, Herts, WD24 4WH
Activities: Wholesale of wine, beer, spirits and other alcoholic beverages
Parent: Majestic Wine PLC
Officers: Alex Iapichino, Secretary; Nicholas James Bell [1985] Director; James Crawford [1977] Director; Olivia FitzGenerald [1972] Director/Businesswoman; Rowan Gormley [1962] Director/Chief Executive [Irish]; Stuart Christopher Lane [1981] Finance Director; Joshua Benjamin Geoffrey Lincoln-Creese [1984] Managing Director; Suzanne Louise Roberts [1974] Supply Chain Director; Natalie Th'ng [1986] Customer Director

Major Properties London Limited
Incorporated: 16 March 1999
Net Worth: £539,090 *Total Assets:* £7,139,904
Registered Office: FWP House, 17 Bourne Court, Southend Road, Woodford Green, Essex, IG8 8HD
Activities: Other business support service activities n.e.c.
Major Shareholder: Gary Mark Stein
Officers: Gary Mark Stein [1960] Director

Maker Properties Ltd
Incorporated: 11 September 2001
Net Worth: £4,558,761 *Total Assets:* £5,565,570
Registered Office: Maker House, 33 Brighton Road, South Croydon, Surrey, CR2 6EB
Activities: Other letting and operating of own or leased real estate
Major Shareholder: Amar Subhag Maker
Officers: Amar Maker [1946] Director/Manager

Mala Engineering Limited
Incorporated: 12 March 1971 *Employees:* 72
Net Worth: £1,872,679 *Total Assets:* £8,066,138
Registered Office: Nicholas House, River Front, Enfield, Middlesex, EN1 3FG
Activities: Plumbing, heat and air-conditioning installation
Shareholders: Keith Crane; Maureen Agnes Crane; Paul Zumeris
Officers: Lee Spong, Secretary; Dean Crane [1961] Director/Building Services Engineer; Keith Crane [1943] Director/Building Services Engineer; Lee Spong [1963] Financial Director; Paul Zumeris [1952] Director/Building Services Engineer

Malibu Health Products Limited
Incorporated: 13 April 1999
Net Worth: £1,099,033 *Total Assets:* £7,536,565
Registered Office: 23 Dennis Lane, Stanmore, Middlesex, HA7 4JS
Activities: Manufacture of soap and detergents
Officers: Stuart Anthony Spurling [1965] Director

Mall School Trust (The)
Incorporated: 11 July 1986 *Employees:* 74
Net Worth: £6,815,542 *Total Assets:* £9,840,333
Registered Office: The Mall School, 185 Hampton Road, Twickenham, Middlesex, TW2 5NQ
Activities: Primary education
Officers: Glen Jones, Secretary; Dr Deborah Clark [1965] Managing Director - Corporate Responsibility; Kanwaljeet Kaur Mahajan [1966] Director; John Owen Morris [1974] Director/Teacher; John Alaister Fraser Short Ring [1982] Director/Teacher; Charmian Louise Paula Smith [1967] Director/Retired GP; Rupert Justin Houlihan Walker [1968] Programme Director

Mallinckrodt Chemical Holdings (U.K.) Limited
Incorporated: 17 January 1992
Net Worth: £13,528,329 *Total Assets:* £16,942,422
Registered Office: 3 Lotus Park, The Causeway, Staines upon Thames, Middlesex, TW18 3AG
Activities: Activities of head offices
Parent: Mallinckrodt Equinox Limited
Officers: Dean Leslie Erdal [1956] Finance Director [American]; Stephen Andrew Welch [1977] Director/Senior Staff Liaison to The President and CEO [American]

Mallinckrodt Chemical Limited
Incorporated: 11 August 1987
Net Worth: £56,340,488 *Total Assets:* £72,142,376
Registered Office: 3 Lotus Park, The Causeway, Staines upon Thames, Middlesex, TW18 3AG
Activities: Manufacture of other organic basic chemicals
Parent: Mallinckrodt UK Ltd
Officers: Dean Leslie Erdal [1956] Finance Director [American]; Stephanie Dorn Miller [1974] Director/Corporate Secretary [American]; Jason Tilly [1973] Director/Attorney [American]; Stephen Andrew Welch [1977] Director/Senior Staff Liaison to The President and CEO [American]

Mallinckrodt Enterprises UK Limited
Incorporated: 17 June 2014 *Employees:* 3
Net Worth: £181,436,656 *Total Assets:* £181,503,984
Registered Office: 3 Lotus Park, The Causeway, Staines upon Thames, Middlesex, TW18 3AG
Activities: Activities of other holding companies n.e.c.
Parent: Mushi UK Holdings Limited
Officers: Alan Catterson [1961] Director/Financial Controller; Stephanie Dorn Miller [1974] Director/Corporate Secretary [American]; Stephen Andrew Welch [1977] Director/Senior Staff Liaison to The President and CEO [American]

Mallinckrodt Equinox Limited
Incorporated: 11 March 2016
Net Worth: £13,584,298 *Total Assets:* £13,596,565
Registered Office: 3 Lotus Park, The Causeway, Staines upon Thames, Middlesex, TW18 3AG
Activities: Activities of other holding companies n.e.c.
Officers: Stephanie Dorn Miller [1974] Director/Corporate Secretary [American]; Stephen Andrew Welch [1977] Director/Senior Staff Liaison to The President and CEO [American]

Mallinckrodt Medical Holdings (UK) Limited
Incorporated: 17 January 1992
Net Worth: £20,057,250 *Total Assets:* £20,057,250
Registered Office: 3 Lotus Park, The Causeway, Staines upon Thames, Middlesex, TW18 3AG
Activities: Activities of head offices
Parent: Mallinckrodt Enterprises UK Limited
Officers: Dean Leslie Erdal [1956] Finance Director [American]; Stephen Andrew Welch [1977] Director/Senior Staff Liaison to The President and CEO [American]

Mallinckrodt Pharmaceuticals Limited
Incorporated: 16 September 2015 *Employees:* 11
Net Worth: £4,698,839,040 *Total Assets:* £4,702,202,368
Registered Office: 3 Lotus Park, The Causeway, Staines upon Thames, Middlesex, TW18 3AG
Activities: Management consultancy activities other than financial management
Parent: Mallinckrodt UK Ltd
Officers: Stephanie Dorn Miller, Secretary; Stephanie Dorn Miller [1974] Director/Corporate Secretary [American]; Josh Schafer [1971] Director/Pharmaceutical Executive [American]; Mark Trudeau [1961] Director/President and Chief Executive Officer [American]

Mallinckrodt UK Finance LLP
Incorporated: 22 September 2015
Net Worth: £1,035,037,952 *Total Assets:* £1,142,992,384
Registered Office: 3 Lotus Park, The Causeway, Staines upon Thames, Middlesex, TW18 3AG

Mallinckrodt UK Ltd
Incorporated: 23 June 1986
Net Worth: £4,961,617,408 *Total Assets:* £9,481,590,784
Registered Office: 3 Lotus Park, The Causeway, Staines upon Thames, Middlesex, TW18 3AG
Activities: Non-trading company
Officers: Stephanie Dorn Miller [1974] Director/Corporate Secretary [American]; Stephen Andrew Welch [1977] Director/Senior Staff Liaison to The President and CEO [American]

Manak Lawyers Limited
Incorporated: 18 November 2015 *Employees:* 32
Net Worth: £280,892 *Total Assets:* £8,573,651
Registered Office: 265 & 271a High Street, Orpington, Kent, BR6 0NW
Activities: Solicitors
Major Shareholder: Surinder Singh Manak
Officers: Saeeda Nosheen Bukhari [1972] Director; Jasdeep Singh Jandu [1984] Director/Solicitor; Aneeta Kaur Kang [1986] Director/Solicitor; Kemesha Simone Lynch [1978] Director/Solicitor [Jamaican]; Surinder Singh Manak [1969] Director/Solicitor

Manchester Jetline Limited
Incorporated: 5 June 1989
Net Worth: £23,017,000 *Total Assets:* £29,029,000
Registered Office: 3 Water Lane, Richmond, Surrey, TW9 1TJ
Activities: Transport via pipeline
Parent: Penspen Limited
Officers: Susan Jane McDonald, Secretary; Robert Lawson [1954] Director of Asset Management; Carl Richard Mook [1966] Director/Engineer

Mane Contract Services Limited
Incorporated: 21 September 1993 *Employees:* 62
Net Worth: £1,958,028 *Total Assets:* £11,432,055
Registered Office: 3rd Floor, 6 Hercules Way, Watford, Herts, WD25 7GS
Activities: Temporary employment agency activities
Major Shareholder: Luigi Pacelli
Officers: Hema Patel, Finance Director; Luigi Pacelli [1963] Director/Executive Chairman

Manelia Limited
Incorporated: 8 August 1979 *Employees:* 2
Net Worth: £3,010,974 *Total Assets:* £5,016,539
Registered Office: Richardson House, Moor Lane, Staines upon Thames, Middlesex, TW19 6EQ
Activities: Roofing activities
Parent: Manelia Holdings Limited
Officers: Dawn Willmont, Secretary; Conor Michael Richardson [1993] Director; George Martin Richardson [1956] Director; Simon David Wright [1963] Director/Roofing

Mangrove Global Limited
Incorporated: 3 September 2013 *Employees:* 22
Net Worth: £1,132,809 *Total Assets:* £7,298,294
Registered Office: 53 Redbridge Lane East, Ilford, Essex, IG4 5EY
Activities: Wholesale of wine, beer, spirits and other alcoholic beverages
Shareholders: John Maitland Coe; Nicholas James Gillett
Officers: John Maitland Coe [1955] Director/Wine and Spirit Merchant; Nicholas James Gillett [1972] Managing Director

Manichem Limited
Incorporated: 2 January 2007 *Employees:* 188
Net Worth Deficit: £3,600,441 *Total Assets:* £9,575,481
Registered Office: 109-111 Field End Road, Pinner, Middlesex, HA5 1QG
Activities: Wholesale of pharmaceutical goods
Parent: Merrygood Ltd
Officers: Krishma Vikash Patel [1981] Director/Pharmacist; Niral Narendra Patel [1981] Director; Vikash Patel [1982] Director; Viresh Patel [1985] Director

Manor Farm Solar Limited
Incorporated: 20 April 2011
Net Worth Deficit: £2,867,554 *Total Assets:* £11,456,423
Registered Office: Beaufort Court, Egg Farm Lane, off Station Road, Kings Langley, Herts, WD4 8LR
Activities: Production of electricity
Parent: European Investments (Cornwall) Limited
Officers: Dominic Hearth, Secretary; Steven William Hughes [1972] Global Support Services Director, UK&I - Commercial; Mitesh Raj Patel [1982] Director/Chartered Accountant; Tracy Jane Scott [1976] Director/Delivery Project Manager; Mark Christopher Wayment [1958] Director

Manor IT (UK) Ltd
Incorporated: 12 June 2007 *Employees:* 15
Net Worth: £449,304 *Total Assets:* £12,924,616
Registered Office: Unit 7, 1st Floor, Roding House, 2 Cambridge Road, Barking, Essex, IG11 8NL
Activities: Other telecommunications activities
Shareholders: Mohammed Nazrul Islam; Fahima Akther
Officers: Mohammed Nazrul Islam, Secretary; Fahima Akther [1980] Director; Mohammed Nazrul Islam [1975] Director

Manor Lodge School
Incorporated: 22 June 1993 *Employees:* 87
Net Worth: £6,900,102 *Total Assets:* £10,201,621
Registered Office: Manor Lodge School, Rectory Lane, Ridge Hill, Shenley, Radlett, Herts, WD7 9BG
Activities: Primary education
Officers: Anne-Marie Claire Ridler, Secretary; David Arnold [1939] Director; Graham Thomas Black [1943] Director/Retired Bursar; Trudy Capaldo [1970] Director/Chartered Accountant; Mark Christopher Cherry [1962] Director/Property Development; Sonia Kaya Coventry [1978] Director/Teacher; Helen Marie Gunasekera [1971] Director/Lawyer; Sarah Ann Hollis [1966] Director/Headmistress; Melody Jones [1975] Director/Teacher; Dr Mohammed Shahzad Ahmed Malik [1967] Director/Venture Capitalist; James Adam Segal [1970] Director/Solicitor; Andrew Monro Williams [1966] Director/Teacher; Stephen Wilson [1947] Director/Retired

The Manor Trust
Incorporated: 11 November 2011 *Employees:* 152
Previous: Norbury Manor Business and Enterprise College for Girls
Net Worth: £19,024,000 *Total Assets:* £20,544,000
Registered Office: Norbury Manor Business and Enterprise College, Kensington Avenue, Thornton Heath, Croydon, Surrey, CR7 8BT
Activities: General secondary education
Officers: Roger Charles Lowe, Secretary; Alan Chambers [1989] Director/Business Consultant; Jane Rosemary Chandler [1960] Director/Accountant; Amanda Jane Compton [1961] Director/Headteacher; Clare Cranham [1970] Director/Headmistress; Richard Trevor McIntosh [1953] Director/Retired; Maria Miller [1964] Director/Self Employed; Desmond Leslie Ogg [1947] Director/Retired; Mary Eileen Turner [1942] Director

Manors Sales and Lettings Limited
Incorporated: 8 April 2004 *Employees:* 6
Net Worth: £2,845,819 *Total Assets:* £7,481,970
Registered Office: 114-116 Goodmayes Road, Ilford, Essex, IG3 9UZ
Activities: Hotels and similar accommodation
Shareholders: Sukhbinder Singh Takhar; Sukhbinder Singh Takhar
Officers: Iqbal Kaur Takhar, Secretary; Iqbal Kaur Takhar [1960] Director; Pirthipal Singh Takhar [1982] Director; Sukhbinder Singh Takhar [1954] Director

Manpower Direct (UK) Ltd.
Incorporated: 9 January 2003 *Employees:* 268
Net Worth: £1,340,744 *Total Assets:* £6,612,683
Registered Office: Unit 20 Dagenham Business Centre, Rainham Road North, Dagenham, Essex, RM10 7FD
Activities: Private security activities
Major Shareholder: Mohammad Sharjeel Bhatti
Officers: Graham Peter Allison [1969] Director; Mohammad Sharjeel Bhatti [1975] Director; Mohammad Raheel Bhatti [1975] Director; Muhammad Kashif Bhatti [1975] Director

Manpower Public Limited Company
Incorporated: 9 May 1956 *Employees:* 1
Net Worth: £133,964,000 *Total Assets:* £168,376,000
Registered Office: Capital Court, Windsor Street, Uxbridge, Middlesex, UB8 1AB
Activities: Activities of head offices
Parent: Manpower Holdings Limited
Officers: Damian Paul Whitham, Secretary; Mark Anthony Cahill [1958] Director; Donald Mondano [1971] Director [American]; Damian Paul Whitham [1967] Director

Manpower Services Limited
Incorporated: 4 April 1968 *Employees:* 19
Net Worth: £8,871,000 *Total Assets:* £14,417,000
Registered Office: Capital Court, Windsor Street, Uxbridge, Middlesex, UB8 1AB
Activities: Other business support service activities n.e.c.
Parent: Manpower Public Limited Company
Officers: Damian Paul Whitham, Secretary; Mark Anthony Cahill [1958] Director; Mark Joseph Donnelly [1968] Director; Damian Paul Whitham [1967] Director

Manpower UK Limited
Incorporated: 15 September 1999 *Employees:* 19,215
Net Worth: £70,881,000 *Total Assets:* £220,271,008
Registered Office: Capital Court, Windsor Street, Uxbridge, Middlesex, UB8 1AB
Activities: Temporary employment agency activities
Parent: Manpower Public Limited Company
Officers: Lee Anthony Paul Graham, Secretary; Christopher Arthur [1966] Director; Mark Anthony Cahill [1958] Director; Mark Joseph Donnelly [1968] Director; James Hick [1968] Director; Damian Paul Whitham [1967] Director

Henry Mansfield Limited
Incorporated: 31 January 1945
Net Worth: £6,014,444 *Total Assets:* £6,798,638
Registered Office: Devonshire House, 582 Honeypot Lane, Stanmore, Middlesex, HA7 1JS
Activities: Development of building projects
Shareholder: Diana Sandra Samis
Officers: John Hennessy, Secretary; John Hennessy [1954] Director/Chartered Surveyor; Diana Sandra Samis [1954] Director

Mapal Limited
Incorporated: 5 February 1993 *Employees:* 66
Net Worth: £8,258,878 *Total Assets:* £11,589,465
Registered Office: Palmerston House, 814 Brighton Road, Purley, Surrey, CR8 2BR
Activities: Manufacture of other machine tools
Shareholder: Dieter Georg August Kress
Officers: Dr Ralf Herkenhoff [1962] Director [German]; Dr Jochen Kress [1975] Director [German]; Wayne Edward Whitehouse [1966] Director

Mapcargo International Limited
Incorporated: 31 May 1995 *Employees:* 3
Net Worth: £1,022,927 *Total Assets:* £8,359,301
Registered Office: 3 Brook Business Centre, Cowley Mill Road, Uxbridge, Middlesex, UB8 2FX
Activities: Other transportation support activities
Parent: Elmex Sales Corporation Limited
Officers: Mark Anthony Hawkins [1972] Director; Daryl Andrew Hill [1964] Director; Howard Michael Charles Jupp [1965] Director/Freight Forwarder

Mapeley Columbus II Limited
Incorporated: 25 August 2000
Net Worth Deficit: £63,861,000 *Total Assets:* £15,750,000
Registered Office: Cambridge House, Clarendon Road, Watford, Herts, WD17 1HP
Activities: Other letting and operating of own or leased real estate
Officers: Michael Anthony Wilson, Secretary; Simon David Ainslie Jones [1970] Director/Chief Financial Officer; Mark Julian Smith [1970] Director; Edward Michael Swales [1979] Director; Michael Anthony Wilson [1956] Director/Solicitor

Mapeley Estates Limited
Incorporated: 10 March 1999
Net Worth Deficit: £25,719,000 *Total Assets:* £7,438,000
Registered Office: Cambridge House, Clarendon Road, Watford, Herts, WD17 1HP
Activities: Other letting and operating of own or leased real estate
Officers: Michael Anthony Wilson, Secretary; Simon David Ainslie Jones [1970] Director/Chief Financial Officer; Mark Julian Smith [1970] Director; Edward Michael Swales [1979] Director; Michael Anthony Wilson [1956] Director/Solicitor

Mapeley Steps Contractor Limited
Incorporated: 12 October 2000
Net Worth Deficit: £73,247,000 *Total Assets:* £46,538,000
Registered Office: Cambridge House, Clarendon Road, Watford, Herts, WD17 1HP
Activities: Other letting and operating of own or leased real estate
Officers: Michael Anthony Wilson, Secretary; Simon David Ainslie Jones [1970] Director/Chief Financial Officer; Mark Julian Smith [1970] Director; Edward Michael Swales [1979] Director; Michael Anthony Wilson [1956] Director/Solicitor

Maple Hotels Management Company Limited
Incorporated: 28 January 1982
Net Worth: £8,076,963 *Total Assets:* £9,606,547
Registered Office: Maple Court, Central Park, Reeds Crescent, Watford, Herts, WD24 4QQ
Activities: Other accommodation
Parent: Hilton Worldwide Limited
Officers: Stuart Beasley [1971] Director/Financial Controller; Richard Geoffrey Beeston [1982] Director/Chartered Accountant; Stephen Patrick Cassidy [1968] Director/SVP Operations UK & Ireland; Michelle Momdjian [1976] Director/Attorney; George Christopher Ogle [1974] Director/Attorney; James Owen Percival [1968] Director/Accountant; Simon Robert Vincent [1963] Director

Marande Limited
Incorporated: 15 September 1987
Net Worth: £5,027,720 *Total Assets:* £7,713,589
Registered Office: 114 Meridian House, Oak Hill Crescent, Woodford Green, Essex, IG8 9PQ
Activities: Other letting and operating of own or leased real estate
Shareholder: Andrew Cushway
Officers: Mark Vernon Cushway, Secretary; Andrew Cushway [1958] Director/Builder; Denise Cushway [1960] Director; Mark Vernon Cushway [1955] Director/Builder; Caterina Tedeschi [1962] Director

Marbank Construction Limited
Incorporated: 2 February 1994 *Employees:* 30
Net Worth: £6,480,000 *Total Assets:* £20,111,000
Registered Office: 2 Wintersells Road, Byfleet, West Byfleet, Surrey, KT14 7LF
Activities: Construction of commercial buildings
Major Shareholder: Mark James Edward Woods
Officers: Stephen Andrew Brown, Secretary; Stephen Andrew Brown [1954] Director/Chartered Accountant; Wayne Ian Harris [1975] Construction Director; Glenn Wensley [1968] Project Director; Mark James Edward Woods [1964] Director/Quantity Surveyor

Marble Lending Limited
Incorporated: 1 April 2016
Net Worth: £2 *Total Assets:* £5,251,412
Registered Office: Elder House, St Georges Business Park, 207 Brooklands Road, Weybridge, Surrey, KT13 0TS
Activities: Activities of venture and development capital companies
Shareholders: Puma VCT 11 PLC; Puma VCT 12 PLC
Officers: Eliot Charles Kaye [1974] Investment Director; Jon Morton-Smith [1951] Director

Marblefloor Limited
Incorporated: 1 August 2000
Net Worth: £4,794,756 *Total Assets:* £6,991,290
Registered Office: 1 Brook Court, Blakeney Road, Beckenham, Kent, BR3 1HG
Activities: Other letting and operating of own or leased real estate
Shareholders: Sandra Sargent; Robert Sargent
Officers: Robert Sargent, Secretary; Robert Sargent [1964] Director/Property Consultant; Sandra Sargent [1969] Director/Journalist

Marcantonio Foods Limited
Incorporated: 6 April 1945 *Employees:* 153
Previous: Marcantonio Foods.Limited
Net Worth: £1,813,411 *Total Assets:* £10,779,802
Registered Office: 20 Thames Road, Barking, Essex, IG11 0HZ
Activities: Manufacture of other food products n.e.c.
Officers: Nicholas Philip Venditti, Secretary; John Patrick Aalhuizen [1965] Director [Swedish]; Thomas Ernst Bruck [1962] Director [German]; Riccardo Antonio Marcantonio [1980] Director; Nadia Millar [1968] Director; Tor Agner Osmundsen [1978] Director of Subsidiaries [Norwegian]; Bernard Bertram Pooley [1957] Finance Director; Nicholas Philip Venditti [1971] Director/Salesperson; Michael Wodskou [1967] Director [Danish]

Marchanson Limited
Incorporated: 20 November 1972 *Employees:* 4
Net Worth: £7,877,851 *Total Assets:* £13,118,397
Registered Office: York House, Empire Way, Wembley, Middlesex, HA9 0FQ
Activities: Operation of arts facilities
Shareholders: Richard Phillip Marchant; Stuart Julian Marchant
Officers: Stuart Julian Marchant, Secretary; Richard Phillip Marchant [1936] Director/Antique Dealer; Stuart Julian Marchant [1963] Director/Antique Dealer

Marchase Limited
Incorporated: 17 August 2005 *Employees:* 221
Net Worth: £21,805,892 *Total Assets:* £34,260,184
Registered Office: Riverside Place, 1-9 Lea Road, Waltham Abbey, Essex, EN9 1AS
Activities: Activities of distribution holding companies
Shareholder: Charles William Smith
Officers: Martin Stewart Earle, Secretary; Martin Stewart Earle [1946] Director/Manager; Charles William Valens Smith [1949] Director/Manager

Marchent Limited
Incorporated: 2 April 2003
Net Worth: £3,023,599 *Total Assets:* £7,448,284
Registered Office: 28 Church Road, Stanmore, Middlesex, HA7 4XR
Activities: Development of building projects
Shareholder: Zeev Zi Pear
Officers: Anita Mehra, Secretary/Director; Anita Mehra [1953] Director; Vidhur Mehra [1975] Director/Accountant

Marco Polo Properties Limited
Incorporated: 3 February 2015
Net Worth: £314,677 *Total Assets:* £5,392,937
Registered Office: 56 Wolsey Road, Northwood, Middlesex, HA6 2EH
Activities: Other letting and operating of own or leased real estate
Shareholders: Thavatheva Thevarajah; Kalaimagalselvi Thevarajah
Officers: Kalaimagalselvi Thevarajah [1963] Director; Thavatheva Thevarajah [1964] Director

Marcus & Marcus Limited
Incorporated: 15 October 2002 *Employees:* 314
Net Worth: £6,156,019 *Total Assets:* £8,390,412
Registered Office: 142 St Marks Road, Enfield, Middlesex, EN1 1BJ
Activities: Residential care activities for learning difficulties, mental health and substance abuse
Major Shareholder: Edward William Marcus
Officers: Matthew John Byatt, Secretary; Edward William Marcus [1958] Director [Malaysian]

Marden Oak Limited
Incorporated: 28 April 1995 *Employees:* 3
Net Worth: £8,561,140 *Total Assets:* £13,144,341
Registered Office: Marden Oak Ltd, P O Box 3196, Caterham, Surrey, CR3 4BZ
Activities: Buying and selling of own real estate
Shareholders: Claire Joanne Dunn; Lynne Susan Norris
Officers: Claire Joanne Dunn [1976] Director/Consultant; Lynne Susan Norris [1978] Director/IT Project Manager & Accountant; Paul Wesley Norris [1944] Director/Retired

Margiberg LLP
Incorporated: 13 September 2013
Net Worth: £6,142,265 *Total Assets:* £6,142,265
Registered Office: 1st Floor, Midas House, 2 Knoll Rise, Orpington, Kent, BR6 0EL
Officers: Henrique de Loyola Rodrigues Alves [1982] Member

Marine Point Property LLP
Incorporated: 22 June 2016
Net Worth: £14,048,415 *Total Assets:* £14,048,415
Registered Office: Aprirose House, 48a High Street, Edgware, Middlesex, HA8 7EQ
Officers: Manish Mansukhlal Gudka [1970] Member; Gareth Jones [1973] Member; Suraj Rashmikant Shah [1982] LLP Member

Marke Creative Merchandise Ltd
Incorporated: 16 December 1977 *Employees:* 47
Previous: Staples Promotional Products Europe Limited
Net Worth: £629,111 *Total Assets:* £6,561,200
Registered Office: Units 6-8 Liongate Enterprise Park, Mitcham, Surrey, CR4 4NY
Activities: Non-specialised wholesale trade
Shareholders: Staples Promotional Products Canada Ltd; Staples Inc
Officers: Lisa Jane Munro, Secretary; John William Caldwell [1957] Director/Accountant [American]; Lisa Jane Munro [1972] Director

Marlborough Isleworth Properties Limited
Incorporated: 13 August 2003 *Employees:* 2
Net Worth: £8,018,994 *Total Assets:* £8,033,768
Registered Office: Osborne House, 143-145 Stanwell Road, Ashford, Middlesex, TW15 3QN
Activities: Other letting and operating of own or leased real estate
Major Shareholder: William Thompson
Officers: William Thompson, Secretary; William Thompson [1953] Director

Marron Civil Engineering Limited
Incorporated: 27 January 1987 *Employees:* 18
Net Worth: £5,162,228 *Total Assets:* £9,641,226
Registered Office: Unit 39 Sheraton Business Centre, Wadsworth Close, Greenford, Middlesex, UB6 7JB
Activities: Construction of other civil engineering projects n.e.c.
Parent: M C Marron Group Limited
Officers: Colin Joseph Marron, Secretary; Claire Marron [1970] Director [Irish]; Colin Joseph Marron [1964] Director; John Francis Marron [1971] Director; Paul Martin Marron [1972] Director; Sandra Marron [1963] Director [Irish]

Marsdens Caterers of Sheffield Limited
Incorporated: 28 December 1939 *Employees:* 587
Net Worth: £8,579,723 *Total Assets:* £13,265,836
Registered Office: 34-36 London Road, Wembley, Middlesex, HA9 7EX
Activities: Other food services
Parent: Marz Limited
Officers: Mohammed Adil, Secretary; Raja Jameel Adil [1971] Director/Solicitor

Marsh Wall Limited
Incorporated: 23 July 2007 *Employees:* 239
Net Worth: £2,449,663 *Total Assets:* £37,376,164
Registered Office: 6 Shield Drive, Brentford, Middlesex, TW8 9EX
Activities: Sale of new cars and light motor vehicles
Shareholder: Wayne Berry
Officers: Deborah Ann Lowles, Secretary; Wayne Robert Berry [1966] Director; Deborah Ann Lowles [1975] Director/Chartered Accountant; John Barry Naylor [1952] Director Corporate Sales

Martello (Holdings) Limited
Incorporated: 15 February 2016 *Employees:* 4
Net Worth: £7,414,682 *Total Assets:* £9,914,682
Registered Office: 76 Powder Mill Lane, The Questor Estate, Dartford, Kent, DA1 1JA
Activities: Activities of other holding companies n.e.c.
Parent: Franki Foundations UK Limited
Officers: James Blackwell [1956] Director/Civil Engineer; Maurice Jean Marcel Bottiau [1963] Director [Belgian]; Wim Peter Bart Claesen [1971] Director [Belgian]; Alistair James MacDonald [1980] Director; Craig Macklin [1976] Director

Martin-Baker Aircraft Company Limited
Incorporated: 3 January 1966 *Employees:* 827
Net Worth: £109,292,000 *Total Assets:* £161,972,992
Registered Office: Lower Road, Higher Denham, Uxbridge, Middlesex, UB9 5AJ
Activities: Manufacture of metal structures and parts of structures
Parent: Killinchy Aerospace Holdings Limited
Officers: William John Henderson Deeves, Secretary; Andrew James Martin [1973] Director; James William Martin [1942] Director; John Stephen Martin [1942] Director; Robert John Martin [1969] Director/Engineer; Robert Keith Morgan [1975] Director

Martlane Limited
Incorporated: 30 January 2001 *Employees:* 98
Net Worth: £14,333,626 *Total Assets:* £16,817,976
Registered Office: 9 Spareleaze Hill, Loughton, Essex, IG10 1BS
Activities: Residential nursing care facilities
Parent: Abbey Total Care Group Ltd
Officers: Devyani Jayanti Patel, Secretary/Director; Devyani Jayanti Patel [1953] Director; Jayanti Mohanlal Patel [1949] Director

Marwin Securities Limited
Incorporated: 6 October 1955 *Employees:* 10
Net Worth: £16,194,382 *Total Assets:* £19,456,530
Registered Office: 28 Church Road, Stanmore, Middlesex, HA7 4XR
Activities: Development of building projects
Shareholders: Michael Stephen Winkler; Richard Anthony Winkler; Mark Jonathan Winkler
Officers: Michael Stephen Winkler, Secretary; Mark Jonathan Winkler [1955] Director; Michael Stephen Winkler [1949] Director

Marylebone Finco Limited
Incorporated: 5 February 2016
Net Worth: £45,646 *Total Assets:* £61,022,936
Registered Office: Regent House, Allum Gate, Theobald Street, Elstree, Borehamwood, Herts, WD6 4RS
Activities: Other letting and operating of own or leased real estate
Officers: Rishi Ramesh Sachdev [1976] Director; Uday Vyas [1978] Director

Marylebone Square Holdings Ltd
Incorporated: 4 January 2017
Net Worth: £14,836,221 *Total Assets:* £15,528,017
Registered Office: Alpha House, 176a High Street, Barnet, Herts, EN5 5SZ
Activities: Buying and selling of own real estate
Major Shareholder: David Warwicker
Officers: David Warwicker [1949] Director

Marylebone Square Property Group Ltd
Incorporated: 4 January 2017
Net Worth: £7,015,478 *Total Assets:* £7,018,478
Registered Office: Alpha House, 176a High Street, Barnet, Herts, EN5 5SZ
Activities: Other letting and operating of own or leased real estate
Parent: Marylebone Square Holdings Ltd
Officers: David Warwicker [1949] Director

Marymount International School
Incorporated: 6 January 2005 *Employees:* 87
Net Worth: £7,761,682 *Total Assets:* £15,182,470
Registered Office: Marymount International School, 65 George Road, Kingston upon Thames, Surrey, KT2 7PE
Activities: General secondary education
Officers: Andre Theo Paul Maria Brenninkmeijer [1959] Director/Chairman [Dutch]; Professor Francis Martin Campbell [1970] Director/Vice Chancellor St Mary's University; Julie Darwent [1973] Director/Retired Investment Banker; Karina Govindji [1977] Director/Group Head of Diversity & Inclusion; Sister Mary Jo Martin [1947] Deputy Director; Paloma Martinez Alvaro [1970] Director/Solicitor [Spanish]; Helena Reimnitz Zu Hohenlohe [1960] Director/Executive Search Consultant [German]; Mark Rigotti [1964] Director/Chief Executive Officer; Cristina Serrano [1971] Executive Director, FIG, Santander Global Bank [Spanish]; Lorraine Ann Smiley [1959] Director/General Counsel [American]; Sister Catherine Vincie [1951] Director/Religious Sister [American]

Marz Limited
Incorporated: 24 October 2005 *Employees:* 587
Net Worth Deficit: £634,860 *Total Assets:* £13,388,672
Registered Office: 34-36 London Road, Wembley, Middlesex, HA9 7EX
Activities: Activities of head offices
Major Shareholder: Raja Jameel Adil
Officers: Mohammed Adil, Secretary; Raja Jameel Adil [1971] Director/Solicitor

Mashco Limited
Incorporated: 21 March 1997 *Employees:* 15
Net Worth: £5,641,555 *Total Assets:* £6,896,520
Registered Office: 17 Colonial Way, Watford, Herts, WD24 4PT
Activities: Wholesale of radio, television goods & electrical household appliances (other than records, tapes, CDs)
Major Shareholder: Jayant Kumar Gokaldas Mashru
Officers: Alka Jayant Mashru, Secretary; Alka Jayant Mashru [1960] Director/Secretary; Jayant Kumar Gokaldas Mashru [1958] Director

R. Maskell (Holdings) Limited
Incorporated: 23 December 2011 *Employees:* 23
Net Worth: £2,824,957 *Total Assets:* £13,072,307
Registered Office: Watergate, Broxhill Road, Havering-atte-Bower, Romford, Essex, RM4 1QH
Activities: Dormant company
Major Shareholder: Richard Henry Maskell
Officers: Nicholas Richard Maskell, Secretary; Lawrence Jefferson Gilbert [1948] Sales Director; Nicholas Richard Maskell [1974] Director/Businessman

R. Maskell Limited
Incorporated: 20 June 1972 *Employees:* 6
Net Worth: £8,758,561 *Total Assets:* £13,745,360
Registered Office: Watergate, Broxhill Road, Havering-atte-Bower, Romford, Essex, RM4 1QH
Activities: Wholesale of household goods (other than musical instruments) n.e.c
Major Shareholder: Richard Henry Maskell
Officers: Nicholas Richard Maskell, Secretary; Justin Simon Gilbert [1975] Director/Businessman; Lawrence Jefferson Gilbert [1948] Sales Director; Nicholas Richard Maskell [1974] Director/Businessman; Richard Henry Maskell [1943] Director

Mason Pearson Bros. Limited
Incorporated: 11 January 1973 *Employees:* 77
Net Worth: £8,554,603 *Total Assets:* £9,241,883
Registered Office: 7 Easter Park, Ferry Lane South, Rainham, Essex, RM13 9BP
Activities: Other manufacturing n.e.c.
Officers: Michael John Pearson, Secretary; Juliette Mary Boulton [1954] Director; Anthony James Jackson [1938] Director; Michael John Pearson [1951] Director

Mastermind Trading Limited
Incorporated: 28 March 2001
Net Worth: £5,996,033 *Total Assets:* £7,197,928
Registered Office: Knapdale Nursery, Cattlegate Road, Enfield, Middlesex, EN2 9ED
Activities: Other letting and operating of own or leased real estate
Parent: Esmeralda Ltd
Officers: Rahul Patel, Secretary; Hendricus Renatus Tamerus [1967] Director [Dutch]

Masters of Beckenham Limited
Incorporated: 31 October 1952 *Employees:* 125
Net Worth: £13,483,212 *Total Assets:* £25,524,862
Registered Office: 150-164 Upper Elmers End Road, Beckenham, Kent, BR3 3DZ
Activities: Sale of new cars and light motor vehicles
Shareholders: Scott David Stoneham; Christian William Stoneham
Officers: Brian Geoffrey Cotton, Finance Director; Brian Geoffrey Cotton [1953] Director; Christian William Stoneham [1968] Director; Scott David Stoneham [1967] Director

Masters Pharmaceuticals Limited
Incorporated: 17 October 1984 *Employees:* 85
Net Worth: £485,273 *Total Assets:* £9,841,748
Registered Office: 380 Centennial Avenue, Centennial Park, Elstree, Herts, WD6 3TJ
Activities: Manufacture of pharmaceutical preparations
Officers: Suzad Masters [1958] Director; Zulfikar Masters [1956] Director/Chairman

Masterson Holdings Limited
Incorporated: 29 June 2001 *Employees:* 268
Net Worth: £24,080,776 *Total Assets:* £78,976,696
Registered Office: Atlantic House, 7 Stirling Way, Borehamwood, Herts, WD6 2BT
Activities: Activities of head offices
Shareholder: Michael Masterson
Officers: Michael Masterson, Secretary; Keith Leonard Masterson [1973] Director/Surveyor [Irish]; Margaret Masterson [1976] Director/Accountant [Irish]; Michael Christian Masterson [1980] Director [Irish]; Michael Masterson [1950] Director Construction Company [Irish]; Mona Ann Masterson [1952] Director; Sean Masterson [1977] Director/Construction Manager [Irish]; Nigel Mark Warnes [1955] Construction Director

Mawpart Commercial Limited
Incorporated: 8 December 1987 *Employees:* 2
Net Worth: £1,903,125 *Total Assets:* £6,648,147
Registered Office: York House, Empire Way, Wembley, Middlesex, HA9 0FQ
Activities: Non-trading company
Parent: Mawpart Properties Limited
Officers: LEA Anne Frances Newman, Secretary; LEA Anne Frances Newman [1950] Director; Michael Levi Weinstein [1948] Director

Maxco London Limited
Incorporated: 6 March 2015
Previous: JCG Investments Limited
Net Worth: £4,395,347 *Total Assets:* £6,596,168
Registered Office: 69-71 East Street, Epsom, Surrey, KT17 1BP
Activities: Other business support service activities n.e.c.
Major Shareholder: James Clifford Gregory
Officers: Charles James Peter Gregory [1983] Director; James Clifford Gregory [1948] Director

Maxen Homes Limited
Incorporated: 5 April 2016
Net Worth: £4,412,855 *Total Assets:* £7,874,786
Registered Office: Coopers House, 65a Wingletye Lane, Hornchurch, Essex, RM11 3AT
Activities: Other letting and operating of own or leased real estate
Shareholders: Michael Xenakis; Adeline Xenakis
Officers: Adeline Xenakis [1969] Director [French]; Michael Xenakis [1960] Director

Maxwelton House Property Company Limited
Incorporated: 8 March 1973 *Employees:* 6
Net Worth: £5,479,183 *Total Assets:* £5,973,850
Registered Office: 1 Beauchamp Court, Victors Way, Barnet, Herts, EN5 5TZ
Activities: Buying and selling of own real estate
Shareholders: Vic Jamieson; Gillian Diana Jamieson
Officers: Sara Jamieson, Secretary; Gillian Diana Jamieson [1936] Director/Executive; Sara Jamieson [1962] Director/Commercial Designer; Simon Charles Jamieson [1961] Director/Accountant; Victor Charles Jamieson [1928] Director/Surveyor

Maybour Logistics Global Limited
Incorporated: 16 February 1998 *Employees:* 1
Previous: Maybour Limited
Net Worth: £4,764,351 *Total Assets:* £7,544,238
Registered Office: Palmerston House, 814 Brighton Road, Purley, Surrey, CR8 2BR
Activities: Sea and coastal freight water transport
Shareholders: Nicholas John Maybour; Natalie Jane Maybour
Officers: Nicholas John Maybour [1959] Director/Franchisee McDonalds Restaurant

Maybury Media LLP
Incorporated: 9 May 2003
Net Worth: £11,513,930 *Total Assets:* £11,514,990
Registered Office: 99 Kenton Road, Harrow, Middlesex, HA3 0AN
Officers: Rt Hon Lord Kenneth Wilfred Baker [1934] LLP Member; Anthony John Bethell [1957] LLP Member; Steven Astley Brown [1959] LLP Member; Stuart Andrew Brydson [1966] LLP Member; Panayotis Christoforou [1957] LLP Member; Mark Gerard Clough [1953] LLP Member; Peter David Cook [1964] LLP Member; David John Courtley [1957] LLP Member; Paul Duffy [1959] LLP Member; David Ereira [1956] LLP Member; Roderick Clifford Evans [1964] LLP Member; David Hill [1954] LLP Member; Mark Hollister [1962] LLP Member; Andrew Hough [1971] LLP Member; Paul McPhie Johnston [1972] LLP Member; Bruce Douglas King [1955] LLP Member; Andrew Christopher Lapping [1963] LLP Member; Gary Lloyd [1961] LLP Member; Christopher John Loynes [1947] LLP Member; Angus John Elsom MacCormick [1965] LLP Member; Deborah Jean Marshall [1961] LLP Member; Dominic Kevin O'Carroll [1960] LLP Member; Christopher Hugh Adrian Oakley [1956] LLP Member; Nicholas John Preston [1955] LLP Member; Linda Ann Reid [1942] LLP Member; Peter Eric Reid [1936] LLP Member; Stewart Martin Robertson [1966] LLP Member; Barrie David Sheers [1963] LLP Member; Robin Turner Shelton [1947] LLP Member; Donald Arthur Starr [1948] LLP Member; Jacqueline Stephens [1960] LLP Member; Mark Paul Stradling [1965] LLP Member; Richard Terley [1912] LLP Member; Paul John Trowbridge [1955] LLP Member; Garry Tibbott Veale [1960] LLP Member; Simon John Wilders [1953] LLP Member; Nicholas Ian Wilson [1960] LLP Member; Robert Harold Youngjohns [1951] LLP Member

Mayday Healthcare PLC
Incorporated: 3 December 2003 *Employees:* 78
Net Worth: £18,303,404 *Total Assets:* £21,135,084
Registered Office: Hygeia, 66-68 College Road, Harrow, Middlesex, HA1 1BE
Activities: Temporary employment agency activities
Major Shareholder: Kevin Michael Coyle
Officers: Howard Pepperdine, Secretary; Anna Louise Cooper [1978] Director; Christopher John Coyle [1984] Director; Kevin Michael Coyle [1956] Managing Director; Sean Deslandes [1974] Director; Michael Howard Helleur [1981] Director; Nicolas Poturicich [1978] Director

Mayfair Carpet Gallery Limited
Incorporated: 22 April 1981 *Employees:* 3
Net Worth: £4,799,775 *Total Assets:* £10,941,125
Registered Office: c/o Syedain & Co, 2nd Floor, Heron House, 109 Wembley Hill Road, Wembley, Middlesex, HA9 8DA
Activities: Wholesale of furniture, carpets and lighting equipment
Officers: Mahmood Anwar, Secretary; Ahmed Hassan Khawaja [1946] Director/Carpet Dealer; Ahmen Khawaja [1984] Director; Arfah Khawaja [1985] Director

Mayfair Housing & Commercial Investments Ltd.
Incorporated: 18 March 1949
Net Worth: £6,459,291 *Total Assets:* £9,642,696
Registered Office: Kings Parade, Lower Coombe Street, Croydon, Surrey, CR0 1AA
Activities: Development of building projects
Parent: Tregony Investments Limited
Officers: Athar Ahmad, Secretary; Athar Ahmad [1939] Director; Salim Ahmed [1963] Director; Samira Ahmed [1968] Director/Journalist; Saira MacNicol [1970] Director/Teacher

Mayfield Grammar School, Gravesend
Incorporated: 6 January 2012 *Employees:* 135
Net Worth: £9,283,907 *Total Assets:* £10,527,136
Registered Office: Mayfield Grammar School, Pelham Road, Gravesend, Kent, DA11 0JE
Activities: General secondary education
Officers: Martin Fielder-White [1950] Director/Finance Officer; Dawn Marie Foulger [1966] Director/Business Improvement Manager; Valerie Ann Green [1946] Director; David Philip Holton [1959] Finance Director; Paresh Kumar Patel [1955] Director/Pharmacist; Ann Elizabeth Sewell [1958] Director/Teacher; David John Wesley [1945] Director/Retired; Melanie Weston [1973] Director/Teacher; Ray Douglas Wickens [1960] Director/Premises Manager; Elaine Dawn Wilson [1968] Director

Maylands Green Limited
Incorporated: 22 November 1991 *Employees:* 62
Net Worth: £8,235,202 *Total Assets:* £12,394,912
Registered Office: 84 Market Place, Romford, Essex, RM1 3JE
Activities: Development of building projects
Shareholders: Nicholas Hilbery Chaplin; Paul William Hodge; Malcolm Hilbery Chaplin
Officers: Nicholas Hilbery Chaplin, Secretary; Sir Malcolm Hilbery Chaplin [1934] Director/Chartered Surveyor; Nicholas Hilbery Chaplin [1965] Director/Chartered Surveyor

Maysor LLP
Incorporated: 8 February 2012
Net Worth: £3,409,705 *Total Assets:* £7,520,503
Registered Office: 505 Pinner Road, Harrow, Middlesex, HA2 6EH
Officers: Nabeel Yunis Soroya [1971] Member; Shahila Samina Soroya [1968] Member

Mazda Motors UK Limited
Incorporated: 8 May 2001 *Employees:* 136
Net Worth: £7,402,000 *Total Assets:* £106,210,000
Registered Office: Victory Way, Crossways Business Park, Dartford, Kent, DA2 6DT
Activities: Sale of new cars and light motor vehicles
Parent: Mazda Motor Corporation
Officers: Ian Fraser, Secretary; Martijn Ten Brink [1973] Director/Vice President, Sales [Dutch]; Colin Maddocks [1969] Director, Financial Services; Jeremy Andrew Thomson [1966] Managing Director

MBH Finco. Limited
Incorporated: 31 October 2013
Net Worth: £58,152 *Total Assets:* £75,860,288
Registered Office: 505 Pinner Road, Harrow, Middlesex, HA2 6EH
Activities: Other letting and operating of own or leased real estate
Officers: Rishi Ramesh Sachdev [1976] Director; Uday Vyas [1978] Director

MBM Forest Products Limited
Incorporated: 23 June 1966 *Employees:* 12
Net Worth: £7,970,225 *Total Assets:* £14,699,267
Registered Office: Clock House, Station Approach, Shepperton, Surrey, TW17 8AN
Activities: Wholesale of wood, construction materials and sanitary equipment
Parent: Consolidated Timber Holdings Ltd
Officers: Andrew James Caldwell [1983] Sales Director; David John Colman [1962] Director/Chartered Accountant; Simon David Holdsworth [1956] Director/Chartered Accountant; Aidan George Hudson [1969] Operations Director; Stephen Peter Sabine [1963] Director/Timber Distributor; Andrew Peter Smith [1959] Director

MC Power Limited
Incorporated: 14 December 2011
Net Worth Deficit: £2,921,000 *Total Assets:* £15,195,000
Registered Office: Beaufort Court, Egg Farm Lane, Kings Langley, Herts, WD4 8LR
Activities: Production of electricity
Parent: Trafalgar Wind Holdings Limited
Officers: Dominic James Hearth, Secretary; Steven William Hughes [1972] Generation & Asset Management Director; Fraser Stephen Merry [1968] Director/Chartered Surveyor; Mitesh Raj Patel [1982] Director/Group Financial Controller

MC Treasury Limited
Incorporated: 23 October 2007
Net Worth: £763,508,992 *Total Assets:* £1,086,730,624
Registered Office: Maple Court, Central Park, Reeds Crescent, Watford, Herts, WD24 4QQ
Activities: Other business support service activities n.e.c.
Parent: HIC Treasury Limited
Officers: Stuart Beasley [1971] Director/Financial Controller; Richard Geoffrey Beeston [1982] Director/Chartered Accountant; James Owen Percival [1968] Director/Accountant; Brian McKay Wilson [1962] Director/Company Secretary

McGee Civil Engineering Limited
Incorporated: 6 November 1963 *Employees:* 123
Previous: McGee Group Limited
Net Worth: £6,887,510 *Total Assets:* £16,900,368
Registered Office: 340-342 Athlon Road, Wembley, Middlesex, HA0 1BX
Activities: Construction of commercial buildings
Parent: McGee Group (Holdings) Limited
Officers: John Paul McGee, Secretary; John Joseph Hennessey [1960] Director/Safety Officer; Brian James McGee [1964] Group Managing Director; John Paul McGee [1966] Director - Head of Group Resources; Michael Thomas McGee [1963] Director [Irish]

McGee Group (Holdings) Limited
Incorporated: 13 June 1968 *Employees:* 353
Net Worth: £15,257,771 *Total Assets:* £48,231,040
Registered Office: 340-342 Athlon Road, Wembley, Middlesex, HA0 1BX
Activities: Construction of commercial buildings
Parent: MFCOIL Limited
Officers: Paul Hickey, Secretary; Sebastian Fossey [1981] Director; John Joseph Hennessy [1960] Director/Safety Professional; Paul Hickey [1965] Director/Chartered Accountant [Irish]; Brian James McGee [1964] Group Managing Director; John Paul McGee [1966] Director - Head of Group Resources; Michael Thomas McGee [1963] Director/Plant Manager [Irish]; Nicholas Mark Taylor [1967] Director; Darren Wayne Wickins [1972] Director

McGinley Aviation Holdings Limited
Incorporated: 2 September 2016 *Employees:* 9
Net Worth: £991,772 *Total Assets:* £11,717,253
Registered Office: 56 Clarendon Road, Watford, Herts, WD17 1DA
Activities: Other activities of employment placement agencies
Major Shareholder: Colm John McGinley
Officers: Donnacha Sean Holly [1984] Director [Irish]; Colm John McGinley [1982] Director [Irish]; Seamus Patrick McGinley [1955] Director [Irish]

McGinley Cep Ltd
Incorporated: 8 April 2010 *Employees:* 34
Previous: McGinley Human Resources Limited
Net Worth: £917,527 *Total Assets:* £7,420,922
Registered Office: 56 Clarendon Road, Watford, Herts, WD17 1DA
Activities: Temporary employment agency activities
Major Shareholder: Colm John McGinley
Officers: Grant Henderson [1978] Director; Donnacha Sean Holly [1984] Finance Director [Irish]; Colm John McGinley [1982] Director [Irish]; Seamus McGinley [1955] Director [Irish]; Peter Rooke [1957] Director

McGrath Bros. (Environmental) Ltd.
Incorporated: 21 December 2005
Net Worth: £2,262,237 *Total Assets:* £26,192,572
Registered Office: 62 River Road, Barking, Essex, IG11 0DS
Activities: Other letting and operating of own or leased real estate
Parent: McGrath Brothers (Holdings) Ltd
Officers: David Oliver McGrath, Secretary [Irish]; David Oliver McGrath [1952] Director/Builder [Irish]; Michael McGrath [1950] Director/Waste Management Executive [Irish]; Patrick McGrath [1958] Director/Builder [Irish]

McGrath Bros. (Waste Control) Limited
Incorporated: 30 November 1981 *Employees:* 92
Net Worth: £13,550,247 *Total Assets:* £22,663,392
Registered Office: 62 River Road, Barking, Essex, IG11 0DS
Activities: Recovery of sorted materials
Officers: David Oliver McGrath, Secretary [Irish]; Tara Katherine Donaghy [1975] Director/Business Manager; John Martin McDaid [1967] Transport Director; David Gerard McGrath [1978] Director/Plant Manager [Irish]; David Oliver McGrath [1952] Director/Builder [Irish]; Michael McGrath [1950] Director/Builder [Irish]; Patrick McGrath [1958] Director/Builder [Irish]; Stephen McGrath [1981] Director/Manager [Irish]; James Roland Oliver [1966] Director/Accountant; Gerard Edward Vines [1961] Plant Director

McGrath Brothers (Holdings) Limited
Incorporated: 2 July 1982 *Employees:* 101
Net Worth: £38,739,484 *Total Assets:* £54,844,800
Registered Office: 62 River Road, Barking, Essex, IG11 0DS
Activities: Activities of other holding companies n.e.c.
Shareholders: David Oliver McGrath; Michael McGrath
Officers: David Oliver McGrath, Secretary [Irish]; David Oliver McGrath [1952] Director/Builder [Irish]; Michael McGrath [1950] Director/Builder [Irish]; Patrick McGrath [1958] Director/Builder [Irish]; Stephen McGrath [1981] Director/Manager [Irish]

MCM Central Limited
Incorporated: 10 September 2015 *Employees:* 2
Net Worth: £4,682,203 *Total Assets:* £6,793,812
Registered Office: Gateway House, 28 The Quadrant, Richmond, Surrey, TW9 1DN
Activities: Other service activities n.e.c.
Parent: Reed Exhibitions Limited
Officers: Jacqueline Mary Poole, Secretary; Alexander David Stuart Bowden [1967] Director/Accountant; Richard John Norman Mortimore [1960] Director; Michele Ruth Tiley-Hill [1972] Director/Chief Financial Officer

MCPA Limited
Incorporated: 18 February 2013
Net Worth: £17,797,238 *Total Assets:* £25,347,940
Registered Office: 2 Castle Business Village, Station Road, Hampton, Surrey, TW12 2BX
Activities: Buying and selling of own real estate
Shareholders: Christopher Paul Anthony; Mark Christopher Cherry
Officers: Christopher Paul Anthony [1958] Director/Fund Manager; Mark Christopher Cherry [1962] Director/Property Developer

MCPE LLP
Incorporated: 14 October 2013
Net Worth: £5,816,667 *Total Assets:* £5,841,596
Registered Office: Salisbury House, 20 Queens Road, Weybridge, Surrey, KT13 9XE

MDJ Group Ltd.
Incorporated: 5 July 2017
Net Worth: £40,000 *Total Assets:* £5,040,000
Registered Office: Eagle House, Stonebridge Road, Eagle Way, Northfleet, Gravesend, Kent, DA11 9BJ
Activities: Activities of other holding companies n.e.c.
Shareholder: Nachhattar Kaur Dhillon
Officers: Manga Singh Dhillon [1958] Director

MDJ Investments Limited
Incorporated: 9 May 2017
Net Worth: £247,999 *Total Assets:* £5,432,072
Registered Office: Eagle House, Stonebridge Road, Eagle Way, Northfleet, Gravesend, Kent, DA11 9BJ
Activities: Other food services
Parent: MDJ Group Ltd.
Officers: Manga Singh Dhillon [1958] Director

ME Construction Limited
Incorporated: 15 June 2007 *Employees:* 36
Net Worth: £1,637,839 *Total Assets:* £8,899,760
Registered Office: Suite D, The Business Centre, Faringdon Avenue, Romford, Essex, RM3 8EN
Activities: Construction of commercial buildings
Parent: Mecon Holdings Limited
Officers: Dennis William Barnard [1957] Director; Paul Alan Driver [1960] Director; Peter McCullagh [1959] Director; Sean William O'Connor [1965] Director; Barry William O'Sullivan [1967] Director; John Jih-Jong Yeo [1959] Director [Singaporean]

Meadvine Limited
Incorporated: 2 August 1999
Net Worth: £1,500,195 *Total Assets:* £7,805,421
Registered Office: 632 Eastern Avenue, Gants Hill, Ilford, Essex, IG2 6PG
Activities: Buying and selling of own real estate
Shareholders: Noam Margolin; Louise Devora Margolin
Officers: Louise Devora Margolin, Secretary; Louise Devora Margolin [1961] Director/Finance Consultant; Noam Margolin [1961] Director/Finance Controller

Mechanical Services Limited
Incorporated: 11 March 1985 *Employees:* 126
Net Worth: £5,140,115 *Total Assets:* £9,582,701
Registered Office: Merlin House, 606 Purley Way, Croydon, Surrey, CR0 4RF
Activities: Other business support service activities n.e.c.
Parent: Mechanical Services EOT Limited
Officers: Margaret Mary Ivory, Secretary; Generald Anthony Ivory [1957] Director/Engineer

Mecon Holdings Limited
Incorporated: 1 November 2012 *Employees:* 38
Net Worth: £1,678,510 *Total Assets:* £8,900,836
Registered Office: Suite D, The Business Centre, Faringdon Avenue, Romford, Essex, RM3 8EN
Activities: Activities of construction holding companies
Major Shareholder: Sean William O'Connor
Officers: Dennis William Barnard [1957] Director; Paul Alan Driver [1960] Director; Peter McCullagh [1959] Director; Sean William O'Connor [1965] Director; Barry William O'Sullivan [1967] Director; John Jih-Jong Yeo [1959] Director [Singaporean]

Medequip Assistive Technology Limited
Incorporated: 11 April 2001 *Employees:* 703
Net Worth: £21,679,000 *Total Assets:* £43,960,000
Registered Office: Unit 2 Summit Centre, Skyport Drive, Harmondsworth, West Drayton, Middlesex, UB7 0LJ
Activities: Retail sale of medical and orthopaedic goods in specialised stores (not incl. hearing aids) n.e.c.
Parent: Siddall Group Limited
Officers: Jonathan Paul Cockroft [1969] Director; Nigel Stewart Paul Cook [1963] Director of Human Resources; Andrew Paul Firth [1964] Operations Director; Michael Frank Greenwood [1965] Director/Chartered Accountant; David Griffiths [1961] Managing Director; James Ibbotson [1977] Director; Adrienne Helen Siddall [1958] Non-Executive Director; Andrew John Siddall [1959] Director/Group Chief Executive; Clive Philip Siddall [1962] Director; Jeremy Charles Siddall [1958] Director; Susan Tracey Siddall [1962] Non-Executive Director; Lyndsey Jane Wainwright [1961] Non-Executive Director; Mike West [1963] Procurement Director

Medequip Group Limited
Incorporated: 21 April 2015 *Employees:* 703
Net Worth: £42,295,000 *Total Assets:* £69,806,000
Registered Office: Unit 2 Summit Centre, Skyport Drive, Harmondsworth, West Drayton, Middlesex, UB7 0LJ
Activities: Retail sale of medical and orthopaedic goods in specialised stores (not incl. hearing aids) n.e.c.
Parent: Medequip Holdings Limited
Officers: Jonathan Paul Cockroft [1969] Director; Nigel Stewart Paul Cook [1963] Director; Andrew Paul Firth [1964] Director; Michael Frank Greenwood [1965] Director/Chartered Accountant; David Griffiths [1961] Director; James Ibbotson [1977] Director; Andrew John Siddall [1959] Director; Clive Philip Siddall [1962] Director; Jeremy Charles Siddall [1958] Director; Mike West [1963] Procurement Director

Medi-Shop Limited
Incorporated: 2 August 1984 *Employees:* 44
Net Worth: £7,095,172 *Total Assets:* £9,360,398
Registered Office: 3rd Floor, Scottish Provident House, 76-80 College Road, Harrow, Middlesex, HA1 1BQ
Activities: Dispensing chemist in specialised stores
Officers: Nikunj Shantilal Malde, Secretary; Deepakkumar Shantilal Malde [1960] Director/Pharmacist; Nikunj Shantilal Malde [1958] Director/Doctor

Media 10 Holdings Limited
Incorporated: 10 June 2009 *Employees:* 288
Net Worth: £2,136,577 *Total Assets:* £22,715,204
Registered Office: Crown House, 151 High Road, Loughton, Essex, IG10 4LF
Activities: Activities of head offices
Shareholder: Lee Steven Newton
Officers: Jane Louise Musgrove, Secretary; Richard John Morey [1965] Director/Publisher; Daren John Newton [1968] Director/Publisher; Lee Steven Newton [1965] Director; Eric John William Wenham [1950] Director

Media 10 Limited
Incorporated: 12 December 2002 *Employees:* 257
Net Worth: £1,908,944 *Total Assets:* £19,237,392
Registered Office: Crown House, 151 High Road, Loughton, Essex, IG10 4LF
Activities: Publishing of consumer and business journals and periodicals
Parent: Media 10 Holdings Limited
Officers: Jane Louise Musgrove, Secretary; Richard John Morey [1965] Director/Publisher; Daren John Newton [1968] Director/Sales Manager; Lee Steven Newton [1965] Director; Eric John William Wenham [1950] Director/Accountant

Medico-Dental Holdings Limited
Incorporated: 20 September 2011 *Employees:* 154
Net Worth Deficit: £15,544,952 *Total Assets:* £5,643,314
Registered Office: 3rd Floor, Chancery House, St Nicholas Way, Sutton, Surrey, SM1 1JB
Activities: Activities of other holding companies n.e.c.
Shareholder: Lisa Margaret Flanagan
Officers: Dominick James Trevelyn Flanagan [1964] Director; Lisa Margaret Flanagan [1963] Director; Salvatore Martin Gatto [1950] Director; David Charles Spencer Harman [1973] Director; David Vogel [1948] Director/Solicitor

Medicrest Limited
Incorporated: 10 July 1995
Net Worth: £3,579,871 *Total Assets:* £5,657,388
Registered Office: 104 High Street, West Wickham, Kent, BR4 0NF
Activities: Other service activities n.e.c.
Major Shareholder: Kanagaratnam Sathananthan
Officers: Shanthini Sathananthan, Secretary; Kanagaratnam Sathananthan [1939] Director/Medical Practitioner

Medipharmacy Limited
Incorporated: 11 March 2004 *Employees:* 113
Net Worth: £3,522,278 *Total Assets:* £12,058,420
Registered Office: 66 Church Street, Croydon, Surrey, CR0 1RB
Activities: Dispensing chemist in specialised stores
Shareholders: Naveen Khosla; Sadhna Khosla
Officers: Naveen Khosla, Secretary; Naveen Khosla [1959] Director/Manager; Sadhna Khosla [1961] Director/Pharmacist

Medivet Group Limited
Incorporated: 16 December 1997 *Employees:* 1,298
Net Worth: £17,021,080 *Total Assets:* £128,100,616
Registered Office: 4 Mowat Industrial Estate, Sandown Road, Watford, Herts, WD24 7UY
Activities: Veterinary activities
Parent: Medivet Partnership LLP
Officers: Arnold Stephen Levy, Secretary/Veterinary Surgeon; Dr Guy Richard Carter [1964] Director/Veterinary Surgeon; Arnold Stephen Levy [1959] Director/Veterinary Surgeon; Kevin Lance Morris [1973] Director; John William Hampden Smithers [1963] Director/Veterinary Surgeon

Medivet Partnership LLP
Incorporated: 20 March 2009 *Employees:* 1,297
Net Worth Deficit: £160,000 *Total Assets:* £72,368,000
Registered Office: 4 Mowat Industrial Estate, Sandown Road, Watford, Herts, WD24 7UY
Officers: David Abratt [1973] Member; Yorram Ariel [1966] Member; Dr Guy Richard Carter [1964] Member; Jan Harold Doedens [1966] Member; Erwin Wilhelm Hohn [1959] Member; Matthew James Holgate [1974] Member; Nitzan Kroter [1969] Member; Jeffrey Stephen Langberg [1958] Member; Richard Mary Leonard [1958] Member; Arnold Stephen Levy [1959] Member; Kevin Lance Morris [1973] Member; Adi Nell [1968] Member; Daniel Preter [1967] Member; Gareth Richardson [1970] Member; John William Hampden Smithers [1963] Member

Medlock Electrical Distributors Limited
Incorporated: 27 March 1947 *Employees:* 241
Net Worth: £22,618,216 *Total Assets:* £45,418,612
Registered Office: 109-115 Eleanor Cross Road, Waltham Cross, Herts, EN8 7NT
Activities: Wholesale of radio, television goods & electrical household appliances (other than records, tapes, CDs)
Major Shareholder: Alan Leslie Moore
Officers: Alan Leslie Moore, Secretary/Director [Irish]; Alan Leslie Moore [1950] Director [Irish]; Ben Patrick Moore [1983] Director [Irish]; Christine Leslie Moore [1952] Marketing Director; David Scott Moore [1972] Director [Irish]; Peter Robert Moore [1978] Sales Director [Irish]

Medreich PLC
Incorporated: 7 November 1995 *Employees:* 58
Net Worth: £20,507,924 *Total Assets:* £40,756,208
Registered Office: Ibex House, Baker Street, Weybridge, Surrey, KT13 8AH
Activities: Wholesale of pharmaceutical goods
Officers: Ashish Gupta, Secretary; Shinya Katafuchi [1960] Director [Japanese]; John McCullough [1970] Director; Yuji Sasaki [1958] Director [Japanese]; Hiromasa Takizawa [1964] Director [Japanese]

Medtronic Limited
Incorporated: 8 September 1972 *Employees:* 763
Net Worth: £31,142,000 *Total Assets:* £212,692,992
Registered Office: Building 9, Croxley Park, Hatters Lane, Watford, Herts, WD18 8WW
Activities: Manufacture of medical and dental instruments and supplies
Parent: Medtronic Public Limited Company
Officers: Philip John Albert [1965] Director/Vice-President of Corporate Tax [American]; Helen Louise Brown [1975] HR Director; Mark Justin Elsey [1967] Finance Director; Jacqueline Fielding [1964] VP & Regional Director, UK/Ireland

Meekland Limited
Incorporated: 21 December 1981 *Employees:* 3
Net Worth: £5,125,966 *Total Assets:* £5,790,732
Registered Office: Aissela, 46 High Street, Esher, Surrey, KT10 9QY
Activities: Other letting and operating of own or leased real estate
Officers: Kim Hurd [1962] Director

Mega Fabrications Group Ltd
Incorporated: 19 March 2012 *Employees:* 87
Net Worth: £6,052,832 *Total Assets:* £10,413,398
Registered Office: Enterprise House, Beesons Yard, Bury Lane, Rickmansworth, Herts, WD3 1DS
Activities: Other building completion and finishing
Shareholders: Nicola Mimoni; Rafi Moshe Mimoni
Officers: Nicola Mimoni, Secretary; Rafi Moshe Mimoni [1963] Group Managing Director

Megnum Limited
Incorporated: 5 March 2003
Net Worth: £3,679,119 *Total Assets:* £10,416,754
Registered Office: 2 Hathaway Close, Stanmore, Middlesex, HA7 3NR
Activities: Buying and selling of own real estate
Major Shareholder: Meena Chotai
Officers: Pradip Khodidas Dhamecha, Secretary/Director; Meena Chotai [1960] Director/Cash Officer Manager; Pradip Khodidas Dhamecha [1958] Director; Shantilal Ratanshi Dhamecha [1931] Director Businessman

MEI Properties Limited
Incorporated: 2 October 2012 *Employees:* 3
Net Worth: £23,563 *Total Assets:* £7,319,123
Registered Office: 16 South End, Croydon, Surrey, CR0 1DN
Activities: Management of real estate on a fee or contract basis
Shareholder: Jesus Bravo Mendez
Officers: Jesus Bravo Mendez [1976] Director/Property Consultant [Spanish]; Peter Michael Nellemose [1952] Director/Chartered Accountant [Danish]

Melford Commercial Properties Ltd.
Incorporated: 3 June 1980
Net Worth: £2,582,000 *Total Assets:* £6,488,000
Registered Office: Purfleet By Pass, Purfleet, Essex, RM19 1TT
Activities: Other letting and operating of own or leased real estate
Parent: Carpetright PLC
Officers: Neil Lloyd Page [1963] Director/Accountant; Jeremy Andrew Sampson [1968] Director/Solicitor

The Meller Educational Trust
Incorporated: 12 June 2009 *Employees:* 284
Net Worth: £48,465,204 *Total Assets:* £50,062,852
Registered Office: The Bushey Academy, London Road, Bushey, Herts, WD23 3AA
Activities: General secondary education
Officers: David Robert Hughes, Secretary; Kate Prudence Bearman [1971] Director; Richard Arthur Elms [1947] Director/Chief Executive; Rita Susan Halbright [1961] Director/School Administrator [British/American]; David Robert Hughes [1970] Director of Finance and Operations; Clive Ashley Ross [1949] Director/Chartered Surveyor; Andrew Jonathan Sheach [1963] Director/Solicitor; Gillian Elizabeth Wiscarson [1954] Director/University Lecturer

Melton House Investments Limited
Incorporated: 7 March 2011 *Employees:* 43
Net Worth: £8,949,815 *Total Assets:* £26,362,588
Registered Office: Melton House, 65-67 Clarendon Road, Watford, Herts, WD17 1DS
Activities: Hotels and similar accommodation
Shareholders: Gursharan Singh Chadha; Jasbir Chadha
Officers: Gursharan Singh Chadha [1960] Director; Vivek Singh Chadha [1988] Director

Melville Hotel Limited
Incorporated: 11 January 2001
Net Worth: £2,296,586 *Total Assets:* £5,755,474
Registered Office: c/o AZR Limited, 79 College Road, Harrow, Middlesex, HA1 1BD
Activities: Hotels and similar accommodation
Shareholders: Anupam Parekh; Shahkuntala Parekh
Officers: Pratik Parekh, Secretary/Director; Anupam Parekh [1944] Director; Pratik Parekh [1975] Director; Shakuntala Parekh [1949] Director

Mentfield UK Limited
Incorporated: 14 September 2004 *Employees:* 70
Net Worth: £522,278 *Total Assets:* £7,646,787
Registered Office: Unit B2, Parkway, Cranford Lane, Heston, Middlesex, TW5 9QA
Activities: Scheduled passenger air transport
Parent: Myone Limited
Officers: Omer Izhari, Secretary; Omer Izhari [1978] Managing Director [Israeli]; Yoav Izhari [1980] Director/Freight Agent [Israeli]

Mentmore Limited
Incorporated: 23 November 1935 *Employees:* 2
Net Worth: £130,272,000 *Total Assets:* £376,945,984
Registered Office: c/o Safestore Holdings PLC, Brittanic House, Stirling Way, Borehamwood, Herts, WD6 2BT
Activities: Activities of other holding companies n.e.c.
Parent: Safestore Acquisition Limited
Officers: Andrew Brian Jones [1966] Director/Chartered Accountant; Federico Vecchioli [1966] Director [French]

John Menzies (108) Limited
Incorporated: 10 November 1994
Net Worth: £54,400,000 *Total Assets:* £77,400,000
Registered Office: 2 World Business Centre Heathrow, Newall Road, London Heathrow Airport, Hounslow, Middlesex, TW6 2SF
Activities: Activities of head offices
Parent: Menzies Group Holdings Limited
Officers: John Francis Alexander Geddes, Secretary; John Francis Alexander Geddes [1968] Director/Company Secretary; Giles Robert Bryant Wilson [1973] Director/Accountant

Menzies Aviation (ASIG Ground Handling) Limited
Incorporated: 12 May 2004 *Employees:* 825
Previous: ASIG Ground Handling Limited
Net Worth Deficit: £3,350,000 *Total Assets:* £15,657,000
Registered Office: 2 World Business Centre Heathrow, Newall Road, London Heathrow Airport, Hounslow, Middlesex, TW6 2SF
Activities: Service activities incidental to air transportation
Parent: Menzies Aviation (ASIG) Limited
Officers: John Francis Alexander Geddes, Secretary; Deon Van Niekerk [1972] Director/Accountant [South African]; Laura Relf [1982] Director/Accountant; Sheena Robertson [1956] Operations Director

Menzies Aviation (ASIG) Limited
Incorporated: 14 February 1984 *Employees:* 872
Previous: ASIG Limited
Net Worth: £23,200,000 *Total Assets:* £39,800,000
Registered Office: 2 World Business Centre Heathrow, Newall Road, London Heathrow Airport, Hounslow, Middlesex, TW6 2SF
Activities: Scheduled passenger air transport
Parent: ASIG Holdings Limited
Officers: John Francis Alexander Geddes, Secretary; Deon Van Niekerk [1972] Director/Accountant [South African]; Laura Relf [1982] Director/Accountant; Sheena Robertson [1956] Operations Director

Menzies Aviation (NL) Limited
Incorporated: 23 February 1999
Net Worth: £13,217,000 *Total Assets:* £13,282,000
Registered Office: 2 World Business Centre Heathrow, Newall Road, London Heathrow Airport, Hounslow, Middlesex, TW6 2SF
Activities: Service activities incidental to air transportation
Parent: Menzies Aviation PLC
Officers: Tristan George Turnbull, Secretary; Matthew Brook McCreath [1978] Director/Accountant; David Alastair Trollope [1960] Director/Accountant

Menzies Aviation (UK) Limited
Incorporated: 27 April 2000 *Employees:* 4,396
Net Worth: £5,200,000 *Total Assets:* £39,600,000
Registered Office: 2 World Business Centre Heathrow, Newall Road, London Heathrow Airport, Hounslow, Middlesex, TW6 2SF
Activities: Service activities incidental to air transportation
Parent: Menzies Aviation PLC
Officers: Tristan George Turnbull, Secretary/Solicitor; Deon Van Niekerk [1972] Director [South African]; David Alastair Trollope [1960] Director/Accountant

Menzies Aviation Holdings Limited
Incorporated: 17 August 2000 *Employees:* 68
Net Worth: £6,600,000 *Total Assets:* £151,800,000
Registered Office: 2 World Business Centre Heathrow, Newall Road, London Heathrow Airport, Hounslow, Middlesex, TW6 2SF
Activities: Service activities incidental to air transportation
Parent: Menzies Group Holdings Limited
Officers: John Francis Alexander Geddes, Secretary; Forsyth Rutherford Black [1969] Director; John Francis Alexander Geddes [1968] Director/Company Secretary; David Alastair Trollope [1960] Director/Accountant; Giles Robert Bryant Wilson [1973] Director/Accountant

Menzies Aviation PLC
Incorporated: 23 August 1994 *Employees:* 5
Net Worth: £49,700,000 *Total Assets:* £609,699,968
Registered Office: 2 World Business Centre Heathrow, Newall Road, London Heathrow Airport, Hounslow, Middlesex, TW6 2SF
Activities: Service activities incidental to air transportation
Parent: Menzies Aviation Holdings Limited
Officers: John Francis Alexander Geddes, Secretary; Forsyth Rutherford Black [1969] Director; John Francis Alexander Geddes [1968] Director/Company Secretary; David Alastair Trollope [1960] Director/Accountant; Giles Robert Bryant Wilson [1973] Director/Accountant

John Menzies Finance Limited
Incorporated: 11 June 2007
Net Worth: £60,100,000 *Total Assets:* £80,100,000
Registered Office: 2 World Business Centre Heathrow, Newall Road, London Heathrow Airport, Hounslow, Middlesex, TW6 2SF
Activities: Financial intermediation not elsewhere classified
Parent: John Menzies PLC
Officers: John Francis Alexander Geddes, Secretary; John Francis Alexander Geddes [1968] Director/Company Secretary; Giles Robert Bryant Wilson [1973] Director/Accountant

Menzies Group Holdings Limited
Incorporated: 31 January 1963
Net Worth: £38,900,000 *Total Assets:* £203,200,000
Registered Office: 2 World Business Centre Heathrow, Newall Road, London Heathrow Airport, Hounslow, Middlesex, TW6 2SF
Activities: Non-trading company
Parent: John Menzies PLC
Officers: John Francis Alexander Geddes, Secretary; John Francis Alexander Geddes [1968] Director/Company Secretary; Giles Robert Bryant Wilson [1973] Director/Accountant

Menzies World Cargo Limited
Incorporated: 4 December 1969 *Employees:* 202
Net Worth Deficit: £14,297,000 *Total Assets:* £12,020,000
Registered Office: 2 World Business Centre Heathrow, Newall Road, London Heathrow Airport, Hounslow, Middlesex, TW6 2SF
Activities: Freight transport by road
Parent: Menzies Aviation PLC
Officers: Tristan George Turnbull, Secretary; Michael Richard Ladd [1963] Director/GM Cargo Process & Planning UK/1; Deon Van Niekerk [1972] Director [South African]

Meraj Limited
Incorporated: 25 January 2000 *Employees:* 32
Net Worth: £4,515,374 *Total Assets:* £7,421,019
Registered Office: Suite 3.17a, Q West, Great West Road, Brentford, Middlesex, TW8 0GP
Activities: Dispensing chemist in specialised stores
Officers: Faruque Hussain Gani, Secretary; Faruque Hussain Gani [1969] Director/Pharmacist; Jusna Gani [1971] Director/Teacher

Merchant Taylors' School
Incorporated: 30 July 1997 *Employees:* 355
Net Worth: £33,755,376 *Total Assets:* £39,653,028
Registered Office: Sandy Lodge, Northwood, Middlesex, HA6 2HT
Activities: General secondary education
Officers: Ian Douglas Williams, Secretary; Richard John Brooman [1955] Director/Chartered Accountant; Dr Jonathan Mark Cox [1966] Director/Headmaster; Guy Beetham Maurice Henry Du Parc Braham [1966] Director/Chief Risk Officer; Alan Roy Eastwood [1955] Director/Retired Chartered Accountant; Lynn Barbara Gadd [1953] Director/Principal; Georgina Jayne Gardiner [1985] Director/Assistant Professor; Christopher Peter Hare [1947] Director Lloyds Managing Agent; Deepak Haria [1963] Director/Chartered Accountant; Sarah Angharad Morgan [1978] HR Director; Andrew Graham Moss [1958] Director/Chartered Accountant; Jane Katherine Mary Redman [1957] Director/Solicitor [Irish]; Dipesh Jayantilal Shah [1953] Director; Robert John Temmink [1973] Director/Barrister; Sir Michael John Tomlinson [1942] Director/Retired; James Douglas Robert Twining [1972] Director/Chief Executive

Merck Consumer Healthcare Limited
Incorporated: 28 August 1979 *Employees:* 9
Net Worth Deficit: £43,683,000 *Total Assets:* £32,178,000
Registered Office: Bedfont Cross, Stanwell Road, Feltham, Middlesex, TW14 8NX
Activities: Non-trading company
Parent: Merck KGaA
Officers: Anthony Joseph Appleton [1962] Director & General Counsel; Alexander George Buckthorp [1973] Finance Director; Vijay Indroo Sitlani [1975] Finance Director [Singaporean]; Christopher John Young [1974] HR Director

Merck Holding Ltd.
Incorporated: 16 May 2013
Net Worth: £1,130,476,928 *Total Assets:* £1,389,846,400
Registered Office: Bedfont Cross, Stanwell Road, Feltham, Middlesex, TW14 8NX
Activities: Activities of other holding companies n.e.c.
Parent: Merck KGaA
Officers: Peter Biro [1967] Director/US Certified Public Accountant [Dutch]; Victor Mark Jackson [1962] Director/Operations Manager

Merck Serono Limited
Incorporated: 2 October 1970 *Employees:* 173
Net Worth: £20,986,000 *Total Assets:* £60,114,000
Registered Office: Bedfont Cross, Stanwell Road, Feltham, Middlesex, TW14 8NX
Activities: Wholesale of pharmaceutical goods
Parent: Merck KGaA
Officers: Peter Biro [1967] Director/US Certified Public Accountant [Dutch]; Charles William Dring [1962] Director; Mary Elizabeth Henderson [1971] Managing Director [Irish]

Merck Sharp & Dohme (Holdings) Limited
Incorporated: 29 September 1928
Net Worth: £455,592,992 *Total Assets:* £455,840,992
Registered Office: Hertford Road, Hoddesdon, Herts, EN11 9BU
Activities: Activities of head offices
Parent: Schering-Plough Holdings Limited
Officers: Richard Robinski, Secretary; Louise Jane Houson [1976] Director; Simon Nicholson [1975] Director; Ebru Can Temucin [1972] Director [Turkish]

Merck Sharp & Dohme Finance Europe Limited
Incorporated: 21 October 1993 *Employees:* 3
Net Worth: £324,069,280 *Total Assets:* £1,183,533,696
Registered Office: Hertford Road, Hoddesdon, Herts, EN11 9BU
Activities: Other business support service activities n.e.c.
Parent: Merck & Co., Inc.
Officers: Richard Robinski, Secretary; Michael Hobbs [1960] Director; Richard Robinski [1958] Director/Secretary; Ebru Can Temucin [1972] Director [Turkish]

Merck Sharp & Dohme Limited
Incorporated: 25 September 1964 *Employees:* 1,162
Net Worth: £440,820,992 *Total Assets:* £607,619,008
Registered Office: Hertford Road, Hoddesdon, Herts, EN11 9BU
Activities: Manufacture of basic pharmaceutical products
Parent: Merck Sharp & Dohme (Holdings) Limited
Officers: Richard Robinski, Secretary; Louise Jane Houson [1976] Director; Simon Nicholson [1975] Director; Ebru Can Temucin [1972] Director [Turkish]

Mercurius Synergy LLP
Incorporated: 23 March 2010
Net Worth: £1,785,275 *Total Assets:* £5,300,906
Registered Office: Ground Floor, Unit 501 Centennial Park, Centennial Avenue, Elstree, Borehamwood, Herts, WD6 3FG

Mercury Land Holdings Limited
Incorporated: 18 November 2015 *Employees:* 1
Net Worth: £8,166,816 *Total Assets:* £23,169,784
Registered Office: 2 River Chambers, High Street, Romford, Essex, RM1 1HR
Activities: Other letting and operating of own or leased real estate
Parent: London Borough of Havering
Officers: Keith Oliver, Secretary; Andrew Blake-Herbert [1970] Director; Garry Kevin Green [1955] Director/Chartered Surveyor; Anthony Vincent Huff [1961] Assistant Director; Ian Philip Rhodes [1963] Director

Meridian Hospital Company (Holdings) Limited
Incorporated: 7 November 1997
Net Worth: £21,808,000 *Total Assets:* £116,998,000
Registered Office: 8 White Oak Square, London Road, Swanley, Kent, BR8 7AG
Activities: Combined facilities support activities
Shareholders: Innisfree M & G PPP LLP; JLIF (GP) Limited
Officers: Graham Beazley - Long [1960] Investment Managing Director; David John Brooking [1975] Investment Director; Carl Harvey Dix [1966] Operations Director; Julian Denzil Sutcliffe [1968] Life Cycle Asset Director; Sir John Wickerson [1937] Director/Solicitor

Meridian Hospital Company PLC
Incorporated: 7 November 1997
Net Worth: £21,808,000 *Total Assets:* £116,998,000
Registered Office: 8 White Oak Square, London Road, Swanley, Kent, BR8 7AG
Activities: Combined facilities support activities
Parent: Meridian Hospital Company (Holdings) Limited
Officers: Graham Maurice Beazley-Long [1960] Investment Managing Director; David John Brooking [1975] Investment Director; Carl Harvey Dix [1966] Operations Director; Julian Denzil Sutcliffe [1968] Life Cycle Asset Director; Sir John Wickerson [1937] Director/Solicitor

Meridian Residential Developments Limited
Incorporated: 18 December 2012 *Employees:* 5
Net Worth: £23,950,626 *Total Assets:* £34,862,720
Registered Office: World Business Centre, 3 Newall Road, London Heathrow Airport, Hounslow, Middlesex, TW6 2TA
Activities: Buying and selling of own real estate
Parent: Grove Acquisitions Limited
Officers: Surinder Arora [1958] Director; Carlton Jeffrey Brown [1972] Director/Chartered Accountant

Meridian Wood Products Ltd.
Incorporated: 21 July 1993
Net Worth: £1,930,691 *Total Assets:* £9,467,976
Registered Office: Clock House, Station Approach, Shepperton, Surrey, TW17 8AS
Activities: Other letting and operating of own or leased real estate
Shareholders: Consolidated Timber Holdings Ltd; Consolidated Timber Holdings Ltd
Officers: David John Colman [1962] Director; Simon David Holdsworth [1956] Director/Chartered Accountant; Andrew Peter Smith [1959] Director

Meritcape Limited
Incorporated: 11 May 1988 *Employees:* 18
Net Worth: £169,602,288 *Total Assets:* £300,435,936
Registered Office: Hadley Hurst, Hadley Common, Barnet, Herts, EN5 5QG
Activities: Development of building projects
Parent: Blendhall Limited
Officers: Anna Victoria Kinsman, Secretary; Anthony George Bunker [1944] Director/Tax Consultant; Alexander Mahboubian [1972] Director/Designer; Enid Mahboubian [1943] Director; Farrokh Mahboubian [1932] Director [Iranian]

Merligen Investments Limited
Incorporated: 26 September 2011 *Employees:* 2
Net Worth: £1,255,108 *Total Assets:* £6,992,358
Registered Office: Suite 2e, 2nd Floor, Phoenix House, Pyrford Road, West Byfleet, Surrey, KT14 6RA
Activities: Other business support service activities n.e.c.
Major Shareholder: Simon Roy Jones
Officers: Paul Faithfull [1970] Director; Simon Roy Jones [1961] Director

Merton Acquisitions Limited
Incorporated: 20 December 2016
Net Worth Deficit: £7,466,808 *Total Assets:* £39,461,368
Registered Office: 3rd Floor, Sterling House, Langston Road, Loughton, Essex, IG10 3TS
Activities: Development of building projects
Shareholders: Luke Oliver Johnson; Galliard Holdings Limited
Officers: Allan William Porter, Secretary; Donagh O'Sullivan [1968] Construction Director [Irish]; Ben John Redmond [1968] Director

Merz Pharma UK Limited
Incorporated: 19 March 2003 *Employees:* 54
Net Worth: £2,726,564 *Total Assets:* £9,142,150
Registered Office: 260 Centennial Park, Elstree Hill South, Elstree, Herts, WD6 3SR
Activities: Wholesale of pharmaceutical goods
Parent: Merz Pharmaceuticals GmbH
Officers: Stefan Brinkmann [1966] Managing Director [German]; Stuart Matthew Rose [1964] Pharmaceutical Managing Director

Mesa Investment Limited
Incorporated: 20 October 2015
Net Worth: £886,186 *Total Assets:* £6,056,051
Registered Office: Alton House, 66 High Street, Northwood, Middlesex, HA6 1BL
Activities: Activities of other holding companies n.e.c.
Major Shareholder: Mattew John Atkinson
Officers: Matthew John Atkinson [1967] Director

Metam Properties Limited
Incorporated: 18 April 2002
Net Worth: £2,471,042 *Total Assets:* £6,071,924
Registered Office: First Floor, 4-10 College Road, Harrow, Middlesex, HA1 1BE
Activities: Other letting and operating of own or leased real estate
Major Shareholder: Mitul Shah
Officers: Mitul Shah [1976] Director/IT Consultant

Metaswitch Networks Ltd
Incorporated: 10 August 1981 *Employees:* 494
Net Worth Deficit: £24,459,660 *Total Assets:* £97,042,192
Registered Office: 100 Church Street, Enfield, Middlesex, EN2 6BQ
Activities: Information technology consultancy activities
Officers: Jason Aaron Brein [1984] Director [American]; Ian Stewart Ferguson [1943] Director; James Goetz [1965] Director/Managing Partner [American]; Hans Martin Nielsen Lund [1968] Director/Business Executive [American]; Graeme MacArthur [1963] Director; Stephen Patrick Mullaney [1963] Director [American]; Deep Shah [1979] Director

Method Products Limited
Incorporated: 11 April 2006
Net Worth Deficit: £2,343,000 *Total Assets:* £6,552,000
Registered Office: The Ministry of Clean, 1 Eton Street, Richmond, Surrey, TW9 1AG
Activities: Wholesale of household goods (other than musical instruments) n.e.c
Parent: People Against Dirty Holdings Limited
Officers: Timothy Earl Bailey [1962] Director/Executive VP [American]; Audrey Sue Ditter [1962] Director/Senior Vice President [American]; Christoph Wolfgang Schulze-Melander [1974] Managing Director

Metier Healthcare Limited
Incorporated: 16 January 1997
Net Worth Deficit: £1,223,367 *Total Assets:* £34,452,380
Registered Office: 4 Estates Yard, Wellhouse Lane, Barnet, Herts, EN5 3DG
Activities: Activities of other holding companies n.e.c.
Parent: Metier Holdings Limited
Officers: Mark John Griffiths [1967] Regional Director; Simon Hayman [1966] Director; Mark Geoffrey David Holden [1957] Investment Director; Mark Christopher Wayment [1958] Director; Elena Giorgiana Wegener [1975] Investment Director

Metier Holdings Limited
Incorporated: 24 November 1998
Net Worth Deficit: £1,223,367 *Total Assets:* £34,452,380
Registered Office: 4 Estates Yard, Wellhouse Lane, Barnet, Herts, EN5 3DG
Activities: Hospital activities
Parent: Infrastructure Investments Holdings Limited
Officers: Mark John Griffiths [1967] Regional Director; Simon Hayman [1966] Director; Mark Geoffrey David Holden [1957] Investment Director; Mark Christopher Wayment [1958] Director; Elena Giorgiana Wegener [1975] Investment Director

Metis Homes Limited
Incorporated: 16 November 2007 *Employees:* 18
Previous: Burton Property Ventures Limited
Net Worth: £2,938,310 *Total Assets:* £25,263,516
Registered Office: Graham House, 7 Wyllyotts Place, Potters Bar, Herts, EN6 2JD
Activities: Development of building projects
Parent: RO Trading Limited
Officers: Anthony William Rawes Burton [1961] Director; Alistair Harris [1977] Planning Director; Adam John O'Brien [1980] Director; Rupert Adam Joleyn Price [1960] Director; Edward Thomas Morton Rowlandson [1974] Director; Andrew John Ormiston Sinclair [1968] Director/Property Developer; Richard Woodman-Bailey [1950] Director

Metra Non-Ferrous Metals Limited
Incorporated: 29 August 1973 *Employees:* 12
Net Worth: £5,072,841 *Total Assets:* £8,738,862
Registered Office: Unit N7, R D Park, Essex Road, Hoddesdon, Herts, EN11 0FB
Activities: Wholesale of wood, construction materials and sanitary equipment
Officers: Trevor Goodey [1954] Director; Dr Armin Wilhelm Emil Melzer [1964] Director/Head of Metal Division [German]

Metro Global Holdings Limited
Incorporated: 16 July 2010 *Employees:* 116
Net Worth: £8,787,381 *Total Assets:* £31,833,718
Registered Office: Upminster Court, 133 Hall Lane, Upminster, Essex, RM14 1AL
Activities: Combined office administrative service activities
Officers: Barry George Tuck, Secretary; Paul Carlile [1955] Director; Stephen William George Ireland [1966] Director; Iain Robert Liddell [1963] Director; Andrew White [1965] Director/General Manager

Metro Investments (Stevenage) LLP
Incorporated: 25 July 2016
Net Worth: £1,040,357 *Total Assets:* £8,568,294
Registered Office: Congress House, 14 Lyon Road, Harrow, Middlesex, HA1 2EN
Officers: Amit Kumar Shantilal Dhamecha [1969] Member; Manish Shantilal Dhamecha [1959] Member; Pradip Khodidas Dhamecha [1958] Member; Rupen Shantilal Dhamecha [1967] Member; Ashok Mathuradas Lakhani [1946] Member; Bharat Lakhani [1951] Member

Metro Mechanical Services Limited
Incorporated: 29 November 1989 *Employees:* 125
Net Worth: £6,074,940 *Total Assets:* £9,246,596
Registered Office: Unit A3, Lion Business Park, Dering Way, Gravesend, Kent, DA12 2DN
Activities: Plumbing, heat and air-conditioning installation
Parent: Hillgate (1234) Ltd
Officers: Nicholas Gaisman [1989] Director; Michael Marks [1989] Director; Timothy Paul Sampson [1957] Director/Operations Manager; Lewis White [1985] Director

Metro Partners LLP
Incorporated: 1 April 2008 *Employees:* 6
Net Worth: £6,869,295 *Total Assets:* £16,880,308
Registered Office: Congress House, 14 Lyon Road, Harrow, Middlesex, HA1 2EN
Officers: Pradip Khodidas Dhamecha [1958] Member; Ashok Mathuradas Lakhani [1946] Member; Amit Kumar Shantilal Dhamecha [1969] LLP Member; Manish Shantilal Dhamecha [1959] LLP Member; Rupen Shantilal Dhamecha [1967] LLP Member; Bharat Mathuradas Lakhani [1951] LLP Member

Metro Properties Limited
Incorporated: 9 September 1999 *Employees:* 4
Net Worth: £6,046,998 *Total Assets:* £11,234,227
Registered Office: 251 Ilford Lane, Ilford, Essex, IG1 2SB
Activities: Hotels and similar accommodation
Officers: Abdul Wahid, Secretary/Director; Abdul Wahid [1954] Director Chief Executive; Ikram Wahid [1977] Director

Metrolink RATP Dev Limited
Incorporated: 11 October 2005 *Employees:* 745
Net Worth: £1,302,000 *Total Assets:* £7,630,000
Registered Office: Busways House, Wellington Road, Twickenham, Middlesex, TW2 5NX
Activities: Other urban, suburban or metropolitan passenger land transport (not underground, metro or similar)
Parent: RATP DEV UK Ltd
Officers: Geraud Martial Boursin [1967] Bid Development Director, RATP Development [French]; Howard Charles Goodbourn [1961] Director/Chief Financial Officer; Peter Richardson [1974] Director

Metropolis Group Holdings Limited
Incorporated: 16 April 2013
Net Worth: £26,025,700 *Total Assets:* £50,160,608
Registered Office: 7th Floor, Vantage London, Great West Road, Brentford, Middlesex, TW8 9AG
Activities: Publishing of consumer and business journals and periodicals
Parent: M New Holdings Limited
Officers: Richard Hutchinson, Secretary; Richard Hutchinson [1966] Finance Director; Robert Andrew Marr [1965] Director/Chief Executive Officer

Metropolis International Group Ltd
Incorporated: 7 April 1994 *Employees:* 194
Net Worth: £2,014,080 *Total Assets:* £40,544,320
Registered Office: 7th Floor, Vantage London, Great West Road, Brentford, Middlesex, TW8 9AG
Activities: Publishing of consumer and business journals and periodicals
Parent: Metropolis Group Holdings Ltd
Officers: Richard Hutchinson, Secretary/Accountant; Richard Hutchinson [1966] Finance Director; Robert Andrew Marr [1965] Director/Chief Executive

Metropolitan Electrical Services Limited
Incorporated: 11 December 1985 *Employees:* 77
Net Worth: £1,876,263 *Total Assets:* £8,281,332
Registered Office: Lynwood House, Crofton Road, Orpington, Kent, BR6 8QE
Activities: Electrical installation
Shareholders: Robert Warner; Maurice Henry Exall
Officers: Jean Georgina Exall, Secretary; Jean Georgina Exall [1949] Director/Secretary; Maurice Henry Exall [1949] Director/Electrical Engineer; Simon Richard Lee [1983] Operations Director; Robert Warner [1965] Director/Electrical Engineer

Metrosold Limited
Incorporated: 7 May 1999
Net Worth: £1,797,083 *Total Assets:* £14,919,094
Registered Office: 3rd Floor, Sterling House, Langston Road, Loughton, Essex, IG10 3TS
Activities: Other business support service activities n.e.c.
Parent: Galliard Holdings Limited
Officers: Allan William Porter, Secretary; David Edward Conway [1976] Director; Stephen Stuart Solomon Conway [1948] Director

Metsa Tissue Limited
Incorporated: 5 August 1993 *Employees:* 15
Net Worth: £3,072,923 *Total Assets:* £8,878,979
Registered Office: 2 Walton Lodge, Bridge Street, Walton on Thames, Surrey, KT12 1BT
Activities: Wholesale of other intermediate products
Parent: Metsa Tissue Oyj
Officers: Alice Olsson, Secretary; Mark Dewick [1963] Director/Vice President Sales & Marketing UK; Arno Simon [1962] Director/Accountant [German]

Mew Investments Ltd
Incorporated: 15 October 2012
Net Worth Deficit: £157,138 *Total Assets:* £5,548,671
Registered Office: The Old Cottage, 125 Shepherds Hill, Romford, Essex, RM3 0NR
Activities: Other letting and operating of own or leased real estate
Major Shareholder: Alan Webb
Officers: Alan John Webb [1980] Director/Businessman; Stacey Denise Webb [1986] Director/Operations Manager

MFG Parentco Limited
Incorporated: 18 August 2016
Net Worth: £34,000 *Total Assets:* £40,391,000
Registered Office: Millbank House, 171-185 Ewell Road, Surbiton, Surrey, KT6 6AP
Activities: Activities of head offices
Parent: MFG Midco Limited
Officers: Justin Christopher Bowman [1972] Director; Christopher Denis Stephen Leach [1949] Director; Adrian Paul Lurie [1973] Director; Stewart Pitt [1972] Director; Mark Henry Storey [1961] Director

MGT Teesside Limited
Incorporated: 23 April 2008
Net Worth Deficit: £13,288,000 *Total Assets:* £544,942,976
Registered Office: 8 White Oak Square, London Road, Swanley, Kent, BR8 7AG
Activities: Production of electricity
Parent: Chaptre Holdings Limited
Officers: Matthew James Spencer Booth [1971] Director; Jens Christian Clausen [1948] Director/Consultant [Danish]; Matthew John Edgar [1985] Director/Senior Vice President [Australian]; Kasper Hansen [1978] Director [Danish]; Andrew Horsley Clifford Hartley [1958] Director; David Jensen [1974] Director/Senior Asset Manager [Danish]

MH Foods Limited
Incorporated: 19 October 1977 *Employees:* 50
Previous: Morehands Limited
Net Worth: £3,789,000 *Total Assets:* £8,404,000
Registered Office: Claygate House, Littleworth Road, Esher, Surrey, KT10 9PN
Activities: Manufacture of condiments and seasonings
Parent: Dairy Crest
Officers: Isobel Jean Hinton, Secretary; Thomas Alexander Atherton [1970] Director/Chartered Accountant; Antony Trevor Hinds [1968] Director

MH Star UK Ltd
Incorporated: 31 August 2010
Net Worth Deficit: £2,227,492 *Total Assets:* £7,686,471
Registered Office: MH Star, 27 Perivale Business Park, Horsenden Lane South, Perivale, Greenford, Middlesex, UB6 7RH
Activities: Retail sale via mail order houses or via Internet
Officers: Colin Leslie Harold Alexander, Secretary; Chunhua Wang [1971] Director [Chinese]

Micro Plus Software Limited
Incorporated: 6 August 1993 *Employees:* 33
Net Worth: £7,959,336 *Total Assets:* £8,556,457
Registered Office: 10 Moorcroft, Harlington Road, Uxbridge, Middlesex, UB8 3HD
Activities: Other business support service activities n.e.c.
Officers: Carl Martin Boraman [1964] Commercial Director; Russell Cozens [1973] Technical Director; Shivender Dhillon [1980] Director/Chief Technology Officer [Indian]; Alison Martino [1969] Marketing Director; Antonio Martino [1969] Managing Director [Italian]; Hilary Louisa Oliver [1973] Marketing Director; Simon Whatley [1969] Sales Director

Microlease Limited
Incorporated: 28 December 1973 *Employees:* 220
Previous: Microlease PLC
Net Worth: £16,805,000 *Total Assets:* £88,697,000
Registered Office: Unit 1 Waverley Business Park, Hailsham Drive, Harrow, Middlesex, HA1 4TR
Activities: Renting and leasing of other machinery, equipment and tangible goods n.e.c.
Parent: Newmir Limited
Officers: Nigel Brown [1957] Director; John Joseph Hafferty [1956] Director/Chief Financial Officer [American]; Paul Joseph McCloskey [1960] Director; Nigel Rennie [1960] Director; David Whitfield [1959] Director

Mid Holding Co UK Limited
Incorporated: 16 May 2014 *Employees:* 1,415
Net Worth: £15,383,396 *Total Assets:* £102,321,984
Registered Office: Hapag-Lloyd House, Cambridge Road, Barking, Essex, IG11 8HH
Activities: Construction of commercial buildings
Major Shareholder: Sahel Majali
Officers: Jacqueline Margaret Diane Adams-Hooker [1969] Director/Accountant; Sahel Majali [1962] Director/Entrepreneur; Shaker Sahel Majali [1988] Director/Architect; Andrew David Shepherd [1978] Director

Middlesex Learning Partnership
Incorporated: 26 July 2011 *Employees:* 327
Previous: The Barnhill Partnership Trust
Net Worth: £21,085,800 *Total Assets:* £26,233,772
Registered Office: Barnhill Community High School, Yeading Lane, Hayes, Middlesex, UB4 9LE
Activities: General secondary education
Officers: Joanne Day, Secretary; Akin Akintola [1956] Director; Simon Arnold [1973] Director/Business Consultant; Ian Thomas Comfort [1953] Director; Poonam Gorania [1982] Director/Accountant; Tracey Carole Hemming [1962] Director/Executive Headteacher; Russell Middleton [1968] Director/Principal Engineer; Teresa St Catherine [1964] Director/Head of HR [Irish]

Midgard Ltd
Incorporated: 22 February 2006 *Employees:* 100
Net Worth: £4,822,688 *Total Assets:* £71,057,872
Registered Office: 4 Elstree Way, Borehamwood, Herts, WD6 1RN
Activities: Construction of commercial buildings
Parent: JRL Group Ltd
Officers: Ronan Joseph Gleeson, Secretary/Director [Irish]; Ronan Joseph Gleeson [1976] Director [Irish]; Kevin William Keegan [1963] Director/Estimator [Irish]; John James Reddington [1972] Director/Formwork [Irish]

Miko Coffee Limited
Incorporated: 12 November 1982 *Employees:* 60
Net Worth: £4,325,348 *Total Assets:* £7,834,074
Registered Office: St Ann's House, St Anns Road, Chertsey, Surrey, KT16 9EH
Activities: Wholesale of coffee, tea, cocoa and spices
Parent: Miko Koffie NV
Officers: Adrian Leonard Stagg, Secretary; Willem Van Gemart [1964] Director [Belgian]; Frans Celesta Van Tilborg [1965] Managing Director [Belgian]; Johannes Petrus Catharina Vandervee [1959] Director [Belgian]

Milcars (Radlett) Limited
Incorporated: 10 July 1978 *Employees:* 34
Net Worth: £580,163 *Total Assets:* £5,202,368
Registered Office: Milcars Building, Otterspool Way, Watford, Herts, WD25 8HL
Activities: Sale of new cars and light motor vehicles
Parent: Milcars Limited
Officers: Anthony Robert Boothby, Secretary; Christopher Leslie Ward [1969] Director

Milcars Limited
Incorporated: 16 July 2003 *Employees:* 37
Net Worth: £884,029 *Total Assets:* £7,533,655
Registered Office: Milcars Building, Otterspool Way, Watford, Herts, WD25 8HL
Activities: Activities of head offices
Major Shareholder: Christopher Leslie Ward
Officers: Anthony Robert Boothby, Secretary; Christopher Leslie Ward [1969] Director

Mill Hill Properties Limited
Incorporated: 14 September 1998 *Employees:* 1
Net Worth: £24,507 *Total Assets:* £10,449,145
Registered Office: 105 Viglen House, Alperton Lane, London, HA0 1HD
Activities: Management of real estate on a fee or contract basis
Shareholders: Bijan Sheibani; Azadeh Majlesi
Officers: Azadeh Majlesi, Secretary/Manager [Iranian]; Bijan Sheibani [1947] Director/Manager [Iranian]; Seyed Ahmad Zolfaghari [1946] Director/Businessman

The Mill Hotel Limited
Incorporated: 28 February 1995 *Employees:* 163
Net Worth: £2,406,904 *Total Assets:* £9,555,213
Registered Office: DVS House, Spring Villa Road, Edgware, Middlesex, HA8 7EB
Activities: Hotels and similar accommodation
Parent: Chester Mill Limited
Officers: Julan Shah [1977] Director; Prag Shah [1989] Director; Priyan Dhirajlal Shah [1980] Director

Millcroft Services P.L.C.
Incorporated: 15 November 1972 *Employees:* 80
Net Worth: £4,080,854 *Total Assets:* £7,746,336
Registered Office: Upper Deck Admirals Quarters, Portsmouth Road, Thames Ditton, Surrey, KT7 0XA
Activities: Scaffold erection
Shareholders: Billy Jones; Denise Jones; Lucy Jones; Roy Frederick Jones; Sam Jones
Officers: Denise Jones, Secretary; Billy Jones [1979] Director/Businessman; Roy Frederick Jones [1946] Director; Sam Jones [1983] Director/Businessman; Melvyn Nicholls [1957] Director; Mark Stimpson [1961] Director of Operations

Millennium Care Homes Limited
Incorporated: 22 June 1995 *Employees:* 278
Net Worth: £8,383,017 *Total Assets:* £9,133,727
Registered Office: 253 Hertford Road, Enfield, Middlesex, EN3 5JL
Activities: Other business support service activities n.e.c.
Shareholders: Mansoor Esmail; Karim Velji
Officers: Mansoor Esmail, Secretary/Dentist; Mansoor Esmail [1961] Director/Dentist; Karim Velji [1960] Director/Dentist

Millennium Cash & Carry Limited
Incorporated: 8 December 1999 *Employees:* 73
Net Worth: £20,582,116 *Total Assets:* £53,710,732
Registered Office: 364-368 Cranbrook Road, Gants Hill, Ilford, Essex, IG2 6HY
Activities: Wholesale of wine, beer, spirits and other alcoholic beverages
Major Shareholder: Panna Mashru
Officers: Rishi Lakhani [1982] Director

Millennium Property (London) Limited
Incorporated: 28 July 2015
Net Worth Deficit: £142,621 *Total Assets:* £5,039,644
Registered Office: 164a Kenton Road, Kenton, Middlesex, HA3 8BL
Activities: Other letting and operating of own or leased real estate
Major Shareholder: Vijendra Nath Malhotra
Officers: Monica Malhotra [1975] Director/Educationalist; Vijendra Nath Malhotra [1950] Director/Chartered Accountant [Indian]

Millennium Seacon Properties Limited
Incorporated: 23 January 2003
Net Worth: £4,263,986 *Total Assets:* £9,474,587
Registered Office: 88 Edgware Way, Edgware, Middlesex, HA8 8JS
Activities: Other letting and operating of own or leased real estate
Officers: Chavi Moskovitz, Secretary; Israel Moskovitz [1964] Director [Canadian]

Miller & Miller (Chemicals) Limited
Incorporated: 4 November 1977 *Employees:* 18
Net Worth: £8,437,924 *Total Assets:* £9,843,544
Registered Office: Haslers, Old Station Road, Loughton, Essex, IG10 4PL
Activities: Wholesale of pharmaceutical goods
Shareholder: John Simon Miller
Officers: Natalie Laura Livingston, Secretary; Natalie Laura Livingston [1972] Director; David Miller [1974] Sales Director; John Simon Miller [1943] Director/Chemist

Millers Bespoke Bakery Limited
Incorporated: 6 June 1996
Net Worth: £5,079,070 *Total Assets:* £6,912,377
Registered Office: 8 Peterborough Road, Harrow, Middlesex, HA1 2BQ
Activities: Manufacture of bread; manufacture of fresh pastry goods and cakes
Major Shareholder: William Marcus Miller
Officers: William Marcus Miller, Secretary/Baker; William Marcus Miller [1967] Director/Baker; Alessandra Maria Luigia Anna Polizzi di Sorrentino [1971] Director; Olga Marie Louise Anna Polizzi di Sorrentino [1946] Director

Millharbour Developments Limited
Incorporated: 22 December 2005
Net Worth: £2,227,962 *Total Assets:* £9,549,624
Registered Office: 3rd Floor, Sterling House, Langston Road, Loughton, Essex, IG10 3TS
Activities: Buying and selling of own real estate
Parent: Raceguide Limited
Officers: Allan William Porter, Secretary; Stephen Stuart Solomon Conway [1948] Director; Donagh O'Sullivan [1968] Construction Director [Irish]

Millipore (U.K.) Limited
Incorporated: 22 December 2000 *Employees:* 175
Net Worth: £122,555,000 *Total Assets:* £129,667,000
Registered Office: Bedfont Cross, Stanwell Road, Feltham, Middlesex, TW14 8NX
Activities: Other research and experimental development on natural sciences and engineering
Shareholders: Sigma Chemical Company Limited; SAFC Biosciences Limited
Officers: Peter Biro [1967] Director/US Certified Public Accountant [Dutch]; Victor Mark Jackson [1962] Director/Operations Manager

Millipore UK Holdings LLP
Incorporated: 26 August 2009
Net Worth: £314,939,008 *Total Assets:* £314,942,016
Registered Office: Bedfont Cross, Stanwell Road, Feltham, Middlesex, TW14 8NX

Mills Family Limited
Incorporated: 1 July 1998 *Employees:* 123
Net Worth: £8,466,482 *Total Assets:* £10,508,873
Registered Office: The Old Exchange, 3 London Road, Farningham, Kent, DA4 0JP
Activities: Residential care activities for the elderly and disabled
Officers: Martin Gregory Mills, Secretary/Care Home Manager; Andrew Timothy Mills [1953] Director; Martin Gregory Mills [1963] Director; Jane Karen Partridge [1956] Director/Care Manager; Sara Ann Pepper [1962] Director

Milpharm Limited
Incorporated: 11 April 1997 *Employees:* 31
Net Worth: £12,127,246 *Total Assets:* £27,974,948
Registered Office: Ares Block, Odyssey Business Park, West End Road, South Ruislip, Middlesex, HA4 6QD
Activities: Wholesale of pharmaceutical goods
Parent: Agile Pharma B.V.
Officers: Thomas Broeer [1960] Director [German]; Venugopalan Muralidharan [1955] Director; Gorla Phaneemdra Prasad [1957] Finance Director [Indian]

Milsom Hotels Limited
Incorporated: 10 June 1982 *Employees:* 251
Net Worth: £9,334,240 *Total Assets:* £16,689,450
Registered Office: 400 Dashwood Lang Road, Weybridge, Surrey, KT15 2HJ
Activities: Hotels and similar accommodation
Major Shareholder: Paul John Milsom
Officers: Michael Henry Gooding, Secretary; Stasos Demetris Anastasiades [1971] Director/Hotelier; Michael Henry Gooding [1964] Director/Chartered Accountant; David Richard Milsom [1958] Director/Education Manager; Generaldine Margaret Dalzell Milsom [1964] Director/Designer; Paul John Milsom [1964] Director/Hotelier & Restaurateur

Minesoft Ltd
Incorporated: 14 August 1996 *Employees:* 27
Net Worth: £3,674,829 *Total Assets:* £7,362,435
Registered Office: Boston House, Little Green, Richmond, Surrey, TW9 1QE
Activities: Other information technology service activities
Shareholders: Ann Frances Chapman-Daniel; Ophir Daniel
Officers: Ophir Daniel, Secretary/Software Engineer [German/Israeli]; Ann Frances Chapman-Daniel [1959] Director; Ophir Daniel [1963] Director/Software Engineer [German/Israeli]; Rahman Andreas Hyatt [1969] Sales Director

Mingold Limited
Incorporated: 31 December 2015
Net Worth: £2 *Total Assets:* £44,881,000
Registered Office: Hill House, Lowlands Road, Harrow, Middlesex, HA1 3EQ
Activities: Buying and selling of own real estate
Parent: Denland Limited
Officers: Brian Martin Comer [1960] Director [Irish]; Luke Andrew Comer [1957] Director [Irish]

Mini Club UK Limited
Incorporated: 28 December 1983
Net Worth Deficit: £31,318,000 *Total Assets:* £5,007,000
Registered Office: Cherry Tree Road, Watford, Herts, WD24 6SH
Activities: Wholesale of clothing and footwear
Parent: The Mothercare Group Limited
Officers: Lynne Samantha Medini, Secretary; Taimoor Anwar [1980] Director/Chartered Accountant [Pakistani]; Kirsty Rowena Homer [1974] HR Director

Minster Care Group Limited
Incorporated: 11 April 2017
Net Worth: £658,786 *Total Assets:* £27,477,660
Registered Office: 238 Station Road, Addlestone, Surrey, KT15 2PS
Activities: Residential care activities for the elderly and disabled
Shareholders: Alka Patel; Mahesh Shivabhai Patel
Officers: John Neal Alflatt, Secretary; John Neal Alflatt [1967] Director/Businessman; Colin William Farebrother [1965] Director/Businessman; Alka Patel [1960] Director/Businesswoman; Mahesh Shivabhai Patel [1953] Director/Businessman

Minster Care Management Limited
Incorporated: 1 December 1998 *Employees:* 1,037
Net Worth Deficit: £1,551,080 *Total Assets:* £60,828,656
Registered Office: 238 Station Road, Addlestone, Surrey, KT15 2PS
Activities: Residential care activities for the elderly and disabled
Parent: Minster Care Group Limited
Officers: John Neal Alflatt, Secretary; Colin William Farebrother [1965] Director; Mahesh Shivabhai Patel [1953] Director

Minton Holdings Limited
Incorporated: 19 March 1953 *Employees:* 3
Net Worth: £8,973,836 *Total Assets:* £10,979,686
Registered Office: Treviot House, 186-192 High Road, Ilford, Essex, IG1 1LR
Activities: Development of building projects
Major Shareholder: Ivor Spiro
Officers: Denise Spiro, Secretary/Director; Denise Spiro [1939] Director; Ivor Spiro [1940] Director; Mandy Susan Spiro [1964] Director/Property Manager

Minverport Enterprises Limited
Incorporated: 25 April 1983
Net Worth: £659,949 *Total Assets:* £6,110,945
Registered Office: 5 Theobald Court, Theobald Street, Elstree, Herts, WD6 4RN
Activities: Non-trading company
Officers: Aamer Johar, Secretary; Aamer Johar [1959] Director

MIQ Logistics EU Limited
Incorporated: 21 January 2004 *Employees:* 346
Net Worth: £12,137,600 *Total Assets:* £23,101,756
Registered Office: Unit 1 Alpha Way, Thorpe Industrial Estate, Egham, Surrey, TW20 8RZ
Activities: Activities of head offices
Officers: Brenda Jean Stasiulis [1966] Director/Accountant [American]; Darren Ross Williams [1966] Director

MIQ Logistics Limited
Incorporated: 15 December 1992 *Employees:* 324
Net Worth: £17,476,296 *Total Assets:* £24,334,236
Registered Office: Unit 1 Alpha Way, Thorpe Industrial Estate, Egham, Surrey, TW20 8RZ
Activities: Other transportation support activities
Parent: MIQ Logistics EU Limited
Officers: Darren Ross Williams, Secretary; Andrew Giles Martin [1962] Managing Director; Brenda Jean Stasiulis [1966] Director/Accountant [American]; Darren Ross Williams [1966] Financial Director

Miriad Property Investments Limited
Incorporated: 4 August 2016
Net Worth: £12,647,237 *Total Assets:* £26,427,208
Registered Office: Haslers, Old Station Road, Loughton, Essex, IG10 4PL
Activities: Development of building projects
Officers: Adam Lopez Dias [1973] Director; Mark Iestyn Lewis [1974] Director/Manager; Simon Emanuel Raine [1981] Director/Manager

Mission Foods UK Limited
Incorporated: 23 April 1992 *Employees:* 267
Previous: Gruma Seaham Limited
Net Worth: £20,112,000 *Total Assets:* £31,083,000
Registered Office: Second Floor, Heathrow Boulevard 4, 282 Bath Road, Sipson, West Drayton, Middlesex, UB7 0DQ
Activities: Manufacture of bread; manufacture of fresh pastry goods and cakes
Shareholders: Mayra Adela Gonzalez Moreno; Graciela Silvia Gonzalez Moreno; Juan Antonio de Jesus Gonzalez Moreno
Officers: Amy Lucy Ashman, Secretary; Dannie Lee Burke [1969] Director/Treasurer [American]; Simon Mark Colaco [1975] Procurement Director; Peter Hall Ellis [1965] Managing Director; Rodolfo Maldonado [1953] Director/Chief Executive Officer [American]; Mohamme Saeed [1969] Human Resources Director

Mission Recordings Limited
Incorporated: 5 August 2009
Net Worth Deficit: £222,220 *Total Assets:* £5,047,515
Registered Office: Wickham House, 2 Upper Teddington Road, Kingston upon Thames, Surrey, KT1 4DY
Activities: Sound recording and music publishing activities
Parent: Mission Entertainment Group Limited
Officers: Norman Lott, Secretary; Harry Edmund Cowell [1960] Director

Mister Dee International Limited
Incorporated: 2 March 1976 *Employees:* 2
Net Worth: £3,895,418 *Total Assets:* £7,488,006
Registered Office: 27 Elms Road, Harrow Weald, Middlesex, HA3 6BB
Activities: Other letting and operating of own or leased real estate
Major Shareholder: Chandrakant Jeshang Shah
Officers: Sheenal Kothari, Secretary; Sheenal Kothari [1979] Director/Accounts; Gina Mistry [1985] Director

Mitcham Garden Village
Incorporated: 27 March 1930
Net Worth: £7,515,405 *Total Assets:* £7,816,407
Registered Office: 151 Wickham Road, Croydon, Surrey, CR0 8TE
Activities: Other accommodation
Officers: Ian Ronald Johnson, Secretary; Elliot James Brunton [1975] Director/Local Government Officer; Sue Dark [1956] Director/Solicitor; Paul Edward Flowers [1973] Director/Residential Housing; Anthony David Halstead [1951] Director/Lawyer; Siobhain McDonagh [1960] Director; Thomas Ian Munn [1942] Director/Retired Town Planner; Sandra Kay Vogel [1964] Director/Journalist; Colin Peter Worley [1947] Director/Retired

Mitchells Holding Limited
Incorporated: 3 August 2015 *Employees:* 149
Net Worth: £3,533,916 *Total Assets:* £8,930,617
Registered Office: Ashcombe House, 5 The Crescent, Leatherhead, Surrey, KT22 8DY
Activities: Activities of other holding companies n.e.c.
Shareholders: Bibi Afroze Mitchell; Brian Geoffrey Mitchell
Officers: Bibi Afroze Mitchell [1953] Director; Brian Geoffrey Mitchell [1953] Director; Natasha Daisy Victoria Mitchell [1988] Director

Mitsubishi Electric Finance Europe PLC
Incorporated: 8 January 1990 *Employees:* 4
Net Worth: £19,754,000 *Total Assets:* £1,049,174,016
Registered Office: Harman House, 1 George Street, Uxbridge, Middlesex, UB8 1QQ
Activities: Financial intermediation not elsewhere classified
Officers: Keiichi Tobinaga, Secretary; Masayuki Nakajima [1968] Director [Japanese]; Masaki Okamoto [1970] Director [Japanese]; Keiichi Tobinaga [1960] Director and Company Secretary [Japanese]

Mitsubishi Heavy Industries Air-Conditioning Europe, Ltd.
Incorporated: 6 February 2013 *Employees:* 32
Net Worth: £63,458,848 *Total Assets:* £104,789,312
Registered Office: 5 The Square, Stockley Park, Uxbridge, Middlesex, UB11 1ET
Activities: Wholesale of other machinery and equipment
Parent: Mitsubishi Heavy Industries, Ltd.
Officers: Henrieta Marcincinova, Secretary; Ryoichi Kariya [1972] Managing Director [Japanese]; Shinichiro Morisaki [1975] Director/Business Executive [Japanese]; Nobuaki Suzuki [1970] Director/Business Executive [Japanese]; Yusuke Tsunashima [1968] Director/Business Executive [Japanese]

Mizen (Nether Street) Limited
Incorporated: 17 November 2016
Net Worth Deficit: £500,762 *Total Assets:* £7,594,383
Registered Office: No 1 Railshead Road, Old Isleworth, Middlesex, TW7 7EP
Activities: Buying and selling of own real estate
Parent: Mizen Properties Limited
Officers: Barry Bernard Tansey, Secretary; Alan Joseph Tansey [1972] Director/Economist [Irish]; Bernard Joseph Tansey [1944] Director/Engineer [Irish]

Mizen Design/Build Ltd.
Incorporated: 1 July 1986 *Employees:* 30
Net Worth: £4,372,203 *Total Assets:* £9,377,231
Registered Office: No 1 Railshead Road, St Margarets, Isleworth, Middlesex, TW7 7EP
Activities: Development of building projects
Parent: Mizen Properties Limited
Officers: Barry Bernard Tansey, Secretary/Accountant [Irish]; Colm Anthony Cronin [1983] Construction Director [Irish]; Gerard Martin Friel [1962] Commercial Director [Irish]; Alan Joseph Tansey [1972] Director/Economist [Irish]; Bernard Joseph Tansey [1944] Director/Engineer [Irish]

Mizen Properties Limited
Incorporated: 15 April 1988 *Employees:* 30
Net Worth: £11,094,804 *Total Assets:* £41,955,016
Registered Office: No 1 Railshead Road, St Margarets, Isleworth, Middlesex, TW7 7EP
Activities: Buying and selling of own real estate
Officers: Barry Bernard Tansey, Secretary/Accountant [Irish]; Alan Joseph Tansey [1972] Director/Economist [Irish]; Bernard Joseph Tansey [1944] Director/Engineer [Irish]

Mizzen Bidco Limited
Incorporated: 25 July 2012
Net Worth: £34,521,000 *Total Assets:* £175,308,992
Registered Office: Ermyn House, Ermyn Way, Leatherhead, Surrey, KT22 8UX
Activities: Fund management activities
Parent: Mizzen Mezzco 2 Limited
Officers: Elizabeth Sarah Annys, Secretary; Andrew Phillip Chapman [1969] Director/Chief Financial Officer; Anthony Santospirito [1984] Director [Australian]; Thomas Woolgrove [1970] Director/Chief Executive Officer

Mizzen Mezzco 2 Limited
Incorporated: 26 September 2012
Net Worth: £158,323,008 *Total Assets:* £165,444,000
Registered Office: Ermyn House, Ermyn Way, Leatherhead, Surrey, KT22 8UX
Activities: Activities of other holding companies n.e.c.
Parent: Mizzen Midco Limited
Officers: Elizabeth Sarah Annys, Secretary; Andrew Phillip Chapman [1969] Director/Chief Financial Officer; Anthony Santospirito [1984] Director [Australian]; Thomas Woolgrove [1970] Director/Chief Executive Officer

Mizzen Mezzco Limited
Incorporated: 14 August 2012 *Employees:* 417
Net Worth Deficit: £59,343,000 *Total Assets:* £1,551,892,992
Registered Office: Ermyn House, Ermyn Way, Leatherhead, Surrey, KT22 8UX
Activities: Activities of other holding companies n.e.c.
Parent: Pomegranate Acquisitions Limited
Officers: Elizabeth Sarah Annys, Secretary; Andrew Phillip Chapman [1969] Director/Chief Financial Officer; Anthony Santospirito [1984] Director [Australian]; Thomas Woolgrove [1970] Director/Chief Executive Officer

Mizzen Midco Limited
Incorporated: 14 April 2014
Net Worth: £218,204,992 *Total Assets:* £232,080,992
Registered Office: Ermyn House, Ermyn Way, Leatherhead, Surrey, KT22 8UX
Activities: Fund management activities
Parent: Mizzen Mezzco Limited
Officers: Elizabeth Sarah Annys, Secretary; Andrew Phillip Chapman [1969] Director/Chief Financial Officer; Anthony Santospirito [1984] Director [Australian]; Thomas Woolgrove [1970] Director/Chief Executive Officer

MJA Investments Limited
Incorporated: 16 July 1991 *Employees:* 3
Net Worth: £4,932,976 *Total Assets:* £13,410,765
Registered Office: 9 Cheam Road, Epsom, Surrey, KT17 1SP
Activities: Other letting and operating of own or leased real estate
Shareholder: Michael Edward Garrett
Officers: Michael Edward Garrett, Secretary; Adam James Garrett [1984] Director/Business Person

MJF Business Services Limited
Incorporated: 14 January 1998 *Employees:* 42
Net Worth: £1,737,306 *Total Assets:* £6,154,860
Registered Office: River House, Riverside Way, Uxbridge, Middlesex, UB8 2YF
Activities: Other building completion and finishing
Parent: MJF Group Ltd
Officers: Christopher Michael Jennings, Secretary; Christopher Michael Jennings [1962] Finance Director; Jonathan Charles Moreland [1965] Director; John Martin Power [1977] Director/Accountant [Irish]; Michael William Power [1970] Director [Irish]

MJF Group Limited
Incorporated: 13 September 1991 *Employees:* 7
Net Worth: £6,380,183 *Total Assets:* £12,850,067
Registered Office: River House, Riverside Way, Uxbridge, Middlesex, UB8 2YF
Activities: Other letting and operating of own or leased real estate
Parent: MJF UK Holdings Ltd
Officers: Christopher Michael Jennings, Secretary; Christopher Michael Jennings [1962] Finance Director; John Martin Power [1977] Director/Accountant [Irish]; Michael William Power [1970] Director [Irish]

MJF UK Holdings Limited
Incorporated: 15 November 1996 *Employees:* 58
Net Worth: £10,472,408 *Total Assets:* £18,834,488
Registered Office: River House, Riverside Way, Uxbridge, Middlesex, UB8 2YF
Activities: Activities of head offices
Officers: Christopher Michael Jennings, Secretary; Christopher Michael Jennings [1962] Finance Director; John Martin Power [1977] Director/Accountant [Irish]; Michael William Power [1970] Director [Irish]

MK Windfarm Limited
Incorporated: 23 March 2004 *Employees:* 5
Net Worth: £10,151,076 *Total Assets:* £13,539,583
Registered Office: Munro House, Portsmouth Road, Cobham, Surrey, KT11 1PP
Activities: Production of electricity
Parent: Danu II Holdings Limited
Officers: Stephen Campbell Joseph Ellis [1959] Director; Rollo Andrew Johnstone Wright [1976] Director; Philip William Kent [1984] Director; Ronan Niall Kierans [1978] Director [Irish]; Nicholas Simon Parker [1969] Director

MND Construction Services Limited
Incorporated: 28 December 2007 *Employees:* 8
Net Worth: £3,755,118 *Total Assets:* £8,916,024
Registered Office: Heasleigh House, 79a South Road, Southall, Middlesex, UB1 1SQ
Activities: Other service activities n.e.c.
Officers: Harprite Dulai, Secretary; Harprite Dulai [1982] Director; Gavin Richard Mayles [1969] Director/Surveyor; Peter Charles Needham [1946] Director/Builder

MNS Care PLC
Incorporated: 11 March 1997 *Employees:* 165
Net Worth: £5,764,783 *Total Assets:* £15,414,494
Registered Office: 116 Headstone Drive, Harrow, Middlesex, HA1 4UH
Activities: Residential nursing care facilities
Parent: SAI Ram Care Limited
Officers: Sandip Ruparelia, Secretary/Care Home Operator; Priti Ruparelia [1963] Director/Care Home Operator; Sandip Ruparelia [1963] Director/Care Home Operator

Moat Homes Finance PLC
Incorporated: 17 August 2011
Net Worth: £50,000 *Total Assets:* £153,255,008
Registered Office: Mariner House, Galleon Boulevard, Dartford, Kent, DA2 6QE
Activities: Activities of other holding companies n.e.c.
Shareholder: Moat Homes Limited
Officers: Gregory Robert Taylor, Secretary; Hazel Anne Sharp [1961] Director/Accountant; Gregory Robert Taylor [1959] Executive Director - Finance

Mobil Trading and Supply Limited
Incorporated: 18 December 1958 *Employees:* 4
Net Worth: £13,878,135 *Total Assets:* £24,515,328
Registered Office: Ermyn House, Ermyn Way, Leatherhead, Surrey, KT22 8UX
Activities: Agents involved in the sale of fuels, ores, metals and industrial chemicals
Parent: Esso UK Limited
Officers: Fiona Harness, Secretary; Per-Erik Aasum [1964] Director/Oil Company Executive [Norwegian]; Robert Michael Cooper [1961] Director/Oil Company Executive; Andrew Mark Johnson [1976] Director/Oil Company Executive; Alex Volkov [1972] Director/Oil Company Executive [American]

Modern Schools (Barnsley) Limited
Incorporated: 14 October 2004
Net Worth Deficit: £4,717,000 *Total Assets:* £29,249,000
Registered Office: 8 White Oak Square, London Road, Swanley, Kent, BR8 7AG
Activities: Construction of commercial buildings
Parent: Modern Schools (Barnsley) Holdings Limited
Officers: Benjamin Christopher Jacob Dean [1979] Director/Portfolio Manager; Alastair James Watson [1974] Investment Director

Modern Schools (Exeter) Limited
Incorporated: 18 February 2004
Net Worth Deficit: £10,123,000 *Total Assets:* £60,781,000
Registered Office: 8 White Oak Square, London Road, Swanley, Kent, BR8 7AG
Activities: Development of building projects
Parent: Modern Schools (Exeter) Holdings Limited
Officers: Benjamin Christopher Jacob Dean [1979] Director/Investment Manager; Richard Keith Sheehan [1975] Investment Director

Mohan Building Services Limited
Incorporated: 3 April 1984
Net Worth: £8,904,373 *Total Assets:* £14,630,588
Registered Office: 3a Manor Road, Gravesend, Kent, DA12 1AA
Activities: Other service activities n.e.c.
Major Shareholder: Mohan Singh Dulai
Officers: Jaswinder Kaur Dulai, Secretary; Mohan Singh Dulai [1956] Director

Mokarabia Limited
Incorporated: 19 November 1998 *Employees:* 8
Net Worth: £786,307 *Total Assets:* £5,034,080
Registered Office: Unit 1 Moor Mead Road, St Margarets Business Centre, Twickenham, Middlesex, TW1 1JS
Activities: Wholesale of coffee, tea, cocoa and spices
Major Shareholder: Marco Zanetti
Officers: Gertrudis Laurel Sami, Secretary; Fabrizio Omoboni [1970] Director [Italian]; Marco Zanetti [1968] Director [Italian]

Mollart Engineering Limited
Incorporated: 26 May 1981 *Employees:* 127
Net Worth: £6,006,246 *Total Assets:* £11,490,883
Registered Office: 106 Roebuck Road, Chessington, Surrey, KT9 1EU
Activities: Manufacture of other special-purpose machinery n.e.c.
Parent: Mollart Holdings Limited
Officers: Jonathan James Upton, Secretary; Christopher Charles Barker [1956] Director/Tooling Manager; Ian Petitt [1958] Sales Director; Wayne Justin Thomas [1976] Director; Jonathan James Upton [1978] Finance Director

Mollart Group Limited
Incorporated: 22 January 2016 *Employees:* 129
Net Worth: £2,270,114 *Total Assets:* £13,630,071
Registered Office: 106 Roebuck Road, Chessington, Surrey, KT9 1EU
Activities: Activities of head offices
Major Shareholder: Neil John Murphy
Officers: Jonathan James Upton, Secretary; Christopher Charles Barker [1956] Tooling Director; Neil John Murphy [1963] Director; Mark Peter Perryman [1973] Director; Ian Petitt [1958] Sales Director; Wayne Justin Thomas [1976] Director; Jonathan James Upton [1978] Finance Director

Monarock Limited
Incorporated: 31 December 2001
Net Worth: £11,233,374 *Total Assets:* £16,269,961
Registered Office: 34 West Drive, Harrow Weald, Middlesex, HA3 6TS
Activities: Buying and selling of own real estate
Shareholders: Sheetal Dalia-Patel; Heena Rajiv Sodha
Officers: Chandrabala Dalia, Secretary/Director; Sheetal Dalia-Patel [1972] Director; Heena Rajiv Sodha [1969] Director

Mondelez UK Biscuit Financing Limited
Incorporated: 11 November 2013
Net Worth: £2,820,495,616 *Total Assets:* £2,820,495,616
Registered Office: Uxbridge Business Park, Sanderson Road, Uxbridge, Middlesex, UB8 1DH
Activities: Activities of head offices
Parent: Mondelez UK Limited
Officers: Adrian John Paul Arrighi [1978] Tax Director; Michael Brendan Foye [1965] Treasury Director; John Michael Hladusz [1972] Director/Chartered Accountant; Carole Noelle Keene [1966] Director

Mondelez UK Finance Company Limited
Incorporated: 26 April 2016
Net Worth: £4,029,776 *Total Assets:* £329,451,520
Registered Office: Cadbury House, Uxbridge Business Park, Sanderson Road, Uxbridge, Middlesex, UB8 1DH
Activities: Activities of head offices
Parent: Kraft Foods Investment Holdings UK Limited
Officers: Adrian John Paul Arrighi [1978] Tax Director; Michael Brendan Foye [1965] Treasury Director; John Michael Hladusz [1972] Director/Chartered Accountant; Carole Noelle Keene [1966] Director

Mondelez UK Holdings & Services Limited
Incorporated: 6 May 1897 *Employees:* 185
Net Worth: £4,284,000,000 *Total Assets:* £4,785,999,872
Registered Office: Cadbury House, Sanderson Road, Uxbridge, Middlesex, UB8 1DH
Activities: Manufacture of cocoa and chocolate confectionery
Parent: Cadbury Limited
Officers: Adrian John Paul Arrighi [1978] Tax Director; Simon Ashbell [1985] Director/Finance Manager; Michael Brendan Foye [1965] Treasury Director; John Michael Hladusz [1972] Director/Chartered Accountant; Darren Redhead [1964] Director; Jason Bryan Vickery [1968] Director/Accountant

Mondelez UK Limited
Incorporated: 6 February 1925 *Employees:* 585
Net Worth: £2,479,772,928 *Total Assets:* £2,928,550,912
Registered Office: Uxbridge Business Park, Sanderson Road, Uxbridge, Middlesex, UB8 1DH
Activities: Other business support service activities n.e.c.
Parent: Mondelez International, Inc
Officers: Jonathan Briscoe [1984] Sales Director; Claire Parkes [1974] Category Development & Market Activation Director; Mark Henry Stananought [1971] Customer Development Director; Louise Anne Stigant [1967] Managing Director

Mondi Finance PLC
Incorporated: 25 August 2006
Net Worth: £367,182,048 *Total Assets:* £2,212,484,352
Registered Office: 1st Floor, Building 1, Aviator Park, Station Road, Addlestone, Surrey, KT15 2PG
Activities: Credit granting by non-deposit taking finance houses and other specialist consumer credit grantors
Parent: Mondi Investments Limited
Officers: Jennifer Louise Hampshire, Secretary; Jennifer Louise Hampshire [1983] Director/Chartered Secretary; Andrew Charles Wallis King [1969] Director/Chief Financial Officer [South African]; Maureen Angela McHugh [1960] Director/Group Head of Tax; James Campbell Paterson [1964] Director/Treasurer

Mondi German Investments Limited
Incorporated: 21 October 2004
Net Worth: £19,787,698 *Total Assets:* £19,792,326
Registered Office: 1st Floor, Building 1, Aviator Park, Station Road, Addlestone, Surrey, KT15 2PG
Activities: Other business support service activities n.e.c.
Parent: Mondi Investments Limited
Officers: Jennifer Louise Hampshire, Secretary; Jennifer Louise Hampshire [1983] Director/Chartered Secretary; Andrew Charles Wallis King [1969] Director/Chief Financial Officer [South African]; James Campbell Paterson [1964] Director/Treasurer; Paul Wessels [1962] Director/Group Head of Reward [South African]

Mondi Investments Limited
Incorporated: 23 January 2004
Net Worth: £3,313,024,256 *Total Assets:* £3,314,483,712
Registered Office: 1st Floor, Building 1, Aviator Park, Station Road, Addlestone, Surrey, KT15 2PG
Activities: Activities of head offices
Parent: Mondi PLC
Officers: Jennifer Louise Hampshire, Secretary; Jennifer Louise Hampshire [1983] Director/Chartered Secretary; Andrew Charles Wallis King [1969] Director/Chief Financial Officer [South African]; James Campbell Paterson [1964] Director/Treasurer; Paul Wessels [1962] Director/Group Head of Reward [South African]

Mondi PLC
Incorporated: 11 April 2007 *Employees:* 26,300
Net Worth: £3,288,762,880 *Total Assets:* £6,383,600,640
Registered Office: 1st Floor, Building 1, Aviator Park, Station Road, Addlestone, Surrey, KT15 2PG
Activities: Activities of head offices
Officers: Jennifer Louise Hampshire, Secretary; Tanya Dianne Fratto [1960] Director [American]; Stephen Clive Harris [1958] Director/CEO, Bodycote PLC; Andrew Charles Wallis King [1969] Director/Chief Financial Officer [South African]; Peter Josef Oswald [1962] Director/CEO Europe & International Div [Austrian]; Tshamano Mohau Frederik Phaswana [1944] Director [South African]; Dominique Jacqueline Nicole Reiniche [1955] Director [French]; David Michael Williams [1946] Director; Stephen Gareth Young [1955] Director

Mongas Kids Wear Limited
Incorporated: 27 July 2009 *Employees:* 18
Net Worth: £1,898,754 *Total Assets:* £11,421,086
Registered Office: 60-66 The Broadway, Southall, Middlesex, UB1 1QB
Activities: Retail sale of clothing in specialised stores
Shareholders: Ankit Monga; Arun Monga
Officers: Ankit Monga, Secretary; Ankit Monga [1988] Director [Indian]; Arun Monga [1960] Director

A.E.Monk & Co.(London) Limited
Incorporated: 21 August 1931 *Employees:* 2
Net Worth: £3,986,053 *Total Assets:* £6,472,971
Registered Office: 7 Beechwood Drive, Cobham, Surrey, KT11 2DX
Activities: Other letting and operating of own or leased real estate
Shareholders: Diana Mary Peacock; Julie Elizabeth Allman
Officers: Diana Mary Peacock, Secretary/Lecturer; Julie Elizabeth Allman [1957] Director; Diana Mary Peacock [1963] Director

Monks Way Development Limited
Incorporated: 10 September 2015
Net Worth Deficit: £48,138 *Total Assets:* £5,965,534
Registered Office: Kajaine House, 57-67 High Street, Edgware, Middlesex, HA8 7DD
Activities: Development of building projects
Major Shareholder: Kamal Abdulla Nozad
Officers: Kamal Abdulla Nozad [1967] Director

Mono Holdings Limited
Incorporated: 26 November 1999
Net Worth: £8,449,775 *Total Assets:* £14,510,316
Registered Office: Unit 4 Baird Road, Enfield, Middlesex, EN1 1SJ
Activities: Activities of head offices
Shareholder: Angelo Yianni
Officers: Maria Yianni, Secretary/Director; Andronikki Yianni [1978] Director; Angelo Yianni [1958] Director [Greek]; Maria Yianni [1980] Director

Mono Properties Limited
Incorporated: 3 February 1999
Net Worth: £7,407,436 *Total Assets:* £9,513,597
Registered Office: Unit 4 Baird Road, Enfield, Middlesex, EN1 1SJ
Activities: Development of building projects
Parent: Mono Holdings Limited
Officers: Maria Yianni, Secretary/Director; Andronikki Yianni [1978] Director; Angelo Yianni [1958] Director/Manufacturer [Greek]; Maria Yianni [1980] Director

Monster Energy Europe Limited
Incorporated: 9 October 2007 *Employees:* 389
Net Worth: £31,493,468 *Total Assets:* £53,013,208
Registered Office: Unit 51 Metropolitan Park, Bristol Road, Greenford, Middlesex, UB6 8UP
Activities: Manufacture of soft drinks; production of mineral waters and other bottled waters
Officers: Neil Shirley, Secretary; Guy Philip Carling [1977] Director; Rodney Cyril Sacks [1949] Director [American]; Hilton Schlosberg [1952] Director; Neil Shirley [1962] Director/VP Finance

Mont Rose College of Management and Sciences Limited
Incorporated: 8 May 2006
Net Worth: £4,621,299 *Total Assets:* £5,364,673
Registered Office: Shakespeare House, South Campus, 267 Cranbrook Road, Ilford, Essex, IG1 4TG
Activities: First-degree level higher education
Major Shareholder: Behjat Sheikh
Officers: Behjat Bilal Sheikh [1976] Director/Education

Montpelier Properties Limited
Incorporated: 2 June 2010 *Employees:* 2
Net Worth: £1,897,260 *Total Assets:* £11,720,902
Registered Office: Central House, 124 High Street, Hampton Hill, Hampton, Surrey, TW12 1NS
Activities: Other letting and operating of own or leased real estate
Major Shareholder: Gregory John Fry
Officers: Gordon James Haxton, Secretary; Cassandra Jill Fry [1973] Director [Australian]; Gregory John Fry [1957] Director

Montreaux Maidenhead Limited
Incorporated: 12 October 2016
Net Worth Deficit: £145,814 *Total Assets:* £8,370,225
Registered Office: Montreaux House, The Hythe, Staines upon Thames, Middlesex, TW18 3JQ
Activities: Buying and selling of own real estate
Major Shareholder: David Burke
Officers: David Burke [1965] Director

Montreaux Redhill Limited
Incorporated: 5 May 2017
Net Worth Deficit: £39,861 *Total Assets:* £6,642,553
Registered Office: Montreaux House, The Hythe, Staines upon Thames, Middlesex, TW18 3JQ
Activities: Buying and selling of own real estate
Major Shareholder: David Burke
Officers: David Burke [1965] Director

Monument Assets Limited
Incorporated: 5 February 1998
Net Worth: £5,181,082 *Total Assets:* £5,184,438
Registered Office: 22 Barn Rise, Wembley, Middlesex, HA9 9NQ
Activities: Development of building projects
Shareholders: Anthony David Chambers; Sarah Davies
Officers: Anthony David Chambers, Secretary/Director; Anthony David Chambers [1955] Director; Sarah Davies [1976] Director/Chartered Accountant

Mood Media Limited
Incorporated: 30 November 1956 *Employees:* 67
Net Worth: £13,840,000 *Total Assets:* £24,609,000
Registered Office: West House, 46 High Street, Orpington, Kent, BR6 0JQ
Activities: Reproduction of sound recording
Parent: Mood Media UK Holdings Limited
Officers: Caroline Sarah Trenter, Secretary; Mick Bennett [1965] Managing Director; Kenneth H Eissing [1970] Director/President in Store Media [American]; Caroline Trenter [1977] Finance Director

Moove Lubricants Limited
Incorporated: 19 November 1986 *Employees:* 162
Previous: Comma Oil & Chemicals Limited
Net Worth: £25,383,000 *Total Assets:* £99,059,000
Registered Office: Moove, Dering Way, Gravesend, Kent, DA12 2QX
Activities: Other treatment of petroleum products (excluding petrochemicals manufacture)
Parent: Cosan Lubes Investments Limited
Officers: Gary Michael Sands, Secretary/Accountant; Filipe Affonso Ferreira [1965] Director [Brazilian]; Marcos Marinho Lutz [1969] Director [Brazilian]; Rubens Ometto Silveira Mello [1950] Director [Brazilian]

Moreland House Care Home Limited
Incorporated: 12 March 2003 *Employees:* 70
Net Worth: £2,562,442 *Total Assets:* £6,722,343
Registered Office: 9 Spareleaze Hill, Loughton, Essex, IG10 1BS
Activities: Residential care activities for the elderly and disabled
Parent: Abbey Total Care Group Limited
Officers: Devyani Jayanti Patel, Secretary/Director; Devyani Jayanti Patel [1953] Director; Jayanti Mohanlal Patel [1949] Director

Morelli Group Limited
Incorporated: 5 May 1992 *Employees:* 210
Net Worth: £7,778,253 *Total Assets:* £15,901,264
Registered Office: Unit 2 Baird Road, Enfield, Middlesex, EN1 1SJ
Activities: Non-specialised wholesale trade
Officers: Robert Cohen, Secretary; Robert Paul Cohen [1977] Director; Joan Laybourn [1941] Director; Michele Laybourn [1965] Director; Andrew Moring [1967] Director; David Moring [1940] Director; John Moring [1948] Director; Julie Moring [1953] Director; Mark Moring [1973] Director; Phyllis Moring [1940] Director; Ruth Rosina Moring-Beale [1962] Director; Stuart Morning [1965] Director; Graham Robert Parker [1968] Director; Allan John Toms [1947] Financial Director; Linda Toms [1950] Director

Moriarty Haulage Limited
Incorporated: 2 February 2007 *Employees:* 2
Net Worth: £2,067,403 *Total Assets:* £5,197,901
Registered Office: Unit C21 Ensign Industrial Estate, Botany Way, Purfleet, Essex, RM19 1TB
Activities: Freight transport by road
Shareholders: Denis Joseph Moriarty; Dennis Patrick Moriarty
Officers: Bridget Moriarty, Secretary; Denis Joseph Moriarty [1976] Director

Morley Finco Limited
Incorporated: 23 April 2014
Net Worth: £6,428 *Total Assets:* £40,970,660
Registered Office: 505 Pinner Road, Harrow, Middlesex, HA2 6EH
Activities: Other letting and operating of own or leased real estate
Officers: Rishi Ramesh Sachdev [1976] Director; Uday Vyas [1978] Director

A.J. Morrisroe & Sons Limited
Incorporated: 1 March 1977 *Employees:* 83
Net Worth: £27,699,638 *Total Assets:* £83,417,040
Registered Office: Unit 4 Oaks Court, Warwick Road, Borehamwood, Herts, WD6 1GS
Activities: Construction of commercial buildings
Major Shareholder: Brian Quinlan Morrisroe
Officers: Brian Quinlan Morrisroe, Secretary; Daniel James Bannister [1976] Health & Safety Director; Michael Ioannou [1968] Commercial Director; Gerard Olaivar Marapao [1961] Director/Accountant; Brian Quinlan Morrisroe [1955] Managing Director

Morrisroe Group Limited
Incorporated: 14 November 2006 *Employees:* 208
Net Worth: £43,130,848 *Total Assets:* £108,799,408
Registered Office: Unit 4 Oaks Court, Warwick Road, Borehamwood, Herts, WD6 1GS
Activities: Other professional, scientific and technical activities n.e.c.
Major Shareholder: Brian Quinlan Morrisroe
Officers: Gerard Olaivar Marapao, Secretary/Chartered Accountant; Daniel James Bannister [1976] Health & Safety Director; Michael Ioannou [1968] Commercial Director; Gerard Olaivar Marapao [1961] Director/Certified Chartered Accountant; Brian Quinlan Morrisroe [1955] Managing Director

Morrisroe UK Ltd
Incorporated: 20 March 2008 *Employees:* 1
Net Worth: £5,008,168 *Total Assets:* £9,663,343
Registered Office: Unit 4 Oaks Court, Warwick Road, Borehamwood, Herts, WD6 1GS
Activities: Construction of commercial buildings
Major Shareholder: Brian Quinlan Morrisroe
Officers: Gerard Olaivar Marapao, Secretary/Accountant; Brian Quinlan Morrisroe [1955] Director

Mortgage Guarantee Limited
Incorporated: 27 March 1980 *Employees:* 4
Previous: Mortgage Guarantee PLC
Net Worth: £11,218,144 *Total Assets:* £11,380,622
Registered Office: Lynwood House, 373-375 Station Road, Harrow, Middlesex, HA1 2AW
Activities: Activities of mortgage finance companies
Major Shareholder: Kenneth Johnson
Officers: Linda Joyce Perrin, Secretary; Kenneth Johnson [1942] Director/Financier

Mosaic Estates Ltd
Incorporated: 14 June 1999 *Employees:* 2
Net Worth Deficit: £4,923,337 *Total Assets:* £8,128,177
Registered Office: Ridgecourt, The Ridge, Epsom, Surrey, KT18 7EP
Activities: Activities of head offices
Officers: Christopher Paul Baker, Secretary; Jeremy Graham Paul Campling [1969] Director/Chartered Surveyor; Sandra Jane Pope [1963] Director/Accountant

Moss Electrical Co. Limited
Incorporated: 28 July 1992 *Employees:* 64
Net Worth: £8,500,961 *Total Assets:* £17,127,676
Registered Office: Maxmor House, Sandpit Road, Dartford, Kent, DA1 5BU
Activities: Wholesale of electronic and telecommunications equipment and parts
Major Shareholder: Robert Jospeh Moss
Officers: Andrew Porter, Secretary; Lindsay Claire Goubel [1971] Operations Director; Christopher John Homer [1959] Commercial Director; Stefan Michael Paul Kemp [1985] Marketing Director; Robert Joseph Moss [1953] Director Executive; Andrew Porter [1963] Finance Director; Domenico Giovanni Raffa [1968] Business Development Director

Moss Electrical Holdings Limited
Incorporated: 26 March 2003 *Employees:* 95
Net Worth: £9,272,191 *Total Assets:* £20,248,884
Registered Office: Maxmor House, Sandpit Road, Dartford, Kent, DA1 5BU
Activities: Financial leasing
Major Shareholder: Robert Jospeh Moss
Officers: Andrew Porter, Secretary; Lindsay Claire Goubel [1971] Operations Director; Christopher John Homer [1959] Commercial Director; Robert Joseph Moss [1953] Director; Andrew Porter [1963] Finance Director

Moss Europe Limited
Incorporated: 23 February 2000 *Employees:* 101
Net Worth: £6,897,978 *Total Assets:* £8,344,625
Registered Office: 16 Hampton Business Park, Bolney Way, Feltham, Middlesex, TW13 6DB
Activities: Wholesale trade of motor vehicle parts and accessories
Major Shareholder: Glen Douglas Adams
Officers: Nigel Lavender, Secretary; Glen Douglas Adams [1948] Director/Executive [American]; Alexander Jocelyn Chaperlin [1972] Commercial Director; Robert Alan Goldman [1962] Director/Executive [American]; Nigel Lavender [1963] Finance Director; Fred Lynch [1951] Director [American]

Mostell Limited
Incorporated: 13 June 2000 *Employees:* 4
Net Worth: £1,244,000 *Total Assets:* £7,548,000
Registered Office: Berth 29-30 Tilbury Freeport, Tilbury, Essex, RM18 7SX
Activities: Wholesale of meat and meat products
Parent: Importo Limited
Officers: Wayne Godfrey [1971] Director; Alan George Hill [1967] Finance Director

Mothercare Group Limited (The)
Incorporated: 21 July 1927
Net Worth Deficit: £13,809,000 *Total Assets:* £70,013,000
Registered Office: Cherry Tree Road, Watford, Herts, WD24 6SH
Activities: Activities of head offices
Parent: Mothercare PLC
Officers: Lynne Samantha Medini, Secretary; Taimoor Anwar [1980] Director/Chartered Accountant [Pakistani]; Kirsty Rowena Homer [1974] HR Director

Mothercare PLC.
Incorporated: 26 September 1985 *Employees:* 4,737
Net Worth: £4,600,000 *Total Assets:* £276,700,000
Registered Office: Cherry Tree Road, Watford, Herts, WD24 6SH
Activities: Other retail sale of new goods in specialised stores (not commercial art galleries and opticians)
Officers: Lynne Samantha Medini, Secretary; William Glyn Lawrence Hughes [1976] Director/Chief Financial Officer; Gillian Dawn Celia Kent [1963] Director; Mark Newton-Jones [1967] Director; Nicholas Barry Edward Wharton [1966] Director; Clive Peter Whiley [1960] Director/Executive Chairman

Mothercare UK Limited
Incorporated: 8 May 1954 *Employees:* 2,604
Net Worth Deficit: £183,600,000 *Total Assets:* £231,000,000
Registered Office: Cherry Tree Road, Watford, Herts, WD24 6SH
Activities: Other retail sale of new goods in specialised stores (not commercial art galleries and opticians)
Parent: Mothercare (Holdings) Limited
Officers: Lynne Samantha Medini, Secretary; Kirsty Rowena Homer [1974] HR Director; William Glyn Lawrence Hughes [1976] Director/Chief Financial Officer; Mark Newton-Jones [1967] Director; Kevin Jonathan Rusling [1977] Managing Director, International

Mothers Ltd
Incorporated: 29 July 2005
Net Worth: £8,873,576 *Total Assets:* £18,980,012
Registered Office: 19-20 Bourne Court, Southend Road, Woodford Green, Essex, IG8 8HD
Activities: Buying and selling of own real estate
Parent: Spacious Developments Ltd
Officers: Jacob Schreiber, Secretary/Company Officer; Israel Moskovitz [1964] Director [Canadian]

Motherwell Holdings Limited
Incorporated: 7 November 2003 *Employees:* 63
Net Worth: £15,917,140 *Total Assets:* £24,807,754
Registered Office: Solus 31, Motherwell Way, West Thurrock, Essex, RM20 3LB
Activities: Activities of head offices
Shareholders: Andrew Douglas Hill; James Douglas Hill
Officers: James Douglas Hill, Secretary/Director; Andrew Douglas Hill [1931] Director; James Douglas Hill [1968] Director

Motivair Compressors Limited
Incorporated: 19 October 1967 *Employees:* 120
Net Worth: £3,033,690 *Total Assets:* £8,746,272
Registered Office: Victoria House, Britannia Road, Waltham Cross, Herts, EN8 7NU
Activities: Other manufacturing n.e.c.
Major Shareholder: Julian Paul Leach
Officers: Iain Beadle [1967] Director; Julian Paul Leach [1953] Director; Jon Andrew Victor Sopher [1965] Director/Consultant

Motor Parts Direct Limited
Incorporated: 28 July 1998 *Employees:* 1,015
Net Worth: £12,447,331 *Total Assets:* £45,425,640
Registered Office: Unit 7 Optima Business Park, Pindar Road, Hoddesdon, Herts, EN11 0DY
Activities: Maintenance and repair of motor vehicles
Officers: Ninna Shah, Secretary; Darshni Shah [1994] Director; Kiran Zaverchand Shah [1957] Director/Business Manager; Mukesh Zaverchand Shah [1960] Director/Business Partner; Neeta Shah [1980] Director; Ninna Shah [1964] Director and Company Secretary; Priyen Shah [1996] Director; Sagar Shah [1988] Director

Motorsport Vision Limited
Incorporated: 8 October 1997 *Employees:* 640
Net Worth: £14,988,437 *Total Assets:* £30,917,884
Registered Office: Motorsport Vision Centre, Brands Hatch, Fawkham, Longfield, Kent, DA3 8NG
Activities: Operation of sports facilities
Parent: MSV Group Limited
Officers: Philip Graham Hopkins, Secretary; Dr Jonathan Charles Palmer [1956] Director

Mott MacDonald Group Limited
Incorporated: 30 April 1973 *Employees:* 14,730
Net Worth: £124,305,000 *Total Assets:* £712,019,968
Registered Office: Mott MacDonald House, 8-10 Sydenham Road, Croydon, Surrey, CR0 2EE
Activities: Other engineering activities
Officers: Paul Edward Ferguson, Secretary; Nicholas Mauro Denichilo [1952] Executive Director [American]; Ian Martin Richard Galbraith [1963] Director; Michael David Haigh [1960] Director/Chartered Engineer; James Huw Keir Harris [1968] Director/Civil Engineer; Keith John Howells [1953] Director/Engineer; Guy William Ingledew Leonard [1955] Director/Chartered Quantity Surveyors; Edwin George Roud [1963] Finance Director

Mott MacDonald International Limited
Incorporated: 15 October 1986
Net Worth: £26,927,146 *Total Assets:* £80,366,896
Registered Office: Mott MacDonald House, 8-10 Sydenham Road, Croydon, Surrey, CR0 2EE
Activities: Other engineering activities
Parent: Mott MacDonald Group Limited
Officers: Diana Zivko, Secretary; Ian Martin Richard Galbraith [1963] Director; Michael David Haigh [1960] Director/Chartered Engineer; James Huw Keir Harris [1968] Director; Keith John Howells [1953] Director/Engineer; Guy William Ingledew Leonard [1955] Director/Chartered Quantity Surveyors; Edwin George Roud [1963] Finance Director

Mott MacDonald Limited
Incorporated: 11 February 1976 *Employees:* 6,619
Net Worth: £337,348,000 *Total Assets:* £732,182,016
Registered Office: Mott MacDonald House, 8-10 Sydenham Road, Croydon, Surrey, CR0 2EE
Activities: Other engineering activities
Parent: Mott MacDonald Group Limited
Officers: Diana Zivko, Secretary; Ian Martin Richard Galbraith [1963] Director/Engineer; Michael David Haigh [1960] Director/Chartered Engineer; James Huw Keir Harris [1968] Director/Civil Engineer; Keith John Howells [1953] Director/Engineer; Guy William Ingledew Leonard [1955] Chief Executive Director; Edwin George Roud [1963] Finance Director

Mount Grace School
Incorporated: 6 July 2011 *Employees:* 108
Net Worth: £11,566,370 *Total Assets:* £12,742,163
Registered Office: Mount Grace School, Church Road, Potters Bar, Herts, EN6 1EZ
Activities: General secondary education
Officers: Paul Seymour, Secretary; Peter Robert Baker [1959] Director/Headteacher; Christopher Cardell-Williams [1946] Director; Janice Diane Couzens [1949] Director/Deputy CEO; Colin Ronald Daniel [1960] Director/Electrical Engineer; Karis Anne Folan [1975] Director; Helen Margaret Frost [1945] Director/Retired; Dawn Gamble [1965] Director/HR Manager; Philip Harding [1960] Finance Director; Sarah Julia Haws [1971] Director/Finance Assistant; Victoria Horne [1983] Director/Teacher; Jean Evelyn Mackie [1949] Director; Paul Michael Pytches [1959] Director/Teacher; David Redington [1952] Director

Mountbrook Properties Limited
Incorporated: 27 June 2002
Net Worth: £2,614,963 *Total Assets:* £7,016,105
Registered Office: Japonica House, 8 Spring Villa Park, Edgware, Middlesex, HA8 7XT
Activities: Other letting and operating of own or leased real estate
Officers: Joel Samuel Storfer, Secretary; Joel Samuel Storfer [1977] Managing Director; Michael Storfer [1950] Director/Chartered Accountant

Mountcharm (S.E.) Limited
Incorporated: 6 October 2000
Net Worth: £9,094,645 *Total Assets:* £11,910,514
Registered Office: Northside House, Mount Pleasant, Barnet, Herts, EN4 9EE
Activities: Buying and selling of own real estate
Shareholder: Melvyn Frank Cooper
Officers: Jason Robert Cooper, Secretary/Director; Adam Cooper [1971] Director; Jason Robert Cooper [1967] Director; Melvyn Frank Cooper [1941] Director

Mountcharm Limited
Incorporated: 12 December 1994 *Employees:* 4
Net Worth: £32,150,532 *Total Assets:* £59,818,216
Registered Office: Northside House, Mount Pleasant, Barnet, Herts, EN4 9EE
Activities: Other service activities n.e.c.
Shareholder: Melvyn Frank Cooper
Officers: Jason Robert Cooper, Secretary/Director; Adam Cooper [1971] Director; Jason Robert Cooper [1967] Director; Melvyn Frank Cooper [1941] Director

Mouskos & Sons Co. Limited
Incorporated: 7 February 1969 *Employees:* 3
Net Worth: £8,024,588 *Total Assets:* £9,782,518
Registered Office: 1st Floor, Woodgate Studios, 2-8 Games Road, Cockfosters, Herts, EN4 9HN
Activities: Hotels and similar accommodation
Parent: Mouskos Holdings Limited
Officers: Christopher Mouskos, Secretary; Christopher Mouskos [1961] Director/Businessman; John Mouskos [1964] Director/Businessman

Mouskos Capital Limited
Incorporated: 17 February 2016
Net Worth: £23,987,352 *Total Assets:* £23,990,352
Registered Office: 1st Floor, Woodgate Studios, 2-8 Games Road, Cockfosters, Barnet, Herts, EN4 9HN
Activities: Activities of head offices
Shareholders: Christopher Mouskos; John Michael Mouskos; Geraldina Mouskos
Officers: Generaldina Mouskos, Secretary; Christopher Mouskos [1961] Director; Generaldina Mouskos [1936] Director; John Michael Mouskos [1964] Director

Mouskos Holdings Limited
Incorporated: 17 February 2016
Net Worth: £27,218,164 *Total Assets:* £27,300,036
Registered Office: 1st Floor, Woodgate Studios, 2-8 Games Road, Cockfosters, Barnet, Herts, EN4 9HN
Activities: Activities of head offices
Shareholders: Christopher Mouskos; John Michael Mouskos; Geraldina Mouskos
Officers: Generaldina Mouskos, Secretary; Christopher Mouskos [1961] Director; Generaldina Mouskos [1936] Director; John Michael Mouskos [1964] Director

Mouskos LLP
Incorporated: 12 December 2012
Net Worth: £49,189,968 *Total Assets:* £49,201,652
Registered Office: 1st Floor, Woodgate Studios, 2-8 Games Road, Cockfosters, Herts, EN4 9HN

Movesell Limited
Incorporated: 28 August 2014
Net Worth: £1,115,529 *Total Assets:* £5,829,247
Registered Office: 10 Sunderland Grove, Leavesden, Watford, Herts, WD25 7GL
Activities: Dormant company
Major Shareholder: Eric Walton
Officers: Edward Walton [1968] Director/Marketing Consultant; Eric Walton [1945] Property and Planning Director

Moyvale Properties Limited
Incorporated: 20 April 1976 *Employees:* 2
Net Worth: £1,833,423 *Total Assets:* £5,316,824
Registered Office: 149-151 Sparrows Herne, Bushey Heath, Watford, Herts, WD23 1AQ
Activities: Development of building projects
Shareholders: Caroline Ann Cooney; Christopher Patrick Cooney
Officers: Christopher Patrick Cooney, Secretary; Caroline Ann Cooney [1964] Director/Office Manager [Irish]; Christopher Patrick Cooney [1966] Director/Property Administrator

MPM Connect Limited
Incorporated: 6 April 2010
Net Worth: £6,252,411 *Total Assets:* £11,764,475
Registered Office: Genville House, 4 Grenville Avenue, Broxbourne, Herts, EN10 7DH
Activities: Activities of head offices
Major Shareholder: Peter John Hearn
Officers: Peter John Hearn [1953] Director; Simon James Murphy [1964] Director

Mr. Plant Hire PLC
Incorporated: 16 March 1982 *Employees:* 65
Net Worth: £7,385,783 *Total Assets:* £8,898,142
Registered Office: Lynwood House, 373-375 Station Road, Harrow, Middlesex, HA1 2AW
Activities: Renting and leasing of other machinery, equipment and tangible goods n.e.c.
Parent: AER Rents Limited
Officers: Siobhan Shaw, Secretary; Martin Lawrence [1960] Director; Ciaran Mahon [1967] Director [Irish]; Stephen O'Flaherty [1961] Director [Irish]

MRB Holdings Ltd
Incorporated: 20 December 2004
Net Worth: £2,232,355 *Total Assets:* £18,909,664
Registered Office: Hunters House, 109 Snakes Lane West, Woodford Green, Essex, IG8 0DY
Activities: Other business support service activities n.e.c.
Major Shareholder: Martin Roderick Brown
Officers: Anne Brown, Secretary; Martin Roderick Brown [1947] Director

MSC Cruises Limited
Incorporated: 6 October 1994 *Employees:* 64
Net Worth: £1,957,205 *Total Assets:* £16,397,508
Registered Office: 5 Roundwood Avenue, Stockley Park, Uxbridge, Middlesex, UB11 1AF
Activities: Travel agency activities
Shareholders: Rafaela Aponte-Diamant; Gianluigi Aponte
Officers: Domenico Ferrara, Secretary; Jean-Plilippe Jacques Francois Neau [1968] Director [French]; Antonio Paradiso [1981] Managing Director [Italian]; Pierfrancesco Vago [1961] Director [Italian]

MSHA International Ltd.
Incorporated: 13 September 1991 *Employees:* 930
Net Worth: £10,422,072 *Total Assets:* £35,705,724
Registered Office: The Pavilion, Rosslyn Crescent, Harrow, Middlesex, HA1 2SZ
Activities: Activities of head offices
Parent: MSHA Holdings Ltd
Officers: Hamid Ali [1956] Director

MSI Property Investments Limited
Incorporated: 8 May 2013
Net Worth: £3,740,817 *Total Assets:* £8,671,877
Registered Office: Unit 1 Firtree House, Creek Road, Barking, Essex, IG11 0JH
Activities: Other letting and operating of own or leased real estate
Major Shareholder: Idris Abdullah
Officers: Idris Abdullah [1977] Director/Property Development

MSK Holdings Limited
Incorporated: 12 April 2006 *Employees:* 154
Net Worth: £25,194,872 *Total Assets:* £33,842,548
Registered Office: Numeric House, 98 Station Road, Sidcup, Kent, DA15 7BY
Activities: Activities of other holding companies n.e.c.
Shareholders: David John Guildford; Anthony Richard Stone
Officers: Maureen Elizabeth Stone, Secretary; Mark Doughty [1964] Director; David John Guildford [1952] Director; Anthony Richard Stone [1950] Director; Richard Mark Stone [1977] Director

MSV Group Limited
Incorporated: 25 November 2003 *Employees:* 734
Net Worth: £23,351,000 *Total Assets:* £43,991,000
Registered Office: Motorsport Vision Centre, Brands Hatch Circuit, Fawkham, Longfield, Kent, DA3 8NG
Activities: Operation of sports facilities
Major Shareholder: Jonathan Charles Palmer
Officers: Philip Graham Hopkins, Secretary; Sir Peter James Ogden [1947] Director; Dr Jonathan Charles Palmer [1956] Director

MTALX Limited
Incorporated: 23 February 2010 *Employees:* 8
Previous: Prospero Metals Limited
Net Worth: £7,229,434 *Total Assets:* £28,795,316
Registered Office: Lynwood House, 373-375 Station Road, Harrow, Middlesex, HA1 2AW
Activities: Management consultancy activities other than financial management
Parent: Prospero Global Holdings Limited
Officers: Daniel Harvey Goldberg [1960] Director/Commodity Trader; Isaac Goldberg [1991] Director; Amos Jessurun Wittenberg [1951] Director [Dutch]

Mulalley & Co. Limited
Incorporated: 15 December 1980 *Employees:* 507
Net Worth: £61,513,000 *Total Assets:* £107,964,000
Registered Office: Teresa Gavin House, Woodford Avenue, Woodford Green, Essex, IG8 8FA
Activities: Construction of commercial buildings
Parent: Sherrygreen Ltd
Officers: Eamon O'Malley, Secretary; Brendan O'Malley [1954] Director; Eamon O'Malley [1955] Director; Vincent O'Malley [1951] Director; Teresa Taylor [1963] Director

Mulcroft Limited
Incorporated: 31 October 1989 *Employees:* 293
Net Worth: £3,307,172 *Total Assets:* £8,559,722
Registered Office: First Floor, Kirkland House, 11-15 Peterborough Road, Harrow, Middlesex, HA1 2AX
Activities: Unlicenced restaurants and cafes
Parent: Fieldrose Limited
Officers: Maya Bharat Patel, Secretary; Bharat Chandubhai Patel [1964] Director/Businessman; Maya Bharat Patel [1965] Director/Secretary

Mullan Partnership Limited
Incorporated: 15 April 2010
Net Worth: £5,811,806 *Total Assets:* £7,463,764
Registered Office: The Gate House, Manford Industrial Estate, Manor Road, Erith, Kent, DA8 2AJ
Activities: Other business support service activities n.e.c.
Officers: Mary Mullan [1938] Director/Property Developer

J P C Mulligan Properties Limited
Incorporated: 6 April 2011
Net Worth: £3,829,937 *Total Assets:* £16,566,412
Registered Office: 15 Dover Road, Northfleet, Gravesend, Kent, DA11 9PH
Activities: Other letting and operating of own or leased real estate
Major Shareholder: Cyril Mulligan
Officers: Richard John Hughes [1956] Director/Chartered Surveyor; Cyril Mulligan [1946] Director [Irish]

Multi Services Kent Limited
Incorporated: 29 August 1996 *Employees:* 46
Net Worth: £4,069,243 *Total Assets:* £10,117,161
Registered Office: Numeric House, 98 Station Road, Sidcup, Kent, DA15 7BY
Activities: Other business support service activities n.e.c.
Parent: MSK Holdings Limited
Officers: Linzi Mountcastle, Secretary; Mark Doughty [1964] Director; David John Guildford [1952] Director; Anthony Richard Stone [1950] Director

Multi Trade Links (UK) Ltd
Incorporated: 4 April 2008 *Employees:* 4
Net Worth: £2,182,741 *Total Assets:* £13,167,877
Registered Office: 5-9 Headstone Road, Harrow, Middlesex, HA1 1PD
Activities: Wholesale of waste and scrap
Shareholders: Manoj, Maganlal Mehta; Maganlal, Moolchand Mehta
Officers: Shriniwas Bajaj [1973] Director; Yogesh Shah [1960] Director

Multitrust Property Investments Limited
Incorporated: 23 May 1991
Net Worth: £218,791 *Total Assets:* £15,567,156
Registered Office: Unicorn House, Station Close, Potters Bar, Herts, EN6 1TL
Activities: Buying and selling of own real estate
Parent: Panther Securities PLC
Officers: Simon Jeffrey Peters, Secretary; Andrew Stewart Perloff [1944] Director; John Henry Perloff [1968] Director; Simon Jeffrey Peters [1977] Director

Mundays LLP
Incorporated: 24 June 2005 *Employees:* 76
Net Worth: £3,021,515 *Total Assets:* £5,171,278
Registered Office: 400 Dashwood Lang Road, Weybridge, Surrey, KT15 2HJ
Officers: Neale Alan Andrews [1962] Member; Kevin Patrick Healy [1963] Member; Valerie Ann Toon [1963] Member; David Ian Willis [1972] Member; Victor Ernest Barker [1957] LLP Member; Sarah Louise Duckworth [1958] LLP Member; Miranda Jane Green [1973] LLP Member; David Patrick Irving [1958] LLP Member; Oliver James Faux Jackson [1970] LLP Member; Gemma Ann James [1980] LLP Member; Nish Kapoor [1979] LLP Member; Joseph Francis Kean [1966] LLP Member; Andrew Mark David Knorpel [1971] LLP Member; James Thomas Lawrence [1980] LLP Member; Pui Pui Manager [1977] LLP Member; Fiona Ruth McAllister [1961] LLP Member; Michael Paul Nixon [1977] LLP Member; James Richard Picknell [1979] LLP Member; Alexander Wing Kin Young [1972] LLP Member

Muniment Limited
Incorporated: 12 September 2013
Net Worth: £35,053 *Total Assets:* £6,793,889
Registered Office: Milton House, 33a Milton Road, Hampton, Surrey, TW12 2LL
Activities: Buying and selling of own real estate
Major Shareholder: Trevor Iain Walker
Officers: Daniel Peter Inman [1986] Director/Property Management and Construction; Trevor Iain Walker [1962] Director/Property Developer

Munnelly Group PLC
Incorporated: 8 June 2005 *Employees:* 108
Previous: Munnelly Group Limited
Net Worth: £6,690,000 *Total Assets:* £22,497,000
Registered Office: Munnelly House, 84-88 Pinner Road, Harrow, Middlesex, HA1 4LP
Activities: Activities of head offices
Major Shareholder: Philip Anthony Munnelly
Officers: Gareth Brewerton, Secretary; Christopher Mark Harrison [1981] Director/Chief Financial Officer; James Philip Munnelly [1983] Director; Paul David Munnelly [1986] Director; Paul Vincent Munnelly [1960] Director/Building Contractor; Philip Anthony Munnelly [1955] Director; William James Walter Noble [1979] Director

Munnelly Support Services Limited
Incorporated: 23 March 1982 *Employees:* 85
Net Worth: £5,791,000 *Total Assets:* £15,170,000
Registered Office: Munnelly House, 84-88 Pinner Road, Harrow, Middlesex, HA1 4LP
Activities: Other specialised construction activities n.e.c.
Parent: Munnelly Group PLC
Officers: Gareth Brewerton, Secretary; Christopher Mark Harrison [1981] Director/Chief Financial Officer; James Philip Munnelly [1983] Commercial Director; Paul David Munnelly [1986] Director/Procurement; Paul Vincent Munnelly [1960] Director/Building Contractor; Philip Anthony Munnelly [1955] Director/Building Contractor; William James Walter Noble [1979] Director/Commercial Executive

Munster Limited
Incorporated: 7 April 1998
Net Worth: £2,058,435 *Total Assets:* £5,631,508
Registered Office: 9a The Broadway, Stanmore, Middlesex, HA7 4DA
Activities: Real estate agencies
Shareholders: Mahesh Raojibhai Patel; Hitenkumar Mansukhlal Shah
Officers: Mahesh Raojibhai Patel, Secretary/Financial Accountant; Mahesh Raojibhai Patel [1968] Director/Financial Accountant; Hitenkumar Mansukhlal Shah [1968] Director/Business Manager

Gerry Murphy Ltd
Incorporated: 29 February 2016 *Employees:* 2
Net Worth: £3,312,442 *Total Assets:* £7,201,928
Registered Office: Archway House, 81-82 Portsmouth Road, Surbiton, Surrey, KT6 5PT
Activities: Other letting and operating of own or leased real estate
Major Shareholder: Gerald Murphy
Officers: Generald Antony Murphy [1968] Director; Kathryn Murphy [1966] Director

Gordon Murray Design Limited
Incorporated: 19 February 2007 *Employees:* 86
Net Worth: £4,434,630 *Total Assets:* £6,425,639
Registered Office: Ashcombe House, 5 The Crescent, Leatherhead, Surrey, KT22 8DY
Activities: Engineering related scientific and technical consulting activities
Major Shareholder: Professor Ian Gordon Murray
Officers: Simon Mark Lewis, Secretary; Meyrick Cox [1964] Director/Fund Manager; Jonathan Feiber [1957] Director [American]; Carl-Peter Edmund Moriz Forster [1954] Director [German]; Professor Ian Gordon Murray [1946] Director/Designer

Musco (St Albans Place) Ltd
Incorporated: 25 January 2013
Net Worth Deficit: £2,183,054 *Total Assets:* £12,563,735
Registered Office: Wood Hall Farm Office, Woodhall Lane, Shenley, Herts, WD7 9AA
Activities: Development of building projects
Shareholders: Musco Developments Ltd; Roca Investments Ltd
Officers: Iain Williamson, Secretary; Andrew Lynton Cohen [1953] Director; Walid Wasfi Wasif Musmar [1974] Director; Iain Williamson [1972] Director/Chartered Accountant

Mushi UK Holdings Limited
Incorporated: 17 June 2014 *Employees:* 3
Net Worth: £181,436,656 *Total Assets:* £181,503,984
Registered Office: 3 Lotus Park, The Causeway, Staines upon Thames, Middlesex, TW18 3AG
Activities: Activities of other holding companies n.e.c.
Parent: Mallinckrodt ARD Holdings Limited
Officers: Alan Catterson [1961] Director/Financial Controller; Stephanie Dorn Miller [1974] Director/Corporate Secretary [American]; Stephen Andrew Welch [1977] Director/Senior Staff Liaison to The President and CEO [American]

MWL International Limited
Incorporated: 2 March 1999 *Employees:* 8
Net Worth: £6,177,266 *Total Assets:* £9,711,590
Registered Office: 80 Lower Road, Fetcham, Leatherhead, Surrey, KT22 9NG
Activities: Activities of head offices
Officers: Mark David Walpole, Secretary/Director; Charles David Murch [1956] Director; David Kenneth Michael Walpole [1941] Director; Mark David Walpole [1970] Director

MY Construction & Carpentry Limited
Incorporated: 31 January 2005 *Employees:* 38
Net Worth: £5,761,134 *Total Assets:* £18,180,600
Registered Office: 103 High Street, Waltham Cross, Herts, EN8 7AN
Activities: Development of building projects
Shareholder: Yoav Tal
Officers: Yoav Tal [1970] Director/Civil Engineer [Israeli]

Myatt's Field Development LLP
Incorporated: 16 March 2012
Net Worth: £227,968 *Total Assets:* £23,142,160
Registered Office: 1 Langston Road, Loughton, Essex, IG10 3SD

Myddleton London Limited
Incorporated: 20 September 2011 *Employees:* 23
Net Worth: £19,099,908 *Total Assets:* £21,065,404
Registered Office: Francis House, 2 Park Road, High Barnet, Barnet, Herts, EN5 5RN
Activities: Activities of other holding companies n.e.c.
Major Shareholder: Philip Silver
Officers: Debra Silver, Secretary; Philip Silver [1959] Director

Mylan Pharma UK Limited
Incorporated: 8 November 2011 *Employees:* 141
Net Worth: £29,811,000 *Total Assets:* £44,497,000
Registered Office: 20 Station Close, Potters Bar, Herts, EN6 1TL
Activities: Other research and experimental development on natural sciences and engineering
Parent: McDermott Laboratories Limited
Officers: Caroline Rebecca Louise Dixon, Secretary; Dr Walter Grant Cook [1967] Managing Director; Caroline Rebecca Louise Dixon [1968] Finance Director

Mylan UK Healthcare Limited
Incorporated: 28 August 2014 *Employees:* 29
Previous: BGP Products Ltd.
Net Worth: £18,299,000 *Total Assets:* £94,587,000
Registered Office: 20 Station Close, Potters Bar, Herts, EN6 1TL
Activities: Wholesale of pharmaceutical goods
Parent: Mylan Holdings Ltd
Officers: Falk Patrick Nuernberger, Secretary; Jean-Yves Brault [1967] Director/General Manager [Canadian]; Caroline Rebecca Louise Dixon [1968] Finance Director

MyTime Active
Incorporated: 24 June 2003 *Employees:* 1,125
Net Worth: £16,326,235 *Total Assets:* £20,130,700
Registered Office: Linden House, 153-155 Masons Hill, Bromley, Kent, BR2 9HY
Activities: Other education n.e.c.
Officers: Grace Obiageli Oforiokuma, Secretary; Cllr Aisha Vance Cuthbert [1987] Director/Councillor; Michael Rhys Evans [1976] Director/Consultant; Robert John Evans [1943] Director/Retired School Teacher; Isobel Mary Gowan [1958] Director/Consultant; Johnny Heald [1970] Director/Marketing; Adrian Hollands [1952] Director/Chartered Accountant; Dr Val Lowman OBE [1953] Non-Executive Director of Be Onsite; Andrew Muzzelle [1972] Digital Media Director; Mark David Oakley [1965] Director/Solicitor; Christine Anne Whatford [1947] Director/Education Consultant

Mywalit (UK) Limited
Incorporated: 7 March 2007 *Employees:* 64
Net Worth: £4,250,244 *Total Assets:* £5,811,363
Registered Office: Unit 3 Beechen Grove, Watford, Herts, WD17 2AD
Activities: Non-specialised wholesale trade
Officers: Karl Thyge Enevoldson, Secretary; Karl Thyge Enevoldson [1967] Director/Secretary; Christopher Rodney Howell [1951] Director; Thomas Paul Irving [1980] Finance Director; Alan Mark Warner [1949] Director

N & C Building Products Limited
Incorporated: 30 September 1856 *Employees:* 324
Net Worth: £15,855,892 *Total Assets:* £23,468,466
Registered Office: 41-51 Freshwater Road, Chadwell Heath, Romford, Essex, RM8 1SP
Activities: Wholesale of wood, construction materials and sanitary equipment
Parent: Nicholls & Clarke Limited
Officers: Geraint David Cooper, Secretary; Geraint David Cooper [1958] Director/Accountant; David Ian Forbes [1965] Director; Kenneth Stuart Alexander Forbes [1937] Director; Stephen Andrew Forbes [1963] Director; Gary Kenneth Gingell [1968] Director; Keith David Hall [1965] Director; Richard John Hill [1971] Director

N.R.C. Plant Limited
Incorporated: 13 January 1997 *Employees:* 33
Net Worth: £7,642,994 *Total Assets:* £19,035,140
Registered Office: Neagron House, Stanford Road, Orsett, Essex, RM16 3BX
Activities: Renting and leasing of other machinery, equipment and tangible goods n.e.c.
Parent: Joseph Gallagher Limited
Officers: Paul Joseph Gallagher, Secretary; Joseph Jude Gallagher [1945] Managing Director [Irish]; Steven Keith Harvey [1963] Director/Civil Engineer; Anthony Andrew Matheson [1968] Group Commercial Director

Nacropolis (Langley) Ltd
Incorporated: 7 October 2016
Net Worth Deficit: £192,710 *Total Assets:* £8,042,739
Registered Office: Suite 1, Stanmore Towers, 8-14 Church Road, Stanmore, Middlesex, HA7 4AW
Activities: Development of building projects
Shareholders: Bhaman Ltd; Nacropolis Developments Ltd
Officers: Amar Pankhania, Secretary; Amar Pankhania [1989] Director; Ravi Pankhania [1977] Director

Naga UK Bidco Limited
Incorporated: 27 June 2013
Net Worth: £235,443,008 *Total Assets:* £364,713,984
Registered Office: Dagger Lane, Elstree, Herts, WD6 3BX
Activities: Other human health activities
Parent: Naga UK Topco Limited
Officers: Kieu Hoang [1944] Director [American]; Kevin Lane [1961] Director/President [American]; Xu Wu [1967] Director/Businessman [Chinese]

Naga UK Topco Limited
Incorporated: 27 June 2013 *Employees:* 2,893
Net Worth: £157,711,008 *Total Assets:* £409,176,992
Registered Office: Dagger Lane, Elstree, Herts, WD6 3BX
Activities: Other human health activities
Parent: Tiancheng International Investment Limited
Officers: Kieu Hoang [1944] Director [American]; Lars Holmqvist [1959] Director/Senior Advisor [Swedish]; Kevin Patrick Lane [1961] Director/Consultant [American]; Xu Wu [1967] Director/Manager [Hong Kong]; Tan Yang [1972] Director/Business Executive [Chinese]

Naked Fine Wine Bonds PLC
Incorporated: 18 July 2013 *Employees:* 2
Net Worth Deficit: £120,000 *Total Assets:* £6,093,000
Registered Office: Majestic House, The Belfry, Colonial Way, Watford, Herts, WD24 4WH
Activities: Wholesale of wine, beer, spirits and other alcoholic beverages
Parent: Naked Wines International Limited
Officers: Alex Iapichino, Secretary; James Crawford [1977] Finance Director; Rowan Gormley [1962] Director [Irish]

Naked Wines International Limited
Incorporated: 24 November 2011 *Employees:* 2
Net Worth: £10,049,000 *Total Assets:* £18,161,000
Registered Office: Majestic House, The Belfry, Colonial Way, Watford, Herts, WD24 4WH
Activities: Activities of head offices
Parent: Majestic Wine PLC
Officers: Alex Iapichino, Secretary; James Crawford [1977] Director; Eamon William FitzGenerald [1984] Director/COO, Naked Wines [Irish]

Naked Wines Prepayments Trustee Company Limited
Incorporated: 13 November 2008
Net Worth Deficit: £10,000 *Total Assets:* £13,361,000
Registered Office: Majestic House, The Belfry, Colonial Way, Watford, Herts, WD24 4WH
Activities: Wholesale of wine, beer, spirits and other alcoholic beverages
Parent: www.nakedwines.com Limited
Officers: Alex Iapichino, Secretary; James Crawford [1977] Director; Eamon William FitzGenerald [1984] Director/COO, Naked Wines [Irish]

Namco UK Limited
Incorporated: 7 June 1993 *Employees:* 318
Previous: Namco Operations Europe Limited
Net Worth: £10,254,000 *Total Assets:* £21,594,000
Registered Office: 37-39 Kew Foot Road, Richmond, Surrey, TW9 2SS
Activities: Other amusement and recreation activities n.e.c.
Parent: Bandai Namco Holdings UK Ltd.
Officers: Raymond Bradley, Secretary; Raymond Bradley [1965] Financial Director; Tomohiro Hattori [1971] Managing Director [Japanese]; Philip Mark Millward [1962] Director

Namu Limited
Incorporated: 4 December 2012
Net Worth: £936,210 *Total Assets:* £9,363,888
Registered Office: 3 Lowther Close, Elstree, Herts, WD6 3PY
Activities: Other letting and operating of own or leased real estate
Major Shareholder: Nadia Parvez
Officers: Shakeel Ahmed [1959] Director; Nadia Parvez Manzoor [1982] Director

Nasco (UK) Ltd
Incorporated: 20 October 2003 *Employees:* 62
Net Worth: £5,514,315 *Total Assets:* £8,447,178
Registered Office: Unit K, Dean Way, Great Western Industrial Park, Southall, Middlesex, UB2 4SB
Activities: Non-specialised wholesale of food, beverages and tobacco
Major Shareholder: Suresh Vidani
Officers: Sushma Suresh Vidani, Secretary; Ashish Vidani [1986] Director; Suresh Vidani [1955] Director

National Animal Welfare Trust
Incorporated: 12 July 2001 *Employees:* 131
Net Worth: £6,454,691 *Total Assets:* £6,747,599
Registered Office: National Animal Welfare Trust, Tyler's Way, Watford Bypass, Watford, Herts, WD25 8WT
Activities: Other business support service activities n.e.c.
Officers: Dawn Elizabeth Webster, Secretary; Diana Margaret Brown [1944] Director/Veterinary Receptionist; Harvey Robert Galloway Carruthers [1967] Director/Veterinary Surgeon; Susan Jane Francombe [1964] Director/Barrister; Lynley Griffiths [1958] Director/Health & Safety Consultant [New Zealander]; Claire Elizabeth James [1955] Director/Retired; Laura Ann Magee [1966] Director/Project Manager; Debbie Matthews [1955] Director; John Richard Pearce [1964] Director/Chartered IT Professional

National Football Centre Limited
Incorporated: 18 July 1990 *Employees:* 278
Net Worth Deficit: £26,993,000 *Total Assets:* £69,510,000
Registered Office: Wembley Stadium, Wembley, Middlesex, HA9 0WS
Activities: Operation of sports facilities
Parent: The Football Association Limited
Officers: Richard James McDermott, Secretary; Mark Paul Burrows [1969] Director/Chief Financial Officer; Martin Richard Glenn [1960] Director/Chief Executive Officer

The National Fostering Agency (Scotland) Limited
Incorporated: 14 June 2005 *Employees:* 20
Net Worth: £1,279,000 *Total Assets:* £32,132,000
Registered Office: Frays Court, 71 Cowley Road, Uxbridge, Middlesex, UB8 2AE
Activities: Other social work activities without accommodation n.e.c.
Parent: NFAG Limited
Officers: Helen Elizabeth Lecky, Secretary; Antony Vincent Holt [1959] Director/Chartered Accountant; Isabella Mary Hutchison [1956] Managing Director; Jean-Luc Emmanuel Janet [1970] Director [French]; David Jon Leatherbarrow [1969] Director/Group Chief Executive Officer

The National Fostering Agency Limited
Incorporated: 17 November 1995 *Employees:* 224
Net Worth: £27,798,000 *Total Assets:* £54,551,000
Registered Office: Frays Court, 71 Cowley Road, Uxbridge, Middlesex, UB8 2AE
Activities: Other social work activities without accommodation n.e.c.
Parent: NFAG Limited
Officers: Helen Elizabeth Lecky, Secretary; Antony Vincent Holt [1959] Director/Chartered Accountant; Isabella Mary Hutchison [1956] Managing Director; Jean-Luc Emmanuel Janet [1970] Director [French]; David Jon Leatherbarrow [1969] Director/Group Chief Executive Officer

National Instruments Corporation (UK) Limited
Incorporated: 8 December 1994 *Employees:* 115
Net Worth: £3,369,480 *Total Assets:* £15,154,573
Registered Office: Elder House, St Georges Business Park, 207 Brooklands Road, Weybridge, Surrey, KT13 0TS
Activities: Manufacture of electronic measuring, testing etc. equipment, not for industrial process control
Officers: Karen Marie Rapp [1967] Director [American]

The Natural Woodfloor Company Limited
Incorporated: 19 September 1994 *Employees:* 17
Net Worth: £5,309,673 *Total Assets:* £6,851,067
Registered Office: 54 Sun Street, Waltham Abbey, Essex, EN9 1EJ
Activities: Manufacture of other products of wood; manufacture of articles of cork, straw and plaiting materials
Shareholders: Nial Gerard Keane; Peter Michael Keane
Officers: Nial Gerard Keane, Secretary; Nial Gerard Keane [1959] Director/Flooring Consultant; Peter Michael Keane [1966] Director [Irish]

Nature Delivered Limited
Incorporated: 17 October 2007 *Employees:* 250
Net Worth: £45,124,320 *Total Assets:* £56,597,200
Registered Office: Palm Court, 4 Heron Square, Richmond, Surrey, TW9 1EW
Activities: Other food services
Parent: ND4A Limited
Officers: Anthony Fletcher [1981] Director; Andrew Gibbs [1978] Director/Accountant

Nature's Finest Food Products Limited
Incorporated: 1 September 2011 *Employees:* 6
Previous: SPC Nature's Finest Limited
Net Worth: £3,904,310 *Total Assets:* £5,175,766
Registered Office: 2nd Floor, Chancery House, St Nicholas Way, Sutton, Surrey, SM1 1JB
Activities: Non-specialised wholesale of food, beverages and tobacco
Parent: World Wise Foods Limited
Officers: John Richard Burton [1955] Director; Phillip James Upex [1963] Finance Director; Ian Wingate [1960] Director

Navblue Limited
Incorporated: 8 October 2002 *Employees:* 109
Previous: European Aeronautical Group UK Limited
Net Worth Deficit: £4,728,000 *Total Assets:* £5,246,000
Registered Office: Hersham Place Technology Park, Molesey Road, Walton on Thames, Surrey, KT12 4RZ
Activities: Service activities incidental to air transportation
Parent: Airbus Group SE
Officers: Sean Doherty [1972] Director/Vice President Finance [Canadian]; Fabrice Hamel [1967] Director [French]; Pierre Madrange [1966] Managing Director & VP [French]

Navigator Terminals Midco Limited
Incorporated: 18 November 2015
Net Worth: £76,242,000 *Total Assets:* £209,240,000
Registered Office: Oliver Road, West Thurrock, Grays, Essex, RM20 3ED
Activities: Support activities for petroleum and natural gas mining
Officers: Mark Roy Charles Shaha, Secretary; Michael David Brennan [1969] Director [Irish]; Tamara Gail Earley [1968] Director/Deputy Chief Executive; Roderick John Gadsby [1969] Director/Investment Professional; Robin William Gisby [1956] Director; James McPhillimy [1964] Director/Chartered Engineer/Consultant; Grant Daniel Rayner [1982] Director [Australian]

Navigator Terminals North Tees Limited
Incorporated: 25 November 2015 *Employees:* 29
Net Worth: £17,123,000 *Total Assets:* £32,549,000
Registered Office: Oliver Road, Grays, Essex, RM20 3ED
Activities: Support activities for petroleum and natural gas mining
Parent: Navigator Terminals Limited
Officers: Mark Roy Charles Shaha, Secretary; Jason Ralph Hornsby [1973] Managing Director; Mark Roy Charles Shaha [1979] Director/Chartered Accountant

Navigator Terminals Seal Sands Limited
Incorporated: 27 November 1964 *Employees:* 75
Previous: Vopak Terminal Teesside Limited
Net Worth: £22,345,000 *Total Assets:* £49,185,000
Registered Office: Navigator Terminals Seal Sands Limited, Oliver Road, Grays, Essex, RM20 3ED
Activities: Operation of warehousing and storage facilities for land transport activities
Parent: Navigator Terminals UK Limited
Officers: Mark Roy Charles Shaha, Secretary; Jason Ralph Hornsby [1973] Managing Director; Mark Roy Charles Shaha [1979] Director/Chartered Accountant

Navigator Terminals UK Limited
Incorporated: 25 November 1977 *Employees:* 5
Previous: Vopak Holding Logistics UK Limited
Net Worth: £35,067,000 *Total Assets:* £36,138,000
Registered Office: Oliver Road, West Thurrock, Grays, Essex, RM20 3ED
Activities: Activities of head offices
Parent: Navigator Terminals Limited
Officers: Mark Roy Charles Shaha, Secretary; Jason Ralph Hornsby [1973] Managing Director; Mark Roy Charles Shaha [1979] Director/Chartered Accountant

Navigator Terminals Windmill Limited
Incorporated: 25 June 1946 *Employees:* 14
Previous: Vopak Terminal Windmill Limited
Net Worth: £4,422,000 *Total Assets:* £6,315,000
Registered Office: Navigator Terminals Windmill Limited, Oliver Road, Grays, Essex, RM20 3ED
Activities: Operation of warehousing and storage facilities for land transport activities
Parent: Navigator Terminals UK Limited
Officers: Mark Roy Charles Shaha, Secretary; Jason Ralph Hornsby [1973] Managing Director; Mark Roy Charles Shaha [1979] Director/Chartered Accountant

Navitas Petroleum Limited
Incorporated: 21 February 2013
Net Worth Deficit: £9,301,000 *Total Assets:* £25,953,000
Registered Office: Elm Park House, Elm Park Court, Pinner, Middlesex, HA5 3NN
Activities: Extraction of crude petroleum
Parent: Navitas Petroleum Limited Partnership
Officers: Benjamin Cuby [1975] Director/Business Development Manager; Adrian Gerard John Olivero [1967] Director; Chanan Reichman [1977] Director [Israeli]; Gideon Abraham Tadmor Cohen [1963] Director/Company Executive [Israeli]

NBC Europe Ltd.
Incorporated: 16 November 2011
Net Worth: £8,566,000 *Total Assets:* £14,784,000
Registered Office: 50 Clarendon Road, Watford, Herts, WD17 1TX
Activities: Activities of other holding companies n.e.c.
Parent: TJX Europe Limited
Officers: Susan Beaumont, Secretary; Alicia Colarte Kelly, Secretary; Lisa Schwartz, Secretary; David Lawrence Averill [1967] SVP Corporate Tax Director [American]; John Joseph Klinger [1964] Director/SVP, Corporate Controller [American]; Mary Blier Reynolds [1955] Director/SVP Treasurer [American]

NBS Trade and Investment Limited
Incorporated: 9 April 2013
Net Worth: £751,199 *Total Assets:* £1,501,340,416
Registered Office: Aquis House, 27-37 Station Road, Hayes, Middlesex, UB3 4DX
Activities: Non-specialised wholesale trade
Officers: Muhammad Abdulwahab Dastagir [1970] Director [American]

NCMT Holdings Limited
Incorporated: 10 July 2007 *Employees:* 114
Net Worth: £7,130,000 *Total Assets:* £33,940,000
Registered Office: Unit 1 Ferry Works, Summer Road, Thames Ditton, Surrey, KT7 0QJ
Activities: Activities of head offices
Officers: David Burley, Secretary; David Burley [1959] Director/CD; Laurence Howard Ireland [1961] Director/CD; Adrian Joseph Maughan [1956] Director/CD; Michael Roland Terry [1955] Director/CD

NCMT Limited
Incorporated: 6 March 1964 *Employees:* 114
Net Worth: £9,364,000 *Total Assets:* £35,459,000
Registered Office: Unit 1 Ferry Works, Summer Road, Thames Ditton, Surrey, KT7 0QJ
Activities: Agents involved in the sale of machinery, industrial equipment, ships and aircraft
Officers: David Burley, Secretary; David Burley [1959] Director; Laurence Howard Ireland [1961] Director; Adrian Joseph Maughan [1956] Director; Michael Roland Terry [1955] Director

NCQ Developments Limited
Incorporated: 3 November 2016
Net Worth: £3,876 *Total Assets:* £5,177,353
Registered Office: 3rd Floor, Sterling House, Langston Road, Loughton, Essex, IG10 3TS
Activities: Other business support service activities n.e.c.
Parent: Galliard Homes Limited
Officers: Allan William Porter, Secretary; David Edward Conway [1976] Director; Michael William Watson [1952] Architectural Director

ND1T Limited
Incorporated: 9 October 2012 *Employees:* 386
Net Worth Deficit: £44,311,156 *Total Assets:* £80,257,536
Registered Office: Palm Court, 4 Heron Square, Richmond, Surrey, TW9 1EW
Activities: Activities of other holding companies n.e.c.
Officers: Andrew David Gibbs, Secretary; Mr Graham James Bosher [1981] Director; Christopher Paul Britton [1957] Director; Fernando Chueca [1971] Director [Spanish]; Dr. Robert James Campbell Easton [1963] Director; Anthony Fletcher [1981] Director; Charlotte Lucy Elizabeth Lawrence [1984] Director; Alexander Ian Macpherson [1964] Director

ND2F Limited
Incorporated: 9 October 2012
Net Worth Deficit: £30,627,408 *Total Assets:* £77,814,816
Registered Office: Palm Court, 4 Heron Square, Richmond, Surrey, TW9 1EW
Activities: Activities of other holding companies n.e.c.
Parent: ND1T Limited
Officers: Anthony Fletcher [1981] Director; Andrew Gibbs [1978] Director

ND3M Limited
Incorporated: 9 October 2012
Net Worth: £2,612,103 *Total Assets:* £77,729,696
Registered Office: Palm Court, 4 Heron Square, Richmond, Surrey, TW9 1EW
Activities: Activities of other holding companies n.e.c.
Parent: ND2F Limited
Officers: Anthony Fletcher [1981] Director; Andrew Gibbs [1978] Director

NDEMIC Creations Ltd
Incorporated: 30 January 2012 *Employees:* 8
Net Worth: £14,858,374 *Total Assets:* £15,878,876
Registered Office: First Floor, Healthaid House, Marlborough Hill, Harrow, Middlesex, HA1 1UD
Activities: Business and domestic software development
Major Shareholder: Thomas James Vaughan
Officers: Rosanna Louise Vaughan [1986] Director; Thomas James Vaughan [1987] Director/Consultant

NDK Europe Limited
Incorporated: 29 June 1988 *Employees:* 29
Net Worth: £2,435,509 *Total Assets:* £16,436,566
Registered Office: River Reach, 31-35 High Street, Kingston upon Thames, Surrey, KT1 1LF
Activities: Wholesale of electronic and telecommunications equipment and parts
Parent: Nihon Dempa Kogyo Company Limited
Officers: Hideyuki Oikawa, Secretary; Yosuke Ito [1970] Director [Japanese]; Hideyuki Oikawa [1970] Managing Director [Japanese]

NEC (UK) Ltd.
Incorporated: 19 June 1973 *Employees:* 92
Net Worth Deficit: £32,641,000 *Total Assets:* £40,467,000
Registered Office: Athene Odyssey Business Park, West End Road, South Ruislip, Middlesex, HA4 6QE
Activities: Wholesale of computers, computer peripheral equipment and software
Parent: NEC Europe Ltd
Officers: Hiroshi Komazaki, Secretary; Chris Richard Jackson [1967] Director/IT Professional; Hiroshi Komazaki [1963] Director [Japanese]; Hironobu Kurosaki [1960] Director [Japanese]

NEC Capital (UK) PLC
Incorporated: 17 February 1987 *Employees:* 3
Net Worth: £9,959,000 *Total Assets:* £154,100,000
Registered Office: Athene Odyssey Business Park, West End Road, South Ruislip, Middlesex, HA4 6QE
Activities: Other service activities n.e.c.
Parent: NEC Corporation
Officers: Hiroshi Komazaki, Secretary; Hiroshi Komazaki [1963] Director/Senior Vice President, CFO [Japanese]; Hironobu Kurosaki [1960] Director/President & CEO [Japanese]; Koji Suwahara [1962] Director/General Manager of Finance Division of NEC Corporation [Japanese]

NEC Europe Ltd
Incorporated: 25 June 1993 *Employees:* 248
Net Worth: £18,872,468 *Total Assets:* £151,679,792
Registered Office: Athene Odyssey Business Park, West End Road, South Ruislip, Middlesex, HA4 6QE
Activities: Wholesale of electronic and telecommunications equipment and parts
Parent: NEC Corporation
Officers: Hiroshi Komazaki, Secretary; Yukio Hioki [1968] Director/Deputy General Manager, Corporate Strategy [Japanese]; Hironobu Kurosaki [1960] Director/President & CEO [Japanese]; Toshiya Matsuki [1960] Director/Executive Vice President, NEC Corporation [Japanese]; Sir Richard Francis Needham [1942] Director; Toshiyuki Otake [1963] Director/Deputy Corporate Controller [Japanese]

Necessity Supplies Limited
Incorporated: 15 April 1986 *Employees:* 21
Net Worth: £18,206,732 *Total Assets:* £23,210,598
Registered Office: Unit 4-5 Northolt Trading Estate, Belvue Road, Northolt, Middlesex, UB5 5QS
Activities: Wholesale of pharmaceutical goods
Officers: Vandana Wadhar, Secretary; Bharat Himatlal Mehta [1952] Director; Ketan Himatlal Mehta [1958] Director/Pharmacist

Needspace? Limited
Incorporated: 28 April 2005 *Employees:* 9
Net Worth: £12,409,716 *Total Assets:* £50,340,344
Registered Office: Wates House, Station Approach, Leatherhead, Surrey, KT22 7SW
Activities: Other letting and operating of own or leased real estate
Parent: Wates Group Limited
Officers: David Owen Allen [1972] Director/Chief Financial Officer; David Alexander Bowen [1967] Finance Director; Richard Maurice Trimming [1954] Director/Chartered Surveyor; Philip Michael Wainwright [1965] Director/Chief Financial Officer; Charles William Randag Wates [1976] Director

Neelkanth Safe Deposit Ltd
Incorporated: 17 July 2012 *Employees:* 5
Net Worth Deficit: £530,888 *Total Assets:* £6,906,889
Registered Office: Bank House, 335-337 Harrow Road, Wembley Triangle, Wembley, Middlesex, HA9 6BB
Activities: Other business support service activities n.e.c.
Shareholders: Kumar Vinodrai Pujara; Manisha Kumar Pujara
Officers: Harikrishna Jani, Secretary; Kumar Vinodrai Pujara [1967] Director [New Zealander]; Manisha Kumar Pujara [1969] Director [New Zealander]; Shivani Vipinchandra Sawjani [1960] Director/Payroll Administrator

Neilcott Construction Limited
Incorporated: 14 December 1973 *Employees:* 159
Net Worth: £9,357,819 *Total Assets:* £57,488,768
Registered Office: Excel House, Cray Avenue, Orpington, Kent, BR5 3ST
Activities: Development of building projects
Parent: Neilcott Construction Services Ltd
Officers: Malcolm Charles Elster, Secretary; Malcolm Charles Elster [1957] Director; Joseph Gissane [1956] Director [Irish]; Neil Eric Harrison [1960] Director; Robert Weatherston [1967] Divisional Construction Director

Neilcott Construction Services Limited
Incorporated: 29 April 1986
Net Worth: £462,640 *Total Assets:* £12,258,663
Registered Office: Excel House, Cray Avenue, Orpington, Kent, BR5 3ST
Activities: Activities of head offices
Parent: Neilcott Holdings Ltd
Officers: Malcolm Charles Elster, Secretary; Malcolm Charles Elster [1957] Managing Director; Joseph Gissane [1956] Director [Irish]; Neil Eric Harrison [1960] Director; Robert Weatherston [1967] Divisional Construction Director

Neilcott Group Holdings Limited
Incorporated: 29 November 2012
Net Worth: £3,375,000 *Total Assets:* £15,166,838
Registered Office: Excel House, Cray Avenue, Orpington, Kent, BR5 3ST
Activities: Activities of head offices
Shareholders: Tyrolese 751 Ltd; James Gerard O'Shea
Officers: Malcolm Charles Elster [1957] Director; James Gerard O'Shea [1961] Director [Irish]

Neilcott Holdings Limited
Incorporated: 6 May 1986
Net Worth: £700,975 *Total Assets:* £13,172,340
Registered Office: Excel House, Cray Avenue, Orpington, Kent, BR5 3ST
Activities: Activities of head offices
Parent: Neilcott Group Holdings Ltd
Officers: Malcolm Charles Elster, Secretary; Malcolm Charles Elster [1957] Director; Joseph Gissane [1956] Director [Irish]; Neil Eric Harrison [1960] Director; Robert Weatherston [1967] Divisional Construction Director

NeilMed Holding Company Limited
Incorporated: 23 June 2016 *Employees:* 18
Net Worth: £6,346,587 *Total Assets:* £11,773,630
Registered Office: 221 Kenton Lane, Kenton, Harrow, Middlesex, HA3 8RP
Activities: Wholesale of pharmaceutical goods
Major Shareholder: Ketan Chandrakant Mehta
Officers: Dr Ketan Chandrakant Mehta [1956] Director/Physician [American]; Nina Mehta [1961] Director [American]

Neilmed Limited
Incorporated: 30 June 2006 *Employees:* 8
Net Worth: £4,547,108 *Total Assets:* £6,988,272
Registered Office: 221 Kenton Lane, Kenton, Harrow, Middlesex, HA3 8RP
Activities: Wholesale of pharmaceutical goods
Officers: Dr Ketan Mehta [1956] Director/Physician [American]; Nina Mehta [1961] Director/Chairman [American]

Nella Holdings Limited
Incorporated: 22 February 2017 *Employees:* 158
Net Worth: £1,195,034 *Total Assets:* £10,737,274
Registered Office: Murray House, Murray Road, Orpington, Kent, BR5 3QY
Activities: Non-trading company
Shareholder: Mark Paul Peter Nella
Officers: Noemi Lucia Nella, Secretary; Caroline Frances Nella [1966] Director; Mario Franco Nella [1988] Operations Director; Mark Paul Peter Nella [1967] Director/Manufacturer; Noemi Lucia Nella [1993] Director; Sacha Nella [1990] Director/Sales Manager; Stefano Nella [1993] Director/Manager

Nellsar Limited
Incorporated: 6 July 1999 *Employees:* 712
Net Worth: £12,801,256 *Total Assets:* £44,493,512
Registered Office: 147a High Street, Waltham Cross, Herts, EN8 7AP
Activities: Other residential care activities n.e.c.
Shareholders: Arinesarajah Ragumoorthy; Jegathambikai Ragumoorthy
Officers: Jegathambikai Ragumoorthy, Secretary; Arinesarajah Ragumoorthy [1945] Director

Nelly Films (Christmas) Limited
Incorporated: 10 November 2016
Net Worth: £8 *Total Assets:* £7,018,021
Registered Office: 1 Brook Court, Blakeney Road, Beckenham, Kent, BR3 1HG
Activities: Motion picture production activities
Parent: Nelly Films Limited
Officers: Ian Robert Sharples [1966] Director/Producer; Simon Robert Williams [1982] Director

Nemo (UK) Holdco, Ltd.
Incorporated: 2 November 2015 *Employees:* 595
Net Worth Deficit: £51,749,000 *Total Assets:* £71,130,000
Registered Office: The Lodge, 92 Uxbridge Road, Harrow Weald, Middlesex, HA3 6DQ
Activities: Activities of other holding companies n.e.c.
Officers: Michael Stephan Haringman, Secretary; James Michael Chu [1958] Director/Managing Partner of Catterton Management Company [American]; Leonard Fluxman [1958] Director/President and Chief Executive Officer [American]; Marc Magliacano [1974] Director/Partner of Catterton Management Company [American]

Neogene Limited
Incorporated: 19 March 2015 *Employees:* 19
Net Worth: £3,354,609 *Total Assets:* £6,455,214
Registered Office: 14 Caxton Way, Watford, Herts, WD18 8UJ
Activities: Manufacture of paints, varnishes and similar coatings, mastics and sealants
Parent: Neogene Holdings Limited
Officers: David Kershaw, Secretary; Paul William Brown [1966] Director; David Jourdain Kershaw [1964] Director; Paul Jourdain Kershaw [1935] Director; Dave Seeley [1965] Operations Director; Graham Charles Webb [1963] Sales Director

Neopost Technologies Limited
Incorporated: 3 October 1963 *Employees:* 172
Net Worth: £10,885,000 *Total Assets:* £13,761,000
Registered Office: Oakwood Hill Industrial Estate, Oakwood Hill, Loughton, Essex, IG10 3TZ
Activities: Manufacture of office machinery and equipment (except computers and peripheral equipment)
Officers: Danny Westlake, Secretary/Accountant; Emmanuelle de Groote [1971] Director/Business Executive [French]; Jean Francois Labadie [1967] Group Supply Chain Director [French]; Thierry Le Jaoudour [1964] Director/Business Executive [French]; Danny Westlake [1965] Director/Accountant

Neptune Hotels Limited
Incorporated: 4 January 1999 *Employees:* 71
Net Worth: £3,112,066 *Total Assets:* £13,372,689
Registered Office: 1 Towers Place, Eton Street, Richmond, Surrey, TW9 1EG
Activities: Hotels and similar accommodation
Parent: China National Travel Service Group Corporation
Officers: Jameson Andrew Lamb, Secretary; Jameson Andrew Lamb [1972] Finance Director; Alex Edward Pritchard [1976] Director

Neptune Subsea IP Limited
Incorporated: 30 January 2017 *Employees:* 3
Net Worth: £2,838,344 *Total Assets:* £7,753,757
Registered Office: Bates House, Church Road, Harold Wood, Romford, Essex, RM3 0SD
Activities: Other telecommunications activities
Officers: Dr Stuart Robert Barnes [1953] Director/Chairman; Carl Michael Steve Harring [1976] Managing Director [Swedish]; Dr James George Mitchell [1981] Director/Investment Manager [Irish]

Ness Global Services Limited
Incorporated: 1 October 1998 *Employees:* 20
Net Worth: £348,145 *Total Assets:* £10,285,147
Registered Office: Squires House, 205a High Street, West Wickham, Kent, BR4 0PH
Activities: Other information technology service activities
Officers: Edward Galati [1967] Director/Chief Financial Officer [American]; Paul Lombardo [1965] Business Manager and Director [American]; Peter John Rogers [1953] Director/Business Development Consultant

Nestates Limited
Incorporated: 10 November 2015
Net Worth Deficit: £916,589 *Total Assets:* £10,346,541
Registered Office: Portland House, 69-71 Wembley Hill Road, Wembley, Middlesex, HA9 8BU
Activities: Other letting and operating of own or leased real estate
Parent: Solai Holdings Limited
Officers: Bhupendra Shantilal Kansagra, Secretary; Bhupendra Shantilal Kansagra [1956] Director; Ramesh Shantilal Kansagra [1950] Director

Neston Court Limited
Incorporated: 14 November 1983 *Employees:* 2
Net Worth: £826,730 *Total Assets:* £6,078,685
Registered Office: 167 Turners Hill, Cheshunt, Herts, EN8 9BH
Activities: Construction of other civil engineering projects n.e.c.
Parent: Dudley Properties Ltd
Officers: Katie Jane Dudley, Secretary/Designer; Christopher Sean Wickman Dudley [1968] Director/Consultant Engineer; Katie Jane Dudley [1970] Director/Designer

Net Pay (EUR) Limited
Incorporated: 29 December 2004 *Employees:* 2
Net Worth: £54,959 *Total Assets:* £35,109,772
Registered Office: 5 Elstree Gate, Elstree Way, Borehamwood, Herts, WD6 1JD
Activities: Information technology consultancy activities
Major Shareholder: Alon Elbaz
Officers: Alon Elbaz [1971] Director/Computer Consultant [Israeli]

NetApp UK Ltd
Incorporated: 6 December 1994 *Employees:* 325
Net Worth: £5,544,023 *Total Assets:* £69,980,512
Registered Office: Rivermead, Oxford Road, Uxbridge, Middlesex, UB9 4BF
Activities: Wholesale of computers, computer peripheral equipment and software
Parent: NetApp, Inc.
Officers: Stephen Peter Faulkner [1973] Director/International Field Operations Finance

Netherhall Gardens Ltd
Incorporated: 17 July 2014
Net Worth Deficit: £64,796 *Total Assets:* £37,621,308
Registered Office: Suite 2, Fountain House, 1a Elm Park, Stanmore, Middlesex, HA7 4AU
Activities: Development of building projects
Parent: Netherhall Gardens Hampstead Ltd
Officers: Robert Stephen Godfrey [1954] Director/Clothing Manufacturer; Tal Orly [1963] Director/Property Developer [Israeli]

Netmac Limited
Incorporated: 15 March 1989 *Employees:* 4
Net Worth: £2,279,335 *Total Assets:* £5,239,671
Registered Office: Evergreens, 15 Hall Road, Wallington, Surrey, SM6 0RT
Activities: Buying and selling of own real estate
Shareholders: Visva Nadesan; Shankari Nadesan
Officers: Shankari Nadesan, Secretary; Shankari Nadesan [1961] Director/Accountant; Visva Nadesan [1961] Director/Accountant

Network Homes Investments (Stockwell) Limited
Incorporated: 14 February 2007
Previous: Community Housing Development Ltd
Net Worth Deficit: £187,782 *Total Assets:* £11,853,693
Registered Office: Olympic Office Centre, 8 Fulton Road, Wembley, Middlesex, HA9 0NU
Activities: Buying and selling of own real estate
Officers: Tabitha Kassem, Secretary; Graham Gregg [1975] Director/Head of Accounting Services; Jennifer Ann Hodgkins [1956] Director/Head of Treasury; Colin James Mitchell [1958] Director/Head of Corporate Finance

Network Homes Investments Limited
Incorporated: 14 February 2007
Previous: Network Stadium Investments Limited
Net Worth: £66,928,128 *Total Assets:* £92,629,920
Registered Office: Olympic Office Centre, 8 Fulton Road, Wembley, Middlesex, HA9 0NU
Activities: Buying and selling of own real estate
Officers: Tabitha Kassem, Secretary; David Howard Gooch [1964] Executive Director of Development; Jonathan Michael Gooding [1953] Director/Chartered Surveyor; Graham Gregg [1975] Director/Head of Accounting Services; Jennifer Ann Hodgkins [1956] Director/Head of Treasury; Colin James Mitchell [1958] Director/Head of Corporate Finance

Network New Build Limited
Incorporated: 19 September 2000
Net Worth: £20,224 *Total Assets:* £22,708,172
Registered Office: Olympic Office Centre, 8 Fulton Road, Wembley, Middlesex, HA9 0NU
Activities: Other letting and operating of own or leased real estate
Officers: Tabitha Kassem, Secretary; Graham Gregg [1975] Director/Head of Accounting Services; Jennifer Ann Hodgkins [1956] Director/Head of Treasury; Colin James Mitchell [1958] Director/Head of Corporate Finance

Network Treasury Services Limited
Incorporated: 12 November 2007
Net Worth: £10,005,763 *Total Assets:* £506,721,056
Registered Office: Olympic Office Centre, 8 Fulton Road, Wembley, Middlesex, HA9 0NU
Activities: Financial intermediation not elsewhere classified
Officers: Tabitha Kassem, Secretary; Bernadette Sarah Conroy [1966] Director/Board Member; Helen Elizabeth Evans [1959] Director/Chief Executive Officer; Patricia Anne Turner [1956] Director/Housing Association Chief Operating Officer; Sean Allan West [1977] Director, Treasury [British/Australian]; Philip Williams [1966] Director/Banker

Neville UK PLC
Incorporated: 8 December 2000 *Employees:* 63
Net Worth: £6,154,406 *Total Assets:* £9,318,385
Registered Office: Unit 6 Viking Way, Erith, Kent, DA8 1EW
Activities: Wholesale of other intermediate products
Parent: Neville UK Trading Holdings Limited
Officers: John David Pompei, Secretary/Director; Andrew Jonathan Neville [1972] Director; Heather Maureen Neville [1938] Director; Ann Louise Pompei [1945] Director; John David Pompei [1946] Director

Neville UK Trading Holdings Limited
Incorporated: 16 July 2012 *Employees:* 63
Net Worth: £6,757,934 *Total Assets:* £10,216,238
Registered Office: Unit 6 Viking Way, Erith, Kent, DA8 1EW
Activities: Wholesale of china and glassware and cleaning materials
Shareholders: Ann Louise Pompei; Heather Maureen Neville
Officers: John David Pompei, Secretary; Heather Maureen Neville [1938] Director; Ann Louise Pompei [1945] Director; John David Pompei [1946] Director

New Demipower Limited
Incorporated: 24 May 2002 *Employees:* 1,385
Net Worth: £4,639,528 *Total Assets:* £37,636,804
Registered Office: Jubilee House, 7-9 The Oaks, Ruislip, Middlesex, HA4 7LF
Activities: Activities of head offices
Shareholders: Amirali Hassanali Moledina Janmohamed; Alim Amirali Janmohamed
Officers: Alim Amirali Janmohamed, Secretary; Alim Amirali Janmohamed [1981] Director; Amirali Hassanali Moledina Janmohamed [1952] Director

New England Seafood International Limited
Incorporated: 6 December 1990 *Employees:* 560
Net Worth: £14,991,000 *Total Assets:* £44,779,000
Registered Office: 48 Cox Lane, Chessington, Surrey, KT9 1TW
Activities: Processing and preserving of fish, crustaceans and molluscs
Shareholder: Michael Richard Colin Stroyan
Officers: Iain Murray Imray, Secretary; Daniel Thomas Aherne [1977] Managing Director; Andrew James McKinlay Crawford [1965] Director; Sophie Crawford [1969] Director; Geoffrey Dennis Eaton [1958] Director; Terence Henry Faulkner [1958] Director; Iain Murray Imray [1957] Director; James Robinson [1971] Sales Director; Johanna Louise Ropner [1963] Director/Part-Time Marketing Consultant; Catharine Stroyan [1963] Director; Michael Richard Colin Stroyan [1965] Director/Wholesale Fish Merchant

New Ladderswood LLP
Incorporated: 23 June 2011
Net Worth: £57,338,856 *Total Assets:* £61,847,616
Registered Office: Teresa Gavin House, Woodford Avenue, Woodford Green, Essex, IG8 8FA

New Landmark Investment Limited
Incorporated: 19 April 2013 *Employees:* 2
Net Worth: £999,644 *Total Assets:* £22,262,130
Registered Office: 72 Darlands Drive, Barnet, Herts, EN5 2DF
Activities: Other business support service activities n.e.c.
Major Shareholder: Peter Breier
Officers: Richard Derrick Bridges [1954] Director; Bradley Paul Kramer [1950] Director

New River Holdings Limited
Incorporated: 19 September 1950 *Employees:* 221
Net Worth: £21,697,232 *Total Assets:* £34,151,528
Registered Office: Riverside Place, 1-9 Lea Road, Waltham Abbey, Essex, EN9 1AS
Activities: Activities of distribution holding companies
Parent: Marchase Limited
Officers: Martin Stewart Earle, Secretary; Martin Stewart Earle [1946] Director/Manager; Matthew Richard Earle [1973] Managing Director; Charles William Valens Smith [1949] Director/Manager

The New Victoria Hospital Limited
Incorporated: 11 August 2006 *Employees:* 260
Net Worth Deficit: £29,835,000 *Total Assets:* £24,828,000
Registered Office: The New Victoria Hospital, 184 Coombe Lane West, Kingston upon Thames, Surrey, KT2 7EG
Activities: Hospital activities
Officers: Graham Arthur Ridgeway Ball [1950] Director; Mark James Curtis [1959] Director/Consultant Surgeon; John Alan Hamblin [1949] Director/Chartered Accountant; Catriona Ann MacKay [1963] Director/Executive Coach; Martin Anthony Matthews [1950] Director

New Way International Ltd
Incorporated: 3 July 2003 *Employees:* 41
Net Worth: £3,062,315 *Total Assets:* £17,938,606
Registered Office: Britannia House, Pier Road, Feltham, Middlesex, TW14 0TW
Activities: Wholesale of electronic and telecommunications equipment and parts
Major Shareholder: Mandeep Singh
Officers: Rupinder Singh, Secretary; Nigel Prince [1967] Director

Newacc (2014) Limited
Incorporated: 12 August 2014 *Employees:* 43
Net Worth: £3,205,715 *Total Assets:* £21,972,700
Registered Office: Belgrave House, 39-43 Monument Hill, Weybridge, Surrey, KT13 8RN
Activities: Other service activities n.e.c.
Parent: Newacc (2018) Limited
Officers: Phillip John Aird-Mash [1975] Director; Philip John Mathews [1966] Director

Newfield Information Technology Limited
Incorporated: 24 May 2000 *Employees:* 24
Net Worth: £5,780,199 *Total Assets:* £5,786,559
Registered Office: Riverview, Oxford Road, Uxbridge, Middlesex, UB8 1HS
Activities: Information technology consultancy activities
Parent: Xerox Limited
Officers: Nigel Ian Bainsfair [1968] Managing Director; Richard Stuart Pitceathly [1965] Director/Lawyer

Newham Family Dental Care Limited
Incorporated: 27 September 2006 *Employees:* 23
Net Worth: £8,589,969 *Total Assets:* £9,064,949
Registered Office: 141 Kings Avenue, Woodford Green, Essex, IG8 0JL
Activities: Dental practice activities
Shareholder: Mahendrakumar Rajnikant Patel
Officers: Nalini Patel, Secretary; Amish Patel [1980] Director/Dentist; Dr Mahendrakumar Rajnikant Patel [1949] Director/Dentist; Nalini Mahendrakumar Patel [1948] Director

Newhospitals (St Helens and Knowsley) Finance PLC
Incorporated: 2 November 2005
Net Worth: £50,000 *Total Assets:* £355,201,984
Registered Office: 8 White Oak Square, London Road, Swanley, Kent, BR8 7AG
Activities: Financial intermediation not elsewhere classified
Parent: Newhospitals (St Helens and Knowsley) Holdings Limited
Officers: David John Brooking [1967] Investment Director; Nicholas John Edward Crowther [1960] Director/Chartered Accountant; Michael Davis [1946] Director

Newhospitals (St Helens and Knowsley) Holdings Limited
Incorporated: 26 October 2005
Net Worth Deficit: £36,655,000 *Total Assets:* £327,828,992
Registered Office: 8 White Oak Square, London Road, Swanley, Kent, BR8 7AG
Activities: Activities of head offices
Shareholders: Innisfree Secondary Partners 1 LLP; Innisfree Secondary Partners 2 LLP
Officers: David John Brooking [1967] Investment Director; Nicholas John Edward Crowther [1960] Director/Chartered Accountant

Newhospitals (St Helens and Knowsley) Limited
Incorporated: 26 October 2005
Net Worth Deficit: £36,705,000 *Total Assets:* £327,828,992
Registered Office: 8 White Oak Square, London Road, Swanley, Kent, BR8 7AG
Activities: Hospital activities
Parent: Newhospitals (St Helens and Knowsley) Holdings Limited
Officers: David John Brooking [1967] Investment Director; Nicholas John Edward Crowther [1960] Director

Newincco 1270 Limited
Incorporated: 13 November 2013 *Employees:* 4
Net Worth: £61,679,296 *Total Assets:* £123,700,328
Registered Office: 3rd Floor, Premier House, Elstree Way, Borehamwood, Herts, WD6 1JH
Activities: Other business support service activities n.e.c.
Parent: Galene Bidco Limited
Officers: Emily Henrietta Gestetner [1967] Director; Harry Leon Landy [1978] Director; Stephen Bryan Wasserman [1984] Director; Danny Stephen Waters [1984] Director

W.R.Newland & Sons Limited
Incorporated: 3 October 1962 *Employees:* 12
Net Worth: £9,731,887 *Total Assets:* £10,122,471
Registered Office: 129 Croydon Road, Caterham, Surrey, CR3 6PE
Activities: Construction of domestic buildings
Officers: Stephen Derek Newland, Secretary; Brian Charles Newland [1945] Director/Builder; James William Newland [1970] Director/Electrician; Nigel Brian Newland [1968] Director/Carpenter; Stephen Derek Newland [1957] Director/Builder

Newland House School Trust Limited
Incorporated: 12 March 1971 *Employees:* 84
Net Worth: £7,040,331 *Total Assets:* £12,030,060
Registered Office: Newland House School, Waldegrave Park, Twickenham, Middlesex, TW1 4TQ
Activities: Primary education
Officers: Geoff Huw Arthur, Secretary; Matthew Duncan Battle [1965] Director/Property Consultant; Richard Lewis Burden [1959] IT Programme Director; Belinda Canham [1951] Director/Headmistress; Dr Henry Howard Cook [1956] Director/Engineering Consultant; Andrew Gumpert [1963] Director/Solicitor; Julia Louise Higgins [1954] Director/Administrator; Adrian Warwick Hughes QC [1955] Director/QC; Jane Teresa Lunnon [1969] Director/Headmistress; Henry Kilpatrick Mann [1960] Director/Chartered Accountant; Dee Suzanne Masters [1981] Director/Barrister; David Howard Ridgeon [1952] Director/Chartered Accountant; James Michael Aitken Ross [1974] Director/Teacher

Newman Street Hotel Limited
Incorporated: 17 February 2016
Net Worth: £48,262,764 *Total Assets:* £48,265,764
Registered Office: 1st Floor, Woodgate Studios, 2-8 Games Road, Cockfosters, Barnet, Herts, EN4 9HN
Activities: Activities of head offices
Parent: Mouskos Capital Limited
Officers: Generaldina Mouskos, Secretary; Christopher Mouskos [1961] Director; Generaldina Mouskos [1936] Director; John Michael Mouskos [1964] Director

Newmarket Holidays Limited
Incorporated: 31 March 1988
Previous: Newmarket Air Holidays Limited
Net Worth: £5,553,363 *Total Assets:* £20,701,376
Registered Office: Cantium House, Railway Approach, Wallington, Surrey, SM6 0BP
Activities: Tour operator activities
Parent: Newmarket Promotions Limited
Officers: Simon Charles Hibbs, Secretary/Director; Toni Paul Frei [1956] Director; Jeremy Charles Griffin [1954] Director; Simon Charles Hibbs [1956] Director

Newmarket Promotions Limited
Incorporated: 22 March 1983 *Employees:* 236
Net Worth: £11,712,941 *Total Assets:* £28,809,550
Registered Office: Cantium House, Railway Approach, Wallington, Surrey, SM6 0BP
Activities: Tour operator activities
Shareholders: Toni Paul Frei; Jeremy Charles Griffin
Officers: Simon Charles Hibbs, Secretary/Director; Toni Paul Frei [1956] Director; Jeremy Charles Griffin [1954] Director; Simon Charles Hibbs [1956] Director; Alan James McWalter [1953] Director; Marc Thomas Raymond Vincent [1969] Finance Director

Newmarket Transport Limited
Incorporated: 14 December 1995
Net Worth: £158,283 *Total Assets:* £5,590,001
Registered Office: Cantium House, Railway Approach, Wallington, Surrey, SM6 0BP
Activities: Other passenger land transport
Parent: Newmarket Holidays Limited
Officers: Simon Charles Hibbs, Secretary/Director; Toni Paul Frei [1956] Director; Jeremy Charles Griffin [1954] Director; Simon Charles Hibbs [1956] Director

Newmarston Ltd
Incorporated: 7 August 2001
Net Worth: £56,238,772 *Total Assets:* £83,385,696
Registered Office: 41 Walsingham Road, Enfield, Middlesex, EN2 6EY
Activities: Other business support service activities n.e.c.
Officers: David Newirth, Secretary; Jacob Adler [1969] Director/Property Manager; Refoel Halpern [1971] Director/Secretary; David Neuwirth [1970] Director; Sir Weis [1981] Director

Newmir Limited
Incorporated: 8 October 1986
Net Worth: £5,692,000 *Total Assets:* £5,714,000
Registered Office: Unit 1 Waverley Business Park, Hailsham Drive, Harrow, Middlesex, HA1 4TR
Activities: Activities of head offices
Parent: Test Equipment Asset Management Ltd
Officers: Nigel Brown [1957] Director; John Joseph Hafferty [1956] Director/Chief Financial Officer [American]

Newport Group (Holdings) Limited
Incorporated: 9 July 2003 *Employees:* 27
Net Worth: £4,759,007 *Total Assets:* £23,408,532
Registered Office: 2nd Floor, Spencer House, 23 Sheen Road, Richmond, Surrey, TW9 1BN
Activities: Activities of head offices
Major Shareholder: Rajesh Kumar Patel
Officers: Rajesh Kumar Patel [1970] Managing Director

Newport Industries Limited
Incorporated: 22 July 1997 *Employees:* 21
Net Worth: £3,669,871 *Total Assets:* £19,454,540
Registered Office: 2nd Floor, Spencer House, 23 Sheen Road, Richmond, Surrey, TW9 1BN
Activities: Agents involved in the sale of fuels, ores, metals and industrial chemicals
Parent: Newport Group (Holdings) Limited
Officers: Rajesh Kumar Patel [1970] Managing Director; Sonal Patel [1972] Director

Newport School Solutions (Holdings) Limited
Incorporated: 3 October 2003
Net Worth Deficit: £3,126,000 *Total Assets:* £14,298,000
Registered Office: Astral House, Imperial Way, Watford, Herts, WD24 4WW
Activities: Activities of head offices
Parent: Infrastructure Investments Holdings Limited
Officers: Ian Hudson, Secretary; David Wyn Davies [1968] Director/Accountant; Hannah Holman [1980] Director

Newport School Solutions Limited
Incorporated: 2 April 2002
Net Worth Deficit: £3,126,000 *Total Assets:* £14,298,000
Registered Office: Astral House, Imperial Way, Watford, Herts, WD24 4WW
Activities: Activities of head offices
Parent: Newport School Solutions (Holdings) Limited
Officers: Ian Hudson, Secretary; David Wyn Davies [1968] Director/Accountant; Hannah Holman [1980] Director

Newschools (Leyton) Limited
Incorporated: 29 November 1999
Net Worth: £1,207,000 *Total Assets:* £10,445,000
Registered Office: 8 White Oak Square, London Road, Swanley, Kent, BR8 7AG
Activities: Combined facilities support activities
Parent: Newschools (Leyton) Holdings Limited
Officers: Sheila Jamieson Clark [1973] Director; Benjamin Christopher Jacob Dean [1979] Director/Investment Manager

Newschools (Merton) Limited
Incorporated: 27 June 2002
Net Worth: £1,985,000 *Total Assets:* £39,979,000
Registered Office: 8 White Oak Square, London Road, Swanley, Kent, BR8 7AG
Activities: Combined facilities support activities
Parent: Newschools (Merton) Holdings Limited
Officers: Sheila Jamieson Clark [1973] Director; Benjamin Christopher Jacob Dean [1979] Director/Investment Manager

Newschools (Swanscombe) Limited
Incorporated: 23 February 2001
Net Worth: £743,000 *Total Assets:* £11,997,000
Registered Office: 8 White Oak Square, London Road, Swanley, Kent, BR8 7AG
Activities: Combined facilities support activities
Parent: Newschools (Swanscombe) Holdings Limited
Officers: Sheila Jamieson Clark [1973] Director; Benjamin Christopher Jacob Dean [1979] Director/Investment Manager

Newserge Limited
Incorporated: 8 January 2013
Net Worth: £4,076,000 *Total Assets:* £7,373,000
Registered Office: Grant Way, Isleworth, Middlesex, TW7 5QD
Activities: Other service activities n.e.c.
Parent: Ciel Bleu 6 Limited
Officers: Christopher Jon Taylor, Secretary; Karl Holmes [1973] Director/Finance Professional; Colin Robert Jones [1964] Director; Christopher Jon Taylor [1971] Director/Company Secretary

Newship Group Limited
Incorporated: 3 August 1978 *Employees:* 601
Net Worth: £37,125,000 *Total Assets:* £109,240,000
Registered Office: Fernside Place, 179 Queens Road, Weybridge, Surrey, KT13 0AH
Activities: Activities of head offices
Major Shareholder: John Watson Newman
Officers: Andrew St Clair Harrison, Secretary/Accountant; Jeremy David Clarkson [1961] Director; Sarah Elizabeth Leach [1975] Director; John Watson Newman [1945] Director/Accountant; Lesley Jean Newman [1948] Director; Richard John Newman [1979] Director/Accountant; Amanda Jane Parker [1974] Director/Accounts Executive

Newship Limited
Incorporated: 31 January 2001 *Employees:* 599
Net Worth: £45,223,000 *Total Assets:* £111,119,000
Registered Office: Fernside Place, 179 Queens Road, Weybridge, Surrey, KT13 0AH
Activities: Activities of head offices
Parent: Newship Group Limited
Officers: Andrew Paul Bale, Secretary/Director; Andrew Paul Bale [1957] Director; Jeremy David Clarkson [1961] Director/Accountant; Stephen Edwin John Compson [1954] Director; John Watson Newman [1945] Director/Chartered Accountant; Richard John Newman [1979] Director/Accountant; David Anthony Thornton [1971] Finance Director

Newship Products Group Limited
Incorporated: 26 September 1977 *Employees:* 207
Net Worth: £10,062,000 *Total Assets:* £20,071,000
Registered Office: Fernside Place, 179 Queens Road, Weybridge, Surrey, KT13 0AH
Activities: Activities of head offices
Shareholder: John Watson Newman
Officers: Andrew St Clair Harrison, Secretary/Accountant; Jeremy David Clarkson [1961] Director; Sarah Elizabeth Leach [1975] Director; John Watson Newman [1945] Director/Accountant; Lesley Jean Newman [1948] Director; Richard John Newman [1979] Director; David Anthony Thornton [1971] Finance Director

Newstone International Limited
Incorporated: 17 December 1996 *Employees:* 2
Net Worth: £1,875,936 *Total Assets:* £6,768,214
Registered Office: c/o M Jaffer & Co, Stamore BIC, Stanmore Place, Howard Road, Stanmore, Middlesex, HA7 1GB
Activities: Other service activities n.e.c.
Shareholders: Cara Simone Kliman; Deborah Joan Wides
Officers: Cara Simone Kliman, Secretary; Deborah Joan Wides [1949] Director

Nexen Petroleum U.K. Holdings Limited
Incorporated: 14 October 2004
Net Worth: £314,124,288 *Total Assets:* £315,630,880
Registered Office: Prospect House, 97 Oxford Road, Uxbridge, Middlesex, UB8 1LU
Activities: Other business support service activities n.e.c.
Parent: CNOOC UK Limited
Officers: Jamie David Doyle, Secretary; Jamie David Doyle [1975] Director; Ray Christopher John Riddoch [1961] Managing Director; Brent Christian Tilford [1978] Finance Director

Nextonline Limited
Incorporated: 13 April 2000
Net Worth: £21,201,784 *Total Assets:* £24,053,180
Registered Office: Compass House, Guildford Street, Chertsey, Surrey, KT16 9BQ
Activities: Non-trading company
Parent: Compass Overseas Holdings No.2 Limited
Officers: Sarah Jane Sergeant [1973] Director/Accountant

Nexus Education Schools Trust
Incorporated: 29 October 2013 *Employees:* 351
Previous: Farnborough Primary School
Net Worth: £61,906,000 *Total Assets:* £65,345,000
Registered Office: Worsley Bridge Primary School, Brackley Road, Beckenham, Kent, BR3 1RF
Activities: Primary education
Officers: Samantha Jane Dossetter, Secretary; Paul Martin Chandler [1947] Director/Retired; Paula Ann Farrow [1966] Director/Headteacher; Naomi Ann Kimber [1956] Director/Retired; Jennifer Ann Millins [1979] Director/Solicitor; Roger Parks [1955] Director/Management Consultant; David Raymond Stacey [1953] Director/Marketing Consultant; Deepti Townsend [1963] Director/Chartered Accountant; Alison Youd [1960] Director/University Lecturer

NFAG Limited
Incorporated: 6 November 2006
Net Worth: £5,803,000 *Total Assets:* £60,975,000
Registered Office: Frays Court, 71 Cowley Road, Uxbridge, Middlesex, UB8 2AE
Activities: Other social work activities without accommodation n.e.c.
Parent: NFAH Limited
Officers: Helen Elizabeth Lecky, Secretary; Antony Vincent Holt [1959] Director/Chartered Accountant; Isabella Mary Hutchison [1956] Managing Director; Jean-Luc Emmanuel Janet [1970] Director/Chief Financial Officer [French]; David Jon Leatherbarrow [1969] Director/Group Chief Executive Officer

NFAH Limited
Incorporated: 6 November 2006
Net Worth: £3,627,000 *Total Assets:* £9,714,000
Registered Office: Frays Court, 71 Cowley Road, Uxbridge, Middlesex, UB8 2AE
Activities: Other social work activities without accommodation n.e.c.
Parent: Belton Associates Limited
Officers: Helen Elizabeth Lecky, Secretary; Antony Vincent Holt [1959] Director/Chartered Accountant; Isabella Mary Hutchison [1956] Managing Director; Jean-Luc Emmanuel Janet [1970] Director [French]; David Jon Leatherbarrow [1969] Director/Group Chief Executive Officer

NFAP Limited
Incorporated: 4 March 2009
Net Worth Deficit: £2,327,000 *Total Assets:* £19,188,000
Registered Office: Frays Court, 71 Cowley Road, Uxbridge, Middlesex, UB8 2AE
Activities: Other social work activities without accommodation n.e.c.
Parent: NFA Partnerships Limited
Officers: Helen Elizabeth Lecky, Secretary; Antony Vincent Holt [1959] Director/Chartered Accountant; Isabella Mary Hutchison [1956] Managing Director; Jean-Luc Emmanuel Janet [1970] Director [French]; David Jon Leatherbarrow [1969] Director/Group Chief Executive Officer

Anthony Nicholas (UK) Limited
Incorporated: 5 July 2007
Net Worth: £16,890,974 *Total Assets:* £58,186,260
Registered Office: 3rd Floor, Premier House, Elstree Way, Borehamwood, Herts, WD6 1JH
Activities: Activities of head offices
Officers: Noel Coyle [1962] Director [Irish]; Mark Naughton-Rumbo [1960] Director; Tony Obernik [1943] Director [Irish]

Nicholls & Clarke Glass Limited
Incorporated: 13 April 1938 *Employees:* 154
Net Worth: £5,154,958 *Total Assets:* £9,004,226
Registered Office: 41-51 Freshwater Road, Chadwell Heath, Romford, Essex, RM8 1SP
Activities: Other manufacturing n.e.c.
Parent: Nicholls & Clarke Limited
Officers: Geraint David Cooper, Secretary; Geraint David Cooper [1958] Director/Accountant; David Ian Forbes [1965] Director; Kenneth Stuart Alexander Forbes [1937] Director; Stephen Andrew Forbes [1963] Director

Nicholls & Clarke Limited
Incorporated: 18 July 1900 *Employees:* 568
Net Worth: £41,292,204 *Total Assets:* £51,268,684
Registered Office: 41-51 Freshwater Road, Chadwell Heath, Romford, Essex, RM8 1SP
Activities: Activities of head offices
Officers: Geraint David Cooper, Secretary; Geraint David Cooper [1958] Director/Accountant; David Ian Forbes [1965] Director; Kenneth Stuart Alexander Forbes [1937] Director; Stephen Andrew Forbes [1963] Director; Gary Kenneth Gingell [1968] Director; Richard John Hill [1971] Director

Nicon Developments Limited
Incorporated: 8 February 1967
Net Worth: £1,793,990 *Total Assets:* £6,612,531
Registered Office: Nicon House, 45 Silver Street, Enfield, Middlesex, EN1 3EF
Activities: Construction of commercial buildings
Shareholders: Alan Hugh Nicholas; Andrew Calder Nicholas; Robert James Nicholas
Officers: Andrew Calder Nicholas, Secretary; Alan Hugh Nicholas [1929] Director; Andrew Calder Nicholas [1955] Director; Robert James Nicholas [1962] Director

Niemans Holdings Limited
Incorporated: 25 June 2002
Net Worth: £3,467,953 *Total Assets:* £7,538,275
Registered Office: 5 Theobald Court, Theobald Street, Elstree, Herts, WD6 4RN
Activities: Dispensing chemist in specialised stores
Officers: Rohit Dwarkadas Kotecha, Secretary; Rohit Dwarkadas Kotecha [1955] Director

Florence Nightingale Aid in Sickness Trust
Incorporated: 30 May 2014
Net Worth: £11,774,694 *Total Assets:* £11,793,590
Registered Office: Room F35, Community House, South Street, Bromley, Kent, BR1 1RH
Activities: Other business support service activities n.e.c.
Officers: Ann Elizabeth Griffiths, Secretary; Lady Tessa Suzanne Mary Brewer [1950] Director; Lady Katharine Elizabeth Brooke [1964] Director; Nicola Joanna Brooksbank [1953] Director/Bookkeeper; Dr Karin Margaret Englehart [1941] Director/HM Dept Coroner Surrey; Peter William Fane [1939] Director; Flora Hood [1959] Director; Fiona Charlotte Hughes [1959] Director; Charlotte Ann Loyd [1946] Director/Retired Charity Manager; Michael Henry Parker [1955] Director/Tour Operator; Helen Margaret Raikes [1955] Director; Suzy Richardson [1963] Director/Physiotherapist

Nikon UK Limited
Incorporated: 17 September 1979 *Employees:* 124
Net Worth: £19,801,028 *Total Assets:* £36,741,208
Registered Office: Nikon House, 380 Richmond Road, Kingston upon Thames, Surrey, KT2 5PR
Activities: Wholesale of household goods (other than musical instruments) n.e.c
Parent: Nikon Holdings Europe B.V.
Officers: Toru Iwaoka [1958] Director [Japanese]; Takaharu Sasaoka [1971] Director/President Nikon Instruments Europe BV [Japanese]; John Kevin Walshe [1965] Director

Nine Heathrow Ventures Limited
Incorporated: 11 December 2014 *Employees:* 5
Net Worth Deficit: £1,943,331 *Total Assets:* £19,260,404
Registered Office: Melton House, 65-67 Clarendon Road, Watford, Herts, WD17 1DS
Activities: Development of building projects
Parent: Chadha Capital Investments Limited
Officers: Gursharan Singh Chadha [1960] Director; Vivek Chadha [1988] Director

Nine Hospitality 3 Ltd
Incorporated: 9 January 2014 *Employees:* 29
Net Worth: £272,790 *Total Assets:* £5,618,570
Registered Office: Melton House, 65-67 Clarendon Road, Watford, Herts, WD17 1DS
Activities: Management of real estate on a fee or contract basis
Parent: Nine Ventures Limited
Officers: Jasbir Kaur Chadha [1962] Director; Vivek Singh Chadha [1988] Director

Nine Hotel Investments Limited
Incorporated: 1 July 2015 *Employees:* 57
Net Worth: £653,258 *Total Assets:* £5,094,129
Registered Office: 65-67 Clarendon Road, Watford, Herts, WD17 1DS
Activities: Hotels and similar accommodation
Shareholders: R & R Asset Management Limited; Vivek Chadha
Officers: Vivek Singh Chadha [1988] Director

Nine Hotel Ventures Limited
Incorporated: 22 October 2014 *Employees:* 2
Net Worth: £1,183,999 *Total Assets:* £5,705,190
Registered Office: Melton House, 65-67 Clarendon Road, Watford, Herts, WD17 1DS
Activities: Buying and selling of own real estate
Shareholders: Gursharan Singh Chadha; Vivek Chadha; R & R Asset Management Limited
Officers: Gursharan Singh Chadha [1960] Director; Vivek Singh Chadha [1988] Director

Nine Reading Hotel Limited
Incorporated: 9 November 2016 *Employees:* 28
Net Worth: £230,298 *Total Assets:* £11,058,695
Registered Office: 65-67 Clarendon Road, Watford, Herts, WD17 1DS
Activities: Hotels and similar accommodation
Parent: Chadha Capital Investments Limited
Officers: Vivek Singh Chadha [1988] Director

Nippon Express (U.K.) Limited
Incorporated: 11 December 1980 *Employees:* 288
Net Worth: £8,518,215 *Total Assets:* £30,495,964
Registered Office: Heathrow 360, 2 Millington Road, Hayes, Middlesex, UB3 4AZ
Activities: Other transportation support activities
Officers: Toshinori Sakai [1961] Director [Japanese]

Nissan Motor (GB) Limited
Incorporated: 21 June 1990 *Employees:* 196
Net Worth: £183,110,000 *Total Assets:* £767,649,024
Registered Office: The Rivers Office Park, Denham Way, Maple Cross, Rickmansworth, Herts, WD3 9YS
Activities: Sale of new cars and light motor vehicles
Parent: Nissan Holdings (UK) Limited
Officers: Steven Neil Tiffin, Secretary; Laurent Franck Christian David [1971] Director/Senior Vice President - Administration and Finance [French]; Gareth John Main [1967] Director/General Manager; Kenneth Alexander Ramirez [1968] Director [American]; Alan David Tennant [1954] Director

Nissin (U.K.) Limited
Incorporated: 6 October 1983 *Employees:* 176
Net Worth: £8,019,000 *Total Assets:* £14,769,000
Registered Office: Unit 5 Horton Industrial Park, Horton Road, West Drayton, Middlesex, UB7 8JD
Activities: Other transportation support activities
Parent: Nissin Corporation
Officers: Kiyoshi Kamata [1956] Managing Director [Japanese]; Noboru Mizutani [1961] Director/EU Sales Executive [Japanese]; Yoshihide Sakamoto [1967] Managing Director [Japanese]; Tetsuo Sakurai [1961] Director/General Manager [Japanese]

NK Image Limited
Incorporated: 3 September 1997 *Employees:* 6
Net Worth: £5,201,690 *Total Assets:* £6,958,479
Registered Office: 16 Arlington Road, Richmond, Surrey, TW10 7BY
Activities: Other specialist photography
Shareholders: Charlotte Knight; Nicholas David Gordon Knight
Officers: Charlotte Knight, Secretary/Photographic Agent; Charlotte Knight [1965] Director/Photographic Agent

NNR Global Logistics UK Limited
Incorporated: 7 November 1991 *Employees:* 112
Net Worth: £8,295,593 *Total Assets:* £15,637,087
Registered Office: Nnr House, Stanwell Road, Feltham, Middlesex, TW14 8NG
Activities: Freight transport by road
Parent: Nishi Nippon Railroad Co
Officers: Apputhurai Chandrakumar, Secretary; Hiroki Anai [1964] Managing Director [Japanese]; Apputhurai Chandrakumar [1967] Director; Lee Anthony Griffiths [1969] Director; Shinji Kitamura [1959] Director [Japanese]

Noahs Ark Chemicals Limited
Incorporated: 19 June 2001 *Employees:* 10
Net Worth: £562,203 *Total Assets:* £9,640,393
Registered Office: 2nd Floor Office, 253-269 High Road, Woodford Green, Essex, IG8 9FB
Activities: Wholesale of chemical products
Major Shareholder: Bharat Bhardwaj
Officers: Rashmi Bhardwaj, Secretary/Chartered Accountant; Dr Bharat Bhardwaj [1968] Director/Chemical Engineer; Rashmi Bhardwaj [1961] Director/Chartered Accountant

Noble Gift Packaging Limited
Incorporated: 26 June 1992 *Employees:* 42
Net Worth: £5,065,652 *Total Assets:* £11,711,019
Registered Office: 73 Lockfield Avenue, Enfield, Middlesex, EN3 7QL
Activities: Other business support service activities n.e.c.
Shareholders: David Stobiecki; Samuel Herzog
Officers: Miriam Stobiecki, Secretary; David Stobiecki [1964] Director/Sales; Peter Weiner [1947] Director/Accountant [Canadian]

Nomad Foods BondCo PLC
Incorporated: 19 June 2014
Previous: Iglo Foods BondCo PLC
Net Worth: £2,765,430 *Total Assets:* £621,933,056
Registered Office: 1 New Square, Bedfont Lakes Business Park, Feltham, Middlesex, TW14 8HA
Activities: Other business support service activities n.e.c.
Parent: Nomad Foods Europe Midco Limited
Officers: Johanna Maria Van Kruijsbergen, Secretary; Stefan Descheemaeker [1960] Director [Belgian]; Johanna Maria Van Kruijsbergen [1961] Director/General Counsel [Dutch]; Samy Rene Zekhout [1962] Director/Chief Financial Officer [French]

Nomad Foods Europe Finco Limited
Incorporated: 18 July 2006
Previous: Iglo Foods Finco Limited
Net Worth: £15,984,400 *Total Assets:* £1,585,529,856
Registered Office: 1 New Square, Bedfont Lakes Business Park, Feltham, Middlesex, TW14 8HA
Activities: Non-trading company
Parent: Nomad Foods Europe Holdco Limited
Officers: Stefan Descheemaeker [1960] Director [Belgian]; Samy Rene Zekhout [1962] Director/Chief Financial Officer [French]

Nomad Foods Europe Holdco Limited
Incorporated: 18 July 2006
Previous: Iglo Foods Holdco Limited
Net Worth: £126,698,944 *Total Assets:* £1,348,299,264
Registered Office: 1 New Square, Bedfont Lakes Business Park, Feltham, Middlesex, TW14 8HA
Activities: Non-trading company
Parent: Nomad Foods Europe Holdings Limited
Officers: Stefan Descheemaeker [1960] Director [Belgian]; Samy Rene Zekhout [1962] Director/Chief Financial Officer [French]

Nomad Foods Europe Holdings Limited
Incorporated: 18 July 2006
Previous: Iglo Foods Holdings Limited
Net Worth: £394,835,936 *Total Assets:* £394,835,936
Registered Office: 1 New Square, Bedfont Lakes Business Park, Feltham, Middlesex, TW14 8HA
Activities: Other business support service activities n.e.c.
Shareholders: Nomad Foods Limited; Nomad Foods Limited
Officers: Stefan Descheemaeker [1960] Director [Belgian]; Samy Rene Zekhout [1962] Director/Chief Financial Officer [French]

Nomad Foods Europe Limited
Incorporated: 18 July 2006 *Employees:* 196
Previous: Iglo Foods Group Limited
Net Worth: £504,436,960 *Total Assets:* £2,627,912,960
Registered Office: 1 New Square, Bedfont Lakes Business Park, Feltham, Middlesex, TW14 8HA
Activities: Manufacture of other food products n.e.c.
Parent: Nomad Foods Europe Midco Limited
Officers: Stefan Descheemaeker [1960] Director [Belgian]; Jason Musk [1971] Director; Sarah Pollard [1974] Finance Director; Samy Rene Zekhout [1962] Director/Chief Financial Officer [French]

Nomad Foods Europe Midco Limited
Incorporated: 18 July 2006
Previous: Iglo Foods Midco Limited
Net Worth: £742,139,136 *Total Assets:* £2,808,313,600
Registered Office: 1 New Square, Bedfont Lakes Business Park, Feltham, Middlesex, TW14 8HA
Activities: Non-trading company
Parent: Nomad Foods Europe Finco Limited
Officers: Stefan Descheemaeker [1960] Director [Belgian]; Jason Musk [1971] Director; Samy Rene Zekhout [1962] Director/Chief Financial Officer [French]

Noodle Properties Limited
Incorporated: 2 March 2015 *Employees:* 2
Net Worth: £461,751 *Total Assets:* £9,237,281
Registered Office: 28 Watersfield Way, Edgware, Middlesex, HA8 6RZ
Activities: Other letting and operating of own or leased real estate
Officers: Adam Kaye [1968] Director; Samantha Sanson [1970] Director

Noon Products Limited
Incorporated: 17 September 1987 *Employees:* 1,927
Net Worth: £58,443,284 *Total Assets:* £224,222,848
Registered Office: Thorpe Lea Manor, Thorpe Lea Road, Egham, Surrey, TW20 8HY
Activities: Other processing and preserving of fruit and vegetables
Parent: Noon Group Limited
Officers: Ronan Deasy, Secretary; Ronan Deasy [1964] Director/Accountant [Irish]; Trevor James Horan [1972] EMEA Country Compliance Director [Irish]; Marguerite Larkin [1971] Director/Chief Financial Officer [Irish]

Nordic Properties Limited
Incorporated: 19 August 2015 *Employees:* 3
Net Worth Deficit: £405,288 *Total Assets:* £7,440,993
Registered Office: Unit 4, 8 Walmgate Road, Perivale, Greenford, Middlesex, UB6 7LH
Activities: Other letting and operating of own or leased real estate
Major Shareholder: Kristian Sibast
Officers: Glenn Elliott [1972] Director; Kristian Sibast [1979] Director [Danish]

Norfolk Capital Group Limited
Incorporated: 4 July 1946
Net Worth: £18,913,000 *Total Assets:* £18,913,000
Registered Office: Queens Court, 9-17 Eastern Road, Romford, Essex, RM1 3NG
Activities: Non-trading company
Parent: BPH Finance Number 1 Limited
Officers: Jonathan Patrick Braidley [1965] Director/Investment Professional; Christopher Andre Kula [1983] Director/Chartered Accountant [German/Canadian]

Norfolk Capital Hotels Limited
Incorporated: 6 October 1927 *Employees:* 14
Net Worth: £10,648,000 *Total Assets:* £10,649,000
Registered Office: Queens Court, 9-17 Eastern Road, Romford, Essex, RM1 3NG
Activities: Hotels and similar accommodation
Parent: Norfolk Capital Group Limited
Officers: Jonathan Patrick Braidley [1965] Director/Investment Professional; Christopher Andre Kula [1983] Director/Chartered Accountant [German/Canadian]

Norgine Pharmaceuticals Limited
Incorporated: 13 March 1998 *Employees:* 63
Net Worth: £8,854,000 *Total Assets:* £16,059,000
Registered Office: Norgine House, Widewater Place, Moorhall Road, Harefield, Uxbridge, Middlesex, UB9 6NS
Activities: Wholesale of pharmaceutical goods
Officers: Alison Philamin Moses, Secretary; Christopher William Bath [1974] Director/Chief Financial Officer; Andy Crichton [1970] Director/General Manager UK & Ireland; Jeremy John Cuffe [1966] Director/General Manager UK; Peter Martin [1956] Director/Chief Operating Officer; Kenneth Eric Scrimgeour [1960] Director/Chief Commercial Officer

Normandy Court Development Limited
Incorporated: 23 June 2016
Net Worth: £135,415 *Total Assets:* £5,687,711
Registered Office: 5 Holmesdale Road, Teddington, Middlesex, TW11 9LJ
Activities: Buying and selling of own real estate
Shareholders: Wessex Green Developments Limited; Westmede Properties Limited
Officers: Jonathan Peter Lynch [1967] Director; Martin John Lynch [1959] Director

Norpap Property (Telford) Ltd
Incorporated: 31 July 2015
Net Worth: £188,488 *Total Assets:* £9,556,848
Registered Office: 4 Warner House, Bessborough Road, Harrovian Business Village, Harrow, Middlesex, HA1 3EX
Activities: Other letting and operating of own or leased real estate
Shareholder: Paul Fecher
Officers: Paul King, Secretary; Adam Scott Fecher [1974] Director; Marc Darren Fecher [1971] Director; Paul Fecher [1946] Director; Paul Edward King [1974] Director/Accountant

Norsette Investment Co. Limited
Incorporated: 27 November 1964 *Employees:* 8
Net Worth: £7,055,193 *Total Assets:* £8,420,374
Registered Office: 436 Hook Road, Chessington, Surrey, KT9 1LY
Activities: Other letting and operating of own or leased real estate
Parent: Brockett Investment Co Ltd
Officers: Ghiselaine Cavaree, Secretary; Sarah Ann Perdita Dawkins [1960] Director; Paula Lucia GAssistanton [1955] Director/Equestrian Management; Kelsey Sharron Marshall [1961] Director; Helena Claire Massow [1952] Director; Ann Leslie Morris [1933] Director; Gareth Leslie Ransom [1962] Director/Building Manager; Janys Wendy Ransom [1964] Director; Richard Leslie Martin Wohanka [1952] Director

North Atlantic (Holdings) Limited
Incorporated: 4 November 1993 *Employees:* 8
Net Worth: £31,771,244 *Total Assets:* £36,138,724
Registered Office: The Naafi Building, Weston Drive, Caterham, Surrey, CR3 5XY
Activities: Marine fishing
Officers: Stewart Norman Harper, Secretary/Director; Matthew James Cox [1972] Director; Stewart Norman Harper [1949] Director; Annerieke Vrolijk [1970] Director [Dutch]

North Atlantic Fishing Company Limited
Incorporated: 6 March 1922 *Employees:* 8
Net Worth: £25,178,780 *Total Assets:* £34,485,000
Registered Office: The Naafi Building, Weston Drive, Caterham, Surrey, CR3 5XY
Activities: Marine fishing
Officers: Stewart Norman Harper, Secretary/Director; Matthew James Cox [1972] Director; Stewart Norman Harper [1949] Director/Fish Trading; Annerieke Vrolijk [1970] Director [Dutch]

The North London Collegiate School
Incorporated: 17 May 1993 *Employees:* 45
Net Worth: £28,371,208 *Total Assets:* £39,737,320
Registered Office: Canons Drive, Edgware, Middlesex, HA8 7RJ
Activities: General secondary education
Officers: Keith Breslauer [1966] Director/Banker [American]; Sophie Christine Carter [1970] Director/School Governor; Elaine Davis [1968] Director; Dr Anton Vignaraj Emmanuel [1965] Director/Doctor; Dr Adam Tobias Fox [1972] Director/Doctor; John Stuart Herlihy [1954] Director; Steven Harold Jaffe [1950] Director/Chartered Accountant; Peter John Nicholas Linthwaite [1956] Director/Investment Manager; Peter David Needleman [1955] Director/Actuary; Eileen Annabelle Raperport [1951] Director/Accountant; Timothy John Suter [1956] Director; Professor Brian Young [1963] Director/University Professor

North Star (2000) Limited
Incorporated: 2 December 1997
Net Worth: £1,996,345 *Total Assets:* £6,972,074
Registered Office: North Star House, 11 London Road, Bromley, Kent, BR1 1BY
Activities: Construction of commercial buildings
Major Shareholder: Marco Williams
Officers: Sara Copper, Secretary; Marco Williams [1963] Director/Developer

Northamber PLC
Incorporated: 3 June 1980 *Employees:* 85
Net Worth: £17,520,000 *Total Assets:* £24,484,000
Registered Office: Namber House, 23 Davis Road, Chessington, Surrey, KT9 1HS
Activities: Wholesale of computers, computer peripheral equipment and software
Major Shareholder: David Michael Phillips
Officers: Sivapragasam Yoganathan, Secretary/Accountant; John Phelim Henry [1962] Director; David Michael Phillips [1945] Director/Company Chairman; Colin Mark Thompson [1960] Director/IT Consultant [British/American]; Geoffrey Paul Walters [1952] Director

Northfield Avenue (Holdings) Limited
Incorporated: 9 July 2004 *Employees:* 2
Net Worth: £6,084,658 *Total Assets:* £18,292,048
Registered Office: First Floor, Radius House, 51 Clarendon Road, Watford, Herts, WD17 1HP
Activities: Development of building projects
Parent: Northfield Avenue Properties Limited
Officers: Richard David Swaine, Secretary; Richard David Swaine [1962] Director; Jonathan James Willoughby [1966] Director

Northstar Property Investment Limited
Incorporated: 18 October 1996
Net Worth: £4,362,721 *Total Assets:* £7,456,388
Registered Office: Unicorn House, Station Close, Potters Bar, Herts, EN6 1TL
Activities: Buying and selling of own real estate
Parent: Panther Securities PLC
Officers: Simon Jeffrey Peters, Secretary; Andrew Stewart Perloff [1944] Director; John Henry Perloff [1968] Director; Simon Jeffrey Peters [1977] Director

Northwood Paper Sales Limited
Incorporated: 15 July 1998 *Employees:* 21
Net Worth: £2,994,494 *Total Assets:* £36,769,968
Registered Office: 4 Warner House, Harrovian Business Village, Bessborough Road, Harrow, Middlesex, HA1 3EX
Activities: Agents specialised in the sale of other particular products
Major Shareholder: Paul Fecher
Officers: Kishor Vekaria, Secretary/Accountant; Adam Scott Fecher [1974] Director/Sales; Paul Fecher [1946] Director

Norwood Green Junior School
Incorporated: 8 May 2013 *Employees:* 49
Net Worth: £8,144,209 *Total Assets:* £9,567,811
Registered Office: Norwood Green Junior School, Thorncliffe Road, Southall, Middlesex, UB2 5RN
Activities: Primary education
Officers: Dawn Blakeburn, Secretary; Ranjit Singh Berdesha [1970] Director/Headteacher; Dawn Blakeburn [1963] Director/School Business Manager; Balwinder Kaur Kalyan [1958] Director/Retail Assistant [Singaporean]; Abdirisak Keynan [1987] Director/Train Inspector; Rajesh Khosla [1965] Director/Entrepreneur; Sukhminder Mann [1960] Director/Processing Officer Accountancy; Catherine Shelagh Norfolk [1966] Director/Headteacher; Dushani Parker [1968] Director/Teacher; Priya Kaur Sehgal [1967] Director/Deputy Headteacher; Samir Vohra [1981] Director/Civil Servant

Norwood Ravenswood
Incorporated: 9 October 1996 *Employees:* 648
Net Worth: £43,448,000 *Total Assets:* £52,817,000
Registered Office: Broadway House, 80-82 The Broadway, Stanmore, Middlesex, HA7 4HB
Activities: Educational support services
Officers: Abiola Yusuf, Secretary; Yonni Leslie Spiero Abramson [1984] Director/Property Developer; Julia Sarah Chain [1957] Director/Solicitor; Tamara Margaret Finkelstein [1967] Director/Civil Servant; Linda Goldberg [1942] Director/Retired; Philip Lee Hertz [1967] Director/Global Head of Restructuring and Insolvency; Angela Hodes [1956] Director/Barrister; Glynnis Joffe [1952] Director/Retired; Neville Kahn [1963] Director/Managing Partner; Mark Pollack [1961] Director; Anthony Leon Philip Rabin [1955] Director; Lady Elaine Sacks [1949] Director; Gary Hilton Sacks [1965] Director; David Mark Smith [1970] Director/Group Head of Tax and Corporate Finance; David Mark Stanton [1969] Board Director and Deputy Chairman

Norwood Schools Ltd.
Incorporated: 9 March 1953 *Employees:* 616
Net Worth: £29,180,000 *Total Assets:* £38,106,000
Registered Office: Broadway House, 80-82 The Broadway, Stanmore, Middlesex, HA7 4HB
Activities: Residential care activities for learning difficulties, mental health and substance abuse
Officers: Abiola Yusuf, Secretary; Neville Kahn [1963] Director/Managing Partner; David Mark Smith [1970] Director/Group Head of Tax and Corporate Finance; David Mark Stanton [1969] Board Director/Deputy Chairman

Notonthehighstreet Enterprises Ltd
Incorporated: 13 October 2005 *Employees:* 190
Net Worth: £10,913,214 *Total Assets:* £22,616,844
Registered Office: 63 Kew Road, Richmond, Surrey, TW9 2NQ
Activities: Other service activities n.e.c.
Shareholder: Hurbert Burda
Officers: Kate Burns, Secretary; Davor Hebel [1976] Director/Venture Capital [Croatian]; Benjamin John Bieder Holmes [1973] Director; Tamara Lohan [1972] Director; Barrie Anne Seidenberg [1965] Director/Chief Executive [American]; Darren Mark Shapland [1966] Director; Christian Kevin Teichmann [1978] Director [German]

Notre Dame School Cobham
Incorporated: 22 December 1999 *Employees:* 134
Net Worth: £10,362,000 *Total Assets:* £11,855,000
Registered Office: Notre Dame School, Burwood House, Burwood Park, Cobham, Surrey, KT11 1HA
Activities: Pre-primary education
Officers: Georgina Louise Ayling, Secretary; Susan Bailes [1953] Director/Consultant; Sister Maria Nieves Escalada Gallego [1957] Director/Religious Sister [Spanish]; Simon Frost [1955] Director; Sr Anne Gill [1946] Director/Sister of The Order; Karl Justin Kieran McCloskey [1962] Director/School Principal [Irish]; Wanda Lorraine Nash [1948] Development and Alumnae Director; Sister Maria Quinn [1942] Director/Sister of a Religious Order; Generald William Russell [1950] Director/Chartered Accountant; Sister Kathy Lynn Schneider [1962] Director/Education [American]; Suzanne Doreen Ware [1963] Director/Barrister (QC); Rev John Mervyn Williams [1946] Director/Priest

Nower Hill High School
Incorporated: 1 July 2011 *Employees:* 189
Net Worth: £22,000,092 *Total Assets:* £25,637,360
Registered Office: George V Avenue, Pinner, Middlesex, HA5 5RP
Activities: General secondary education
Officers: Ian Peter Noutch, Secretary; Janet Beverley Buckingham [1960] Director; Christina Byrne [1969] Director/Community Leadership Manager [Irish]; Adeela Chowdhry [1971] Director/Project Manager; Julie Ann Gardner [1984] Director/Teacher; Janet Herson [1953] Director/Teacher; Abdeslam Ahmed Karmoun [1963] Director/IT Risk Manager [British/Moroccan]; Sukaina Kassam [1975] Director/Housewife; Diana Mary MacLeod La Rue [1951] Director; Andrew Simon Lane [1966] Director; Christopher James Livesey [1964] Director/Headteacher; Roy McKerracher [1956] Director/Accountant; Kala Nair [1967] Director/Teacher [Singaporean]; Asad Omar [1944] Director/Retired; Chandreyi Parkin [1967] Director/Teaching and Learning Assistant; Kevin Mark Ward [1965] Director/Manager; Michelle Weerasekera [1969] Director/Voluntary Sector

NPL Management Limited
Incorporated: 10 June 1994 *Employees:* 769
Net Worth: £84,963,000 *Total Assets:* £128,708,000
Registered Office: National Physical Laboratory, Hampton Road, Teddington, Middlesex, TW11 0LW
Activities: Other service activities n.e.c.
Parent: Secretary of State for Business, Energy and Industrial Strategy
Officers: Andrew John Armstrong, Secretary; Dr David Grant [1947] Director; Penelope Jane Holt [1972] Director/Chief Financial Officer; Dr Paul John Arton Howarth [1970] Managing Director; Dr Stephanie Hurst [1961] Director/Senior Civil Servant; Professor Gaoqing Max Lu [1963] Director/Vice-Chancellor [Australian]; Professor Sir James Rufus McDonald [1957] Director/University Principal; Nigel John Perry [1957] Director/Chief Executive; Martyn Russell Sene [1957] Director; Brigid Ann Sutcliffe [1959] Director; Doctor Peter Anthony Thompson [1967] Director/Chief Executive Officer

NPT Finance Limited
Incorporated: 23 July 2015 *Employees:* 12
Net Worth Deficit: £6,726 *Total Assets:* £7,908,908
Registered Office: 2c Southbridge House, Southbridge Place, Croydon, Surrey, CR0 4HA
Activities: Buying and selling of own real estate
Shareholders: Cormac Henderson; Shane David Miller-Bourke
Officers: Cormac Henderson [1980] Director/Property [Irish]; Shane David Miller-Bourke [1980] Director/Property [Irish]; Oliver Mark Russell [1979] Director/Property

NSL (Holdings) Limited
Incorporated: 17 March 2014 *Employees:* 108
Net Worth: £17,830,518 *Total Assets:* £23,043,112
Registered Office: Unit 4-5 Northolt Trading Estate, Belvue Road, Northolt, Middlesex, UB5 5QS
Activities: Wholesale of pharmaceutical goods
Shareholder: Ketan Himatlal Mehta
Officers: Ketan Mehta, Secretary; Bharat Himatlal Mehta [1952] Director; Ketan Himatlal Mehta [1958] Director

NSL Group Limited
Incorporated: 7 March 2008 *Employees:* 2
Net Worth: £11,481,177 *Total Assets:* £11,843,620
Registered Office: Unit 4-5 Northolt Trading Estate, Belvue Road, Northolt, Middlesex, UB5 5QS
Activities: Wholesale of pharmaceutical goods
Officers: Ketan Himatlal Mehta, Secretary; Bharat Himatlal Mehta [1952] Director; Ketan Himatlal Mehta [1958] Director/Pharmacist

NTS Retail Limited
Incorporated: 5 March 2012
Net Worth: £2,915,661 *Total Assets:* £7,913,368
Registered Office: 57 Blakes Avenue, New Malden, Surrey, KT3 6RF
Activities: Retail sale in non-specialised stores with food, beverages or tobacco predominating
Major Shareholder: Nalliah Thayaparan
Officers: Nalliah Thayaparan [1973] Director

The Nuance Group (UK) Limited
Incorporated: 29 August 1973 *Employees:* 259
Net Worth: £10,762,000 *Total Assets:* £22,405,000
Registered Office: 4 New Square, Bedfont Lakes, Feltham, Middlesex, TW14 8HA
Activities: Other retail sale in non-specialised stores
Officers: Paul Henry Donaldson, Secretary/Financial Controller; Christopher David Bouttle [1968] Director; Frederick Robert Creighton [1958] Director; Benjamin Harmstorf [1976] Director/Chief Financial Officer [German]

Nucleus Financial Group PLC
Incorporated: 29 July 2005 *Employees:* 180
Net Worth: £16,182,000 *Total Assets:* £28,785,000
Registered Office: Elder House, St Georges Business Park, 207 Brooklands Road, Weybridge, Surrey, KT13 0TS
Activities: Financial intermediation not elsewhere classified
Officers: Nicola Megaw, Secretary; Tracy Dunley-Owen [1972] Director; David Ritchie Ferguson [1969] Director; Stuart James Geard [1974] Director/Chartered Accountant [South African]; Jeremy Paul Gibson [1973] Director/Chartered Accountant; Margaret Grace Hassall [1961] Director; John Anthony Levin [1963] Director; Jonathan Charles Polin [1959] Director/Chief Executive Officer, Sanlam UK; James Anthony Angus Samuels [1950] Director

Nucleus Financial Services Limited
Incorporated: 21 November 2005 *Employees:* 157
Net Worth: £12,926,000 *Total Assets:* £23,524,000
Registered Office: Elder House, St Georges Business Park, 207 Brooklands Road, Weybridge, Surrey, KT13 0TS
Activities: Financial intermediation not elsewhere classified
Parent: Nucleus Financial Group Limited
Officers: Nicola Megaw, Secretary; Tracy Dunley-Owen [1972] Director; David Ritchie Ferguson [1969] Director; Stuart James Geard [1974] Director/Chartered Accountant [South African]; Jeremy Paul Gibson [1973] Director/Chartered Accountant; Margaret Grace Hassall [1961] Director; John Anthony Levin [1963] Director; Jonathan Charles Polin [1959] Director/Chief Executive Officer, Sanlam UK; James Anthony Angus Samuels [1950] Director

Nucleus Limited
Incorporated: 3 February 1993 *Employees:* 42
Net Worth: £647,593 *Total Assets:* £6,912,219
Registered Office: John Loftus House, Summer Road, Thames Ditton, Surrey, KT7 0RD
Activities: Management consultancy activities other than financial management
Shareholder: Peter Nicholas Matthews
Officers: Michael John Stannard, Secretary; Peter Nicholas Matthews [1957] Designer/Director; Adam Charles Smith [1964] Director [Australian]; Michael John Stannard [1962] Director/Accountant

Nuffield Health
Incorporated: 14 January 1957 *Employees:* 16,198
Net Worth: £64,100,000 *Total Assets:* £737,299,968
Registered Office: Epsom Gateway, Ashley Avenue, Epsom, Surrey, KT18 5AL
Activities: Other human health activities
Officers: Toby Newman, Secretary; Martin Warwick Bryant [1952] Director; Fiona Elizabeth Driscoll [1958] Director; Patrick Adam Fernesley Figgis [1957] Director; Russell Stephen Mons Hardy [1960] Director; David William Lister [1958] Director/Chief Information Officer; Dr Natalie-Jane Anne MacDonald [1962] Director/Chief Executive; Stephen Maslin [1957] Director/Chartered Accountant; Philip Guy McCracken [1948] Director; Nilesh Sachdev [1958] Director

Nuffield Health Pension Trustees Limited
Incorporated: 12 February 2016
Net Worth: £5,087,696 *Total Assets:* £76,287,696
Registered Office: Epsom Gateway, Ashley Avenue, Epsom, Surrey, KT18 5AL
Activities: Other business support service activities n.e.c.
Parent: Nuffield Health
Officers: Toby Newman, Secretary; Alan Davies [1950] Director/Retired Pharmacist; Michael Haffenden [1960] Director/Hospital Doctor; John Edward Jones [1947] Director/Retired; David McNair [1963] Director/Hospital Doctor; Colin Roderick Miller [1955] Director/Accountant; Jose Perez [1949] Director/Retired [Spanish]

NUR Limited
Incorporated: 14 March 1997 *Employees:* 2
Net Worth: £4,714,932 *Total Assets:* £7,985,634
Registered Office: 7-9 The Oaks, Ruislip, Middlesex, HA4 7LF
Activities: Renting and operating of Housing Association real estate
Major Shareholder: Amirali Hassanali Moledina Janmohamed
Officers: Alim Amirali Janmohamed, Company Secretary; Alim Amirali Janmohamed [1981] Director/BSL Economics and Business; Amirali Hassanali Moledina Janmohamed [1952] Director

nVent International (UK) Ltd
Incorporated: 25 August 2015
Previous: Pentair International (UK) Ltd
Net Worth: £749,903,168 *Total Assets:* £749,903,168
Registered Office: 8th Floor, The Mille, 1000 Great West Road, Brentford, Middlesex, TW8 9DW
Activities: Financial management
Parent: nVent Electric PLC
Officers: Neil Stuart Mackintosh [1959] Director of Tax; Marek Tapsik [1974] Director/Associate General Counsel [Czech]; Roman Zubinski [1980] Director/Europe Controller [French]

NVSM Limited
Incorporated: 29 March 2001 *Employees:* 2
Net Worth: £11,677,186 *Total Assets:* £17,151,288
Registered Office: 4th Floor, Metroline House, 118-122 College Road, Harrow, Middlesex, HA1 1BQ
Activities: Buying and selling of own real estate
Major Shareholder: Vasam Shabnem Ibrahim
Officers: Vasam Shabnem Ibrahim [1970] Director/Stockbroker; Sadia Zafar [1976] Director

NW3 Capital Ltd
Incorporated: 26 October 2012 *Employees:* 2
Net Worth: £3,314,826 *Total Assets:* £12,304,672
Registered Office: c/o Jarvis & Co Business Services, 75 Main Road, Gidea Park, Romford, Essex, RM2 5EL
Activities: Construction of domestic buildings
Major Shareholder: Robbi Malandreniotis
Officers: Dimitri Malandreniotis [1977] Director; Robbi Malandreniotis [1977] Director/Property Developer

O G Holdings Limited
Incorporated: 6 June 2000 *Employees:* 3
Previous: Offer Group Holdings Limited
Net Worth: £10,558,185 *Total Assets:* £11,902,151
Registered Office: Burgoine House, 8 Lower Teddington Road, Hampton Wick, Kingston upon Thames, Surrey, KT1 4ER
Activities: Other letting and operating of own or leased real estate
Parent: Livid Dare Limited
Officers: Daisy Offer, Secretary/Director; Claire Offer [1969] Director; Daisy Offer [1933] Director; Harry John Miles Offer [1962] Director/Chartered Surveyor

O'Halloran & O'Brien Limited
Incorporated: 11 April 1972 *Employees:* 75
Net Worth: £61,027,696 *Total Assets:* £113,127,728
Registered Office: O'Brien House, 197-199 Garth Road, Morden, Surrey, SM4 4NE
Activities: Other specialised construction activities n.e.c.
Shareholder: OHOB Group Ltd
Officers: Colin David Southey, Secretary; Brian Hector Bonnyman [1958] Director/Group MD; Steve John Burke [1973] Director/Civil Engineer [Irish]; Martin Walter Alfred Francis [1959] Health & Safety Director; Leslie John Gosling [1959] Director/Contracts Manager; Thomas Jason O'Brien [1976] Director/Company Manager; Thomas Francis O'Brien [1947] Director/Builder [Irish]; Stephen John Richards [1972] Director/Surveyor; Colin David Southey [1959] Director

O'Hara Bros. Surfacing Limited
Incorporated: 23 September 1975 *Employees:* 52
Net Worth: £5,236,955 *Total Assets:* £9,380,980
Registered Office: 101 Rowlands Avenue, Hatch End, Middlesex, HA5 4AW
Activities: Construction of roads and motorways
Parent: Rowlands 2014 Limited
Officers: Noreen O'Hara, Secretary; Colin Hambling [1953] Director/Civil Engineer; Christopher Patrick O'Hara [1986] Director [Irish]; John O'Hara [1950] Director/Manager [Irish]; Lawrence O'Hara [1954] Director/Manager [Irish]; Michael O'Hara [1947] Director/Manager [Irish]; Seamus O'Hara [1957] Director/Contractor [Irish]; John Sanders [1967] Director/Engineer

O'Hara Property Investment Holding Company Limited
Incorporated: 21 February 1985
Net Worth: £10,962,729 *Total Assets:* £15,568,922
Registered Office: 101 Rowlands Avenue, Hatch End, Middlesex, HA5 4AW
Activities: Other letting and operating of own or leased real estate
Shareholders: Patrick Joseph O'Hara; Michael O'Hara
Officers: Patrick Joseph O'Hara, Secretary; Patrick Joseph O'Hara [1944] Director/Manager [Irish]; Michael O'Hara [1947] Director/Manager [Irish]

O'Hara Transport Limited
Incorporated: 30 October 1997 *Employees:* 6
Net Worth: £2,064,792 *Total Assets:* £7,025,443
Registered Office: 101 Rowlands Avenue, Hatch End, Pinner, Middlesex, HA5 4AW
Activities: Freight transport by road
Major Shareholder: Michael O'Hara
Officers: Noreen O'Hara, Secretary; Christopher Patrick O'Hara [1986] Director [Irish]; John James Frances O'Hara [1979] Director/Chartered Surveyor [Irish]; Michael Joseph O'Hara [1980] Director/Civil Engineer; Michael O'Hara [1947] Director/Public Works Contractor [Irish]

O'Malley Haulage Limited
Incorporated: 22 June 2005 *Employees:* 5
Net Worth: £5,635,022 *Total Assets:* £10,745,246
Registered Office: Hilfield Lane, Aldenham, Watford, Herts, WD25 8DT
Activities: Freight transport by road
Parent: New ACH Limited
Officers: Thomas O'Malley [1947] Director [Irish]; Adrian Thomas Omalley [1980] Director

O'Neill Investments Limited
Incorporated: 18 March 2002 *Employees:* 4
Net Worth: £22,025,076 *Total Assets:* £31,838,832
Registered Office: 1 Beauchamp Court, Victors Way, Barnet, Herts, EN5 5TZ
Activities: Other letting and operating of own or leased real estate
Shareholders: Sean James O'Neill; Jean Therese Wheeler
Officers: Sean James O'Neill, Secretary; Sean James O'Neill [1963] Director/Property Investor/Developer; Jean Therese Wheeler [1963] Director/Administrator [Irish]

R.O'Rourke & Son Limited.
Incorporated: 17 December 1991
Net Worth: £4,521,000 *Total Assets:* £12,234,000
Registered Office: Bridge Place, Anchor Boulevard, Admirals Park, Crossways, Dartford, Kent, DA2 6SN
Activities: Construction of commercial buildings
Parent: Laing O'Rourke Holdings Limited
Officers: Robert Edward Turner, Secretary; Declan James McGeeney [1978] Director/General Manager [Irish]; Alexander Stewart McIntyre [1956] Director

O'Rourke Civil & Structural Engineering Limited
Incorporated: 1 August 1977
Net Worth: £6,815,000 *Total Assets:* £6,815,000
Registered Office: Bridge Place, Anchor Boulevard, Admirals Park, Crossways, Dartford, Kent, DA2 6SN
Activities: Construction of commercial buildings
Parent: R O'Rourke & Son Limited
Officers: Robert Edward Turner, Secretary; Alexander Stewart McIntyre [1956] Director; Hubert Desmond O'Rourke [1949] Director/Structural Engineer [Irish]; Raymond Gabriel O'Rourke [1947] Director/Structural Engineer [Irish]

O'Rourke Investments Holdings (UK) Limited
Incorporated: 14 June 2004
Net Worth: £307,433,984 *Total Assets:* £400,808,000
Registered Office: Bridge Place, Anchor Boulevard, Admirals Park, Crossways, Dartford, Kent, DA2 6SN
Activities: Activities of head offices
Major Shareholder: James Fairweather Edmondson
Officers: Robert Edward Turner, Secretary; Barry Dye [1958] Director/Quantity Surveyor; Gerard Loftus [1960] Director; Declan James McGeeney [1978] Director/General Manager [Irish]; Alexander Stewart McIntyre [1956] Director; Paul William McNerney [1977] Director/Business Unit Leader; John Christopher O'Connor [1965] Commercial Director; Hubert Desmond O'Rourke [1949] Director/Building Contractor [Irish]; Raymond Gabriel O'Rourke [1947] Director/Structural Engineer [Irish]

O.B.C. (Europe) Limited
Incorporated: 20 February 1998 *Employees:* 4
Net Worth: £8,949,323 *Total Assets:* £9,564,465
Registered Office: York House, Empire Way, Wembley, Middlesex, HA9 0FQ
Activities: Other letting and operating of own or leased real estate
Shareholders: Alan Richard Bekhor; Julia Ruth Bekhor
Officers: Julia Ruth Bekhor, Secretary; Alan Richard Bekhor [1960] Director; Julia Ruth Bekhor [1960] Director

O.S.T.C. Limited
Incorporated: 30 September 2004 *Employees:* 459
Net Worth: £13,181,628 *Total Assets:* £52,668,920
Registered Office: 2nd Floor, Imperial House, 21-25 North Street, Bromley, Kent, BR1 1SD
Activities: Activities auxiliary to financial intermediation n.e.c.
Officers: Justina Naik, Secretary; Jonathan Dean Aucamp [1968] Director; Robert James Brophy [1968] Director; Dr Ian Paul Firla [1970] Director [Polish]; Lee Antony Hodgkinson [1972] Director/Chief Executive; Danny Langley [1972] Director; Michael Peter Saunter [1969] Director; Michael Jose Shirley [1975] Managing Director; Mark Adam Slade [1969] Director/Futures Trader

Oak Narwana LLP
Incorporated: 28 June 2016
Net Worth: £8,154,027 *Total Assets:* £13,316,127
Registered Office: 1 Pelhams Walk, Esher, Surrey, KT10 8QA
Officers: Dr Ruchika Barathan [1980] Member; Akash Neil Gupta [1983] Member; Dr Nirmal Gupta [1955] Member; Vinod Kumar Gupta [1950] Member; Aarav Rohan Barathan [2012] LLP Member; Kush Vinod Barathan [2010] LLP Member; Dr Vijay Prakash Barathan [1980] LLP Member

Oak Tree Schools Holdings Limited
Incorporated: 15 March 1995 *Employees:* 270
Net Worth: £7,025,651 *Total Assets:* £14,004,221
Registered Office: 6 Albion Hill, Loughton, Essex, IG10 4RA
Activities: Other business support service activities n.e.c.
Shareholders: Matthew Hagger; Nicholas Osborne Hagger; Madeline Ann Hagger
Officers: Matthew Hagger, Secretary; Madeline Ann Hagger [1950] Director; Matthew Hagger [1974] Director; Nicholas Osborne Hagger [1939] Director

Oakburn European Properties Limited
Incorporated: 23 March 1998
Net Worth: £11,178,230 *Total Assets:* £17,665,056
Registered Office: Riverside House, 1-5 Como Street, Romford, Essex, RM7 7DN
Activities: Development of building projects
Parent: Oakburn Properties Limited
Officers: Simon Ansel Blausten, Secretary/Surveyor; Benjamin Blausten [1986] Director; Deborah Elizabeth Blausten [1990] Director; Douglas Blausten [1951] Director/Chartered Surveyor; Hannah Blausten [1991] Director; Jonathan Andrew Blausten [1992] Director; Samuel Blausten [1991] Director; Simon Ansel Blausten [1956] Director/Chartered Surveyor

Oakburn Investment Holdings Limited
Incorporated: 10 June 1986
Net Worth: £3,486,682 *Total Assets:* £5,100,000
Registered Office: Riverside House, 1-5 Como Street, Romford, Essex, RM7 7DN
Activities: Activities of other holding companies n.e.c.
Shareholders: Douglas Blausten; Simon Ansel Blausten
Officers: Simon Ansel Blausten, Secretary; Douglas Blausten [1951] Director/Chartered Surveyor; Simon Ansel Blausten [1956] Director/Chartered Surveyor

Oakburn Properties Limited
Incorporated: 31 July 1959
Net Worth: £6,551,017 *Total Assets:* £13,053,889
Registered Office: Riverside House, 1-5 Como Street, Romford, Essex, RM7 7DN
Activities: Other letting and operating of own or leased real estate
Shareholders: Douglas Blausten; Simon Ansel Blausten
Officers: Simon Ansel Blausten, Secretary/Surveyor; Douglas Blausten [1951] Director/Chartered Surveyor; Simon Ansel Blausten [1956] Director/Chartered Surveyor

Oakdene Holdings Limited
Incorporated: 10 August 2007
Net Worth: £7,074,266 *Total Assets:* £7,074,628
Registered Office: 59 Victoria Road, Surbiton, Surrey, KT6 4NQ
Activities: Activities of head offices
Major Shareholder: Andrew Morris Davies
Officers: Jane Mariette Wright, Secretary; Andrew Morris Davies [1962] Director

Oakfield (Foods) Limited
Incorporated: 24 February 1987 *Employees:* 52
Net Worth: £23,582,060 *Total Assets:* £44,994,880
Registered Office: 1st Floor, 3 Elstree Gate, Elstree Way, Borehamwood, Herts, WD6 1JD
Activities: Production of meat and poultry meat products
Officers: David Lee Burr, Secretary; David Lee Burr [1971] Finance Director; Mark David Glass [1967] Sales Director; Thomas Matthew Greaney [1988] Director; Daniel Ian Hargreaves [1981] Technical Director; Harvey Philip Ingram [1947] Director/Solicitor; Alison Levy [1959] Director; Miles Ivor Levy [1956] Sales Director; Darren John Short [1966] Director

Oakray Limited
Incorporated: 31 October 1979 *Employees:* 196
Net Worth: £11,856,817 *Total Assets:* £15,224,925
Registered Office: 1 Warner House, The Harrovian Business Village, Bessborough Road, Harrow, Middlesex, HA1 3EX
Activities: Plumbing, heat and air-conditioning installation
Officers: Maureen Franklin, Secretary; Andrew Clark [1962] Director; Wayne John Dejager [1966] Director; Keith Sidney Mottram [1957] Director

Oaks Academy Trust
Incorporated: 5 March 2014 *Employees:* 103
Net Worth: £4,998,000 *Total Assets:* £6,169,000
Registered Office: Banstead Infant School, The Horseshoe, Banstead, Surrey, SM7 2BQ
Activities: Primary education
Officers: Tomos Lewis Davies [1958] Property Director; Joan Mary Hornsby [1958] Director/Retired; Stephen Leslie Mann [1957] Director/Care Home Operator; Deborah Matthews [1962] Director; John Stephenson [1947] Director/Retired; Richard Frederick Charles Wagner [1943] Director/Retired; Joyce Walter [1951] Director/Chartered Secretary

Oaktree Property Company Limited
Incorporated: 14 July 2009 *Employees:* 2
Net Worth: £42,715 *Total Assets:* £5,248,149
Registered Office: c/o Barnes Roffe LLP, 3 Brook Business Centre, Cowley Mill Road, Uxbridge, Middlesex, UB8 2FX
Activities: Activities of other holding companies n.e.c.
Major Shareholder: Denis O'Brien
Officers: Brendan Christoph Hayes, Secretary; Brendan Christoph Hayes [1974] Director; Mark George Polychronakis [1974] Director

Oakwood Finance London Limited
Incorporated: 16 September 2005 *Employees:* 1
Net Worth: £1,956,829 *Total Assets:* £10,161,086
Registered Office: Unit 3 Elstree Gate, Elstree Way, Borehamwood, Herts, WD6 1JD
Activities: Wholesale of meat and meat products
Major Shareholder: Miles Ivor Levy
Officers: David Lee Burr, Secretary; Jay Bradley Levy [1990] Director; Miles Ivor Levy [1956] Director

Oasis Lending LLP
Incorporated: 4 November 2016
Net Worth: £16,915,680 *Total Assets:* £16,915,680
Registered Office: Elder House, St Georges Business Park, 207 Brooklands Road, Weybridge, Surrey, KT13 0TS

Oatfield Limited
Incorporated: 27 April 2001
Net Worth: £9,235,670 *Total Assets:* £15,303,548
Registered Office: Melbury House, 34 Southborough Road, Bickley, Kent, BR1 2EB
Activities: Other letting and operating of own or leased real estate
Shareholders: Rohit Singh Jawaheer; Sherine Ruth Jawaheer
Officers: Sherine Ruth Jawaheer, Company Secretary; Rohit Singh Jawaheer [1953] Director; Sherine Ruth Jawaheer [1952] Director

Oatlands Investments Limited
Incorporated: 12 May 1986 *Employees:* 94
Net Worth: £12,786,145 *Total Assets:* £16,471,685
Registered Office: Oatlands Park Hotel, Oatlands Drive, Weybridge, Surrey, KT13 9HB
Activities: Hotels and similar accommodation
Shareholder: Swissco Investments Limited
Officers: Nawaz Ismail Ebrahim Jamal, Secretary; Karam Dhala [1953] Director/Hotelier; Karim Nawaz Ismail Jamal [1978] Director/Surgeon; Nawaz Ismail Ebrahim Jamal [1953] Director; Rehmetullah Amirally Hasham Jamal [1955] Director/Economist [Kenyan]; Alim Somji [1959] Director; Shafin Alimudin Somji [1989] Director

Oblue Limited
Incorporated: 20 March 2012
Net Worth: £6,190,328 *Total Assets:* £8,407,542
Registered Office: Portland House, 69-71 Wembley Hill Road, Wembley, Middlesex, HA9 8BU
Activities: Sea and coastal freight water transport
Parent: Union Maritime Limited
Officers: Bhupendra Shantilal Kansagra, Secretary; Laurent Elie Cadji [1977] Director/Businessman; Lewis Levy Cadji [1938] Director/Businessman; Bhupendra Shantilal Kansagra [1956] Director/Businessman; Ramesh Shantilal Kansagra [1950] Director/Businessman

Ocean Gateway LLP
Incorporated: 19 February 2009
Net Worth: £13,218,958 *Total Assets:* £13,291,004
Registered Office: Upminster Court, 133 Hall Lane, Upminster, Essex, RM14 1AL
Officers: Iain Robert Liddell [1963] Member

Ocean Holidays Limited
Incorporated: 18 June 2013 *Employees:* 145
Net Worth: £831,498 *Total Assets:* £25,649,200
Registered Office: Floor 9, North House, St Edwards Way, Romford, Essex, RM1 3AE
Activities: Tour operator activities
Officers: George Hardie Hastings [1977] Director; Harry Rawson Hastings [1983] Director; Daniel James Ox [1979] Director; David John Ox [1978] Director

The Ockendon Academy
Incorporated: 25 November 2010 *Employees:* 185
Net Worth: £22,698,648 *Total Assets:* £25,208,908
Registered Office: Erriff Drive, South Ockendon, Essex, RM15 5AY
Activities: General secondary education
Officers: Jacqueline Insole, Secretary; Kathleen Ann Cooney [1949] Director; Donna Driscoll [1978] Director/Learning Base Supervisor; Lorraine Jean Hodges [1958] Director/Support-Cover Supervisor; Samantha Kahn [1973] Director; James Lepine [1993] Director/Casework Assistant Crown Prosecution Service; Richard Charles Milligan [1954] Director/Retired; Olubunmi Adefunke Bisola Obisesan [1992] Director/Company Secretary; Kifwanakene Pupe [1975] Director/Financial Consultant; Joanne Edgeworth Rainey [1974] Director/Principal; Richard Douglas Haydon Wickens [1990] Director/Technical Specialist - Data - Banking

OCO Limited
Incorporated: 8 May 1979 *Employees:* 179
Net Worth: £4,383,747 *Total Assets:* £8,243,899
Registered Office: Meersbrook House, 15 Essex Road, Dartford, Kent, DA1 2AU
Activities: Electrical installation
Officers: Philip John Cowdery, Secretary; Philip John Cowdery [1956] Director/Engineer; Anthony John Harrison [1948] Director/Engineer; Christopher Oborne [1950] Director/Engineer; George Oborne [1950] Director/Engineer

Ocobase Limited
Incorporated: 14 December 1978 *Employees:* 2
Net Worth: £106,970,032 *Total Assets:* £111,565,152
Registered Office: 198 Lower Addiscombe Road, Croydon, Surrey, CR0 7AB
Activities: Buying and selling of own real estate
Shareholders: Paul David Upward; Simon Leslie Upward
Officers: Simon Leslie Upward, Secretary; Paul David Upward [1962] Director; Simon Leslie Upward [1961] Director

Ocourage Limited
Incorporated: 5 November 2012
Net Worth: £10,713,758 *Total Assets:* £15,176,342
Registered Office: Portland House, 69-71 Wembley Hill Road, Wembley, Middlesex, HA9 8BU
Activities: Sea and coastal freight water transport
Parent: Union Maritime Limited
Officers: Bhupendra Shantilal Kansagra, Secretary; Laurent Elie Cadji [1977] Director/Businessman; Lewis Levy Cadji [1938] Director/Businessman; Bhupendra Shantilal Kansagra [1956] Director/Businessman; Ramesh Shantilal Kansagra [1950] Director/Businessman

Octagon Developments Limited
Incorporated: 18 December 1979 *Employees:* 61
Net Worth: £37,877,000 *Total Assets:* £44,604,000
Registered Office: Weir House, Hurst Road, East Molesey, Surrey, KT8 9AY
Activities: Construction of commercial buildings
Parent: Octagon Group Limited
Officers: Timothy David Robert Banks, Secretary/Director; Timothy David Robert Banks [1967] Director; Robert John Birch [1961] Director; David John James [1943] Director; Angus Jason McQuhae [1966] Director; Jonathan Valentine Pope [1955] Regional Director; Colin Tutt [1956] Director; Roger Stanley Wyatt [1937] Director

Octagon Group Holdings Limited
Incorporated: 11 July 2007 *Employees:* 61
Net Worth: £7,558,000 *Total Assets:* £40,730,000
Registered Office: Weir House, Hurst Road, East Molesey, Surrey, KT8 9AY
Activities: Activities of head offices
Officers: Timothy David Robert Banks, Secretary/Director; Timothy David Robert Banks [1967] Director; David John James [1943] Director; Angus Jason McQuhae [1966] Director; Colin Tutt [1956] Director; Roger Stanley Wyatt [1937] Director

Octagon Group Limited
Incorporated: 7 June 2001
Net Worth: £20,855,000 *Total Assets:* £47,297,000
Registered Office: Weir House, Hurst Road, East Molesey, Surrey, KT8 9AY
Activities: Activities of head offices
Parent: Octagon Group Holdings Limited
Officers: Timothy David Robert Banks, Secretary/Director; Timothy David Robert Banks [1967] Director; David John James [1943] Director; Angus Jason McQuhae [1966] Director; Colin Tutt [1956] Director

Odessa Print Group Ltd
Incorporated: 1 March 1983 *Employees:* 85
Net Worth: £613,992 *Total Assets:* £6,861,207
Registered Office: Lynwood House, Crofton Road, Orpington, Kent, BR6 8QE
Activities: Printing n.e.c.
Shareholders: Robert Michael Charles; Laurence Scott Matthews
Officers: Janet Charles, Secretary; Robert Michael Charles [1972] Director; Laurence Scott Matthews [1962] Sales Director

Odris Holdings Limited
Incorporated: 15 April 2016
Net Worth: £5,000,200 *Total Assets:* £5,000,200
Registered Office: 166 College Road, Harrow, Middlesex, HA1 1RA
Activities: Activities of other holding companies n.e.c.
Major Shareholder: Sean Peter O'Driscoll
Officers: Sean Peter O'Driscoll [1971] Director [Irish]

Odris Investments Limited
Incorporated: 8 December 2015
Net Worth: £4,997,792 *Total Assets:* £5,825,632
Registered Office: 166 College Road, Harrow, Middlesex, HA1 1RA
Activities: Other business support service activities n.e.c.
Parent: Odris Holdings Limited
Officers: Sean Peter O'Driscoll [1971] Director [Irish]

Odyssey Trust for Education
Incorporated: 11 November 2011 *Employees:* 185
Previous: Townley Grammar School
Net Worth: £23,206,000 *Total Assets:* £25,015,000
Registered Office: Townley Grammer School, Townley Road, Bexleyheath, Kent, DA6 7AB
Activities: General secondary education
Officers: Kal Joshi, Secretary; Steven Thomas Darsey [1958] Director/Group Chairman; Desmond Deehan [1967] Director/Headteacher; Professor Stephen Mark Vernon Hailes [1965] Director/Lecturer; Emily Elizabeth Larson [1990] Director of International Positive Education [American]; Daniel Southon Morrow [1978] Director/CEO of Multi Academy Trust; John Paterson [1951] Director/Environmental Health Officer; Yunita Ramgoolam [1973] Director/Accountant; Aamer Mirza Mohammed Safdar [1971] Director/Pharmacist

The Offer Group Ltd
Incorporated: 5 September 1986 *Employees:* 4
Net Worth: £19,492,774 *Total Assets:* £24,458,782
Registered Office: Burgoine House, 8 Lower Teddington Road, Hampton Wick, Surrey, KT1 4ER
Activities: Other letting and operating of own or leased real estate
Officers: Daye Offer, Secretary; Daye Offer [1933] Director; Lucy Elizabeth Offer [1961] Director/Home Economist; Timothy Henry Miles Offer [1959] Director/Chartered Surveyor

Offerco Limited
Incorporated: 18 May 2009
Net Worth: £10,621,678 *Total Assets:* £10,707,692
Registered Office: Grenville House, 4 Grenville Avenue, Broxbourne, Herts, EN10 7DH
Activities: Activities of head offices
Major Shareholder: Peter John Hearn
Officers: Peter John Hearn, Secretary; Peter John Hearn [1953] Director; Simon James Murphy [1964] Director

Office Overload Limited
Incorporated: 15 February 1966
Net Worth: £752,837 *Total Assets:* £5,222,438
Registered Office: 429-433 Pinner Road, Harrow, Middlesex, HA1 4HN
Activities: Temporary employment agency activities
Officers: Susan Jane Orchard, Secretary/Executive; Michael Anthony Whitelegg, Secretary; Susan Jane Orchard [1956] Director/Executive; Robert William Pollock [1928] Director/President Drake International [Canadian]

Officeteam Group Limited
Incorporated: 4 March 2004 *Employees:* 886
Net Worth: £21,184,000 *Total Assets:* £70,184,000
Registered Office: Unit 4, 500 Purley Way, Croydon, Surrey, CR0 4NZ
Activities: Activities of head offices
Major Shareholder: Jonathan Paul Moulton
Officers: Philippa Anne Maynard, Secretary; Nicholas Robin Hodges [1959] Director; Andrew Graham Mobbs [1978] Finance Director; Robert James Moore [1970] Director

Officeteam Limited
Incorporated: 6 April 2004 *Employees:* 844
Net Worth Deficit: £3,430,000 *Total Assets:* £104,854,000
Registered Office: c/o Oyezstraker, Unit 4, 500 Purley Way, Croydon, Surrey, CR0 4NZ
Activities: Non-specialised wholesale trade
Major Shareholder: Jonathan Paul Moulton
Officers: Philippa Anne Maynard, Secretary; David John Harvell [1966] Director; Nicholas Robin Hodges [1959] Director; Andrew Graham Mobbs [1978] Director; Robert James Moore [1970] Director

The Offie Limited
Incorporated: 26 March 2003 *Employees:* 1
Net Worth: £2,011,597 *Total Assets:* £5,089,589
Registered Office: 34 Queensbury Station Parade, Edgware, Middlesex, HA8 5NN
Activities: Wholesale of wine, beer, spirits and other alcoholic beverages
Officers: Bhavna Jasraj, Secretary; Rajesh Hargovind Jasraj [1964] Director

Offshore Containers Holdings Limited
Incorporated: 8 February 2008
Net Worth: £3,248,164 *Total Assets:* £85,758,864
Registered Office: 298 Sandycombe Road, Kew, Richmond, Surrey, TW9 3NG
Activities: Support activities for petroleum and natural gas mining
Parent: OCHL (Globe) Limited
Officers: John Miller Heiton [1976] Director

Oforce Limited
Incorporated: 20 February 2012
Net Worth: £1,385,508 *Total Assets:* £5,890,976
Registered Office: Portland House, 69-71 Wembley Hill Road, Wembley, Middlesex, HA9 8BU
Activities: Sea and coastal freight water transport
Parent: Union Maritime Limited
Officers: Bhupendra Shantilal Kansagra, Secretary; Laurent Elie Cadji [1977] Director/Businessman; Lewis Levy Cadji [1938] Director/Businessman; Bhupendra Shantilal Kansagra [1956] Director/Businessman; Ramesh Shantilal Kansagra [1950] Director/Businessman

OGE Drilling & Investment Ltd
Incorporated: 26 June 2003
Net Worth: £5,214,723 *Total Assets:* £18,709,168
Registered Office: Spirit House, 8 High Street, West Molesey, Surrey, KT8 2NA
Activities: Agents involved in the sale of machinery, industrial equipment, ships and aircraft
Officers: Juan Carlos Hincapie Carvajal, Secretary; Luis Alberto Hincapie Carvajal [1975] Director [Colombian]

OH Logistics International (UK) Ltd
Incorporated: 12 March 2008
Net Worth: £26,990,280 *Total Assets:* £55,658,144
Registered Office: Unit 1 Action Court, Ashford Road, Ashford, Middlesex, TW15 1XS
Activities: Freight air transport
Parent: Geodis Wilson UK Ltd
Officers: Matthias Hansen [1964] Director/Regional Vice President EMEA [German]; Gunnar Kind [1970] Finance Director [German]; Christopher John Packwood [1975] Director

Oki Europe Limited
Incorporated: 7 December 1987 *Employees:* 530
Net Worth: £14,551,730 *Total Assets:* £128,627,400
Registered Office: Blays House, Wick Road, Englefield Green, Egham, Surrey, TW20 0HJ
Activities: Wholesale of computers, computer peripheral equipment and software
Parent: Oki Data Corporation
Officers: Rakesh Ramniklal Rabheru, Secretary; Takaaki Hagiwara [1967] Director [Japanese]; Hiroshi Ito [1955] Director [Japanese]; Kazuo Kawahara [1967] Director [Japanese]; Akira Ogasawara [1963] Director [Japanese]; Shigeru Ogasawara [1966] Director [Japanese]; Tsukasa Takasawa [1964] Director [Japanese]

Old Vicarage School Trust
Incorporated: 26 January 1973 *Employees:* 42
Net Worth: £3,350,254 *Total Assets:* £5,113,541
Registered Office: 48 Richmond Hill, Richmond upon Thames, Surrey, TW10 6QX
Activities: Primary education
Officers: Christopher James King, Secretary; Mekhla Barua [1983] Director/Teacher; Sarah Marina Brown [1973] Director/Lawyer; Greg Caplan [1961] Director; Guy Cowley [1949] Director/Retired; Christian Michael Heidl [1969] Director/Investment Advisor [German]; Dr Bryony Henderson [1981] Director/Doctor; Suzanne Kathryn Longstaff [1969] Director/Headteacher; Judith Claire Nightingale [1966] Director/Solicitor; Simon Waldman [1956] Director/Journalist; Sally Yeadon [1964] Director/Auditor

Oleoland Hotel Company Limited
Incorporated: 26 October 1990 *Employees:* 1
Net Worth: £10,921,244 *Total Assets:* £12,656,068
Registered Office: 7 Redbridge Lane East, Ilford, Essex, IG4 5ET
Activities: Other accommodation
Officers: Panna Unadkat, Secretary; Panna Unadkat [1954] Director

Olivanna Ltd
Incorporated: 19 March 1997 *Employees:* 1
Net Worth: £876,210 *Total Assets:* £7,895,756
Registered Office: 12 Hatherley Road, Sidcup, Kent, DA14 4DT
Activities: Development of building projects
Major Shareholder: Paul Hughes Skeates
Officers: Paul Hughes Skeates [1961] Director/Developer

Olivegate Properties Limited
Incorporated: 4 March 2002 *Employees:* 2
Net Worth: £24,097,736 *Total Assets:* £36,333,076
Registered Office: Hadley Hurst, Hadley Common, Barnet, Herts, EN5 5QG
Activities: Other business support service activities n.e.c.
Parent: Blendhall Limited
Officers: Anna Victoria Kinsman, Secretary; Alexander Mahboubian [1972] Director/Developer; Farrokh Mahboubian [1932] Director [Iranian]

Olivewood Limited
Incorporated: 20 March 1995 *Employees:* 20
Net Worth: £3,955,603 *Total Assets:* £8,748,244
Registered Office: Unit B2, Neptune Road, Harrow, Middlesex, HA1 4HX
Activities: Agents involved in the sale of timber and building materials
Shareholders: Laxman Lalji Murji; Sanjay Laxman Murji
Officers: Amratben Laxman Murji [1960] Director; Laxman Lalji Murji [1961] Director; Sanjay Laxman Murji [1984] Director

OLM Group Limited
Incorporated: 25 July 1996 *Employees:* 204
Net Worth: £6,228,877 *Total Assets:* £20,030,796
Registered Office: Cairns House, 10 Station Road, Teddington, Middlesex, TW11 9AA
Activities: Activities of head offices
Major Shareholder: Peter Cairns O'Hara
Officers: Christine Margaret Hicks, Company Secretary; Peter Cairns O'Hara [1956] Director/Computer Professional

OLM Systems Limited
Incorporated: 30 May 1991 *Employees:* 154
Net Worth: £8,243,502 *Total Assets:* £21,406,962
Registered Office: Cairns House, 10 Station Road, Teddington, Middlesex, TW11 9AA
Activities: Business and domestic software development
Major Shareholder: Peter Cairns O'Hara
Officers: Christine Margaret Hicks, Secretary; Peter Cairns O'Hara [1956] Director/Computer Professional

OLR (UK) Limited
Incorporated: 2 June 2008 *Employees:* 30
Net Worth: £2,347,605 *Total Assets:* £10,314,193
Registered Office: 137 Ireton Avenue, Walton on Thames, Surrey, KT12 1EN
Activities: Management consultancy activities other than financial management
Major Shareholder: James Hugh Ferguson Spalding
Officers: James Hugh Ferguson Spalding [1966] Director/Chief Executive

Omavale Limited
Incorporated: 27 October 1977 *Employees:* 1
Net Worth: £13,624,618 *Total Assets:* £19,027,584
Registered Office: The Coach House, Powell Road, Buckhurst Hill, Essex, IG9 5RD
Activities: Other letting and operating of own or leased real estate
Officers: James Thomas Jordan [1957] Director

OMEC Holdings Limited
Incorporated: 21 September 2015 *Employees:* 35
Net Worth: £6,631,783 *Total Assets:* £7,962,508
Registered Office: 108 Ripon Way, Borehamwood, Herts, WD6 2JA
Activities: Activities of other holding companies n.e.c.
Major Shareholder: Clifford Sydney Cooper
Officers: Patricia Jane Whiteford, Secretary; Clifford Sydney Cooper [1942] Director/Chairman

Omni Serv Limited
Incorporated: 16 September 2003 *Employees:* 4,155
Net Worth: £13,666,000 *Total Assets:* £61,331,000
Registered Office: World Business Centre, 2 Newall Road, London Heathrow Airport, Hounslow, Middlesex, TW6 2SF
Activities: Service activities incidental to air transportation
Parent: ABM International (Holdings) Limited
Officers: John King, Secretary; John David King [1966] Finance Director; Antony Richard Marke [1966] Director

Oncoland Limited
Incorporated: 2 December 1965 *Employees:* 8
Net Worth: £5,770,101 *Total Assets:* £13,710,360
Registered Office: Gay Dawn Offices, Pennis Lane, Fawkham, Longfield, Kent, DA3 8LZ
Activities: Mixed farming
Parent: F.C. Stark Limited
Officers: Stephen John Billings, Secretary; Andrew John Billings [1964] Director; Clive John Billings [1955] Director/Farm Manager; Ronald John Billings [1960] Director/Manager; Stephen John Billings [1961] Director/Manager

One for All (UK) Ltd.
Incorporated: 13 May 1992 *Employees:* 8
Net Worth: £4,290,146 *Total Assets:* £6,195,421
Registered Office: 79 College Road, Harrow, Middlesex, HA1 1BD
Activities: Wholesale of electronic and telecommunications equipment and parts
Parent: Universal Electronics B.V.
Officers: Paul Joseph Bennett, Secretary; Orhan Acar [1975] Director/Manager of Finance [Dutch]; Paul Joseph Bennett [1955] Managing Director [Irish]

One World Express Inc. Limited
Incorporated: 4 August 1998 *Employees:* 80
Net Worth: £2,795,905 *Total Assets:* £9,706,528
Registered Office: One World House, Pump Lane, Hayes, Middlesex, UB3 3NB
Activities: Other information technology service activities
Parent: One World Group Services Limited
Officers: Atul Surendra Bhakta [1971] Director; Ravinder Jessel [1964] Director

One YMCA
Incorporated: 3 May 2002 *Employees:* 266
Previous: Watford & District YMCA
Net Worth: £13,349,513 *Total Assets:* £16,558,202
Registered Office: Charter House, Charter Place, Watford, Herts, WD17 2RT
Activities: Other accommodation
Officers: David Martin, Secretary; John Peter Ball [1978] Director/Chief Executive; Max Beddard [1960] Director/Accountant; Simon Box [1967] Director/Management Consultant; Jane Catherine Cotton [1959] Director; Clare Hearnshaw [1965] Director/Charity Executive; Benjamin Peter Johnson [1978] Director/Chartered Surveyor; John Robert Knight [1960] Director; Nicola Lucas [1987] Director/Solicitor; Dionne McCalla [1971] Director/Manager; Nicholas Claud Mourant [1958] Director/Chartered Accountant; Andrew Newell [1956] Director; Christine Maria Josepha Neyndorff [1953] Director/Senior Manager [Dutch]; Sal Thirlway [1973] Director; Javier Uriarte [1975] Director/Auditor [Spanish]

Oneclickhr Limited
Incorporated: 19 September 1996
Net Worth Deficit: £22,177,000 *Total Assets:* £9,241,000
Registered Office: Syward Place, Pyrcroft Road, Chertsey, Surrey, KT16 9JT
Activities: Information technology consultancy activities
Parent: ADP Network Services Limited
Officers: Michael Anthony Bonarti [1965] Director/Attorney [American]; Jeffrey Lewis Phipps [1968] Managing Director; Lorna Wake [1976] Director/Accountant

Onix Investments UK Ltd
Incorporated: 25 August 2017
Net Worth: £379,004,064 *Total Assets:* £795,908,160
Registered Office: 2nd Floor, Building 1, Imperial Place, Maxwell Road, Borehamwood, Herts, WD6 1JN
Activities: Activities of financial services holding companies
Parent: Pilgrim's Pride Corporation
Officers: Jose Jardim [1975] Director; Fabio Sandri [1971] Director/Chief Financial Officer [Brazilian]

Onkar International Limited
Incorporated: 5 March 1980 *Employees:* 40
Net Worth: £88,944,200 *Total Assets:* £140,223,632
Registered Office: 19 South Road, Southall, Middlesex, UB1 1SU
Activities: Development of building projects
Officers: Donna Bahia, Secretary; Donna Bahia [1974] Director; Kuljinder Singh Bahia [1972] Director

Only Care Limited
Incorporated: 12 January 2009
Net Worth: £1,555,199 *Total Assets:* £8,694,155
Registered Office: 5 Churchill Court, 58 Station Road, North Harrow, Harrow, Middlesex, HA2 7SA
Activities: Residential care activities for the elderly and disabled
Shareholders: Amit Kumar Shantilal Dhamecha; Rupen Shantilal Dhamecha
Officers: Amit Kumar Shantilal Dhamecha [1969] Director

Onslow Inc. Ltd
Incorporated: 13 January 2017 *Employees:* 1
Net Worth Deficit: £71,200 *Total Assets:* £9,831,311
Registered Office: 5 Elstree Gate, Elstree Way, Borehamwood, Herts, WD6 1JD
Activities: Other service activities n.e.c.
Major Shareholder: Sheila Marie Labatt
Officers: Sheila Marie Labatt [1960] Director [Canadian]

Opal (Earlsfield) LLP
Incorporated: 25 October 2013
Net Worth: £8,313,000 *Total Assets:* £11,231,000
Registered Office: Cowley Business Park, Cowley, Uxbridge, Middlesex, UB8 2AL

Opal (Silvertown) LLP
Incorporated: 8 December 2014
Net Worth Deficit: £1,754,000 *Total Assets:* £80,879,000
Registered Office: Cowley Business Park, Cowley, Uxbridge, Middlesex, UB8 2AL

OPD Group Limited
Incorporated: 21 May 1996
Net Worth: £37,256,848 *Total Assets:* £37,850,904
Registered Office: Grenville House, 4 Grenville Avenue, Broxbourne, Herts, EN10 7DH
Activities: Activities of other holding companies n.e.c.
Shareholders: Offerco Limited; MPM Connect
Officers: Peter Hearn, Secretary; Peter John Hearn [1953] Director/Chartered Accountant; Simon James Murphy [1964] Director

Opecprime Development Limited
Incorporated: 19 March 1987 *Employees:* 21
Net Worth: £1,081,984 *Total Assets:* £13,186,159
Registered Office: Hill House, Lowlands Road, Harrow, Middlesex, HA1 3EQ
Activities: Development of building projects
Shareholders: Luke Andrew Comer; Brian Martin Comer
Officers: Brian Martin Comer [1960] Director [Irish]; Luke Andrew Comer [1957] Director [Irish]; Thomas Donnellan [1960] Director [Irish]

Opecprime Properties Limited
Incorporated: 17 December 1985 *Employees:* 3
Net Worth: £11,356,132 *Total Assets:* £22,600,000
Registered Office: Hill House, Lowlands Road, Harrow, Middlesex, HA1 3EQ
Activities: Development of building projects
Shareholders: Luke Andrew Comer; Brian Martin Comer
Officers: Brian Martin Comer [1960] Director [Irish]; Luke Andrew Comer [1957] Director [Irish]; Thomas Donnellan [1960] Director [Irish]

Openview Group Limited
Incorporated: 28 April 2004 *Employees:* 307
Net Worth: £8,792,224 *Total Assets:* £22,470,132
Registered Office: Openview House, Chesham Close, Romford, Essex, RM7 7PJ
Activities: Non-trading company
Shareholders: Mark Philip Ingleson; Kevin Charles Hall; Paul Bullen
Officers: Paul Bullen [1969] Director; Kevin Charles Hall [1956] Director; Mark Philip Ingleson [1961] Director

Openview Security Solutions Limited
Incorporated: 27 May 1997 *Employees:* 295
Net Worth: £10,469,136 *Total Assets:* £24,037,484
Registered Office: Openview House, Chesham Close, Romford, Essex, RM7 7PJ
Activities: Electrical installation
Parent: Openview Group Limited
Officers: Paul Bullen [1969] Director; Kevin Charles Hall [1956] Director; Mark Philip Ingleson [1961] Director

Operations Holdings Ltd
Incorporated: 9 January 2017 *Employees:* 869
Net Worth Deficit: £3,623,741 *Total Assets:* £7,225,985
Registered Office: Gidar House, 13 The Crossway, Uxbridge, Middlesex, UB10 0JH
Activities: Activities of other holding companies n.e.c.
Shareholders: Ravinder Gidar; Sukhvinder Singh Gidar
Officers: Ravinder Singh Gidar [1959] Director; Sukhvinder Singh Gidar [1968] Director

Optima Chemical Ltd
Incorporated: 16 August 2012
Net Worth: £1,063,033 *Total Assets:* £19,829,948
Registered Office: 80 Strafford Gate, Potters Bar, Herts, EN6 1PG
Activities: Agents involved in the sale of fuels, ores, metals and industrial chemicals
Major Shareholder: Artur Khikhlya
Officers: Christopher Engeham [1950] Director/Company Consultant; Artur Khikhlya [1964] Director/Business Consultant [Cypriot]; Valery Tayim [1988] Director/Secretary [Cypriot]

Optimal Limited
Incorporated: 23 May 1994 *Employees:* 2
Net Worth: £3,515,377 *Total Assets:* £7,605,870
Registered Office: Commonwood Farm, Commonwood, Kings Langley, Herts, WD4 9BB
Activities: Other letting and operating of own or leased real estate
Shareholders: Heather Anne Lench; Michael Anthony Lench
Officers: Heather Anne Lench, Secretary/Director; Heather Anne Lench [1957] Director; Michael Anthony Lench [1954] Director

Optimum Group Services PLC
Incorporated: 3 May 1989 *Employees:* 439
Net Worth: £2,656,944 *Total Assets:* £16,675,437
Registered Office: Jebsen House, 53-61 High Street, Ruislip, Middlesex, HA4 7BD
Activities: Other business support service activities n.e.c.
Shareholders: John Francis Crehan; Annette Crehan
Officers: Annette Crehan, Secretary; John Francis Crehan [1961] Director/Air Conditioning; James Edward Moore [1962] Director/Chief Executive

Optivo Development Services Limited
Incorporated: 4 October 2004
Previous: Viridian Development Services Limited
Net Worth: £3,630,000 *Total Assets:* £10,715,000
Registered Office: Grosvenor House, 125 High Street, Croydon, Surrey, CR0 9XP
Activities: Construction of commercial buildings
Officers: Alison Jane Wignall, Secretary; Kerry Kyriacou [1958] Executive Director; Josephine Kay Robinson [1958] Executive Director Governance and Compliance; Sarah Anne Smith [1966] Executive Director Finance & Resources

Optivo Finance PLC
Incorporated: 2 February 2012
Previous: AmicusHorizon Finance PLC
Net Worth: £100,000 *Total Assets:* £302,900,000
Registered Office: Grosvenor House, 125 High Street, Croydon, Surrey, CR0 9XP
Activities: Financial intermediation not elsewhere classified
Officers: Josephine Kay Robinson, Secretary; David Phillimore Clifford [1952] Director; Paul Denniston Hackett [1966] Director/Chief Executive; Thomas James Paul [1984] Director of Treasury & Commercial; Sarah Anne Smith [1966] Finance and Resources Director

Opus 2 International Limited
Incorporated: 16 August 2006 *Employees:* 93
Net Worth: £13,343,205 *Total Assets:* £19,423,704
Registered Office: Winton Place, 16 Blackhills, Esher, Surrey, KT10 9JW
Activities: Other professional, scientific and technical activities n.e.c.
Parent: Opus 2 Magnum Holdings Limited
Officers: Martin Graham Bangs, Secretary/Accountant; Martin Graham Bangs [1964] Director/Accountant; Graham Francis Smith [1958] Director/Chief Executive

Opus 2 Magnum Holdings Limited
Incorporated: 8 December 2011 *Employees:* 145
Net Worth: £6,266,351 *Total Assets:* £12,786,475
Registered Office: Winton Place, 16 Blackhills, Esher, Surrey, KT10 9JW
Activities: Activities of head offices
Shareholder: Graham Francis Smith
Officers: Martin Graham Bangs, Secretary; Martin Graham Bangs [1964] Director/Accountant; Graham Francis Smith [1958] Director/Consultant

Orange Music Electronic Company Limited
Incorporated: 9 December 1976 *Employees:* 20
Net Worth: £6,508,087 *Total Assets:* £7,707,820
Registered Office: 108 Ripon Way, Borehamwood, Herts, WD6 2JA
Activities: Manufacture of other electrical equipment
Parent: OMEC Holdings Limited
Officers: Patricia Jane Whiteford, Secretary; Charles Kingsley Cooper [1987] Director; Chloe Cooper [1983] Director; Clifford William Cooper [1981] Director; Clifford Sydney Cooper [1942] Director/Chairman; Adrian Gwyn Emsley [1967] Director/Electronics Engineer

Orbis Protect Limited
Incorporated: 5 March 1990 *Employees:* 421
Net Worth: £9,761,000 *Total Assets:* £15,612,000
Registered Office: Beaufort House, Cricket Field Road, Uxbridge, Middlesex, UB8 1QG
Activities: Private security activities
Parent: Project Cube Bidco Limited
Officers: Stephen John Crabb, Secretary; Stephen John Crabb [1956] Finance Director; Robert Ian Freer [1964] Director; Benjamin William Howard [1975] Director/Accountant; Guy Anthony Other [1965] Director/Chief Executive

Orbit Investment Securities Services PLC
Incorporated: 4 July 2000 *Employees:* 8
Net Worth: £8,168,637 *Total Assets:* £8,273,677
Registered Office: Suite 2, 5th Floor, Congress House, 14 Lyon Road, Harrow, Middlesex, HA1 2EN
Activities: Security dealing on own account
Officers: Sakshi Shah, Secretary; Brian Page Constant [1937] Director; Jayechund Jingree [1947] Non-Executive Director Chairman [Mauritian]; Sudip Shah [1982] Director/Chief Executive

Orbital Equipment Limited
Incorporated: 30 March 1999 *Employees:* 18
Net Worth: £2,502,137 *Total Assets:* £8,346,485
Registered Office: 18 Galleyhill Road, Waltham Abbey, Essex, EN9 2AG
Activities: Other business support service activities n.e.c.
Shareholders: Noel Patrick Smith; S & W Plant Limited
Officers: Noel Patrick Smith [1950] Director [Irish]; Darren Michael Williams [1969] Director/Plant Hire

Orbital Fasteners Holdings Limited
Incorporated: 31 October 2012 *Employees:* 78
Net Worth: £9,872,712 *Total Assets:* £14,158,778
Registered Office: Olds Approach, Tolpits Lane, Watford, Herts, WD18 9XT
Activities: Activities of distribution holding companies
Shareholders: Jonathan David Wilson; Peter Thomas Wilson; Christine Agnes Wilson
Officers: Jonathan David Wilson [1961] Director/Manager; Peter Thomas Wilson [1932] Director

Orbital Fasteners Limited
Incorporated: 27 July 1976 *Employees:* 78
Net Worth: £9,495,547 *Total Assets:* £10,853,972
Registered Office: Olds Approach, Tolpits Lane, Watford, Herts, WD18 9XT
Activities: Non-specialised wholesale trade
Shareholders: Jonathan David Wilson; Peter Thomas Wilson; Christine Agnes Wilson
Officers: Peter Thomas Wilson, Secretary; Christine Wilson [1936] Director/Accounts Supervisor; Jonathan David Wilson [1961] Director/General Manager; Peter Thomas Wilson [1932] Director/Wholesaler

Orchard Hill College Academy Trust
Incorporated: 5 April 2013 *Employees:* 569
Net Worth: £72,848,000 *Total Assets:* £88,169,000
Registered Office: Quadrant House, The Quadrant, Brighton Road, Sutton, Surrey, SM2 5AS
Activities: Other education n.e.c.
Officers: Tracey Goodsell, Secretary; Dr Caroline Allen OBE [1963] Director/Principal; Yolande Burgess [1965] Strategic Director; Kevin Francis Finnigan [1949] Director of Employment and Training; Stephen Finlay Heron Lawes [1956] Director/College Vice Principal; Barbara Elizabeth McIntosh [1951] Director/Retired; Jay Huntley Mercer [1953] Director & Local Government Officer; David Winkler [1953] Director/Dentist

Orchard Plumbing Limited
Incorporated: 15 April 1999 *Employees:* 14
Net Worth: £5,949,796 *Total Assets:* £8,328,928
Registered Office: Trinity House, 3 Bullace Lane, Dartford, Kent, DA1 1BB
Activities: Retail sale of electrical household appliances in specialised stores
Major Shareholder: Paul Thomas
Officers: Paul Thomas, Secretary; Paul Thomas [1967] Director/Plumber

Original Additions (Beauty Products) Limited
Incorporated: 5 April 2004 *Employees:* 96
Net Worth: £23,715,480 *Total Assets:* £27,130,652
Registered Office: Ventura House, Bullsbrook Road, Hayes, Middlesex, UB4 0UJ
Activities: Wholesale of perfume and cosmetics
Parent: Original Additions Topco Limited
Officers: James Rogers [1966] Director [American]; James Stammer [1974] Director/President [American]; Mark Alexander Wood [1973] Director

The Original Bedstead Co Limited
Incorporated: 5 November 1998 *Employees:* 14
Net Worth: £5,922,619 *Total Assets:* £6,654,791
Registered Office: c/o Price Mann & Co, 447 Kenton Road, Harrow, Middlesex, HA3 0XY
Activities: Manufacture of other furniture
Officers: Neeraj Nagpal, Secretary; Dhruv Nagpal [1987] Director/Import/Export [Indian]; Kavita Nagpal [1960] Director/Import/Export [Indian]; Neeraj Nagpal [1955] Director/Import/Export [Indian]

The Original London Sightseeing Tour Limited
Incorporated: 14 December 1988 *Employees:* 236
Net Worth: £4,899,000 *Total Assets:* £10,163,000
Registered Office: Busways House, Wellington Road, Twickenham, Middlesex, TW2 5NX
Activities: Other urban, suburban or metropolitan passenger land transport (not underground, metro or similar)
Parent: RATP DEV UK Ltd
Officers: Ronan Bois [1971] Director [French]; Thierry Claude Henry Alexandre Couturier [1966] Operations Director [French]; Romain Ferriere [1975] Director/Chief Financial Officer [French]

Orlando Limited
Incorporated: 24 June 1987 *Employees:* 1
Net Worth: £7,408,269 *Total Assets:* £7,487,465
Registered Office: c/o TG Associates Ltd, 7 Jardine House, Harrovian Business Village, Bessborough Road, Harrow, Middlesex, HA1 3EX
Activities: Performing arts
Major Shareholder: Helena Bonham Carter
Officers: Thomas David Bonham Carter, Secretary; Edward Henry Bonham Carter [1960] Director/Fund Manager; Helena Bonham Carter [1966] Director/Actress; Thomas David Bonham Carter [1961] Director/Management Consultant

Orleans Park School
Incorporated: 2 August 2012 *Employees:* 138
Net Worth: £29,629,432 *Total Assets:* £31,701,936
Registered Office: Orleans Park School, Richmond Road, Twickenham, Middlesex, TW1 3BB
Activities: General secondary education
Officers: Kelly Louise Wallis, Secretary; Elaine Margaret Ball [1966] Director/Headteacher; Jennifer Kim Baskerville [1984] Director/Corporate Responsibility Senior Manager; Julian Bell [1962] Director/Teacher; Jeanette Best [1962] Director; Adam Andrew Dunlop [1964] Director/Editor; Adam Steuart Gladstone [1973] Director/Teacher; Sarah Kate MacKenzie [1966] Director/Homemaker; Laurence Norman Mann [1960] Director/Solicitor; Karen Jane Miller [1971] Director/Partner in a Wholesaler; Stuart Nevill [1970] Director/Charity CEO; Katie O'Connor [1979] Director/Head of Mathematics; Elizabeth Pawsey [1967] Director/Executive Coach & Facilitator; John Martin Riglin [1962] Director/Manager; Anthony Charles Shoebridge [1948] Director/Retired; Eleanor Catherine Stewart [1970] University Programme Director; Sir David Whitlock Tanner [1947] Performance Director (British Rowing)

Orley Farm School Trust
Incorporated: 21 May 1959 *Employees:* 108
Net Worth: £11,316,055 *Total Assets:* £15,772,453
Registered Office: South Hill Avenue, Harrow, Middlesex, HA1 3NU
Activities: Primary education
Officers: Trishna Kamal Vaid, Secretary; Michael John Andrews [1958] Chartered Surveyor and Director; Colin John Hayfield [1955] Director/Chartered Accountant; Kim Louise Hill [1964] Director/Headteacher; Philippa Jackson [1950] Director/Company Secretary; Shivani Kothari [1971] Director/Certified Chartered Accountant; Leena Malde [1966] Director/Company Secretary; Dilip Navapurkar [1961] Director/Property Developer; Rajesh Mansukhlal Raithatha [1972] Managing Director; Doctor Mary Elizabeth Short [1958] Director/Headmistress; Alan Nigel Smith [1962] Director/Banker; Anil Sofat [1972] Commercial Director

Orthene Chemicals Limited
Incorporated: 18 March 1976 *Employees:* 41
Net Worth: £5,027,357 *Total Assets:* £10,497,679
Registered Office: Brember Road, South Harrow Industrial Estate, Harrow, Middlesex, HA2 8UJ
Activities: Manufacture of other chemical products n.e.c.
Parent: Orthene Holdings Ltd
Officers: David Mark Edwards [1966] Production Director; Stephen Walter Jay [1965] Technical Director; Charles James Ker [1967] Managing Director; Roger Brett Ker [1978] Sales Director; Benjamin Hugh Remmington [1966] Operations Director

Orthene Holdings Limited
Incorporated: 17 August 2010 *Employees:* 57
Net Worth: £6,638,203 *Total Assets:* £11,594,368
Registered Office: Unit 13 South Harrow Industrial Estate, Brember Road, Harrow, Middlesex, HA2 8UJ
Activities: Manufacture of other chemical products n.e.c.
Major Shareholder: Charles James Ker
Officers: Charles James Ker [1967] Director

Orthopaedic Research UK
Incorporated: 6 October 2005 *Employees:* 5
Net Worth: £25,502,792 *Total Assets:* £28,451,824
Registered Office: c/o Brayne Williams & Barnard Limited, Rosemount House, Rosemount Avenue, West Byfleet, Surrey, KT14 6LB
Activities: Other business support service activities n.e.c.
Officers: Anthony John Edge [1944] Director/Orthopaedic Surgeon; Peter Evans Harrison [1962] Managing Director; Patrick Latham [1945] Director/Chartered Accountant; David Simeon Martin [1949] Director; Robert Ross Vallings [1943] Director/Solicitor

Osborn Securities (Braintree) Limited
Incorporated: 29 June 2009
Net Worth: £448,187 *Total Assets:* £5,812,744
Registered Office: 1 Towers Place, Eton Street, Richmond, Surrey, TW9 1EG
Activities: Hotels and similar accommodation
Parent: China National Travel Sevices Group Corporation
Officers: Jameson Andrew Lamb [1972] Director; Alex Edward Pritchard [1976] Director

Ospirit Limited
Incorporated: 20 February 2012
Net Worth: £1,899,611 *Total Assets:* £6,453,463
Registered Office: Portland House, 69-71 Wembley Hill Road, Wembley, Middlesex, HA9 8BU
Activities: Sea and coastal freight water transport
Parent: Union Maritime Limited
Officers: Bhupendra Shantilal Kansagra, Secretary; Laurent Elie Cadji [1977] Director/Businessman; Lewis Levy Cadji [1938] Director/Businessman; Bhupendra Shantilal Kansagra [1956] Director/Businessman; Ramesh Shantilal Kansagra [1950] Director/Businessman

Ostrider Limited
Incorporated: 5 November 2012
Net Worth: £1,705,664 *Total Assets:* £6,071,151
Registered Office: Portland House, 69-71 Wembley Hill Road, Wembley, Middlesex, HA9 8BU
Activities: Sea and coastal freight water transport
Parent: Union Maritime Limited
Officers: Bhupendra Shantilal Kansagra, Secretary; Laurent Elie Cadji [1977] Director/Businessman; Lewis Levy Cadji [1938] Director/Businessman; Bhupendra Shantilal Kansagra [1956] Director/Businessman; Ramesh Shantilal Kansagra [1950] Director/Businessman

OTC Direct Limited
Incorporated: 27 October 1995
Net Worth: £59,200,000 *Total Assets:* £111,000,000
Registered Office: 43 Cox Lane, Chessington, Surrey, KT9 1SN
Activities: Wholesale of pharmaceutical goods
Parent: Alliance Boots Holdings Limited
Officers: Lucie Charlotte Massart, Secretary; Alexandro Depau [1970] Director [American]; Pablo Cortes Rivas [1972] Director [Spanish]

Ouhla Properties Limited
Incorporated: 1 September 2000 *Employees:* 5
Net Worth: £16,250,662 *Total Assets:* £19,251,248
Registered Office: Cranfields, First Floor, 43 Friends Road, Croydon, Surrey, CR0 1ED
Activities: Development of building projects
Officers: Fazia Ouhla, Secretary; Fazia Ouhla [1962] Director/Property Manager; Mozamil Ouhla [1930] Director/Property Investor

Outlook Fostering Services Limited
Incorporated: 22 January 2002 *Employees:* 6
Net Worth: £688,000 *Total Assets:* £7,653,000
Registered Office: 5th Floor, Metropolitan House, 3 Darkes Lane, Potters Bar, Herts, EN6 1AG
Activities: Other social work activities without accommodation n.e.c.
Parent: Caretech Community Services Ltd
Officers: Gareth Dufton, Secretary; Gareth Dufton [1976] Director/Chartered Accountant; Farouq Rashid Sheikh [1958] Director; Haroon Rashid Sheikh [1956] Director

Oval Quarter Developments Limited
Incorporated: 8 December 2011 *Employees:* 4
Net Worth: £6,462,949 *Total Assets:* £6,462,950
Registered Office: One Langston Road, Loughton, Essex, IG10 3SD
Activities: Management of real estate on a fee or contract basis
Parent: Myatt's Field Development LLP
Officers: Mark Kevin Francis [1980] Director; Richard Graham Higgins [1956] Director; Peregrine Murray Addison Lloyd [1956] Director; Christopher Muir Turnbull [1986] Development Director

Ovationdata Limited
Incorporated: 23 October 1986
Previous: DPTS Limited
Net Worth: £5,160,973 *Total Assets:* £6,273,280
Registered Office: Unit 10 Crayfields Industrial Park, Main Road, St Pauls Cray, Orpington, Kent, BR5 3HP
Activities: Computer facilities management activities
Parent: Ovationdata Group Holdings Limited
Officers: Susann McCarrick, Secretary; Gregory Gary Servos [1962] Director/Manager [American]; Mark Anthony Wildig [1961] Director

Overseas Air Travel Limited
Incorporated: 22 November 1995 *Employees:* 5
Net Worth: £3,237,000 *Total Assets:* £121,246,000
Registered Office: P O Box 365, Waterside, Harmondsworth, Middlesex, UB7 0GB
Activities: Travel agency activities
Parent: British Airways Holidays Limited
Officers: Katie Louise Bishop, Secretary; Claire Marie Elizabeth Bentley [1968] Director/Airline Executive; Andrew Peter David Brem [1968] Director [Swiss]; Henry James Adam Daniels [1969] Director; Colm Leo Lacy [1970] Director/Airline Executive [Irish]; Sarah Elizabeth Mussenden [1965] Director; Jack Robert Smith [1977] Director

Overton Grange School
Incorporated: 9 May 2011 *Employees:* 138
Net Worth: £22,666,000 *Total Assets:* £26,386,000
Registered Office: Overton Grange School, Stanley Road, Sutton, Surrey, SM2 6TQ
Activities: General secondary education
Officers: Karen Brown, Secretary; Charlotte Susan Auger [1974] Director/Teacher; Aaron Michael Banham [1972] Director; Generald Bennett [1959] Director/Teacher; Shelene Louise Brown [1981] Director/Teacher; Simon David Michael Doubell [1963] Director/IT Analyst; Peter Michael Duus [1973] Director/Teacher [Danish]; James Christopher Eales [1989] Director/NHS Manager; Stephen Gillmore [1964] Director; Brenda Pauline Morley [1943] Director; David John Nicholls [1965] Director/Driving Instructor; Karthik Sankaran [1975] Director/Associate Manager [Indian]; Mohan Shekar [1981] Director/Chief Advisor; Keith Benjamin Stride [1964] Director/Headteacher (Acting); Marion Helen Williams [1953] Director

Oyezstraker Group Limited
Incorporated: 4 April 1996
Net Worth: £601,000 *Total Assets:* £51,260,000
Registered Office: Unit 4, 500 Purley Way, Croydon, Surrey, CR0 4NZ
Activities: Activities of head offices
Major Shareholder: Jonathan Paul Moulton
Officers: Philippa Anne Maynard, Secretary; Andrew Graham Mobbs [1978] Finance Director

P & R Installation Company Limited
Incorporated: 3 November 1997 *Employees:* 192
Net Worth: £2,052,463 *Total Assets:* £10,594,075
Registered Office: 6-8 Powerscroft Road, Sidcup, Kent, DA14 5DT
Activities: Plumbing, heat and air-conditioning installation
Parent: Bilby PLC
Officers: David Thomas Ellingham [1954] Financial Director; Matthew Hobbs [1973] Managing Director; David Richardson [1971] Director/Contracts Manager

P Energy Limited
Incorporated: 28 June 2013
Net Worth: £5,512,433 *Total Assets:* £8,619,584
Registered Office: Portland House, 69-71 Wembley Hill Road, Wembley, Middlesex, HA9 8BU
Activities: Sea and coastal freight water transport
Parent: Focus Tankers Ltd
Officers: Bhupendra Shantilal Kansagra, Secretary; Laurent Elie Cadji [1977] Director/Businessman; Lewis Levy Cadji [1938] Director/Businessman; Bhupendra Shantilal Kansagra [1956] Director/Businessman; Ramesh Shantilal Kansagra [1950] Director/Businessman

P G S International Limited
Incorporated: 27 February 2006 *Employees:* 3
Net Worth Deficit: £22,679,598 *Total Assets:* £184,642,336
Registered Office: 2-4 Eastern Road, Romford, Essex, RM1 3PJ
Activities: Other reservation service activities n.e.c.
Parent: PGS Otelcilik Turizm Ticaret A.S.
Officers: Nicola Jane Cheater [1978] Director

P.I.E. Pharma Limited
Incorporated: 8 January 1996
Net Worth: £139,906 *Total Assets:* £10,276,358
Registered Office: 39a Joel Street, Northwood Hills, Northwood, Middlesex, HA6 1NZ
Activities: Manufacture of basic pharmaceutical products
Major Shareholder: Anuj Somchand Shah
Officers: Anuj Somchand Shah [1966] Director/Actuary

P.I.G. Holdings Limited
Incorporated: 23 September 2015
Net Worth Deficit: £1,679,000 *Total Assets:* £15,448,000
Registered Office: 5th Floor, The Shipping Building, Old Vinyl Factory, 252-254 Blyth Road, Hayes, Middlesex, UB3 1HA
Activities: Activities of head offices
Parent: Host Europe Group Limited
Officers: Richard Anthony Winslow [1979] Director; Jonathan Ying Kit Wong [1976] Director

P.S.V. Transport Systems Limited
Incorporated: 15 February 1994 *Employees:* 75
Net Worth: £4,671,422 *Total Assets:* £6,284,917
Registered Office: 21 Impresa Park, Pindar Road, Hoddesdon, Herts, EN11 0DL
Activities: Manufacture of other electronic and electric wires and cables
Shareholders: Leigh Barnwell; John King
Officers: Leigh Charles Barnwell [1971] Director/Engineer; John Charles King [1959] Sales Director

PAAM Investments Limited
Incorporated: 22 July 2005
Net Worth: £1,730,907 *Total Assets:* £7,494,018
Registered Office: Unit B2, Ullswater Crescent, Ullswater Industrial Estate, Coulsdon, Surrey, CR5 2HR
Activities: Other retail sale in non-specialised stores
Shareholders: Just Another Property Ltd; Tannegate Ltd
Officers: Rajan Virendrabhai Patel, Secretary; Bhavini Udhyam Amin [1963] Director/Pharmacist; Udhyam Babubhai Amin [1961] Director/Businessman; Dipesh Virendrabhai Patel [1966] Director; Kiren Virendrabhai Patel [1970] Director; Rajan Virendrabhai Patel [1972] Director/IT Consultant; Virendra Chhotabhai Patel [1938] Director

Pace Academy Trust
Incorporated: 12 February 2014 *Employees:* 208
Previous: Chipstead Valley Academy Trust
Net Worth: £24,362,088 *Total Assets:* £26,805,070
Registered Office: c/o Chipstead Valley Primary School, Chipstead Valley Road, Coulsdon, Surrey, CR5 3BW
Activities: Primary education
Officers: Lisa Beach [1980] Director/Accountant; Kevin Stuart Bright [1961] Director/Business Psychologist; Roger George Capham [1939] Director/Retired; Edward Stephen Denley [1956] Director/Accountant; Michael Douglas Fuller [1957] Director/Company Secretary; Linda Iris Hall [1948] Director/Retired Headteacher; Hannah Hamilton [1976] Finance Director; Dipa Patel [1976] Director/Civil Engineer; Mark Rosewell [1958] Director/Executive Headteacher

Pact Educational Trust Limited
Incorporated: 29 February 1996 *Employees:* 107
Net Worth: £6,692,653 *Total Assets:* £16,542,914
Registered Office: The Cedars School, Coombe Road, Croydon, Surrey, CR0 5RD
Activities: Primary education
Officers: Eleanor Sorel Leonard, Secretary; Alexander George Frans Maria Alting Von Geusau [1962] Director/Banker [Dutch]; Xavier Bosch [1964] Director/Accountant; Sarah Margaret Cassidy [1967] Director/Project Manager; Eleanor Sorel Leonard [1969] Director/Solicitor; Philip James Leonard [1967] Director/Management Consultant; Peter Millington [1971] Director/Banker; Doctor Anthony Paul Gerard Newman Sanders [1962] Director/Medical Practitioner; Maria Louise Newman Sanders [1964] Director; Jane Claire Phillips [1961] Director; Mark Philip Selby Stables [1966] Director/Teacher; Edward Allen Victor Thompson [1948] Director/Solicitor

Padwicks Travel (Wembley) Limited
Incorporated: 21 October 1981 *Employees:* 36
Net Worth: £7,229,062 *Total Assets:* £30,341,244
Registered Office: 523 High Road, Wembley, Middlesex, HA0 2DH
Activities: Travel agency activities
Shareholders: Pramila Patel; Rashmi Chhotabhai Patel
Officers: Pramila Ashok Patel, Secretary; Pramila Ashok Patel [1952] Director/Travel Agent; Rashmi Chhotabhai Patel [1955] Director/Travel Agent

Michael Page Holdings Limited
Incorporated: 8 June 1984 *Employees:* 141
Net Worth: £14,283,000 *Total Assets:* £948,027,008
Registered Office: Page House, 1 Dashwood Lang Road, Bourne Business Park, Addlestone, Surrey, KT15 2QW
Activities: Other activities of employment placement agencies
Parent: Michael Page Recruitment Group Limited
Officers: Kaye Maguire, Secretary; Kaye Elizabeth Maguire [1977] Director/General Counsel and Company Secretary; Kelvin John Stagg [1971] Director/Accountant; Jeremy Paul Tatham [1969] Director/Accountant

Michael Page International Holdings Limited
Incorporated: 12 December 1988 *Employees:* 2
Net Worth: £8,502,000 *Total Assets:* £48,638,000
Registered Office: Page House, 1 Dashwood Lang Road, Bourne Business Park, Addlestone, Surrey, KT15 2QW
Activities: Activities of other holding companies n.e.c.
Parent: Michael Page Partnership Limited
Officers: Kaye Maguire, Secretary; Kaye Elizabeth Maguire [1977] Director/General Counsel and Company Secretary; Kelvin John Stagg [1971] Director/Accountant; Jeremy Paul Tatham [1969] Director/Accountant

Michael Page International Recruitment Limited
Incorporated: 27 December 2000 *Employees:* 1,274
Net Worth: £833,841,024 *Total Assets:* £1,333,287,936
Registered Office: Page House, 1 Dashwood Lang Road, Bourne Business Park, Addlestone, Surrey, KT15 2QW
Activities: Other activities of employment placement agencies
Parent: Pagegroup PLC
Officers: Kaye Maguire, Secretary; Kaye Elizabeth Maguire [1977] Director/General Counsel and Company Secretary; Kelvin John Stagg [1971] Director/Accountant; Jeremy Paul Tatham [1969] Director/Accountant

Michael Page International Southern Europe Limited
Incorporated: 14 December 2000 *Employees:* 5
Net Worth: £1,248,000 *Total Assets:* £106,235,000
Registered Office: Page House, 1 Dashwood Lang Road, The Bourne Business Park, Addlestone, Surrey, KT15 2QW
Activities: Activities of head offices
Parent: Pagegroup PLC
Officers: Kaye Maguire, Secretary; Geoffroy Marie Humbert de Beaucorps [1974] Finance Director [French]; Patrick Pierre Hollard [1968] Director [French]; Kaye Elizabeth Maguire [1977] Director/General Counsel and Company Secretary; Kelvin John Stagg [1971] Director/Accountant; Jeremy Paul Tatham [1969] Director/Accountant

Michael Page Partnership Limited
Incorporated: 30 September 1983 *Employees:* 2
Net Worth: £3,426,000 *Total Assets:* £43,563,000
Registered Office: Page House, Dashwood Lang Road, Bourne Business Park, Addlestone, Surrey, KT15 2QW
Activities: Activities of head offices
Parent: Michael Page Holdings Limited
Officers: Kaye Maguire, Secretary; Kaye Elizabeth Maguire [1977] Director/General Counsel and Company Secretary; Kelvin John Stagg [1971] Director/Accountant; Jeremy Paul Tatham [1969] Director/Accountant

Michael Page Recruitment Group Limited
Incorporated: 15 April 1988 *Employees:* 2
Net Worth: £13,001,000 *Total Assets:* £104,353,000
Registered Office: Page House, 1 Dashwood Lang Road, The Bourne Business Park, Addlestone, Surrey, KT15 2QW
Activities: Management consultancy activities other than financial management
Parent: Michael Page International Recruitment Limited
Officers: Kaye Maguire, Secretary; Kaye Elizabeth Maguire [1977] Director/General Counsel and Company Secretary; Kelvin John Stagg [1971] Director/Accountant; Jeremy Paul Tatham [1969] Director/Accountant

Pagegroup PLC
Incorporated: 30 January 1997 *Employees:* 6,549
Previous: Michael Page International PLC
Net Worth: £270,056,992 *Total Assets:* £499,812,000
Registered Office: Page House, 1 Dashwood Lang Road, The Bourne Business Park, Addlestone, Surrey, KT15 2QW
Activities: Activities of head offices
Officers: Kaye Elizabeth Maguire, Secretary; Simon Boddie [1960] Finance Director; Patrick Jean-Marie de Smedt [1955] Director [Belgian]; Michelle Miriam Healy [1968] Director/HR Professional [Irish]; Stephen John Ingham [1962] Executive Director; David Soutar Lowden [1957] Director; Sylvia Metayer [1960] Director [French]; Angela Charlotte Seymour-Jackson [1966] Director; Kelvin John Stagg [1971] Director/Management Accountant

Paje Limited
Incorporated: 11 May 2009 *Employees:* 3
Net Worth Deficit: £158,763 *Total Assets:* £5,336,165
Registered Office: 2nd Floor, 215 Lower Addiscombe Road, Croydon, Surrey, CR0 6RB
Activities: Buying and selling of own real estate
Officers: Maxine Deacon, Secretary; Ade Fabunmi-Stone [1964] Director/General Manager; Pauline Jennifer Fabunmi-Stone [1957] Director/Administrator

Palacath Limited
Incorporated: 11 September 1972
Net Worth: £29,606,992 *Total Assets:* £35,614,168
Registered Office: Atlas House, 28 Great Cambridge Road, Enfield, Middlesex, EN1 1UU
Activities: Development of building projects
Officers: Judith Erlich, Secretary; Baruch Erlich [1962] Director/Solicitor; Judith Erlich [1960] Director/Secretary

Palace Street Developments Limited
Incorporated: 23 November 1993 *Employees:* 2
Net Worth: £8,709,248 *Total Assets:* £9,913,686
Registered Office: Ashcombe House, 5 The Crescent, Leatherhead, Surrey, KT22 8DY
Activities: Other letting and operating of own or leased real estate
Parent: Palace Street Investments Limited
Officers: William Michael Fellows, Secretary/Surveyor; Nicholas George Mensforth Eyles [1947] Director/Surveyor; William Michael Fellows [1949] Director/Surveyor

The Palace Theatre Watford Limited
Incorporated: 1 July 1996 *Employees:* 38
Net Worth: £6,062,637 *Total Assets:* £6,404,190
Registered Office: Palace Theatre, 20 Clarendon Road, Watford, Herts, WD17 1JZ
Activities: Artistic creation
Officers: Jamie Arden, Secretary; Karen Ann Collett [1962] Director/Learning Support Assistant; Kenny Rebecca Dada [1995] Director/Account Executive; Anne Beverley Fenton [1953] Director/Executive Search Consultant; John Brian Hunt [1951] Director/Retired; Mark Phillip Lawrence [1959] Executive Director; Deborah Lincoln [1960] Director/Senior Vice-President, Corporate Communications; Carol Lingwood [1962] Director/Head of Costume, Royal National Theatre; Binita Mehta-Parmar [1990] Director/Corporate Communications Consultant; John Douglas Pritchard [1994] Director/Artist; Georgina Rae [1984] Director/Production Associate; Brett Scott Spencer [1968] Director/Broadcast; Patrick Thomas Stoddart [1944] Director/Lecturer; Jayne Trotman [1965] Director; Timothy James Williams [1965] Director/Credit Manager

Palladio Estates Limited
Incorporated: 14 March 1986
Net Worth: £6,548,367 *Total Assets:* £7,937,870
Registered Office: 2 AC Court, High Street, Thames Ditton, Surrey, KT7 0SR
Activities: Development of building projects
Parent: Trenvale Limited
Officers: Darren Matthew Johns, Secretary; Darren Matthew Johns [1971] Director/Banker; David Edwin Johns [1938] Director

Palmera Holdings Limited
Incorporated: 17 June 2014
Net Worth Deficit: £354,856 *Total Assets:* £5,356,071
Registered Office: 5 Elstree Gate, Elstree Way, Borehamwood, Herts, WD6 1JD
Activities: Activities of other holding companies n.e.c.
Shareholders: Saad Audeh; Bassam Audeh
Officers: Saad Audeh [1966] Director/Chairman

Pamina Estates Limited
Incorporated: 6 February 2015
Net Worth: £5,279,249 *Total Assets:* £8,188,296
Registered Office: 50 Lancaster Road, Enfield, Middlesex, EN2 0BY
Activities: Other letting and operating of own or leased real estate
Major Shareholder: Michael Blakey
Officers: Michael Blakey [1963] Director; Paula May Blakey [1963] Director

Pan United Ltd
Incorporated: 4 September 1979 *Employees:* 12
Net Worth: £6,199,392 *Total Assets:* £7,889,665
Registered Office: 4th Floor, 15 College Road, Harrow, Middlesex, HA1 1BA
Activities: Wholesale of fruit and vegetables
Major Shareholder: Ashok Kumar Parekh
Officers: Prakash Mehta, Secretary; Praful Shah [1951] Director/Accountant

Panalpina World Transport Limited
Incorporated: 15 November 1939 *Employees:* 356
Net Worth Deficit: £815,000 *Total Assets:* £47,638,000
Registered Office: Panalpina House, Great South West Road, Feltham, Middlesex, TW14 8NU
Activities: Operation of warehousing and storage facilities for water transport activities
Parent: Panalpina World Transport (Holding) Ltd.
Officers: Caterina Rossi Herdman, Secretary; Christopher David Cooper [1968] Director/Freight Forwarder; Caterina Rossi Herdman [1954] Director/Human Resources [Italian]; Frank Simmen [1965] Director/Accountant [Swiss]; Rachel Wilton [1974] Director/Country Head of Marketing and Sales UK and Ireland

Panavision Europe Limited
Incorporated: 17 August 1990 *Employees:* 713
Net Worth Deficit: £7,115,000 *Total Assets:* £108,122,000
Registered Office: Corporate Office, Metropolitan Centre, Bristol Road, Greenford, Middlesex, UB6 8GU
Activities: Renting and leasing of media entertainment equipment
Shareholder: Stephen Andrew Feinberg
Officers: Jeffrey Thomas Allen [1953] Director; Mark Vincent Furssedonn [1965] Group Operations Director; Jasminder Singh Kalsey [1974] Director; Kimberly Ann Snyder [1962] Director [American]

Pancredit Systems Ltd.
Incorporated: 1 February 1988 *Employees:* 56
Net Worth: £7,742,000 *Total Assets:* £12,178,000
Registered Office: Elder House, St Georges Business Park, Brooklands Road, Weybridge, Surrey, KT13 0TS
Activities: Business and domestic software development
Parent: Equiniti Holdings Limited
Officers: Katherine Cong, Secretary; Seema Sangar [1976] Finance Director; John Stier [1966] Director/Chief Financial Officer; Guy Richard Wakeley [1970] Director

PandoraExpress 2 Limited
Incorporated: 6 March 2003
Net Worth: £3,444,000 *Total Assets:* £248,162,000
Registered Office: Hunton House, Highbridge Estate, Oxford Road, Uxbridge, Middlesex, UB8 1LX
Activities: Licenced restaurants
Parent: PandoraExpress 1 Limited
Officers: Andrew David Pellington, Secretary; Andrew David Pellington [1964] Director; Jinlong Wang [1957] Director [American]

PandoraExpress 3 Limited
Incorporated: 6 March 2003
Net Worth Deficit: £1,815,000 *Total Assets:* £244,707,008
Registered Office: Hunton House, Highbridge Estate, Oxford Road, Uxbridge, Middlesex, UB8 1LX
Activities: Licenced restaurants
Parent: PandoraExpress 2 Limited
Officers: Andrew David Pellington, Secretary; Andrew David Pellington [1964] Director; Jinlong Wang [1957] Director [American]

PandoraExpress 4 Limited
Incorporated: 6 March 2003 *Employees:* 2
Net Worth: £239,012,000 *Total Assets:* £246,580,000
Registered Office: Hunton House, Highbridge Estate, Oxford Road, Uxbridge, Middlesex, UB8 1LX
Activities: Licenced restaurants
Parent: PandoraExpress 3 Limited
Officers: Andrew David Pellington, Secretary; Andrew David Pellington [1964] Director; Jinlong Wang [1957] Director [American]

PandoraExpress 7 Limited
Incorporated: 11 December 2003 *Employees:* 2
Net Worth: £54,686,000 *Total Assets:* £83,505,000
Registered Office: Hunton House, Highbridge Industrial Estate, Oxford Road, Uxbridge, Middlesex, UB8 1LX
Activities: Non-trading company
Parent: PizzaExpress Operations Limited
Officers: Andrew David Pellington, Secretary; Andrew David Pellington [1964] Director; Jinlong Wang [1957] Director [American]

Pandrol (Vortok) Limited
Incorporated: 16 May 1975 *Employees:* 27
Previous: Multiclip Company Limited
Net Worth: £10,155,000 *Total Assets:* £12,715,000
Registered Office: Osprey House, 63 Station Road, Addlestone, Surrey, KT15 2AR
Activities: Manufacture of other fabricated metal products n.e.c.
Parent: Pandrol International
Officers: Jonathan Baxter, Secretary; Neil Algar [1975] Director; Olivier Vincent Antille [1971] Director [French]; Wayne Martin Peacock [1958] Director; Richard Smith Robertson [1964] Director

Pandrol Finance Limited
Incorporated: 30 July 1999 *Employees:* 2
Net Worth: £104,517,000 *Total Assets:* £110,940,000
Registered Office: Osprey House, 63 Station Road, Addlestone, Surrey, KT15 2AR
Activities: Activities of production holding companies
Parent: Pandrol Group Limited
Officers: Jonathan Baxter, Secretary; Olivier Vincent Antille [1971] Director [French]; Brian Forster [1953] Director

Pandrol Group Limited
Incorporated: 30 July 1999 *Employees:* 2
Net Worth: £79,568,000 *Total Assets:* £85,962,000
Registered Office: Osprey House, 63 Station Road, Addlestone, Surrey, KT15 2AR
Activities: Activities of production holding companies
Parent: Pandrol Holdings Limited
Officers: Jonathan Baxter, Secretary; Olivier Vincent Antille [1971] Director [French]; Brian Forster [1953] Director

Pandrol Holdings Limited
Incorporated: 15 September 1999
Net Worth: £84,916,000 *Total Assets:* £85,686,000
Registered Office: Osprey House, 63 Station Road, Addlestone, Surrey, KT15 2AR
Activities: Activities of production holding companies
Parent: HRT UK Limited
Officers: Jonathan Baxter, Secretary; Olivier Vincent Antille [1971] Director [French]; Brian Forster [1953] Director

Pandrol International Limited
Incorporated: 14 September 1945 *Employees:* 2
Net Worth: £2,645,000 *Total Assets:* £126,180,000
Registered Office: Osprey House, 63 Station Road, Addlestone, Weybridge, Surrey, KT15 2AR
Activities: Activities of production holding companies
Parent: Pandrol Finance Limited
Officers: Jonathan Baxter, Secretary; Olivier Vincent Antille [1971] Director [French]; Brian Forster [1953] Director

Pandrol Limited
Incorporated: 4 July 1953 *Employees:* 229
Net Worth: £20,706,000 *Total Assets:* £54,439,000
Registered Office: Osprey House, 63 Station Road, Addlestone, Weybridge, Surrey, KT15 2AR
Activities: Manufacture of other fabricated metal products n.e.c.
Parent: Pandrol International Limited
Officers: Jonathan Baxter, Secretary; Olivier Vincent Antille [1971] Director [French]; Stephen John Cox [1961] Director; Brian Forster [1953] Director; Wayne Martin Peacock [1958] Director; Guy Henri Jean Paul Talbourdet [1965] Managing Director [French]

Paneurosys Limited
Incorporated: 30 September 1992 *Employees:* 2
Net Worth: £3,157,158 *Total Assets:* £6,894,992
Registered Office: Flat A, 6 Riverdale Gardens, East Twickenham, Middlesex, TW1 2BZ
Activities: Other letting and operating of own or leased real estate
Shareholders: Ronald Edward Crick; Carol Anne Holdsworth
Officers: Carol Anne Holdsworth, Secretary; Ronald Edward Crick [1947] Director; Carol Anne Holdsworth [1957] Director

Pantheon Hotels and Leisure Limited
Incorporated: 8 June 1981 *Employees:* 124
Net Worth: £10,223,317 *Total Assets:* £17,291,444
Registered Office: The Barn Hotel, West End Road, Ruislip, Middlesex, HA4 6JB
Activities: Hotels and similar accommodation
Parent: SNB Holdings Limited
Officers: Kathirgamathamby Jegeswaran, Secretary/Accountant; Nor Fazlina Bhattessa [1963] Director [Malaysian]; Shalil Nalin Bhattessa [1968] Director/Businessman

Panther (VAT) Properties Limited
Incorporated: 25 June 1996
Net Worth: £14,378,993 *Total Assets:* £55,986,056
Registered Office: Unicorn House, Station Close, Potters Bar, Herts, EN6 1TL
Activities: Buying and selling of own real estate
Parent: Panther Securities PLC
Officers: Simon Jeffrey Peters, Secretary; Andrew Stewart Perloff [1944] Director; John Henry Perloff [1968] Director; Simon Jeffrey Peters [1977] Director

Panther AL (VAT) Limited
Incorporated: 11 March 2009
Net Worth: £1,843,507 *Total Assets:* £5,279,398
Registered Office: Unicorn House, Station Close, Potters Bar, Herts, EN6 1TL
Activities: Other letting and operating of own or leased real estate
Parent: Panther Securities PLC
Officers: Simon Jeffrey Peters, Secretary; Andrew Stewart Perloff [1944] Director; John Henry Perloff [1968] Director; Simon Jeffrey Peters [1977] Director/Accountant

Panther Hinckley (VAT) Ltd
Incorporated: 27 September 2017
Net Worth Deficit: £199,151 *Total Assets:* £5,625,048
Registered Office: Unicorn House, Station Close, Potters Bar, Herts, EN6 1TL
Activities: Buying and selling of own real estate
Parent: Panther Securities PLC
Officers: Simon Jeffrey Peters, Secretary; Andrew Stewart Perloff [1944] Director; John Henry Perloff [1968] Director; Simon Jeffrey Peters [1977] Director

Panther Investment Properties Limited
Incorporated: 9 April 1973
Net Worth: £12,678,165 *Total Assets:* £27,539,376
Registered Office: Unicorn House, Station Close, Potters Bar, Herts, EN6 1TL
Activities: Buying and selling of own real estate
Parent: Panther Securities PLC
Officers: Simon Jeffrey Peters, Secretary; Andrew Stewart Perloff [1944] Director; John Henry Perloff [1968] Director; Simon Jeffrey Peters [1977] Director

Panther Securities P L C
Incorporated: 17 October 1934 *Employees:* 21
Net Worth: £91,212,000 *Total Assets:* £211,962,000
Registered Office: Unicorn House, Station Close, Potters Bar, Herts, EN6 1TL
Activities: Buying and selling of own real estate
Officers: Simon Jeffrey Peters, Secretary/Director; Bryan Richard Galan [1943] Director/Chartered Surveyor; Peter Michael Kellner [1942] Director; Andrew Stewart Perloff [1944] Director; John Henry Perloff [1968] Director; Simon Jeffrey Peters [1977] Director

Panther Shop Investments Limited
Incorporated: 22 February 1934
Net Worth: £2,480,655 *Total Assets:* £6,016,560
Registered Office: Unicorn House, Station Close, Potters Bar, Herts, EN6 1TL
Activities: Buying and selling of own real estate
Parent: Panther Securities PLC
Officers: Simon Jeffrey Peters, Secretary; Andrew Stewart Perloff [1944] Director; John Henry Perloff [1968] Director; Simon Jeffrey Peters [1977] Director

Panther Trading Limited
Incorporated: 9 July 1974
Net Worth: £8,727,900 *Total Assets:* £16,531,522
Registered Office: Unicorn House, Station Close, Potters Bar, Herts, EN6 1TL
Activities: Buying and selling of own real estate
Parent: Panther Securities PLC
Officers: Simon Jeffrey Peters, Secretary; Andrew Stewart Perloff [1944] Director; John Henry Perloff [1968] Director; Simon Jeffrey Peters [1977] Director

Papa Entertainment Limited
Incorporated: 12 May 2011 *Employees:* 1
Previous: Papa Entertainment PLC
Net Worth: £9,580,352 *Total Assets:* £9,841,621
Registered Office: Wickham House, 2 Upper Teddington Road, Kingston upon Thames, Surrey, KT1 4DY
Activities: Video production activities
Major Shareholder: Dermod Owen Hynes
Officers: Harry Edmund Cowell [1960] Director; Eoghan Hynes [1948] Director [Irish]; Norman Alec Charles Lott [1955] Director; Korda Jerome Roberts Marshall [1960] Director

Papa Midco Limited
Incorporated: 23 October 2014 *Employees:* 87
Net Worth Deficit: £63,689,000 *Total Assets:* £133,035,000
Registered Office: Johnston House, 8 Johnston Road, Woodford Green, Essex, IG8 0XA
Activities: Financial management
Parent: Papa Topco Limited
Officers: Michael Douglas Comish [1965] Operations Director [British/Canadian]; Dirk Gustaf Eller [1972] Director/Partner [American]; Peter William James [1983] Director; Karen Elisabeth Dind Jones [1956] Director

Papa Topco Limited
Incorporated: 23 October 2014 *Employees:* 4,311
Net Worth Deficit: £273,806,016 *Total Assets:* £133,039,000
Registered Office: Johnston House, 8 Johnston Road, Woodford Green, Essex, IG8 0XA
Activities: Financial management
Shareholders: David Bonderman; James George Coulter
Officers: Michael Douglas Comish [1965] Operations Director [British/Canadian]; Dirk Gustaf Eller [1972] Director/Partner [American]; Peter William James [1983] Director; Karen Elisabeth Dind Jones [1956] Director

Paradine Holdings Limited
Incorporated: 11 August 2015
Net Worth: £9,499,622 *Total Assets:* £10,175,627
Registered Office: 5 Elstree Gate, Elstree Way, Borehamwood, Herts, WD6 1JD
Activities: Activities of other holding companies n.e.c.
Shareholders: George Frost; Wilfred Paradine Frost
Officers: George Frost [1987] Director; Wilfred Paradine Frost [1985] Director

Paragon Internet Group Limited
Incorporated: 22 March 2011 *Employees:* 52
Net Worth: £3,598,000 *Total Assets:* £23,931,000
Registered Office: 5th Floor, The Shipping Building, Old Vinyl Factory, 252-254 Blyth Road, Hayes, Middlesex, UB3 1HA
Activities: Information technology consultancy activities
Parent: P.I.G. Holdings Limited
Officers: Sara Silveira Da Costa Da Cunha Rego [1973] Director [Portuguese]; Jonathan Ying Kit Wong [1976] Director

Paragon Treasury PLC
Incorporated: 30 October 2014
Net Worth: £13,000 *Total Assets:* £224,140,000
Registered Office: Case House, 85-89 High Street, Walton on Thames, Surrey, KT12 1DZ
Activities: Financial intermediation not elsewhere classified
Parent: Paragon Asra Housing Ltd
Officers: Marion Hall, Secretary; Stephen David Amos [1957] Director/Retired Banker; David Edgar Hunter [1955] Director; Curtis Mark Juman [1968] Finance Director

Parallel Learning Trust
Incorporated: 11 July 2013 *Employees:* 293
Net Worth: £11,721,000 *Total Assets:* £23,066,000
Registered Office: Suite 1, Baker House, Horsley Road, Bromley, Kent, BR1 3LB
Activities: Primary education
Officers: Richard Francis Pugh, Secretary; Mark Peter Jordan [1977] Director/Chief Executive Officer; Michael Martell [1952] Director/Education Consultant; Ross Alexander Neal [1956] Director/Youth Engagement Manager; Rosemary Newlove [1952] Director/Retired Headteacher; Richard Francis Pugh [1975] Director/Solicitor; Andrea Smith [1969] Director/Parenting Support Worker; Bhaavin Wallia [1993] Director/Management Consultant

Paramount 26 Limited
Incorporated: 4 April 1989 *Employees:* 33
Net Worth: £3,919,352 *Total Assets:* £8,201,855
Registered Office: Unit 7 Eurocourt, Cosgrove Road, Oliver Close, West Thurrock, Essex, RM20 3EE
Activities: Manufacture of other fabricated metal products n.e.c.
Officers: Ailbhe Weldon, Secretary; David Weldon [1974] Director [Irish]

Parcelhero Group Limited
Incorporated: 4 April 2013
Net Worth: £5,067,697 *Total Assets:* £7,977,296
Registered Office: 3-6 Canute House, Durham Wharf Drive, Brentford, Middlesex, TW8 8HR
Activities: Unlicensed carriers
Major Shareholder: Roger Sumner Rivers
Officers: Roger Sumner Rivers [1976] Director/Business Executive; Gavin FitzGenerald Wynne [1964] Director/Business Executive

The Park Federation Academy Trust
Incorporated: 17 July 2012 *Employees:* 798
Net Worth: £56,272,000 *Total Assets:* £67,274,000
Registered Office: Botwell Common Road, Hayes, Middlesex, UB3 1JA
Activities: Primary education
Officers: Elaine Armstrong, Secretary; Jasjit Sohal, Secretary; Simon Neil Carter [1964] Director/Government Servant; Afsheen Chowdhry [1980] Director/Solicitor; Ranisha Dhamu [1973] Director/Corporate Information Governance Officer; Peter John Dollimore [1956] Director/Retired; Anoop Kumar Ghai [1958] Director/Banker; Muralee Nair [1965] Director/Banker; Dr Adel Ben Mohamed Rouz [1965] Director/Business/HR [Tunisian]; Nicola Jane Tranter [1968] Director/Deputy Headteacher; Dr Martin John Young [1960] Director/Executive Headteacher

Park Garage Group PLC
Incorporated: 16 January 1998 *Employees:* 17
Net Worth: £20,167,968 *Total Assets:* £46,549,408
Registered Office: 1-3 Station Approach, Hayes, Bromley, Kent, BR2 7EQ
Activities: Retail sale in non-specialised stores with food, beverages or tobacco predominating
Shareholder: Sunil Tandon
Officers: Balraj Tandon, Secretary; Balraj Tandon [1959] Director/Businessman; Sunil Tandon [1962] Director/Businessman

Park Green Investments Limited
Incorporated: 13 July 1993
Net Worth: £509,574 *Total Assets:* £5,461,071
Registered Office: Onslow Hall, Little Green, Richmond, Surrey, TW9 1QS
Activities: Other letting and operating of own or leased real estate
Major Shareholder: Stephen Thompson
Officers: Robert Stephen Thompson, Secretary; Robert Stephen Thompson [1983] Director/Chartered Surveyor; Stephen Thompson [1959] Director/Chartered Surveyor

Park Grove Residential Limited
Incorporated: 12 January 2017
Net Worth Deficit: £42,707 *Total Assets:* £6,241,196
Registered Office: No 1 Railshead Road, St Margarets, Old Isleworth, Middlesex, TW7 7EP
Activities: Other letting and operating of own or leased real estate
Officers: Barry Bernard Tansey, Secretary; Alan Joseph Tansey [1972] Director [Irish]; Bernard Joseph Tansey [1944] Director/Engineer [Irish]

Park High School
Incorporated: 1 July 2011 *Employees:* 182
Net Worth: £20,294,172 *Total Assets:* £23,561,744
Registered Office: Park High School, Thistlecroft Gardens, Stanmore, Middlesex, HA7 1PL
Activities: Technical and vocational secondary education
Officers: Marilyn Joy Ashton [1953] Director/Planning Consultant; Sean Guiheen [1985] Director/Teacher; Bhupendra Vishram Hirani [1971] Director/Self Employed; Karen Elaine Hogge [1969] Director/Teaching Assistant; David Emlyn Lumley [1958] Director; Sam Methuen [1959] Director/Solicitor; Josephine Muir [1948] Director/Retired; Naresh Patel [1966] Director/Mechanical Engineer; Sangita Hitesh Patel [1965] Director/Accountant; Toral Patel [1968] Director/ICT, Data & Library Manager; Hayley Louise Perren [1988] Director/Teacher; Richard Samuels [1986] Director/Pastoral Support Assistant; Ramesh Shah [1955] Director/Finance Manager; Dr John Phillip Wise [1945] Director; John Woodgate [1959] Director/Retired Fire Officer

Park House Residential Developments Limited
Incorporated: 10 December 2015
Net Worth Deficit: £313,182 *Total Assets:* £5,570,006
Registered Office: Park House, 87 Burlington Road, New Malden, Surrey, KT3 4QP
Activities: Other business support service activities n.e.c.
Major Shareholder: David Alexander King
Officers: Joanne Elizabeth Lamont, Secretary; David Alexander King [1945] Director/Property Developer; Steven Perez [1963] Director/House Builders

Park Rutland Investments (London) Limited
Incorporated: 12 April 1957
Net Worth: £15,922,064 *Total Assets:* £16,587,068
Registered Office: Kingfisher House, 21-23 Elmfield Road, Bromley, Kent, BR1 1LT
Activities: Other letting and operating of own or leased real estate
Officers: Julian Davies Gregory [1966] Director/Publisher; Micheal Judge Judge [1934] Director/Solicitor; Steven Taylor [1962] Director/Solicitor

Park Score Ltd
Incorporated: 7 February 2005 *Employees:* 2
Net Worth: £7,916,394 *Total Assets:* £15,513,085
Registered Office: Unit 39 Sheraton Business Centre, Wadsworth Close, Greenford, Middlesex, UB6 7JB
Activities: Other professional, scientific and technical activities n.e.c.
Shareholder: Thomas Henry James
Officers: Kevin Guidera, Secretary; Thomas Henry James [1961] Director; Sandra Marron [1963] Director [Irish]

Parkdale Investments Limited
Incorporated: 9 June 1961
Net Worth: £3,838,464 *Total Assets:* £38,207,036
Registered Office: Atlas House, 28 Great Cambridge Road, Enfield, Middlesex, EN1 1UU
Activities: Buying and selling of own real estate
Officers: Judith Erlich, Secretary; Baruch Erlich [1962] Director/Solicitor; Judith Erlich [1960] Director/Secretary

Parklight Properties Limited
Incorporated: 27 February 2012 *Employees:* 4
Net Worth: £1,963,513 *Total Assets:* £11,039,246
Registered Office: 30 Campion Close, Croydon, Surrey, CR0 5SN
Activities: Other letting and operating of own or leased real estate
Officers: Ashok Patel [1959] Director/Businessman; Priti Patel [1963] Director/Businesswoman; Ramanbhai Patel [1932] Director/Businessman

The Parkside Group (Holdings) Limited
Incorporated: 18 May 2015 *Employees:* 95
Net Worth: £3,163,658 *Total Assets:* £12,784,806
Registered Office: Unit 5 The Willow Centre, 17 Willow Lane, Mitcham, Surrey, CR4 4NX
Activities: Aluminium production
Officers: Peter Thomas Dziurzynski [1966] Managing Director; Martyn David Hayward [1968] Operations Director; Simon John Jones [1959] Director

Parkside Group Limited (The)
Incorporated: 7 November 1967 *Employees:* 95
Net Worth: £4,871,349 *Total Assets:* £12,473,392
Registered Office: Unit 5, 17 Willow Lane, Mitcham, Surrey, CR4 4NX
Activities: Aluminium production
Officers: Peter Thomas Dziurzynski, Secretary; Lisa Alexander [1971] Director of Finance & HR; Alison Davey [1973] Commercial Director; Peter Thomas Dziurzynski [1966] Director; Martyn David Hayward [1968] Director; Simon John Jones [1959] Director; Richard Reeve [1962] Sales Director

Parkside Leisure Limited
Incorporated: 26 March 1965 *Employees:* 82
Net Worth: £7,290,507 *Total Assets:* £8,252,080
Registered Office: Paradise Park, White Stubbs Lane, Broxbourne, Herts, EN10 7QA
Activities: Activities of other holding companies n.e.c.
Shareholders: Peter Charles Sampson; Grace Florence Sampson
Officers: Grace Florence Sampson, Secretary/Director; Grace Florence Sampson [1940] Director; Peter Charles Sampson [1939] Director; Lynn Kathleen Whitnall [1964] Director

Parkside School Trust
Incorporated: 16 August 1960 *Employees:* 75
Net Worth: £4,312,806 *Total Assets:* £6,194,034
Registered Office: The Manor, Stoke Road, Stoke D'Abernon, Cobham, Surrey, KT11 3PX
Activities: Primary education
Officers: Eve-Lucille McCann, Secretary; John Generald Cahill [1950] Director/Retired; Kerry Gallagher [1977] Audit Director; Celia Jane Gregory [1956] Director of St George's Hill Lawn Tennis Club; Monique Herne [1969] Director/Housewife [Dutch]; Edward Luke Kesterton [1992] Director/Senior Specialist; Roger MacDonald Morris [1947] Director/Chartered Accountant; Andrew Shilton [1959] Director; Robin Simon Southwell [1960] Director; Michael Joseph Stevens [1962] Director/Group Chief Executive Officer; Pauline Jean Stoffberg [1955] Director/Partner; Jonathan Brian Vincent Wood [1965] Director/Retired

Parkview Treasury Services (UK) Limited
Incorporated: 22 October 2007
Net Worth: £241,660,000 *Total Assets:* £1,834,680,960
Registered Office: 1st Floor, Ash House, Littleton Road, Ashford, Middlesex, TW15 1TZ
Activities: Activities of head offices
Parent: United Technologies Holdings Limited
Officers: Lynn Banis, Secretary; Christian Bruno Jean Idczak [1963] Director/Business Executive [French]; James Terence George Laurence [1964] Financial Director; Patricia Catherine Moran [1964] Finance Director [American]; Peter Ross [1964] Finance Director; Louise Kay Thompson [1983] Director/Chartered Management Accountant

Parkwood Hall Co-operative Academy Trust
Incorporated: 17 March 2015 *Employees:* 142
Net Worth: £4,896,000 *Total Assets:* £6,968,000
Registered Office: Parkwood Hall Cooperative Academy, Beechenlea Lane, Swanley, Kent, BR8 8DR
Activities: Other education n.e.c.
Officers: Joanne Elizabeth Nyland, Secretary; Abidemi Agidee-Adekunle [1975] Director/Governor; Richard Leonard Allalouf [1970] Director/Governor; Soshana Sabeena Wijeratne Austin [1972] Director; Simon Joseph Blackburn [1963] Director/Network Traffic Controller; Libby Merle Blake [1957] Director/Consultant; Steve Finch [1970] Director/Contracts Manager; Barbara McBrien [1955] Director/School Business Manager; Kolawole Olounbanjo [1965] Director/Governor; Katherine Priestley [1968] Director/Human Resources; Elisa Valdez [1978] Director/Governor [Argentinian]; Robert Stanley Walkington [1943] Director/Retired; Kirsty Louise Wiseman [1975] Director/Teacher

Parrsouth Limited
Incorporated: 28 September 1998 *Employees:* 1
Net Worth: £3,136,650 *Total Assets:* £10,205,603
Registered Office: 1 Parkshot, Richmond, Surrey, TW9 2RD
Activities: Buying and selling of own real estate
Shareholders: Barbara Anne Ivie; Kevin Campbell Ivie
Officers: Barbara Anne Ivie, Secretary; Kevin Campbell Ivie [1949] Director/Tour Operator

Parry Murray & Company Limited
Incorporated: 13 December 1929 *Employees:* 19
Net Worth: £9,220,107 *Total Assets:* £10,604,473
Registered Office: 3rd Floor, Simpson House, 6 Cherry Orchard Road, Croydon, Surrey, CR0 6BA
Activities: Wholesale of textiles
Parent: Ambadi Enterprises Limited
Officers: Eoin Michael Campbell, Secretary; Murugappa Arunachalam [1967] Director/Industrialist; Richard Anthony Chamberlain [1942] Director; Peter Edward Driscoll [1943] Director; Ajit Akkara Veetil Kumar [1954] Director/Company Executive; Ramesh Kizhakepatt Menon [1960] Director [Indian]; Venkatachalam Muthiah [1958] Director/Company Executive [Indian]

Parthenon Entertainment Limited
Incorporated: 19 February 2002 *Employees:* 63
Net Worth: £9,545,000 *Total Assets:* £95,502,000
Registered Office: Grant Way, Isleworth, Middlesex, TW7 5QD
Activities: Television programme distribution activities
Parent: Parthenon Media Group Limited
Officers: Christopher Jon Taylor, Secretary; Karl Holmes [1973] Director/Finance Professional; Colin Robert Jones [1964] Director; Christopher Jon Taylor [1971] Director/Company Secretary

Party Invitation Limited
Incorporated: 3 July 1997 *Employees:* 5
Net Worth: £3,777,345 *Total Assets:* £5,784,211
Registered Office: 616D Green Lane, Ilford, Essex, IG3 9SE
Activities: Other retail sale in non-specialised stores
Major Shareholder: Aiyub Machhada
Officers: Rukhsana Machhada, Secretary; Aiyub Machhada [1957] Director

Pass J. Holdings Limited
Incorporated: 20 September 1985 *Employees:* 112
Net Worth: £5,007,681 *Total Assets:* £11,181,216
Registered Office: Online House, 240 Freshwater Road, Dagenham, Essex, RM8 1RX
Activities: Freight transport by road
Officers: Pamela Rose Oleary, Secretary; Juanita Dora Oleary [1965] Director/Controller Staff Agency; Pamela Rose Oleary [1940] Director/Office Manager; Steven James Oleary [1961] Director/Transport Operations Manager

Passportcard Limited
Incorporated: 3 October 2014 *Employees:* 187
Net Worth: £6,156,567 *Total Assets:* £14,473,239
Registered Office: 43 Bushfield Crescent, Edgware, Middlesex, HA8 8XQ
Activities: Other business support service activities n.e.c.
Officers: Eyal Ben Chelouce [1961] Director [Israeli]; Teresa Chia [1981] Director [American]; Alon Ketzef [1967] Director [Israeli]; Robert L Seelig [1968] Director [American]

Pattinson Green Limited
Incorporated: 5 December 2009 *Employees:* 2
Net Worth: £7,213,526 *Total Assets:* £7,255,889
Registered Office: Norman House, 8 Burnell Road, Sutton, Surrey, SM1 4BW
Activities: Other letting and operating of own or leased real estate
Major Shareholder: Frances Caelia Nicholson
Officers: Frances Caelia Nicholson [1957] Director/Research Consultant; Francoise Stichelbaut [1967] Director/Translator/Trainer [Belgian]

Payless Group Limited
Incorporated: 14 August 1996 *Employees:* 3
Net Worth: £6,577,992 *Total Assets:* £14,698,229
Registered Office: c/o Danmirr Consultants, 170 Church Road, Mitcham, Surrey, CR4 3BW
Activities: Retail sale in non-specialised stores with food, beverages or tobacco predominating
Shareholder: Iftikhar Ahmed
Officers: Mahomed Erfan Abdul Gaffar, Secretary; Parveen Ahmed, Secretary; Iftikhar Ahmed [1967] Director/Businessman

PB Bidco Limited
Incorporated: 1 July 2013
Net Worth: £34,403,000 *Total Assets:* £115,077,000
Registered Office: Two Bridges, Guildford Street, Chertsey, Surrey, KT16 9AU
Activities: Business and domestic software development
Officers: Jason Phillip Conley [1975] Finance Director [American]; Robert Christopher Crisci [1975] Finance Director [American]; Robin Tarquinn Morris-Weston [1970] Director; John Kenneth Stipancich [1968] Director/Vice President, General Counsel and Secretary [American]

PB Holdco Limited
Incorporated: 5 July 2013
Net Worth: £41,625,000 *Total Assets:* £114,291,000
Registered Office: Two Bridges, Guildford Street, Chertsey, Surrey, KT19 9AU
Activities: Business and domestic software development
Officers: Jason Phillip Conley [1975] Finance Director [American]; Robert Christopher Crisci [1975] Finance Director [American]; Robin Tarquinn Morris-Weston [1970] Director; John Kenneth Stipancich [1968] Director/Vice President, General Counsel and Secretary [American]

PB Midco Limited
Incorporated: 1 July 2013 *Employees:* 4
Net Worth: £105,528,000 *Total Assets:* £114,290,000
Registered Office: Two Bridges, Guildford Street, Chertsey, Surrey, KT16 9AU
Activities: Business and domestic software development
Officers: Jason Phillip Conley [1975] Finance Director [American]; Robert Christopher Crisci [1975] Finance Director [American]; Robin Tarquinn Morris-Weston [1970] Director; John Kenneth Stipancich [1968] Director/Vice President, General Counsel and Secretary [American]

PB Topco Limited
Incorporated: 1 July 2013 *Employees:* 4
Net Worth: £128,494,000 *Total Assets:* £131,370,000
Registered Office: Two Bridges, Guildford Street, Chertsey, Surrey, KT16 9AU
Activities: Business and domestic software development
Officers: Jason Phillip Conley [1975] Finance Director [American]; Robert Christopher Crisci [1975] Finance Director [American]; Robin Tarquinn Morris-Weston [1970] Director; John Kenneth Stipancich [1968] Director/Vice President, General Counsel and Secretary [American]

PCL Bidco Limited
Incorporated: 29 October 2012
Net Worth Deficit: £50,806,000 *Total Assets:* £109,900,000
Registered Office: Grove House, Guildford Road, Leatherhead, Surrey, KT22 9DF
Activities: Activities of head offices
Parent: PCL Holdco Limited
Officers: Christopher Michael Higgs, Secretary; Christopher Michael Higgs [1956] Finance Director; Uwe Nickel [1958] Director/Chief Executive Officer [German]; Duncan Paul Stonehouse [1970] Operations Director

PCL Holdco Limited
Incorporated: 29 October 2012
Net Worth: £68,861,000 *Total Assets:* £68,861,000
Registered Office: Grove House, Guildford Road, Leatherhead, Surrey, KT22 9DF
Activities: Activities of head offices
Parent: HCS Group GmbH
Officers: Christopher Michael Higgs, Secretary; Christopher Michael Higgs [1956] Finance Director; Uwe Nickel [1958] Director/Chief Executive Officer [German]; Duncan Paul Stonehouse [1970] Operations Director

PCL Transport Limited
Incorporated: 15 January 2002 *Employees:* 6
Net Worth: £8,333,116 *Total Assets:* £30,098,416
Registered Office: 57-59 High Street, Hoddesdon, Herts, EN11 8TQ
Activities: Freight transport by road
Shareholders: Giuseppe Ricotta; Giuseppina Ricotta
Officers: Joe Ricotta, Secretary; Cristina Ricotta [1995] Director; Giuseppe Ricotta [1966] Director; Giuseppina Ricotta [1969] Director

PDC Brands UK Limited
Incorporated: 22 March 2016 *Employees:* 96
Net Worth: £3,490,904 *Total Assets:* £48,029,652
Registered Office: Ventura House, Bullsbrook Road, Hayes, Middlesex, UB4 0UJ
Activities: Other service activities n.e.c.
Officers: James Rogers [1966] Director/Chief Operating Officer [American]; James Stammer [1974] Director/President & Chief Executive Officer, PDC Brands [American]; Mark Alexander Wood [1973] Director

PE (Mount Carmel) Limited
Incorporated: 1 February 2016
Net Worth Deficit: £132,256 *Total Assets:* £9,179,248
Registered Office: Salisbury House, 20 Queens Road, Weybridge, Surrey, KT13 9XE
Activities: Development of building projects
Shareholders: Glyn Watkin Jones; Portchester Estates Limited
Officers: Paul David Anthony Schiavo [1975] Director; Glyn Watkin Jones [1944] Director

Peace Hospice Care
Incorporated: 24 April 1991 *Employees:* 138
Net Worth: £6,055,075 *Total Assets:* £6,556,619
Registered Office: Peace Hospice Care, Peace Drive, Watford, Herts, WD17 3PH
Activities: Other human health activities
Officers: Ragen Ramanbhai Amin [1963] Director/Accountant; Patrick James Brennan [1959] Director/Banking Executive; Virginia Ruth Edwards [1956] Director/Clinician and Manager; Alan Philip Graham [1947] Director/Retired Merchant Banker; Jarmo Pentti Ensio Kesanto [1955] Director/Chief Executive [Finnish]; Terence Benjamin Ritchie [1976] Director/Solicitor; Dr Jeremy Stephen Shindler [1959] Director/General Practitioner; Yolanda Woolf [1963] Director/Consultant

Peacock Homes Limited
Incorporated: 26 September 1968 *Employees:* 7
Net Worth: £14,557,790 *Total Assets:* £16,250,122
Registered Office: Beechwood, 57 Church Street, Epsom, Surrey, KT17 4PX
Activities: Financial intermediation not elsewhere classified
Parent: Aviary Investment Holdings Limited
Officers: Karen Mary Crosby, Secretary; Mervyn Llewellyn Sheen [1944] Director; Penelope Jane Sheen [1947] Director

Peak Securities Limited
Incorporated: 25 September 1961 *Employees:* 3
Net Worth: £50,514,408 *Total Assets:* £108,068,072
Registered Office: Russell House, 140 High Street, Edgware, Middlesex, HA8 7LW
Activities: Other letting and operating of own or leased real estate
Parent: Regentsmead Limited
Officers: Lee Robert Mesnick [1968] Director/Accountant; Richard Alan Ross [1942] Director

Pearl Properties Limited
Incorporated: 30 November 1993 *Employees:* 6
Net Worth: £3,591,628 *Total Assets:* £11,731,613
Registered Office: College House, 17 King Edwards Road, Ruislip, Middlesex, HA4 7AE
Activities: Management of real estate on a fee or contract basis
Major Shareholder: Gideon Ian Israel
Officers: Gideon Ian Israel, Secretary/Engineer; Adam Israel [1989] Director/Researcher; Denise Israel [1951] Director/Housewife; Gideon Ian Israel [1948] Director/Engineer; Joanna Israel [1986] Director/Fine Arts Valuer; Rachile Israel [1924] Director/Teacher; Ben Benjamin Kfir [1975] Director/Property Manager; Alexandra Lucie Van Someren [1968] Director/Administrator

Pearl River Delta Investments Limited
Incorporated: 20 December 2002
Net Worth: £98,322,296 *Total Assets:* £98,754,248
Registered Office: Chertsey Road, Sunbury on Thames, Middlesex, TW16 7BP
Activities: Activities of head offices
Parent: BP Global Investments Limited
Officers: David William Knipe [1974] Director/Oil Company Executive

Pebble Beach Systems Group PLC
Incorporated: 27 September 2000 *Employees:* 84
Previous: Vislink PLC
Net Worth Deficit: £6,065,000 *Total Assets:* £13,047,000
Registered Office: 12 Horizon Business Village, Brooklands Road, Weybridge, Surrey, KT13 0TJ
Activities: Activities of head offices
Officers: Alison Unitt, Secretary; Robin Beatham Howe [1947] Director; Peter Michael Mayhead [1972] Finance Director; John Charles Varney [1956] Director

Pebble Beach Systems Ltd
Incorporated: 10 March 2000 *Employees:* 71
Net Worth: £6,426,000 *Total Assets:* £10,006,000
Registered Office: Unit 12 Horizon Business Village, 1 Brooklands Road, Weybridge, Surrey, KT13 0TJ
Activities: Other information technology service activities
Parent: Pebble Beach Systems Group PLC
Officers: Peter Michael Mayhead, Secretary; Peter Michael Mayhead [1972] Director/Chief Financial Officer and Chief Operating Officer; John Charles Varney [1956] Director

The Pegasus Academy Trust
Incorporated: 24 February 2011 *Employees:* 332
Net Worth: £31,267,000 *Total Assets:* £35,930,000
Registered Office: Whitehorse Manor School, Brigstock Road, Thornton Heath, Surrey, CR7 7JN
Activities: Primary education
Officers: Josephine Mary Ridge, Secretary; Shelley Davies [1972] Director/Educationalist; Fiona Fearon [1980] Director/HR Consultant; Gary Griffin [1959] Director/Retired School Teacher; Richard Henry Hill [1948] Director; Sylvia Ann McNamara [1953] Director/Education Consultant; Ian Patterson [1956] Director/Retired; Nina Pogossova [1981] Managing Director; Matthew Jolyon Roberts [1965] Director/Headteacher; Lynne Diane Sampson [1964] Director/Headteacher; Kevin Paul Smith [1959] Director/Fire Officer

Pegrid Limited
Incorporated: 1 April 2014
Net Worth: £1,141,777 *Total Assets:* £5,347,549
Registered Office: 52 Queens Road, Twickenham, Middlesex, TW1 4EX
Activities: Other letting and operating of own or leased real estate
Shareholders: Richard Ignatius Ryan; Paula Elizabeth Ryan
Officers: Paula Elizabeth Ryan [1963] Director/Accountant [Irish]; Richard Ignatius Ryan [1962] Director/Accountant [Irish]

Pelham Academy Trust
Incorporated: 11 March 2013 *Employees:* 176
Previous: Pelham Primary School
Net Worth: £16,191,067 *Total Assets:* £17,813,396
Registered Office: Pelham Primary School, Pelham Road, Bexleyheath, Kent, DA7 4HL
Activities: Pre-primary education
Officers: Morayo Akinduro [1994] Director/Accountant [Nigerian]; Richard Bain [1981] Director/Project Manager; Derek Clements [1945] Director; Melanie Davids [1961] Director/Deputy Headteacher; James Michael George Green [1982] Director/Business Manager; Jill Louise Hayman [1969] Director; Andrew Ian Hogarth [1961] Director/Headteacher; Irene Margaret Holliss [1957] Director; Berenice Larbi [1979] Director/Administrator; Nigel Richard Marchant [1960] Director/Clerk; Rory Owen McDonnell [1969] Director; Joanne Moulton [1971] Director/Education Welfare Officer; David Mummery [1984] Director/Admissions Officer; Dr Abutaleb Muhammed Fazlur Rashid [1937] Director; Gary David Streatfield [1976] Director/Teacher; Joseph Andrew Wood [1985] Director/Senior Associate

Penasul UK Limited
Incorporated: 27 October 2003 *Employees:* 3
Net Worth: £5,467,000 *Total Assets:* £5,723,000
Registered Office: 2nd Floor, Building 1, Imperial Place, Maxwell Road, Borehamwood, Herts, WD6 1JN
Activities: Processing and preserving of poultry meat
Officers: Wesley Mendonca Batista Filho [1991] Director/Business Executive [Brazilian]

Penenden Heath Investments LLP
Incorporated: 27 January 2009
Net Worth: £5,053,694 *Total Assets:* £7,559,659
Registered Office: 54 St Marys Lane, Upminster, Essex, RM14 2QT
Officers: Anthony David Thorogood [1962] Member; Roger Wright [1955] Member

Penn Place Investments Limited
Incorporated: 14 March 2013 *Employees:* 3
Net Worth Deficit: £1,049,678 *Total Assets:* £6,167,780
Registered Office: First Floor, Radius House, 51 Clarendon Road, Watford, Herts, WD17 1HP
Activities: Other business support service activities n.e.c.
Major Shareholder: Thomas Richard MacBride Price
Officers: Marie Louise Price [1975] Director/Solicitor; Thomas Richard MacBride Price [1973] Director/Financier

The Penspen Group Limited
Incorporated: 27 May 1970
Net Worth: £5,002,000 *Total Assets:* £67,325,000
Registered Office: 3 Water Lane, Richmond, Surrey, TW9 1TJ
Activities: Activities of head offices
Parent: Dar Al-Handasah (UK) Limited
Officers: Susan Jane McDonald, Secretary; Dany Aoun [1970] Director [Lebanese]; Gillian Anne Empringham [1974] Director/HR; Peter Bernard O'Sullivan [1969] Director/Chief Executive [Irish]; Talal Shair [1967] Director/Executive [Jordanian]

Penspen Limited
Incorporated: 23 May 1957 *Employees:* 249
Net Worth: £4,332,000 *Total Assets:* £63,387,000
Registered Office: 3 Water Lane, Richmond, Surrey, TW9 1TJ
Activities: Engineering related scientific and technical consulting activities
Parent: The Penspen Group Limited
Officers: Susan Jane McDonald, Secretary; Neale Carter [1968] Director/Business Development; Nigel St John Thomas Curson [1961] Director/Engineer; Gillian Anne Empringham [1974] HR Director; Peter Bernard O'Sullivan [1969] Director/Chief Executive [Irish]; Timothy Webber [1964] Finance Director

Penta Consulting Limited
Incorporated: 11 March 1998 *Employees:* 95
Net Worth: £15,853,825 *Total Assets:* £20,861,136
Registered Office: Crosspoint House, 28 Stafford Road, Wallington, Surrey, SM6 9AA
Activities: Human resources provision and management of human resources functions
Shareholders: Penta Ultimate Holdings Ltd; Penta Consulting Holdings Limited
Officers: Jamie Brookes, Secretary; Paul Richard Clark [1964] Managing Director; John Robert Foley [1955] Director; Robert Harverson [1961] Director; Ian Michael O'Neill [1976] Sales Director; Adam David Olver [1982] Sales Director; Aminash Patel [1981] Sales Director; Fraser Wyman Searle [1962] Director/Accountant; Jamie Andrew Sobrany [1972] Director; Richard Anthony Wilson [1966] Sales Director

Pentagon Freight Services PLC
Incorporated: 6 March 1974 *Employees:* 126
Net Worth: £29,182,128 *Total Assets:* £39,823,044
Registered Office: Pentagon House, Unit 1.02 Crayfields Industrial Estate, Main Road, Orpington, Kent, BR5 3HP
Activities: Other transportation support activities
Parent: Pentagon Holdings Limited
Officers: Kim Lesley Ochiltree, Secretary; Kim Lesley Ochiltree [1969] Finance Director; Ashley Paul Taylor [1972] Director [Australian]

Pentagon Holdings Limited
Incorporated: 30 October 2000 *Employees:* 728
Net Worth: £44,689,576 *Total Assets:* £85,540,848
Registered Office: Unit 1.02, Crayfield Industrial Estate, Main Road, Orpington, Kent, BR5 3HP
Activities: Activities of other holding companies n.e.c.
Officers: Clare Madeleine Smith [1938] Director; Ashley Paul Taylor [1972] Director [Australian]

Pentair UK Holdings Limited
Incorporated: 10 January 2014
Net Worth: £133,198,552 *Total Assets:* £133,198,552
Registered Office: Regal House, 70 London Road, Twickenham, Middlesex, TW1 3QS
Activities: Activities of head offices
Parent: Pentair PLC
Officers: Grant William O'Grady [1970] Director [Australian]; Andrew Gary Smyth [1976] Director/Tax Planning; Henning Wolfgang Wistorf [1982] Director [German]

People Against Dirty Holdings Limited
Incorporated: 17 November 2015 *Employees:* 406
Net Worth: £117,970,552 *Total Assets:* £232,747,920
Registered Office: The Ministry of Clean, 1 Eton Street, Richmond, Surrey, TW9 1AG
Activities: Activities of production holding companies
Officers: Brian Patrick Tippett, Secretary; Timothy Earl Bailey [1962] Director/Executive VP [American]; Audrey Sue Ditter [1962] Director/Senior Vice President [American]

Pepkor UK Retail Limited
Incorporated: 30 October 2014 *Employees:* 283
Net Worth Deficit: £38,717,488 *Total Assets:* £27,856,412
Registered Office: Oak House, Reeds Crescent, Watford, Herts, WD24 4QP
Activities: Other retail sale in non-specialised stores
Parent: Poundland Limited
Officers: Mathew David Ankers, Secretary; Mathew David Ankers [1986] Director/Accountant; Sean Nicholas Nennens Cardinaal [1967] Director/Business Executive; Darren Vernon [1968] Retail Director

Pepper (UK) Limited
Incorporated: 29 March 2008 *Employees:* 312
Net Worth: £8,841,009 *Total Assets:* £16,696,472
Registered Office: Harman House, 1 George Street, Uxbridge, Middlesex, UB8 1QQ
Activities: Activities of mortgage finance companies
Parent: Pepper Homeloans Limited
Officers: Roger Stephen Lansdowne, Secretary/Accountant; Warren Henry Justice [1966] Director/Accountant; Richard Eugene Klemmer [1960] Director [American]; Generald Martin McHugh [1964] Director; Laurence Morey [1974] Director; Joy Laina Warner [1965] Director

Peppercorn Investments Limited
Incorporated: 20 December 2004 *Employees:* 2
Net Worth: £4,922,567 *Total Assets:* £11,360,579
Registered Office: c/o Messrs Elliot Woolfe & Rose, Equity House, 128-136 High Street, Edgware, Middlesex, HA8 7TT
Activities: Management of real estate on a fee or contract basis
Parent: Peppercorn Property Investments Ltd
Officers: Elisabeth MacHugh, Secretary; Stephen Melville [1949] Director/Property Consultant; Martin Anthony Nathan [1948] Director/Lawyer

Peppercorn Property Investments Limited
Incorporated: 11 April 1985 *Employees:* 3
Net Worth: £17,702,836 *Total Assets:* £22,478,208
Registered Office: c/o Messrs Elliot Woolfe & Rose, 1st Floor, Equity House, 128-136 High Street, Edgware, Middlesex, HA8 7TT
Activities: Development of building projects
Shareholders: Bedford Square Properties Limited; Woodfield House Properties Limited; Bedford Square Properties Limited
Officers: Elisabeth MacHugh, Secretary; Stephen Melville [1949] Director/Property Consultant; Martin Anthony Nathan [1948] Director/Lawyer

Perfect Practices Group Limited
Incorporated: 6 April 2017 *Employees:* 2
Net Worth Deficit: £631,688 *Total Assets:* £9,160,334
Registered Office: Nicholas House, River Front, Enfield, Middlesex, EN1 3FG
Activities: Dental practice activities
Parent: Dentex Healthcare Group Limited
Officers: Bhavna Doshi [1970] Director; Rahul Rohit Doshi [1968] Director; Barry Koors Lanesman [1959] Director [South African]; Michael Brent Zurowski [1965] Director

Perfect Smile Group Holding Limited
Incorporated: 21 May 2014 *Employees:* 180
Net Worth: £1,117,887 *Total Assets:* £15,048,207
Registered Office: Perfect Smile Dental Surgery, 25-27 Kew Road, Richmond, Surrey, TW9 2NQ
Activities: Dental practice activities
Officers: Palvesh Patel, Secretary; Chirag Subhashchandra Patel [1977] Director/Dentist

Perfect Smile Newcastle Limited
Incorporated: 24 January 2014 *Employees:* 55
Net Worth Deficit: £362,740 *Total Assets:* £5,114,778
Registered Office: 25-27 Kew Road, Richmond, Surrey, TW9 2NQ
Activities: Dental practice activities
Officers: Palvesh Patel, Secretary; Chirag Patel [1977] Director/Dentist

Perform Group Financing PLC
Incorporated: 17 July 2015
Net Worth Deficit: £406,000 *Total Assets:* £205,448,000
Registered Office: Hanover House, Plane Tree Crescent, Feltham, Middlesex, TW13 7BZ
Activities: Other professional, scientific and technical activities n.e.c.
Parent: Perform Sports Media Limited
Officers: Benedict Luke Barlow, Secretary; Stuart Joel Epstein [1963] Director [American]; Paul Oszkar David Morton [1979] Director

Perform Group Limited
Incorporated: 25 July 2007 *Employees:* 2,445
Previous: Perform Group PLC
Net Worth Deficit: £232,350,000 *Total Assets:* £892,328,000
Registered Office: Hanover House, Plane Tree Crescent, Feltham, Middlesex, TW13 7BZ
Activities: Other professional, scientific and technical activities n.e.c.
Parent: AI Perform Holdings LLP
Officers: Lincoln Eduardo Benet [1963] Director [American]; Simon Cristofer Denyer [1974] Director; Stuart Joel Epstein [1963] Director [American]; John Mark Gleasure [1970] Director; Herman Siegfried Jorg Mohaupt [1966] Director/Investment Executive [German]; Kiyoshi Nakamura [1959] Director/Businessman [Japanese]; John Skipper [1955] Director/Executive Chairman [American]; Paul Ashton Walker [1957] Director

Perform Investment Limited
Incorporated: 8 July 2015
Net Worth Deficit: £343,655,008 *Total Assets:* £464,953,984
Registered Office: Hanover House, Plane Tree Crescent, Feltham, Middlesex, TW13 7BZ
Activities: Other professional, scientific and technical activities n.e.c.
Parent: Perform Media Channels Ltd
Officers: Paul Oszkar David Morton [1979] Director; James David Rushton [1978] Director

Perform Media Channels Ltd
Incorporated: 6 December 2005
Net Worth Deficit: £34,189,000 *Total Assets:* £369,636,992
Registered Office: Hanover House, Plane Tree Crescent, Feltham, Middlesex, TW13 7BZ
Activities: Other professional, scientific and technical activities n.e.c.
Parent: Perform Media Services Ltd
Officers: Simon Cristofer Denyer [1974] Director/Sports Marketing; Paul Oszkar David Morton [1979] Director

Perform Media Sales Ltd
Incorporated: 23 June 2004
Net Worth Deficit: £19,947,000 *Total Assets:* £114,639,000
Registered Office: Sussex House, Plane Tree Crescent, Feltham, Middlesex, TW13 7HE
Activities: Media representation services
Parent: Perform Media Services Ltd
Officers: Simon Cristofer Denyer [1974] Director/Sports Marketing; Paul Oszkar David Morton [1979] Director

Perform Media Services Ltd
Incorporated: 29 August 1997 *Employees:* 947
Net Worth: £25,153,000 *Total Assets:* £360,615,008
Registered Office: Hanover House, Plane Tree Crescent, Feltham, Middlesex, TW13 7BZ
Activities: Other professional, scientific and technical activities n.e.c.
Parent: Perform Sports Media Limited
Officers: Simon Cristofer Denyer [1974] Director/Sports Marketing; Paul Oszkar David Morton [1979] Director

Perform Sporting News Limited
Incorporated: 1 March 2013
Net Worth Deficit: £14,342,510 *Total Assets:* £36,441,864
Registered Office: Sussex House, Plane Tree Crescent, Feltham, Middlesex, TW13 7HE
Activities: Other professional, scientific and technical activities n.e.c.
Parent: Perform Media Channels Ltd
Officers: David Baddeley [1983] Financial Director; Juan Carlos Delgado Vesga [1978] Managing Director [Colombian]; Simon Cristofer Denyer [1974] Director

Perform Sports Media Limited
Incorporated: 17 July 2015
Net Worth: £348,784,000 *Total Assets:* £595,744,000
Registered Office: Hanover House, Plane Tree Crescent, Feltham, Middlesex, TW13 7BZ
Activities: Other professional, scientific and technical activities n.e.c.
Parent: Perform Group Limited
Officers: Paul Oszkar David Morton [1979] Director

Periworld Limited
Incorporated: 27 March 1986 *Employees:* 5
Net Worth: £9,666,682 *Total Assets:* £16,285,444
Registered Office: Allen House, 1 Westmead Road, Sutton, Surrey, SM1 4LA
Activities: Other letting and operating of own or leased real estate
Officers: Andrew Carmel Delicata, Secretary/Director; Andrew Carmel Delicata [1977] Director; Antoinette Francesca Delicata [1987] Director/Businesswoman; David Gerrard Delicata [1985] Director/Businessman; James Michael Delicata [1978] Director/Property Developer

Perpetuum Construction Limited
Incorporated: 17 February 2014
Net Worth Deficit: £529,274 *Total Assets:* £7,619,679
Registered Office: Ground Floor, 189 Richmond Road, Kingston upon Thames, Surrey, KT2 5DD
Activities: Development of building projects
Parent: Perpetuum Development Limited
Officers: Dina Dos Santos Figueira, Secretary; Stephen Donovan [1969] Director [Irish]; Christopher William Ward [1969] Director [Irish]

PES Group Limited
Incorporated: 4 August 1993 *Employees:* 43
Previous: Maintest Engineering Limited
Net Worth: £3,124,239 *Total Assets:* £7,369,898
Registered Office: The Shipping Building, The Old Vinyl Factory, Blyth Road, Hayes, Middlesex, UB3 1HA
Activities: Non-specialised wholesale trade
Shareholders: Kevin McDermot; James Wallace McConachie
Officers: Kevin McDermot, Secretary; Phillip King [1960] Director; Kevin McDermot [1962] Director

Pet and Aquatics Properties Limited
Incorporated: 25 February 2009
Net Worth: £5,606,000 *Total Assets:* £10,580,000
Registered Office: Tropical Marine Centre, Solesbridge Lane, Chorleywood, Herts, WD3 5SX
Activities: Renting and operating of Housing Association real estate
Parent: Tropical Marine Centre (2012) Ltd
Officers: Amanda Kathryn Taylor, Secretary; Amanda Kathryn Taylor [1959] Director and Company Secretary; Christopher John Thomas [1955] Director; Paul Desmond West [1957] Managing Director

Pet Mate Limited
Incorporated: 13 December 1985 *Employees:* 32
Net Worth: £7,872,425 *Total Assets:* £8,430,761
Registered Office: Lyon Road, Hersham, Surrey, KT12 3PU
Activities: Manufacture of other plastic products
Shareholders: Christopher Peter Kirk; Barbara Melvin Kirk
Officers: Barbara Melvin Kirk, Secretary/Managing Director; Barbara Melvin Kirk [1957] Director; Christopher Peter Kirk [1955] Managing Director

Petco Trading (UK) Limited
Incorporated: 11 September 2008 *Employees:* 15
Net Worth: £32,146,588 *Total Assets:* £205,126,992
Registered Office: 1 Blake Mews, Richmond upon Thames, Surrey, TW9 3GA
Activities: Other business support service activities n.e.c.
Officers: Alan Michael Jones, Secretary; Ahmad Hakimi Bin Muhammad Radzi [1973] Director/Head of Finance & Accounts [Malaysian]; Shamsul Bahari Salleh [1966] Director [Malaysian]; Emry Mohd Tamrin [1970] Director [Malaysian]

Peterborough (Progress Health) Holdings Limited
Incorporated: 15 January 2007
Net Worth Deficit: £57,614,000 *Total Assets:* £415,440,992
Registered Office: 8 White Oak Square, London Road, Swanley, Kent, BR8 7AG
Activities: Activities of construction holding companies
Shareholders: JLIF Holdings (Peterborough Hospital) Limited; Peterborough Hospital Investments Limited
Officers: Andrew Brian Deacon [1980] Portfolio Director; Carl Harvey Dix [1966] Operations Director; Julian Denzil Sutcliffe [1968] Life Cycle Asset Director; Mark Christopher Wayment [1958] Director

Peterborough (Progress Health) Nominee Limited
Incorporated: 15 January 2007
Total Assets: £27,749,000
Registered Office: 8 White Oak Square, London Road, Swanley, Kent, BR8 7AG
Activities: Activities of construction holding companies
Parent: Peterborough (Progress Health) Holdings Limited
Officers: Andrew Brian Deacon [1980] Portfolio Director; Carl Harvey Dix [1966] Operations Director; Julian Denzil Sutcliffe [1968] Life Cycle Asset Director; Mark Christopher Wayment [1958] Director

Peterborough (Progress Health) PLC
Incorporated: 16 January 2007
Net Worth Deficit: £57,614,000 *Total Assets:* £415,440,992
Registered Office: 8 White Oak Square, London Road, Swanley, Kent, BR8 7AG
Activities: Development of building projects
Parent: Peterborough (Progress Health) Holdings Limited
Officers: Andrew Brian Deacon [1980] Portfolio Director; Carl Harvey Dix [1966] Operations Director; Anthony Robert Faulkner [1973] Director; Julian Denzil Sutcliffe [1968] Life Cycle Asset Director; Mark Christopher Wayment [1958] Director

The Petersham Hotel Limited
Incorporated: 19 November 1987 *Employees:* 320
Net Worth: £14,470,878 *Total Assets:* £28,215,508
Registered Office: Nightingale Lane, Richmond, Surrey, TW10 6UZ
Activities: Hotels and similar accommodation
Officers: Greville Richard Hugh Dare, Secretary/Hotel Ownership; Greville Richard Hugh Dare [1963] Director/Hotelier; Luana Carol Luchterhand [1961] Director/Interior Designer

Petrocell Holdings Limited
Incorporated: 18 November 1974 *Employees:* 177
Net Worth: £12,741,437 *Total Assets:* £19,946,964
Registered Office: 274-8 Wickham Road, Shirley, Croydon, Surrey, CR0 8BJ
Activities: Maintenance and repair of motor vehicles
Major Shareholder: Jeremiah Bernard Dowling
Officers: Elaine Read, Secretary; Elizabeth Dawson [1980] Director; Jeremiah Bernard Dowling [1946] Director [Irish]; John Timothy Dowling [1975] Director/Manager; Patrick Ronald Dowling [1980] Garage Director; Thomas Andrew Dowling [1984] Director; Elaine Read [1963] Financial Director

Petroleum Geo-Services (UK) Limited
Incorporated: 23 November 1993
Net Worth: £96,148,000 *Total Assets:* £130,185,000
Registered Office: 4 The Heights, Brooklands, Weybridge, Surrey, KT13 0NY
Activities: Support activities for petroleum and natural gas mining
Parent: Petroleum Geo-Services ASA
Officers: Gottfred Langseth [1966] Director [Norwegian]; Rune Olav Pedersen [1970] Director [Norwegian]; Christin Steen Nilsen [1953] Director/VP Chief Accountant [Norwegian]

Petrolvalves (G.B.) Limited
Incorporated: 26 September 1984 *Employees:* 16
Net Worth: £5,915,973 *Total Assets:* £19,184,008
Registered Office: 18-22 Church Street, Hampton, Surrey, TW12 2EG
Activities: Other manufacturing n.e.c.
Officers: Emiliano Veronesi, Secretary; Luca Barsella [1970] Director/Area Sales Manager [Italian]; Filippo Rinaldi [1973] Director/Area Sales Manager [Italian]; Emiliano Veronesi [1973] Finance Director [Italian]

Pexhurst Services Limited
Incorporated: 30 January 1990 *Employees:* 40
Net Worth: £2,314,239 *Total Assets:* £7,939,112
Registered Office: Haslers, Old Station Road, Loughton, Essex, IG10 4PL
Activities: Construction of commercial buildings
Parent: Vella Holdings Limited
Officers: Alberto Marco Vella, Secretary; Stuart Christopher Byles [1973] Director; Penelope Anne Dew [1977] Finance Director; Lee Paul Stuart [1973] Director; Nicolo Giuseppe Tagliarini [1973] Director/Marketer; Martino John Vella [1969] Director

PFU (EMEA) Limited
Incorporated: 7 August 1981 *Employees:* 107
Previous: PFU Imaging Solutions Europe Limited
Net Worth: £34,858,572 *Total Assets:* £63,459,240
Registered Office: Hayes Park Central, Hayes End Road, Hayes, Middlesex, UB4 8FE
Activities: Wholesale of computers, computer peripheral equipment and software
Parent: Fujitsu Limited
Officers: Akihisa Kamata [1963] Director/Corporate Senior Vice President, PFU Limited [Japanese]; Hiroaki Kashiwagi [1964] Director/General Manager, PFU (EMEA) Limited [Japanese]; Toru Maki [1959] Director/President and CEO, PFU (EMEA) Limited [Japanese]; Yasunori Miyauchi [1965] Director/Corporate Senior Vice President, PFU Limited [Japanese]; Michael Paul Nelson [1961] Director/Vice President; Shigeaki Suzuki [1962] Director/CFO, PFU (EMEA) Limited [Japanese]

PGG Properties Limited
Incorporated: 9 June 2014 *Employees:* 2
Net Worth: £4,401,996 *Total Assets:* £14,451,077
Registered Office: 102-104 Park Lane, Croydon, Surrey, CR0 1JB
Activities: Buying and selling of own real estate
Shareholders: Sunil Tandon; Balraj Tandon
Officers: Balraj Tandon [1959] Director/Businessman; Sunil Tandon [1962] Director/Businessman

PGS Exploration (UK) Limited
Incorporated: 3 March 1994 *Employees:* 201
Net Worth: £62,412,024 *Total Assets:* £94,821,744
Registered Office: 4 The Heights, Brooklands, Weybridge, Surrey, KT13 0NY
Activities: Support activities for petroleum and natural gas mining
Parent: Petroleum Geo-Services (UK) Limited
Officers: Gottfred Langseth [1966] Director [Norwegian]; Olav Rune Pedersen [1970] Director [Norwegian]; Christin Steen Nilsen [1953] Director/VP Chief Accountant [Norwegian]

Phalarope Limited
Incorporated: 16 December 2014
Net Worth: £11,586,009 *Total Assets:* £11,599,656
Registered Office: Salisbury House, 20 Queens Road, Weybridge, Surrey, KT13 9XE
Activities: Non-trading company
Major Shareholder: Martin Richard Tracey Church
Officers: Martin Richard Tracey Church [1962] Director/Doctor

Pharmacare (Europe) Limited
Incorporated: 24 October 2007 *Employees:* 36
Net Worth Deficit: £2,150,795 *Total Assets:* £6,085,796
Registered Office: The Old Rectory, Church Street, Weybridge, Surrey, KT13 8DE
Activities: Wholesale of perfume and cosmetics
Major Shareholder: Toby Rowley Browne
Officers: Toby Rowley Browne, Secretary/Director [Australian]; Toby Rowley Browne [1953] Director [Australian]; Anthony John Robertson [1973] Director [Australian]

Pharmaceuticals Direct Limited
Incorporated: 25 November 1999 *Employees:* 18
Net Worth: £18,600,224 *Total Assets:* £33,313,492
Registered Office: Old Station Road, Loughton, Essex, IG10 4PL
Activities: Wholesale of pharmaceutical goods
Parent: Pharmadent Holdings lmited
Officers: Hital Patel, Secretary; Bemal Patel [1973] Director; Hital Patel [1974] Director/Company Secretary

Pharmadent Holdings Limited
Incorporated: 15 June 2010 *Employees:* 44
Net Worth: £11,048,828 *Total Assets:* £28,510,594
Registered Office: c/o Haslers, Old Station Road, Loughton, Essex, IG10 4PL
Activities: Activities of head offices
Parent: SIP Trustees Limited
Officers: Hital Patel, Secretary; Bemal Patel [1973] Director

Pharmasure Limited
Incorporated: 21 February 2000 *Employees:* 35
Net Worth: £2,817,653 *Total Assets:* £5,113,464
Registered Office: Lentcroft, 10 Cassiobury Park Avenue, Watford, Herts, WD18 7LB
Activities: Wholesale of pharmaceutical goods
Shareholders: Terence Sullivan; Christine Olga Sullivan
Officers: Terence Sullivan, Secretary; Christine Olga Sullivan [1955] Director/Chairman; Terence Sullivan [1956] Managing Director

Pharmvit Limited
Incorporated: 23 October 1979 *Employees:* 24
Net Worth: £120,960 *Total Assets:* £5,199,113
Registered Office: 177 Bilton Road, Greenford, Middlesex, UB6 7HQ
Activities: Manufacture of basic pharmaceutical products
Major Shareholder: Khalid Latif
Officers: Khalid Latif [1954] Director/Management Accountant

Pheechool Holdings Limited
Incorporated: 2 September 2014
Net Worth: £9,225,841 *Total Assets:* £10,060,241
Registered Office: Numeric House, 98 Station Road, Sidcup, Kent, DA15 7BY
Activities: Activities of other holding companies n.e.c.
Major Shareholder: Samir Pheechool Boulis
Officers: Dr Samir Pheechool Boulis [1975] Director/Dentist

PHH 1 Limited
Incorporated: 2 November 2012 *Employees:* 8,038
Net Worth: £22,300,000 *Total Assets:* £87,468,000
Registered Office: Building 1, Imperial Place, Elstree Way, Borehamwood, Herts, WD6 1JN
Activities: Licenced restaurants
Parent: HWS 3 Limited
Officers: Maria Rachael Watkins, Secretary; Jens Tjeerd Hofma [1966] Managing Director [Dutch]; Andrew Mark Platt [1967] Director/Accountant

PHH 2 Limited
Incorporated: 2 November 2012
Net Worth Deficit: £12,585,291 *Total Assets:* £18,859,400
Registered Office: Building 1, Imperial Place, Elstree Way, Borehamwood, Herts, WD6 1JN
Activities: Licenced restaurants
Parent: PHH 1 Limited
Officers: Maria Rachael Watkins, Secretary; Jens Tjeerd Hofma [1966] Managing Director [Dutch]; Andrew Mark Platt [1967] Director/Accountant

J.A. Phillips Holdings Limited
Incorporated: 20 August 1991 *Employees:* 20
Net Worth: £18,046,756 *Total Assets:* £20,419,454
Registered Office: Unit 8 Trafalgar Business Centre, 77-89 River Road, Barking, Essex, IG11 0JU
Activities: Activities of head offices
Major Shareholder: James Albert Phillips
Officers: Emma Margaret Warran, Secretary; James Daniel Phillips [1981] Director; James Albert Phillips [1959] Director; Matthew John Phillips [1988] Director

Philmont Properties UK Limited
Incorporated: 19 June 2006
Net Worth: £124,235 *Total Assets:* £6,207,040
Registered Office: Elm Park House, Elm Park Court, Pinner, Middlesex, HA5 3NN
Activities: Buying and selling of own real estate
Officers: David Dennis Cuby [1948] Director/Company Executive

Phivco UK II Limited
Incorporated: 25 June 2009
Net Worth: £229,423,008 *Total Assets:* £287,228,992
Registered Office: 980 Great West Road, Brentford, Middlesex, TW8 9GS
Activities: Other business support service activities n.e.c.
Parent: ViiV Healthcare Limited
Officers: Jill Dawn Anderson [1964] Director; Karen Marion Grainger [1978] Director/Pharmaceutical Regulatory Executive [Irish]; Deborah Jayne Waterhouse [1967] Director

Phoenix Property Development Co. Ltd.
Incorporated: 15 May 1998
Net Worth: £16,159,190 *Total Assets:* £16,242,471
Registered Office: 1st Floor, Midas House, 2 Knoll Rise, Orpington, Kent, BR6 0EL
Activities: Other professional, scientific and technical activities n.e.c.
Officers: Ann-Marie Philpot [1994] Director; Helen Louise Roue [1967] Director; Fabio Stampanoni [1976] Director/Lawyer [Swiss]

Phoenix Property Investment Company Limited
Incorporated: 16 November 1995
Net Worth: £7,224,248 *Total Assets:* £12,054,792
Registered Office: 2nd Floor, 29 Dingwall Road, Croydon, Surrey, CR0 2NB
Activities: Other letting and operating of own or leased real estate
Parent: Axcel Group Limited
Officers: Sunil Patel, Secretary/Businessman; Shamir Patel [1970] Director/Businessman; Sunil Patel [1968] Director/Businessman

Phoenix Software Limited
Incorporated: 15 October 1990 *Employees:* 163
Net Worth: £7,374,000 *Total Assets:* £32,899,000
Registered Office: Bytes House, Randalls Way, Leatherhead, Surrey, KT22 7TW
Activities: Wholesale of computers, computer peripheral equipment and software
Parent: Blenheim Group Limited
Officers: Paul David Emms [1967] Director; Clare Lucy Metcalfe [1968] Director; Samantha Jayne Mudd [1969] Director; Neil Robert Murphy [1964] Director; Keith Alan Richardson [1959] Director; Robert Eben Venter [1960] Director [South African]

Photo - Me International P L C
Incorporated: 14 September 1962 *Employees:* 1,371
Net Worth: £143,256,992 *Total Assets:* £238,908,992
Registered Office: Unit 3b Blenheim Road, Epsom, Surrey, KT19 9AP
Activities: Other service activities n.e.c.
Officers: Delmo Rinaldo Vincenzo Primo Mansi, Secretary; Yitzhak Apeloig [1959] Director/Manager and Investor [Israeli]; Francoise Rose Georgette Coutaz-Replan [1957] Finance Director [French]; Serge Paul Crasnianski [1942] Director [French]; Jean Marcel Denis [1938] Director/Chartered Accountant [French]; John Henry James Lewis [1940] Director; Eric Armand Mergui [1955] Director/Chief Operating Officer [French]; Emmanuel John Olympitis [1948] Director

Photo-Me Limited
Incorporated: 15 August 2016 *Employees:* 7
Net Worth: £26,564,876 *Total Assets:* £73,950,312
Registered Office: Unit 3b Blenheim Road, Epsom, Surrey, KT19 9AP
Activities: Other business support service activities n.e.c.
Parent: Photo-Me International PLC
Officers: Delmo Rinaldo Vincenzo Primo Mansi, Secretary; Serge Paul Crasnianski [1942] Director [French]

Photon Properties Limited
Incorporated: 6 February 2014
Net Worth: £33,806 *Total Assets:* £5,511,915
Registered Office: GPF Lewis House, Olds Approach, Tolpits Lane, Watford, Herts, WD18 9AB
Activities: Development of building projects
Shareholder: Kalpna Budhdeo
Officers: Shamir Pravinchandra Budhdeo [1967] Director

Piazza Property LLP
Incorporated: 19 February 2015
Net Worth: £5,701,206 *Total Assets:* £5,701,206
Registered Office: 3 Park Court, Pyrford Road, West Byfleet, Surrey, KT14 6SD
Officers: Calogero Paolino Piazza [1966] Member; Giuseppina Piazza [1970] Member

Pickering Dental Surgeries Limited
Incorporated: 16 March 1950 *Employees:* 21
Net Worth: £5,395,145 *Total Assets:* £5,763,539
Registered Office: York House, Empire Way, Wembley, Middlesex, HA9 0FQ
Activities: Dental practice activities
Major Shareholder: Gregory Stephen Ireland
Officers: Kristina Kidmose, Secretary; Gregory Stephen Ireland [1958] Director/Dental Surgeon [Australian/British]

Pickhurst Infant Academy
Incorporated: 8 July 2011 *Employees:* 65
Previous: Pickhurst Infant School
Net Worth: £6,253,467 *Total Assets:* £6,678,411
Registered Office: Pickhurst Infant School, Pickhurst Lane, West Wickham, Kent, BR4 0HL
Activities: Primary education
Officers: Kate Morgan Ambrosi [1974] Director/Council Officer; Catherine Craven [1976] Director/Child Workforce Mentor; Lynn Key [1949] Director/Retired Headteacher; Jane Alexandra Knight [1958] Director/Accountant; Elizabeth Gwendolin Laws [1975] Director/Headteacher; Christina Moody [1970] Director/Education Adviser; Paul Osborne [1976] Director/Firefighter; Stephen Harold Shooman [1949] Director/Retail Senior Management; Tushar Srivastava [1980] Director; Rachael Swarbrick [1974] Director/Teacher

Picturehouse Cinemas Limited
Incorporated: 28 October 1988 *Employees:* 689
Net Worth: £5,283,227 *Total Assets:* £38,594,624
Registered Office: 8th Floor, Vantage London, Great West Road, Brentford, Middlesex, TW8 9AG
Activities: Motion picture projection activities
Parent: Cineworld Holdings Limited
Officers: Fiona Smith, Secretary; Clare Louise Binns [1954] Director; Israel Greidinger [1961] Director/Cinema Proprietor [Israeli]; Mr Moshe Joseph Greidinger [1952] Director/Cinema Proprietor [Israeli]; Roei Kaufman [1985] Director/Accountant

Pinden Limited
Incorporated: 2 August 2004 *Employees:* 102
Net Worth: £3,144,645 *Total Assets:* £14,831,102
Registered Office: Waldens Depot, Waldens Road, Orpington, Kent, BR5 4EU
Activities: Quarrying of ornamental and building stone, limestone, gypsum, chalk and slate
Shareholder: Terence Malcolm Bishop
Officers: Stephen Edward Bishop [1959] Director/Estimating Manager; Sydney Michael Bishop [1956] Director/Contracts Manager; Terrence Malcolm Bishop [1941] Director/Demolition Contractor; Thomas James Bishop [1965] Director/Manager

Pinder Developments Co. (Chislehurst) Limited
Incorporated: 2 April 1973 *Employees:* 4
Net Worth: £4,454,506 *Total Assets:* £6,287,922
Registered Office: 24 Eynsford Close, Petts Wood, Orpington, Kent, BR5 1DP
Activities: Renting and operating of Housing Association real estate
Major Shareholder: Trevor Alfred Ferris
Officers: Linda Ferris, Secretary; Nigel John Ferris [1963] Director/Engineer

Pineridge Investments Limited
Incorporated: 13 May 1991
Net Worth: £10,748,772 *Total Assets:* £24,892,824
Registered Office: 28 Church Road, Stanmore, Middlesex, HA7 4XR
Activities: Other letting and operating of own or leased real estate
Shareholders: Franco Pietro Giovanni Sidoli; Charterhouse Square Holdings Limited
Officers: Jacqueline Smith, Secretary; Martin Keith Rodwell [1961] Director/Architect; Franco Sidoli [1963] Director/Chartered Surveyor

Ping Pong Limited
Incorporated: 12 May 2004 *Employees:* 308
Net Worth: £3,001,698 *Total Assets:* £9,527,504
Registered Office: Elder House, St Georges Business Park, Brooklands Road, Weybridge, Surrey, KT13 0TS
Activities: Licenced restaurants
Officers: James Michael Alexander Horler [1965] Director/Chairman; Artem Sagiryan [1981] Director; Timothy Paul Thorpe [1970] Director

Pink Fortress Limited
Incorporated: 1 October 2007
Net Worth: £1,840,804 *Total Assets:* £5,297,371
Registered Office: 3 Park Court, Pyrford Road, West Byfleet, Surrey, KT14 6SD
Activities: Development of building projects
Parent: Pink Fortress Holdings Ltd
Officers: Maya Al-Khalil [1971] Director

Pinnacle Foods Limited
Incorporated: 2 May 2007 *Employees:* 49
Net Worth: £5,579,996 *Total Assets:* £10,280,604
Registered Office: Windsor House, Britannia Road, Waltham Cross, Herts, EN8 7NX
Activities: Processing and preserving of meat
Parent: GPS Food Group (UK) Limited
Officers: Padraig Anthony McCarthy [1967] Director [Irish]; Fergus Quinn-Smith [1965] Director; Graham Reed [1964] Director; Christopher John Wilson [1961] Director

Pinnacle Insurance PLC
Incorporated: 14 April 1971
Net Worth: £158,516,992 *Total Assets:* £332,326,016
Registered Office: Pinnacle House, A1 Barnet Way, Borehamwood, Herts, WD6 2XX
Activities: Life insurance
Parent: Cardif Pinnacle Insurance Holdings PLC
Officers: Matthew Justin Lorimer, Secretary; Gerard Binet [1953] Development and Strategy Director [French]; Peter John Box [1952] Director; Stanislas Louis Paul Francois Chevalt [1961] Director/Exco Member - Co - BNPPC [French]; Marie Haderer [1979] Director/Actuary [French]; Matthew Justin Lorimer [1967] Director/Solicitor; Nicholas Dutfield Rochez [1954] Director; Andrew Miles Wigg [1972] Director

Pinnacle Schools (Fife) Limited
Incorporated: 24 October 2000
Net Worth: £3,569,000 *Total Assets:* £32,899,000
Registered Office: 8 White Oak Square, London Road, Swanley, Kent, BR8 7AG
Activities: Other business support service activities n.e.c.
Parent: Pinnacle Schools (Fife) Holdings Limited
Officers: John Stephen Gordon [1962] Director; Matthew Templeton [1973] Director

Pinns Wharf Limited
Incorporated: 7 November 1991 *Employees:* 8
Net Worth: £5,774,631 *Total Assets:* £6,356,519
Registered Office: Treviot House, 186-192 High Road, Ilford, Essex, IG1 1LR
Activities: Operation of warehousing and storage facilities for water transport activities
Shareholders: Gary Albert Widdowson; Beverley Ann Widdowson; Robert Gibbs (Contracting) Company Limited
Officers: Howard Victor Jones, Secretary; Barry Albert Elvidge [1949] Director; Howard Victor Jones [1950] Director; Duncan Alexander Ross [1967] Director; Gary Albert Widdowson [1958] Managing Director

Pioneer DJ Europe Limited
Incorporated: 23 September 2014 *Employees:* 64
Net Worth: £12,357,470 *Total Assets:* £54,872,156
Registered Office: Artemis, Odyssey Business Park, West End Road, South Ruislip, Middlesex, HA4 6QE
Activities: Manufacture of other electrical equipment
Parent: Pioneer DJ Corporation
Officers: Anita Toni Wilkinson, Secretary; Kei Aikawa [1975] Director [Japanese]; Anita Toni Wilkinson [1970] Director/Solicitor

Piramal Critical Care Limited
Incorporated: 22 June 2004 *Employees:* 16
Previous: Piramal Life Sciences (UK) Limited
Net Worth: £18,122,694 *Total Assets:* £276,387,680
Registered Office: Ground Floor, Suite 4, Heathrow Boulevard East Wing, 280 Bath Road, West Drayton, Middlesex, UB7 0DQ
Activities: Manufacture of basic pharmaceutical products
Officers: Kaushik Upadhyay, Secretary; Peter Daniel Deyoung [1978] Director/Chief Executive Officer of Piramal Critical Care B [American]; William John Hargan [1958] Director/VP Sales and Marketing; Kaushik Upadhyay [1980] Director [Indian]

Pirin Ltd
Incorporated: 7 March 1972
Previous: Pirin PLC
Net Worth: £12,490,393 *Total Assets:* £18,658,932
Registered Office: Sage House, New Ford Business Centre, New Ford Road, Waltham Cross, Herts, EN8 7PG
Activities: Other letting and operating of own or leased real estate
Parent: Pirin Holdings Limited
Officers: Joyce Kathleen Hammond, Secretary; Thea Patricia Buisson [1971] Director/Administrator; Neal Peter Hammond [1973] Director/Builder

Pitchset Limited
Incorporated: 23 June 2010
Net Worth: £6,200,989 *Total Assets:* £10,778,681
Registered Office: Northside House, Mount Pleasant, Barnet, Herts, EN4 9EE
Activities: Other service activities n.e.c.
Shareholders: Melvyn Frank Cooper; Jason Robert Cooper
Officers: Adam Cooper, Secretary; Adam Cooper [1971] Director; Jason Robert Cooper [1967] Director; Melvyn Frank Cooper [1941] Director

Pizza Gogo Ltd
Incorporated: 21 September 1995 *Employees:* 94
Net Worth: £7,733,404 *Total Assets:* £14,916,840
Registered Office: Unit 6 Teakcroft, Fairview Industrial Park, Marsh Way, Rainham, Essex, RM13 8UH
Activities: Butter and cheese production
Officers: Hamid Haghighat, Secretary/General Manager; Homayoun Aminnia [1963] Director/General Manager; Hamid Haghighat [1960] Director/General Manager

Pizza Hut (U.K.) Limited
Incorporated: 21 September 1972 *Employees:* 8,033
Net Worth: £53,007,000 *Total Assets:* £97,308,000
Registered Office: Building 1, Imperial Place, Elstree Way, Borehamwood, Herts, WD6 1JN
Activities: Licenced restaurants
Parent: PHH 2 Limited
Officers: Maria Rachael Watkins, Secretary; Kathryn Elizabeth Austin [1976] HR Director; Jens Tjeerd Hofma [1966] Director [Dutch]; Susan Marshall [1973] Chief Director for Operations; Andrew Mark Platt [1967] Director/Accountant; Michael William Edward Spencer [1969] Director of Operations - Dine-In

PizzaExpress (Franchises) Limited
Incorporated: 30 March 1993
Net Worth: £11,598,000 *Total Assets:* £13,942,000
Registered Office: Hunton House, Highbridge Estate, Oxford Road, Uxbridge, Middlesex, UB8 1LX
Activities: Licenced restaurants
Parent: PizzaExpress Group Limited
Officers: Andrew David Pellington, Secretary; Liam John Collette [1978] Director [Australian]; Andrew David Pellington [1964] Director; Jinlong Wang [1957] Director [American]

PizzaExpress (Restaurants) Limited
Incorporated: 31 March 1993 *Employees:* 10,646
Net Worth: £714,636,992 *Total Assets:* £983,900,032
Registered Office: Hunton House, Highbridge Estate, Oxford Road, Uxbridge, Middlesex, UB8 1LX
Activities: Licenced restaurants
Parent: PizzaExpress Limited
Officers: Andrew David Pellington, Secretary; Nicola Zoe Bowley [1971] Director; David Roger Murphy [1974] Director; Andrew David Pellington [1964] Director; Jinlong Wang [1957] Director [American]

PizzaExpress (Wholesale) Limited
Incorporated: 28 April 1993 *Employees:* 17
Net Worth: £22,347,000 *Total Assets:* £82,605,000
Registered Office: Hunton House, Highbridge Estate, Oxford Road, Uxbridge, Middlesex, UB8 1LX
Activities: Licenced restaurants
Parent: PizzaExpress Limited
Officers: Andrew David Pellington, Secretary; Andrew David Pellington [1964] Director; Jinlong Wang [1957] Director [American]

PizzaExpress Financing 1 PLC
Incorporated: 4 July 2014 *Employees:* 14,510
Net Worth Deficit: £57,921,000 *Total Assets:* £1,233,755,008
Registered Office: Hunton House, Highbridge Estate, Oxford Road, Uxbridge, Middlesex, UB8 1LX
Activities: Non-trading company
Parent: PizzaExpress Group Holdings Limited
Officers: Andrew David Pellington, Secretary; Andrew David Pellington [1964] Director; Xiaoxin Shao [1981] Director [Chinese]; Jinlong Wang [1957] Director [American]; Bing Yuan [1968] Director [Chinese]

PizzaExpress Financing 2 PLC
Incorporated: 7 July 2014
Net Worth Deficit: £5,454,000 *Total Assets:* £1,280,556,032
Registered Office: Hunton House, Highbridge Estate, Oxford Road, Uxbridge, Middlesex, UB8 1LX
Activities: Non-trading company
Parent: PizzaExpress Financing 1 PLC
Officers: Andrew David Pellington, Secretary; Andrew David Pellington [1964] Director; Xiaoxin Shao [1981] Director [Chinese]; Jinlong Wang [1957] Director [American]; Bing Yuan [1968] Director [Chinese]

PizzaExpress Group Holdings Limited
Incorporated: 3 July 2014 *Employees:* 14,510
Net Worth Deficit: £57,921,000 *Total Assets:* £1,233,755,008
Registered Office: Hunton House, Highbridge Estate, Oxford Road, Uxbridge, Middlesex, UB8 1LX
Activities: Non-trading company
Officers: Andrew David Pellington, Secretary; Jianzhong Gong [1962] Director/Banker [Chinese]; Ma Mingju [1961] Director/VP of Jin Jiang International (Holdings) Co., Ltd [Chinese]; Andrew David Pellington [1964] Director; Xiaoxin Shao [1981] Director [Chinese]; Jinlong Wang [1957] Director [American]; Bing Yuan [1968] Director [Chinese]

PizzaExpress Group Limited
Incorporated: 14 July 2014 *Employees:* 228
Net Worth Deficit: £212,971,008 *Total Assets:* £1,113,291,008
Registered Office: Hunton House, Highbridge Estate, Oxford Road, Uxbridge, Middlesex, UB8 1LX
Activities: Activities of head offices
Parent: PizzaExpress Financing 2 PLC
Officers: Andrew David Pellington, Secretary; Andrew David Pellington [1964] Director; Xiaoxin Shao [1981] Director [Chinese]; Jinlong Wang [1957] Director [American]; Bing Yuan [1968] Director [Chinese]

PizzaExpress International Holdings Limited
Incorporated: 25 March 2015 *Employees:* 2
Net Worth Deficit: £10,510,000 *Total Assets:* £65,241,000
Registered Office: Hunton House, Highbridge Estate, Oxford Road, Uxbridge, Middlesex, UB8 1LX
Activities: Activities of other holding companies n.e.c.
Parent: PizzaExpress Group Limited
Officers: Andrew David Pellington, Secretary; Andrew David Pellington [1964] Director; Jinlong Wang [1957] Director [American]

PizzaExpress Limited
Incorporated: 11 December 1978 *Employees:* 4
Net Worth: £106,198,000 *Total Assets:* £824,732,032
Registered Office: Hunton House, Highbridge Estate, Oxford Road, Uxbridge, Middlesex, UB8 1LX
Activities: Licenced restaurants
Parent: PizzaExpress Operations Limited
Officers: Andrew David Pellington, Secretary; Nicola Zoe Bowley [1971] Director; David Roger Murphy [1974] Director; Andrew David Pellington [1964] Director; Jinlong Wang [1957] Director [American]

PizzaExpress Merchandising Limited
Incorporated: 29 November 1996
Net Worth: £106,751,000 *Total Assets:* £118,259,000
Registered Office: Hunton House, Highbridge Estate, Oxford Road, Uxbridge, Middlesex, UB8 1LX
Activities: Licenced restaurants
Parent: PizzaExpress Limited
Officers: Andrew David Pellington, Secretary; Andrew David Pellington [1964] Director; Jinlong Wang [1957] Director [American]

PizzaExpress Operations Limited
Incorporated: 18 July 2003
Net Worth Deficit: £272,502,016 *Total Assets:* £1,203,827,968
Registered Office: Hunton House, Highbridge Industrial Estate, Oxford Road, Uxbridge, Middlesex, UB8 1LX
Activities: Financial management
Parent: PizzaExpress Group Limited
Officers: Andrew David Pellington, Secretary; Nicola Zoe Bowley [1971] Director; Andrew David Pellington [1964] Director; Jinlong Wang [1957] Director [American]

PJG Developments Limited
Incorporated: 23 October 1992
Net Worth: £4,375,199 *Total Assets:* £10,000,778
Registered Office: 11-12 Hallmark Trading Centre, Fourth Way, Wembley, Middlesex, HA9 0LB
Activities: Buying and selling of own real estate
Major Shareholder: Martin Joseph Finnerty
Officers: Martin Joseph Finnerty [1951] Director

PKA WLWF Holding (UK) Limited
Incorporated: 19 June 2017
Net Worth: £119,903,000 *Total Assets:* £242,544,000
Registered Office: 8 White Oak Square, London Road, Swanley, Kent, BR8 7AG
Activities: Activities of other holding companies n.e.c.
Officers: James Edward Burbidge [1975] Director/Chartered Accountant; Mark Alan Cade [1972] Director/Chartered Engineer; Domenico Tripodi [1984] Director [Italian]

The Placement Group Healthcare Limited
Incorporated: 17 January 2006 *Employees:* 87
Net Worth: £579,476 *Total Assets:* £5,524,426
Registered Office: 110 Brooker Road, Waltham Abbey, Essex, EN9 1JH
Activities: Other human health activities
Parent: The Placement Group (Holdings) PLC
Officers: Steven Porter, Secretary; Steven Porter [1968] Director; Edward Clive Simpson [1972] Director

Pladis Foods Limited
Incorporated: 4 November 2014 *Employees:* 8,093
Net Worth: £936,300,032 *Total Assets:* £5,041,800,192
Registered Office: United Biscuits, Hayes Park, Hayes End Road, Hayes, Middlesex, UB4 8EE
Activities: Activities of head offices
Major Shareholder: Murat Ulker
Officers: Mark Oldham, Secretary; Richard Handscombe [1954] Director/Accountant; Simon Edward Munir [1964] Director/Fund Manager; Murat Ulker [1959] Director/Chairman [Turkish]

Plan B Healthcare PLC
Incorporated: 11 February 2009 *Employees:* 29
Net Worth: £4,575,660 *Total Assets:* £5,591,085
Registered Office: Hygeia Building, 66-68 College Road, Harrow, Middlesex, HA1 1BE
Activities: Temporary employment agency activities
Major Shareholder: Kevin Michael Coyle
Officers: Howard Pepperdine, Secretary; Anna Louise Cooper [1978] Director; Christopher John Coyle [1984] Director/Accountant; Kevin Michael Coyle [1956] Director/Accountant; Michael Howard Helleur [1981] Director; Nicolas Poturicich [1978] Director

Planetree Developments Limited
Incorporated: 1 February 2017 *Employees:* 1
Net Worth: £1 *Total Assets:* £18,765,816
Registered Office: c/o Blossom House School Limited, Station Road, Motspur Park, New Malden, Surrey, KT3 6JJ
Activities: Development of building projects
Parent: Lanend Limited
Officers: Joanna Briant Burgess [1950] Director/Teacher

Planshore Limited
Incorporated: 14 October 1988 *Employees:* 73
Net Worth: £11,142,473 *Total Assets:* £12,753,003
Registered Office: 9 Spareleaze Hill, Loughton, Essex, IG10 1BS
Activities: Residential nursing care facilities
Officers: Devyani Jayanti Patel, Secretary; Devyani Jayanti Patel [1953] Director/Administrator; Jayanti Mohanlal Patel [1949] Director/Secretary

Plastico Limited
Incorporated: 26 October 1984 *Employees:* 84
Net Worth: £51,777 *Total Assets:* £9,692,827
Registered Office: First Floor, 110-112 Morden Road, Mitcham, Surrey, CR4 4DA
Activities: Manufacture of other plastic products
Officers: Eileen June Wiggins, Secretary/Business Owner; Caroline Alicia Wiggins [1960] Director/Chief Executive Officer; Eileen June Wiggins [1930] Director/Chairman

Platinum Acquisition Limited
Incorporated: 22 August 2016 *Employees:* 3
Net Worth: £70,676,224 *Total Assets:* £149,896,496
Registered Office: Catalyst House, 720 Centennial Court, Centennial Park, Elstree, Herts, WD6 3SY
Activities: Other business support service activities n.e.c.
Parent: Platinum Midco Limited
Officers: Thomas Christopher Barnds [1968] Director [American]; Maurice Andre Hernandez [1981] Director [American]; Jason Michael Klein [1973] Director [American]

Platinum Gold Homes Limited
Incorporated: 17 February 2011
Net Worth: £1,574,607 *Total Assets:* £5,260,407
Registered Office: Malvern Lodge, London Road, Swanley, Kent, BR8 7HA
Activities: Buying and selling of own real estate
Major Shareholder: Kultar Singh Vagha
Officers: Rajinder Kaur, Secretary; Kultar Singh Vagha [1979] Director/Estate Agents

Platinum Investments Surrey Limited
Incorporated: 10 October 2011
Net Worth Deficit: £609,672 *Total Assets:* £9,385,228
Registered Office: First Floor Office, 4 Ashley Road, Epsom, Surrey, KT18 5AX
Activities: Activities of head offices
Shareholders: Antonie Bouwer; Gerhard Swart
Officers: Antonie Bouwer [1940] Director/Accountant [South African]; Jan Hendrik Munnik [1981] Director/Quantity Surveyor

Platinum Midco 2 Limited
Incorporated: 1 September 2016 *Employees:* 3
Net Worth: £90,332,704 *Total Assets:* £90,332,704
Registered Office: Catalyst House, 720 Centennial Court, Centennial Park, Elstree, Herts, WD6 3SY
Activities: Other business support service activities n.e.c.
Parent: Platinum Topco Limited
Officers: Thomas Christopher Barnds [1968] Director [American]; Maurice Andre Hernandez [1981] Director [American]; Jason Michael Klein [1973] Director [American]

Platinum Midco Limited
Incorporated: 22 August 2016 *Employees:* 3
Net Worth: £90,332,704 *Total Assets:* £90,332,704
Registered Office: Catalyst House, 720 Centennial Court, Centennial Park, Elstree, Herts, WD6 3SY
Activities: Other business support service activities n.e.c.
Parent: Platinum Midco 2 Limited
Officers: Thomas Christopher Barnds [1968] Director [American]; Maurice Andre Hernandez [1981] Director [American]; Jason Michael Klein [1973] Director [American]

Platinum Newco II Limited
Incorporated: 1 August 2016 *Employees:* 1
Net Worth: £119,901,816 *Total Assets:* £125,000,000
Registered Office: Catalyst House, 720 Centennial Court, Centennial Park, Elstree, Herts, WD6 3SY
Activities: Activities of other holding companies n.e.c.
Parent: Platinum Newco III Limited
Officers: James Brown [1971] Director; Jon Stratford [1970] Director

Platinum Topco Limited
Incorporated: 22 August 2016 *Employees:* 176
Net Worth Deficit: £50,161,772 *Total Assets:* £171,971,168
Registered Office: Catalyst House, 720 Centennial Court, Centennial Park, Elstree, Herts, WD6 3SY
Activities: Other business support service activities n.e.c.
Officers: Thomas Christopher Barnds [1968] Director [American]; James Brown [1971] Director; Maurice Andre Hernandez [1981] Director [American]; Jason Michael Klein [1973] Director [American]; Rachel Spasser [1967] Director/Operating Principal [American]

Plaut International Limited
Incorporated: 20 December 1988 *Employees:* 19
Net Worth: £2,957,026 *Total Assets:* £11,955,962
Registered Office: 8c Bourne Court, Southend Road, Woodford Green, Essex, IG8 8HD
Activities: Agents involved in the sale of timber and building materials
Shareholders: Edward James Lindenberg; Peter Lindenberg
Officers: Dominic Higman, Secretary; Dominic Higman [1977] Finance Director; Edward James Lindenberg [1946] Director/Chairman; James Edward Charles Lindenberg [1971] Director; Peter Karl Lindenberg [1987] Sales Director; Stephen Paul Pinder [1971] Sales Director; John Stephen Yates [1960] Managing Director

Playags UK Limited
Incorporated: 3 June 2015
Net Worth: £7,112,105 *Total Assets:* £9,624,531
Registered Office: 1st Floor, Healthaid House, Marlborough Hill, Harrow, Middlesex, HA1 1UD
Activities: Publishing of computer games
Officers: David Lopez [1973] Director [American]

Playpower UK Limited
Incorporated: 24 August 2005 *Employees:* 3
Net Worth Deficit: £16,178,092 *Total Assets:* £7,575,839
Registered Office: Clockhouse Nurseries, Clockhouse Lane East, Egham, Surrey, TW20 8PG
Activities: Activities of head offices
Parent: Littlejohn Fund V, LP
Officers: Anne Coleman, Secretary; Morland Joseph Copeland [1961] Director [American]; Mark Leslie Hoskins [1964] Director; Stephen Geoffrey Lyon [1966] Financial Director

Pledream Properties Limited
Incorporated: 22 July 1971 *Employees:* 3
Net Worth: £9,729,355 *Total Assets:* £13,850,547
Registered Office: 32 Phipps Hatch Lane, Enfield, Middlesex, EN2 0HN
Activities: Other letting and operating of own or leased real estate
Major Shareholder: Richard Morris Jenkins
Officers: Maureen Matilda Susan Amar, Secretary/Director; Maureen Matilda Susan Amar [1944] Director/Marketing Manager; Richard Morris Jenkins [1944] Director; Michael Samuel Sheridan [1945] Director/Solicitor

Plexus Europe Limited
Incorporated: 28 March 1983
Net Worth: £3,330,000 *Total Assets:* £6,812,000
Registered Office: Baronsmede, The Avenue, Egham, Surrey, TW20 9AB
Activities: Other professional, scientific and technical activities n.e.c.
Officers: Mark Donald Fairchild [1959] Director/Corporation Executive; Andrej Jonovic [1980] Managing Director [Swedish]

Plexus Holdings PLC
Incorporated: 24 February 1997 *Employees:* 54
Net Worth: £40,916,000 *Total Assets:* £46,154,000
Registered Office: Elder House, St Georges Business Park, 207 Brooklands Road, Weybridge, Surrey, KT13 0TS
Activities: Activities of head offices
Officers: Kerin Williams, Secretary; Craig Francis Bryce Hendrie [1973] Director; Charles Jones [1959] Director [American]; Kunming Liu [1977] Director [Chinese]; Graham Paul Stevens [1958] Director; Jerome Jeffrey Thrall [1949] Director [American]; Bernard Herman Van Bilderbeek [1948] Executive Director [Dutch]

Pleythorne Limited
Incorporated: 20 December 1966
Net Worth: £15,294,359 *Total Assets:* £17,479,726
Registered Office: 8 Tavistock Court, Tavistock Road, Croydon, Surrey, CR9 2ED
Activities: Renting and operating of Housing Association real estate
Parent: Brymore Holdings Limited
Officers: Lucinda Jane Lewis, Secretary; Leonard Sidney Lewis [1956] Director; Miles Jason Webber [1969] Director

Plotplan Limited
Incorporated: 15 October 2007
Net Worth Deficit: £1,790,268 *Total Assets:* £11,041,436
Registered Office: 3rd Floor, Sterling House, Langston Road, Loughton, Essex, IG10 3TS
Activities: Development of building projects
Shareholders: David Edward Conway; Richard Matthew Conway; Gary Alexander Conway
Officers: David Edward Conway, Secretary; David Edward Conway [1976] Director; Gary Alexander Conway [1973] Director

Plutus Estates (Braintree) Limited
Incorporated: 15 March 2016
Net Worth Deficit: £218,774 *Total Assets:* £7,960,062
Registered Office: 7 St John's Road, Harrow, Middlesex, HA1 2EY
Activities: Other letting and operating of own or leased real estate
Parent: Plutus Estates Limited
Officers: Shailesh Virendra Patel [1963] Director; Pankaj Keshavlal Rajani [1963] Director

Plutus Estates Limited
Incorporated: 14 May 2014
Net Worth: £498,684 *Total Assets:* £10,229,884
Registered Office: 7 St John's Road, Harrow, Middlesex, HA1 2EY
Activities: Other letting and operating of own or leased real estate
Shareholders: Pankaj Keshavlal Rajani; Shailesh Virendra Patel
Officers: Shailesh Virendra Patel [1963] Director/Accountant; Pankaj Keshavlal Rajani [1963] Director/Accountant

Plymouth (Notte Street) Limited
Incorporated: 31 March 2016
Net Worth Deficit: £876,691 *Total Assets:* £17,104,904
Registered Office: 2nd Floor, Unicorn House, Station Close, Potters Bar, Herts, EN6 1TL
Activities: Other letting and operating of own or leased real estate
Parent: Harouni Group of Companies Limited
Officers: David Samuel Harouni [1977] Director; Jeremiah Harouni [1949] Director; Philip James Saunders [1947] Director

PMP Recruitment Limited
Incorporated: 24 December 1997 *Employees:* 22,537
Net Worth: £9,126,477 *Total Assets:* £138,570,784
Registered Office: Chevron House, Long Lane, Hillingdon, Uxbridge, Middlesex, UB10 9PF
Activities: Temporary employment agency activities
Parent: Cordant People Limited
Officers: Alan Connor, Secretary/Director; Chris Martin Kenneally [1960] Director; Jack Rainer Ullmann [1928] Director; Phillip Lionel Ullmann [1964] Director/Group Managing

Derek Pobjoy Investments Limited
Incorporated: 11 September 1969
Net Worth: £4,699,801 *Total Assets:* £7,188,864
Registered Office: Millennia House, Kingswood Park, Bonsor Drive, Tadworth, Surrey, KT20 6AY
Activities: Precious metals production
Shareholders: Derek Charles Pobjoy; Taya Christa Pobjoy
Officers: Timothy John Warner, Secretary; Derek Charles Pobjoy [1933] Director; Taya Christa Pobjoy [1969] Director

Pod-Trak Limited
Incorporated: 8 August 2007 *Employees:* 70
Net Worth: £4,822,904 *Total Assets:* £10,283,354
Registered Office: Crove House, 14 Aintree Road, Perivale, Greenford, Middlesex, UB6 7LA
Activities: Construction of railways and underground railways
Major Shareholder: Paul O'Donnell
Officers: Brenda O'Donnell, Secretary; Stephen Francis Given [1983] Director; Brenda O'Donnell [1980] Director [Irish]; Paul O'Donnell [1982] Director/Electrician [Irish]

Poland Street Properties Limited
Incorporated: 23 June 1949 *Employees:* 3
Net Worth: £3,286,247 *Total Assets:* £26,280,136
Registered Office: Landmark Chartered Accountants, Leavesden Park 5, Hercules Way, Watford, Herts, WD25 7GS
Activities: Other letting and operating of own or leased real estate
Parent: Salmon Management and Finance Limited
Officers: Maurice Bertram Gluck [1930] Director/Chartered Accountant; Paul Jeremy Roger Newman [1951] Director

Polar Audio Limited
Incorporated: 3 July 1969 *Employees:* 27
Net Worth: £6,625,120 *Total Assets:* £8,193,030
Registered Office: 19 Montpelier Avenue, Bexley, Kent, DA5 3AP
Activities: Wholesale of audio tapes, records, CDs and video tapes and the equipment on which these are played
Shareholders: Beyer Dynamic (G.B.) Limited; Beyer Dynamic (G.B.) Limited
Officers: Stuart Matthew Leader [1975] Director; John Nigel Midgley [1953] Executive Director; Timothy Sean Riley [1963] Director

Polaris Ventures Ltd
Incorporated: 12 December 2001
Net Worth: £3,515,395 *Total Assets:* £7,489,138
Registered Office: Compton House, 20A Selsdon Road, South Croydon, Surrey, CR2 6PA
Activities: Development of building projects
Officers: Kalpana Magecha, Secretary; Dilip Magecha [1956] Director

Pole To Win International Limited
Incorporated: 5 January 2016
Net Worth: £15,906,937 *Total Assets:* £19,717,092
Registered Office: Second Floor, Vantage London, Great West Road, Brentford, Middlesex, TW8 9AG
Activities: Activities of other holding companies n.e.c.
Officers: Stephen Moseley, Secretary; Masaru Harada [1961] Director/Secretary [Japanese]; Deborah Lynn Kirkham [1971] Director [American]; Stephen Moseley [1967] Director [American]; Tamiyoshi Tachibana [1951] Director [Japanese]; Teppei Tachibana [1974] Director [Japanese]; Tetsuji Tsuda [1973] Director [Japanese]

Pole To Win UK Limited
Incorporated: 19 December 2012 *Employees:* 731
Previous: Pole To Win Europe Limited
Net Worth: £3,506,110 *Total Assets:* £6,925,578
Registered Office: Second Floor, Vantage London, Great West Road, Brentford, Middlesex, TW8 9AG
Activities: Other business support service activities n.e.c.
Parent: Pole To Win International Limited
Officers: Michihiro Suzuki, Secretary; Andrew Simon Emery [1972] Director; Masaru Harada [1961] Director/Secretary [Japanese]; Deborah Lynn Kirkham [1971] Director [American]; Stephen Moseley [1967] Director [American]; Teppei Tachibana [1974] Director [Japanese]

Poliform UK Limited
Incorporated: 14 May 2001 *Employees:* 43
Net Worth: £1,712,047 *Total Assets:* £6,780,912
Registered Office: Lawfords Limited, Union House, Walton Lodge, Bridge Street, Walton on Thames, Surrey, KT12 1BT
Activities: Wholesale of household goods (other than musical instruments) n.e.c
Shareholder: Poliform SpA
Officers: Marie Therese Khachfe, Secretary; Giovanni Anzani [1950] Director/Entrepreneur [Italian]; Bronwen Sarah Harris [1970] Director; Georges Youssef Khachfe [1946] Director/Design Consultant; Marie Therese Khachfe [1953] Director/Designer; Alberto Spinelli [1946] Director/Entrepreneur [Italian]

Polybags Limited
Incorporated: 19 July 1961 *Employees:* 70
Net Worth: £5,533,132 *Total Assets:* £7,130,483
Registered Office: 1 Lyon Way, Greenford, Middlesex, UB6 0AQ
Activities: Manufacture of other plastic products
Major Shareholder: Geoffrey Walter Davies
Officers: Geoffrey Walter Davies, Secretary; Sally Maria Arbuthnott [1967] Director/Personnel Manager; Joanna Clare Phyllis Copley [1965] Director/Solicitor; Geoffrey Walter Davies [1931] Director/Chartered Accountant; Jonathan Walter Davies [1970] Director; Jonathan Howard Lomax [1971] Director/Manager

Popat Stores Limited
Incorporated: 21 March 2011
Net Worth: £6,000,222 *Total Assets:* £6,825,539
Registered Office: 138 Ealing Road, Alperton, Wembley, Middlesex, HA0 4PY
Activities: Wholesale of household goods (other than musical instruments) n.e.c
Officers: Neeta Modi [1959] Director/Businesswoman; Anillal Gordhandas Sunderji Popat [1945] Director/Businessman; Jagdish Gordhandas Sunderji Popat [1946] Director/Businessman; Ramnik Gordhandas Sunderji Popat [1940] Director/Businessman

Popsoda Limited
Incorporated: 15 October 2003 *Employees:* 25
Net Worth: £9,065,348 *Total Assets:* £9,522,041
Registered Office: 48-50 Fowler Road, Hainault Business Park, Ilford, Essex, IG6 3UT
Activities: Wholesale of clothing and footwear
Parent: Popsoda Holdings Limited
Officers: Shelly Kudhail, Secretary; Balraj Kudhail [1965] Director/Sales Person

Porcelanosa (South East) Limited
Incorporated: 6 December 1995 *Employees:* 162
Net Worth: £8,815,000 *Total Assets:* £19,179,000
Registered Office: Units 1-6 Otterspool Way, Bushey, Watford, Herts, WD25 8HL
Activities: Wholesale of wood, construction materials and sanitary equipment
Parent: Porcelanosa Group Limited
Officers: Deep Shah, Secretary; Silvestre Segarra [1966] Director [Spanish]; Igor Vazquez [1976] Director/Manager [Spanish]

Porcelanosa Group Limited
Incorporated: 6 January 1989 *Employees:* 37
Net Worth: £5,557,000 *Total Assets:* £6,537,000
Registered Office: Units 1-6 Otterspool Way, Bushey, Watford, Herts, WD25 8HL
Activities: Activities of other holding companies n.e.c.
Parent: Porcelanosa U.K. Limited
Officers: Deep Shah, Secretary; Hector Maria Colonques [1942] Director [Spanish]; Manuel Colonques [1942] Director [Spanish]

Porcelanosa U.K. Limited
Incorporated: 5 September 1995 *Employees:* 456
Net Worth: £110,485,000 *Total Assets:* £134,772,000
Registered Office: Units 1-6 Otterspool Way, Bushey, Watford, Herts, WD25 8HL
Activities: Leasing of intellectual property and similar products, except copyright works
Shareholder: Asuncion Manzanet
Officers: Deep Shah, Secretary; Manuel Colonques [1942] Director [Spanish]

Port of London Properties Limited
Incorporated: 24 November 1982
Net Worth: £15,685,000 *Total Assets:* £15,710,000
Registered Office: London River House, Royal Pier Road, Gravesend, Kent, DA12 2BG
Activities: Buying and selling of own real estate
Parent: Port of London Authority
Officers: Susan Jane Grundy, Secretary; Robin John David Mortimer [1972] Director/Chief Executive; Julie Tankard [1966] Director/Chief Financial Officer

Port of Tilbury London Limited
Incorporated: 25 October 1991 *Employees:* 641
Net Worth: £119,671,000 *Total Assets:* £711,844,992
Registered Office: Leslie Ford House, Tilbury Freeport, Tilbury, Essex, RM18 7EH
Activities: Service activities incidental to water transportation
Parent: International Transport Limited
Officers: Pamela June Smyth, Secretary; Carole Jean Cran [1970] Director/Chief Financial Officer; Paul Stuart Dale [1971] Asset and Site Director; Charles Graham Hammond [1961] Director/Solicitor; Stuart James Wallace [1970] Director/Chief Operating Officer; Peter John Ward [1964] Commercial Director

Portico UK Holdco Limited
Incorporated: 16 November 2015
Net Worth Deficit: £2,164,924 *Total Assets:* £7,704,637
Registered Office: Buckingham House East, Buckingham Parade, Stanmore, Middlesex, HA7 4EB
Activities: Other holiday and other collective accommodation
Parent: 21NS Investments Limited
Officers: Darren Arman, Secretary; Darren Mark Arman [1968] Director; John Neil Stewart [1953] Director

Portnall House Ltd
Incorporated: 20 December 2016 *Employees:* 1
Net Worth: £87,635 *Total Assets:* £6,515,047
Registered Office: Munro House, Portsmouth Road, Cobham, Surrey, KT11 1PP
Activities: Activities of other holding companies n.e.c.
Major Shareholder: Nigel Duncan Taee
Officers: Nigel Duncan Taee [1961] Director

Positive Entertainment Ltd
Incorporated: 19 November 2013
Net Worth: £8,340,216 *Total Assets:* £10,110,334
Registered Office: 30 Station Lane, Hornchurch, Essex, RM12 6NJ
Activities: Sound recording and music publishing activities
Major Shareholder: Andrew Paul Green
Officers: Andrew Paul Green [1965] Director; Niall Green [1993] Director; Jamie Duncan McGilvray [1983] Director/Business Development Manager; Albert Steven Turner [1970] Director/Accountant

Postgrad Limited
Incorporated: 26 August 1997
Net Worth: £1,958,270 *Total Assets:* £9,250,281
Registered Office: Zone G, Salamander Quay West, Park Lane, Harefield, Middlesex, UB9 6NZ
Activities: Other letting and operating of own or leased real estate
Parent: Handsale Limited
Officers: Bindu Sodha, Secretary; Bharat Chunilal Sodha [1959] Director

George Potter House Ltd
Incorporated: 26 June 2009
Net Worth: £2,478,589 *Total Assets:* £6,998,965
Registered Office: 69-70 Castle House, Victoria Street, Englefield Green, Surrey, TW20 0QX
Activities: Residential nursing care facilities
Shareholders: Amar Sheikh; Momin Sheikh
Officers: Amar Sheikh, Secretary; Sheikh Amar [1961] Director; Momin Sheikh [1963] Director

Pourshins Limited
Incorporated: 27 July 1981 *Employees:* 64
Net Worth: £8,670,000 *Total Assets:* £31,332,000
Registered Office: Ash House, Littleton Road, Ashford, Middlesex, TW15 1TZ
Activities: Operation of warehousing and storage facilities for water transport activities
Officers: Willem Hendrik Human, Secretary; Stephen Philip Corr [1960] Managing Director; Thomas William Fountain [1969] Director/Chief Financial Officer; Willem Hendrik Human [1982] Finance Director [British/South African]

Powerbase Management Company Limited
Incorporated: 29 March 2001 *Employees:* 2
Net Worth: £3,234,754 *Total Assets:* £5,489,501
Registered Office: 5 Elstree Gate, Elstree Way, Borehamwood, Herts, WD6 1JD
Activities: Renting and operating of Housing Association real estate
Shareholders: Afshin Fouladbakhsh; Joseph Khavari
Officers: Afshin Fouladbakhsh, Secretary/Director; Afshin Fouladbakhsh [1970] Director; Joseph Khavari [1954] Director/Architect

Powergas Africa Limited
Incorporated: 10 September 2014 *Employees:* 72
Net Worth: £18,993,298 *Total Assets:* £37,415,864
Registered Office: Unit 7 Chancery Gate Close, Stonefield Way, South Ruislip, Middlesex, HA4 0JS
Activities: Manufacture of gas
Officers: Navaratnarajah Navendrha, Secretary; Riya Grover [1988] Director; Aditya Khilnani [1990] Director; Deepak Khilnani [1959] Director

PPP Capital Limited
Incorporated: 2 February 2016 *Employees:* 6
Net Worth: £20,761,856 *Total Assets:* £35,069,812
Registered Office: 9 Bridle Close, Kingston upon Thames, Surrey, KT1 2JW
Activities: Other letting and operating of own or leased real estate
Shareholders: Chandrakant Babubhai Patel; Pratima Chandrakant Patel; Sanjeev Charles Patel; Rajeev Charles Patel
Officers: Kenneth Bradley, Secretary; Chandrakant Babubhai Patel [1939] Director; Pratima Chandrakant Patel [1941] Director; Dr Rajeev Charles Patel [1972] Director; Sanjeev Charles Patel [1974] Director

PQW Brenley Corner Limited
Incorporated: 29 November 2007
Net Worth Deficit: £227,399 *Total Assets:* £8,399,154
Registered Office: 147a High Street, Waltham Cross, Herts, EN8 7AP
Activities: Residential nursing care facilities
Shareholders: Arinesarajah Ragumoorthy; Jegathambikai Ragumoorthy
Officers: Jegathambikai Ragumoorthy, Secretary; Arinesarajah Ragumoorthy [1945] Director

PRA Group (UK) Limited
Incorporated: 9 August 2001 *Employees:* 300
Net Worth: £24,391,000 *Total Assets:* £492,511,008
Registered Office: Wells House, 15-17 Elmfield Road, Bromley, Kent, BR1 1LT
Activities: Financial intermediation not elsewhere classified
Parent: PRA Group Inc
Officers: Steven Edward Daws [1969] Director; Richard Owen James [1967] Managing Director; Per Martin Sjolund [1972] Director [Swedish]

Dr Michael Prager Holdings Limited
Incorporated: 18 November 2011
Net Worth: £7,071,336 *Total Assets:* £11,820,336
Registered Office: 195a Kenton Road, Harrow, Middlesex, HA3 0HD
Activities: Activities of head offices
Major Shareholder: Frank Michael Prager
Officers: Christina Christoforou, Secretary; Dr Frank Michael Prager [1968] Director [German]

Prax Petroleum Limited
Incorporated: 20 November 2002
Net Worth: £16,705,960 *Total Assets:* £188,040,848
Registered Office: Prax House, Horizon Business Village, 1 Brooklands Road, Weybridge, Surrey, KT13 0TJ
Activities: Wholesale of petroleum and petroleum products
Officers: Arani Soosaipillai, Secretary; Don Camillo Emilio Borneo [1957] Director/Oil Trader; Winston Sanjeevkumar Soosaipillai [1973] Director

Precision Engineering Plastics Ltd
Incorporated: 17 March 1986 *Employees:* 101
Net Worth: £5,339,181 *Total Assets:* £6,361,024
Registered Office: 1063 Mollison Avenue, Enfield, Middlesex, EN3 7NJ
Activities: Manufacture of other plastic products
Parent: Precision Engineering Plastics (Holdings) Limited
Officers: Padraic Doheny, Secretary [Irish]; Padraic Doheny [1966] Production Director [Irish]; Vince Marino [1967] Director/Engineer [Italian]

Precision Printing Co. Limited
Incorporated: 14 December 1979 *Employees:* 167
Net Worth: £1,496,706 *Total Assets:* £15,753,570
Registered Office: Unit 15 Thames Gateway Park, Chequers Lane, Dagenham, Essex, RM9 6PR
Activities: Printing n.e.c.
Shareholders: Clive David Cooper; Gary Ian Peeling
Officers: Margaret Anne Howell, Secretary/Accountant; Clive David Cooper [1947] Director; Gloria Cooper [1953] Director/Marketing Executive; Margaret Anne Howell [1948] Director/Accountant; Paul Brian Mason [1971] Commercial Director; Gary Ian Peeling [1971] Managing Director; Andrew Skarpellis [1973] Director; Edward Allan Steward [1947] Director

Prefect Software LLP
Incorporated: 9 December 2004
Net Worth: £21,970,278 *Total Assets:* £43,967,152
Registered Office: 166 College Road, Harrow, Middlesex, HA1 1RA
Officers: Barry Belasco [1940] LLP Member; Helen Belasco [1940] LLP Member; Joseph Gabriel Bowman [1968] LLP Member; Patrick Doherty [1942] LLP Member; Andrea Longhi [1968] LLP Member; Alastair Keith MacKeith [1958] LLP Member; Malik Moiz [1958] LLP Member; Paresh Patel [1977] LLP Member; Richard Derek Platt [1976] LLP Member; Priya Nalin Kantilal Shah [1972] LLP Member

Premier Decorations Limited
Incorporated: 4 February 1988 *Employees:* 82
Net Worth: £1,021,388 *Total Assets:* £10,791,078
Registered Office: Premier House, Braintree Road, Ruislip, Middlesex, HA4 0EJ
Activities: Wholesale of household goods (other than musical instruments) n.e.c
Shareholder: Jarnail Singh Athwal
Officers: Michael Geoffrey Sancto, Secretary/Accountant; Jarnail Singh Athwal [1953] Director; Jasmin Athwal [1977] Director/H & S Training; Jason Jaswinder Athwal [1980] Director/IT Manager; Jito Kaur Athwal [1955] Director/Administrator; Heny Lachman Mahtani [1964] Director; Vinod Lachman Mahtani [1961] Director; Pravin Patel [1961] Director/General Manager

Premier Euro Hotels Limited
Incorporated: 23 April 2015 *Employees:* 4
Net Worth: £1,970,074 *Total Assets:* £36,904,408
Registered Office: Kirkland Hose, 11-15 Peterborough Road, Harrow, Middlesex, HA1 2AX
Activities: Hotels and similar accommodation
Officers: Dinesh Gordhandas Bhattessa [1946] Director/Businessman; Haider Ladhu Jaffer [1940] Director; Dr Manoj Raman [1960] Director/Businessman; Hassanali Amirali Dawood Suleman [1954] Director

Premier Fleet Management and Contract Hire Limited
Incorporated: 12 December 2006 *Employees:* 114
Net Worth: £317,008 *Total Assets:* £47,869,992
Registered Office: Venson House, 1 AC Court, High Street, Thames Ditton, Surrey, KT7 0SR
Activities: Activities of other holding companies n.e.c.
Major Shareholder: Dermot Fachtna Desmond
Officers: John Gerard Bateson [1963] Director [Irish]; Mark William Gerard [1965] Finance Director; Samantha Jane Roff [1968] Director; Simon John Staton [1973] Sales Director

Premier Fruit & Nut Limited
Incorporated: 24 October 1986
Net Worth: £42,394,444 *Total Assets:* £45,135,876
Registered Office: Premier House, 56-59 Leslie Park Road, Croydon, Surrey, CR0 6TP
Activities: Wholesale of fruit and vegetables
Shareholders: Narendra Hirji Shah; Minaxi Narendra Shah
Officers: Minaxi Narendra Shah, Secretary; Minaxi Narendra Shah [1952] Director; Narendra Hirji Shah [1950] Director; Rajeev Narendra Shah [1981] Director/Trader

Premier Lotteries Capital UK Limited
Incorporated: 17 March 2010 *Employees:* 963
Net Worth Deficit: £137,000,000 *Total Assets:* £815,200,000
Registered Office: Tolpits Lane, Watford, Herts, WD18 9RN
Activities: Activities of head offices
Parent: Premier Lotteries Investments UK Limited
Officers: John Edward Michael Dillon, Secretary; John Edward Michael Dillon [1963] Legal Director and Company Secretary; Ilya Kachko [1979] Director/Portfolio Manager [Canadian]; Andrew Jonathan Mark Taylor [1961] Director/Private Equity Investor

Premier Lotteries UK Limited
Incorporated: 17 March 2010 *Employees:* 963
Net Worth Deficit: £19,800,000 *Total Assets:* £814,899,968
Registered Office: Tolpits Lane, Watford, Herts, WD18 9RN
Activities: Non-trading company
Parent: Premier Lotteries Capital UK Limited
Officers: John Edward Michael Dillon, Secretary; John Edward Michael Dillon [1963] Legal Director and Company Secretary; Ilya Kachko [1979] Director/Portfolio Manager [Canadian]; Andrew Jonathan Mark Taylor [1961] Director/Private Equity Investor

Premier Moves Limited
Incorporated: 17 September 1996 *Employees:* 219
Net Worth: £4,341,865 *Total Assets:* £7,657,564
Registered Office: Heritage House, 345 Southbury Road, Enfield, Middlesex, EN1 1TW
Activities: Removal services
Major Shareholder: Sally Anne Barrington Thompson
Officers: Francis Vivian Hopping, Secretary; Robert James Foote [1955] Director/CFO EMEA [Canadian]; Stephen Hardie [1972] Managing Director; Barry Anthony Koolen [1966] Director

Premier PLC
Incorporated: 3 February 1988 *Employees:* 82
Net Worth: £7,540,387 *Total Assets:* £14,417,769
Registered Office: Premier House, Braintree Road, Ruislip, Middlesex, HA4 0EJ
Activities: Activities of distribution holding companies
Shareholder: Jarnail Singh Athwal
Officers: Michael Geoffrey Sancto, Secretary/Accountant; Jarnail Singh Athwal [1953] Director; Jito Kaur Athwal [1955] Director; Heny Lachman Mahtani [1964] Director; Vinod Lachman Mahtani [1961] Director

Premier Quilting Company Limited
Incorporated: 6 July 1959 *Employees:* 41
Net Worth: £5,178,334 *Total Assets:* £8,675,334
Registered Office: York House, Empire Way, Wembley, Middlesex, HA9 0FQ
Activities: Wholesale of textiles
Officers: David Lobenstein, Secretary; David Hochhauser [1981] Director; Ronald Edward Hochhauser [1959] Director

Premier Rugby Limited
Incorporated: 31 August 1995 *Employees:* 30
Net Worth: £30,650 *Total Assets:* £24,510,050
Registered Office: Regal House, 70 London Road, Twickenham, Middlesex, TW1 3QS
Activities: Activities of sport clubs
Officers: Adrian Alli, Secretary; Christopher Arthur Booy [1952] Director; Bruce Timothy Craig [1962] Director; Michael Rowland Crossan [1956] Director/President; Nicholas John Eastwood [1959] Director/Chief Executive; Ismail Walid Kurdi [1968] Director; David John Morgan [1957] Director; Simon Sebastian Orange [1967] Director/Chairman; Anthony George Edward Rowe [1948] Director/Chairman; Martin George St Quinton [1957] Director; Peter William Gregory Tom [1940] Director; Mitesh Velani [1982] Director; John White [1951] Director/Chairman; Jason Whittingham [1971] Director/Financier

Premier Work Support Limited
Incorporated: 27 May 2004 *Employees:* 52
Net Worth: £1,566,184 *Total Assets:* £6,452,410
Registered Office: 19-20 Bourne Court, Southend Road, Woodford Green, Essex, IG8 8HD
Activities: Temporary employment agency activities
Shareholders: Joseph Brian Green; Darren Liebman
Officers: Joseph Brian Green, Secretary; Joseph Brian Green [1969] Director/Recruitment; Darren Liebman [1967] Director/Recruitment

Premiere Coffee Limited
Incorporated: 17 June 2004 *Employees:* 632
Net Worth: £2,931,028 *Total Assets:* £8,348,895
Registered Office: Finance Office, Costa Coffee, 311-313 Collier Row Lane, Romford, Essex, RM5 3ND
Activities: Unlicenced restaurants and cafes
Shareholders: Scoffs Group Ltd; Antony Francesco Tagliamonti
Officers: Carlo Jawed [1965] Director/Certified Chartered Accountant; Antony Francesco Tagliamonti [1979] Director/Businessman

Premiere Employment Group Limited
Incorporated: 13 November 2003 *Employees:* 3,446
Net Worth: £5,923,020 *Total Assets:* £20,152,888
Registered Office: Chevron House, 346 Long Lane, Hillingdon, Middlesex, UB10 9PF
Activities: Temporary employment agency activities
Parent: Cordant People Limited
Officers: Alan Connor, Secretary; Chris Martin Kenneally [1960] Director; Jack Rainer Ullmann [1928] Director; Phillip Lionel Ullmann [1964] Director

Premium Credit Limited
Incorporated: 29 April 1986 *Employees:* 417
Net Worth: £182,362,000 *Total Assets:* £1,533,364,992
Registered Office: Ermyn House, Ermyn Way, Leatherhead, Surrey, KT22 8UX
Activities: Credit granting by non-deposit taking finance houses and other specialist consumer credit grantors
Parent: Vendcrown Limited
Officers: Elizabeth Sarah Annys, Secretary; Christopher Stephen Burke [1960] Director; Peter Anthony Colin Catterall [1968] Director; Andrew Phillip Chapman [1969] Director/Chief Financial Officer; Maxim Devin Crewe [1980] Director; Colin Denis Keogh [1953] Director/Chairman; John Reeve [1944] Director; Anthony Santospirito [1984] Director [Australian]; Thomas Woolgrove [1970] Director/Chief Executive Officer; David Thomas McAree Young [1961] Director

Prestige Nursing Limited
Incorporated: 5 April 1971 *Employees:* 1,227
Net Worth: £2,407,173 *Total Assets:* £7,982,079
Registered Office: Greenview House, 5 Manor Road, Wallington, Surrey, SM6 0BW
Activities: Activities of head offices
Parent: Sodexo Holdings Ltd
Officers: Laurent Paul Joseph Arnaudo [1967] Director/Region CFO UK&I at Sodexo [French]; Sarosh Mistry [1969] Director/CEO Home Care Sodexo [American]; Nicolas Jean-Pierre Boudouin Morel [1973] Director [French]; Didier Jean-Marie Bernard Sandoz [1962] Director [French]

Prestolite Electric Limited
Incorporated: 31 October 1974 *Employees:* 99
Net Worth: £6,792,000 *Total Assets:* £15,957,000
Registered Office: 12-16 Bristol Road, Greenford, Middlesex, UB6 8UP
Activities: Manufacture of electric motors, generators and transformers
Officers: Beverley Anne Hounslow, Secretary; Dennis Chelminski [1952] Director/Vice President [American]; Ference Laszlo Gemesi [1965] Sales Director [Hungarian]; Beverley Anne Hounslow [1969] Finance Director; Terence Rom [1956] Director/Engineer

Preston Manor Academy Trust
Incorporated: 14 January 2013 *Employees:* 251
Net Worth: £27,444,716 *Total Assets:* £31,668,798
Registered Office: Preston Manor School, Carlton Avenue East, Wembley, Middlesex, HA9 8NA
Activities: General secondary education
Officers: Jonathan Richard Bach [1956] Director/Education Consultant; Badrun Nessa Salina Chowdhury [1973] Director; Everton Counsell [1966] Director; Sandra Eismann [1978] Director; Beth Ann Kobel [1971] Director/Headteacher; Susan Estella Lawrence [1963] Director/Headteacher; Vivek Luthra [1971] Director; Shiraz Nasrabadi [1968] Director; Donald Balford Palmer [1962] Director/Lecturer; Kinna Patel [1988] Director/Product Manager; Leela Paul [1990] Director/Teacher; Deborah Margaret Sloan [1988] Director [Irish]

Preziosa Cruise Limited
Incorporated: 6 December 2016
Net Worth: £21,322,380 *Total Assets:* £386,967,136
Registered Office: 5 Roundwood Avenue, Stockley Park, Uxbridge, Middlesex, UB11 1AF
Activities: Sea and coastal passenger water transport
Shareholders: Gianluigi Aponte; Rafaela Aponte-Diamant
Officers: Domenico Ferrara, Secretary; Jonathan Francis Campbell [1971] Director/Chartered Accountant; Emilio La Scala [1960] Director [Italian]; Pierfrancesco Vago [1961] Director [Italian]

M.Price Limited
Incorporated: 6 May 1958 *Employees:* 146
Net Worth: £6,959,844 *Total Assets:* £18,238,488
Registered Office: 1 Haslemere Business Centre, Lincoln Way, Enfield, Middlesex, EN1 1DX
Activities: Glazing
Parent: M Price Group Limited
Officers: Colin Frank Chapman, Secretary; Beverley Pauline Chapman [1972] Director; Colin Frank Chapman [1965] Director; Daren Robert Fletcher [1970] Construction Director; Adam Waring [1977] Managing Director

Pricketts Limited
Incorporated: 22 November 1945 *Employees:* 6
Net Worth: £36,536,624 *Total Assets:* £38,022,408
Registered Office: 225 London Road, Staines upon Thames, Middlesex, TW18 4HR
Activities: Buying and selling of own real estate
Officers: Judith Margaret Prickett, Secretary; Jennifer Eileen Cross [1955] Director; Christopher Charles Prickett [1949] Director; Judith Margaret Prickett [1953] Director

Pridenature Limited
Incorporated: 21 June 1995 *Employees:* 4
Net Worth: £4,664,981 *Total Assets:* £9,487,002
Registered Office: Holbrook House, 34-38 Hill Rise, Richmond, Surrey, TW10 6UA
Activities: Buying and selling of own real estate
Major Shareholder: Robert Leigh
Officers: Robert Elliott Leigh [1960] Director/Estate Agent

Prima Tapes & Labels Ltd
Incorporated: 8 October 1979 *Employees:* 30
Net Worth: £4,920,221 *Total Assets:* £5,644,624
Registered Office: Prima House, Faraday Way, St Mary Cray, Orpington, Kent, BR5 3QW
Activities: Other business support service activities n.e.c.
Parent: Prima Tapes and Labels Group Limited
Officers: Sara Elizabeth Downey [1980] Director; David James Lee [1978] Director; Jonathan Paul Lee [1983] Director; Mark Richard Lee [1971] Director; Ryan Jonathan Lee [1978] Director; Stewart David Lee [1972] Director

The Primary First Trust
Incorporated: 18 October 2013 *Employees:* 354
Net Worth: £16,677,000 *Total Assets:* £22,201,000
Registered Office: The White House, Clifton Marine Parade, Gravesend, Kent, DA11 0DY
Activities: Primary education
Officers: Dr Branwen Mary Bingle [1973] Director/University Lecturer; Sandra Margaret Connington [1963] HR Director; William John Harwood [1965] Director; Stephen Rumbles [1964] Managing Director; Paul Stingmore [1981] Director/Management Consultant

Primat Recruitment Limited
Incorporated: 16 December 1980 *Employees:* 117
Net Worth: £13,122,000 *Total Assets:* £17,174,000
Registered Office: 27 Great West Road, Brentford, Middlesex, TW8 9BW
Activities: Human resources provision and management of human resources functions
Parent: AFW UK Oil & Gas Limited
Officers: Victor Jibuike, Secretary; Alan Stewart Gordon [1964] Director; Thomas Francis Honan [1962] Director/Chief Financial Officer [Australian]; James Arnold Lenton [1967] Managing Director; Nicola Dawn Mason [1971] Operations Director; Shaun Poll [1968] Director/Chartered Mechanical Engineer

Prime Care Solutions (Kingston) Holdings Limited
Incorporated: 22 December 2003
Net Worth Deficit: £11,429,000 *Total Assets:* £38,657,000
Registered Office: 8 White Oak Square, London Road, Swanley, Kent, BR8 7AG
Activities: Activities of head offices
Shareholders: Palio (No 3) Limited; Dolphin One Limited
Officers: Carl Harvey Dix [1966] Operations Director; Paul Allyn Edwards [1976] Director/Tax Adviser; Gary William Mills [1956] Director/Project Manager

Prime Care Solutions (Kingston) Limited
Incorporated: 11 June 2003
Net Worth Deficit: £11,429,000 *Total Assets:* £38,657,000
Registered Office: 8 White Oak Square, London Road, Swanley, Kent, BR8 7AG
Activities: Construction of commercial buildings
Parent: Prime Care Solutions (Kingston) Holdings Limited
Officers: Carl Harvey Dix [1966] Operations Director; Paul Allyn Edwards [1976] Director/Tax Adviser; Gary William Mills [1956] Director/Project Manager

Primeeng Group Limited
Incorporated: 25 March 2014 *Employees:* 1,049
Previous: Ricardo Carvalho Investments Limited
Net Worth: £4,411,176 *Total Assets:* £21,590,238
Registered Office: Suite A3:25, Vista Centre, 50 Salisbury Road, Hounslow, Middlesex, TW4 6JQ
Activities: Activities of other holding companies n.e.c.
Major Shareholder: Ricardo Bruno Pereira Carvalho
Officers: Ricardo Bruno Pereira Carvalho [1978] Director [Portuguese]; Malcolm John Steward [1941] Director/Chartered Secretary

Princess Alice Hospice
Incorporated: 25 November 1981 *Employees:* 434
Net Worth: £15,895,144 *Total Assets:* £17,396,758
Registered Office: West End Lane, Esher, Surrey, KT10 8NA
Activities: Other education n.e.c.
Officers: Diane Elizabeth Rickwood, Secretary; Gail Mack Cookson [1957] Fundraising Director; Despina Don-Wauchope [1969] Director/Accountant; Professor Sean Robert Hilton [1949] Director/Emeritus Professor; Jane Tannahill Hogg [1957] Director/Head of Governance NHS Trust; Andrew Jennings [1950] Director/Accountant; Jeannine Marie Nolan [1959] Director/Communication Consultant; Dr Heather Frances Patel [1959] Director/GP; Karen Suzanne Roberts [1963] Director/Head of Talent and Executive Development; Christopher Edward Roshier [1946] Director/Retired; Professor Fiona Mary Ross [1951] Director/Dean and Professor; Sean Michael Watson [1948] Director/Solicitor; Peter Anthony West [1950] Director/Health Economist

The Principal Edinburgh George Street Limited
Incorporated: 15 April 2005 *Employees:* 270
Previous: Troy Management Services (George) Limited
Net Worth: £12,946,000 *Total Assets:* £21,181,000
Registered Office: Broadwater Park, Denham, Uxbridge, Middlesex, UB9 5HR
Activities: Hotels and similar accommodation
Parent: IHC May Fair Hotel Limited
Officers: Catherine Elizabeth Lindsay, Secretary; Michael Todd Glover [1971] Director/Financial Controller [American]; Nicolette Henfrey [1969] Director; Geoffrey Howard Lee [1955] Director [Australian]; Daisy Eleanor Loveday Caroline Llewellyn [1976] Director; David James Taylor [1976] Director; Matthew Woollard [1985] Director

The Principal London Limited
Incorporated: 26 November 2003 *Employees:* 34
Previous: Troy Management Services (Russell) Limited
Net Worth: £6,548,000 *Total Assets:* £63,768,000
Registered Office: Broadwater Park, North Orbital Road, Denham, Uxbridge, Middlesex, UB9 5HR
Activities: Hotels and similar accommodation
Parent: IHC May Fair Hotel Limited
Officers: Catherine Elizabeth Lindsay, Secretary; Michael Todd Glover [1971] Director/Financial Controller [American]; Nicolette Henfrey [1969] Director; Geoffrey Howard Lee [1955] Director [Australian]; Daisy Eleanor Loveday Caroline Llewellyn [1976] Director; David James Taylor [1976] Director; Matthew Woollard [1985] Director

The Principal Manchester Limited
Incorporated: 26 November 2003 *Employees:* 347
Previous: Troy Management Services (Manchester Palace) Limited
Net Worth Deficit: £4,980,000 *Total Assets:* £35,954,000
Registered Office: Broadwater Park, North Orbital Road, Denham, Uxbridge, Middlesex, UB9 5HR
Activities: Hotels and similar accommodation
Parent: IHC May Fair Hotel Limited
Officers: Catherine Elizabeth Lindsay, Secretary; Michael Todd Glover [1971] Director/Financial Controller [American]; Nicolette Henfrey [1969] Director; Geoffrey Howard Lee [1955] Director [Australian]; Daisy Eleanor Loveday Caroline Llewellyn [1976] Director; David James Taylor [1976] Director; Matthew Woollard [1985] Director

The Principal York Limited
Incorporated: 26 November 2003 *Employees:* 207
Previous: Troy Management Services (Royal York) Limited
Net Worth Deficit: £4,129,000 *Total Assets:* £12,133,000
Registered Office: Broadwater Park, Denham, Uxbridge, Middlesex, UB9 5HR
Activities: Hotels and similar accommodation
Parent: IHC May Fair Hotel Limited
Officers: Catherine Elizabeth Lindsay, Secretary; Michael Todd Glover [1971] Director/Financial Controller [American]; Nicolette Henfrey [1969] Director; Geoffrey Howard Lee [1955] Director [Australian]; Daisy Eleanor Loveday Caroline Llewellyn [1976] Director; David James Taylor [1976] Director; Matthew Woollard [1985] Director

Prinhold Limited
Incorporated: 1 August 2011 *Employees:* 1
Net Worth: £3,164,371 *Total Assets:* £23,869,468
Registered Office: c/o Hillier Hopkins LLP, Radius House, 51 Clarendon Road, Watford, Herts, WD17 1HP
Activities: Other letting and operating of own or leased real estate
Major Shareholder: Jonathan Russell Beck
Officers: Jonathan Russell Beck [1967] Director/Investor

L.E. Pritchitt & Company Limited
Incorporated: 18 May 1983 *Employees:* 223
Net Worth: £3,959,000 *Total Assets:* £24,888,000
Registered Office: 2nd Floor, Kingfisher House, 21-23 Elmfield Road, Bromley, Kent, BR1 1LT
Activities: Liquid milk and cream production
Officers: Tom Griffin, Secretary; Dermot Farrell [1966] Director/Manager [Irish]; Thomas Anthony Griffin [1978] Director [Irish]; Peter Sheridan [1962] Director/Financial Controller [Irish]

ProAV Holdings Limited
Incorporated: 26 February 2014 *Employees:* 323
Net Worth: £498,325 *Total Assets:* £25,243,768
Registered Office: ProAV House, Omega Way, Egham, Surrey, TW20 8RD
Activities: Wholesale of other intermediate products
Major Shareholder: Richard Brookes
Officers: LEA Brookes [1966] Director; Richard James Brookes [1964] Managing Director; Francesca Hazell [1969] Director

ProAV Limited
Incorporated: 28 January 1992 *Employees:* 323
Net Worth: £3,581,153 *Total Assets:* £26,596,152
Registered Office: ProAV House, Omega Way, Egham, Surrey, TW20 8RD
Activities: Wholesale of other intermediate products
Parent: ProAV Holdings Limited
Officers: LEA Brookes [1966] Director; Richard James Brookes [1964] Director/Sales; Francesca Hazell [1969] Director

Procter & Gamble (Health & Beauty Care) Limited
Incorporated: 6 June 1947
Net Worth: £325,384,000 *Total Assets:* £411,360,000
Registered Office: The Heights, Brooklands, Weybridge, Surrey, KT13 0XP
Activities: Non-trading company
Parent: Procter & Gamble UK Group Holdings Limited
Officers: Anthony Joseph Appleton, Secretary; Anthony Joseph Appleton [1962] Director/Solicitor; Gianluca Branda [1970] Director/Product Supply Leader [Italian]; Alexander George Buckthorp [1973] Finance Director; Aimee Karen Goldsmith [1973] Associate Director, Communications P&G Northern Europe; Rebecca Jane Goodall [1976] Customer Accounts Director; Daisy Victoria Gray [1980] Sales Director; Ian Douglas Morley [1966] Group Sales Director; Aileen Louise Nathan [1981] Commercial Operations Associate Director; Vijay Indroo Sitlani [1975] Finance Director [Singaporean]; Christopher John Young [1974] HR Director

Procter & Gamble (L & CP) Limited
Incorporated: 5 December 1996
Net Worth: £112,389,000 *Total Assets:* £125,951,000
Registered Office: The Heights, Brooklands, Weybridge, Surrey, KT13 0XP
Activities: Other service activities n.e.c.
Parent: Procter & Gamble UK Group Holdings Limited
Officers: Anthony Joseph Appleton, Secretary; Anthony Joseph Appleton [1962] Director/Solicitor; Gianluca Branda [1970] Director/Product Supply Leader [Italian]; Alexander George Buckthorp [1973] Finance Director; Aimee Karen Goldsmith [1973] Associate Director, Communications P&G Northern Europe; Rebecca Jane Goodall [1976] Customer Accounts Director; Daisy Victoria Gray [1980] Sales Director; Ian Douglas Morley [1966] Group Sales Director; Aileen Louise Nathan [1981] Commercial Operations Associate Director; Vijay Indroo Sitlani [1975] Finance Director [Singaporean]; Christopher John Young [1974] HR Director

Procter & Gamble Finance (UK) Limited
Incorporated: 30 April 2004
Net Worth: £1,474,711,936 *Total Assets:* £1,474,711,936
Registered Office: The Heights, Brooklands, Weybridge, Surrey, KT13 0XP
Activities: Non-trading company
Parent: Procter & Gamble Investment Company (UK) Limited
Officers: Anthony Joseph Appleton, Secretary; Anthony Joseph Appleton [1962] Director/Solicitor; Alexander George Buckthorp [1973] Finance Director; Vijay Indroo Sitlani [1975] Finance Director [Singaporean]

Procter & Gamble Holdings (UK) Limited
Incorporated: 30 April 2004
Net Worth: £1,450,305,536 *Total Assets:* £1,450,305,536
Registered Office: The Heights, Brooklands, Weybridge, Surrey, KT13 0XP
Activities: Activities of head offices
Officers: Anthony Joseph Appleton, Secretary; Anthony Joseph Appleton [1962] Director/Solicitor; Alexander George Buckthorp [1973] Finance Director; Vijay Indroo Sitlani [1975] Finance Director [Singaporean]

Procter & Gamble Investment Company (UK) Limited
Incorporated: 30 April 2004
Net Worth: £1,430,648,704 *Total Assets:* £1,430,648,704
Registered Office: The Heights, Brooklands, Weybridge, Surrey, KT13 0XP
Activities: Non-trading company
Parent: Procter & Gamble Holdings (UK) Limited
Officers: Anthony Joseph Appleton, Secretary; Anthony Joseph Appleton [1962] Director/Solicitor; Alexander George Buckthorp [1973] Finance Director; Vijay Indroo Sitlani [1975] Finance Director [Singaporean]

Procter & Gamble Limited
Incorporated: 1 March 1905
Net Worth: £307,371,008 *Total Assets:* £307,380,992
Registered Office: The Heights, Brooklands, Weybridge, Surrey, KT13 0XP
Activities: Non-trading company
Officers: Anthony Joseph Appleton, Secretary; Anthony Joseph Appleton [1962] Director/Solicitor; Alexander George Buckthorp [1973] Finance Director; Vijay Indroo Sitlani [1975] Finance Director [Singaporean]

Procter & Gamble Overseas Limited
Incorporated: 30 April 2004
Net Worth: £1,509,418,752 *Total Assets:* £1,509,418,752
Registered Office: The Heights, Brooklands, Weybridge, Surrey, KT13 0XP
Activities: Non-trading company
Parent: Procter & Gamble Finance (UK) Limited
Officers: Anthony Joseph Appleton, Secretary; Anthony Joseph Appleton [1962] Director/Solicitor; Alexander George Buckthorp [1973] Finance Director; Vijay Indroo Sitlani [1975] Finance Director [Singaporean]

Procter & Gamble Product Supply (U.K.) Limited
Incorporated: 27 June 1995 *Employees:* 839
Net Worth: £290,435,008 *Total Assets:* £432,592,992
Registered Office: The Heights, Brooklands, Weybridge, Surrey, KT13 0XP
Activities: Manufacture of soap and detergents
Parent: Procter & Gamble (Health & Beauty Care) Limited
Officers: Anthony Joseph Appleton, Secretary; Anthony Joseph Appleton [1962] Director/Solicitor; Gianluca Branda [1970] Director/Product Supply Leader [Italian]; Alexander George Buckthorp [1973] Finance Director; Adina Pascu [1971] Director/Plant Manager [Romanian]; Vijay Indroo Sitlani [1975] Finance Director [Singaporean]; Gary Kenneth Wightman [1971] Director/Plant Manager; Christopher John Young [1974] HR Director

Procter & Gamble Technical Centres Limited
Incorporated: 20 November 1996 *Employees:* 1,029
Net Worth: £110,775,000 *Total Assets:* £234,520,000
Registered Office: The Heights, Brooklands, Weybridge, Surrey, KT13 0XP
Activities: Other professional, scientific and technical activities n.e.c.
Parent: Procter & Gamble (Health & Beauty Care) Limited
Officers: Anthony Joseph Appleton, Secretary; Anthony Joseph Appleton [1962] Director/Solicitor; Alexander George Buckthorp [1973] Finance Director; Claire Elaine Long [1969] Finance Director; Vasiliki Poulopoulou [1965] R&D Associate Director [Greek/British]; Scott Anthony Rodrigue [1963] Research Director [American]; Vijay Indroo Sitlani [1975] Finance Director [Singaporean]; Christopher John Young [1974] HR Director

Procter & Gamble UK Group Holdings Limited
Incorporated: 9 March 1994 *Employees:* 4
Previous: Procter & Gamble UK Holdings Limited
Net Worth: £251,771,008 *Total Assets:* £251,772,000
Registered Office: The Heights, Brooklands, Weybridge, Surrey, KT13 0XP
Activities: Operation of warehousing and storage facilities for land transport activities
Parent: Procter & Gamble Limited
Officers: Anthony Joseph Appleton, Secretary; Anthony Joseph Appleton [1962] Director/Solicitor; Alexander George Buckthorp [1973] Finance Director; Vijay Indroo Sitlani [1975] Finance Director [Singaporean]

Procter & Gamble UK Parent Company Limited
Incorporated: 7 April 2011 *Employees:* 3
Net Worth: £1,013,041,408 *Total Assets:* £1,013,041,408
Registered Office: The Heights, Brooklands, Weybridge, Surrey, KT13 0XP
Activities: Non-trading company
Officers: Anthony Joseph Appleton, Secretary; Anthony Joseph Appleton [1962] Director/Solicitor; Alexander George Buckthorp [1973] Finance Director; Vijay Indroo Sitlani [1975] Finance Director [Singaporean]

Professor Puzzle Limited
Incorporated: 20 March 2002 *Employees:* 42
Net Worth: £2,655,539 *Total Assets:* £6,237,858
Registered Office: The Puzzle Academy, Messom Mews, Twickenham, Middlesex, TW1 4DP
Activities: Non-specialised wholesale trade
Major Shareholder: Benjamin Neil Meldrum
Officers: Adam David Langley [1987] Sales Director; Ben Neil Meldrum [1976] Director/Puzzle Wholesaler; Ruth Lesley Meldrum [1976] Director

Profresh Solutions Limited
Incorporated: 22 April 2004
Net Worth Deficit: £111,768 *Total Assets:* £5,012,472
Registered Office: Thames House, Thames Road, Crayford, Dartford, Kent, DA1 4QP
Activities: Freight transport by road
Shareholders: Solstor UK Limited; Turners (Soham) Limited
Officers: Kevin Stuart Dechaine, Secretary; David Alex Aichen [1969] Director; Leon Aichen [1941] Director; Paul Edwin Day [1958] Director; Winifred Mary Day [1934] Director

Project Tristar Limited
Incorporated: 22 November 2007
Net Worth Deficit: £574,000 *Total Assets:* £24,763,000
Registered Office: Unit 1 Horton Road, West Drayton, Middlesex, UB7 8BQ
Activities: Other passenger land transport
Parent: Addison Lee Group Limited
Officers: Lee Gage, Secretary; Andrew Kenneth Boland [1969] Director/Chief Executive Officer; Simon Gordon [1970] Director

Promede Limited
Incorporated: 19 April 2006
Net Worth Deficit: £111,822 *Total Assets:* £7,977,948
Registered Office: 36 Railway Approach, Station Road, Harrow, Middlesex, HA3 5AA
Activities: Development of building projects
Parent: TLC Group Limited
Officers: Gagan Puri, Secretary; William Charles Neal [1986] Director; Paavan Popat [1985] Managing Director; Honourable Shivaan Shillin Popat [1988] Director; Gagan Puri [1978] Finance Director

Pronovias UK Limited
Incorporated: 8 February 2006
Net Worth: £10,403,903 *Total Assets:* £11,436,852
Registered Office: 1st Floor, Healthaid House, Marlborough Hill, Harrow, Middlesex, HA1 1UD
Activities: Retail sale of clothing in specialised stores
Officers: Lucilla Talamazzi Bongioanni, Secretary; Amandine Julie Marceline Ohayon [1975] Managing Director [French]

Proper Music Distribution Limited
Incorporated: 7 April 1993 *Employees:* 107
Net Worth: £740,400 *Total Assets:* £9,507,494
Registered Office: c/o Myrus Smith, Norman House, 8 Burnell Road, Sutton, Surrey, SM1 4BW
Activities: Other service activities n.e.c.
Parent: Proper Music Group Limited
Officers: Miriam Bernadette Brigid Mills, Company Secretary; Andrew Steven Hill [1977] Managing Director; Malcolm Stuart Mills [1950] Director

Property Finance Capital (No 2) Limited
Incorporated: 19 November 2014
Net Worth: £2,300 *Total Assets:* £10,636,145
Registered Office: 1st Floor, Healthaid House, Marlborough Hill, Harrow, Middlesex, HA1 1UD
Activities: Financial intermediation not elsewhere classified
Parent: Alternative Bridging Corporation Limited
Officers: Robert Jeffrey Piper, Secretary; Stephen Daniel Meller [1967] Director; Brian Leslie Rubins [1939] Director; Jonathan Rubins [1967] Director

Property Finance Capital (No 3) Limited
Incorporated: 8 April 2016
Net Worth: £2,800 *Total Assets:* £7,562,722
Registered Office: 1st Floor, Healthaid House, Marlborough Hill, Harrow, Middlesex, HA1 1UD
Activities: Financial intermediation not elsewhere classified
Parent: Alternative Bridging Corporation Limited
Officers: Robert Jeffrey Piper, Secretary; Stephen Daniel Meller [1967] Director; Brian Leslie Rubins [1939] Director; Jonathan Rubins [1967] Director

Property Finance Capital Limited
Incorporated: 21 July 2010 *Employees:* 1
Net Worth: £23,820 *Total Assets:* £60,334,692
Registered Office: 1st Floor, Health Aid House, Marlborough Hill, Harrow, Middlesex, HA1 1UD
Activities: Financial intermediation not elsewhere classified
Parent: Alternative Bridging Corporation Limited
Officers: Robert Jeffrey Piper, Secretary; Giovanni Primo Losi [1948] Director [Italian]; Stephen Daniel Meller [1967] Director/Finance Broker; Melvin Frank Robinson [1956] Director; Brian Leslie Rubins [1939] Director; Jonathan Rubins [1967] Director

Property Finance Nominees (No.3) Limited
Incorporated: 29 May 1996
Net Worth: £100 *Total Assets:* £57,545,068
Registered Office: 1st Floor, Health Aid House, Marlborough Hill, Harrow, Middlesex, HA1 1UD
Activities: Financial intermediation not elsewhere classified
Parent: Alternative Bridging Corporation Limited
Officers: Robert Jeffrey Piper, Secretary; Stephen Daniel Meller [1967] Director/Finance Broker; Brian Leslie Rubins [1939] Director; Jonathan Rubins [1967] Director

Property Plus Investments Limited
Incorporated: 23 February 2005
Net Worth: £4,202,071 *Total Assets:* £5,576,700
Registered Office: 75 Midsummer Avenue, Hounslow, Middlesex, TW4 5AY
Activities: Buying and selling of own real estate
Shareholders: Mujahid Ali; Ruheda Khanom
Officers: Ruheda Khanom, Secretary; Mujahid Ali [1965] Director/Manager Restaurant

Property Support Services UK Limited
Incorporated: 14 November 2005 *Employees:* 765
Net Worth: £2,742,108 *Total Assets:* £6,170,109
Registered Office: 249 Cranbrook Road, Ilford, Essex, IG1 4TG
Activities: General cleaning of buildings
Major Shareholder: Michael John Rust
Officers: Michael John Rust, Secretary; Michael John Rust [1947] Director

The Property Warehouse Limited
Incorporated: 22 October 2003 *Employees:* 1
Net Worth Deficit: £1,183,714 *Total Assets:* £10,018,453
Registered Office: 19-20 Bourne Court, Southend Road, Woodford Green, Essex, IG8 8HD
Activities: Development of building projects
Parent: AVDIME Limited
Officers: Tracey Joanna Aviram, Secretary; David Aviram [1953] Director

Propertycoe Limited
Incorporated: 23 December 2015 *Employees:* 1
Net Worth Deficit: £894,548 *Total Assets:* £5,449,220
Registered Office: 53 Redbridge Lane East, Ilford, Essex, IG4 5EY
Activities: Development of building projects
Shareholders: John Maitland Coe; Jacqueline Coe
Officers: Jacqueline Coe [1957] Director; John Maitland Coe [1955] Director

Proppertunity Limited
Incorporated: 3 December 2007
Net Worth Deficit: £245,382 *Total Assets:* £6,147,803
Registered Office: 2nd Floor, Unicorn House, Station Close, Potters Bar, Herts, EN6 1TL
Activities: Buying and selling of own real estate
Major Shareholder: Michael Glassman
Officers: Jordan Luke Glassman [1991] Director; Michael Glassman [1963] Director

Prosidion Limited
Incorporated: 25 November 2002 *Employees:* 1
Net Worth: £5,477,000 *Total Assets:* £5,491,000
Registered Office: 2000 Hillswood Drive, Chertsey, Surrey, KT16 0RS
Activities: Research and experimental development on biotechnology
Parent: Astellas Pharma Inc.
Officers: Stephen Shea Knowles [1963] Director/SVP Chief Financial Officer [American]; Collette Taylor [1963] Director/SVP HR & Corporate Administration [American]

Prospect Healthcare (Hairmyres) Group Limited
Incorporated: 7 April 2003
Net Worth Deficit: £9,561,000 *Total Assets:* £84,352,000
Registered Office: 8 White Oak Square, London Road, Swanley, Kent, BR8 7AG
Activities: Activities of head offices
Officers: David John Brooking [1967] Investment Director; Christopher James [1968] Investment Director; Jeffrey Michael Thornton [1953] Director/Consultant

Prospect Healthcare (Hairmyres) Holdings Limited
Incorporated: 10 February 1998
Total Assets: £9,462,000
Registered Office: 8 White Oak Square, London Road, Swanley, Kent, BR8 7AG
Activities: Activities of head offices
Officers: David John Brooking [1967] Investment Director; Christopher James [1968] Investment Director; Jeffrey Michael Thornton [1953] Director/Consultant

Prospect Healthcare (Hairmyres) Limited
Incorporated: 11 February 1998
Net Worth Deficit: £9,056,000 *Total Assets:* £84,789,000
Registered Office: 8 White Oak Square, London Road, Swanley, Kent, BR8 7AG
Activities: Hospital activities
Officers: David John Brooking [1967] Investment Director; Christopher James [1968] Investment Director; Jeffrey Michael Thornton [1953] Director/Consultant

Prospect Healthcare (Hairmyres) Resources
Incorporated: 10 August 2004
Net Worth: £13,522,000 *Total Assets:* £13,522,000
Registered Office: 8 White Oak Square, London Road, Swanley, Kent, BR8 7AG
Activities: Other credit granting n.e.c.
Parent: Prospect Healthcare (Hairmyres) Holdings Limited
Officers: David John Brooking [1967] Investment Director; Christopher James [1968] Investment Director; Jeffrey Michael Thornton [1953] Director/Consultant

Prospect Healthcare (Hinchingbrooke) Limited
Incorporated: 24 July 2003
Net Worth Deficit: £67,000 *Total Assets:* £23,405,000
Registered Office: 8 White Oak Square, London Road, Swanley, Kent, BR8 7AG
Activities: Combined facilities support activities
Parent: Prospect Healthcare (Hinchingbrooke) Holdings Limited
Officers: Ross William Driver [1981] Director; Julian Mark Rudd-Jones [1955] Director/Property Developer; Mark Christopher Wayment [1958] Investment Director Infrastructure

Prospect Healthcare (Reading) Limited
Incorporated: 19 July 1999
Net Worth: £2,890,000 *Total Assets:* £29,903,000
Registered Office: 8 White Oak Square, London Road, Swanley, Kent, BR8 7AG
Activities: Combined facilities support activities
Parent: Prospect Healthcare (Reading) Holdings Limited
Officers: David John Brooking [1967] Investment Director; Sabrina Sidhu [1979] Director

Prospects Group 2011 Limited
Incorporated: 18 July 2011 *Employees:* 1,219
Net Worth Deficit: £32,012,000 *Total Assets:* £37,933,000
Registered Office: Shaw Trust House, 19 Elmfield Road, Bromley, Kent, BR1 1LT
Activities: Activities of head offices
Parent: The Shaw Trust Limited
Officers: Nicholas Oliver Carey, Secretary; Paul Michael Baldwin [1965] Director; James Nicholas Bell [1966] Director; Victoria Blakeman [1968] Director; Brenda Patricia Cabras [1955] Director; Nicholas Oliver Charles Carey [1986] Director; Peter David Holmes [1953] Director; Vanessa Helen Miner [1962] Director; Jacqueline Maria Oughton [1964] Director; David George Phipps [1970] Director/Chief Finance Officer; Alison Ruth Williams [1965] Director

Prospects Services
Incorporated: 30 March 1995 *Employees:* 1,154
Net Worth Deficit: £31,112,000 *Total Assets:* £37,111,000
Registered Office: Shaw Trust House, 19 Elmfield Road, Bromley, Kent, BR1 1LT
Activities: Educational support services
Parent: Prospects Services Midco Limited
Officers: Catherine Joanne Trevorrow, Secretary; Paul Michael Baldwin [1965] Director; James Nicholas Bell [1966] Director; Victoria Blakeman [1968] Director; Brenda Patricia Cabras [1955] Director; Nicholas Oliver Charles Carey [1986] Director; Peter David Holmes [1953] Director; Vanessa Helen Miner [1962] Director; Jacqueline Maria Oughton [1964] Director; David George Phipps [1970] Finance Director; Alison Ruth Williams [1965] Director

PRP Architects LLP
Incorporated: 25 January 2011 *Employees:* 236
Net Worth: £8,313,447 *Total Assets:* £14,317,796
Registered Office: Ferry Works, Summer Road, Thames Ditton, Surrey, KT7 0QJ
Officers: Neil Timothy Griffiths [1965] Member; Brendan Anthony Kilpatrick [1963] Member; Anne-Marie Marie Nicholson [1969] Member; Manisha Patel [1971] Member; Justin Bannister [1968] LLP Member; Marco Santos Baptista [1973] LLP Member; Andrew William Black [1981] LLP Member; Ian Bott [1961] LLP Member; Richard William Burgess [1954] LLP Member; Jennifer Anne Buterchi [1968] LLP Member; Clare Louise Cameron [1972] LLP Member; Bhupinder Singh Chawla [1966] LLP Member; James Andrew Chubb [1978] LLP Member; Scott Cromack [1975] LLP Member; John Dawkins [1976] LLP Member; Thomas Delharity [1970] LLP Member; Nicolas Dunn [1966] LLP Member; Sajna Angeli Ganoo [1975] LLP Member; James Hackett [1982] LLP Member; Richard Harvey [1977] LLP Member; Michael Hawkins [1961] LLP Member; Robert High [1984] LLP Member; Mary Louise Hutchison [1972] LLP Member; Stephen Hynds [1954] LLP Member; Adrian Peter Charles Judd [1963] LLP Member; Spyridon Katsaros [1980] LLP Member; Graham Locke [1963] LLP Member; Toby Martin-Jay [1973] LLP Member; Ezekiel Osho [1965] LLP Member; Philip Michael Pamment [1961] LLP Member; Steven Phillips [1971] LLP Member; Richard James Price [1978] LLP Member; Marylis Ramos [1975] LLP Member; Andrew Robson [1973] LLP Member; Scott Sanderson [1973] LLP Member; Craig Sheach [1972] LLP Member; Robert Squibb [1977] LLP Member; Mark Walker [1978] LLP Member; Alistair James Weir [1964] LLP Member

PS Foundation
Incorporated: 5 March 2008
Net Worth: £15,380,015 *Total Assets:* £15,382,721
Registered Office: Warren House, Warreners Lane, Weybridge, Surrey, KT13 0LQ
Activities: General secondary education
Shareholders: Vinodka Murria; Sunil Bhalla; Mark Richard Butt
Officers: Sunil Bhalla [1959] Director/Teacher; Mark Richard Butt [1960] Director; Vinodka Murria [1962] Director

PSN Holdco Limited
Incorporated: 9 March 2015
Net Worth Deficit: £869,000 *Total Assets:* £27,428,000
Registered Office: Hanover House, Plane Tree Crescent, Feltham, Middlesex, TW13 7BZ
Activities: Non-trading company
Parent: Perform Sports Media Limited
Officers: Paul Oszkar David Morton [1979] Director

PSSG Group Limited
Incorporated: 8 May 2015 *Employees:* 1,502
Net Worth: £5,062,579 *Total Assets:* £15,548,770
Registered Office: 249 Cranbrook Road, Ilford, Essex, IG1 4TG
Activities: Other service activities n.e.c.
Major Shareholder: Michael John Rust
Officers: Michael John Rust [1947] Director

Pudfield Investments Ltd
Incorporated: 11 August 1983
Net Worth: £4,877,966 *Total Assets:* £5,711,650
Registered Office: 52 High Street, Pinner, Middlesex, HA5 5PW
Activities: Other business support service activities n.e.c.
Officers: Natalie Goldstone [1980] Director; Marc Adam Jackson [1972] Director/IT Analyst Consultant; Marilyn Rochelle Jackson [1951] Director/Designer

Puma Heritage PLC
Incorporated: 7 November 2012
Net Worth: £51,462,000 *Total Assets:* £53,540,000
Registered Office: Elder House, St Georges Business Park, Brooklands Road, Weybridge, Surrey, KT13 0TS
Activities: Activities of financial services holding companies
Officers: James Ednie Brydie [1959] Director; Michael David Posen [1944] Director; Michael Laurent Van Messel [1964] Director/Accountant

Punjab House Associated Ltd
Incorporated: 13 October 2011 *Employees:* 2
Net Worth: £7,387,622 *Total Assets:* £13,301,499
Registered Office: 232a Northolt Road, Harrow, Middlesex, HA2 8DU
Activities: Other letting and operating of own or leased real estate
Shareholders: Surinder Kaur Chopra; Surinder Kaur Chopra
Officers: Waryam Singh Kakol [1970] Director/Consultant [Dutch]

Pura Foods Limited
Incorporated: 28 August 1987 *Employees:* 174
Net Worth: £62,272,000 *Total Assets:* £110,393,752
Registered Office: ADM International Offices, Church Manorway, Erith, Kent, DA8 1DL
Activities: Manufacture of oils and fats
Shareholders: ADM Pura Limited; Archer Daniels Midland (UK) Limited
Officers: Douwe Alserda [1968] Director/Financial Controller [Dutch]; Marcus Degen [1966] Director/General Manager [Dutch]; Lance Thomas Rogers [1973] Director/Financial Controller

Purcell School (The)
Incorporated: 30 April 1963 *Employees:* 142
Net Worth: £13,554,334 *Total Assets:* £14,567,751
Registered Office: The Purcell School, Aldenham Road, Bushey, Watford, Herts, WD23 2TS
Activities: General secondary education
Officers: Aideen Catherine McNamara, Secretary; Charles Esmond Beer [1956] Director/Tax Adviser; Professor Timothy James Blinko [1965] Director/Academic; Jonathan Edward Eley [1971] Director/Solicitor; James Christopher Fowler [1962] Director/Headmaster; Janice Graham [1968] Director/Violinist; Sir Roger Tustin Jackling [1943] Director/Retired; Professor Colin James Lawson [1949] Director/Academic; William Rufus Benjamin McDonnell [1973] Director/Group Chief Risk Officer; Dr Rebecca Mooney [1968] Director/Solicitor; Ian Hearle David Odgers [1938] Director/Executive Search; Mark Edmund Racz [1955] Director/Academic [American]; Joanna Van Heyningen [1945] Director/Architect; Kirsty Von Malaise [1974] Director/Headmistress

G.Purchase Construction Limited
Incorporated: 27 March 2002 *Employees:* 145
Net Worth: £6,877,000 *Total Assets:* £8,955,000
Registered Office: Wates House, Station Approach, Leatherhead, Surrey, KT22 7SW
Activities: Construction of domestic buildings
Parent: Purchase Group Limited
Officers: Philip Michael Wainwright, Secretary; David Owen Allen [1972] Director/Chief Financial Officer; David Keir Ewart Morgan [1974] Managing Director; Paul Campbell Rowan [1964] Group HR Director; Philip Michael Wainwright [1965] Director/Chief Financial Officer

Purchase Group Limited
Incorporated: 30 December 2004
Net Worth: £9,056,000 *Total Assets:* £10,320,000
Registered Office: Wates House, Station Approach, Leatherhead, Surrey, KT22 7SW
Activities: Activities of head offices
Parent: Wates Living Space (Maintenance) Limited
Officers: Philip Michael Wainwright, Secretary; David Owen Allen [1972] Director/Chief Financial Officer; David Keir Ewart Morgan [1974] Managing Director; Paul Campbell Rowan [1964] Group HR Director; Philip Michael Wainwright [1965] Director/Chief Financial Officer

Pure Bricks Limited
Incorporated: 29 September 2016 *Employees:* 2
Net Worth: £236,370 *Total Assets:* £5,112,774
Registered Office: Concept House, Home Park Road, Kings Langley, Herts, WD4 8UD
Activities: Buying and selling of own real estate
Shareholder: Ing. Christian Trapl
Officers: Johann Hager [1949] Director [Austrian]; Sir Hossein Yassaie [1956] Director/Chairman

Pure International Limited
Incorporated: 23 September 2016 *Employees:* 61
Net Worth: £5,263,746 *Total Assets:* £12,681,089
Registered Office: Concept House, Home Park Road, Kings Langley, Herts, WD4 8UD
Activities: Manufacture of consumer electronics
Shareholder: Ing. Christian Trapl
Officers: Johann Hager [1949] Director [Austrian]; Martin Muller [1988] Director [Austrian]; Sir Hossein Yassaie [1956] Director/Chairman

Purebond Limited
Incorporated: 9 July 1991
Net Worth: £8,761,799 *Total Assets:* £9,725,268
Registered Office: Portland House, 69-71 Wembley Hill Road, Wembley, Middlesex, HA9 8BU
Activities: Other service activities n.e.c.
Parent: Solai Holdings Limited
Officers: Bhupendra Shantilal Kansagra, Secretary; Bhupendra Shantilal Kansagra [1956] Director; Ramesh Shantilal Kansagra [1950] Director; Rishi Ramesh Kansagra [1981] Director

Purelake Investments Limited
Incorporated: 1 April 1998
Net Worth: £34,220,308 *Total Assets:* £85,338,672
Registered Office: Purelake House, Plaistow Lane, Bromley, Kent, BR1 4DS
Activities: Other letting and operating of own or leased real estate
Parent: Purelake Properties Ltd
Officers: Sara Ann White, Secretary; Generald Anthony Dowd [1962] Finance Director; Barry John White [1962] Director/Property Developer; Sara Ann White [1965] Director/Company Secretary

Purelake New Homes Limited
Incorporated: 9 March 1992 *Employees:* 49
Net Worth: £38,515,208 *Total Assets:* £44,710,352
Registered Office: Purelake House, Plaistow Lane, Bromley, Kent, BR1 4DS
Activities: Construction of other civil engineering projects n.e.c.
Parent: Purelake Properties Ltd
Officers: Sara Ann White, Secretary; Noel Robert Convert [1971] Construction Director; Generald Anthony Dowd [1962] Finance Director; Tracey Ann Wheelan [1978] Sales Director; Barry John White [1962] Director/Property Developer; Sara Ann White [1965] Director/Secretary

Purelake Properties Limited
Incorporated: 10 July 1991 *Employees:* 49
Net Worth: £59,287,748 *Total Assets:* £109,685,592
Registered Office: Purelake House, Plaistow Lane, Bromley, Kent, BR1 4DS
Activities: Other letting and operating of own or leased real estate
Shareholders: Barry John White; Sara Ann White
Officers: Sara Ann White, Secretary; Barry John White [1962] Director/Property Developer; Sara Ann White [1965] Director/Secretary

Purfleet Commercials Limited
Incorporated: 1 June 1984 *Employees:* 108
Net Worth: £3,201,071 *Total Assets:* £5,002,097
Registered Office: 601 London Road, West Thurrock, Grays, Essex, RM20 4AU
Activities: Maintenance and repair of motor vehicles
Parent: Harris Holdings (Grays) Limited
Officers: Peter James Harlow, Secretary; Peter Joseph Greenyer [1956] Director/Certified Accountant; Francesca Emma Harlow [1986] Director; Peter James Harlow [1985] Director/Accountant; Frank Douglas Harris [1964] Director; James Daniel Selway [1989] Director; Danielle Elizabeth Van Der Wiel [1962] Director; John Robert Vickery [1959] Director/Engineer

Purism Properties Limited
Incorporated: 21 September 2010
Previous: Duplo Property Limited
Net Worth: £2,458,528 *Total Assets:* £7,002,459
Registered Office: Automated Precision House, Hamm Moor Lane, Addlestone, Surrey, KT15 2SD
Activities: Other letting and operating of own or leased real estate
Officers: Alan David John Greenhalgh [1954] Director; Philip William Greenhalgh [1956] Director; Robin David Vincent Greenhalgh [1962] Director; Glyn Adrian Nutting [1959] Director

Purley Baptist Church
Incorporated: 29 September 2009 *Employees:* 12
Net Worth: £5,372,613 *Total Assets:* £6,823,335
Registered Office: Admin Office, Purley Baptist Church, Banstead Road, Purley, Surrey, CR8 3EA
Activities: Activities of religious organisations
Officers: Michele Jane Bailey [1963] Director/Manager; David John Clarke [1958] Director/Civil Servant; Rev Dr James Michael Collins [1970] Director/Church Minister; Ben Quartey-Papafio [1960] Director/Retired; Ian Jeremy Roberts [1961] Director; Joanna Claire Walker [1973] Director/Accountant; Rev Marilyn Webb [1955] Director/Minister of Religion

Purley Point Limited
Incorporated: 22 May 2008
Net Worth: £269,133 *Total Assets:* £5,023,712
Registered Office: 786 London Road, Thornton Heath, Surrey, CR7 6JB
Activities: Other letting and operating of own or leased real estate
Parent: Goldstar Healthcare Ltd
Officers: Anilkumar Jivraj Shah, Secretary; Pravinchandra Jivraj Shah [1954] Director

Purple Surgical Holdings Limited
Incorporated: 26 April 1973 *Employees:* 143
Net Worth: £5,076,322 *Total Assets:* £12,701,356
Registered Office: 2 Chestnut House, Farm Close, Shenley, Herts, WD7 9AD
Activities: Activities of head offices
Major Shareholder: Robert Sharpe
Officers: Philip David Franklin, Secretary; Richard Lampert [1948] Director/Chartered Accountant; Jane Eddy Sharpe [1967] Director/Executive; Robert Sharpe [1963] Director

Purslow Investments Limited
Incorporated: 3 April 2012
Previous: New Malden Golf Centre Limited
Net Worth: £4,433,190 *Total Assets:* £11,433,935
Registered Office: 1st Floor, 5 Century Court, Tolpits Lane, Watford, Herts, WD18 9PX
Activities: Operation of sports facilities
Major Shareholder: Christian Mark Cecil Purslow
Officers: Christian Mark Cecil Purslow [1963] Director; Jayne Elizabeth Purslow [1962] Director

Pyramid Builders Limited
Incorporated: 23 November 1994 *Employees:* 4
Net Worth: £6,169,893 *Total Assets:* £8,950,507
Registered Office: 38a Fourth Way, Wembley, Middlesex, HA9 0LH
Activities: Other construction installation
Major Shareholder: Liam Clear
Officers: Liam Clear [1961] Director/General Builder/Civil Engineer [Irish]

Pyramid Schools (Sheffield) Limited
Incorporated: 17 February 2000
Net Worth Deficit: £1,623,000 *Total Assets:* £33,368,000
Registered Office: 8 White Oak Square, London Road, Swanley, Kent, BR8 7AG
Activities: Other business support service activities n.e.c.
Parent: Sheffield Schools Services Holdings Limited
Officers: David John Brooking [1967] Investment Director; Alastair James Watson [1974] Investment Director

Q.F.S. Scaffolding Limited
Incorporated: 9 July 2003 *Employees:* 130
Net Worth: £3,672,053 *Total Assets:* £8,313,443
Registered Office: Westminster House, Denton Wharf, Mark Lane, Gravesend, Kent, DA12 2PL
Activities: Scaffold erection
Shareholder: Kevin James Clifford
Officers: Keely Baker, Secretary; Kevin James Clifford [1963] Director/Scaffolding Contractor; Peter Alan Reade [1955] Managing Director

Q.N. Hotels (Wrexham) Limited
Incorporated: 18 February 2004 *Employees:* 66
Net Worth: £455,137 *Total Assets:* £5,572,337
Registered Office: QN House, Loughton Business Centre, 5 Langston Road, Loughton, Essex, IG10 3FL
Activities: Hotels and similar accommodation
Officers: Qamar Ahmed, Secretary/Hotelier; Aftab Ahmed [1944] Director/Hotelier; Qamar Ahmed [1973] Director/Hotelier

Q.N. Hotels Limited
Incorporated: 6 September 1993 *Employees:* 120
Net Worth: £11,607,775 *Total Assets:* £19,404,120
Registered Office: QN House, Unit 4 Loughton Business Centre, 5 Langston Road, Loughton, Essex, IG10 3FL
Activities: Hotels and similar accommodation
Officers: Qamar Ahmed, Secretary/Hotelier; Aftab Ahmed [1944] Director/Hotelier; Qamar Ahmed [1973] Director/Hotelier

QBS Software Limited
Incorporated: 3 April 1987 *Employees:* 37
Net Worth: £3,290,522 *Total Assets:* £15,515,417
Registered Office: 7 Wharfside, Rosemont Road, Wembley, Middlesex, HA0 4QB
Activities: Wholesale of computers, computer peripheral equipment and software
Parent: GNR Technology Ltd
Officers: Graham David Stevinson [1971] Director

QED (Clacton) Limited
Incorporated: 14 May 2003
Net Worth: £2,552,000 *Total Assets:* £30,126,000
Registered Office: 8 White Oak Square, London Road, Swanley, Kent, BR8 7AG
Activities: Combined facilities support activities
Parent: QED (Clacton) Holdings Limited
Officers: David John Brooking [1967] Investment Director; Benjamin Christopher Jacob Dean [1979] Director/Investment Manager

QED (Leeds) Limited
Incorporated: 19 December 2003
Net Worth: £1,317,000 *Total Assets:* £28,176,000
Registered Office: 8 White Oak Square, London Road, Swanley, Kent, BR8 7AG
Activities: Combined facilities support activities
Parent: QED (Leeds) Holdings Limited
Officers: Benjamin Christopher Jacob Dean [1979] Director/Investment Manager; Alastair James Watson [1974] Investment Director

QH Estates Ltd
Incorporated: 22 February 2011
Net Worth: £11,582,685 *Total Assets:* £22,161,596
Registered Office: 2 Peterwood Way, Croydon, Surrey, CR0 4UQ
Activities: Other letting and operating of own or leased real estate
Major Shareholder: Naliniben Kiritkumar Patel
Officers: Ameet Patel, Secretary; Kirit Chimanbhai Patel Junior [1980] Director; Heena Patel [1963] Finance Director; Rupa Patel [1981] Director; Jayanti Chimanbhai Patel Junior [1984] Director

QOTD Film Investment Limited
Incorporated: 11 October 2013
Net Worth Deficit: £134,285 *Total Assets:* £8,769,251
Registered Office: 3rd Floor, Vyman House, 104 College Road, Harrow, Middlesex, HA1 1BQ
Activities: Motion picture production activities
Officers: Michael Benaroya [1981] Director [American]

QSC 1208 Limited
Incorporated: 4 December 2006
Net Worth: £5,520,317 *Total Assets:* £56,909,872
Registered Office: Two Bridges, Guildford Street, Chertsey, Surrey, KT16 9AU
Activities: Business and domestic software development
Parent: PB Bidco Limited
Officers: Jason Phillip Conley [1975] Finance Director [American]; Robert Christopher Crisci [1975] Finance Director [American]; Robin Tarquinn Morris-Weston [1970] Director; John Kenneth Stipancich [1968] Director/Vice President, General Counsel and Secretary [American]

QSC 1209 Limited
Incorporated: 4 December 2006 *Employees:* 4
Net Worth: £78,974,000 *Total Assets:* £79,262,000
Registered Office: Two Bridges, Guildford Street, Chertsey, Surrey, KT16 9AU
Activities: Business and domestic software development
Parent: QSC 1208 Limited
Officers: Jason Phillip Conley [1975] Finance Director [American]; Robert Christopher Crisci [1975] Finance Director [American]; Robin Tarquinn Morris-Weston [1970] Director; John Kenneth Stipancich [1968] Director/Vice President, General Counsel and Secretary [American]

Quad Building Services (Southern) Limited
Incorporated: 1 July 1994 *Employees:* 20
Net Worth: £4,404,431 *Total Assets:* £6,011,935
Registered Office: Springfield House, 99-101 Crossbrook Street, Waltham Cross, Herts, EN8 8JR
Activities: Construction of commercial buildings
Officers: Sciovane Loretta Shephard, Secretary; Martin Sydney Shephard [1958] Director; Sciovane Loretta Shephard [1962] Director/Admin Assistant; Anne Marie Treacy [1970] Director; Mark Michael Treacy [1970] Director/Commercial Manager

Quality Line Transport Limited
Incorporated: 25 November 1933 *Employees:* 367
Previous: H.R. Richmond Limited
Net Worth: £4,655,000 *Total Assets:* £8,589,000
Registered Office: Busways House, Wellington Road, Twickenham, Middlesex, TW2 5NX
Activities: Other passenger land transport
Parent: RATP DEV UK Ltd
Officers: Catherine Marie-Jeanne Chardon [1970] Transformation Director [French]; Romain Ferriere [1975] Director/Chief Financial Officer [French]; Karen Rose Fuller [1968] HR Director; Howard Charles Goodbourn [1961] Director/Chief Financial Officer; David Andrew Kaye [1962] Director; Kuldeep Singh Nothey [1965] Service Delivery Director; Peter Richardson [1974] Finance Director; Florence Rodet [1969] Director/Secretary General - Public Relations [French]; Fiona Jacqueline Taylor [1962] Managing Director

Quality Spirits International Limited
Incorporated: 3 March 1986 *Employees:* 12
Net Worth: £112,124,000 *Total Assets:* £116,992,000
Registered Office: Independence House, 84 Lower Mortlake Road, Richmond, Surrey, TW9 2HS
Activities: Wholesale of wine, beer, spirits and other alcoholic beverages
Parent: William Grant & Sons Enterprises Limited
Officers: Karen Louise Forbes, Secretary; Alexander John Davies [1982] Director/Head of Finance & Business Development; John Michael Harvey [1956] Managing Director; Ewan John Henderson [1968] Director; Michael Lamont [1960] Director

Quebec Court Freehold Limited
Incorporated: 11 May 2010 *Employees:* 4
Net Worth: £169,318 *Total Assets:* £9,496,658
Registered Office: Kajaine House, 57-67 High Street, Edgware, Middlesex, HA8 7DD
Activities: Other letting and operating of own or leased real estate
Major Shareholder: Tariq Mahmood Chaudhry
Officers: Ali Sattar Chaudri, Secretary; Kalim Ahmad Tahir [1956] Director/Finance Manager

Queen Elizabeth's Girls' School (Barnet)
Incorporated: 8 July 2011 *Employees:* 119
Net Worth: £17,166,906 *Total Assets:* £18,958,656
Registered Office: High Street, Barnet, Herts, EN5 5RR
Activities: General secondary education
Officers: Professor Ashley Braganza [1961] Director/University Professor; Dr Susan Cottam [1967] Director/Clinical Psychologist; Alison Davis [1963] Director/Chief Information Officer; Royden Gothelf [1960] Director/IT Production Manager; Rebecca Eloise Hanley [1967] Director/Broadcast Journalist; Lisa Hartshorn [1979] Director/Deputy Company Secretary; Alan James Jenner [1951] Director/Retired; Deborah Lane [1958] Director/Landscape Gardener; Dr Dewi Lewis [1967] Director/Chemist and Tutor; Bhavin Mistry [1984] Director/Head of Financial Operations; Uzoamaka Joy Nwamuu [1970] Director/Housewife; Rebecca Elizabeth Peer [1975] Director/Housewife; Hannah Ross [1980] Director/Lawyer; Carrie Arboleda Scott [1987] Director/Senior Auditor [American]; Violet Walker [1958] Director/Headteacher

Queen Elizabeth's School Barnet
Incorporated: 19 August 2010 *Employees:* 115
Net Worth: £24,766,726 *Total Assets:* £26,613,764
Registered Office: Queen Elizabeth's School Barnet, Queen's Road, Barnet, Herts, EN5 4DQ
Activities: General secondary education
Officers: Emine Aghdiran, Secretary; Matthew Beard [1968] Director/Public Relations; Anthony Michael Binstock [1983] Director/Self Employed; Martyn Henry Stewart Bradish [1951] Director/Chartered Accountant; David James Burton [1959] Director/Chartered Accountant; Kenneth Reginald Cooper [1931] Director; Roger Anthony Delves [1957] Director; Neil James Dominic Enright [1977] Director/Headmaster; David John Farrer [1943] Director; Jane Elizabeth Ferguson [1950] Director; Reverend Christopher Ferris [1977] Director/Clerk of Holy Orders; Andrew Nicholas Gaskell [1949] Director/Chartered Accountant; Maureen Janet Hooley [1952] Operations Director; Eric Houston [1952] Director; Anne MacDonald [1979] Director/Teacher; Barrie Robert Martin [1934] Director/Chartered Surveyor; Dr Caroline Martin [1969] Director/Science Adviser; Colin William Price [1961] Director/Teacher; Naresh Harsadray Raval [1957] Director/Architect; Patricia Reid [1967] Director/Health Visitor; Dr Voi Shim Wong [1961] Director/Medicine (Specialist) [Malaysian]

Queenring Limited
Incorporated: 5 August 1980 *Employees:* 2
Net Worth: £947,235 *Total Assets:* £5,549,835
Registered Office: 28 Lindsay Drive, Kenton, Harrow, Middlesex, HA3 0TD
Activities: Other retail sale of new goods in specialised stores (not commercial art galleries and opticians)
Major Shareholder: Rohit Babulal Mehta
Officers: Pravina Rohitkumar Mehta, Secretary; Rohit Babulal Mehta [1953] Director/Pharmacist

Queens' School (Bushey)
Incorporated: 27 May 2011 *Employees:* 175
Net Worth: £39,479,916 *Total Assets:* £41,587,780
Registered Office: Queens' School, Aldenham Road, Bushey, Herts, WD23 2LX
Activities: General secondary education
Officers: Tracy Anne Jenner, Secretary; Catherine Agnihotri [1965] Director/Support Worker (SEND); Lyndsey Rebecca Billinge [1984] Director/Teacher; Keith Burberry Cook [1963] Director/Accountant; Susan Mary Gorton [1960] Director/Examinations Officer; Gillian Sarah Kate Gray [1966] Director/Librarian; David Charles Hall [1944] Director/Retired; Sian Elizabeth Ann Henry [1969] Director/Social Work; Stephen Robert Jakeman [1956] Director/Accountant; Sunil Jobanputra [1989] Director/Civil Servant; Jonathan Morrell [1973] Director/Headteacher; Jayesh Jayantilal Patel [1982] Director/Train Operator; Rakesh Patel [1972] Director/Bank Manager; Julie Raybould [1967] Director/Recruitment Consultant; Clare Jean Rose [1975] Director/Service Delivery Manager; Carole Watson [1952] Director/Retired

Queenscourt Limited
Incorporated: 9 January 1995 *Employees:* 294
Net Worth: £4,928,245 *Total Assets:* £9,379,244
Registered Office: First Floor, Kirkland House, 11-15 Peterborough Road, Harrow, Middlesex, HA1 2AX
Activities: Unlicenced restaurants and cafes
Shareholders: Bharat Chandubhai Patel; Maya Bharat Patel
Officers: Maya Bharat Patel, Secretary; Bharat Chandubhai Patel [1964] Director/Businessman; Maya Bharat Patel [1965] Director/Secretary

Queensgate Finco Ltd
Incorporated: 9 December 2015
Net Worth: £10,434 *Total Assets:* £10,264,102
Registered Office: 505 Pinner Road, Harrow, Middlesex, HA2 6EH
Activities: Other letting and operating of own or leased real estate
Parent: Queensgate Mezz Hold Co Ltd
Officers: Jiten Rameshchandra Kantaria [1973] Director; Rupal Jiten Kantaria [1979] Director; Ramesh Chandra Govindji Sachdev [1945] Director

Queensway Associates Limited
Incorporated: 3 April 1998
Net Worth: £3,966,052 *Total Assets:* £5,769,975
Registered Office: 35 Glanleam Road, Stanmore, Middlesex, HA7 4NW
Activities: Buying and selling of own real estate
Shareholders: Lexadmin Trust Reg. Schaan; Palm Tree Properties Limited
Officers: Stephen Messias, Secretary; Orion Benjamin Tamary, Secretary; Shaoul Houri [1957] Director; Orion Benjamin Tamary [1960] Director/Property Consultant

Queenwood Golf Club Limited
Incorporated: 21 April 1999 *Employees:* 72
Net Worth: £14,885,660 *Total Assets:* £17,762,472
Registered Office: Stonehill Road, Ottershaw, Surrey, KT16 0AQ
Activities: Activities of sport clubs
Officers: Gerard Ivers, Secretary; Lurana Churchill Green [1948] Director/Interior Designer [American]; Frederick D. Green [1939] Director/Real Estate Developer [American]; David Otway Haythe [1944] Director/MD Investment Bank; John James Moore [1967] Executive Managing Director [Canadian]; Gerard Tvedt [1954] Director

The Quest Academy - Coloma Trust
Incorporated: 9 June 2010 *Employees:* 69
Net Worth: £12,637,000 *Total Assets:* £14,101,000
Registered Office: The Quest Academy-Coloma Trust, Farnborough Avenue, South Croydon, Surrey, CR2 8HD
Activities: General secondary education
Officers: Dr Rosemary Ekong [1960] Director/Scientist; Ronald James Huggett [1950] Director/Retired; Graham Jennings [1961] Director/Data Compliance Manager; Jacqueline Rose Johnson [1964] Director/Headteacher; Carol Lesley Kinch [1962] Director/Circuit Judge; Laura Louise Lloyd [1977] Director/Teacher; Dr Arthur Naylor [1949] Director; Sister Agnes Mary O'Shea [1937] Director [Irish]; Louise Stotesbury [1955] Director/Pastoral Manager; Christine Patricia Gainsborough Waring [1943] Director/Retired; Sister Felice Anne Bowker Wright [1943] Director

Questmoor Limited
Incorporated: 21 April 1980 *Employees:* 15
Net Worth: £5,090,115 *Total Assets:* £5,493,129
Registered Office: 96 High Street, Potters Bar, Herts, EN6 5AT
Activities: Dispensing chemist in specialised stores
Parent: Goldquest Limited
Officers: Smita Morjaria, Secretary; Yogesh Chhotalal Morjaria [1954] Director/Pharmacist

Quickdrop Limited
Incorporated: 2 September 2003
Net Worth Deficit: £5,668,109 *Total Assets:* £67,552,240
Registered Office: 3rd Floor, Sterling House, Langston Road, Loughton, Essex, IG10 3TS
Activities: Buying and selling of own real estate
Parent: Galliard Holdings Limited
Officers: Allan William Porter, Secretary; David Edward Conway [1976] Director; Stephen Stuart Solomon Conway [1948] Director; Donagh O'Sullivan [1968] Construction Director [Irish]

Quinn Investment Holdings (London) Limited
Incorporated: 9 December 2013 *Employees:* 115
Net Worth: £6,975,182 *Total Assets:* £19,140,008
Registered Office: Suite D, The Business Centre, Faringdon Avenue, Romford, Essex, RM3 8EN
Activities: Activities of other holding companies n.e.c.
Shareholders: Marian Ann Quinn; Seamus Anthony Quinn
Officers: Marian Ann Quinn [1954] Director; Seamus Anthony Quinn [1958] Director

Quivira Bridging No.1 LLP
Incorporated: 4 May 2012
Net Worth: £6,583,121 *Total Assets:* £8,255,121
Registered Office: 1st Floor, Monument House, 215 Marsh Road, Pinner, Middlesex, HA5 5NE
Officers: Rajiv Dhirendra Nathwani [1988] Member; Vishal Adatia [1978] LLP Member; James Brian Busche [1958] LLP Member; Ella Chandarana [1960] LLP Member; Dr Paul Groves [1960] LLP Member; Aditi Karia [1959] LLP Member; Ashoka Kavi [1953] LLP Member; Deepak Kavi [1961] LLP Member; Kieran Kavi [1994] LLP Member; Shona Nadia Kavi [1990] LLP Member; Dr Supriy Kavi [1964] LLP Member; Dhanibai Kerai [1955] LLP Member; Dhanji Kerai [1956] LLP Member; Sandeep Kotecha [1962] LLP Member; Sharda Kotecha [1941] LLP Member; Sonia Kotecha [1964] LLP Member; Vinodchandra Kotecha [1936] LLP Member; Eva Susanne Maguire [1956] LLP Member; Jaisukh Devji Patel [1955] LLP Member; Neil Prajay Patel [1993] LLP Member; Rikin Popat [1985] LLP Member; Anjali Rishi Raja [1983] LLP Member; Harshila Raja [1952] LLP Member; Mahendra Raja [1946] LLP Member; Rishi Raja [1982] LLP Member; Bhavisha Shah [1980] LLP Member; Mitesh Shah [1978] LLP Member; Nileshkumar Ratilal Shah [1968] LLP Member

R & R Asset Management Limited
Incorporated: 24 June 2014
Net Worth: £590,652 *Total Assets:* £7,443,654
Registered Office: Sun House, 428 Long Drive, Greenford, Middlesex, UB6 8UH
Activities: Activities of other holding companies n.e.c.
Shareholder: Raminder Singh Ranger
Officers: Harmeet Singh Ahuja [1972] Director; Raminder Singh Ranger [1948] Director/Freight Consultant; Renu Ranger [1955] Director/Head of Human Resources

R A Insurance Brokers Limited
Incorporated: 10 September 1996 *Employees:* 50
Net Worth: £5,471,762 *Total Assets:* £10,000,237
Registered Office: 2nd Floor, 29 Dingwall Road, Croydon, Surrey, CR0 2NB
Activities: Non-life insurance
Shareholders: Sunil Patel; Shamir Patel
Officers: Sunil Patel, Secretary; Shamir Patel [1970] Director/Insurance Broker; Sunil Patel [1968] Director/Insurance Broker

R K Property Investments Ltd.
Incorporated: 13 July 1979 *Employees:* 3
Net Worth: £4,630,944 *Total Assets:* £8,951,534
Registered Office: Unit 10 Loughton Business Centre, Langston Road, Loughton, Essex, IG10 3FL
Activities: Other construction installation
Major Shareholder: Ranjit Singh
Officers: Deepak Rani, Secretary; Inderpal Singh Matharu [1972] Director/Quantity Surveyor; Deepak Rani [1950] Director/Housewife; Ranjit Singh [1939] Director

R O Ventures Limited
Incorporated: 10 October 1963
Net Worth: £28,223,264 *Total Assets:* £91,076,080
Registered Office: Graham House, 7 Wyllyotts Place, Potters Bar, Herts, EN6 2JD
Activities: Activities of head offices
Parent: RO Enterprises Limited
Officers: Edward Thomas Morton Rowlandson [1974] Director; Richard Graham St John Rowlandson [1939] Director/Chartered Accountant

R S L (Slough) Limited
Incorporated: 19 February 2001 *Employees:* 1
Net Worth: £1,490,147 *Total Assets:* £6,600,238
Registered Office: 9 Bell Weir Close, Wraysbury, Middlesex, TW19 6HF
Activities: Other letting and operating of own or leased real estate
Shareholders: Inderpal Singh Laly; Ravinder Singh Laly
Officers: Ravinder Laly, Secretary; Inderpal Singh Laly [1986] Director/Financial Analyst; Jaswant Laly [1953] Director/Optician; Ravinder Laly [1952] Director

R V Moat House Limited
Incorporated: 15 October 2007 *Employees:* 81
Net Worth: £3,711,771 *Total Assets:* £13,077,738
Registered Office: 1st Floor, Brunswick House, Regent Park, 297-299 Kingston Road, Leatherhead, Surrey, KT22 7LU
Activities: Other business support service activities n.e.c.
Parent: Retirement Villages Limited
Officers: Sally Irene Rees, Secretary; Sarah Denise Burgess [1971] Director; William Edwin John Crawford [1970] Director/Development; Neil Donaldson [1966] Director/Accountant; Andrew George Esmond Ovey [1971] Director/Investment Manager

RA Securities London Limited
Incorporated: 17 November 2016 *Employees:* 1
Net Worth: £100 *Total Assets:* £13,602,942
Registered Office: 166 College Road, Harrow, Middlesex, HA1 1RA
Activities: Other business support service activities n.e.c.
Major Shareholder: Roy Derek Allan
Officers: Roy Derek Allan [1957] Director

Raban Holdings Limited
Incorporated: 3 March 2006
Net Worth Deficit: £10,111 *Total Assets:* £5,946,833
Registered Office: 5-9 Eden Street, Kingston upon Thames, Surrey, KT1 1BQ
Activities: Buying and selling of own real estate
Major Shareholder: Simon Anthony Talbot-Williams
Officers: Simon Anthony Talbot Williams, Secretary; Simon Anthony Talbot Williams [1961] Director/Chartered Surveyor

Racal Acoustics Limited
Incorporated: 19 January 2004 *Employees:* 83
Net Worth: £63,774,000 *Total Assets:* £66,500,000
Registered Office: Waverley Industrial Estate, Hailsham Drive, Harrow, Middlesex, HA1 4TR
Activities: Manufacture of other electrical equipment
Parent: Weston Aerospace Limited
Officers: Stephen Nolan [1969] Director [American]; Curtis Carl Reusser [1960] Director/President and Chief Executive Officer [American]; Albert Scott Yost [1965] Director/Group Vice President [American]

Rackspace Limited
Incorporated: 20 December 1999 *Employees:* 1,046
Net Worth: £59,453,228 *Total Assets:* £236,999,472
Registered Office: Unit 8 Millington Road, Hayes, Middlesex, UB3 4AZ
Activities: Data processing, hosting and related activities
Officers: Christopher Rosas, Secretary; Darren George Norfolk [1977] Managing Director; Christopher Rosas [1977] Director/VP Global Tax [American]; Reinhard Waldinger [1976] Director [Swiss]

Rackspace UK Leasing Limited
Incorporated: 3 September 2015
Net Worth: £47,380,000 *Total Assets:* £66,431,580
Registered Office: Unit 8 Millington Road, Hayes, Middlesex, UB3 4AZ
Activities: Renting and leasing of office machinery and equipment (including computers)
Parent: Rackspace Hosting, Inc.
Officers: Darren George Norfolk [1977] Managing Director; Christopher Rosas [1977] Director/VP of Global Tax [American]; Reinhard Waldinger [1976] Director [Swiss]

Radia Estates Limited
Incorporated: 13 July 2001 *Employees:* 13
Net Worth: £3,089,788 *Total Assets:* £11,398,139
Registered Office: Rosslyn House, 34 Railway Approach, Harrow, Middlesex, HA3 5AA
Activities: Other letting and operating of own or leased real estate
Major Shareholder: Mukesh Kumar Radia
Officers: Tina Ghelani, Secretary; Mukesh Kumar Radia [1959] Director/Solicitor

Radiation Limited
Incorporated: 10 November 1998 *Employees:* 4
Net Worth: £1,481,413 *Total Assets:* £5,178,419
Registered Office: 9a The Broadway, Stanmore, Middlesex, HA7 4DA
Activities: Other letting and operating of own or leased real estate
Shareholders: Mahesh Raojibhai Patel; Hitenkumar Mansukhlal Shah; Alpa Mahesh Patel; Navika Hitenkumar Shah
Officers: Mahesh Patel, Secretary; Alpa Mahesh Patel [1972] Director/Pharmacist; Mahesh Raojibhai Patel [1968] Director/Accountant; Hitenkumar Mansukhlal Shah [1968] Director/Accountant; Navika Hitenkumar Shah [1972] Director/Pharmacist

Radical Investments Limited
Incorporated: 28 October 2015
Net Worth: £2 *Total Assets:* £17,080,976
Registered Office: 3rd Floor, Sterling House, Langston Road, Loughton, Essex, IG10 3TS
Activities: Financial intermediation not elsewhere classified
Shareholders: Galliard Holdings Limited; Allied Commercial Exporters Limited
Officers: Allan William Porter, Secretary; Edward Azouz [1949] Director; Stephen Stuart Solomon Conway [1948] Director; Michael William Watson [1952] Director

Radio Developments Ltd
Incorporated: 13 August 2013 *Employees:* 2
Net Worth: £5,683,140 *Total Assets:* £12,430,948
Registered Office: Haslers, Old Station Road, Loughton, Essex, IG10 4PL
Activities: Other letting and operating of own or leased real estate
Shareholders: Simon Emanuel Raine; Adam Lopez Dias
Officers: Adam Lopez Dias [1973] Director; Simon Emanuel Raine [1981] Director/Manager

Radnor House School (Holdings) Limited
Incorporated: 5 August 2010 *Employees:* 182
Net Worth: £30,950,608 *Total Assets:* £54,664,096
Registered Office: Pope's Villa, Cross Deep, Twickenham, Middlesex, TW1 4QG
Activities: General secondary education
Shareholders: David Paton; Josephine Claire Paton; Albion Venture Capital Trust PLC; Albion Development VCT PLC; Crown Place VCT PLC; Albion Technology & General VCT PLC; Albion Enterprise VCT PLC; David Paton; Josephine Claire Paton; Albion Ventures LLP
Officers: Eleanor Rose Allen [1981] Director/Education Consultant; Dr Colin Diggory [1954] Director; Emil Slavchev Gigov [1970] Director/Banker [British/Bulgarian]; Barry Robert Martin [1950] Non-Executive Director; Neil Moulding [1970] Finance Director; David Paton [1977] Director

Radnor House School (Property) Limited
Incorporated: 6 August 2010
Net Worth: £24,153,904 *Total Assets:* £36,183,008
Registered Office: Popes Villa, Cross Deep, Twickenham, Middlesex, TW1 4QG
Activities: General secondary education
Parent: Radnor House School (Holdings) Limited
Officers: Neil Moulding [1970] Finance Director; David Paton [1977] Director

Radnor House Sevenoaks (Holdings) Limited
Incorporated: 15 January 2015 *Employees:* 94
Net Worth: £5,499,897 *Total Assets:* £18,054,304
Registered Office: Popes Villa, Cross Deep, Twickenham, Middlesex, TW1 4QG
Activities: General secondary education
Parent: Radnor House School (Holdings) Limited
Officers: Neil Moulding, Secretary; Eleanor Rose Allen [1981] Director/Education Consultant; Dr Colin Diggory [1954] Director; Emil Slavchev Gigov [1970] Director/Banker [British/Bulgarian]; Barry Robert Martin [1950] Non-Executive Director; Neil Moulding [1970] Finance Director; David Paton [1977] Director/Headteacher

Radnor House Sevenoaks (Property) Limited
Incorporated: 15 January 2015
Net Worth: £8,614,331 *Total Assets:* £16,933,416
Registered Office: Pope's Villa, Cross Deep, Twickenham, Middlesex, TW1 4QG
Activities: General secondary education
Parent: Radnor House Sevenoaks (Holdings) Limited
Officers: Neil Moulding, Secretary; Neil Moulding [1970] Finance Director; David Paton [1977] Director/Headteacher

Raedex Consortium Limited
Incorporated: 15 February 2012 *Employees:* 27
Net Worth Deficit: £2,895,384 *Total Assets:* £10,360,206
Registered Office: 1 Bell Parade, Glebe Way, West Wickham, Kent, BR4 0RH
Activities: Activities of other holding companies n.e.c.
Major Shareholder: Reginald Larry-Cole
Officers: Reginald Larry-Cole [1970] Director/Car Salesman; Scott Andrew Martin [1978] Director/Car Salesman

Raffingers Advisory Limited
Incorporated: 13 January 2014
Previous: Contemporary Tailors Ltd
Net Worth: £2,640,654 *Total Assets:* £5,193,460
Registered Office: 19-20 Bourne Court, Southend Road, Woodford Green, Essex, IG8 8HD
Activities: Accounting and auditing activities
Shareholders: Gary Paul Inglis; Lee Elliot Manning; Graham Barry Soraff
Officers: Katie Brill, Secretary; Sarah Inglis, Secretary; Paula Manning, Secretary; Amanda Jane Moody, Secretary; Bremini Sudarshan, Secretary; Gary Paul Inglis [1959] Director/Accountant; Lee Elliot Manning [1968] Director/Accountant; Adam Howard Moody [1971] Director/Accountant; Graham Barry Soraff [1972] Director/Accountant; Thurairatnam Sudarshan [1970] Director/Accountant

Raglan Primary School
Incorporated: 29 July 2013 *Employees:* 86
Net Worth: £6,120,000 *Total Assets:* £6,948,000
Registered Office: Raglan Primary School, Raglan Road, Bromley, Kent, BR2 9NL
Activities: Primary education
Officers: Jessica Benning [1976] Director/School Administration Assistant; Martin Brian Daniels [1972] Director/Management Accountant; Alison Gaynor Dumper [1963] Director/Teacher; Rachael Ezinwa [1986] Director/Teacher; James Henry Faiers [1986] Director/Maths Teacher; Scott Anthony George [1973] Director/IT Administrator; Kathleen Margetts [1961] Director/Headteacher; Helena Michelle Smith [1970] Director/Higher Education Manager

Railsite Holdings Limited
Incorporated: 11 March 2008 *Employees:* 4
Net Worth: £6,837,283 *Total Assets:* £6,869,107
Registered Office: 10 The Street, Epsom Road, West Horsley, Leatherhead, Surrey, KT24 6AU
Activities: Other telecommunications activities
Shareholder: Andrew Charles Elliman
Officers: Louise Margaret Elliman, Secretary; Andrew John Charles Elliman [1964] Director; Louise Margaret Elliman [1963] Director; Peter Michael Hinchcliffe [1959] Director; Paul Innes [1957] Director; Simon Douglas Ralph [1954] Director/Engineer

Rainham Industrial Services Limited
Incorporated: 5 November 2002 *Employees:* 554
Net Worth: £583,000 *Total Assets:* £12,320,000
Registered Office: 795 London Road, Grays, Essex, RM20 3LH
Activities: Construction of commercial buildings
Shareholder: Timothy Edward McCarthy
Officers: Tim McCarthy [1960] Director; David Paget [1970] Director/Engineer; Andrew Phillip Pearson [1958] Director; Karen Louise Richards [1964] Director/Financial Controller; Andrew Mark Rynston [1965] Director; Michael Anthony Scaife [1959] Director/Engineer; Nicholas Paul David Winks [1948] Director

Raisio UK Limited
Incorporated: 19 January 2010 *Employees:* 2
Net Worth: £44,273,000 *Total Assets:* £58,564,000
Registered Office: Benecol Limited, The Mille, 1000 Great West Road, Brentford, Middlesex, TW8 9DW
Activities: Activities of head offices
Parent: Raisio Oyj
Officers: Merja Sisko Lumme [1961] Director/VP Human Resources [Finnish]; Iiro Tapio Wester [1963] Director/Chief Commercial Officer [Finnish]

RAK Petroleum PLC
Incorporated: 17 June 2013
Net Worth: £504,105,472 *Total Assets:* £1,310,131,840
Registered Office: Elder House, St Georges Business Park, Brooklands Road, Weybridge, Surrey, KT13 0TS
Activities: Activities of other holding companies n.e.c.
Officers: Kevin Toner, Secretary; Sultan Abdulla Ahmad Majid Al Ghurair [1980] Director/Chief Executive Officer [Emirati]; Bjorn Kenneth Dale [1974] Managing Director DNO ASA [Norwegian]; Amirali Handjani [1977] Director/Business Executive [American]; Ahmed Jamal Jawa [1956] Director/Businessman [Saudi Arabian]; Bijan Mossavar-Rahmani [1952] Director/Business Executive [American]

Ram Parkash Sunderdass & Sons Ltd
Incorporated: 7 November 2008 *Employees:* 32
Net Worth: £7,507,778 *Total Assets:* £12,899,200
Registered Office: 108 The Broadway, Southall, Middlesex, UB1 1QF
Activities: Other retail sale in non-specialised stores
Officers: Harish Roy Babber, Secretary; Harish Roy Babber [1953] Director; Suneel Ram Parkash Babber [1958] Director/Jeweller

Rambert School of Ballet and Contemporary Dance Trust
Incorporated: 5 December 2005
Net Worth: £4,437,321 *Total Assets:* £7,638,594
Registered Office: Clifton Lodge, St Margaret's Drive, Twickenham, Middlesex, TW1 1QN
Activities: Other letting and operating of own or leased real estate
Officers: Clare Erica Buckle, Secretary; Richard Butler Adams [1944] Director/Retired; Philip Cazenove Lawford [1957] Director/Charity Administrator; Nigel William Reid [1954] Director/Solicitor; Katie Elizabeth Thorpe [1979] Director/Chartered Accountant

Rambler Metals and Mining PLC
Incorporated: 14 April 2004 *Employees:* 185
Net Worth: £46,771,196 *Total Assets:* £70,515,392
Registered Office: Salatin House, 19 Cedar Road, Sutton, Surrey, SM2 5DA
Activities: Other mining and quarrying n.e.c.
Major Shareholder: Bradford Alan Mills
Officers: Peter Mercer, Secretary; Terrell Iver Ackerman [1953] Director/Consultant [American]; Eason Cong Chen [1981] Director/Corporate Controller [Canadian]; Belinda Labatte [1974] Director/Mining [American]; Bradford Alan Mills [1954] Director/Mining Executive [American]; Glenn Robert Poulter [1964] Director/Consultant; Mark Vandyke Sander [1955] Director/Mining Executive [American]; Norman Patrick Williams [1974] Director/Chief Executive [Canadian]

Ranbaxy (U.K.) Limited
Incorporated: 21 November 1994 *Employees:* 19
Net Worth: £15,061,894 *Total Assets:* £28,360,372
Registered Office: 5th Floor, Hyde Park Hayes 3, 11 Millington Road, Hayes, Middlesex, UB3 4AZ
Activities: Wholesale of pharmaceutical goods
Officers: Hellen de Kloet [1965] Director/Business Executive [Dutch]; Prashant Savla [1974] Director [Dutch]; Neeraj Sharma [1972] Director [Indian]

Ranbaxy Holdings (UK) Limited
Incorporated: 23 May 1995 *Employees:* 2
Net Worth: £32,087,286 *Total Assets:* £32,096,450
Registered Office: 5th Floor, Hyde Park Hayes 3, 11 Millington Road, Hayes, Middlesex, UB3 4AZ
Activities: Financial intermediation not elsewhere classified
Officers: Prashant Lakhamshi Savla [1974] Finance Director [Indian]; Neeraj Sharma [1972] Director [Indian]

RANC Care Homes Limited
Incorporated: 6 December 1988 *Employees:* 936
Net Worth: £38,889,360 *Total Assets:* £41,548,828
Registered Office: Coopers House, 65a Wingletye Lane, Hornchurch, Essex, RM11 3AT
Activities: Residential nursing care facilities
Parent: RANC Holdings Limited
Officers: Aneet Rai, Secretary; Aneet Rai [1967] Director; Rabinder Singh Rai [1960] Director

RANC Holdings Limited
Incorporated: 27 June 2014
Net Worth: £87,942,552 *Total Assets:* £148,106,368
Registered Office: Coopers House, 65a Wingletye Lane, Hornchurch, Essex, RM11 3AT
Activities: Residential nursing care facilities
Shareholders: Aneet Kaur Rai; Rabinder Singh Rai
Officers: Aneet Rai [1967] Director; Rabinder Singh Rai [1960] Director

Randall Watts Construction Ltd
Incorporated: 15 June 2000
Net Worth: £898,894 *Total Assets:* £7,827,101
Registered Office: 34 Westway, Caterham on the Hill, Caterham, Surrey, CR3 5TP
Activities: Construction of commercial buildings
Shareholders: Mark Anthony James Watts; Kenneth Ronald Watts
Officers: Deborah Anita Thake, Secretary; Kenneth Ronald Watts [1952] Director; Mark Anthony James Watts [1976] Director/Sub Contractor

Randall Watts London Limited
Incorporated: 25 February 2014
Net Worth Deficit: £3,117,663 *Total Assets:* £18,847,888
Registered Office: 34 Westway, Caterham on the Hill, Caterham, Surrey, CR3 5TP
Activities: Construction of commercial buildings
Shareholders: Mark Anthony James Watts; Kenneth Ronald Watts
Officers: Deborah Anita Thake, Secretary; Kenneth Ronald Watts [1952] Director; Mark Anthony James Watts [1976] Director

Rangemist Limited
Incorporated: 19 December 2008
Net Worth: £4,282,556 *Total Assets:* £11,854,180
Registered Office: 24 Carfax Road, Hornchurch, Essex, RM12 4BA
Activities: Other letting and operating of own or leased real estate
Major Shareholder: Osman Yusuf
Officers: Osman Yusuf [1970] Director/Developer

Ranks Enterprises Limited
Incorporated: 16 December 1999 *Employees:* 9
Net Worth: £2,357,014 *Total Assets:* £5,243,576
Registered Office: Ranks House, Unit B4 Neptune Road, Harrow, Middlesex, HA1 4HX
Activities: Wholesale of textiles
Parent: Ranks Property Holdings Ltd
Officers: Kalpna Lakhani, Company Secretary; Attul Kumar Lakhani [1962] Managing Director; Kalpna Lakhani [1964] Director/Company Secretary

Ranola Properties Limited
Incorporated: 12 August 2011 *Employees:* 2
Net Worth: £6,241,301 *Total Assets:* £19,371,308
Registered Office: Brook House, 54a Cowley Mill Road, Uxbridge, Middlesex, UB8 2QE
Activities: Management of real estate on a fee or contract basis
Parent: Ranola Holdings Limited
Officers: Jay Dave [1981] Director; Gerard John Smith [1962] Director [Irish]; Simon Smith [1992] Director [Irish]

Rapid Action Packaging Limited
Incorporated: 22 April 1996 *Employees:* 233
Net Worth: £9,878,884 *Total Assets:* £22,018,086
Registered Office: Elder House, St Georges Business Park, 207 Brooklands Road, Weybridge, Surrey, KT13 0TS
Activities: Artistic creation
Shareholders: Joint Funding Partners Limited; Ludgate Environmental Fund Limited
Officers: Andrew Robert Drummond, Secretary; Lord Martin Beaver [1965] Director/Salesman; Andrew Robert Drummond [1965] Finance Director; John Hedley McKimmie [1948] Director; Julian David Kyrle Money [1959] Director/Designer; Katherine Elizabeth Pethick [1961] Director/Graphic Designer; Ekaterina Alexandra Sharashidze [1974] Director [American/Georgian]; Gijs-Jan Hein Voskamp [1977] Director/Chief Executive Officer [Dutch]; Graham Bernard Williams [1952] Director

Rapiergroup Limited
Incorporated: 26 May 2017 *Employees:* 61
Net Worth: £2,046,773 *Total Assets:* £6,058,819
Registered Office: Nicholas House, River Front, Enfield, Middlesex, EN1 3FG
Activities: Activities of other holding companies n.e.c.
Shareholders: Helen Rosemary Seaman; Christopher Whittaker
Officers: Paul Stuart Denny [1972] Director; Helen Rosemary Seaman [1967] Director; Christopher Whittaker [1971] Director

Rashmian Limited
Incorporated: 6 October 1976 *Employees:* 24
Net Worth: £5,919,537 *Total Assets:* £10,162,573
Registered Office: Unit J, Braintree Industrial Estate, Braintree Road, Ruislip, Middlesex, HA4 0EJ
Activities: Non-specialised wholesale trade
Officers: Kirankumar Chhabildas Patel, Secretary; Kirankumar Chhabildas Patel [1950] Director/Businessman; Kunal Kiran Patel [1984] Director; Pradeepkumar Chhabildas Patel [1948] Director/Businessman; Rashmikant Chhabildas Patel [1946] Director/Businessman; Setu Rashmi Patel [1970] Buying Director

R.T.Rate Limited
Incorporated: 30 August 1955 *Employees:* 76
Net Worth: £4,899,521 *Total Assets:* £11,092,069
Registered Office: Hogg Lane Service Station, Hogg Lane, Grays, Essex, RM17 5QL
Activities: Sale of new cars and light motor vehicles
Shareholders: Colin John Rate; Catharina Adriana Maria Rate
Officers: Michael Day [1967] Aftermarket Director; Luke Padbury-Clark [1980] Sales Director; Catharina Adriana Maria Rate [1953] Director [Dutch]; Colin John Rate [1946] Managing Director; Sebastiaan John Rate [1980] Director

RATP DEV UK Ltd
Incorporated: 11 June 2010 *Employees:* 40
Net Worth: £60,347,000 *Total Assets:* £195,572,992
Registered Office: Busways House, Wellington Road, Twickenham, Middlesex, TW2 5NX
Activities: Other service activities incidental to land transportation, n.e.c.
Officers: Laurence Batlle [1971] Director [French]; Romain Ferriere [1975] Director/Chief Financial Officer [French]; Howard Charles Goodbourn [1961] Director/Chief Financial Officer

Raue LLP
Incorporated: 8 April 2010 *Employees:* 158
Net Worth: £12,181,574 *Total Assets:* £13,365,174
Registered Office: Elder House, St Georges Business Park, 207 Brooklands Road, Weybridge, Surrey, KT13 0TS
Officers: Dr Jan Hegemann [1963] Member; Dr. Wolfram Hertel [1971] Member; Dr. Bernd Beckmann [1973] LLP Member; Dr. Maren Bedau [1974] LLP Member; Dr Michael Bergmann [1975] LLP Member; Dr Friedemann Eberspacher [1978] LLP Member; Annette Feissel [1971] LLP Member; Dr. Klaus Goecke [1967] LLP Member; Dr Cornelia Gorn [1976] LLP Member; Dr Robert Heine [1974] LLP Member; Dr. Sascha Herms [1969] LLP Member; Judith Heyn [1971] LLP Member; Dr Joerg Jaecks [1971] LLP Member; Dr. Kornelius Kleinlein [1959] LLP Member; Dr. Stephan Bernhard Koch [1971] LLP Member; Dr Wolfgang Kuhia [1953] LLP Member; Dr. Gernod Meinel [1960] LLP Member; Georg Miggel [1958] LLP Member; Andreas Nelle [1962] LLP Member; Dr. Markus Plesser [1968] LLP Member; Peter Raue [1941] LLP Member; Dr. Justus Schmidt-Ott [1961] LLP Member; Friedrich Tobias Schoene [1966] LLP Member; Dr. Carl-Stephan Schweer [1963] LLP Member; Dr. Hans Seiler [1957] LLP Member; Dr Valentin Todorow [1975] LLP Member; Dr. Bettina Tugendreich [1973] LLP Member; Christian Von Hammerstein [1965] LLP Member; Dr Katharina Wodarz [1973] LLP Member

Raven Promotions Limited
Incorporated: 29 May 2001
Net Worth: £7,662,083 *Total Assets:* £9,104,190
Registered Office: Onega House, 112 Main Road, Sidcup, Kent, DA14 6NE
Activities: Other business support service activities n.e.c.
Major Shareholder: William Howard Porter
Officers: Andrew James Rooke, Secretary; William Howard Porter [1963] Director

Raven Roofing and Building Supplies Limited
Incorporated: 10 July 1974 *Employees:* 60
Net Worth: £1,012,536 *Total Assets:* £6,776,495
Registered Office: Head Office, Applemor House, Campbell Road, Twickenham, Middlesex, TW2 5BY
Activities: Agents involved in the sale of timber and building materials
Shareholders: Mark William Applebee; Andrew Nicholas Morris
Officers: Mark William Applebee, Company Secretary; Mark William Applebee [1966] Director; Mandy Humm [1978] Financial Director; Andrew Nicholas Morris [1961] Director; Adrian John Tansley [1967] Sales Director

Ravensale Limited
Incorporated: 1 February 1980 *Employees:* 8
Net Worth: £32,260,092 *Total Assets:* £53,164,788
Registered Office: 115 Wembley Commercial Centre, East Lane, North Wembley, Middlesex, HA9 7UR
Activities: Activities of head offices
Officers: Sandra Clarissa Jarvis, Secretary; Bruce Darrel Grayston Jarvis [1948] Director; Joseph Richard Jarvis [1974] Director; Sandra Clarissa Jarvis [1950] Director

RBC Investments (Surrey) Limited
Incorporated: 23 January 2015 *Employees:* 7
Net Worth: £714,593 *Total Assets:* £11,156,863
Registered Office: Runnymede Civic Centre, Station Road, Addlestone, Surrey, KT15 2AH
Activities: Other letting and operating of own or leased real estate
Shareholders: Runnymede Borough Council; Runnymede Borough Council
Officers: Paul Robert Green, Secretary; Cllr Mark James Maddox [1959] Managing Director; Peter James McKenzie [1956] Finance Director; John Noel Rice [1955] Director/Chief Executive

RBH Hotel Management Limited
Incorporated: 15 July 2010 *Employees:* 273
Previous: Redefine Hotel Management Limited
Net Worth: £1,569,464 *Total Assets:* £7,558,867
Registered Office: 10th Floor, The Mille, 1000 Great West Road, Brentford, Middlesex, TW8 9DW
Activities: Management of real estate on a fee or contract basis
Parent: Redefine BDL Hotel Group Ltd
Officers: Paula Ross, Secretary; David Hart [1978] Director/Chartered Accountant; Helder Ricardo Silva Pereira [1955] Director/Businessman [Portuguese]

RBH Hotels UK Limited
Incorporated: 7 October 2010 *Employees:* 200
Previous: Redefine BDL Hotels UK Limited
Net Worth: £2,433,000 *Total Assets:* £6,509,000
Registered Office: 10th Floor, The Mille, 1000 Great West Road, Brentford, Middlesex, TW8 9DW
Activities: Management of real estate on a fee or contract basis
Parent: Redefine BDL Hotel Group
Officers: Paula Ross, Secretary; Susan Bland [1970] Director; David Hart [1978] Director/Chartered Accountant; Helder Ricardo Silva Pereira [1955] Director/Businessman [Portuguese]

RBR Property Investments Limited
Incorporated: 14 June 2006 *Employees:* 3
Net Worth: £1,096,751 *Total Assets:* £8,021,086
Registered Office: 962 Eastern Avenue, Newbury Park, Ilford, Essex, IG2 7JD
Activities: Buying and selling of own real estate
Major Shareholder: Jamil Raja
Officers: Paul Nicholas Boughtwood [1962] Director

RCI Financial Services Limited
Incorporated: 15 January 1997 *Employees:* 268
Net Worth: £304,297,984 *Total Assets:* £5,533,118,976
Registered Office: Rivers Office Park, Denham Way, Maple Cross, Rickmansworth, Herts, WD3 9YS
Activities: Credit granting by non-deposit taking finance houses and other specialist consumer credit grantors
Parent: RCI Banque SA
Officers: Sukhraj Jouhal, Secretary; Jean-Louis Labauge [1968] Managing Director [French]; Peter McEvoy [1978] Finance Director [Irish]; Enrico Rossini [1970] Director [Italian]

RCL (UK) Ltd.
Incorporated: 11 June 2002 *Employees:* 87
Net Worth: £9,037,450 *Total Assets:* £107,839,368
Registered Office: 3 The Heights, Brooklands, Weybridge, Surrey, KT13 0NY
Activities: Sea and coastal passenger water transport
Officers: Ruth Generaldine Marshall, Secretary; Ruth Generaldine Marshall [1964] Director/Solicitor; Gavin Stuart Smith [1966] Director/Senior Vice President [Australian]

RCL Cruises Ltd
Incorporated: 6 September 2010 *Employees:* 529
Net Worth: £403,416,640 *Total Assets:* £945,661,312
Registered Office: 3 The Heights, Brooklands, Weybridge, Surrey, KT13 0NY
Activities: Sea and coastal passenger water transport
Officers: Ruth Marshall, Secretary; Captain Manolis Kasselas [1965] Director/AVP Marine Operations [Greek]; Stuart Leven [1968] Director/Vice President EMEA; Ruth Generaldine Marshall [1964] Director/Solicitor; Gavin Stuart Smith [1966] Director/Senior Vice President [Australian]

RCL Investments Ltd
Incorporated: 20 June 2005
Net Worth: £17,750,832 *Total Assets:* £17,751,788
Registered Office: 3 The Heights, Brooklands, Weybridge, Surrey, KT13 0NY
Activities: Sea and coastal passenger water transport
Officers: Ruth Generaldine Marshall, Secretary; Jason Liberty [1975] Director/Chief Financial Operator [American]; Gavin Stuart Smith [1966] Director/Senior Vice President [Australian]

RDL1 Limited
Incorporated: 2 November 2016 *Employees:* 2
Net Worth Deficit: £2,653,296 *Total Assets:* £9,522,393
Registered Office: Batchworth House, Church Street, Rickmansworth, Herts, WD3 1JE
Activities: Development of building projects
Shareholders: Christopher John Leslie Burdge; Alan Francis Springford
Officers: Christopher John Leslie Burdge, Secretary; Christopher John Leslie Burdge [1955] Director/Accountant; Alan Francis Springford [1956] Director

RDT Limited
Incorporated: 6 February 1991 *Employees:* 83
Net Worth: £5,266,671 *Total Assets:* £8,359,214
Registered Office: Lynwood House, Crofton Road, Orpington, Kent, BR6 8QE
Activities: Information technology consultancy activities
Major Shareholder: Mark William Bates
Officers: Andrew John Hardy, Secretary; Mark William Bates [1962] Director/Computer Systems Design; Andrew John Hardy [1964] Director/Computer Systems Development; Holger Hasenstrauch [1963] Director/Analyst Programmer [German]

Reach Academy Trust
Incorporated: 13 May 2011 *Employees:* 99
Previous: Reach Academy
Net Worth: £17,798,974 *Total Assets:* £19,028,760
Registered Office: 53-55 High Street, Feltham, Middlesex, TW13 4AB
Activities: Pre-primary education
Officers: David William Dowding, Secretary; Jennifer Anne Baxter [1980] Director/Management Consultant; Rebecca Cramer [1983] Director; David William Dowding [1983] Director; Emma Caroline Luxton [1971] Director/Lawyer; Jonathan McGoh [1980] Director; Thomas Henry Sawbridge [1984] Director/Assistant Headteacher; Judith Sarah Tacon [1977] Director/Chartered Accountant; Edward Vainker [1981] Director

Reach Active Group Limited
Incorporated: 10 June 2005 *Employees:* 159
Net Worth: £2,216,075 *Total Assets:* £8,969,035
Registered Office: Printing House, 66 Lower Road, Harrow, Middlesex, HA2 0DH
Activities: Other specialised construction activities n.e.c.
Shareholders: John Thomas Gallagher; Seamus Andrew Gallagher
Officers: John Thomas Gallagher [1968] Director [Irish]; Seamus Andrew Gallagher [1966] Director [Irish]

Readie Construction Limited
Incorporated: 26 January 2007 *Employees:* 104
Net Worth: £920,742 *Total Assets:* £27,932,864
Registered Office: Unit 18 Falcon Business Centre, Ashton Road, Romford, Essex, RM3 8UR
Activities: Construction of commercial buildings
Parent: Readie Management Limited
Officers: Jessica McCarthy [1978] Finance Director; Glenn Stuart Read [1970] Director/Construction; David Ian Stephens [1982] Director/Construction; Paul Michael Stephens [1979] Construction Director

Reading Scientific Services Limited
Incorporated: 19 November 1962 *Employees:* 346
Net Worth: £11,932,000 *Total Assets:* £18,645,000
Registered Office: Cadbury House, Sanderson Road, Uxbridge, Middlesex, UB8 1DH
Activities: Other research and experimental development on natural sciences and engineering
Parent: Mondelez UK Holdings & Services Limited
Officers: Helena May McKenzie Brennan [1958] Science Director; Jacinta Maria George [1967] Commercial Director RSSL [Irish]; Rachel Ann Henton [1969] Director/General Manager

Realmpark Health Care (Petworth) Limited
Incorporated: 18 November 1996
Net Worth: £2,515,783 *Total Assets:* £6,231,796
Registered Office: 110-112 Lancaster Road, New Barnet, Herts, EN4 8AL
Activities: Other residential care activities n.e.c.
Officers: Carol Jane Piper, Secretary; Daniel Philip Harvey [1985] Director/Property Development Manager; Rebecca Louise Harvey [1987] Director/Accounts Manager

Red Circle Security Services Limited
Incorporated: 24 December 1985 *Employees:* 3
Net Worth: £18,267,732 *Total Assets:* £25,980,226
Registered Office: 792 Wickham Road, Croydon, Surrey, CR0 8EA
Activities: Other letting and operating of own or leased real estate
Shareholders: Veena Bahl; Bashir Ahmed Rana
Officers: Veena Bahl, Secretary; Bashir Ahmed Rana [1940] Director

The Red Lion Hotel (Henley) Limited
Incorporated: 3 April 2007 *Employees:* 24
Net Worth: £1,327,330 *Total Assets:* £5,589,669
Registered Office: 38a High Street, Northwood, Middlesex, HA6 1BN
Activities: Hotels and similar accommodation
Parent: M G Hotels Limited
Officers: Kulbir Singh Gill, Secretary; Mandip Gill [1967] Director/Hotelier; Sukhdip Gill [1975] Director/Hotelier

Redab PLC
Incorporated: 10 January 1989 *Employees:* 4
Net Worth: £2,530,043 *Total Assets:* £6,910,246
Registered Office: 167 Turners Hill, Cheshunt, Herts, EN8 9BH
Activities: Other business support service activities n.e.c.
Parent: Cotton Limited
Officers: John Laurence Lovell McKenzie, Secretary; Karl Gustav Pettersson [1948] Managing Director [Swedish]; Berit Maria Sundgren [1955] Director/Financial Controller [Swedish]

Redbridge Sports Centre Trust Limited
Incorporated: 22 January 1971 *Employees:* 165
Net Worth: £7,706,628 *Total Assets:* £8,929,152
Registered Office: Forest Road, Barkingside, Essex, IG6 3HD
Activities: Activities of sport clubs
Officers: Carolynne Spencer, Secretary; Eric William Brown [1941] Director; Paul Robert Fawssett Clarke [1950] Director/Bank Executive; John Cecil Fortescue [1928] Director/Retired Brewer; Judith Anne Naomi Garfield [1966] Director/Trustee; Rasmita Gohil [1964] Director; Jayna Jogia [1988] Director/Trustee; Jane Kelloe [1952] Director/Solicitor (Non Practising); Martin Lawrence [1965] Director/Badminton Development Officer; Kenneth Stewart Leggate [1962] Director; Councillor Robert Charles Littlewood [1952] Director/Teacher; John Norman [1962] Director; Clive Beverly Rippon [1944] Director; Joyce Ellen Ryan [1941] Director/Teacher; Kartar Singh [1955] Director/Trustee; Carolynne Spencer [1967] Director/Accountant

J. Reddington Ltd
Incorporated: 23 July 1996 *Employees:* 123
Net Worth: £32,858,140 *Total Assets:* £85,098,440
Registered Office: 4 Elstree Way, Borehamwood, Herts, WD6 1RN
Activities: Construction of commercial buildings
Parent: JRL Group Ltd
Officers: Ronan Joseph Gleeson, Secretary/Director [Irish]; Ronan Joseph Gleeson [1976] Director [Irish]; Kevin William Keegan [1963] Director/Estimator [Irish]; John James Reddington [1972] Director/Formwork [Irish]

The Alec Reed Academy
Incorporated: 22 May 2002 *Employees:* 210
Net Worth: £36,593,000 *Total Assets:* £40,347,000
Registered Office: Bengarth Road, Northolt, Middlesex, UB5 5LQ
Activities: Pre-primary education
Officers: Marghanita Helen Muris, Secretary; Baba Abu [1966] Director/Banker; Sofina Bhatti [1982] Director/Teacher; Heather Flint [1951] Director/Education Consultant; Claudia Lashmore-Bennett [1980] Director/Teacher; Dee Martin [1962] Director/Campus Operation Manager; Allison Janice Moise-Dixon [1976] Director/Principal & CEO; Dee Morrison [1969] Director/Legal PA; Mike Phillips [1961] Managing Director; Emma Price [1990] Director/Programme Lead, Teach First; Louise Prince [1969] Director/Rights Executive; Tamana Sayed [1979] Director/Registered Nurse; Richard Antony Taylor [1969] Divisional Director Recruitment

Reed Business Information Limited
Incorporated: 27 September 1918 *Employees:* 1,514
Net Worth: £678,201,984 *Total Assets:* £946,572,992
Registered Office: Quadrant House, The Quadrant, Sutton, Surrey, SM2 5AS
Activities: Other information technology service activities
Parent: Reed Business Information (Holdings) Limited
Officers: Mark Vickers Kelsey [1960] Director; Jamie Andrew O'Sullivan [1971] Director/Chief Finance Officer

Reed Exhibitions Limited
Incorporated: 21 December 1960 *Employees:* 475
Net Worth: £32,753,048 *Total Assets:* £236,997,920
Registered Office: Gateway House, 28 The Quadrant, Richmond, Surrey, TW9 1DN
Activities: Activities of exhibition and fair organisers
Parent: RELX (UK)
Officers: Jacqueline Mary Poole, Secretary/Company Lawyer; Alexander David Stuart Bowden [1967] Director/Accountant; Darren Geoffrey Johnson [1966] Director; Richard John Norman Mortimore [1960] Director/Chief Executive; Michele Ruth Tiley-Hill [1972] Director

Dennis Reed Limited
Incorporated: 1 February 1936 *Employees:* 1
Net Worth: £2,799,518 *Total Assets:* £7,782,264
Registered Office: 172 Greenford Road, Sudbury Hill, Harrow, Middlesex, HA1 3QZ
Activities: Other business support service activities n.e.c.
Shareholders: Leigh of Hurley; Trevor Quentin Leigh
Officers: Lord Leigh of Hurley, Secretary; Jacqueline Maureen Harris [1935] Director; Trevor Quentin Leigh [1960] Director; Lord Leigh of Hurley [1959] Director/Chartered Accountant

The Reedham Children's Trust
Incorporated: 29 June 1904 *Employees:* 8
Net Worth: £9,283,263 *Total Assets:* £9,309,253
Registered Office: The Lodge, 23 Old Lodge Lane, Purley, Surrey, CR8 4DJ
Activities: Other social work activities without accommodation n.e.c.
Officers: Sarah Jane Smart, Secretary; Peter John Allen [1949] Retired Investment Director; Rawle Emerson Beckles [1964] Director/Head of Fundraising & Communications; Lucille Francis-Hume [1971] Director/Kindred Support Officer; Jeremy Carl Groombridge [1955] Director/Retired Civil Servant; Anne-Marie Emmeline Headley [1976] Director/Human Resources Professional; Sonia Jenkins [1966] Director/Consultant in Child Protection; Veronica Martin [1965] Director; Michael John Nevill [1947] Director; Jameson Robert Mark Smith [1962] Director; Deborah Anne Welham [1959] Director/Retail Management

D.B. Rees (Builders) Limited
Incorporated: 28 November 1968 *Employees:* 8
Net Worth: £4,739,988 *Total Assets:* £7,768,971
Registered Office: 62a Station Road, Kings Langley, Herts, WD4 8LB
Activities: Construction of domestic buildings
Shareholder: Glyn Nicholas Rees
Officers: Gary Rees, Secretary; David Balfour Rees [1934] Building Director; Gary Rees [1957] Director/Quantity Surveyor; Glyn Nicholas Rees [1961] Director/Contracts Manager; Michael James Hemingway Rees [1987] Director

Regal Trading Ltd
Incorporated: 14 May 2014
Net Worth Deficit: £1,026,939 *Total Assets:* £7,949,834
Registered Office: 30 Station Road, Orpington, Kent, BR6 0SA
Activities: Residential care activities for the elderly and disabled
Major Shareholder: Kanagaratnam Rajakanthan
Officers: Kanagaratnam Rajakanthan [1955] Director

The Regard ACH Holdco Limited
Incorporated: 2 August 2016
Net Worth: £21,416,000 *Total Assets:* £22,046,000
Registered Office: Unit 6 & 7 Princeton Mews, 167-169 London Road, Kingston upon Thames, Surrey, KT2 6PT
Activities: Other business support service activities n.e.c.
Parent: Galaxy Group Bidco Limited
Officers: Garry John Fitton, Secretary; Garry John Fitton [1972] Finance Director; Nicola Rosemary Lucy Hopkins [1968] Director/Chartered Accountant; Peter Kinsey [1964] Director

The Regard Partnership Limited
Incorporated: 31 January 1996 *Employees:* 1,561
Net Worth: £66,339,000 *Total Assets:* £89,982,000
Registered Office: Unit 6 Princeton Mews, 167-169 London Road, Kingston upon Thames, Surrey, KT2 6PT
Activities: Residential care activities for learning difficulties, mental health and substance abuse
Parent: Ruby Topco Limited
Officers: Garry John Fitton, Secretary; Garry John Fitton [1972] Finance Director; Nicola Rosemary Lucy Hopkins [1968] Director/Chartered Accountant; Peter Kinsey [1964] Director

Regenter B3 Holdco Limited
Incorporated: 6 February 2002
Net Worth Deficit: £5,005,000 *Total Assets:* £57,194,000
Registered Office: 8 White Oak Square, London Road, Swanley, Kent, BR8 7AG
Activities: Activities of head offices
Parent: Palio (No 5) Limited
Officers: Carl Harvey Dix [1966] Operations Director; Edward Mountney [1985] Director/Investment Professional

Regenter B3 Limited
Incorporated: 6 February 2002
Net Worth Deficit: £5,005,000 *Total Assets:* £57,194,000
Registered Office: 8 White Oak Square, London Road, Swanley, Kent, BR8 7AG
Activities: Other business support service activities n.e.c.
Parent: Regenter B3 Holdco Limited
Officers: Carl Harvey Dix [1966] Operations Director; Edward Mountney [1985] Director/Investment Professional

Regenter Bentilee District Centre (Holding) Limited
Incorporated: 24 March 2003
Net Worth: £298,000 *Total Assets:* £10,035,000
Registered Office: 8 White Oak Square, London Road, Swanley, Kent, BR8 7AG
Activities: Activities of head offices
Parent: JLIF (GP) Limited
Officers: Edward Mountney [1985] Director/Investment Professional; Neil Woodburn [1979] Director/Chartered Building Surveyor

Regenter Bentilee District Centre Limited
Incorporated: 15 March 2004
Net Worth: £298,000 *Total Assets:* £10,035,000
Registered Office: 8 White Oak Square, London Road, Swanley, Kent, BR8 7AG
Activities: Construction of commercial buildings
Parent: Regenter Bentilee District Centre (Holding) Limited
Officers: Edward Mountney [1985] Director/Investment Professional; Neil Woodburn [1979] Director/Chartered Building Surveyor

Regenter LCEP Holdco Limited
Incorporated: 24 January 2005
Net Worth Deficit: £2,878,000 *Total Assets:* £19,889,000
Registered Office: 8 White Oak Square, London Road, Swanley, Kent, BR8 7AG
Activities: Activities of head offices
Parent: Palio (No. 6) Limited
Officers: Carl Harvey Dix [1966] Operations Director; Edward Mountney [1985] Director/Investment Professional

Regenter LCEP Limited
Incorporated: 24 January 2005
Net Worth Deficit: £2,878,000 *Total Assets:* £19,889,000
Registered Office: 8 White Oak Square, London Road, Swanley, Kent, BR8 7AG
Activities: Construction of commercial buildings
Officers: Carl Harvey Dix [1966] Operations Director; Edward Mountney [1985] Director/Investment Professional

Regenter Myatts Field North Holding Company Limited
Incorporated: 7 January 2011
Net Worth Deficit: £5,025,000 *Total Assets:* £78,731,000
Registered Office: 8 White Oak Square, London Road, Swanley, Kent, BR8 7AG
Activities: Activities of head offices
Parent: JLIF Holdings (Lambeth Social Housing) Limited
Officers: David Richard Bradbury [1969] Asset Director; Vikki Louise Everett [1971] Director/Project Manager

Regenter Myatts Field North Limited
Incorporated: 11 January 2011
Net Worth Deficit: £5,025,000 *Total Assets:* £78,731,000
Registered Office: 8 White Oak Square, London Road, Swanley, Kent, BR8 7AG
Activities: Other business support service activities n.e.c.
Parent: Regenter Myatts Field North Holding Company Limited
Officers: David Richard Bradbury [1969] Asset Director; Vikki Louise Everett [1971] Director/Project Manager

Regentrealm Limited
Incorporated: 29 November 1999
Net Worth: £8,800,000 *Total Assets:* £439,400,000
Registered Office: Hayes Park, Hayes End Road, Hayes, Middlesex, UB4 8EE
Activities: Non-trading company
Parent: United Biscuits Bidco Limited
Officers: Mark Oldham, Secretary/Barrister; Helen Josephine McCarthy [1966] Director; Mark Oldham [1959] Director

Regentsmead Limited
Incorporated: 14 October 1991 *Employees:* 12
Net Worth: £51,465,568 *Total Assets:* £63,029,272
Registered Office: Russell House, 140 High Street, Edgware, Middlesex, HA8 7LW
Activities: Financial intermediation not elsewhere classified
Shareholders: Richard Alan Ross; Lee Richard Joseph Portnoi
Officers: Lee Robert Mesnick [1968] Director/Accountant; Richard Alan Ross [1942] Director

Regina 2015 Limited
Incorporated: 29 June 2015 *Employees:* 1
Net Worth: £131,346 *Total Assets:* £5,826,872
Registered Office: 28 Watersfield Way, Edgware, Middlesex, HA8 6RZ
Activities: Other letting and operating of own or leased real estate
Shareholders: Adam Kaye; Jonathan Kaye
Officers: Jonathan Kaye [1978] Director

Regis 2000 Limited
Incorporated: 13 November 2000 *Employees:* 1
Net Worth: £6,432,728 *Total Assets:* £17,150,980
Registered Office: 28 Watersfield Way, Edgware, Middlesex, HA8 6RZ
Activities: Other letting and operating of own or leased real estate
Major Shareholder: Jonathan Kaye
Officers: Arun Maganlal Bathia, Secretary; Jonathan Samuel Kaye [1978] Director

Reichhold UK Limited
Incorporated: 3 September 1986 *Employees:* 44
Net Worth: £19,457,000 *Total Assets:* £24,140,000
Registered Office: 54 Willow Lane, Mitcham, Surrey, CR4 4NA
Activities: Manufacture of plastics in primary forms
Officers: Munir Ahmed [1958] Director; Richard Thomas Donovan [1965] Director

Reichmann Properties PLC
Incorporated: 22 April 1998 *Employees:* 13
Previous: Glenville Investments PLC
Net Worth: £5,063,965 *Total Assets:* £18,139,238
Registered Office: 5 Elstree Gate, Elstree Way, Borehamwood, Herts, WD6 1JD
Activities: Other letting and operating of own or leased real estate
Officers: Dov Reichmann, Secretary; Daniel Naftali Reichmann [1988] Director; Dov Reichmann [1930] Director

Reliance Communications (U.K.) Limited
Incorporated: 13 December 2002 *Employees:* 1
Net Worth: £31,973,284 *Total Assets:* £37,609,052
Registered Office: Sovereign Court, 635 Sipson Road, Sipson, West Drayton, Middlesex, UB7 0JE
Activities: Wired telecommunications activities
Shareholder: Anil Dhirubhai Ambani
Officers: Andrew Peter Goldie, Secretary; Andrew Peter Goldie [1960] Director/Service

Reliance Entertainment Productions 12 Ltd
Incorporated: 7 July 2015
Net Worth: £5,171,250 *Total Assets:* £5,471,271
Registered Office: 99 Kenton Road, Harrow, Middlesex, HA3 0AN
Activities: Motion picture production activities
Officers: Deepak Nayar [1959] Director/Film Producer [American]; Laure Marie Vaysse [1984] Director/Chief Operating Officer [French]

Reliance Entertainment Productions 5 Ltd
Incorporated: 15 December 2011
Net Worth: £4,253,714 *Total Assets:* £5,878,711
Registered Office: 99 Kenton Road, Harrow, Middlesex, HA3 0AN
Activities: Motion picture production activities
Officers: Deepak Nayar [1959] Director/Film Producer [American]; Laure Marie Vaysse [1984] Director/Chief Operating Officer [French]

Reliance Entertainment Productions 7 Ltd
Incorporated: 15 December 2011
Net Worth: £6,749,562 *Total Assets:* £13,636,532
Registered Office: 99 Kenton Road, Harrow, Middlesex, HA3 0AN
Activities: Motion picture production activities
Officers: Deepak Nayar [1959] Director/Film Producer [American]; Laure Marie Vaysse [1984] Director/Chief Operating Officer [French]

Reliance Entertainment Productions Scandi Ltd
Incorporated: 7 July 2015
Previous: Cuckoo Lane Productions No. 5 Limited
Net Worth: £4,956,568 *Total Assets:* £5,269,034
Registered Office: 99 Kenton Road, Harrow, Middlesex, HA3 0AN
Activities: Motion picture production activities
Officers: Deepak Nayar [1959] Director/Film Producer [American]; Laure Marie Vaysse [1984] Director/Chief Operating Officer [French]

Reliance Globalcom (UK) Limited
Incorporated: 2 February 1998 *Employees:* 16
Net Worth: £8,321,702 *Total Assets:* £25,962,996
Registered Office: Sovereign Court, 635 Sipson Road, Sipson, West Drayton, Middlesex, UB7 0JE
Activities: Human resources provision and management of human resources functions
Shareholder: Anil Dhirubhai Ambani
Officers: Rodney Hardwicke Riley, Secretary; Andrew Peter Goldie [1960] Director/Service in Private Sector; Bipendra Kumar Sinha [1971] Director/Service [Indian]

Reliance Infra Projects (UK) Limited
Incorporated: 12 May 2008
Net Worth: £159,158 *Total Assets:* £118,668,744
Registered Office: Amba House, 4th Floor, Kings Suite, 15 College Road, Harrow, Middlesex, HA1 1BA
Activities: Other business support service activities n.e.c.
Officers: Hussaini Jawadwala [1979] Director/Service [Indian]

Reliance Investments Ltd
Incorporated: 7 February 2007
Net Worth: £2,405,480 *Total Assets:* £5,467,239
Registered Office: Top Floor, Bridgewater House, 866-868, Uxbridge Road, Hayes, Middlesex, UB4 0RR
Activities: Buying and selling of own real estate
Shareholders: Rajinder Singh Makkar; Inderpal Kaur Makkar
Officers: Rajinder Singh Makkar, Secretary; Inderpal Kaur Makkar [1967] Director

Reliance Vanco Group Limited
Incorporated: 9 April 1992
Net Worth: £56,389,056 *Total Assets:* £129,491,488
Registered Office: Sovereign Court, 635 Sipson Road, Sipson, West Drayton, Middlesex, UB7 0JE
Activities: Activities of head offices
Major Shareholder: Anil Dhirajlal Ambani
Officers: Andrew Peter Goldie [1960] Director

Remington Partners Ltd
Incorporated: 9 September 2002
Net Worth: £5,757,082 *Total Assets:* £6,179,502
Registered Office: 62 Lime Grove, Ruislip, Middlesex, HA4 8RY
Activities: Other letting and operating of own or leased real estate
Major Shareholder: David Daniel Lubel
Officers: Dr David Daniel Lubel, Secretary; Gillian Diane Lubel [1960] Director/Company Secretary

Remus Construction & Development Limited
Incorporated: 2 July 2003
Net Worth Deficit: £119,084 *Total Assets:* £8,117,962
Registered Office: Marden Manor, 1 The Crescent, Station Road, Woldingham, Surrey, CR3 7DB
Activities: Construction of domestic buildings
Major Shareholder: Tor Graves
Officers: Tor Sriachavanon Graves, Secretary/Manager; Tor Sriachavanon Graves [1972] Director/Manager

Remus White Limited
Incorporated: 7 September 1993 *Employees:* 110
Net Worth: £2,123,811 *Total Assets:* £9,537,541
Registered Office: 54 Frensham Close, Southall, Middlesex, UB1 2YG
Activities: Primary education
Major Shareholder: Melissa Katharyn Remus
Officers: Melissa Katharyn Remus [1967] Director/Teacher [American]

Remy's Limited
Incorporated: 13 January 1984 *Employees:* 22
Net Worth: £15,590,877 *Total Assets:* £29,172,980
Registered Office: Unit 6 ZK Park, 23 Commerce Way, Croydon, Surrey, CR0 4ZS
Activities: Buying and selling of own real estate
Officers: Arvindkumar Devji Shah, Secretary; Arvindkumar Devji Shah [1946] Director/Clothing Merchant; Mansukhlal Devji Shah [1941] Director/Clothing Merchant; Sailesh Devji Shah [1958] Director/Clothing Merchant; Suresh Devji Shah [1949] Director/Clothing Merchant

Renatus Property Management Limited
Incorporated: 29 November 2011 *Employees:* 9
Net Worth Deficit: £3,819 *Total Assets:* £37,320,448
Registered Office: Suite 2, West Hill House, West Hill, Epsom, Surrey, KT19 8JD
Activities: Other letting and operating of own or leased real estate
Parent: Street Family Group of Companies (Holdings) Limited
Officers: Andrew Mark Munday, Secretary; Patricia Jane French [1951] Director; Rivkah Hazel McCullough [1980] Director/Commercial Portfolio Executive; Andrew Mark Munday [1969] Director/Property Manager

Renault Group U.K. Limited
Incorporated: 18 October 1990
Net Worth: £16,670,781 *Total Assets:* £16,671,500
Registered Office: Renault Group UK Limited, The Rivers Office Park, Denham Way, Maple Cross, Rickmansworth, Herts, WD3 9YS
Activities: Accounting and auditing activities
Parent: Renault SA
Officers: James Alexander Blendis, Secretary; El-Hassan Aitsaid [1964] Finance Director [Belgian]; Thierry Antoine Joseph Cognet [1955] Director [French]

Renault Institute of Quality Management Limited
Incorporated: 13 November 1995 *Employees:* 147
Net Worth: £865,805 *Total Assets:* £7,275,986
Registered Office: The Rivers Office Park, Denham Way, Maple Cross, Rickmansworth, Herts, WD3 9YS
Activities: Management consultancy activities other than financial management
Shareholders: Renault SA; Renault UK Limited
Officers: James Britton Mitchell, Secretary; Farid Aractingi [1953] Director/VP RNSR Audit & Organisation [French]; Mark Alexander Crockett [1967] Director; Timothy Peter Marriott [1969] Director/Manager; Claire Martin [1962] Managing Director [French]; Nicholas Roy Tame [1965] Sales Director; Vincent Tourette [1969] Managing Director [French]

Renault U.K. Limited
Incorporated: 19 December 1904 *Employees:* 230
Net Worth: £26,936,000 *Total Assets:* £300,583,008
Registered Office: The Rivers Office Park, Denham Way, Maple Cross, Rickmansworth, Herts, WD3 9YS
Activities: Sale of new cars and light motor vehicles
Parent: Renault Group UK Limited
Officers: James Alexander Blendis, Secretary; El-Hassan Aitsaid [1964] Finance Director [Belgian]; Mark Alexander Crockett [1967] Director, Services and Quality; Lucy Kate Jones [1976] HR Director; Jean-Louis Labauge [1968] Managing Director [French]; Timothy Peter Mariott [1969] Aftersales Director; Nicholas Roy Tame [1965] Sales Director; Vincent Noel Tourette [1969] Managing Director [French]; Adam Vance Thomas Wood [1983] Marketing Director

Renewable Energy Centre Limited
Incorporated: 8 December 1995
Net Worth Deficit: £1,313,000 *Total Assets:* £7,632,000
Registered Office: Beaufort Court, Egg Farm Lane, Kings Langley, Herts, WD4 8LR
Activities: Construction of commercial buildings
Parent: Renewable Energy Systems Limited
Officers: Dominic James Hearth, Secretary; Donald Crawford Joyce [1973] Director/Chief Financial Officer; Mitesh Raj Patel [1982] Director/Group Financial Controller; Richard Paul Russell [1981] Finance Director

Renewable Energy Systems Holdings Limited
Incorporated: 26 September 2003 *Employees:* 1,683
Net Worth: £296,894,016 *Total Assets:* £620,592,000
Registered Office: Beaufort Court, Egg Farm Lane, off Station Road, Kings Langley, Herts, WD4 8LR
Activities: Activities of head offices
Shareholders: Douglas James McAlpine; Richard Hugh McAlpine; Andrew William McAlpine; Gavin Malcolm McAlpine; Robert Edward Thomas William McAlpine; Hector George McAlpine
Officers: Dominic James Hearth, Secretary; Ivor Douglas Catto [1966] Director/Deputy CEO; Donald Crawford Joyce [1973] Director/Chief Financial Officer; Chris Michael Marsh [1963] Director; Douglas James McAlpine [1983] Director; Dr Gavin Malcolm McAlpine [1976] Director; Marco Perona [1967] Director [French]; Graham Matthew Reid [1962] Director/Chief Executive Officer, Americas; Rachel Ruffle [1967] Managing Director, UK & Ireland

Renewable Energy Systems Limited
Incorporated: 8 October 1981 *Employees:* 357
Net Worth: £193,522,000 *Total Assets:* £336,766,016
Registered Office: Beaufort Court, Egg Farm Lane, Station Road, Kings Langley, Herts, WD4 8LR
Activities: Construction of commercial buildings
Parent: Renewable Energy Systems Holdings Limited
Officers: Dominic James Hearth, Secretary; Ivor Douglas Catto [1966] Director/Deputy CEO; Dominic James Hearth [1966] Director/General Counsel; Steven William Hughes [1972] Generation & Asset Management Director; Donald Crawford Joyce [1973] Director/Chief Financial Officer; Chris Michael Marsh [1963] Director; Rachel Ruffle [1967] Projects Director, Western Europe and Deputy MD; Richard Paul Russell [1981] Finance Director

Rent 2 Own Cars Ltd
Incorporated: 12 May 2011
Net Worth Deficit: £7,493,578 *Total Assets:* £15,669,892
Registered Office: 1 Bell Parade, Glebe Way, West Wickham, Kent, BR4 0RH
Activities: Renting and leasing of cars and light motor vehicles
Shareholders: Reginald Larry-Cole; Raedex Consortium Limited
Officers: Reginald Larry-Cole [1970] Director/Car Salesman; Scott Andrew Martin [1978] Director/Car Salesman

Repair Funding Limited
Incorporated: 6 October 2011 *Employees:* 2
Net Worth: £4,467,144 *Total Assets:* £55,964,520
Registered Office: Enterprise House, Vicarage Road, Egham, Surrey, TW20 9FB
Activities: Management consultancy activities other than financial management
Parent: Enterprise Rent-a-Car UK Limited
Officers: Teresa Holderer, Secretary; Ricky Allan Short [1958] Director [American]

RES UK & Ireland Limited
Incorporated: 26 September 2003
Net Worth: £54,556,000 *Total Assets:* £78,506,000
Registered Office: Beaufort Court, Egg Farm Lane, off Station Road, Kings Langley, Herts, WD4 8LR
Activities: Other business support service activities n.e.c.
Parent: Renewable Energy Systems Limited
Officers: Dominic James Hearth, Secretary; Jasbir Singh Bains [1966] Director/Commercial Manager; Steven William Hughes [1972] Generation & Asset Management Director; Rachel Ruffle [1967] Projects Director, Western Europe and Deputy MD; Richard Paul Russell [1981] Finance Director

Resham PLC
Incorporated: 25 March 1986 *Employees:* 4
Net Worth: £7,336,939 *Total Assets:* £21,289,094
Registered Office: c/o Parker Cavendish, 28 Church Road, Stanmore, Middlesex, HA7 4XR
Activities: Buying and selling of own real estate
Major Shareholder: Davinder Singh Mander
Officers: Pritpal Kaur Mander, Secretary; Balwinder Kaur Mander [1975] Director/Secretary; Dr Davinder Singh Mander [1965] Director/Travel Agent; Harinder Singh Mander [1970] Director/Travel Agent; Pritpal Kaur Mander [1938] Director/Travel Agent

Residential Care Services Limited
Incorporated: 4 June 1993 *Employees:* 31
Net Worth: £4,031,952 *Total Assets:* £6,482,979
Registered Office: 9 Grand Avenue, Wembley, Middlesex, HA9 6LS
Activities: Other residential care activities n.e.c.
Shareholder: Lynda Osarieme Eribo
Officers: Frank Idemudia Eribo, Secretary; Dr Frank Eribo [1951] Director/Medical Consultant; Dr Lynda Osarieme Eribo [1952] Director

Residential Land Holdings Limited
Incorporated: 24 October 2006 *Employees:* 45
Net Worth: £14,338,465 *Total Assets:* £21,526,836
Registered Office: 19-20 Bourne Court, Southend Road, Woodford Green, Essex, IG8 8HD
Activities: Activities of head offices
Major Shareholder: Bruce Weir Ritchie
Officers: Jonathan Simon David Anthony Rust, Company Secretary; Bruce Weir Ritchie [1965] Director

Residential Land Limited
Incorporated: 4 November 1987 *Employees:* 50
Net Worth Deficit: £22,166,022 *Total Assets:* £6,344,970
Registered Office: 19-20 Bourne Court, Southend Road, Woodford Green, Essex, IG8 8HD
Activities: Development of building projects
Parent: Residential Land Holdings Limited
Officers: Jonathan Simon David Anthony Rust, Secretary; Abdolkhalegh Khalid Al Sharifi [1945] Director; Bruce Weir Ritchie [1965] Director; Jonathan Simon David Anthony Rust [1973] Director/Company Secretary

Residential Land Management 2 Ltd
Incorporated: 16 April 2010
Net Worth: £10,410,065 *Total Assets:* £15,896,826
Registered Office: 19-20 Bourne Court, Southend Road, Woodford Green, Essex, IG8 8HD
Activities: Development of building projects
Parent: Residential Land Holdings Limited
Officers: Bruce Weir Ritchie [1965] Director

Residential Land Management Limited
Incorporated: 5 December 2006 *Employees:* 1
Net Worth: £4,811,231 *Total Assets:* £5,896,533
Registered Office: 19-20 Bourne Court, Southend Road, Woodford Green, Essex, IG8 8HD
Activities: Development of building projects
Parent: Residential Land Holdings Limited
Officers: Bruce Weir Ritchie [1965] Director

Residential Loans Ltd.
Incorporated: 10 August 1998 *Employees:* 1
Net Worth: £5,030,329 *Total Assets:* £9,312,835
Registered Office: c/o Richards Solicitors, 1st Floor, Grosvenor House, 1 High Street, Edgware, Middlesex, HA8 7TA
Activities: Other credit granting n.e.c.
Officers: David Levitus, Secretary; Dorothy Fleming [1956] Director/Administration Manager; David Levitus [1968] Director; Susan Adele Levitus [1968] Director/Administrator; Allan Smith [1981] Director

Residential Management Group Limited
Incorporated: 21 August 1980 *Employees:* 406
Net Worth: £5,594,000 *Total Assets:* £9,818,000
Registered Office: RMG House, Essex Road, Hoddesdon, Herts, EN11 0DR
Activities: Management of real estate on a fee or contract basis
Parent: Places for People Ventures Operations Limited
Officers: Christopher Paul Martin, Secretary; David Cowans [1957] Director; Alan James Inglis [1958] Finance Director; Hugh Jordan McGeever [1960] Director/Manager; Christopher Robin Leslie Phillips [1950] Director/Chairman

Residential Properties Funds Limited
Incorporated: 17 May 2004
Net Worth: £2,113,703 *Total Assets:* £6,478,264
Registered Office: 505 Pinner Road, Harrow, Middlesex, HA2 6EH
Activities: Buying and selling of own real estate
Major Shareholder: Ramji Bechar Kerai
Officers: Ramji Bechar Kerai, Secretary; Ramji Bechar Kerai [1960] Director/Accountant; Ramesh Mavji Pindoria [1977] Director

Residual and Brand Management Limited
Incorporated: 5 September 1994 *Employees:* 20
Previous: Residual Brand Management Limited
Net Worth: £2,276,872 *Total Assets:* £7,155,733
Registered Office: Unit 8 Trafalgar Business Centre, 77-89 River Road, Barking, Essex, IG11 0JU
Activities: Non-specialised wholesale of food, beverages and tobacco
Parent: J. A. Phillips Holdings Limited
Officers: Emma Margaret Warran, Secretary; James Albert Phillips [1959] Director

Restate Management Ltd
Incorporated: 25 July 2013
Net Worth Deficit: £26,160 *Total Assets:* £17,690,850
Registered Office: 4 The Mews, Bridge Road, Twickenham, Middlesex, TW1 1RF
Activities: Wholesale of pharmaceutical goods
Major Shareholder: Valerii Los
Officers: Katherine Anne Hickson [1978] Director/Consultant

RET Becket Keys Church of England Free School Trust
Incorporated: 7 June 2012 *Employees:* 100
Net Worth: £15,612,000 *Total Assets:* £16,578,000
Registered Office: Manor House, The Crescent, Leatherhead, Surrey, KT22 8DY
Activities: General secondary education
Officers: Daniel Christopher Lynch, Secretary; John Chambers [1951] Director/Education Consultant; Pauline Davidson [1961] Director/Administrator; Jenny Downs [1969] Director/IT Consultancy; Iain Andrew William Gunn [1973] Director/Primary School Headteacher; Paul Hamilton [1969] Director/Vicar; Karen Lynch [1957] Director; Adam Pope [1969] Director/IT Consultant; Christine Savage [1969] Director/Lecturer; Andy Scott Evans [1975] Director/Headteacher

Retallack Holidays Limited
Incorporated: 7 February 2012 *Employees:* 127
Previous: Retallack Holiday Lettings Limited
Net Worth Deficit: £7,117,854 *Total Assets:* £5,599,709
Registered Office: 3rd Floor, Sterling House, Langston Road, Loughton, Essex, IG10 3TS
Activities: Other business support service activities n.e.c.
Parent: Galliard Resorts Limited
Officers: Allan William Porter, Secretary; David Edward Conway [1976] Director; Stephen Stuart Solomon Conway [1948] Director

Retirement Villages Group Limited
Incorporated: 18 January 2005 *Employees:* 633
Net Worth: £132,932,000 *Total Assets:* £160,166,000
Registered Office: 1st Floor, Brunswick House, Regent Park, 297-299 Kingston Road, Leatherhead, Surrey, KT22 7LU
Activities: Activities of head offices
Shareholder: Harvitour Limited
Officers: Sally Irene Rees, Secretary; Sarah Denise Burgess [1971] Director; William Edwin John Crawford [1970] Director; Neil Donaldson [1966] Director/Accountant; Christina Elizabeth Edwards [1943] Director; Emmanuel Lefebvre [1974] Director/Fund Management [French]; Andrew George Esmond Ovey [1971] Director/Investment Manager; Oscar Russell [1987] Director

Retirement Villages Limited
Incorporated: 29 June 1999 *Employees:* 3
Net Worth: £21,071,008 *Total Assets:* £65,107,568
Registered Office: 1st Floor, Brunswick House, Regent Park, 297-299 Kingston Road, Leatherhead, Surrey, KT22 7LU
Activities: Other business support service activities n.e.c.
Parent: Retirement Villages Group Limited
Officers: Sally Irene Rees, Secretary; William Edwin John Crawford [1970] Director/Development; Neil Donaldson [1966] Director/Accountant; Andrew George Esmond Ovey [1971] Director/Investment Banker

Rex Partners LLP
Incorporated: 20 December 2006
Net Worth: £27,939,492 *Total Assets:* £28,973,348
Registered Office: Harmile House, 54 St Marys Lane, Upminster, Essex, RM14 2QT
Officers: Hilary Ann Williams [1946] Member; Stuart Kenneth Mathieson Williams [1944] Member

Rex Trade Associates Limited
Incorporated: 26 March 2007
Net Worth: £1,530,163 *Total Assets:* £8,937,277
Registered Office: Harmile House, 54 St Mary's Lane, Upminster, Essex, RM14 2QT
Activities: Other business support service activities n.e.c.
Major Shareholder: Stuart Kenneth Mathieson Williams
Officers: Lisa Sheppard, Secretary; Andrew Mathieson Williams [1972] Director/TV Producer; Hilary Ann Williams [1946] Director/Theatre/Theatrical Producer; Stuart Kenneth Mathieson Williams [1944] Director/Property Developer/Retailer

Rex Venture Resources Limited
Incorporated: 2 February 2007
Net Worth: £9,590,554 *Total Assets:* £9,591,554
Registered Office: 54 St Marys Lane, Upminster, Essex, RM14 2QT
Activities: Fund management activities
Major Shareholder: Stuart Kenneth Mathieson Williams
Officers: Lisa Sheppard, Secretary; Andrew Mathieson Williams [1972] Director/Retailer; Hilary Ann Williams [1946] Director/Theatre Producer; Stuart Kenneth Mathieson Williams [1944] Director/Property Developer

Reyhold Limited
Incorporated: 30 November 2015 *Employees:* 927
Net Worth: £3,257,000 *Total Assets:* £53,438,000
Registered Office: National Distribution Centre, Britannia Road, Waltham Cross, Herts, EN8 7RQ
Activities: Activities of head offices
Major Shareholder: Antony William Reynolds
Officers: Antony William Reynolds [1964] Director

Reynolds Catering Supplies Limited
Incorporated: 4 August 1994 *Employees:* 927
Net Worth: £5,516,000 *Total Assets:* £53,377,000
Registered Office: National Distribution Centre, Britannia Road, Waltham Cross, Herts, EN8 7RQ
Activities: Wholesale of fruit and vegetables
Parent: Reyhold Limited
Officers: Andrew David Austin [1973] Finance Director; Richard Alexander Calder [1963] IT Director; Paul James Collins [1965] Commercial Director; Stephen David High [1971] Director; Paul Stephen William Pegg [1957] Director; Antony William Reynolds [1964] Director/Caterer; Linda Sarah Simons [1969] Director

RFU Injured Players Foundation
Incorporated: 27 November 2007
Net Worth: £7,793,057 *Total Assets:* £10,297,275
Registered Office: Rugby House, Twickenham Stadium, 200 Whitton Road, Twickenham, Middlesex, TW2 7BA
Activities: Other human health activities
Parent: Rugby Football Union
Officers: Angus Roch Bujalski, Secretary; Evan Davies [1966] Director/Consultant Spinal Surgeon; Dr Stephen Charles Duckworth [1960] Director of Disability Assessments; Nigel John Henderson [1951] Director/Consultant Orthopaedic Surgeon; Dr Margaret Mary Emer McGilloway [1967] Director/Clinical Lead for Neurorehabilitation; Judith Mary Metcalfe [1958] Director; Doctor Frederick Riach Ironside Middleton [1942] Director/Retired Physician; Paul Edward Murphy [1950] Director/Product Manager; Stephen Brian Pearson [1963] Investment Director; Nigel Arthur Tarrant [1953] Director/Solicitor - Partner; Robert Fraser Udwin [1959] Director

Rhenus High Tech UK Limited
Incorporated: 23 November 2004 *Employees:* 128
Previous: LCE U.K. Limited
Net Worth: £248,438 *Total Assets:* £7,283,392
Registered Office: Keiler House, Challenge Road, Ashford, Middlesex, TW15 1AX
Activities: Activities of other holding companies n.e.c.
Parent: Rhenus Beteiligungen International GmbH
Officers: Richard Kennerley, Secretary; Michael Paatz [1970] Managing Director [German]; Nicolas Rottmann [1974] Director [German]

Rhenus Lupprians Limited
Incorporated: 12 February 1990 *Employees:* 128
Previous: Lupprian's Computer Express Limited
Net Worth: £486,398 *Total Assets:* £7,520,852
Registered Office: Keiler House, Challenge Road, Ashford, Middlesex, TW15 1AX
Activities: Freight transport by road
Parent: Rhenus High Tech UK Limited
Officers: Richard Kennerley, Secretary; Graham Atcheson Barrow [1965] Director; Carsten Braune [1966] Director [German]; Richard Kennerley [1973] Managing Director

Rhiannon Properties Limited
Incorporated: 26 October 1987 *Employees:* 5
Net Worth: £1,922,335 *Total Assets:* £8,473,616
Registered Office: c/o Fenleys, 1st Floor, 168 High Street, Watford, Herts, WD17 2EG
Activities: Buying and selling of own real estate
Major Shareholder: Malcolm James Ablett
Officers: Rachel Ablett, Secretary/Administrator; Malcolm James Ablett [1952] Director/Property Dealer

Rhodehurst Limited
Incorporated: 28 April 2004
Net Worth: £1,953,581 *Total Assets:* £6,591,610
Registered Office: 102 High Street, West Wickham, Kent, BR4 0NF
Activities: Buying and selling of own real estate
Officers: Alan Terrence Manuel, Secretary; Alan Terrance Manuel [1942] Director/Managing Consultant; Arif Badrudin Virani [1960] Director/Accountant

Rhodia Holdings Limited
Incorporated: 22 November 1995
Net Worth: £249,571,008 *Total Assets:* £501,308,992
Registered Office: 34 Clarendon Road, Watford, Herts, WD17 1JJ
Activities: Activities of head offices
Officers: Alison Murphy, Secretary; Alexis Michel Brouhns [1955] Director/Manager [Belgian]; Melvin John Dawes [1967] Director/Solicitor; Nathan Mills [1977] Director/Engineer [American]; Alison Murphy [1965] Director/Financial Controller

Rhodia International Holdings Limited
Incorporated: 27 July 1898
Net Worth: £55,610,000 *Total Assets:* £55,991,000
Registered Office: 34 Clarendon Road, Watford, Herts, WD17 1JJ
Activities: Activities of head offices
Parent: Rhodia Holdings Limited
Officers: Alison Murphy, Secretary; Melvin John Dawes [1967] Director/Solicitor; Tom Dutton [1964] Director/Health, Safety & Environment Manager; Alison Murphy [1965] Director/Financial Controller

Rhodia Limited
Incorporated: 6 May 1926
Net Worth: £150,058,000 *Total Assets:* £211,896,000
Registered Office: 34 Clarendon Road, Watford, Herts, WD17 1JJ
Activities: Manufacture of other inorganic basic chemicals
Parent: Rhodia Holdings Limited
Officers: Alison Murphy, Secretary; Tom Dutton [1964] Director/Health, Safety & Environment Manager; John Stuart Moorhouse [1951] Director/Chemical Engineer; Alison Murphy [1965] Director/Financial Controller

Rhombi Holdings Limited
Incorporated: 22 June 2011 *Employees:* 5
Net Worth: £78,694,320 *Total Assets:* £528,601,536
Registered Office: Aviation House, The Lodge, Harmondsworth Lane, West Drayton, Middlesex, UB7 0LQ
Activities: Activities of head offices
Parent: Teledyne Technologies Incorporated
Officers: Nicholas James Wargent, Secretary; Stephen F. Blackwood [1962] Director/Corporate Treasurer [American]; Susan Lee Main [1958] Director/Senior Vice President and Chief Financial Officer [American]; Edwin Roks [1964] Director/Corporate President [Dutch]; Nicholas James Wargent [1973] Director/Solicitor

RHP Finance PLC
Incorporated: 27 November 2014
Net Worth: £13,000 *Total Assets:* £138,651,008
Registered Office: 8 Waldegrave Road, Teddington, Middlesex, TW11 8GT
Activities: Financial intermediation not elsewhere classified
Officers: Corinna Jayne Bishopp, Secretary; Corinna Jayne Bishopp [1973] Finance Director; David Done [1962] Director/Chief Executive; John Edward Newbury [1949] Director; Stephen Geoffrey Michael Speak [1963] Director/Councillor

Rian Properties Limited
Incorporated: 25 April 1960
Net Worth: £5,347,954 *Total Assets:* £6,800,188
Registered Office: 28 Elmgate Gardens, Edgware, Middlesex, HA8 9RT
Activities: Other letting and operating of own or leased real estate
Shareholders: John Howard Harris; Marilyn Podro
Officers: John Howard Harris, Secretary; Jason Marc Gee [1969] Director/Property Consultant; John Howard Harris [1943] Director/Solicitor; Marilyn Podro [1940] Director/Property Manager

Rican Securities Limited
Incorporated: 4 November 1993 *Employees:* 3
Net Worth: £11,725,455 *Total Assets:* £15,836,983
Registered Office: Ground Floor, rear The Estate House, 201 High Road, Chigwell, Essex, IG7 5BJ
Activities: Other service activities n.e.c.
Major Shareholder: Andrew Paul Klein
Officers: Howard Malcolm Klein, Secretary; Andrew Paul Klein [1966] Director/Businessman; Howard Malcolm Klein [1940] Director

Richardson Roofing Company Limited
Incorporated: 19 May 1980 *Employees:* 45
Net Worth: £4,938,477 *Total Assets:* £9,955,317
Registered Office: Richardson House, Moor Lane, Staines upon Thames, Middlesex, TW19 6EQ
Activities: Roofing activities
Parent: Richardson Roofing Holdings Limited
Officers: Dawn Willmont, Secretary; Patrick Joseph MacSweeney [1957] Director; George Martin Richardson [1956] Director; Simon David Wright [1963] Director/Roofing

Richardson Roofing Holdings Limited
Incorporated: 18 December 1998 *Employees:* 51
Net Worth: £6,512,361 *Total Assets:* £12,888,130
Registered Office: Richardson House, Moor Lane, Staines upon Thames, Middlesex, TW19 6EQ
Activities: Activities of head offices
Major Shareholder: George Martin Richardson
Officers: Dawn Willmont, Secretary; George Martin Richardson [1956] Director; Simon David Wright [1963] Director/Roofing

Riches Ilford Ltd
Incorporated: 24 July 2014
Net Worth: £2,393,792 *Total Assets:* £7,327,717
Registered Office: 148 Cranbrook Road, Ilford, Essex, IG1 4LZ
Activities: Buying and selling of own real estate
Major Shareholder: Herjit Singh Kataria
Officers: Herjit Singh Kataria [1967] Director

Richmond & Hampshire Limited
Incorporated: 15 May 2001
Net Worth: £2,276,333 *Total Assets:* £10,829,678
Registered Office: The Petersham, Nightingale Lane, Richmond, Surrey, TW10 6UZ
Activities: Other business support service activities n.e.c.
Officers: Greville Richard Hugh Dare, Secretary/Hotel Owner; Sir Euan Hamilton Anstruther-Gough-Calthorpe BT [1966] Director/Principal; Greville Richard Hugh Dare [1963] Director/Hotelier; Simon James Scarr [1965] Director/Accountant; Philip David Warden [1963] Director/Hotelier

Richmond and Hillcroft Adult and Community College
Incorporated: 6 November 1924 *Employees:* 160
Previous: Hillcroft College (Incorporated) Limited
Net Worth: £51,009,000 *Total Assets:* £59,180,000
Registered Office: Hillcroft College, South Bank, Surbiton, Surrey, KT6 6DF
Activities: Post-secondary non-tertiary education
Officers: Sara George, Secretary; Mark Desmond Albrow [1952] Director/Retired; Richard David Brewster [1946] Director/Retired; Helen Patricia Darracott [1961] Director/Regulatory Compliance; Gabrielle Nina Flint [1968] Director/Principal and Chief Executive; Christine Louise Fluker [1953] Director/Retired; Professor Andrew John Timothy George [1963] Director/University Professor; Professor Linda Joyce Jones [1948] Director; Nicola Jane O'Shea [1947] Director/Retired; Farah Rachlin [1963] Director/Solicitor; Lisa Claire Sharp [1977] Director/Economic Development Consultant; Graham John Tharp [1968] Director/Educational Programme Manager; Nigel Digby Ware [1947] Director/Chartered Accountant

Richmond Green Developments Limited
Incorporated: 3 February 2012 *Employees:* 6
Net Worth: £775,037 *Total Assets:* £8,688,500
Registered Office: Westminster Business Centre, Printing House Lane, Hayes, Middlesex, UB3 1AP
Activities: Development of building projects
Major Shareholder: Colin Hugh Deehan
Officers: Colin Hugh Deehan [1964] Director

The Richmond West Schools Trust
Incorporated: 23 March 2016 *Employees:* 225
Net Worth: £32,253,784 *Total Assets:* £36,118,740
Registered Office: Twickenham School, Percy Road, Twickenham, Middlesex, TW2 6JW
Activities: General secondary education
Officers: Adele Suzanne Kimber [1961] Director/Editor; Claire Little [1967] Group HR Director; Annmarie Loughlin [1968] Director/Certified Accountant; Joanne Merritt [1966] Director; Philippa Jane Nunn [1965] Director/Headteacher; Charis Laura Jane Penfold [1963] Director/Teacher; Siobhan Peters [1970] Director/Chief Financial Officer; Neil Philip Smith [1981] Director/Head of Strategic & Business Development; Angela Mary Thomas [1957] Director [Irish]; Brian Winstanley [1964] Director/Programme Manager

Richstone Properties Limited
Incorporated: 2 May 2014
Net Worth: £23,092,330 *Total Assets:* £46,332,496
Registered Office: Gladstone House, 77-79 High Street, Egham, Surrey, TW20 9HY
Activities: Other letting and operating of own or leased real estate
Shareholders: David Graham Peter Rich-Jones; Laura Elizabeth Rich-Jones
Officers: David Graham Peter Rich-Jones [1961] Director [British/Canadian]; Laura Elizabeth Rich-Jones [1966] Director

Rickmansworth School
Incorporated: 14 March 2011 *Employees:* 143
Net Worth: £16,730,769 *Total Assets:* £18,782,918
Registered Office: Rickmansworth School, Scots Hill, Rickmansworth, Herts, WD3 3AQ
Activities: General secondary education
Officers: David Wilson, Secretary; Jonathon Peter Nicholas James Bowers [1968] Director/Police Officer; Harvey Alan Frederick Collyer [1946] Director/Retired; Geoffrey Cox [1952] Director/Senior HR Consultant; John Andrew de Braux [1950] Director/Recruitment Consultant; Keith Charles Deboice Douglas [1964] Director/Headteacher; Jennifer Ellen Dufton [1969] Director/IT Manager; Mark Fletcher [1968] Director/Bank Officer [Australian]; Peter Harman [1946] Director/Retired; Timothy John Lester Harrison [1954] Director/Chartered Surveyor; Ubaid Hassan [1971] Director/IT and Finance Consultant; Neeshat Hussein [1960] Director; Ashley Lagrange [1952] Director/Teacher [Zimbabwean]; Qasim Latif [1982] Director/Professional Services Consultant; Josanne Leon [1964] Director/Head of Human Resources; Ian Anthony Martin [1963] Director/Teacher; Gillian Robson [1965] Director/School Secretary; Anthony Robert Walker [1958] Director/Company Secretary; Dr David Wellings [1965] Director/Teacher/Researcher; Susan Helen Wilson [1968] Director/Teacher

Ridgeland Properties Limited
Incorporated: 22 December 1997
Net Worth: £30,934,108 *Total Assets:* £73,175,928
Registered Office: Hill House, Lowlands Road, Harrow, Middlesex, HA1 3EQ
Activities: Development of building projects
Major Shareholder: Donovan Gijsbertus Wijsmuller
Officers: Brian Martin Comer [1960] Director [Irish]; Luke Andrew Comer [1957] Director [Irish]

RIG Medical Recruit Limited
Incorporated: 4 September 2002 *Employees:* 95
Net Worth: £1,114,000 *Total Assets:* £5,103,000
Registered Office: Northside House, 69 Tweedy Road, Bromley, Kent, BR1 3WA
Activities: Temporary employment agency activities
Parent: CPL Resources Public Limited Company
Officers: Robert Bryan [1979] Director; Mark Buckley [1973] Finance Director [Irish]; Anne Heraty [1960] Director [Irish]; Aftab Khan [1985] Director

Right Choice Insurance Brokers Limited
Incorporated: 9 November 2007 *Employees:* 306
Net Worth: £8,412,678 *Total Assets:* £18,314,632
Registered Office: St James House, 27-43 Eastern Road, Romford, Essex, RM1 3NH
Activities: Non-life insurance
Parent: Right Choice Holdings Limited
Officers: Michael Paul Joseph, Secretary; Darren Jason Joseph [1969] Director/Operations Manager; Michael Paul Joseph [1971] Director; Robert John Taberner [1957] Director/Chartered Accountant

Right Choice Property Holdings Limited
Incorporated: 14 October 2010
Net Worth Deficit: £599,071 *Total Assets:* £5,309,494
Registered Office: St James House, 27-43 Eastern Road, Romford, Essex, RM1 3NH
Activities: Other letting and operating of own or leased real estate
Major Shareholder: Michael Paul Joseph
Officers: Darren Jason Joseph [1969] Director/Operations Manager; Michael Paul Joseph [1971] Director; Robert John Taberner [1957] Director/Chartered Accountant

Rijac Properties Limited
Incorporated: 21 November 1977 *Employees:* 2
Net Worth: £7,825,495 *Total Assets:* £9,321,262
Registered Office: York House, Empire Way, Wembley, Middlesex, HA9 0FQ
Activities: Other letting and operating of own or leased real estate
Parent: Lindsay Drive General Investment Company Limited
Officers: Alexander Terence Shields, Secretary; Alexander Terence Shields [1981] Director; Michael George Shields [1943] Director/Chartered Surveyor

Rilla Properties Limited
Incorporated: 5 October 2010
Net Worth: £3,256,208 *Total Assets:* £6,101,841
Registered Office: 52 Cedar Drive, Hatchend, Pinner, Middlesex, HA5 4DE
Activities: Buying and selling of own real estate
Major Shareholder: Martin Derek Edward Bayntun
Officers: Martin Derek Edward Bayntun [1974] Director/Hotelier

Rimex Metals (U.K.) Limited
Incorporated: 18 December 1959 *Employees:* 86
Net Worth: £3,542,555 *Total Assets:* £10,193,596
Registered Office: 17 Aden Road, Enfield, Middlesex, EN3 7SU
Activities: Manufacture of other fabricated metal products n.e.c.
Parent: Rimex Metals Group Ltd
Officers: Barbara Ellen Brandt, Secretary; Nicholas Edward Stanley Barnes [1962] Sales Director; Timothy John Childs [1966] Director; Richard John Watson [1965] Production Director

Rina Consulting Ltd
Incorporated: 26 October 2010 *Employees:* 253
Previous: Era Technology Limited
Net Worth: £6,098,000 *Total Assets:* £16,201,000
Registered Office: Era Building, Cleeve Road, Leatherhead, Surrey, KT22 7SA
Activities: Engineering related scientific and technical consulting activities
Shareholders: Edif Group Management Limited; Edif Group Management Ltd
Officers: Adam Crocker, Secretary; Fabio Bagnoli [1972] Director/Division Manager [Italian]; Simon Timothy Brown [1961] Managing Director; Adam George Crocker [1975] Director; Stefano Socci [1973] Director [Italian]

Ripmax Limited
Incorporated: 7 April 1949 *Employees:* 60
Net Worth: £4,103,665 *Total Assets:* £9,129,936
Registered Office: 241 Green Street, Enfield, Middlesex, EN3 7SJ
Activities: Wholesale of other intermediate products
Parent: Ultimate Model Corporation Limited
Officers: Mark Henley, Secretary; Graham John Hales [1948] Director; Robert Allan Hales [1953] Director; Peter Alan Halman [1945] Director/Engineer; Mark David Henley [1971] Director/Chartered Accountant; Matthew Hull [1981] Commercial Director; Jason Harvey Metcalf [1968] Director/Corporate Financier; Nicholas Julian Moss [1964] Managing Director; Colin Mark Peter Straus [1960] Director/Export Executive; Mark Wood [1957] Purchasing Director

Riposte Limited
Incorporated: 18 July 2003 *Employees:* 2
Net Worth: £273,600,992 *Total Assets:* £275,720,992
Registered Office: Hunton House, Highbridge Industrial Estate, Oxford Road, Uxbridge, Middlesex, UB8 1LX
Activities: Financial management
Parent: PandoraExpress 7 Limited
Officers: Andrew David Pellington, Secretary; Andrew David Pellington [1964] Director; Jinlong Wang [1957] Director [American]

Rise Park Academy Trust
Incorporated: 21 May 2014 *Employees:* 102
Net Worth: £7,002,794 *Total Assets:* £8,047,842
Registered Office: Rise Park Infant School, Annan Way, Rise Park, Romford, Essex, RM1 4UD
Activities: Primary education
Officers: Nicholas Robert Bone [1979] Director/Banker; Victoria Natalie Botham [1978] Director/Accounts/Administration; Carolyn Emma Fox [1961] Director/Primary Headteacher; Kevin Stuart Johns [1957] Director/IT Consultant; Denis Henry Stevens [1941] Director/Retired

Riso (U.K.) Limited
Incorporated: 26 May 1992 *Employees:* 85
Net Worth: £1,742,036 *Total Assets:* £6,247,527
Registered Office: 610 Centennial Park, Centennial Avenue, Elstree, Herts, WD6 3TJ
Activities: Manufacture of computers and peripheral equipment
Parent: Riso Kagaku Corporation
Officers: Stephen Edmund Thomas Root, Secretary; Tomiyama Fumiya [1964] Director [Japanese]; Toshihiko Kawatsu [1967] Director [Japanese]; Tatsuo Murakami [1976] Managing Director [Japanese]

Riverdale Developments Limited
Incorporated: 20 April 2004 *Employees:* 16
Net Worth: £7,438,065 *Total Assets:* £37,863,328
Registered Office: O'Brien House, 197-199 Garth Road, Morden, Surrey, SM4 4NE
Activities: Development of building projects
Parent: OHOB Group Ltd
Officers: Colin David Southey, Secretary; Brian Hector Bonnyman [1958] Director/Group MD; Richard John Matthews [1960] Managing Director; Thomas Francis O'Brien [1947] Director/Builder [Irish]; Louise Patricia O'Brien Smith [1979] Director; Colin David Southey [1959] Director

Rivers Finance Group PLC
Incorporated: 18 October 2002 *Employees:* 9
Net Worth: £1,090,958 *Total Assets:* £16,517,509
Registered Office: Amba House, 15 College Road, Harrow, Middlesex, HA1 1BA
Activities: Renting and leasing of office machinery and equipment (including computers)
Major Shareholder: Ratankumar Daryani
Officers: John Nicholson, Secretary; Ratankumar Daryani [1960] Director; Michael David Friend [1958] Director

Rivers Leasing PLC
Incorporated: 14 September 2010 *Employees:* 9
Previous: Rivers Leasing Limited
Net Worth: £453,160 *Total Assets:* £16,499,837
Registered Office: Amba House, 15 College Road, Harrow, Middlesex, HA1 1BA
Activities: Renting and leasing of office machinery and equipment (including computers)
Major Shareholder: Ratankumar Daryani
Officers: John Roger Nicholson, Secretary; Stephen Charles Bassett [1953] Director; Ratankumar Daryani [1960] Director; Michael David Friend [1958] Director

Riverside Bio Limited
Incorporated: 14 June 2012 *Employees:* 18
Net Worth: £601,040 *Total Assets:* £8,039,764
Registered Office: 10 Osier Way, Mitcham, Surrey, CR4 4NF
Activities: Other food services
Parent: Bio Collectors Holdings Ltd
Officers: Paul Killoughery, Secretary; Paul Killoughery [1963] Director/Accountant

Riverstone Europe LLP
Incorporated: 30 April 2007 *Employees:* 14
Net Worth: £8,098,227 *Total Assets:* £9,803,717
Registered Office: 5 Elstree Gate, Elstree Way, Borehamwood, Herts, WD6 1JD
Officers: Robin Joseph Alexander Duggan [1966] LLP Member; Christopher Barton Hunt [1963] LLP Member

Riverstone Pictures (CMP) Limited
Incorporated: 25 April 2017
Net Worth: £128 *Total Assets:* £5,352,066
Registered Office: 99 Kenton Road, Harrow, Middlesex, HA3 0AN
Activities: Motion picture production activities
Parent: Riverstone Pictures Limited
Officers: Nicholas Anthony Crosfield Bower [1975] Director/Film Producer; Deepak Nayar [1959] Director/Film Producer [American]

Riverstone Pictures (Show Dogs) Limited
Incorporated: 19 May 2016
Net Worth: £87 *Total Assets:* £19,864,386
Registered Office: 99 Kenton Road, Harrow, Middlesex, HA3 0AN
Activities: Motion picture production activities
Parent: Riverstone Pictures Limited
Officers: Nicholas Anthony Crosfield Bower [1975] Director/Film Producer; Deepak Nayar [1959] Director/Film Producer [American]

Riverstone Solutions 2 Limited
Incorporated: 5 May 2016
Net Worth: £636 *Total Assets:* £14,035,968
Registered Office: 99 Kenton Road, Harrow, Middlesex, HA3 0AN
Activities: Motion picture production activities
Parent: Riverstone Pictures Limited
Officers: Nicholas Anthony Crosfield Bower [1975] Director/Film Producer; Deepak Nayar [1959] Director/Film Producer [American]

Riverstore Limited
Incorporated: 27 September 2005
Net Worth: £2,510,305 *Total Assets:* £6,237,838
Registered Office: Phoenix Wharf, Eel Pie Island, Twickenham, Middlesex, TW1 3DY
Activities: Development of building projects
Major Shareholder: Henry William Cope Harrison
Officers: Kim James Hawkins, Secretary/Chartered Surveyor; Henry William Cope Harrison [1950] Director/Architect; Kim James Hawkins [1962] Director/Chartered Surveyor

Riverway Investments Limited
Incorporated: 8 April 2014 *Employees:* 160
Net Worth: £7,929,581 *Total Assets:* £11,138,222
Registered Office: Haslers, Old Station Road, Loughton, Essex, IG10 4PL
Activities: Other letting and operating of own or leased real estate
Parent: Riverway Investments Holdings Limited
Officers: Jon Warren Crosby, Secretary; Jon Warren Crosby [1978] Director; Stephen Douglas Crosby [1974] Director; Stephen Clive Crosby [1950] Director

RKPE Limited
Incorporated: 16 December 2014
Net Worth Deficit: £870,013 *Total Assets:* £6,804,483
Registered Office: Salisbury House, 20 Queens Road, Weybridge, Surrey, KT13 9XE
Activities: Development of building projects
Shareholders: Portchester Estates Limited; Richard Koch
Officers: Paul David Anthony Schiavo [1975] Director

RL Retail Services Limited
Incorporated: 23 December 1999 *Employees:* 1,748
Net Worth: £15,512,272 *Total Assets:* £27,429,290
Registered Office: 46 Clarendon Road, Watford, Herts, WD17 1HE
Activities: Other business support service activities n.e.c.
Parent: Ralph Lauren Corporation
Officers: Aldo Alex Fleri [1961] Director/Vice President Sales UK; Carmel Ann Pedatella [1974] Director/Business Executive [American]; Robert Patrick Ranftl [1971] Director/Business Executive [American]; Andrew Howard Smith [1971] Director/Business Executive

RO Enterprises Limited
Incorporated: 4 April 2003
Net Worth: £7,966,160 *Total Assets:* £7,966,160
Registered Office: Graham House, 7 Wyllyotts Place, Potters Bar, Herts, EN6 2JD
Activities: Non-trading company
Parent: RO Financing Company Limited
Officers: Edward Thomas Morton Rowlandson [1974] Director; Richard Graham St John Rowlandson [1939] Director/Chartered Accountant

RO Financing Company Limited
Incorporated: 11 February 2011
Net Worth: £46,587,744 *Total Assets:* £46,587,744
Registered Office: Graham House, 7 Wyllyotts Place, Potters Bar, Herts, EN6 2JD
Activities: Non-trading company
Parent: RO Trading Limited
Officers: Edward Thomas Morton Rowlandson [1974] Director

RO Properties Limited
Incorporated: 11 October 2004 *Employees:* 4
Net Worth Deficit: £14,342,000 *Total Assets:* £38,183,000
Registered Office: Graham House, 7 Wyllyotts Place, Potters Bar, Herts, EN6 2JD
Activities: Activities of other holding companies n.e.c.
Shareholders: Richard Graham St John Rowlandson; Edward Thomas Morton Rowlandson; Richard Woodman-Bailey
Officers: David Colin Roberts [1962] Director/Solicitor; Edward Thomas Morton Rowlandson [1974] Director; Richard Graham St John Rowlandson [1939] Director/Chartered Accountant; Richard Woodman-Bailey [1950] Director

RO Property Management Limited
Incorporated: 8 September 1966 *Employees:* 8
Net Worth: £9,884,277 *Total Assets:* £59,752,972
Registered Office: Graham House, 7 Wyllyotts Place, Potters Bar, Herts, EN6 2JD
Activities: Development of building projects
Parent: RO Trading Limited
Officers: Edward Thomas Morton Rowlandson [1974] Director; Richard Graham St John Rowlandson [1939] Director/Chartered Accountant

RO Regional Properties Limited
Incorporated: 5 March 2002
Net Worth: £6,268,940 *Total Assets:* £21,486,416
Registered Office: Graham House, 7 Wyllyotts Place, Potters Bar, Herts, EN6 2JD
Activities: Development of building projects
Parent: RO Properties Limited
Officers: Edward Thomas Morton Rowlandson [1974] Director; Richard Graham St John Rowlandson [1939] Director

RO Trading Limited
Incorporated: 19 November 2004 *Employees:* 61
Net Worth: £84,494,000 *Total Assets:* £111,794,000
Registered Office: Graham House, 7 Wyllyotts Place, Potters Bar, Herts, EN6 2JD
Activities: Activities of other holding companies n.e.c.
Shareholders: Richard Graham St John Rowlandson; Edward Thomas Morton Rowlandson; Richard Woodman-Bailey
Officers: David Colin Roberts [1962] Director/Solicitor; Edward Thomas Morton Rowlandson [1974] Director; Richard Graham St John Rowlandson [1939] Director/Chartered Accountant; Richard Woodman-Bailey [1950] Director

Road Tech Computer Systems Limited
Incorporated: 7 May 1986 *Employees:* 64
Net Worth: £5,145,236 *Total Assets:* £8,350,735
Registered Office: First Floor, Radius House, 51 Clarendon Road, Watford, Herts, WD17 1HP
Activities: Other software publishing
Parent: Road Tech Holdings Limited
Officers: Bernadette Beevor, Secretary; Adrian Paul Barrett [1965] Director; Bernadette Beevor [1958] Director; Derek Anthony Beevor [1955] Director; Benjamin Samuel Clewett [1971] Director; Daren Anthony Cole [1967] Director; Diane Alice Dooling [1964] Director; Tony Paul Jeffree [1982] Director; Philip David Thornhill [1982] Director

Road Tech Holdings Limited
Incorporated: 23 February 2016 *Employees:* 64
Net Worth: £5,145,236 *Total Assets:* £8,350,735
Registered Office: c/o Hillier Hopkins LLP, First Floor, Radius House, 51 Clarendon Road, Watford, Herts, WD17 1HP
Activities: Activities of other holding companies n.e.c.
Major Shareholder: Derek Anthony Beevor
Officers: Adrian Paul Barrett [1965] Director; Bernadette Beevor [1958] Director; Derek Anthony Beevor [1955] Director; Benjamin Samuel Clewett [1971] Director; Daren Anthony Cole [1967] Director; Diane Alice Dooling [1964] Director; Tony Paul Jeffree [1982] Director; Philip David Thornhill [1982] Director

Roadhouse Building & Civil Engineering Ltd.
Incorporated: 12 July 2011 *Employees:* 16
Net Worth: £1,879,484 *Total Assets:* £6,748,109
Registered Office: 3 Enterprise House, 8 Essex Road, Dartford, Kent, DA1 2AU
Activities: Other specialised construction activities n.e.c.
Shareholders: Samantha Buggy; David George Light
Officers: Samantha Buggy [1980] Director/Service Consultant; David George Light [1974] Director/Manager

Roalco Limited
Incorporated: 6 September 1977 *Employees:* 176
Net Worth: £1,682,748 *Total Assets:* £6,370,382
Registered Office: Turnbull House, 226 Mulgrave Road, Cheam, Surrey, SM2 6JT
Activities: Other building completion and finishing
Shareholders: Adrian Barry Cook; Alan Roy Potter
Officers: Adrian Barry Cook, Secretary; Adrian Barry Cook [1948] Director; Alan Roy Potter [1950] Director

Roamquest Limited
Incorporated: 29 July 1997
Net Worth: £1,446,572 *Total Assets:* £7,386,239
Registered Office: 3rd Floor, Sterling House, Langston Road, Loughton, Essex, IG10 3TS
Activities: Development of building projects
Parent: Galliard Holdings Limited
Officers: Allan William Porter, Secretary; David Edward Conway [1976] Director; Michael William Watson [1952] Architectural Director

William Robinson Gravetye Charity
Incorporated: 14 April 2009
Net Worth: £9,757,733 *Total Assets:* £9,904,080
Registered Office: 1st Floor, 168 High Street, Watford, Herts, WD17 2EG
Activities: Other letting and operating of own or leased real estate
Officers: Sheila Ann Taylor, Secretary; Dr Mary Margaret Barkham [1961] Director/Environmental Research Consultant; Karen Lesley Dukes [1963] Director/Chartered Accountant; Andrew John Martin [1946] Director/FRICS; Michael Harry Walker Neal [1956] Director/Land and Property Consultant; Gillian Hazel Sandham [1947] Director; Sir Henry William Studholme [1958] Director/Forest Manager/Chartered Accountant

Robinson Webster (Holdings) Limited
Incorporated: 4 September 1972 *Employees:* 1,067
Net Worth: £9,573,000 *Total Assets:* £48,406,000
Registered Office: 159 Mortlake Road, Richmond, Surrey, TW9 4AW
Activities: Retail sale of clothing in specialised stores
Shareholders: Best Dressed Group Limited; Robinson Property Company Limited
Officers: Rebecca Sheila Paul, Secretary; Belle Robinson [1964] Director; Kieron Bartholemew Traynor [1960] Director

Robore Cuts Limited
Incorporated: 28 July 1992 *Employees:* 78
Net Worth: £4,828,286 *Total Assets:* £7,629,258
Registered Office: Unit 16 Mitcham Industrial Estate, Streatham Road, Mitcham, Surrey, CR4 2AP
Activities: Other specialised construction activities n.e.c.
Major Shareholder: David Rickus
Officers: Paul Ernest Nattrass, Secretary; David Rickus [1971] Director/Contracts Manager

Rocco Homes Limited
Incorporated: 29 August 2007
Net Worth: £17,659,332 *Total Assets:* £44,745,772
Registered Office: 2nd Floor, 45-47 High Street, Cobham, Surrey, KT11 3DP
Activities: Other business support service activities n.e.c.
Shareholders: Georgina Clarke; Rupert Clarke
Officers: Georgina Clarke, Secretary; Georgina Clarke [1968] Director; Rupert Clarke [1969] Director/Property Developer

Rock & Alluvium Limited
Incorporated: 28 February 1984 *Employees:* 70
Net Worth: £7,357,000 *Total Assets:* £12,198,000
Registered Office: Cowley Business Park, Cowley, Uxbridge, Middlesex, UB8 2AL
Activities: Other specialised construction activities n.e.c.
Parent: Galliford Try Construction & Investments Holdings Limited
Officers: Darren Martin Brockett [1970] Director; Martin Cooper [1971] Director/Chartered Accountant; Bill Hocking [1963] Director

Rocket Medical Group PLC
Incorporated: 2 February 2016 *Employees:* 162
Net Worth: £11,480,740 *Total Assets:* £13,290,275
Registered Office: Bermer House, Imperial Way, Watford, Herts, WD24 4XX
Activities: Activities of head offices
Officers: Jeffrey Donald Jackson, Secretary; Robert Lee Bernberg [1960] Director; Jeffrey Donald Jackson [1962] Finance Director

Rocket Medical PLC
Incorporated: 11 November 1996 *Employees:* 154
Net Worth: £11,593,395 *Total Assets:* £13,167,504
Registered Office: Bermer House, Imperial Way, Watford, Herts, WD24 4XX
Activities: Manufacture of medical and dental instruments and supplies
Officers: Jeffrey Donald Jackson, Secretary; Robert Lee Bernberg [1960] Director; Stuart Hastings [1957] Marketing Director; Jeffrey Donald Jackson [1962] Finance Director; Leslie John Todd [1962] Operations Director

Rockley Dene Homes Limited
Incorporated: 11 March 1987 *Employees:* 302
Net Worth: £53,177,544 *Total Assets:* £88,143,448
Registered Office: 36 Railway Approach, Harrow, Middlesex, HA3 5AA
Activities: Residential nursing care facilities
Parent: TLC Group Limited
Officers: Gagan Puri, Secretary; William Charles Neal [1986] Director; Paavan Popat [1985] Managing Director; Honourable Shivaan Shillin Popat [1988] Director; Gagan Puri [1978] Finance Director

Leslie Rogers Investments Limited
Incorporated: 20 February 1962 *Employees:* 4
Net Worth: £5,191,335 *Total Assets:* £7,049,526
Registered Office: 2nd Floor, Unicorn House, Station Close, Potters Bar, Herts, EN6 1TL
Activities: Development of building projects
Shareholders: Jennifer Olivia Thomas; Samantha Emma Thomas
Officers: Margaret Mary Thomas, Secretary; Oliver William Haines [1941] Director; Margaret Mary Thomas [1951] Director

Rokeby Educational Trust Limited
Incorporated: 25 February 1966 *Employees:* 91
Net Worth: £7,769,940 *Total Assets:* £9,714,597
Registered Office: Coombe Croft, George Road, Kingston on Thames, Surrey, KT2 7PB
Activities: Primary education
Officers: Maureen Elizabeth Adams, Secretary; Ishminder Singh Alg [1979] Director/Chartered Accountant; Bernard Anthony Brenninkmeijer [1968] Director/Investor [Dutch]; Deirdre Anne Davidson [1975] Director/Writer [Irish]; Annabel Henriette Evans-Tovey [1965] Director/Barrister; Dominic Peter FitzGenerald [1974] Director/Deputy Headteacher; Sebastian Henkes [1971] Director/Consultant; Dr Andrew James Mayfield [1964] Director/Teacher; Caroline Norah Newsholme [1967] Director/Solicitor; Janice Lynn Price [1965] Director/Magistrate; James Courtney Thompson [1973] Director/Headmaster

Rollover Limited
Incorporated: 1 May 1991 *Employees:* 44
Net Worth: £12,955,567 *Total Assets:* £28,591,152
Registered Office: Thorpe Lea Manor, Thorpe Lea Road, Egham, Surrey, TW20 8HY
Activities: Other food services
Parent: Rollover Group Limited
Officers: Ronan Deasy, Secretary; Ronan Deasy [1964] Director/Accountant [Irish]; Trevor James Horan [1972] EMEA Country Compliance Director [Irish]; Marguerite Larkin [1971] Director/Chief Financial Officer [Irish]

Roman Investments Limited
Incorporated: 6 June 1989
Net Worth: £8,523,546 *Total Assets:* £17,029,512
Registered Office: Lynwood House, 373-375 Station Road, Harrow, Middlesex, HA1 2AW
Activities: Development of building projects
Major Shareholder: David Jonathan Rosenberg
Officers: David Jonathan Rosenberg [1956] Director/Businessman

Romans International Limited
Incorporated: 13 April 1994 *Employees:* 17
Net Worth: £6,314,331 *Total Assets:* £18,446,572
Registered Office: 103-105 Brighton Road, Coulsdon, Surrey, CR5 2NG
Activities: Sale of used cars and light motor vehicles
Major Shareholder: Paul Alexander Jaconelli
Officers: Paul Alexander Jaconelli [1949] Director/Car Dealer; Tom Jaconelli [1985] Director

Rooff Group Limited (The)
Incorporated: 20 April 1929
Net Worth: £6,997,003 *Total Assets:* £8,047,577
Registered Office: The Granary, 80 Abbey Road, Barking, Essex, IG11 7BT
Activities: Activities of head offices
Parent: Rooff Holdings Limited
Officers: John Anthony Pearson, Secretary; Alan Alfred Horn [1929] Director; Mark Patrick Seebold Horn [1967] Director/Builder; John Anthony Pearson [1954] Finance Director

Rooff Holdings Limited
Incorporated: 2 December 1998 *Employees:* 77
Net Worth: £17,688,318 *Total Assets:* £26,304,592
Registered Office: The Granary, 80 Abbey Road, Barking, Essex, IG11 7BT
Activities: Activities of head offices
Officers: John Anthony Pearson, Secretary; Alan Alfred Horn [1929] Director; Mark Patrick Seebold Horn [1967] Director/Builder; John Anthony Pearson [1954] Finance Director

Rooff Ltd
Incorporated: 20 July 1976 *Employees:* 12
Net Worth: £4,362,061 *Total Assets:* £12,547,066
Registered Office: The Granary, 80 Abbey Road, Barking, Essex, IG11 7BT
Activities: Construction of commercial buildings
Parent: The Rooff Group Limited
Officers: John Anthony Pearson, Secretary; Stephen John Drury [1965] Director/Building & Development; Ghanshyam Hirani [1982] Operations Director; Alan Alfred Horn [1929] Director; Mark Patrick Seebold Horn [1967] Director/Builder; Ronald Nicholls [1959] Commercial Director; Antony Charles Pearce [1963] Construction Director; John Anthony Pearson [1954] Finance Director

Rooff Property LLP
Incorporated: 8 September 2006
Net Worth: £11,513,261 *Total Assets:* £11,712,768
Registered Office: The Granary, 80 Abbey Road, Barking, Essex, IG11 7BT
Officers: Alan Alfred Horn [1929] Member; Mark Patrick Seebold Horn [1967] Member

Roomes Stores,Limited
Incorporated: 13 June 1927 *Employees:* 55
Net Worth: £5,807,538 *Total Assets:* £8,997,605
Registered Office: 22-24 Station Road, Upminster, Essex, RM14 2UB
Activities: Other retail sale in non-specialised stores
Officers: Margaret Generaldine Roome [1927] Director; Michael David Roome [1961] Managing Director; Stephen John Roome [1954] Director

Roos Energy Limited
Incorporated: 17 May 2011
Net Worth Deficit: £2,740,000 *Total Assets:* £33,296,000
Registered Office: Beaufort Court, Egg Farm Lane, Kings Langley, Herts, WD4 8LR
Activities: Production of electricity
Parent: Trafalgar Wind Holdings Limited
Officers: Dominic James Hearth, Secretary; Steven William Hughes [1972] Generation & Asset Management Director; Fraser Stephen Merry [1968] Director/Chartered Surveyor; Mitesh Raj Patel [1982] Director/Group Financial Controller

Rooted Architecture Limited
Incorporated: 5 March 2010 *Employees:* 3
Net Worth Deficit: £48,369 *Total Assets:* £7,430,538
Registered Office: Belgrave House, 39-43 Monument Hill, Weybridge, Surrey, KT13 8RN
Activities: Architectural activities
Shareholders: Lai Chun Clatter Lauener; Jeremy Andrew Scott; Tonja Sabina Scott
Officers: Lai Chun Clatter Lauener [1953] Director/General Manager [Swiss]; Jeremy Andrew Scott [1978] Director/Architect; Tonja Sabina Scott [1977] Director/Architect [Swiss]

Rose Bruford College of Theatre and Performance
Incorporated: 7 June 1952 *Employees:* 80
Previous: Rose Bruford College of Theatre and Performance Ltd.
Net Worth: £7,447,000 *Total Assets:* £10,742,000
Registered Office: Lamorbey Park, Sidcup, Kent, DA15 9DF
Activities: First-degree level higher education
Officers: Ruth Bourne, Secretary; Helen Bowles [1949] Director/Retired; Roderick Brown [1951] Director/Retired Solicitor; Colin Edward Campbell [1946] Director/Self Employed; Paul Bertram Dale [1947] Director/Retired; George Hodge Littlejohn [1952] Director/Chartered Accountant; Hassan Nigel Mahamdallie [1961] Director/Self Employed; Don Frank Massey [1957] Director and Local Councillor; Mike John McCart [1948] Director South Bank; Samantha Kirsty Perez-Lumbreras [1984] Director/Outreach Manager; Professor Michael Paul Saks [1952] Director/University Professor; Monisha Amrit Shah [1969] Non-Executive Board Director - Various; Jennifer Margaret Sims [1950] Director/Retired College Principal; Kathryn Southworth [1952] Director/Semi-Retired Academic, PT Reviewer QAA; Cara Jayne Turtington [1977] Director/Chartered Accountant; Kevin Gerard Wallace [1957] Director/Theatre Producer [Irish]; Thomas James Michael Wilson [1977] Programme Director

Rose Film Partnership LLP
Incorporated: 20 April 2007
Net Worth: £16,761,960 *Total Assets:* £16,761,960
Registered Office: 99 Kenton Road, Harrow, Middlesex, HA3 0AN
Officers: David James Lyndsey Harper [1980] Member; Peter Daniel Arduino [1968] LLP Member; Richard Bernard Charles [1954] LLP Member; Sean Devine [1963] LLP Member; Leslie Gough [1950] LLP Member; Allan Watson Graham [1960] LLP Member; Colin Steuart Grassie [1961] LLP Member; Timothy Charles Robert Henderson [1961] LLP Member; George Heydon [1961] LLP Member; Jamie Hutchin [1975] LLP Member; Jonathan Richard Jeff [1974] LLP Member; Ajitsinh Moahnsinh Kara [1967] LLP Member; Nigel Lindsay Kennedy [1955] LLP Member; John Joseph King [1963] LLP Member; Michael James King [1956] LLP Member; Ian Alexander MacDonald [1939] LLP Member; Calum Neil Forbes MacInnes [1961] LLP Member; Guy Kenneth Peter Marshall [1965] LLP Member; Tom Foulery McGrath [1968] LLP Member; Julian Ralph Stewart Newiss [1953] LLP Member; Adrian Kim Parker [1960] LLP Member; Dr Duncan Fraser Ralston [1962] LLP Member; Alexander George Malcolm Ritchie [1954] LLP Member; Paul Howard Ross [1966] LLP Member; Michael Leslie Says [1960] LLP Member; James Richard Scott [1975] LLP Member; Mark Andrew Wallace [1959] LLP Member; Guy Ian Swinburn Wilson [1972] LLP Member; Christopher Alan Wimhurst [1951] LLP Member

Roseberry Property Development Company Limited
Incorporated: 12 April 1985 *Employees:* 3
Net Worth: £5,006,367 *Total Assets:* £5,134,838
Registered Office: 21 Lodge Lane, Grays, Essex, RM17 5RY
Activities: Development of building projects
Shareholders: Donald Matthew Baker; Sally Juliet Butler
Officers: Candy Suzanne Baker [1957] Director; Donald Matthew Baker [1953] Director/Chartered Accountant; David Lander [1945] Director/Licensed Conveyancer

Rosebery House Developments Limited
Incorporated: 20 May 2016
Net Worth Deficit: £505,321 *Total Assets:* £8,897,434
Registered Office: 3rd Floor, Sterling House, Langston Road, Loughton, Essex, IG10 3TS
Activities: Development of building projects
Parent: Galliard Holdings Limited
Officers: Allan William Porter, Secretary; Stephen Stuart Solomon Conway [1948] Director; Donagh O'Sullivan [1968] Director [Irish]

The Rosedale Hewens Academy Trust
Incorporated: 27 June 2011 *Employees:* 235
Net Worth: £86,428,000 *Total Assets:* £88,925,000
Registered Office: Wood End Green Road, Hayes, Middlesex, UB3 2SE
Activities: Pre-primary education
Officers: Susan Galloway, Secretary; Marie Diane Ashley [1964] Director/Service Manager; Anthony Laurence Cohen [1957] Director/Electrical Engineer; Norman Leslie Deas [1946] Director/Catering Consultant; Sarah Morgan Driscoll [1979] Director/Chief Operating Officer; Stewart John Michie Duguid [1967] Director/ICT Manager; Jane Mary Ellis [1959] Director/Executive Headteacher; Heidi Paula Faure [1975] Director/Executive Principal; Clive Ian Neathey [1955] Director/Executive Principal; Ian O'Connor [1979] Director/Principal; Devard Darien Russell-Jones [1984] Director/Service Manager [Jamaican]

Roseland Parc Limited
Incorporated: 27 August 2003 *Employees:* 5
Net Worth: £3,764,601 *Total Assets:* £9,044,142
Registered Office: 1st Floor, Brunswick House, Regent Park, 297-299 Kingston Road, Leatherhead, Surrey, KT22 7LU
Activities: Development of building projects
Parent: Roseland Village Limited
Officers: Sally Irene Rees, Secretary; Sarah Denise Burgess [1971] Director; William Edwin John Crawford [1970] Director/Development; Neil Donaldson [1966] Director/Accountant; Andrew George Esmond Ovey [1971] Director/Investment Manager

Rosemead Limited
Incorporated: 11 August 2003
Net Worth: £804,302 *Total Assets:* £6,974,386
Registered Office: 65 Westbury Road, Northwood, Middlesex, HA6 3DA
Activities: Dispensing chemist in specialised stores
Shareholders: Dinesh Ramji Ganatra; Dineshkumar Ramji Ganatra
Officers: Nutanbala Dhirajlal Sakaria, Secretary; Jayshree Indravadan Suchak, Secretary; Dineshkumar Ramji Ganatra [1956] Director/Pharmacist

Roseplot Properties Limited
Incorporated: 7 July 2000
Net Worth: £5,241,088 *Total Assets:* £5,241,738
Registered Office: Hill House, Lowlands Road, Harrow, Middlesex, HA1 3EQ
Activities: Development of building projects
Major Shareholder: Donovan Gijsbertus Wijsmuller
Officers: Brian Martin Comer [1960] Director [Irish]; Luke Andrew Comer [1957] Director [Irish]

Rosetree Finance Limited
Incorporated: 11 December 2002 *Employees:* 12
Net Worth: £7,035,834 *Total Assets:* £10,056,309
Registered Office: Russell House, 140 High Street, Edgware, Middlesex, HA8 7LW
Activities: Financial intermediation not elsewhere classified
Shareholders: Richard Alan Ross; Clive Melvyn Winkler
Officers: Lee Robert Mesnick [1968] Director/Accountant; Richard Alan Ross [1942] Director

Rosetta Investments Limited
Incorporated: 22 February 2012
Net Worth: £1,512,322 *Total Assets:* £6,734,044
Registered Office: Queens Court, 9-17 Eastern Road, Romford, Essex, RM1 3NH
Activities: Other letting and operating of own or leased real estate
Officers: Shahzad Asif Mahmood [1977] Director/Consultant; Sergio Ferreira Ramos [1976] Director/Consultant [South African]

Roseview (London) Ltd.
Incorporated: 23 June 2010
Net Worth: £1,511,167 *Total Assets:* £7,704,758
Registered Office: 249 Cranbrook Road, Ilford, Essex, IG1 4TG
Activities: Other business support service activities n.e.c.
Shareholder: Garry Jon Simpson
Officers: Garry Jon Simpson [1967] Director

Rosewell Properties Limited
Incorporated: 16 September 1994 *Employees:* 5
Net Worth: £2,711,868 *Total Assets:* £5,194,984
Registered Office: 78 The Drive, Morden, Surrey, SM4 6DP
Activities: Buying and selling of own real estate
Shareholder: Steven Henry Sidwell
Officers: Henry George Sidwell, Secretary; Henry George Sidwell [1949] Director; Paul Sidwell [1976] Director/Property Developer; Rosabel Ogilvie Downie Sidwell [1947] Director; Steven Henry Sidwell [1974] Director/Property Developer

Rowhurst Limited
Incorporated: 1 June 1987
Net Worth: £5,135,245 *Total Assets:* £7,196,458
Registered Office: 41 Walsingham Road, Enfield, Middlesex, EN2 6EY
Activities: Buying and selling of own real estate
Major Shareholder: Aubrey Weis
Officers: Rachel Weis, Secretary; Rachel Weis [1952] Director/Secretary; Sir Weis [1981] Director; Clifford Donald Wing [1960] Director

Rowlands 2014 Limited
Incorporated: 22 August 2014 *Employees:* 61
Net Worth: £15,997,321 *Total Assets:* £22,445,204
Registered Office: 101 Rowlands Avenue, Hatch End, Pinner, Middlesex, HA5 4AW
Activities: Activities of other holding companies n.e.c.
Major Shareholder: Michael O'Hara
Officers: Colin Hambling, Secretary; Michael O'Hara [1947] Director [Irish]

Rowlandson Investments Limited
Incorporated: 3 November 1961 *Employees:* 7
Net Worth Deficit: £10,899,915 *Total Assets:* £25,810,204
Registered Office: Graham House, 7 Wyllyotts Place, Potters Bar, Herts, EN6 2JD
Activities: Financial intermediation not elsewhere classified
Parent: RO Group Property Ventures Limited
Officers: Edward Thomas Morton Rowlandson [1974] Director; Richard Graham St John Rowlandson [1939] Director/Chartered Accountant

Mary Roxburghe Trust
Incorporated: 25 September 2015 *Employees:* 2
Net Worth: £13,261,608 *Total Assets:* £13,446,895
Registered Office: West Horsley Place, Epsom Road, West Horsley, Leatherhead, Surrey, KT24 6AN
Activities: Activities of other membership organisations n.e.c.
Officers: Arthur Bamber Gascoigne [1935] Director/Historian; Angela Mary Kidner [1948] Director/Designer; Adrian James Lajtha [1957] Director/Company Administration; Giles Alexander MacKenzie Reid [1975] Commercial Director; Patrick Temple Roberts [1957] Director/Bursar; John Nicol Simpson [1947] Director

Royal British Legion Poppy Factory Limited (The)
Incorporated: 11 March 1925 *Employees:* 66
Net Worth: £25,792,162 *Total Assets:* £29,247,398
Registered Office: 20 Petersham Road, Richmond, Surrey, TW10 6UR
Activities: Other manufacturing n.e.c.
Officers: William Robert Kay, Secretary; Michael Francis Bustard [1946] Director/Part Time Training Consultant; Clifford Roderick Stanton Dare [1967] Director/Chartered Surveyor; Peter Richard Gill [1955] Director/Retired; Dr Sridevi Kalidindi [1971] Director/Doctor; Alistair James Kett [1971] Director/Management Consultant; Steven Colin Monger-Godfrey [1952] Director/Chartered Surveyor; Andrew Richard Dawren Sharpe [1960] Director/Army Officer; Simon Anthony Taylor [1962] Director/Chartered Surveyor; Andrew John Truscott [1973] Director/Investment Banker; Andrew Ian Fergusson Wishart [1964] Director; Julius Peregrine Harold Shepherd Wolff-Ingham [1963] Director/Charity Executive

Royal Docks Property LLP
Incorporated: 20 October 2016 *Employees:* 27
Net Worth: £49,646,900 *Total Assets:* £71,380,480
Registered Office: Apirose House, 48a High Street, Edgware, Middlesex, HA8 7EQ
Officers: Manish Mansukhlal Gudka [1970] Member; Gareth Jones [1973] Member; Suraj Rashmikant Rashmikant [1982] LLP Member

The Royal Masonic School for Girls
Incorporated: 22 November 1977 *Employees:* 285
Net Worth: £3,050,685 *Total Assets:* £7,480,872
Registered Office: P O Box 356, Rickmansworth Park, Rickmansworth, Herts, WD3 4HF
Activities: General secondary education
Officers: Diana Elizabeth Deborah Robinson, Secretary; Sean Christopher Brew [1967] Director/Surveyor; John Brewer [1961] Director/Professor of Sport Science; Peta Ruth Alexandra Dyke [1955] Director/Headteacher; David Richard Ellis [1955] Director/Civil Servant; Herbert Keith Emmerson [1939] Director/Retired Police Officer; James William Flecker [1939] Director/Retired; Abigail Chloe Gray [1977] Director/Senior Logistics Manager; Christopher Michael Hayward [1959] Politician and Director; Jonathan Gary Knopp [1944] Director/Retired; Tessa Anne Louise Lemon [1960] Director/H.R. Consultant; Fiona Kirsty Richards [1973] Managing Director; Nicholas Sidney Springer [1948] Director/Consultant; Simon Anthony Staite [1956] Director/Solicitor; Andrew George Wauchope [1962] Director/Investment Manager

The Royal Medical Foundation
Incorporated: 8 June 2000
Net Worth: £7,683,106 *Total Assets:* £7,692,744
Registered Office: Epsom College, College Road, Epsom, Surrey, KT17 4JQ
Activities: Other social work activities without accommodation n.e.c.
Officers: Christopher John Powis Titman, Secretary; Dr Helena Blake [1952] Director/Consultant Radiologist [Irish]; Dr Jeremy Shaw Bolton [1943] Director/Retired; Doctor Hywel Henry Bowen Perkins [1952] Director/GP; Richard Henderson Bruce [1952] Director/Barrister; Andrew John Pianca [1951] Director/Accountant; Karen Elizabeth Thomas [1958] Director/Orthopaedic Surgeon; Dr Alastair James Wells [1960] Director/Doctor; Mark MacGregor Williamson [1972] Director/Solicitor

Royal School of Needlework (The)
Incorporated: 16 April 1878 *Employees:* 24
Net Worth: £5,088,599 *Total Assets:* £5,531,215
Registered Office: Apartment 12a, Hampton Court Palace, East Molesey, Surrey, KT8 9AU
Activities: First-degree level higher education
Officers: Susan Margaret Kay-Williams, Secretary; Elizabeth Ann Braakenburg Dyce [1970] Director/Solicitor; Nicola Ashley Clarke [1959] Director/Retired; Caroline Claire de Guitaut [1969] Director/Curator; Morgan Hixon Seidler Fowles [1981] Director; Samantha Jane Hoe-Richardson [1971] Director/Head of Environment; Deborah Lamb [1962] Director; Prof. John Richard Miles [1944] Director/Designer/Professor; Andrew William Palmer [1953] Director/Accountant; Sharan Janet Elizabeth Wicks [1965] Director/Project Manager; Stephanie Jane Wright [1954] Director/Chartered Accountant

RPSD2 Limited
Incorporated: 12 August 2016
Net Worth: £102 *Total Assets:* £15,011,804
Registered Office: 99 Kenton Road, Harrow, Middlesex, HA3 0AN
Activities: Motion picture production activities
Parent: Riverstone Pictures Limited
Officers: Nicholas Anthony Crosfield Bower [1975] Director/Film Producer; Deepak Nayar [1959] Director/Film Producer [American]

RR Securities Limited
Incorporated: 9 April 2009 *Employees:* 4
Net Worth Deficit: £7,088 *Total Assets:* £7,951,924
Registered Office: Ormonde House, 2 High Street, Epsom, Surrey, KT19 8AD
Activities: Credit granting by non-deposit taking finance houses and other specialist consumer credit grantors
Shareholders: William Robert Ruffler; Myra Margaretha Veronica Ruffler
Officers: Fiona Emily Page, Secretary; Myra Margaretha Veronica Ruffler [1947] Director [Dutch]; William Robert Ruffler [1944] Director

RSA Island Village Limited
Incorporated: 20 March 1997 *Employees:* 3
Net Worth: £6,932,279 *Total Assets:* £9,314,666
Registered Office: 12 Island Centre Way, Enfield, Middlesex, EN3 6GS
Activities: Other service activities n.e.c.
Officers: Alan Charles Ray, Secretary; Martin Frank Jewell [1944] Director/Planning Consultant; Michael Anthony Polledri [1945] Director/Chartered Accountant; Robert Michael Taylor [1942] Director; Gary John Walker [1948] Director; Roger Philip Weeks [1961] Director/Retired; Michael Frederick Wehrmann [1947] Director/Business Consultant

RSD Travel Limited
Incorporated: 27 January 2011 *Employees:* 16
Net Worth: £1,973,623 *Total Assets:* £7,793,221
Registered Office: Chase Green House, 42 Chase Side, Enfield, Middlesex, EN2 6NF
Activities: Travel agency activities
Major Shareholder: Christian Gunter Funk
Officers: Katherine Anne Castleman, Secretary; Katherine Anne Castleman [1971] Director/Tour Operator; Dr Andreas Zangemeister [1968] Director/Entrepreneur [German]; Horst Johann Zsifkovits [1961] Managing Director [Austrian]

RSI Retail Solutions Limited
Incorporated: 17 August 2011 *Employees:* 40
Net Worth Deficit: £795,927 *Total Assets:* £5,200,737
Registered Office: 27 Great West Road, Brentford, Middlesex, TW8 9BW
Activities: Activities of head offices
Officers: Albert Edward Clement [1962] Director [American]; John Laurence Neale [1970] Director [Australian]

Ruby Topco Limited
Incorporated: 12 June 2014
Net Worth Deficit: £419,000 *Total Assets:* £145,100,000
Registered Office: Unit 6 & 7 Princeton Mews, 167-169 London Road, Kingston upon Thames, Surrey, KT2 6PT
Activities: Residential care activities for learning difficulties, mental health and substance abuse
Parent: The Regard (Group) Bidco Limited
Officers: Garry John Fitton, Secretary; Garry John Fitton [1972] Finance Director; Nicola Rosemary Lucy Hopkins [1968] Director/Chartered Accountant; Peter Kinsey [1964] Director

Rubylake Investments Limited
Incorporated: 7 June 2005
Net Worth: £2,300,539 *Total Assets:* £7,247,955
Registered Office: 19-20 Bourne Court, Southend Road, Woodford Green, Essex, IG8 8HD
Activities: Development of building projects
Parent: Alto Property Investments Limited
Officers: Abraham Rosenberg, Secretary/Director; Abraham Aharon Dodi [1963] Director; Abraham Rosenberg [1948] Director

Rugby Football Development Limited
Incorporated: 19 April 2005 *Employees:* 256
Net Worth: £4,780,000 *Total Assets:* £15,349,000
Registered Office: Rugby House, Twickenham Stadium, 200 Whitton Road, Twickenham, Middlesex, TW2 7BA
Activities: Other sports activities
Parent: Rugby Football Union
Officers: Angus Roch Bujalski, Secretary; Susan Margaret Day [1972] Director/Chief Financial Officer

Rugby Football Foundation
Incorporated: 4 December 2002
Net Worth: £1,884,983 *Total Assets:* £19,556,538
Registered Office: Rugby House, Twickenham Stadium, 200 Whitton Road, Twickenham, Middlesex, TW2 7BA
Activities: Other sports activities
Parent: Rugby Football Union
Officers: Angus Roch Bujalski, Secretary; Susan Margaret Day [1972] Director/Chief Financial Officer; Neil Reginald Hagerty [1962] Director; Philip Robert Johnson [1946] Director; Sheila Pancholi [1972] IT Risk Assurance Director; David William Roberts [1956] Director; Malcolm Wharton [1948] Director/Education Business Consultant

Ruislip High School
Incorporated: 3 March 2014 *Employees:* 125
Net Worth: £15,408,638 *Total Assets:* £17,633,988
Registered Office: Ruislip High School, Sidmouth Drive, Ruislip, Middlesex, HA4 0BY
Activities: General secondary education
Officers: Mark Robert Bedwell [1961] Director/Accountant; Emma Flynn [1988] Director/Teacher; John Frederick Garner [1969] Director/Retired; Laura Horton [1990] Director/Teacher; Charles Khan [1972] Director; Edward Francis Lavery [1960] Director/Bank Manager; Martina Anne Bernadette Lecky [1971] Director/Teacher; Anna Leeves [1974] Director/Data Manager; Amarjit Mikulko-Valley [1975] Director/Teacher; Pauline Anne Nixon [1952] Director/Interim Head of Education Borough of Harrow; Maria Penicud [1954] Director/Education Consultant; Dr Mary Richards [1966] Director/University Lecturer; Nicholas Jon Symmons [1956] Director/IT Consultant; Steven Tuckwell [1968] Director/Head of Distribution/Logistics; Joannna Nicola Wagstaffe [1961] Director/Academic Registrar University of Law

Runecorp Limited
Incorporated: 12 November 1999
Net Worth: £444,852,992 *Total Assets:* £571,641,024
Registered Office: Hayes Park, Hayes End Road, Hayes, Middlesex, UB4 8EE
Activities: Non-trading company
Parent: Solvecorp Limited
Officers: Mark Oldham, Secretary/Barrister; Helen Josephine McCarthy [1966] Director; Mark Oldham [1959] Director

Runnymede (Holdings) Limited
Incorporated: 3 September 2013
Net Worth Deficit: £1,314,828 *Total Assets:* £11,685,084
Registered Office: 182 Brooklands Road, Weybridge, Surrey, KT13 0RJ
Activities: Non-life insurance
Major Shareholder: Andrew Stuart Beaumont
Officers: Kirsty Michelle Hunt, Secretary; Andrew Stuart Beaumont [1949] Director; Jeremy Richard Holt Evans [1958] Director

Runnymede Homes Limited
Incorporated: 21 December 2011 *Employees:* 21
Previous: Runnymede Homes (Developments) Limited
Net Worth: £10,332,425 *Total Assets:* £18,157,632
Registered Office: 182 Brooklands Road, Weybridge, Surrey, KT13 0RJ
Activities: Development of building projects
Major Shareholder: Andrew Stuart Beaumont
Officers: Kirsty Michelle Hunt, Secretary; Andrew Stuart Beaumont [1949] Director; Julian Richard Grundy [1959] Director; Mark Timothy Knight [1960] Director; Michael John Weeks [1969] Director

Runnymede Investments Limited
Incorporated: 5 May 1994 *Employees:* 4
Net Worth: £26,498,192 *Total Assets:* £34,758,336
Registered Office: 182 Brooklands Road, Weybridge, Surrey, KT13 0RJ
Activities: Other letting and operating of own or leased real estate
Major Shareholder: Andrew Stuart Beaumont
Officers: Kirsty Michelle Hunt, Secretary; Andrew Stuart Beaumont [1949] Director; Martin Arthur Brown [1946] Director

Rush Hair Group Limited
Incorporated: 4 October 2016 *Employees:* 940
Net Worth Deficit: £1,234,000 *Total Assets:* £25,265,000
Registered Office: 23 George Street, Croydon, Surrey, CR0 1LA
Activities: Other retail sale not in stores, stalls or markets
Major Shareholder: Andrew Panayiotis Phouli
Officers: Stelios Andrew [1964] Director; Gerard Gould [1966] Director/Investor; Stephen Richard Knight [1962] Director; Andreas Panayiotis Phouli [1967] Director; Alastair James Weinel [1965] Director

Rushmon Limited
Incorporated: 26 February 1973 *Employees:* 21
Net Worth: £8,006,789 *Total Assets:* £12,817,257
Registered Office: 2 Esher Road, Hersham, Walton on Thames, Surrey, KT12 4JY
Activities: Construction of domestic buildings
Shareholders: Michael Arthur Ratcliffe; Steven Michael Ratcliffe
Officers: Paul Anthony Robinson, Secretary; Michael Kevin Bicknell [1954] Managing Director; Michael Arthur Ratcliffe [1943] Director; Steven Michael Ratcliffe [1967] Director

Rusjon (UK) Limited
Incorporated: 14 June 1999
Net Worth: £6,139,493 *Total Assets:* £6,299,958
Registered Office: 20 Park Avenue, Farnborough, Orpington, Kent, BR6 8LL
Activities: Buying and selling of own real estate
Officers: Alan Geoffrey Fernback [1947] Director; Denise Wren [1948] Director

Russell & Bromley Limited
Incorporated: 3 November 1952 *Employees:* 948
Net Worth: £73,445,424 *Total Assets:* £86,099,560
Registered Office: 24-34 Farwig Lane, Bromley, Kent, BR1 3RB
Activities: Retail sale of footwear in specialised stores
Shareholder: Roger John Bromley
Officers: Philip Wright, Secretary; Andrew Michael James Bromley [1968] Director; Roger John Bromley [1943] Director; Sebastian Michael Alan Bromley [1986] Director/Business Executive; Stuart Peter William Bromley [1971] Director

A Russell (Farmers) Limited
Incorporated: 3 September 1951 *Employees:* 18
Net Worth: £5,385,182 *Total Assets:* £8,393,092
Registered Office: Pentowan Farm, Church Road, Noak Hill, Romford, Essex, RM4 1LD
Activities: Growing of cereals (except rice), leguminous crops and oil seeds
Major Shareholder: David Guy Russell
Officers: David Guy Russell, Secretary; Daniel Russell [1986] Director; David Guy Russell [1959] Director/Farmer; Lloyd David Russell [1983] Director

Russell Education Trust
Incorporated: 26 November 2010 *Employees:* 292
Net Worth: £13,932,000 *Total Assets:* £17,602,000
Registered Office: Manor House, The Crescent, Leatherhead, Surrey, KT22 8DY
Activities: Educational support services
Officers: Clive James Brazil [1974] Director/House Parent; Mary Helen Karaolis [1947] Director/Retired Headteacher; Daniel Christopher Lynch [1955] Director/Education Consultant; Karen Lynch [1957] Director/Education Consultant; John McDermott [1943] Director/Education Consultant; Christine Smyth [1957] Director/Headteacher; Philip Ward [1948] Director/Retired

Russell Finex Limited
Incorporated: 29 November 1934 *Employees:* 340
Net Worth: £21,434,680 *Total Assets:* £38,615,720
Registered Office: Browells Lane, Feltham, Middlesex, TW13 7EW
Activities: Manufacture of machinery for food, beverage and tobacco processing
Parent: Russell-Hurst Trustees Ltd
Officers: Lisa Jane Harris, Secretary; Kenneth John Armour [1966] Finance Director; Martin William Chipperfield [1960] Sales & Marketing Director; Stanley John Keyworth [1943] Director/Consultant; Robert Joseph O'Connell [1971] Sales & Marketing Director USA & India; Resham Singh [1956] Managing Director; Ian Charles Wardlaw [1968] Manufacturing Director

Donald Russell Holdings Limited
Incorporated: 14 December 2011
Net Worth Deficit: £2,753,000 *Total Assets:* £15,000,000
Registered Office: 29 Ullswater Crescent, Coulsdon, Surrey, CR5 2HR
Activities: Activities of head offices
Parent: Vestey Holdings Limited
Officers: Neil Thornton, Secretary; Colin George Copland [1954] Finance Director; George Moubray William Vestey [1964] Director/Executive Vice Chairman

Donald Russell Limited
Incorporated: 31 May 1984 *Employees:* 230
Net Worth: £5,780,000 *Total Assets:* £13,741,000
Registered Office: 29 Ullswater Crescent, Coulsdon, Surrey, CR5 2HR
Activities: Other food services
Parent: Donald Russell Holdings Limited
Officers: Neil Thornton, Secretary; Paul William Adams [1965] Marketing Director; Colin George Copland [1954] Finance Director; Tazio Gagliardi [1970] Director/Manager [Swiss]; Robert Edmund Patrick McFarlane [1965] Director; Peter Cyril Overton [1967] Supply Chain Director; George Moubray William Vestey [1964] Director/Executive Vice Chairman

Russell School Trust
Incorporated: 15 March 1974 *Employees:* 215
Net Worth: £14,303,798 *Total Assets:* £27,174,608
Registered Office: Royal Russell School, Coombe Lane, Croydon, Surrey, CR9 5BX
Activities: Pre-primary education
Officers: Jane Victoria Burton [1965] Director; Nicholas Cobill [1976] Director/Barrister; Dr Agnelo Teles Fernandes [1960] Director; Lisa Jane Jessup [1970] Director/General Manager Support Services; Simon Henry Kolesar [1948] Director/Chartered Surveyor; James Douglas Lacey [1975] Director/Partner, Planning Consultancy; Andrew Gideon Lorie [1967] Director/Barrister; Anne Martin [1959] Director/Lawyer; Rohit Mathur [1978] Director/Banker; Andrew John Merriman [1966] Finance Director; Sir Philip Drury Moor [1959] Director/QC; James Richard Penny [1965] Director/Banker; Jane Ellen Ann Stevens [1957] Director/Headmistress

Ruxley Holdings Limited
Incorporated: 27 September 1984 *Employees:* 7
Net Worth: £4,438,320 *Total Assets:* £7,218,070
Registered Office: Regus, Wellington Way, Weybridge, Surrey, KT13 0TT
Activities: Activities of head offices
Major Shareholder: William Francis Muddyman
Officers: Jonathan Paul Larbey, Secretary; Jane Hayden-Obadia [1968] Director/Performing Arts; Jonathan Paul Larbey [1969] Director; Andrew Martin Muddyman [1965] Director; William Francis Muddyman [1937] Director; David Everard Shrimpton [1943] Director/Accountant; Alastair Charles Spencer [1948] Director/Company Secretary

RVT Group Limited
Incorporated: 12 January 2012 *Employees:* 53
Previous: Rentavent Limited
Net Worth: £12,768 *Total Assets:* £5,304,061
Registered Office: Prospect House, Riverside Industrial Estate, Riverside Way, Dartford, Kent, DA1 5BS
Activities: Manufacture of non-domestic cooling and ventilation equipment
Officers: Penelope Chattell [1971] Director; Timothy Chattell [1968] Director; Dawn Dupont [1980] Director; Isabel Dupont [1949] Director; Juliet Sarah Dupont [1977] Director; Philip Dupont [1974] Director; Roger Edward Dupont [1948] Director; Timothy Dupont [1980] Director; Deborah Hayward [1978] Director; Julian Hayward [1976] Director

RWW Holdings Limited
Incorporated: 29 May 2015 *Employees:* 3
Net Worth: £6,943,460 *Total Assets:* £6,947,460
Registered Office: Gap Cottage, 3 Croydon Road, Keston, Kent, BR2 6EA
Activities: Administration of financial markets
Major Shareholder: Robert William Walker
Officers: Neil Christopher Rose, Secretary; Neil Christopher Rose [1958] Director/Accountant; Robert William Walker [1939] Director; Sharon Walker [1965] Director

A & J Ryan Holdings Limited
Incorporated: 24 July 2013
Net Worth: £5,706,053 *Total Assets:* £7,585,636
Registered Office: Numeric House, 98 Station Road, Sidcup, Kent, DA15 7BY
Activities: Activities of other holding companies n.e.c.
Shareholders: John Joseph Ryan; Anthony Patrick Ryan
Officers: John Joseph Ryan, Secretary; Anthony Patrick Ryan [1957] Director; John Joseph Ryan [1954] Director

A & J Ryan Mechanical Services Limited
Incorporated: 1 March 1989 *Employees:* 43
Net Worth: £1,983,115 *Total Assets:* £5,339,412
Registered Office: Numeric House, 98 Station Road, Sidcup, Kent, DA15 7BY
Activities: Plumbing, heat and air-conditioning installation
Shareholders: John Joseph Ryan; Anthony Patrick Ryan; A & J Ryan Holdings Limited
Officers: John Joseph Ryan, Secretary; Anthony Patrick Ryan [1957] Director; John Joseph Ryan [1954] Director

Rycote Microphone Holdings Limited
Incorporated: 7 March 2013 *Employees:* 3
Net Worth: £5,589,196 *Total Assets:* £5,589,196
Registered Office: Bridge House, Heron Square, Richmond, Surrey, TW9 1EN
Activities: Activities of head offices
Parent: Vitec Investments Limited
Officers: Jonathan Mark Bolton [1966] Director; Martin Jon Green [1968] Director; Katharina Helen Marie Kearney-Croft [1974] Director

Rye Plant Hire Limited
Incorporated: 31 March 1994 *Employees:* 2
Net Worth: £799,360 *Total Assets:* £6,028,577
Registered Office: c/o Cox Costello, Basing House, 46 High Street, Rickmansworth, Herts, WD3 1HP
Activities: Demolition
Major Shareholder: Simon Barlow
Officers: Karen Barlow [1967] Director; Simon Barlow [1965] Director/Plant and Transport Manager

S & B Herba Foods Limited
Incorporated: 4 July 1919 *Employees:* 101
Net Worth: £60,955,000 *Total Assets:* £79,704,000
Registered Office: 2nd Floor, North Block, Central Court, 1b Knoll Rise, Orpington, Kent, BR6 0JA
Activities: Grain milling
Officers: Peter John Cattaneo, Secretary; Antonio Hernandez Callejas [1955] Director [Spanish]; Felix Hernandez Callejas [1958] Director [Spanish]; Peter John Cattaneo [1949] Director; Robert Leslie Holben [1946] Director; Rafael Angel Lopez Relimpio [1971] Director [Spanish]

S & D Pharma Limited
Incorporated: 17 December 1990 *Employees:* 4
Net Worth: £6,273,521 *Total Assets:* £6,941,872
Registered Office: Unit 10 Delta Court, Manor Way, Borehamwood, Herts, WD6 1FJ
Activities: Wholesale of pharmaceutical goods
Parent: London Pharma & Chemicals Group Ltd
Officers: Andrea Nemcokova [1964] Director [Slovak]; Daniel Reuben Straus [1972] Director/Business Manager

S A Designer Parfums Limited
Incorporated: 11 April 2001 *Employees:* 58
Net Worth: £9,479,150 *Total Assets:* £38,092,696
Registered Office: Amertrans Park, Bushey Mill Lane, Watford, Herts, WD24 7JG
Activities: Wholesale of perfume and cosmetics
Parent: Shaneel Enterprises Ltd
Officers: Hitesh Bhogilal Mehta, Secretary; Dilesh Bhogilal Mehta [1960] Director; Hitesh Bhogilal Mehta [1956] Director

S and J Investments (Delivery Office Southall) Limited
Incorporated: 5 August 2011 *Employees:* 1
Net Worth: £2,772,253 *Total Assets:* £9,803,563
Registered Office: Melton House, 65-67 Clarendon Road, Watford, Herts, WD17 1DS
Activities: Activities of open-ended investment companies
Shareholder: Gursharan Singh Chadha
Officers: Gursharan Singh Chadha [1960] Finance Director; Vivek Singh Chadha [1988] Director/Businessman

S M E Enterprise Limited
Incorporated: 2 April 1985 *Employees:* 77
Net Worth: £5,133,831 *Total Assets:* £6,159,836
Registered Office: Runway House, The Runway, Ruislip, Middlesex, HA4 6SE
Activities: Unlicenced restaurants and cafes
Parent: SME Investments Ltd
Officers: Aly Mohamed Esmail, Secretary; Sayed Mohamed Esmail, Secretary; Aly Mohamed Esmail [1982] Director; Sayed Mohamed Esmail [1986] Director

S N B Holdings Limited
Incorporated: 15 March 2002 *Employees:* 167
Net Worth: £11,704,291 *Total Assets:* £18,470,068
Registered Office: The Barn Hotel, West End Road, Ruislip, Middlesex, HA4 6JB
Activities: Non-trading company
Major Shareholder: Shalil Nalin Bhattessa
Officers: Kathirgamathamby Jeggswaran, Secretary; Shalil Nalin Bhattessa [1968] Director/Hotelier

S-P RIL Limited
Incorporated: 14 July 1961
Net Worth: £52,179,000 *Total Assets:* £52,808,000
Registered Office: West Hill, Hertford Road, Hoddesdon, Herts, EN11 9BU
Activities: Non-trading company
Parent: Schering-Plough Holdings Limited
Officers: Richard Robinski, Secretary; Louise Jane Houson [1976] Director; Simon Nicholson [1975] Director; Ebru Can Temucin [1972] Director [Turkish]

S.A.T.V. Publishing Limited
Incorporated: 8 December 1972
Net Worth: £13,718,000 *Total Assets:* £14,630,000
Registered Office: Grant Way, Isleworth, Middlesex, TW7 5QD
Activities: Non-trading company
Parent: Sky Television Limited
Officers: Christopher Jon Taylor, Secretary; Karl Holmes [1973] Director/Finance Professional; Colin Robert Jones [1964] Director; Christopher Jon Taylor [1971] Director/Company Secretary

S.J.M. Alloys & Metals Limited
Incorporated: 23 April 1993 *Employees:* 21
Net Worth: £4,712,839 *Total Assets:* £18,553,084
Registered Office: 98 Westbury Lane, Buckhurst Hill, Essex, IG9 5PW
Activities: Wholesale of metals and metal ores
Shareholders: Stephen James Midgley; Caroline Mary Midgley
Officers: Caroline Mary Midgley, Secretary; Stephen James Midgley [1963] Director/Metal Trading

S.L.E. Limited
Incorporated: 9 July 1982 *Employees:* 107
Net Worth: £8,549,384 *Total Assets:* £10,597,272
Registered Office: Twin Bridges Business Park, 232 Selsdon Road, South Croydon, Surrey, CR2 6PL
Activities: Manufacture of medical and dental instruments and supplies
Major Shareholder: Bernard John Nelligan
Officers: Susan Nelligan, Secretary; Michael David Donovan [1939] Director; Bernard John Nelligan [1959] Director; Martin James Pearcy [1969] Sales & Marketing Director; Peter Malcolm Richards [1958] Financial Director

S.S.A.T. Property Investments Limited
Incorporated: 2 May 2013
Net Worth: £1,548,314 *Total Assets:* £7,373,126
Registered Office: 166 College Road, Harrow, Middlesex, HA1 1RA
Activities: Other business support service activities n.e.c.
Parent: Aliom Holdings Limited
Officers: Andrew Lawrence Tullie [1969] Director

S.S.S.Gears Limited
Incorporated: 1 June 1950 *Employees:* 43
Net Worth: £81,394,520 *Total Assets:* £93,697,616
Registered Office: Park Road, Sunbury on Thames, Middlesex, TW16 5BL
Activities: Other engineering activities
Parent: Synchro Clutch Company Ltd
Officers: James Michael George Neeves, Secretary/Sales Engineer; Paul Stuart Bizzill [1973] Director of Engineering; Morgan Leland Hendry [1950] Director/Engineer [American]; James Michael George Neeves [1962] Director/Sales Engineer

S.T.C.Plumbing & Heating Merchants Limited
Incorporated: 4 May 1972 *Employees:* 40
Net Worth: £9,488,906 *Total Assets:* £17,098,472
Registered Office: Hopson House, Breakspear Road, Ruislip, Middlesex, HA4 7SE
Activities: Wholesale of hardware, plumbing and heating equipment and supplies
Major Shareholder: Terence John Clyne
Officers: Jason Clyne [1972] Director/Manager; Terence John Clyne [1943] Director/Heating Consultant

SAB Properties (London) Limited
Incorporated: 10 March 1997 *Employees:* 1
Net Worth: £4,082,302 *Total Assets:* £5,414,420
Registered Office: 18 Silver Street, Enfield, Middlesex, EN1 3EG
Activities: Renting and operating of Housing Association real estate
Major Shareholder: Julia Mary Burke
Officers: Julia Mary Burke, Secretary; Martin Gerard Burke [1950] Director/Publican [Irish]

Saba Infra Cambridgeshire Limited
Incorporated: 9 October 2012
Previous: Indigo Infra Cambridgeshire Limited
Net Worth Deficit: £1,176,686 *Total Assets:* £13,827,983
Registered Office: Oak House, Reeds Crescent, Watford, Herts, WD24 4PH
Activities: Other transportation support activities
Parent: Saba Infra UK Limited
Officers: Gary Charles Pickard, Secretary; Phillip David Herring [1970] Managing Director; Josep Oriol Carreras [1961] Director [Spanish]; Gary Charles Pickard [1965] Director/Chartered Accountant

Saba Infra Cardiff Limited
Incorporated: 2 February 1996
Previous: Indigo Infra Cardiff Limited
Net Worth: £8,628,463 *Total Assets:* £10,321,327
Registered Office: Oak House, Reeds Crescent, Watford, Herts, WD24 4PH
Activities: Other transportation support activities
Parent: Saba Infra Holdings UK Limited
Officers: Gary Charles Pickard, Secretary; Phillip David Herring [1970] Managing Director; Josep Oriol Carreras [1961] Director [Spanish]; Gary Charles Pickard [1965] Finance Director

Saba Infra Gloucestershire Limited
Incorporated: 7 August 2009
Previous: Indigo Infra Gloucestershire Limited
Net Worth: £3,857,069 *Total Assets:* £11,914,174
Registered Office: Oak House, Reeds Crescent, Watford, Herts, WD24 4PH
Activities: Other transportation support activities
Parent: Saba Infra UK Limited
Officers: Gary Charles Pickard, Secretary; Phillip David Herring [1970] Managing Director; Josep Oriol Carreras [1961] Director [Spanish]; Gary Charles Pickard [1965] Finance Director

Saba Infra Hertfordshire Limited
Incorporated: 28 May 2010
Previous: Indigo Infra Hertfordshire Limited
Net Worth: £3,128,728 *Total Assets:* £10,594,414
Registered Office: Oak House, Reeds Crescent, Watford, Herts, WD24 4PH
Activities: Other transportation support activities
Parent: Saba Infra UK Limited
Officers: Gary Charles Pickard, Secretary; Phillip David Herring [1970] Managing Director; Josep Oriol Carreras [1961] Director [Spanish]; Gary Charles Pickard [1965] Finance Director

Saba Infra Holdings UK Limited
Incorporated: 31 October 1991
Previous: Indigo Infra Holdings UK Limited
Net Worth: £14,647,520 *Total Assets:* £28,750,320
Registered Office: Oak House, Reeds Crescent, Watford, Herts, WD24 4PH
Activities: Activities of head offices
Parent: Saba Group UK Limited
Officers: Gary Charles Pickard, Secretary; Phillip David Herring [1970] Managing Director; Josep Oriol Carreras [1961] Director [Spanish]; Gary Charles Pickard [1965] Finance Director

Saba Infra UK Limited
Incorporated: 1 March 1995
Previous: Indigo Infra UK Limited
Net Worth: £3,111,696 *Total Assets:* £6,418,772
Registered Office: Oak House, Reeds Crescent, Watford, Herts, WD24 4PH
Activities: Other transportation support activities
Parent: Saba Infra Holdings UK Limited
Officers: Gary Charles Pickard, Secretary; Phillip David Herring [1970] Managing Director; Josep Oriol Carreras [1961] Director [Spanish]; Gary Charles Pickard [1965] Finance Director

Saba Park Services UK Limited
Incorporated: 17 March 1989 *Employees:* 832
Previous: Indigo Park Services UK Limited
Net Worth: £7,544,901 *Total Assets:* £18,971,592
Registered Office: Oak House, Reeds Crescent, Watford, Herts, WD24 4PH
Activities: Other transportation support activities
Parent: Saba Infra Holdings UK Limited
Officers: Gary Charles Pickard, Secretary; Phillip David Herring [1970] Managing Director; Josep Oriol Carreras [1961] Director [Spanish]; Gary Charles Pickard [1965] Finance Director

Saba Park Solutions UK Limited
Incorporated: 5 July 1990
Previous: Indigo Park Solutions UK Limited
Net Worth Deficit: £3,789,903 *Total Assets:* £6,705,591
Registered Office: Oak House, Reeds Crescent, Watford, Herts, WD24 4PH
Activities: Other transportation support activities
Parent: Saba Park Services UK Limited
Officers: Gary Charles Pickard, Secretary; Phillip David Herring [1970] Managing Director; Josep Oriol Carreras [1961] Director [Spanish]; Gary Charles Pickard [1965] Finance Director

Sabichi Homewares Limited
Incorporated: 12 July 1994 *Employees:* 41
Net Worth: £6,589,993 *Total Assets:* £8,405,660
Registered Office: Sabichi House, 5 Wadsworth Road, Perivale, Middlesex, UB6 7JB
Activities: Agents involved in the sale of furniture, household goods, hardware and ironmongery
Officers: Mukesh Lata Bagga, Secretary/Administrator; Mukesh Lata Bagga [1956] Director/Administrator; Sabrina Bagga [1981] Director/Manager; Sachin Bagga [1982] Director; Tarsem Bagga [1953] Director/Manufacturer and Importer

Sabre EMEA Marketing Limited
Incorporated: 24 April 2001 *Employees:* 3
Net Worth: £6,690,470 *Total Assets:* £9,196,465
Registered Office: 1 Church Road, Richmond, Surrey, TW9 2QE
Activities: Other business support service activities n.e.c.
Parent: Sabre International B.V.
Officers: Roshan Mendis [1972] Director/Senior Vice President [Sri Lankan]; Laurence Woodhouse [1981] Director/Vice President

Sabre Global Technologies Limited
Incorporated: 2 February 1995 *Employees:* 154
Previous: Sabre Europe Management Services Limited
Net Worth: £19,891,016 *Total Assets:* £108,301,144
Registered Office: 1 Church Road, Richmond, Surrey, TW9 2QE
Activities: Activities of head offices
Parent: Sabre International B.V.
Officers: Gina Nouri, Secretary; Roshan Mendis [1972] Director/Senior Vice President [Sri Lankan]; Laurence Woodhouse [1981] Director/Vice President

Sabre UK Marketing Limited
Incorporated: 2 February 1995 *Employees:* 91
Net Worth: £11,811,101 *Total Assets:* £20,741,318
Registered Office: 1 Church Road, Richmond, Surrey, TW9 2QE
Activities: Other information technology service activities
Parent: Sabre International B.V.
Officers: Richard Addey [1976] Country Director [French]; Roshan Mendis [1972] Director/Senior Vice President [Sri Lankan]; Antonella Vecchio [1960] Director/Vice President [Italian]

Safe Haven London
Incorporated: 11 January 2005 *Employees:* 2
Net Worth: £29,279,716 *Total Assets:* £53,576,304
Registered Office: GO5, Thorncroft Manor, Thorncroft Drive, Leatherhead, Surrey, KT22 8JB
Activities: Other letting and operating of own or leased real estate
Officers: Edward John Chesterman [1966] Director; Nicholas Francis Markham [1968] Director/Chief Operating Officer

Safe Properties Limited
Incorporated: 29 May 2003
Net Worth Deficit: £1,925,268 *Total Assets:* £6,063,988
Registered Office: 13 Brantwood Gardens, Enfield, Middlesex, EN2 7LY
Activities: Other letting and operating of own or leased real estate
Officers: Nabil Hussain, Secretary; Awlad Hussain [1948] Director; Rukea Begum Hussain [1963] Director

Safedale Limited
Incorporated: 3 October 1991 *Employees:* 139
Net Worth: £4,543,385 *Total Assets:* £19,517,820
Registered Office: Safedale House, 1 Aden Road, Enfield, Middlesex, EN3 7SE
Activities: Dispensing chemist in specialised stores
Officers: Kumud Balubhai Patel, Secretary; Amit Balubhai Patel [1966] Director/Pharmacist; Balubhai Khushalbhai Patel [1942] Director/Pharmacist; Dr. Piyushbhai Khushalbhai Patel [1952] Director/Chemist

Safegold Properties Limited
Incorporated: 19 September 1986 *Employees:* 2
Net Worth: £18,110,116 *Total Assets:* £24,876,724
Registered Office: 5 Chartwell Place, Middle Road, Harrow, Middlesex, HA2 0HE
Activities: Other letting and operating of own or leased real estate
Officers: Kiran Dalia, Secretary; Kiran Dalia [1959] Director/Property Dealer; Rasiklal Chatrabhuj Dalia [1952] Director/Property Dealer

Safestand Limited
Incorporated: 2 March 2004 *Employees:* 2
Net Worth: £7,291,254 *Total Assets:* £7,456,059
Registered Office: 38a Fourth Way, Wembley, Middlesex, HA9 0LH
Activities: Other specialised construction activities n.e.c.
Major Shareholder: Liam Clear
Officers: Liam Clear [1961] Director [Irish]

Safestore Acquisition Limited
Incorporated: 16 July 2003 *Employees:* 2
Net Worth: £251,432,992 *Total Assets:* £576,177,024
Registered Office: Brittanic House, Stirling Way, Borehamwood, Herts, WD6 2BT
Activities: Activities of head offices
Parent: Safestore Group Limited
Officers: Andrew Brian Jones [1966] Director/Chartered Accountant; Federico Vecchioli [1966] Director [French]

Safestore Group Limited
Incorporated: 16 July 2003 *Employees:* 2
Net Worth: £8,886,000 *Total Assets:* £543,182,976
Registered Office: Brittanic House, Stirling Way, Borehamwood, Herts, WD6 2BT
Activities: Activities of head offices
Parent: Safestore Investments Limited
Officers: Andrew Brian Jones [1966] Director/Chartered Accountant; Federico Vecchioli [1966] Director [French]

Safestore Holdings PLC
Incorporated: 8 April 2003 *Employees:* 584
Net Worth: £637,699,968 *Total Assets:* £1,156,600,064
Registered Office: Brittanic House, Stirling Way, Borehamwood, Herts, WD6 2BT
Activities: Activities of head offices
Officers: Helen Mary Bramall, Secretary; Claire Balmforth [1967] Director; Andrew Brian Jones [1966] Director/Chartered Accountant; Joanne Louise Kenrick [1966] Director; Ian Stephen Krieger [1952] Director; Alan Stuart Lewis [1952] Director/Investment Banker; William Alder Oliver [1956] Director; Federico Vecchioli [1966] Director [French]

Safestore Investments Limited
Incorporated: 23 November 2006 *Employees:* 2
Net Worth: £1,256,000 *Total Assets:* £150,000,000
Registered Office: Brittanic House, Stirling Way, Borehamwood, Herts, WD6 2BT
Activities: Activities of other holding companies n.e.c.
Parent: Safestore Holdings PLC
Officers: Andrew Brian Jones [1966] Director/Chartered Accountant; Federico Vecchioli [1966] Director [French]

Safestore Limited
Incorporated: 19 July 2005 *Employees:* 453
Net Worth: £156,804,992 *Total Assets:* £447,948,000
Registered Office: Brittanic House, Stirling Way, Borehamwood, Herts, WD6 2BT
Activities: Other letting and operating of own or leased real estate
Parent: Safestore Acquisition Limited
Officers: Andrew Brian Jones [1966] Director/Chartered Accountant; David Roy Penniston [1958] Property Director; Federico Vecchioli [1966] Director [French]

Safestore Properties Limited
Incorporated: 15 January 1996 *Employees:* 3
Net Worth: £126,238,000 *Total Assets:* £223,668,992
Registered Office: Brittanic House, Stirling Way, Borehamwood, Herts, WD6 2BT
Activities: Other letting and operating of own or leased real estate
Parent: Mentmore Limited
Officers: Andrew Brian Jones [1966] Director/Chartered Accountant; David Roy Penniston [1958] Property Director; Federico Vecchioli [1966] Director [French]

Safetell Limited
Incorporated: 28 July 1989 *Employees:* 78
Net Worth: £1,546,780 *Total Assets:* £6,158,809
Registered Office: Unit 46 Fawkes Avenue, Dartford, Kent, DA1 1JQ
Activities: Other manufacturing n.e.c.
Parent: Newmark Security PLC
Officers: Marie-Claire Dwek [1964] Director; Paul Lovell [1955] Director/Chartered Accountant; Anton Johannes Pieterse [1964] Director [South African]

Safety-Kleen Europe Limited
Incorporated: 15 December 1998 *Employees:* 2
Net Worth: £33,205,000 *Total Assets:* £66,915,000
Registered Office: Profile West, 950 Great West Road, Brentford, Middlesex, TW8 9ES
Activities: Activities of head offices
Parent: WP SK Limited
Officers: Andrew Gregory Firth, Secretary; Andrew Patrick Griffith [1968] Director; Philippe Robert Francis Mauguy [1960] Director [French]

Safety-Kleen U.K. Limited
Incorporated: 8 November 1974 *Employees:* 551
Net Worth: £151,648,992 *Total Assets:* £164,420,000
Registered Office: Profile West, 950 Great West Road, Brentford, Middlesex, TW8 9ES
Activities: Repair of other equipment
Officers: Andrew Gregory Firth, Secretary; Mark Stephen Cawley [1971] Director; Andrew Patrick Griffith [1968] Director; Philippe Robert Francis Mauguy [1960] Director [French]

Safety-Kleen UK (Europe) Limited
Incorporated: 25 November 1998 *Employees:* 2
Net Worth: £22,381,000 *Total Assets:* £84,911,000
Registered Office: Profile West, 950 Great West Road, Brentford, Middlesex, TW8 9ES
Activities: Activities of head offices
Parent: Safety-Kleen Europe Limited
Officers: Andrew Gregory Firth, Secretary; Andrew Patrick Griffith [1968] Director; Philippe Robert Francis Mauguy [1960] Director [French]

Safety-Kleen UK (France) Limited
Incorporated: 25 November 1998
Net Worth: £19,341,000 *Total Assets:* £19,722,000
Registered Office: Profile West, Great West Road, Brentford, Middlesex, TW8 9ES
Activities: Activities of head offices
Shareholders: WP SK Limited; Safety-Kleen Europe Limited
Officers: Andrew Gregory Firth, Secretary; Andrew Patrick Griffith [1968] Director; Philippe Robert Francis Mauguy [1960] Director [French]

Safetykleen Group Services Limited
Incorporated: 26 March 2008 *Employees:* 44
Net Worth Deficit: £259,104,000 *Total Assets:* £710,739,008
Registered Office: Profile West, 950 Great West Road, Brentford, Middlesex, TW8 9ES
Activities: Activities of head offices
Parent: WP Midco 3 Limited
Officers: Andrew Gregory Firth, Secretary; Andrew Gregory Firth [1964] Director/Chartered Accountant; Andrew Patrick Griffith [1968] Director; Philippe Robert Francis Mauguy [1960] Director [French]

Saffie Investments Limited
Incorporated: 15 January 2016 *Employees:* 2
Net Worth: £1,234,559 *Total Assets:* £11,110,722
Registered Office: JPB Harris, Harmile House, 54 St Mary's Street, Upminster, Essex, RM14 2QT
Activities: Activities of investment trusts
Shareholders: Damon Marcus Buffini; Lady Deborah Si Yin Buffini
Officers: Sir Damon Marcus Buffini [1962] Director/Venture Capitalist; Lady Deborah SI Yin Buffini [1962] Director/Solicitor

Fredereck Sage Holdings Limited
Incorporated: 18 May 2016
Net Worth: £91,700 *Total Assets:* £5,867,409
Registered Office: Sage House, New Ford Business Centre, New Ford Road, Waltham Cross, Herts, EN8 7PG
Activities: Activities of construction holding companies
Officers: Joyce Kathleen Hammond, Secretary; Petra Diane Bernkopf [1968] Director; Thea Patricia Buisson [1971] Director/Administrator; Joyce Kathleen Hammond [1944] Director; Neal Peter Hammond [1973] Director; Donna Louise White [1967] Director

Sagoo & Takhar Limited
Incorporated: 8 March 1976 *Employees:* 2
Net Worth: £10,972,276 *Total Assets:* £14,367,279
Registered Office: 120 The Green, Southall, Middlesex, UB2 4BQ
Activities: Other letting and operating of own or leased real estate
Officers: Paramjit Singh Takhar, Secretary; Sardara Singh Sagoo [1930] Director [Indian]; Harjit Sandhu [1957] Director/Housewife; Paramjit Singh Takhar [1945] Director [Indian]

Sahara Care Limited
Incorporated: 28 February 2000 *Employees:* 137
Previous: Sahara Care Homes Limited
Net Worth: £6,628,119 *Total Assets:* £8,354,130
Registered Office: Haslers, Old Station Road, Loughton, Essex, IG10 4PL
Activities: Residential care activities for the elderly and disabled
Shareholders: Terence William Brown; Hurjinder Sharon Kaur
Officers: Darren Scott Turner, Secretary; Terence William Brown [1942] Director; Sharon Lynn Bye [1963] Director/Chief Executive; Hurjinder Sharon Kaur [1967] Director/Manager; Christopher Brian Charles Manhire [1955] Director/Chartered Surveyor; Darren Scott Turner [1969] Director/Certified Accountant

Sahara Holdings Limited
Incorporated: 14 March 2000 *Employees:* 79
Net Worth: £14,430,047 *Total Assets:* £22,246,394
Registered Office: Europa House, Littlebrook DC1, Shield Road, Dartford, Kent, DA1 5UR
Activities: Wholesale of electronic and telecommunications equipment and parts
Shareholders: Kevin Batley; Nigel Batley
Officers: Nigel Batley, Secretary/Financial Director; Annette Batley [1959] Director/IT; Kevin Batley [1954] Sales Director; Nigel Batley [1957] Financial Director; Sheila Elizabeth Batley [1956] Company Secretary/Director

Sahara Presentation Systems PLC
Incorporated: 21 October 1977 *Employees:* 75
Net Worth: £15,223,568 *Total Assets:* £23,098,064
Registered Office: Europa House, Littlebrook DC1, Shield Road, Dartford, Kent, DA1 5UR
Activities: Wholesale of other machinery and equipment
Parent: Sahara Holdings Limited
Officers: Nigel Batley, Secretary/Director; Kevin Batley [1954] Director; Nigel Batley [1957] Financial Director; Simon Barratt Chidsey [1964] Business Development Director; Samantha Jane Hartop [1971] Director/Salesperson; Shaun David Marklew [1974] Sales Director

SAI Commodities Limited
Incorporated: 1 March 2007 *Employees:* 8
Net Worth: £1,147,105 *Total Assets:* £6,339,885
Registered Office: 65 Delamere Road, Hayes, Middlesex, UB4 0NN
Activities: Agents involved in the sale of a variety of goods
Major Shareholder: Deepak Lal Rupchandani
Officers: Ishwar Lal Ashoka [1935] Director/Manager; Deepak Lal Rupchandani [1962] Director/Manager [Indian]

Sail Croatia Adventures Limited
Incorporated: 21 February 2005 *Employees:* 19
Net Worth: £4,124,648 *Total Assets:* £5,616,618
Registered Office: 188 High Street, Egham, Surrey, TW20 9ED
Activities: Tour operator activities
Shareholders: Grant Seuren; Helle Bramsen Seuren
Officers: Helle Bramsen Seuren, Secretary [Danish]; Grant Seuren [1974] Director [New Zealander]; Helle Bramsen Seuren [1971] Director [Danish]

Saint Francis Hospice
Incorporated: 11 May 1978 *Employees:* 296
Net Worth: £12,996,000 *Total Assets:* £13,928,000
Registered Office: The Hall, Broxhill Road, Havering-atte-Bower, Romford, Essex, RM4 1QH
Activities: Hospital activities
Officers: Lynn Bryan, Secretary; Peter Adams [1944] Director/Retired; Peter John Batt [1974] Divisional Managing Director; Peter Desmond Crutchett [1951] Director/Actuary; David Thomas Forster [1948] Director/Retired; Paul Gwinn [1946] Director/Retired; Amanda Camille Hallums [1958] NHS Director (Interim); Linda Ann Huggett [1952] Director/Councillor; Malcolm Paul Miller [1949] Director/Retired; Pauline Margaret Russell [1951] Director/Retired; Dr Gurdev Singh Saini [1947] Director/GP; Dr Robert MacKenzie Weatherstone [1946] Director/Consultant Physician; Colin Robert Wilkins [1981] Director/Account Manager

Saints Transport (Holdings) Limited
Incorporated: 30 November 2016 *Employees:* 312
Net Worth Deficit: £988,127 *Total Assets:* £14,327,330
Registered Office: Templar House, 1 The Summit Centre, Skyport Drive, Harmondsworth, West Drayton, Middlesex, UB7 0LJ
Activities: Freight transport by road
Shareholder: Piers Carroll
Officers: Kevin John Beeches [1956] Director; Stephen Leonard Beeches [1946] Director; Martin Carroll [1948] Director; Piers Carroll [1978] Director

Saints Transport GRP Limited
Incorporated: 23 November 2007 *Employees:* 312
Net Worth: £1,175,722 *Total Assets:* £14,438,034
Registered Office: Templar House, 1 The Summit Centre, Skyport Drive, Harmondsworth, West Drayton, Middlesex, UB7 0LJ
Activities: Freight transport by road
Major Shareholder: Martin Carroll
Officers: Kevin John Beeches, Secretary; Piers Carroll [1978] Director

Saints Transport Limited
Incorporated: 12 September 1968 *Employees:* 312
Net Worth: £1,178,222 *Total Assets:* £14,438,034
Registered Office: Templar House, 1 The Summit Centre, Skyport Drive, Harmondsworth, West Drayton, Middlesex, UB7 0LJ
Activities: Freight transport by road
Shareholder: Piers Carroll
Officers: Kevin John Beeches, Secretary; Kevin John Beeches [1956] Director; Stephen Leonard Beeches [1946] Director; Martin Carroll [1948] Director; Piers Carroll [1978] Director

Saipem Limited
Incorporated: 18 March 2010 *Employees:* 596
Net Worth: £146,761,664 *Total Assets:* £251,528,448
Registered Office: Saipem House, 12-42 Wood Street, Kingston upon Thames, Surrey, KT1 1TG
Activities: Other construction installation
Officers: Lisa Cooper, Secretary; Paolo Formica [1967] Managing Director [Italian]; Massimiliano Guerra [1967] Director [Italian]; Dominique Jean Seng [1957] Director/Chairman [French]

Saiwil Limited
Incorporated: 9 February 2006
Net Worth: £1,701,160 *Total Assets:* £5,549,344
Registered Office: 5a Parr Road, Stanmore, Middlesex, HA7 1NP
Activities: Information technology consultancy activities
Shareholders: Rajiv Singh Arora; Sabina Arora
Officers: Sabina Arora, Secretary; Rajiv Singh Arora [1964] Director/Consultant; Sabina Arora [1966] Director/Lecturer

Salaft Properties Limited
Incorporated: 15 May 1959 *Employees:* 5
Net Worth: £57,556,992 *Total Assets:* £79,544,768
Registered Office: Aissela, 46 High Street, Esher, Surrey, KT10 9QY
Activities: Development of building projects
Shareholders: Russell Gavin Baum; Lincoln Fraser Small
Officers: Lincoln Fraser Small, Secretary; Abigail Sarah Baum [1970] Director/PA; Russell Gavin Baum [1970] Director/Accountant; Suzanne Ferreira [1976] Director; Lincoln Fraser Small [1944] Director

Sale Service and Maintenance Ltd.
Incorporated: 8 December 2000 *Employees:* 35
Net Worth: £3,577,794 *Total Assets:* £7,168,501
Registered Office: Sale House, 25 Upper Mulgrave Road, Cheam, Sutton, Surrey, SM2 7AY
Activities: Plumbing, heat and air-conditioning installation
Major Shareholder: Peter John Sale
Officers: Claire Louise Bradford, Secretary; Sean Dailey [1966] Director/Operations Manager; Mark Johnson [1957] Director/Estimator; Peter John Sale [1961] Director

Salient Investments Ltd.
Incorporated: 19 January 1994
Net Worth: £4,279,515 *Total Assets:* £8,179,708
Registered Office: 2nd Floor, 29-33 Church Road, Stanmore, Middlesex, HA7 4AR
Activities: Buying and selling of own real estate
Officers: Mukesh Kanubhai Patel, Secretary; Minaben Mahesh Patel [1961] Director

Salisbury Holdings Limited
Incorporated: 11 March 2014 *Employees:* 407
Net Worth: £11,356,000 *Total Assets:* £22,835,000
Registered Office: Cambridge House, 47 Clarendon Road, Watford, Herts, WD17 1HP
Activities: Combined facilities support activities
Officers: Michael Anthony Wilson, Secretary; Simon David Ainslie Jones [1970] Director/Chief Financial Officer; Mark Julian Smith [1970] Director; Edward Michael Swales [1979] Director; Michael Anthony Wilson [1956] Director/Solicitor

Salisbury Workplace Services Limited
Incorporated: 6 March 2012 *Employees:* 137
Previous: Salisbury FM Limited
Net Worth: £10,552,000 *Total Assets:* £21,566,000
Registered Office: Cambridge House, Clarendon Road, Watford, Herts, WD17 1HP
Activities: Combined facilities support activities
Parent: Salisbury Holdings Limited
Officers: Michael Anthony Wilson, Secretary; Simon David Ainslie Jones [1970] Director/Chief Financial Officer; Mark Julian Smith [1970] Director; Edward Michael Swales [1979] Director; Michael Anthony Wilson [1956] Director/Solicitor

Salmon Management and Finance Limited
Incorporated: 30 September 1949 *Employees:* 3
Previous: Foumar Properties Limited
Net Worth: £23,117,916 *Total Assets:* £23,369,664
Registered Office: c/o Landmark Chartered Accountants, Leavesden Park, 5 Hurcules Way, Watford, Herts, WD25 7GS
Activities: Other credit granting n.e.c.
Shareholders: Cripps Trust Corporation Limited; Isobel Jean Hunter; Jacqueline Mary Oates; Penelope Jacqueline Warr; Maurice Bertram Gluck
Officers: Maurice Bertram Gluck [1930] Director/Chartered Accountant; Paul Jeremy Roger Newman [1951] Director; Harold Charles Wilson [1955] Director/Accountant

Samaritans
Incorporated: 11 April 1963 *Employees:* 178
Net Worth: £19,771,000 *Total Assets:* £21,331,000
Registered Office: The Upper Mill, Kingston Road, Ewell, Surrey, KT17 2AF
Activities: Activities of other membership organisations n.e.c.
Officers: Christopher John Ward Sparrow, Secretary; Laura Bunt [1984] Director/Deputy CEO; Dr Jackie Craissati [1960] Director/Psychology; Eleanor Ruth Farrell [1977] Director/General Manager [Irish]; Amanda Jayne Finch [1958] Director/Teacher; Andrew Ian Kean [1957] Director/Accountant; Ana Laing [1968] Director/Local Government Officer [Spanish]; Gaia Federica Francesca Marcus [1986] Director/Strategist; Jennifer Margaret McCartney [1948] Director/Chair; Amanda Louise Perrin [1959] Director/Volunteer; Simon Salem [1957] Director/Retired; John Charles Roger Tennent [1964] Director/Chartered Accountant; Monica Josephine Turner [1961] Director/HR Consultant; Giles Wilmore [1967] Director/Civil Servant

Samax Resources Limited
Incorporated: 20 July 1989
Net Worth: £17,384,000 *Total Assets:* £19,018,806
Registered Office: 4th Floor, Communications House, South Street, Staines upon Thames, Surrey, TW18 4PR
Activities: Activities of head offices
Officers: Kevin Patrick Ernest Davies, Secretary; Kevin Patrick Ernest Davies [1957] Director/Transitional Manager

Samsung C & T U.K. Limited
Incorporated: 24 June 1975 *Employees:* 14
Net Worth: £9,280,000 *Total Assets:* £27,098,000
Registered Office: 5th Floor, Profile West, 950 Great West Road, Brentford, Middlesex, TW8 9ES
Activities: Non-specialised wholesale trade
Officers: DOO Yul Lee [1976] Director [South Korean]; Hyun Suk Lee [1973] Director

Samsung Electronics (UK) Limited
Incorporated: 28 July 1995 *Employees:* 1,129
Net Worth: £361,736,000 *Total Assets:* £1,121,426,048
Registered Office: Samsung House, 1000 Hillswood Drive, Chertsey, Surrey, KT16 0PS
Activities: Manufacture of consumer electronics
Parent: Samsung Electronics Co. Limited
Officers: Sung Wuk Kang, Secretary; Byung June Chun [1966] Director/President - UK/ROI [South Korean]; Sung Wuk Kang [1971] Director [South Korean]; Taekwan Kim [1965] Director/European CFO [South Korean]

Samsung SDS Europe Limited
Incorporated: 30 March 2000 *Employees:* 286
Net Worth: £80,362,000 *Total Assets:* £100,519,000
Registered Office: 1st Floor, No 5 The Heights, Brooklands, Weybridge, Surrey, KT13 0NY
Activities: Data processing, hosting and related activities
Officers: Jong Cheel Im, Secretary; Jongcheel Im [1968] Managing Director [South Korean]; Dong Kyu Kim [1982] Director [South Korean]

Samsung Semiconductor Europe Limited
Incorporated: 3 March 1997
Net Worth: £61,102,300 *Total Assets:* £61,102,300
Registered Office: 1st Floor, No 5 The Heights, Brooklands, Weybridge, Surrey, KT13 0NY
Activities: Manufacture of other electrical equipment
Officers: Dermot John Ryan [1962] Director/Company President [Irish]

Sancroft Properties Limited
Incorporated: 5 November 1997
Net Worth: £4,743,978 *Total Assets:* £6,848,588
Registered Office: Hill House, Lowlands Road, Harrow, Middlesex, HA1 3EQ
Activities: Development of building projects
Major Shareholder: Donovan Gijsbertus Wijsmuller
Officers: Brian Martin Comer [1960] Director [Irish]; Luke Andrew Comer [1957] Director [Irish]

Sandhill Homes Limited
Incorporated: 25 January 1999
Net Worth: £1,345,958 *Total Assets:* £16,372,683
Registered Office: Unit 5 Charlton Mead Lane, Hoddesdon, Herts, EN11 0DJ
Activities: Construction of domestic buildings
Parent: The Sandhill Homes Corporation Limited
Officers: Nicholas David Cooper, Secretary; David John Cooper [1953] Director; Nicholas David Cooper [1977] Director/Builder

Sandhill Park Limited
Incorporated: 20 November 1991 *Employees:* 6
Net Worth: £7,400,632 *Total Assets:* £8,041,243
Registered Office: York House, Empire Way, Wembley, Middlesex, HA9 0FQ
Activities: Other letting and operating of own or leased real estate
Officers: Sylvia Frances Fineberg, Secretary; David Fineberg [1940] Director/Chartered Surveyor; Paul Francis Fineberg [1963] Director; Simon Vivian Fineberg [1966] Director; Sylvia Frances Fineberg [1942] Director

Sandkot Limited
Incorporated: 7 February 1984 *Employees:* 2
Net Worth: £4,546,236 *Total Assets:* £8,366,568
Registered Office: Ballward House, 3 Liberty Centre, Mount Pleasant, Wembley, Middlesex, HA0 1TX
Activities: Development of building projects
Shareholders: Shayko Limited; Ballward Limited
Officers: Prafulla Kotecha, Secretary; Vipul Suresh Kotecha [1968] Director

Saniflo Limited
Incorporated: 21 February 1979 *Employees:* 31
Net Worth: £4,521,623 *Total Assets:* £8,017,655
Registered Office: Howard House, The Runway, South Ruislip, Middlesex, HA4 6SE
Activities: Wholesale of hardware, plumbing and heating equipment and supplies
Major Shareholder: Claude Perdriel
Officers: Arnaud Corbier [1961] Director [French]; Tim Pestell [1957] Managing Director

Santray Limited
Incorporated: 30 October 2007 *Employees:* 3
Net Worth Deficit: £65,765 *Total Assets:* £36,447,964
Registered Office: 2nd Floor, Hygeia House, 66 College Road, Harrow, Middlesex, HA1 1BE
Activities: Other business support service activities n.e.c.
Officers: Leisha Ann Joyce Frett [1987] Director [Guyanese]; Dr Christoph Bernhard Gutmann [1976] Director [Swiss]; Jerome Rubin-Delanchy [1980] Director [French]

SAP (UK) Limited
Incorporated: 31 July 1987 *Employees:* 1,567
Net Worth Deficit: £24,664,000 *Total Assets:* £431,924,000
Registered Office: Clockhouse Place, Bedfont Road, Feltham, Middlesex, TW14 8HD
Activities: Other software publishing
Parent: SAP SE
Officers: Jens Claus Amail [1967] Managing Director [German]; Yu-Ho Cheung [1970] Director/General Counsel; Peter David [1965] Director/Financial Officer [German]; Renaud Valery Heyd [1972] Director/Chief Financial Officer [French]

Sapiens (UK) Limited
Incorporated: 23 December 1987 *Employees:* 84
Net Worth: £2,016,359 *Total Assets:* £22,822,872
Registered Office: Harman House, 1 George Street, Uxbridge, Middlesex, UB8 1QQ
Activities: Other information technology service activities
Officers: Patrick Slattery, Secretary; Ron Al Dor [1960] Director [Israeli]; Patrick Slattery [1954] Finance Director

Sapna Caterers Limited
Incorporated: 1 June 1998 *Employees:* 35
Net Worth: £2,854,401 *Total Assets:* £7,924,180
Registered Office: Ground Floor, Elizabeth House, 54-58 High Street, Edgware, Middlesex, HA8 7EJ
Activities: Event catering activities
Shareholder: Kamran Tariq
Officers: Asma Tariq, Secretary; Asma Tariq [1952] Director/Secretary; Kamran Tariq [1972] Director/IT Consultant; Mohammad Tariq [1949] Director/Catering Executive; Rizwan Tariq [1980] Director/Administrator; Zeeshan Tariq [1981] Director/Sales/Marketing

Sara (London) Limited
Incorporated: 23 May 1984 *Employees:* 3
Net Worth: £5,683,722 *Total Assets:* £11,542,600
Registered Office: First Floor, Kirkland House, 11-15 Peterborough Road, Harrow, Middlesex, HA1 2AX
Activities: Agents specialised in the sale of other particular products
Parent: Eastern Focus Investments Ltd.
Officers: Ashok Ramchand Mohinani [1963] Director/Businessman [Indian]; Ramchand Udharam Mohinani [1935] Director [Indian]

Sardar Properties (U.K.) Limited
Incorporated: 25 May 1993
Net Worth: £21,656,040 *Total Assets:* £23,952,000
Registered Office: 50 Ollards Grove, Loughton, Essex, IG10 4DW
Activities: Other letting and operating of own or leased real estate
Officers: Charanjit Singh, Secretary/Salesman; Balbir Singh Doal [1956] Director/Manufacturer; Sadhu Ram [1953] Director/Manufacturer; Charanjit Singh [1950] Director/Salesman; Diyal Singh [1925] Director/Manufacturer; Harbans Singh [1958] Director/Manufacturer; Tarsem Singh [1947] Director/Manufacturer

Sarena House LLP
Incorporated: 18 November 2014 *Employees:* 2
Net Worth: £1,395,071 *Total Assets:* £58,106,640
Registered Office: 3rd Floor, Sterling House, Langston Road, Loughton, Essex, IG10 3TS

Sarr Hotels (Luton) Ltd
Incorporated: 12 April 2016 *Employees:* 75
Net Worth Deficit: £257,020 *Total Assets:* £7,857,898
Registered Office: 428 Long Drive, Greenford, Middlesex, UB6 8UH
Activities: Hotels and similar accommodation
Officers: Harmeet Singh Ahuja [1972] Director; Ravinder Singh Gidar [1959] Director

Sarr Investments Limited
Incorporated: 8 July 2015 *Employees:* 3
Net Worth: £3,113,372 *Total Assets:* £12,895,621
Registered Office: 428 Long Drive, Greenford, Middlesex, UB6 8UH
Activities: Hotels and similar accommodation
Officers: Harmeet Singh Ahuja [1972] Director; Ravinder Singh Gidar [1959] Director; Anil Kumar Sharma [1952] Director

Sarr Noke Hospitality Limited
Incorporated: 20 July 2016 *Employees:* 1
Net Worth Deficit: £340,729 *Total Assets:* £9,005,375
Registered Office: 428 Long Drive, Greenford, Middlesex, UB6 8UH
Activities: Hotels and similar accommodation
Officers: Harmeet Singh Ahuja [1972] Director; Ravinder Singh Gidar [1959] Director

Sartorius Stedim UK Limited
Incorporated: 12 December 2006 *Employees:* 50
Net Worth: £8,259,992 *Total Assets:* £13,602,207
Registered Office: Longmead Business Centre, Blenheim Road, Epsom, Surrey, KT19 9QQ
Activities: Wholesale of electronic and telecommunications equipment and parts
Parent: Sartorius Stedim Biotech SA
Officers: David Campbell, Secretary; Bettina Berendsen [1963] Director/Vice President [German]; David Campbell [1967] Director/Accountant

Sartra International Limited
Incorporated: 29 April 1983 *Employees:* 27
Net Worth: £4,028,233 *Total Assets:* £7,003,218
Registered Office: 71 Hayes Hill, Hayes, Bromley, Kent, BR2 7HN
Activities: Non-specialised wholesale trade
Major Shareholder: Brian George Groves
Officers: Sarah Jane Groves, Secretary; Michael John Clark [1948] Director/Sales Manager; Brian George Groves [1945] Director/Export Manager

Satair UK Limited
Incorporated: 27 December 1995 *Employees:* 17
Net Worth: £5,930,221 *Total Assets:* £8,531,809
Registered Office: Unit 3 Space Waye, North Feltham Trading Estate, Feltham, Middlesex, TW14 0TH
Activities: Other business support service activities n.e.c.
Parent: Airbus SE
Officers: Hendrik Brand [1971] Director [German]; Jonathan Paul Ravenhall [1959] Managing Director; Hubertus Johannes Dorotheus Reijnen [1972] Director/Chairman [Dutch]

Satco Investments Limited
Incorporated: 25 September 1987
Net Worth: £16,537,554 *Total Assets:* £22,797,708
Registered Office: Aprirose House, 48a High Street, Edgware, Middlesex, HA8 7EQ
Activities: Other letting and operating of own or leased real estate
Parent: Satco Investments Holding Limited
Officers: Mansukhlal Gosar Gudka, Secretary; Kumud Mansukhlal Gudka [1945] Director/Company Secretary; Manish Mansukhlal Gudka [1970] Director; Mansukhlal Gosar Gudka [1941] Director; Parag Mansukhlal Gudka [1971] Director

Sauvello Limited
Incorporated: 4 November 2016 *Employees:* 2
Net Worth Deficit: £265,829 *Total Assets:* £27,625,672
Registered Office: Rosebank, Claremont Park Road, Esher, Surrey, KT10 9LT
Activities: Activities of open-ended investment companies
Shareholders: Ross William Snape; Lisa Search
Officers: Lisa Snape [1965] Director; Ross William Snape [1964] Director

Saville Services Limited
Incorporated: 6 February 2009
Net Worth: £4,499,058 *Total Assets:* £6,738,240
Registered Office: Elder House, St Georges Business Park, 207 Brooklands Road, Weybridge, Surrey, KT13 0TS
Activities: Other service activities n.e.c.
Shareholder: Puma VCT 9 PLC
Officers: Eliot Charles Kaye, Secretary; Lee Marcus Josephs [1982] Director; Michael Edward Jourdain [1964] Director; Tony Kumar Throp [1985] Director/Investment Manager

Saxonchart Limited
Incorporated: 10 September 2007 *Employees:* 2
Net Worth Deficit: £3,336,778 *Total Assets:* £30,768,108
Registered Office: 19-20 Bourne Court, Southend Road, Woodford Green, Essex, IG8 8HD
Activities: Development of building projects
Shareholder: Residential Land Holdings Limited
Officers: Jonathan Simon David Anthony Rust, Company Secretary; Deepak Jalan [1974] Director; Bruce Weir Ritchie [1965] Director

Saxton Limited
Incorporated: 10 June 2009 *Employees:* 66
Net Worth: £13,469,662 *Total Assets:* £29,712,904
Registered Office: 249 Cranbrook Road, Ilford, Essex, IG1 4TG
Activities: Other business support service activities n.e.c.
Shareholders: Jane Catherine Austin; SIP Trustees Ltd; Alan Austin
Officers: Alan Austin [1950] Director; Janice Catherine Austin [1952] Director/Secretary

Saya Enterprises Limited
Incorporated: 7 February 1992 *Employees:* 36
Net Worth: £1,506,390 *Total Assets:* £7,719,311
Registered Office: Unit 1, 372 Ealing Road, Alperton, Wembley, Middlesex, HA0 1BH
Activities: Manufacture of other food products n.e.c.
Parent: Sarjudas Foundation
Officers: Rakesh Ramesh Patel, Secretary; Chandresh Patel [1958] Director; Himakshu Arvindbhai Patel [1967] Director [British Virgin Islander]; Jitendrakumar Maganbhai Patel [1952] Managing Director; Rakesh Ramesh Patel [1963] Director/Certified Accountant; Krishnakumar Pattani [1959] Director/Accountant

Sazerac UK Limited
Incorporated: 28 February 2003 *Employees:* 25
Net Worth Deficit: £368,640 *Total Assets:* £33,908,028
Registered Office: 60 Marina Place, Hampton Wick, Kingston upon Thames, Surrey, KT1 4BH
Activities: Wholesale of wine, beer, spirits and other alcoholic beverages
Major Shareholder: William Alan Goldring
Officers: Rebecca Lucy Martin [1958] Managing Director; Christopher Douglas Ritchie [1972] Director [Canadian]; Christopher Robin Skinger [1974] Director [American]; Magdalena Ewa Tadych [1978] Finance Director [Polish]

SC Leisure Group Limited
Incorporated: 11 May 1960
Net Worth: £166,655,008 *Total Assets:* £168,168,992
Registered Office: Broadwater Park, Denham, Bucks, UB9 5HR
Activities: Other service activities n.e.c.
Parent: Six Continents Investments Limited
Officers: Fiona Cuttell, Secretary; Michael Jon Cockcroft [1974] Director/Accountant; Michael Todd Glover [1971] Director/Financial Controller [American]; Nicolette Henfrey [1969] Director

Scalable Software Ltd
Incorporated: 20 February 2008 *Employees:* 20
Net Worth Deficit: £9,826,317 *Total Assets:* £5,760,396
Registered Office: The Old Rectory, Church Street, Weybridge, Surrey, KT13 8DE
Activities: Business and domestic software development
Parent: JMI Services LLC
Officers: Mark Jonathan Cresswell [1965] Director/Manager; Christopher Gomersall [1959] Director; Charles Edwards Noell [1952] Director/Investment Manager [American]

Scan Corporation Limited
Incorporated: 1 November 1990
Net Worth Deficit: £717,913 *Total Assets:* £6,111,041
Registered Office: 1021 Harrow Road, Sudbury, Middlesex, HA0 2SJ
Activities: Wholesale of other intermediate products
Shareholders: Farhad Davarzani; Ladan Davarzani
Officers: Lili Davarzani, Secretary; Farhad Davarzani [1970] Director/Computer Engineer

Scape Opportunities Dublin Limited
Incorporated: 22 October 2015
Net Worth Deficit: £599,205 *Total Assets:* £20,804,240
Registered Office: Munro House, Portsmouth Road, Cobham, Surrey, KT11 1PP
Activities: Other business support service activities n.e.c.
Shareholder: Nigel Duncan Taee
Officers: Ronan Niall Kierans [1978] Director [Irish]; Nigel Duncan Taee [1961] Director; Thomas Ward [1978] Director

Scentrics Information Security Technologies Limited
Incorporated: 19 March 2008 *Employees:* 4
Net Worth: £405,525,984 *Total Assets:* £505,965,952
Registered Office: 238 Station Road, Addlestone, Surrey, KT15 2PS
Activities: Information technology consultancy activities
Officers: Guruparan Chandrasekaran [1967] Director/Business Executive; Jerome Jehan Mohamed [1975] Director/Consultant; Phillip John Price [1952] Director/Business Executive; David Edward Svendsen [1948] Director [Australian]

Schenker Limited
Incorporated: 16 November 1943 *Employees:* 624
Net Worth: £12,137,000 *Total Assets:* £68,653,000
Registered Office: Schenker House, Unit 3 LHR Portal, Scylla Road, London Heathrow Airport, Hounslow, Middlesex, TW6 3FE
Activities: Freight transport by road
Parent: DB (UK) Investments Ltd
Officers: Declan Joseph Byrne, Secretary; Declan Joseph Byrne [1967] Finance Director [Irish]; Doug John Coull [1956] Air Product Director UK & Ireland; Steve Cuddeford [1965] Director; Julie Heard [1969] Sales Director UK & Ireland; Ray Hennessy [1961] Director/Chief Executive Officer [Irish]; Adrian Mark Jennings [1970] Ocean Product Director UK & Ireland; Deborah Jane Mansfield [1971] HR Director

Schering-Plough Holdings Limited
Incorporated: 15 September 1988
Net Worth: £436,287,008 *Total Assets:* £498,076,992
Registered Office: West Hill, Hertford Road, Hoddesdon, Herts, EN11 9BU
Activities: Activities of head offices
Parent: Merck & Co., Inc.
Officers: Richard Robinski, Secretary; Louise Jane Houson [1976] Director; Simon Nicholson [1975] Director; Ebru Can Temucin [1972] Director [Turkish]

Schindler Ltd.
Incorporated: 21 June 1960 *Employees:* 734
Net Worth: £27,782,000 *Total Assets:* £92,323,000
Registered Office: 205 Brooklands Road, Weybridge, Surrey, KT13 0BG
Activities: Manufacture of other special-purpose machinery n.e.c.
Officers: Frederik Jacobus Van Rensburg Wepener, Secretary; Aldo Braccetti [1961] Managing Director [Italian]; Frederik Jacobus Van Rensburg Wepener [1975] Director/Chief Financial Officer

Schinvest Limited
Incorporated: 23 March 1984
Net Worth: £24,086,000 *Total Assets:* £26,172,000
Registered Office: 205 Brooklands Road, Weybridge, Surrey, KT13 0BG
Activities: Manufacture of lifting and handling equipment
Officers: Frederik Jacobus Van Rensburg Wepener, Secretary; Aldo Braccetti [1961] Managing Director [Italian]; Frederik Jacobus Van Rensburg Wepener [1975] Director/Chief Financial Officer

Schweppes Limited
Incorporated: 6 November 1958
Net Worth: £389,079,008 *Total Assets:* £389,079,008
Registered Office: Cadbury House, Sanderson Road, Uxbridge, Middlesex, UB8 1DH
Activities: Activities of head offices
Parent: Mondelez International, Inc
Officers: Adrian John Paul Arrighi [1978] Tax Director; Michael Brendan Foye [1965] Treasury Director; John Michael Hladusz [1972] Director/Chartered Accountant; Carole Noelle Keene [1966] Director

Schwing Stetter (UK) Ltd
Incorporated: 3 June 1946 *Employees:* 21
Net Worth: £5,198,000 *Total Assets:* £5,813,000
Registered Office: Unit 11 Perivale Industrial Estate, Horsenden Lane South, Greenford, Middlesex, UB6 7RL
Activities: Manufacture of pumps
Parent: Schwing GmbH
Officers: Neil Anthony Coupe, Secretary; John Hugh Byrne [1963] Director; Neil Anthony Coupe [1967] Director; Klaus Heinrich Wilhelm Kappelmann [1955] Director/Financial Controller [German]

Science, Engineering and Manufacturing Technologies Alliance
Incorporated: 5 December 1988
Net Worth: £29,402,000 *Total Assets:* £35,358,000
Registered Office: Unit 2 The Orient Centre, Greycaine Road, Watford, Herts, WD24 7GP
Activities: Technical and vocational secondary education
Officers: Andrew Stephen McLachrie, Secretary; Paul Adrian Birt [1961] HR Director; Karen Boswell [1963] Managing Director; Michael James Evans [1963] Managing Director; Dame Judith Elizabeth Hackitt [1954] Director/Chair; Selma Hunter [1964] Director; Jose Luis Martins Dos Santos Lopes [1964] Director/Manager Product Development; Indro Mario Mukerjee [1960] Director/Chief Executive Officer; Sharron Alexandra Pamplin [1969] Director/HR; Sarah Louise Sandle [1969] Director/VP Strategy; Mark Ian Tarry [1971] Director/Accountant; Ian Waddell [1965] Director/National Officer of Unite

SCIH Branston 3
Incorporated: 9 August 2002
Net Worth: £1,545,063,040 *Total Assets:* £1,545,536,000
Registered Office: Broadwater Park, Denham, Bucks, UB9 5HR
Activities: Activities of head offices
Shareholder: Six Continents Limited
Officers: Fiona Jane Littlebury-Cuttell, Secretary; Michael Jon Cockcroft [1974] Director/Accountant; Michael Todd Glover [1971] Director/Financial Controller [American]; Nicolette Henfrey [1969] Director

Scimitar Care Hotels PLC
Incorporated: 14 August 1978 *Employees:* 357
Net Worth: £33,259,680 *Total Assets:* £37,530,288
Registered Office: The Lodge, Coopers Lane Road, Potters Bar, Herts, EN6 4AD
Activities: Residential care activities for the elderly and disabled
Officers: Valerie Irene Gerrard, Secretary; Valerie Irene Gerrard [1946] Director of Care; Joanne Maria Mason [1963] Director/Residential Care; Luke Matthew Sargeant [1978] Operations Director; Paul David Sargeant [1966] Finance Director

Scimitar House (Holdings) Limited
Incorporated: 24 June 2016 *Employees:* 2
Net Worth Deficit: £43,215 *Total Assets:* £8,663,172
Registered Office: 166 College Road, Harrow, Middlesex, HA1 1RA
Activities: Development of building projects
Parent: Estates and Lets 2 LLP
Officers: Michael Spencer Docker [1963] Director; Michele Docker [1965] Director

Scimitar House Limited
Incorporated: 16 June 2014 *Employees:* 1
Net Worth: £4,205,012 *Total Assets:* £7,487,943
Registered Office: 166 College Road, Harrow, Middlesex, HA1 1RA
Activities: Buying and selling of own real estate
Parent: Scimitar House (Holdings) Limited
Officers: Michael Docker, Secretary; Michael Spencer Docker [1963] Director

Scotline Limited
Incorporated: 27 January 1983 *Employees:* 20
Net Worth: £5,397,575 *Total Assets:* £9,884,397
Registered Office: 75 Main Road, Gidea Park, Romford, Essex, RM2 5EL
Activities: Sea and coastal freight water transport
Shareholder: Peter Thomas Millatt
Officers: Peter Thomas Millatt, Secretary; Marion Terase Frances Osborne, Secretary/Director; Roy John Brooks [1949] Director/Ship Manager; Cindy Lee Crancher [1962] Director/Manager; Peter Thomas Millatt [1949] Director; Marion Terase Frances Osborne [1960] Director

T.E.Scudder Limited
Incorporated: 27 May 1958 *Employees:* 91
Net Worth: £8,946,292 *Total Assets:* £20,308,644
Registered Office: Carey House, Great Central Way, Wembley, Middlesex, HA9 0HR
Activities: Demolition
Parent: Carey Group PLC
Officers: Fiona Mary O'Donnell, Secretary; John Carey [1941] Director [Irish]; Denis Patrick Deacy [1965] Director; Gary Whyton [1961] Director

SDJ Enterprises Limited
Incorporated: 22 December 2009 *Employees:* 155
Net Worth: £9,981,322 *Total Assets:* £14,420,452
Registered Office: Second Floor, Ashdon House, Moon Lane, Barnet, Herts, EN5 5YL
Activities: Activities of financial services holding companies
Shareholders: Joshus Steven Landy; Dewayne Walter Bridges; Stephen Craig Mitchem
Officers: Joshus Steven Landy [1969] Director [American]; Jeremy Dean Shaffer [1971] Director [American]

Sea Cloud 1 Limited
Incorporated: 7 April 2016 *Employees:* 112
Net Worth: £9,353,129 *Total Assets:* £22,157,740
Registered Office: Elder House, St Georges Business Park, Brooklands Road, Weybridge, Surrey, KT13 0TS
Activities: Activities of head offices
Major Shareholder: Andrea Susan Greystoke
Officers: John David Clarke [1953] Director/Solicitor; Andrea Susan Greystoke [1946] Director [American/British]; David William Morse [1960] Director/Education Consultant; Sheila Patricia Redrupp [1959] Director/Chartered Accountant; Abigail Melinda Fawn Snell [1978] Director

Sea Cloud 2 Limited
Incorporated: 7 April 2016 *Employees:* 77
Net Worth Deficit: £4,495,780 *Total Assets:* £8,158,525
Registered Office: Elder House, St Georges Business Park, Brooklands Road, Weybridge, Surrey, KT13 0TS
Activities: Activities of head offices
Major Shareholder: Andrea Susan Greystoke
Officers: John David Clarke [1953] Director/Solicitor; Andrea Susan Greystoke [1946] Director [American/British]; David William Morse [1960] Director/Education Consultant; Sheila Patricia Redrupp [1959] Director/Chartered Accountant; Abigail Melinda Fawn Snell [1978] Director

Sea, Air & Land Forwarding Limited
Incorporated: 13 March 1987 *Employees:* 24
Net Worth: £7,355,436 *Total Assets:* £11,804,356
Registered Office: Sun House, 428 Long Drive, Greenford, Middlesex, UB6 8UH
Activities: Other transportation support activities
Shareholder: Raminder Singh Ranger
Officers: Renu Ranger, Secretary; Harmeet Singh Ahuja [1972] Director; Reena Ahuja [1978] Director; Raminder Singh Ranger [1948] Director

Seabrook Holdings Limited
Incorporated: 6 November 1989 *Employees:* 132
Net Worth: £8,853,284 *Total Assets:* £33,100,808
Registered Office: Admiral House, 853 London Road, West Thurrock, Essex, RM20 3LG
Activities: Activities of head offices
Major Shareholder: Michael Ronald Seabrook
Officers: Stuart Michael Seabrook, Secretary; Michael Ronald Seabrook [1950] Director/Freight Forwarder; David Lee Tanner [1952] Director/Freight Forwarder

Seabrook Warehousing Limited
Incorporated: 18 April 1995 *Employees:* 88
Net Worth: £4,073,068 *Total Assets:* £10,200,498
Registered Office: Admiral House, 853 London Road, West Thurrock, Essex, RM20 3LG
Activities: Operation of warehousing and storage facilities for water transport activities
Parent: Seabrook Holdings Limited
Officers: Stuart Michael Seabrook, Secretary; Stuart Michael Seabrook [1973] Director; David Lee Tanner [1952] Director

Seacon Group Limited
Incorporated: 22 May 2001 *Employees:* 84
Net Worth: £13,555,767 *Total Assets:* £17,670,420
Registered Office: Tower Wharf, Lower Road, Northfleet, Kent, DA11 9BD
Activities: Other transportation support activities
Officers: Kevin Jeeves, Secretary; Manjit Dale [1965] Director; James Albert Roth [1966] Director

Seacon Terminals Limited
Incorporated: 25 February 1981 *Employees:* 28
Net Worth: £8,954,619 *Total Assets:* £13,904,799
Registered Office: Tower Wharf, Lower Road, Northfleet, Gravesend, Kent, DA11 9BD
Activities: Operation of warehousing and storage facilities for water transport activities
Parent: Seacon Group Limited
Officers: Kevin Jeeves, Secretary; Patrick Terence Cockerton [1974] Director/Manager Steel Services; Michael Anthony Collins [1956] Director/Chartered Ship Broker; Kevin Jeeves [1958] Director/Accountant; James Albert Roth [1966] Director

Searchfield (Oatlands Court) Limited
Incorporated: 2 August 2016 *Employees:* 2
Net Worth Deficit: £256,240 *Total Assets:* £8,207,585
Registered Office: Gladstone House, 77-79 High Street, Egham, Surrey, TW20 9HY
Activities: Construction of domestic buildings
Shareholders: Searchfield Developments Limited; Springmark Ltd
Officers: Andrew Nicholas Searchfield [1969] Director; Michaela Searchfield [1971] Director

Seasoned Events Limited
Incorporated: 17 August 2000 *Employees:* 123
Net Worth: £3,394,195 *Total Assets:* £5,236,040
Registered Office: Crown House, 855 London Road, Grays, Essex, RM20 3LG
Activities: Event catering activities
Parent: Crown Holdings Limited
Officers: Javed Taher, Secretary; Charles Nicholas Beer [1971] Director/Catering Hospitality; Deirdre Morgan [1952] Director; Russell Lee Christopher Morgan [1952] Director/Co Chairman; Colin Sayers [1971] Director/Catering; Christopher John Sullivan [1956] Director

Secom PLC
Incorporated: 26 February 1991 *Employees:* 778
Net Worth: £30,498,000 *Total Assets:* £43,885,000
Registered Office: Secom House, 52 Godstone Road, Kenley, Surrey, CR8 5JF
Activities: Security systems service activities
Officers: Neil Fanthome-Hodgson, Secretary; Alan Blake [1965] Director; Neil Fanthome-Hodgson [1965] Director; Sadahiro Sato [1960] Director [Japanese]; Minoru Takezawa [1963] Director [Japanese]; Paul Arnold Weaver [1969] Director

Secomak Limited
Incorporated: 16 September 1930 *Employees:* 34
Net Worth: £4,279,899 *Total Assets:* £6,751,012
Registered Office: Unit 330 Centennial Park, Elstree, Herts, WD6 3TJ
Activities: Manufacture of other special-purpose machinery n.e.c.
Parent: Secomak Holdings Ltd
Officers: John Francis Moore, Secretary; John Francis Moore [1954] Director/Chief Executive Officer; David Stuart Palmer [1985] Managing Director

Second Shurgard UK Camberley Limited
Incorporated: 4 November 2004
Net Worth: £6,186,216 *Total Assets:* £6,195,606
Registered Office: 2 AC Court, High Street, Thames Ditton, Surrey, KT7 0SR
Activities: Operation of warehousing and storage facilities for land transport activities
Parent: Shurgard UK Limited
Officers: Marc Pierre Francois Oursin [1962] Director [French]

Security Monitoring Centres Limited
Incorporated: 4 September 1936 *Employees:* 1
Net Worth: £21,526,000 *Total Assets:* £42,449,000
Registered Office: Littleton Road, Ashford, Middlesex, TW15 1TZ
Activities: Private security activities
Parent: Chubb Group Security Limited
Officers: Laura Wilcock, Secretary; Craig Alexander Forbes [1963] Finance Director; Colin Walters [1965] Director/General Manager

Seebeck 133 Limited
Incorporated: 9 November 2006
Previous: Axis Group Integrated Services Limited
Net Worth: £714,000 *Total Assets:* £14,420,000
Registered Office: Ground Floor Suite, River House, Maidstone Road, Sidcup, Kent, DA14 5RH
Activities: Activities of head offices
Officers: Simon Kenneth Giles, Secretary; Roger Leonard Burdett [1950] Director; Simon Kenneth Giles [1974] Finance Director; Jonathan Stephen Levine [1952] Director; David John Mundell [1957] Director

Sega Amusements International Limited
Incorporated: 31 March 1983 *Employees:* 67
Previous: Sega Amusements Europe Limited
Net Worth: £15,762,000 *Total Assets:* £22,663,000
Registered Office: 42 Barwell Business Park, Leatherhead Road, Chessington, Surrey, KT9 2NY
Activities: Manufacture of professional and arcade games and toys
Parent: Sega Sammy Holdings Inc
Officers: Roger Stuart Pennington, Secretary; Mikio Ina [1964] Director/Business Executive [Japanese]; Morio Moriya [1968] Director/Business Executive [Japanese]; Takeshi Nakayama [1959] Director/Deputy Department Manager [Japanese]; Roger Stuart Pennington [1961] Finance Director; Paul Williams [1964] Director/Chief Executive Officer

Sega Europe Limited
Incorporated: 4 October 1982 *Employees:* 154
Net Worth: £15,846,000 *Total Assets:* £60,303,000
Registered Office: 27 Great West Road, Brentford, Middlesex, TW8 9BW
Activities: Other service activities n.e.c.
Parent: Sega Sammy Holdings Inc
Officers: Nicola Ormrod, Secretary; Gary Robert Dale [1961] Director/Chief Operating Officer; Kenji Matsubara [1962] Director [Japanese]; Tatsuyuki Miyazaki [1967] Director/Chief Executive Officer [Japanese]; David Jonathon Ward [1965] Director/Chief Financial Officer

Sega Publishing Europe Limited
Incorporated: 13 September 2005 *Employees:* 61
Net Worth Deficit: £50,000 *Total Assets:* £39,371,000
Registered Office: 27 Great West Road, Brentford, Middlesex, TW8 9BW
Activities: Publishing of computer games
Parent: Sega Sammy Holdings Inc
Officers: Nicola Ormrod, Secretary; Gary Robert Dale [1961] Director/Chief Operating Officer; Kenji Matsubara [1962] Director [Japanese]; Tatsuyuki Miyazaki [1967] Director/Chief Executive Officer [Japanese]; David Jonathon Ward [1965] Director/Chief Financial Officer

Seismic Exploration (Canada) Ltd
Incorporated: 7 July 1995
Net Worth: £5,655,183 *Total Assets:* £6,950,169
Registered Office: 4 The Heights, Brooklands, Weybridge, Surrey, KT13 0NY
Activities: Support activities for petroleum and natural gas mining
Parent: Petroleum Geo-Services (UK) Limited
Officers: Gottfred Langseth [1966] Director [Norwegian]; Rune Olav Pedersen [1970] Director [Norwegian]; Christin Steen Nilsen [1953] Director/VP Chief Accountant [Norwegian]

SEJ Assets Limited
Incorporated: 27 May 2014 *Employees:* 45
Net Worth: £9,715,689 *Total Assets:* £15,391,768
Registered Office: Unit 5a Caxton Trading Estate, Printing House Lane, Hayes, Middlesex, UB3 1BE
Activities: Other letting and operating of own or leased real estate
Shareholders: Anish Kumar Aggarwal; Sejal Mahesh Aggarwal
Officers: Anish Kumar Aggarwal [1980] Director; Sejal Mahesh Aggarwal [1980] Director

SEJ Distribution Ltd
Incorporated: 19 May 2008 *Employees:* 36
Net Worth: £2,098,057 *Total Assets:* £6,960,997
Registered Office: SEJ House, 5 Caxton Trading Estate, Printing House Lane, Hayes, Middlesex, UB3 1BE
Activities: Non-specialised wholesale trade
Parent: SEJ Assets Limited
Officers: Sejal Aggarwal, Secretary; Anish Kumar Aggarwal [1980] Director/Tax Consultant; Sejal Mahesh Aggarwal [1980] Director

Selborne Care Limited
Incorporated: 19 July 2005 *Employees:* 534
Net Worth: £8,646,126 *Total Assets:* £14,845,953
Registered Office: 5th Floor, Metropolitan House, 3 Darkes Lane, Potters Bar, Herts, EN6 1AG
Activities: Other human health activities
Parent: Caretech Community Services Limited
Officers: Gareth Dufton, Secretary; Gareth Dufton [1976] Director/Chartered Accountant; John Joseph Ivers [1962] Director; Farouq Rashid Sheikh [1958] Director

Select Enterprises (Holdings) Limited
Incorporated: 12 January 2011
Net Worth: £5,425,217 *Total Assets:* £14,678,742
Registered Office: Crown House, 227 Aldborough Road South, Ilford, Essex, IG3 8HZ
Activities: Pre-primary education
Shareholders: Savinderjit Singh Kalsi; Balvinder Kalsi
Officers: Balvinder Kalsi, Secretary; Balvinder Kalsi [1967] Director/Chartered Accountant; Sarup Singh Kalsi [1939] Director; Savinderjit Kalsi [1964] Director/Chartered Surveyor

Select Enterprises Limited
Incorporated: 4 April 2005
Net Worth: £1,402,625 *Total Assets:* £13,570,220
Registered Office: Crown House, 227 Aldborough Road South, Ilford, Essex, IG3 8HZ
Activities: Other letting and operating of own or leased real estate
Shareholders: Savinderjit Singh Kalsi; Balvinder Kalsi
Officers: Balvinder Kalsi, Secretary/Director; Balvinder Kalsi [1967] Director; Savinderjit Singh Kalsi [1964] Director

Select Plant Hire Company Limited
Incorporated: 20 December 1985
Net Worth: £183,522,000 *Total Assets:* £259,896,992
Registered Office: Bridge Place, Anchor Boulevard, Admirals Park, Crossways, Dartford, Kent, DA2 6SN
Activities: Other specialised construction activities n.e.c.
Parent: R O'Rourke & Son Limited
Officers: Robert Edward Turner, Secretary; Matthew Clement Hugh Gill [1971] Director/Group Financial Controller; Stephen John Harley [1951] Director; Alexander Stewart McIntyre [1956] Director; Paul William McNerney [1977] Director/Business Unit Leader; Hubert Desmond O'Rourke [1949] Director/Structural Engineer [Irish]

Select Poultry & Meat Ltd
Incorporated: 12 May 2003 *Employees:* 96
Net Worth: £1,665,923 *Total Assets:* £6,272,146
Registered Office: 467 Rainham Road South, Dagenham, Essex, RM10 7XJ
Activities: Retail sale of meat and meat products in specialised stores
Parent: ORG Holdings Limited
Officers: James Charles George [1975] Director/Butcher; Rosina Alexandra George [1977] Director/Businesswoman

Selecta Holding Limited
Incorporated: 14 June 2007
Net Worth: £14,375,000 *Total Assets:* £18,314,000
Registered Office: Apollo House, West End Road, Odyssey Business Park, Ruislip, Middlesex, HA4 6QD
Activities: Activities of head offices
Parent: KKR & Co.L.P.
Officers: Daniel Henry Abrahams [1973] Director; Jan Marck Vrijlandt [1965] Managing Director [Dutch]

Selecta U.K. Limited
Incorporated: 25 April 1991 *Employees:* 1,088
Previous: Pelican Rouge Coffee Solutions Limited
Net Worth: £9,668,000 *Total Assets:* £73,467,000
Registered Office: Apollo House, Odyssey Business Park, West End Road, Ruislip, Middlesex, HA4 6QD
Activities: Other food services
Parent: Selecta UK Holding Limited
Officers: Daniel Henry Abrahams [1973] Director/Accountant; David Christophe Marc Flochel [1973] Director [French]; Wesley Mulligan [1963] Managing Director [Irish]

Selecta UK Holding Limited
Incorporated: 19 October 1925
Previous: Pelican Rouge Coffee Solutions Group Limited
Net Worth Deficit: £84,711,000 *Total Assets:* £83,043,000
Registered Office: Apollo House, Odyssey Business Park, West End Road, Ruislip, Middlesex, HA4 6QD
Activities: Other food services
Parent: KKR & Co.L.P.
Officers: Daniel Henry Abrahams [1973] Director; David Christophe Marc Flochel [1973] Director [French]; Wesley Mulligan [1963] Managing Director [Irish]; Gabriel Pirona [1970] Director [French]

Selwyns Travel Limited
Incorporated: 24 August 1978 *Employees:* 242
Net Worth: £4,916,968 *Total Assets:* £9,679,364
Registered Office: Busways House, Wellington Road, Twickenham, Middlesex, TW2 5NX
Activities: Other passenger land transport
Parent: RATP DEV UK Ltd
Officers: Cyril Herve Carniel [1961] Director/Consultant [French]; Howard Charles Goodbourn [1961] Director/Chief Financial Officer; Selwyn Alun Jones [1947] Director; Carl Andrew Ogden [1982] Service Delivery Director; Ann Marie Pauline Slavin [1969] Finance Director [Irish]

SEM Limited
Incorporated: 17 October 1914 *Employees:* 205
Net Worth: £26,317,848 *Total Assets:* £36,391,328
Registered Office: One Hundred House, Brunel Way, Dartford, Kent, DA1 5TH
Activities: Manufacture of electric motors, generators and transformers
Parent: Westec Holding Company Limited
Officers: Michael Alexander Laming, Company Secretary; Fiona Blyth [1967] Joint Managing Director; Michael Alexander Laming [1953] Director; Thomas Peter Walther [1963] Joint Managing Director [German]

Seneca Environmental Solutions Ltd
Incorporated: 16 December 2008 *Employees:* 47
Net Worth: £3,452,341 *Total Assets:* £29,532,112
Registered Office: Carey House, Great Central Way, Wembley, Middlesex, HA9 0HR
Activities: Recovery of sorted materials
Parent: Carey Group PLC
Officers: Fiona Mary O'Donnell, Secretary; John Anthony Carey [1964] Director [Irish]; Patrick Joseph Carey [1945] Director [Irish]; Denis Patrick Deacy [1965] Director; Kenneth Eamon Doran [1978] Director [Irish]

Senior Engineering Investments Limited
Incorporated: 17 September 1968
Net Worth: £669,816,000 *Total Assets:* £1,019,582,976
Registered Office: 59-61 High Street, Rickmansworth, Herts, WD3 1RH
Activities: Activities of head offices
Parent: Senior PLC
Officers: Andrew John Bodenham, Secretary; Andrew John Bodenham [1966] Director and Company Secretary; Bindi Jayantilal Jivraj Foyle [1973] Director; David Hamilton Squires [1963] Director

Senior Finance Four Limited
Incorporated: 12 June 2009
Net Worth: £43,373,000 *Total Assets:* £183,024,992
Registered Office: 59-61 High Street, Rickmansworth, Herts, WD3 1RH
Activities: Activities of head offices
Parent: Senior Engineering Investments Limited
Officers: Andrew John Bodenham, Secretary; Andrew John Bodenham [1966] Director; Bindi Jayantilal Jivraj Foyle [1973] Director

Senior Finance Seven Limited
Incorporated: 13 March 2014
Net Worth: £12,720,575 *Total Assets:* £12,720,575
Registered Office: 59-61 High Street, Rickmansworth, Herts, WD3 1RH
Activities: Activities of head offices
Parent: Senior Engineering Investments Limited
Officers: Andrew John Bodenham, Secretary; Andrew John Bodenham [1966] Director; Bindi Jayantilal Jivraj Foyle [1973] Director

Senior Finance Six Limited
Incorporated: 16 November 2011
Net Worth: £86,993,320 *Total Assets:* £130,925,520
Registered Office: 59-61 High Street, Rickmansworth, Herts, WD3 1RH
Activities: Activities of head offices
Parent: Senior Engineering Investments Limited
Officers: Andrew John Bodenham, Secretary; Andrew John Bodenham [1966] Director; Bindi Jayantilal Jivraj Foyle [1973] Director

Senior Five Limited
Incorporated: 13 September 2011
Net Worth: £283,276,704 *Total Assets:* £570,557,504
Registered Office: 59-61 High Street, Rickmansworth, Herts, WD3 1RH
Activities: Activities of head offices
Parent: Senior US Holdings Inc.
Officers: Andrew John Bodenham, Secretary; Andrew John Bodenham [1966] Director and Company Secretary; Bindi Jayantilal Jivraj Foyle [1973] Director

Senior PLC
Incorporated: 18 December 1933 *Employees:* 7,658
Net Worth: £531,600,000 *Total Assets:* £950,800,000
Registered Office: 59-61 High Street, Rickmansworth, Herts, WD3 1RH
Activities: Activities of head offices
Officers: Andrew John Bodenham, Secretary; Dr Celia Frances Baxter [1958] Director; Susan Brennan [1962] Director [American]; Bindi Jayantilal Jivraj Foyle [1973] Director; Giles Frances Bertram Kerr [1959] Director; Ian Graham King [1956] Director; Rajiv Sharma [1966] Director [Singaporean]; David Hamilton Squires [1963] Director; Mark Edward Vernon [1953] Director [American]

Senior UK Limited
Incorporated: 3 July 1985 *Employees:* 1,299
Net Worth: £66,473,000 *Total Assets:* £149,584,000
Registered Office: 59-61 High Street, Rickmansworth, Herts, WD3 1RH
Activities: Manufacture of other special-purpose machinery n.e.c.
Parent: Senior Engineering Investments Limited
Officers: Andrew John Bodenham, Company Secretary; Andrew John Bodenham [1966] Director and Company Secretary; Bindi Jayantilal Jivraj Foyle [1973] Director; Michael Sheppard [1959] Director/President-APD [American]; David Hamilton Squires [1963] Director

Sensormatic Limited
Incorporated: 15 June 1992
Net Worth Deficit: £19,705,000 *Total Assets:* £9,149,000
Registered Office: Security House, The Summit, Hanworth Road, Sunbury on Thames, Middlesex, TW16 5DB
Activities: Other business support service activities n.e.c.
Parent: Johnson Controls International PLC
Officers: Mark Ayre [1963] Finance Director; Peter Schieser [1967] Director [German]

Services Support (Cleveland) Holdings Limited
Incorporated: 12 January 2000
Net Worth: £584,000 *Total Assets:* £6,605,000
Registered Office: 8 White Oak Square, London Road, Swanley, Kent, BR8 7AG
Activities: Activities of head offices
Parent: Amalie PFI (UK) Limited
Officers: Clement David Baptiste Leverd [1986] Director/Investment Executive [French]; Elena Giorgiana Wegener [1975] Director/Investment Executive

Services Support (Cleveland) Limited
Incorporated: 12 January 2000
Net Worth: £584,000 *Total Assets:* £6,605,000
Registered Office: 8 White Oak Square, London Road, Swanley, Kent, BR8 7AG
Activities: Other business support service activities n.e.c.
Parent: Services Support (Cleveland) Holdings Limited
Officers: Clement David Baptiste Leverd [1986] Director/Investment Executive [French]; Elena Giorgiana Wegener [1975] Director/Investment Executive

Services Support (Gravesend) Holdings Limited
Incorporated: 20 January 2000
Net Worth: £4,293,000 *Total Assets:* £39,864,000
Registered Office: 8 White Oak Square, London Road, Swanley, Kent, BR8 7AG
Activities: Activities of head offices
Shareholders: Palio (No.1) Limited; Amalie PFI (UK) Limited
Officers: David Richard Bradbury [1969] Asset Director; James Christopher Heath [1975] Director; Elena Giorgiana Wegener [1975] Director/Investment Executive

Services Support (Gravesend) Limited
Incorporated: 20 January 2000
Net Worth: £4,293,000 *Total Assets:* £39,864,000
Registered Office: 8 White Oak Square, London Road, Swanley, Kent, BR8 7AG
Activities: Other business support service activities n.e.c.
Parent: Services Support (Gravesend) Holdings Limited
Officers: David Richard Bradbury [1969] Asset Director; James Christopher Heath [1975] Director; Elena Giorgiana Wegener [1975] Director/Investment Executive

Services Support (Manchester) Holdings Limited
Incorporated: 24 August 2001
Net Worth Deficit: £12,344,000 *Total Assets:* £83,626,000
Registered Office: 8 White Oak Square, London Road, Swanley, Kent, BR8 7AG
Activities: Activities of head offices
Shareholders: Palio (No 1) Limited; Amalie PFI (UK) Limited
Officers: James Christopher Heath [1975] Director; Clement David Baptiste Leverd [1986] Director/Investment Executive [French]; Neil Woodburn [1979] Director/Chartered Building Surveyor

Services Support (Manchester) Limited
Incorporated: 24 August 2001
Net Worth Deficit: £12,344,000 *Total Assets:* £83,626,000
Registered Office: 8 White Oak Square, London Road, Swanley, Kent, BR8 7AG
Activities: Other business support service activities n.e.c.
Parent: Services Support (Manchester) Holdings Limited
Officers: James Christopher Heath [1975] Director; Clement David Baptiste Leverd [1986] Director/Investment Executive [French]; Neil Woodburn [1979] Director/Chartered Building Surveyor

Services Support (SEL) Holdings Limited
Incorporated: 20 January 2000
Net Worth Deficit: £4,790,000 *Total Assets:* £77,453,000
Registered Office: 8 White Oak Square, London Road, Swanley, Kent, BR8 7AG
Activities: Activities of head offices
Shareholders: JLIF Holdings (Justice and Emergency Services) Limited; Amalie PFI (UK) Limited
Officers: Farid Barekati [1984] Director/Chartered Accountant; David Richard Bradbury [1969] Director/Senior Investment Manager; James Christopher Heath [1975] Director; Elena Giorgiana Wegener [1975] Director/Investment Executive

Services Support (SEL) Limited
Incorporated: 7 December 1998
Net Worth Deficit: £4,790,000 *Total Assets:* £77,453,000
Registered Office: 8 White Oak Square, London Road, Swanley, Kent, BR8 7AG
Activities: Other business support service activities n.e.c.
Parent: Services Support (SEL) Holdings Limited
Officers: Farid Barekati [1984] Director/Chartered Accountant; David Richard Bradbury [1969] Director/Senior Investment Manager; James Christopher Heath [1975] Director; Elena Giorgiana Wegener [1975] Director/Investment Executive

Servipharm Limited
Incorporated: 22 May 1989 *Employees:* 28
Net Worth: £4,570,605 *Total Assets:* £6,037,450
Registered Office: 39a Joel Street, Northwood Hills, Northwood, Middlesex, HA6 1NZ
Activities: Wholesale of pharmaceutical goods
Major Shareholder: Vipul Shah
Officers: Vipul Shah [1963] Director/Businessman [Kenyan]

Servotest Testing Systems Ltd
Incorporated: 11 June 2007 *Employees:* 37
Net Worth: £3,002,389 *Total Assets:* £6,523,431
Registered Office: Unit 2 Alpha Way, Thorpe Industrial Estate, Egham, Surrey, TW20 8RZ
Activities: Manufacture of electrical and electronic equipment for motor vehicles and their engines
Parent: BBK Test Systems Hongkong Co. Limited
Officers: Brian David Ferris [1944] Director; Jing Lie Li [1959] Director; Jin Tian [1978] Director [Chinese]; Yan Shen Zhang [1971] Director [Chinese]

SES (Engineering Services) Limited
Incorporated: 19 April 1961 *Employees:* 903
Previous: Shepherd Engineering Services Limited
Net Worth Deficit: £3,321,000 *Total Assets:* £62,982,000
Registered Office: Wates House, Station Approach, Leatherhead, Surrey, KT22 7SW
Activities: Construction of commercial buildings
Parent: Wates Construction Limited
Officers: Philip Michael Wainwright, Secretary; David Owen Allen [1972] Director/Chief Financial Officer; Paul Chandler [1964] Managing Director; Simon James Potter [1963] Group Commercial Director; Paul Campbell Rowan [1964] Group HR Director; Philip Michael Wainwright [1965] Director/Chief Financial Officer

Setfirst Limited
Incorporated: 3 January 1989
Net Worth: £15,873,934,336 *Total Assets:* £35,656,830,976
Registered Office: 980 Great West Road, Brentford, Middlesex, TW8 9GS
Activities: Activities of head offices
Parent: GlaxoSmithKline Finance PLC
Officers: Simon Paul Dingemans [1963] Director; Adam Walker [1967] Director

Seven Seas Limited
Incorporated: 6 April 1939 *Employees:* 44
Net Worth Deficit: £25,302,000 *Total Assets:* £16,648,000
Registered Office: Bedfont Cross, Stanwell Road, Feltham, Middlesex, TW14 8NX
Activities: Manufacture of basic pharmaceutical products
Parent: Merck Consumer Healthcare Limited
Officers: Anthony Joseph Appleton [1962] Director & General Counsel; James David Binnington [1968] Director; Alexander George Buckthorp [1973] Finance Director; Heidrun Gresle [1966] Director/General Manager UK & Ireland [German]; Vijay Indroo Sitlani [1975] Finance Director [Singaporean]; Christopher John Young [1974] HR Director

Sevita (UK) Limited
Incorporated: 20 May 2008
Net Worth: £24,309,000 *Total Assets:* £38,614,000
Registered Office: Compass House, Guildford Street, Chertsey, Surrey, KT16 9BQ
Activities: Other business support service activities n.e.c.
Parent: Compass Overseas Holdings No.2 Limited
Officers: Sarah Jane Sergeant [1973] Director/Accountant

Seymour House Residential Care Homes Limited
Incorporated: 24 February 2003 *Employees:* 74
Net Worth: £3,041,362 *Total Assets:* £8,594,592
Registered Office: Seymour House, 13-17 Rectory Road, Rickmansworth, Herts, WD3 1FH
Activities: Residential care activities for the elderly and disabled
Parent: Seymour House Investments Limited
Officers: Salim Rhemtulla, Secretary; Murad Rhemtulla [1944] Director; Salim Rhemtulla [1977] Director; Yasmin Rhemtulla [1972] Director

SF11 Limited
Incorporated: 5 August 2011
Net Worth: £500,581 *Total Assets:* £23,523,460
Registered Office: Kinetic Business Centre, The Kinetic Centre, Theobald Street, Borehamwood, Herts, WD6 4PJ
Activities: Financial intermediation not elsewhere classified
Parent: Spring Finance Limited
Officers: Moshe Moses, Secretary; George Leo Benninger [1946] Director/Attorney [American]; Martin David Chesler [1973] Director/Accountant; Christopher Charles Chew [1972] Director/Head of Lending; Paul Julian Mann [1968] Investment Director; Graeme Edward Wade [1979] Director/Head of Sales

SFAET Ltd
Incorporated: 1 July 2011 *Employees:* 191
Previous: Success for All Educational Trust
Net Worth: £25,028,000 *Total Assets:* £27,800,000
Registered Office: Redden Court School, Cotswold Road, Harold Wood, Romford, Essex, RM3 0TS
Activities: General secondary education
Officers: Justin Paul Barrett, Secretary; Parminder Kohli [1971] Director; Quenton Shiel Lennon [1970] Director/Businessman; Anita Stewart [1980] Director/Virtual Headteacher; Joanna Wilkinson [1977] Director; Neil Yeomans [1962] Director/Retired

SG Equipment Finance (December) Limited
Incorporated: 19 November 1980
Net Worth: £4,080,969 *Total Assets:* £22,868,920
Registered Office: Parkshot House, Kew Road, Richmond, Surrey, TW9 2PR
Activities: Financial leasing
Parent: Societe Generale Equipment Finance Limited
Officers: Timothy Edward Goodship, Secretary; Stephen John Bowden [1964] Director/Senior Account Manager; Timothy Edward Goodship [1979] Director/Certified Chartered Accountant; Dominic Lawson Hughes [1972] Director/Financier; David Robert George Yates-Mercer [1964] Director/Accountant

SG Technologies Group Limited
Incorporated: 1 December 2011 *Employees:* 188
Previous: S G Technologies Group Limited
Net Worth: £3,853,000 *Total Assets:* £14,823,000
Registered Office: 85 Ferry Lane, Rainham, Essex, RM13 9YH
Activities: Other manufacturing n.e.c.
Shareholder: John Stephen Taylor
Officers: Stuart Andrew Hutcheon [1970] Sales Director; Timothy George Robinson [1973] Operation Director; Jonathan Clark Swift [1975] Director/Engineer; John Stephen Taylor [1963] Director; Stephen Thomas Quentin Williams [1951] Director

SG Technologies Limited
Incorporated: 11 September 1987 *Employees:* 187
Previous: S G Technologies Limited
Net Worth: £5,431,000 *Total Assets:* £16,504,000
Registered Office: Tesla House, 85 Ferry Lane, Rainham, Essex, RM13 9YH
Activities: Other manufacturing n.e.c.
Officers: Stuart Andrew Hutcheon [1970] Director/Sales Manager; Timothy George Robinson [1973] Operations Director; Jonathan Clark Swift [1975] Director/Engineer; John Stephen Taylor [1963] Director/Development; Stephen Thomas Quentin Williams [1951] Director

SGB Infrastructure Middle East Limited
Incorporated: 15 August 2007
Previous: Harsco Infrastructure Middle East Limited
Net Worth: £67,126,000 *Total Assets:* £67,144,000
Registered Office: Regent Park, 299 Kingston Road, Leatherhead, Surrey, KT22 7SG
Activities: Activities of head offices
Major Shareholder: Donald Gogel
Officers: Andreas Akhtar [1974] Director/Lawyer [German]; Christopher McGalpine [1972] Director/Accountant

Shadowgrade Developments Limited
Incorporated: 19 February 1988 *Employees:* 28
Net Worth: £9,376,252 *Total Assets:* £20,069,988
Registered Office: Wraysbury Hall, Ferry Lane, Staines upon Thames, Middlesex, TW19 6HG
Activities: Hotels and similar accommodation
Major Shareholder: David Winn
Officers: Colin Higgins, Secretary; Joanna Cross [1980] Director; Scott Hamilton [1953] Managing Director; Colin Higgins [1965] Director/Accountant

Shakoor Capital Limited
Incorporated: 12 February 1998 *Employees:* 1
Previous: Handsel Limited
Net Worth: £8,887,165 *Total Assets:* £9,465,524
Registered Office: Premier Suite, 4 Churchill Court, 58 Station Road, North Harrow, Middlesex, HA2 7ST
Activities: Security dealing on own account
Major Shareholder: Was Shakoor
Officers: Waseem Shakoor [1967] Director/Management Consultant

Shaneel Enterprises Limited
Incorporated: 30 September 1987 *Employees:* 150
Net Worth: £55,743,016 *Total Assets:* £92,480,160
Registered Office: 78 Wembley Park Drive, Wembley, Middlesex, HA9 8HE
Activities: Wholesale of perfume and cosmetics
Officers: Chetna Dilesh Mehta, Secretary; Dilesh Bhogilal Mehta [1960] Director/Businessman Wholesaler; Hitesh Bhogilal Mehta [1956] Director/Pharmacist

Sharan Properties Limited
Incorporated: 24 October 1984 *Employees:* 3
Net Worth: £10,794,672 *Total Assets:* £11,806,635
Registered Office: 106 Sudbury Court Drive, Harrow, Middlesex, HA1 3TG
Activities: Buying and selling of own real estate
Shareholder: Usha Gupta
Officers: Usha Gupta, Secretary; Prashant Gupta [1970] Director; Usha Gupta [1945] Director

Share and Debenture Trust Limited (The)
Incorporated: 19 February 1914 *Employees:* 7
Net Worth: £6,652,837 *Total Assets:* £7,668,025
Registered Office: 43 Market Place, Romford, Essex, RM1 3AB
Activities: Buying and selling of own real estate
Officers: Conor O'Mahony, Secretary; Rosemary Ann Fisher [1935] Director/Housewife; Lawrence Alan Knott [1942] Director/Retired Estate Agent; John Frederick Waley Sanderson [1954] Director/Business Analyst; David Lingen Sunnucks [1961] Director/Farmer; Lucinda Jane Frances Sunnucks [1962] Director; William D'Urban Sunnucks [1956] Director

Sharish Properties Limited
Incorporated: 6 October 2010
Net Worth Deficit: £71,698 *Total Assets:* £6,420,497
Registered Office: Lynx House, Ferndown, Northwood, Middlesex, HA6 1PQ
Activities: Buying and selling of own real estate
Major Shareholder: Aarti Patel
Officers: Arati Patel [1964] Director

Sharp Electronics (Europe) Limited
Incorporated: 8 May 2012 *Employees:* 208
Net Worth: £73,973,384 *Total Assets:* £202,510,208
Registered Office: 4 Furzeground Way, Stockley Park, Uxbridge, Middlesex, UB11 1EZ
Activities: Other manufacturing n.e.c.
Parent: Sharp Corporation
Officers: Gosia Grant-Lipinska, Secretary; Jun Ashida [1966] Director [Japanese]; Seitaro Nomura [1976] Director [Japanese]

Sharp International Finance (U.K.) PLC
Incorporated: 2 May 1990 *Employees:* 3
Net Worth: £33,154,948 *Total Assets:* £116,652,608
Registered Office: 4 Furzeground Way, Stockley Park, Uxbridge, Middlesex, UB11 1EZ
Activities: Financial intermediation not elsewhere classified
Officers: Tatsuaki Watanabe, Secretary; Satoshi Sakakibara [1958] Director/Businessman [Japanese]; Tatsuaki Watanabe [1965] Director/Businessman [Japanese]

Shazam Productions Limited
Incorporated: 18 November 2003 *Employees:* 5
Net Worth: £7,893,610 *Total Assets:* £9,265,620
Registered Office: 34 Anyards Road, Cobham, Surrey, KT11 2LA
Activities: Artistic creation
Major Shareholder: Sharon Gillian Sullivan
Officers: Sharon Gillian Sullivan, Secretary; Amy Louise Sullivan [1983] Director; Daniel John Charles Sullivan [1975] Director/Musician; James David Thomas Sullivan [1978] Director/Musician; Sharon Gillian Sullivan [1953] Director

Sheargold Limited
Incorporated: 5 September 1991 *Employees:* 17
Net Worth: £6,958,270 *Total Assets:* £8,574,457
Registered Office: Unit 1 Imperial Park, Stonefield Way, Ruislip, Middlesex, HA4 0JW
Activities: Agents involved in the sale of a variety of goods
Shareholders: Nitinkumar Vanechand Mehta; Jyotsna Nitin Mehta; Hemal Nitinkumar Mehta
Officers: Jyotsna Nitin Mehta, Secretary; Hemal Nitinkumar Mehta [1986] Procurement Director; Jyotsna Nitin Mehta [1956] Director/Operations; Nitinkumar Vanechand Mehta [1953] Managing Director; Sapna Nitinkumar Mehta [1981] Financial Director; Amar Anil Shah [1980] Commercial Director

Sheikh Holdings Group (Investments) Limited
Incorporated: 26 May 2011 *Employees:* 63
Net Worth: £26,006,516 *Total Assets:* £51,078,424
Registered Office: 7th Floor, Metropolitan House, 3 Darkes Lane, Potters Bar, Herts, EN6 1AG
Activities: Activities of other holding companies n.e.c.
Shareholders: Haroon Rashid Sheikh; Farouq Rashid Sheikh
Officers: Gareth Dufton, Secretary; Matthew James Davis [1970] Director; Gareth Norman Dufton [1976] Director/Chartered Accountant; Akbar Sheikh [1989] Director; Farouq Rashid Sheikh [1958] Director; Haroon Rashid Sheikh [1956] Non-Executive Director Chairman; Yusuf Rashid Sheikh [1992] Director

Shelfside (Holdings) Limited
Incorporated: 20 December 2000 *Employees:* 93
Net Worth: £7,114,410 *Total Assets:* £37,585,772
Registered Office: 166 College Road, Harrow, Middlesex, HA1 1RA
Activities: Renting and operating of Housing Association real estate
Parent: Best Holdings (UK) Limited
Officers: Ian Michael Farr, Secretary; Alfred William Best [1970] Director; Waseem Hanif [1967] Director

Shelfside Group LLP
Incorporated: 10 August 2016 *Employees:* 2
Net Worth: £38,964,948 *Total Assets:* £50,248,940
Registered Office: 166 College Road, Harrow, Middlesex, HA1 1RA
Officers: Alfred William Best [1970] Member

Shelfside Holding (Northern) Ltd
Incorporated: 13 January 2011 *Employees:* 2
Net Worth: £3,576,408 *Total Assets:* £10,345,071
Registered Office: 166 College Road, Harrow, Middlesex, HA1 1RA
Activities: Other business support service activities n.e.c.
Parent: Best Holdings (UK) Limited
Officers: Waseem Hanif, Secretary; Alfred William Best [1970] Managing Director

Shellen Construction Limited
Incorporated: 7 March 1996 *Employees:* 2
Net Worth: £4,281,088 *Total Assets:* £5,468,128
Registered Office: College House, 17 King Edwards Road, Ruislip, Middlesex, HA4 7AE
Activities: Other construction installation
Shareholders: Leonard William Pitt; Michelle Jane Pitt
Officers: Michelle Jane Pitt, Secretary; Leonard William Pitt [1962] Director/Security Fitter

Shelly Motors Limited
Incorporated: 8 December 2006 *Employees:* 43
Previous: Barry Shelley Limited
Net Worth Deficit: £519,059 *Total Assets:* £5,573,710
Registered Office: Warren Place, Birch Vale, Cobham, Surrey, KT11 2PX
Activities: Sale of used cars and light motor vehicles
Major Shareholder: Lesley Shelly
Officers: Andrew Shelly, Secretary; Andrew James Shelly [1974] Director/Business Manager; Lesley Shelly [1948] Director [New Zealander]

Shenley Park Trust
Incorporated: 23 May 1990 *Employees:* 5
Net Worth: £10,191,887 *Total Assets:* £10,235,764
Registered Office: The Bothy, Shenley Park, Radlett Lane, Shenley, Radlett, Herts, WD7 9DW
Activities: Other amusement and recreation activities n.e.c.
Officers: Glyn Stewart Dredge, Secretary; Glyn Stewart Dredge [1966] Park Director; Rosemary Elizabeth Gilligan [1957] Director; Warren Barry Gordon [1968] Director/Solicitor; Steve James Harrington-Smith [1974] Director; Anthony Charles Harris [1976] Director/Solicitor; Neil James Hibbert [1962] Director/Accountant; Seamus Quilty [1951] Director/Councillor; Natalie Rowan [1980] Director; Anthony Philip Spencer [1948] Director; William Susman [1967] Director/Estate Agent; Howard Wand [1955] Director/Printer; Simon Ward [1963] Director/IT Consultant

Shepherd Harris & Co Limited
Incorporated: 15 July 2014 *Employees:* 22
Net Worth: £398,338 *Total Assets:* £6,749,598
Registered Office: 96 Silver Street, Enfield, Middlesex, EN1 3EL
Activities: Solicitors
Major Shareholder: Duncan Ferguson Ritchie
Officers: Duncan Ferguson Ritchie, Secretary; Gennaro Giuseppe Baffa [1972] Director/Chartered Legal Executive; Tazeen Roohi Khaliq [1966] Director/Solicitor; Duncan Ferguson Ritchie [1959] Director/Solicitor

Sheplord Limited
Incorporated: 11 September 1985
Net Worth: £3,146,720 *Total Assets:* £6,658,804
Registered Office: Vellum Hall Farm, 28 Church Lane, Northaw, Herts, EN6 4NX
Activities: Development of building projects
Officers: Juanita Obrien, Secretary; Casey Edward O'Brien [1980] Director/Foreman; Jamie Francis O'Brien [1976] Director/Project Manager; Juanita Ellen O'Brien [1952] Director/Secretary; Francis Obrien [1944] Director/Garage Proprietor [Irish]

Shepperton Hotels Holdings Limited
Incorporated: 7 October 1997
Net Worth: £13,215,829 *Total Assets:* £16,885,998
Registered Office: Warren Lodge Hotel, Church Square, Shepperton on Thames, Surrey, TW17 9JZ
Activities: Hotels and similar accommodation
Officers: Patrick William Strachan Gordon, Secretary; Alison Ruth Gordon [1967] Director/Hotelier; David George Strachan Gordon [1965] Director/Solicitor; James Douglas Strachan Gordon [1961] Director/Solicitor; Patrick William Strachan Gordon [1960] Director/Chartered Surveyor

Shepperton Hotels Limited
Incorporated: 3 January 1966 *Employees:* 70
Net Worth: £9,961,016 *Total Assets:* £13,060,999
Registered Office: Warren Lodge Hotel, Church Square, Shepperton on Thames, Surrey, TW17 9JZ
Activities: Hotels and similar accommodation
Officers: Patrick William Strachan Gordon, Secretary; Alison Ruth Gordon [1967] Director/Hotelier; David George Strachan Gordon [1965] Director/Solicitor; James Douglas Strachan Gordon [1961] Director/Solicitor; Patrick William Strachan Gordon [1960] Director

Sherrygold No.1 Limited
Incorporated: 5 December 2002
Net Worth: £5,950,404 *Total Assets:* £14,630,546
Registered Office: Jubilee House, 7-9 The Oaks, Ruislip, Middlesex, HA4 7LF
Activities: Other letting and operating of own or leased real estate
Major Shareholder: Amiran Hassan Moledina Janmohamed
Officers: Alim Amirali Janmohamed, Secretary; Alim Amirali Janmohamed [1981] Director; Amirali Hassanali Moledina Janmohamed [1952] Director

Sherrygreen Homes Ltd
Incorporated: 9 February 2006 *Employees:* 10
Net Worth: £6,163,197 *Total Assets:* £26,906,754
Registered Office: Teresa Gavin House, Woodford Avenue, Woodford Green, Essex, IG8 8FA
Activities: Development of building projects
Parent: Sherrygreen Ltd
Officers: Eamon O'Malley, Secretary; Brendon O'Malley [1954] Director; Eamon O'Malley [1955] Director; Martin Taylor [1952] Director/Manager; Teresa Taylor [1963] Director

Sherrygreen Limited
Incorporated: 19 October 1983 *Employees:* 527
Net Worth: £103,762,000 *Total Assets:* £171,018,000
Registered Office: Teresa Gavin House, Woodford Avenue, Woodford Green, Essex, IG8 8FA
Activities: Activities of head offices
Officers: Eamon O'Malley, Secretary; Brendon O'Malley [1954] Managing Director; Eamon O'Malley [1955] Director; Shaun O'Malley [1966] Director; Vincent O'Malley [1951] Director; Teresa Taylor [1963] Director

Shetson Property Developments Limited
Incorporated: 14 May 1993 *Employees:* 4
Net Worth: £6,342,526 *Total Assets:* £19,743,774
Registered Office: Unit 2 Westpoint, 328 Bath Road, Hounslow, Middlesex, TW4 7HW
Activities: Development of building projects
Shareholder: Santokh Singh
Officers: Triya Maicha, Secretary; Santokh Singh, Secretary/Retired; Santokh Singh [1935] Director/Retired; Sarabjit Singh [1951] Director/Administration Officer [Indian]

Shields Environmental Group (Holdings) Ltd.
Incorporated: 14 May 2015 *Employees:* 138
Net Worth Deficit: £4,866,000 *Total Assets:* £20,411,000
Registered Office: Shields Environmental, Kerry Avenue, Aveley, South Ockendon, Essex, RM15 4YE
Activities: Activities of head offices
Shareholder: William Anthony Rice
Officers: David Harry Challis [1962] Director/Chief Financial Officer; Daniel Jones [1982] Director; William Anthony Rice [1952] Director

Shields Environmental Investment (Holdings) Limited
Incorporated: 15 May 2015 *Employees:* 4
Net Worth Deficit: £3,059,000 *Total Assets:* £19,212,000
Registered Office: Shields Environmental, Kerry Avenue, Aveley, South Ockendon, Essex, RM15 4YE
Activities: Activities of head offices
Parent: Shields Environmental Group (Holdings) Ltd
Officers: David Harry Challis [1962] Director; Daniel Jones [1982] Director; William Anthony Rice [1952] Director

Shilton Bidco Limited
Incorporated: 28 April 2017 *Employees:* 3
Net Worth: £106,638,000 *Total Assets:* £1,029,436,992
Registered Office: Profile West, 950 Great West Road, Brentford, Middlesex, TW8 9ES
Activities: Non-trading company
Parent: Shilton Holdco Limited
Officers: Andrew Gregory Firth [1964] Director; Andrew Patrick Griffith [1968] Director; Philippe Robert Francis Mauguy [1960] Director [French]

Shilton Holdco Limited
Incorporated: 28 April 2017
Net Worth: £211,656,992 *Total Assets:* £439,038,016
Registered Office: Profile West, 950 Great West Road, Brentford, Middlesex, TW8 9ES
Activities: Non-trading company
Officers: Andrew Gregory Firth [1964] Director; Andrew Patrick Griffith [1968] Director; Philippe Robert Francis Mauguy [1960] Director [French]

Shimtech Industries Group Limited
Incorporated: 17 December 2014 *Employees:* 457
Previous: Auctus Scorpion Topco Limited
Net Worth: £48,860,720 *Total Assets:* £194,229,792
Registered Office: 7 A/B, Millington Road, Hayes, Middlesex, UB3 4AZ
Activities: Activities of head offices
Officers: Andrew David Caffyn [1964] Director/Business Executive; Alastair Scott Fanning [1967] Director/Business Executive; John Frederik Hartz [1973] Director/Investment Professional [Danish]; Prince Valerio Camillo Francesco Massimo [1973] Director/Business Executive; Catherine Allingham Richards [1973] Director/Investment Professional; Lord Edward Albert Charles Spencer-Churchill [1974] Director/Business Executive; Brian Williams [1957] Director [American]

Shimtech Industries Holdco Limited
Incorporated: 17 December 2014
Previous: Auctus Scorpion Holdco Limited
Net Worth: £3,163,000 *Total Assets:* £108,458,000
Registered Office: 7 A/B, Millington Road, Hayes, Middlesex, UB3 4AZ
Activities: Activities of head offices
Parent: Auctus Scorpion Midco Limited
Officers: Heath Denis Batwell [1983] Director/Accountant [Irish]; Andrew David Caffyn [1964] Director/Business Executive; Alastair Scott Fanning [1967] Director/Business Executive; John Frederik Hartz [1963] Director/Investment Professional [Danish]; Prince Valerio Camillo Francesco Massimo [1973] Director/Business Executive; Catherine Allingham Richards [1973] Director/Investment Professional; Lord Edward Albert Charles Spencer-Churchill [1974] Director/Business Executive; Brian Williams [1957] Director [American]

Shimtech Industries Holdco2 Limited
Incorporated: 17 December 2014 *Employees:* 1
Previous: Auctus Industries Limited
Net Worth Deficit: £17,760,000 *Total Assets:* £248,446,000
Registered Office: 7 A/B, Millington Road, Hayes, Middlesex, UB3 4AZ
Activities: Activities of head offices
Parent: Auctus Scorpion Holdco Limited
Officers: Heath Denis Batwell [1983] Director/Accountant [Irish]; Andrew David Caffyn [1964] Director/Business Executive; Alastair Scott Fanning [1967] Director/Business Executive; John Frederik Hartz [1963] Director/Investment Professional [Danish]; Prince Valerio Camillo Francesco Massimo [1973] Director/Business Executive; Catherine Allingham Richards [1973] Director/Investment Professional; Lord Edward Albert Charles Spencer-Churchill [1974] Director/Business Executive; Brian Williams [1957] Director [American]

Shimtech Industries Limited
Incorporated: 4 February 2011 *Employees:* 4
Net Worth Deficit: £21,796,152 *Total Assets:* £74,196,240
Registered Office: 7A/B Millington Road, Hayes, Middlesex, UB3 4AZ
Activities: Activities of head offices
Parent: Shimtech Industries Holdco2 Limited
Officers: Heath Denis Batwell [1983] Director/Accountant [Irish]; Alastair Scott Fanning [1967] Director/Accountant; Christopher Eric Smith [1971] Director

Shire Properties (South East) Limited
Incorporated: 19 March 1997 *Employees:* 1
Net Worth: £3,971,265 *Total Assets:* £7,179,683
Registered Office: Haslers, Old Station Road, Loughton, Essex, IG10 4PL
Activities: Buying and selling of own real estate
Major Shareholder: Christopher Mark Relph
Officers: Julie Powell, Secretary; Christopher Mark Relph [1956] Director

Shirley High School
Incorporated: 7 November 2011 *Employees:* 132
Net Worth: £17,857,532 *Total Assets:* £19,622,708
Registered Office: Shirley High School, Shirley Church Road, Croydon, Surrey, CR0 5EF
Activities: General secondary education
Officers: Maeve Celeste Garcia, Secretary; Nigel Mark Barrow [1959] Director/Headteacher; Elizabeth Anne Daniels [1981] Director/Financial Regulation, Governance & Professionalism; Robert David Farquharson [1968] Director/Chief Operating Officer; Gillian Manson [1965] Director/Accounts Manager Construction; Raymond Tod Munn [1976] Director/Mentor; Colin Benjamin Nicholson [1985] Director/Teacher; Oumaduth Sauba [1978] Director/Chartered Management Accountant; Sarah Smith [1971] Director/Chartered Accountant; Paul James Templeman-Wright [1959] Director/Senior Vice Principal; Michael West [1949] Director/Retired

Shiva Kingsway Limited
Incorporated: 10 September 2014 *Employees:* 88
Net Worth: £429,304 *Total Assets:* £117,024,896
Registered Office: 505 Pinner Road, Harrow, Middlesex, HA2 6EH
Activities: Hotels and similar accommodation
Officers: Rishi Ramesh Sachdev [1976] Director; Uday Vyas [1978] Director

SHL Group Limited
Incorporated: 5 September 1977 *Employees:* 469
Net Worth: £54,856,000 *Total Assets:* £73,779,000
Registered Office: The Pavilion, 1 Atwell Place, Thames Ditton, Surrey, KT7 0NE
Activities: Activities of head offices
Parent: SHL International Management Limited
Officers: Andrew James Bradshaw [1971] Director/General Manager; Michael Edmondson [1976] Director/Head of Finance; Andrew William Myers [1964] Director/Chief Financial Officer; David Edward Ryell [1971] Director/Head of Financial Controller

SHL People Solutions Group Holdings Ltd.
Incorporated: 13 February 1997
Net Worth: £5,147,000 *Total Assets:* £5,147,000
Registered Office: The Pavilion, 1 Atwell Place, Thames Ditton, Surrey, KT7 0NE
Activities: Activities of other holding companies n.e.c.
Parent: SHL International Management Limited
Officers: Michael Edmondson [1976] Director/Head of Finance; Andrew William Myers [1964] Director/Chief Financial Officer; David Edward Ryell [1971] Director/Head of Financial Controller

SHL Product Ltd
Incorporated: 31 March 2008 *Employees:* 30
Net Worth: £813,499 *Total Assets:* £5,236,234
Registered Office: The Pavilion, 1 Atwell Place, Thames Ditton, Surrey, KT7 0NE
Activities: Activities of other holding companies n.e.c.
Parent: SHL International Management Limited
Officers: Michael Edmondson [1976] Director/Head of Finance; Andrew William Myers [1964] Director/Chief Financial Officer; David Edward Ryell [1971] Director/Head of Financial Controller

Shogun Finance Limited
Incorporated: 22 November 1985 *Employees:* 12
Net Worth: £5,886,000 *Total Assets:* £227,207,008
Registered Office: 116 Cockfosters Road, Barnet, Herts, EN4 0DY
Activities: Financial intermediation not elsewhere classified
Shareholders: Spitalgate Dealer Services Limited; Black Horse Group Limited
Officers: David Dermot Hennessey, Secretary; Christopher Michael Adams [1982] Director; Paul Andrew Brigden [1966] Director; Masami Ichiki [1968] Director [Japanese]; Richard Andrew Jones [1972] Marketing Director; David William Ramsey [1963] Managing Director; Dr Nagla Thabet [1974] Director

Shooting Star Chase
Incorporated: 11 May 1994 *Employees:* 174
Net Worth: £13,335,888 *Total Assets:* £14,121,439
Registered Office: Bridge House, Addlestone Road, Addlestone, Surrey, KT15 2UE
Activities: Other human health activities
Officers: Jennifer Johnson, Secretary; Paul Victor Boughton [1955] Director; Andrew Peter Cosslett [1955] Director/Business Executive; Dr Jonathan Paul Craig [1969] Medical Director; Kenneth George Hanna [1953] Director; Jonathan Alexander Kembery [1967] Global Legal Director; Dr Jayne Price [1968] Director/Associate Professor Children's Nursing; Catherine Helen Van't Riet [1967] Director/Clinical Team Leader

Shopfittings Direct Limited
Incorporated: 12 June 1998 *Employees:* 74
Net Worth: £3,495,894 *Total Assets:* £10,263,358
Registered Office: 186-192 High Road, Ilford, Essex, IG1 1LR
Activities: Non-specialised wholesale trade
Shareholder: David Neil Brooks
Officers: Paul Martin Brooks, Secretary; Paul Martin Brooks [1963] Director

Shoppertrak Limited
Incorporated: 16 October 1987 *Employees:* 58
Previous: Footfall Limited
Net Worth Deficit: £5,792,000 *Total Assets:* £23,559,000
Registered Office: Security House, The Summit, Hanworth Road, Sunbury on Thames, Middlesex, TW16 5DB
Activities: Other service activities n.e.c.
Parent: Tyco Holdings (UK) Limited
Officers: Mark Ayre [1963] Finance Director; Nicholas Dominic Pompa [1963] Director

Shoreland Limited
Incorporated: 28 July 1997
Net Worth: £2,361,254 *Total Assets:* £5,566,853
Registered Office: Kimberley House, 31 Burntoak Broadway, Edgware, Middlesex, HA8 5LD
Activities: Other letting and operating of own or leased real estate
Shareholders: Mark Gerald Collins; Iain James Collins
Officers: Mark Generald Collins, Secretary/Director; Iain James Collins [1966] Director; Mark Generald Collins [1968] Director

Shorterm Group Limited
Incorporated: 21 September 1998 *Employees:* 2
Net Worth: £4,882,000 *Total Assets:* £12,796,000
Registered Office: The Barn, Philpots Close, Yiewsley, Middlesex, UB7 7RY
Activities: Temporary employment agency activities
Parent: Grouse Bidco Limited
Officers: Stephen Gallucci [1969] Director; Patrick Finbarr Keenan [1967] Director/Accountant [Irish]

Shorterm Limited
Incorporated: 4 August 1972 *Employees:* 112
Net Worth: £15,046,000 *Total Assets:* £35,267,000
Registered Office: The Barn, Philpots Close, Yiewsley, Middlesex, UB7 7RY
Activities: Temporary employment agency activities
Parent: Shorterm Group Limited
Officers: Stephen Gallucci [1969] Director; Patrick Finbarr Keenan [1967] Director/Accountant [Irish]

Shotfield Development Business Partnership Limited
Incorporated: 12 January 2009
Net Worth Deficit: £1,972,558 *Total Assets:* £10,867,554
Registered Office: Jubilee Health Centre West, Shotfield, Wallington, Surrey, SM6 0HY
Activities: General medical practice activities
Shareholder: Muhammad Mansoor Ahmed
Officers: Dr Muhammad Mansoor Ahmed [1962] Director/GP; Dr Bernard Patrick Lewis [1962] Director/Doctor; Dr Heather Ruth Lings [1961] Director/GP; Dr Joanna Elizabeth Munden [1962] Director/GP; Dr Ian Martin Wilson [1956] Director/Doctor

Shrewsbury Hotel Limited
Incorporated: 6 November 2007
Net Worth: £965,963 *Total Assets:* £7,414,865
Registered Office: 1 Towers Place, Eton Street, Richmond, Surrey, TW9 1EG
Activities: Buying and selling of own real estate
Parent: China National Travel Service Group Corporation
Officers: Jameson Andrew Lamb [1972] Director; Alex Edward Pritchard [1976] Director

Shrewsbury House School Trust Limited
Incorporated: 25 January 1979 *Employees:* 120
Net Worth: £9,003,865 *Total Assets:* £17,830,712
Registered Office: 107 Ditton Road, Surbiton, Surrey, KT6 6RL
Activities: Primary education
Officers: Peter Norman Leslie Dart, Secretary; Susan Clarke [1978] Director/Headmistress; Darren Matthew Johns [1971] Director/Investment Banker; Louis Victor Ralph Laville [1959] Director/Chartered Accountant; Joanna Jane Le Grice [1965] Director/Consultant; Andrew Lawrence Lee [1951] Director/Chartered Accountant; Clare Linney [1968] Director/Speech and Language Therapist; Miles Roger Millard [1965] Director/Retired; David Ian Sanders [1967] Director/Leadership Coach; Jane Lesley Whittingham [1962] Director/Headmistress

Shun Cheong Lung Holding Company Limited
Incorporated: 22 April 2002 *Employees:* 1
Net Worth: £7,461,304 *Total Assets:* £7,816,680
Registered Office: Scla House, 21-25 River Road, Barking, Essex, IG11 0DA
Activities: Activities of head offices
Major Shareholder: Kwok Keung Wong
Officers: Jan Wong, Secretary; Jan Mary Wong [1954] Director/Company Secretary; Kwok Keung Wong [1950] Director

Shure Europe Holdings Limited
Incorporated: 4 November 2010 *Employees:* 765
Net Worth: £103,405,272 *Total Assets:* £124,386,464
Registered Office: Unit 2 The IO Centre, Lea Road, Waltham Abbey, Essex, EN9 1AS
Activities: Activities of other holding companies n.e.c.
Officers: Paul Lance Applebaum [1963] Director/Executive VP and General Counsel [American]; Christine Marie Schyvinck [1967] Director [American]; Bruce Douglas Skof [1971] Director/Accountant [American]

Shure UK Limited
Incorporated: 3 February 2003 *Employees:* 45
Net Worth: £8,243,641 *Total Assets:* £10,435,757
Registered Office: Unit 2 The I O Centre, Lea Road, Waltham Abbey, Essex, EN9 1AS
Activities: Wholesale of electronic and telecommunications equipment and parts
Parent: Shure Europe Holdings Limited
Officers: Robert Lackey, Secretary; Raymond Joseph Crawford [1963] Director/Chief Marketing and Sales Officer [American]; Robert Geoffrey Lackey [1965] Director/Accountant; Bruce Douglas Skof [1971] Director [American]

Shurgard UK Limited
Incorporated: 11 April 2003 *Employees:* 77
Net Worth: £166,884,784 *Total Assets:* £194,987,392
Registered Office: 2 AC Court, High Street, Thames Ditton, Surrey, KT7 0SR
Activities: Operation of warehousing and storage facilities for land transport activities
Parent: Shurgard Holding Luxembourg SARL
Officers: Marc Pierre Francois Oursin [1962] Director [French]

Shurgard UK West London Limited
Incorporated: 21 June 2004 *Employees:* 3
Net Worth: £2,183,040 *Total Assets:* £8,097,269
Registered Office: 2 AC Court, High Street, Thames Ditton, Surrey, KT7 0SR
Activities: Operation of warehousing and storage facilities for land transport activities
Parent: Public Storage
Officers: Jean Louis Henri Kreusch [1964] Director/Executive Manager [Belgian]; Marc Pierre Francois Oursin [1962] Director [French]

SI Electrical Limited
Incorporated: 11 December 1997 *Employees:* 2
Net Worth: £2,119,348 *Total Assets:* £6,800,209
Registered Office: 12 Hatherley Road, Sidcup, Kent, DA14 4DT
Activities: Electrical installation
Officers: Sinead Norris [1980] Director [Irish]; Simon Peter Wyeth [1962] Director

Sian Formwork Limited
Incorporated: 9 May 2003
Net Worth: £3,207,131 *Total Assets:* £5,927,820
Registered Office: Sian Formwork Limited, Stonebridge Road, Northfleet, Gravesend, Kent, DA11 9BA
Activities: Construction of other civil engineering projects n.e.c.
Shareholders: Jugjit Singh Sian; Ajit Singh Sian
Officers: Jugjit Singh Sian, Secretary; Ajit Singh Sian [1974] Director; Jugjit Singh Sian [1976] Director

Sidan Trading Holdings Limited
Incorporated: 19 July 2017 *Employees:* 3
Net Worth: £5,195,507 *Total Assets:* £5,195,867
Registered Office: Amshold House, Goldings Hill, Loughton, Essex, IG10 2RW
Activities: Other business support service activities n.e.c.
Shareholders: Daniel Paul Sugar; Simon Sugar
Officers: Jonathan Dumont, Secretary; Roger George Adams [1950] Director; Daniel Paul Sugar [1971] Director; Simon Sugar [1969] Director

Siddharth Jewellery (U.K.) Limited
Incorporated: 8 April 2004 *Employees:* 2
Net Worth: £1,849,051 *Total Assets:* £6,240,844
Registered Office: 1 Oxhey Ridge Close, Northwood, Middlesex, HA6 3JU
Activities: Wholesale of watches and jewellery
Shareholders: Rajan Kohli; Neelja Kohli
Officers: Neelja Kohli, Secretary/Self Employed; Neelja Kohli [1964] Director/Self Employed; Rajan Kohli [1962] Director/Jeweller; Siddharth Kohli [1990] Director

Siem Shipping UK Limited
Incorporated: 27 September 1993 *Employees:* 27
Previous: Star Reefers UK Limited
Net Worth: £3,948,564 *Total Assets:* £13,486,472
Registered Office: 40 Brighton Road, Sutton, Surrey, SM2 5BN
Activities: Sea and coastal freight water transport
Major Shareholder: Kristian Siem
Officers: Charles Bondi, Secretary [Norwegian]; Charles Bondi [1972] Director/Accountant; Kenneth Reid Ross [1968] Director/Chief Operating Officer

The Siemon Company Limited
Incorporated: 12 April 1991 *Employees:* 68
Net Worth: £8,757,415 *Total Assets:* £14,080,926
Registered Office: Siemon House, 36-48 Windsor Street, Chertsey, Surrey, KT16 8AS
Activities: Other telecommunications activities
Officers: Neil Peter Edwards, Secretary; Keith Vincent Astin [1948] Managing Director; Neil Peter Edwards [1970] Finance Director; Steven Paul Foster [1974] Managing Director; Carl Neill Siemon [1951] Director [American]

Sienna Real Estate Ltd
Incorporated: 24 October 2012
Net Worth: £46,379 *Total Assets:* £5,322,799
Registered Office: 11th Floor, The Mille, 1000 Great West Road, Brentford, Middlesex, TW8 9DW
Activities: Buying and selling of own real estate
Parent: Citycom Technologies Group Limited
Officers: Vinod Zada Kakkar [1984] Director

Sifcon International PLC
Incorporated: 25 October 1946 *Employees:* 58
Net Worth: £6,634,617 *Total Assets:* £16,430,931
Registered Office: New Ford Road, Brittania Road Industrial Estate, Waltham Cross, Herts, EN8 7PG
Activities: Wholesale of household goods (other than musical instruments) n.e.c
Major Shareholder: Nicholas Stephen Tiffin
Officers: Alan Charles Pimm, Secretary; Alan Charles Pimm [1949] Director; John Pugh [1955] Director/Sales; Tracy Frances Storan [1965] Director/Chartered Accountant; Nicholas Stephen Tiffin [1960] Director; Peter Michael Tuck [1954] Director/Credit Controller

Sigma Sports Limited
Incorporated: 23 July 2003 *Employees:* 88
Previous: Sigma Sport Limited
Net Worth: £3,805,219 *Total Assets:* £11,647,652
Registered Office: 37-43 High Street, Hampton Wick, Kingston upon Thames, Surrey, KT1 4DA
Activities: Other retail sale of new goods in specialised stores (not commercial art galleries and opticians)
Shareholder: Bradshaw Taylor Limited
Officers: Ian Whittingham, Secretary; Corry Edward Bradshaw Cavell-Taylor [1961] Director/Retailer and Distributor; James Stewart McEuen [1969] Director; Andrew Herbert Noel [1948] Director/Chartered Accountant in General Practice; Jason Brian Turner [1971] Director/Retailer; Ian Whittingham [1971] Director/Retailer

Signet Direct Diamond Sourcing Limited
Incorporated: 12 April 2011
Net Worth: £79,225,376 *Total Assets:* £86,724,216
Registered Office: Imperial Place, 3 Maxwell Road, Borehamwood, Herts, WD6 1JN
Activities: Other business support service activities n.e.c.
Parent: Signet Holdings Limited
Officers: Benjamin Harris [1983] Director/Attorney; Rory O'Donnell [1977] Director/Financial Controller [American]; Michele Santana [1970] Director/Chief Financial Officer [American]

Signet Group Limited
Incorporated: 27 January 1950 *Employees:* 1
Net Worth: £631,923,072 *Total Assets:* £1,798,029,184
Registered Office: Imperial Place, 3 Maxwell Road, Borehamwood, Herts, WD6 1JN
Activities: Activities of head offices
Parent: Signet Jewelers Limited
Officers: Benjamin Harris, Secretary; Marianne Kelly [1974] Director/Head of Finance; Raina Margaret Miles [1962] Director/Chartered Accountant; Michele Santana [1970] Director/Chief Financial Officer [American]

Signet Group Services Limited
Incorporated: 13 May 1999 *Employees:* 7
Net Worth: £3,711,000 *Total Assets:* £17,505,000
Registered Office: Imperial Place, 3 Maxwell Road, Borehamwood, Herts, WD6 1JN
Activities: Other business support service activities n.e.c.
Parent: Signet Holdings Limited
Officers: Benjamin Harris, Secretary; Marianne Kelly [1974] Director/Head of Finance; Raina Margaret Miles [1962] Director/Chartered Accountant; Michele Santana [1970] Director/Chief Financial Officer [American]

Signet Holdings Limited
Incorporated: 13 May 1999
Net Worth: £1,155,329,152 *Total Assets:* £1,202,115,712
Registered Office: Imperial Place, 3 Maxwell Road, Borehamwood, Herts, WD6 1JN
Activities: Non-trading company
Parent: Signet Group Limited
Officers: Benjamin Harris, Secretary; Marianne Kelly [1974] Director/Head of Finance; Raina Margaret Miles [1962] Director/Chartered Accountant; Michele Santana [1970] Director/Chief Financial Officer [American]

Signet Trading Limited
Incorporated: 12 May 1999 *Employees:* 3,255
Net Worth: £290,904,000 *Total Assets:* £369,443,008
Registered Office: Imperial Place, 3 Maxwell Road, Borehamwood, Herts, WD6 1JN
Activities: Other business support service activities n.e.c.
Parent: Signet Holdings Limited
Officers: Benjamin Harris, Secretary; Shaun David Carney [1966] Finance Director; Benjamin Harris [1983] Director/Attorney

Signet UK Finance PLC
Incorporated: 17 April 2014
Net Worth: £4,957,018 *Total Assets:* £306,881,696
Registered Office: Imperial Place, 3 Maxwell Road, Borehamwood, Herts, WD6 1JN
Activities: Other business support service activities n.e.c.
Parent: Signet Group Limited
Officers: Benjamin Harris, Secretary; Marianne Kelly [1974] Director/Head of Finance; Raina Margaret Miles [1962] Director/Chartered Accountant; Michele Santana [1970] Director/Chief Financial Officer [American]

Silixa Ltd
Incorporated: 10 April 2007 *Employees:* 56
Net Worth: £7,139,280 *Total Assets:* £8,589,637
Registered Office: Silixa House, 230 Centennial Park, Elstree, Herts, WD6 3SN
Activities: Other business support service activities n.e.c.
Officers: Rasheed Abayomi Amunikoro, Secretary; Trevor Michael Burgess [1954] Director; Mahmoud Farhadiroushan [1962] Director/Engineer; Alison Jane Patricia Goligher [1965] Director; Ingebright Masvie [1966] Director [Norwegian]; Dr Tom Parker [1969] Director/Engineer; Glynn Richard Williams [1955] Director/Chief Executive Officer

M & D Silk Properties Ltd
Incorporated: 10 November 2010
Net Worth: £25,173,256 *Total Assets:* £31,327,848
Registered Office: 2 Fauna Close, Stanmore, Middlesex, HA7 4PX
Activities: Buying and selling of own real estate
Officers: David Christopher Leslie Silk [1961] Director; Lynne Carol Silk [1962] Director

Silnat Holdings Limited
Incorporated: 23 May 2014
Net Worth: £16,285,834 *Total Assets:* £16,500,291
Registered Office: York House, Empire Way, Wembley, Middlesex, HA9 0FQ
Activities: Activities of other holding companies n.e.c.
Shareholders: David Rothman; Harold Rothman
Officers: David Rothman [1959] Director; Harold Rothman [1956] Director

Silvermead Properties Ltd
Incorporated: 14 May 2002 *Employees:* 1
Net Worth: £640,680 *Total Assets:* £5,283,786
Registered Office: Aaron House, Island Farm Avenue, West Molesey, Surrey, KT8 2RG
Activities: Construction of other civil engineering projects n.e.c.
Major Shareholder: Samuel Gary Nagioff
Officers: Samuel Gary Nagioff [1959] Director/Printer

Silvermere Golf & Leisure Limited
Incorporated: 31 August 1984 *Employees:* 62
Net Worth: £7,344,852 *Total Assets:* £13,344,884
Registered Office: Downs Farm, Reigate Road, Ewell, Surrey, KT17 3BX
Activities: Operation of sports facilities
Parent: Dwellcourt Ltd
Officers: Jeffrey Thomas Hilliard, Secretary; James Michael Bowry [1987] Finance Director; Jeffrey Thomas Hilliard [1964] Director/Development Manager; Douglas William McClelland [1949] Director; Terry Kirk Sims [1971] Director; Steven John Turnbull [1976] Director

Silverson Machines Holdings Limited
Incorporated: 23 May 2014 *Employees:* 113
Net Worth: £21,838,684 *Total Assets:* £29,534,494
Registered Office: York House, Empire Way, Wembley, Middlesex, HA9 0FQ
Activities: Activities of production holding companies
Shareholders: Harold Rothman; David Rothman
Officers: David Rothman [1959] Director; Harold Rothman [1956] Director

Silverson Machines Limited
Incorporated: 26 July 1946 *Employees:* 113
Net Worth: £14,293,701 *Total Assets:* £16,510,545
Registered Office: York House, Empire Way, Wembley, Middlesex, HA9 0FQ
Activities: Manufacture of other special-purpose machinery n.e.c.
Parent: Silverson Machines Holdings Limited
Officers: David Rothman, Secretary; David Rothman [1959] Director; Harold Rothman [1956] Director

Silvertime Amusements Limited
Incorporated: 4 July 1995 *Employees:* 61
Net Worth: £3,928,439 *Total Assets:* £5,879,011
Registered Office: 107 Hindes Road, Harrow, Middlesex, HA1 1RU
Activities: Activities of amusement parks and theme parks
Major Shareholder: Edward James Reed
Officers: Edward James Reed, Secretary; Edward James Reed [1977] Director; Ian James Reed [1940] Director

Silverton Property Investments Limited
Incorporated: 25 July 1997
Previous: Silverton Developments Limited
Net Worth: £9,721,678 *Total Assets:* £14,247,594
Registered Office: 9-11 High Beech Road, Loughton, Essex, IG10 4BN
Activities: Other accommodation
Major Shareholder: Mohammed Iqbal Vesamia
Officers: Munira Banu Vesamia, Secretary; Aamir Mohammed Vesamia [1996] Director; Abdul Rehman Vesamia [1944] Director; Fatima Vesamia [1972] Director; Mohammed Iqbal Vesamia [1967] Director; Munira Banu Vesamia [1947] Director; Saniya Vesamia [1997] Director

Simat Properties Limited
Incorporated: 8 November 1963 *Employees:* 5
Net Worth: £1,735,487 *Total Assets:* £12,479,319
Registered Office: 2nd Floor, Hygeia House, 66 College Road, Harrow, Middlesex, HA1 1BE
Activities: Development of building projects
Shareholders: June Viiolet Beckley; Simon Charles Derek Beckley
Officers: Simon Charles Derek Beckley, Secretary; June Violet Beckley [1931] Director; Simon Charles Derek Beckley [1959] Director

Simm Tronic Limited
Incorporated: 25 September 1992 *Employees:* 104
Net Worth: £5,400,862 *Total Assets:* £8,387,818
Registered Office: Unit 3 Waterside Industrial Estate, Charlton Mead Lane, Hoddesdon, Herts, EN11 0QR
Activities: Manufacture of electric lighting equipment
Officers: Mario Costanzo, Secretary; Mario Costanzo [1963] Director; Steven Terence Goskie [1963] Director; Giacomo Russo [1955] Director; Vincenzo Russo [1959] Director; Raymond Arthur Vos [1964] Director

Simmons & Hawker Limited
Incorporated: 10 November 1934 *Employees:* 8
Net Worth: £24,730,974 *Total Assets:* £31,467,332
Registered Office: Falcon House, Central Way, Feltham, Middlesex, TW14 0UQ
Activities: Other letting and operating of own or leased real estate
Officers: Robert William Assael [1950] Director/Solicitor; Heather Dorice Hawker [1941] Director; John Flory Hawker [1970] Director; Barry Andrew Judd [1941] Director/Chartered Surveyor; Bryony Clare Stevens [1960] Director/Primary Teacher

Simon Holdings PLC
Incorporated: 14 June 1967 *Employees:* 95
Net Worth: £9,056,532 *Total Assets:* £13,095,738
Registered Office: The Clock Tower, Bridge Street, Walton on Thames, Surrey, KT12 1AY
Activities: Activities of head offices
Officers: Graham Patrick Harmes, Secretary; Martyn Roland Harmes [1954] Director; Patrick Francis Murphy [1943] Director; Simon John Murphy [1971] Director/Sales and Recruitment

Simpson Marketing Limited
Incorporated: 14 October 1997
Net Worth: £14,957,590 *Total Assets:* £14,996,613
Registered Office: 4 The Mews, Bridge Road, Twickenham, Middlesex, TW1 1RF
Activities: Buying and selling of own real estate
Shareholders: Oleksandr Tytarenko; Ievgen Bilash
Officers: Anthony Curran [1942] Director/Businessman [Irish]

Sims Milling Services Limited
Incorporated: 22 October 2009 *Employees:* 57
Net Worth: £4,204,742 *Total Assets:* £12,635,793
Registered Office: Burrows Farm, Brentwood Road, Bulphan, Essex, RM14 3TL
Activities: Other specialised construction activities n.e.c.
Major Shareholder: Geoffrey Anthony Sims
Officers: Geoffrey Anthony Sims [1966] Director

Sinai (Antiques) Limited
Incorporated: 11 July 1977 *Employees:* 7
Net Worth: £2,964,505 *Total Assets:* £9,345,633
Registered Office: Lynwood House, 373-375 Station Road, Harrow, Middlesex, HA1 2AW
Activities: Retail sale of other second-hand goods in stores (not incl. antiques)
Parent: Mount Sinai Holdings Limited
Officers: Sylvia Sinai, Secretary; Elcana Sinai [1947] Director/Antique Dealer [Israeli]

Sinclair House Properties Limited
Incorporated: 15 June 1998 *Employees:* 6
Net Worth: £5,078,130 *Total Assets:* £5,245,409
Registered Office: Bridge House, 11 Creek Road, Hampton Court, Surrey, KT8 9BE
Activities: Development of building projects
Shareholder: Martin Sinclair Rutter
Officers: Stella Rutter, Secretary; Stella Smith, Secretary; Clive Patrick Farrell [1946] Director; Martin Sinclair Rutter [1948] Director/Chartered Surveyor

Thomas Sinden Limited
Incorporated: 28 January 1997 *Employees:* 107
Net Worth: £5,178,521 *Total Assets:* £20,384,588
Registered Office: 137-145 Church Road, Harold Wood, Romford, Essex, RM3 0SH
Activities: Development of building projects
Shareholders: Desmond Francis Thomas; Graeme Sinden
Officers: Jonathan Neil Taylor, Secretary; Stephen Thomas McMahon [1969] Director; Graeme Sinden [1965] Director; Desmond Francis Thomas [1960] Director

Sinek Global Finance & Trading LLP
Incorporated: 21 July 2008
Net Worth: £20,152,748 *Total Assets:* £30,981,460
Registered Office: First Floor, Healthaid House, Marlborough Hill, Harrow, Middlesex, HA1 1UD

Sines LLP
Incorporated: 13 January 2009 *Employees:* 10
Net Worth: £6,638,991 *Total Assets:* £12,040,737
Registered Office: 166 College Road, Harrow, Middlesex, HA1 1RA
Officers: Elaine Ann Sines [1965] Member; Maurice Sines [1962] Member

Sines Parks (S.E.) Limited
Incorporated: 2 February 2007 *Employees:* 6
Net Worth: £4,183,018 *Total Assets:* £9,846,920
Registered Office: 166 College Road, Harrow, Middlesex, HA1 1RA
Activities: Other business support service activities n.e.c.
Major Shareholder: Maurice Sines
Officers: Elaine Ann Sines, Secretary; Elaine Ann Sines [1965] Director; Maurice Sines [1962] Director

Sines Parks Holdings Limited
Incorporated: 6 December 2012
Net Worth: £6,884,420 *Total Assets:* £18,351,088
Registered Office: 166 College Road, Harrow, Middlesex, HA1 1RA
Activities: Activities of other holding companies n.e.c.
Major Shareholder: Maurice Sines
Officers: Elaine Ann Sines [1965] Director; Maurice Sines [1962] Director

Sines Parks Ltd
Incorporated: 27 January 2003 *Employees:* 2
Net Worth: £2,109,031 *Total Assets:* £20,432,996
Registered Office: 166 College Road, Harrow, Middlesex, HA1 1RA
Activities: Recreational vehicle parks, trailer parks and camping grounds
Parent: Sines Parks Holdings Limited
Officers: Elaine Ann Sines, Secretary; Elaine Ann Sines [1965] Director; Maurice Sines [1962] Director

Singer & James Limited
Incorporated: 28 October 1976 *Employees:* 12
Net Worth: £4,068,491 *Total Assets:* £5,210,532
Registered Office: Roebuck Road, Hainault, Ilford, Essex, IG6 3TZ
Activities: Manufacture of metal structures and parts of structures
Officers: Gregory John Taylor, Secretary; Jack Ernest Bell [1957] Director; Graham Shaw James [1960] Director; Gregory John Taylor [1960] Director/Company Secretary

SintecMedia Global Ltd
Incorporated: 22 December 2000
Net Worth: £18,999,208 *Total Assets:* £19,009,208
Registered Office: Artemis House, Odyssey Business Park, West End Road, Ruislip, Middlesex, HA4 6QE
Activities: Business and domestic software development
Officers: Elad Lustig, Secretary; Lorne Brown [1975] Director [American]; Paul Nicholas Bryan-Harris [1970] Director

SintecMedia LON Ltd
Incorporated: 20 November 2005 *Employees:* 13
Net Worth: £6,116,877 *Total Assets:* £46,466,108
Registered Office: Artemis House, Odyssey Business Park, West End Road, Ruislip, Middlesex, HA4 6QE
Activities: Other professional, scientific and technical activities n.e.c.
Officers: Lorne Brown [1975] Director [American]; Paul Nicholas Bryan-Harris [1970] Director

SintecMedia WEM Ltd
Incorporated: 2 December 1999 *Employees:* 41
Net Worth: £1,731,650 *Total Assets:* £25,215,930
Registered Office: Artemis House, Odyssey Business Park, West End Road, Ruislip, Middlesex, HA4 6QE
Activities: Business and domestic software development
Officers: Elad Lustig, Secretary; Lorne Brown [1975] Director [American]; Paul Nicholas Bryan-Harris [1970] Director

SIP Group Limited
Incorporated: 10 May 2004
Net Worth: £10,713,801 *Total Assets:* £19,897,728
Registered Office: 114-116 Goodmayes Road, Ilford, Essex, IG3 9UZ
Activities: Activities of head offices
Shareholders: Sukhbinder Singh Takhar; Iqbal Kaur Takhar; Pirthipal Singh Takhar
Officers: Iqbal Kaur Takhar, Secretary; Iqbal Kaur Takhar [1960] Director/Company Secretary; Pirthipal Singh Takhar [1982] Director; Sukhbinder Singh Takhar [1954] Director

Sirhowy Enterprise Way (Holdings) Limited
Incorporated: 6 October 2003
Net Worth Deficit: £3,398,000 *Total Assets:* £39,123,000
Registered Office: 8 White Oak Square, London Road, Swanley, Kent, BR8 7AG
Activities: Activities of head offices
Parent: JLIF (GP) Limited
Officers: Carl Harvey Dix [1966] Operations Director; Johannes Petrus Heemelaar [1956] Director [Dutch]

Sirhowy Enterprise Way Limited
Incorporated: 3 October 2003
Net Worth Deficit: £3,398,000 *Total Assets:* £39,123,000
Registered Office: 8 White Oak Square, London Road, Swanley, Kent, BR8 7AG
Activities: Construction of commercial buildings
Parent: Sirhowy Enterprise Way (Holdings) Limited
Officers: Carl Harvey Dix [1966] Operations Director; Johannes Petrus Heemelaar [1956] Director [Dutch]

SITA Information Networking Computing UK Limited
Incorporated: 16 May 2000 *Employees:* 396
Net Worth Deficit: £90,415,984 *Total Assets:* £89,077,264
Registered Office: c/o Sita Legal, 1 London Gate, 252-254 Blyth Road, Hayes, Middlesex, UB3 1BW
Activities: Other information service activities n.e.c.
Parent: SITA N.V.
Officers: Alain Brodeur, Secretary; Aileen Teresa Mary McEntee, Secretary; Nicolas Emmanuel Husson [1969] Director/Chief Financial Officer [French]; Barbara Marguerite Ploux Dalibard [1958] Director/Chief Executive Officer [French]; Jeremy Colin Springall [1968] Director/Senior Vice President

Site Sales Marketing Limited
Incorporated: 19 July 1989 *Employees:* 53
Net Worth: £20,688,224 *Total Assets:* £22,387,996
Registered Office: Haslers, Old Station Road, Loughton, Essex, IG10 4PL
Activities: Real estate agencies
Shareholders: Denise Lorraine Smith; Murray George Smith
Officers: Denise Lorraine Smith, Secretary; Murray George Smith [1963] Director/Estate Agent

Sitecrest Limited
Incorporated: 23 July 1984 *Employees:* 5
Net Worth: £13,801,840 *Total Assets:* £14,391,378
Registered Office: Harmile House, 54 St Mary's Lane, Upminster, Essex, RM14 2QT
Activities: Other letting and operating of own or leased real estate
Major Shareholder: Robert David Hagger
Officers: Tracey Lynn Hagger, Secretary; Robert David Hagger [1959] Director; Tracey Lynn Hagger [1967] Director

Six Continents Holdings Limited
Incorporated: 12 June 1996
Net Worth: £1,027,502,976 *Total Assets:* £1,028,201,984
Registered Office: Broadwater Park, Denham, Bucks, UB9 5HR
Activities: Activities of head offices
Shareholders: Six Continents Limited; Asia Pacific Holdings Limited
Officers: Fiona Cuttell, Secretary; Paul Russell Edgecliffe-Johnson [1972] Director/Accountant; Michael Todd Glover [1971] Director/Financial Controller [American]; Nicolette Henfrey [1969] Director

Six Continents Hotels International Limited
Incorporated: 26 April 1962
Net Worth: £5,885,918,208 *Total Assets:* £5,887,932,928
Registered Office: Broadwater Park, Denham, Bucks, UB9 5HR
Activities: Activities of head offices
Parent: Six Continents Limited
Officers: Fiona Jane Littlebury-Cuttell, Secretary; Colin Philip Garwood [1961] Director; Michael Todd Glover [1971] Director/Financial Controller [American]; Nicolette Henfrey [1969] Director; George Turner [1971] Director/Company Secretary

Six Continents Investments Limited
Incorporated: 1 June 1961
Net Worth: £271,105,984 *Total Assets:* £271,191,008
Registered Office: Broadwater Park, Denham, Bucks, UB9 5HR
Activities: Other business support service activities n.e.c.
Parent: Six Continents Limited
Officers: Fiona Jane Littlebury-Cuttell, Secretary; Michael Jon Cockcroft [1974] Director/Accountant; Michael Todd Glover [1971] Director/Financial Controller [American]; Nicolette Henfrey [1969] Director

Six Continents Limited
Incorporated: 17 August 1967 *Employees:* 192
Net Worth: £2,916,999,936 *Total Assets:* £10,364,999,680
Registered Office: Broadwater Park, Denham, Bucks, UB9 5HR
Activities: Other business support service activities n.e.c.
Parent: Intercontinental Hotels Limited
Officers: Fiona Cuttell, Secretary; Paul Russell Edgecliffe-Johnson [1972] Director/Certified Chartered Accountant; Michael Todd Glover [1971] Director/Financial Controller [American]; Nicolette Henfrey [1969] Director; George Turner [1971] Director

Six Continents Overseas Holdings Limited
Incorporated: 7 November 1991
Net Worth: £2,179,664,896 *Total Assets:* £2,185,080,064
Registered Office: Broadwater Park, Denham, Bucks, UB9 5HR
Activities: Other business support service activities n.e.c.
Parent: Six Continents Limited
Officers: Fiona Cuttell, Secretary; Michael Jon Cockcroft [1974] Director/Accountant; Michael Todd Glover [1971] Director/Financial Controller [American]; Nicolette Henfrey [1969] Director; George Turner [1971] Director

Six Continents Restaurants Limited
Incorporated: 13 June 1962
Net Worth: £61,081,000 *Total Assets:* £61,100,000
Registered Office: Broadwater Park, Denham, Bucks, UB9 5HR
Activities: Other business support service activities n.e.c.
Parent: Six Continents Limited
Officers: Fiona Jane Littlebury-Cuttell, Secretary; Michael Jon Cockcroft [1974] Director/Accountant; Michael Todd Glover [1971] Director/Financial Controller [American]; Nicolette Henfrey [1969] Director

Siya Properties Limited
Incorporated: 30 September 1999 *Employees:* 22
Net Worth: £4,561,084 *Total Assets:* £8,075,574
Registered Office: 50 Field End Road, Eastcote, Pinner, Middlesex, HA5 2QN
Activities: Hotels and similar accommodation
Shareholders: Jaipal Gupta; Ruchir Gupta
Officers: Ved Prakash Yadav, Secretary; Charu Gupta [1968] Director/Hotelier [Indian]; Ruchir Gupta [1974] Director/Self Employed [Indian]; Shashi Gupta [1947] Director [Indian]

SK Hynix UK Limited
Incorporated: 5 July 1995 *Employees:* 12
Net Worth: £10,931,376 *Total Assets:* £216,451,216
Registered Office: Unit 4 Horizon Business Village, 1 Brooklands Road, Weybridge, Surrey, KT13 0TJ
Activities: Wholesale of computers, computer peripheral equipment and software
Parent: SK Hynix Inc.
Officers: Jae Kwon Hwang, Secretary; Jae Kwon Hwang [1980] Director/General Manager [South Korean]; Ho Sang Lee [1966] Managing Director [South Korean]; Dong Hui Son [1970] Director/General Manager [South Korean]

Skanska Cementation International Holdings Limited
Incorporated: 5 February 1969
Net Worth: £18,565,000 *Total Assets:* £18,610,000
Registered Office: Maple Cross House, Denham Way, Maple Cross, Rickmansworth, Herts, WD3 9SW
Activities: Activities of head offices
Parent: Skanska Construction Holdings UK Limited
Officers: Steven Leven, Secretary; Mark Lawson Galloway [1955] Director/Solicitor; Culdip Kelly Kaur Gangotra [1970] Director/Accountant

Skanska Cementation International Limited
Incorporated: 26 July 1948
Net Worth: £20,569,000 *Total Assets:* £33,210,000
Registered Office: Maple Cross House, Denham Way, Maple Cross, Rickmansworth, Herts, WD3 9SW
Activities: Construction of commercial buildings
Parent: Skanska Construction Holdings UK Limited
Officers: Steven Leven, Secretary; Mark Lawson Galloway [1955] Director/Solicitor; Culdip Kelly Kaur Gangotra [1970] Director/Accountant

Skanska Construction (Regions) Limited
Incorporated: 24 October 1927
Net Worth: £4,604,000 *Total Assets:* £11,881,000
Registered Office: Maple Cross House, Denham Way, Maple Cross, Rickmansworth, Herts, WD3 9SW
Activities: Construction of commercial buildings
Parent: Skanska UK PLC
Officers: Steven Leven, Secretary; David William Kyriacos [1976] Director; Steven Leven [1967] Director/Company Secretary; Steven Edward Lindsay [1975] Director

Skanska Construction Holdings UK Limited
Incorporated: 30 October 2000
Net Worth: £2,960,000 *Total Assets:* £314,691,008
Registered Office: Maple Cross House, Denham Way, Maple Cross, Rickmansworth, Herts, WD3 9SW
Activities: Activities of head offices
Parent: Skanska AB
Officers: Mark Lawson Galloway, Secretary; Gregor Lawrence Craig [1963] Managing Director; Culdip Kelly Kaur Gangotra [1970] Director/Accountant

Skanska Construction UK Limited
Incorporated: 19 July 1923 *Employees:* 5,125
Net Worth: £250,718,000 *Total Assets:* £774,459,008
Registered Office: Maple Cross House, Denham Way, Maple Cross, Rickmansworth, Herts, WD3 9SW
Activities: Construction of commercial buildings
Parent: Skanska UK PLC
Officers: Steven Leven, Secretary; Gregor Lawrence Craig [1963] Managing Director; Katrina Mary Dowding [1970] Director; Thomas Peter Faulkner [1974] Director; Culdip Kelly Kaur Gangotra [1970] Director/Accountant; Martin George Neeson [1968] Director/Manager

Skanska Infrastructure Development UK Limited
Incorporated: 21 February 1995 *Employees:* 39
Net Worth Deficit: £50,734,000 *Total Assets:* £22,338,000
Registered Office: Maple Cross House, Denham Way, Maple Cross, Rickmansworth, Herts, WD3 9SW
Activities: Development of building projects
Parent: Skanska AB
Officers: Steven Leven, Secretary; Paul Alan Bannister [1959] Director; Simon Richard Thorpe Beauchamp [1973] Commercial Director

Skanska Infrastructure Investment UK Limited
Incorporated: 23 December 2002
Net Worth: £71,613,000 *Total Assets:* £91,503,000
Registered Office: Maple Cross House, Denham Way, Maple Cross, Rickmansworth, Herts, WD3 9SW
Activities: Other business support service activities n.e.c.
Parent: Skanska AB
Officers: Steven Leven, Secretary; Paul Alan Bannister [1959] Director; Simon Richard Thorpe Beauchamp [1973] Commercial Director

Skanska J.V. Projects Ltd
Incorporated: 18 December 1998 *Employees:* 30
Net Worth: £46,048,000 *Total Assets:* £97,344,000
Registered Office: Maple Cross House, Denham Way, Maple Cross, Rickmansworth, Herts, WD3 9SW
Activities: Other business support service activities n.e.c.
Parent: Skanska Construction UK Limited
Officers: Steven Leven, Secretary; Katrina Mary Dowding [1970] Director; Thomas Peter Faulkner [1974] Director; Culdip Kelly Kaur Gangotra [1970] Director/Accountant

Skanska Major Projects Limited
Incorporated: 9 November 1970 *Employees:* 8
Net Worth: £13,079,000 *Total Assets:* £22,816,000
Registered Office: Maple Cross House, Denham Way, Maple Cross, Rickmansworth, Herts, WD3 9SW
Activities: Other specialised construction activities n.e.c.
Parent: Skanska Construction UK Limited
Officers: Steven Leven, Secretary; Katrina Mary Dowding [1970] Director; Culdip Kelly Kaur Gangotra [1970] Director/Accountant

Skanska Project Developments Limited
Incorporated: 24 November 2006 *Employees:* 9
Net Worth: £20,098,000 *Total Assets:* £115,084,000
Registered Office: Maple Cross House, Denham Way, Maple Cross, Rickmansworth, Herts, WD3 9SW
Activities: Development of building projects
Parent: Skanska UK PLC
Officers: Steven Leven, Secretary; Culdip Kelly Kaur Gangotra [1970] Director/Accountant; Helen Katherine Martin [1975] Director/Civil Engineer; Martin George Neeson [1968] Director/Manager

Skanska Rashleigh Weatherfoil Limited
Incorporated: 26 March 1964 *Employees:* 1,074
Net Worth: £66,226,000 *Total Assets:* £202,738,000
Registered Office: Maple Cross House, Denham Way, Maple Cross, Rickmansworth, Herts, WD3 9SW
Activities: Electrical installation
Parent: Skanska Construction UK Limited
Officers: Steven Leven, Secretary; Katrina Mary Dowding [1970] Director; Adam Michael McDonald [1983] Director

Skanska Residential Development UK Limited
Incorporated: 14 June 2010
Net Worth: £3,333,000 *Total Assets:* £6,849,000
Registered Office: Maple Cross House, Denham Way, Maple Cross, Rickmansworth, Herts, WD3 9SW
Activities: Development of building projects
Parent: Skanska AB
Officers: Steven Leven, Secretary; Culdip Kelly Kaur Gangotra [1970] Director/Accountant; Helen Katherine Martin [1975] Director/Civil Engineer

Skanska TAM Limited
Incorporated: 1 March 2013
Net Worth: £42,658,000 *Total Assets:* £87,536,000
Registered Office: Maple Cross House, Denham Way, Maple Cross, Rickmansworth, Herts, WD3 9SW
Activities: Development of building projects
Parent: Skanska Construction Services Trustee Limited
Officers: Nigel John Pitchers, Secretary; Harvey James Francis [1965] Director; Philippa Jane Smith [1958] Director; David Ian Wills [1962] Director

Skanska UK PLC
Incorporated: 16 December 1963 *Employees:* 5,741
Net Worth: £261,776,000 *Total Assets:* £891,872,000
Registered Office: Maple Cross House, Denham Way, Maple Cross, Rickmansworth, Herts, WD3 9SW
Activities: Construction of commercial buildings
Parent: Skanska Construction Holdings UK Limited
Officers: Mark Lawson Galloway, Secretary; Gregor Lawrence Craig [1963] Managing Director; Katrina Mary Dowding [1970] Director; Thomas Peter Faulkner [1974] Director; Harvey James Francis [1965] Director; Mark Lawson Galloway [1955] Director/Solicitor; Culdip Kelly Kaur Gangotra [1970] Director/Accountant; Martin George Neeson [1968] Director/Manager

Ski Solutions Limited
Incorporated: 9 January 1985 *Employees:* 40
Net Worth: £2,252,482 *Total Assets:* £5,261,821
Registered Office: 2nd Floor, Nucleus House, 2 Lower Mortlake Road, Richmond, Surrey, TW9 2JA
Activities: Travel agency activities
Parent: Ski Solutions Holdings Limited
Officers: Craig Murray Burton [1979] Director

Skillcrown Holdings Limited
Incorporated: 29 October 2013 *Employees:* 39
Net Worth: £8,138,446 *Total Assets:* £37,200,196
Registered Office: Terrance House, 151 Hastings Road, Bromley, Kent, BR2 8NQ
Activities: Development of building projects
Parent: Skillcrown Holdings (2018) Limited
Officers: Yalpiray Osman, Secretary; Angela Anne Osman [1952] Director/Secretary [Irish]; Arif Salik Osman [1980] Director/Builder; Yalpiray Osman [1951] Director/Builder; Steven Taylor [1962] Director/Solicitor

Skillcrown Homes (UK) LLP
Incorporated: 5 June 2009
Net Worth: £14,792,657 *Total Assets:* £22,443,164
Registered Office: Terrance House, 151 Hastings Road, Bromley, Kent, BR2 8NQ
Officers: Zoe Emine Clein [1974] Member; Angela Anne Osman [1952] Member; Arif Salik Osman [1980] Member; Sener Louise Osman [1977] Member; Yalpiray Osman [1951] Member

Sky Comedy Limited
Incorporated: 13 July 1995
Previous: BSkyB Comedy Limited
Net Worth: £34,004,000 *Total Assets:* £35,250,000
Registered Office: Grant Way, Isleworth, Middlesex, TW7 5QD
Activities: Non-trading company
Parent: Sky Ventures Limited
Officers: Christopher Jon Taylor, Secretary; Karl Holmes [1973] Director/Finance Professional; Colin Robert Jones [1964] Director; Christopher Jon Taylor [1971] Director/Company Secretary

Sky CP Limited
Incorporated: 27 March 2015 *Employees:* 1,170
Net Worth: £1,575,000,064 *Total Assets:* £1,830,000,000
Registered Office: Grant Way, Isleworth, Middlesex, TW7 5QD
Activities: Television programme production activities
Parent: Sky UK Limited
Officers: Christopher Jon Taylor, Secretary; Robin John Crossley [1958] Director/Technology Consultant; Karl Holmes [1973] Director/Finance Professional; Didier Lebrat [1960] Director/Chief Technology Officer [French]; Colin Smith [1973] Director/CFO, UK & Ireland; Alun David Webber [1966] Managing Director

Sky Finance Europe Limited
Incorporated: 18 February 2015
Total Assets: £727,587,968
Registered Office: Grant Way, Isleworth, Middlesex, TW7 5QD
Activities: Other business support service activities n.e.c.
Parent: Sky PLC
Officers: Christopher Jon Taylor, Secretary; Karl Holmes [1973] Director/Finance Professional; Colin Robert Jones [1964] Director; Christopher Jon Taylor [1971] Director/Company Secretary

Sky Group Finance PLC
Incorporated: 28 September 2005 *Employees:* 2
Previous: BSkyB Finance UK PLC
Net Worth: £451,200,992 *Total Assets:* £1,193,028,992
Registered Office: Grant Way, Isleworth, Middlesex, TW7 5QD
Activities: Other business support service activities n.e.c.
Parent: Sky Limited
Officers: Christopher Jon Taylor, Secretary; Tanya Claire Richards [1971] Director/Group Financial Controller; Colin Smith [1973] Director/CFO, UK & Ireland; Christopher Jon Taylor [1971] Director/Company Secretary

Sky History Limited
Incorporated: 23 June 1995
Previous: BSkyB History Limited
Net Worth: £5,950,000 *Total Assets:* £20,690,000
Registered Office: Grant Way, Isleworth, Middlesex, TW7 5QD
Activities: Activities of head offices
Parent: Sky Ventures Limited
Officers: Christopher Jon Taylor, Secretary; Karl Holmes [1973] Director/Finance Professional; Colin Robert Jones [1964] Director; Christopher Jon Taylor [1971] Director/Company Secretary

Sky Home Communications Limited
Incorporated: 18 October 2004 *Employees:* 3
Net Worth: £30,687,000 *Total Assets:* £34,752,000
Registered Office: Grant Way, Isleworth, Middlesex, TW7 5QD
Activities: Wired telecommunications activities
Parent: Sky UK Limited
Officers: Christopher Jon Taylor, Secretary; Karl Holmes [1973] Director/Finance Professional; Colin Robert Jones [1964] Director; Christopher Jon Taylor [1971] Director/Company Secretary

Sky In-Home Service Limited
Incorporated: 24 October 1986 *Employees:* 3,325
Net Worth: £298,203,008 *Total Assets:* £689,548,032
Registered Office: Grant Way, Isleworth, Middlesex, TW7 5QD
Activities: Television programme production activities
Parent: Sky UK Limited
Officers: Christopher Jon Taylor, Secretary; Denise Elizabeth Catherine Allan [1966] Director Customer Service; Colin Smith [1973] Director/CFO, UK & Ireland; Andrew Christopher Stylianou [1966] Director/Chartered Accountant; Christopher Jon Taylor [1971] Director/Company Secretary

Sky Insurance Services Group Limited
Incorporated: 18 October 2006 *Employees:* 70
Net Worth: £1,751,391 *Total Assets:* £6,245,438
Registered Office: 167 Turners Hill, Cheshunt, Herts, EN8 9BH
Activities: Activities of insurance agents and brokers
Parent: Sky Holdings (UK) Limited
Officers: Michael James Daly [1955] Director/Broker; Paul Desmond Daly [1971] Director/Insurer; Scott Forrester [1980] Director/Insurance Brooker; Jae LEA Pearse [1975] Director/Insurance Broker

Sky International Operations Limited
Incorporated: 2 May 2012
Net Worth: £2,932,312,832 *Total Assets:* £8,306,297,344
Registered Office: Grant Way, Isleworth, Middlesex, TW7 5QD
Activities: Activities of head offices
Parent: Sky UK Limited
Officers: Christopher Jon Taylor, Secretary; Karl Holmes [1973] Director/Finance Professional; Colin Robert Jones [1964] Director; Christopher Jon Taylor [1971] Director/Company Secretary

Sky IQ Limited
Incorporated: 6 May 2010
Net Worth: £15,606,000 *Total Assets:* £24,724,000
Registered Office: Grant Way, Isleworth, Middlesex, TW7 5QD
Activities: Data processing, hosting and related activities
Parent: Sky Ventures Limited
Officers: Christopher Jon Taylor, Secretary; Karl Holmes [1973] Director/Finance Professional; Colin Robert Jones [1964] Director; Christopher Jon Taylor [1971] Director/Company Secretary

Sky Limited
Incorporated: 25 April 1988 *Employees:* 28,927
Previous: Sky PLC
Net Worth: £4,016,000,000 *Total Assets:* £18,001,999,872
Registered Office: Grant Way, Isleworth, Middlesex, TW7 5QD
Activities: Activities of head offices
Parent: Comcast Bidco Limited
Officers: Christopher Jon Taylor, Secretary; Arthur R Block [1955] Director/General Counsel [American]; Michael J Cavanagh [1966] Director/Senior Executive Vice President & CFO [American]; David L Cohen [1955] Director/Senior Executive VP & Chief Diversity Officer [American]

Sky LLU Assets Limited
Incorporated: 13 December 1995 *Employees:* 3
Previous: BSkyB LLU Assets Limited
Net Worth: £14,628,000 *Total Assets:* £14,633,000
Registered Office: Grant Way, Isleworth, Middlesex, TW7 5QD
Activities: Other information technology service activities
Parent: Sky UK Limited
Officers: Christopher Jon Taylor, Secretary; Karl Holmes [1973] Director/Finance Professional; Colin Robert Jones [1964] Director; Christopher Jon Taylor [1971] Director/Company Secretary

Sky Operational Finance Limited
Incorporated: 10 March 1994
Previous: BSkyB Finance Limited
Net Worth: £168,471,008 *Total Assets:* £9,861,266,432
Registered Office: Grant Way, Isleworth, Middlesex, TW7 5QD
Activities: Financial intermediation not elsewhere classified
Parent: Sky Limited
Officers: Christopher Jon Taylor, Secretary; Karl Holmes [1973] Director/Finance Professional; Colin Robert Jones [1964] Director; Christopher Jon Taylor [1971] Director/Company Secretary

Sky Retail Stores Limited
Incorporated: 11 May 2000 *Employees:* 782
Net Worth: £11,230,000 *Total Assets:* £16,616,000
Registered Office: Grant Way, Isleworth, Middlesex, TW7 5QD
Activities: Other business support service activities n.e.c.
Parent: Sky UK Limited
Officers: Christopher Jon Taylor, Secretary; Karl Holmes [1973] Director/Finance Professional; Colin Robert Jones [1964] Director; Christopher Jon Taylor [1971] Director/Company Secretary

Sky SNI Limited
Incorporated: 22 March 2013
Net Worth: £44,752,000 *Total Assets:* £47,161,000
Registered Office: Grant Way, Isleworth, Middlesex, TW7 5QD
Activities: Other information service activities n.e.c.
Parent: Sky UK Limited
Officers: Christopher Jon Taylor, Secretary; Colin Robert Jones [1964] Director; Christopher Jon Taylor [1971] Director/Company Secretary

Sky Subscribers Services Limited
Incorporated: 27 January 1989 *Employees:* 8,604
Net Worth: £616,659,008 *Total Assets:* £858,601,024
Registered Office: Grant Way, Isleworth, Middlesex, TW7 5QD
Activities: Other service activities n.e.c.
Parent: Sky UK Limited
Officers: Christopher Jon Taylor, Secretary; Denise Elizabeth Catherine Allan [1966] Director Customer Service; Colin Smith [1973] Director/CFO, UK & Ireland; Andrew Christopher Stylianou [1966] Director/Chartered Accountant; Christopher Jon Taylor [1971] Director/Company Secretary

Sky Telecommunications Services Limited
Incorporated: 21 December 1993
Previous: BSkyB Telecommunications Services Limited
Net Worth: £1,259,000,064 *Total Assets:* £1,444,999,936
Registered Office: Grant Way, Isleworth, Middlesex, TW7 5QD
Activities: Other business support service activities n.e.c.
Parent: Sky UK Limited
Officers: Christopher Jon Taylor, Secretary; Colin Smith [1973] Director/CFO, UK & Ireland; Andrew Christopher Stylianou [1966] Director/Chartered Accountant; Christopher Jon Taylor [1971] Director/Company Secretary

Sky Television Limited
Incorporated: 24 September 1980
Net Worth: £84,776,000 *Total Assets:* £1,006,201,024
Registered Office: Grant Way, Isleworth, Middlesex, TW7 5QD
Activities: Activities of head offices
Parent: Sky PLC
Officers: Christopher Jon Taylor, Secretary; Karl Holmes [1973] Director/Finance Professional; Colin Robert Jones [1964] Director; Christopher Jon Taylor [1971] Director/Company Secretary

Sky UK Limited
Incorporated: 10 March 1994 *Employees:* 6,038
Previous: British Sky Broadcasting Limited
Net Worth: £1,123,000,064 *Total Assets:* £18,364,999,680
Registered Office: Grant Way, Isleworth, Middlesex, TW7 5QD
Activities: Television programme production activities
Parent: Sky PLC
Officers: Christopher Jon Taylor, Secretary; Colin Smith [1973] Finance Director; Andrew Christopher Stylianou [1966] Director/Chartered Accountant; Christopher Jon Taylor [1971] Director/Company Secretary; Stephen John Van Rooyen [1973] Director/Chief Executive Officer, UK & Ireland

Sky Ventures Limited
Incorporated: 17 August 1995
Net Worth: £383,636,992 *Total Assets:* £647,968,000
Registered Office: Grant Way, Isleworth, Middlesex, TW7 5QD
Activities: Activities of head offices
Parent: Sky UK Limited
Officers: Christopher Jon Taylor, Secretary; Karl Holmes [1973] Director/Finance Professional; Colin Robert Jones [1964] Director; Christopher Jon Taylor [1971] Director/Company Secretary

Skylight Investments Limited
Incorporated: 14 June 2011
Net Worth: £100 *Total Assets:* £17,019,638
Registered Office: Flat 201, Ramsey House, Central Square, Wembley, Middlesex, HA9 7AH
Activities: Other professional, scientific and technical activities n.e.c.
Officers: Diane Patricia Sanger [1960] Director

Skyline Arcomet Limited
Incorporated: 14 April 2004 *Employees:* 28
Previous: Skyline Tower Crane Services Ltd
Net Worth: £11,751,480 *Total Assets:* £15,667,716
Registered Office: 609 London Road, West Thurrock, Grays, Essex, RM20 3BJ
Activities: Other specialised construction activities n.e.c.
Shareholders: Darren Lee Whitford; Arcomet Tower Cranes Limited
Officers: Philippe Andre Marie Cohet [1961] Director [French]; Sven Pieter Vrancken [1975] Commercial Director [Belgian]; Darren Lee Whitford [1971] Director

Skylord Travel PLC
Incorporated: 25 November 1988 *Employees:* 28
Net Worth: £2,475,964 *Total Assets:* £9,513,370
Registered Office: 208 Field End Road, Eastcote, Pinner, Middlesex, HA5 1RD
Activities: Travel agency activities
Shareholders: Rajan Kumar Sehgal; Dalip Kumar Kewalramani
Officers: Kartick Kumari Sehgal, Secretary; Dalip Kumar Kewalramani [1969] Director/Travel Agent; Manjinder Seehra [1970] Director/Travel Agent; Kartick Kumari Sehgal [1956] Director/Travel Agent; Rajan Kumar Sehgal [1951] Director/Accountant; Ujjwal Sehgal [1981] Director/Businessman

Skynet (London) Limited
Incorporated: 5 December 2001 *Employees:* 7
Net Worth: £15,522,935 *Total Assets:* £21,945,900
Registered Office: Skynet House, 18-21 Pulborough Way, Hounslow, Middlesex, TW4 6DE
Activities: Unlicensed carriers
Shareholder: Dianne Joy Ellis
Officers: Dianne Joy Ellis, Secretary/Manager; Dianne Joy Ellis [1956] Director/Manager; John Barry Ellis [1939] Director/General Manager

Sliabh Construction Limited
Incorporated: 24 March 2006 *Employees:* 4
Net Worth: £3,753,612 *Total Assets:* £7,016,944
Registered Office: 47 Woodland Road, Maple Cross, Rickmansworth, Herts, WD3 9ST
Activities: Construction of domestic buildings
Shareholder: Joseph Moran
Officers: Joseph Moran, Secretary/Builder [Irish]; John Prior, Secretary/Builder [Irish]; Joseph Moran [1968] Director/Construction Worker [Irish]; John Prior [1968] Director/Construction Worker [Irish]

Sloggett Group Limited
Incorporated: 12 October 1988 *Employees:* 6
Net Worth: £28,511,648 *Total Assets:* £41,359,968
Registered Office: 1 Mount Mews, High Street, Hampton, Surrey, TW12 2SH
Activities: Activities of head offices
Officers: Gerard Raymond Sloggett, Secretary; Christopher Anthony Grady [1960] Director/Chartered Surveyor; Samuel Jennings [1971] Director/Chartered Surveyor; Angus Mervyn Sloggett [1969] Director/Building Manager; Dudley Harold Sloggett [1936] Director; Gerard Raymond Sloggett [1940] Director; Ian Charles Sloggett [1970] Director/Sales Executive

SLS Holding Company Limited
Incorporated: 1 September 2009
Net Worth Deficit: £15,738,000 *Total Assets:* £91,498,000
Registered Office: 8 White Oak Square, London Road, Swanley, Kent, BR8 7AG
Activities: Activities of head offices
Shareholders: JLIF Holdings (Street Lighting) Limited; Skanska TAM Limited
Officers: Paul Alan Bannister [1959] Director/Accountant; David Richard Bradbury [1969] Director/Senior Investment Manager; Jennifer Kathryn Fegan [1973] Director/Lawyer; Katherine Mary Rae [1980] Director/Legal Advisor; Paul Sydney Shadbolt [1957] Asset Management Director; Keerthana Sivanathan [1988] Director/Senior Management Accountant

SM Global Consultancy Limited
Incorporated: 17 September 2013
Net Worth: £239,954 *Total Assets:* £6,273,002
Registered Office: 1st Floor, Bradley's Business Centre, Central Way, North Feltham Trading Estate, Feltham, Middlesex, TW14 0XQ
Activities: Other activities of employment placement agencies
Shareholder: Salmab Iftikhar
Officers: Daniel Carlin [1977] Business Director; Michael Dennis Roy Gadsby [1989] Director; Salman Iftikhar [1987] Director; Erum Salman [1986] Director/Consultancy [Pakistani]

Smart Card Software Limited
Incorporated: 13 October 2004 *Employees:* 3
Net Worth: £9,409,732 *Total Assets:* £11,382,703
Registered Office: 5 White Oak Square, London Road, Swanley, Kent, BR8 7AG
Activities: Business and domestic software development
Parent: Rambus Inc
Officers: Jae Kyung Kim, Secretary; Jae Kyung Kim [1970] Director/SVP, Legal Counsel and HR [American]; Rahul Mathur [1973] Director/SVP, CFO [American]; Martin Philip Scott [1955] Director/SVP, CTO [American]

Smart Transactions Group Limited
Incorporated: 1 March 2000 *Employees:* 1
Net Worth: £10,443,000 *Total Assets:* £10,473,000
Registered Office: John Loftus House, Summer Road, Thames Ditton, Surrey, KT7 0QQ
Activities: Business and domestic software development
Parent: Acre 1144 Limited
Officers: Thomas MacKenzie Newton, Secretary/Accountant; John Michael Morgan Holland [1963] Director; Peter Nicholas Matthews [1957] Director; Duncan McNeil [1952] Director; Jens Peter Montanana [1960] Director; Adam Charles Smith [1964] Director [Australian]

Smartcomms SC Limited
Incorporated: 11 October 2001 *Employees:* 117
Previous: Thunderhead Limited
Net Worth Deficit: £8,505,000 *Total Assets:* £15,767,000
Registered Office: Catalyst House, 720 Centennial Court, Centennial Park, Elstree, Herts, WD6 3SY
Activities: Business and domestic software development
Parent: Platinum Newco I Limited
Officers: James Brown [1971] Director; Jon Stratford [1970] Director

SMC Investcorp Limited
Incorporated: 14 May 2015 *Employees:* 5
Net Worth Deficit: £432,991 *Total Assets:* £13,316,588
Registered Office: Lower Ground Floor, The Old Station, Moor Lane, Staines upon Thames, Middlesex, TW18 4BB
Activities: Development of building projects
Major Shareholder: Billy Kwok Kee Yung
Officers: Pik Mui Cindy Li [1962] Director [Hong Kong]; Mustafa Aziz Taher [1983] Director; Billy Kwok Kee Yung [1953] Director

SME (Coffee) Limited
Incorporated: 26 September 2006 *Employees:* 78
Net Worth: £1,047,767 *Total Assets:* £12,153,441
Registered Office: Runway House, The Runway, Ruislip, Middlesex, HA4 6SE
Activities: Unlicenced restaurants and cafes
Parent: SME Holdings Ltd
Officers: Aly Mohamed Esmail, Secretary; Sayed Mohamed Esmail, Secretary; Aly Mohamed Esmail [1982] Director; Sayed Mohamed Esmail [1986] Director

SME (Pizza) Limited
Incorporated: 19 December 2000 *Employees:* 355
Net Worth Deficit: £2,521,296 *Total Assets:* £5,442,398
Registered Office: Runway House, The Runway, Ruislip, Middlesex, HA4 6SE
Activities: Unlicenced restaurants and cafes
Parent: SME Holdings Ltd
Officers: Aly Mohamed Esmail, Secretary; Sayed Mohamed Esmail, Secretary; Aly Mohamed Esmail [1982] Director; Sayed Mohamed Esmail [1986] Director/Mediator

SME Corporation Limited
Incorporated: 1 June 2007 *Employees:* 80
Net Worth: £3,033,510 *Total Assets:* £8,170,117
Registered Office: Runway House, The Runway, Ruislip, Middlesex, HA4 6SE
Activities: Unlicenced restaurants and cafes
Parent: SME Investments Ltd
Officers: Aly Mohamed Esmail, Secretary; Sayed Mohamed Esmail, Secretary; Aly Mohamed Esmail [1982] Director; Sayed Mohamed Esmail [1986] Director

SME Fast Foods Limited
Incorporated: 19 October 1987 *Employees:* 52
Net Worth: £3,929,699 *Total Assets:* £5,645,431
Registered Office: Runway House, The Runway, Ruislip, Middlesex, HA4 6SE
Activities: Unlicenced restaurants and cafes
Parent: SME Investments Ltd
Officers: Aly Mohamed Esmail, Secretary; Sayed Mohamed Esmail, Secretary; Aly Mohamed Esmail [1982] Director; Sayed Mohamed Esmail [1986] Director

SME Group PLC
Incorporated: 13 April 1988 *Employees:* 1,620
Net Worth: £55,596,000 *Total Assets:* £111,588,000
Registered Office: Runway House, The Runway, Ruislip, Middlesex, HA4 6SE
Activities: Activities of head offices
Officers: Aly Mohamed Esmail, Secretary; Sayed Mohamed Esmail, Secretary; Aly Esmail [1982] Director; Sayed Mohamed Esmail [1986] Director

SME Holdings Limited
Incorporated: 14 December 2001 *Employees:* 1,012
Net Worth: £23,182,824 *Total Assets:* £63,635,392
Registered Office: Runway House, The Runway, Ruislip, Middlesex, HA4 6SE
Activities: Activities of head offices
Officers: Sayed Mohamed Esmail, Secretary; Aly Mohamed Esmail [1982] Director; Sayed Mohamed Esmail [1986] Director

SME Investments Limited
Incorporated: 10 May 2005 *Employees:* 529
Net Worth: £27,143,268 *Total Assets:* £71,963,288
Registered Office: Runway House, The Runway, Ruislip, Middlesex, HA4 6SE
Activities: Activities of head offices
Parent: SME Group PLC
Officers: Aly Mohamed Esmail, Secretary; Sayed Mohamed Esmail, Secretary; Aly Mohamed Esmail [1982] Director; Sayed Mohamed Esmail [1986] Director

SME Properties Limited
Incorporated: 10 March 2005
Net Worth: £3,134,435 *Total Assets:* £16,102,450
Registered Office: Runway House, The Runway, Ruislip, Middlesex, HA4 6SE
Activities: Other accommodation
Officers: Aly Mohamed Esmail, Secretary; Sayed Mohamed Esmail, Secretary; Aly Mohamed Esmail [1982] Director; Sayed Mohamed Esmail [1986] Director

SME Trading Limited
Incorporated: 17 May 1989 *Employees:* 205
Net Worth: £4,051,813 *Total Assets:* £10,123,182
Registered Office: Runway House, The Runway, Ruislip, Middlesex, HA4 6SE
Activities: Unlicenced restaurants and cafes
Parent: SME Holdings Ltd
Officers: Aly Mohamed Esmail, Secretary; Sayed Mohamed Esmail, Secretary; Aly Mohamed Esmail [1982] Director; Sayed Mohamed Esmail [1986] Director

Smith and Byford Limited
Incorporated: 29 September 1972 *Employees:* 370
Net Worth: £7,106,293 *Total Assets:* £12,542,890
Registered Office: St George House, Station Approach, Cheam, Sutton, Surrey, SM2 7AT
Activities: Electrical installation
Shareholders: William Smith; Hazel Rosemary Smith
Officers: Paula McLachlan, Secretary; Brian Grove [1962] Director/Install Manager; Melanie Herridge [1984] Business Director; Paula McLachlan [1969] Office Director; David Ovington [1971] Director/Chief Technology Officer; Hazel Rosemary Smith [1941] Director; William Smith [1967] Managing Director; William Smith [1942] Director/Chairman; Andrew Richard Wilson [1977] Finance Director

H. Smith Food Group PLC
Incorporated: 22 January 1990 *Employees:* 33
Net Worth: £4,419,886 *Total Assets:* £17,509,352
Registered Office: 24 Easter Industrial Park, Ferry Lane South, Rainham, Essex, RM13 9BP
Activities: Wholesale of meat and meat products
Major Shareholder: Christopher Jamie Smith
Officers: Phillip Trevor Wheater, Secretary; Daniel Lawrence Fallis [1976] Sales Director; David Keith Howe [1967] Director/Sales; Richard James Murray [1965] Finance Director; Christopher Jamie Smith [1959] Director/Poultry Merchant; Shaun Daniel Smith [1989] Director/Frozen Food Wholesaler

Drew Smith Homes Limited
Incorporated: 21 September 1994
Net Worth: £1,565,857 *Total Assets:* £23,192,174
Registered Office: Cowley Business Park, High Street, Cowley, Uxbridge, Middlesex, UB8 2AL
Activities: Buying and selling of own real estate
Parent: Galliford Try Partnerships Limited
Officers: Kevin Allan Corbett [1960] Director; Mark Robert Farnham [1965] Director/Accountant; Stuart Daniel Munro [1967] Director; Stephen John Teagle [1959] Director; Peter Martin Truscott [1962] Director

Smith Kline & French Laboratories Limited
Incorporated: 21 April 1897
Net Worth: £464,864,000 *Total Assets:* £464,873,984
Registered Office: 980 Great West Road, Brentford, Middlesex, TW8 9GS
Activities: Manufacture of basic pharmaceutical products
Parent: SmithKline Beecham Limited
Officers: Simon Paul Dingemans [1963] Director

Drew Smith Limited
Incorporated: 19 October 1989 *Employees:* 89
Net Worth: £3,055,412 *Total Assets:* £19,102,560
Registered Office: Cowley Business Park, High Street, Cowley, Uxbridge, Middlesex, UB8 2AL
Activities: Construction of domestic buildings
Parent: Galliford Try Partnerships Limited
Officers: Kevin Allan Corbett [1960] Director; Mark Robert Farnham [1965] Director/Accountant; Stuart Daniel Munro [1967] Director; Stephen John Teagle [1959] Director; Peter Martin Truscott [1962] Director

Smithers Information Limited
Incorporated: 13 October 1999 *Employees:* 40
Net Worth: £7,365,000 *Total Assets:* £9,543,000
Registered Office: Main Building, Cleeve Road, Leatherhead, Surrey, KT22 7RU
Activities: Other professional, scientific and technical activities n.e.c.
Parent: Smithers UK Holdings Limited
Officers: John Michael Hochschwender [1960] Director/Executive [American]; Ravinderjeet Singh Lally [1975] Managing Director

SmithKline Beecham (Export) Limited
Incorporated: 8 October 1993
Net Worth: £3,403,000 *Total Assets:* £9,255,000
Registered Office: 980 Great West Road, Brentford, Middlesex, TW8 9GS
Activities: Other business support service activities n.e.c.
Parent: SmithKline Beecham Limited
Officers: Adam Walker [1967] Director

SmithKline Beecham (H) Limited
Incorporated: 18 December 1996
Net Worth: £69,482,000 *Total Assets:* £69,504,000
Registered Office: 980 Great West Road, Brentford, Middlesex, TW8 9GS
Activities: Activities of head offices
Parent: Wellcome Limited
Officers: Adam Walker [1967] Director

SmithKline Beecham (Investments) Limited
Incorporated: 21 June 1935
Net Worth: £471,728,992 *Total Assets:* £495,331,008
Registered Office: 980 Great West Road, Brentford, Middlesex, TW8 9GS
Activities: Financial intermediation not elsewhere classified
Shareholders: Setfirst Limited; SmithKline Beecham Limited
Officers: Adam Walker [1967] Director

SmithKline Beecham (SWG) Limited
Incorporated: 26 May 1923
Net Worth: £7,054,000 *Total Assets:* £7,072,000
Registered Office: 980 Great West Road, Brentford, Middlesex, TW8 9GS
Activities: Other human health activities
Parent: SmithKline Beecham Limited
Officers: Adam Walker [1967] Director

SmithKline Beecham Limited
Incorporated: 24 January 1989 *Employees:* 1,333
Net Worth: £1,310,000,000 *Total Assets:* £2,496,000,000
Registered Office: 980 Great West Road, Brentford, Middlesex, TW8 9GS
Activities: Manufacture of soft drinks; production of mineral waters and other bottled waters
Parent: GlaxoSmithKline Finance PLC
Officers: Victoria Anne Whyte, Secretary; Simon Paul Dingemans [1963] Director

SmithKline Beecham Marketing and Technical Services Limited
Incorporated: 16 April 1951
Net Worth: £2,885,000 *Total Assets:* £16,581,000
Registered Office: 980 Great West Road, Brentford, Middlesex, TW8 9GS
Activities: Other business support service activities n.e.c.
Parent: SmithKline Beecham Limited
Officers: Adam Walker [1967] Director

SmithKline Beecham Overseas Limited
Incorporated: 29 October 1990
Net Worth: £40,316,000 *Total Assets:* £56,486,000
Registered Office: 980 Great West Road, Brentford, Middlesex, TW8 9GS
Activities: Activities of head offices
Parent: SmithKline Beecham Limited
Officers: Simon Paul Dingemans [1963] Director

SmithKline Beecham Research Limited
Incorporated: 21 March 1928 *Employees:* 107
Net Worth: £15,345,000 *Total Assets:* £25,847,000
Registered Office: 980 Great West Road, Brentford, Middlesex, TW8 9GS
Activities: Activities of head offices
Parent: GlaxoSmithKline Consumer Healthcare Holdings Limited
Officers: Richard Green [1974] Director; Richard Philip Tattershall [1982] Director/Accountant

Smiths Business Information Services Limited
Incorporated: 24 September 1996 *Employees:* 83
Net Worth: £9,371,000 *Total Assets:* £18,836,000
Registered Office: First Floor, Building 7, Croxley Business Park, Hatters Lane, Watford, Herts, WD18 8PA
Activities: Information technology consultancy activities
Parent: Smiths Group International Holdings Limited
Officers: Vanya Katreece Hughes, Secretary; Martin James Fox [1965] Director/Accountant; Vanya Katreece Hughes [1978] Director/Solicitor

Smiths Industries Industrial Group Limited
Incorporated: 31 October 1968 *Employees:* 49
Net Worth: £65,134,000 *Total Assets:* £68,211,000
Registered Office: Unit 130 Centennial Park, Elstree, Herts, WD6 3TJ
Activities: Other service activities n.e.c.
Parent: Smiths Interconnect Group Limited
Officers: Eric Lakin, Secretary; Paul Harris [1957] Director/President Smiths Connectors; Giuseppe Lancella [1961] Managing Director [Italian]

Smiths Interconnect Group Limited
Incorporated: 9 July 2008 *Employees:* 6
Net Worth: £269,216,992 *Total Assets:* £474,943,008
Registered Office: Unit 130 Centennial Park, Elstree, Herts, WD6 3TJ
Activities: Activities of head offices
Parent: Smiths Group International Holdings Limited
Officers: Eric Lakin, Secretary; Karen Maria Bomba [1964] Director/President [American]; Eric Daniel Lakin [1970] Director/Vice President, Finance; Simon James Price [1974] Director

SNC-Lavalin (GB) Holdings Limited
Incorporated: 7 April 2017
Net Worth: £913,605,888 *Total Assets:* £2,316,271,872
Registered Office: Woodcote Grove, Ashley Road, Epsom, Surrey, KT18 5BW
Activities: Activities of head offices
Officers: Arden Furlotte, Secretary; Louise Mary McAllister, Secretary; Elliot Michael Nobelen, Secretary; Mark Stephen Anderson [1965] Finance Director; Simon Glenister Cole [1965] Director/Accountant

SNC-Lavalin (GB) Limited
Incorporated: 6 May 2014
Net Worth: £2,242,508,800 *Total Assets:* £2,262,006,272
Registered Office: Woodcote Grove, Ashley Road, Epsom, Surrey, KT18 5BW
Activities: Activities of head offices
Officers: Louise Mary McAllister, Secretary; Elliot Michael Nobelen, Secretary; Mark Stephen Anderson [1965] Finance Director; Simon Glenister Cole [1965] Director/Accountant; James Richard Compston [1965] Director/SVP - Customer Relationships & Business; Richard Thomas Glandon George [1955] Director/MD

SNC-Lavalin Co. Ltd.
Incorporated: 13 November 2013
Net Worth: £23,589,672 *Total Assets:* £23,647,700
Registered Office: Woodcote Grove, Ashley Road, Epsom, Surrey, KT18 5BW
Activities: Other professional, scientific and technical activities n.e.c.
Officers: Louise Mary McAllister, Secretary; Elliot Michael Nobelen, Secretary; Simon Glenister Cole [1965] Director/Accountant; James Richard Compston [1965] Director/SVP Customer Relationships & Business Development; Richard Thomas Glandon George [1955] Director/MD

SNC-Lavalin Rail & Transit Limited
Incorporated: 24 May 1995 *Employees:* 442
Previous: Interfleet Technology Limited
Net Worth Deficit: £4,917,000 *Total Assets:* £29,885,000
Registered Office: Woodcote Grove, Ashley Road, Epsom, Surrey, KT18 5BW
Activities: Engineering related scientific and technical consulting activities
Parent: Interfleet Holdings Ltd
Officers: Louise Mary McAllister, Secretary; Elliot Michael Nobelen, Secretary; Richard Thomas Glandon George [1955] Director/MD; Michael John Grace [1963] Director

SNC-Lavalin UK Holding Limited
Incorporated: 22 September 2011
Net Worth: £2,332,000 *Total Assets:* £6,251,000
Registered Office: Woodcote Grove, Ashley Road, Epsom, Surrey, KT18 5BW
Activities: Engineering design activities for industrial process and production
Officers: Louise Mary McAllister, Secretary; Elliot Michael Nobelen, Secretary; Olivier D'Ambra [1980] Director [Canadian]

Snowden Developments Limited
Incorporated: 11 October 2016
Net Worth Deficit: £32,852 *Total Assets:* £6,583,988
Registered Office: 14 Oxford Road, Wealdstone, Harrow, Middlesex, HA3 7RG
Activities: Development of building projects
Officers: Dhiraj Samji Dabasia [1984] Director/Businessman; Hitesh Samji Dabasia [1980] Director/Doctor; Sundip Samji Dabasia [1983] Director/Businessman; Samji Shivji Patel [1956] Director/Businessman; Gaurang Babulal Velani [1973] Director/Businessman

Snowflake 145 Limited
Incorporated: 17 June 2003
Net Worth Deficit: £214,190 *Total Assets:* £8,306,165
Registered Office: NJHco, Suite 1, The Sanctuary, 23 Oak Hill Grove, Surbiton, Surrey, KT6 6DU
Activities: Activities of other holding companies n.e.c.
Major Shareholder: Klaas Johannes Zwart
Officers: Simon Graham [1970] Alternate Director; Nicola Claire McGall [1973] Alternate Director; Paul Emmanuel O'Neill [1978] Director [Irish]; Adrian Relph [1967] Director

Societe Generale Equipment Finance Limited
Incorporated: 7 July 1998 *Employees:* 96
Net Worth: £48,127,000 *Total Assets:* £977,971,968
Registered Office: Parkshot House, 5 Kew Road, Richmond, Surrey, TW9 2PR
Activities: Financial leasing
Parent: Societe Generale SA
Officers: Timothy Edward Goodship, Secretary; Stephen John Bowden [1964] Director/Senior Account Manager; Timothy Edward Goodship [1979] Director/Certified Chartered Accountant; Dominic Lawson Hughes [1972] Director/Financier; David Robert George Yates-Mercer [1964] Director/Accountant

Soda Studios Limited
Incorporated: 2 April 2007
Net Worth: £1 *Total Assets:* £12,020,679
Registered Office: 42 Lytton Road, Barnet, Herts, EN5 5BY
Activities: Development of building projects
Parent: Investland Limited
Officers: Joseph Peter Gerrard [1954] Director/Property Developer; Michael Gerrard [1957] Director/Property Developer

Softwareone UK Limited
Incorporated: 25 June 2008 *Employees:* 141
Net Worth: £3,700,108 *Total Assets:* £55,639,360
Registered Office: 1 Parkshot, Richmond, Surrey, TW9 2RD
Activities: Information technology consultancy activities
Parent: SoftwareOne AG
Officers: Andrew Martin, Secretary; Dr Hans Grueter [1959] Director [Swiss]; Pascal Rene Hungerbuehler [1985] Director/Head of Legal [Swiss]; Andrew Martin [1972] Finance Director; Satpaul Virdi [1970] Managing Director

Sogea Holdings (UK) Limited
Incorporated: 6 May 1997
Net Worth: £166,660,992 *Total Assets:* £186,660,992
Registered Office: Astral House, Imperial Way, Watford, Herts, WD24 4WW
Activities: Activities of head offices
Parent: Vinci Construction SAS
Officers: Bruno Michel Dupety [1956] Director/Engineer [French]; Yann Paul Grolimund [1959] Director/Chief Financial Officer [French]

Soho Loop Limited
Incorporated: 11 May 2017
Net Worth Deficit: £310,160 *Total Assets:* £8,645,959
Registered Office: 3rd Floor, Sterling House, Langston Road, Loughton, Essex, IG10 3TS
Activities: Development of building projects
Shareholders: Galliard Holdings Limited; Apsley House Capital PLC
Officers: Allan William Porter, Secretary; Stephen Stuart Solomon Conway [1948] Director; Gerard Nock [1947] Director/Company Chairman; Carl Robin Norstrom [1984] Director [Swedish]; Donagh O'Sullivan [1968] Construction Director [Irish]

SOL Electronics Limited
Incorporated: 31 October 2001 *Employees:* 8
Net Worth: £857,146 *Total Assets:* £9,210,482
Registered Office: Unit 2 The Bridge Business Centre, Bridge Road, Southall, Middlesex, UB2 4AY
Activities: Non-specialised wholesale trade
Officers: Steven Mark Ellis [1976] Sales Director

Solai Holdings Limited
Incorporated: 31 January 1985 *Employees:* 328
Net Worth: £211,682,000 *Total Assets:* £745,441,984
Registered Office: Portland House, 69-71 Wembley Hill Road, Wembley, Middlesex, HA9 8BU
Activities: Other service activities n.e.c.
Officers: Bhupendra Shantilal Kansagra, Secretary; Bhupendra Shantilal Kansagra [1956] Director; Rajni Shantilal Kansagra [1942] Director/Engineer; Ramesh Shantilal Kansagra [1950] Director

Solai House Limited
Incorporated: 18 May 2017
Net Worth: £31,627 *Total Assets:* £5,462,655
Registered Office: Portland House, 69-71 Wembley Hill Road, Wembley, Middlesex, HA9 8BU
Activities: Other letting and operating of own or leased real estate
Parent: Solai Holdings Ltd
Officers: Bhupendra Kansagra, Secretary; Bhupendra Shantilal Kansagra [1956] Director; Rajni Shantilal Kansagra [1942] Director; Ramesh Shantilal Kansagra [1950] Director; Rishi Ramesh Kansagra [1981] Director; Sunil Rajni Kansagra [1976] Director

Solight Limited
Incorporated: 21 December 2000
Net Worth: £2,540,548 *Total Assets:* £9,505,534
Registered Office: World Business Centre, 3 Newall Road, London Heathrow Airport, Hounslow, Middlesex, TW6 2TA
Activities: Other letting and operating of own or leased real estate
Officers: Surinder Arora, Secretary; Sunita Arora [1964] Director; Surinder Arora [1958] Director

The Solihull Hotel Company Limited
Incorporated: 4 September 1987 *Employees:* 70
Net Worth: £14,771,000 *Total Assets:* £19,835,000
Registered Office: Queens Court, 9-17 Eastern Road, Romford, Essex, RM1 3NG
Activities: Hotels and similar accommodation
Parent: BPH Finance Number 1 Limited
Officers: Jonathan Patrick Braidley [1965] Director/Investment Professional; Christopher Andre Kula [1983] Director/Chartered Accountant [German/Canadian]

Soloberry Limited
Incorporated: 8 January 2004 *Employees:* 31
Previous: CPM (Retail) Limited
Net Worth: £2,689,000 *Total Assets:* £9,104,000
Registered Office: Thames House, Thames Road, Crayford, Kent, DA1 4QP
Activities: Wholesale of fruit and vegetables
Parent: A G Thames Holdings Limited
Officers: Christopher Oakley, Secretary; David Alex Aichen [1969] Director; Leon Aichen [1941] Director/Chairman; Gary Raymond Linsell [1970] Director; Christopher Richard Oakley [1963] Finance Director

Solstor Holdings Limited
Incorporated: 10 February 2016 *Employees:* 120
Net Worth: £8,462,952 *Total Assets:* £19,573,160
Registered Office: Thames House, Thames Road, Crayford, Kent, DA1 4QP
Activities: Freight transport by road
Major Shareholder: Leon Aichen
Officers: Kevin Stuart Dechaine, Secretary; David Alex Aichen [1969] Director; Kevin Stuart Dechaine [1979] Director; Graham Neville Doe [1971] Director

Solstor UK Limited
Incorporated: 20 September 1999 *Employees:* 116
Net Worth: £8,498,063 *Total Assets:* £19,627,498
Registered Office: Thames House, Thames Road, Crayford, Kent, DA1 4QP
Activities: Freight transport by road
Major Shareholder: Leon Aichen
Officers: Kevin Stuart Dechaine, Secretary; David Alex Aichen [1969] Director; Kevin Stuart Dechaine [1979] Director; Graham Neville Doe [1971] Director

Solvay Solutions UK Limited
Incorporated: 15 July 1892 *Employees:* 283
Net Worth Deficit: £536,819,008 *Total Assets:* £207,010,000
Registered Office: 34 Clarendon Road, Watford, Herts, WD17 1JJ
Activities: Manufacture of other chemical products n.e.c.
Parent: Rhodia Holdings Limited
Officers: Alison Murphy, Secretary; Tom Dutton [1964] Director/Health, Safety & Environment Manager; Michael Neil Holland [1971] Market Director HPC EMEA; Nathan Mills [1977] Director/Engineer [American]; Alison Murphy [1965] Director/Financial Controller

Solvecorp Limited
Incorporated: 12 November 1999
Net Worth Deficit: £281,971,008 *Total Assets:* £464,835,008
Registered Office: Hayes Park, Hayes End Road, Hayes, Middlesex, UB4 8EE
Activities: Non-trading company
Parent: Deluxestar Limited
Officers: Mark Oldham, Secretary/Barrister; Helen Josephine McCarthy [1966] Director; Mark Oldham [1959] Director

Somers Hills Limited
Incorporated: 27 June 2017 *Employees:* 23
Net Worth: £282,721 *Total Assets:* £5,712,764
Registered Office: EPP House, 8-9 Epsom Business Park, Epsom, Surrey, KT17 1JF
Activities: Installation of industrial machinery and equipment
Shareholder: Stephen Charles Merritt
Officers: Melissa James [1966] Director; Stephen Charles Merritt [1965] Managing Director; Josephine Dorothy Mitchell [1949] Director; Stewart William Morris [1966] Director; Roger William Mott [1954] Director; Peter Trevor Samuels [1946] Director/Chartered Accountant; Keith James Stalker [1951] Director

Sonata Europe Limited
Incorporated: 25 September 2006 *Employees:* 4
Net Worth: £6,187,799 *Total Assets:* £7,755,917
Registered Office: 11th Floor West, The Mille, 1000 Great West Road, Brentford, Middlesex, TW8 9HH
Activities: Information technology consultancy activities
Officers: Kundan K Lal, Secretary; Sathyanarayana Ramarao [1965] Director/Service [Indian]; Tridip Saha [1973] Director/Employee

The Sons of Divine Providence
Incorporated: 10 July 2001 *Employees:* 71
Net Worth: £6,697,493 *Total Assets:* £6,922,356
Registered Office: 13 Lower Teddington Road, Hampton Wick, Kingston upon Thames, Surrey, KT1 4EU
Activities: Renting and operating of Housing Association real estate
Officers: Michael Thomas Healy, Secretary; Father Stephen Peter Beale [1959] Director/Priest; Bernadette Mary Griffin [1940] Director; Rev Christopher Philip Kehoe [1955] Director/Priest; Rev John Perrotta [1938] Director/Minister of Religion [Italian]; Jose Luis Simionato [1962] Director/Priest [Argentinian/Italian]

Sony Europe Limited
Incorporated: 14 September 1989 *Employees:* 2,730
Net Worth Deficit: £604,445,248 *Total Assets:* £1,102,010,112
Registered Office: c/o Legal Department, The Heights, Brooklands, Weybridge, Surrey, KT13 0XW
Activities: Manufacture of consumer electronics
Parent: Sony Overseas Holding B.V.
Officers: Katherine Bromley, Secretary; Shigeru Kumekawa [1963] Director/President [Japanese]; Masaki Kurebayashi [1967] Director [Japanese]; Ricky Londema [1964] Director/Business Executive [Dutch]

Sony Global Treasury Services PLC
Incorporated: 30 November 2000
Net Worth: £742,964,544 *Total Assets:* £14,148,797,440
Registered Office: Sony Europe Limited, The Heights, Brooklands, Weybridge, Surrey, KT13 0XW
Activities: Other business support service activities n.e.c.
Parent: Sony Overseas Holding BV
Officers: Jane Helen Lawrence, Secretary; Jiro Aikawa [1963] Managing Director [Japanese]; Hiroyuki Ishiguro [1968] Director/General Manager [Japanese]; Masaki Kurebayashi [1967] Director [Japanese]; Atsuko Murakami [1958] Director/Business Executive [Japanese]

Sotherby LLP
Incorporated: 26 October 2015 *Employees:* 2
Net Worth: £9,555,702 *Total Assets:* £18,917,582
Registered Office: 166 College Road, Harrow, Middlesex, HA1 1RA
Officers: Michael Spencer Docker [1963] Member; Michele Docker [1965] Member

Soul Coffee House (London) Limited
Incorporated: 18 March 2016 *Employees:* 166
Net Worth Deficit: £782,039 *Total Assets:* £6,485,169
Registered Office: 64 Wolsey Road, Northwood, Middlesex, HA6 2EH
Activities: Unlicenced restaurants and cafes
Major Shareholder: Aly Hassanali Moleaina Janmohamed
Officers: Aly Hassanali Moleaina Janmohamed [1957] Director; Shehzad Janmohamed [1984] Director

Soul Coffee House (South) Limited
Incorporated: 2 January 2015 *Employees:* 275
Net Worth Deficit: £1,819,618 *Total Assets:* £5,742,139
Registered Office: 64 Wolsey Road, Moor Park, Northwood, Middlesex, HA6 2EH
Activities: Unlicenced restaurants and cafes
Major Shareholder: Aly Hassanali Moleaina Janmohamed
Officers: Aly Hassanali Moleaina Janmohamed [1957] Director; Shehzad Janmohamed [1984] Director

Soul Coffee House (West) Limited
Incorporated: 2 January 2015 *Employees:* 235
Net Worth: £508,004 *Total Assets:* £5,933,998
Registered Office: 64 Wolsey Road, Moor Park, Northwood, Middlesex, HA6 2EH
Activities: Unlicenced restaurants and cafes
Major Shareholder: Aly Hassanali Moleaina Janmohamed
Officers: Aly Hassanali Moleaina Janmohamed [1957] Director; Shehzad Janmohamed [1984] Director

Soul Coffee House Limited
Incorporated: 2 January 2015 *Employees:* 1,103
Net Worth Deficit: £2,860,860 *Total Assets:* £27,126,388
Registered Office: 64 Wolsey Road, Moor Park, Northwood, Middlesex, HA6 2EH
Activities: Activities of head offices
Major Shareholder: Aly Hassanali Moleaina Janmohamed
Officers: Aly Hassanali Moleaina Janmohamed [1957] Director; Shehzad Janmohamed [1984] Director

Soul Foods Limited
Incorporated: 26 March 2002 *Employees:* 777
Net Worth: £4,015,281 *Total Assets:* £17,520,264
Registered Office: 64 Wolsey Road, Northwood, Middlesex, HA6 2EH
Activities: Activities of head offices
Major Shareholder: Aly Hassanali Moleaina Janmohamed
Officers: Samirah Janmohamed, Secretary; Aly Hassanali Moleaina Janmohamed [1957] Director; Shehzad Janmohamed [1984] Director

Sourcecode UK Limited
Incorporated: 23 July 2003 *Employees:* 41
Net Worth Deficit: £7,021,702 *Total Assets:* £34,420,536
Registered Office: Number 1 The Heights, Brooklands, Weybridge, Surrey, KT13 0NY
Activities: Other information technology service activities
Officers: Shelley Hall, Secretary; John Ederer [1969] Director [American]; Loyd Evan Ellis [1955] Director [American]

South Central Property Limited
Incorporated: 25 January 1993 *Employees:* 46
Net Worth: £75,370,016 *Total Assets:* £268,950,304
Registered Office: Portland House, 67-71 Wembley Hill Road, Wembley, Middlesex, HA9 8BU
Activities: Other letting and operating of own or leased real estate
Officers: Monique Francoise Cadji, Company Secretary; Laurent Elie Cadji [1977] Director/Trader; Lewis Levy Cadji [1938] Director; Monique Francoise Cadji [1949] Director/Company Secretary; Sarita Michele Kraljevic [1971] Director/Housewife; Miriam Martine Taylor [1973] Director/Housewife

South Coast Watch Fair Limited
Incorporated: 31 March 1994
Net Worth: £1,431,822 *Total Assets:* £6,626,735
Registered Office: 2nd Floor, Unicorn House, Station Close, Potters Bar, Herts, EN6 1TL
Activities: Other letting and operating of own or leased real estate
Major Shareholder: Jeremiah Harouni
Officers: David Samuel Harouni [1977] Director; Jeremiah Harouni [1949] Director

South Darenth Farms and Cold Store Company Limited
Incorporated: 27 May 1960 *Employees:* 11
Net Worth: £15,853,690 *Total Assets:* £24,169,964
Registered Office: St Margarets Farm, St Margarets Road, South Darenth, Dartford, Kent, DA4 9LB
Activities: Growing of cereals (except rice), leguminous crops and oil seeds
Parent: Favourquick Ltd
Officers: Alison Eleanor Hawkins, Secretary; Alison Eleanor Hawkins [1958] Director; Derek George Hawkins [1955] Director; Lisa Jane Alexandra Hawkins [1969] Director; Yvonne Suzette Maria Hawkins Houiller [1962] Director; Sharon Claretta Angela Kirby [1957] Director; Fiona Kathryn Louise Taylor [1964] Director/CD/Research Scientist

South Manchester Energy Limited
Incorporated: 20 December 2016 *Employees:* 2
Net Worth Deficit: £2,404,717 *Total Assets:* £6,424,504
Registered Office: Munro House, Portsmouth Road, Cobham, Surrey, KT11 1PP
Activities: Other business support service activities n.e.c.
Parent: GCP Biogas 1 Limited
Officers: David George Conlon [1978] Director

South Mimms Services Limited
Incorporated: 30 August 1951
Net Worth: £9,528,421 *Total Assets:* £9,763,739
Registered Office: Plantagenet House, 4 Plantagenet Road, New Barnet, Herts, EN5 5JQ
Activities: Other letting and operating of own or leased real estate
Major Shareholder: Christopher Edward Scarfe
Officers: Nicholas James Scarfe, Secretary; Nicholas James Scarfe [1992] Director

South Orpington Learning Alliance Multi-Academy Trust
Incorporated: 9 February 2012 *Employees:* 391
Previous: Tubbenden Primary School
Net Worth: £29,454,432 *Total Assets:* £33,824,152
Registered Office: Tubbenden Primary School, Sandy Bury, Orpington, Kent, BR6 9SD
Activities: Pre-primary education
Officers: Carole Ann Booker, Secretary; Adrian Karl David Fisher [1969] Director/Self Employed Consultant; Sarah Anne Gardiner [1972] Director; Clive Stephen Howse [1963] Managing Director of Media Planning Agency; June Christine Riley [1957] Director/School Business Manager; Robert Matthew Sampson [1962] Director/Bank Manager; Robert Michael Summers [1976] Director/Consultant; Pradeep Kumar Thatai [1951] Director/Accountant; James Turvey [1963] Director/Headmaster

South West Essex Community Education Trust Limited
Incorporated: 5 July 2011 *Employees:* 455
Previous: WESCD Community Education Trust Limited
Net Worth: £34,847,000 *Total Assets:* £43,314,000
Registered Office: Stifford Clays Road, Orsett, Grays, Essex, RM16 3NJ
Activities: Pre-primary education
Officers: Peter James Melville, Secretary; Duncan James Gotobed [1970] Director of Training Consultancy; John King [1950] Director/Education Consultant; Raymond John Moore [1957] Senior Bank Manager and Director; Stephen James Munday [1976] Director/Headteacher; David Robert Pavitt [1966] Director/Retired; Christina Louise Pumfrey [1968] Director/Executive Headteacher; Garry Tapsell [1972] Director/Fitness Manager

Southall Travel Limited
Incorporated: 6 December 1984 *Employees:* 38
Net Worth: £44,537,160 *Total Assets:* £92,942,480
Registered Office: 19 South Road, Southall, Middlesex, UB1 1SU
Activities: Travel agency activities
Officers: Donna Bahia, Secretary; Donna Bahia [1974] Director; Kuljinder Singh Bahia [1972] Director; Jaymin Dhirajlal Borkhatria [1965] Director

Southbeck Investment Company Limited
Incorporated: 27 December 1963 *Employees:* 3
Net Worth: £4,713,299 *Total Assets:* £5,143,405
Registered Office: Trinity House, 3 Bullace Lane, Dartford, Kent, DA1 1BB
Activities: Other letting and operating of own or leased real estate
Parent: Inca Property Enterprises Limited
Officers: Gillian Campbell Fraser Noach, Secretary; Robert Lewis Noach [1951] Director/Financial Service Executive; Doctor Avigdor Manuel Saks [1958] Director/Doctor [South African]; Dr Sarya Alon Saks [1956] Director/Doctor [South African]

Southborough High School
Incorporated: 16 September 2011 *Employees:* 80
Net Worth: £10,369,795 *Total Assets:* £12,097,168
Registered Office: Southborough High School, Hook Road, Surbiton, Surrey, KT6 5AS
Activities: General secondary education
Officers: Brian Burns, Secretary; Michael Patrick Armstrong [1953] Director/Teacher; Sampa Bhasin [1965] Director/Financial Consultant; Malcolm Gregory [1958] Director/Retired; Clare Anne Henderson [1966] Director; Otto Frederick Houwen [1973] Director/Civil Servant [Dutch]; Junaid Kazi [1980] Director/Senior Manager, Product Management; Robin Kent [1964] Director; Jamie-Lee King [1986] Director/Teacher; Joannis Michael Phillips [1953] Director/IT Manager; Sarfraz Ahmad Rahman [1961] Director; Michael Rose [1965] Director/Teacher; Niall Raith Le Fleming Smith [1970] Director; Robert Miles Steed [1949] Director/Kingston Councillor Retired; Nicholas James Tassell [1973] Director/Head of Risk & Compliance; Christopher James Upton [1959] Director/Coffee Shop Proprietor; Dr Rebecca White [1988] Director/Teacher

Southcrown Limited
Incorporated: 12 March 1985 *Employees:* 3
Net Worth: £4,112,750 *Total Assets:* £6,413,976
Registered Office: 1 Town Quay Wharf, Abbey Road, Barking, Essex, IG11 7BZ
Activities: Development of building projects
Parent: Westcrown Investments Limited
Officers: Nina Louise Anderson [1974] Director/Administration Manager; Barry Stewart [1943] Director

Southdown Holdings Limited
Incorporated: 26 June 2000 *Employees:* 3
Net Worth: £6,653,674 *Total Assets:* £14,352,874
Registered Office: Ermyn Lodge Stud, Shepherds Walk, Epsom, Surrey, KT18 6DF
Activities: Other letting and operating of own or leased real estate
Parent: Timesquare Holdings Limited
Officers: Lesley Jean Smith, Secretary; Anthony James Smith [1947] Director

Southern Counties Care Limited
Incorporated: 22 January 1988 *Employees:* 52
Net Worth: £5,593,518 *Total Assets:* £9,234,864
Registered Office: Image Court, 328-334 Moseley Road, Walton-on-Thames, Surrey, KT12 3LT
Activities: Residential care activities for the elderly and disabled
Shareholder: Sheth Sonachand Dharmanan Singh Jeebun
Officers: Zainah Jeebun, Secretary; Sheth Sonachand Dharmanan Singh Jeebun [1961] Director/Entrepreneur; Zainah Jeebun [1961] Director/Entrepreneur

The Southern Motor Group Limited
Incorporated: 2 May 1967 *Employees:* 91
Net Worth: £4,112,904 *Total Assets:* £21,786,532
Registered Office: 22 Lansdowne Road, Croydon, Surrey, CR0 2BD
Activities: Retail trade of motor vehicle parts and accessories
Officers: Stephen Paul Price, Secretary; Peter John Price [1966] Director/Sales Manager; Stephen Paul Price [1964] Director/Accountant

Southfleet Investments Limited
Incorporated: 4 December 1962 *Employees:* 2
Net Worth: £5,416,791 *Total Assets:* £6,081,901
Registered Office: 4th Floor, Joynes House, New Road, Gravesend, Kent, DA11 0AT
Activities: Development of building projects
Officers: Susan Rowe, Secretary; Alan Henry George Rowe [1937] Director; Susan Rowe [1942] Director/Married Woman

Sovereign Business Integration Group PLC
Incorporated: 16 November 1994 *Employees:* 62
Net Worth: £2,678,727 *Total Assets:* £5,129,243
Registered Office: Metro Point, Chalk Lane, Cockfosters, Barnet, Herts, EN4 9JQ
Activities: Information technology consultancy activities
Major Shareholder: Richard David Barker
Officers: Heather Margaret Barker, Secretary; Richard David Barker [1946] Director; Jason Dickens [1983] Managing Director SBR; Joanna Clare Sedley-Burke [1968] Managing Director

Sovereign Equity Holdings Limited
Incorporated: 20 December 2012
Net Worth: £601,844 *Total Assets:* £16,624,164
Registered Office: 7-9 Stafford Road, Wallington, Surrey, SM6 9AN
Activities: Activities of head offices
Major Shareholder: Parminder Singh Dosanjh
Officers: Arjan Singh Dosanjh [1987] Director; Parminder Singh Dosanjh [1955] Director; Sarvjeet Kaur Dosanjh [1960] Director/Accounts Manager

Sovereign Recovery (UK) Limited
Incorporated: 15 December 2006
Net Worth: £98,400 *Total Assets:* £9,582,107
Registered Office: 6c Ocean House, Bentley Way, New Barnet, Herts, EN5 5FP
Activities: Maintenance and repair of motor vehicles
Officers: Douglas Pope [1964] Director; Edward Pope [1963] Director

SP Macbeth 5 Limited
Incorporated: 12 April 2012 *Employees:* 55
Net Worth: £9,250,149 *Total Assets:* £12,689,862
Registered Office: Unit 3 Shepperton Business Park, Govett Avenue, Shepperton, Surrey, TW17 8BA
Activities: Activities of other holding companies n.e.c.
Shareholders: Thomas William Hamlett; Trevor John Brain
Officers: Trevor John Brain [1954] Director/Accountant; Paul Cuthill [1962] Director; Thomas William Hamlett [1972] Director

Space Truust UK Ltd
Incorporated: 8 April 2011
Net Worth: £96,942,280 *Total Assets:* £96,950,280
Registered Office: Unit 2 Popin Business Centre, South Way, Wembley, Middlesex, HA9 0HB
Activities: Financial intermediation not elsewhere classified
Officers: Peter Albert Koley [1965] Director/Entrepreneur [Swiss]

Spacemaker Group Limited
Incorporated: 17 November 1997 *Employees:* 104
Net Worth: £6,081,880 *Total Assets:* £7,613,709
Registered Office: Westgate Chambers, 8a Elm Park Road, Pinner, Middlesex, HA5 3LA
Activities: Activities of head offices
Major Shareholder: Malcolm John Harrison
Officers: Laura Harrison, Secretary; Jack Harrison [1985] Director; Laura Harrison [1956] Director/Administration Manager; Malcolm John Harrison [1951] Director; William Harrison [1987] Director

Spaces Personal Storage Limited
Incorporated: 12 February 1998 *Employees:* 3
Net Worth: £53,262,000 *Total Assets:* £53,262,000
Registered Office: c/o Safestore Holdings Limited, Brittanic House, Stirling Way, Borehamwood, Herts, WD6 2BT
Activities: Other letting and operating of own or leased real estate
Parent: Safestore Acquisition Limited
Officers: Andrew Brian Jones [1966] Director/Chartered Accountant; David Roy Penniston [1958] Property Director; Federico Vecchioli [1966] Director [French]

Spar (UK) Limited
Incorporated: 4 August 1959 *Employees:* 74
Net Worth: £13,187 *Total Assets:* £24,605,934
Registered Office: Hygeia Building, 66-68 College Road, Harrow, Middlesex, HA1 1BE
Activities: Wholesale of wine, beer, spirits and other alcoholic beverages
Officers: Mark Steven Keeley [1962] Director/Retail; Christopher William Lewis [1968] Trading Director; Jacqueline Elizabeth MacKenzie [1967] Director/Chief Information Officer; Deborah Mary Robinson [1965] Director; Ian David Taylor [1965] Retail Director

Spar Food Distributors Limited
Incorporated: 4 April 1975 *Employees:* 74
Net Worth: £13,436 *Total Assets:* £24,605,884
Registered Office: Mezzanine Floor, Hygeia Building, 66-68 College Road, Harrow, Middlesex, HA1 1BE
Activities: Retail sale in non-specialised stores with food, beverages or tobacco predominating
Officers: Martin John Agnew [1962] Director; Mike Boardman [1972] Director; Michael Dominic Wells Hall [1972] Director; Jeremy Charles Marwood [1958] Director; Colin Gibson McLean [1965] Director; Deborah Mary Robinson [1965] Director

Spark Property Assets LLP
Incorporated: 28 April 2010
Net Worth: £22,454,656 *Total Assets:* £28,140,584
Registered Office: 7-9 Stafford Road, Wallington, Surrey, SM6 9AN
Officers: Arjan Singh Dosanjh [1987] Member; Parminder Singh Dosanjh [1955] Member; Karen Deep Kaur Aujla [1981] LLP Member; Sarvjeet Kaur Dosanjh [1960] LLP Member; Raman Deep Kaur Sandhu [1983] LLP Member

Sparquote Limited
Incorporated: 27 October 1982 *Employees:* 3
Net Worth: £15,630,194 *Total Assets:* £19,368,620
Registered Office: Cavendish House, 369 Burnt Oak Broadway, Edgware, Middlesex, HA8 5AW
Activities: Activities of religious organisations
Officers: Anne-Mette Reichmann [1966] Director; David Reichmann [1962] Director; Dov Reichmann [1930] Director

SPD Moorgate Limited
Incorporated: 18 November 2014
Net Worth Deficit: £2,356,000 *Total Assets:* £30,092,000
Registered Office: Maple Cross House, Denham Way, Maple Cross, Rickmansworth, Herts, WD3 9SW
Activities: Development of building projects
Parent: Skanska Project Developments Limited
Officers: Steven Leven, Secretary; Culdip Kelly Kaur Gangotra [1970] Director/Accountant; Helen Katherine Martin [1975] Director/Civil Engineer; Martin George Neeson [1968] Director/Manager

Speakerbus Limited
Incorporated: 13 March 1987 *Employees:* 19
Net Worth: £3,259,755 *Total Assets:* £7,443,590
Registered Office: Hanover House, Britannia Road, Queens Gate, Waltham Cross, Herts, EN8 7TF
Activities: Other telecommunications activities
Parent: Speakerbus Group PLC
Officers: Robert James Connolly, Secretary; Gwen Ventris [1952] Director/Executive Chairman; Andrew Wodhams [1957] Managing Director

Specialist Equipment Solutions Limited
Incorporated: 23 July 1976 *Employees:* 57
Net Worth: £22,976,000 *Total Assets:* £24,535,000
Registered Office: 27 Great West Road, Brentford, Middlesex, TW8 9BW
Activities: Renting and leasing of construction and civil engineering machinery and equipment
Parent: AFW UK Oil & Gas Limited
Officers: Victor Jibuike, Secretary; Alan Stewart Gordon [1964] Director; Thomas Francis Honan [1962] Director/Chief Financial Officer [Australian]; James Arnold Lenton [1967] Managing Director; Nicola Dawn Mason [1971] Operations Director; Shaun Poll [1968] Director/Chartered Mechanical Engineer

Specialist Learning Trust
Incorporated: 21 July 2017
Net Worth: £6,842,496 *Total Assets:* £8,229,906
Registered Office: Hawes Lane, West Wickham, Kent, BR4 9AE
Activities: Primary education
Officers: Tara-Jane Brodie [1969] Director/Company Secretary; Susan Emily Colquhoun [1953] Director/Retired; Theresa Gillen [1956] Director/Social Worker/Safeguarding Consultancy; Barbara Florence Hart [1949] Director/Retired; Dr Khadija Himid-Wilson [1958] Director/Medical Doctor; Samantha Jane McKale [1977] Director/Housewife; Mary Louise Paddon [1953] Director/Retired; Geoffrey Frederick Parsons [1950] Director/Retired; John Nigel Plummer [1956] Director/Retired

Specialist Plant Associates Limited
Incorporated: 19 April 1988 *Employees:* 16
Net Worth: £3,433,217 *Total Assets:* £6,163,456
Registered Office: Neagron House, Stanford Road, Orsett, Essex, RM16 3BX
Activities: Other specialised construction activities n.e.c.
Parent: Joseph Gallagher Limited
Officers: Agnes Theresa Gallagher, Secretary; Joseph Jude Gallagher [1945] Managing Director [Irish]; Paul Joseph Gallagher [1981] Director; Steven Harvey [1963] Director/Civil Engineer; Anthony Andrew Matheson [1968] Group Commercial Director; Ian George Matthews [1964] Director/Mechanical Engineer Engineering Manager

Spectris Group Holdings Limited
Incorporated: 27 March 1973
Net Worth: £1,131,335,040 *Total Assets:* £1,745,929,984
Registered Office: Heritage House, Church Road, Egham, Surrey, TW20 9QD
Activities: Activities of head offices
Parent: Spectris PLC
Officers: Rebecca Louise Dunn, Secretary; Eoghan Pol O'Lionaird [1966] Director [Irish]; Clive Graeme Watson [1958] Director

Spectris PLC
Incorporated: 4 June 1986 *Employees:* 8,713
Net Worth: £1,204,099,968 *Total Assets:* £1,798,899,968
Registered Office: Heritage House, Church Road, Egham, Surrey, TW20 9QD
Activities: Activities of head offices
Officers: Mark Janos Serfozo, Secretary; Karim Bitar [1965] Director [American]; Derek John Harding [1973] Director; Andrew James Heath [1964] Director; Russell John King [1957] Director; Ulf Quellmann [1965] Director/Treasurer [German]; William Claire Seeger Jr [1951] Director [American]; Clive Graeme Watson [1958] Finance Director; Kjersti Wiklund [1962] Director [Norwegian]; Mark David Williamson [1957] Director; Martha Brown Wyrsch [1958] Director/President [American]

Spectris UK Holdings Limited
Incorporated: 30 May 2002
Net Worth: £114,803,000 *Total Assets:* £146,976,992
Registered Office: Heritage House, Church Road, Egham, Surrey, TW20 9QD
Activities: Activities of head offices
Parent: Spectris Group Holdings Limited
Officers: Rebecca Louise Dunn, Secretary; Anthony William Dumpleton [1969] Director/Accountant; Clive Graeme Watson [1958] Director

Spectris US Holdings Limited
Incorporated: 30 May 2002
Net Worth: £284,519,008 *Total Assets:* £455,179,008
Registered Office: Heritage House, Church Road, Egham, Surrey, TW20 9QD
Activities: Activities of head offices
Parent: Spectris Group Holdings Limited
Officers: Rebecca Louise Dunn, Secretary; Anthony William Dumpleton [1969] Director/Accountant; Clive Graeme Watson [1958] Director

Spectrum Franchising Limited
Incorporated: 11 May 1987 *Employees:* 52
Net Worth: £24,667,000 *Total Assets:* £27,182,000
Registered Office: Velocity, 1 Brooklands Drive, Brooklands, Weybridge, Surrey, KT13 0SL
Activities: Other cleaning services
Parent: Spectrum Holdings Limited
Officers: Matthew Edward Stanley Brabin [1965] Director/Chief Executive Officer; Kenneth Ian Mackintosh [1962] Director; Stephen Graham Mitchell [1964] Managing Director; Barbara Plucnar Jensen [1971] Director/Chief Financial Officer [Danish]

Spedition Services Limited
Incorporated: 19 December 1990 *Employees:* 45
Net Worth: £7,073,008 *Total Assets:* £10,552,391
Registered Office: Spedition House, 1-2 Blenheim Court, Brook Way, Leatherhead, Surrey, KT22 7NA
Activities: Freight rail transport
Parent: PSC Logistics SPRL
Officers: Jennine Helen Garner, Secretary; Yasmin Fazal [1966] Director/General Manager; Zakaria Rastorp Fazal [1995] Director/Student; Cormac David Tracey [1973] Director [Irish]

Speed 9395 Limited
Incorporated: 30 October 2002
Net Worth: £4,755,772 *Total Assets:* £8,195,488
Registered Office: Zone G, Salamader Quay West, Park Lane, Harefield, Middlesex, UB9 6NZ
Activities: Buying and selling of own real estate
Parent: Starcare Homes Limited
Officers: Bharat Chunilal Sodha, Secretary/Director; Bharat Chunilal Sodha [1959] Director

Spence Refit Ltd
Incorporated: 15 June 2005 *Employees:* 42
Net Worth: £2,056,924 *Total Assets:* £9,874,049
Registered Office: First Floor, Radius House, 51 Clarendon Road, Watford, Herts, WD17 1HP
Activities: Construction of commercial buildings
Parent: Jean-Luc Developments Limited
Officers: Denise Carr [1960] Financial Director; Andrew Hill [1966] Director; Luke Johnson Spence [1988] Director; Russell Jonathon James Spence [1985] Director

Spencers Property Investments Limited
Incorporated: 12 August 1996 *Employees:* 4
Net Worth: £10,883,390 *Total Assets:* £21,419,826
Registered Office: 249 Cranbrook Road, Ilford, Essex, IG1 4TG
Activities: Other letting and operating of own or leased real estate
Shareholders: Alan Austin Spencer; Roger Ashley Spencer
Officers: Roger Spencer, Secretary/Director; Alan Austin Spencer [1961] Director; Roger Ashley Spencer [1966] Director

Speyside Renewable Energy Finance PLC
Incorporated: 19 June 2014
Net Worth: £64,000 *Total Assets:* £46,536,000
Registered Office: 8 White Oak Square, London Road, Swanley, Kent, BR8 7AG
Activities: Production of electricity
Parent: Speyside Renewable Energy Partnership Hold Co Limited
Officers: Maxwell Francis Aitken [1977] Director; David Richard Bradbury [1969] Asset Director; Benjamin Matthew Cashin [1972] Director; Paul John Ireland [1979] Director; David Adam Whitehurst [1971] Director/Investment Professional

Spicers Limited
Incorporated: 16 December 1946 *Employees:* 419
Net Worth: £37,327,000 *Total Assets:* £95,105,000
Registered Office: c/o The Spicers-Officeteam Group Limited, Unit 4, 500 Purley Way, Croydon, Surrey, CR0 4NZ
Activities: Wholesale of office furniture
Major Shareholder: Jonathan Paul Moulton
Officers: Philippa Anne Maynard, Secretary; Edwin Richard Ford [1967] Director; Richard Ashley Jones [1965] Director; Andrew Graham Mobbs [1978] Director

The Spicers-Officeteam Group Limited
Incorporated: 5 June 2014 *Employees:* 1,352
Net Worth Deficit: £30,774,000 *Total Assets:* £153,911,008
Registered Office: Unit 4, 500 Purley Way, Croydon, Surrey, CR0 4NZ
Activities: Activities of head offices
Major Shareholder: Jonathan Paul Moulton
Officers: Philippa Anne Maynard, Secretary; Robert Alexander Asplin [1979] Director; Edwin Richard Ford [1967] Director; Richard Ashley Jones [1965] Director; Andrew Graham Mobbs [1978] Director; Octavia Kate Morley [1968] Director

Michael Spiers (Jewellers) Limited
Incorporated: 14 April 1961 *Employees:* 56
Net Worth: £4,826,149 *Total Assets:* £9,059,541
Registered Office: 3 Theobald Court, Theobald Street, Borehamwood, Herts, WD6 4RN
Activities: Retail sale of watches and jewellery in specialised stores
Shareholder: Adam Matheson Spiers
Officers: Keith Anthony White, Secretary; Michael Goldwell Cox [1946] Director/Manager; Adam Matheson Spiers [1966] Director/Chartered Accountant; Elizabeth Ann Spiers [1940] Director/Jeweller; James Walker [1969] Director/Manager; Keith Anthony White [1940] Director/Jeweller; Rita White [1940] Director/Display Designer

Spirit Energy North Sea Limited
Incorporated: 19 November 2002
Previous: Centrica North Sea Limited
Net Worth: £70,212,000 *Total Assets:* £956,955,008
Registered Office: 1st Floor, 20 Kingston Road, Staines upon Thames, Middlesex, TW18 4LG
Activities: Extraction of crude petroleum
Parent: Centrica Newco 123 Limited
Officers: Nicola MacLeod, Secretary; Generald Martin Harrison [1954] Director; Andrew Daryl Le Poidevin [1958] Director; Nicola Jane MacLeod [1974] Director/General Counsel; Neil James McCulloch [1970] Director/EVP Technical and Operated Production

Spirit Energy Production UK Limited
Incorporated: 18 October 1995 *Employees:* 263
Previous: Hydrocarbon Resources Limited
Net Worth: £924,329,984 *Total Assets:* £1,535,412,992
Registered Office: 1st Floor, 20 Kingston Road, Staines upon Thames, Middlesex, TW18 4LG
Activities: Extraction of crude petroleum
Shareholders: GB Gas Holdings Limited; Centrica Newco 123 Limited
Officers: Nicola MacLeod, Secretary; Generald Martin Harrison [1954] Director; Andrew Daryl Le Poidevin [1958] Director; Nicola Jane MacLeod [1974] Director/General Counsel; Neil James McCulloch [1970] Director/EVP Technical and Operated Production

Spirit Energy Resources Limited
Incorporated: 21 September 1993
Previous: Spirit Norway Limited
Net Worth Deficit: £597,174,976 *Total Assets:* £488,572,992
Registered Office: 1st Floor, 20 Kingston Road, Staines upon Thames, Middlesex, TW18 4LG
Activities: Extraction of crude petroleum
Parent: Spirit Energy Limited
Officers: Nicola MacLeod, Secretary; Generald Martin Harrison [1954] Director; Andrew Daryl Le Poidevin [1958] Director; Nicola Jane MacLeod [1974] Director/General Counsel; Neil James McCulloch [1970] Director/EVP Technical and Operated Production

Spirit Energy Southern North Sea Limited
Incorporated: 8 March 2006 *Employees:* 1
Previous: Bayerngas Europe Limited
Net Worth: £208,274,464 *Total Assets:* £300,243,456
Registered Office: 1st Floor, 20 Kingston Road, Staines upon Thames, Middlesex, TW18 4LG
Activities: Support activities for petroleum and natural gas mining
Parent: Spirit Europe Ltd
Officers: Nicola MacLeod, Secretary; Generald Martin Harrison [1954] Director; Andrew Daryl Le Poidevin [1958] Director; Nicola Jane MacLeod [1974] Director/General Counsel; Neil James McCulloch [1970] Director/EVP Technical and Operated Production

Spirit Europe Limited
Incorporated: 30 March 2004 *Employees:* 11
Previous: Spirit Europe Ltd
Net Worth: £221,987,536 *Total Assets:* £271,979,104
Registered Office: 1st Floor, 20 Kingston Road, Staines upon Thames, Middlesex, TW18 4LG
Activities: Other mining and quarrying n.e.c.
Parent: Spirit Energy Limited
Officers: Nicola MacLeod, Secretary; Generald Martin Harrison [1954] Director; Nicola Jane MacLeod [1974] Director/General Counsel; Neil James McCulloch [1970] Director/EVP Technical and Operated Production

Spirit Norway Limited
Incorporated: 17 March 2006 *Employees:* 119
Previous: Centrica Norway Limited
Net Worth: £340,781,088 *Total Assets:* £1,857,423,872
Registered Office: 1st Floor, 20 Kingston Road, Staines upon Thames, Middlesex, TW18 4LG
Activities: Activities of head offices
Parent: Spirit Energy Limited
Officers: Andrew Daryl Le Poidevin [1958] Director; Nicola Jane MacLeod [1974] Director/General Counsel; Dag Halvard Omre [1958] Regional Director [Norwegian]

Spirit Resources (Armada) Limited
Incorporated: 16 March 2001
Previous: Spirit Energy Resources (Armada) Limited
Net Worth: £37,379,000 *Total Assets:* £50,855,000
Registered Office: 1st Floor, 20 Kingston Road, Staines upon Thames, Middlesex, TW18 4LG
Activities: Extraction of crude petroleum
Parent: Centrica Newco 123 Limited
Officers: Nicola MacLeod, Secretary; Generald Martin Harrison [1954] Director; Nicola Jane MacLeod [1974] Director/General Counsel; Neil James McCulloch [1970] Director/EVP Technical and Operated Production

Splash Damage Limited
Incorporated: 30 April 2001 *Employees:* 236
Net Worth: £26,772,126 *Total Assets:* £32,278,618
Registered Office: Royal Court, 81 Tweedy Road, Bromley, Kent, BR1 1RG
Activities: Ready-made interactive leisure and entertainment software development
Parent: Radius Maxima Limited
Officers: Ross Arthur William Farrow, Secretary; Ross Arthur William Farrow [1983] Finance Director; Gruffydd Randal Jenkins [1974] Director; Richard Jolly [1979] Director/Chief Executive; Jamarson Kong [1978] Director/Senior Management [Chinese]; Alex Xu Yiran [1972] Director/Senior Management [Chinese]

Splendid Hospitality Group LLP
Incorporated: 5 October 2007 *Employees:* 805
Previous: Sojourn Hotels LLP
Net Worth: £296,313,312 *Total Assets:* £593,888,832
Registered Office: Haydon House, 296 Joel Street, Pinner, Middlesex, HA5 2PY
Officers: Nadeem Shirazali Boghani [1978] Member; Shiraz Noormohamed Boghani [1950] Member

Sports Gambling Committee Ltd
Incorporated: 9 January 2017
Net Worth: £7,695,740 *Total Assets:* £7,695,740
Registered Office: 25 Forest Road, Loughton, Essex, IG10 1EB
Activities: Other business support service activities n.e.c.
Major Shareholder: Billy David Clark
Officers: Billy David Clark [1996] Director

Sports Interactive Limited
Incorporated: 21 July 1994 *Employees:* 93
Net Worth: £2,279,346 *Total Assets:* £9,807,884
Registered Office: 27 Great West Road, Brentford, Middlesex, TW8 9BW
Activities: Other service activities n.e.c.
Parent: Sega Sammy Holdings Inc
Officers: Nicola Ormrod, Secretary; Gary Robert Dale [1961] Director/Chief Operating Officer; Tatsuyuki Miyazaki [1967] Director [Japanese]; David Jonathon Ward [1965] Director/Chief Financial Officer

Sportsworld Group Limited
Incorporated: 13 September 1982 *Employees:* 8
Net Worth: £3,813,000 *Total Assets:* £9,915,000
Registered Office: The Studios, Rosedale Road, Richmond, Surrey, TW9 2SX
Activities: Travel agency activities
Parent: Sportsworld Holdings International Limited
Officers: Nathan John Wilson [1972] Director

Spring Finance Limited
Incorporated: 5 February 1999 *Employees:* 12
Net Worth: £38,160 *Total Assets:* £26,494,268
Registered Office: Kinetic Business Centre, The Kinetic Centre, Theobald Street, Borehamwood, Herts, WD6 4PJ
Activities: Credit granting by non-deposit taking finance houses and other specialist consumer credit grantors
Officers: Moshe Moses, Secretary; George Leo Benninger [1946] Director/Attorney [American]; Martin David Chesler [1973] Director/Accountant; Christopher Charles Chew [1972] Director/Head of Lending; Paul Julian Mann [1968] Investment Director; Graeme Edward Wade [1979] Director/Head of Sales

The Spring Partnership Trust
Incorporated: 2 June 2011 *Employees:* 350
Previous: HPS MAT
Net Worth: £32,122,352 *Total Assets:* £35,905,352
Registered Office: George Lane, Hayes, Bromley, Kent, BR2 7LQ
Activities: Primary education
Officers: Verity Mary Bolton, Secretary; Carolyn Ann Barenbrug [1964] Director/Consultant; Joanna Patricia Brinkley [1964] Director/Headteacher; John Christopher Cliff [1952] Director/Retired; Lindsay Jane Falk [1979] Compliance Director; Kelly Hawker [1977] Director/Deputy Headteacher; Clive Hilton Lees [1963] Director/Student; James Martin [1977] Director/Teacher; David Chuma Okafor [1967] Director/IT Management; Ruth Helen Punter [1977] Director/Tax Consultant; Robert Wesley James Taylor [1980] Director/Risk Manager

Springhill Property Investments Limited
Incorporated: 27 May 2016
Net Worth: £3,439,805 *Total Assets:* £6,607,496
Registered Office: 36 Goodmayes Road, Ilford, Essex, IG3 9UR
Activities: Other letting and operating of own or leased real estate
Shareholder: Mohammad Ishaq
Officers: Irshad Ishaq [1980] Director; Manzoor Begum Ishaq [1950] Director; Mohammad Ishaq [1940] Director

Spruce Investments Limited
Incorporated: 5 December 1997
Net Worth: £4,167,923 *Total Assets:* £5,733,506
Registered Office: 15-17 Pound Lane, Epsom, Surrey, KT19 8RY
Activities: Other letting and operating of own or leased real estate
Shareholders: Stephen Richard Pavey; Sharon Julia Pavey
Officers: Christopher Michael Shepherd, Secretary; Sharon Julia Pavey [1961] Marketing Director; Stephen Richard Pavey [1961] Managing Director

D.J.Squire & Co.,Limited
Incorporated: 8 July 1936 *Employees:* 821
Net Worth: £33,790,000 *Total Assets:* £49,522,000
Registered Office: Sixth Cross Road, Twickenham, Middlesex, TW2 5PA
Activities: Retail sale of flowers, plants, seeds, fertilizers, pet animals and pet food in specialised stores
Shareholder: Colin Squire
Officers: Mark Alastair Wilson, Secretary; Martin Nicholas Breddy [1961] Director; Janet Deirdre Elaine Cody [1932] Director/Administrator; Darran Oakley [1966] Director; Adrian Humphrey Austen Osborn [1944] Director; Colin Stuart Squire [1936] Director/Horticulturalist; Sarah Catherine Elaine Squire [1965] Director; Mark Alastair Wilson [1962] Finance Director

Squire Energy Limited
Incorporated: 4 June 2003 *Employees:* 22
Net Worth: £2,985,669 *Total Assets:* £7,862,338
Registered Office: 25-29 High Street, Leatherhead, Surrey, KT22 8AB
Activities: Construction of utility projects for fluids
Officers: John Burke [1947] Engineering Director [Irish]; John Charles Clifton [1967] Director/Project Manager; Mark Harold Halsey [1959] Director/Project Engineer; Stuart Howard Thomas [1963] Director/Gas Consultant

SR Developers Limited
Incorporated: 17 July 2014
Net Worth: £800,780 *Total Assets:* £7,778,150
Registered Office: 1st Floor, 44-50 The Broadway, Southall, Middlesex, UB1 1QB
Activities: Development of building projects
Major Shareholder: Sant Ram Ghai
Officers: Sant Ram Ghai [1966] Director

SRCH Limited
Incorporated: 11 February 2005 *Employees:* 27
Net Worth: £6,750,953 *Total Assets:* £9,445,218
Registered Office: Charles Lake House, Claire Causeway, Crossways Business Park, Dartford, Kent, DA2 6QA
Activities: Activities of construction holding companies
Shareholders: Alan Dean Swift; Stephen Carl Swift
Officers: Stephen Carl Swift, Secretary; Alan Dean Swift [1967] Director; Stephen Carl Swift [1968] Director

SSCP Spring Midco 2 Limited
Incorporated: 28 March 2015 *Employees:* 2
Net Worth Deficit: £955,000 *Total Assets:* £148,200,992
Registered Office: Frays Court, 71 Cowley Road, Uxbridge, Middlesex, UB8 2AE
Activities: Other professional, scientific and technical activities n.e.c.
Parent: SSCP Spring Midco 1 Limited
Officers: Helen Elizabeth Lecky, Secretary; Jean-Luc Emmanuel Janet [1970] Director/Chief Financial Officer [French]; David Jon Leatherbarrow [1969] Director/Group Chief Executive Officer

SSCP Spring Topco Limited
Incorporated: 3 October 2014 *Employees:* 1,717
Net Worth Deficit: £69,611,000 *Total Assets:* £450,452,992
Registered Office: Frays Court, 71 Cowley Road, Uxbridge, Middlesex, UB8 2AE
Activities: Activities of head offices
Officers: Helen Elizabeth Lecky, Secretary; Iain James Anderson [1955] Director/Chief Executive; Enrico Biale [1977] Director [Italian]; Jonathan Lister Heathcote [1961] Director; Benjamin Hopper [1985] Director/Investment Executive; Jean-Luc Emmanuel Janet [1970] Director/Chief Financial Officer [French]; David Jon Leatherbarrow [1969] Director/Group Chief Executive Officer; Douglas John Quinn [1955] Director/Chairman

St Catherine's Catholic School
Incorporated: 5 July 2011 *Employees:* 125
Net Worth: £8,547,000 *Total Assets:* £9,974,000
Registered Office: St Catherine's Catholic School, Watling Street, Bexleyheath, Kent, DA6 7QJ
Activities: General secondary education
Officers: Sarah Brame [1974] Director/Bursar and Clerk to Trustees; Lynne Brooks [1956] Director/Retired; Esther Generaldine Cato Sargeant [1972] Director/Teacher; Barry John Connell [1947] Director/Retired; Yvonne Marie Connolly [1976] Director/Headteacher; Steven Paul Fox [1978] Operations Director; Thomas Kennedy [1971] Director/Civil Servant; Ian Laponder [1971] Director/Procurement Manager; Karen Mary Laponder [1963] Director/Local Government Officer; Kathryn Monin [1982] Director/Teacher; Yvonne Uttley-Wright [1957] Director/Retired Teacher

St Catherine's School Twickenham
Incorporated: 27 January 1992 *Employees:* 78
Net Worth: £6,784,337 *Total Assets:* £13,257,218
Registered Office: St Catherine's School Twickenham, Cross Deep, Twickenham, Middlesex, TW1 4QJ
Activities: Pre-primary education
Officers: Ian Graham Stewart, Secretary/Chartered Accountant; Pauline Isabella Alldridge [1956] Director/Retired; Paul Leighton Clifford [1952] Director/Chartered Accountant; Michael John Edwards [1958] Director/Retired, Formerly a Solicitor; Sylvia Rosamund Hamilton [1956] Director/HR and Marketing Consultant; Stephen Jefferson [1952] Director/Retired; Elizabeth Morris [1958] Director/Solicitor; Maria Teresa Patterson [1953] Director/Retired; Alan Perrier [1948] Director/Retired; Sean Skehan [1964] Director/Deputy Head; Edward Charles Awdeley Sparrow [1953] Director/Solicitor

St Cross Developments Limited
Incorporated: 18 January 1996
Net Worth Deficit: £1,081,742 *Total Assets:* £6,987,972
Registered Office: Unit 4 Limes Court, Conduit Lane, Hoddesdon, Herts, EN11 8EP
Activities: Development of building projects
Shareholders: Brian Henry Mahoney; Michael John Lodge; Gary Stephen Mahoney
Officers: Sarah Jane Jacobsen, Company Secretary; Michael John Lodge [1952] Director/Accountant; Brian Henry Mahoney [1935] Director/Printer; Gary Stephen Mahoney [1963] Director/Printer

St Edward Homes Limited
Incorporated: 26 June 2006
Net Worth: £5,343,000 *Total Assets:* £28,772,000
Registered Office: Berkeley House, 19 Portsmouth Road, Cobham, Surrey, KT11 1JG
Activities: Construction of commercial buildings
Shareholders: The Berkeley Group PLC; The Prudential Assurance Company Limited
Officers: Jared Stephen Philip Cranney, Secretary; Trevor John Hankin [1959] Director; David Geoffrey Morris [1967] Director/Chartered Surveyor; Robert Charles Grenville Perrins [1965] Director; Anthony William Pidgley [1947] Director; Tom Edward Pocock [1983] Director; Frances Luisa Ruocco [1985] Director

St Edwards Court (Romford) Limited
Incorporated: 8 July 2016
Net Worth Deficit: £2,429,335 *Total Assets:* £8,667,196
Registered Office: 3rd Floor, Sterling House, Langston Road, Loughton, Essex, IG10 3TS
Activities: Development of building projects
Parent: Galliard Holdings Limited
Officers: Allan William Porter, Secretary; Stephen Stuart Solomon Conway [1948] Director; Donagh O'Sullivan [1968] Construction Director [Irish]

St George Blackfriars Limited
Incorporated: 4 March 2005
Net Worth: £206,874,432 *Total Assets:* £514,294,368
Registered Office: Berkeley House, 19 Portsmouth Road, Cobham, Surrey, KT11 1JG
Activities: Construction of domestic buildings
Parent: St George South London Limited
Officers: Jared Stephen Philip Cranney, Secretary; Benjamin James Marks, Secretary; Marcus Giles Blake [1971] Director; Piers Martin Clanford [1970] Director; Mark Richard Elgar [1974] Director; Paul Roger Kimber [1977] Director; Benjamin James Marks [1977] Director; James Paul Nicolson [1980] Director [Finnish]; Edward Villiers Noble [1979] Director; Robert Charles Grenville Perrins [1965] Director; Anthony William Pidgley [1947] Director; Richard James Stearn [1968] Director

St George Ealing Limited
Incorporated: 18 June 2013
Previous: LS Ealing Leisure Limited
Net Worth: £4,016,044 *Total Assets:* £39,087,736
Registered Office: Berkeley House, 19 Portsmouth Road, Cobham, Surrey, KT11 1JG
Activities: Development of building projects
Parent: St. George West London Limited
Officers: Jared Stephen Philip Cranney, Secretary; Benjamin James Marks, Secretary; Neil Finlay Bowron [1977] Director; Piers Martin Clanford [1970] Director; Mark Richard Elgar [1974] Director; Robert William Elliott [1981] Director; Stephen Alan Kirwan [1974] Director [New Zealander]; Benjamin James Marks [1977] Director; Edward Villiers Noble [1979] Director; Robert Charles Grenville Perrins [1965] Director; Anthony William Pidgley [1947] Director; Andrew John Pollock [1962] Director; Austen Grant Runnicles [1976] Director; Richard James Stearn [1968] Director

St George Healthcare Limited
Incorporated: 26 July 1999 *Employees:* 124
Net Worth: £57,503 *Total Assets:* £12,615,239
Registered Office: 2 Imperial Place, Maxwell Road, Borehamwood, Herts, WD6 1JN
Activities: Hospital activities
Parent: Elysium Healthcare (Ultimate Care) Limited
Officers: Sarah Juliette Livingston, Secretary; Lesley Joy Chamberlain [1963] Director/Group Chief Executive; Dr Quazi Shams Mahfooz Haque [1968] Executive Medical Director; Steven John Woolgar [1955] Director of Policy and Regulation

St George PLC
Incorporated: 11 March 1991 *Employees:* 466
Net Worth: £639,779,968 *Total Assets:* £1,104,471,040
Registered Office: Berkeley House, 19 Portsmouth Road, Cobham, Surrey, KT11 1JG
Activities: Activities of head offices
Shareholders: The Berkeley Group PLC; The Berkeley Group PLC
Officers: Jared Stephen Philip Cranney, Secretary; Benjamin James Marks, Secretary; Piers Martin Clanford [1970] Director; Benjamin James Marks [1977] Director; Robert Charles Grenville Perrins [1965] Director; Anthony William Pidgley [1947] Director; Richard James Stearn [1968] Director; David Gregory Tillotson [1964] Director

St George's Weybridge
Incorporated: 11 February 1993 *Employees:* 574
Net Worth: £38,261,220 *Total Assets:* £49,638,200
Registered Office: St George's College, Weybridge Road, Addlestone, Surrey, KT15 2QS
Activities: Pre-primary education
Officers: Gregory Cole, Secretary; David Joseph Alfred Anderson [1943] Retired Managing Director; Sarah Helen Conrad [1969] Director/Headteacher; Diane Lesley Ewart [1961] Director/Investment Banker; Caroline Louise Gordon [1956] Director/Retired Medical Academic; Jason Matthew Hood [1970] Director; Christopher Trevor Peter Jansen [1970] Managing Director; Timothy Joseph Kirkham [1965] Sales Director; John Michael Lewin [1960] Director/Banker; Prof Ann Helen Muggeridge [1962] Director/Professor; Father William MacKenzie Muir [1945] Director/RC Priest; Denis Nowlan [1954] Director/Senior Manager; Karen Lacovara Patterson [1969] Director/Counsellor [American/British]; Charles Stanley William Prescott [1952] Director/Financial Analyst; Catherine Shevlin [1976] Director/Accountant; Simon Patrick Willis [1963] Director

St James Contracts Limited
Incorporated: 24 June 2002
Net Worth: £625,707 *Total Assets:* £6,646,083
Registered Office: Unit 17 Capstan Centre, Thurrock Park Way, Tilbury, Essex, RM18 7HH
Activities: Other letting and operating of own or leased real estate
Shareholders: David Andrew McCartney; Michelle McCartney
Officers: Michelle McCartney, Secretary; David Andrew McCartney [1971] Director/Tiler

St James Group Limited
Incorporated: 24 April 1996 *Employees:* 312
Net Worth: £590,302,016 *Total Assets:* £744,556,992
Registered Office: Berkeley House, 19 Portsmouth Road, Cobham, Surrey, KT11 1JG
Activities: Development of building projects
Parent: The Berkeley Group PLC
Officers: Jared Stephen Philip Cranney, Secretary; Alison Jane Dowsett [1966] Director; Sean Ellis [1968] Director; Paul Ivan Hopkins [1961] Director; Peter Kemkers [1971] Director; Robert Charles Grenville Perrins [1965] Director; Anthony William Pidgley [1947] Director; Richard James Stearn [1968] Director; Clive Nicholas Walter [1969] Director

St James Homes (Grosvenor Dock) Limited
Incorporated: 8 December 2000
Net Worth: £3,145,316 *Total Assets:* £23,036,194
Registered Office: Berkeley House, 19 Portsmouth Road, Cobham, Surrey, KT11 1JG
Activities: Development of building projects
Parent: St James Group Limited
Officers: Jared Stephen Philip Cranney, Secretary; Sean Ellis [1968] Director; Paul Ivan Hopkins [1961] Director; Peter Kemkers [1971] Director; Robert Charles Grenville Perrins [1965] Director; Anthony William Pidgley [1947] Director; Richard James Stearn [1968] Director; Clive Nicholas Walter [1969] Director

St James Media LLP
Incorporated: 6 September 2002
Net Worth: £12,236,442 *Total Assets:* £12,236,442
Registered Office: 99 Kenton Road, Harrow, Middlesex, HA3 0AN
Officers: Rt Hon Lord Kenneth Wilfred Baker [1934] LLP Member; Lady Mary Elizabeth Baker [1937] LLP Member; Bernard Samuel Baron [1950] LLP Member; Peter Lincoln Breitenbach [1954] LLP Member; Jonathan MacNee Carswell [1967] LLP Member; Duncan Duckett [1944] LLP Member; Enrico Filiberto Eusebi [1962] LLP Member; David Paul Grant [1961] LLP Member; Peter Brown Grant [1954] LLP Member; Margaret Harrison [1944] LLP Member; Nicholas Lorraine Edmund Hill [1948] LLP Member; Lois Elizabeth Kerrison [1969] LLP Member; Andrew Christopher Lapping [1963] LLP Member; Gary Lloyd [1961] LLP Member; Christopher John Loynes [1947] LLP Member; Michele Luzi [1956] LLP Member; Steven Morgan [1966] LLP Member; John Culverhouse Muncey [1962] LLP Member; Gordon Climson Perry [1955] LLP Member; Paul Charles Hargrave Pheysey [1962] LLP Member; Hugh Alexander Rutherford [1958] LLP Member; Jonathan Darell Seal [1962] LLP Member; Anil Sri Pathmanathan [1958] LLP Member; Jeremy James Swift [1965] LLP Member; Richard Terley [1912] LLP Member; Andrew Robert Thornhill [1943] LLP Member; Joanna Trollope [1943] LLP Member; Simon John Wilders [1953] LLP Member

St John's School, Northwood
Incorporated: 30 July 1997 *Employees:* 78
Net Worth: £7,029,068 *Total Assets:* £7,869,374
Registered Office: Potter Street Hill, Northwood, Middlesex, HA6 3QY
Activities: Primary education
Officers: Nigel Edward Stone, Secretary; Simon John Everson [1965] Director/Headmaster; Elizabeth Kate Fenwick [1965] Director; James Christopher Fowler [1962] Director/Headteacher; Lady Patricia Anne Harding [1951] Director; Paul Robert Henson [1961] Director/Accountant; Peter Ramsay MacDougall [1955] Director/Retired; Martin Andrew Lewis Robb [1970] Director/Chartered Surveyor; Richard Alexander Dermot Sullivan [1961] CEO and Managing Director; Nicola Walker [1970] Director/Catering Business Owner

St Mark Homes PLC
Incorporated: 10 August 1999 *Employees:* 4
Net Worth: £5,879,850 *Total Assets:* £8,401,370
Registered Office: No 1 Railshead Road, St Margarets, Isleworth, Middlesex, TW7 7EP
Activities: Development of building projects
Officers: Barry Bernard Tansey, Secretary [Irish]; John Connolly [1959] Director; William Cortis Gair [1942] Director; Sean Anthony Ryan [1966] Director/Accountant [Irish]; Barry Bernard Tansey [1970] Director [Irish]; Bernard Joseph Tansey [1944] Director [Irish]

St Mary's CE Academy, Cheshunt
Incorporated: 21 March 2012 *Employees:* 180
Net Worth: £29,748,000 *Total Assets:* £31,793,000
Registered Office: St Mary's CE Academy, Lieutenant Ellis Way, Cheshunt, Herts, EN7 5FB
Activities: General secondary education
Officers: Stephanie Benbow [1963] Director/Headteacher; Maureen Bruce [1949] Director; Debra Ann Chilton [1963] Director/Banker; Peter Leonard Chorley [1962] Director/Qualifying Manager; Paul George Daniel [1959] Director/Health, Safety and Environment Manager; Natasha Shaneen Graham [1977] Director/Business Manager; Sarah Murphy [1972] Director/Headteacher; Rebecca Clare Shah [1985] Director/Teacher; Nicola Jane Smith [1971] Director/Pre School Leader; Steven John Warner [1973] Director/Teacher

St Mary's University, Twickenham
Incorporated: 25 October 2006 *Employees:* 738
Net Worth: £101,973,000 *Total Assets:* £130,741,000
Registered Office: Waldegrave Road, Strawberry Hill, Twickenham, Middlesex, TW1 4SX
Activities: First-degree level higher education
Officers: Andrew Murray Browning, Secretary; Professor Edward David Joseph Acton [1949] Director/Higher Education Consultant; Professor Francis Martin Campbell [1970] Director/Vice-Chancellor; Jeffery William Cottle [1964] Director/Lawyer [American/British]; Noreen Doyle [1949] Director [Irish]; Richard Damian Finn [1963] Director/Priest; David Anthony Hartnett [1951] Director/Independent Taxation Advisor; Natalie Mary-Jean Hobkirk [1997] Director; Claire McDonnell [1971] Director; Professor Anne Moran [1950] Director; Charles Philip Richard Moth [1958] Director/Bishop of The Armed Forces; June Patricia Mulroy [1949] Director/Chartered Accountant; Kristen Pilbrow [1975] Director/International Student Experience Manager; Professor Anthony Towey [1959] Director

St William Homes LLP
Incorporated: 7 November 2014
Net Worth: £129,159,000 *Total Assets:* £269,284,000
Registered Office: Berkeley House, 19 Portsmouth Road, Cobham, Surrey, KT11 1JG

St. Aubyn's (Woodford Green) School Trust
Incorporated: 8 July 1975 *Employees:* 127
Net Worth: £8,080,006 *Total Assets:* £9,000,073
Registered Office: St Aubyn's School, Woodford New Road, Woodford Green, Essex, IG8 9DU
Activities: Primary education
Officers: Maureen Patricia Foakes, Secretary; Abraham Jacobus Botha [1959] Director/Consultant Surgeon; Debra Elaine Davidson-Smith [1963] Director/Magistrate; Susan Evans [1964] Director/Chartered Accountant; Michael Robert Foster [1941] Director/Architect; Rajesh Kalia [1969] Director/Lawyer; Judith Mary Lunn [1957] Director/Teacher; Joanne Elizabeth Ruff [1962] Director/Solicitor; Dilipkumar Shah [1946] Director/Accountant; Jonathan Scott Williams [1971] Director/Consultant Project Manager

St. Dominic's Ltd.
Incorporated: 7 September 1989 *Employees:* 136
Net Worth: £4,747,076 *Total Assets:* £11,126,769
Registered Office: Image Court, 328-334 Moseley Road, Walton-on-Thames, Surrey, KT12 3LT
Activities: Residential care activities for the elderly and disabled
Shareholder: Sheth Sonachand Dharmanan Singh Jeebun
Officers: Zainah Jeebun, Secretary/Director; Sheth Jeebun [1961] Director; Zainah Jeebun [1961] Director

St. George's Hill Lawn Tennis Club Limited
Incorporated: 12 October 1971 *Employees:* 123
Net Worth: £5,674,876 *Total Assets:* £7,155,003
Registered Office: St Georges Hill Lawn Tennis Club, St Georges Hill, Weybridge, Surrey, KT13 0LL
Activities: Operation of sports facilities
Officers: Miles Hill, Secretary; John David Bevington [1947] Director/Coach & Mentor; Richard Scott Foster [1950] Director/Chairman CCRC; Patricia Carol Franklin-Bruce [1953] Director; Howard Graham McDowell House [1952] Director/Solicitor; Christopher Martin Jenkins [1986] Director/Office & Project Manager; Charles Graham Menzies-Smith [1950] Director; Annika Ratcliffe [1961] Director/Independent Change Leadership Consultant; Terri Estelle Sheperdigian [1958] Director/Senior Business Development Manager; James Ashley Dyson Stephens [1960] Director

St. James The Great R.C. Primary and Nursery School
Incorporated: 6 February 2012 *Employees:* 76
Net Worth: £7,255,000 *Total Assets:* £8,618,000
Registered Office: Windsor Road, Thornton Heath, Surrey, CR7 8HJ
Activities: Primary education
Officers: Lavinia Owen, Secretary; Edwin Abreo [1951] Director/Retired Banker; Christopher John Andrew [1971] Director/Headteacher

St. John's Preparatory & Senior School Limited
Incorporated: 4 February 2004 *Employees:* 76
Net Worth: £3,640,085 *Total Assets:* £7,148,655
Registered Office: 5 Elstree Gate, Elstree Way, Borehamwood, Herts, WD6 1JD
Activities: Primary education
Shareholders: Andrew Tardios; Calliope Tardios
Officers: Andrew Tardios, Secretary/School Master; Andrew Tardios [1948] Director/Headmaster; Calliope Tardios [1952] Director/Headmistress

St. Luke's Hospice (Harrow & Brent) Ltd.
Incorporated: 22 June 1987 *Employees:* 164
Net Worth: £9,713,000 *Total Assets:* £10,918,000
Registered Office: Kenton Grange, Kenton Road, Harrow, Middlesex, HA3 0YG
Activities: Hospital activities
Officers: Carolyn Bennett [1976] Director/Fundraiser; Rajesh Bhatia [1963] Director/Banker; Norma Susan Brier [1949] Director; Cheryl Jeanette Brodie [1955] Director/Learning & Development Consultant; Professor Robert Samuel Elkeles [1942] Director/Consultant Physician; Christine Mary Glenn [1952] Director/Barrister; Dr Reena Zivia Majus [1954] Director/General Practitioner; Claire Victoria Melia-Tompkins [1978] Director/Head of Stakeholder Communications; Julia Newland [1959] Director/Solicitor; Dr Gillian Ida Schiller [1955] Director/Partner Gateway Consulting Group

St. Margaret's School Bushey
Incorporated: 20 May 1996 *Employees:* 173
Net Worth: £21,346,244 *Total Assets:* £23,384,684
Registered Office: St Margaret's School, Merry Hill Road, Bushey, Herts, WD23 1DT
Activities: Primary education
Officers: Dr Kenneth Victor Young, Secretary/Bursar; Justin Alford [1970] Director/Lawyer; David Clout [1941] Director/Retired; Brian Thomas Coulshed [1950] Director/Retired Headmaster; Judith Elizabeth Fenn [1966] Director/Business Executive; Rev William John Morris Gibbs [1971] Director/Clerk in Holy Orders; Ellen Hill [1952] Director/Retired; Rachel Floretta Hodgson [1969] Director/Marketing Consultant; Malcolm Spooner [1955] Director/Head of Markets

St. Vincent's Charitable Trust
Incorporated: 9 June 1992 *Employees:* 78
Previous: St Vincent's Hospital
Net Worth: £9,140,273 *Total Assets:* £10,010,634
Registered Office: St Vincent's Nursing Home, Wiltshire Lane, Eastcote, Pinner, Middlesex, HA5 2NB
Activities: Medical nursing home activities
Officers: Patricia Kathleen Black [1947] Director/Senior Lecturer (Academic Institute & University); Fergal Davern [1966] Director; Revd John Patrick Deehan [1949] Director/Roman Catholic Priest; Alan Joseph Edmondson [1931] Director/Retired; Kathleen Fox [1953] Director; Dr Robert Christopher Richmond Horsburgh [1949] Director; Linda Ann Martin [1963] Director/Florist; Katie Frances O'Brien [1983] Director; William Parisutham [1951] Director; Neville George Ransley [1945] Director/Retired; Jacqueline Ann Redrup [1954] Director; John Charles Steinitz [1950] Director/Retired

St.Helen's School Northwood
Incorporated: 4 October 1946 *Employees:* 330
Net Worth: £20,457,000 *Total Assets:* £24,897,000
Registered Office: Eastbury Road, Northwood, Middlesex, HA6 3AS
Activities: Primary education
Officers: Mark Richard MacKenzie Crooks, Secretary; Monica Bhandari [1980] Director/Senior Lecturer in Law; Nadeem Shirazali Boghani [1978] Director/Vice Chairman; Dr Sara Rhianydd Gordon [1985] Director/Research Assistant; Puneeta Mongia [1973] Assistant Director Strategy; Alison Mary Phillipson [1952] Director/Retired; Dr Susan Mary Pitts [1955] Director/Lecturer; Elizabeth Radice [1951] Director/Retired; Vivek Sapra [1966] Senior Director; Michelle Weerasekera [1969] Director/Voluntary Worker; Suzanne Lindsay Woolfson [1964] Director/Chartered Accountant

St.Martins' (Northwood) Preparatory School Trust Limited
Incorporated: 28 November 1961 *Employees:* 77
Net Worth: £10,893,608 *Total Assets:* £13,108,400
Registered Office: 40 Moor Park Road, Northwood, Middlesex, HA6 2DJ
Activities: Primary education
Officers: Alison Claire Curran, Secretary; Simon John Everson [1965] Director/Headmaster; James Christopher Fowler [1962] Director/Headteacher; Vernon William Hales [1961] Director/Headmaster; Andrew Simon Harris [1966] Director/Chartered Accountant; Neil Alexander Hinds [1960] Director/Chartered Surveyor; Mark Richard Jordan [1968] Director; Christine Anne Marks [1958] Director/Consultant; Jeremy William Peter Richards [1962] Director/Investment Manager; Christopher Ralph Scott [1959] Director/Consultant; Dr Rabia Yaqoob [1967] Director/General Practitioner - Partner

St.Michael's Manor Limited
Incorporated: 2 June 1965 *Employees:* 59
Net Worth: £6,532,398 *Total Assets:* £8,589,856
Registered Office: 1 Beauchamp Court, 10 Victors Way, Barnet, Herts, EN5 5TZ
Activities: Hotels and similar accommodation
Parent: Avon Lake Holdings Limited
Officers: Devika Gunputh, Secretary; Devika Gunputh [1957] Director [Mauritian]; Munundev Gunputh [1958] Director [Mauritian]

Stafford-Miller Limited
Incorporated: 14 September 1936
Net Worth: £5,089,000 *Total Assets:* £5,100,000
Registered Office: 980 Great West Road, Brentford, Middlesex, TW8 9GS
Activities: Non-trading company
Officers: Victoria Anne Whyte, Secretary; Richard Green [1974] Director; Richard Philip Tattershall [1982] Director/Accountant

Stag Group Limited
Incorporated: 18 April 2008 *Employees:* 95
Net Worth: £4,365,451 *Total Assets:* £20,386,756
Registered Office: 1 Lyon Road, Walton on Thames, Surrey, KT12 3PU
Activities: Activities of other holding companies n.e.c.
Parent: ALA (Advanced Logistics Aerospace) SpA
Officers: Gennaro di Capua [1954] Director [Italian]; Vittorio Genna [1961] Director [Italian]; Fulvio Scannapieco [1952] Director [Italian]; Adolfo Varini [1964] Director [Italian]

H.Stain Limited
Incorporated: 14 April 1949 *Employees:* 10
Net Worth: £15,567,278 *Total Assets:* £18,329,352
Registered Office: York House, Empire Way, Wembley, Middlesex, HA9 0FQ
Activities: Retail sale of watches and jewellery in specialised stores
Major Shareholder: Martin Sydney Stain
Officers: Delia Sherry Stain, Secretary; Sara Melanie Joffe [1963] Director; Lynn Susan Kaye [1961] Director; Delia Sherry Stain [1934] Director; Martin Sydney Stain [1934] Director

Staines Preparatory School Trust
Incorporated: 23 March 1987 *Employees:* 81
Net Worth: £4,394,158 *Total Assets:* £6,487,510
Registered Office: Staines Preparatory School, 3 Gresham Road, Staines upon Thames, Middlesex, TW18 2BT
Activities: Primary education
Officers: Rachel McLennan, Secretary; Richard Frank Adams [1964] Director/Digital Strategist; Penelope Anne Austin [1960] Director/Headteacher; Michael Bannister [1949] Director/Senior Executive British Airways; Sarah Jane Caulfield [1973] Director/Solicitor; Richard Howard Chadburn [1935] Director/Consultant; Robert Allan Davies [1939] Director/Architectural Consultant; Matthew Richard Hall [1977] Director/Accountant; Anthony Madigan [1961] Director; Wendy Jane Ransom [1967] Director/Admissions Officer; Mary Robinson [1961] Director/Project Manager; Jennifer Margaret Sice [1936] Director/Health Visitor

Stair Tread Holdings Limited
Incorporated: 3 June 2008 *Employees:* 90
Net Worth: £2,516,572 *Total Assets:* £7,822,533
Registered Office: Unit 5-6 Orpington Trade Centre, Murray Road, Orpington, Kent, BR5 3SS
Activities: Activities of distribution holding companies
Shareholders: Stuart Malcolm Gay; Raymond Jose Colgate
Officers: Stuart Malcolm Gay, Secretary; Raymond Jose Colgate [1965] Director; Stuart Malcolm Gay [1958] Director/Accountant; Barry Pitt [1954] Director

Stanbreck Properties Ltd
Incorporated: 22 November 2001
Net Worth: £4,546,882 *Total Assets:* £5,101,975
Registered Office: Atlas House, 28 Great Cambridge Road, Enfield, Middlesex, EN1 1UU
Activities: Other letting and operating of own or leased real estate
Shareholders: Baruch Erlich; Jufith Erlich
Officers: Baruch Erlich, Secretary/Solicitor; Baruch Erlich [1962] Director/Solicitor

Standard Plant Hire Limited
Incorporated: 28 January 2009 *Employees:* 9
Net Worth: £4,021,575 *Total Assets:* £7,662,427
Registered Office: 9 Limes Road, Beckenham, Kent, BR3 6NS
Activities: Renting and leasing of construction and civil engineering machinery and equipment
Shareholders: Michael Derek Fleming; Michael David Fleming
Officers: Michael Derek Fleming [1960] Director; Michael David Fleming [1991] Director/Civil Engineer

Standard Wharf Limited
Incorporated: 1 November 2013
Net Worth: £2,382,103 *Total Assets:* £7,847,730
Registered Office: 189 Manor Road, Erith, Kent, DA8 2AD
Activities: Operation of warehousing and storage facilities for land transport activities
Officers: George William Harvey, Secretary; Peter Andrew Alexander [1958] Director; Peter Francis Connolly [1967] Director; George William Harvey [1946] Director; Mark Harvey [1974] Director

Standley Holdings Limited
Incorporated: 7 December 2016
Net Worth Deficit: £103,834 *Total Assets:* £17,044,232
Registered Office: 9 Cheam Road, Epsom, Surrey, KT17 1SP
Activities: Activities of other holding companies n.e.c.
Major Shareholder: Roland Barrie Standley
Officers: Roland Barrie Standley [1969] Director

Stanley Dock Properties Limited
Incorporated: 6 November 2009 *Employees:* 2
Net Worth Deficit: £2,184,988 *Total Assets:* £15,561,307
Registered Office: Devonshire House, Manor Way, Borehamwood, Herts, WD6 1QQ
Activities: Development of building projects
Officers: Gerard Michael Comaskey [1970] Director/Property Manager [Irish]; Patrick John Power [1973] Director/Surveyor [Irish]

Stanmore Contractors Limited
Incorporated: 9 October 1992 *Employees:* 241
Net Worth: £23,930,244 *Total Assets:* £44,200,124
Registered Office: Stanmore House, Gyproc Park, Church Manorway, Erith, Kent, DA8 1DE
Activities: Plastering
Major Shareholder: Rajbir Singh Manak
Officers: Tanya Maria Barrett, Secretary; Rajbir Singh Manak, Secretary [Indian]; Rajbir Singh Manak [1966] Managing Director [Indian]; Surinder Singh Manak [1969] Director

Stanmore Implants Worldwide Limited
Incorporated: 19 February 1996 *Employees:* 98
Net Worth: £3,219,000 *Total Assets:* £8,373,000
Registered Office: Unit 210 Centennial Park, Centennial Avenue, Elstree, Herts, WD6 3SJ
Activities: Manufacture of medical and dental instruments and supplies
Shareholders: Stryker Corporation; SIW Holdings Limited
Officers: Peter Ewart Bradley [1961] Director/Business Executive; Robert Craig Cohen [1961] Director/Business Executive

Stanmore Law Practice Limited
Incorporated: 14 September 2016 *Employees:* 13
Net Worth: £163,764 *Total Assets:* £6,134,805
Registered Office: 51-53 The Broadway, Stanmore, Middlesex, HA7 4DJ
Activities: Solicitors
Major Shareholder: Peter Simon Elliston
Officers: Genene Laura Collins [1955] Director/Solicitor; Peter Simon Elliston [1948] Director/Solicitor; Graham Bennett Morrison-Wood [1955] Director/Solicitor; Sital Dipul Patel [1974] Director/Solicitor; Stuart David Turney [1979] Director/Chartered Legal Executive

R Stanton-Gleaves UK Limited
Incorporated: 25 August 2015
Net Worth: £28,472,620 *Total Assets:* £29,330,048
Registered Office: 19-20 Bourne Court, Southend Road, Woodford Green, Essex, IG8 8HD
Activities: Activities of other holding companies n.e.c.
Major Shareholder: Robin James Stanton-Gleaves
Officers: Robin James Stanton-Gleaves [1968] Director

Stapleford Commercial Group Limited
Incorporated: 15 October 1992 *Employees:* 4
Net Worth: £14,557,801 *Total Assets:* £26,114,722
Registered Office: Charles Lake House, Claire Causeway, Crossways Business Park, Dartford, Kent, DA2 6QA
Activities: Buying and selling of own real estate
Shareholders: Royston John Searle; Neil Royston Searle
Officers: Natalie Jane Conroy, Secretary; Natalie Jane Conroy [1969] Director; Carole Ann Searle [1945] Director; Neil Royston Searle [1971] Director; Royston John Searle [1945] Director

Stapleford Frog Island (Rainham) Limited
Incorporated: 14 October 2008 *Employees:* 4
Net Worth: £2,856,364 *Total Assets:* £12,603,535
Registered Office: Charles Lake House, Claire Causeway, Crossways Business Park, Dartford, Kent, DA2 6QA
Activities: Other letting and operating of own or leased real estate
Parent: Stapleford Commercial Group Limited
Officers: Natalie Jane Conroy, Secretary; Natalie Jane Conroy [1969] Director; Carole Ann Searle [1945] Director; Neil Royston Searle [1971] Director; Royston John Searle [1945] Director

Star Reefers Trading Limited
Incorporated: 10 December 1991 *Employees:* 2
Net Worth: £7,160,950 *Total Assets:* £7,405,564
Registered Office: 40 Brighton Road, Sutton, Surrey, SM2 5BN
Activities: Sea and coastal freight water transport
Officers: Charles Bondi, Secretary [Norwegian]; Charles Bondi [1972] Director/Accountant [Norwegian]; Kenneth Reid Ross [1968] Director/Chief Operating Officer

Starbones Limited
Incorporated: 6 February 2007
Net Worth Deficit: £2,989,096 *Total Assets:* £16,362,519
Registered Office: 3rd Floor, Sterling House, Langston Road, Loughton, Essex, IG10 3TS
Activities: Development of building projects
Parent: GDL (Chiswick) LLP
Officers: Allan William Porter, Secretary; Edward Azouz [1949] Director/Chartered Accountant; Jeffrey Azouz [1947] Director/Chartered Surveyor; John Cole [1971] Director; Stephen Stuart Solomon Conway [1948] Director; Jonathan Simon Goldstein [1966] Director; Kim Alexander Gottlieb [1957] Director/Surveyor; Donagh O'Sullivan [1968] Construction Director [Irish]

Starcare Homes Limited
Incorporated: 30 June 2000
Net Worth: £2,189,586 *Total Assets:* £7,298,812
Registered Office: Zone G, Salamander Quay West, Park Lane, Harefield, Middlesex, UB9 6NZ
Activities: Other letting and operating of own or leased real estate
Parent: Handsale Limited
Officers: Bharat Chunilal Sodha, Secretary; Bharat Chunilal Sodha [1959] Director

Starglade Parks Limited
Incorporated: 20 December 2005 *Employees:* 2
Net Worth: £5,597,123 *Total Assets:* £8,391,390
Registered Office: 2b Highstone House, 165 High Street, Barnet, Herts, EN5 5SU
Activities: Construction of domestic buildings
Major Shareholder: Royston Cooper
Officers: Royston Cooper [1967] Director

F.C. Stark Limited
Incorporated: 20 May 1936 *Employees:* 12
Net Worth: £38,788,268 *Total Assets:* £86,386,232
Registered Office: Gay Dawn Offices, Pennis Lane, Fawkham, Longfield, Kent, DA3 8LZ
Activities: Development of building projects
Officers: Stephen John Billings, Secretary; Andrew John Billings [1964] Director/Manager; Clive John Billings [1955] Director/Manager; Ronald John Billings [1960] Director; Stephen John Billings [1961] Director

Starna Limited
Incorporated: 29 November 1971 *Employees:* 98
Net Worth: £6,812,441 *Total Assets:* £8,149,187
Registered Office: Hainault Business Park, 52-54 Fowler Road, Hainault, Essex, IG6 3UT
Activities: Other business support service activities n.e.c.
Major Shareholder: Alan Keith Hulme
Officers: Nathan Richard Hulme, Secretary; Alan Keith Hulme [1943] Director; Nathan Richard Hulme [1984] Director

Starna Scientific Limited
Incorporated: 28 February 1964 *Employees:* 96
Net Worth: £6,879,286 *Total Assets:* £7,965,248
Registered Office: 52-54 Fowler Road, Hainault Business Park, Hainault, Essex, IG6 3UT
Activities: Manufacture and processing of other glass, including technical glassware
Officers: Nathan Richard Hulme, Secretary; Alan Keith Hulme [1943] Director; Nathan Richard Hulme [1984] Director

Startling Music Limited
Incorporated: 15 July 1968 *Employees:* 1
Net Worth: £16,371,089 *Total Assets:* £16,666,777
Registered Office: 5 Elstree Gate, Elstree Way, Borehamwood, Herts, WD6 1JD
Activities: Sound recording and music publishing activities
Parent: Cornwall
Officers: Bruce Victor Grakal [1940] Director [American]; Graham David Hill [1946] Director/Self Employed

Stat Holding International Limited
Incorporated: 24 September 2002 *Employees:* 3
Net Worth: £3,220,656 *Total Assets:* £6,083,324
Registered Office: Premier Suite, 4 Churchill Court, 58 Station Road, Harrow, Middlesex, HA2 7ST
Activities: Other engineering activities
Parent: Doris Engineering SA
Officers: Darren Michael Love, Secretary; Michel Emile Albert Caplain [1956] Director [French]; Nicolas Francoise Parsloe [1960] Director/Engineer; Cyrille Hubert Sailly [1974] Director [French]; Francois Eurgene Paul Thiebaud [1959] Director/Doris Operation Manager [French]

Stat Marine Limited
Incorporated: 30 March 1993 *Employees:* 83
Net Worth: £8,499,510 *Total Assets:* £12,380,829
Registered Office: Premier Suite, 4 Churchill Court, 58 Station Road, North Harrow, Middlesex, HA2 7ST
Activities: Other professional, scientific and technical activities n.e.c.
Parent: Stat Holding International Limited
Officers: Darren Michael Love, Secretary; Luc Guy Delclos [1964] Director/Engineer [French]; Guy Rene Facon [1958] Director [French]; Jerome Samson Raffaelli [1962] Director [French]

State Oil Limited
Incorporated: 22 November 2000 *Employees:* 114
Net Worth: £25,545,760 *Total Assets:* £286,220,000
Registered Office: Prax House, Horizon Business Village, 1 Brooklands Road, Weybridge, Surrey, KT13 0TJ
Activities: Extraction of crude petroleum
Officers: Arani Soosaipillai, Secretary; Don Camillo Emilio Borneo [1957] Director/Oil Trader; Winston Sanjeevkumar Soosaipillai [1973] Director/Accountant

State Street HCL Holdings (UK) Limited
Incorporated: 9 December 2011
Net Worth: £6,359,102 *Total Assets:* £6,386,137
Registered Office: Axon Centre, Church Road, Egham, Surrey, TW20 9QB
Activities: Other service activities n.e.c.
Parent: HCL Investments (UK) Limited
Officers: Richard Mark Batey, Secretary; Prahlad Rai Bansal [1957] Director [Indian]; Samuel Michael Brager [1963] Director [Australian]; Subramanian Gopalakrishnan [1967] Director [Indian]; David Patrick Keohane [1960] Director/Corporate Executive [American]; John Lehner [1965] Director [American]

Staten Investments Limited
Incorporated: 15 March 2006
Net Worth Deficit: £22,464 *Total Assets:* £22,459,124
Registered Office: Formacompany & Co Ltd, 11 Church Road, Great Bookham, Leatherhead, Surrey, KT23 3PB
Activities: Other information technology service activities
Major Shareholder: Gennady Kotlyarov
Officers: Gennadiy Konstantinovich Kotlyarov [1936] Director/Businessman [Russian]

Stealth Leisure Limited
Incorporated: 29 May 1996
Net Worth: £6,656,742 *Total Assets:* £6,663,126
Registered Office: 65a Station Road, Edgware, Middlesex, HA8 7HX
Activities: Gambling and betting activities
Shareholder: Graham Victor Coomes
Officers: Gemma Alison Coomes, Secretary; Graham Victor Coomes [1965] Director/Turf Accountant

Stebiz Limited
Incorporated: 8 August 2000
Net Worth: £1,532,721 *Total Assets:* £10,777,422
Registered Office: 23 George Street, Croydon, Surrey, CR0 1LA
Activities: Other letting and operating of own or leased real estate
Officers: Andrew Panayiotis Phouli, Secretary/Director; Stelios Andrew [1964] Director; Andrew Panayiotis Phouli [1967] Director; George Costa Phouli [1965] Director

Steel Yard Trading LLP
Incorporated: 9 January 2012
Net Worth: £5,358,324 *Total Assets:* £5,358,324
Registered Office: Suite 1, The Studio, St Nicholas Close, Elstree, Herts, WD6 3EW

Steiner UK Limited
Incorporated: 24 September 2009 *Employees:* 3
Net Worth Deficit: £6,617,531 *Total Assets:* £9,136,322
Registered Office: The Lodge, 92 Uxbridge Road, Harrow Weald, Middlesex, HA3 6DQ
Activities: Activities of head offices
Parent: Nemo (UK) Holdco, Ltd.
Officers: Robert Boehm, Secretary [American]; Michael Stephan Haringman, Secretary; Michael Stephan Haringman [1944] Director/Solicitor; Marc Magliacano [1974] Director/Investor [American]; Robert Barry John Schaverien [1964] Managing Director

Stem Healthcare Limited
Incorporated: 30 March 2007 *Employees:* 76
Previous: Stem Marketing Limited
Net Worth: £14,305,428 *Total Assets:* £21,893,588
Registered Office: 1 Parkshot, Richmond, Surrey, TW9 2RD
Activities: Management consultancy activities other than financial management
Parent: UDG Healthcare (UK) Holdings Limited
Officers: Damien Moynagh, Secretary; Martin Curry [1967] Director; Nigel John Mansford [1961] Director; Grainne McAleese [1979] Director [Irish]; Robert Wood [1965] Marketing Director

Stema Shipping (UK) Limited
Incorporated: 11 January 1995 *Employees:* 25
Net Worth: £2,669,259 *Total Assets:* £20,056,992
Registered Office: Alexandra House, Waterfront, Lakeside, Grays, Essex, RM20 1WL
Activities: Other business support service activities n.e.c.
Parent: Stema Shipping A/S
Officers: Martin Berby Johansen, Secretary; Claus Boisen [1981] Director [Danish]; Martin Berby Johansen [1973] Managing Director [Norwegian]

Step Academy Trust
Incorporated: 21 April 2011 *Employees:* 673
Previous: The Step Academy Trust
Net Worth: £86,502,000 *Total Assets:* £93,763,000
Registered Office: Gonville Road, Thornton Heath, Surrey, CR7 6DL
Activities: Primary education
Officers: Kirstie Martin, Secretary; Alan Michael Armstrong [1947] Director/Retired; Dr Katherine Sarah Chhatwal [1976] Director/Chief Programme Officer; Isabelle Dennigan [1968] Director/Banking Professional [French]; Mark Ducker OBE [1965] Director/Chief Executive Officer; Ross Gardner [1972] Director/Global Delivery & Business Engagement Lead; Navdeep Sanghara [1981] Director/Executive Headteacher, Inspire Partnership

Sterling Relocation Limited
Incorporated: 11 December 1991 *Employees:* 118
Net Worth: £4,571,000 *Total Assets:* £13,950,000
Registered Office: Hallmark House, Rowdell Road, Northolt, Middlesex, UB5 6AG
Activities: Removal services
Parent: Sterling International Group Limited
Officers: Michael Joseph Brannigan [1966] Director/Executive [American]; Kevin Patrick Gannon [1970] Director/Executive Management [American]

H.Stern (Jewellery) Limited
Incorporated: 12 May 1964 *Employees:* 9
Net Worth Deficit: £162,468 *Total Assets:* £8,128,656
Registered Office: York House, Empire Way, Wembley, Middlesex, HA9 0FQ
Activities: Retail sale of watches and jewellery in specialised stores
Major Shareholder: Ruth Stern
Officers: Liu Loo Ly de Oliveira, Secretary; Liu Loo Ly de Oliveira [1955] Director [Chinese]; Oscar Luiz Goldemberg [1956] Director [Brazilian]

Sterndale Systems Limited
Incorporated: 17 December 1992 *Employees:* 1
Net Worth: £10,570,879 *Total Assets:* £14,628,791
Registered Office: Batchworth House, Batchworth Place, Church Street, Rickmansworth, Herts, WD3 1JE
Activities: Other letting and operating of own or leased real estate
Major Shareholder: Peter Nicholas Kopik
Officers: John Kopik, Secretary; Peter Nicholas Kopik [1954] Director/Architect [Irish]

John Steward Transport Limited
Incorporated: 11 August 1981
Net Worth: £5,389,221 *Total Assets:* £7,162,291
Registered Office: 94 Brook Street, Erith, Kent, DA8 1JF
Activities: Freight transport by road
Major Shareholder: John Charles Steward
Officers: John Charles Steward [1946] Director/Haulier

Barry Stewart & Sons Limited
Incorporated: 20 July 1983 *Employees:* 20
Net Worth: £2,722,462 *Total Assets:* £5,592,325
Registered Office: 1 Town Quay Wharf, Abbey Road, Barking, Essex, IG11 7BZ
Activities: Other specialised construction activities n.e.c.
Parent: Stewart Castle Limited
Officers: Glen Matthew Anderson [1969] Director; Nina Louise Anderson [1974] Director/Administrator; Barry Stewart [1943] Director

Stiefel Consumer Healthcare (UK) Limited
Incorporated: 2 February 2015
Net Worth: £156,755,008 *Total Assets:* £226,192,000
Registered Office: 980 Great West Road, Brentford, Middlesex, TW8 9GS
Activities: Activities of other holding companies n.e.c.
Parent: GlaxoSmithKline Consumer Healthcare Holdings Limited
Officers: Richard Green [1974] Director; Tobias Hestler [1972] Director [German/Swiss]

Stirling Civil Engineering Limited
Incorporated: 14 October 1963
Net Worth: £8,468,000 *Total Assets:* £18,700,000
Registered Office: 310 Harrow Road, Wembley, Middlesex, HA9 6LL
Activities: Development of building projects
Parent: Hadden Shipping Limited
Officers: Sudhir Bhatt [1956] Director [Kenyan]; Maurice Mathias de Souza [1943] Director/Contracts Manager [Kenyan]; Gilbert Josiah Mungu [1962] Director [Kenyan]; Pragnesh Jitendra Patel [1970] Director; Jonathan Reading [1962] Director/Artist; Guiseppe Sabatini [1942] Director/Civil Servant [Italian]; Ashu Tosh Sharma [1969] Director; Gennaro Sirgiovanni [1950] Director [Italian]

STM Group (UK) Limited
Incorporated: 28 May 2005 *Employees:* 1,195
Previous: STM Security Group (UK) Limited
Net Worth: £1,210,927 *Total Assets:* £7,816,021
Registered Office: 3rd Floor Northside, Argyle House, Joel Street, Northwood Hills, Northwood, Middlesex, HA6 1NW
Activities: Private security activities
Shareholder: Perry Bernard Simpson
Officers: Hannah Louisa Bridgman, Secretary; Perry Bernard Simpson [1958] Director [New Zealander]

Stokes Marsh Solar Limited
Incorporated: 12 September 2012
Net Worth: £430,833 *Total Assets:* £14,536,924
Registered Office: Lynwood House, Crofton Road, Orpington, Kent, BR6 8QE
Activities: Production of electricity
Parent: Stokes Marsh Solar Holdco Limited
Officers: Cesar Gonzalez Otalora [1974] Director/Chief Executive Officer [Spanish]

Stonebourne Properties Limited
Incorporated: 17 March 1958
Net Worth: £4,725,084 *Total Assets:* £5,351,899
Registered Office: 28 Church Road, Stanmore, Middlesex, HA7 4XR
Activities: Development of building projects
Major Shareholder: Adrienne Linda Hirshman
Officers: Adrienne Hirshman, Secretary; Geoffrey Robin Hirshman [1940] Director; Richard James Hirshman [1971] Director

Stonemanor Limited
Incorporated: 13 September 2002 *Employees:* 238
Net Worth: £7,905,040 *Total Assets:* £15,797,151
Registered Office: Suite 2, Fountain House, 1a Elm Park, Stanmore, Middlesex, HA7 4AU
Activities: Retail sale of clothing in specialised stores
Major Shareholder: Philip Michael Chaimo
Officers: Hugh Kelly, Secretary/Retail; Philip Michael Chaimo [1960] Director/Buyer

Stonplan Limited
Incorporated: 29 August 1958
Net Worth: £12,576,170 *Total Assets:* £12,579,420
Registered Office: Park Place House, 24 Church Street, Epsom, Surrey, KT17 4QB
Activities: Activities of head offices
Major Shareholder: Albert Richard Perry
Officers: Alison Higgins, Secretary; James Perry Hallam [1978] Director; Michael Stuart Hastings [1942] Director/Certified Accountant; Albert Richard Perry [1924] Director

Stora Enso Holdings UK Limited
Incorporated: 16 July 1901 *Employees:* 19
Net Worth Deficit: £5,355,000 *Total Assets:* £10,573,000
Registered Office: 1 Kingfisher House, New Mill Road, Orpington, Kent, BR5 3QG
Activities: Activities of head offices
Parent: Stora Enso Oyj
Officers: Ville Valtteri Valikangas, Secretary; James Ford Barr [1972] Director/Accountant; Pasi Kyckling [1978] Director/Group Accountant [Finnish]

Stora Enso Timber UK Limited
Incorporated: 11 August 1926 *Employees:* 10
Net Worth: £5,722,000 *Total Assets:* £10,799,000
Registered Office: 1 Kingfisher House, New Mill Road, Orpington, Kent, BR5 3QG
Activities: Agents involved in the sale of timber and building materials
Parent: Stora Enso Holdings UK Ltd
Officers: Ville Valtteri Valikangas, Secretary; James Ford Barr [1972] Director/Accountant; Howard Mark Sidney-Wilmot [1967] Sales Director

Storefast Limited
Incorporated: 23 October 1987 *Employees:* 6
Net Worth: £6,169,393 *Total Assets:* £10,481,264
Registered Office: Orchard House, Courtyard V, Springhead Enterprise Park, Northfleet, Kent, DA11 8HN
Activities: Operation of warehousing and storage facilities for land transport activities
Shareholders: Sharon Claretta Angela Kirby; John Kirby
Officers: Sharon Claretta Angela Kirby, Secretary; John Kirby [1955] Director/Cold Storage; Sharon Claretta Angela Kirby [1957] Director/Cold Storage

Storm Technologies Limited
Incorporated: 22 May 2000 *Employees:* 138
Net Worth: £2,368,221 *Total Assets:* £21,701,044
Registered Office: 2 The Boulevard, Blackmoor Lane, Croxley Business Park, Watford, Herts, WD18 8YW
Activities: Other information technology service activities
Parent: Storm Technologies Group Limited
Officers: Soraya Brooker, Secretary; John Robert Brooker [1967] Director; Randers Manuel Marquis [1970] Director/Accountant; Trevor John Nickolls [1975] Sales Director; Mark Raymond Smith [1973] Operations Director; Nicholas Marc Umney [1979] Software Sales Director

J.A. Stott (Carpentry) Limited
Incorporated: 29 July 1993 *Employees:* 48
Net Worth: £5,245,880 *Total Assets:* £6,835,187
Registered Office: Jubilee House, 7-9 The Oaks, Ruislip, Middlesex, HA4 7LF
Activities: Joinery installation
Major Shareholder: Michael Joseph Tierney
Officers: John Kevin Michael Kane [1962] Construction Director; Brian Kearney [1982] Commercial Director [Irish]; Michael Joseph Tierney [1962] Managing Director [Irish]

Strand Court Properties Limited
Incorporated: 22 February 1946
Net Worth: £22,533,000 *Total Assets:* £25,068,000
Registered Office: 889 Greenford Road, Greenford, Middlesex, UB6 0HE
Activities: Other letting and operating of own or leased real estate
Parent: Thorntons Limited
Officers: Tim John Shirley, Secretary; David Stuart Murby [1965] Director/Accountant; Tim John Shirley [1979] Director/Solicitor

Strandhaven Limited
Incorporated: 7 February 1979 *Employees:* 63
Net Worth: £2,582,577 *Total Assets:* £6,682,171
Registered Office: 600 High Road, Seven Kings, Ilford, Essex, IG3 8BS
Activities: Dispensing chemist in specialised stores
Shareholders: Dhirendra Somaiya; Harsha Somaiya
Officers: Harsha Somaiya, Secretary; Dhirendra Somaiya [1953] Director/Pharmacist

Strategic Imperatives Limited
Incorporated: 4 October 2005 *Employees:* 19
Net Worth: £5,044,464 *Total Assets:* £5,140,402
Registered Office: Birch House, Fairfield Avenue, Staines upon Thames, Middlesex, TW18 4AB
Activities: Information technology consultancy activities
Officers: Wail Sabbagh, Secretary; Wail Sabbagh [1967] Director

Strategic Shipping Company Limited
Incorporated: 7 June 1984 *Employees:* 41
Net Worth: £3,814,122 *Total Assets:* £6,474,720
Registered Office: Centrum House, 36 Station Road, Egham, Surrey, TW20 9LF
Activities: Other transportation support activities
Shareholders: Mervyn John Griffiths; Peter Howard Philip O'Rorke
Officers: Mervyn John Griffiths, Secretary; Janice Ann Griffiths [1953] Director; Mervyn John Griffiths [1952] Director/Freight Forwarder; Peter Howard Philip O'Rorke [1956] Director/Freight Forwarder; Susan Loraine O'Rorke [1957] Director

Stratford High Street Ventures Limited
Incorporated: 5 March 2014
Net Worth: £3,256,899 *Total Assets:* £7,979,251
Registered Office: 3rd Floor, Sterling House, Langston Road, Loughton, Essex, IG10 3TS
Activities: Other business support service activities n.e.c.
Parent: Galliard Holdings Limited
Officers: Stephen Stuart Solomon Conway [1948] Director; Vincent Daniel Goldstein [1960] Director/JV Partner; Donagh O'Sullivan [1968] Construction Director [Irish]

John Street & Company (Surrey) Limited
Incorporated: 10 September 1949 *Employees:* 3
Net Worth: £1,348,773 *Total Assets:* £43,769,624
Registered Office: Suite 2, West Hill House, West Hill, Epsom, Surrey, KT19 8JD
Activities: Other letting and operating of own or leased real estate
Parent: Street Family Group of Companies (Holdings) Limited
Officers: Andrew Mark Munday, Secretary; Patricia Jane French [1951] Director; Rivkah Hazel McCullough [1980] Director/Commercial Portfolio Executive; Andrew Mark Munday [1969] Director/Property Manager; Jonathan Justin Selig Symons [1949] Director

Street Family Group of Companies (Holdings) Limited
Incorporated: 16 October 2012 *Employees:* 3
Net Worth: £63,992,172 *Total Assets:* £65,420,112
Registered Office: Suite 2, West Hill House, West Hill, Epsom, Surrey, KT19 8JD
Activities: Non-trading company
Parent: Rothschild & Co
Officers: Andrew Mark Munday, Secretary; Patricia Jane French [1951] Director; Joanna Hudaly [1955] Director/Counsellor; Rivkah Hazel McCullough [1980] Director/Commercial Portfolio Executive; Andrew Mark Munday [1969] Director/Property Manager

Street Property (Holdings) Limited
Incorporated: 17 October 2012 *Employees:* 2
Net Worth: £9,572,812 *Total Assets:* £44,051,604
Registered Office: Suite 2, West Hill House, West Hill, Epsom, Surrey, KT19 8JD
Activities: Other letting and operating of own or leased real estate
Parent: Street Family Group of Companies (Holdings) Limited
Officers: Andrew Mark Munday, Secretary; Patricia Jane French [1951] Director; Rivkah Hazel McCullough [1980] Director/Commercial Portfolio Executive; Andrew Mark Munday [1969] Director/Property Manager

Paul Strickland Scanner Centre
Incorporated: 3 July 1986 *Employees:* 56
Net Worth: £11,655,830 *Total Assets:* £13,635,338
Registered Office: Paul Strickland Scanner Centre, Rickmansworth Road, Northwood, Middlesex, HA6 2RN
Activities: Hospital activities
Officers: Catherine Ruth Williams, Secretary; Dr Roberto Alonzi [1973] Director/Doctor; Patrick John Kelly [1949] Director/Banker [Irish]; Dilip Manek [1953] Director of Finance [Indian]; Daniel Jonathan Ross [1964] Director/Chief Executive; Palvi Shah [1961] Executive Director and Assistant General Council; Catherine Ruth Williams [1959] Director/Retired NHS Manager and Therapy Radiographer; Dr Terence Richard Wright [1945] Director/Self Employed Business Consultant

Strides Arcolab International Ltd
Incorporated: 10 November 2004 *Employees:* 1
Net Worth: £19,537,040 *Total Assets:* £48,504,460
Registered Office: Unit 4 Metro Centre, Tolpits Lane, Watford, Herts, WD18 9SS
Activities: Other business support service activities n.e.c.
Officers: Vikesh Kumar [1984] Director/Service [Indian]; Krishnan Tirucherai Parthasarathy [1971] Director [Indian]; Mohana Kumar Pillai [1956] Director/Service [Indian]; Rajasekar Visvanathan [1961] Director/Service

Strides Pharma Global (UK) Ltd
Incorporated: 29 July 2015 *Employees:* 2
Net Worth: £16,483,671 *Total Assets:* £20,348,244
Registered Office: Unit 4 Metro Centre, Tolpits Lane, Watford, Herts, WD18 9SS
Activities: Wholesale of pharmaceutical goods
Parent: Strides Arcolab International Limited
Officers: Vikesh Kumar [1984] Director/Service [Indian]; Krishnan Tirucherai Parthasarathy [1971] Director [Indian]; Mohana Kumar Pillai [1956] Director [Indian]

Strongholding Limited
Incorporated: 9 March 2016
Net Worth Deficit: £413,016 *Total Assets:* £9,400,342
Registered Office: 2nd Floor, Unicorn House, Station Close, Potters Bar, Herts, EN6 1TL
Activities: Other letting and operating of own or leased real estate
Parent: Apexbrook Limited
Officers: David Samuel Harouni [1977] Director; Jeremiah Harouni [1949] Director

STS Flooring Distributors Limited
Incorporated: 8 October 1996 *Employees:* 90
Net Worth: £6,544,882 *Total Assets:* £11,852,623
Registered Office: Unit 5-6 Orpington Trade Centre, Murray Road, Orpington, Kent, BR5 3SS
Activities: Wholesale of furniture, carpets and lighting equipment
Parent: Stair Tread Investments Limited
Officers: Raymond Colegate, Secretary; Raymond Jose Colgate [1965] Director; James Charles Flockhart [1954] Sales Director; Stuart Malcolm Gay [1958] Finance Director; Barry Pitt [1954] Director; Clifford Edward Wallman [1942] Company Secretary/Director

Stubbins Marketing Limited
Incorporated: 26 June 1987 *Employees:* 1
Net Worth: £6,243,295 *Total Assets:* £6,696,084
Registered Office: 147a High Street, Waltham Cross, Herts, EN8 7AP
Activities: Wholesale of fruit and vegetables
Officers: Onofria Dicarlo [1963] Director/Secretary; Antonio Giuseppe Difrancesco [1987] Director; Mario Difrancesco [1948] Director [Italian]; Michele Difrancesco [1983] Director/Senior Video Editor; Stephen Andrew Randall [1962] Director/Management Accountant; Giuseppe Ricotta [1966] Director

Stulz U.K. Limited
Incorporated: 23 March 1987 *Employees:* 47
Net Worth: £4,765,207 *Total Assets:* £6,804,769
Registered Office: First Quarter, Blenheim Road, Epsom, Surrey, KT19 9QN
Activities: Steam and air conditioning supply
Officers: Brendan Leonard, Secretary; Brendan Anthony Leonard [1965] Managing Director; Jurgen Stulz [1947] Director [German]

Subex (UK) Limited
Incorporated: 30 March 2001 *Employees:* 47
Net Worth: £2,722,000 *Total Assets:* £12,333,000
Registered Office: First Floor, Rama, 17 St Anns Road, Harrow, Middlesex, HA1 1JU
Activities: Other software publishing
Officers: Anil Chandanmal Singhvi [1959] Director [Indian]; Venkataraman Gopalasamudram Srinivasan [1969] Director [Indian]; Vinod Kumar Padmanabhan [1970] Director/Service [Indian]

Subsea 7 Crewing Limited
Incorporated: 21 August 1973
Net Worth: £15,510,612 *Total Assets:* £63,792,680
Registered Office: 40 Brighton Road, Sutton, Surrey, SM2 5BN
Activities: Other service activities n.e.c.
Parent: Subsea 7 Senior Holdings (UK) Limited
Officers: Lorna Helen Peace, Secretary; Simon David Ellis [1975] Group Legal Director - Commercial; John Alexander Gordon [1967] Finance Director; Neil McDonald [1961] Director/Vice President - Offshore Resources

Subsea 7 Engineering Limited
Incorporated: 18 April 2006
Net Worth: £23,708,000 *Total Assets:* £72,891,000
Registered Office: 40 Brighton Road, Sutton, Surrey, SM2 5BN
Activities: Other business support service activities n.e.c.
Parent: Subsea 7 Limited
Officers: Lorna Helen Peace, Secretary; James Richard Haylock [1974] Director/Senior Counsel; Paul Thomas Rosier [1960] Director/Chartered Engineer; David Robert Williams [1971] Director/Vice President - AFGOM

Subsea 7 Finance (UK) PLC
Incorporated: 28 August 2014
Net Worth: £4,980,038 *Total Assets:* £224,045,200
Registered Office: 40 Brighton Road, Sutton, Surrey, SM2 5BN
Activities: Other business support service activities n.e.c.
Parent: Subsea 7 International Holdings (UK) Limited
Officers: Andrew Hayward, Secretary; Alexandre Armand Bringer [1975] Director/VP & Group Controller [French]; Mark Austin Hodgkinson [1961] Director/Head of Treasury [Australian]; Nathalie Veronique Jacqueline Ghislaine Louys [1963] Director/General Counsel [Belgian]; Ricardo Horacio Rosa [1956] Director/Chief Financial Officer

Subsea 7 Interim UK Holdings Limited
Incorporated: 24 August 2011
Net Worth: £2,575,193,856 *Total Assets:* £2,577,399,296
Registered Office: 40 Brighton Road, Sutton, Surrey, SM2 5BN
Activities: Activities of other holding companies n.e.c.
Parent: Subsea 7 International Holdings (UK) Limited
Officers: Alexandre Armand Bringer [1975] Director/VP & Group Controller [French]; Nathalie Veronique Jacqueline Ghislaine Louys [1963] Director/General Counsel [Belgian]; Douglas James Young [1964] Director/Group Financial Controller

Subsea 7 International Contracting Limited
Incorporated: 23 June 1995
Net Worth: £135,740,112 *Total Assets:* £247,003,392
Registered Office: 40 Brighton Road, Sutton, Surrey, SM2 5BN
Activities: Other specialised construction activities n.e.c.
Parent: Subsea 7 Senior Holdings (UK) Limited
Officers: Lorna Helen Peace, Secretary; Simon David Ellis [1975] Legal Director; John Alexander Gordon [1967] Finance Director; Marcelo Lopes Xavier [1980] Director/Vice President [Brazilian]; Neil McDonald [1961] Director/Vice President - Offshore Resources

Subsea 7 Investments (UK) Limited
Incorporated: 2 September 2014
Net Worth: £1,144,120,576 *Total Assets:* £1,149,899,776
Registered Office: 40 Brighton Road, Sutton, Surrey, SM2 5BN
Activities: Other business support service activities n.e.c.
Parent: Subsea 7 Interim UK Holdings Limited
Officers: Lorna Helen Peace, Secretary; Alexandre Armand Bringer [1975] Director/VP & Group Controller [French]; Mark Austin Hodgkinson [1961] Director/Head of Treasury [Australian]; Jihane Karim [1983] Finance Director [French]; Nathalie Veronique Jacqueline Ghislaine Louys [1963] Director/General Counsel [Belgian]; Douglas James Young [1964] Director

Subsea 7 Limited
Incorporated: 5 November 2001
Net Worth: £884,398,976 *Total Assets:* £1,134,483,968
Registered Office: 40 Brighton Road, Sutton, Surrey, SM2 5BN
Activities: Support activities for petroleum and natural gas mining
Parent: Subsea 7 Interim UK Holdings Limited
Officers: Lorna Helen Peace, Secretary; Simon David Ellis [1975] UK Legal Director; John Alexander Gordon [1967] Director/Finance Manager; David Lowther [1966] Director/Vice President - Middle East; Graham Christopher Sharland [1961] Director/VP - Life of Field/Itech; Philip John Simons [1966] Director/VP Canada, Med & Russia; Colin Strachan [1965] Finance Director; Jonathan Richard Tame [1965] Director/Vice President - UK & Canada; Stephen George Wisely [1962] Director/EVP Northern Hemisphere and Life of Field

Subsea 7 Offshore Resources (UK) Limited
Incorporated: 5 September 2011
Net Worth: £2,456,738,560 *Total Assets:* £2,468,395,520
Registered Office: 40 Brighton Road, Sutton, Surrey, SM2 5BN
Activities: Support activities for petroleum and natural gas mining
Parent: Subsea 7 Senior Holdings (UK) Limited
Officers: Simon David Ellis [1975] Group Legal Director - Commercial; John Alexander Gordon [1967] Finance Director; Neil McDonald [1961] Director/Vice President - Offshore Resources

Subsea 7 Senior Holdings (UK) Limited
Incorporated: 24 August 2011
Net Worth: £1,719,828,480 *Total Assets:* £4,240,687,360
Registered Office: 40 Brighton Road, Sutton, Surrey, SM2 5BN
Activities: Activities of other holding companies n.e.c.
Parent: Subsea 7 International Holdings (UK) Limited
Officers: Alexandre Armand Bringer [1975] Director/VP & Group Controller [French]; Nathalie Veronique Jacqueline Ghislaine Louys [1963] Director/General Counsel [Belgian]; Douglas James Young [1964] Director/Group Financial Controller

Subsea 7 Treasury (UK) Limited
Incorporated: 17 March 1970
Net Worth: £938,905,472 *Total Assets:* £5,851,809,280
Registered Office: 40 Brighton Road, Sutton, Surrey, SM2 5BN
Activities: Other business support service activities n.e.c.
Parent: Subsea 7 International Holdings (UK) Limited
Officers: Lorna Helen Peace, Secretary; Alexandre Armand Bringer [1975] Director/VP & Group Controller [French]; Mark Austin Hodgkinson [1961] Director/Head of Treasury [Australian]; Nathalie Veronique Jacqueline Ghislaine Louys [1963] Director/General Counsel [Belgian]; Ricardo Horacio Rosa [1956] Director/Chief Financial Officer

Subsea 7 West Africa Contracting Limited
Incorporated: 5 March 1993
Net Worth: £5,525,424 *Total Assets:* £17,845,574
Registered Office: 40 Brighton Road, Sutton, Surrey, SM2 5BN
Activities: Other specialised construction activities n.e.c.
Parent: Subsea 7 Senior Holdings (UK) Limited
Officers: Lorna Helen Peace, Secretary; James Richard Haylock [1974] Legal Director; Justin Richard Parfett [1976] Finance Director; David Robert Williams [1971] Director/VP - AFGOM London

Sudbury Plastering Services Limited
Incorporated: 2 September 1988 *Employees:* 5
Net Worth: £6,222,107 *Total Assets:* £7,979,707
Registered Office: Suite 1, 5 Hercules Way, Leavesden Park, Watford, Herts, WD25 7GS
Activities: Plastering
Shareholders: Theresa Duffy; Paschal Duffy
Officers: Theresa Duffy, Secretary; Conor Patrick Duffy [1991] Director/Projects Manager; Paschal Duffy [1955] Managing Director [Irish]

Sugarman Family Limited
Incorporated: 28 August 2014 *Employees:* 2
Net Worth: £428,347 *Total Assets:* £8,130,931
Registered Office: Haslers, Old Station Road, Loughton, Essex, IG10 4PL
Activities: Financial intermediation not elsewhere classified
Shareholders: Marlene Sugarman; Paul Sugarman
Officers: Marlene Sugarman [1948] Director/Recruitment Consultant; Paul Sugarman [1944] Director/Recruitment Consultant

Sugarman Group Limited
Incorporated: 14 April 1998 *Employees:* 369
Net Worth: £9,900,993 *Total Assets:* £15,749,438
Registered Office: Chevron House, 346 Long Lane, Hillingdon, Uxbridge, Middlesex, UB10 9PF
Activities: Other business support service activities n.e.c.
Parent: Cordant People Limited
Officers: Alan Connor, Secretary; Chris Martin Kenneally [1960] Director; Jack Rainer Ullmann [1928] Director; Philip Lionel Ullmann [1964] Director

Sukanya Holdings Limited
Incorporated: 21 April 2017 *Employees:* 1
Net Worth Deficit: £28,149 *Total Assets:* £6,078,417
Registered Office: c/o N M Shah & Company, Miller House, Rosslyn Crescent, Harrow, Middlesex, HA1 2RZ
Activities: Activities of financial services holding companies
Officers: Sandeep Kalhan [1964] Director

Sumitomo Electric Europe Limited
Incorporated: 29 February 1996 *Employees:* 46
Net Worth: £7,014,000 *Total Assets:* £43,287,000
Registered Office: Unit 220 Centennial Avenue, Centennial Park, Elstree Hill South, Elstree, Borehamwood, Herts, WD6 3SL
Activities: Wholesale of electronic and telecommunications equipment and parts
Parent: Sumitomo Electric Industries Limited
Officers: Koji Kimura, Secretary; Koji Kimura [1969] Director [Japanese]; Eizo Mitani [1961] Director/General Manager - Electron Devices [Japanese]; Yasuyuki Shibata [1964] Director [Japanese]; Masakazu Watanabe [1961] Managing Director [Japanese]

Summerhill Birmingham Limited
Incorporated: 11 September 2017
Net Worth Deficit: £36,330 *Total Assets:* £14,644,183
Registered Office: 3rd Floor, Sterling House, Langston Road, Loughton, Essex, IG10 3TS
Activities: Development of building projects
Shareholders: Galliard Holdings Limited; Apsley House Capital PLC
Officers: Allan William Porter, Secretary; Stephen Stuart Solomon Conway [1948] Director; Gerard Nock [1947] Director/Company Chairman; Carl Robin Norstrom [1984] Director [Swedish]; Donagh O'Sullivan [1968] Construction Director [Irish]

Ann Summers Ltd.
Incorporated: 10 December 1971 *Employees:* 1,242
Net Worth: £48,093,220 *Total Assets:* £82,357,000
Registered Office: Gold Group House, Godstone Road, Whyteleafe, Surrey, CR3 0GG
Activities: Retail sale of clothing in specialised stores
Major Shareholder: David Gold
Officers: John Edward Boyle [1963] Director/Chief Operating Officer; Jacqueline Gold [1960] Director/Chief Executive; Vanessa Gold [1967] Managing Director

Summit Asset Management Limited
Incorporated: 2 March 1992 *Employees:* 12
Net Worth: £2,513,000 *Total Assets:* £6,833,000
Registered Office: Melita House, 124 Bridge Road, Chertsey, Surrey, KT16 8LA
Activities: Financial leasing
Major Shareholder: Christopher Neil Hunter Gordon
Officers: Simon James Knevett Barratt, Secretary; Simon James Knevett Barratt [1958] Finance Director; Christopher Neil Hunter Gordon [1958] Managing Director; Neil Anthony Roberts [1949] Director/Financier; Timothy Rodney Spring [1958] Commercial Director

Summit Media Limited
Incorporated: 27 August 1992 *Employees:* 106
Previous: Summit Records Ltd.
Net Worth Deficit: £403,269 *Total Assets:* £15,199,332
Registered Office: Heathrow House, Bath Road, Hounslow, Middlesex, TW5 9AT
Activities: Other information technology service activities
Parent: TCC Global N.V
Officers: Antonie Johannes Theodorus Schipperijn, Secretary; Hedley James Roger Aylott [1971] Managing Director; Antonie Johannes Theodorus Schipperijn [1961] Director [Dutch]; Petrus Adrianus Valkenburg [1961] Director [Dutch]

Sun Hotel Limited
Incorporated: 4 March 2004 *Employees:* 38
Net Worth: £6,065,292 *Total Assets:* £21,087,584
Registered Office: Unit 7 & 8c Kingston House Estate, Portsmouth Road, Long Ditton, Surbiton, Surrey, KT6 5QG
Activities: Hotels and similar accommodation
Major Shareholder: Sampathkumar Mallaya
Officers: Komathy Sampathkumar [1959] Director/Company Secretary; Mallaya Sampathkumar [1958] Director

Sun Mark Limited
Incorporated: 16 January 1995 *Employees:* 77
Net Worth: £38,094,772 *Total Assets:* £73,485,520
Registered Office: Sun House, 428 Long Drive, Greenford, Middlesex, UB6 8UH
Activities: Agents involved in the sale of food, beverages and tobacco
Shareholders: Raminder Singh Ranger; Renu Ranger
Officers: Renu Ranger, Secretary; Harmeet Singh Ahuja [1972] Director; Raminder Singh Ranger [1948] Director

Sun Valley Foods Limited
Incorporated: 19 December 1960 *Employees:* 2,225
Net Worth: £6,344,000 *Total Assets:* £177,972,000
Registered Office: Velocity V1, Brooklands Drive, Weybridge, Surrey, KT13 0SL
Activities: Raising of poultry
Parent: Cargill PLC
Officers: Dena Michelle L O'Bue, Secretary; Peter Michael Allan [1968] Director/General Manager; Christopher John Shooter [1957] Director/BU FP&A Lead; Federico Urquidi Negron [1965] Director/UK & Ireland Controller [Spanish]

Sunbury Manor School
Incorporated: 28 February 2011 *Employees:* 113
Net Worth: £5,789,137 *Total Assets:* £7,955,217
Registered Office: Sunbury Manor School, Nursery Road, Sunbury on Thames, Middlesex, TW16 6LF
Activities: General secondary education
Officers: Chiara Dawn Crichard, Secretary; Christopher William Burch [1955] Director/IT Consultant; Allan David Cottle [1976] Director/Teacher; Anne Louise Duncan [1966] Director/Headteacher; David Lloyd Evans [1953] Director/Retired; Carol Ann Fagan [1954] Director/Head of Inclusion; Sandra Christine Flint [1960] Director/Accounts Administrator; Emily Flippance [1969] Director/Telecoms Consultant; Louise Claire Hirst [1957] Director/Teacher; Debra Christine Johnson [1962] Director/Teacher; Penelope Ann Jones [1946] Director/Retired; Margaret Anne Lamey [1947] Director; Mark Daniel McCartney [1984] Director/Project Manager; Christopher William Webber [1974] Director/Bank Manager

Sunflower Healthcare (Greenford) LLP
Incorporated: 26 June 2006 *Employees:* 65
Net Worth: £544,021 *Total Assets:* £6,119,106
Registered Office: Canjayar, Tydcombe Road, Warlingham, Surrey, CR6 9LU
Officers: Manish Vinod Khiroya [1972] Member; Bhagirath Rasiklal Patel [1958] Member; Rupane Sunil Patel [1969] Member; Hashit Mahendra Shah [1969] Member; Meera Hashit Shah [1970] Member; Nimeet Dodhia [1978] LLP Member; Monica Khiroya [1971] LLP Member; Sajani Mittal [1975] LLP Member; Seetal Nilay Patel [1976] LLP Member; Parul Vinod Scampion [1970] LLP Member; Thomas Scampion [2011] LLP Member

Sungard Availability Services (DR) Limited
Incorporated: 22 November 1994
Net Worth: £33,489,000 *Total Assets:* £54,004,000
Registered Office: Unit B, Heathrow Corporate Park, Green Lane, Hounslow, Middlesex, TW4 6ER
Activities: Activities of head offices
Parent: Guardian IT
Officers: Susan Diane Lynch [1961] Director/Chief Financial Officer [American]; Michael John Threlfall [1961] Director/Senior Vice President - Global Consulting

Sungard Availability Services (UK) Limited
Incorporated: 4 April 1989
Net Worth: £21,577,000 *Total Assets:* £137,739,008
Registered Office: Unit B, Heathrow Corporate Park, Green Lane, Hounslow, Middlesex, TW4 6ER
Activities: Other information technology service activities
Parent: Sungard Availability Services (Holdings) Europe, Inc.
Officers: Susan Diane Lynch [1961] Director/Chief Financial Officer [American]; Michael John Threlfall [1961] Director/Senior Vice President - Global Consulting

Sunlight PV Ltd
Incorporated: 17 October 2007
Net Worth: £26,473,280 *Total Assets:* £29,480,514
Registered Office: 1 Olympic Way, Wembley, Middlesex, HA9 0NP
Activities: Production of electricity
Shareholders: Liberty Venture Limited; LEM Holdings Limited
Officers: Larisa Nikolaos Kolpidou, Secretary; Sergey Kolpidi [1960] Director/Engineer [Russian]; Michail Sergios Kolpidis [1991] Director/Businessman [Greek]

Sunny Bidco Limited
Incorporated: 3 August 2016 *Employees:* 103
Net Worth Deficit: £21,973,488 *Total Assets:* £107,374,400
Registered Office: Salamander Quay, West Park Lane, Harefield, Middlesex, UB9 6NZ
Activities: Activities of financial services holding companies
Parent: Sunny Midco Limited
Officers: Simon James Banks [1967] Director; Edward Heale [1973] Director; Philip Hollett [1961] Director; Thomas William Elliott Leigh [1971] Director

Sunny Midco Limited
Incorporated: 3 August 2016
Net Worth: £27 *Total Assets:* £67,133,896
Registered Office: Salamander Quay, West Park Lane, Harefield, Middlesex, UB9 6NZ
Activities: Activities of financial services holding companies
Parent: Sunny Topco Limited
Officers: Simon James Banks [1967] Director; Edward Heale [1973] Director; Philip Hollett [1961] Director; Thomas William Elliott Leigh [1971] Director

Sunny Topco Limited
Incorporated: 3 August 2016 *Employees:* 103
Net Worth Deficit: £22,143,228 *Total Assets:* £107,375,296
Registered Office: Salamander Quay, West Park Lane, Harefield, Uxbridge, Middlesex, UB9 6NZ
Activities: Activities of financial services holding companies
Officers: Simon James Banks [1967] Director; Paraag Dave [1975] Director/Investment Manager; Edward Heale [1973] Director; Philip Hollett [1961] Director; Kassir Huassin Kayani [1971] Director; Thomas William Elliott Leigh [1971] Director; Simon David Pitcher [1972] Director/Chartered Accountant; Mateusz Michal Szeszkowski [1972] Director/Investor [Canadian]

Sunnyfield Veg Limited
Incorporated: 4 April 1996 *Employees:* 28
Net Worth: £4,155,914 *Total Assets:* £7,552,427
Registered Office: Lynwood House, 373-375 Station, Harrow, Middlesex, HA1 2AW
Activities: Wholesale of fruit and vegetables
Shareholders: Ronny Wai Kin Liu; Sue Shuk Yin Liu
Officers: Sue Shuk Yin Liu, Secretary; Michael Chan Tong Fong [1963] Director; Ronny Wai Kin Liu [1960] Director; Sue Shuk Yin Liu [1961] Director

Sunray Estates Limited
Incorporated: 15 March 2004 *Employees:* 4
Net Worth: £8,306,802 *Total Assets:* £15,948,466
Registered Office: 5 Elstree Gate, Elstree Way, Borehamwood, Herts, WD6 1JD
Activities: Development of building projects
Shareholders: Ady Doron; David Azouri; Ronit Azouri
Officers: Ady Doron, Secretary; David Azouri [1961] Director; Tal Azouri [1989] Director; Ady Doron [1956] Director [British/Israeli]; Dana Doron [1989] Director

Sunrose Property Limited
Incorporated: 24 June 2005
Net Worth: £2,795,607 *Total Assets:* £9,322,711
Registered Office: 616D Green Lane, Ilford, Essex, IG3 9SE
Activities: Buying and selling of own real estate
Officers: Echewodo Lambert Nwawudu, Secretary/Engineer; Dorothy Ihuoma Nwawudu [1963] Director/IT Consultant; Echewodo Lambert Nwawudu [1964] Director/Engineer

Sunsave 12 (Derriton Fields) Ltd
Incorporated: 30 August 2012
Net Worth: £2,900,000 *Total Assets:* £12,917,000
Registered Office: Beaufort Court, Egg Farm Lane, off Station Road, Kings Langley, Herts, WD4 8LR
Activities: Production of electricity
Parent: European Investments Solar Holdings Limited
Officers: Dominic James Hearth, Secretary; Steven William Hughes [1972] Global Support Services Director, UK&I - Commercial; Mitesh Raj Patel [1982] Director/Group Financial Controller; Tracy Jane Scott [1976] Director/Delivery Project Manager - New Technologies UK&I; Mark Christopher Wayment [1958] Director

Sunsave 25 (Wix Lodge Farm) Limited
Incorporated: 24 May 2013
Net Worth: £8,788,000 *Total Assets:* £19,526,000
Registered Office: Beaufort Court, Egg Farm Lane, off Station Road, Kings Langley, Herts, WD4 8LR
Activities: Production of electricity
Parent: European Investments Solar Holdings Limited
Officers: Dominic James Hearth, Secretary; Steven William Hughes [1972] Global Support Services Director, UK&I - Commercial; Mitesh Raj Patel [1982] Director/Group Financial Controller; Tracy Jane Scott [1976] Director/Delivery Project Manager - New Technologies UK&I; Mark Christopher Wayment [1958] Director

Sunset Travel Limited
Incorporated: 28 May 1981 *Employees:* 20
Net Worth: £2,306,321 *Total Assets:* £6,319,660
Registered Office: 6 Bedford Park, Croydon, Surrey, CR0 2AP
Activities: Tour operator activities
Major Shareholder: Harvin Kaumaya
Officers: Sarita Kaumaya, Secretary; Hamish Kaumaya [1974] Marketing Director; Harvin Kaumaya [1944] Director/Travel Agent; Sarita Kaumaya [1951] Director/Secretary

Sunshine Properties Limited
Incorporated: 30 August 1956 *Employees:* 6
Net Worth: £5,653,359 *Total Assets:* £7,711,588
Registered Office: Ground Floor, Unit 501 Centennial Park, Centennial Avenue, Elstree, Borehamwood, Herts, WD6 3FG
Activities: Other letting and operating of own or leased real estate
Shareholders: Adrian Aubrey Marks; Janice Rosalind Rainsbury
Officers: Sara Estelle Saville, Secretary; Adrian Aubrey Marks [1949] Director/Retired Solicitor; Benjamin James Marks [1977] Director/Chartered Accountant; Janice Rosalind Rainsbury [1947] Director; Simon Michael Rainsbury [1976] Director/Civil Engineer

Sunstar Group Limited
Incorporated: 31 May 1990
Net Worth: £9,515,890 *Total Assets:* £17,213,568
Registered Office: c/o Danmirr Consultants, 170 Church Road, Mitcham, Surrey, CR4 3BW
Activities: Retail sale in non-specialised stores with food, beverages or tobacco predominating
Major Shareholder: Najib Khan
Officers: Mahomed Erfan Abdul Gaffar, Secretary; Mohammed Najib Khan, Secretary/Businessman; Akhtar Jan Khan [1959] Director; Mohammed Najib Khan [1958] Director/Businessman

Suntory UK Holdings Limited
Incorporated: 10 August 2016
Net Worth: £2,240,600,320 *Total Assets:* £2,312,583,424
Registered Office: 2 Longwalk Road, Stockley Park, Uxbridge, Middlesex, UB11 1BA
Activities: Activities of production holding companies
Officers: Akira Haraguchi [1959] Director/Executive Officer [Japanese]; Shinichiro Hizuka [1955] Senior Managing Director [Japanese]

Sunvil International Sales Limited
Incorporated: 17 July 1970 *Employees:* 66
Net Worth: £2,409,705 *Total Assets:* £10,197,099
Registered Office: Sunvil House, Upper Square, Isleworth, Middlesex, TW7 7BJ
Activities: Tour operator activities
Shareholders: Noel Christie Luciano Josephides; Nourbar John Der Parthog
Officers: Ismet Emin, Secretary; Peter Vasken Dudley Der Parthog [1957] Director/Travel Agent/Tour Operator; Noel Christie Luciano Josephides [1948] Director/Tour Operator; Christopher Wright [1974] Director/Tour Operator

Super Industries DMCC Metals Limited
Incorporated: 31 March 2015
Net Worth: £1,509,970 *Total Assets:* £7,756,200
Registered Office: 19 Edinburgh Drive, Staines upon Thames, Middlesex, TW18 1PJ
Activities: Wholesale of metals and metal ores
Officers: Rajesh Satija [1967] Director [Indian]; Renu Satija [1972] Commercial Director [Indian]

Super Toughened Glass Limited
Incorporated: 1 October 1998 *Employees:* 145
Net Worth: £32,237,848 *Total Assets:* £44,073,320
Registered Office: 65-67 Wembley Hill Road, Wembley, Middlesex, HA9 8DP
Activities: Shaping and processing of flat glass
Shareholders: Karsan Kanji Hirani; Dhanbhai Karsan Hirani; Devji Khimji Meghani; Laxmiben Devji Meghani
Officers: Karsan Kanji Hirani, Secretary; Karsan Kanji Hirani [1959] Director; Devji Khimji Meghani [1953] Director; Sanjay Devji Meghani [1976] Director

Supercraft Holdings Limited
Incorporated: 17 February 2004 *Employees:* 164
Net Worth: £2,314,744 *Total Assets:* £7,647,385
Registered Office: Canada Road, Oyster Lane, Byfleet, Surrey, KT14 7JL
Activities: Activities of other holding companies n.e.c.
Officers: Jeffrey Dosser, Secretary; Paul Barber [1965] Managing Director; Geoffrey Alan Green [1950] Director; David McDougall [1968] Director/Engineer; Jeremiah Riordan [1953] Director/Engineer

Supercraft Limited
Incorporated: 24 March 1982 *Employees:* 159
Net Worth: £2,399,469 *Total Assets:* £7,925,783
Registered Office: Canada Road, Oyster Lane, Byfleet, Surrey, KT14 7JL
Activities: Machining
Parent: Supercraft Holdings Ltd
Officers: Jeffrey Dosser, Secretary; Paul Barber [1965] Director/Engineer; David McDougall [1968] Director/Engineer; Jeremiah Riordan [1953] Director/Engineer

Superdrug Stores PLC
Incorporated: 28 May 1964 *Employees:* 6,644
Net Worth: £254,990,000 *Total Assets:* £753,222,016
Registered Office: 51 Sydenham Road, Croydon, Surrey, CR0 2EU
Activities: Dispensing chemist in specialised stores
Parent: A.S. Watson (Health & Beauty UK) Limited
Officers: Edith Shih, Secretary; Richard Alexander Fleming [1971] Finance Director; Dr Alan John Heaton [1962] Director; Dominic Kai Ming Lai [1953] Director [Canadian]; Peter William MacNab [1957] Director

Supreme Hotels LLP
Incorporated: 20 December 2011 *Employees:* 137
Net Worth: £2,797,612 *Total Assets:* £16,153,491
Registered Office: Haydon House, 296 Joel Street, Pinner, Middlesex, HA5 2PY
Officers: Nadeem Boghani [1978] Member; Shiraz Boghani [1950] Member

Surebay Developments Limited
Incorporated: 11 March 2016 *Employees:* 9
Net Worth: £389,563 *Total Assets:* £19,714,984
Registered Office: 1st Floor, 44-50 The Broadway, Southall, Middlesex, UB1 1QB
Activities: Buying and selling of own real estate
Major Shareholder: Sant Ram Ghai
Officers: Sant Ram Ghai [1966] Director/Businessman

Surrey Blue Limited
Incorporated: 30 April 2010 *Employees:* 25
Net Worth: £7,720,521 *Total Assets:* £38,712,928
Registered Office: Allen House, 1 Westmead Road, Sutton, Surrey, SM1 4LA
Activities: Other business support service activities n.e.c.
Major Shareholder: Justin Douglas William Barnes
Officers: Justin Douglas William Barnes [1965] Director

Surrey Lighting Services Limited
Incorporated: 2 September 2009
Net Worth Deficit: £15,738,000 *Total Assets:* £91,498,000
Registered Office: 8 White Oak Square, London Road, Swanley, Kent, BR8 7AG
Activities: Other business support service activities n.e.c.
Parent: SLS Holding Company Limited
Officers: Paul Alan Bannister [1959] Director/Accountant; David Richard Bradbury [1969] Director/Senior Investment Manager; Jennifer Kathryn Fegan [1973] Director/Lawyer; Katherine Mary Rae [1980] Director/Legal Advisor; Paul Sydney Shadbolt [1957] Asset Management Director; Keerthana Sivanathan [1988] Director/Senior Management Accountant

Surrey Rest Homes Limited
Incorporated: 7 May 2003
Net Worth: £340,531 *Total Assets:* £6,897,092
Registered Office: Oak House, 19 Queens Road, Weybridge, Surrey, KT13 9UE
Activities: Residential nursing care facilities
Shareholders: Ajit Prasad; Nishi Prasad
Officers: Dr Ajit Prasad, Secretary/Health Care; Nishi Prasad, Secretary/Health Care; Anchal Bouri [1983] Director of Administration and Development; Ajit Prasad [1949] Director/Health Care; Nishi Prasad [1958] Director/Health Care

Sussex Gardens Hotels Limited
Incorporated: 2 May 1973 *Employees:* 3
Net Worth: £19,258,724 *Total Assets:* £21,618,956
Registered Office: 1st Floor, Woodgate Studios, 2-8 Games Road, Cockfosters, Herts, EN4 9HN
Activities: Hotels and similar accommodation
Parent: Mouskos Holdings Limited
Officers: Generaldina Mouskos, Secretary; Christopher Mouskos [1961] Director/Businessman; Generaldina Mouskos [1937] Director/Hotelier; John Mouskos [1964] Director/Businessman

Sutton Business Centre Limited
Incorporated: 17 July 1991 *Employees:* 7
Net Worth: £5,706,213 *Total Assets:* £6,893,231
Registered Office: Ermyn Lodge Stud, Shepherds Walk, Epsom, Surrey, KT18 6DF
Activities: Development of building projects
Parent: Southdown Holdings Limited
Officers: Lesley Jean Smith, Secretary; Anthony James Smith [1947] Director

Sutton Grammar School Trust
Incorporated: 13 May 2011 *Employees:* 107
Net Worth: £16,637,000 *Total Assets:* £18,337,000
Registered Office: Sutton Grammar School, Manor Lane, Sutton, Surrey, SM1 4AS
Activities: General secondary education
Officers: Dr Neville Stuart Wrench, Secretary; Felicity Hilary Evelyn Alexander [1956] Director/Solicitor; Paul Stewart Chambers [1957] Director/Bank Official; Paul Simon Davis [1979] Director/Teacher; Julian Robert Edwards [1949] Director/Management Consultant; Gordon Douglas Ironside [1955] Director/Teacher; Gareth Wilson Jones [1956] Director/Surveyor; Robert William Murrill [1955] Director/Consultant; Amanda Jane Nobel [1964] Director/Educational Psychologist; Raymond Ashley Pletts [1984] Director/Teacher; Nayana Prasad [1971] Director; Peter Julian Ritson [1949] Director/Chartered Gas Engineer; Devkant Rustagi [1975] Director

Sutton Group Holdings Limited
Incorporated: 4 December 1989 *Employees:* 158
Net Worth: £4,169,407 *Total Assets:* £14,986,647
Registered Office: St James House, Grosvenor Road, Twickenham, Middlesex, TW1 4AJ
Activities: Activities of insurance agents and brokers
Officers: Kimberley Lyle, Secretary; Michael Bouchier Baldwin [1945] Director/Insurance Broker; Peter Ivan Jones [1942] Director/Company Chief Executive; Kimberley Lyle [1961] Director/Accountant; Kevin MacEvoy [1951] Director/Insurance Broker

Sutton Winson Limited
Incorporated: 29 March 1955 *Employees:* 125
Net Worth: £2,077,000 *Total Assets:* £9,823,000
Registered Office: St James House, Grosvenor Road, Twickenham, Middlesex, TW1 4AJ
Activities: Activities of insurance agents and brokers
Officers: Russell John Gray, Secretary; Russell John Gray [1976] Finance Director; Andrew Clive Jonas [1966] Director/Project Manager; Grahame Michael Lamb [1965] Director/Insurance Broker; Kimberley Lyle [1961] Director/Accountant; Kevin MacEvoy [1951] Director/Insurance Broker; Richard John Morley [1967] Director/Insurance Broker; Gareth David Roberts [1968] Director; David Alexander Thomson [1961] Director/Insurance Broker

Suzo International (UK) Limited
Incorporated: 1 December 2004 *Employees:* 25
Net Worth: £4,196,294 *Total Assets:* £7,406,789
Registered Office: Unit 1 & 2 King Georges Trading Estate, Davis Road, Chessington, Surrey, KT9 1TT
Activities: Non-specialised wholesale trade
Parent: Global Investments Holding B.V.
Officers: Charles Thomas Frederick Sines, Secretary; Kenneth Ross Brotman [1965] Director/Banker [American]; Charles Thomas Frederick Sines [1977] Director

Swakeleys Properties Limited
Incorporated: 7 August 1954 *Employees:* 8
Net Worth: £6,972,789 *Total Assets:* £7,185,590
Registered Office: Wimborne House, 4 Pump Lane, Hayes, Middlesex, UB3 3NB
Activities: Other letting and operating of own or leased real estate
Officers: Clare Cecelia Francis, Secretary; Josephine Lesley Bridel [1957] Director; Doctor John Alexander Milne Davidson [1955] Director; James Curzon Farr [1944] Director/Chartered Surveyor; Clare Cecelia Francis [1957] Director

Swakeleys School for Girls
Incorporated: 18 March 2011 *Employees:* 136
Net Worth: £32,878,026 *Total Assets:* £34,289,056
Registered Office: Swakeleys School for Girls, Clifton Gardens, Uxbridge, Middlesex, UB10 0EJ
Activities: General secondary education
Officers: Helen Manwaring, Secretary; Susan Elizabeth Caldwell [1967] Director/Exams Officer; Dean Crosby Charles [1970] Director/Bank Manager; John Fox [1940] Director/Retired; Theresa Gruber Miller [1974] Director/Secretary; Bandhana Jakhu [1978] Director/Administrator; David Paul McLauchlan [1974] Director/Railway Worker; Sylvia Proctor [1971] Director/Administrator; Susan Elizabeth Pryor [1959] Director/Headteacher; Debra Sadeh [1974] Director/Administrator; Rajpal Sall [1965] Director/Accountant; Hardip Singh [1956] Director/Civil Servant; Ruby Lestacia Stephen [1978] Director/Teacher; Anne Torrent [1952] Director/Teacher

Swan Mill (Holdings) Limited
Incorporated: 19 June 1930 *Employees:* 266
Net Worth: £36,570,000 *Total Assets:* £44,979,000
Registered Office: Swan Mill, Goldsel Road, Swanley, Kent, BR8 8EU
Activities: Activities of head offices
Shareholders: Stephen Richard Lewin; John William Williams; Richard Alexander Jennings
Officers: James Bryan [1962] Manufacturing Director; David Charles Byk [1967] Managing Director; Graham Rogers [1968] Finance Director; Tom Aiden Worton [1965] Welsh Operations Director

Swan Mill Paper Company Limited
Incorporated: 14 September 1983 *Employees:* 175
Net Worth: £31,525,000 *Total Assets:* £37,843,000
Registered Office: Swan Mill, Goldsel Road, Swanley, Kent, BR8 8EU
Activities: Manufacture of other articles of paper and paperboard n.e.c.
Parent: Swan Mill (Holdings) Limited
Officers: James Bryan [1962] Manufacturing Director; David Charles Byk [1967] Managing Director; Graham Rogers [1968] Finance Director; Tom Aiden Worton [1965] Director Wales

Swanbrae Limited
Incorporated: 27 April 1970 *Employees:* 2
Net Worth: £5,483,778 *Total Assets:* £12,828,343
Registered Office: Raffingers, 19-20 Bourne Court, Southend Road, Woodford Green, Essex, IG8 8HD
Activities: Development of building projects
Major Shareholder: James Patrick Tye
Officers: Lauren Rose Tye, Secretary; James Patrick Tye [1953] Director

Swanlea Limited
Incorporated: 5 February 1990
Net Worth: £14,839,733 *Total Assets:* £19,301,774
Registered Office: Unit 5 Charlton Mead Lane, Hoddesdon, Herts, EN11 0DJ
Activities: Other letting and operating of own or leased real estate
Shareholder: David John Cooper
Officers: Susan Jane Cooper, Secretary; David John Cooper [1953] Director; Susan Jane Cooper [1952] Director

Swanvale Management Limited
Incorporated: 7 March 2002
Net Worth: £1,228,961 *Total Assets:* £6,758,181
Registered Office: 5 Margaret Road, Romford, Essex, RM2 5SH
Activities: Development of building projects
Shareholder: Graham Joseph Toomey
Officers: Graham Joseph Toomey [1961] Director

J.J. Sweeney Limited
Incorporated: 22 October 1996 *Employees:* 25
Net Worth: £4,493,571 *Total Assets:* £7,130,090
Registered Office: 5 Hockley Drive, Gidea Park, Romford, Essex, RM2 6NL
Activities: Joinery installation
Shareholders: John Joseph Sweeney; Helen Marie Sweeney
Officers: John Joseph Sweeney, Secretary; Helen Marie Sweeney [1953] Director/Part Time Secretary [Irish]; John Paul Sweeney [1983] Director [Irish]; John Joseph Sweeney [1950] Director/Builder [Irish]; Patrick Christopher Sweeney [1981] Director [Irish]

Sweetland Properties Limited
Incorporated: 6 February 1967 *Employees:* 2
Net Worth: £5,368,102 *Total Assets:* £5,448,002
Registered Office: The Old Rectory, Church Street, Weybridge, Surrey, KT13 8DE
Activities: Other letting and operating of own or leased real estate
Shareholders: Brian David Douthwaite; Barbara Ann Douthwaite
Officers: Barbara Ann Douthwaite, Secretary; Barbara Ann Douthwaite [1945] Director/Property Management; Brian David Douthwaite [1942] Director/Property Management; Mark David Douthwaite [1967] Director/Fitness Manager; Stuart Simon Douthwaite [1971] Director

Swift 100 Limited
Incorporated: 21 July 2016 *Employees:* 2
Net Worth: £367,454 *Total Assets:* £7,243,120
Registered Office: Ground Floor, Irene House, Five Arches Business Park, Maidstone Road, Sidcup, Kent, DA14 5AE
Activities: Buying and selling of own real estate
Shareholder: Michael Reuben Warren
Officers: Mark Anthony Allen [1964] Director; Michael Reuben Warren [1969] Director

Swift Roofing Contracts Limited
Incorporated: 2 February 1995 *Employees:* 27
Net Worth: £1,516,433 *Total Assets:* £7,355,988
Registered Office: Charles Lake House, Claire Causeway, Crossways Business Park, Dartford, Kent, DA2 6QA
Activities: Roofing activities
Parent: SRCH Limited
Officers: Stephen Carl Swift, Secretary/Financial Director; Paul Leslie Lewis [1955] Contractors Director; Alan Dean Swift [1967] Contracts Director; Stephen Carl Swift [1968] Financial Director

Swiss Post Solutions Ltd
Incorporated: 10 July 2002 *Employees:* 1,555
Net Worth: £11,434,000 *Total Assets:* £39,237,000
Registered Office: Parkshot House, 5 Kew Road, Richmond, Surrey, TW9 2PR
Activities: Other business support service activities n.e.c.
Parent: Die Schweizerische Post
Officers: Adam Cater, Secretary/Accountant; Gary Harrold [1972] Director; Jorg Vollmer [1967] Director [German]

Sword Charteris Limited
Incorporated: 27 March 2014 *Employees:* 199
Previous: Sword IT Solutions Limited
Net Worth: £2,743,536 *Total Assets:* £12,313,559
Registered Office: 1000 Great West Road, Brentford, Middlesex, TW8 9DW
Activities: Information technology consultancy activities
Officers: David Bruce [1968] Director; John Douglas Innes [1957] Director; Jacques Francis Mottard [1952] Director [French]; Philip Neil Norgate [1973] Director/Chief Financial Officer

Sword Soft Limited
Incorporated: 22 February 2007
Net Worth: £49,338,144 *Total Assets:* £49,414,896
Registered Office: 1000 Great West Road, Brentford, Middlesex, TW8 9DW
Activities: Other information technology service activities
Officers: Frederic Goosse [1969] Director [Belgian]; Jacques Francois Mottard [1952] Director [French]

Symbio Energy Limited
Incorporated: 21 March 2012 *Employees:* 2
Net Worth Deficit: £4,331,773 *Total Assets:* £9,278,916
Registered Office: Room 103, Mansion House, Bucknalls Lane, Watford, Herts, WD25 9XX
Activities: Production of electricity
Parent: Dispensary Holdings Limited
Officers: Shamir Pravinchandra Budhdeo [1967] Director

Symmetry Logistics Holdings Limited
Incorporated: 28 June 2013 *Employees:* 604
Net Worth: £676,569 *Total Assets:* £51,057,244
Registered Office: Littlebrook DC1, Shield Road, Dartford, Kent, DA1 5UR
Activities: Activities of head offices
Officers: Robert William Gilbert Ross, Secretary; Andrew Neville Baxter [1975] Director; Robert William Gilbert Ross [1982] Finance Director

Symmetry Logistics Limited
Incorporated: 28 June 2013 *Employees:* 6
Net Worth Deficit: £3,898,456 *Total Assets:* £12,882,725
Registered Office: Littlebrook DC1, Shield Road, Dartford, Kent, DA1 5RU
Activities: Activities of head offices
Major Shareholder: Andrew Neville Baxter
Officers: Robert William Gilbert Ross, Secretary; Andrew Neville Baxter [1975] Director; Daniel Paul Cook [1974] Director; Angus Hind [1980] Director; Richard Litchfield [1976] Director; Dionne Redpath [1973] Director; Robert William Gilbert Ross [1982] Finance Director

Synamedia Limited
Incorporated: 18 July 1995
Previous: NDS Limited
Net Worth: £165,757,840 *Total Assets:* £369,984,768
Registered Office: One London Road, Staines upon Thames, Middlesex, TW18 4EX
Activities: Other information technology service activities
Parent: Triton UK Bidco Limited
Officers: Ismat Levin [1967] Director; Charles Richard Kenneth Medlock [1960] Director; Yves Padrines [1976] Director [French]

Synaptic Trust
Incorporated: 1 April 2011 *Employees:* 315
Net Worth: £33,559,000 *Total Assets:* £38,895,000
Registered Office: West Thornton Primary Academy, Rosecourt Road, Croydon, Surrey, CR0 3BS
Activities: Primary education
Officers: Julie Anne Newman, Secretary; Keith Kirby [1961] Director/PR and Communications; Remi Ladega [1964] Director/Company Secretary; Anthony Stuart Roberts [1964] Director/Executive Headteacher; Keith Harold Robinson [1947] Director/Retired; Roger White [1949] Director/Retired; Muyideen Olufemi Oluwole Yusoof [1972] Director/Recruitment Manager

Synbra UK Limited
Incorporated: 1 May 1996
Net Worth: £23,563,152 *Total Assets:* £36,775,304
Registered Office: Infinity House, Anderson Way, Belvedere, Kent, DA17 6BG
Activities: Other business support service activities n.e.c.
Parent: Jablite Holdings Ltd
Officers: Matthew David Groom, Secretary; Wayne Robert Brown [1961] Manufacturing Director; Richard Peter Simon Lee [1968] Director

Synchro Clutch Company Limited
Incorporated: 24 July 1979 *Employees:* 77
Net Worth: £88,795,216 *Total Assets:* £96,960,448
Registered Office: Synchro House, Park Road, Sunbury on Thames, Middlesex, TW16 5BL
Activities: Activities of head offices
Officers: Paul Stuart Bizzill, Secretary; Paul Stuart Bizzill [1973] Director of Engineering; Morgan Leland Hendry [1950] Director [American]; James Michael George Neeves [1962] Managing Director

Syner-Med (Pharmaceutical Products) Limited
Incorporated: 14 July 1994
Net Worth: £3,418,042 *Total Assets:* £5,802,189
Registered Office: DS House, 306 High Street, Croydon, Surrey, CR0 1NG
Activities: Other business support service activities n.e.c.
Major Shareholder: Dipak Devji Bhatti
Officers: Pratima Dipak Bhatti, Secretary; Antony Han-Liang NG, Secretary; Dipak Devji Bhatti [1956] Director/Pharmaceutical Market; Pratima Dipak Bhatti [1960] Director/Secretary; Lindsay Ruth Westwood [1965] Finance Director

Syscap Leasing Limited
Incorporated: 28 May 1992
Net Worth: £8,020,463 *Total Assets:* £20,508,788
Registered Office: CI Tower, St Georges Square, New Malden, Surrey, KT3 4TE
Activities: Financial leasing
Parent: Syscap Limited
Officers: Selena Jane Pritchard, Secretary; Andrew James D'Arcy [1959] Director

Syscap Limited
Incorporated: 19 February 1990
Net Worth: £8,665,082 *Total Assets:* £10,834,499
Registered Office: CI Tower, St George's Square, New Malden, Surrey, KT3 4TE
Activities: Financial leasing
Parent: Wesleyan Bank Limited
Officers: Selena Jane Pritchard, Secretary; Andrew James D'Arcy [1959] Director

SZ & W Limited
Incorporated: 1 February 2013 *Employees:* 45
Net Worth: £1,230,765 *Total Assets:* £7,186,782
Registered Office: 249 Cranbrook Road, Ilford, Essex, IG1 4TG
Activities: Retail sale of electrical household appliances in specialised stores
Major Shareholder: Craig Leslie Davies
Officers: Craig Leslie Davies [1960] Director; Ricky Davies [1982] Director/Operations Manager

T G Commodities Limited
Incorporated: 16 December 1998
Net Worth: £1,008,816 *Total Assets:* £19,073,816
Registered Office: Waters Meet, Willow Avenue, New Denham, Uxbridge, Middlesex, UB9 4AF
Activities: Wholesale of metals and metal ores
Major Shareholder: Sanjeev Gupta
Officers: Surinder Jolly, Secretary; Parduman Kumar Gupta [1943] Director [Indian]

T G Products Limited
Incorporated: 17 December 1992 *Employees:* 19
Net Worth: £20,500,000 *Total Assets:* £74,453,000
Registered Office: Littleton Road, Ashford, Middlesex, TW15 1TZ
Activities: Other manufacturing n.e.c.
Parent: Chubb Group Security Limited
Officers: Robert John Sloss, Secretary/Solicitor; Anthony Brennan [1966] Finance Director [Irish]; Craig Alexander Forbes [1963] Finance Director

T. Bro Investment Limited
Incorporated: 20 March 1995
Net Worth: £2,165,003 *Total Assets:* £10,973,910
Registered Office: Argyle House, Northside Level 3, Joel Street, Northwood, Middlesex, HA6 1NW
Activities: Other letting and operating of own or leased real estate
Major Shareholder: Bharat Kumar Hirji Thakrar
Officers: Bharat Kumar Hirji Thakrar [1957] Director/Businessman

T.C & D Construction Ltd.
Incorporated: 17 May 2006 *Employees:* 5
Net Worth: £4,596,683 *Total Assets:* £5,960,834
Registered Office: 1a Station Road, Sidcup, Kent, DA15 7EN
Activities: Construction of commercial buildings
Officers: Daiva Staniukynaite [1977] Director/Accountant [Lithuanian]

T.C. Racing (Leisure) Limited
Incorporated: 29 March 1983 *Employees:* 2
Net Worth: £5,565,164 *Total Assets:* £6,503,667
Registered Office: Dawes Court House, Dawes Court, High Street, Esher, Surrey, KT10 9QD
Activities: Other letting and operating of own or leased real estate
Officers: Kenneth Seakens, Secretary; Tracy MacRitchie [1965] Director

T.H.G. & C.C. Limited
Incorporated: 1 September 1988 *Employees:* 1
Net Worth: £6,561,595 *Total Assets:* £7,875,000
Registered Office: c/o Prohal Ltd, 54 Clarendon Road, Watford, Herts, WD17 1DU
Activities: Operation of sports facilities
Officers: Allan Saud, Secretary; Allan Saud [1986] Director

T.S.G. Building Services PLC
Incorporated: 18 January 2000 *Employees:* 259
Net Worth: £7,502,118 *Total Assets:* £16,224,464
Registered Office: TSG House, Cranborne Industrial Estate, Cranborne Road, Potters Bar, Herts, EN6 3JN
Activities: Construction of domestic buildings
Shareholder: Adam James Thrussell
Officers: Robert Joseph Glendinning, Secretary; Robert Joseph Glendinning [1969] Director/Chartered Management Accountant; Stephen James Gwynn [1957] Director/Surveyor; John Philip Holloway [1947] Contracts Director; Bryan Lloyd Rees [1968] Construction Director; Adam James Thrussell [1979] Managing Director

T.S.L. Finance Limited
Incorporated: 30 August 2000 *Employees:* 14
Net Worth: £1,031,533 *Total Assets:* £35,641,412
Registered Office: Unit 8 West London Industrial Park, Iver Lane, Uxbridge, Middlesex, UB8 2JG
Activities: Sale of used cars and light motor vehicles
Major Shareholder: Fil Levi Gray
Officers: Fil Levi Gray [1958] Director

The Tabor Group Ltd
Incorporated: 10 March 2000 *Employees:* 239
Net Worth: £3,451,602 *Total Assets:* £12,393,842
Registered Office: Regency House, 33 Wood Street, Barnet, Herts, EN5 4BE
Activities: Other business support service activities n.e.c.
Major Shareholder: Edward Tabor
Officers: Georgina Hill, Secretary; Julie Patmore [1958] Director; Edward James Tabor [1948] Director; Katriona Jane Tabor [1966] Director

Tackle Guru Limited
Incorporated: 16 December 2008 *Employees:* 5
Net Worth: £3,292,940 *Total Assets:* £5,262,109
Registered Office: Orbital House, 20 Eastern Road, Romford, Essex, RM1 3PJ
Activities: Other retail sale not in stores, stalls or markets
Major Shareholder: Andrew John Reynolds
Officers: Damian Keith Clarke [1971] Director/Head of Operations; Daniel William Fairbrass [1970] Director; Andrew John Reynolds [1970] Director

Taj Securities Company Number Two Limited
Incorporated: 23 May 2017
Net Worth Deficit: £117,684 *Total Assets:* £5,247,047
Registered Office: Kirkland House, 11-15 Peterborough Road, Harrow, Middlesex, HA1 2AX
Activities: Hotels and similar accommodation
Major Shareholder: Haider Ladhu Jaffer
Officers: Haider Ladhu Jaffer [1940] Director; Dr Manoj Raman [1960] Director; Hassanali Amirali Dawood Suleman [1954] Director

Talbot House Business Centre Limited
Incorporated: 3 March 1999 *Employees:* 6
Net Worth: £9,236,597 *Total Assets:* £15,386,373
Registered Office: Kajaine House, 57-67 High Street, Edgware, Middlesex, HA8 7DD
Activities: Other letting and operating of own or leased real estate
Shareholders: Stephen Michael Glynne; Stephen Michael Cole
Officers: Stephen Michael Glynne, Secretary/Director; Stephen Michael Cole [1952] Director; Stephen Michael Glynne [1951] Director

Tallentire Energy Limited
Incorporated: 17 January 2012
Net Worth Deficit: £4,980,000 *Total Assets:* £20,532,000
Registered Office: Beaufort Court, Egg Farm Lane, Kings Langley, Herts, WD4 8LR
Activities: Production of electricity
Parent: Trafalgar Wind Holdings Limited
Officers: Dominic James Hearth, Secretary; Steven William Hughes [1972] Generation & Asset Management Director; Fraser Stephen Merry [1968] Director/Chartered Surveyor; Mitesh Raj Patel [1982] Director/Group Financial Controller

Tan Sales (London) Limited
Incorporated: 23 September 1982 *Employees:* 20
Net Worth: £4,545,687 *Total Assets:* £5,814,732
Registered Office: Kimberley House, 31 Burnt Oak Broadway, Edgware, Middlesex, HA8 5LD
Activities: Non-specialised wholesale trade
Officers: Rameshchandra Shah, Secretary; Ankit Shah [1986] Sales Director; Parit Ramesh Shah [1980] Director; Rameshchandra Shah [1949] Director

Tancia (Holdings) Limited
Incorporated: 22 March 2010 *Employees:* 165
Net Worth: £5,158,128 *Total Assets:* £7,723,485
Registered Office: Charles Lake House, Claire Causeway, Crossways Business Park, Dartford, Kent, DA2 6QA
Activities: Activities of other holding companies n.e.c.
Major Shareholder: Nicholas Joseph Cleere
Officers: Nicholas Joseph Cleere, Secretary; Amanda Jane Cleere [1966] Director; Nicholas Joseph Cleere [1952] Director [Irish]

Tancia Limited
Incorporated: 8 September 1994 *Employees:* 165
Net Worth: £4,553,307 *Total Assets:* £7,172,905
Registered Office: Charles Lake House, Claire Causeway, Crossways Business Park, Dartford, Kent, DA2 6QA
Activities: Other business support service activities n.e.c.
Parent: Tancia (Holdings) Limited
Officers: Helen Louise Marin Dyl, Secretary; Amanda Jane Cleere [1966] Marketing Director; Nicholas Joseph Cleere [1952] Director/Partner [Irish]; Helen Louise Marin Dyl [1986] Director/Solicitor, Manager

Tandridge Learning Trust
Incorporated: 10 October 2012 *Employees:* 354
Previous: Warlingham School
Net Worth: £32,195,000 *Total Assets:* £37,693,000
Registered Office: Tandridge Learning Trust, Tithepit, Shaw Lane, Warlingham, Surrey, CR6 9YB
Activities: Primary education
Officers: Paula Chowdhury, Secretary; Richard Calverley Baker [1963] Finance Director; Steven Burn [1961] Director/Finance and Marketing; Alex Ghattas [1971] Director/Finance Manager; David Humphrey Prothero [1946] Director/Education; Karen Jayne Quinton [1959] Director

Tanita International Ltd.
Incorporated: 9 September 1997 *Employees:* 27
Net Worth: £41,427,496 *Total Assets:* £43,626,796
Registered Office: 5th Floor, Hyde Park Hayes 3, 11 Millington Road, Hayes, Middlesex, UB3 4AZ
Activities: Wholesale of other machinery and equipment
Officers: Shinsuke Nakagawa, Secretary; Isamu Kobayashi [1961] Director [Japanese]; Senri Tanida [1972] Director/President of Tanita Corporation [Japanese]; Shunji Tanida [1971] Director [Japanese]

Tanjong Public Limited Company
Incorporated: 2 January 1926
Net Worth: £187,762,768 *Total Assets:* £444,819,264
Registered Office: Elder House, St Georges Business Park, 207 Brooklands Road, Weybridge, Surrey, KT13 0TS
Activities: Activities of head offices
Officers: Wai Ping Goh, Secretary; Ashwin Kumar Das [1976] Director/General Manager of Usaha Tegas Sdn Bhd [Malaysian]; Mazita Binti Mokty [1972] Director/General Counsel of Usaha Tegas Sdn Bhd [Malaysian]; Rohan Rajan Rajasooria [1972] Director/Group Treasurer of Usaha Tegas Sdn Bhd [Malaysian]

O.C. Tanner Limited
Incorporated: 9 March 2001 *Employees:* 37
Net Worth: £4,110,299 *Total Assets:* £8,276,004
Registered Office: 6a Imprimo Park, Lenthall Road, Loughton, Essex, IG10 3UF
Activities: Other business support service activities n.e.c.
Parent: OC Tanner Company
Officers: Scott Nielsen Archibald [1974] Director [American]; Ty Darren Brown [1967] Director [American]; Ian Feaver [1963] Director; Joanna Morley [1979] Director; Robert Mark Ordever [1975] Director; David Allan Petersen [1957] Director/Executive Vice President [American]; Scott David Sperry [1966] Director/Vice President Finance [American]

Tapi Carpets & Floors Limited
Incorporated: 3 October 2014 *Employees:* 398
Net Worth: £8,427,268 *Total Assets:* £40,078,868
Registered Office: 1a Spur Road, Orpington, Kent, BR6 0PH
Activities: Retail sale of carpets, rugs, wall and floor coverings in specialised stores
Officers: Paul Jacobs, Secretary; Neil James Anscomb [1978] Director; William Jack Barker [1989] Director; Graham Roger Betts [1970] Director; Andrew James Brown [1971] Director; Johanna Constantinou [1971] Director; Stephen Charles Davies [1964] Director; Brian Deen [1952] Director; Antony James Evans [1970] Director; Jeremy Christopher Alan Garrish [1960] Director; Charles William Harris [1963] Director; Christine Mary Harris [1956] Director; Martin James Harris [1969] Director; Peter Alexander Harris [1963] Director; Paul Jacobs [1968] Director; Karen Knighton [1961] Director; Terry Collin Moore [1959] Director; Garry Arthur Postle [1967] Director; Deborha Powell [1968] Director; Tracey Carol Skea [1972] Director; Lee James Styles [1968] Director; Michael Thomas Sweeney [1967] Director; Jason Turner [1971] Director

Tara Mobile Ltd
Incorporated: 23 December 2011
Net Worth: £7,498,986 *Total Assets:* £7,504,500
Registered Office: Battle House, East Barnet Road, Barnet, Herts, EN4 8RR
Activities: Other mining and quarrying n.e.c.
Officers: Dipak Darbari [1951] Director/Management Consultant

Tarian Investment Co. Limited
Incorporated: 8 April 1953 *Employees:* 3
Net Worth: £7,924,884 *Total Assets:* £8,991,018
Registered Office: Unit 5 Manor Farm, Manor Road North, Thames Ditton, Surrey, KT7 0BH
Activities: Other letting and operating of own or leased real estate
Officers: Simon Harvey Jones, Secretary/Property Manager; Denis Rossiter Carpenter [1938] Director/Retired RAF Officer; Rodney Duncan Jones [1940] Director/Builder; Simon Harvey Jones [1967] Director/Property Investment

TASIS The American School in England
Incorporated: 15 December 1981 *Employees:* 239
Net Worth: £3,160,710 *Total Assets:* £20,860,680
Registered Office: Coldharbour Lane, Thorpe, Surrey, TW20 8TE
Activities: Pre-primary education
Officers: David Riley, Secretary; Fernando Gonzalez [1948] Administrative Director [American]; Chawki Karam [1985] Director/Banker; David Harold King [1951] Director/Chartered Accountant; Fiona Elisabeth Stafford Loveridge [1962] Director; Laurence Eric McKell [1964] Director/Teacher; Teresa Ferguson McLaughlin [1964] Director/Homemaker [American]; John Stuurman Wyper [1950] Managing Director Hines Europe [American]

TASIS UK Limited
Incorporated: 30 October 1981 *Employees:* 239
Net Worth: £3,160,710 *Total Assets:* £20,860,670
Registered Office: Coldharbour Lane, Thorpe, Surrey, TW20 8TE
Activities: Pre-primary education
Officers: David Riley, Secretary; Lynn Fleming Aeschlimann [1945] Director/Company Administrator [American]; William Thomas Fleming [1943] Director [American]; Fernando Gonzalez [1948] Director [American]

Tata Global Beverages Capital Limited
Incorporated: 12 September 2006
Net Worth: £89,858,000 *Total Assets:* £162,334,000
Registered Office: 325 Oldfield Lane North, Greenford, Middlesex, UB6 0AZ
Activities: Activities of other holding companies n.e.c.
Parent: Tata Global Beverages Limited
Officers: Miles Thomas Bailey, Secretary; Miles Thomas Bailey [1974] Director/General Counsel & Company Secretary; John Jacob [1962] Director/Vice President-Group Finance [Indian]; Krishna Kumar Lakshmanan [1958] Director [Indian]; Ajoy Kumar Misra [1957] Director [Indian]; Shirish Amratlal Shah [1959] Director/Chartered Accountant; Manesh Thakrar [1961] Director

Tata Global Beverages GB Limited
Incorporated: 9 February 1995 *Employees:* 359
Net Worth: £202,342,000 *Total Assets:* £241,331,008
Registered Office: 325 Oldfield Lane North, Greenford, Middlesex, UB6 0AZ
Activities: Non-specialised wholesale of food, beverages and tobacco
Parent: Tata Global Beverages Holdings Limited
Officers: Miles Thomas Bailey, Secretary; Adil Ahmad [1962] Director/Service, Global CMO [Indian]; John Mark Edward Burdett [1967] Director/Chartered Engineer; Krishna Kumar Lakshmanan [1958] Director [Indian]; Manesh Thakrar [1961] Director

Tata Global Beverages Group Limited
Incorporated: 3 September 1999 *Employees:* 624
Net Worth: £506,776,992 *Total Assets:* £683,667,008
Registered Office: 325 Oldfield Lane North, Greenford, Middlesex, UB6 0AZ
Activities: Other credit granting n.e.c.
Shareholder: Tata Global Beverages Capital Limited
Officers: Miles Thomas Bailey, Secretary; Adil Ahmad [1962] Director/Service, Global CMO [Indian]; John Mark Edward Burdett [1967] Director/Chartered Engineer; Krishna Kumar Lakshmanan [1958] Director [Indian]; Ajoy Kumar Misra [1957] Director [Indian]; Shirish Amratlal Shah [1959] Director/Chartered Accountant; Manesh Thakrar [1961] Director/Chief Financial Officer - EMEA

Tata Global Beverages Holdings Limited
Incorporated: 18 October 1996
Net Worth: £174,531,008 *Total Assets:* £189,515,008
Registered Office: 325 Oldfield Lane North, Greenford, Middlesex, UB6 0AZ
Activities: Activities of other holding companies n.e.c.
Parent: Tata Global Beverages Group Limited
Officers: Miles Thomas Bailey, Secretary; Miles Thomas Bailey [1974] Director/General Counsel & Company Secretary; John Jacob [1962] Director/Vice President-Group Finance [Indian]; Krishna Kumar Lakshmanan [1958] Finance Director [Indian]; Manesh Thakrar [1961] Director

Tata Global Beverages Investments Limited
Incorporated: 12 September 2006 *Employees:* 5
Net Worth: £365,472,992 *Total Assets:* £371,004,000
Registered Office: 325 Oldfield Lane North, Greenford, Middlesex, UB6 0AZ
Activities: Activities of other holding companies n.e.c.
Parent: Tata Global Beverages Group Limited
Officers: Miles Thomas Bailey, Secretary; Krishna Kumar Lakshmanan [1958] Director [Indian]; Ajoy Kumar Misra [1957] Director [Indian]; Shirish Amratlal Shah [1959] Director/Chartered Accountant; Manesh Thakrar [1961] Director/Chief Financial Officer - EMEA

Tata Global Beverages Overseas Holdings Limited
Incorporated: 3 February 1995
Net Worth Deficit: £44,601,000 *Total Assets:* £51,138,000
Registered Office: 325 Oldfield Lane North, Greenford, Middlesex, UB6 0AZ
Activities: Activities of other holding companies n.e.c.
Parent: Tata Global Beverages Holdings Limited
Officers: Miles Thomas Bailey, Secretary; John Jacob [1962] Director/Vice President-Group Finance [Indian]; Krishna Kumar Lakshmanan [1958] Director [Indian]; Ajoy Kumar Misra [1957] Director [Indian]; Manesh Thakrar [1961] Director

Tata Global Beverages Services Limited
Incorporated: 9 January 1995 *Employees:* 53
Net Worth: £345,663,008 *Total Assets:* £529,515,008
Registered Office: 325 Oldfield Lane North, Greenford, Middlesex, UB6 0AZ
Activities: Activities of head offices
Parent: Tata Global Beverages Holdings Limited
Officers: Miles Thomas Bailey, Secretary; Krishna Kumar Lakshmanan [1958] Director [Indian]; Ajoy Kumar Misra [1957] Director [Indian]; Manesh Thakrar [1961] Director

Tati Company Limited
Incorporated: 6 March 1914
Net Worth: £395,462,976 *Total Assets:* £407,121,664
Registered Office: York House, Empire Way, Wembley, Middlesex, HA9 0FQ
Activities: Buying and selling of own real estate
Officers: David Alan Nathan [1949] Director/Senior Partner - Grant Thornton Accountants [South African]; Neville Sweidan [1941] Director/Head of Forensic Services - Grant Thornton [South African]; Sifelani Thapelo [1965] Director/Lawyer [Botswanan]

The Taunton Linac Company Limited
Incorporated: 16 March 2005
Net Worth Deficit: £6,899,000 *Total Assets:* £27,053,000
Registered Office: 8 White Oak Square, London Road, Swanley, Kent, BR8 7AG
Activities: Combined facilities support activities
Parent: The Taunton Linac (Holdings) Company Limited
Officers: Benjamin Christopher Jacob Dean [1979] Director/Investment Manager; Richard Keith Sheehan [1975] Investment Director

Tavern Quay Developments LLP
Incorporated: 18 July 2013
Net Worth: £1,148,902 *Total Assets:* £8,811,165
Registered Office: CKR House, East Hill, Dartford, Kent, DA1 1RZ

Tax Computer Systems Limited
Incorporated: 31 January 2005 *Employees:* 71
Net Worth: £2,983,258 *Total Assets:* £13,543,293
Registered Office: Ground Floor, Magna House, 18-32 London Road, Staines upon Thames, Middlesex, TW18 4BP
Activities: Business and domestic software development
Parent: Tax Systems Holdings Limited
Officers: Kevin Paul Goggin [1962] Director/Chartered Accountant; Gavin Anthony Peter Lyons [1977] Director

Tax Systems Holdings Limited
Incorporated: 6 June 2017
Net Worth: £73,252,864 *Total Assets:* £76,449,880
Registered Office: Ground Floor, Magna House, 18-32 London Road, Staines upon Thames, Middlesex, TW18 4BP
Activities: Activities of other holding companies n.e.c.
Parent: Tax Systems PLC
Officers: Kevin Paul Goggin [1962] Finance Director; Gavin Anthony Peter Lyons [1977] Director

Tax Systems PLC
Incorporated: 17 December 2003 *Employees:* 82
Previous: Eco City Vehicles PLC
Net Worth: £47,279,000 *Total Assets:* £88,376,000
Registered Office: Ground Floor, Magna House, 18-32 London Road, Staines upon Thames, Middlesex, TW18 4BP
Activities: Activities of distribution holding companies
Shareholder: MXC Capital Limited
Officers: Kevin Goggin, Secretary; Linda Janice Beal [1961] Director; Clive Nathan Carver [1961] Director; Paul David Gibson [1964] Director/Business Development; Kevin Paul Goggin [1962] Finance Director; Gavin Anthony Peter Lyons [1977] Director

John A.Taylor & Sons Limited
Incorporated: 29 December 1955 *Employees:* 7
Net Worth: £2,522,355 *Total Assets:* £8,263,199
Registered Office: 1 Penta Court, Station Road, Borehamwood, Herts, WD6 1SL
Activities: Non-specialised wholesale of food, beverages and tobacco
Major Shareholder: Ron Auerbach
Officers: Roni Auerbach, Secretary; Chantal Auerbach [1960] Director; Roni Auerbach [1955] Director

R.G. Taylor Engineering Limited
Incorporated: 7 December 1967 *Employees:* 24
Net Worth: £3,096,484 *Total Assets:* £6,271,519
Registered Office: 71 Goldings Road, Loughton, Essex, IG10 2QW
Activities: Plumbing, heat and air-conditioning installation
Shareholders: Ian John Berney; Angela Ivy Taylor
Officers: Andrew Richard Taylor, Secretary; Ian John Berney [1968] Director/Engineer; Julie Angela Kelley [1974] Director; Savvas Stephen Matheou [1980] Director; Christopher Monk [1962] Director/Heating Engineer; Andrew Richard Taylor [1972] Director; Angela Ivy Taylor [1944] Director

Taylor Mac Limited
Incorporated: 25 February 2011 *Employees:* 4
Net Worth: £21,227 *Total Assets:* £5,584,204
Registered Office: Batchworth House, Batchworth Place, Church Street, Rickmansworth, Herts, WD3 1JE
Activities: Construction of domestic buildings
Shareholders: Catherine Elizabeth McArdle; Christopher Paul Taylor
Officers: Catherine Elizabeth McArdle [1978] Director; James McArdle [1942] Director [Irish]; Christopher Paul Taylor [1980] Director

Taylor Wentworth Limited
Incorporated: 25 February 1999
Net Worth: £3,536,156 *Total Assets:* £6,173,196
Registered Office: Epic House, 128 Fulwell Road, Teddington, Middlesex, TW11 0RQ
Activities: Renting and operating of Housing Association real estate
Shareholders: Susan Deborah Daniel; William Wentworth Daniel
Officers: William Wentworth Daniel, Secretary/Director; Susan Deborah Daniel [1964] Director; William Wentworth Daniel [1965] Director

Taylor Woodrow Construction
Incorporated: 19 June 1996 *Employees:* 154
Net Worth: £84,972,000 *Total Assets:* £132,612,000
Registered Office: Astral House, Imperial Way, Watford, Herts, WD24 4WW
Activities: Development of building projects
Parent: Vinci Construction UK Limited
Officers: Bruno Michel Dupety [1956] Director/Engineer [French]; Julian Paul Gatward [1966] Director/Civil Engineer; Anthony Kennedy Raikes [1964] Director/Chartered Civil Engineer

Taylors Legal Limited
Incorporated: 28 January 2016 *Employees:* 44
Net Worth: £237,828 *Total Assets:* £8,566,699
Registered Office: 184 Manor Road, Chigwell, Essex, IG7 5PZ
Activities: Activities of patent and copyright agents; other legal activities n.e.c.
Shareholders: Nicola Clare Mercer; Elliott Robert Costa
Officers: Elliott Robert Costa [1975] Director; Nicola Daniel [1980] Director; Shamma Kambo [1989] Director; Nicola Clare Mercer [1972] Director

Tazaki Foods Limited
Incorporated: 27 July 1978 *Employees:* 84
Net Worth: £10,340,511 *Total Assets:* £15,858,909
Registered Office: 12 Innova Way, Innova Park, Enfield, Middlesex, EN3 7FL
Activities: Wholesale of meat and meat products
Parent: T. Tazaki & Company Limited
Officers: Masumi Uetsuji, Secretary; Chikahiro Furukawa [1961] Director/Food Importer [Japanese]; Kazuyoshi Ito [1961] Director [Japanese]; Masumi Uetsuji [1963] Director [Japanese]

TBC Bank Group PLC
Incorporated: 26 February 2016 *Employees:* 6,993
Net Worth: £724,201,920 *Total Assets:* £5,045,101,056
Registered Office: Elder House, St Georges Business Park, 207 Brooklands Road, Weybridge, Surrey, KT13 0TS
Activities: Activities of financial services holding companies
Officers: Vakhtang Butskhrikidze [1970] Director [Georgian]; Maria Luisa Cicognani [1964] Director [Italian]; Nikoloz Enukidze [1970] Director; Nicholas Dominic Haag [1958] Director; Badri Japaridze [1960] Director [Georgian]; Tsira Kemularia [1977] Director; Mamuka Khazaradze [1966] Director [Georgian]; Eric Jeyarajan Rajendra [1958] Director [American]; Giorgi Shagidze [1975] Director [Georgian]

TBE (Southern) Limited
Incorporated: 8 June 1983
Net Worth: £32,340,068 *Total Assets:* £38,875,668
Registered Office: 2nd Floor, The Atrium, 31 Church Road, Ashford, Middlesex, TW15 2UD
Activities: Other letting and operating of own or leased real estate
Parent: JWL Property Finance Limited
Officers: Marie Annick Avis, Secretary; Adrian Eyre Lloyd [1979] Director; Britta Adrienne Lloyd [1945] Director/Psychotherapist [Swiss]; Jeremy William Lloyd [1942] Director/Banker; Bryan Kevin Meehan [1968] Director/Entrepreneur [Irish]; Antonia Gillian Silcock [1985] Director; Colin Laird Walker-Robson [1952] Director/Chartered Accountant

TBG (1) 2009 Limited
Incorporated: 14 October 2009
Net Worth: £507,999,008 *Total Assets:* £507,999,008
Registered Office: Berkeley House, 19 Portsmouth Road, Cobham, Surrey, KT11 1JG
Activities: Development of building projects
Parent: The Berkeley Group PLC
Officers: Jared Stephen Philip Cranney, Secretary; David Martin Lowry [1981] Director; Robert Charles Grenville Perrins [1965] Director; Anthony William Pidgley [1947] Director; Richard James Stearn [1968] Director

TBG (3) 2009 Limited
Incorporated: 14 October 2009
Net Worth: £555,097,984 *Total Assets:* £1,382,528,000
Registered Office: Berkeley House, 19 Portsmouth Road, Cobham, Surrey, KT11 1JG
Activities: Development of building projects
Parent: The Berkeley Group PLC
Officers: Jared Stephen Philip Cranney, Secretary; David Martin Lowry [1981] Director; Robert Charles Grenville Perrins [1965] Director; Anthony William Pidgley [1947] Director; Richard James Stearn [1968] Director

TBG (4) Limited
Incorporated: 5 October 2010
Net Worth: £525,227,008 *Total Assets:* £525,227,008
Registered Office: Berkeley House, 19 Portsmouth Road, Cobham, Surrey, KT11 1JG
Activities: Other business support service activities n.e.c.
Shareholders: TBG (1) 2009 Limited; The Berkeley Group PLC
Officers: Jared Stephen Philip Cranney, Secretary; David Martin Lowry [1981] Director; Robert Charles Grenville Perrins [1965] Director; Anthony William Pidgley [1947] Director; Richard James Stearn [1968] Director

TBG Holding C Limited
Incorporated: 13 August 2013 *Employees:* 371
Net Worth: £6,148,267 *Total Assets:* £16,413,738
Registered Office: 24 High Street, Ewell, Surrey, KT17 1SJ
Activities: Activities of other holding companies n.e.c.
Shareholder: Jonathan Daniel Brown
Officers: Jonathan Daniel Brown [1967] Director/Heating Engineer

TC Facilities Management Limited
Incorporated: 11 December 1990 *Employees:* 4,243
Net Worth: £4,617,561 *Total Assets:* £24,822,880
Registered Office: Sapphire House, 74-76 Walton Street, Walton on the Hill, Tadworth, Surrey, KT20 7RU
Activities: General cleaning of buildings
Major Shareholder: Trevor George Cripps
Officers: Simon James Cripps [1970] Director; Trevor George Cripps [1944] Director; Daniel Jacobus Jacobs [1976] Finance Director; Anthony William Reed [1963] Director

TCA Investments Limited
Incorporated: 27 October 2011
Net Worth: £558,391 *Total Assets:* £7,467,735
Registered Office: High Street Centre, 137-139 High Street, Beckenham, Kent, BR3 1AG
Activities: Management of real estate on a fee or contract basis
Shareholders: Mary McGrath; Patrick Joseph McGrath
Officers: Quraish Sajjad Hussain Adamally [1980] Director; Mary McGrath [1963] Director [Irish]; Patrick Joseph McGrath [1955] Director [Irish]

Tchibo Coffee International Limited
Incorporated: 23 May 1963 *Employees:* 149
Net Worth: £24,446,268 *Total Assets:* £28,856,822
Registered Office: Tchibo House, 7-8 Blenheim Road, Epsom, Surrey, KT19 9BE
Activities: Non-specialised wholesale of food, beverages and tobacco
Officers: Kate Asamoa, Secretary; Kate Elizabeth Jane Asamoa [1976] Finance Director; Paul Chadderton [1963] Managing Director

TCL Manufacturing Limited
Incorporated: 26 January 1990 *Employees:* 149
Net Worth: £8,647,676 *Total Assets:* £10,205,224
Registered Office: Unit 1 Gateway XIII, Ferry Lane, Rainham, Essex, RM13 9JY
Activities: Manufacture of other fabricated metal products n.e.c.
Parent: Fortune Brands Home & Security, Inc.
Officers: Angela Pla, Secretary; Nicholas Ian Fink [1974] Director/President [American]; Steven James Geary [1966] Director/Business Executive; John D Lee [1972] Director [American]; Ian Ross Walker [1977] Director

TCR New Limited
Incorporated: 10 February 2017
Net Worth Deficit: £3,480,386 *Total Assets:* £48,970,824
Registered Office: 22 Barn Rise, Wembley, Middlesex, HA9 9NQ
Activities: Other letting and operating of own or leased real estate
Parent: TCR Finance Limited
Officers: Sarah Davies, Secretary; Anthony David Chambers [1955] Director/Property Developer; Sarah Davies [1976] Director/Property Investor

TCR UK Limited
Incorporated: 5 October 2001 *Employees:* 218
Net Worth: £6,047,381 *Total Assets:* £46,323,968
Registered Office: Dixcart House, Addlestone Road, Bourne Business Park, Addlestone, Surrey, KT15 2LE
Activities: Renting and leasing of freight air transport equipment
Parent: Envol Investments Limited
Officers: Patrice de Hemptinne, Secretary; Tom Joeri W Bellekens [1978] Director/Chief Operating Officer [Belgian]; Benoit Biebuyck [1972] Director/Chief Finance Officer [Belgian]; Jan de Leeuw [1974] Managing Director [Belgian]; Kristof Philips [1980] Director/General Manager [Belgian]

Tearfund
Incorporated: 13 November 1970 *Employees:* 878
Net Worth: £32,632,000 *Total Assets:* £37,725,000
Registered Office: 100 Church Road, Teddington, Middlesex, TW11 8QE
Activities: Other social work activities without accommodation n.e.c.
Officers: Mary Ann Drew, Secretary; Stephanie Clare Biden [1980] Director/Solicitor; William Ian Curtis [1953] Director/International Development Consultant; John Davidson [1959] Director/Solicitor; Stephanie Jane Heald [1963] Director/Publisher, Editor & Writer; Sally Ann Jones-Evans [1966] Director; Anna Elisabeth Laszlo [1969] Director; Philip Duncan Loney [1964] Director; Rev Mark Melluish [1959] Director/Vicar; Reverend Harold Creeth Miller [1950] Director/Bishop of Down and Dromore; Jillian Mills [1958] Director/Consultant; Rosemary Winifred Nuamah Williams [1974] Director/Self Employed; Anthony Dangasuk Poggo [1964] Director/Bishop [South Sudanese]; Craig Rowland [1956] Director; John Shaw [1951] Director

Tech 21 UK Limited
Incorporated: 20 November 2005 *Employees:* 81
Net Worth: £19,051,154 *Total Assets:* £64,286,460
Registered Office: Syds Quay, Eel Pie Island, Twickenham, Middlesex, TW1 3DY
Activities: Other manufacturing n.e.c.
Major Shareholder: Jason Lloyd Roberts
Officers: Peter Vernon Charles Cass, Secretary; Peter Vernon Charles Cass [1955] Director/Accountant; Jason Lloyd Roberts [1969] Director

Technical Staffing Resources Limited
Incorporated: 14 January 2011 *Employees:* 5
Net Worth: £556,124 *Total Assets:* £66,808,688
Registered Office: Hill Park Court, Springfield Drive, Leatherhead, Surrey, KT22 7NL
Activities: Other activities of employment placement agencies
Parent: Kellogg Brown & Root International Group Holdings LLP
Officers: Susan Meirion Owen, Secretary; David Lindsay Gibson [1962] Director/Vice President Operations-EMEA; Jalal Jay Ibrahim [1960] Director [American]; Martin Nelhams [1960] Director

Teddington 2 Limited
Incorporated: 22 December 2009 *Employees:* 2
Net Worth: £223,000,992 *Total Assets:* £350,064,000
Registered Office: LGC, Queens Road, Teddington, Middlesex, TW11 0LY
Activities: Other business support service activities n.e.c.
Parent: LGC Science Group Limited
Officers: Navneet Kaur Ogle, Secretary; Simon Lawrence Parsons [1969] Finance Director; Timothy Michael Robinson [1963] Director

Teddington School
Incorporated: 4 July 2012 *Employees:* 141
Net Worth: £42,265,624 *Total Assets:* £44,062,220
Registered Office: Teddington School, Broom Road, Teddington, Middlesex, TW11 9PJ
Activities: General secondary education
Officers: Andrea Louise Arbiter, Secretary; Carl Ainley [1969] Director/Chartered Civil Engineer & Project Manager; Catherine Balfour-Roberts [1971] Director/Senior Lecturer; Anne Davison [1969] Director/Head of Finance; Daryl Greenwood [1959] Director/Marketing Manager; Juliet Claire Hartridge [1970] Director/Gardener; Trevor Alexander Huggins [1958] Director/Journalist; Andrew Oliva-Hauxwell [1973] Director/Charity Executive; Sarah Tate [1963] Director/Teacher; Katie Wade [1973] Finance Director; Marie Wylde [1983] Director/Accountant

Tees Limited
Incorporated: 16 March 1981 *Employees:* 12
Net Worth: £2,262,331 *Total Assets:* £5,817,848
Registered Office: Unit 1-8 Centenary Industrial Estate, Jeffreys Road, Enfield, Middlesex, EN3 7UF
Activities: Non-specialised wholesale of food, beverages and tobacco
Parent: TFC Holdings London Limited
Officers: Sercan Erkarslan, Secretary/Manager [French]; Ercan Ucur [1970] Director; Huseyin Ucur [1945] Director

Telbridge Motor Company Limited
Incorporated: 21 February 2003 *Employees:* 2
Net Worth: £1,237,708 *Total Assets:* £5,443,740
Registered Office: Allen House, 1 Westmead House, Sutton, Surrey, SM1 4LA
Activities: Sale of new cars and light motor vehicles
Major Shareholder: Terry Richard Pestell
Officers: Terry Richard Pestell [1958] Director

Telecoms World (Group) Limited
Incorporated: 15 December 2014
Net Worth: £10,024,450 *Total Assets:* £10,033,451
Registered Office: 2 Kingfisher House, Crayfields Business Park, New Mill Road, Orpington, Kent, BR5 3QG
Activities: Other telecommunications activities
Shareholders: David William Noble; Kelly Ellen Noble
Officers: Neil Anthony Barrall [1966] Director; David William Noble [1962] Director; Kelly Ellen Noble [1969] Director

Teledyne Limited
Incorporated: 19 October 1999 *Employees:* 540
Net Worth: £98,531,000 *Total Assets:* £139,464,992
Registered Office: Aviation House, The Lodge, Harmondsworth Lane, West Drayton, Middlesex, UB7 0LQ
Activities: Manufacture of electronic components
Parent: Rhombi Holdings Limited
Officers: Nicholas James Wargent, Secretary; Susan Lee Main [1958] Director/Senior Vice President and Chief Financial Officer [American]; Robert Mehrabian [1941] Director/Corporate Executive [American]; Ian Michael Skiggs [1967] Director/General Manager; Nicholas James Wargent [1973] Director/Solicitor

Telford Homes City North Limited
Incorporated: 3 February 2014
Net Worth: £18,768,000 *Total Assets:* £35,179,000
Registered Office: Telford House, Queens Gate, Britannia Road, Waltham Cross, Herts, EN8 7TF
Activities: Development of building projects
Shareholder: Telford Homes Regeneration Developments Holdings Limited
Officers: Monique Chantal Woudberg, Secretary; David Myles Campbell [1965] Group Sales and Marketing Director; Jonathan Graham Di-Stefano [1974] Director/Chief Executive; John Anthony FitzGenerald [1971] Director/Chief Executive; Katie Rogers [1981] Finance Director

Telford Homes PLC
Incorporated: 1 December 2000 *Employees:* 265
Net Worth: £231,091,008 *Total Assets:* £427,688,000
Registered Office: Telford House, Queensgate, Britannia Road, Waltham Cross, Herts, EN8 7TF
Activities: Development of building projects
Officers: Monique Chantal Woudberg, Secretary; David Myles Campbell [1965] Sales and Marketing Director; Jonathan Graham di Stefano [1974] Financial Director Property; Jane Margaret Earl [1957] Director/Charity Chief Executive; John Anthony FitzGenerald [1971] Managing Director Telford Home; Jerome Patrick Geoghegan [1967] Group Land and Planning Director; Katie Rogers [1981] Financial Director; Andrew Graham Wiseman [1956] Director

Telida Limited
Incorporated: 23 May 2013
Net Worth: £1,538,822 *Total Assets:* £8,044,808
Registered Office: Hill House, Lowlands Road, Harrow, Middlesex, HA1 3EQ
Activities: Development of building projects
Major Shareholder: Donovan Gijsbertus Wijsmuller
Officers: Brian Martin Comer [1960] Director [Irish]; Luke Andrew Comer [1957] Director [Irish]

Templecare Limited
Incorporated: 29 June 1995
Net Worth: £978,938 *Total Assets:* £43,912,432
Registered Office: 238 Station Road, Addlestone, Surrey, KT15 2PS
Activities: Activities of other holding companies n.e.c.
Parent: Minster Care Management Limited
Officers: John Neal Alflatt, Secretary; Mahesh Shivabhai Patel [1953] Director; Surendra Shivabhai Patel [1945] Director

Templefields House LLP
Incorporated: 17 December 2015
Net Worth: £7,954,156 *Total Assets:* £7,956,809
Registered Office: Wrencote House, 123 High Street, Croydon, Surrey, CR0 0XJ

Tempur Sealy International Limited
Incorporated: 14 March 2003 *Employees:* 38
Net Worth: £3,160,000 *Total Assets:* £8,056,000
Registered Office: Tempur House, Caxton Point, Printing House Lane, Hayes, Middlesex, UB3 1AP
Activities: Activities of head offices
Officers: David Montgomery, Secretary; David Montgomery [1960] Director/General Manager; Bhaskar Rao [1965] Director/Chief Financial Officer [American]

Tempur UK Limited
Incorporated: 16 September 1992 *Employees:* 106
Net Worth: £9,528,000 *Total Assets:* £26,838,000
Registered Office: Caxton Point, Printing House Lane, Hayes, Middlesex, UB3 1AP
Activities: Retail of furniture, lighting, and similar (not musical instruments or scores) in specialised store
Parent: Dan Foam AS
Officers: Paula Lesley Thomas, Secretary; Tobin David James [1970] Managing Director; David Montgomery [1960] Director/General Manager; Bhaskar Rao [1965] Director/Chief Financial Officer [American]

Ten Levels Ltd
Incorporated: 19 November 2014 *Employees:* 1
Net Worth: £2,922,146 *Total Assets:* £6,155,892
Registered Office: 14a Farwig Lane, Bromley, Kent, BR1 3RB
Activities: Other letting and operating of own or leased real estate
Major Shareholder: Lucy Pitham
Officers: Lucy Pitham [1985] Director

Ten Motives Limited
Incorporated: 25 November 2008 *Employees:* 22
Net Worth: £4,700,000 *Total Assets:* £5,173,000
Registered Office: 1 Eton Street, Richmond, Surrey, TW9 1EF
Activities: Other retail sale of new goods in specialised stores (not commercial art galleries and opticians)
Parent: Nicoventures Holdings Limited
Officers: Jessica Munday, Secretary; Nigel Graeme Hardy [1968] Director/Head of Sales, UK & Ireland; William Richard Darvell Hill [1977] Director; Alexander Kolpakov [1981] Director; Dimitri Alexandros Tounis [1980] Director; Gemma Bridget Webb [1963] Director [Irish]

Tennay Properties Limited
Incorporated: 2 March 1962 *Employees:* 11
Net Worth: £14,095,664 *Total Assets:* £16,681,209
Registered Office: Terminal House, Station Approach, Shepperton, Surrey, TW17 8AS
Activities: Other letting and operating of own or leased real estate
Parent: Ian Allan Group Limited
Officers: Derek Arthur Hart, Secretary; David Ian Allan [1954] Executive Director; Edwin Paul Allan [1957] Executive Director

Teoco UK Limited
Incorporated: 12 November 2013
Net Worth Deficit: £23,983,700 *Total Assets:* £28,921,400
Registered Office: c/o Aircom International Ltd, Pascal Place, Randalls Way, Leatherhead, Surrey, KT22 7TW
Activities: Other telecommunications activities
Major Shareholder: Atul Jain
Officers: Philip Merritt Giuntini [1946] Director [American]; Atul Jain [1960] Director/CEO - Chairman [American]

TER AG Ltd.
Incorporated: 8 December 2011
Net Worth: £5,156,906 *Total Assets:* £5,205,477
Registered Office: Office 184, Regico Offices, The Old Bank, 153 The Parade, High Street, Watford, Herts, WD17 1NA
Activities: Other service activities n.e.c.
Major Shareholder: Maksims Ter-Oganesov
Officers: Maksims Ter-Oganesovs [1967] Director [Latvian]

Terminus House Harlow LLP
Incorporated: 28 April 2016
Net Worth: £9,754,025 *Total Assets:* £10,221,978
Registered Office: Wrencote House, 123 Croydon High Street, Croydon, Surrey, CR0 0XJ

Terra Trade and Engineering LLP
Incorporated: 16 July 2007
Net Worth: £7,806,530 *Total Assets:* £7,939,795
Registered Office: Wayman House, 141 Wickham Road, Shirley, Croydon, Surrey, CR0 8TE

TES Enterprise Solutions Ltd
Incorporated: 27 November 2012 *Employees:* 1
Previous: Tectre Enterprise Solutions Ltd
Net Worth: £783,964 *Total Assets:* £28,815,054
Registered Office: 10 Western Road, Romford, Essex, RM1 3JT
Activities: Agents specialised in the sale of other particular products
Major Shareholder: Ronald William James Argent
Officers: Ronald William James Argent [1953] Director; Stephen Southern [1953] Director

TES-AMM Europe Holdings Ltd
Incorporated: 17 September 2009 *Employees:* 9
Previous: Dataserv Group Holdings Limited
Net Worth Deficit: £257,093 *Total Assets:* £11,549,366
Registered Office: Unit 5 Radius Park, Faggs Road, Feltham, Middlesex, TW14 0NG
Activities: Activities of head offices
Parent: TES-AMM (Singapore) Pte. Ltd
Officers: Stephen Maxwell Graham [1970] Director; Gary Bewick Steele [1971] Director

TES-AMM UK Ltd
Incorporated: 23 May 1995 *Employees:* 36
Previous: Dataserv Limited
Net Worth: £4,401,975 *Total Assets:* £7,622,408
Registered Office: Unit 5 Radius Park, Faggs Road, Feltham, Middlesex, TW14 0NG
Activities: Wholesale of computers, computer peripheral equipment and software
Shareholders: TES-AMM Europe Holdings Ltd; Dataserv Group Holdings Limited
Officers: Gary Alan Chesterman, Secretary; Stephen Maxwell Graham [1970] Director

Tesla Motors Limited
Incorporated: 28 February 2002 *Employees:* 432
Net Worth: £17,905,932 *Total Assets:* £314,548,416
Registered Office: 197 Horton Road, West Drayton, Middlesex, UB7 8JD
Activities: Manufacture of motor vehicles
Parent: Tesla, Inc.
Officers: Marc Jesus Cerda [1966] Director/Business Executive [American]; Vaibhav Taneja [1978] Director/Business Executive [American]; Stephan William Werkman [1973] Director/Business Executive [Dutch]

Test Equipment Asset Management Limited
Incorporated: 29 March 2006
Net Worth Deficit: £28,093,000 *Total Assets:* £39,761,000
Registered Office: Unit 1 Waverley Industrial Estate, Hailsham Drive, Harrow, Middlesex, HA1 4TR
Activities: Other professional, scientific and technical activities n.e.c.
Officers: Nigel Brown [1957] Director; John Joseph Hafferty [1956] Director/Chief Financial Officer [American]; Paul Joseph McCloskey [1960] Sales Director

Texcel (2011) Limited
Incorporated: 22 February 2011 *Employees:* 114
Net Worth: £3,224,932 *Total Assets:* £6,148,046
Registered Office: Parkside Works, Thames Road, Crayford, Kent, DA1 4SB
Activities: Activities of other holding companies n.e.c.
Shareholders: William Heaney Bryce; Andrew Nigel McLeod; Peter John Shawyer
Officers: Luke Vincett, Secretary; William Heaney Bryce [1947] Director; Andrew Nigel McLeod [1964] Director; Peter John Shawyer [1957] Director; Luke John Vincett [1973] Director

Texcel Developments Ltd
Incorporated: 22 November 1982 *Employees:* 4
Net Worth: £4,826,506 *Total Assets:* £9,087,953
Registered Office: Parkside Works, Thames Road, Crayford, Kent, DA1 4SB
Activities: Other letting and operating of own or leased real estate
Shareholder: Graham William Bryce
Officers: Graham William Bryce [1979] Director/Property Administrator; William Heaney Bryce [1947] Director/Engineer; Peter John Shawyer [1957] Director/Engineer

Texcel Technology PLC
Incorporated: 3 May 1991 *Employees:* 114
Net Worth: £3,146,272 *Total Assets:* £6,148,036
Registered Office: Thames Road, Crayford, Kent, DA1 4SB
Activities: Manufacture of electronic components
Parent: Texcel (2011) Limited
Officers: Luke John Vincett, Secretary; William Heaney Bryce [1947] Director/Chairman; Andrew Nigel McLeod [1964] Managing Director; Peter John Shawyer [1957] Director; Luke John Vincett [1973] Finance Director

TFC Holdings London Limited
Incorporated: 26 September 2011 *Employees:* 254
Net Worth: £11,990,166 *Total Assets:* £35,875,512
Registered Office: Unit 1-8 Centenary Industrial Estate, Jeffreys Road, Enfield, Middlesex, EN3 7UF
Activities: Activities of other holding companies n.e.c.
Shareholders: UCAR Investment Ltd; Huseyin Ucur
Officers: Ercan Ucur, Secretary; Ercan Ucur [1970] Director; Huseyin Ucur [1945] Director

TFC Properties Limited
Incorporated: 23 October 2007 *Employees:* 1
Net Worth: £829,395 *Total Assets:* £5,533,989
Registered Office: 66 Lancaster Avenue, Hadley Wood, Barnet, Herts, EN4 0EU
Activities: Buying and selling of own real estate
Shareholders: Floros Christodoulou; Theodora Christodoulou
Officers: Floros Christodoulou, Secretary/Managing Director; Floros Christodoulou [1958] Managing Director; Theodora Christodoulou [1962] Director/Property Developer

TGS Geophysical Company (UK) Limited
Incorporated: 6 March 2006
Net Worth Deficit: £14,329,054 *Total Assets:* £43,833,228
Registered Office: 1 The Crescent, Surbiton, Surrey, KT6 4BN
Activities: Support activities for petroleum and natural gas mining
Parent: TGS-Nopec Geophysical Company ASA
Officers: Paul William Bradbury [1978] Director/Business Executive; Erik Finnstrom [1957] Director/Business Executive [American]; Tanya Flor Herwanger [1973] Director/Businesswoman [Belizean]

TH UK & Ireland Limited
Incorporated: 29 July 2016 *Employees:* 113
Net Worth: £24,321,048 *Total Assets:* £29,562,736
Registered Office: Fortune House, Crabtree Office Village, Eversley Way, Egham, Surrey, TW20 8RY
Activities: Unlicenced restaurants and cafes
Officers: Gurprit Dhaliwal [1982] Director; Jaipal Singh Dhillon [1990] Director; Kevin John Hydes [1978] Director/Chief Financial and Commercial Officer; Surinderjit Singh Kandola [1965] Director; Alexandre Grein de Macedo [1977] Director/President, Tim Hortons [American]; Lucas Lopes Muniz [1986] Director/President, Tim Hortons International [Canadian]

Thames Ditton Sports and Squash Club Limited
Incorporated: 12 January 1977 *Employees:* 159
Net Worth: £4,612,340 *Total Assets:* £7,496,442
Registered Office: Colets, St Nicholas Road, Thames Ditton, Surrey, KT7 0PW
Activities: Fitness facilities
Officers: Richard John Gawen Holman, Secretary; Nicholas John Carr [1949] Director/Chartered Surveyor; John Middleton Dennis [1946] Director/Business Consultant; John Hilary Mortlock East [1947] Director/Solicitor; Andrew John Holder [1968] Director/Investment Manager; Richard John Gawen Holman [1943] Director/Chartered Accountant; Lincoln Peter Munro Jopp [1968] Director/Army Officer; Basil David Moss [1935] Director/Actor; Peter David Alan Mothersill [1957] Director/Material Manager; Andrew James Bryce Riley [1962] Director; Benjamin Mabon Roberts [1969] Director/Teacher; Jehan Sherjan [1976] Director/Management Consultant

Thames Honda Limited
Incorporated: 4 March 2002 *Employees:* 101
Net Worth: £2,777,454 *Total Assets:* £6,231,192
Registered Office: Ruislip Honda, Victoria Road, South Ruislip, Middlesex, HA4 0LJ
Activities: Other retail sale of new goods in specialised stores (not commercial art galleries and opticians)
Parent: Thames Honda Holdings Limited
Officers: Thomas Forbes, Secretary; Susan Ellen Clark [1982] Director [Irish]; Conor James Forbes [1989] Director [Irish]; Linda Bridget Forbes [1984] Director [Irish]; Gemma Mary Lalayiannis [1985] Director [Irish]

Thames Industrial Estate Limited
Incorporated: 2 January 2001 *Employees:* 2
Net Worth: £2,175,239 *Total Assets:* £14,454,908
Registered Office: 1st Floor, Sheraton House, Lower Road, Chorleywood, Rickmansworth, Herts, WD3 5LH
Activities: Development of building projects
Major Shareholder: Raymond Valentine Mawhood
Officers: Lisa Jane Ashton-Jones, Secretary; Lisa Jane Ashton-Jones [1966] Director/Landlord & Property Developer; Philip Ashton-Jones [1964] Director/Barrister; Raymond Valentine Mawhood [1942] Director

Thames Properties Ltd.
Incorporated: 2 December 1988
Net Worth: £46,987,732 *Total Assets:* £53,337,912
Registered Office: 6 Forge Lane, Petersham Road, Richmond, Surrey, TW10 7BF
Activities: Buying and selling of own real estate
Shareholders: Barbara Anderman; Margaret Ann Fruchter; Tessa Frances Goldstein
Officers: Margaret Ann Fruchter, Secretary/College Lecturer; Barbara Anderman [1948] Director/Professor; Margaret Ann Fruchter [1945] Director; Simon Maurice Fruchter [1976] Director/Property Developer; Tessa Frances Goldstein [1954] Director

Thames Recycling Limited
Incorporated: 26 April 2012 *Employees:* 2
Net Worth: £2,005,116 *Total Assets:* £7,398,556
Registered Office: Northside House, 69 Tweedy Road, Bromley, Kent, BR1 3WA
Activities: Collection of non-hazardous waste
Shareholders: Dean Anthony Gregory; David Kenneth Barrett
Officers: David Kenneth Barrett [1957] Director; Dean Anthony Gregory [1964] Director

Thames Reinforcements Limited
Incorporated: 14 February 2006 *Employees:* 140
Net Worth: £7,659,173 *Total Assets:* £20,254,036
Registered Office: 4 Elstree Way, Borehamwood, Herts, WD6 1RN
Activities: Other specialised construction activities n.e.c.
Parent: JRL Group Ltd
Officers: Ronan Joseph Gleeson, Secretary/Director [Irish]; Ronan Joseph Gleeson [1976] Director [Irish]; Kevin William Keegan [1963] Director [Irish]; John James Reddington [1972] Director/Builder [Irish]

Thamesfield Limited
Incorporated: 31 May 2005 *Employees:* 53
Net Worth: £7,254,065 *Total Assets:* £7,970,297
Registered Office: 1st Floor, Brunswick House, Regent Park, 297-299 Kingston Road, Leatherhead, Surrey, KT22 7LU
Activities: Other business support service activities n.e.c.
Parent: Retirement Villages Management Limited
Officers: Sally Irene Rees, Secretary; Sarah Denise Burgess [1971] Director; Neil Donaldson [1966] Director/Accountant; Andrew George Esmond Ovey [1971] Director/Investment Manager

Thamesmead School
Incorporated: 28 June 2011 *Employees:* 127
Net Worth: £8,857,000 *Total Assets:* £11,314,000
Registered Office: Thamesmead School, Manygate Lane, Shepperton, Surrey, TW17 9EE
Activities: General secondary education
Officers: Jennifer Burtsell [1980] Director/Teacher; Michael Oliver Coombs [1950] Director; Nikki Jenkins [1969] Director/Event Coordinator; William Lancelot Kerr [1959] Director/Chartered Accountant; Gregory Martin [1947] Director/Retired; Michael Frederick Martin [1939] Director/Retired; David Munby [1952] Director/Business Engagement Manager; Ruth Helen Murton [1957] Director/Company Owner; Rory Keir Jonathan Pogson [1966] Director/Army Officer; Philip Reeves [1974] Director/Headteacher; Gemma Seabrook [1963] Director/Administrator; Jason Tendler [1970] Director/Bank Manager; David John Theaker [1943] Associate Director Manufacturer; Alexander John Warner [1971] Director/Consultant

Thenhurst Agricultural Limited
Incorporated: 8 March 1977 *Employees:* 10
Net Worth: £12,383,000 *Total Assets:* £12,624,000
Registered Office: Bridge House, 69 London Road, Twickenham, Middlesex, TW1 3SP
Activities: Mixed farming
Parent: Haymarket Group Limited
Officers: Brian John Freeman [1964] Director/Accountant; Lord Michael Ray Dibdin Heseltine [1933] Director/Publisher; Hon Rupert Heseltine [1967] Director/Publisher

Therakos (UK), Ltd
Incorporated: 9 October 2012 *Employees:* 23
Net Worth: £6,315,817 *Total Assets:* £26,275,732
Registered Office: 3 The Causeway, Lotus Park, Staines upon Thames, Middlesex, TW18 3AG
Activities: Activities of other holding companies n.e.c.
Parent: Mallinckrodt PLC
Officers: Paul Robert Coiante [1969] Director [American]; Thomas Joseph Englese [1974] Director [American]; Alasdair John Fenlon [1966] Director [Irish]; Christopher Hirt [1968] VP and Managing Director [German]; Gary James McCutcheon [1959] Finance Director

Thew Arnott Group Limited
Incorporated: 20 May 2009 *Employees:* 35
Net Worth: £3,962,283 *Total Assets:* £6,483,862
Registered Office: Aissela, 46 High Street, Esher, Surrey, KT10 9QY
Activities: Activities of other holding companies n.e.c.
Major Shareholder: Richard Froude Newman
Officers: Anthony Edward Froude Newman [1930] Director; Richard Froude Newman [1959] Director; Vivien Anne Newman [1955] Director

Thirsk Winton LLP
Incorporated: 2 June 2009 *Employees:* 9
Net Worth: £405,515 *Total Assets:* £6,846,768
Registered Office: Swan House, 9-12 Johnston Road, Woodford Green, Essex, IG8 0XA
Officers: Stephen Bernard Thirsk [1945] Member; Jason Martin Winton [1980] Member; Matthew Stephen Barrett [1986] LLP Member

THMG Limited
Incorporated: 23 October 2014 *Employees:* 136
Net Worth Deficit: £4,828,725 *Total Assets:* £5,903,035
Registered Office: 2 AC Court, High Street, Thames Ditton, Surrey, KT7 0SR
Activities: Other human health activities
Shareholder: James Edward Hugh Farquharson
Officers: Peter Ashley Boddy [1965] Director; James Edward Hugh Farquharson [1961] Director

Thomas,Arthur & Gordon,Limited
Incorporated: 28 February 1946 *Employees:* 4
Net Worth: £4,892,562 *Total Assets:* £8,091,394
Registered Office: Unit 4 Limes Court, Conduit Lane, Hoddesdon, Herts, EN11 8EP
Activities: Renting and operating of Housing Association real estate
Shareholders: Russell Arthur Gordon Thomas; Barry Adrian Southey Thomas; Louise Laurel Barber
Officers: Louise Laurel Barber [1947] Director; Barry Adrian Southey Thomas [1941] Director

Thompson Bros. (Esher) Limited
Incorporated: 14 May 1955 *Employees:* 225
Net Worth: £11,586,039 *Total Assets:* £16,894,208
Registered Office: Garson Farm, Winterdown Road, Esher, Surrey, KT10 8LS
Activities: Growing of other tree and bush fruits and nuts
Shareholder: Derek Michael Richardson
Officers: Clare Patricia James [1973] Director/Horticultural Retailer; Alan Paul Richardson [1974] Director/Retail; Derek Michael Richardson [1938] Director/Horticulturist; Ian Lance Richardson [1967] Director/Horticulturalist; Ben Thompson [1980] Director/Marketing Manager; Peter Roy Thompson [1948] Director/Horticulturist

Thompsons (UK) Holdings Limited
Incorporated: 3 August 2015 *Employees:* 235
Net Worth: £12,201,453 *Total Assets:* £22,517,220
Registered Office: Rutland Works, Vulcan Way, New Addington, Croydon, Surrey, CR9 0DE
Activities: Activities of head offices
Major Shareholder: Margaret Elizabeth Burton
Officers: Trevor David Russell, Secretary; Margaret Elizabeth Burton [1949] Director; Scott Leigh Burton [1974] Director; Simon Karl Shields [1973] Director; Patrick Allen Thomas [1946] Director [Irish]

Thompsons (UK) Limited
Incorporated: 12 March 1973 *Employees:* 152
Net Worth: £10,960,950 *Total Assets:* £19,549,700
Registered Office: Vulcan Way, New Addington, Croydon, Surrey, CR9 0DE
Activities: Manufacture of other fabricated metal products n.e.c.
Parent: Thompsons (UK) Holdings Ltd
Officers: Patrick Allen Thomas, Secretary [Irish]; Margaret Elizabeth Burton [1949] Director/Purchasing Manager; Scott Leigh Burton [1974] Director/Sales Manager; Simon Karl Shields [1973] Director/Sales Manager; Patrick Allen Thomas [1946] Director/Manager [Irish]

Thompsons Nursery Limited
Incorporated: 7 March 1984 *Employees:* 111
Net Worth: £4,877,064 *Total Assets:* £6,194,973
Registered Office: Perry Street, Chislehurst, Kent, BR7 6HA
Activities: Growing of other perennial crops
Shareholder: Ursula Margarete Thompson
Officers: Ursula Margarete Thompson, Secretary; Michele Bramley [1966] Director; John Thompson [1970] Director; Peter Thompson [1973] Director/Garden Centre Manager; Ursula Margarete Thompson [1944] Director/Nurseryman

Thorn Security Group Limited
Incorporated: 16 February 1994
Net Worth: £4,894,000 *Total Assets:* £13,155,000
Registered Office: Security House, The Summit, Hanworth Road, Sunbury on Thames, Middlesex, TW16 5DB
Activities: Activities of head offices
Parent: Tyco Holdings (UK) Limited
Officers: Mark Ayre [1963] Finance Director; Peter Schieser [1967] Director [German]

Thorn Security Limited
Incorporated: 28 June 1962 *Employees:* 232
Net Worth: £32,056,000 *Total Assets:* £61,857,000
Registered Office: Security House, The Summit, Hanworth Road, Sunbury on Thames, Middlesex, TW16 5DB
Activities: Other manufacturing n.e.c.
Parent: Thorn Security Group Limited
Officers: Mark Ayre [1963] Finance Director; Moosa Farook Meah [1965] Director

Thorney Leys Developments Limited
Incorporated: 3 May 2017
Net Worth: £176,221 *Total Assets:* £10,282,169
Registered Office: 3rd Floor, Sterling House, Langston Road, Loughton, Essex, IG10 3TS
Activities: Development of building projects
Parent: Galliard Holdings Limited
Officers: Allan William Porter, Secretary; David Edward Conway [1976] Director; Stephen Stuart Solomon Conway [1948] Director; Jonathan Michael Morgan [1978] Director; Donagh O'Sullivan [1968] Construction Director [Irish]

Thorntons Limited
Incorporated: 13 May 1921 *Employees:* 2,962
Previous: Thorntons PLC
Net Worth Deficit: £47,468,000 *Total Assets:* £125,707,000
Registered Office: 889 Greenford Road, Greenford, Middlesex, UB6 0HE
Activities: Manufacture of cocoa and chocolate confectionery
Parent: Ferholding UK Ltd
Officers: Tim John Shirley, Secretary; Salvatore Castelli [1971] Finance Director [Italian]; Pieraldo Oldano [1965] Managing Director [Italian]; Marco Pescarolo [1957] Director/Global Treasurer [Italian]

A.E. Thorogood Investments Limited
Incorporated: 26 February 1964
Net Worth: £3,233,518 *Total Assets:* £7,570,718
Registered Office: The Old Rectory, Church Street, Weybridge, Surrey, KT13 8DE
Activities: Development of building projects
Shareholders: A.E. Thorogood Ltd; Gareth Edward Grant; Philip John Munk
Officers: Gareth Edward Grant [1968] Director/Manager; Jill Marion Grant [1935] Director; Matthew Charles Truelove [1967] Director/Solicitor

A.E.Thorogood Limited
Incorporated: 21 August 1954
Net Worth: £7,871,319 *Total Assets:* £16,702,256
Registered Office: The Old Rectory, Church Street, Weybridge, Surrey, KT13 8DE
Activities: Development of building projects
Major Shareholder: Jill Marian Grant
Officers: Gareth Edward Grant [1968] Director; Jill Marion Grant [1935] Director; Matthew Charles Truelove [1967] Director/Solicitor

Thothaal Group Limited
Incorporated: 1 April 2005
Net Worth: £1,511,159 *Total Assets:* £5,409,309
Registered Office: c/o Danmirr Consultants, 170 Church Road, Mitcham, Surrey, CR4 3BW
Activities: Retail sale in non-specialised stores with food, beverages or tobacco predominating
Officers: Mahomed Erfan Abdul Gaffar, Secretary; Asad Manzoor, Secretary; Majed Ismail Chaudhry [1961] Director; Atif Hussain [1976] Director; Asad Manzoor [1974] Director

Threshold Land & Estates Limited
Incorporated: 16 April 1968 *Employees:* 3
Net Worth: £6,436,276 *Total Assets:* £13,671,013
Registered Office: North Wing, Burgoine House, 8 Lower Teddington Road, Hampton Wick, Surrey, KT1 4ER
Activities: Other letting and operating of own or leased real estate
Parent: O G Holdings Limited
Officers: Daye Offer, Secretary; Claire Offer [1969] Director; Daye Offer [1933] Director; Harry John Miles Offer [1962] Director/Chartered Surveyor

THS Group Limited
Incorporated: 15 January 2016 *Employees:* 9
Net Worth: £5,210,916 *Total Assets:* £5,290,555
Registered Office: c/o Hillier Hopkins LLP, First Floor, Radius House, 51 Clarendon Road, Watford, Herts, WD17 1HP
Activities: Web portals
Major Shareholder: Sebastien Goldenberg
Officers: Sebastien Goldenberg [1972] Director/Consultant [French]

Thumbzup UK Limited
Incorporated: 16 March 2015 *Employees:* 2
Net Worth: £1,272,899 *Total Assets:* £18,839,764
Registered Office: Suite 105, Viglen House, Alperton Lane, Wembley, Middlesex, HA0 1HD
Activities: Other business support service activities n.e.c.
Officers: Aviad Eyal [1970] Director [Israeli]; Saul Jacob Gorin [1965] Director [South African]

Tican (Chilled) Limited
Incorporated: 26 May 2000 *Employees:* 78
Net Worth: £5,014,000 *Total Assets:* £17,086,000
Registered Office: 3rd Floor, Crown House, 151 High Road, Loughton, Essex, IG10 4LG
Activities: Other business support service activities n.e.c.
Parent: Tican UK Limited
Officers: Matthew McGeough, Secretary/Director; Richard Neil Burke [1956] Director; Simon Robert Halliday [1965] Director; Andrew Jones [1958] Director; Matthew McGeough [1976] Director; Jason Wilkie [1969] Director

Tican (UK) Holdings Limited
Incorporated: 26 September 2007
Net Worth: £6,109,925 *Total Assets:* £8,861,939
Registered Office: Crown House, 151 High Road, Loughton, Essex, IG10 4LG
Activities: Activities of head offices
Shareholders: Clemens Tonnies; Robert Tonnies
Officers: Matthew McGeough, Secretary; Matthew McGeough [1976] Director; Niels Jorgen Villesen [1966] Finance Director [Danish]

Ticketgrange Limited
Incorporated: 12 July 1983 *Employees:* 61
Net Worth: £9,156,707 *Total Assets:* £10,623,406
Registered Office: The Downshire, 71 Baldwins Lane, Croxley Green, Rickmansworth, Herts, WD3 3LT
Activities: Gambling and betting activities
Shareholders: John Harris; Richard Harris
Officers: John Harris, Secretary; John Harris [1958] Director/Amusement Caterer; Richard Harris [1954] Director/Amusement Caterer

The Tiffin Girls' School
Incorporated: 22 February 2011 *Employees:* 127
Net Worth: £15,339,000 *Total Assets:* £16,959,000
Registered Office: The Tiffin Girls' School, Richmond Road, Kingston upon Thames, Surrey, KT2 5PL
Activities: General secondary education
Officers: Saira Barakzai [1964] Director/Teacher; Sarah Beeching [1969] Director/Economist; Kate Bevan [1981] Director/Teacher; Dr Alexandra Buckle [1980] Director/Academic; Caroline Calascione [1961] Director; Shelley Frost [1973] Director/Chartered Surveyor; Giuliano Giovannetti [1967] Director/CEO, Arch Mortgage Insurance [Italian]; Fazl-E Hasnain [1945] Director/Chartered Accountant [Dutch]; Tara Suzanne Holt [1969] Director/Tax Accountant; Adrian Trevor Howe [1961] Finance Director; Ian John Keary [1969] Director/Teacher; Alice Nabi [1966] Director/Barrister; Donna Newell [1971] Director/Teacher; Carol Perry [1958] Director

TIGI International Limited
Incorporated: 30 July 1996 *Employees:* 147
Net Worth Deficit: £5,702,556 *Total Assets:* £33,217,912
Registered Office: Unilever House, Springfield Drive, Leatherhead, Surrey, KT22 7GR
Activities: Hairdressing and other beauty treatment
Parent: TIGI Holdings Limited
Officers: James Oliver Earley, Secretary; Richard Clive Hazell, Secretary; Mark Bleathman [1969] Director/TIGI Global GM; Philip James Cheadle [1977] Director/General Manager TIGI Western Europe; Bijal Vikram Sheth [1970] Finance Director

Tilda Limited
Incorporated: 25 September 1970 *Employees:* 244
Net Worth: £59,872,000 *Total Assets:* £83,850,000
Registered Office: Coldharbour Lane, Rainham, Essex, RM13 9YQ
Activities: Grain milling
Parent: Hain Frozen Foods UK Limited
Officers: Nicholas Keen, Secretary; Robert Bailie [1972] Finance Director; Denise Menikheim Faltischek [1973] Director/General Counsel [American]; James Michael Langrock [1965] Director [American]; Umesh Parmar [1965] Director; Mark Lawrence Schiller [1961] Director/CEO Hain Celestial [American]

Timeboard Industrial Properties LLP
Incorporated: 6 August 2013
Net Worth: £10,824,037 *Total Assets:* £15,028,699
Registered Office: 28 Church Road, Stanmore, Middlesex, HA7 4XR

Timeboard Investments LLP
Incorporated: 28 March 2012
Net Worth: £2,011,769 *Total Assets:* £43,800,520
Registered Office: 28 Church Road, Stanmore, Middlesex, HA7 4XR

Times Square Estates Limited
Incorporated: 2 February 2001 *Employees:* 2
Net Worth: £5,034,383 *Total Assets:* £5,641,898
Registered Office: 5 Mountwood Close, South Croydon, Surrey, CR2 8RJ
Activities: Buying and selling of own real estate
Major Shareholder: Josephine Anthea Otnes
Officers: Dudley Sharratt Mead, Secretary; Danielle Otnes [1976] Director/Teacher; Josephine Anthea Otnes [1945] Director

Titan Containers Limited
Incorporated: 7 June 1993 *Employees:* 41
Net Worth: £1,699,950 *Total Assets:* £7,427,944
Registered Office: Europa Trading Centre, London Road, Grays, Essex, RM20 4DB
Activities: Other service activities n.e.c.
Parent: Titan Containers A/S
Officers: Layland Barker [1954] Director; Robin Mark Staunton [1957] Director/Lawyer

Tithe Academy
Incorporated: 29 June 2011 *Employees:* 171
Previous: Rooks Heath College
Net Worth: £16,703,750 *Total Assets:* £21,301,552
Registered Office: Eastcote Lane, South Harrow, Middlesex, HA2 9AH
Activities: General secondary education
Officers: Pauline Ann Hughes [1954] Director; Pinakin Vithalji Katbamna [1962] Director/Science Teacher; Dr John Reavley [1958] Director; Nicola Roger [1963] Director/Administrator; Savvas Savva [1958] Director; Robin Brownrigg Tullo [1950] Director/Retired

TJX Europe Buying (Deutschland) Limited
Incorporated: 24 February 1995
Net Worth: £222,000 *Total Assets:* £16,075,000
Registered Office: 50 Clarendon Road, Watford, Herts, WD17 1TX
Activities: Agents involved in the sale of a variety of goods
Parent: TJX UK
Officers: Susan Beaumont, Secretary; Alicia Colarte Kelly, Secretary; Lisa Schwartz, Secretary; David Lawrence Averill [1967] SVP, Corporate Tax Director [American]; John Joseph Klinger [1964] Director/SVP, Corporate Controller [American]; Mary Blier Reynolds [1955] Director/SVP, Treasurer [American]

TJX Europe Buying Limited
Incorporated: 24 January 2011
Net Worth: £268,000 *Total Assets:* £55,088,000
Registered Office: 50 Clarendon Road, Watford, Herts, WD17 1TX
Activities: Other business support service activities n.e.c.
Parent: TJX UK
Officers: Alicia Colarte Kelly, Secretary; David Lawrence Averill [1967] SVP Corporate Tax Director [American]; John Joseph Klinger [1964] Director/SVP, Corporate Controller [American]; Mary Blier Reynolds [1955] Director/SVP Treasurer [American]

TJX Europe Limited
Incorporated: 18 August 1995
Net Worth: £207,720,992 *Total Assets:* £643,612,992
Registered Office: 50 Clarendon Road, Watford, Herts, WD17 1TX
Activities: Other retail sale of new goods in specialised stores (not commercial art galleries and opticians)
Parent: The TJX Companies, Inc.
Officers: Susan Beaumont, Secretary; Alicia Colarte Kelly, Secretary; Lisa Schwartz, Secretary; David Lawrence Averill [1967] SVP, Corporate Tax Director [American]; John Joseph Klinger [1964] Director/SVP, Corporate Controller [American]; Mary Blier Reynolds [1955] Director/SVP Treasurer [American]

TJX Germany Ltd.
Incorporated: 25 July 2013
Net Worth: £36,442,000 *Total Assets:* £36,500,000
Registered Office: 50 Clarendon Road, Watford, Herts, WD17 1TX
Activities: Activities of other holding companies n.e.c.
Parent: TJX Europe Limited
Officers: Susan Beaumont, Secretary; Alicia Colarte Kelly, Secretary; Lisa Schwartz, Secretary; David Lawrence Averill [1967] SVP, Corporate Tax Director [American]; John Joseph Klinger [1964] Director/SVP, Corporate Controller [American]; Mary Blier Reynolds [1955] Director/SVP, Treasurer [American]

TJX UK
Incorporated: 18 August 1995 *Employees:* 20,177
Net Worth: £645,600,000 *Total Assets:* £1,234,300,032
Registered Office: 50 Clarendon Road, Watford, Herts, WD17 1TX
Activities: Other retail sale of new goods in specialised stores (not commercial art galleries and opticians)
Parent: TJX Europe Limited
Officers: Susan Beaumont, Secretary; Alicia Colarte Kelly, Secretary; Lisa Schwartz, Secretary; David Lawrence Averill [1967] SVP Corporate Tax Director [American]; John Joseph Klinger [1964] Director/SVP, Corporate Controller [American]; Mary Blier Reynolds [1955] Director/SVP Treasurer [American]

TJX UK Property Limited
Incorporated: 10 November 2015 *Employees:* 3
Net Worth Deficit: £150,000 *Total Assets:* £16,295,000
Registered Office: 50 Clarendon Road, Watford, Herts, WD17 1TX
Activities: Other letting and operating of own or leased real estate
Parent: The TJX Companies, Inc.
Officers: Susan Beaumont, Secretary; Alicia Colarte Kelly, Secretary; Lisa Schwartz, Secretary; David Lawrence Averill [1967] SVP, Corporate Tax Director [American]; John Joseph Klinger [1964] Director/SVP, Corporate Controller [American]; Mary Blier Reynolds [1955] Director/SVP, Treasurer [American]

TK Maxx
Incorporated: 17 December 1992
Net Worth: £4,907,000 *Total Assets:* £11,160,000
Registered Office: 50 Clarendon Road, Watford, Herts, WD17 1TX
Activities: Retail of furniture, lighting, and similar (not musical instruments or scores) in specialised store
Parent: TJX Europe Limited
Officers: Susan Beamont, Secretary; Alicia Colarte Kelly, Secretary; Lisa Schwartz, Secretary; David Lawrence Averill [1967] SVP, Corporate Tax Director [American]; John Joseph Klinger [1964] Director/SVP, Corporate Controller [American]; Mary Blier Reynolds [1955] Director/SVP, Treasurer [American]

TLC Group Limited
Incorporated: 19 February 1999 *Employees:* 784
Net Worth: £120,999,840 *Total Assets:* £203,683,040
Registered Office: 36 Railway Approach, Harrow, Middlesex, HA3 5AA
Activities: Residential nursing care facilities
Major Shareholder: Lady Sandhya Popat
Officers: Gagan Puri, Secretary; William Charles Neal [1986] Director; Paavan Popat [1985] Managing Director; Lady Sandhya Popat [1954] Director; Honourable Shivaan Shillin Popat [1988] Director; Gagan Puri [1978] Finance Director

TMD Holdings Limited
Incorporated: 21 April 2005 *Employees:* 186
Net Worth: £12,058,000 *Total Assets:* £22,778,000
Registered Office: Unit 3 Swallowfield Way, Hayes, Middlesex, UB3 1DQ
Activities: Activities of head offices
Shareholders: Peter John Butcher; Victor Howard Smith
Officers: David Alan Brown [1969] Director; Peter John Butcher [1946] Director; Victor Howard Smith [1945] Director; Martin John Treemoon Woolley [1958] Director

TMD Technologies Limited
Incorporated: 21 April 1969 *Employees:* 177
Net Worth: £13,571,000 *Total Assets:* £23,829,000
Registered Office: Unit 3 Swallowfield Way, Hayes, Middlesex, UB3 1DQ
Activities: Manufacture of other electrical equipment
Officers: David Alan Brown [1969] Director; Peter John Butcher [1946] Director; Michael John Clark [1955] Quality Director; Tracey Jane Ledwell [1965] Engineering Programme Director; Jane Ann McAlister [1963] Director; David Marshall Pike [1960] Operations Director; Victor Howard Smith [1945] Director; Martin John Treemoon Woolley [1958] Director

TN (UK) Consultancy Ltd
Incorporated: 2 February 2011
Net Worth: £347,883 *Total Assets:* £8,001,449
Registered Office: 902 Eastern Avenue, Newbury Park, Ilford, Essex, IG2 7HZ
Activities: Development of building projects
Officers: Naresh Kumar Chopra [1959] Director/Property Developer; Tina Chopra [1963] Director/Bookkeeper

The Tobacco Pipe Makers and Tobacco Trade Benevolent Fund
Incorporated: 25 February 2010
Net Worth: £7,710,016 *Total Assets:* £7,755,936
Registered Office: Suffolk House, George Street, Croydon, Surrey, CR0 0YN
Activities: Other social work activities without accommodation n.e.c.
Officers: Ralph Agust Valdimar Edmondson, Secretary; Fiona Josephine Alder [1964] Director/Hypnotherapist; Nicholas Mark Gower-Smith [1955] Director/Chartered Accountant; David Gwynder Lewis [1942] Director; Roger Lewis Harold Merton [1941] Director/Consultant; Simon George Orlik [1946] Director/Retired; Martine Alice Petetin [1952] Director/Retired [French]; Nigel Mervyn Sutherland Rich [1945] Director; Antony Vincent Scanlan [1957] Director

Todd Doors Limited
Incorporated: 5 September 1985 *Employees:* 86
Net Worth: £1,019,078 *Total Assets:* £5,968,875
Registered Office: Suite 1, 5 Hercules Way, Leavesden Park, Watford, Herts, WD25 7GS
Activities: Agents involved in the sale of timber and building materials
Parent: The Todd Group Limited
Officers: Virginia Todd, Secretary; James Lee Dean [1977] Director; Shelagh Gail Doyle [1959] Director; Robert Henry Mitchell [1962] Director; Matthew Charles Todd [1974] Director; Richard James Verrico [1964] Director

The Todd Group Limited
Incorporated: 19 October 2004 *Employees:* 86
Net Worth: £1,138,364 *Total Assets:* £6,089,086
Registered Office: Suite 1, 5 Hercules Way, Leavesden Park, Watford, Herts, WD25 7GS
Activities: Activities of head offices
Shareholders: Matthew Charles Todd; Virginia Todd
Officers: Virginia Todd, Secretary; Matthew Charles Todd [1974] Director

Togher Construction Limited
Incorporated: 13 January 2004 *Employees:* 19
Net Worth: £5,534,104 *Total Assets:* £10,937,303
Registered Office: 3 Wharf Road, Enfield, Middlesex, EN3 4TA
Activities: Development of building projects
Shareholder: William Christopher Togher
Officers: William Christopher Togher, Secretary/Carpenter; David Gerard Togher [1970] Director; William Christopher Togher [1968] Director

Toll Global Forwarding (UK) Limited
Incorporated: 9 February 1987
Net Worth: £15,622,000 *Total Assets:* £15,702,000
Registered Office: Australis House, Unit 2 Heron Way, Feltham, Middlesex, TW14 0AR
Activities: Other transportation support activities
Parent: Japan Post Holdings Co. Ltd
Officers: Bruce James Chaplin [1976] Director [South African]; Thomas Riber Knudsen [1970] Director [Danish]; Mark Steven Kurzeja [1957] Director

Toll Investments (NA) Ltd
Incorporated: 25 March 2010
Net Worth: £77,613,328 *Total Assets:* £77,613,328
Registered Office: Australis House, Unit 2 Heron Way, Feltham, Middlesex, TW14 0AR
Activities: Activities of head offices
Parent: Japan Post Holdings Co. Ltd
Officers: Bruce James Chaplin [1976] Director [South African]; Mark Steven Kurzeja [1957] Director

Toly Products (U.K.) Limited
Incorporated: 16 April 1973 *Employees:* 12
Net Worth: £2,387,426 *Total Assets:* £7,595,494
Registered Office: Aissela, 46 High Street, Esher, Surrey, KT10 9QY
Activities: Manufacture of other plastic products
Officers: Andrew Imre Gatesy [1964] Director; Peter Stefan Gatesy [1966] Director; Nicholas Xuereb [1970] Director [Maltese]

Tomo Motor Parts Limited
Incorporated: 20 September 2005 *Employees:* 50
Net Worth: £2,731,603 *Total Assets:* £8,171,865
Registered Office: Unit 1 Tomo Industrial Estate, Packet Boat Lane, Cowley, Middlesex, UB8 2JP
Activities: Wholesale trade of motor vehicle parts and accessories
Parent: Tomo Motor Group Limited
Officers: Darren Perkins, Secretary; Darren Perkins [1973] Director; David Alan Donald Perkins [1946] Director; Dean David Perkins [1970] Director; James Lee Spencer [1981] Finance Director

Tone Group Limited
Incorporated: 14 February 2002 *Employees:* 211
Net Worth: £4,067,987 *Total Assets:* £8,504,401
Registered Office: c/o McBrides Accountants LLP, Nexus House, 2 Cray Road, Sidcup, Kent, DA14 5DA
Activities: Activities of other holding companies n.e.c.
Major Shareholder: Andrew Stewart Needham
Officers: Madhu Ahluwalia, Secretary; Madhu Ahluwalia [1966] Director; Andrew Stewart Needham [1970] Director/Scaffolding Consultant

Tone Scaffolding Services Limited
Incorporated: 12 April 1999 *Employees:* 185
Net Worth: £3,556,453 *Total Assets:* £6,115,418
Registered Office: c/o McBrides Accountants LLP, Nexus House, Cray Road, Sidcup, Kent, DA14 5DA
Activities: Scaffold erection
Parent: Tone Group Limited
Officers: Madhu Ahluwalia, Secretary; Madhu Ahluwalia [1966] Director; Andrew Stewart Needham [1970] Director/Scaffolding Consultant

Topfib Limited
Incorporated: 6 July 1992
Net Worth: £8,659,864 *Total Assets:* £9,139,298
Registered Office: Coopers House, 65a Wingletye Lane, Hornchurch, Essex, RM11 3AT
Activities: Financial intermediation not elsewhere classified
Major Shareholder: Keith Robert Carnelley
Officers: Marilyn Joy Payne, Secretary; Keith Robert Carnelley [1949] Director/Businessman

Topgolf Group Limited
Incorporated: 2 September 2002
Net Worth: £38,909,356 *Total Assets:* £51,660,136
Registered Office: Kinetic House, Theobald Street, Elstree, Herts, WD6 4PJ
Activities: Other sports activities
Parent: Baydrive Group Limited
Officers: Kieren Charles Mildwaters, Secretary; Eldridge Allen Burns [1969] Director/General Counsel [American]; William Barry Davenport [1971] Finance Director [American]

Topgolf Limited
Incorporated: 2 March 1999 *Employees:* 518
Net Worth: £51,981,752 *Total Assets:* £63,387,980
Registered Office: Kinetic House, Theobald Street, Elstree, Herts, WD6 4PJ
Activities: Operation of sports facilities
Parent: Topgolf Group Limited
Officers: Kieren Charles Mildwaters, Secretary; Eldridge Allen Burns [1969] Director/General Counsel [American]; William Barry Davenport [1971] Finance Director [American]

Toroce Investments Ltd
Incorporated: 22 July 2016 *Employees:* 2
Net Worth: £908,122 *Total Assets:* £5,399,144
Registered Office: Munro House, Portsmouth Road, Cobham, Surrey, KT11 1PP
Activities: Fund management activities
Shareholders: Thomas Peter Campbell Ellis; Rosanna Jane Ellis; Celia Rose Ellis
Officers: Sarah Louise Ellis [1961] Director; Stephen Campbell Joseph Ellis [1959] Director

Toshiba Global Commerce Solutions (U.K.) Limited
Incorporated: 24 July 2012 *Employees:* 73
Net Worth Deficit: £11,942,470 *Total Assets:* £26,720,284
Registered Office: Abbey Cloisters, Abbey Green, Chertsey, Surrey, KT16 8RB
Activities: Other information technology service activities
Parent: TGCS Holdings Corporation
Officers: Valerie Anne Jacqueline Amand [1965] Director/Office Worker (Finance Operating Officer) [Belgian]; Toshiharu Higuchi [1969] Director/Office Worker [Japanese]; Adam Nicholas Sheppard [1961] Director/President & CEO Toshiba TEC Retail Operations

Toshiba Information Systems (UK) Limited
Incorporated: 19 October 1967 *Employees:* 11
Net Worth: £29,776,600 *Total Assets:* £37,230,544
Registered Office: Consort House, 1 Princes Road, Weybridge, Surrey, KT13 9TU
Activities: Wholesale of computers, computer peripheral equipment and software
Parent: Toshiba Corporation, Japan
Officers: Patrick Emmanuel Whelan, Secretary/Head of Legal Services [Irish]; Thomas Peter Cunliffe [1973] Director/Chief Operating Officer & Chief Financial Officer; Masato Kaneko [1970] Director [Japanese]; Hitoshi Otsuka [1958] Managing Director [Japanese]; Patrick Emmanuel Whelan [1971] Legal Director & Company Secretary [Irish]

Toshiba of Europe Limited
Incorporated: 13 November 1997 *Employees:* 51
Net Worth: £14,561,434 *Total Assets:* £318,844,928
Registered Office: 3 Furzeground Way, Stockley Park, Uxbridge, Middlesex, UB11 1EZ
Activities: Other business support service activities n.e.c.
Parent: Toshiba Corporation
Officers: Masato Kaneko [1970] Director [Japanese]; Hitoshi Otsuka [1958] Director [Japanese]; Takuya Tsukuda [1963] Director [Japanese]

Toshiba Tec U.K. Imaging Systems Limited
Incorporated: 13 December 2000 *Employees:* 286
Net Worth: £24,373,000 *Total Assets:* £43,535,000
Registered Office: Abbey Cloisters, Abbey Green, Chertsey, Surrey, KT16 8RB
Activities: Manufacture of other electrical equipment
Parent: Toshiba TEC Corporation
Officers: Martin Andrew Langridge, Secretary/Accountant; Martin Andrew Langridge [1963] Director/Chartered Accountant; Tatsuya Ogawa [1979] Deputy Managing Director [Japanese]; Adam Nicholas Sheppard [1961] Director; Toshiyasu Takahashi [1963] Director [Japanese]; Masayuki Takesue [1981] Director [Japanese]

Total Support Services Limited
Incorporated: 26 May 1993 *Employees:* 2,452
Net Worth: £5,325,438 *Total Assets:* £10,676,703
Registered Office: Lynwood House, Crofton Road, Orpington, Kent, BR6 8QE
Activities: General cleaning of buildings
Shareholders: Katrina Gostt; Daniel Gostt
Officers: Susan Mary Hadjidakis, Secretary; James Christian Alexander [1979] Operations Director; Daniel Gostt [1973] Operations Director

Tour Partner Group Limited
Incorporated: 5 October 2015 *Employees:* 3
Previous: Mayfair Fox Bidco Limited
Net Worth: £136,076 *Total Assets:* £47,284,208
Registered Office: 5th Floor, Hygeia Building, 66-68 College Road, Harrow, Middlesex, HA1 1BE
Activities: Activities of other holding companies n.e.c.
Parent: Mayfair Fox Midco Limited
Officers: Paul John Maine [1965] Director/Chief Executive; Mark David Mayhew [1959] Director; Mark Pharoah [1964] Finance Director

Tour Partner Group Midco Limited
Incorporated: 5 October 2015
Previous: Mayfair Fox Midco Limited
Net Worth Deficit: £6,170,447 *Total Assets:* £66,387,204
Registered Office: 5th Floor, Hygeia Building, 66-68 College Road, Harrow, Middlesex, HA1 1BE
Activities: Activities of other holding companies n.e.c.
Officers: Paul John Maine [1965] Director/Chief Executive; Mark David Mayhew [1959] Director; Mark Pharoah [1964] Finance Director

Toureen Contractors Limited
Incorporated: 3 July 1992 *Employees:* 164
Net Worth: £5,086,975 *Total Assets:* £27,035,496
Registered Office: 25 Cecil Road, Harrow, Middlesex, HA3 5QY
Activities: Construction of commercial buildings
Parent: Toureen Group Ltd
Officers: Daniel Nolan, Secretary/Construction Manager; Daniel Nolan [1971] Director/Construction Manager; Denis Nolan [1962] Director; David Graham Parker [1969] Director/Quantity Surveyor

Toureen Group Limited
Incorporated: 7 August 2006 *Employees:* 219
Net Worth: £12,908,236 *Total Assets:* £38,441,624
Registered Office: 25 Cecil Road, Wealdstone, Harrow, Middlesex, HA3 5QY
Activities: Other business support service activities n.e.c.
Major Shareholder: Denis Nolan
Officers: David Graham Parker, Secretary; Nicholas Mark Gibson [1971] Director/Quantity Surveyor; Mouwafak Asad Kassir [1972] Director; Daniel Nolan [1971] Director/Construction Manager; Denis Nolan [1962] Director; David Graham Parker [1969] Director/Quantity Surveyor

Toureen Plant Limited
Incorporated: 7 August 2006 *Employees:* 26
Net Worth: £3,270,338 *Total Assets:* £7,938,777
Registered Office: 25 Cecil Road, Wealdstone, Harrow, Middlesex, HA3 5QY
Activities: Other specialised construction activities n.e.c.
Parent: Toureen Group Ltd
Officers: Daniel Nolan, Secretary; Denis Nolan [1962] Director

Tower Bridge Homes Care Limited
Incorporated: 20 June 1996 *Employees:* 1,094
Net Worth: £24,133,836 *Total Assets:* £64,816,460
Registered Office: 228 St Mary's Lane, Upminster, Essex, RM14 3DH
Activities: Other business support service activities n.e.c.
Officers: Indumati Lakhani, Company Secretary; Sharifa Lakhani [1987] Managing Director; Shiraz Lakhani [1945] Director

Tower Hill Investment Partners Limited
Incorporated: 14 April 1999
Net Worth: £4,849,840 *Total Assets:* £16,623,895
Registered Office: 219 Croydon Road, Caterham, Surrey, CR3 6PH
Activities: Financial management
Major Shareholder: Anthony Granville Mallin
Officers: Martina Lyons [1965] Director [Irish]; Anthony Granville Mallin [1955] Director; Marie-Louise Mallin-Poels [1961] Director [Dutch]

Tower Hill Suffolk Limited
Incorporated: 16 February 1998
Net Worth: £8,155,454 *Total Assets:* £17,103,280
Registered Office: 219 Croydon Road, Caterham, Surrey, CR3 6PH
Activities: Buying and selling of own real estate
Major Shareholder: Anthony Granville Mallin
Officers: Martina Lyons [1965] Director/Accountant [Irish]; Anthony Granville Mallin [1955] Director

The Tower, One St George Wharf Limited
Incorporated: 6 August 2002
Net Worth: £67,077,000 *Total Assets:* £201,730,000
Registered Office: Berkeley House, 19 Portsmouth Road, Cobham, Surrey, KT11 1JG
Activities: Construction of commercial buildings
Parent: The Berkeley Group PLC
Officers: Jared Stephen Philip Cranney, Secretary; Piers Martin Clanford [1970] Director; Mark Richard Elgar [1974] Director; Benjamin James Marks [1977] Director; Ian Antony Pearcey [1969] Director; Robert Charles Grenville Perrins [1965] Director; Anthony William Pidgley [1947] Director; Richard James Stearn [1968] Director

Towers & Co.,Limited
Incorporated: 28 July 1898 *Employees:* 117
Net Worth: £11,352,000 *Total Assets:* £29,375,000
Registered Office: 3-5 Tower House, Amwell Street, Hoddesdon, Herts, EN11 8UR
Activities: Wholesale of meat and meat products
Parent: Towers Thompson Holdings Ltd
Officers: Paul Dolan [1953] Director/Company Secretary; Terry George Goddard [1957] Director/Chartered Accountant

Towers Thompson Holdings Limited
Incorporated: 18 November 1997 *Employees:* 154
Net Worth: £6,057,000 *Total Assets:* £26,248,000
Registered Office: 3-5 Tower House, Amwell Street, Hoddesdon, Herts, EN11 8UR
Activities: Wholesale of meat and meat products
Officers: Paul Dolan [1953] Director/Executive Chairman; Terry George Goddard [1957] Director/Chartered Accountant

Townhold Limited
Incorporated: 4 June 1999 *Employees:* 2
Net Worth: £19,678,856 *Total Assets:* £25,175,964
Registered Office: Hadley Hurst, Hadley Common, Barnet, Herts, EN5 5QG
Activities: Development of building projects
Parent: Blendhall Limited
Officers: Anna Victoria Kinsman, Secretary; Alexander Mahboubian [1972] Director; Farrokh Mahboubian [1932] Director [Iranian]

Toyota (G.B.) PLC
Incorporated: 28 September 1967 *Employees:* 272
Net Worth: £14,392,000 *Total Assets:* £721,769,024
Registered Office: Great Burgh, Burgh Heath, Epsom, Surrey, KT18 5UX
Activities: Sale of new cars and light motor vehicles
Parent: Toyota Motor Corporation
Officers: Darren Paul Morris, Secretary; Matthew Peter Harrison [1968] Director/Chairman; Akito Takami [1967] Director [Japanese]; Paul Michael Van Der Burgh [1964] Director

Toyota Financial Services (UK) PLC
Incorporated: 26 September 1988 *Employees:* 405
Net Worth: £576,649,984 *Total Assets:* £6,119,365,120
Registered Office: Great Burgh, Burgh Heath, Epsom, Surrey, KT18 5UZ
Activities: Other credit granting n.e.c.
Parent: Toyota Financial Services Corporation
Officers: Rupert Charles Wentworth-Jessop, Secretary; Douglas Frank Gillies [1959] Managing Director; Yoshiyuki Hiramine [1973] Director [Japanese]; Ivo Josko Ljubica [1967] Director/Chief Executive Officer [Croatian]; Christian Ties Ruben [1967] Director/Chief Financial Officer [German]; Paul Michael Van Der Burgh [1964] Managing Director

A.L.Tozer Limited
Incorporated: 21 November 1944 *Employees:* 91
Net Worth: £7,265,687 *Total Assets:* £10,671,845
Registered Office: Pyports, Downside Bridge Road, Cobham, Surrey, KT11 3EH
Activities: Growing of vegetables and melons, roots and tubers
Major Shareholder: Peter Dawson
Officers: Debra Barr, Secretary; Debra Lynn Barr [1968] Director/Accountant; Laurence Charles Rangdale Dawson [1983] Director; Dr Peter Robert Dawson [1940] Director/Plant Breeder; Frances Mary Gawthrop [1955] Director/Plant Breeder; Steven James Winterbottom [1959] Director

Tozer Seeds Limited
Incorporated: 7 September 1998 *Employees:* 43
Net Worth: £3,018,249 *Total Assets:* £7,308,062
Registered Office: Pyports, Downside Bridge Road, Cobham, Surrey, KT11 3EH
Activities: Other service activities n.e.c.
Parent: A.L. Tozer Limited
Officers: Debra Barr, Secretary; Debra Lynn Barr [1968] Director/Accountant; Laurence Charles Rangdale Dawson [1983] Director; Dr Peter Robert Dawson [1940] Director/Seedsman; Steven James Winterbottom [1959] Managing Director

TPS Abbeydale Archway Limited
Incorporated: 8 February 2016
Net Worth Deficit: £29,817 *Total Assets:* £5,126,106
Registered Office: The Lodge, Heriots, The Common, Stanmore, Middlesex, HA7 3HG
Activities: Buying and selling of own real estate
Officers: Marc Simon Franks [1981] Director; Caroline Tessa Portnoi [1961] Director; Lee Richard Joseph Portnoi [1959] Director

Track Technology Limited
Incorporated: 16 January 1958 *Employees:* 3
Net Worth: £13,742,000 *Total Assets:* £13,974,000
Registered Office: Osprey House, 63 Station Road, Addlestone, Weybridge, Surrey, KT15 2AR
Activities: Activities of production holding companies
Parent: Pandrol International Limited
Officers: Jonathan Baxter, Secretary; Olivier Vincent Antille [1971] Director [French]; Brian Forster [1953] Director; Guy Henri Jean Paul Talbourdet [1965] Managing Director [French]

Tracker Network (UK) Limited
Incorporated: 26 July 1991 *Employees:* 110
Net Worth Deficit: £5,088,000 *Total Assets:* £5,062,000
Registered Office: 6-9 The Square, Stockley Park, Uxbridge, Middlesex, UB11 1FW
Activities: Other business support service activities n.e.c.
Shareholders: Tantalum Innovations Limited; Tantalum Innovations Limited
Officers: Hugh Wolley, Secretary; Greig Hilton [1974] Director; Bengt Erik Ramberg [1976] Executive Director [Swedish]

TRAD Group Limited
Incorporated: 8 September 1997
Net Worth: £5,960,739 *Total Assets:* £6,607,299
Registered Office: 1 Elmfield Park, Bromley, Kent, BR1 1LU
Activities: Activities of head offices
Parent: TRAD Hire & Sales Limited
Officers: James Arthur Fassenfelt, Secretary; Dr Mohed Altrad [1948] Director [French]; James Arthur Fassenfelt [1975] Finance Director; Madame Isabelle Marie Andree Montfort Epouse Garcia [1966] Director [French]; Louis Marie Maurice Roger Huetz [1970] Director [French]; Desmond Anthony Moore [1956] Director; Raymond Kennedy Neilson [1966] Director

TRAD Hire & Sales Limited
Incorporated: 12 January 1998 *Employees:* 99
Net Worth: £33,305,510 *Total Assets:* £92,950,464
Registered Office: 1 Elmfield Park, Bromley, Kent, BR1 1LU
Activities: Other specialised construction activities n.e.c.
Major Shareholder: Mohamed Altrad
Officers: James Arthur Fassenfelt, Secretary; Dr Mohed Altrad [1948] Director [French]; James Arthur Fassenfelt [1975] Finance Director; Madame Isabelle Marie Andree Montfort Epouse Garcia [1966] Director [French]; Louis Marie Maurice Roger Huetz [1970] Director [French]; Desmond Anthony Moore [1956] Managing Director; Raymond Kennedy Neilson [1966] Director; John Paterson [1964] Director

TRAD Properties LLP
Incorporated: 22 December 2011
Net Worth: £13,536,436 *Total Assets:* £26,020,592
Registered Office: Haslers, Old Station Road, Loughton, Essex, IG10 4PL
Officers: Christopher Hayden Smith [1974] Member; Jacqueline Walker [1959] Member

TRAD Safety Systems Limited
Incorporated: 29 February 1988 *Employees:* 150
Net Worth: £5,745,935 *Total Assets:* £12,939,934
Registered Office: 1 Elmfield Park, Bromley, Kent, BR1 1LU
Activities: Other specialised construction activities n.e.c.
Parent: TRAD Hire & Sales Limited
Officers: James Arthur Fassenfelt, Secretary; Dr Mohed Altrad [1948] Director [French]; James Arthur Fassenfelt [1975] Finance Director; Madame Isabelle Marie Andree Montfort Epouse Garcia [1966] Director [French]; Louis Marie Maurice Roger Huetz [1970] Director [French]; Desmond Anthony Moore [1956] Director/Manager; Raymond Kennedy Neilson [1966] Director

TRAD Scaffolding Co.Limited
Incorporated: 17 November 1971 *Employees:* 304
Net Worth: £16,203,635 *Total Assets:* £22,854,960
Registered Office: 1 Elmfield Park, Bromley, Kent, BR1 1LU
Activities: Other specialised construction activities n.e.c.
Parent: TRAD Group Limited
Officers: James Arthur Fassenfelt, Secretary; Dr Mohed Altrad [1948] Director [French]; Gary Mark Checketts [1968] Divisional Director; James Arthur Fassenfelt [1975] Finance Director; Madame Isabelle Marie Andree Montfort Epouse Garcia [1966] Director [French]; Neil Stephen Garner [1963] Director; Rosalind Anne Howe [1970] Human Resources Director; Louis Marie Maurice Roger Huetz [1970] Director [French]; Steve Laurence Kearney [1961] Director/Safety, Health and Environment Manager; Peter McShane [1972] Director; Desmond Anthony Moore [1956] Director; Raymond Kennedy Neilson [1966] Director

Trade Sale (Slough) Limited
Incorporated: 22 March 2002 *Employees:* 1
Net Worth: £11,749,150 *Total Assets:* £13,916,787
Registered Office: Unit 8 West London Industrial Park, Iver Lane, Uxbridge, Middlesex, UB8 2JG
Activities: Sale of used cars and light motor vehicles
Officers: Fil Levi Gray [1958] Director

Trade Sale Ltd
Incorporated: 10 November 1997 *Employees:* 4
Net Worth: £14,548,128 *Total Assets:* £62,124,796
Registered Office: Unit 8 West London Industrial Park, Iver Lane, Uxbridge, Middlesex, UB8 2JG
Activities: Sale of used cars and light motor vehicles
Major Shareholder: Fil Levi Gray
Officers: Fil Levi Gray [1958] Director

Tradewise Group of Companies Limited
Incorporated: 22 November 2013 *Employees:* 197
Net Worth: £8,921,113 *Total Assets:* £47,179,276
Registered Office: 300 Southbury Road, Enfield, Middlesex, EN1 1TS
Activities: Activities of financial services holding companies
Shareholders: North Atlantic Value GP 4 Limited; James William Humphreys
Officers: Jennifer Ann Jones, Secretary; Marcus Charles Killick [1962] Director/Chief Executive; Christopher Mills [1952] Director; David John Ratledge [1970] Director/Chartered Certified Accountant; Michael Robert Tyler [1966] Director/Chief Executive

Tradewise Insurance Services Limited
Incorporated: 23 May 2002 *Employees:* 155
Net Worth: £2,320,088 *Total Assets:* £28,386,768
Registered Office: 300 Southbury Road, Enfield, Middlesex, EN1 1TS
Activities: Activities of insurance agents and brokers
Shareholders: North Atlantic Value GP 4 Limited; James William Humphreys; Tradewise Group of Companies Limited
Officers: Jennifer Ann Jones, Secretary; Paul George Bates [1976] Claims Director; Wayne Michael Bradshaw [1958] Sales & Marketing Director; Bernard Wayne Martin [1975] Claims Director; Alison Claire Middleton [1973] Director; David John Ratledge [1970] Director/Accountant; Annette Bridget Tyler [1972] Director; Michael Robert Tyler [1966] Director

Tradex Insurance Company Limited
Incorporated: 27 October 1994 *Employees:* 30
Net Worth: £18,395,000 *Total Assets:* £224,964,000
Registered Office: 7 Eastern Road, Romford, Essex, RM1 3NH
Activities: Non-life insurance
Parent: Tradex Insurance Holdings Limited
Officers: Steven Jonathon Moore, Secretary; Deborah Ann Austin [1967] Director/Underwriter; Stephen Richard Braine [1954] Director/Chief Financial Officer; Garry Michael Fearn [1950] Director; Nicholas John Taylor [1958] Director/Chief Executive Officer; Andrew Peter Whitehouse [1962] Director

Tradex Insurance Holdings Limited
Incorporated: 3 February 2012 *Employees:* 30
Net Worth: £18,410,000 *Total Assets:* £224,988,992
Registered Office: 7 Eastern Road, Romford, Essex, RM1 3NH
Activities: Non-life insurance
Major Shareholder: Royston William Clegg
Officers: Steven Jonathon Moore, Secretary; Deborah Ann Austin [1967] Director/Underwriter; Stephen Richard Braine [1954] Director/Chief Financial Officer; Garry Michael Fearn [1950] Director; Nicholas John Taylor [1958] Director/Chief Executive Officer; Andrew Peter Whitehouse [1962] Director

Trading Post Limited (The)
Incorporated: 21 September 1938 *Employees:* 12
Net Worth: £2,287,622 *Total Assets:* £6,580,669
Registered Office: 1 Beresford Avenue, Wembley, Middlesex, HA0 1NU
Activities: Other business support service activities n.e.c.
Shareholders: Varsha Girdhar Mulchandani; Girdhar Devidas Mulchandani
Officers: Varsha Girdhar Mulchandani, Secretary; Girdhar Devidas Mulchandani [1958] Director/Accountant

Trading Scents (2014) Limited
Incorporated: 14 April 2014
Net Worth: £3,246,614 *Total Assets:* £5,596,729
Registered Office: 2 Park Court, Pyrford Road, West Byfleet, Surrey, KT14 6SD
Activities: Wholesale of perfume and cosmetics
Shareholders: Eoin Alan MacLeod; Trading Scents Group Limited
Officers: Eoin Alan MacLeod [1962] Director

Trading Scents Group Limited
Incorporated: 14 April 2014
Net Worth: £4,554,895 *Total Assets:* £6,196,438
Registered Office: 2 Park Court, Pyrford Road, West Byfleet, Surrey, KT14 6SD
Activities: Wholesale of perfume and cosmetics
Major Shareholder: Eoin Alan MacLeod
Officers: Eoin Alan MacLeod [1962] Director

Trafalgar Leisure Ltd
Incorporated: 2 February 1999 *Employees:* 58
Net Worth: £19,594,476 *Total Assets:* £40,114,984
Registered Office: Lynwood House, 373-375 Station Road, Harrow, Middlesex, HA1 2AW
Activities: Public houses and bars
Major Shareholder: Sameir Talib Hamadi
Officers: Sheila Louise Hamadi, Secretary; Rashied Hamadi [1969] Director; Sameir Talib Hamadi [1970] Director/Jeweller

Trafalgar Square Investments Limited
Incorporated: 20 August 2003
Net Worth: £4,586,543 *Total Assets:* £7,033,219
Registered Office: Ground Floor, rear The Estate House, 201 High Road, Chigwell, Essex, IG7 5BJ
Activities: Other business support service activities n.e.c.
Major Shareholder: Andrew Paul Klein
Officers: Howard Malcolm Klein, Secretary; Andrew Paul Klein [1966] Director/Businessman; Howard Malcolm Klein [1940] Director

Trafficinvest Limited
Incorporated: 6 May 2016 *Employees:* 39
Net Worth: £13,781,325 *Total Assets:* £28,090,748
Registered Office: 1 Parkshot, Richmond, Surrey, TW9 2RD
Activities: Activities of other holding companies n.e.c.
Officers: Erik Langaker [1963] Director/Investment Professional [Norwegian]; Anders Christian Wilhelmsen [1987] Director/Investment Professional [Norwegian]; Oscar Alexander Garmann Wilhelmsen [1991] Director/Student [Norwegian]

Tram Operations Limited
Incorporated: 1 September 1995 *Employees:* 218
Net Worth: £3,094,000 *Total Assets:* £9,873,000
Registered Office: Tramlink Depot, Coomber Way, Croydon, Surrey, CR0 4TQ
Activities: Other urban, suburban or metropolitan passenger land transport (not underground, metro or similar)
Parent: Centrewest Limited
Officers: Michael Hampson, Secretary; Nicholas Keith Chevis [1964] Director; Andrew Mark James [1966] Director; Stephen Montgomery [1962] Director; Jacqueline Susan Townsend [1958] Managing Director; Adrian Mark Wlodarski [1961] Director/Accountant

Trans Global Freight Management Limited
Incorporated: 11 August 1976 *Employees:* 187
Net Worth: £4,284,668 *Total Assets:* £37,289,880
Registered Office: Woodlands, 79 High Street, Greenhithe, Kent, DA9 9RD
Activities: Other transportation support activities
Parent: Trans Global Limited
Officers: Dilsher SEN, Secretary; Lee Andrew Bolsover [1966] Director/Freight Forwarder; David Carpentier [1972] Director/Information Technology Management [French]; Prasad Santosh Chogle [1972] Director/Freight Forwarder; Stephen Knight [1960] Director/Shipping Agent; Simon David Rawlinson [1967] Director/Freight Forwarder; Barry John Ruck [1959] Director; Dilsher SEN [1968] Director/Company Solicitor

Trans Global Group Limited
Incorporated: 25 November 1970 *Employees:* 11
Previous: Excel Shipping Group Limited
Net Worth: £2,333,987 *Total Assets:* £6,082,895
Registered Office: Woodlands, 79 High Street, Greenhithe, Kent, DA9 9RD
Activities: Other transportation support activities
Shareholders: Trans Global Limited; Trans Global Limited
Officers: Dilsher SEN, Secretary; Subir Ranjan Dasgupta [1945] Director [Singaporean]; Stephen Knight [1960] Director; Barry John Ruck [1959] Director/Accountant; Suvamoy Saha [1958] Director/Service [Indian]; Dilsher SEN [1968] Director/Company Solicitor

Trans Global Limited
Incorporated: 31 December 1963 *Employees:* 231
Net Worth: £4,642,000 *Total Assets:* £37,490,000
Registered Office: Woodlands, 79 High Street, Greenhithe, Kent, DA9 9RD
Activities: Activities of head offices
Shareholder: Dunstan Trust Nominee Ltd
Officers: Dilsher SEN, Secretary/Lawyer; Subir Ranjan Dasgupta [1945] Director [Singaporean]; Kevin Leon Jones [1952] Director; Padam Kumar Khaitan [1953] Director/Advocate [Indian]; Stephen Knight [1960] Director; Barry John Ruck [1959] Director/Accountant; Suvamoy Saha [1958] Director [Indian]; Dilsher SEN [1968] Director

Trans-Britannia Properties Limited
Incorporated: 26 July 1979 *Employees:* 16
Net Worth Deficit: £1,975,245 *Total Assets:* £6,047,043
Registered Office: c/o Parker Cavendish, 28 Church Road, Stanmore, Middlesex, HA7 4XR
Activities: Development of building projects
Parent: Sandringham Investments Limited
Officers: Zalina Dewan, Secretary; Ramesh Dewan [1947] Director/Publisher; Sheena Selina Dewan [1973] Director

Transcar Projects (Holdings) Ltd
Incorporated: 6 November 1996 *Employees:* 20
Net Worth: £2,193,400 *Total Assets:* £6,506,643
Registered Office: 1 Crayside, Five Arches Business Park, Maidstone Road, Sidcup, Kent, DA14 5AG
Activities: Activities of other holding companies n.e.c.
Shareholders: Dean Rossiter; Lyn Elizabeth Salter
Officers: Lyn Elizabeth Salter, Secretary; Dean Rossiter [1968] Director; Lyn Elizabeth Salter [1956] Director

Transcar Projects Limited
Incorporated: 13 April 1977 *Employees:* 20
Net Worth: £622,297 *Total Assets:* £5,240,367
Registered Office: 1 Crayside, Five Arches Business Park, Maidstone Road, Sidcup, Kent, DA14 5AG
Activities: Other transportation support activities
Parent: Transcar Projects (Holdings) Ltd
Officers: Lyn Elizabeth Salter, Secretary; Dean Rossiter [1968] Director; Lyn Elizabeth Salter [1956] Director

Transeur Properties Limited
Incorporated: 25 February 2002
Net Worth: £9,388,332 *Total Assets:* £26,975,800
Registered Office: Overseas House, 66-68 High Road, Bushey Heath, Herts, WD23 1GG
Activities: Renting and operating of Housing Association real estate
Major Shareholder: Philip Nandwani
Officers: Philip Nandwani, Secretary/General Manager; Gobind Hemandas Nandwani [1931] Director/Marketing Manager; Philip Nandwani [1963] Director/General Manager

Transfleet Properties Limited
Incorporated: 12 February 2015 *Employees:* 6
Net Worth: £3,658,902 *Total Assets:* £6,319,710
Registered Office: 4th Floor, Metroline House, 118-122 College Road, Harrow, Middlesex, HA1 1BQ
Activities: Other letting and operating of own or leased real estate
Major Shareholder: Jayman Chhotalal Badiani
Officers: Jayman Chhotalal Badiani [1959] Director; Rahuel Hemang Badiani [1993] Director; Rajan Jayman Badiani [1989] Director

Transform Housing & Support
Incorporated: 13 June 1972 *Employees:* 143
Previous: Surrey Community Development Trust
Net Worth: £20,369,000 *Total Assets:* £45,192,000
Registered Office: Bradmere House, Brook Way, Leatherhead, Surrey, KT22 7NA
Activities: Other accommodation
Officers: Ratna Sukumaran, Secretary; Mark Edward Austen [1949] Director; Jane Bolton [1957] Director; Christopher James Deacon [1954] Director/Management Consultant; Sally Ann Dubery [1964] Director/Charity Chief Executive; Lee Harris [1962] Director; Nickie Johnson [1984] Director; Robert William Mills [1969] Director; Christopher John Relleen [1948] Director; David John Turner [1936] Director

Transform Schools (Bassetlaw) Limited
Incorporated: 3 February 2005
Net Worth Deficit: £12,648,000 *Total Assets:* £84,582,000
Registered Office: 8 White Oak Square, London Road, Swanley, Kent, BR8 7AG
Activities: Other business support service activities n.e.c.
Parent: Transform Schools (Bassetlaw) Holdings Limited
Officers: Todd Malcolm Anderson [1980] Director/Accountant [New Zealander]; Christopher James [1968] Investment Director; Richard Keith Sheehan [1975] Investment Director

Transform Schools (Birmingham) Holdings Limited
Incorporated: 12 September 2005
Net Worth Deficit: £20,047,000 *Total Assets:* £80,415,000
Registered Office: 8 White Oak Square, London Road, Swanley, Kent, BR8 7AG
Activities: Activities of construction holding companies
Parent: Innisfree Schools (Secondary) Limited
Officers: Gaynor Birley-Smith [1966] Investment Director; Richard Keith Sheehan [1975] Investment Director

Transform Schools (Birmingham) Limited
Incorporated: 12 September 2005
Net Worth Deficit: £20,047,000 *Total Assets:* £80,415,000
Registered Office: 8 White Oak Square, London Road, Swanley, Kent, BR8 7AG
Activities: Development of building projects
Parent: Transform Schools (Birmingham) Holdings Limited
Officers: Gaynor Birley-Smith [1966] Investment Director; Richard Keith Sheehan [1975] Investment Director

Transform Schools (Knowsley) Holdings Limited
Incorporated: 29 May 2007
Net Worth Deficit: £39,047,000 *Total Assets:* £186,576,992
Registered Office: 8 White Oak Square, London Road, Swanley, Kent, BR8 7AG
Activities: Activities of other holding companies n.e.c.
Parent: PPDI Assetco Limited
Officers: Stephen Gordon [1962] Director; Roger Thompson [1954] Director

Transform Schools (Knowsley) Intermediate Limited
Incorporated: 30 May 2007
Total Assets: £14,414,000
Registered Office: 8 White Oak Square, London Road, Swanley, Kent, BR8 7AG
Activities: Other business support service activities n.e.c.
Parent: Transform Schools (Knowsley) Holdings Limited
Officers: Stephen Gordon [1962] Director; Roger Thompson [1954] Director

Transform Schools (Knowsley) Limited
Incorporated: 29 May 2007
Net Worth Deficit: £39,047,000 *Total Assets:* £186,576,992
Registered Office: 8 White Oak Square, London Road, Swanley, Kent, BR8 7AG
Activities: Other business support service activities n.e.c.
Parent: Transform Schools (Knowsley) Holdings Limited
Officers: Stephen Gordon [1962] Director; Roger Thompson [1954] Director

Transform Schools (North Lanarkshire) Funding PLC
Incorporated: 9 February 2005
Net Worth: £50,000 *Total Assets:* £175,468,992
Registered Office: 8 White Oak Square, London Road, Swanley, Kent, BR8 7AG
Activities: Financial intermediation not elsewhere classified
Parent: Transform Schools (North Lanarkshire) Holdings Limited
Officers: David John Brooking [1967] Investment Director; Robert Alistair Martin Gillespie [1990] Director/Financial Controller; Christopher James [1968] Investment Director; Kirsty O'Brien [1982] Director/Operations Manager

Transform Schools (North Lanarkshire) Holdings Limited
Incorporated: 16 February 2005
Net Worth: £8,004,000 *Total Assets:* £185,952,992
Registered Office: 8 White Oak Square, London Road, Swanley, Kent, BR8 7AG
Activities: Activities of head offices
Shareholders: Equitix Education 2 Limited; Innisfree Secondary Partners 2 LLP
Officers: David John Brooking [1967] Investment Director; Robert Alistair Martin Gillespie [1990] Director/Financial Controller; Christopher James [1968] Investment Director; Kirsty O'Brien [1982] Director/Operations Manager

Transform Schools (North Lanarkshire) Limited
Incorporated: 9 February 2005
Net Worth: £7,954,000 *Total Assets:* £185,952,992
Registered Office: 8 White Oak Square, London Road, Swanley, Kent, BR8 7AG
Activities: Other building completion and finishing
Parent: Transform Schools (North Lanarkshire) Holdings Limited
Officers: David John Brooking [1967] Investment Director; Robert Alistair Martin Gillespie [1990] Director/Financial Controller; Christopher James [1968] Investment Director; Kirsty O'Brien [1982] Director/Operations Manager

Transform Schools (Rotherham) Holdings Limited
Incorporated: 25 March 2003
Net Worth: £1,000 *Total Assets:* £9,600,000
Registered Office: 8 White Oak Square, London Road, Swanley, Kent, BR8 7AG
Activities: Activities of head offices
Parent: Innisfree Schools (F2C) Limited
Officers: Todd Malcolm Anderson [1980] Director/Accountant [New Zealander]; Christopher James [1968] Investment Director; Richard Keith Sheehan [1975] Investment Director

Transform Schools (Rotherham) Limited
Incorporated: 25 March 2003
Net Worth: £1,710,000 *Total Assets:* £95,697,000
Registered Office: 8 White Oak Square, London Road, Swanley, Kent, BR8 7AG
Activities: Other business support service activities n.e.c.
Parent: Transform Schools (Rotherham) Holdings Limited
Officers: Todd Malcolm Anderson [1980] Director/Accountant [New Zealander]; Christopher James [1968] Investment Director; Richard Keith Sheehan [1975] Investment Director

Transform Schools (Stoke) Holdings Limited
Incorporated: 22 September 2000
Net Worth Deficit: £2,416,000 *Total Assets:* £36,008,000
Registered Office: 8 White Oak Square, London Road, Swanley, Kent, BR8 7AG
Activities: Activities of construction holding companies
Parent: Innisfree Schools (F2C) Limited
Officers: David John Brooking [1975] Investment Director; Richard Keith Sheehan [1975] Investment Director

Transform Schools (Stoke) Limited
Incorporated: 22 September 2000
Net Worth Deficit: £2,416,000 *Total Assets:* £36,008,000
Registered Office: 8 White Oak Square, London Road, Swanley, Kent, BR8 7AG
Activities: Development of building projects
Parent: Transform Schools (Stoke) Holdings Limited
Officers: David John Brooking [1975] Investment Director; Richard Keith Sheehan [1975] Investment Director

Transmec Properties Limited
Incorporated: 11 July 2007 *Employees:* 3
Net Worth: £3,952,516 *Total Assets:* £14,407,471
Registered Office: Transmec Building, London Road, West Thurrock, Essex, RM20 3LH
Activities: Other letting and operating of own or leased real estate
Shareholder: Massimo Montecchi
Officers: Mohammed Imran [1978] Director; Danilo Montecchi [1952] Director [Italian]

Transmec UK Limited
Incorporated: 7 August 1990 *Employees:* 174
Net Worth: £4,856,212 *Total Assets:* £11,061,722
Registered Office: Transmec Building, London Road, West Thurrock, Essex, RM20 3LH
Activities: Freight transport by road
Shareholders: Danilo Montecchi; Massimo Montecchi
Officers: Mohammad Imran, Secretary; Danilo Montecchi [1952] Director/Freight Forwarder [Italian]

Transputec Limited
Incorporated: 2 October 1997 *Employees:* 50
Net Worth: £5,218,938 *Total Assets:* £7,198,086
Registered Office: Transputec House, 19 Heather Park Drive, Wembley, Middlesex, HA0 1SS
Activities: Computer facilities management activities
Shareholders: Anil Bharti Sehgal; Sunil Kumar Sehgal
Officers: Anil Sehgal, Secretary; Mark Norman Nightingale [1967] Director/Chief Operating Officer; Anil Seghal [1961] Director; Sunil Sehgal [1964] Director

Travel Blue Limited
Incorporated: 18 March 1987 *Employees:* 12
Net Worth: £6,315,532 *Total Assets:* £7,732,154
Registered Office: Magnolia House, Spring Villa Park, 11 Spring Villa Road, Edgware, Middlesex, HA8 7EB
Activities: Other manufacturing n.e.c.
Major Shareholder: Avi Levin
Officers: Avi Levin, Secretary/Managing Director; Avi Levin [1954] Managing Director; Hadassa Levin [1954] Director [German]; Jonathan Smith [1952] Director

Travel Nation Limited
Incorporated: 11 December 2001 *Employees:* 50
Net Worth: £429,709 *Total Assets:* £5,961,508
Registered Office: 2nd Floor, Nucleus House, Lower Mortlake Road, Richmond, Surrey, TW9 2JA
Activities: Travel agency activities
Major Shareholder: Haydn Gordon Wrath
Officers: Jonathan Mark Goodall [1974] Commercial Director

Travel Republic Holdings Ltd.
Incorporated: 20 June 2007
Net Worth: £26,314,000 *Total Assets:* £69,617,000
Registered Office: Clarendon House, 147 London Road, Kingston upon Thames, Surrey, KT2 6NH
Activities: Other business support service activities n.e.c.
Parent: Travel Technology Investments Limited
Officers: Iain Charles Richard Andrew [1965] Director; Asif Hamza Parkar [1974] Director/Finance Manager

Travel Republic Ltd
Incorporated: 1 August 2003 *Employees:* 352
Net Worth: £17,588,000 *Total Assets:* £118,592,000
Registered Office: Clarendon House, 147 London Road, Kingston upon Thames, Surrey, KT2 6NH
Activities: Travel agency activities
Parent: Dnata Travel Holdings UK Limited
Officers: Iain Charles Richard Andrew [1965] Director; John Constantine Bevan [1965] Director; Joshua Wilfrid Gubbay [1969] Director; Asif Hamza Parkar [1974] Director/Finance Manager; Frank Fouad Rejwan [1970] Director

Travel Technology Investments Limited
Incorporated: 16 June 2010
Net Worth: £23,877,000 *Total Assets:* £81,911,000
Registered Office: Clarendon House, 147 London Road, Kingston upon Thames, Surrey, KT2 6NH
Activities: Activities of head offices
Parent: Dnata World Travel Limited
Officers: Iain Charles Richard Andrew [1965] Director; Asif Hamza Parkar [1974] Director/Finance Manager

Travellanda Ltd
Incorporated: 1 March 2010 *Employees:* 17
Net Worth: £69,080 *Total Assets:* £6,419,920
Registered Office: Stanmore Business & Innovation Centre, Stanmore Place, Howard Road, Stanmore, Middlesex, HA7 1GB
Activities: Other reservation service activities n.e.c.
Shareholders: Ahmad Alkatib; Mohammad Javad Gharizadeh; Bruno Alexandre Laranjeiro
Officers: Ahmad Alkatib [1983] Director; Mohammad Javad Gharizadeh [1983] Director [Italian]; Bruno Alexandre Laranjeiro [1977] Director [French]

Travelpack Marketing & Leisure Services Limited
Incorporated: 23 July 1985 *Employees:* 36
Net Worth: £598,434 *Total Assets:* £20,189,584
Registered Office: 523 High Road, Wembley, Middlesex, HA0 2DH
Activities: Travel agency activities
Parent: Padwicks Travel (Wembley) Limited
Officers: Ashokkumar Chhotabhai Patel [1949] Director/Travel Agent; Rashmi Chhotabhai Patel [1955] Director/Travel Agent

Treasury Wine Estates EMEA Limited
Incorporated: 26 September 1986 *Employees:* 113
Net Worth: £110,482,000 *Total Assets:* £205,760,000
Registered Office: Regal House, 70 London Road, Twickenham, Middlesex, TW1 3QS
Activities: Manufacture of wine from grape
Officers: Michelle Elizabeth Brampton [1972] Finance Director; Richard John Renwick [1969] Director/Chief Financial Officer Europe

Treasury Wine Estates UK Brands Limited
Incorporated: 25 February 2011
Net Worth: £92,093,024 *Total Assets:* £92,878,672
Registered Office: 9th Floor, Regal House, 70 London Road, Twickenham, Middlesex, TW1 3QS
Activities: Manufacture of wine from grape
Parent: FBL Holdings Limited
Officers: Michelle Elizabeth Brampton [1972] Finance Director; Richard John Renwick [1969] Director/Chief Financial Officer Europe

Treebond Limited
Incorporated: 9 January 2003 *Employees:* 5
Net Worth: £7,356,529 *Total Assets:* £15,179,623
Registered Office: First Floor, Radius House, 51 Clarendon Road, Watford, Herts, WD17 1HP
Activities: Buying and selling of own real estate
Parent: JDM Investments Limited
Officers: Eithne Bridget McGowan, Secretary [Irish]; John Denis McGowan [1966] Director/Publican & Property Developer [Irish]

Treetops Capital Limited
Incorporated: 26 October 2012
Net Worth: £2,923,694 *Total Assets:* £18,612,568
Registered Office: 34 Croydon Road, Caterham, Surrey, CR3 6QB
Activities: Financial management
Major Shareholder: Arkadiy Rachkov
Officers: Arkadiy Rachkov [1974] Director [Russian]

Trellis Acquisitions Limited
Incorporated: 20 December 2011
Net Worth Deficit: £165,554,000 *Total Assets:* £610,833,984
Registered Office: Wyevale Garden Centres, Syon Park, London Road, Brentford, Middlesex, TW8 8JF
Activities: Activities of other holding companies n.e.c.
Parent: Trellis Investments Limited
Officers: Laura Harradine-Greene, Secretary; Charlotte Broadbent [1990] Director; Alexander Rupert Gavin [1954] Director; Anthony Generald Jones [1973] Director; Justin Matthew King [1961] Director

Trellis Finance Limited
Incorporated: 9 February 2012 *Employees:* 6,290
Net Worth: £71,927,000 *Total Assets:* £422,680,000
Registered Office: Wyevale Garden Centres, Syon Park, London Road, Brentford, Middlesex, TW8 8JF
Activities: Activities of other holding companies n.e.c.
Parent: Trellis Holdco Limited
Officers: Laura Harradine-Greene, Secretary; Charlotte Broadbent [1990] Director; Anthony Generald Jones [1973] Director; Justin Matthew King [1961] Director

Trellis Holdco Limited
Incorporated: 9 February 2012
Net Worth Deficit: £97,384,000 *Total Assets:* £189,350,000
Registered Office: Wyevale Garden Centres, Syon Park, London Road, Brentford, Middlesex, TW8 8JF
Activities: Activities of other holding companies n.e.c.
Parent: Wyevale Garden Centres Capital Limited
Officers: Laura Harradine-Greene, Secretary; Charlotte Broadbent [1990] Director; Anthony Generald Jones [1973] Director; Justin Matthew King [1961] Director

Trellis Investments Limited
Incorporated: 9 February 2012 *Employees:* 6,290
Net Worth: £120,332,000 *Total Assets:* £422,860,992
Registered Office: Wyevale Garden Centres, Syon Park, London Road, Brentford, Middlesex, TW8 8JF
Activities: Activities of other holding companies n.e.c.
Parent: Trellis Finance Limited
Officers: Laura Harradine-Greene, Secretary; Charlotte Broadbent [1990] Director; Anthony Generald Jones [1973] Director; Justin Matthew King [1961] Director

Trend Machinery & Cutting Tools Limited
Incorporated: 14 November 1977 *Employees:* 76
Net Worth: £4,722,323 *Total Assets:* £10,083,295
Registered Office: Unit 6 Odhams Trading Estate, Watford, Herts, WD24 7TR
Activities: Wholesale of other machinery and equipment
Shareholders: Annette Kelly; Stephen Julius Phillips
Officers: Christopher Robert Lamb, Secretary; Christopher James Carter [1975] Marketing Director; Grant John Davidson [1965] Operations Director; Christopher Robert Lamb [1973] Finance Director; Neil McMillan [1969] Technical Director; Stephen Julius Phillips [1966] Director/Chairman; Alistair Roberts [1968] CEO & Managing Director; Michael Phillip Tideswell [1976] Sales Director

Treno Investments Ltd
Incorporated: 20 January 2015 *Employees:* 5
Net Worth Deficit: £678,376 *Total Assets:* £8,250,949
Registered Office: 1B, First Floor, 142 Johnson Street, Southall, Middlesex, UB2 5FD
Activities: Buying and selling of own real estate
Major Shareholder: Amit Hasmukhbhai Patel
Officers: Amit Hasmukh Raojibhai Patel [1975] Director

Trentpeak Limited
Incorporated: 18 June 1976 *Employees:* 1
Net Worth: £2,892,372 *Total Assets:* £13,564,798
Registered Office: Garnault, Bulls Cross, Enfield, Middlesex, EN2 9HD
Activities: Buying and selling of own real estate
Major Shareholder: Omiros Marovouniotis
Officers: Seija Heinonen, Secretary; Omiros Mavrovouniotis [1948] Director

TRG Logistics Ltd
Incorporated: 17 April 2000 *Employees:* 620
Net Worth: £1,073,792 *Total Assets:* £7,383,882
Registered Office: 2nd Floor, Pathtrace House, 91-99 High Street, Banstead, Surrey, SM7 2NL
Activities: Temporary employment agency activities
Parent: NLGordon Ltd
Officers: Steven John Imber, Secretary; Nicholas Lucien Gordon [1975] Director; Steven John Imber [1963] Managing Director

Tri-Continental Limited
Incorporated: 29 September 1987 *Employees:* 23
Net Worth: £7,157,492 *Total Assets:* £17,101,246
Registered Office: Tricon Plaza, Braintree Road, Ruislip, Middlesex, HA4 0EJ
Activities: Other information technology service activities
Shareholder: Israel Lwanga
Officers: Joseph Nsambu Musisi, Secretary [Ugandan]; Edward Katimbo-Mugwanya [1948] Director/Accountant [Ugandan]; Israel Lwanga [1948] Director [Ugandan]; Joy Namuli-Lule Lwanga [1955] Director [Ugandan]; Joseph Nsambu Musisi [1949] Director/Engineer [Ugandan]

Tricomm Housing (Portsmouth) Limited
Incorporated: 18 May 2005
Net Worth Deficit: £8,737,449 *Total Assets:* £51,347,824
Registered Office: 8 White Oak Square, London Road, Swanley, Kent, BR8 7AG
Activities: Development of building projects
Parent: Tricomm Housing (Portsmouth) Holdings Limited
Officers: Neeti Mukundrai Anand [1984] Director; Stewart Chalmers Grant [1951] Director; Adam George Waddington [1974] Investment Director

Trident Garages Limited
Incorporated: 14 June 1963 *Employees:* 84
Net Worth: £6,166,310 *Total Assets:* £8,666,887
Registered Office: Trident House, Guildford Road, Ottershaw, Chertsey, Surrey, KT16 0NZ
Activities: Sale of new cars and light motor vehicles
Officers: Christopher John Roberts, Secretary; Stephen Norman Henderson [1949] Commercial Director; Christopher John Roberts [1968] Finance Director; James Barnaby Roberts [1970] Director; Richard Michael Roberts [1963] Managing Director

Triland Properties Limited
Incorporated: 21 January 2002
Net Worth: £238,806 *Total Assets:* £5,737,134
Registered Office: 68 St Margarets Road, Edgware, Middlesex, HA8 9UU
Activities: Other letting and operating of own or leased real estate
Shareholders: Shivani Jarrett; Shreya Sheth; Shailee Sheth
Officers: Nila Dilip Sheth, Secretary; Shivani Jarrett [1982] Director/Administrator; Dilip Shantilal Sheth [1954] Director

Trimite Limited
Incorporated: 27 May 1981 *Employees:* 66
Previous: Weilburger Coatings (UK) Limited
Net Worth: £154,962 *Total Assets:* £5,919,281
Registered Office: Unit 3 Silverdale Road Industrial Estate, Silverdale Road, Hayes, Middlesex, UB3 3BL
Activities: Manufacture of paints, varnishes and similar coatings, mastics and sealants
Parent: Trimite Bid Co Limited
Officers: Catherine Lorraine Hopkins [1972] Director; Richard William Marston [1966] Director; David Gareth Roberts [1952] Director; Philip John Westwood [1962] Director

Trinitas Academy Trust
Incorporated: 7 March 2011 *Employees:* 397
Net Worth: £6,724,000 *Total Assets:* £12,525,000
Registered Office: Trinity Church of England School, Erith Road, Belvedere, Kent, DA17 6HT
Activities: Primary education
Officers: Katharine Elizabeth MacKenzie, Secretary; Beverley Joy Gardner [1965] Director/Executive Headteacher; David Herbert [1939] Director/Clerk in Holy Orders; Rev Michael James Leader [1946] Director/Pastor; Matthew David Phillips [1971] Managing Director; Frederick William Price [1926] Director/Retired Engineer; Thomas Saul Ward [1957] Director/Chartered Accountant

Triplehigh Limited
Incorporated: 5 December 1990
Net Worth: £10,070,259 *Total Assets:* £13,952,020
Registered Office: 27a Maxwell Road, Northwood, Middlesex, HA6 2XY
Activities: Development of building projects
Major Shareholder: Mary Flannery
Officers: Mary Flannery, Company Secretary [Irish]; Mary Flannery [1953] Director/Company Secretary [Irish]; Patrick Flannery [1950] Director [Irish]

Triplerose Limited
Incorporated: 20 February 1996
Net Worth: £65,902,736 *Total Assets:* £123,471,992
Registered Office: 88 Edgware Way, Edgware, Middlesex, HA8 8JS
Activities: Buying and selling of own real estate
Officers: Chavi Moskovitz, Secretary; Chavi Moskovitz [1964] Director/Housewife; Israel Moskovitz [1964] Director/Property [Canadian]

Tristmire Limited
Incorporated: 7 February 1995
Net Worth: £15,295,904 *Total Assets:* £28,489,294
Registered Office: Unit 7 Horizon Business Village, 1 Brooklands Road, Weybridge, Surrey, KT13 0TJ
Activities: Development of building projects
Officers: Sandra Joanne Brownlie, Secretary; Lauren Atkins [1976] Director/Manager; Malcolm Paul Atkins [1952] Director/Property Developer

Trochair Limited
Incorporated: 10 March 1930
Net Worth: £2,365,000 *Total Assets:* £26,068,000
Registered Office: 5 Queensway, Croydon, Surrey, CR9 4DL
Activities: Other letting and operating of own or leased real estate
Officers: Paul Stuart Gaff, Secretary; Alberto Fasanotti [1974] Finance Director [Italian]; Martin Hamilton [1953] Company Secretary/Solicitor/Director; Steven Antony Wright [1980] Director/Accountant

Trollope & Colls Limited
Incorporated: 30 November 1903
Net Worth: £1,646,000 *Total Assets:* £8,326,000
Registered Office: Maple Cross House, Denham Way, Maple Cross, Rickmansworth, Herts, WD3 9SW
Activities: Construction of commercial buildings
Parent: Skanska UK PLC
Officers: Steven Leven, Secretary; David William Kyriacos [1976] Director; Steven Leven [1967] Director/Company Secretary; Steven Edward Lindsay [1975] Director

Tropical Marine Centre (2012) Ltd
Incorporated: 14 November 2012 *Employees:* 94
Net Worth: £2,559,000 *Total Assets:* £6,838,000
Registered Office: Tropical Marine Centre, Solesbridge Lane, Chorleywood, Herts, WD3 5SX
Activities: Marine aquaculture
Major Shareholder: Paul Desmond West
Officers: Amanda Kathryn Taylor, Secretary; Amanda Kathryn Taylor [1959] Company Secretary/Director; Christopher John Thomas [1955] Director; Paul Desmond West [1957] Director

Tropical Marine Centre Limited
Incorporated: 28 January 2009 *Employees:* 94
Net Worth: £2,611,000 *Total Assets:* £10,168,000
Registered Office: Tropical Marine Centre, Solesbridge Lane, Chorleywood, Herts, WD3 5SX
Activities: Marine aquaculture
Parent: Pet & Aquatics Properties Ltd
Officers: Amanda Kathryn Taylor, Secretary; Nicholas Grant Bridel [1974] Director; Brian Joao Schaff [1980] Managing Director [Portuguese]; Amanda Kathryn Taylor [1959] Director and Company Secretary; Derek Thomson [1964] Director; Paul Desmond West [1957] Managing Director

Tropical Sky Limited
Incorporated: 15 April 2005 *Employees:* 77
Net Worth: £1,657,177 *Total Assets:* £13,528,517
Registered Office: 2nd Floor, Nucleus House, 2 Lower Mortlake Road, Richmond, Surrey, TW9 2JA
Activities: Tour operator activities
Parent: Vivid Skies Ltd
Officers: Michael Gregory Collins, Secretary/Director; Jacqueline Collins [1968] Finance Director; Michael Gregory Collins [1969] Director; David Anthony Hennessy [1958] Director [Irish]

TRSL Limited
Incorporated: 10 October 1991 *Employees:* 119
Previous: Townends (Lettings & Management) Limited
Net Worth: £7,837,413 *Total Assets:* £9,014,810
Registered Office: Unit 2 Wintersells Road, Byfleet, West Byfleet, Surrey, KT14 7LF
Activities: Real estate agencies
Shareholders: Alchemy Special Opportunities LLP; Badger Holdings Limited
Officers: Vincent Edward Corley [1963] Director; Nicholas Anthony Robert Dunning [1962] Director; Graham Martin Harrison [1957] Director; Julian Matthew Irby [1966] Director/Chief Financial Officer; Timothy Pierre Van Der Schyff [1979] Managing Director, Group Lettings

True World Foods (UK) Ltd
Incorporated: 4 November 1994
Previous: Sun Ocean Limited
Net Worth: £3,808,911 *Total Assets:* £7,951,042
Registered Office: Unit 10b Beaver Industrial Park, Brent Road, Southall, Middlesex, UB2 5FB
Activities: Wholesale of other food, including fish, crustaceans and molluscs
Officers: Alexander J Choi [1974] Director [American]; Bongjin Jung [1974] Director; Shunichiro Yoshida [1950] Director [Japanese]

Trueform Engineering Limited
Incorporated: 3 August 1977 *Employees:* 165
Net Worth: £3,447,190 *Total Assets:* £12,883,560
Registered Office: Unit 12 Pasadena Trading Estate, Pasadena Close, Pump Lane, Hayes, Middlesex, UB3 3NQ
Activities: Manufacture of other fabricated metal products n.e.c.
Officers: Robert Ian MacNaughton [1978] Finance Director; Jonathan Morley [1970] Design-Engineering Director

W.A. Truelove & Son Limited
Incorporated: 15 October 1934 *Employees:* 80
Net Worth: £5,630,300 *Total Assets:* £10,867,317
Registered Office: 118 Carshalton Road, Sutton, Surrey, SM1 4RL
Activities: Funeral and related activities
Shareholders: David Alexander Hyde Truelove; Simon Andrew Truelove
Officers: David Alexander Hyde Truelove, Secretary; Geoffrey Michael Peck [1952] Director/Accountant; David Alexander Hyde Truelove [1959] Director/Accountant; Simon Andrew Truelove [1955] Funeral Director

Truly Holdings Limited
Incorporated: 12 February 2016 *Employees:* 66
Net Worth: £5,550,675 *Total Assets:* £38,307,680
Registered Office: 2nd Floor, Nucleus House, 2 Lower Mortlake Road, Richmond, Surrey, TW9 2JA
Activities: Activities of other holding companies n.e.c.
Shareholders: Krishna Veni Edara; Sridhar Kumar Edara
Officers: Sridhar Kumar Edara [1971] Director

Truly Travel Limited
Incorporated: 24 March 2009 *Employees:* 16
Net Worth: £8,692,597 *Total Assets:* £14,463,172
Registered Office: 2nd Floor, Nucleus House, 2 Lower Mortlake Road, Richmond, Surrey, TW9 2JA
Activities: Travel agency activities
Parent: Truly Holdings Limited
Officers: Sridhar Kumar Edara [1971] Director [Indian]; Petrakis Panteli [1963] Director

Truman Securities Limited
Incorporated: 20 June 2015
Net Worth: £41,822 *Total Assets:* £17,147,800
Registered Office: Kirkland House, 11-15 Peterborough Road, Harrow, Middlesex, HA1 2AX
Activities: Hotels and similar accommodation
Officers: Haider Ladhu Jaffer [1940] Director; Hassanali Amirali Dawood Suleman [1954] Director

Try Homes Limited
Incorporated: 1 May 1991
Net Worth: £27,414,000 *Total Assets:* £27,716,000
Registered Office: Cowley Business Park, Cowley, Uxbridge, Middlesex, UB8 2AL
Activities: Construction of commercial buildings
Parent: Linden Holdings Limited
Officers: Kevin Allan Corbett [1960] Director/Solicitor; Andrew James Duxbury [1975] Director/Accountant

TT Skate Properties Limited
Incorporated: 8 April 2010 *Employees:* 35
Net Worth: £776,473 *Total Assets:* £7,683,083
Registered Office: High Street Centre, 137-139 High Street, Beckenham, Kent, BR3 1AG
Activities: Management of real estate on a fee or contract basis
Shareholders: Mary McGrath; Patrick Joseph McGrath
Officers: Quraish Sajjad Hussain Adamally [1980] Director; Mary McGrath [1963] Director [Irish]; Patrick Joseph McGrath [1955] Director [Irish]

Tudor Bank Limited
Incorporated: 23 October 2003 *Employees:* 140
Net Worth: £4,691,242 *Total Assets:* £5,169,856
Registered Office: 1st Floor, 44-50 The Broadway, Southall, Middlesex, UB1 1QB
Activities: Residential nursing care facilities
Officers: Palani Ketheeswaran [1968] Director; Sharmili Seevarajah [1977] Director; Nadarajah Bernard Suresparan [1959] Director/Company Secretary; Vathsala Suresparan [1961] Director; Shan Vivian [1993] Director

Tudor Court Primary Academy Trust
Incorporated: 4 June 2014 *Employees:* 150
Net Worth: £7,595,230 *Total Assets:* £9,942,944
Registered Office: Tudor Court Primary School, Bark Burr Road, Grays, Essex, RM16 6PL
Activities: Primary education
Officers: Julia Mary Violet Edmeades [1974] Director/Human Resources Manager; Riham Ahmed Moustafa Moustafa El Maghraby [1975] Director/Classroom Support Assistant; Chinyere Emuche Eruchalu [1984] Director/Project Manager; Philip Brian Peter Kyriacou [1973] Director/Executive Principal; Cheryl Anne Mason [1979] Director/Chartered Accountant; Andrew McLeod [1975] Director/Security Risk Manager; Kim Lorraine Moore [1972] Director/Sports Injury & Massage Therapist; Paul Robert Raymond [1990] Director/Teacher; Keeley Michele Shelton [1972] Director/Bookkeeper; Emily Louise Sheppard [1988] Director; Kelly Ann Stevens [1978] Director/Teacher

Tudor Investments Limited
Incorporated: 1 February 1999
Net Worth: £2,271,766 *Total Assets:* £6,636,222
Registered Office: Tudor House, 185 Kenton Road, Harrow, Middlesex, HA3 0EY
Activities: Buying and selling of own real estate
Officers: Sonal Ashar, Secretary; Rasila Ashwin Shah, Secretary; Meera Rupani [1988] Director; Ashwin MoTlchand Shah [1955] Director; Rasila Ashwin Shah [1953] Director

Tudor Williams (Holdings) Limited
Incorporated: 9 September 2004 *Employees:* 137
Net Worth: £7,588,251 *Total Assets:* £11,896,893
Registered Office: 53-59 High Street, New Malden, Surrey, KT3 4BU
Activities: Other retail sale in non-specialised stores
Officers: John Charles Morris, Secretary/Retailer; John Charles Morris [1963] Director/Retailer; Trevor Kenneth Tudor Williams [1930] Director/Retailer

Tulip Properties & Real Estate Ltd
Incorporated: 21 July 2015
Net Worth: £3,304,673 *Total Assets:* £11,042,356
Registered Office: 35 Gabrielle House, 332-336 Perth Road, Ilford, Essex, IG2 6FF
Activities: Other letting and operating of own or leased real estate
Officers: Varun Chadha [1982] Director; Nikkita Kewal Mahajan [1983] Director

Tumi (UK) Limited
Incorporated: 20 September 2006 *Employees:* 43
Net Worth: £1,372,581 *Total Assets:* £6,370,563
Registered Office: Palmerston House, 814 Brighton Road, Purley, Surrey, CR8 2BR
Activities: Other retail sale of new goods in specialised stores (not commercial art galleries and opticians)
Parent: Samsonite Limited
Officers: Patrick Baele [1957] Director [Belgian]; Kyle Gendreau [1969] Director [American]; Damien Marie Albert Mignot [1966] Director [French]

Turner Properties Limited
Incorporated: 28 August 1986 *Employees:* 4
Net Worth: £7,197,425 *Total Assets:* £12,023,430
Registered Office: Tudor House, 185 Kenton Road, Harrow, Middlesex, HA3 0EY
Activities: Buying and selling of own real estate
Shareholders: Ashwin Motichand Shah; Rasila Ashwin Shah
Officers: Sonal Ashar, Secretary; Rasila Ashwin Shah, Secretary; Meera Rupani [1988] Director; Ashwin MoTlchand Shah [1955] Director/Chartered Accountant; Rasila Ashwin Shah [1953] Director

Turnhold Properties Limited
Incorporated: 6 February 1991 *Employees:* 13
Net Worth: £15,579,005 *Total Assets:* £18,473,580
Registered Office: 249 Cranbrook Road, Ilford, Essex, IG1 4TG
Activities: Development of building projects
Shareholder: Garry Jon Simpson
Officers: Michele Suzanne Simpson, Secretary; David Ronald Elliott [1974] Director; Garry Jon Simpson [1967] Director/Commercial Agent; Michele Suzanne Simpson [1968] Director; Elise Ruth Summers [1966] Director

Turnlet Films (JN) Limited
Incorporated: 30 May 2017
Net Worth: £1 *Total Assets:* £9,366,773
Registered Office: 99 Kenton Road, Harrow, Middlesex, HA3 0AN
Activities: Motion picture production activities
Parent: Turnlet Films Limited
Officers: Simon Horsman [1967] Director; Andrea Scarso [1984] Director [Italian]; Simon Robert Williams [1982] Director

Tuskerdirect Limited
Incorporated: 25 October 1999 *Employees:* 171
Net Worth: £26,149,160 *Total Assets:* £185,849,040
Registered Office: Building 4, Hatters Lane, Croxley Green Business Park, Watford, Herts, WD18 8YF
Activities: Renting and leasing of cars and light motor vehicles
Parent: Hamsard 3353 Limited
Officers: Laura Catherine Elizabeth Alexander [1979] Director/Chief Financial Officer; Clive Andrew Whistler Baker [1974] Director [British/South African]; Simon English [1960] Director; Paul Gilshan [1975] Director

P.C. Tustin & Company Limited
Incorporated: 3 March 1986 *Employees:* 3
Net Worth: £4,779,175 *Total Assets:* £5,785,387
Registered Office: Suite 2, Fountain House, 1a Elm Park, Stanmore, Middlesex, HA7 4AU
Activities: Development of building projects
Parent: C.V.J. Properties Ltd
Officers: Charles William Vaughan-Jones, Secretary; Margaret Maria Therese Brown [1951] Director/Theatre Nurse; Jane Elizabeth Putt [1953] Director; Charles William Vaughan-Jones [1953] Director

Tustin Properties Ltd
Incorporated: 22 March 2010 *Employees:* 3
Net Worth: £9,658,567 *Total Assets:* £11,390,600
Registered Office: Suite 2, Fountain House, 1a Elm Park, Stanmore, Middlesex, HA7 4AU
Activities: Buying and selling of own real estate
Shareholder: Alexander Charles Tustin
Officers: Catherine Takhtay [1971] Director/Property Consultant; Alexander Charles Tustin [1973] Director/Sales Executive; Brie Kirsty Tustin [1978] Director/Property Consultant; Elsa Tustin [1947] Director/Textile Artist

TVH Fizzy Holdings Limited
Incorporated: 21 March 2012
Net Worth Deficit: £1,923,000 *Total Assets:* £26,628,000
Registered Office: Premier House, 52 London Road, Twickenham, Middlesex, TW1 3RP
Activities: Other letting and operating of own or leased real estate
Officers: Patricia Etter, Secretary; Guy John Burnett [1969] Group Development Director; Ian Roderick Johnson [1965] Finance Director; Nicholas John Lloyd [1967] Director/Head of Keyworker Rented Housing; Kush Rawal [1982] Commercial Director

TWE Finance (UK) Limited
Incorporated: 31 January 2011
Net Worth: £3,446,432 *Total Assets:* £60,580,812
Registered Office: 9th Floor, Regal House, London Road, Twickenham, Middlesex, TW1 3QS
Activities: Manufacture of wine from grape
Parent: Treasury Wine Estates EMEA Limited
Officers: Michelle Elizabeth Brampton [1972] Finance Director; Richard John Renwick [1969] Director/Chief Financial Officer Europe

Twentieth Century Fox Television Distribution (U.K.), Ltd.
Incorporated: 24 June 2016
Net Worth: £161,836,432 *Total Assets:* £209,570,784
Registered Office: 99 Kenton Road, Harrow, Middlesex, HA3 0AN
Activities: Motion picture distribution activities
Parent: Twentieth Century Fox International Television Inc
Officers: Jonathan Gottlieb [1972] Director/Lawyer [American]; Jane Waxman [1965] Director/Executive Vice President, Twenty-First Century Fox [American]

TWG Europe Limited
Incorporated: 27 May 2009 *Employees:* 345
Net Worth: £126,431,000 *Total Assets:* £519,175,008
Registered Office: Twenty Kingston Road, Staines upon Thames, Surrey, TW18 4LG
Activities: Activities of financial services holding companies
Parent: Assurant, Inc.
Officers: Natalie Ann Paddock, Secretary; George Derek Wilson Bartlett [1948] Director; Michael John Carter [1981] Director; Colin Martin Kersley [1956] Director; Ricardo Jesus Morales-Gomez [1970] Director [American]; Andrew James Morris [1971] Director/Chief Executive; Claude Kwasi Sarfo-Agyare [1969] Director

TWG Services Limited
Incorporated: 6 February 1985 *Employees:* 344
Net Worth: £1,556,000 *Total Assets:* £73,476,000
Registered Office: Twenty Kingston Road, Staines upon Thames, Surrey, TW18 4LG
Activities: Activities of insurance agents and brokers
Parent: TWG Europe Limited
Officers: Natalie Ann Paddock, Secretary; George Derek Wilson Bartlett [1948] Director; Michael John Carter [1981] Director; Colin Martin Kersley [1956] Director; Ricardo Jesus Morales-Gomez [1970] Director [American]; Andrew James Morris [1971] Director/Chief Executive Officer; Claude Kwasi Sarfo-Agyare [1969] Director

Twickenham Experience Ltd
Incorporated: 13 April 2000 *Employees:* 18
Net Worth: £40,696,000 *Total Assets:* £53,160,000
Registered Office: Rugby House, Twickenham Stadium, 200 Whitton Road, Twickenham, Middlesex, TW2 7BA
Activities: Event catering activities
Shareholders: Compass Services (UK) Limited; Rugby Football Union
Officers: Angus Roch Bujalski, Secretary; Robert Thomas Johnson Briers [1951] Director/Retired; Susan Margaret Day [1972] Director/Chief Financial Officer; Michael Andrew Jones [1982] Finance Director; Simon Edwin Massie-Taylor [1980] Director/Chief Commercial Officer; Helen Alison Weir [1962] Independent Director

Twickenham Studios Limited
Incorporated: 6 June 2012 *Employees:* 52
Net Worth: £522,917 *Total Assets:* £16,749,533
Registered Office: Twickenham Studios, The Barons, Twickenham, Middlesex, TW1 2AW
Activities: Motion picture production activities
Officers: Dr Zulfikar Masters [1956] Director; Roger Michael Sewell [1957] Director/Certified Chartered Accountant; Sanjit Singh Vohra [1957] Director

Twilight Real Estate Limited
Incorporated: 2 March 2017
Net Worth Deficit: £3,152 *Total Assets:* £17,772,256
Registered Office: Unit 4 Imperial Park, Stonefield Way, South Ruislip, Middlesex, HA4 0JW
Activities: Buying and selling of own real estate
Shareholder: Nayan Thakrar
Officers: Nayan Thakrar [1960] Director

Twinglobe Limited
Incorporated: 20 June 1983 *Employees:* 4
Net Worth: £3,945,454 *Total Assets:* £10,668,499
Registered Office: 7 Coombehurst Close, Hadley Wood, Herts, EN4 0JU
Activities: Other letting and operating of own or leased real estate
Shareholders: Twinglobe 2008 Ltd; Nineacre Limited
Officers: Mihir Kantilal Thakerar, Secretary/Businessman/Director; Dipak Thakerar [1965] Businessman/Director; Mihir Kantilal Thakerar [1963] Businessman/Director

TX Group Europe Ltd.
Incorporated: 12 July 1991 *Employees:* 59
Net Worth: £3,549,000 *Total Assets:* £10,658,000
Registered Office: Suite 32, 4th Floor, 1000 Great West Road, Brentford, Middlesex, TW8 9HH
Activities: Wholesale of watches and jewellery
Officers: David Thomas Payne, Secretary; Yves Paul di Benedetto [1958] Director/Business Executive [French]; Annika Katarina Forsberg [1969] Director/Business Executive [Swedish]; Paul Martin [1966] Director/Business Executive; David Thomas Payne [1971] Director/Business Executive [American]

Ty Danjuma Family Office Limited
Incorporated: 15 June 2009 *Employees:* 9
Net Worth: £72,400,000 *Total Assets:* £91,351,000
Registered Office: 1st Floor, Two Furlongs, Esher, Surrey, KT10 9AA
Activities: Activities auxiliary to financial intermediation n.e.c.
Major Shareholder: Theophilus Yakubu Danjuma
Officers: Gloria Amina Atta [1971] Executive Director [Nigerian]; Daniel Pontoppidan Broby [1964] Director; Theophilus Yakubu Danjuma [1938] Director/Retired [Nigerian]; Simon Miles Foster [1968] Director/Chief Executive Officer; Hannatu Kizeya Gentles [1975] Director/Chief Operating Officer; Dipankar Shewaram [1973] Director/Asset Management Banking & Finance

TY Properties (UK) Limited
Incorporated: 12 February 2010 *Employees:* 4
Net Worth: £38,902,000 *Total Assets:* £49,173,000
Registered Office: 1st Floor, Two Furlongs, Esher, Surrey, KT10 9AA
Activities: Buying and selling of own real estate
Parent: Ty Danjuma Family Office Limited
Officers: Theophilus Danjuma [1985] Director [Nigerian]; Simon Miles Foster [1968] Director/Accountant; Hannatu Kizeya Gentles [1975] Director/Family Officer

TY Ventures (UK) Limited
Incorporated: 10 November 2009
Net Worth: £1,242,761 *Total Assets:* £6,285,605
Registered Office: 1st Floor, Two Furlongs, Portsmouth Road, Esher, Surrey, KT10 9AA
Activities: Other business support service activities n.e.c.
Parent: Ty Danjuma Family Office Limited
Officers: Hulkar Azam [1983] Director/Governance & Compliance Manager [Uzbek]; Simon Miles Foster [1968] Director/Accountant; Hannatu Kizeya Gentles [1975] Director/Family Officer

Tyco Building Services Products (UK) Limited
Incorporated: 15 November 1990 *Employees:* 74
Net Worth Deficit: £2,770,000 *Total Assets:* £35,127,000
Registered Office: Security House, The Summit, Hanworth Road, Sunbury on Thames, Middlesex, TW16 5DB
Activities: Non-specialised wholesale trade
Parent: Johnson Controls International PLC
Officers: Mark Ayre [1963] Finance Director; Laurens Swennenhuis [1965] Managing Director [Dutch]

Tyco European Metal Framing Limited
Incorporated: 29 January 1999
Net Worth Deficit: £629,000 *Total Assets:* £5,113,000
Registered Office: Security House, The Summit, Hanworth Road, Sunbury on Thames, Middlesex, TW16 5DB
Activities: Manufacture of metal structures and parts of structures
Parent: Tyco Holdings (UK) Limited
Officers: Mark Ayre [1963] Finance Director; Peter Schieser [1967] Director [German]

Tyco Fire Products Manufacturing Limited
Incorporated: 16 August 1984 *Employees:* 175
Net Worth: £68,420,000 *Total Assets:* £84,488,000
Registered Office: Security House, The Summit, Hanworth Road, Sunbury on Thames, Middlesex, TW16 5DB
Activities: Non-specialised wholesale trade
Parent: Tyco European Metal Framing Limited
Officers: Joseph Paul Harvey-Nimmo [1978] Manufacturing Operations Director; Mark James MacMichael [1966] Director; Damien Morris [1960] Director

A.E. Tyler Limited
Incorporated: 18 August 1972 *Employees:* 112
Net Worth: £2,195,056 *Total Assets:* £7,026,779
Registered Office: Crown House, 30a Commerce Road, Brentford, Middlesex, TW8 8LE
Activities: Other service activities n.e.c.
Major Shareholder: William Antony Tyle
Officers: Michael Edward Freely [1971] Marketing Director; Charlotte Joy Tyler [1971] Director; William Antony Tyler [1968] Managing Director

Tyrolese (751) Limited
Incorporated: 14 December 2012 *Employees:* 159
Net Worth: £5,455,091 *Total Assets:* £45,411,928
Registered Office: Excel House, Cray Avenue, Orpington, Kent, BR5 3ST
Activities: Activities of head offices
Major Shareholder: Malcolm Charles Elster
Officers: Malcolm Charles Elster [1957] Director

U K Insurance Business Solutions Limited
Incorporated: 3 August 2004
Net Worth: £4,784,274 *Total Assets:* £7,408,279
Registered Office: Churchill Court, Westmoreland Road, Bromley, Kent, BR1 1DP
Activities: Activities of insurance agents and brokers
Parent: Direct Line Insurance Group PLC
Officers: Roger Cheston Clifton, Secretary; Jonathan Paul Greenwood [1968] Director/Bank Official; Michael Anthony Holliday-Williams [1970] Director; Neil Manser [1974] Director/Accountant

Uavend Exeter LLP
Incorporated: 14 April 2015 *Employees:* 3
Net Worth: £4,687,173 *Total Assets:* £12,522,000
Registered Office: Unit 2 Langley Wharf, Railway Terrace, Kings Langley, Herts, WD4 8JE
Officers: Eamon Mark O'Connor [1962] Member; Viviane O'Connor [1971] Member

Uavend Norris Castle Ltd
Incorporated: 3 June 2016 *Employees:* 2
Net Worth: £5,451,230 *Total Assets:* £6,060,357
Registered Office: Lady Capels Wharf, Hempstead Road, Watford, Herts, WD17 3NL
Activities: Development of building projects
Shareholders: Eamon Mark John O'Connor; Edward Wellington
Officers: Eamon Mark O'Connor [1962] Managing Director; Edward Wellington [1988] Director/Property Developer/Contractor

UB Overseas Limited
Incorporated: 13 May 1980
Net Worth: £1,216,610,048 *Total Assets:* £1,367,154,048
Registered Office: Hayes Park, Hayes End Road, Hayes, Middlesex, UB4 8EE
Activities: Activities of head offices
Parent: United Biscuits (Holdings) Limited
Officers: Mark Oldham, Secretary/Director; Helen Josephine McCarthy [1966] Director; Mark Oldham [1959] Director

UCAR Properties Limited
Incorporated: 22 September 1993 *Employees:* 5
Net Worth: £3,998,961 *Total Assets:* £7,816,139
Registered Office: Unit 1-8 Centenary Industrial Estate, Jeffreys Road, Enfield, Middlesex, EN3 7UF
Activities: Buying and selling of own real estate
Parent: TFC Holdings London Limited
Officers: Ercan Ucur [1970] Director; Huseyin Ucur [1945] Director/Merchant

UCL Albion Limited
Incorporated: 14 June 2016
Net Worth: £7,316,847 *Total Assets:* £7,597,164
Registered Office: Portland House, 69-71 Wembley Hill Road, Wembley, Middlesex, HA9 8BU
Activities: Sea and coastal freight water transport
Parent: Union Carriers Limited
Officers: Bhupendra Shantilal Kansagra, Secretary; Laurent Elie Cadji [1977] Director/Businessman; Lewis Levy Cadji [1938] Director/Businessman; Bhupendra Shantilal Kansagra [1956] Director/Businessman; Ramesh Shantilal Kansagra [1950] Director/Businessman

UCL Frognal Limited
Incorporated: 18 April 2017
Net Worth: £4,467,897 *Total Assets:* £8,496,399
Registered Office: Portland House, 69-71 Wembley Hill Road, Wembley, Middlesex, HA9 8BU
Activities: Other business support service activities n.e.c.
Officers: Bhupendra Shantilal Kansagra, Secretary; Laurent Elie Cadji [1977] Director/Businessman; Lewis Levy Cadji [1938] Director/Businessman; Bhupendra Shantilal Kansagra [1956] Director/Businessman; Ramesh Shantilal Kansagra [1950] Director/Businessman

UCL Harrow Limited
Incorporated: 27 October 2016
Net Worth: £3,716,272 *Total Assets:* £5,996,053
Registered Office: Portland House, 69-71 Wembley Hill Road, Wembley, Middlesex, HA9 8BU
Activities: Other business support service activities n.e.c.
Parent: Union Carriers Limited
Officers: Bhupendra Shantilal Kansagra, Secretary; Laurent Elie Cadji [1977] Director/Businessman; Lewis Levy Cadji [1938] Director/Businessman; Bhupendra Shantilal Kansagra [1956] Director/Businessman; Ramesh Shantilal Kansagra [1950] Director/Businessman

Ugo Foods Group Limited
Incorporated: 30 September 1938 *Employees:* 131
Net Worth: £1,579,172 *Total Assets:* £7,561,803
Registered Office: 1 Hertsmere Industrial Park, Warwick Road, Borehamwood, Herts, WD6 1GT
Activities: Manufacture of macaroni, noodles, couscous and similar farinaceous products
Major Shareholder: Paul Luigi Ugo
Officers: Andrew Blackett [1973] Director; Sophia Louise Cooke [1980] Commercial Director; Bernard Philip Klug [1939] Director; Paul Luigi Ugo [1966] Director/Food Manufacturer

UHP Investments Limited
Incorporated: 23 December 2003
Net Worth: £7,635,067 *Total Assets:* £17,104,812
Registered Office: Bank House, 81 St Judes Road, Englefield Green, Surrey, TW20 0DF
Activities: Other letting and operating of own or leased real estate
Major Shareholder: Nigel William Wray
Officers: Carel Jacobus Engelbrecht [1979] Director; Kamal Somchand Shah [1959] Director/Chartered Accountant; Daniel Johannes Van Den Heever [1979] Director

UIDUK Ltd
Incorporated: 9 August 2011
Net Worth: £927,243 *Total Assets:* £12,182,200
Registered Office: 3 Lowther Close, Elstree, Borehamwood, Herts, WD6 3PY
Activities: Development of building projects
Major Shareholder: Kay Manzoor
Officers: Kay Manzoor [1982] Director

UK 786 Limited
Incorporated: 3 June 2015
Net Worth: £6,017 *Total Assets:* £6,459,313
Registered Office: 85 Shaftesbury Avenue, South Harrow, Middlesex, HA2 0PP
Activities: Development of building projects
Officers: Mohammed Pyarali Bandali [1962] Director; Abbas Liyakatali Datoo [1974] Director [Grenadian]; Liyakatali Mohamed Abdalla Datoo [1947] Director [Grenadian]; Murtaza Liakatali Datoo Pardan [1974] Director

UK Addiction Treatment Group Limited
Incorporated: 1 October 2012 *Employees:* 17
Previous: The Recovery Clinic Limited
Net Worth: £1,242,552 *Total Assets:* £5,210,883
Registered Office: c/o UK Addiction Treatment Group Ltd, 1st Floor, Unit 1 Imperial Place, Maxwell Road, Borehamwood, Herts, WD6 1JN
Activities: Activities of other holding companies n.e.c.
Parent: UKAT Investments Limited
Officers: Colin John O'Connor, Secretary; Eytan Leigh Alexander [1971] Director/Broker; Howard Beggs [1968] Director [Irish]; Rory Cremin [1976] Director [Irish]; Daniel Gerrard [1970] Director; Sean Connall Higgins [1981] Director/Doctor [Irish]; Gerard Hunt [1959] Director [Irish]

UK Assistance Accident Repair Centres Limited
Incorporated: 13 December 1990
Net Worth: £50,241,000 *Total Assets:* £80,181,000
Registered Office: Churchill Court, Westmoreland Road, Bromley, Kent, BR1 1DP
Activities: Maintenance and repair of motor vehicles
Parent: Direct Line Insurance Group PLC
Officers: Roger Cheston Clifton, Secretary; Cormac Bradley [1973] Director [Irish]; Jessie Burrows [1968] Director; Stuart Robert Forrester [1970] Director of Legal Services and Claims; Steven Maddock [1968] Director/Bank Official; Paul Nightingale [1964] Director; Helen Clare O'Murchu [1967] Director

UK Highways A55 (Holdings) Limited
Incorporated: 20 July 1998
Net Worth: £22,878,000 *Total Assets:* £92,167,000
Registered Office: 8 White Oak Square, London Road, Swanley, Kent, BR8 7AG
Activities: Activities of other holding companies n.e.c.
Parent: JLIF (Holdings) A55 Limited
Officers: David Richard Bradbury [1969] Director/Senior Investment Manager; Johannes Petrus Heemelaar [1956] Director [Dutch]

UK Highways A55 Limited
Incorporated: 20 July 1998
Net Worth: £22,881,000 *Total Assets:* £92,167,000
Registered Office: 8 White Oak Square, London Road, Swanley, Kent, BR8 7AG
Activities: Construction of roads and motorways
Parent: UK Highways A55 (Holdings) Limited
Officers: David Richard Bradbury [1969] Director/Senior Investment Manager; Johannes Petrus Heemelaar [1956] Director [Dutch]

UK Highways M40 (Holdings) Limited
Incorporated: 16 June 1994
Net Worth: £1,491,000 *Total Assets:* £105,969,000
Registered Office: 8 White Oak Square, London Road, Swanley, Kent, BR8 7AG
Activities: Other business support service activities n.e.c.
Shareholders: Palio (No. 7) Limited; Semperian Subholdings M40 Limited
Officers: David Richard Bradbury [1969] Director/Senior Investment Manager; Ian Richard Gethin [1971] Director/Investment Banker; Johannes Petrus Heemelaar [1956] Director [Dutch]; Neil Rae [1971] Director

UK Highways M40 Limited
Incorporated: 12 April 1995
Net Worth: £1,326,000 *Total Assets:* £105,964,000
Registered Office: 8 White Oak Square, London Road, Swanley, Kent, BR8 7AG
Activities: Other business support service activities n.e.c.
Officers: David Richard Bradbury [1969] Director/Senior Investment Manager; Ian Richard Gethin [1971] Director/Investment Banker; Johannes Petrus Heemelaar [1956] Director [Dutch]; Neil Rae [1971] Director

UK Real Estate Limited
Incorporated: 6 March 1986 *Employees:* 12
Net Worth: £107,743,128 *Total Assets:* £189,299,520
Registered Office: York House, Empire Way, Wembley, Middlesex, HA9 0FQ
Activities: Development of building projects
Major Shareholder: Nicholas John Capstick-Dale
Officers: Jeremy Louis Landau, Secretary; Nicholas John Capstick-Dale [1962] Director

UK Salads Investments Limited
Incorporated: 13 May 2014
Net Worth: £934,575 *Total Assets:* £5,094,427
Registered Office: 1st Floor, 87-89 High Street, Hoddesdon, Herts, EN11 8TL
Activities: Buying and selling of own real estate
Officers: Giuseppina Colletti [1963] Director; Vito Colletti [1960] Director [Italian]; Leonora Milazzo [1966] Director; Pasquale Milazzo [1963] Director [Italian]; Franca Schillaci [1970] Director; Giuseppe Schillaci [1969] Director [Italian]

ULS Living Limited
Incorporated: 1 February 2001
Previous: UHG Limited
Net Worth: £6,907,000 *Total Assets:* £9,118,000
Registered Office: Media House, Azalea Drive, Swanley, Kent, BR8 8HU
Activities: Activities of head offices
Parent: United Livign (South) Holdings Limited
Officers: Ian George Burnett [1959] Director; Stuart Wilson Laird [1953] Director; David Masters [1971] Finance Director; Timothy Nicholas Wood [1965] Commercial Director

Ultimate Care Limited
Incorporated: 1 August 2006 *Employees:* 62
Net Worth: £1,923,456 *Total Assets:* £5,674,592
Registered Office: 1st Floor, 44-50 The Broadway, Southall, Middlesex, UB1 1QB
Activities: Other accommodation
Shareholder: Nadarajah Bernard Suresparan
Officers: Nadarajah Bernard Suresparan, Secretary/Consultant; Nadarajah Bernard Suresparan [1959] Director/Consultant; Vathsala Suresparan [1961] Director

Ultimate Holdings Limited
Incorporated: 3 July 2008
Previous: Ultimate Opportunities Limited
Net Worth: £68,859 *Total Assets:* £20,565,496
Registered Office: Typhoon Building, Oakcroft Road, Chessington, Surrey, KT9 1RH
Activities: Other business support service activities n.e.c.
Parent: Ultimate Capital Funding Ltd
Officers: Mark Julian Hugo Holden, Secretary; Mark Julian Hugo Holden [1960] Director; Palinda Samarasinghe [1970] Director

Ultimate Model Corporation Limited
Incorporated: 8 August 1996 *Employees:* 98
Net Worth: £1,702,622 *Total Assets:* £7,016,030
Registered Office: 241 Green Street, Enfield, Middlesex, EN3 7SJ
Activities: Activities of head offices
Major Shareholder: Nicholas Julian Moss
Officers: Mark Henley, Secretary; Mark David Henley [1971] Director/Chartered Accountant; Jason Harvey Metcalf [1968] Director/Corporate Financier; Nicholas Julian Moss [1964] Director/Businessman

Ultra Electronics Holdings PLC
Incorporated: 25 June 1993 *Employees:* 4,172
Net Worth: £512,172,000 *Total Assets:* £1,083,816,960
Registered Office: 417 Bridport Road, Greenford, Middlesex, UB6 8UA
Activities: Activities of head offices
Officers: Brenda Louise Ruppel, Secretary; Martin Tilston Broadhurst [1953] Director; Douglas Caster [1953] Director/Chairman; Geeta Gopalan [1964] Director; John Raymond Hirst [1952] Director; Victoria Mary Hull [1962] Director; Simon Charles Conrad Pryce [1961] Director; William Anthony Rice [1952] Director; Amitabh Sharma [1967] Finance Director; Sir Robert Walmsley [1941] Director

Ultra Electronics Limited
Incorporated: 25 June 1993 *Employees:* 1,878
Net Worth: £144,234,000 *Total Assets:* £447,919,008
Registered Office: 417 Bridport Road, Greenford, Middlesex, UB6 8UA
Activities: Other manufacturing n.e.c.
Parent: Ultra Electronics Holdings PLC
Officers: Anant Prakash, Secretary; Michael Baptist [1965] Divisional Managing Director; Simon Charles Conrad Pryce [1961] Director; Carlos Ricardo Santiago [1955] Director [American]; Amitabh Sharma [1967] Finance Director; Graeme David Stacey [1965] Director

Ultrabrook Limited
Incorporated: 3 November 2003
Net Worth: £5,624,514 *Total Assets:* £6,109,083
Registered Office: c/o Messors RSB Associates, 101 Wanstead Park Road, Ilford, Essex, IG1 3JH
Activities: Other letting and operating of own or leased real estate
Officers: Lolita Sanger, Secretary; Dalbir Singh Sanger [1965] Director/Businessman

UML Blandford Limited
Incorporated: 27 April 2015
Net Worth: £6,221,663 *Total Assets:* £10,650,281
Registered Office: Portland House, 69-71 Wembley Hill Road, Wembley, Middlesex, HA9 8BU
Activities: Sea and coastal freight water transport
Parent: Focus Tankers Ltd
Officers: Bhupendra Shantilal Kansagra, Secretary; Laurent Elie Cadji [1977] Director/Businessman; Lewis Levy Cadji [1938] Director/Businessman; Bhupendra Shantilal Kansagra [1956] Director/Businessman; Ramesh Shantilal Kansagra [1950] Director/Businessman

UML Chiltern Limited
Incorporated: 27 April 2015
Net Worth: £5,129,875 *Total Assets:* £9,020,699
Registered Office: Portland House, 69-71 Wembley Hill Road, Wembley, Middlesex, HA9 8BU
Activities: Sea and coastal freight water transport
Parent: Union Maritime Limited
Officers: Bhupendra Shantilal Kansagra, Secretary; Laurent Elie Cadji [1977] Director/Businessman; Lewis Levy Cadji [1938] Director/Businessman; Bhupendra Shantilal Kansagra [1956] Director/Businessman; Ramesh Shantilal Kansagra [1950] Director/Businessman

UML Eagle Limited
Incorporated: 30 June 2014
Net Worth: £5,421,567 *Total Assets:* £10,039,261
Registered Office: Portland House, 69-71 Wembley Hill Road, Wembley, Middlesex, HA9 8BU
Activities: Sea and coastal freight water transport
Parent: Focus Tankers Ltd
Officers: Bhupendra Shantilal Kansagra, Secretary; Laurent Elie Cadji [1977] Director/Businessman; Lewis Levy Cadji [1938] Director/Businessman; Bhupendra Shantilal Kansagra [1956] Director/Businessman; Ramesh Shantilal Kansagra [1950] Director/Businessman

UML Hinde Limited
Incorporated: 14 April 2015
Net Worth: £5,516,461 *Total Assets:* £8,028,726
Registered Office: Portland House, 69-71 Wembley Hill Road, Wembley, Middlesex, HA9 8BU
Activities: Sea and coastal freight water transport
Parent: Focus Tankers Ltd
Officers: Bhupendra Shantilal Kansagra, Secretary; Laurent Elie Cadji [1977] Director/Businessman; Lewis Levy Cadji [1938] Director/Businessman; Bhupendra Shantilal Kansagra [1956] Director/Businessman; Ramesh Shantilal Kansagra [1950] Director/Businessman

UML Marylebone Limited
Incorporated: 12 May 2015
Net Worth: £8,332,677 *Total Assets:* £15,011,344
Registered Office: Portland House, 69-71 Wembley Hill Road, Wembley, Middlesex, HA9 8BU
Activities: Sea and coastal freight water transport
Parent: Union Maritime Limited
Officers: Bhupendra Shantilal Kansagra, Secretary; Laurent Elie Cadji [1977] Director/Businessman; Lewis Levy Cadji [1938] Director/Businessman; Bhupendra Shantilal Kansagra [1956] Director/Businessman; Ramesh Shantilal Kansagra [1950] Director/Businessman

UML Mayfair Limited
Incorporated: 25 January 2016
Net Worth: £3,594,846 *Total Assets:* £8,264,092
Registered Office: Portland House, 69-71 Wembley Hill Road, Wembley, Middlesex, HA9 8BU
Activities: Sea and coastal freight water transport
Parent: Union Maritime Limited
Officers: Bhupendra Shantilal Kansagra, Secretary; Laurent Elie Cadji [1977] Director/Businessman; Lewis Levy Cadji [1938] Director/Businessman; Bhupendra Shantilal Kansagra [1956] Director/Businessman; Ramesh Shantilal Kansagra [1950] Director/Businessman

UML Moxon Limited
Incorporated: 27 April 2015
Net Worth: £6,972,699 *Total Assets:* £10,108,995
Registered Office: Portland House, 69-71 Wembley Hill Road, Wembley, Middlesex, HA9 8BU
Activities: Sea and coastal freight water transport
Parent: Focus Tankers Ltd
Officers: Bhupendra Shantilal Kansagra, Secretary; Laurent Elie Cadji [1977] Director/Businessman; Lewis Levy Cadji [1938] Director/Businessman; Bhupendra Shantilal Kansagra [1956] Director/Businessman; Ramesh Shantilal Kansagra [1950] Director/Businessman

UML Portman Limited
Incorporated: 29 July 2015
Net Worth: £3,465,544 *Total Assets:* £7,045,995
Registered Office: Portland House, 69-71 Wembley Hill Road, Wembley, Middlesex, HA9 8BU
Activities: Sea and coastal freight water transport
Parent: Union Maritime Limited
Officers: Bhupendra Shantilal Kansagra, Secretary; Laurent Elie Cadji [1977] Director/Businessman; Lewis Levy Cadji [1938] Director/Businessman; Bhupendra Shantilal Kansagra [1956] Director/Businessman; Ramesh Shantilal Kansagra [1950] Director/Businessman

UML Wembley Limited
Incorporated: 22 December 2015
Net Worth: £2,338,520 *Total Assets:* £12,715,205
Registered Office: Portland House, 69-71 Wembley Hill Road, Wembley, Middlesex, HA9 8BU
Activities: Sea and coastal freight water transport
Parent: Focus Tankers Ltd
Officers: Bhupendra Shantilal Kansagra, Secretary; Laurent Elie Cadji [1977] Director/Businessman; Lewis Levy Cadji [1938] Director/Businessman; Bhupendra Shantilal Kansagra [1956] Director/Businessman; Ramesh Shantilal Kansagra [1950] Director/Businessman

UML Westminster Limited
Incorporated: 19 January 2016
Net Worth: £3,068,397 *Total Assets:* £9,067,016
Registered Office: Portland House, 69-71 Wembley Hill Road, Wembley, Middlesex, HA9 8BU
Activities: Sea and coastal freight water transport
Parent: Union Maritime Limited
Officers: Bhupendra Shantilal Kansagra, Secretary; Laurent Elie Cadji [1977] Director/Businessman; Lewis Levy Cadji [1938] Director/Businessman; Bhupendra Shantilal Kansagra [1956] Director/Businessman; Ramesh Shantilal Kansagra [1950] Director/Businessman

UML Wigmore Limited
Incorporated: 19 March 2015
Net Worth: £2,448,032 *Total Assets:* £9,117,172
Registered Office: Portland House, 69-71 Wembley Hill Road, Wembley, Middlesex, HA9 8BU
Activities: Sea and coastal freight water transport
Parent: Union Maritime Limited
Officers: Bhupendra Shantilal Kansagra, Secretary; Laurent Elie Cadji [1977] Director/Businessman; Lewis Levy Cadji [1938] Director/Businessman; Bhupendra Shantilal Kansagra [1956] Director/Businessman; Ramesh Shantilal Kansagra [1950] Director/Businessman

UML Wimpole Limited
Incorporated: 17 September 2015
Net Worth: £4,562,951 *Total Assets:* £7,610,585
Registered Office: Portland House, 69-71 Wembley Hill Road, Wembley, Middlesex, HA9 8BU
Activities: Sea and coastal freight water transport
Parent: Union Maritime Limited
Officers: Bhupendra Shantilal Kansagra, Secretary; Laurent Elie Cadji [1977] Director/Businessman; Lewis Levy Cadji [1938] Director/Businessman; Bhupendra Shantilal Kansagra [1956] Director/Businessman; Ramesh Shantilal Kansagra [1950] Director/Businessman

UMV Global Foods Company Ltd.
Incorporated: 30 October 2014
Net Worth: £1,028,400,000 *Total Assets:* £2,077,799,936
Registered Office: United Biscuits, Hayes Park, Hayes End Road, Hayes, Middlesex, UB4 8EE
Activities: Activities of head offices
Parent: UMV Global Foods Holding Company Limited
Officers: Baris Oner, Secretary; Richard Handscombe [1954] Director/Accountant; Simon Edward Munir [1964] Director/Fund Manager; Murat Ulker [1959] Director/Chairman [Turkish]

UMV Global Foods Holding Company Ltd.
Incorporated: 30 October 2014 *Employees:* 8,093
Net Worth: £1,106,400,000 *Total Assets:* £2,754,500,096
Registered Office: United Biscuits, Hayes Park, Hayes End Road, Hayes, Middlesex, UB4 8EE
Activities: Activities of head offices
Parent: Pladis Foods Limited
Officers: Mark Oldham, Secretary; Richard Handscombe [1954] Director/Accountant; Simon Edward Munir [1964] Director/Fund Manager; Murat Ulker [1959] Director/Chairman [Turkish]

Unbar Rothon Limited
Incorporated: 25 February 1921 *Employees:* 74
Net Worth: £6,964,191 *Total Assets:* £7,604,267
Registered Office: 44-54 Orsett Road, Grays, Essex, RM17 5ED
Activities: Manufacture of condiments and seasonings
Officers: Carol Doreen Rothon, Secretary; Carol Doreen Rothon [1952] Director/Administrator; Matthew Lewis Rothon [1979] Director/Manager; Patrick Leonard Rothon [1951] Director/Factory Manager; Richard Michael Rothon [1980] Director/Manager; William Lewis Rothon [1945] Director/Food Technologist

Uncle Buck Finance LLP
Incorporated: 1 July 2010 *Employees:* 66
Previous: Uncle Buck Payday Loans LLP
Net Worth Deficit: £1,439,995 *Total Assets:* £6,677,132
Registered Office: River Bridge House, Anchor Boulevard, Crossways Business Park, Dartford, Kent, DA2 6SL
Officers: Steven George Murray [1966] Member

Uneek Forwarding Limited
Incorporated: 30 April 1981 *Employees:* 48
Net Worth: £2,501,940 *Total Assets:* £8,658,383
Registered Office: Unit 1 & 2 Renwick Industrial Estate, Renwick Road, Barking, Essex, IG11 0SD
Activities: Other transportation support activities
Officers: Varsha Prakash Patel, Secretary; Avinash Raojibhai Patel [1950] Director; Prakash Raojibhai Patel [1954] Director; Rajesh Raojibhai Patel [1957] Director; Varsha Prakash Patel [1955] Director

Unicorn Ingredients Ltd
Incorporated: 28 March 2008 *Employees:* 17
Net Worth: £486,540 *Total Assets:* £9,658,763
Registered Office: 9 Bridle Close, Surbiton Road, Kingston upon Thames, Surrey, KT1 2JW
Activities: Wholesale of other food, including fish, crustaceans and molluscs
Shareholders: Nicola Janice Divers; Francis James Horan
Officers: Sally Claire Horan, Secretary; Nicola Janice Divers [1960] Director; Francis James Horan [1962] Director

Unicourt Properties Limited
Incorporated: 7 May 1998
Net Worth: £7,902,236 *Total Assets:* £8,332,172
Registered Office: Little Acre, East End Way, Pinner, Middlesex, HA5 3BS
Activities: Buying and selling of own real estate
Major Shareholder: Jonathan Bradley Coren
Officers: Generald Coren, Secretary/Director; Generald Coren [1927] Director; Joel Anthony Coren [1982] Director/Surveyor; Jonathan Bradley Coren [1956] Director/Chartered Surveyor

Unifruit Group Limited
Incorporated: 7 June 2011 *Employees:* 10
Net Worth: £8,675,038 *Total Assets:* £11,405,024
Registered Office: 155 High Street, Rickmansworth, Herts, WD3 1AR
Activities: Activities of other holding companies n.e.c.
Shareholders: Mukesh Dayalal Tolia; Jayshree Mukesh Tolia
Officers: Jayshree Mukesh Tolia [1958] Director; Mukesh Dayalal Tolia [1954] Director

Unifruit Limited
Incorporated: 21 February 1984 *Employees:* 10
Net Worth: £8,690,137 *Total Assets:* £11,420,123
Registered Office: Unifruit House, 155 High Street, Rickmansworth, Herts, WD3 1AR
Activities: Wholesale of fruit and vegetables
Parent: Unifruit Group Limited
Officers: Jayshree Mukesh Tolia, Secretary/Housewife; Jayshree Mukesh Tolia [1958] Director; Mukesh Dayalal Tolia [1954] Director

Unilever UK Limited
Incorporated: 9 December 1937 *Employees:* 2,976
Net Worth: £1,239,565,952 *Total Assets:* £1,671,614,976
Registered Office: Unilever House, Springfield Drive, Leatherhead, Surrey, KT22 7GR
Activities: Manufacture of ice cream
Parent: Unilever UK Group Limited
Officers: James Oliver Earley, Secretary; Richard Clive Hazell, Secretary; Hazel Karen Detsiny [1972] Managing Director FMCG; Paul William Fenwick [1970] Director/Accountant; Placid Oriol Jover Goma [1981] Director/VP HR UK & Ireland [Spanish]; Sebastian John Munden [1968] Director/EVP & GM Unilever UK & Ireland; Jonathan David Strachan [1964] Director/Manager; Marc John Woodward [1974] Director/VP Customer Development

Union Carriers Limited
Incorporated: 7 June 2016
Net Worth: £17,289,696 *Total Assets:* £22,164,462
Registered Office: Portland House, 69-71 Wembley Hill Road, Wembley, Middlesex, HA9 8BU
Activities: Sea and coastal freight water transport
Shareholders: Solai Holdings Limited; Samilau Limited
Officers: Bhupendra Shantilal Kansagra, Secretary; Laurent Elie Cadji [1977] Director/Businessman; Lewis Levy Cadji [1938] Director/Businessman; Bhupendra Shantilal Kansagra [1956] Director/Businessman; Ramesh Shantilal Kansagra [1950] Director/Businessman

Union Glory Limited
Incorporated: 29 April 2008
Net Worth Deficit: £4,095,446 *Total Assets:* £11,452,143
Registered Office: Portland House, 69-71 Wembley Hill Road, Wembley, Middlesex, HA9 8BU
Activities: Sea and coastal freight water transport
Parent: Union Maritime Limited
Officers: Bhupendra Shatilal Kansagra, Secretary; Laurent Elie Cadji [1977] Director/Businessman; Lewis Levy Cadji [1938] Director/Businessman; Bhupendra Shantilal Kansagra [1956] Director/Businessman; Ramesh Shantilal Kansagra [1950] Director/Businessman

Union Investcorp Limited
Incorporated: 18 April 2008
Net Worth: £27,243,118 *Total Assets:* £30,790,780
Registered Office: Portland House, 69-71 Wembley Hill Road, Wembley, Middlesex, HA9 8BU
Activities: Other business support service activities n.e.c.
Shareholders: Solai Holdings Limited; South Central Property Limited
Officers: Bhupendra Shatilal Kansagra, Secretary; Laurent Elie Cadji [1977] Director/Businessman; Lewis Levy Cadji [1938] Director/Businessman; Bhupendra Shantilal Kansagra [1956] Director/Businessman; Ramesh Shantilal Kansagra [1950] Director/Businessman

Union Maritime Limited
Incorporated: 12 January 2006 *Employees:* 67
Net Worth: £102,587,064 *Total Assets:* £292,708,416
Registered Office: Portland House, 69-71 Wembley Hill Road, Wembley, Middlesex, HA9 8BU
Activities: Sea and coastal freight water transport
Shareholders: Solai Holdings Limited; South Central Property Limited
Officers: Bhupendra Shantilal Kansagra, Secretary; Laurent Elie Cadji [1977] Director/Businessman; Lewis Levy Cadji [1938] Director/Businessman; Bhupendra Shantilal Kansagra [1956] Director/Businessman; Ramesh Shantilal Kansagra [1950] Director/Businessman; Sarita Michele Kraljevic [1971] Director/Housewife

Unique Atlantic Seafood Limited
Incorporated: 23 January 2013 *Employees:* 1
Net Worth: £338,839 *Total Assets:* £5,070,586
Registered Office: Lygon House, 50 London Road, Bromley, Kent, BR1 3RA
Activities: Wholesale of other food, including fish, crustaceans and molluscs
Shareholder: Unique Seafood Holdings Limited
Officers: Morten Wad Dethlefsen [1969] Managing Director [Danish]; Harald Nissen [1965] Director [Danish]; Inger Marie Sperre [1971] Director [Norwegian]; Kjetil Sperre [1961] Director [Norwegian]

Unique Seafood Limited
Incorporated: 27 January 1997 *Employees:* 13
Net Worth: £3,283,313 *Total Assets:* £9,598,757
Registered Office: Lygon House, 50 London Road, Bromley, Kent, BR1 3RA
Activities: Wholesale of fruit and vegetables
Parent: Unique Seafood Holdings Limited
Officers: Harald Nissen, Secretary; Harald Nissen [1965] Director/Seafood Wholesaler [Danish]; Inger Marie Sperre [1971] Director [Norwegian]; Kjetil Sperre [1961] Director [Norwegian]

Uniquehelp Limited
Incorporated: 30 November 1987 *Employees:* 106
Net Worth: £13,636,709 *Total Assets:* £15,501,395
Registered Office: 30 Station Road, Orpington, Kent, BR6 0SA
Activities: Residential nursing care facilities
Officers: Kanagaratnam Rajakanthan [1955] Director

Uniserve (Air Freight) Limited
Incorporated: 23 March 1988 *Employees:* 47
Net Worth: £24,624,976 *Total Assets:* £33,466,564
Registered Office: Upminster Court, Hall Lane, Upminster, Essex, RM14 1AL
Activities: Freight air transport
Major Shareholder: Iain Robert Liddell
Officers: Barry George Tuck, Secretary; Leighton Bonnett [1967] Director; Iain Robert Liddell [1963] Director

Uniserve (Europe) Limited
Incorporated: 13 June 1985 *Employees:* 15
Net Worth: £7,919,139 *Total Assets:* £9,889,359
Registered Office: Upminster Court, 133 Hall Lane, Upminster, Essex, RM14 1AL
Activities: Freight transport by road
Parent: Uniserve Holdings Limited
Officers: Barry George Tuck, Secretary; Iain Robert Liddell [1963] Director

Uniserve (U.K.) Limited
Incorporated: 16 April 1985 *Employees:* 108
Net Worth Deficit: £9,283,453 *Total Assets:* £9,081,439
Registered Office: Upminster Court, 133 Hall Lane, Upminster, Essex, RM14 1AL
Activities: Freight transport by road
Parent: Uniserve Holdings Limited
Officers: Barry George Tuck, Secretary; Iain Robert Liddell [1963] Director

Uniserve Holdings Limited
Incorporated: 23 March 1988 *Employees:* 684
Net Worth: £74,631,000 *Total Assets:* £116,781,000
Registered Office: Upminster Court, Hall Lane, Upminster, Essex, RM14 1AL
Activities: Activities of distribution holding companies
Major Shareholder: Iain Robert Liddell
Officers: Barry George Tuck, Secretary; Stephen William George Ireland [1966] Director; Iain Robert Liddell [1963] Director; Paul Stone [1958] HR Director

Uniserve Limited
Incorporated: 21 June 1984 *Employees:* 54
Net Worth: £48,612,580 *Total Assets:* £59,599,056
Registered Office: Upminster Court, 133 Hall Lane, Upminster, Essex, RM14 1AL
Activities: Sea and coastal freight water transport
Parent: Uniserve Holdings Limited
Officers: Barry George Tuck, Secretary; Stephen William George Ireland [1966] Director; Iain Robert Liddell [1963] Director

Unit 2 (Rickmansworth) Limited
Incorporated: 1 July 2013
Net Worth: £469,665 *Total Assets:* £5,025,641
Registered Office: Olds Approach, Tolpits Lane, Watford, Herts, WD18 9XT
Activities: Other letting and operating of own or leased real estate
Shareholders: Peter Thomas Wilson; Christine Agnes Wilson
Officers: Jonathan David Wilson [1961] Director/Salesman; Peter Thomas Wilson [1932] Director/Salesman

United Biscuits (UK) Limited
Incorporated: 25 May 1990 *Employees:* 4,514
Net Worth: £1,566,000,000 *Total Assets:* £3,558,799,872
Registered Office: Hayes Park, Hayes End Road, Hayes, Middlesex, UB4 8EE
Activities: Manufacture of rusks and biscuits; manufacture of preserved pastry goods and cakes
Parent: McVitie & Price Limited
Officers: Mark Oldham, Secretary/Director; Ahmed Salman Amin [1959] Director [American]; Nicholas Robert Bunker [1964] Managing Director; Richard Handscombe [1954] Director; Helen Marie Pitcher [1958] Director; Mustafa Tercan [1974] Director/Chief Financial Officer [Turkish]; Ali Ulker [1969] Director [Turkish]; Murat Ulker [1959] Director/Chairman [Turkish]; Jim Nafez Zaza [1957] Director/Executive Vice Chairman-Chief Operating Officer [American]

United Biscuits Bidco Limited
Incorporated: 5 October 2006
Net Worth: £220,300,000 *Total Assets:* £2,108,099,968
Registered Office: Hayes Park, Hayes End Road, Hayes, Middlesex, UB4 8EE
Activities: Activities of head offices
Parent: United Biscuits Holdco 2 Limited
Officers: Mark Oldham, Secretary/Director; Helen Josephine McCarthy [1966] Director; Huseyin Avni Metinkale [1963] Director [Turkish]

United Biscuits BondCo Limited
Incorporated: 5 October 2006
Net Worth Deficit: £395,300,000 *Total Assets:* £331,800,000
Registered Office: Hayes Park, Hayes End Road, Hayes, Middlesex, UB4 8EE
Activities: Activities of head offices
Parent: United Biscuits Topco Limited
Officers: Mark Oldham, Secretary/Director; Helen Josephine McCarthy [1966] Director; Huseyin Avni Metinkale [1963] Director [Turkish]

United Biscuits Holdco 2 Limited
Incorporated: 5 October 2006
Net Worth: £219,000,000 *Total Assets:* £1,658,300,032
Registered Office: Hayes Park, Hayes End Road, Hayes, Middlesex, UB4 8EE
Activities: Activities of head offices
Parent: United Biscuits Holdco Limited
Officers: Mark Oldham, Secretary/Director; Helen Josephine McCarthy [1966] Director; Mark Oldham [1959] Company Secretary/Director; Murat Ulker [1959] Director/Chairman [Turkish]

United Biscuits Holdco Limited
Incorporated: 5 October 2006
Net Worth Deficit: £294,200,000 *Total Assets:* £1,439,299,968
Registered Office: Hayes Park, Hayes End Road, Hayes, Middlesex, UB4 8EE
Activities: Activities of head offices
Parent: United Biscuits VLNCo Limited
Officers: Mark Oldham, Secretary/Director; Helen Josephine McCarthy [1966] Director; Huseyin Avni Metinkale [1963] Director [Turkish]

United Biscuits VInco Limited
Incorporated: 5 October 2006
Net Worth: £600,000,000 *Total Assets:* £600,000,000
Registered Office: Hayes Park, Hayes End Road, Hayes, Middlesex, UB4 8EE
Activities: Activities of head offices
Parent: United Biscuits BondCo Limited
Officers: Mark Oldham, Secretary/Director; Helen Josephine McCarthy [1966] Director; Huseyin Avni Metinkale [1963] Director [Turkish]

United Distributing Company (Coin Machine Sales) Limited (The)
Incorporated: 6 March 1984 *Employees:* 25
Net Worth: £2,591,328 *Total Assets:* £5,996,973
Registered Office: 10 Western Road, Romford, Essex, RM1 3JT
Activities: Other business support service activities n.e.c.
Major Shareholder: Mark Nicholas Horwood
Officers: Sheila Helena Horwood, Secretary; Derek Norman Horwood [1933] Director/Coin Machine Distributor; Lisa Beverly Horwood [1965] Director; Mark Nicholas Horwood [1964] Director/Sales Manager

United Healthcare (South Buckinghamshire) Group Limited
Incorporated: 4 June 2001
Net Worth: £8,085,000 *Total Assets:* £55,167,000
Registered Office: 8 White Oak Square, London Road, Swanley, Kent, BR8 7AG
Activities: Combined facilities support activities
Parent: Innisfree Nominees Limited
Officers: Ellen Charlotte Le Breton Schroder [1957] Director; Richard Keith Sheehan [1975] Investment Director; Alastair James Watson [1974] Investment Director

United Healthcare (South Buckinghamshire) Holdings Limited
Incorporated: 27 February 1997
Net Worth: £123,000 *Total Assets:* £24,603,000
Registered Office: 8 White Oak Square, London Road, Swanley, Kent, BR8 7AG
Activities: Combined facilities support activities
Parent: United Healthcare (South Buckinghamshire) Group Limited
Officers: Ellen Charlotte Le Breton Schroder [1957] Director; Richard Keith Sheehan [1975] Investment Director; Alastair James Watson [1974] Investment Director

United Healthcare (South Buckinghamshire) Limited
Incorporated: 28 August 1997
Net Worth: £3,631,000 *Total Assets:* £45,954,000
Registered Office: 8 White Oak Square, London Road, Swanley, Kent, BR8 7AG
Activities: Combined facilities support activities
Parent: United Healthcare (South Buckinghamshire) Holdings Limited
Officers: Ellen Charlotte Le Breton Schroder [1957] Director; Richard Keith Sheehan [1975] Investment Director; Alastair James Watson [1974] Investment Director

United Kingdom Accreditation Service
Incorporated: 30 June 1995 *Employees:* 255
Net Worth: £7,631,831 *Total Assets:* £14,726,102
Registered Office: 2 Pine Trees, Chertsey Lane, Staines upon Thames, Middlesex, TW18 3HR
Activities: Other professional, scientific and technical activities n.e.c.
Officers: Georgia Alsop, Secretary; Georgia Alsop [1970] Finance Director; James Randolph Lindsay [1955] Director; Dr Jeffery William Llewellyn [1947] Director/Chief Executive; Professor Michael Raymond Mainelli [1958] Director/Accountant [Irish]; Professor Adrian Charles Newland [1949] Director; Sir Duncan Kirkbride Nichol [1941] Director/Professor; Jeffrey David Ruddle [1977] Director; Lorraine Michelle Turner [1977] Director; Sarah Veale [1953] Director/Member of Regulatory Policy Committee

United Living (North) Group Limited
Incorporated: 13 September 2011
Previous: Pyper Construction Limited
Net Worth Deficit: £3,238,000 *Total Assets:* £19,465,000
Registered Office: Media House, Azalea Drive, Swanley, Kent, BR8 8HU
Activities: Activities of head offices
Parent: United Living Group Limited
Officers: Ian George Burnett [1959] Director; Christopher Richard Hurley [1974] Director; Stuart Wilson Laird [1953] Director; David Masters [1971] Finance Director; Christopher John Thomas [1955] Director; Timothy Nicholas Wood [1965] Commercial Director

United Living (North) Holdings Limited
Incorporated: 30 June 2005 *Employees:* 4
Previous: DTB Holdings Limited
Net Worth: £26,000 *Total Assets:* £42,618,000
Registered Office: Media House, Azalea Drive, Swanley, Kent, BR8 8HU
Activities: Activities of head offices
Parent: United Living (North) Group Limited
Officers: Ian George Burnett [1959] Director; Stuart Wilson Laird [1953] Director; David Masters [1971] Finance Director; Timothy Nicholas Wood [1965] Director

United Living (North) Limited
Incorporated: 10 March 1955 *Employees:* 183
Previous: Bullock Construction Limited
Net Worth: £13,789,000 *Total Assets:* £35,102,000
Registered Office: Media House, Azalea Drive, Swanley, Kent, BR8 8HU
Activities: Development of building projects
Parent: United Living (North) Holdings Limited
Officers: Ian George Burnett [1959] Director/Chief Executive; Steve Denis Carden [1958] Director; Charles Neil Dunn [1962] Director; Joanne Jamieson [1975] Director; Stuart Wilson Laird [1953] Director; David Masters [1971] Finance Director; Daren Moseley [1970] Director; Anne Catherine Newman [1960] People Services Director

United Living (South) Group Limited
Incorporated: 9 February 2010
Previous: UHG Holdings Limited
Net Worth: £2,086,000 *Total Assets:* £55,203,000
Registered Office: Media House, Azalea Drive, Swanley, Kent, BR8 8HU
Activities: Activities of head offices
Parent: United Living Group Limited
Officers: Ian George Burnett [1959] Director; Stuart Wilson Laird [1953] Director; David Masters [1971] Finance Director; Timothy Nicholas Wood [1965] Commercial Director

United Living (South) Limited
Incorporated: 28 August 1964 *Employees:* 325
Previous: United House Limited
Net Worth: £41,196,000 *Total Assets:* £114,285,000
Registered Office: Media House, Azalea Drive, Swanley, Kent, BR8 8HU
Activities: Development of building projects
Parent: ULS Living Limited
Officers: Ian George Burnett [1959] Director; Steve Denis Carden [1958] Director; Joanne Jamieson [1975] Director; Stuart Wilson Laird [1953] Director; David Masters [1971] Finance Director; Daren Moseley [1970] Director; Anne Catherine Newman [1960] People Services Director

United Living Group Limited
Incorporated: 22 August 2014 *Employees:* 520
Net Worth: £13,828,000 *Total Assets:* £132,833,000
Registered Office: Media House, Azalea Drive, Swanley, Kent, BR8 8HU
Activities: Activities of head offices
Officers: Ian George Burnett [1959] Director; Charles Neil Dunn [1962] Director; Christopher Richard Hurley [1974] Director; Stuart Wilson Laird [1953] Director; David Masters [1971] Director/Chartered Accountant; Christopher John Thomas [1955] Director; Martyn John Vitty [1975] Director; Timothy Nicholas Wood [1965] Director

The United Reformed Church (Southern Synod) Trust Limited
Incorporated: 21 November 1980 *Employees:* 8
Net Worth: £25,661,556 *Total Assets:* £26,063,498
Registered Office: The Synod Office, East Croydon URC, Addiscombe Grove, Croydon, Surrey, CR0 5LP
Activities: Activities of religious organisations
Officers: Catherine Elizabeth Kingdom, Secretary; Linda Margaret Austin [1956] Director/Manager & Chartered Engineer; Revd Bridget Jane Banks [1965] Director/Minister of Religion; Rev Michael John Davies [1933] Director/Retired; John Harold Denison [1948] Director/Retired [American]; Revd Derrick Sena Dzandu-Hedidor [1953] Director/Synod Clerk [Ghanaian]; Revd Nicola Jayne Furley-Smith [1961] Director/Minister of Religion; Alan David Kirby [1946] Director/Retired; David Henry Walters [1946] Director; Revd Helen Amy Elizabeth Warmington [1959] Director/Minister; Revd George Donald Watt [1961] Director/Minister

United Technologies Finance (U.K.) Limited
Incorporated: 5 October 1922
Net Worth: £237,822,000 *Total Assets:* £237,822,000
Registered Office: 1st Floor, Ash House, Littleton Road, Ashford, Middlesex, TW15 1TZ
Activities: Non-trading company
Parent: Parkview Treasury Services (UK) Limited
Officers: Lynn Banis, Secretary; Christian Bruno Jean Idczak [1963] Director/Business Executive [French]; James Terence George Laurence [1964] Financial Director; Patricia Catherine Moran [1964] Director [American]; Michael Patrick Ryan [1969] Director/Businessman [American]

United Technologies Holdings Limited
Incorporated: 18 December 1963
Net Worth: £326,270,016 *Total Assets:* £768,590,016
Registered Office: 1st Floor, Ash House, Littleton Road, Ashford, Middlesex, TW15 1TZ
Activities: Activities of head offices
Parent: Goodrich Aftermarket Services Limited
Officers: Lynn Banis, Secretary; Christian Bruno Jean Idczak [1963] Director/Business Executive [French]; James Terence George Laurence [1964] Financial Director; Patricia Catherine Moran [1964] Finance Director [American]; Louise Kay Thompson [1983] Director/Chartered Management Accountant

Unitruc Limited
Incorporated: 12 March 1984 *Employees:* 111
Net Worth: £2,324,669 *Total Assets:* £6,992,959
Registered Office: Greytown House, 221-227 High Street, Orpington, Kent, BR6 0NZ
Activities: Freight transport by road
Major Shareholder: Richard Kenneth Horsfall
Officers: Richard Kenneth Horsfall, Secretary; Alexander Richard Horsfall [1994] Director; Richard Kenneth Horsfall [1959] Managing Director

Unity Academy Trust
Incorporated: 7 September 2016 *Employees:* 165
Net Worth: £14,566,910 *Total Assets:* £15,904,869
Registered Office: Upland Primary School, Church Road, Bexleyheath, Kent, DA7 4DG
Activities: Primary education
Officers: Stuart James Doubleday [1980] Director/Civil Servant; Emma Johnson [1974] Director/Personal Secretary; Victoria Jane Marsh [1976] Director/Executive Headteacher; Bola Ibilola Ojo [1955] Director/Retired; Dr Steven John Smith [1955] Director/Retired; Nii Okai Tagoe [1990] Director/Compliance Officer; Thea Eleri Tanner [1987] Director/Chartered Accountant

Unity Schools Trust
Incorporated: 4 July 2011 *Employees:* 252
Previous: The Magna Carta School
Net Worth: £31,003,000 *Total Assets:* £35,321,000
Registered Office: The Magna Carta School, Thorpe Road, Staines upon Thames, Surrey, TW18 3HJ
Activities: General secondary education
Officers: Elizabeth Simmons, Secretary; Jennifer Anne Febry [1964] Director/Accountant; Paul Allen Green [1963] Director/Civil Servant; Christopher Paul Howorth [1965] Director/University Lecturer; Robin Michael Kent [1964] Director/Retired; Jessica McMichael [1966] Director/Teacher; Suresh Pillai [1969] Director/Banker; David Benjamin Wales [1975] Director/Management Consultant

Universal Dispense Systems Limited
Incorporated: 28 October 2003 *Employees:* 54
Net Worth: £1,036,481 *Total Assets:* £6,667,852
Registered Office: Universal Buildings, Green Lane, Hounslow, Middlesex, TW4 6DF
Activities: Manufacture of taps and valves
Parent: Wilman Universal Group Limited
Officers: Robert Bernard Cook, Secretary/Engineer; Robert Bernard Cook [1947] Director/Engineer; Colin Brian Elvidge [1953] Director; Neil Robert Tanner [1972] Director

Universal Tyre Company (Deptford) Limited (The)
Incorporated: 22 August 1933 *Employees:* 167
Net Worth: £9,702,545 *Total Assets:* £18,616,326
Registered Office: Units 8 & 9 Orbital One, Green Street, Green Road, Dartford, Kent, DA1 1QG
Activities: Maintenance and repair of motor vehicles
Officers: Matthew James Abbott [1985] Director/Chartered Accountant; Rupert Eastell [1961] Director/Accountant; Andrew Aubrey Wright [1957] Director/Tyre Distributor; Simon Paul Wright [1974] Director/Tyre Distributor

Universal Tyres and Spares Limited
Incorporated: 22 May 1957 *Employees:* 48
Net Worth: £3,338,897 *Total Assets:* £6,186,844
Registered Office: Units 18-19 Crown Trading Estate, Clayton Road, Hayes, Middlesex, UB3 1DU
Activities: Non-specialised wholesale trade
Major Shareholder: Adrian Richard Tennant
Officers: Michael Christopher Jackson [1977] Director/General Manager; Thomas Mark Phipps [1975] Director/Purchasing Manager; Adrian Richard Tennant [1944] Director; Margaret Ann Tennant [1949] Director

The Unstuffy Hotel Co Limited
Incorporated: 19 March 2003 *Employees:* 29
Net Worth Deficit: £3,673,752 *Total Assets:* £13,732,529
Registered Office: Dixcart House, Addlestone Road, Bourne Business Park, Addlestone, Surrey, KT15 2LE
Activities: Hotels and similar accommodation
Shareholders: Neelu Singh; Analjit Singh
Officers: Laurence Binge, Secretary; Laurence Binge [1959] Director; Peter Anthony Robertson [1980] Director; Analjit Singh [1954] Director [Indian]; Sahil Vachani [1983] Director [Indian]; Tara Singh Vachani [1987] Director [Indian]

Up Offshore (UK) Limited
Incorporated: 4 August 2005 *Employees:* 2
Net Worth: £2,288,983 *Total Assets:* £12,396,296
Registered Office: Fourth Floor, 18-20 Hill Rise, Richmond, Surrey, TW10 6UA
Activities: Sea and coastal freight water transport
Parent: Scapef IV LP
Officers: Malcolm Fraser Keen, Secretary; Peter Banghart Evensen [1958] Director [American]; Jesus Llorca [1975] Director [American]; Alejandro Romano [1979] Director [Mexican]

Upgrade Investments Limited
Incorporated: 9 January 1997
Net Worth: £2,891,946 *Total Assets:* £5,685,491
Registered Office: c/o Parker Cavendish, 28 Church Road, Stanmore, Middlesex, HA7 4XR
Activities: Development of building projects
Shareholder: Zeev Zi Pear
Officers: Anita Mehra, Secretary; Anita Mehra [1953] Director; Vidhur Mehra [1975] Director/Accountant

Upminster Academies Trust
Incorporated: 14 September 2012 *Employees:* 89
Net Worth: £8,481,000 *Total Assets:* £9,326,000
Registered Office: Upminster Infant School, St Mary's Lane, Upminster, London, RM14 3BS
Activities: Primary education
Officers: Dr Deborah Lee Birrell [1977] Director/Medical Advisor; Heidi Clarke [1977] Director/Accountant; Ann Louise Cooke [1962] Director/School Librarian; Alison Edgcombe [1973] Director/Headteacher; Matthew James Pepper [1972] Director/IT Manager; Jane Elizabeth Margaret Phillips [1974] Director/Accountant; Keri Denise Pitt [1973] Director/Accountant; Jackie Theresa Woodgate [1958] Director/Registered Childminder

Uponor Limited
Incorporated: 7 July 1997 *Employees:* 37
Net Worth: £2,728,000 *Total Assets:* £6,110,000
Registered Office: The Pavillion, Blackmoor Lane, Croxley Business Park, Watford, Herts, WD18 8GA
Activities: Wholesale of hardware, plumbing and heating equipment and supplies
Parent: Uponor Corporation
Officers: John Patrick Fahy, Secretary; Reetta Elina Harkki [1965] Director/Lawyer [Finnish]; Maija Strandberg [1969] Director/Chief Financial Officer [Finnish]

Upper Street Investments LLP
Incorporated: 29 August 2014
Net Worth: £2,173,016 *Total Assets:* £5,135,076
Registered Office: 119 High Road, Loughton, Essex, IG10 4LT
Officers: Vincent Daniel Goldstein [1960] Member

UPS (UK Holding) Limited
Incorporated: 10 November 2003
Net Worth: £149,615,408 *Total Assets:* £239,067,920
Registered Office: UPS House, Forest Road, Feltham, Middlesex, TW13 7DY
Activities: Activities of head offices
Parent: United Parcel Service, Inc.
Officers: Elisabel Rodriguez Marquez, Secretary; Louis Anthony Rivieccio Jr [1965] Director [American]; Elisabel Rodriguez Marquez [1980] Finance Director [Spanish]; Peter Raoul Stewardson [1964] Director/Legal Attorney; Mark Simon Vale [1965] Director

UPS (UK) Limited
Incorporated: 2 October 1984 *Employees:* 21
Net Worth: £588,991,488 *Total Assets:* £2,179,633,664
Registered Office: UPS House, Forest Road, Feltham, Middlesex, TW13 7DY
Activities: Activities of head offices
Parent: United Parcel Service, Inc.
Officers: Peter Raoul Stewardson, Secretary; Ronald Woo-Sung Chang [1965] Director/Corporate Finance, President [American]; Tim Regis Helsen [1979] Director/Manager [Belgian]; Elisabel Rodriguez Marquez [1980] Finance Director [Spanish]; Peter Raoul Stewardson [1964] Director/Legal Attorney

UPS Air Couriers of America Limited
Incorporated: 11 February 1969 *Employees:* 33
Net Worth: £10,709,000 *Total Assets:* £14,312,000
Registered Office: UPS House, Forest Road, Feltham, Middlesex, TW13 7DY
Activities: Freight air transport
Parent: UPS (UK Holding) Limited
Officers: Elisabel Rodriguez Marquez, Secretary; Tim Regis Helsen [1979] Director/Manager [Belgian]; Louis Anthony Rivieccio Jr [1965] Director [American]; Elisabel Rodriguez Marquez [1980] Finance Director [Spanish]; Peter Raoul Stewardson [1964] Director/Legal Attorney; Mark Simon Vale [1965] Director

UPS Global Treasury PLC
Incorporated: 6 March 1985 *Employees:* 21
Net Worth: £80,841,776 *Total Assets:* £2,141,116,800
Registered Office: UPS House, Forest Road, Feltham, Middlesex, TW13 7DY
Activities: Financial intermediation not elsewhere classified
Parent: UPS (UK) Limited
Officers: Peter Raoul Stewardson, Secretary; Ronald Woo-Sung Chang [1965] Director/Corporate Finance, President [American]; Parvinder Singh Gill [1973] Treasury Director; Tim Regis Helsen [1979] Director/Manager [Belgian]; Jennifer Leigh Powers [1970] Director/Treasury Manager [American]; Peter Raoul Stewardson [1964] Director/Legal Attorney

UPS Limited
Incorporated: 24 July 1985 *Employees:* 8,145
Net Worth: £262,695,008 *Total Assets:* £664,441,984
Registered Office: UPS House, Forest Road, Feltham, Middlesex, TW13 7DY
Activities: Unlicensed carriers
Parent: UPS (UK Holding) Limited
Officers: Elisabel Rodriguez Marquez, Secretary; Louis Anthony Rivieccio Jr [1965] Director [American]; Elisabel Rodriguez Marquez [1980] Finance Director [Spanish]; Peter Raoul Stewardson [1964] Director/Legal Attorney; Mark Simon Vale [1965] Director

Urban Enhance Limited
Incorporated: 19 July 2000 *Employees:* 2
Net Worth: £2,888,047 *Total Assets:* £10,705,299
Registered Office: The Old Barn, off Wood Street, Swanley Village, Swanley, Kent, BR8 7PA
Activities: Development of building projects
Shareholders: Paul Dereck Martin; Paula Elizabeth Martin
Officers: Paula Elizabeth Martin, Secretary; Paul Dereck Martin [1965] Director; Paula Elizabeth Martin [1966] Director/Administrator

Urbanicity (No. 16) LLP
Incorporated: 27 April 2012
Net Worth: £10,447,041 *Total Assets:* £13,404,916
Registered Office: 2nd Floor, 45-47 High Street, Cobham, Surrey, KT11 3DP

The Ursuline Academy Ilford
Incorporated: 11 August 2011 *Employees:* 80
Net Worth: £8,628,732 *Total Assets:* £9,295,986
Registered Office: The Ursuline Academy, Morland Road, Ilford, Essex, IG1 4JU
Activities: General secondary education
Officers: Mariano Scotti, Secretary; Joanna Abazari [1976] Director/Bank Clerk [Polish]; John Anthony [1949] Director/Retired; Louise Bath [1989] Director/Chartered Accountant; Father Matthew Bemand-Qureshi [1976] Director/Parish Priest; Sarah Bergin McCarthy [1972] Director/Human Resources; David Burge [1948] Director/Retired; Robert Caldeira [1963] Director/Consultant Business Analyst; Sister Kathleen Colmer [1948] Director/Provincialate; Jacqueline Da Prato [1955] Director/Retired; Ingrid Doves [1972] Director/Civil Servant; Maureen Duncan [1958] Director/Teacher; Lady Deniece Elizabeth Grant [1959] Director/Teacher; Emma Jakob [1990] Director/Banker; Heather Mackie [1988] Director/Teacher; Karen Reilly [1964] Director/Headteacher; Luke Robertson [1970] Director/Teacher; Angela St Ville [1958] Director/Health Professional

UT (UK) Limited
Incorporated: 8 February 2005
Net Worth: £6,927,770 *Total Assets:* £6,927,770
Registered Office: 1st Floor, Ash House, Littleton Road, Ashford, Middlesex, TW15 1TZ
Activities: Activities of head offices
Parent: United Technologies Corporation
Officers: Lynn Banis, Secretary; Christian Bruno Jean Idczak [1963] Director/Business Executive [French]; James Terence George Laurence [1964] Financial Director; Patricia Catherine Moran [1964] Finance Director [American]; Louise Kay Thompson [1983] Director/Chartered Management Accountant

Uxbridge High School Academy Trust
Incorporated: 5 May 2011 *Employees:* 136
Net Worth: £22,468,504 *Total Assets:* £24,446,592
Registered Office: Uxbridge High School Academy Trust, The Greenway, Uxbridge, Middlesex, UB8 2PR
Activities: General secondary education
Officers: Norwena Thomas, Secretary; David Andrew Aldridge [1978] Director of Research; Ben Beadle [1981] Director of Customer Relations; Jessica Timandra Beishon [1964] Director/Medical Communications Manager; Jennifer Bull [1988] Director/Local Government Officer; Rajiv Harry Deo Cahannac [1987] Director/Senior Internal Auditor; Nigel Brian Clemens [1963] Director/Principal; Samuel Frederick Michael Head [1994] Director/Teacher; Avril Ann James [1965] Director/Office Manager; Ada Jarvis-Kanayo [1964] Director/Teacher; Nigel McGreeghan [1965] Director/Prison Officer; Ian Fergus Moules [1965] Director/Civil Servant; Susan Elaine O'Sullivan [1942] Director/Project Manager; Minesh Parmar [1964] Director/Independent Financial Advisor; Peter Neil Waine [1954] Director

V.B. Investments Limited
Incorporated: 2 July 2003
Net Worth Deficit: £6,584,000 *Total Assets:* £31,251,000
Registered Office: Astral House, Imperial Way, Watford, Herts, WD24 4WW
Activities: Financial management
Parent: Vinci Pensions Limited
Officers: Christopher Carl Brennan [1969] Director/Accountant; Ian David Hudson [1964] Director/Chartered Accountant

V.I.P. Limited
Incorporated: 29 October 1982
Net Worth: £7,854,261 *Total Assets:* £8,646,623
Registered Office: Unit 21 Schooner Park, Crossways Business Park, Dartford, Kent, DA2 6NW
Activities: Activities of head offices
Shareholders: George David Allen; Leslie Allen
Officers: George David Allen, Secretary; George David Allen [1945] Director

V.S. Properties Limited
Incorporated: 25 April 1968 *Employees:* 8
Net Worth: £3,495,736 *Total Assets:* £7,849,039
Registered Office: 28 Church Road, Stanmore, Middlesex, HA7 4RX
Activities: Hotels and similar accommodation
Parent: Instyle Apartments Limited
Officers: Vidhur Mehra, Secretary/Director; Anita Mehra [1953] Director; Vidhur Mehra [1975] Director

Vadsala Limited
Incorporated: 18 December 1995
Net Worth: £3,898,033 *Total Assets:* £5,874,752
Registered Office: c/o S Syedain & Co, 2nd Floor, Heron House, 109 Wembley Hill Road, Wembley, Middlesex, HA9 8DA
Activities: Other letting and operating of own or leased real estate
Officers: John Patrick Gallagher, Secretary; Michael Joseph Gallagher [1943] Director [Irish]

Vahnea Marolda Investments LLP
Incorporated: 15 January 2014
Net Worth: £15,133,396 *Total Assets:* £15,168,396
Registered Office: 3 Valencia Road, Stanmore, Middlesex, HA7 4JL
Officers: Abhay Varma [1971] Member; Lord Philip Esme Howard [1945] LLP Member; Sarah Sophia Howard [1950] LLP Member; Robin Lawther [1961] LLP Member; Alberto Marolda [1961] LLP Member; Jan Stephen Pethick [1947] LLP Member; Vera Reimann-Dubbers [1962] LLP Member

The Valentine Group Limited
Incorporated: 22 November 2002
Net Worth: £9,082,854 *Total Assets:* £14,636,649
Registered Office: Global House, 1 Ashley Avenue, Epsom, Surrey, KT18 5FL
Activities: Buying and selling of own real estate
Shareholders: The Valentine Group Holdings Limited; Jennifer Burgess; Catherine Ruth Poole
Officers: Joanna Katie Hunt, Secretary; Richard John Burgess [1946] Director/Chartered Accountant; John Charles Bentlif South [1937] Director/Retired

Valeo Limited
Incorporated: 26 October 2000 *Employees:* 272
Net Worth: £3,210,000 *Total Assets:* £7,717,000
Registered Office: 5th Floor, Metropolitan House, 3 Darkes Lane, Potters Bar, Herts, EN6 1AG
Activities: Other human health activities
Officers: Gareth Dufton, Secretary; Gareth Dufton [1976] Director/Chartered Accountant; Farouq Rashid Sheikh [1958] Director

Valiant Holdings Limited
Incorporated: 21 April 2008 *Employees:* 41
Net Worth: £9,742,043 *Total Assets:* £12,875,541
Registered Office: First Floor, North Argyle House, Joel Street, Northwood Hills, Northwood, Middlesex, HA6 1LN
Activities: Activities auxiliary to financial intermediation n.e.c.
Shareholders: Prescient Capital Limited; Suvak Holdings Limited
Officers: Kirenjeet Kaur [1972] Director; Ajay Pabari [1959] Managing Director; Bharat Kumar Hirji Thakrar [1957] Director; Sanjay Thakrar [1979] Director

Valley Primary School
Incorporated: 6 July 2011 *Employees:* 60
Net Worth: £4,975,000 *Total Assets:* £5,540,000
Registered Office: Beckenham Lane, Bromley, Kent, BR2 0DA
Activities: Dormant company
Officers: Soraya Shahnaz Crowley [1966] Director/Teaching Assistant; Stephen Jackson [1976] Director; William John Mitchell [1963] Director; Helen Ann Randell [1965] Director; Toby Mark Reid [1972] Director/Banker

Valley Trucks Holdings Limited
Incorporated: 19 June 2009 *Employees:* 1
Net Worth: £754,021 *Total Assets:* £14,455,042
Registered Office: 57-59 High Street, Hoddesdon, Herts, EN11 8TQ
Activities: Activities of other holding companies n.e.c.
Major Shareholder: Giuseppe Ricotta
Officers: Giuseppe Ricotta [1966] Director

Valley Wholesale Carpets (2004) Limited
Incorporated: 4 March 2004 *Employees:* 112
Net Worth: £14,219,362 *Total Assets:* £19,697,338
Registered Office: Unit 1 Turpin Lane, Erith, Kent, DA8 2AT
Activities: Activities of distribution holding companies
Major Shareholder: Stephen Mitchell
Officers: Kate Mitchell, Secretary/Director; Kate Mitchell [1979] Director; Stephen Mitchell [1975] Director

Valley Wholesale Carpets Limited
Incorporated: 21 July 1982 *Employees:* 112
Net Worth: £17,212,600 *Total Assets:* £19,690,298
Registered Office: Turpin Lane, Erith, Kent, DA8 2AT
Activities: Wholesale of furniture, carpets and lighting equipment
Officers: Kate Mitchell, Secretary/Director; Kate Mitchell [1979] Director/Secretary; Stephen Mitchell [1975] Director/Salesman

Van Ameyde UK Holding Limited
Incorporated: 6 December 1994 *Employees:* 2
Net Worth: £18,494,420 *Total Assets:* £18,504,096
Registered Office: 34 The Mall, Bromley, Kent, BR1 1TS
Activities: Activities auxiliary to financial intermediation n.e.c.
Parent: Vanameyde International BV
Officers: Lisa Karen Caton, Secretary; Piet Middelkoop [1965] Director [Dutch]; David Robert Wilson [1963] Managing Director

Van Ameyde UK Limited
Incorporated: 3 April 1973 *Employees:* 75
Net Worth: £1,872,835 *Total Assets:* £11,288,703
Registered Office: 34 The Mall, Bromley, Kent, BR1 1TS
Activities: Activities auxiliary to financial intermediation n.e.c.
Officers: Lisa Karen Caton, Secretary; Karel Johannes Berends [1966] Finance Director [Dutch]; Piet Middelkoop [1965] Director [Dutch]; David Robert Wilson [1963] Managing Director

Van Gastel Beheer Limited
Incorporated: 22 August 2006
Net Worth: £5,332,293 *Total Assets:* £5,432,310
Registered Office: 262 Bedfont Lane, Feltham, Middlesex, TW14 9NU
Activities: Activities of other holding companies n.e.c.
Major Shareholder: Marcus Christiaan Antonius Hubertus Van Gastel
Officers: Marcus Christiaan Antonius Hubertus Van Gastel [1960] Director/Manager [Dutch]

Vanco UK Limited
Incorporated: 15 September 1988 *Employees:* 68
Net Worth Deficit: £41,398,512 *Total Assets:* £7,690,985
Registered Office: Sovereign Court, 635 Sipson Road, Sipson, West Drayton, Middlesex, UB7 0JE
Activities: Other telecommunications activities
Parent: Reliance Vanco Group Limited
Officers: Andrew Peter Goldie [1960] Director

Vandemoortele (U.K.) Limited
Incorporated: 9 April 1973 *Employees:* 23
Net Worth: £1,858,000 *Total Assets:* £9,783,000
Registered Office: Charta House, 30-38 Church Street, Staines upon Thames, Surrey, TW18 4EP
Activities: Retail sale in non-specialised stores with food, beverages or tobacco predominating
Parent: Vandemoortele
Officers: Dirk Durez, General Secretary/Director [Belgian]; Bart Jozef Bruyneel [1960] Managing Director [Belgian]; Dirk Durez [1955] Director/General Secretary [Belgian]; Filip Jeanne Goethals [1965] Commercial Director [Belgian]

Vanderbilt Hotels Limited
Incorporated: 8 April 1993 *Employees:* 128
Net Worth: £14,917,000 *Total Assets:* £38,533,000
Registered Office: 140 Bath Road, Hayes, Middlesex, UB3 5AW
Activities: Hotels and similar accommodation
Parent: Edwardian Group Limited
Officers: Vijay Wason, Secretary; John Robert Morley [1945] Director/Financial Consultant; Jasminder Singh [1951] Director/Hotelier

Vanguard Holdings Limited
Incorporated: 31 July 1964 *Employees:* 17
Net Worth: £31,352,484 *Total Assets:* £35,381,472
Registered Office: The Vanguard Business Centre, Alperton Lane, off Western Avenue, Greenford, Middlesex, UB6 8AA
Activities: Activities of head offices
Shareholder: Edward McKim Lyell McCullagh
Officers: Denise McCullagh, Secretary; Charlotte Alison McCullagh [1984] Marketing Director; Edward McKim Lyell McCullagh [1935] Director; William Alistair McCullagh [1985] Logistics and IT Director

Vanguard Learning Trust
Incorporated: 4 October 2011 *Employees:* 217
Previous: Vyners Learning Trust
Net Worth: £17,313,000 *Total Assets:* £20,323,000
Registered Office: Vyners School, Warren Road, Ickenham, Uxbridge, Middlesex, UB10 8AB
Activities: Pre-primary education
Officers: Janet Anne Beater, Secretary; Peter Wynne Davies [1949] Director; William Henry Gardner [1945] Director/Retired Teacher; Mark Hague [1958] Director/Accountant; Edward Francis Lavery [1960] Director; Dr Martina Anne Bernadette Lecky [1971] Director/Headteacher; Pamela Nash [1968] Director/ICT Account Manager; Pauline Anne Nixon [1952] Director; Andrew Jeremy Sykes [1963] Director/IT Programme Manager; David Peter Trood [1971] Director/Solicitor; Colin Peter Tucker [1973] Director/Headteacher

Vanneck Bros Limited
Incorporated: 29 September 2014
Net Worth: £348,561 *Total Assets:* £7,307,832
Registered Office: 28 Church Road, Stanmore, Middlesex, HA7 4XR
Activities: Activities of open-ended investment companies
Officers: Alexander Stevenson [1974] Director/Writer; Charles Dennistoun Stevenson [1980] Director/Civil Service; Heneage John Stevenson [1978] Director/Investor/Entrepreneur; William Beckford James Stevenson [1984] Director/Fund Manager

Vanneck Residential LLP
Incorporated: 18 July 2014
Net Worth: £8,747,208 *Total Assets:* £15,878,174
Registered Office: Parker Cavendish, 28 Church Road, Stanmore, Middlesex, HA7 4XR
Officers: Alexander Albert Henry Fraser [1984] Member; Heneage John Stevenson [1978] Member

Vantage Volante Limited
Incorporated: 25 November 1999
Net Worth: £7,513,686 *Total Assets:* £13,718,099
Registered Office: Amwell House, 19 Amwell Street, Hoddesdon, Herts, EN11 8TS
Activities: Management of real estate on a fee or contract basis
Shareholders: Carol Williams; Helen Goate
Officers: Carol Williams, Secretary/Director; Helen Elizabeth Goate [1958] Director/Management; Rachel Marion Susan Hahn [1953] Director/Management; Carol Williams [1947] Director; Richard Stewart Williams [1945] Director

Vantas International Limited
Incorporated: 13 January 1977
Net Worth: £9,365,630,976 *Total Assets:* £9,697,094,656
Registered Office: Cadbury House, Sanderson Road, Uxbridge, Middlesex, UB8 1DH
Activities: Activities of head offices
Parent: Mondelez UK Holdings & Services Limited
Officers: Adrian John Paul Arrighi [1978] Tax Director; Michael Brendan Foye [1965] Treasury Director; John Michael Hladusz [1972] Director/Chartered Accountant; Carole Noelle Keene [1966] Director

Vanwise Group Limited
Incorporated: 22 September 2003 *Employees:* 37
Net Worth: £2,069,445 *Total Assets:* £6,722,487
Registered Office: Treviot House, 186-192 High Road, Ilford, Essex, IG1 1LR
Activities: Sale of new cars and light motor vehicles
Major Shareholder: Declan Matthew O'Driscoll
Officers: Declan Matthew O'Driscoll [1971] Director

VASBP Limited
Incorporated: 6 January 2014
Net Worth: £5,129,309 *Total Assets:* £5,347,255
Registered Office: 42 Christchurch Avenue, Kenton, Harrow, Middlesex, HA3 8NJ
Activities: Other service activities n.e.c.
Shareholders: Shamir Karsandas Popat; Bhavan Shamir Popat
Officers: Bhavna Shamir Popat, Secretary; Bhavna Shamir Popat [1965] Director; Shamir Karsandas Popat [1961] Director/Pharmacists

Vashisht Surgical Limited
Incorporated: 7 April 1999 *Employees:* 2
Net Worth: £5,375,523 *Total Assets:* £5,652,167
Registered Office: 4 Red Lion Court, Alexandra Road, Hounslow, Middlesex, TW3 1JS
Activities: Specialists medical practice activities
Officers: Dr Shubha Vashisht, Secretary; Rajiv Vashisht [1957] Director/Doctor/Surgeon

Vassall Ventures Limited
Incorporated: 24 July 2006
Net Worth: £8,691,216 *Total Assets:* £8,730,016
Registered Office: 4 The Mews, Bridge Road, Twickenham, Middlesex, TW1 1RF
Activities: Management of real estate on a fee or contract basis
Major Shareholder: Andrii Vasyl'ovych Khirsin
Officers: Anthony Curran [1942] Director/Businessman [Irish]

Vectra Limited
Incorporated: 13 March 2000
Net Worth: £527,107 *Total Assets:* £16,518,368
Registered Office: 36 Paradise Road, Richmond, Surrey, TW9 1SE
Activities: Management consultancy activities other than financial management
Officers: Deepti Rishi [1959] Director/Business Executive; Rati Rishi [1987] Director; Swati Rishi [1982] Director

Vega Industries Limited
Incorporated: 14 April 1999 *Employees:* 18
Net Worth: £4,958,907 *Total Assets:* £11,210,557
Registered Office: Suite 3, 1st Floor, Concress House, 14 Lyon Road, Harrow, Middlesex, HA1 2EN
Activities: Installation of industrial machinery and equipment
Officers: Paryank Ramesh Shah, Secretary; Rizwan Gilani [1965] Director [Indian]; Himanshu Patel [1966] Director; Bhadresh Shah [1951] Director/Engineer [Indian]; Paryank Ramesh Shah [1956] Director/Chartered Accountant [Indian]

Velani & Velani Ltd
Incorporated: 18 October 1996 *Employees:* 2
Net Worth: £2,583,794 *Total Assets:* £5,382,199
Registered Office: 62 The Drive, Ickenham, Middlesex, UB10 8AQ
Activities: Other letting and operating of own or leased real estate
Shareholders: Allen Jaku Velani; Kirit Velani; Suresh Velani
Officers: Allen Jaku Velani, Secretary/Director; Allen Jaku Velani [1967] Director/Software Engineer; Kirit Jaku Velani [1962] Director/Management Consultant; Suresh Jaku Velani [1965] Director/Software Support

Vendcrown Limited
Incorporated: 5 June 1996
Net Worth: £50,669,000 *Total Assets:* £58,671,000
Registered Office: Ermyn House, Ermyn Way, Leatherhead, Surrey, KT22 8UX
Activities: Other business support service activities n.e.c.
Parent: Mizzen Bidco Limited
Officers: Elizabeth Sarah Annys, Secretary; Andrew Phillip Chapman [1969] Director/Chief Financial Officer; Anthony Santospirito [1984] Director [Australian]; Thomas Woolgrove [1970] Director/Chief Executive Officer

Venson Automotive Solutions Limited
Incorporated: 13 May 1992 *Employees:* 80
Net Worth: £13,348,766 *Total Assets:* £50,620,388
Registered Office: Venson House, 1 AC Court, High Street, Thames Ditton, Surrey, KT7 0SR
Activities: Sale of new cars and light motor vehicles
Parent: Premier Fleet Management and Contract Hire Limited
Officers: John Gerard Bateson, Secretary/Director [Irish]; John Gerard Bateson [1963] Director [Irish]; Mark William Gerard [1965] Finance Director; Brian Michael O'Sullivan [1963] Director [Irish]; Samantha Jane Roff [1968] Director; Simon John Staton [1973] Director

Ventford Limited
Incorporated: 11 December 2012
Net Worth: £2,678,610 *Total Assets:* £5,643,158
Registered Office: 5 Theobald Court, Theobald Street, Elstree, Herts, WD6 4RN
Activities: Other letting and operating of own or leased real estate
Major Shareholder: Torlork Singh
Officers: Dilip Singh [1982] Director; Pushpa Singh [1959] Director; Torlork Singh [1957] Director

Venture Lighting Europe Limited
Incorporated: 27 March 1997 *Employees:* 50
Net Worth Deficit: £1,227,123 *Total Assets:* £14,589,358
Registered Office: Trinity Court, Batchworth Island, Church Street, Rickmansworth, Herts, WD3 1RT
Activities: Non-specialised wholesale trade
Parent: Advanced Lighting Technologies Europe Limited
Officers: Philip Colin Croker [1978] Managing Director; Sabu Krishnan [1958] Director/Engineer [American]

Verde Agritech PLC
Incorporated: 14 August 2006 *Employees:* 11
Previous: Verde Potash PLC
Net Worth: £14,466,844 *Total Assets:* £14,730,166
Registered Office: 19 Salatin House, Cedar Road, Sutton, Surrey, SM2 5DA
Activities: Other mining and quarrying n.e.c.
Officers: Timothy William Slater, Secretary; Michael Henry Hicks Beach Earl St Aldwyn [1950] Director; Getulio Lamartine de Paula Fonseca [1937] Director [Brazilian]; Renato Couto Gomes [1979] Director/Lawyer [Brazilian]; Alysson Paulinelli [1936] Director/Agronomy Engineer [Italian]; Paulo Sergio Machado Ribeiro [1961] Director/Engineer [Brazilian]; Cristiano Botelho Veloso [1981] Director [Brazilian]

Verex Group Limited
Incorporated: 3 June 2008 *Employees:* 111
Net Worth Deficit: £3,912,944 *Total Assets:* £10,738,675
Registered Office: Batchworth House, Batchworth Place, Church Street, Rickmansworth, Herts, WD3 1JE
Activities: Activities of head offices
Shareholder: James Richard Hallett
Officers: Crispin Peter Burdett, Secretary; Mark Jonathan Aplin [1978] Director; Crispin Peter Burdett [1967] Director; Peter de Rousset Hall [1952] Director/Consultant; Brian Richard Hallett [1953] Director; James Richard Hallett [1980] Director/IT Consultant; Andrew Christopher Long [1963] Director; Duncan Robert Perritt [1963] Director/Accountant

Verex Insurance Services Limited
Incorporated: 25 January 2006 *Employees:* 92
Previous: Original Insurance Services Limited
Net Worth: £3,243,105 *Total Assets:* £10,754,122
Registered Office: Batchworth House, Batchworth Place, Church Street, Rickmansworth, Herts, WD3 1JE
Activities: Activities of insurance agents and brokers
Shareholder: James Richasrd Hallet
Officers: Crispin Peter Burdett, Secretary; Crispin Peter Burdett [1967] Director; Andrew Christopher Long [1963] Director; Duncan Robert Perritt [1963] Director/Accountant

Verico Europe Holding Limited
Incorporated: 22 August 1985 *Employees:* 33
Previous: Presstek Europe Limited
Net Worth: £5,087,000 *Total Assets:* £5,948,000
Registered Office: Unit 30 Riverside Way, Uxbridge, Middlesex, UB8 2YF
Activities: Agents involved in the sale of machinery, industrial equipment, ships and aircraft
Officers: John Becker [1952] Director/Investment Professional [American]; Yuval Sascha Dubois [1966] Director/President & CEO [Israeli]

Verifone (U.K.) Limited
Incorporated: 15 March 1988 *Employees:* 174
Net Worth: £10,336,000 *Total Assets:* £32,080,000
Registered Office: 3 Roundwood Avenue, Stockley Park, Uxbridge, Middlesex, UB11 1AF
Activities: Other information technology service activities
Officers: Vikram Kalidindi Varma, Secretary; Marc Evan Rothman [1964] Director [American]; Vikram Kalidindi Varma [1978] Director/Attorney [American]

Verifone Services UK & Ireland Limited
Incorporated: 16 September 1992 *Employees:* 134
Net Worth: £8,696,199 *Total Assets:* £16,786,518
Registered Office: 3 Roundwood Avenue, Stockley Park, Uxbridge, Middlesex, UB11 1AF
Activities: Other software publishing
Officers: Vikram Kalidindi Varma, Secretary; Marc Evan Rothman [1964] Director [American]; Vikram Kalidindi Varma [1978] Director/Attorney [American]

Verint Systems UK Limited
Incorporated: 18 April 1991 *Employees:* 440
Net Worth: £30,895,000 *Total Assets:* £91,495,000
Registered Office: 241 Brooklands Road, Weybridge, Surrey, KT13 0RH
Activities: Information technology consultancy activities
Parent: Verint WS Holdings Limited
Officers: Peter Demian Fante [1967] Director/General Counsel [American]; Nicola Guiseppe Nonini [1961] Director; Douglas Edward Robinson [1956] Director/Chief Financial Officer [American]

Verint Technology UK Limited
Incorporated: 7 October 2011 *Employees:* 3
Net Worth: £245,266,640 *Total Assets:* £333,026,240
Registered Office: 241 Brooklands Road, Weybridge, Surrey, KT13 0RH
Activities: Other information technology service activities
Parent: Verint Systems Inc
Officers: Peter Demian Fante [1967] Director/General Counsel [American]; David Peter Outram [1962] Director; Douglas Edward Robinson [1956] Director/Chief Financial Officer [American]

Verint WS Holdings Limited
Incorporated: 22 April 2003 *Employees:* 4
Net Worth: £211,632,000 *Total Assets:* £257,842,000
Registered Office: 241 Brooklands Road, Weybridge, Surrey, KT13 0RH
Activities: Business and domestic software development
Parent: Verint Technology UK Limited
Officers: Peter Demian Fante [1967] Director/General Counsel [American]; Nicola Guiseppe Nonini [1961] Director; David Peter Outram [1962] Director; Douglas Edward Robinson [1956] Director/Chief Financial Officer [American]

Verisk International Holdings Limited
Incorporated: 9 February 2000 *Employees:* 852
Previous: Healix International Holdings Limited
Net Worth: £2,322,953 *Total Assets:* £16,769,658
Registered Office: Healix House, Esher Green, Esher, Surrey, KT10 8AB
Activities: Activities of other holding companies n.e.c.
Parent: Verisk Analytics Inc
Officers: Kenneth Thompson, Secretary; Dr Paul Geoffrey Hassan Beven [1959] Director/Medical Practitioner; Maroun Mourad [1973] Director/Business Executive [American]; Kenneth Edward Thompson [1959] Director/Attorney [American]

Veritas Educational Trust
Incorporated: 1 August 2011 *Employees:* 156
Previous: Bishop Ramsey Church of England Academies Trust
Net Worth: £12,109,699 *Total Assets:* £14,484,234
Registered Office: Bishop Ramsey Church of England School, Hume Way, Ruislip, Middlesex, HA4 8EE
Activities: General secondary education
Officers: Karen Ball [1961] Director/Civil Servant; Jonathan Chu [1993] Director/Management Consultant; Helen Mary Dimmock [1965] Director/Civil Servant; Catherine Patrice Gower [1968] Director/Lecturer; Elizabeth Ann Richardson [1961] Director/Headteacher; Alison Mary Straszewski [1963] Director/Banker; Susan Elizabeth Vale [1958] Director; Andrew John Wilcock [1955] Director/Headteacher

Veriton Pharma Limited
Incorporated: 21 January 1997 *Employees:* 36
Previous: Special Products Limited
Net Worth: £4,870,489 *Total Assets:* £6,863,314
Registered Office: Unit 16 Trade City, Avro Way, Brooklands Business Park, Weybridge, Surrey, KT13 0YF
Activities: Wholesale of pharmaceutical goods
Parent: March Medical Limited
Officers: Dr Hannah Mary Talbot Aiken [1979] Director; Chris James Grimes [1975] Director; Dr Stephen Philip Jones [1957] Director/Pharmacist; Carole Iris March [1949] Director; Dr Graham Alan March [1945] Director/Pharmacist; Jason Asnam Saiban [1972] Director/Solicitor; Theresa Anne Wallis [1957] Director; Roderick William Wild [1967] Director/Chartered Accountant

The Vernon Educational Trust Limited
Incorporated: 18 December 1974 *Employees:* 161
Net Worth: £32,141,448 *Total Assets:* £40,220,160
Registered Office: Danes Hill School, Leatherhead Road, Oxshott, Leatherhead, Surrey, KT22 0JG
Activities: Primary education
Officers: Richard Quinn, Secretary; Dr Adrian Fairbank [1961] Director/Medical Doctor; Ian Michael Hunt [1960] Director/Chief Executive Officer; Alexandra Mary Selina Hutchinson [1971] Director/Headmistress; Timothy William Jones [1957] Director/Solicitor; Anthony John Lunn [1964] Director; Robert George Mansfield [1950] Director/Chief Executive; John Andrew McLaren [1963] Communications Director; Andrew Hugh Monro [1950] Director/Educational Consultant; Doctor Heather Frances Patel [1959] Director/General Medical Practitioner; Mark Anthony Smith [1962] Director/Educational Consultant; Dr Marc Van Grondelle [1970] Director/Partner Professional Services Firm

Vestey Foods International Limited
Incorporated: 11 August 2010 *Employees:* 25
Net Worth: £1,416,000 *Total Assets:* £17,628,000
Registered Office: 29 Ullswater Crescent, Coulsdon, Surrey, CR5 2HR
Activities: Wholesale of meat and meat products
Parent: Vestey Foods International Holdings Ltd
Officers: Neil Thornton, Secretary; Colin George Copland [1954] Director; Kenneth Hermanson [1968] Director/Meat Trader [Danish]; Soren Jakobsson [1969] Managing Director [Danish]; George Moubray William Vestey [1964] Director

Vestey Foods Limited
Incorporated: 16 November 1994
Previous: Vestey Foods Group Limited
Net Worth: £22,165,000 *Total Assets:* £22,644,000
Registered Office: 29 Ullswater Crescent, Coulsdon, Surrey, CR5 2HR
Activities: Activities of head offices
Parent: Vestey Holdings Limited
Officers: Neil Thornton, Secretary; Colin George Copland [1954] Director; Neil Thornton [1968] Director; George Moubray William Vestey [1964] Director

Vestey Foods UK Limited
Incorporated: 12 April 2000 *Employees:* 243
Net Worth: £15,999,000 *Total Assets:* £53,420,000
Registered Office: 29 Ullswater Crescent, Coulsdon, Surrey, CR5 2HR
Activities: Wholesale of meat and meat products
Parent: Vestey Foods UK (Holdings) Limited
Officers: Neil Thornton, Secretary; Colin George Copland [1954] Finance Director; Matthew William Flood [1983] Director/Chief Executive Officer; Kenneth Hermansen [1968] Director; George Moubray William Vestey [1964] Director; Neal Wakeham [1970] Director/Accountant

Vestey Group Limited
Incorporated: 24 July 2002
Net Worth: £88,246,000 *Total Assets:* £95,996,000
Registered Office: 29 Ullswater Crescent, Coulsdon, Surrey, CR5 2HR
Activities: Activities of head offices
Parent: Western United Investment Company Limited
Officers: Neil Thornton, Secretary; George Moubray William Vestey [1964] Director/Retail Butchery; Lord Samuel George Armstrong Vestey [1941] Director/Merchant; Honourable William Guy Vestey [1983] Director; Robin John Henry Vesty [1968] Director

Vestey Holdings Limited
Incorporated: 28 May 1900 *Employees:* 940
Net Worth: £74,299,000 *Total Assets:* £168,658,000
Registered Office: 29 Ullswater Crescent, Coulsdon, Surrey, CR5 2HR
Activities: Activities of head offices
Parent: Vestey Group Limited
Officers: Neil Thornton, Secretary; Colin George Copland [1954] Director; James Alexander Scott [1940] Director/Chartered Accountant; George Moubray William Vestey [1964] Director/Retail Butchery; Robin John Henry Vestey [1968] Director

Vetex Limited
Incorporated: 1 February 2016 *Employees:* 2
Net Worth Deficit: £1,536,129 *Total Assets:* £15,314,148
Registered Office: 166 College Road, Harrow, Middlesex, HA1 1RA
Activities: Other business support service activities n.e.c.
Officers: Michael Ackenson [1945] Director/Chartered Accountant; David Geoffrey White [1959] Director/Accountant

VFS Legal Limited
Incorporated: 11 July 2011
Net Worth: £878,919 *Total Assets:* £26,235,670
Registered Office: Kingfisher House, 21-23 Elmfield Road, Bromley, Kent, BR1 1LT
Activities: Other business support service activities n.e.c.
Parent: Vertical Financial Services Limited
Officers: Alan Irving [1944] Director; Norman John Kenvyn [1957] Director; Robert Andrew Norman [1956] Director; Kathryn Thomson [1978] Director/Lawyer

VGC Group Limited
Incorporated: 14 March 2006 *Employees:* 1,297
Net Worth: £17,196,830 *Total Assets:* £26,583,700
Registered Office: Cardinal House, Bury Street, Ruislip, Middlesex, HA4 7GD
Activities: Activities of head offices
Shareholders: Matthew John Fitzpatrick; Laurence Richard McKidd
Officers: Olivia Fitzpatrick, Secretary; Sinnathamby Balasundaram [1953] Director/Accountant; Stephen Burns [1970] Business Development Director; Sudarshan Deshmukh [1978] IT Director [Indian]; Terence Roy Dutton-Wells [1948] Director; Matthew John Fitzpatrick [1945] Director [Irish]; Jacques Kriel [1980] Director [South African]; Laurence Richard McKidd [1955] Director; Ciara Melanie Pryce [1979] Director; Andrew Rogers [1946] Director/Consultant [Irish]; Christopher Edward Ryan [1979] Director; Robert John Webb [1949] Director

Via Global Limited
Incorporated: 13 July 2006 *Employees:* 24
Net Worth: £798,868 *Total Assets:* £8,025,002
Registered Office: 5 Elstree Gate, Elstree Way, Borehamwood, Herts, WD6 1JD
Activities: Other business support service activities n.e.c.
Major Shareholder: Charlie Chun Kee Lee
Officers: Sai Min Timothy Lam [1957] Director [Canadian]; Arnold Lee [1975] Director [Canadian]; Carol Lee [1978] Director [American]; Charlie Chun Kee Lee [1929] Director [Chinese]; Mark Royden [1960] Director/Logistics

Via-Vox Limited
Incorporated: 24 January 2003 *Employees:* 62
Net Worth: £11,459,925 *Total Assets:* £14,821,082
Registered Office: Vectra House, 36 Paradise Road, Richmond, Surrey, TW9 1SE
Activities: Other telecommunications activities
Parent: PGI Services (UK) Holdings Limited
Officers: Alice Riviezzo, Secretary; Kevin James McAdams [1964] Director/Chief Finance Officer [American]; Alice Riviezzo [1961] Director/Senior Vice President Tax [American]; John Daniel Stone [1963] Director [Irish]

Viadex Limited
Incorporated: 6 September 2000 *Employees:* 57
Net Worth: £3,826,299 *Total Assets:* £15,767,877
Registered Office: Unit 20 Red Lion Road Business Park, Red Lion Road, Surbiton, Surrey, KT6 7QD
Activities: Other information technology service activities
Shareholder: Elliot Read
Officers: Catherine Helen Hutson, Secretary; Pascale Bull [1969] Director/Chief Operating Officer; Constantine Martin Cooper [1970] Managing Director; Dan Hayden Hammond [1975] Sales Director; Damon Osborne [1971] Accounts Director; Elliot Read [1969] Founder Director; Karen Anne Read [1970] HR & Project Director

J M W Vicary Limited
Incorporated: 14 August 2002 *Employees:* 40
Net Worth: £166,751 *Total Assets:* £6,013,005
Registered Office: Lynton House, 304 Bensham Lane, Thornton Heath, Surrey, CR7 7EQ
Activities: Dispensing chemist in specialised stores
Shareholders: Neepa Patel; Yogesh Patel
Officers: Neepa Patel, Secretary; Dr Neepa Patel [1972] Director/Company Secretary; Yogesh Patel [1972] Director

Victoria Docks Hotel Company (Number Two) Limited
Incorporated: 8 August 2006 *Employees:* 4
Net Worth: £48,293,472 *Total Assets:* £54,760,104
Registered Office: Kirkland House, 11-15 Peterborough Road, Harrow, Middlesex, HA1 2AX
Activities: Other letting and operating of own or leased real estate
Officers: Haider Ladhu Jaffer [1940] Director/Businessman; Dr Manoj Raman [1960] Director/Businessman; Hassanali Amirali Dawood Suleman [1954] Director/Businessman; Cameron Beresford Sunter [1956] Director/Solicitor

Victoria Docks Hotel Company Limited
Incorporated: 8 February 2001 *Employees:* 3
Net Worth: £7,481,308 *Total Assets:* £33,074,908
Registered Office: Kirkland House, 11-15 Peterborough Road, Harrow, Middlesex, HA1 2AX
Activities: Hotels and similar accommodation
Officers: Haider Ladhu Jaffer [1940] Director/Businessman; Hassanali Amirali Dawood Suleman [1954] Director/Businessman; Cameron Beresford Sunter [1956] Director/Solicitor

The Victoria Foundation
Incorporated: 11 September 1985 *Employees:* 261
Net Worth Deficit: £4,511,000 *Total Assets:* £25,976,000
Registered Office: St Davids House, 15 Worple Way, Richmond, Surrey, TW10 6DG
Activities: Hospital activities
Officers: Graham Arthur Ridgeway Ball, Secretary/Director; Graham Arthur Ridgeway Ball [1950] Director; Anthony Ralph Cooke [1948] Director; John Alan Hamblin [1949] Director/Chartered Accountant; Henry Peter Hope [1942] Director/Retired Veterinary Surgeon; Christopher Peter Lyons [1951] Director; Martin Anthony Matthews [1950] Director

Victory Lighting (UK) Limited
Incorporated: 18 April 1991 *Employees:* 21
Net Worth: £5,079,020 *Total Assets:* £5,814,978
Registered Office: Ground Floor, Unit 501 Centennial Park, Centennial Avenue, Elstree, Borehamwood, Herts, WD6 3FG
Activities: Manufacture of electric lighting equipment
Shareholders: Alan Penman; Jacqueline Penman
Officers: Jacqueline Penman, Secretary/Training Officer; Alan Penman [1951] Director; Jacqueline Penman [1962] Director; Jordan Penman [1988] Director/Logistics Manager; Matthew Joseph Tyler Penman [1989] Director/General Manager

Victorygame Limited
Incorporated: 10 February 1983 *Employees:* 3
Net Worth: £10,347,781 *Total Assets:* £36,794,544
Registered Office: 7 The Triangle Centre, Uxbridge Road, Southall, Middlesex, UB1 3ED
Activities: Development of building projects
Officers: Valveer Kaur Pandher, Secretary; Jaswinder Singh Pandher [1977] Director; Surjit Singh Pandher [1954] Director; Tersham Singh Pandher [1975] Director; Valveer Kaur Pandher [1956] Director

Vidafresh Limited
Incorporated: 7 January 2010 *Employees:* 20
Net Worth: £1,353,276 *Total Assets:* £10,753,041
Registered Office: Regus House, Victory Way, Crossways Business Park, Dartford, Kent, DA2 6QD
Activities: Wholesale of fruit and vegetables
Shareholder: Terence Robert Watts
Officers: Scott Gregory Davies [1979] Commercial Director; Christopher Gerard Rawlins [1974] Commercial Director; Robert Joel Watts [1980] Director/Senior Software Engineer; Terence Robert Watts [1952] Director

Viewrose Limited
Incorporated: 26 April 2011 *Employees:* 2
Net Worth: £3,549,942 *Total Assets:* £8,103,932
Registered Office: First Floor, Radius House, 51 Clarendon Road, Watford, Herts, WD17 1HP
Activities: Buying and selling of own real estate
Shareholders: Richard Spencer Frank; J F S Estates Limited
Officers: Richard Spencer Frank [1967] Director; Jonathan Floyd Schuman [1969] Director/Surveyor

ViiV Healthcare Finance 2 Limited
Incorporated: 28 October 2015
Net Worth: £849,372,096 *Total Assets:* £861,767,552
Registered Office: 980 Great West Road, Brentford, Middlesex, TW8 9GS
Activities: Financial intermediation not elsewhere classified
Parent: ViiV Healthcare Limited
Officers: Joceyln Brown [1974] Director/Head of HR; Rebecca Elizabeth Hall [1982] Director, Financial Controller; Timothy Andrew Tordoff [1964] Director/Senior Vice President VIIV Healthcare Europe

ViiV Healthcare Finance Limited
Incorporated: 11 January 2016
Net Worth: £202,044,000 *Total Assets:* £2,271,303,936
Registered Office: 980 Great West Road, Brentford, Middlesex, TW8 9GS
Activities: Financial intermediation not elsewhere classified
Parent: ViiV Healthcare UK (No.3) Limited
Officers: Jill Dawn Anderson [1964] Director; Karen Marion Grainger [1978] Director/Pharmaceutical Regulatory Executive [Irish]; Deborah Jayne Waterhouse [1967] Director

ViiV Healthcare Limited
Incorporated: 14 April 2009
Net Worth: £1,488,999,936 *Total Assets:* £7,080,999,936
Registered Office: 980 Great West Road, Brentford, Middlesex, TW8 9GS
Activities: Activities of head offices
Parent: GlaxoSmithKline Mercury Limited
Officers: Agnieszka Moskal Gallagher, Secretary; Douglas Ernest Giordano [1962] Director [American]; Dr John Apeler Keller [1964] Director/President and CEO Shionogi Inc [American]; John Joseph Lepore [1966] Director [American]; Dr Sabine Luik [1969] Director/Chief Medical Officer [German]; Alexander Roderick MacKenzie [1959] Director/Head of Pharmatherapeutics R & D; Luke Victor Miels [1974] Director/President, Global Pharmaceuticals [Australian]; David Simon Redfern [1966] Director/Chief Strategy Officer; Regis Jean-Pierre Simard [1965] Director/Head of Supply Chain [French]; Deborah Jayne Waterhouse [1967] Director; Dr Pauline Margaret Williams [1967] Director

ViiV Healthcare Overseas Limited
Incorporated: 23 September 2009
Net Worth: £131,093,000 *Total Assets:* £131,581,000
Registered Office: 980 Great West Road, Brentford, Middlesex, TW8 9GS
Activities: Wholesale of pharmaceutical goods
Parent: ViiV Healthcare Limited
Officers: Jill Dawn Anderson [1964] Director; Karen Marion Grainger [1978] Director/Pharmaceutical Regulatory Executive [Irish]; Deborah Jayne Waterhouse [1967] Director

ViiV Healthcare Trading Services UK Limited
Incorporated: 5 August 2009
Net Worth: £52,910,000 *Total Assets:* £3,306,328,064
Registered Office: 980 Great West Road, Brentford, Middlesex, TW8 9GS
Activities: Wholesale of pharmaceutical goods
Parent: ViiV Healthcare Limited
Officers: Jill Dawn Anderson [1964] Director; Karen Marion Grainger [1978] Director/Pharmaceutical Regulatory Executive [Irish]; Deborah Jayne Waterhouse [1967] Director

ViiV Healthcare UK (No.3) Limited
Incorporated: 26 October 2012
Net Worth: £3,944,185,088 *Total Assets:* £4,336,324,096
Registered Office: 980 Great West Road, Brentford, Middlesex, TW8 9GS
Activities: Activities of other holding companies n.e.c.
Shareholders: ViiV Healthcare UK Limited; ViiV Healthcare Limited
Officers: Jill Dawn Anderson [1964] Director; Karen Grainger Marion [1978] Director/Pharmaceutical Regulatory Executive [Irish]; Deborah Jayne Waterhouse [1967] Director

ViiV Healthcare UK (No.4) Limited
Incorporated: 18 December 2015
Net Worth: £210,515,008 *Total Assets:* £256,428,992
Registered Office: 980 Great West Road, Brentford, Middlesex, TW8 9GS
Activities: Other professional, scientific and technical activities n.e.c.
Parent: ViiV Healthcare Limited
Officers: Jill Dawn Anderson [1964] Director; Karen Marion Grainger [1978] Director/Pharmaceutical Regulatory Executive [Irish]; Deborah Jayne Waterhouse [1967] Director

ViiV Healthcare UK (No.5) Limited
Incorporated: 18 January 2016
Net Worth: £13,046,000 *Total Assets:* £77,537,000
Registered Office: 980 Great West Road, Brentford, Middlesex, TW8 9GS
Activities: Other professional, scientific and technical activities n.e.c.
Parent: ViiV Healthcare Limited
Officers: Jill Dawn Anderson [1964] Director; Karen Marion Grainger [1978] Director/Pharmaceutical Regulatory Executive [Irish]; Deborah Jayne Waterhouse [1967] Director

ViiV Healthcare UK Limited
Incorporated: 13 August 2009 *Employees:* 175
Net Worth: £4,456,565,248 *Total Assets:* £7,015,779,840
Registered Office: 980 Great West Road, Brentford, Middlesex, TW8 9GS
Activities: Wholesale of pharmaceutical goods
Parent: ViiV Healthcare Limited
Officers: Jill Dawn Anderson [1964] Director; Karen Marion Grainger [1978] Director/Pharmaceutical Regulatory Executive [Irish]; Deborah Jayne Waterhouse [1967] Director

Villachase Limited
Incorporated: 19 January 1988
Net Worth: £4,714,429 *Total Assets:* £20,990,900
Registered Office: Unit 17 Hallmark Trading Estate, Fourth Way, Wembley, Middlesex, HA9 0LB
Activities: Other letting and operating of own or leased real estate
Officers: Parminder Gupta [1968] Director/Property Management; Ved Parkash Gupta [1937] Director/Property Developer

Vinayak Properties Limited
Incorporated: 17 March 2009 *Employees:* 2
Net Worth: £4,430,484 *Total Assets:* £21,953,264
Registered Office: 98 Pinner Road, Harrow, Middlesex, HA1 4GZ
Activities: Other letting and operating of own or leased real estate
Shareholders: Khushma Dalia; Rushma Dalia; Trushma Dalia
Officers: Khushma Dalia, Secretary; Khushma Dalia [1982] Director/Businesswoman; Rushma Dalia [1983] Director/Businesswoman; Trushma Dalia [1988] Director/Businesswoman

Vinci Construction UK Limited
Incorporated: 13 September 1988 *Employees:* 3,298
Net Worth: £120,806,000 *Total Assets:* £546,112,000
Registered Office: Astral House, Imperial Way, Watford, Herts, WD24 4WW
Activities: Construction of commercial buildings
Parent: Vinci PLC
Officers: Jean-Pierre Bonnet, Secretary; Christopher Carl Brennan [1969] Director/Accountant; Bruno Michel Dupety [1956] Director/Engineer [French]; Julian Paul Gatward [1966] Director/Civil Engineer; Christopher Michael Hamer [1959] Director/Civil Engineer; Anthony Kennedy Raikes [1964] Director/Chartered Civil Engineer

Vinci Environment UK Limited
Incorporated: 15 May 2007
Net Worth: £46,000 *Total Assets:* £14,973,000
Registered Office: Astral House, Imperial Way, Watford, Herts, WD24 4WW
Activities: Other specialised construction activities n.e.c.
Shareholders: Vinci Construction UK Limited; Vinci Environnement
Officers: Bruno Michel Dupety [1956] Director/Engineer [French]; Francois de Gassart [1977] Director of Operations [French]; Julian Paul Gatward [1966] Director/Civil Engineer; Frederic Yves Marie Peigne [1967] Director [French]; Hughes Guy Marie Patrick Seutin [1974] Director [Belgian]; Luc Valaize [1955] Commercial and Offers Director [French]

Vinci Fleet Services Limited
Incorporated: 22 June 1983
Net Worth: £8,660,000 *Total Assets:* £13,580,000
Registered Office: Astral House, Imperial Way, Watford, Herts, WD24 4WW
Activities: Renting and leasing of construction and civil engineering machinery and equipment
Parent: Vinci PLC
Officers: Mark Blanchard [1959] Director/Accountant; Christopher Carl Brennan [1969] Director/Accountant; Ruth Elizabeth Tilbrook [1968] Director/Accountant

Vinci PLC
Incorporated: 5 October 1962 *Employees:* 3,482
Net Worth: £80,003,000 *Total Assets:* £556,436,992
Registered Office: Astral House, Imperial Way, Watford, Herts, WD24 4WW
Activities: Activities of head offices
Parent: Sogea Holdings (UK) Limited
Officers: Ruth Elizabeth Tilbrook, Secretary; Bruno Michel Dupety [1956] Director/Engineer [French]; Richard Michel Rene Francioli [1959] Director/Company Chairman [French]; Yann Paul Grolimund [1959] Director [French]

Vinci Property Limited
Incorporated: 6 May 1960
Net Worth Deficit: £2,275,000 *Total Assets:* £7,563,000
Registered Office: Astral House, Imperial Way, Watford, Herts, WD24 4WW
Activities: Other letting and operating of own or leased real estate
Parent: Vinci PLC
Officers: Christopher Carl Brennan [1969] Director/Accountant; Ruth Elizabeth Tilbrook [1968] Director/Accountant

Vinci UK Developments Limited
Incorporated: 13 January 1960 *Employees:* 5
Previous: Vinci Investments Limited
Net Worth: £14,502,000 *Total Assets:* £58,511,000
Registered Office: Astral House, Imperial Way, Watford, Herts, WD24 4WW
Activities: Activities of head offices
Parent: Vinci Construction UK Limited
Officers: Bruno Michel Dupety [1956] Director/Engineer [French]; Graham Lambert [1969] Director

Vine Investment Company Limited (The)
Incorporated: 12 August 1957 *Employees:* 3
Net Worth: £5,485,627 *Total Assets:* £6,036,134
Registered Office: Capital Court, 30 Windsor Street, Uxbridge, Middlesex, UB8 1AB
Activities: Other letting and operating of own or leased real estate
Officers: Hugh William Try, Secretary; Hugh William Try [1937] Director/Builder; John Andrew Try [1942] Director/Builder; Richard Thomas Try [1956] Director/Gardener

Vinepost Limited
Incorporated: 16 October 2007
Net Worth: £1,306,152 *Total Assets:* £18,481,164
Registered Office: 3rd Floor, Sterling House, Langston Road, Loughton, Essex, IG10 3TS
Activities: Activities of open-ended investment companies
Shareholders: David Edward Conway; Gary Alexander Conway; Richard Matthew Conway
Officers: David Edward Conway, Secretary; David Edward Conway [1976] Director; Gary Alexander Conway [1973] Director; Richard Matthew Conway [1978] Director

Viners Capital Properties Limited
Incorporated: 8 April 2014 *Employees:* 5
Net Worth: £690,951 *Total Assets:* £15,850,952
Registered Office: 1 Wall Hall Mansion, Wall Hall Drive, Aldenham, Watford, Herts, WD25 8BZ
Activities: Other letting and operating of own or leased real estate
Officers: Ian Alistair McGregor, Secretary; Anthea Rose Novak [1949] Director; Edna Novak [1954] Director; Leon Beverly Novak [1949] Director; Melvyn Ian Novak [1944] Director

Vink UK Limited
Incorporated: 25 July 1975 *Employees:* 436
Previous: Vink UK PLC
Net Worth: £23,877,000 *Total Assets:* £46,216,000
Registered Office: Holmes House, 24-30 Baker Street, Weybridge, Surrey, KT13 8AU
Activities: Wholesale of wood, construction materials and sanitary equipment
Parent: Vink Holdings Limited
Officers: Robin Michael Howard, Finance Director; Anthony Michael Bird [1965] Finance Director; Keith Whiting Colburn [1948] Director [American]; Roger David Goddard [1953] Director/Chartered Accountant; Robin Michael Howard [1961] Finance Director; Douglas Talbot McNair [1947] Director; David Whittow Williams [1957] Director/General Manager; William Sones Woof [1951] Director/Solicitor

Vinstrata Builders (London) Limited
Incorporated: 14 March 1983 *Employees:* 9
Net Worth: £6,015,004 *Total Assets:* £6,687,975
Registered Office: 4 Lakes Road, Keston, Kent, BR2 6BN
Activities: Construction of commercial buildings
Shareholder: Keith Marshall
Officers: Linda Anne Conway, Secretary; Keith Marshall [1961] Director

T. Visaman & Sons Limited
Incorporated: 24 October 2006 *Employees:* 2
Net Worth: £5,622,532 *Total Assets:* £12,199,468
Registered Office: 616D Green Lane, Ilford, Essex, IG3 9SE
Activities: Dispensing chemist in specialised stores
Officers: Preeti Pattni, Secretary; Pravin Pattani [1957] Director/Chemist

Vision Homes Limited
Incorporated: 16 November 1999
Net Worth: £2,927,301 *Total Assets:* £7,469,897
Registered Office: 70 East Hill, Dartford, Kent, DA1 1RZ
Activities: Buying and selling of own real estate
Shareholders: Grahame Donald Crisp Seaman; Permjit Singh Sulh
Officers: Permjit Singh Sulh, Secretary/Property Developer; Grahame Donald Crisp Seaman [1946] Director/Property Developer; Permjit Singh Sulh [1968] Director/Property Developer

Vista Al Mar Limited
Incorporated: 11 May 2004 *Employees:* 2
Net Worth Deficit: £949,585 *Total Assets:* £5,732,761
Registered Office: c/o Barnes Roffe Chartered Accountants, 3 Brook Business Centre, Cowley Mill Road, Uxbridge, Middlesex, UB8 2FX
Activities: Activities of other holding companies n.e.c.
Major Shareholder: Denis O'Brien
Officers: Brendan Christoph Hayes, Secretary; Brendan Christoph Hayes [1974] Director; Mark George Polychronakis [1974] Director

Visual Impact (UK) Limited
Incorporated: 7 April 1987 *Employees:* 125
Net Worth: £20,098,052 *Total Assets:* £29,229,290
Registered Office: Unit 3 Teddington Business Park, Station Road, Teddington, Middlesex, TW11 9BQ
Activities: Television programme production activities
Major Shareholder: Neil Jonathan Quincey
Officers: Graham Hawkins [1967] Director; Paresh Jani [1966] Director/Accountant; Tim Sparrock [1968] Sales Director

Visual Response Limited
Incorporated: 13 February 1991 *Employees:* 27
Net Worth: £1,598,527 *Total Assets:* £7,047,536
Registered Office: Numeric House, 98 Station Road, Sidcup, Kent, DA15 7BY
Activities: Other information technology service activities
Parent: V R Holdings Limited
Officers: Lesley Ann Waters, Secretary; Mark Michael Waters [1960] Director

Vitec Group Holdings Limited
Incorporated: 5 July 1999
Net Worth: £82,590,000 *Total Assets:* £162,190,000
Registered Office: Bridge House, Heron Square, Richmond, Surrey, TW9 1EN
Activities: Activities of head offices
Parent: The Vitec Group PLC
Officers: Jonathan Mark Bolton, Secretary; Jonathan Mark Bolton [1966] Director/Company Secretary; Martin Jon Green [1968] Director/Head of Business Development; Katharina Helen Marie Kearney-Croft [1974] Finance Director

The Vitec Group PLC.
Incorporated: 30 January 1928 *Employees:* 1,675
Net Worth: £135,600,000 *Total Assets:* £289,700,000
Registered Office: Bridge House, Heron Square, Richmond, Surrey, TW9 1EN
Activities: Activities of head offices
Officers: Jonathan Mark Bolton, Secretary; Stephen Clive Bird [1960] Director/Chief Executive; Martin Jon Green [1968] Director/Business Development; Christopher John Humphrey [1957] Director/Accountant; Katharina Helen Marie Kearney-Croft [1974] Finance Director; John McDonough [1951] Director; Ian Philip McHoul [1960] Director; Duncan John Penny [1963] Director/Chief Executive; Caroline Agnes Morgan Thomson [1954] Director; John Richard Tyson [1970] Director

Vitec Imaging Solutions UK Limited
Incorporated: 15 November 1985 *Employees:* 68
Previous: Manfrotto UK Limited
Net Worth: £4,162,000 *Total Assets:* £9,751,000
Registered Office: Bridge House, Heron Square, Richmond, Surrey, TW9 1EN
Activities: Other manufacturing n.e.c.
Parent: Vitec Investments Limited
Officers: Jonathan Mark Bolton, Secretary; Jonathan Mark Bolton [1966] Director/Company Secretary; Christopher William Carr [1975] Director; Loris Frizzo [1970] Director [Italian]; Martin Jon Green [1968] Director; Katharina Helen Marie Kearney-Croft [1974] Finance Director; Neil Keith Martin [1969] Director/Site Manager; Marco Pezzana [1969] Director/Divisional CEO [Italian]

Vitec Investments Limited
Incorporated: 19 August 1998
Net Worth: £131,802,000 *Total Assets:* £260,059,008
Registered Office: Bridge House, Heron Square, Richmond, Surrey, TW9 1EN
Activities: Activities of head offices
Parent: Vitec Group Holdings Limited
Officers: Jonathan Mark Bolton, Secretary; Jonathan Mark Bolton [1966] Director/Company Secretary; Martin Jon Green [1968] Director/Head of Business Development; Katharina Helen Marie Kearney-Croft [1974] Finance Director

Vitec Production Solutions Limited
Incorporated: 11 July 1983 *Employees:* 180
Previous: Vitec Videocom Limited
Net Worth: £129,394,000 *Total Assets:* £164,204,000
Registered Office: Bridge House, Heron Square, Richmond, Surrey, TW9 1EN
Activities: Machining
Parent: The Vitec Group PLC
Officers: Jonathan Mark Bolton, Secretary; Jonathan Mark Bolton [1966] Director/Company Secretary; Martin Jon Green [1968] Director/Head of Business Development; Dr Alan Charles Hollis [1964] Managing Director; Katharina Helen Marie Kearney-Croft [1974] Finance Director; Andrew John Kelly [1977] Director/Chartered Accountant; Richard Graham Satchell [1980] Director

Vivo Medical Care Limited
Incorporated: 4 February 2011 *Employees:* 9
Net Worth Deficit: £225,003 *Total Assets:* £6,641,173
Registered Office: 10 Bourne End Road, Northwood, Middlesex, HA6 3BS
Activities: General medical practice activities
Shareholder: Hewawasamge Ravindranath Srilal Wijeratne
Officers: Maheepala Akrapkuruppu Wickramasinghe Ekneligoda [1965] Director/Doctor [Sri Lankan]; Arumugadas Kumaradas [1957] Director; Rasitha Kumaradas [1969] Director/Doctor [Sri Lankan]; Kiran Nandkumar Purandare [1969] Director/Doctor [Indian]; Oswald Deepa Ratnayake [1948] Director/Doctor; Somil Devendra Wijendra [1948] Director/Doctor; Dr Hewanasamge Wijitha Kumara Wijeratne [1966] Director/Doctor; Hewawasamge Ravindranath Srilal Wijeratne [1959] Director/Doctor [Sri Lankan]; Dr Jayantha Jayasiri Wijeratne [1947] Director/Doctor

Vizual Business Tools Limited
Incorporated: 16 December 1999
Net Worth: £3,764,000 *Total Assets:* £5,815,000
Registered Office: Syward Place, Pyrcroft Road, Chertsey, Surrey, KT16 9JT
Activities: Other information technology service activities
Parent: OneClickHR Limited
Officers: Michael Anthony Bonarti [1965] Director/Attorney [American]; Jeffrey Lewis Phipps [1968] Managing Director; Lorna Wake [1976] Director/Accountant

Vlasak Holdings Limited
Incorporated: 10 July 1959 *Employees:* 3
Net Worth: £5,262,081 *Total Assets:* £5,358,957
Registered Office: First Floor, Radius House, 51 Clarendon Road, Watford, Herts, WD17 1HP
Activities: Activities of head offices
Shareholders: Josef Maurer; Vitezslava Maurer
Officers: Vitezslava Maurer, Secretary; Josef Maurer [1950] Director [British/Czech]; Monica Susan Maurer [1970] Director [British/Czech]; Vitezslava Maurer [1950] Director/Company Secretary [British/Czech]

J. Van Vliet London Cash & Carry Limited
Incorporated: 10 November 1994 *Employees:* 331
Net Worth: £2,402,265 *Total Assets:* £11,620,717
Registered Office: Knapdale Nursery, Cattlegate Road, Enfield, Middlesex, EN2 9ED
Activities: Wholesale of flowers and plants
Parent: Esmeralda Limited
Officers: Rahul Patel, Secretary; Jo-Anne Newham [1973] Director [Irish]

Voicevale Limited
Incorporated: 1 June 1981 *Employees:* 71
Net Worth: £28,011,732 *Total Assets:* £82,394,624
Registered Office: Voicevale House, Spring Villa Park, Edgware, Middlesex, HA8 7EB
Activities: Non-specialised wholesale trade
Major Shareholder: Robert Teddy Danon
Officers: Linda Christine Barrett, Secretary; Linda Christine Barrett [1966] Director/Financial Controller [Irish]; Edward Danon [1984] Director; Naomi Danon [1957] Director/Marketing Consultant; Roby Teddy Danon [1956] Director; Cho Yin Ho [1964] Director/Commodity Trader; Chiaki Onozuka [1970] Director [Japanese]

Volante Limited
Incorporated: 6 October 1981 *Employees:* 41
Net Worth: £9,180,194 *Total Assets:* £11,360,618
Registered Office: Units 3 & 4 Fairfield Trade Park, Villiers Road, Kingston upon Thames, Surrey, KT1 3AY
Activities: Wholesale of other intermediate products
Parent: Brookvale Ltd
Officers: Keith Michael Ball, Secretary; David Evans [1969] Operations Director; Stephen Philip Holmes [1956] Director; Nicholas Charles Clegg Treasure [1964] Sales Director

Volex Group Holdings Limited
Incorporated: 24 June 1993
Net Worth: £13,814,000 *Total Assets:* £19,312,000
Registered Office: c/o Volex PLC, Holbrook House, 34-38 Hill Rise, Richmond, Surrey, TW10 6UA
Activities: Activities of other holding companies n.e.c.
Parent: Volex PLC
Officers: Daren John Morris, Secretary; Nicolas Henry Holland [1971] Director; Daren John Morris [1970] Director

Volex PLC
Incorporated: 19 September 1919 *Employees:* 6,466
Net Worth: £36,625,332 *Total Assets:* £117,791,552
Registered Office: Holbrook House, 34-38 Hill Rise, Richmond, Surrey, TW10 6UA
Activities: Manufacture of electronic components
Officers: Daren John Morris, Secretary; Adrian Chamberlain [1957] Director; Dean Roderick Moore [1957] Director; Daren John Morris [1970] Director; Nathaniel Rothschild [1971] Director [Canadian]

Volga-Dnepr UK Ltd.
Incorporated: 3 August 1999 *Employees:* 45
Net Worth: £93,069,952 *Total Assets:* £105,627,016
Registered Office: 3 Roundwood Avenue, Stockley Park, Uxbridge, Middlesex, UB11 1AF
Activities: Freight air transport
Major Shareholder: Alexey Ivanovich Isaykin
Officers: Elena Lebedeva, Secretary; Alexey Isaykin [1952] Director/Businessman [Cypriot]

VolkerFitzpatrick Limited
Incorporated: 22 May 1989 *Employees:* 998
Net Worth: £57,666,000 *Total Assets:* £179,503,008
Registered Office: Hertford Road, Hoddesdon, Herts, EN11 9BX
Activities: Construction of commercial buildings
Parent: Volkerwessels Limited
Officers: Naomi Anne Connell [1965] Director; John Anthony Cox [1964] Managing Director [Irish]; David John Griffin [1973] Commercial Director; Ceri Suzanne Humphrey [1971] Director; Richard Andrew Offord [1964] Director; Alan Robert Robertson [1962] Director

Volkerhighways Limited
Incorporated: 1 October 1959 *Employees:* 320
Net Worth: £9,604,000 *Total Assets:* £41,902,000
Registered Office: Hertford Road, Hoddesdon, Herts, EN11 9BX
Activities: Other specialised construction activities n.e.c.
Parent: VolkerFitzpatrick Limited
Officers: Naomi Anne Connell [1965] Director; Jonathon Michael Humphries [1967] Director; Alan Robert Robertson [1962] Director

Volkerinfra Limited
Incorporated: 19 January 1933 *Employees:* 34
Net Worth: £3,678,000 *Total Assets:* £7,537,000
Registered Office: Hertford Road, Hoddesdon, Herts, EN11 9BX
Activities: Construction of utility projects for electricity and telecommunications
Parent: Volkerstevin Group Limited
Officers: Naomi Anne Connell [1965] Director; Robert Damian Coupe [1965] Director; Alan Robert Robertson [1962] Director; Lynsey Taylor [1975] Finance Director; Anthony Richard Towse [1968] Director

Volkerlaser Ltd
Incorporated: 13 December 1999 *Employees:* 119
Net Worth: £6,492,000 *Total Assets:* £14,555,000
Registered Office: Hertford Road, Hoddesdon, Herts, EN11 9BX
Activities: Other specialised construction activities n.e.c.
Parent: Volkerwessels Limited
Officers: Naomi Anne Connell [1965] Director; Alan Robert Robertson [1962] Director; Michael James Weaver [1962] Director/Quantity Surveyor

Volkerrail Group Limited
Incorporated: 13 October 2003 *Employees:* 794
Net Worth: £22,881,000 *Total Assets:* £106,023,000
Registered Office: Hertford Road, Hoddesdon, Herts, EN11 9BX
Activities: Activities of construction holding companies
Parent: Volkerwessels UK Limited
Officers: Stephen Jeffrey Cocliff [1958] Director; Naomi Anne Connell [1965] Director; Paul Howard Nolan [1966] Director; Alan Robert Robertson [1962] Director; Andrew Michael Wilkins [1964] Director

Volkerrail Limited
Incorporated: 11 April 1996 *Employees:* 342
Net Worth: £10,877,000 *Total Assets:* £84,958,000
Registered Office: Hertford Road, Hoddesdon, Herts, EN11 9BX
Activities: Construction of roads and motorways
Parent: Volkerrail Group Limited
Officers: Stephen Jeffrey Cocliff [1958] Director; Naomi Anne Connell [1965] Director; Paul Howard Nolan [1966] Director; Alan Robert Robertson [1962] Director; Andrew Michael Wilkins [1964] Director

Volkerrail Specialist Businesses Limited
Incorporated: 10 April 2001 *Employees:* 452
Net Worth: £11,852,000 *Total Assets:* £28,070,000
Registered Office: Hertford Road, Hoddesdon, Herts, EN11 9BX
Activities: Other specialised construction activities n.e.c.
Parent: Volkerrail Group Limited
Officers: Stephen Jeffrey Cocliff [1958] Director; Naomi Anne Connell [1965] Director; Paul Howard Nolan [1966] Director; Alan Robert Robertson [1962] Director; Andrew Michael Wilkins [1964] Director

Volkerservices Limited
Incorporated: 22 May 2000 *Employees:* 243
Net Worth: £4,327,000 *Total Assets:* £26,081,000
Registered Office: Hertford Road, Hoddesdon, Herts, EN11 9BX
Activities: Construction of roads and motorways
Parent: Volkerwessels Limited
Officers: Naomi Anne Connell [1965] Director; Ceri Suzanne Humphrey [1971] Director; Richard Andrew Offord [1964] Director; Alan Robert Robertson [1962] Director

Volkerstevin Group Limited
Incorporated: 9 December 2011 *Employees:* 579
Net Worth: £17,715,000 *Total Assets:* £78,214,000
Registered Office: Hertford Road, Hoddesdon, Herts, EN11 9BX
Activities: Construction of other civil engineering projects n.e.c.
Parent: Volkerwessels UK Limited
Officers: Naomi Anne Connell [1965] Director; Robert Damian Coupe [1965] Director; Alan Robert Robertson [1962] Director; Lynsey Taylor [1975] Finance Director; Anthony Richard Towse [1968] Director

Volkerstevin Limited
Incorporated: 24 May 1934 *Employees:* 436
Net Worth: £19,771,000 *Total Assets:* £58,728,000
Registered Office: Hertford Road, Hoddesdon, Herts, EN11 9BX
Activities: Construction of other civil engineering projects n.e.c.
Parent: Volkerstevin Group Limited
Officers: Naomi Anne Connell [1965] Director; Robert Damian Coupe [1965] Director; Alan Robert Robertson [1962] Director; Lynsey Taylor [1975] Finance Director; Anthony Richard Towse [1968] Director

Volkerwessels Limited
Incorporated: 19 March 1986 *Employees:* 1,360
Net Worth: £70,130,000 *Total Assets:* £211,092,992
Registered Office: Hertford Road, Hoddesdon, Herts, EN11 9BX
Activities: Activities of head offices
Parent: Volkerwessels UK Limited
Officers: Naomi Anne Connell [1965] Director; Richard Andrew Offord [1964] Director; Alan Robert Robertson [1962] Director; Michael James Weaver [1962] Director/Quantity Surveyor

Volkerwessels UK Limited
Incorporated: 31 July 1974 *Employees:* 2,733
Net Worth: £88,947,000 *Total Assets:* £351,801,984
Registered Office: Hertford Road, Hoddesdon, Herts, EN11 9BX
Activities: Construction of commercial buildings
Officers: Naomi Anne Connell, Secretary; Stephen Jeffrey Cocliff [1958] Director; Naomi Anne Connell [1965] Director; Robert Damian Coupe [1965] Director; Hendrik Willem Renier August Maria Janssen [1954] Director/General Counsel [Dutch]; Richard Andrew Offord [1964] Director; Alan Robert Robertson [1962] Director; Alfred Vos [1969] Director [Dutch]

Voluntary Service Overseas
Incorporated: 18 September 1961 *Employees:* 730
Net Worth: £22,137,000 *Total Assets:* £47,489,000
Registered Office: 100 London Road, Kingston upon Thames, Surrey, KT2 6QJ
Activities: Other education n.e.c.
Officers: Jennifer Margaret Owen, Secretary; Charles Paul Abani [1960] Director/International Development Practitioner [Nigerian/British]; Gustaaf Teunis Franciscus Eskens [1949] Director/Company Chair [Dutch]; Hardeep Jhutty [1982] Director; Dr Noerine Kaleeba [1951] Director/HIV & Aids Campaigner (Retired) [Ugandan]; Christopher James Merry [1961] Director/Chief Executive; Stephen Meredith Pidgeon [1947] Director/Fundraising Consultant; Amanda Rowlatt [1962] Director/Economist; Biranchi Naryan Upadhyaya [1964] Director/Development Expert [Indian]; James Samuel Younger [1951] Director

VS Alliance Limited
Incorporated: 10 August 2012
Net Worth: £103,472,256 *Total Assets:* £103,512,560
Registered Office: Dixcart House, Addlestone Road, Bourne Business Park, Addlestone, Surrey, KT15 2LE
Activities: Activities of other holding companies n.e.c.
Major Shareholder: Victor Shkulev
Officers: Laurence Binge [1959] Director/Accountant; Simon Peter Barry Horne [1963] Director/Chief Financial Officer Hearst; Peter Anthony Robertson [1980] Director/Lawyer; Victor Shkulev [1958] Director/CEO of Media Group [Russian]

Vulcan Wharf Limited
Incorporated: 23 June 2017
Net Worth Deficit: £8,100 *Total Assets:* £7,554,665
Registered Office: One York Road, Uxbridge, Middlesex, UB8 1RN
Activities: Development of building projects
Shareholder: Broadwick Estates Ltd
Officers: Scott Brown [1968] Director [Australian]; Susan Hickey [1963] Director/Chief Financial Officer; Adam Lawrence [1970] Director; Richard Howard Mortimer [1953] Director for Development and Sales

Vvoosh Limited
Incorporated: 7 May 2010 *Employees:* 2
Net Worth: £6,074,820 *Total Assets:* £6,234,973
Registered Office: 5 Stirling Court Yard, Stirling Way, Borehamwood, Herts, WD6 2FX
Activities: Web portals
Shareholder: Manuel Fernandez
Officers: Jeff Mendlesohn, Secretary; Manuel Fernandez [1968] Director; Jeffrey Howard Mendlesohn [1953] Director/Chartered Accountant

VXR Imaging Limited
Incorporated: 4 May 2010 *Employees:* 11
Net Worth: £5,039,021 *Total Assets:* £6,302,189
Registered Office: Gladstone House, 77-79 High Street, Egham, Surrey, TW20 9HY
Activities: Other professional, scientific and technical activities n.e.c.
Shareholders: Stephen Dorrell; Tina Jane Dorrell
Officers: Stephen Dorrell [1962] Director; Tina Jane Dorrell [1967] Director

W & L Investments LLP
Incorporated: 2 April 2016
Net Worth: £12,073,404 *Total Assets:* £15,752,335
Registered Office: 42 Lytton Road, Barnet, Herts, EN5 5BY
Officers: Julia Selt [1963] Member; Lauren Selt [1960] Member; Lewis Selt [1963] Member; Wayne Michael Selt [1958] Member

W.T. Partnership Limited
Incorporated: 23 August 1973 *Employees:* 116
Net Worth: £1,685,456 *Total Assets:* £6,668,090
Registered Office: Amp House, Dingwall Road, Croydon, Surrey, CR0 2LX
Activities: Quantity surveying activities
Parent: WT Partners Ltd
Officers: Nicholas John Day, Secretary; Stephen Paul Beard [1957] Director/Quantity Surveyor; Alan Robert Chapman [1953] Director/Consultant; Alastair Cunningham [1982] Director/Quantity Surveyor; Nicholas John Day [1957] Director/Consultant; Geoffrey Keith Driver [1959] Director/Quantity Surveyor; Gary Brian Elkes [1977] Finance Director; Martin Fantl [1966] Director/Project Manager; Mr Paul Edward Goldstraw [1965] Director/Quantity Surveyor; Paul Henson [1961] Director/Quantity Surveyor; Timothy Hill [1978] Director/Project Manager; John Leslie Hinchliffe [1949] Director/Consultant; Steven Lester [1962] Director/Quantity Surveyor; Andrew Mannion [1973] Director/Quantity Surveyor; Gary Payne [1955] Director/Consultant; Antony Perry [1971] Director/Quantity Surveyor; Christopher Peyman [1956] Director/Chartered Surveyor; Jonathan Lee Pickles [1971] Director/Quantity Surveyor; Ian Matthew Rhodes [1974] Director/Quantity Surveyor; Andrew John Richardson [1969] Director/Surveyor; Dean Anthony Smith [1970] Director/Surveyor; Nicholas Tyler [1960] Director/Quantity Surveyor

W3 Insights Ltd
Incorporated: 19 February 2002
Net Worth: £4,738,000 *Total Assets:* £8,303,000
Registered Office: 1st Floor, Vantage London, Great West Road, Brentford, Middlesex, TW8 9AG
Activities: Other business support service activities n.e.c.
Parent: GL Education Group Limited
Officers: Robert Dargue [1975] Director/Chartered Accountant; Gregor Stanley Watson [1965] Director

Wadlow Energy Holdings Limited
Incorporated: 23 June 2011
Net Worth: £1,000 *Total Assets:* £23,460,000
Registered Office: Beaufort Court, Egg Farm Lane, Kings Langley, Herts, WD4 8LR
Activities: Activities of head offices
Parent: DIF Infra 4 UK Limited
Officers: Dominic James Hearth, Secretary; David Lau [1981] Director/Originator [German]; Helen Mary Murphy [1981] Director/Asset Manager [Irish]

Wadlow Energy Limited
Incorporated: 30 November 2010
Net Worth Deficit: £12,638,000 *Total Assets:* £47,619,000
Registered Office: Beaufort Court, Egg Farm Lane, Kings Langley, Herts, WD4 8LR
Activities: Other specialised construction activities n.e.c.
Parent: Wadlow Energy Holdings Limited
Officers: Dominic James Hearth, Secretary; David Lau [1981] Director/Originator [German]; Helen Mary Murphy [1981] Director/Asset Manager [Irish]

Wagermotion Limited
Incorporated: 12 July 1996 *Employees:* 1
Net Worth: £8,757,737 *Total Assets:* £20,276,084
Registered Office: Unit E6, Bridge Close, Crossways Business Park, Dartford, Kent, DA2 6QN
Activities: Other letting and operating of own or leased real estate
Officers: Muir Martin Ologhlen, Secretary; Noel Furlong [1937] Director [Irish]

The Waldegrave Trust
Incorporated: 4 July 2012 *Employees:* 154
Net Worth: £22,315,844 *Total Assets:* £24,606,262
Registered Office: Waldegrave School, Fifth Cross Road, Twickenham, Middlesex, TW2 5LH
Activities: General secondary education
Officers: Alexandra Clare Warburton, Secretary; Karen Janette Oliver [1969] Director/Home; Frances Joy Perrow [1964] Director/Communications Consultant; Tracy Victoria Royle [1970] Director/Employee at Microsoft; Andrew Michael Tanner [1968] Director/IT Consultant; Elizabeth Tongue [1973] Director/Headteacher; Michael Barry Wilkinson [1957] Director/Employee at BP

Walgreens Boots Alliance Services Limited
Incorporated: 11 November 2009 *Employees:* 299
Previous: Alliance Boots Management Services Limited
Net Worth: £40,490,000 *Total Assets:* £82,593,000
Registered Office: 2 The Heights, Brooklands, Weybridge, Surrey, KT13 0NY
Activities: Other business support service activities n.e.c.
Parent: Alliance Boots Holdings Limited
Officers: Frank Standish, Secretary; Claude Louis Bahoshy [1973] Director; Martin Christopher Delve [1967] Director/Accountant; Mark Francis Muller [1964] Director; Frank Standish [1963] Director [Irish]

Walker Greenbank PLC.
Incorporated: 3 May 1899 *Employees:* 686
Net Worth: £61,612,000 *Total Assets:* £99,653,000
Registered Office: Chalfont House, Oxford Road, Denham, Bucks, UB9 4DX
Activities: Activities of head offices
Officers: Caroline Geary, Secretary; Michael David Gant [1969] Director; Christopher Charles Bevan Rogers [1960] Director; Terry George Stannard [1950] Director/Consultant; Vijaykumar Champaklal Thakrar [1961] Director; Dame Ila Dianne Thompson [1950] Director

Wallacespace Limited
Incorporated: 19 February 1993 *Employees:* 125
Net Worth: £4,793,370 *Total Assets:* £9,803,414
Registered Office: Salatin House, 19 Cedar Road, Sutton, Surrey, SM2 5DA
Activities: Other service activities n.e.c.
Shareholders: Roy James Gilmore Kerr; Renata Kim Wallace
Officers: Roy James Gilmore Kerr, Secretary; Roy James Gilmore Kerr [1955] Director/Marketing Executive; Renata Kim Wallace [1966] Director/Training Executive

Walnut Estates Limited
Incorporated: 2 December 1998 *Employees:* 1
Net Worth: £6,507,833 *Total Assets:* £9,276,954
Registered Office: Walnut Cottage, Lovelands Lane, Lower Kingswood, Surrey, KT20 6XG
Activities: Other letting and operating of own or leased real estate
Parent: Walnut Holdings Limited
Officers: Andrea Lewis, Secretary; Henry Norman Lewis [1939] Director

The Walsall Hospital Company (Holdings) Limited
Incorporated: 10 July 2007
Net Worth Deficit: £8,427,000 *Total Assets:* £164,771,008
Registered Office: 8 White Oak Square, London Road, Swanley, Kent, BR8 7AG
Activities: Activities of head offices
Shareholders: BIIF Hold Co III Limited; Innisfree Secondary Partners 2 LLP
Officers: Bryan Michael Acutt [1979] Director/Investment Manager; Gaynor Birley-Smith [1966] Investment Director; David John Brooking [1967] Investment Director; John Ivor Cavill [1972] Director; Benjamin Christopher Jacob Dean [1979] Director/Investment Manager

The Walsall Hospital Company PLC
Incorporated: 31 August 2007
Net Worth Deficit: £8,427,000 *Total Assets:* £164,771,008
Registered Office: 8 White Oak Square, London Road, Swanley, Kent, BR8 7AG
Activities: Combined facilities support activities
Parent: The Walsall Hospital Company (Holdings) Limited
Officers: Bryan Michael Acutt [1979] Director/Investment Manager; Gaynor Birley-Smith [1966] Investment Director; David John Brooking [1967] Investment Director; John Ivor Cavill [1972] Director; Benjamin Christopher Jacob Dean [1979] Director/Investment Manager; Michael Edward Fry [1958] Director

Walsall Public Lighting Holding Company Limited
Incorporated: 10 January 2001
Net Worth Deficit: £370,000 *Total Assets:* £10,374,000
Registered Office: 8 White Oak Square, London Road, Swanley, Kent, BR8 7AG
Activities: Activities of head offices
Parent: JLIF (GP) Limited
Officers: Carl Harvey Dix [1966] Operations Director; Carlos Vela Lazaga [1989] Director/Junior Valuation Analyst [Spanish]

Walsall Public Lighting Limited
Incorporated: 10 January 2001
Net Worth Deficit: £370,000 *Total Assets:* £10,374,000
Registered Office: 8 White Oak Square, London Road, Swanley, Kent, BR8 7AG
Activities: Construction of commercial buildings
Parent: Walsall Public Lighting Holding Company Limited
Officers: Carl Harvey Dix [1966] Operations Director; Carlos Vela Lazaga [1989] Director/Junior Valuation Analyst [Spanish]

Walsingham Care
Incorporated: 12 May 2006 *Employees:* 1
Net Worth: £6,150,914 *Total Assets:* £6,160,904
Registered Office: c/o Brayne Williams & Barnard Limited, Rosemount House, Rosemount Avenue, West Byfleet, Surrey, KT14 6LB
Activities: Other business support service activities n.e.c.
Officers: Jonathan William Andrew [1950] Director/Bishops Trustee; Ruth Mary Bruce [1959] Director/Psychotherapist; John Deal [1934] Director; Ian Roger Ford [1957] Director/Solicitor; Robert David Hewitt [1955] Director/Chartered Accountant; Nicolette Joy Shaw [1961] Director/Chief Executive of a Charity; Tannia Shipley [1948] Director/Charity Trustee

Wandale Limited
Incorporated: 31 January 2012
Net Worth: £89,437 *Total Assets:* £86,751,960
Registered Office: Hill House, Lowlands Road, Harrow, Middlesex, HA1 3EQ
Activities: Development of building projects
Major Shareholder: Donovan Gijsbertus Wijsmuller
Officers: Brian Martin Comer [1960] Director [Irish]; Luke Andrew Comer [1957] Director [Irish]

Wandle Valley School
Incorporated: 10 August 2011 *Employees:* 43
Net Worth: £3,460,902 *Total Assets:* £5,469,279
Registered Office: Wandle Valley School, Welbeck Road, Carshalton, Surrey, SM5 1LW
Activities: Other education n.e.c.
Officers: Michelle Evans [1981] Director/Teacher; Maldwyn Fjord-Roberts [1979] Director/Headmaster; Natoya Ivey [1983] Director/Mature Student; David Nicholas Conrad Johnson [1962] Director/DJ Outreach/Sporting Chances; Tariro Edith Madzima [1989] Director/Compliance Officer; Christopher Rupert Henry Phillips [1963] Director/Site Supervisor; Suzanne Marie Rowson [1971] Director/Teacher; Gary Wright [1963] Director/School Governor

Warborough Investments Limited
Incorporated: 30 March 1962 *Employees:* 2
Net Worth: £58,755,496 *Total Assets:* £61,271,024
Registered Office: 198 Lower Addiscombe Road, Croydon, Surrey, CR0 7AB
Activities: Other letting and operating of own or leased real estate
Parent: Ocobase Limited
Officers: Simon Leslie Upward, Secretary; Paul David Upward [1962] Director; Simon Leslie Upward [1961] Director

Warchest Limited
Incorporated: 22 September 2011 *Employees:* 17
Net Worth Deficit: £9,701,142 *Total Assets:* £12,903,055
Registered Office: Royal Court, 81 Tweedy Road, Bromley, Kent, BR1 1RG
Activities: Publishing of computer games
Parent: Radius Maxima Limited
Officers: Ross Arthur William Farrow, Secretary; Ross Arthur William Farrow [1983] Finance Director; Richard Jolly [1979] Director; Jamarson Kong [1978] Director/Senior Management [Chinese]; Alex Xu Yiran [1972] Director/Senior Management [Chinese]

Warm Hearth Limited
Incorporated: 5 October 2015 *Employees:* 75
Net Worth: £1,753,976 *Total Assets:* £5,752,265
Registered Office: Elder House, St Georges Business Park, 207 Brooklands Road, Weybridge, Surrey, KT13 0TS
Activities: Public houses and bars
Shareholders: Puma VCT 11 PLC; Puma VCT 10 PLC
Officers: Ian Seath Lishman [1979] Director; Alexander Rupert West [1981] Director/Investment Manager

Warrant Investments PLC
Incorporated: 22 March 1994 *Employees:* 5
Net Worth: £19,620,204 *Total Assets:* £42,415,112
Registered Office: One Wellstones, Watford, Herts, WD17 2AE
Activities: Other business support service activities n.e.c.
Shareholder: Jeremy Laurence Stevens
Officers: Jeremy Laurence Stevens, Secretary; Anthony Ian Fine [1938] Director/Chartered Surveyor; Jeremy Laurence Stevens [1959] Director/Surveyor

Warrant Properties Limited
Incorporated: 23 May 2003 *Employees:* 5
Net Worth: £7,046,807 *Total Assets:* £19,209,212
Registered Office: One Wellstones, Watford, Herts, WD17 2AE
Activities: Other business support service activities n.e.c.
Major Shareholder: Jeremy Laurence Stevens
Officers: Lesley Anne Stevens, Secretary; Jeremy Laurence Stevens [1959] Director/Surveyor; Lesley Anne Stevens [1963] Director/Interior Designer

Warren House Conference Centre Limited
Incorporated: 15 August 2005 *Employees:* 54
Net Worth: £8,739,411 *Total Assets:* £9,299,501
Registered Office: Warren House, Warren Road, Kingston upon Thames, Surrey, KT2 7HY
Activities: Hotels and similar accommodation
Shareholders: Patricia Mary Brown; Philip Joseph Brown
Officers: Patricia Mary Brown, Secretary/Investor; Patricia Mary Brown [1938] Director/Investor; Victoria Kathleen Louise Good [1965] Director/Author; Oliver Liam O'Callaghan-Brown [1967] Director/Osteopath

Warren Road Primary School
Incorporated: 24 May 2011 *Employees:* 136
Net Worth: £9,536,279 *Total Assets:* £10,589,741
Registered Office: Warren Road Primary School, Warren Road, Orpington, Kent, BR6 6JF
Activities: Primary education
Officers: Natasha Charles-Lewis [1976] Director/Accountant [Caribbean]; Andrew James Corstorphine [1986] Director/Teacher; Richard Alexander Edmonds [1963] Director; Richard Thomas Hulme [1973] Director/Civil Servant; Antony Johnson [1976] Director/Building Contractor; Fadzayi Musanhu [1976] Director/Corporate Finance [Zimbabwean]; Sarah Palmer [1979] Director/Deputy Headteacher; Paula Jayne Reddin [1976] Director; Joanne Salacinski [1981] Director/Commercial Manager; Jamie Thomas [1981] Director/Deputy Headteacher; Haibin Yu [1975] Director

Warrens Warehousing Group Limited
Incorporated: 10 November 2009 *Employees:* 379
Net Worth: £9,789,030 *Total Assets:* £18,960,614
Registered Office: Ground Floor, Irene House, Maidstone Road, Sidcup, Kent, DA14 5AE
Activities: Operation of warehousing and storage facilities for land transport activities
Parent: Culina Group Limited
Officers: Mark Anthony Allen, Secretary; Mark Anthony Allen [1964] Director; Nigel Stephen Jury [1950] Director; Christian Lee Price [1975] Director/Chartered Accountant; Thomas Van Mourik [1963] Director [Dutch]; Michael Reuben Warren [1969] Director

Warrens' Warehousing & Distribution (Midlands) Limited
Incorporated: 18 November 1992 *Employees:* 379
Net Worth: £9,468,963 *Total Assets:* £18,717,320
Registered Office: Ground Floor, Irene House, Maidstone Road, Sidcup, Kent, DA14 5AE
Activities: Operation of warehousing and storage facilities for land transport activities
Parent: Warrens Warehousing Group Limited
Officers: Mark Anthony Allen, Secretary/Finance; Mark Anthony Allen [1964] Director/Finance; Nigel Stephen Jury [1950] Director; Christian Lee Price [1975] Director/Chartered Accountant; Thomas Van Mourik [1963] Director [Dutch]; Michael Reuben Warren [1969] Director

Wasteland Group Limited
Incorporated: 14 November 2000 *Employees:* 3
Net Worth: £3,174,415 *Total Assets:* £7,541,768
Registered Office: 2nd Floor, Nucleus House, 2 Lower Mortlake Road, Richmond, Surrey, TW9 2JA
Activities: Real estate agencies
Shareholders: Edward William Penrose Cartlidge; Matilda Anne Cartlidge
Officers: Edward William Penrose Cartlidge [1970] Director Tour Operator; Matilda Anne Cartlidge [1972] Director/Housewife

Watch It Come Down Limited
Incorporated: 30 July 1956 *Employees:* 141
Net Worth: £8,141,835 *Total Assets:* £19,672,172
Registered Office: Waldens Depot, Waldens Road, Orpington, Kent, BR5 4EU
Activities: Renting and leasing of construction and civil engineering machinery and equipment
Shareholder: Terence Malcolm Bishop
Officers: Stephen Edward Bishop [1959] Director/Estimating Manager; Sydney Michael Bishop [1956] Director/Contracts Manager; Terrence Malcolm Bishop [1941] Director/Demolition Contractor; Thomas James Bishop [1965] Director/Manager

Watches International Limited
Incorporated: 4 February 1997 *Employees:* 26
Net Worth: £4,660,764 *Total Assets:* £6,509,667
Registered Office: FWP House, 17 Bourne Court, Southend Road, Woodford Green, Essex, IG8 8HD
Activities: Manufacture of jewellery and related articles
Parent: Watches International Holdings Limited
Officers: Gary Mark Stein [1960] Director

Watchingwell Farms Limited
Incorporated: 24 February 1964 *Employees:* 9
Net Worth: £6,640,035 *Total Assets:* £7,632,809
Registered Office: Gay Dawn Farm, Pennis Lane, Fawkham, Dartford, Kent, DA3 8LY
Activities: Raising of dairy cattle
Parent: F.C. Stark Limited
Officers: Stephen John Billings, Secretary; Andrew John Billings [1964] Director; Clive John Billings [1955] Director; Ronald John Billings [1960] Director/Manager; Stephen John Billings [1961] Director/Manager

Water Incorporated
Incorporated: 5 July 2006
Net Worth: £40,492 *Total Assets:* £10,041,309
Registered Office: Northside House, Mount Pleasant, Barnet, Herts, EN4 9EE
Activities: Activities of other membership organisations n.e.c.
Officers: Adam Kaoru Herwegh Vonk [1997] Director [Dutch]; Chiara Yuki Herwegh Vonk [1995] Director [Dutch]; Scipio Akira Herwegh Vonk [1999] Director [Dutch]; Peter Lawrence Ulrich [1958] Director/Administrator

Waterfront Cafe Benson Limited
Incorporated: 6 July 2016
Net Worth: £5,786,399 *Total Assets:* £6,034,674
Registered Office: 122a Nelson Road, Twickenham, Middlesex, TW2 7AY
Activities: Licenced restaurants
Major Shareholder: Christopher John Price
Officers: Christopher John Price [1964] Director; Gemma Price [1988] Director; Jennifer Price [1983] Director

Waterlow Business Supplies Limited
Incorporated: 15 May 1989 *Employees:* 2
Net Worth: £7,574,782 *Total Assets:* £7,620,913
Registered Office: Unit 4, 500 Purley Way, Croydon, Surrey, CR0 4NZ
Activities: Other business support service activities n.e.c.
Major Shareholder: Jonathan Paul Moulton
Officers: Philippa Anne Maynard, Secretary; Nicholas Robin Hodges [1959] Director; Andrew Graham Mobbs [1978] Finance Director

Waters Limited
Incorporated: 24 March 1994 *Employees:* 156
Net Worth: £8,637,000 *Total Assets:* £36,251,000
Registered Office: 610 Centennial Park, Centennial Avenue, Elstree, Herts, WD6 3TJ
Activities: Manufacture of electronic measuring, testing etc. equipment, not for industrial process control
Parent: Micromass Limited
Officers: James Hallam [1973] Director/General Manager, Northern Europe; Michael Cornelius Harrington [1960] Director [Irish]; Gary Joseph Murphy [1960] Director [American]; Columbanus Patrick O'Mahony [1964] Director [Irish]

Wates Construction Limited
Incorporated: 15 January 1986 *Employees:* 3,683
Net Worth: £101,108,000 *Total Assets:* £591,993,024
Registered Office: Wates House, Station Approach, Leatherhead, Surrey, KT22 7SW
Activities: Construction of commercial buildings
Parent: Wates Group Limited
Officers: Philip Michael Wainwright, Secretary; David Owen Allen [1972] Director/Chief Financial Officer; Stephen James Beechey [1968] Group Strategy Director; Helen Patricia Bunch [1965] Group Strategic Director; Paul Chandler [1964] Director/Construction Group MD; David Keir Ewart Morgan [1974] Managing Director; Simon James Potter [1963] Group Commercial Director; Paul Campbell Rowan [1964] Group HR Director; Philip Michael Wainwright [1965] Director/Chief Financial Officer

Wates Developments Limited
Incorporated: 30 August 1947 *Employees:* 30
Net Worth: £46,175,000 *Total Assets:* £95,624,000
Registered Office: Wates House, Station Approach, Leatherhead, Surrey, KT22 7SW
Activities: Development of building projects
Parent: Wates Group Limited
Officers: David Owen Allen [1972] Director/Chief Financial Officer; David Alexander Bowen [1967] Finance Director; David Michael Brocklebank [1970] Director; Martin Geoffrey Leach [1965] Operations Director; Timothy Andrew de Burgh Wates [1966] Director

Wates Foundation Limited (The)
Incorporated: 23 December 1981 *Employees:* 4
Net Worth: £18,882,376 *Total Assets:* £19,036,852
Registered Office: Wates House, Station Approach, Leatherhead, Surrey, KT22 7SW
Activities: Other social work activities without accommodation n.e.c.
Officers: Jeremy Wright, Secretary; Nicholas Edwards [1954] Director; Oliver John Charles Heynes [1971] Director/Helicopter Pilot; Claire Alexandra Joy Spotswood Brown [1974] Director/Housewife; Andrew Eugene Paul Wates [1969] Director; Neil Edward Wates [1986] Director/Chartered Surveyor

Wates Group Limited
Incorporated: 14 June 1984 *Employees:* 3,972
Net Worth: £119,415,000 *Total Assets:* £702,764,032
Registered Office: Wates House, Station Approach, Leatherhead, Surrey, KT22 7SW
Activities: Activities of construction holding companies
Shareholders: Annabelle Louisa Mary Elliott; Andrew Eugene Paul Wates; Annette Beatrice Therese Wates; Paul Christopher Ronald Wates
Officers: Philip Michael Wainwright, Secretary; David Owen Allen [1972] Director/Chief Financial Officer; David Martin Barclay [1954] Director; Paul Chandler [1964] Director/Construction Group MD; Jeremy Henry Moore Newsum [1955] Director/Chartered Surveyor; Jonathan Mark Oatley [1968] Director/Chief Executive; Philip Michael Wainwright [1965] Director/Chief Financial Officer; Andrew Eugene Paul Wates [1969] Managing Director; Charles William Randag Wates [1976] Managing Director; James Garwood Michael Wates [1960] Director; Jonathan Giles MacArtney Wates [1967] Director; Timothy Andrew de Burgh Wates [1966] Director

Wates Group Services Limited
Incorporated: 1 June 1938 *Employees:* 250
Net Worth Deficit: £30,531,000 *Total Assets:* £48,559,000
Registered Office: Wates House, Station Approach, Leatherhead, Surrey, KT22 7SW
Activities: Other business support service activities n.e.c.
Parent: Wates Group Limited
Officers: Philip Michael Wainwright, Secretary; David Owen Allen [1972] Director/Chief Financial Officer; Simon James Potter [1963] Group Commercial Director; Paul Campbell Rowan [1964] Group HR Director; Philip Michael Wainwright [1965] Director/Chief Financial Officer; Timothy Andrew de Burgh Wates [1966] Managing Director

Wates Living Space (Maintenance) Limited
Incorporated: 26 October 1973 *Employees:* 852
Net Worth: £20,481,000 *Total Assets:* £60,934,000
Registered Office: Wates House, Station Approach, Leatherhead, Surrey, KT22 7SW
Activities: Other service activities n.e.c.
Parent: Wates Constructon Limited
Officers: Philip Michael Wainwright, Secretary; David Owen Allen [1972] Director/Chief Financial Officer; Helen Patricia Bunch [1965] Managing Director; David Keir Ewart Morgan [1974] Business Unit Managing Director; Simon James Potter [1963] Group Commercial Director; Paul Campbell Rowan [1964] Group HR Director; Philip Michael Wainwright [1965] Director/Chief Financial Officer

Watford Association Football Club Limited (The)
Incorporated: 22 July 1909 *Employees:* 254
Net Worth: £2,859,090 *Total Assets:* £168,852,896
Registered Office: Vicarage Road Stadium, Vicarage Road, Watford, Herts, WD18 0ER
Activities: Other sports activities
Parent: Hornets Investment Limited
Officers: Peter James Wastall, Secretary; Scott Ian Duxbury [1972] Director; David Bernard Fransen [1951] Director; Professor Stuart Read Timperley [1943] Director

Watford FC's Community Sports & Education Trust
Incorporated: 18 September 2003 *Employees:* 87
Net Worth: £6,085,219 *Total Assets:* £6,531,742
Registered Office: Vicarage Road Stadium, Vicarage Road, Watford, Herts, WD18 0ER
Activities: Sports and recreation education
Officers: Peter James Wastall, Secretary; Paul Anthony Clark [1951] Director/Retired; Edmund James Coan [1957] Marketing Director; Justin Paul Davis Smith [1961] Charity Director; Christopher John Luff [1964] Director; Simon James MacQueen [1975] Director/Strategic Services; Christopher James Norton [1955] Director; Professor Stuart Read Timperley [1943] Director

Watford Grammar School for Boys
Incorporated: 17 August 2010 *Employees:* 200
Net Worth: £18,300,976 *Total Assets:* £20,789,344
Registered Office: Watford Grammar School for Boys, Rickmansworth Road, Watford, Herts, WD18 7JF
Activities: General secondary education
Officers: Caroline Brown, Secretary; Milan Bavisi [1971] Director/Telecommunication Manager; Susan Margaret Branch [1942] Director/Retired; Ian Alexander Cooksey [1974] Director/Headmaster; Caroline Cox [1969] Director/Teacher; Rajesh Gordhandas Dawda [1972] Director/Chartered Accountant; Rachel Dunsby [1966] Director/Exams Officer; Stuart David Hart [1972] Director/Financial Planner; Stephen Anthony Nokes [1952] Director/Headmaster; Adam Edouard Parsons [1970] Director/Journalist; Sameena Riaz [1974] Director/Teacher; Rev Anthony William Rindl [1964] Director/Vicar; Professor David Alastair Ritchie [1959] Director/University Professor; Stephanie Emma Rodgers [1975] Director/Teacher; Stephen Shannon [1957] Financial Director; Andrew William Speirs [1965] Director/Investment Banker; Terry John Sweeney [1968] Finance Director; Anne Watson [1963] Director/Learning Support Assistant

Watford Grammar School for Girls
Incorporated: 17 August 2010 *Employees:* 161
Net Worth: £13,673,997 *Total Assets:* £15,644,219
Registered Office: Watford Grammar School for Girls, Lady's Close, Watford, Herts, WD18 0AE
Activities: General secondary education
Officers: Philip Beasley, Secretary; Sylvia Lucy Chong-Tai [1969] Director/Teacher; Dr Nigel Corp [1952] Director/GP; Russell Guy Deane [1959] Director; Harvey Spencer Griffiths [1968] Director/Investment Manager; Prakash Jani [1970] Director/Consultant; Mr Stephen Ernest Johnson [1953] Director; Clare Kirwan [1977] Director/Teacher; Michael Duncan Lewis [1972] Director/Army Officer; Mary Patricia Meerabux [1954] Director/Teacher; Nicholas John Moorhouse [1955] Director; Akintomide Idowu Oyesola [1963] IT Programme Director; Zia Al Rehman [1977] Director/Electronics Engineer; Rev Anthony William Rindl [1964] Director; Fiona Shore [1953] Director/Teacher; Jane Willis [1955] Director; Camilla Woods [1967] Director

The Watford UTC
Incorporated: 5 July 2013 *Employees:* 31
Net Worth: £8,392,721 *Total Assets:* £10,003,247
Registered Office: 18 Colonial Way, Watford, Herts, WD24 4PT
Activities: Technical and vocational secondary education
Officers: Alexander Hall, Secretary; Christopher John Francis Andrews [1961] Director; Kate Prudence Bearman [1971] Director/Communications Consultant; Richard Arthur Elms [1947] Director; Stephen Peter Hunt [1959] Director/University Lecturer; Celeste Jones [1973] Director/University Manager; Sir Leigh Warren Lewis [1951] Director/Part-Time Consultant; Claire Elaine Lish [1973] Director/Head of Human Resources; Emma Jane Loveland [1969] Director/Principal [Irish]; Mohan Deep Raj Luthra [1979] Director; Ashok Shankar Patil [1945] Director/IT Sales Consultant; Ian Smithson [1970] Director/Regional Officer

Watling Tyre Service Limited (The)
Incorporated: 26 March 1965 *Employees:* 137
Net Worth: £3,613,923 *Total Assets:* £10,993,567
Registered Office: 1-3 Pelham Road, Gravesend, Kent, DA11 0HN
Activities: Maintenance and repair of motor vehicles
Shareholders: Karen Frances Flury; Norman Frederick Flury
Officers: Karen Frances Flury [1944] Director; Norman Frederick Flury [1933] Director; Roger James Flury [1965] Director

Watmough Brothers Investments Limited
Incorporated: 28 February 1975 *Employees:* 4
Net Worth: £3,821,140 *Total Assets:* £7,115,685
Registered Office: 118 Upper Wickham Lane, Welling, Kent, DA16 3DR
Activities: Activities of open-ended investment companies
Shareholders: Nicholas Alexander Watmough; Christopher Charles Watmough
Officers: Christopher Charles Watmough, Secretary; Christopher Charles Watmough [1953] Director/Mortor Accessory Dealer; Nicholas Alexander Watmough [1951] Director/Motor Accessory Dealer

Watts Farms (Sales) Limited
Incorporated: 11 April 2003 *Employees:* 3
Net Worth: £689,153 *Total Assets:* £10,635,286
Registered Office: Sondix House, Sandpit Road, Dartford, Kent, DA1 5BU
Activities: Wholesale of fruit and vegetables
Parent: Watts Farms Fresh Produce Holdings Limited
Officers: Joseph Cottingham [1973] Director; Avril Marion Gray [1952] Director/Farmer; Dr Edward Donald Berkerley Gray [1984] Director; Michael Berkeley Gray [1947] Director/Farmer

Watts Farms Catering Limited
Incorporated: 31 October 2011 *Employees:* 168
Net Worth: £721,467 *Total Assets:* £7,267,568
Registered Office: Sondix House, Sandpit Road, Dartford, Kent, DA1 5BU
Activities: Other food services
Parent: Watts Farms Fresh Produce Holdings Limited
Officers: Joseph Cottingham [1973] Director; Avril Marion Gray [1952] Director; Dr Edward Donald Berkerley Gray [1984] Director; Michael Berkeley Gray [1947] Director

Watts Farms Fresh Produce Holdings Limited
Incorporated: 11 November 2011
Net Worth: £2,645,531 *Total Assets:* £15,553,254
Registered Office: Sondix House, Sandpit Road, Dartford, Kent, DA1 5BU
Activities: Activities of agricultural holding companies
Shareholders: Avril Marion Gray; Michael Berkeley Gray
Officers: Joseph Cottingham [1973] Director; Avril Marion Gray [1952] Director; Dr Edward Donald Berkerley Gray [1984] Director; Michael Berkeley Gray [1947] Director

Watts Farms Packers Limited
Incorporated: 29 March 2007 *Employees:* 190
Net Worth: £1,638,538 *Total Assets:* £8,116,563
Registered Office: Sondix House, Sandpit Road, Dartford, Kent, DA1 5BU
Activities: Packaging activities
Parent: Watts Farms Fresh Produce Holdings Limited
Officers: Joseph Cottingham [1973] Director; Avril Marion Gray [1952] Director/Farmer; Dr Edward Donald Berkerley Gray [1984] Director; Michael Berkeley Gray [1947] Director/Farmer

Waverley House Hotel Limited
Incorporated: 27 November 1995 *Employees:* 48
Net Worth: £42,155,576 *Total Assets:* £69,639,704
Registered Office: Kanta House, Victoria Road, South Ruislip, Middlesex, HA4 0JQ
Activities: Hotels and similar accommodation
Officers: Bhasker Tailor, Secretary/Chairman; Jawahar Jamnadas Chatwani [1948] Director; Rashmi Jamnadas Chatwani [1954] Director; Satish Jamnadas Chatwani [1953] Director

Waystone 32 Limited
Incorporated: 14 December 1995 *Employees:* 7
Net Worth: £2,859,370 *Total Assets:* £5,591,806
Registered Office: CP House, Otterspool Way, Watford Bypass, Watford, Herts, WD25 8JJ
Activities: Construction of commercial buildings
Parent: Waystone Limited
Officers: Eric Lewis, Secretary; Paul Andrew Filer [1957] Director/Chartered Accountant; Iris Gibbor [1951] Director; Philip Hoffbrand [1967] Director; Alistair James McLoughlin [1968] Director/Business Executive; Helen McLoughlin [1964] Director/Business Manager; Stuart McLoughlin [1939] Director; Alexei James Schreier [1976] Director

Waystone Limited
Incorporated: 11 December 1989 *Employees:* 23
Net Worth: £3,426,714 *Total Assets:* £13,491,168
Registered Office: CP House, Otterspool Way, Watford Bypass, Watford, Herts, WD25 8JJ
Activities: Construction of commercial buildings
Parent: Waystone (Holdings) Limited
Officers: Eric Lewis, Secretary; Paul Andrew Filer [1957] Director/Chartered Accountant; Iris Gibbor [1951] Director; Philip Hoffbrand [1967] Director; Alistair James McLoughlin [1968] Director/Business Executive; Helen McLoughlin [1964] Director/Business Manager; Stuart McLoughlin [1939] Director/Engineer; Alexei James Schreier [1976] Director

WD1A Limited
Incorporated: 13 March 2014
Net Worth: £3,214,083 *Total Assets:* £9,054,424
Registered Office: The Hive, Camrose Avenue, London, HA8 6AG
Activities: Buying and selling of own real estate
Parent: Double A Group Ltd
Officers: Mahendra Patel, Secretary; Anthony Andrew Kleanthous [1966] Director

WDFG UK Holdings Limited
Incorporated: 28 February 1996 *Employees:* 14
Net Worth: £166,526,000 *Total Assets:* £429,328,000
Registered Office: Bedfont Lakes, 4 New Square, Feltham, Middlesex, TW14 8HA
Activities: Retail sale of beverages in specialised stores
Officers: Christopher David Bouttle [1968] Director; Frederick Robert Creighton [1958] Director; Benjamin Harmstorf [1976] Director [German]; Eugenio Miguel Andrades Yunta [1986] Director [Spanish]

WDFG UK Limited
Incorporated: 11 November 1993 *Employees:* 3,698
Net Worth: £150,624,000 *Total Assets:* £340,180,000
Registered Office: 4 New Square, Bedfont Lakes, Feltham, Middlesex, TW14 8HA
Activities: Retail sale of beverages in specialised stores
Parent: WDFG UK Holdings Limited
Officers: Christopher David Bouttle [1968] Director; Frederick Robert Creighton [1958] Director; Benjamin Harmstorf [1976] Director [German]; Eugenio Miguel Andrades Yunta [1968] Director [Spanish]

We Are Pentagon Limited
Incorporated: 28 December 2012 *Employees:* 8
Net Worth: £5,560,518 *Total Assets:* £6,359,886
Registered Office: 11 The Green, Richmond, Surrey, TW9 1PX
Activities: Other service activities n.e.c.
Parent: We Are Pentagon Group Ltd
Officers: Graham Broughton [1981] Director; Laurence John Ashley Guy [1976] Director; Benjamin James Morris [1976] Director/Chartered Accountant; Chrystalla Spire [1956] Director; Silvia Yaneva [1984] Finance Director [Bulgarian]

Wealmoor Limited
Incorporated: 6 March 1973 *Employees:* 940
Net Worth: £25,666,690 *Total Assets:* £55,834,576
Registered Office: Unit 5 Jetha House, Auriol Drive, Greenford Park, Greenford, Middlesex, UB6 0TP
Activities: Post-harvest crop activities
Officers: Leena Avnish Malde, Secretary; Vilasgauri Ratilal Dhanani [1937] Director; Avnish Amritlal Malde [1965] Director; Leena Avnish Malde [1966] Director

Wear Point Wind Limited
Incorporated: 5 January 2012
Net Worth: £10,000 *Total Assets:* £13,410,000
Registered Office: 8 White Oak Square, London Road, Swanley, Kent, BR8 7AG
Activities: Production of electricity
Parent: Wear Point Wind Holdco Limited
Officers: Joseph Mark Linney [1958] Director/Chartered Quantity Surveyor; Simon Owen Vince [1963] Construction & Operations Director

Webley Holdings (UK) Limited
Incorporated: 11 April 2014 *Employees:* 2
Net Worth: £12,485,246 *Total Assets:* £13,016,285
Registered Office: Lynwood House, Crofton Road, Orpington, Kent, BR6 8QE
Activities: Activities of other holding companies n.e.c.
Major Shareholder: Andrew Charles Webley
Officers: Kimberley Anne Brazill [1961] Director; Andrew Charles Webley [1962] Director

W K Webster & Co Ltd
Incorporated: 24 February 1972 *Employees:* 191
Net Worth: £8,404,073 *Total Assets:* £37,320,556
Registered Office: Webster House, 207 Longlands Road, Sidcup, Kent, DA15 7JH
Activities: Other business support service activities n.e.c.
Shareholders: Anthony Steven Smith; Gregg Victor Newman; Christopher John Osman
Officers: Ann Castle, Secretary; Timothy Ross Champkins [1979] Director/Chartered Accountant; Gregg Victor Newman [1961] Director/Claims Agent; Christopher John Osman [1959] Director/Marine Claims Adjuster; Anthony Steven Smith [1979] Director/Claims Agent

Wedge Investments Limited
Incorporated: 16 August 2005 *Employees:* 4
Net Worth: £6,855,969 *Total Assets:* £8,677,694
Registered Office: Unit 11 Worton Court, Worton Hall Industrial Estate, Worton Road, Isleworth, Middlesex, TW7 6ER
Activities: Other letting and operating of own or leased real estate
Major Shareholder: James Richard Wedge
Officers: David Howard Turner, Secretary/Accountant; John Rees James [1934] Director/Lawyer; David Howard Turner [1962] Director/Accountant; Anna Helen Wedge [1968] Director; James Richard Wedge [1966] Director

Weekes Brothers (Welling) Limited
Incorporated: 20 November 1947 *Employees:* 7
Net Worth: £5,151,450 *Total Assets:* £5,616,207
Registered Office: Fruit Distribution Depot, Darenth Hill, Dartford, Kent, DA2 7QY
Activities: Other letting and operating of own or leased real estate
Officers: Peter Mark Cumins, Secretary; Lisa Helen Bain [1974] Director; Gail Elizabeth Bryan [1975] Director; Sally Louise Hone [1976] Director; Janice Gail Weekes [1946] Director/Company Secretary; Jill Marie Weekes [1978] Commercial Director

Welcome To England (Hotels) Limited
Incorporated: 15 April 1977 *Employees:* 3
Net Worth: £4,659,349 *Total Assets:* £5,023,045
Registered Office: Suite 2, West Hill House, West Hill, Epsom, Surrey, KT19 8JD
Activities: Other letting and operating of own or leased real estate
Parent: Street Family Group of Companies (Holdings) Limited
Officers: Andrew Mark Munday, Secretary; Patricia Jane French [1951] Managing Director; Rivkah Hazel McCullough [1980] Director/Commercial Portfolio Executive; Andrew Mark Munday [1969] Director/Property Manager; Jonathan Justin Selig Symons [1949] Director

Wellcome Foundation Limited (The)
Incorporated: 1 January 1924
Net Worth: £293,239,008 *Total Assets:* £457,700,992
Registered Office: 980 Great West Road, Brentford, Middlesex, TW8 9GS
Activities: Activities of head offices
Parent: Wellcome Limited
Officers: Victoria Anne Whyte, Secretary; Simon Paul Dingemans [1963] Director

Wellcome Limited
Incorporated: 6 November 1985
Net Worth: £1,804,000,000 *Total Assets:* £1,843,000,064
Registered Office: 980 Great West Road, Brentford, Middlesex, TW8 9GS
Activities: Activities of head offices
Parent: GlaxoSmithKline Finance PLC
Officers: Victoria Anne Whyte, Secretary; Simon Paul Dingemans [1963] Director

Wellmode Limited
Incorporated: 3 April 2001 *Employees:* 2
Net Worth Deficit: £19,485,876 *Total Assets:* £57,800,000
Registered Office: Hadley Hurst, Hadley Common, Barnet, Herts, EN5 5QG
Activities: Non-trading company
Officers: Anna Victoria Kinsman, Secretary; Anthony George Bunker [1944] Director/Tax Consultant; Alexander Mahboubian [1972] Director/Designer

Wellsborough Developments Limited
Incorporated: 28 August 1998
Net Worth: £9,023,040 *Total Assets:* £12,513,400
Registered Office: 131-133 Red Lion Road, Surbiton, Surrey, KT6 7RQ
Activities: Other letting and operating of own or leased real estate
Shareholders: Cuffe Holdings Ltd; Regalmain Ltd
Officers: Arthur Charles Cowdery, Secretary/Director; Arthur Charles Cowdery [1953] Director; Christopher Anthony O'Callaghan [1954] Director/Designer [Irish]

Wellstone Management Ltd
Incorporated: 18 August 2014
Net Worth: £1,047,468 *Total Assets:* £7,941,923
Registered Office: Bath Road, Harlington, Hayes, Middlesex, UB3 5AL
Activities: Other retail sale not in stores, stalls or markets
Major Shareholder: Darbara Singh Dhanoa
Officers: Darbara Singh Dhanoa [1961] Director

Wembley Multi Academy Trust
Incorporated: 10 July 2012 *Employees:* 149
Previous: Wembley High Technology College
Net Worth: £33,675,544 *Total Assets:* £35,774,840
Registered Office: Wembley High Technology College, East Lane, Wembley, Middlesex, HA0 3NT
Activities: Primary education
Officers: Harjagbir Kaur Bal [1959] Director/Headteacher; Jennifer Betterton [1987] Director/Solicitor; Christopher John Caulkin [1980] Director/Investment Analyst; Kishor Mistry [1970] Director/Charity Chief Executive; Councillor James Moher [1946] Director/Lecturer [Irish]; Roderic Henry Patrick Rennison [1955] Director; Bhavik Shah [1964] Director/Sales Manager

Wembley National Stadium Limited
Incorporated: 18 June 1997 *Employees:* 112
Net Worth: £161,159,008 *Total Assets:* £589,750,976
Registered Office: Wembley Stadium, Wembley, Middlesex, HA9 0WS
Activities: Operation of sports facilities
Parent: Football Association Limited
Officers: Richard James McDermott, Secretary; Mark Paul Burrows [1969] Director/Chief Financial Officer; Martin Richard Glenn [1960] Director/Chief Executive Officer; Jonathan Robert Sellins [1963] Operations Director

Wembley Tyres Limited
Incorporated: 16 December 1996 *Employees:* 6
Net Worth: £6,771,616 *Total Assets:* £7,453,510
Registered Office: 28 Church Road, Stanmore, Middlesex, HA7 4XR
Activities: Other retail sale not in stores, stalls or markets
Shareholders: Marcus Webb; Sylvana Webb
Officers: Marcus Webb [1966] Director/Motor Mechanic

Wenta
Incorporated: 8 August 1983 *Employees:* 44
Net Worth: £6,121,330 *Total Assets:* £11,234,375
Registered Office: Colne Way, Watford, Herts, WD24 7ND
Activities: Other information service activities n.e.c.
Officers: Simon Robert Arbon [1954] Director/Chartered Surveyor; Alfred Anthony Bond [1948] Director; Samantha Jane Chaney [1982] Director/Solicitor; Zoe Julie Hancock [1974] Director/Principal; Graham William Lane [1962] Director/IT Consultant; Paul Owen Layte [1980] Director; Peter Duncan Oxley [1976] Director; Helen Webb [1965] Director/Management Consultant

Wenta Business Centres Limited
Incorporated: 9 July 1990 *Employees:* 7
Net Worth: £3,022,185 *Total Assets:* £10,438,055
Registered Office: Colne Way, Watford, Herts, WD24 7ND
Activities: Development of building projects
Parent: Wenta
Officers: Simon Robert Arbon [1954] Director/Chartered Surveyor; Edward Christopher Jordan [1963] Director

Wesco Distribution-International Limited
Incorporated: 25 March 1998 *Employees:* 53
Net Worth: £16,859,000 *Total Assets:* £32,930,000
Registered Office: 1 Princeton Mews, 167-169 London Road, Kingston upon Thames, Surrey, KT2 6PT
Activities: Other business support service activities n.e.c.
Officers: Brian M Begg, Secretary; Gary J. Habsburg, Secretary; Domenic Anthony Macioce III, Secretary; Samantha L O'Donoghue, Secretary; Brian M Begg [1973] Director/Treasurer [American]; Domenic Anthony Macioce III [1967] Director/Vice-President, Tax [American]

West & Coe Limited
Incorporated: 10 September 1982 *Employees:* 97
Net Worth: £5,992,934 *Total Assets:* £7,376,552
Registered Office: 620 Rainham Road South, Dagenham, Essex, RM10 8YP
Activities: Other human health activities
Shareholder: Edward Jeremy West
Officers: William Gillanders, Secretary; Jennifer Gillanders [1957] Director; Daphne Mary West [1928] Director; Edward Jeremy West [1956] Director

West Bridgford JV LLP
Incorporated: 6 October 2016
Net Worth Deficit: £121,000 *Total Assets:* £14,975,000
Registered Office: Cowley Business Park, Cowley, Uxbridge, Middlesex, UB8 2AL

West Dorset Leisure Holidays Limited
Incorporated: 24 April 1978
Net Worth: £4,592,385 *Total Assets:* £6,588,743
Registered Office: The Old School House, Bridge Road, Hunton Bridge, Kings Langley, Herts, WD4 8SZ
Activities: Recreational vehicle parks, trailer parks and camping grounds
Major Shareholder: Vanessa Anne Cox
Officers: Martin John Cox, Secretary; Patricia Doreen Butcher [1928] Director/Caravan Site Operator; Martin John Cox [1953] Director/Caravan Site Operator; Vanessa Anne Cox [1958] Director/Caravan Site Operator

West Hatch High School Academy Trust
Incorporated: 10 May 2011 *Employees:* 199
Net Worth: £11,230,000 *Total Assets:* £15,242,000
Registered Office: West Hatch High School, High Road, Chigwell, Essex, IG7 5BT
Activities: General secondary education
Officers: Lisa Catherine Barker, Secretary; Kulvarn Atwal [1974] Director/Headteacher; Stephanie Field [1954] Director/Teacher; John William Haley [1948] Director/Chartered Surveyor; Carl Frederick Hansen [1958] Director; Adrian Samuel Harris [1955] Director/Accountant; Sheila Jones [1958] Director/Private Client Administrator; Harpreet Kaur Kahlon [1979] Director/Cover Supervisor; Daniel Leonard [1978] Director/Headteacher; Matthew Armstrong Lopez-Dias [1970] Director/Web Developer Camera Grip; Marcella Lord [1976] Director; Nancy Janet Lycett [1967] Director; Melanie Frances Marsden [1994] Director/Teacher; Julie Ann Pearce [1964] Director/Clerical Officer; Stephen Barry Phillips [1949] Director; Mohammed Siraj Sait [1965] Director/University Reader [Indian]; Leanne Claire Smith [1968] Director/Catering Manager; David Paul Solomons [1955] Director/Teacher; Justin James Van Wijngaarden [1967] Director/Chartered Accountant; Bertrand Pierre Marie Florent Vandermarcq [1981] Director/Technical Officer [French]; Samantha Ann Vandermarcq [1970] Director; Sheila Weeden [1959] Director/Local Government

West Herts Community Free School Trust
Incorporated: 10 December 2012 *Employees:* 86
Net Worth: £10,876,478 *Total Assets:* £11,487,138
Registered Office: Lanchester Community Free School, Hempstead Road, Watford, Herts, WD17 3HD
Activities: Primary education
Officers: Gayle Cook [1966] Director; Angela Olasubomi Daniel [1975] Director/Head of Finance; Leonard David Gelernter [1945] Director/Judge of The Family Court; Martin Glick [1954] Director/Accountant; John Howard Harris [1956] Director/Self Employed Management Consultant; Gregory Holmes [1985] Director/Local Government Officer; Dr Phillip Mason [1987] Director/Lecturer; Isobel Louise Maxwell [1966] Human Resources Director; Kristian Alexander MacArthur North [1981] Business Director; Anne Lucy Punter [1952] Director/Retired; Amandip Sidhu [1976] Director

West London YMCA
Incorporated: 2 September 1996 *Employees:* 144
Net Worth: £7,179,414 *Total Assets:* £28,731,302
Registered Office: St James House, 9-15 St James Road, Surbiton, Surrey, KT6 4QH
Activities: Other accommodation
Officers: Gwynne Myfanwy Price Jarvis, Secretary; Generald Chifamba [1992] Director; Howard Peter Dawson [1970] Housing Director; Louise Hedges [1981] Director/Civil Servant; Andrew John Palmer [1956] Director/Charity Chief Executive; Helen Posner [1981] Director/Principal Investment; Albin Andrew Stadtmiller [1966] Director/Charity Manager Fundraiser [American/British]; Edward Louis Samuel Weiss [1932] Director/Retired; Kenneth John Youngman [1956] Finance Director

West One Bathrooms Limited
Incorporated: 7 March 1978 *Employees:* 65
Net Worth: £870,457 *Total Assets:* £6,684,310
Registered Office: Unit D, Davis Road Industrial Park, Davis Road, Chessington, Surrey, KT9 1TQ
Activities: Other retail sale of new goods in specialised stores (not commercial art galleries and opticians)
Officers: Susan Stanley, Secretary; Duncan James Waters [1967] Director/General Manager; Kevin Anthony Stewart Waters [1965] Director/Sales Manager

West One Technology Ltd
Incorporated: 31 July 1998 *Employees:* 166
Net Worth: £6,050,517 *Total Assets:* £14,308,900
Registered Office: 153 Brooker Road, Waltham Abbey, Essex, EN9 1JH
Activities: Other telecommunications activities
Shareholders: Kern Ronald Judge; Nicola Pauline Judge
Officers: Nicola Pauline Judge, Secretary; Kern Ronald Judge [1965] Director/Electronics Engineer

West Ten Properties (UK) Limited
Incorporated: 30 May 2006
Net Worth: £1,668,065 *Total Assets:* £7,036,975
Registered Office: Waters Meet, Willow Avenue, Denham, Uxbridge, Middlesex, UB9 4AF
Activities: Buying and selling of own real estate
Shareholder: Sanjiv Nahar
Officers: Sanjiv Nahar, Secretary/Legal Assistant; Rajan Nahar [1968] Director/Solicitor; Sanjiv Nahar [1972] Director/Estate Agent; Sarwan Singh Nahar [1948] Director/Businessman

West Thurrock Academy
Incorporated: 18 October 2012 *Employees:* 87
Net Worth: £3,893,253 *Total Assets:* £5,119,315
Registered Office: West Thurrock Academy, Schoolfield Road, Grays, Essex, RM20 3HR
Activities: Primary education
Officers: Michael Okon Antai [1964] Director; William Bart-Plange [1978] Director/Solicitor; Susan Cook [1967] Director/Headteacher; Dawn Davies [1972] Director/Teacher; Angelicque Eastman-Owhoka [1975] Director; Dilip Jethwa [1965] Director/Train Driver; Isaac Kamweru [1969] Director/Minister; Cecilia Klemen [1976] Director/Secretary; Herbert Masamba [1973] Director/Banker; Jessica Pitcher [1985] Director/Teacher; Michael Prue [1985] Director/School Governor; Shona Stronach [1961] Director/Retired

Westbourne Academy Trust
Incorporated: 9 May 2011 *Employees:* 67
Previous: Westbourne Primary School
Net Worth: £6,608,442 *Total Assets:* £7,398,280
Registered Office: Westbourne Primary School, Anton Crescent, Collingwood Road, Sutton, Surrey, SM1 2NT
Activities: Primary education
Officers: Diane Slack, Secretary; Joanna Elizabeth Bolton [1970] Director/Teacher; Ian Martin Cobbold [1945] Director/Retired; Julie Ann Craig [1976] Director/Teacher; Mandy Gillian Hanford [1969] Director/Business Consultant; Bernie Francis Higgins [1962] Director of Training; Mehnaz Fatima Khan [1979] Director; Daniel Miracapillo [1974] Director/Headteacher [British/Italian]; Nigel Povey [1969] Director/Civil Servant; Edward Gwynn Prothero [1958] Director; Louise Natalie Smith [1986] Director/Civil Servant; Xing Wang [1970] Director and Consultant [Chinese]

Westbrook Primary School
Incorporated: 10 May 2013 *Employees:* 61
Net Worth: £7,686,513 *Total Assets:* £10,569,545
Registered Office: Westbrook Primary School, Westbrook Road, Hounslow, Middlesex, TW5 0NB
Activities: Primary education
Officers: Sarah Margaret Vass, Secretary; Manpreet Singh Babbra [1982] Director/Technical Analyst; Carly Elizabeth Benton [1979] Director/Deputy Headteacher; Marie Coffey [1952] Director/Health Visiting Specialist Practice Teacher; Laura Hannah Gallagher [1986] Director/Assistant Headteacher; Angela Khungar [1979] Director; Alex Leggett [1972] Director/Deputy Headteacher; Pooja Pabari [1986] Director/Radiographer; Dalvir Singh Roop [1975] Director/Chartered Accountant; Melvyn Tatters [1971] Director/Headmaster

Western United Investment Company Limited
Incorporated: 26 August 1918 *Employees:* 944
Net Worth: £80,600,000 *Total Assets:* £188,700,000
Registered Office: 29 Ullswater Crescent, Coulsdon, Surrey, CR5 2HR
Activities: Activities of head offices
Shareholders: Carl Hermann Konrad Friedlaender; Russell Clark; Michael John Seymour Eades
Officers: Neil Thornton, Secretary; George Moubray William Vestey [1964] Director/Retail Butchery; Robin John Henry Vestey [1968] Director/Agricultural Consultant; Lord Samuel George Armstrong Vestey [1941] Director/Merchant; Honourable William Guy Vestey [1983] Director

Western Wines Holdings Limited
Incorporated: 15 July 2002
Net Worth: £114,755,000 *Total Assets:* £114,755,000
Registered Office: Thomas Hardy House, 2 Heath Road, Weybridge, Surrey, KT13 8TB
Activities: Non-trading company
Parent: Accolade Wines Europe No. 2 Limited
Officers: Anthony Graham Wood, Secretary; Adrian Francis McKeon [1963] Regional Managing Director, UKIR; Andrew Peter Smith [1974] Director/Accountant; Anthony Graham Wood [1975] Director/Financial Controller [Australian]

Westfield Academy
Incorporated: 13 May 2013 *Employees:* 102
Net Worth: £28,316,524 *Total Assets:* £30,417,196
Registered Office: Westfield Academy, Tolpits Lane, Watford, Herts, WD18 6NS
Activities: General secondary education
Officers: Timothy Body [1967] Director/Teacher; Louise Everett [1969] Director/Retired; Andrew Leslie Farrer [1961] Director/Senior Marketing Manager; Bruce Mallett [1954] Director/Finance; David William Yuill [1960] Director/Civil Servant

Westfields Homes Limited
Incorporated: 19 December 2005 *Employees:* 4
Net Worth: £37,686 *Total Assets:* £5,098,134
Registered Office: 1-3 Old Mill Road, Hunton Bridge, Herts, WD4 8RD
Activities: Construction of commercial buildings
Officers: Ben Taylor, Secretary; Ben Taylor [1973] Director; Ivan Reginald George Toscani [1959] Director/Property Developer; Brian Cecil Frederick Varley [1946] Director; James Nathan Varley [1976] Director/Surveyor

Westgate House Developments Limited
Incorporated: 22 March 2016
Net Worth Deficit: £3,758,031 *Total Assets:* £39,558,556
Registered Office: 3rd Floor, Sterling House, Langston Road, Loughton, Essex, IG10 3TS
Activities: Development of building projects
Shareholders: Galliard Developments Limited; C.J.O'Shea and Company Limited
Officers: Allan William Porter, Secretary; Edward Azouz [1949] Director/Chartered Accountant; Stephen Stuart Solomon Conway [1948] Director; Jonathan Simon Goldstein [1966] Director; Rory O'Connor [1959] Director; Donagh O'Sullivan [1968] Construction Director [Irish]

Westlake Estates Limited
Incorporated: 14 January 1998
Net Worth: £10,508,914 *Total Assets:* £16,449,147
Registered Office: 148 Cranbrook Road, Ilford, Essex, IG1 4LZ
Activities: Other letting and operating of own or leased real estate
Major Shareholder: Devinderjit Singh Kataria
Officers: Inderjit Kaur Sethi, Secretary; Devinderjit Singh Kataria [1965] Director

Westway Services Holdings (2010) Ltd.
Incorporated: 2 July 2008
Net Worth: £771,939 *Total Assets:* £13,072,953
Registered Office: Artemis Building, Odyssey Business Park, West End Road, South Ruislip, Middlesex, HA4 6QE
Activities: Activities of head offices
Parent: Westway Services Holdings (2014) Ltd
Officers: Mike Bindeman [1958] Director [American]; Colin Andrew Stevenson [1963] Finance Director

J D Wetherspoon PLC
Incorporated: 25 March 1983 *Employees:* 38,384
Net Worth: £286,561,984 *Total Assets:* £1,476,313,984
Registered Office: Wetherspoon House, Reeds Crescent, Watford, Herts, WD24 4QL
Activities: Public houses and bars
Officers: Nigel Connor, Secretary; Sir Richard Gervase Beckett [1944] Director; Susan Alina Cacioppo [1966] Personnel & Legal Director; John David Hutson [1965] Director/Chief Executive Officer; Timothy Randall Martin [1955] Non-Executive Director Chairman; Elizabeth McMeikan [1962] Director; Harry Michael Charles Morley [1965] Director; Debra Van Gene [1954] Director/Executive Research Consultant; Benjamin Newton Whitley [1978] Finance Director

Wheatland Cheese Co. Limited
Incorporated: 19 June 1984 *Employees:* 16
Net Worth: £9,537,600 *Total Assets:* £11,550,367
Registered Office: 3a Livingstone Court, 55 Peel Road, Harrow, Middlesex, HA3 7QT
Activities: Non-specialised wholesale trade
Officers: Jayant Manishanker Upadhyay [1948] Managing Director; Ravindra Manishanker Upadhyay [1950] Director

Whelan & Grant (Contractors) Limited
Incorporated: 26 July 1966 *Employees:* 34
Net Worth: £8,000,004 *Total Assets:* £11,389,643
Registered Office: Clare House, 4 Thames Street, Walton on Thames, Surrey, KT12 2PU
Activities: Construction of commercial buildings
Parent: Whelan & Grant Holdings Ltd
Officers: John Joseph Whelan, Secretary; Simon Edward George [1960] Director/Quantity Surveyor; Brian James Gilbert [1970] Director/Surveyor; Russell Harvey White [1965] Director/Construction

Whelan & Grant (Holdings) Limited
Incorporated: 5 April 1974 *Employees:* 89
Net Worth: £14,388,686 *Total Assets:* £18,338,496
Registered Office: Clare House, 4 Thames Street, Walton on Thames, Surrey, KT12 2PU
Activities: Other business support service activities n.e.c.
Shareholders: Susan Whelan; Catherine Grant
Officers: Catherine Grant, Secretary; Simon Edward George [1960] Director/Quantity Surveyor; Laurence Noel Grant [1953] Managing Director; John Joseph Whelan [1957] Director/Accountant [Irish]

Whisper Films Limited
Incorporated: 18 October 2010 *Employees:* 29
Net Worth: £2,862,032 *Total Assets:* £6,052,070
Registered Office: Unit B, South Avenue Studios, 7 South Avenue, Richmond, Surrey, TW9 3EL
Activities: Motion picture production activities
Officers: David Marshall Coulthard [1971] Director; Harriet Felicity Alice Humphrey [1981] Director/Production Manager; Jacob John Humphrey [1978] Director; Sunil Ramanbhai Patel [1977] Director/TV Producer; Laura Elizabeth Tree-Patel [1977] Director/Fashion Buyer

T.W. White & Sons (Holdings) Limited
Incorporated: 7 October 1976 *Employees:* 103
Net Worth: £3,032,683 *Total Assets:* £11,857,114
Registered Office: 242 Lower Road, Great Bookham, Leatherhead, Surrey, KT23 4DE
Activities: Dormant company
Shareholder: Neil Peter White
Officers: Karen Elizabeth Basson, Secretary; Karen Elizabeth Basson [1958] Director/Estate Agent; Neil Peter White [1955] Director/Garage Proprietor

T.W. White & Sons Limited
Incorporated: 14 December 1970 *Employees:* 103
Net Worth: £2,159,986 *Total Assets:* £11,857,114
Registered Office: 242 Lower Road, Great Bookham, Leatherhead, Surrey, KT23 4DE
Activities: Sale of new cars and light motor vehicles
Shareholder: Neil Peter White
Officers: Karen Elizabeth Basson, Secretary; Karen Elizabeth Basson [1958] Director; Neil Peter White [1955] Director/Garage Proprietor

The White Brasserie Company Ltd
Incorporated: 7 January 2010 *Employees:* 456
Net Worth Deficit: £3,163,518 *Total Assets:* £15,049,314
Registered Office: Wizard House, 2a Cambridge Road, Teddington, Middlesex, TW11 8DR
Activities: Licenced restaurants
Parent: Brasserie Bar Co Limited
Officers: Jeremy Brown [1966] Property Director; Mark Derry [1960] Director; Christopher Patrick Edward Guy [1981] Finance Director; Helen Louise Melvin [1968] Director/Accountant

White Lodge Centre
Incorporated: 20 October 1981 *Employees:* 76
Net Worth: £6,067,000 *Total Assets:* £6,196,000
Registered Office: White Lodge Centre, Holloway Hill, Lyne, Chertsey, Surrey, KT16 0AE
Activities: Child day-care activities
Officers: David Brian Meller, Secretary; Tim Bevans [1969] Director/Management Consultant; Stephen Charles Carrodus [1952] Director; Jean Choules [1966] Director; Sarah Louise Dade [1974] Director/Administrator; Victoria Ellen Jones [1980] Director/Lawyer; David Brian Meller [1966] Finance Director; Alison Sarah Raw [1975] Director/Occupational Therapist; Jane Stuart-Palikira [1973] Director; Kathleen Taylor [1954] Director/Consultant; Lisa Walsh [1966] Director

White Rock Land LLP
Incorporated: 23 August 2013
Net Worth: £2,392,000 *Total Assets:* £48,318,000
Registered Office: Cowley Business Park, Cowley, Uxbridge, Middlesex, UB8 2AL

The Whiteley Homes Trust
Incorporated: 10 November 2003 *Employees:* 148
Net Worth: £48,317,912 *Total Assets:* £57,607,644
Registered Office: Octagon Road, Whiteley Village, Walton on Thames, Surrey, KT12 4EH
Activities: Other accommodation
Officers: Dr Beverly Ann Castleton [1948] Director/Consultant Physician; Roger Myles Formby [1938] Director/Solicitor; Keith John Hiscock [1958] Director/Stockbroker/Investment Banker; Michael Alan Pomery [1944] Director/Consulting Actuary; Michael George Sadler [1947] Director/Retired; Jason Shaw [1973] Director/Chartered Accountant; Jackie Stevens [1963] Director/NHS Executive; Duncan Alan Mordue Straughen [1954] Director; Michael Frederick Arthur Tolley [1947] Director/Semi-Retired Consultant Surveyor; Aileen Woollhead [1959] Director

Whiteoak Developments Limited
Incorporated: 13 April 1993 *Employees:* 6
Net Worth: £11,921,253 *Total Assets:* £12,796,009
Registered Office: Allen House, 1 Westmead Road, Sutton, Surrey, SM1 4LA
Activities: Construction of commercial buildings
Major Shareholder: Anthony William Whitby
Officers: Alan William Payne, Secretary/Accountant; Martin Charles Armstrong [1955] Director/Registered Auditor; Alan William Payne [1951] Director/Accountant; Anthony William Whitby [1954] Director; Rachel Whitby [1967] Director

The Whiter Smile Limited
Incorporated: 14 September 2001 *Employees:* 45
Net Worth: £204,004 *Total Assets:* £5,241,175
Registered Office: 98 Station Road, Sidcup, Kent, DA15 7BY
Activities: Dental practice activities
Shareholders: Pheechool Holdings Limited; Samir Pheechool Boulis
Officers: Samir Pheechool Boulis, Secretary; Dr Samir Pheechool Boulis [1975] Director/Dentist

Whitestone Property Services Limited
Incorporated: 25 April 2017 *Employees:* 2
Net Worth: £3,663,985 *Total Assets:* £8,164,258
Registered Office: 74 Shenley Hill, Radlett, Herts, WD7 7BD
Activities: Activities of other holding companies n.e.c.
Shareholders: Pritpal Singh Millan; Rajpreet Millan
Officers: Pritpal Singh Millan [1971] Director; Rajpreet Millan [1972] Director

Whitstable Homes Ltd
Incorporated: 4 May 2012
Net Worth: £33,464 *Total Assets:* £5,566,109
Registered Office: 30 Station Road, Orpington, Kent, BR6 0SA
Activities: Development of building projects
Major Shareholder: Kanagaratnam Rajakanthan
Officers: Kanagaratnam Rajakanthan [1955] Managing Director

WHTC Ltd
Incorporated: 6 September 2012 *Employees:* 138
Net Worth: £3,435,016 *Total Assets:* £10,884,137
Registered Office: North House, St Edwards Way, Romford, Essex, RM1 3PP
Activities: Other business support service activities n.e.c.
Shareholders: Anthony Edward Chapman; William James Hughes
Officers: Anthony Edward Chapman [1962] Director; William James Hughes [1971] Director

Wickland (Holdings) Limited
Incorporated: 24 December 1981
Net Worth: £14,327,537 *Total Assets:* £19,022,956
Registered Office: Lyon House, Lyon Road, Romford, Essex, RM1 2BG
Activities: Other letting and operating of own or leased real estate
Shareholders: David Michael Collins; David Michael Collins
Officers: David Michael Collins, Secretary; David Michael Collins [1963] Director

WIH UK Limited
Incorporated: 21 April 2016
Net Worth: £2,882,777,856 *Total Assets:* £2,882,777,856
Registered Office: Pemberton House, Bakers Road, Uxbridge, Middlesex, UB8 1EZ
Activities: Activities of other holding companies n.e.c.
Parent: Coca-Cola European Partners PLC
Officers: Paul Van Reesch, Secretary; Frank Govaerts [1961] Director [Belgian]; Joyce Marie King-Lavinder [1959] Director [American]; Paul Van Reesch [1976] Director; Edward Owen Walker [1967] Director

Wildview Limited
Incorporated: 10 November 1999 *Employees:* 3
Net Worth: £5,470,795 *Total Assets:* £5,957,525
Registered Office: York House, Empire Way, Wembley, Middlesex, HA9 0FQ
Activities: Development of building projects
Parent: Newcroft Investments Limited
Officers: Vivian Emmy Taylor, Secretary; Simon Mark Collins [1974] Director; Allan Raymond Taylor [1948] Director; Vivian Emmy Taylor [1949] Director/Company Secretary

Willco Properties Ltd
Incorporated: 13 August 2014
Net Worth: £2,350,493 *Total Assets:* £5,223,241
Registered Office: Crown House Mews, Chequers Lane, Walton on the Hill, Tadworth, Surrey, KT20 7ST
Activities: Development of building projects
Major Shareholder: William MacKenzie Morris
Officers: David Mark Pay, Secretary; Martin James Morris [1963] Director; William MacKenzie Morris [1997] Director/Property Manager

William Willett Learning Trust
Incorporated: 7 February 2011 *Employees:* 182
Net Worth: £37,125,000 *Total Assets:* £39,579,000
Registered Office: Coopers School, Hawkwood Lane, Chislehurst, Kent, BR7 5PS
Activities: General secondary education
Officers: Robert Carling, Secretary; Andrew Downes [1950] Director/Consultant Engineer; Shirley Puxty [1959] Director/School Principal; Claire Agnes Singleton [1956] Director/Solicitor; Lorraine Anne Stuart [1955] Director/Local Government Officer

Willhay Management Limited
Incorporated: 7 November 2007 *Employees:* 4
Net Worth: £3,559,816 *Total Assets:* £5,145,235
Registered Office: Willhay House, 37-39 Roebuck Road, Hainault Business Park, Hainault, Essex, IG6 3TU
Activities: Other business support service activities n.e.c.
Officers: Hadrien Salin [1982] Director/Corporate Finance [French]

Williams and Hill Group Ltd
Incorporated: 30 April 2015 *Employees:* 116
Net Worth: £4,616,902 *Total Assets:* £8,673,165
Registered Office: Unit 9 Space Waye, Feltham, Middlesex, TW14 0TH
Activities: Activities of head offices
Shareholders: Deborah Louise Hill; Aneta Dorota Williams; Clifford Paul Williams; Kerry John Hill
Officers: Deborah Louise Hill, Secretary; Aneta Dorota Williams, Secretary; Kerry John Hill [1966] Director; Clifford Paul Williams [1960] Director

The Willow Learning Trust
Incorporated: 16 May 2011 *Employees:* 257
Previous: Glenthorne High School
Net Worth: £45,442,000 *Total Assets:* £50,639,000
Registered Office: Glenthorne High School, Sutton Common Road, Sutton, Surrey, SM3 9PS
Activities: General secondary education
Officers: Dr Kerry Guest, Secretary; Dayo Balogun [1974] Director/Marketing Consultant; Simon Brown [1956] Director/Retired; Stephan Cook [1960] Director/Headteacher; Nigel Edward Griffiths [1947] Director/Retired; Marilyn Antoinette Holness [1959] Director/Head of Department; Stephen John Hume [1961] Director/Headteacher; Tom Magill [1969] Director/Social Care Manager; Isabelle Paget [1948] Director/Retired; Grant Alan Stonell [1974] Director/Financial Controller; Stephen Waring [1945] Director; Janet Elizabeth Flett Wright [1952] Director/Retired

Wilman Marine Limited
Incorporated: 5 October 1981
Net Worth: £3,405,827 *Total Assets:* £5,546,963
Registered Office: Universal Buildings, Green Lane, Hounslow, Middlesex, TW4 6DF
Activities: Machining
Major Shareholder: Robert Bernard Cook
Officers: Robert Bernard Cook, Secretary; Robert Bernard Cook [1947] Director/Engineer

Wilman Universal Group Limited
Incorporated: 23 September 2002 *Employees:* 118
Net Worth: £4,352,302 *Total Assets:* £15,017,031
Registered Office: Universal Buildings, Green Lane, Hounslow, Middlesex, TW4 6DF
Activities: Other manufacturing n.e.c.
Major Shareholder: Robert Bernard Cook
Officers: Robert Bernard Cook, Secretary/Engineer; Robert Bernard Cook [1947] Director/Engineer

Wilman Universal Industries Limited
Incorporated: 25 February 1997 *Employees:* 62
Net Worth: £5,115,178 *Total Assets:* £11,267,816
Registered Office: Universal Buildings, Green Lane, Hounslow, Middlesex, TW4 6DF
Activities: Installation of industrial machinery and equipment
Officers: Robert Bernard Cook, Secretary; David William Budge [1958] Director; Cherill Duboc Cook [1948] Director; Robert Bernard Cook [1947] Director/Engineer; Elizabeth Kathleen Denham [1973] Director

Wilsons Automobiles and Coachworks Limited
Incorporated: 3 February 1933 *Employees:* 223
Net Worth: £25,710,900 *Total Assets:* £47,490,304
Registered Office: Nonsuch Business Park, Kiln Lane, Epsom, Surrey, KT17 1DH
Activities: Sale of new cars and light motor vehicles
Shareholders: Teresa Wilson; Ian Anthony Wilson
Officers: Teresa Wilson, Secretary; John Patrick Butler [1970] Director; Maria Fenwick [1966] Director/Manager; Wojciech Gumienny [1983] Director [Polish]; Gina Storr [1959] Projects Director; David Michael Wheatcroft [1973] Sales Director; Ian Anthony Wilson [1940] Director/Chairman; Teresa Wilson [1940] Sales Director; Toni Wilson [1961] Sales Director

Wind Assets LLP
Incorporated: 21 December 2009
Net Worth: £6,191,000 *Total Assets:* £13,288,000
Registered Office: 8 White Oak Square, London Road, Swanley, Kent, BR8 7AG

Wind Farm Holdings Limited
Incorporated: 26 September 2003
Previous: RES Wind Farm Holdings Limited
Net Worth: £9,735,000 *Total Assets:* £39,600,000
Registered Office: Beaufort Court, Egg Farm Lane, off Ststion Road, Kings Langley, Herts, WD4 8LR
Activities: Activities of head offices
Parent: The Renewables Infrastructure Group (UK) Investments Limited
Officers: Dominic James Hearth, Secretary; Caroline Elizabeth Gilpin [1977] Director/PPA Origination Manager; Steven William Hughes [1972] Generation & Asset Management Director; Mitesh Raj Patel [1982] Director/Group Financial Controller

Windcrest (U.K.) Limited
Incorporated: 6 September 1995
Net Worth: £11,685,602 *Total Assets:* £12,035,480
Registered Office: Unit 8 Abbey Industrial Estate, Mount Pleasant, Wembley, Middlesex, HA0 1NR
Activities: Manufacture of other electrical equipment
Officers: Nilima Patel, Secretary; Hansaraj Santuram Patel [1957] Director

Windmill Organics Limited
Incorporated: 28 April 1998 *Employees:* 90
Net Worth: £36,343,552 *Total Assets:* £44,271,744
Registered Office: 34a Clifton Road, Kingston upon Thames, Surrey, KT2 6PH
Activities: Wholesale of other food, including fish, crustaceans and molluscs
Shareholders: Noel McDonald; Donata Berger
Officers: Donata Berger, Secretary; Noel McDonald [1947] Director [Irish]

D.W. Windsor Limited
Incorporated: 21 April 1977 *Employees:* 126
Net Worth: £6,427,687 *Total Assets:* £10,049,681
Registered Office: DW Windsor, Pindar Road, Hoddesdon, Herts, EN11 0DX
Activities: Manufacture of electric lighting equipment
Parent: DW Windsor Group Limited
Officers: Terence Albert Dean [1959] Director/Chief Executive Officer; Alan Richard Grant [1963] Design Director

Winscales Moor Windfarm Limited
Incorporated: 23 March 2004 *Employees:* 3
Net Worth: £2,708,555 *Total Assets:* £5,217,476
Registered Office: Munro House, Portsmouth Road, Cobham, Surrey, KT11 1PP
Activities: Production of electricity
Parent: Danu Holding Limited
Officers: Stephen Campbell Joseph Ellis [1959] Director; Rollo Andrew Johnstone Wright [1976] Director; Philip William Kent [1984] Director; Ronan Niall Kierans [1978] Director [Irish]; Nicholas Simon Parker [1969] Director

Wintertime Properties Limited
Incorporated: 24 March 2004
Net Worth: £2,716,220 *Total Assets:* £9,776,739
Registered Office: The Barn, 1 Watford House Lane, Watford, Herts, WD17 1BJ
Activities: Other letting and operating of own or leased real estate
Shareholder: Manoj Mahendra Raithatha
Officers: Sarojini Raithatha, Secretary; Manoj Mahendra Raithatha [1972] Director

Wise Trading Limited
Incorporated: 13 December 1988 *Employees:* 15
Net Worth: £8,364,867 *Total Assets:* £16,904,696
Registered Office: Long Drive, Station Approach, South Ruislip, Middlesex, HA4 0HN
Activities: Wholesale of wine, beer, spirits and other alcoholic beverages
Officers: Iqbal Singh Johal, Secretary; Balkar Singh Johal [1946] Director; Balraj Singh Johal [1948] Director; Iqbal Singh Johal [1954] Director; Jasbir Singh Johal [1953] Director; Sarnpal Singh Johal [1957] Director

WJ Groundwater Limited
Incorporated: 21 September 1981 *Employees:* 149
Net Worth: £10,728,998 *Total Assets:* £15,310,471
Registered Office: Unit 5 Abbotts Business Park, Primrose Hill, Kings Langley, Herts, WD4 8FR
Activities: Test drilling and boring
Officers: Stevyn David Michael Harris, Secretary; Richard Michael Fielden [1964] Director/Civil Engineer; Stevyn David Michael Harris [1976] Director/Accountant; Dr Gary John Holmes [1970] Director/Engineer; Paul David Adinolfi Judge [1960] Director/Engineer; Dr Toby Ouvry Linfield Roberts [1958] Director/Civil Engineer; Paul Francis Turner [1975] Director/Engineering

WJ Management Limited
Incorporated: 14 July 1997 *Employees:* 248
Net Worth: £9,786,126 *Total Assets:* £15,991,835
Registered Office: Unit 5 Abbotts Business Park, Primrose Hill, Kings Langley, Herts, WD4 8FR
Activities: Non-trading company
Officers: Stevyn David Michael Harris, Secretary; Richard Michael Fielden [1964] Director/Civil Engineer; Stevyn David Michael Harris [1976] Director/Accountant; Dr Gary John Holmes [1970] Director/Engineer; Dr Toby Ouvry Linfield Roberts [1958] Director/Civil Engineer; Paul Francis Turner [1975] Director/Engineering

WK Properties Limited
Incorporated: 19 May 2010 *Employees:* 2
Net Worth: £2,669,168 *Total Assets:* £5,149,714
Registered Office: Bank House, 81 St Judes Road, Englefield Green, Surrey, TW20 0DF
Activities: Management of real estate on a fee or contract basis
Shareholders: Amanda Jane Kerrison; Debra Michelle Williams
Officers: Amanda Jane Kerrison [1973] Director; Debra Michelle Williams [1969] Marketing Director

WLHC Projectco Limited
Incorporated: 22 October 2009
Net Worth Deficit: £21,195 *Total Assets:* £37,067,272
Registered Office: 8 White Oak Square, London Road, Swanley, Kent, BR8 7AG
Activities: Library activities
Parent: WLHC Holdco Limited
Officers: Neeti Mukundrai Anand [1984] Director; Adam George Waddington [1974] Director

WLMG Limited
Incorporated: 31 July 1996 *Employees:* 81
Previous: Hanif Automotive Limited
Net Worth: £452,592 *Total Assets:* £6,920,921
Registered Office: 313 Field End Road, Eastcote, Middlesex, HA4 9NT
Activities: Sale of new cars and light motor vehicles
Shareholders: Neal David Benstead; Andrew Paul James Mortimer
Officers: Natalie Culhane, Secretary; Neal David Benstead [1970] Managing Director; Andrew Paul James Mortimer [1977] Commercial Director

WMF United Kingdom Limited
Incorporated: 30 December 1998 *Employees:* 75
Net Worth: £11,481,204 *Total Assets:* £15,209,381
Registered Office: 31 Riverside Way, Uxbridge, Middlesex, UB8 2YF
Activities: Agents specialised in the sale of other particular products
Parent: SEB S.A.
Officers: Julie Anne Green [1971] Director

WNDirect Limited
Incorporated: 14 July 2011 *Employees:* 83
Net Worth: £6,007,965 *Total Assets:* £21,585,420
Registered Office: 2 AC Court, High Street, Thames Ditton, Surrey, KT7 0SR
Activities: Other transportation support activities
Parent: DPDgroup UK Ltd
Officers: Robert Anthony Betts, Secretary; Simon Batt [1977] Director; Gwenael Clement [1981] Director [French]; Francois Copigneaux [1963] Director [French]

Woldingham School
Incorporated: 2 July 2008 *Employees:* 211
Net Worth: £20,665,518 *Total Assets:* £27,910,932
Registered Office: Woldingham School, Marden Park, Woldingham, Caterham, Surrey, CR3 7YA
Activities: General secondary education
Officers: Simon David William Hopkins, Secretary; Ian Edward Baker [1961] Director/Chartered Accountant; Ciara Mary Brown [1962] Director/Communications Consultant [Irish]; Simon Dempster Collins [1959] Director/Headmaster; Nicholas Paul Le Cuirot Crapp [1963] Managing Director; William Crothers [1960] Director/Civil Servant; Heather Gail Hanbury [1960] Director/Headmistress; Alexandra Sara Christine Maule [1965] Director; Robert Henry Parkinson [1956] Director/Recruitment Consultant; Martin Louis Redman [1955] Director; Christopher Scattergood [1969] Director; Tim Woffenden [1953] Director/Teacher; James Nicholas Wright [1971] Director/Chartered Accountant

Wolters Kluwer (UK) Limited
Incorporated: 9 March 1948 *Employees:* 257
Net Worth: £31,772,484 *Total Assets:* £97,016,512
Registered Office: 145 London Road, Kingston upon Thames, Surrey, KT2 6SR
Activities: Other software publishing
Parent: Wolters Kluwer Holdings (UK) PLC
Officers: John Goudie, Secretary; Samantha Joanne Bond [1972] Finance Director; Claire Louise Carter [1973] Managing Director; John Goudie [1965] Director/Chartered Accountant

Wolters Kluwer Health (Europe) Limited
Incorporated: 14 February 1991
Net Worth: £1,922,000 *Total Assets:* £12,451,000
Registered Office: 145 London Road, Kingston upon Thames, Surrey, KT2 6SR
Activities: Publishing of consumer and business journals and periodicals
Parent: Wolters Kluwer Holdings (UK) PLC
Officers: John Goudie, Secretary; Kevin Joseph [1974] Director and Regional Controller [Malaysian]

Wolters Kluwer Health (Medical Research) Limited
Incorporated: 7 December 1983 *Employees:* 113
Net Worth: £7,211,000 *Total Assets:* £24,669,000
Registered Office: Croner House, 145 London Road, Kingston upon Thames, Surrey, KT2 6SR
Activities: Other publishing activities
Parent: Wolters Kluwer Health (Europe) Limited
Officers: John Goudie, Secretary; Roy Mulder [1971] Director/VP Finance [Dutch]; Philip Warren [1953] Finance Director; Gareth Robert Williams [1971] Director

Wolters Kluwer Health (Professional & Education) Limited
Incorporated: 2 September 1999 *Employees:* 40
Net Worth: £254,000 *Total Assets:* £12,578,000
Registered Office: 145 London Road, Kingston upon Thames, Surrey, KT2 6SR
Activities: Book publishing
Parent: Wolters Kluwer Health (Europe) Limited
Officers: John Goudie, Secretary; Roy Mulder [1971] Director/VP Finance [Dutch]; Philip Warren [1953] Finance Director; Gareth Robert Williams [1971] Director

Wolters Kluwer Holdings (UK) PLC
Incorporated: 8 September 1977
Net Worth Deficit: £28,851,976 *Total Assets:* £146,081,552
Registered Office: 145 London Road, Kingston upon Thames, Surrey, KT2 6SR
Activities: Activities of other holding companies n.e.c.
Parent: Wolters Kluwer International Holding BV
Officers: John Goudie, Secretary; Samantha Joanne Bond [1972] Finance Director; Claire Louise Carter [1973] Managing Director

Wolters Kluwer Tax and Accounting Limited
Incorporated: 21 July 1995 *Employees:* 44
Net Worth: £13,565,940 *Total Assets:* £22,932,704
Registered Office: 145 London Road, Kingston upon Thames, Surrey, KT2 6SR
Activities: Business and domestic software development
Parent: Wolters Kluwer Holdings (UK) PLC
Officers: John Goudie, Secretary; Dimiter Dimitrov [1973] Managing Director EMEA [Bulgarian]; James Barron Dunham [1963] Director/Business Executive [American]; James Michael Mundis [1970] Director [American]

Wood End Academy
Incorporated: 12 April 2011 *Employees:* 67
Net Worth: £10,672,370 *Total Assets:* £11,642,451
Registered Office: Wood End Academy, Vernon Rise, Greenford, Middlesex, UB6 0EQ
Activities: Primary education
Officers: Sarah Margaret Lindsey, Secretary; Mohammad Arshad [1969] Director; Julie Ann Evans [1972] Director; Matt Haresnape [1970] Director/Deputy Head [South African]; Rev Maureen Catherine Hider [1956] Director/Minister; Angie Howard [1979] Director/Training Co-ordinator; Imran Iqbal Khan [1980] Director/Business Executive; Janice Elizabeth Phillpot [1962] Director/Teaching Assistant; Lynette Smith [1955] Director/Admin Officer; Lee Warner Dudley Liversedge Stainbank [1975] Director; Gabriela Vince [1977] Director/Teaching Assistant [Venezuelan]

Wood Farm (Stanmore) Limited
Incorporated: 23 June 2011
Net Worth Deficit: £1,365,843 *Total Assets:* £18,215,322
Registered Office: 14 Oxford Road, Wealdstone, Middlesex, HA3 7RG
Activities: Development of building projects
Officers: Kiran Bhudia [1984] Director/London Property Developers; Dhiraj Dabasia [1984] Director/London Property Developers; Samji Shivji Patel [1956] Director/London Property Developers

Wood Green Investments Limited
Incorporated: 3 July 2005 *Employees:* 2
Net Worth: £4,198,212 *Total Assets:* £8,237,548
Registered Office: Treviot House, 186-192 High Road, Ilford, Essex, IG1 1LR
Activities: Buying and selling of own real estate
Shareholder: Leslie Steven Gilbert
Officers: Leslie Steven Gilbert [1964] Director

Wood Group Industrial Services Limited
Incorporated: 22 June 2004 *Employees:* 2,001
Net Worth: £39,458,000 *Total Assets:* £80,461,000
Registered Office: Compass Point, 79-87 Kingston Road, Staines upon Thames, Middlesex, TW18 1DT
Activities: Other specialised construction activities n.e.c.
Parent: Wood Group Engineering & Operations Support Limited
Officers: Iain Angus Jones, Secretary; Derek Byrne [1972] Director/President - Industrial Services [Irish]; Richard Manson Duff [1958] Director; Andrew James Findlay [1974] Director/Financial Controller; Alan James Johnstone [1963] Director; Stephen James Nicol [1975] Director/Chief Financial Officer; Craig Shanaghey [1971] Director/SVP Industrial Services

Wood Group Kenny Limited
Incorporated: 7 November 1978 *Employees:* 30
Net Worth: £20,270,000 *Total Assets:* £22,648,000
Registered Office: Compass Point, 79-87 Kingston Road, Staines upon Thames, Middlesex, TW18 1DT
Activities: Construction of other civil engineering projects n.e.c.
Parent: Wood Group Kenny Corporate Limited
Officers: Iain Angus Jones, Secretary; Grant Rae Angus [1970] Director; Alan Rae Fotheringham [1966] Director; Robert Alexander MacDonald [1968] Director

Wood Group Kenny UK Limited
Incorporated: 29 December 1988 *Employees:* 454
Previous: Wood Group Kenny Caledonia Limited
Net Worth: £10,027,000 *Total Assets:* £10,190,000
Registered Office: Compass Point, 79-87 Kingston Road, Staines upon Thames, Middlesex, TW18 1DT
Activities: Engineering related scientific and technical consulting activities
Parent: Wood Group Kenny Corporate Limited
Officers: Iain Angus Jones, Secretary; Grant Rae Angus [1970] Director; Alan Rae Fotheringham [1966] Director; Robert Alexander MacDonald [1968] Director

Wood Hall Investments Limited
Incorporated: 11 August 1999
Net Worth: £1,951,365 *Total Assets:* £18,096,462
Registered Office: Wood Hall Lane, Shenley, Radlett, Herts, WD7 9AA
Activities: Financial management
Major Shareholder: Andrew Lynton Cohen
Officers: Iain Williamson, Secretary/Chartered Accountant; Andrew Lynton Cohen [1953] Director; Wendy Philippa Cohen [1950] Director; Iain Williamson [1972] Director/Chartered Accountant

Wood Hall Land & Properties Limited
Incorporated: 20 July 2012
Net Worth: £4,574,605 *Total Assets:* £28,376,944
Registered Office: Wood Hall Farm Office, Woodhall Lane, Shenley, Herts, WD7 9AA
Activities: Activities of head offices
Major Shareholder: Andrew Lynton Cohen
Officers: Iain Williamson, Secretary; Andrew Lynton Cohen [1953] Director

E Wood Holdings Limited
Incorporated: 13 August 1946 *Employees:* 2
Net Worth: £4,688,000 *Total Assets:* £7,321,000
Registered Office: Unit 3, 207 Brooklands Road, Weybridge, Surrey, KT13 0TS
Activities: Activities of other holding companies n.e.c.

Woodcote Estates Limited
Incorporated: 31 March 2003
Net Worth: £18,661,508 *Total Assets:* £45,316,128
Registered Office: Crown House Mews, Chequers Lane, Walton on the Hill, Tadworth, Surrey, KT20 7ST
Activities: Other letting and operating of own or leased real estate
Major Shareholder: Martin James Morris
Officers: David Mark Pay, Secretary; Martin James Morris [1963] Director

Woodcote High School
Incorporated: 1 May 2012 *Employees:* 155
Net Worth: £15,085,000 *Total Assets:* £17,383,000
Registered Office: Woodcote High School, Meadow Rise, Coulsdon, Surrey, CR5 2EH
Activities: General secondary education
Officers: Rosemary Vivien Viggiani, Secretary; Stephen David Cooper [1962] Director/Principal Highway Officer; Dr Paul Charlton Driscoll [1961] Director/Research Scientist; Suzanne Michelle Dudman [1969] Director/Mother; Lyton Mark Ferron [1967] Director/Retail Store Owner; Judith Frances Lowson [1983] Director/Deputy Headteacher; Sandra Janice Parsons [1965] Director/HR Consultant; Emma Louise Pattison [1977] Director/Headmistress; James Alexander Porter [1984] Director/Chartered Accountant; Thomas Justin Russell [1966] Director/School Teacher; Hiten Panachand Savla [1966] Director/Chartered Accountant; Emily Jade Sexton [1990] Director/Digital Optimisation Manager; Mark Anthony Southworth [1959] Director/Headteacher; Chidi Ifejika Umezurike [1977] Director/Solicitor; Alison Margaret Utting [1974] Director/ELP Co-ordinator; Kristian Edward Witherington [1973] Director/Local Government Officer

Woodford Heating & Energy Limited
Incorporated: 2 November 1993 *Employees:* 129
Net Worth: £6,210,683 *Total Assets:* £13,368,076
Registered Office: First Floor, Oakwood House, Oakwood Industrial Estate, Loughton, Essex, IG10 3TZ
Activities: Plumbing, heat and air-conditioning installation
Parent: Woodford Heating Holdings Limited
Officers: Stephen Thomas Abbott [1978] Operations Director; Roy Steven Alderslade [1960] Director/Plumber

Woodford Heating Holdings Limited
Incorporated: 6 September 2013 *Employees:* 130
Net Worth: £8,846,079 *Total Assets:* £17,343,320
Registered Office: First Floor, Oakwood House, Oakwood Industrial Estate, Loughton, Essex, IG10 3TZ
Activities: Activities of construction holding companies
Major Shareholder: Roy Steven Alderslade
Officers: Roy Steven Alderslade [1960] Director

A & A Woodford Limited
Incorporated: 27 May 1983 *Employees:* 57
Previous: A. & A. Electrical Distributors Limited
Net Worth: £8,887,202 *Total Assets:* £13,066,474
Registered Office: 3rd Floor, Crown House, 151 High Road, Loughton, Essex, IG10 4LG
Activities: Non-specialised wholesale trade
Parent: A. & A. 2000 Limited
Officers: Ann Kathleen Warren, Secretary; Alan Michael Warren [1957] Director/Electrician; Ann Kathleen Warren [1956] Director/Secretary

Woodgavil Estates Limited
Incorporated: 16 July 2009 *Employees:* 3
Net Worth: £14,442,024 *Total Assets:* £18,272,468
Registered Office: 9 Cheam Road, Ewell, Epsom, Surrey, KT17 1SP
Activities: Other letting and operating of own or leased real estate
Parent: Woodgavil Properties Ltd
Officers: Paul Edward Morris [1954] Director

Woodgavil Limited
Incorporated: 16 July 2009
Net Worth: £19,324,168 *Total Assets:* £24,964,550
Registered Office: Crown House Mews, Chequers Lane, Walton on the Hill, Tadworth, Surrey, KT20 7ST
Activities: Other letting and operating of own or leased real estate
Parent: Woodgavil Properties Ltd
Officers: David Mark Pay, Secretary; Martin James Morris [1963] Director

Woodgavil Properties Limited
Incorporated: 23 December 1954
Net Worth: £27,082,972 *Total Assets:* £29,440,504
Registered Office: Crown House Mews, Chequers Lane, Walton on the Hill, Tadworth, Surrey, KT20 7ST
Activities: Other letting and operating of own or leased real estate
Shareholders: Martin James Morris; Paul Edward Morris
Officers: Martin James Morris [1963] Director; Paul Edward Morris [1954] Director

The Woodland Academy Trust
Incorporated: 5 July 2011 *Employees:* 222
Net Worth: £19,845,000 *Total Assets:* £22,939,000
Registered Office: Northumberland Heath Primary School, Wheelock Close, Byron Drive, Erith, Kent, DA8 1JE
Activities: Primary education
Officers: Dr Deborah Joan Absalom [1955] Director/Retired; Chika Chukwujekwu [1974] Director/Forensic Accountant; Heather Rosanne Daley [1963] Director/HR Professional; Kamaldeen Giwa [1978] Director/Chartered Surveyor; Rebecca Johnson [1985] Director/Learning & Events Manager; Daniel Morrow [1978] Director/Executive Principal/CEO [Irish]; Neil Howard Riddington [1965] Director/Insurance Clerical; Jim Rouncefield [1951] Director/Retired

Woodledge Limited
Incorporated: 4 December 1995
Net Worth: £4,014,122 *Total Assets:* £8,275,650
Registered Office: 5 Elstree Gate, Elstree Way, Borehamwood, Herts, WD6 1JD
Activities: Activities of head offices
Officers: Eldad Aizenberg, Secretary; Eldad Aizenberg [1957] Managing Director; Naomi Braybrooke [1967] Director/Day Centre Manager; Daniel Cigman [1969] Director/Designer; Julie Cigman [1954] Director/Teacher/Writer; Dr Ruth Cigman [1951] Director/Writer

Woodside Road Limited
Incorporated: 5 December 2000
Net Worth: £872,825 *Total Assets:* £8,578,726
Registered Office: Berkeley House, 19 Portsmouth Road, Cobham, Surrey, KT11 1JG
Activities: Non-trading company
Parent: Berkeley Commercial Investments Limited
Officers: Jared Stephen Philip Cranney, Secretary; Robert Charles Grenville Perrins [1965] Director; Anthony William Pidgley [1947] Director; Richard James Stearn [1968] Director

Workout Limited
Incorporated: 19 September 2003 *Employees:* 7
Net Worth: £479,127 *Total Assets:* £13,325,661
Registered Office: 3rd Floor, Sterling House, Langston Road, Loughton, Essex, IG10 3TS
Activities: Other letting and operating of own or leased real estate
Parent: Galliard Homes Limited
Officers: Allan William Porter, Secretary; Keith Alder Barber [1962] Director/Property Buyer; Stephen Stuart Solomon Conway [1948] Director; Donagh O'Sullivan [1968] Construction Director [Irish]

World Duty Free Limited
Incorporated: 30 July 1997
Net Worth: £21,245,000 *Total Assets:* £21,408,000
Registered Office: The Compass Centre, Nelson Road, Hounslow, Middlesex, TW6 2GW
Activities: Other retail sale of new goods in specialised stores (not commercial art galleries and opticians)
Parent: LHR Airports Limited
Officers: Christopher John Annetts [1972] Director; Ross Findlay Scott Baker [1974] Director

World Mission Agency - Winners Chapel International
Incorporated: 19 August 2009 *Employees:* 40
Net Worth: £21,502,440 *Total Assets:* £24,500,488
Registered Office: 1 Churchill Close, Green Street, Green Road, Dartford, Kent, DA1 1QE
Activities: Activities of religious organisations
Officers: Dr. Olumuyiwa John Olumoroti, Secretary; Alakoro Syrenius Abaya [1956] Director/Administration; Adebayo Arowolo [1972] Director/Accountant; Abosede Olufunke Obanobi [1964] Director/Accountant; Mamiroro Christine Ogunkanmi [1965] Director/Chartered Architect/Project Manager; Olumuyiwa Olufote [1980] Director/Certified Chartered Accountant; Dr. Olumuyiwa John Olumoroti [1968] Director/Medical Doctor

World Transport Agency Limited
Incorporated: 16 May 1913 *Employees:* 62
Net Worth: £2,057,274 *Total Assets:* £8,690,108
Registered Office: Thameside House, Kingsway Business Park, Oldfield Road, Hampton, Middlesex, TW12 2HD
Activities: Other transportation support activities
Parent: World Transport Agency Group Limited
Officers: Charles Eric Wegener, Secretary; Antony Raymond Butler [1959] Director/Freight Forwarding; Elaine Christine Evans [1973] Director; Thomas Kuehn [1970] Director [German]; John David Sommer [1977] Director

World Wise Foods Limited
Incorporated: 6 April 2010 *Employees:* 41
Net Worth: £5,179,496 *Total Assets:* £28,088,864
Registered Office: Second Floor, Chancery House, St Nicholas Way, Sutton, Surrey, SM1 1JB
Activities: Non-specialised wholesale of food, beverages and tobacco
Major Shareholder: John Richard Burton
Officers: John Richard Burton [1955] Director; Andrew Paul Mylrea [1962] Director/Retired; Phillip James Upex [1963] Finance Director

Worldwide Energy Logistics Group Limited
Incorporated: 24 March 2009 *Employees:* 28
Net Worth: £6,747,245 *Total Assets:* £10,519,601
Registered Office: Grosvenor House, 4-7 Station Road, Sunbury on Thames, Surrey, TW16 6SB
Activities: Freight transport by road
Shareholders: Martin Burt; Sevinc Burt
Officers: Sevinc Burt, Secretary; Martin Burt [1961] Managing Director; Sevinc Burt [1969] Commercial Director

Worldwide Energy Logistics Limited
Incorporated: 5 February 2004 *Employees:* 16
Net Worth: £5,474,745 *Total Assets:* £8,926,375
Registered Office: Grosvenor House, 4-7 Station Road, Sunbury on Thames, Surrey, TW16 6SB
Activities: Freight transport by road
Parent: Worldwide Energy Logistics Group Ltd
Officers: Sevinc Burt, Secretary/Commercial Director; Martin Burt [1961] Managing Director; Sevinc Burt [1969] Commercial Director

Worldwide Flight Services Limited
Incorporated: 2 December 1999 *Employees:* 459
Net Worth: £13,058,354 *Total Assets:* £37,583,808
Registered Office: Building 552, Shoreham Road East, London Heathrow Airport, Hounslow, Middlesex, TW6 3UA
Activities: Operation of warehousing and storage facilities for air transport activities
Officers: Steven Greenhalgh [1974] Finance Director; Francois Jean Pierre Mirallie [1962] Director/Group CFO [French]; Patrick Ian Roberts [1950] Managing Director

Worldwide Product Sourcing Limited
Incorporated: 17 February 2009 *Employees:* 2
Net Worth: £8,002,402 *Total Assets:* £10,001,640
Registered Office: Bentinck House, Bentinck Road, West Drayton, Middlesex, UB7 7RQ
Activities: Other business support service activities n.e.c.
Shareholders: Pamela Mabel Bellis; Jennifer Mary Benson
Officers: Pamela Mabel Bellis [1948] Director; Jennifer Mary Benson [1948] Director

WorleyParsons Europe Limited
Incorporated: 5 December 2001 *Employees:* 505
Net Worth: £317,726,016 *Total Assets:* £401,252,992
Registered Office: 27 Great West Road, Brentford, Middlesex, TW8 9BW
Activities: Architectural activities
Officers: Victor Jibuike, Secretary; John Robert Creasy [1970] Director/Finance Manager; Werner Dorfling [1970] Director; Alan Stewart Gordon [1964] Director; Thomas Francis Honan [1962] Director/Chief Financial Officer [Australian]; Andrew Wood [1959] Director [Australian]

WorleyParsons UK Finance Sub Limited
Incorporated: 21 February 2008
Net Worth: £333,431,008 *Total Assets:* £426,903,008
Registered Office: 27 Great West Road, Brentford, Middlesex, TW8 9BW
Activities: Financial management
Parent: WorleyParsons Europe Limited
Officers: Victor Jibuike, Secretary; Alan Stewart Gordon [1964] Managing Director; Thomas Francis Honan [1962] Director/Chief Financial Officer [Australian]; Andrew Wood [1959] Director [Australian]

WorleyParsons UK Finance Sub No. 2 Ltd
Incorporated: 8 December 2016
Net Worth: £328,763,520 *Total Assets:* £330,134,528
Registered Office: 27 Great West Road, Brentford, Middlesex, TW8 9BW
Activities: Financial management
Parent: WorleyParsons UK Finance Sub Limited
Officers: Victor Jibuike, Secretary; Alan Stewart Gordon [1964] Director; Thomas Francis Honan [1962] Director/Chief Financial Officer [Australian]; Andrew Peter Wood [1959] Director/Chief Executive Officer [Australian]

Worth More Limited
Incorporated: 14 March 2005
Net Worth: £2,955,740 *Total Assets:* £6,350,088
Registered Office: 6th Floor, Amp House, Dingwall Road, Croydon, Surrey, CR0 2LX
Activities: Other letting and operating of own or leased real estate
Major Shareholder: Satinder Pal Kaur Sidhu
Officers: Manmohan Singh Sidhu [1960] Director/General Manager

Worthing Retail Limited Liability Partnership
Incorporated: 6 May 2005
Net Worth Deficit: £4,018,830 *Total Assets:* £8,927,249
Registered Office: Philip Harris House, 1a Spur Road, Orpington, Kent, BR6 0PH

WP Midco1 Limited
Incorporated: 26 March 2008 *Employees:* 2
Net Worth Deficit: £467,728,000 *Total Assets:* £280,068,992
Registered Office: Profile West, 950 Great West Road, Brentford, Middlesex, TW8 9ES
Activities: Activities of head offices
Parent: WP Safetykleen Limited
Officers: Andrew Gregory Firth, Secretary; Andrew Patrick Griffith [1968] Director; Philippe Robert Francis Mauguy [1960] Director [French]

WP Midco2 Limited
Incorporated: 26 March 2008
Net Worth: £267,900,000 *Total Assets:* £267,900,000
Registered Office: Profile West, 950 Great West Road, Brentford, Middlesex, TW8 9ES
Activities: Activities of head offices
Parent: WP Midco 1 Limited
Officers: Andrew Gregory Firth, Secretary; Andrew Patrick Griffith [1968] Director; Philippe Robert Francis Mauguy [1960] Director [French]

WP Midco3 Limited
Incorporated: 26 March 2008 *Employees:* 2
Net Worth: £391,524,992 *Total Assets:* £752,249,984
Registered Office: Profile West, 950 Great West Road, Brentford, Middlesex, TW8 9ES
Activities: Activities of head offices
Parent: WP Midco 2 Limited
Officers: Andrew Gregory Firth, Secretary; Andrew Patrick Griffith [1968] Director; Philippe Robert Francis Mauguy [1960] Director [French]

WP Safety-Kleen Limited
Incorporated: 26 March 2008
Net Worth: £303,664,000 *Total Assets:* £310,040,000
Registered Office: Profile West, 950 Great West Road, Brentford, Middlesex, TW8 9ES
Activities: Activities of head offices
Officers: Andrew Gregory Firth, Secretary; Andrew Patrick Griffith [1968] Director; Philippe Robert Francis Mauguy [1960] Director [French]

WP SK Holdings Limited
Incorporated: 21 May 2004
Net Worth: £46,000,000 *Total Assets:* £46,000,000
Registered Office: Profile West, 950 Great West Road, Brentford, Middlesex, TW8 9ES
Activities: Activities of head offices
Parent: Safetykleen Group Services Limited
Officers: Andrew Gregory Firth, Secretary; Andrew Patrick Griffith [1968] Director; Philippe Robert Francis Mauguy [1960] Director [French]

WP SK Limited
Incorporated: 21 May 2004 *Employees:* 2
Net Worth: £112,267,000 *Total Assets:* £224,239,008
Registered Office: Profile West, 950 Great West Road, Brentford, Middlesex, TW8 9ES
Activities: Activities of head offices
Parent: WP SK Midco Limited
Officers: Andrew Gregory Firth, Secretary; Andrew Patrick Griffith [1968] Director; Philippe Robert Francis Mauguy [1960] Director [French]

WP SK Midco Limited
Incorporated: 8 March 2005 *Employees:* 2
Net Worth Deficit: £101,056,000 *Total Assets:* £176,288,992
Registered Office: Profile West, 950 Great West Road, Brentford, Middlesex, TW8 9ES
Activities: Activities of head offices
Parent: WP SK Holdings Limited
Officers: Andrew Gregory Firth, Secretary; Andrew Patrick Griffith [1968] Director; Philippe Robert Francis Mauguy [1960] Director [French]

WPA Support Services Limited
Incorporated: 31 October 2003
Net Worth Deficit: £5,043,000 *Total Assets:* £19,869,000
Registered Office: Astral House, Imperial Way, Watford, Herts, WD24 4WW
Activities: Other specialised construction activities n.e.c.
Parent: WPA Support Services (Holdings) Limited
Officers: Ian David Hudson [1964] Director/Chartered Accountant; Rory John Murphy [1969] Director/Chartered Surveyor

Wren Buyerco Limited
Incorporated: 16 May 2015 *Employees:* 7
Net Worth Deficit: £25,434,450 *Total Assets:* £94,009,480
Registered Office: 32 Crown Road, Enfield, Middlesex, EN1 1TH
Activities: Renting and leasing of construction and civil engineering machinery and equipment
Officers: Francois Dekker [1975] Director [Dutch]; Jeremy Peter Fish [1965] Director/Chief Executive Officer; Greg Paul FitzGenerald [1964] Director/Chairman; Debbie Mantzouridis [1991] Director/Investment Executive; Stuart Russell McMinnies [1968] Investment Director; Julian Alexander O'Neill [1971] Director

Wren Midco Limited
Incorporated: 15 May 2015 *Employees:* 2
Net Worth: £21,730,244 *Total Assets:* £100,600,096
Registered Office: 32 Crown Road, Enfield, Middlesex, EN1 1TH
Activities: Renting and leasing of construction and civil engineering machinery and equipment
Officers: Francois Dekker [1975] Director [Dutch]; Stuart Russell McMinnies [1968] Investment Director

Wren Topco Limited
Incorporated: 14 May 2015 *Employees:* 282
Net Worth Deficit: £28,396,000 *Total Assets:* £200,296,992
Registered Office: 32 Crown Road, Enfield, Middlesex, EN1 1TH
Activities: Renting and leasing of construction and civil engineering machinery and equipment
Officers: Francois Dekker [1975] Director [Dutch]; Jeremy Peter Fish [1965] Chief Executive Director; Greg Paul FitzGenerald [1964] Director/Chairman; Jonathan Laloum [1986] Director/Investment Professional [French]; Debbie Mantzouridis [1991] Director/Investment Executive; Stuart Russell McMinnies [1968] Investment Director; Julian Alexander O'Neill [1971] Director

Wrest Park Limited
Incorporated: 26 August 2008 *Employees:* 14
Net Worth: £7,036,386 *Total Assets:* £22,351,964
Registered Office: 1st Floor, Sheraton House, Lower Road, Chorleywood, Herts, WD3 5LH
Activities: Development of building projects
Major Shareholder: Raymond Valentine Mawhood
Officers: Lisa Jane Ashton Jones, Secretary; Philip Ashton Jones [1964] Director/Barrister; Raymond Valentine Mawhood [1942] Director

G.R.Wright & Sons Limited
Incorporated: 25 June 1913 *Employees:* 115
Net Worth: £34,885,784 *Total Assets:* £39,198,168
Registered Office: Ponders End Mills, Enfield, Middlesex, EN3 4TG
Activities: Grain milling
Major Shareholder: David Andrew Wright
Officers: Lorraine Joanne Kaye, Secretary; Alan Cave [1958] Director/Flour Miller; Simon Robert Clack [1950] Director/Project Manager; Lorraine Joanne Kaye [1965] Finance Director; Julian Alastair Woodgate [1970] Director/Bakery Technologist; David Andrew Wright [1962] Director/Miller; James Wright [1989] Production Director/Miller

Richard Wright Music Limited
Incorporated: 15 August 1972 *Employees:* 2
Net Worth: £12,520,923 *Total Assets:* £17,229,790
Registered Office: 5 Elstree Gate, Elstree Way, Borehamwood, Herts, WD6 1JD
Activities: Artistic creation
Parent: Ramogan Limited
Officers: Gala Wright [1970] Director/Designer; Jamie Wright [1971] Director/Property Manager

Wrist Holding UK Limited
Incorporated: 14 April 2011
Previous: Wrist Europe (UK) Limited
Net Worth: £39,997,000 *Total Assets:* £56,484,000
Registered Office: 3rd Floor, South Wing, St James House, 27-43 Eastern Road, Romford, Essex, RM1 3NH
Activities: Activities of other holding companies n.e.c.
Officers: Soeren Juul Joergensen [1974] Director/Vice President [Danish]; Robert Steen Kledal [1969] Director/President [Danish]; Anders Skipper [1967] Director/Executive Vice President and CFO [Danish]

Wryde Croft Wind Farm Limited
Incorporated: 27 September 2004
Net Worth Deficit: £6,705,000 *Total Assets:* £42,107,000
Registered Office: Beaufort Court, Egg Farm Lane, off Station Road, Kings Langley, Herts, WD4 8LR
Activities: Production of electricity
Parent: Notos Energy Limited
Officers: Dominic James Hearth, Secretary; Peter Edward Dias [1981] Director; Christopher Peter Gaydon [1978] Director [Hungarian]; Paul Stephen Latham [1956] Director; Thomas James Rosser [1985] Director

Wurth Holding UK Ltd
Incorporated: 20 April 1990 *Employees:* 2
Net Worth: £10,045,000 *Total Assets:* £10,084,000
Registered Office: 1 Centurion Way, Erith, Kent, DA18 4AF
Activities: Activities of head offices
Officers: Andrew Richard Dagnall [1963] Director; Joachim Kaltmaier [1962] Director [German]

Wurth UK Limited
Incorporated: 26 July 1973 *Employees:* 569
Net Worth: £4,037,000 *Total Assets:* £21,901,000
Registered Office: 1 Centurion Way, Erith, Kent, DA18 4AF
Activities: Wholesale trade of motor vehicle parts and accessories
Parent: Wurth Holding UK Limited
Officers: Andrew Richard Dagnall, Secretary; Andrew Richard Dagnall [1963] Finance Director; Ivor Laurence Morgan Jones [1974] Director/Operations Manager; Jason Murphy [1969] Managing Director

WVC Land & Developments Limited
Incorporated: 1 November 1993
Net Worth: £5,725,431 *Total Assets:* £10,575,458
Registered Office: Felstead Manor, Long Lane, Stanwell, Staines upon Thames, Middlesex, TW19 7AN
Activities: Buying and selling of own real estate
Major Shareholder: William Robert James Dowling
Officers: William Dowling [1948] Director/Motor Trader; William Robert James Dowling [1972] Director/Commercial Vehicle Trader

WVC Vehicle Solutions Limited
Incorporated: 20 September 1999 *Employees:* 18
Net Worth: £2,604,827 *Total Assets:* £8,399,972
Registered Office: Felstead Manor, Long Lane, Stanwell, Staines upon Thames, Middlesex, TW19 7AN
Activities: Sale of used cars and light motor vehicles
Major Shareholder: William Robert James Dowling
Officers: William Alfie Dowling [1999] Director/Motor Trader; William Robert James Dowling [1972] Director

WWW Sunoptic Com UK Limited
Incorporated: 16 April 1996 *Employees:* 4
Net Worth: £333,785 *Total Assets:* £21,345,202
Registered Office: Regus Suite, Level 3, 79 College Road, Harrow, Middlesex, HA1 1BD
Activities: Wholesale of other intermediate products
Officers: Alan Roy Kentish [1966] Director/Chartered Accountant

Www.Nakedwines.Com Limited
Incorporated: 13 August 2008 *Employees:* 120
Net Worth: £2,487,000 *Total Assets:* £23,975,000
Registered Office: Majestic House, The Belfry, Colonial Way, Watford, Herts, WD24 4WH
Activities: Retail sale of beverages in specialised stores
Parent: Naked Wines International Limited
Officers: Alex Iapichino, Secretary; James Crawford [1977] Director; Eamon William FitzGenerald [1984] Director/COO, Naked Wines [Irish]

Wyevale Acquisitions Borrower Limited
Incorporated: 15 August 2007
Net Worth Deficit: £3,137,000 *Total Assets:* £134,244,992
Registered Office: Wyevale Garden Centres, Syon Park, London Road, Brentford, Middlesex, TW8 8JF
Activities: Buying and selling of own real estate
Parent: Wyevale Garden Centres Holdings Limited
Officers: Laura Harradine-Greene, Secretary; Anthony Generald Jones [1973] Director; Richard MacLachlan [1976] Director

Wyevale Garden Centres Acquisitions Limited
Incorporated: 21 May 2013
Net Worth: £3,139,000 *Total Assets:* £66,081,000
Registered Office: Wyevale Garden Centres, Syon Park, London Road, Brentford, Middlesex, TW8 8JF
Activities: Activities of other holding companies n.e.c.
Parent: Wyevale Garden Centres Limited
Officers: Laura Harradine-Greene, Secretary; Anthony Generald Jones [1973] Director; Richard MacLachlan [1976] Director

Wyevale Garden Centres Capital Limited
Incorporated: 9 February 2012 *Employees:* 6,290
Net Worth: £82,242,000 *Total Assets:* £422,868,000
Registered Office: Wyevale Garden Centres, Syon Park, London Road, Brentford, Middlesex, TW8 8JF
Activities: Activities of other holding companies n.e.c.
Major Shareholder: Guy Hands
Officers: Laura Harradine-Greene, Secretary; Charlotte Broadbent [1990] Director; David Browne [1979] Director [American]

Wyevale Garden Centres G & L Limited
Incorporated: 10 November 1997
Net Worth: £16,892,000 *Total Assets:* £70,126,000
Registered Office: Wyevale Garden Centres, Syon Park, London Road, Brentford, Middlesex, TW8 8JF
Activities: Other retail sale of new goods in specialised stores (not commercial art galleries and opticians)
Parent: EHGT Limited
Officers: Laura Harradine-Greene, Secretary; Anthony Generald Jones [1973] Director; Richard MacLachlan [1976] Director

Wyevale Garden Centres Holdings Limited
Incorporated: 18 December 1985
Net Worth: £299,280,000 *Total Assets:* £455,476,992
Registered Office: Wyevale Garden Centres, Syon Park, London Road, Brentford, Middlesex, TW8 8JF
Activities: Activities of head offices
Parent: Garden Centre Holdings Limited
Officers: Laura Harradine-Greene, Secretary; Anthony Generald Jones [1973] Director; Richard MacLachlan [1976] Director

Wyevale Garden Centres Limited
Incorporated: 15 June 1960
Net Worth: £11,174,000 *Total Assets:* £528,996,000
Registered Office: Wyevale Garden Centres, Syon Park, London Road, Brentford, Middlesex, TW8 8JF
Activities: Retail sale of flowers, plants, seeds, fertilizers, pet animals and pet food in specialised stores
Parent: Wyevale Garden Centres Holdings Limited
Officers: Laura Harradine-Greene, Secretary; Anthony Generald Jones [1973] Director; Richard MacLachlan [1976] Director

WYM Legal Limited
Incorporated: 15 June 2015 *Employees:* 23
Previous: When You Move Limited
Net Worth Deficit: £1,315,361 *Total Assets:* £6,321,915
Registered Office: The Junction, Station Road, Watford, Herts, WD17 1ET
Activities: Solicitors
Parent: WYM Holdings Limited
Officers: Russell James Darvill, Secretary; Grant William Ambridge [1977] Director/Lawyer; Simon John Bath [1974] Managing Director; Russell Darvill [1975] Director; Peter James Goodman [1978] Director; Robert McKellar [1987] Director/Lawyer; Ian Leslie Weaver [1953] Director

Xavier Catholic Education Trust
Incorporated: 16 June 2016 *Employees:* 635
Net Worth: £51,365 *Total Assets:* £9,923,462
Registered Office: Salesian School, Guildford Road, Chertsey, Surrey, KT16 9LU
Activities: General secondary education
Officers: Reverend Peter Maurice Andrews [1948] Director/Catholic Priest; Maria Philomena Bridgette Dineen [1960] Director/Retired; Miroslaw Jerzy Feliks Gliniecki [1967] Director/Management Consultant; Michael Patrick Harrington [1961] Director/HR Operations Manager; Peter John O'Brien [1953] Director/Retired; John Bernard Wells [1947] Director/Accountant

Xerox (UK) Limited
Incorporated: 16 August 1937 *Employees:* 1,594
Net Worth: £390,800,000 *Total Assets:* £667,699,968
Registered Office: Riverview, Oxford Road, Uxbridge, Middlesex, UB8 1HS
Activities: Wholesale of other office machinery and equipment
Parent: Xerox Capital (Europe) Limited
Officers: Richard Stuart Pitceathly, Secretary; David Brian Dyas [1963] Director/President, UK & Ireland, Eurasia, India, MEA; Julie Hesselgrove Ward [1963] Director/Senior Vice President; Rodney Noonoo [1962] Director/CFO, UK & Ireland, Eurasia, India, MEA [American]; Richard Stuart Pitceathly [1965] Director/Lawyer

Xerox Capital (Europe) Limited
Incorporated: 20 June 1995
Net Worth: £512,366,016 *Total Assets:* £807,499,008
Registered Office: Riverview, Oxford Road, Uxbridge, Middlesex, UB8 1HS
Activities: Financial intermediation not elsewhere classified
Parent: Xerox Limited
Officers: Richard Pitceathly, Secretary; Anthony William Arthurton [1972] Director/Accountant; Daniel Marc Benoit [1967] Director/International Operations CFO [French]; Stuart William Kirk [1960] Director EMEA Treasury Operations [Irish]

Xerox Finance Limited
Incorporated: 16 August 1937 *Employees:* 27
Net Worth: £123,226,000 *Total Assets:* £309,790,016
Registered Office: Riverview, Oxford Road, Uxbridge, Middlesex, UB8 1HS
Activities: Renting and leasing of office machinery and equipment (including computers)
Parent: Xerox (UK) Limited
Officers: Richard Pitceathly, Secretary; Martin Boyle [1976] Director/General Manager; Rodney Noonoo [1962] Director/CFO, UK & Ireland, Eurasia, India, MEA [American]

Xerox Limited
Incorporated: 19 December 1956
Net Worth: £2,796,000,000 *Total Assets:* £3,376,000,000
Registered Office: Riverview, Oxford Road, Uxbridge, Middlesex, UB8 1HS
Activities: Wholesale of other office machinery and equipment
Parent: Xerox Overseas Holdings Limited
Officers: Richard Pitceathly, Secretary; Daniel Marc Benoit [1967] Director/International Operations CFO [French]; Lisa Marie Oliver [1966] HR Director; Richard Stuart Pitceathly [1965] Director/Lawyer; Herve Tessler [1963] Director/President, International Operations [French]

Xerox Overseas Holdings Limited
Incorporated: 7 November 1996
Net Worth: £4,630,000,128 *Total Assets:* £7,706,999,808
Registered Office: Riverview, Oxford Road, Uxbridge, Middlesex, UB8 1HS
Activities: Activities of head offices
Parent: Xerox UK Holdings Limited
Officers: Richard Pitceathly, Secretary; Anthony William Arthurton [1972] Director/Accountant; Daniel Marc Benoit [1967] Director/International Operations CFO [French]; Lisa Marie Oliver [1966] HR Director

Xerox Products UK Limited
Incorporated: 1 December 2016
Net Worth: £3,661,950 *Total Assets:* £9,866,195
Registered Office: Riverview, Oxford Road, Uxbridge, Middlesex, UB8 1HS
Activities: Wholesale of computers, computer peripheral equipment and software
Officers: Mohamed Hareb Al Otaiba [1973] Director [Emirati]; Mohamed Amer [1976] Director/Regional General Manager [Egyptian]; Jason Wakefield [1969] Director/Financial Controller

Xerox UK Holdings Limited
Incorporated: 14 April 1998
Net Worth: £4,295,000,064 *Total Assets:* £4,295,000,064
Registered Office: Riverview, Oxford Road, Uxbridge, Middlesex, UB8 1HS
Activities: Activities of other holding companies n.e.c.
Parent: Xerox Investments Europe BV
Officers: Richard Pitceathly, Secretary; Anthony William Arthurton [1972] Director/Accountant; Daniel Marc Benoit [1967] Director/International Operations CFO [French]; Lisa Marie Oliver [1966] HR Director

Xstro Investments Limited
Incorporated: 11 January 2006 *Employees:* 4
Net Worth: £5,621,281 *Total Assets:* £7,352,916
Registered Office: 6th Floor, Amp House, Dingwall Road, Croydon, Surrey, CR0 2LX
Activities: Renting and operating of Housing Association real estate
Parent: Express Property Investments Limited
Officers: Michelle Bean, Secretary; Sudhir Dwarkadas Hathi [1952] Director

Xtera Topco Limited
Incorporated: 24 January 2017 *Employees:* 60
Net Worth: £2,004,485 *Total Assets:* £31,366,754
Registered Office: Bates House, Church Road, Harold Wood, Romford, Essex, RM3 0SD
Activities: Activities of other holding companies n.e.c.
Officers: Dr Stuart Robert Barnes [1953] Director/Chairman; Carl Michael Steve Harring [1976] Director [Swedish]; Dr James George Mitchell [1981] Director [Irish]

XTO UK, Ltd
Incorporated: 20 May 2005
Net Worth Deficit: £8,931,994 *Total Assets:* £9,759,258
Registered Office: Ermyn House, Ermyn Way, Leatherhead, Surrey, KT22 8UX
Activities: Other business support service activities n.e.c.
Parent: Exxon Mobil Corporation
Officers: Fiona Henderson Harness, Secretary; Robert Michael Cooper [1961] Director/Oil Company Executive; Jay Loren Jackson [1962] Director/Oil Company Executive [American]; Andrew Mark Johnson [1976] Director/Oil Company Executive

Y.A. Property Investments Limited
Incorporated: 8 November 2009 *Employees:* 1
Net Worth: £1,740,182 *Total Assets:* £16,903,558
Registered Office: 19 Edinburgh Drive, Staines upon Thames, Middlesex, TW18 1PJ
Activities: Other letting and operating of own or leased real estate
Major Shareholder: Yunis Abasov
Officers: Yunis Abasov [1985] Director

Yang Ming (UK) Ltd
Incorporated: 29 January 1997 *Employees:* 63
Net Worth Deficit: £71,830,496 *Total Assets:* £169,668,224
Registered Office: 210 South Street, Romford, Essex, RM1 1TR
Activities: Sea and coastal freight water transport
Officers: Simon John Williams, Secretary; Chao-Feng Chang [1964] Director/Shipping Manager [Taiwanese]; Hsien-Chien Chang [1973] Director [Taiwanese]; Yi-TA Wu [1972] Director [Taiwanese]

Yavneh College Academy Trust
Incorporated: 23 May 2011 *Employees:* 131
Previous: Yavneh College
Net Worth: £30,547,060 *Total Assets:* £31,446,916
Registered Office: Hillside Avenue, Borehamwood, Herts, WD6 1HL
Activities: General secondary education
Officers: Hayley Ann Fraser, Secretary; Daniel Iain Album [1963] Director/Fund Manager; Mark Elliot Frazer [1985] Director/PR; Richard Michael Gilbert [1969] Director/Solicitor; Rolanda Gail Hyams [1955] Director/Chartered Accountant; Roz Levin [1950] Director/Retired; Spencer Lewis [1967] Director/Headteacher; Doreen Morris [1946] Director/Academic Standards Manager; Susan Neale [1952] Director/Retired; Susan Annette Nyman [1956] Director/Chartered Accountant; Daniel Paul Summerfield [1969] Director/Investment Manager

Yehudi Menuhin School Limited (The)
Incorporated: 3 September 1964 *Employees:* 39
Net Worth: £22,650,024 *Total Assets:* £23,135,464
Registered Office: Millfield, Cobham Road, Stoke D'Abernon, Cobham, Surrey, KT11 3QQ
Activities: General secondary education
Officers: Shelley Thurman Twitchin, Secretary; Dominic Benthall [1976] Director/Barrister; Lord Norman Roy Blackwell [1952] Director/Bank Chairman; Jonathan Deakin [1983] Director/Consultant; John Ellis Everett [1947] Director/Consultant; Andrew Malcolm Hunter Johnston [1953] Director; Anna Jane Rebecca Joseph [1964] Managing Director; Oscar Max Lewisohn [1938] Director [Danish]; Stuart Walter Mitchell [1964] Director/Fund Manager; Richard Francis Maxwell Morris [1944] Director/Chief Executive; John Clovis Pagella [1943] Director/Chartered Surveyor; Alice Mary Phillips [1960] Director/Headteacher; Anthea Vanessa Richards [1947] Director; Geoffrey William Richards [1948] Director/Lawyer; Veronica Judith Colleton Wadley [1952] Director; Jonathan Peter Willcocks [1953] Director/Musician

Yellow Brick Developments Limited
Incorporated: 31 January 1996
Net Worth: £4,376,936 *Total Assets:* £7,506,531
Registered Office: TK House, 69 Banstead Road, Carshalton, Surrey, SM5 3NP
Activities: Other business support service activities n.e.c.
Major Shareholder: Aart-Jan Timmer
Officers: Aart-Jan Timmer, Secretary; Aart-Jan Timmer [1960] Director [Dutch]

Yendall Hunter Limited
Incorporated: 28 January 2015 *Employees:* 16
Net Worth: £7,115,286 *Total Assets:* £8,776,678
Registered Office: 75 Park Lane, Croydon, Surrey, CR9 1XS
Activities: Management consultancy activities other than financial management
Parent: YH Holdings (UK) Limited
Officers: Martin James Hunter [1967] Director/Chartered Surveyor; Andrew Edward Yendall [1970] Director/Chartered Surveyor

YMCA St Pauls Group
Incorporated: 28 September 1994 *Employees:* 248
Previous: YMCA London South West
Net Worth: £13,459,745 *Total Assets:* £43,328,256
Registered Office: St James House, 9-15 St James Road, Surbiton, Surrey, KT6 4QH
Activities: Other accommodation
Officers: Gwynne Myfanwy Price Jarvis, Secretary; Generald Chifamba [1992] Director; Howard Peter Dawson [1970] Director; Louise Hedges [1981] Director/Civil Servant; Andrew John Palmer [1956] Director/Chief Executive, Housing Association; Helen Gill Posner [1981] Director; Albin Andrew Stadtmiller [1966] Director [American/British]; Edward Louis Samuel Weiss [1932] Director/Retired; Kenneth John Youngman [1956] Director of Finance

Yomans (London) Limited
Incorporated: 19 March 1965 *Employees:* 2
Net Worth: £6,645,765 *Total Assets:* £8,925,338
Registered Office: 21 Jesmond Way, Stanmore, Middlesex, HA7 4QR
Activities: Other letting and operating of own or leased real estate
Major Shareholder: Michael Robin Sitton
Officers: Paula Sitton, Secretary; Michael Robin Sitton [1960] Director/Accountant

Yoplait UK Limited
Incorporated: 2 April 1991 *Employees:* 13
Net Worth: £69,666,000 *Total Assets:* £89,322,000
Registered Office: Floor 5, Harman House, 1 George Street, Uxbridge, Middlesex, UB8 1QQ
Activities: Non-specialised wholesale of food, beverages and tobacco
Parent: General Mills, Inc.
Officers: Jana Marie-Rose Gaffaney [1980] Legal Director [American]; Anne-Laure Jacquemart [1969] Finance Director [French]; Benjamin John Pearman [1972] Managing Director

York Apartments Limited
Incorporated: 21 May 2001
Net Worth: £5,396,739 *Total Assets:* £10,688,985
Registered Office: 88 Edgware Way, Edgware, Middlesex, HA8 8JS
Activities: Other letting and operating of own or leased real estate
Shareholder: Zeev Zi-Pear
Officers: Vidhur Mehra, Secretary; Anita Mehra [1953] Director; Vidhur Mehra [1975] Director

York House Centre Limited
Incorporated: 24 November 2014 *Employees:* 12
Net Worth: £417,210 *Total Assets:* £5,864,904
Registered Office: Nicholas House, River Front, Enfield, Middlesex, EN1 3FG
Activities: Dental practice activities
Parent: SD Dentco Limited
Officers: Stuart John Bowen-Davies [1960] Director/Dentist; Barry Koors Lanesman [1959] Director [South African]; Michael Brent Zurowski [1965] Director [Australian]

Yorkshire Dales Country Park Limited
Incorporated: 31 March 2009 *Employees:* 3
Net Worth: £7,034,984 *Total Assets:* £9,524,737
Registered Office: 166 College Road, Harrow, Middlesex, HA1 1RA
Activities: Other holiday and other collective accommodation
Parent: Leisure Parks Real Estate (Holdings) Limited
Officers: Colin Crickmore [1958] Director/Businessman; James Robert Crickmore [1980] Director/Businessman; Maurice Sines [1962] Director/Businessman

Yorkshire Transformations Limited
Incorporated: 18 May 2003
Net Worth Deficit: £7,361,000 *Total Assets:* £32,537,000
Registered Office: 8 White Oak Square, London Road, Swanley, Kent, BR8 7AG
Activities: Construction of commercial buildings
Parent: Yorkshire Transformations Holdings Limited
Officers: Neeti Mukundrai Anand [1984] Director; David Bolton [1968] Director; Stewart Chalmers Grant [1951] Director; Guy Christopher Millichamp [1964] Director; Angela Louise Roshier [1975] Director/Finance; Martin Timothy Smith [1967] Director/Banker; Christopher Thomas Solley [1970] Director/Investment Manager

Your Healthcare Community Interest Company
Incorporated: 1 December 2008 *Employees:* 582
Net Worth: £5,154,988 *Total Assets:* £12,803,966
Registered Office: 22 Hollyfield Road, Surbiton, Surrey, KT5 9AL
Activities: Other human health activities
Shareholders: Siobhan Elizabeth Clarke; Edward William Montgomery; Kanapathy Pillai Siva Samboo Sivakumaran
Officers: Julie Sherlock, Secretary; Kevin Richard Barrett [1970] Director; Shane Brennan [1962] Director; Jeremy David Budd [1965] Director; Siobhan Elizabeth Clarke [1960] Managing Director of Provider Services [Irish]; Elizabeth Frances Corrado [1965] Director; Edward William Montgomery [1979] Director/Board Lead for IT & PMO; Anne Nazemetz [1986] Director [American]; Julie Sherlock [1961] Director/Board Lead for Customer Care & Facilities; Kanapathy Pillai Siva Samboo Siva Kumaran [1957] Director/Board Lead for Finance

Yourway Transport Limited
Incorporated: 16 January 2004 *Employees:* 16
Net Worth: £3,117,514 *Total Assets:* £23,926,840
Registered Office: 2 Pulborough Way, Hounslow, Middlesex, TW4 6DE
Activities: Unlicensed carriers
Major Shareholder: Gulamali Jaffer
Officers: Maliha Jaffer, Secretary; Gulamali Jaffer [1975] Director/President [American]

Yparho Investments Limited
Incorporated: 6 September 2002
Net Worth: £14,660,658 *Total Assets:* £21,981,840
Registered Office: 2nd Floor, Katherine House, 11 Wylyotts Place, Potters Bar, Herts, EN6 2JD
Activities: Activities of open-ended investment companies
Major Shareholder: Antonakis Chrysostomou
Officers: Chrystalla Chrysostomou, Secretary; Antonakis Chrysostomou [1941] Director/Hotelier

Yparho Limited
Incorporated: 29 November 1996 *Employees:* 15
Net Worth: £4,808,666 *Total Assets:* £5,193,124
Registered Office: 2nd Floor, Katherine House, 11 Wyllyotts Place, Potters Bar, Herts, EN6 2JD
Activities: Hotels and similar accommodation
Shareholders: Antonakis Chrysostomou; Yparho Investments Limited
Officers: Chrystalla Chrysostomou, Secretary; Antonakis Chrysostomou [1941] Director/Hotelier

Z Hotel Poland Street Property LLP
Incorporated: 12 July 2016
Net Worth: £15,058,413 *Total Assets:* £15,058,413
Registered Office: Aprirose House, 48a High Street, Edgware, Middlesex, HA8 7EQ
Officers: Manish Mansukhlal Gudka [1970] Member; Gareth Jones [1973] Member; Suraj Rashmikant Shah [1982] LLP Member

Zameen Ltd
Incorporated: 31 July 2012
Net Worth: £9,772,038 *Total Assets:* £9,837,838
Registered Office: Spirit House, 8 High Street, West Molesey, Surrey, KT8 2NA
Activities: Activities of head offices
Officers: Gilles Christophe Marc Blanchard [1964] Director/Businessman [French]; Shiao Mae Chan [1975] Director [Malaysian]; Shaun Antony di Gregorio [1972] Director/Financier [Australian]; Imran Ali Khan [1978] Director/Businessman; Zeeshan Ali Khan [1977] Director/Businessman; Ali Shahid Rana [1980] Director/Investment Banker

Zandera Ltd
Incorporated: 6 March 2009 *Employees:* 22
Net Worth: £721,000 *Total Assets:* £5,480,000
Registered Office: Members Hill, Brooklands Road, Weybridge, Surrey, KT13 0QU
Activities: Wholesale of electronic and telecommunications equipment and parts
Parent: Japan Tobacco Inc.
Officers: Andrew Chamberlain [1965] Director/Accountant; Nicholas Charles David Craig [1977] Director/Solicitor; Jason Robert Melling [1971] HR Director

Zebrak London Limited
Incorporated: 19 July 2011 *Employees:* 2
Net Worth: £374,811 *Total Assets:* £5,287,860
Registered Office: Lynwood House, 373-375 Station Road, Harrow, Middlesex, HA1 2AW
Activities: Other business support service activities n.e.c.
Shareholders: Adam Philip Zebrak; Tracy Jane Zebrak
Officers: Adam Philip Zebrak [1965] Director; Tracy Jane Zebrak [1959] Director

Zeco Limited
Incorporated: 8 October 1997 *Employees:* 20
Net Worth: £4,445,858 *Total Assets:* £5,394,586
Registered Office: Enterprise House, 34 Faringdon Avenue, Harold Hill, Romford, Essex, RM3 8SU
Activities: Agents involved in the sale of textiles, clothing, fur, footwear and leather goods
Officers: Arwin Taheam, Secretary/Management Consultant; Ajay Taheam [1970] Director/Marketing Consultant; Arwin Taheam [1974] Director/Management Consultant

Zenoffice Limited
Incorporated: 31 October 1974 *Employees:* 76
Net Worth: £640,084 *Total Assets:* £5,746,638
Registered Office: Unit 4, 500 Purley Way, Croydon, Surrey, CR0 4NZ
Activities: Printing n.e.c.
Major Shareholder: Jonathan Paul Moulton
Officers: Philippa Maynard, Secretary; George Bruce Davie [1969] Commercial Director; Stephanie Hitchman [1965] Director; Leslie John Kerr [1967] Director; Andrew Graham Mobbs [1978] Finance Director; Octavia Kate Morley [1968] Director/Chairman; Dale Vincent Needham [1973] Director; Martyn Shaun Waterhouse [1964] Director

The Zentropa Film Partnership LLP
Incorporated: 1 September 2003
Net Worth: £6,554,950 *Total Assets:* £6,984,795
Registered Office: 99 Kenton Road, Harrow, Middlesex, HA3 0AN
Officers: Robert William Adams [1948] LLP Member; Mary Catherine Best [1960] LLP Member; Christopher Jordan Carlson [1978] LLP Member; Stuart Douglas Cooper [1966] LLP Member; Paul Francis Fraser [1960] LLP Member; Jason Nicholas Galbraith-Marten [1967] LLP Member; Andrew Hagan [1969] LLP Member; Andrew James Hartley [1946] LLP Member; Dr David Anthony Hett [1955] LLP Member; David Edmund Hoggett [1962] LLP Member; Jennifer Pamela Houghton [1946] LLP Member; Prof Howard Saul Jacobs [1938] LLP Member; Rachel Daisy Jones [1968] LLP Member; Karl Roderick Knipe [1966] LLP Member; The Estate of Nico Lethbridge [1949] LLP Member; Leighton Richard Lloyd [1963] LLP Member; David Rugbinder Singh Mattu [1958] LLP Member; Jarlath James McHale [1958] LLP Member; Bryan Edward Mouat [1967] LLP Member; Robert Thomas Newham [1966] LLP Member; Thomas Paine [1966] LLP Member; Marcus Ewart Ronksley Potts [1960] LLP Member; Samantha Jane Smith [1974] LLP Member; Gary Peter Tailby [1963] LLP Member; Adrian Mark Williamson [1957] LLP Member; Stephen John Yarwood [1961] LLP Member

Zest Living Limited
Incorporated: 1 October 1982 *Employees:* 3
Net Worth: £3,765,521 *Total Assets:* £20,862,288
Registered Office: 4 Elstree Gate, Elstree Way, Borehamwood, Herts, WD6 1JD
Activities: Other letting and operating of own or leased real estate
Officers: Ronan Patrick Murphy, Secretary; Daniel Gerard Durkan [1964] Director [Irish]; Ronan Patrick Murphy [1969] Director/Chartered Accountant [Irish]

Zian Hi-Tech (U.K.) Limited
Incorporated: 22 June 1998 *Employees:* 2
Net Worth Deficit: £39,504 *Total Assets:* £8,086,581
Registered Office: Mulberry Cottage, Clamp Hill, Stanmore, Middlesex, HA7 3JQ
Activities: Wholesale of textiles
Major Shareholder: Haian Ma
Officers: Jianhua Huang, Secretary; Haian Ma [1966] Director/Importer and Exporter

Ziegler UK Limited
Incorporated: 25 November 2005 *Employees:* 105
Net Worth: £3,829,453 *Total Assets:* £16,594,064
Registered Office: 609 London Road, Grays, Essex, RM20 3BJ
Activities: Other service activities incidental to land transportation, n.e.c.
Parent: Eaglets Limited
Officers: William Geoffrey Craig, Secretary; William Geoffrey Craig [1963] Director/Chartered Management Accountant; Diane Govaerts [1984] Director [Belgian]; Lee James Marshall [1969] Director; Alain Robert Ziegler [1956] Director [Swiss]

Ziji Productions Limited
Incorporated: 18 July 2000 *Employees:* 2
Net Worth: £9,331,060 *Total Assets:* £11,230,180
Registered Office: 5 Elstree Gate, Elstree Way, Borehamwood, Herts, WD6 1JD
Activities: Other service activities n.e.c.
Shareholders: Leila Ansari; Francis George Roddam
Officers: Samantha Hill, Secretary; Leila Ansari [1973] Director [German]; Francis George Roddam [1946] Director

Zing Leisure Limited
Incorporated: 9 July 2004 *Employees:* 425
Net Worth: £2,591,453 *Total Assets:* £7,592,303
Registered Office: 4 Redwing Court, Ashton Road, Romford, Essex, RM3 8QQ
Activities: Unlicenced restaurants and cafes
Major Shareholder: Django King Man Fung
Officers: Django King Man Fung, Secretary; Django King Man Fung [1961] Director & Secretary; Tony Sanderson [1968] Director/Accountant

Zionstone Limited
Incorporated: 16 November 1982 *Employees:* 10
Net Worth: £15,589,543 *Total Assets:* £42,309,000
Registered Office: Unit 7 Horizon Business Village, 1 Brooklands Road, Weybridge, Surrey, KT13 0TJ
Activities: Buying and selling of own real estate
Officers: Sandra Joanne Brownlie, Secretary; Lauren Atkins [1976] Director/Manager; Malcolm Paul Atkins [1952] Director

Zoom Gas Pipelines Limited
Incorporated: 11 April 2006 *Employees:* 74
Net Worth Deficit: £76,977,000 *Total Assets:* £376,759,008
Registered Office: First Floor, Bluebird House, Mole Business Park, Randalls Road, Leatherhead, Surrey, KT22 7BA
Activities: Activities of other holding companies n.e.c.
Parent: Zoom Infrastructure Limited
Officers: Thomas William Butler [1959] Director [Irish]; Anna Louise Dellis [1973] Director; Nicholas Horler [1959] Director/Chairman; Paul Miles [1971] Director/Chief Financial Officer; Kevin O'Connor [1976] Director/Chief Executive Officer; Sebastian Schwengber [1979] Director/Investment Professional [German]; Bernardo de SA Braamcamp Sobral Sottomayor [1973] Director [Portuguese]

Zoom Holding Limited
Incorporated: 11 April 2006 *Employees:* 74
Net Worth Deficit: £159,046,000 *Total Assets:* £375,684,992
Registered Office: First Floor, Bluebird House, Mole Business Park, Randalls Road, Leatherhead, Surrey, KT22 7BA
Activities: Activities of other holding companies n.e.c.
Parent: 3i MIA Holdings Limited
Officers: Thomas William Butler [1959] Director [Irish]; Anna Louise Dellis [1973] Director; Nicholas Horler [1959] Director/Chairman; Paul Miles [1971] Director/Chief Financial Officer; Kevin O'Connor [1976] Director/Chief Executive Officer; Sebastian Schwengber [1979] Director/Investment Professional [German]; Bernardo de SA Braamcamp Sobral Sottomayor [1973] Director [Portuguese]

Zoom Infrastructure Limited
Incorporated: 11 April 2006 *Employees:* 74
Net Worth Deficit: £175,252,000 *Total Assets:* £375,833,984
Registered Office: First Floor, Bluebird House, Mole Business Park, Leatherhead, Surrey, KT22 7BA
Activities: Activities of other holding companies n.e.c.
Parent: Zoom Holding Limited
Officers: Thomas William Butler [1959] Director [Irish]; Anna Louise Dellis [1973] Director; Nicholas Horler [1959] Director/Chairman; Paul Miles [1971] Director/Chief Financial Officer; Kevin O'Connor [1976] Director/Chief Executive Officer; Sebastian Schwengber [1979] Director/Investment Professional [German]; Bernardo de SA Braamcamp Sobral Sottomayor [1973] Director [Portuguese]

The Zoroastrian Trust Funds of Europe (Incorporated)
Incorporated: 1 December 1978 *Employees:* 4
Net Worth: £6,662,190 *Total Assets:* £6,673,256
Registered Office: Zoroastrian Centre, 440 Alexandra Avenue, Harrow, Middlesex, HA2 9TL
Activities: Other social work activities without accommodation n.e.c.
Officers: Kobad Savak Avari [1955] Director; Gav Dara Buhariwala [1955] Director; Javid Canteenwala [1970] Director/Chartered Accountant; Malcolm Minoo Deboo [1963] Director/Consultant Engineer; Behram Rustomji Kapadia [1944] Director/Senior Financial Consultant; Darius Jal Karkaria [1959] Director/IT Programme Manager; Parivash Kiani [1969] Director/Travel Consultant; Dorab Erach Mistry OBE [1953] Director/Chartered Accountant; Rohinton Firoze Munshi [1973] Director/Legal Advisor; Shazneen Yazdi Munshi [1987] Director/Legal Adviser; Shernaz Bomi Sadri JP [1959] Director; Jesmin Fahrookh Sorab [1955] Director/Travel Consultant

Zotefoams International Limited
Incorporated: 14 May 1992
Net Worth: £21,849,356 *Total Assets:* £21,849,356
Registered Office: 675 Mitcham Road, Croydon, Surrey, CR9 3AL
Activities: Non-trading company
Parent: Zotefoams PLC
Officers: Alex Charles Small, Secretary; Gary Christopher McGrath [1967] Director/Chartered Accountant; David Burns Stirling [1966] Director

Zotefoams PLC
Incorporated: 14 May 1992 *Employees:* 360
Net Worth: £59,090,000 *Total Assets:* £100,264,000
Registered Office: 675 Mitcham Road, Croydon, Surrey, CR9 3AL
Activities: Manufacture of other plastic products
Officers: Alex Charles Small, Secretary; Angela Claire Bromfield [1962] Director; Jonathan Douglas Carling [1965] Director; Stephen Paul Good [1961] Director; Gary Christopher McGrath [1967] Director/Chartered Accountant; Douglas Grant Robertson [1953] Director; David Burns Stirling [1966] Director/Accountant

This page is intentionally left blank

Standard Industrial Classification

01110 Growing of cereals (except rice), leguminous crops and oil seeds

Bhaggo Limited
A Russell (Farmers) Limited
South Darenth Farms and Cold Store Co

01130 Growing of vegetables and melons, roots and tubers

A.L.Tozer Limited

01160 Growing of fibre crops

Cargill Cotton Limited

01190 Growing of other non-perennial crops

Abbey View Produce Limited

01250 Growing of other tree and bush fruits and nuts

Thompson Bros. (Esher) Limited

01290 Growing of other perennial crops

Thompsons Nursery Limited

01410 Raising of dairy cattle

Watchingwell Farms Limited

01430 Raising of horses and other equines

Fishdance Limited

01470 Raising of poultry

Sun Valley Foods Limited

01500 Mixed farming

Oncoland Limited
Thenhurst Agricultural Limited

01629 Support activities for animal production (other than farm animal boarding)

EWOS Limited

01630 Post-harvest crop activities

Wealmoor Limited

02400 Support services to forestry

John Deere Forestry Limited
Gristwood and Toms Limited

03110 Marine fishing

North Atlantic (Holdings) Ltd
North Atlantic Fishing Co Ltd

03210 Marine aquaculture

Tropical Marine Centre (2012) Ltd
Tropical Marine Centre Limited

06100 Extraction of crude petroleum [31]

Amoco (Fiddich) Limited
BP Amoco Exploration (Faroes) Ltd
BP Exploration (Algeria) Ltd
BP Exploration (Alpha) Limited
BP Exploration (Angola) Ltd
BP Exploration (Azerbaijan) Ltd
BP Exploration (Caspian Sea) Ltd
BP Exploration (Delta) Limited
BP Exploration (Epsilon) Ltd
BP Exploration (Shah Deniz) Ltd
BP Exploration Beta Limited
BP Exploration Indonesia Ltd
BP Exploration Libya Limited
BP Exploration North Africa Ltd
BP Exploration Operating Co Ltd
BP Exploration Orinoco Limited
CNOOC Ettrick U.K. Limited
CNOOC Petroleum Europe Limited
CNOOC Petroleum Farragon U.K. Ltd
Esso Exploration and Production UK
Esso Petroleum Co Ltd
Esso UK Limited
ExxonMobil International Ltd
Impact Africa Limited
Impact Oil & Gas Limited
Navitas Petroleum Limited
Spirit Energy North Sea Ltd
Spirit Energy Production UK Ltd
Spirit Energy Resources Ltd
Spirit Resources (Armada) Ltd
State Oil Limited

06200 Extraction of natural gas

Impact Oil & Gas Limited
Navitas Petroleum Limited

07290 Mining of other non-ferrous metal ores

Euromax Resources (Macedonia) UK Ltd
Flintridge Resources Limited

08110 Quarrying of ornamental and building stone, limestone, gypsum, chalk and slate

Pinden Limited

08120 Operation of gravel and sand pits; mining of clays and kaolin

William Boyer & Sons, Limited
J Clubb Limited
J.& J.Franks Limited

08990 Other mining and quarrying n.e.c.

Ahern Land Reclamation Limited
Rambler Metals and Mining PLC
Spirit Europe Limited
Tara Mobile Ltd
Verde Agritech PLC

09100 Support activities for petroleum and natural gas mining [21]

BP (Abu Dhabi) Limited
BP Containment Response Ltd
BP Exploration China Limited
BP Exploration Company (Middle East)
BP Gas Marketing Limited
BP Kuwait Limited
BP Senegal Investments Limited
BP Shafag-Asiman Limited
Bowland Resources (No.2) Ltd
Bowland Resources Limited
Impact Oil & Gas Limited
Navigator Terminals Midco Ltd
Navigator Terminals North Tees Ltd
Offshore Containers Holdings Ltd
PGS Exploration (UK) Limited
Petroleum Geo-Services (UK) Ltd
Seismic Exploration (Canada) Ltd
Spirit Energy Southern North Sea Ltd
Subsea 7 Limited
Subsea 7 Offshore Resources (UK) Ltd
TGS Geophysical Company (UK) Ltd

10110 Processing and preserving of meat

Freshasia Foods Ltd
Pinnacle Foods Limited

10120 Processing and preserving of poultry meat

Penasul UK Limited

10130 Production of meat and poultry meat products

Freshasia Foods Ltd
Kerry Foods Limited
Oakfield (Foods) Limited
Sun Valley Foods Limited

10200 Processing and preserving of fish, crustaceans and molluscs

New England Seafood International

10390 Other processing and preserving of fruit and vegetables

Archer Daniels Midland Erith Ltd
Chelmer Foods Limited
Del Monte Europe Limited
Eda Quality Foods Limited
Noon Products Limited

10410 Manufacture of oils and fats

Archer Daniels Midland Erith Ltd
Pura Foods Limited

10420 Manufacture of margarine and similar edible fats

Dairy Crest Group PLC
Dairy Crest Limited
Pura Foods Limited

10511 Liquid milk and cream production

Dairy Crest France Holdings 2 Ltd
Dairy Crest Group PLC
Dairy Crest Limited
L.E. Pritchitt & Co Ltd

10512 Butter and cheese production
Dairy Crest Limited
Pizza Gogo Ltd

10519 Manufacture of other milk products
Dairy Crest Limited

10520 Manufacture of ice cream
L.E. Pritchitt & Co Ltd
Unilever UK Limited

10611 Grain milling
ADM Milling Limited
S & B Herba Foods Limited
Tilda Limited
G.R.Wright & Sons Limited

10612 Manufacture of breakfast cereals and cereals-based food
Honey Monster Foods Limited

10710 Manufacture of bread; manufacture of fresh pastry goods and cakes
Bonne Bouche Catering Limited
Coughlans Bakeries Limited
Gruma Europe Limited
Millers Bespoke Bakery Limited
Mission Foods UK Limited

10720 Manufacture of rusks and biscuits; manufacture of preserved pastry goods and cakes
United Biscuits (UK) Limited

10730 Manufacture of macaroni, noodles, couscous and similar farinaceous products
Ugo Foods Group Limited

10821 Manufacture of cocoa and chocolate confectionery
Cargill Chocolate UK Limited
Ferrero UK Limited
Ernest Jackson & Co. Limited
Mondelez UK Holdings & Services Ltd
Thorntons Limited

10822 Manufacture of sugar confectionery
Ernest Jackson & Co. Limited

10840 Manufacture of condiments and seasonings
MH Foods Limited
Unbar Rothon Limited

10890 Manufacture of other food products n.e.c. [11]
Adelie Foods Limited
Appetite Holdings Limited
Aunt Bessie's Limited
Benecol Limited
Birds Eye Limited
Gruma Europe Limited
Jain International Foods Ltd
MH Foods Limited
Marcantonio Foods Limited
Nomad Foods Europe Limited
Saya Enterprises Limited

10920 Manufacture of prepared pet foods
Tropical Marine Centre Limited

11010 Distilling, rectifying and blending of spirits
Beam Suntory UK Limited
Distell International Holdings Ltd

11020 Manufacture of wine from grape
Accolade Wines Limited
Cellarmaster Wines Holdings (UK) Ltd
FBL Holdings Limited
TWE Finance (UK) Limited
Treasury Wine Estates EMEA Ltd
Treasury Wine Estates UK Brands Ltd

11030 Manufacture of cider and other fruit wines
Distell International Holdings Ltd

11040 Manufacture of other non-distilled fermented beverages
Distell International Holdings Ltd

11070 Manufacture of soft drinks; production of mineral waters and other bottled waters
Coca-Cola European Partners GB Ltd
Coca-Cola European Partners PLC
Lucozade Ribena Suntory Ltd
Monster Energy Europe Limited
SmithKline Beecham Limited

12000 Manufacture of tobacco products
Gallaher Limited
Karelia Tobacco Company (UK) Ltd

13931 Manufacture of woven or tufted carpets and rugs
Latif International Limited

13950 Manufacture of non-wovens and articles made from non-wovens, except apparel
Saul D Harrison & Sons PLC

14132 Manufacture of other women's outerwear
Armondi UK Limited
Kara Designs Ltd

14190 Manufacture of other wearing apparel and accessories n.e.c.
Cover Up Clothing Limited

14310 Manufacture of knitted and crocheted hosiery
Covidien UK Limited

14390 Manufacture of other knitted and crocheted apparel
Barrie Knitwear Limited

16290 Manufacture of other products of wood; manufacture of articles of cork, straw and plaiting materials
Natural Woodfloor Co Ltd

17290 Manufacture of other articles of paper and paperboard n.e.c.
Swan Mill Paper Co Ltd

18129 Printing n.e.c.
Bible and Gospel Trust
Howard Hunt (City) Limited
LE Packaging Ltd
Leading Edge Labels Limited
Magnet Harlequin Limited
Odessa Print Group Ltd
Precision Printing Co. Limited
Zenoffice Limited

18140 Binding and related services
Bible and Gospel Trust

18201 Reproduction of sound recording
Mood Media Limited

19201 Mineral oil refining
BP Oil UK Limited
BP Turkey Refining Limited
ExxonMobil Marine Limited
Lubricants UK Limited

19209 Other treatment of petroleum products (excluding petrochemicals manufacture)
Moove Lubricants Limited

20110 Manufacture of industrial gases
Air Products (BR) Limited
Air Products PLC

20130 Manufacture of other inorganic basic chemicals
BP Aromatics Limited
BP Chemicals Limited
Industrial Chemicals Limited
Jablite Limited
Rhodia Limited

20140 Manufacture of other organic basic chemicals
Bimax Chemicals Limited
ExxonMobil Chemical Limited
Mallinckrodt Chemical Limited

20160 Manufacture of plastics in primary forms
Advanced Elastomer Systems Ltd
Reichhold UK Limited

20301 Manufacture of paints, varnishes and similar coatings, mastics and sealants
Fujichem Sonneborn Limited
Kromachem Limited
Neogene Limited
Trimite Limited

20411 Manufacture of soap and detergents

Industrial Chemicals Limited
Malibu Health Products Limited
Procter & Gamble Product Supply (U.K.)
Unilever UK Limited

20420 Manufacture of perfumes and toilet preparations

Combe International Limited
Firmenich UK Limited
Gillette U.K. Limited

20590 Manufacture of other chemical products n.e.c. [10]

Aeropak (Chemical Products) Ltd
Apatech Limited
Haltermann Carless UK Limited
ITW Limited
Industrial Chemicals Group Ltd
Industrial Chemicals Limited
Moove Lubricants Limited
Orthene Chemicals Limited
Orthene Holdings Limited
Solvay Solutions UK Limited

21100 Manufacture of basic pharmaceutical products [20]

A1 Pharmaceuticals Holdings Ltd
Bristol-Myers Squibb Pharmaceuticals
Chemidex Pharma Limited
Colorcon Limited
D.D.D. Limited
Diomed Developments Limited
Eco Animal Health Ltd.
Ennogen Healthcare Ltd
Essential Pharma Limited
Generics (U.K.) Limited
Ernest Jackson & Co. Limited
Laxmi BNS Holdings Limited
Macarthys Laboratories Limited
Merck Sharp & Dohme Limited
P.I.E. Pharma Limited
Pharmvit Limited
Piramal Critical Care Limited
Seven Seas Limited
Smith Kline & French Laboratories
SmithKline Beecham Limited

21200 Manufacture of pharmaceutical preparations

Accord Healthcare Limited
Brown & Burk UK Limited
Chemidex Pharma Limited
Combe International Limited
Dermal Laboratories Limited
Glaxo Operations UK Limited
GlaxoSmithKline Consumer Healthcare (UK) Trading
Masters Pharmaceuticals Ltd

22290 Manufacture of other plastic products

Crystal Clear Group Limited
John Guest Limited
ITW Limited
Pet Mate Limited
Plastico Limited
Polybags Limited
Precision Engineering Plastics Ltd
Toly Products (U.K.) Limited
Zotefoams PLC

23110 Manufacture of flat glass

Crystal Clear Group Limited

23120 Shaping and processing of flat glass

F A Firman (Harold Wood) Ltd
Super Toughened Glass Limited

23190 Manufacture and processing of other glass, including technical glassware

John Artis Limited
Lubkowski Saunders and Associates
Starna Scientific Limited

23490 Manufacture of other ceramic products n.e.c.

John Artis Limited

23510 Manufacture of cement

Imerys Aluminates Limited

23610 Manufacture of concrete products for construction purposes

Laing O'Rourke Manufacturing Ltd

23630 Manufacture of ready-mixed concrete

J Clubb Limited

23990 Manufacture of other non-metallic mineral products n.e.c.

Armstrong World Industries Ltd
Day Group Limited

24100 Manufacture of basic iron and steel and of ferro-alloys

Kubach & Sambrook (Metals) Ltd

24410 Precious metals production

Britannia Refined Metals Ltd
Derek Pobjoy Investments Ltd

24420 Aluminium production

Parkside Group (Holdings) Ltd
Parkside Group Limited

24430 Lead, zinc and tin production

Britannia Refined Metals Ltd

25110 Manufacture of metal structures and parts of structures

Hy-Ten Group Limited
Hy-Ten Limited
Killinchy Aerospace Holdings Ltd
Knight Precision Metals Ltd
Knight Strip Metals Limited
Lee-Warren Fabrication and Design
Martin-Baker Aircraft Co Ltd
Singer & James Limited
Tyco European Metal Framing Ltd

25400 Manufacture of weapons and ammunition

Boss & Co.Limited

25610 Treatment and coating of metals

Knight Precision Metals Ltd
Knight Strip Metals Limited

25620 Machining

Fundamental Engineering Ltd
Kenard Engineering Co Ltd
Supercraft Limited
Vitec Production Solutions Ltd
Wilman Marine Limited

25710 Manufacture of cutlery

John Artis Limited

25930 Manufacture of wire products, chain and springs

European Springs and Pressings Ltd

25940 Manufacture of fasteners and screw machine products

Forgefix Limited

25990 Manufacture of other fabricated metal products n.e.c. [13]

Armstrong Metal Ceilings Ltd
Ergonomic Solutions Limited
London Fluid System Technologies Ltd
Lymington Precision Engineering (LPE)
Lymington Precision Engineers Co.
M.A.C.-RK Precision Engineering Ltd
Pandrol (Vortok) Limited
Pandrol Limited
Paramount 26 Limited
Rimex Metals (U.K.) Limited
TCL Manufacturing Limited
Thompsons (UK) Limited
Trueform Engineering Limited

26110 Manufacture of electronic components

Analog Devices Limited
Centronic Limited
Fujikura Europe Limited
ITW Limited
Integrated Electronic Technologies
Teledyne Limited
Texcel Technology PLC
Volex PLC

26200 Manufacture of computers and peripheral equipment

A. & G. P. Trading Limited
Riso (U.K.) Limited

26301 Manufacture of telegraph and telephone apparatus and equipment

Gulmay Limited
Teledyne Limited

26309 Manufacture of communication equipment other than telegraph, and telephone apparatus and equipment

Digico Europe Limited
Eskan Electronics Limited

26400 Manufacture of consumer electronics

Eskan Electronics Limited
Integrated Electronic Technologies
Pure International Limited
Samsung Electronics (UK) Ltd
Sony Europe Limited

26511 Manufacture of electronic measuring, testing etc. equipment, not for industrial process control

Applied Laser Engineering Ltd
Centronic Limited
Linkam Scientific Instruments Ltd
National Instruments Corporation (UK)
Waters Limited

26512 Manufacture of electronic industrial process control equipment

Chromalox (UK) Limited

26701 Manufacture of optical precision instruments

Starna Scientific Limited

26702 Manufacture of photographic and cinematographic equipment

Sony Europe Limited

27110 Manufacture of electric motors, generators and transformers

Prestolite Electric Limited
SEM Limited

27120 Manufacture of electricity distribution and control apparatus

Automated Technology Group Ltd
Blakley Electrics Limited

27320 Manufacture of other electronic and electric wires and cables

P.S.V. Transport Systems Ltd

27400 Manufacture of electric lighting equipment

Designplan Lighting Limited
Simm Tronic Limited
Victory Lighting (UK) Limited
D.W. Windsor Limited

27510 Manufacture of electric domestic appliances

Beko PLC

27900 Manufacture of other electrical equipment [18]

Canon Europe Limited
Dewhurst PLC
Digico UK Limited
Electrosonic Limited
FT Technologies (UK) Ltd
Fujitsu General (U.K.) Co. Ltd
Gulmay Holdings Limited
Kelvin Hughes Limited
Kentec Electronics Limited
Kidde Safety Europe Limited
Orange Music Electronic Co Ltd
Pioneer DJ Europe Limited
Racal Acoustics Limited
Samsung Semiconductor Europe Ltd
TMD Technologies Limited
Toshiba Tec U.K. Imaging Systems Ltd
Volex PLC
Windcrest (U.K.) Limited

28131 Manufacture of pumps

Charles Austen Pumps Limited
Schwing Stetter (UK) Ltd

28140 Manufacture of taps and valves

Hale Hamilton (Valves) Limited
Universal Dispense Systems Ltd

28220 Manufacture of lifting and handling equipment

Schinvest Limited

28230 Manufacture of office machinery and equipment (except computers and peripheral equipment)

Ergonomic Solutions Limited
Neopost Technologies Limited

28250 Manufacture of non-domestic cooling and ventilation equipment

J & E Hall Limited
RVT Group Limited

28290 Manufacture of other general-purpose machinery n.e.c.

Harsco Rail Limited

28490 Manufacture of other machine tools

Atlanta Trust Limited
Coborn Engineering Co Ltd
Horn Cutting Tools Limited
Mapal Limited

28930 Manufacture of machinery for food, beverage and tobacco processing

Russell Finex Limited

28990 Manufacture of other special-purpose machinery n.e.c. [10]

Aerospace Tooling Limited
HAGS-SMP Limited
Ilapak Limited
Integrated Design Limited
Mollart Engineering Limited
Russell Finex Limited
Schindler Ltd.
Secomak Limited
Senior UK Limited
Silverson Machines Limited

29100 Manufacture of motor vehicles

Caterham Cars Group Limited
Caterham Cars Ltd.
Tesla Motors Limited

29201 Manufacture of bodies (coachwork) for motor vehicles (except caravans)

Fasttrax Limited

29310 Manufacture of electrical and electronic equipment for motor vehicles and their engines

Servotest Testing Systems Ltd

30920 Manufacture of bicycles and invalid carriages

Brompton Bicycle Limited

31020 Manufacture of kitchen furniture

Commodore Kitchens Limited

31090 Manufacture of other furniture

Burgess Furniture Ltd
Original Bedstead Co Limited

32120 Manufacture of jewellery and related articles

Watches International Limited

32300 Manufacture of sports goods

Cobra Industries Limited
Dunlop International Europe Ltd

32401 Manufacture of professional and arcade games and toys

Sega Amusements International Ltd

32409 Manufacture of other games and toys, n.e.c.

Flair Leisure Products PLC

32500 Manufacture of medical and dental instruments and supplies

Otto Bock Healthcare PLC
Gulmay Limited
Kimal PLC
Medtronic Limited
Rocket Medical PLC
S.L.E. Limited
Stanmore Implants Worldwide Ltd

32990 Other manufacturing n.e.c. [41]

Air Products (Chemicals) Teesside
Allen (Concrete) Limited
Attewell Limited
Babcock Wanson UK Limited
Biz Karts Limited
CSL (Dualcom) Limited
Clivnars Limited
Cremer (UK) Manufacturing Co. Ltd
Crystal Group Limited
Crystal Home Improvements Group Ltd
Crystal Home Improvements Holdings
Crystal Windows & Doors Ltd
D3O Holdings Ltd
Danly UK Limited
Daylighting Power Limited
ET Enterprises Limited
Express Toughening Ltd
Fibron BX Limited
Giesecke+Devrient Mobile Security GB Ltd
Gillette U.K. Limited
ITW Limited
KS SPV 3 Limited
KS SPV 4 Limited
Kone PLC
Malibu Health Products Limited
Mason Pearson Bros. Limited
Motivair Compressors Limited
Nicholls & Clarke Glass Ltd
Petrolvalves (G.B.) Limited
Royal British Legion Poppy Factory
SG Technologies Group Limited
SG Technologies Limited
Safetell Limited
Sharp Electronics (Europe) Ltd
T G Products Limited
Tech 21 UK Limited
Thorn Security Limited
Travel Blue Limited
Ultra Electronics Limited
Vitec Imaging Solutions UK Ltd
Wilman Universal Group Limited

33120 Repair of machinery

Aerzen Machines Limited
Arcus Solutions Limited
BEC (London) Limited
Coyle Equipment Services Ltd
Duplo International Limited
Schwing Stetter (UK) Ltd

33140 Repair of electrical equipment

BEC (London) Limited
Brownings Electric Co Ltd

33160 Repair and maintenance of aircraft and spacecraft

British Airways Avionic Engineering
British Airways Maintenance Cardiff
Lufthansa Technik Landing Gear Services UK

33170 Repair and maintenance of other transport equipment n.e.c.

Harsco Rail Limited
Keltbray Aspire Limited

33190 Repair of other equipment

Business Systems (U.K.) Ltd
Coyle Equipment Services Ltd
J & E Hall Limited
High Point Solutions Limited
Kelvin Hughes Limited
Safety-Kleen U.K. Limited

33200 Installation of industrial machinery and equipment

Beck & Pollitzer Engineering Ltd
Coyle Equipment Services Ltd
European Process Plant Limited
Heidelberg Graphic Equipment Ltd
Koenig & Bauer (UK) Limited
Safety-Kleen U.K. Limited
Somers Hills Limited
Vega Industries Limited
Wilman Universal Industries Ltd

35110 Production of electricity [35]

Air Products Renewable Energy Ltd
Amber Solar Parks (Holdings) Ltd
Amber Solar Parks Limited
Atlantica Yield PLC
B K S Energy Limited
BL Wind Limited
Barking Power Limited
Bradenstoke Solar Park Limited
Branden Solar Parks (Holdings) Ltd
Branden Solar Parks Limited
Burton Wold Wind Farm (Trading) Ltd
Churchtown Farm Solar Limited
Cummins Cogeneration Limited
Earlseat Wind Farm Ltd
East Langford Solar Limited
Garves Wind Limited
Glenchamber Wind Energy Ltd
Grange Renewable Energy Ltd
Hazel Renewables Limited
Kenwyn Solar Limited
MC Power Limited
MGT Teesside Limited
MK Windfarm Limited
Manor Farm Solar Limited
Roos Energy Limited
Speyside Renewable Energy Finance PLC
Stokes Marsh Solar Limited
Sunlight PV Ltd
Sunsave 12 (Derriton Fields) Ltd
Sunsave 25 (Wix Lodge Farm) Ltd
Symbio Energy Limited
Tallentire Energy Limited
Wear Point Wind Limited
Winscales Moor Windfarm Ltd
Wryde Croft Wind Farm Limited

35120 Transmission of electricity

Atlantica Yield PLC

35130 Distribution of electricity

ESP Electricity Limited

35140 Trade of electricity

Corona Energy Retail 4 Limited
Cummins ESB Nigeria Limited

35210 Manufacture of gas

Powergas Africa Limited

35220 Distribution of gaseous fuels through mains

Corona Energy Retail 4 Limited

35230 Trade of gas through mains

Corona Energy Retail 1 Limited

35300 Steam and air conditioning supply

Daikin Airconditioning UK Ltd
Healy's ACR Limited
Stulz U.K. Limited

37000 Sewerage

Hydro Cleansing Limited

38110 Collection of non-hazardous waste

Clover Environmental Solutions Ltd
Erith Haulage Co Ltd
Hydro Cleansing Limited
Pinden Limited
Safety-Kleen U.K. Limited
Thames Recycling Limited

38120 Collection of hazardous waste

Erith Haulage Co Ltd
Hydro Cleansing Limited
Safety-Kleen U.K. Limited

38210 Treatment and disposal of non-hazardous waste

BNS Company (Property Holdings) Ltd
Pinden Limited

38220 Treatment and disposal of hazardous waste

ATK Energy EU Services Limited
Erith Contractors Limited
Pinden Limited

38320 Recovery of sorted materials

F.J. Church & Sons Limited
Day Group Limited
FBM Metals (UK) Limited
McGrath Bros. (Waste Control) Ltd
Seneca Environmental Solutions Ltd

39000 Remediation activities and other waste management services

ACM Environmental PLC
Econometric Limited
Erith Contractors Limited
FJC Topco Limited
Hydro Cleansing Limited
P. Johnson & Son (1976) Ltd

41100 Development of building projects [364]

66 Queen Square Limited
A A Homes and Housing (Exchange Court)
AP Asset Management Limited
Ability Developments Limited
Ability Hotels (Luton Inn) Ltd
Abode Hallam Ltd
Acqua Plus Developments Ltd
Adelmill Limited
Aldis of Barking Limited
Alfreds Way Investments (No. 2) Ltd
Allois Properties (Leatherhead) Ltd
Ambika Investments Limited
Andgrove Property Investments Ltd
Anglia Secure Homes (South East) Ltd
Anita Impex Limited
Apollo Property Investment Ltd
Aquila Maldon Limited
Artillery Properties Limited
Asha (Camberley) Ltd
Asino Limited
Assetsky Limited
Thomas Aston Homes Limited
Astonpalm Limited
Avocado Developments Limited
Avocado Developments Wealdstone Ltd
Balcraft Properties Limited
Barnardo Developments Limited
Bath Road Properties Limited
Belgrave Land (Armley) Limited
Belgrave Land (Kilmarnock) Ltd
Belgrave Land (Management) Ltd
Belgrave Land (Perth) Limited
Bellecity Limited
Bellis Homes Limited
Berkeley Homes (Fleet) Limited
Berkeley Homes (Southall) Ltd
Berkeley Ryewood Limited
Betcrown Limited
Birmingham Schools Partnership Ltd
Blackwater Securities Limited
Blenheim Barnes Limited
Blessville Limited
Blitzfair Limited
Blue Prop Ltd
Boleyn Phoenix Limited
Bostall Estates Limited
Bourne Court Properties Ltd
Bridge Road Southall Limited
Brinor Investments Limited
Brookpass Limited
Brookstream Properties Limited
Buckmead Limited
Bugler Developments Limited
Bugler Group Limited
Buildvantage Limited
Buxton Building Contractors Ltd
CK Property Developments Ltd
CNM Estates (Tolworth Tower MB) Ltd
CNM Estates (Tolworth Tower MBP) Ltd
CNM Estates (Tolworth Tower SBP) Ltd
CNM Estates Holdings Limited
CS Property and Consultancy Ltd.
Calda Limited
Camden Development Co Ltd
Canterbury Homes Ltd
Careys New Homes Limited
Carlton House Developments Ltd
Carrain Limited
Castledene Investments Limited
Castlestone Investments Ltd
Cathedral Holdings Limited
Central Developments (UK) Ltd
Central Office and Commercial Properties
Centro Group Limited
Ceros (Bradford) Limited
Chantry Securities Limited
Charlie Properties Limited
Charterhouse Ilford Limited
Cherubond Limited
Chesside Homes Limited
Chiltern Court Properties Ltd
Cibi Investments Limited
Citigate Homes (UK) Ltd
City & Docklands (W3) Limited
City & Southern Limited
City & Westminster Developments Ltd
Clarence Estates (London) Ltd
Clearview Homes Limited
Collins 2017 Limited
Commercial Freeholds & Investments Ltd
Cooper Estates Limited
Corumbe Investments Limited
Country Rhythm Limited
Owen Coyle Managements Ltd
Craneshaw House Limited
Crest Nicholson (Henley-on-Thames)
Crest Nicholson Operations Ltd
Cricklewood Developments Ltd
Crickmore Developments Limited
Croudace Strategic Limited
Cuffe PLC
Cygnet Street Developments Ltd
DKH Investments Limited
Dakota Developments Limited
Dalco Developments Limited
Dalin Limited
De Vere Homes Limited
Decadent Properties Limited
Dee Gee Properties Limited
Delamere (Chelmsford) Limited
Delbanco Meyer & Co Ltd
Denecroft Estates Limited
Denland Limited
Dependable Homes Limited
Derby Healthcare PLC
Dimehome Limited
Dip Systems (UK) Limited
Dock and Let Limited
Doncaster School Solutions Ltd
Durkan Estates Limited
Durkan Holdings Limited
Durkan Limited
Elektron Tower 3 Limited
Elmbridge Village Limited
Explore Living Limited
Fairmile Homes One Limited
Fairmile Homes Three Limited
Fairview Enfield Limited
Fairview Homes Limited
Fairview New Homes (Charlton) Ltd
Fairview New Homes (Chase Road) Ltd
Fairview New Homes (Colindale) Ltd
Fairview New Homes (Developments)
Fairview New Homes (Properties) Ltd
Fairview New Homes (South East) Ltd
Fairview New Homes (Willow Way) Ltd
Fairview Ventures Limited
Falcon Investment Ltd
Fascroft Limited
Feabrex Limited
Fieldgrange Properties Limited
Fieldside Associates Limited
Filross Securities Limited
Fitzjohns Avenue Ltd
Freshplant Limited
Fulca Limited
GDL (Aylesbury) Limited
GDL (Luton) Developments Ltd
GDL (Millharbour) Limited
GDL (Romford) Limited
GDL (Slough Developments) Ltd
GHL (Crescent Lane) Limited
GHL (Kilmorie) Limited
GHL (Summerstown) Limited
Gade Property Developments Ltd
Galliard Construction Limited
Galliard Estates Limited
Galliard Homes Limited
Galliford Try Services Limited
Ganco Limited
J. Gardner Holdings Limited
Garfwish Limited
Garratt Services (Tooting) Ltd
Gateway Hotel Dunstable Ltd
Ghai & Co. Limited
Glansevern Properties Limited
Goldings Estates Limited
Goodwin Associates Limited
Gracechurch Sports Management Ltd
Grafton Flats Limited
Graham Land & Developments Ltd
Gravesend and District Real Estate Co
Grays Thurrock Properties Ltd
Greencourt Property Group Ltd
Grove Developments Limited
Grovepoint Properties Limited
Hamilcourt Industrial Holdings Ltd
Hawthorn Crow Limited
Higgins Construction PLC
Higgins Homes PLC
Hildo Limited
Hincroft Limited
Hollyhedge Limited
Hooper Homes West Well Limited
Hoopers Homes Limited
Howarth Homes (Farnham Close) Ltd
Howarth Homes PLC
J. B. Developments & Construction
J.C.S. Developments Ltd.
JEDS Investments Ltd
JSA Properties (UK) Limited
James Development Co Ltd
Jessica House Developments Ltd
K K Investment Ltd
KGN Developments Limited
Kent EHFA Projectco Limited
Kewbridge Trading Limited
W.D.King Limited
LSQ (Crimscott Street) Holdings Ltd
Lakedale Developments Limited
Lanend Limited
Lavender Property Investments Ltd
Lee Savell Properties Limited
Limesquare Business Parks Ltd
Thomas Lipton Ltd
Littlecroft Properties Limited
Lodestar Properties Limited
London Residential Healthcare Ltd
London Square (Crimscott Street) Ltd
London Square (Fulham) Limited
London Square (Holdings) Ltd
London Square (Putney) Limited
London Square (Streatham) Ltd
London Square Development Management

London Square Developments (Ventures)
London Square Developments Ltd
London Square Limited
Longford Securities & Equities (K & T)
Longford Securities & Equities Ltd
Lowen Homes Limited
Loxleigh Investments Limited
MY Construction & Carpentry Ltd
Henry Mansfield Limited
Marchent Limited
Marwin Securities Limited
Mayfair Housing & Commercial Investments
Maylands Green Limited
Meritcape Limited
Merton Acquisitions Limited
Metis Homes Limited
Minton Holdings Limited
Miriad Property Investments Ltd
Mizen Design/Build Ltd.
Modern Schools (Exeter) Ltd
Monks Way Development Limited
Mono Properties Limited
Monument Assets Limited
Moyvale Properties Limited
Musco (St Albans Place) Ltd
Nacropolis (Langley) Ltd
Neilcott Construction Limited
Netherhall Gardens Ltd
Nine Heathrow Ventures Limited
Northfield Avenue (Holdings) Ltd
Oakburn European Properties Ltd
Olivanna Ltd
Onkar International Limited
Opecprime Development Limited
Opecprime Properties Limited
Ouhla Properties Limited
PE (Mount Carmel) Limited
Palacath Limited
Palladio Estates Limited
Peppercorn Property Investments Ltd
Perpetuum Construction Limited
Peterborough (Progress Health) PLC
Photon Properties Limited
Pink Fortress Limited
Planetree Developments Limited
Plotplan Limited
Polaris Ventures Ltd
Promede Limited
Property Warehouse Limited
Propertycoe Limited
RDL1 Limited
RKPE Limited
RO Property Management Limited
RO Regional Properties Limited
Residential Land Limited
Residential Land Management 2 Ltd
Residential Land Management Ltd
Richmond Green Developments Ltd
Ridgeland Properties Limited
Riverdale Developments Limited
Riverstore Limited
Roamquest Limited
Leslie Rogers Investments Ltd
Roman Investments Limited
Roseberry Property Development Co Ltd
Rosebery House Developments Ltd
Roseland Parc Limited
Roseplot Properties Limited
Rubylake Investments Limited
Runnymede Homes Limited
SMC Investcorp Limited
SPD Moorgate Limited
SR Developers Limited
Salaft Properties Limited
Sancroft Properties Limited
Sandkot Limited
Saxonchart Limited
Scimitar House (Holdings) Ltd
Sheplord Limited
Sherrygreen Homes Ltd
Shetson Property Developments Ltd
Simat Properties Limited
Sinclair House Properties Ltd
Thomas Sinden Limited
Skanska Infrastructure Development UK
Skanska Project Developments Ltd
Skanska Residential Development UK
Skanska TAM Limited
Skillcrown Holdings Limited
Snowden Developments Limited
Soda Studios Limited
Soho Loop Limited
Southcrown Limited
Southfleet Investments Limited
St Cross Developments Limited
St Edwards Court (Romford) Ltd
St George Ealing Limited
St James Group Limited
St James Homes (Grosvenor Dock) Ltd
St Mark Homes PLC
Stanley Dock Properties Ltd
Starbones Limited
F.C. Stark Limited
Stirling Civil Engineering Ltd
Stonebourne Properties Limited
Summerhill Birmingham Limited
Sunray Estates Limited
Sutton Business Centre Limited
Swanbrae Limited
Swanvale Management Limited
TBG (1) 2009 Limited
TBG (3) 2009 Limited
TN (UK) Consultancy Ltd
Taylor Woodrow Construction
Telford Homes City North Ltd
Telford Homes PLC
Telida Limited
Thames Industrial Estate Ltd
Thorney Leys Developments Ltd
A.E. Thorogood Investments Ltd
A.E.Thorogood Limited
Togher Construction Limited
Townhold Limited
Trans-Britannia Properties Ltd
Transform Schools (Birmingham) Ltd
Transform Schools (Stoke) Ltd
Tricomm Housing (Portsmouth) Ltd
Triplehigh Limited
Tristmire Limited
Turnhold Properties Limited
P.C. Tustin & Co Ltd
UIDUK Ltd
UK 786 Limited
UK Real Estate Limited
Uavend Norris Castle Ltd
United Living (North) Limited
United Living (South) Limited
Upgrade Investments Limited
Urban Enhance Limited
Victorygame Limited
Vulcan Wharf Limited
Wandale Limited
Wates Developments Limited
Wenta Business Centres Limited
Westgate House Developments Ltd
Whitstable Homes Ltd
Wildview Limited
Willco Properties Ltd
Wood Farm (Stanmore) Limited
Wrest Park Limited

41201 Construction of commercial buildings [130]

AHL Holdings (Manchester) Ltd
Alder Hey (Special Purpose Vehicle)
Amey Highways Lighting (Manchester)
Austin (GB) Limited
Austin Company of (U.K.) Ltd
Aylesbury Vale Parkway Limited
BDL Group PLC
Barrowfen Properties Limited
Bishopswood Estates Limited
Blenheim House Construction Ltd
M.& R.Bowman Limited
Boxtrent Limited
Bynorth Limited
P.J. Carey (Contractors) Ltd
Cementation Skanska Limited
V.G.Clements (Contractors) Ltd
Collaborative Services Support NE
P. Colohan & Co. Limited
Crispin & Borst Limited
Crown House Technologies Ltd
Dalton Resources Limited
Defence Support (St Athan) Ltd
Designer M & E Services UK Ltd
J P Dunn Construction Limited
Gordon Durham & Co.Limited
Education Support (Enfield 2) Holdings
Education Support (Enfield 2) Ltd
Education Support (Newham) Holdings
Education Support (Newham) Ltd
Education Support (Swindon) Ltd
Explore Manufacturing Limited
Exterior Plas Limited
Flahive Brickwork Limited
Forth Health Holdings Limited
Forth Health Limited
GT NEPS (Holdings) Limited
GT NEPS Limited
Galliford Try Building Limited
Galliford Try Employment Ltd
Galliford Try HPS Limited
Galliford Try Homes Limited
Galliford Try PLC
Galliford Try Partnerships Ltd
Harrington (Properties) Ltd
Healthcare Support (Newcastle) Holdings
Healthcare Support (Newcastle) Ltd
Healthcare Support (North Staffs)
Henry Construction Projects Ltd
Hiretest Limited
Jean-Luc Developments Ltd
Kelly Rail U.K. Ltd
Kirkman and Jourdain Construction
LSQ (Crimscott Street) Holdings Ltd
Laing Construction Limited
John Laing Construction Ltd
John Laing International Ltd
Laing Limited
Laing O'Rourke Construction Ltd
Laing O'Rourke Holdings Ltd
Laing O'Rourke PLC.
Laing O'Rourke Services Ltd
Landmark Civil Engineering Ltd
Landmark Groundworks Limited

Leander Build Limited
Leander Construction Limited
Linden Limited
Linden Wates (Westbury) Ltd
London Square (Streatham) Ltd
London Wharf Limited
ME Construction Limited
Marbank Construction Limited
McGee Civil Engineering Ltd
McGee Group (Holdings) Limited
Mid Holding Co UK Limited
Midgard Ltd
Mizen Design/Build Ltd.
Modern Schools (Barnsley) Ltd
A.J. Morrisroe & Sons Limited
Morrisroe UK Ltd
Mulalley & Co. Limited
Nicon Developments Limited
North Star (2000) Limited
R.O'Rourke & Son Limited.
O'Rourke Civil & Structural Engineering
Octagon Developments Limited
Optivo Development Services Ltd
Pexhurst Services Limited
Prime Care Solutions (Kingston) Ltd
Quad Building Services (Southern)
Rainham Industrial Services Ltd
Randall Watts Construction Ltd
Randall Watts London Limited
Readie Construction Limited
J. Reddington Ltd
Regenter Bentilee District Centre
Regenter LCEP Limited
Renewable Energy Centre Ltd
Renewable Energy Systems Ltd
Rooff Ltd
SES (Engineering Services) Ltd
Sherrygreen Homes Ltd
Thomas Sinden Limited
Sirhowy Enterprise Way Limited
Skanska Cementation International
Skanska Construction (Regions) Ltd
Skanska Construction UK Ltd
Skanska UK PLC
Spence Refit Ltd
St Edward Homes Limited
T.C & D Construction Ltd.
Togher Construction Limited
Toureen Contractors Limited
Tower, One St George Wharf Ltd
Transform Schools (Birmingham) Ltd
Transform Schools (Stoke) Ltd
Trollope & Colls Limited
Try Homes Limited
United Living (South) Limited
Vinci Construction UK Limited
Vinstrata Builders (London) Ltd
VolkerFitzpatrick Limited
Volkerwessels UK Limited
Walsall Public Lighting Ltd
Wates Construction Limited
Waystone 32 Limited
Waystone Limited
Westfields Homes Limited
Whelan & Grant (Contractors) Ltd
Whiteoak Developments Limited
Yorkshire Transformations Ltd

41202 Construction of domestic buildings [90]

3 Torland Drive Ltd
78A SW48BH Limited
Abbey Developments Limited
A.S. Ashcroft Limited
Ashley Homes Limited
BH (City Forum) Limited
Belsize Garages Project Ltd
Bishopswood Estates Limited
Boxtrent Limited
Breyer Group PLC
Brookpass Limited
CALA 1 Limited
CALA Group (Holdings) Limited
P.J. Carey (Contractors) Ltd
Careys New Homes Limited
Clancy Developments Limited
Croudace Homes Group Limited
Croudace Homes Limited
Croudace Portland Limited
Denton Homes Limited
Devine Homes PLC
Evolution (Woking) Limited
Exterior Plas Limited
Fairview Estates (Housing) Ltd
Flahive Brickwork Limited
GH Land Developments Limited
Giggs Hill Green Homes Limited
Glansevern Properties Limited
Great Park Developments Ltd
Hart Homes Limited
Hill Partnerships Limited
Hive 1 Ltd
JFD Developments Ltd
Jaysam Contractors Limited
Jaysam Developments Borehamwood Ltd
Jaysam Developments Wembley Ltd
Kaybridge Construction (Barnet) Ltd
Kearns Premier Homes Ltd
Kearns Property Management & Development
L.W. (Developments) Limited
LSQ (Crimscott Street) Holdings Ltd
LSQ Holdco 3 Limited
Leander Build Limited
Leven Wharf Limited
Linden Wates (Kempshott) Ltd
Linden Wates (The Frythe) Ltd
Lint (Redington Road) Limited
London Square (Crimscott Street) Ltd
London Square (Fulham) Limited
London Square (Holdings) Ltd
London Square (Putney) Limited
London Square (Streatham) Ltd
London Square Development Management
London Square Developments (Holdings)
London Square Developments (Ventures)
London Square Developments Ltd
London Square Limited
London Wharf Limited
Lowen Homes Limited
Marbank Construction Limited
McGee Civil Engineering Ltd
McGee Group (Holdings) Limited
Midgard Ltd
Mizen Design/Build Ltd.
Mulalley & Co. Limited
NW3 Capital Ltd
W.R.Newland & Sons Limited
Nicon Developments Limited
North Star (2000) Limited
G.Purchase Construction Ltd
Randall Watts Construction Ltd
Randall Watts London Limited
J. Reddington Ltd
D.B. Rees (Builders) Limited
Remus Construction & Development Ltd
Rooff Ltd
Rushmon Limited
Sandhill Homes Limited
Searchfield (Oatlands Court) Ltd
Thomas Sinden Limited
Sliabh Construction Limited
Drew Smith Limited
St George Blackfriars Limited
St Mark Homes PLC
Starglade Parks Limited
T.C & D Construction Ltd.
T.S.G. Building Services PLC
Taylor Mac Limited
United Living (North) Limited
United Living (South) Limited

42110 Construction of roads and motorways [10]

Aylesbury Vale Parkway Limited
P.J. Carey (Contractors) Ltd
Connect Plus (M25) Limited
Countyroute (A130) PLC.
Countyroute Limited
Galamast Limited
O'Hara Bros. Surfacing Limited
UK Highways A55 Limited
Volkerrail Limited
Volkerservices Limited

42120 Construction of railways and underground railways

Pod-Trak Limited

42130 Construction of bridges and tunnels

Joseph Gallagher Limited

42210 Construction of utility projects for fluids

Ashby & Croft Limited
Flowstop Services Limited
Squire Energy Limited

42220 Construction of utility projects for electricity and telecommunications

P.J. Carey (Contractors) Ltd
Fourway Communication Limited
JSM Construction Limited
Volkerinfra Limited

42910 Construction of water projects

J.Browne Construction Co Ltd
Clancy Docwra Limited
Flowstop Services Limited

42990 Construction of other civil engineering projects n.e.c. [29]

Charteroak Estates Limited
Coniston Limited
Oliver Connell and Son Ltd
Deco Design and Build Co. Ltd
J Devine Civil Engineering Ltd
Durkin and Sons Limited
Etcetera Construction Services Ltd
Flowstop Services Limited
Granherne Limited
Houlihan & Co. (Excavations) Ltd
Keltbray Group (Holdings) Ltd
Killoughery Holdings Limited
Laing O'Rourke Infrastructure Ltd

Lowery Limited
Marron Civil Engineering Ltd
Neston Court Limited
O'Hara Bros. Surfacing Limited
Purelake New Homes Limited
Residential Land Limited
Sian Formwork Limited
Silvermead Properties Ltd
Taylor Woodrow Construction
Toureen Contractors Limited
Transform Schools (Birmingham) Ltd
Transform Schools (Stoke) Ltd
Vinci Construction UK Limited
Volkerstevin Group Limited
Volkerstevin Limited
Wood Group Kenny Limited

43110 Demolition [12]

Syd Bishop & Sons (Demolition) Ltd
Brown and Mason Limited
CIKU Construction Services Ltd
Cantillon Limited
Erith Contractors Limited
John F Hunt Limited
Keltbray Group (Holdings) Ltd
Keltbray Limited
McGee Civil Engineering Ltd
Rye Plant Hire Limited
T.E.Scudder Limited
Toureen Contractors Limited

43120 Site preparation

Aitch Demolition Co. Ltd
CIKU Construction Services Ltd
Erith Contractors Limited
J & J Transport Limited
McGee Civil Engineering Ltd
McGee Group (Holdings) Limited
Togher Construction Limited
Toureen Contractors Limited

43130 Test drilling and boring

BP Exploration Angola (Kwanza Benguela)
WJ Groundwater Limited

43210 Electrical installation [23]

AMD Environmental Limited
Artic Building Services Ltd
Boon Building Services Ltd
Carmel (UK) Limited
ESSCI Ireland Limited
ESSCI Limited
ESSCI Technical Services Ltd
Emcor Group (UK) PLC
Essex Services Group Limited
Healy Refrigeration & Air Conditioning Services
Imtech Engineering Services London and South
Kirkman and Jourdain Construction
Lorne Stewart PLC
Metropolitan Electrical Services Ltd
OCO Limited
Openview Security Solutions Ltd
G.Purchase Construction Ltd
Rainham Industrial Services Ltd
SI Electrical Limited
Skanska Rashleigh Weatherfoil Ltd
Smith and Byford Limited
T.C & D Construction Ltd.
Walsall Public Lighting Ltd

43220 Plumbing, heat and air-conditioning installation [28]

AMD Environmental Limited
Artic Building Services Ltd
Aston Heating Limited
BSW Heating Ltd
Boon Building Services Ltd
T Brown Group Limited
ESSCI Ireland Limited
ESSCI Limited
ESSCI Technical Services Ltd
Emcor Group (UK) PLC
H & V Serviceplan Limited
Robert Heath Heating Limited
Imtech Engineering Services London and South
Kirkman and Jourdain Construction
Lorne Stewart PLC
Mala Engineering Limited
Metro Mechanical Services Ltd
OCO Limited
Oakray Limited
P & R Installation Co Ltd
G.Purchase Construction Ltd
A & J Ryan Mechanical Services Ltd
Sale Service and Maintenance Ltd.
Smith and Byford Limited
Stulz U.K. Limited
T.S.G. Building Services PLC
R.G. Taylor Engineering Ltd
Woodford Heating & Energy Ltd

43290 Other construction installation [18]

Architectural Decorators Ltd
Boon Building Services Ltd
Breyer Group PLC
Cellecta Limited
Celtic Contractors Limited
Corley + Woolley Limited
Falco Construction Limited
Fire Design Solutions Limited
GPF Lewis PLC
Kelly Communications Limited
Liftec Lifts Limited
G.Purchase Construction Ltd
Pyramid Builders Limited
R K Property Investments Ltd.
Rainham Industrial Services Ltd
Saipem Limited
Shellen Construction Limited
Spence Refit Ltd

43310 Plastering

Stanmore Contractors Limited
Sudbury Plastering Services Ltd

43320 Joinery installation

Architectural Decorators Ltd
Beck Interiors Limited
Cie PLC
Jaysam Contractors Limited
J.A. Stott (Carpentry) Ltd
J.J. Sweeney Limited

43330 Floor and wall covering

DMC Contracts Limited

43341 Painting

Architectural Decorators Ltd

43342 Glazing

Everest Limited
Everglade Holdings Limited
Everglade Windows Limited
M.Price Limited

43390 Other building completion and finishing [17]

Architectural Decorators Ltd
Bryen & Langley Limited
Celtic Contractors Limited
Copley Limited
Exterior Plas Limited
Gypcraft Drylining Contractors Ltd
Harringtons Builders PLC
Hayre Builders Co Ltd
Johalian Property Limited
Mark Luck Limited
MJF Business Services Limited
Mega Fabrications Group Ltd
Richmond Green Developments Ltd
Roalco Limited
Spence Refit Ltd
Togher Construction Limited
Transform Schools (North Lanarkshire)

43910 Roofing activities

Breyer Group PLC
Manelia Limited
Richardson Roofing Co Ltd
Swift Roofing Contracts Ltd

43991 Scaffold erection

Aerial Scaffolding Limited
Alandale Plant & Scaffolding Ltd
Lyndon Scaffolding PLC
Millcroft Services P.L.C.
Q.F.S. Scaffolding Limited
Tone Scaffolding Services Ltd

43999 Other specialised construction activities n.e.c. [87]

AMD Environmental Limited
Advanced Access Platforms Ltd
Alandale Holdings Limited
Alandale Logistics Limited
Aldis of Barking Limited
Ansa UK Limited
Ansa Utilities Limited
Apex Lift & Escalator Engineers Ltd
Area Sq. Limited
B & T Plant Hire Limited
BML Utility Contractors Ltd
Beck Interiors Limited
Beck MBI Limited
Boost Homes Ltd
Breyer Group PLC
Brisko Scaffolding Limited
Bronzeshield Lifting Limited
J.Browne Construction Co Ltd
Celtic Contractors Limited
City Lifting Limited
J. Coffey Construction Ltd
Collins Construction Ltd
Concept Developments (Cobham) Ltd
Corley + Woolley Limited
Denver Building Services Ltd
Easymix Concrete UK Ltd
Erith Plant Services Limited
P. Flannery Plant Hire (Oval) Ltd
Foundation Developments Ltd

Galldris Construction Limited
Grupotec Renewables Limited
Guideline Lift Services Ltd
H & S Contractors (Kent) Ltd
H & S Contractors Limited
Hayre Builders Co Ltd
Healy Refrigeration & Air Conditioning Services
John F Hunt Group Ltd
John F. Hunt Plant Hire Ltd
Imperial Ductwork Services Ltd
Instalcom Limited
Kellogg Brown & Root (U.K.) Ltd
Kellogg Brown & Root Overseas Ltd
Kelly Communications Group Ltd
Kelly Communications Limited
Kelly Fleet Services Limited
Kelly Rail Group Ltd
George Killoughery Limited
LDD Construction Limited
Levolux Limited
Lorclon Limited
McGrath Bros. (Waste Control) Ltd
Millcroft Services P.L.C.
Munnelly Support Services Ltd
O'Halloran & O'Brien Limited
Pink Fortress Limited
Reach Active Group Limited
Roadhouse Building & Civil Engineering
Robore Cuts Limited
Rock & Alluvium Limited
Rye Plant Hire Limited
SES (Engineering Services) Ltd
Safestand Limited
Select Plant Hire Co Ltd
Sian Formwork Limited
Sims Milling Services Limited
Skanska Major Projects Limited
Skyline Arcomet Limited
Specialist Plant Associates Ltd
Spence Refit Ltd
Barry Stewart & Sons Limited
Subsea 7 International Contracting
Subsea 7 West Africa Contracting Ltd
TRAD Hire & Sales Limited
TRAD Safety Systems Limited
TRAD Scaffolding Co.Limited
Thames Reinforcements Limited
Tone Scaffolding Services Ltd
Toureen Plant Limited
Vinci Environment UK Limited
Volkerhighways Limited
Volkerinfra Limited
Volkerlaser Ltd
Volkerrail Specialist Businesses Ltd
WJ Groundwater Limited
WPA Support Services Limited
Wadlow Energy Limited
Wood Group Industrial Services Ltd

45111 Sale of new cars and light motor vehicles [31]

Altomart Limited
Aprite (GB) Limited
Burwater Holdings Limited
Citygate Automotive Limited
Currie Motors UK Limited
Drift Bridge Garage Limited
Essex Motor Co Ltd
GVE London Ltd
Geyfords Limited
H.W.M. Limited
Hill's Garages (Woodford) Ltd
Stephen James (Automotive) Ltd
Kia Motors (UK) Limited
W.J.King (Garages) Limited
Marsh Wall Limited
Masters of Beckenham Limited
Mazda Motors UK Limited
Milcars (Radlett) Limited
Nissan Motor (GB) Limited
R.T.Rate Limited
Renault U.K. Limited
Tara Mobile Ltd
Telbridge Motor Co Ltd
Tesla Motors Limited
Toyota (G.B.) PLC
Trident Garages Limited
Vanwise Group Limited
Venson Automotive Solutions Ltd
WLMG Limited
T.W. White & Sons Limited
Wilsons Automobiles and Coachworks

45112 Sale of used cars and light motor vehicles [19]

Aprite (GB) Limited
Citygate Automotive Limited
Currie Motors UK Limited
Drift Bridge Garage Limited
Geyfords Limited
Hill's Garages (Woodford) Ltd
Michael James Autos PLC
Marsh Wall Limited
Milcars (Radlett) Limited
R.T.Rate Limited
Romans International Limited
Shelly Motors Limited
T.S.L. Finance Limited
Trade Sale (Slough) Limited
Trade Sale Ltd
Trident Garages Limited
WVC Vehicle Solutions Limited
T.W. White & Sons Limited
Wilsons Automobiles and Coachworks

45190 Sale of other motor vehicles

Fuller Leisure Limited
Geyfords Limited
Harris Commercial Repairs Ltd
Harris Commercial Sales Ltd

45200 Maintenance and repair of motor vehicles [22]

Acorn Truck Sales Limited
Aprite (GB) Limited
Citygate Automotive Limited
Currie Motors UK Limited
Fasttrax Limited
Geyfords Limited
Harry Motors Ltd
Hill's Garages (Woodford) Ltd
Lantern Recovery Specialists PLC
Marsh Wall Limited
Motor Parts Direct Limited
Petrocell Holdings Limited
Purfleet Commercials Limited
Sovereign Recovery (UK) Ltd
Tesla Motors Limited
Trident Garages Limited
UK Assistance Accident Repair Centres
Universal Tyre Company (Deptford)
Venson Automotive Solutions Ltd
WLMG Limited
Watling Tyre Service Limited
T.W. White & Sons Limited

45310 Wholesale trade of motor vehicle parts and accessories [14]

Acorn Truck Sales Limited
Aprite (GB) Limited
Bharat Forge International Ltd
Brigade Electronics Group PLC
Calbrook Cars Limited
Continental Tyre Group Ltd.
Mazda Motors UK Limited
Moss Europe Limited
P.S.V. Transport Systems Ltd
Tesla Motors Limited
Tomo Motor Parts Limited
WLMG Limited
T.W. White & Sons Limited
Wurth UK Limited

45320 Retail trade of motor vehicle parts and accessories [12]

Citygate Automotive Limited
Currie Motors UK Limited
Harris Commercial Repairs Ltd
Marsh Wall Limited
Milcars (Radlett) Limited
Moss Europe Limited
Motor Parts Direct Limited
Purfleet Commercials Limited
Southern Motor Group Limited
Tomo Motor Parts Limited
Universal Tyre Company (Deptford)
Watling Tyre Service Limited

45400 Sale, maintenance and repair of motorcycles and related parts and accessories

Bike Alert PLC

46110 Agents selling agricultural raw materials, livestock, textile raw materials and semi-finished goods

Agrofertrans Ltd.
K2 Trading Limited
A.L.Tozer Limited

46120 Agents involved in the sale of fuels, ores, metals and industrial chemicals

Mobil Trading and Supply Ltd
Newport Industries Limited
Optima Chemical Ltd

46130 Agents involved in the sale of timber and building materials [11]

Anchor Bay Construction Products Ltd
CED Limited
E. T. Clay Products Limited
Davroc Limited
Harris & Bailey Limited
McGrath Bros. (Waste Control) Ltd
Olivewood Limited
Plaut International Limited
Raven Roofing and Building Supplies
Stora Enso Timber UK Limited
Todd Doors Limited

46140 Agents involved in the sale of machinery, industrial equipment, ships and aircraft

All Metal Services Limited
Citizen Machinery UK Ltd
Communications & Power Industries Europe
Gentec Energy PLC
Hawkspare Limited
NCMT Limited
OGE Drilling & Investment Ltd
Verico Europe Holding Limited

46150 Agents involved in the sale of furniture, household goods, hardware and ironmongery

Cort Business Services UK Ltd
Sabichi Homewares Limited

46160 Agents involved in the sale of textiles, clothing, fur, footwear and leather goods

Zeco Limited

46170 Agents involved in the sale of food, beverages and tobacco

All World Foods Limited
Cellarmaster Wines Holdings (UK) Ltd
General Mills UK Limited
A C Georgiades Ltd
Interlink Direct Limited
Sun Mark Limited

46180 Agents specialised in the sale of other particular products

Aprirose Trading Limited
CP Kelco UK Limited
Delta Membrane Systems Limited
John Guest Speedfit Limited
Northwood Paper Sales Limited
Sara (London) Limited
TES Enterprise Solutions Ltd
Vega Industries Limited
WMF United Kingdom Limited

46190 Agents involved in the sale of a variety of goods

Agility Project Logistics Ltd
Apex Medical Respiratory Ltd
Engineering, Logistics and Trading International UK
Farsound Aviation Limited
SAI Commodities Limited
Sheargold Limited
TJX Europe Buying (Deutschland) Ltd

46210 Wholesale of grain, unmanufactured tobacco, seeds and animal feeds

ADM Arkady Limited
Archer Daniels Midland (UK) Ltd

46220 Wholesale of flowers and plants

J. Van Vliet London Cash & Carry

46310 Wholesale of fruit and vegetables [19]

A.G. Thames Holdings Limited
Best Foods Limited
Chingford Fruit Limited
Compagnie Fruitiere UK Limited
Del Monte (UK) Limited
Del Monte Foods International Ltd
Fortuna Frutos (UK) Limited
Grapes Direct Limited
Pan United Ltd
Premier Fruit & Nut Limited
Reynolds Catering Supplies Ltd
A Russell (Farmers) Limited
Soloberry Limited
Stubbins Marketing Limited
Sunnyfield Veg Limited
Unifruit Limited
Unique Seafood Limited
Vidafresh Limited
Watts Farms (Sales) Limited

46320 Wholesale of meat and meat products [18]

Anzco Foods UK Limited
Best Foods Limited
Cherryfield (Croydon) Limited
Cherryfield Holdings Limited
Cook's Delights Limited
Eda Quality Foods Limited
GPS Food Group (UK) Limited
W W Giles (Smithfield) Ltd
Interlink Direct Limited
JBS Global (UK) Limited
Mostell Limited
Oakwood Finance London Limited
H. Smith Food Group PLC
Tazaki Foods Limited
Towers & Co.,Limited
Towers Thompson Holdings Ltd
Vestey Foods International Ltd
Vestey Foods UK Limited

46330 Wholesale of dairy products, eggs and edible oils and fats

ADM Trading (UK) Limited
All World Foods Limited
Eda Quality Foods Limited
Foodspeed Limited

46341 Wholesale of fruit and vegetable juices, mineral water and soft drinks

Eda Quality Foods Limited

46342 Wholesale of wine, beer, spirits and other alcoholic beverages [23]

Dhamecha Foods Limited
Distell International Holdings Ltd
Ellis of Richmond (Holdings) Ltd
Ellis of Richmond Limited
Eurochoice Limited
John E.Fells & Sons Limited
William Grant & Sons Brands Ltd
Hi - Line Wines Limited
Hi-Spirits Ltd
Hills Prospect PLC
Lay & Wheeler Limited
Maison Maurice Limited
Majestic Wine PLC
Majestic Wine Warehouses Ltd
Mangrove Global Limited
Millennium Cash & Carry Ltd
Naked Fine Wine Bonds PLC
Naked Wines Prepayments Trustee Co Ltd
Offie Limited
Quality Spirits International Ltd
Sazerac UK Limited
Spar (UK) Limited
Wise Trading Limited

46350 Wholesale of tobacco products

British American Tobacco UK Ltd

46360 Wholesale of sugar and chocolate and sugar confectionery

ADM Trading (UK) Limited
Bazooka Candy Brands International
Cargill Weybridge Limited
Empire Bespoke Foods Limited
Lindt & Sprungli (U.K.) Ltd

46370 Wholesale of coffee, tea, cocoa and spices

Cargill Weybridge Limited
Complete Coffee Limited
Equatorial Traders Limited
Food Brands Group Limited
Miko Coffee Limited
Mokarabia Limited

46380 Wholesale of other food, including fish, crustaceans and molluscs

Cook's Delights Limited
Empire Bespoke Foods Limited
Interlink Direct Limited
True World Foods (UK) Ltd
Unicorn Ingredients Ltd
Unique Atlantic Seafood Ltd
Windmill Organics Limited

46390 Non-specialised wholesale of food, beverages and tobacco [23]

ADM Trading (UK) Limited
Velji Bhovan & Sons (Trading) Ltd
T.Choithram & Sons (London) Ltd
Delice de France Limited
Dhamecha Foods Limited
Donatantonio Limited
Gima (UK) Limited
Golden Meadows Limited
Heley International Limited
Hi - Line Wines Limited
JJ Food Service Limited
Korea Foods Co Ltd
Lituanica UK Ltd
Nasco (UK) Ltd
Nature's Finest Food Products Ltd
Residual and Brand Management Ltd
Tata Global Beverages GB Ltd
John A.Taylor & Sons Limited
Tazaki Foods Limited
Tchibo Coffee International Ltd
Tees Limited
World Wise Foods Limited
Yoplait UK Limited

46410 Wholesale of textiles

Excelsior Textiles Limited
Globaltex Limited
Parry Murray & Co Ltd
Premier Quilting Co Ltd
Ranks Enterprises Limited
Zian Hi-Tech (U.K.) Limited

46420 Wholesale of clothing and footwear [10]

By Malene Birger UK Ltd.
Chi-Chi Collection Limited
Cover Up Clothing Limited
Dennys Uniforms Limited
Direct Boot and Shoe Supplies Ltd
E. Feldman Limited
Gaat International Ltd
Ralph Lauren UK Limited
Mini Club UK Limited
Popsoda Limited

46431 Wholesale of audio tapes, records, CDs and video tapes and the equipment on which these are played

Pioneer DJ Europe Limited
Polar Audio Limited
Sony Europe Limited

46439 Wholesale of radio, television goods & electrical household appliances (other than records, tapes, CDs)

Alba Broadcasting Corporation Ltd
D & M Audiovisual Ltd
Mashco Limited
Medlock Electrical Distributors Ltd

46440 Wholesale of china and glassware and cleaning materials

John Artis Limited
CBee (Europe) Limited
Donovan Bros. Limited
E.F.G. Housewares Limited
Lesser & Pavey Ltd.
Neville UK Trading Holdings Ltd

46450 Wholesale of perfume and cosmetics [18]

Almirall Limited
Beauty Wholesale Limited
Bluestar Enterprise Limited
Brand Agency (London) Limited
CBee (Europe) Limited
Dermalogica (UK) Limited
Direct Supplies (2014) Limited
Kenneth Green Associates Ltd
Imperial Pharmaceuticals Ltd
KMI Brands Limited
Karium Ltd
Mashco Limited
Original Additions (Beauty Products)
Pharmacare (Europe) Limited
S A Designer Parfums Limited
Shaneel Enterprises Limited
Trading Scents (2014) Limited
Trading Scents Group Limited

46460 Wholesale of pharmaceutical goods [65]

A1 Pharmaceuticals Holdings Ltd
A1 Pharmaceuticals PLC
Accord Healthcare Limited
Alium Medical Limited
Alliance Healthcare (Distribution)
Almirall Limited
Astellas Pharma Europe Ltd.
Astellas Pharma Ltd.
BR Pharma International Ltd
Celgene Limited
Chemidex Generics Limited
Chemilines Group Holdings Ltd
Chemilines Limited
G. D. Cooper & Co Ltd
Dallas Burston Ashbourne Holdings
Davis and Dann Limited
Durbin PLC
Eco Animal Health Group PLC
Ennogen Healthcare Ltd
Essential Pharma Limited
Ethypharm UK Limited
Ferring Pharmaceuticals Ltd
Galderma (U.K.) Limited
Garusa Solutions U.K. Limited
Genesis Pharmaceuticals Ltd
Glaxo Wellcome UK Limited
GlaxoSmithKline Caribbean Ltd
GlaxoSmithKline Consumer Trading Services
GlaxoSmithKline Export Limited
GlaxoSmithKline UK Limited
Glenmark Pharmaceuticals Europe Ltd
Gowrie Laxmico Limited
Grunenthal Limited
Interport Limited
Kanta Enterprises Limited
Laxmi BNS Holdings Limited
Laxmico Limited
Manichem Limited
Masters Pharmaceuticals Ltd
Medreich PLC
Merck Serono Limited
Merz Pharma UK Limited
Miller & Miller (Chemicals) Ltd
Milpharm Limited
Mylan UK Healthcare Limited
NSL (Holdings) Limited
NSL Group Limited
Necessity Supplies Limited
NeilMed Holding Co Ltd
Neilmed Limited
Norgine Pharmaceuticals Ltd
OTC Direct Limited
P.I.E. Pharma Limited
Pharmaceuticals Direct Limited
Pharmasure Limited
Piramal Critical Care Limited
Ranbaxy (U.K.) Limited
Restate Management Ltd
S & D Pharma Limited
Servipharm Limited
Strides Pharma Global (UK) Ltd
Veriton Pharma Limited
ViiV Healthcare Overseas Ltd
ViiV Healthcare Trading Services UK
ViiV Healthcare UK Limited

46470 Wholesale of furniture, carpets and lighting equipment

Furlong Flooring (Southern) Ltd.
Mayfair Carpet Gallery Limited
Medlock Electrical Distributors Ltd
Parry Murray & Co Ltd
STS Flooring Distributors Ltd
Valley Wholesale Carpets Ltd

46480 Wholesale of watches and jewellery

Condor Group Limited
Eran Diamonds (UK) Limited
Siddharth Jewellery (U.K.) Ltd
TX Group Europe Ltd.

46499 Wholesale of household goods (other than musical instruments) n.e.c [22]

ARRI (GB) Limited
Aandatta Limited
F & J Arpino Limited
Bandai UK Limited
Bic U.K. Limited
CBee (Europe) Limited
Countrywide Electrical Distributors
Ecover (UK) Limited
Elia International Limited
Epoch-Making Toys Limited
S. Franses Limited
C.P. Hart & Sons Limited
Himalaya Carpets Limited
R. Maskell Limited
Method Products Limited
Nikon UK Limited
Original Bedstead Co Limited
Poliform UK Limited
Popat Stores Limited
Premier Decorations Limited
Residual and Brand Management Ltd
Sifcon International PLC

46510 Wholesale of computers, computer peripheral equipment and software [19]

Acer U.K. Limited
Broadberry Data Systems Ltd
Bromcom Computers PLC
Creative Distribution Limited
E92 Plus Limited
Frontline Technology Limited
High Point Solutions Limited
NEC (UK) Ltd.
NetApp UK Ltd
Northamber PLC
Oki Europe Limited
PFU (EMEA) Limited
Phoenix Software Limited
QBS Software Limited
SK Hynix UK Limited
Sony Europe Limited
TES-AMM UK Ltd
Toshiba Information Systems (UK) Ltd
Xerox Products UK Limited

46520 Wholesale of electronic and telecommunications equipment and parts [21]

Bosch Service Solutions Ltd
Click Entertainment Limited
Future Electronics Limited
Hanwha Techwin Europe Limited
High Point Solutions Limited
LG Electronics U.K. Ltd
Moss Electrical Co. Limited
NDK Europe Limited
NEC (UK) Ltd.
NEC Europe Ltd
New Way International Ltd
One for All (UK) Ltd.
Pioneer DJ Europe Limited
Sahara Holdings Limited
Samsung Electronics (UK) Ltd
Sartorius Stedim UK Limited
Sharp Electronics (Europe) Ltd
Shure UK Limited
Sumitomo Electric Europe Ltd
Toshiba Information Systems (UK) Ltd
Zandera Ltd

46610 Wholesale of agricultural machinery, equipment and supplies

Agri-Chemicals Limited
KM Products Europe Limited
Sunlight PV Ltd

46620 Wholesale of machine tools

Geo. Kingsbury Machine Tools Ltd
Mapal Limited

46630 Wholesale of mining, construction and civil engineering machinery

KM Products Europe Limited

46650 Wholesale of office furniture

Spicers Limited

46660 Wholesale of other office machinery and equipment

QBS Software Limited
Spicers Limited
Xerox (UK) Limited
Xerox Limited

46690 Wholesale of other machinery and equipment [13]

A T & T (GB) Limited
Aerzen Machines Limited
Brymec Ltd
Duplo International Limited
J & E Hall Limited
Medlock Electrical Distributors Ltd
Mitsubishi Heavy Industries Air-Conditioning Europe,
Sahara Presentation Systems PLC
Sartorius Stedim UK Limited
Tanita International Ltd.
Tchibo Coffee International Ltd
Trend Machinery & Cutting Tools Ltd
Xerox Products UK Limited

46711 Wholesale of petroleum and petroleum products

Harvest Energy Limited
Prax Petroleum Limited

46719 Wholesale of other fuels and related products [14]

Agri-Chemicals Limited
Air BP Limited
BNK (UK) Limited
BP Eastern Mediterranean Ltd
BP Exploration Company (Middle East)
BP International Limited
BP Marine Limited
BP Middle East Limited
BP Oil International Limited
BP Oil Vietnam Limited
BP+Amoco International Limited
Corona Gas Management Limited
ExxonMobil Gas Marketing Europe Ltd
Fuel Oils (Holdings) Limited

46720 Wholesale of metals and metal ores

Ardour World Limited
Associated Lead Mills Ltd.
EID Limited
Euro Alloys Limited
S.J.M. Alloys & Metals Limited
Super Industries DMCC Metals Ltd
T G Commodities Limited

46730 Wholesale of wood, construction materials and sanitary equipment [17]

Alsford Timber Limited
Brausch & Co (UK) Limited
Cembrit Limited
A.W.Champion Limited
A.W. Champion Timber Limited
Compass Forest Products Ltd
Day Group Limited
Falcon Panel Products Limited
Gilray Plant Limited
KFM Holdings Limited
Robert Lee Distribution Ltd
MBM Forest Products Limited
Metra Non-Ferrous Metals Ltd
N & C Building Products Ltd
Porcelanosa (South East) Ltd
Vink UK Limited
Wurth UK Limited

46740 Wholesale of hardware, plumbing and heating equipment and supplies [11]

A P P Wholesale PLC
Bathroom Brands Holdings UK Ltd
Crosswater Limited
M.E. Duffell Limited
Grohe Limited
Hansgrohe Limited
Robert Lee Distribution Ltd
S.T.C.Plumbing & Heating Merchants
Saniflo Limited
Uponor Limited
Wurth UK Limited

46750 Wholesale of chemical products

Aprirose Trading Limited
Attwell Business Inc. Limited
Gantrade Europe Limited
IMCD UK Limited
Noahs Ark Chemicals Limited
Orthene Holdings Limited

46760 Wholesale of other intermediate products [16]

Advanced Logistics for Aerospace (UK)
Batt Cables PLC
Cargill PLC
Gould International UK Limited
Gould Paper Sales UK Limited
Gould Publication Papers UK Ltd
Jain (Europe) Limited
Metsa Tissue Limited
Neville UK PLC
ProAV Holdings Limited
ProAV Limited
Ripmax Limited
STS Flooring Distributors Ltd
Scan Corporation Limited
Volante Limited
WWW Sunoptic Com UK Limited

46770 Wholesale of waste and scrap

Aprirose Trading Limited
Benfleet Scrap Co Limited
Robert Gibbs (Contracting) Co Ltd
Global Metcorp Limited
Multi Trade Links (UK) Ltd

46900 Non-specialised wholesale trade [72]

Anglo-Dal Limited
Ballward Limited
Balton CP Limited
Bamboo Distribution Limited
Bandai Namco Holdings UK Ltd
Bernlite Limited
Best Foods Limited
Bio-Rad Laboratories Limited
Bosch Automotive Service Solutions Ltd
Boyden & Co.Limited
A.Martin Bunzl Limited
Chartco Limited
Chemox Pound Limited
Cimbali UK Limited
Communications & Power Industries Europe
Company of Animals Limited
Costco Online UK Limited
Costco UK Holdings Limited
Costco Wholesale UK Limited
Cousins Material House Limited
William Croxson & Son,Limited
Curtis Holt Limited
D.K. Tools Limited
Deal Partners Limited
Dhiman Enterprises Limited
Donovan Bros. Limited
Elite Mobile Limited
Fedrigoni U.K. Limited
Furlong Flooring (Southern) Ltd.
Godiva Bearings (Southern) Ltd
Grant & Bowman Limited
Greenyard Prepared UK Limited
F.W. Hipkin Limited
Hoo Hing Holdings Limited
Hoo Hing Limited
Huxley Global Limited
IIAA Limited
Interport Limited
Katsouris Brothers Limited
L & M (Heating) Supplies Ltd
Lee Industrial Limited
Lefroy Brooks Diffusion Ltd
Lesaffre UK and Ireland Ltd
Longmill Realty Limited
Marke Creative Merchandise Ltd
Mashco Limited
Masters Pharmaceuticals Ltd
Morelli Group Limited
Mywalit (UK) Limited
NBS Trade and Investment Ltd
Officeteam Limited
Orbital Fasteners Limited
PES Group Limited
Plastico Limited
Professor Puzzle Limited
Rashmian Limited
SEJ Distribution Ltd
SOL Electronics Limited
STS Flooring Distributors Ltd
Samsung C & T U.K. Limited
Sartra International Limited
Shopfittings Direct Limited

Suzo International (UK) Ltd
Tan Sales (London) Limited
Tchibo Coffee International Ltd
Tyco Building Services Products (UK)
Tyco Fire Products Manufacturing Ltd
Universal Tyres and Spares Ltd
Venture Lighting Europe Ltd
Voicevale Limited
Wheatland Cheese Co. Limited
A & A Woodford Limited

47110 Retail sale in non-specialised stores with food, beverages or tobacco predominating [13]

Elbrook (Cash & Carry) Limited
Esin Cash & Carry Limited
J P & S Servicess Ltd
Kavanagh Retailing (UK) Ltd
LB Enterprises Limited
NTS Retail Limited
Park Garage Group PLC
Payless Group Limited
Spar Food Distributors Limited
Sunstar Group Limited
Tazaki Foods Limited
Thothaal Group Limited
Vandemoortele (U.K.) Limited

47190 Other retail sale in non-specialised stores [13]

Velji Bhovan & Sons (Trading) Ltd
Oliver Bonas Limited
Chessington Nurseries Holdings Co Ltd
H.K.S. Retail Limited
Hi-Tec Europe Limited
J H Lorimer Limited
Nuance Group (UK) Limited
PAAM Investments Limited
Party Invitation Limited
Pepkor UK Retail Limited
Ram Parkash Sunderdass & Sons Ltd
Roomes Stores,Limited
Tudor Williams (Holdings) Ltd

47210 Retail sale of fruit and vegetables in specialised stores

LB Enterprises Limited
Spar (UK) Limited
Thompson Bros. (Esher) Limited

47220 Retail sale of meat and meat products in specialised stores

Select Poultry & Meat Ltd
Spar Food Distributors Limited

47230 Retail sale of fish, crustaceans and molluscs in specialised stores

Albert Darnell Limited
Spar Food Distributors Limited

47250 Retail sale of beverages in specialised stores

Payless Group Limited
WDFG UK Holdings Limited
WDFG UK Limited
Www.Nakedwines.Com Limited

47260 Retail sale of tobacco products in specialised stores

Spar (UK) Limited
WDFG UK Holdings Limited
WDFG UK Limited

47290 Other retail sale of food in specialised stores

Herbalife (U.K.) Limited
KFG Quickserve Limited
Spar (UK) Limited
Spar Food Distributors Limited

47300 Retail sale of automotive fuel in specialised stores

Brobot Petroleum Limited
J P & S Servicess Ltd
NTS Retail Limited
Trident Garages Limited

47410 Retail sale of computers, peripheral units and software in specialised stores

Elegant Electronics Limited
Phoenix Software Limited
QBS Software Limited

47429 Retail sale of telecommunications equipment other than mobile telephones

EDC Systems Limited

47430 Retail sale of audio and video equipment in specialised stores

Brighthouse Group Limited
Brighthouse Holdings Limited

47510 Retail sale of textiles in specialised stores

Asiatic Carpets Holdings Ltd

47530 Retail sale of carpets, rugs, wall and floor coverings in specialised stores

Euro Services Limited
Mayfair Carpet Gallery Limited
Tapi Carpets & Floors Limited

47540 Retail sale of electrical household appliances in specialised stores

Brighthouse Group Limited
Brighthouse Holdings Limited
Brighthouse Limited
Caversham Finance Limited
Caversham Trading Limited
Orchard Plumbing Limited
Poliform UK Limited
SZ & W Limited

47599 Retail of furniture, lighting, and similar (not musical instruments or scores) in specialised store

Brighthouse Limited
Caversham Finance Limited
Caversham Trading Limited
Chard Properties (UK) Limited
Fishpools Limited
C.P. Hart & Sons Limited
Medlock Electrical Distributors Ltd
TK Maxx
Tempur UK Limited

47620 Retail sale of newspapers and stationery in specialised stores

J H Lorimer Limited
Zenoffice Limited

47650 Retail sale of games and toys in specialised stores

Epoch-Making Toys Limited

47710 Retail sale of clothing in specialised stores [10]

Dennys Uniforms Limited
Kidiliz Group UK Ltd
Ralph Lauren London Limited
Ralph Lauren UK Limited
Mongas Kids Wear Limited
Pronovias UK Limited
Robinson Webster (Holdings) Ltd
Stonemanor Limited
Ann Summers Ltd.
TK Maxx

47721 Retail sale of footwear in specialised stores

Direct Boot and Shoe Supplies Ltd
Russell & Bromley Limited

47722 Retail sale of leather goods in specialised stores

Direct Boot and Shoe Supplies Ltd
Fleetmill Limited

47730 Dispensing chemist in specialised stores [21]

ABC Drug Stores Limited
AMG Healthcare Limited
Avicenna Holdings Ltd
Badiani & Co Ltd
Day Lewis PLC
Elgon (Enfield) Limited
Michael Franklin (Chemists) Ltd
Jalaram Limited
Manichem Limited
Medi-Shop Limited
Medipharmacy Limited
Meraj Limited
Niemans Holdings Limited
Pharmasure Limited
Questmoor Limited
Rosemead Limited
Safedale Limited
Strandhaven Limited
Superdrug Stores PLC
J M W Vicary Limited
T. Visaman & Sons Limited

47749 Retail sale of medical and orthopaedic goods in specialised stores (not incl. hearing aids) n.e.c.

K2M UK Limited
Medequip Assistive Technology Ltd
Medequip Group Limited

47750 Retail sale of cosmetic and toilet articles in specialised stores

Superdrug Stores PLC
WDFG UK Holdings Limited
WDFG UK Limited

47760 Retail sale of flowers, plants, seeds, fertilizers, pet animals and pet food in specialised stores

Leonard F.Jollye (Brookmans Park)
D.J.Squire & Co.,Limited
Wyevale Garden Centres Limited

47770 Retail sale of watches and jewellery in specialised stores

Eran Diamonds (UK) Limited
Michael Spiers (Jewellers) Ltd
H.Stain Limited
H.Stern (Jewellery) Limited

47781 Retail sale in commercial art galleries

Thomas Gibson Fine Art Ltd

47789 Other retail sale of new goods in specialised stores (not commercial art galleries and opticians) [24]

AG Retail Cards Limited
CP Kelco UK Limited
Chessington Nurseries Limited
D & M Tools Limited
Early Learning Centre Limited
Elec-Mec (Wholesale) Limited
Emson Haig Limited
FPI Limited
F.Hinds Limited
Jewellery Channel Limited
Mothercare PLC.
Mothercare UK Limited
Popat Stores Limited
Queenring Limited
Sigma Sports Limited
TJX Europe Limited
TJX UK
Ten Motives Limited
Thames Honda Limited
Thompson Bros. (Esher) Limited
Tumi (UK) Limited
West One Bathrooms Limited
World Duty Free Limited
Wyevale Garden Centres G & L Ltd

47791 Retail sale of antiques including antique books in stores

Butchoff Antiques Limited

47799 Retail sale of other second-hand goods in stores (not incl. antiques)

Sinai (Antiques) Limited

47910 Retail sale via mail order houses or via Internet

Baker Ross Limited
Buyagift PLC
D & M Tools Limited
MH Star UK Ltd
Mothercare UK Limited
Robinson Webster (Holdings) Ltd
SEJ Distribution Ltd
Tan Sales (London) Limited

47990 Other retail sale not in stores, stalls or markets [15]

Atlanta Trust Limited
Bates Wharf Marine Sales Ltd
Beko PLC
Catalyst Corporate Development Ltd
Continuity Co Ltd
Danjuma Collection Ltd
Duplo International Limited
Fairway of Course Limited
Korda Developments Limited
Olivewood Limited
Rush Hair Group Limited
Tackle Guru Limited
WDFG UK Holdings Limited
Wellstone Management Ltd
Wembley Tyres Limited

49100 Passenger rail transport, interurban

Heathrow Express Operating Co Ltd

49200 Freight rail transport

Spedition Services Limited

49319 Other urban, suburban or metropolitan passenger land transport (not underground, metro or similar)

London Sovereign Limited
London United Busways Limited
Metrolink RATP Dev Limited
Original London Sightseeing Tour Ltd
Tram Operations Limited

49320 Taxi operation

Colts Cabs Limited

49390 Other passenger land transport [12]

Agility Project Logistics Ltd
Anderson Travel Limited
Chalfont Coaches of Harrow Ltd
City Circle UK Limited
Ealing Community Transport
Ensign Bus Co Ltd
Golden Tours Sightseeing Ltd
Intercede 2052 Limited
Newmarket Transport Limited
Project Tristar Limited
Quality Line Transport Limited
Selwyns Travel Limited

49410 Freight transport by road [45]

A.G. Thames Holdings Limited
P.F. Ahern (London) Limited
Arcese UK Limited
Chalfont Coaches of Harrow Ltd
Cosco Shipping Crystal Logistics (UK) Co
Croydon Logistics Limited
Day Group Limited
EC Logistics Limited
Erith Haulage Co Ltd
Europa Road Limited
Explore Transport Limited
Express Freight Services (U.K.) Ltd
FTX Logistics Limited
Forest Freight Limited
Geodis FF United Kingdom Ltd.
Glengall Limited
W. Humphreys Transport (London) Ltd
Industrial Chemicals Limited
J & J Transport Limited
Lenham Storage Co Ltd
Mark Luck Limited
M3J Solutions Ltd
Menzies World Cargo Limited
Moriarty Haulage Limited
NNR Global Logistics UK Ltd
O'Hara Transport Limited
O'Malley Haulage Limited
PCL Transport Limited
Pass J. Holdings Limited
Profresh Solutions Limited
Rhenus Lupprians Limited
Saints Transport (Holdings) Ltd
Saints Transport GRP Limited
Saints Transport Limited
Schenker Limited
Solstor Holdings Limited
Solstor UK Limited
Spedition Services Limited
John Steward Transport Ltd
Transmec UK Limited
Uniserve (Europe) Limited
Uniserve (U.K.) Limited
Unitruc Limited
Worldwide Energy Logistics Group Ltd
Worldwide Energy Logistics Ltd

49420 Removal services

Bishop & Sons' Depositories Ltd
J & J Transport Limited
Kelerbay Limited
Premier Moves Limited
Sterling Relocation Limited

49500 Transport via pipeline

BP Gas Marketing Limited
E.S. Pipelines Limited
ESP Networks Limited
Manchester Jetline Limited

50100 Sea and coastal passenger water transport

Preziosa Cruise Limited
RCL (UK) Ltd.
RCL Cruises Ltd
RCL Investments Ltd

50200 Sea and coastal freight water transport [50]

Alcedo Shipping Limited
B Crystal Limited
B Emerald Limited
BP Eastern Mediterranean Ltd
BP Shipping Limited
Clion Limited
Container Providers International (UK)
Cosco Maritime (UK) Limited
Cosco Shipping Lines (UK) Ltd
Fulton Maritime Holdings Ltd
Fulton Maritime Limited
Geodis FF United Kingdom Ltd.
Hudson Kensington Limited
Hudson Lisse Limited
Hudson Richmond Limited
International Marine Transportation
Maybour Logistics Global Ltd
NNR Global Logistics UK Ltd
Oblue Limited
Ocourage Limited
Oforce Limited
Ospirit Limited
Ostrider Limited
P Energy Limited
Schenker Limited
Scotline Limited
Siem Shipping UK Limited
Spedition Services Limited
Star Reefers Trading Limited
UCL Albion Limited
UML Blandford Limited
UML Chiltern Limited
UML Eagle Limited
UML Hinde Limited
UML Marylebone Limited
UML Mayfair Limited
UML Moxon Limited
UML Portman Limited
UML Wembley Limited
UML Westminster Limited
UML Wigmore Limited
UML Wimpole Limited
Union Carriers Limited
Union Glory Limited
Union Maritime Limited
Uniserve Limited
Up Offshore (UK) Limited
Worldwide Energy Logistics Group Ltd
Worldwide Energy Logistics Ltd
Yang Ming (UK) Ltd

51101 Scheduled passenger air transport [11]

ASIG Holdings Limited
B & H Worldwide (Holdings) Ltd
BA Cityflyer Limited
British Airways Holidays Ltd
British Airways PLC
Heathrow Airport Limited
KLM Cityhopper UK Limited
LHR Airports Limited
Mentfield UK Limited
Menzies Aviation (ASIG) Ltd
Worldwide Energy Logistics Ltd

51102 Non-scheduled passenger air transport

Air Charter Service Group Ltd
Air Charter Service Limited
Amsair Aircraft Limited
British Airways PLC
Jato Aviation Limited
London Executive Aviation Ltd

51210 Freight air transport [12]

Air Charter Service Group Ltd
Air Charter Service Limited
Dunwoody Airline Services Ltd
Geodis FF United Kingdom Ltd.
IAG Cargo Limited
NNR Global Logistics UK Ltd
OH Logistics International (UK) Ltd
Schenker Limited
UPS Air Couriers of America Ltd
Uniserve (Air Freight) Limited
Volga-Dnepr UK Ltd.
Worldwide Energy Logistics Group Ltd

52101 Operation of warehousing and storage facilities for water transport activities

Bulk Powder Terminals Limited
Panalpina World Transport Ltd
Pinns Wharf Limited
Pourshins Limited
Seabrook Warehousing Limited
Seacon Terminals Limited

52102 Operation of warehousing and storage facilities for air transport activities

Panalpina World Transport Ltd
Seabrook Warehousing Limited
Worldwide Flight Services Ltd

52103 Operation of warehousing and storage facilities for land transport activities [19]

Croydon Logistics Limited
Europa Road Limited
Garrets International Limited
Gibbs & Ball Limited
Hasbro U.K. Limited
London City Bond Limited
Navigator Terminals Seal Sands Ltd
Navigator Terminals Windmill Ltd
Procter & Gamble UK Group Holdings
Seabrook Warehousing Limited
Second Shurgard UK Camberley Ltd
Shurgard UK Limited
Shurgard UK West London Ltd
Standard Wharf Limited
Storefast Limited
Transmec UK Limited
Warrens Warehousing Group Ltd
Warrens' Warehousing & Distribution (Midlands)
Wealmoor Limited

52219 Other service activities incidental to land transportation, n.e.c.

Balgores Motors (1982) Limited
Bucci Freight Services Limited
Clece Care Services Limited
H.& G.Car Parks Limited
Landmark Global (UK) Limited
MJF Business Services Limited
RATP DEV UK Ltd
Ziegler UK Limited

52220 Service activities incidental to water transportation

FLW Holding Limited
Port of Tilbury London Limited
Ziegler UK Limited

52230 Service activities incidental to air transportation [16]

Aerospares 2000 Limited
Aviation Business Continuity Ltd
Bickerton's Aerodromes Limited
British Airways Holidays Ltd
British Airways PLC
Cobalt Ground Solutions Ltd
GH London Ground Handling Services
Landmark Global (UK) Limited
Menzies Aviation (ASIG Ground Handling)
Menzies Aviation (NL) Limited
Menzies Aviation (UK) Limited
Menzies Aviation Holdings Ltd
Menzies Aviation PLC
Navblue Limited
Omni Serv Limited
Ziegler UK Limited

52241 Cargo handling for water transport activities

Gefco Forwarding UK Ltd.
Panalpina World Transport Ltd

52242 Cargo handling for air transport activities

Aviation Servicing Co Ltd
British Airways PLC
Delivered on Time Limited
Gefco Forwarding UK Ltd.
Heathrow Cargo Handling Ltd
IAG Cargo Limited
Landmark Global (UK) Limited
Panalpina World Transport Ltd

52243 Cargo handling for land transport activities

Gefco Forwarding UK Ltd.
Landmark Global (UK) Limited

52290 Other transportation support activities [48]

Agility Logistics Limited
Allport Cargo Services Limited
B & H Worldwide (Holdings) Ltd
Bollore Logistics UK Ltd
Roberto Bucci (U.K.) Limited
CHEP Pallecon Solutions Ltd
Concordia International Forwarding
Cosco Shipping (UK) Co Ltd
Cosco Shipping Crystal Logistics (UK) Co
DHL Global Forwarding (UK) Ltd
Delivered on Time Limited
Exel Freight Management (UK) Ltd
Expeditors International (UK) Ltd
FTX Logistics Limited
Geodis FF United Kingdom Ltd.
Hapag-Lloyd (U.K.) Limited
JF Hillebrand UK Limited
Jas Forwarding (UK) Limited
Kuehne + Nagel Limited
MIQ Logistics Limited
Mapcargo International Limited
NNR Global Logistics UK Ltd
Nippon Express (U.K.) Limited
Nissin (U.K.) Limited
Pentagon Freight Services PLC
SEJ Distribution Ltd
Saba Infra Cambridgeshire Ltd
Saba Infra Cardiff Limited
Saba Infra Gloucestershire Ltd
Saba Infra Hertfordshire Ltd
Saba Infra UK Limited
Saba Park Services UK Limited
Saba Park Solutions UK Limited
Schenker Limited
Sea, Air & Land Forwarding Ltd
Seacon Group Limited
Sterling Relocation Limited
Strategic Shipping Co Ltd
Toll Global Forwarding (UK) Ltd
Trans Global Freight Management Ltd
Trans Global Group Limited
Transcar Projects Limited
Uneek Forwarding Limited
WNDirect Limited
World Transport Agency Limited
Worldwide Energy Logistics Group Ltd
Worldwide Energy Logistics Ltd
Ziegler UK Limited

53100 Postal activities under universal service obligation

Key Mail (UK) Limited

53201 Licensed carriers

Citipost Mail Limited
Direct Link Worldwide Limited
G3 Worldwide Mail (UK) Limited

53202 Unlicensed carriers

Deltec International Courier Ltd
Parcelhero Group Limited
Skynet (London) Limited
UPS Limited
Yourway Transport Limited

55100 Hotels and similar accommodation [154]

12 Property FE Limited
Ability Hotels (Aberdeen) Ltd
Ability Hotels (Cambridge) Ltd
Ability Hotels (Dunblane) Ltd
Ability Hotels (Liverpool) Ltd
Ability Hotels (Luton Inn) Ltd
Ability Hotels (Peterborough) Ltd
Ability Hotels (Syon Park) Ltd
Ability Hotels (Syon) Limited
Ace Investments Limited
Adda Hotels
Algonquin Management Partners (UK) Ltd
Alhambra Hotel Limited
Ariyan Hotels Limited
Avantis Hotels Limited
Axcel Hospitality (Manchester) Ltd
Banks Hotel Limited
Bath Resorts Limited
Beale's Hotels Limited
Beale's Limited
R. J. and D. E. Billings Ltd
Brook Hotels Group Limited
Brook Hotels No. 1 Limited
Bryant Park Hospitality UK Ltd
Buckinghamshire Park Resort (Holdings)
Buxton Crescent Hotel and Thermal Spa Co
CP Regents Park Two Limited
CTS Metropark Limited
Caesar Management Limited
Carnarvon Hotels Limited
Castle Green Kendal Limited
Chester International Hotel Ltd
Chilworth Manor Limited
Comfort Hotels Limited
Derbyshire Hotel Derby Limited
Ebury 106 Limited
Edwardian Bloomsbury Street Ltd
Edwardian Canary Wharf Hotel Ltd
Edwardian Exclusive Hotels Ltd
Edwardian Free Trade Hall Ltd
Edwardian Grafton Hotel Ltd
Edwardian Hampshire Hotels Ltd
Edwardian International Hotels Ltd
Edwardian Ltd
Edwardian Mercer Street Ltd
Edwardian Pastoria Hotels Ltd
Elgon Hotels Limited
Elvetham Hall (Property) Ltd
FIC Grand Plaza Ltd
Fairview Hotels Limited
Falcon Hotels Limited
Five Star Inns Limited
Goodwill SIP Limited
Grand Central Hotel Glasgow Ltd
Grove HR Limited
Grove T5 Limited
HLT London Manage Limited
HLT Stakis Operator Limited
Harrogate International Hotel Ltd
Heathrow Edwardian Hotel Ltd
Highrak Limited
Hilton International Hotels (UK) Ltd
Hilton International IP Holding 2
Hilton International IP Holding Ltd
Hilton UK Hotels Limited
Hilton UK Manage Limited
Hilton Worldwide Holding 2 Ltd
Hilton Worldwide Manage Branchco Ltd
Hilton Worldwide Manage Ltd
Hollin Hill Properties Limited
Hoole Hall Country Club Ltd
Hotel Inter-Continental London Ltd
Hotel Management International Ltd
Hungerburger Limited
Intercontinental Hotels Group PLC
Kesgrave Hall Limited
Kew Green (LRG Property) Ltd
Kew Green (LRG1) Limited
Kew Green (LRG2) Limited
Kew Green (Norwich Property) Ltd
Kew Green (Square) Limited
Kew Green Group Limited
Kew Green Hotels (Ashford) Ltd
Kew Green Hotels (Birmingham LRG1)
Kew Green Hotels (Chester) Ltd
Kew Green Hotels (Colchester) Ltd
Kew Green Hotels (Derby/Nottingham)
Kew Green Hotels (Gatwick) Ltd
Kew Green Hotels (Haydock) Ltd
Kew Green Hotels (Lancaster) Ltd
Kew Green Hotels (Norwich LRG1) Ltd
Kew Green Hotels (Portsmouth LRG1)
Kew Green Hotels (Portsmouth) Ltd
Kew Green Hotels (Speke) Ltd
Kew Green Hotels (Taunton) Ltd
Kew Green Hotels (Warrington) Ltd
Kew Green Hotels (York) Ltd
Kew Green Hotels Limited
Kew Green Intermediate One Ltd
Kingston Lodge Hotel Limited
Kingsway Hall Hotel Limited
LQAL UK Limited
Leena Plaza Limited
Leeu London Limited
Lester Hotels (Finchley) Ltd
Letchworth Hall Hotel (Trading) Ltd
Lodge Hotels (London) Limited
London Inn Hotels (Stratford) Ltd
London May Fair Hotel Limited
Manors Sales and Lettings Ltd
Melton House Investments Ltd
Melville Hotel Limited
Metro Properties Limited
Mill Hotel Limited
Milsom Hotels Limited
Mouskos & Sons Co. Limited
Neptune Hotels Limited
Nine Heathrow Ventures Limited
Nine Hotel Investments Limited
Nine Reading Hotel Limited
Norfolk Capital Hotels Limited
Oatlands Investments Limited
Osborn Securities (Braintree) Ltd
Pantheon Hotels and Leisure Ltd
Petersham Hotel Limited
Premier Euro Hotels Limited
Principal Edinburgh George Street
Principal London Limited
Principal Manchester Limited
Principal York Limited
Q.N. Hotels (Wrexham) Limited
Q.N. Hotels Limited
Red Lion Hotel (Henley) Ltd
Sarr Hotels (Luton) Ltd
Sarr Investments Limited
Sarr Noke Hospitality Limited
Shadowgrade Developments Ltd
Shepperton Hotels Holdings Ltd
Shepperton Hotels Limited
Shiva Kingsway Limited
Siya Properties Limited
Solihull Hotel Co Ltd

St.Michael's Manor Limited
Sun Hotel Limited
Sussex Gardens Hotels Limited
Taj Securities Company Number Two
Truman Securities Limited
Unstuffy Hotel Co Limited
V.S. Properties Limited
Vanderbilt Hotels Limited
Victoria Docks Hotel Co Ltd
Warren House Conference Centre Ltd
Waverley House Hotel Limited
Yparho Limited

55209 Other holiday and other collective accommodation

Portico UK Holdco Limited
Yorkshire Dales Country Park Ltd

55300 Recreational vehicle parks, trailer parks and camping grounds

Lee Park Estates Ltd
Leisure Parks Real Estate Ltd
Sines Parks Ltd
West Dorset Leisure Holidays Ltd

55900 Other accommodation [19]

Aldwych Leisure Limited
Assured Services Limited
Cobham Hall
Grange Centre for People with Disabilities
Grovehawk Ltd
Hart Homes (Watford) Limited
Isleworth & Hounslow Charity Ltd
Maple Hotels Management Co Ltd
Mitcham Garden Village
Oleoland Hotel Co Ltd
One YMCA
SME Properties Limited
Shadowgrade Developments Ltd
Silverton Property Investments Ltd
Transform Housing & Support
Ultimate Care Limited
West London YMCA
Whiteley Homes Trust
YMCA St Pauls Group

56101 Licenced restaurants [23]

Blanc Brasseries Limited
Bookcash Trading Limited
Brasserie Bar Co Limited
CK Property Developments Ltd
Caskade Caterers Limited
DP Poland PLC
KFG Restaurants Limited
Kesgrave Hall Limited
PHH 1 Limited
PHH 2 Limited
PandoraExpress 2 Limited
PandoraExpress 3 Limited
PandoraExpress 4 Limited
Ping Pong Limited
Pizza Hut (U.K.) Limited
PizzaExpress (Franchises) Ltd
PizzaExpress (Restaurants) Ltd
PizzaExpress (Wholesale) Ltd
PizzaExpress Limited
PizzaExpress Merchandising Ltd
Scan Corporation Limited
Waterfront Cafe Benson Limited
White Brasserie Co Ltd

56102 Unlicenced restaurants and cafes [30]

APPT Corporation Limited
Adil Catering Limited
Alderforce Limited
Alderforce North Limited
Alderforce SC Limited
Alim Caterers Limited
Alim Investments Limited
Chicken Cabins Limited
Davton Holdings Ltd
Demipower (1991) Limited
Demipower Limited
Fazal Fast Foods Limited
Fieldrose Limited
Goldex Investments Limited
ISS Facility Services Limited
Mulcroft Limited
Pizza Hut (U.K.) Limited
Premiere Coffee Limited
Queenscourt Limited
S M E Enterprise Limited
SME (Coffee) Limited
SME (Pizza) Limited
SME Corporation Limited
SME Fast Foods Limited
SME Trading Limited
Soul Coffee House (London) Ltd
Soul Coffee House (South) Ltd
Soul Coffee House (West) Ltd
TH UK & Ireland Limited
Zing Leisure Limited

56103 Take-away food shops and mobile food stands

Adil Catering Limited
Full House Restaurants Holdings Ltd
Full House Restaurants Limited
KMP Taste Limited

56210 Event catering activities [13]

Clay Oven UK Limited
Cobham Hall
Compass Group Holdings PLC
Compass Group Procurement Ltd
Do & Co. International Catering Ltd
Eventist Group Limited
Gate Gourmet London Limited
Kudos Catering (UK) Limited
LSG/Sky Chefs Europe Holdings Ltd
Pizza Gogo Ltd
Sapna Caterers Limited
Seasoned Events Limited
Twickenham Experience Ltd

56290 Other food services [18]

Ali UK Limited
Bartlett Mitchell Limited
DPSK Limited
Do & Co. Event & Airline Catering
Harro Foods Limited
ISS Mediclean Limited
Innovate Services Limited
MDJ Investments Limited
Marsdens Caterers of Sheffield Ltd
Nature Delivered Limited
Pourshins Limited
Riverside Bio Limited
Rollover Limited
Donald Russell Limited
Selecta U.K. Limited
Selecta UK Holding Limited
Tara Mobile Ltd
Watts Farms Catering Limited

56302 Public houses and bars

Brimheath Developments Limited
CK Property Developments Ltd
Derby Pub Co Ltd
JDM Investments Limited
Maida Vale Leisure Limited
Trafalgar Leisure Ltd
Warm Hearth Limited
J D Wetherspoon PLC
White Brasserie Co Ltd

58110 Book publishing

Bible and Gospel Trust
Paula Hawkins Limited
Kays Limited
Wolters Kluwer Health (Professional & Education)

58142 Publishing of consumer and business journals and periodicals

Autosport Media UK Ltd
Bible and Gospel Trust
Haymarket Media Group Ltd.
Media 10 Limited
Metropolis Group Holdings Ltd
Metropolis International Group Ltd
Wolters Kluwer Health (Europe) Ltd

58190 Other publishing activities

EMAP Publishing Limited
GL Assessment Limited
GL Education Group Limited
Kodak Limited
Wolters Kluwer Health (Medical Research)

58210 Publishing of computer games

Playags UK Limited
Sega Publishing Europe Limited
Warchest Limited

58290 Other software publishing

Filemaker International
Frontline Technology Limited
Road Tech Computer Systems Ltd
SAP (UK) Limited
Subex (UK) Limited
Verifone Services UK & Ireland Ltd
Wolters Kluwer (UK) Limited

59111 Motion picture production activities [14]

Creative Video Productions Ltd
Nelly Films (Christmas) Ltd
QOTD Film Investment Limited
RPSD2 Limited
Reliance Entertainment Productions 12
Reliance Entertainment Productions 5 Ltd
Reliance Entertainment Productions 7 Ltd
Reliance Entertainment Productions Scandi
Riverstone Pictures (CMP) Ltd
Riverstone Pictures (Show Dogs) Ltd
Riverstone Solutions 2 Limited
Turnlet Films (JN) Limited
Twickenham Studios Limited
Whisper Films Limited

59112 Video production activities

Baby Network Limited
Chrome Dreams Media Ltd
John Laing International Ltd
Papa Entertainment Limited

59113 Television programme production activities [13]

ATP Media Operations Limited
BBC Studioworks Limited
Beecham Productions Limited
Input Video Ltd
Love Productions Limited
Reliance Entertainment Productions 12
Reliance Entertainment Productions 5 Ltd
Reliance Entertainment Productions 7 Ltd
Reliance Entertainment Productions Scandi
Sky CP Limited
Sky In-Home Service Limited
Sky UK Limited
Visual Impact (UK) Limited

59120 Motion picture, video and television programme post-production activities

Twickenham Studios Limited

59131 Motion picture distribution activities

Cine-UK Limited
Cineworld Cinemas Limited
Twentieth Century Fox Television Distribution (U.K.),

59133 Television programme distribution activities

ATP Media Operations Limited
Baby Network Limited
Indiacast UK Ltd
Parthenon Entertainment Ltd

59140 Motion picture projection activities

Bell Theatre Services Limited
Picturehouse Cinemas Limited

59200 Sound recording and music publishing activities

Mission Recordings Limited
Papa Entertainment Limited
Positive Entertainment Ltd
Startling Music Limited

60200 Television programming and broadcasting activities

ATP Media Operations Limited
Al Jazeera International Ltd
BBC Studioworks Limited
Baby Network Limited
CML Projects Technology Ltd
Gearhouse Broadcast Limited
Input Video Holdings Ltd
Islam Channel Limited

61100 Wired telecommunications activities

Capital City Service Limited
Flag Atlantic UK Limited
Kinetic IT Limited
Reliance Communications (U.K.) Ltd
Sky Home Communications Ltd

61200 Wireless telecommunications activities

CML Projects Technology Ltd
Capital City Service Limited
Cellxion Ltd
Fourway Communication Limited
Reliance Communications (U.K.) Ltd
Sky Home Communications Ltd

61300 Satellite telecommunications activities

7e Communications Limited
CML Projects Technology Ltd
Giga Communications Limited

61900 Other telecommunications activities [25]

Aircom International Limited
Aspect Software UK Limited
Business Systems (U.K.) Ltd
Chartco Limited
Clickatell Limited
Cloud Networks Limited
Epsilon Telecommunications Ltd
Giesecke+Devrient Mobile Security GB Ltd
Manor IT (UK) Ltd
NEC (UK) Ltd.
Neptune Subsea IP Limited
Railsite Holdings Limited
SOL Electronics Limited
Samsung Electronics (UK) Ltd
Siemon Co Ltd
Sky Home Communications Ltd
Sky UK Limited
Speakerbus Limited
Subex (UK) Limited
Tara Mobile Ltd
Telecoms World (Group) Limited
Teoco UK Limited
Vanco UK Limited
Via-Vox Limited
West One Technology Ltd

62011 Ready-made interactive leisure and entertainment software development

Creative Assembly Limited
Global Draw Limited
Hawk-Eye Innovations Limited
Splash Damage Limited

62012 Business and domestic software development [48]

3pillar Global UK Limited
ACI Global Limited
Arcplan UK Limited
Bandai Namco Entertainment UK Ltd.
Basis Technologies International Ltd
Bromcom Computers PLC
Cadline Limited
Campaign Master (UK) Limited
Casewise Systems Limited
Clinisys Group Limited
Clinisys Solutions Limited
Cyberscience PLC
E2X Limited
Excitech Limited
Exela Technologies Limited
FSI (FM Solutions) Limited
FSI Global PLC
GBST Limited
GBST Wealth Management Limited
Hawk-Eye Innovations Limited
IGT U.K. Limited
Intuitive Holding Limited
Intuitive Limited
Invigia Limited
Longview Holding Hedge UK Ltd
Longview Holding Parent UK Ltd
Longview Holding UK 2 Limited
Longview Holding UK Limited
NDEMIC Creations Ltd
OLM Systems Limited
PB Bidco Limited
PB Holdco Limited
PB Midco Limited
PB Topco Limited
Pancredit Systems Ltd.
Phoenix Software Limited
QSC 1208 Limited
QSC 1209 Limited
Scalable Software Ltd
SintecMedia Global Ltd
SintecMedia WEM Ltd
Smart Card Software Limited
Smart Transactions Group Ltd
Smartcomms SC Limited
Tax Computer Systems Limited
Verint WS Holdings Limited
Wolters Kluwer (UK) Limited
Wolters Kluwer Tax and Accounting

62020 Information technology consultancy activities [55]

ACI Worldwide (EMEA) Limited
Allocate Bidco Limited
Allocate Holdco Limited
Allocate Midco Limited
Allocate Software Limited
Allocate Topco Limited
Amphora Acquisitions Limited
Arcplan UK Limited
Axon Solutions Limited
Basis Technologies International Ltd
Bytes Security Partnerships Ltd
Bytes Technology Group Limited
Cadline Limited
Casewise Limited
Casewise Systems Limited
CeleritiFinTech Limited
Charter UK Limited
Comparex UK Limited
Corbus Europe Limited
Cyberscience PLC
DST Process Solutions Limited
EMC Consulting (UK) Limited
EMC Europe Limited
Ensono Limited
Equiniti Data Limited
Ergonomic Solutions International
Excelredstone Converged Solutions
Excitech Limited
Fusion Business Solutions (UK) Ltd
Go Daddy Europe Limited
HCL Great Britain Limited
HCL Investments (UK) Ltd
Hawk-Eye Innovations Limited
Longview Holding Hedge UK Ltd
Longview Holding Parent UK Ltd
Longview Holding UK 2 Limited
Longview Holding UK Limited
Metaswitch Networks Ltd
Net Pay (EUR) Limited

Newfield Information Technology Ltd
Oneclickhr Limited
Paragon Internet Group Limited
RDT Limited
SAP (UK) Limited
Saiwil Limited
Scentrics Information Security Technologies
Smiths Business Information Services
Softwareone UK Limited
Sonata Europe Limited
Sovereign Business Integration Group PLC
Strategic Imperatives Limited
Subex (UK) Limited
Sword Charteris Limited
TES Enterprise Solutions Ltd
Verint Systems UK Limited

62030 Computer facilities management activities [14]

Amphora Acquisitions Limited
Arcplan UK Limited
Ensono Limited
Excelredstone Converged Solutions
Excitech Limited
Longview Holding Hedge UK Ltd
Longview Holding Parent UK Ltd
Longview Holding UK Limited
NetApp UK Ltd
Newfield Information Technology Ltd
Ovationdata Limited
Smiths Business Information Services
Sovereign Business Integration Group PLC
Transputec Limited

62090 Other information technology service activities [81]

3pillar Global UK Limited
Academia Limited
Agfa Healthcare UK Limited
Alliance Healthcare (IT Services)
Amphora Acquisitions Limited
Arcplan UK Limited
Automatic Data Processing Ltd
Boston Limited
Bytes Software Services Ltd
CAE Technology Services Ltd
Champ Cargosystems (UK) Ltd
Channeladvisor UK Limited
Cisilion (Group) Limited
Cisilion Limited
Computer Financial Consultants Ltd
Crestron (UK) Limited
Cyberscience PLC
D-Link (Europe) Limited
D4T4 Solutions PLC
DST Process Solutions Limited
EMC Computer Systems (U.K.) Ltd
Endace Europe Limited
Ensono Limited
Excelredstone Converged Solutions
Excelredstone Services Limited
Excitech Limited
Experis Group Limited
F5 Networks Limited
GD UK Holdings, Ltd
Go Daddy Europe Limited
Hansen Holdings Europe Ltd
ISG Technology Holdings Ltd
ISG Technology Limited
Ikarim Business Services Ltd
Ikon Science Limited
Imagination Technologies Ltd
Intelliflo Limited
Interdist Alliances Limited
Juniper Networks (UK) Limited
Lenta 2 Limited
Longview Holding Hedge UK Ltd
Longview Holding Parent UK Ltd
Longview Holding UK 2 Limited
Longview Holding UK Limited
Minesoft Ltd
NEC (UK) Ltd.
Ness Global Services Limited
NetApp UK Ltd
Newfield Information Technology Ltd
One World Express Inc. Limited
Oneclickhr Limited
Pebble Beach Systems Ltd
Phoenix Software Limited
QBS Software Limited
Reed Business Information Ltd
Sabre UK Marketing Limited
Sapiens (UK) Limited
Scentrics Information Security Technologies
Sky LLU Assets Limited
Smartcomms SC Limited
Smiths Business Information Services
Sourcecode UK Limited
Sovereign Business Integration Group PLC
Staten Investments Limited
Storm Technologies Limited
Stulz U.K. Limited
Summit Media Limited
Sungard Availability Services (UK)
Sword Soft Limited
Synamedia Limited
TES Enterprise Solutions Ltd
Toshiba Global Commerce Solutions (U.K.)
Tri-Continental Limited
Verifone (U.K.) Limited
Verint Systems UK Limited
Verint Technology UK Limited
Verint WS Holdings Limited
Viadex Limited
Visual Response Limited
Vizual Business Tools Limited
Xerox (UK) Limited

63110 Data processing, hosting and related activities [15]

123-Reg Limited
Amphora Acquisitions Limited
Classic Cinemas Limited
E Y C Limited
Ensono Limited
GX Technology EAME Limited
Gartner U.K. Limited
HCL Great Britain Limited
Heart Internet Limited
Rackspace Limited
Samsung SDS Europe Limited
Sky IQ Limited
Smiths Business Information Services
Sovereign Business Integration Group PLC
Subex (UK) Limited

63120 Web portals

E Y C Limited
THS Group Limited
Vvoosh Limited

63990 Other information service activities n.e.c. [11]

CEB Global Limited
Chartco Limited
E Y C Limited
Earth-I Ltd
Erwin Technologies UK Limited
IGD Services Limited
Imagination Technologies Group Ltd
Ovationdata Limited
SITA Information Networking Computing UK
Sky SNI Limited
Wenta

64191 Banks

Counties Home Loan Management Ltd
Enterprise Finance Limited
First Rate Exchange Services Holdings
First Rate Exchange Services Ltd
Healthcare Support (North Staffs) Finance
Jabac Finances Limited

64201 Activities of agricultural holding companies

Borelli Tea Holdings Limited
Watts Farms Fresh Produce Holdings

64202 Activities of production holding companies [17]

ADM Pura Limited
Amber Solar Parks (Holdings) Ltd
Branden Solar Parks (Holdings) Ltd
Domino Investments Limited
John Guest Holdings Limited
John Guest International Ltd
HRT UK Limited
Jain International Foods Ltd
LGX Holdings Limited
Pandrol Finance Limited
Pandrol Group Limited
Pandrol Holdings Limited
Pandrol International Limited
People Against Dirty Holdings Ltd
Silverson Machines Holdings Ltd
Suntory UK Holdings Limited
Track Technology Limited

64203 Activities of construction holding companies [33]

Breyer Holdings Limited
Bryen & Langley (Holdings) Ltd
City North (Telford Homes) Ltd
Clancy Group PLC
Connect Plus (M25) Holdings Ltd
Deneep Limited
Fairview Holdings Limited
Fairview New Homes Limited
Frankham Holdings Limited
GDL Holdco Limited
P.C. Harrington Holdings Ltd
Hill Holdings Limited
IHS Lothian Holdings Limited
JRL Group Holdings Limited
JRL Group Limited
Kellogg Brown & Root (Services) Ltd
Kellogg Brown & Root Group Ltd
Kellogg Brown & Root Holdings (U.K.)
Kellogg Brown & Root Holdings Ltd
Kellogg Brown & Root International Group
Keltbray Group Limited

Kent EHFA Holdco Limited
Kone PLC
Mecon Holdings Limited
Peterborough (Progress Health) Holdings
Peterborough (Progress Health) Nominee
SRCH Limited
Fredereck Sage Holdings Ltd
Transform Schools (Birmingham) Holdings
Transform Schools (Stoke) Holdings
Volkerrail Group Limited
Wates Group Limited
Woodford Heating Holdings Ltd

64204 Activities of distribution holding companies [13]

E. Christian & Company (Holdings)
Global Logistics Group Ltd
Grant & Bowman International Ltd
Loudwater Management Limited
Marchase Limited
New River Holdings Limited
Orbital Fasteners Holdings Ltd
Premier PLC
Stair Tread Holdings Limited
Tax Systems PLC
Uniserve Holdings Limited
Valley Wholesale Carpets (2004) Ltd
ViiV Healthcare Overseas Ltd

64205 Activities of financial services holding companies [20]

BMAK FX Limited
Belmont Green Ltd
Birmingham Schools Partnership (Group)
CDB (U.K.) Limited
Coats Group Finance Co Ltd
Coventry and Rugby Hospital Company (Holdings)
H & T Group PLC
Honister Capital Holdings I Ltd
Independent Commercial Broking Group
KSEYE Capital Holdings Limited
Onix Investments UK Ltd
Puma Heritage PLC
SDJ Enterprises Limited
Sukanya Holdings Limited
Sunny Bidco Limited
Sunny Midco Limited
Sunny Topco Limited
TBC Bank Group PLC
TWG Europe Limited
Tradewise Group of Companies Ltd

64209 Activities of other holding companies n.e.c. [330]

A T & T (GB) Holdings Limited
A6 Audio Bidco Limited
AER Rents Limited
ATP Media Holdings Limited
Ability Hotels (Cambridge) Ltd
Ability Hotels (Dunblane) Ltd
Ability Hotels (Glasgow) Ltd
Ability Hotels (III) Finance Ltd
Ability Hotels (III) Group Ltd
Ability Hotels (III) Holdings Ltd
Ability Hotels (III) UK Ltd
Ability Hotels (IV) Finance Ltd
Ability Hotels (IV) Holdings Ltd
Ability Hotels (IV) UK Limited
Ability Hotels (Luton) Limited
Ability Hotels (Syon) Limited
Adelie Foods Group Limited
Airclaims Group (Overseas) Ltd
Albain Bidco UK Limited
Albrin Capital Limited
Amshold Securities Limited
Anella Limited
Anno 2017 Joint Holding (UK) Ltd
Apex Lifts (Group) Limited
Apollo RPL Limited
Aquila MB2 Limited
Aquila MB3 Limited
Arora Hotels Limited
Artemis Interiors Limited
Asap Growth Limited
Ashcoe Holdings Limited
Audbern Limited
Audio UK 2 Limited
Audio UK 3 Limited
Audiotonix Group Limited
Audiotonix Limited
Audley Group Limited
Augustus 1 Limited
Augustus 2 Limited
Axiom Education (Edinburgh) Holdings
Axiom Education (Perth & Kinross) Holdings
B & P Acquisitionco Limited
B & P Holdings II Limited
B & P Midco Limited
BFIM Limited
BIP Industries Limited
BL Bottling Holdings UK Ltd
BP Mauritania Investments Ltd
Bal Holdings Limited
Bathroom Brands Group Limited
Bathroom Brands Limited
Beam Suntory UK Holdings Ltd
Beck & Pollitzer Engineering Holdings
Beck & Pollitzer Holdings Ltd
Best Holdings (UK) Limited
Blackstown Holdings Limited
Blenheim Group Limited
Boon Group Limited
Bottling Holdings Europe Ltd
Brambles Holdings Unlimited
Brambles Investment Ltd.
Brambles Nominees Limited
Brambles U.K. Limited
Brenray Holdings Ltd
C.V.J. Properties Ltd
CAE Technology Holdings Ltd
CCEP Holdings UK Limited
CEB Global Holdings Limited
Capital Dairy Company (Holdings) Ltd
Capsicum Motorsport Holdings Ltd
Carpetright of London Limited
Caterham Cars Group Limited
Caterham Enterprises Limited
Central Nottinghamshire Hospitals (Holdings)
Chromium Acquisitions Limited
Cineworld Group PLC
Citipost Holdings Limited
Clearwater Property Estates Ltd
Cloud Possibilities Limited
Colorcon European Holdings (No.5)
Console Midco Limited
Cornwall
J J Coughlan (Holdings) Ltd
Country House Weddings Holdings Ltd
Cramlington Renewable Energy
Developments Hold Co
Crislex Limited
Crumlin Capital Limited
Cyan Logistics Limited
Donamount Limited
Donatantonio Group Limited
EACG Holdings Limited
ESPUG Finance Limited
Education Management Corporation Ltd
Edwardian Exclusive Ltd
Edwardian Finance Ltd
Edwardian Group Limited
Edwardian Hotel Finance Ltd
Edwardian Hotel Investments Ltd
Edwardian Investments Ltd
Edwardian New Finance Limited
Elite Mobile (Holdings) Ltd
Ellenbrook Holdings Limited
Elmex Sales Corporation Ltd
Endeavour SCH Holdings Limited
Equiniti Services Limited
Europe Incoming Holdings Ltd
FSI Global PLC
Fairview Hotels Limited
Fasttrax Holdings Limited
Ferholding UK Ltd
Firebolt RB Holdings Limited
Fitton & Co Ltd
Flight Centre Travel Group (European Holdings)
Flowercloud Limited
Forth Ports Finance PLC
Fourfront Holdings Limited
G S A R Holdings Limited
GAIAE Limited
GCH Corporation Limited
GR Bottling Holdings UK Ltd
Galaxy Group Bidco Limited
Gall Holdings Limited
Galldris Holdings Limited
Galliard Group Limited
Garrets Bidco 2 Limited
Gate Gourmet Holdings U.K. Ltd
Geieonline Dafconsulting (UK) Ltd.
Gibson Bidco Limited
Gibson Propco Limited
T Gilmartin Holdings Limited
GlaxoSmithKline Consumer Healthcare (Overseas)
GlaxoSmithKline Consumer Healthcare (UK) IP
GlaxoSmithKline Intellectual Property (No.2)
GlaxoSmithKline Intellectual Property Development
GlaxoSmithKline Intellectual Property Holdings
GlaxoSmithKline Intellectual Property
Glorious Solutions Limited
Gosselin Mobility UK Limited
Granitte Investments (UK) Ltd
Green Flag Holdings Limited
Grey Bridge Holdings Limited
Grouse Bidco Limited
Grouse Midco Limited
Grouse Topco Limited
Grovetowns Southern Limited
Gym Group Midco1 Limited
Gym Group Midco2 Limited
Gym Group PLC
HEB Real Estate Limited
HH Global Group Limited
HH Global Limited
Harlequin FC Holdings Limited
Houlihan & Co (Holdings) Ltd
Howitzer Acquisition Limited

Howard Humphreys & Partners Ltd
Hunn Holdings Limited
IHS Lothian Investments Ltd
IM Estates Limited
ITW Holdings I Limited
ITW Holdings II Limited
ITW Holdings III Limited
ITW Holdings IV Limited
ITW Holdings V Limited
ITW Holdings VI Limited
ITW Holdings VII Limited
Imperial Ductwork Services Holdings
Innisfree Schools (F2C) Ltd
Innisfree Schools (Secondary) Ltd
Intelliflo Bidco Limited
Intelliflo Holdings 2013 Ltd
Intelliflo Intermediate Holdings Ltd
Intelliflo Midco Limited
International Transport Ltd
JPO Communications Limited
JRL Group (Ireland) Limited
JRL Property Holdings Limited
JSM Group Holdings Limited
Jennor Holdings Limited
Leonard F Jollye (Holdings) Ltd
Jollyes Group Limited
Jollyes Retail Group Limited
Jupiter Midco 1 Limited
Jupiter Midco 2 Limited
KBR (U.K.) Investments Limited
KFG Holdings Limited
KSEYE Group Limited
Kanta Enterprises Limited
Kedleston Wings Holdco Ltd
Kellogg Brown & Root DH Ltd
Kellogg Brown & Root Group Ltd
Kellogg Brown & Root Holdings (U.K.)
Kellogg Brown & Root Holdings Ltd
Kellogg Brown & Root International Group
Kellogg Brown & Root London Ltd
Keswick European Holdings Ltd
Kilofrequency Limited
Kingsway Asset Co Limited
Kingsway Mezz Co Limited
Kingsway Mezz Hold Co Limited
Kingsway Senior Hold Co Ltd
Kout Food Group Restaurants UK Ltd
Lantern Services (Holdings) Ltd
Laser Holdings Limited
Leisure Parks Real Estate (Holdings)
Lint Group Limited
London Arena Investments Ltd
M New Holdings Limited
MDJ Group Ltd.
MSK Holdings Limited
Mallinckrodt Enterprises UK Ltd
Mallinckrodt Equinox Limited
Martello (Holdings) Limited
McGrath Brothers (Holdings) Ltd
Medico-Dental Holdings Limited
Mentmore Limited
Merck Holding Ltd.
Mesa Investment Limited
Metier Healthcare Limited
Mitchells Holding Limited
Mizzen Mezzco 2 Limited
Mizzen Mezzco Limited
Moat Homes Finance PLC
Mushi UK Holdings Limited
Myddleton London Limited
NBC Europe Ltd.
ND1T Limited
ND2F Limited
ND3M Limited
Nemo (UK) Holdco, Ltd.
OMEC Holdings Limited
OPD Group Limited
Oakburn Investment Holdings Ltd
Oaktree Property Co Ltd
Odris Holdings Limited
Onix Investments UK Ltd
Operations Holdings Ltd
PKA WLWF Holding (UK) Limited
Michael Page International Holdings
Palmera Holdings Limited
Paradine Holdings Limited
Parkside Leisure Limited
Pentagon Holdings Limited
Pheechool Holdings Limited
PizzaExpress International Holdings
Platinum Newco II Limited
Pole To Win International Ltd
Porcelanosa Group Limited
Portnall House Ltd
Premier Fleet Management and Contract Hire
Primeeng Group Limited
Quinn Investment Holdings (London)
R & R Asset Management Limited
RAK Petroleum PLC
RO Properties Limited
RO Trading Limited
Raedex Consortium Limited
Rapiergroup Limited
Rhenus High Tech UK Limited
Road Tech Holdings Limited
Rowlands 2014 Limited
A & J Ryan Holdings Limited
SHL People Solutions Group Holdings Ltd.
SHL Product Ltd
SP Macbeth 5 Limited
Safestore Investments Limited
Fredereck Sage Holdings Ltd
Sheikh Holdings Group (Investments)
Shure Europe Holdings Limited
Silnat Holdings Limited
Sines Parks Holdings Limited
Snowflake 145 Limited
Stag Group Limited
Standley Holdings Limited
R Stanton-Gleaves UK Limited
Stiefel Consumer Healthcare (UK) Ltd
Subsea 7 Interim UK Holdings Ltd
Subsea 7 Senior Holdings (UK) Ltd
Sukanya Holdings Limited
Supercraft Holdings Limited
TBG Holding C Limited
TFC Holdings London Limited
TJX Germany Ltd.
Tancia (Holdings) Limited
Tata Global Beverages Capital Ltd
Tata Global Beverages Holdings Ltd
Tata Global Beverages Investments
Tata Global Beverages Overseas Holdings
Tax Systems Holdings Limited
Templecare Limited
Texcel (2011) Limited
Therakos (UK), Ltd
Thew Arnott Group Limited
Tone Group Limited
Tour Partner Group Limited
Tour Partner Group Midco Ltd
Trafficinvest Limited
Transcar Projects (Holdings) Ltd
Transform Schools (Birmingham) Holdings
Transform Schools (Knowsley) Holdings
Transform Schools (Stoke) Holdings
Trellis Acquisitions Limited
Trellis Finance Limited
Trellis Holdco Limited
Trellis Investments Limited
Truly Holdings Limited
UK Addiction Treatment Group Ltd
UK Highways A55 (Holdings) Ltd
Unifruit Group Limited
VS Alliance Limited
Valley Trucks Holdings Limited
Van Gastel Beheer Limited
Verint Technology UK Limited
Verint WS Holdings Limited
Verisk International Holdings Ltd
ViiV Healthcare UK (No.3) Ltd
Vista Al Mar Limited
Volex Group Holdings Limited
WIH UK Limited
Webley Holdings (UK) Limited
Whitestone Property Services Ltd
Wolters Kluwer Holdings (UK) PLC
E Wood Holdings Limited
Wrist Holding UK Limited
Wyevale Garden Centres Acquisitions
Wyevale Garden Centres Capital Ltd
Xerox UK Holdings Limited
Xtera Topco Limited
Zoom Gas Pipelines Limited
Zoom Holding Limited
Zoom Infrastructure Limited

64301 Activities of investment trusts

Fidelity Asian Values PLC
Fidelity China Special Situations PLC
Fidelity European Values PLC
Fidelity Japan Trust PLC
Fidelity Special Values PLC
Gargonay Limited
Saffie Investments Limited

64303 Activities of venture and development capital companies

Anglo Suisse Investments Ltd
B & P Buyco Limited
B & P Midco 1 Limited
B & P Midco 2 Limited
Beck & Pollitzer Limited
European Property Development Ltd
Flexibon Limited
HSP Investments Limited
Marble Lending Limited

64304 Activities of open-ended investment companies

Catalina Investments Limited
Eclerx Investments (UK) Ltd
S and J Investments (Delivery Office Southall)
Sauvello Limited
Vanneck Bros Limited
Vinepost Limited
Watmough Brothers Investments Ltd
Yparho Investments Limited

64306 Activities of real estate investment trusts

Fairview Hotels Investments (2) Ltd

64910 Financial leasing [23]

BP Car Fleet Limited
Black Arrow Group Limited
Brighthouse Group Limited
Brighthouse Holdings Limited
Brighthouse Limited
British Airways 777 Leasing Ltd
CHG-Meridian Computer Leasing UK Ltd
CHG-Meridian UK Limited
Capsicum Leasing Limited
Caversham Finance Limited
Cross London Trains Finance Co Ltd
Cross London Trains Holdco 2 Ltd
Cross London Trains Holdco Ltd
Cross London Trains Limited
De Lage Landen Leasing Limited
Hitachi Capital (UK) PLC
Moss Electrical Holdings Ltd
SG Equipment Finance (December) Ltd
Societe Generale Equipment Finance
Summit Asset Management Ltd
Syscap Leasing Limited
Syscap Limited
Venson Automotive Solutions Ltd

64921 Credit granting by non-deposit taking finance houses and other specialist consumer credit grantors [12]

Aura Finance (Holdco) Limited
Bluestar Enterprise Limited
Conance Limited
Counties Home Loan Management Ltd
E.G.T. Bridging Finance Ltd
HFSI Limited
Hitachi Capital (UK) PLC
Mondi Finance PLC
Premium Credit Limited
RCI Financial Services Limited
RR Securities Limited
Spring Finance Limited

64922 Activities of mortgage finance companies

Aura Finance (Holdco) Limited
Belmont Green Finance Ltd
Belmont Green Funding 2 Ltd
Counties Home Loan Management Ltd
FBSE Finance Limited
Innotrade Europe Limited
Mortgage Guarantee Limited
Pepper (UK) Limited
TN (UK) Consultancy Ltd

64929 Other credit granting n.e.c. [17]

CRK Finance Limited
Capital Hospitals (Issuer) PLC
E.G.T. Finance Limited
Exmoore Financial Credit Co Ltd
First Atlantic Finance Limited
Flight Centre Robin Limited
Garusa Solutions U.K. Limited
Greenlight Credit Ltd
IBRC Asset Finance Limited
KSEYE Capital No.1 Limited
KSEYE Capital No.2 Limited
Kimberley Capital Limited
Prospect Healthcare (Hairmyres) Resources
Residential Loans Ltd.
Salmon Management and Finance Ltd
Tata Global Beverages Group Ltd
Toyota Financial Services (UK) PLC

64991 Security dealing on own account

Afinacorp Limited
Crownstar Limited
Daleham Finance Limited
Equicap Estates Limited
Orbit Investment Securities Services PLC
Shakoor Capital Limited

64992 Factoring

Hertz UK Receivables Ltd
Hitachi Capital (UK) PLC

64999 Financial intermediation not elsewhere classified [98]

ADT Finance Limited
AGCO Finance Limited
Allandale Investments Limited
Alternative Bridging (UK 1) Ltd
Alternative Bridging (UK 2) Ltd
Alternative Bridging Corporation Ltd
Atlanta Trust Limited
BP Australia Swaps Management Ltd
BP Capital Markets P.L.C.
BP Finance P.L.C
Beechwood Investments Limited
Belmont Green Funding 2 Ltd
Bizy Investments Limited
Brambles Finance PLC
British Danubian Trade Development Co
CFS-Zipp Limited
Canada Life Finance (U.K.) Ltd
Cargill Financial Markets Ltd
Cargill Global Funding PLC
Cargill Investments
Cargill UK Finance Limited
Chaptre Finance PLC
Chaptre Investments Limited
City & Commercial Holdings Ltd
Citybond Holdings Limited
Connect Plus (M25) Intermediate Ltd
Corncrake Limited
Counties Home Loan Management Ltd
Crown Agents Bank Limited
Distinction Investments Ltd
East Mediterranean Trading Ltd
Equiniti Global Payments Ltd
European Investments (Cornwall) Holdings
First Rate Exchange Services Holdings
First Rate Exchange Services Ltd
Foster Denovo Limited
Frithsden Finance (Birmingham) Ltd
GE Money Home Finance Limited
Garusa Solutions U.K. Limited
GlaxoSmithKline Capital PLC
GlaxoSmithKline Consumer Healthcare Finance
GlaxoSmithKline Consumer Healthcare Finance No. 2
GlaxoSmithKline Finance PLC
GlaxoSmithKline IHC Limited
Glaxochem (UK) Unlimited
Green Hercules Trading Limited
HFMC Group Holdings Ltd
Harvey & Thompson Limited
Hastoe Capital PLC
Healthcare Support (Newcastle) Finance
Henley Group Finance Limited
Heritage Square Limited
Ilot Capital UK Ltd
Ilot Investments UK Ltd
Innotech Advisers Limited
Kent Capital Ltd
Kimberley Peer Ventures One Ltd
Kingrose Limited
Kinsat Enterprises Ltd
Kodak International Finance Ltd
Legolas Debt Holdco Limited
John Menzies Finance Limited
Mitsubishi Electric Finance Europe PLC
Mondi Finance PLC
Network Treasury Services Ltd
Newhospitals (St Helens and Knowsley) Finance
Nucleus Financial Group PLC
Nucleus Financial Services Ltd
Optivo Finance PLC
Orbit Investment Securities Services PLC
PRA Group (UK) Limited
Paragon Treasury PLC
Peacock Homes Limited
Property Finance Capital (No 2) Ltd
Property Finance Capital (No 3) Ltd
Property Finance Capital Ltd
Property Finance Nominees (No.3) Ltd
RHP Finance PLC
Radical Investments Limited
Ranbaxy Holdings (UK) Limited
Regentsmead Limited
Rosetree Finance Limited
Rowlandson Investments Limited
SF11 Limited
Sharp International Finance (U.K.) PLC
Shogun Finance Limited
Sky Operational Finance Ltd
SmithKline Beecham (Investments) Ltd
Space Truust UK Ltd
Sugarman Family Limited
Syscap Leasing Limited
Topfib Limited
Transform Schools (North Lanarkshire) Funding
UPS Global Treasury PLC
ViiV Healthcare Finance 2 Ltd
ViiV Healthcare Finance Ltd
Walsall Public Lighting Ltd
Xerox Capital (Europe) Limited

65110 Life insurance

Canada Life Limited
Cardif Pinnacle Insurance Holdings PLC
Forester Life Limited
London General Life Co Ltd
Pinnacle Insurance PLC

65120 Non-life insurance [19]

Churchill Insurance Co Ltd
Citybond Holdings Limited
Complete Cover Group Limited
DL Insurance Services Limited
Grove & Dean (Holdings) Ltd
Grove & Dean Limited
HFIS PLC
Hyperformance Limited
Independent Commercial Broking Ltd
International Passenger Protection
Key Bidco Limited
Key Midco Limited
London General Insurance Co Ltd
Pinnacle Insurance PLC
R A Insurance Brokers Limited
Right Choice Insurance Brokers Ltd
Runnymede (Holdings) Limited

Tradex Insurance Co Ltd
Tradex Insurance Holdings Ltd

65202 Non-life reinsurance

International Passenger Protection

65300 Pension funding

BP Pension Trustees Limited

66110 Administration of financial markets

Bamrose Enterprises Limited
Nucleus Financial Group PLC
RWW Holdings Limited
TN (UK) Consultancy Ltd

66120 Security and commodity contracts dealing activities

Aliunde Limited
Arcus Investment Limited
Axiom Wealth Management Ltd
Canada Life Asset Management Ltd
Crownstar Limited
Gupta Brothers & Co Limited

66190 Activities auxiliary to financial intermediation n.e.c.

Cargill Financial Services Europe
Nucleus Financial Group PLC
O.S.T.C. Limited
Onix Investments UK Ltd
Ty Danjuma Family Office Ltd
Valiant Holdings Limited
Van Ameyde UK Holding Limited
Van Ameyde UK Limited

66220 Activities of insurance agents and brokers [13]

Avantia Insurance Limited
Daly Holdings Limited
Devitt Insurance Services Ltd
Direct Chauffeur Line Limited
Ingenie Services Limited
KGM Underwriting Services Ltd
Sky Insurance Services Group Ltd
Sutton Group Holdings Limited
Sutton Winson Limited
TWG Services Limited
Tradewise Insurance Services Ltd
U K Insurance Business Solutions Ltd
Verex Insurance Services Ltd

66290 Other activities auxiliary to insurance and pension funding

4th Dimension Innovation Ltd
HCL Insurance BPO Services Ltd
TWG Services Limited

66300 Fund management activities

Black River Asset Management (UK)
Choice Wealth Management Ltd
DBCN Limited
Films & Equipments Limited
Mizzen Bidco Limited
Mizzen Midco Limited
Rex Venture Resources Limited
Toroce Investments Ltd

68100 Buying and selling of own real estate [298]

155 Staines Road Ltd
78A SW48BH Limited
A E Properties Limited
AGP Holdings (1) Limited
AKA London Limited
Abbey Mills Properties Ltd
Acre Invest (Sydenham) Limited
Actionmanor Limited
Altomart Limited
Ambika Investments Limited
Amshold Group Limited
Amshold International Limited
Amsik Limited
Amsprop Bishopsgate Limited
Amsprop Central Limited
Amsprop City Properties Ltd
Amsprop Estates Limited
Amsprop Investments Limited
Amsprop London Limited
Amsprop Portland Limited
Anthony Property Co. Limited
Archway Apartments Limited
Ares Properties Ltd
Arugula Spruce Limited
Asha (Camberley) Ltd
Ashill Land Limited
Assetsky Limited
Audley Binswood Limited
Audley Chalfont Limited
Audley Clevedon Limited
Audley Coopers Hill Limited
Audley Court Limited
Audley Ellerslie Limited
Audley Group Developments 1 Ltd
Audley Inglewood Limited
Audley St Elphins Limited
Audley St George's Limited
Audley Stanbridge Earls Ltd
Aurient Investments Limited
Avamore Limited
Avocado Developments Limited
Avocado Developments Wealdstone Ltd
Avon Estates (London) Limited
Aylmer Road Limited
BMG (Ashford) General Partner Ltd
BP Properties Limited
Bal Holdings Limited
Bamrose Properties Limited
Thomas Bates & Son Limited
Becontree Estates Ltd
Berwen Limited
Best Commercial Properties Ltd
R. J. and D. E. Billings Ltd
G E Bowra Group Limited
Braycote Ltd
Brembury Properties Limited
Buildvantage Limited
Burhill Estates Co Ltd
Burnt Common Nurseries Limited
Bushey Developments Ltd
Butlers Walsall Ltd
CS Property and Consultancy Ltd.
Campmoss Property (Tangley Place)
Campmoss Property Co Ltd
Canadian & Arcadia Limited
Canadian & West End Limited
Capedeal Limited
Capital Investment and Finance Ltd
Cardiff Property PLC
Caskade Properties Limited
Caunton Management Limited
Central Office and Commercial Properties
Cergold Limited
Chalford Property Co Ltd
Chesterhill Investments Ltd
Cheyne Assets Ltd
Clearview Homes (Western Avenue) Ltd
Clifford Property Co Ltd
Combined Counties Properties Ltd
Comwood Holdings Ltd.
Richard Cook Limited
Cooper Estates Limited
Corumbe Investments Limited
Countrywide Developments (UK) PLC
Court Lodge Epsom Limited
Owen Coyle Managements Ltd
Cranfield Technology Park Investments
D and D Property Co Ltd
DBA Advisors Limited
DSJ Homes Limited
DST Global Solutions (Realty) Ltd
Delbanco Meyer & Co Ltd
Deltec Citimail Limited
Demiland Limited
Denbourne Investments Limited
Denton Homes Surrey Limited
Dernagree Properties Limited
Desilu Estates Limited
Desilu Group Limited
Dimehome Limited
Dip Systems (UK) Limited
Directfield Limited
Dow Properties Limited
Ebonyhill Limited
Ebury 106 Limited
Elmswood Properties Limited
Enfield Innovations Ltd
Equicap Estates Limited
Essex Road Development Limited
Eurocity Properties (Central) Ltd
Falcon Investment Ltd
First Investments (UK) Limited
First Rented Housing Group Ltd
Fishnet Properties Limited
Four Quarters (Ingestre Road) Ltd
Friend's Property Portfolio Ltd
G & O Properties (London) Ltd
G & O Securities Limited
GHH Estate Limited
Garden Centre Property Development Trading
Ghai & Co. Limited
Giggs Hill Green Homes Limited
Gita Properties Limited
Glansevern Properties Limited
Goldfield Homes Limited
Grafton Flats Limited
Gravesend and District Real Estate Co
Greenbond Properties Limited
H & H Care Home Investments Ltd
F.H. Hale & Sons (Builders) Ltd
Handsale Limited
Handspan Limited
Harlington Chambers Limited
Heartlands Hotel Limited
Heatpoint Limited
Hedgemans Limited
Helius Investments Limited
Higgins Investments PLC
Highassets Limited
Hill Residential Limited
Housing Gateway Limited

J P Investments London Ltd
Java Asset Management Limited
Daniel Johns Ltd
KBR Property Investments Ltd
Kallar Investments Limited
Kallarview Homes Limited
Katana Property Limited
Kenville Limited
H.H.Keys Estates Limited
Khakharia Properties Limited
Khosla Investments Limited
Killoughery Properties Limited
Kimberley Real Estate Limited
Kitewood (Creekside) Limited
Lamrose Properties Limited
Land Finance & Mortgage Corporation
Larkspur Investments Limited
Lightwood Strategic Limited
Lionel Road Coalyard Ltd
Lionel Road Developments Ltd
Lixmere Properties Limited
London Square (Crimscott Street) Ltd
London Square (Fulham) Limited
London Square (Holdings) Ltd
London Square (Putney) Limited
London Square Development Management
London Square Developments (Ventures)
London Square Developments Ltd
London Square Limited
London and Hertfordshire Ltd
Longmill Rickbost Ltd
Lowen Homes Limited
MCPA Limited
Maidensgrove Limited
Marden Oak Limited
Marwin Securities Limited
Marylebone Square Holdings Ltd
Maxwelton House Property Co Ltd
Meadvine Limited
Megnum Limited
Melton House Investments Ltd
Meridian Residential Developments
Millharbour Developments Ltd
Mingold Limited
Mizen (Nether Street) Limited
Mizen Properties Limited
Monarock Limited
Monks Way Development Limited
Montreaux Maidenhead Limited
Montreaux Redhill Limited
Mothers Ltd
Mountcharm (S.E.) Limited
Multitrust Property Investments Ltd
Muniment Limited
NPT Finance Limited
NVSM Limited
Netmac Limited
Network Homes Investments (Stockwell)
Network Homes Investments Ltd
Nine Hotel Ventures Limited
Normandy Court Development Ltd
Northstar Property Investment Ltd
Oakburn European Properties Ltd
Ocobase Limited
Olivanna Ltd
PGG Properties Limited
PJG Developments Limited
Paje Limited
Panther (VAT) Properties Ltd
Panther Hinckley (VAT) Ltd
Panther Investment Properties Ltd
Panther Securities P L C
Panther Shop Investments Ltd
Panther Trading Limited
Parkdale Investments Limited
Parrsouth Limited
Philmont Properties UK Limited
Photon Properties Limited
Platinum Gold Homes Limited
Port of London Properties Ltd
Pricketts Limited
Pridenature Limited
Property Plus Investments Ltd
Proppertunity Limited
Pure Bricks Limited
Queensway Associates Limited
Quickdrop Limited
RBR Property Investments Ltd
Raban Holdings Limited
Reliance Investments Ltd
Remy's Limited
Resham PLC
Residential Properties Funds Ltd
Rhiannon Properties Limited
Rhodehurst Limited
Riches Ilford Ltd
Rilla Properties Limited
Leslie Rogers Investments Ltd
Rosewell Properties Limited
Rowhurst Limited
Rusjon (UK) Limited
Salient Investments Ltd.
Sandkot Limited
Scan Corporation Limited
Scimitar House Limited
Sharan Properties Limited
Share and Debenture Trust Ltd
Sharish Properties Limited
Shire Properties (South East) Ltd
Shrewsbury Hotel Limited
Sienna Real Estate Ltd
M & D Silk Properties Ltd
Simpson Marketing Limited
Sinclair House Properties Ltd
Drew Smith Homes Limited
Space Truust UK Ltd
Speed 9395 Limited
Stapleford Commercial Group Ltd
F.C. Stark Limited
Sunrose Property Limited
Surebay Developments Limited
Swanvale Management Limited
Swift 100 Limited
TFC Properties Limited
TN (UK) Consultancy Ltd
TPS Abbeydale Archway Limited
TY Properties (UK) Limited
Tati Co Ltd
Thames Properties Ltd.
Times Square Estates Limited
Tower Hill Suffolk Limited
Trans-Britannia Properties Ltd
Treebond Limited
Treno Investments Ltd
Trentpeak Limited
Triplerose Limited
Tristmire Limited
Tudor Investments Limited
Turner Properties Limited
P.C. Tustin & Co Ltd
Tustin Properties Ltd
Twilight Real Estate Limited
UCAR Properties Limited
UK Salads Investments Limited
Unicourt Properties Limited
Valentine Group Limited
Victorygame Limited
Viewrose Limited
Vision Homes Limited
Vulcan Wharf Limited
WD1A Limited
WVC Land & Developments Ltd
Watchingwell Farms Limited
West Ten Properties (UK) Ltd
Wood Green Investments Limited
Wyevale Acquisitions Borrower Ltd
Zionstone Limited

68201 Renting and operating of Housing Association real estate [43]

Ability Housing Association
Ahmed Property Limited
Blackwater Securities Limited
Brymore Estates Limited
Brymore Investments Limited
Caunton Management Limited
Central Office and Commercial Properties
Charlie Properties Limited
Cibi Investments Limited
Dhamecha Property Limited
Dimehome Limited
E & J Properties Limited
Excellent Properties Ltd.
Feabrex Limited
A.A.Fisher (Properties) Ltd
Heathcrest Limited
Highassets Limited
Himelight Limited
Hurstlane Limited
John S. Miller Limited
Kallarview Homes Limited
Khakharia Properties Limited
Lapid Developments Limited
Megnum Limited
NUR Limited
PJG Developments Limited
Pet and Aquatics Properties Ltd
Pinder Developments Co. (Chislehurst)
Pleythorne Limited
Polaris Ventures Ltd
Powerbase Management Co Ltd
SAB Properties (London) Ltd
Sandkot Limited
Shelfside (Holdings) Limited
Sons of Divine Providence
Taylor Wentworth Limited
Thomas,Arthur & Gordon,Limited
Times Square Estates Limited
Trans-Britannia Properties Ltd
Transeur Properties Limited
Treebond Limited
Wildview Limited
Xstro Investments Limited

68202 Letting and operating of conference and exhibition centres

Brandon House Limited

68209 Other letting and operating of own or leased real estate [556]

1 Big Data Management Limited
A A Homes and Housing (5 Sydenham Road)
A A Homes and Housing (Cygnet House)
A A Homes and Housing (Metro Point)
Property

A A Homes and Housing Ltd
A E Properties Limited
A L Properties Limited
AA Property and Construction Services
ABSL1 Limited
ACR Investments Limited
AMB Property Ltd
APFS Property Ltd
Abbey Investments Limited
Abbey Mills Properties Ltd
Abbeyman Investments Limited
Ability Developments Limited
Ability Hotels (Liverpool Plaza) Ltd
Ability Hotels (Manchester) Ltd
Ability Hotels (Newcastle) Ltd
Ability Hotels (Southport) Ltd
Acclaim Handling Group Ltd
Acre 1176 Limited
Adil Property Investment Ltd
Adilsons Properties Limited
Alimar Limited
Alphalarch Limited
Amalgamated Property Holdings Ltd
Angel Property Investments Ltd
Angelica Estates Limited
Anitass Limited
Antoniou Investments Limited
Anya House Limited
Aquila BTE 1 Limited
Aquila Chelmsford Limited
Aquila EHS Limited
Aquila Estates Limited
Arcese Real Estate UK Limited
Arem Investments Limited
Arihant Limited
Armitage BC1 Limited
Arora Heathrow Holdings Ltd
Astor Lodge Holdings Limited
Atkins Properties Limited
Atlanta Trust Limited
Aurient Investments Limited
Aurient Investments N16 Ltd
Avon Estates (London) Limited
Avon Freeholds Limited
B.A.T.S. Ilford Limited
Badger BC Investments Limited
Bagga Holdings Limited
Bamrose Enterprises Limited
Bamrose Properties Limited
Barilone Properties Limited
Barrowfen Properties Limited
Baruch Holdings Limited
Thomas Bates & Son Limited
Bayside Investment Co Ltd
Bayti Properties Limited
Beacon (Mimms) Limited
Becontree Estates Ltd
Belgrave Land (Sheffield) Ltd
Benacre Investments Limited
Benja Properties Limited
Berea Limited
Berrite Limited
Berwen Limited
Biggin Hill Hangar Co Ltd
Black Arrow Group Limited
Black Katz Eddy (Holdings) Ltd
Blackfriars Securities (Brighton)
Blackstone City Ltd
Blenheim Estates Limited
Blenheim Property Management Ltd
Bostall Estates Limited
Bourn Investments Limited
M.& R.Bowman Limited
Brandon House Limited
Brent Housing Ltd
Brianco Services Limited
Brick Projects (Marland) Ltd
Bricklehampton Classic Care Ltd
Brickline Properties Limited
Broadrich Limited
Brookpass Limited
J.Browne Properties (UK) Ltd
C.L.T. Timber and Transport Ltd
CS Property and Consultancy Ltd.
Camgate Holdings Limited
Campmoss Property (Tangley Place)
Campmoss Property Co Ltd
Canadian & Arcadia Limited
Canadian & West End Limited
Cardiff Ground Rents Limited
Cardiff Property PLC
Caredeal Limited
Caretech Estates (No 2) Ltd
Caretech Estates (No 3) Ltd
Caretech Estates (No 7) Ltd
Caretech Estates (No. 5) Ltd
Caretech Estates (No.4) Ltd
Caretech Estates Limited
Carigluz Investment Co Limited
Carpetright of London Limited
Cathedral Holdings Limited
Centaur Property Estates Ltd
Centaur Property Group Limited
Central Developments (UK) Ltd
Central Property Investments Ltd
Centre for Engineering and Manufacturing Excellence
Chainkey Limited
Chalford Property Co Ltd
A.W. Champion Properties Ltd
Chantry Securities Limited
Charter Court (New Malden) Ltd
Charterhouse Simon Limited
Chellbrook Properties Limited
Chicken Villas Limited
Churton Property Developments Ltd
City & Commercial Holdings Ltd
City of London Holdings & Investments
Clearwater Property Co Ltd
Cloverton Property Ltd
Cobalt Limited
Harry A.Coff,Limited
Coldunell Limited
Consolidated Equities Limited
Richard Cook Limited
Cooper Estates Limited
Coopers Investments Limited
F. Copson Limited
Cossam Investment Co Ltd
Costco Limited
Countrywide Developments (UK) PLC
Courtlands Estate (Richmond) Ltd
Owen Coyle Managements Ltd
Crane Apartments Limited
Crane Investments Ltd
Cranfield Technology Park Investments
Cresta Estates Limited
Cromwell (Egham) Limited
Cromwell (Wandsworth) Limited
Cromwell Investments (Richmond) Ltd
Crown House (Tadworth) Limited
Crown House Investments Ltd
Croydon House Ltd
Cuffe Holdings Limited
Culham Limited
Currie Motors Kingston Limited
Currie Motors Limited
D.B.T. (Holdings) Limited
DC Management Services Limited
DSJ Homes Limited
DST Global Solutions (Realty) Ltd
Datamede Limited
Datamust Co Ltd
Deanplan Limited
Robert Deards Limited
Deards Services Limited
Dedalo1 Limited
Deekay Investments Limited
Demiland Limited
Dentoptic Limited
Dependable Homes Limited
Dial Investments Limited
Dialgreen Estates Limited
Diamond Corporation Limited
Dilawar & Sons Limited
Dilawar Property Ltd.
Dip Systems (UK) Limited
Directfield Limited
District One Estates Ltd
Dow Properties Limited
Drayton Kirk Ltd
Dudley Properties Limited
E.D.S. Holdings Limited
EC Logistics Limited
Eagle 456 Limited
Earndrive Limited
East Central Limited
Ebenezer Bethel UK Limited
Elcot Service Flats Limited
Empire Investment Capital Ltd
Enfield Innovations Ltd
Envirotech Properties Limited
Epoch RJK Limited
Erindale Limited
Essential Harvest Limited
Etcetera Construction Services Ltd
Eurocity Properties (Central) Ltd
Euron Developments (France) Ltd
Everguard Limited
Excelsior Property Investments Ltd
Fairmont Property Developers UK Ltd
Fairview Hotels Investments (2) Ltd
Finer Limited
First Network Properties Ltd
First Rented Housing Group Ltd
Fishpools (Finance) Limited
Flahive Developments Limited
Fleetwood Developments Limited
Forextra Developments Limited
Frattro Limited
Frelene Limited
Fresh Wharf Estates Limited
G & O Properties (London) Ltd
G & O Securities Limited
Gable Homes Lettings Limited
Gada Limited
Gardeners' Royal Benevolent Society
J. Gardner Holdings Limited
Garusa Solutions U.K. Limited
Gatehall Services Limited
Gathercrest Properties Limited
Gita Properties Limited
Glansevern Properties Limited
Glengall Limited
Globegold Limited
Good Harvest Group Limited

Good Harvest Properties (Hammersmith)
Good Harvest Properties (Southwark)
Good for Food Limited
Goodmayes Properties Ltd
Goodshoeman Limited
Gouhari Enterprises Limited
Gracilis Ltd.
Grafton Flats Limited
Grant & Boyd Limited
R. & I. Grant & Co. Limited
Gratia (Abbey Care Home) Ltd
Grays Thurrock Properties Ltd
Grayshott Investments Limited
Green Homes Investment Ltd
Greenfield Property Developments Ltd
Greenstone Oxford Limited
Greystead Properties Limited
Griffon Land & Estates Limited
Griffon Land Holdings Limited
Gunpowder Mill Developments Ltd
H & H Care Home Investments Ltd
Hadgate Limited
Haig Housing Trust
Halcyon Offices Limited
F.H. Hale & Sons (Builders) Ltd
Handsale Limited
Harlequin Estates (Twickenham) Ltd
Harlington Chambers Limited
William Hartley Group Limited
Hayre Investments (Ealing) Ltd.
Hedgemans Limited
G.A.F. Heley (Properties) Ltd
High Park Investments Limited
S.Hille & Co.(Holdings) Ltd
Hillingdon House (UK) Limited
Hoddesdon Developments Ltd
Homeguard Properties Limited
Honeycroft Hill Ltd
Housing Gateway Limited
Humberside Land Limited
Humphrey & Stretton (Properties) Ltd
Hunn Holdings Limited
ILB Investments Limited
Iceport Limited
Inner Town Homes Limited
J. Isaacs Management Limited
Ist Developments Limited
J J Food Service Holdings Ltd
JRL Property Limited
JTC Ventures Limited
P. Johnson & Son (1976) Ltd
Johnson Group Limited
H.C. Jones & Co (Surrey) Ltd
Jopate Estates Limited
K 2 Properties Limited
K.C.Y. Limited
KBR Property Investments Ltd
KECS Investments Limited
KM Estates Limited
Kailas Hotel Finance Co Ltd
Kalbro Investments Limited
Kallar Investments Limited
Kap Homes Ltd.
Kara Management Ltd
Katrin Properties Limited
Keash Properties Limited
Kelly Property Co Ltd
Kestates Limited
Kewstone Limited
Kimberley Property Investments Ltd
Klassik Property Ltd
Kolajola UK Ltd

L.M.H. Properties Limited
La Nu-Range Ltd
Lamrose Properties Limited
Land Management Limited
Hugh Langmead Limited
Lasted Limited
Leitrim Properties Limited
Lenta Properties Limited
Linkhaven Estates Ltd
Livid Dare Limited
Lixmere Properties Limited
London & District Limited
London Urban Investments Ltd
Lord Street Properties (Southport)
Luce Limited
Luna Estates Limited
M & H Properties London Ltd
M D Properties Limited
MBH Finco. Limited
MJA Investments Limited
MJF Group Limited
MSI Property Investments Ltd
Maker Properties Ltd
Mapeley Columbus II Limited
Mapeley Estates Limited
Mapeley Steps Contractor Ltd
Marande Limited
Marblefloor Limited
Marco Polo Properties Limited
Marden Oak Limited
Marlborough Isleworth Properties Ltd
Marylebone Finco Limited
Marylebone Square Property Group Ltd
Mastermind Trading Limited
Maxen Homes Limited
McGrath Bros. (Environmental) Ltd.
Meekland Limited
Melford Commercial Properties Ltd.
Mercury Land Holdings Limited
Meridian Wood Products Ltd.
Metam Properties Limited
Mew Investments Ltd
Millennium Property (London) Ltd
Millennium Seacon Properties Ltd
Mister Dee International Ltd
Monarock Limited
A.E.Monk & Co.(London) Ltd
Montpelier Properties Limited
Morley Finco Limited
Mothers Ltd
Mountbrook Properties Limited
Mountcharm (S.E.) Limited
J P C Mulligan Properties Ltd
Multitrust Property Investments Ltd
Gerry Murphy Ltd
Namu Limited
Needspace? Limited
Nestates Limited
Netmac Limited
Network Homes Investments Ltd
Network New Build Limited
Noodle Properties Limited
Nordic Properties Limited
Norpap Property (Telford) Ltd
Norsette Investment Co. Ltd
Northstar Property Investment Ltd
O G Holdings Limited
O'Hara Property Investment Holding Co
O'Neill Investments Limited
O.B.C. (Europe) Limited
Oakburn European Properties Ltd
Oakburn Properties Limited

Oatfield Limited
Ocobase Limited
Offer Group Ltd
Omavale Limited
Onkar International Limited
Optimal Limited
PPP Capital Limited
Paje Limited
Palacath Limited
Palace Street Developments Ltd
Pamina Estates Limited
Paneurosys Limited
Panther (VAT) Properties Ltd
Panther AL (VAT) Limited
Panther Securities P L C
Park Green Investments Limited
Park Grove Residential Limited
Park Rutland Investments (London)
Parkdale Investments Limited
Parklight Properties Limited
Parkside Leisure Limited
Parrsouth Limited
Pattinson Green Limited
Peak Securities Limited
Pegrid Limited
Periworld Limited
Phoenix Property Investment Co Ltd
Photon Properties Limited
Pineridge Investments Limited
Pirin Ltd
Pledream Properties Limited
Plutus Estates (Braintree) Ltd
Plutus Estates Limited
Plymouth (Notte Street) Ltd
Poland Street Properties Ltd
Postgrad Limited
Pricketts Limited
Prinhold Limited
Proppertunity Limited
Punjab House Associated Ltd
Purelake Investments Limited
Purelake Properties Limited
Purism Properties Limited
Purley Point Limited
QH Estates Ltd
Quebec Court Freehold Limited
Queenring Limited
Queensgate Finco Ltd
Quickdrop Limited
R S L (Slough) Limited
RBC Investments (Surrey) Ltd
RBR Property Investments Ltd
Radia Estates Limited
Radiation Limited
Radio Developments Ltd
Rambert School of Ballet and Contemporary Dance Trust
Rangemist Limited
Red Circle Security Services Ltd
Regina 2015 Limited
Regis 2000 Limited
Reichmann Properties PLC
Reliance Investments Ltd
Remington Partners Ltd
Renatus Property Management Ltd
Residential Properties Funds Ltd
Rex Venture Resources Limited
Rhiannon Properties Limited
Rhodehurst Limited
Rian Properties Limited
Richstone Properties Limited
Right Choice Property Holdings Ltd

Rijac Properties Limited
Riverway Investments Limited
William Robinson Gravetye Charity
Leslie Rogers Investments Ltd
Rosetta Investments Limited
Rosewell Properties Limited
Rowhurst Limited
Royal British Legion Poppy Factory
Runnymede Investments Limited
SEJ Assets Limited
SMC Investcorp Limited
Safe Haven London
Safe Properties Limited
Safegold Properties Limited
Safestore Limited
Safestore Properties Limited
Sagoo & Takhar Limited
Saiwil Limited
Sandhill Park Limited
Sardar Properties (U.K.) Ltd
Satco Investments Limited
Scan Corporation Limited
Select Enterprises Limited
Shadowgrade Developments Ltd
Sharan Properties Limited
Share and Debenture Trust Ltd
Sherrygold No.1 Limited
Shetson Property Developments Ltd
Shoreland Limited
Sienna Real Estate Ltd
Silverson Machines Holdings Ltd
Simmons & Hawker Limited
Sitecrest Limited
Solai House Limited
Solight Limited
South Central Property Limited
South Coast Watch Fair Limited
South Mimms Services Limited
Southbeck Investment Co Ltd
Southdown Holdings Limited
Spaces Personal Storage Ltd
Speed 9395 Limited
Spencers Property Investments Ltd
Springhill Property Investments Ltd
Spruce Investments Limited
St James Contracts Limited
Stanbreck Properties Ltd
Stapleford Frog Island (Rainham) Ltd
Starcare Homes Limited
Stebiz Limited
Sterndale Systems Limited
Strand Court Properties Ltd
John Street & Company (Surrey) Ltd
Street Property (Holdings) Ltd
Strongholding Limited
Sunshine Properties Limited
Swakeleys Properties Limited
Swanlea Limited
Swanvale Management Limited
Sweetland Properties Limited
Swift 100 Limited
T. Bro Investment Limited
T.C. Racing (Leisure) Limited
TBE (Southern) Limited
TCR New Limited
TFC Properties Limited
TJX UK Property Limited
TVH Fizzy Holdings Limited
Talbot House Business Centre Ltd
Tarian Investment Co. Limited
Ten Levels Ltd
Tennay Properties Limited
Texcel Developments Ltd
Threshold Land & Estates Ltd
Tower Hill Suffolk Limited
Transfleet Properties Limited
Transmec Properties Limited
Triland Properties Limited
Triplerose Limited
Tristmire Limited
Trochair Limited
Tudor Investments Limited
Tulip Properties & Real Estate Ltd
Turner Properties Limited
Tustin Properties Ltd
Twinglobe Limited
UHP Investments Limited
UK Salads Investments Limited
Ultrabrook Limited
Unit 2 (Rickmansworth) Limited
Vadsala Limited
Velani & Velani Ltd
Ventford Limited
Victoria Docks Hotel Company (Number Two)
Victorygame Limited
Villachase Limited
Vinayak Properties Limited
Vinci Property Limited
Vine Investment Co Ltd
Viners Capital Properties Ltd
WVC Land & Developments Ltd
Wagermotion Limited
Walnut Estates Limited
Warborough Investments Limited
Wedge Investments Limited
Weekes Brothers (Welling) Ltd
Welcome To England (Hotels) Ltd
Wellsborough Developments Ltd
West Ten Properties (UK) Ltd
Westlake Estates Limited
Wickland (Holdings) Limited
Wintertime Properties Limited
Woodcote Estates Limited
Woodgavil Estates Limited
Woodgavil Limited
Woodgavil Properties Limited
Workout Limited
Worth More Limited
Y.A. Property Investments Ltd
Yomans (London) Limited
York Apartments Limited
Zest Living Limited

68310 Real estate agencies [15]

Acorn Limited
Badger Holdings Limited
Chawla's Limited
Dow Properties Limited
Gibbs Gillespie Sales Limited
Headstart 4 Life Limited
Jenga (UK) Limited
Jenga House Limited
Lipman Properties Limited
Munster Limited
Netmac Limited
Radiation Limited
Site Sales Marketing Limited
TRSL Limited
Wasteland Group Limited

68320 Management of real estate on a fee or contract basis [60]

Al-Mubarakia Limited
Amar Property Services Limited
Applepeach Limited
Arcus FM Limited
Arlen Properties Limited
Audley Willicombe Limited
Avon Estates (London) Limited
Avon Lake Holdings Limited
Axiom Education (Edinburgh) Ltd
Axiom Education (Perth & Kinross)
Bayside Investment Co Ltd
Bereta Investments Limited
Birchwood Commercial Ltd
Blenheim Consultancy Services Ltd
Bow Village Limited
Carlton Group Developments Ltd
HJ Dhillon Ltd.
Dow Properties Limited
Elliot Leigh Property Investments 2 Ltd
Esso Property Management Company,
First Wave Housing Limited
Greensea Real Estate Management Ltd
HML PM Ltd
Harouni Group of Companies Ltd
Hayre Investments & Developments Ltd
K.E.M. Property Services Ltd
Kailash Estates Limited
Kallarview Homes Limited
Kenville Limited
Khakharia Properties Limited
Kingston University Service Co Ltd
Letting International Limited
Lingerham Properties Limited
MEI Properties Limited
Mapeley Steps Contractor Ltd
Marylebone Square Property Group Ltd
Mill Hill Properties Limited
Modern Schools (Exeter) Ltd
Netmac Limited
Nine Hospitality 3 Ltd
Ocobase Limited
Oval Quarter Developments Ltd
Pearl Properties Limited
Peppercorn Investments Limited
RBH Hotel Management Limited
RBH Hotels UK Limited
RBR Property Investments Ltd
Ranola Properties Limited
Residential Management Group Ltd
Salmon Management and Finance Ltd
Sandkot Limited
Space Truust UK Ltd
John Street & Company (Surrey) Ltd
TCA Investments Limited
TK Maxx
TT Skate Properties Limited
Tulip Properties & Real Estate Ltd
Vantage Volante Limited
Vassall Ventures Limited
WK Properties Limited

69102 Solicitors

Duncan Lewis Solicitors Ltd
Manak Lawyers Limited
Shepherd Harris & Co Limited
Stanmore Law Practice Limited
WYM Legal Limited

69109 Activities of patent and copyright agents; other legal activities n.e.c.

Taylors Legal Limited

69201 Accounting and auditing activities

CS Property and Consultancy Ltd.
JSA Services Limited
Raffingers Advisory Limited
Renault Group U.K. Limited

69202 Bookkeeping activities

London Pharma & Chemicals Group Ltd
Raffingers Advisory Limited

69203 Tax consultancy

Bluecastle Enterprises Limited
Raffingers Advisory Limited

70100 Activities of head offices [692]

360shareholders Limited
3VS UK Limited
A-Roads Investments Limited
A. & A. 2000 Limited
ACI Worldwide (EMEA) Limited
AD Construction Group Limited
ADI Finance 1 Limited
ADI Finance 2 Limited
ADT (UK) Limited
ADT Group Limited
AERL Holding Limited
AHL Holdings (Manchester) Ltd
ATK Energy EU Limited
AVM Vision Investments Ltd
AVMI Group Limited
Abaris Holdings Limited
Abbey Group Limited
Abbey Total Care Group Limited
Abriand Limited
Accolade Wines Holdings Europe Ltd
Adelie Foods Bidco Limited
Advanced Group Holdings Ltd
Advanced Lighting Technologies Europe
P.F. Ahern & Sons Limited
Air Products Group Limited
Akaal Group PLC
Alder Hey Holdco 1 Limited
Alder Hey Holdco 2 Limited
Alder Hey Holdco 3 Limited
Ian Allan Group Limited
Allport Group Limited
Aluminium Services (UK) Ltd
Amshold Trading Limited
Anglogold Ashanti International Exploration Holdings
Archer Daniels Midland (UK) Ltd
Arcus Solutions (Holdings) Ltd
Arora Management Services Ltd
Arora T5 Holdings Limited
Aryzta UK Holdings I Limited
Associated Coffee Merchants (International)
Athena Care Homes (UK) Limited
Atkins Holdings Limited
WS Atkins Limited
Automated Technology Group Holdings
Avalon Cellars Two Limited
Axon Group Limited
BA and AA Holdings Limited
BECAP Spicers (UK) Limited
BP Absheron Limited
BP Africa Limited
BP Alternative Energy Investments
BP America Limited
BP Asia Pacific Holdings Ltd
BP Biofuels Brazil Investments Ltd
BP Chemicals (Korea) Limited
BP Chemicals East China Investments
BP Chemicals Investments Ltd
BP Corporate Holdings Limited
BP Exploration Operating Co Ltd
BP Global Investments Limited
BP Greece Limited
BP Holdings Canada Limited
BP Holdings North America Ltd
BP Indonesia Investment Ltd
BP International Limited
BP Investments Asia Limited
BP Pipelines (BTC) Limited
BP Pipelines (SCP) Limited
BP Pipelines Tap Limited
BP Russian Investments Limited
BP Technology Ventures Limited
BPH Finance Number 1 Limited
BTC Pipeline Holding Co Ltd
Baik Agency Limited
Bartlett Mitchell Services Ltd
Baruch Investments Limited
Beck MBI Limited
Belron International Limited
Benson & Hedges Limited
Berkeley Group Holdings PLC
Berkeley Group PLC
Berkeley Homes PLC
Berkeley Residential Limited
Big Bear Group Limited
Black Katz Eddy (Holdings) Ltd
Blendhall Limited
Robert Bosch UK Holdings Ltd
Bottling Great Britain Limited
Brambles Enterprises Limited
Brambles Holdings (UK) Limited
Brasserie Bar Co Limited
Bricklehampton Classic Care Ltd
Brigade Electronics Group PLC
Brigade Holdings Limited
Bristol-Myers Squibb Holdings 2002
Britair Holdings Limited
Britannia Security Group Ltd
British Airways Associated Companies
Broadway Malyan Holdings Ltd
Brymore Holdings Limited
Martin Bunzl International Ltd
Burhill Group Limited
Burlodge Group Limited
Burroughs Wellcome International Ltd
By Chelmer (Holdings) Limited
Bycentral Holdings Limited
Bynorth (Holdings) Limited
Bywest (Holdings) Limited
CDK U.K. Limited
CP Holdings Limited
CSL Communications Group Ltd
CSPH Limited
Cadbury Limited
Cadbury Schweppes Finance Ltd
Cadbury Schweppes Overseas Ltd
Cadbury South Africa (Holdings)
Canada Life (U.K.) Limited
Cardif Pinnacle Insurance Holdings PLC
Cardinal International Limited
Care Expertise Limited
Care Management Group (Acquisition)
Caretech Holdings PLC
Castle Bidco PLC
Caunton Management Limited
Ceesail Limited
Centro Group Limited
Chelsea Stores Holdings Ltd
Chevaning Mining Co Ltd
Chigwell (London) Limited
Chromium Assets Limited
Chubb Fire & Security Limited
Chubb Group (International) Ltd
Chubb Group Limited
Chubb Group Properties Limited
Chubb Group Security Limited
Chubb International Holdings Ltd
Chubb Limited
Churchgate Estates Limited
Cineworld Cinemas Holdings Ltd
Cineworld Holdings Limited
City Link (Cardiff) Holdings Ltd
City Link (Cardiff) Limited
City of London Holdings & Investments
Citygate Holdings Limited
I.P. Clarke & Co. Limited
Cluff Oil Limited
Coats Global Services Limited
Coats Group PLC
Coats Industrial Thread Ltd
Coats Limited
Coca-Cola European Partners Holdings Great Britain
Coca-Cola European Partners Services Europe
Collaborative Services Support (NE) Holdings
Community Stores Limited
Compass Group Finance No. 3 Ltd
Compass Group Finance No.2 Ltd
Compass Group Holdings PLC
Compass Group PLC
Compass Overseas Holdings Ltd
Compass Overseas Holdings No.2 Ltd
Coniston Dartford Limited
Consolidated Timber Holdings Group
Consolidated Timber Holdings Ltd
Consort Healthcare (Blackburn) Holdings
Continental U.K. Group Holdings Ltd
Richard Cook Limited
Corona Energy Limited
Cosan Lubes Investments Ltd
Cousins Holdings Limited
Crest Nicholson Holdings PLC
Crest Nicholson PLC
Cromwell Holdings Limited
Cromwell Investments Limited
Crown Holdings Limited
Croydon and Lewisham Lighting Services (Holdings)
Currie Finance and Leasing Co Ltd
DC Management Services Limited
DDD Investments Limited
DPA Support Services Limited
DS (Holdings) 2 Limited
DS (Holdings) 3 Limited
DSTI Holdings Limited
Dashtag
Davroc Limited
De Lage Landen Limited
Defence Support (St Athan) Holdings
Delta Limited
Derby School Solutions (Holdings)
Devine Holdings Limited
Dhamecha Group Limited
Dhamecha Holdings Limited
Direct Line Group Limited
Direct Line Insurance Group PLC
Dnata World Travel Limited

Doncaster School Solutions (Holdings)
Dormole Limited
Dunlop International Holdings Ltd
Durbin PLC
Dwellcourt Limited
EHGT Limited
EPI Group Holdings Ltd
ESP Utilities Group Limited
Eastbury Park (Holdings) Ltd
Edif Group Finance Limited
Edif Group Management Limited
Education Support (Enfield 2) Holdings
Education Support (Enfield) Holdings
Education Support (Newham) Holdings
Education Support (Newham) Ltd
Education Support (Swindon) Holdings
Elysium Healthcare (Lighthouse) Ltd
Embee Holdings Limited
Emcor (UK) Limited
Enfield Fancy Goods Limited
Ensign Holdco 1 Limited
Ensign Holdco 3 Limited
Ensign Holdco 4 Limited
Entel Communications Holdings Ltd
Enterprise Rent-a-Car European Holdings
Enterprise Rent-a-Car UK Holdings
Epsomedical (Acquisitions) Ltd
Equiniti Holdings Limited
Equion Health (Newcastle) Ltd
Erith Holdings Limited
Europa Worldwide Group Limited
H.Evans & Sons Limited
Excess Baggage Group Limited
Excess Baggage Holdings Ltd
Exel Freight Management (UK) Ltd
Expanded Limited
Experis Group Limited
Exploration Service Co Ltd
Explore Capital Limited
FGP Topco Limited
FJJ Limited
Faber Prest Limited
Facilicom UK Limited
Ferring Laboratories Limited
Finance Ireland Limited
Finefrance Holdings Limited
A.A. Fisher (Holdings) Ltd
A.A.Fisher Limited
Fishpools Holdings Limited
Forester Holdings (Europe) Ltd
Forth Health Holdings Limited
Alexander Fraser Holdings Ltd
Fusion Global Limited
Future Electronics Management Services
GDC (Holdings) Ltd
GE Money Home Lending Holdings Ltd
GGI Holdings Limited
GL Education (No.3) Limited
GMK Pepper Holdings Limited
GPG (UK) Holdings Limited
Gada Limited
Gade Investments Limited
Gallaher Group Limited
Gallaher Overseas (Holdings) Ltd
Gallaher Overseas Limited
Galldris Services Ltd
Galliard Holdings Limited
Galliford Try Construction & Investments Holdings
Galliford Try Investments Ltd
Galliford Try PLC
Genuine Solutions Group Ltd
Genuine Solutions International Ltd
Gillette Industries Limited
Glasgow Learning Quarter (Holdings)
Glaxo Group Limited
GlaxoSmithKline Consumer Healthcare Holdings
GlaxoSmithKline Holdings (One) Ltd
GlaxoSmithKline Holdings Ltd
GlaxoSmithKline Investment Holdings
GlaxoSmithKline Mercury Ltd
GlaxoSmithKline PLC
GlaxoSmithKline Services Unlimited
Glendola Leisure (Holdings) Ltd
Gold Group International Ltd
Gold Group Properties Limited
Gould International UK Limited
Grant Family Holdings Limited
Grant Family Investments Ltd
Gravity Media Group Holdings Ltd
Gravity Media Group Limited
D.Green & Co.(Stoke Newington) Ltd
Guangdong Investments Limited
Guardian DR (Overseas Holdings) Ltd
Guardian IT
Guru Nanak Limited
Gym Group Operations Limited
H & D Support Services (Holdings)
HCL EAS Ltd
HCL Technologies UK Limited
HCP Holdings Limited
HEL Bidco Ltd
HML Holdings PLC
HRS Investments Limited
Harris Holdings (Grays) Ltd
Harsco (U.K.) Limited
Harsco (UK) Group Limited
Harsco Infrastructure Group Ltd
Harsco Investment Limited
Harsco Leatherhead Limited
Harsco Metals 385 Limited
Harsco Metals Group Limited
Harsco Metals Holdings Limited
Harsco Mole Valley Limited
Harvard International Limited
Harvest Midco Limited
Haymarket Group Limited
Haymarket Publishing Services Ltd
Healthcare Drugstores Limited
Healthcare Support (Erdington) Holdings
Healthcare Support (Newcastle) Holdings
Healthcare Support (North Staffs) Holdings
Heathrow (AH) Limited
Heathrow (DSH) Limited
Heathrow (SP) Limited
Heathrow Airport Holdings Ltd
Heathrow Enterprises Limited
Heathrow Finance PLC
Heathrow Holdco Limited
Heathrow T5 Hotel Limited
Heathrow Top Limited
Henley Group Holdings Limited
Hexagon Positioning Intelligence Ltd
Higgins Group PLC
Hillary Bidco Limited
Hills Group Enterprises Ltd
Hilton HHC Limited
Hinds Ltd
Holmes Care (Group) Limited
Hospital Company (Southmead) Holdings
Hospitality Holdings Limited
Host Europe Group Limited
Host Europe Limited
Hotel Management International (Holdings)
Hybrid Dining Limited
IBA Group Holdings Limited
IHC Hotel Limited
IHC May Fair (Holdings) Ltd
IHC May Fair Hotel Limited
IHC Overseas (U.K.) Limited
IHC UK (Holdings) Limited
IMCD Holding UK Ltd
IMCD UK Acquisitions Limited
IMCD UK Investments Ltd
ISS UK Holding Limited
ISS UK Limited
Independent Group (UK) Limited
Insignia Investments Limited
Inspiral Oldham Holding Co Ltd
Intercontinental (PB) 1
Intercontinental (PB) 3 Ltd
Intercontinental Hotels Group PLC
Interfleet Holdings Limited
JDM Investments Limited
JLW Excellent Homes for Life Holding Co
JTI (UK) Management Ltd
Jablite Holdings Limited
Jankel Group Limited
KBC Advanced Technologies Ltd
KH Finance Limited
KH Finance No.2 Limited
KH Holdco Limited
KMP Holdings Limited
KMS Holdings Limited
Kalbro Investments Limited
Kane Group Limited
Kaysail Limited
Kedleston Group Limited
Kenard Group Limited
Kennford Group Limited
Kentex Group Limited
Kerry Holdings (U.K.) Limited
Kidde International Limited
Kidde Limited
Kidde UK
Kidsprog Limited
Kimal Holdings Limited
Geo. Kingsbury Holdings Ltd
Kingswood Corporation Limited
Kluman and Balter Holdings Ltd
Kraft Foods Investment Holdings UK
Kraft Foods UK IP & Production Holdings
Kromachem Holdings Limited
L & M Holding Ltd
LGC Group Holdings Limited
LGC Science Group Holdings Ltd
LGC Science Group Limited
LPM Acquisitions Limited
Lanvin Trading Ltd
Lapid Developments Limited
Lascelles Leisure Limited
Lea Redway Limited
Legacy Broadcast Group Holdings Ltd
Leonardo Holdings Limited
Lynn Lewis Limited
Lighthouse Healthcare Group Ltd
Limje Holdings Limited
Livingston Group Limited
London Airports 1992 Limited
London Irish Holdings Limited
London Pharma & Chemicals Group Ltd
London Pharma & Chemicals Holdings Ltd
Lotus Flower Holdings Limited
M.H.J. Limited
M.M.C. Investments Limited

MFG Parentco Limited
MIQ Logistics EU Limited
MJF Group Limited
MJF UK Holdings Limited
MPM Connect Limited
MSHA International Ltd.
MWL International Limited
Macquarie Corona Energy Holdings Ltd
Majestic Securities Limited
Mallinckrodt Chemical Holdings (U.K.)
Mallinckrodt Medical Holdings (UK)
Manpower PLC
Marz Limited
Masterson Holdings Limited
McGee Group (Holdings) Limited
McGrath Brothers (Holdings) Ltd
Media 10 Holdings Limited
John Menzies (108) Limited
Merck Sharp & Dohme (Holdings) Ltd
Milcars Limited
Mollart Group Limited
Mondelez UK Biscuit Financing Ltd
Mondelez UK Finance Co Ltd
Mondelez UK Holdings & Services Ltd
Mondi Finance PLC
Mondi Investments Limited
Mondi PLC
Mono Holdings Limited
Mosaic Estates Ltd
Mothercare Group Limited
Motherwell Holdings Limited
Mouskos Capital Limited
Mouskos Holdings Limited
Munnelly Group PLC
NCMT Holdings Limited
Naked Wines International Ltd
Navigator Terminals UK Limited
Neilcott Construction Services Ltd
Neilcott Group Holdings Ltd
Neilcott Holdings Limited
New Demipower Limited
Newhospitals (St Helens and Knowsley) Holdings
Newman Street Hotel Limited
Newmir Limited
Newport Group (Holdings) Ltd
Newport School Solutions (Holdings)
Newport School Solutions Ltd
Newship Group Limited
Newship Limited
Newship Products Group Limited
Anthony Nicholas (UK) Limited
Nicholls & Clarke Limited
Niemans Holdings Limited
O'Rourke Investments Holdings (UK)
OLM Group Limited
Oakdene Holdings Limited
Ocobase Limited
Octagon Group Holdings Limited
Octagon Group Limited
Offerco Limited
Officeteam Group Limited
Oki Europe Limited
Opus 2 Magnum Holdings Limited
Oyezstraker Group Limited
P.I.G. Holdings Limited
PCL Bidco Limited
PCL Holdco Limited
Michael Page International Southern Europe
Michael Page Partnership Ltd
Pagegroup PLC
Parkview Treasury Services (UK) Ltd
Pearl River Delta Investments Ltd
Pebble Beach Systems Group PLC
Penspen Group Limited
Pentair UK Holdings Limited
Petroleum Geo-Services (UK) Ltd
Pharmadent Holdings Limited
J.A. Phillips Holdings Ltd
PizzaExpress Group Limited
Pladis Foods Limited
Platinum Investments Surrey Ltd
Playpower UK Limited
Plexus Holdings PLC
Dr Michael Prager Holdings Ltd
Premier Lotteries Capital UK Ltd
Prestige Nursing Limited
Prime Care Solutions (Kingston) Holdings
Procter & Gamble Holdings (UK) Ltd
Prospect Healthcare (Hairmyres) Group
Prospect Healthcare (Hairmyres) Holdings
Prospects Group 2011 Limited
Purchase Group Limited
Purple Surgical Holdings Ltd
R O Ventures Limited
RSI Retail Solutions Limited
Raedex Consortium Limited
Raisio UK Limited
Ravensale Limited
Regenter B3 Holdco Limited
Regenter Bentilee District Centre (Holding)
Regenter LCEP Holdco Limited
Regenter Myatts Field North Holding Co
Reliance Vanco Group Limited
Renewable Energy Systems Holdings
Residential Land Holdings Ltd
Retirement Villages Group Ltd
Reyhold Limited
Rhodia Holdings Limited
Rhodia International Holdings Ltd
Rhombi Holdings Limited
Richardson Roofing Holdings Ltd
Riverway Investments Limited
Rocket Medical Group PLC
Rooff Group Limited
Rooff Holdings Limited
Rowlandson Investments Limited
Donald Russell Holdings Ltd
Ruxley Holdings Limited
Rycote Microphone Holdings Ltd
SCIH Branston 3
SGB Infrastructure Middle East Ltd
SHL Group Limited
SIP Group Limited
SLS Holding Co Ltd
SME Group PLC
SME Holdings Limited
SME Investments Limited
SNC-Lavalin (GB) Holdings Ltd
SNC-Lavalin (GB) Limited
SSCP Spring Topco Limited
Saba Infra Holdings UK Limited
Sabre Global Technologies Ltd
Safestore Acquisition Limited
Safestore Group Limited
Safestore Holdings PLC
Safety-Kleen Europe Limited
Safety-Kleen UK (Europe) Ltd
Safety-Kleen UK (France) Ltd
Safetykleen Group Services Ltd
Samax Resources Limited
Schering-Plough Holdings Ltd
Schweppes Limited
Sea Cloud 1 Limited
Sea Cloud 2 Limited
Seabrook Holdings Limited
Seebeck 133 Limited
Selecta Holding Limited
Senior Engineering Investments Ltd
Senior Finance Four Limited
Senior Finance Seven Limited
Senior Finance Six Limited
Senior Five Limited
Senior PLC
Services Support (Cleveland) Holdings
Services Support (Gravesend) Holdings
Services Support (Manchester) Holdings
Services Support (SEL) Holdings Ltd
Setfirst Limited
Sherrygreen Limited
Shields Environmental Group (Holdings)
Shields Environmental Investment (Holdings)
Shimtech Industries Group Ltd
Shimtech Industries Holdco Ltd
Shimtech Industries Holdco2 Ltd
Shimtech Industries Limited
Shun Cheong Lung Holding Co Ltd
Signet Group Limited
Simon Holdings PLC
Sirhowy Enterprise Way (Holdings)
Six Continents Holdings Ltd
Six Continents Hotels International
Skanska Cementation International Holdings
Skanska Construction Holdings UK Ltd
Sky History Limited
Sky International Operations Ltd
Sky Limited
Sky Television Limited
Sky Ventures Limited
Sloggett Group Limited
SmithKline Beecham (H) Limited
SmithKline Beecham Overseas Ltd
SmithKline Beecham Research Ltd
Smiths Interconnect Group Ltd
Sogea Holdings (UK) Limited
Soul Coffee House Limited
Soul Foods Limited
Sovereign Equity Holdings Ltd
Spacemaker Group Limited
Spectris Group Holdings Ltd
Spectris PLC
Spectris UK Holdings Limited
Spectris US Holdings Limited
Spicers-Officeteam Group Ltd
Spirit Norway Limited
St George PLC
Steiner UK Limited
Stonplan Limited
Stora Enso Holdings UK Limited
Sungard Availability Services (DR)
Swan Mill (Holdings) Limited
Symmetry Logistics Holdings Ltd
Symmetry Logistics Limited
Synchro Clutch Co Ltd
TES-AMM Europe Holdings Ltd
TMD Holdings Limited
TRAD Group Limited
Tanjong PLC
Tata Global Beverages Group Ltd
Tata Global Beverages Investments
Tata Global Beverages Overseas Holdings
Tata Global Beverages Services Ltd
Tempur Sealy International Ltd
Thompsons (UK) Holdings Ltd
Thorn Security Group Limited
Tican (UK) Holdings Limited

Todd Group Limited
Toll Investments (NA) Ltd
Trans Global Limited
Transform Schools (North Lanarkshire) Holdings
Transform Schools (Rotherham) Holdings
Travel Technology Investments Ltd
Tyrolese (751) Limited
UB Overseas Limited
ULS Living Limited
UMV Global Foods Co Ltd.
UMV Global Foods Holding Co Ltd.
UPS (UK Holding) Limited
UPS (UK) Limited
UT (UK) Limited
Ultimate Model Corporation Ltd
Ultra Electronics Holdings PLC
United Biscuits Bidco Limited
United Biscuits BondCo Limited
United Biscuits Holdco 2 Ltd
United Biscuits Holdco Limited
United Biscuits Vlnco Limited
United Living (North) Group Ltd
United Living (North) Holdings Ltd
United Living (South) Group Ltd
United Living Group Limited
United Technologies Holdings Ltd
V.I.P. Limited
VGC Group Limited
Vanguard Holdings Limited
Vantas International Limited
Verex Group Limited
Vestey Foods Limited
Vestey Group Limited
Vestey Holdings Limited
ViiV Healthcare Limited
ViiV Healthcare UK Limited
Vinci PLC
Vinci UK Developments Limited
Vitec Group Holdings Limited
Vitec Group PLC.
Vitec Investments Limited
Vlasak Holdings Limited
Volkerrail Group Limited
Volkerwessels Limited
Volkerwessels UK Limited
WP Midco1 Limited
WP Midco2 Limited
WP Midco3 Limited
WP SK Holdings Limited
WP SK Limited
WP SK Midco Limited
WP Safety-Kleen Limited
Wadlow Energy Holdings Limited
Walker Greenbank PLC.
Walsall Hospital Company (Holdings)
Walsall Public Lighting Holding Co Ltd
Wellcome Foundation Limited
Wellcome Limited
Western United Investment Co Ltd
Westway Services Holdings (2010) Ltd.
Williams and Hill Group Ltd
Wind Farm Holdings Limited
Wood Hall Land & Properties Ltd
Woodledge Limited
Wurth Holding UK Ltd
Wyevale Garden Centres Holdings Ltd
Xerox Overseas Holdings Ltd
Zameen Ltd
Zotefoams PLC

70210 Public relations and communications activities

Future Electronics Management Services
H H Associates Limited

70221 Financial management [22]

Active Travel Group Bidco Ltd
Cummins Associates Limited
Erac UK Finance Limited
Financial Management Limited
Future Electronics Management Services
GlaxoSmithKline Holdings (Ireland)
Hexagon Corporate Management Ltd
Hexagon Manufacturing Intelligence Management
JBG Enterprises Limited
Lefa Enterprises Limited
London Pharma & Chemicals Group Ltd
Papa Midco Limited
Papa Topco Limited
PizzaExpress Operations Ltd
Riposte Limited
Tower Hill Investment Partners Ltd
Treetops Capital Limited
V.B. Investments Limited
Wood Hall Investments Limited
WorleyParsons UK Finance Sub Ltd
WorleyParsons UK Finance Sub No. 2 Ltd
nVent International (UK) Ltd

70229 Management consultancy activities other than financial management [50]

ATK Energy EU Limited
Arora Management Services Ltd
Atkins Limited
Axcorp Limited
BMT Group Limited
BMT Hi-Q Sigma Limited
Bayut Ltd
Belron Finance Issuer Limited
Belron Finance Limited
Belron Lending UK Limited
Blenheim Consultancy Services Ltd
CEB Holdings UK 1 Limited
CEB Holdings UK 2 Limited
Console Bidco Limited
Corero Network Security PLC
Corporate Solutions Consulting Ltd
Court Cavendish Limited
EA Consulting Group Ltd
Faithful+Gould Limited
Future Electronics Management Services
Glastry Advisory Partners Ltd
Goal Group Limited
HCL Insurance BPO Services Ltd
Hadgate Limited
Harvest Investments Solutions Ltd
Highplus Limited
Hystead Limited
IZH Holdings Ltd
Investors in Ideas Ltd
JB & Ace Limited
Keswick Enterprises Group Ltd
L.M.H. (Management Services) Ltd
Lefa Enterprises Limited
Lexcross Limited
Liberata UK Limited
MTALX Limited
Mallinckrodt Pharmaceuticals Ltd
Monument Assets Limited
Nucleus Limited
OLR (UK) Limited
Michael Page Recruitment Group Ltd
Renault Institute of Quality Management
Repair Funding Limited
Riverway Investments Limited
St James Contracts Limited
Stem Healthcare Limited
Tata Global Beverages Services Ltd
Vectra Limited
T. Visaman & Sons Limited
Yendall Hunter Limited

71111 Architectural activities

Austin (GB) Limited
Austin Company of (U.K.) Ltd
Rooted Architecture Limited
T.S.G. Building Services PLC
WorleyParsons Europe Limited

71112 Urban planning and landscape architectural activities

Atkins Limited

71121 Engineering design activities for industrial process and production

Granherne Limited
SNC-Lavalin UK Holding Limited
WorleyParsons Europe Limited

71122 Engineering related scientific and technical consulting activities

Edif Group Limited
Granherne Limited
Gordon Murray Design Limited
Penspen Limited
Rina Consulting Ltd
SNC-Lavalin Rail & Transit Ltd
SNC-Lavalin UK Holding Limited
Wood Group Kenny UK Limited
WorleyParsons Europe Limited

71129 Other engineering activities [26]

Aston Heating Limited
Atkins Limited
Austin Company of (U.K.) Ltd
BMT Defence and Security UK Ltd
BMT Group Limited
Beck & Pollitzer Engineering Ltd
Broadway Malyan Holdings Ltd
Broadway Malyan Limited
Butler & Young Approved Inspectors
Frankham Consultancy Group Ltd
ITC Concepts Limited
JGC New Energy UK Limited
KBC Process Technology Limited
Kellogg Brown & Root Limited
Kellogg Brown & Root Overseas Operations
Kellogg Brown & Root Overseas Projects
Kellogg Brown & Root Projects Ltd
Kirby Group Engineering (UK) Ltd
Mott MacDonald Group Limited
Mott MacDonald International Ltd
Mott MacDonald Limited
Precision Engineering Plastics Ltd
S.S.S.Gears Limited
SNC-Lavalin UK Holding Limited
Servotest Testing Systems Ltd
Stat Holding International Ltd

71200 Technical testing and analysis

BRE Global Limited
Lambda Therapeutic Limited
SNC-Lavalin UK Holding Limited

72110 Research and experimental development on biotechnology

Action Potential Venture Capital Ltd
Exagon Industries Limited
LGC Genomics Limited
Magdi Yacoub Institute
Prosidion Limited

72190 Other research and experimental development on natural sciences and engineering [19]

BMT Defence and Security UK Ltd
BMT Group Limited
BRE Trust
Beko PLC
Brigade Electronics Group PLC
Building Research Establishment Ltd
Celgene Europe Limited
Centre for Engineering and Manufacturing Excellence
Cobird Limited
Domantis Limited
Galvani Bioelectronics Limited
GlaxoSmithKline Research & Development
HEL Limited
Millipore (U.K.) Limited
Mylan Pharma UK Limited
Reading Scientific Services Ltd
SmithKline Beecham Limited
Sunlight PV Ltd
TGS Geophysical Company (UK) Ltd

73110 Advertising agencies

Agency Press Limited
David Allen Holdings Limited
Cherry Advertising Limited
IDG International Marketing Services Europe
JCDecaux UK Limited
JCDecaux United Limited
Jobladder Limited
Kingpin Communications Limited

73120 Media representation services

ATP Media Licensing Limited
MacFarlane Media Limited
Perform Media Sales Ltd

73200 Market research and public opinion polling

Jato Dynamics Limited

74100 Specialised design activities

WJ Groundwater Limited

74202 Other specialist photography

NK Image Limited

74901 Environmental consulting activities

Carbon Solutions Global Ltd

74902 Quantity surveying activities

Faithful+Gould Limited
T.S.G. Building Services PLC
W.T. Partnership Limited

74909 Other professional, scientific and technical activities n.e.c. [51]

AVM Impact Ltd
Abhaya Limited
Brand Reputation Compliance Ltd
British Board of Agrement
Butterworth Laboratories Ltd
Crest Plus Operations Limited
Cromsource Ltd
Design Blue Limited
E P I Limited
Field Marketing (UK) Holdings Ltd
Field Marketing (UK) Limited
Fujitsu General Air Conditioning (UK)
GX Technology EAME Limited
Geomac Limited
Grigny (UK) Limited
Institute of Grocery Distribution
Intermay Management Ltd
KLDiscovery Ontrack Limited
Kellogg Brown & Root (Greenford) Ltd
Kinedexe UK Limited
Kromachem Holdings Limited
LGC Limited
Land & Water Services Ltd
M.H.J. Limited
Morrisroe Group Limited
Opus 2 International Limited
Park Score Ltd
Perform Group Financing PLC
Perform Group Limited
Perform Investment Limited
Perform Media Channels Ltd
Perform Media Services Ltd
Perform Sporting News Limited
Perform Sports Media Limited
Phoenix Property Development Co Ltd
Plexus Europe Limited
Procter & Gamble Technical Centres
Remington Partners Ltd
SNC-Lavalin Co Ltd
SSCP Spring Midco 2 Limited
SintecMedia LON Ltd
Skylight Investments Limited
Smithers Information Limited
Stat Marine Limited
Test Equipment Asset Management Ltd
United Kingdom Accreditation Service
VXR Imaging Limited
ViiV Healthcare UK (No.3) Ltd
ViiV Healthcare UK (No.4) Ltd
ViiV Healthcare UK (No.5) Ltd
ViiV Healthcare UK Limited

74990 Non-trading company [114]

ADT South Africa Holding Ltd
Accolade Wines Europe No. 2 Ltd
Alestra Limited
Armstrong (U.K.) Investments
Atlantic 2/3 UK Holdings Ltd
Avantia Limited
BP Exploration Personnel Co Ltd
BP Services International Ltd
BPE Polandco Limited
Berkeley (SQP) Limited
Berkeley Homes (PCL) Limited
Berkeley Seventy-Six Limited
By Chelmer PLC
Cargill Holdings
Cargill Investments Holdings Ltd
Cargill UK Holdings Limited
Ceragon (UK) Limited
Cerestar UK Ltd
Charco 2010 Limited
Clarges Pharmaceuticals Ltd
Compass Group Finance No.4 Ltd
Compass Group North America Investments
Compass Group North America Investments No.2
Compass Hotels Chertsey
Continental Investment Limited
Cressdene Limited
Crest Nicholson Developments (Chertsey)
Dairy Crest (Services) Limited
Derrin Brothers Properties Ltd
Dhamecha Group Limited
Dunlop International Group Ltd
Early Learning Holdings Ltd
Elysium Healthcare Holdings 2 Ltd
Elysium Healthcare Holdings 3 Ltd
Elysium Healthcare LC Limited
Endon Europe Power 1 Limited
Endon Europe Power 3 Limited
Endon Europe Power 6 Limited
Ensco 1212 Limited
Ensco 1214 Limited
Ferring Asset Management Ltd
Foray 414 Limited
Forester Investments Limited
Fraserfort Limited
Joseph Gallagher Group Ltd
Galleon Investments (Dartford) Ltd
GlaxoSmithKline Consumer Healthcare (UK) (No.1)
Godrej UK Limited
Goodman Family Investments Ltd
Goodrich Inertial Limited
Green Lane Goose Limited
HIC Racing (Chiswick) Limited
HIC Treasury Limited
Heathrow Airport Fuel Co Ltd
Hel Group Limited
Heley Holdings Limited
Kelly Communications Enterprises Ltd
Kelly Communications Trading Group
Kerneos Holding Northern Europe Ltd
Kewsaw Limited
Kingston Bidco Limited
Kingston Midco Limited
Kingston Topco Limited
Knight Noise Limited
Knowledge & Merchandising Inc. Ltd
LGC (Teddington) Limited
Laser Holdings Limited
Lester Hotels Group Limited
Mallinckrodt UK Ltd
Mawpart Commercial Limited
Menzies Group Holdings Limited
Merck Consumer Healthcare Ltd
Minverport Enterprises Limited
Nella Holdings Limited
Nextonline Limited
Nomad Foods Europe Finco Ltd
Nomad Foods Europe Holdco Ltd
Nomad Foods Europe Midco Ltd
Norfolk Capital Group Limited
Openview Group Limited
PSN Holdco Limited
PandoraExpress 7 Limited
Phalarope Limited
PizzaExpress Financing 1 PLC
PizzaExpress Financing 2 PLC
PizzaExpress Group Holdings Ltd

Premier Lotteries UK Limited
Procter & Gamble (Health & Beauty Care)
Procter & Gamble Finance (UK) Ltd
Procter & Gamble Investment Company (UK)
Procter & Gamble Limited
Procter & Gamble Overseas Ltd
Procter & Gamble UK Parent Co Ltd
RO Enterprises Limited
RO Financing Co Ltd
Regentrealm Limited
Runecorp Limited
S N B Holdings Limited
S-P RIL Limited
S.A.T.V. Publishing Limited
Shilton Bidco Limited
Shilton Holdco Limited
Signet Holdings Limited
Sky Comedy Limited
Solvecorp Limited
Stafford-Miller Limited
Street Family Group of Companies (Holdings)
United Technologies Finance (U.K.)
Upgrade Investments Limited
WJ Management Limited
Wellmode Limited
Western Wines Holdings Limited
Woodside Road Limited
Zotefoams International Ltd

75000 Veterinary activities

Kynoch Vets Limited
Medivet Group Limited

77110 Renting and leasing of cars and light motor vehicles [16]

Apex Car Rental (Norwich) Ltd
Burnt Tree Group Limited
Buy 2 Let Cars Ltd
P.J. Carey Plant Hire (Oval) Ltd
Cargobull Finance Limited
Enterprise Rent-a-Car UK Holdings
Enterprise Rent-a-Car UK Ltd
Erac UK Finance Limited
Hamsard 3352 Limited
Hamsard 3353 Limited
Hertz (U.K.) Limited
Hertz Accident Support Ltd
Limesquare Finance Limited
Limesquare Vehicle Rental Ltd
Rent 2 Own Cars Ltd
Tuskerdirect Limited

77120 Renting and leasing of trucks and other heavy vehicles

Burnt Tree Group Limited
Cargobull Finance Limited
DGC Limited
Denton Wharf Properties Ltd
Galliford Try Plant Limited
John F. Hunt Hire Centres Ltd

77291 Renting and leasing of media entertainment equipment

Britannia Row Productions Ltd
Panavision Europe Limited

77299 Renting and leasing of other personal and household goods

Cort Business Services UK Ltd

77310 Renting and leasing of agricultural machinery and equipment

Sunlight PV Ltd

77320 Renting and leasing of construction and civil engineering machinery and equipment [19]

Ardent Hire Solutions Limited
P.J. Carey Plant Hire (Oval) Ltd
City Tool Hire Limited
Clancy Plant Limited
J. Devine Plant Hire Limited
Emerson Crane Hire Limited
Fork Rent Limited
John F Hunt Power Limited
JRL Plant and Logistics Ltd
Keltbray Plant Limited
London Tower Crane Hire & Sales Ltd
Specialist Equipment Solutions Ltd
Standard Plant Hire Limited
Tone Group Limited
Vinci Fleet Services Limited
Watch It Come Down Limited
Wren Buyerco Limited
Wren Midco Limited
Wren Topco Limited

77330 Renting and leasing of office machinery and equipment (including computers)

Business Systems (U.K.) Ltd
Econocom Limited
Rackspace UK Leasing Limited
Rivers Finance Group PLC
Rivers Leasing PLC
Xerox (UK) Limited
Xerox Finance Limited

77351 Renting and leasing of air passenger transport equipment

British Airways Leasing Ltd
British Midland Airways Ltd
Lufthansa Technik Landing Gear Services UK

77352 Renting and leasing of freight air transport equipment

TCR UK Limited

77390 Renting and leasing of other machinery, equipment and tangible goods n.e.c. [14]

ARRI Rental Services UK Ltd
Acclaim Handling Limited
Alandale Scaffolding Group Ltd
Chartco Limited
Chep Intercontinental Containers Ltd
Chep UK Limited
Clearway Environmental Services (U.K)
Kingscote Construction Services Ltd
Land & Water Plant Limited
Livingston Ltd
Microlease Limited
Mr. Plant Hire PLC
N.R.C. Plant Limited
Specialist Equipment Solutions Ltd

77400 Leasing of intellectual property and similar products, except copyright works

Porcelanosa U.K. Limited

78109 Other activities of employment placement agencies [10]

Day Webster Limited
Eurostaff Group Limited
L P M (Professional Recruitment) Ltd
McGinley Aviation Holdings Ltd
Michael Page Holdings Limited
Michael Page International Recruitment
Prestige Nursing Limited
Royal British Legion Poppy Factory
SM Global Consultancy Limited
Technical Staffing Resources Ltd

78200 Temporary employment agency activities [24]

1st Step Solutions Limited
A24 Group Limited
Antal International Limited
Arabella Health Staffing Ltd
Athona Limited
Cordant People Limited
Coyle Personnel PLC
EA Consulting Group Ltd
Experis Resource Support Services
Kelly Services (UK) Limited
Mane Contract Services Limited
Manpower UK Limited
Mayday Healthcare PLC
McGinley Cep Ltd
Office Overload Limited
PMP Recruitment Limited
Plan B Healthcare PLC
Premier Work Support Limited
Premiere Employment Group Ltd
Prestige Nursing Limited
RIG Medical Recruit Limited
Shorterm Group Limited
Shorterm Limited
TRG Logistics Ltd

78300 Human resources provision and management of human resources functions

Omni Serv Limited
Penta Consulting Limited
Primat Recruitment Limited
Reliance Globalcom (UK) Ltd

79110 Travel agency activities [24]

Ian Allan Travel Limited
Brightsun Travel (UK) Limited
CWT Holdco Limited
Carlson Wagonlit New Holdco Ltd
Carlson Wagonlit UK Ltd
E.F.R. Travel Limited
Flight Centre (UK) Limited
Flight Centre (UK) Wholesale Ltd
Imagine Cruising Limited
Jetclub Limited
MSC Cruises Limited
Onkar International Limited
Overseas Air Travel Limited
Padwicks Travel (Wembley) Ltd
RCL Cruises Ltd
RSD Travel Limited
Ski Solutions Limited
Skylord Travel PLC
Southall Travel Limited
Sportsworld Group Limited
Travel Nation Limited

Travel Republic Ltd
Travelpack Marketing & Leisure Services
Truly Travel Limited

79120 Tour operator activities [14]

Ian Allan Travel Limited
Cosmos Tours Limited
DTW (Holdings) Limited
Discover The World Limited
Dnata Travel (U.K.) Ltd.
Hebridean Island Cruises Ltd
Newmarket Holidays Limited
Newmarket Promotions Limited
Ocean Holidays Limited
Sail Croatia Adventures Ltd
Sunset Travel Limited
Sunvil International Sales Ltd
Travelpack Marketing & Leisure Services
Tropical Sky Limited

79909 Other reservation service activities n.e.c.

ATD Travel Services Limited
Insurance Claims Accommodation Bureau
Kreutzer Touristik GB Limited
P G S International Limited
Travellanda Ltd

80100 Private security activities [12]

Clearway Environmental Services (U.K)
G4S Aviation Services (UK) Ltd
G4S Cash Centres (UK) Limited
G4S Cash Solutions (UK) Ltd
G4S Secure Solutions (UK) Ltd
G4S Security Services (UK) Ltd
ISS Facility Services Limited
Manpower Direct (UK) Ltd.
Omni Serv Limited
Orbis Protect Limited
STM Group (UK) Limited
Security Monitoring Centres Ltd

80200 Security systems service activities

Axis Security Services Limited
Chubb (NI) Limited
Chubb Fire & Security Limited
Frontline Security Solutions Ltd
Openview Security Solutions Ltd
Secom PLC

81100 Combined facilities support activities [33]

Academy Services (Tendring) Ltd
Academy Services (Waltham Forest)
Affinity (Reading) Limited
Artic Building Services Ltd
Capital Hospitals (Holdings) Ltd.
Capital Hospitals Ltd.
Coventry and Rugby Hospital Company PLC
Derby Healthcare (Holdings) Ltd
Derby School Solutions Limited
Emcor Group (UK) PLC
H & D Support Services Limited
Hamton Environmental Services Ltd
ISS Facility Services Limited
ISS Mediclean Limited
Kingston University Service Co Ltd
LHR Business Support Centre Ltd
Mapeley Steps Contractor Ltd
Meridian Hospital Company (Holdings)
Meridian Hospital Company PLC
Newschools (Leyton) Limited
Newschools (Merton) Limited
Newschools (Swanscombe) Ltd
Prospect Healthcare (Hinchingbrooke)
Prospect Healthcare (Reading) Ltd
QED (Clacton) Limited
QED (Leeds) Limited
Salisbury Holdings Limited
Salisbury Workplace Services Ltd
Taunton Linac Co Ltd
United Healthcare (South Buckinghamshire) Group
United Healthcare (South Buckinghamshire) Holdings
United Healthcare (South Buckinghamshire)
Walsall Hospital Company PLC

81210 General cleaning of buildings [12]

Atlas Contractors Limited
Axis Cleaning and Support Services
Chem-Dry U.K. Limited
Clece Care Services Limited
Cordant Cleaning Limited
Facilicom Cleaning Services Ltd
Hamton Environmental Services Ltd
ISS Facility Services Limited
Property Support Services UK Ltd
Rainham Industrial Services Ltd
TC Facilities Management Ltd
Total Support Services Limited

81222 Specialised cleaning services

ISS Damage Control Limited

81229 Other building and industrial cleaning activities

Atlas Cleaning Limited
ISS Damage Control Limited

81299 Other cleaning services

Apollo Cleaning Services Ltd
Atlas Cleaning Limited
ISS Damage Control Limited
Spectrum Franchising Limited

82110 Combined office administrative service activities

Biz Group Holdings Limited
G & O Securities Limited
I-Catering Management Services Ltd
Metro Global Holdings Limited

82190 Photocopying, document preparation and other specialised office support activities

Advanced Business Equipment Ltd

82200 Activities of call centres

Harte Hanks UK Limited

82301 Activities of exhibition and fair organisers

Media 10 Limited
Reed Exhibitions Limited

82911 Activities of collection agencies

G & O Securities Limited

82920 Packaging activities

Kendon Packaging Group PLC
Kendon Rope & Twine Co Limited
Watts Farms Packers Limited

82990 Other business support service activities n.e.c. [485]

ABP Packaging Limited
ACC Aviation Limited
ACM Eco Holdings Limited
AHL Holdings (Wakefield) Ltd
APCOA Parking (UK) Limited
APCOA Parking Holdings (UK) Ltd
AVM Impact Ltd
Acre 1144 Limited
Aequitas Estates (Poyle) Ltd
P.F. Ahern & Sons Limited
P.F. Ahern (London) Limited
Ahern Land Reclamation Limited
Aitch Care Homes (London) Ltd
Aitco Management Limited
Akari Therapeutics, PLC
Alestra Group Holdings Limited
Alexen Avocats (UK) Limited
Alexion Pharma UK Limited
Alliance BMP Limited
Alliance Healthcare Management Services
Almus Pharmaceuticals Limited
Alto Property Investments Ltd
Amery Construction Limited
Amey Highways Lighting (Wakefield)
Amshold Securities Limited
Annes Gate Property PLC
Apexpost Limited
Aquifer Limited
Asia Pacific Holdings Limited
Aston Heating Limited
Atkins ATK Investments Limited
Atkins International Holdings Ltd
W.S. Atkins International Ltd
Atkins Investments UK Limited
Atkins Limited
Aura Finance Limited
Avonpark Village (Care Homes) Ltd
Axis Group Integrated Services Ltd
Azurie Blue Limited
B & A Group Liverpool Street Ltd
B F Design Solutions Limited
BP Gas Marketing Limited
BP Investment Management Ltd
BP Petrochemicals India Investments
BP Subsea Well Response Ltd
BPC Interiors Limited
Bandai Namco Amusement Europe Ltd
Beam Suntory Operations Ltd
Beecham Group P L C
Berkeley Two Hundred and Three Ltd
Bet Invest Ltd
Bio Products Laboratory Ltd
Bio-Rad Services UK Limited
Black Twig Limited
Blackfriars Land Co Ltd
Blossom House School Limited
James Blunt Limited
Bold-Rock Management and Investments Ltd
Brentwick Limited
Bristol-Myers Squibb Business Services
Britannic Trading Limited
Broadway Malyan Employee Ownership Trustees
Bromley Business Centre (Holdings) Ltd.

Brown and Mason Holdings Ltd
J.Browne Construction Co Ltd
Burney Realty Limited
Burnfield Limited
Bute Capital Limited
CLFIS (U.K.) Limited
CNOOC UK Limited
CWR Capital Ltd
Canada Life Group (U.K.) Ltd
Cappagh Browne Utilities Ltd
Capsicum Motorsport Limited
Caravel Trading Ltd
Cardif Pinnacle Insurance Management Services
Castle Village Limited
Cegal Limited
Centro PLC
Ceros No.1 Limited
Chrysalis (Stanhope) Limited
Churchgate Estates Limited
Cineworld Estates Limited
Cipla (EU) Limited
Civil Service Benevolent Fund
Clinical Pathology Accreditation (UK)
Cloudview Holdings Limited
Coats Finance Co. Limited
Consort Healthcare (Blackburn) Funding
Consort Healthcare (Blackburn) Holdings
Consort Healthcare (Blackburn) Ltd
Construction Workers Guild Ltd
Consulco Finance Ltd
Continua Limited
Contracting Made Easy Ltd
Corbus Europe Limited
Corinthian Land (West Kent) Ltd
Cosan Lubes Investments Ltd
Country House Weddings Limited
Creative Car Park Ltd
Crockford Park Properties Ltd
Crosswater Holdings Limited
Crown Agents Bank Limited
Crown Design and Development Ltd
Croydon Logistics Limited
Croydon and Lewisham Lighting Services
DB Investments Limited
DF Group Limited
DNC UK Limited
DW Windsor Group Limited
Dairy Crest France Holdings 1 Ltd
Dairy Crest UK Limited
Danu Holding Limited
Danu II Holdings Limited
Deacons Associates Limited
Dealcyber Limited
Dexter House Limited
Diamed (G.B.) Ltd.
Direct Supplies (2014) Group Ltd
Direct Supplies (London) Ltd
Dynama Solutions Ltd
E-Nova Healthcare Limited
ENRA Group Limited
EPI Global Ltd
ESP Connections Limited
Easyfairs UK Limited
Ecohomes Development Limited
Ecover (UK) Limited
Education Support (Enfield 2) Holdings
Education Support (Enfield 2) Ltd
Education Support (Enfield) Ltd
Edwardian London Management Services
Eight Investment Limited
Ellenbrook Developments PLC
Elwy 2 Limited
Elwy 3 Limited
Energypro Asset Management Ltd
Eskaylab Limited
European Investments (Cornwall) Ltd
European Investments (Earlseat) Ltd
European Investments (SCEL) Ltd
ExxonMobil Chemical Investment Co Ltd
ExxonMobil Finance Co Ltd
ExxonMobil Financial Investment Co Ltd
ExxonMobil Holding Co Ltd
ExxonMobil Investment Co Ltd
ExxonMobil UK Limited
Ezra Attia Limited
FC JB Co Limited
FTE & M Limited
Faithful+Gould Limited
Far East & Co Limited
First City Care (London) Ltd
First Rate Exchange Services Holdings
First Rate Exchange Services Ltd
Florin Industrial Services Holdings
Former Reichmann Properties PLC
Forss Wind Farm Limited.
Foster & Allen Holdings Ltd
Francotyp-Postalia Limited
Friars Developments Limited
Frontline Security Solutions Ltd
Fulton Central Limited
Fulton Clover Limited
Fulton Grand Limited
Fulton Hyde Limited
Fulton Lincoln Limited
Fulton Regent Limited
Fulton St James Limited
GCP Asset Finance 1 Limited
GCP Biomass 1 Ltd
GCP Biomass 2 Limited
GCP Biomass 3 Limited
GCP Biomass 4 Limited
GCP Cardale PFI Ltd
GCP Education 1 Limited
GCP Green Energy 1 Limited
GCP Healthcare 1 Limited
GCP Hydro 1 Limited
GCP Onshore Wind 1 Limited
GCP Onshore Wind 3 Limited
GCP Programme Funding 1 Ltd
GCP RHI Boiler 1 Limited
GCP Rooftop Solar 1 Limited
GCP Rooftop Solar 2 Limited
GCP Rooftop Solar 3 Limited
GCP Rooftop Solar 4 Limited
GCP Rooftop Solar 5 Ltd
GCP Rooftop Solar 6 PLC
GCP Rooftop Solar Finance PLC
GCP Social Housing 1 Limited
GDL (Luton) Developments Ltd
GE Money Servicing Limited
GHL (Hackney Wick) Limited
GL Assessment Limited
GMK Pepper Holdings Limited
Galliard Developments Limited
Garreg Lwyd Energy Limited
Genie Energy UK Ltd
Gerrard International Limited
Gilead Sciences Europe Ltd.
Giles Homes Limited
Gladstone Court Developments Ltd
Glasgow Learning Quarter Ltd
GlaxoSmithKline Intellectual Property Management
GlaxoSmithKline International Ltd
GlaxoSmithKline Investment Services
Goal Global Recoveries Limited
Goal Group Limited
Grantol Investments Limited
Green Hill Energy Limited
Green Mountain Estates Ltd
Green Space London Limited
Grovestream Limited
Guild of Construction Workers Ltd
HCL Insurance BPO Services Ltd
HCT Portland Limited
HFS Investment Properties Ltd
HH Global Corporate Services Ltd
Haemonetics Asia UK Ltd
Harlequin Direct Limited
Harsco (U.K.) Limited
Harsco Rail Limited
Hasbro U.K. Limited
Hayes Point (Sully) Limited
Haymarket UK2 Limited
Healthcare Support (North Staffs) Finance
Robert Heath Group Limited
Heathrow Airport Limited
Herbalife (U.K.) Limited
Hertz Holdings III UK Limited
Highway Stops Retail Limited
Hill Group Services Limited
Hill of Towie Limited
Hilton Finance (UK) Limited
Hilton Worldwide FS Treasury Ltd
Holmes Care (Group) Limited
Homepines Investments Limited
Horlicks Limited
Hotel Intercontinental London (Holdings)
Hudson Almere Limited
Hudson Arnhem Limited
Hudson Brent Limited
Hudson Camden Limited
Hudson Chemical Tankers Ltd
Howard Hunt Mail Limited
Hunters Contracts Limited
I.C.F. Finance Limited
I4B Holdings Limited
IAG GBS Limited
ICS Incorporation Limited
IGUK Support Services Limited
IHG Hotels Limited
Igroup 8 Limited
Information Security Forum Ltd
Infotech Trade Services Ltd
Inspiral Oldham Limited
Interchemprod and Invest Ltd
Intercontinental Adjusters (Europe)
Intercontinental Hotels Ltd
Interiors with Art Limited
Intralot Finance UK Limited
Investland Limited
Islandbridge Chigwell Limited
JLW Excellent Homes for Life Ltd
JTI (RMS) Ltd
Jasper Morrison Limited
Jupiter Topco Limited
K.E.M. Property Services Ltd
KPIT Technologies (UK) Limited
Kelly Comms Limited
Kidde Finance Limited
Kore Wireless UK PLC
Kristal Enterprises Limited
Kuehne + Nagel (UK) Limited
Kuflink Bridging Ltd
LGC (Holdings) Limited

LGC Investments Limited
LGC Science Holdings Limited
LGC Science Investments Ltd
LGC Whirlwind Limited
LRH Care Homes Limited
Langdon Foundation
Laridge Investments Limited
Leez Priory Limited
Leyton Clubs (London) Limited
Liberata UK Limited
Lime Tree Village Limited
Lineside Logistics (Southern) Ltd
Link Asset Services (Holdings) Ltd
Link Corporate Trustees (UK) Ltd
Link Market Services Limited
Linkmart Limited
Local Boy'z Group Holding Ltd
London Irish Consortium (2013) Ltd
London Outpost Limited
M G 111 Ltd
MA Securities London Limited
MC Treasury Limited
MJF Business Services Limited
MRB Holdings Ltd
Major Properties London Ltd
Manpower Services Limited
Masterson Holdings Limited
Maxco London Limited
Mechanical Services Limited
Merck Sharp & Dohme Finance Europe
Merligen Investments Limited
Merton Acquisitions Limited
Metrosold Limited
Micro Plus Software Limited
Millennium Care Homes Limited
Mondelez UK Limited
Mondi German Investments Ltd
Mullan Partnership Limited
Multi Services Kent Limited
NCQ Developments Limited
National Animal Welfare Trust
Navigator Terminals Midco Ltd
Neelkanth Safe Deposit Ltd
New Landmark Investment Ltd
Newincco 1270 Limited
Newmarston Ltd
Nexen Petroleum U.K. Holdings Ltd
Florence Nightingale Aid in Sickness Trust
Noble Gift Packaging Limited
Nomad Foods BondCo PLC
Nomad Foods Europe Finco Ltd
Nomad Foods Europe Holdco Ltd
Nomad Foods Europe Holdings Ltd
Nomad Foods Europe Midco Ltd
Nuffield Health Pension Trustees Ltd
Oak Tree Schools Holdings Ltd
Odris Investments Limited
Olivegate Properties Limited
Optimum Group Services PLC
Orbital Equipment Limited
Orthopaedic Research UK
Park House Residential Developments
Passportcard Limited
Penn Place Investments Limited
Petco Trading (UK) Limited
Pharmacare (Europe) Limited
Pharmasure Limited
Phivco UK II Limited
Photo-Me Limited
Pinnacle Schools (Fife) Ltd
Platinum Acquisition Limited
Platinum Midco 2 Limited
Platinum Midco Limited
Platinum Topco Limited
Pole To Win UK Limited
Prima Tapes & Labels Ltd
Procter & Gamble Technical Centres
Pudfield Investments Ltd
Pyramid Schools (Sheffield) Ltd
R V Moat House Limited
RA Securities London Limited
RES UK & Ireland Limited
RL Retail Services Limited
Raven Promotions Limited
Redab PLC
Dennis Reed Limited
Regard ACH Holdco Limited
Regenter B3 Limited
Regenter Myatts Field North Ltd
Reliance Infra Projects (UK) Ltd
Retallack Holidays Limited
Retirement Villages Limited
Rex Trade Associates Limited
Richmond & Hampshire Limited
Rocco Homes Limited
Roseview (London) Ltd.
Rush Hair Group Limited
S A Designer Parfums Limited
S.S.A.T. Property Investments Ltd
SCIH Branston 3
Sabre EMEA Marketing Limited
Samsung Electronics (UK) Ltd
Santray Limited
Satair UK Limited
Saxton Limited
Scape Opportunities Dublin Ltd
Sensormatic Limited
Services Support (Cleveland) Ltd
Services Support (Gravesend) Ltd
Services Support (Manchester) Ltd
Services Support (SEL) Limited
Servipharm Limited
Sevita (UK) Limited
Shelfside Holding (Northern) Ltd
Sidan Trading Holdings Limited
Signet Direct Diamond Sourcing Ltd
Signet Group Services Limited
Signet Trading Limited
Signet UK Finance PLC
Silixa Ltd
Sines Parks (S.E.) Limited
Six Continents Investments Ltd
Six Continents Limited
Six Continents Overseas Holdings Ltd
Six Continents Restaurants Ltd
Skanska Infrastructure Investment UK
Skanska J.V. Projects Ltd
Sky Finance Europe Limited
Sky Group Finance PLC
Sky Retail Stores Limited
Sky Telecommunications Services Ltd
Sky UK Limited
SmithKline Beecham (Export) Ltd
SmithKline Beecham Marketing and Technical Services
Sonata Europe Limited
Sony Global Treasury Services PLC
South Central Property Limited
South Manchester Energy Ltd
Sports Gambling Committee Ltd
Starna Limited
Stema Shipping (UK) Limited
Stratford High Street Ventures Ltd
Strides Arcolab International Ltd
Subsea 7 Engineering Limited
Subsea 7 Finance (UK) PLC
Subsea 7 Investments (UK) Ltd
Subsea 7 Treasury (UK) Limited
Sugarman Group Limited
Surrey Blue Limited
Surrey Lighting Services Ltd
Swiss Post Solutions Ltd
Synbra UK Limited
Syner-Med (Pharmaceutical Products)
TBG (4) Limited
TJX Europe Buying (Deutschland) Ltd
TJX Europe Buying Limited
TWG Services Limited
TY Ventures (UK) Limited
Tabor Group Ltd
Tancia Limited
O.C. Tanner Limited
Taylor Wentworth Limited
Teddington 2 Limited
Thamesfield Limited
Thumbzup UK Limited
Tican (Chilled) Limited
Toshiba of Europe Limited
Toureen Group Limited
Tower Bridge Homes Care Ltd
Tracker Network (UK) Limited
Trading Post Limited
Trafalgar Square Investments Ltd
Transform Schools (Bassetlaw) Ltd
Transform Schools (Knowsley) Intermediate
Transform Schools (Knowsley) Ltd
Transform Schools (North Lanarkshire) Holdings
Transform Schools (Rotherham) Ltd
Travel Republic Holdings Ltd.
UCL Frognal Limited
UCL Harrow Limited
UK Highways M40 (Holdings) Ltd
UK Highways M40 Limited
Ultimate Holdings Limited
Union Investcorp Limited
United Distributing Company (Coin Machine Sales)
VFS Legal Limited
Vendcrown Limited
Vetex Limited
Via Global Limited
ViiV Healthcare UK Limited
W3 Insights Ltd
WHTC Ltd
Walgreens Boots Alliance Services
Walsingham Care
Warrant Investments PLC
Warrant Properties Limited
Waterlow Business Supplies Ltd
Wates Group Services Limited
W K Webster & Co Ltd
Wesco Distribution-International Ltd
Western United Investment Co Ltd
Whelan & Grant (Holdings) Ltd
Willhay Management Limited
Woodledge Limited
Worldwide Product Sourcing Ltd
XTO UK, Ltd
Yellow Brick Developments Ltd
Zebrak London Limited

84110 General public administration activities

Achieving for Children CIC
BMT Defence and Security UK Ltd

Liberata UK Limited

84220 Defence activities

BMT Defence and Security UK Ltd
BMT Group Limited
Eastbury Park Limited
Jankel Armouring Limited

84240 Public order and safety activities

Guarding UK Ltd

84250 Fire service activities

Chubb Fire & Security Limited
Chubb Fire Limited
Fire Design Solutions Limited

85100 Pre-primary education [28]

Aldenham Foundation
Aquinas Church of England Education Trust
Avanti Schools Trust
Bellevue Education International Ltd
Bentley Wood Trust
Caterham School Limited
Claremont Fan Court Foundation Ltd
Dicky Birds Pre School Nurseries Ltd
Ewell Castle School
Feltonfleet School Trust Ltd
German School Association Ltd
Hampton School
Heathland Whitefriars Federation
E. Ivor Hughes Educational Foundation
Notre Dame School Cobham
Pelham Academy Trust
Reach Academy Trust
The Alec Reed Academy
Rosedale Hewens Academy Trust
Russell School Trust
Select Enterprises (Holdings) Ltd
South Orpington Learning Alliance Multi-Academy Trust
South West Essex Community Education Trust
St Catherine's School Twickenham
St George's Weybridge
TASIS The American School in England
TASIS UK Limited
Vanguard Learning Trust

85200 Primary education [128]

Abercorn Education Ltd
Abercorn School Limited
Al-Noor Foundation Limited
Aldenham Foundation
Alexandra Infant School
Amadeus Primary Academies Trust
Aquinas Church of England Education Trust
Atwood Primary Academy
Avanti Schools Trust
Babington House School Limited
Balgowan Primary School
Bancroft's School
Beddington Park Academy Trust
Bellevue Education International Ltd
Belmont Castle Academy
Bentley Wood Trust
Bishopsgate School Limited
Bourne Education Trust
Broadfields Academy Trust
Burnt Ash Primary School
Bushey St James Trust
Catalyst Academies Trust
Caterham School Limited
Chancery Education Trust
Charles Kalms, Henry Ronson Immanuel College
Chesterton Education Limited
Chigwell School
Children's Trust
Claremont Fan Court Foundation Ltd
Cleves Academy Trust
Connect Schools Academy Trust
Cranmore School
Cygnus Academies Trust
Days Lane Primary School
Drapers' Multi-Academy Trust
Eden Academy
Edge Grove School Trust Ltd
Edmonton Academy Trust
Ewell Castle School
Excellence in Education Trust
Fairchildes Academy Community Trust
Feltonfleet School Trust Ltd
GLF Schools
Galaxy Trust
Gateway Learning Community
German School Association Ltd
Hampton School
Harrow Academies Trust
Heathland Whitefriars Federation
Highfield Infants' School
Highfield Junior School
Hindu Education Authority Ltd
Hoddesdon School Trust
Homefield Preparatory School Trust
Howard Partnership Trust
E. Ivor Hughes Educational Foundation
Hurst Primary School
Inclusive Multi Academy Trust
Inspired Learning Group (UK) Ltd
Kew College
King's House School Trust (Richmond)
Krinvest Limited
LDBS Frays Academy Trust
Lady Eleanor Holles School
Langley Park Learning Trust
Latchmere Academy Trust
Lumen Learning Trust
Lycee International de Londres
Mall School Trust
Manor Lodge School
Newland House School Trust Ltd
Nexus Education Schools Trust
Norwood Green Junior School
Notre Dame School Cobham
Oaks Academy Trust
Old Vicarage School Trust
Orley Farm School Trust
Pace Academy Trust
Pact Educational Trust Limited
Parallel Learning Trust
Park Federation Academy Trust
Parkside School Trust
Pegasus Academy Trust
Pelham Academy Trust
Pickhurst Infant Academy
Primary First Trust
Raglan Primary School
Reach Academy Trust
The Alec Reed Academy
Remus White Limited
Rise Park Academy Trust
Rokeby Educational Trust Ltd
Rosedale Hewens Academy Trust
Russell School Trust
Shrewsbury House School Trust Ltd
South Orpington Learning Alliance Multi-Academy Trust
South West Essex Community Education Trust
Specialist Learning Trust
Spring Partnership Trust
St Catherine's School Twickenham
St George's Weybridge
St John's School, Northwood
St. Aubyn's (Woodford Green) School Trust
St. James The Great R.C. Primary and Nursery School
St. John's Preparatory & Senior School
St. Margaret's School Bushey
St.Helen's School Northwood
St.Martins' (Northwood) Preparatory School Trust
Staines Preparatory School Trust
Step Academy Trust
Synaptic Trust
TASIS The American School in England
TASIS UK Limited
Tandridge Learning Trust
Trinitas Academy Trust
Tudor Court Primary Academy Trust
Unity Academy Trust
Upminster Academies Trust
Vanguard Learning Trust
Vernon Educational Trust Ltd
Warren Road Primary School
Wembley Multi Academy Trust
West Herts Community Free School Trust
West Thurrock Academy
Westbourne Academy Trust
Westbrook Primary School
Wood End Academy
Woodland Academy Trust

85310 General secondary education [182]

ACS International Schools Ltd
Aim Academies Trust
Al-Khair Foundation
Aldenham Foundation
Alperton Community School
Aquinas Church of England Education Trust
Archbishop Lanfranc Academy - Coloma Trust
Arete Trust
Avanti Schools Trust
Babington House School Limited
Bancroft's School
Beacon Multi-Academy Trust Ltd
Bentley Wood Trust
Beths Grammar School
Bexley Grammar School
Bishop Wand Church of England School
Bishopshalt School
Blackfen School for Girls
Blenheim High School
Bourne Education Trust
Brentford School for Girls
Broxbourne School
Bullers Wood Multi Academy Trust
Bushey St James Trust
Campion School
Canons High School
Carshalton Boys Sports College
Caterham School Limited
Chadwell Heath Academy

Charles Kalms, Henry Ronson Immanuel College
Cheam Academies Network
Chigwell School
Children's Trust
Chislehurst School for Girls
Chislehurst and Sidcup Grammar School
Chobham School Academy (Stratford)
Chrysalis Multi Academy Trust
Claremont Fan Court Foundation Ltd
Collegiate Trust
Coombe Academy Trust
Cranford Community College
Dame Alice Owen's School
Danes Educational Trust
Darrick Wood School
Dartford Grammar School
Davenant Foundation School
Decus Educational Trust
Drapers' Multi-Academy Trust
East Barnet School
Eden Academy
Edmonton Academy Trust
Education for The 21st Century
Elmwey Learning Trust
Elstree UTC
Emerson Park Academy
Empower Learning Academy Trust
Endeavour MAT
Epsom College
Erith School
Every Child, Every Day Academy Trust
Ewell Castle School
Folio Education Trust
GLF Schools
Gateway Learning Community
Generations Multi Academy Trust
German School Association Ltd
Girls' Learning Trust
Good Shepherd Catholic Trust
Grand Union Multi Academy Trust
Greenshaw Learning Trust
Guru Nanak Sikh Academy Ltd
Halliford School Limited
Hampton School
Harefield Academy Trust
Harrodian School Limited
Harrow Academies Trust
Harrow High School
Hatch End High School
Haydon School
Heathland Whitefriars Federation
Heathrow Aviation Engineering UTC
Hertswood Academy
Hinchley Wood School
Hindu Education Authority Ltd
Hoddesdon School Trust
Homefield Preparatory School Trust
Howard Partnership Trust
Hurstmere School
Impact Multi Academy Trust
Isleworth and Syon School for Boys
Jewish Community Secondary School Trust
Kedleston (OS Education) Ltd
Kedleston (Wings Education) Ltd
Kings Langley School
Kingsmead School
Kingston Grammar School
Lady Eleanor Holles School
Lampton School Academy Trust
Langley Park Learning Trust
Langley Park School for Boys Academy Trust
Life Education Trust
Lycee International de Londres
Manor Trust
Marymount International School
Mayfield Grammar School, Gravesend
Meller Educational Trust
Merchant Taylors' School
Middlesex Learning Partnership
Mount Grace School
North London Collegiate School
Notre Dame School Cobham
Nower Hill High School
Ockendon Academy
Odyssey Trust for Education
Orleans Park School
Orley Farm School Trust
Overton Grange School
PS Foundation
Pact Educational Trust Limited
Parallel Learning Trust
Preston Manor Academy Trust
Purcell School
Queen Elizabeth's Girls' School (Barnet)
Queen Elizabeth's School Barnet
Queens' School (Bushey)
Quest Academy - Coloma Trust
RET Becket Keys Church of England Free School Trust
Radnor House School (Holdings) Ltd
Radnor House School (Property) Ltd
Radnor House Sevenoaks (Holdings)
Radnor House Sevenoaks (Property)
Reach Academy Trust
The Alec Reed Academy
Richmond West Schools Trust
Rickmansworth School
Rosedale Hewens Academy Trust
Royal Masonic School for Girls
Ruislip High School
Russell School Trust
SFAET Ltd
Shirley High School
South West Essex Community Education Trust
Southborough High School
Specialist Learning Trust
St Catherine's Catholic School
St Catherine's School Twickenham
St George's Weybridge
St Mary's CE Academy, Cheshunt
St. Aubyn's (Woodford Green) School Trust
St. John's Preparatory & Senior School
St. Margaret's School Bushey
St.Helen's School Northwood
Summit Media Limited
Sunbury Manor School
Sutton Grammar School Trust
Swakeleys School for Girls
TASIS The American School in England
TASIS UK Limited
Tandridge Learning Trust
Teddington School
Thamesmead School
Tiffin Girls' School
Tithe Academy
Trinitas Academy Trust
Unity Schools Trust
Ursuline Academy Ilford
Uxbridge High School Academy Trust
Vanguard Learning Trust
Veritas Educational Trust
Waldegrave Trust
Watford Grammar School for Boys
Watford Grammar School for Girls
Wembley Multi Academy Trust
West Hatch High School Academy Trust
Westfield Academy
William Willett Learning Trust
Willow Learning Trust
Woldingham School
Woodcote High School
Xavier Catholic Education Trust
Yavneh College Academy Trust
Yehudi Menuhin School Limited

85320 Technical and vocational secondary education [12]

Alperton Community School
Brit School Limited
Centre for Engineering and Manufacturing Excellence
Elstree UTC
Heathrow Aviation Engineering UTC
JTL
Jancett Childcare & Jace Training
PS Foundation
Park High School
Science, Engineering and Manufacturing Technologies Alliance
Summit Media Limited
Watford UTC

85410 Post-secondary non-tertiary education

Avanti Schools Trust
Davenant Foundation School
PS Foundation
Richmond and Hillcroft Adult and Community College
Veritas Educational Trust
Willow Learning Trust

85421 First-degree level higher education

GL Assessment Limited
London School of Theology
Mont Rose College of Management and Sciences
Rose Bruford College of Theatre and Performance
Royal School of Needlework
St Mary's University, Twickenham

85422 Post-graduate level higher education

London School of Theology
Rose Bruford College of Theatre and Performance
St Mary's University, Twickenham

85510 Sports and recreation education

One YMCA
Royal School of Needlework
Watford FC's Community Sports & Education Trust

85520 Cultural education

Backstage Centre Limited
Brit School Limited
Pact Educational Trust Limited
Royal School of Needlework

85590 Other education n.e.c. [17]

Able Skills Limited
Aldro School Educational Trust Ltd
The John Apthorp Charity
Beacon Hill Academy
Harris Federation
Institute of Grocery Distribution
Kemnal Academies Trust
Learning Tree International Ltd
London South East Academies Trust
Loxford School Trust Limited
MyTime Active
Orchard Hill College Academy Trust
Pact Educational Trust Limited
Parkwood Hall Co-operative Academy Trust
Princess Alice Hospice
Voluntary Service Overseas
Wandle Valley School

85600 Educational support services

Achieving for Children CIC
Bellevue Education Group Ltd
GLF Schools
Kedleston Schools Limited
Norwood Ravenswood
Prospects Group 2011 Limited
Prospects Services
Russell Education Trust

86101 Hospital activities [20]

Central Nottinghamshire Hospitals PLC
Central Surrey Health Limited
Consort Healthcare (Mid Yorkshire) Funding
Consort Healthcare (Mid Yorkshire) Holdings
Consort Healthcare (Mid Yorkshire)
Elysium Healthcare (St Mary's) Ltd
Elysium Healthcare No. 2 Ltd
Elysium Healthcare Property 2 Ltd
Elysium Healthcare Property 3 Ltd
Endeavour SCH PLC
ISS Mediclean Limited
Metier Holdings Limited
New Victoria Hospital Limited
Newhospitals (St Helens and Knowsley)
Prospect Healthcare (Hairmyres) Ltd
Saint Francis Hospice
St George Healthcare Limited
St. Luke's Hospice (Harrow & Brent) Ltd.
Paul Strickland Scanner Centre
Victoria Foundation

86102 Medical nursing home activities

Claremont Care Services Ltd
Dalemead Care Home Limited
Dovestone Estates Limited
Forth Health Limited
Hazeldell Ltd
Hospital Company (Southmead) Ltd
Millennium Care Homes Limited
St. Vincent's Charitable Trust

86210 General medical practice activities

Central Surrey Health Limited
Ellenor
Health & Case Management Ltd
La Nu-Range Ltd
Shotfield Development Business Partnership
Sugarman Group Limited
Vivo Medical Care Limited

86220 Specialists medical practice activities

Combat Stress
Elysium Healthcare (Acorn Care) Ltd
Elysium Healthcare (Healthlinc) Ltd
Vashisht Surgical Limited

86230 Dental practice activities

Dentex Healthcare Group Ltd
Kavo Dental Limited
Newham Family Dental Care Ltd
Perfect Practices Group Ltd
Perfect Smile Group Holding Ltd
Perfect Smile Newcastle Ltd
Pickering Dental Surgeries Ltd
Whiter Smile Limited
York House Centre Limited

86900 Other human health activities [50]

Agfa Healthcare UK Limited
Alina Care Limited
Avenues Trust Group
Bio Products Laboratory Holdings Ltd
Otto Bock Healthcare PLC
Bramley Health Holding Co Ltd
Bromley Healthcare CIC
Caretech Community Services (No.2)
Caretech Community Services Ltd
Central Surrey Health Limited
Chai-Lifeline Cancer Care
Clinisupplies Limited
Cochlear Europe Limited
Cochlear Research and Development
Thomas H. Collison Limited
Cranstoun
Elysium Healthcare (Farndon) Ltd
Elysium Healthcare (Ultimate Care)
Elysium Healthcare No. 3 Ltd
Elysium Healthcare No. 4 Ltd
Frasers and Son Ltd
Galvani Bioelectronics Limited
Gittisham Care Limited
Handsale Limited
Health & Case Management Ltd
Holmes Care Limited
Imaging Centre Holdings Ltd
Inspire Community Trust
Langford Clinic Limited
Leprosy Mission International
Medtronic Limited
MyTime Active
Naga UK Bidco Limited
Naga UK Topco Limited
Nuffield Health
PS Foundation
Peace Hospice Care
Placement Group Healthcare Ltd
Postgrad Limited
Prestige Nursing Limited
Princess Alice Hospice
RFU Injured Players Foundation
Selborne Care Limited
Shooting Star Chase
SmithKline Beecham (SWG) Ltd
THMG Limited
Valeo Limited
Voluntary Service Overseas
West & Coe Limited
Your Healthcare CIC

87100 Residential nursing care facilities [40]

A.G.E. Nursing Homes Limited
AMS Care Limited
Abbey Care Complex Limited
Abbey Ravenscroft Park Limited
Angel Care (Orchid Care Homes) Ltd
Angel Care PLC
Askham Village Community Ltd
Assured Services Limited
Aster Healthcare Ltd.
Berkeley Healthcare Limited
Camberley Care Limited
Clavering Care Limited
Cooperscroft Care Home Limited
Custodes Acqco Limited
Custodes Midco Limited
De Vere Care Limited
Esteem Care Ltd
Farrington Care Homes Limited
GCH (St Katharine's) Limited
Graham Care (YB) Limited
Greenswan Consultants Limited
Heritage Care Homes Limited
Huntington House Limited
Nicholas James Care Homes Ltd
Karuna Care (TLC) Limited
Loughton Care Centre Limited
MNS Care PLC
Martlane Limited
Millennium Care Homes Limited
PQW Brenley Corner Limited
Planshore Limited
George Potter House Ltd
RANC Care Homes Limited
RANC Holdings Limited
Rockley Dene Homes Limited
Surrey Rest Homes Limited
TLC Group Limited
Tudor Bank Limited
Uniquehelp Limited
Whiteley Homes Trust

87200 Residential care activities for learning difficulties, mental health and substance abuse [12]

Avenues Trust Group
CMG Holdco Limited
Care Management Group Limited
Clece Care Services Limited
Cranstoun
Homes Caring for Autism Ltd
Marcus & Marcus Limited
Norwood Ravenswood
Norwood Schools Ltd.
Regard Partnership Limited
Ruby Topco Limited
Sons of Divine Providence

87300 Residential care activities for the elderly and disabled [31]

AMS Care Wiltshire Limited
Abbey Care Complex Limited
Abbey Ravenscroft Park Limited
Aitch Care Homes Holdco Ltd
Aitch Care Homes Topco Limited
Ashdown Care Limited
Assured Services Limited
Avenues Trust Group
Broadham Care Limited
Brownlow Enterprises Limited
Careprogress Limited
Children's Trust
Chislehurst Care Limited
Clece Care Services Limited
Denville Hall 2012
Krinvest Limited
Martlane Limited
Mills Family Limited
Minster Care Group Limited
Minster Care Management Ltd
Moreland House Care Home Ltd
Only Care Limited
Planshore Limited
Regal Trading Ltd
Sahara Care Limited
Scimitar Care Hotels PLC
Seymour House Residential Care Homes
Sons of Divine Providence
Southern Counties Care Limited
St. Dominic's Ltd.
Whiteley Homes Trust

87900 Other residential care activities n.e.c. [17]

Abbeyfield Southern Oaks
Action for Children Services Ltd
Care Providers Recruitment Ltd
Caretech Community Services (No.2)
Caretech Community Services Ltd
Children's Trust
Community Support Project Ltd
Coxwell Care Limited
Croftwood Care (Cheshire) Ltd
Crossways Care (UK) Limited
Hawthorne Trust Limited
Laurels Care Limited
London Care Partnership Ltd
Nellsar Limited
Realmpark Health Care (Petworth) Ltd
Residential Care Services Ltd
Valeo Limited

88100 Social work activities without accommodation for the elderly and disabled

Heritage Care Limited
Inspire Community Trust

88910 Child day-care activities

Action for Children
Action for Children Services Ltd
Jancett Childcare & Jace Training
Norwood Schools Ltd.
One YMCA
West London YMCA
White Lodge Centre

88990 Other social work activities without accommodation n.e.c. [33]

Achieving for Children CIC
Barnardo Services Limited
Barnardo's
Belton Associates (Group Holdings)
Belton Associates Holdings Ltd
Belton Associates Limited
Congregation of The Daughters of The Cross International Generalate
Cranstoun
Davenant Centre
Dewan Foundation Limited
Foster Care Agency Limited
Gardeners' Royal Benevolent Society
Hawthorne Trust Limited
JCA Charitable Foundation
Jay Fostering Limited
NFAG Limited
NFAH Limited
NFAP Limited
National Fostering Agency (Scotland)
National Fostering Agency Ltd
Norwood Ravenswood
Norwood Schools Ltd.
Outlook Fostering Services Ltd
Princess Alice Hospice
Reedham Children's Trust
Royal Medical Foundation
Saint Francis Hospice
St. Luke's Hospice (Harrow & Brent) Ltd.
Tearfund
Tobacco Pipe Makers and Tobacco Trade Benevolent Fund
Wates Foundation Limited
West London YMCA
Zoroastrian Trust Funds of Europe (Incorporated)

90010 Performing arts

Orlando Limited
Yehudi Menuhin School Limited

90020 Support activities to performing arts

Backstage Centre Limited

90030 Artistic creation

Fifty Shades Ltd
First Network Ltd.
Palace Theatre Watford Limited
Rapid Action Packaging Limited
Shazam Productions Limited
Summit Media Limited
Richard Wright Music Limited

90040 Operation of arts facilities

Backstage Centre Limited
Danjuma Collection Ltd
Davenant Centre
Inspireall Leisure and Family Support Services
Latif International Limited
Marchanson Limited
Palace Theatre Watford Limited
Twickenham Studios Limited

91011 Library activities

WLHC Projectco Limited

91012 Archives activities

Hill Co Ltd

91030 Operation of historical sites and buildings and similar visitor attractions

Asgill House Trust Limited

91040 Botanical and zoological gardens and nature reserves activities

Gardeners' Royal Benevolent Society
William Robinson Gravetye Charity

92000 Gambling and betting activities

Barcrest Group Limited
Camelot Business Solutions Ltd
Camelot Global Lottery Solutions Ltd
Camelot UK Lotteries Limited
Stealth Leisure Limited
Ticketgrange Limited

93110 Operation of sports facilities [23]

Buckinghamshire Golf Co Ltd
Burhill Golf and Leisure Ltd
Burhill Group Limited
Double A Group Services Ltd
FL Property Management Limited
Football First Limited
Fulham Stadium Limited
Golf Entertainment International Ltd
Hive Football Centre Holdings Ltd
Impulse Leisure
Inspireall Leisure and Family Support Services
Kingswood Golf & Country Club Ltd
MSV Group Limited
Motorsport Vision Limited
MyTime Active
National Football Centre Ltd
Purslow Investments Limited
Silvermere Golf & Leisure Ltd
St. George's Hill Lawn Tennis Club
St. Margaret's School Bushey
T.H.G. & C.C. Limited
Topgolf Limited
Wembley National Stadium Ltd

93120 Activities of sport clubs [11]

Brentford FC Limited
Buckinghamshire Golf Co Ltd
Fulham Football Club Limited
Fulham Football Leisure Ltd
Lensbury Limited
London Irish Rugby Football Ground
London Irish Scottish Richmond Ltd
Premier Rugby Limited
Purslow Investments Limited
Queenwood Golf Club Limited
Redbridge Sports Centre Trust Ltd

93130 Fitness facilities

Gym Limited
National Football Centre Ltd
Thames Ditton Sports and Squash Club
YMCA St Pauls Group

93191 Activities of racehorse owners

Fishdance Limited

93199 Other sports activities [12]

Cougar Holdco London Limited
Double A Group Services Ltd
Football Association Limited
Harlequin Football Club Ltd
Inspireall Leisure and Family Support Services
Maia Leisure Limited
Motorsport Vision Limited
National Football Centre Ltd
Rugby Football Development Ltd
Rugby Football Foundation
Topgolf Group Limited
Watford Association Football Club

93210 Activities of amusement parks and theme parks

Silvertime Amusements Limited

93290 Other amusement and recreation activities n.e.c.

Anglo Scottish Leisure Limited
Body Works West at Lambton Place Ltd
Davenant Centre
HAGS-SMP Limited
Inspireall Leisure and Family Support Services
Kidspace Adventures Holdings Ltd
Namco UK Limited
Shenley Park Trust
Trafalgar Leisure Ltd

94110 Activities of business and employers membership organisations

British Marine Federation

94120 Activities of professional membership organisations

Leisure and Outdoor Furniture Association

94910 Activities of religious organisations [14]

Amana Trust
Anoopam Mission
BW Foundation
Church of Pentecost - UK
Duke Street Church (Richmond-upon-Thames)
Erinastar Limited
Grace Baptist Trust Corporation
International Society for Krishna Consciousness
Purley Baptist Church
Sons of Divine Providence
Sparquote Limited
United Reformed Church (Southern Synod) Trust
World Mission Agency - Winners Chapel International
YMCA St Pauls Group

94990 Activities of other membership organisations n.e.c.

British Limbless Ex-Service Men's Association
Foundation and Friends of The Royal Botanic Gardens, Kew
One YMCA
Premier Rugby Limited
Mary Roxburghe Trust
Royal School of Needlework
Samaritans
Water Incorporated

95110 Repair of computers and peripheral equipment

C.C. (Engineering) Limited
HCL Great Britain Limited

96010 Washing and (dry-)cleaning of textile and fur products

Essex County Laundry,Limited

96020 Hairdressing and other beauty treatment

Headmasters Partnership Ltd
Headmasters Salons Limited
TIGI International Limited

96030 Funeral and related activities

Family Funerals Trust Limited
Golden Leaves Limited
Lodge Bros. (Funerals) Limited
W.A. Truelove & Son Limited

96040 Physical well-being activities

IAH Charity Co Ltd
MyTime Active

96090 Other service activities n.e.c. [113]

ABM Technical Solutions Ltd
ADT Fire and Security PLC
ATC Holdings Limited
Acclaim DMW Holdings Limited
Acqua Plus Developments Ltd
Advanced Industrial Technology Corporation
Air Menzies International Ltd
Alder Hey (Special Purpose Vehicle)
All World Foods Limited
Amaze Capital Limited
Automatic Sales Limited
BW Foundation
Barrett Industrial Limited
Beam Global Finance UK Limited
Bellman Property Group Limited
Blackstone City Ltd
Book Trade Charity (BTBS)
Brand Energy & Infrastructure Services UK,
Martin Bunzl International Ltd
Bycentral Limited
Bynorth Limited
Bywest Limited
Caligor Opco UK, Ltd
Cedars Village Limited
Chart Forte Holdings Ltd
Charters Village Limited
Chawla & Gulati Property Investments
Chem-Dry Franchising Limited
Citipost Limited
Conneely Drylining Limited
Cordant Group PLC
Cordant Security Limited
Corinthia Investments Limited
D.M.C. Business Machines Ltd
Davenant Centre
Dovestone Estates Limited
Dunkeld Trading Limited
Finepoint Broadcast Limited
Fineraid Limited
Focus Tankers Limited
Frisco (U.K.) Sales Limited
Gago Invest Limited
Garrets Bidco Limited
H. K. S. Holdings Limited
H.K.S. Motors Limited
Harsco (U.K.) Limited
Healthcare Support (Erdington) Ltd
Heathrow Hydrant Operating Co Ltd
Herbalife Europe Limited
Hertz Europe Limited
Higgs International Limited
Highway Care Group Limited
Highway Care Limited
Home and Comforts Limited
I E Music Limited
IAH Charity Co Ltd
Independent Inspections Ltd
Intercontinental Hotels Group Services Company
KBR (Aspire Construction) Ltd
KBR (Aspire Services) Limited
LNOC Limited
Laxkan Holdings Ltd
Laxkan Ltd
Link Market Services Trustees Ltd
London Residential Healthcare Ltd
M - Integrated Solutions PLC
M.W. Helicopters Limited
MCM Central Limited
MND Construction Services Ltd
Maison Moti Limited
Marz Limited
Medicrest Limited
Mohan Building Services Ltd
Mountcharm Limited
NEC Capital (UK) PLC
NPL Management Limited
Newacc (2014) Limited
Newserge Limited
Newstone International Limited
Notonthehighstreet Enterprises Ltd
Onslow Inc. Ltd
Openview Security Solutions Ltd
PDC Brands UK Limited
PSSG Group Limited
Photo - Me International P L C
Pitchset Limited
Procter & Gamble (L & CP) Ltd
Proper Music Distribution Ltd
Purebond Limited
Purley Baptist Church
RSA Island Village Limited
Rican Securities Limited
SC Leisure Group Limited
Saville Services Limited
Sega Europe Limited
Shoppertrak Limited
Sky Subscribers Services Ltd
Smiths Industries Industrial Group
Solai Holdings Limited
Sports Interactive Limited
State Street HCL Holdings (UK) Ltd

Subsea 7 Crewing Limited
TER AG Ltd.
Teledyne Limited
Titan Containers Limited
Tozer Seeds Limited
A.E. Tyler Limited
VASBP Limited
Voluntary Service Overseas
Wallacespace Limited
Wates Living Space (Maintenance) Ltd
We Are Pentagon Limited
Ziji Productions Limited

98000 Residents property management

Ash Properties Limited
Courtlands Estate (Richmond) Ltd
Easyoffice Rental Limited
G & O Properties (London) Ltd
Sherrygreen Limited

99000 Activities of extraterritorial organisations and bodies

Amal Investments Limited

99999 Dormant company [17]

Active Travel Group Limited
Active Travel Group Midco Ltd
Arora Manchester Limited
Besimcho Limited
Cablesheer Group Limited
Chubb Group (International) Ltd
Console Lowco Limited
Digico Global Limited
Ethypharm Holdings UK Ltd
Etonbrook Properties PLC
Gapsun Properties Limited
Host Europe Investments Ltd
Lowery Group Limited
R. Maskell (Holdings) Limited
Movesell Limited
Valley Primary School
T.W. White & Sons (Holdings) Ltd

Printed in 8pt Nimbus Sans L

Designed by URW++ Design and Development GmbH

Dellam Publishing Limited

2 Heath Drive, Sutton, Surrey, SM2 5RP

Fax: 020 8770 7478 email: enquiries@dellam.com

SAN: 0177881 EAN/GLN: 5030670177882

www.ingramcontent.com/pod-product-compliance
Lightning Source LLC
LaVergne TN
LVHW082005200926
848481LV00010B/2807
* 9 7 8 1 9 1 2 7 3 6 2 5 6 *